CONCISE ENCYCLOPEDIA OF PSYCHOLOGY

SECOND EDITION

CONCISE ENCYCLOPEDIA OF PSYCHOLOGY

SECOND EDITION

RAYMOND J. CORSINI
and
ALAN J. AUERBACH

Editors

CONSULTING EDITORS

Anne Anastasi
Albert Bandura
William Bevan
Theodore Blau
Nicholas Cummings
Florence Denmark
Raymond Fowler
Stanley Graham
E. R. Hilgard
Joseph Matarazzo
W. J. McKeachie
Paul Meehl
Robert Perloff
M. Brewster Smith
Janet Spence
Charles Spielberger
Bonnie Strickland
Logan Wright

ASSOCIATE EDITORS

Mary Allen
Carol Austad
Kent Berridge
Gordon Bower
Carl Eisdorfer
H. J. Freudenberger
Elaine Hatfield
Stephen Haynes
Arthur Kovacs
Mary Beth Leisen
Anthony Marsella
Melvin Marx
William McGuire
J. Bruce Overmier
Donald Peterson
A. R. Prakanis
K. Werner Schaie
Alice D. Scheuer
Roger Walsh
Michael Wertheimer

Managing Editor: Becky Ozaki

JOHN WILEY & SONS

New York • Chichester • Brisbane • Toronto • Singapore

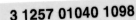
Library of Congress Cataloging-in-Publication Data:

Concise Encyclopedia of psychology / Raymond J. Corsini, Alan J. Auerbach, editors:
  consulting editors, Anne Anastasi . . . [et al.] : associate editors,
Mary Allen . . . [et al.]. -- 2nd ed.
    p. cm.
  "A Wiley-Interscience publication."
  ISBN 0-471-13159-8 (alk. paper)
  1. Psychology—Encyclopedias. I. Corsini, Raymond J.
II. Anastasi, Anne, 1908-. III. Allen, Mary.
BF31.E553 1996
150′.3–dc20   95–26497
                                                    CIP

Printed in the United States of America

10 9 8 7 6 5 4 3 2 1

To Carl R. Rogers and B. F. Skinner

CONTRIBUTORS

Theodora M. Abel, Ph.D., *University of New Mexico, Albuquerque, New Mexico,* Culture and Psychotherapy; Quadraplegics: Psychological Aspects

Norman Abeles, Ph.D., *Michigan State University, East Lansing, Michigan,* Competency in Psychology; Credentialing; Ethical Problems in Psychology; Late-Life Forgetting; Older Adults: Mood and Memory; Prescription Privileges; Pseudodementia

Rosemary C. Adam-Terem, Ph.D., *University of Hawaii, Honolulu, Hawaii,* Introspection

Jack R. Adams-Webber, Ph.D., *Brock University, St. Catherines, Ontario, Canada,* Cognitive Complexity; Personal Construct Theory; Repertory Grid Technique

Lewis R. Aiken, Ph.D., *Pepperdine University, Malibu, California,* Aptitude Testing; Field Research; Interest Inventories; Item Analysis; Observational Methods; Rating Scales; Selection Tests

Icek Ajzen, Ph.D., *University of Massachusetts, Amherst, Massachusetts,* Attitudes; Interpersonal Attraction

George W. Albee, Ph.D., *University of Vermont, Burlington, Vermont,* Primary Prevention of Psychopathology

James E. Alcock, Ph.D., *York University, Toronto, Ontario, Canada,* Barnum Effect; Cooperation/Competition; Frustration–Aggression Hypothesis; Gambler's Fallacy; Irritable Bowel Syndrome; Mass Hysteria; Occultism

Lynn E. Alden, Ph.D., *University of British Columbia, Vancouver, British Columbia, Canada,* Avoidant Personality

Theron Alexander, Ph.D., *Temple University, Philadelphia, Pennsylvania,* Acculturation; Biological Rhythms; Childhood Neurosis; Cultural Determinism; Cultural Differences

Mary J. Allen, Ph.D., *California State College, Bakersfield, California,* Central Limit Theorem; Curvilinear Relationship; Experimental Methods; Intervening Variable; Performance Tests; Porteus Maze Test; Power of Tests; Random Numbers; Scientific Method; Strong–Campbell Interest Inventory; Testing Methods

G. Hugh Allred, Ed.D., *Brigham Young University, Provo, Utah,* Marital Interaction Styles; Physics and the Behavioral Sciences

Louise Bates Ames, Ph.D., *Gesell Institute of Human Development, New Haven, Connecticut,* Academic Success and Grouping; Aging: Behavior Changes

Anne Anastasi, Ph.D., *Fordham University, Bronx, New York,* Differential Psychology

Nancy S. Anderson, Ph.D., *University of Maryland, College Park, Maryland,* Coding; Cognition; Forgetting; Form/Shape Perception; Memory Experiments; Mnemonics

John L. Andreassi, Ph.D., *City University of New York, New York, New York,* Neurotoxic Substances; Phenylketonuria; Pituitary Disorders; Sensory Deprivation; Somatotypes; Split-Brain Research

I. Robert Andrews, Ph.D., *Simon Fraser University, Burnaby, British Columbia, Canada,* Employee Productivity; Leadership Styles; Leadership Training

Richard S. Andrulis, Ph.D., *Industrial Psychologist, West Chester, Pennsylvania,* Employment Practices; Hidden Figures Test; Myers–Briggs Type Indicator; Operations Research

Hymie Anisman, Ph.D., *Carleton University, Ottawa, Ontario, Canada,* Amphetamine Effects; Immunological Functioning; Neurochemistry; Stimulants; Stress Consequences

Heinz L. Ansbacher, Ph.D., *University of Vermont, Burlington, Vermont,* Masculine Protest

Hal R. Arkes, Ph.D., *Ohio University, Athens, Ohio,* Clinical Judgment

Robert B. Armstrong, Ph.D., *University of British Columbia, Vancouver, British Columbia, Canada,* Early Recollections; Parent Education

Rudolf Arnheim, Ph.D., *University of Michigan, Ann Arbor, Michigan,* Gestalt Psychology; Psychology of the Arts

Magda B. Arnold, Ph.D., *Retired, Tucson, Arizona,* Cognitive Theories of Emotion

Philip Ash, Ph.D., *Private Practice, Blacksburg, Virginia,* Honesty Tests; Testing and Legislation

Richard M. Ashbrook, M.A., *Ohio State University, Columbus, Ohio,* Character Disorders; Immature Personality

William Asher, Ph.D., *Purdue University, West Lafayette, Indiana,* Experimental Controls; Miller Analogies Test; Mooney Problem Checklist; Research Methodology

Alan J. Auerbach, *Wilfrid Laurier University, Waterloo, Ontario, Canada,* Industrial/Organizational Psychology

Carol Shaw Austad, Ph.D., *Central Connecticut State University, New Britain, Connecticut,* Managed Mental Health Care; Psychotherapy Effectiveness

John J. B. Ayres, Ph.D., *University of Massachusetts, Amherst, Massachusetts,* Backward Conditioning; Inhibitory Conditioning; Selective Attention

Kurt W. Back, Ph.D., *Duke University, Durham, North Carolina,* Altruism; Communication Processes; Conformity; Group Dynamics; Rites de Passage

Albert Bandura, Ph.D., *Stanford University, Stanford, California,* Self-Efficacy

Augustine Barón, Jr., Psy.D., *University of Texas, Austin, Texas,* Communication Theory; Ethnic Minorities; Loss and Grief; Morale in Organizations; Need–Press Theory; Negotiation; Sociology of Psychological Knowledge; Telephone Counseling

Daniel Bar-Tal, Ph.D., *Tel-Aviv University, Tel-Aviv, Israel,* Helping Behavior; Pygmalion Effect

S. Howard Bartley, Ph.D., *Memphis State University, Memphis, Tennessee,* Experimental Psychology; Fatigue; Hypothalamus; Stimulus; Taste Perception; Visual Perception

Bernard M. Bass, Ph.D., *State University of New York, Binghamton, New York,* Leadership and Supervision; Management Development; Team Performance

Andrew S. Baum, Ph.D., *U.S. University of the Health Sciences, Bethesda, Maryland,* Crowding; Emotions; Environmental Psychology; Territoriality I

Gary S. Belkin, Ed.D., *Long Island University, Brooklyn, New York,* Phobias; Sexual Abstinence

Alan S. Bellack, Ph.D., *The Medical College of Pennsylvania, Philadelphia, Pennsylvania,* Behavioral Contracts; Flooding; Role-Play Tests

Camilla Persson Benbow, Ed.D., *Iowa State University, Ames, Iowa,* Sex Differences in Mathematics

Thomas S. Bennett, Ph.D., *University of South Alabama, Mobile, Alabama,* Brain Laterality; Divorce; Enuresis; Group Psychotherapy; Lateral Dominance; Privileged Communications; Professional Ethics; Tantrums

Philip G. Benson, Ph.D., *New Mexico State University, Las Cruces, New Mexico,* Creativity Measures; Exit Interviews; General Aptitude Test Battery; Hawthorne Effect; Mixed Standard Scale

Peter M. Bentler, Ph.D., *University of California, Los Angeles, California,* Multivariate Analysis Methods

Stanley Berent, Ph.D., *University of Michigan, Ann Arbor, Michigan,* Fight/Flight Reaction; Group Cohesiveness; Group Pressure; Power; Vocational Rehabilitation

Robert C. Berg, Ed.D., *North Texas State University, Denton, Texas,* Directive Counseling; Group Counseling; Interpersonal Skills Development; Premarital Counseling

Kathleen Stassen Berger, Ph.D., *City University of New York, New York, New York,* Birth Trauma; Breast-Feeding; Child Neglect; Imaginary Companions; Language Development; Marasmus; Middle Childhood

Leonard Berger, Ph.D., *Clemson University, Clemson, South Carolina,* Behaviorally Anchored Rating Scales; Halo Effect; Least Preferred Coworker Scale; Likert Scaling; Rater Errors; Task Analysis; Unobtrusive Measures; Wonderlic Personnel Test

Michael D. Berzonsky, Ph.D., *State University of New York, Cortland, New York,* Adolescent Identity Formation; Deviant Maturation; Eriksonian Developmental Stages; Moral Development

James Bieri, Ph.D., *University of Texas, Austin, Texas,* Literature and Psychology

Karen Linn Bierman, Ph.D., *Pennsylvania State University, University Park, Pennsylvania,* Child Guidance Clinics; Play Therapy; School Adjustment; School Gangs; Skill Learning; Social Isolation

Jerry Binder, Ph.D., *Behavioral Health Consultant, Corona del Mar, California,* Mental Health Teams; Mental Illness: Attitudes Toward; Sleep Treatment

Paul Bindrim, Ph.D., *Bindrim Institute, Hollywood, California,* Nude Group Therapy; Vector Approach to Psychotherapy

Thomas Blass, Ph.D., *University of Maryland, Catonsville, Maryland,* Biography; Interactionism

Theodore H. Blau, Ph.D., *Private Practice, Tampa, Florida,* American Psychological Foundation; Expert Testimony; Independent Practice; Police Psychology; Smoking Behavior

Milton S. Bloombaum, Ph.D., *University of Hawaii, Honolulu, Hawaii,* Guttman Scale; Role Playing; Role Taking

Gerald S. Blum, Ph.D., *University of California, Santa Barbara, California,* Blacky Pictures; Hypnosis as a Research Tool

C. Alan Boneau, Ph.D., *George Mason University, Fairfax, Virginia,* Psychological Science

Edward S. Bordin, Ph.D., *University of Michigan, Ann Arbor, Michigan,* Developmental Counseling; Time-Limited Psychotherapy; Work and Play

Edgar F. Borgatta, Ph.D., *University of Washington, Seattle, Washington,* Social Psychology

Marie L. Borgatta, Ph.D., *University of Washington, Seattle, Washington,* Background Characteristics; Clinical Versus Statistical Prediction

Dale E. Bowen, Ph.D., *Hilltop Rehabilitation Hospital, Grand Junction, Colorado,* Contamination (Statistical); Instrument Design; Sensorimotor Processes; Vision (Theories of); Weight Control

C. Reginald Brasington, Ph.D., *University of South Carolina, Columbia, South Carolina,* Birth Order

Sharon S. Brehm, Ph.D., *Harpur College of Arts & Sciences, SUNY Binghamton, Binghamton, New York,* Reactance Theory

Margaret Brenman-Gibson, Ph.D., *Harvard Medical School, Cambridge, Massachusetts,* Psychoanalysis

Frederick D. Breslin, Ph.D., *Glassboro State College, Glassboro, New Jersey,* Children's Behavioral Stages; Individual Differences; Maternal Deprivation

Marilynn B. Brewer, Ph.D., *University of California, Santa Barbara, California,* Ingroups/Outgroups

Arthur P. Brief, Ph.D., *Tulane University, New Orleans, Louisiana,* Occupational Stress; Task Design

Richard W. Brislin, Ph.D., *East-West Center, Honolulu, Hawaii,* Cross-Cultural Psychology; Cross-Cultural Training Programs; Power: Strategies and Tactics

Frederick G. Brown, Ph.D., *Iowa State University, Ames, Iowa,* Cluster Analysis; Differential Aptitude Tests; Edwards Personal Preference Schedule; Measurement; Response Bias; Test Anxiety

Robert T. Brown, Ph.D., *University of North Carolina, Wilmington, North Carolina,* Congenital Infections; Crucial Experiments in Psychology; Fetal Alcohol Syndrome; Fragile X Syndrome; Inborn Errors of Metabolism; Lesch–Nyhan Syndrome

Sheldon S. Brown, Ph.D., *North Shore Community College, Beverly, Massachusetts,* Handedness; Homelessness; Montessori Method; Neonatal Development; Surface Transportation

William F. Brown, Ed.D., *Southwest Texas State University, San Marcos, Texas,* Study Methods

Josef Brožek, Ph.D., *Massachusetts Institute of Technology, Cambridge, Massachusetts,* Malnutrition and Human Behavior

B. R. Bugelski, Ph.D., *State University of New York, Buffalo, New York,* Extrasensory Perception; Imageless Thought: The Würzburg School; Imagery; Imitative Learning; Memory; Rewards; Thorndike's Laws of Learning; Work–Rest Cycles

John T. Cacioppo, Ph.D., *Ohio State University, Columbus, Ohio,* Social Psychophysiology

John B. Campbell, Ph.D., *Colgate University, Hamilton, New York,* Central Traits; Cognitive Dissonance; Personal Documents; Personality Changes

Samuel S. Cardone, M.D., Ph.D., *Illinois Department of Mental Health, Chicago, Illinois,* Alcoholism Treatment; Assessing Children for Psychotherapy; Psychologists as Mental Health Consultants

Mark S. Carich, Ph.D., *Adler School of Professional Psychology, Chicago, Illinois,* Automatic Thoughts; Cybernetics; The Unconscious

Peter Carich, Ph.D., *Retired,* Paradigms

John G. Carlson, Ph.D., *University of Hawaii, Honolulu, Hawaii,* Social Phobia

J. Douglas Carroll, Ph.D., *Bell Laboratories, Murray Hill, New Jersey,* Multidimensional Scaling

John B. Carroll, Ph.D., *Rutgers State University, Newark, New Jersey,* Cognitive Abilities; Foreign Language Aptitude; School Learning; Word Frequency

A. Charles Catania, Ph.D., *Private Practice, Lancaster, California,* Natural Selection

Fairfid M. Caudle, Ph.D., *College of Staten Island, Staten Island, New York,* Infant Perceptual Abilities; Magical Number Seven; Memory Retrieval Processes; Memory Span; Rehearsal

Joseph R. Cautela, Ph.D., *Boston College, Chestnut Hill, Massachusetts,* Covert Conditioning; Endorphins/Enkephalins

Paul F. Chapman, Ph.D., *University of Minnesota, Minneapolis, Minnesota,* Neural Mechanisms of Learning

Gordon J. Chelune, Ph.D., *Retired, Cleveland, Ohio,* Conversion Disorder; Convulsive Shock Therapy; Delirium Tremens; Epilepsy; Hysteria; Organic Syndromes

Martin M. Chemers, Ph.D., *Claremont McKenna College, Claremont, California,* Leadership Effectiveness

Irvin L. Child, Ph.D., *Yale University, New Haven, Connecticut,* Anthropology; Anthropomorphic Thinking; Free Will; Primitive Mentality; Psychokinesis; Rankian Psychology; Witchcraft

Margaret M. Clifford, Ph.D., *University of Iowa, Iowa City, Iowa,* Academic Ability Grouping; Academic Underachievement; Curriculum Development; Educational Psychology

George A. Clum, Ph.D., *Virginia Polytechnic Institute and State University, Blackburg, Virginia,* Panic Disorders

Richard Welton Coan, Ph.D., *Tucson, Arizona,* Archetypes; Complexes; Extraversion/Introversion; Personality Types

William C. Coleman, D.Min., *United Methodist Church, Newton, Massachusetts,* Biography

Gary R. Collins, Ph.D., *Trinity Evangelical Divinity School, Deerfield, Illinois,* Pastoral Counseling; Religion and Psychology

Gerald Cooke, Ph.D., *Private Practice, Plymouth Meeting, Pennsylvania,* Forensic Psychology

Irving M. Copi, Ph.D., *University of Hawaii, Honolulu, Hawaii,* Mill's Canons

Stanley Coren, Ph.D., *University of British Columbia, Vancouver, British Columbia, Canada,* Choice Reaction Time; Lens Model (Brunswik); Neuropsychological Development; Set; Subliminal Perception

Gerald Corey, Ed.D., *California State University, Fullerton, California,* Alternative Educational Systems; Body Image; Constitutional Types; Neopsychoanalytic School; Psychodrama; Role Expectations; Self-Esteem; Small Group Therapies; Therapy Trainees; Transactional Analysis

Raymond J. Corsini, Ph.D., *Private Practice, Honolulu, Hawaii,* Innovative Psychotherapies

John F. Corso, Ph.D., *Las Cruces, New Mexico,* Auditory Discrimination; Auditory Disorders; Auditory Localization; Auditory Perception; Ear; Psychophysical Laws

James W. Croake, Ph.D., *Knollwood Park Hospital, Mobile, Alabama,* Fears Throughout the Life Span; Normal Development

Nicholas A. Cummings, Ph.D., *Biodyne Institute, San Francisco, California,* Universal Health Care

Arnold E. Dahlke, Ph.D., *Private Practice, Los Angeles, California,* Factor Analysis

John G. Darley, Ph.D., *University of Minnesota, Minneapolis, Minnesota,* Vocational Interest Measurement

Linda Lee Davidoff, Ph.D., *Essex Community College, Baltimore, Maryland,* Childhood Psychoses; Experimenter Effects; Facial Expressions; Noise Effects

William S. Davidson II, Ph.D., *Michigan State University, East Lansing, Michigan,* Crime; Deviance; Labeling Theory; Violence

Deborah Davis, Ph.D., *University of Nevada, Reno, Nevada,* Attitude Measurement

Hymie I. Day, Ph.D., *York University, Downsview, Ontario, Canada,* Exploratory Behavior; Play

Edward L. Deci, Ph.D., *University of Rochester, Rochester, New York,* Control of Behavior; Intrinsic Motivation; Self-Determination

Patrick DeLeon, Ph.D., J.D., *U.S. Senate, Hawaii,* Public Policy

F. E. Denison, Short-Term Therapy

Florence L. Denmark, Ph.D., *Hunter College, New York, New York,* International Organizations of Psychology; Prejudice and Discrimination; Zeĭgarnik Effect

M. Ray Denny, Ph.D., *Michigan State University, East Lansing, Michigan,* Age Differences; Animals Raised as Humans; Cognitive Maps; Conditioning of Compensatory Reactions; Down Syndrome (Mongolism); Ecological Validity; Emotion and Memory; Escape–Avoidance Learning; Evolution; Expectancy Theory; Instinctive Behavior; Mnemonic Systems; Neobehaviorism; State-Dependent Learning

Donald R. Denver, Ph.D., *Quebec, Montreal, Canada,* Intelligence Measures

Norman K. Denzin, Ph.D., *University of Illinois, Urbana, Illinois,* Controlled Drinking; Idiographic–Nomothetic Psychology; James–Lange Theory of Emotions; Ritual Behavior; Self—Looking-Glass Concept; Symbolic Interaction

Francine Deutsch, Ph.D., *San Diego State University, San Diego, California,* Career Choices; Day-Care Centers; Life Events; Pets; Sibling Relationships

Donald A. Dewsbury, Ph.D., *University of Florida, Gainesville, Florida,* American Psychological Association II; Animal Aggressive Behavior; Animal Communication; Animal Intelligence; Animal Parental Behavior; Animal Sexual Behavior; Animal Sociobiology; Genetic Fitness; Hormones and Behavior; Insight Learning; Species-Specific Behavior; Territoriality II

Esther E. Diamond, Ph.D., *Educational/Psychological Consultant, Evanston, Illinois,* Forced-Choice Testing; Job Satisfaction; Kuder Occupational Interest Survey; Sex Bias in Measurement; Surveys

Milton Diamond, Ph.D., *University of Hawaii, Honolulu, Hawaii,* Sexuality: Orientation and Identity

Ernest Dichter, Ph.D., *Deceased,* Consumer Psychology; Level of Aspirations; Persuasive Communications

John W. Donahoe, Ph.D., *University of Massachusetts, Amherst, Massachusetts,* Behavior Analysis; Learning Theories; Operant Conditioning; Schedules of Reinforcement; Selectionism

E. Thomas Dowd, Ph.D., *Kent State University, Kent, Ohio,* Counseling Psychology; Leisure Counseling

Peter W. Dowrick, Ph.D., *University of Pennsylvania, Philadelphia, Pennsylvania,* Behavioral Modeling; Video Psychology

Clifford J. Drew, Ph.D., *University of Utah, Salt Lake City, Utah,* Dependent Variables; Longitudinal Studies; Statistical Significance; Vineland Social Maturity Scale

Robert E. Driscoll, Psy.D., *The University of Humanistic Studies, San Diego, California,* Birth Order and Personality

Philip H. DuBois, Ph.D., *Washington University, St. Louis, Missouri,* Army Tests, World War I; Opinion Polls; Q-Sort Technique; Stanford–Binet Intelligence Scale; Vocabulary Tests

Jean E. Dumas, Ph.D., *Purdue University, West Lafayette, Indiana,* Conduct Disorder

Bruce R. Dunn, Ph.D., *University of West Florida, Pensacola, Florida,* Cocktail Party Phenomenon; Free Recall; Learning Strategies

Daniel G. Eckstein, Ph.D., *U.S. International University, San Diego, California,* Birth Order and Personality; Lifestyle Assessment; Movement Therapy

Thomas E. Edgar, Ed.D., *Idaho State University, Pocatello, Idaho,* Soft Determinism

William E. Edmonston, Jr., Ph.D., *Colgate University, Hamilton, New York,* Hypnotic Age Regression; Organic Psychoses; Second-Signal System; Senile Psychoses; Toxic Psychoses

Lyle J. Eide, Ph.D., *University of Manitoba, Winnipeg, Manitoba, Canada,* Biographies

Albert Ellis, Ph.D., *Institute for Rational-Emotive Therapy, New York, New York,* Current Psychotherapies; Sex Therapies

Roger E. Enfield, Ph.D., *New Mexico Bureau of Mental Health, Albuquerque, New Mexico,* Central Nervous System; Double Bind; Homeostasis; Rational–Emotive Behavior Therapy; Sullivan's Interpersonal Theory

John W. Engel, Ph.D., *University of Hawaii, Honolulu, Hawaii,* Punishment; Spouse Abuse

N. J. Entwistle, *University of Edinburgh, Edinburgh, Scotland,* Approaches to Learning

Franz R. Epting, Ph.D., *University of Florida, Gainesville, Florida,* Optimal Functioning

David R. Evans, Ph.D., *University of Western Ontario, London, Ontario, Canada,* Accident Proneness and Prevention; Communication Skills Training; Computer Software; Computer-Assisted Instruction; Microtraining; Quality of Life

Frederick J. Evans, Ph.D., *Carrier Foundation, Belle Mead, New Jersey,* Hypnosis; Placebo

Craig A. Everett, Ph.D., *Conciliation Court, Tucson, Arizona,* Marriage Counseling

Robert B. Ewen, Ph.D., *Private Practice, Miami, Florida,* Horney's Theory; Oedipus Complex; Personality Theories; Sublimation

Hans J. Eysenck, Ph.D., D.Sc., *Institute of Psychiatry, Denmark Hill, London, England,* Behavioral Genetics

Benjamin Fabrikant, Ph.D., *Fairleigh Dickinson University, Teaneck, New Jersey,* Psychological Assessment; Psychotherapy

Dennis G. Faust, Ed.D., *Science Applications, Inc., McLean, Virginia,* Behavioral Intervention; Instructional Systems Development

Herman Feifel, Ph.D., *Veterans Administration Outpatient Clinic, Los Angeles, California,* Thanatology

Robert D. Felner, Ph.D., *University of Illinois, Urbana, Illinois,* Day Hospitals; Mental Health Programs; Professional Consultations; Psychiatric Clinics; Reliability of Diagnoses; Terminally Ill People

Eva Dreikurs Ferguson, Ph.D., *Southern Illinois University, Edwardsville, Illinois,* Motivation; Social Equality

Fred E. Fiedler, Ph.D., *University of Washington, Seattle, Washington,* Leadership Effectiveness

Erik E. Filsinger, Ph.D., *University of Alabama, University, Alabama,* Marital Adjustment; Social Class

Frank W. Finger, Ph.D., *University of Virginia, Charlottesville, Virginia,* Circadian Rhythm; Human Behavioral Rhythms

Stanley Finger, Ph.D., *Washington University, St. Louis, Missouri,* Cerebral Localization

Harold Kenneth Fink, Ph.D., *Private Practice, Honolulu, Hawaii,* Cafeteria Feeding; Chromosome Disorders; Genetic Disorders; Genetic Dominance and Recessiveness; Obesity

Norman J. Finkel, Ph.D., *Georgetown University, Washington, DC,* Psychology and the Courts; Right to Refuse Treatment; Right to Treatment

Chet H. Fischer, Ph.D., *Radford University, Radford, Virginia,* Assertiveness Training; Exorcism

Dennis F. Fisher, Ph.D., *U.S. Army Human Engineering Laboratory, Aberdeen Proving Ground, Maryland,* Eye Movements; Fear; Learning Disabilities; Loneliness; Memory Disorders; Short-Term Memory; Thought Disturbances

Stuart G. Fisher, Ph.D., *Holy Cross College, Worcester, Massachusetts,* Counterconditioning; Experimental Neurosis; Nonprofessionals in Mental Health; Sleep Disorders

James L. Fobes, Ph.D., *Army Research Institute for the Behavioral Sciences, Presidio of Monterey, California,* Color Vision; Transfer of Training

Vincent Foley, Ph.D., *Private Practice, New York, New York,* Family Therapy; Multiple Family Therapy

John P. Foreyt, Ph.D., *Baylor College of Medicine, Houston, Texas,* Cognitive Behavior Therapy; Obesity Treatments

Barbara Forisha-Kovach, Ph.D., *University of Michigan, Dearborn, Michigan,* Adolescent Development; Organizational Climate; Women, Psychology of

W. Rodney Fowler, Ed.D., *University of Tennessee, Chattanooga, Tennessee,* Hostage Negotiations

Paul Fraisse, Ph.D., *Université Rene Descartes, Paris, France,* Rhythm

Jerome D. Frank, M.D., Ph.D., *Johns Hopkins University School of Medicine, Baltimore, Maryland,* Effective Components of Psychotherapy; Sociopsychological Determinants of War and Peace

Viktor E. Frankl, M.D., Ph.D., *University of Vienna Medical School, Vienna, Austria,* Logotherapy

Cyril M. Franks, Ph.D., *Rutgers University, Piscataway, New Jersey,* Behavior Therapy: Problems and Issues

Calvin J. Frederick, Ph.D., *University of California, Los Angeles, California,* Disaster Analysis; Psychopharmacology; Speech Disorders; Stuttering

M. J. Friedman, Ph.D., *Montclair State College, Montclair, New Jersey,* Posttraumatic Stress Disorder

Benjamin Fruchter, Ph.D., *University of Texas, Austin, Texas,* Multiple Correlation; Multiple Regression

Dorothy A. Fruchter, Ph.D., *Educational Development Corporation, Austin, Texas,* Driver's License Testing

Robert M. Gagné, Ph.D., *Florida State University, Tallahassee, Florida,* Learning Outcomes, I

Sol L. Garfield, Ph.D., *Washington University, St. Louis, Missouri,* Brief Psychotherapy; Effectiveness of Psychotherapy; Emerging Psychotherapies

Kurt F. Geisinger, Ph.D., *Fordham University, New York, New York,* Bogardus Social Distance Scale; Psychometrics; Questionnaires; Test Standardization

Eugene T. Gendlin, Ph.D., *University of Chicago, Chicago, Illinois,* Focusing

Dianne Gerard, Ph.D., *Private Practice, Kauai, Hawaii,* Female Sexual Dysfunction; Human Sexuality

Kenneth J. Gergen, Ph.D., *Swarthmore College, Swarthmore, Pennsylvania,* Diachronic Versus Synchronic Models; Ethnic Groups; Ethnocentrism; Social Constructionism

Mary M. Gergen, Ph.D., *Swarthmore College, Swarthmore, Pennsylvania,* Ethnocentrism

Karen M. Gil, Ph.D., *Duke University Medical Center, Durham, North Carolina,* Pain: Coping Strategies; Sickle Cell Disease

Amedeo P. Giorgi, Ph.D., *University of Quebec at Montreal, Quebec, Canada,* Descriptive Psychology; Existentialism; Geisteswissenschaftliche Psychologie; Metapsychology

Rita T. Giubilato, R.N., M.S.N., *Thomas Jefferson University, Philadelphia, Pennsylvania,* Cerebral Blood Flow Studies; Cerebral Palsy; Health Care Services; Multiple Sclerosis; Parkinson's Disease

Thomas A. Glass, Ph.D., *Private Practice, Honolulu, Hawaii,* Gestalt Therapy

William Glasser, M.D., *Institute for Reality Therapy, Los Angeles, California,* Reality Therapy; Schools without Failure

Charles J. Golden, Ph.D., *Private Practice, Milford, Pennsylvania,* Neuropsychology

Arnold P. Goldstein, Ph.D., *Syracuse University, Syracuse, New York,* Aggression

G. Ken Goodrick, Ph.D., *University of Houston, Houston, Texas,* Cognitive Behavior Therapy

Leonard D. Goodstein, Ph.D., *Washington, DC,* Human Relations Training; Industrial Consultants; Self-Disclosure

Richard E. Goranson, *York University, Toronto, Ontario, Canada,* Functional Autonomy

Bernard S. Gorman, Ph.D., *Nassau Community College, Garden City, New York,* Manic-Depressive Personality; Rigidity

Stanley R. Graham, Ph.D., P.C., *New School for Social Research, New York, New York,* National College of Professional Psychology

Donald L. Grant, Ph.D., *University of Georgia, Athens, Georgia,* Performance Appraisal; Personnel Selection

Martin S. Greenberg, Ph.D., *University of Pittsburgh, Pittsburgh, Pennsylvania,* Bystander Involvement; Galilean/Aristotelian Thinking; Mob Psychology

William A. Greene, Ph.D., *Eastern Washington University, Cheney, Washington,* Biofeedback

James Lynn Greenstone, Ed.D., *Southwestern Academy of Crisis Interveners, Dallas, Texas,* Conflict Mediation; Crisis Intervention; Hostage Negotiations; Intervener Survival

William Edgar Gregory, Ph.D., *University of the Pacific, Stockton, California,* Animism; Attention Span; Authoritarian Personality; College Academic Prediction; General Systems; National Character; Religious Behavior; Scapegoating; Simulation; Sleep Learning; Taboos

Bruce Greyson, M.D., *University of Connecticut Health Center School of Medicine, Farmington, Connecticut,* Near-Death Experiences

Sebastian P. Grossman, Ph.D., *University of Chicago, Chicago, Illinois,* Chemical Brain Stimulation; Hunger; Physiological Needs

J. P. Guilford, Ph.D., *Deceased,* Human Intelligence; Structure-of-Intellect Model

Robert M. Guion, Ph.D., *Bowling Green State University, Bowling Green, Ohio,* Clerical Aptitude Testing; Interviewing (Selection); Job Analysis; Job Evaluation; Null Hypothesis Testing

Harold O. Gulliksen, Ph.D., *Educational Testing Service, Princeton, New Jersey,* Scaling

Jay Gurian, Ph.D., *Retired, Washington, DC,* Dependency

Giselher Guttmann, Ph.D., *University of Vienna, Vienna, Austria,* Ergopsychometry

Russell A. Haber, Ph.D., *University of South Carolina, Columbia, South Carolina,* Parental Permissiveness

Frederick P. Haehnlen, Ph.D., *University of Hawaii, Honolulu, Hawaii,* Counselor Education

Natalie R. Haimowitz, Ph.D., *Private Practice, Evanston, Illinois,* Deprivation Effects; Middle Age

Calvin S. Hall, Ph.D., *Retired, Santa Cruz, California,* Dreams

Harold V. Hall, Ph.D., *Private Practice, Honolulu, Hawaii,* Correctional Institutions; Deception; Hallucinations

Forest W. Hansen, Ph.D., *Lake Forest College, Lake Forest, Illinois,* Catharsis; Existential Psychotherapy; Implosive Therapy; Self-Help Groups

James M. Harper, Ph.D., *Brigham Young University, Provo, Utah,* Marital Interaction Styles; Physics and the Behavioral Sciences

Robert S. Harper, Ph.D., *Private Practice, Charleston, South Carolina,* Graduate Training in Psychology; Psychological Laboratories; Teaching Undergraduate Psychology

Albert J. Harris, Ph.D., *Deceased,* Reading Disabilities

Joseph T. Hart, Ph.D., *Private Practice, Los Angeles, California,* Eclectic Psychotherapy; Functional Psychology; Phyloanalysis; Sales Psychology; Sports Psychology

Eugene L. Hartley, Ph.D., *Scottsdale, Arizona,* Canalization; Plant Behavior

Elaine Hatfield, Ph.D., *University of Hawaii, Honolulu, Hawaii,* Emotional Contagion; Equity; Love; Physical Attractiveness

L. J. Hatterer, M.D., *Cornell University Medical School, Ithaca, New York,* Addictive Process

Stephen N. Haynes, Ph.D., *University of Hawaii, Honolulu, Hawaii,* Computer-Assisted Assessment; Halfway Houses; Heroin Addiction; Symptom Remission Therapy

Nancy Ann Haynie, Ph.D., *Deceased,* Cognitive Learning Styles; Neurolinguistics; Peer Counseling

Bert Hayslip, Jr., Ph.D., *University of North Texas, Denton, Texas,* Aging and Intelligence; Cognitive Interventions with Older Persons; Death Anxiety

R. Jock Hearn, Ph.D., *University of Oriental Studies, Los Angeles, California,* Altruistic Suicide; Artistic Morphology; Zen Buddhism

Verda T. Heisler, Ph.D., *Private Practice, San Diego, California,* Analytical Psychology

Gregory M. Herek, Ph.D., *University of California, Davis, California,* Homosexuality

Allen K. Hess, Ph.D., *Auburn University, Auburn, Alabama,* American Board of Professional Psychology; Marathon Therapy; Psychotherapy Training; Relationship Therapy

Ernest R. Hilgard, Ph.D., *Stanford University, Stanford, California,* American Psychological Association I

Julian E. Hochberg, Ph.D., *Columbia University, New York, New York,* Constancy; Perception; Unconscious Inference

Jeanne S. Hoffmann, Ph.D., *Private Practice, Honolulu, Hawaii,* Munchausen Syndrome by Proxy; Pediatric Psychology

Ronald R. Holden, Ph.D., *Queen's University, Kingston, Ontario, Canada,* Face Validity; Hopelessness; Moderated Multiple Regression; Social Desirability

David L. Holmes, Ed.D., *The Eden Institute, Princeton, New Jersey,* Idiot Savant; Residential Alternatives; Toilet Training

David S. Holmes, Ph.D., *University of Kansas, Lawrence, Kansas,* Defense Mechanisms

Wayne H. Holtzman, Ph.D., *University of Texas, Austin, Texas,* International Psychology

John L. Horn, Ph.D., *University of Denver, Denver, Colorado,* Cross-Sectional Research; Ipsative Scaling; The Sixteen Personality Factor Questionnaire

Charles H. Huber, Ph.D., *New Mexico State University, Las Cruces, New Mexico,* Environmental Measures; Prosocial Behavior; School Truancy

Eugene L. Hudson, J.D., *Private Practice, Monte Sereno, California,* Jury Psychology

Bradley E. Huitema, Ph.D., *Western Michigan University, Kalamazoo, Michigan,* Single-Subject Research Designs; Time-Series Analysis

Lloyd G. Humphreys, Ph.D., *University of Illinois, Champaign, Illinois,* Heredity and Intelligence

Thelma Hunt, M.D., Ph.D., *Deceased,* Psychological Testing: Its Survival Problems

Elizabeth B. Hurlock, Ph.D., *Private Practice, Atlanta, Georgia,* Dress

Richard W. Husband, Ph.D., *Florida State University, Tallahassee, Florida,* Criterion in Employment; Scholarship and Achievement

Max L. Hutt, Ph.D., *Deceased,* Block Design Test; Michigan Picture Test; Microdiagnosis

George W. Hynd, Ed.D., *University of Georgia, Athens, Georgia,* Alexia/Dyslexia; Dementia; Neuromuscular Disorders

James R. Iberg, Ph.D., *Private Practice, Chicago, Illinois,* Experiential Psychotherapy; Reflective Listening

Daniel R. Ilgen, Ph.D., *Michigan State University, East Lansing, Michigan,* Industrial Psychology; Personnel Evaluation

Lee A. Jackson, Jr., Ph.D., *University of North Carolina, Wilmington, North Carolina,* Group Problem Solving

Finn K. Jellestad, Ph.D., *University of Bergen, Bergen, Norway,* Heterosynaptic Facilitation

Arthur R. Jensen, Ph.D., *University of California, Berkeley, California,* Cultural Bias in Tests; General Intelligence Factor; Heritability; Inbreeding and Human Factors; Law of Filial Regression; Reaction Time

David W. Johnson, Ed.D., *University of Minnesota, Minneapolis, Minnesota,* Individualism; Peer Influences; Social Influence

Orval G. Johnson, Ph.D., *Weld County BOCES, La Salle, Colorado,* Comrey Personality Scales; Speech Development

Roger T. Johnson, Ed.D., *University of Minnesota, Minneapolis, Minnesota,* Individualism; Peer Influences

Eve Jones, Ph.D., *Los Angeles City College, Los Angeles, California,* Nonverbal Therapies

James W. Kalat, Ph.D., *North Carolina State University, Raleigh, North Carolina,* Antabuse; Electroconvulsive Therapy; Huntington's Chorea; Peptic Ulcer; Specific Hungers

Barry H. Kantowitz, Ph.D., *Purdue University, West Lafayette, Indiana,* Information Processing

Richard P. Kappenberg, Ph.D., *Rehabilitation Hospital of the Pacific, Honolulu, Hawaii,* Conjoint Therapy; Family Crises; Hallucinogenic Drugs; Interdisciplinary Treatment; Rehabilitation

Werner Karle, Ph.D., *Private Practice, Corona del Mar, California,* Mental Health Teams; Mental Illness: Attitudes Toward; Sleep Treatment

Richard A. Kasschau, Ph.D., *University of Houston, Houston, Texas,* Flesch Formulas; Reading Measures; Semantic Differential; Teaching Machines

Robert Kastenbaum, Ph.D., *Arizona State University, Tempe, Arizona,* Logical Positivism; Time Perspective

Albert J. Kearney, Ph.D., *Behavior Therapy Institute, Sudbury, Massachusetts,* Covert Conditioning; Endorphins/Enkephalins

Nira Kefir, Ph.D., *Alfred Adler Institute, Tel-Aviv, Israel,* Dispositional Sets; Impasse/Priority Therapy; Mechanisms of Group Psychotherapy

E. James Kehoe, Ph.D., *University of New South Wales, Kensington, Australia,* Neural Network Models

Timothy Keith-Lucas, Ph.D., *The University of the South, Sewanee, Tennessee,* Biographies

E. Lowell Kelly, Ph.D., *Deceased,* Astrology; Graphology

F. Donald Kelly, Ph.D., *Florida State University, Tallahassee, Florida,* Social Interest

Roy M. Kern, Ed.D., *Georgia State University, Atlanta, Georgia,* Cognitive Therapies; Personality and Illness

Carolin Keutzer, Ph.D., *University of Oregon, Eugene, Oregon,* Transpersonal Psychology (I)

Gregory A. Kimble, Ph.D., *Duke University, Durham, North Carolina,* Acquired Drives; Crespi Effect; Distribution of Practice; Double-Alternation Learning; Gross Motor Skill Learning; Higher-Order Conditioning; Incentives; Learning Curves; Limen; Reinforcement

James E. King, Ph.D., *University of Arizona, Tucson, Arizona,* Comparative Psychology; Ethology

Diana L. Kitch, M.A., *Private Practice, Wichita, Kansas,* Burnout; Hospice

Herbert J. Klausmeier, Ed.D., *San Diego, California,* Conceptual Learning and Development

Walter G. Klopfer, Ph.D., *Deceased,* Personality Assessment; Psychological Reports; Rorschach Technique

Sibylle Klosterhalfen, Ph.D., *Institute for Medical Psychology, Düsseldorf, Germany,* Anticipatory Nausea

Thomas A. Kochan, Ph.D., *Massachusetts Institute of Technology, Cambridge, Massachusetts,* Arbitration; Job Security; Labor–Management Relations

Joan W. Koff, Ph.D., *Forest Institute of Professional Psychology, Honolulu, Hawaii,* Cross-Cultural Psychological Assessment; Delusional Disorders

Albert T. Kondo, Ph.D., *University of Houston, Houston, Texas,* Obesity Treatments

Richard Royal Kopp, Ph.D., *California School of Professional Psychology, Los Angeles, California,* Neglected Children; Purposive Behavior

Sheldon J. Korchin, Ph.D., *Deceased,* Clinical Assessment; Ethics of Psychological Research

Leonard Krasner, Ph.D., *Stanford School of Medicine, Stanford, California,* Behavior Therapy; Behaviorism: History

David R. Krathwohl, Ph.D., *Syracuse University, Syracuse, New York,* Control Groups; Criterion Measures; Double-Blind Research; Experimental Designs; Sampling

Alan G. Kraut, Ph.D., *American Psychological Society, Washington, DC,* American Psychological Society

Stanley Krippner, Ph.D., *Saybrook Institute, San Francisco, California,* Alternative Doctoral Programs; Creativity; Personology; Psychoneuroimmunology

Irwin L. Kutash, Ph.D., *Private Practice, Maplewood, New Jersey,* Anxiety; Victimology

Steinar Kvale, Ph.D., *University of Aarhus, Risskov, Denmark,* Postmodernism

Marianne S. La Croce, Ph.D., *St. John's University, New York, New York,* Biographies

Roy Lachman, Ph.D., *University of Houston, Houston, Texas,* Information-Processing Theory

Jesse Lair, Ph.D., *Montana State University, Bozeman, Montana,* Peer Group Therapy

Lev N. Landa, Ph.D., *Columbia University Teachers College, New York, New York,* Algorithmic-Heuristic Theory

Carol Landau, Ph.D., *Brown University Division of Medicine, Providence, Rhode Island,* Antipsychotic Drugs; Marijuana; National Training Laboratory; Obsessive-Compulsive Personality; Substance Abuse; Walk-in Clinics

Ted Landsman, Ph.D., *University of Florida, Gainesville, Florida,* Peak Experiences

Eugene E. Landy, Ph.D., *Private Practice, Honolulu, Hawaii,* Disjunctive Therapies

Ellen J. Langer, Ph.D., *Harvard University, Cambridge, Massachusetts,* Mindlessness–Mindfulness

Arnold A. Lazarus, Ph.D., *Rutgers University, New Brunswick, New Jersey,* Multimodal Therapy

Richard S. Lazarus, Ph.D., *University of California, Berkeley, California,* Coping

Thomas H. Leahey, Ph.D., *Virginia Commonwealth University, Richmond, Virginia,* Associationism; Behaviorism; Empiricism; Faculty Psychology; Mechanistic Theory; Medieval Thinking; Operationalism; Philosophy of Science; Positivism; Psychic Research

Robert A. Leark, Ph.D., *College Hospital, Cerritos, California,* American Association of Humanistic Psychology; Infantilism; Precocious Development

George R. Leddick, Ph.D., *Indiana-Purdue Universities, Fort Wayne, Indiana,* Marriage Counseling; Psychotherapy Supervision

Arthur Lerner, Ph.D., *Los Angeles City College, Los Angeles, California,* Bibliotherapy; Human Services; Poetry Therapy

Harry Levinson, Ph.D., *The Levinson Institute, Belmont, Massachusetts,* Executive Selection; Organizational Diagnosis

Sharon Leviton, Ph.D., *Southwestern Academy of Crisis Interveners, Dallas, Texas,* Conflict Mediation; Crisis Intervention; Intervener Survival

Eugene E. Levitt, Ph.D., *Indiana University School of Medicine, Indianapolis, Indiana,* Bisexuality; Exhibitionism; Incest; Male Sexual Dysfunction; Nymphomania; Sadomasochism

Parker E. Lichtenstein, Ph.D., D.Sc., *Denison University, Granville, Ohio,* Biographies

Carol Schneider Lidz, Psy.D., *United Cerebral Palsy Association, Philadelphia, Pennsylvania,* Early Childhood Education; Educational Assessment; Educational Mainstreaming

Morton A. Lieberman, Ph.D., *University of Chicago, Chicago, Illinois,* Change Induction Groups

Martin S. Lindauer, Ph.D., *State University of New York, Brockport, New York,* Experimental Aesthetics; Phenomenological Method; Physiognomic Perception

Henry Clay Lindgren, Ph.D., *San Francisco State University, San Francisco, California,* Achievement Need; Affiliation Need; Discovery Learning; Open Education; Peer Tutoring; Psychology of Money; Sociometry; Stereotyping

Ronald Lippitt, Ph.D., *Deceased,* Action Research; Social Climate Research; T-Groups

Mark W. Lipsey, Ph.D., *Claremont Graduate School, Claremont, California,* Program Evaluation

George K. Lockwood, Ph.D., *Palo Alto, California,* Beck Depression Inventory, Deprogramming; Hypothesis Testing; Leary Interpersonal Checklist

John C. Loehlin, Ph.D., *University of Texas, Austin, Texas,* Nature–Nurture Controversy

Jane Loevinger, Ph.D., *Washington University, St. Louis, Missouri,* Ego Development

Donald N. Lombardi, Ph.D., *Seton Hall University, South Orange, New Jersey,* Drug Addiction; Inferiority Feelings; Juvenile Delinquency

Samuel Long, Ph.D., *Business Alienation Research, New York, New York,* Alienation (Political); Conservatism/Liberalism; Political Values

Ivar Lovaas, Ph.D., *University of California, Los Angeles, California,* Autism

James O. Lugo, Ph.D., *Fullerton College, Fullerton, California,* Adult Development; Human Development; Infant Development

Robert W. Lundin, Ph.D., *The University of the South, Sewanee, Tennessee,* Act Psychology; Biographies; Functionalism; Hormic Psychology; Humoral Theory; Psychology of Music; Structuralism; Superstition

David T. Lykken, Ph.D., *University of Minnesota, Minneapolis, Minnesota,* Lie Detection; Psychoneurology, Psychopathic Personality; Psychophysiology

Salvatore Maddi, Ph.D., *University of California, Irvine, California,* Existential Psychology; Personality Research

Peter A. Magaro, Ph.D., *New York, New York,* Character Disorders; Immature Personality

Michael P. Maloney, Ph.D., *University of Southern California School of Medicine, Los Angeles, California,* Abstract Intelligence; Leiter International Performance Scale; Malingering; Mental Retardation

Guy J. Manaster, Ph.D., *University of Texas, Austin, Texas,* Gerontology; Gifted and Talented Children; Only Children; Retirement; Runaway Behavior

John H. Mann, Ph.D., *Private Practice, Carson City, Nevada,* Human Potential; Yoga

Anthony J. Marsella, Ph.D., *University of Hawaii, Honolulu, Hawaii,* Culture-Bound Disorders; Depression

Ference I. Marton, Ph.D., *University of Göteborg, Göteborg, Sweden,* Learning Outcomes, II

Robert C. Marvit, M.D., *Private Practice, Honolulu, Hawaii,* American Psychiatric Association; Criminal Responsibility; Cyclothymic Personality; Nonconforming Personality

Melvin H. Marx, Ph.D., *Retired, Cullouhee, North Carolina,* Connectionism; Control of Variables; Eclecticism; Frequency Judgment; Implicit Learning and Memory; Inferential Bias in Memory; Information Processing (Unconscious); Law of Parsimony; Operational Definition; Systems and Theories; Theoretical Constructs

Joseph D. Matarazzo, Ph.D., *University of Oregon Health Sciences Center, Portland, Oregon,* Diagnoses; Intelligence Measures

Barbara B. Mates, Ph.D., *American Diagnostic Learning and Reading Center, New York, New York,* Accommodation; Cutaneous Senses; Speech and Hearing Measures

Kenneth B. Matheny, Ph.D., *Georgia State University, Atlanta, Georgia,* Cognitive Therapies; Personality and Illness

Margaret W. Matlin, Ph.D., *State University of New York, Genesco, New York,* Anticipation Method; Apparent Movement; Apparent Size; Concept Learning; Figure/Ground; Perceptual Development

Kathleen A. McCluskey, Ph.D., *University of Kansas, Lawrence, Kansas,* Birth Injuries; Embryo and Fetus

F. J. McGuigan, Ph.D., *United States International University, San Diego, California,* Cognitive Psychophysiology

John Paul McKinney, Ph.D., *Michigan State University, East Lansing, Michigan,* Child Psychology; Identity Formation; Masturbation; Psychosexual Stages; Sexual Development; Sexual Intercourse, Human

James H. McMillan, Ph.D., *Virginia Commonwealth University, Richmond, Virginia,* Academic Aptitude Tests; Classroom Dynamics; Culture Fair Tests; Grading in Education; Rote Learning

Werner M. Mendel, M.D., *Private Practice, Los Angeles, California,* Schizophrenia; Supportive Care; Treatment Outcome

Ivan N. Mensh, Ph.D., *University of California–Los Angeles, School of Medicine, Los Angeles, California,* Therapies for Institutionalized Elderly Psychiatric Patients

Peter F. Merenda, Ph.D., *University of Rhode Island, Kingston, Rhode Island,* Chi Square Test; Computerized Adaptive Testing; Confidence Limits; Correlation Methods; Empirical Research Methods; Parametric Statistical Tests; Probability; Small-Sample Statistics; Variables in Research

Stanley Milgram, Ph.D., *Deceased,* Obedience

Neal E. Miller, Ph.D., *Yale University, New Haven, Connecticut,* Behavioral Medicine

Theodore Millon, Ph.D., *University of Miami, Coral Gables, Florida,* Borderline Personality; Compulsive Personality; Dependent Personality; Diagnostic and Statistical Manual of Mental Disorders; Histrionic Personality; Millon Behavioral Health Inventory; Millon Clinical Multiaxial Inventory; Narcissistic Personality; Paranoid Personality; Passive–Aggressive Personality; Personality Disorders; Schizotypal Personality

Henryk Misiak, Ph.D., *Fordham University, New York, New York,* Psychoendocrinology

Tae-Im Moon, Ph.D., *Department of Health, Honolulu, Hawaii,* Appetite Disorders; Dermatitis; Reevaluation Counseling; Shyness

Stewart Moore, M.S.W., *University of Windsor, Windsor, Ontario, Canada,* Meditation; Relaxation Training

Harold H. Mosak, Ph.D., *Private Practice, Chicago, Illinois,* Adlerian Psychology

Dan Motet, Ph.D., *Private Practice, Honolulu, Hawaii,* Identity Crisis; Music Therapy; Suggestion Therapy

Robert Murison, Ph.D., *University of Bergen, Bergen, Norway,* Animal Models

Frank B. Murray, Ph.D., *University of Delaware, Newark, Delaware,* Piaget's Theory

Anne Myers, Ph.D., *State University College, New Paltz, New York,* Fiducial Limits; Statistical Inference; Statistics in Psychology

Kathleen M. Myers, M.D., *University of Washington, Seattle, Washington,* Normal Development

Thomas F. Nagy, Ph.D., *Stanford University School of Medicine, Stanford, California,* The Ethical Principles of Psychologists and Code of Conduct (1992 Revision)

Terri L. Needles, Ph.D., *Forest Institute of Professional Psychology, Honolulu, Hawaii,* Feminist Therapy II

Arthur Nelson, M.D., *Private Practice, New York, New York,* Orgone Therapy

David G. Nickinovich, Ph.D., *University of Washington, Seattle, Washington,* Causal Reasoning; Cohort Differences; Metaanalysis; Structural Equation Modeling

Rafael Nuñez, Ph.D., *University of Mexico, Cholula, Puebla, Mexico,* Fromm's Theory

J. Nuttin, Ph.D., *University of Leuven, Louvain, Belgium,* Task

Michael S. Nystul, Ph.D., *Eastern New Mexico University, Portales, New Mexico,* Single Parenthood; Transcendental Meditation

William H. O'Brien, Ph.D., *Bowling Green State University, Bowling Green, Ohio,* Functional Analysis; Medical Model of Psychotherapy

Ruth Ochroch, Ph.D., *New York University, New York, New York,* Minimal Brain Dysfunction (Diagnosis); Minimal Brain Dysfunction (Intervention)

Walter E. O'Connell, Ph.D., *Retired, Houston, Texas,* Humor

Merle H. Ohlsen, Ph.D., *Indiana State University, Terre Haute, Indiana,* Marriage Counseling in Groups

Laurel W. Oliver, Ph.D., *U.S. Army Research Institute, Alexandria, Virginia,* Military Psychology

Marlene Oscar-Berman, Ph.D., *Boston University Medical Center, Boston, Massachusetts,* Brain; Brain Injuries; Central Nervous System Disorders; Psychosurgery

Charles E. Osgood, Ph.D., *University of Illinois, Urbana, Illinois,* Grit

Samuel H. Osipow, Ph.D., *Ohio State University, Columbus, Ohio,* Career Counseling; Dictionary of Occupational Titles; Occupational Interests

Thomas Ostrom, Ph.D., *Ohio State University, Columbus, Ohio,* Attitude Measurement; Attitude Theory; Impression Formation; Social Cognition

J. Bruce Overmier, Ph.D., *University of Minnesota, Minneapolis, Minnesota,* Animal Models; Behavioral Inhibition; Models

B. Ozaki-James, M.A., *Honolulu, Hawaii,* Waldorf Education

Richard C. Page, Ph.D., *University of Georgia, Athens, Georgia,* Drug Users' Treatment; Unstructured Therapy Groups

Edward L. Palmer, Ph.D., *Davidson College, Davidson, North Carolina,* Advertising; Applied Research; Consumer Research

Loren D. Pankratz, Ph.D., *University of Oregon, Portland, Oregon,* Diagnoses; Factitious Disorders

Louis V. Paradise, Ph.D., *University of New Orleans, New Orleans, Louisiana,* Academic Achievement Tests; American Council on Education; Classroom Discipline; Graduate Education; National Education Association; Project Talent; School Phobia

Susan M. Parry, Ph.D., *University of North Carolina, Charlotte, North Carolina,* Feminist Therapy I

H. McIlvanie Parsons, Ph.D., *Essex Corporation, Alexandria, Virginia,* Automation; Engineering Psychology; Human Factors

Sandra Paulsen, Ph.D., *University of Hawaii, Honolulu, Hawaii,* Eye Movement Desensitization and Reprocessing

Paul B. Pedersen, Ph.D., *Syracuse University, Syracuse, New York,* Cross-Cultural Counseling; Culture Shock; International Conferences; Multicultural Counseling

Lawrence A. Pervin, Ph.D., *Rutgers University, New Brunswick, New Jersey,* Dynamic Psychology

Donald R. Peterson, Ph.D., *Rutgers University, New Brunswick, New Jersey,* Doctor of Psychology Degree; Schools of Professional Psychology

Charles S. Peyser, Ph.D., *The University of the South, Sewanee, Tennessee,* Pseudopsychology; Psychotherapy Techniques

E. Jerry Phares, Ph.D., *Kansas State University, Manhattan, Kansas,* Incomplete Sentences; Locus of Control; Social Learning Theories

E. Lakin Phillips, Ph.D., *George Washington University, Washington, DC,* Conflict Resolution Therapy; Expressive Arts

Chris Piotrowski, M.A., *University of West Florida, Pensacola, Florida,* Adolescent Sex Offenders

John M. Platt, Ed.D., *Elk Grove School District, Elk Grove, California,* Encouragement

Thomas G. Poplawski, Ph.D., *Private Practice, Northampton, Massachusetts,* Anthroposophy; Camphill Movement

Anthony R. Pratkanis, Ph.D., *University of California, Santa Cruz, California,* Sleeper Effect; Subliminal Influence

Ann B. Pratt, Ph.D., *Capital University, Columbus, Ohio,* Genius; Graduate Record Examinations (GREs); Hypothetical-Deductive Reasoning; Nonverbal Intelligence Tests; Objective Psychology; Vitalism

Robert Alan Prentky, Ph.D., *Brandeis University, Waltham, Massachusetts,* Antisocial Personality; Heritability of Personality; Mental Illness: Early History; Productive Thinking; Taxonomic Systems

N. H. Pronko, Ph.D., *Wichita State University, Wichita, Kansas,* Interbehavioral Psychology; Physiological Psychology (Nonreductionism); Reflex Arc Concept

Anthony Quagliano, Ph.D., *University of Hawaii, Honolulu, Hawaii,* Signs and Symbols

A. I. Rabin, Ph.D., *Michigan State University, East Lansing, Michigan,* Clinical Psychology Graduate Training; Projective Techniques; Wechsler Intelligence Tests

Victor Raimy, Ph.D., *Deceased,* Actualizing Therapy; Autogenic Training; Bioenergetics; Eidetic Psychotherapy; Fixed-Role Therapy; Mainstreaming (Psychotics); Nondirective Psychoanalysis; Primal Therapy; Psychosynthesis

K. Ramakrishna Rao, Ph.D., *Duke University, Durham, North Carolina,* Consciousness; Parapsychology

Julian Rappaport, Ph.D., *University of Illinois, Champaign, Illinois,* Community Psychology

Mark Rapport, Ph.D., *University of Hawaii, Honolulu, Hawaii,* Attention-Deficit Hyperactivity Disorder; Psychostimulant Treatment for Children

Nathaniel J. Raskin, Ph.D., *Northwestern University, Chicago, Illinois,* Client-Centered Therapy; Psychotherapy Research

Herb Reich, M.A., *Private Practice, New York, New York,* Abreaction; z-Score; Zwaademaker Odor System

Daniel Reisberg, Ph.D., *Reed College, Portland, Oregon,* Eyewitness Testimony; Synesthesia; Visual Imagery; Working Memory

Mary E. Reuder, Ph.D., *Queens College, New York, New York,* Field Dependency; Field Theory; Mind–Body Problem; Monism–Dualism; Phrenology; Sin

Cecil R. Reynolds, Ph.D., *Texas A & M University, College Station, Texas,* Crucial Experiments in Psychology; Employment Tests; Group Problem Solving; Race Bias in Testing; Sociodrama

David K. Reynolds, Ph.D., *To Do Institute, Los Angeles, California,* Morita Therapy; Naikan Therapy

Harriet L. Rheingold, Ph.D., *University of North Carolina, Chapel Hill, North Carolina,* Development of Human Social Behavior

George F. Rhoades, Ph.D., *Olo Hou Clinic, Honolulu, Hawaii,* Sadistic Ritualistic Abuse

Edward J. Rickert, Ph.D., *University of Alabama, Birmingham, Alabama,* Behavioral Contrast; Blocking; Contextual Association; Stimulus Generalization; Two-Process Learning Theory

Lynn Ries, Ph.D., *University of Washington, Seattle, Washington,* Social Exchange Theory

Arthur J. Riopelle, Ph.D., *Louisiana State University, Baton Rouge, Louisiana,* Adaptation; Habituation; Imprinting; Instinct; Primate Behavior; Tool Using

Donald Robbins, Ph.D., *Fordham University, New York, New York,* Language in Great Apes; Mathematical Learning Theory

Gary J. Robertson, Ph.D., *American Guidance Service, Circle Pines, Minnesota,* Act Assessment; Bayley Scales of Infant Development (Bayley Scales); Columbia Mental Maturity Scale; Mental Measurements Yearbooks; Merrill–Palmer Scales; Pencil-and-Paper Intelligence Tests; Progressive Matrices (Raven's); Scholastic Aptitude Test; Stanford Achievement Test

Richard J. Robertson, Ph.D., *Northeastern Illinois University, Chicago, Illinois,* Control Theory

George H. Robinson, Ph.D., *University of North Alabama, Florence, Alabama,* Audiometry; Depth Perception; Fechner's Law; Magnitude Estimation; Psychophysical Methods; Psychophysics; Weber's Law

Ronald Roesch, Ph.D., *Blaine, Washington,* Competency to Stand Trial; Psychology and the Law

Carl R. Rogers, Ph.D., *Deceased,* Person-Centered Approach Foundations

Michael Rohrbaugh, Ph.D., *College of William and Mary, Williamsburg, Virginia,* Paradoxical Intervention

Joseph C. Rook, Ph.D., *Castle Rock, Colorado,* Acupuncture; Antidepressive Drugs; Cranial Nerves; Pain

Saul Rosenzweig, Ph.D., *Washington University, St. Louis, Missouri,* Idiodynamics; Rosenzweig Picture–Frustration (P–F) Study

Helen Warren Ross, Ph.D., *San Diego State University, San Diego, California,* Infant Socialization

Joseph R. Royce, Ph.D., *Deceased,* Epistemology, Psychological; Individuality Theory; Molar–Molecular Constructs; Philosophical Problems in Psychology; Systems Theory; Theoretical Psychology

Joseph F. Rychlak, Ph.D., *Loyola University, Chicago, Illinois,* Dialectic; Teleological Psychology

William S. Sahakian, Ph.D., *Deceased,* Infection Theory; Philosophical Psychotherapy

Andrew Salter, B.S., *Private Practice, New York, New York,* Conditioned Reflex Therapy

William Samuel, Ph.D., *California State University, Sacramento, California,* A-Type Personality; B-Type Personality; Conforming Personality; Internalization; Learned Helplessness; Schizoid Personality

John W. Santrock, Ph.D., *University of Texas, Richardson, Texas,* Adolescence; Life-Span Development; Parent–Child Relations; Stepchildren; Stepparents

Edward P. Sarafino, Ph.D., *Trenton State College, Trenton, New Jersey,* Children's Fears; Infant Play Behavior; Personal Space; Rewards and Intrinsic Interest

William I. Sauser, Jr., Ph.D., *Auburn University, Auburn, Alabama,* Allport–Vernon–Lindzey Scale; Critical Incident Technique; Man-to-Man Scale; Thurstone Scaling

Joseph M. Scandura, Ph.D., *University of Pennsylvania, Philadelphia, Pennsylvania,* Instructional Theory; Structural Learning Theory

K. Warner Schaie, Ph.D., *Pennsylvania State University, State College, Pennsylvania,* Adult Intellectual Development; Primary Mental Abilities; Sequential Methods

Candace G. Schau, Ph.D., *University of New Mexico, Albuquerque, New Mexico,* Sex Differences: Developmental; Sex-Role Development

Alice D. Scheuer, Ph.D., *University of Hawaii, Honolulu, Hawaii,* Anhedonia; Paranoia; Peace Psychology

Harold V. Schmitz, Ph.D., *Consolidated Edison Company, New York, New York,* Occupational Clinical Psychologist; Occupational Clinical Psychology; Outplacement Counseling

D. Schuldberg, Clinical Assessment

Julius Seeman, Ph.D., *Vanderbilt University, Nashville, Tennessee,* Personality Integration

Saul B. Sells, Ph.D., *Texas Christian University, Fort Worth, Texas,* Drug Rehabilitation; Employee Attitude Surveys; Factor-Analyzed Personality Questionnaires

James Shanteau, Ph.D., *Kansas State University, Manhattan, Kansas,* Agricultural Psychology; Management Decision Making

Deane H. Shapiro, Jr., Ph.D., *University of California, Irvine, California,* Psychological Health; Self-Control

Kenneth J. Shapiro, Ph.D., *Psyeta, Washington Grove, Maryland,* Ethical Treatment of Animals; Hot Line Services; Rolfing; Temperaments

Marvin E. Shaw, Ph.D., *University of Florida, Gainesville, Florida,* Responsibility and Behavior

Robert A. Shaw, Ph.D., *Brown University, Providence, Rhode Island,* Praise; Reinforcement Schedules; Reinforcers; Self-Fulfilling Prophecies; Tabula Rasa

Anees A. Sheikh, Ph.D., *Marquette University, Milwaukee, Wisconsin,* Mental Imagery

Steven D. Sherrets, Ph.D., *Omaha, Nebraska,* Battered People; Child Abuse; Climate and Personality; Sociobiology; Surrogate Parents (Animals)

Edwin S. Shneidman, Ph.D., *University of California–Los Angeles, School of Medicine, Los Angeles, California,* Make-a-Picture-Story Test; Suicide; Suicide Prevention

Varda Shoham, Ph.D., *University of Arizona, Tucson, Arizona,* Paradoxical Intervention

Bernard H. Shulman, M.D., *Northwestern University Medical School, Chicago, Illinois,* Adlerian Psychotherapy

Miguel Siguan, Ph.D., *University of Barcelona, Barcelona, Spain,* Bilingualism; Psycholinguistics

Elsa M. Siipola, Ph.D., *Smith College, Northampton, Massachusetts,* Bender Gestalt; Holtzman Inkblot Technique; House–Tree–Person Test; Sentence Completion Test; Thematic Apperception Test; Word Association Test

Hirsch Lazaar Silverman, Ph.D., *Private Practice, West Orange, New Jersey,* Geriatric Psychology

Alan Simpkins, Ph.D., *University of Hawaii, Honolulu, Hawaii,* Peabody Picture Vocabulary Test

B. F. Skinner, Ph.D., *Deceased,* Operant Behavior

M. Brewster Smith, Ph.D., *University of California, Santa Cruz, California,* Humanistic Psychology

William Paul Smith, Ph.D., *Vanderbilt University, Nashville, Tennessee,* Conflict Resolution; Distributive Justice; Exchange Theory; Prisoner's Dilemma; Rivalry

Subhash R. Sonnad, Ph.D., *Western Michigan University, Kalamazoo, Michigan,* Gender Role Stress; Naturalistic Observation

E. H. Spain, Epidemiology of Mental Disorders

Arnold R. Spokane, Ph.D., *Lehigh University, Bethlehem, Pennsylvania,* Occupational Adjustment; Occupational Counseling; Work Efficiency; Work-Space Designs

Robert P. Sprafkin, Ph.D., *VA Medical Center, Syracuse, New York,* Social Skills Training

Julian C. Stanley, Ed.D., *Johns Hopkins University, Baltimore, Maryland,* Precocious Mathematical Reasoners

Robert H. Stensrud, Ed.D., *University of Northern Iowa, Cedar Falls, Iowa,* Environmental Stress; Holistic Health; Self-Actualization

Robert M. Stern, Ph.D., *Pennsylvania State University, University Park, Pennsylvania,* Digestive System; Electrodermal Activity; General Adaptation Syndrome; Parasympathetic Nervous System; Sympathetic Nervous System

Gerald L. Stone, Ph.D., *University of Iowa, Iowa City, Iowa,* Counseling

Hugh A. Storrow, M.D., *University of Kentucky, Lexington, Kentucky,* Eating Disorders; Psychosomatics; Respiratory Disorders

Ezra Stotland, Ph.D., *University of Washington, Seattle, Washington,* Empathy; Stress

Richard B. Stuart, D.S.W., *Weight Watchers International, Manhasset, New York,* Human Courtship Patterns; Spouse Selection

David I. Suchman, Ph.D., *University of Florida, Gainesville, Florida,* Optimal Functioning

Norman D. Sundberg, Ph.D., *University of Oregon, Eugene, Oregon,* Biographical Inventories; Boredom; Buffering Hypothesis; Fundamental Attribution Error; Nonverbal Behavior; Trait Psychology; Transpersonal Psychology (I)

Donald E. Super, Ph.D., *Savannah, Georgia,* Career Development

R. J. Sutherland, *The University of Lethbridge, Lethbridge, Alberta, Canada,* Electroencephalography

William S. Sutton, Ph.D., *Bowie State College, Bowie, Maryland,* Consequences, Natural and Logical; Determinism/Indeterminism; Naturwissenschaftliche Psychologie

Thomas Szasz, M.D., *State University of New York, Syracuse, New York,* Myth of Mental Illness

Julian I. Taber, Ph.D., *VA Medical Center, Reno, Nevada,* Gambling Behavior

James T. Tedeschi, Ph.D., *State University of New York, Albany, New York,* Deindividuation; Displacement; Interpersonal Communication; Interpersonal Perception

Alex Thomas, Ph.D., *School Psychologist, Port Clinton, Ohio,* Handicapped (Attitudes Toward); Play Development; School Psychologists; School Readiness

Beverly E. Thorn, Ph.D., *Ohio State University, Columbus, Ohio,* Antianxiety Drugs; Electrical Nervous System Stimulation; Neurosurgery; Pseudohermaphrodism; Sex Chromosome Disorders; Sexual Dysfunction

B. Michael Thorne, Ph.D., *Mississippi State University, Mississippi State, Mississippi,* All-or-None Law; Alzheimer's Disease; Behavioral Toxicology; Food Deprivation; Introversion–Extroversion; Lobotomy; Neurotransmitters; Olfaction; Paradoxical Sleep; Pituitary

Eleanor Reardon Tolson, Ph.D., *University of Washington, Seattle, Washington,* Psychiatric Social Work

Louis G. Tornatzky, Ph.D., *National Science Foundation, Washington, DC,* Ecological Psychology; Field Experimentation; Innovation Processes

William T. Tsushima, Ph.D., *Straub Clinic and Hospital, Honolulu, Hawaii,* Luria–Nebraska Neuropsychological Battery; Minnesota Multiphasic Personality Inventory; Psychosomatic Disorders

Leonard P. Ullmann, Ph.D., *Jacksonville Beach, Florida,* Behavior Modification; Token Economies

Rhoda K. Unger, Ph.D., *Montclair State College, Upper Montclair, New Jersey,* Androgyny; Sex Differences; Sex Roles; Sexism

Susana P. Urbina, Ph.D., *University of North Florida, Jacksonville, Florida,* Amnesia; Attention; Benton Visual Retention Scale; Educational Testing Service; Errors (Type I and II); Pick's Disease

Adrian van Kaam, Ph.D., *Duquesne University, Pittsburgh, Pennsylvania,* Formative Theory of Personality

Rodney D. Vanderploeg, Ph.D., *James A. Haley Veterans Hospital, Tampa, Florida,* Neuropsychological Assessment

Anthony J. Vattano, Ph.D., *University of Illinois, Urbana, Illinois,* GROW; Integrity Groups; Social Casework

Frances E. Vaughan, Ph.D., *California Institute of Transpersonal Psychology, Menlo Park, California,* Transpersonal Psychology (II)

Alan Vaux, Ph.D., *Southern Illinois University, Carbondale, Illinois,* Needs Assessment; Social Interventions; Social Support

Philip E. Vernon, Ph.D., *Deceased,* Biographies

W. Edgar Vinacke, Ph.D., *State University of New York, Buffalo, New York,* Healthy Personality; Independent Personalities; Inner/Outer-Directed Behavior

Rex Alvon Wadham, Ph.D., *Brigham Young University, Provo, Utah,* Marital Interaction Styles; Physics and the Behavioral Sciences

Morton Wagman, Ph.D., *University of Illinois, Urbana, Illinois,* Artificial Intelligence

Edwin E. Wagner, Ph.D., *Forest Institute of Professional Psychology, Huntsville, Alabama,* Hand Test; Internal Validity; Rationalism; Reductionism

Richard D. Walk, Ph.D., *George Washington University, Washington, DC,* Illusions; Perceptual Distortions; Perceptual Organization; Perceptual Style; Perceptual Transactionalism

Patricia M. Wallace, Ph.D., *University of Maryland, Far East Division, Japan,* Aphasia; Autonomic Nervous System; Brain Waves

Susan Frieder Wallock, Ph.D., *John F. Kennedy University, Orinda, California,* East–West Psychology; Gestures; Movement Therapy

Roger Walsh, M.D., Ph.D., *University of California, Irvine, California,* Global Crises; Shamanism; Transpersonal Psychology (II)

Zhong-Ming Wang, Ph.D., *Hangzhou University, Zheijiang, China,* Judgment and Decision Making; Organizational Psychology

Helen H. Watkins, M.A., *University of Montana, Missoula, Montana,* Ego-State Theory and Therapy

John G. Watkins, Ph.D., *University of Montana, Missoula, Montana,* Hypnotherapy; Multiple Personality

Wilse B. Webb, Ph.D., *University of Florida, Gainesville, Florida,* Ancient Theories of Dreams; Sleep; Theories of Sleep

Danny Wedding, Ph.D., *Missouri Institute of Mental Health, St. Louis, Missouri,* Computed Tomography; Halstead–Reitan Battery

Joel Lee Weinberger, Ph.D., *Adelphi University, Garden City, New Jersey,* Psychotherapy: Common Factors; Subliminal Psychodynamic Activation

Arnold D. Well, Ph.D., *University of Massachusetts, Amherst, Massachusetts,* Analysis of Covariance; Analysis of Variance; Central Tendency Measures; Correlation and Regression; Factorial Designs; Nonparametric Statistical Tests

W. W. Wenrich, Ph.D., *North Texas State University, Denton, Texas,* Brief Therapy; Hypertension; Muscle Relaxation

Michael Wertheimer, Ph.D., *University of Colorado, Boulder, Colorado,* Isomorphism; Topological Psychology

Donald L. Wertlieb, Ph.D., *Tufts University, Medford, Massachusetts,* Affective Development; Early Childhood Development; Handicaps; Health Psychology; Hyperactivity; Libido

Malcolm R. Westcott, Ph.D., *York University, Toronto, Ontario, Canada,* Freedom; Intuition

Ian Q. Whishaw, Ph.D., *University of Lethbridge, Lethbridge, Alberta, Canada,* Animal Hypnosis; Decortication; Electroencephalography

Erika Wick, Ph.D., *St. John's University, New York, New York,* Adopted Children; Fantasy; Somatopsychics

Delos Wickens, Ph.D., *Ohio State University, Columbus, Ohio,* Classical Conditioning

Douglas A. Williams, *University of Winnipeg, Manitoba, Canada,* Behavioral Inhibition

Richard H. Willis, Ph.D., *University of Pittsburgh, Pittsburgh, Pennsylvania,* Surprise

Charles Winick, Ph.D., *City University of New York, New York, New York,* Fads and Fashions; Propaganda

Michael L. Woodruff, Ph.D., *East Tennessee State University, Johnson City, Tennessee,* Acetylcholinesterase; Action Potential; Adrenal Glands; Encopresis; Eye; Glands and Behavior; Limbic System; Reflexes; Reticular Activating System; Tranquilizing Drugs

Ruth C. Wylie, Ph.D., *Goucher College, Towson, Maryland,* Self-Concept

Sylvia Yuen, Ph.D., *University of Hawaii, Honolulu, Hawaii,* Job Status, Racial Differences

O. L. Zangwill, Ph.D., *University of Cambridge, Cambridge, England,* Biography

R. W. Zaslow, Ph.D., *Deceased,* Bonding and Attachment; Myths; Z-Process

Reni Zazzo, Ph.D., *Retired, Paris, France,* Biography

Daniel J. Ziegler, Ph.D., *Villanova University, Villanova, Pennsylvania,* Pedophilia; Psychoanalytic Stages; Sexual Deviations; Transsexualism; Transvestism

Marvin Zuckerman, Ph.D., *University of Delaware, Newark, Delaware,* Sensation Seeking

FOREWORD

In the foreword to the first edition of the *Concise Encyclopedia of Psychology,* published in 1987, Hans J. Eysenck wrote: "The authors are exceptionally knowledgeable, the editing is impeccable, and overall, of all one-volume compendiums of psychology, this is undubitably the book of choice." The second edition of the encyclopedia continues the tradition of excellence established in the first and extends it to a higher level of quality and distinction.

The second edition has set new standards that will be hard to match. The publishing experience of Raymond J. Corsini and the scholarly contributions of Alan Auerbach are immediately apparent in both the comprehensive scope of the entries and the crisp, yet detailed, writing that characterizes them. Psychology owes Auerbach and Corsini a debt of gratitude for summarizing and defining the current state of knowledge in this expanding and influential discipline that is constantly achieving new levels of scientific and professional insight and application.

The *Concise Encyclopedia of Psychology* contains abbreviated versions of most of the entries of the four-volume encyclopedia, having lost only historical entries and some biographies, while maintaining the clarity, scope, and depth of coverage that resulted in The American Library Association naming the first edition "Reference Book of the Year." It is indeed remarkable how easily the concise version reads from "Abreac-tion" to "Zwaardemaker Odor System." From A to Z, readers will find themselves turning page after page with the delight that accompanies both the discovery and affirmation of knowledge.

Since the first edition of the *Concise Encyclopedia of Psychology* was published, psychology has entered a new era of theory, research, and practice. There are new faces, new thoughts, and enduring issues. Readers of the second edition will find it all here: new, updated, and revised entries that capture the challenge, progress, and tradition of psychology's past and present. There is little more that can be asked. The entries are authoritative, the coverage is comprehensive, and the exposition is clear.

As the field of psychology enters the dawn of a new century, the *Concise Encyclopedia of Psychology* will continue to be the standard desktop reference for psychologists and others seeking definitive statements on virtually every aspect of the field. It should be found on the desk of serious students, scholars, and others seeking an understanding of the myriad of terms, concepts, and people that comprise the contemporary discourse community of psychology.

ANTHONY J. MARSELLA, PH.D.
Honolulu, Hawaii

PREFACE

In a world of burgeoning psychological research accessible by electronic search machines, we wanted to add another traditional book—a volume that balances erudition and clarity, depth and compactness, breadth and focus, and currentness and classicism. In this book, we wanted to serve all those interested in psychology, from the layperson and neophyte student to the professional researcher and practitioner. In this second edition, we took inspiration from Albert Ellis, who had told one of us (R. C.) that he read the entire first concise edition to refresh his global understanding of psychology, and from Alan Hess, who said, "I keep the four-volume on my shelf and the *Concise* on my desk."

Through careful editing of the four-volume second edition of the *Encyclopedia of Psychology,* we retained more than 95% of the entries and an estimated 80% of the contents. As encyclopedias, more than other books, are expected to endure, we respected the authors' emphasis on historical precedent and on landmark or classic work. Recent works are not ignored (indeed, we updated a number of entries), but we were mindful of their not having stood the test of time; and given our academic experience (more than 80 years between us), we know that today's revelation may become yesterday's fad.

Of all the social sciences, psychology is the one that attracts the most research, study, and public interest. Hence, the many consumers of psychological information deserve a modestly priced, authoritative, single-volume source for much of the material they seek. We hope that this book will be such a source, well into the 2000s.

RAYMOND J. CORSINI AND ALAN J. AUERBACH
Honolulu, Hawaii and Waterloo, Ontario, Canada
March 1996

ACKNOWLEDGMENTS

A work of 1.2 million words is not a one- or even a two-person undertaking. The counsel of Rosemary C. Adams-Terem, Eugene E. Landy, Anthony J. Marsella, and Neal Pinckney was indispensable, as was the condensing work of Robert W. Lundin, Danny Wedding, and associate editor Mary Beth Leisen.

We are most indebted to Becky Ozaki for her editorial help and to John Wiley staffers Herb Reich (senior editor, now retired), Jo Ann Miller (executive editor), and Mintrue Gonzalez (editorial assistant). The indexing team included Krystyna Felczak and Martina Zalac.

Our wives, Kleona Rigney, M.D., and Trudy Trudel, M.A., respectively, advised on medical matters and supervised the indexing. Besides being tolerant, supportive, and always helpful, they provided the *most* essential of contemporary services: Sometimes only they—computer experts both—could uncrash our equipment!

HOW TO USE THIS ENCYCLOPEDIA

This encyclopedia has four distinct parts:

1. The front matter contains a list of all contributors and the topics they have written on, a foreword by Dr. Anthony Marsella, and our preface, which provides information on, and our intentions for, this book.

2. Entries, the main part of this book, include almost 1000 pages of articles condensed from the full four-volume encyclopedia. We re-moved a number of items of historical interest that can be read in their entirety in the full version. Virtually all entries end in cross-references to other entries in the volume.

3. Biographies, summarizing major contributions of the 1000 psychologists who had been nominated for inclusion by historians William Sahakian, Robert Lundin, and Parker Lichtenstein.

4. Name and subject indexes that permit easy location of topics or names within the 2000-odd entries.

A

ABREACTION

The term *abreaction* was first used in psychoanalytic literature by Joseph Breuer and Sigmund Freud in their *Studies in hysteria.* According to Clara Thompson, Freud "established abreaction through free association as a means of undoing the process of repression." It is now recognized, however, that abreactions can also occur in hypnosis, either spontaneously or with guidance, or be drug induced.

The beneficial consequence of rediscovering the submerged memory is probably due to the release of the pent-up emotional content of the memory that had never been fully expressed or recognized but that, nevertheless, affects the person's thinking and behavior. The discharge of affect is probably an epiphenomenon, because most certainly the cognitive element is more important in leading to changes in thought and behavior than the emotional reaction. By bringing previously repressed and unknown conflicts to consciousness the problem is, in the terms of psychoanalytic theory, "worked through" (i.e., the patient in reliving the experience is freed from the "strangled" emotion).

Abreaction is ordinarily thought of as a part of the more general phenomenon of catharsis. Some authorities equate the two terms, others reserve *catharsis* for the process and *abreaction* for the result. Various interpretations of the place of abreaction in psychotherapy have spawned a variety of methodologies among psychotherapeutic innovators that attempt to achieve abreactive effects. Among them are the primal therapy of Arthur Janov and J. L. Moreno's psychodrama.

CATHARSIS
EMOTIONS
INTROSPECTION
MEMORY
UNCONSCIOUS

H. REICH

ABSTRACT INTELLIGENCE

Nearly all persons use classificatory schemes to reduce, clarify, and adjust to environmental and interpersonal events. To develop such schemes, it is necessary to search for similarities in meaning among some elements. Most people would recognize that an apple and a banana are alike because they are both fruit. This process of developing classificatory schemata is referred to as abstract reasoning or abstract intelligence.

Abstract reasoning is measured and evaluated in a number of ways. On the Stanford–Binet Intelligence Scale, the examinee is read a short passage and then asked to reconstruct in consecutive order its main thoughts. It is believed that the key element in this task is the subject's ability to comprehend the "drift" of an abstract passage. Other methods include the Similarities subtest of the Wechsler Adult Intelligence Scale, which requires the examinee to state how pairs of items are "alike," and the Object Sorting Test of the Goldstein–Scheerer Battery, which assesses abstraction by determining, for example, whether objects are sorted on the basis of color or shape (concrete) or function (abstract).

CLINICAL ASSESSMENT
INTELLIGENCE MEASURES
TESTING METHODS

M. P. MALONEY

ACADEMIC ABILITY GROUPING

The practice of organizing students within a grade or subject area into subgroups according to ability was initiated in the 1920s and has since been referred to as ability grouping. Developments in intelligence testing and the widespread use of aptitude measures undoubtedly contributed to the introduction of this practice. Since its initiation, the merits and demerits of ability grouping have been vigorously debated.

As of 1926, nearly 90% of elementary schools in cities with populations of 100,000 or more used some form of ability grouping. Toward the end of the 1930s, proponents of progressive education began to voice their objections to this "stigmatizing" practice and in part effected a temporary decrease in its use between the early 1940s and mid-1950s. However, an increase in the use of ability grouping was observed shortly thereafter.

The most definitive evaluation, made by a task force commissioned and funded by the U. S. Office of Education in 1969, reviewed research studies published between 1920 and 1970, as well as questionnaire responses. Among the findings and conclusions were the following:

1. On the basis of two surveys conducted in the late 1960s and early 1970s, approximately 77% of the country's school districts used some form of ability grouping; furthermore, many respondents expressed an intention to increase the use of this practice.

2. The use of ability grouping was positively correlated with size of school district and grade level and was widely endorsed by teachers and administrators.

3. Barely 37% of the teachers expressed a preference for teaching low-ability students over average-ability, high-ability, or mixed groups.

4. High socioeconomic groups and Whites were overrepresented in high-ability groups.

5. Some research studies provided evidence of increased scholastic achievement among high-ability students because of grouping, but few studies showed similar trends for average- and low-ability groups.

6. Ability grouping tended to increase the self-concept of students assigned to high-ability groups and lower the self-concept of those assigned to low-ability groups. Furthermore, the deficits associated with low self-concept appeared to be most observable among students of low socioeconomic status and minority groups.

The task force recommended the development of alternatives to ability grouping. But even before the final report was released, federally funded research and development centers were engaged in designing, developing, and exploring just such alternatives. The objectives of pacing, sequencing, and tailoring instruction in accordance with the ability and achievement level of the learner will undoubtedly always be judged as psychologically and pedagogically sound. It is the *methods* by which these objectives are attained, and the social, cognitive, and psychological effects of such methods, that may occupy researchers and educators indefinitely.

Individualized instruction appears to be slowly replacing ability grouping. The extent to which this occurs in the years ahead is likely to depend on the ability of researchers and curriculum developers to identify effective, efficient, and economic processes and products for individualized instruction. Implementing such programs has proven difficult, and the end results have been less than fully satisfying. Individualized instruction as presently conceptualized overlooks the need for and potential of student interaction. Elimination of the social dimensions of learning could prove to be as unsatisfactory as the clustering and stigmatizing of students by ability.

ACADEMIC SUCCESS AND GROUPINGS
LEARNING SCHEDULES

M. M. CLIFFORD

ACADEMIC ACHIEVEMENT TESTS

Academic achievement tests are designed to measure the specific effects of a program of study. Generally, they represent the terminal evaluation of what was learned or accomplished by the student. For example, a final examination taken by students after completing a course in algebra would be considered an achievement test. There is some confusion between academic achievement tests and academic aptitude tests. The latter are defined as tests to measure what students have learned across a cumulative area, so that predictions concerning their future performance can be made.

There are two general types of academic achievement tests in use: standardized academic achievement tests and teacher-made tests. A standardized test is meant to be given under the same conditions—as for instance the time allowed to everyone who takes it—so that scores can be compared across groups of test takers. Considerable time and expertise go into the development of standardized tests, making a variety of information and comparisons available to the testing personnel. In contrast, the teacher-made test is developed by the teacher to measure the achievement of the instruction objectives to be accomplished by the unit of instruction. Here the questions are based on the material taught, so as to determine how well the student has learned. While teacher-made tests are common in education and serve an irreplaceable function, standardized testing at times provides accurate and meaningful comparisons between students and the instruction they receive.

Most school systems utilize some form of general academic achievement test batteries throughout the elementary and secondary school years. The most widely used achievement test batteries focus on educational skills and knowledge of content such as reading, arithmetic, language usage, and work-study skills. Many tests are available to measure general educational achievement or specific course subject matter. Careful critiques and evaluations of the major published tests of academic achievement can be found in O. K. Buros' *Mental measurements yearbooks.* At the college level, the College Board's Advanced Placement Program develops academic achievement tests in a variety of subject-matter fields to help students gain admission to college with advanced standing in one or more subject areas. Also, the College Board's College-Level Examination Program facilitates the granting of college credit by examination of college-level education acquired through independent study and other nontraditional means.

Another approach to academic achievement testing is criterion-referenced testing, which, though comparatively new, is gaining in usage for assessing educational achievement. Essentially, a criterion-referenced test indicates at what level an individual is able to perform. The items in a criterion-referenced test are directly keyed to specific educational objectives to be accomplished in the instruction. Thus, the score on the test would reflect what the test taker has specifically achieved. This is similar to the purpose underlying teacher-made tests. However, there is considerably greater specificity in linking the educational objectives of the instruction to the subsequent measure of their achievement. Often a minimum level of achievement is specified, but rather than designate this by some arbitrary score such as 70%, it is identified by the minimum competency level judged to be acceptable. The growing importance that school systems are placing on minimum levels of competency to complete a particular grade or be awarded a high school diploma has further advanced the development of criterion-referenced testing.

ACADEMIC UNDERACHIEVERS
EDUCATIONAL ASSESSMENT

L. V. PARADISE

ACADEMIC APTITUDE TESTS

There are many types of academic aptitude tests. Global tests, such as measures of intelligence, assess a wide variety of cognitive capabilities and predict, in a general way, degree of success in most academic pursuits. Specific tests, however, predict degree of success in more limited areas, such as mathematics, music, English, or art, and are appropriate for making placements in these areas.

Aptitude tests frequently have broader coverage than achievement tests, but very often it is difficult to distinguish the tests on the basis of specific items. The primary difference is in purpose: Aptitude tests predict learning, whereas achievement tests assess past learning and present knowledge. Confusion is understandable since many achievement tests predict subsequent learning better than some aptitude tests, especially when the predicted achievement is in a narrowly defined area. According to Anne Anastasi in *Psychological testing* and Lee Cronbach in *Essentials of psychological testing,* the difference between aptitude and achievement tests can be represented on a continuum from specific, school-focused achievements (e.g., teacher-made tests) to general capabilities (e.g., intelligence). Aptitude tests such as the Scholastic Aptitude Test (SAT) and the Graduate Record Examination (GRE) would fall in the middle.

RELIABILITY AND VALIDITY OF APTITUDE TESTS

Aptitude tests should possess particular types of validity and reliability. It is essential that an aptitude test demonstrate predictive validity, that is, the extent to which test scores can predict a given criterion. Thus aptitude test scores are used not to determine performance on the items, but rather to predict a relevant criterion (e.g., the Miller Analogies Test might be used to predict graduate school success). Generally, correlation coefficients are used to describe the predictive relationship, and correlations of .40 to .50 are considered acceptable. For some aptitude tests, especially general tests of intelligence such as the Stanford–Binet, it is also desirable to have construct validity.

IQ TESTS

In 1917 the U.S. War Department, with the assistance of the American Psychological Association, developed and administered group intelligence tests called Army Alpha and Army Beta. These tests could be administered to a large number of individuals at one time and proved helpful in selecting commissioned and noncommissioned officers. Many other group intelligence tests were developed for school use following the same pattern as the Army Alpha.

When intelligence test scores of a large group of children are graphed to show the frequency of each score, the result is a bell-shaped normal curve. The mean, or average score, is always 100, and the standard deviation is about 15. Children who score less than 70 (lower 2% of population) may be diagnosed as mentally retarded, while scores higher than 130 (upper 2% of population) are sometimes placed in the gifted category.

MULTIFACTOR APTITUDE TESTS

Multifactor aptitude tests contain a number of subtests that measure different aptitudes. The subtests assess a wider range of aptitudes than is found in the IQ test. The results can be useful in vocational and educational counseling. The entire battery of tests is standardized on the same individuals, which permits comparisons across subtests and the identification of relatively strong and weak aptitudes.

One of the most widely used multiple aptitude batteries is the Differential Aptitude Test (DAT). The DAT has eight subtests: verbal reasoning, numerical ability, abstract reasoning, clerical speed and accuracy, mechanical reasoning, space relations, spelling, and language usage. The verbal reasoning and numerical ability subtests are combined to give a score comparable to a Wechsler Intelligence Scale for Children—Revised (WISC-R) or Stanford–Binet general IQ score. The DAT is used in grade 8 or 9 to provide relevant information to students as they plan for future education.

Other multifactor aptitude tests include the U. S. Employment Service General Aptitude Battery (GATB), which has 12 tests and reports 9 scores; the Armed Services Vocational Aptitude Battery (ASVAB); the Nonreading Aptitude Test (NATB); the Comprehensive Ability Battery; the Guilford–Zimmermann Aptitude Battery; the International Primary Factors Test Battery; the Metropolitan Readiness Tests; and the Boehm Test of Basic Concepts (BTBC).

Specific aptitude tests are available to predict success in such areas as clerical and stenographic aptitude, vision and learning, vision and hearing, mechanical aptitude, musical and artistic aptitudes, and creativity. Aptitude tests that are used for selection into a course of study or profession include the Scholastic Aptitude Test (SAT), the American College Testing Program Test Battery (ACT), the Law School Admissions Test (LSAT), and the Medical College Admissions Test (MCAT).

Knowledge of aptitude test scores may assist teachers in forming realistic expectations for students and in individualizing learning experiences. Comparing aptitude with achievement scores can identify discrepancies that suggest attention to either learner or instructional inadequacies. In vocational counseling, aptitude tests help point out differential aptitudes and compare relative strengths to skills required in different vocations. The results also help counselors to diagnose the reasons for student misbehavior. For example, an IQ test may indicate that a child is bored or frustrated in a class.

Perhaps the most important use of aptitude tests involves selection, classification, and placement. Aptitude tests are used to determine whether a child is mentally retarded. In situations where only a limited number of students may be admitted from a large group of applicants, aptitude tests provide a common basis of comparison for all students; in conjunction with other information, the scores are used to decide which students will be admitted.

APTITUDE TESTING
CLINICAL/STATISTICAL PREDICTION
COLLEGE ACADEMIC PREDICTION
DIFFERENTIAL APTITUDE TESTS
PENCIL AND PAPER IQ TESTS

J. H. McMILLAN

ACADEMIC SUCCESS AND GROUPING

Since neither the policy of entering children in school chiefly on the basis of their chronological age, nor the policy of allowing highly intelligent children to start school early, seemed to guarantee school success, a new criterion for readiness was sought. Largely due to the work of Dr. Frances L. Ilg, a policy was proposed that by the 1970s had been rather widely accepted. This was that children should be started in school, and subsequently promoted, on the basis of their behavioral age rather than of their chronological age or their mental age as based on tests.

This notion came directly from clinical practice. In the 1950s it was observed that almost 100% of the boys and girls referred to the Gesell

Institute clinical service because of school difficulties were overplaced in school. This led investigators to ask if this unusual amount of overplacement occurred mostly among children who were in trouble enough that their parents brought them to a clinical service. If one checked the behavior age of children in an ordinary middle-class public school, would one also find that many of the boys and girls were in a grade that fit their chronological age but was too advanced for their actual behavior age or developmental level?

Research was carried out at the Hurlbutt School in Weston, Connecticut, over a 3-year period during the 1950s. All kindergarten, first-grade, and second-grade children were examined to determine (a) How many, if any, of these children were "ready" for the work of the grade to which their chronological age and the law assigned them? (b) Did immature or unready children catch up as time went on? and (c) On the basis of a 20-minute readiness test in the fall of a given year, to what extent could faculty predict those children who by the end of the school year would fail the grade and thus be unready for promotion?

Gesell Institute staff have trained psychologists and educators in giving the tests and have helped school systems to set up so-called Developmental Placement Programs. In carrying out a Developmental Placement Program, a school gives a brief (about 10-minute) Gesell Developmental Examination to all children old enough chronologically to enter kindergarten. Those fully up to their age *in behavior* are entered into kindergarten with the presumption that they will go into first grade the following year. Less mature boys and girls are put into a prekindergarten, with the assumption that they will spend 2 years in kindergarten. There will in all likelihood be some children so immature that they may need to wait an additional year before starting school. In such a program it is also recommended that the school provide a prefirst grade. Thus some of the more immature children spend 3 years in the school setting before getting to the full first grade.

Developmental placement programs in various school systems throughout the country have proved successful from several points of view. They can sharply reduce the number of children who need remedial help.

Developmental placement can also increase reading level in a group. In Garden Grove, California, one year's first graders were used as a control group while the next year all kindergarten children were placed developmentally. In first grade, 65% of the control group had read below grade level in contrast to only 8% of the developmentally placed children.

In Convall, New Hampshire, a check on the actual school success of 300 children evaluated on the Gesell scale as ready or not ready to begin kindergarten showed that, of those who later needed to repeat the grade, only 3% had been judged by Gesell as ready, while 56% had been judged as unready. An Oklahoma study showed that the mean rating on the Metropolitan tests of the 1979 kindergarten class, in which the children had been entered on the basis of birthday age, was 40.21. The mean rating for the next year's class, which had been grouped on the basis of behavior age, was 64.44.

The Gesell Institute experience indicates that being certain that each child is developmentally ready for the school situation can prevent unreasonable and unnecessary failure.

ACADEMIC ABILITY GROUPINGS
ACADEMIC UNDERACHIEVERS

L. B. AMES

ACADEMIC UNDERACHIEVEMENT

Underachievement is the attainment of a level of performance below an expected or predicted level. Traditionally, IQ measures have been used to predict a level of achievement, and standardized achievement tests, to establish the criterion. A discrepancy of some stated magnitude expressed in standard scores frequently has served as the operational definition of underachievement for both research and field-classification activities.

The primary purpose of identifying underachievers is to enable instructors to tailor and target instruction to reduce or eliminate underachieving. The definition as well as the rationale associated with underachievement appears simple, sound, and practical. A more critical examination, however, reveals numerous problems.

R. L. Thorndike suggested that underachievement can theoretically be viewed as a reflection of a system's inability to make accurate predictions; perfect predictions of achievement would, after all, preclude discrepancies and eliminate underachievement as well as overachievement. Aptitude–achievement discrepancies that serve as indices of under- and overachievement are explained by Thorndike in terms of four major factors:

1. *Errors of measurement.* A student's performance on both the criterion and predictor variable may produce two scores or composites on one day, and two different scores or composites the following day.

2. *Heterogeneity of criterion.* Performance on teacher-made tests, grade-point average, course grades, and rank in class are all indicators of academic achievement and, as such, constitute potential criteria to be used in determining underachievement. However a grade of B, a GPA of 3.26, and a class ranking will have very different meanings, depending on the group of students and the teacher involved.

3. *Scope of predictors.* Preoccupation with IQ and other scholastic aptitude measures has handicapped educators in diagnosing and responding to underachievement problems. They must identify other stable factors related to aptitude-achievement discrepancies and thereby increase the validity of our predictors.

4. *Manipulate variables.* Some percentage of school underachievement can be eliminated by making changes in students' environments. Changes in texts, teachers, seating, or form of feedback may reduce underachievement.

Farquhar and Payne evaluated techniques commonly used to identify under- and overachievers. They concluded that there were four primary and distinctive categories into which these techniques could be classified:

1. *Central tendency splits.* These methods dichotomize a distribution of combined aptitude and achievement scores.

2. *Arbitrary partitioning.* This technique contrasts extreme groups and eliminates the central part of a distribution.

3. *Relative discrepancy splits.* Here a comparison is made of individuals' ranks on an aptitude measure and achievement measure (grade-point average).

4. *Regression.* This approach measures the discrepancy between actual and predicted achievement when the latter is determined from an aptitude measure.

Although Thorndike facetiously suggested that we might even wish to relabel the phenomena of under- and overachievement as "over- and underintelligence," respectively, there was no intimation in his treatise that the concept of under achievement had outlived its usefulness.

ACADEMIC ACHIEVEMENT TESTS
EDUCATIONAL ASSESSMENT
HUMAN INTELLIGENCE
LEARNING OUTCOMES
SCHOOL LEARNING

M. M. CLIFFORD

ACCIDENT PRONENESS AND PREVENTION

Accidents are a major cause of death, acute hospitalization, and incapacitation among all age groups. Studies in psychology have tended to focus upon three areas in which accidents are of particular concern: accidents in childhood and adolescence, accidents in occupational settings, and accidents associated with motor vehicles. The National Center for Health Statistics, in their publication *U.S. national health survey,* and Marc Lalonde, in *A new perspective on the health of Canadians,* indicate that accidents are a major cause of death among individuals between the ages of 5 and 19 years. Accidents account for the majority of acute hospitalizations, emergency room visits, and physician visits for this age group. Similar statistics suggest that accidents are a prominent cause of death, acute hospitalization, and incapacity among members of the labor force. In the occupational sphere, accidents are significant in both human terms and lost productivity. In the Lalonde report, accidents associated with motor vehicles account for a significant proportion of deaths and acute hospitalizations in all age groups prior to 50 years of age. Given the pervasive impact of accidents on human functioning, it is not unreasonable that psychologists are involved in studies of accident proneness and prevention.

There is some dispute as to who first introduced the term "accident proneness." Bakwin and Bakwin state that the term was first introduced in 1926 by Karl Marbe. A number of other authors have attributed the term to H. F. Dunbar in an article published in 1944. Epidemiological studies have indicated that a small group of individuals tend to have a disproportionately high level of accidents, while the majority of persons have very few. This finding, taken together with the repeated observation that between 80 and 90% of all accidents are due to human error, led to the concept of accident proneness. The assumption was made that those individuals accounting for repeated accidents were accident prone—that is, they possessed a personality trait or traits that predisposed them to have repeated accidents. A number of authors, arguing that the term *accident proneness* lacks precision and tends to be defined differentially by each researcher, have preferred the term *accident repetitiveness,* which indicates that an individual has accidents at a rate greater than chance.

There is considerable disagreement in the literature concerning what trait or traits lead to accident repetitiveness. Traits such as inward-turning aggression, psychological maladjustment, sensation seeking, impulsiveness, and inability to cope with accident-provoking situations have been shown to be associated with accident repetitiveness. Despite considerable research on accident proneness and repetitiveness, results concerning the importance of personality traits in this phenomenon remain inconclusive. As personality theorists have become disenchanted with the trait approach, they have developed models of accident proneness and repetitiveness reflecting an interactional point of view.

The interactional position argues that both long-term and more immediate personal and environmental characteristics contribute to such phenomena as accident repetitiveness. The general models proposed by Moos and Dohrenwend are applicable to accident proneness and repetitiveness. Studies such as those by Whitlock, Stoll, and Rekhdahl, and Mehrabian and Ross, have supported the use of more complex interactional models to explain accident repetitiveness. Another important argument in favor of these more complex models is that they tend to agree with the models developed in the area of accident prevention. For example, Dohrenwend indicates the various remedial activities that can be taken with respect to each factor in her model. Her general analysis is similar to others suggested in the more specific area of accident prevention.

One of the most informative works on accident prevention is an edited book by Margolis and Kroes entitled *The human side of accident prevention.* The book comprises four chapters that develop guidelines to effect safe working conditions and hence prevent accidents in the work environment. The first chapter, by Tuttle, Dachler, and Schneider, presents guidelines developed from the organizational psychology perspective. The authors suggest that facets of organizational objectives and policies, the interface between the job and the individual, group and interpersonal processes, leadership, and feedback systems should all be designed to facilitate safety in the workplace. In short, safety should be an important priority to the organization, and hence should be considered in all aspects of the person/organization interaction. The second chapter, by Grether, presents guidelines predicated in engineering psychology. Specific guidelines relating to work organization, job characteristics and demands, workplace design and layout, task characteristics and demands, and control-display characteristics are presented. The author argues that these various aspects of the work activity should be designed to minimize human-initiated errors. Goldstein's chapter on training outlines a set of guidelines applicable to the development and evaluation of safety training programs. In the final chapter McIntire and White present guidelines developed from a behavior modification orientation that are pertinent to the development and maintenance of safe working conditions. While the guidelines presented in this book are oriented toward occupational settings, they can be easily extrapolated to other settings—the home, leisure activities, and so forth.

A second orientation to accident prevention involves task analysis of accidents and near accidents in order to rectify the conditions that led to the occurrence. Ricketson, Brown, and Graham report the outcome of such a study. They advocate analyzing accidents in terms of what task error occurred, what system inadequacies produced the task error, and hence what remedial measures are necessary to prevent recurrence. Cost-benefit analysis suggested that remedial actions cost only one-tenth the cost of the accidents. F. D. Fowler used a similar methodology to derive recommendations for accident prevention based on a single fatal accident. He recommended that accidents be analyzed using systems analysis in which aspects of the total system are considered rather than the individual parts of the system. A further analytic strategy is advocated by Richter, Gordon, Halamish, and Gribetz, who recommend that accidents be analyzed in terms of three temporal points (precrash, crash, and postcrash) to develop procedures that will either prevent an accident or, should it occur, lessen its impact.

Given the importance of accident prevention, it is evident that this area of research has not received the attention it deserves by psychologists. Early efforts to explain accident repetitiveness as the result of certain accident-prone traits has perhaps hindered rather than enhanced the development of this area. Studies focusing on the interaction of long-term and more immediate environmental and personal factors in accident occurrences are beginning to emerge. Once the relative importance of these factors has been determined, a variety of interventions can be employed to either offset the occurrence of accidents or reduce their impact. Methods derived from organizational development, engineering psychology, instructional psychology, behavior modification, and community psychology are tenable as means of accident prevention.

APPLIED RESEARCH
ERGOPSYCHOMETRY
INDUSTRIAL CONSULTANTS
NOISE EFFECTS
TASK DESIGN
TOOL USING
WORK/SPACE DESIGNS

D. R. EVANS

ACCOMMODATION

VISUAL ACCOMMODATION
Visual accommodation is the automatic adjustment process by which the lens of the eye adjusts to focus on objects at different distances. When the eye is at rest, the *suspensory ligaments* hold the lens firmly in a relatively flattened position. The resting eye is then in a far-point vision position and can focus on objects that are at least 20 feet distant. Light rays passing through the cornea and aqueous humor then enter the pupil of the eye and pass through the lens, after which they pass through the vitreous humor and reach the retina in focus.

For near vision, closer than 20 feet, the *ciliary muscles,* located around and attached to the suspensory ligaments, contract. This causes relaxation of the suspensory ligaments, which then allow the flattened lens, which is elastic and soft, to thicken and bulge. The light rays are thus bent and fall, sharply focused, on the retina. Illumination level has been found to have an effect on accommodation. There have been various theories of the physiological mechanism for accommodation. Bartley notes as most likely the view that the sympathetic nervous system is responsible for a basic tonal background, through vascular innervation. The oculomotor nerve, through increased or decreased innervation, leads to positive and negative accommodation, or specific adjustment for focusing.

NERVE ACCOMMODATION
When a constant stimulus, such as an electric current, is applied to a nerve, the excitability of the nerve under the cathode, or negative electrode, increases quickly. With continued stimulation by current flow, there is a slow decrease in nerve excitability, known as accommodation, followed by a sudden drop when the current is stopped. Following cessation of the stimulating current, the nerve briefly becomes less sensitive to stimulation than it was before the current was turned on.

ACCOMMODATION IN INFANT DEVELOPMENT
The term *accommodation* was also used by Jean Piaget as part of his theoretical view of how infants develop cognitively. Accommodation refers to the infant's modification of concepts or of notions of the world as a response to new experiences or to experiences inconsistent with a previously held notion. *Assimilation* refers to the incorporation into the child's cognitive structure of notions from elements of environmental experience. When an organized cognitive pattern develops through the processes of accommodation and assimilation, a *schema* or *scheme* (pl. *schemata*) is said to have developed. Schemata develop, according to Piaget, during the first 2 years, or *sensorimotor period,* during which the infant develops mainly through sensorimotor activities. Piaget differentiated six stages of sensorimotor development.

ADAPTATION
DEPTH PERCEPTION
EYE
PERCEPTION
PIAGET'S THEORY

B. B. MATES

ACCULTURATION
Acculturation is a process whereby individuals learn about the rules for behavior characteristic of a certain group of people. The term *culture* refers to the way of life of a people and includes the tools or methods with which they extract a livelihood from their environment. It also includes the web of social relations, understandings, and customs, and rules or attitudes about supernatural or supreme beings. These influences on a person's behavior determine ways of thinking, choices, and life goals. Customs and traditions for solving problems are passed from one generation to the next through pathways in the family and in the social institutions of the society.

Culture continues to influence people's lives over the entire life span. Some writers such as Margaret Mead have maintained as she did in *From the south seas* that individuals in the process of acculturation internalize the rules of the culture. Such internalization can have profound and lasting influence even on the physical functioning of people's bodies; it can even affect the traits passed on to the next generation through dictation of choices of mates.

Acculturation has broad meaning as an abstraction. With children, it means that they must conform to the patterns of behavior accepted and valued by the parents. Thus some freedom of choice must be forfeited by the child because of parental cajolery to internalize the prescribed codes of conduct.

Anthropologists see cultural patterns as fixed and as part of the personality. Ruth Benedict in *Patterns of culture* emphasized that human behavior comes to exemplify the culture in which the child grows up. To some degree, therefore, the culture lays out life's destiny and direction: Its ways become the child's ways. Eventually the child and adult see no other way or course of action save that dictated by the culture. An extreme emphasis on the concept allows little belief in individuality or freedom except within cultural rules.

CROSS-CULTURAL PSYCHOLOGY
ENVIRONMENTAL PSYCHOLOGY
ETHNOCENTRISM
GROUP COHESIVENESS
RITES OF PASSAGE
SOCIAL PSYCHOLOGY

T. ALEXANDER

ACETYLCHOLINESTERASE

Acetylcholinesterase (AChE) is a membrane-bound enzyme associated with neurons and synaptic junctions in both the central and peripheral nervous systems. It inactivates the neurotransmitter acetylcholine (ACh) by hydrolyzing it to choline and acetic acid. Its distribution within the brain is assumed to reflect the distribution of acetylcholine containing neurons. Since special stains allow AChE to be seen with the light microscope, this enzyme has been used as a "marker" in the development of neuroanatomic maps of the cholinergic pathways within the brain.

Blockade of the action of AChE leads to an accumulation of ACh at the postjunctional receptor sites. Anti-AChE agents are usually categorized as either reversible or irreversible. Physostigmine (eserine) is the premier example of a reversible agent, while the organophosphates, such as diisopropyl phosphorofluoride (DFP), are irreversible. The organophosphates, initially developed during World War II for their potential in chemical warfare, are deadly poisons and are used primarily as insecticides. However, some of the reversible anti-AChE agents are used both as therapeutic agents and as tools to learn more about brain function. Clinically, physostigmine is used to treat glaucoma. Neostigmine, an anti-AChE compound that does not readily cross the blood-brain barrier, is useful in treating the symptoms of myasthenia gravis, a disorder of ACh production at the neuromuscular junction.

The reversible anti-AChE agents decrease locomotor activity in animals. Conversely, agents that block ACh activity increase locomotor activity, suggesting an inhibitory role for brain ACh in control of locomotion. Administration of AChE inhibitors may also impair acquisition and performance of shock-avoidance tasks and other forms of learned behavior. Finally, AChE inhibitors alter brain electrical activity. For example, physostigmine produces a desynchronized neocortical electroencephalogram and a synchronous theta rhythm within the hippocampus.

BRAIN
CENTRAL NERVOUS SYSTEM
CHEMICAL BRAIN STIMULATION
NEUROCHEMISTRY

M. L. WOODRUFF

ACHIEVEMENT NEED

The most thoroughly studied of the 20 psychological needs identified by H. A. Murray in his seminal study, *Explorations in personality*, is what Murray termed "need achievement." In early research studies, the need to achieve (n Ach) was assumed to be present in any situation marked by competition with a standard of excellence. (The standard of excellence could of course be set by others' performance or by one's own aspirations.) In most of these studies, especially the ones conducted by D. C. McClelland and his associates, n Ach was measured by analyses of stories told by subjects in response to pictures included in or resembling those of the Thematic Apperception Test (TAT). The concurrent validity of the TAT measure was shown by a study in which McClelland and Atkinson found that naval cadets who had been made to "fail" (because of false information given them about their performance on seemingly important tests) introduced more achievement themes in their TAT stories than did members of a control group. The predictive validity of the TAT method was demonstrated by McClelland, who found that college students who made high n Ach scores were more likely to enter entrepreneurial occupations in later years than were students who scored low.

McClelland maintained that the level of economic achievement attained by a society is determined by the way it raises its children. This is the theme of his best-known work, *The achieving society*, in which he maintained that achievement themes identified in such diverse modes of expression as pottery designs, literature, and children's textbooks predicted levels of economic achievement decades later in various countries and cultures, ancient, medieval, and modern. The effect of child-rearing practices can, however, be reversed. McClelland and Winter report field studies conducted in India of businessmen with initially low levels of n Ach who were coached in order to raise their levels of aspiration, and who consequently expanded their business activities and made significant economic contributions to their community.

The work of McClelland and his associates has been criticized on a number of grounds. M. S. Weinstein observed that he, as well as other researchers, found TAT measures to be of low reliability and questionable validity. Maehr and Nicholls objected to the McClelland group's emphasis on personality as a critical variable in determining behavior, to the narrowness of their achievement criteria, and to their failure to obtain significant results regarding achievement motivation in women.

Many researchers have also been unable to find significant relationships between women's n Ach scores and achievement-related variables. Horner suggested that women are likely to believe that ambition is inappropriate for them, especially in fields dominated by men, and that, as a consequence, they are inhibited by a "fear of success." Subsequent research by Sid and Lindgren, however, indicated that fear of success has inhibiting effects on men as well as women.

One reason for researchers' inability to relate n Ach scores to women's achievement may lie in the way n Ach is usually assessed. These measures, both of the TAT and questionnaire type, have typically attempted to cover all components of what has come to be recognized as achievement motivation: task orientation, positive attitudes toward problems and challenges, responsiveness to the Zeigarnik effect, preference for medium-risk ventures (as contrasted with high- or low-risk ventures), competitiveness, and the desire to work independently for self-determined goals rather than for group goals. The unsatisfactory reliability and validity of n Ach measures may be the result of attempting to measure too broad a spectrum of traits. Lindgren proposed that problems inherent in such measures could be bypassed by employing a forced-choice questionnaire in which subjects would be required to choose between achievement-related personal styles and those that were affiliation-related. The rationale for this juxtaposition of factors was found in a number of studies that showed needs for achievement and affiliation to be negatively correlated. Research by Lindgren and by Sadd et al. with the resulting questionnaire reported (a) no significant differences between mean scores of men and women undergraduates, and (b) positive correlations between n Ach scores and academic performance.

The strong emphasis on cognitive psychology that appeared in the 1970s had a marked effect on achievement motivation research. During this period, Maehr and Nicholls pointed out, researchers became interested in subjects' cognitions about the nature of achievement, their purposes in performing achievement-related acts, and their attributions as to causes of outcomes. Cross-cultural studies, for example, turned up both differences and similarities between national cultures and the way in which their members interpreted "success" and "failure" and attributed the antecedents and consequences of success.

By the early 1980s, the question of whether achievement motivation may be appropriately studied as a personality trait or whether it should be studied cognitively had not been resolved, thus personality and cognitive psychologists continued to pursue their separate ways. The earlier questions that had been raised by Weinstein as to whether achievement motivation could be measured, or indeed whether it existed at all, seemed to have been resolved, for research activity in this area actually increased during the 1970s and 1980s. Weinstein's criticism of the reliability of TAT measures may, however, have stimulated the development of questionnaire measures, for the majority of studies of achievement motivation in the 1980s employed this potentially more reliable type of assessment.

AFFILIATION NEED
EXHIBITIONISM
INADEQUATE PERSONALITY
JOB STATUS
LEVEL OF ASPIRATION
OPTIMAL FUNCTIONING

H. C. LINDGREN

ACQUIRED DRIVES

One of the raging controversies in the history of psychology once centered on the aspect of the nature–nurture issue, which asks whether motives are inborn or learned. Some psychologists, of whom William McDougall was the most important, took the instinctivist position that motives are inborn, unlearned, universal within species, and at least to a degree, continuous between species. Other psychologists, for whom John B. Watson was the most important spokesman, argued that motives are acquired through learning and therefore differ from individual to individual, culture to culture, and species to species. As generally with the nature–nurture issue, the intensity of this controversy has lessened with time. It is now clear that all motives are a joint product of biological and environmental forces. If the question is asked at all, it is in terms of the relative importance of these two contributions.

Certain motives, sometimes called *primary drives,* are chiefly biological. Hunger, thirst, pain avoidance, and sex are examples. Even in these cases, however, experience plays a part. Rhythms of feeding and drinking, sensitivity to pain, and preferences in sexual partners are all influenced in this way. Other motives, sometimes called *secondary* or *acquired drives,* are determined primarily by experience, as for instance fears, affection for parents, drug addictions, and functionally autonomous habits such as

miserliness. These examples show something of the variety of acquired drives. They also suggest that different acquired drives may depend on forms of learning that differ at least superficially.

ACQUISITION OF FEAR

One of the forms of learning just referred to is *classical conditioning.* Experimental evidence that some motives are acquired as the result of this process dates at least to the famous study of Watson and Rayner, who conditioned the boy "little Albert" to fear a white rat. The rat (CS) was shown to the child, simultaneously with a loud and unpleasant sound (US) produced by striking a steel bar behind his head. The sound caused the child to cry (UR). After a few repetitions, Albert cried at the sight of the rat (CR), and this fear generalized to other furry objects, such as a fur neckpiece or a Santa Claus mask. Attempts to repeat the Watson and Rayner study were not always successful, and Valentine made the cogent point that fears might be much more easily conditioned to furry objects such as a caterpillar or a rat, than to others such as a pair of opera glasses. In spite of these criticisms, the impact of the Watson and Rayner study on the history of psychology was considerable. It indicated that reactions once thought to be instinctive were more properly seen as the result of learning.

AFFECTIONAL RESPONSES

The young of many species come to treat the first large, moving, noisy object they see as if it were a parent. In most cases this object is in fact a parent, but the process of *imprinting,* as it is called, may produce such attachments to other species and even inanimate objects.

Various lines of evidence indicate that an essential component of imprinted reactions is motivational. The hatchlings of precocial birds, if imprinted on any object, stay near that object and will climb over obstacles to get near it; further, they make distress calls in its absence. The process of learning involved in imprinting bears a strong resemblance to classical conditioning and may be the same thing.

SOCIAL TECHNIQUES

Literature in the area of acquired motivation suggests that some motives may be acquired by a process that is more like instrumental learning. E. C. Tolman has given us an account that is fairly representative. Figure 1 summarizes his view, which holds that, in infancy, the individual has only a set of biological drives. Inevitably these drives are subjected to frustration, and new techniques are developed to satisfy them. Whatever techniques lead to relief from frustration are learned, and they become characteristic of the individual's repertory of responses to the world. As Tolman's drive-conversion diagram (Figure 1) also suggests, these first primitive adjustments achieved by the individual are not adequate to deal with all situations. They too are frustrated, with the result that new learning occurs and the individual's reactions to the world are modified further.

It should be noted that, so far in this account, nothing has been said about motives. Yet a glance at Figure 1 will reveal that several of the social techniques are ones that we often describe in motivational terms. Aggression, hostility, social approval, loyalty, identification, and self-punishment are all terms that probably occur more often in psychological literature in the context of motive than in that of habit. This suggests that there must be some sense in which habits are, or can become, motives. Gordon Allport once suggested in an article that such is the case, and he offered the concept of functional autonomy, whereby well-established habits become ends in themselves—that is, motives. It should be noted, however, that functional autonomy does not explain such effects; it only describes them.

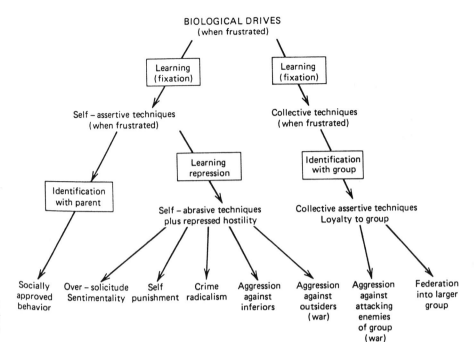

Figure 1. Tolman's drive-conversion diagram. From G. A. Kimble, *Hilgard and Marquis' conditioning and learning,* 1961. Based on E. C. Tolman, *Drives toward war,* 1942.

ADDICTIONS

Addictions to tobacco, alcohol, and other substances are of special interest because they dramatize certain features of the psychology of acquired motivation. The motivational power of the addictions is obvious: Lives have been devoted to, and even lost to, activities performed to support an addiction. Established addictions no doubt represent a change in the physiology of the addicted person, probably a change in how certain neurotransmitters function. But at the same time, addictions are clearly acquired. This testifies to the power that experience may sometimes have over biological processes.

The mechanism of learning an addiction appears to be a two-stage process. In the first stage, the future addict experiments with the addictive substance out of curiosity or a yielding to peer pressure, or for some other reason that soon becomes irrelevant. In the case of some drugs like the opiates, only a few such encounters are required to leave the individual with a powerful craving after the initial euphoria produced by the drug wears off. The only ways to relieve this craving are either painful waiting for the craving to subside or taking more of the substance in question. People who become addicted choose the latter alternative, thus beginning the vicious circle: drug—euphoria—agonized craving—drug again. In abstract terms, the learning process appears to be of the operant or instrumental variety, with the relief from craving and the agony of abstinence playing a greater role than the positively reinforcing euphoric experience initiated by the drug.

MOTIVATION AND EMOTION

The literature on the various acquired drives and drugs provides a particularly straightforward way of making a methodological point. Although common speech and some psychological theories make a distinction between motives and emotions, it is clear that these terms refer to different aspects of the same process. Motivation refers to the power of an acquired drive to promote certain kinds of behavior, chiefly those of reaching certain goals—relief from fear, being near a parent, achieving certain social goals, or avoiding withdrawal symptoms. Emotion refers to the subjective experiences associated with the arousal of these states.

These points are all very nicely integrated in R. L. Solomon's *opponent-process theory* of emotion. The essential ideas in this theory

are the following: (a) the conditions that arouse a motivational/emotional state (State A) also call out a more sluggishly acting opposed state (State B); (b) State B is a "slave" state, which occurs as an inevitable accompaniment of State A; (c) termination of the original emotional circumstances leaves State B as the individual's dominating emotional state; and (d) State B, but not State A, increases with use and decreases with disuse.

Solomon and others have applied this opponent-process theory to many different motivational/emotional reactions. The application provides a rich account of the details of such behavior and a means of understanding the changes in such reactions after many arousals of the emotion. In opiate addiction, for instance, at first the effect of the drug (State A) is a feeling of euphoria, a "rush"; when the drug wears off, its aftereffect (State B) is craving. With continued usage and the strengthening of State B, the effect of the drug is less intense and is often described as a feeling of contentment. Its aftereffect is now much more intense—an excruciatingly painful set of withdrawal symptoms. Similar accounts are put forward for other emotional experiences.

**CLASSICAL CONDITIONING
CONDITIONING
FUNCTIONAL AUTONOMY
HIGHER ORDER CONDITIONING
SPECIFIC HUNGERS**

G. A. KIMBLE

ACT ASSESSMENT

The ACT Assessment is a comprehensive college admissions testing program developed and administered by the American College Testing Program. Three separate measures constitute the program offering: an interest inventory, a student profile, and four academic tests. First administered in 1959, the ACT Assessment is currently completed by more than 1 million students annually.

The ACT Interest Inventory, taken by the candidate at the time of registration for the academic test battery, contains 90 items measuring student preferences in six areas: Science, Creative Arts, Social Service,

Business Contact, Business Detail, and Technical. The Student Profile Section, also completed at the time of registration, is a questionnaire designed to elicit information in five areas: biographical, educational-vocational plans, out-of-class accomplishments, factors influencing college choice, and special needs. Results of the two self-report instruments are integrated with the test results and reported to high schools, colleges, and candidates.

The core of the ACT Assessment is the 2-hour and 40-minute battery of four academic tests: English Usage (75 items, 40 minutes), Mathematics Usage (40 items, 50 minutes), Social Studies Reading (52 items, 35 minutes), and Natural Sciences Reading (52 items, 35 minutes). The academic tests are administered nationally on five different test dates (four dates abroad) in more than 3000 approved test centers. All operational test forms are secure. Standard scores ranging from 1 to 36 are reported for each of the four tests, and a composite summarizing performance on the entire battery. Percentile ranks are available for various reference groups.

An impressive array of research reports are available to colleges requiring the ACT Assessment. For example, percentile ranks are prepared periodically by type of institution, type of students, and geographic region, and for individual colleges. Various expectancy tables and other data designed to predict candidate success in specific institutions are gathered and published regularly. Interpretive information is functionally and attractively packaged. A recent study conducted in 290 colleges requiring the ACT Assessment found median correlations of .50 for ACT test scores alone versus college grades, .50 for self-reported high school grades alone versus college grades, and .58 for ACT test scores combined with self-reported high school grades versus college grades.

ACADEMIC APTITUDE TESTS
APTITUDE TESTING
ATTITUDE MEASUREMENT
COLLEGE ACADEMIC PREDICTION
INTEREST INVENTORIES

G. J. ROBERTSON

ACTION POTENTIAL

The action potential is a self-propagating change in membrane voltage conducted sequentially along the axon of a neuron transmitting information from the neuron cell body to the axon terminal. In the normal flow of neuronal communication, the action potential is initiated as a consequence of summation of local graded potentials in the region where the axon arises from the neuron cell body. This region is called the *axon hillock*. Once initiated at the axon hillock, the action potential will be conducted without change in magnitude along the axon until it invades the axon terminal and causes release of quanta of neurotransmitter molecules.

To understand the action potential it is necessary to begin with an explanation of the voltage difference that exists across the neuronal membrane in the absence of any external influence. This voltage difference is caused by separation of ions by the cell membrane and is known as the resting membrane potential. To record the voltage across the neuronal membrane one microelectrode remains outside the cell while a second penetrates the cell. The voltage potential between the two electrodes is amplified and measured. For most neurons the measured resting membrane potential is from -60 to -70 millivolts (mV); the inside of the cell is negative relative to the outside.

The resting membrane potential is determined by the relative distribution of positively or negatively charged ions near the extracellular and intracellular surface of the cell membrane. Positive sodium (Na^+) and potassium (K^+) ions and negative chloride (Cl^-) and organic (A^-) ions are important for both the resting membrane potential and the action potential. The positively charged ions are called *cations* and the negatively charged ions are called *anions*. The organic anions are mostly proteins and organic acids.

During the resting state, Na^+ and Cl^- have higher extracellular than intracellular concentrations, and K^+ and A^- are more highly concentrated within the cell. The organic anions never leave the intracellular compartment, and in most neurons Cl^- is relatively free to pass through the membrane. Three factors contribute to determining the ionic distribution across the membrane. The first is the relative permeability of the membrane to each ion species. The second factor is the concentration gradient of each ion species, and the third is the electromotive force created by the separation of charges.

Because the inside of the cell is negative relative to the outside and there is a lower intracellular concentration of Na^+, the sodium cations would flood into the cell if the membrane were freely permeable to Na^+. At rest, however, the cell membrane is not freely permeable to Na^+. Permeability of a membrane to any given ion species is controlled by the number of membrane channels available for that particular species. These channels are made of membrane-spanning proteins and may be always open, or nongated, or only open under certain conditions. Channels that open or close depending on conditions are called gated channels. Whether the gated channels are open or closed depends on the conformation of the proteins that form the walls of the channel. When the neuron membrane is at rest there are few open gated channels for Na^+. The Na^+ that does enter the cell flows through the nongated, nonspecific channels in the membrane, but is actively extruded from the cell by the sodium–potassium pump. This pump is made of carrier proteins (compared with channel proteins) and uses metabolic energy to export Na^+ and import K^+. The Na^+–K^+ pump maintains the intracellular and extracellular concentrations of these ions, which are necessary for cell homeostasis and creation of the resting membrane potential. During the resting state, then, Na^+ enters the cell because it has a higher concentration outside than inside, and the electromotive force created by the relative intracellular negativity propels these cations inward. However, few channels through which Na^+ may pass are available and what Na^+ does enter is actively extruded. Potassium cations seek to leave the inside of the cell, following their concentration gradient, but the electromotive force resists this movement. There is a relative lack of open K^+ channels, and many K^+ ions that do leave the cell are returned to the intracellular compartment by the Na^+–K^+ pump. The paucity of open membrane channels for Na^+ and K^+ in the resting state and the Na^+–K^+ pump serve to maintain an excess of extracellular Na^+ and intracellular K^+. The magnitude of the resting membrane potential is thus the result of the degree of separation of these cations and the presence of the organic anions within the cell.

The Na^+ and K^+ channels are of the voltage-gated variety. This means that a change in voltage across the membrane changes the conformation of the channel proteins to either open or close the channel. If the membrane potential becomes more positive (i.e., the membrane depolarizes), Na^+ channels begin to open. Depolarization is caused by flow of ions through channels. On dendrites and cell bodies, channels are open by neurotransmitters released at the synapse from other cells. The neurotransmitters bind to receptors on the target neuron and open chemically gated ion channels. If the neurotransmitter is excitatory, an influx of cations occurs and the postsynaptic membrane depolarizes in the area of the synapse. This depolarization is less than required for generation of an action potential. However, summation at the axon hillock of excitatory postsynaptic potentials (EPSPs) when any hyperpolarizing inhibitory postsynaptic potentials (IPSPs) occur in the same region of the cell at about the same time as the EPSPs may result in an action potential if the summed voltage is a large enough depolarization (about $+10$ mV).

If the depolarization at the axon hillock is about $+10$ mV, voltage-gated Na^+ channels open and Na^+ rushes into the cell. This causes the transmembrane voltage to move rapidly toward the $+55$ mV, which is the voltage when Na⁺ is in concentration equilibrium across the membrane. Electrically, this sudden depolarization caused by the Na⁺ current is the rising phase of the action potential. As the depolarization advances (about 0.5 ms) the Na⁺ channels begin to close and voltage-gated K⁺ channels open. K⁺ leaves the cell, and in combination with decreased Na⁺ conductance, this reverses the depolarization. Because K⁺ rushes from the cell, there is a brief overshoot hyperpolarization before the K⁺ channels close. The hyperpolarization lasts about 2 ms. During the first part of this hyperpolarization the membrane Na⁺ channels will not open and an action potential cannot be generated (absolute refractory period). During the final milliseconds, Na⁺ channels are less able to open and a stronger stimulus is needed to elicit an action potential (relative refractory period). Within 2.5 ms after the peak of the action potential the Na⁺–K⁺ pump has restored the resting Na⁺–K⁺ concentrations and the system is ready for reactivation.

The action potential propagates because the ionic current flow at one point of the membrane causes changes in capacitance current flow in the adjacent membrane toward the axon terminal. The capacitance current flow changes the transmembrane voltage potential and opens Na⁺ channels, and the entire sequence just described begins again. In myelinated axons, the current flow occurs only at the nodes of Ranvier and the action potential jumps from one node to the next (saltatory conduction). This produces more rapid conduction of the nerve action potential than is possible in nonmyelinated axons.

ACETYLCHOLINESTERASE
CENTRAL NERVOUS SYSTEM
NEUROCHEMISTRY
PSYCHOPHYSIOLOGY

M. L. WOODRUFF

ACTION RESEARCH

It is important to distinguish three different meanings denoted by the term *action research*. First, it may be diagnostic research concerning some ongoing aspect of an action process such as community anomie, organizational morale, or group productivity—research focused on action. Second, it designates a procedure of collecting data from the participants of some group system, and then providing feedback about the findings from the data as an intervention to influence, presumably in some helpful way, the ongoing action process of the group. Third, it is a procedure in which the participants in some social system are involved in a data collection process about themselves, and then utilize the data generated to review the facts about themselves in order to take remedial or developmental action.

RESEARCH DIAGNOSIS OF ONGOING ACTION

In social work it is typical for community organization researchers to make survey studies of some aspect of the community and to write up their findings and sometimes their recommendations to the community leaders or agency administrators. In business it is typical for consultants to make studies of organizational morale or productivity, and to prepare the findings and recommendations for the top leadership of the company. In this type of research there is no particular focus on feedback of the findings to the workers in the system as an intervention to influence the social or work process. Typically, the findings are written reports, with one or two copies for the top administrator or chairman of the board or some other part of the leadership system to whom the researchers are accountable.

Kurt Lewin and his students conceptualized and operationalized the other two meanings of action research following the founding of the

Research Center for Group Dynamics at MIT in 1945. At that time there was a great deal of intellectual and operational interest in the processes of feedback. Norbert Wiener, a professor at MIT, developed his system of cybernetics. Also, the field of guided missile research had become active, with its technology of feedback guidance to correct direction toward the goal. Lewin saw the potential applications of these technological developments to the areas of social research and social action.

This was a deliberately planned intervention to influence attitude change through feedback of information. During this period an even more influential development was occurring in the development of the T-Group or Training Group developed at the National Training Laboratory for Group Development at Bethel, Maine. With his collaborators, Bradford, Benne, and Lippitt, Lewin developed a procedure of providing groups with a group process observer who had responsibility for making data available to groups about themselves as they studied their own process and worked on their development in such areas as leadership, decision making, dealing with hidden agendas, opening up communication, improvement of goal setting, and similar phenomena. During one period of this development, each group was provided with two observers. One was a research observer whose responsibility and accountability was to a research director who was carrying on basic research on the group process, while the other was the group process observer whose accountability was to the group and who collected data for them and reported findings only to them.

The conceptualization and reporting of the significance of this type of feedback process led to the program of organizational feedback interventions and studies conducted by Floyd Mann and others under the leadership of Rensis Likert at the University of Michigan. In these experiments a survey of morale and group functioning was conducted and departmental groups in the company were provided with selected feedback of the findings, with trained discussion leaders helping them develop interpretations, implications, and plans for improvement from the findings.

PARTICIPATIVE INVOLVEMENT IN DATA COLLECTION AND FEEDBACK

Social researchers who have been the most interested in creating conditions for personal and social change as a result of data collection and feedback have discovered three advantages to the involvement of group members in the data collection and feedback process. First, the more persons involved in planning and collecting the data, the more they acquire a psychological ownership of the facts and accept their credibility and relevance as intervention for change. Second, data collection by volunteer group members is far more economical. Third, the training of group members to conduct their own research inquiries develops an internal capability for research and development that continues as a resource for the group after external research resources have withdrawn.

In many T-Groups and other types of study groups, the external group process observer has been replaced by a rotating process observer chosen from the group. Usually some type of initial consultation on group observation procedures and feedback techniques has been conducted to build this type of competence into the group and its membership, but from then on the group provides its own data collection feedback resources as part of the ongoing life of the group.

Again, in a study of the attitudes and expectations of parents, pupils, and teachers, three research squads of volunteers were trained to conduct the questionnaires: a team of teachers, a team of parents, and a team of students. Not only did they collect the data effectively, but volunteer squads also worked with the researcher on the analysis of the findings and preparations of feedback charts. But most important, teams of a parent, student, and teacher conducted the feedback sessions in all schools, presenting their findings and leading discussions of the meanings of the results for the improvement of relationships between parents, teachers, and students. The follow up indicated a significant impact of this type of action research procedure.

Finally, in a large community the research focus was on the manner in which children and youth were developed, educated, and treated by all parts of the community. There was need for intensive interviews with large samples of about 800 adults, youth, and children. Within 3 weeks 300 volunteer interviewers were recruited from all age levels, both sexes, and relevant racial and ethnic backgrounds. These volunteers were trained in an intensive 3-hour training session, with role-playing practice, to use the interview schedule and to discover the traps in their own procedures. They then did one trial interview and had a second follow-up training session a week later.

All interviews were collected within a 3-week period with the respondents being interviewed by somebody of the same age, sex, and racial or ethnic characteristics. The interviews were coded by a university research center that indicated that the data were of just as high a quality as the interviews from the national professional interviewing staff.

Several types of feedback sessions were conducted with the findings of the survey. The data "belonged" to the community and had credibility and impact. In one series of six meetings, the 75 influential leaders of the community most involved with determining how children and youth were handled, participated in a series of six sessions to derive implications from the findings and to plan improvement through collaborative action. Also, open sessions were conducted for all those who had participated in the study and for other citizens of the community.

It seems clear that the third meaning of action research is the most sophisticated and the most successful in ensuring the effective linkage between fact finding and fact utilization, which is the most basic purpose of the idea of action research.

COMMUNICATION THEORY
EMPIRICAL RESEARCH METHODS
FIELD RESEARCH
RESEARCH METHODOLOGY

R. LIPPITT

ACT PSYCHOLOGY

The principles of Act Psychology were first set forth by a Catholic priest, Franz Brentano (1838–1917) in a book entitled, *Psychologie vom empirischen Standpunkt* (*Psychology from an empirical standpoint*). Brentano thought psychology should follow the method of empirical observation and separate itself from the philosophical quagmire into which it had fallen under Immanuel Kant, whom Brentano considered to be a mystic. For Brentano, "empirical meant sensory experience with emphasis on activity." He believed that the experience should always directly relate to the object.

Wundt contended that psychology should study the contents of experience (the mind), and the task of the psychologist was to analyze these mental contents into their discrete elements. Brentano objected to this approach and became one of Wundt's severest critics. For Brentano, psychological processes became significant only when they constituted the *acts* of the mind. If one saw the color "red," the color itself was not mental, but the act of "experiencing red" was the significant event.

Brentano identified three classes of acts: (a) ideating, consisting of sensing and imagining; (b) judging, comprising acknowledging, evaluating, and reflecting; and (c) feeling, involving attitudes toward or against an object, as in loving or hating.

Perhaps Act Psychology influenced later psychological systems only in an indirect way. The functionalists of the early twentieth century also

objected to Wundt's elemental analysis of consciousness and stressed psychological activity as a function of the mind. Later, the Gestalt psychologists shared Brentano's objection to a psychology of elemental content.

EMPIRICISM
MIND/BODY PROBLEM
PHENOMENOLOGICAL METHOD
STRUCTURALISM

R. W. LUNDIN

ACTUALIZING THERAPY

This approach is said to be a creative synthesis of a variety of viewpoints about therapy. It puts equal emphasis on thinking, feeling, and the bodily aspects of being. Everett Shostrom, who developed the system with its emphasis on normal human growth, published his most comprehensive book, *Actualizing therapy: Foundations for a scientific ethic,* in 1976.

The goal of this therapy is the achievement of self-actualization rather than curing illness or solving immediate problems. Shostrom states that the polarities of anger–love and strength–weakness are essentially universal values that support personal growth and interpersonal fulfillment when expressed in living. Self-actualization occurs when clients find the strength through therapy to trust their core selves despite negative influences from life.

The techniques employed were drawn from a number of sources. Reflection of feeling attempts to reexpress in fresh words the client's essential attitudes. Reflection of experience attempts to provide feedback in order to expand awareness of the body during therapy. Self-disclosure by the therapist is said to provide a genuine human encounter. Interpretation provides the client with hypotheses about relationships and meanings. In body awareness techniques, clients engage in body exercises that develop contact with anger, love, strength, and weakness. Further techniques used are value clarification, analysis of the client's manipulative behavior patterns, and character analysis. Actualizing therapy has been used most extensively with normal or mildly disturbed persons in either individual or group therapy.

INNOVATIVE PSYCHOTHERAPIES
PSYCHOTHERAPY

V. RAIMY

ACUPUNCTURE

For centuries acupuncture has been used in China as an analgesic, and more recently as an anesthetic. Its original application was for pains of arthritis and gastrointestinal disturbances.

The process involves inserting needles of various lengths to various depths at one or more sites in the body. After insertion, these might be stimulated, left in place, or immediately withdrawn. The history of acupuncture is philosophical rather than anatomic. Traditional Chinese belief is that when the two life forces, *yin* and *yang,* are in disharmony, they create disturbances in nature and disease in man. Human ailments can be treated if the equilibrium of the forces is restored through the needling technique at significant points (meridians) of the body.

Skeptics maintain that acupuncture's effectiveness is psychological and/or hypnotic. However, since the technique has apparently been successful with infants and animals such as horses, and because the relief often continues long after the needling, neither of these explanations seems acceptable.

Probably the most adequate explanation is the gate-control theory. Needling large neural fibers transmits sensory signals that compete with pain signals of small neural fibers, thus "closing the gate." Moreover, portions of the brainstem that have an inhibitory influence on pain transmission are stimulated, thus operating via descending fibers on areas distant from the locus of the needle.

Finally, there is reason to believe that stimulation of this nature facilitates increased levels of endorphins. Much-needed research is currently being initiated that will undoubtedly contribute to a greater understanding of this technique.

PAIN
PSYCHOPHYSIOLOGY

J. C. ROOK

ADAPTATION

Like many other words in psychology, *adaptation* has multiple meanings. At the basis of all the meanings, however, is the concept carried by its Latin root, *adaptare,* to fit.

Among ethologists, who think that characteristic species-typical behaviors are distillations of evolutionary processes, each physical and behavioral characteristic of a species is the product of and contributes to its adaptive radiation, the multiplication of individuals that can survive in the changing environment, and the diversification of the species in a diverse environment. Such adaptation is genetically based and requires numerous generations to be accomplished.

In contrast to this genetic adaptation are phenotypic adaptations, often only seconds in duration, which occur within the life span of an individual. The results of these adaptations are not transmitted to the offspring, although the capacity for such adaptation is. Implicit in the concept is the alteration of an individual by the presence of a persistent, nontoxic or nontraumatic, nonfatiguing stimulus, or by the prolonged cessation and absence of a customary, persistent stimulus, such as weightlessness. Further examples of such adaptation include the gradual diminution in the coldness of water after we immerse our hand in it; the reduction in loudness of a tone after a few seconds; and the return of sight (though colorless) after a period in a darkened room following exposure to bright lights, and the return of comfortable color vision after reexposure to a brightly lighted environment. The mechanisms involved in these examples are all different: stimulus (receptor) failure in the cold; activation of an acoustic reflex (plus receptor change); and bleaching and regeneration of photopigments plus neural change in the retina. In general, scientists tend to think of this kind of adaptation as occurring in or affecting the receptor, whereas the term for a similar phenomenon—*habituation*—is reserved for those situations in which more central events are at least involved if not prominent.

A so-called "General Adaptation Syndrome" was proposed by Selye as part of our typical response to dangerous environmental challenge. This syndrome is an extension of Cannon's Emergency Syndrome, the "flee, fright, or fight" syndrome, consisting of a rapid total body response to the challenge. Many manifestations of the adaptation syndrome have been observed in lower animals, but they often are difficult to detect in humans. Other concepts (e.g., acclimatization) have been proposed to account for many of the data.

ACCOMMODATION
GENERAL ADAPTATION SYNDROME
HABITUATION

A. J. RIOPELLE

ADDICTIVE PROCESS

The word "addicted" has become generalized and is no longer confined to the World Health Organization's definition of addiction as

A state of periodic or chronic intoxication produced by the repeated consumption of a natural or synthetic drug for which one has an overpowering desire or need (i.e., compulsion) . . . with the presence of a tendency to increase the dose and evidences of phenomena of tolerance, abstinence and withdrawal, in which there is always psychic and physical dependence on the effects of the drug.

In common parlance addiction relates to almost any substance, activity, or interaction. People are now said to be "addicted" to food, smoking, gambling, buying, work, play, and sex.

No single addictive personality type exists. Specific ethnic, familial, intra- or interpersonal, peer, environmental, constitutional, and genetic factors collectively contribute to vulnerability to the addictive process. The individual in whom this process is operant has an overpowering desire or need for a substance, object, action or interaction, fantasy, and/or milieu that produces a psychophysiologic "high." This desire or need is repetitive, impulsive, and compulsive in nature. The high is a pleasurable coping mechanism for any physical or psychic pressure, conflict, stress, or pain. Over the life span of the process, the high diminishes. The individual experiences progressively less relief with increasing degrees of tolerance, abstinence, and withdrawal phenomena. In the end stages there is no relief, masking, coping, or resolution of pain, and only vestigial pleasure is derived from the process.

Psychic and physical dependence may occur. Character defects (dishonesty, manipulation, blaming others, insatiability, irresponsibility, grandiosity, etc.) can provoke the process or emerge from it. The addictive process can be continuous, cyclic, sporadic, or periodic, depending on the individual's life history. It remains predictable, being based on specific historical, psychodynamic, and environmental *trigger mechanisms.* Shifts can occur from one addiction to another, or several addictions can coexist.

An individual can become an *addictive complement* (i.e., provocateur) not necessarily addicted to an agent, but nonetheless an integral part of the process. An addictive complement is any person, group, or environment that keeps the addictive process alive. For example, a work-addicted, nagging parent becomes the complement of a drug- or play-addicted child. Many addicts find another person whose addiction feeds into and seems to justify their own. Addicts need people who provide what they feel they lack, or interact with others who reflect their own inadequacies. They become bound to such people—relatives, spouses, lovers, peers—with the addictive substance or practice as the catalyst. When addicts find a subculture, they find not only partners to support their addictive cycle, but a steady source of complements. The addictive agent/process can also be utilized as a means of dealing with untreated and painful psychotic symptoms, often masking the psychosis or bringing temporary relief.

THE ETIOLOGY OF ADDICTIVENESS

Shifting etiologic factors at different stages of a person's life breeds addictiveness. These factors become complex and elusive, once vulnerability evolves into a full-blown identifiable addiction. The process is then autonomous and self-perpetuating. The initial causes often remain unrevealed and unrelated to the perpetuation of the process, which has developed a life of its own.

The addict is commonly a person who early in life experienced one or many polarized excesses, inconsistencies, or deprivations in the following significant areas: intimacy, discipline, parental role models (gender-erotic), passivity–aggressivity, work–play functions, frustration tolerance, and ability to delay gratification or to live with moderation. Impairment in these areas is responsible for varying degrees of destruction of self-esteem and control.

The addicted individual finds relationships progressively more painful, resulting in a high incidence of provoked, imposed, or actual rejections. The adolescent often becomes involved in the addictive process as a means of rebellion. Sadomasochistic interactions can emerge. There is always a high degree of narcissism and shifting from overevaluations to self-contempt as a defense against society's reactions to the addictive practice. It is not easy to determine which came first—the current destructive interpersonal interactions and self-contempt, or the addictive practice. In any event, the process is perpetuated by polarized excesses in inter- or intrapersonal interactions and self-perceptions.

The peer group can be a central etiologic factor in the addictive process. A need to establish peer status and to be accepted can provoke emergence into the process. Youngsters who have been excessively passive are vulnerable to peer pressures. The practice can also occur from a need for peer leadership, which they are unable to attain. The practice can become a form of pseudoleadership. Problems in an adolescent's ability to establish, identify, and cope with a society's prototypic gender-erotic role and currently valued sexual practices can be a core provocative factor of the process. Not uncommonly the individual is introduced into the addictive practice in a one-to-one secret addictive peer collusion to deal with fear, guilt, or anxiety.

The media can contribute by promoting addictive practices as ways to cope with or resolve pain, conflict, pressure, or stress, or to attain success. The media often reflect the many parental polarized excesses by delivering double-bind (contradictory) messages. The public is inundated with both the values and dangers of addictive agents and practices. Typical are advertisements promoting in large print the joy of smoking, with small print noting that cigarettes are carcinogenic.

To understand and treat addictions, one must go beyond the specific agent and examine the multivariant etiologies, dynamics, and interpersonal interactions. One must examine the *addictive process.* This process can be defined and diagnosed. It entails common etiologies and psychodynamics. It always involves more than the addictive person and agent. One must look for the *addictive complement* and *trigger mechanisms.* The process has a life history in which there may be shifts from one addiction to another, or multiple addictions at different stages. Understanding these factors is essential to establishing a diagnosis and engaging in effective treatment.

DRUG EDUCATION
DRUG REHABILITATION
DRUG USERS' TREATMENT
HEROIN ADDICTION

L. J. Hatterer

ADLERIAN PSYCHOLOGY

Adlerian psychology, also known as Individual Psychology, was developed by Alfred Adler after his separation from the Vienna Psychoanalytic Society in 1911. Individual Psychology is often misinterpreted as a psychology of the individual or of individual differences, when it actually refers to the indivisibility of the person, to the person viewed as a totality.

Alfred Adler (1870–1937) was a Viennese ophthalmologist–turned-*Nervenarzt* (psychiatrist) whom Freud invited to participate in his Wednesday night discussions. In 1907 Adler published his *Study of organ inferiority and its psychical compensation,* which Freud applauded as a significant contribution to Freudian psychology. While the concepts of organ inferiority and compensation found a place in later Adlerian theory, they are no longer regarded as the cornerstones of Adlerian theory. In 1908 Adler advanced the notion of the aggressive instincts to complement Freud's sexual instincts. While Freud initially rejected Adler's introduc-

tion of the aggressive instincts, he later integrated them into the corpus of psychoanalytic theory in 1923.

Adler rose in the ranks of the Vienna Psychoanalytic Society, becoming editor of its journal and president. During this period Adler engaged Freud in controversy over Freud's concept of penis envy. Freud considered penis envy as the universal wish among women. Adler substituted for it the concept of masculine protest, which held that women wish to have equal status with men (which for some means having a penis) or even a status superior to them, while some men strive for the status of "real" men. After acrimonious debate, a vote was taken. Adler and his followers, losing the vote, left the society and founded the Society for Free Psychoanalytic Research. Shortly thereafter Adler's first Adlerian book, *The neurotic constitution,* was published.

After a suspension of the new society's activities during World War I, when Adler served in the Austrian army, it resumed as the Society of Individual Psychology and introduced its journal, the *Zeitschrift für Individualpsychologie.* The movement flourished in Vienna and elsewhere in Europe until the advent of the Nazi era. Adler during the last decade of his life divided his time between Europe and the United States. The umbrella organization for the Adlerian movement is the International Association of Individual Psychology. National societies exist in the United States, Germany, Switzerland, Austria, France, the Netherlands, Italy, and Great Britain.

BASIC ASSUMPTIONS
Adlerian theory is predicated on and follows several basic assumptions.

1. Following Smuts, it views the person holistically, rather than reductionistically. All part-functions of the person are seen as being in the service of the whole person.

2. People are not determined nor are they victims of their past, their heredity, or their environments. People have and make choices. The theory teaches individual responsibility.

3. All behavior is goal-directed and can best be understood in terms of the person's goal strivings, the person's unique line of movement. The person is always in the process of becoming. This movement toward the goal is designed to move the person from a minus to a plus situation.

4. Since people can choose, they are seen as proactive rather than merely reactive. They can perceive events, appraise them, and arrive at conclusions about these events.

5. People are not merely adaptive to their environments, events, or stimuli. They can create, modify, or alter these stimuli objectively or subjectively.

6. People apprehend the world subjectively; therefore, to understand the person "we must be able to see with his eyes and listen with his ears" (Alfred Adler).

7. Adlerian psychology is a social psychology: All behavior must be understood within the social context. People move about, as the early Gestalt school described it, within a phenomenal field. Adlerian psychology is often described as a field theory.

8. Adler introduced a psychology of values. The highest value—the ideal value for people—lay in social interest, which many view as a psychological reformulation of such religious precepts as "Love thy neighbor as thyself" and "Do not keep thyself aloof from the community." Much of Adlerian thought and practice conveys norms for living. Adler was the forerunner of current existentialism in that he emphasized such concepts as choice, individual responsibility, and the meaning of life.

9. Adlerian psychology may be described as an idiographic psychology. Nomothetic descriptions may also be utilized for teaching purposes,

but whenever Adler indulged in such formulations, he would caution his students, "But then, it could also be entirely different."

10. Adlerian psychology is a psychology of use rather than a psychology of possession. It is functional, it is dynamic. Except for heuristic purposes, Adlerians do not categorize. Diagnostic nomenclature is not particularly congenial to Adlerian practice.

PERSONALITY THEORY

The human infant is the most helpless of the animal species. In order to survive it must learn how to size up the environment and form correct conclusions about it. The family constellation constitutes the primary social environment for the child, and the child attempts to find a place within it. Each child wants to belong, to be significant, to count, and to be taken account of, first within the family and subsequently in the larger society. Children's perceptions of their positions in the family help create their evaluations of both self and others. These evaluations are incorporated into a cognitive map, the lifestyle, which influences the person's line of movement in life.

For teaching purposes, the convictions within the lifestyle may be categorized in many ways. One schema divides them into the categories of self-concept, self-ideal, *Weltbild* or picture of the world, and the personal ethical convictions. Noncongruence among convictions may lead to inferiority feelings. For example, a person holding the convictions that "in order to have a place, I should be Number 1" (self-ideal), "but I am Number 2" (self-concept), will feel inferior. These convictions, the primary inferiority feelings resulting from the helplessness of infancy, and the secondary inferiority feelings derived from the noncongruence of convictions, constitute the person's lifestyle. Although most of the convictions are nonconscious (in Adlerian terms, the person is not centrally aware of attending to them), the person's behavior is nevertheless generally consonant with them. Within the same lifestyle one can also behave usefully in life if one is encouraged, and uselessly if one is discouraged.

Emotions, being behavior, have purpose. They are generated in order to move people in the direction of their goals. People are the creators, not the victims, of their emotions. Emotions, in Adlerian theory as in rational-emotive theory, are cognitively based.

The inferiority feeling is normal in that all know that they fall short of what they should be. When people act as if they were inferior, develop symptoms, act sick, or act out, they demonstrate an inferiority complex, a term encompassing all of what is generally referred to as "psychopathology" and what Adlerians term "discouragement."

Since mastery of the environment is vital, the person creates a lifestyle that will assist in meeting this goal. The general goals of the lifestyle are to understand, predict, and control life and self. Life calls upon people to find solutions for three life tasks. The first is work, which for children and many adults includes school. Work comprises such subtasks as vocational choice, preparation, and satisfaction; use of leisure time; and retirement. The second is the social task, which includes two subtasks—the subtask of belonging and one that Berne used in his title *Games people play*. The third task, Adler indicated, is based on the fact that we exist in two sexes, and each sex must do something about the other sex. Adler frowned upon the term "opposite sex," since as an advocate of sexual equality he believed it might connote an adversarial relationship between the sexes. Subtasks in this group center about sex-role definition and identification, negotiating the sexual developmental phases (e.g., puberty, menopause), courtship, love, marriage, living together, and for some people, divorce.

Confronted with the life tasks, people assume three stances: "yes," "yes, but" (this also appears in the Adlerian literature as "if only"), and "no." People who respond to the life tasks with a "yes" demonstrate social interest or *Gemeinschaftsgefühl*. This affirmative response does not connote a passive adaptation to life. Adlerian psychology, being a normative psychology, demands of people that they accept the personal obligation to make changes in society when the latter falls short. Social interest is a construct that incorporates such characteristics as commitment to life, social cooperation, contribution to the common welfare, and caring. People who demonstrate social interest face life with courage, confidence, and optimism. The quantity of social interest displayed provides an index of mental health or normality.

People who reply with "yes, but" acknowledge the necessity of solving the life tasks, but simultaneously are alert to the necessity of protecting themselves, their reputations, and their self-esteem. They answer "yes" to the life tasks, "but" they cannot solve them in a direct problem-solving fashion. Those who continually use "yes, but" are the neurotics: those who announce "yes, but I'm sick" (or have a block or a hangup) are labeled psychoneurotic, while those who proclaim, "Yes, I know the task is there, but I defy it" (i.e., act out) compose the character neurotic group. Neurosis, so regarded, is the effort of discouraged individuals to meet the life tasks by avoiding direct problem solving. In doing so, neurotics avoid the subjective failure or success that would render them vulnerable to threats to the self, the self-esteem, or their place.

The third group meets the life tasks by turning its back on them and saying "no" to the consensually validated tasks and solutions of their culture. These people are regarded as psychotic. Since Adlerians operate in a growth-model psychology, people with so-called psychopathology are viewed as discouraged rather than mentally ill.

APPLICATIONS

The major interests of Adlerians have been in the clinical and educational areas, but almost the entire spectrum of individual and group behavior has been the object of Adlerian scrutiny.

In the area of diagnosis the foci of attention have been the family constellation and early recollections. Both are investigated in the construction of lifestyle summaries. Early recollections, according to R. L. Munroe, were "actually the first approach toward the projective-test method now so widely used." Early recollections are important because they are remembered, not because they occurred. They can actually be nonconscious fabrications. The interpretation of early recollections is based on the assumption that memory is selective, and that we recall from the many possible events available for recollection only those that reflect our current stance in life. They are for each person "the story of my life." Parenthetically, if a patient changes in psychotherapy, his or her early recollections will also change, and this provides a measure of progress and outcome in psychotherapy.

To gain an appreciation of why a person developed particular convictions in lifestyle, we study the person's family constellation—the web of relationships between siblings, and between siblings and parental figures. Some Adlerians understand these relationships in terms of birth order or ordinal position; others, in more idiographic fashion, attempt to understand them in terms of psychological position.

Adlerians rely less on psychological testing than do other practitioners. When they do use tests, they choose "dynamic" tests that are consonant with their theoretical position or translate the variables into Adlerian terms.

Adlerian psychotherapy is a growth-model psychotherapy whose stated goal is to enhance the expression of social interest. The therapy has been variously described as cognitive, behavioral, existential, humanistic, and transactional, as well as an insight therapy. Adlerians engage in group therapy, psychodrama, marital therapy, and family therapy. Rudolf Dreikurs introduced group therapy into a private-practice setting in the mid-1920s and pioneered in the concurrent treatment of marital partners. Family therapy was an offshoot of the public family counseling offered through the Vienna schools before the Nazi occupation.

While Freud initially reconstructed the life of childhood from the free associations of his adult patients, Adler studied children directly. Because of his focus, his child psychology was normative rather than developmental. This posture was translated into applications in family counseling and education. In the former area he introduced public family counseling into the Vienna schools. Twenty-eight such *Erziehungsberatungsstellen* offered services until they were disbanded when the Nazis entered Austria. The typical procedure, still in use with some modifications, was to interview a family before an audience of parents and teachers, after which the counselor offered some practical suggestions for improving the family situation. The process was considered educational rather than clinical. In conjunction with this family counseling, parent study groups have flourished throughout the United States and Canada. Interested parents meet with a study group leader, usually on a weekly schedule, for study and discussion of child-rearing methods. The discussion generally centers on an Adlerian textbook on such methods.

In the field of education Adler's theories were first implemented by Oskar Spiel, who founded the Individual Psychological Experimental School in Vienna, which is described in his *Discipline without punishment*. Phyllis Bottome, the novelist and biographer of Adler, conducted a similar school in Kitzbühel, Austria. In the United States, Dreikurs and his coworkers carried on this work in schools throughout the country.

Adlerian psychology has steadily found an increasing number of adherents. Simultaneously, many of its concepts and methods have penetrated other systems of psychology. The concepts of inferiority feeling and inferiority complex have become household words.

ADLERIAN PSYCHOTHERAPY
INDIVIDUAL EDUCATION
PERSONALITY THEORIES
SOCIAL INTEREST
SOFT DETERMINISM

H. H. MOSAK

ADLERIAN PSYCHOTHERAPY

Adlerian psychotherapy was originally developed by Alfred Adler while a member of Sigmund Freud's group. After their separation in 1911, Adler rapidly expanded the outline of his theory and continued to elaborate it until his death in 1937. Since then, his followers have further developed the theory and procedures.

Adler's theory shared some of psychoanalysis's tenets: psychic determinism, the purposive nature of behavior, the existence of many motives outside conscious awareness, and the notions that dreams could be understood as a mental product, and that insight into one's own unconscious motives and assumptions had curative power. Adler, however, rejected the energy model of libido and replaced it with a future-oriented model of striving toward a subjectively determined position of significance, which was much more teleological. He rejected the tripartite structure of personality (id–ego–superego), replacing it with a holistic personality-as-unity model.

THE MODEL OF MAN

Adlerians visualize the organism as an open system striving for fulfillment and completeness with continuous development. The manner of striving is determined by the interaction between innate programs and early life experiences. Feedback from early life experiences leads to various perceptual discriminations, which become an organized perceptual system with core constructs guiding further perceptual processing of incoming information. The perceptual system, a subsystem of the organism, has the task of organizing stimuli into a meaningful Gestalt in order to facilitate

organismic striving. This subsystem functions as a *creative self,* a self-directing principle that creates a set of subjective assumptions that begin as a rule of thumb for coping with the world and grow into a set of rules for perceiving and acting in the world. These rules are consistent over time and become more fixed and generally function outside conscious awareness. Adler called these rules the *lifestyle*—the overall master program the perceptual system has created. The presence of a master plan makes the personality a unity. The elucidation of the lifestyle becomes an important part of psychotherapy.

The right meaning of life, according to Adler, is the recognition that humans need each other, must respect each other and learn to bond and cooperate in common tasks, rather than engage in destructive competition or narcissistic vanities. Appropriate values, appropriate aspirations, open-mindedness toward life, self-understanding, reasonable interpersonal skills, and *Gemeinschaftsgefühl* (social interest) all help to give the right meaning to life.

THE THEORY OF THERAPY

In spite of its flexible approach, Adlerian therapy is as systematic as psychoanalysis. The therapist has specific goals and specific diagnostic methods for understanding the patient. The goals of the therapist are to reveal the person to him- or herself and to encourage the person to make useful changes in coping with life. To do this, the therapist has four tasks: (a) to establish a therapeutic relationship, (b) to understand the person's assumptive universe, (c) to reveal these assumptions to the person in such a way that (d) they become subject to self-correction and facilitate change.

THE PRACTICE OF THERAPY

Assessment
Because the goal of therapy includes changing crucial mistakes in the person's assumptive universe, most Adlerians try to understand this aspect of the person at or near the beginning of the therapeutic relationship. This can be done in a systematized set of formal interviews, if the person is capable of and ready for such cooperation, or it can be done in a more casual way with the less ready person, to allow the relationship to grow while relief is provided for immediate distress, symptoms, and life situation stresses. The two main areas of investigation that lead to an understanding of these basic assumptions (the lifestyle) are the family constellation and early childhood recollections.

In line with his holistic view of the mental life, Adler considered memories of early life to be retrospectively constructed under the influence of the lifestyle. The purpose of memory is to aid adaptation to the tasks of life. Therefore examination of the childhood situation reveals how the person reconstructed the past to be an aid in the present. The story of the patient's childhood provides the keys to understanding the lifestyle. The family constellation is the story of early experiences with parents and siblings, and shows the adaptive movements the person made in responding to the challenges of these early interpersonal relationships. In effect, it shows how the person found a niche in the family ecological system: who the models were, which behaviors were reinforced by the environment, and the directions in which the person as child began to train for future adaptive movements. Early difficulties, loss of or rejection by a parent, areas of successful striving, and areas of life in which the person met early discouragement, all shed light on future adaptive behavior.

The *earliest childhood recollections* are of special significance, because they constitute a projective technique for direct assessment of the meaning that the person has given to life. They reveal the child's interpretation and response to the early challenges of life, its ability or lack of it to overcome difficulties, and the master plan for coping with the contingencies of existence.

From this material, the therapist tries to understand the person's master plan and specifically to recognize where this plan leads to maladaptive behaviors. If the therapist has understood well, he or she can relate the person's present difficulties to these errors of perception—the mistaken conclusions about life as portrayed in the lifestyle. In essence, the therapist should now know the personality factors that contribute to the current difficulty. Having understood these factors and their effects, the therapist is ready to impart understanding to the person. Assessment, however, remains a continuing process all through therapy, both in continually refining the therapist's understanding and in continually applying the understanding to the patient's behavior in life and productions in therapy.

This continuous assessment requires the therapist to be sensitive to all the patient's behavior, both verbal and nonverbal. Adler specifically recommended that the therapist learn to use empathy and intuition in order to become an expert guesser—to try to see events from the person's point of view and to look for future evidence to test the accuracy of his or her own assumptions about the person. The technique of guessing consists of finding parts that fit together into a comprehensible whole that reveals the person as engaging in consistent movement toward a subjective chosen goal of significance. In this sense, Adlerians are holistic and teleological. All behavior, even symptoms, is considered adaptive in intent.

Adler's term for nonconsensual assumptions is *private logic*. These assumptions are usually outside immediate awareness. What one experiences consciously is ideas, emotions, interests, urges, and impulses, which one explains by various rationalizations, or denies or ignores. What the therapist sees are hidden motives, safeguarding tendencies, and movements to preserve the more or less fictional values of the lifestyle.

Promoting Insight

The person is largely unaware of his or her private logic, of the master plan, and of many underlying motives for thoughts, feelings, and actions. While it is possible for personality change to take place without insight into one's own dynamics, insight is usually a requirement for change, and interpretation is the chief tool for promoting insight. The therapist operates from the assumption that the patient does not know what is wrong; it is the therapist's job to reveal it. Adlerians interpret very specific items: the hidden motives behind behavior, the direction of movement, and the self-defeating and unrealistic assumptions.

Hidden Motives

Motives are interpreted in terms of purpose. The purpose of a symptom may be to safeguard against a defeat of one's plans, to neutralize expected antagonism from another, to gain a spurious victory, or to otherwise safeguard self-esteem. The purpose of an intense emotion is to facilitate an action, sometimes against one's better judgment.

Direction of Movement

The underlying movements are either advances toward appropriate solutions to the challenges of life, retreats from these tasks, or attempts to detour around them.

Self-Defeating and Unrealistic Assumptions

The basic mistakes found in the lifestyle can all be understood as mistakes in common-sense thinking. These include misfocusing, closed-mindedness, constricted categories of thought, overabstract rather than denotative thinking, reification of idiosyncratic ideas, failure to validate premises, excessively high expectations or aspirations, and inaccurate characterization of events, all the result of failure to make appropriate perceptual discriminations.

Technique of Interpretation

Insight, while not always leading to change, provides information about what ought to be changed. Some interpretations are readily accepted by the person because they provide a welcome clarification of what has been happening to him or her and a gratifying self-understanding. Other interpretations are resisted because they confront the person with aspects of the self that threaten self-esteem or the sense of self-control. Adlerians often couch interpretations in tentative language such as "Perhaps . . ." or "Could it be that . . . ?" and so allow the person to disagree. Where appropriate, dramatic illustrations, metaphors, or aphorisms may be used to help the person toward self-discovery.

Real insight arouses affect. Recognizing one's real intentions often makes it impossible for the person to continue to feel like a victim or to demand special privilege. Recognizing one's own mistaken assumptions helps the person to stop misconstruing life and devise more effective coping strategies.

Relationship

Therapy is a dialogue that requires cooperation. The first task of the therapist is to develop a meaningful cooperation with the patient. Using the patient's own desire to be helped, the therapist behaves like an interested friend who shows that he or she understands the patient and accepts the patient as worthwhile. The therapist does this by making no pejorative judgments concerning the patient's behavior, by making remarks that show understanding and respect for the patient's feelings, and by finding something positive in the patient on which to comment. By sympathetic attitude and carefully constructed questions, the therapist inquires further and further into the patient's life, thoughts, feelings, dreams, fantasies, and problems. The good relationship is one of open discussion, with the patient being attentive to interpretations and open to self-examination.

Transference

The therapist will expect that, when therapy goes well, the patient will have fond feelings for him or her. These fond feelings are treated as the natural tendency for human beings to bond to each other when cooperating in a common task. In addition, however, the patient will bring into the therapy situation his or her characteristic ways of coping with tasks and relationships, as well as distorted assumptions and unconscious expectations. These are treated as lifestyle phenomena and are interpreted as such, especially where they interfere with learning new, improved adaptive behavior. While the transference neurosis may provide opportunity for additional self-learning, the Adlerian considers it an artificial product of therapy itself, and a private agreement between patient and therapist for the patient to behave in an infantile way. To deliberately encourage it would in most cases make therapy unnecessarily long-lasting.

Resistance

There are many reasons for the phenomenon of resistance; of these, four are major. A common cause of resistance is failure of the therapist and patient to share common goals. If the patient is not in the market to buy what the therapist has for sale, no sale will take place. A second reason for resistance is the patient's use of the *depreciation tendency* (devaluing what others have to offer) as a major safeguarding tendency to preserve his or her positive self-esteem. A third cause is the natural resistance of the patient to any intervention that threatens to invalidate his or her constructs, and a fourth, the ingrained perceptual set of some people that rigidly resists discrepant information (cf. George Kelly's "impermeable constructs"). Handling resistance requires continued sensitivity by the therapist to the current frame of mind of the patient, and the ability to track the patient's movement back and forth between openness and defensiveness.

Facilitating Change

Change is made possible by the creative power of the patient to reconstruct his or her own perceptual system through increased understanding. The desired direction of change is toward increased awareness of unconscious motives and self-defeating behaviors; increased sense of personal competence; increased ability to understand others and relate to them effectively; realistic self-identification and self-acceptance; replacement of inappropriate self-aggrandizing values with prosocial values (social interest); recognizing one's real needs in place of the fantasied goals of personal superiority; and active courageous engagement with the tasks of life.

The insight into the mistaken assumptive universe and its consequences is only the first step toward change. Overcoming the reluctance to confront life directly is just as important. Active engagement includes the willingness to try alternative behaviors, to give up special safeguards and special demands for entitlement, and the willingness to accept setbacks in the process of learning new coping strategies. The therapist acts as guide, counselor, supporter, and encourager of these new behaviors. Some of these straightforward behaviors are modeled by the therapist. The therapist's unqualified support of courageous movement provides the patient with some security even in the face of difficulties (the therapist shows faith in the patient). In addition, the therapist judiciously suggests tasks that will provide an experience of success and warns against tasks for which the patient does not seem ready.

THERAPEUTIC PROCESS

So long as new learning continues and behavior change ensues, the therapist is satisfied to continue the same way. As different problems come into focus, the understanding of the lifestyle is applied again to their resolution. Dreams are important signals of pending movements and often foreshadow the emergence into awareness of new insights or new difficulties. The increase or diminution of symptomatic complaints shows the back-and-forth movements of the patient in therapeutic progress. Plateaus are respites between tasks. New behavior takes a certain amount of time to learn. As the patient proceeds, he or she eventually learns to understand symptoms, emotions, behavior, and dreams and so becomes much more knowledgeable about him- or herself. At these times, intervals between therapy sessions become longer and eventually the patient is ready to terminate.

Termination does not mean the end of personal growth. In therapy the patient has learned a method for self-understanding and continues to use this method. Years after therapy has ended the patient may continue to discover new insights and continue the process of personal growth. By the same token, therapy never has an absolute end. The patient may return to the therapist in the future to cope better with a life stress or to take up some previously unfinished business.

THERAPEUTIC MODALITIES

Adlerian therapists work in all settings including schools, drug and alcohol programs, and correctional institutions. Adlerian techniques of child rearing and child education have become especially widespread, and Adlerian insights have been used in personnel counseling, management programs, and resolution of disputes among conflicting groups.

ADLERIAN PSYCHOLOGY
DREAMS
EARLY RECOLLECTIONS
PSYCHOANALYSIS
PSYCHOTHERAPY

B. H. Shulman

ADOLESCENCE

Adolescence is the period of transition from childhood to early adulthood, entered at approximately 11 to 13 years of age and ending at 18 to 21 years of age—the exact time period, however, depending on such diverse factors as the surrounding culture and biological development. The transition involves changes in biological, cognitive, and social development.

While the scientific study of adolescence usually is dated to the work of G. Stanley Hall, the quantity and quality of empirical work focused on adolescents has lagged behind comparable efforts to study children. Child development research centers, graduate training programs, and journals have far outnumbered such efforts directed at improving our knowledge about adolescents.

While pubertal changes are well defined (spurt in growth, changes in sex characteristics and endocrine levels), these are gradual changes. Pinpointing when one actually enters and leaves adolescence is not easy. However, puberty does seem to be occurring earlier than in past decades, probably because of improved health and nutrition. The discipline of behavior genetics is starting to be usefully applied to such changes.

Not only do adolescents undergo biological changes, but they experience cognitive changes as well. Most researchers agree that the onset of adolescence does not signal the appearance of full-blown formal operational thought. One alternative view, expressed in the branch model, holds that the dominant path of adolescent thought is formal operational in nature (more abstract and organized than concrete thought), but that alternative routes are possible as well. Another perspective suggests that formal operational thought should be divided into early and late phases. Many applications of Piaget's theory to adolescent education have followed the assumption that most adolescents are concrete operational thinkers and, therefore, should be taught in less abstract, more concrete ways.

The social transitions of adolescents focus on such diverse areas of personality as identity, independence, sex roles, morals and values, and achievement. The construct of identity, more than any other, seems to intuitively capture some of the most important changes that occur during adolescence.

Researchers have been interested in two contexts that most influence adolescent development: peers and parents. One recent investigation suggests that conformity to antisocial peers peaks around the ninth grade, and that by the twelfth grade there is less conflict between parent and peer norms. While authoritarian discipline seems to repress the development of independence in adolescence and democratic parenting seems to promote it, researchers might pay closer attention to such concepts as reciprocal socialization and synchrony-asynchrony. The latter concept—namely, that a competent parent follows in order to lead—seems especially pertinent to successful parenting during adolescence.

HISTORICAL TRANSITION

Some writers and researchers believe that too much attention has been given to the problems and disturbances of adolescence. The majority of adolescents, even in the so-called "rebellious" late 1960s, move along efficiently and competently toward mature adulthood.

While it is easy to stereotype adolescents in any period of time, some changes do appear to have occurred. Conger indicates several: (a) Regarding sex roles, more mothers are providing a role model who works and makes money, and more adolescent girls are being reared to be androgynous rather than traditionally feminine; (b) many more adolescents are growing up in families in which the mother works, and many more are being reared in families fractured by divorce; and (c) a subtler change appears to be occurring—one difficult to pinpoint, but which may be best described as an increased interest in self.

**ADOLESCENT DEVELOPMENT
HUMAN DEVELOPMENT
LIFE-SPAN DEVELOPMENT**

J. W. SANTROCK

ADOLESCENT DEVELOPMENT

The first conceptualization of adolescence occurred in G. Stanley Hall's monumental two-volume work, *Adolescence,* published in 1904. Hall's work coincided with increasing popular concern about teenage individuals. Growing in the early 1900s, this concern exploded after World War I when youthful soldiers returned from the front disillusioned with the world their elders had handed them. Emphasis on youth was strong in the 1920s and it became clear that the young were a separate generation. The decade of the 1960s was again a time when youth activities were prominent, when the "under 30" generation became a subject of popular concern. During this latter decade research on adolescence came into its own.

CHANGE AND CRISIS

The view of adolescence as change and crisis received formal recognition with the work of Erik Erikson. His *Childhood and society* proposed that the major event of adolescence was an "identity crisis." He defined an identity crisis as a time of searching for a new sense of self that encompassed all that one had been as well as what one would become. An identity crisis might be mild or acute, but generally Erikson characterized this time of self-searching as one of anxiety and confusion.

BIOLOGY

Biologically oriented scientists have documented the physical growth and sexual maturation that occurs at the beginning of the teen years (give or take a year or two). At this time, young people rather quickly shoot up several inches in height. This "growth spurt" occurs simultaneously with the beginning of sexual maturation, during which time reproductive organs develop and the sexual attributes that will characterize youth as men and women occur. Biological change in early adolescence is dramatic and may have resounding implications for other aspects of development.

The impact of biological development is seen in the studies of early- and late-maturing boys and girls whose timetable for growth is out of synchrony with a majority of their peers. Both early- and late-maturing boys and girls show evidence of psychological and social differences from their peers, but the evidence in the case of boys is more clear-cut. For example, boys who mature early often have an advantage over other boys that lasts through adolescence and early adulthood. They demonstrate social poise, leadership potential, and a variety of other valued characteristics. Late-maturing boys, however, are often at a disadvantage side by side with their peers. They are often aggressive, irresponsible, and dependent all at the same time. Although these differences even out, and in some cases reverse themselves later in life, the impact of biological development is clearly seen in these cases where young people are not in accord with the normative timetable.

COGNITION

The study of cognitive development in adolescence has relied heavily on the theoretical work of Jean Piaget. Piaget saw children and adolescents as moving through cognitive stages. At each stage, thinking patterns are shaped by a particular view of reality. The stage of cognitive development associated with adolescence he called "formal operations." Thinking now becomes abstract and hypothetical. Adolescents become able to distinguish inner feelings from outer events and to explore subjective and objective worlds with greater range.

The stage of formal operations, according to Piaget, opens up wider possibilities for adolescents and affects their psychological and social development. Adolescents are now able to imagine "being in love" and, as a consequence, fall in love with all the emotional pangs attendant on this state. Adolescents can also imagine ideal worlds better than their own, and thus become impatient with the fallibility of the real world. Adolescents now have the capacity to imagine how they appear to others, and their ability to see their own reflection (however distorted) in the eyes of others increases their self-consciousness. Cognitive changes may also account for psychological and social changes in adolescence and they may predispose some young people to experience a "crisis" of self-understanding.

Other researchers are less insistent on the dramatic nature of cognitive change than Piaget. They argue that change is gradual, occurring over time, and that psychological changes may be phased in at different times as young people mature. Although many psychologists are not strongly impressed with the dramatic nature of change, they nonetheless rely on Piaget's stages as guideposts for exploring adolescent cognitive development.

PERSONALITY

Other theorists attribute the crises to different causes. Erik Erikson places the "identity crisis" in center stage. Harry Stack Sullivan saw adolescent conflicts as emerging when young people sought to develop relationships first with same-sex and later with other-sex peers. Loevinger has described adolescence as a time in which young people struggle to reconcile new contradictions introduced by their increased awareness of self and others.

Many psychologists, however, have noted that the personality growth may not show any of these signs of struggle. It is a moot point whether the complacency of many adolescents is due to successful adaptation to their social setting or to avoidance of important psychological issues. It is clear, however, that many adolescents experience tranquillity rather than tumult as they shape a view of themselves during adolescence and beyond.

MORALITY

The area of moral development in adolescence became prominent with the work of Lawrence Kohlberg in the 1960s. Kohlberg stated that every adolescent is a philosopher and has a certain orientation to the world that shapes moral decisions and consequent behavior. Building on the cognitive work of Piaget, Kohlberg developed a model of moral development: As adolescents move into the cognitive stage of formal operations, they are also equipped to move from the conventional to the postconventional moral stage. In the conventional stage, young people learn to follow the rules of their community and society, honoring traditional customs and laws. In the postconventional stage they move beyond the laws of their society to consider what is best for people at large. In the postconventional stage moral decisions are based on principle.

The study of cognitive, personal, and moral growth has been strongly influenced by the work of important theorists such as Freud, Erikson, Piaget, and Kohlberg. In each of these areas, models of development have been constructed that imply that adolescent growth is largely an individual matter, motivated by forces within the young person. With the exception of Sullivan, most theorists in these areas have paid little attention to the social environment or the cultural experience of the adolescent.

SEXUALITY

In the study of sexual development and behavior, psychologists and other social scientists enter social/cultural arenas. Sexual behavior is usually a social act, involving others as well as self. In most societies sexual behavior is governed by strong cultural norms and expectations that vary from culture to culture, or within social groups and geographic regions of a single culture.

In our own culture, adolescent sexuality has assumed a special significance. Adolescents mature sexually in the early teen years, developing capacity for sexual intercourse. Young people are then faced with two sets of conflicting norms. More recent ones condone youthful sexual activity under certain conditions. Older, more entrenched norms, however, forbid adolescent sexual activity. As a result, adolescents may experience ambivalence about sexual expression owing to conflicting norms. The concurrent maturation of sexual capacities and the injunctions against sexual expression create tension. For many adults, as well as young people, adolescent sexuality thus comes to symbolize the changes occurring in adolescence.

Two prominent interpretations of adolescent sexual behavior take opposite points of view in describing the causes of sexual behavior and explaining differences in adolescent sexual experience between males and females. One is that of Freud; the other is that of W. Simon and J. H. Gagnon. The Freudian viewpoint argues that adolescent sexual behavior is a result of increasingly strong inner drives not yet channeled and controlled. These drives are postulated to be stronger in males than in females. The fact that traditionally there has been more and earlier male sexual activity is used to support this point of view.

Simon and Gagnon, however, argue that sexuality is not a response to inner drives but rather a *learned* response to cultural expectations. For example, in our society people expect boys to be sexual and they become so. People expect girls, in contrast, to be more interested in love than sex, and so girls meet these expectations. Consequently, each sex follows a cultural script and learns the behaviors expected by their culture.

THE FAMILY AND SOCIETY

Adolescent development is affected by young people's experience in their families, with their peers, and in the schools. Each setting has an impact on whether changes occurring in adolescence result in positive or negative developments for the individual and society at large.

THE PEER GROUP

Adolescent peer groups are a source of popular concern. Adults fear that peers will lead young people astray and that adult influence will wane as peers become more important. In general, this has not been substantiated by research. For most adolescents, the family influence surpasses peer influence on major questions throughout this developmental period.

In general, adolescents benefit in a number of ways from association with their peer group. First, friends their own age give adolescents a place to develop their social skills and provide a buffer against the aloneness often experienced during the teen years. Second, the peer group provides a setting, first with same-sex friends and later with opposite-sex pairings, in which they explore their own identity and discover who they are. Finally, although the peer group exacts conformity to its own standards, particularly in the early teens, the group provides an anchorage for adolescents as they move from dependence on their family to adult independence.

Some young people, however, become completely dependent on their peer group for social support and behavioral expectations. These youth, a minority, are termed peer-oriented adolescents and often experience themselves as forsaken by the adult world. In many ways, this smaller group illustrates adult fears about groups of same-age adolescents, for they often defy the established order, engage in antisocial acts, and attempt to create a world that meets their own needs as opposed to others'.

SCHOOLS

In the school setting much of peer group activity is most evident, for particularly in the middle teens, the school becomes the life setting of adolescents. Different peer groups may be identified in terms of their identification with school as well as their intellectual or social orientation. For each peer group, then, school will have a different meaning and affect their development in different ways.

Students who are not school-oriented fall into two groups, depending on whether their orientation is more intellectual or social. In some schools there is a small group of intellectual students who do not identify with the school or the adult establishment. These are often the rebels or philosophers. A larger group of nonschool-identified youth have a social orientation. They spend time together for social reasons and may prompt each other to experiment with drugs, alcohol, and crime.

In the same suburban high school where the "jocks" reigned, the nonschool-identified students were the "burn-outs." They too had their own territory, controlled the flow of marijuana, and spoke only with each other. Their standards were different from the jocks and they chose to thumb their noses at mainstream practices. Other students who identified with neither the jocks nor the burn-outs were in between and developed their own less distinctive orientation.

ADOLESCENCE
ADOLESCENT IDENTITY FORMATION
HUMAN DEVELOPMENT
MORAL DEVELOPMENT
SEX ROLE DEVELOPMENT

B. Forisha-Kovach

ADOLESCENT IDENTITY FORMATION

Modern psychology owes a major debt to William James' insightful theorizing in his *Principles of psychology* on the self as the integrator of experience and the locus of personal identity. Erik Erikson's views on ego identity have inspired most contemporary research on identity formation. According to his rather general formulation, adolescents consciously attempt to synthesize their previous experiences and make personal commitments in order to resolve fundamental questions about the meaning of their lives. Erikson has not provided an explicit definition of identity, fearing that the overall meaning might be lost in the narrowness of operational specificity.

Several investigators have used self-report questionnaires or the sorting of self-descriptive adjectives as operational measures of Eriksonian identity. However, such instruments typically fail to provide information about the process by which individuals have developed their identities. The majority of recent investigations, therefore, have employed the identity-status paradigm developed in 1964 by James Marcia. Marcia assumed that two dimensions were central in Erikson's theory of identity: the presence or absence of firm commitments and the presence or absence of a personal crisis.

An identity-status interview is used to ascertain an individual's reported prior (or current) crises and existing commitments in vocation and ideology. Of the four status classifications that can be made, two indicate the presence of a firm personal identity: *Achievers* and *Foreclosures*. These statuses differ from each other in the process by which their identities were developed. Achievers have formed their own personal commitments following an active decision-making period. Foreclosures, in contrast, have more passively (without crisis) adopted the goals and values prescribed for them by others, especially former caregivers. The remaining status classifications include uncommitted individuals. *Diffusions* lack a firm sense of identity and are not currently involved in a decision-making crisis. *Moratoriums* are actively engaged with vocational and ideological issues; they are attempting to forge their own commitments.

Research with the identity-status paradigm has revealed some sex differences. When males are classified into the statuses, Achievers have fared the best in most comparisons. Edmund Bourne concludes that Achievers score relatively high on measures such as moral reasoning, personal control over their lives, adaptability, intimacy, and conceptual reflectivity. Male Moratoriums appear to be most similar to their achieved counterparts. However, their relatively high performance variability and self-reported anxiety seem consistent with the assumption that they are in the process of actively trying to formulate their own commitments. Male Foreclosures fare poorly in status comparisons and have been found to be relatively rigid, inflexible, externally controlled, and conventional in their moral reasoning. While male Diffusions have proved consistently less effective than Achievers in most investigations, they do not appear to fit the picture of severe identity confusion portrayed in Erikson's theory. In most comparisons, however, male Diffusions are not statistically distinguishable from their foreclosed counterparts.

Marcia notes that female Achievers and Foreclosures are the most resistant to conformity pressure, the most field-independent, and the least anxious. On measures of authoritarianism, female Foreclosures do, however, appear to be as rigid and inflexible as their male counterparts. Gallatin suggested that an identity-crisis model may be an inappropriate view of optimal female personality development. Instead—given the stereotypic expectations for reactive, nurturing behavior—the stability of the female's identity may be the critical concern. Thus having a firm identity, regardless of whether it is a personal achievement or a passive foreclosure, may be the key issue. Because of societal expectations for males to be independent and instrumental, the proximity to personally achieving an identity may be the most critical aspect of personality development in male youth.

ADOLESCENCE
CENTRAL TRAITS

M. D. Berzonsky

ADOLESCENT SEX OFFENDERS

Historically, sexual offenses by adolescents have been minimized and viewed as innocent sex play, experimentation, curiosity, or a normal aspect of sexual development. In the early 1980s, clinicians and the judicial system determined that aberrant juvenile sexual behaviors were unacceptable and considered criminal actions in need of appropriate psychological treatment. Although incidence rates vary, Uniform Crime Report (UCR) statistics indicate that 20% of rapes and about 50% of reported cases of child molestation are committed by adolescents. Confirmatory data from treatment settings show that child victims of sexual abuse report an adolescent perpetrator in 40 to 60% of cases. Most adolescent sex offenders are male. The incidence rate is about 5% for females; such offenses predominantly occur with siblings or in baby-sitting situations.

The most common offenses among male offenders are fondling, rape, and exhibitionism, with 50% of the offenses involving some form of penetration. Nearly 66% of the victims are children under 10 years of age. Most of the victims of adolescent sexual offenses are known by the offender; the majority are either family members, extended family members, or acquaintances. Noteworthy, the majority of adolescent sex offenders had themselves been sexually abused as children or come from families where spousal violence, child abuse, or sexual molestation had occurred. The high incidence of childhood victimization suggests a reactive, conditioned behavior pattern that demonstrates the cyclical nature of sexual abuse. There is no evidence that adolescent sex offenders are

more prevalent in the lower socioeconomic strata, although several studies implicate the problems of the father-absent household.

Earlier studies on the etiologies of juvenile sexual abuse revealed that the adolescent child molester is a loner, has few friends or social peers, prefers interaction with younger children, has a limited occupational history, is an underachiever, is immature, and identifies with a dominating mother. More recent research has suggested other clinical dimensions of the adolescent offender (i.e., feelings of male inadequacy; low self-esteem; fear of rejection; anger toward women; aberrant erotic fantasies; identification with adult models of aggression, violence, and intimidation). A central characteristic of the offender is poor psychological adjustment and adaptation, which is evident in poor social skills, social isolation, lack of appropriate assertiveness, and deficits in communication skills.

Differential diagnosis is a major concern in the evaluation of sex offenders. It is difficult to distinguish between the diagnosis of "sex offender" and related disorders of delinquency, impulsivity, conduct disturbances, hyperactivity, and substance abuse. Frequently, a dual diagnosis seems in order. A related problem arises when clinicians or researchers must differentiate between the psychological and criminal nature of the offense. A review of the literature by G. E. Davis and H. Leitenberg emphasizes that empirical research on the characteristics and profile of the adolescent sex offender is still at the rudimentary stage.

In recent years, several studies have reported on the psychological assessment of juvenile sex offenders versus nonsex adolescent offenders. Studies using the Minnesota Multiphasic Personality Inventory and the Rorschach Inkblot Test found few differences between sex offenders and juvenile offenders. This has led researchers to conclude that adolescent sex offenders are actually a subgroup of juvenile delinquents or sociopaths. On the Rorschach, however, the former group gave more anatomy responses, which reflected repressed hostility and destructive impulses.

An increasing number of rehabilitation programs are now available for the specific treatment of the adolescent sex offender. A National Adolescent Perpetrator Network has been established with guidelines for treatment components and goals. These include confronting denial and accepting responsibility, understanding the pattern or cycle of sexually offensive behaviors, development of empathy for victims, control of deviant sexual arousal, combating cognitive distortions that trigger offending, expression of emotions and self, development of trust, remediation of social skills deficits, and relapse prevention. In addition, these intensive treatment programs focus on didactic instruction on normal human sexuality, training in interpersonal and dating skills, and teaching anger control techniques. Psychodynamic-oriented therapy has shown disappointing results, whereas various behavioral, cognitive-behavioral, and prescriptive approaches have proved to be most efficacious. Many programs use a multicomponent treatment approach, which usually includes family therapy. However, biological treatment modalities such as antiandrogenic medications are not indicated in the treatment of adolescent offenders. Residential treatment and community-based programs are showing much promise. J. Bingham and C. Piotrowski discuss the usefulness and rehabilitative aspects of a house arrest program in Florida as an option to incarceration for young sex offenders. Unfortunately, few controlled outcome studies have been reported on the long-term effectiveness of these types of treatment programs.

ADOLESCENT DEVELOPMENT
ANTISOCIAL PERSONALITY
BATTERED PEOPLE
CHILD ABUSE
SEXUAL DEVIATIONS

C. Piotrowski

ADOPTED CHILDREN

There are two kinds of adopted children: the intrafamilially adopted and the extrafamilially adopted.

In intrafamilial adoption, children are adopted either by blood relatives or by family members by marriage, frequently a stepparent of the adopted child. In intrafamilial adoption the desire to adopt a child is usually not the primary motivating force. Adoption may result from the marriage of a child's parent, from the wish to provide equal status to children coming from two single-parent households into one new family, or from the perceived necessity or duty of family members to adopt a child left to them by the biological parent or parents under adverse circumstances. The benefit of intrafamilial adoption lies in the child's remaining in touch with family roots and growing up within a familial environment, where family history is available.

Children adopted as infants may need to be told about their adoptive status. In some cases children have not been told until adulthood. Even then, prudent timing of the adoption disclosure is of psychological importance.

The child adopted into an extrafamilial setting is confronted with specific problems in terms of acceptance, rejection, identification, and separation. Adoptees have to deal with the reasons for the rejection by their biological parents and at times also with the reasons—not always merely altruistic—for being wanted by their new parents. Identifying with the adopting parents may be a complex task, if truth and fantasy about the lost parents interferes. The identification issue may be complicated by parental counteridentification problems, especially if the child is of much different appearance (ethnically or racially) or of a different IQ level, or if the parents ever imply or state that the child's unacceptable behavior is attributable to biological heritage. Adoptees appear especially vulnerable to any semblance of rejection. Even normal parental limit setting can be interpreted as parental rejection. Being sensitive to weak, unstable, or conditional parent–child bonding, adopted children act out reality testing of parental love, often precipitating the very rejection they feared while seeking the confirmation of acceptance they had hoped for. Children traumatized by separation and maternal deprivation are likely to cling to their adoptive parents, then go through a turbulent time when seeking to separate from their parents in adolescence.

The adoptee's experienced degree of wantedness by the adoptive parents is a powerful defense against the perceived rejection by the biological parents. Although being unwanted and rejected can lead to low self-esteem, a comparison with normal children—both adopted and nonadopted—revealed no difference in self-concept between the two groups. Other studies concur with the finding that adoption becomes a negligible factor in individuals with positive adjustments. Despite the presumed rejection factor, many adopted children—especially while feeling misunderstood by their parents during adolescence—develop a need for their "real" parents. In their struggle for independence they seek the projection of their lost parent, with which they can identify. Some adoptees initiate actual searches for their natural parents.

Sibling rivalries in split families are of special significance, when adopted children have to compete with biological children, whose parents underscore the difference by favoring their natural children. The issue here is status and power, not blood. The same type of rivalry responses have been observed in families including adopted and foster children. Being an adopted child turns into a status symbol, when compared to the mere foster child who is "not really" the adoptive parents' child.

Adoptees are overrepresented among the children presented for psychotherapeutic services. This may not be due to an implied higher incident of emotional problems in that population, but seems to reflect the adoptive parents' greater willingness to seek professional assistance. They are freer to accept a difficulty as the child's problem rather than as a reflection on themselves. A report by W. Huth compiling the results of major studies on adopted children concluded that the total of psychological problems, as well as of psychopathology, in adopted and nonadopted children is about the same.

BONDING AND ATTACHMENT
CHARACTER DEVELOPMENT
HERITABILITY
IDENTITY FORMATION

E. WICK

ADRENAL GLANDS

The adrenal glands (often called suprarenal glands in humans) are paired structures located just above the kidneys. Each adrenal is composed of an outer cortex and an inner medulla. Secretions of the cortex are controlled by circulatory hormones produced in the anterior pituitary gland (adenohypophysis), while medullary output is under direct control of the sympathetic nervous system. The adrenal cortex has three layers, the outer zona glomerulosa, the intermediate zona fasciculata, and the inner zona reticularis.

Several steroid hormones, synthesized from cholesterol, are secreted by the adrenal cortex and are important in the maintenance of blood volume, blood pressure, and blood glucose levels, as well as the response of the organism to stress. These hormones are so crucial to the organism that death quickly follows removal of the adrenal cortices. Cortisol is the primary glucocorticoid secreted by the adrenal in humans. Corticosterone is secreted in small quantities in humans, but is the primary glucocorticoid secreted in the rat. These substances are classified as glucocorticoids because of their effect on glucose metabolism and because they are secreted by the zonae fasciculata and reticularis. The glucocorticoids also suppress inflammatory responses.

Aldosterone is secreted by the zona glomerulosa and is categorized as a mineralcorticoid because of its ability to alter electrolyte balance in the body. Aldosterone stimulates the distal tubule of the kidney to resorb sodium ions and causes a decrease in sodium concentration in sweat.

Adrenocorticotropic hormone (ACTH), released by the adenohypophysis, maintains the structural integrity of the outer two layers of the adrenal cortex and stimulates secretion of the glucocorticoids. Synthesis and release of ACTH are controlled by corticotropin-releasing factor (CRF). CRF is produced in the hypothalamus. Levels of glucocorticoid in the circulation provide negative feedback for secretion rate of CRF and, therefore, ultimately of the glucocorticoids themselves. The renin-angiotensin system produces complex feedback regulation between the adrenal and the kidney to control the secretion of aldosterone.

Chromaffin cells in the adrenal medulla synthesize and release the catecholamines epinephrine (adrenaline) and norepinephrine (noradrenaline). Secretion of norepinephrine and epinephrine is under control of sympathetic preganglionic fibers from the eighth through the eleventh thoracic vertebral segments. The chromaffin cells act as postganglionic neurons. Secretion of the catecholamines depends on the behavioral state of the organism. Secretion is very low during sleep, increases during emission of routine, nonstressful activities, and surges markedly during physical or psychological stress.

ENDORPHINS/ENKEPHALINS
NEUROCHEMISTRY
PSYCHOENDOCRINOLOGY

M. L. WOODRUFF

ADULT DEVELOPMENT

The life-span approach to adult development includes the study of (a) the phase of life from the end of formal education to the beginning of retirement, (b) the effects of preadulthood life on adult development and the subsequent effect of adult development on old age and dying, (c) adulthood development as such, (d) the interdisciplinary approach to development across different cultural settings and over historical time, and (e) the search for goals and means for optimizing both adult development and its childhood precursors and its subsequent effect on later life.

DEFINITION OF ADULT DEVELOPMENT

In technologically advanced societies there are no clear guideposts for entering adulthood such as the initiation rites among primitive societies. According to Aries, infants, children, and adults were for centuries considered to be only quantitatively or physically different; infants were viewed as scaled-down adults who merely needed to get big. It was not until the seventeenth and eighteenth centuries, with the emergence of modern concepts of childhood, family care, and education, that the distinction between childhood and adulthood began.

Adulthood is usually divided into three segments—early, middle, and mature—with increasing awareness of a new "substage" to characterize those on the threshold of full adulthood (usually college students) based on the analysis of R. W. White and Keniston. The criteria for deciding on the age limits of each substage depend on whether one is interested in chronological or legal age (years since birth), functional age (measures of skills and competencies), existential age (how old one feels), or other measure such as skeletal age, hormonal age, emotional age, social age, moral age, and so forth.

The age range for youth is typically from 16 through 21 years, although the upper limits often reach into the mid-20s. Characteristics of the special subculture of youth include:

1. *Deepening of interests.* From a large pool of interests, hobbies, and explorations, youth must now focus on occupational and lifestyle choices and begin to develop required competencies, sustained interests, and long-term commitments to choices.
2. *Humanizing of values.* There is a gradual realization that to connect with the adult society one must begin to break away from sole participation in youth's culture, and to realize the unity of all humanity regardless of age, background, and geographic location. Young people sense the need to care for others as an extension of caring for self. Concern for improving world conditions is part of the idealism and romantism of youth.
3. *Stabilizing of self-concept.* Young people need to test out their "real selves" in the arena of initimate and relatively stable human relationships. The more assured youths are about their values, the less risk they run being overwhelmed during the give-and-take of social interactions. Eventually youth must see themselves as separate individuals who are capable of union with others while still maintaining their own individualities.

The age when important life events occur is a significant means for defining adult development. A chronological listing of life events may be referred to as a human lifeline and may serve as a "social and biological clock."

LIFE-SPAN ADULT DEVELOPMENT

Adulthood is the least explored age span, even though it extends over two-thirds of the human life span.

Search for stability of identity in terms of occupation and lifestyles: exploration and increasing commitments to adult roles. Search for greater independence from parents and teachers: making one's own decisions even when it is precarious to establish self-reliance. Search for intimacy with a partner: learning that intimacy requires mutual trust, support, and sharing of both positive and negative feelings; possible beginning of family or single-life cycle.

Taking stock of life and deciding on rededication or a search for new identity. Extending qualities of caring and responsibility to the community at large and directing and assisting younger people not in the family. Becoming more of one's own person on the job, within the family, and in fulfilling one's talents and dreams.

Change of life signaled by menopause in women and climacteric in men. Increased awareness of life's mortality and that one's dreams must be achieved now or become a "never never." General physical decline with corresponding bodily concerns; decline in speed of movements and rate of learning and thinking and short-term memory (about 30 seconds). Reasoning and thinking continue to improve.

The life-span adult development viewpoint is based on the observation that there are both stability and change throughout the course of human life. The non–life-span view is that significant development is over by about age 20 as measured by "increments," that adulthood is a long plateau, and that development in terms of "decrements" typifies life until death.

CHARACTERISTICS OF ADULT DEVELOPMENT

The long stretch of adulthood is more influenced by a diversity of "social clocks" than the fairly "universal biological clocks" that gave the major impetus to early development. In general, although adult developmental changes are more gradual and less sequential and predictable than those at the extreme ends of the human life span, they are just as essential for continual growth, whether they be happy or unhappy experiences. Change seems to be the natural state of affairs of the mind, body, and self.

Biological Development

The muscles, skeleton, and inner organs reach their maximum potentials during the mid-20s, except for the thymus and brain. The thymus gland and other lympnoid-type tissues, essential components of the body's disease- and stress-fighting system, reach maximum growth before adolescence and continue declining throughout the life course. It seems that there is an urgent need for developing the immune system's ability to withstand stress early in life. Other vital organs begin their decline about age 40. Brain cell formation, 90 to 95% complete by year one, seems to be over by age 3, along with myelinization, which influences the speed of nerve impulses. Continued development for another 10 to 15 years occurs among the interconnections of brain cells, the dendrites, and the supporting glial cells.

Beginning with early adulthood there are slow, almost imperceptible changes with age. These gradual declines become more apparent after age 30 in such functions as reaction time, body strength, and cardiovascular work performance, whereas other body declines such as vision and audition do not become disturbing until about age 50. There is a nearly linear decline in most body functions occurring at the rate of about 1% per year during adulthood and old age. Nevertheless, regular exercise and proper nutrition seem to extend longevity, happiness, and sexual activities, as observed in the Vilcabamba people of Ecuador and the Abkhazians in Russia's Caucasus.

SOCIAL DEVELOPMENT

The concept of adult socialization emerged gradually during the 1950s as research demonstrated that the socialization process continued beyond adolescence. Adult socialization may be viewed as a sequence of learned social roles in terms of major life events.

Thus far, adult socialization has revealed two major life-span characteristics. B. L. Neugarten suggests that there is a predictable progression from an outward-directed orientation to life heavily influenced by external controls, toward *interiority*, a more passive, introverted, self-directed existence in which the maturing adult depends more and more on a developing inner system of beliefs. Thus, over time, human beings tend to become more unique and self-actualizing. The second trend, reported both by Neugarten and by Jung in "The stages of life," is a gradual reversal of sex roles after middle age. Men tend to become more passive and nuturant, whereas women tend to become more domineering and outgoing.

PSYCHOLOGICAL DEVELOPMENT
Research reveals significant personality improvements toward higher levels of competencies as evidenced in *The growth of logical thinking* by Inhelder and Piaget, in moral development by Kohlberg, in higher-order motivational drives as described by Kuhlen, and even in the kinds of defense mechanisms employed when under pressure as proposed by Vaillant. When under stress mature adults tend to use humor, provide assistance to others, plan for the future, and postpone reacting to current unavoidable conflicts.

LIFE-SPAN DEVELOPMENT
MIDDLE AGE

J. O. LUGO

ADULT INTELLECTUAL DEVELOPMENT
Why do some individuals retain their behavioral competence well into advanced old age, whereas others show early decline? This question has long been a central topic in the psychology of adult development and aging. Other questions being studied include:

1. Does intelligence change uniformly through adulthood or are there different life-course ability patterns?
2. At what age is there a reliably detectable age decrement in ability, and what is the magnitude of that decrement?
3. What are the patterns of generational differences, and what are their magnitudes?
4. What accounts for individual differences in age-related change in adulthood?
5. Can cognitive decline in old age be reversed?

THE MEASUREMENT OF ADULT INTELLIGENCE
Most large-scale studies of adult intelligence conducted during the past few decades have used either the Wechsler Adult Intelligence Scale (WAIS) or one of its derivatives or a derivative of Thurstone's work on the primary mental abilities. Findings of these studies differ markedly, however, depending on whether age comparisons have been made in a cross-sectional manner or whether the same individuals have been followed longitudinally.

DIFFERENTIAL PATTERNS OF CHANGE
There does not seem to be a uniform pattern of age-related changes across all intellectual abilities: studies of overall intellectual ability (IQ) have, therefore, been found insufficient to monitor age changes and age differences in intellectual functioning for either individuals or groups. Age difference work with the WAIS suggests that verbal abilities are maintained well, whereas performance tests early on show age differences favoring younger adults. Longitudinal data on the WAIS also show high

levels of stability of verbal behaviors into advanced old age, while performance scales begin to decline in midlife, with substantial decline into old age. Data from studies with the primary mental abilities lend some support to the notion that active or fluid abilities tend to decline earlier than passive or crystallized abilities. There are, however, important ability-by-age and ability-by-cohort interactions that complicate matters. For example, women tend to decline earlier in the active abilities, whereas men do so on the passive abilities. In addition, although fluid abilities begin to decline earlier, crystallized abilities appear to show steeper decrement once the late 70s are reached. More fine-grained analyses suggest substantial gender differences and differential changes for those who decline compared with those who remain stable when age changes are decomposed into loss in accuracy or speed.

AGE LEVEL AND MAGNITUDE OF AGE-RELATED INTELLECTUAL DECLINE
Cross-sectional studies with the WAIS suggest that significant age differences favoring young adults can be found by the 30s for performance tests and by the 60s for verbal tests. These differences, however, confound cohort effects in education and health status. By contrast, in longitudinal studies, reliably replicable average age decrements in intellectual abilities are rarely found before age 60 but are observed for all intellectual functions at least by age 74. Analyses of individual differences in intellectual change, however, demonstrate that even at age 81 less than half of all observed individuals showed reliable decremental change over the preceding 7 years.

With respect to magnitude of decline, average decrement until age 60 amounts to less than 0.2 standard deviation (SD), but by age 81, average decrement reaches a magnitude of at least 1 SD for most intellectual abilities.

GENERATIONAL DIFFERENCES
The existence of generational differences in intellectual abilities has been conclusively demonstrated. Almost linear positive cohort shifts have been observed for inductive reasoning, with more spasmodic positive shifts for verbal ability and spatial orientation. A curvilinear cohort pattern has been found for number skills, which reach a peak for birth cohorts born in the 1920s and then follow a largely negative slope. A similar curvilinear cohort pattern has been observed also for word fluency. As a consequence, using cross-sectional studies of intellectual aging tends to underestimate age changes before age 60 for abilities with negative cohort gradients and to overestimate age changes for abilities with positive cohort gradients.

INDIVIDUAL DIFFERENCES IN AGE-RELATED CHANGE IN ADULTHOOD
Individual differences are large at all ages, such that substantial overlap among samples can be found from young adulthood into the mid-70s. Very few individuals decline on all or most abilities. Indeed, maintenance of functioning on one or more abilities is characteristic for most individuals well into advanced old age. Longitudinal data permit investigation of individual differences in antecedent variables that differentiate persons who experience early decrement from others who maintain high levels of functioning into advanced age. A number of factors have been identified that account for such individual differences, some of which have been shown to be amenable to experimental intervention. Variables found to be predictive of favorable cognitive aging include (a) absence of cardiovascular and other chronic disease, (b) favorable environment as indicated by high socioeconomic status, (c) involvement in a complex and intellectually stimulating environment, (d) flexible personality style at midlife, (e) high cognitive status of spouse, and (f) maintenance of level of perceptual processing speed.

REVERSIBILITY OF COGNITIVE DECLINE

The effectiveness of cognitive interventions has been demonstrated in various laboratory studies. Cognitive decline in many older people may well be the result of disuse of specific skills that can be reserved by appropriate training regimens. In two studies, approximately 66% of the experimental subjects showed significant improvement, and about 40% of those who had declined significantly over 14 years were returned to their predecline level. Moreover, it was shown that training occurred at the ability (latent-construct) level and that training did not disturb the ability factor structure.

ADULT DEVELOPMENT
AGE DIFFERENCES
VOCABULARY TESTS

K. W. SCHAIE

ADVERTISING

Advertising is a communication tool designed to inform an audience (usually a mass one) of available or forthcoming services and especially products. . . . presenting the product or service as effectively as possible within prevailing constraints of accuracy, completeness, and good taste.

Effective advertising depends heavily on effective consumer research. A research knowledge of consumer characteristics, desires, buying habits, and lifestyles enables the advertiser to tailor the message and target the audience for maximum receptivity and impact. This knowledge further enables the advertiser to skillfully select the appropriate communication channel, to monitor consumer satisfaction after the sale, and to initiate future product modifications or new product entries.

HISTORY

The earliest ad on record is a sheet of papyrus in Thebes (3000 B.C.), advertising for a runaway slave. Advertising and its function have moved through several stages of development since that time. Brand names and trademarks (i.e., shields) emerged during the Middle Ages, and newspaper advertising had its formal beginnings in seventeenth-century England.

The time period 1875 to 1905 has been called an "Era of Bold Enterprise" in advertising. With transcontinental railroads came the development of national markets and national advertising plans. With rapid growth in national advertising, ethics concerns were soon to follow. In 1911 the Associated Advertising Clubs of America adopted a code of ethics for truthful advertising, and *Printer's Ink* magazine drew up legal statutes for penalizing false and misleading advertising practices. In 1914 the Federal Trade Commission was established to "stop unfair competition" through advertising. The first two decades of the twentieth century had been an "Era of Reexamination."

The 1920s spawned rapid and dramatic growth in advertising. With radio emerged a major new medium, and the nation's first sponsored radio network broadcast was made in 1924. By the late 1940s television brought a vast new media dimension, and the rapid growth of the television market brought equally rapid growth in advertising revenues.

Two periods of general consumer unrest surfaced within this rapid growth picture. The 1930s brought attacks on the existence of advertising and led to the Wheeler—Lea amendment to the Federal Trade Commission Act of 1938. With consumer resistance came polling techniques and attention to consumer thoughts, values, wants, and needs. The 1960s brought consumer unrest relating to a range of product and environmental issues. Spearheaded by Ralph Nader's *Unsafe at any speed: The designed-in dangers of the American automobile*, the concerns included environmental and personal harm from pesticide use, population growth, ecology

awareness, and food/hunger/nutrition issues. The effect of consumerism in each instance was to heighten advertiser awareness and sensitivity to consumer thoughts and feelings. Revenues themselves continued their general and dramatic growth.

PSYCHOLOGY OF ADVERTISING

Walter Dill Scott's pioneering work, *The psychology of advertising*, set the stage and tone for the relationship between the academic discipline and the applied field. What had been an awkward new relationship in 1908 had become a generally accepted union by 1930, and Scott commented that virtually every field of psychology was prominently involved in advertising. Sharon Bridwell noted that two models of psychology's involvement emerged over time. The early model expressed an attention-association-action sequence, whereas the more sophisticated later model included attention-comprehension/understanding-association-memory-action. While both models encompassed the concept of motivation, the later model added the elements of perception, image, and cueing. The models shared the common goal of action and a product or service association/satisfaction that would lead to a repeated action pattern.

SELECTION OF MEDIA

From an advertising perspective each of the media has characteristic strengths and weaknesses. If one feasibly could reach every consumer in person—in effect, talk to each individual—it would maximize personal sales effectiveness. With a capacity to bring "lifelike" visual/auditory communication into the consumer's own home, television is the most personalized of the mass media. It is limited by the need for brief, clear messages and its transitory nature, so it must rely on other media to provide information-intensive and later-reference functions. Its expense renders it unavailable to the small or neighborhood business. Both radio and television are high-saturation media, in that virtually every consumer household owns a receiver and, therefore, has the potential to be reached.

ROLE OF ADVERTISING IN MARKETING

By the 1950s the refinement of data-gathering techniques and data analysis prompted economists to take seriously the role of advertising in marketing. It became clear that advertising stimulated competition and could lower unit costs by increasing demand and production. It also served to standardize prices by providing consumers with comparative-cost information within ads. In addition, it was "labor saving" and could reach a targeted audience at a very low "cost per thousand" figure. But economists were not uniformly agreed on the benefits of advertising. John Kenneth Galbraith viewed advertising in negative terms because he believed it created synthetic wants and needs, fueling a production cycle to meet the consumer demand that advertising had created. In his view, "A man who is hungry need never be told of his need for food," and the creation of synthetic wants negatively affected the economy. F. A. Hayeck considered the fulfillment of wants beyond the innate to be "cultural achievement." The role of advertising in developing and fulfilling acquired needs was viewed as a positive cultural contribution and a healthy force in the economy.

ETHICS IN ADVERTISING

There has been considerable diversity of opinion regarding responsibility for advertising and how, to what extent, and by whom that responsibility should be assumed. D. M. Potter saw advertising as an institution that exerted social control without any sense of social responsibility. H. E. Burtt indicated that technically the role of an applied science "is to determine how a particular result may be accomplished and not whether that result ought to be achieved." Despite its technical qualification as an applied science, Burtt saw the influence of advertising as so widespread that it must assume responsibility.

Special Audience

The case of a special television viewing audience—children—enjoined government regulatory agencies, consumer groups, broadcasters, and advertisers in a 10-year struggle beginning in 1970. Section 5 of the Federal Trade Commission Act stated that "It is both unfair and deceptive within the meaning of this Act to address television advertising for any product to young children who are still too young to understand the selling purpose or otherwise comprehend and evaluate the advertising." Through the citizen-group effort of the Council for Children, Media and Merchandising, improvements were made in the nutrition content of cereals advertised to children, and the effort of Action for Children's Television resulted in the removal of vitamin ads, a ban on having a program-related character sell a product (host-selling), program/commercial separation, and reduction in the commercial-time-per-hour allowed in children's programs. In 1978 the Federal Trade Commission issued a staff report recommending: (a) a ban on all television advertising directed to children "too young to understand the selling purpose of, or otherwise comprehend or evaluate, the advertising" ("too young" being defined as less than 8 years of age); (b) a ban on television advertising directed to older children "for sugared products, the consumption of which poses the most serious dental health risks" ("older" being defined as 8 to 11 years); (c) a requirement that televised advertising directed to older children for sugared products not included in proposals "be balanced by nutritional and/or health disclosures funded by advertisers."

APPLIED RESEARCH
CONSUMER RESEARCH

E. L. Palmer

AFFECTIVE DEVELOPMENT

Affect, as a feature or type of behavior, and hence a focus of psychology, is one of the least understood and most difficult problems in the field. "Affect" relates to and/or encompasses a wide range of concepts and phenomena including feelings, emotions, moods, motivation, and certain drives and instincts. Anger, joy, fear, laughter, sadness, anxiety, pride, love, hate, and so on—all are so central to human experience, yet so little understood by psychology. Theorists and researchers have approached affect in numerous ways, often using idiosyncratic, contradictory, or mutually exclusive conceptualizations and operational definitions that have resulted in confusion and limited progress in our understanding of affect or any of these other related or synonymous constructs.

The psychology of *affective development* seeks to describe, map out, and explain the processes, continuities, and changes in the experience, differentiation, and expression of affect. Most often, affective development is placed in dichotomy, or even counterpoint, with cognitive development, reflecting an age-old concern with mind-body dualism, thinking versus feeling. Much of the discussion centers around the primacy of one over the other and/or the nature of their interaction or mutual influence. Referents and resolutions are often sought in the social domain, whether in terms of social cognition or object relations, because of the complexity and salience of interpersonal and intrapersonal relations for ideas, attitudes, feelings, and behavior. Whatever categorizations may be hypothesized for the sake of theory building or empirical inquiry, it is important to bear in mind the complexity of affective development and the limited state of our current knowledge.

From its early days, psychoanalysis as a clinical and developmental psychology has centered on affective development. Psychologists influenced by the organismic developmental psychology proposed by Heinz Werner in 1940 have also had a long-standing interest in affective development. In the 1970s and 1980s a number of conceptual and methodological advances converged, bringing about a resurgence of interest, priority, and legitimacy for the study of affective development.

Models of affective development vary in the degree to which they emphasize biological elements or socialization elements. Darwinian and ethological models are especially interested in unlearned complex behavior and often posit central nervous system specificity, and correspondence between stimulus or elicitors and an individual's affective response. Socialization models emphasize learning processes, especially in the infant–caregiver interaction, and situational or environmental influences on affective experience or expression. Reliance on one or the other model type, of course, influences the manner in which affective development is understood or studied. For instance, biological researchers might be more likely to measure electrophysiological responsiveness or neurophysiological correlates of specific emotions, whereas socialization researchers might be more interested in observing the quality of parent–child attachment and separation reactions over time. It is likely that multiple models and perspectives will be essential to furthering our understanding of affective development, and indeed such comprehensive and integrative approaches are evident in current theories of affective development such as Sroufe's organizational perspective and Tomkins' and Izard's differential emotions theory.

In his review of current knowledge on affective development, Yarrow states:

> Emotional expression can best be understood in a developmental context, in the framework of psychological changes accompanying the infant's increased autonomy, increasing awareness of a capacity to control people, objects, and self, and in the context of cognitive changes associated with a developing memory and the acquisition of object permanence. Similarly motor expression of emotion and the ability to inhibit and modulate responses to emotional stimuli are dependent on the maturation of the central nervous system. In examining the developmental course of emotional expression, it becomes evident that some aspects of emotional and cognitive development are on parallel lines; in other instances the cognitive skill is a prerequisite for emotional expression. Chronological age is not a simple variable; it is only a rough index of the psychological changes associated with the changing capacities of the child . . .

COGNITIVE THEORIES OF EMOTIONS
EMOTIONS

D. L. Wertlieb

AFFILIATION NEED

Need for affiliation (*n Aff*) was 1 of 20 psychological needs identified by H. A. Murray and measured through his Thematic Apperception Test (TAT). The *n Aff* is scored when one or more of the characters in a subject's TAT story shows concern "over *establishing, maintaining, or restoring a positive affective relationship with another person*" (italics in the original). Individuals scoring high on *n Aff* on Gough's Adjective Check List tend to describe themselves in such terms as friendly, warm, trusting, talkative, cheerful, kind, loyal, helpful, praising, accepting, and generous. These characteristics are more likely to be associated with feminine than with masculine personality stereotypes. S. Miller and K. M. Nardini found, for example, that women scored higher than men on a measure of affiliation tendency, while Bose, Das Gupta, and Lindgren observed that female undergraduates in Calcutta, who took a Bengali test measuring *n Aff* and need for achievement (*n Ach*), scored higher on *n Aff* and lower on *n Ach* than male undergraduates did.

There is considerable evidence to show that *n Ach* and *n Aff* are negatively correlated, probably because the two motives are generally expressed in mutually incompatible forms of behavior.

Studies generally confirm hypotheses based on *n Aff* theory. Lansing and Heyns, for instance, found that *n Aff* was significantly related to frequency of local telephone calls made by subjects, although it was only weakly related to numbers of letters written or frequency of visits to relatives and close friends living at a distance. Sid and Lindgren found that women students majoring in nursing and education rated higher on a measure of *n Aff* than did students in other major fields, and that the *n Aff* of expectant mothers was higher than that of any other group tested.

The possibility that affiliation tendency is characterized by sensitivity to rejection was explored by Mehrabian, who found the two traits to be essentially unrelated. Both variables were negatively correlated with a measure of achieving tendency, but affiliation tendency was positively correlated with measures of empathy and arousal-seeking tendency, whereas sensitivity to rejection was negatively correlated with arousal-seeking tendency and social desirability. Mehrabian found, however, that scores on measures of affiliative tendency and sensitivity to rejection could be combined to produce a single measure of dependency.

NEED/PRESS THEORY
PROSOCIAL BEHAVIOR

H. C. LINDGREN

AGE DIFFERENCES

Behavioral changes with age are as striking as changes in physical appearance. Both training and altered structures contribute to these psychological differences. Differences that occur throughout the life span are mainly studied by *cross-sectional* and *longitudinal* methods.

Age differences in intelligence have been extensively studied. Mental age (MA) as measured by standard intelligence tests increases with chronological age (CA), and because of the way age scales are constructed, the relation is linear. An average child shows an increase of 1 year in MA for each year of CA until about 15 to 18 years of age, when MA is assumed to level off. There is evidence, however, that the intellectual ability of some individuals may continue to increase at least until they are in their early 20s.

The question of the growth of MA with age is complicated by two factors: (a) the difficulty level of items for young adults, and (b) the different composition of abilities tested at different age levels. If there are few difficult items at the upper end of the scale, older subjects cannot show improvement: The "ceiling" of the test is too low. If the same functions are not being tested at different age levels, what does it mean to say that MA *increases* with age?

The constancy of IQ across time has long been an age-related issue. In general, IQ's of schoolchildren and adults have been found to be constant enough to allow satisfactory prediction over several years. And within limits, the older the subjects, the longer the test scores remain relatively constant (within 4 to 5 IQ points). At the opposite extreme, preschool IQ's are very poor predictors of scores obtained later in life. It should be emphasized, however, that, even when test-retest correlations are high for a group, sizable systematic shifts in IQ can occur in particular individuals. A change of 30 or more points in a mean of 12 years has been found in 9% of the cases studied by Honzik, Macfarlane, and Allen.

Interestingly, there is often a large drop in IQ a few years before death, regardless of when death occurs. Such a drop in IQ can even be used to predict death.

The fact that recognition memory and recall show decided improvement in children, say, between ages 6 and 9 is probably related to an increase in mental age. The older children use implicit verbalization more—labeling, rehearsing, and comparing stimuli. Age seems to affect recall performance more than recognition, improving performance in children and hindering it in old age.

A fair number of generalizations can be made about behavior changes in later life.

1. Since behavior is in part a product of the central nervous system, the loss of brain cells with age is probably a relevant consideration. By the age of 80 or 90, 40% of cortical cells may be lost. Also, water content declines and fats increase in the brain over the life span.

2. Older people definitely have more health problems than the young, which inevitably modifies their behavior.

3. Visual acuity and accommodation decline because of the increase in opacity and loss of elasticity of the lens of the eye in middle age. Changes in the retina later in life also impair color vision and increase sensitivity to glare.

4. Similarly in audition, perception of higher frequencies disappears in the middle years, and after 65 many adults require, although they do not necessarily use, hearing aids. Stress due to hearing loss can produce depression and other emotional disorders.

5. There is also declining sensitivity in taste, smell, and pain in the later years.

6. Older people seem to take longer to learn verbal material than do the young. However, when the learning of older people is self-paced and meaningful, they perform well. They also improve in learning and long-term memory when instructed to use mediating or mnemonic devices.

7. Older people's deficit in long-term memory seems to be mainly one of retrieval; short-term memory is impaired only when the task requires divided attention (e.g., dichotic listening). Span remains essentially intact until very advanced years.

8. Individual variability in all intellectual tasks increases over the life span, but this does not pose an educational problem until around 70 years of age or later.

9. With increasing age the central nervous system slows down. This change appears to account for the gradual decrease in speed of responding across the life span for a wide range of tasks, including reaction time, sorting objects, copying, canceling, and other similar processing functions.

10. Although there are few studies on problem solving and creativity as a function of aging, some hypotheses have emerged:

    (a) Older subjects tend to ask uninformative questions, to be disrupted by irrelevant and redundant information, and to treat both positive and negative instances of a concept as positive. Failure to profit from negative information can make a person seem rigid.

    (b) If memory load is kept low and older people are given strategy hints and the like, age-related deficits in problem solving can be substantially reduced (Sanders et al., 1975).

    (c) Although Lehman (1953) concluded that most creative achievements occur early in a scientist's or artist's career, considerable evidence indicates that some of the most valuable contributions come late in life. For example, Claude Monet began his famed "Water Lily" series at age 73; Benjamin Franklin invented the bifocal lens at 78; Sophocles wrote *Oedipus rex* at 75; and George Bernard Shaw wrote his first play at 48. When the quality of works by Bach and Beethoven is assessed by the number of times a piece has been recorded, the latest works excel.

11. As one grows older, interests change; for example, the participant in sports becomes a spectator, and the incidence of crime declines steadily.

12. Finally, well-conducted sequential studies suggest that a person's personality is characterized more by continuity than by change. Cohort differences appear to be more prevalent than age changes.

ALZHEIMER'S DISEASE
HUMAN DEVELOPMENT
LIFE-SPAN DEVELOPMENT
LONGITUDINAL STUDIES

M. R. DENNY

AGGRESSION

Aggression is complex and multiply determined in its causes, difficult to predict, and in many instances hard to control.

Aggression as Instinct

The belief that aggression is instinctive is popular among the general American public. In the 1960s three books championing the instinctive basis of aggression were widely received in the United States: Lorenz's *On aggression,* Ardrey's *The territorial imperative,* and Morris' *The naked ape.* Each espoused the view that aggression springs primarily from an innate fighting instinct. According to this view, aggressive energy growing from this instinct is spontaneously generated within the person continuously and at a constant rate. As time passes, aggressive energy is said to build up. The more that has accumulated, the weaker the stimulus necessary to set it off or release it into overt aggressive behavior. If enough time has passed since its last expression, overt aggression may occur spontaneously, with no apparent releasing stimuli. In this view, aggressive energy inexorably accumulates and inexorably must be expressed.

Instinct theory, a blend of anecdote, analogical leaps, unsystematic journalism, and undefined concepts, is seductively appealing. It is irresponsible, in the sense that, according to the theory, aggressive urges accumulate and must be expressed independent of the individual's choice. The theory is comprehensive, in that it can sweepingly "explain" diverse forms and rates of aggression when no other single cause, by itself, can do so. Most contemporary scientific views of aggression in America agree that one contributing factor is a genetic-physiological capacity to aggress.

Aggression as Drive

As scientific interest in the purported instinctual basis of aggressive behavior waned, it was replaced by the concept of drive. For over two decades, American scientific efforts relative to aggression focused on drive concepts.

The course of much of the research on the frustration-aggression hypothesis and its derivative propositions often proved not to be smooth. While much was learned about frustration and aggression, definitional problems persisted and the relationship of these two variables suffered from a largely insoluble circularity. As R. N. Johnson notes, "The presence of frustration was taken to mean that subsequent behavior was likely to be aggressive, and the presence of aggression was used as evidence that the preceding experience had been frustrating." Leonard Berkowitz and Seymour Feshbach focused largely on drive theory, and both were active in efforts to revise and extend frustration-aggression thinking. Berkowitz suggested that stimuli regularly associated with aggression may gradually acquire the capacity to elicit aggressive actions from individuals previously provoked. Frustration, he proposed, induces anger that by itself leads not to overt aggression, but instead to a readiness or set to respond aggressively. Actual overt aggression, Berkowitz suggested, will not occur unless suitable aggression-relevant cues are present. These cues are usually stimuli (people, places, objects, etc.) associated with current or previous anger instigators.

Aggression as Social Learning

Much of American psychology after the 1950s shifted its concern away from unobservable, purported inner determinants of behavior toward external influences on overt responses. Human behavior has been studied extensively in terms of eliciting stimuli and reinforcing consequences.

Social learning theory is a cognitive/stimulus-response view not only of aggression, but also of a wide variety of other behaviors. The processes responsible for aggression are, according to this view, essentially identical to the processes relevant to the learning, performance, and maintenance of most forms of overt behavior. Table 1 is a summary statement of the processes that, according to social learning theory, are responsible for the individual's *acquisition* or original learning of aggressive behaviors, the *instigation* of overt acts of aggression at any given point in time, and the *maintenance* of such behavior.

Social learning theory acknowledges that a given individual's potential to behave aggressively probably stems from neurophysiological characteristics. Genetic, hormonal, central nervous system, and resultant physical characteristics of the individual, it is held, all influence one's capacity or potential to aggress, as well as the likelihood that specific forms of aggression will, in fact, be learned.

Given the neurophysiological capacity to acquire and retain aggression in one's behavioral repertoire, Bandura suggests that such acquisition proceeds by means of direct or vicarious experiences. In both instances, the role of reinforcement looms large. Overtly aggressive acts, occurring in the context of trial-and-error behavior or under instructional control of others, are likely, when reinforced, to increase the probability that aggression will be learned or acquired by the individual. Bandura views reinforced practice as a particularly consequential event in the learning of aggression via direct experiences, be it childhood pushing and shoving, adolescent fighting, or adult military combat.

But heaviest emphasis for the acquisition of aggression is placed on vicarious processes. Such observational learning is held to emanate from three types of modeling influences: familial, subcultural, and symbolic. The physically abused child who strikes out at peers and, as an adult, batters his or her own child, may have acquired such behaviors via observation of his or her own parents. Subcultural modeling influences on the acquisition of aggression are exemplified by the behavior of adolescents in response to their observation of peer aggression. Vicarious symbolic modeling on television, in the papers, and in comic books is apparently also a major source for learning aggression. Crucial is the fact that such aggression usually "works." The aggressive model, be it parent, peer, or television character, is often reinforced for behaving aggressively. Individuals tend to acquire those behaviors for which they observe others being rewarded. The likelihood of such acquisition is enhanced by certain characteristics of the model (e.g., perceived expertness; high status; same sex, age, and race as the observer), of the behavior being modeled (e.g., clarity, repetition, difficulty, detail, enactment by several models), and of the observer—that is, the person viewing and learning from the model (e.g., similarity to the model, friendliness toward the model, instructions to imitate, and—most important, as noted—reward for imitating).

In summary, of the three diverse American approaches to understanding the origins and nature of aggressive behavior, the instinct view was, and remains, largely a detour away from an empirically based and societally useful comprehension of aggression and its control. Drive theory was also inadequate in many particulars, but served, and continues to serve, a major heuristic function via the research and theoretical efforts to which it has given rise. Social learning theory, in our view, represents the most theoretically sound, empirically supported, and pragmatically useful view of aggression available. As a good scientific stance should

Table 1 Social Learning Theory of Aggression

Acquisition	Instigation	Maintenance

I. *Neurophysiological*
Genetic
Hormonal
C.N.S. (e.g., hypothalamus, limbic
system)
Physical characteristics
	I. *Aversive*
	Frustration
	Adverse reductions in reinforcement
	  Relative deprivation
	  Unjustified hardships
	Verbal threats and insults
	Physical assaults
		I. *Direct External Reinforcement*
		Tangible (material)
		Social (status, approval)
		Alleviation of aversiveness
		Expression of injury

II. *Observational Learning* Family influences (e.g., abuse) Subcultural influences (e.g., delin- quency) Symbolic modeling (e.g., television)	II. *Modeling Influences* Disinhibitory-reduced restraints Facilitative Emotional arousal Stimulus-enhancing (attentional)	II. *Vicarious Reinforcement* Observed reward (Receipt- facilitation effect) Observed punishment (Escape- disinhibitory effect)
III. *Direct Experience* Combat Reinforced practice	III. *Incentives Inducements* Instrumental aggression Anticipated consequences IV. *Instructional Control* V. *Delusional Control* VI. *Environmental Control* Crowding Ambient temperature Noise Physical environment	III. *Neutralization of Self-Punishment* Moral justification Palliative comparison Euphemistic labeling Displacement of responsibility Diffusion of responsibility Dehumanization of victims Attribution of blame to victims Misrepresentation of consequences Graduated desensitization

be, it is a testable, logically consistent set of constructs of increasingly demonstrable validity.

INSTIGATION

Once having learned how to aggress—and when, where, with whom, and so on—what determines whether the individual will in fact do so? According to social learning theory, the actual performance of aggressive behaviors is multiply determined.

Aversive events may serve as an evocation of aggression. Frustration is seen as one such aversive instigator, as in drive theory. But, unlike in drive theory, frustration is at the same time but one instigator among several, and also a phenomenon recognized to have several generally equipotential possible consequences in addition to aggression, such as regression, withdrawal, dependency, psychosomatization, self-anesthetization with drugs and alcohol, and constructive problem solving. Adverse reductions in reinforcement are a second purported type of aversive instigation to aggression. Commentators on collective aggression have pointed to this instigation, especially in the form of a perceived sense of deprivation relative to others or hardship perceived as unjustified—rather than deprivation or hardship in an absolute sense—as a major source of mob violence, riots, and the like. Verbal insults and physical assaults are additional, and particularly potent, aversive instigators to aggression. Toch has shown that insults most likely to evoke physical assault include threats to reputation and manly status, and public humiliation. Physical assault as an aversive instigation to reciprocal behavior is most likely to occur when avoidance is difficult and the level of instigating assaultiveness is both high and frequent.

Just as modeling influences are a major means by which new patterns of aggression are acquired, so they can also function as significant instigators to overt aggressive behavior. If we observe another person (the model) behaving aggressively and not being punished for it, this observation can have a *disinhibitory effect*. Through a process akin to vicarious extinction of fear, such disinhibition can result in overt aggression by the observer. Should the model be rewarded for the displayed aggression, a

response facilitation effect may occur. The model's behavior now functions as an inducement to engage in matching behavior. The sight of others behaving aggressively often engenders *emotional arousal* in the observer, and considerable empirical evidence exists that arousal facilitates the occurrence of aggressive behavior, especially in persons for whom such a response is well-practiced and readily available.

Incentive Inducements

S. Feshbach and others have drawn the distinction between angry aggression and instrumental aggression. The goal of the former is to hurt another individual; the latter is an effort to obtain rewards. Incentive inducements to aggression relate to this second definition.

Aggression very often pays, incentive-induced aggression often lets the aggressor obtain the sought-after incentive, and therein lies one of the obstacles—perhaps the most fundamental one—to successful, widespread aggression control.

Instructional Control

Individuals may aggress against others because they are told to do so. Obedience is taught and differentially rewarded by family and school during childhood and adolescence, and by many social institutions during adulthood (at work, in military service, etc.).

Bizarre beliefs, inner voices, paranoid suspiciousness, perceptions of divine messages, delusions of grandeur—may all function as apparent instigators to aggression. The aggression may be justified in self-defensive terms, in messianic terms, as an expression of heroic responsibility, or on similar bases. While delusional control is not to be minimized, it is probable that the frequency of this form of instigation is greatly overestimated.

Environmental Control

As psychologists in recent years have become increasingly interested in the effects on behavior of external events, even "founding" the subfield of environmental psychology, there has been an increased examination of external events as instigators to aggression. Crowding, temperature, noise, and other characteristics of the environment have been studied. Evidence reveals that each may instigate aggression. Whether aggressive behavior does in fact grow from crowded conditions, hot days and nights, high noise levels, or the like, appears to be a somewhat complicated function of the physical intensity of these environmental qualities, their personalogical attributes, the levels of emotional arousal they engender, and their interaction, external constraints, and other considerations.

MAINTENANCE

Aggressive behavior is influenced by the extrinsic rewards it elicits. Such rewards may be tangible or social, or may consist of the alleviation of aversive treatment, or possibly the inducing of expressions of pain by the person against whom one is aggressing.

Vicarious processes are important for the maintenance of aggression. The aggression-maintaining effects of observing others receiving rewards for aggressing comes about, Bandura suggests, via (a) its informational function, (b) its motivational function, and (c) its disinhibitory effect, as when the observer sees others escaping punishment for their aggressive behavior.

Social learning theory proposes that there are also self-produced consequences by which individuals regulate their own behavior. With regard to aggression, most persons learn that aggressive behavior should be negatively sanctioned, and they do so by what they say, do, or feel about themselves following their own aggressive behavior. There also exist persons whose self-reinforcement is such that overt aggression is a rewardable source of pride. They are prone to combativeness and derive enhanced feelings of self-worth from its success.

PREDICTION OF AGGRESSION

The timing and target of aggression prevention efforts may be optimally guided when one knows who is going to be aggressive, and where and when such behavior will occur. High levels of accurate prediction have proven difficult to obtain. On a broad level of inquiry, it has been established that aggressive criminal behavior consistently correlates with such demographic and related variables as past criminal behavior, age, sex, race, socioeconomic status, and opiate or alcohol abuse. But such actuarial probabilities are of modest value in predicting the overt behavior of any given individual or individuals.

In *The clinical prediction of violent behavior,* Monahan critically reviewed the five major investigations that have sought to examine the utility of psychological test and interview data for predicting aggression. The outcomes of these predictive efforts are summarized in Table 2.

It is clear from Table 2 that clinical prediction of adult aggression yields a dismaying number of mispredictions. False positives, in particular—predicted to be aggressive, but with no actual aggression ensuing—are very high across all five studies. Monahan notes that "the 'best' clinical research currently in existence indicates that psychiatrists and psychologists are accurate in no more than one out of three predictions of violent behavior over a several-year period."

AGGRESSION CONTROL

Relaxation training is rooted historically in decades-old techniques originated by E. Jacobson, is popular in contemporary therapeutic usage—especially as a component of systematic desensitization procedures—and is empirically demonstrated to be effective in an extended series of investigations. It is an effective means for reducing the tension and arousal states so often viewed as precursors to overt aggression.

Self-control training as an approach to anger and aggression control has taken several forms, chief among them being to teach the target person to engage in a process variously termed rational restructuring, cognitive self-instruction, and stress inoculation, the central feature of which is learning to make verbal self-statements that effectively self-instruct the person to respond to feelings of anger and arousal with more reflective and less aggressive behavior. It is an aggression-control intervention of demonstrated efficacy and growing utilization.

Communication skills training utilizes didactic techniques to literally teach constructive communication behaviors. Targeted focus on an especially useful approach to conflict resolution by means of *negotiation training,* follows the more general communication skills training. Finally, to maximize the likelihood that conflict-resolving, negotiated agreements are in fact lived up to, the parties to the conflict are taught to draw up and execute written agreements known as *behavioral contracts.* This commonly grouped-together triad of interventions appears to be an especially promising approach to aggression control and the consequent reduction of interpersonal conflict.

Contingency management, the use of rewards and nonphysical punishment, has the longest investigative history of the interventions considered here. Contingency management is an especially potent aggression-control intervention, particularly in those applications that combine rewards to increase constructive or prosocial behaviors.

Psychotherapy has not proven especially effective. Psychotherapeutic applications responsive to salient patient characteristics—such as peer group responsiveness among aggressive adolescents—proved more effective in reducing aggression. Instructional therapies, which usually derive their specific procedures from social learning theory, have quite consistently demonstrated their behavior-change effectiveness.

Small-Group Interventions

Psychological skill training uses a series of psychoeducational procedures to teach aggression-management skills. Teaching procedures often include modeling, behavioral rehearsal, and performance feedback. The skill-enhancement effectiveness of this intervention has been broadly and reliably demonstrated.

Character education—in the form of its major, contemporary expression, the Character Education Curriculum—is a comprehensive series of lessons in prosocial character traits designed especially for elementary school utilization.

Values clarification, seeking to enhance prosocial values without resorting to indoctrination, rests on rather different assumptions and techniques. The goals are to help students develop, clarify, and apply their

Table 2   Validity Studies of the Clinical Prediction of Violent Behavior

Study	Percent True Positive	Percent False Positive	Percent True Negative	Percent False Negative	Number Predicted Violent	Number Predicted Nonviolent	Follow-up Years
Kozol et al. (1972)	34.7	65.3	92.0	8.0	49	386	5
Steadman & Cocozza (1974)	20.0	80.0	—	—	967	—	4
Cocozza & Steadman (1976)	14.0	86.0	84.0	16.0	154	103	3
Steadman (1977)	41.3	58.7	68.8	31.2	46	106	3
Thornberry & Jacoby (1979)	14.0	86.0	—	—	438	—	4

own values by freely and thoughtfully choosing among alternative values. Empirical research has provided some tentative and partial support for the effectiveness of values clarification in decreasing destructive attitudes and behavior and in increasing constructive alternatives.

Moral education, reflected especially in the work of Kohlberg, is a particularly prominent small-group intervention designed to teach prosocial alternatives to aggression.

ENVIRONMENTAL STRESS
PERSONALITY DISORDERS
PROSOCIAL BEHAVIOR
SELF-CONTROL
TANTRUMS
VIOLENCE

A. P. GOLDSTEIN

AGING AND INTELLIGENCE

Intelligence has been both an interesting and controversial topic of research in the field of adult development. The topic of intellectual change in adulthood is a complex one, characterized by different theoretical outlooks and many methodological concerns.

The data indicate that intelligence is best considered as multidimensional (multifaceted) and that IQ is not an adequate or accurate estimate of adult intelligence. Therefore, statements about whether intelligence grows or declines with age must recognize the complexity of intellectual functioning in adulthood. Because intelligence is complex, it should not be surprising to observe that different aspects of intelligence change in different ways (and for different reasons) in different people with age.

Among the earliest studies of the effects across age on intellectual functioning are the cross-sectional studies of Miles and Miles and Jones and Conrad, for which noticeable declines in performance with increasing age were obtained. Early cross-sectional studies also found overall Wechsler Adult Intelligence Scale (WAIS) performance with increased age (relative to the standard reference group of those 20 to 34 years old) to peak between ages 20 and 34 and to decline slowly until about age 60, with more severe declines afterward. Longitudinal studies, however, typically display an increase in overall performance with age.

Botwinick notes that the patterns of uncorrected scores do reflect age trends, subject to the "appropriateness" of the testing content and the state of the person tested. Moreover, individual differences in intelligence may outweigh such age-related differences, accounting for the relatively low correlations between age and intelligence.

On the basis of cross-sectional data, a *classic aging pattern* of intelligence has been found: Both WAIS verbal and performance subtests decline with age, but the decrement for performance is a great deal more severe. This finding, as noted by Botwinick has been replicated in at least nine other principal studies. Using the Stanford–Binet, Terman obtained cross-sectional standardization data that yielded similar results. Papalia and coworkers and Hornblum and Overton also have reported decrements in Piagetian conservation tasks with increasing chronological age, arguing that this decline is paralleled by the observed decrement in fluid abilities. Each is relatively unaffected by formal schooling, culture, or specific life experiences. It may be that older adults' thinking is of a different *quality* than that of younger adults, causing the former to redefine the Piagetian tasks put to them so that the answers will differ. Rather than assume an age-related decline in Piagetian intelligence a new stage of intellectual development termed *postformal reasoning* may emerge. Postformal reasoning is relative, or temporary, and highly dependent on the immediate context.

Longitudinal designs have failed to support an age-related decrement in intellectual performance, generally finding increases up to a point followed by a leveling off. Owens found gains in army alpha total scores with age up to approximately age 40 or 50. Schaie's longitudinal data over the adult life span suggest that there is gain in intellectual abilities through one's 40s followed by relative stability for most skills through the 50s and early 60s; average losses for most abilities become significant after age 60. Such declines are greater for persons with significant health difficulties, when performance is speeded, for those who are poorly educated, and for those who live in intellectually deprived environments. Moreover, there are individual differences in the extent of declines in abilities after the age of 60. Less than 33% experience decrement until age 74, and only 30 to 40% experience significant losses in intellectual skills by age 81. Though many individuals "selectively optimize" certain skills after age 80, the reduction in intellectual abilities becomes more apparent into one's 80s and 90s. Other longitudinal investigations yield similarly positive data on adult developmental change in intelligence.

One of the most important findings in adult intelligence is the recognition of cohort effects in intellectual functioning. For some abilities, cohort differences are positive (younger cohorts perform more adequately), as in the case of the primary mental abilities (PMA) of verbal meaning, spatial orientation, and inductive reasoning, largely due to higher levels of education and better health for such persons. For other skills, cohort effects are negative, as in the case of PMA number skills or word fluency. Indeed, when controls for level of education are made, age differences in WAIS verbal scores are affected more strongly than are WAIS performance scores, supporting education as a major factor influencing intelligence that is cohort specific.

A most recent development is the search for everyday intelligence. Everyday intelligence possesses what might be called ecological or functional validity in that it reflects the skills adults actually use to function on an everyday basis in situations indigenous to them. Relative to formal measures of intellectual functioning, the everyday context in which individuals exercise their abilities may be a more accurate reflection of their intellectual prowess. Dealing with other people in relationships, making decisions, weighing options in ambiguous life-planning situations, and evaluating one's standing in various life domains (e.g., disease, death, financial matters) may indeed be reasonable estimates of intelligence. Much work remains to be done in this relatively new area of intellectual functioning in adulthood.

AGING AND BEHAVIOR CHANGES
INTELLIGENCE MEASURES

B. HAYSLIP, JR.

AGING: BEHAVIOR CHANGES

Until the twentieth century, relatively little was known about the patterning of human behavior. Strong environmentalists had maintained that behavior was a result of environmental forces impinging on the individual. In past centuries even hereditarians, although believing that the way people behave is to a large extent dependent on inherited factors, did not go so far as to outline or emphasize the possibility that human behavior changes in a highly patterned way with age.

That older people behaved differently from when they were young was, of course, generally accepted. But the notion that behavior changed in so patterned a way that this patterning could be objectively measured and charted seems not to have been considered.

Arnold Gesell was perhaps the first scientist to attempt to chart in detail the minute progressions of age development; to a large extent, it became his life's work.

Gesell's work and that of his staff always focused primarily on the changes in behavior expected to occur as the organism ages. Through

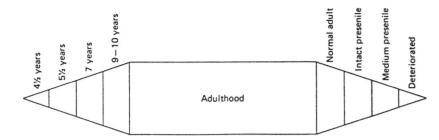

Figure 1. Human life span as a diamond.

some 300 publications, Gesell outlined the specific behavior changes that might be expected from infancy through the first 16 years of life and developed behavior tests that he and his staff perfected.

Evaluation of the age level of any given individual's behavior was arrived at by subjecting the person (infant or child) to a series of graded behavior tests such as reaction to 1-inch cubes, the copying of geometric forms, the completion of the incompleted figure of a man, and other similar tasks. After many years of research, graded norms were published to cover behavior from 4 weeks of age through 10 years. The Gesell studies suggest that behavior characteristic of any age amounts to more than just the sum of specific abilities which the individual can master or express at that age. Each advancing age appears also to have its own individuality. There are ages of equilibrium and ages of disequilibrium, ages of inward and ages of expansive behavior. These follow each other in an apparently systematic and predictable order.

AFTER SIXTEEN

During the first year of life it has been possible to categorize changes on a monthly basis. This slows down to six monthly intervals from 2 through 6 years of age and to yearly intervals from 6 to 16 years of age. After that the intervals become much greater and thus increasingly difficult to define.

In addition, the relative contributions of heredity and environment to any person's behavior might be different at different times of life. Observations suggested that in the earliest years and again in old age, hereditary factors might play a major role. In midlife and even as early as the early 20s, environmental factors seem to play a relatively larger role. For all these reasons, age changes in the years following 16 seem difficult to determine.

SEVENTY AND OVER

The *normal adult* elderly person, regardless of chronological age, responds both on behavior tests and in everyday life as does the hypothetically "normal" younger adult. The *intact presenile* individual shows some slippage but still in most instances can maintain daily routines, including the handling of finances, and is quite capable of living alone. The modest onset of presenility can be observed in small ways. The elderly person tends to be mildly forgetful, somewhat egocentric, and set in his or her ways.

The *medium presenile* individual shows a good deal of slippage and will do best if living in a protected atmosphere, even though such an individual may superficially appear quite alert and even moderately capable. People falling in this category are often greatly misunderstood by those around them. Superficially they may be able to behave in a quite "normal" way, make a reasonably good appearance, and carry on usual conversations. They then confound and disturb relatives, friends, and those caring for them by behaving in a childish or irrational way. Others are then apt to become impatient, feeling that these individuals could do better if they would only try. However, the *deteriorated presenile*

person obviously needs protection, although even here the person falls short of sheer senile dementia.

BEHAVIOR CHANGES IN THE ENTIRE LIFE SPAN

Gesell studies of aging led to the diagrammatic expression of the course of intellectual function during the human life span as an elongated diamond (see Figure 1). Schematically, one may say that cognitive and other functions increase and improve through perhaps the first 20 years or so of life, and then may be assumed to hold their own for the next 40 to 60 years. Finally, there appears to be in most a gradual closing and narrowing down, with behavior reverting systematically to ways characteristic of ever earlier age levels.

Gesell researchers have long maintained that young children should start school and be subsequently promoted on the basis of their behavior age rather than their chronological age. The same principle seems to hold for old age. In old age as in childhood, the behavior age rather than the chronological age should guide our expectations of function—a consideration that could change retirement practices in this country. Such practices might, effectively, be based on the way the person functions rather than on the chronological age as such.

ALZHEIMER'S DISEASE
PERSONALITY CHANGES

L. B. AMES

AGRICULTURAL PSYCHOLOGY

In contrast to other social sciences that have developed specialized interests and/or applications in agriculture, psychology has had relatively little interaction with agricultural or rural issues. Thus, there has not been any psychological counterpart to such social science specialities as rural sociology, farm marketing, agricultural economics, and rural geography. Nonetheless, psychological and agricultural issues have overlapped in several domains: (a) the investigation of farming tasks and skills, (b) the analysis of expert agricultural judges, (c) the evaluation of farm management decisions, and (d) some miscellaneous other areas.

FARMING SKILLS

Traditionally, farm workers were expected to have a wide variety of manual and mechanical skills, and psychologists were concerned with examining those skills. For instance, R. W. Tomlinson reported that dairy workers must be proficient in over nine separate tasks ranging from operating milking machines to evaluating the health of cows. In short, a traditional farm worker was a jack-of-all-trades with general skills in a great many areas.

However, with the increased mechanization of farms and farm machinery, there has been a shift in the skills needed. Instead of many general abilities, more specialized abilities became necessary.

With the trend away from smaller family farms toward larger corporate farms, a greater need has developed for farmers with judgment and management abilities and less need for manual/mechanical abilities. Accordingly, behavioral researchers have turned toward analysis of the cognitive skills needed in agricultural judgment and management.

AGRICULTURAL JUDGMENT

Apparently the first analysis of expert judgment in any area was conducted in 1917 by H. D. Hughes, who observed that the corn rated highest by expert corn judges did not always produce the highest crop yields. Subsequently, Henry Wallace—later vice president under Franklin Roosevelt—extensively reanalyzed the data collected by Hughes and reported that, although there was fairly high agreement among the corn judges, the ratings correlated only slightly with crop yields.

Trumbo, Adams, Milner, and Schipper asked licensed grain inspectors to judge samples of grain. Nearly one-third of the samples were misgraded, and when graded a second time, more than one-third of the samples were given a different grade. Finally, the investigators found that increased experience made judges more confident, but did not make them more accurate; instead, more experienced judges had a tendency to overgrade (i.e., grade inflation).

A similar analysis of soil judges by Shanteau and Gaeth revealed validity and reliability values of about 50%. One source of errors was reported to be interference caused by the presence of irrelevant materials in the soils. In a follow-up, Gaeth and Shanteau attempted to reduce this interference. They found that training not only reduced the effect of irrelevant materials, but also increased the accuracy of the judgments.

There have been several psychological investigations of livestock judges. Phelps and Shanteau found that the judges not only used almost all the information provided, but did so in a reliable manner. Gaeth and Shanteau compared six groups of livestock judges varying in background and training. There were three major results: (a) the experienced judges were able to extract more information and use it in more complex ways; (b) experts tended to judge each case on an individual basis, whereas less experienced judges were more likely to use the same strategy for all cases; and (c) experienced judges were more reliable than those with less experience.

FARM MANAGEMENT

There has been a considerable amount of research on the decisions necessary to manage a farm. The majority of this work has been concerned with how the decisions should be made optimally. However, there has been some consideration as to how to modify decision situations to reflect the psychological limitations and abilities of farmers. For instance, Rajala and Sage considered a variety of methods intended to help farmers make more effective decisions.

Investigations have also been conducted to determine what factors are used by farmers in making various marketing decisions. Foxall reported that farmers' buying decisions are similar to the strategies used by industrial buyers. Specifically, farmers rely heavily on past experience and relatively little on word of mouth and other interpersonal factors.

Psychological analyses have proved particularly useful in constructing better techniques for evaluating and managing food quality. Based on such research, an improved instrument was developed for the evaluation of dairy goods.

MISCELLANEOUS

In summary, although "agricultural psychology" is not normally recognized as a subfield of psychology, there have nevertheless been a wide variety of applications of behavioral research in agricultural settings.

APPLIED RESEARCH
EXPERIMENTAL DESIGNS
FIELD EXPERIMENTATION
MANAGEMENT DECISION MAKING
PLANT BEHAVIOR

J. SHANTEAU

ALCOHOLISM TREATMENT

Recovery from alcoholism would best be facilitated by the continuum of treatment that a service delivery system provides. There are many variables to examine when designing this type of system. An initial concern should be the scope of the geographic area to be serviced, which can range from a worldwide perspective down to a specific neighborhood. Upon determining the geographic area, an assessment of alcoholism service needs is called for. This includes identifying the population in need of services, identifying existing services, recognizing service gaps, and examining the resources needed to complete the service delivery system.

The largest percentage of available alcoholism services is for adult males. There has been some recognition of the need for increased services for women, adolescents, families of alcohol abusers and alcoholics, and other groups. The economic situation may dictate more accountability of existing services and an examination of possible duplication of programming in any designated geographic area. Finally, the need for new services such as day care and vocational training for women, has become apparent. When an alcoholism program is being planned for a particular community, stereotyped attitudes toward alcohol abuse or alcoholism often appear.

TREATMENT SYSTEM COMPONENTS

Emergency Services

Emergency services is the first level of care for the person who is acutely ill or in crisis. The services can include medical evaluation, treatment and supervision, diagnostic evaluation, treatment planning, and triage to the appropriate level of care, if necessary. There are three types of emergency services generally available for the individual with an alcohol abuse or alcoholism problem.

1. *Medical.* Medical services are usually provided in a hospital emergency room. Generally, there is variation in the methods used in hospital emergency rooms to provide some level of detoxification. An alternative setting is a community-based medical detoxification facility not within a hospital.

2. *Nonmedical.* Community-based, social-setting detoxification agencies are examples of an emergency care model. There is an emphasis on supportive counseling, medical stabilization, and preparation for the next level of care within the network of services. Staffing is usually by a combination of alcoholism counselors, paramedics, and individuals identified with a specific health care discipline. The usual length of stay is a maximum of five days.

3. *Psychological.* Often individuals who are abusing alcohol experience a high level of stress and anxiety and, therefore, seek out a crisis intervention program to alleviate these feelings. Alcoholism issues often emerge as a person begins treatment for an initial psychiatric disorder. In this kind of setting, it is important to arrive at a differential diagnosis to effect an appropriate referral and treatment plan.

Inpatient Care

Inpatient care provides for 24-hour supervised care under the direction of a physician in a medical setting. In a hospital setting, this service is usually provided on the general medical floor. The three primary referral categories are (a) individuals who are in need of medical detoxification; (b) medical conditions associated with alcoholism such as ulcers, hepatitis, pancreatitis, etc.; (c) psychiatric emergencies due to alcoholism.

Intermediate Care

Intermediate care is usually referred to as residential care. It is designed for people who cannot reside in an independent living situation while attempting to deal with their alcohol abuse or alcoholism problem. Examples of residential care for alcohol abuse or alcoholism are the following.

1. *Residential Rehabilitation.* Residential rehabilitation is intensive treatment, usually using an array of treatment modalities such as individual, group, and family therapy; Alcoholics Anonymous (AA); vocational and recreation therapy; and a variety of treatment techniques. Lengths of stay generally vary from 21 to 30 days. Some residential rehabilitation programs are designed for special populations such as chronic recidivists. The issue of a client's motivation or readiness for treatment usually arises when there is an intake assessment. Controversy continues regarding the criteria for determining motivation, and whether applicants for admission can deal with this issue relative to their current state of recovery.

2. *Halfway Houses.* A halfway house is a residential facility that is viewed as a step between an intensive inpatient program and independent living. There is usually a minimum amount of treatment offered within the halfway house, with an emphasis on linking into community-based agencies and support systems. Generally, there is a resident manager who often lives within the facility. There are house rules, and a structured environment is provided for the residents. A halfway house is often an alternative to returning to a stressful home situation before developing the skills and confidence to cope with those stresses. The average length of stay is usually 3 to 12 months, with a range of treatment approaches. The 12 steps of AA are an integral, and sometimes focal, treatment modality.

3. *Partial Hospitalization.* Partial hospitalization is viewed as serving the client who needs more intensive treatment but can be maintained in an independent living situation for a portion of the day. *Day treatment* is designed for the client who has a living situation and is not in need of this level of intensive treatment in a residential setting. *Intensive outpatient rehabilitation* is similar to day treatment but can be offered in the evening as well, for those who are employed or otherwise occupied during the daytime hours. The number of hours varies from 2 to 8 per day, for from 1 to 7 days per week. The traditional modalities of psychotherapy are used as part of the treatment plan. Partial hospitalization programs recognize the need for assessing the clients' ability to manage their lives and sobriety during the hours that they are not in treatment. Backup and supportive services are considered vital in developing a treatment plan for individuals in these programs.

Other Services

There is an array of other services not offered directly but that may significantly influence the delivery of services to the client. *Prevention* provides the correct information in a meaningful fashion, so that an individual will not begin to abuse alcohol. A secondary goal would be to identify issues and problems that a person might be experiencing, so they would not lead to alcohol abuse. Information can be disseminated through written materials, discussions with various groups, and media presentations. *Training* is an ongoing delivery of basic information in all aspects of alcohol abuse or alcoholism. Many alcoholism and related programs have continuous training for their staff, identified as "in-service training." Of course, basic training in the alcohol abuse and alcoholism area is offered to many groups, individuals, agencies, and organizations.

TREATMENT METHODS

The choice of treatment system usually depends on the population, resources, and program philosophy.

Alcoholics Anonymous

Alcoholics Anonymous (AA) is based on 12 steps and 12 traditions offered as a guide for recovery from the disease of alcoholism. Each individual is encouraged to develop and work on his or her "own program" for recovery. Usually, a person is coupled with a "sponsor," a recovering AA alcoholic who has sustained sobriety over a long period of time.

Alanon

Alanon is designed for spouses of recovering or practicing alcoholics and for significant others in the alcoholic's life. It is based on the 12 steps and 12 traditions of AA, and the format is a regular group meeting.

Alateen

Alateen is offered to the children of alcoholic parents, the age level usually being adolescence. The 12 steps and 12 traditions are used as a base for these group meetings.

Alatot

Alatot focuses on younger children of recovering or practicing alcoholics or significant others in the alcoholic's life. Like Alateen, it is based on the 12 steps and 12 traditions of AA. The format is a group setting.

Adult Children of Alcoholics

Adults who acknowledged that one or both parents or caregiver were abusing or addicted to alcohol have become active members of Adult Children of Alcoholics (ACOA) self-help groups, which are based on the 12-step philosophy. In addition to the self-help model, individual, group, and family therapy have been used by this population.

Psychotherapy

Psychotherapy provides a therapist-counselor to assist the patient-client in understanding his or her feelings and thoughts in individual or group psychotherapy. The psychodynamic approach to the treatment of alcohol abuse and alcoholism assumes that the drinking behavior is but a symptom of an underlying pathology that must be specifically treated. An alternative model assumes that alcoholism is a disease or illness and that, even though sobriety is achieved, basic issues that may impede one from being comfortable and happy as a sober person are in need of exploration and resolution.

Family therapy is designed to examine the relationships and communication patterns within a family structure. There is a basic assumption that dynamics are present in the family system that let each family member assume an integral role in maintaining a balance within the family unit. The goal of family therapy is to identify this system of relationships and agreements and then use interventions that will lead to well-functioning, productive interactions.

A primary concept within the framework of family therapy is *codependence*. Codependence has been defined as a primary disease and as a disease within every member of an alcoholic family. It can be viewed as a dysfunctional pattern of living and problem solving, which is nurtured by an unreasonable set of rules within the family system. A codependent person can be one who is human-relationship dependent and focuses his or her life around an addictive agent. Some characteristics of codependents are (a) not trusting one's own perceptions, (b) caretaking, (c) lacking boundaries, (d) becoming indispensable, and (e) becoming a martyr.

Children's therapeutic play groups are intended to provide an educational and supportive environment for children of alcoholic parents or caretakers. The age range is typically 2 to 11 years. Activities, some of which are specifically related to alcohol use and abuse, are introduced to engage the children. Materials are sensitive to the child's development.

Therapeutic workshops are typically a short-term, time-limited approach, focusing on specific problem areas. They are often weekend experiences, career-planning workshops, or problem-solving meetings. Terms such as *sensitivity groups* and *marathon* are used in this treatment method.

Recreational and occupational therapy is an activity-oriented process designed to reduce tensions through exercise, athletics, and other endeavors. Occupational therapy typically involves a work-related project, with the construction of a specific item.

Behavior therapy emphasizes two goals regarding alcohol abuse and alcoholism: (a) to eliminate excessive alcohol consumption as a dominant response to stress and other aversive situations and (b) to establish alternative adaptive models of coping behavior. Behavior therapists often view alcohol abuse and alcoholism within a social learning framework. Behavioral approaches include (a) aversion conditioning to shift the perception of drinking-related stimuli from positive to negative, by associating drinking with uncomfortable or aversive events; (b) operant conditioning to change the drinking response as well as those variables that have influenced the drinking behavior; (c) cognitive behavior therapy to assist individuals cognitively to restructure their maladaptive thoughts in an effort to eliminate dysfunctional behavior such as excessive drinking; and (d) multidimensional behavioral approaches to focus on the antecedents and consequences of drinking patterns.

Drug therapy can provide drugs specific to alcohol abuse and alcoholism—namely, disulfiram (Antabuse) and cyanamide (Temposil). The ingestion of alcohol while one of these drugs is present in the body will cause an aversive reaction such as facial flushing, nausea, heart palpitations, and vertigo—reactions that are not usually life threatening. There are various ways to distribute these drugs, such as having a "helping person"—usually a counselor—administer the drug at a specified meeting time, so as to provide a personal interchange. The most destructive use of these drugs would be as a punitive measure, under the guise of "setting limits." An individual with poor impulse control or bad judgment would not be a good candidate for this therapeutic intervention. Psychoactive drugs such as Valium, Librium, Lithium, and Thorazine have also been used in the treatment of alcohol abuse and alcoholism. These drugs are viewed either as a primary therapeutic intervention or, more commonly, as one component of a total treatment plan. Medications are used with this population as a means of stabilizing their physical being.

ADDICTIVE PROCESS
BEHAVIOR THERAPY
CHANGE INDUCTION GROUPS
DRUG USERS' TREATMENT
HEALTH CARE SERVICES
PEER GROUP THERAPY
PROGRAM EVALUATION
SELF-CONTROL

S. S. CARDONE

ALEXIA/DYSLEXIA

In an increasingly literate world the inability to read becomes a serious disability affecting academic success, employment, and self-concept. Since widespread literacy is a recent historical development, it should not be surprising that it was only about 100 years ago that the first case of alexia or "word blindness" was described. Much of the early literature discussing cases of reading disability due to brain damage (alexia) resulted from the interest generated over the neuroanatomic basis of aphasia.

Jules Dejerine in 1891 first provided an in-depth clinical and pathological investigation of alexia. He described a patient who had suffered a stroke that resulted in aphasia, alexia, and agraphia. Although the severe language disturbance cleared up over several years, the severe reading disability did not. After the patient died, a postmortem examination revealed a large infarct in the region known as the angular gyrus in the left parieto-temporal-occipital region. Later reports by clinicians throughout Europe and England confirmed Dejerine's observations regarding the possible etiology of alexia.

Alexia describes an acquired reading disability due to brain insult and may be conceptualized in numerous ways. The alexia can be categorized according to the site of the injury, the nature of the reading disturbance, and, of course, according to one's own theoretical orientation.

D. F. Benson proposed that the alexias be conceptualized into three categorizations. *Posterior alexia* is due primarily to occlusion of the left posterior cerebral artery resulting in destruction of some of the left occipital cortex. Alexia without agraphia best describes the condition, in that a very serious disturbance of word recognition and comprehension exists in the absence of a writing deficit. Although these patients cannot read, they experience no difficulty in writing. Typically, a right homonymous hemianopia exists as well as a color-naming deficit.

Central alexia is generally due to damage in the dominant parietal region similar to Dejerine's case, where the region of the angular gyrus was damaged. Alexia with agraphia typifies central alexia. A right-sided sensory loss may also occur, owing to the damage in the left parietal region.

Anterior alexia, D. F. Benson has argued, is due to lesions in the region of Broca's area and is typified by some limited comprehension of words. However, a literal alexia for the naming of letters may exist. The symptoms of aphasia also appear concurrently with anterior alexia. Severe anomia or a word-finding deficit may be present, as well as a right-sided weakness due to the involvement of the left motor strip.

By definition, the alexias describe a condition where reading ability was lost as the result of some neurological insult. An understanding of the clinical and experimental literature on alexia has greatly increased understanding of dyslexia. The term *dyslexia* refers to an inborn or congenital inability to learn to read. Many educators and psychologists would prefer the term *developmental reading disorders,* because it avoids the implication that the etiology of the reading disorder is due to neurological deficits. Consequently, dyslexia is the most appropriate term when it describes a reading disability presumed to be of neurologic origin.

Drake and Galaburda, and Kemper, have provided convincing evidence as to the neurological basis for dyslexia through their postmortem studies of the brains of dyslexics. Drake found in his patient atrophy of the corpus callosum, many ectopic neurons in the white matter, and abnormal convolutional patterns in the parietal lobe. Galaburda and Kemper reported that the brain they examined showed a lack of normal asymmetry between the left and right planum temporale, and polymicrogyri were observed in the region known to subserve reading and language functions. Microscopically, they found fused molecular layers, no cellfree layer, and dysplasia. Other investigators have reported that the brains of dyslexics may also evidence a reversal of normal hemispheric asymmetries as revealed on computed tomography (CT) scans.

From a clinical perspective, it is now recognized that at least two and quite possibly several distinct subtypes of dyslexia exist. Boder was the first to clearly articulate what she termed the "dysphonetic" and "dyseidetic" dyslexic. The dysphonetic dyslexic experiences difficulty interpreting and integrating written symbols with their corresponding sound. The dyseidetic dyslexic performs deficiently on tasks requiring visual perception and is unable to develop a sight word vocabulary.

Pirozzolo, through his more experimental research, has furthered the understanding of the subtypes of dyslexia. He proposed that the two major subtypes of dyslexia were better conceptualized as "auditory-linguistic" and "visual-spatial." The auditory-linguistic dyslexic was characterized by developmentally delayed language onset, expressive speech deficits, anomia, low verbal intelligence relative to performance intelligence and reading using a letter-by-letter decoding strategy. The visual-spatial dyslexic had a relatively better verbal intelligence quotient in comparison to the performance intelligence quotient, had poor handwriting and faulty eye movements, and used a phonetic decoding strategy in reading.

Regarding intervention with alexic and dyslexic patients, the research has yet to provide a convincing paradigm for successful treatment. Individual recovery rates for alexic patients vary considerably; the educational literature offers some hope for successful remediation, depending primarily on the severity of the dyslexic condition.

APHASIA
BRAIN INJURIES
LEARNING DISABILITIES
ORGANIC BRAIN SYNDROMES
READING DISABILITIES

G. W. HYND

ALGORITHMIC-HEURISTIC THEORY

The notion of algorithm was considered solely a mathematical concept until the early 1950s. The term *algorithm* usually means a precise, unambiguous, and generally comprehensible *prescription* for carrying out, in each particular case, a defined sequence of relatively elementary operations to solve any problem belonging to a certain class or type.

The Algorithmic-Heuristic Theory (AHT) has demonstrated how to do the following: (a) identify quasi-algorithmic processes (similar to algorithmic processes in mathematics) in subjects other than mathematics; (b) develop and teach algorithms for solving these nonmathematical problems; (c) find algorithms for many types of problems that were never regarded as algorithmic in nature, and for which algorithms were never known or taught; (d) make more specific many of the overly general and ambiguous heuristics that were known and occasionally used in instruction, by devising more specific heuristics and heuristic prescriptions; (e) teach these more specific heuristics systematically to students, thus developing in them the ability to effectively solve nonalgorithmic problems; (f) discover heuristics that were not previously known and teach them to students; (g) design a new type of instructional methodology and materials, based on the knowledge of algo-heuristic processes, which are directed at the explicit and systematic formation of such processes in students; (h) develop in students general algorithmic and nonalgorithmic methods of thinking, and related general cognitive skills and abilities underlying intelligence; and (i) increase considerably the overall effectiveness and efficiency of performance, learning, and instruction.

In terms of its application, the AHT has as its major task creating instructional processes capable of developing expert performers, learners, and decision makers in any area where such tasks arise.

COGNITIVE COMPLEXITY
INFORMATION PROCESSING THEORY

L. N. LANDA

ALIENATION (POLITICAL)

Political alienation, or disaffection, is basically a feeling of dissatisfaction, disillusionment, and detachment regarding political leaders, governmental policies, and the political system.

Feelings of political disaffection comprise at least five components: *powerlessness* ("People like me don't have any say about what the government does"); *discontentment* ("For the most part, the government serves the interests of a few organized groups such as business or labor, and isn't very concerned about the needs of people like me"); *distrust* ("A large number of city and county politicians are political hacks"); *estrangement* ("When I think about the government in Washington, I don't feel as if it's my government"); and *hopelessness* ("The future of this country seems dark to me").

Three research findings seem germane to this conceptualization of political disaffection. First, these five components of disaffection are highly interrelated, with high levels of disaffection in one component correlating with high levels of disaffection in the other four. Second, two attitudinal dimensions appear to underlie these five components, with political powerlessness and estrangement forming a personal dimension of disaffection, while political discontentment, distrust, and hopelessness constitute a systemic dimension of disaffection. Third, in exploring the attribution of responsibility for political disaffection, one finds that individuals attribute the condition of the political system to the unintentional behavior of private citizens ("Citizens are uninformed about politics and public affairs because the government lies to them"), rather than to the intentional behavior of public officials ("Politicians are unqualified for the positions they hold").

Two demographic factors have been rather consistently found to relate to feelings of political disaffection: socioeconomic status and race. Thus political alienation is more prevalent among the lower and working classes than among the middle and upper classes, and Blacks are more politically alienated than Whites.

THEORIES

At least seven explanations have been advanced to account for people's feelings of political alienation. *Complex organization theory* states that political disaffection will occur when people are unable or unwilling to participate politically in society, large formal organizations, or their communities. Two key causes of political alienation in society are a lack of primary relationships and an inability to belong to and participate in voluntary associations. When these two phenomena occur, feelings of political alienation result. *Mass society theory*, the principal variant of this explanation, suggests that modern society cannot be understood, does not offer achievable goals, is composed of people with dissimilar values, permits few personal satisfactions, and offers no sense of personal control. These societal characteristics lead in turn to political disaffection.

Social disadvantages theory, by comparison, holds that people's social positions do not produce political disaffection, but rather that disaffection results from the perceptions that people occupying social positions have of their relations with other people and other social entities. This theory would be supported by the evidence that socioeconomic status—that is, education, income, and occupation—is related to political disaffection, with such feelings occurring more frequently among individuals with less formal education, lower income levels, and blue-collar, manual occupations.

Personal failure theory postulates three preconditions for political alienation: (a) the individual must occupy a social position that limits his or her actions, (b) these limited opportunities must preclude the achievement of major life goals, and (c) the individual must perceive him- or herself as a failure in these attempts at goal attainment. In this case, failure to attain personal life goals does not engender political alienation; such a failure must be both socially caused and recognized by the individual, for political alienation to occur.

Social isolation theory of alienation suggests that feelings of political disaffection are related to isolation from, or a lack of assimilation to, the political system. This lack of assimilation pertains to any social ties to any social object, not necessarily to society itself, and can be either cognitive or behavioral in nature. In addition, the social isolation can be either involuntary or voluntary, unconscious or conscious. In this instance, disaffection would be predicted from disinterest in politics, political apathy, weak partisanship, political ignorance, and a failure to vote.

In contrast to these sociological theories of political alienation, the *social deprivation model of disaffection* postulates that personal feelings of social deprivation lead to low self-esteem, which in turn results in high levels of political alienation. The two key elements in this theory—the linkage between perceived social deprivation and feelings of low self-esteem, and between low self-esteem and felt political alienation—have not been supported in surveys of White and Black adolescents.

Conversely, the *sociopolitical reality explanation of political disaffection* has been repeatedly supported in empirical research. This theory posits a direct link between perceptions of the sociopolitical system's functioning and feelings of political disaffection, with critical views of the system's operation being directly linked to felt disaffection. While the sociopolitical reality model of political disaffection receives strong support, it manifests a major shortcoming, in that no account is provided for the nexus between a person's critical perceptions of systemic functioning and that person's feelings of political disaffection.

This connection is provided by the *systemic disaffection theory*, which suggests that three causal factors contribute to political alienation. First, critical perceptions of sociopolitical reality—that is, of economic and racial discrimination—must occur. Second, a politically irrational, perfectionistic response to the operations of the sociopolitical system must next occur, typically of a moralistic, rigid, grandiose nature. Third, psychological reactance, or perceived threat from the sociopolitical system, must also be elicited. This perceived threat to and/or loss of freedom will be particularly salient if the individual feels particularly susceptible to such a threat or loss, or views himself or herself as being comparable to others who have experienced a threat or loss of freedom.

These three preconditions follow a specific causal sequence. Thus critical perceptions of sociopolitical reality not only directly contribute to feelings of alienation from the sociopolitical system, but also lead to irrational political ideation and to psychological reactance. Next, irrational political ideation fosters high levels of psychological reactance and generates political alienation. Then, feelings of psychological reactance also contribute to political alienation.

CONSEQUENCES

A major concern among theories on the political disaffection process is the consequences of disaffection for the political system. Of the four attitudinal and behavioral consequences of political disaffection that are most frequently cited in the literature—attitudinal rightism and negativism, and behavioral apathy and extremism—only behavioral apathy has been firmly established in the research literature on conventional political activity. Thus it can be concluded that the politically disaffected, in their political attitudes and behavior, differ little from the politically allegiant. It also follows that the stability and viability of democratic political systems are not jeopardized by politically alienated segments of the population who may remain more politically apathetic than their peers.

CONSERVATISM/LIBERALISM
EQUITY THEORY
NATIONAL CHARACTER
POLITICAL VALUES

S. Long

ALL-OR-NONE LAW

A typical neuron or nerve cell consists of a cell body, dendrites, and an axon. The axon is generally a relatively long process that extends away from the cell body. To carry information from the beginning of the axon to its end, most neurons generate action or spike potentials. The all-or-none law refers to the action potential; thus it is a characteristic of axonal transmission.

The all-or-none law states that the size, shape, and speed of the action potential are independent of the intensity of the stimulus that triggers it. In other words, it doesn't matter to a neuron whether the stimulus that elicits the action potential is very mild (e.g., a soft touch) or very strong (e.g., a shark bite). As long as the stimulus is strong enough to trigger the action potential, it is transmitted from one end of the axon to the other nondecrementally (i.e., without any decrease in size, shape, or speed).

A neuron's action potentials are analogous to signals from a telegraph key; a neuron cannot send bigger or faster action potentials any more than a telegraph operator can send bigger or faster signals with the telegraph key. What a neuron can do is send more signals per unit of time to indicate the strength of a stimulus. Thus a soft touch might trigger 10 impulses per second in a given neuron, whereas a shark bite might elicit 200 impulses per second in the same neuron.

The all-or-none concept was first demonstrated in 1871 in the heart muscle by American physiologist Henry P. Bowditch. In 1902, English physiologist F. Gotch found evidence for an all-or-none effect in nerves, but the effect was not definitively proven until the work of Edgar Douglas Adrian. For his work, Adrian was awarded a Nobel prize in physiology in 1932. Actually, Adrian's work was preceded by many studies performed by K. Lucas. Lucas named the law in his article "The All or None Contraction of the Amphibian Skeletal Muscle Fibre."

Like most "laws" of the nervous system, the all-or-none law has exceptions. Some neurons can produce a series of action potentials that grow successively smaller, thus disobeying the law.

ACTION POTENTIAL
CHEMICAL BRAIN STIMULATION
ELECTRICAL NERVOUS SYSTEM STIMULATION
ELECTROENCEPHALOGRAPHY
NEUROCHEMISTRY

B. M. Thorne

ALLPORT–VERNON–LINDZEY SCALE

The Allport–Vernon–Lindzey scale is based on the classification of basic motives in personality formulated by Eduard Spranger in *Types of men*. The six values are: (a) *theoretical:* empirical, critical, rational interest in the discovery of truth; (b) *economic:* interest in what is useful, practical, applicable; (c) *aesthetic:* interest in form, harmony, grace, symmetry, fitness; (d) *social:* altruistic or philanthropic love of people; (e) *political:* interest in personal power, influence, and renown; and (f) *religious:* the mystical motive that seeks to understand the unity of the cosmos.

PERSONALITY ASSESSMENT

W. I. Sauser, Jr.

ALTERNATIVE DOCTORAL PROGRAMS

In the United States, most individuals aspiring toward a doctoral degree in psychology and related fields (e.g., Ph.D., psy. D., Ed.D., D.S.W.) enter a program at a state or private university in which psychology is one of several graduate programs. However, some students select doctoral programs considered *alternative* rather than *traditional*. Spence has called for "mutual tolerance" between programs rather than "a single, ideal model that all training institutions should be expected to adopt."

Some programs are alternative in the sense that they are neither state approved nor accredited by either a regional accrediting agency or the American Psychological Association (APA). Council of Social Work Accreditation is comparable with APA accreditation. The quality of doctoral programs varies considerably, some being nothing but diploma mills (where a student literally writes a check and receives a diploma through the mail) to serious attempts at innovative education that offer a legal degree but lack certain requirements for state approval. Other programs are alternative in the sense that they are freestanding (i.e., they are not departments of accredited universities but "stand apart" from traditional schools). Some of these schools are APA accredited, whereas others have only state or regional approval.

Another group of schools look on themselves as alternative because they are nonresidential in nature. Students do their course work in their homes, communicating with their instructors through telephone, the postal service, or electronic mail (users of which often make the case that contemporary computer technology undercuts the necessity for lengthy residential requirements). They attend short-term residential seminars several times a year, allowing them to meet their family and job responsibilities while working toward a doctorate. Some of these schools provide opportunities for clinical training, whereas others are theory and research oriented.

An additional way that schools may be alternative is in terms of their perspective toward psychology. Most doctoral programs in psychology are cognitive–behavioral, psychoanalytic–psychodynamic, or electric in orientation. Others are specifically humanistic, existential–phenomenological, transpersonal, or cross-cultural. Some take a spirited political and social stance, and others reflect a religious orientation or the world view of their founder. At the master's degree level, there is an even wider choice of alternative programs with diverse orientations.

Students considering alternative doctoral programs need to consider their motivations and professional needs. If an individual hopes to apply for licensing in his or her state and to practice psychotherapy, it is essential that the school of choice at least be state approved. If that individual is considering leaving the state, it is preferable that the school of choice be regionally accredited. Moreover, government-backed student loans are only available for students enrolled in regionally accredited programs. A wider range of choices exists if the doctoral program also has APA accreditation (graduates of some alternative programs are denied a listing in the National Register of Health Service Providers in Psychology), and some states will not allow graduates of nonresidential schools to sit for licensing examinations. Some people do not plan to use their doctorate for professional advancement but simply as a way of symbolizing completion of their life work; these individuals often opt to write a doctoral dissertation for a nonaccredited school that has few residential or course work requirements. A few students opt for alternative programs in other countries; again, the problem of equivalency needs to be considered if these individuals intend to use their degrees for professional purposes in the United States.

A number of alternative schools have formed the Consortium for Diversified Psychology Programs. This consortium has filed complaints against APA for purported exclusion of alternative programs in psychology and gives graduates of its member schools legal advice in regard to obtaining permission to take state licensing examinations. A related activist organization, the National Psychology Advisory Association, consists of students and alumni of alternative schools. The dialectic in psychological graduate schools between diversity and conformity, between the values and principles embedded in established programs and those embodied by those alternative schools that challenge the status quo, is reflected in these struggles, and the outcome will be a signal as to the future of American psychology.

CLINICAL PSYCHOLOGY GRADUATE TRAINING
COLLEGE OF PROFESSIONAL PSYCHOLOGY
GRADUATE TRAINING IN PSYCHOLOGY

S. KRIPPNER

ALTERNATIVE EDUCATIONAL SYSTEMS

During the 1960s and the 1970s there was considerable emphasis on alternative educational systems and humanistic forms of teaching/learning. This was a reaction against the restrictions of traditional education, which focuses on intellectual aspects of learning and on mastery of basic skills and content. The alternative approaches have tended to stress the affective side of the teaching/learning process, including attention given to the learners' feelings, values, interests, beliefs, and life experiences. While many of these alternative approaches—frequently labeled "humanistic education"—have focused on the *process* of learning, the main aim is the integration of the cognitive and affective domains. Education is not seen as strictly "cultivating the intellect," but rather as helping the individual become a full and complete person. While basic content and factual material are not necessarily ignored in the humanistic approach, the emphasis is on the concerns of the learner as a person. The assumption is that if the learner is actively engaged in discovery, then learning is of a significant nature.

In *Freedom to learn,* Carl Rogers stated that teaching is a vastly overrated function. Teaching—seen as the imparting of knowledge—does not take into consideration the rapidly and changing nature of modern society. According to Rogers, the goal of education is best viewed as the facilitation of change and learning.

One model of an alternative educational system is described by A. S. Neill in *Summerhill: A radical approach to child rearing.* Neill vividly describes what children are like who come to his school from repressive, authoritarian backgrounds. Neill's philosophy is much like Rogers' in that both have a deep faith in the capacity of the individual to grow and learn, if given the freedom to do so. Neill believes that children will become self-regulated individuals, if granted genuine freedom. Thus his educational system is grounded on the assumption that children have a desire to learn about life. While Neill's approach to education has been called extreme by some critics, his methods seem to produce results. His residential school had no required subjects and few rules (most of the latter developed by the children themselves), and children were free to pursue their interests.

Other writers have made a case for alternative forms of learning, even though their approaches have not been as extreme as Neill's. George Leonard's *Education and ecstasy* is devoted to the theme that there is such a thing as sheer joy of learning. Leonard's premise is that if children were allowed to continue an intrinsic search for making new discoveries, both learning and life would be more ecstatic than the drudgery it often is. He indicated that individuals have all the basic know-how to allow for joyful learning *now,* but that certain encrusted notions of what education should be prevent it from becoming a personally enriching experience.

John Holt's *How children learn* makes essentially the same point. Children *do* learn, because it is a basic human need and it is fun. Curiosity, exploration, the need to manipulate, the need to discover how things work, are parts of the growth of healthy children. Competition, threats, and external motivation are not needed to entice the unschooled. For Holt, classrooms can be a place where children experience the connection of learning with real life. Holt believes that teaching approaches should provide the opportunities for children to follow their natural interests, and that education should consist of far more than memorizing factual material and learning basic skills.

INDIVIDUAL EDUCATION
MONTESSORI METHOD
SCHOOLS WITHOUT FAILURE
WALDORF EDUCATION

G. COREY

ALTRUISM

In the technical language of evolutionary biologists, altruistic behavior is behavior by one organism such that the chances of its own survival—or of the survival of its offspring—are diminished in favor of that of other members of the species. The standard interpretation of this behavior is that it is advantageous for the whole genetic pool protected by adaptive behavior, but not for the individual. Thus altruistic behavior will be more frequent, the higher the common heredity; close relations show higher altruism than more distant relations, family higher than nonfamily, and so on. Altruism in this way is connected with group selection, the theory that evolution proceeds at the group, not the individual, level; groups that include altruistic behavior would have improved survival chances.

The term itself, altruism, was coined by Auguste Comte as part of his accounting for social units; altruism in this sense means selfless concern for the welfare of others and may occur without any risk to the altruist. Altruism—like imitation, suggestion, and sympathy—was used in early sociology as a general explanation of social behavior. Like these other terms, altruism fell into disuse when the unitary explanation of society was abandoned; in the meantime the term had entered the common language from its sociological origin.

Altruism has become a topic in experimental social psychology under the general heading of prosocial behavior. Research interest in the field arose after much work had been done on antisocial behavior, especially aggression. As an applied problem the reduction of aggression was important, but so was the promotion of prosocial behavior. Two types of action that have been studied extensively are helping behavior and bystander intervention. In both these fields the conditions of this behavior have to be specified: We know that both of them occur and do not occur, so that the question of a universal does not arise. Altruistic behavior can thus be seen as exchange behavior, as a function of the relationship—that is, as dependent on relative status, familiarity with the environment, and the availability of alternate actors who could do the appropriate act.

AFFILIATION NEED
ALIENATION
LOVE

K. W. BACK

ALTRUISTIC SUICIDE

The sociologist Emile Durkheim, in his classic work, *Suicide,* defined altruistic suicide as that form of self-destruction in which the person gives up his or her life on behalf of the group and its belief system. He cited its widespread occurrence in various cultures, describing those in which it commonly occurs as "primitive." "They can only persist," he said, "if the individual has no interests of his own, he must be trained to renunciation to an unquestioned abnegation."

Durkheim divided altruistic suicide into three categories: *obligatory altruistic suicide,* a term he suggested might be better applied to the whole category as, on all occasions, a measure of coercion exists; *optional altruistic suicide,* where one commits self-murder to avoid disgrace; and *acute altruistic suicide,* as in the self-obliteration of certain mystics. All three categories were viewed by Durkheim as rooted in the common source of inadequate differentiation from the group.

He contrasted this form of self-destruction with *anomic suicide,* in which the individual suffers from social dislocation and lack of regulation by society, and from *egoistic suicide,* in which the victim suffers from lack of integration with the society, as in those holding extreme individualistic positions. While Durkheim viewed the subject as a purely sociological phenomenon, more recent research indicates the simultaneous presence of psychological, cultural, and political variables.

Altruistic suicide has occurred throughout the world since antiquity. Examples include the Kamikaze pilots of World War II, the self-immolation of the protesting monks in Vietnam, and the deaths by starvation of I.R.A. prisoners in Northern Ireland. Franco Fornari, in *The psychoanalysis of war,* cites the death of the Kamikaze pilots as illustrating the "paranoid elaboration of mourning," in which denied hostility to "parental" figures combined with an externally threatening reality to produce acts of suicide and murder. Using a psychodynamic model, one might interpret the actions of the pilots as involving "splitting" and "projection," while the deaths of the Vietnamese monks could be seen as "depressive" in nature, with rage turned against the introjected "bad object."

Jock Hearn, in *The soldier and the monk,* a study of the two suicidal Asian populations, identified cultural and philosophical factors, including a devaluation of the personal, and a tradition of self-sacrifice among certain role bearers—the military and the religious. It was precisely these two groups that Freud's *Group psychology and the analysis of the ego* cited as examples of group psychology wherein a number of individuals have substituted the same object for their ego ideal, and have thus identified with one another in their ego.

Threatened groups have encouraged the fantasy that members about to commit altruistic suicide are "already dead." Herbert Hendin has referred to such fantasies in his *Suicide and Scandinavia.* The suicide of selected group representatives has been used as a final political weapon by groups at an earlier level of economic development, which are on the point of being overwhelmed by superior military technology. Altruistic suicide, then, is a multiply determined phenomenon, which may be best understood by utilizing a comprehensive cross-disciplinary approach.

SUICIDE
THANATOLOGY

R. J. HEARN

ALZHEIMER'S DISEASE

Alzheimer's disease (AD) is a dementing disorder occurring in middle age (45–60 or 65 years of age), and characterized by relatively consistent cellular changes in the aging brain. It is sometimes called presenile dementia to distinguish it from senility or senile dementia (older than 65 years of age).

The clinical symptomatology is characterized by progressive mental impairment, usually beginning with a defect in recent memory. There is a failure to register current events, although the past may be fairly well preserved. As the disease progresses, there is a loss of remote memory and a decline in reasoning capacity. Nominal (naming) aphasia may be present also in later stages.

Depression is common in early stages of the disorder, although euphoria is occasionally seen. It is very important to distinguish between depression unaccompanied by dementia and depression with AD, since the prognosis and prospects for treatment are much better if there is no organic brain damage. In cases where a differential diagnosis cannot be made, the patient should be treated for depression.

Personality changes often seem to be an exaggeration of premorbid tendencies. Thus a slightly suspicious person may become paranoid. In some cases, however, there is a reversal of predisease tendencies.

Neurophysiologically, AD is characterized by marked cortical atrophy with ventricular dilatation. Alzheimer's disease is not really a diffuse brain disorder. Rather, there seems to be selective vulnerability of certain areas including association areas of the parietal, temporal, and frontal cortex. By contrast, primary motor and sensory areas are relatively well preserved. Of subcortical areas, the hippocampus and amygdala seem to be especially vulnerable.

Under microscopic examination, three unique pathological changes in brain tissue characterize AD: neurofibrillary tangles, senile plaques, and granulovacuolar degeneration. *Neurofibrillary tangles* (NFT) are composed of bundles of paired helical filaments that differ in size and composition from unpaired filaments found in normal neurons. The number of NFT has been found to be correlated with the degree of mental impairment. *Senile plaques* are basically clusters of abnormal neuronal processes. Degree of plaque formation is also correlated with the degree of intellectual deterioration. *Granulovacuolar degeneration* is a form of neuronal degenerative change often seen only in the hippocampus. All three changes in brain tissue may be found in the nondemented elderly, but the numbers and degree of severity are generally much greater in the demented.

A variety of possible causes have been suggested. For example, a genetic basis has been suggested by the high incidence of AD in certain families. A possible viral origin has been investigated, since studies have shown that plaques are induced in mouse brains when the animals are injected with the causative agent of scrapie. An autoimmune basis has been hypothesized in which brain protein leaks into circulation through a defective blood brain barrier. In circulation, antibrain antibodies are formed that then recross the defective barrier to attack the brain.

The possibility that toxicity from trace metals may be involved has been theorized. One of the leading candidates is aluminum, which has been shown to produce NFT when injected into the brains of susceptible species. Elevated aluminum levels have been found in the brains of patients who died from AD, and its distribution matched the distribution of NITY but not of senile plaques.

A variety of therapies have been applied in AD, but the results have been disappointing. Unsuccessful treatments have included hyperbaric oxygen and chemical agents of many types such as vitamins, vasodilators, and numerous psychotropic drugs.

BRAIN
CENTRAL NERVOUS SYSTEM DISORDERS
MINIMAL BRAIN DYSFUNCTIONS (DIAGNOSIS AND INTERVENTION)

B. M. THORNE

AMERICAN ASSOCIATION OF HUMANISTIC PSYCHOLOGY

Founded in 1962, the American Association of Humanistic Psychology (AAHP) seeks to encourage study in the problems of living that confront human existence. The humanistic school grew out of a reaction to behaviorism's narrowness and ivy tower approach. The association is a process of that growth.

AAHP has as its aim a focus on the human being as an experiencing person. The emphasis on the person also evaluates the process of becoming as well as the ability to make rational choices. It upholds humanity's meaningfulness in life and values human dignity and worth. Individuals involved in the founding of AAHP included Kurt Goldstein, Andras Angyl, Abraham Maslow, Henry A. Murray, Anthony J. Sutich, Carl Rogers, and James F. T. Bugental, who served as AAHP's first president. AAHP's *Journal of Humanistic Psychology* communicates research, theory, and commentaries to its members.

AMERICAN PSYCHOLOGICAL ASSOCIATION
HUMANISTIC PSYCHOLOGY

R. A. LEARK

AMERICAN BOARD OF PROFESSIONAL PSYCHOLOGY

The American Board of Professional Psychology (ABPP) began as an outgrowth of the post-World War II popularity of psychology, and the subsequent need for standards of excellence. The American Psychological Association (APA) accepted a report by an appointed committee in September 1946, recommending that an independent examining committee award diplomate status to qualified psychologists. The American Board of Examiners in Professional Psychology (ABEPP) was incorporated in April 1947, separate from APA, to ensure competence in fee-for-service activities. It was empowered to (a) "grant, issue, and control the use of its diploma of special competence in fields of professional psychology" (clinical, counseling, and industrial); and (b) to "arrange, conduct and control investigations and examinations to determine the qualifications of individuals who make voluntary application for such diplomas."

THE CREDENTIALING PROCESS

To attain diplomate candidate status, a psychologist must be an APA (or Canadian Psychological Association) member, hold a Ph.D. in psychology, and have 5 years of professional postgraduate experience, 1 year of which can be a predoctoral internship or equivalent experience. Until December 31, 1949, a "grandfather" clause operated whereby a person who had functioned as a psychologist for 10 or more years with a B.A. degree earned before 1936, or for 5 years or more with a Ph.D., could be awarded diplomate status.

AMERICAN PSYCHOLOGICAL ASSOCIATION
COMPETENCY IN PSYCHOLOGY

A. K. HESS

AMERICAN COUNCIL ON EDUCATION

Fourteen national organizations joined in establishing the Emergency Council on Education in 1918 to coordinate education efforts during World War I. With the success of this cooperative effort in education, later that year the Council changed its name to the American Council on Education (ACE) and began its role in education. The council now provides many services to higher education. Its primary function is to coordinate and organize colleges and universities in the United States. Located in Washington, DC, it includes almost 1400 member colleges and universities and more than 170 member educational associations.

A number of divisions focus on specific concerns, including external relations, government relations, international educational relations, and policy and research.

L. V. PARADISE

AMERICAN PSYCHIATRIC ASSOCIATION

The American Psychiatric Association, founded in 1844, is the oldest national medical society in the United States. For the first 50 years it remained a small organization of medical superintendents of American institutions for the insane. In 1892 the name was changed to the American Medico-Psychological Association, and the present name was adopted in 1921. Membership has grown from 900 in 1918 to more than 26,000 in 1981. This represents 70% of the estimated 31,000 psychiatrists in the United States. More than 400 members are from other countries. All members other than honorary must be physicians with some specialized training and experience in psychiatry.

The objectives of the association are to improve the treatment, rehabilitation, and care of the mentally retarded and emotionally disturbed; to promote research, professional education in psychiatry and allied fields, and the prevention of psychiatric disabilities; to advance the standards of all psychiatric services and facilities; to foster the cooperation of all who are concerned with the medical, psychological, social, and legal aspects of mental health and illness; to make psychiatric knowledge available to other practitioners of medicine, to scientists in other fields, and to the public; and to promote the best interests of patients and those actually or potentially making use of mental health services.

AMERICAN PSYCHOLOGICAL ASSOCIATION

R. C. MARVIT

AMERICAN PSYCHOLOGICAL ASSOCIATION I

The American Psychological Association (APA) is the recognized inclusive organization for those with academic credentials in psychology—usually a master's or doctoral degree from an accredited university. The classes of membership changed from time to time, but in the bylaws as amended through 1980 there were three classes: associates, members, and fellows. The associates are primarily at the master's level; members are primarily those with doctoral degrees; and fellows are those with at least 5 years of experience beyond the doctoral degree, and sufficient evidence of unusual and outstanding contributions as to receive nomination by a division of the APA and election by the Council of Representatives. Fellows and members vote and may hold office, but associates achieve these privileges only after five consecutive years as associate.

The statement of the objectives of the APA in the first article of its bylaws begins: "The objects of the American Psychological Association shall be to advance psychology as a science and as a profession and as a means of promoting human welfare by the encouragement of psychology in all its branches in the broadest and most liberal manner." The statement goes on to explain how this includes research, high standards of ethical conduct, the diffusion of psychological knowledge, and the application of research findings to the promotion of the public welfare.

The APA publishes scientific journals and a monthly newsletter. The central office also manages the annual convention, which commonly attracts upwards of 15,000 members and has numerous functions, such as conducting the annual election of officers in the APA and its divisions and representing APA to governmental and other agencies.

The growth in membership in the APA proceeded by nearly equal small increments until about 1925, when an exponential growth began, partly after World War I but more impressively after World War II. A number of psychological journals began publication, but the APA did not acquire its own journals until 1922, when it purchased all the stock of the Psychological Review Company, until then privately held by Howard C. Warren.

There had been some conflicts of interest within the APA from the early years, represented at first by the debate between psychology as science and as philosophy, then tests versus laboratory, later basic research versus applied research, and concurrently the extent to which psychology was to remain rooted in the university or outside in professional practice. In the effort to resolve these issues, a constitutional convention was held in New York on May 29 to 31, 1943, while World War II was still in progress, under the chairmanship of E. G. Boring. The result was a new APA constitution with a divisional structure that would satisfy the special interests of the members and a central office to take over the managerial duties.

On the whole, the new constitution worked rather well for three decades. After that new tensions developed, particularly with the decreasing representation of the academically oriented psychologists and the increasing representation of those in professional practice with their many problems of legal licensing and relations to other professions, such as psychiatry and medicine. A number of smaller organizations of psychologists developed outside the APA to represent the special interests, but in most instances members of these groups retained their membership in the APA. Adjustments were made from time to time, but the APA remained the covering organization for qualified psychologists in America.

AMERICAN BOARD OF PROFESSIONAL PSYCHOLOGY
AMERICAN PSYCHOLOGICAL FOUNDATION
INTERNATIONAL PSYCHOLOGICAL ORGANIZATIONS

E. R. HILGARD

AMERICAN PSYCHOLOGICAL ASSOCIATION II

With a 1996 membership of more than 100,000, the American Psychological Association (APA) is the premier organization of psychologists in North America and, indeed, the world. It is a complex organization, with multiple functions and a complicated organizational structure dedicated to advancing psychology as a profession and as a science.

ORGANIZATION

The APA is a corporation with a constitution and bylaws, chartered in the District of Columbia. The principal organizational units of the APA include the council of representatives, the board of directors, the officers, the boards and committees, and the central office, with its chief executive officer (CEO).

The council of representatives is the major legislative body in the APA. The representatives are elected by the various divisions and state psychological associations, with the number of representatives from each unit determined by an annual apportionment ballot. The council sets the policies of the APA and elects some of its officers.

The 12-person board of directors is composed of six council members elected to serve along with the elected APA officers, the president, past president, president elect, treasurer, recording secretary, and CEO. This small group does much of the management of the APA during the year. It has particular responsibility for financial affairs.

The central office is headed by the CEO's executive office. The primary units within the central office are various directorates: communications, education, practice, science, public interest, and finance and administration. The central office runs the APA on a day-to-day basis. It has more than 400 employees that provide staff for the various boards and committees and conduct other business. The central office is involved in controlling a major publishing unit, managing stocks and real estate, and collecting more than $10 million per year in membership dues.

ACTIVITIES

Among the many activities of the APA, the annual conventions and publication activities are especially visible. The APA generally conducts one annual convention. In its early years, the annual convention was held in December, timed to occur in association with that of the AAAS, with which it became formally affiliated in 1902. The APA eventually met with the AAAS only in alternate years, and finally became an independent annual convention, held in the late summer, beginning in 1929. Before World War II, the annual convention was held on college campuses and used dormitories for housing. As the APA grew after the war, it became necessary to meet in downtown hotels in major cities. Today, the annual convention is a major 5-day event of papers and other presentations, which are listed in a thick program book. The convention is typically scattered among a cluster of large hotels and is attended by more than 13,000 psychologists.

In the early years of organized psychology in North America, the principal journals were privately owned. Various APA committees considered the possibility of a publishing effort at different times during the early part of the twentieth century. However, it was not until 1923 that the APA became involved in publishing journals. In 1922, the APA council voted to accept the offer made by Howard C. Warren to sell all shares of stock in the Psychological Review Company to the APA. The sale included five journals: *Psychological Review, Psychological Bulletin, Journal of Experimental Psychology, Psychological Monographs,* and *Psychological Index.* The *Journal of Abnormal and Social Psychology* was donated by its founder, Morton Prince, in 1926. APA publications in 1990 included 20 primary journals plus the *American Psychologist* and *Contemporary Psychology,* as well as secondary journals, newsletters, and the like. In addition, various APA divisions publish their own journals, such as the *Journal of Social Issues,* published by the Society for the Psychological Study of Social Issues (Division 9), and *The Teaching of Psychology,* published by the Division of the Teaching of Psychology (Division 2).

Among the services provided by the APA is the maintenance of a system of abstracts of published articles in journals and books. This began in various publications, including the *Psychological Index* and *Psychological Bulletin* and evolved into *Psychological Abstracts,* begun in 1927. This work is now overseen by PsychINFO, a department of the APA charged with the acquisition, storage, retrieval, and dissemination of information from the literature in psychology. An extensive program of modernization was implemented with the advent of computer technology, leading to the release of *PsychLit,* a CD-ROM–based system, in 1986.

Throughout its history, the APA has published various materials in booklike formats. The publication of its *Ethical standards for psychologists, Publication manual,* and *America's psychologists: A survey of a growing profession* were landmarks in the development of a program of book publishing by the APA. A serious book program was begun in 1965; by 1992, it included more than 100 titles of books and other materials.

D. A. DEWSBURY

AMERICAN PSYCHOLOGICAL FOUNDATION

Founded in 1953, the American Psychological Foundation was conceived by the board of directors of the American Psychological Association (APA) as an instrument for the continued development of psychology in the public weal. Contributions were to be sought from the membership at large, and management of the foundation was placed by the bylaws in the hands of a board of trustees built around a nucleus of the seven most recent past presidents of APA. From the beginning, the executive officer and the treasurer of APA have served as officers of the APF.

Over the years, the board of trustees has made an effort to award grants in such a way that the science, the profession, and the public good are served.

The American Psychological Foundation has recognized the importance of keeping documents and research materials readily available and so has sought to preserve relevant archives. The first grant in this area was made to protect and update the G. Stanley Hall papers contributed by APA to Clark University. In 1979 the foundation donated a substantial sum from the Rosen Fund to support the child development aspect of the Archives Foundation located at the University of Akron in Ohio. This foundation is devoted to developing and advancing the Archives of the History of American Psychology.

Many distinguished psychologists have contributed to the foundation through either direct financial aid or the assignment of royalties to the foundation. Donors of substantial contributions may specify a particular use for their gift.

AMERICAN PSYCHOLOGICAL ASSOCIATION

T. H. BLAU

AMERICAN PSYCHOLOGICAL SOCIETY

The American Psychological Society (APS) is the national organization devoted to scientific psychology. Established in 1988, APS's membership exceeded 15,000 in 5 years, making it probably the fastest growing scientific society in the world. The society's mission is to promote, protect, and advance the interests of scientifically oriented psychology in research, application, and improvement of human welfare.

APS members include psychologists engaged in scientific research or the application of scientifically grounded research findings without regard for specialities. APS represents members—including nearly 500 outside the United States—whose interests span the entire gamut of psychological science subdisciplines. Requirements of membership are a doctoral degree or evidence of sustained and significant contributions to scientific psychology; student affiliates are also accepted. Distinguished contributions are recognized by fellow status or, in cases of superior achievement, by specific awards.

PUBLICATIONS

APS publishes two bimonthly scholarly journals, *Psychological Science* and *Current Directions in Psychological Science. Psychological Science* presents the latest developments in psychological science for the purposes of promoting interdisciplinary knowledge among psychologists as well as presenting scientific psychology to nonpsychologists. *Current Directions in Psychological Science* publishes minireview articles, spanning the range of cutting-edge psychological research. The society also publishes *The APS Observer,* a newsletter that features the current activities of the society, national and international events that affect the society or psychology, noteworthy psychological research, and employment listings.

STUDENT CAUCUS

APS offers its student affiliates the opportunity to serve in a leadership role within the society. The APS Student Caucus (APSSC) elects its own officers and advocates who advise the board of directors on issues of student membership recruitment, retention, and conversion as well as accreditation and employment concerns. The APSSC also oversees the formation of student chapters and administers a mentorship program, guest lecture program, and a student travel award fund.

ACHIEVEMENT AWARDS

APS recognizes exceptional contributions to scientific psychology with its William James Fellow Award, two of which are awarded each year. Two new awards—the James McKeen Cattell Award in applied psychology and a still unnamed award for significant contributions to the discipline during the early stages of one's career—are scheduled to be awarded beginning in 1993.

FORMATION

The impetus for creating APS came from the recognition that (a) the needs and interests of scientific and academic psychologists were distinct from those in clinical practice, and (b) that there was a strong need for a society that would advance the interests of the discipline in ways that specialized organizations were not intended to do. An interim group, the Assembly for Scientific and Applied Psychology (ASAP), had sought repeatedly to reform the American Psychological Association (APA) from within, but efforts to increase the autonomy of academically oriented psychologists within the APA framework were rejected by a membership-wide vote of that organization. Following the failure of these reorganization efforts, the APS became the official embodiment of the ASAP reform effort, and the new organization was launched August 12, 1988, when a mail ballot of the membership was approved 419 to 13.

SUMMITS

One of APS's first activities was to convene the Summit of Scientific Psychological Societies in January 1989. Attendees, representing more than 40 psychological organizations, addressed the role of science advocacy, how to enhance the identity of psychology as a coherent scientific discipline, the protection of scientific values in education and training, the use of science in the public interest, and scientific values in psychological practice. Subsequent summit meetings, involving representatives of 70 organizations, produced the *Human Capital Initiative (HCI),* a national behavioral science research agenda. The document targets six critical contemporary problems facing the nation, communities, and families that can be helped by psychological science: worker productivity, schooling and literacy, the aging society, drug and alcohol abuse, mental and physical health, and violence in American society. The *HCI* is intended as guidance for Congress and federal research agencies in planning behavioral science research activities. Future summits will formulate specific research initiatives, addressing other cross-cutting concerns.

The APS-sponsored summit of 1992 addressed accreditation criteria and procedures for graduate psychology education programs. Although the suggested accreditation system applies only to doctoral programs aimed at training clinical, counseling, or school psychologists, accreditation affects graduate education in psychology in numerous ways and, therefore, is an issue of concern to all psychologists. The most direct influence is on the content and curriculum of the programs themselves, but accreditation requirements also affect the distribution of resources across different programs, the use of faculty time, and the priorities of graduate students within those departments.

ADVOCACY

A primary reason APS was founded was to provide a distinct Washington presence for scientific psychology. APS is widely recognized as an active leader in advancing the interests of basic and applied psychological, behavioral, and social science research in the legislative arena and in the federal agencies that support these areas of research.

A. G. KRAUT

AMNESIA

Amnesia, a general term, refers to a partial or total loss of memory functions, which, in contrast with ordinary forgetfulness, is considered pathological. Two major types of amnesia are recognized on the basis of the timing of forgotten events or material. *Anterograde amnesia,* also known as acquisition amnesia, refers to an inability to form new long-term memories and has been repeatedly linked to injury or atrophy in the hippocampal and medial temporal areas of the brain. *Retrograde amnesia* refers to a loss of memory for past events that were once remembered. The latter can be *episodic* or *epochal,* depending on whether the memory loss covers only specific, isolated events or longer periods of time.

Most amnestic disorders do not occur in isolation, but are usually accompanied by some confusion and disorientation and, depending on their source, loss of additional intellectual functions. The course, duration, and reversibility of amnestic disorders vary greatly, depending on the condition that precipitated them.

ALZHEIMER'S DISEASE
APHASIA
MEMORY DISORDERS
ORGANIC BRAIN SYNDROMES
STRESS CONSEQUENCES

S. P. URBINA

AMPHETAMINE EFFECTS

Amphetamine, a potent sympathomimetic amine, has pronounced stimulant effects on the central and peripheral nervous systems. This compound produces a variety of physiological effects, including alterations in systolic and diastolic blood pressures, contraction of smooth muscles and, in high doses, increased oxygen consumption. Behaviorally, the drug is known to produce appetite suppression, hyperthermia, wakefulness, alertness, decreased sense of fatigue, improved concentration, elevations of mood, elation, euphoria, and increased speech and motor activity. In infrahuman animals the most prominent effects of the drug are increased locomotor activity, the induction of stereotypy consisting mainly of repeated grooming, licking, gnawing, and sniffing, as well as the induction of stimulus perseveration in which animals repeatedly visit places or objects previously explored.

Prolonged use of amphetamine, or high doses of the drug, may result in fatigue and depression, and some individuals may experience headache, dizziness, vasomotor disturbances, agitation, confusion, dysphoria, apprehension, or delirium. Moreover, it has been reported that the behavioral consequences of repeated amphetamine consumption may be virtually indistinguishable from the symptom profile that characterizes paranoid schizophrenia. This latter effect, it seems, has been largely responsible for the attention devoted to the analysis of amphetamine actions, and repeated attempts have been made to develop animal models of schizophrenia using acute and repeated treatments of amphetamines and other catecholamine stimulants.

Prolonged exposure to amphetamine was reported to result in apparent tolerance to the mood-altering, anorexigenic, and hyperthermic effects of the drug. In contrast, the motor consequences and altered cognitive patterns associated with amphetamine intoxication are exacerbated with repeated drug intake. Various propositions have been advanced to account for the response enhancements seen after chronic amphetamine treatment, including conditioned drug effects, alterations in catecholamine synthesis, and hypersensitivity of dopamine receptors. In addition, it is possible that chronic amphetamine produces receptor proliferation, which ultimately results in receptor supersensitivity. A similar view has been forwarded to account for mechanisms subserving the schizophrenic symptomatology. It is also possible that chronic treatment with amphetamine alters activity in the striatal-nigral pathway or reduces the sensitivity of autoreceptors (self-inhibitory) present on presynaptic dopamine neurons.

CHEMICAL BRAIN STIMULATION
NEUROCHEMISTRY
PSYCHOENDOCRINOLOGY
PSYCHOPHARMACOLOGY

H. ANISMAN

ANALYSIS OF COVARIANCE

The analysis of covariance is a statistical technique, closely related to the analysis of variance, in which the dependent variable is statistically adjusted on the basis of other related information in order to remove extraneous variability and thus increase the efficiency of the analysis.

As an example, consider an experimental design in which three different methods of teaching arithmetic are compared. Students are randomly assigned to one of the instruction conditions and the dependent variable is the score obtained on a standardized achievement test administered at the end of the instruction period. The decision about whether the teaching methods are equally effective is obscured by random "error" variability present in the situation. Even if the teaching methods were equally good, we would not expect the average achievement score in each of the three groups to be exactly the same. Each individual's achievement score is determined not only by the teaching method but also by the ability of the student and a host of variables, such as how well he or she was feeling on the day of testing. The more these sources of variability can be reduced, the easier it will be to assess the effects of the teaching methods.

One way of experimentally reducing variability would be to restrict the range of intelligence of the students participating in the study. The approach of analysis of covariance, however, is to control for such sources of variability *statistically*. The assumption is made that some portion of the usual error component is predictable from the individual's score on a related measure referred to as the *covariate*. For example, if we have intelligence scores for each of the students, we can use this information to adjust the achievement scores in such a way as to reduce the variability due to individual differences in ability. The simplest set of computations assumes a linear relationship between the dependent variable and the covariate or covariates.

Analysis of covariance involves more assumptions than does the corresponding analysis of variance and the procedure is more frequently misused.

ANALYSIS OF VARIANCE
STATISTICS IN PSYCHOLOGY

A. D. WELL

ANALYSIS OF VARIANCE

The analysis of variance is a general statistical technique developed mainly by R. A. Fisher. While the technique involves dealing with different estimates of variability, its purpose is to assess differences in group means. The technique allows statistical analysis of the effects of factors and combinations of factors (main effects and interactions) on the dependent variable. (For definitions of these terms, see the entry on factorial designs.)

As an example of the logic of analysis of variance, consider a simple design in which we have a single independent variable or factor A and, say, three groups of subjects. The goal of such a design would generally be to determine whether the dependent variable varied as a function of factor A. However, because of random variability (e.g., individual differences, measurement error), we would not expect the average score to be exactly the same for each group of subjects, even if factor A had no real effect. Analysis of variance would allow us to test the null hypothesis that there are no real effects of the factor, so that the differences among scores are due only to random variability.

Assuming that the null hypothesis is true, it is possible to obtain two different estimates of the variance of the population. One of these estimates is based on the variability in the group means, and the other on the variances of the scores within each of the groups in the design.

If the null hypothesis is true, both measures will estimate the same population variance. As a consequence, the measures will have the same value except for random variability, and the ratio of the measures will have a known theoretical distribution (the *F* distribution, named after Fisher).

If the null hypothesis is not true, the two measures will not estimate the same population variance, because the first measure will be influenced by any real effects of the factor while the second will not be. The ratio of the first measure to the second will tend to be larger than would be expected if the ratio were truly distributed as *F*. If the ratio is large enough, the null hypothesis can be rejected.

ANALYSIS OF COVARIANCE
STATISTICS IN PSYCHOLOGY

A. D. WELL

ANALYTICAL PSYCHOLOGY

Analytical psychology is the work of Carl Gustav Jung (1875–1961) and his followers, who continue the development and clinical application of his theory. About 1907 he became a supporter of Freud and an active colleague within the psychoanalytic circle, but he withdrew about 1913 because of philosophical and theoretical differences.

Jung's theory is philosophically based in a teleological assumption of organismic purposivism, through which the transformative processes of individuation unfold within the person in ways already inherent in the unique potential carried by that psychological center that Jung called the Self. Jung's concepts were initially rejected by American psychology for the very reasons that made them an honored voice in the Zeitgeist of holistic and self-actualization theory initiated by American writers of the 1950s. Jung's notion of the Self emphasizes the importance of balance and wholeness, but also goes far beyond this in its recognition of the spiritual dimension and transcendent source of the creative power inherent in the growth potential within each individual psyche.

Jung's concept of the Self cannot be clearly defined or fully elucidated without reference to his overall theory. It is an unusually comprehensive and unifying theory, presenting a psychology of the individual rooted in an evolutionary history carried as archetypal image and predisposition within the collective unconscious. Symbolized by the ocean as the primary source and container of biological evolution, the collective unconscious antedates and contains humankind's emergent consciousness. The ego as the carrier of differentiated consciousness is therefore a latecomer in human development, an island risen out of the ocean. Jung sees the true center of the individual psyche as the creative source from which life and development spring, and this source is the Self, which is simultaneously and paradoxically unique and universal, biological and transcendental.

Jung's concept of the unconscious includes the individual realm of the personal unconscious derivative from childhood experience, but goes beyond this into the oceanic depths of the collective unconscious (also called the objective psyche, as distinguished from personal and subjective), which carries both the individual's connection with the transcendent Source of his or her unique creative potential, and also the psychological legacy of human experience from the earliest primeval beginnings. The language of the unconscious is symbolic imagery, which presents an intangible inner reality *as if* it were the scene depicted. The symbolic mode is applicable to that which can never be fully known, and the essential mystery of the human soul is honored in Jungian psychology. The enigmatic aspect of dreams is viewed, not as the product of censoring by the ego, but rather as a function of our lack of conversance with the primal language, combined with the essential mystery of the never completely knowable.

While dreams from the level of the personal unconscious use known people and places as vehicles of expression, motifs beyond the level of personal experience are conveyed through archetypal images that reach into all those world mythologies that have symbolized the evolution of the human psyche.

While the Self constitutes the archetypal Totality and carries the central organizing principle of the psyche, it is too comprehensive ever to be confronted directly, and the confrontations of the ego with the archetypal realm occur primarily through the *persona,* the *shadow,* and the *anima* or *animus.* While the Self represents the archetypal unity toward which persons strive in their attempts to achieve union of the opposites, the more immanent archetypal forces carry the paradoxical nature of life as opposites calling for reconciliation.

The persona and the shadow are a pair of opposites. While rooted in the archetypal necessity for collective cultural adaptation, the *persona* develops closer to consciousness than do other archetypal forces and produces the social mask appropriate to social roles. It is shaped through training by representatives of collective authority. In opposition to it lies the *shadow,* constituted partially by personal attributes hidden from awareness through repression when complexes were formed, but also compounded by archetypal nuclei, which carry both the darkness of universal "evil" and the creative potential of generative energy.

Psychological difficulties are intensified by increasing polarization between persona and shadow. The individual who identifies with the idealized imagery of the persona is in danger of eruptions from the neglected and rejected shadow realm, which becomes intensified as an inner enemy because of the lack of recognition and relatedness by the ego. Entering consciousness through projection either onto other people or through imagery in dreams and imaginative products, the shadow is an unwanted intruder that nevertheless brings the possibility of facilitating individuation through opening the doors of the unconscious into that which calls for redemption and transformation.

Jung refers to the masculine principle within the psyche of the woman as the *animus,* and to the feminine principle within the psyche of the man as the *anima.* Bridging the distance between earth (feminine) and spirit (masculine), the sexual polarity carries a basic creative dynamism of the individuation urge. Analogous to the positive and negative energies of electricity, the sexual opposites carry a powerful reciprocal attraction. These opposites are perhaps most readily characterized through reference to the Chinese principles of yang (masculine) and yin (feminine). The yang represents the aggressive, initiating, penetrating power of the phallus and the sword. The yin represents the receptive, yielding, containing, and pulsating rhythms of the womb and the tides.

An important aspect of the individuation process is the achievement of conscious acceptance of the attributes coming from "the other within." The man thus individuated is enriched in his masculine functioning by an inner source of inspiration, creativity, and emotional involvement. The anima enables him to relate with a flow of spontaneous feeling. Without such utilization of his feminine side as an inner resource, he tends to fall into unconscious identification with the image of an "inferior woman," expressed through moodiness and depression or inflation and primitive irrationality.

The woman who has achieved conscious acceptance of her animus attributes is able to use her Logos powers effectively in dealing with the outer world. She is able to make discriminations with objectivity, her capacities for observation and reasoning are enhanced, and she may become adept in the perception of meaning. Without such utilization of her masculine side as a differentiated resource, she may fall into unconscious identification with the image of the "superior man," pronouncing judgments as if they were fact, making assumptions without examination, and proclaiming opinions in a self-righteous or dogmatic way.

In honoring the unconscious as a source of wisdom and potential growth, Jung provided a new valuing of introversion as a way of relating to life. The introversion–extroversion polarity is the base of Jung's typology, which presents the ways in which the ego orients toward living. The individual with an introverted orientation functions more naturally and spontaneously in terms of the inner world, while the individual with an extroverted orientation functions more naturally and spontaneously in terms of the outer world. Neither orientation is superior to the other, but each has its own advantages and limitations.

Serving the ego in conjunction with the basic *Erlebnistyp* of introversion–extroversion are the four functions, which exist as dualities. They form a cross, of which intuition and sensation are the perceptual or information-gathering functions, and thinking and feeling are the ordering or evaluating functions. Each person has one leading or superior function, which is aided by an auxiliary function from the other polarity. The superior and auxiliary functions are used through the prevailing *Erlebnistyp;* that is, if an individual is introverted, his or her superior and auxiliary functions are introverted, while the third and fourth functions are extroverted. The fourth function, the opposite of the leading function, is called the inferior function because it is least developed. It is the function most likely to be used in manifestations of the shadow.

Each of the four functions relates to personality characteristics specific both to their introverted or extroverted form and also to their degree of development. Differences in typology may make it very difficult for one person to understand another, and this is a common source of interpersonal problems. Jungian typology is useful therapeutically inasmuch as it is not a schema of static characteristics but a system of dynamics.

Although all people possess all these components, the variations in combinations and degrees of development result in much diversity. While some people are decidedly introverted or extroverted, others are closer to center on this dimension. All four functions operate spontaneously without conscious direction, but the more differentiated ones are more amenable to creative utilization by the ego, while the less developed ones operate more primitively and compulsively. Although more balance among the functions may be achieved with increasing individuation, the hierarchical order is always retained, with the third and fourth functions exerting a compensatory influence on the conscious ego.

ARCHETYPES
EAST/WEST PSYCHOLOGY
PERSONALITY THEORIES
PHILOSOPHICAL PSYCHOLOGY
PSYCHOANALYSIS
TRANSPERSONAL PSYCHOLOGY

V. T. Heisler

ANCIENT THEORIES OF DREAMS

There is no doubt about the salience of dreams in the ancient world. The written records provide profuse evidence of their prophetic, religious, and curative significance to the people of those times.

One of the first existing writings of importance was the Assyrian epic of Gilgamesh, which was written in the third millennium. This half-divine hero was introduced to his companion Enkidu in two dreams. Enkidu became the interpreter of Gilgamesh's dreams, which were messages from the gods and guided the two in their human adventures. The continuing importance of dreams in Assyria is seen in use of dreams by Ashurbanipal in his campaigns in the 7th century B.C. The cuneiform libraries of the Babylonian and Chaldean peoples contain large numbers of dream recordings and translations.

The earliest known papyri of the Egyptians contained many formulas for obtaining and interpreting dreams, and the continuation of their central role in Egypt is seen in the Old Testament descriptions of the important part played by Joseph in the interpretation of the pharaoh's dreams.

The Upanishad writings of India from about 1000 B.C. contain long passages about dreams and their importance in spiritual life.

In the opening of the *Iliad,* Zeus sends a dream figure to Agamemnon, which urged the attack on Troy. The presence of dreams directs much of the continued action and continues in the *Odyssey* with the dreams of Penelope about the return of her husband, Odysseus. It was the uncertainty of these latter dreams that led to the description of dreams that passed through the gates of ivory (true dreams) and those that passed through the obscure gates of horn (false dreams).

The Old Testament speaks of the important role of dreams from Genesis through Zechariah. God spoke to Abraham in the night informing him of the Covenant between God and his people and reiterated his message to Jacob. Joseph seemed to have received his dreams less directly and dreamed in a more symbolic form. His ability to interpret dreams placed him in a position of authority in Egypt. The great Hebrew kings— Samuel, David, and Solomon—dreamed great dreams. Dreams are crucial in the chapters about Job and Daniel. In the prophets, we see some of the underlying complexities that must be associated with dreams. These were the relationships between visions, dreams, and prophecy and the problem of distinguishing between true and false among these. The only true touchstone lay in the relationship between the dreamer and God.

The important role of the dream continues in the New Testament as exemplified by the annunciation dream of the birth of Christ: "But when he thought on these things, behold an angel of the Lord appeared unto him in a dream, saying, Joseph, thou son of David, fear not to take unto thee Mary thy wife; for that which is conceived in her is of the Holy Ghost."

The Greek tradition moves away from the archaic form expressed in the works of Homer, which portrayed dreams as supernatural revelations from gods or great figures from the past. Beginning in about the 5th century B.C., the Orphic idea of seeking an individual communication with gods who would yield information for interpretation or use was developed. By the 3rd century B.C., this Orphic tradition had become institutionalized in the presence of more than 400 "temples" where individuals could bring their dreams or where they could sleep and "incubate" dreams that would be interpreted in terms of cures or future plans.

The treatment of dreams can be found in the writing of most of the great early Greek philosophers (e.g., Pythagoras, Heraclitus, Democritus). Plato clearly took dreams quite seriously as seen in his dialogue *Crito.* Here he describes Socrates' dream about his impending death. In the *Republic* he discusses the emergence of the dark, instinctual aspects of persons in dreams.

In this pervasively supernatural dream world there are two remarkable exceptions: the writings of Aristotle and Cicero. Each flatly denied the supernatural prophetic role of dreams. Aristotle viewed dreams as residual sensory impressions and accounted for their unusual quality in terms of our reduced level of "reasoning" during sleep and their uncontrolled "running" and "collisions." Cicero considered dreams to be "phantoms and apparitions." He suggests that we should pay no more attention to dreams than we do to the products of drunks or the insane. He suggested

that to solve a problem, such as whether a voyage would be successful, consult an expert, such as a navigator.

DREAMS
MYTHS

W. B. WEBB

ANDROGYNY

Although the idea that a single individual can embody components of both masculinity and femininity was introduced to psychology by Carl Jung in his essay on "Anima and animus," modern psychology paid little attention to this idea until the concept of androgyny was introduced by Sandra Bem, who argued that masculinity and femininity constitute complementary domains of positive traits and behaviors and that, in principle, it is possible for a person to be both masculine and feminine, agentic and communal, instrumental and expressive, depending on the situational appropriateness of these various modalities.

Although researchers have abandoned the original concept of androgyny as a prescription for mental health, the concept of androgyny has been useful to psychology. In particular, dialogues in the area have sensitized psychologists to the multidimensional aspects of sex and gender. Future research in the area may suggest ways that social definitions about sex roles are incorporated into personal identity, into the self, and into the way people process their perceptions about social reality.

ROLE EXPECTANCIES
SEX ROLE DEVELOPMENT
SEX ROLES

R. K. UNGER

ANHEDONIA

The term *anhedonia,* as its Greek roots indicate, refers to the absence of hedonism, or a lack of desire to experience pleasure and avoid pain. Coined in 1896 by Theodule Ribot to refer to the absence of emotion in patients with hepatic disease, anhedonia was equated with a type of pathological depression or melancholy by William James, who believed that it was on a continuum with anguish but was less serious. Nevertheless, the concept of anhedonia was given little further attention in the medical or psychological literature.

Eugen Bleuler observed that the disappearance of affect signaled the onset of dementia praecox or schizophrenia, and Sandro Rado specified that the affect in question was a diminished capacity for pleasure. Paul Meehl provided a name for the phenomenon by resurrecting the term *anhedonia* and proposed that measures for it be developed to identify persons at risk for schizophrenia.

In line with Meehl's proposal, Chapman, Chapman, and Rawlin published three true–false scales to measure physical and social anhedonia and to indicate psychosis-proneness: the Physical Anhedonia Scale, the Perceptual Aberration Scale, and the Nonconformity Scale. Items in the scales had been selected from a large pool of rationally developed statements, according to how well they discriminated between hospitalized schizophrenic and nonschizophrenic patients in regard to levels of anhedonia. Norms were obtained for gender, age, and social groups among university undergraduates; persons whose scores were 2 standard deviations (SDs) above the mean were considered to be at higher than normal risk for the development of psychosis.

Scores on the physical and social anhedonia scales have been found to be positively correlated with each other and negatively correlated with scores for social competence, social desirability, sensation seeking, and effective coping behaviors, among others. They have also been significantly correlated with several patterns of Minnesota Multiphasic Personality Inventory (MMPI) subscale scores. However, some studies have not found a relationship between anhedonia levels and responses to specific emotion-provoking stimuli and have suggested that anhedonia is not a consistent sign of schizophrenia, but a consequence of mental disturbance, poor status, and low educational levels.

Longitudinal studies to address the basic question of whether high anhedonia scores reliably predict psychosis remain to be done. Ethical as well as practical questions about obtaining and using such scores, and particularly any potentially harmful effects of such use, also remain to be asked and answered. Norms for anhedonia levels in various ethnocultural groups also need to be obtained; in fact, normal differences already have been observed among Caucasian and Asian-American groups.

Overall, the relationship of anhedonia and psychosis appears to be clinically significant but insufficiently researched; it has diagnostic value but, at present, uncertain predictive value, and unexplored preventive or therapeutic value.

Although anhedonia has been of interest mainly as a possible predictor of schizophrenia, it was early observed in other disorders, both physical and psychological, and deficits in the ability to experience pleasure are recognized as parts of syndromes ranging from dementia to posttraumatic stress disorder. Anhedonia is not considered to be a disorder in itself but only a symptom of disorder, and, in fact, the term has not yet appeared in either most professional manuals or standard dictionaries. Its usefulness as a concept, however, has become apparent.

DEPRESSION
EMOTIONS
HOPELESSNESS
PERSONALITY TYPES
SCHIZOPHRENIA

A. D. SCHEUER

ANIMAL AGGRESSIVE BEHAVIOR

The term *aggression* is difficult to define. In general it refers to behavioral patterns in which an animal either delivers or threatens to deliver some noxious stimulus to another animal.

KINDS OF AGGRESSION

Intertwined with the problem of defining aggression is that of determining motivational bases. If one believes in a unified definition of aggression, one can postulate a unitary drive underlying aggression. For example, the ethologist Lorenz, in *On aggression*, proposed a hydraulic model of aggression: associated with aggression is an internal energy source; the tendency to aggress increases as a function of time since the last aggressive encounter. Lorenz proposed that attendance at violent spectator sports might drain aggressive energy.

An alternative approach was proposed by Moyer, who argued that there are many kinds of aggression, each with its own set of predisposing conditions, eliciting stimuli, physiological bases, and consequences. Moyer proposed a list including predatory aggression, intermale aggression, fear-induced aggression, irritable aggression, territorial defense, maternal aggression, instrumental aggression, and sex-related aggression—a preliminary list that he recognized would require refinement. Wittenberger distinguished intrasexual aggression, intersexual aggression, parental aggression, infanticide aggression, peer aggression, defensive aggression, redirected aggression, and predatory aggression. Some combination of these two lists may be useful.

EVOLUTION OF AGGRESSION

Aggressive encounters often occur in situations of conflict over resources, such as food and mating partners. Various evolutionary theorists have assessed the selective pressures associated with intrasexual aggression in relation to such resources. When two animals fight over a resource, the winner gets the resource but suffers a cost in time and possible injury. The loser may incur the same or greater losses without reaping any benefits. The extent to which a prolonged aggressive encounter would be beneficial to an animal will depend on many factors including its fighting ability, the fighting ability of the opponent, and the value of the resource to each. Where the payoff of varying behavioral patterns varies according to the strategies utilized by one's opponents, theorists use a version of game theory to determine an *evolutionarily stable strategy*. An evolutionarily stable strategy is one which, once it becomes common in a population, will lead to a greater level of fitness than any of a series of defined alternative strategies.

DEVELOPMENT OF AGGRESSION

The development of aggressive behavior can be seen as a function of both genetic and environmental influences. Inbred strains of mice display different levels of aggressive behavior in tests of intermale aggression even if reared in similar environments. Indeed, one can cross-foster young animals so that individuals of each strain are reared by parents of the opposite strain; little effect is seen on the level of aggressive behavior. However, environmental factors are also important. For example, rhesus monkeys reared by aggressive mothers develop into especially aggressive adults.

PHYSIOLOGICAL CONTROL

Hormonal factors are very important in the regulation of intrasexual aggression, although they may be of little importance for other behavioral patterns such as predation. As is the case for sexual behavior, hormones affect aggressive behavior in two distinct ways. The presence of androgens or estrogens in mice, rats, or hamsters around the time of birth has pervasive and long-term importance for the occurrence of aggression in the adult animal. If a young female house mouse is exposed to androgen during the critical period, she will show adult levels of aggressive behavior comparable to normal males. Conversely, if a male is deprived of androgen during this period, his adult levels of aggression will be reduced. Whereas the actions of hormones during critical periods are irreversible, hormonal actions in adults are generally reversible. Thus if a male is castrated as an adult, his level of intermale aggression will decrease. The original level may be restored, however, with exogenous hormones. This is not the case with perinatal hormonal action.

As noted by Moyer, different forms of aggression have different neural bases. For example, predatory aggression (if classed as aggression at all) is triggered by electrical stimulation of the lateral hypothalamus, an area also associated with eating and drinking. Irritable aggression is that form related to pain or frustration; there are indications that the ventromedial hypothalamus may play an important role in its regulation.

As might be expected, drugs have different effects on different types of aggressive behavior. For example, predatory aggression has been shown to be facilitated by a drug that decreases levels of the neurotransmitter serotonin; irritable aggression is altered by manipulation of norepinephrin levels; and spontaneous aggression appears affected by yet another substance, dopamine.

The opportunity to engage in aggressive behavior often has reinforcing value to animals. Thus a mouse or Siamese Fighting Fish will learn to perform an arbitrary operant response when the reinforcement is the opportunity to engage in an aggressive encounter.

AGGRESSION
ECOLOGICAL PSYCHOLOGY
GESTURES
TERRITORIALITY
VIOLENCE

D. A. DEWSBURY

ANIMAL COMMUNICATION

Animal communication has occurred when one animal has been shown to influence the behavior of another. The kinds of influence generally subsumed under the category of "communication" are those mediated via the sense organs of the animal receiving the signal. A situation wherein one animal responds to another's call is an instance of communication, whereas an animal altering another's behavior by injuring it would not be regarded as having communicated.

COMMUNICATION SYSTEMS

A communication system entails the interaction of several elements. There must first be a *signal*—generally some behavioral pattern emitted by an organism that is the *sender*. Signals are emitted in varying *contexts,* and the significance of the signal can vary with the context in which it is emitted. Signals travel in various *channels,* such as a vocal-auditory channel, and must be discriminated from the other *noise,* or irrelevant background activity, in that channel. The signal must reach another animal, the *receiver,* whose behavior is altered. The sender and receiver can be said to share a *code,* which includes the complete set of all possible signals.

Sensory Modalities

Communication can occur in any sensory modality to which the organisms are responsive. Fireflies provide an excellent example of communication in a visual channel. They are active at night, with females generally remaining on the ground and males flying about. Flying males emit flashes of a color, intensity, frequency of occurrence, and duration that are characteristic of the species. Females answer in a similarly specific manner after a latency dependent on the species and temperature. Gradually, the male hones in on the female's signal and pairing takes place. Many of the courtship and aggressive displays of birds, which have been much studied by ethologists, function primarily in the visual modality.

Perhaps the best-known signals in the auditory modality are the songs of birds and the calls of such animals as frogs and crickets. Perhaps the most dramatic signals are those of humpback whales. The elements constituting these "songs" last between 7 and 30 minutes before they are repeated. These signals can be transmitted for many miles in the oceanic sound channel.

Tactile signals require close proximity but are common in social species such as many primates. Chimpanzees, for example, convey relatively subtle messages via their sense of touch. Many other species utilize tactile signals during courtship and copulation to achieve appropriate timing and orientation of the events surrounding reproduction.

Chemical signals are quite important in many species, especially mammals and insects, but are less generally recognized. *Pheromones* are chemical signals that function within species, and *allomones* communicate among species, as between prey and predator. *Hormones* mediate chemical "communication" within an organism. There are many examples of important mammalian social odors. The rate at which mice reach puberty is affected by the presence of pheromones; in general, pheromones from animals of the same sex retard, and those from the opposite sex accelerate, the appearance of puberty. A female mouse that has mated with one male will display a blockage of pregnancy, or *Bruce effect,* if exposed to a strange male or the odor of a strange male a couple of days later. Female rats emit a maternal pheromone that aids young pups in finding them. The estrous cycles of female rats housed near each other tend to become synchronized; a similar menstrual synchrony has been found in humans.

Other communication channels are used by specialized species. The ultrasonic systems of bats and dolphins are well-known. Some species of fishes use an electrical system both to locate objects and to communicate.

Different modalities have particular advantages for communicative signals. Chemical signals, for example, are slow to fade, move around corners, can be used at night, and are useful at long range. However, their rates of transmission are slow and they are difficult to localize. Auditory and visual signals travel much faster and are more easily localizable. Auditory signals are much more effective at night and in the presence of barriers, such as trees, than are visual signals.

Significant Examples

Perhaps the most famous example of naturally occurring animal communication is the "dance language" of honeybees. Foraging bees that have located a rich food source return to the hive and communicate the location of the food sources to their hive mates. If the food is less than 100 meters away a simple round dance is used. To communicate longer distances, a waggle dance is utilized. The waggle is performed on a vertical surface and assumes a pattern that approximates a figure eight. Between the two loops of the eight is a "straight run" that communicates much. The duration of the straight run correlates with the distance of the food source. The direction of the straight run, relative to gravity, indicates the direction to the food source, relative to the sun. Thus the forager performs a straight run oriented straight up when the receiver is to fly directly toward the sun, and straight down when the food source is in the opposite direction. Like many communication systems, the honeybee "language" is multimodal, with visual, tactile, auditory, and chemical aspects. Although the communication value of the dance aspect has been questioned, it does appear to be highly specific under many circumstances.

Perhaps the most publicized examples of animal communication in psychology are studies of "language" in chimpanzees. Early researchers met with limited success when attempting to condition chimps to vocalize. More recently, however, several researchers have trained animals to use rather complicated communication systems by relying on gestures and operant responses. Gardner and Gardner employed American Sign Language, the system used by many deaf humans, and succeeded in establishing a complex signal repertoire. The chimp, Washoe, could both send and receive an impressive catalogue of such signals. Premack and Premack taught their chimp, Sarah, to position plastic symbols in particular order so as to convey messages. Rumbaugh and Gill used a computerized system with Lana, who had to depress a set of operant response keys in the appropriate order as part of her language system. The extent to which these systems represent true language, and especially the use of grammatical rules, remains quite controversial.

ANIMAL SOCIOBIOLOGY
ETHOLOGY
COMMUNICATION PROCESSES

D. A. DEWSBURY

ANIMAL HYPNOSIS

Should you have both the time and a rabbit, try the following experiment. Lift the animal up gently and place it on its back on a flat surface. Within a few moments its head and hindquarters will relax, its breathing will become regular, and it will remain in that position for as long as 5 minutes

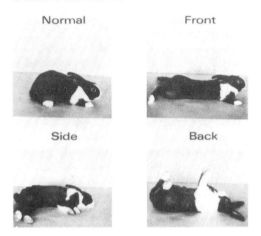

Figure 1. Postures in which Dutch belt rabbits can be placed to display animal hypnosis. From K. P. Flannigan and I. Q. Whishaw. The effects of some pharmacological agents on the duration of immobility shown by rabbits placed in various postures (1977). With permission.

after being released. The rabbit will also remain immobile after being placed in a number of other positions such as those illustrated in Figure 1. This behavior is called *animal hypnosis*. The term has its origins in the early belief that the immobile animal was in a state resembling human hypnosis—a belief reinforced both by the length of time that animals remained immobile and by the bizarre nature of their posture. Not all scientists are happy with the term animal hypnosis: There has been an ongoing search for a better name. The behavior has also been called mesmerism, death feint, playing possum, tonic immobility, paroxysmal inhibition, akinesis, Totstell reflex, immobility reflex, catalepsy, cataplexy, restraint-induced immobility, and so on.

Darwin first suggested that hypnosis or "playing dead" serves as protection from predation. Ratner elaborated this idea into a theory stating that a prey's responses change in proportion to the distance of a predator. If the predator is far away, the prey may run; if the predator is closer, the prey may stand still to avoid being seen; and if the predator is very close, the prey may lie immobile to prevent attack. There is growing support for this theory.

Very little is known about what the nervous system is doing during animal hypnosis. The first suggestion advanced to account for hypnosis came from the Russian psychologist, Pavlov, who argued that hypnotized animals are asleep. The results of many studies recording the electrical activity of the brain show quite clearly that brain activity of hypnotized animals is no different from that of normal, alert animals. This finding, coupled with naturalistic studies showing that hypnotized animals are alert to the possibilities of escape, and with more formal studies showing that hypnotized animals can learn, argues strongly against the idea that the hypnotized animal is asleep.

Apart from interest in understanding the phenomena in its own right, many people suggest that information obtained about animal hypnosis may have relevance for understanding a number of human medical conditions. Included among these are catatonia, or waxy immobility, displayed by some schizophrenics; catalepsy associated with Parkinson's disease; and the paralysis, called narcolepsy, that sometimes strikes people when they are awake. It is also thought that the study may shed some light on how terror prevents people from acting either defensively or offensively in combat situations, or when threatened by other types of attack. Finally, it is thought that an understanding of immobility will help clarify the nature of some human disorders characterized by excessive activity, such as mania or childhood hyperactivity. Certainly, whether or not these goals are realized, understanding animal hypnosis will provide further

understanding of how animals, including humans, are able to remain still in the many contexts in which immobility is adaptive.

HYPNOSIS

I. Q. WHISHAW

ANIMAL INTELLIGENCE

The view that animal species differ with respect to their levels of intelligence is firmly entrenched in the popular mind. In numerous articles in the popular press and on varied television programs, the intelligence levels of cats and dogs, cows and pigs, or other groups of species are compared. Even Aristotle sought to rank species on a single scale of intelligence, the *scala natura*. Some tend to view comparative psychology as entailing little more than the generation of such comparisons. Implicit in this approach is the belief that there exists some unitary trait, "intelligence," and that some species have more of it than do others. Yet there appears to be little support for such a view.

HISTORY

Throughout much of the history of philosophy one finds the view that fundamentally different processes are involved in the regulation of behavior in human versus nonhuman animals. Thus Descartes wrote that "after the error of atheism, there is nothing that leads weak minds further astray from the paths of virtue than the idea that the minds of other animals resemble our own." With Darwin the continuity of mental processes arose. Darwin, Romanes, and others cited numerous anecdotes emphasizing humanlike behavior in nonhuman animals. In reaction to this approach, C. Lloyd Morgan, Jacques Loeb, and others called for careful experimental analyses of learning to replace reliance on unsubstantiated anecdotes.

An important innovator in the early study of animal intelligence was E. L. Thorndike. Thorndike noted that "dogs get lost hundreds of times and no one ever notices it or sends an account of it to a scientific magazine. But let one find his way from Brooklyn to Yonkers and the fact immediately becomes a circulating anecdote." In his brief career as a comparative psychologist Thorndike studied a variety of species. He concluded: "Formally the crab, fish, turtle, dog, cat, monkey and baby have very similar intellects and characters. All are systems of connections subject to change by the law of exercise and effect." Although species were viewed as differing with respect to the kinds of connections they make and their abilities to do so, a single process was implied. Thorndike had little use for simple comparisons of "intelligence." He believed that one function of comparative psychology was to trace the evolution of the human intellect and that "this aim is helped little by knowing that dogs are brighter than cats, or whales than seals, or horses than cows."

Thorndike's views tended to dampen research on the evolution of intelligence and to foster concentration on the study of a few species. However, a sufficient number of studies was completed, so that a reasonable view of animal intelligence is possible. Undoubtedly, humans and apes can succeed in feats of learning unmatched by other species. However, there appears to be no simple method for ordering the species on a scale. Nor is there any solid indication that the processes underlying human learning are fundamentally different from those in nonhuman species.

LEARNING IN INVERTEBRATES

Many studies have been conducted in an attempt to demonstrate learning in single-celled organisms such as paramecia and amoebae. Changes in performance correlated with practice, quite similar to the changes in multicellular organisms, have been demonstrated. In no case, however, is it clear that true associative learning has occurred. Single-celled organisms are sensitive to such factors as the pH, polarization, and carbon dioxide content of their water. Many of the manipulations used in studying learning (e.g., shock, food delivery) affect these factors. Thus it is impossible to determine whether learning has occurred or the medium has been altered.

Flatworms (or planarians) are the simplest organisms with bilateral symmetry. More definitive evidence of their ability to learn has been provided. If a 1-second shock is delivered while a flatworm is gliding along the surface of water, it will turn its body or contract. If a light or a vibration occurs just prior to shock onset and many trials are run, the flatworm begins to respond to that stimulus prior to the shock. This is a simple instance of classical conditioning. By randomly presenting vibrations and light, only one of which was associated with shock, investigators demonstrated that true learning was involved in these response changes. Comparative psychologists have demonstrated learning in many other invertebrate species including snails, crabs, earthworms, and various species of insects.

QUANTITATIVE COMPARISONS OF VERTEBRATES

Many tasks have been used in attempts to scale learning ability in different species. Although there are tasks that some species, but not others, have been found to learn, there is no simple way in which to scale intelligence.

The simplest approach to the study of intelligence would be through the simplest problems. One can compare the rate of response acquisition in classical and instrumental learning in a variety of species. The learning of mazes or other simple discriminations also could be studied. Unfortunately, such comparisons reveal no orderly scale of intelligence. Some species with relatively complex brains are slower to learn certain tasks than are animals with simpler brains.

In the search for tasks that differentiate species, greater complexity must be added to the stimuli to be discriminated or to the responses to be made. The most widely studied such problem is the *learning set task*. Learning sets generally involve the capacity to discriminate between two objects. Food is hidden under one of the two, and the task of the animal is simply to choose which of the two covers the food. Animals of many species can learn this task readily. Once the first such task is learned, another is given, and this is followed by another, until hundreds of discriminations may be learned. Many animals get better and better with successive discriminations; they "learn to learn" or display a "learning set." Others are as slow to learn the last discrimination as they were with the first. Rats, squirrels, and tree shrews show little improvement over hundreds of problems, whereas chimpanzees, gorillas, and rhesus monkeys show rapid improvement. Other primates and carnivores are intermediate. These results led to the view that the learning set task may provide a means with which to scale intelligence levels across many species. One problem with this approach is that some species perform at levels quite unexpected from their neuroanatomy. For example, both pigeons and ferrets improve at about the same rate as do squirrel monkeys. Myna birds and blue jays perform at levels comparable to those of cats, marmosets, and squirrel monkeys, but crows show only marginal improvement.

The major difficulty with use of the learning set problem, as well as many other complex tasks, in comparing species, is that it is difficult, if not impossible, to create conditions that are not biased in favor of some species and against others. First is the problem of differences in sensory function. Humans, nonhuman primates, and birds rely very heavily on visual information, whereas other species rely more heavily on other modalities. Learning set problems, being designed by humans, generally utilize stimuli easily discriminated visually because they differ in size, shape, color, and other such characteristics. The reason that primates and birds perform so well may relate more to the development of their visual systems than to their intelligence levels. It is equally difficult to equate problems for different species with regard to the level of motivation, the magnitude of reinforcement, and the motor capabilities of each species. It is a small wonder that no simple scale of intelligence has been generated.

REASONING AND INSIGHT

Thorndike found little evidence of reasoning or insight in his studies of animal learning. Others have argued that such a conclusion was inevitable, given the testing conditions used by Thorndike. Köhler devised a variety of tasks in which chimpanzees had their path to a goal blocked by some problem in need of solution. In some tasks the chimps had to pile up boxes to reach a banana suspended from the ceiling. In other problems, sticks had to be joined together or otherwise manipulated, if the reward was to be obtained. Köhler's apes appeared to reach sudden, insightful solutions to the problems they faced. Others have noted that the performance of chimps in these tasks is affected by naturally occurring responses to such stimuli and by previous exposure and play. The occurrence of insight is difficult to demonstrate.

SPECIFIC LEARNING ABILITIES

One cannot but be struck by the ease with which certain animals learn some tasks and by the difficulty they have with others. Digger wasps are able to perform a kind of complex delayed response learning with respect to the contents of several burrows. Indigo buntings attend to patterns of movement of the stars and fixate on a "North Star" in relation to the relative movement by different stars. Rats that have been poisoned are unlikely to eat the same tasting food again, although they may return to the location at which they were poisoned and eat food that looks similar. Although it is easy to train a rat to run to escape electric shock, it is harder to train it to stay and depress a lever to escape from shock.

In each of these situations animals appear "prepared" to learn certain things and "contraprepared" to learn others. In adapting to particular niches, each species must solve certain problems. Learning is a part of that adaptation, and the capacity to learn—indeed, to learn certain things—is as subject to the action of natural selection as are other traits.

There is a growing view that evolution has not produced a gradual increase in a unidimensional level of intelligence, but rather that species have evolved specific learning abilities relevant to their survival and reproduction in specific niches. The underlying processes may—or may not—be identical across species. What natural selection has ensured is that animals can learn those things critical for life as they live it. Any generalized abstract "intelligence" may be the creation of the scientist and not relevant to the differential survival and reproduction of organisms in their natural habitats.

PERSPECTIVE

Humans are a very visual species adept at learning. We tend to value other species in relation to our own proclivities and to assess them in terms appropriate to our own mode of adaptation. It should be recognized, however, that complex learning is but one means of adapting. Where the situation and appropriate response are both highly predictable and stable over evolutionary time, it may be best to have a response rigidly determined by genotype rather than one subject to the vagaries of learning. Other species have adapted in ways different from our own. We should not be surprised that we cannot force them into a set of pigeon holes along a unidimensional scale. Further, as noted by Harlow, "There is no evidence of an intellectual gulf at any point, and there are no existing data that would justify the assumption that there is a greater gap between men and monkeys than there is between monkeys and their closest kin."

ANIMAL SOCIOBIOLOGY
HUMAN INTELLIGENCE
INSTINCTIVE BEHAVIOR

D. A. Dewsbury

ANIMAL MODELS

Animal models are widely used in psychology (a) to promote a conceptual framework in which it might be possible to recognize new relationships and interactions among the environment, central nervous system, and behavior; (b) to promote the generation of testable hypotheses important for understanding human behavior; and (c) to study psychological phenomena under simpler and more controlled conditions than can be achieved in research with humans.

Animal models have a long and distinguished history in studies of both normal and abnormal behavior. However, while other life scientists (e.g., anatomists, physiologists, pharmacologists) broadly accept both the homological and analogical bases for the use of animal models, some contemporary analysts—often with little grounding in biology—see less value and occasionally deride animal models as tools for understanding human behavior. The schism between those recognizing the value of animal research and those who do not parallels the divide between the mechanistic and humanistic traditions of psychology and between accepting the evolutionary theory of Charles Darwin versus accepting the psychophysical dualism of René Descartes. Evolutionary theory projects a continuity of mind and emotions from animals to humans, whereas Cartesian dualism argues that even though organs and brains might be similar across species, the mental products are different. The Cartesian position has been argued to pose a conundrum for the use of animal models—if the animal is "like" a human, the same ethical constraints apply to studies on animals as apply to studies on humans, whereas if the animal is "unlike" the human, there is little reason to study animals within the context of human behavior and psychopathology. But this position and the common demand for a priori assurances that research with a given model will advance a specific therapy reflect a fundamental failure to understand the nature and function of models and the accumulative nature of scientific progress.

At the more biological end of the continuum of psychological research and application, the use of animal models finds general acceptance and is largely noncontroversial: These include research on neural mechanisms of learning, perceptual–cognitive mechanisms of the brain, memory dysfunction in aging populations, mechanisms of drug dependency and addiction, and psychopharmacology. Application of animal models is an established integral component of the successes in these research areas.

Studies of nervous transmission in the giant axon of the squid form a cornerstone for our knowledge of the workings of the central nervous system in higher organisms. At the neural network level, in-depth studies of long-term potentiation in hippocampal slice preparations of rats has led to highly promising advances in the understanding of the molecular and neurophysiological bases of learning in humans. At the level of whole nonmammalian organisms, experiments on learning and memory in mollusks form a basis for studying mechanisms of short- and long-term memory at the molecular level as well as offering advances in understanding "simple" mechanisms of learning and the neurochemical basis thereof.

Animal modeling also has played an important role in studies of the biological bases of complex behavioral traits through the development of behavior genetics. For example, use of fast-breeding rats and mice in selective breeding has demonstrated that individual differences in complex behavioral traits such as aggression reflect heritable differences in strategies in coping with the environment. This difference in coping is paralleled by a difference in the animals' sensitivity to the dopamine agonist apomorphine. Such studies suggest possible biological bases for complex human behavior. Animal models help us to make educated guesses as to which traits in humans might be worth pursuing from a behavior genetic perspective. The best known contemporary human examples are the Minnesota Twin Studies, which have shown in twins reared apart that genetic factors contribute significantly to personality, including religiosity.

In understanding psychosomatic disorders and disease, animal models have provided guides as to some of the predisposing factors. For example, animal studies definitely established the association between plasma pepsinogen levels and stress gastrointestinal pathology parallel to that suggested in humans. This, in turn, prompted research into personality factors associated with plasma pepsinogen and ulcers. A direct line runs through studies of individual differences in behavioral coping with stress in rats, the studies of coping and gastric pathology in primates, through to more recent research on human differences in autonomic reactivity to stress. More recently, the use of animal models has provided a solid scientific basis for the "new" field of psychoneuroimmunology. Despite a significant body of anecdotal evidence, a link between the psychological state, immunity, and cancer was fiercely opposed by the medical establishment until the publication of numerous controlled studies that used animal models in which behavioral stress was directly observed to modulate immunocompetence.

Animal modeling becomes more difficult and more controversial as it attempts to address behavioral issues in psychopathology. Animal models promise an understanding of psychopathology, not as bizarre distortions of behavior but rather as the consequence of lawful psychological processes whose principles and mechanisms can be elucidated scientifically. Ivan Pavlov was the first to argue that experimentally induced behavioral dysfunction in animals might teach us about human dysfunction: In appetitive classical conditioning experiments with dogs, he observed that presenting a series of increasingly difficult discriminations between a circle and an ellipse resulted in the animals' behavior finally becoming so agitated and erratic that the dysfunction was designated experimental neurosis. In subsequent parallel work with children in an auditory discrimination task, an analogous manipulation led to somewhat similar results. More important, Pavlov and his associates found bromide salts to be an effective "therapy" for both the dogs and the children. There followed a number of efforts to create animal models of psychopathology. Two of Pavlov's American students, Horsley Gantt and Howard Liddell, contributed greatly in this regard.

These observations by Pavlov and his students that maladaptive behavior patterns could be conditioned in animals and that these were analogous to human neuroses inspired others to explore the possibility of a new study of psychopathology based in animal research.

Some scientists have proposed the essential features that animal models of human psychopathology should strive toward: there should be similarity of symptoms, essential causes and cures, underlying physiology, and a specificity to the particular disorder and not simply a model of general psychopathology. But it should be clear that these criteria are impossible to fulfill, rather they reflect an ideal. In fact, should they ever be attained, the "model" would no longer be a model but something with considerably greater significance: One will have moved from a state of analogy to identity.

Numerous models of human psychopathology have been developed, some more complete and useful than others. Perhaps most well-known to the general reader is Harry Harlow's report of the effects of maternal separation in nonhuman primates and his experimental differentiation between the suckling and comforting functions fulfilled by the mother. The dramatic consequences of this separation for the young nonhuman primate (i.e., behavioral withdrawal and loss of appetite and sleep) were likened to the psychopathological effects of neglect in institutionalized human infants (i.e., anaclitic depression). This model of depression is of particular importance for helping to understand the psychological problems of orphans raised in unstimulating environments. Later studies on the psychophysiological responses of young nonhuman primates separated from their mothers lead to understanding behavioral and social factors that modulate and buffer the stressfulness of human mother–infant separations.

The learned helplessness model of depression based on behavioral research with dogs has been important both in the development of therapeutic regimes and in understanding the etiology of some forms of depression. Perhaps of equal long-term importance is the impetus the model has provided for (a) active hypothesis testing within its framework, (b) studies of the neurochemistry of depression, and (c) its usefulness in screening for therapeutic drugs. Models of depression have blossomed. Many of these rely on some *behavioral* manipulation of the animal that also have known biological consequences. It is a common misunderstanding that psychobiologists focus their work on animal models because they believe that the root of human psychopathology is biological. As exemplified by the learned helplessness model, the comparative psychologist might start with a nonphysiological environmental–behavioral manipulation that induces a set of behavioral and physiological symptoms with similarities to the human condition he or she wishes to model. The same symptoms also will have behavioral consequences, which in turn have additional biological consequences.

Aging and its commonly associated dementias, in which neurophysiological changes have far-reaching and devastating psychological effects, may be an area of special future promise for animal models. At present, the nature of senile dementia is not understood from the cognitive, behavioral, or physiological perspective. Animal models can contribute to identification of all these to determine and reduce the risk factors and the degrees of expressed disability.

Behavioral dysfunctions and psychiatric disorders must continue to be studied to bring relief to literally tens of millions of sufferers. Until some significant grasp on the processes involved are understood, scientists are deterred from some classes of research with human subjects and patient populations—in particular those experimenting with etiologies or with therapies that involve not yet understood physiological changes.

Animal research may help, because this grasp is to be gained only through the use of animal models. It is particularly surprising that animal models should today be the focus of intellectual hostility in a society in which psychological problems and mental disease pose such a large threat to human well-being.

There are ethical considerations in the use of animals for such research. The animal employed must be chosen with care and knowledge of its basic physiology, and the numbers of animals required for an experiment should be carefully evaluated. Experiments should be performed strictly within the guidelines laid down by the respective authorities after prior peer review.

Despite the conceptual and scientific challenges associated with the use of animal models, the demand for advances in psychology (and other life sciences) through these models necessitate that they continue to be used when appropriate.

ANIMAL PARENTAL BEHAVIOR MODELS
NEURAL NETWORK MODELS
PERCEPTUAL ORGANIZATIONS
PSYCHOPHARMACOLOGY

R. Murison
J. B. Overmier

ANIMAL PARENTAL BEHAVIOR

Parental behavior includes all behaviors directed at the care and maintenance of one's young or the young of close relatives. Although it is common to view parental behavior as beginning with the birth or hatching of the young, such behavior may actually begin at conception or even earlier. The building of nests, alteration of feeding patterns, and acquisition and storage of needed resources all can occur early in a reproductive sequence but function for the care and maintenance of the young.

Parental behaviors vary greatly among different species. Whereas some species never see their own offspring, others display elaborate and intricately controlled parental patterns. Among insects, digger wasps have been much studied. The female digs a burrow and then provides each egg with a paralyzed prey in that burrow. When the young hatch, the mother is gone but the young have both shelter and food awaiting them. By contrast, the parental behaviors of honeybees are elaborate and continuous. Eggs are deposited in hexagonal-shaped cells in the hive; a steady stream of workers visits the cells, inspects them, cleans them, and feeds the developing young.

Fishes are remarkably varied in their parental patterns. Carp scatter eggs on plants; trout often deposit them in sand or gravel; in other species unattended eggs simply float to the surface and disperse. Contrast such minimal behavior with the elaborate nests of other species, such as the bubble nests of the Siamese fighting fish. Cichlid fishes of the genus *Tilapia* may carry and brood eggs in their mouths. In some species of fishes the male cares for the young, as with the ethologists' favorite species, the three-spined stickleback.

Amphibians have evolved various ways to cope with the problem of maintaining moist conditions while they spend part of their lives on land. Many lay eggs in water. Others carry their eggs with them, as do Surinam toads, in which eggs hatch in a specialized fold in the female's back, and midwife toads, in which males carry eggs around their waists.

Most birds incubate their eggs by sitting on them. As many species are monogamous, male and female may each take turns incubating the eggs. Australian mallee fowl females build elaborate mounds for their eggs and devote much time to ensuring that a proper temperature is maintained inside the mound. Only brood parasites, such as cuckoos and cowbirds, are emancipated from parental behavior, laying eggs in the nests of host species which proceed to care for them.

Ring doves have been a favorite species in the study of parental behavior. Male and female share in the duties of nest building and sitting on the eggs. There is a dramatic shift in behavior during this time: Early in the sequence birds do not sit on eggs; later, one lifts the whole nest if one tries to lift the female—her grip is that tight. When the young hatch, the parents feed them with "crop milk," regurgitated material from the epithelial lining of their crops.

Parental care is highly developed in mammals and generally entails parturition, nursing, grooming, nest building, transport of the young, defense of the young, play, and tuition. Because of the evolution of mammary glands, parental care in mammals is performed disproportionately by females to a greater extent than in many other taxa. The sequence of mother–young interactions during the period of nursing is similar in many species, such as cats and laboratory rats. When the young are quite small the mother initiates the nursing bout, often by approaching the young and assuming a specific posture. In a second stage there is often a mutual approach by mother and young. In the final stage the young approach and the mother may actively avoid their solicitations. The sequence ends with weaning. The extent of male involvement can be minimal, as in many rodents and ungulates, or quite elaborate, as in some carnivores and primates.

The occurrence of parental behavior is dependent on hormonal secretions, neural mechanisms, and sensory factors. In ring doves, nest building can be induced with injections of estrogen; progesterone injections produce incubation behavior. Fluctuations in the naturally occurring levels of these hormones are consistent with the view that estrogens are especially important for nest building and progesterone for incubation—at least in females.

There is no one hormone responsible for the induction of parental behavior in mammals. Throughout her pregnancy the female normally shows substantial and predictable fluctuations in her hormonal milieu. By using carefully planned sequences of injections of estrogen, progesterone, and prolactin, various workers have succeeded in eliciting maternal behavior in nulliparous females—but only hours after introduction of the young rat pups. Cross-transfusion of blood from females that had recently delivered litters to nulliparous females has been found to induce maternal behavior in rats. Mere exposure of adult rats to young pups for 10 to 15 days elicits a complete, but nonhormonally based, complement of parental behaviors. Of course, in nature the young would die in that time. Hormones appear to synchronize the appearance of the young and the onset of parental behavior.

SOCIOBIOLOGICAL PERSPECTIVE

As each individual has been selected to maximize its own fitness level, parent and young should be in conflict with regard to the allocation of parental resources. Each offspring would be expected to demand a greater share of parental resources than the parent is prepared to give. This demand should be curbed only when excessive demands decrease the young's inclusive fitness by substantially interfering with the survival and reproduction of their kin. The changing pattern through development of parent and young, initiation of parental care, and ultimately weaning conflict may reflect the differential interests of parent and young.

The final effect of adequate parental care is the survival, growth, and reproductive success of the young. The disturbances seen in young mammals raised without their parents are testimony to the importance of parental care.

ANIMAL SEXUAL BEHAVIOR
ANIMAL SOCIOBIOLOGY
ETHOLOGY
INSTINCTIVE BEHAVIOR

D. A. DEWSBURY

ANIMAL SEXUAL BEHAVIOR

Although not all animal species reproduce sexually, it is through sexual reproduction that the genes of most species are passed from generation to generation. A complete sequence of sexual activity entails initiation, copulation, and sequelae, and can be analyzed with respect to questions of both short-term causation and evolution.

INITIATION

Breeding is seasonal in many species. As the time of breeding approaches there may be major changes in both the behavior and the appearance of the animals. Thus males that were gregarious and protectively colored may become quite aggressive toward each other and assume a bright coloration.

Copulation is generally preceded by some form of courtship activity. In monogamous species, such as many birds, there may be little courtship immediately before mating. In more promiscuous species, however, courtship can be quite elaborate. The complex aerobatics of the queen butterfly, the zigzag dances of stickleback fish, and the ritualized displays of many species of ducks provide dramatic examples.

Courtship signals may be communicated through any of several sensory modalities. Fiddler crabs use a prominent visual display as they wave their enlarged claws in species-specific patterns. Crickets and bullfrogs use prominent mating calls as part of their vocal displays. Olfaction is especially important in many mammalian species: Various patterns of following, nuzzling, and licking of the anogenital region are common.

Courtship appears to function to bring both partners to the appropriate stage of readiness for copulation in synchrony and to permit both male and female to select an appropriate partner.

COPULATION

Sperm transfer patterns are even more diverse in nonmammalian species. In insects the partners of some species may remain coupled for hours. In other species, however, the partners may never meet; the male simply leaves a package of sperm, the spermatophore, on the substrate and the female picks it up later. Sperm transfer in most birds entails a simple "cloacal kiss." Fertilization may be external in the case of many fishes and other aquatic species, with male and female simply shedding gametes into the water.

The ultimate consequence of sexual activity is successful reproduction. However, there are many more immediate consequences of sexual activity. The readiness of male and female to engage in further sexual behavior may be markedly altered. In some species there is a postcopulatory display, such as the "after-reaction" in which female cats roll on their backs and display marked alterations in EEG pattern.

The females of some species, such as rabbits and cats, are induced ovulators: Ovulation occurs only after mating. In others it is the neuroendocrine events necessary to prepare the uterus for the implantation of a fertilized ovum that occur only after mating. In species such as these, critical events in female reproductive physiology are triggered by male stimulation, which must be delivered in the appropriate amount and pattern.

IMMEDIATE CAUSATION

Many factors influence a given episode of sexual activity. Hormones are a major determinant. Males generally copulate only when appreciable levels of male hormones, androgens, are circulating in their systems; females become responsive in the presence of titers of such hormones as estrogen and progesterone. A different hormone action occurs developmentally. In general, developing male mammals must have appropriate levels of male hormone and females an absence of such hormone during a critical developmental period (prenatal in primates), if sexual activity is to be normal. The latter effect appears irreversible.

The developmental pattern of sexual behavior varies from species to species. Genetic influences have been demonstrated in a variety of species. The importance of early experience has been demonstrated repeatedly; for example, the sexual activity of rhesus monkeys reared in isolation is profoundly disturbed. Puberty is associated with the onset of sexual activity; such activity may decline in old age.

EVOLUTION AND ADAPTIVE SIGNIFICANCE

There are few clear trends in the evolution of sexual behavior patterns. Although sexual activity is generally rather invariant within species and variable across species, its evolution appears to have been characterized by repeated adaptations to particular selective pressures rather than by unidimensional progress.

The divergent behavioral patterns of different species appear adapted to permit successful reproduction under the environmental pressures and constraints with which each lives. Thus, for example, locking patterns, which would render partners vulnerable to predation, are not generally found among prey species mating in the open. In such species brief copulations with ejaculation on a single insertion are common. In addition, individuals are selected, so that it is their genes that are passed on to the next generation. As several males may mate with a given female, various patterns have evolved that act to increase the likelihood that a given animal will be successful, in competition with others, at inseminating females and ensuring gene survival. Thus the patterns of male and female are adapted to ensure successful reproduction by each under the conditions in which they live.

ANIMAL SOCIOBIOLOGY
INSTINCTIVE BEHAVIOR

D. A. DEWSBURY

ANIMAL SOCIOBIOLOGY

Sociobiology is an attempt to apply principles from evolutionary and population biology to the understanding of social behavior. Its formulation can be understood in historical context. In the early part of this century, principles from genetics, population biology, and evolution were fused into the "modern synthetic theory" of evolution. In 1962, Wynne-Edwards proposed that much social behavior can be explained because it is advantageous to the group. Thus, for example, once a certain number of territories are used, birds without territories might refrain from breeding to avoid overexploitation of available resources, thus acting for the good of the group. The fallacy of this approach was soon revealed. If genes are associated with such behavior, how could they spread? The very birds acting for the good of the group are the ones not breeding, hence their genes will be selected against. This recognition forced and stimulated scientists from various disciplines to reexamine the evolution of social behavior and to think more clearly about the ways in which natural selection works. The result was a flurry of research and theoretical activity that had far-reaching consequences for many biological and social sciences.

Much misunderstanding has stemmed from sociobiological postulates about the ways in which genes are viewed as influencing behavior. That genes influence some behavior is incontrovertible. Sociobiological principles apply only to behavior that is influenced by genes to some degree; by no means does this imply either that genes "determine" behavior or that environmental factors are not important. Further misunderstanding of the field results from the shorthand used in describing gene action. When, for example, a sociobiologist proposes that a bird may refrain from breeding for the good of the group, in no way does this imply conscious assessment by the animal. Rather, one could hypothesize that the behavior is the result of natural selection's past operation to permit the survival of genes which, in the present environment, create birds that refrain from breeding. The nature of the immediate stimuli controlling the behavior is left open; it is the evolutionary pressures that are of interest to the sociobiologist. Although this interest requires genetic influence, it does not necessitate or require either genetic determinism or postulated conscious choice.

FOUNDATIONS OF SOCIOBIOLOGY

The "bottom line" in evolutionary theory is the survival of genes and their replicates. Organisms are viewed as the genes' way of making more genes. Dawkins treats the organism as a "survival machine" constructed by the genes for their protection and reproduction.

Genetic fitness may be measured as the relative contribution to the whole gene pool of future generations made by a given individual as compared with other individuals. Natural selection must work, by definition, to maximize the levels of fitness of organisms. By the term fitness, then, the sociobiologist means nothing about the appearance or physical prowess of an animal; the term refers only to the degree to which the individual is effective in getting the genes in his or her genotype transmitted for future generations. Natural selection, then, must work at the level

of the individual. The bird that refrains from breeding has a low fitness and its genotype is not transmitted.

If one assumes that natural selection works at the level of the individual, several puzzles are solved but others are created. One must wonder, as did Darwin, about the sterile castes of insects. One might also wonder why young adult birds in some species stay with their parents and help rear their brothers and sisters, rather than breeding on their own. A major impetus for the development of sociobiology, and the solution of these puzzles, came with the proposal by W. D. Hamilton of the notions of kin selection and inclusive fitness.

Close relatives share many genes. Indeed, people on the average share half of their genes with their parents, siblings, and offspring. The proportion of genes shared decreases as one moves to individuals of more distant relation. Hamilton recognized that this presented an alternative route through which individuals might get their genes represented in future generations—through their kin. *Kin selection* is the action of natural selection on genes because of their effect in increasing the fitness of close relatives. A sister's children share one-fourth of her brother's genes. Therefore, his overall reproductive success will be as effectively increased if he can ensure that she bears two children as if he had one of his own. The extent of kin selection will vary with the benefits to the kin, the costs to the individual, and the degree of relatedness between the donor and the beneficiary. The term *inclusive fitness* refers to the overall, total level of fitness of an individual. This is the result of personal or classical fitness (or direct fitness) as defined above, plus a component resulting from kin selection (i.e., indirect fitness).

Altruistic behavior is any behavior that produces an increase in the personal, classical fitness of another organism at the cost of a decrease in the personal fitness of the donor. The bottom line, as in all sociobiology, is fitness—the relative effectiveness in transmitting genes to future generations. By this definition, care of one's own young would not be considered altruistic because it contributed to one's personal fitness. However, if one aids a close relative at a cost to one's own direct fitness level, that would be altruistic. Clearly, altruistic behavior can evolve through kin selection, because it may increase the inclusive fitness of the animal concerned. Thus the birds helping at the nest and sterile insect workers are contributing to the reproductive success of their kin, since this behavior increases inclusive fitness. If the term "ultimate altruism" refers to behavior that increases the inclusive fitness of another organism at a cost to the inclusive fitness of the donor, ultimate altruism ought never to occur.

Sometimes apparently altruistic behavior is displayed toward individuals that are not close relatives. One way in which this might occur is through *reciprocal altruism*. An organism might engage in altruistic behavior toward another in exchange for the "promise" that the other will do the same under like circumstances at a future time. If the costs to both are small and the benefits large, this behavior could contribute to the fitness of each, even though the individuals are not closely related. It may be beneficial for a person to throw a life preserver to a nonrelative because later the same may be done for the rescuer. It is generally agreed that reciprocal altruism can be important only among animals with complex social structures and individual recognition. Enforcement against "cheaters" must be continuous. Otherwise, one would expect the appearance of individuals who accrued the benefits of reciprocal altruism without reciprocating and hence without suffering the costs.

STRATEGIES IN REPRODUCTIVE BEHAVIOR

In sociobiological perspective, the reproductive efforts of a pair of animals are seen not as the result of the cooperation of two individuals to perpetuate the species, but rather as the action, and perhaps manipulation, of each acting to increase its own level of inclusive fitness. The term *parental investment* refers to the sum of all investments by an individual in an offspring at the cost of the ability to invest in other offspring. Often, females make a greater investment in offspring than males. In mammals with promiscuous breeding systems, for example, females produce large ova, carry the young to term, nurse the young, and provide most of the parental care. Males provide sperm and, in some species, little else. In general, the sex investing more (generally females) becomes a limiting "resource" for the sex investing less. It has even been proposed that males "parasitize" the investments of females. Thus males generally compete for females, as with dominance hierarchies, territoriality, or complex courtship displays. Females generally are more selective in their choice of mates. Whereas the females of many species are coy, males may be ardent. Thus the major components of what Darwin termed "sexual selection" are female choice and male-male competition. Whereas most females produce a relatively small number of young in their lifetimes, males are more variable, some siring many offspring and others few or none. Male and female strategies in reproductive endeavors can be quite different.

Like the conflict between male and female, the conflict between parents and offspring has important consequences. It is in the interest of the parent to maximize its own level of inclusive fitness by distributing its investment among its young. An individual offspring will be selected to maximize its fitness by accruing a greater share of those resources than would be optimal for the parent. An individual offspring should be selected to secure more than its share of resources, up to the point where it hurts its own inclusive fitness because of reduced survival and reproduction of its siblings. Many conflicts, such as the weaning conflict between parent and young, can be seen as the interaction between two individuals acting in ways that have been selected to maximize levels of inclusive fitness.

Parents should generally be selected to restrict parental care to their own offspring. Where this is not the case, as with helping birds and "aunting" monkeys, other explanations are required. Practice in caring for young may benefit individuals when they eventually have their own. Participating in a family unit as an active helper may protect a young adult bird from predators and may help it later establish a breeding territory of its own. The complexity of hormone interaction necessary to elicit parental behavior in rodents may have been selected to ensure that such behavior occurs only under a restricted set of conditions when it can be directed at one's own young.

SOCIAL STRUCTURE AND BREEDING SYSTEMS

The social structure of a species or population can be viewed as the product of the actions of all individuals operating to increase their inclusive fitness levels. Where the distribution of food, predators, and other factors render it difficult for one parent to rear young alone, monogamy may be selected. Under different circumstances one parent may be able to rear the young, and the second parent may leave soon after mating. In many mammals it is the female that cares for young; in many fishes it is the male.

Among the most intriguing social units are those of the eusocial insects. In these animals there are sterile worker castes, an overlap of two or more generations of young in the colony, and a complex division of labor. One might wonder why kin selection produced such an extreme form of social behavior as in the worker females that sacrifice their own reproductive abilities to help their mother raise their siblings. The most prevalent explanation of the evolution of this structure is the *haplodiploid* hypothesis. Haplodiploidy is the mode of reproduction among certain hymenopteran insects. Although females arise from fertilized eggs, males arise from unfertilized eggs. Males are haploid and females are diploid; this means that, whereas females have two of each kind of chromosome (one from their mother and one from their father), males have just one. If the queen of the colony mates with just one male, then, all females will get exactly the same genes from their father. In species lacking

haplodiploidy, females share only half the genes from their father. As a result, females share three-fourths of their genes with their sisters rather than the usual half. However, they share only half their genes with their own offspring. Because of haplodiploidy, then, females are more closely related to their sisters than to their offspring. If they are to maximize their inclusive fitness, perhaps it is not surprising that these females care for their sisters rather than their own offspring. It should be recognized that there are other hypotheses for the evolution of eusociality and that haplodiploidy cannot provide the total explanation. However, it is surely one important factor. The evolution of eusociality in insects provides one example of the way in which sociobiological principles can shed new light on old problems.

OVERVIEW

The advantage of sociobiological thinking parallels that which has been the basis of the success of evolutionary approaches in general. The theory provides a way in which to understand many diverse phenomena in the light of a few general theoretical principles. However, the field is young. There is much theory and not enough data. Much more empirical research is needed. Further, some excesses have been apparent in the application and extrapolation of the theory. Animal sociobiology offers the possibility of integrating a rich array of behavioral phenomena within a broad theory.

ALTRUISM
COOPERATION-COMPETITION
ECOLOGICAL PSYCHOLOGY
PROSOCIAL BEHAVIOR

D. A. Dewsbury

ANIMALS RAISED AS HUMANS

There are three prominent studies in which young chimpanzees were raised as human children. Other projects involve a gorilla and an orangutan in homelike environments. In the earliest study, W. N. Kellogg and his wife raised a female chimpanzee infant (Gua) together with their infant son Donald for 9 months. Gua was dressed in clothing, kissed and cuddled, and otherwise treated as an ordinary young child.

Gua was introduced into the home at the age of 7½ months, 2 months younger than Donald. In this context Gua acquired numerous types of human behavior, including upright locomotion, skipping, kissing for forgiveness, eating with a spoon, drinking from a glass, and some bladder and bowel control. Although chronologically younger than Donald, she outdistanced Donald in learning these skills and was also superior in strength, sound localization, and following verbal commands. Doubtless, Gua's superiority was due to a faster rate of maturation in these early months. Toward the end of the experiment Donald began to catch up in everything except strength and to surpass Gua in many activities, especially language behavior. In short, although humans are very slow to reach maturity, they typically attain a level well in excess of their nearest primate relative.

The next study was conducted by Keith and Cathy Hayes with a home-raised female chimpanzee named Viki. The chief aim of this study was to teach Viki to speak, but in 6 years she only learned three words (papa, mama, and cup). Even this learning required an arduous procedure in which most of the sounds had to be artificially produced by experimenter manipulation of Viki's lips. However, the study did confirm the Kelloggs' finding that a chimpanzee raised in a human environment does acquire many human responses. For example, Viki spontaneously imitated the following behaviors: operating a spray gun, prying lids off cans with a screwdriver, sharpening a pencil, and applying cosmetics to face and lips. Viki could also solve certain mechanical problems after a single demonstration, whereas caged chimpanzees took much longer or failed altogether. Unfortunately, Viki died of a virus infection before the limits of the attempt to humanize her were tested.

The third ambitious project involving a chimpanzee raised as a human was the Gardners' research with a young female chimpanzee they called Washoe. Because chimpanzees make very few sounds—that is, they lack the biological equipment for speech but have a rich gestural language in the wild—Allen and Beatrice Gardner at the University of Nevada attempted to teach Washoe standard American Sign Language, a system whereby deaf people use signs that stand for whole words rather than letters.

From about 1 year of age, Washoe was raised in her own house trailer in the Gardners' backyard. This trailer was fitted out like a home with crib, high chair, bibs, washcloths, toothbrushes, and a great deal of human interaction, including even a graduate student "baby-sitter" in the evening. Communication was conducted solely by means of sign language. In Washoe's presence everyone talked to each other or to Washoe by "signing." Washoe was only minimally confined and was taken for walks around the yard and occasionally into the Gardners' house. She was played with and tickled frequently, often in the context of learning sign language.

By the end of the 22nd month of this project, Washoe could appropriately use at least 30 signs, and in all she learned more than 160 signs. The signs she used did not remain specific to the original referents but transferred to new and different referents (e.g., a particular book was the original referent for the sign "book," but later any book elicited the appropriate sign). Washoe strung signs together but mainly into two-sign combinations like a 2-year-old child; spontaneously named objects; and occasionally created new combinations of signs. The Gardners also claimed that she learned elementary rules of grammar, roughly at the level of a 2- or 3-year-old child.

According to the investigators at the University of Oklahoma, Washoe occasionally "taught" sign language to her youngster. For example, she placed a chair before her adopted youngster and then made the standard sign for "This is" and the sign for "chair." Other chimpanzees at the University of Oklahoma that started to learn sign language at a younger age than Washoe seemed to learn to sign much faster than Washoe, and they learned without the experimenters' having to communicate with each other in sign language in their presence and without any special efforts to humanize them.

COMPARATIVE PSYCHOLOGY
PRIMATE BEHAVIOR

M. R. Denny

ANIMISM

Animism is the attribution of human characteristics to inanimate objects, or to plants and animals not normally manifesting such characteristics (as in attributing hostility to a tree or benevolent influence to a fish). Most frequently it is an artifact of man: a carved stone or wooden figure. Whatever the object, the animist believes that it thinks and feels as a human. Like a human, it has a "soul."

The term *animism* comes from the Latin *animus*, or "spirit." At first it was used to describe the pantheistic concept of the "world soul," but very early it became an anthropological term referring to the attitudes of primitive religion, which saw particular places and things as having special powers. To explain these special powers, they were assumed to have "souls" even as human beings did, whose souls were independent of the owners' bodies and permanently left them at death. Often these spirits had special powers—powers, for instance, to influence the outcome of the hunt—or had *only* special powers.

RELIGION AND PSYCHOLOGY
SUPERSTITIONS

W. E. Gregory

ANTABUSE

Antabuse (disulfiram) is a drug often employed to combat alcoholism. It was originally used in the manufacture of rubber; the low rate of alcoholism among workers in rubber-manufacturing plants led to its medical application, beginning in the late 1940s.

Antabuse affects alcohol consumption through an alteration of alcohol metabolism. Ethyl alcohol is metabolized in the liver by the enzyme alcohol dehydrogenase into aldehyde, then by the enzyme aldehyde NAD-oxidoreductase into acetate. Antabuse and a similar drug, Temposil (calcium carbimide), inactivate the latter enzyme by binding its copper ion. Consequently, after someone has taken Antabuse, alcohol can be converted to aldehyde, but aldehyde cannot be converted to acetate. Aldehyde accumulates, causing toxic effects including flushing of the face, increased heart rate and pulse pressure, nausea and vomiting, headache, and difficulty in breathing. It is intended that the alcoholic will learn to avoid alcohol because of these unpleasant aftereffects.

Learned taste aversions to alcohol may occur under these conditions, but they are likely to be weak, because alcoholic beverages have already become so familiar to the drinker. The main effectiveness of Antabuse, according to a study by Fuller and Roth, comes from the threat of illness rather than actual illness. The rate of total abstinence for 1 year was as high in patients who only thought they were getting a therapeutic dose of Antabuse (25%) as in those who were actually getting it (21%).

The effectiveness of an Antabuse tablet declines over time; for the treatment to be effective, one must take a tablet daily. Compliance is voluntary; an alcoholic who wishes to drink with impunity can simply stop taking the pills for a day or two before returning to alcohol. The drug, then, helps only the drinker who wishes to reinforce a decision to abstain; it is no substitute for a motivation to abstain.

ALCOHOLISM TREATMENT
CHEMICAL BRAIN STIMULATION
NEUROTOXIC SUBSTANCES
PSYCHOPHARMACOLOGY

J. W. Kalat

ANTHROPOLOGY

Anthropology, the science of humans, is a label that might have been attached to what is instead called *psychology*. Like psychology, anthropology has developed as a broad discipline devoted to scientific study of humanity; like psychology, too, it is a diverse discipline whose members are not always sharply distinguishable from members of other disciplines engaged in the scientific study of humanity.

The interest that most consistently distinguishes it from sister disciplines is concentration on the comparison of societies with each other (especially preliterate or so-called "primitive" societies), an interest expressed both in detailed characterization of specific societies and in formulation of principles that are genuinely cognizant of intersocietal variation. This interest is expressed very differently in three broad subdisciplines:

1. *Archaeology,* the study of the prehistory of human societies by controlled inference from the physical evidence recoverable by excavation.

2. *Physical anthropology,* the study of the origins of human groups by investigating the distribution of bodily characteristics (including not

only gross characteristics but such subtle ones as blood chemistry and genes), and the comparative study of other species related to human beings genetically or in conditions of life. Interspecies comparison is extended to behavioral studies, which are similar to some research in comparative psychology and behavioral zoology.

3. *Sociocultural anthropology,* which concentrates on the culture and social structure of human societies. Among the many special fields included here is anthropological linguistics, whose practitioners may have more in common with linguists than with other kinds of anthropologists.

All the subdisciplines of anthropology are potentially relevant to one or another aspect of psychology. The rest of this article is confined, however, to sociocultural anthropology, which has the most fully developed interrelations with psychology, and stresses its relevance to psychology. A scholarly introduction to many topics in social and cultural anthropology is available in a handbook edited by Honigmann.

ANTHROPOLOGICAL METHOD

Anthropologists may and do use a great variety of methods, some of them originating in other social science disciplines. The method distinctively associated with anthropology, however, is fieldwork in which an outside investigator lives in a community for an extended period, participating so far as is possible in its ordinary activities, observing even when he cannot actively participate, and interviewing members of the community not only as individuals to be learned about but also as informants—that is, providers of information about the community and its customary activities and beliefs.

ANTHROPOLOGICAL THEORY

The history of culture is what most anthropological theory seeks to explain. In various and sometimes distinctive forms, the concept of evolution underlies much of the theorizing. Nineteenth-century anthropologists built an overly simple picture of uniform progression of culture through dependable stages. Early in the twentieth century this was largely replaced by *functionalism,* which concentrated on the way in which present features of a successful culture sustain each other. Psychologists will recognize in functionalist writings underlying ideas similar to those of much psychological theorizing, and it is not surprising that some anthropological theorists have found behavioristic and psychoanalytic concepts useful in developing their accounts of culture. There is less of a clear relation to psychological theory, and sometimes an avoidance of theory, in two other anthropological movements: *diffusionism,* which attempts to guide the development of systematic knowledge about the spread of cultural features from one society to another, and *cognitive or structural anthropology,* which sees a culture as a web of meanings to be interpreted.

FIELDWORK FINDINGS AS DATA

Fieldwork may be motivated by the anthropologist's theoretical interests and curiosity about a specific area or people. The cumulating body of fieldwork findings, portraying the culture of many societies around the world, forms a lasting contribution of anthropology to the theoretical concerns and broad curiosity of all social scientists. This body of ethnographies (as scholarly studies of cultures are called) has been drawn on in an attempt to answer many questions of interest to psychology; for many questions it is the only source of answer, since the ethnographies include information about many societies now extinct or greatly modified by prolonged contact with industrial societies.

Do all human societies engage in warfare? Is warfare always carried on primarily by men rather than women? Is belief in an afterlife found everywhere? Are all communities organized into families? Is incest always

prohibited? The recorded ethnographies can yield answers to questions such as these. Although the answers are not always simple, they provide better knowledge about universalities of human nature than can be obtained by naive generalization from knowledge only of one's own society and the few others one may come to know something about at first hand.

Knowledge of universalities of human nature helps in understanding individual development in any one society, or in planning psychological research. Universality does not, of course, imply that a tendency is inborn and not learned. Everyone develops within a society, and societies may all have arrived at certain rules that control the socialization of new members.

Modes of Thought

Anthropologists have devoted much energy to an effort to understand the meaning of rituals, myths, magical procedures, and the like, and to characterize the modes of thought involved. Like literary critics seeking to understand a specific poem, they are more inclined toward intensive study of the specific material and its context, than toward abstraction and generalized theory. Thus the outcome of such research is often a detailed elucidation of a particular set of data from a particular society, rather than a theory purporting to be universally valid, and the elucidation is no easier to test empirically than is a literary critic's interpretation of a poem. Yet this work of cognitive anthropologists is concerned with aspects of thought to which cognitive psychologists have given little attention, and the writings that have emerged have implications for human thought generally.

Universality of Process

A serious criticism of much psychological research is that the conclusions may be culture-bound: If the principles arrived at have been tested only within a single culture, perhaps they are valid only for it. Psychologists may deal with this criticism by repeating research in other cultural settings; outcomes of this sort of replication are summarized for many topics in a handbook of cross-cultural psychology. But for some conclusions a less direct approach, with broader implications, is available. Some features of a culture set conditions for human learning that may lead to development of other features in a way that seems predictable from principles derived from within-cultural research.

Anthropologists' knowledge is primarily a product of the twentieth century. As their research proceeded through the century, however, the opportunities for field work in preliterate societies, especially in ones not yet radically altered by interaction with industrial societies, greatly diminished. The methods and theories developed by anthropologists are now increasingly being applied to study our own and other industrial societies.

ACCULTURATION
ASIAN PSYCHOLOGIES
CROSS-CULTURAL PSYCHOLOGY
CULTURAL DIFFERENCES
RITES DE PASSAGE
SOCIAL PSYCHOLOGY
TABOOS

I. L. CHILD

ANTHROPOMORPHIC THINKING

Anthropomorphic thinking interprets the actions of animals and physical objects as the outcome of processes similar to those a person is aware of as leading to some of his or her own actions: knowledge, motivation, planning, and choice. In the nineteenth and early twentieth century many Westerners considered the thought of preliterate peoples to be dominated by anthropomorphism; religious beliefs and practices of such peoples seemed generally to fit this pattern. But its extension to all "primitive thought" was a serious exaggeration. The efficiency of preliterate peoples in securing nourishment, shelter, and transportation with simple technologies suggests a basic realism of thought, and many fieldworkers confirm this inference on the basis of their informants' explanations of beliefs and practices. Anthropomorphic thinking seems most characteristic at points where realistic knowledge and techniques are inadequate; some aspects of religion, in all periods and cultures, seem to arise from this principle. In recent centuries the advance of objective scientific knowledge and its extension to new fields has diminished the occasion for anthropomorphic thinking, and in this fact lies some of the warfare between science and religion.

Three kinds of psychological study of thinking have especially contributed to an appreciation of how widespread are anthropomorphic tendencies, and to an understanding of the processes responsible: (a) Piagetian analysis of children's thinking; (b) the psychoanalytic interpretation of some thought distortions as *projection,* and (c) analysis, in social psychology and cognitive science, of judgment in the face of uncertainty.

Psychologists have sometimes viewed the extension of science to their field as requiring the total abandonment of anthropomorphic thinking in trying to understand animals and, by extension, even persons. The rigid objectivism of the behavioristic movement has gradually given way, through lively controversy, to wide acceptance of some degree of anthropomorphism in scientific interpretation of both persons and animals.

ANIMISM
ANTHROPOLOGY
OCCULTISM
PIAGET'S THEORY

I. L. CHILD

ANTHROPOSOPHY

The anthroposophy system of thought was formulated early in the twentieth century by Austrian Rudolf Steiner. The term *anthroposophy* translates from the Greek as "wisdom of man," although Steiner once said that the term should be understood to mean "awareness of one's humanity." Anthroposophy teaches that an individual's usual knowledge and thinking are valuable but that they must be transformed to affect permeation and thereby gain access to a knowledge of higher worlds, a superconscious realm beyond that of our normal senses. This is the realm of imagination, intuition, inspired thinking, and even clairvoyant experience—forms of cognition that Steiner attributed to a human spirit or to the spiritual worlds.

From the research methodology of anthroposophy, there stems an impressive (though sometimes difficult to understand) body of research beginning with Steiner's 60 books and almost 6000 published lectures. This work bears the title *spiritual science.* These teachings and research have found application in the numerous anthroposophic endeavors around the world—the Waldorf or Rudolf Steiner schools, the Camphill schools and communities for emotionally and mentally disabled children and adults, the biodynamic method of organic agriculture, and a school of architecture, to name but a few.

Anthroposophy expands into a true Weltanschauung, which strives to explain on a deeper level the workings of most aspects of the world and the human's being. The traditional thinker may find these principles difficult to accept, especially when paired with topics like karma and rebirth, talk of spiritual beings, or Atlantis. The practical applications of this phenomenological or empirical approach to the spiritual world, however, are more difficult to dispute. The evidence they provide compels

one to take a closer look at Steiner's attempt to seek long-term solutions to the problems of individual and social life through the development by men and women of a sense-free or spiritual cognition.

CAMPHILL MOVEMENT
RUDOLF STEINER
WALDORF EDUCATION

T. G. POPLAWSKI

ANTIANXIETY DRUGS

Anxiety, a subjective emotional state, is characterized by pervasive feelings such as apprehension and dread, and often accompanied by physical symptoms such as muscle tension, tremors, palpitations, chest pain, headache, dizziness, and gastrointestinal distress. Anxiety may or may not be connected to stressful or fearful stimuli. Most antianxiety agents (called anxiolytics, daytime sedatives, minor tranquilizers) belong to a larger class of psychoactive substances, the sedative-hypnotics. While differing in chemical structure and potency, all sedative-hypnotics are capable of producing a continuum of depressive states, including relief of anxiety, disinhibition, sedation, sleep, anesthesia, coma, and death (the result of depression of respiratory centers in the brain). All sedative-hypnotics function as antianxiety agents, but historical, marketing, and safety considerations, and slight differences in mechanism of action, led to the use of certain substances over others.

The oldest anxiolytic drug, ethyl alcohol, is similar in many respects to other sedative-hypnotics, but is used primarily for social and recreational, rather than medical, purposes. Three other substances with a long history are the alcohols chloral hydrate and paraldehyde, and a nonalcohol, bromide. Barbiturates, first synthesized in the late 1800s, are prescribed to produce drowsiness or sedation. Because barbiturates produce rapid tolerance (larger doses are needed to maintain the effect) and physical dependence (evidenced by withdrawal syndrome upon cessation of drug taking), and because they are potent respiratory depressants, synthesis of nonbarbiturate sedative-hypnotics in the 1950s was welcomed. In fact, nonbarbiturate sedative-hypnotics—a prototype of which is meprobamate (Miltown, Equanil)—are equally dangerous in terms of tolerance, dependence, and respiratory depression. These drugs were marketed as minor tranquilizers, falsely implying a safer and more specific treatment of anxiety. In addition, use of the term "minor tranquilizer" implies that these drugs are on a spectrum with antipsychotic medications (known as major tranquilizers), whereas they are very different in mechanism and behavioral action.

In the 1960s benzodiazepines (Valium, Librium) were synthesized, and soon became the most widely prescribed drugs in the United States. Benzodiazepines are more selective than other sedative-hypnotics in suppressing anxiety, probably due to a selective affinity for specific receptors in the limbic system (known as benzodiazepine receptors). Although tolerance is a problem with all sedative-hypnotics, benzodiazepines, stimulating less production of metabolic enzymes in the liver than do other sedative-hypnotics, are less likely to produce tolerance. Physical dependence on benzodiazepines does occur, but only with high doses over a long period of time. Duration of action of the benzodiazepines, being longer than that of other sedative-hypnotics, enables fewer doses to be taken, but increases the risk of buildup if frequent doses are taken. The most important advantage of the benzodiazepines is the large dose, much greater than anxiolytic doses, required to produce respiratory depression; this wide safety margin makes the drug almost nonlethal. However, behavioral depressant effects of the benzodiazepines, if combined with effects of other sedative-hypnotics (e.g., alcohol), may depress respiration in a supraadditive or synergistic manner (i.e., more than the sum of the respiratory depression of the single drugs added together).

A few substances not included in the sedative-hypnotic class are sometimes used as antianxiety agents. Antihistamines such as hydroxyzine (Vistaril) are particularly useful in anxiety-related skin conditions; anticholinergic side effects of dry mouth and blurred vision reduce potential for abuse. Tricyclic antidepressants such as doxepin (Sinequan) are used when anxiety accompanies depression. Beta-adrenergic blockers such as propranolol (Inderal) are usually prescribed when anxiety accompanies a medical condition such as hypertension or tachycardia. Newer drugs are being used, such as alprazolam for panic attacks.

ANTIDEPRESSIVE DRUGS
ANTIPSYCHOTIC DRUGS
ANXIETY
NEUROPSYCHOLOGY
PSYCHOPHARMACOLOGY
TRANQUILIZING DRUGS

B. E. Thorn

ANTICIPATION METHOD

The anticipation method in verbal learning is a popular technique for presenting items for paired-associate and serial-learning tasks.

When the anticipation method is applied to *paired-associate tasks,* subjects are told that, whenever a stimulus is presented, they must supply the appropriate response. Several seconds later, the stimulus and the response are presented together. Thus subjects alternate between anticipating responses and receiving feedback. The pairs are presented in different random orders on each trial. Learning continues until the criterion (e.g., correct anticipation of all responses) is reached. The anticipation method for paired-associate tasks is to be contrasted with the study-test (also called blocking or recall) method for paired-associate tasks, in which subjects are exposed to an entire list of pairs before supplying a response to each stimulus.

When the anticipation method is applied to *serial-learning tasks,* subjects are initially exposed to a list of items to be learned in order. On subsequent trials, subjects try to anticipate an item on the list before it is exposed several seconds later. The items are presented in constant order on each trial. Learning continues until the criterion (typically, one perfect recitation) is reached. The anticipation method for serial-learning tasks is to be contrasted with the study-test method for serial-learning tasks, in which subjects alternate between exposure to the entire list and attempted recall of the entire list.

An advantage of the anticipation method is that it provides subjects with immediate feedback about the correctness of their responses. However, a disadvantage is that the anticipation method combines learning and performance. Performance is typically somewhat better with the study-test method than with the anticipation method, although this superiority may depend on list characteristics.

LEARNING
RESEARCH METHODOLOGY

M. W. Matlin

ANTICIPATORY NAUSEA

The application of chemotherapy (CT) in cancer patients frequently results in side effects such as nausea and vomiting, occurring as a direct consequence of cytotoxic drugs. Usually, post-therapeutic nausea is reduced by antiemetic or anxiolytic therapy. In several CT patients, nausea occurs before the drug is actually applied. Patients seem to react to the

smell of the clinic, to nurses who are preparing the skin for injection, or even to the sight of the hospital. This effect is called anticipatory nausea (AN). Occasionally, AN and post-therapeutic nausea and vomiting may lead to refusal of CT.

The first model of personality characteristics allows for a psychological intervention strategy aimed at the prevention of post-therapeutic nausea. Patients should learn to limit their side effects of CT, to cope with specific anxiety-inducing situations, and to minimize their physiological arousal. Results of treatment by hypnosis, progressive muscle relaxation, systematic desensitization, biofeedback in combination with muscle relaxation, and attentional distraction techniques have been reported. Effects of such treatment on AN have been seen in some studies, but not all of these strategies accept the specific assumption of AN as being a learned response.

Because conditioned stimulus–unconditioned stimulus (CS–US) associations are built in the CNS, AN is mediated by the CNS. Consequently, AN does not respond to serotoninergic antiemetics, which primarily act on vagal afferents. But AN should respond to stimuli that downgrade the contingency between the signaling cues and nausea. Because certain CS–US associations are unavoidable in a clinical setting, the intervention procedure is to block such associations.

A well-established paradigm of classical conditioning to achieve this is that of overshadowing. Instead of a single CS, combinations of stimuli are predictable with the US. Typically, these stimuli are CS_1 and CS_2. If CS_1 is presented with the US, the conditioned response (CR) is assumed to be strong; that is, when a nurse applies alcohol to a patient's skin (CS) preceding the CT (US), the patient may become nauseated (CR) before the US acts directly on the gastrointestinal tract and/or the chemoreceptor trigger zone in the brain. If, however, a seldom and strong odor or taste (CS_2) is presented with the smell of alcohol (CS_1), then the CS_1 is overshadowed by CS_2. In other words, the internal representation of the smell of alcohol is prevented from becoming associated with the US. The CS_2 must be varied from trial to trial because CS_2 will itself become a strong stimulus to elicit the CR. It should not be concealed that antiemetics given to prevent nausea and vomiting may gain CS properties by signaling cytotoxic infusion and, therefore, become associated with CT.

The efficacy of overshadowing is supported by experiences made with conditioned taste avoidance in cancer patients. Their daily food avoidance could be at least reduced using a similar intervention technique. Patients who have been exposed to a novel taste before CT exhibited rejection of their clinical diet less often.

ANTICIPATORY METHOD
CLASSICAL CONDITIONING
LOCUS OF CONTROL

S. Klosterhalfen

ANTIDEPRESSIVE DRUGS

Confusion and controversy in the diagnostic differentiation of depressions has made it difficult to conduct controlled studies for evaluating drug therapy. Many experts believe that many depressions are due to a biochemical abnormality.

The discovery of drug therapy for endogenous depression was, as in many medical discoveries, serendipitous. In the 1950s, it was observed that the monoamine oxidase inhibitors used in treating patients suffering from tuberculosis had an elevating effect on some of the depressed individuals. Around the same time, it was found that the treatment of hypertension with reserpine caused patients to become depressed. This led J. J. Schildkraut to postulate a "catecholamine hypothesis of affective disorders." To understand his theory and the biochemistry of depression, a brief knowledge of neural transmission is required.

Because nerves in the body do not physically connect but are separated by a *synaptic cleft,* impulses must pass from one to another by a chemical

Table 1 Antidepressive Drugs

Generic Name	Commercial Name
Tricyclic Group	
Imipramine	Tofranil
Desipramine	Norpramin
Amitriptyline	Elavil
Protriptyline	Vivactil
Doxepin	Sinequan
Nortriptyline	Aventyl
MAO Inhibitor Group	
Isocarboxazid	Marplan
Phenelzine	Nardil
Tranylcypramine	Parnate
Stimulant Amines	
Amphetamine	Benzedrine
Dextroamphetamine	Dexedrine
Methamphetamine	Methedrine
Methylphenidate	Ritalin

ADRENAL GLANDS
ANTIANXIETY DRUGS
DEPRESSION
HABITUATION
NEUROCHEMISTRY
PSYCHOPHARMACOLOGY
PSYCHOPHYSIOLOGY
TRANQUILIZING DRUGS

J. C. ROOK

ANTIPSYCHOTIC DRUGS

Antipsychotic drugs were introduced in the United States in about 1956. For centuries there was anecdotal information concerning *rauwolfia serpentia*, a root used in India for a whole range of psychological problems. Reserpine, a rauwolfia alkaloid, was reported in the treatment of schizophrenia in India as early as 1943.

As more effective classes of antipsychotic drugs were developed, they were used on a large scale in psychiatric institutions to treat schizophrenia. Accompanied by changes in public policy, these medications were partially responsible for the reduction in the number of people in veteran and state hospitals. The control of psychotic symptoms made ambulatory care, as well as individual, group, family, and milieu therapy, more accessible to people with schizophrenia. Greenblatt and his colleagues found that patients treated with antipsychotic medication showed more improvement than those treated without medication. However, the highest rate of improvement was reported by patients who received a combination of chemotherapy and intensive social therapy. Many studies have replicated these results, and most authorities recommend that antipsychotic medication be prescribed as only one part of an overall treatment plan.

The major classes of antipsychotic drugs and some trade names are listed in Table 1 on page 60. Reserpine, a rauwolfia alkaloid, is rarely used. The phenothiazines are by far the most widely researched of the antipsychotic medications, but J. M. Davis concluded that there is little evidence to support the use of one specific type of antipsychotic drug over another. Effective daily doses range considerably, based on individual differences.

Although antipsychotic drugs can be used to treat certain organic psychoses such as amphetamine intoxication, their primary use has been in treating the symptoms of schizophrenia. The antipsychotic drugs usually control agitation and combative behavior within days, but changes in cognition such as psychotic thinking, hallucinations, and delusions may require 4 to 6 weeks. Greater therapeutic results have been reported in people who have been ill less than 2 years.

Side effects vary with the class of medication, but most of the antipsychotic drugs can produce extrapyramidal effects. The parkinsonian syndrome includes muscular rigidity, tremor, changes in posture, shuffling gait, and psychomotor retardation. Bizarre movements of the tongue, facial movements, and restlessness are also commonly reported, in addition to these extrapyramidal reactions. A rare but very serious side effect is agranulocytosis. A dramatic side effect of long-term use of antipsychotic medication is tardive dyskinesia, characterized by grimacing, jerky arm movements, and lip smacking.

Many side effects can be controlled by the administration of antiparkinsonian drugs, careful monitoring, and sensitive dosage scheduling by the physician. In a volume of *Schizophrenia Bulletin*, several psychiatrists recommended the use of brief drug-free periods, the lowest possible dosage, and greater emphasis on psychosocial treatment of schizophrenia in order to prevent and reduce the tardive dyskinesia.

Given the side effects, it is clear that although antipsychotic drugs can benefit schizophrenics greatly, they must be used conservatively and with attention to the individual's response.

called a neurotransmitter. At least nine chemical substances have been identified as neurotransmitters (also called biogenic amines), with two strongly implicated in depression: norepinepherine and serotonin. With the transmission of a neural impulse, a neurotransmitter is released into the synaptic cleft. It briefly binds to the postsynaptic receptor, then is released back into the cleft, with a large portion eventually reabsorbed into the original (presynaptic) storage vesicles. A small portion is metabolized by an enzyme called monoamine oxidase, and an even lesser amount metabolized by a second enzyme.

There are three classes of antidepressive medications: (a) tricyclics, (b) monoamine oxidase inhibitors, and (c) sympathomimetic stimulants. These are discussed in reverse order. See Table 1 above for examples of each.

Sympathomimetic stimulants promote the release of the stored neurotransmitter as well as block its reuptake from the synapse. Since these drugs have only a short effect and can become habit-forming, they are no longer the drug of choice for depression.

As their name suggests, *monoamine oxidase inhibitors* work by inhibiting the metabolic activity of the enzyme. This, in effect, causes an increased concentration of the neurotransmitter in the cleft. Because of potential side effects and restrictions in diet, these drugs are not used very frequently.

Tricyclics prevent the reuptake of the neurotransmitter from the synapse. Not all tricyclics act equally on norepinephrine and serotonin. Desipramine apparently blocks the reuptake of norepinephrine; amitriptyline blocks serotonin; and imipramine inhibits both norepinephrine and serotonin, but at half the potency of either of these other drugs.

Finally, there is indication that urinary levels of MHPG (3-methoxy-4-hydroxyphenyl glycol) correlate strongly with brain levels of norepinephrine. Investigations are beginning to suggest two biochemical subtypes of depression: (a) those with low urinary MHPG who seem to respond to desipramine and imipramine (the "norepinephrine depression"); and (b) those with normal or elevated MHPG who, in turn, respond to amitriptyline treatment (a "serotonin depression"). The latter have also been adequately treated with chlorimipramine or doxepin hydrochloride.

At the present time, most antidepressive drug therapy stems from this catecholamine hypothesis. However, the possibility of other etiologic factors (steroids, electrolytes, nutrition, etc.) has not and cannot yet be excluded.

Table 1   Antipsychotic Drugs

Class	Name		Manufacturer
	Generic	Trade	
I Butyrophenones	Haloperidol	Haldol	McNeil
II Dibenzoxapines	Loxapine	Loxitane	Lederle
III Dihyroindolones	Molindone	Moban	Endo
IV Raawolfia alkaloid	Reserpine	Serpasial	Ciba
		Rau-sed	Squibb
		Sandril	Lilly
		Raurine	Westerfield
		Vio-serpine	Rowell
		Reserpoid	Upjohn
V Thioxanthenes	Chlorprothixene	Taractan	Roche
	Thiothizene	Navane	Roerig
VI Phenothiazines			
A. Aliphatic	Chlorpromazine	Thorazine	Smith, Kline & French
	Triflupromazine	Vesprin	Squibb
	Promazine	Sparine	Wyeth
B. Piperazine	Prochlorperazine	Compazine	Smith, Kline & French
	Perphenazine	Trilafon	Schering
	Trifluoperazine	Stelazine	Smith, Kline & French
	Fluphenazine	Prolixin	Squibb
		Permitil	Schering
	Acetophenazine	Tindal	Schering
	Butaperazine	Repoise	Robins
	Carphenazine	Proketazine	Wyeth
C. Piperidine	Thioridazine	Mellaril	Sandoz
	Mesoridazine	Serentil	Boehringer
	Piperacetazine	Quide	Dow

CHEMICAL BRAIN STIMULATION
NEUROCHEMISTRY
PSYCHOPHARMACOLOGY

C. LANDAU

ANTISOCIAL PERSONALITY

The search for biological factors underlying antisocial personality has increasingly become a major focus of research. One aspect of this research that has stirred considerable interest as well as controversy concerns the effect of abnormal genotypes on antisocial behavior. Of all the tales of "bad genes," the two most famous are the Jukes and the Kallikaks.

Richard L. Dugdale, a New York prison inspector, meticulously scoured the archives in his thorough genealogic investigation of the Juke family. His 1877 report, *The Jukes: A study in crime, pauperism, disease, and heredity,* covered seven generations, 540 blood relatives, and 169 persons related by marriage or cohabitation. Contrary to popular belief, Dugdale did not find the Jukes' criminality to be the product of a long chain of bad genes, but asserted the importance of the environment: "Environment is the ultimate controlling factor in determining careers, placing heredity itself as an organized result of invariable environment. . . . They are not an exceptional class of people: their like may be found in every county in this State. . . . In the Jukes it was shown that heredity depends upon the permanence of the environment." A. H. Estabrook, who came into possession of Dugdale's original notes, painted a very different picture of the family in his book *The Jukes* in 1915. Whereas Dugdale characterized the Jukes as poor, ignorant, and having great vitality, Estabrook described them as indolent, dishonest, licentious, and feeble-minded.

The story of the Kallikaks is no less fascinating. The Kallikak family was studied by Henry H. Goddard, director of a school for the mentally retarded in New Jersey. Goddard's *The Kallikak family,* traced two lineages, both descending from the same Revolutionary War soldier. The "good Kallikaks" were descendants of the soldier's marriage to a Quaker woman of presumably "good blood." The "bad Kallikaks" were descendants of the soldier's impious union with a feeble-minded young woman. The offspring of this union was so horrible that he became known as "Old Horror." Old Horror fathered ten young horrors, who in turn grew up and became responsible for hundreds of additional horrors. It was Goddard's mission to trace the lives of these bad Kallikaks. Since the two Kallikak families originated with the same male, it is curious that none of the "bad genes" were reflected in any degenerate behavior among the good Kallikaks. While there may in fact have been a genetic contribution to some of the Kallikaks' antisocial behavior, Goddard's disregard of the environment renders this study meaningless from a scientific standpoint; however, it still makes for interesting reading.

The scientific association between the abnormal XYY genotype and antisocial behavior was first made in 1965 by P. A. Jacobs and her colleagues at Western General Hospital in Edinburgh. The theoretical importance of an extra Y chromosome for human aggression can be understood in terms of the heightened masculinity deriving from an extra male-determining chromosome. One might expect unusual tallness and robust physique as well as increased aggressive tendencies from altered testosterone metabolism.

Jacobs and her colleagues examined 197 prison hospital inmates, all of whom were in some manner dangerous. Seven inmates (3.5%) had an XYY chromosome configuration. Since the frequency of XYY males at birth ranges between 0.5 and 3.5/1000 (0.005–0.035%), the reported incidence in the Western General Hospital sample was "highly significant." The investigators also identified two other key features of the XYY syndrome (tall stature and mental subnormality), which, along with tendency to antisocial conduct, have been referred to as the XYY triad. Another study surveyed a representative sample of 2538 males in various penal institutions in Scotland, finding only 2.76 XYY cases/1000, a frequency which did not significantly differ from the expected rate of 1.3/1000.

In a comprehensive survey of the then current literature, Jarvik, Klodin, and Matsuyama reported a total frequency of XYYs in the criminal population of 1.9% (98 out of 5066 men from 20 studies). The authors stated that this frequency is 15 times greater than that found in newborn males (.13%) and normal adults (.13%) and almost 3 times greater than that found in mental patients (.7%). Jarvik, Klodin, and Matsuyama concluded that while an "extra Y chromosome predisposes to aggressive behavior . . . it is safe to predict that persons with an extra Y chromosome will constitute but an insignificant proportion of the perpetrators of violent crimes."

While the incidence of an abnormal chromosome configuration occurs 20 times more often in male inmates of prisons and psychiatric hospitals than in male infants in the normal population, there is as yet little that can be concluded about the behavioral implications of aberrant genotypes. It is premature to assign any causal role for antisocial behavior to chromosomal aberrations, since the contribution of the environment remains interwoven with endogenous factors in the complex matrix of elements producing the behavior. In this regard, adoptee studies that investigate children born to antisocial or criminal parents but raised in prosocial homes provide evidence that genetics does play some role in human aggression. In conclusion, it is important to keep in mind that the behavioral phenotypes of XYY males, just as of normal XY males, are the result of *both* genotypic *and* environmental factors.

CRIME
CULTURAL DETERMINISM
HERITABILITY
HERITABILITY OF PERSONALITY TRAITS

R. A. PRENTKY

ANXIETY

Anxiety will be covered from two major psychological points of view, the psychodynamic and the behavioral.

Freud described such in the following chronological sequence as early sources of anxiety: (a) absence of the mother, (b) punishments that lead to fear of loss of parental love, (c) castration fear or the female equivalent during the Oedipal period, and (d) disapproval by the superego or self-punishment for actions a person takes that he or she does not accept as right, just, or moral. In these cases the ego of the child can react with anxiety. A child may come to fear his own instinctual wishes and react with anxiety, which allows him or her to oppose the instinctual wish by compelling the ego to oppose the wish that raised his or her anxiety.

Other theories include that of Melanie Klein, who on the basis of the actual analysis of young children felt that anxiety has its origin in fear of death. She distinguished two types of anxiety: persecutory, deriving from fear of annihilation of the ego; and depressive, related to fear of the harm done to internal and external loved objects by the child's destructive impulses.

Rollo May described anxiety as apprehension caused by the threat to values that the individual holds essential to his or her existence as a personality. H. S. Sullivan described anxiety as an intensely unpleasant state of tension due to experiencing disapproval in interpersonal relationships. He describes how, through an empathic link between baby and mother, tension and anxiety in the mother induces anxiety in the infant.

Samuel Kutash developed a theory of anxiety that utilizes research on both anxiety and stress. Anxiety or a state of disequilibrium occurs when one is not experiencing the optimal level of stress for one's constitution. Tranquillity, or a state of equilibrium or malequilibrium, results when one is experiencing the optimal stress level for one's constitution, either in a healthy balance (equilibrium) or in an unhealthy balance (malequilibrium). Anxiety can be adaptive if at a level that can signal a need for change to an individual, and maladaptive if so high as to be immobilizing or so low as to be nonmotivating.

LEARNING AND BEHAVIORAL THEORIES

H. S. Kaplan described the basic difference between learning and behavioral theories of anxiety on the one hand, and psychodynamic or psychoanalytic theories on the other hand, seeing the former as focusing on proximal stimuli while the latter as focusing on distal causes. Bootzin and Max describe it thus: "In psychodynamic theory, anxiety or avoidance behavior is interpreted as a sign of underlying intrapsychic conflict (a distal stimulus); in learning and behavioral theories, anxiety is taken as a response to some immediately preceding stimulus and is maintained by reinforcing consequences (proximal stimuli)." The proximal stimuli can be external, as for instance an upcoming examination or a rejection by a significant other, or internal, such as self-devaluation or imaginary dangers.

Important data from the behavioral point of view include Pavlovian conditioning studies like the first such study by J. B. Watson and R. Rayner, done with an infant. More recent modifications of Pavlovian conditioning theory emphasize information processing and expectancy, and not association through contiguity alone. According to A. R. Wagner and R. A. Rescorla, for example, Pavlovian conditioning of a conditioned stimuli is due to the new information the stimuli provides about the unconditioned stimulus, such as its magnitude or frequency of occurrence. Avoidance learning studies have also clarified this, beginning with Mowrer's dual-process theory with regard to the first process, Pavlovian conditioning of fear to a conditioned stimulus; the second process occurs when the organism escapes, which is reinforced by fear reduction. Later research, however, has led to conclusions such as Herrnstein's that conditioned stimuli signal the occasion for reinforcement or punishment but do not reinforce or punish. Bandura stresses the predictive value of neutral stimuli that have been paired with aversive stimuli. Once established, defensive behavior remains, because avoidance prevents the subject from ever learning that the original stimuli may have changed and may no longer be dangerous.

A second set of behavioral studies of import come out of the operant conditioning model, where the reinforcement or punishment is dependent on the response of the subject. These theorists focus on avoidance behavior, and its results and treatments involve positive reinforcements of progressively closer approximations of a desired approach behavior. Stimuli that signal reinforcement or discriminative stimuli are stressed, not conditioned stimuli.

EMOTIONS
STRESS
STRESS CONSEQUENCES

I. L. KUTASH

APHASIA

A language disturbance produced by lesion or disease in the brain is called aphasia. These disorders are distinguished from those produced by other causes such as mental retardation, paralysis of the vocal apparatus, or sense organ disorders. Several different systems have been proposed to categorize various types of language disturbances, based on symptomatology. Most of these proposals make at least a general distinction between disturbances that primarily affect the ability to speak (expressive, or Broca's aphasia), and the ability to understand language (receptive, or Wernicke's aphasia). Aphasias that affect a very limited speech ability (such as the ability to read written language) are rarely seen, but their existence has provided information about the relationship between different brain areas and specific language functions.

Paul Broca was the first to link types of aphasia with specifically located lesions in the brain. He demonstrated an association between damage in the left hemisphere and aphasia.

Carl Wernicke identified another kind of aphasia that produces disturbances in the ability to understand language (receptive aphasia) as well as in the ability to speak. Patients typically have fluent and rapid speech, but their utterances are devoid of content or meaning. They choose inappropriate words and add nonsensical syllables. This kind of aphasia is also usually associated with brain damage on the left side, but the damage is posterior to Broca's area.

Wernicke proposed a theory of language production that is still valid. The underlying utterance originates in Wernicke's area and then is transferred to Broca's area, where a coordinated program for the utterance is produced. This program is then passed to the motor cortex, which activates the appropriate motor sequences required for the specific utterance. The fiber pathways between the two language areas, and the cortical areas for vision and audition, play critical roles. Damage to them can produce unusual types of aphasia, such as word deafness.

**BRAIN
COMMUNICATION PROCESSES
CRANIAL NERVES**

P. M. WALLACE

APPARENT MOVEMENT

In apparent or illusory movement, an object appears to move even though it is really stationary. Apparent movement is therefore to be contrasted with real movement. There are four major kinds of apparent movement: autokinetic movement, induced movement, stroboscopic movement, and movement aftereffects.

Autokinetic movement occurs when a stationary object is viewed against a background that is not well-defined; the stationary object appears to move. This phenomenon may explain reports of UFOs.

In *induced movement,* a frame of reference undergoes real movement in one direction, producing an illusion that a stationary object is moving in the opposite direction. A common example of induced movement happens when quickly moving clouds induce apparent movement in the relatively stationary moon.

Stroboscopic movement (or the phi phenomenon) occurs when two adjacent lights are flashed sequentially. If the interstimulus interval is too brief, observers report that the lights flashed simultaneously. If the interstimulus interval is too long, the lights appear to go on and off in turn. Stroboscopic movement occurs, however, if the interstimulus interval is about 30–200 msec. Motion pictures and television make use of stroboscopic motion.

Movement aftereffects occur when an observer has been watching continuous motion in one direction and then shifts the gaze to a different textured surface; this surface appears to move in the opposite direction. For example, if one stares at a waterfall and then gazes at the bank, the bank appears to move upward.

**PERCEPTION
PERCEPTUAL DISTORTION**

M. W. MATLIN

APPARENT SIZE

Apparent size, or judged size, is an important topic in visual perception. Three aspects of apparent size have attracted the most attention. One aspect is size constancy, or the tendency for apparent size to remain constant despite changes in retinal size. Another aspect is size illusions, or incorrect perceptions of an object's size, and the third area of interest involves explanations for how an object's size is perceived.

Three major theories have been proposed regarding size perception. The size-distance invariance hypothesis proposes that we derive an object's apparent size by considering both retinal size and apparent distance. Thus we know how big an object is by considering the size of the image it occupies on the retina, taking into account how far away the object appears to be. Cues to an object's apparent distance include both monocular factors (e.g., accommodation, linear perspective, atmospheric perspective, shading, interposition, height cues, and motion parallax) and binocular factors (e.g., convergence and binocular parallax). This classical hypothesis is widely accepted despite some negative evidence.

The other two theories stress that apparent size is a function of the relationship between visual stimuli. According to Rock and Ebenholtz's relative size explanation, the apparent size of an object depends on the relative size of other objects. Thus we use nearby objects as a frame of reference. According to J. J. Gibson's theory, the apparent size of an object depends on the number of texture units that the object covers. The greater the number of texture units, the larger the apparent size.

The two latter theories argue that the proximal stimulus contains all the information necessary for size perception, whereas the size-distance invariance hypothesis states that additional cues are necessary. All three theories may be at least partially correct. We may use all three sources of information to judge apparent size.

**CONSTANCY
ILLUSIONS**

M. W. MATLIN

APPETITE DISORDERS

Appetite disorders are characterized by gross disturbances in eating behaviors; they include anorexia nervosa and bulimia. The essential feature of anorexia nervosa is reduction of total food intake followed by life-threatening weight loss. Initially, anorectics restrict food intake for fear of becoming obese, but in later stages of the illness there is loss of appetite. Clinical symptoms include intense fear of gaining weight, preoccupation with food, amenorrhea in females, distorted body image, and bizarre eating habits. Anorexia nervosa usually occurs between ages 10 and 30 and is more prevalent among females. Adequate studies have not been conducted to establish definite predisposing factors in anorexia nervosa.

Bulimia is characterized by recurrent episodes of binge eating. The term bulimia means voracious appetite; during the binge these individuals rapidly consume large quantities of high caloric foods. Bulimics are preoccupied with their weight and make repeated attempts to control it through dieting, vomiting, and laxatives. They are aware of their abnormal eating behaviors and often experience remorse and depression following a binge. Though some anorexic individuals engage in binge eating, bulimia is not considered a subcategory of anorexia nervosa. Onset of illness occurs usually in adolescence and is more prevalent among females. The predisposing factors in bulimia are unknown.

**OBESITY
WEIGHT CONTROL**

T.-I. MOON

APPLIED RESEARCH

Applied research is oriented toward outcomes rather than concepts, and the research will be conducted in the problem-based setting rather than in the laboratory. Because that situation is complex and most likely encompasses a vast diversity of people, the research finding is very difficult to generalize beyond the setting in which it was conducted. As Anastasi pointed out, the basic researcher may be asking a question about the nature of learning, while the applied researcher may be asking which of several instructional methods is most effective for training airplane pilots. Because basic researchers work with a tightly defined, simple study in a laboratory setting, they can better pinpoint specific factors that account for differences found. This simplicity gives basic research a greater likelihood of making causal linkages.

EARLY HISTORY

As early as 1908, Hugo Munsterberg stated: "The time for . . . Applied Psychology is surely near, and work has been started from most various sides. Those fields of practical life which come first in question may be said to be education, medicine, art, economics, and law." Hailed as "the first all-around applied psychologist in America," Munsterberg shaped the field, brought definition to it, and outlined its potential uses in business and industry. Equally significant was the pioneering influence of Walter Dill Scott. In the same year that Munsterberg predicted Applied Psychology's era, Scott was bringing that era still closer to fruition with his book *The psychology of advertising.* Seven years later he again pioneered as he became the first psychologist to receive an appointment as professor of applied psychology at an American university (Carnegie Institute of Technology).

The early branches of applied research reflected closely the industrial orientation of their pioneers. Three of the basic research disciplines gave early birth to applied research offspring. Psychological testing produced personnel selection and classification; experimental psychology parented human factors engineering; and personality/social psychology provided the background setting for work in employee relations. One can readily see that the early history of applied research is, in effect, the history of industrial psychology as well.

PSYCHOLOGY PROFESSION: TENSION AND GROWTH

The formally stated goal of the American Psychological Association (APA) gives testimony to the tension and growth that applied research has brought to the discipline. APA's goal is "to advance psychology as a science, a profession, and as a means of promoting human welfare."

No members of the profession felt this implication more prominently than did clinical psychologists. Unable to meet their applied-research and psychotherapy-orientation needs within the APA, they formed state and national splinter groups (e.g., the American Association of Applied Psychology, Psychologists Interested in the Advancement of Psychotherapy) where their applied research interests and involvements could be effectively and meaningfully shared. The fact that splinter groups and their members now live under the APA roof is prominent evidence of the professional growth that has occurred within the association. It is also a tribute to the efforts of pioneers such as Carl Rogers who devoted extensive time and personal energy to the task of unifying. The threefold goal—science, profession, and human welfare—has attained a visible balance within the professional activity and commitments of the APA.

CURRENT STATUS

The first applied research areas—personnel selection, human factors, and employee relations—have now branched well beyond their early beginnings. Employee relations and personnel selection now come within the heading of industrial and organizational psychology, a rapidly growing field that directs extensive attention to management problems and employee training programs. Human factors are now an entry within the general framework of engineering psychology, focusing on problems of work and fatigue, efficiency in work methods, and improvement in the working and living environment. This latter focus has developed into the currently emerging field of environmental psychology, which looks upon the person's environment as an active, organized system that restricts some behaviors and encourages others. To understand a community or an organization, the environmental or ecological psychologist seeks to identify and describe the behavior settings that occur within that milieu. A third entry—consumer psychology—has gained its own separate and distinct identity. Initially a part of business and industrial psychology, the field first concentrated on specific features in advertising. Now it has expanded to include research into consumer characteristics, wants, and preferences. Because it combines research into economic behavior on the one hand and product design on the otherhand, it frequently touches the fields of economics and sociology.

Research Trends

Applied research trends have paralleled the change patterns which have occurred within the applied branches themselves. In a 20-year study, one of the most notable changes found in *Journal of Applied Psychology* articles was an increase in the number of field studies and a corresponding decrease in the number of experimental studies. Part of this change may have been due to increases in the availability of external funding, but there were strong signs that focus shifts within applied research itself also had played a major role. In addition to the research format itself, areas of interest also had notably changed in *Journal of Applied Psychology* coverage during that time period. While personnel selection, interest measurement, psychometrics, and test development and theory had been prominent in early coverage, the areas of motivation, leadership, organizational psychology, and job satisfaction dominated the contemporary research attention. In a 20-year period all the leading research interests had dramatically changed.

CONSUMER RESEARCH
FIELD EXPERIMENTATION

E. L. PALMER

APPROACHES TO LEARNING

One of the distinctive features of recent work in the field of educational psychology is the much greater importance given to ecological validity. Instead of looking to mainstream psychology to supply principles of learning applicable across a wide sweep of contrasting situations, there is now a tendency to develop explanatory constructs out of specific educational contexts. Resnick provides illustrations of this type of work in classroom situations. A new area of research in Europe and Australia has been exploring *student* learning and has developed sets of categories used to construct descriptions of learning firmly rooted in the experiences of students.

One starting point was a series of learning experiments carried out by Ference Marton and his colleagues in Gothenburg, Sweden. Marton was interested in how students tackled the task of reading an academic article. His work differed from traditional experiments in the use of realistically complex learning materials (an article of at least 1500 words), and in the application of rigorous qualitative analyses to interview protocols in which students reported their reading strategies and described what they had learned from the articles.

Analysis of the protocols identified qualitatively different levels of understanding and contrasting intentions and processes. One particularly strong distinction was found in the way students tackled the reading task. Some students set out with the intention actively to seek out the author's meaning. They interacted with the text as a whole, challenging the author's argument by examining and reorganizing the evidence in relation to the conclusions; they also related the ideas to previous knowledge and their own experiences. In short, these students were seeking to *reconstruct* a personal understanding of the article. This has been termed a *deep approach* to learning, and can be compared with David Ausubel's idea of a meaningful learning set. Other students, in contrast, adopted a *surface approach.* They focused their attention on the words in the text, apparently believing that learning implied the exact recall of important facts or ideas, as presented by the author. Their approach was thus narrowly focused on the details and often included an attempt to "spot" questions. They often failed to appreciate the hierarchical structure in the text, and so confused examples with principles. Above all, they concentrated on rote learning techniques to *reproduce* aspects of the article about which they expected to be questioned.

A study by Svensson reported a relationship between the general approach to learning used in everyday studying and examination performance. Most of the students who consistently adopted a deep approach passed all their examinations, whereas less than a quarter of those using a surface approach were fully successful. This marked difference partly results from the additional fact that students adopting a deep approach put in longer hours of independent studying. It appears that the deep approach, by focusing on understanding, is likely to make work more interesting and rewarding. There is thus a functional relationship linking approach to learning and the number of hours spent in studying.

Most of the extensions of Marton's work have involved qualitative analyses of interview protocols, but at the University of Lancaster, questionnaires and inventories were also used by Entwistle and Ramsden to measure approaches to studying. One outcome of this work has been the suggestion that a deep approach is itself carried out in different ways. Some students, particularly in science subjects, concentrate initially on factual detail, building a broader perspective only later on, while other students prefer to start with this broader view.

Two interesting problems are associated with the description of contrasting learning styles and approaches. First, to what extent are styles distinct from approaches, and second, are they stable attributes of the individual or are they mainly dependent on the specific learning task or context? Conceptually it is possible to separate two styles of learning—comprehension and operation learning—both of which will often be necessary for understanding. But empirically, a close correlation is found between a deep approach and comprehension learning, and between a surface approach and operation learning. It appears that while operation learning can be the initial strategy in seeking understanding, in practice it is more likely to be part of an instrumental approach that relies not just on identifying evidence, but also on rote learning it. Again, while the deep approach ought to involve attention to detail, a majority of students using that approach are beguiled by their search for personal meaning and fail to give sufficient attention to supportive evidence.

Marton and his colleagues argue persuasively that the approach to learning is *not* a stable characteristic of the individual, but a specific response to the particular task and learning context. The evidence is, however, equivocal. As Entwistle argues, people show evidence of both consistency and variability, depending on the methods of measurement used and the perspective adopted by the researcher. Although it might seem that intellectual ability was likely to be one of those relatively stable characteristics associated with approach to learning, what evidence there is from work by Säljö suggests that there is no such relationship, at least among university students. The Lancaster work does, however, suggest personality correlates of comprehension learning that might hint at possible roots in cerebral dominance.

The research group at Gothenburg examined factors likely to influence approaches to learning. Säljö showed that narrow factual questions shifted most students toward a surface approach. Questions demanding understanding had less effect on students initially adopting a surface approach: They simply redefined the task requirements and tried to reproduce summaries of the author's message without providing evidence of having come to grips with the arguments. In another experiment Fransson showed that content perceived as interesting or personally relevant appeared to facilitate deep learning, while a learning situation perceived as anxiety-provoking was likely to induce a surface approach. Ramsden and Entwistle have shown similar effects in relation to students' perceptions of their academic departments. Students adopting a deep approach and having positive attitudes to learning were likely to categorize their department as having good teaching and allowing freedom in learning. Departments perceived as imposing a heavy workload and denying freedom in learning contained an above-average number of students reporting surface approaches. It is interesting to note that departmental ratings were not related to organized study methods or to levels of achievement motivation. Totally independent work carried out by Biggs in Newcastle, Australia, has identified similar dimensions of studying by making use only of quantitative methods. Using a Study Processes Questionnaire, Biggs identified three main factors. Further work at Lancaster using an Approaches to Studying Inventory has led Entwistle and Ramsden to describe four such factors, the first three of which closely resemble those reported by Biggs. They have been described as *study orientations,* which comprise orientation, meaning, reproducing orientation, strategic orientation, and nonacademic orientation. The first two of these orientations are *general* tendencies to utilize deep or surface approaches to studying respectively. The third represents an achievement orientation that makes use of both approaches strategically to acquire high grades, while the final orientation reflects little evidence of the use of either of those approaches to studying.

Table 1 summarizes the anticipated relationships between orientations, motives, and learning processes. There are good logical and conceptual reasons for all these categories, and some empirical support for the implied relationships. But since this research area is both new and rapidly developing, the relationships should be viewed as tentative and be reconsidered in the light of subsequent work.

CLASSROOM DYNAMICS
DISCOVERY LEARNING
INSTRUCTIONAL THEORY
LEARNING OUTCOMES

N. J. Entwistle

APTITUDE TESTING

Broadly defined, an aptitude test is any psychometric instrument used to predict what an individual is "apt" to do. Measures of achievement, special abilities, interests, personality traits, or of any other human characteristic or behavior could qualify as an aptitude test. This broad definition, however, is seldom applied. The term aptitude test is usually restricted to single tests or batteries of tests of special abilities that purportedly measure the ability to learn or be trained in a specific skill or occupational area.

Dozens of standardized measures of aptitudes, including entire batteries, are now commercially available. Examples of aptitude test batteries are the Differential Aptitude Tests, which are used extensively in academic counseling at the junior-high level and beyond, and the General Aptitude Test Battery, which employs an occupational ability pattern approach to vocational counseling.

Table 1 Approaches to Learning

Educational Orientation	Study Orientation	Predominant Motivation	Learning Processes
Personal	Meaning	Intrinsic: interest in what is being learned	Active, holistic attempts to incorporate new ideas with existing knowledge
Vocational	Reproducing	Extrinsic: concern for qualifications or fear of failure	Narrow, serialist concentration on learning details by rote and following syllabus closely
Academic	Strategic	Need for achievement and affiliation with staff	Structuring and organizing work, using either rote or meaningful learning as required to earn high grades
Social	Nonacademic	Need for affiliation with peers	Little concern for academic requirements; main activities and interests extracurricular

GENERAL VERSUS SPECIFIC APTITUDES

General intelligence tests such as the Stanford–Binet Intelligence Scale and the Wechsler Adult Intelligence Scale measure a composite of specific aptitudes. In Cronbach's terminology, these tests have a broad *bandwidth,* because they correlate significantly with performance in a broad range of areas. However, such tests have low *fidelity*—that is, their correlations with performance in specific areas are usually low. Further, special aptitude tests have lower bandwidths but, hopefully, higher fidelity. Their average correlation with success in a wide range of fields is typically lower than that of general intelligence tests, but the correlation of a specific test with performance in a given field is higher.

As was true for general intelligence tests, psychologists who pioneered in the construction of aptitude tests assumed that such tests measure innate potential to learn. Consequently, scores on these tests should not be greatly affected by specific learning experiences. As J. B. Carroll has demonstrated, scores on certain aptitude tests do not change with training. However, scores on other aptitude tests—for example, measures of motor dexterity—improve significantly with practice.

VALIDITY OF APTITUDE TESTS

Some psychologists such as Vernon have maintained that general intelligence is more important than specific aptitudes as a determinant of vocational success. It has been demonstrated, however, that scores on tests of mechanical and clerical aptitudes, in particular, do contribute to the prediction of success in various occupations. The value of tests of art and musical aptitudes for predictive purposes is not as clear, but even here some positive results have been obtained.

In general, aptitude tests are better predictors of success in training programs than for on-the-job performance.

Many aptitude-testing practices that were current before the validity and fairness of employment testing became a legal issue during the 1960s were questionable. But today, because of the difficulty of meeting the Equal Employment Opportunity Commission's employee selection guidelines, many companies have discontinued the use of aptitude tests.

**EMPLOYMENT PRACTICES
INDUSTRIAL PSYCHOLOGY
SELECTION TESTS**

L. R. AIKEN

ARBITRATION

Arbitration is a procedure whereby a third party resolves a dispute between two or more parties by issuing a decision or award that is binding on each party. Arbitration is used in a wide variety of civil, financial, and industrial disputes. It is most widely used in industrial relations to resolve disputes between workers or labor organizations and employers.

Arbitration can either be *voluntary* or *compulsory.* Voluntary arbitration is a process in which both parties agree privately that they will settle any future unresolved disputes by arbitration.

The structure of arbitration can vary in a number of ways. The arbitrator can be an individual or a panel composed of several members. If a panel is used, the individuals can either be all neutral members, or *tripartite*—that is, the panel is composed of one or more representatives of each party to the dispute and one or more neutrals. The decision-making process can also vary. Under a conventional arbitration decision-making process, the arbitrator can fashion any award he or she deems appropriate. Under a newer form of arbitration called *final offer arbitration,* the parties each submit a final offer to the arbitrator; the arbitrator must then pick one or the other and cannot fashion a compromise award. Final offer arbitration is an innovation that was first proposed by C. M. Stevens as a way of overcoming the belief that conventional arbitration carries with it strong disincentives for disputing parties to make the compromises necessary to resolve their disputes on their own. The hypothesis is that, because the parties believe the arbitrator will choose a compromise position somewhere between their final offers, they hold back making compromise offers lest the arbitrator take their final offers and impose a further compromise in the final award. Final offer arbitration is designed to overcome this disincentive by taking away the opportunity for the arbitrator to issue a compromise award. Instead, each negotiator has an incentive to make an offer that the arbitrator will find more equitable than the offer of the other party.

The arbitration process normally is initiated when one or both parties file a petition for arbitration, noting the parties to the dispute, the issues in dispute, and the contract, law, or prior agreement that specifies that arbitration is available. Various agencies exist to administer arbitration agreements and to aid in selecting an arbitrator. The largest private agency is the American Arbitration Association. Each year this agency handles more than 20,000 labor arbitrations and thousands of nonlabor cases. After an arbitrator is appointed, a hearing is conducted in which the representatives of each party present their proposals and offer evidence to support their case. The nature of these proceedings varies; however, they tend to follow the general format of a legal proceeding with the arbitrator serving as the judge and conducting the hearing and with the representatives of each party calling witnesses and arguing their case. After the hearing is completed, the arbitrator examines both the written documents introduced at the hearing, and the oral arguments of the parties and their witnesses, and issues a written award. If either party then fails to comply with the award, the other party normally is free to seek a court order to enforce the award.

BEHAVIORAL CONTRACTS
HUMAN RELATIONS TRAINING
JURY PSYCHOLOGY

T. A. KOCHAN

ARCHETYPES

Carl Jung introduced this term into psychological theory, and he is primarily responsible for the development of the concept to which it refers. He recognized two basic layers in the unconscious: the personal unconscious, whose contents are derived from present lifetime experience, and the collective unconscious, whose contents are inherited and essentially universal within the species. The collective unconscious consists of archetypes. Jung described these as primordial images that have existed from the remotest times but lack clear content. Their specific content as realized images is supplied by the material of conscious experience. Thus the archetype as such is an empty form that must be inferred, or derived by abstraction, from a class of experienced images or symbols.

Jung contends that his use of the term *archetypes* is more empirical and less metaphysical than the term used by idealistic philosophers. He arrived at the concept initially through a study of psychotic patients and augmented his understanding through a more comprehensive study of symbol systems.

Jung began to develop the archetype concept during his early work at the Burghölzli Mental Hospital, where he observed that some of his relatively uneducated psychotic patients experienced universal religious and mythological symbols. In many instances it was clear that the patient could not have learned of the symbol through formal study; hence the appearance of the symbol in the patient's ideation or imagery had to represent a spontaneous eruption of unconscious material not derived throughout present lifetime experience. Jung subsequently explored the archetypal realm through an intensive examination of his own dreams and waking fantasies.

The archetypes to which Jung devotes the greatest amount of attention in his writings include the shadow, the anima and animus, the wise old man, the magna mater (or great earth mother), the child, and the self.

The archetypes just noted tend to be experienced in personified form. They may appear as figures in dreams, and they provide the source of such cultural symbols as gods and goddesses. They also enter extensively into interpersonal experience, being frequently projected onto other people. Each archetype can be expressed in a great variety of personifications. A given anima image may be positive or negative and may emphasize any of a number of possible qualities: sexuality, beauty, wisdom, spirituality, moral virtue, destructiveness, and so forth. Other archetypes, which Jung calls archetypes of transformation, do not appear in a personal form. They are expressed in many of the situations, places, implements, and events of our dreams, and they govern corresponding motifs in folklore. Jung believed he had identified the most important archetypes, but it may be assumed that the total number of archetypes is indefinitely large and that an exhaustive inventory of them is not feasible.

ANALYTICAL PSYCHOLOGY

R. W. COAN

ARMY TESTS, WORLD WAR I

World War I opened a new era in American applied psychology. When the United States entered the war in April 1917, Robert M. Yerkes, president of the American Psychological Association (APA), took energetic steps to involve psychologists in the war effort. He made an immediate visit to Canada, where authorities advocated psychological methods

for the selection of recruits and treatment of incapacitated soldiers. Working through the APA and the National Research Council, he interested the U. S. Army in the development of a screening examination. The committee he assembled for the purpose included three men who had published versions of the Binet test; H. H. Goddard, who had made the first American translation; L. M. Terman, who had just completed the Stanford revision; and Yerkes himself, coauthor of a Binet point scale.

The original plan of the committee was to devise a form of the Binet suitable for military use—a suggestion which had been firmly turned down by the French army when proposed by Alfred Binet several years earlier. The proposal to make a short test for individual administration was quickly abandoned when the committee examined a group intelligence test made available by Arthur S. Otis, Terman's graduate student.

Examination A was administered to approximately 140,000 soldiers prior to May 1918, when, on the basis of extensive statistical analysis and further test development, it was replaced by a revision—the famous Army Alpha. Two subtests were eliminated; directions were modified; a weighting system was dropped; certain items were revised, some omitted, others added; and within each test the items were arranged in order of difficulty—all in accordance with psychometric procedures for which there was little precedent, but that became standard for later test developers. Examination Army Alpha was used to classify some 1,250,000 individuals in the U. S. Army. It was published for civilian use after World War I and led directly to the use of mental testing for college admissions and in personnel selection in business and industry. While group mental alertness tests currently used in education, business, industry, and the armed services differ considerably from Examination A, they are all of direct descent.

The Army psychologists also developed a nonverbal test for illiterates—the Army Beta—and an individual scale somewhat similar to the Binet.

INTELLIGENCE MEASURES
NONVERBAL INTELLIGENCE TESTS
PENCIL/PAPER INTELLIGENCE TESTS
TEST STANDARDIZATION

P. H. DuBois

ARTIFICIAL INTELLIGENCE

In its broadest sense, artificial intelligence is the abstract science of human, animal, and machine cognition. A unified theory of cognition constitutes its ultimate objective.

As a theoretical psychology, artificial intelligence is the continuation of a research program initiated by George Boole: "The mathematics we have to construct are the mathematics of the human intellect." The mathematics referred to is known as Boolean algebra and is a system for representing propositions in binary notation. Boolean symbolic logic, together with the development of programming languages, made possible the computational science of artificial intelligence.

E. L. Post established the mathematical foundations of production systems that were later employed in the information-processing psychology of A. Newell and H. A. Simon.

The production system was one of those happy events, though in minor key, that historians of science often talk about: a rather well-prepared formalism, sitting in wait for a scientific mission. Production systems have a long and diverse history. Their use of symbolic logic starts with Post, from whom the name is taken. They also show up as Markov algorithms. Their use in linguistics, where they are also called rewrite rules, dates from Chomsky. As with so many other notions in computer science, they really entered into wide currency when they became operationalised in programming languages.

The strength and limitations of artificial intelligence are best explored by comparing it with human cognitive ability in a number of intellectual domains. The domains selected for comparison are mathematical theorem proving, legal reasoning, problem solving in the physical sciences, and the processes of scientific discovery.

MATHEMATICAL THEOREM PROVING

From the time of Euclid, human intelligence sufficed for the establishment of mathematical theorems in geometry, algebra, calculus, and more advanced topics. For the proof of the four-color theorem, human intelligence required the intellectual contribution of artificial intelligence. The most creative minds in mathematics had struggled in vain to prove the validity of the four-color conjecture and it was only when Appel and Haken accepted the computer as a full intellectual partner that the century-old enigma could be resolved with precision and completeness.

Moreover, whereas the validity of mathematical proofs depended on confirmation in replication by human mathematicians, the validity of the Appel and Haken proof could be established only by the independent verification of other computer programs. A foundational shift had taken place in the exclusive reliance on human mathematical reasoning as the ultimate authority.

The four-color conjecture was originally advanced by Francis Guthrie in 1852, and although subjected to many ingenious mathematical methods, it remained resistant to proof until Appel and Haken, a century later, brought to bear the acumen of artificial intelligence. The four-color conjecture asserts that "four colors are sufficient to color every map so that neighboring countries sharing a common border have different colors."

The solution of the four-color problem depended on the availability of sophisticated methods for the systematic analysis of thousands of configurations of maps, countries, and colors. To manage this immense complexity, Appel and Haken developed advanced computer programs. Far from being restricted to a mechanical analysis of possible configurations, the intelligent computer made original intellectual contributions to the solution of the four-color problem. In the following passage, Appel and Haken present a dramatic account of the increasing sophistication of the computer program and of its mathematical ideas that sometimes exceeded their own in quality.

At this point the program, which had by now absorbed our ideas and improvements for two years, began to surprise us. At the beginning we would check its arguments by hand so we could always predict the course it would follow in any situation; but now it suddenly started to act like a chess-playing machine. It would work out compound strategies based on all the tricks it had been "taught" and often these approaches were far more clever than those we would have tried. Thus it began to teach us things about how to proceed that we never expected. In a sense it had surpassed its creators in some aspects of the "intellectual" as well as the mechanical parts of the task.

The mathematical proof of the four-color theorem entailed immense amounts of computation by both human and computer intelligence, but the intellectual intricacies of the latter could be independently verified only by other computer programs.

The revolutionary employment of artificial intelligence stirred controversy in both mathematical and philosophical disciplines. Appel and Haken responded to the issues of proof by the mathematician and proof by the computer in the following terms:

When proofs are long and highly computational, it may be argued that even when hand checking is possible, the probability of human error is considerably higher than that of machine error; moreover, if the computations are sufficiently routine, the validity of programs themselves is easier to verify than the correctness of hand computations.

In any event, even if the Four-Color Theorem turns out to have a simpler proof, mathematicians might be well advised to consider more carefully other problems that might have solutions of this new type, requiring computation or analysis of a type not possible for humans alone. There is every reason to believe that there are a large number of such problems.

Traditionally, the mathematical sciences have upheld the criterion of lucid deductive reasoning in the establishment of proofs, and reasoning was the exclusive product of human mathematical minds. According to the philosopher Tymoczko, the proof of the four-color theorem by its very dependency on a computer whose operations cannot be humanly corroborated is unacceptable.

If we accept the four-color theorem as a theorem, then we are committed to changing the sense of "theorem", or more to the point, to changing the sense of the underlying concept of "proof."

Whether the "sense of the underlying concept of proof" is changed, or only the agent of proof is changed, constitutes a strategic issue for mathematicians and philosophers, but the intellectual implications of artificial mathematical intelligence may well extend to the cannons of acceptable research in all disciplines.

LEGAL REASONING

The concept of computer jurisprudence originated with Gottfried Leibniz who, although, famous for his work in the development of the differential and integral calculus, also was a brilliant philosopher and an international lawyer. Leibniz conceived of a mathematically directed machine that would replace legal disputations between lawyer and lawyer or judge and judge with a computationally based resolution in a manner analogous to the settlement of disputes among accountants regarding sums: "Let us calculate."

Several centuries later, Anne Gardner developed a computer program directed not toward the replacement of legal disputations by calculation but the modeling of legal reasoning in a computer program. Gardner's legal reasoning program was assigned a problem in contract law. The contract law problem was part of a final examination taken by first-year Harvard Law School students. The legal acumen of the computer program and that of Harvard students could thereby be compared. The examination problem in contract law dealt with the discernment of legal issues in an offer and acceptance problem.

The Gardner legal-reasoning program contains complex knowledge hierarchies that represent the facts in the contract problem and a set of 100 rules for reasoning about the facts and reaching legal conclusions. The reasoning of the program resulted in a total of nine analyses of the law school contract problem, each accompanied by the specific determination that a contract was or was not in effect at various points during the offer and acceptance negotiations. In contrast to the nine analyses produced by the computer program, the Harvard Law School students produced only four analyses.

The Gardner legal-reasoning program represents an initial foray into the domain of legal reasoning. The program focuses on clear issues in contract law, but only at the elementary level. In addition, although the program can negotiate among its facts and its rules to reach decisions, it cannot respond to more complex aspects of the law or to legal policy or to multiple judicial interpretations. Statutory regulations can, at the present time, be embodied in expert legal systems, but they will require immense advances in artificial intelligence to approach the speculation of Leibniz that the resolution of disputations among lawyers and judges can be obtained by means of the procedures of computation.

PROBLEM SOLVING IN THE PHYSICAL SCIENCES

The artificial intelligence problem-solving system, flexible expert reasoner with multidomain inferencing (FERMI), combines scientific principles, general methods, and domain-specific knowledge to solve problems in particular areas of physical science. The architecture of FERMI contains two mutually accessible hierarchical structures of knowledge schemas and method schemas that provide the capacity for generality of application across domains. The general knowledge schema includes the principle of decomposition and the principle of invariance. These are intellectual principles of great scope and power in science and mathematics generally and are the most interesting aspects of FERMI.

The principle of decomposition had its philosophical origin in Descartes who advised the partitioning of any difficult problem into simple solvable component problems and its mathematical origin and in Leibniz who demonstrated that difficult problems in integral calculus could be solved by decomposing the mathematical function into a series of simple integratable functions. The principle of decomposition in the FERMI system is applied to such problems as computing the total pressure drop to a fluid system by decomposing the total path in the system into a series of component paths and computing their pressure drops.

The decomposition principle and associated decomposition methods apply to functions of many types of entities. For example, decomposition applies to pressure drops or potential drops as functions of paths, to areas or centers of mass as functions of regions, and to temporal functions expressed as functions of frequency.

The principle of invariance is ubiquitous in mathematics and science. Equations for physical laws typically involve a set of variables and one or more invariant constants. In FERMI, the principle of invariance is used in conjunction with a method of comparison of invariance to set up an equation for solving a physical science problem.

For example, the energy of a particle can be expressed in terms of its position and velocity. If the particle's energy is invariant, a consideration of the particle at two different times (corresponding to different positions and velocities of the particle) yields an equation relating these positions and velocities.

In FERMI, the quantity schema contains general knowledge hierarchically organized with the capacity for lower and more specific levels to inherit knowledge from higher and more general levels. In the hierarchy, the top node is quantity, and it has three children: type, difference quantity, and property. Type has two children: vector field and scalar field. Property has two children: decomposable quantity and invariant quantity. Decomposable quantity has two children: path and region. Invariant quantity has three children: path, input–output, and time. The path child of decomposable quantity and the path child of invariant quantity share a common descendent: invariant sum/path. Invariant sum/path has two children: pressure drop and potential drop. Pressure drop has two children: PD and PD^2.

In FERMI, problem-solving methods are contained in the method schema hierarchy. In this hierarchy, the root node is method, and it has three children: property-related method, algebraic method, and analogy. Property-related method has two children: decomposition and comparison of invariants. Decomposition has two children: control structure and entity type. Comparison of invariants has two children: path and input–output. Control structure has three children: known, iterative, and recursive. Entity type has two children: path and region. Path child of comparison of invariants has two children: constrained path and preferred direction.

FERMI's ability to solve problems in domains of physical science are summarized in the following terms:

Problems about pressures in liquids. FERMI can find the pressure difference between any two points in one or more liquids at rest. . . .

Problems about centers of mass. FERMI can find the center of mass of any planar object which is rectangular or decomposable into rectangular parts.

Problems about electric circuits. FERMI can find time-independent potential drops of currents in electric circuits consisting of any small number of wires, resistors, and batteries interconnected in various ways.

FERMI can also now apply invariance of energy to relate the mass and speeds of a satellite or a falling object at two different locations.

The extension of the general principles of decomposition and invariance together with specific domain knowledge can result in impressive future development of FERMI. The authors of the FERMI system plan extensions of the decomposition principle to the following domains: mechanics, geometry, electricity and magnetism, heat and thermodynamics, chemistry, and waves. According to the developers of FERMI, the principle of invariance can be extended to quantitative problems in the conservation of momentum, angular momentum, and energy.

The hierarchical structure of quantity schema and method schema, including especially the intellectual principles of invariance and decomposition, appear to accord to FERMI the capacity for flexibility and generality of application. These capacities, however, are rigidly circumscribed by its own fixed hierarchical structure. It is lacking in the type of ingenuity and intelligent finesse that characterized the problem-solving cognitions of its namesake, Enrico Fermi.

THE PROCESS OF SCIENTIFIC DISCOVERY

There are two artificial intelligence approaches to the processes of scientific discovery. In the first approach, no attempt is made to model the cognitive processes of human scientists; rather, the technical methods of artificial intelligence are deployed. In the second approach, the intellective processes of scientific discovery are computationally modeled.

The first approach is represented by computer programs that discovered or rediscovered scientific and mathematical knowledge. Using a set of sophisticated heuristics written in a mere two pages of LISP code, the automatic mathematician program made a number of mathematical discoveries, including the concept of prime numbers, the conjecture that every even number can be represented as the sum of two prime numbers, and the fundamental theorem of arithmetic. Shen has developed a broad computational architecture of artificial intelligence discovery systems that subsumes both the AM program and its successor EURISCO. Langley, Simon, Bradshaw, and Zytkow present an account of a number of sophisticated programs that rediscovered quantitive laws in physics and astronomy. For example, the BACON.3 program rediscovered, among others, Galileo's laws of acceleration. Ohm's laws of electricity, and Kepler's third law of planetary motion. In the chemical sciences, the MetaDendral program made a number of significant discoveries that were later published in a highly selective scientific journal.

The second approach is represented by the KEKADA program that directly modeled, in detail, the experimental procedures and scientific discoveries of the eminent biochemist Hans Krebs, credited with the establishment of the nature of the ornithine effect and the urea cycle. Krebs made his discoveries in 1932, and later Holmes—on the basis of Krebs's laboratory records and interviews with him—produced a reconstruction, in fine detail, of the cognitive and experimental sequences involved in Krebs's metabolic discoveries. Based on the accounts of Holmes, Kulkarni and Simon created KEKADA, an artificial intelligence program that emulated Krebs's biochemical discoveries.

KEKADA's discovery processes include a high-level control structure based on the two-space model of problem solving. The model searches, systematically and cyclically, through an instance space composed of a set of experiments and their results and of a rule space composed of hypotheses and their embedded knowledge structures. Heuristic operators are coordinated to carry out searches in the instance space and the rule space.

A comparative analysis of KEKADA's performance with that of Krebs indicated near identity in the intricate course of experimentation that led to the discovery of the ornithine cycle. From this near identity of performance, Kulkarni and Simon conclude that KEKADA "constitutes a theory of Krebs' style of experimentation." Kulkarni and Simon also conclude that due to the large number of widely applicable domain-independent heuristics, KEKADA constitutes a general simulator and general theory of the scientific discovery process.

Computational theories of the processes of scientific discovery can be broadly conceived in terms of a general logic that embraces a set of basic assumptions.

The research of Kulkarni and Simon on the KEKADA system will be used to examine these assumptions and, to that extent, to evaluate the logic of computational theories of scientific discovery.

The assumption that the processes of creativity in scientific discovery has a knowable character can be supported once it is granted that some degree of confidence can be placed in Holmes's account. . . . The assumption that the creative processes of scientific discovery are definable can be supported given KEKADA's definitional heuristics which include the capacity for planning and executing experiments, the recognition of surprising experimental results, and the consequent revision of hypotheses and continuation of the control strategies of systematic experimentation.

The assumption that scientific discovery processes represent subsets of general problem-solving strategies is supported by the two-space model of problem solving which provided the general superstructure for the development of the control logic in the KEKADA system. . . .

The assumption that scientific discovery processes can be modelled by the standard heuristics of computational problem-solving systems is supported by . . . KEKADA's possession of a large set of general heuristics, potentially applicable to scientific discovery problems beyond those of Krebs.

Computational theories of the scientific discovery process are essentially directed at the emulation of cognitive processes in contrast to theories of human scientific discovery processes that include motivational and affective processes.

Guiding our investigations is what we have termed the *intrinsic motivation principle of creativity:*
People will be most creative when they feel motivated primarily by the interest, enjoyment, satisfaction, and challenge of the work itself—not by external pressures.

In essence, we are saying that the love people feel for their work has a great deal to do with the creativity of their performances. This proposition is clearly supported by accounts of the phenomenology of creativity. Most reports from and about creative individuals are filled with notions of an intense involvement in and unrivaled love for their work.

Intrinsic motivation, required for human creativity, is not essential for computational discovery systems. In the artificial intelligence approach to scientific discovery, the mechanisms of algorithms and heuristic operators are sufficient.

It is clear that impressive results such as those from KEKADA and BACON. 3 can emerge from computational scientific discovery systems. It should be noted, however, that these systems are inductive and data driven. Radically new computational systems that go beyond the limits imposed by the inductive method will be required to attain the imaginative heights of advanced theoretical physics.

ALGORITHMIC–HEURISTIC THEORY
CAUSAL REASONING
COMPUTER SOFTWARE
GENERAL SYSTEMS
SYSTEMS AND THEORIES
THEORETICAL PSYCHOLOGY

M. WAGMAN

ARTISTIC MORPHOLOGY
Artistic morphology refers to the scientific study of form and structure in art. The emphasis is on form in the visual arts. Since the last century, psychologists have been involved in the related study of perception. Franz Boas in his *Primitive art* cites Wilhelm Wundt as declaring, "For the psychological study, art stands in a position between language and myth."

One may conceive of visual form as developing from an interaction of four factors. The first is the structure of the images of objects projected upon the eyes. Such forms, in a sense, represent aspects of arrested processes. They possess a certain dynamism deriving from the forces inherent within them.

The second factor consists of the formative powers existing within the visual apparatus. Percepts are ordered by means of the structures of that apparatus. The Gestalt psychologist, Max Wertheimer, had formulated "principles of articulation," which Rudolf Arnheim, in his *Art and visual perception,* reduced to a single "principle of similarity," an example of a hypothesized general law in which forces of a single psychological or physiological field tend toward the simplest symmetrical distribution.

The third factor is the organism's motivation for observing, selecting, and understanding. This is originally related to biological survival. Form and subject matter in art are related to what the artists and those who support them consider significant. From the bison silhouettes of the Paleolithic caves to the "nonobjective" rhythms of Mondrian, artists have expressed their personal concerns and those of their particular milieu. Earlier assumptions of inferior ability among "primitive" artists have been dispelled by the recognition that the function of such creations differs from that of "representational" work.

The last factor relates to the expression of attitudes, temperament, and inner conflicts in the artist. The art critic Herbert Read, in his *Education through art,* has commented on the profound affinity between the artist and the form he or she selects.

Clinicians attempt to interpret such works in two basic ways: One uses the method of Freudian psychoanalysis. Ernst Kris, in his *Psychoanalytic explorations in art,* has made a significant contribution from this viewpoint. A second approach, known as "isomorphic symbolism," is based on the assumption that the structural qualities of visual form are related to similar characteristics in human behavior; thus children who prefer "warm" colors have been found to be of more "social" temperament.

Form and structure in art, then, are not static elements, but derive from a dynamic interaction of processes within the artist and the objects of his or her perception.

ART THERAPY
GESTALT PSYCHOLOGY
PSYCHOLOGY OF ART

R. J. HEARN

ASSERTIVENESS TRAINING
Assertiveness training (AT) was introduced by Andrew Salter and popularized by Joseph Wolpe and Arnold Lazarus. AT is most frequently included as one aspect of a broader therapeutic program. Its goals include (a) increased awareness of personal rights; (b) differentiating between nonassertiveness, assertiveness, and aggressiveness; and (c) learning both verbal and nonverbal skills. The latter category involves saying "no"; asking favors or making requests; expressing positive and negative feelings; and initiating, continuing, and terminating conversations.

Assertiveness training, as generally practiced, requires determining the specific situations in which the client characteristically behaves maladaptively—that is, either unassertively or aggressively. There is little evidence supporting a generalized trait of assertiveness. A number of self-report inventories are available for assessing the client's responses to various situations. Among these are the Assertion Inventory, the Assertiveness Self-Statement Inventory, the College Self-Expression Inventory, the Conflict Resolution Inventory, the Rathus Assertiveness Schedule, and the Wolpe-Lazarus Assertion Inventory. Behaviorally, while it is desirable to observe the client in the troublesome situation, it is typical to assess behavior in response to a simulated (usually audio- or videotaped) situation similar to the problematic situation, or to role play the unproductive interaction.

If assessment demonstrates that the client is always unassertive or aggressive, then alternative, more general therapies are suggested. However, if there are specific situations in which the client could perform with increased assertiveness, AT is recommended.

There is no universally agreed-upon program called assertiveness training. The personal preferences of the therapist determine the course of therapy. However, the following five procedures are commonly utilized to generate increased assertiveness. First, response acquisition learning, increasing assertiveness through modeling (both overt and covert) and instruction. The focus is on both the verbal and nonverbal components of assertiveness. Second, response reproduction, performing the new responses using role playing, behavior rehearsal, or response practice. Third, response refining, shaping and strengthening the new behavior with appropriate feedback, criticism, and coaching. Fourth, cognitive restructuring, challenging irrational beliefs that interfere with assertiveness and introducing cognitions that enhance assertiveness. Finally, generalization instruction, attempting new behaviors *in vivo* and encouraging generalizability to new situations. These techniques, often used in groups, are continued until the client demonstrates appropriate assertiveness.

COUNSELING
FEMINIST THERAPY
PSYCHOTHERAPY

C. H. FISCHER

ASSESSING CHILDREN FOR PSYCHOTHERAPY

The process of assessing a child as being in need of psychotherapy is typically initiated by a request, usually identified as a referral. It may be activated by parents, significant individuals in a child's life, schools, health care agencies, health care professionals, law enforcement, and, in some instances, the child. The information, in both content and detail, can vary, usually depending on the referral source. A general statement regarding the child's problem is the minimum data usually reported. This can be supplemented and enriched by prior medical, neurological, psychological, educational, and other evaluations. Of course, developmental and social histories are invaluable. In addition, determination of attendees of the psychodiagnostic interview, explanation of the format, and the establishment of fee for the first session, should be clarified.

The next phase of this process is the arranging of the psychodiagnostic interview.

A typical initial psychodiagnostic session would include the mother, the father, and the child. One approach is to meet with them individually, with the most time devoted to the child. A wrap-up meeting for feedback and recommendations can include the three of them. The sequence might be the mother, the father, and then the child. The focus of the individual interview should be on obtaining some information on the person, their perception of the child's problem, and their relationship and interaction with the child. Often, the mother offers the most detailed developmental history of the child, while the father shares an alternative perspective of the child's problem. The time spent with the child should follow the

cues of the child, with respect to his or her most comfortable vehicle of expression. This can include verbal interchanges, play, drawing, or assembling something like a puzzle or a toy. Variables such as age, intellectual and social development, and apparent level of disturbance will be critical in determining interactional methods with the child.

The goal of the psychodiagnostic interviewing process is to integrate all the information to date, in order to provide a sound recommendation. Prior to the offering of a recommendation, feedback is given to the participants from the psychodiagnostic interview process. This can include the sharing of observations and impressions of the interactions, relative to the presenting problem. Time should be allowed for a reaction and discussion of these comments. The assessor should then take the responsibility of explaining the psychotherapeutic process, with an emphasis on the therapeutic relationship and the "fit" between the therapist and the client. There can be some discussion of the goals of psychotherapy and the means of attaining those goals.

The final phase of this process is an integration of the total input to arrive at a productive recommendation regarding possible need for psychotherapy.

CHILD GUIDANCE CLINICS
DIAGNOSES
FAMILY COUNSELING
PSYCHOTHERAPY

S. S. CARDONE

ASSOCIATIONISM

Association of ideas is the intuitive notion that ideas are grouped together, or associated, in explicable ways. For example, if someone says "horse," one is likely to think "animal," "rider," or "race," but not "shelf," "battery," or "floor." The first set of ideas are all associated with horses, the latter are not. Associationism embraces association of ideas and makes it into a general systematic account of mind or behavior.

John Locke coined the phrase "association of ideas" in the fourth edition of his *Essay concerning human understanding.* He regarded associations as a kind of "madness," as they get in the way of rational, directed thinking. Notwithstanding Locke's condemnation, several eighteenth-century philosophers turned association of ideas into associationism, a view of mind and behavior that places association at the heart of thinking and tends to reduce all psychological principles to the principle of association.

Foremost among these philosophers were David Hume and David Hartley. Hume proudly reduced the mind to the association of ideas, maintaining that the mind contains either perceptions or their copies and ideas, and that ideas are glued together by two laws of association, similarity and contiguity (whereby two ideas that occur together become linked).

The tendency signaled by Hume and Hartley to elevate the principle of associative learning was continued by the nineteenth-century British associationists James Mill, his son John Stuart Mill, and his son's friend, Alexander Bain. James Mill proposed a mechanical theory of association in which ideas are stuck together like tinkertoys. J. S. Mill recognized the unwieldiness of this arrangement and proposed mental chemistry, in which several ideas can merge into one and reveal emergent properties, as when hydrogen and oxygen merge to make water. Bain placed Hartley's project on a better foundation, uniting association philosophy with up-to-date physiology to produce a real association psychology.

It was then only a short step to psychological experiments on association formation, or learning and memory. Thomas Brown had already put forward an empirically researchable form of associationism in his secondary laws of association, which further specified the operation of the primary laws (contiguity, similarity). For example, Brown argued that the more frequently two ideas were contiguously experienced, the stronger would be the associative bond between them, which law of frequency is open to empirical test.

In the twentieth century, association of ideas transmuted into association of stimulus and response under the influence of behaviorism. The laws of association became the laws of learning; the law of frequency became the gradually rising learning curve; the law of similarity, the generalization gradient; and contiguity of ideas, contiguity of unconditioned and conditioned stimuli. More recently, eighteenth-century concepts have revived with cognitive psychology, which views memory as an associative network of ideas (e.g., in J. R. Anderson and G. H. Bower's *Human associative memory*) embedded in a complex information-processing system, rather like the old mental faculties.

The doctrine of association has not gone unchallenged. The Gestalt psychologists completely renounced it, and various psychologists have periodically attacked it. Nevertheless, association of ideas has proven the most durable of psychological concepts, having maintained an unbroken record of influence from Plato to cognitive science.

INFORMATION PROCESSING
MEMORY
THORNDIKE'S LAWS OF LEARNING

T. H. LEAHEY

ASTROLOGY

Astrology is the divining of the future of human affairs and other events on the earth from observations of the relative positions and movements of the sun, moon, and planets. Such practices date back to the earliest periods of recorded history. Early observations of the positions and movements of these celestial bodies formed the basis for the development of the present science of astronomy. While separation of objective observation and the art of prophecy occurred before the Christian era, astrologers continued to hold important positions in the courts of Europe up to the fourteenth and fifteenth centuries.

All varieties of astrological forecasting are based on a presumed relationship between patterns of the positions of the sun, moon, and planets at a specific time (e.g., the birth of an individual). This pattern is referred to as the individual's horoscope.

Although generally discredited by practically all scientifically trained persons, astrology still fascinates and is believed in by a substantial portion of the population. Many major newspapers publish a daily horoscope, and many books are published each year purporting to instruct the individual in maintaining the unity of his or her personal rhythm with that of the celestial cycles.

FREE WILL
MEDIEVAL THINKING
PSEUDOPSYCHOLOGY

E. L. KELLY

ATTENTION

Attention can be defined as a readiness on the part of the organism to perceive stimuli that surround it. Historically, the concept of attention has occupied a central position in the field of psychology. In the late nineteenth and early twentieth centuries, the functionalist and structuralist schools of psychology regarded attention as a core problem in the field, while emphasizing different aspects of it. The functionalists centered on the selective nature of attention as an active function of the organism based on its motivational state. Thus, while recognizing that attention can sometimes be passive or reflexive, they concentrated on its volitional aspects and on the fact that attention determines that which the organism experiences. The structuralists, however, saw attention as a state of consciousness that consists of increased concentration and results in sensory clearness. They, therefore, chose to study the conditions that tend to maximize the prominence or clearness of a sensation.

Gestalt psychologists, associationists, behaviorists, and psychoanalytic theorists tended to neglect attention in their postulations or to relegate it to a relatively unimportant role. Thus, little significant progress was made in the field of attention through the years when these various schools were vying for preeminence in psychology.

Modern Russian psychologists pioneered the study of the *orienting reflex* or *orienting response,* which consists of a cluster of physiological changes that occur in an organism as a response to changes in its surroundings and which are conceived as physiological correlates of attention. These correlates include changes in electrical brain activity, and in the electrical activity of the skin, pupillary dilation, tightening of the skeletal muscles, increased cerebral blood volume, and postural shifts. The orienting reflex results in improved reception of stimulation and increased learning. In the United States, the work initiated by the Russians has been pursued through intense study of individual differences in the strength of the orienting reflex and the concomitants of those differences.

The work of neurophysiologists and neuroanatomists such as Hernández-Péon and others has resulted in the identification of a diffuse structure in the brain stem, called the reticular formation, which appears to mediate the processes of arousal, attention, and stimulus selection. The study of the reticular formation, also known as the reticular activating system, and its connections to other important brain regulatory systems has provided a basis for physiological explanations of the influence of motivation, sleep, sensory input, learning, and endogenous, as well as exogenous, chemical substances on the process of attention.

ATTENTION SPAN
INFORMATION PROCESSING
PERCEPTION
SELECTIVE ATTENTION

S. P. URBINA

ATTENTION-DEFICIT HYPERACTIVITY DISORDER

Attention-deficit hyperactivity disorder (ADHD) is a complex and chronic disorder of brain, behavior, and development whose behavioral and cognitive consequences pervade multiple areas of functioning. Although the cause(s) of ADHD remain obscure, current research suggests that a primary component of the disorder involves the brain's inability to regulate itself appropriately (which involves both the initiation and inhibition of behavior and activity) on an ongoing basis and under a range of normally occurring circumstances and conditions. Individuals with ADHD experience a wide range of behavioral, cognitive, and interpersonal difficulties that interfere with their everyday functioning and well-being. The extent to which these difficulties are manifested are influenced by other factors such as what the individual is asked to do (or not to do), for how long, and the prevailing environmental conditions. Individuals with ADHD can behave and perform normally in many circumstances and under a variety of conditions but lack the ability to do so consistently over extended periods of time. Instead, they rely on others to provide them with the necessary external (behavioral) and internal (medication) mechanisms by which they regulate their behavior.

ETIOLOGY

Speculations concerning the cause or causes of ADHD range from brain-based mechanisms to environmental toxins. Although definitive answers remain elusive, recent discoveries suggest several possible factors. Neurochemical abnormalities, particularly those involving the monoamines—comprising the catecholamines (dopamine and norepinephrine) and the indoleamine serotonin—have been implicated as potential contributing factors. The evidence to date remains speculative, but suggests a possible selective deficiency in the availability of dopamine and/or norepinephrine.

More promising results have emerged in three recent studies. Lou, using single-photon-emission computed tomography to measure cerebral blood flow, reported hypoperfusion and low neural activity in the striatal and orbital prefrontal regions of children with ADHD compared with controls, whereas the primary sensory and sensorimotor regions were hyperperfused. Studies by Satterfield, using EEG brain electrical activity mapping (BEAM) techniques, have been relatively consistent with Lou's findings in showing abnormality in information processing in the frontal lobes of children with ADHD. Finally, Zametkin et al., in studying adults who had been hyperactive since childhood, reported reduced glucose metabolism in various areas of the brain, particularly the premotor and superior prefrontal regions—areas known to be associated with the regulation of attention, motor activity, and information processing. Collectively, these findings implicate a central nervous system mechanism in the development of ADHD, most likely involving connections between the prefrontal areas and the limbic system.

DIAGNOSING ADHD

Diagnosing ADHD in children is currently a cumbersome and complex task for which few professionals are adequately trained. A comprehensive clinical workup usually involves (a) a structured or semistructured clinical interview with the child's parents; (b) detailed historical information concerning the child's prenatal, perinatal, and postnatal development; accomplishment of developmental milestones; and medical, education, and behavioral history; (c) the use of broad- and narrow-band standardized behavioral rating scales obtained from both the child's teacher(s) and parents; and (d) direct observations of the child while interacting in the classroom or in a clinic-based simulated classroom. Several computerized, neurocognitive instruments have also been shown to be helpful to the diagnostic process, but their specific usefulness in terms of differential diagnosis remains unproven at present.

TREATMENT REGIMENS FOR CHILDREN WITH ADHD

Current treatment regimens for children with ADHD must be considered as "maintenance" therapies at present, as no single or combined treatment renders the child normalized once withdrawn. Nevertheless, a variety of new behavioral approaches have cropped up in the last few years. Although psychostimulants remain the first-line defense, behavioral and pharmacological approaches are often combined to produce maximum benefit for the child. The impact of these new approaches on the clinical status of children with ADHD will not be known for several years, and one can only hope that they will have a greater impact than has been described in recent long-term outcome studies.

ACADEMIC UNDERACHIEVEMENT
BEHAVIORAL GENETICS
EARLY CHILDHOOD EDUCATION
DIAGNOSIS
STRESS CONSEQUENCES

M. Rapport

ATTENTION SPAN

Attention span is the length of time a subject can keep an object or topic under consideration. Put another way, it is the length of time an object or topic can be kept "in focus." Novelty, or changes, seems to be the prime factor in capturing and holding attention. Attention rapidly wanes in a fixed, unchanging stimulus situation, but is immediately aroused with change or novelty. Attention span refers to the length of time the organism can find material of interest in the situation. This will be partly influenced by the amount and degree of distractive stimulation present. Genetic factors will also be significant, as a "pointer" has a prolonged attention span toward specific "targets." Personality factors will also be significant, in terms of what will be of interest to the subject. The more elements of interest in the stimulus situation, the greater the attention span is apt to be.

A major problem in educational practice is represented by differences in expectations by adults of children's "staying power" in terms of their attention span and children's actual capacities to attend.

ABSTRACT INTELLIGENCE
FATIGUE

W. E. Gregory

ATTITUDE MEASUREMENT

In many areas of psychological test construction (e.g., personality, ability, or intelligence testing), the aim is to produce a single, thoroughly validated test that will become widely adopted by the field. The area of attitude measurement has not followed that tradition. Although several compendia of validated scales are available, researchers often prefer to devise new scales for each new research project. One reason for this difference in approach is that there are a near infinite number of attitudes, and ones of potential interest seem to change each year. Second, attitude is such a robust human characteristic that different measures of the same attitude—even when the scales are produced by different researchers—usually intercorrelate very highly.

THEORETICAL CONSIDERATIONS

When constructing or selecting an attitude measure, one must specify (a) the attitude object, (b) the conceptual attributes of the attitude construct relevant to the aims of the research, and (c) the response domain.

One can measure attitudes toward any of a variety of behaviors, ideas, concepts, or entities. An attitude may be very specific and concrete (attitudes toward a specific person or movie), may refer to a social category (Irish or gamblers), or be quite broad and abstract (war or conservatism).

Prior to developing or selecting a measure of attitude, it is necessary to define what is meant by the concept. Most authorities view an attitude as a hypothetical construct, the most prominent attribute, which is its evaluative character.

Attitudes have other attributes that the researcher may wish to measure. Attitude-relevant beliefs may vary, for example, in their extensiveness, consistency, or dimensionality. Attitudes may also vary in the extent to which they are related to the person's central values and basic personal needs. This may produce differences in the level of ego involvement.

As a hypothetical construct, attitude is not available for direct observation. Its existence is revealed by its effects on the person's observable responses. Historically, attitude researchers have identified three categories of response. *Affective responses* refer to the feelings and physiological reactions one has to the attitude object. *Cognitive responses* include the information, beliefs, and inferences made about the object. *Conative responses* refer to the behaviors one initiates—or intends to initiate—in regard to the attitude object.

PRACTICAL CONSIDERATIONS

Research goals will dictate the degree of *structure* used in the measurement instrument. For example, in the most unstructured and open-ended format, the person might be asked, "What do you think of X?" In contrast, in the most structured format, the person is presented with a set of alternatives in multiple-choice format. If the research is exploratory in nature, the open format is often preferable. It will provide more information about subjects' thoughts, often identifying issues the researcher had not previously considered. In addition, the unstructured format provides subjects with greater freedom of expression, thus often enhancing rapport. Structured formats, however, are much easier to score, provide less opportunity for distortion in coding, focus responses more directly on the issues of primary concern, and may be administered to larger groups of people. Thus, when the researcher has clearly identified the particular feelings, beliefs, and behaviors of interest, the closed format is generally preferable.

Most research uses of attitude scales assume that the person is aware of his or her attitude and is also willing to fully and accurately convey it. For many attitude issues and research settings, this assumption is reasonably accurate.

Unobtrusive techniques are designed to prevent persons from being aware that they are being formally observed in any way. For example, the seating distance between two persons may provide an index of their attitudes toward each other, while hair or dress style may provide an index of political conservatism, and carpet wear may reflect public liking for an art exhibit.

When *indirect techniques* are used, persons are usually aware that they are being evaluated. However, they should not be aware that it is their attitude that is of interest to the test giver. Instead, they are under the assumption that the evaluator is interested in some other aspect of their behavior such as logical thinking ability, moral judgments, or perceptual abilities. For example, attitudes have been indirectly assessed through errors in tests of factual knowledge and logical thinking. This approach is based on the assumption that people, when they err, perceive those conclusions with which they agree as being based in fact or logically derived, and conversely for those with which they disagree. In the case of racial and ethnic attitudes, the testees can be asked to make judgments of the personality, motives, or intelligence of the target group. This is done in the guise of evaluating the testees' ability to make accurate character judgments.

Finally, one must consider the limitations of time and resources available for scale construction, administration, and scoring. If time is in short supply, self-report techniques involving few items in a structured format are generally preferable. Such techniques require less time both for administration and for scoring. Most structured scales can also be administered in large groups; whereas indirect, unobtrusive, or physiological measures often cannot. In addition, self-report measures are often cheaper and do not require the complex materials sometimes necessary for other methods.

Both unobtrusive and indirect measures are believed to be less susceptible to efforts to conceal an attitude or to convey only socially desirable beliefs than are the more typical direct self-report techniques. This is because people are either unaware of being tested or are focusing on other dimensions of evaluation (e.g., abilities). While this sort of deception may make it possible for the researcher to more accurately index the attitudes of interest, it is important to remember that this is being done without the person's informed consent. In such cases, every consideration must be given to the person's right to privacy. Anonymity should be maintained in any dissemination of results.

MEASURING THE UNOBSERVABLE

Defining attitude as a hypothetical (and therefore unobservable) construct seems to directly contradict the view that attitude can be measured on the basis of observable responses. Two strategies have been used to deal with this dilemma. A *single measure* (e.g., the single-item self-rating) of attitude is adopted, but extensive background research is done to learn about that measure's potential biases and the circumstances under which these lead to distortions. The investigator either adjusts the circumstances of the scale's uses or adds control conditions to the study that minimize or eliminate the contribution of scale bias. The *multiple operationism strategy* involves measuring attitude in two or more operationally distinct ways. For example, separate measures might be constructed for the affective, cognitive, and conative categories of attitudinal response. The separate indices would then be combined into one overall measure of attitude. This strategy assumes that the bias in any one index will be canceled out by opposite biases in the other indices.

ATTITUDES
ATTITUDE THEORY
SCALING

D. Davis
T. Ostrom

ATTITUDE THEORY

Positive and negative attitudes are shown by people of all ages and from all cultures. This ubiquity of attitudes has long been a source of fascination to social theorists.

From its beginnings in the early years of this century, social psychology was concerned with studying attitudes. The term has encompassed a variety of psychological and behavioral dispositions. People can have an "expectant attitude" (like a foot racer waiting for the starting gun), a "disgruntled attitude" (as when our request for a salary raise is denied), a "cooperative attitude" (as when we are asked for help), or an "authoritarian attitude" (in relation to out-groups and interpersonal relations).

The earliest theoretical efforts were directed toward devising sets of categories into which different attitudes could be classified. A number of dichotomies were proposed for distinguishing between fundamental "types" of attitudes, including "mental/physical," "voluntary/nonvoluntary," and "conscious/unconscious." Discussions of the attitude concept during the 1930s were dominated by such distinctions.

This diversity in usage of "attitude" and these categorical distinctions are still found in nontechnical discussions of attitudes. Since the 1930s, however, the technical usage has employed a much more restricted definition. The attitude concept is distinguished from other dispositions such as situation-specific expectancies (e.g., set), personality characteristics (e.g., authoritarianism), traits (e.g., cooperativeness), or moods (e.g., happiness).

CONCEPTUAL PROPERTIES OF AN ATTITUDE

The most prominent feature of an attitude is its evaluative character, the disposition to respond toward an "object" in a positive or negative manner. Attitudes thus can range from very favorable to very unfavorable on an evaluative continuum.

Theory attempts to relate this hypothetical construct to observables. Attitude theorists assume that attitudes are *acquired through experience*. One important enterprise is to establish antecedents of attitude formation and change. All theorists assume that attitudes *exert a directive influence* on overt responses. Thus, a second descriptive enterprise now is to determine the consequences of attitude; a fully comprehensive theory of attitudes would provide an understanding of both antecedents and consequences.

Approaches to the development of attitude theory focus on the *processes* through which attitudes develop and affect our lives. These theories draw on the various psychological processes that have been studied in the areas of reinforcement and learning, cognition and memory, and needs and motivation. To a lesser extent, attitude theories may also draw on work by perceptual, physiological, and genetic researchers. The aim of this "process" approach is to develop a theory transportable across all attitude objects and across all settings in which attitudes are affected or expressed. Consequently, one does not find theories specific to "racial attitudes," "peer group influences," or "television advertisements." A single theory anchored in basic psychological processes should accommodate all such specific concerns.

ANTECEDENTS

Attitude researchers have invested far more effort in studying the antecedents of attitudes than the consequences. Perhaps the widespread belief in the relevance of attitudes to social behavior has inspired greater interest in how attitudes can be changed (and therefore manipulated) to improve society. An extensive array of antecedent variables have been explored, most of which relate to the effects of persuasive communications. The communication process can be divided into five components: *source* (e.g., communicator credibility), *message* (e.g., use of fear appeals), *channel* (e.g., direct experience vs. mass media), *receiver* (e.g., intelligence of the audience), and *destination* (e.g., temporal decay of induced change).

A comprehensive attitude theory should be able to explain findings in all these areas. Unfortunately, no single, unifying theory of attitude is accepted by all researchers in the field. Textbooks on attitude theory describe well over 30 distinct theoretical formulations. Four separate classes of attitude theory can be identified. They have in common the view that attitudes can be represented as an evaluative disposition falling somewhere on a pro-to-anti continuum. They differ, however, in the extent to which supplementary features are integral to the hypothetical construct.

The undifferentiated view defines attitude as being nothing more or less than an *evaluative disposition*. Attitude is an unelaborated concept referring only to a location on the evaluative continuum. Past experiences, informational influences, reinforcements, and motivational pressures all contribute to the attitude at the time they occur. The resulting attitude is the cumulative accretion of those past events. Each life experience makes its contribution at the time of occurrence and thereafter remains irrelevant to the status of the attitude. Theories that draw heavily on principles of classical conditioning and reinforcement often adopt this undifferentiated approach. So, too, do theories that view attitudes as the result of sequential information integration processes or concept formation processes.

The second category of theory views attitude as the *set of beliefs* the person holds about the attitude object. In this case, the basic elements of an attitude are the individual beliefs or cognitions. The overall evaluative disposition is but one of several attributes that characterize the attitude. The evaluative disposition is the resultant of all those beliefs that are salient at the time the observed response is initiated. In this view of attitude, there is no single "true" evaluative disposition, only an average that emerges over a variety of responses. Each response derives from a different sample of the belief set; evaluative consistency emerges because all samples are taken from the same population of beliefs.

A third point of view refers to the *set of motivational forces* operating on the person that are relevant to the attitude object. The basic elements of an attitude consist of the values, needs, drives, motives, and personality dispositions of the person. Typically, this set contains only the more enduring (rather than situationally determined) motivational dispositions. This view is sometimes referred to as the functional approach, since attitudes (their formation and change) are seen as functionally satisfying the person's more basic motivational needs.

A wide variety of these attitude-relevant functions have been identified. Attitudes can serve an *instrumentality* function, in which they are used to obtain rewards and avoid punishments in our social world. People often espouse attitudes as a way of managing the impressions others form of them. Attitudes can serve a *value-maintenance function,* in which they are viewed as deriving from (and providing sustenance to) more basic values like "equality" and "financial security." Attitudes can serve a *knowledge* function, helping us deal effectively with the complex and overwhelming flow of information encountered in life. Attitudes allow us to simplify this information by reducing it to categories specific to each attitude object and then attaching a positive or negative response disposition to the category.

Attitudes can serve a *consistency* function, since people need to view themselves as reasonable and consistent in their attitudes and beliefs; awareness of inconsistencies is uncomfortable and motivates the person to restore cognitive equilibrium. Attitudes can serve a *uniqueness* function, letting people develop attitudes that distinguish them from others in their social group. Attitudes can serve an *ego-defensive* function, defending the person against unflattering self-truths deriving from antisocial impulses and inner conflicts, and from sources of information external to the self. Attitudes can serve a *reactance* function: Because people resist threats to their freedom to think and feel as they choose, they adopt attitudes directly opposite to those advocated by a coercive source.

The evaluative characteristic of attitudes operates in the service of these motives: Positive attitudes emerge only if basic motivational needs are satisfied by positive responses toward the attitude object. The observed attitudinal response will be determined by whatever set of motives is dominant at the time of the response. Thus, like the "set of beliefs" conception, the "set of motives" view assumes there is no single "true" attitude; consistency over responses derives from the stability of the person's underlying motive structure.

The fourth category of attitude theory takes the position that *attitudes are nonexistent.* Whereas other theorists agree that attitudes are unobservable, this category of theorist believes them to be social fictions. Being nonexistent, attitudes should not be given the scientific status of a hypothetical construct. These theorists readily acknowledge that people can and do describe themselves as possessing attitudes. However, they maintain that this does not mean that a concept of attitude must be invoked to explain these responses. Instead, it is argued that self-reports of attitudes are the result of "self-perception" processes in which people review their own past behaviors relevant to the attitude object and induce what their attitude must be.

CONSEQUENCES

The ideal attitude theory should encompass both antecedents and consequences, but most theoretical efforts have focused on the antecedents. Regarding consequences, theories would need to show how an attitude combines with other theoretical variables to affect the particular response system being observed. Instead, most theories are content with the unelaborated assertion that an attitude will have a directive influence (in a positive or negative direction) on the observed response. Rarely does a theory designate what categories of overt response should and should not be affected, nor do they usually indicate the circumstances under which attitudes exert their influence.

Two kinds of consequences have received special attention. Most reasearchers who have developed theories of antecedents have used verbal measures of attitude. They have accepted the premise that people can accurately describe their own beliefs and attitudes. Some researchers, however, have examined the circumstances under which such verbal reports do and do not accurately reflect the underlying attitude. The results of this response bias research have been used primarily to improve the research methods used in testing predictions regarding the antecedents of attitudes.

A great deal of work has been done on how attitudes affect behaviors. Some important factors are whether the attitude was formed on the basis of direct experience with the attitude object, and how salient the attitude is at the time of the behavior. Some authorities have argued that overall attitude is only marginally relevant to specific actions. More important is the attitude toward the act itself, since that attitude incorporates feelings about the attitude object, the type of behavior, and the temporal-social context in which the behavior is elicited.

When the hypothetical construct includes more than just an evaluative disposition (as with the "set of beliefs" and "set of motives" approaches), other properties of attitudes also provide a conceptual basis for studying consequences. For example, internally consistent attitudes have a stronger effect on behavior than do inconsistent ones. Organized belief sets should have the same effects as cognitive schemas. Ego-involved attitudes (i.e., those closely linked to central values) are viewed as affecting responses more strongly than less personally relevant attitudes.

Several attitudinal phenomena are not yet well understood by attitude theorists. Little is known about the sudden and intense emotional arousal that attitudes sometimes produce. Little is known about how attitudes lead people to make enormous personal sacrifices in behalf of their loved ones and ideals. Little is known about the massively dramatic reversals in attitude that sometimes occur (as in the case of emotional trauma, religious conversion, and love at first sight). Although enormous strides in understanding attitudes have been made since the early years of this century, these and other unresolved issues indicate that fundamental questions are still unanswered.

ATTITUDE MEASUREMENT
PERSONALITY
SELECTIVE ATTENTION
SOCIAL COGNITION

T. OSTROM

ATTITUDES

Throughout the history of social psychology, attitude has played a central role in the explanation of social behavior. It is usually defined as a disposition to respond favorably or unfavorably to an object, person, institution, or event. People can hold attitudes of varying degrees of favorability toward themselves and toward any discriminable aspect of their environment. Widely shared, positive attitudes toward relatively abstract goals (freedom, honesty, security) are known as values.

Attitude is considered a hypothetical construct; being unobservable, it must be inferred from measurable responses that reflect positive or negative evaluations of the attitude object. Three categories of responses are distinguished, following a classification that goes back at least to Plato: Attitudes can be inferred from *cognitive responses* or beliefs (reflecting the individual's perception of, and information about, the attitude object); *affective responses* (evaluations of, and feelings toward, the object); and *conative responses* (behavioral intentions, tendencies, and actions with respect to the object).

Although attitudes are sometimes viewed as containing all three response classes or components, most social psychologists identify and define attitudes in terms of affect or evaluation.

ATTITUDE FORMATION

Early attempts to identify the origins of attitudes focused on the needs or functions that attitudes may serve. Thus, attitudes were assumed to have instrumental or utilitarian functions (helping people attain rewards and avoid punishments); knowledge functions (organizing and simplifying people's experiences); expressive functions (enabling emotional release); and ego-defensive functions (protecting and enhancing the self). Although it generated considerable interest, the functional approach to attitudes has been of limited practical value. Its limitations can be traced in part to a built-in circularity of reasoning: We infer attitude-related needs from the attitudes people are known to hold, and we then use these inferred needs to explain the observed attitudes.

Defining attitude as an implicit, evaluative response to a stimulus, behaviorally oriented social psychologists have used principles of classical conditioning to describe and explain attitude formation. Repeated and systematic association between the attitude object (conditioned stimulus) and a positively or negatively valued event (unconditioned stimulus) is assumed to produce a favorable or unfavorable affective reaction (attitude) to the object.

A general trend toward cognitive or information-processing explanations of social behavior has brought a concomitant decline in the importance accorded to needs and automatic conditioning processes. Instead, stress is now placed on the role of information as a basis of attitude formation. According to this view, beliefs—representing people's subjective knowledge about themselves and their world—are the primary determinants of attitudes. Each belief links the attitude object to a positively or negatively valued attribute: Thus smoking (the object) causes lung cancer (the attribute). Generally speaking, the greater the number of beliefs that associate the object with positive attributes, and the smaller the number of beliefs that associate it with negative attributes, the more favorable is the resultant attitude toward the object. More precise formulations are provided by expectancy value or expected utility models of attitude. According to these models, the value or utility of each attribute contributes to the attitude in direct proportion to the person's subjective probability (strength of belief) that the object has the attribute in question. The sum or average of these weighted attribute utilities is said to determine the overall attitude toward the object.

ORIGINS OF BELIEFS

The assumption that attitudes have an informational foundation ties the question of attitude formation to the origins of our beliefs about ourselves and about our social environment.

One important source of information about objects, people, and events is direct experience. Thus one may learn that cigarette smoking produces unpleasant odors, that a certain television program portrayed a great deal of violence, or that overweight reduces physical stamina. Based on personal experience, beliefs of this kind tend to be held with great confidence and to resist change. Often, they reflect reality quite accurately. Over time, however, many factors tend to distort memory for events and thus reduce the accuracy of beliefs based on direct experience. As a general rule, these distortions serve to increase the internal consistency and coherence of remembered events.

There are limits to the number and kinds of beliefs that can be formed by way of direct experience. Much of our information is acquired through conversation with other people or is communicated to us by a variety of sources such as television, radio, newspapers, and books. Many factors are found to influence acceptance of such second-hand information and its incorporation into the receiver's belief system. First and foremost is the coherence and persuasive power of the information provided in the communication. Additional factors include credibility of the source, type of appeal (e.g., appeals based on fear or humor), and personality characteristics of the receiver.

Information obtained by means of direct experience or verbal communication can provide the basis for a variety of inferences. Many of our beliefs are the result of such inference processes. For example, people form far-ranging impressions of another person on the basis of one or two items of information about that person. An individual described as responsible tends also to be viewed as persevering, honest, tidy, careful, and so on. These inferences are said to follow from intuitive or implicit theories of personality.

ATTITUDES AND BEHAVIOR

From its inception, the attitude concept has been invoked to explain social behavior. Since attitudes are considered behavioral dispositions, it is natural to assume that they direct, and in some sense determine, social action. Racial prejudice (negative attitudes toward racial or ethnic groups) is blamed for discriminatory behavior, political actions are traced to liberal or conservative attitudes, and many behaviors related to sex and the family are explained by reference to religiosity. As a general rule, positive attitudes are expected to produce favorable behaviors toward the attitude object, while negative attitudes are expected to produce unfavorable behaviors.

Casual observation appears to support the idea of a close association between attitudes and behavior. In fact, the assumption that attitudes can be used to predict and explain social actions went largely unchallenged until the late 1960s. By that time, however, there was growing evidence that a strong relation between verbal expressions of attitude and overt behavior could not be taken for granted. Controlled studies failed to find relations between racial attitudes and such actions as accepting members of the racial group in a hotel or restaurant, conforming with their views or behaviors, or extending an invitation to members of that group. Among many other negative findings, it was reported that attitudes toward cheating failed to predict actual cheating behavior; that attitudes toward another person were unrelated to cooperation or competition with that person; and that work-related attitudes had little to do with absenteeism, tardiness, or turnover.

Under the weight of this negative evidence, social psychologists were forced to reexamine the nature of attitude and its relation to social behavior. Increased understanding resulted from renewed recognition that attitude is an unobservable, hypothetical construct that must be inferred from measurable responses to the attitude object.

Single behaviors, however, can be predicted from attitudes toward the behaviors themselves—for example, attitudes toward smoking marijuana (rather than global attitudes toward the counterculture), attitudes toward attending church services (as opposed to attitudes toward the church), or attitudes toward donating blood (instead of global attitudes concerning altruism). There is growing evidence, however, that response tendencies reflected in attitudes toward specified actions can change as a result of situational demands or unanticipated events. Moreover, individuals are found to vary in their susceptibility to the influence of such external factors. Thus, while attitudes toward behaviors tend to produce corresponding behavioral intentions, the extent to which these intentions are actually carried out is moderated by situational factors and individual difference variables. Nevertheless, barring unforeseen events, behavioral attitudes and intentions are usually found to be quite accurate predictors of subsequent actions.

ATTITUDE MEASUREMENT
INTERPERSONAL PERCEPTIONS
STEREOTYPING

I. Ajzen

A-TYPE PERSONALITY

Research on the A-type, coronary-prone personality is probably the most comprehensive investigation ever conducted into how a person's mental and behavioral characteristics can influence his or her likelihood of devel-

oping a life-threatening physical ailment. The risk factors frequently cited by physicians as contributing to an individual's susceptibility to coronary heart disease (CHD) are fat intake, cigarette smoking, lack of exercise, and various physiological indicators. M. Friedman and R. H. Rosenman reported, however, that these factors often do not satisfactorily account for differences in the prevalence of CHD between various groups— American men and women, for example. These cardiologists described a pattern of behavior that made a contribution to coronary risk somewhat independent of the foregoing factors. The pattern, subsequently elaborated and defined by the development of standardized interview procedures and questionnaires, was called Type A personality. It is "characterized by attributes such as hard-driving effort, striving for achievement, competitiveness, aggressivity, haste, impatience, restlessness, alertness, uneven bursts of amplitude in speech, and hurried motor movement. Individuals with this pattern are usually conscientiously committed to their occupation, and whatever its level, often have achieved success in it." The contrasting pattern, defined as a relative absence of Type A behaviors, is called Type B.

In a longitudinal study begun in 1963, nearly 3000 men initially showing no evidence of CHD were followed up over 8 and a half years. It was found that of the 257 men who developed coronary disease, more than twice as many were Type A as were Type B. The association between Type A characteristics and CHD remained significant even after other risk factors—blood pressure, serum cholesterol levels, cigarette smoking, and so forth—were statistically controlled for.

The results of laboratory research have suggested that Type As perceive time to be passing more rapidly than do Type Bs and, perhaps for this reason, work at a near-maximum pace even when there is no specified deadline. Type As seem better able than Type Bs to focus their attention on a primary task; as a result, their performance may actually improve when they are simultaneously exposed to a secondary, distracting task. It has been suggested that the Type A person's initial response to feedback that he or she is *not* coping successfully with a problem-solving task, is to intensify his or her efforts but also to show a collapse of effective coping—called "learned helplessness"—when failure feedback is very salient or prolonged.

Studies using physiological indicators of stress have typically found no differences in resting levels between As and Bs, but a tendency for As to outstrip Bs in increases in heart rate or blood pressure when presented with a difficult or competitive task. Type As may also be more stressed than Bs by *under*stimulation, as indicated by greater secretion of adrenalin during an absence of involving tasks. While the physiological data are complex and not entirely consistent, it has been proposed that the greater variability in autonomic reactivity shown by Type As may be a causative element in their greater susceptibility to CHD.

Evidence concerning sex differences suggests that Type A personalities appear less frequently among women than men.

B-TYPE PERSONALITY
HOMEOSTASIS
LEARNED HELPLESSNESS
PSYCHOSOMATIC DISORDERS

W. Samuel

AUDIOMETRY

Accurate measurement of hearing, the primary concern of audiometry, has become possible as a result of the application of psychophysical methods permitting behavioral precision, and the development of electronic instruments permitting accurate, stable, replicable, and precise stimulus specification. Measurement of human hearing typically utilizes an oscillator (e.g., electron tube or transistor), amplifier, calibrated headphones, and measuring devices (e.g., a voltmeter for signal amplitude and a frequency counter for tone frequency determinations). In addition, a quiet environment, such as is provided by a sound-attenuating acoustic booth, is necessary for threshold measurement.

The frequency range of normal human hearing is from approximately 20 Hz (cycles per second) to 20,000 Hz, with sensitivity varying over this range. Maximal sensitivity occurs between 1000 and 4000 Hz with a minimum absolute pressure threshold of 20 micronewtons per square meter (or, in older terminology, 0.0002 dyne/cm^2).

Clinical (or medical) audiology takes this sensitivity variation into account when evaluating heating for diagnostic purposes. By using clinical audiometers, which produce a standard set of preadjusted frequencies at discrete amplitude steps, and abbreviated psychophysical methods, it is possible to get hearing measures for each ear. These are plotted as an audiogram, which shows normal hearing (as a function of frequency) as a horizontal line near the top ("audiometric zero"), and the hearing level of the examinee as points above or below this line. Defective hearing is indicated by points far below the horizontal line.

AUDITORY DISCRIMINATION
AUDITORY DISORDERS
AUDITORY PERCEPTION
EAR

G. H. ROBINSON

AUDITORY DISCRIMINATION

Sound waves have duration and can be described in three physical characteristics: frequency, intensity, and phase. The auditory system with its anatomic and neurophysiological functions not only detects acoustic stimuli by means of these characteristics, but can analyze their suprathreshold differences as a basis for discriminating between stimuli.

Within the typical range of normal hearing, approximately 20 to 20,000 Hz, all frequencies are not equally audible in quiet. Frequencies in the region of 1000 to 2000 Hz require less energy to be heard; as frequencies depart from this region, there is a slight increase in threshold sound pressure level (SPL) toward the upper end of the audible range, but a marked increase for frequencies approaching the lower end.

When the frequency of a pure tone is below 1000 Hz, absolute changes as small as 3 Hz can be discriminated; above 1000 Hz, absolute changes as small as 0.2 to 0.3% of the test frequency can be reported accurately. The smallest absolute change in frequency that can be discriminated is called the just noticeable difference (jnd or Δf). This value can be expressed in terms of a relative frequency change, $\Delta f/f$, where f is the frequency of the test tone. Above 1000 Hz, $\Delta f/f$ (the Weber ratio) remains constant at approximately 0.003; below 1000 Hz, the Weber ratio increases as frequency decreases. Thus the ear is less sensitive to changes in low frequency tones. Frequency discrimination improves as the intensity of the test tone is increased above threshold, with enormous decrements in the jnd above 2000 Hz. There are at least 1500 jnds in frequency between the lowest and highest audible tones, given SPL as a parameter.

Intensity discrimination of two tones depends on the frequency and the intensity of the test tones. The size of the jnd in intensity (ΔI) is minimal in the frequency region of greatest auditory sensitivity, approximately 2000 Hz. As the frequency departs above and below this region, the value of ΔI gradually increases, particularly for lower frequencies. With frequency held constant, AI decreases markedly as the intensity of the test tone is increased above threshold. The Weber ratio ($\Delta I/I$) is not constant, but varies between 1/20 for 2500 Hz at 100 dB above threshold and 7.5 for 35 Hz at 5 dB above threshold.

For 1000 Hz and an interaural phase difference (θ) of 45°, a change ($\Delta\theta$) of approximately 3° can be detected. For frequencies up to 900 Hz, $\Delta\theta$ remains constant, but as frequency increases above 1000 Hz and θ changes from 0° to 180° or from 360° to 180°, the value of $\Delta\theta$ increases to approximately 30° for 2000 Hz.

For time (t), the Weber ratio ($\Delta t/t$) is not constant, but declines as the duration of the standard signal is lengthened. For tones with t values from 0.4 msec to 4 msec, the Weber ratio decreases rapidly from 2.0 to 0.4; as the standard varies from 4.0 msec to 400 msec, the Weber ratio continues to decline, but less markedly. If the ability to make temporal judgments is determined by presenting silent intervals between two auditory stimuli, a pair of clicks presented monaurally can be heard as double for intervals as small as 3 to 6 msec, as shown by S. M. Abel.

Volume refers to the judged size of a sound (not loudness) and depends on frequency and intensity. Low-frequency tones are judged as big; high-frequency tones, as small. As intensity is increased, the volume of low frequencies increases slowly, but that of high-frequency tones changes more rapidly. At very high intensity levels, all frequencies appear equal in volume.

Tones can be judged in terms of density independently of their pitch, loudness, and volume. Density refers to the judged compactness or hardness of a sound. Loud high-frequency tones are judged to be denser than softer low-frequency tones.

The quality of pure tones that resembles vowels is termed vocality. For example, a tone of 263 Hz is judged to sound like *u* in true; 1053 Hz has the quality of *a* as in father; and 4200 Hz is judged as *i* in machine.

AUDITORY DISORDERS
AUDITORY LOCALIZATION
AUDITORY PERCEPTION
EAR

J. F. CORSO

AUDITORY DISORDERS

Auditory disorders may consist of hearing loss, otorrhea, pain, and tinnitus.

Conductive Hearing Loss

This type occurs when there is a disease or obstruction in the auditory conductive mechanism: the external auditory canal, the tympanic membrane, or the middle ear space and structures. A conductive loss is evidenced in an ear that shows a greater than 10 dB difference in pure tone air and bone conduction audiograms averaged over frequencies in the speech range; however, speech discrimination is normal.

Sensorineural Hearing Loss

The designation "sensorineural" represents two different sites of lesions in the auditory system. A sensory loss is produced by damage, degeneration, or developmental failure of hair cells in the organ of Corti or any structure within the cochlear duct. A neural loss is produced by similar deficiencies central to the cochlear duct, including the spiral ganglion, the cochlear nucleus, and the acoustic portion of the VIIIth cranial nerve. Unless a definite site of lesion is determined by specific diagnostic tests for a given hearing loss, the term sensorineural is used to cover both possibilities.

Progressive hearing loss occurs primarily with aging and is termed presbycusis. As shown by J. F. Corso in *Aging sensory systems and perception*, presbycusis may begin in the early 30s and affects both ears similarly. For frequencies above approximately 1000 Hz, men have poorer hearing for pure tones than women, age held constant; below approximately 500 Hz, women have poorer hearing. Four subclasses of presbycusis have been identified by Gacek and Schuknecht (1969); these involve degeneration or disorders in the sensory or neural structures of the cochlea, or in its associated mechanical and metabolic processes.

A second etiological factor in progressive hearing loss is exposure to excessive noise over long time periods, as in a work environment. Noise-induced hearing loss affects mostly the frequencies in the region of 4000 Hz. However, continued noise exposure gradually deepens and widens the audiogram "notch," so that hearing sensitivity becomes progressively worse and extends to frequencies in the speech range—below 4000 Hz. Thus speech discrimination is impaired, with poor speech understanding especially in noisy environments.

Ménière's disease, syphilis, tumors of the VIIIth cranial nerve, and hereditary factors may produce progressive sensorineural hearing losses of the unilateral or bilateral type. The degree of impairment in speech discrimination depends on the severity of the prevalent disorder.

Nonprogressive hearing loss of the sensorineural type may be associated with congenital factors including maternal rubella, family history of early deafness, parental blood incompatability, prematurity, and ear infections. Audiological tests usually show bilateral hearing loss and reduced speech discrimination.

A mixed hearing loss has a conductive and a sensorineural component. Thus, both air and bone conduction thresholds are depressed. Ordinarily this type of loss is associated with chronic otitis media or otosclerosis. In either case, speech discrimination may be reduced and hearing loss is progressive.

Otorrhea is defined as the drainage of fluid from the external auditory canal and may be the presenting symptom of ear disease. Diseases can occur in the external auditory canal or the middle ear and may be acute or chronic. The hearing loss related to acute otitis media is usually mild to moderate, and conductive in type. When chronic otitis media establishes itself, the hearing loss is typically conductive and progressive, and may be quite severe. If complications occur involving the labyrinth, an associated sensorineural hearing loss may occur.

TINNITUS

Tinnitus is the hearing of sounds within a person's head. In objective tinnitus the sound originates within the individual and may be heard by an examiner; in subjective tinnitus the sound is heard only by the individual. Tinnitus may develop suddenly or slowly, over several hours or days; it may be present constantly or intermittently; it may be unilateral, bilateral, or central in localization. The sound may be heard as loud or soft and may be high or low in pitch. The temporal pattern of the auditory experience may be pulsatile with the heartbeat, steady, clicking, or blowing with respiration. Tinnitus is a typical concomitant of sensorineural hearing loss; however, it may be associated with a vast number of other etiological factors, such as external otitis, otitis media, Eustachian tube dysfunction, vascular anomalies, hypertension, and muscular spasms.

AUDITORY DISCRIMINATION
AUDITORY LOCALIZATION
AUDITORY PERCEPTION
EAR

J. F. CORSO

AUDITORY LOCALIZATION

Auditory localization refers to the ability of a listener to determine the spatial position of a sound source, in terms of direction and distance.

This ability depends primarily on interaural differences in sound input due to the interposition of the head and the distance between the two ears.

CUES FOR DIRECTION

The acoustic pathway between the ears of an average person is approximately 0.75 feet. Since sound travels through air at approximately 1100 feet/second, a sound directly from the right will arrive at the right ear about 0.7 msec sooner than the left and is localized to the right. Interaural time differences as small as 0.01 msec can be detected by a normal listener. The temporal difference at the two ears varies as a function of direction of the sound source. When the sound source is directly in front of, above, or behind the listener, the interaural time difference is zero, so that head movements must be initiated to provide the necessary cues for sound localization.

Two factors produce interaural intensity differences as a directional cue: (a) sound traveling in air decreases in intensity according to the inverse square law, so that sounds are louder in the ear nearer to the sound source than in the other, because of the distance around the head; (b) the head acts as a sound barrier, leaving the ear away from the sound source in an acoustical shadow.

When a sound source is located anywhere in the median plan of the body, binaural cues are equalized and accurate localization depends on the generation of interaural differences by head movement. Movements around a vertical axis lead to binaural differences for sources located ahead or behind the listener, but not for sources above or below. Tilting the head assists localization for sources above or below, but not in front or in back. Head movements produce simultaneous changes in the cues for sound localization: interaural intensity differences, time relations, and phase.

Auditory cues to distance involve four factors: (a) the inverse square law of sound transmission, by which the sound from a more distant source is heard more softly; (b) timbre, in that complex sounds from a more distant source contain fewer high-frequency components because of their attenuation while traveling through air; (c) interaural intensity and phase patterns, which decrease in complexity as a function of distance from the source; and (d) reverberation patterns, which vary in time and involve both the sound source and the environmental surroundings. The auditory judgment of distance is less accurate than that of direction.

AUDITORY DISORDER
AUDITORY DISCRIMINATION
AUDITORY PERCEPTION
EAR

J. F. CORSO

AUDITORY PERCEPTION

The process of auditory perception involves the generation of behavioral responses to simple and complex acoustic stimuli: pure tones, music, speech, and noise.

A pure tone is a sound that has a pressure change that is a simple sinusoidal function of time; it can be described by frequency, amplitude, and phase. Physical changes on the frequency continuum from low to high produce corresponding changes in psychological pitch, while changes in physical amplitude are related directly to psychological loudness. However, pitch is affected secondarily by the intensity and duration of a sound; loudness, by frequency and duration. Pure tones can also be discriminated by the psychological dimensions of volume, density, and vocality.

Musical tones are complex sounds with repetitive waveforms that can be described in terms of a fundamental frequency and its multiples (harmonics or overtones), together with their relative amplitudes and phase relations. As the fundamental frequency of a complex tone increases from approximately 20 Hz to 5000 Hz, the pitch (and tone height) increases monotonically. Musical tones separated by an octave are perceived as similar in tone chroma.

Speech sounds consist of complex, variable waveforms formulated into words perceived and understood on the basis of their acoustical properties and linguistic context. In English there are 15 phonemes having vowel sounds and 24 phonemes having consonant sounds, with distinctive acoustical features from which all words are formed. The different parts of each word contain different bands of frequencies (formant regions) with differing amounts of energy per band. Primary speech frequencies range from approximately 125 Hz to 3500 Hz. In conversational speech there are no clear boundaries between words, but the listener's knowledge of the language gives meaning to the speech sounds; this produces segmentation (apparent separations) between words. Sentences are easier to understand if they are semantically and syntactically correct.

Noise is a complex sound that consists of numerous frequencies and has no periodicity in pressure changes with time. When the frequencies extend over a wide portion of the audible range, the result is called "white noise," which is heard as the sound of escaping steam. The annoyance value of noise is determined primarily by its high-frequency components and their relative intensities, in conjunction with the continuity-intermittency characteristics of the noise.

AUDITORY DISCRIMINATION
AUDITORY DISORDERS
AUDITORY LOCALIZATION
EAR

J. F. CORSO

AUTHORITARIAN PERSONALITY

The "authoritarian personality" is a term applied to a particular personality pattern studied by a team of researchers at the University of California, Berkeley, during the 1940s.

The researchers at first sought to identify an "anti-Semitic" personality, but found themselves broadening the concept to "ethnocentric" personality. This, in turn, was broadened to "fascist personality." The scale became known as the "F" scale, even when the concept was relabeled "antidemocratic" personality and "authoritarian" personality. (The ethnocentric scale was retained in the final battery as the "E" scale.)

Although the Berkeley researchers found a high correlation between ethnocentrism and authoritarianism, Richard Christie discovered that the correlations found in California did not hold in Texas, where ethnocentrism was more deeply ingrained culturally. With Maria Jahoda he later edited a critique of the authoritarian personality research. Frenkel-Brunswik found "intolerance of ambiguity" to be a characteristic of this personality type.

The authoritarian personality by Adorno et al. is undoubtedly one of the most comprehensive studies of personality yet made. There can be little doubt that the research pointed to personality configurations of a complex nature related to social rigidity and lack of adaptation. When defined in such terms as "rigidity," "dogmatism," "two-valuedness," "intolerance of ambiguity," and "authority-dependence," the concept obviously touches on one of the major problems of personality and functioning.

CENTRAL TRAITS
CONSERVATISM/LIBERALISM
PERSONALITY THEORIES

W. E. GREGORY

AUTISM

Infantile autism is considered to be the most severe psychological disorder affecting children. Characterized by early onset, it is estimated to involve 6 children in 10,000 births, with a ratio of males to females of 5:1. The etiology is unknown. The prognosis is poor, although behavioral (learning based) therapy offers some help. It is customary to diagnose autism on the basis of a set of behavioral deficiencies, excesses, and the presence of certain normal behaviors.

BEHAVIORAL DEFICIENCIES

1. The autistic child has little or no language, either receptive or expressive. The child may be mute, or if speech is present it is echolalic in the sense that the child will echo other people's voices or what he hears on television. Receptive speech is also deficient, in that the child may be able to respond only to simple commands ("sit down," "eat," "shut the door," etc.), and not to abstract speech such as pronouns (yours, mine, his and hers, etc.) or to temporal terms (first and last, etc.). The child's failure to express or understand language is the most common complaint that the parents have when they bring their child for examination. The problems with language can be identified during the child's second year of life.

2. The child behaves as if he or she has an apparent sensory/perceptual deficit—that is, behaves *as if* blind and deaf—but closer examinations reveal intact sensory modalities. The parents of autistic children complain that the children have extreme difficulty in paying attention. Usually, autistic children will not maintain eye-to-eye contact with the parents and/or will not orient their head in a reliable manner to other people's speech.

3. Autistic children usually do not develop close love relationships with their parents. This can be evidenced during their first few months of life, when parents complain that the child was not cuddly, and may in fact have resisted physical contact by stiffening the back and attempting to slide away from the parent's embrace.

4. Autistic children do not develop toy play the way average children do. They show no particular interest in toys and do not usually spend their spare time playing with them. If they do play with toys, it is often in a peculiar and idiosyncratic fashion, such as when they turn a toy truck upside down and spin its wheels, or carry a piece of string that they compulsively twirl, or carry a doll to smell or suck. The failure to develop toy play can be identified during the second year of life.

5. Play with friends may be missing or markedly reduced. The child may have no interest or skill in playing games, being largely unaware of other children without being involved in the give-and-take type play. This sign is also quite noticeable during the second year of life.

6. Autistic children often are delayed or fail to develop common self-help skills. They have problems in learning to dress themselves, toilet themselves, and eat unassisted. Similarly, they show a gross deficiency in recognizing common dangers, and may have to be closely guarded so that they do not get hurt by crossing the street in heavy traffic, playing with electrical equipment, and so forth.

Of these various deficiencies, numbers 2, 3, and 5 are perhaps most significant. Some children have reasonably good development in areas 1, 4, and 6, but are still diagnosed as autistic.

BEHAVIORAL EXCESSES

1. Autistic children have a considerable amount of tantrums and aggression. This aggression may be directed toward themselves, as when

they bite themselves or hit their head against the floor or furniture or punch themselves in the face. Sometimes the aggression is directed toward others, as when they bite, scratch, or hit their parents. Most parents complain that autistic children are very hard to manage, have low frustration tolerance, and respond to even minor frustrations with a great deal of anger.

2. Autistic children may show a great deal of "self-stimulatory" behavior in the form of ritualistic, repetitive, and stereotyped acts such as rocking the body in a standing and sitting position, flapping the arms at the wrists, spinning objects, gazing at lights, lining objects in neat rows, observing rotating fans or other appliances that revolve, or jumping up and down or twirling the body for long periods of time.

These two behavioral excesses are almost always present in autism, but do not really emerge in full form until the second year of life.

NORMAL BEHAVIORS

The autistic child does show a set of normal behaviors that are labeled "splinter-skills" or "islets of intact intellectual functioning." These normal behaviors center on:

1. Autism is often diagnosed when the child has met the normal developmental milestones, such as walking unassisted by 15 months of age. It is frequently reported that autistic children have *unusually good motor development,* so that they walk and balance with a great deal of ease.

2. It similarly has become customary to look for signs of *adequate memory* in order to diagnose autism. For example, the autistic child may be able to echo or otherwise repeat other people's voices, or commercials heard on television. Or the child may have a good memory for visual details.

3. Autistic children may show certain *special and well-developed interests,* as in playing with mechanical objects such as appliances or motorized toys. Some autistic children evidence a great deal of interest in music and dance. Others show considerable ability to put together puzzles, a liking for numbers or alphabet letters, and so forth.

4. Some autistic children do evidence limited but *special fears* that exist in more transient forms in average children. For example, some autistic children may have unusual fear of the noise generated by a vacuum cleaner or of the siren of a passing ambulance.

DIFFERENTIAL DIAGNOSIS

1. It is difficult to draw the distinction between autism and other forms of developmental disabilities such as mental retardation, because children with mental retardation will evidence many of these characteristics. When a distinction is made between autistic children and other kinds of children with mental retardation, it is usually based on the following behaviors: behavioral deficiencies 1, 2, 3, and 5; behavioral excesses 1 and 2; normal behavior 1, and one of 2, 3, or 4.

2. Some writers view autism and childhood schizophrenia as one disorder, while others separate them. The separation is based on: (a) age, with age of onset for autism placed within the first year, while childhood schizophrenia requires normal development for at least the first 2 years of life; and (b) the "thought-disorder" (hallucinations, delusions, etc.) usually presupposed in the diagnosis of childhood schizophrenia, which may necessitate the presence of language.

BONDING AND ATTACHMENT
MENTAL RETARDATION
SCHIZOPHRENIA
Z PROCESS

I. LOVAAS

AUTOGENIC TRAINING

This method of training people to reduce stress and control body functions was developed in Germany near the turn of the century by the neuropathologist Oskar Vogt, who observed that many of his patients were able to induce a hypnosis-like state in which they could control such things as stress, tension, fatigue, headaches, and backaches. The present-day authority on this training is Wolfgang Luthe (e.g., 1969). Many practitioners of autogenic training in the United States are working in medical settings on psychophysiological disorders. The approach is also said to be helpful in treating behavior disorders of most kinds, but it is not recommended for psychosis and some forms of heart disease.

HYPNOSIS
PSYCHOTHERAPY
RELAXATION TRAINING

V. RAIMY

AUTOMATIC THOUGHTS

Automatic thoughts are spontaneous ideas–ideations or thoughts typically indicated by internal self-statements or self-talk. Cognitive theories emphasize the roles of belief systems, cognitive schematas, intellectual processes, and automatic thoughts in behavioral operations. Each individual has a frame of reference, variously called personality, lifestyle, worldview, and so on, within which one copes with life. One's inner belief structure depends on past experiences, learnings, goals, purposes, and core belief structures. Automatic thoughts differ from belief structures. Merluzzi and Boltwood state, "an important distinction between automatic thoughts or self statements and underlying schemata or belief systems [is] automatic thoughts are spontaneous self statements or ruminations. . . . In contrast cognitive schematas are seen as relatively stable, enduring traits like cognitive patterns." Similarly, Beck and Weishaar distinguish between automatic and voluntary thoughts. Voluntary thoughts are fully conscious self-determined decisions. Automatic thoughts "are more stable and less accessible than voluntary thoughts [and] are generally quite powerful." Both voluntary thoughts and automatic thoughts are consistent with one's core beliefs or schematas.

UNCONSCIOUS PROCESSES

Automatic thoughts are considered to be unconscious or lying below the surface of immediate conscious awareness. They are spontaneous self-statements, stemming from core beliefs out of conscious awareness.

APPLICATIONS

In cognitive and cognitive-behavioral therapies, the primary focus is on changing the clients "distorted" or dysfunctional belief systems. Clients' belief systems are explored and accessed. Albert Ellis outlines 12 irrational beliefs, and Beck outlines primarily six cognitive distortions or distorted thoughts-belief processes. Others have added to and modified irrational beliefs and cognitive distortions.

Core beliefs can be accessed by having people monitor their own spontaneous self-statements or automatic thoughts. These are then challenged and changed. Therapy problems can be resolved by changing one's views of the problems via automatic thoughts, a kind of paradigmatic shift in thinking, known in psychotherapy jargon as *reframing*.

COGNITIVE COMPLEXITY
CONSCIOUSNESS
DEFENSE MECHANISMS
FREE WILL
IDEODYNAMICS
UNCONSCIOUS, THE

M. S. CARICH

AUTOMATION

Though automation affects human beings in many ways—and they in turn influence its adoption—this term has seldom appeared in psychological writings. From a psychological perspective, automation can affect people in at least six areas: (a) activities (performance) at work or at home—their jobs; (b) emotions—enjoyment of life or job satisfaction; (c) motivational variables, such as intrinsically reinforcing or deterring feedback; (d) social relationships or interactions and organizational structure or conflict; (e) school learning and skill training; and (f) health and safety.

Automation has received some attention—if less than it deserved—from engineering psychology and human factors research in analyzing task allocations between people and machines, and in symbiotically combining them. For example, it has proved difficult to automate such complex human performance as continuous voice recognition (although not single words alone or linked), language translation (unless vocabulary and syntax are restricted), and decision making or choice (except in standardized situations such as checkers or chess). However, humans and machines operating suitably together can become very effective.

Sociologists and others have attributed to industrial automation presumably emotional or arousal effects under labels such as anomie, alienation, disaffection, and estrangement, and psychologists have discussed job satisfaction, stress, boredom, and morale; but the picture has remained unclear owing to conceptual ambiguities, lack of data, and indications of many individual differences among workers.

Automation has had varying effects on social relationships and organizational factors. For example, assembly-line automation reduced the skills needed, isolated workers from each other, and simplified assembly jobs. Computer automation raised the skills needed, created interdependence among workers, and made their jobs more complex, with more job sharing and rotation; it also led to changes in management structures, job losses and changes, and management and labor resistance. Automation in the home through labor-saving devices has given homemakers more leisure time or capability to work elsewhere and may well have influenced the quality of family life, parental care, and sexual relationships between wives and husbands.

"Automation" can reasonably be said to mean a replacement of or substitution for some human competence by means of a device. Simply augmenting human capability or introducing a capability that humans lack does not constitute automation, although the distinctions may at times be hard to draw. Automation can replace any of the three elements involved in human competence: sensors (vision is automated through a remote TV, and thermal sensing by a thermostat); effectors (a forklift or a robot replaces lifting and carrying, and an automobile substitutes for walking); and a central nervous system for integrating both the preceding (as a computer does with its memory and control functions). Automa-

tion can increase in the degree that such replacements or substitutions can be increased—for example, through refinements in machine vision, mechanical fingers, and artificial intelligence in robots.

It will increase further for the same reasons it has already become so prevalent. In one sense, it has been needed to match increases in population; earlier, nonautomated methods of agriculture, transportation, communication, and production could not support current population levels. Psychologically, automation is adopted owing to a number of motivational factors. Because it reduces costs, management and investors reap more financial gain. It often prevents accidents, ill health, and discomfort—although it may bring other kinds of these in its wake. Automation also reduces effort and inconvenience in daily living—an incentive for its adoption that should not be underestimated.

ACCIDENT PRONENESS AND PREVENTION
INSTRUMENT DESIGN
JOB ANALYSIS

H. M. PARSONS

AUTONOMIC NERVOUS SYSTEM

The autonomic nervous system supplies motor fibers to the heart, the stomach, the pancreas, the small and large intestines, the sweat glands, peripheral blood vessels, and other internal organs, tissues, and glands. Its main functions are to regulate physiological processes involving these internal organs, such as blood pressure and body temperature, and to prepare the body for emergencies by initiating appropriate physiological adjustments.

The pathways of the autonomic nervous system include neurons in both the central and peripheral nervous systems. They begin with nerve cells in the brain stem and spinal cord. The axons of these cells, called preganglionic fibers, leave the central nervous system through cranial nerves (in the brain) or ventral roots (in the spinal cord) and travel to autonomic ganglia. These neurons then synapse with postganglionic fibers, which are distributed to various organs and glands.

The autonomic nervous system has two divisions, based on the anatomic distribution of the autonomic fibers: the sympathetic division and the parasympathetic division. These two components also have different functions. The preganglionic fibers of the *sympathetic division* begin in the spinal cord, leave through the ventral roots, and travel to the ganglia in the sympathetic trunks, located along either side of the vertebral column. These two elongated trunks extend from the base of the skull to the end of the vertebral column. The preganglionic fibers synapse in the ganglia of these sympathetic trunks. Then the postganglionic fibers leave the trunks and travel to the various organs and glands innervated by the sympathetic division. Some of these include the heart, the stomach, the small intestine, the pancreas, the large intestine, the salivary glands, the eye, and numerous blood vessels throughout the body.

The *parasympathetic division* of the autonomic nervous system is also called the craniosacral system because of its anatomic distribution. The preganglionic fibers leave the central nervous system through certain cranial nerves (oculomotor, facial, glossopharyngeal, vagus, and accessory) and also through the sacral (lower) part of the spinal cord. They travel to their visceral destinations and synapse in ganglia located in or near their target organs. Parasympathetic fibers reach many of the same organs and glands as sympathetic fibers, including the heart, the stomach, the small intestine, and the pancreas. However, there are several exceptions. For example, the parasympathetic fibers do not innervate peripheral blood vessels.

The autonomic nervous system is primarily under the control of nuclei in the hypothalamus. This area of the brain is involved in many activities, including the control of body temperature, eating, drinking, sexual behavior, and many emotional behaviors. The autonomic nervous system participates in some of these activities under the direction of the hypothalamus.

FUNCTIONS

The two primary functions of the autonomic nervous system are (a) to maintain homeostasis in the body, and (b) to prepare the body for emergencies. The sympathetic and parasympathetic divisions play important roles in these functions. In general, activation of the sympathetic division produces more widespread effects throughout the body, and its activation is important in the body's response to stress. Parasympathetic fibers, however, usually have more localized effects on individual target organs and glands. When both sympathetic and parasympathetic fibers innervate the same organ, they usually have opposite effects. For example, parasympathetic activation causes a slowing of cardiac contractions, whereas sympathetic activation causes heart rate to increase.

The homeostatic function of the autonomic nervous system is illustrated by its role in several physiological processes, including the control of blood pressure, thermoregulation, and pupil dilation. For example, a decrease in room temperature stimulates the sensory neurons in the skin that are sensitive to temperature. These neurons send impulses to the spinal cord and brain. The hypothalamus, which also contains cells sensitive to blood temperature, triggers activities designed to conserve heat, such as constriction of peripheral blood vessels and shivering. As body temperature rises, these processes are reversed.

The autonomic nervous system's response to stress is primarily due to widespread sympathetic activation and the accompanying changes in many body organs. In the presence of a stressor, sympathetic activation produces an increase in heart rate, increase in blood pressure, pupil dilation, inhibition of peristalsis, increase in sweat gland activity in the palms, release of hormones from the adrenal glands, and other changes. These physiological adjustments concentrate the body's resources in functions that are important during a physical threat, particularly the muscles. Blood supply to the skin and to the internal organs is reduced, while blood supply to the heart and muscles is increased. Physiological processes that are less important during an emergency, such as digestion, are inhibited. Sympathetic activation, and the changes in the endocrine system that accompany it, prepare the organism to fight or flee by mobilizing energy resources and temporarily increasing physical strength. Chronic sympathetic activation, however, is known to be associated with health problems.

The term *autonomic* implies that this component of the nervous system is automatic and not under voluntary control. However, many autonomic functions can be regulated by conscious activity, using appropriate procedures. Biofeedback, for example, enables many hypertensive patients to reduce their blood pressure.

BRAIN
CENTRAL NERVOUS SYSTEM
NEUROPSYCHOLOGY
SYMPATHETIC NERVOUS SYSTEM

P. M. WALLACE

AVOIDANT PERSONALITY

The diagnostic label *avoidant personality,* or *avoidant personality disorder,* was first included in the third edition of the *Diagnostic and statistical manual (DSM-III)* to describe individuals who desire friends but whose concerns about criticism and rejection lead to social inhibition and avoidance. The American Psychiatric Association DSM-IV work group revised earlier diagnostic criteria for avoidant personality disorder to clarify distinctions between this condition and related disorders. According to these criteria, the avoidant person:

1. Frequently anticipates and worries about being criticized or disapproved of in social situations.

2. Has few friends despite the desire to relate to others.

3. Avoids social or occupational activities that involve significant interpersonal contact.

4. Is inhibited in the development of intimate relationships for fear of being seen as foolish and ridiculed or being exposed and shamed.

5. Possesses low self-esteem because he or she feels socially inept and/ or unappealing.

The avoidant pattern typically onsets in childhood or preadolescence, and many avoidant individuals report that they have been timid as long as they can remember. The avoidant person experiences recurrent periods of anxiety and depression, for which he or she may receive concomitant diagnoses and treatment. Some of these individuals use alcohol or prescription medications to calm themselves before social encounters. At least some of these attempts at self-medication lead to abusive patterns of substance use.

Personality types characterized by social sensitivity and withdrawal appear in earlier clinical descriptions of personality disorders, most notably in depictions of the schizoid and phobic character styles. For example, Kretschmer described a hyperaesthetic variant of the schizoid personality that was marked by sensitive susceptibility, shyness, and psychic conflict. Fenichel's descriptions of the phobic character include features, such as the phobic avoidance of desired objects, that parallel current descriptions of the avoidant individual.

Clinical observation and empirical studies suggest that avoidant personality disordered patients display social fears of greater severity and in a broader range of situations than patients with generalized social phobia, but that many of the core features of the two conditions (e.g., fear of negative evaluation) are similar.

There are also similarities between avoidant personality and traits such as shyness and social timidity, which characterize individuals in the general (i.e., nonclinical) population. Writers such as Stephen Briggs suggest that avoidant individuals and shy individuals differ primarily in terms of the severity, rather than the nature, of the symptoms they display. Shyness and social timidity are generally believed to stem from innate differences in physiological reactivity. This raises the possibility that the avoidant individual has stronger dispositional tendencies than the shy individual or that negative social experiences aggravate dispositional factors to produce the more severe avoidant condition.

A variety of treatment strategies have been tried with avoidant individuals. Several empirical studies provide support for the effectiveness of behavioral and cognitive-behavioral regimens; avoidant individuals have been found to display significant improvements in social comfort and activity following such programs.

L. E. ALDEN

B

BACKGROUND CHARACTERISTICS

Background characteristics refer to a broad array of descriptive variables sometimes referred to as *demographic variables.* Demographic variables include sex, age, race, ethnic background, place and type of residence, household and family composition, occupation, income, education, and so on.

Comparative study of societies and cultures has focused attention on variations in racial/biological characteristics, and on political, economic, religious, family/kinship, and other institutional systems. Some cultural differences may be linked, implicitly or explicitly, to biological factors, presumably owing to constriction of genetic pools through geographic isolation, restrictive marriage patterns, the definition of particular physiological or physical attributes as desirable (or rejected), and so forth. But in general, the transmission of cultural patterns has been visualized as a result of social learning.

Social and psychological scientists have focused on various sets of background characteristics. One may examine whether groups have similar or different backgrounds and try to relate background variables to psychological factors or outcomes.

Background characteristics are frequently labeled as "ascribed" or "achieved." "Ascribed" characteristics are viewed generally as nonmodifiable. For example, subgroup membership is derived in part from the race and ethnic origins of one's parents, but in addition to such physical characteristics, parents usually pass on religious affiliation to their offspring. Within heterogeneous societies, different racial, ethnic, and religious membership are category attributes derived from the family of origin, and these ascriptions may have ramifications for behavior. Further, one is born into a family that has some social position allocated according to other characteristics such as family income, integration into the community, and prestige. Also important are family makeup variables such as family size, family composition, sex of siblings, and number of siblings and their spacing. Other family variables considered salient for psychological outcomes concern process, rather than structure, such as interaction patterns and socialization practices. Through these processes the family may transmit general cultural values, but it also provides experiences directed by the attitudes and expectations associated with the particular cultural subgroup and family constellation.

A person's sex and age are also "ascribed" characteristics, although conceptually somewhat different from those variables previously described. The importance of sex and contingent gender roles continue to receive attention in the study of psychological factors. Age of an individual is considered a basic variable of importance for behavior in every society. Age is one measure of the fact that concomitant and broader experiences continue to add to the social and psychological matrix first supplied by the family of origin. As a result, "achieved" characteristics accrue to the individual, adding to the store of what becomes added background for future events and stages of life. Thus a person's education, occupation, income, current family, and status in the community become important variables in understanding personality and behavior. At one time or another, *any* or *all* of the characteristics previously discussed, whether ascribed or achieved, may be conceptualized as being background to psychological outcomes.

RACE, ETHNICITY, AND SOCIAL CLASS

Race (biological characteristics) should be distinguishable from ethnicity (cultural characteristics). In practice, however, it is difficult to determine unequivocally either race or ethnic characteristics. Differences in behavioral outcomes among racial and/or ethnic groups are not easy to interpret because of the confounding influences of other background factors.

SEX

Much of earlier psychological research accumulated knowledge predominantly from the study of male subjects (especially college students). Reported differences between the sexes—for example, strength, spatial abilities, and verbal abilities, which may have specific biological components—are difficult to evaluate without considering early and continuing skills training and general socialization into culturally defined "feminine" and "masculine" orientations. Sex is a biological variable, and most psychological research strongly suggests that the roles and status contingent on biological sex identifications (i.e., gender socialization) are central to explaining differences that may occur between males and females relative to psychological variables such as conformity, aggression, and emotional behavior. The difficulty in separating sex from gender complicates the resolution of issues concerning sex differences, and important questions remain concerning male and female behaviors.

ACCULTURATION
ANDROGYNY
CROSS-CULTURAL PSYCHOLOGY
FIELD DEPENDENCY
NATIONAL CHARACTER

M. L. Borgatta

BACKWARD CONDITIONING

A backward conditioning procedure is one in which the unconditioned stimulus (US) begins before the conditioned stimulus (CS) begins. Procedures in which the CS begins after US onset but before US termination, are a subclass of backward conditioning procedures called "cessation conditioning procedures." This term derives from the fact that the CS onset "predicts" the cessation of the US. Backward procedures, including the cessation type, are distinguished from "simultaneous conditioning procedures," in which the CS and US begin at the same time, and from "forward conditioning procedures," in which the CS begins before the US.

In any conditioning procedure, be it backward or otherwise, any one of three outcomes is logically possible: (a) the CS may remain neutral; (b) the CS may become "excitatory," acquiring the ability to excite some change in behavior; or (c) the CS may become "inhibitory," acquiring the ability to oppose that same behavioral change. Over the years each of these effects has been claimed for backward conditioning, and it turns out that all three results can occur in succession as the number of backward pairings increases. Thus, before the first backward pairing, the CS may be relatively neutral; with only a few pairings the CS may become excitatory; and with still more pairings the CS may lose its excitatory powers, passing through a neutral point and then eventually acquiring inhibitory properties.

CLASSICAL CONDITIONING
HIGHER ORDER CONDITIONING
OPERANT CONDITIONING

J. J. B. Ayres

BARNUM EFFECT

In the right circumstance, most people will readily accept a generalized personality description as being a remarkably accurate description of their own personalities. Such a description might be the product of an astrological analysis, a palm reading, a psychic reading, or even a personality assessment carried out by a professional psychologist. The only circumstance that seems to matter is that the individual believes that the description was produced specifically in reference to oneself.

Paul Meehl, following the example of his colleague (D. G. Patterson, labeled this phenomenon the *Barnum effect,* after P. T. Barnum, the bombastic showman whose credo was "There is a sucker born every minute.") Meehl was not particularly concerned with astrologers, psychics, and other purveyors of putative occult wisdom. Rather, he was alarmed by the occurrence of this phenomenon in the context of clinical psychological assessment. He chose to use Barnum's name in the deliberate effort to stigmatize what he called *pseudosuccessful clinical procedures* in which personality analyses generated from tests and interviews were made to fit the patient largely because they were trivial in nature. They elicit positive responses from the client because population base rates ensure their applicability to almost anyone.

Research into the Barnum effect has generally involved leading subjects to believe that their personality has been analyzed in some manner and then giving them a written personal assessment. Unbeknownst to the subjects, everyone receives identical feedback. Subjects are then asked to rate the accuracy and the specificity of the feedback. Rarely do subjects fail to judge the assessment as accurate, so long as it is general enough.

Forer used the following generalized personality description in his classic demonstration of this phenomenon, and it, or a variant of it, has been used in most of the ensuing research:

> You have a great need for other people to like and admire you. You have a tendency to be critical of yourself. You have a great deal of unused capacity which you have not used to your advantage. While you have some personality weaknesses, you are generally able to compensate for them. Your sexual adjustment has presented problems for you. Disciplined and self-controlled outside, you tend to be worrisome and insecure inside. At times you have serious doubts as to whether you have made the right decision or done the right thing. You prefer a certain amount of change and variety and become dissatisfied when hemmed in by restrictions and limitations. You pride yourself as an independent thinker and do not accept others' statements without satisfactory proof. You have found it unwise to be too frank in revealing yourself to others. At times, you are extroverted, affable, sociable, while at other times you are introverted, wary, reserved. Some of your aspirations tend to be pretty unrealistic. Security is one of your major goals in life.

Such a "reading" succeeds in leading people to accept it as an accurate personal assessment for two reasons: (a) most of the statements are general enough to apply to anyone, and (b) in such a description, which contains many elements, it is likely that there are some that the individual can interpret as being quite specific to what he or she believes to be his or her own character. Each such descriptor may prompt the individual to think about some specific instance in their own life for which the descriptor applies, and finding such an instance may lead to the impression that the descriptor was more specific than it was. The significant correspondence is between the descriptor and what the individual *believes* to be his or her character, because people rarely are totally objective about their personalities and may well be reluctant to accept undesirable descriptors, even if objective analysis were to show their applicability.

Once the reading is accepted as accurate, the passage of time may enhance its apparent accuracy, especially if it was orally presented so that rereading is not available. In a description containing many elements, it is easy to ignore and subsequently forget those descriptors that seem to not at all apply and to focus on and remember only those that seem close to the mark.

The more generally favorable the overall description, the greater the likelihood that the reading will be taken to be accurate. Indeed, subjects who were initially skeptical about astrology have been reported to waver in their skepticism when given flattering horoscopes.

Readings offered by astrologers and psychics, although on the surface often appearing to be more specific than the description previously detailed, commonly invoke the Barnum effect.

The danger of the Barnum effect for clinical psychologists and other professional diagnosticians is that such people may come to attribute too much significance, either to their own clinical inferences or to the results of personality tests, because of the client's positive feedback. Personal validation is a fallacious procedure, but one that can produce powerful convictions in both the assessor and the assessed of the efficacy of even an ineffective diagnostic approach.

ADVERTISING
ASTROLOGY
CAUSAL REASONING
PERSONALITY ASSESSMENT
PHRENOLOGY
SALES PSYCHOLOGY

J. E. ALCOCK

BATTERED PEOPLE

Within the United States the sanctity of the family and the rights of family members—particularly parents and especially fathers—to guide the family without outside interference or intrusion is valued. This concern for the privacy and independence of the family has placed a barrier between it and the outside world. Protection of this position has at times insulated families from the police, the courts, and the probing eye of the researcher. However, the American family experiences a considerable amount of internal violence. The severity of the problem is at least partially reflected in known statistics presented in a review of violence in the American family by Murray Straus, Richard Gelles, and Suzanne Steinmetz. These statistics indicate that violence within the family is one of the leading causes of death, injury, and emotional pathology.

The problem appears to cut across all races and levels of socioeconomic status. All forms of violence within the family are less detectable at the higher levels of social and economic positions.

The 1960s saw a rapid growth in concern and legislation to address the problem of child abuse. By 1968 protective services for children, and laws requiring the reporting of suspected cases, were provided universally in all 50 states. While some states also provided for protective services for adults who cannot adequately advocate for themselves, general attention to other forms of family violence was—and in many ways still is—lacking. Abuse of older parents and grandparents by family members and abuse among siblings has still received almost no attention in our laws and our research, and not enough in our social concern.

The situation is somewhat brighter in the area of spouse abuse. In 1971, a woman named Erin Pizzey started a refuge for abused women in England. The first organized efforts in the United States relative to spouse abuse came in 1972, when a group called Women's Advocates began a telephone information and referral service for battered women in St. Paul, Minnesota. Two years later this group set up the first known refuge in the United States for battered wives and their children.

Despite the growing focus on violence within the family, little good research across the spectrum is available. Yet some general facts are known. First and maybe foremost, violence begets violence. Regardless of the type of battering or the target, individuals who were or are themselves abused are more likely than nonbattered people to resort to violence in the future. This appears to be especially true for males, and not surprisingly, males are more likely to commit the abuse.

Where the abuse is exclusively between adults, nearly 50% of the time there is mutual violence. It is impossible to completely understand the role of such violence. It may involve self-defense or a jointly escalating pattern. Males tend to inflict graver injuries and use more dangerous instruments of violence such as a gun or knife.

In most cases, the injuries inflicted are not premeditated. Frequently, they are, however, the result of exaggerated efforts to gain or maintain control over the other person. Violence in these households tends to be taken for granted; the abuser is often impulsive and unable to control emotions. Emotions rapidly build to an extreme, although sufficient control is generally maintained to avoid inflicting serious permanent injury or death.

Each type of abuse can and does exist independent of the other forms, although they do seem to be frequently related. Some authorities on family violence believe these findings indicate that abuse—in some forms and to some degree—is sanctioned within the context of the family home and that the "loss of control" is learned or of lesser importance.

All forms of abuse are much more likely with the presence of alcohol. Abuse also appears to become more likely when the family is under stress or when the abuser has a poor history of dealing with stress, although the majority of abusive individuals are not so emotionally disturbed as to be diagnosed as psychotic. The environment is also a factor: Abuse is more likely in homes where there are more than two children, where there is considerable stress, and where decision making is largely in the hands of one person.

A more global focus on the role of violence in our culture and the socioeconomic pressures will be required to address the problem within the larger society. Reducing the social isolation of families and the sexist attitudes within the society should help set the stage for more general intervention and prevention.

AGGRESSION
CHILD ABUSE
STRESS
VICTIMOLOGY
VIOLENCE

S. D. SHERRETS

BAYLEY SCALES OF INFANT DEVELOPMENT (Bayley Scales)

The Bayley Scales are measures for assessing the development of infants and young children, ages 1 to 30 months. Test content is organized into two separate scales: the Mental Scale and the Motor Scale. The Mental Scale assesses the precursors of cognitive development, including perceptual acuity, discrimination, acquisition of object constancy, memory, rudimentary problem solving, early verbal communication, classification, and generalization. The Motor Scale assesses body control, large muscle coordination, and manipulation of the hands and fingers. A third component, the Infant Behavior Record (IBR), is a rating scale completed after administration of the Mental and Motor Scales and provides the clinician a means of evaluating the child's environmental interaction and response.

INFANT DEVELOPMENT
INTELLIGENCE MEASURES

G. J. ROBERTSON

BECK DEPRESSION INVENTORY

The Beck Depression Inventory (BDI) was designed as a standardized measure of the depth of depression. Its items were based on observations of attitudes and symptoms characteristic of depressed patients. All significant symptoms and attitudes associated with depression were accounted for, since the number of reported symptoms was found to be associated with the depth of depression. Represented within the inventory are 21 categories of symptoms and attitudes: sadness, pessimism, sense of failure, dissatisfaction, guilt, sense of punishment, self-dislike, self-accusations, suicidal ideation, crying spells, irritability, social withdrawal, indecision, distorted body image, work inhibition, sleep disturbance, fatigability, loss of appetite, weight loss, somatic preoccupation, and loss of libido.

DEPRESSION
MEASUREMENT

G. K. LOCKWOOD

BEHAVIOR ANALYSIS

Behavior analysis is a comprehensive approach to the study of behavior pioneered by B. F. Skinner and developed by other behavioral scientists. Its goal is to provide a conceptually integrated account of the full range of behavior, ranging from the relatively simple behavior of animals in highly controlled laboratory studies to the complex behavior of humans in the everyday world. The breadth of behavior analysis is illustrated by Skinner's writings, which range from laboratory studies of basic behavioral processes of rats and pigeons to nonlaboratory investigations of verbal behavior in humans to philosophical and societal issues of more general concern. In its claimed breadth, behavior analysis contrasts with much current theorizing in psychology, which most often takes the form of limited theories—so-called miniature theories—that seek to integrate information from more narrowly defined domains (e.g., classical conditioning, memory, or language).

Behavior analysis is characterized by several other features that distinguish it from alternative approaches. Among these are a commitment to a selectionist approach to complexity, an exclusive reliance on experimental analysis as the source of principles for understanding behavior, a focus on the behavior of individuals rather than groups as the proper subject matter of psychology, and a central interest in applying the science to the amelioration of the human condition.

SELECTIONIST APPROACH TO COMPLEXITY

This approach to the explanation of complexity began with Charles Darwin's efforts to account for the development of complex and diverse life forms as the result of the repeated action of relatively simple processes summarized by the principle of natural selection. In the case of behavior analysis, complexity—here, complex behavior—arises as the cumulative effect of selection by reinforcers. Thus if a hungry rat presses a lever and food appears thereafter, then the rat is more likely to press the lever when it next sees the lever. Similarly, if a person speaks with another and the other attends to and reacts warmly to the words of the speaker, the speaker is more likely to continue talking. In the first example, food functions as a reinforcer for lever pressing; in the second, attentive listening functions as a reinforcer for speaking.

The view that complex behavior arises from the cumulative effect of selection by reinforcement, which progressively alters the environmental guidance of behavior, is seen as strictly analogous to the Darwinian view that complex structure arises from the cumulative effect of natural selection. Thus behavior analysis favors what might be called a bottom-up approach in which complexity emerges as a consequence of the cumulative effect of lower-level processes, notably selection by reinforcement. This account of the origins of complex behavior differs from most psychological theorizing in which complexity is seen as the expression of higher order principles—what might be called a top-down approach. For the behavior analyst, to attribute the orderliness of behavior to an idealized set of rules, or to higher order principles in general, is to fall prey to the same error as Darwin's contemporaries who attributed the orderliness of species to an idealized design or plan, reflecting special acts of creation rather than the cumulative effects of natural selection.

ANALYSIS AND INTERPRETATION
Behavior analysis is not the only approach within psychology that attempts to account for complex behavior as the emergent product of lower level processes. Within cognitive psychology, an approach known as parallel-distributed processing also seeks to understand complex behavior as the result of simpler processes. The distinction between behavior analysis and other bottom-up approaches is that in behavior analysis the lower-level processes are identified through experimental analysis. In experimental analysis, observations are obtained under conditions that permit all the variables of which the behavior is a function to be manipulated and/or measured by the experimenter. Although no experimental analysis is perfectly realized, the conditions of observation must approximate this ideal closely enough so that orderly relations between variables may be observed to a high degree of precision with a single organism. Thus accounts of complex behavior as the product of simpler processes (e.g., those summarized by a principle of reinforcement) may only use processes that are directly based on independent experimental analyses. This contrasts with other bottom-up approaches in psychology in which the lower-level processes are *inferences* from the complex behavior itself. Thus cognitive psychologists might infer "short-term memory processes and structures" from a study of the recall of verbal responses.

The behavior analyst, like most psychologists, appeals to unobserved processes in accounts of complex behavior. However, unlike most psychologists, the unobserved processes are accorded only those characteristics that have been determined through independent experimental analyses. The characteristics are not the result of inferences from the complex behavior itself.

For the behavior analyst, because the conditions under which complex phenomena are observed rarely meet the demands of experimental analysis, the understanding of complex phenomena is usually not the province of experimental analysis but of scientific interpretation. Scientific interpretation makes use of principles based directly on experimental analysis to account for complex phenomena. If complex phenomena can be generated as the cumulative effect of simpler processes, then these processes constitute explanations of the complex phenomena. The situation is much the same as in evolutionary biology in which the origin of a particular species is said to be explained if the processes of natural selection could have produced that species. Thus the goal of scientific interpretation in understanding complex phenomena—whether complex behavior in psychology or complex structure in evolutionary biology—is to demonstrate that the lower-level processes acting over time are sufficient to produce the observed complexity.

INDIVIDUAL AS THE FOCUS OF STUDY
Because complex behavior is the result of the cumulative effect of lower-level processes—such as selection by reinforcers—and those processes act in different sequences for different individuals, the individual organism is the focus of study in behavior analysis. More specifically, because selection by reinforcement acts on a population of responses from a single organism, experimental analysis must be directed at uncovering regularities in the behavior of the individual.

APPLIED BEHAVIOR ANALYSIS
In many other theoretical perspectives in experimental psychology, tensions and even incompatibilities exist between the science and its application. Tensions arise principally because many applications are viewed as insufficiently "scientific" by laboratory investigators. Incompatibilities exist principally because much of experimental psychology is based on averaging findings across different individuals whereas applications are most often directed at the individual case. For the behavior analyst, the application of basic principles is a type of scientific interpretation. Thus application provides a major means for evaluating the fruitfulness of the lower-level processes uncovered through experimental analysis. Furthermore, because experimental analysis is based on the intensive study of the behavior of individual organisms, the application of the principles to individuals is a natural extension of basic research. The lower-level principles uncovered through experimental analysis have been successfully applied to many areas of human functioning—including education, behavior disorders, developmental disabilities, business management, and public policy.

BEHAVIOR MODIFICATION
CLASSICAL CONDITIONING
COGNITIVE COMPLEXITY
OPERANT BEHAVIOR

J. DONAHOE

BEHAVIOR MODIFICATION
What is common to the many different formulations and techniques of behavior modification is direct intervention to alter a person's reactions to situations that this person or some significant others deem changeworthy. There are many implications in this definition that touch upon the nature of behavior considered changeworthy, the formulation of the bases of action (personality) and the justification for professional intervention.

DEVIANT OR CHANGEWORTHY BEHAVIOR
The behavioral approach is properly named because the focus is overt behavior. Such behavior is real rather than symbolic or symptomatic. There are no separate rules for the development, maintenance, or alteration of changeworthy (abnormal) or acceptable (normal) behavior.

Behavior is always in reaction to situations. While the limits imposed by physiological abilities such as injuries or heredity are not to be ignored, the major variance in changeworthy behavior lies in reactions to situations and the evaluation of these responses. The relevant fields of study, then, are those of behavioral science in general and social, personality, learning, and organizational psychology in particular. All material on the social influence process is useful.

INTERVENTION: DIRECT OR INDIRECT
Based on this intellectual position, behavior modification procedures are direct. This is a crucial point both in theory and practice. In biochemical reductionist medical models and in pseudomedical models or analogs such as psychoanalysis, disturbing and changeworthy behavior is presumed symptomatic and indicative of an "underlying" disorder. The locus of the problem is seen as lying within the individual. An example of the medical model analog is the ascription of almost all adult sexual problems such as impotence to poor resolution of the Oedipus complex, with the result that the person's realistic difficulty was not dealt with while the Oedipus complex was investigated. The success of direct retraining in sexual experience, pioneered by many but mostly associated with the names of Masters and Johnson, argues against such an avoidance of direct treatment. Behavior modification procedures are direct and reeducative,

and provide experiences to help the person learn more socially effective ways to deal with situations. *The object is the reaction to the situation, not the reaction alone.* A person may deal poorly with a situation for many reasons. It is not the avoidance or other inappropriate reaction that is the necessary focus of treatment, but rather the development of effective ways of dealing with the situation.

Measurement is crucial to behavior modification. It occurs first by an analysis of the conditions leading to changeworthy behavior. Next, it provides feedback as to the adequacy of the intervention procedure. Measuring the original changeworthy behavior and the new alternative methods of dealing with the situation provide objective information as to whether the program undertaken is working or requires modification. The process of behavior modification follows the same rules applied to the person being modified; evaluation of overt behavior, decision, and reprogramming. Just as no behaviors are laudatory or changeworthy in themselves, no behavior modification procedures are good or bad, effective or ineffective in themselves. All procedures must be evaluated in terms of the person and situation to which they are applied.

HISTORY OF BEHAVIOR MODIFICATION

If behavior modification is defined as the education of people to deal effectively with social situations, behavior modification is as old as socialization itself. All institutions, from family to government, intervene and alter human behavior.

Deliberate use of direct procedures to alter a person's responses to situations has been reported in ethnographic studies of preliterate societies and in such Greco-Roman writings as Ovid's *Remedies of love.* Jean-Jacques Rousseau devised situations to provide his fictional student, Emile, with experiences, and pioneer educators such as John Locke, John Dewey, and William James may all be identified as precursors of behavior modification.

In 1954, P. E. Meehl's *Clinical versus statistical prediction* was published, indicating that psychological tests using dynamic formulations or trait theories were not more effective (and frequently less) than simple demographic or formal measures, and in 1952 H. J. Eysenck challenged the value of the psychotherapeutic procedures then in use. The development of both the behavior modification and encounter/sensitivity/Gestalt movements should be considered in this historical context in which psychologists were looking for either justification of what they did or new ways to attain the benefits they claimed to provide.

Among other sources that prepared the ground for behavior modification were J. D. Frank's analysis of behavior influence in psychological treatment, T. S. Szasz's attack on biochemical reductionist thinking, applied social interactions, and the work of sociologists such as H. S. Becker.

Behavior therapy was associated with direct treatment, applying concepts from learning theory. The behavior therapy involved treatment, but did not necessarily reformulate the very nature of changeworthy behavior. It was a new procedure rather than a necessarily new approach.

Throughout the late 1950s and early 1960s, material testing out direct rather than indirect treatment appeared, and the very success of the process, without symptom substitution, led to a questioning not only of psychoanalytic and biochemical reductionist theories, but of the very nature of so-called abnormal, deviant, or pathological behavior.

There are many streams of behavior modification. While specification oversimplifies the reality, four may be considered. The first two are associated, respectively, with the Skinnerian operant conditioning theory and with Pavlovian/Hullian respondent conditioning and drive reduction theories. The outstanding investigators are Teodoro Ayllon and Joseph Wolpe, whose work made direct treatment in the clinical setting a demonstrable, effective alternative to other procedures.

BEHAVIOR MODIFICATION TECHNIQUES

Within the Skinnerian or operant framework, the frequency of acts is a function of consequences. A pleasant event subsequent to an act is likely to increase the frequency of that act in future similar circumstances and is called *positive reinforcement.* Escape or avoidance of an unpleasant consequence is also likely to increase the future emission of an act; because the event does not occur, this is called *negative reinforcement.* Withdrawal of a positive subsequent event for certain acts is likely to reduce the frequency of that act and is called *extinction.* When an unpleasant consequence is introduced contingent on an act, the frequency of that act is likely to decrease and the paradigm is called *punishment.* New, complex acts may be developed by reinforcing successive approximations, and this is called *shaping. Chaining,* a way in which complex sequences of acts may be developed, works backward from the final act toward earlier acts in the final sequence. A third way in which novel or complex acts may be developed is called *prompting and fading.* In this instance, the instructor guides the learner in making the target response, and as the learner increases in skill, the teacher reduces or fades the amount of help given. Much seemingly "abnormal" behavior may result when people such as parents or spouses reinforce behavior that has short-term advantages to them, but which in the long run is counterproductive. Other conditions that may be involved in the development or maintenance of changeworthy behaviors are negative reinforcement where an irrelevant or self-defeating act keeps one from the situation that is difficult to deal with, and superstitious behavior where fortuitous reinforcement leads to a behavior maintained by further fortuitous pleasant events on a schedule that is difficult to extinguish.

A *discriminative stimulus* marks the time and place when an act will have reinforcing consequences. Discriminative stimuli, such as a mother's attention or money, may become reinforcing stimuli, and are then called acquired, secondary, or generalized reinforcers. Such acquired reinforcers may be extinguished, as money in a time of high inflation, or even become aversive when they signal a removal or time out from reinforcement, as in the case of a mother's attention when she acts as chaperon. The establishment of culturally approved acquired reinforcers, and emission of behavior under culturally expected discriminative stimuli, are major elements of socialization. However, primary reinforcing stimuli such as food may satiate—that is, lose their effectiveness when in surplus.

A stimulus that has been previously neutral may, by occurring shortly before or contiguous with another, come to elicit the response of the latter. A stimulus such as alcohol may come to elicit a response of avoidance, disgust, or anxiety if paired with an electric shock or nausea induced by a chemical such as apomorphine. This is called *aversive conditioning.* Conversely, if elements of a feared stimulus or situation are presented when the person is so relaxed that the relaxation is stronger than the physiological correlates of anticipated punishment (anxiety), the person's fearful or avoidant response may be reduced. This is the operational basis of Wolpe's *systematic desensitization.* Presentation of a feared stimulus without the subsequent fearful experience may lead to a reduction of irrelevant or avoidant behavior—that is, extinction—and is the rationale of treatments such as flooding, implosion, and reactive inhibition therapy.

Just as pairing elements of a situation with a physically unpleasant event may reduce approach to the situation, in *covert sensitization*—the opposite of systematic desensitization—the person visualizes unpleasant and anxiety-provoking events in such situations as inappropriate drinking. *Aversion relief* is a technique in which a stimulus that has repeatedly signaled the escape or avoidance of an unpleasant situation is used as a positive stimulus. For example, for purposes of altering sexual preference, a picture of a member of the opposite sex may signal the termination or avoidance of an unpleasant odor or electric shock.

H. L. Hollingworth wrote about *reintegration,* in which one aspect of a situation brought it back in its entirety. The differentiation of situations, and of elements in or out of context, is an area that may be dealt with by the procedures previously mentioned, or may also respond to procedures of cognitive behavior modification of a more global nature. At a first level, one may provide oneself with an unpleasant consequence whenever one has a "thought" or "desire" that is changeworthy. For example, there are pocket-size shock apparati that can be used contingent on the thought of a cigarette. One may introduce various response costs contingent on thoughts or feelings such as red-taping, in which the person must engage in a long series of acts before being allowed a pleasant but changeworthy experience. For example, prior to smoking, the person enters in a diary the time, place, thoughts, and activities, then does ten push ups, then gazes for a minute at a picture of diseased lungs. After this, the person is allowed the cigarette. The cost frequently exceeds the perceived value of the event, and even if not, there has been an increased period of time between the impulse and activity. Related to this is the procedure of *thought-stopping* in which the person has acquired a strong and obtrusive stimulus that interferes with "the stream of thought." A similar procedure is *overcorrection*, which may be used for overt behavior or cognitions; the individual must make restitution far beyond the act.

The variants applying fundamental psychological principles are limited only by the ingenuity of the worker in tailoring ideas to fit the needs of specific clients in particular situations.

BEHAVIOR THERAPY
BEHAVIOR THERAPY: PROBLEMS AND ISSUES
COVERT CONDITIONING
EFFECTIVENESS COMPONENTS OF PSYCHOTHERAPY
PSYCHOTHERAPY
TOKEN ECONOMIES

L. P. ULLMANN

BEHAVIOR THERAPY

A series of terms often used interchangeably in psychology with somewhat different origins and meanings are behavior therapy, behavior modification, behavioral engineering, behavior influence, applied behavior analysis, behaviorism, cognitive behavior modification, conditioning, operant conditioning, S–R approach, social learning, vicarious learning, reinforcement, contingency management, stimulus control, and multimodal therapy.

The first known use of the term *behavior therapy* in the literature was in a 1953 status report by Lindsley, Skinner, and Solomon, referring to their application of operant conditioning research (on a plunger-pulling response) with psychotic patients. O. R. Lindsley had suggested the term to B. F Skinner, based on the simplicity of "behavior" and the linkage, via "therapy," to other treatment procedures.

Independent of this early usage and of each other, Arnold Lazarus used the term to refer to Joseph Wolpe's application of the "reciprocal inhibition" technique to neurotic patients, and Hans Eysenck used it to refer to the application of "modern learning theory" to the behavior of neurotic patients. Eysenck based his observations on the procedures of a group of investigators then working at the Maudsley Hospital in London. These early investigators consistently defined behavior therapy in terms of "learning theory."

In the first article devoted to "behavior therapy" published in the *Annual review of psychology,* Krasner argued that 15 streams of development within the science of psychology came together during the 1950s and 1960s to form this new approach to behavior change. These streams may be briefly summarized as follows:

1. The concept of behaviorism in experimental psychology.
2. The research in instrumental (operant) conditioning.
3. The development of the technique of reciprocal inhibition as a "treatment" procedure.

4. The experimental studies by a group of investigators at Maudsley Hospital in London.
5. The application of conditioning and learning concepts to human behavior problems in the United States, from the 1920s through the 1950s.
6. Interpretations of psychoanalysis in terms of learning theory, enhancing learning theory as a respectable base for clinical work.
7. The concept of classical conditioning derived from Ivan Pavlov as the basis for explaining and changing both normal and deviant behavior.
8. Theoretical concepts and research studies of social role learning and interactionism in social psychology and sociology.
9. Research in developmental and child psychology emphasizing vicarious learning and modeling.
10. Social influence studies of demand characteristics, experimenter bias, hypnosis, and placebo.
11. An environmentally based social learning model as an alternative to the "disease" model of human behavior.
12. Dissatisfaction with psychotherapy and the psychoanalytic model, as evidenced by strong critiques.
13. The development of the idea of the clinical psychologist within the scientist–practitioner model.
14. A movement within psychiatry away from the then orthodox focus on internal dynamics and pathology, toward concepts of human interaction and environmental influence.
15. A utopian emphasis on the planning of social environments to elicit and maintain the best of human behavior.

The elements of the belief system common to behavior therapy adherents include a statement of concepts, so they could be tested experimentally; the notion of the "laboratory" as ranging from animal mazes through the basic human learning studies to hospitals, schools, homes, and the community; research as treatment and treatment as research; and an explicit strategy of therapy or change.

The unifying factor in behavior therapy is its derivation from experimentally established procedures and principles. The specific experimentation varies widely but has in common all the attributes of scientific investigation, including control of variables, presentation of data, replicability, and a probabilistic view of behavior.

Kanfer and Phillips classified four types of behavior therapy, a categorization still in use: interactive therapy, requiring extended series of personal interviews using the therapists' verbal behavior to catalyze changes in the patient; instigation therapy, using suggestions and tasks to teach the patient to become his or her own therapist; replication therapy, changing behavior by replicating a critical segment of the patient's life within the therapy setting; and intervention therapy, disruption by the therapist of narrow response classes as they appear in the patient's interactions with his or her natural environment.

Applied behavior analysts utilize environmental variables to effect behavioral changes. A wide range of intervention techniques have been developed on the basis of principles generally derived from laboratory research, such as reinforcement, stimulus control, punishment, and extinction. Many, if not most, of the techniques used in community applications illustrate applied behavior analysis.

A second approach labeled by Kazdin and Wilson as the *neobehavioristic mediational S–R model* applies the principles of classical conditioning derived from the earlier works of Ivan Pavlov, C. L. Hull, E. R. Guthrie, O. H. Mowrer, and N. E. Miller. Wolpe has been most responsible for integrating this material into a systematic treatment approach. Concepts of intervening variables and hypothetical constructs (e.g., Hull and Mowrer) warrant the use of a mediational terminology. This is further exemplified by the use of unobservable processes, such as the imagined representation of anxiety-eliciting stimuli in systematic desensitization.

The newest group of behavior therapists use the term *cognitive-behavior modification* and the concept of cognition to denote their approach to intervention procedures. These investigators emphasize the importance of, and focus on, cognitive processes and private events as mediators of behavior change. Key concepts of this group include assumptive models of reality, attributions of one's own behavior and that of others, thoughts, images, self-statements, self-instruction, sets, response strategies, and other constructs to account for "cognitive processes."

The *social learning approach* to behavior therapy has been conceptualized by Bandura. Behavioral response patterns are influenced by external stimulus events (primarily through classical conditioning), by external reinforcement, and most important, by cognitive mediational processes. Behavior change is effected primarily through a symbolic modeling process in which learning occurs through the observation and coding of representational processes based on these observations or even on imagined material.

Social learning theory emphasizes the reciprocal interaction between the individual's behavior and the environment. The individual is considered capable of self-directed behavior change. Bandura has integrated the social learning approach in the concept of "self-efficacy," which emphasizes individuals' expectations about their own behavior as they are influenced by performance-based feedback, vicarious information, and psychological changes.

Krasner and his collaborators use the concept of *environmental design* in an approach to behavior change that links applied behavior analysis and social learning concepts with elements of environmental psychology, "open education," architecture, and social planning.

The behaviorists are stressing a new-old theme: the urgency of finding solutions to environmental problems of our society and the belief that the behaviorists can contribute to those solutions. The postwar theme of a "better society" as the goal of the behaviorists thus returns, although it has really been part of the behavioral stream throughout its history.

Virtually all the early investigators in this field believed that there was a very close linkage between their research and the social and ethical applications and implications of this research. The controversy as to whether science is value-free or value-laden has been an integral part of the behavior therapy history. The view of an integral research–societal linkage was most clearly influenced and led by Skinner's writings, particularly *Walden two*. This novel, written by a scientist whose basic research itself had not yet had very much impact on the field of psychology, raised issues pertaining to social systems, ethics, and morality; it anticipated the social and ethical issues arising from behavior therapy that became concerns in the 1970s and 1980s. Throughout, the growing concern on the part of both professionals and public has been "behavior therapy for what?" What is desirable behavior on the part of a human being in a given set of circumstances and who is to decide?

BEHAVIOR MODIFICATION
COGNITIVE THERAPIES
COVERT CONDITIONING
MULTIMODAL THERAPY
PSYCHOTHERAPY

L. KRASNER

BEHAVIOR THERAPY: PROBLEMS AND ISSUES

Behavior therapy is an increasingly accepted part of the mental health establishment, bringing with it an influx of professional issues pertaining to clinical strategies, training, licensing, guidelines, accountability, legal constraints, and a host of problems encountered in the hurly-burly of daily practice.

Behavioral procedures go back to antiquity. What is new is the systematic application and formulation of the principles in terms of scientific methodology. This methodology contains within it the following features: objectivity, quantification, replicability, validation, hypothesis testing, reliance on data and reason rather than appeal to authority, and an obligation to submit feasible alternative explanations to scientific scrutiny.

For some behavior therapists, the conceptual framework is Pavlovian classical conditioning translated into practice by such techniques as aversion therapy and systematic desensitization. For other behavior therapists, the primary influence is Skinnerian operant conditioning and an empirical analysis of behavior, leading to behavioral shaping, token economies, and so forth. For yet others, the uniqueness of behavior therapy lies in its emphasis on the application of experimental methodology to individual cases. For social learning theorists, modeling and conditioning principles have been incorporated into a performance-based schema with the individual and the environment exerting reciprocal and interactive influences.

Some behavior therapists accept trait theories, others do not. For some, the environment is all-encompassing; for others, physiological and constitutional factors are paramount. Some view behavior therapy as in large part an exercise in self-actualization, but for others, self-control is a delusion. For this latter group, there is no such thing as a self; the guiding principle is radical or metaphysical behaviorism, with a complete denial of any intervening variable between stimulus and response. For some behavior therapists, data are sufficient and theory is of little or no consequence; for others, theory is essential if behavior therapy is to advance.

Most behavior therapists share certain characteristics in addition to or arising out of methodology. These include a focus on current rather than historical determinants of behavior, an emphasis on overt behavior change as a main criterion by which treatment is to be evaluated, the delineation of treatment in objective terms to make replication possible, a reliance on basic research as a source of hypotheses about treatment and specific techniques of intervention, and a specificity in defining, treating, and measuring target populations.

The definition of behavior therapy tentatively adopted by the Association for Advancement of Behavior Therapy in the early 1970s was as follows:

Behavior therapy involves primarily the application of principles derived from research in experimental and social psychology for the alleviation of human suffering and the enhancement of human functioning. Behavior therapy involves a systematic evaluation of the effectiveness of these applications. Behavior therapy involves environmental change and social interaction rather than the direct alteration of bodily processes by biological procedures. The aim is primarily educational. The techniques facilitate improved self-control. In the conduct of behavior therapy, a contractual agreement is negotiated, in which mutually agreeable goals and procedures are specified. Responsible practitioners using behavior therapy are guided by generally accepted principles.

Behavior therapy started in the 1950s. Its first decade was characterized by ideology and polemics, the second by consolidation, and the third by the development of sophisticated methodology, innovative conceptual models, and a search for new horizons. These developments involve an increasing acceptance of inner processes (the so-called cognitive revolution), a growing interdisciplinary basis, and a broadening interface with the community. Because of this expanded domain, and because behavior therapy is not a unitary system with circumscribed therapeutic procedures, conceptual problems and issues arise.

S–R LEARNING THEORY AND CONDITIONING IN BEHAVIOR THERAPY

There is increasing evidence that behavior therapy is firmly based on neither theories nor principles of conditioning. Conditioning is devoid of precise meaning. The differentiation between classical and operant conditioning remains equivocal. The relationships between conditioning in the laboratory, conditioning in the clinic, and conditioning in daily life are complex and open to diverse interpretations. No general factor of conditionability has as yet been demonstrated, even though it is an implicit assumption underlying much of behavior therapy. Neither classical conditioning, operant conditioning, nor applied behavioral analysis account adequately for the many complexities of neuroses. Attempts to update conditioning theory in terms of cognition, subjective experience, or interaction response patterns could complicate rather than clarify the issue. Thus the evidence for conditioning as an explanatory concept in behavior therapy is, at best, equivocal.

Were it to be granted that behavior therapy is based on theories of learning, there is still little agreement about which learning theories or principles are applicable. Whether the prevailing concepts of conditioning are adequate to account for covert, inner-directed processes is yet unresolved. It is occasionally proposed that the foundation of behavior therapy be broadened to include knowledge drawn from social psychology, physiology, and sociology rather than relying exclusively on conditioning-based learning theory. To do so would be to change radically some of the premises on which behavior therapy is based.

A unifying factor in behavior therapy is generally considered to be its derivation from experimentally established procedures and principles that conform to the characteristic methodology of the behavioral scientist. Unfortunately, much of behavior therapy rests on limited scientific evidence. At best, behavior therapy is based on empirical validation rather than derivation from theory, and occasionally on little more than prevailing notions arising out of the clinical experience of the practitioner. Swan and MacDonald found that behavior therapy as actually conducted is not always consistent with the theories and principles espoused by the practitioners concerned.

ROLE OF COGNITION IN BEHAVIOR THERAPY

Perhaps because of a desire to discard anything that smacked of mentalism or inner processes, early behavior therapists resolutely rejected all forms of cognitive influence. Within two decades this situation changed drastically, so that behavior therapy in the 1980s was in the throes of what was termed the "cognitive revolution." The emphasis on the role of cognition aroused considerable dispute and dialogue within the ranks of behavior therapy. For some behavior therapists, cognitions are not behaviors, but are hypothetical constructs used to account for relationships between the environment and behavior. For others, cognition is an integral part of behavior therapy, to be accounted for either in terms of some form of conditioning or by the introduction of an as yet undetermined additional explanatory concept.

The precise relationship between cognition and behavior remains equivocal. All therapies are probably simultaneously cognitive and behavioral to a greater or lesser extent. Further clarification must await the development of an appropriate technology of brain–behavior–cognitive function.

Virtually all current procedures in behavior therapy involve some cognitive influence. Most behavior therapists reject the radical or metaphysical approach in favor of some form of methodological behaviorism. It is more appropriate to regard contemporary behavior therapists as behavioral rather than behavioristic. Nevertheless, the debate about the behaviorism in behavior therapy is far from resolved, and the issue of what is and what is not philosophically legitimate remains a matter of lively controversy.

Certain individuals recognize the impossibility of philosophical or conceptual integration between psychoanalysis and behavior therapy but insist that some form of interaction is both feasible and desirable at the level of practice.

BEHAVIORISM
BEHAVIOR MODIFICATION
BEHAVIOR THEORY
CLASSICAL CONDITIONING
COGNITIVE THERAPIES
OPERANT CONDITIONING

C. M. Franks

BEHAVIORAL CONTRACTS

One of the fundamental guideposts of behavior therapy is the functional law of effect: Behavior is generally under the control of reinforcement contingencies. The term *functional* here implies that most important human behaviors are not governed by precise, one-to-one relationships with environmental consequences. However, contingent stimuli and events do exert a powerful influence. Many of the most effective behavior therapy strategies, such as token economies and parent management training, operate primarily by the systematic control of contingencies: reinforcement of desirable behavior and punishment or extinction of undesirable behavior. These operant approaches are most useful with captive populations, such as young children or psychiatric inpatients, for whom the therapist or his or her agent (e.g., the parent) controls many patient reinforcers.

Manipulative operant strategies are not useful with noncaptive groups or those who have many sources of reinforcement, such as adolescents and adult outpatients. Operant principles are still applicable, but they can be applied only if the individual enters into a contingent agreement voluntarily. *Behavioral contracts* are therapeutic agreements in which the parties agree to place a problem behavior under contingent control. One person consents to perform behavior X or refrain from behavior Y, in return for which another person agrees to administer a positive consequence or withhold a negative consequence. As with any operant intervention, the critical element is thought to be the contingent relationship between behavior and consequence. The only unique feature is that *both* parties have agreed to the contingency in advance, rather than one imposing it on the other.

Behavioral contracts have been widely used in three areas: therapeutic planning, marital therapy, and family therapy with adolescents. Goals, strategies, anticipated treatment duration, and methods of evaluation are all discussed in advance and specified in a therapeutic contract. The agreement may be written or oral, and typically is reexamined and renegotiated after a trial period. Thus patients know what treatment will entail, the rationale, and what to expect in terms of cost, time, and possible outcomes. They can make informed decisions about whether or not to participate.

Behavioral contracts are widely employed in behavioral marital therapy. Their role is based on the *behavioral exchange* model of marital happiness. Marriage, like all interpersonal relationships, is governed by reciprocity. Spouses provide each other with positive reinforcement or punishment as a function of what they receive from each other. Happy marriages are marked by the widespread interchange of positive reinforcers. The spouses cooperate, assist each other, and are satisfied because of the frequent exchange of favors, considerate behavior, affection, and so forth.

Anecdotal clinical data support the use of marital contracts, but there is little empirical data documenting their effectiveness. It has been suggested that the primary benefit of contracts comes from the problem solving and negotiation that are involved in formulating contract terms, and that the specific contingencies are superfluous. In addition, contracting may even have negative effects by overly objectifying problems and raising questions about the partners' motives for behavior change. Some behaviors (e.g., affection, sex) are valued only if they appear to be spontaneous and sincere and show "caring." Contracted behaviors obviously do not have these characteristics; hence, they may be devalued. Considering these uncertainties, the role and practice of contracting must be studied further, before firm conclusions can be made about its utility.

The third area in which behavioral contracts are frequently used is family therapy. Contracts seem to be especially useful with families with adolescents and delinquents. The process of contracting teaches problem solving, negotiation, and compromise. The contracts themselves specify behavioral goals for the child and reasonable consequences (positive and negative) to be provided by parents. They eliminate the arbitrary nature of discipline, and define privileges and restrictions on the adolescent that are fair to parents and child. A typical contract might be: "John will be home by 10:00 P.M. every school night. If he is not, he is grounded on Saturday night. If he is, he can use the family car on Saturday night, and remain out until 2:00 A.M. If he violates the Saturday curfew, he cannot use the car on the next two Saturdays." As in the case of marital contracts, such family contracts seem to be useful clinically. Because the goals of parent–adolescent therapy are focused more on reducing overt conflict and reaching accommodations than on reestablishing love and affection, questions about motivation are less critical. But it is difficult to separate the effects of contracts from other aspects of therapy, and there are no definitive data about their impact.

CONSEQUENCES

A. S. BELLACK

BEHAVIORAL CONTRAST

Behavioral contrast refers to a behavioral change that occurs as a consequence of a transition from one condition of reinforcement to another. The phenomenon is studied with either discrete-trial or free-responding (operant) procedures. A discrete-trial procedure such as an alley runway restricts responding to a specific, externally determined situation, whereas in an operant setting responses are unrestrained at least within broad spatial and temporal limits. With discrete-trials animals are reinforced in a particular situation and then receive a more or a less favorable condition of reinforcement in the same situation. Successive positive contrast is present when performance to the now more favorable reinforcement is enhanced because of the previous experience with the less favorable reinforcer. Successive negative contrast is observed following a change from a more to a less favorable condition of reinforcement; performance is suppressed relative to a group that always experienced the smaller reward.

Simultaneous contrast is present when responding to a stimulus is altered, following a change in the condition of reinforcement to another stimulus.

While simultaneous positive contrast is reliably obtained with operant procedures, simultaneous negative contrast is found only under special conditions with this training procedure. In most operant experiments, responding does not change to the stimulus correlated with the unchanged reinforcement schedule, following a more favorable change in the other schedule. In summary, positive rather than negative contrast is found in free-responding situations when the conditions of reinforcement are contrasted, whereas negative contrast is present when reinforcement is contrasted in discrete-trial settings.

Behavioral contrast continues to attract interest because it appears as an exception to the laws of extinction and stimulus generalization. For example, if the condition of reinforcement is made less favorable to a stimulus following training where the two stimuli are correlated with equivalent schedules of reinforcement, then, depending on the similarity of the two stimuli and the law of extinction responding to the stimulus signaling, the unchanged component of reinforcement might be expected to decline rather than increase.

CLASSICAL CONDITIONING
OPERANT BEHAVIOR
REINFORCERS

E. J. RICKERT

BEHAVIORAL GENETICS

Behavioral genetics is the application of genetic principles to the study of behavioral variables. The major areas of psychology that have been studied along these lines have been intelligence, personality, and psychological abnormality. Behavioral genetics is essentially a subsection of biometrical genetics—that is, that part of genetics concerned with the application of Mendelian principles to polygenic inheritance. Mendelian principles were supposed (erroneously) to apply only to characters determined by single gene action; biometrical genetics extends these principles to characters whose expression is determined by two or more genes.

A single gene gives rise essentially to one of two expressions such as tall/short, red/green, and large seeds/small seeds. When a character is determined by more than one gene, a continuum is created along which different characters are spaced in a way that resembles the normal distribution more and more as the number of genes involved becomes larger.

The essential features of the multiple factor hypothesis are (a) the governing factors or genes are inherited in the Mendelian fashion; and (b) they have effects on the character under observation similar to one another, supplementing each other and being sufficiently small in relation to the nonheritable variation—or at least in relation to the total variation—for discontinuities to become indiscernible in the phenotypic distribution. In this way smooth, continuous variation of the phenotype could arise from discontinuous, quantal variation of the genotype. Clearly, there are dangers in postulating these multifactorial or polygenic systems. The constituent genes postulated in polygenic segregation are so alike in their effects, and so readily mimicked by nonheritable factors, that they cannot easily be identified individually within the systems. Accordingly, it is difficult and may be impossible to follow such genes by the simple Mendelian technique, which creates doubt about their being borne on the chromosomes and so being subject to Mendelian inheritance.

It is often assumed that the major aim of behavioral genetics is the determination of the heritability of a given trait, but this is not true. Behavioral geneticists see the method as a clue to the genetic and environmental architecture of behavior, and are as much interested in environmental factors and their contribution as they are in genetic factors. Furthermore, they partition the genetic variance into different components such as the additive genetic variance, dominance effects, effects due to assortative mating, and effects due to epistasis. The dominant-recessive nature of inheritance is too well known to require discussion. Assortative mating simply means that the mating system is not one of panmixia (random mating), but that mate selection either favors like marrying like (positive assortative mating), or else that like marries unlike (negative assortative mating). Practically all mating patterns are either positive or approach panmixia; negative assortative mating is exceedingly rare in humans. Epistasis is nonadditive genetic variance due to interaction between different gene loci.

Generally, geneticists also look at the interaction between environment and heredity, distinguishing carefully between two types of interaction. In the first place we have what may be called the statistical interaction—the fact that different genotypes may respond differently to the same environmental effect. If a particular change in the environment raises the IQ of every genotype by an equal number of points, the environmental effect is said to be *additive*. If, however, some genotypes gain 20 points, some 10 points, and some nothing at all, we talk about the environmental change interacting with genotypes to produce different phenotypic effects in different genotypes.

Another type of interaction is the so-called *covariance* of genotypes and environments, which arises when genotypic values and environmental values are *correlated* in the population.

We can now define heritability as the ratio of genetic variance divided by total or phenotypic variance: $h^2 = V_G/V_P$. The genetic variance, V_G, is divided into four components: additive genetic variance, nonadditive genetic variance due to dominance at the same gene loci, nonadditive genetic variance due to interaction between different gene loci (epistasis), and genetic variance due to assortative mating. Thus,

$$V_G = V_A + V_D + V_{E_p} + V_{AM}$$

The phenotypic variance, V_P—the variation in the particular character that is observed—is made up as follows:

$$V_P = V_G + V_E + V_{GE} + \text{Cov GE} + V_e$$

where V_G is again the genetic variance, V_E additive environmental variance independent of the genotype, V_{GE} variance due to interaction (i.e., nonadditive effects) of genotypes and environments, Cov GE the covariance of genotypes and environments, and V_e error variance due to unreliability of measurements.

It is sometimes said in textbooks that it is impossible to estimate the relative importance of heredity and environment, just as it is impossible to say which is more important in defining the area of a field, the length or the width. This indicates the lack of understanding that many people have of the problems and methods of behavioral genetics. We are dealing throughout with apportioning *variance;* clearly, a single field has no variance and so is completely irrelevant to the discussion. If we took a thousand fields varying in area, length, and width, then by a simple application of analysis of variance we could tell which factor—length or width—was more important in determining the differences in area, and assign relative weights to these two factors. Exactly the same can be done in the case of genetic analysis.

The fact that we are dealing with variances throughout indicates that our findings will be measures of *population parameters;* they will be relevant to a particular clearly defined population. The findings cannot be extended to other groups. Strictly speaking, the findings should not be generalized beyond the population studied.

It will also be clear that the concept of *heritability* applies to groups, not to individuals.

The fundamental model that underlies all the formulae given previously is based on the simple fact that the phenotype for any given trait will be determined by both the individual's genetic makeup and the environmental circumstances. In its basic form, the phenotype (P) is expressed quite simply as the sum of the genetic effects (G) and the environmental effects (E) : $P = G + E$. In laboratory animals, we can measure the values of G and E without difficulty by rearing animals from a number of strains in a range of environments and then observing mean performances. In humans, assessing the effects of G and E is more difficult because we have only limited control over both genetic makeup and the environment. However, the situation is no more difficult than in many other branches of social science where complete experimental control is impossible. Indeed, it is considerably better, since the biological mechanisms of Mendelian inheritance guarantee a substantial measure of randomization of genetic and environmental influences.

The logic of the twin studies is straightforward. Twins are divided into monozygotic and dizygotic on the basis of similarity (MZ) or dissimilarity (DZ) of obvious physical characteristics known to be very highly genetically determined, such as fingerprints or a variety of blood group factors. Individuals are then measured on the trait in question, and the extent to which MZ twins are found to resemble each other more than DZs is taken as an indication of the relative importance of genetic influences.

The analysis of variance of twin pairs partitions total IQ variation into two sources, that between pairs (BP) and that within (W). To the extent that pairs resemble each other, the mean square between (B) will be greater than that within (W), the ratio $(B - W)/(B + W)$ being a measure of this resemblance known as the *intraclass correlation*. It is to these mean squares, or to the correlations derived from them, that we equate our genetic and environmental components $V(G)$ and $V(E)$.

E has to be replaced by two components, one reflecting the effects of home background together with shared or common experiences, and the other reflecting experiences that typically differ for siblings even though they are reared together. The between-families environmental variance will be referred to as common environment (CE) and the within-families environmental variance as specific environment (SE), respectively. This gives us the phenotypic variance

$$V(P) = V(G) + V(CE) + V(SE)$$

Analysis of variance of twin data allows us to separate these components.

Unreliability variation, which equals one minus the reliability coefficient, can be corrected for by simply subtracting the unreliability variance from $V(SE)$, then calculating the new total variation and expressing $V(G)$ as a fraction of this new total.

Many other approaches have been used in the field of intelligence, personality, attitudes, and abnormal behavior to supplement twin studies of this kind, among them studies of MZ twins brought up in separation, adoption studies, the study of genetic regression to the mean, familial intercorrelations, and so forth. The major findings cannot of course be summarized here, but they do indicate that genetic factors have a powerful influence on human abilities, personality, temperament, social attitudes, and abnormal behavior in general. Methods and designs are constantly being improved, and the margin for error of the statistical estimates reduced. Behavioral genetics is a very powerful tool for the study of human behavior; it is regrettable that it is not taught more widely to students of psychology.

HERITABILITY
LAW OF FILIAL REGRESSION
GENETIC DOMINANCE AND RECESSIVENESS

H. J. EYSENCK

BEHAVIORAL INHIBITION

The concept of inhibition was introduced into behavior theory from physiology where it had been discussed and studied for more than 100 years. René Descartes, who provided foundations for modern physiology, discussed the possibility of physiological inhibition—inhibition that might be manifest in observable behavior. The first experimental demonstration of inhibition was provided in 1823 by Charles Bell who was studying the control of the eye muscles. In 1838, A. W. Volkmann showed that the pumping action of the heart could be reduced by the action of the vagus nerve. But a key experiment—key less for the observation itself than the conclusions it led to—was the demonstration in 1863 by Ivan Sechenov, that spinal reflexes could be inhibited by application of a stimulus (salt) applied to the transected midbrain. From this, Sechenov inferred that inhibition of behavior was a central nervous system function and that mental processes were excitatory and inhibitory reflexes organized as antagonistic functions. These ideas elaborated in his *Reflexes of the brain* greatly influenced Pavlov. Sechenov's book suffered a long period of censorship because the concept of inhibition was seen as a challenge to volition and free will.

"By inhibition we mean the arrest of the functions of the structure or organ, by the action upon it of another, while its power to execute those functions is still retained, and can be manifest as soon as the restraining function is removed" has been given as a definition of inhibition in physiology. When extended to psychology by Pavlov, the essence of this definition—inhibition as an antagonist to excitatory processes—was retained.

Pavlov, in 1927, distinguished four experimental procedures under which the behavioral reductions observed were believed to produce "internal" or conditioned inhibition: (a) the reduction of responding to an established conditioned excitatory stimulus (CS$^+$) when that CS$^+$ occurred in a serial or simultaneous compound with a second stimulus and the *compound* was *not* reinforced, (b) extinction of a previously learned response, (c) reduction of responding to the unreinforced CS$^-$ in a CS$^+$ versus CS$^-$ discrimination, and (d) diminution of the amplitude of a conditioned response, during the early portion of a lengthy CS paired with a US. The first procedure is now the paradigmatic instance of what is called conditioned inhibition.

It has been an issue of controversy as to whether the other three instances of internal behavioral inhibition (especially c and d) are manifestations of the same processes as those that produce the paradigmatic conditioned inhibition. Two general types of alternatives have been offered. One harks back to Descartes and invokes competition between incompatible reactions, although little direct evidence is ever adduced to show that there is another competing behavior. The other harks back to Thomas Hobbes and is not a matter of inhibition but rather simply less excitation.

To resolve such a controversy, it is necessary to divine a definition of conditioned inhibition and ways of independently testing for it. Such a step was long in coming because despite the substantial early attention, Pavlovian conditioning phenomena soon were relegated to a minor place in psychology as more attention was given to the learning that occurred in the paradigms pioneered by Thorndike and by Skinner in which behavior was instrumental in garnering rewards for the organism. It was only when so-called two-process theories to explain this instrumental learning began relying on embedded Pavlovian learning that interest in the latter was reawakened.

One promoter of two-process accounts, Rescorla (1969), offered an operational "definition" of conditioned inhibition and suggested tests that could be applied to detect its presence independently of the conditions under which it was observed. It was hypothesized that inhibition was based on the learning that occurred when a CS and US were negatively correlated (i.e., the US was more likely in the absence of the CS than in its presence). Such a CS was designated *CS$^-$*, and its properties as a conditioned inhibitor were argued to be opposite to those of an excitatory CS$^+$ that was paired with or positively correlated with the occurrence of the US. Two tests were suggested for a putative conditioned inhibitor to determine if its properties were opposite those of a CS$^+$. To ensure that the initially observed behavioral inhibition was attributable to inferred conditioned inhibition and not some other process (e.g., attentional distraction), the CS$^-$ was required to pass both tests. One test was the summation test in which the CS$^-$ was directly compounded with a CS$^+$; the required result was that the behavior eliciting power of the CS$^+$ had

to be reduced by virtue of this compounding. The second was a retardation of acquisition test in which the CS$^-$ was now paired with the US to transform it into a CS$^+$; the required result was that the transformation of the CS$^-$ into a CS$^+$ had to proceed more slowly than the transformation of a neutral stimulus into a CS$^+$. Indeed, it turns out that if one uses Pavlov's procedure of reinforcing the CS$^+$ when it occurs alone but not when it occurs in a compound with the putative inhibitor (CS$^-$), the CS$^-$ will suppress the response eliciting actions of another excitatory CS$^+$, and the CS$^-$ will be more slowly transformed into a CS$^+$.

Nonetheless, there remains a reluctance by some to infer that the reduced behavior that accompanies presentations of a putative conditioned inhibitor is in fact attributable to inhibitory mechanisms. A contemporary example of a Hobbesian theory would suggest that when a CS that is very excitatory, by virtue of its pairing with a US, is compounded with a CS that has little excitatory power, because it has not been paired with a US, the result is an intermediate level of excitation due to the averaging of the values of the two CSs. Such an average level should elicit less behavior than the excitatory CS alone (i.e., this predicts a reduction in elicited behavior without reference to inhibition). The appeal of such an analysis is that it might permit accounting for behavior without invoking the additional concept of inhibition. It seems, however, that this "averaging" model itself relies on some kind of "computational" inhibition (else one should see additivity of the reactions to the stimuli).

Although, Rescorla's definition provides a set of operations for producing a conditioned inhibitor and for verifying its status as one, the psychological basis for the learning is not clear. On the basis of Pavlov's procedures, one might suggest that conditioned inhibition is based on the CS$^-$ signaling a period during which the US will not appear. This can be shown to be false: If one CS is reliably paired with a given US, then a second CS also is reliably paired with the same US and then, if both CSs together are combined with a third CS and this triplet is paired with the same US, it turns out that this third CS acquires the properties of a conditioned inhibitor, even though it did not signal a period in which the US would not occur. However, this procedure also suggests an answer. When two independently established CS$^+$s are compounded, unusually high levels of excitation are elicited—higher than can be conditioned by the single US; thus in the triplet, the third stimulus occurs in a context of greater excitation than can be sustained by the US. Hence, although the third stimulus does not predict the nonoccurrence of the US, it does predict a US that is less than what the two CS$^+$s in the compound taken together predict. A conditioned inhibitor, therefore, seems to result when a CS is unreinforced or *under*reinforced in the presence of other excitatory stimuli or contexts. This is currently the most accepted psychological account. The principles of this account are captured in the well-corroborated contemporary quantitative conditioning model proposed by Wagner and Rescorla.

Conditioned inhibition continues to be a central concept in the explanation of learned behaviors and their performance over a variety of conditions.

ACQUIRED DRIVES
BACKWARD CONDITIONING
BLOCKING
BRAIN
CONNECTIONISM
COVERT CONDITIONING
HOMEOSTASIS
IMPLICIT LEARNING
LEARNING THEORIES
STIMULUS

J. B. Overmier
D. A. Williams

BEHAVIORAL INTERVENTION

Intervention is a generic term referring to any treatment intended to alter another's immediate behavior or course of behavior. Intervention seeks to alter behavior by influencing it directly, by manipulating the environment, or by some combination of both. Typically, the term is used to refer to the process of ameliorating a symptom, concern, or problem of behavior impinging on human growth, functioning, or well-being. Intervention may also serve to prevent behavioral dysfunction or develop human potential. Psychotherapy, marriage counseling, and employee development consultation are examples of applications of behavioral intervention.

Behavioral intervention can be defined along two dimensions. The first is the *context* in which it occurs. Context consists of the respective parties who participate in the intervention process and the roles they fulfill. The second dimension is the *process* itself—the actual activities carried on by those who participate.

CONTEXT

Intervention can only be considered when some symptom, concern, or problem of behavior is evidenced by some person hereafter to be called the *client*. The client is the party to whom intervention services are then provided by the *interventionist* (i.e., therapist, counselor, consultant, etc.). In most cases the client is a voluntary, self-referred participant in the intervention process who has solicited assistance to resolve a concern. The interventionist is expected to apply understanding and expertise to treat and ameliorate the client's problem. Thus at least one client and one interventionist must be involved for intervention to be effected. More than one client or interventionist can participate, however. Group psychotherapy, for example, involves multiple clients and sometimes co-therapists.

PROCESS

Many different theoretical orientations and corresponding treatment techniques exist, as for instance *psychodynamic theory, client-centered theory,* and *behaviorism,* by which to describe and effect the process. Numerous researchers have aptly pointed out the seeming contradiction and lack of cohesion apparent across many of the different approaches to practice. Consequently, the field lacks mutually acceptable concepts and terminology by which to describe the intervention process at an operational level of detail.

The various approaches share a common aim. All seek to ameliorate or resolve problems of human behavior, be they remedial, preventative, or developmental problems in nature. In light of this common aim, more recently there has been a trend toward describing intervention as a *problem-solving process.* From the problem-solving point of view, intervention is seen as a process that seeks to resolve a discrepancy between the client's existing life status, and some more desirable status, which represents a solution to the presenting problem. At this level of abstraction, intervention can be described independently of any particular theoretical orientation while reflecting the process activities common to most.

Defining the client's presenting status. The initial activities of the intervention process seek to develop a realistic, detailed appraisal of how things are presently operating in the client's problem situation (i.e., what symptoms, behaviors, social or environmental factors define the presenting concern). Typically, the client tends to volunteer this information early in the intervention process. The interventionist will usually help clarify the client's perceptions of the concern and may employ first-hand observation or other measures to amplify and validate what the client reports. An important aspect of this process component is developing knowledge of the client's personal characteristics, since such attributes as health, personality, and intelligence may contribute to the problem or rule out certain treatment approaches. In the final analysis, these initial activities permit the interventionist to develop a baseline description of the specific nature of the client's presenting concern.

Forming a concept of the problem resolved. Once the client's presenting status has been clarified and defined, activities next focus on forming a concept of how things would be operating in the client's life if the problem were resolved. The purpose of this process component is to identify the goals that intervention should achieve to overcome the client's presenting concern. Here the interventionist draws on some established concept of what would be normal or more desirable behavior (tempered by knowledge of the client's specific needs and ability to change) to develop intervention goals. Often the interventionist will collaborate with the client to negotiate interim goals for resolving the concern. Once the concept of what represents problem resolution is formed, it becomes the goal status that the intervention process seeks to help the client achieve.

Determining what maintains the problem. When the client's present behavioral status differs from the goal status, then a status discrepancy exists. This process component is concerned with determining what maintains that discrepancy—that is, what blocks the client from resolving the incongruency between present circumstances as opposed to how things could be operating if the problem were resolved. Here the interventionist will analyze all diagnostic information available to identify the cause of the status discrepancy. This component of the intervention process makes possible the link between problem cause and treatment strategies appropriate to resolving the presenting concern.

Identifying and selecting treatment. Once the interventionist has determined what causes and maintains the problem, the range of treatment strategies is considerably narrowed. Client factors such as maturity, intelligence, social skills, health, and so on, will be considered to further narrow the treatment options to those most compatible with the client. Ultimately, the interventionist will identify one or more treatments for resolving the concern and may even collaborate with the client to select the specific treatment approach with which the client is most confident.

Applying the intervention treatment. With the treatment strategy selected, this process component takes direct action to resolve the presenting problem. The interventionist implements the treatment to bring about client behavior change and thus achieve the intervention goals. Certain treatment activities may involve the client and interventionist collaborating to bring about the desired change. Other activities may be effected independently and subtly by the interventionist—activities that are intended to provide clarification, direction, reinforcement, and other support to the client. By whatever the balance of responsibility for effecting the treatment, intervention will take action on the problem by directly influencing client behavior, by manipulating the environment, or by some combination of both.

Evaluating case progress. Once any aspect of the intervention treatment is applied, the interventionist begins to monitor the client's response. Case evaluation is employed to provide continual feedback as to how the treatment is taking effect. To monitor treatment progress, the interventionist may use informal methods such as personal observation or structured methods such as tests. By whatever method, case evaluation is essential to maintaining treatment effectiveness and determining when treatment goals have been attained.

Interventionist–client relationship. When problem solving is engaged in by two or more persons, an interpersonal relationship is inherent in the process. Maintaining positive, productive relations with the client is thus essential to effect collaborative problem solving. Such a relationship fosters the supportive environment necessary for client change and also client trust in the interventionist.

PROCESS DYNAMICS

The components of the intervention process are a highly interdependent set of elements. Thus it would be rare to find the process effected as straightforwardly as the foregoing suggests. Rather, each client's case has its own influence on the manner in which the process is implemented by the interventionist. Generally, however, the first phase of intervention can be characterized as a *diagnostic phase*. It involves the first four process components concerned with problem analysis. The second or *action phase* involves implementing the intervention treatment to resolve the problem. The third or *feedback phase* provides data to the interventionist and client as to the efficacy of the intervention treatment. If the action phase has been successful, case evaluation confirms this, and the intervention process can cease with respect to the presenting problem. If unsuccessful in whole or in part, the process may be recycled by the interventionist in search of new inputs to determine treatment adjustments. Concurrent with these three phases of activity, the interventionist–client relationship is maintained in ongoing fashion to provide the supportive conditions necessary to collaborative problem solving.

CLINICAL PSYCHOLOGY
COUNSELING
PSYCHOTHERAPY
PSYCHOTHERAPY TECHNIQUES
SOCIAL CASEWORK

D. G. FAUST

BEHAVIORAL MEDICINE

Behavioral medicine integrates behavioral with biomedical knowledge relevant to physical health and disease. It brings together the relevant parts of the behavioral sciences of psychology, epidemiology, sociology, and anthropology with the biomedical sciences of physiology, endocrinology, immunology, pharmacology, anatomy, nutrition, and the branches of medicine and public health, along with the related professions of dentistry, nursing, social work, and health education. It involves basic and applied research, the application of its knowledge and techniques to prevention, diagnosis, therapy, and rehabilitation, and the evaluation of these applications.

The Surgeon General's Report, *Healthy people*, presented the following key challenge to behavioral medicine. At the beginning of this century the leading causes of death were influenza, pneumonia, diphtheria, tuberculosis, and gastrointestinal infections. Since then, the yearly death rate from these diseases per 100,000 people has been reduced from 580 to 30! As a result of these and other advances, the burden of illness has changed to deaths and disabilities in which behavior plays an important role, as for example heart attacks, cancer, cirrhosis of the liver, and injuries from accidents, violence, or poisons. The report quoted an estimate that 50% of mortality from the ten leading causes of death in the United States can be traced to lifestyles, and concluded that the major opportunity for further improvements in health is in the area of changing unhealthy behaviors.

RECALCITRANT TYPES OF UNHEALTHY BEHAVIOR

Smoking is one of the important lifestyle factors harmful to health. Converging lines of evidence show that cigarettes are causal factors in producing cardiovascular disease; cancer of the mouth, lungs, and esophagus; and respiratory conditions such as emphysema, bronchitis, and chronic obstructive lung disease. The effects depend on the dose, and the risk is reduced by quitting. Experiments on several different species of animals prove that cigarette smoke causes cancer in the lungs and other organs. Nicotine has been found to be a primary reinforcer for smoking, because most people report little satisfaction from smoke that lacks nicotine, even if it contains all the other constituents of tobacco smoke. When the nicotine content of smoke is reduced, most people change their smoking behavior, inhaling more, smoking each cigarette nearer to the end, and/or consuming more cigarettes in ways that tend to maintain the previous dose of nicotine. Thus low-nicotine cigarettes may be more harmful than helpful. The withdrawal symptoms and difficulties that many people encounter in trying to quit smoking indicate that nicotine can be addictive.

Sixty percent of the regular smokers in the United States have tried to quit at some time, and 30% more would like to quit. But only one in ten who try to quit succeed for more than a short time. While various Quit Clinics may achieve up to 70% short-term success, the long-term success rate in this possibly different population is no better than that of those who go it alone. Emotions such as anger or frustration count for many first instances of backsliding, and one slip, or at the most two, cause continued resumption of the addictive behavior.

The extreme difficulty of permanently breaking the smoking habit has caused investigators to concentrate on trying to understand the factors that cause children to start smoking and on using this understanding to design programs to prevent them from starting. Such programs have actively involved young people in developing strategies to counteract pressures from peers, adults, and the media.

Alcohol abuse contributes to cirrhosis of the liver, pancreatitis, several types of cancer, accidents, violence, fires, and lost production. Studies have shown that genetic and cultural and other psychosocial factors contribute to alcoholism, although we need to learn far more about the specific details. While a number of different treatment programs are successful for some people, the average rate of long-term success is discouragingly low, a fact that suggests emphasis on prevention.

Diet can also affect health. Anorexia nervosa, an extreme form of self-starvation occurring mostly in young girls, can be extremely damaging to health and causes death in a significant number of cases. Unbalanced diets deficient in proteins, vitamins, or essential elements are also harmful. A larger national problem, however, is obesity. Compared with those of average weight, men and women 20 to 30% overweight have a mortality 20 to 40% greater, and those 50 to 60% overweight have a mortality 150 to 250% greater. Obesity increases the risk of hypertension, diabetes, and heart disease, and complicates surgery; losing weight can be a significant factor in treating certain cases of hypertension and diabetes.

The fact that the incidence of obesity in people born into the upper social classes is less than in those born into the lower ones suggests that obesity is subject to control by some sort of influence in the social environment; there is also evidence for hereditary factors. Treatments as different as psychoanalysis and behavior therapy can cause some obese people to return permanently to normal weight. But, as in the case of smoking and alcoholism, relapse rates for many patients are discouragingly high. Because the goal of loss of weight can be measured objectively, the problem of obesity provides a challenging opportunity to test the effectiveness of different forms of intervention.

Type A behavior has been defined as hard-driving, competitive, impatient, and hostile. Studies following up those with this kind of behavior have shown that they are approximately two-and-a-half times as likely to have heart attacks as those with less evidence of such traits, who are designated as Type B.

Noncompliance is another problem. If everyone followed their doctor's recommendations, it would be easy to get rid of those behaviors known to be unhealthy. But in many cases, following the doctor's orders involves giving up some immediate gratification or encountering some immediate inconvenience or extra effort to achieve a greater but remote satisfaction, or to avoid a severe but remote consequence. Thus the fact that immediate outcomes are more effective than delayed ones works strongly against compliance. For example, studies have estimated that approximately one-third to one-half of patients do not take the drugs that are prescribed. Psychologists who study such problems have found that having the reason for the prescribed procedure adequately explained does help some, but often this is not enough.

EFFECTS OF EMOTIONAL STRESS AND OTHER PSYCHOSOCIAL FACTORS

Epidemiological, clinical, and life-change studies have shown that conditions that loosely may be described as stressful increase the likelihood of a wide range of medically undesirable consequences. Among the many conditions studied are rapid social change, social disorganization, migration to a radically different environment, bombing raids and disasters, loss of a spouse, overstimulation, monotony, and lack of control over important aspects of work or the environment. Instead of any specific psychosomatic effect to be predicted from any specific type of stressor, typical results have been increased risks for a wide variety of disorders such as sudden cardiac death, myocardial infarction, hypertension, stroke, diabetes, gastrointestinal problems, multiple sclerosis, tuberculosis, influenza, pneumonia, headaches, and insomnia.

Often, stressful conditions that have a disastrous effect on some people may have little or no effect on others. Some of these individual differences probably are innate, but others depend on psychosocial factors such as how a threat is perceived and the coping responses performed to deal with it. Coping responses and their consequences have been studied in patients subjected to drastic stresses such as paralysis from a spinal lesion, severe burns, open-heart surgery, or cancer.

Experimental Confirmation

While the evidence in the foregoing studies is impressive, much of it is subject to alternative interpretation. For example, there are at least 20 studies showing that people living in certain stable, relatively simple societies have blood pressure that is unusually low and does not increase with age. But when people of the same genetic stock migrate to the radically different conditions of cities, they have higher blood pressure that does increase with age. While these results show that some environmental factor must be involved—and increased stress is a probable one—other explanations such as decreased exercise or increased salt and fat in the diet are difficult to rule out.

Controlled experiments, however, can rule out alternative interpretations. For example, an experiment has shown that if mice raised in isolation are put into a colony composed of narrow passageways designed to produce repeated conflicts, they develop high blood pressure through a series of stages apparently analogous to those in human essential hypertension, and die prematurely of strokes, kidney damage, and other types of cardiovascular pathology associated with high blood pressure. When mice that have not been reared in isolation are placed in this same colony, they develop a stable social organization with far fewer conflicts and do not develop hypertension or die prematurely.

Many other experiments have shown that conditions that may be described as stressful can reduce the effectiveness of the immune system as measured directly and also as measured by resistance to experimental infections and implanted tumors. The latter effects are especially complex and not yet well understood; in some cases, stress can have the opposite effect of increasing the effectiveness of the immune system.

Mechanisms for the Effect of the Brain on the Body

It has long been known that the brain and its neurohumoral systems control vital functions such as breathing, heart rate, blood pressure, blood flow, temperature, digestion, intestinal motility, and fluid and electrolyte balance.

Evidence has increasingly shown the degree to which functions of lower centers of the brain can be modified by functions of higher ones. For example, when blood pressure goes up in the emotionally calm animal, stimulation of the baroreceptors in the carotid artery elicits reflexes that cause the heart to slow down and the arterioles to dilate, so that blood pressure returns to normal. But under conditions of fear or rage, impulses from higher centers inhibit these reflexes, so that blood pressure is free to continue to increase. In addition to their implications for behavioral

medicine, results like these mean that reflex pathways in the nervous system cannot be understood without taking account of the behavioral state of the organism.

It has long been known that psychological factors can have a strong effect on pain. With susceptible patients, deep hypnosis has been used as a substitute for a general anesthetic in major surgery. The readily observable behavioral and physiological responses that a very hungry dog makes to a painful stimulus can be eliminated, if that stimulus is made a signal for food. This phenomenon has been called counterconditioning. When, after lengthy exposure to deadly combat, a soldier is severely wounded and being evacuated to the rear as the first step in being sent home, he may show little signs of pain and not request morphine, in contrast with a similarly injured civilian for whom the injury means serious problems instead of merciful escape. These phenomena may be explained by pathways that have been discovered in which nerve impulses inhibit pain. These pathways involve the release of opiate-like peptides whose action is intermediate between the brief ones of neurotransmitters and the longer-lasting ones of hormones.

Massive discharges from the sympathetic nervous system, occurring for example during fear, have been shown to cause damaged hearts to fibrillate and thus produce sudden death. A number of the different cells in the immune system have been found to have receptors for, and be affected by, a number of different hormones and peptides that are under the control of the brain and are released during emotional stresses.

Effects of Stress via Behavior

Another of the effects of stressful situations, especially when they cannot be controlled, is depression. Mild discouragement or depression can cause neglect of personal hygiene, diet, and other ways of taking good care of oneself. Severe depression can cause catastrophic neglect or positively harmful behaviors, including suicide. In addition to these behavioral factors, it is possible that there are as yet poorly understood physiologically adverse effects of depression and giving up, and conversely, positive effects of a strong will to live.

PSYCHOLOGICAL PROBLEMS PRODUCED BY INJURY, DISEASE, AND AGING

Another aspect of behavioral medicine is taking care of the psychological problems induced by injury or illness. Some patients may be stressed and depressed by their injury or their illness, and thus add to their condition adverse physiological and behavioral effects that can make their condition worse, leading to further stresses and discouragement in a continuing downward spiral. This is especially likely to occur with an injury or chronic illness, the initial effects of which are not rapidly counteracted by a natural healing process. Conversely, if patients who have slid downhill in this way can be mobilized to cope with stresses and take better care of themselves, they can be started on an upward spiral toward making the most of what is left of their potentialities. Some of the conditions creating strong emotional and behavioral problems for the patient are paralysis from high lesions of the spinal cord, crippling injuries, severe burns, diagnosis of cancer, anticipation of major surgery, a heart attack, dialysis for kidney failure, epilepsy, hemophilia, and diabetes. Such conditions, especially in childhood, can pose severe problems of anxiety, of feeling stigmatized, and of compliance with inconvenient or aversive medical regimes. Old age can produce manifold problems of adjustment to radically changed circumstances of life. In the elderly, feelings of weakness may cause depression, or symptoms of depression may be mistaken for senility. Behavioral medicine is making increasing contributions to such problems.

THERAPY AND REHABILITATION

In applications to physical medicine, an important advance has been the development of behavioral techniques useful in therapy and rehabilitation. An attractive feature of many of these techniques is that, instead of the patients having something done to them, they teach the patients to do something for themselves.

Given the effects of stressful conditions on health and the fact that illness can be a strong stressor, it is understandable that providing comfort and support has always been an important part of the art of medicine. But, with the development of effective technologies, this time-consuming function has tended to be neglected by specialists in physical medicine, creating a need for the services of specialists in behavioral medicine. For a considerable number of cases that come into a health care facility, social and emotional problems lie behind the somatic complaint. Thus it has been found that providing suitable forms of brief psychotherapy can reduce the total load on the clinic.

Many different forms of psychological therapy have been found useful in medical settings. A general eclectic understanding of learning theory, cognitive processes, psychodynamics, social factors, and the specific medical details of the condition being treated, is a useful and often essential background for applying any specific behavioral technique. Three general approaches—behavior therapy, relaxation training, and biofeedback— are described, but they by no means exhaust the possibilities.

Behavior Therapy

Behavior therapy applies a variety of experimentally derived principles of learning, and also clinically derived techniques, to the modification of behavior. A central idea in applications to physical medicine is that when sickness behavior is reinforced more strongly than health behavior, it will persist after the organic cause has disappeared. Powerful reinforcers for such behaviors are the sympathy and attention of family members and care-facility staff, relief from aversive responsibilities and duties, disability payments, and pain-killing or sleep-inducing medications. A sample of the type of sickness behaviors commonly reinforced in this way includes signs of pain such as wincing, limiting physical activity, asking for pain-killing drugs, extreme dependence, fatigue, weakness, headaches, dizziness, and various other complaints that are either without an organic cause or are disproportionate, so that the patient is not making full use of his or her potential capabilities. It is profitable to try behavior therapy when adequate organic causes are absent, strong reinforcement for sickness behavior is evident, and it is practicable to withhold these reinforcements and to provide reinforcements for health behavior first in the health care situation and then in the patient's normal environment.

Behavior therapy has been useful in many medical settings. One of the earliest and best-evaluated uses has been in treating pain that has no discoverable organic basis. It also has been used to teach patients to control symptoms as diverse as vomiting and enuresis, to minimize the deficit of patients whose ability to perform activities of daily living has been reduced by physical illness or injury, and to help the elderly achieve greater independence. It has helped patients to comply with medical regimes—for example, to take prescribed medications, to improve the use of atrophied muscles by conscientiously exercising, and to participate in other forms of physical therapy. Phobias of medical procedures such as having blood drawn, injections, dialysis, and dental work have been eliminated by training patients to relax and then introducing them gradually to progressively more fear-inducing steps of the procedure, in combination with demonstrations by the therapist or other calm models. But the foregoing examples do not begin to exhaust the diverse applications.

Relaxation Training

Relaxation training was developed by E. Jacobson in the 1930s. He taught patients to go systematically through the body from the fingers to the toes, tensing muscle groups and then relaxing them, concentrating on the sensations produced by relaxation, and then learning to become progressively more and more relaxed. To this procedure have been added concentration on relaxing imagery, monotonous repetition of a word,

regular deep breathing, and passive concentration on producing sensations of warmth and heaviness. Patients are instructed to practice at home, often with the help of tape recordings, so as to canvass life situations (waiting for a red light, hearing the telephone ring) that elicit tension, and to make these become cues for eliciting rapid relaxation. For many patients, such procedures appear to reduce stress and have been found to reduce hormonal and other physiological indices of stress. But in some patients deep relaxation produces feelings of disorientation, of being out of control, or it arouses frightening images—effects that must be handled by more traditional psychotherapeutic procedures. It is possible to be completely relaxed but panic-stricken.

Conscientious practice of relaxation has been found to be helpful in treating patients with a variety of conditions such as headaches, Raynaud's disease (a painful and eventually injurious vasoconstriction of the fingers in response to stress or cold), asthma, and cardiac arrhythmias. It is a helpful component of natural childbirth.

Biofeedback

Biofeedback uses measuring instruments to give patients and their therapists better information (i.e., feedback) about what is happening in their bodies. It is useful where (a) the medically desirable direction of change is clear, (b) a response that can produce such a change is potentially learnable, (c) the response that can produce that change has been prevented by the patient's poor or mistaken perception of what is being done, and (d) where moment-to-moment measurements can provide better information.

Many patients who apparently had reached the limit of improvement by traditional physical therapy methods (themselves a type of behavioral treatment) have been helped by biofeedback to make further significant improvement. When the training aided by biofeedback enables reasonably young patients or birth-injured children, who previously had been unable to do so, to feed and dress themselves or to work and support themselves, the accumulative financial savings in health care costs over the years of expected life make the treatment enormously cost-effective.

Biofeedback has been found useful in treating a variety of other conditions such as fecal incontinence, drug-resistant epilepsy, and painfully poor circulation in the legs. Advances in miniaturized electronic technology are providing portable measuring devices that allow more extensive therapeutic training in normal life, as well as the identification of situations especially stressful to the patients as a first step toward teaching them to cope better.

ACUPUNCTURE
A-TYPE BEHAVIOR
BEHAVIOR MODIFICATION
BIOFEEDBACK
ENDORPHINS/ENKEPHALINS
HEALTH CARE SERVICES
HEALTH PSYCHOLOGY
HOLISTIC HEALTH
MUSCLE RELAXATION
PSYCHOPHYSIOLOGY
PSYCHOSOMATIC DISORDERS
REHABILITATION CENTERS
SOCIOPSYCHOPHYSIOLOGY
STRESS MANAGEMENT
WEIGHT CONTROL

N. E. MILLER

BEHAVIORAL MODELING

Modeling may be defined as the process by which an individual (the model) serves to illustrate behavior that can be imitated or adapted in the thoughts, attitudes, or overt behaviors of another individual (the observer). The model may be live, filmed, described in any other medium such as print, or even imagined. When intended observers are used as their own models, the process is called self-modeling. These applications are quite different procedurally and in theoretical basis.

GENERAL PRINCIPLES

Albert Bandura, the foremost proponent of modeling strategies, has identified four elements necessary for success: attention to modeled events, retention of what is observed, ability to imitate modeled behaviors, and motivation to reproduce those behaviors. The characteristics of the model contribute to the effectiveness of the procedure. The use of similar models, multiple models, and coping (as opposed to "mastery") performances have all been shown to assist effectiveness. The ability of the viewer "to identify" somehow with the model is often cited as an important factor.

When the model is similar, the observer will pay more attention and is more likely able to replicate the demonstrated behavior. Because it is the behavior that is important, behavioral similarity counts more than looks, social background, etc., and unusual models can be more distracting than effective. The use of multiple models can improve the magnitude of effect and its generalization to other settings.

Coping or "struggling" models are sometimes more effective than mastery models (which demonstrate only superior or expert performance), but the results of research have been mixed, especially given that higher status models also can be more effective. It may be best not to consider model status or coping versus mastery as factors in their own right, but to consider their contribution to attention getting and to examine how clearly they demonstrate skills that are appropriate and manageable for the trainee.

The characteristics of the observer and the setting also affect the efficacy of modeling. Sometimes observational learning must first be taught as a skill in itself (e.g., for children with autism). Emphasizing a positive outcome or reward for the target behavior can enhance the effectiveness of a model. But it is important to note the frequent failure of "negative outcome modeling" to act as a deterrent. The reverse is often the case, sometimes tragically. For example, more than once televised dramatizations of teenage suicides have been followed by increases in suicides by young people.

Modeling will normally take place early in the learning sequence: basic information, *modeling,* practice, feedback, and feedforward. It also can be used as a sophisticated component in advanced learning applications.

APPLICATIONS

Modeling has been widely applied and researched in a number of areas. Representative examples are described below in six broad categories.

Professional Training

Modeling is often used in the training of human services personnel. For example, videotaped modeling has been used as the major component in training health care personnel to handle psychiatric emergencies and as a smaller but key component in the training of job coaches. Other popular areas include the training of teachers and counselors, where it accounts for larger gains in specific skills than role playing or feedback.

Social Skills and Daily Living

Modeling as *in vivo* demonstrations are widely used as part of social skills training. Video modeling is the staple of many packaged programs and is underused in other situations. It has been the primary component in training programs as diverse as teaching young, isolated children to overcome their shyness, to providing alternatives to social behavior re-

lated to drug abuse, aggression, and other illicit or unhealthy activities. For example, films of age-appropriate students coping with social pressure to smoke cigarettes have been effective in programs at junior high schools. The programs with greatest effectiveness are those that illustrate adaptive coping (resisting coercion without destroying friendships) not those that show negative consequences (early death by cancer).

Parent and Child

Different forms of modeling have been widely used in programs for parent training. Although there is no substitute for realistic practice in acquiring skills for child care and management, it is equally clear that observing effective models is almost essential even to begin such practice. Most parent training is precipitated by conduct problems of children. Another approach is to address the child's problems directly by teaching self-management. Modeling also proves effective for this purpose, using either peers or adults.

Preparing for Medical and Dental Treatment

The need to prepare people (especially children) for scary treatment procedures has been extensively served by modeling strategies. Information (e.g., what steps are involved in the procedure) is important to emotional and long-term attitudes, but modeling is more essential to immediate behavioral change.

Motor Performance

Sport and other body coordination skills are widely taught using some form of demonstration by coaches, peers, and experts. Physical therapists also use modeling as the principal component in rehabilitation through therapeutic exercises. The commercial video market is replete with examples, usually by experts, for the development of individual skills.

Special Populations

Appropriately designed modeling has obvious application to "special" populations, who by definition may lack relevant models in their natural environment. Examples exist in the teaching of daily living skills, such as shopping for young adults with autism. Other types of skills for which modeling-based training has been developed include social skills, recreation, communication (especially sign language), vocational skills, and, to a lesser extent, academics. Whereas it would seem most appropriate to use peers as models, often the models are experts (or typically developing adults) who perform demonstrations carefully constructed to match the disability or developmental level of the trainees.

APPROACHES TO LEARNING
ASSERTIVENESS TRAINING
HUMAN RELATIONS TRAINING
PEER INFLUENCES
SOCIAL SKILLS TRAINING
SOCIODRAMA

P. W. DOWRICK

BEHAVIORAL TOXICOLOGY

Behavioral toxicology is the study of behavioral changes induced by exposure to environmental substances. It is a hybrid science, its foundations coming from the behavioral sciences and from toxicology. With an increasing association between the behavioral sciences and neurology, *neurobehavioral toxicology* may be an appropriate term to describe the field.

Studies of the behavioral effects on humans of exposure to toxic substances have lagged behind animal research for at least two reasons.

First, there are ethical limitations on exposing humans to potentially harmful substances. Second, most of the available techniques for measuring the effects of exposure have not proven to be sensitive to low-level exposure. The potential importance of behavioral toxicology lies in the realization that behavioral changes may be the earliest indicator of excessive exposure to a toxic substance.

The earliest symptoms of mercury poisoning in humans include irritability, anxiety, insomnia, hyperreactivity, shyness, and emotional instability. The gradual mood and character changes go unnoticed by the victim, while producing increasing problems in social relationships, a tendency toward depression, and signs of hypochondria. Psychological testing has shown a positive correlation between length of mercury exposure and neuroticism and introversion.

Organic solvents have been investigated extensively to see if they produce early neurobehavioral effects. This research led to the establishment of the new disease organic solvent syndrome (OSS), recognized in Scandinavia as a consequence of exposure to solvents. The symptoms are nearly identical to complaints following heavy-metal exposure and include lack of initiative, inability to concentrate, excessive fatigue, emotional instability, headache, and sexual dysfunction.

One of the most difficult issues confronting behavioral toxicology is the possibility that some individuals may be hypersusceptible to particular substances. There have been claims that certain kinds of food additives and food dyes may cause hyperactivity in children; this is known as the Feingold hypothesis after its discoverer. A small number of hyperactive children do show extreme hypersusceptibility to certain food additives.

Behavioral teratology, a subarea of behavioral toxicology, is defined as the study of the functional effects of toxicant exposure during the development of the nervous system. The exposure may either occur prenatally or postnatally. Some toxicants studied include food additives, therapeutic and drugs of abuse, hormones, alcohol, heavy metals, and pesticides. The early postnatal rat is often used as an animal model, because the development of the rat's brain in the first week of postnatal life is comparable with the developmental stage of the human brain at the end of the third trimester of pregnancy. Thus, according to Ruppert, "behavioral evaluation in rats following postnatal exposure to potential neurotoxicants can be a useful strategy for assessing the functional consequences of neurotoxic insult during later stages of brain development."

Drugs ingested prenatally may affect fetal development and produce physical and/or behavioral impairment. For example, the ingestion of alcohol during pregnancy may produce fetal alcohol syndrome (FAS).

A number of studies have pointed to the possibility of a neurotoxic effect of aluminum exposure as a potential cause of Alzheimer's disease (AD). Some evidence supporting such a notion includes the finding of elevated aluminum concentrations in the brains of AD victims, the report that aluminum intoxication may play a role in the phenomenon of dialysis dementia (altered behavior and dementia in kidney disease patients undergoing dialysis), and a variety of animal studies with cats, rabbits, and rats.

As one example of an animal study that found evidence for behavioral changes following aluminum ingestion, Thorne et al. fed adult rats chow containing different amounts of aluminum and found that heightened brain levels of aluminum were correlated with poor performance on a passive–avoidance task and with difficulties on a visual discrimination task with reversal. The highest concentrations of aluminum in the animals were found in the hippocampus; apparently the hippocampus has an affinity for concentrating metals such as lead and zinc.

Because of the enormous quantity of potentially neurotoxic substances, both synthetic and natural, to which humans are routinely exposed, the field of behavioral toxicology has burgeoned since its inception in 1975.

ACETYLCHOLINESTERASE
ALCOHOLISM TREATMENT

DRUG USERS' TREATMENT
NEUROCHEMISTRY
PSYCHOPHARMACOLOGY

B. M. THORNE

BEHAVIORALLY ANCHORED RATING SCALES

Behaviorally Anchored Rating Scales (BARS) is an approach developed by Patricia C. Smith and L. M. Kendall in 1963 to develop a well-defined, job-related rating scale. This approach was based on the critical incident approach of J. C. Flanagan, which outlined actual behavioral incidents indicative of successful or unsuccessful performance.

Behaviorally anchored rating scales have developed along two lines: behavioral expectation scales (BES) and behavioral observation scales (BOS). Both approaches can take long periods of time for development and involve many people, so that these techniques are usually limited to large organizations having job categories with many positions in each.

Both BARS techniques begin alike. Subject-matter experts (usually supervisors or employees in the specific job) are asked to participate in various group sessions. In the BES technique, the first group writes the major dimensions of the job, and a second group then develops performance incidents of varying levels of performance statements in each of these dimensions. A third group is asked to retranslate the work of the first two groups, that is, to put a randomized list of performance statements in the proper categories. Incidents that are not placed into the proper job category or dimension are dropped because of their ambiguity. A fourth group is then asked to put a value on the incidents that remain. Again, items with disagreement (high standard deviation) are eliminated. Finally, two supervisors are asked to rate each employee, and an analysis is completed to determine if the job dimensions are independent.

The BOS technique also starts by having a group of experts develop behavioral incidents. Subsequent group meetings involve rewriting and clarifying incidents, placing the incidents into job dimension, and determining if the incidents and dimensions are as independent as possible. Then a subordinate is evaluated on each incident or item on a scale ranging from 7 (very frequently) to 1 (rare or seldom). Incidents can all be worked in the same direction and a total score given. The basic advantage of the BARS technique seems to be the organizational involvement and support developed during implementation of the process.

JOB ANALYSIS
LIKERT SCALING
SCALING
THURSTONE SCALING

L. BERGER

BEHAVIORISM

Behaviorism was the most significant movement in experimental psychology for the first three quarters of the twentieth century. It was launched by John B. Watson in 1913, but had already begun in the work of psychologists such as E. L. Thorndike and Ivan Pavlov, and remains influential today despite an increasing chorus of criticism after about 1960.

Prior to behaviorism, experimental psychologists studied the mind, which they defined as conscious experience, and their research tool was one or another form of introspection. All were mentalists in taking mind as the subject matter of psychology to be described by introspection, and some were explanatory mentalists in seeking to explain conscious events as the result of underlying mental processes. Behaviorism rejects both mentalist tenets and mentalism's method of introspection.

METHODOLOGICAL VERSUS METAPHYSICAL BEHAVIORISM

Philosophically, one must distinguish two main justifications for rejecting mentalism and choosing behaviorism. A methodological behaviorist concedes that mental events and processes are real, but maintains that they cannot be studied scientifically. The data of science, says the methodological behaviorist, must be public events, such as the motions of the planets or chemical reactions, that all researchers can observe. Conscious experience, however, is necessarily private; introspection may describe it (often inaccurately), but does not make it public for all to see. Therefore, to be scientific, psychology must study only overt behavior and reject introspection. However real and fascinating, consciousness, methodologically speaking, cannot be scientific psychology's subject matter.

The metaphysical behaviorist makes a more sweeping assertion: Just as the physical sciences have rejected demons, spirits, and gods, showing them to be myths, so the psychologist must reject mental events and mental processes as mythical. This is not to say that mental concepts such as "idea" are necessarily meaningless (though they may be), any more than the concept "Zeus" is meaningless. We can describe Zeus and account for why people believed in him, while nevertheless asserting that the name Zeus never referred to anything that ever existed. Similarly, says the radical behaviorist, we can describe the conditions under which people use "idea" or any other mental concept, and account for why they believe they have minds, and still assert that "idea" or "mind" and so on do not refer to anything that really exists, except perhaps certain behaviors and certain stimuli. Therefore psychology must be behavioristic, because there is no mind to investigate: Behavior is all there is.

VARIETIES OF NEOBEHAVIORISM

The major varieties of neobehaviorism are formal behaviorism, including logical behaviorism and purposive (or cognitive) behaviorism; informal behaviorism; and radical behaviorism. All but the last are forms of methodological behaviorism; radical behaviorists uphold metaphysical behaviorism.

Formal Behaviorism

While the behaviorist takes the subject matter of psychology to be behavior, he does not necessarily rule out talking about unobserved processes that may be used to explain observed behavior. Indeed, under the influence of logical positivism and operationism, the formal behaviorist made it his job to explain observed behavior in terms of a theory consisting of just such unobserved entities. A given unobserved theoretical construct was operationally defined in terms of either manipulations performed on the animal, or some aspect of its stimulus environment, or a measurable aspect of its behavior. In this way formal behaviorists hoped to gain scientific status by accepting methodological behaviorism, while aspiring to the same kind of explanatory theory found in physics or chemistry, where unobserved theoretical terms are commonplace.

The *logical behaviorism* of Clark L. Hull and his associates was the most completely developed program of formal behaviorism. Following the lead of Newton and physics generally, Hull set out a hypothetico-deductive learning theory proposed to be valid for all mammals. The theory was stated as a set of axioms from which, via operational definition, predictions about behavior were derived that could then be put to the test.

E. C. Tolman's *purposive* or *cognitive behaviorism,* when contrasted with Hull's logical behaviorism, shows how different two behaviorisms can be in detail while retaining allegiance to Watson's broad creed. Tolman rejected the mechanistic muscle-twitchism of Watson and Hull. For them, learning consisted in associating certain stimuli with specific motor responses, thus eliminating reference to purpose or cognition, which they regarded as mysterious and mentalistic. Tolman, however, conceived of behavior as ineluctably *purposive,* in that animals are always acting to move toward or away from some goal; and of learning as ineluctably *cognitive;* its purpose being not to respond to stimuli, but to learn about one's environment.

Informal Behaviorism

After the golden age of theory in the 1930s and 1940s, behaviorism went through further evolution. The neo-Hullian behaviorism of the post-World War II era is sometimes called neobehaviorism, but a more descriptive phrase would be *informal behaviorism* or "liberalized S–R theory." The major hallmark of the movement was lessened concern with axiomatic grand theory and increased willingness to talk about the higher mental processes in human beings, if done in S–R mediational terms. Formal behaviorism thus became less rigidly formal and more flexible in handling important human phenomena such as language and problem solving.

The informal behaviorists conceived r–s pairs as central brain processes that nevertheless followed the usual laws of S–R learning, and so could be incorporated into operational S–R theories of learning with no abandonment of behaviorism.

The informal behaviorists were thus able to talk about thinking, memory, problem solving, and language in S–R behavior theory terms, treating them as covert parts of learned S–R connections. In this way the range of behavior explicable in S–R terms was increased. One notable result was social learning theory, a marriage of neo-Hullian behaviorism and psychoanalysis, with some of Freud's postulated mental mechanisms being treated as covert mediating behaviors.

Radical Behaviorism

The purest form of behaviorism is B. F. Skinner's radical behaviorism. Skinner rejected methodological behaviorism for the more radical assertion of metaphysical behaviorism: Mind and mental talk are cultural myths to be exploded and discarded.

Ordinary, everyday mentalistic talk is explained in three ways. First, some alleged mental events like a toothache are really just physical processes in the body that we have learned to label. There is no difference in principle between a public stimulus like a pinprick, and a private one like a toothache, except that one person alone has access to the latter stimulating event. Second, some mental events, especially feelings, are just collateral by-products of environmental influence and resulting behavior, but play no role in determining behavior. So one may "feel satisfied" if praised by one's boss, but what controls the behavior is the praise itself—the reinforcer—and not the collateral feeling. Unlike private stimuli, which may exert control over behavior, collateral feelings do not, and may be ignored by scientific psychology, however much they fascinate the phenomenologist. Finally, many mentalistic terms are simply rejected outright as myths, being regarded as verbal operants taught by our culture and entirely devoid of reference.

In its essence, though not at all in its details, radical behaviorism is the closest of all the neobehaviorisms to Watson's classical behaviorism.

BEHAVIORISM TODAY

Radical behaviorism is the only behaviorism exerting serious influence today. The other behaviorisms have passed into history, their founders' intellectual descendents having altered them beyond recognition.

But behaviorism as a philosophy and a historical movement remains an object of interest to psychologists, philosophers, and historians.

BEHAVIORISM: HISTORY
LOGICAL POSITIVISM
MECHANISTIC THEORY
MIND/BODY PROBLEM

PURPOSIVE BEHAVIOR
TELEOLOGICAL PSYCHOLOGY

T. H. Leahey

BEHAVIORISM: HISTORY

Behaviorism has a highly complex history within the broader context of developments in psychology, science, and American society. A simple starting place is a straightforward and succinct dictionary definition of it as "the psychological school holding that objectively observable organismic behavior constitutes the essential or exclusive scientific basis of psychological data and investigation and stressing the role of environment as a determinant of human and animal behavior" (*American heritage dictionary*).

Within psychology, the origins of behaviorism are generally attributed to the opening paragraph of a paper published by John B. Watson.

> Psychology as the behaviorist views it is a purely objective experimental branch of natural science. Its theoretical goal is the prediction and control of behavior. Introspection forms no essential part of its methods, nor is the scientific value of its data dependent upon the readiness with which they lend themselves to interpretation in terms of consciousness. The behaviorist, in his efforts to get a unitary scheme of animal response, recognizes no dividing line between man and brute. The behavior of man, with all of its refinement and complexity, forms only a part of the behaviorist's total scheme of investigation.

Watson's statement directly addressed the issue of the *control* of behavior that, more than any other, has pervaded the psychology and society in the last part of the twentieth century.

Skinner argued that behaviorism was "not the scientific study of behavior, but a philosophy of science concerned with the subject matter and methods of psychology."

As is true of every aspect of psychology, controversy abounds as to the origins and prehistory of behaviorism. Historians of psychology who were contemporaries of Watson (e.g., E. G. Boring, Edna Heidbreder, R. S. Woodworth) clearly credit Watson as being the "founder" of behaviorism. Later writers on the subject (e.g., A. E. Kazdin, F. Samelson) see Watson as a "catalyst" of a movement—toward "objectivism," away from "consciousness"—that was already well in progress. They note that Watson was not quite unique in the new approach that he called "behaviorism"—neither in terminology nor in what it stood for.

Some elements of the public reaction to Watson's *Behaviorism* must be noted particularly as commented on by leading newspapers of the era. The references may be a reaction to the most famous of Watson's assertions, widely quoted and misquoted through the years: "Give me a dozen healthy infants, well-formed, and my own specified world to bring them up in and I'll guarantee to take any one at random and train him to become any type of specialist I might select—doctor, lawyer, artist, merchant-chief, and, yes, even beggarman and thief, regardless of his talents, penchants, tendencies, abilities, vocations, and race of his ancestors."

The implications of this statement for behaviorism, and for American society, were of course enormous. Unfortunately, this quotation has usually been taken out of context, and the lines that follow are ignored: "I am going beyond my facts and I admit it, but so have the advocates of the contrary and they have been doing it for many thousands of years. Please note that when this experiment is made I am to be allowed to specify the way the children are to be brought up and the type of world they have to live in."

The behavioral movement in American psychology can be approached as a *scientific/social movement* influenced by, and in turn influencing, the broader society in which it developed. Behaviorism evolved in the context of the social, political, cultural, educational, economic, and intellectual history of twentieth-century America. Conversely, as the pragmatic philosophy of the behavioral movement spread beyond the bounds of the psychology laboratory, it influenced virtually every aspect of American life.

Historians of the psychology of the early twentieth century emphasize the growth of materialism, determinism, mechanism, and even anti-intellectualism as pervasive forces in American society as it moved from a predominantly rural to an urban base. These forces were compatible with, and articulated with, what have been seen as the major philosophical tenets of behaviorism.

There has been an affinity and mutual influence between behaviorism as embodied in Watson and the field of animal psychology. Animal psychology was presumably objective in the sense that the observer—like the astronomer, physicist, or botanist—necessarily stands outside the material he studies.

Yet later scholarship of early behaviorism, particularly that of Samelson, labels it a myth that behaviorism developed out of animal psychology because working with animals forced researchers into behavioral studies. For example, the major animal psychologists of the period, R. M. Yerkes and M. F. Washburn, rejected Watson and his theories. There already was a trend in psychology prior to and contemporaneously with Watson—especially in animal psychology—to question the usefulness of the concept of "consciousness."

The research and theoretical formulations of early investigators, particularly Watson, in their emphasis on environmental influences on behavior, brought to the fore the concepts of "learning" that became the central focus of experimental psychology through the subsequent decades. A series of investigators—E. L. Thorndike, E. R. Guthrie, E. C. Tolman, C. L. Hull, K. W. Spence, O. H. Mowrer, B. F. Skinner, A. Bandura, and others—attempted to construct theories or models of learning and postulated a variety of principles and mechanisms to explain "learning."

BEHAVIOR MODIFICATION
BEHAVIORISM
HISTORY OF PSYCHOLOGY
LOGICAL POSITIVISM

L. Krasner

BENDER GESTALT

In 1938 Lauretta Bender published a monograph entitled *A visual motor Gestalt test and its clinical use*. This simple test consists of nine geometric patterns consisting of dots, lines, angles, and curves. The designs are presented singly in a specified order to the subject, who is asked to copy each of them. The patterns were borrowed from Max Wertheimer's classical study on the theory of Gestalt psychology. These patterns were designed to illustrate the Gestalt principles of normal perceptual organization (e.g., proximity, continuity, closure) as applied to the grouping and patterning of stimuli. Deviations from these normal laws are considered symptoms in the Bender Gestalt. Since Bender was interested in the maturation of these laws from early childhood to adulthood, the simplest method of testing how the patterns were perceived was by having the subject copy them. Thus a critical motor factor was introduced that has its own laws of maturation; the task was transformed into a perceptual motor task.

Several adaptations of the original Bender test appeared in an effort to standardize the administration and scoring. By far the most innovative adaptation was Hutt's development of the test as a tool for evaluating personality dynamics, including symbolic psychoanalytic interpretation. The end result of all these conflicting adaptations has been great variability in the findings obtained from one study to the next, little agreement on the critical indices for differential diagnosis, and failures in the validation of the test. However, most clinicians agree that the Bender Gestalt is a useful tool for detecting the presence of brain damage and psychoses.

CLINICAL ASSESSMENT
GESTALT PSYCHOLOGY
PROJECTIVE TECHNIQUES

E. M. SIIPOLA

BENTON VISUAL RETENTION SCALE

Arthur L. Benton originally devised the Visual Retention Test to supplement auditory-vocal measures of retention. The present version of the test, known as the Revised Visual Retention Test, is designed to assess visual-spatial perception, and visuoconstructive abilities as well as memory.

There are three alternate equivalent forms of the test, each consisting of ten designs made up of one or more geometric figures. Each form may be administered under four different conditions, including copying the designs and reproducing them from memory, with variations in the time of exposure and in the amount of delay until actual reproduction of the designs.

The Benton Scale, like the Bender Gestalt and the Graham–Kendall Memory for Designs tests, has frequently been used by itself to screen for organicity. Although it has generally been found more effective than these and other comparable measures, the hit rates achieved vary a great deal depending on the characteristics of the samples used, such as psychiatric status and the extent and location of brain lesions. The Benton Scale appears to be an effective tool for assessing those brain functions that it was designed to tap, and when used knowledgeably in combination with supplementary measures, can make a significant contribution to the discriminating power of a neuropsychological battery.

BENDER GESTALT TEST
BRAIN
HALSTEAD-REITAN BATTERY
LURIA-NEBRASKA SCALE
ORGANIC BRAIN SYNDROMES

S. P. URBINA

BIBLIOTHERAPY

The term bibliotherapy is derived from two Greek words—*biblion* (book) and *therapeia* (healing)—and designates a form of supportive psychotherapy. Bibliotherapy has come to mean the application of all literary genres to the therapeutic process, including printed and nonprinted matter and audiovisual aids.

Bibliotherapy is sometimes practiced on a one-to-one basis. Usually, however, it is practiced on a group basis in hospitals, in clinics, and in educational, gerontological, mental health, and correctional centers.

Bibliotherapy materials can be powerful and dynamic tools for tapping large vistas of unknown feelings and for clarifying unresolved conflicts. The reading matter selected may be for purposes of sharing information or of addressing emotional needs, and is particularly effective when geared to the level of feeling and understanding of the individual.

The field of bibliotherapy is an expanding one, and in addressing itself to standards, ethics, and training, it appears to be gaining wider acceptance as a therapeutic tool.

POETRY THERAPY
LITERATURE AND PSYCHOLOGY

A. LERNER

BILINGUALISM

The bilingual individual knows two languages to the same extent and depth and is able to use them on any occasion with the same effectiveness. Besides commanding two languages, what characterizes a bilingual person is the capacity to keep the two linguistic systems separate, so as to switch easily from one to the other.

This definition refers to the perfect or ideal bilingual. What we encounter in real life are individuals who approach this definition in varying degrees. Any study on bilingualism must start by determining the degree of bilingualism of the subjects under study, the knowledge they have of each language, and the way they use them. Language tests specially designed for academic or clinical examinations and questionnaires can be used for that purpose. The subjects' familiarity with each language can also be measured by laboratory techniques.

The oldest and to a certain extent most interesting studies on bilingualism refer to children learning to speak in two languages at the same time. A child who grows up in a bilingual context learns to speak the two languages without difficulty, although with some slowness. Bilingual children internalize both languages very early, but normally adopt one of them as their first language.

For many years studies on bilingualism have sought to determine whether bilingualism favors or impairs intellectual development. Saers' research with Welsh children seemed to prove that it was harmful. Similar results were inferred from studies carried out in the United States with immigrant children. But in the 1960s Peal and Lambert presented results that showed a favorable influence, and other research confirms them. On the whole today it is thought that in well-balanced social circumstances and with a correct teaching, bilingualism is not detrimental and may even help develop certain intellectual aspects such as flexibility and creativity. However, very often these social and pedagogical conditions are not fulfilled, because bilinguals are at the same time generally members of underprivileged social groups.

COGNITIVE COMPLEXITY
CROSS-CULTURAL PSYCHOLOGY
LANGUAGE LEARNING
PSYCHOLINGUISTICS

M. SIGUAN

BIOENERGETICS

This system of psychotherapy developed by Alexander Lowen concentrates on releasing the body from tensions related to and resulting from defective body postures. These postural rigidities are theorized to inhibit a free flow of energies.

Bioenergetics issues from and relates to Wilhelm Reich's *Character analysis* and his system of Orgone Therapy. Lowen, a student of Reich, retained some of his teacher's concepts, but added others, especially "grounding."

Basic bioenergetics theory asserts we are only bodies in which tensions are stored and discharged. The optimal individual is firmly grounded and experiences pleasure in living. The disturbed person has a flow-block due to body rigidities, shown by stiffness and areas of tension in the body. Therapy calls for releasing these tensions through body work.

Therapy consists mainly of removal of blocks through exercises and postures antagonistic to the blocked areas. Rigid persons may be asked to howl and toss their arms about to loosen their muscular armor. In addition, they are taught to become grounded, to relax with nature.

INNOVATIVE PSYCHOTHERAPIES
PSYCHOTHERAPY

V. RAIMY

BIOFEEDBACK

Biofeedback is best understood as consisting of a closed feedback loop. The loop is composed of the organism as a control system, the response produced by the organism, and a means to detect and display the response for the control system. The control system is either programmed by instructions or influenced by rewards or punishments to modify the detected responses. For example, a person is instructed to increase the heart rate (the programmed phase); the heart rate is then detected by a monitor and fed back to the person. A feedback loop is thereby established, so that increases in heart rate can be indicated. Biological systems are replete with such feedback loops. In biofeedback the control system may be thought of as closely allied to the central nervous system and the learning process, rather than the more reflexive controls operating for homeostatic integrity.

There have been many attempts to develop voluntary control over processes considered automatic and self-regulatory in nature. Processes such as heart rate, blood pressure, and gastric secretion change along their respective dimensions, depending on metabolic needs and emotional states. But when such processes move beyond certain limits, then the health and proper functioning of the organism are compromised. Self-control can be viewed as a therapeutic method, with perhaps little of the side effects of more traditional therapies. A second stimulus for the development of biofeedback came from theorists concerned with disproving the hypothesis that responses innervated by the autonomic nervous system were not modifiable by reward learning. This position held that such responses were capable of being modified only through the conditional response techniques developed by I. P. Pavlov. A third impetus came from the interest in self-control of conscious states. The fact that electroencephalographic (EEG) rhythms could be modified by providing information to a person regarding EEG activity led to increased biofeedback research. Finally, the notion that self-regulation of neuromuscular function might help alleviate certain types of pain like a headache, or lead to recovery of muscular function following trauma or disease, further helped the development of biofeedback.

CONTROL OF AUTONOMIC RESPONSES

Early experimental reports indicated that human subjects might be able to voluntarily control the vasomotor response, electrodermal activity, and heart rate. Following these early studies, a number of laboratories began publishing data claiming to have effected instrumental learning on a variety of autonomically mediated responses, using different schedules of reinforcement, with both human and animal subjects.

Besides the usual methodological objections, criticism centered on the mechanism underlying the changes. The mediation issue was formulated, holding that true instrumental learning was not occurring. Instead, the subjects were somehow mediating the autonomic response either through some type of cognition (e.g., thinking calming or emotional thoughts) or some type of covert striate muscular activity, either intended or actual. Although this issue remains unresolved, recent work on subjects paralyzed by spinal lesions and plagued by hypotension indicates that neither cognitions, intended movement, nor actual movements can account entirely for the blood pressure increases learned. Autonomic instrumental learning is also influenced by such variables as type of feedback, awareness, instruc-

tions, and homeostatic restraints linking separate response systems both autonomic and somatic.

Biofeedback has been applied to Raynaud's disease, cardiac abnormalities, migraine headache, hypertension, functional diarrhea, asthma, as well as other problems with autonomic involvement such as anxiety, eczema, and sexual arousal. Evaluation of the therapeutic efficacy of biofeedback regarding these disorders remains controversial.

The application of biofeedback techniques to problems resulting from neuromuscular dysfunction has shown considerable promise. Neuromuscular feedback has shown impressive specificity of control by successfully training subjects to either activate or inhibit the activity of single motor muscle units.

ELECTROENCEPHALOGRAPHIC FEEDBACK

Attempts have been made to change EEG activity either through instrumental learning or through manipulation of cognitive states thought to underlie a specific range of EEG frequencies. Results of such studies argued that the amount of alpha did change and led to changes in the psychological state. Increased alpha was related to feelings of relaxed attention and absence of anxiety. Whether increases in alpha produced psychological changes or the psychological states produced the EEG changes became part of the mediation issue. Evidence available strongly implicates the role of eye movement in the production or suppression of alpha. This oculomotor hypothesis is the most salient explanation regarding alpha control. Convergence, divergence, and focusing of the eyes are related to the amount of alpha produced. Correlated psychological states with such changes are at least partly due to expectations.

Evaluation of the biofeedback research and its clinical applications reveal problems closely parallel to other areas of scientific psychology and its application. Theory development, mechanism of action, experimenter bias, placebo, and long-term benefits have all received attention and merit more.

ADAPTATION
BEHAVIORAL MEDICINE
THORNDIKE'S LAWS OF LEARNING

W. A. GREENE

BIOGRAPHICAL INVENTORIES

Taking a case history or obtaining a record of education and employment is almost always part of applied psychological work, and to some extent the experimental psychologists must also obtain something of a history on a subject. In psychological lore, it is often said that the best prediction of future behavior is past behavior in similar circumstances. Surprisingly, there are few structured tests for systematic scoring of personal history.

Four major sources for constructing scores or indexes from life history data are the following: (a) interviews with the target person or acquaintances, (b) personal documents and products such as diaries or works of an artist, (c) application blanks, and (d) biographical inventories. The first three may be used informally and impressionistically, or they may be quantified by rating or coding the frequency of use for categories of events or problems. Standardized application blanks may be quantified by attaching weights to items.

Most quantitative work on biodata have been done in connection with industrial or business purposes. Perhaps the only published biographical inventory constructed in a clinical context is the M-B History Record. A special quantified clinical use of biodata is to be found in *life changes* studies. These typically ask the subject to check a list of occurrences within the last 6 months or a year. The weighted results have been shown to correlate with problems of health or mental health.

CLINICAL ASSESSMENT
PERSONAL DOCUMENTS

N. D. Sundberg

BIOLOGICAL RHYTHMS

Biological rhythms are cyclic processes taking place within organisms. They have to do with much of the activity of life on earth. Their cycles may be circadian (lasting about a day) or may last longer, such as the monthly menstrual cycle. This rhythmic activity is determined by processes and forces both inside and outside the body. An example of a biological rhythm is that of the change from sleep to a wakened state. Such a change between sleep and wakeful behavior comes from "biological clocks" in the cells and organs of the body. Accordingly, the cells of our bodies contain timers or "individual clocks," which in association with RNA (ribonucleic acid) process proteins in a cyclic 24-hour period.

But not all the biological clocks' dynamics come from in-processes. Some influences come from the environment, as for example the effects of the rotation of the earth and moon. Most human activity is affected by the revolutions of the earth around the sun and the moon's orbit around the earth.

In human beings, circadian rhythms are often changed by physical processes taking place internally. Variation, for example, in body temperature follows a circadian rhythm with the low parts of the cycle occurring in the early morning and late at night. At the highest point, midday, one finds the best performance on complex tasks.

When we change our activity from our normal rhythm we cause confusion in our bodies, as when we experience "jet lag." The change from east to west or west to east interrupts the usual pattern of sleep and activity our bodies are accustomed to. We do not feel well until our body functioning adapts to a new cycle of sleep and wakefulness.

Biological rhythms are just beginning to be understood in their importance in our lives since, as in other areas of human behavior, we have difficulty in separating biological from environmental influences.

CIRCADIAN RHYTHMS

T. Alexander

BIRTH INJURIES

The occurrence of severe injuries to the infant during labor and delivery has greatly decreased, owing primarily to marked improvements in the obstetrical management of at-risk pregnancies. Techniques such as ultrasound scanning to determine fetal position prior to labor, and the use of internal fetal heart monitoring during labor, have significantly reduced the incidence of mortality and morbidity caused by the process of birth. The total elimination of injury, however, has not been achieved. Approximately 5% of deliveries in the United States end in some degree of injury to the infant. The two most common injuries are anoxia and structural damage to the brain or body of the infant.

Anoxia is any type of oxygen deprivation to the brain or other tissues. Severe, prolonged oxygen deprivation may result in fetal or neonatal death. Effects on surviving infants are clearly related to the duration and degree of oxygen deprivation. Deprivation of less than a few minutes usually causes no apparent damage to the infant. Longer periods are linked to brain damage, which may be manifested behaviorally as learning disabilities, psychomotor impairment, intellectual impairment, cerebral palsy, seizure disorders, speech defects, and paralysis. The causes of anoxia during birth are many, the most common being lengthy labor, premature birth, umbilical cord accidents, premature separation of the placenta from the uterine wall, and obstetrical management.

Prolonged labor (longer than 20 to 24 hours) can cause decreases in maternal blood oxygen level, resulting in oxygen deprivation in the fetus. Premature delivery of the infant (prior to 38 weeks gestational age) is a frequent cause of anoxia. The infant is often incapable of unassisted respiration because of an immature respiratory system. Resuscitation and mechanical assistance for respiration are often necessary to keep the infant alive and to prevent further oxygen deprivation. Accidents to the umbilical cord may cause anoxia in a number of ways. Prior to birth, the cord may be wrapped around the neck of the fetus and constrict during labor and delivery, restricting blood flow to the brain. Any obstruction of blood flow through the umbilical cord, the only source of oxygen to the fetus, itself causes oxygen deprivation until independent respiration is established. A prolapsed cord, where a section of the cord is delivered through the birth canal before the infant, is the most common type of obstruction. The cord becomes wedged between the maternal pelvis and fetal head, thereby blocking blood flow. Severing of the umbilical cord after delivery prior to established, independent neonatal respiration can also lead to anoxia.

Newborn infants may also fail to establish independent respiration after delivery because of drugs used by the mother for pain control during labor and delivery. Obstetrical medication passes quickly to the fetus through the placenta and umbilical cord. Many of these drugs have been shown to depress the infant's respiratory system and impair the infant's ability to breathe. Assistance is necessary to prevent serious oxygen deprivation. Excessive amniotic fluid in the throat and lungs can also hinder oxygen intake. Immediate removal of the fluid by suctioning is necessary to allow the infant to breathe independently.

Infants delivered by forceps may suffer intercranial injury and hemorrhage. The effects of this intercranial damage depend on the extent of the damage and hemorrhaging. In severe cases the infant may die within minutes of the injury. In relatively mild cases, no apparent after effects are evident.

EMBRYO AND FETUS
INFANT DEVELOPMENT
MINIMAL BRAIN DYSFUNCTION

K. A. McCluskey

BIRTH ORDER

Empirical studies of birth order have involved a search for correlates between personality variables and ordinal position in the family. Birth-order research has a disconnected character, being almost always atheoretical, so that many conflicting findings appear in the literature.

The typical research procedure is to ask for birth-order, without accounting for variables in the order itself such as age, separation between siblings, sex differences, abortions, miscarriages, or stillborns. The reported findings are often inconclusive because the researchers do not compare persons born in similar positions. The most critical need is that a birth-order research model be established. Most researchers do not view birth order as a determinant of personality, but believe that the order itself describes an influencing environment for the individual.

The following represent empirical studies reporting birth-order differences statistically significant at or beyond the 0.05 confidence level. More than 3000 birth-order research studies were examined, but only a very small sample of published reports can be summarized. Research findings suggest five psychological positions, and this review is prepared along these divisions: first-, second-, middle-, last-, and only-born child in the family.

FIRST-BORN

First-borns have better high school grades than the later-born students; are most vulnerable to stress; attend college in greater number than their later-born peers; and show the greatest representation among problem children.

SECOND-BORN

The second-born child represents a distinct birth-order category. Such children manifest greater dependency behavior than either first- or later-borns; seek more adult help and approval than first- or later-borns; spend more time in individual activity; are generally more talkative; and express more negative affect than other subjects. Many seemingly effeminate boys are first- or especially second-born. Second-borns in same-sex dyads appear to imitate the same-sex parent more than their older sibling.

MIDDLE-BORN

Middle children tend to be better adjusted emotionally if from large families; have the greatest feeling of not belonging; are most sensitive to injustices and feelings of being slighted; are most successful in team sports; are most likely to study music and languages and to practice the creative arts; have aesthetic interests; and are overrepresented among actors.

LAST-BORN

Last-borns affiliate with a fraternity more than first-borns and only children; appear to have the highest self-esteem; are best adjusted if from large families; have the greatest overrepresentation of psychiatric disorders if from small families; and are most likely to have the lowest IQ and to experience school failure. Later-born females tend to have significantly lower self-esteem than expected.

ONLY-BORN

Growing up without siblings has no unusual impact on personality development. Only-borns are overrepresented in regard to emotional disturbance, and the only son has the strongest need for nurturance. Only-borns appear to assume less responsibility for success than do first- or later-borns; are most likely to be referred for clinical help; and are most likely to return for more clinical help.

SPACING

Like-sexed siblings with closer age spacing get higher scores on tests of cognitive abilities. First-borns having siblings less than 3 years younger show greater need for affiliation and help than first-borns not having close siblings.

PARENTAL INFLUENCE

First-borns report higher parental control than those born later. In a study of Norwegian families, males have a higher value than females in the parents' eyes.

The authority of parents is accepted more fully by first-born than by later-born male adolescents. Paternal authority is perceived to be most important in the academic and economic interest of first-born children.

Mothers are perceived as more accepting than fathers; and younger parents are perceived as more accepting than older parents; and younger children perceive their parents to be more accepting and more firmly controlling than do older children.

SIBLING INFLUENCE

Older siblings are perceived as more powerful, while younger siblings are perceived as showing more resentment and appealing more to parents for help. In a study of two-sibling families, highest conformity was found for later-born females with a same-sex sibling. Men who express special fondness for an older sister tend to marry women who had only younger brothers.

Both first- and later-born females tend to be more socially oriented than first- and later-born males. First-born and only children are significantly more self-disclosing, and both sexes disclose more to friends than to siblings, with preference for disclosure to siblings of the same sex. The highest discloser is one who has available a sibling of the same sex who is 1 or 2 years older.

Intelligence scores rise with increasing maternal age and fall with increasing birth order.

Last-borns are overrepresented among heavy drinkers. Only children are overrepresented on skid row. The first-born in a family—or at least the first male in the family—had a greater tendency toward alcoholism than other children, where the first-born male has had to help provide for the family at the earliest possible age.

ACADEMIC ACHIEVEMENT

First-borns attend college more than expected, and score higher in intellectual and academic performance. When differences in level of motivation are controlled, differences between first-borns and last-borns disappear.

Test scores on the National Merit Scholarship Qualifying Test decrease as the size of family increases and decrease within the same family with the order of birth. There is an increased preoccupation with intellectual achievement among first-borns with brothers. On measures of intelligence, first-borns score higher; education of the mother or father, family income, and the mother's age do not alter the relationship.

MENTAL HEALTH

In a study of schizophrenia there was an overrepresentation of cases from the second half of the birth order, especially among patients from very large families. In a study of schizophrenia there was an overrepresentation of early ranks in sibships of five and larger. A peak of schizophrenia occurs at the second from last position, and this was true consistently for each of five studies.

In a military training camp, only children were more likely than first children to consult the psychiatrist, to be diagnosed as psychoneurotic, and to be discharged from the service. Diagnoses of first children were almost equally divided between psychoneurosis and personality disorder. Few second children were diagnosed as psychoneurotic; usually they were diagnosed as having personality disorder.

First-borns are highest in paranoia tendency, while middle-born groups are high on anxiety. When first-borns have an audience, they display poorer recall than later-borns. First-borns report higher fear than later-borns. First-borns and only children are more sensitive to pain, and first-borns are more affiliative.

MARRIAGE

First-born women are more likely to attend prenatal classes than later-borns. First-born males are younger at marriage than later-born males. Dyads of first-born spouses are closer together in age than dyads of later-born spouses. More first-born women are married in June than later-borns. No significant difference is found between first-borns and later-borns in age of wives at marriage and length of engagement.

A higher proportion of ever-marrieds is found among both eldest sons and eldest children. The lowest proportions of ever-marrieds are found among youngest sons. Marriages consisting of a first-born and a later-born are more successful than marriages composed of two first-borns or two later-borns.

DELINQUENCY

Delinquent children come from larger than average-size families. First-borns and delinquents from smaller families are better socialized or have better socialization resources than last-borns and those from larger families. Middle children have the greatest risk of delinquency. First-borns are underrepresented among delinquents and are more likely to successfully complete the parole period, as compared with later-borns.

OCCUPATION

First-born women express significantly greater interest in a college profession career than later-born women, while first-born and later-born men show about the same degree of interest.

Women employed in occupations that are not sex-typical are younger and more likely to be first-born, to have had working mothers, and to mention males as important career influences.

TWINS

Girl twins are more often premature on the basis of weight; incidence of prematurity is seven times that of singletons; physical defects occur most frequently in the most premature; teachers' ratings indicate no significant difference between the health of twins and singletons; mothers of fraternal twins are older at the birth of their babies than mothers of identical twins; lesser weight of twins tends to persist into early school years.

Twins raised singly from birth have higher scores on measures of intelligence than twins raised together, and lower scores than those of single births. The twin born first develops psychomotor skills better, regardless of birth weight. The psychomotor development in the first 6 months of life is more similar in monozygotic than in dizygotic twin partners. Developmental patterns are better associated with birth weight than with birth order.

Twins show immature solitary play patterns. A first-born twin has a 15% greater probability of having a higher IQ than his or her partner; being the heavier twin raises by 65% the probability of having a higher IQ.

ADLERIAN PSYCHOLOGY
BIRTH ORDER AND PERSONALITY
FIELD DEPENDENCY
PERSONALITY THEORIES

C. R. BRASINGTON

BIRTH ORDER AND PERSONALITY

One of Alfred Adler's most significant contributions to psychology has been the relationship between birth order and personality development. Adler hypothesized that the position of the child in the family introduces specific problems that are handled in generally the same way. Such experiences associated with birth order result in a characteristic personality for each ordinal birth position.

There has been a plethora of research on birth order. Despite the highly empirical nature of most of the research, results are often restricted to isolated phenomena and incomplete explanations, as there is an absence of an underlying and comprehensive theory of birth order. There appears to be much documentation that the psychological ramifications of being raised in a certain ordinal position account for relationships between birth order and other phenomena, but little has been done toward understanding or explaining birth-order results. It appears that the birth order alone cannot explain the obtained results.

The amount of research on birth order reflects its importance, however. Even when contradictory research results are obtained, the methodology or a poor theoretical basis on which the research was built can account for the findings. Allman, and R. L. Greene and J. R. Clark, found few differences in personality profiles when all factors other than birth-order were eliminated. Even with that damning of birth-order research, it continues with significant results being achieved, especially when the various critical factors are controlled. What is becoming increasingly clear is that "influences of birth order are more general than has been suggested by Adler," prompting Mosak to suggest that one's own *subjective psychological* birth-order perception is more important than mere biological birth position.

Adler stated that, to understand a human being, the entire context of the family atmosphere needs to be understood and that an important issue within that rearing is the birth position in the family constellation. As the family group develops, different needs arise and the fulfillment of these needs is assigned to each child in order of birth. The style of coping is never the same for any two children as the situation changes. Adler pointed out that the needs or demands that influence a particular style of life correspond to the child's perceived particular birth order.

What follows are the four birth-order categories with corresponding descriptions and research findings. It should be stressed that such descriptions indicate general trends to assist psychologists in making *guesses* relative to birth order and personality dynamics rather than only the labeling of individuals.

FIRST-BORN

First-born children occupy a unique position in the family. Parents have more time and attention to devote to their first child and are apt to be more cautious, indulgent, and protective. The first-born does not have to compete with older siblings and, for a while, has only adult models to copy and adult standards of conduct to emulate.

Research indicates that these factors do have an effect. First-born children are more likely to score at the upper extremes on intelligence tests, be highly motivated, achieve eminence, and have a high need for achievement. There are just as many first-born National Merit Scholarship winners as second- and third-borns combined. They are the most frequent in *Who's Who* and are most likely to be found in leadership positions.

Such children tend to be very responsible and are production-minded in order to meet the adult standards. They are conservative, conscientious, and cooperative, reflecting the desire to maintain their privileged position with their parents after a rival appears.

MIDDLE CHILDREN

Second-born and/or middle children never experience the uniqueness of being the only one. They strive harder and will often compete to "take over." The middle child may walk in the shadow of the older sibling whom he or she seeks to overtake. The middle child often feels less competent than the older child (not realizing that his or her inadequacies are a function of age) and may try to excel in other areas. For example, if the oldest child has an intellectual bent, the middle child may be athletically or artistically inclined.

Research indicates that middle children are sensitive to injustices, unfairness, and feelings of being wronged. They are likely to be found in aesthetic endeavors. Middle children, being very sociable and accepting, are good diplomats, work well as team members, relate well to older and younger people, and are able to maintain good relationships.

YOUNGEST CHILDREN

The youngest child also occupies a unique position in the family. He or she never has a pursuer and, being the "baby of the family," will never be dethroned. The early socialization of last-borns more frequently involves indulgent, pampering treatment by other family members, resulting in a dependent-impulsive personality type.

The youngest child tends to be spoiled, as the older siblings join in with the parents to attend to all of his or her needs. Frequently, the result of this is a sense of security and a noncompetitive nature; he or she will strive to be always supported by others. The youngest child is frequently the most "powerful" in the family, resorting to the *aggressive* acting out or crying.

The youngest have a more developed lighter side to their personalities and are fun loving. Youngest children tend to be the most popular and affiliative and have the highest self-esteem of all birth positions. They are creative and humanitarian and have the highest appreciation of humor. When from a very large family, last-borns have the strongest need to achieve and are the best adjusted. However, they are most likely to experience school failure, to be alcoholic (a dependent personality), and to have the lowest IQ. Nonetheless, the last-born position is the best-liked of all possible birth positions.

ONLY CHILDREN
Only children share with youngest children the fact that they are never dethroned or displaced; they are never pursued. They also share the uniqueness of the first-born and do not have to compete for attention, having only adult behaviors and standards to emulate. Only children tend also to be spoiled by parents and may devote later years attempting to regain the favored position, having occupied stage center without having had to do anything for it. The result for the only child is that he or she will either remain dependent and helpless or will strive to meet adult competency.

Research indicates that only children have problems with close relationships, tending to be loners and lonely. Onlys tend to be selfish, with the lowest need for affiliation. They are most eager to please, yet maintain the most autonomy and are the least afraid of failure. Such children are most likely to go to college and are academically successful. Next to the first-born, the only child has the highest IQ and the highest need for achievement. In fact, the only child does achieve academically as a leader, and makes the best teacher or composer. Psychologically, only children have the most problems, being most likely to be referred for clinical help with psychiatric disorders and to be repeaters for such help.

Investigation will continue, since the merits and potential of our present knowledge and hoped-for future research data play an important role in the understanding of human behavior.

BIRTH ORDER
CHILD PSYCHOLOGY
EARLY CHILDHOOD DEVELOPMENT
SIBLING RELATIONSHIPS

R. E. Driscoll
D. G. Eckstein

BIRTH TRAUMA
Birth trauma is the idea that birth is a physically difficult and psychologically terrifying experience for the infant, and that memory of this experience remains buried in the unconscious. This idea is at least as old as Buddha, who considered birth one of the five inevitable sufferings of human life. The psychoanalyst Otto Rank, one of Freud's disciples, elaborated on the basic concept in *The trauma of birth.* He explained that leaving the uterus, where food, warmth, quiet, and oxygen are abundant, to enter the harsh world of hunger, cold, noise, and breathing difficulties was bound to be traumatic. According to psychoanalytic theory, any traumatic experience leaves a scar on the individual's mind that interferes with normal, rational thinking; Rank proposed that birth was such a trauma.

Some psychologists and psychiatrists, among them R. D. Laing, agree with Rank's formulation. As a result, they encourage adults to attempt to reexperience their own births, in order to bring to consciousness the buried memories that may be warping the person's adult development.

Some physicians have attempted to reduce the newborn's pain at the sudden transition from the womb. Foremost among these is Frederick Leboyer who, in *Birth without violence,* describes the "torture of the innocent" that is modern hospital birth, asking, "what futility to believe that so great a cataclysm will not leave its mark?" Leboyer suggests that several things can be done to create a "gentle birth," among them postponing the cutting of the umbilical cord, dimming the lights and stilling the noise of the delivery room, and bathing the newborn in lukewarm water—all to slow down the rapid transition from one world to another.

Other psychologists and physicians believe birth trauma is more fantasy than fact. They point out, for example, that medical procedures that are very painful for older children, such as circumcision or the setting of a broken bone, produce very few cries from newborns. In addition, if newborns are held securely next to their mother's body, or are wrapped snugly in a soft blanket immediately after birth, they quickly become peaceful and curious—not the usual reaction after a traumatic experience.

Nevertheless, while birth trauma remains unproven, many parents and medical personnel have attempted to make the newborn's first moments after birth more pleasant. Holding the newborn upside down and slapping it, or whisking it away before the mother and father can hold it, are much less common than they once were.

PSYCHOANALYSIS
RANKIAN PSYCHOLOGY
REBIRTHING

K. S. Berger

BISEXUALITY
Bisexuality is a word applied to an adult whose desire for, and/or choice of, sexual partners includes persons of both the opposite and the same sex. In conception, the bisexual person should have no preference, being equally attracted to both males and females, but the term is often misapplied to individuals who have partners of both sexes and also have a clear preference for one or the other sex.

The prototype bisexual is the "3" on the 7-point scale of sexual preference proposed by Alfred Kinsey and his associates in their classic book, *Sexual behavior in the human male.*

While individuals who have sexual contact with persons of both sexes are not uncommon, true bisexuals are relatively rare. Kinsey and his colleagues found that just more than 3% of adult White males fit his definition of bisexual. Among females, a little more than 1% of the single females were 3s.

HOMOSEXUALITY
SEXUAL DEVIATION

E. E. Levitt

BLACKY PICTURES
Designed as a tool for investigating psychodynamic dimensions of personality, the Blacky Pictures can be classed as a modified projective technique. The pictures are a series of dog cartoons, the first portraying a cast of characters that includes the hero Blacky (described as male or female, according to the sex of the test taker), the parents Mama and

Papa, and a sibling of unspecified age and sex named Tippy. In the 11 test cartoons Blacky is shown in settings intended to tap stages of psychosexual development, types of defense mechanisms, and forms of interpersonal relationships.

The subject's task is first to make up a vivid, imaginative story for each of the cartoons and then to respond to a series of multiple-choice and short-answer inquiry items pertaining to that cartoon.

PERSONALITY
PSYCHOANALYSIS
ROSENZWEIG PICTURE FRUSTRATION STUDY

G. S. BLUM

BLOCK DESIGN TEST

This test developed by Samuel C. Kohs was based on an extensive 1921 study and published in 1923. It was intended as a nonverbal test of intelligence that presumably tapped analytic and synthetic aspects of cognitive functions. Kohs' findings demonstrated that the test correlated reasonably well with results obtained on the Stanford–Binet Test of Intelligence ($r = 0.81$) in a wide age range from 2 years 7 months to adulthood (although applicable norms are not reliable below 5 years of age). Revision of both the directions for the test and the norms continued by other workers for a number of years.

This test is still used extensively as part of intelligence test batteries, as by Wechsler in his Wechsler Adult Intelligence Test (WAIS). The test has also been found to be highly useful in analyzing aspects of "constructive" intelligence involving the conversion of perceptual impressions into planned constructive behavior.

INTELLIGENCE MEASURES
LURIA-NEBRASKA SCALE
WECHSLER TESTS

M. L. HUTT

BLOCKING

The inference that the temporal contiguity between events is not sufficient for an association to be formed between them is by now commonplace. An outstanding example of this conclusion is the phenomenon of blocking. Blocking occurs when conditioning to a stimulus is attenuated or "blocked" because that stimulus signals an outcome previously predicted by another cue. Specifically, a subject trained to a conditioned stimulus (A) prior to conditioning to a compound stimulus (AB), that was formed from the original element (A) and an added element (B), does not evidence learning when tested to B alone. The previous training to A somehow blocks or prevents conditioning to the new stimulus.

The theories which have superseded the Rescorla–Wagner model may be distinguished on the basis of whether they focus attention on the processing of the unconditioned stimulus (US) or on the processing of the conditioned stimulus (CS). In accounting for blocking, A. R. Wagner's information-processing theory retains the crucial feature of the Rescorla–Wagner model, namely, that associations are established between events because of the processing devoted to the US. By this account, an event that resides in memory prior to its actual occurrence is not processed to the same extent as an event that is unexpected—that is, one that is not in memory when it actually occurs. Thus the loss of associability to the new CS in blocking occurs because the initial stimulus during compound conditioning evokes the memory of the US; the US is now represented in memory with the new element and the compound stimulus. Thus when

the US actually occurs, less processing takes place between it and the new cue.

Mackintosh's attentional theory offers an alternative account of blocking by positing a stimulus-specific rate parameter that is decremented in the face of no change in reinforcement. Stimuli that consistently track and so predict emotional outcomes (US) tend to be heeded on subsequent trials; conversely, stimuli that signal no change in the nature of the US are eventually ignored. Since the qualitative and quantitative properties of the US remain unchanged during the second stage of the blocking paradigm, there is a loss in the associability to the new but redundant cue.

The basic notion of Mackintosh's theory is that the associative strength of a particular CS depends on the extent to which it is a reliable predictor of the US relative to other stimuli. It assumes that the salience of the stimulus continues to increase as long as that stimulus remains a good predictor. Peace and Hall have modified this counterintuitive notion of Mackintosh's theory by proposing that the CS will continue to be processed to the extent that it is paired with an unpredicted or surprising US. Blocking is explained by suggesting that the new CS will not be processed, because it has been paired with an unsurprising US. While none of these theories can accommodate all the observations made from the blocking paradigm, they have stimulated considerable research and new, promising avenues of conceptualizing the learning process.

CONDITIONING
INFORMATION PROCESSING

E. J. RICKERT

BODY IMAGE

People are affected in a very fundamental way by how they perceive their bodies and how they think others perceive them. This perception is related to societal standards and cultural concepts. Thus, in certain cultures, a hefty body is considered attractive, while in other cultures the ideal is a slim and trim figure. Persons are not simply affected by the social and cultural standards of physical beauty; rather, their attitudes and evaluations of certain body traits determine how they feel about themselves.

If persons feel basically unattractive, unappealing, or in some way physically inferior, these self-perceptions are likely to have a powerful effect on other areas of their lives.

In discussing the relationship between body image and the healthy personality, Sidney Jourard commented that a healthy body ideal is one that is not too discrepant from the cultural concept of an ideal body, but that is revised by the person to make allowances for uniqueness and individuality. His and Landsman's *Healthy personality* points out that people modify their views of the ideal body to make allowances for increasing age, so they can continue to regard themselves as reasonably attractive at each stage of life. This adjustment is important, since otherwise one may aspire to unrealistic and unattainable goals. In Sidney Jourard's view, an accurate body concept is essential for achieving a healthy personality. Unfortunately, many people have been taught erroneous beliefs about their bodies. They may become alienated from their bodies and lose the capacity to pay attention to the messages their bodies are sending to themselves and to others.

One's body image—the picture and evaluation of one's body—is a basic part of one's self-concept. While cultural standards of beauty are critical in forming this self-evaluation, one's attitudes are even more influential in determining one's self-concept. One of the problems with uncritically accepting cultural norms of the ideal body is that few people really attain them. For those who fall drastically short of these cultural ideals, the result can be devastating in terms of self-worth as it relates to body image. It is thus essential for individuals to make an honest assessment of how they see their bodies and how they feel about them. This subjective evaluation of their bodies is at least as powerful as their objective physical traits and fortunately is open to change.

CONSTITUTIONAL TYPES
DRESS
FACIAL EXPRESSIONS
GESTURES

G. COREY

BOGARDUS SOCIAL DISTANCE SCALE

The Bogardus Social Distance Scale was one of the first techniques for measuring attitudes toward racial and ethnic groups. Underlying the scale is the basic concept that the more prejudiced an individual is against a particular group, the less that person will wish to interact with members of the group. Thus the items that compose a Bogardus scale describe relationships into which a respondent might be willing to enter with a member of the specified cultural group (e.g., spouse, friend, neighbor, coworker, citizen, visitor to our country, etc.). Items are worded in terms of either inclusion or exclusion. "Would you accept an X as a spouse?" is an inclusion-type question. "Would you keep all Ys out of America?" is an exclusion-type question. The respondent's attitude toward the specified group is defined by how close a relationship the respondent is willing to accept with a member of that group. In E. S. Bogardus' early work, he found that White Americans maintained relatively small social distances toward the British, Canadians, and northern Europeans, but greater social distances toward southern Europeans. Groups that differed racially were subject to even larger social distances. Extending the typical use of Bogardus scales, Triandis and Triandis used multifactor experimental designs to separate the independent effects of varying aspects of group membership (e.g., race, religion, and occupation). They later showed that various aspects of group membership of the respondents interact with the social distances they assign various other groups. Thus Americans were found to consider race an important variable, while Greeks considered religion to be more critical. Personality factors such as dogmatism have also been shown to be related to one's desire to maintain relatively large social distances with groups other than one's own.

ATTITUDE MEASUREMENT
GUTTMAN SCALING
PREJUDICE/DISCRIMINATION
RACE BIAS IN TESTING
SCALING
STEREOTYPING

K. F. GEISINGER

BONDING AND ATTACHMENT

John Bowlby introduced the term *attachment,* which was established as the essential concept for a new theoretical approach that combines ethology and psychoanalysis for understanding the origins of a child's bond to the mother.

ETHOLOGICAL THEORY AND ATTACHMENT

Animal studies suggest that lasting attachments are formed by a process of *imprinting* that occurs in a short time span at an early critical period of life. Ethology assumes that genetically preprogrammed behaviors im-

portant for species survival interact with the environment to produce bonding.

Konrad Lorenz, a pioneer in the study of imprinting, demonstrated that newly hatched fowl such as goslings would become fixed upon and follow the first moving proximal object or person they encountered shortly after birth. Niko Tinbergen demonstrated that the fight-flight response in animals evolves into socialized ritualistic behaviors. Robert Zaslow concluded from studies of the pathology of attachment found in infantile autism that the formation of attachment depends on two bonding networks of behavior: (a) the body–contact bond, necessary for intimacy and basic trust; and (b) the eye–face–contact bond, necessary for integration, focus, and direction of behavior.

LEARNING THEORY AND ATTACHMENT

Learning theorists have stressed the importance of feeding as a primary drive-reducing reinforcement mechanism for the development of attachment to the mother as a learned process. The satisfaction of the primary drive of hunger results in a positive attachment to the mother through a secondary reinforcement in the feeding situation. A new development in learning theory appeared when Harry Harlow stated that oral gratification through feeding was not sufficient to develop attachment and affection when mannequin monkey mothers were used.

DEVELOPMENT OF ATTACHMENT

In general, attachment emerges in a series of developmental steps that are species-specific. In the beginning, the infant is attached to all humans who exhibit species behaviors that are effectively compatible. Bowlby describes the development of attachment behavior as having four phases: (a) orientation and signals as a general reaction with no discrimination of a specific person, (b) orientation and signals directed to one or more discriminated people, (c) maintenance of proximity to a person by means of locomotion and signals, and (d) formation of a reciprocal relationship with people. Strong attachments to specific persons appear at approximately 7 months of age and are exhibited as a fear of strangers. Infants display protest behavior in the form of anger and resistance when separated from a person to whom they are attached. The protest behavior is increased in an unfamiliar environment, indicating attachment to place as well as people. As cognition and memory develop in the child, the intensity of protest and the need for physical proximity are reduced because the separation is seen as temporary.

QUALITY OF ATTACHMENT

The stability and strength of attachment depends on the quality of parental–infant interaction patterns. A positive attachment is developed by a combination of nuturant-affectionate behaviors and the expression of resistant-angry behaviors in the infant and child. Chronic unresolved anger in parent and child disturbs attachment formation. Rhythm and timing have been found to affect the quality of attachment. Infants are more attached to the parent who responds quickly and spontaneously initiates interactions. Later studies by Ainsworth reveal that the quality of attachment depends on stimulation and control of the environment and child. Ainsworth stated that infants may be securely or anxiously attached, thus affecting the quality and stability of attachment.

ATTACHMENT AND PSYCHOPATHOLOGY

Bowlby showed that after the initial positive bond is formed between mother and infant at about 6 months, the infant reacts to loss of the mother in three characteristic stages. First, there is "protest"—crying and anger that serve to bring mother back. If this is unsuccessful, a period of "despair" follows, characterized by withdrawal, depression, and decrease in activity. Finally, a stage of "detachment" appears in which the infant is relatively unresponsive to people. The child's anger toward the mother figure is a central feature of this pattern. The anger is expressed openly in the protest phase and indirectly in the detachment phase. Bowlby stated that the separation experience elicits intense and violent hatred of the mother figure.

Bowlby's observations on separation and loss are supported by the infant studies of Ainsworth and a number of infrahuman primate studies. René Spitz described anaclitic depression as a condition in which the infant, when separated from the mother, dies because of hospitalization. Zaslow and Breger made an attachment analysis of early infantile autism, which is followed by separation and loss. They derived several theoretical conclusions applicable to normal human attachment and the psychopathology of attachment. The first was that holding a child in a state of protest behavior, characteristic of infant-child crying, forms a stress-to-relaxation cycle that is a fundamental unit of positive attachment. The greater the intensity of "protest," the greater the relaxation and the stronger the bond between child and parent. The second conclusion was that social-affective human attachment is to the face and not to the breast. The human species-specific behaviors important for the maintenance of face-to-face interactions, such as smiling, crying with tears, talking, and listening, are not found in the autistic child, who strongly resists eye-face contact. These provide an alternative behavioral network to the fight-flight response that results from the stress of prolonged eye-face contact found in lower species.

Bowlby reached a general conclusion about attachment theory and its relationship to psychopathology with the view that attachment theory is a scientifically valid system that incorporates concepts derived from psychoanalysis, ethology, cognitive theory, and control theory.

AFFILIATION NEED
AUTISM
AVOIDANT PERSONALITY
DEINDIVIDUATION
IMPRINTING
INFANT DEVELOPMENT
INFANTILISM
Z PROCESS

R. W. ZASLOW

BORDERLINE PERSONALITY

Recognizing that many patients do exhibit mixed symptoms of indeterminant seriousness and changing character, certain theorists proposed that the borderline concept be formally employed to represent a midrange level of personality cohesion or prognostic severity.

The most salient symptom ascribed to these personalities is the depth and variability of their moods. Borderlines typically experience extended periods of dejection and disillusionment, interspersed on occasion with brief excursions of euphoria and significantly more frequent episodes of irritability, self-destructive acts, and impulsive anger. Most individuals with this personality will have had checkered histories in either personal relationships or in school or work performance. Few persevere to attain mature goals, and many exhibit an extreme unevenness in fulfilling normal social functions and responsibilities. Their histories show repeated setbacks, a lack of judgment and foresight, tendencies to digress from earlier aspirations, and failures to utilize their natural aptitudes. Most appear not to learn from their troubled experiences and involve themselves in the same imbroglios and quandaries as before. Disturbances in identity and goals are extremely common, evident in uncertainties regarding self-esteem, gender, and vocational aims. Their periodic moody contrariness often alternates with subjective feelings and complaints of isolation, emptiness, or boredom.

Because of its newness as a formal diagnostic designation, the label "borderline" has no historical tradition or clinical literature. Nevertheless, there are precursors that refer to essentially the same constellation of traits. Drawing on a biosocial-learning approach to personality, Theodore Millon formulated the following diagnostic criteria for the borderline individual in *Disorders of personality:*

1. Intense endogenous moods (e.g., continually fails to accord mood with external events; is either depressed or excited or has recurring periods of dejection and apathy interspersed with spells of anger, anxiety, or euphoria)

2. Dysregulated activation (e.g., experiences desultory energy level and irregular sleep-wake cycle; describes time periods that suggest that affective-activation equilibrium is constantly in jeopardy)

3. Self-condemnatory conscience (e.g., reveals recurring self-mutilating and suicidal thoughts; periodically redeems moody behavior through contrition and self-derogation)

4. Dependency anxiety (e.g., is preoccupied with securing affection and maintaining emotional support; reacts intensely to separation and reports haunting fear of isolation and loss)

5. Cognitive-affective ambivalence (e.g., repeatedly struggles to express attitudes contrary to inner feelings; simultaneously experiences conflicting emotions and thoughts toward self and others, notably love, rage, and guilt)

DIAGNOSTIC AND STATISTICAL MANUAL
PERSONALITY DISORDERS

T. MILLON

BOREDOM

Although boredom is an emotion that probably everyone has experienced, it has received little research attention as compared with emotions such as depression and anger.

There are important theoretical reasons to understand boredom as a motivational concept connecting inner feelings and motives with environmental conditions. A variety of theories relate boredom to attention, arousal, information processing, and stimulus underload. The most common theoretical approach construes boredom as occurring in situations with less than the optimal level of stimulation. Theorists tend to emphasize either external conditions or internal characteristics. Berlyne stated that boredom is "a drive that is reduced through divertive exploration and aroused when external stimuli are excessively scarce or excessively monotonous." Industrial research tends to emphasize external conditions as they affect productivity. In contrast, Zuckerman emphasized internal elements and saw boredom susceptibility as a part of a stimulus-seeking model. O'Hanlon relates boredom to arousal, habituation, effort, and stress. Laird asserts that the experience of boredom results at least partially from perceiving oneself as inattentive with no alternative explanations.

Csikszentmihalyi explored the balance of boredom with anxiety, both being mismatches between environmental challenge and personal competence. Boredom is considered to occur in situations in which a person's capabilities are greater than situational opportunities for expression, whereas anxiety comes when the environment demands more of the person that he or she is able to perform or give at the time. The achievement of balance occurs in "flow," a condition of pleasurable absorbed interest in an activity. Plutchik's structural model of eight basic emotions places boredom as being close to, but milder than, loathing and disgust and bordering the other mild emotions, annoyance and pensiveness. For existentialists, a distinction may be made between existential boredom and neurotic boredom. Psychoanalytic thought emphasizes problems of conflict or control; for instance, Fenichel stated that boredom occurs "when we must not do what we want to do, or must do what we do not want to do." Cross-cultural issues also offer possible theoretical challenges for exploring boredom as an important relation between person and environment.

One kind of research consists of experiments in which conditions are manipulated; a stimulus situation is created that is assumed to be boring, such as the monotonous task of crossing out a given letter on pages of random letters. Another research approach involves studying the experience of daily life; this has been mainly done by Csikszentmihalyi and his associates. The third approach is to correlate ratings or questionnaires about boredom with other measures or conditions.

In research, the most commonly used measure of boredom and boredom proneness, as with many internal emotions such as depression and anxiety, is some form of self-report. Behavioral indicators of the state of boredom include yawning, "glaze" eyes, slumped posture, restlessness, and such signs of inattention as looking around the room. Emotions or states opposite to boredom include interest, enthusiasm, involvement, engagement, flow, and optimal stimulation.

In devising his stimulus-seeking scale, Zuckerman included a boredom susceptibility subscale, which has been used in many studies. Another of a few relevant measures is the boredom proneness (BP) scale, a 28-item self-report scale, that shows good reliability and some evidence of validity but does not correlate significantly with the Zuckerman subscale. Vodanovich and Kass identified five factors in the BP scale that were conceptually quite similar to those discussed in the literature: external stimulation, internal stimulation, affective responses to boredom, perception of time, and constraints. Males appear to be more boredom prone than females, and cultural differences have been observed. Among other things, BP has been found to relate to disinclination to vote and pathological gambling. Several studies have shown a moderate overlap between depression and boredom. Interpersonal elements, such as loneliness, also seem to be related to boredom.

Coping with boredom is another area of study. Fantasy is one way of coping with monotonous situations, and a paucity of fantasy may be related to BP. There is evidence that addictive behaviors are used in coping with boredom, including overeating. Robinson has shown that boredom is important in school performance and postulates a system-oriented model. A number of clinicians have been concerned about coping with boredom during psychotherapy either on the part of the patient or the therapist; boredom is seen as an indicator of problems in transference or countertransference. Boredom also appears to be a signal of problems with creativity. The positive function of boredom may be to alert a person to do something different. Certainly there is sufficient evidence to indicate that boredom is an emotion deserving a great deal more research attention. Disentangling boredom from other emotions and fitting it into a larger theory of emotions is an unfinished task.

ACADEMIC UNDERACHIEVEMENT
COGNITIVE COMPLEXITY
DISPOSITIONAL SETS
INTERVENING VARIABLES
MOTIVATION
SENSATION SEEKING

N. D. SUNDBERG

BRAIN

The human brain is a complex aggregate of billions of cells working together to sustain life in a unique and fluid yet stable way, despite changing stimuli, changing needs, and changes in behavior. As life progresses from infancy through childhood, adolescence, adulthood, and senescence, so does the body. Likewise the brain changes in a characteristic fashion to correspond with predetermined internal ontogenetic and developmental patterns, as well as to accommodate interactions between the body and the external environment. Developmentally, the brain begins at the most rostral extension of the neural tube; it bends over and convolutes as it expands within the confines of the cranium. The brain's expansion is disproportionate relative to the growth of the spinal cord, the most caudal extension of the central nervous system. Figure 1 illustrates the development of the human brain, showing its major subdivisions.

THREE MAJOR SECTIONS OF THE BRAIN: FOREBRAIN, MIDBRAIN, AND HINDBRAIN

The first of the three major sections of the developing brain is the largest and most expansive; it is called the *prosencephalon* or forebrain and is made up of two subdivisions: the telencephalon (endbrain) and the diencephalon (interbrain). Telencephalic structures account for about 75% of the weight of the entire human central nervous system. These structures include the two cerebral hemispheres that, although separated by a large interhemispheric fissure, are connected by a mass of crossing fiber tracts (in the corpus callosum and the preoptic area). The surface of the hemispheres is a multicellular layer of brain tissue about 4.5 centimeters thick, called the cerebral cortex. The cortex is divided into subregions according to gross anatomic landmarks called sulci (creases in the surface of the brain less deep than fissures) and gyri (the convolutions or folds bounded by sulci). The largest subregions are called lobes, of which there are four in each hemisphere: frontal, parietal, temporal, and occipital. The location of the four lobes and other major brain structures can be seen in Figures 1 and 2.

In the cerebral hemispheres the cortex has a laminar architecture with the different neuronal cell types organized in layers. From an evolutionary standpoint, the layered cortical areas have changed in complexity across the phylogenetic scale.

The cerebral hemispheres are attached to the diencephalon by massive fiber bundles, the corona radiata. Major structural components present in the diencephalon include the thalamus (a way station for neurons coming in from outside the thalamus, as well as from within the thalamus itself); the subthalamus (a way station between the thalamus and the cortex); the hypothalamus (literally, "under the thalamus"); and the epithalamus (containing the pineal body and the habenular complex).

The middle section of the developing brain is called the *mesencephalon* or midbrain. The mesencephalon is made up of three main parts, the tectum (containing auditory and visual relay stations, called the inferior and superior colliculi); the tegmentum (containing the midbrain reticular formation that activates attention, the substantia nigra that subserves motor functions, and numerous other nuclear groups); and the crus cerebri (a descending bundle of fibers).

The third major section of the brain, part of which eventually exits into the spinal cord at the base of the skull, is the hindbrain. It is composed of two subparts, the metencephalon (consisting of the pons and cerebellum) and the myelencephalon (the medulla oblongata). The cerebellum is a prominent eminence and is the center for motor skills. The pons and medulla oblongata contain clusters of cranial nerve nuclei that connect the nerves going to and from the face and head. Because of the shape and position of the pons and medulla at the base of the brain, they often are referred to as the brain stem, although this term usually includes structures in the midbrain and lower diencephalon as well.

The various components of the brain are interconnected through a very complicated network of neuronal pathways, with neurons in continuous communication. Nuclei within the brain seldom act autonomously. Instead, several nuclei and their fiber tracts may act together to organize

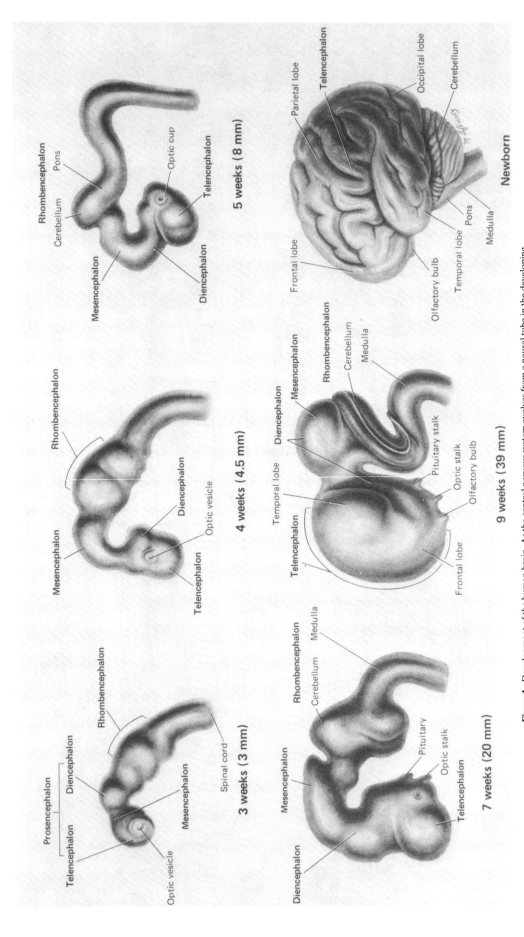

Figure 1. Development of the human brain. As the central nervous system evolves from a neural tube in the developing fetus, the prosencephalon—especially its telencephalic extreme—becomes enlarged relative to the mesencephalon and rhombencephalon. By the time of birth the telencephalon has surrounded the rest of the brain, with the exception of the cerebellum and the most caudal part of the brainstem.

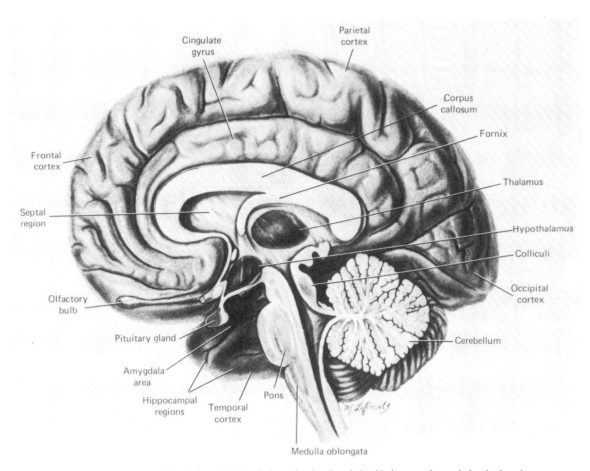

Figure 2. Medial view of the right cerebral hemisphere, showing the relationship between the cortical and subcortical regions.

and modulate complex behaviors, and through their interaction form the basis for life. The functions subserved by these many diverse structures and systems are generally similar in all normal, healthy adults. Sensory systems regulate information coming from outside and inside the body; attentional systems not only keep us alert, but also allow us to ignore stimulus information that may be irrelevant and to rest when we need to; motor systems regulate how we respond and move about; and motivational systems monitor drives and needs and homeostasis. Other systems help us to learn and to remember or forget.

Brain structures that are part of one system may, at the same time, play a role in the activities of another system or systems. To exemplify this interwoven interplay among subparts of the brain, the neural connections of cortex in the anterior portion of the frontal lobes (prefrontal cortex) will be traced to other brain regions.

PREFRONTAL CORTEX CONNECTIONS TO OTHER NEOCORTICAL REGIONS

The prefrontal cortex, postulated to be important in vaguely defined functions such as judgment, tact, impulse control, and abstract thinking, is located in the rostral extreme of the telencephalon. During phylogeny, the human prefrontal cortex evolved into its current configuration and large size relative to the rest of the brain. Other cortical areas are connected to this large prefrontal region by many fibers and fiber bundles, or fasciculi. In general, the cortico-cortical connections tend to be reciprocal, with both outgoing (efferent) and incoming (afferent) influences to and from the same regions.

PREFRONTAL CONNECTIONS WITH THE LIMBIC SYSTEM

Also providing a network of reciprocal interactions with prefrontal cortex is the limbic system. Afferents from limbic areas have a diffuse distribution throughout the prefrontal cortex. In the most restricted sense, the limbic system refers to the hippocampal formation, the amygdala, the cingulate gyrus, and cortex located behind the corpus callosum and extending around the hippocampus. Nauta and Domesick have presented extensive evidence for a widely expanded concept of the limbic system that includes mesencephalic connections and has influence on the septum, the basal ganglia, the hypothalamus, frontal cortex, and temporal cortex. The authors conclude that the limbic system "not only monitors the sensory processes of the cerebral cortex, but can also reach out to intervene in these processes." In this manner the limbic system has input to visceral and endocrine functions, motivational states, and perceptual/learning processes.

The prefrontal cortex appears to have two distinct sets of limbic system connections, but within them there is considerable overlap. Medial and dorsolateral prefrontal cortex send fibers to cingulate cortex and, around and behind the corpus callosum, to the hippocampal areas; orbital prefrontal cortex sends fibers to the septal region, which has direct connections with the amygdala. The septum also connects with the hippocampus by way of a large band of fibers, the fornix.

Although there are connections throughout the thalamus going to and from prefrontal cortex, emphasis is placed on the most numerous, those in the dorsomedial thalamic nucleus. One portion of this nucleus sends fibers to and receives fibers from orbital prefrontal cortex and the amygdaloid complex; another part connects reciprocally with dorsolateral prefrontal cortex. Thalamic nuclei that communicate with prefrontal cortex also receive impulses along fibers coming from the hypothalamus; similarly, connections from orbital prefrontal cortex directly to the lateral sector of the hypothalamus have been identified.

Not all subcortical and limbic inputs to prefrontal cortex are relayed through the thalamus and hypothalamus. Connections exist between prefrontal cortex and the substantia nigra, the midbrain tegmentum, and the central gray portion of the midbrain. The reticular formation is probably one of several stations relaying sensory information to and from the frontal lobes, in some cases by way of the limbic system; other midbrain structures serve as part of a motor pathway.

Inputs to prefrontal cortex from the thalamus, hypothalamus, and midbrain seem to provide information about the internal emotional and motivational state of the organism in much the same way as inputs from the limbic system. These internally synthesized influences, together with the influences that prefrontal cortex assimilates from incoming sensory information, help to give meaning and significance to external events.

The subthalamus, a way station between the thalamus and the cortex, also receives prefrontal input. The subthalamus is part of a motor system that has reciprocal connections with the caudate nucleus, and there are strong efferent connections from prefrontal cortex to the caudate, with additional connections to the putamen. Although there are many efferents from prefrontal cortex to the basal ganglia, there seem to be no afferent inputs from basal ganglia upward to prefrontal areas.

SYNTHESIS OF PREFRONTAL CONNECTIONS

J. M. Fuster has postulated that prefrontal cortex plays a role in the temporal structuring of behavior by (a) aiding in the preparation of sensory and motor systems for action, (b) holding some information in a flexible memory store, and (c) suppressing the interfering influences of internal and external information that might otherwise disrupt formative behavioral sequences. Investigation has indicated an enormously complex interaction between this area and other areas of the brain. However, even when it is damaged, no clearly definable single function appears to be lost; instead, an essential element or quality of being human is missing.

BRAIN INJURIES
CENTRAL NERVOUS SYSTEM DISORDERS
HYPOTHALAMUS
LIMBIC SYSTEM
NEUROPSYCHOLOGY
RETICULAR ACTIVATING SYSTEMS
SPLIT-BRAIN RESEARCH

M. OSCAR-BERMAN

BRAIN INJURIES

The brain can suffer injury in diverse ways: metabolic or structural abnormalities genetically inherited or perinatally induced; trauma from civilian accidents or military combat; toxicity from drugs, heavy metals, or poisonous gases; malnutrition; infections or diseases; tumors; cerebrovascular accidents; surgical removal of brain tissue for relief of epilepsy, intractable pain, or serious psychiatric symptomatology; and normal aging.

Early perinatal brain lesions tend to be more extensive and diffuse than those incurred later in life. Early lesions often are detected by abnormalities in behavior observed during later development, and the time of onset of the damage can only be approximated in relation to presumed prenatal events. By contrast, lesions incurred beyond infancy often can be linked to a specific event or to an approximate onset in the symptomatology, and premorbid behavior can be compared with postinjury behavior. Certain patterns of injury usually produce clearer

abnormalities than others. However, brain damage does not always result in immediately apparent symptoms, and localization of the site and extent of damage may be difficult.

A variety of imaging techniques for visualizing the lesion may be used to measure parameters such as ventricular size, cerebral blood-flow patterns, regional glucose utilization, and the presence of abnormal tissue masses. These techniques include echoencephalography, pneumoencephalography, angiography, X-rays, CT (computed tomography) scans, PET (positron emission tomography) scans, and NMR (nuclear magnetic resonance) imaging.

Damage to specific regions of the brain also produces behavioral abnormalities that can be measured quantitatively and qualitatively by employing sensitive tests of impaired or lost functions. Cognitive and intellectual defects can be measured through the skillful administration and interpretation of tests specifically designed to elucidate organically based impairments.

BRAIN
LOBOTOMY
ORGANIC BRAIN SYNDROMES
PSYCHOSURGERY

M. OSCAR-BERMAN

BRAIN LATERALITY

Laterality refers to the functional asymmetry of the two cerebral hemispheres of the brain. That is, although the two halves of the brain work as a coordinated whole, many functions are subserved more by one hemisphere than by the other.

Wide interest in the functional lateralization of the human cerebrum dates from the 1860s, when the French physician Paul Broca made public his findings that several patients with speech dysfunctions were found on autopsy to have lesions in the left frontal lobe. It has gradually become apparent that each hemisphere has functions in which it plays a more dominant role than the other.

The most obvious asymmetry related to the human brain is handedness, which is often related to the lateralization of other functions. In right-handers, it is almost always true that speech functions are found primarily in the left hemisphere. While this is also true in the majority of left-handers, the latter are more likely than right-handers to have speech functions either primarily in the right hemisphere or distributed between both hemispheres. Left-handers apparently are likely to have less functional asymmetry than right-handers.

Structural asymmetries have been found in the human brain, with some areas being larger on one side than on the other, particularly in the areas associated with speech. While there is often speculation about the functional effects of these structural asymmetries, the exact connections have not yet been demonstrated.

There are a variety of methods for studying hemisphere asymmetries. One is by autopsy, which reveals lesions associated with behavioral dysfunction observed prior to the subject's death. Another is by observation of functional deficits present in people with identifiable lesions. Lesions can be identified by neurosurgery, X-ray, or computed tomography.

Exceptions exist for every rule pertaining to asymmetrically represented functions. However, there are functions that are more commonly lateralized. The most obvious of these is language, that in most right-handed people is represented predominantly in the left hemisphere. For this reason, the left hemisphere has long been called the "dominant" one, while the right has been called the "minor" or "silent" hemisphere. Damage to the left hemisphere, or unilateral presentation of information to the right hemisphere, often causes difficulty in speaking, reading, naming, or understanding spoken language. Functions that are most often under primarily right-hemisphere control include visual-spatial reasoning and memory, tactile and visual recognition of form, musical ability, and copying and drawing geometric figures.

Nebes described differences in the ways the two hemispheres process information. Left-hemisphere processing involves analysis of information in a logical sequential manner, while right-hemisphere processing involves more synthesis of information in a simultaneous manner. M. D. Lezak's review of the findings of several studies indicates that there may be some differences in emotional functioning involving the two hemispheres as well, as reflected in different patterns of emotional response to unilateral brain damage.

Even in split-brain subjects, the functions usually represented in one hemisphere can be accessed by the other through use of peripheral nervous system mechanisms. Gazzaniga and his colleagues labeled this process "cross-cuing." One example is when a stimulus presented to the right hemisphere results in some emotional response that is interpreted by the left hemisphere in such a way that the person can make a verbal response. Information may therefore pass from one hemisphere through peripheral nerve fibers to the other hemisphere, even when direct interhemispheric transfer across the corpus callosum is impossible.

Despite the evidence for laterality in the human cerebrum, the normal brain operates in a coordinated, unified manner. Kinsbourne emphasizes that lateralized functioning of one hemisphere is complementary to that of the other. The laterality of the brain provides a means of processing different components of information, rather than performance of separate types of activity.

BRAIN
BRAIN INJURIES
COMPUTED TOMOGRAPHY
NEUROPSYCHOLOGY
SPLIT-BRAIN RESEARCH

T. S. BENNETT

BRAIN WAVES

Neuronal activity, partly electrical in nature, can be recorded by using an electroencephalograph (EEG). The record of the changes in electrical activity in the brain across time is the electroencephalogram, commonly called brain waves. H. Berger (1873–1941), a German psychiatrist, first developed the technique.

In the normal person, brain waves vary dramatically. The frequency of brain waves ranges between 1 and 100 cycles/second. The magnitude of voltage changes within the waveforms is usually about 50 microvolts, although some waves as high as 1 millivolt have been found in normal individuals. The pattern of a person's brain waves is a global and rather crude measure of brain function, but it has been related loosely to states of consciousness and also to abnormalities in the brain.

In human beings, brain waves are recorded from electrodes placed in several locations on the scalp. The potential differences between the electrodes are amplified and recorded on moving chart paper as a function of time. These potential differences originate from neurons in the cerebral cortex, and are almost certainly due to synaptic field potentials. These are the excitatory and inhibitory postsynaptic potentials produced in response to the release of neurotransmitter substance by the presynaptic neuron. Neurons oriented at right angles to the surface of the cortex probably play the major role in the production of brain wave patterns.

Brain waves have been grouped according to their frequencies and labeled with Greek letters. The most common frequencies include alpha (8–12 cps), beta (13 cps and faster), theta (4–7 cps), and delta (3 cps and slower).

Certain rhythmical brain waves are present in different areas of the brain.

BRAIN WAVES AND SLEEP

Brain wave records have proven useful in investigations of sleep. During sleep the pattern of brain wave activity reflects the person's state of consciousness fairly accurately. The waking state is usually characterized by a high degree of beta activity. As the person falls asleep, the brain waves begin to show higher amplitude and lower frequency, passing through several stages. These stages merge into one another and are not entirely distinct. Stage 0 is a waking state just preceding sleep, characterized by the presence of the alpha rhythm. Stage 1 shows similar wave patterns, but somewhat lower voltage activity, and loss of alpha rhythm. Stage 2 is identified by the appearance of "sleep spindles": very brief (½ to 2 second) bursts of 13- to 16-cycle-per-second brain wave activity. This stage also shows "K complexes," or sharp rises and falls in the waveform. Stage 3 is a transition stage, containing both spindles and K complexes of Stage 2, and some of the slower waves predominant in Stage 4. The final and deepest stage is Stage 4, which contains mainly delta waves ranging from one-half to three cycles/second.

Another waveform that appears during sleep is called REM. The pattern is similar to Stage 1, but the individual is clearly asleep. This stage is associated with rapid eye movements (REMs) of one or two per second, which occur in short bursts. It is also accompanied by complete loss of muscle tonus in the antigravity muscles, penile erections in males, and rapid spiking activity in the pons, geniculate bodies, and occipital cortex. REM sleep probably represents periods of dreaming, since most subjects report a dream if they are awakened during this stage of sleep. In contrast, only about 20% of subjects awakened during other stages of sleep report dreaming.

BRAIN WAVES AND CLINICAL DIAGNOSIS

Despite their limitations, brain waves have also been valuable in clinical diagnosis of brain abnormalities. There are no waveforms or frequencies that are clearly abnormal, and brain waves are interpreted in the entire context of behavior and other neurological tests. Brain waves are particularly useful in the diagnosis and evaluation of disorders such as epilepsy, brain tumors, cerebral infections, coma, and brain death. Serial brain wave recordings are used to follow the course of recovery after traumatic head injuries, strokes, or other brain injuries.

Computerization has contributed enormously to the usefulness of brain wave records. The computer can filter particular frequencies, analyze lengthy records, and average records. One important advance in the computerization of brain wave records is the evoked potential. The presentation of an abrupt environmental stimulus produces no visible change in an EEG record, because the electrodes are recording from a huge neuron population and the neuronal response to the stimulus might only affect a small fraction of that population. The spontaneous activity in all the other neurons whose electrical activity is contributing to the brain wave pattern, masks the activity in the neurons of interest. However, if the stimulus is presented repeatedly, the brain wave records can be averaged by computer. The spontaneous and random activity in the records will eventually average to zero and "wash out." The consistent response of the neuron population to the repeated presentation of the stimulus will remain. This residual waveform pattern is the evoked potential. It is widely used in research on the auditory and visual systems.

BRAIN
CENTRAL NERVOUS SYSTEM
NEUROPSYCHOLOGY

PSYCHOPHYSIOLOGY

P. M. WALLACE

BREAST-FEEDING

Physicians all agree that breast milk is the best nourishment for infants in the first months of life. Compared to formula-fed babies, breast-fed babies have fewer digestive problems, fewer allergies, fewer illnesses, and a lower incidence of sudden infant death syndrome (crib death). Nutritionally, there is no perfect substitute for human milk.

Many psychologists believe that breast-feeding confers psychological benefits as well, as it may strengthen the bond between mother and infant. Physiologically, mother and infant share pleasure and discomfort: Both sucking and suckling are satisfying experiences, and an empty stomach and overfull breasts are painful. Thus the mother not only receives the psychic satisfaction that she is meeting her infant's needs with her own body, but also finds that she and the infant are enmeshed in a natural symbiotic relationship. In addition, the amount of breast milk produced is directly related to the vigor, duration, and frequency of sucking, thus establishing another link between mother and child. Finally, the natural skin-to-skin contact may help bond the two.

However, many psychologists believe that other ways of strengthening the mother–infant bond provide adequate substitutes for breast-feeding. The particular mode of feeding, psychologically, is not crucial, whereas the overall pattern of interaction is.

K. S. BERGER

BRIEF PSYCHOTHERAPY

The proper length of psychotherapy has been a subject for discussion since Sigmund Freud, who was concerned about the length of time required for psychoanalysis and believed that as the knowledge of human personality and psychopathology increased, the time required solely for therapy would gradually diminish. However, his expectations were not confirmed. Instead, in the United States at least, psychoanalysis increased in length. Although precise and reliable statistics are not readily available, it appears that most analyses take from 4 to 6 years.

Because of the historical development of psychoanalysis and psychodynamic therapy in general, for many years it was a commonly held view that psychotherapy required a moderately long period of time to secure positive results. The belief was that the individual's neurotic problems developed over a period of many years and that the underlying causative factors were repressed unconscious conflicts. Consequently, the therapist could not force therapeutic progress by being overly directive but had to play a patient and passive role. In fact, to proceed too quickly could be detrimental because the clients would be forced to confront their conflicts before they were ready to do so.

A number of events occurring in the 1960s, however, led to some significant changes in the mental health area in the United States. The Joint Commission on Mental Illness and Health appointed by the U.S. Congress came up with a number of conclusions and recommendations after 5 years of study and deliberation. Among them was the view that psychoanalysis was both too expensive and time-consuming to meet the needs of the majority of people requiring psychotherapeutic services. It also was recommended that community mental health centers be set up to meet these needs and along with this development a number of innovative programs featuring crisis intervention and brief psychotherapy were developed. Instead of long waiting lists for conventional psychotherapy, walk-in clinics and emergency clinics provided round-the-clock services with brief therapy lasting from 6 to 10 sessions. The rationale was that treatment provided at the time of crisis would be briefer, would help the

individual return to his or her previous level of functioning, and would prevent the problem from becoming chronic.

Some research reports indicated that the median length of therapy in outpatient clinics was only around six to eight sessions. The reality was that most patients did not want long-term therapy and terminated their therapy after a relatively few sessions. Over time, there was an increasing awareness that therapists should modify their expectations about the required length of therapy and provide briefer forms of therapy, and this is what has occurred.

Brief therapy differs from long-term psychotherapy in a number of ways. Although no absolute number of sessions defines brief psychotherapy, most appear to be in the range of 16 to 25 sessions, although some are as brief as 1 session and some may extend to about 40 sessions. Brief therapy may be time limited, for which a specific number of sessions or period of time is announced in advance, or there may be no specific time limit but a general time frame provided by the therapist. In this way, the client at the outset of therapy has a clear idea of how long therapy is expected to last.

Brief psychotherapy is more focused than traditional psychotherapy. The various forms of brief psychodynamic therapy tend to emphasize a specific focus for therapy, although there are variations among them. Although operating from a different theoretical perspective, cognitive-behavioral therapies tend to focus on specific problems or symptomatic behaviors. The role of therapists in brief psychotherapy is quite different from the more traditional therapeutic role in that to a significant degree the therapist assumes a more directive role and responsibility for leading the course of therapy.

In brief therapy, attention is focused on the patient's current life situation. The here and now become the focus instead of the events in the distant past. The goal is to help clients with the problems that brought them to therapy and not with a more lofty hypothetical goal of "personality reconstruction." Some forms of brief psychotherapy, particularly cognitive-behavioral ones, try to teach clients coping mechanisms and procedures that can be used to prevent and overcome problems in the future.

Brief psychotherapy is the most popular form of psychotherapy today, and it is the type preferred by most people who seek help for their problems of adjustment.

Several studies have shown that brief forms of psychotherapy have secured outcomes comparable with those reported for therapies of longer duration. Brief psychotherapy is not a panacea for all psychological ills, but it is an effective form of therapy for depression, anxiety disorders, marital problems, and related difficulties. For such reasons it appears to be the first choice for most individuals.

ALTERNATIVE PSYCHOTHERAPIES
ECLECTIC PSYCHOTHERAPY
HISTORICAL ROOTS OF PSYCHOTHERAPY
INNOVATIVE PSYCHOTHERAPIES

S. L. GARFIELD

BRIEF THERAPY

Brief therapy denotes any of a wide variety of psychotherapeutic procedures with relatively limited and delineated objectives. It is employed to contrast intervention techniques that are more time-consuming and that propose goals that are more therapeutically global.

While classical psychoanalysis was at first comparatively brief, developing interest in repressed memories and the analysis of a patient's character structure greatly extended the time required for its successful completion. According to F. G. Alexander and T. M. French in *Psychoan-*

alytic therapy, most classical psychoanalyses require a minimum of 500 sessions, while brief therapy may be completed in 10 to 65 sessions. Although these estimates of therapeutic duration may vary, classical analysis, when compared with many other therapy procedures and techniques, is a lengthy enterprise.

In addition to the time differential between psychoanalysis and other psychotherapies, other factors typically offer a delineation. These include the goals of therapy, focus of treatment, and role of the therapist. In psychoanalysis the goal is to restructure the patient's personality with a focus on the individual's early history and liberation of unconscious content, so that this content can be better addressed through the mediations of a mature ego. The role of the therapist in this activity is one of an exploratory, passive, nondirective, and interpretive observer.

In brief psychotherapy such as biofeedback, behavior therapy, or rational-emotive therapy, the goal is usually rather specific. Specific goal orientation would be exemplified by therapeutic intervention. Brief psychotherapy also focuses on the present malady and a modification of the current variables that precipitate or maintain a presenting complaint, rather than giving extensive attention to the patient's early history. Finally, in brief therapy, the therapist will often assume a rather active role and offer directives, suggestions, and strategies intended to expedite a complete and satisfactory resolution of the problem or problems that the patient has presented.

INNOVATIVE PSYCHOTHERAPIES
PSYCHOTHERAPY

W. W. WENRICH

B-TYPE PERSONALITY

Although the A-type, coronary-prone personality has been extensively researched and written about, people exhibiting the contrasting B-type personality have served mainly as a control group against which the characteristics of Type A individuals may be compared. Thus a thorough review of the literature on Type A behavior by K. A. Matthews notes that Bs speak less quickly, loudly, and explosively than As and describe themselves as less aggressive, active, hardworking, or achievement-oriented. Relative to As, Type Bs regard themselves as more self-controlled and more satisfied with their work, life achievements, and marriage. Psychophysiological studies have usually found Bs to be less autonomically responsive than As during aversive stimulation or exposure to a difficult problem-solving task.

A few studies have outlined some distinguishing features of the B personality type. Type Bs excel, relative to As, on tasks requiring deliberation and patience, and Bs are more likely to persist in their problem-solving efforts in the face of highly salient feedback that these efforts are not succeeding. Peculiarly, though, *moderately* salient failure feedback may actually undermine the problem-solving efforts of Bs, both in comparison with As exposed to moderately salient feedback, and Bs exposed to highly salient feedback. Finally, Bs seem to have a broader focus of attention than As, and for this reason may outperform As on a task intended to distract attention from a primary task.

In the original research validating the Type A/B distinction, nearly one third of the men who developed coronary heart disease were classified as Type B. Therefore the Type B personality is by no means coronary-immune, merely less coronary-prone than the Type A. Furthermore, the description of the Type B personality in terms *opposite* to those used to characterize Type A may sometimes be misleading.

A-TYPE PERSONALITY
PSYCHOSOMATIC DISORDERS

W. SAMUEL

BUFFERING HYPOTHESIS

A *buffer* is a protective barrier—a cushion or procedure for reducing shock. The buffering hypothesis, as specifically applied in psychology, is the assertion that social support serves as a protection against stress that produces psychological or physiological disorder or disease.

Several issues emerge when one attempts to do research on the buffering hypotheses. One is the measurement of the variables, stress, social support, and the outcome. Psychological *stress* is often measured by a person's report of major life events of the last few months, such as changes in work or family relations, weighted to give a total score. A less used kind of measure is called "daily hassles," such as household chores and having to wait in traffic. *Social support* is measured in three ways: (a) social network membership (often called social integration), such as living with a family, belonging to a club, or attending a church; (b) perceived social support, such as self-report of availability of people with whom to talk about problems and people to provide material aid if one is in need; and (c) support behaviors, such as reported or observed actions of helping the person in need. The first two methods have received the most research attention. The *outcome* or dependent variables are physical or psychological disorders (or health), such as depression, recovery from surgery, smoking cessation, and development of cancer or AIDS symptoms in infected people.

Findings across many studies with the first two social support measures have been positive. Sheldon Cohen concluded, "The epidemiological data on the role of social integration in morbidity and mortality have clearly established that the social environment plays an important role in health and well being . . . [and] when a perceived availability of social support measure is used, these effects reliably occur in the prediction of psychological and physical symptoms."

Beyond these generally positive findings, many theoretical and research questions remain. One is the issue of whether findings are the result of main effects or buffering effects. Is social support a true buffering effect having no influence of its own but being entirely conditional on the presence of stress? Another related issue is the place of social support in the chain of multiple cause and effect as represented in the diathesis-stress theories of psychopathology. Diathesis refers to predispositions to disorder from biological or early experiential causes. Social "support" and "nonsupport" interact with other variables throughout the life cycle.

The integration of the many possible variables into a model explaining why social support works clarifies the buffering hypothesis. Cohen has presented a transactional model that includes core concepts about social networks, stressful events, personality factors including perceived social support, stress appraisal, and support behaviors ultimately affecting the development of a disorder. Cohen indicates that one personality feature that seems particularly important to include in addition to social support is the sense of internalized control or self-efficacy. Coping styles are other psychological variables that need to be included in an integrated theory of the relation between stress and disorder around the buffering hypothesis. On a larger than individual scale, community settings are potential buffers for stress.

ADAPTATION
COGNITIVE COMPLEXITY
COPING
ENVIRONMENTAL STRESS
GENERAL ADAPTATION SYNDROME
HEALTH PSYCHOLOGY

LOCUS OF CONTROL
PERCEPTUAL DISTORTIONS
PERSONALITY INTEGRATION
STRESS
STRESS CONSEQUENCES

N. D. SUNDBERG

BURNOUT

"Burnout" describes a specific dysfunction among helping professionals believed to be the result of excessive demands made upon their energy, strength, and resources. Although a clear, agreed-upon definition does not exist, burnout is characterized by the inability to be sufficiently concerned about and involved with service recipients. Symptoms among affected workers include low worker morale, impaired performance, high job turnover, increased alcohol and drug abuse, more reported mental illness, greater marital and family conflict, and cynical, "dehumanized" attitudes.

The evolution of burnout as a separate job stress syndrome is partly due to employer concern about turnover, deterioriation of quality service, absenteeism, accidents, and overutilization of sick leave. It is also due to worker concern about emotional exhaustion and apathy, physical fatigue, psychosomatic illness, increased alcohol and drug consumption, cynicism, inappropriate anger, and depression. Treatment of burnout can be given at any point in the process. Various personal and environmental variables can be manipulated to decrease the likelihood that burnout will occur.

OCCUPATIONAL STRESS
STRESS
STRESS CONSEQUENCES

D. L. KITCH

BYSTANDER INVOLVEMENT

In March 1964, Kitty Genovese was brutally murdered in New York while 38 of her neighbors watched from their apartment windows. Even though the attack lasted over a half hour, no one called the police until it was over. At that time psychologists knew little about the dynamics of bystander involvement. As a direct result of the Genovese murder, a great deal of empirical and theoretical knowledge has been generated on the topic.

One of the most widely accepted models of bystander involvement in emergency situations is the model developed by Latané and Darley. In their book, *The unresponsive bystander: Why doesn't he help?*, the model was presented. Rather than involving a single decision to intervene or not, bystanders must make a series of decisions. First, the bystander must notice that something is happening. Second, the bystander must interpret or label what has been noticed as an emergency. Third, the bystander must decide that he or she has a responsibility to become involved. Fourth, the bystander must decide what form of assistance to render. Fifth, a decision must be made on how to implement the previous decision. The model has been supported by a great deal of laboratory and field research conducted by Latané and Darley as well as others.

Findings point to the important role played by social influence factors at two particular stages of the model—labeling the event as an emergency, and feeling responsible for becoming involved. Bystanders may use the actions of others in the situation to help them interpret the event. Factors relating to the bystander's personality and demographic characteristics have been found to provide a poorer accounting of bystander involvement than have features of the situation.

ATTITUDES
CONFORMITY
PROSOCIAL BEHAVIOR
SOCIAL CLIMATE EXPERIMENTS
VIOLENCE

M. S. GREENBERG

C

CAFETERIA FEEDING

Clara M. Davis discovered that if an assortment of foods is set, cafeteria-style, in front of an infant, in a week's time or so the infant normally will have selected a balanced diet, even though at one meal he or she might fill up on starch (e.g., mashed potatoes) and at the next meal on proteins (e.g., chopped meat and lima beans). As specific hungers for certain nutrients develop, the baby chooses appropriate foods or liquids, not because the baby "knows" the need for a balanced diet, but simply because they make him or her *feel good.*

Davis further noted that although babies went on "binges" of eating one food at a time, they switched choices enough to obtain a balanced diet in the long run. Children, through trial and error, learn through their smell and taste senses which foods to select to satisfy their current physiological needs.

EARLY CHILD DEVELOPMENT

INFANCY DEVELOPMENT

H. K. FINK

CAMPHILL MOVEMENT

The Camphill Movement is an international network of therapeutic communities, including schools for mentally and emotionally challenged children, training colleges for young adults, and villages for adults. The first Camphill School for Children in Need of Special Care was founded in 1940 in Aberdeen, Scotland, by Karl Koenig. Koenig believed that by living in a community with "disabled" people, "normal" persons would have something to gain. He decried the "three great errors" of modern times—agnosticism, the Darwinian notion of "the survival of the fittest," and the psychological theory of measurable intelligence.

CAMPHILL SCHOOLS

Camphill Schools seek to educate children in accordance with their potentials—the challenge of handicapped children is that often the physical body has malformities or imperfections that prevent the spiritual being, or energy, from entering children. Children live in familylike settings, in households with staff who live there with their own families. There is no shift work, and staff are not usually paid salaries. Rather, their needs are met as long as they are members of the community. This economic arrangement stems from Steiner's belief that in a healthy social life, people work because they like their work and find it rewarding. In turn, community members deserve to be supported as a basic right.

CAMPHILL VILLAGES

Camphill villages were intended to address the specific concerns of parents who want their disabled children to make meaningful contributions to society. The first Camphill village was founded in 1954 on an estate gifted by the publisher W. E. Macmillan when the U. S. government would not allow Macmillan's mentally retarded son to emigrate to America to join him.

As much as possible, villagers have the same rights and responsibilities as staff. Long before the current consumer rights movement among the disabled today, villagers of Camphill sat on the governance committees of the community and took part in the social and cultural life of the community.

The Camphill movement is most established in Britain, where it was founded, and is the largest private provider of services to persons with special needs there and the greatest recipient of awards for quality care. Since its inception, it has grown to become a worldwide movement including Africa, South America, and the United States.

ANTHROPOSOPHY
RUDOLF STEINER
WALDORF EDUCATION

T. G. POPLAWSKI

CANALIZATION

Gardner Murphy borrowed the term from Pierre Janet and over several decades gave it prominence as an important learning theory. As it is now conceived, the canalization hypothesis provides a conceptualization of drive modification as a function of repeated satisfaction by stimuli within a limited range. It is differentiated from conditioning in that the latter, both S-type and R-type (classical and operant), refers to what Sherrington has called preparatory responses, whereas canalization refers to consummatory responses. A child may be canalized into a high preference for ice cream in one culture and for whale blubber in another culture. Both canalizations would lead to satisfaction of human hungers, but the first child, after the canalization, would be unlikely to accept the blubber, just as the second might find the ice cream far from desirable. Essentially, the canalization hypothesis attempts to account for the process whereby an originally neutral stimulus takes on positive value as a satisfier, and for the narrowing of the range from within which a drive may be satisfied.

As long as there is some actual satisfaction of a drive, some degree of canalization will occur. Obviously, however, there will be variations in the strength of canalizations induced as a function of a variety of factors. Murphy identified a number of these variables in general terms. The first variable relates to the strength of the needs: The stronger the need, the greater the effect of a satisfier in producing canalization. The range of the variation in strength of needs is considerable, and different canalizations may be established at different points in the range. Another theorem related to strength of needs is as follows: The stronger the drive,

the broader the range of satisfiers that will be accepted, and the greater the generalization of the canalizations. Also, the stronger the drive, the more the readiness to accept less preferred satisfiers.

A second major variable is defined in terms of the intensity of gratification: The greater the satisfaction induced, the stronger the canalization, and the more rapidly the rate of canalization will proceed. Need satisfaction is not necessarily accompanied by tension reduction. Canalizations are a function of satisfactions that may relate to tension increase rather than reduction.

A third variable is the developmental stage of the individual. Earliest canalizations in the infant represent relatively independent needs and satisfiers as mediated by the parents and other attendants. The first really consistent source of gratification is the child's own body. Another (almost) omnipresent satisfier is the mother or mother-substitute, the most intense satisfier among all the social personal objects in the surroundings. As the child continues growing and expanding in the world, needs expand and new wants are established. With this development, the self-concept expands and the patterning of canalizations is given direction and individuality. Preferences are expressed for experiences congruent with the self, and satisfactions are derived from such encounters.

The fourth major variable is frequency of gratification: Other things being equal, the greater the frequency of specific forms of gratification, the stronger the canalizations established. With very strong drives and very intense gratifications, one experience might establish a strong canalization. With more moderate drives and satisfiers in the middle or weak range, a number of trials would be needed before the canalization effects would be perceptible. It is here that the formulation would apply and studies of the effects of familiarization would be relevant. It should be remembered, however, that among the human drives are curiosity and the need to expand and grow; there is perceived challenge and the need for mastery. The drives so identified provide a pull away from the familiar and represent a demand for novelty and adventure. This countervailing constellation is still poorly understood, but it represents a fundamental force as significant as the canalization processes.

Confirmation and elaboration of the canalization theory in controlled studies have been slow to develop. Some of the best verification of the fundamental hypothesis has come from animal studies such as Paul Young's experiments on familiarization as a factor in animal choices of food. Studies of humans typically focus on modification of liking for esoteric foods as a function of familiarity.

CLASSICAL CONDITIONING
PERSONALITY

E. L. HARTLEY

CAREER CHOICES

Conventional wisdom dictates that a career is something possessed. Activities are often judged relative to a career. During the entry process, efforts usually go toward preparation—developing skills, values, concepts, or whatever is appropriate to assuming an occupational identity. During the exit process, energies typically focus on determining the degree of success.

HISTORICAL CONTEXT

The empirical study of work began in the early twentieth century. Career guidance was the province of settlement houses prior to the vocational and educational movements in the United States. World War I created employment opportunities, expanded and varied job situations, and an urgency for identifying efficient procedures to recruit, screen, train, classify, and evaluate performance. In response to that need, industrial psychology and psychometrics were conceived. Efforts focused on worker behavior and labor-management interaction. The Great Depression forced the study of the unemployed as a sociological phenomenon and stimulated assessments of marginal occupational groups such as waitresses, cab drivers, and railroaders. During World War II, a burgeoning national scientific and economic capacity promoted the study of work and careers. Individuals were linked to society via their social roles and, in the case of work, by their jobs and careers.

To explain career development various interpretations of findings generated theories ranging from conservative to radical in the political sense.

INDIVIDUAL AND SOCIAL CONTEXT APPROACHES

Studies by D. E. Super, J. L. Holland, and A. Roe have supported a trait-factor position that assumes that jobs and careers are environments reflecting the personality and interest differences among people, or have advanced the notion of life stage. The personality-environment fit model posits that individual motivation accounts for career choices and for variations in careers. Initial, trial, and stable work phases emerged as concepts. *Initial* referred to jobs held while pursuing a formal education; *trial* meant indexed form or employer-imposed changes in a 3-year time frame or less; and *stable* designated time periods of longer than 3 years. Data showed that individuals with advantaged backgrounds and white-collar, skilled, and supervisory occupations evidenced a longer stable phase, whereas manual, unskilled, blue-collar individuals from disadvantaged backgrounds lingered for a longer time in the trial phase. D. E. Super proposed a more elaborate scheme: ages 14 to 18, crystallization; ages 18 to 21, specification; ages 21 to 24, implementation; ages 25 to 35, stabilization; and ages 35 and up, consolidation. Daniel J. Levinson and others stated that stages are part of both the biological and social aging process, hence they are preprogrammed while influenced by societal factors.

In a classical study, certain personality factors and situational pressures were shown to be related to whether or not an individual would change or remain in an occupation. Four occupational patterns emerged: routine career, flexible career, disjointed career, and orderly, sequential career.

Certain factors seem related to determining the degree of liking a job and hence making successful career choices. These include (a) familiarity with the occupation, (b) match between an individual's characteristics and those of the environment, (c) good occupational role models, (d) challenging but not threatening job requirements and expectations, (e) reduced concern with prestige, (f) match between personnel and work values, and (g) the socialization context of the work environment. Besides these variables, researchers have identified two major orientations—money-related and work-satisfaction-related—expressed by workers and used by them to make career choices. The first group derives little satisfaction from the work process itself, either in terms of accomplishments or feelings of self-fulfillment, but gains satisfaction and makes career decisions according to the direct status benefits associated with salary. The second group has a strong work orientation. The process of work is satisfying, and choices are made related to attaining accomplishments.

Both orientations exist across all fields of work, although there is a higher proportion of work-oriented white-collar individuals. Blue-collar workers tend to be more dissatisfied with their jobs than white-collar workers, but often have fewer chances for selecting interesting and varied tasks.

Thus people work for different reasons: money, status, prestige, companionship, satisfaction, and so on, and career choices are often made with some, if not all, of these reasons in mind. An individual's perceptions of work and associated reasons for working are determined largely by previous experiences and prevailing societal attitudes.

A LIFE COURSE APPROACH

Since life in industrial societies is depicted by significant social transitions, a life course perspective considers multiple roles as sets of complex interrelationships that must be studied within their contexts, and posits that events in life are normatively timed with synchronies and asynchronies having consequences for subsequent events. Individuals are viewed as actors on their environments: They negotiate, decide, and adapt. Also, individual needs, interests, expectations, and even options change over time. Applied to the study of careers, life course considerations introduce additional complexity.

A sharp increase in holding power over the work course was noted regardless of socioeconomic status or gender. Career lines followed by males were made up of higher-status jobs and had more holding power than those followed by females or lower-status career lines. Career lines were more differentiated during young adulthood (late 20s and early 30s) and then became less differentiated during the middle years, reflecting a settling-in pattern. Data for career ports of entry and exit varied markedly by occupational group and gender.

A decline in ports of entry and an increase in ports of exit were found during the last decade of the work course—explained by the marked decline in recruitment sources available for older individuals, and by the more widely accepted attitude that supports early retirement. For lower-status career lines, a U-shaped pattern emerged over the work course: both entries and exits were greater at the beginning and end of the work course than at any other time.

In general, research on career choice within a life course framework suggests that choice may not play as major a role in an initial entrance decision. However, choosing to leave a job or career entirely may be a decision with far more statistically significant social and psychological consequences, in light of trends that support wanting to be happy with one's work. Tremendous variations in rates of progression, patterns of entry and exit, opportunities for advancement, and returns on personal growth highlight the literature and are influenced by gender, age, socioeconomic and skill levels, and job sector. The concept of choice is considered more multifaceted and dynamic than it has been in past, and career research efforts, according to Robert J. Havighurst's review of "The world of work," have become systematically more interested in theory and methodology; in the timing, sequencing, and patterning of careers; and in the interactive effects of a multitude of individual, familial, and societal factors.

CAREER DEVELOPMENT
EMPLOYMENT PRACTICES
JOB STATUS
OCCUPATIONAL ADJUSTMENT
WORK EFFICIENCY

F. DEUTSCH

CAREER COUNSELING

Career counseling is a major psychological intervention that focuses on separate functions including career planning, career decision making, career adjustment, and career effectiveness. These interventions may be delivered individually, in groups, programmatically, or in various combinations of the three. The interventions draw heavily upon techniques of vocational assessment, occupational information, and labor market trends, and information about personal attributes as they relate to work.

Individual approaches to career counseling and career development have been characterized by a series of interactions with clients that usually range from two to five interviews. These interviews are typically phased as follows:

1. An intake interview in which the counselor and client establish a working relationship to the point where the counselor can begin

to develop some working hypotheses about the client's needs and well-being.

2. A phase involving what might be called "problem definition," in which the client's major concerns are made more explicit than originally, and a priority order of these concerns is established.

3. An assessment phase that involves some more or less systematic appraisal of the client's attributes that seem to be most closely related to the defined problem or problems. This assessment can be done using interview methods, or might involve a rather extensive variety of psychological tests and inventories. Furthermore, the assessment phase can include work simulation or job sample tasks and techniques.

4. A feedback phase in which the counselor reports back to the client the results and the potential meaning of the previous phases, particularly the assessment phase.

5. Finally, an implementation phase in which the client's main responsibility, with the help of the counselor, is to make decisions pertinent to putting into action, in appropriate ways, some of the major information and attitudes implication of the previous four phases.

Career counseling generally involves emotionally charged content and attitudes that the counselor must deal with appropriately. Originally, group approaches to career counseling and career development were instigated as a time- and money-saving device. While this remains true, advances in group career counseling have indicated that one counselor may not be as effective as several counselors working with a group of individuals, thus reducing the cost savings somewhat.

Programmatic interventions are based on the assumption of a predictable sequence of events as one matures. This predictable sequence allows the anticipation of client needs at various stages of life. The result of that anticipation is the development of programs designed to enhance an individual's passage through these staged events.

Comparing individual, group, and programmatic approaches, one is likely to find that programmatic approaches are used anticipating normal growth and development and without the presence of a problem; that individual approaches are typically used with individuals who seem to need some extra help in dealing with normal career-decision problems; and that group approaches include a high proportion of both normally developing individuals and individuals with problems.

ISSUES IN CAREER COUNSELING AND DEVELOPMENT

Certain major issues concern occupational information, indecision/indecisiveness, career patterns, approaches to understanding career development, and problems in career development, counseling, and adjustment.

Occupational Information

Occupational information has been a cornerstone of interventions in career counseling for many years. It remains an important aspect in the armament of the career counselor. Sources of occupational information include the *Dictionary of occupational titles,* the *Occupational outlook handbook,* various occupational flyers that report up-to-date attributes of occupations of various sorts, and more recently a number of computer-based occupational search and simulation systems such as SIGI, which allow the user to explore occupational activities independently.

Understanding the way individuals move through their career lives is an important content area for career counselors. Although Donald Super did not initially devise them, he popularized and brought wide attention to issues concerning career patterns. The idea of maturation through career stages is inherent in the notion of career patterns. Observation suggests that career patterns have changed over the years and a once relatively rare pattern—the serial or multiple career—is becoming

increasingly common. In addition, there appear to be gender issues related to career patterns and more subtle changes during mid-life than earlier approaches assumed.

Some of the practical reasons why career counseling has emerged as a specialty include problems of selection entry and adjustment to work. Selection is a major problem largely for the school-age person who is trying to sort out the extensive array of occupational responsibilities into a manageable subset about which appropriate educational and career decisions can be made. Therefore, much of the research has focused on how these decisions are made—on the indecision scales previously mentioned, the measurement of occupational interests, and the establishment of occupational information-based systems. A large number of studies have examined the transition from school to work.

STATE OF THE ART

Most career counseling occurs either in the context of schools, employee assistance programs, or settings in which other psychological services are delivered, such as private practice or rehabilitation clinics of various sorts. As a consequence, the range of ethics and appropriate practice is quite diverse. Fundamentally, career counseling should be pursued following the same basic ethics as any other psychological intervention, emphasizing as systematic an approach as the practitioner can provide, privacy and confidentiality, appropriate record keeping and evaluation, and follow-up of client outcomes for the purpose of improving future services. Unfortunately, settings outside the usual psychological service setting do not emphasize these principles to the degree desirable, and workers in schools and industries might at times be subjected to conflicting demands by their institutional employers. As a professional field that has been emerging for many years, career counseling remains somewhat rudimentary in its systematic ethical approaches and principles.

CAREER DEVELOPMENT
COUNSELING
EMPLOYMENT PRACTICES
INDUSTRIAL PSYCHOLOGY
OCCUPATIONAL COUNSELING

S. H. Osipow

CAREER DEVELOPMENT

Career development denotes the process, sequences, and tasks of moving from one position to another. Theory and research, and hence applications, in vocational psychology can be divided into four major categories: matching, phenomenological, developmental, and decision-making approaches.

MATCHING APPROACHES

This category includes theories and methods based on *differential psychology* and *situational theories,* the latter including structural, contextual, and socialization approaches.

DIFFERENTIAL APPROACHES

For practical purposes these approaches were developed during World War I, when U. S. Army psychologists using group tests found significant differences between men who had had differing civilian occupations, which led them to establish a rough hierarchy of occupations based on intellectual levels. This in turn led to work with special aptitudes, culminating in the 1930s in the aptitude profiles of men and women for a variety of skilled, clerical, managerial, and professional occupations.

The method was especially useful in short-term counseling and in personnel classification, as in dealing with veterans returning to civilian life in search of peacetime employment.

But aptitudes, as exemplified in the GATB and the DAT, were not the only basis for matching people and occupations. Psychoanalysts had been pointing out that aptitudes alone do not account for job success or failure; indeed, no one had ever claimed that they did, although some had made the point that aptitudes are more readily measured and studied than personality.

The first to do more than point out the importance of personality was Anne Roe, who applied Maslovian theory and child development research findings to occupational choice. Although hers was a neat and appealing theory, postulating the importance of the psychological climate of the childhood home, subsequent studies failed to support it, as S. H. Osipow pointed out in *Theories of career development.* The experiences of later childhood and adolescence—contrary to Sigmund Freud and Abraham Maslow—are too important and have too much of a modifying effect on the results of early childhood for Roe's theory to be valid.

Situational Theories

It is a well-documented commonplace that parental socioeconomic status is a major determinant of one's eventual adult occupational status. Studies by William Sewell and others confirm that, although parental status is a major determinant of how much education a youth gets and therefore of where one enters the world of work, youth in school and college do a good deal to establish their own independent socioeconomic status and to make their own places higher on the vocational ladder.

Structural approaches put the emphasis on the opportunities made available by being born into a given social level.

Contextual approaches reflect the attempt by some theorists to seek a more balanced view of the impact of situational factors by placing individual qualities in the social context.

Socialization approaches have filled the gap to some degree, Orville Brim having pointed out in 1966 that socialization is viewed as a process whereby the individual (a) adjusts to society, even if that requires modifying the social structure in some way; and (b) conforms to social role expectations. Socialization theory is interested in how labor is developed so that the work of society gets done and should therefore be considered as more applicable to labor development than to career development.

PHENOMENOLOGICAL APPROACHES

Self-concept theory has been applied to career development by Super and by many others. It has focused on the individual as the decider, recognizing that concepts of oneself are not of the self in a vacuum, but in a situation. Individuals act in terms of their concept of the situation as well as of themselves. The approach appealed to the *Zeitgeist* of the 1950s and 1960s, and triggered a great deal of research with high school and college students.

Self-concept theory has also been open to criticism as an approach applicable to mobile, relatively autonomous middle-class youth, but not to those who are less free to choose, to whom structural theory may more often apply.

Congruence theory postulates a dynamic, to some implicit degree developmental, quality in vocational choice, in which the individual makes a series of successive approximations in the fitting of the self into a preoccupational or occupational situation congenial with personality traits, which Holland views as stable bases of choice. Choice is therefore seen as a process of matching one's personality traits with those of an occupation. If there is freedom to move, it results in leaving an uncongenial situation for one that may prove more congenial. For this reason this approach is called congruence theory: a special case of matching that

is theoretically more complete and possibly more powerful than self-concept theory.

DEVELOPMENTAL APPROACHES

Matching theories, of whatever type, have focused on occupational choice, or at most on a series of occupational choices in which it is the current choice that is of interest. They have therefore tended to neglect the nature of the series of choices, implicitly viewing them as all of the same order while neglecting the personal and situational developments or processes that link each choice in the series in some meaningful way. Dissatisfaction with this neglect of developmental psychology, and in particular of developmental perspectives and methods, led in the 1950s to research and theorizing of a different type.

The first work on occupational careers was strictly empirical: Paul Lazarsfeld and Charlotte Bühler collected and analyzed data on the careers of Austrian subjects, the former focusing on youth, but the latter dealing with the entire life span and including occupational roles along with other life-career roles. Donald Super sought to weave this work, various other lesser studies, and his own observations into a systematic treatment of occupational career development. When Eli Ginzberg and associates published *Occupational choice,* counseling psychologists, vocational counselors, and certain others began to look at careers developmentally.

Super conceptualized a career as a rainbow in which each band of color represents a different life-career role, ranging from the first role, child (usually the only role from birth to entry into school), through the roles of pupil-student, leisurite, worker, spouse, homemaker, parent, citizen, and eventually annuitant. The amount of space colored or shaded in a band represents the time given to the role, while the depth of the color or shading shows the degree of commitment to each of the roles. The roles are interactive, and may be *extensive* or supportive as one carries over into and is helped by another; or *complementary,* when talents not used in one are happily used in another; or *compensatory,* when one role provides desired outlets not found in the customary role. In addition, any of the preceding may be *competitive* with other roles, creating conflict if the time or emotional commitment devoted to a given role has a negative impact on another major role. This has been called a *life-span, life-space approach* to career development.

Growth is the childhood stage, when self-concepts are developing but when identification with key figures and fantasy are dominant in thinking about occupations.

Exploration proceeds through tentative and trial stages, leading in due course to *Establishment,* which at first involves trial with little commitment, and in due course a greater degree of commitment if the trial is rewarding.

Establishment having taken place, consolidation, advancement, or perhaps transfer and a new establishment process may take place. These are normally in due course followed by the plateau of midcareer, when men and women have peaked and enter the stage of *Maintenance.* But some never peak; rather, they keep on climbing because they are innovators who remain creative. Some who do peak keep updating themselves and truly maintain their places in the world of work, while still others stagnate, perhaps keeping their jobs through organizational and personal inertia, or becoming deadwood and in due course being released as such prior to retirement. Such men and women have prematurely entered the *Decline* stage, which normally begins in the 60s with substages of tapering off, disengagement, and adjusting to retirement.

The Life Career Rainbow also seeks to depict the various social and personal determinants that affect careers. Although this may be a useful graphic method of conveying the complexity over time and space of a career, *Path Models* have been developed, along with path analysis methods of using statistical regression analysis, which have more heuristic and research value.

DECISION-MAKING APPROACHES

During the 1970s a new focus on career development emerged. Jepsen identified several "decision types," but Harren and Arroba used methods that enabled them to define these as decision styles, any one of which might be used at some point by a given person, even though one might have context- or content-related styles. Thus a choice of an elective course in college might be made impulsively by a person whose selection of major field or summer vacation job might follow the steps of classical, logical problem solving, whereas another person might make even definitive career decisions impulsively. It is perhaps not unexpected that logical career decision-making processes have been most thoroughly studied, although the *methods* rather than their *outcomes* have been the subjects of research.

CAREER DEVELOPMENT
INDUSTRIAL PSYCHOLOGY
OCCUPATIONAL INTERESTS

D. E. SUPER

CATHARSIS

Catharsis is used in aesthetics and the psychology of art with reference to spectator response, and in psychotherapy with reference to the release of repressed affect or psychic energy.

In ancient Greek *katharsis* most commonly meant "purgation," especially of guilt. But its most notable use in ancient times occurs in Aristotle's cryptic definition of tragedy as drama which "accomplishes through pity and fear the catharsis of such feelings."

In psychoanalytic literature the term first appears in *Studies on hysteria* by Josef Breuer and Sigmund Freud, although both the naming and the therapeutic method initially associated with it are credited to Breuer. Breuer had apparently cured patients of hysterical symptoms by inducing them, under hypnosis, to relive or remember forgotten childhood events—often but not always traumatic—and the affects associated with them. Freud hypothesized that in such cases the mental or nervous energy that would have led to the original affect was diverted into hysterical symptoms and that memories of the experiences were repressed into the unconscious. When under hypnosis both the memory and the associated affect were brought into consciousness, the affect was thereby discharged and the symptom eliminated. The process of affective discharge was also called "abreaction."

Freud stated that the cathartic method was both the precursor and the ongoing nucleus of psychoanalysis.

In contemporary psychotherapy outside the psychoanalytic tradition, "catharsis" often refers in a general way to the therapeutic release of emotions or tensions, including some that might be conscious or related to conscious experiences. It is a central concept in psychodrama and a major aspect of most brief and crisis-oriented therapies. Sometimes it is called "talking out," "acting out," or "ventilation." In implosive therapy, there is a deliberate attempt to elicit strong emotions in order to bring about cathartic release of tension.

BRIEF THERAPY
CRISIS INTERVENTION
IMPLOSIVE THERAPY

F. W. HANSEN

CAUSAL REASONING

Interest in causes range from the cursory and often trivial inquisitiveness of everyday wonder to the systematic rigor of scientific investigation. Due to this wide-range interest in cause–effect relationships, it is essential that the principal constituent features of causal reasoning be clearly specified. As an epistemological process, the attribution of causality (i.e., the designation of certain events as causes and other events as effects) requires special consideration. Hume cited three criteria for causation: (a) the contiguous occurrence of the presumed cause and effect in both space and time; (b) a temporal ordering of events such that the presumed cause precedes the effect; and (c) the covariation of presumed cause and effect such that whenever one varies, the other will also vary. Hume concluded that causality cannot be empirically demonstrated but rather is inferred from observed events.

Spurious causality refers to the situation in which the inferred relationship between a specified cause (A) and effect (B) is actually the result of the effect of a third unspecified factor (C) that is the cause of both A and B. Thus, rather than A causing B, another factor (C) may be the cause of both A and B. To ensure that a causal relationship does indeed appear to exist between A and B, other causal factors such as C must be identified and incorporated in the analysis. If a causal relationship in fact appears to be evident between A and B, then the covariation between A and B will persist, controlling for the confounding effects of causally prior variables such as C. Necessary for the inference of causality, these four conditions underlie causal reasoning in the behavioral sciences. Hence, the claim "A causes B" actually means that A and B have been found to covary in the proper time sequence and that there are compelling theoretical and methodological reasons to believe that B is an effect of A.

Causal reasoning in the behavioral sciences is distinct from what can be regarded as more of a common view of causal reasoning. Commonly, causality is perceived as the occurrence of cause-and-effect events in a necessary and sufficient manner much like the action of one billiard ball directly striking another. The works of Hume and Mill cited previously reflect such an intellectual disposition. Subsequently, the necessary and sufficient criteria for the inference of causality evident in these early works have been replaced by more of a contributory and partial view of causation. Events are viewed probabilistically and "causes" of these events are regarded as sufficient (but not both necessary and sufficient) to produce a specified effect. In the abstract, causal reasoning is bound only by the skill and imagination of the investigator; however, when used to inform and guide research, certain constraints are inherent in causal analysis, two of which are mentioned.

First, the factors identified as "causes" do not represent final, complete, or ultimate causes in any epistemological sense. Hence, research into causes of human behavior represents an inherently tentative and incomplete process of inquiry. Within any field of scientific inquiry, the search for causes is restricted in a variety of ways; however, the comparatively complex, indeterminate, and dynamic nature of human behavior, as presently understood, represents an added challenge to the behavioral sciences. Second, although the presumed relations between causes and effects derived from this line of reasoning can never be proven empirically, causal reasoning nevertheless requires an explicit research framework and, in particular, dictates that the implications of each of the theoretical arguments used be stated as precisely as possible. In light of this mandated explicitness, causal reasoning represents a powerful and compelling means of studying human behavior. Moreover, causal reasoning entails the formal attempt to bridge the hiatus between the development of theory, on the one hand, and the refinement of research methodologies, on the other hand; an effort most succinctly revealed by the causal modeling approach of Blalock and others. In light of this hiatus, effective operationalization of theoretically derived propositions represents a crucial process with profound implications.

The inferential nature of causal reasoning represents a core concern among behavioral scientists and has admittedly lead to a certain confusion in the field as to the meaning of causality and a questioning of whether the notion of causality serves a necessary and productive role in science. Further debate has arisen questioning whether causal reasoning should be limited to experimental and quasi-experimental research in which variables of interest can reportedly be "manipulated." It has been argued that a clearer understanding of underlying causal dynamics can only be realized when the research design permits the manipulation of variables. However, the actual degree of manipulation realized in experimental designs may be appreciably less than envisioned or anticipated. Moreover, while experimental designs do permit a simpler set of *a priori* assumptions, the principal features of causal analyses based on experimental research designs, on the one hand, and nonexperimental or observational research designs, on the other hand, have been found to be identical. The exact role of causal reasoning in behavioral research will continue to be debated; however, to the extent that the investigation of human behavior remains at least implicitly guided by the question of causation, causal reasoning and causal models provide a precise and exacting framework for such inquiry.

DETERMINISM/INDETERMINISM
MILL'S CANONS

D. G. NICKINOVICH

CENTRAL LIMIT THEOREM

The Central Limit Theorem concerns the distribution of a linear composite. Y is a linear composite of a set of variables (X_1, X_2, X_3, etc.) if $Y = a_1X_1 + a_2X_2 + a_3X_3 + \ldots$, where the as are weights. For example, if Y equals $3X_1 + 4X_2$, then a_1 equals 3 and a_2 equals 4. The Central Limit Theorem states that the shape of the distribution of Y becomes more and more like the normal distribution as the number of variables included in the composite increases. Specifically, the Central Limit Theorem states that Y is asymptotically normal as the number of composited variables approaches infinity. The Central Limit Theorem is one of the principal reasons that psychologists and statisticians make regular use of the normal distribution.

Notice that the theorem does not require that the variables in the composite are normally distributed. Y is asymptotically normal even when the composited variables have very non-normal distributions. Perhaps this is most easily illustrated by compositing a set of coin tosses. Imagine tossing a fair (unbiased) coin one time, recording 0 for a tail and 1 for a head. This experiment has two possible outcomes, each equally likely. If we call the experiment's outcome X, it can be concluded that P ($X = 0$) = 0.5 and P ($X = 1$) = 0.5. The distribution of X is illustrated in Figure 1.

Repeat this simple experiment ten times, generating values for X_1, $X_2, X_3, \ldots X_{10}$. Each of the Xs has the same distribution. It is possible to create a new variable that is a linear composite of the Xs. Let $Y = X_1 + X_2 + X_3 \ldots + X_{10}$. Y is the number of heads in ten tosses of a fair coin, and the distribution of Y is shown in Figure 2. Notice that with only ten variables in our composite, Y resembles the normal distribution. If the coin were tossed 1000 times and the outcomes were summed, the distribution would be almost indistinguishable from the normal distribution.

The Central Limit Theorem frequently is introduced as a special case, to describe the distribution of the sample mean. The sample mean is a linear composite of the scores in the sample, with each score weighted by $1/N$, where N is the sample size. If N is large enough, the distribution of the sample mean will be normal, so the normal distribution can be used to build confidence interval estimates of the population mean and to test hypotheses concerning the sample mean. Researchers generally assume the sample mean has a normal distribution of N is at least 30, but how quickly the distribution assumes the normal shape depends on how normal the Xs are. If the X scores are normally distributed, their mean will always be normally distributed. If the X scores are very nonnormal, N may have to be larger than 30 for the Central Limit Theorem to apply.

The Central Limit Theorem also can explain why many physical measurements are normally distributed. Human heights and weights are determined by many factors, probably including hundreds of genes and thousands of variables related to nutritional and psychological history. Heights or weights can be thought of as a composite of thousands of variables, so should be normally distributed. Many psychological traits, such as intelligence, also are normally distributed, probably because they are influenced by thousands of genes and prenatal and postnatal events. Deviations from normality suggest the heavy influence of one event that overrides the linear composite. For example, extremely short people, so extreme that their presence is not consistent with the normal distribution, may have heights determined by a pituitary problem. Their heights are not influenced by the genes and events that under other circumstances would have made them taller. Similarly, people with extremely low intelligence may have a rare genetic defect or may have been subject to some trauma that damaged the central nervous system.

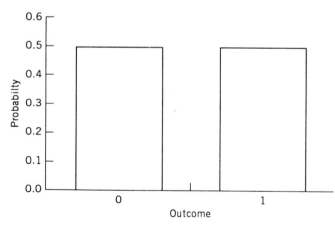

Figure 1. Distribution of X.

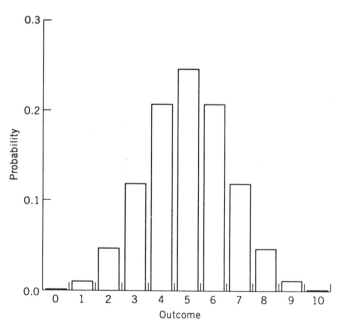

Figure 2. Distribution of Y.

NULL HYPOTHESIS TESTING
STATISTICS IN PSYCHOLOGY

M. J. ALLEN

CENTRAL NERVOUS SYSTEM

The central nervous system (CNS) refers to that portion of the nervous system that lies within the skull and spinal column and receives nervous impulses from sense receptors throughout the organism, regulates bodily processes, and organizes and directs behavior. Anatomically, the CNS comprises the brain and spinal cord, which float within the cranial cavity of the skull and the vertebral canal of the spinal column in a liquid matrix called cerebrospinal fluid, which also fills their hollows and serves as a protective cushion against damage. CNS tissue is further protected by three enfolding membranes called the meninges. The outer and toughest, the *dura mater,* attaches to skull and spine, encasing the spongy *arachnoid* membrane, interior to which the cerebrospinal fluid circulates. The soft *pia mater* is contiguous with the outer layer of brain and cord.

The basic structural unit of nervous tissue is the nerve cell or *neuron,* a specialized body cell of elongated shape (from a few microns to several feet in length), whose enhanced reactivity and conductivity permit it to propagate or conduct an electrical impulse along its length, and to chemically stimulate adjacent neurons to do likewise at specialized junctions called *synapses.* The nervous system is made up of *billions* of neurons, which interconnect every part of the organism to monitor and regulate it. *Receptor* neurons lead like the twigs of a tree inward to branches and thence to great trunks, called nerves, which enter the CNS and ascend into the brain. There also, *effector* neurons originate and descend to exit the CNS as nerves branching repeatedly out to regulate all muscle tissue and therefore all bodily activity. Twelve bilateral pairs of *cranial* nerves enter the brain directly. The cord is the origin of 31 bilateral pairs of *spinal* nerves, which exit the CNS through openings between adjacent vertebrae. Each spinal nerve contains both entering receptor fibers and departing effector fibers, but divides on reaching the cord, sensory fibers entering on the back, motor fibers exiting on the front.

The spinal cord is thus a great pathway for ascending and descending nerve tracts, but connectedness is a property of the CNS. A third type of neuron, the *interneuron,* is found here. Interneurons connect effector and receptor neurons, and by repeated branchings of their tips may synapse at either end with many hundreds of other neurons. The *functional* unit of the nervous system is the *reflex arc,* which so links receptor and effector neurons that a stimulus at a sense receptor capable of causing its nerve to conduct will automatically trigger an effector neuron to produce a response in a muscle or gland. Some reflexes are extremely simple, but most are not. The CNS is *hierarchically organized* with higher centers being stimulated by and acting upon lower centers, so that progressively more complex reflexes are organized progressively higher in the CNS. Certain muscle stretch reflexes operate for the most part spinally. Respiratory reflexes are largely centered in the brain stem, that part of the brain that is contiguous to the spinal cord. Homeostatic reactions depend on reflexes organized higher yet, in the hypothalamus, which may give rise to motivational states such as hunger and thirst. It is thought that by means of progressively more complex reflexes (some inborn, but most acquired through learning) all functions of the CNS are conducted, including the higher mental functions, the seat of which is the brain. The CNS is also symmetrically organized. Midline structures like the cord have two symmetrical halves. Other structures are duplicated, like the two cerebral hemispheres. Most fibers cross the midline (e.g., the left brain controls the right hand).

The brain is an organ of unparalleled complexity of parts and function, a reality that may be obscured by summary description. A great deal has nevertheless been learned about the pathways followed by ascending and descending nerve tracts. Much of the CNS is white matter, being the encased *processes* or extensions of nerve cells, bundles of which indicate pathways called *tracts.* The nerve bodies are not encased and are present as gray matter, clusters of which indicate centers of activity called *nuclei.*

The gross anatomy of the brain, in very greatly oversimplified summary, may be divided into three regions: (a) the *brain stem,* the parts of which (medulla, pons, mesencephalon) contain the nuclei of the *brain stem reticular formation,* which is vital in consciousness and the level of arousal of the brain above; (b) the *cerebellum,* a center for the smooth regulation of motor behavior; and (c) the *cerebrum,* which is of greatest interest to psychology for its organizing role in the higher mental functions and emotion. Between brain stem and cerebrum are the *thalamus* and *hypothalamus.* Thalamic nuclei largely integrate and relay sensory impulses upward to the cerebrum. Hypothalamic nuclei, however, are vital in the regulation of homeostatic reactions and in integrating the reflexes of the nuclei of the *limbic system,* structures embedded deep within the cerebrum that give rise to emotional experience and expression.

The cerebrum's deeply fissured gray outer surface, the hemispheres of its *cerebral cortex,* are the terminus of sensory processes and the origin of motor processes. Much of this area is given over to *association areas* of interneurons, whose complex interconnections give rise to memory, speech, purposive behavior, and, generally, the higher mental functions.

The pathways, relays, and sensory and motor areas of the brain have been mapped by largely physical and physiological methods. But the nature of the higher mental processes of humans remains elusive because they cannot be charted thus. As J. Minckler observed, the structure and function of nervous tissue are so intertwined that they must be studied together. At some levels of the CNS, the appropriate units of function are physiological. Other levels are best studied through discrete behaviors. Still more complex functions of the brain, however, require the scrutiny of complex patterns or styles of behavior, and the highest levels of brain function shade into issues of intelligence, logic, purpose, and consciousness, themselves as little understood as the brain.

The study of the CNS in humans is thus the study of brain behavior and brain–mind relationships, a field in which psychology is heavily involved. That there is a relationship between brain and mind is well established and has been observed for a very long time. C. J. Golden noted that Pythagoras, in 500 B.C., linked brain and human reasoning. In the second century A.D., Galen of Pergamum observed the effects on consciousness of brain injury in gladiators and described animals rendered senseless by pressure on their brains.

Galen was incorrect in attributing mental processes to the fluid-filled hollows of the brain, a view that nevertheless endured until the Renaissance. Modern concepts regarding brain functions did not begin to develop until the 1800s. This delay resulted from vitalistic and imprecise views of both brain and mind, and endured until a more scientific and reductionistic view of both brain and behavior emerged. Ramón y Cajal forwarded neuron theory in the late 1800s and received a Nobel Prize in physiology in 1906, the same year that C. S. Sherrington, who developed the concept of the reflex arc, published on integrative mechanisms of the nervous system. Galton's work with the behavioral measurement of individual differences contributed greatly to the emerging science of *psychometrics* or mental measurement. J. B. Watson moved psychology toward the study of behavior rather than mental states; he and B. F. Skinner both contributed to a science and technology of behavior that has meshed well with biology in permitting brain-behavior studies.

The nervous system, so simple in basic elements, is so complex in arrangements. As J. I. Hubbard observed, it is easy to imagine neuronal arrangements capable of causing muscles to contract or glands to empty, but difficult to imagine such arrangements permitting the aging Beethoven to compose works he could no longer hear. The sheer complexity of interconnections, which could well permit such complex behaviors, virtually defies understanding. Some 5 million neurons, for example, may lie beneath a single square centimeter of brain surface, each of which synapses with perhaps 600 other neurons. Virtually the entire depth and surface of the brain may be involved in any given behavior: "although very basic skills can be localized, all observable behavior is a complex interaction of numerous basic skills so that the brain as a whole is involved in most actual behavior."

To be understood, the brain (and possibly all the CNS) must be understood as a whole. Yet owing to limits in theory, knowledge, and perhaps capacity, we must approach the whole through study of the parts, viewed at many levels and from many perspectives. Full understanding of the CNS thus lies beyond any one discipline. Psychologists have put forward or contributed to models of mind compatible with known facts of brain function. They have used neuroscientific findings to develop models of human behavior, and they commonly contribute directly to knowledge of brain-behavior relationships through experimental and clinical neuropsychology.

Experimental neuropsychologists have long studied such things as the behavioral derangements caused by known lesions and other disturbances of CNS tissue in animals. *Clinical neuropsychologists* have increasingly used qualitative and quantitative aspects of behavior on special tasks to deduce or infer the probable locus and nature of brain tissue impairments in humans. The accuracy of such assessment has reached very substantial levels, and the behavioral mappings of strengths and deficits have found a growing role in treatment and rehabilitation efforts.

BRAIN
CRANIAL NERVES
HYPOTHALAMUS
LIMBIC SYSTEM
RETICULAR ACTIVATING SYSTEM

R. E. ENFIELD

CENTRAL NERVOUS SYSTEM DISORDERS

Psychological processes such as attention, perception, motivation, emotion, language, cognition, and action are controlled by the brain. When certain parts of the brain are damaged, specific functions may be lost, with the degree of loss related to lesion size and location. For example, damage to a strip of cortex in the frontal lobes that control movement of parts of the body will result in paralysis of those body parts. Lesions within relay stations along the visual sensory system will result in visual field defects such as scotomas ("blind spots"). Lesions deep in the hypothalamus may produce hunger, uncontrolled eating, and obesity. Also, destruction of areas involved in arousal may result in a permanent comatose state.

Disorders of the central nervous system can be classified according to lesion location or according to symptomatology and functional loss (although this distinction is not meant to be a mutually exclusive one). An example of the former would be a *frontal-lobe syndrome*, involving perseverative responding, difficulty with impulse control, and inappropriate emotional expression; an example of the latter would be *apraxia*, defined as an inability to carry out, when asked, complex skilled movements despite normal comprehension and absence of paralysis.

The term *amnesia* refers to disorders of memory, including memory for recent events (anterograde amnesia) and memory for events long ago (retrograde amnesia). *Dementia* is usually defined as a global impairment of cognition and personality without impairment of consciousness. *Aphasia* refers to language disturbances. Korsakoff's syndrome represents a type of amnesia; Huntington's disease leads to a form of dementia that is combined with a movement disorder; Broca's and Wernicke's aphasias exemplify different aspects of disturbances in verbal communication. The

salient symptoms of each of these are described in turn. However, it must always be acknowledged that the complexity of behavioral abnormalities associated with exemplars, such as amnesias, dementias, and aphasias, points out the need to give attention to a wide spectrum of perceptual and cognitive deficits that may be integral to the presenting symptom of any disorder of the central nervous system.

ALCOHOLIC KORSAKOFF'S DISEASE

George Talland linked the etiology of Korsakoff's disease most frequently with the polyneuropathy of chronic alcoholism and associated malnutrition. The critical brain lesions are thought to include the mammillary bodies of the hypothalamus and/or medial thalamic nuclei. Damage to these or to other regions of the brain (hippocampus, fornix, anterior thalamus) identified with the classic interconnected circuit described by J. W. Papez, has been associated with memory impairment, including severe anterograde amnesia for recent events, and some retrograde amnesia for events prior to the appearance of obvious symptomatology. The verbal memory deficits exhibited by these patients have received wide attention from experimental neuropsychologists.

Although anterograde amnesia is the most obvious presenting symptom in Korsakoff patients, it has been suggested that, in addition to having severe memory problems, these individuals also suffer from impaired cognitive functioning as well. Oscar-Berman has indicated that restricted attention, retarded perceptual processing, decreased sensitivity to reward contingencies, and perseverative response tendencies may be deficits independent of memory loss. These additional abnormalities probably reflect widespread cerebral atrophy accompanying sustained alcohol abuse. Thus, emphasis should be given to sensory and cognitive deficits that may be integral to the disease process caused by chronic alcoholism.

HUNTINGTON'S DISEASE

Huntington's disease results from an inherited biochemical error of metabolism, the mechanics of which are largely unknown. Exhaustive genealogical documentation has determined that each offspring of a carrier has a 50% chance of developing the disease. Symptoms usually do not begin to appear until the patient's thirties, well into the child-bearing years. Progressive deterioration (mental and motoric) mounts slowly for about 15 years and is relieved only by death. Lesions are well localized bilaterally in the caudate nucleus of the neostriatum, although additional diffuse damage to the frontal and temporal lobes also is noted. The effects described clinically are choreathetosis and dementia (in the most common variant of the disease).

Huntington's disease usually becomes manifest by the appearance of choreic movements involving the extremities, trunk, and face. Early in the disease the choreic patient may be able to incorporate involuntary movements into purposeful actions, but this ability gradually gives way to continual exaggerated movement. Sleep, respiration, and speech are also affected. "Mental alterations" usually appear subsequent to the onset of involuntary movements, although they may develop simultaneously with or even prior to the movement disorder.

APHASIA

The term *aphasia* literally means "no language." More realistically, aphasic patients suffer from an impairment in their previous level of ability to use language expressively or receptively. There are many different forms of aphasia, and classification schemes can be found in *Selected papers on language and the brain* by Norman Geschwind, and in *The assessment of aphasia and related disorders* by Harold Goodglass and Edith Kaplan. Pathology is almost always within the left hemisphere of both right-handed as well as left-handed patients. It is frequently located in either the frontal lobe (Broca's aphasia) or the temporal lobe (Wernicke's aphasia), and usually is the result of a cerebrovascular accident, tumor, or trauma.

There are components of aphasia that can be considered as language-specific amnesias. If a lesion is in the neighborhood of a cortical sensory projection zone, the resulting disorder may involve one or another of the sensory modalities (audition or vision), but if it is in a polysensory integration zone, it will cause a disorder of more highly elaborate functions (e.g., spatial recognition, language, and/or voluntary movement). It has been argued that aphasia is a mere loss of certain linguistic abilities, and that the "intellect" remains intact. Others, however, regard aphasia either as the manifestation of a primary intellectual loss or as the loss of a restricted aspect of intelligence.

BRAIN
BRAIN INJURIES
ORGANIC BRAIN SYNDROMES

M. OSCAR-BERMAN

CENTRAL TENDENCY MEASURES

The purpose of measures of central tendency is to provide a single summary number that best describes a set of observations or scores. The terms "measure of central tendency" and "average" are often used interchangeably, although some authors restrict the use of "average" to the arithmetic mean. Although there are many measures of central tendency, those most commonly encountered are the mode, median, and mean.

The *mode* of a set of scores is simply the score that occurs with the greatest frequency. In grouped data, the mode is the midpoint of the class interval that contains the greatest number of scores.

The *median* is simply the score value below which 50% of the scores fall. If there are an odd number of scores, the median is taken as the middle score. If there are an even number of scores, the median is taken to be halfway between the middle two scores. The median is a more useful measure than the mode and is frequently used with skewed data. It should be noted, however, that the median is insensitive to extreme scores.

The *arithmetic mean* of a set of scores is the most commonly encountered measure of central tendency and can be obtained by adding up the scores and dividing by the number of scores. (In this section, the term "mean" is taken to represent the arithmetic mean.) There are a number of advantages to using the mean. Unlike other measures of central tendency, the mean is responsive to the exact position of each score in the distribution. It is, however, extremely sensitive to extreme scores and for this reason is sometimes not used for highly skewed distributions of scores.

The mean is particularly useful in inferential statistics, because the sample mean is a relatively efficient estimator of the population mean. If a large number of samples were randomly selected from a population of scores, one would not expect the sample means to be exactly the same as one another or the mean of whole population. However, the variability of the sample means about the population mean can be shown to be less than the variability of the sample medians about the population median. In addition, it can be shown (the central limit theorem) that the sampling distribution of the mean approaches a normal distribution as sample size increases.

STATISTICS IN PSYCHOLOGY

A. D. WELL

CENTRAL TRAITS

The assumption that personality can be construed as a set of central traits, or relatively enduring behavioral predispositions, has largely structured traditional, nonpsychodynamic personality theory, measurement, and research. Trait models have come under increasing logical and empirical attack since the mid-1960s; however, a close reading of major "classic" trait positions and their reformulations tempers these critiques substantially.

The original trait model of personality was that of Gordon Allport, who, in *Pattern and growth in personality,* proposed traits as the central structural units of personality. A trait was described as a "broad system of similar action tendencies," incorporating the concepts of "equivalence of stimuli" and "equivalence of response"; that is, any of a variety of situations that are equivalent in meaning to the individual trigger the disposition, which in turn gives rise to any of a variety of behaviors, all with equivalent meaning. In more formal terms, trait was described as "a neuropsychic structure having the capacity to render many stimuli functionally equivalent, and to initiate and guide equivalent (meaningfully consistent) forms of adaptive and expressive behavior." Allport's position on traits was a reasoned and cautious one. For example, he acknowledged that "no trait theory can be sound unless it allows for, and accounts for, the variability of a person's conduct"; that is, environmental pressures, roles, and antagonistic intrapsychic factors may suspend, distort, or inhibit the expression of traits.

Allport's distinction between common traits, dimensions along which most people within a culture can be compared, and personal dispositions, which have the same operating characteristics as common traits but are "peculiar to the individual," is well known. His idiographic orientation hinged on the belief that personal dispositions "reflect the personality accurately, whereas common traits are categories into which the individual is forced." Only by studying a single life exhaustively can these personal dispositions be identified. Once identified, they can be catalogued in terms of relative intensity as a *cardinal* disposition or pervasive influence; *central* dispositions such as appear in a letter of recommendation; or less important and less consistent *secondary* dispositions. Personal dispositions were also seen to vary in degree of intentionality.

Allport described "trait" as a generic term referring to "cortical, subcortical, or postural dispositions having the capacity to gate or guide specific phasic reactions. It is only the phasic reaction that is visible; the tonic is carried somehow in the still mysterious realm of neurodynamic structure." Allport conceded that trait theory could not be "so simple-minded as it once was," that his earlier position had underemphasized social and situational factors, and that an adequate theory must relate the inside (trait) and outside (situational) systems.

The second dominant trait position has been that of Raymond B. Cattell. This position, in which traits refer to general behavior tendencies, was linked with that of Allport by virtue of Cattell's assumption that the Language Personality Sphere (i.e., the 4500 trait names abstracted from the English language by Allport) encompassed the totality of personality.

An additional relevant model is provided by J. P. Guilford, who defined a trait as "any enduring way in which one person differs from others." In an article published in 1975 he proposed a three-level hierarchical model based on ten factor traits.

David McClelland provides a final example of a personality model in which traits play a central, albeit not exclusive, role. McClelland proposed that three classes of constructs are necessary to describe personality: motives, schemas, and traits. McClelland defined a trait as "the learned tendency of an individual to react as he has reacted more or less successfully in the past in similar situations when similarly motivated." He identified 15 basic traits, grouped according to the response systems of Moving, Thinking, Performing, Emoting, Interacting, and Conforming. This concept of trait as a consistent response system is analogous to Allport's concept of expressive traits and Cattell's concept of temperament traits. Notice also that the qualifiers in the definition preclude any facile expectation that a person will behave in a constant fashion across all situations and circumstances.

Ross Stagner advocated the legitimacy and necessity of traits as psychological variables. Sounding much like Allport and McClelland, Stagner suggested that "a trait be conceived as a schema, or a cognitive rule, that guides behavior in a variety of situations perceived as belonging to this schema or subject to this rule. . . . a cognitive process that equates otherwise different situations in terms of their attributes or consequences." Thus trait scores "correspond to the magnitudes of situational pressures the person will resist in order to hold to his preferred mode of behavior." Echoing Cattell, Stagner referred to a trait as a "cognitive-affective 'deep structure'" (i.e., source trait) that may be transformed into a variety of overt behavioral consistencies (i.e., surface trait). Furthermore, the trait concept has utility for Stagner: "behavior often is predicted more accurately by a knowledge of established trait patterns than by a knowledge of the specific situation."

CRITICISM OF TRAIT THEORIES

Walter Mischel stated that "with the possible exception of intelligence, highly generalized behavioral consistencies have not been demonstrated, and the concept of personality traits as broad response predispositions is thus untenable." Mischel proposed that traits are insufficient as causes owing to their circular nature: a trait is inferred from behavior, then that trait is employed to "explain" the behavior. In addition, Mischel concluded that trait theories "largely ignore the role of environmental conditions or stimulus situations in the regulation of behavior."

These and subsequent criticisms have had a salutary impact on the field; however, the trait models described previously provide three grounds for response. First, Allport and McClelland have made it clear that there is no theoretical reason to expect a person to behave consistently, or even to maintain a given rank order within a sample, on all traits in all situations. Consistency of behavior across situations is perhaps most meaningfully considered as a within-subject, rather than an across-subjects, phenomenon; furthermore, perhaps we should expect consistency only on those few traits that are "central" or "cardinal" for a person. In spite of these objections, Mischel's challenge remains an empirical one: Trait consistency, however defined and constrained, must be demonstrated.

A second answer to criticism notes that the argument that trait theorists impute causal significance to traits appears to be overstated. For example, in *The structure of human personality,* Eysenck referred to a trait "simply as a *descriptive* variable, very much in the manner in which physicists elaborated the periodic table of the elements. . . . [A trait of sociability] does not pretend to explain why some people are more sociable than others. But the causal question could not even be raised unless some answer to the descriptive problem had been found." Furthermore, the charge of causal circularity is weakened by the designation of traits as generalized tendencies encompassing various situations and generating diverse behaviors.

A third response to criticism argues that the charge that trait models largely ignore the environment is also open to dispute. It is true that trait psychologists such as Allport and Cattell have assigned preeminence to traits, but they also acknowledged the crucial role of the situation—Cattell through his specification equation and statement that trait intensity equals response magnitude divided by stimulus magnitude, and Allport through the concept of equivalence of stimuli and such statements as "we should think of traits as *ranges of possible behavior.*" Trait theorists rely on traits for the description of personality structure, but they are cognizant that prediction of behavior entails a combination of personality and situational variables.

Although criticisms of trait formulations make it clear that psychology has left what Allport termed "the age of innocence," it can be argued that the sophisticated trait models described previously retain utility for the analysis and description of personality, for the prediction of behavior, and for the formulation of general principles of human behavior.

ARCHETYPES
A-TYPE PERSONALITY
B-TYPE PERSONALITY
DISPOSITIONAL SETS

J. B. CAMPBELL

CEREBRAL BLOOD FLOW STUDIES

Cerebral blood flow studies measure the total or regional brain blood flow to determine areas of normal, increased, or decreased blood supply.

Evaluation of cerebral blood studies may be indicated for any of the following reasons: (a) to estimate the risk of lack of blood supply to the brain (cerebral ischemia) prior to a surgical procedure; (b) to estimate cerebral blood flow during a surgical procedure; (c) to indicate potential for recovery and effectiveness of the surgical procedure after an operation; (d) to determine the state of the cerebral blood supply in situations of increased brain fluid pressure, as well as to see the effect of therapeutic measures; (e) to study changes in cerebral blood flow in victims of stroke and evaluate its abnormal process in the course of the disease; (f) to investigate factors that influence cerebral blood flow characteristics and cerebral cellular function; (g) to investigate the effects of drugs on cerebral blood flow; and (h) to investigate the abnormal physiology in various diseases such as migraines, seizures, and states of severe memory dysfunction in which cerebral hemodynamics and metabolic disorders might be involved. Like most neurological diagnostic tests, cerebral blood flow studies provide general information on the presence of an abnormality, but do not indicate the specific nature of the causative lesion.

Cerebral blood flow can be determined through a variety of techniques. The Kety-Schmidt method for determining total cerebral blood flow involves the patient inhaling a mixture of 15% nitrous oxide and air for 10 minutes, following which an arterial and venous blood sample is drawn to measure the clearance of the gas from the cerebral tissue. Another method for determining cerebral blood flow is the use of the Doppler Ultrasonic Directional Flowmeter, which measures carotid blood flow continuously, for the purpose of quantitative assessment of the capacity of cerebral collateral circulation.

BRAIN
BRAIN INJURIES
HYPERTENSION

R. T. GIUBILATO

CEREBRAL LOCALIZATION

Localization of function is the theoretical backbone of modern neuropsychology, neurology, and related disciplines, all of which attempt to correlate behavior with brain function.

In the history of the brain sciences, it is possible to conceive of the theory of localization as being applied to the whole, and then to increasingly smaller parts. At first the question seemed to be, "Why is the brain special and how is it different from other organs?" Aristotle (384–322 B.C.), the greatest of the Greek naturalist philosophers, believed that the heart was the seat of sensory and cognitive functions and that the brain simply tempered "the heat and seething" of the heart. In contrast, Democritus (c. 460–370 B.C.) and Plato (c. 429–348 B.C.) believed that intellect belonged not in the heart, but in the head.

At the time of the Roman empire, most behavioral functions were associated with the brain, although the passions were still regarded by some as "matters of the heart." The most important of the physicians at this time was Galen, who suggested that the front of the brain received sensory impressions while the cerebellar region was responsible for motor functions.

The church of the fourth and fifth centuries A.D. went one step further when they localized imagination, intellect, and memory in the different ventricles of the brain. This early type of localization theory was embraced by St. Augustine and by Posidonius of Byzantium, and was broadly accepted for more than 1000 years.

During the Renaissance, as scientists returned to dissection and experimentation, observation replaced conjecture. Leonardo da Vinci made molds of the ventricles to reveal their true shapes, and Andreas Vesalius showed that the ventricles did not vary much across species. Renewed attention was drawn to differences among the gross anatomic divisions of the brain. Slowly, the idea of ventricular localization gave way.

The events of the Renaissance set the stage for Thomas Willis to publish his *Cerebri anatome* in 1664. Willis proposed that the corpus striatum, which he defined as all white matter between the basal ganglia and the cortex, played a role in sensation, and that the cerebral cortex controlled memory and the will. The cerebellum was thought to regulate the vital and involuntary motor systems. This division of the brain into functional parts, based partly on comparative anatomy, partly on clinical material, and partly on other theories, changed existing thinking about the brain.

The seeds were planted for modern cortical localization theory when Franz Gall presented his theory of phrenology. He maintained that different areas of the cerebral cortex subserved different mental faculties and that cranial features correlated with the development of the specific underlying organs of mind. Gall and the phrenologists were convinced that humanity's highest functions belonged in the front of the cortex.

The theories of the phrenologists stimulated great debate. Some scientists thought the theory had merit, others found it absurd, and still others were led to believe that cortical localization made sense, but that Gall's methods could not show this. The last position was advocated by Jean-Baptiste Bouillaud. He began to localize speech in the frontal lobes in 1825 and spent years collecting autopsy material in support of localization.

The debates in the French scientific academies over cortical localization continued to heat up until 1861, when Paul Broca presented his celebrated case of M. Leborgne. His patient had lost his capacity for articulate language and the autopsy revealed a lesion involving the third frontal convolution of the left hemisphere. Broca's localization of a center for articulate language confirmed Bouillaud's belief and was the first cortical localization to receive broad acceptance.

In 1865, Broca published another landmark paper. His cases revealed that the left hemisphere of the brain is the area that controls speech. This was something that Marc Dax had recognized in 1836. Unfortunately, Dax failed to make his findings public in his lifetime, and his report on more than 40 cases did not appear in print until 1865.

In 1870, Gustav Fritsch and Eduard Hitzig identified the motor cortex in the dog, first by stimulation and then by ablation, showing that cortical localization could be studied in animals under controlled conditions. Lesion studies were conducted to localize not just various sensory functions, such as vision and hearing, but higher "intellectual" functions.

The advancement of localization theory was not based solely on pathological material. It also received good support from other sources. In 1875, Richard Caton reported that cortical electrical activity varied in accord with Ferrier's maps when his animals were chewing, looking at flashing lights, or doing other things. In addition, Paul Flechsig showed that different cortical areas became myelinated at different times. The idea that neurons did not fuse to form massive nets also stimulated

acceptance of cortical localization, as did cytoarchitectonic studies of the cortex.

The dominant trend since 1870 has been to try to divide all parts of the brain into smaller functional units. Some scientists urged caution, arguing that it is important to remember that no part of the brain really functions independently of all other parts. There has also been a concern that individuals have been too quick to equate anatomic markers and "localization of symptoms" with localization of specific "psychological" functions. At present, no one disputes the idea that the central nervous system is made up of specialized parts. Yet it also is clear that the functions of these various parts can only be inferred from lesion material and from anatomic and physiological studies. Because an inference is involved, scientists are likely to continue to debate the exact functions of certain parts of the brain for years to come.

BRAIN
BRAIN INJURIES
BRAIN LATERALITY
CENTRAL NERVOUS SYSTEM
ELECTROENCEPHALOGRAPHY
PHRENOLOGY

S. FINGER

CEREBRAL PALSY

Cerebral palsy is a term for those disorders of impaired brain and motor functioning with onset before or at birth, or during the first year of life. It is the result of a static lesion of the brain that cannot be cured and does not progress. The causes, clinical manifestations, and prognoses are widely variable. Manifestations may include mental retardation, learning disabilities, seizures, sensory and speech deficits, and impaired ability of voluntary muscles. The incidence of cerebral palsy is 1.3 to 5.0 per 1000 live births.

Both genetic and acquired factors may be responsible for these syndromes, although the cause is often obscure or multiple.

Classification of syndromes is commonly based on the predominant motor deficit and includes the following forms: (a) The *spastic* forms comprise approximately 75% of cases, are due to involvement of the upper motor neurons, and are characterized by increased tone of the involved musculature, rhythmic muscle contractions, abnormal reflexes, and a tendency to contractures. Types include spastic hemiplegia, implying that both extremities on one side are involved, and spastic tetraplegia, involving spasticity of all four extremities to approximately the same degree. Spastic paraplegia refers to involvement of both legs but complete sparing of the upper extremities. (b) *Dyskinetic* cerebral palsies imply impaired voluntary activity by uncontrolled and purposeless movements that disappear during sleep. (c) *Ataxic* cerebral palsy is related to a static lesion of the cerebellum or its pathways. Involved children have a wide-based walk and experience difficulty in turning rapidly and performing fast repetitive movements poorly. This type has the best prognosis for functional improvement. (d) *Mixed* forms may be present with clinical manifestations of more than one type.

TREATMENT

The management varies with the child's age, the type and severity of involvement, the presence or absence of seizures, and the degree of intellect. The motor aspects can be modified to a certain degree. Spastic children develop contractures, and this can be counteracted by surgical and nonsurgical means. The physical therapist can produce beneficial results through stretching tight tendons by passive and active exercises and by using certain mechanical devices.

BRAIN INJURIES
NEUROMUSCULAR DISORDERS
NEUROPSYCHOLOGY

R. T. GIUBILATO

CHANGE INDUCTION GROUPS

More than 5 million Americans have participated in groups aimed at personal growth or change; twice that number are members of self-help groups and consciousness-raising groups, and tens of thousands are patients in group psychotherapy.

Goals vary all the way from reducing juvenile delinquency in others to reducing weight in themselves. Some bring problems once taken almost exclusively to mental health professionals—severe personal or interpersonal concerns. Others face no immediate serious stress, but seek a group in hope that it will provide personal enrichment. Another sizable clientele are those who see themselves as limited by specific problems created by their relationship to a social order that suppresses them because of their sex, sexual mores, race, or age. Finally, there are groups whose members claim no motive for belonging other than to widen their experience.

The use of groups for systematically helping people in distress is of relatively recent origin in mental health practice. Small groups, however, have always served as important healing agents. Religious healers have always relied heavily on group forces, but when healing passed from the priestly to the medical profession, the deliberate use of group forces fell into decline. The development of psychiatry as part of medicine was predicated on the idea that "scientific medicine" must distinguish itself from healing that stemmed from nonscientific traditions. For its legitimization as a branch of medical science, the treatment of psychological problems required medical science, a clear differentiation between its methods and those that preceded it in folk societies, where highly developed group-based techniques were used for curing psychological illness within the framework of kith and kin, groups of similar sufferers, or the religious community.

In the early 1900s isolated individuals reported using groups for therapeutic benefit. Joseph Pratt, a Boston internist, organized classes for patients with tuberculosis. In Europe Alfred Adler established guidance centers that used group concepts in treating working-class patients. An early and important influence in the development of group psychotherapy was the use of the healing group by Jacob L. Moreno. In England, Trigant L. Burrow, who coined the term "group analysis," used groups for the analysis of behavior disorders.

Group psychotherapy did not develop in full force until World War II. In time of short supply of psychiatric personnel and increased need for service, the "reasonableness" of treating patients in groups came to the fore. The spread of group forms was much influenced by the social pragmatics of professionally treating large numbers of people efficiently. Also influential was the changing nature of theory about human nature and the genesis of psychological ills. The suggestion that psychological disturbance might be intrinsically related to problems of relationships among people—a social rather than intrapsychic explanation—eased the transition from a dyad to multiperson treatment.

COMPARISONS AMONG CURRENT HEALING GROUPS

There are four major types of groups whose central task is the psychological and behavioral alteration of individuals and the relief of human misery. *Group therapy* explicitly employs a medical model. Its avowed public goal is "cure," or the production of mental health, and it sees as its relevant population those who define themselves as seeking release from psychological misery. The groups' members are generally called "patients," who are thought by the therapist (and probably themselves) to be psychologically "ill" and to exhibit "sick" behavior.

In contrast, a variety of *self-help organizations*—perhaps as many as 250 separate organizations—are by intention not professionally led. As lay movements, however, they share with group psychotherapy restrictive notions of appropriate clientele. The range for any particular self-help organization's attention is limited to people who have a common symptom, problem, or life predicament.

A third set of healing groups, variously labeled as *sensitivity training* and *encounter groups*, is connected to the Human Potential Movement. Usually they are professionally directed. Unlike group therapy, which implies psychological illness and patient status, or self-help programs, which are directed at the members' common problem, the Human Potential Movement considers its activities relevant to all who want to grow, change, and develop.

Finally, *consciousness-raising groups* share with self-help groups the insistence on nonprofessional orientation and peer control, but unlike the self-help groups they have broad criteria for inclusion. The tie that binds is not a common psychological syndrome, but a general social characteristic of a large subgroup of people—sex, race, ethnicity, age, or sexual behavior—permitting wide latitude regarding personal particularities.

Another important difference among the various group systems is their attribution system—the interpretive theories explicitly and implicitly communicated regarding the source of human misery and how one resolves it.

The various types of healing groups differ in how and to what extent they manage psychological distance between the leader and the participants. A variety of methods serves to diminish distance: the transparency of the therapist, the use of an informal setting, the diminution of the importance of the leader's expertise, the presentation of self more nearly as a peer, and the use of physical contact.

PROFESSIONAL THEORIES OF HEALING GROUPS

Behavioral models, best expressed in social learning theory, advance various mechanisms as essential for change induction: arousal enhancement and reduction, modeling, and cognitive restructuring. The leaders are assumed to be in precise control of the situation: They have the power to change, desensitize, model, and so forth, all the behavior that is desired. The failure of most behavior approaches to take into account the complexities of the social system and its unique properties for change reduces the power of change strategies that have demonstrated success in dyads.

Humanistic approaches are represented by diverse settings that share a common view of human nature, the source of one's plight, and what is required for growth or change. Emphasis is placed on the human being as a developing person, and the goal is actualization of latent potential. The most widely known humanistic system is that developed by Carl Rogers.

Although it uses the group quite differently, the *Gestalt approach* also embraces a fundamentally positive view of human nature and its psychosocial needs. Humanistically oriented therapies usually do not emphasize the social system characteristics as of prime importance for inducing change.

Dynamic approaches have historical roots that are psychoanalytic. They view the source of human misery as intrapsychic: It is inner conflicts that an individual has carried over a lifetime. Therapy involves the cognitive mastery, both generically and currently, of these conflicts.

CHARACTERISTICS OF GROUPS THAT FACILITATE LEARNING OR HEALING

Of paramount importance are as follows:

1. The capacity to develop a sense of belonging.
2. The capacity to control a member's behavior by reward and punishment.

3. The capacity to define reality and thereby how members should view themselves, the group as a whole, and others in the group.

4. The capacity to induce and release powerful feelings.

5. The capacity to provide a contrast for social comparison and feedback. Such comparisons facilitate revision of identity by suggesting new possibilities or alternatives.

THERAPEUTICS AND THE ROLE OF THE THERAPIST/LEADER

Underlying all professional theories of group change is the social microcosm assumption that the group will generate feelings, thoughts, or behaviors that are personally troublesome. Whether the theorist assumes that dynamic conflicts are at issue looks at interpersonal relationships as the source of personal problems, or takes a behavioral position, in each case it is believed that the initial step in change is the elicitation of troublesome issues. The display of these issues in a context that is in some important ways different from ordinary life constitutes the first step of the therapeutic process. Next, the behavior, thought, or feeling must be experienced in ways different from previous history; participants need to "learn" that the feared consequence will not necessarily occur.

An examination of the variety of theoretical positions would reveal a large number of terms or concepts to describe things that therapists or leaders do: They interpret, resist, confront, reflect, support, develop role-playing scenes, act as the observing ego, precipitate crises for the group by not acting in accord with expectations, reinforce, model, make contracts, set up ground rules, protect, express acceptance, communicate genuineness and positive regard, analyze transference, express feelings, interpret group dynamics, teach, act as a whole person, disclose personal feelings, challenge, act provocatively, and so forth. The descriptive and conceptual labels used to describe the role are indeed broad and far-ranging.

M. A. Lieberman, I. D. Yalom, and M. B. Miles, by examining leadership behaviors represented by eight theoretical positions, describe four fundamental leader functions: emotional stimulation, support, meaning attribution, and executive functions. All leaders, no matter what their theoretical orientation, employ some behavior in these four areas, although they differ widely with regard to the amount and particular emphasis on any one.

Sensitivity training leaders see their role as helping members understand themselves and others through understanding the group process. They focus on the group as a whole and on the members' transactions with each other. Such leaders attempt to explain what the group as a whole is doing, focusing on such issues as group maintenance, cohesiveness, power and work distribution, subgrouping, and scapegoating.

Gestalt therapists stress the wholeness of the individual. Change is viewed as a subintellectual process mediated by helping the individual get in touch with the primitive wisdom of the body. There is little use of the group or, for that matter, of the other group members. In the classical practice of this methodology, there is an empty chair, "the hot seat," next to the leader, to which the members come one by one to "work" with the leader.

Transactional analysis leaders work with each of the group members in turn. The term "transactional analysis" refers to the transactions among internal symbols (parent, child, and adult) rather than transactions among individuals. Establishing learning contracts (the setting of specific goals) and formal teaching of the analytic model are typical.

Basic encounter group leaders emphasize the experiencing and deepening of interpersonal relationships and the liberating of somatic restrictions. They believe that by breaking free of social and muscular inhibitions, people can learn to experience their own bodies and other people in a different and fuller sense. The focus is on both the individual's inner states and interpersonal relationships.

Client-centered leaders center their attention on interpersonal or intrapersonal dynamics. Their goal is to behave as a model for personal development, establishing the conditions of genuineness, unconditional positive regard, and empathy—the basic ingredients of the therapeutic relationship.

Attack therapy emphasizes the expression of anger: Each member in turn is systematically attacked and explored by the others in the belief that, if one is attacked long enough in one's weak areas, one will strengthen them. This procedure is called "the game" in Synanon because, once the group meeting is over the atmosphere changes quickly to one of support. The Synanon form of attack therapy differs from other models having a similar emphasis in that the Synanon groups are composed of both experienced and inexperienced members, so that much of the work is done by "experienced game players." In other forms of attack therapy the leader is almost exclusively the confronting agent.

Psychodramatic approaches construct role-playing or psychodramatic exercises so as to let participants act out heretofore blocked behaviors or feared emotional relationships in a "safer" setting. The technology involves the assumption that a person can learn from direct experience as an actor in the role, or vicariously as an observer of the psychodrama.

Psychoanalytically oriented groups focus on the inner dynamics, especially the early history as expressed in the group. Such groups tend to be less emotionally charged, more rationally based, with a focus on intellectual mastery of inter- and intrapersonal forces operating in the group. The therapist acts as an observing ego, interpreting resistance and analyzing defenses of individuals as they are played out in the group social microcosm.

EXPERIENCES THAT MAKE FOR CHANGE

The overall process of change through group methods can be thought of in terms of two central and interdependent aspects of the group experience. Group characteristics prescribe the conditions that define the context in which the sought-for changes are to take place. The other important aspect of the group change-induction system is the "package" of events and experiences—change mechanisms. Some will be quite familiar to readers acquainted with individual therapy; others can take place only in a multiperson situation. None of these events has been shown to be necessarily successful with all people or under all conditions. They represent a distillation of what is generally regarded as important.

Expressiveness. Emotional expression is central in most theories. Some theoretical positions emphasize the expression of positive feelings, while in others the expression of negative feelings is considered critical.

Self-disclosure is the explicit communication of information that a group participant believes other members would be unlikely to acquire unless told, and that the person considers so highly private that great caution in telling is usually exercised.

Feedback. Feedback is the receipt of information about how one is perceived by peers and is unique to the group situation.

The experience of intense emotions. All therapy involves the emotional life of the person. Experiencing strong affects does not necessarily require engaging in the direct expression of feeling. Healing groups offer innumerable stimuli to generate intense emotions in members.

The experience of communion. A unique group attribute is the ability to provide members with a feeling of oneness with others.

Altruism. Unique to group settings is the experience of being facilitative to others.

Spectatorism. It is not uncommon in change-inducing groups that a few people remain quiet and inactive throughout the history of the group, yet benefits from the group may accrue to them. Although not fully understood, spectator-derived gains frequently occur.

Discovering similarity. The relief participants experience when they discover that their problem is not unique appears to be one of the more positive experiences that groups offer.

Experimentation. The group situation offers a setting that permits participants to experiment with new forms of behavior under low risk.

The inculcation of hope. Groups often generate events that inspire hope—a feeling that one can change and that the group can be responsible for such change.

Cognitive factors. Traditional psychotherapeutic systems growing out of dynamic psychiatry clearly emphasize the role of cognitive factors, usually expressed in terms of insight. In general, evidence from reasonably well-controlled studies is encouraging; the variety of healing groups described in this article do provide benefit.

ACTIVITY GROUP THERAPY
ENCOUNTER GROUP THERAPY
GROUP PSYCHOTHERAPY
HUMAN POTENTIAL MOVEMENT
MARATHON THERAPY
MECHANISMS OF GROUP PSYCHOTHERAPY

M. A. LIEBERMAN

CHARACTER DISORDERS

A. A. Roback defined character as the disposition to inhibit impulse and narrow self-seeking in light of some value principle. Included in this meaning of character were the concepts of emotional control, affiliative orientation, and emotional investment in distant goals.

From this traditional definition the concept of character disorders evolved to include four rather diverse patterns of abnormal behavior. These are alcoholism, drug addiction, sexual deviancy, and psychopathy. The behavior patterns typically constitute a violation of the codes and conventions of society.

The most common example of character disorder is the condition classically designated as the psychopathic or sociopathic personality. Current reviews of the experimental literature on the psychopathic personality present distinctions between primary and secondary psychopathy. The former represents individuals with lowered anxiety, guiltlessness, and an inability to form affectional relationships, while the secondary type is more neurotic, experiencing guilt and anxiety, and forming interpersonal relationships.

Alcoholism and drug abuse have traditionally been included under the heading of character disorders. These individuals generally show many dependency-autonomy conflicts, and problems in the area of impulse control, conformity to social expectations, and personal value commitments that are common to a disorder of character. Similar sexual deviations including exhibitionism, transvestism, voyeurism, sadomasochism, fetishism, rape, homosexuality, pedophilia, and incest have historically been included in this category.

In the more recent history of psychology, "character disorder" is used as a generic term referring to disorders of personality. Such disorders represent any deeply ingrained, inflexible, maladaptive patterns of relating to, perceiving, and thinking about the environment and oneself. They may cause either significant impairment in adaptive functioning or subjective distress. Thus they are pervasive personality traits and are exhibited in a wide range of social and personal contexts. Although the classification of character disorders is varied and somewhat subjective, commonly accepted nosological systems of character (personality) disorders exist. *The Diagnostic and statistical manual of mental disorders* is one system of describing these conditions.

IMMATURE PERSONALITY
NONCONFORMING PERSONALITY
PERSONALITY DISORDERS

P. A. MAGARO
R. ASHBROOK

CHEMICAL BRAIN STIMULATION

Since about 1950, attempts have been made to study brain functions in laboratory animals by injecting various chemicals directly into the brain or its ventricular spaces. Most commonly, drugs are used that stimulate or inhibit the synthesis, release, or reaction to the neurotransmitter substances that are responsible for the transfer of information from one nerve cell to another at synaptic junctions. Commonly used drugs include various hormones (including sex, pancreatic, gastrointestinal, and renal hormones) thought to act directly on some portions of the brain, toxins that selectively destroy certain nerve cells, and salt or sugar solutions that may selectively act on so-called osmo- or gluco-receptors. The purpose of these injections is to achieve the selective activation or inactivation of small groups of nerve cells that are characterized not only by a common chemical affinity for certain drugs but also by a common behavioral or physiological function. One of two basic procedures is typically followed.

Most commonly, the subject of the experiment is anesthetized and very thin stainless-steel tubes are implanted into the brain through small holes drilled into the skull. The tubes are held in place by cementing them to the skull. The experimental subject is then allowed to recover from the surgery and is subsequently subjected to a variety of behavioral tests. The second type of procedure involves similar surgical procedures, except that even thinner and more fragile glass pipettes are implanted into the brain. In these experiments, the drugs are injected (or electrophoretically ejected from the pipettes) while the experimental animal remains under deep anesthesia and the electrical activity of individual nerve cells or small groups of nerve cells is recorded.

BRAIN
NEUROCHEMISTRY
NEUROSURGERY

S. P. GROSSMAN

CHI SQUARE TEST

The chi square test (χ^2) was developed in 1900 by Karl Pearson. It is a nonparametric test involving observed and expected frequencies; the latter may be either theoretical (probability) or empirically determined. The basic formula for calculating the chi square statistic is

$$\chi^2 = \sum_1^k \frac{(f_0 - f_e)^2}{f_e}$$

The chi square test is most commonly applied to single groups, $2 \times k$ groups, $k \times 1$ groups, and 2×2 contingency tables, and is used for goodness of fit tests. The χ^2 statistic is related to measures of association such as the phi coefficient (ϕ), contingency coefficient (C), and Cramer's phi (ϕ'). The χ^2 statistic is based on a multinomial distribution that reduces to binomial form when $k = 2$. The chi square test is used in multivariate statistics and in calculating multinomial probabilities, especially from log linear models.

STATISTICS IN PSYCHOLOGY

P. F. MERENDA

CHILD ABUSE

Child abuse is defined as the nonaccidental injury of children by their parent or guardian. Severity of the injury is not included in this definition; however, definitions based on severity vary across states in legal interpretations, the courts, and their rulings, and even across time with the history of childhood. The history of American approaches to child abuse has followed the shifting history of social values and attitudes toward children.

From ancient to colonial times, children were seen as the property of their parents, who had the legal right to treat or mistreat the children in any way they saw fit. In some cases children were castrated or physically mistreated under the sanction or direction of a religious leader. Present-day agencies designed to specifically address the concerns of physical abuse with children trace their origins to a now classic case of a foster child named Mary Ellen in 1874. She had been beaten daily by her stepmother and there appeared to be no legal means to protect her. At the time there were no laws against cruelty to children, although such laws did exist with regard to animals. Mary Ellen's case was brought to the Society for the Prevention of Cruelty to Animals, which referred her to the court as an "animal who is getting mistreated." It was from this case that the society developed the children's division of the American Humane Association.

In 1974, the Federal Child Abuse, Prevention and Treatment Act was passed by Congress, providing direct assistance to states to help them develop child abuse and neglect programs. The act further provided for research in child abuse and neglect, and established the Center for Child Abuse and Neglect with the Children's Bureau in the Department of Health and Human Services' Office of Child Development. By 1968 protective services for children and reporting laws were provided universally in all 50 states. Renewed interest in child abuse came about as the result of several factors, not the least of which was the concern of physicians during the 1960s for the medical and emotional damage being done to children.

As attitudes toward children and violence itself have changed within our society, the problem has developed in distinguishing between discipline that is necessary and legitimate in its own right, and excessive and inappropriate violence toward children. Definitions vary from individual to individual and judge to judge, and even from state to state. The most seriously injured children are usually referred to as "battered children," whereas the term "abused child" is considered less extreme. The physical and psychological neglect of a child is even more difficult to define and has received significantly less attention in social science literature and legal intervention. The exception to this is where the neglect is so extreme as to produce possible physical harm to the child.

Sexual abuse of children is a separate area that deserves attention in its own right. Sexual abuse can take place with or without other physical abuse or neglect.

It is impossible to know the exact incidence of abuse, neglect, and sexual abuse, since only the more serious cases tend to be reported. All states now have laws that mandate official reporting of all forms of abuse; however, the number of cases officially reported are quite conservative. Individuals of higher socioeconomic status are underrepresented in the statistics, since they are most likely to go to private treatment facilities that are the least likely to report incidents of abuse, except in extreme cases.

The majority of physically abused children require no medical treatment, and probably fewer than 1% receive fatal injuries. With the exclusion of sexual abuse, males are the most frequent victims of physical abuse at all age levels. These statistical investigations suggest that the majority of abused children are 6 years of age or older, with a much smaller percentage under 2 years; however, children of preschool age are not as likely to be noticed by outside agencies such as schools.

It appears that most physical abuse of children, excluding sexual abuse, is of an unplanned, unintentional nature, being committed by a parent facing extreme environmental stress. Usually the abuse stems from expectations that the child was unable to meet and an overly punitive parent who relies on corporal punishment for discipline. In some cases the parents expect behaviors or development considerably beyond the age-

specific abilities of the child or are unrealistic within the situation presented. Many parents were found to actually expect the child to care for them: A child that had been crying for an extended period of time was seen as rejecting the parent and unloving.

By far, the majority of abusive acts stem from attempts at discipline that become exaggerated to the point of abuse. In almost all cases the subsequent injuries—particularly if serious—were not intended. Even in cases of sexual abuse, the parent will often report having meant no harm, and may justify the act as an attempt to "educate" the child sexually.

Most parents who abuse their child carry no serious psychiatric diagnosis, but they do often have difficulty with social relationships, and with controlling their temper and impulsive reactions that quickly become violent. Frequently they not only experience considerable stress from their environment, but also—much more important—have difficulty dealing with stress through appropriate nonviolent means.

Most explanations of child abuse revolve around combinations of factors, including an individual who is predisposed to reacting physically when confronted with the need to discipline a child, particularly when that individual is overly stressed. In addition, environmental circumstances often help to stress and disinhibit the individual.

Certain predisposing characteristics of children can enhance the likelihood of abuse as well. Children resulting from an unwanted or particularly stressful pregnancy or delivery are more likely to be abused, as are children who have had low birth weights or are hyperactive or have any types of learning or behavioral difficulties. An extended separation between the parents and the child—particularly within the first year of life—seems to increase the potential for abuse.

A number of methods for treating and preventing abuse have been attempted. The treatment and prevention of physical abuse tends to be more successful than that of sexual abuse or neglect. Certainly the first and most immediate concern is to remove children who are in serious physical danger. In the majority of such cases, children removed from the home because of physical abuse eventually are returned.

Most approaches to abuse revolve around two general areas. The most direct approach is working with the parents themselves to help them cope with stress, modify their behavior, and come to understand the dynamics of the abuse. The second, more general, approach tries to improve the parents' contacts with the larger society. Attempts are made to reduce the amount of stress that the family is experiencing, while increasing the amount of support and facilitative services. In all cases, and particularly in cases of sexual abuse, at least initial outside supervision appears to be extremely important.

With a combination of the intensive individual and broader social interventions, the likelihood of being able to successfully intervene and diminish the chances of severe damage to the child is greatly enhanced.

AGGRESSION
BATTERED PEOPLE
CHILD NEGLECT
VIOLENCE

S. D. SHERRETS

CHILD GUIDANCE CLINICS

The first child guidance clinics were established in the early 1920s by the National Commission for Mental Hygiene. These clinics were inspired by the Mental Hygiene Movement founded by Clifford Beers in 1909. A central goal of this movement was to provide psychiatric services to the greater populace, whereas previously they had been available only to the more affluent. The novel feature of these first clinics was the use of an interdisciplinary team of professionals (psychiatrists, psychologists, and social workers) to provide comprehensive and cost-effective services to children.

Since their initial development, child guidance clinics have undergone many changes in theoretical orientation and therapeutic approach. Child guidance professionals may view a child's problems in terms of a variety of perspectives including the behavioral, family, and community and social. Similarly, the treatments commonly employed range from behavior modification or parent counseling to marital or family therapy and school consultation, in addition to traditional individual child therapy. Referral rates for the various childhood problems have remained much the same, but these same problems are more often conceptualized and treated within an expanded behavioral and social-system (family and community) model of child adjustment and development.

With the coming of the community mental health movement, the majority of child guidance services have been integrated into the broader systems of community mental health services.

COMMUNITY PSYCHOLOGY
COUNSELING
FAMILY THERAPY
SOCIAL CASEWORK

K. L. BIERMAN

CHILD NEGLECT

Child neglect is a failure to meet a child's basic physical or psychological needs. Child maltreatment takes many forms, including brutality and sexual abuse as well as neglect. Ironically, child neglect is the most common and probably the most destructive form of child maltreatment, yet it has received the least attention.

Neglect can take many forms, including inadequate clothing, shelter, or medical care. The three most harmful forms, however, are inadequate food, safety, and love.

Nutrition. Inadequate feeding is the most basic kind of physical neglect. In the extreme form, most common in early infancy, the child is fed so infrequently that he or she starves to death. In North America, more infants die of such severe neglect than of brutality.

Less extreme forms of insufficient feeding result in "failure to thrive," when an infant or child grows at a significantly slower rate than height and weight tables would predict. This can occur when the food offered is too little, or when the feeding situation is so emotionally draining that the child does not consume enough to meet nutritional needs.

Improper feeding is another form of neglect. If a child does not get a well-balanced diet, the child will suffer from specific vitamin and mineral deficiencies and become listless, irritable, and prone to illness.

Safety. In North America, more children die of accidents than the next six causes of childhood death combined, as each year about 1 child in 3000 dies in an accidental death. Inadequate supervision and precaution are examples of child neglect and are present in 90% of the serious accidents that befall children. Factors beyond parental control, such as the lack of safe playgrounds or strict laws about drunk drivers, and the age and sex of the child, also affect the likelihood of serious accidents.

Love. Older children are better able to meet their own needs for nourishment and safety. However, children of all ages need to be loved and respected, and parents may neglect to meet these basic psychological needs even if physical needs are met.

The consequences of psychological neglect of a child also vary with age. In infancy, the most serious consequence is that the normal bond between parent and child will not form. Thus neglected toddlers usually avoid or reject maternal contact. They are even less likely to show evidence of secure attachment to their mothers than do abused infants. Since the parent–child bond provides the framework for other relationships the child will have and acts as a base for later exploration and cognitive development, an impairment in this relationship makes it more likely that the neglected infant will become a friendless, slow-learning child.

Psychological neglect during the preschool years sometimes takes the form of extreme permissiveness, when parents do not set appropriate limits or provide adequate guidelines for behavior. Overly permissive parents tend to have preschool children who are immature and unhappy and show poor self-control.

In middle childhood and adolescence, children whose parents do not seem to love or care about their welfare often seek the attention of others, which can push them into damaging sexual relationships or destructive peer contact. Although even children of good parents can become truants, runaways, delinquents, or suicides, neglected children are much more likely to do so.

INCIDENCE OF NEGLECT

Over 700,000 cases of child neglect are reported in the United States each year. The actual incidence is certainly higher, as many lay and professional people are reluctant to report someone for neglect unless the child is in immediate severe danger. In *Child abuse*, Ruth and Henry Kemp estimate that between 20 and 30% of all parents have difficulty caring for their children adequately.

Although child neglect can occur in any type of home, rich or poor, neglectful parents tend to have little education or money, few friends, and many children. These general characteristics are true for brutal parents as well; indeed, evidence of neglect is present in about one-third of all reported cases of child abuse. However, compared to normal or abusive parents, neglectful parents are more likely to be apathetic and depressed.

PREVENTION AND TREATMENT

Although the direct responsibility for child care in our society falls on parents, indirectly the entire society is responsible. Social measures to lessen the incidence of unwanted pregnancy, poverty, and single parenthood would reduce the incidence of serious neglect. Early signs of neglect, such as a mother who fails to talk to, look at, or hold her newborn, or the infant who fails to gain weight, should become a signal for friends, grandparents, social workers, and psychologists to help the parent care for the child, or to assume child care until the parent becomes more responsive. Currently, researchers know the serious consequences and the early signs of neglect, but more research is needed to know exactly how, and when, to intervene.

BONDING AND ATTACHMENT
CHILD ABUSE
EARLY CHILDHOOD DEVELOPMENT
MARASMUS

K. S. BERGER

CHILD PSYCHOLOGY

Child psychology deals with the personality and behavior of children, typically from conception to puberty. Although some authors and researchers include adolescence in their definition of child psychology, most current writers see adolescence as a separate field. Child psychology has referred in the past to both normal and abnormal behavior, and has historically included both theory and research concerning the development, rearing, and education of children, as well as psychotherapy or counseling of disturbed children.

Among the research interests of child psychologists are social and emotional development, physical growth and motor behavior, learning and intellectual growth, language development, and personality development. Some researchers restrict their work to a particular age period such as infancy, the prenatal period, the newborn era, or the school years. Others emphasize the changes across the years in psychological constructs such as cognition, socialization, aggression, dependency, morality, learning, or achievement. Some topics such as language development have been studied in terms of specific behaviors (e.g., number of words at a given age, the use of given parts of speech, etc.), as well as psychological constructs (e.g., language socialization, language and cognition).

The period of childhood is generally divided for didactic purposes into substages. The prenatal period can be further divided into the periods of the zygote (0 to 2 weeks), embryo (2 weeks to 2 months), and fetus (2 months to birth). Similarly, the postnatal period can be divided into infancy, preschool, middle childhood, and later childhood.

HISTORY OF CHILD PSYCHOLOGY

At least four sorts of history can be considered with respect to child psychology. Ontogenetic history, the history of the organism from conception to death, is the basic material of human development. Phylogenetic history refers to the evolutionary development of the species.

A third sort of history refers to the changes over time of the concept of childhood. Such a notion is related to the sociocultural history of the family. Philippe Muller identified four periods in the cultural history of the family that corresponded to changing conceptions of the child.

First stage, before 1750. Birth and death were "natural." There was no prevention of birth, nor was medicine too effective in delaying death. Since the infant mortality rate was high, children were fragile yet easily replaceable, and therefore not especially important. Under such harsh circumstances children were expected to grow up quickly, and were for the most part treated like miniature adults.

Second stage, 1750 to 1880. Childhood came to be seen as a period of innocence, and children began to be protected from the harsh realities of the adult world and to be considered, as Rousseau suggested in *Emile,* as individuals with their own needs relative to their own stage of development.

Third stage, 1880 to 1930. By the end of the nineteenth century, the birth rate began to drop dramatically. With the emergence of the nuclear family as the unit of recreational, social, and cultural significance, parents took a more direct role in the education of their children. Rewards and punishments were meted out in the hopes of instilling a firm conscience.

Fourth stage, from 1930 until the present. Finally, according to Muller, the family has reached a stage in its development in which the child has been accorded a position of privilege. The child is no longer seen as an easily replaceable, fragile commodity, nor exploited as a member of the work force. Rather, the child has assumed the importance of "a little prince," around whom revolve several professions, considerable marketing efforts, and a certain amount of legislation. As the demographic structure of the human race has changed, so have family characteristics and our resulting concept of what it means to be a child.

A fourth kind of history in child psychology is the history of the field itself. Most research on the processes of development has been concerned with variables or logical constructs whose origins of intellectual interest can be traced to ancient philosophy. The antecedents of psychology lie in philosophy and physiology; child psychology is no exception. Early Greek writers were concerned with the stages of development and with the socialization process, as well as with such practical issues as the proper education of children. The origins of child psychology as a science,

however, can be traced to the careful observations recorded in early "baby biographies," often by parent observers.

More recent influences on child psychology have been the testing movement and the development of child guidance clinics and major university centers for research on child behavior.

THEORIES IN CHILD PSYCHOLOGY

Early theories of child psychology were largely implicit. Children were thought of as miniature adults, and as such no special logical constructs were necessary to explain their behavior. Not until the late nineteenth century and the emergence of a formal discipline of psychology did theories about child behavior become prominent. An early child psychologist was G. Stanley Hall, who proposed a biogenetic theory that behavior was influenced mainly by biological growth and genetic predispositions.

Freud, the father of psychoanalysis, emphasized environmental and especially social factors in the development of child behavior and personality. Freud was one of the first to stress the influence of early experience on later behavior, and to assign a major role to the unconscious in explaining behavior. He postulated that individuals pass through a series of psychosexual stages that are defined by the characteristic way in which libido, or mental sexual energy, gets expressed.

Jean Piaget developed a major theory that seeks to explain cognitive development. The cognitive-developmental position of Piaget is a stage theory, with the stages referring to the increasingly complex way in which the individual can incorporate and process information and assimilate it into his or her own previously developed mental structures.

Learning theorists have tended to view children's behavior as based on environmental rather than organism factors and, like Freud, see the organism as passive rather than active in its own development. The emergence of social learning theory was in some respects a combination of psychoanalytic and learning theory concepts.

RESEARCH METHODS IN CHILD PSYCHOLOGY

Since the days of the baby biographies, child psychology has progressed in both theory and methods. When the issue of concern has been age changes in some trait or behavior, two procedures have been used. With the *longitudinal* approach, investigators follow the same subjects over the years of interest and observe age changes. With the *cross-sectional* approach the researcher tests subjects of different ages. Each of these procedures has its advantages and its limitations. A combination of the two procedures has been suggested by some authors as a more powerful approach with fewer disadvantages.

A variety of research methods have been used, including questionnaires, ratings and rankings by teachers, peers, parents, and oneself, interviews, observation, projective tests, personality and intelligence tests, and direct experimentation.

ISSUES IN DEVELOPMENTAL PSYCHOLOGY

The contrasting views of the child as an active agent or a recipient remains a salient issue in child psychology, and one on which theorists and researchers remain divided. The relative influence of environmental factors, contrasted with genetic predispositions in child behavior, is also a dimension of importance to child psychologists. Finally, child psychologists differ with respect to the importance they place on stages in development: Although some theorists perceive development as proceeding by discrete stages, others assume a more continuous unfolding of personality and behavior.

J. P. McKinney

CHILDHOOD NEUROSIS

Neurosis is a mental disorder of a mild nature usually involving (a) a lack of understanding of the cause of problems, (b) excessive anxiety, and (c) impulsive behavior where impulses often conflict with one another. Neurosis may also include physical symptoms of illness, obsessive or compulsive behavior, and specific fears or phobias. Authorities differ as to diagnostic categories within the classification of neurosis, but common listings include hysteria, involving emotional lability and perhaps conversion of mental problems into physical ones; generalized anxiety, with little understanding of its cause; obsessive-compulsive patterns of behavior—impulses to engage in unreasonable or ritualistic behavior; and phobias.

In studying children's behavior one must ask why children act as they do, why their behavior results in disapproval, and what social processes exist to control their behavior. As Prudence Rains and her associates show, once children are labeled as deviant, they become part of a special status group in our society. Among those placed in such a category, the placement tends to become deterministic or self-fulfilling: They continue to be bad (deviant) because that is the way they are perceived by significant people in their lives.

Thus, a better view would be to see children as having developmental problems and to concentrate efforts to help them build on their potential to accomplish learning requirements and to live within the cultural and social tolerance of society.

T. Alexander

CHILDHOOD PSYCHOSES

Childhood psychoses are a miscellaneous group of severe disturbances with the afflicted deviating grossly from what is expected socially and intellectually for their age. The two most common psychotic disorders of childhood are infantile autism and childhood schizophrenia.

Disagreements about childhood psychoses cover almost every facet, from names and defining criteria to explanations and treatments. Though controversy exists, the impairments in the psychotic disorders are universally described by adjectives such as "profound," "pervasive," and "severe." There also is little question that the conditions tend to be lifelong maladies, although a small percentage of patients do improve substantially. Poor outcomes are associated with performing in the retarded range on intelligence tests at the time of diagnosis, remaining mute beyond the age of 5, showing signs of psychosis before age of 10, and being introverted, shy, and inhibited before the onset of difficulties.

The symptoms of autism and childhood schizophrenia overlap considerably. A group of British psychiatrists have enumerated nine traits that characterize these and other forms of childhood psychosis:

1. Serious sustained impairments of personal relationships. These take the form of withdrawal in autism and of obsessive attachment (often to a mother) in childhood schizophrenia.

2. A seeming lack of awareness of personal identity manifested by grotesque postures and by self-mutilation.

3. Unusual preoccupation with inanimate objects, often without awareness of their usual function.

4. Extreme resistance to any sort of change, and rituals aimed at maintaining sameness.

5. Abnormal perceptual experiences, leading to exaggerated, abbreviated, or unpredictable responses to sensory events. Many psychotic children have difficulty focusing their attention and seem unusually unresponsive to their surroundings.

6. Excessive, acute, illogical anxieties; in some cases, terrors of common household objects.

7. Severe speech impairments—commonly, a loss of, or failure to acquire, speech. Some psychotic children use language oddly: For example, they reverse pronouns or speak without inflections.

8. Peculiar motor behavior, including contortions, immobility, hyperactivity, and repetitive stereotyped mannerisms. Frequently, there are attempts at self-stimulation, like twirling, walking on the toes, flapping the hands, and rocking—especially when psychotic children are confined to institutions with few routines.

9. Retarded general intellectual skills. More than 50% of psychotic children function in the retarded range persistently. Yet autistic children sometimes show near normal or even superior intellectual functioning in specific areas such as memory, music, or arithmetic—talents rarely seen in schizophrenic children.

These nine characteristics are not seen exclusively in the psychoses, nor do they occur in all children considered psychotic. In actuality, it is often difficult to distinguish psychotic conditions from mental retardation, brain damage, and the symptoms accompanying blindness and deafness.

Besides the divergent social maladjustments and intellectual patterns, there are other key contrasts between autism and childhood schizophrenia. Although signs of autism are typically present from the beginning of life, the schizophrenic child usually seems normal until some time after 30 months (up to 12 years). The autistic child goes to great lengths to preserve existing routines and arrangements—something that the schizophrenic child is not concerned with. As regards motor skills, the autistic child is adept while the schizophrenic child is likely to evidence poor coordination and balance. Autistic children show an unusual interest in mechanical objects, which do not fascinate their schizophrenic counterparts. Also, whereas autistic youngsters seem oblivious to the environment, schizophrenic children appear confused.

The backgrounds of autistic and schizophrenic children are characteristically different, too. Autistic children are likely to come from a relatively high social class; their relatives display a low incidence of schizophrenic disorders. Schizophrenic children, however, come predominantly from poor families, and their kin exhibit a high rate of schizophrenic disorders.

ETIOLOGIES

The etiologies of these psychotic conditions are unknown. However, explanations of both autism and childhood schizophrenia assume that the symptoms of these disorders can be acquired in diverse ways. Research emphasizes the contributions of physiology.

Most theorists see childhood schizophrenia as similar to the adult variety and suspect that the same causative agents are at work in both cases. Current theories focus on biochemical abnormalities (in brain dopamine especially). In some cases they appear to be of genetic origin, perhaps triggered by stresses. Although not all youngsters with childhood schizophrenia show signs of birth complications or brain damage, they show a higher incidence of birth difficulties and other signs of defective neural functioning than do their siblings and normal controls. So far, support for specific central nervous system defects is meager.

In autism—especially in cases where symptoms appear pronounced from infancy on—investigators suspect brain pathology due to either heredity or birth complications. There is little agreement as to whether this applies in all cases, whether several different lesions may be involved, or precisely what the pathology is. Nonetheless, there is evidence that prenatal infections like rubella, inherited neurological disorders, bleeding in pregnancy, and an unknown genetic disorder may be involved.

Investigators of environmental causes rarely distinguish between schizophrenia and autism in childhood, seeing them as essentially the same disorder.

Parents of psychotic children are far from a homogeneous group. The mothers and fathers of schizophrenic children often do show pathology, including psychosis, isolation, and introversion. However, there is no evidence confirming that parental disorders precede and precipitate their offspring's disturbances. The parents of autistic children tend to be free of schizophrenia and schizophrenic symptoms. When psychological disturbance is present, it seems to be most often the result of having an autistic child or being scapegoated by mental health professionals.

TREATMENT

Those who view the problem as primarily an organic one rely on both physical and educational therapies. Hormones like thyroid, massive amounts of vitamins, and other drugs can provide symptomatic relief, especially for insomnia, hyperactivity, and aggressiveness. Reeducative efforts—often behavioristic in orientation—try to provide children with coping skills and to remove maladaptive symptoms. Such highly structured educational programs seem to be superior to other forms of social-psychological treatment.

CHILDHOOD NEUROSIS
HERITABILITY
PERSONALITY
PSYCHOENDOCRINOLOGY
SCHIZOID PERSONALITY
SEX CHROMOSOME DISORDERS

L. L. DAVIDOFF

CHILDREN'S BEHAVIORAL STAGES

Studies of human development indicate basic principles underlying all developmental processes that lead to a series of stages that all individuals can be expected to go through. These principles are related to heredity as it interacts with environment and time during critical or sensitive periods and maturation. Indications of a stage development approach can be found in the work of Arnold Gesell, Jean Piaget, Lawrence Kolberg, Sigmund Freud, Erik Erickson, and others. These theorists generally think of development as a genetically determined sequence interacting in a continuous and, so to speak, creative fashion with the environment.

From birth onward there are new stages in motor, cognitive (thinking), and personality development to be considered. The organism is now in a position to be observed and much more rigorous research is possible. At birth every infant has a repertoire of reflex behaviors to carry on everyday activities. In addition, sensory awareness begins to develop at a faster pace. Touch appears to be the only completely active sense at birth, but vision and hearing are even more advanced in their development than specialists considered possible only a short time ago.

Development in the womb and after birth follows three basic sequences. The first goes from the head downward in the body and is known in the literature as cephalocaudal development. The second is from the center of the body outward, known in the literature as proximodistal development. The third is the change from the massive generalized responses seen initially to the more specific later responses, indicated in the literature as a movement from gross to refined movements.

Arnold Gesell, who was interested in the genetically determined or maturational aspects of development, founded the Yale Clinic of Child Development at Yale University. He was concerned with the unfolding of inner tendencies rather than the changes resulting from learning or experience. Gesell concluded that behavior occurred in an unvarying sequence and that maturational changes made new kinds of behavior possible. He believed that knowledge about the maturational readiness of a child was essential for developing the best educational and training programs.

Behavioral norms for many aspects of child development were obtained and published in *Developmental diagnoses: Normal and abnormal child development,* by A. Gesell and C. Amatruda. The behaviors described in this publication are set up on a normative basis in such a way that 50% of the children examined at a particular age level will demonstrate the behavior under consideration, 25% will not have achieved that level of behavior as yet, and 25% will be beyond it. The norms are developed and presented in this form to help parents make decisions in regard to their own children. The norms enable parents to know what normal behavior could be expected and to be aware of developmental problems that might exist. Although Gesell stressed these norms in his work, he was also sensitive to differences among children and did not want the norms to obscure individuality of development.

Some psychologists think that Gesell overgeneralized in reporting his developmental growth stages. Some conclude that his work on sequential levels of development, and his indication that growing stages are major periods of reorganization followed by periods of integration of the changes that have taken place, added a great deal to our understanding of how a child changes while maturing.

Jean Piaget considered development to be a continuous and creative interaction between the organism and the environment. He noted that both body and sensory activities contribute to a child's development of intelligence and stressed the need for adequate stimulation in the early years. Piaget concluded that the child's developmental stages dealt with specific cognitive behaviors that gradually and predictably changed in some specific order.

Piaget found four major stages, each of which contained consistent ways of dealing with the world different from the other three. The stages are sequential and an individual must pass through all four of them. At the same time the stages are not rigidly fixed in a time sequence: They can overlap to some extent, and the ages at which a stage is to appear are only approximate.

The four stages that Piaget identified were: (a) the sensorimotor stage, from birth to approximately 2 years of age; (b) the preoperational stage, from approximately 2 to 7 years of age; (c) the concrete operations stage, from approximately 7 to 11 years of age; and (d) the formal operations stage, from approximately 11 to 15 years of age.

In the *sensorimotor stage* the infant is learning to use the body and is gaining immediate experiences through the senses. All activity is practical and based on immediate experiences.

The *preoperational stage* finds the child beginning to use words and solve more complex problems. Children can move from one- or two-word sentences at age 2 years, to eight- or ten-word sentences at around 5 years of age.

The *concrete operations stage* brings a literal, concrete way of thinking and a tendency to give up the magical thinking of the previous stage. Reasoning during this period is based on concrete examples, and each experience is considered as unique and not related to another experience.

The *formal operations stage* is when rational patterns of thinking are able to develop. Symbolic meanings are understood and abstract strategies are possible. Hidden meanings can be understood, and generalizations from stories and games become a possibility.

Piaget sees these changes as part of an individual's moving toward a state of equilibrium. A well-balanced set of ideas organized into a workable mental system can be used to solve new problems.

Children assimilate particular kinds of experience at each stage of development, as they perform activities they already know how to do by using their new level of awareness. Accommodation occurs when children internalize these experiences and make them a part of their new capability.

Freud is considered a major developmental theorist with a stage-dependent approach. His theory of psychosexual development stresses the fact that certain early experiences during sensitive periods have lasting effects on the individual. He hypothesized five basic stages of development, with each stage characterized by a new socialization problem facing the individual. Stage 1 is the *oral stage*, which goes from birth to $1\frac{1}{2}$ years of age; stage 2 is the *anal stage*, which lasts from $1\frac{1}{2}$ to 3 years of age: stage 3 is the *phallic stage*, which lasts from 3 to 7 years of age, during which the child becomes aware of genital differences and the pleasures related to the genital area such as masturbation. The Oedipus complex and the castration complex appear at this time. Stage 4, the *latency stage*, lasts from 7 to 12 years of age, a period when primary love interests are diverted to individuals outside the home. The basic personality has been formed by this time and becomes more or less stabilized during this stage. This period is often considered a calm before the storm of pubertal change. Stage 5 is the *genital stage*, which lasts from 12 years of age into the adult period of life. This is a period where the instinctual sexual drives increase, parental attachments are dissolved, and adolescent conflicts develop.

Freud believed that if the first three stages are completed without psychic trauma, the individual will tend to be psychologically healthy. If, however, some of the basic needs are frustrated, personality development will be arrested or fixation will occur and the personality will be affected at all later stages.

Similar to Piaget and Freud, the neo-Freudian Erik Erikson believed in a stage-dependent approach. He disagreed with Freud's psychosexual concepts because he believed that they were too narrowly conceived and that personality is not totally defined in early childhood, but continues to develop throughout life. He evolved an eight-stage psychosocial development sequence, with his early childhood stages almost a duplicate of Freud.

Lawrence Kolberg sees moral development as a universal cognitive process that proceeds from one stage to the next in a definite and fixed fashion at a pace determined by the individual's opportunities and experiences.

ADOLESCENT DEVELOPMENT
DEVELOPMENT OF HUMAN SOCIAL BEHAVIOR
ERIKSONIAN DEVELOPMENTAL STAGES
MORAL DEVELOPMENT
NORMAL DEVELOPMENT

F. D. BRESLIN

CHILDREN'S FEARS

Because fear is an emotional response to a perceived threat, it provides a protective survival mechanism by alerting the individual to danger. Mild or moderate fear reactions are viewed as normal and adaptive, promoting caution when real danger is present. However, fears become maladaptive when intense and persistent, alerting the child in the absence of potential danger, and interfering with normal physical, social, and intellectual functioning.

Psychologists generally distinguish between two types of fear: (a) *phobia*, an intense and to some extent irrational fear directly associated with specific objects, events, or situations; and (b) *anxiety*, a vague feeling of apprehension, uneasiness, or impending doom that has a relatively uncertain or unspecific source. Although the particular fears a child will develop—and their severity—cannot be predicted accurately, some generalizations about gender and age factors in the development of fears can be made.

GENDER AND AGE DIFFERENCES

Researchers have found consistently that girls report a greater number of fears than do boys. However, one cannot tell from these studies whether this gender difference is due to a higher inborn fear reactivity in females or whether other factors such as sex-role influences are responsible.

Several studies have found age-related changes in the *type* of fear children report. An overview of this developmental trend reveals that, as children grow older, their fears tend to become (a) more abstract and (b) more anticipatory, rather than being tied to immediate occurrences. For instance, compared to young children, older children tend to be less afraid of animals but more fearful of school and social relations.

Infancy and the toddler stage. Normal babies are born with startle or fright reactions to pain, to loss of physical support, and to sudden loud noises and flashes of light. Two common fears of infancy and the toddler stage are fear of strangers and separations.

Preschool and early school years. Among the more common fears that develop in early childhood are (listed alphabetically): animals and insects; dark, especially at bedtime; death, often related to separation distress; doctors and dentists; heights; monsters and imaginary creatures such as ghosts and witches; school, often related to separation distress; storms and other natural events; and deep water.

Middle childhood to adolescence. In later childhood, a frequent theme underlying children's fears is the threat of physical injury from criminals and from machinery such as cars and airplanes. However, the most distinctive trend during this age period is toward increasing worry about school, individual competence, and social relationships—worries that continue into adolescence.

SOURCES OF FEAR

The process by which fears are acquired seems to involve three factors and are as follows:

1. *Inborn sources.* Each baby enters the world with certain dispositions or basic personality traits, called "temperaments." The temperamental styles of individuals seem to be enduring and appear to make some children vulnerable to the development of fear. These children may be more affected by and less able to cope with stressful experiences.

2. *Experiences.* Direct encounters with negative events can lead to fear by way of classical conditioning: The ability of a previously unfeared stimulus to elicit fear is increased when it becomes associated with an event that already elicits a fear reaction.

3. *Thinking and imagination.* Fears can also arise out of children's imagination, particularly when incorrect ideas and faulty reasoning are involved.

TREATMENT

Children can be helped to cope with fears before they become serious problems. When therapy is needed, two of the most effective treatments for fear reduction are counterconditioning and modeling. In *counterconditioning* a calm, relaxation, or coping response is substituted for the fear response by way of classical conditioning procedures, in which the feared object is gradually paired with pleasant or neutral events. Therapeutic *modeling* is a procedure in which the child observes other people in progressively more active or direct encounters with the feared object.

EMOTIONS
FEAR
FEARS THROUGHOUT THE LIFE SPAN

E. P. SARAFINO

CHOICE REACTION TIME

In a simple reaction time task, the subject simply responds whenever he or she detects a particular stimulus. No decision, other than whether the stimulus is present or absent, is required. In a choice reaction time task, more than one stimulus can be present, and more than one response is required, depending on the nature of stimulus or judgments made about them. Thus subjects might be asked to tap a response key with their right hand if the stimulus is a square and their left hand if it is a circle. The time between the presentation of the stimulus for recognition and the actual response is the choice reaction time.

Experimenters using choice reaction times usually try to arrange the situation so that detection time does not change across the various stimuli by selecting a stimulus presentation procedure in which all stimuli are equally detectable (this can be verified by simple reaction time procedures). They also try to set up the situation so that response selection takes the same amount of time under all conditions (the voice reaction procedure is helpful here, or use of very simple finger or foot taps or even eye blinks can do this). If they are successful at minimizing any variations in detection and response selection, then any changes in the reaction time can be attributed to variations in the difficulty of the decision or the nature of the decisional process.

The inferential process by which mental structure is defined is based on reaction times from several types of tasks. Sometimes these are perceptual recognition tasks. The more difficult the recognition, or the more alternatives involved, the slower the reaction times, hence the reaction time here is a measure of the task difficulty. In other cases the tasks involve comparisons between objects (e.g., whether two stimuli are the same or different) or even evaluation of stimuli along complex dimensions (e.g., beauty, danger, etc.). Some recent work, however, has involved search tasks, for which a target is sought from a collection of distracting nontarget stimuli or the search involves a search through memory for a particular item. It is here that choice reaction times have proven themselves to be particularly useful in determining the nature and sequence of the psychological processes involved.

To see how one infers mental-processing structure from reaction times, consider an example in which there are two stimuli and subjects must compare them. A subject might be asked to tap one key if the stimulus is large and one if it is small. Alternatively, a subject might be asked to respond one way if the stimulus is green and the other way if it is red. Notice that there are two separate tasks involved here (evaluating size and color), each of which takes time. Now suppose that the two tasks are combined, asking subjects to push one key if the stimulus is large and green and another key if it is not. Early researchers who used choice reaction times as their measures simply assumed that because now the judgment involved two stimulus dimensions (size and color) that the reaction time would be longer than judging just one stimulus dimension (e.g., size or color alone). They were startled to find that this was not always the case. The upshot of this confusing result was that researchers began to doubt the usefulness of the reaction time methodology. Sternberg, in the late 1960s, showed that particular patterns of response times corresponded with particular patterns of mental processing. Specifically,

adding stimulus dimensions to be judged will lengthen response times if each stimulus dimension is judged one at a time in a *serial* or sequential manner. If stimulus dimensions are judged all at the same time, that is, in *parallel,* then adding stimuli will not lengthen the processing time. Thus, observing how reaction times change, or fail to change, as stimuli or stimulus dimensions are added tells us whether the decision involves parallel or serial processing. This reasoning is used to determine how items are retrieved from memory. In some cases the reaction times are consistent with parallel processing of many features and in other cases with serial processing.

Choice reaction times also have been used to study other processes, including attention, emotion, and aesthetic judgment and even whether individuals are telling the truth or lying. Complex mathematical modeling systems now have been developed that allow such reaction times to be analyzed in terms of specific processing stages and strategies and the exploration of the effects of the subject's patterns of expectations. It appears that the simple passage of time between the presentation of a stimulus and a subject's decision about some aspect of it may well turn out to be the key to several complex questions about cognitive and perceptual processing.

EXPERIMENTAL METHODS
MEASUREMENT
REACTION TIME

S. COREN

CHROMOSOME DISORDERS

In 1962, after textbooks had proclaimed for 30 years that there were 48 chromosomes in human cells, Joe Hin Tjio and Albert Levan, by growing human cells in their laboratory, discovered that they contained only 23 pairs, or 46 chromosomes! This is important in understanding a chromosomal disorder such as Down syndrome, in which 47 chromosomes exist in each cell.

Most knowledge of chromosomal changes that cause phenotypic or bodily alterations or abnormalities comes from the study of the genotype (gene arrangements) of the salivary gland chromosomes of the common fruit fly, *Drosophila melanogaster,* although the same changes apparently occur also in humans and other organisms. Although many human diseases are inherited, in only a few are the exact chromosomal distortions known. One can only infer from the phenotypic results that chromosome and gene changes have occurred.

Chromosomes are double-spiraled molecules of deoxyribonucleic acid (DNA), the chemical basis of inheritance. Chromosomal disorders are believed to result from rearrangements in the order or number of genes in the chromosomes. These genes are atom clusters within the DNA molecules that determine the nature of ribonucleic acid (RNA) molecules, which serve as "messengers" to determine the structure and function of organic tissues. This primary genetic substance, DNA, acts on and through the cytoplasm as a catalyst for changing the characteristics of cells to form skin and muscles, nerves and blood vessels, bones and connective tissue, and other specialized cells, without the genes themselves being changed in this process. Multiple genes are often involved in the same physical construction in the body; not every physical trait is the result of the action of a single gene.

Various chromosome changes have genetic consequences such as follows:

1. *Chromosome breakage.* Rearrangement of chromosomes can result from X rays, ionizing radiation, perhaps cosmic rays, and many other still unknown biochemical or other environmental influences.

X rays can break a chromosome into one or more pieces, and in the rearrangement process a segment of one chromosome may be *lost,* causing a mutation or phenotypic change. Thus a defective or abnormal recessive gene may now express itself, because the normal allele (corresponding gene on the sister chromosome) is lost and therefore cannot neutralize the impact of the defective gene. When chromosomal deficiencies in the human embryo have a lethal effect, the baby would not be born, so that lethal genes have no bearing on the evolution of a species.

2. *Crossover.* Chromosome pairs are twisted in a spiral around each other like mating earthworms, and may break at any homologous point—that is, on the same level in the two chromosomes of a pair. Meiosis (the reduction division that occurs in developing the gametes or sex cells, ova, and sperm) causes a separation of each pair of chromosomes, so that only one chromosome of each pair enters the egg or sperm. When a break occurs, one end of one chromosome may now connect to a broken end of the second chromosome, with the remaining two pieces also joining together, so as to form two entirely new and different chromosomes. This is called crossing over.

3. *Duplication or loss of genes.* A piece breaks off one chromosome and attaches to its partner, duplicating in the second chromosome genes already present. The extra group of genes is usually less harmful than the loss of genes in the first chromosome, and if benign, may even create new inherited combinations. The chromosome with the deficiency (loss or change of genes) may result in a mutation or phenotypic change.

4. *Translocation.* Chromosome segments are transferred from one chromosome to a nonhomologous one, causing sterility. Thus any negative phenotypic expression at least cannot be passed on to the succeeding generations.

5. *Inversion.* A chromosome is broken in two or more places and a segment becomes inverted (turned end to end) before being reincorporated in the reconstructed chromosome. This is very common, and is the chief natural method for gene rearrangement in species evolution. However, the new hybrid may be isolated in its new form, since it is sterile in reproductive attempts with the original form.

6. *Position effect.* A gene changed to a new chromosomal position on the same chromosome may display a changed phenotypic appearance in the organism.

7. *Polyploidy.* Failure of meiosis (the chromosomal reduction division in preparation for reproduction) to occur in a germ cell may double the normal chromosomal number in a gamete (sperm or egg). Triploids have three complete sets of chromosomes in the gametes instead of the two just mentioned. Or there is a duplication without separation of the chromosomes in mitosis (ordinary cell division), creating a tetraploid cell with four instead of two homologous chromosomes of each kind. We all normally possess polyploid cells in our liver and elsewhere, without their doing any noticeable harm. Where polyploidy occurs in only one chromosome, an extra chromosome appears in the genotype that may cause a serious phenotypic change as in Down syndrome (DS or "mongolism"), where there is an extra #21 chromosome in each cell. A small percentage of abnormal births occurs in DS offspring, in which this extra autosome (non–sex-determining chromosome) causes the affected infant to be smaller and its mental and physical development to be slower. DS victims have 47 chromosomes. In Down syndrome the extra chromosome causes the sufferer to produce too much of an enzyme that breaks down the necessary protein tryptophan, which occurs in milk and aids sleep, and is essential to normal brain function. Only a small percentage of DS births are definitely hereditary, but prebirth detection is possible by amniocentesis.

GENETIC DISORDERS
GENETIC DOMINANCE AND RECESSIVENESS
HERITABILITY

H. K. FINK

CIRCADIAN RHYTHM

It has been known for hundreds of years that daily cycles of leaf and petal movements occur in some plants, and over the past few decades the ubiquity of circadian rhythmicity in animals has been demonstrated. Particularly striking is temporal variation in the organism's response to physiological challenges. The dose of amphetamine that will kill 78% of a group of rats at 0300 hours is lethal for only 7% if injected at 0600; several times as many mice will survive a given exposure to X-ray irradiation at 0800 as at 2000 hours; identical injections of lidocaine hydrochloride given to rodents precipitate convulsions in 6% at 1500 hours and in 83% of rodents at 2100 hours. Time-related variations in therapeutic effectiveness and toxic side effects have been demonstrated for a number of medicinal substances routinely used with human patients.

Early observers assumed that daily rhythms are simply direct responses to such environmental signals as the natural sequence of day and night. This interpretation has been challenged by the discovery that, in the absence of such obvious time cues (*Zeitgebers*) as regularly alternating light and dark, many of the organism's cycles persist or "free run," but with a period deviating significantly from 24 hours and differing from individual to individual. The most widely accepted interpretation is that the organism possesses an intrinsic and innate quality of circadian rhythmicity, as if under the influence of an internal system of self-sustaining oscillators, ordinarily synchronized to exactly 24 hours by recurring external stimuli but not necessarily dependent on them. The ability of many species to use the sun's position as a cue for maintaining directional orientation, constantly correcting for its relative movement during the day (the so-called time-compensated sun compass), seems to imply some sort of internal cycling or time sense.

Most investigators believe that the ontogenetic development of rhythms does not depend on exposure to time-giving cues in the immediate environment—in other words, that learning is not required. This is not to say, however, that the rhythms are immutable. It has clearly been demonstrated in some species that early experience with light/dark cycles a few hours longer or shorter than 24 hours can have a long-lasting effect on the free-running period of an individual's circadian rhythms.

It is hypothesized that loss of the normal temporal relations among the various circadian rhythms ("internal desynchronization") interferes with the bodily economy and impairs psychological functioning. This may account in part for the perturbations experienced following rapid transmeridian travel and during irregular living schedules imposed by shift work.

ACCIDENT PRONENESS AND PREVENTION
HUMAN BEHAVIORAL RHYTHMS
RHYTHM
WORK/REST CYCLES

F. W. FINGER

CLASSICAL CONDITIONING

Classical conditioning is also called conditioned response, conditioned reflex, conditional response, and conditional reflex. Ivan Pavlov was the first to explore its characteristics extensively. The great volume of work done in Pavlov's laboratory showed conditioning to have many unsuspected facets that led to the development of integrated conditioning theory and eventually to the application of conditioning explanations to behavior in general.

Conditioning, a form of learning, consists of the pairing of two stimuli, each of which originally produces a response different from the other. Typically, the response to one consists of little more than attending to it (technically called the orienting response). This is termed the conditioned stimulus (CS). The response to the other, the unconditioned stimulus (UCS), is the response that is measured directly, or occasionally indirectly, and is called the unconditioned response (UCR). The UCS evokes this response consistently and shows little or no adaptation; its occurrence is determined by the experimenter and not by the subject's actions. Conditioned stimuli that are often used include food-producing salivation, a shock that generates a defense or emotional reaction, a puff of air to the eye. Conditioning occurs if the other stimulus (the CS) acquires the capacity to produce a response like the one given to the UCS. This is called the conditioned response (CR). In other words, the original response to the CS has been modified and learning has occurred.

Temporal Relationships of CS and UCS

An important variable in conditionability is the temporal relationship between the onset of the two stimuli—the potential CS and the UCS. The CS precedes the UCS in *forward conditioning;* the onset of CS and UCS coincide in *simultaneous conditioning;* the CS follows the UCS in *backward conditioning.* The bulk of the evidence suggests that conditioning does not occur in the backward or simultaneous situations. Occasionally, an experiment reports some minimal data interpreted as backward or simultaneous conditioning, but such responding may not really represent a conditioned response in the usual meaning of that term. Forward conditioning obviously occurs, but not as a simple relationship between the difference in onset times of the CS and the UCS. Figure 1 shows this relationship much as reported in a number of experiments that have used different responses as well as different species as subjects. Conditioning does not occur until the CS onset precedes the UCS onset by about 0.15 seconds, and then the efficiency of conditioning rises quite steeply to reach a maximum at about 0.5 seconds, from which point it begins a gradual decline. Although experiments differ somewhat in their temporal values, a curve such as that seen in Figure 1 with a maximum at about 0.5 seconds or slightly less has been obtained sufficiently often to lead one to conclude that it describes general and basic characteristics of conditioning that must be considered in any theoretical interpretation of the conditioned response.

In forward conditioning the CS may continue until the UCS occurs, then terminate with it. This is called *delayed conditioning.* In *trace conditioning* the CS continues for a short time, then terminates, and sometime later the UCS occurs. Conditioning develops in this case even though the CS was not physically present with the UCS.

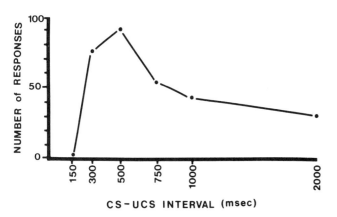

Figure 1. The relationship between time of onset of the CS and the UCS.

It seems that any stimulus that can be properly controlled may serve as a conditioned stimulus. Lights and tones are used most frequently.

The range of conditionable responses is as wide as that of conditioned stimuli, and a variety of unconditioned stimuli have been used successfully to produce varying responses.

Conditioning can also occur even though no response was made to the UCS during pairing. Curare-type drugs, which block the neural impulses to the muscles, are administered during the pairing session, yet on recovery from the drug effect, conditioned responses are given.

What Is Conditioned?

In the laboratory, the CS is a specific stimulus and the UCS another specific stimulus producing a particular response. Actually, on both stimulus and response side what is learned is broad and general in nature as well as specific. On the stimulus side, this is demonstrated in the concept of *stimulus generalization.* If the CS for an acquired conditioned response is a tone of middle value, tests will show that the response is given to tones both higher and lower than the original tone, and that the strength of the response decreases as the tones depart farther and farther from the actual conditioning tone. The principle holds true for other sensory fields and for language as well. What is learned on the stimulus side is to respond to a class of stimuli, even though the experience is limited to a single member of that class.

The term *response generalization* refers to a similar process with regard to the response that is conditioned. Two examples suffice. First, a standing sheep is conditioned to lift its leg with shock as the UCS; when turned on its back, the animal struggles to right itself. Second, a human subject with palm down and fingers on an electrode is conditioned to make an upward-moving extension response to a buzzer; when the arm is turned over so that the palm of the hand is up, the subject responds to the CS alone with a flexion response that leads to an upward movement, although a downward movement can still be made. Clearly, more than a specific muscular movement has been learned. One can assume that what is conditioned represents a schema from which specific responses functionally appropriate to the realities of the current situation can be generated.

The conditioned response is no mere replica of the unconditioned response—no simple substitution of one stimulus for another in producing the same response. This fact is demonstrated by the nature of the response created in forward conditioning to different onset times between the CS and the UCS.

Extinction

If, after a conditioned response has been acquired by the pairing of conditioned and unconditioned stimulus, the CS is presented alone a number of times, responding to it will decline until, with enough presentations, the CR will no longer occur to the CS. This operation is called *experimental extinction,* or simply extinction.

The rate at which a response will extinguish is determined by various factors such as the number of training or reinforced trials that have been given, and the intensity of the unconditioned stimulus. These factors seem obvious, but there is another very potent factor in extinction that is not so obvious, called *partial reinforcement.* If, during the conditioning process, reinforced trials are not given steadily but are randomly mixed with nonreinforced presentations of the CS, the resulting conditioned response will require more trials before extinction occurs than it would have if all trials had been reinforced. The rate of extinction will depend on the ratio of reinforced to nonreinforced trials during the training; to a certain limit, resistance to extinction increases as the proportion of nonreinforced trials increases. This same characteristic is found in many other types of learning; the partial reinforcement effect is a basic characteristic of behavior in general, as is also inconsistency of reinforcement in the world.

If the response is extinguished and some extended period of time passes without interpolated pairing of the CS and the UCS, the conditioned response will again appear. Called *spontaneous recovery,* this is a very pervasive and robust effect. The term "spontaneous recovery" is of course not explanatory; it simply describes the fact that an extinguished response will be revived with the passage of time in spite of lack of further training.

Discrimination

The principle of stimulus generalization indicates that, even though only one CS of a particular value is used, conditioning develops to other stimuli that are along that same psychological dimension. *Differential conditioning* between one stimulus, called the positive, and any other stimulus, the negative, can be obtained by continuing to reinforce the original stimulus while frequently presenting the other without the UCS, thus extinguishing its response. After this response has been extinguished, one can present another stimulus with a value between it and the positive stimulus but closer to the negative one. Some responsiveness will be found to it, but if it is never reinforced, it too will be extinguished. By progressively moving closer and closer to the ever reinforced stimulus, a finer and finer discrimination can be achieved. In some instances, however, not only does the differentiation break down, but the subject may develop an *experimental neurosis.*

Extensions of Conditioning

In the examples of conditioning presented, the UCS has always been one for which the UCR is innately determined. The CS, by virtue of its pairing with the UCS, acquires the ability to elicit a response of that general class. A logical extension is to investigate the possibility that the CS may now be used as an UCS for a new CR. This procedure, termed *higher order conditioning,* was undertaken in Pavlov's laboratory and was followed by more extensive work by others. The process has been generally successful. There have even been demonstrations of extension beyond a single step, wherein the second or new CS has been used to develop a third CR. Conditioning, therefore, is not limited to the use of inborn UCS.

Sensory preconditioning is a further extension of conditioning. In this situation two stimuli, neither of which produces a clearly defined UCS—for example, a light and a tone—are first paired together; then one of them is used as a CS for a response such as leg withdrawal to a shock UCS. After this conditioning has been established, the response of leg withdrawal will be given to the other of the two originally paired stimuli of the preconditioning session. The work completed to date suggests that the principles or rules for this process are the same as those that hold for ordinary conditioning. As with higher order conditioning, sensory preconditioning considerably broadens the potential range of conditioning as a determinant of behavior.

One of the empirical characteristics of the laboratory-produced CR is that, once acquired, it seems to be—in contrast with many other learning activities—quite immune to the forgetting process. It seems likely that the extreme resistance to forgetting that has been noted in the CR may be an artificial consequence of the experimental programs.

CLINICAL APPLICATIONS OF CONDITIONING

Since conditioning essentially consists of changing a response to some stimulus event, its value as a therapeutic tool for eliminating undesirable reactions was recognized very early. Mary Cover Jones was able to eliminate a child's fear reaction to a white rabbit by what is called a *counterconditioning* process. The feared animal was introduced into the room at some distance from the seated child, who was simultaneously given favored food to eat, this serving as a UCS to produce a positive response. The procedure is called counterconditioning rather than simple extinction because the UCS produces a response that is counter to a fear reaction.

A modification of this method, called *systematic desensitization,* uses the gradual introduction of the feared stimulus without a UCS. Conceptually, this is simple extinction.

IMPACT OF CLASSICAL CONDITIONING ON PSYCHOLOGICAL THEORY

An inevitable consequence of the use of the CS was to shift the explanatory emphasis of behavior away from an instinctive one to an environmental one. The lesson to be learned from the conditioning laboratory seemed to be that the response to any stimulus may be modified and a new one substituted for the old by the appropriate pairing of CS and UCS. Watson used this concept to attack the then current extensive usage of instinct as an explanation of much behavior.

Pavlov was a physiologist rather than a psychologist, and his interpretation of the conditioning process used the behavior obtained as an analog of neural processes in the cortex of the brain. His theory paralleled, for these "psychic" reflexes, the theory of I. M. Sechenov, a mid–nineteenth-century Russian physiologist, for the physical or bodily reflexes. Conditioning behavior was a function of two opposing processes, *excitation* and *inhibition,* with excitation resulting primarily from the pairing of CS and UCS, and inhibition from presenting the CS alone, with the magnitude of the CR being the result of the summation of these two independent neural processes. These concepts have been perpetuated and reoccur in one form or another in modern theoretical psychology. Excitation and inhibition formed the basis of Clark L. Hull's influential 1943 behavior theory, which generated a great deal of research.

ASSOCIATION, PERFORMANCE, AND THE CR

What makes the CR of great interest is the fact that the first stimulus produces an overt response highly similar to the response given to the second stimulus. In conditioning, then, the subject acquires not only an association but also a way of acting. This is reminiscent of the distinction between learning and performance made by E. C. Tolman. As he pointed out, a rat may know the correct pathway through a maze, but it will not perform and demonstrate its knowledge unless it is hungry and there is food at the end of the maze. In other words, in many situations an incentive must be added independently to produce the performance that demonstrates knowledge. Just being in the maze is not enough to elicit the running response of threading its alleys without error. In conditioning, the CS evokes both knowledge and action. Inherent in the CS is not only information, but also a command to respond overtly and appropriately. It is this fact that sets conditioning apart from simple associative learning, which requires some additional operation or operations to demonstrate the learning.

CONDITIONING AS AN ADAPTIVE AND FUNCTIONAL PROCESS

Pavlov commented on the potential adaptive value of the CR, and many of its characteristics can be so interpreted. It is a mechanism that permits the organism to prepare for an oncoming event by making an appropriate anticipatory response. The failure to obtain backward or even simultaneous conditioning can be understood in this light, for in neither case does the CS *predict* the UCS and thereby permit some action to be taken prior to its presentation.

A contradiction to the general predictability explanation is introduced by the fact that conditioning also does not develop at very short forward intervals (from simultaneity to about 0.15 seconds). From a logical point of view, predictability of the UCS is possible, so that the simple prediction interpretation needs modification. The difficulty can be met by assuming that time must be added to permit the initiation of the response mechanism prior to the occurrence of the UCS.

If one accepts the view that the generality of conditioning across many species and many responses has evolved because of its functional value as an adaptive mechanism, then the lack of conditioning at the short, forward interval leads to a further stipulation concerning the predictability interpretation. It is simply that prediction of the UCS alone is not sufficient, but that also there must be available, with a moderate degree of consistency, additional time to activate the program that produces the adaptive response prior to the onset of the UCS. Viewed in this light, the CR is seen as a finely tuned and "intelligent" process, a component of the behavior of the entire organism.

BACKWARD CONDITIONING
LEARNING CURVES
OPERANT CONDITIONING

D. WICKENS

CLASSROOM DISCIPLINE

There is considerable disagreement on the definition of classroom discipline. Generally, it is defined as a process involving parents, teachers, and students that seeks to develop students' self-control, character, self-respect, respect for others, and orderliness. Discipline is to be positive and constructive, not negative, not punishment, although punishment may be involved in the discipline process. *Classroom management* is often used as a synonym for classroom discipline. Classroom management refers to all activities and interactions, planned or spontaneous, that occur within a classroom. In recent years there has been an emerging interest in the approaches to classroom management.

With greater concern for discipline coupled with the increasing prevalence of other discipline-related school problems, such as violence, vandalism, and crime, educators have started to focus on this problem, which until recently was neglected by educational theorists. Current research seems to indicate that discipline is multicausal and that parents, teachers, and administrators may differ in their perceptions of its causes.

CLASSROOM DYNAMICS
ENCOURAGEMENT
SCHOOL ADJUSTMENT

L. V. PARADISE

CLASSROOM DYNAMICS

Classroom dynamics encompass a broad array of group processes and teacher–student interactions that affect the nature and amount of student learning. The specific components of the dynamics include such factors as how members of the class communicate with one another, expectations of one another, the degree to which members like and respect one another, and grouping practices. These components affect such learning outcomes as achievement, attitudes, self-concept, and social perspective taking.

COMMUNICATION

The nature of communication in the classroom is the most important and basic aspect of classroom dynamics. Communication involves sending and receiving messages between people. The messages may be verbal or nonveral, and in classrooms the nature of the messages becomes routine and fits self-perpetuating patterns. These patterns of interaction can be categorized in many ways. David and Roger Johnson, in *Learning together and alone: Cooperation, competition, and individualization,* use the term "goal structure" to describe different types of interaction patterns. A cooperative goal structure exists when students perceive that their own achievement goals depend on how well other students achieve their goals. Cooperative goal structures result in the most accurate communication among students, constructive conflict management, decreased fear of failure, trust, acceptance and support, and emotional involvement in learning. Competitive goal structures exist when students are competing, with one another for achievement goals. Competition fosters cautious and defensive interaction and misleading and threatening communication. Individualistic goal structures are organized to separate students, reduce interaction, and allow for independent learning experiences. In individualistic settings, students work by themselves without interacting, with one another. In an ideal classroom, all three goal structures are used.

Nonverbal messages, communicated as facial expression, gestures, and bodily posture, accompany verbal language in social interaction. Nonverbal messages are often inconsistent with verbal content, especially in situations where a person tries to mask feelings. Nonverbal messages are expressed continually in the classroom. Peers are likely to imitate the nonverbal gestures of influential students.

Communication is influenced by the physical setting of the classroom, especially seating arrangements. A circle pattern of seating results in the greatest amount of classroom participation, and students directly facing the instructor participate more than do students to the sides of the instructor. When the seating arrangement is in lines or rows, there is a tendency for students on the periphery to participate less than students in the middle or front, resulting in a lack of involvement and satisfaction. Seating arrangements that are made on the basis of ability levels also affect communication: If all the high readers sit at one table, middle high at another, middle at a third, and so forth, the contact between high- and low-achievement students is lessened. This may encourage status differences among students and make it difficult to have trusting, open, and honest communication.

EXPECTATIONS

Hundreds of studies have examined the idea that teachers' expectations affect the way they treat students, and that different treatment influences what students learn. Expectations affect the way we behave and how we interpret another's behavior, and the way we believe affects how others respond to us. In the classroom the teacher is confronted with a very complex, busy environment. Philip Jackson, in his classic book *Life in classrooms,* pointed out that a single teacher may engage in more than 1000 interpersonal exchanges with students and must constantly respond to students' demands. The pace is rapid and hectic, with very little time to contemplate actions. Thus it is necessary for teachers to selectively attend to and interpret events, since all aspects of the classroom cannot be monitored. Teachers will often develop expectations, because the expectations help in interpretation and selective attention. Teachers form expectations on information received from test scores, siblings' performance, actual behavior of the student, gender, social class background, teacher comments, and other sources. These expectations are then communicated by interacting differentially with individual students, depending on the expectation. Differential behaviors are evident in many areas: seating arrangements (e.g., putting low-expectation students in a group); the amount of time the teacher waits for a response from students; attention; amounts of praise, criticism, and feedback; the type of questions asked; and demands made on students.

ATTRACTION

The extent to which students like and respect one another affects their level of academic performance. Students who are accepted by their peers and like them in turn feel better about being in and participating in class than do students who are rejected by others in the class.

Most friendships begin because of proximity and physical appearance. Students who sit close to one another become friends, as will students who see attractive physical aspects in one another. Communication develops among these students, and as common values and interests are discovered, the relationship deepens. According to Richard and Patricia Schmuck in *Group processes in the classroom,* the development of interpersonal attraction involves a series of "filtering factors," beginning with proximity, physical attraction, and social status as primary factors, followed by granting status and security to others, discovering common values and attitudes, and enhancement of self-esteem by providing and receiving positive reactions.

Teachers who (a) talk to a large variety of students, (b) call on all students, (c) reward individual behavior but reprimand the entire group, (d) enhance the status and security of students by praising them before their peers, (e) do not demean or embarrass students in front of others, and (f) construct small groups so that every student has an opportunity to work with every other student in the class, are generally more effective in creating a positive atmosphere in which important psychological needs are met.

GROUPING

Students are grouped in a variety of ways: by age in first, second, and third grades and so on; by ability (e.g., high, medium, and low achievers); by sex; by interests; by whether they take the bus or walk home; by curriculum (e.g., college preparatory or vocational); and many other criteria. These grouping practices influence the nature of interaction that occurs and, eventually, what students learn.

Grouping and tracking of students into separate classrooms on the basis of ability is a method for reducing the range of ability among students in the same class. This type of grouping is termed "homogeneous," since students of similar ability are placed together. When students are assigned classrooms randomly there is a greater range of ability in each class. Research has demonstrated that homogeneously grouped students do not achieve more than heterogeneously grouped students. In fact, because of the poorer quality of instruction that may result, low-ability students learn less in homogeneously than heterogeneously grouped classes. Low-ability students achieve more in heterogeneous classes because they interact with high-ability students who model better skills, attitudes, and expectations, and because they receive better instruction.

ACADEMIC ABILITY GROUPING
ACADEMIC SUCCESS GROUPING

J. H. McMillan

CLERICAL APTITUDE TESTING

A standard was established for clerical aptitude testing with the 1931 publication of the Minnesota Vocational Test for Clerical Workers, subsequently the Minnesota Clerical Test. Each item consists of a pair of identical or merely similar names or numbers; the examinee is supposed to check those that are identical in a tightly timed test period. The ability measured is perceptual speed and accuracy. Other frequently measured abilities in clerical aptitude testing include verbal comprehension, numerical fluency, memory, and reasoning ability. Work samples of specific clerical skills such as typing, shorthand, spelling, or punctuation are often used in clerical aptitude testing as well.

APTITUDE TESTING
PSYCHOMETRICS

R. M. Guion

CLIENT-CENTERED THERAPY

Client-centered therapy is one of the major approaches to counseling and psychotherapy. It was formulated by Carl Rogers in 1940, based largely on his experience as director of a guidance center in Rochester, New York, during the 1930s.

Central hypothesis. This method of helping people is based on the belief that, given an optimal psychological climate, individuals have within themselves vast resources for self-understanding, for altering their concepts of self and others, and for generating self-directed behavior.

Growth-promoting conditions. In 1957, Rogers published an article, "The necessary and sufficient conditions of therapeutic personality change." Three of these conditions refer to therapist attitudes or therapist-offered conditions: (a) genuineness, realness, or congruence; (b) acceptance, caring, prizing, or unconditional positive regard; and (c) empathic understanding. The other conditions are: (a) that the client and therapist be in psychological contact; (b) that the client be vulnerable, anxious, in a state of incongruence; and (c) that the client perceive or "register" the therapist-offered conditions. The therapist attitudes are defined as follows:

Congruence. This is regarded as the most basic of the attitudinal conditions. The therapist is aware of his or her visceral feelings and is free to express these to the client. There is a willingness to be transparent in the relationship. The therapist is trying to create a person-to-person relationship, rather than adopting a professional posture that causes personal feelings to be hidden or unclear.

Unconditional positive regard. The therapist prizes the client's unique individuality. There is a willingness to hear, understand, and accept all kinds of thoughts, feelings, and behaviors, regardless of whether they agree with the therapist. The therapist cares for the client nonpossessively, and respects attitudes of confusion, hostility, and depression to the same degree as those that evidence clarity, love, and optimism.

Empathic understanding. The therapist listens to what the client is trying to communicate, particularly on a feeling level, and responds by sharing that understanding with the client. This sharing is both verbal and nonverbal; the therapist's regard for the world as experienced by the client is basic, as is the therapist's interest in being a companion as the client explores that world and is willing to share it.

Client changes. The client-centered hypothesis is that if the therapist's attitudes are experienced by the client, the latter will change in predictable ways. Most of these come under the heading of two basic personality theory constructs, *self* and *experiencing,* which are intimately related. Although the changes described come from research and other literature in client-centered therapy, they apply to a large extent to individuals who benefit from many other approaches to psychotherapy. The two most central results of successful client-centered therapy are a raised level of self-esteem and a greater openness to experience. Related changes include: (a) a relaxation in the client's concept of his or her concept of ideal self, contributing to increased congruence between self and ideal; (b) better self-understanding; (c) movement from an external to an internal locus of evaluation; (d) greater self-confidence; (e) increased acceptance of and more positive and comfortable relationships with others; (f) a reduction in defensiveness, concealment, guilt, and insecurity; (g) an increased capacity to experience and to express feelings of the moment; (h) an expansion of what is accepted as part of the self; (i) the acceptance of a greater variety of experiences, which may be negative or positive; (j) increased trust in what feels right to the person; (k) greater willingness "to be a process," to give up fixed goals and expectations, to be aware of the possibility of more than one reality; (l) increased sensitivity and the realization of intuitive and self-transcending capacities; and (m) greater consciousness of being able to influence others and to be a force in the world.

Significance in personality theory and research. In addition to introducing the revolutionary idea that therapy clients could be helped without guidance or interpretation, Rogers, by setting forth a very clear formulation of the new nondirective or client-centered approach, and by publishing complete verbatim transcripts of cases, unlocked the closed doors of therapy rooms and stimulated a vast amount of research. He fostered the attitude that psychotherapy could be studied objectively and, with his students and associates, furnished instrumentation to carry it out.

At Ohio State University in the early 1940s, Bernard J. Covner worked with Rogers to set up a system of electrical recording (wire, discs, and tape were used at different times), while demonstrating the incompleteness of the traditional note-taking method, and E. H. Porter and W. U. Snyder pioneered in devising systems of categorizing client statements and counselor responses. Victor Raimy measured self-attitudes during therapy among many other projects. At the University of Chicago in 1946, ten cases were completely recorded, transcribed, and exhaustively analyzed. The "parallel studies" project was succeeded by a larger and more sophisticated one reported in a book edited by Rogers and Diamond in 1954. This project focused strongly on measures of self-concept, ideal self, and the relationship between the two before, during, and after therapy.

At the University of Wisconsin in 1957, Rogers, Eugene Gendlin, and others tested the client-centered hypothesis in an exhaustive research effort with hospitalized schizophrenic patients. The research and practice at Ohio State and at the universities of Chicago and Wisconsin were accompanied by a continuing process of theory development.

After Rogers' move to California, however, client-centered philosophy branched out on such a vast scale that, increasingly, the terms "person-centered approach" and "a way of being" began to be used in place of "client-centered psychotherapy." Rogers' books and the films made by him and associates following his move to California define the scope of his "quiet revolution." That revolution included leadership in the encounter group movement, helping to humanize entire school systems; integrating experiential and cognitive learning; dealing with tensions between racial, religious, and political groups in the United States, Northern Ireland, Poland, and South Africa; facilitating the development of community in groups approaching 1000 and more coming from as many as 22 countries; and depicting the emerging personal power of individuals in the context of a variety of institutions: psychotherapy, marriage, education, industry, and national governments.

COGNITIVE THERAPIES
EFFECTIVENESS COMPONENTS OF PSYCHOTHERAPY
HISTORY OF CLINICAL PSYCHOLOGY
PERSON-CENTERED THEORY FOUNDATIONS
PSYCHOTHERAPY
REFLECTIVE LISTENING

N. J. RASKIN

CLIMATE AND PERSONALITY

Discussion of the weather and its effects on human beings has been a popular topic ever since ancient times, when Hippocrates and Aristotle concerned themselves with the relationship between types of people and the environment in which they lived. These ancient writers, as well as more recent ones, believed that climate has a "deterministic" effect on humans and their activities. Believers in "climatic determinism" maintain that various aspects of the weather have an impact on the physiological, psychological, and social reactions of human beings. These writers at one time or another have asserted that virtually every aspect of one's social, psychological, and physiological state can be affected by various aspects of the weather. These effects may operate directly through interactions between the weather and one's physiology, which subsequently force emotional and behavioral changes, or indirectly through other factors,

which then affect the personality. Such indirect effects may result from various conditions: loss of production due to weather changes; loss of employment and income; inability to travel; effects on leisure time; stress from extreme weather conditions; changes in food and availability of food that can be grown; effects on the degree of "openness" of the architecture; environmental dictation of what types of work and leisure activities can take place; and constriction of individuals within a geographic area, limiting the available pool of genetic variation.

Interacting climatic factors cited as possible influences include temperature, humidity, solar radiation, wind, barometric pressure, ionic balance, pollution, degree and type of precipitation, air transparency (cloudiness), and electromagnetic fluctuations. Making research in this area even more complex is the fact that these factors can also interact to produce additional effects.

It has long been known that weather conditions affect criminal behavior, including riots. Riots are most likely to take place under intensely hot and humid conditions with relatively little wind. During such conditions tensions build, fatigue and irritability increase, and human aggression is released. The presence of extremely cold temperatures or rain tends to stop such criminal behavior. This research can be seen as reinforcing the notion that colder climates allow for greater vigor in activity in both mental and physical behaviors. It has been suggested that physical work or extreme mental concentration are equally hampered by high temperatures and humidity with little precipitation.

A growing body of literature in biometeorology continues to document the interaction between our basic physiology and the weather. Although this is a controversial area and more research needs to be completed, there do appear to be predictable fluctuations in the incidence and severity of medical conditions as a function of various climatic variations. Research has suggested that the physiological changes are a direct result of such variations. These physiological changes underlie moods and behaviors that change indirectly.

Although many scientists and the lay public alike choose to believe in climatic determinism, hard evidence supporting these beliefs is clearly lacking.

ECOLOGICAL PSYCHOLOGY
ENVIRONMENTAL PSYCHOLOGY
FIELD DEPENDENCY

S. D. SHERRETS

CLINICAL ASSESSMENT

Clinical assessment is the process by which clinicians gain understanding necessary for making informed decisions concerning a patient. The type of knowledge gained from this process depends on the approach of the assessor and the type of instruments used. Usually the intent is description and prediction in order to plan, execute, and evaluate therapeutic interventions and predict future behavior. Assessment may be used to provide an understanding of a particular area of a person's functioning (i.e., cognitive processes, social skills, and emotions), to catalog the type and circumstances of certain behaviors (e.g., symptomatic behaviors), to form a complex description or model of the person, or to assign the client to a particular diagnostic category.

Any number of assessment techniques may be used, singly or in combination, depending on the orientation of the clinician and the specific questions for which answers are sought. Interviews, observations, and tests are commonly used. A typical test battery might include an objective test of cognitive functioning, an objective personality inventory, projective test, and a test that involves psychomotor functioning. When the subject is a child, various play situations may be used.

THREE MODELS OF CLINICAL ASSESSMENT

Psychodiagnosis

Psychodiagnosis, the dominant model of clinical assessment since the postwar era, might better be termed psychodynamic or personological assessment. Psychodiagnosis uses a number of assessment procedures, including both projective techniques and more objective and standardized tests, in order to tap a number of areas of psychological functioning on both conscious and unconscious levels. The goal is to describe individuals in personological rather than normative terms. Although it may involve applying a psychiatric diagnosis, the primary purpose is to describe the particular individual in as full, multifaceted, and multilevel a way as possible. The psychodiagnostic model emphasizes the role of the clinician's judgment and inference in organizing and conceptualizing the questions to be answered and the techniques to be used, as well as integrating diverse findings.

Supporters of the psychometric model are critical of the subjectivism and lack of demonstrated reliability and validity of the tests favored by psychodiagnosticians, especially projective tests. They have also questioned the abilities of clinicians to synthesize assessment data. Others have accused the psychodiagnostic model of putting undue emphasis on intrapsychic processes.

The Psychometric Model

An alternate model of assessment might be termed the *psychometric orientation.* Although clinicians of varying orientations use standardized tests, in the psychometric tradition they are particularly valued as objective measurement instruments allowing individuals to be compared along empirically defined trait dimensions. Clear, structured items are preferred to the less structured stimuli of the projective techniques, and the reliability and validity of the tests are of central importance. The role of judgment and inference on the part of the examiner is minimized.

Adherents of this model believe that test scores should be able to stand on their own without requiring interpretation by an experienced clinician. The psychometric and psychodiagnostic traditions have clashed on this point. The controversy over "clinical versus statistical prediction" debates whether behavior can be better predicted by combining objective test data in empirically derived prediction equations, or whether a clinician can better combine the data and make predictions by more subjective methods.

The Behavioral Model

Behavioral assessment concentrates on measuring overt behaviors, particularly problem behaviors, as well as the contexts in which they occur. The intent is to discover *what* people do, *when, where,* and *under what circumstances.* This is in contrast to searching for the underlying reasons *why* people behave as they do, or seeking to classify people in traditional diagnostic groups. Dispositional constructs, such as traits or personality dynamics, are considered either nonexistent or irrelevant to the prediction and modification of behavior. The emphasis is on data immediately useful for planning and evaluating treatment.

Today behavioral assessment makes use of observations in naturalistic, contrived, and role-playing situations, while also assessing the subject's self-reported behavior by means of inventories and clinical interviews. With the rise of *cognitive-behavioral* approaches to assessment there is increasing concern not only with what clients do and say they do, but also with such phenomena as their feelings, thoughts, goals, internal images, and conversations.

CRITICISMS AND TRENDS

There has been a decided decline of commitment to this role among psychologists and growing criticism of testing. Diagnostic testing has been identified with psychiatric labeling and has been criticized as exemplifying the concepts and role relations of the "medial model." It has been criticized as unreliable and useless, if not harmful.

Others have charged that tests invade privacy and enforce conformity, and deny opportunity to non-mainstream citizens. Minority psychologists have criticized tests developed and standardized on white, largely middle class populations—and often interpreted by clinicians of like background—as unfairly judging minority individuals in work, educational, and clinical situations. Thus clients differing in race—as well as in class, sex, and lifestyle—may be seen as sicker and also less apt to gain from verbal, insight-oriented therapy. This criticism has resulted in a growing tendency to assess strengths as well as weaknesses and to develop culturally appropriate norms and instruments.

In spite of these criticisms, testing appears to be alive and well. In general, the field is changing in a number of ways. Some trends are the development of techniques that focus more directly on *particular* specific questions of relevance to treatment; refinement of the measurement properties of assessment devices of all kinds; more reliance on lower level interpretations of test findings that remain close to the data; greater concern with the situational, interpersonal, and environmental factors relevant to determining behavior; and at the same time, more respectful attention to the person's own views of his or her character, problems, or situation.

As techniques of psychological treatment continue to multiply, assessment techniques are likely to see increasing use in matching clients with the most appropriate form of treatment. They are also valuable for evaluating the effectiveness of therapy. With a greater and more diverse segment of the population needing and seeking psychological help, and with third-party payments and accountability an increasing reality, clinicians must be prepared to evaluate the usefulness of interventions both in general and for specific individuals.

Assessment procedures continue to make contributions to research. They can provide measures of both independent and dependent variables, and are useful for establishing criterion groups (e.g., of subjects with bipolar affective disorders) in studies, for example, of biochemical, psychophysiological, or cognitive processes.

Finally, assessment procedures are valuable in the training of psychologists. They remain one of the best ways to learn about the structure and functioning of humans for research and personality study, and to sharpen the understanding of clinicians.

ATTITUDE MEASUREMENT
CLINICAL/STATISTICAL PREDICTION
CULTURAL BIASES IN TESTING
MEASUREMENT
PENCIL/PAPER IQ TESTS
QUESTIONNAIRES
TESTING AND LEGISLATION

D. Schuldberg
S. J. Korchin

CLINICAL JUDGMENT

The study of clinical judgment can be partitioned into two distinct areas. The first consists of research suggesting that clinicians' judgments are low in reliability and validity. Meehl concluded that an actuarial formula that combines data about a person will predict as well as or better than an experienced clinician could. As long as the same data are provided to the formula as to a human judge, the conclusion that the formula cannot lose the contest seems inescapable. A major reason is that the formula is consistent, whereas human judges are not. Clinicians such as

R. R. Holt have tried to counter this finding by noting that a clinician's judgment is necessary to perform such tasks as selection of the variables to be used as predictors. Thus, although simple mathematical models surpass an unaided clinician in integrating information, clinicians must decide what information to look for in the first place.

This area of clinical judgment research will likely continue indefinitely for two reasons. First, many clinicians base their judgment on tests whose validity has been called into question. Consequently, researchers who examine the validity of judgments based on such tests will continue to report discouraging results. Second, the psychological disorders listed in the *Diagnostic and statistical manual* do not have crisp definitions. When botanists examine a plant, a clear taxonomy governs in which category any specimen must be placed. In classifying psychological disorders, category boundaries are fuzzy. Many clinicians doubt that such an imprecise classificational scheme as in the *DSM* has much utility; therefore, they do not follow its guidelines. Whether clinicians base their judgments on their own idiosyncratic diagnostic criteria (with unknown validity and reliability) or the imperfectly defined categories of the *DSM*, their clinical judgment will suffer. As a result, critics of clinical judgment will not have difficulty in finding examples of weak performance. Some clinicians have heeded the advice of Meehl, Dawes, and other actuarial advocates by developing statistical models of clinical diagnosis.

The second area of research on clinical judgment has dealt with the judgment process itself, identifying factors that impede accurate judgment. Preconceived notions constitute one such factor. They can detract from accurate judgment in at least three ways. First, people tend to distort their memory of prior information so that it becomes more consistent with their preconceived hypotheses. Second, people also distort current information in the direction of their hypotheses, even if the hypotheses are only tentative. Third, the judgment of correlation is warped by preconceived notions. This phenomenon of illusory correlation has been demonstrated many times with different assessment devices.

Subjects' incomplete use of evidence may also contribute to the illusory correlation phenomenon. Consider the prototypic diagnostic situation depicted in Figure 1. Is the presence of the symptom associated with the subsequent outcome? Much of the research indicates that judges making this decision weigh the evidence in cell A too heavily. They base their judgment largely on the number of times the symptom and the outcome have co-occurred. Thus there is no actual relation between the symptom and the outcome depicted in Figure 1, because the outcome is equally likely to occur regardless of whether the symptom is present.

A second impediment to accurate clinical judgment is judges' failure to give adequate consideration to base rates, the proportion of time the event occurs in a given population. Many clinicians ask patients and their families about the presence of these symptoms when a head injury is suspected. Gouvier et al. found that 35% of head-injured patients do report that they often lose their temper. However, 37% of non–head-injured persons also report this symptom. Similarly, 29% of head-injured patients report that they are often irritable, but 31% of the control group subjects also report this symptom. Consequently, impatience and irritability are not diagnostic in determining the presence of a head injury, because their frequency in head-injured patients is almost identical to the base rate. Unless clinicians take base rates into consideration, the accuracy of their judgments suffer.

Two other impediments to good judgment are particularly robust. The hindsight bias refers to the tendency, following an event, for judges to exaggerate the extent to which they could have predicted the event beforehand. The hindsight bias prevents learning as much as one can from the occurrence of an event. Because the occurrence seems not at all surprising in hindsight, the causes of the event or the bases for one's already "accurate" judgment are not examined.

Related to this bias and partially caused by it is the serious overconfidence most people express in their judgments. There also is some evidence that those who judge the least accurately may be the most overconfident. Fischhoff and Slovic suggest that the ability merely to generate some plausible rule (e.g., "Psychotics are often pale") carries with it the conviction that the rule has some validity. Overconfidence is a serious impediment to good judgment, because overconfident judges see no need for assistance, correction, or remediation. A few efforts to decrease overconfidence and the hindsight bias have been somewhat successful.

Another reason why accurate clinical judgment is so difficult to achieve is that we apparently have limited awareness of the bases for our judgments. When interrogated about factors that influenced their decisions, diagnosticians and laypersons were unable to respond accurately. Nisbett and Wilson suggest that when asked why we behaved in a certain way, we provide a cogent reason, even though we may be totally unaware of the real reason. If we cannot reliably identify the factors that influence our judgment, improving judgment becomes more difficult.

Recent research on impediments to accurate clinical judgment has heightened psychologists' appreciation of the immense difficulty of the judgment task. Brehmer comments that it is remarkable that clinicians learn anything from experience, given the probabilistic nature of the many cues that confront them and the dearth of truly informative feedback they receive. Garb and Faust et al. have shown that experience—even enormous experience—does not reliably result in improved judgment performance.

Recent debate about the reliability and validity of clinical judgment plus contemporary research detailing the impediments to good judgment suggest the following recommendations. Taxonomy of disorders should be improved. Assessment devices must meet acceptable standards of reliability and validity. Actuarial formulas should be used whenever sufficient data are available.

CLINICAL ASSESSMENT
CLINICAL VS STATISTICAL PREDICTIONS
DIAGNOSES
DIAGNOSTIC AND STATISTICAL MANUAL OF MENTAL DISORDERS
JUDGMENT AND DECISION MAKING

H. R. ARKES

CLINICAL PSYCHOLOGY GRADUATE TRAINING

Formal, systematic training of clinical psychologists in the United States did not commence until the 1940s, receiving its impetus following World War II, when the need for large numbers of clinical psychologists became evident.

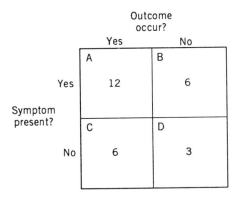

Figure 1. Number of times a symptom and subsequent outcome occur separately and together.

Although the term "clinical psychology" was apparently coined as early as 1896 by Lightner Witmer, there really was not a defined field of study and training that bore that designation until several decades later. Since the days of Witmer, psychologists engaged in remedial work as members of "teams" (with psychiatrists and social workers) in mental health clinics and hospitals, as "psychometrists" or mental testers, and as psychotherapists as well. Their training was in traditional academic psychology at university psychology departments, supplemented by practicum work and "internships" in some of the available mental health installations under the supervision of psychiatrists.

By 1947, a number of universities had been developing graduate training programs in clinical psychology. Early in the same year the American Psychological Association (APA) appointed a special committee, chaired by David Shakow, to do the following:

1. Formulate a recommended program for training in clinical psychology.
2. Formulate standards for institutions giving training in clinical psychology, including both universities and internship and other practicum facilities.
3. Study and visit institutions giving instruction. . . .
4. Maintain liaison with other bodies concerned with these problems.

The committee's full report was published later that year under the title "Recommended graduate training program in clinical psychology." It was based on the deliberations of the special committee and on earlier documents published by the American Association of Applied Psychology, which, founded in the 1930s, was later reintegrated into the APA. The report first concerned itself with "preprofessional requirements" for graduate training in clinical psychology, which included intellectual qualifications in addition to a series of personality attributes, and a broad background in psychology, the physical sciences, and humanities. Second, the report proposed a 4-year graduate training program leading to the Ph.D. degree. The curriculum was to include courses in the following areas: general psychology (physiological-comparative, developmental, history, and social); psychodynamics of behavior (dynamic and experimental dynamic psychology, and psychopathology); diagnostic methods (observation, interviewing, and various intelligence and personality tests); therapy (individual and group); and research methods and related disciplines. In addition to this academic curriculum, practicum experience was recommended for the student, including a full-year internship to facilitate "full-time contact with human clinical material, contact of a much more intensive kind than he can possibly achieve during the clinical clerkships of the second year."

A landmark event in the history of graduate training in clinical psychology took place in the summer of 1949 in Boulder, Colorado. The results of that conference and the formulation of the so-called "Boulder model" of clinical training were of considerable influence more than three decades later. Under the auspices of the National Institute of Mental Health, the APA convened a 2-week meeting to formulate training goals and programs for the preparation of clinical psychologists to meet the burgeoning needs for their services. Most of the conference deliberations focused on the 1947 report of the APA committee, which by and large was endorsed by the conference.

The Boulder conference recommended a core curriculum in clinical psychology that "should be so organized that both diagnostic and therapeutic techniques are taught in integrated relationship to theories of personality and behavior." The areas of the core curriculum proposed by the conference are as follows:

1. Human physiology
2. Personality theory
3. Developmental psychology
4. Social relations
5. Psychopathology
6. Personality appraisal
7. Clinical medicine and clinical psychiatry
8. Psychotherapy and remedial procedures
9. Clinical research methodology
10. Professional and interprofessional relationships
11. Community resources and organization
12. Practicum and internship experience

The overall doctoral program that emerged involved a minimum of 4 years of graduate work. During this period, the course work in general and clinical psychology was to be completed, as well as the practicum experiences, including a year's internship; also, the research for the mandatory doctoral dissertation was to be finished.

Although the need for trained clinical psychologists has been increasing, some difficulties with the training model itself have also become more salient. Even at the Boulder conference some doubts were raised about the realism of the scientist-practitioner goal. Then and in the decades that followed, questions have been raised as to whether the two sets of personal qualities and talents—those of the scientist and the clinician—actually reside in the same person. Increasingly, students have come to training programs with strong interests in clinical practice but with little motivation for research, as the publication record of the graduates of the clinical programs attests.

A new training model had developed in the late 1960s that preceded, and possibly stimulated, the Vail conference—the introduction of the Psychology Doctorate (Psy.D.) program at the University of Illinois in 1968. Clinical psychology training under this program departed from the earlier Ph.D. model, for it attempted to train applied clinicians and not scholars or scientists. This program stressed applied courses in various modes of assessment and intervention, community mental health, and so on. The stringent requirements of the Ph.D. dissertation were eliminated, but training in research evaluation and reporting was retained as part of the program.

Since 1968 a number of universities have begun to offer the Psy.D. degree. In some institutions the Psy.D. program is offered by a separate institute independent of the Psychology Department. Still another development has been the "free-standing" professional school of psychology. By the early 1980s, professional schools entirely independent of existing universities had come into being. Most of these offer the Psy.D. degree, but some offer the Ph.D. as well. These schools usually have very small full-time faculties and rely primarily on part-time faculty recruited from the professional community.

Essentially, the Ph.D. programs in clinical psychology in the first year require courses in statistics, clinical assessment, personality theory, and M.A. research seminar work. In the second year the program is rounded out by psychopathology, introduction to psychotherapy, practicum, and completion of the M.A. thesis research. The third year is devoted to advanced practicum (clerkship), electives, history, and systems and dissertation research. Finally, the fourth year is spent in serving a full-time internship. However, as noted earlier, this ideal time frame is rarely achieved: Most students spend 5 years or more completing the program.

No two doctoral programs in clinical psychology are alike. There is considerable flexibility and variation from one program to another. From the very start, the participants at Boulder wisely refused to carve the clinical training program in stone. They allowed for innovation and creativity, being cognizant of a constantly changing world and changing social conditions.

AMERICAN BOARD OF PROFESSIONAL PSYCHOLOGY
AMERICAN PSYCHOLOGICAL ASSOCIATION

A. I. RABIN

CLINICAL VERSUS STATISTICAL PREDICTION

A common model of clinical therapy includes the therapist as diagnostician. The therapist is expected to have access not only to standardized test data of various kinds, but also to details about the client gathered through direct contact, which presumably increases the potential for refined and accurate evaluation of the client and subsequent outcomes. This view has been questioned by psychometricians.

The issues in the controversy were formalized by Paul Meehl. In his classic book, *Clinical versus statistical prediction,* he discussed the issue of successful prediction of behavior outcomes. Meehl distinguished between (a) the kinds of *data* used for predictive purposes (psychometric versus nonpsychometric information), and (b) the *methods* used for prediction ("formal" or "actuarial" versus "informal" or "clinical"). By psychometric data, Meehl meant information collected under standardized conditions and scored, recorded, or classified objectively by a fixed set of instructions. Under nonpsychometric data (essentially, case-study materials) he included facts of social history, other reported personal information, and materials gleaned from interviews or by observation.

Subsequently, J. O. Sines reviewed 50 studies comparing actuarial and clinical predictions of behavioral outcomes of various types. He reported in some detail 14 studies representative of central concerns in psychopathology. With but one exception, Sines concluded that the actuarial predictions equaled or were superior to clinical prediction. Sines discussed the general low level of success in prediction by either method, and more specifically in psychopathology. He called attention to the fact that unreliability of chosen criteria sets limits on both actuarial and clinical prediction, and to the problem, with either method, of predicting for certain "difficult" types of clients, and for predicting unique or rare behaviors.

Other analysts have concurred with the general conclusions drawn by Meehl and Sines, sometimes suggesting methodological refinements that might improve prediction.

Scholars still continue to make comparisons of the approaches, but in the current era of evaluation research, the visible controversy has abated considerably, even as the theoretical and practical issues remain unresolved.

In summary, proponents and/or critics of any particular approach should avoid polarization of the issue and agree on the standards to be used in comparative evaluations. Agreement is required on what becomes defined as the dependent variable whose outcome is to be predicted (the criterion variable), and then regular predictors of the outcome may be treated as (prior) independent variables. Errors in prediction can occur for any number of reasons, including inappropriate or unreliable measurement of variables, unanticipated interaction between variables, omission of important variables, and so forth. If actuarial models omit variables to which only clinicians can have access, then, theoretically, prediction by the clinician could be made more accurate by including such information.

It should be acknowledged that application of actuarial prediction procedures may not be productive where specifically defined outcomes or diagnoses are not the rule. In those cases, characteristic of many areas in the domain of psychology, approaches based on clinical experience remain the procedure of choice.

CLINICAL ASSESSMENT
OBSERVATIONAL METHODS
PERFORMANCE APPRAISAL

PERSONALITY ASSESSMENT
PSYCHOMETRICS
RATER ERROR
STATISTICAL INFERENCES

M. L. BORGATTA

CLUSTER ANALYSIS

Cluster analysis is a general term applied to any of a wide variety of methods used to classify objects, events, or individuals into groups on the basis of similarity of salient attributes. Although there is no single definition of a cluster, all definitions stress terms such as similarity, likeness, and proximity. In more technical terms, clusters are homogeneous subgroups formed by a method that minimizes variance within groups (clusters) and maximizes variance between groups.

Clustering techniques are used to identify similar subgroups of objects or individuals and to develop taxonomies. Thus they allow the investigator to describe the structure and relationship of objects to each other and to develop laws and statements about classes of objects.

All clustering methods involve four basic steps: (a) obtaining measures of the attributes of the objects or individuals to be classified, (b) deciding on a measure of similarity, (c) developing rules and procedures for forming clusters, and (d) applying these rules to the data to form clusters. As a number of alternative procedures can be used at each step, a wide variety of clustering methods have been developed.

A first decision involves what attributes or properties to use as the basis of classification. This, of course, will vary with the problem and nature of the objects being classified. Also, although each attribute usually is weighted equally, differential weighting can be used

The second decision is the appropriate measure of similarity. This can be the number of common attributes, the correlation between attributes, a distance function, or some other measure.

A third decision involves the method of classification. Agglomerative methods start with individuals and combine them into groups; divisive methods start with a broad group and subdivide it into subgroups. Monothetic classifications involve classes where all members have at least one attribute in common; polythetic classification groups share a number of properties but do not necessarily have a single common attribute.

A fourth decision is how many groups to form. This can be determined by internal criteria (e.g., natural breaks between groups) or by external criteria (i.e., what classification scheme results in the most useful laws). Finally, one must determine whether to use a hierarchical or nonhierarchical classification scheme. In the former, groups are at different levels of generality (as in biological taxonomies); in the latter, groups are at the same level of generality (as in Q factor analysis). The results of these decisions will determine the appropriate method of analysis to use and the nature of the clusters formed.

CRITERION MEASURES
EMPIRICAL RESEARCH METHODS
MEASUREMENT
STATISTICS IN PSYCHOLOGY

F. G. BROWN

COCKTAIL PARTY PHENOMENON

Under some circumstances, we are capable of focusing our attention so intently on a task that we fail to attend to other events occurring simultaneously. However, there are occasions when we are faced with many conflicting inputs and we are compelled to shift our attention. A prime example is a large, crowded party with many loud conversations occurring at the same time. To understand the person with whom we are chatting, we typically have to focus most of our attention to the discussion at hand. Yet, if we suddenly hear our name dropped or a topic of particular interest discussed in a nearby conversation, we shift our attention to that other conversation.

To explain the cocktail party phenomenon, Treisman suggested that, rather than completely filtering out other conversations or rapidly switching our attention among them, we *attenuate* or give them a low level of attention. In this way, even though most of the information from the other attenuated conversations (channels) does not get further processing, it is possible that some information from them can leak through, particularly information having a low detection threshold (e.g., our name). Thus the cocktail party phenomenon illustrates one of the ways we deal with the demands of divided and selected attention.

ATTENTION SPAN
AUDITORY PERCEPTION
BACKGROUND CHARACTERISTICS
SELECTIVE ATTENTION

B. R. DUNN

CODING

Coding is a term used in many content areas of psychology to describe aspects of stimuli and responses. In the study of sensation, one speaks of the accessory sensory structures that gather the environmental physical energies and thereby fashion a better "proximal" stimulus for the sensory receptors to work on. After the physical energies are collected, the next step is a transduction of the physical stimulus energy into a neural impulse, after which coding occurs at further neural centers.

The concept of coding is also used in cognitive psychology in describing memory processes. In *Coding processes in human memory,* Arthur Melton and Edwin Martin indicate that the coding concept and the terminological variants of encoding, recoding, decoding, functional stimuli, subjective units, "chunks," or coding responses refer to activities within the individual. These activities may be iconic or phonemic representational responses, associated meaning responses, translation, or elaboration responses. According to Wayne Wickelgren in *Cognitive psychology,* coding is a system for representing thoughts of any kind, such as ideas, percepts, images, features, segments, responses, concepts, propositions, and schemata. Thus there are many attributes to stimuli, and not all are involved in every thought, memory, or action, but the brain provides the neural codings necessary to record the varied experiences.

APPERCEPTION
COGNITIVE PSYCHOPHYSIOLOGY
CONTEXTUAL ASSOCIATIONS
INFORMATION PROCESSING

N. S. ANDERSON

COGNITION

Cognition is a "generic term used to designate all processes involved in knowing," according to Ernest R. Hilgard in "Consciousness in contemporary psychology." After the word cognition, the index of William James' *Principles of psychology* says, "See *knowing.*" Thus cognition comprises all mental activity or states involved in knowing and the mind's functioning, and includes perception, attention, memory, imagery, language functions, developmental processes, problem solving, and the area of artificial intelligence.

Most cognitive psychologists agree that explanations of how the mind works need not be behaviorally observable, but can include the studies of underlying neural events. Arthur L. Blumenthal pointed out in *The process of cognition* that a distinction is made in the study of two types of questions: one is the content of human knowledge; the other the nature of the mental processes that enable the learning and use of that knowledge. This distinction is the content-versus-process distinction.

Joseph R. Royce has indicated that J. P. Guilford's structure of intellect model includes 28 knowing or cognitive factors, and that his three ways of knowing constitute a class of cognitive processes. Blumenthal also expressed the idea that cognitions can represent anything, are usually presumed to have something to do with reality, and do not qualify as knowledge.

A major theme of contemporary cognitive psychology is the constructivist claim that human cognition is an active process. The information-processing approach analyzes the cognitive processes into a sequence of ordered stages of changes in the information represented in the brain. Each stage in the sequence of processing from perception to action is a particular mental activity or topic of cognition.

APPERCEPTION
INFORMATION PROCESSING
INFORMATION PROCESSING THEORY
MENTAL IMAGERY
PERCEPTUAL ORGANIZATION
STRUCTURE OF INTELLECT MODEL

N. S. ANDERSON

COGNITIVE ABILITIES

Cognitive abilities may be thought of either as characteristics of the human species as a whole, such as the ability to acquire a first language, or as characteristics that vary among individuals or groups of individuals, such as verbal or reasoning ability. Generally, studies of cognitive abilities treat them from the standpoint of individual differences, for there appear to be differences between individuals even in those abilities characteristic of the human species as a whole.

Tests of Cognitive Abilities

James McKeen Cattell proposed the term "mental test" in 1890, but even before that Frances Galton had devised a series of simple mental tests. Cattell's tests, given to American college students, included tests of speed of mental reaction, sensory discrimination, and word association. These tests, however, were found not to relate well to the students' scholastic success. In the early 1900s France's Alfred Binet found that tests of more complex mental functions, such as the ability to memorize prose or to solve simple reasoning problems, were useful in forecasting children's school success and in identifying children regarded as mentally retarded. Early in the twentieth century, British psychologists under the leadership of Charles Spearman developed numerous tests of mental functions that could be given to both children and adults. In the United States the impetus for the "testing movement" came not only through the adaptation of Binet's tests by Lewis M. Terman in 1916, known as the Stanford–Binet test, but also through the extensive use of tests in classifying officer and enlisted recruits mobilized for World War I. All these tests—those of Binet and Terman, as well as the army tests—came to be regarded as tests of "intelligence." They were studied not only for their practical utility but also as measures of important mental characteristics.

The correlation coefficient could also be used to measure the degree with which different tests agreed with one another in measuring the same trait or characteristic. This idea was first proposed by Spearman in 1904. In a series of researches culminating in the publication of his major work in 1927, *The abilities of man,* Spearman developed a theory of intelligence—actually, a theory of cognitive abilities—in which all mental tests were seen as measuring, to varying degrees, a single trait or "factor" of cognitive ability, which Spearman called "g" (for "general" ability). Spearman considered that the "g" factor was measured whenever the mental task required what he called the *eduction* of relationships and correlates—what might be called *inference,* or *induction,* in more common parlance. Some of Spearman's contemporaries, however, were not ready to accept the notion of a single factor of cognitive ability, pointing out that different tests appeared to measure different abilities—special abilities to use language, to manipulate spatial relationships, to remember things learned, and so forth.

With the further development of *factor analysis,* issues about cognitive abilities progressed toward resolution. Leaders in this development were Cyril Burt and Godfrey Thomson in Britain, and Karl Holzinger, Truman L. Kelley, and L. L. Thurstone in the United States.

Factors of Cognitive Ability

A major goal in the study of cognitive abilities is to determine what types of abilities can be identified and to interpret their nature. In 1938, Thurstone published "Primary mental abilities," a factor analysis of a battery of 57 measures of cognitive abilities administered as group paper-and-pencil tests to university students. Many of the measures were of a type found in intelligence tests, but each was designed to tap a single cognitive function. In this battery he found at least eight factors that could be clearly interpreted:

S, space: the ability to perceive spatial patterns and to compare them

V, verbal comprehension: the ability to identify word meanings and, more generally, to understand language and manipulate verbal relationships

W, word fluency: the ability to rapidly produce words fitting certain restrictions as to their spelling

N, number facility: speed and accuracy in performing simple arithmetical operations

I, induction: the ability to infer rules governing given patterns of stimuli

P, perceptual speed: speed and accuracy in finding given visual stimuli in an array of material, or in comparing such stimuli with one another

D, deduction: ability to reason from premises and produce an accurate conclusion

M, rote memory: ability to learn and remember arbitrary associations between stimuli, such as words and numbers

Thurstone regarded his results as supporting the conclusion that there is not *one* kind of intelligence, but *many.* In later studies by Thurstone and many others, this conclusion has been modified to propose that cognitive abilities are organized "hierarchically." That is, there are some cognitive abilities that are very general and enter into a wide variety of mental performances, whereas others are more specialized.

The hierarchical view of cognitive abilities has taken several forms. Favored by British psychologists such as Philip Vernon in *The structure of human abilities* is the view that the major group factor is Spearman's "g," and that minor group factors are "v:ed," a verbal-numerical-educational factor arising primarily as a consequence of schooling, and "k:m," a "practical-mechanical-spatial-physical" factor; in addition, there are fairly numerous specific factors such as verbal, numerical, space, and others comprised under these group factors.

The so-called "structure of intellect" (SI) model has been advocated by J. P. Guilford in *The nature of human intelligence.* Guilford rejected the idea of "g" or general intelligence. Instead, he believed that all cognitive abilities could ultimately be cross-classified with respect to the types of mental operations, contents, and "products" or outcomes they involved. Each type of cognitive ability or factor was claimed to involve a particular process, content, and product. Processes or "operations" were cognition, memory, divergent production, convergent production, and evaluation. Contents could be figural, symbolic, semantic, or behavioral (this last pertaining to gestures, facial expressions, and the like). Products could be units, classes, relations, systems, transformations, and implications. Guilford attempted to provide strict definitions for these categories, which combine to yield at least 120 different factors. Because of various technical considerations, not all researchers in the field have accepted Guilford's model, but it has been useful in guiding further studies, and Guilford claims to have identified some 100 independent factors of ability.

From the vantage point of factor analysis, what is measured by any particular test may be either a single, "pure" factor of cognitive ability, or a conglomerate of several such abilities.

In the 1970s, several cognitive psychologists resurrected from virtual oblivion the study of the very simple cognitive functions that had been explored by J. M. Cattell and others in the late nineteenth century as possible measures of intelligence. Increased technological sophistication and the use of microcomputers made this possible.

Clinical Approaches

Jean Piaget was a major investigator of cognitive abilities using a largely clinical approach. He was interested more in studying these abilities as universal characteristics of the human species, and focused on the development of these abilities over the life span, especially in children. The method was to ask individual children questions about their knowledge and beliefs about the world; it also included the use of certain more or less standard cognitive tasks, such as asking a child to arrange a series of sticks in order of size, or to predict the height of the water in a vessel of narrow diameter after being poured from a wider vessel.

Psychologists have debated whether the kinds of cognitive ability studied by Piaget and his colleagues are related to the factors of intelligence as studied by psychometricians using more formal tests. Undoubtedly they are, but the Piagetian cognitive abilities are probably best regarded as being subtypes of the inductive, deductive, and spatial abilities studied by psychometricians. The rate at which these abilities develop in different children is probably fairly well indexed by measures of general intelligence.

A clinical approach to the study of cognitive abilities was also employed by the Russian psychologist Alexander Luria in his studies of the development of mental functions in different, largely uneducated, groups in the former Soviet Union around 1932, reported in *Cognitive development,* and in his studies of the impairment of mental capacities in aphasics and other brain-damaged individuals. In the latter studies, utilizing a series of informal cognitive tests described in *Higher cortical functions in man,* he developed a theory of how various cognitive functions are performed in different parts of the brain.

DEVELOPMENT AND DECLINE OF COGNITIVE ABILITIES

For the average individual, it appears that all cognitive abilities develop gradually from birth or shortly thereafter up through the age of about 20 to 22 years, but at possibly different rates. Because it is difficult to specify absolute scales or metrics for the different abilities, it has also been difficult to compare abilities with respect to their rate of development. It is certain, however, that there are large differences among individuals with regard to rates of cognitive development, both in general ability as well as in more specialized abilities.

Evidence regarding the possible decline of mental abilities in adulthood and old age is somewhat inconclusive. In general, psychologists report that "crystallized" abilities such as vocabulary continue well into old age with little decline, if any, while "fluid" abilities such as reasoning show some decline, on the average, particularly if the cognitive task requires speed in response. Interpretation of this evidence is difficult because of the possibility that differences among age cohorts are traceable to cultural and educational differences. For many individuals, cognitive abilities appear to persist into old age at their normal levels.

SOURCES OF INDIVIDUAL DIFFERENCES

A major concern of psychology is with the extent to which individual differences are determined biologically, that is, genetically or through natural maturation processes, or by the experiences with the environment—though education, training, and incidental learning generally. This problem has been particularly acute in connection with cognitive abilities.

The question is to what extent cognitive abilities can be improved by special training. There is little doubt that some abilities can be so improved; for example, it is clearly possible for an individual's vocabulary and verbal ability to be increased to some extent by special efforts. Efforts to improve certain other abilities such as spatial ability have been less successful. In general, there is a large gap in our knowledge about the limits to which various cognitive abilities can be improved. A frequent finding is that programs to improve cognitive abilities tend to increase individual differences rather than diminish them.

In view of the acknowledged significance of cognitive abilities in the advancement of democratic and technological civilizations, their scientific study is one of the more important branches of psychology.

GENERAL INTELLIGENCE FACTORS
INTELLIGENCE MEASURES
STRUCTURE OF INTELLECT MODEL

J. B. CARROLL

COGNITIVE BEHAVIOR THERAPY

Cognitive behavior therapy is an approach designed to change mental images, thoughts, and thought patterns so as to help patients overcome emotional and behavioral problems. It is based on the theory that behaviors and emotions are caused in part by cognitions and cognitive processes that one can learn to change. Traditional psychotherapies have always recognized that cognitions play an important role in behavior and emotions; however, cognitive behavior therapy is distinct from previous insight therapies in that it deals only with "here-and-now" cognitions. It also deals with these cognitions in a more systematic way than other therapies. It uses principles of behavior modification to find out what cognitions a patient has and which ones may be causing trouble. Behavioral techniques are then used to reduce the undesired cognitions, to suggest new cognitions and ways of thinking about a problem, and to reinforce these new cognitions. These techniques include: (a) keeping records of desired and undesired cognitions and noting the conditions in which they occur; (b) modeling new cognitions; (c) using the imagination to visualize how new cognitions can be related to desired behaviors and emotional well-being; and (d) practicing in the real world with these new cognitions so that they become the patient's habitual way of thinking.

Cognitions that may need changing include beliefs and belief systems as well as thoughts and images. A person organizes and uses cognitions through cognitive processes. These processes include: (a) ways of evaluating and organizing information about the environment and oneself; (b) ways of processing information for coping with life and solving problems; and (c) ways of predicting and evaluating future events.

HISTORY

Cognitive behavior therapy is an outgrowth of behavior modification and therapy. Behavior therapy of the 1960s attempted to explain and treat emotional and behavioral disorders using the same laws of operant and respondent conditioning that had been used successfully on lower organisms, infants, and retarded persons. However, in dealing with humans, researchers found that even very powerful external manipulations often failed to change behaviors in a consistent way. For example, to treat depressive behaviors one could reward "happy" behaviors and punish "depressive" behaviors. However, if a patient's cognitive processes involved a tendency to self-blame or to label him- or herself a failure, the external manipulations would be ineffective.

Interest in self-control, or the ability to be unaffected by immediate rewards and punishments in order to achieve a goal, helped shift many behaviorists' belief in external control of behavior to theories that postulate that a person can use cognitive skills to solve problems presented by the environment. Thought processes were seen to have an important role in determining behaviors and feelings.

Albert Bandura's *Principles of behavior modification* was a significant event for many behavior therapists searching for more integrative models, in that he presented theoretical interpretations of both operant and classical conditioning while emphasizing the importance of cognitive processes in the regulation of behavior.

THEORY

Cognitions are never considered in research with lower animals. Human life is so complex, and so much of the information we receive comes through language, that it is possible for cognitions and cognitive processes to develop that do not reflect accurately the reality of a person's environment; these cognitions can cause inappropriate and undesirable behaviors and/or emotions. Similar conditions might produce fear or depression in some, and no reaction in others.

Humans learn to satisfy their needs by observing the outcomes of events and behaviors. From these observations they develop expectations about what will happen and about their ability to perform. They also learn to have certain emotions as the result of certain outcomes or events. They compare themselves with others, and make value judgments about their own and other's behaviors. Thus it is not the external conditions alone that determine our behaviors, but the decisions we make based on our cognitions about the conditions. Thus cognitions can result in undesirable behavior or emotions, depending on what cognitions a person has learned to use in various life situations. If people learn to think of themselves as failures, they may become depressed. If they come to believe they cannot cope with a situation, they will attempt to avoid it. The goal of cognitive therapy is to change patients' faulty ways of thinking about themselves and to teach them the skills needed to cope with problem situations. The therapy involves learning experiences designed to change cognitions so that the latter become more appropriate and do not hamper social or emotional development.

OVERVIEW OF COGNITIVE THERAPIES

Rational-Emotive Therapy

Albert Ellis recognized that his patients held irrational beliefs such as "I must be perfect" and "Everyone must love me." These beliefs go hand in hand with a preoccupation about what others think of a person. Whenever reality deviates from these beliefs, the patient interprets it as a terrible thing. Because reality seldom meets the irrational expectations, depression can occur. Therapy involves persuading the patient to adopt more rational cognitions through modeling of appropriate thoughts. Patients are urged to monitor the quality of their thoughts, to become aware of their frequency of occurrence and their effect on emotions.

Cognitive Therapy

Aaron Beck described how persons can become depressed by using distorted thinking. Examples of such thinking include focusing on failure more than success, thinking that one failure means total failure, and other cognitive tendencies to think of oneself in a negative light. Therapy consists of recognizing these tendencies and performing homework exercises designed to give success experiences. Examples of more adaptive, positive thinking are given to the patient, who practices them until they replace the old thinking style.

Self-Instructional Training

Donald Meichenbaum viewed cognitions as self-instructions used in the development of behavioral skills. These instructions were at a conscious level when the behavior was first being learned. After it was learned, the instructions faded from awareness, and the behavior was performed automatically. Abnormal instructions may be learned, leading to undesirable behaviors. If the instructions were faulty or incomplete, the patient will later have anxiety about performing the behaviors adequately. Therapy consists of learning new self-instructions through modeling. The patient imagines using a new set of instructions for a new set of behaviors. This therapy has been used mainly with aggressive children and for test anxiety.

Covert Modeling Therapy

Joseph Cautela has researched ways to help people learn to deal with stressful or anxiety-producing situations by having them mentally rehearse the required behaviors. Patients learn to imagine what will happen as a result of their behavior and what actions they can take to cope with the situation. The patient also practices relaxation techniques, so that anxiety and stress do not interfere with performance of the plan. This therapy has been used with phobias and unassertiveness.

Coping Skills Training

This therapy, described by Marvin Goldfried, is similar to covert modeling. The patient imagines a stressful situation and then imagines coping with the anxiety. However, in coping skills training the visualizing is done in a sequence of images of increasing anxiety. At each stage more anxiety is tolerated through the use of relaxation techniques. In this way the patient never becomes too anxious to persevere with coping responses. The patient may also role-play the problem situation as practice. This therapy has been used for test anxiety and to help persons cope with indecisiveness.

Anxiety Management Training

This therapy, described by Richard Suinn and Frank Richardson, is similar to other therapies in that the imagination of anxiety-arousing events is used. The therapist trains the patient to recognize and use symptoms of anxiety as a signal to utilize coping strategies such as relaxation or thinking success-oriented thoughts. This therapy emphasizes using a variety of imagined situations so that the patient will be better able to cope with an array of real situations. It is generally used with persons who cannot perform in certain situations owing to excessive anxiety.

Stress Inoculation Training

Donald Meichenbaum has described how, in this therapy, fear and anxiety are seen as caused by awareness of heightened physiological arousal and by anxiety-causing thoughts. The training involves learning to relax and changing the anxious thoughts and feelings. These techniques are rehearsed mentally and then used in actual stressful situations set up by the therapist, such as unpredictable electric shock. Experience with these stressful activities allows the patient to develop skill in using relaxation and anxiety-reducing thoughts. The stressful activities are carefully controlled, so that the patient gains self-confidence without being overwhelmed by the stressors.

Problem-Solving Therapies

These therapies assume that problems of life require a set of cognitive skills such as being able to see means-ends relationships, to come up with alternative solutions, and to predict the results of these solutions. Behavioral and emotional problems can occur if a person is lacking in these abilities. In behavioral problem-solving therapy, described by Thomas D'Zurilla and Marvin Goldfried, patients are trained to specify the problems in their life, to generate possible solutions, and to try out the best ones. Patients self-monitor their means-end thinking processes and their ability to evaluate their behavior. This therapy has been used with disturbed children and adults who seem to be deficient in problem-solving skills.

Michael Mahoney suggested that people could adapt better to life if they systematically used a sequence of procedures to arrive at a solution, much the way a scientist or an engineer would. These procedures are: (a) specify the problem; (b) collect information; (c) identify causes or patterns; (d) examine options; (e) narrow the options and try them out; (f) compare the outcomes; and (g) extend and revise them based on the outcomes.

METHODOLOGY

The methodology of cognitive behavior therapy involves identifying and changing specific cognitive processes as they relate to problems of emotions and behavior. The emphasis in therapy is to deal with here-and-now goal-oriented cognitions in a systematic fashion, using the social learning principles of modeling and rehearsal along with self-awareness and relaxation training.

Cognitive Therapy of Depression

Aaron Beck has described his approach to the treatment of depression in *Cognitive therapy and the emotional disorders*. Depressed patients see themselves as losers; therapy is designed to make them feel like winners. The therapist will first select several of the patient's problems, which may be emotional, motivational, cognitive, behavioral, or physiological. Each problem is explored at three levels: in terms of abnormal behavior, such as inactivity or social isolation; in terms of emotional disturbances, such as wanting to escape; and in terms of cognitions of hopelessness and defeat.

Patients are told that keeping busy will make them feel better. The therapist and patient can design a daily activity schedule to fill up each day. These behaviors are graded, so that the patient is motivated to perform a series of tasks of increasing difficulty that are related to the alleviation of a target problem. If difficulty is increased slowly, the patient should meet with a series of successes. The therapist can provide feedback about success, thus reversing the depressive cycle of failure and negative self-evaluation.

For cognitive reappraisal, the patient and therapist look at the relations between depressive cognitions and symptoms. The patient self-monitors thoughts, feelings, and behaviors that occur before, during, and after problem situations. To change cognitive processes, the therapist can have the patient consider alternative explanations of experiences, showing that there are other ways to interpret events besides those that reflect negatively on the self. The therapist gently explores the patient's closed belief system involving negativism toward the world and the self; the therapist questions the reasons for such beliefs and debates the patient, bringing out evidence to the contrary. Cognitive rehearsal involves having the patient imagine a sequence of events related to a problem area. Perceived obstacles and conflicts are brought up for discussion, and cognitive reappraisal and problem-solving techniques are used to work through them.

SUMMARY

Psychotherapeutic approaches have, from the beginning, considered thought processes as important as causes of problem emotions and behaviors. However, the relation between thoughts, emotions, and behaviors was often explained by abstract theories, which made therapy difficult for the patient to understand and difficult for the researcher to evaluate. As a reaction to this emphasis on unseen and mysterious processes, behavior therapy limited itself only to observable and external events. Then cognitive behavior therapy focused on thoughts as behaviors.

However, cognitive behavior therapy was not a return to the traditional insight therapies. Unlike previous therapies, cognitive behavior therapy is systematic in dealing with internal events in that it categorizes thought processes and ties them to external events through careful observation over time of thoughts, feelings, and behaviors.

Cognitive behavior therapy is directed toward the learning through practice of specific skills that have direct relevance to the presenting problem. In cognitive behavior therapy the emphasis on learning skills, and on self-responsibility in the application of these skills, may give the patient a greater sense of self-mastery and coping ability. If cognitive behavior therapy proves ultimately to be an effective treatment method, it will mark the successful application of the scientific method to the analysis and change of our unseen thought processes.

COGNITIVE THERAPY
CURRENT PSYCHOTHERAPIES
EFFECTIVENESS COMPONENTS OF PSYCHOTHERAPY
PSYCHOTHERAPY
SYSTEMATIC DESENSITIZATION

J. P. FOREYT
G. K. GOODRICK

COGNITIVE COMPLEXITY

Cognitive complexity was defined originally by James Bieri as "the tendency to construe social behavior in a multidimensional way." His operational definition of this concept was derived from George Kelly's Role Construct Repertory Grid Test, in which subjects successively categorize personal acquaintances in terms of various bipolar dimensions, or "constructs," elicited from themselves, as for example, reserved/outgoing. Bieri's index of cognitive complexity is based on the extent to which subjects use different constructs independently of each other in categorizing the same persons. This is essentially a measure of differentiation between constructs. He found a test–retest reliability of 0.80 for this index, which correlated with subjects' accuracy in predicting differences between themselves and two acquaintances in terms of their responses to a questionnaire concerned with social behavior.

Subsequently, Bieri developed a new grid test in which subjects rate 10 acquaintances using a 6-point scale from -3 to $+3$ on the basis of a standard list of 10 bipolar constructs. Each set of ratings is compared with every other, assigning 1 point whenever the same person is given identical ratings on two constructs. The higher the total score, the less cognitively complex the subject.

Research based on Bieri's measure of cognitive complexity indicates that subjects tend to differentiate among constructs more in characterizing people with "negative valences"—for instance, "the person with whom you feel least comfortable" or "a disliked character in a play"—than in describing "positive" figures, such as "your best friend" or "the protagonist of your favorite novel." This finding is consistent with his "vigilance hypothesis," which implies that we tend to be more discriminating in construing the behavior of potentially threatening persons so as to isolate our impressions of them.

Other indices of cognitive complexity derived from various repertory grid tests include, among others, the proportion of total variance accounted for by the largest factor or first principal component, the number of significant correlations between constructs, the average correlation between constructs, the average distance between figures, and the extent to which others are characterized as similar to the self.

The main problem encountered in using repertory grids to assess cognitive complexity in normal subjects is reflected by the finding that thought-disordered schizophrenics exhibit a relatively high degree of statistical independence between constructs in characterizing people in grid tests; however, their social judgments are described better as random rather than as complex in organization, in that they are highly unstable from one occasion to the next.

COGNITIVE DISSONANCE
PERSONAL CONSTRUCT THEORY
REPERTORY GRID TEST

J. R. ADAMS-WEBBER

COGNITIVE DISSONANCE

The theory of cognitive dissonance was proposed by Leon Festinger in *A theory of cognitive dissonance.* Festinger predicated the theory on the assumption that a person is motivated to maintain consistency or consonance among pairs of relevant cognitions, where a cognition refers to any knowledge or belief about self, behavior, or the environment. Cognitions X and Y are regarded as dissonant "if not-X follows from Y"; such dissonance is postulated to be "psychologically uncomfortable" and to produce pressure both to reduce the dissonance and to avoid situations or information that would increase the dissonance.

Festinger indicated that the amount of pressure to reduce the dissonance would be a function of the magnitude of the dissonance, where the magnitude of dissonance produced by a given cognition depends both on the importance ascribed to it and other relevant cognitions, and on the proportion of the relevant cognitions that are dissonant. Dissonance may be reduced by altering one of the dissonant cognitions, by reducing the importance of the dissonance, or by adding new information that is consonant with one of the discrepant cognitions or that somehow "reconciles" the two dissonant elements. Dissonance is postulated to produce cognitive activity designed to reduce the dissonance.

Several points must be made at this juncture. First, Festinger postulated a pressure or tendency to reduce dissonance; this effort may not be successful. Therefore Festinger stated that "in the presence of a dissonance, one will be able to observe the *attempts* to reduce it. If attempts to reduce dissonance fail, one should be able to observe the symptoms of psychological discomfort." Second, attempts to reduce dissonance may fail because the cognitions are resistant to change; for example, changing a cognition might contradict reality or change other consonances into dissonances, change might be painful or impossible, or a behavior may be highly satisfying in other respects. Finally, as subsequent researchers have indicated, Festinger's position concerns psychological inconsistency, not formal logical inconsistency; that is, "I smoke" and "Smoking causes cancer" will produce dissonance only with the assumption that the smoker does not want cancer.

Festinger noted the certain existence of individual differences in how and how much people respond to dissonance, and proposed a quantifiable "tolerance for dissonance" continuum. Several studies have demonstrated that existing personality scales can serve as moderators of reactions to dissonance.

In summary, the strength of cognitive dissonance theory has also been its weakness; that is, the postulation of cognitive mechanisms has had a substantial heuristic impact, but the resulting intricate experimental procedures have been subject to alternative interpretations. Attempts to explicate the role of arousal states and the implication of the self-concept promise both to clarify the theory and to enhance its contribution.

COGNITIVE COMPLEXITY
PERCEPTION
SELF-FULFILLING PROPHECY
SURPRISE

J. B. CAMPBELL

COGNITIVE INTERVENTIONS WITH OLDER PERSONS

On the assumption that declines with age in intelligence are not irreversible and that intellectual functioning in old age is characterized by a great deal of plasticity, some investigators have developed training programs to help older adults enhance their intellectual skills. One such project is the Adult Development and Enrichment Project (ADEPT). These investigators have focused on skills required to solve items measuring fluid intelligence, (G_f), which typically demonstrates declines with increased age. By comparing elderly people who received such training with those who received no training or with those who simply practiced (without benefit of any training), they concluded that older persons can in fact enhance their intellectual skills. They based their conclusions about the efficacy of their training program on evidence suggesting (a) a hierarchical pattern of transfer and (b) maintenance of training effects over time. This hierarchical pattern of transfer suggests that tests measuring G_f (near transfer task) should be affected by training to the greatest extent, and those measuring crystallized ability (G_c) (far transfer task) should be least affected. For those who had simply been allowed to practice with items measuring G_f, no hierarchical pattern of transfer to G_f versus G_c was found. Moreover, the magnitude of training effects was greater for training program participants than for those who served as members of the control group, for whom no training, but only practice was provided. These effects were maintained 1 month after training and to a somewhat lesser extent at 6 months.

Indeed, the training data collected by Schaie and Willis using primary mental abilities (PMA) has demonstrated that training can apparently reverse 14-year declines in PMA performance. For persons who had participated in several subsequent training programs over a 7-year interval, intellectual performance still exceeded their original levels 7 years earlier.

Hayslip found that providing older persons with anxiety-reduction techniques, such as substituting success self-statements, for failure self-statements, and relaxation was almost as effective as direct specific rule-based training and superior to persons who were not trained at all. Moreover, practice seemed to help all persons, regardless of whether they were trained.

Another means of enhancing intellectual performance is to allow older people to generate their own intellectual problem-solving strategies versus having to provide such strategies formally to them by a tutor. This research suggests that even in the absence of explicit instruction and feedback, older adults can perform adequately.

Research to date, therefore, indicates that there are a number of ways to ensure that older individuals' intellectual skills do not deteriorate. However, the breadth of these training effects, whether persons respond equally to each type of intervention or whether a combination of the previously mentioned approaches works better, remain as questions to be answered. As not all older persons respond equally to training, one should expect to observe individual differences in training effects as well

as some specificity in terms of what types of older adults respond to distinct varieties of interventions.

These findings demonstrate that cognitive aging need not be characterized by decline and that older adults can continue to grow intellectually. To optimize intellectual performance, older adults can use a number of strategies to help them compensate for declines in their intellectual skills brought on by disease or obsolescence of skills.

Findings in the memory training literature are equally optimistic. Intervening at a process level, wherein encoding and retrieval deficits can be focused, seems to be effective in enhancing short-term memory performance in older adults. In addition, ensuring that learning is adequate before retrieval; pacing the memory task; and using materials that are familiar, concrete, and therefore, more easily organized also seem to be effective. Although there are individual differences in memory training efficacy among older persons, there also is some evidence that memory training techniques may not be spontaneously used by older learners. A learner-in-context approach, incorporating environmental, task, and person-specific factors that also take into consideration the goals and values of the learner, as well as the importance attached to enhancing one's skills, seems to succeed best.

ABSTRACT INTELLIGENCE
AGING AND INTELLIGENCE
COGNITIVE ABILITIES
OLDER ADULTS: MOOD AND MEMORY

B. HAYSLIP, JR.

COGNITIVE LEARNING STYLES

Because cognitive style is a construct representing a domain of observable behaviors, there are inconsistencies in the choice of specific behaviors to be included for investigation and representation. A number of investigators have devised measuring instruments to elicit particular behaviors for analysis of an individual's cognitive style.

A clear distinction must be made between cognitive style and ability or achievement. Initially, they are often considered to be similar, or at least related; this misconception contributes to some confusion surrounding cognitive style. Cognitive style addresses behavior and preference; it is value-free, having no good or bad judgments. Cognitive style is concerned with qualitative rather than quantitative differences of the dimensions.

An individual's cognitive style is determined by the way he or she takes note of the surroundings, seeks meaning, and becomes informed. In addition to identifying the ways of mastering an educational task, a cognitive style map can direct the individual toward realistic career goals. The diagnostic prescription can be augmented to improve missing variables by developing a personalized educational program to account for the individual's strengths and weaknesses.

APPROACHES TO LEARNING
COGNITIVE COMPLEXITY

N. A. HAYNIE

COGNITIVE MAPS

A cognitive map represents the relative locations of points in space, making it possible for an animal to orient itself toward a point that has no distinctive cues. Tolman appears to have coined the term and to have applied it to maze learning in rats. His cognitive map hypothesis was tentatively supported by data from his laboratory, namely the sudden drop in errors with the initial introduction of a food reward in a previously explored complex maze and appropriate responding in so-called insight and alternative path studies. Similarly, Maier's three-table–reasoning problem assumed that a successful rat knew the position of each table with respect to the other two tables.

Later, Olton provided somewhat more convincing evidence for the hypothesis of cognitive maps. Using an eight-arm radial maze, Olton and associates studied spatial memory in the rat by removing the food pellet at the end of each alley once it had been visited on the trial. The rats soon learned, to almost an errorless level, to enter only an arm that had not been previously visited. Rats perform well with controlled odor cues or odor trails, go to the appropriate spatial location even when the maze is rotated, and do not learn fixed sequences that could function independently of spatial memories.

Morris tested the cognitive map hypothesis directly by requiring rats to locate a slightly submerged platform in a tank of water made opaque by adding milk. Once the maze is learned from the one starting point, the rat can be dropped into any point in the tank and it sets a course more or less directly toward the platform, as consistent with a cognitive map.

One animal that clearly has a cognitive map and perhaps has one that may be superior to humans is the chimpanzee. This was first observed by Tinklepaugh in his study of multiple delayed response using 16 different containers situated as equally spaced pairs in a large circle. One member of each pair, on the left or the right, was baited while the subject (chimpanzee, human adult, or human child) watched. After a short delay, the subject was free to find the hidden object for each pair. Children did very poorly on this task, and chimpanzees were slightly superior to human adults, having a success rate of more than 70%, even when the baiting was done in a random fashion, which would seem to rule out unintentional cuing by the experimenters because they did not remember where things were either.

Birds also seem to have cognitive maps. For example, marsh tits exhibit good spatial memory for seeds that they have hoarded in a variety of cache locations. They also avoid earlier used but now empty holes. These memories probably reflect species-specific adaptations. The birds are very poor in finding seeds stored in holes by an experimenter, ruling out smell as a basis for detecting seed locations.

Bees clearly use landmarks around sources of nectar to locate the substance, but recent evidence suggests that this local map consists of route-based memories rather than as a cognitive map of a familiar landscape, as with humans and other vertebrates. A study by Whishaw on latent learning in a swimming pool task raises questions about the rats' use of cognitive mapping, because of strong evidence for the use of associative processing.

Denny provides information on how cognitive maps are established. Visual recognition and ability to move about in a spatial layout were tested following single-route or multiple-route training of the space solely through kinesthesis (by means of blind hand movements among points on a plane). Single-route training, in spite of much more practice on the target route, failed to yield better learning of the route than multiple-route training and produced a much poorer cognitive map, as judged from kinesthetic and visual transfer tasks. Certain conclusions seem justified: (a) the more varied the initial experience, the more abstract and less egocentric (individual-referenced) the representation of space becomes and (b) active experiencing of space produces a representation of the space as a coordinated whole—one that transcends the individual links (paths) between locations. The whole is known better than its parts.

ABSTRACT INTELLIGENCE
COGNITIVE ABILITIES
CRESPI EFFECT
MEMORY EXPERIMENTS

PRIMATE BEHAVIOR
REINFORCEMENT

M. R. DENNY

COGNITIVE PSYCHOPHYSIOLOGY

Cognitive psychophysiology is an interdisciplinary field overlapping psychology and physiology in which efforts are made to solve the classical problem of "mind" through modern electronic technology. The primary thesis is that mental processes are generated when selective bodily systems interact, and that they can be directly studied with sufficiently sensitive equipment. The bodily systems include the receptors (eyes, ears, etc.), central nervous system (principally the brain), skeletal musculature, autonomic system (the gastrointestinal tract, the cardiovascular system, etc.), and their neural interconnections. The field's interdisciplinary nature is exemplified by researchers from psychology, physiology, medicine, and biomedical engineering.

Approaches to the problem of mind, dating from the time of ancient philosophers, may be summarily classified as either *dualistic* or *monistic.* Traditionally, dualistic positions have been the most popular, even as they are today in everyday thinking. The basic assumption of dualism is that there are two kinds of entities in the world, those of a "physical" (material) and those of a "mental" (nonmaterial) nature; furthermore, in dualism only physical events are knowable by science. Monism, however, holds that the universe consists of only one kind of entity. The principle monistic position is that of strict materialism, which holds that there are only physical phenomena in the universe. According to materialistic monism, therefore, mental processes are physical phenomena generated within the body and can therefore be directly observed through scientific technology.

CONTEMPORARY ASSESSMENT OF THE PROBLEM OF MIND

In considering where in the body thoughts occur, objectivity demands that we avoid predisposing biases and consider that any bodily system might serve some cognitive function until empirically established otherwise. However, the reactions of these systems are often so subtle that they are referred to as *covert* (versus *overt*). Covert reactions are such small-scale bodily processes that they cannot be observed with the naked eye; hence they must be amplified in the laboratory to be studied, as in the case of brain waves or heart activity.

Cognitive psychophysiologists, specializing in different bodily systems and using extremely sensitive procedures, have now been successful in measuring covert reactions *throughout* the body during cognitive activities. Furthermore, it has been established that these events occur in close temporal proximity to one another and are systematically (often causally) related. The conclusion is inescapable that widespread covert reactions in the receptors, brain, muscles, and autonomic system are intricately linked through complex neuromuscular circuits that have cybernetic (feedback or servoloop) characteristics.

THE TRANSITION FROM MECHANICAL TO ELECTRONIC METHODS

Around the turn of the twentieth century, researchers eagerly attempted to construct "thought-reading machines" with what tools were then available. With the advent of the vacuum tube, these crude mechanical methods gave way to the sensitive electronic techniques that were critical for the advancement of cognitive psychophysiology. Thus, about 1921, primitive electromyographs for recording electrical components of muscle activity became available. The first recording of electroencephalograms was by Hans Berger in 1929, empirically establishing that the brain generates electrical signals (although Berger's findings were greeted with skepticism for many years). The galvanic skin response and other measures of autonomic activity during emotion had been initiated in the late nineteenth century (especially with Feré in 1888); such autonomic measures were important in the early development of cognitive psychophysiology, as they continue to be today.

There are four essential features of a cognitive psychophysiological laboratory for electrically studying covert bodily events: (a) *sensors,* usually electrodes placed over the brain and on the surface of the skin to detect electrical components of neural, muscular, and glandular phenomena; (b) *amplifiers,* which increase the amplitude of the body signal sensed; (c) *readout devices,* such as cathode ray oscilloscopes or recorders, which can display the covert body signals; and (d) *quantification systems,* which render numerical values for those signals.

A number of the more commonly measured psychophysiological events are classified in Table 1. The primary division is between *responses* of the muscular and glandular systems and *neurophysiological* processes of the central nervous system.

The first two *response* classes in Table 1, those of the skeletal musculature in the speech and somatic regions, are best measured electrically through electromyography. *Myo,* standing for muscle, and *graph,* for writing, form the term for recording electrical components of muscle activity.

Covert eye behavior, the third response category in Table 1, is typically recorded through electrooculography, where *oculo* refers to the eyes.

The last response class, that for autonomic behavior, consists of a variety of subcategories. Common autonomic components include: (a) measures of heart (cardiac) activity through electrocardiography; (b) activity of the intestinal portion of the gastrointestinal tract, which, when electrically recorded, yields the electrogastrogram; and (c) electrodermal measures of skin (dermal) activity, most prominently the galvanic skin response measured with the psychogalvanometer.

The second major category in Table 1 is for electrical signals from the brain. These include such well-known events as alpha waves (large amplitude, cyclical waves) and beta waves (lower in amplitude than alpha waves, but greater in frequency).

With the entrance of the small electronic computer into the laboratory, however, it became possible to *average* brain waves to expose intrinsic signals not discernible in the raw traces.

Table 1   Covert Psychophysiological Events in Humans

I. Covert Responses (muscular and glandular events)
  A. Covert speech responses: electromyographic measures from the tongue, lip, chin, cheek, laryngeal, and jaw regions
  B. Covert somatic responses: electromyographic measures of the skeletal musculature from the fingers, arms, legs, etc.
  C. Covert eye responses, principally through electrooculography
  D. Covert autonomic responses
    1. Cardiovascular measures such as heart rate, electrocardiogram, finger pulse volume, and blood pressure
    2. Visceral muscle activity principally from the intestines, as the electrogastrogram
    3. Electrodermal measures from the surface of the skin (galvanic skin response, skin conductance, etc.)
II. Neurophysiological Processes
  Electrical activity from the brain, recorded with electroencephalography, through signal-averaging, yields average evoked potentials, and the contingent negative variation.

DIRECT ELECTRICAL MEASUREMENT OF MENTAL PROCESSES

Individual experiments have established that each of the events specified in Table 1 occurs during cognitive experiences (though the grand experiment of simultaneously recording all those measures has not been attempted). The various mental events are *similar,* then, in that they all involve covert activities throughout the body, including the brain.

The *unique* mentalistic terms for mental events exist because the experiences occur under different environmental and organismic conditions. Night dreams, daydreams, and directed rational thought all differ, for instance, because of the degree to which they are influenced by environmental input. During "sleep thoughts" or images of night dreams, most environmental stimulation is physiologically "shut off," apparently at the reticular activating system. Consequently, the mental activity of dreaming is chaotic, since it is not directed by external reality, or as one psychiatrist put it, a night dream allows us all to go safely insane for a brief period of time. Similar mental processes occur in the daydream, but they are partially influenced by the external environment. During directed problem solving, rational thought processes are largely controlled by repeated reference to the environment.

Hallucinations—false perceptions that the patient confuses with real ones—are akin to night dreams in that they are controlled by internal stimuli, though they are mistakenly ascribed to external forces. Neuromuscular circuits that generate visual hallucinations presumably include the occipital lobe at the back of the brain and the eyes. Auditory hallucinations are similarly thought to be generated when auditory and linguistic regions of the brain interact with muscles of the ears and speech. Auditory hallucinations, for instance, seem to be produced when the patient subvocalizes, as indicated by auditory and electromyographical recording of covert speech (Figure 1).

Auditory components of night dreams are apparently generated by neuromuscular circuits like those for auditory hallucinations. Figure 2 illustrates small-scale, rapid covert muscle activity in the lips and chin when one experiences conversations in dreams. These covert speech responses are not present during visual dreams or nondreaming periods.

Deaf individuals who are not proficient in oral speech use dactylic ("sign" or "manual") language for communication. The muscles for the fingers therefore are the locus of *their* linguistic response mechanisms. For them, consequently, the speech musculature is not engaged during thought. Instead, they make covert finger responses when thinking. In addition, individuals who are proficient in *both* oral and manual language processes engage both the speech musculature and the fingers covertly during thought.

TECHNOLOGICAL CONSEQUENCES

As from all scientific fields, a number of practical applications flow from cognitive psychophysiology, perhaps the most important being principles for self-regulation. As one continuously meets the stresses of life, there often eventuates some bodily malfunction. The primitive reaction of the body to stress is characterized as the startle reflex, a major component of which is the tensing of the skeletal musculature for fight or flight. Chronic states of excess tension throughout the skeletal musculature can result in two classes of bodily malfunctions: (a) psychiatric difficulties such as anxiety states, phobias, and depression; and (b) psychosomatic maladies such as ulcers, headaches, spastic colon, and elevated blood pressure. The original and apparently most effective method for alleviating these tension maladies is progressive relaxation, developed by Edmund Jacobson from 1908 on. In progressive relaxation one relaxes the skeletal muscle system, which in turn produces a state of tranquillity throughout the central and autonomic nervous systems. Jacobson has shown that habitual relaxation can thereby alleviate many psychiatric and

Figure 1. A sample tracing of the report of a hallucination. The 2-sec intervals before and after the report are marked on the event line at the top. Next in order are the pneumogram, arm electromyogram, chin electromyogram, tongue electromyogram, and the sound record. The increase in chin electromyographic activity and in subvocalization (bottom trace) coincide with the hallucinatory experience.

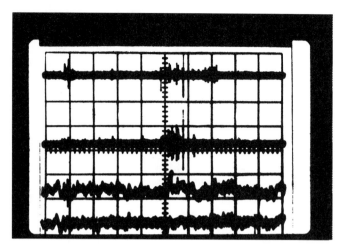

Figure 2. Illustration of signals during a conversational dream. From the top down, the signals are lip electromyogram, chin electromyogram, horizontal eye placement, and frontal electroencephalogram. Amplitude for the top three traces is 50 μV/division, and 100 μV/division for the electroencephalogram. Time is 1 sec/division.

psychosomatic maladies such as those mentioned previously. However, perhaps the prophylactic application of progressive relaxation has even greater beneficial consequences. For this purpose Jacobson has advocated that tension control be universally taught to children while in the primary grades.

Another prominent method aimed at the development of self-regulation is biofeedback, in which internal processes are transduced to make them publicly observable. The strategy is to monitor and thus control such internal events as brain waves, muscle signals, and electrodermal responses by visually observing them as on a cathode ray oscilloscope or by hearing them through an external speaker. Biofeedback holds considerable promise for helping us to better understand our internal world; much research is currently in progress in this important area. There are, however, difficulties in its clinical application such as the dependency of the learner on a biofeedback signal. Consequently, if the desired changes in behavior occur in the clinic, they may not be lasting and generalized to the patient's everyday world. Nevertheless, a revolutionary consequence of biofeedback and progressive relaxation is that they provide the opportunity to study a person's internal world, just as classical psychology has concentrated on our relationship with the external environment.

Another application has been in the understanding of reading and of the teaching of silent reading. It is a common myth that subvocalization—or more technically, covert speech behavior—retards reading proficiency. Popular "speed reading courses," for instance, seek to increase reading rate by short-circuiting the speech musculature. Some teachers have attempted to prevent subvocalization by taping lips or filling the mouths of pupils with marbles, by wrapping the tongue about a pencil, and so forth. However, such efforts to inhibit subvocalization are futile, for the speech musculature still responds during silent reading even when so inhibited. The empirical generalization is that covert speech behavior occurs in all silent readers and is necessary for comprehending what is being read. Actually, as the reading rate becomes faster, the amount of covert speech behavior does not *decrease,* but *increases.* However, if speech muscles are well relaxed during reading through progressive relaxation, the reader fails to understand the meaning of the text. The implication for teachers, therefore, is that they should not tamper with the child's subvocalization, for the child *needs* to subvocalize while reading. Actually, subvocalization becomes naturally reduced over time, although it still persists in the adult at a very reduced level.

Lie detection, or more precisely the detection of deception, is a widespread application for espionage purposes, for the identification of criminals, and even as a criterion for employment. The polygraph, which relies heavily on cardiovascular measures, is the most widely used instrument for these purposes. Unfortunately the traditional polygraph, like newer variations of lie detectors such as the psychological stress evaluator and the voice stress analyzer, do not have sufficient validity to justify their standard use. However, techniques and principles *are* available within the field of cognitive psychophysiology to develop successful deception detection systems and will undoubtedly be made.

AUTOGENIC TRAINING
COGNITIVE COMPLEXITY
LIE DETECTION
NEUROLINGUISTICS
NEUROPSYCHOLOGY
RELAXATION TRAINING

F. J. McGUIGAN

COGNITIVE THEORIES OF EMOTION

Theories of emotion try to explain how emotion is aroused, how it produces physiological changes, and how one emotion differs from another. The answer to the first question distinguishes cognitive theories from other theories of emotion.

Theorists of all persuasions usually agree that anger, fear, or both are aroused when a situation is interpreted as annoying and/or dangerous. Many insist that such arousal is programmed into the nervous system during evolutionary prehistory and serves biological survival. For cognitive psychologists, every emotion is aroused by knowing something and appraising it. No doubt, some appraisals are preprogrammed: Infants like anything sweet the first time they taste it. However, older children and adults appraise what they encounter not only as it affects their bodily well-being but also as it affects them as persons. The child is angry when teased by buddies; the young man, when his pals show him up before his girlfriend. If emotions depend on appraisals, there will be as many different emotions as there are different appraisals. Emotions may be classified, but they need not be derived from one another.

Not surprisingly, cognitive theories have a long history. In the third century B.C., Aristotle suggested in his *De anima* (*About the soul*) that human beings and animals can make sensory judgments (through what he called the *vis estimativa*) of things as being good or bad for them; this estimate arouses an emotion, liking, or dislike. Thomas Aquinas, in his *Commentary,* followed Aristotle in this explanation of emotional arousal.

Descartes insisted that all emotions are aroused directly by exciting the "animal spirits," or by arousing inherent reflex actions together with the physiological changes necessary for survival—a notion shared by Darwin. William James and Carl Lange later reversed the common-sense view that emotion produces bodily changes, by insisting that bodily changes follow directly on the perception of the exciting object: Our sensation of these changes *is* the emotion.

The James–Lange theory of emotion was accepted unquestioningly and soon fatally reduced the interest of academic psychologists in the analysis of emotion.

To say that some situations arouse hereditary patterns is no solution. Fear or anger may arouse flight or attack, but they still depend on a realization that something is threatening or annoying, which is an appraisal, however rudimentary.

M. B. Arnold introduced the notion of appraisal into academic psychology. She defined emotion as "a felt action tendency toward anything intuitively appraised as good, or away from anything intuitively appraised as bad for me here and now," which is "accompanied by a pattern of physiological changes organized toward a specific kind of approach or withdrawal." Arnold distinguished a few basic emotions, simple reactions to the appraisal of basic situations: liking (love), dislike, desire, aversion, joy, sorrow, daring, fear, anger, hope, and despair.

In her book *Emotion and personality,* Arnold pointed out that emotions depend not only on the intuitive appraisal of something as "good or bad for me," but also on the spontaneous appraisal of possible responses as suitable or unsuitable. Something threatening may be seen as difficult to escape and so arouses fear, or it may be appraised as something that can be anticipated by bold action and so is overcome by a daring attack. Arnold emphasized that the intuitive spontaneous appraisal is supplemented by a deliberate value judgment, at least in the older child and adult, just as sensory knowledge is complemented by conceptual knowledge. Because we use intuitive and reflective appraisals concurrently, even our intuitive judgments generating emotion can be educated. Because the person is a unit, every reflective value judgment will be accompanied by an intuitive appraisal. Value judgments are seldom if ever coldly objective: What is valued, attracts. Hence emotions can be socialized, influenced by social attitudes and customs.

Like other cognitive theorists, Arnold realizes the importance of the physiological changes that accompany emotion. When these changes are felt, they are again appraised and may either reinforce or change the original emotion. When a person appraises an increased pulse rate during fear as indicating heart disease, the original fear is now overlaid by a fear of illness. By definition, heart disease weakens the body. The fear aroused by the increased pulse rate then dictates the appraisal that, being ill, one will not be able to cope with the situation, which increases the original fear.

Important research in emotion is reported by Richard Lazarus and his coworkers. These scientists make appraisal the cornerstone of their theory of emotion. Lazarus suggests that each emotion is based on a particular kind of cognitive appraisal accompanied by motor-behavioral and physiological changes. He distinguishes primary appraisal, secondary appraisal, and reappraisal. The secondary appraisal is an evaluation of a person's relation to the environment and so leads to an altered emotional response. Reappraisal can occur as a simple evaluation of the significance of this altered relation to the environment, or it may be a psychological attempt at coping with stress. Such a reappraisal is not necessarily based on factual information, but can be an attempt to look at the situation from a more congenial point of view. In Lazarus' terms, it may be a "defensive reappraisal." A reappraisal may also be an attempt at coping when direct action is impossible.

Lazarus and his associates found that the appraisal of a situation and therefore a person's emotional reaction could be manipulated experimentally. Before they showed a harrowing subincision film to the experimental subjects, they read a passage to one group that described the painful procedure at length, and told another group that the boys in the picture were willing to undergo this initiation ritual and were proud of their stoic endurance. To a third group, finally, they gave "intellectualizing" information that emphasized the anthropological significance of the ritual. The first group was strongly affected by the film, while the other two groups remained comparatively unaffected.

Although the influence of cognition on appraisal is well documented, the distinction between intuitive and reflective appraisal is more difficult to substantiate. In his article "Feeling and thinking: Preferences need no inferences," R. B. Zajonc pointed out that the notion of the primacy of feeling has languished since Wundt's time. In cognitive psychology it has been replaced by an information-processing scheme in which an affective reaction occurs only after considerable processing. Hence major works on cognition disregard affect or feeling and concentrate exclusively on cognitive processing. Yet, says Zajonc, "affect . . . is the major currency in which social intercourse is transacted." Hence, "to arouse affect, objects need to be cognized very little, in fact, minimally." In recall as in perception, the affective reaction is the first element to emerge. As Zajonc points out, although affect may mark the end of considerable cognitive activity (in listening to a joke, for instance), this need not imply that cognitive activity is a necessary component of affect.

According to Zajonc, there is a separation between affect and cognition. Judgments of similarity and judgments of preference have different dimensions. Early in the twentieth century, T. Nakashima reported in his "Contribution to the study of affective processes," that judgments of pleasantness and unpleasantness are independent of sensory qualities and so cannot be mediated by them. Aesthetic judgments and preferences of all kinds do not depend on cognitive analysis. Experimental investigations have shown that judgments of like and dislike are made and recalled with great certainty, while judgments that a given stimulus word is new or a repeat are made with noticeable uncertainty. Hence Zajonc concludes that the perceptual process, starting from sensory experience, arouses first an unconscious affective reaction, and next produces the recognition of familiar features (also unconscious) before the reflective cognitive processing begins.

We may conclude that Zajonc has exposed a chink in the armor of cognitive psychology. Thinking and reflective judgment seem to depend as much on affect as on sensory experience. Because affect is a conscious experience of attraction/repulsion that is not generated by a reflective value judgment, it must be aroused by the spontaneous (unconscious) appraisal of good/bad objects and suitable/unsuitable responses. Emotions are usually accompanied by reflective judgments, can themselves be appraised as suitable/unsuitable, and can be changed by corrective experiences, but rarely by reflection or persuasion.

COGNITIVE COMPLEXITY
LEARNED HELPLESSNESS
THOUGHT DISTURBANCES
UNCONSCIOUS INFERENCES

M. B. ARNOLD

COGNITIVE THERAPIES

Cognitive therapies are a loosely associated group of approaches that stress the importance of cognitive processes as determinants of behavior. They maintain that behavior and emotions result largely from one's appraisal of the situation, and that, because appraisal is influenced by beliefs, assumptions, images, and self-talk, these cognitions become the targets of therapy. Although these therapies differ in regard to specific techniques, they share certain basic assumptions. Michael Mahoney listed three assumptions common to cognitive therapies: (a) behavior and emotions develop through cognitive processes; (b) procedures based on the human learning laboratory are effective in influencing cognitive processes; and (c) the therapist should serve as a "diagnostician-educator" to uncover maladaptive cognitive processes and arrange learning experiences for altering them.

COMPARISON WITH OTHER THERAPIES

Although traditional psychotherapies, such as psychoanalysis and client-centered therapy, acknowledge the importance of beliefs and other mental phenomena in influencing behavior, cognitive therapies differ from them in several important respects. First, they stress the *primacy* of cognitions over emotions and behaviors. Because they believe cognitions instigate behaviors and trigger emotions, they maintain that the alteration of dysfunctional thoughts, assumptions, and beliefs should be the principle concern of therapy.

Most therapies are cognitive therapies, inasmuch as they seek to bring about changes in the client's private views. Most traditional therapies, however, plan for such changes as side effects of other therapeutic goals. Cognitive therapy differs from these therapies in more directly attacking faulty assumptions, beliefs, and thoughts, and in specifically teaching coping skills believed to be missing from the client's repertoire.

Cognitive therapies differ from behavioral ones in assigning greater importance to mental phenomena. *Orthodox* behaviorists ignore cognitions in favor of overt behavior. Their focus is on measurable behaviors, and their procedures are limited to efforts to engineer the environment so as to extinguish undesirable behaviors and reinforce desirable ones. Many cognitive therapists were former behaviorists who became disillusioned with the narrowness of the behavioral position. Their experience taught them that many human problems cannot be adequately treated without taking mental phenomena such as beliefs and self-talk into consideration.

HISTORICAL EVOLUTION OF COGNITIVE THERAPIES

Around the turn of the twentieth century, the Swiss psychologist Paul DuBois wrote in *The psychic treatment of nervous disorders* that emotional distress was caused by erroneous ideas, and that the task of therapy was to disabuse the patient of such ideas by demonstration, logical induction, and reason.

Somewhat later, and more central to the evolution of cognitive therapies, was the work of Alfred Adler. In *What life should mean to you* Adler expressed his conviction that neurotics base their self-defeating behavior on fictional beliefs, such as the necessity of being superior to others. Therapy, according to him, consisted of changing such beliefs. Patients were taught that social interest and cooperativeness are more functional guides for behavior than neurotic needs to be superior and to dominate.

Albert Ellis and Aaron Beck, traditionally trained psychotherapists, evolved distinctively cognitive therapies strongly emphasizing cognitive factors.

Behavioral therapists frustrated with the limitations of environmental engineering in effecting changes in clients began to adopt cognitive positions in the early 1970s. Their skepticism regarding the adequacy of the conditioning therapies as a basis for therapy was abated by changes in learning theory and developmental psychology.

REPRESENTATIVE COGNITIVE THERAPIES

Coping Skills

Cognitive therapists with behavioral backgrounds often teach coping skills that require the manipulation of cognitions. One such coping approach is *covert modeling,* described by Joseph Cautela. Covert modeling refers to mentally rehearsing difficult performances before attempting to handle them in real life. Sports psychologists refer to it as "mental practice." Alan Kazdin concluded that although there is research to support the use of covert modeling with selected clinical problems, the technique does not appear to be as effective as actual practice, so that the use of covert modeling seems particularly appropriate where actual practice is not possible.

Adaptations of Joseph Wolpe's systematic desensitization are being taught as coping skills. Marvin Goldfried describes one such adaptation. Whereas Wolpe's techniques aim for mastery over disturbing stimuli, Goldfried's adaptation uses disturbing stimuli to teach the client to reduce physiological arousal. Although clients are instructed in systematic desensitization to *terminate* images that arouse anxiety, Goldfried's clients are asked to *maintain* the images and relax them away. Goldfried maintains that this coping skill will generalize to a wide range of disturbing situations.

Problem Solving

Some cognitive-behavior therapists believe inadequate problem-solving skills are responsible for such dysphoric emotions as frustration, hostility, anxiety, and depression. Failure to solve significant problems in life, they maintain, leads to these unhappy states. Certain cognitive behaviorists have constructed problem-solving models for use in therapy.

Few would contest the importance of thoughts, assumptions, images, self-talk, and other cognitions in influencing behavior and emotional states. Challenges to cognitive therapy are directed not so much at their emphasis on the importance of these cognitive factors as at the effectiveness of their procedures for altering them. The research on these procedures presents an inconclusive picture of their usefulness.

COGNITIVE BEHAVIOR THERAPY
COGNITIVE COMPLEXITY
INNOVATIVE PSYCHOTHERAPIES
PSYCHOTHERAPY

K. B. MATHENY
R. M. KERN

COHORT DIFFERENCES

The term *cohort* refers to any group or collection of individuals who experience, within a given period of time, a similar type of significant life event. The event used to identify cohorts can vary, ranging from birth to specific experiences such as entry into postsecondary school, retirement from the labor force, or first marriage. The temporal boundaries used to delineate different cohorts are arbitrary; the period of time within which the significant life event occurs can be as little as one day to two decades or more. Because different life experiences can be used in the identification of cohorts, the discussion of cohort differences will be more focused if the most commonly identified cohort is selected for consideration, namely the birth cohort. A birth cohort refers to any group of individuals who were born within an arbitrary period of time.

By identifying individuals who are aging during specific time periods, birth cohorts allow for an assessment of change across time in the attributes of individuals entering or leaving certain age-specific roles and positions of society. Attention can then be directed at similarities and differences between, for example, those who entered college in the 1940s and those who entered college in the mid-1960s. Different birth cohorts typically experience a different set of events that, in turn, may lead to a different set of expectations, attitudes, and behaviors. The cohort of individuals born during the 1920 to 1924 time period and who were in their late teens and early twenties in the 1940s can be compared with the cohort of individuals born in the 1945 to 1949 time period. Unquestionably, a series of pronounced differences are evident between the first cohort, whose adolescent experiences occurred during the Great Depression of the 1930s, and the second cohort of post-World War II baby boomers. However, before attributing any apparent differences in expectations, attitudes, and behavior to cohort differences *per se,* the technical matter of separating the effects of cohort, age, and period must be addressed.

The study of intercohort differences requires the consideration of three possible sources of dissimilarity: (a) actual differences in attitudes and behavior of individuals within the respective cohorts; (b) differences attributable to aging processes within the cohorts; and (c) differences caused by the unique experiences of cohorts during particular historical periods. However, the separation of these three sources of variability (cohort effects, age effects, and period effects) entails as yet unresolved statistical and conceptual difficulties. Apart from the problem of determining the separate effects of sampling variability distinctly attributable to cohort, age, and period effects, two other difficulties remain.

With the passage of time, the compositional characteristics of cohorts may change due to the effects of either attrition or migration. As a birth cohort ages, the effects of mortality can alter the compositional characteristics of the cohort if those who died differed in certain characteristics from those who remained alive. Similarly, at different times in history, the impact of migration can appreciably alter the characteristics of geographically specific cohorts if the characteristics of those who leave are different from those who remain.

Attempts to distinguish between cohort, age, and period effects invariably encounter an identification problem. Due to the linear dependence of cohort, age, and period effects, it is not possible statistically to separate the unique impact of each. The confounding effects of cohort, age, and period influences necessitate that inquiry into cohort differences be predicated on a well-developed theoretical and substantive understanding of phenomena under study and the implications that these three effects have for the study. Because statistical procedures alone are unable to delineate the separate contributions of these three effects, it is incumbent that the study and assessment of cohort differences be theoretically and conceptually precise in its expectations.

AGE DIFFERENCES
AGING: BEHAVIOR CHANGES

CONTROL GROUPS
SOCIAL INFLUENCE

D. G. NICKINOVICH

COLLEGE ACADEMIC PREDICTION

This is the procedure for predicting academic success or failure on the basis of information available at time of entrance. Different institutions and researchers use different combinations of high school grades, aptitude tests, achievement tests, and personality tests to make these predictions. Predictions are usually made for different academic majors and for different institutions. The data that predict an A grade in one institution may predict only a C grade in another, and the data that predict an A for modern languages may predict a C in pharmacy, and so on. Probably this is partly because different institutions attract different personality types, so that even an engineer from one institution is different from an engineer at another. One institution may attract vocationally oriented persons, whereas another attracts individuals interested in research and theory. Also, because the teaching staff of one institution differs from another, they tend to evaluate students differently. The School of Law at the University of California in Berkeley differs markedly from The School of Law at the University of California in San Francisco. The first has full-time faculty, whereas the second has faculty who are practicing lawyers. The first attracts full-time students interested in legal theory; the second, part-time students primarily interested in applications of the law. Personality factors need to be considered more than they are: If one fails to note the characteristics of a "loner," such a student may be considered a potential "C" student, but come out an "A" student because he or she is competing with students who are much more socially oriented. Such tests predict outcome much better than interviews or recommendations; the more specific they are, the better the prediction.

ACADEMIC APTITUDE TESTS
APTITUDE TESTING
SCHOLARSHIP AND ACHIEVEMENT

W. E. GREGORY

COLOR VISION

The visual experience of most vertebrates features sensitivity to the intensity of electromagnetic radiation within their range of visible wavelengths, from about 380 to 760 nanometers (nm). Beyond this achromatic or colorless sensitivity, some fish, birds, reptiles, and mammals (mainly human and nonhuman primates) are also sensitive to a wavelength's color (hue) and apparent purity or strength (saturation). Most human beings see the shorter spectral wavelengths as bluish (near 480 nm), medium wavelengths as greenish (near 510 nm) and yellowish (near 580 nm), and longer wavelengths as reddish (near 700 nm). Along with these differences in hue, a color may be seen as ranging from highly saturated (e.g., dark red) to desaturated (e.g., pink).

TYPES OF COLOR VISION

By definition, color vision permits discrimination between at least one frequency of visible monochromatic light versus white light of a comparable brightness. Beyond this minimal ability, considerable inter- and intraspecies differences exist in the extent of color vision capabilities. For those with normal or trichromatic color vision (trichromats), every wavelength is discriminable from white. Further, for trichromats a combination of three other monochromatic lights (usually a short, medium, and long wavelength) is required to subjectively match all the visible wavelengths.

Not all those with trichromatic color vision necessarily have comparable color vision, however. As depicted in Table 1, various types of color vision anomalies exist for trichromats. Although anomalous trichromats are able to see the entire range of colors perceived by those with normal trichromatic vision, they may require supranormal intensities to recognize colors within their range of decreased sensitivity. In addition, within this anomalous range, colors are often seen as faded or less saturated, and a reduced ability to discriminate between adjacent colors is sometimes found.

Differentiation of the various types of anomalous trichromats—for example, in terms of protanomalous or deuteranomalous—can be made with the Rayleigh match or anomaloscope test. With normal trichromatic vision, there is a unique mixture of green light (535 nm, yellowish green) plus red light (670 nm, yellowish red) that cannot be distinguished from a yellow light (589 nm, reddish yellow). For anomalous trichromats, the combination of red and green that matches yellow differs from that for normal trichromats. Protanomalous viewers need additional red in the mixture to match yellow; similarly, deuteranomalous trichromats require a mixture containing a greater amount of green.

Dichromats evidence a more severe limitation of color vision than do anomalous trichromats; for dichromats, not all the visible wavelengths can be distinguished from white, and all the wavelengths can be matched by a mixture of only two other wavelengths. The classification of dichromatic versus trichromatic vision is based on the neutral point test that examines the ability to discriminate between numerous individual monochromatic wavelengths and white light. Although trichromats can discriminate between each individual wavelength and white light when brightnesses are equated, for dichromats there is a narrow range of wavelengths that cannot be so discriminated.

This narrow band of wavelengths indiscriminable from white light is referred to as the neutral point, and its spectral location determines the particular type of dichromatism. As indicated in Table 1, protanopia and deuteranopia are associated with seeing blue and yellow but not red or green. Conversely, tritanopia and tetartanopia are accompanied by perception of red and green but not blue or yellow.

Monochromats can match any visible wavelength by merely adjusting the intensity of a single other wavelength. With the possible exception of some limited color vision associated with blue-cone monochromatism, monochromats do not see color.

SPECTRAL SATURATION
Subjective saturation can be estimated by determining the extent to which a monochromatic light can be diluted by the addition of white light, before this mixture becomes indiscriminable from a white light of equivalent brightness. The greater the amount of white light that can be added in the mixture (before the combination cannot be discriminated from white), the greater the subjective saturation of the hue.

SPECTRAL DISCRIMINABILITY
The richness of color vision is partially indicated by the number of distinct colors that can be seen. The extent of such uniqueness is estimated by the ability to discriminate between adjacent colors measured in Weber fractions ($\Delta\lambda/\lambda$) for color discriminations.

THEORIES OF COLOR VISION
Recent conceptualizations of the underlying mechanism mediating color vision feature a merger of two accounts initially considered to be in conflict. One approach, trichromatic theory, was advanced by Thomas Young and Hermann von Helmholtz, who stressed the relative activity of cones maximally sensitive to red, green, or blue. The other account, opponent-process theory, was developed by Ewald Hering, Leo Hurvich, and Dorothea Jameson. Their approach considered red-green as well as blue-yellow to be antagonistic processes. These two emphases have now been reconciled so that trichromatic theory describes receptor activity and opponent-process theory applies to higher-order neural integration.

Table 1   Categories of Color Vision

Classification	Percentage Incidence in Human Beings		Appearance of Spectrum
	Males	Females	
Trichromatism			
Normal			Normal
Anomalous			
Protanomalous	1	0.02	Reduced brightness, saturation, and hue discriminability at long wavelengths
Deuteranomalous	4.9	0.38	Reduced brightness, saturation, and hue discriminability at medium wavelengths
Tritanomalous	rare		Reduced brightness, saturation, and hue discriminability at short wavelengths
Dichromatism			
Protanopia	1	0.02	Gray at 494 nm neutral point; blue below, yellow above
Deuteranopia	1.1	0.01	Gray at 499 nm neutral point; blue below, yellow above
Tritanopia	0.002	0.001	Gray at 570 nm neutral point; green below, red above
Tetartanopia	rare		Gray at 470 and 580 nm neutral points; green between, red above and below
Monochromatism			
Rod	0.003	0.002	Gray
Neural			Gray
Blue-cone			Gray; some blue and yellow possibly seen

Data are from G. Wyszecki & W. S. Stiles, *Color science: Concepts and methods, quantitative data and formulas,* and F. A. Geldard, *The human senses.*
A complete description of each deficiency is complex and disputed in some cases. Briefly, a classification may include brightness sensitivity, a neutral point test, a Rayleigh match test, color discrimination ability, and perceived saturation.

NEUROCHEMISTRY
VISION, THEORIES OF
VISUAL PERCEPTION

J. L. FOBES

COLUMBIA MENTAL MATURITY SCALE

The Columbia Mental Maturity Scale (CMMS), developed at Columbia University, is designed for ages 3½ through 10 years and consists of 92 items, each printed on a 6- by 19-inch card. Each item measures pictorial or geometric classification skills. Items use the multimental format, which requires the child to point to the picture or geometric shape that does not belong with the other elements on the card. Items are grouped into eight overlapping levels, each consisting of 56 to 65 items. Examinees are routed to one of these levels based on their chronological age. Administration is individual and requires 15 to 20 minutes.

Although significant correlations have been found between CMMS and individually administered intelligence measures, the CMMS cannot be routinely substituted for these because it measures only one aspect of intellectual functioning.

INTELLIGENCE MEASURES
NONVERBAL INTELLIGENCE TESTS

G. J. ROBERTSON

COMMUNICATION PROCESSES

Communication is essentially a process by which the state of affairs at one place is transmitted to another place by symbolic means. The study of the process has engaged the collaboration of many different disciplines, from electrical engineering to philosophy, from biology to political science. The serious study of communication processes as a separate field of inquiry derived from the realization that different phenomena in each field have something in common, and that application of a unified communications model would be beneficial for each field.

The accepted general form of analysis of the process is due to the need for measuring transmission of information by communications engineers and consists of five steps: (a) the source (the original state of affairs); (b) the transmitter; (c) the channel; (d) the source of noise; and (e) the receiver, leading to the reconstructed state of affairs. The channel has a capacity to vary a certain kind and amount of data; thus the translation of the data into the form acceptable to the channel (coding) and the reverse process for use by the receiver (decoding) become central problems in the analysis and design of communication systems. Noise is defined as the origin of errors in transmission: The signal received by the receiver is a function of the original signal and noise.

The study of communication is divided into interpersonal and mass communication. The main difference is that, in interpersonal communication, the receiver can respond immediately, creating a network of several communication chains. Mass communication is not so responsive and each transmission link is separated; however, some technical advances blur this distinction, making mass communication responsive.

The study of interpersonal communication is the more complex of the two, because the units of communication are not easily differentiated. Theoretical approaches and aims of research in this field are heavily dependent on methods of research, observation, experiments, or field study.

The study of mass communication has been guided mainly by interest in content. Mass media—books, newspapers, broadcasting, plays, movies, and so on—come naturally in large units; the production is little amenable to experimental control or detailed analysis of communication structure.

Thus conditions and consequences are mainly macrosocial; large units of content are the natural targets. The basic method of communication research in mass media is content analysis, but no generally useful systems have emerged as they have in interaction analysis.

Although some work in content analysis has been directed toward microunits of communication, especially in studies applying the mathematical theory of information to measuring style, most techniques of content analysis use large units, either directly or by inference, such as values expressed or conflicts shown. This analysis may select the demographic traits of characters, the kind of plot in a novel or play, the length in column inches or printing of news articles, or the type of heroes in magazine biographies. Mass communication analysis is concerned primarily with the meanings, with what is in the channel, where the record is generally variable. Correspondingly, there has been less concern with the conditions under which the communication process occurred, which are harder to determine. The direction of research is therefore opposite that of interpersonal communication, and frequently evidence from content analysis is taken as proof of effects on the audience.

FACIAL EXPRESSIONS
PERCEPTUAL TRANSACTIONALISM

K. W. BACK

COMMUNICATION SKILLS TRAINING

Therapists of diverse theoretical positions have long realized that numerous clients with a variety of psychopathological complaints are deficient in interpersonal or communication skills. Persons diagnosed as schizophrenic, neurotic, or mildly mentally retarded, as well as alcoholics, those having marital difficulties, and parents with child management problems, have all been seen as having difficulties in interpersonal communication. In the period from 1970 to 1980, three major trends led to the increased emphasis on communication skills training as an important therapeutic and preventive tool. The first and perhaps most important trend was the disenchantment of many psychologists and other therapists with the medical model of therapeutic intervention. As A. P. Goldstein has noted in *Psychological skills training,* an increasing number of therapists turned to a different set of assumptions. Basic to this approach is the assumption that the client is suffering from a skill performance deficit and that the role of the therapist is to teach or train the client to perform the requisite set of skills.

The second trend was the increasing application of behavioral strategies to the treatment of a diversity of behavioral problems. It was quickly recognized that, before psychiatric clients could be deinstitutionalized or normalized, they would have to learn an extensive array of communication skills, such as conversational skills and job acquisition and maintenance skills. Behaviorists working with neurotic clients quickly learned that many of their clients required assertiveness training.

The third trend involved communication skills training that usually focused on two broad sets of interpersonal skills: skills in simply interacting with one or more persons and skills involving interpersonal or shared problem solving. Conversational skills training is directed toward the enhancement of an individual's ability to initiate and maintain conversations with other people. Communication skills training is a central component of most assertiveness-training procedures, because effective communication is seen as an important precursor to assertive behavior.

As the various communication skills training programs developed, it became increasingly obvious that there are perhaps a common set of communication skills that pervade the many and varied interpersonal activities in which people engage. Five basic sets of communication skills apply in most situations: (a) visually and physically responsive behavior, listener sensitivity to the communication of another, and congruent expression; (b) skills designed to encourage others to give information, including the use of silence, minimal encouragements, and questioning; (c) information-giving skills such as self-disclosure, feedback, and inferences; (d) skills providing communications designed to change the behavior of others, such as evaluation, requests, and advice; and (e) skills involved in shared problem solving—communication and problem-solving skills that are used to arrive at mutually satisfactory solutions to problems.

Most communication skills training programs are based on a similar model of training involving an instructional sequence, a practice sequence, and a generalization sequence. R. M. Gagné and L. J. Briggs in *Principles of instructional design* summarize many of the important characteristics of instruction included in various communication skills training programs.

Initial research in this area involved the demonstration that communication skills training methods produced significant increments in performance during training. A second wave of research involved the demonstration that increments in communication skills performance led to changes in other behaviors such as decreased delinquency, improved marital and parent–child relations, and increased academic performance. A subsequent concern of researchers was the demonstration that educationally based methods of communication skills training are superior to methods based on other assumptions, such as sensitivity training. Yet another focus of research has been the specification of the skills that should be included in communication skills training programs and the best methods of training the constituent skills. It can be concluded that communication skills training programs are effective; however, considerable research is required to develop programs that enhance the generalization of the skills to different situations and over time.

MAINSTREAMING (PSYCHOTICS)

D. R. Evans

COMMUNICATION THEORY

In an effort to bring some understanding to the complexities of human interactions, scientists have developed a number of theories dealing with communication processes. The study of communication includes a number of disciplines, each focusing on a variety of factors.

The *dimensional approach* attempts to delineate specific components or elements of communication. Typically these include a communication source, a message, a channel, and a receiver. Once these dimensions are deciphered, scientists then focus their attention on one or more of them to investigate how communication might be constructed.

The *process approach* focuses on the dynamics, both internal and external, to the sender and receiver of a message. Attitudes of the receiver toward the source and the messages transmitted are analyzed to ascertain how they influence the flow of communication. Conversely, perceptions of the source toward the receiver and the message being sent also are viewed as important dimensions for analysis.

The *functional approach* directs attention to the functions or purposes of communication. Three typical types of functions discussed by researchers include syntactics (the structural elements of communications), semantics (the study of meanings), and pragmatics (the practical consequences of communication).

B. A. Fisher discusses four major "perspectives" on the study of communication. The *mechanistic perspective* emphasizes the physical elements of communication, including the transmission and reception of messages along a linear schema starting with a source and ending with a receiver.

The *psychological perspective* primarily entails a conceptualization of communication based on behaviorism. Individuals are assumed to exist in a stimulus field containing a myriad of stimuli that may be attended to by using the various senses. An individual not only receives stimuli but also emits them as well. The concept of reinforcement is employed to explain the qualitative changes that can occur in the communication process. In addition, the way in which an individual processes the stimuli internally also is studied by more cognitively oriented behavioral researchers.

The *interactional perspective* has as its most basic characteristic the notion that "every form of social interactions begins or ends with a consideration of the human self." Thus it is a humanistic perspective focusing on communication as a vehicle for developing one's potential through social interaction. This perspective makes use of such concepts as social roles, cultural symbols, the search for self-understanding, the influence of self-disclosure in human interactions, and so forth. The self is the ultimate reference point from which meaning in communication is derived.

The *pragmatic perspective,* in line with Lin's functional approach, conceptualizes the study of communication as concentrating on outcomes and consequences. Further, these outcomes and consequences are viewed as occurring in an ongoing sequence of interactions. These sequences may then be grouped together into an interpretable pattern. Collections of patterns create an overall integrated system of sequences. At present the pragmatic perspective is the most popular, especially in the field of psychotherapy.

INFORMATION PROCESSING
PSYCHOLINGUISTICS

A. Barón, Jr.

COMMUNITY PSYCHOLOGY

Community psychology entered the lexicon of most psychologists in 1965, following a conference designed to establish a role for psychology in the United States' community mental health movement. The report of the conference called for psychologists to become active in the problems of society by assuming the role of social change agent and "participant–conceptualizer." The term *community mental health* refers to a broad array of mental health service delivery programs loosely thought of as a national social policy designed to reduce the incidence and prevalence of mental illness. This public health goal requires an epidemological rather than a clinical view of mental illness.

The roots of the community mental health movement may be found in many of the early traditions of American psychology, and in the first half of the twentieth century as the "mental hygiene movement." The Mental Health Study Act, passed by the U.S. Congress in 1955, established a Joint Commission on Mental Health and Illness. In 1966 the Division of Community Psychology was established within the American Psychological Association.

The community mental health and community psychology movement was originally driven by a desire to deinstitutionalize the mental hospital population and to extend the reach of services to underserved populations. Since then it has taken a more preventive stance—to keep people out of hospitals altogether by strengthening their social environment; to reduce the negative impact of social institutions on individuals; and to encourage and develop the strengths and competencies of individuals and communities.

The basic approach to community mental health has implied a critique of traditional clinical services that often wait passively for individual clients to seek out a mental health professional who will provide individual psychotherapy, and that isolate people in mental hospitals away from family, friends, jobs, and other community resources. The community mental health concept questions the effectiveness of such services and society's ability to reach large numbers of citizens in need. The concept suggests, instead, a social policy that emphasizes prevention of emotional distress.

The idea of primary prevention has served as a bridge for psychological research on the social conditions of life and how they affect the well-being of individuals. Originally, primary prevention research focused on populations with a high risk for mental illness and on a search for predisposing factors. Later, it included high-risk situations and events such as school transitions, alienating organizations, unemployment, racism, neighborhood resources, and social networks.

As community psychology developed in these later directions, a central theme has emphasized looking toward psychological knowledge that may be useful for social and public policy in fields as diverse as child rearing, law, education, geriatrics, social welfare, and a variety of other "social dilemmas."

CONCEPTIONS OF SOCIETY

Community mental health professionals have assumed that the major social issues confronting people with problems in living involve learning how to adjust, how to acquire new skills, and how to adapt to the demands of society. This classical view of mental health services suggests that society is and should be relatively stable. An alternative to the stability-oriented viewpoint has been put forth by community psychologists. In spite of the reality of individual problems in adjustment, it is suggested that social and community interventions should take place in a context that assumes change.

STYLE OF SERVICE DELIVERY

Mental health professionals have generally assumed that the proper mode of intervention is defined by the "doctor–patient relationship." Even those who reject a disease conception of human behavior tend to accept the medical style of intervention in which the "expert" or authority, who usually holds some sort of advanced degree, is responsible for diagnosis and prescription.

An alternative style of intervention, the *seeking mode,* has been developed by community psychologists to offer services or intervention somewhere other than in a mental health setting. Such services may be delivered by a variety of people, both professional and nonprofessional. It allows professionals to take on a variety of new roles, for instance, as consultants to others who deliver direct service such as college students, volunteers, teachers, or police officers. This mode of intervention lets the professionals help create new settings such as neighborhood drop-in centers for adolescents or the elderly, encourages the formation of self-help groups, and helps create alternative educational experiences, community betterment, and economic development and housing programs.

LEVELS OF ANALYSIS

A social/community perspective suggests that the "social order" may be thought of as a series of increasingly complex levels of organization. Each level serves as a point both for understanding and for intervention. Each level can operate according to variables and conceptions that are self-contained, although each level influences the other. To comprehend the social order community, psychology uses conceptions and principles for understanding individuals, groups, organizations, institutions, communities, and societies, as well as the relationships within and among levels of analysis and how they influence one another. However, far more than in other areas of psychology, there is emphasis on a broad social critique that may be thought of as the institutional, community, or social policy level.

THE AGENT OF TRANSMISSION

Beginning with the pioneering work of people such as Margaret Rioch, Ernest Poser, Robert Reiff and Frank Reissman, Jules Holzberg, Mort Bard, and Emory Cowen and others, the 1960s and 1970s brought recognition of the value of nonprofessionals in the mental health delivery system. A widespread acceptance evolved of the reality that many people who are earning their living in other than one of the mental health professions, such as students, housewives, or retired workers, can be helpful to others with problems in living.

A second consideration bringing recognition to nonprofessional mental health workers has been the observation that certain occupations place people in role relationships that allow them to influence the course of coping with crises for large numbers of people. Such helpers are not hired by the mental health system, nor are they volunteering their services as mental health workers. In fact, they probably do not even think of themselves as having anything to do with mental health. Acknowledging that most people do not seek out professional mental health workers and that help is often wherever one finds it, provides the social/community interventionist with an almost endless set of possibilities for extending influence.

A third way in which the other than professionally trained helpers have been encouraged is through the development of self-help groups. The ideology of the community mental health and community psychology movements has been quite consistent with the rise in legitimacy of self-help groups. In many ways, people coming together out of mutual concern is the ideal of a strength-based, preventively oriented mental health system.

A further extension of the agent of transmission of help involves the natural support systems. These are the less formal, less intentional helping relationships that exist among significant others. The obvious but heretofore largely ignored reality is that family, friends, church and neighborhood groups, clubs, and organizations make up a human fabric in people's lives through which problems in living are often filtered, solved, made more complicated, or altered. Those who take a public health, preventive, or policy-oriented view stress that most people never seek out professional or formal nonprofessional mental health service, but work out their problems living in their own natural support settings. Some of these settings will be effective, helpful ones, and others less so. Recognition of natural support systems has lead to a realization that by studying such settings it may be possible for helping professionals to learn important information about how the process of help proceeds.

CRISIS INTERVENTION
EFFECTIVENESS COMPONENTS OF PSYCHOTHERAPY
MAINSTREAMING (PSYCHOTICS)
NONPROFESSIONALS IN MENTAL HEALTH

J. Rappaport

COMPARATIVE PSYCHOLOGY

The behavior of animals is the subject matter of comparative psychology. Animal behavior research may have either or both of two basic goals. The first is to find principles and theories that govern animal behavior. These may be specific to one or a few closely related animal species, or they may have greater universality and include humans. The second possible goal is to understand if an animal's behavior in the laboratory or in its natural environment contributes to its overall evolutionary fitness, and if it does, how this increased fitness was achieved.

Pre–nineteenth-century literature and natural history are punctuated with assorted stories, anecdotes, and speculations about animal behavior, but until the late nineteenth century no one attempted any systematic and scientific study of animal behavior. Perhaps part of the reason was the assumed chasm between human and animal behavior expressed by the seventeenth-century philosopher René Descartes, who asserted that human behavior was governed by thinking and reasoning processes, while animals were mere creatures of mechanical reflexes and instincts.

This strict separation of animal and human behavior was brought into question by the theory of evolution, which represents the starting point for present-day comparative psychology. Charles Darwin and Alfred Russell Wallace independently discovered the basic tenets of the theory first presented publicly at a meeting of the Linnaean Society in 1858. The theory stated that all naturally occurring populations are constantly and gradually changing as a result of natural selection operating on individuals that vary according to their fitness. This process led to an enormous diversity in plant and animal forms, with one of those lines evolving into hominids and eventually humans. This evolutionary development had two important implications: (a) that elements of human mentality would be found in animals, and (b) that elements of animal mentality would be found in humans. Darwin, well aware of these implications, addressed the first in *The descent of man* and the second in *The expression of emotions in man and animals*. However, in his notebooks Darwin stated a subtler implication: If a scientific psychology of the human mind could be constructed, this would be evidence that the human mind and behavior were as subject to natural law as animal behavior. The underlying assumption was that if an animal's behavior was similar to one's own behavior in some particular setting, then one need only examine one's own mental events to find a good approximation of the animal's thinking.

The extravagant and often colorful interpretations of animal behavior inevitably provoked a counterreaction. C. Lloyd Morgan argued that only directly observable behavior could be used to develop theories and generalizations. Morgan's canon states that we should apply to animal behavior the simplest possible explanation consistent with observations. It was a relatively small step from the objective comparative psychology of Morgan to John B. Watson's behaviorism, which eliminated all reference to unobservable mental events and processes in animals. Morgan's rigorous version of comparative psychology and Watson's behaviorism were in large part responses to overzealous attribution of human intellectual abilities to animals. The case of Clever Hans is the most celebrated illustration of the problem.

Clever Hans: A Horse's Warning to Psychology

In 1904 a retired Berlin schoolteacher, Wilhelm von Osten, captured public attention with evidence that his horse, Clever Hans, could read, spell, and answer an astounding variety of arithmetic problems, including multiplication of fractions. Von Osten's technique was to assign each letter of the alphabet a number that was then presented to Hans on a blackboard. Thus instructed, Hans could respond to questions by tapping out answers with his right front hoof on a board. This case was different from many other similarly performing animals of the time, because von Osten was not deliberately cuing Hans about when to start and stop tapping. Hans' act puzzled numerous authorities who viewed it, and the mystery was not solved until a young psychologist, Oskar Pfungst, subjected Hans and von Osten to a series of systematic observations. Pfungst demonstrated that von Osten was unintentionally cuing the horse. Specifically, subtle changes in von Osten's breathing, facial movements such as flaring of the nostrils, and head movements were being used by Hans as signals to start or stop foot tapping. Pfungst calculated that movements of 1 mm at the edge of von Osten's wide-brimmed hat were detected by the attentive horse. Von Osten was shattered by this revelation, but never admitted that Hans lacked remarkable linguistic and calculating abilities.

THE HOW AND WHY OF ANIMAL BEHAVIOR

Suppose we observe a group of recently hatched goslings eagerly following their mother in single file. The most obvious and basic question that

could be asked is why the goslings are following. Some psychologists would say that the behavior, a result of imprinting, is obviously adaptive. It occurs in birds that have well-developed locomotor and sensory capabilities at or shortly after hatching. Also, the mother typically perambulates on the ground or water during the day, instead of flying. In the past, those goslings with genes predisposing them to follow their mothers closely were more likely to survive than goslings with a weaker following tendency. Furthermore, goslings that were highly precocial (i.e., relatively well developed at hatching) were better equipped to follow their mothers than those that were more immature and weak. Thus, through natural selection, some bird species developed a tendency to be precocial and to follow moving objects presented shortly after hatching.

An experimental psychologist might be somewhat dissatisfied with this evolutionary explanation of imprinting and therefore offer an alternative account. Laboratory experiments have demonstrated that precocial birds' imprinting to a mother or to some other prominent stimulus is formed within the first few hours after hatching; therefore, a rapid conditioning probably underlies the imprinting. One such theory states that the imprinting is acquired because retreating objects evoke a reduction in sympathetic activity and thus become positive reinforcers. According to another theory, moving stimuli are unconditioned stimuli that elicit unconditioned following responses in newly hatched precocial birds. After classical conditioning occurs, visual properties of the moving stimuli become conditioned stimuli and also elicit following.

These two accounts are examples of ultimate and proximate explanations. *Ultimate explanations* emphasize how the behavior contributes to the overall evolutionary fitness of an animal. Thus these explanations are closely associated with the function of a behavior in solving an animal's problems in its natural environment. In other words, ultimate explanations answer *why* a behavior occurs.

Proximate explanations address the question of *how* a behavior occurs. These explanations answer questions about a behavior's ontogenetic development, how it is affected by learning, and how it is affected by physiological, neurological, and other environmental variables. Proximate explanations incorporate mechanisms that exert effects within an individual's lifetime. In contrast, ultimate explanations incorporate mechanisms that have been affecting natural selection long into the phylogenetic past of the individual.

Both ultimate and proximate explanations are clearly legitimate scientific approaches to understanding animal behavior and in no way conflict with each other. Nevertheless, considerable heat and controversy have arisen in the past, caused by failure to appreciate the independence of these two basic approaches.

MIND, SELF-CONCEPTS, AND LANGUAGE IN ANIMALS

The possibilities and manifestations of mind and consciousness in animals were topics of active speculation in the early post-Darwinian period of comparative psychology.

The feat of communicating with animals through language has fascinated humans throughout history. Because chimpanzees are avid imitators of human actions, sign language would seem to be an obvious alternative to speaking. Although, in 1927, Robert Yerkes speculated about the possibility of apes learning a gestured language, it was not until 1966 that a determined effort was made to teach sign language to a chimpanzee. Beatrice and R. Allen Gardner began instructing a young chimpanzee, Washoe, in American Sign Language. The project was more successful than earlier attempts with vocalization. Within the first 3 years of the project, Washoe was reported to have acquired a reliable naming vocabulary in excess of 85 signs. She displayed some skill at putting signs together in short grammatical sentences, but never showed any comprehensive ability to produce sentences in diverse situations.

Washoe's widely publicized accomplishments were shortly followed by several other ape language projects. Francine Patterson successfully trained a young gorilla with American Sign Language, and David Premack taught a chimpanzee to produce and respond to sequences of plastic symbols that followed grammatical rules. Also, Duane Rumbaugh placed the chimpanzee Lana in 24-hour-per-day contact with a keyboard connected to a small computer. Each key displayed a geometrical symbol, termed a lexigram, that signified a word or concept. Lana learned to push the keys to answer questions and make requests in accordance with the grammatical rules of Yerkish, an artificial language created for the Lana project. More recently, Herbert Terrace found no evidence of grammatical understanding in a highly trained chimpanzee who acquired an extensive vocabulary; as the length of sentences increased, there was no corresponding increase in grammatical complexity, as would occur in the language development of the human child.

Are these well-educated apes showing rudiments of true language? It is now clear that much of the initial enthusiasm in attributing human language abilities to apes was incorrect or at least not justified by the evidence. However, it is equally clear that those who dismissed the apes' language-like abilities as mere tricks, or as instances of the Clever Hans error, were equally incorrect. An important set of abilities have been identified that are distinctly different from those described in previous animal learning literature.

One of the characteristics of the human mind is the ability for self-reflection or the ability to perceive oneself as a separate part of the environment. This seems to be a natural part of consciousness to us, but it is not evident that animals have this same self-reflective ability. Because we cannot ask the animal itself what it is thinking about, it might appear that questions about animals' self-awareness would be hopelessly impossible to attack experimentally.

G. G. Gallup, Jr., devised a simple, direct, and clever test for determining whether primates have self-awareness, or at least one type of self-awareness. Many animals respond vigorously to their mirror images. The question Gallup asked was whether a chimpanzee would eventually learn that the image was its own and not that of another animal. He answered the question by first giving chimpanzees extensive experience with a mirror. Then the animals were anesthetized and an odorless red dye painted on their upper eyebrow ridges and ear tops. The chimpanzees could not see these areas directly; they were only visible in the mirror image. After recovering from the anesthesia, the chimpanzees were reintroduced to the mirrors. When seeing their images, they began extensive manual exploration of the dyed areas on their heads. Similar results occurred in orangutans. However, these self-directed head movements did not occur in gorillas or gibbons and several monkey species. Further, chimpanzees reared in isolation also failed to increase their head-directed responses after the red dye application. The clear-cut, all-or-none nature of these results is interesting. They suggest a basic diversion with humans, chimpanzees, and orangutans constituting a self-aware group of primates while the remaining apes and the monkeys are not gifted with self-awareness.

Obviously, the research on cognitive comparative psychology briefly described in this section has much to discover. However, it is an exciting new direction. There is a substantial place for a renewed comparative psychology within the traditional framework of psychology.

ANIMAL COMMUNICATION
ANIMAL INTELLIGENCE
ETHOLOGY
IMPRINTING
LANGUAGE IN GREAT APES

J. E. KING

COMPETENCY IN PSYCHOLOGY

In a consumer-oriented society, competence is of frequent concern. People want a competently built and functioning automobile. They want television sets repaired by competent technicians. When a sink becomes clogged and overflows, a qualified plumber is called. Nowhere is the issue of competence more salient than when it involves physical, emotional, legal, and spiritual well-being. Society absolutely insists that those who provide health services be competent, and there is an assumption that those who teach these professionals are competent to do so.

There appear to be three components to a definition of competence. The first relates to having suitable abilities and skills; the second to being legally qualified; and the third to whether an individual's expertise entitles that individual to belong to a profession. Competence is an elastic term because it does not specify extent. Competence can include minimal, moderate, optimal, and superior qualifications. That is not, however, what is usually meant by competence. Most individuals who state they are seeking a competent physician are thinking of someone whom they expect to be highly competent. Thus in common usage, competence has taken on a strongly evaluative meaning. Similarly, most professional and licensing bodies bar individuals from practice if they are proven incompetent. When considering competency in given skills that require specific performance-based criteria, one can be on somewhat safe ground. When evaluating competency in the profession, the line is more difficult to draw.

For psychologists, competency is usually viewed from the perspective of professional service activities, usually clinical services. Minimal levels of competency are addressed directly by the American Psychological Association's *Standards for providers of psychological services,* professional standards review committees (PSRC), and third-party payer, quality-assurance reviews.

The definition of professional competence calls for a brief review of psychology as a profession. Professions must serve and be essential to society, have a large body of knowledge, and usually be granted some exclusive rights by society. Thus society generally recognizes a profession's right to control the dispensing of its expertise, and also expects the professional organizations to exercise control over their members. An occupation, however, uses more specific knowledge and consists of the possession of specific skills. One can assess those skills directly and employ specific criteria to determine adequate performance. Performance-based assessment requires proof that an individual has mastered a required number of skills. Although these skills may be attained in a school, many individuals learn them by working as apprentices and helpers until they reach a level of competence necessary to perform independent occupational duties.

Some people believe that the same should apply to professional psychologists. They believe that the ultimate criterion for evaluating competence of the practitioner is the client. They suggest that individual competence can be measured through role-playing tasks or recorded therapy sessions that can be evaluated, for example, by supervisors. They emphasize that competence be assessed through the evaluation of performance in therapeutic work. Competence evaluation should be in terms of the degree of benefit provided by the practitioner to the consumer.

Gerald Koocher discusses the meaning of competence and questions whether current credentialing methods in psychology can differentiate between minimal and superior competence. He points out that competence may vary as a function of a given professional service, suggesting that competence could perhaps be viewed as a state rather than a trait.

Daniel B. Hogan, writing about the definition of the practice of psychology and the regulation of psychotherapists, points out that competence is difficult to predict if one cannot adequately define the process of therapy. He believes that until we can specify a clear relationship between credentials and successful treatment, competence will be difficult to define.

Attempting to clarify some of the issues surrounding credentialing and competence, Arthur Wiens and John Menne point out that there are various important stages to establishing eventual competence. First, the graduate education and training program should provide the basic knowledge that all psychologists should possess. Although knowledge itself is an important component of becoming a psychologist, in itself knowledge does not guarantee competence. A concurrent stage is supervised experience, wherein others evaluate the trainee's acquisition of appropriate skills and ability to perform in a professionally competent manner. Within this context one must assume that a profession does have a broad body of knowledge, but that the possession of skills by itself is not sufficient to demonstrate competence. The purpose of licensing is to make sure that every applicant has obtained a basic body of knowledge in psychology and to evaluate the supervised training and experience of applicants, usually through endorsement procedures and often by means of additional written or oral examinations. Licensing also provides assurance to the consumer that incompetent or unethical practitioners will be dealt with properly. Enforcement of licensing depends on the strength of the investigative arm of the licensing board.

The national examination for professional practice simply verifies that candidates have acquired the basic knowledge of psychology. Although it is always possible that a candidate has not learned the required basic knowledge, it is also possible that the program from which an individual has graduated did not provide that basic knowledge sufficiently.

Some people believe that licensing and certification should be optional rather than mandatory. They contend that the public should have the right to seek out the services of a licensed practitioner or—*caveat emptor*—an unlicensed one, just as one can employ the services of a bookkeeper rather than a CPA.

One should differentiate between entry-level competence and continuing competence. Competent professional practice means keeping up with developments in one's field. Many licensing laws for psychologists require participation in continuing education activities, although it is difficult to assess whether this guarantees the assimilation of new knowledge by the participant. Some people believe that the time is soon approaching when professionals should be relicensed periodically. This would probably require developing assessment measures of basic knowledge and the maintenance of skills, as well as evidence of having assimilated new developments in one's specialty. Concern about competence has led to healthy questioning concerning current credentialing and licensing procedures. It has also led to a clearer definition of the content matter of the "core" of psychology, as well as clearer definitions of what constitutes doctoral education. Hopefully, as the profession and science of psychology continue to develop, the definition of competence will continue to encompass emerging trends.

AMERICAN PSYCHOLOGICAL ASSOCIATION
CAREER DEVELOPMENT
PROFESSIONAL ETHICS

N. Abeles

COMPETENCY TO STAND TRIAL

Competency to stand trial refers to provisions in the criminal law whereby defendants may be found incompetent, if it appears that they are unable to fully understand and participate in their defense. Although the criteria for a determination of incompetency vary somewhat from state to state, the constitutional standard was established by the U.S. Supreme Court in *Dusky v. United States* (362 U.S. 402, 1960), which held

It is not enough for the district judge to find that "the defendant is oriented to time and place and has some recollection of events," but that the test must be whether he has sufficient present ability to consult with his lawyer with a reasonable degree of rational understanding—and whether he has a rational as well as factual understanding of the proceedings against him.

Although the criteria established in this standard may seem clear, in practice their application has been fraught with misunderstanding and confusion. It is important to note that the concept of competency is quite different from responsibility or the insanity defense. Although competency is concerned with a defendant's present ability to participate in the defense, responsibility refers to a defendant's mental state at the time of the alleged crime and is used as a trial defense. It is possible to be competent to stand trial and still successfully raise the insanity defense. Conversely, a defendant initially found incompetent, but who later regained competency and was brought to trial, could be judged responsible for the crime.

COMPETENCY MOTIONS

The first step in the competency procedures is a motion to the court. Based on a Supreme Court decision (*Pate v. Robinson*), the principal actors in a trial—judge, prosecutor, and defense attorney—must raise the issue of competency, if evidence is presented that raises a "*bona fide* doubt" of a defendant's competency. The judge has the responsibility to hear the evidence—usually presented in the form of a motion for an evaluation of competency—and decide whether there is sufficient doubt to warrant an evaluation of the defendant.

Once a motion is granted, most courts commit defendants to an institution for periods of up to 60 days. The option available in most jurisdictions to evaluate defendants in jail or on an outpatient basis is exercised infrequently. Psychiatrists and, more recently, psychologists are asked to evaluate a defendant and provide the court with information about mental status.

The validity of the link between psychosis and incompetency has never been established. In fact, the validity of decisions about competency has never been studied. It is quite possible that psychotic defendants may well be competent to stand trial. The possibilities for incorrect decisions is in large part due to the fact that the criteria for evaluating competency are unclear.

The reliability of judgments about competency appears to be quite high. Evaluators trained to conduct competency interviews can usually achieve agreement in 90% or more of cases. However, high levels of reliability do not necessarily mean that the validity of the decision has also been established.

Another controversial issue is the relevance of amnesia as a criterion for finding a defendant incompetent. On the surface, it would seem evident that if a defendant cannot recall the circumstances of the alleged offense and cannot communicate facts or other information to an attorney, he or she is incompetent. However, the courts have usually held that amnesia by itself may not be a basis for a finding of incompetency. The courts have suggested that the evaluators must demonstrate that the amnesia has an effect on the defense. The disallowance of amnesia may in part reflect the concern lest amnesia be used by malingerers as a tactic to avoid or postpone a trial. With respect to amnesia, the courts have taken a strong position about the necessity of supporting information linking an observed symptom or behavior to the actual legal situation. However, the courts have usually not taken this position on other clinical issues.

One significant attempt to develop a standard measure to serve as a guide for evaluators of competency is the Competency Assessment Instrument (CAI).

DISPOSITION OF INCOMPETENT DEFENDANTS

Theoretically, the final decision about competency rests with the courts. A judge may use an evaluator's report or testimony as a basis for the decision, but is not bound to agree with it. In practice, however, the courts almost always accept the evaluators' conclusions and recommendations.

Once found incompetent, a defendant is usually committed to an institution for an indefinite period for treatment. If competency is regained, the trial resumes. In the past, this commitment has been for quite lengthy periods. This practice was challenged in the case of *Jackson v. Indiana,* in which it was held that an incompetent defendant "cannot be held more than the reasonable period of time necessary to determine whether there is a substantial probability that he will attain that capacity in the foreseeable future." This decision has led in some states to changes in the law setting time limits for treatment. The assumption is that if treatment is going to be successful, it will be so in a relatively short time, often with drugs or short-term psychotherapy.

PROPOSED CHANGES

Roesch and Golding have proposed several changes in the evaluation and treatment procedures. First, the motions requesting an evaluation should be specific, detailing the concerns that support the motion. If a motion is considered appropriate, they argue that most evaluations do not have to take place in an institutional setting. In a review of 10 studies they found that an average of only about 30% of evaluated defendants were found incompetent, owing in large part to the inappropriate use of competency evaluations. As a consequence, many cases could be evaluated in the jail or on an outpatient basis. In one of their studies, Roesch and Golding found that a 1- to 2-hour interview that focused primarily on legal issues could form the basis of an initial decision. Further, the conclusions reached as a result of these evaluations were in high agreement with the results of a more lengthy inpatient institutional evaluation lasting an average of 17 days.

Roesch and Golding also proposed that evaluations be conducted by panels made up of mental health and legal professionals, to allow for a more complete assessment of both legal and mental health issues. After the initial evaluation is completed and a court hearing held, competent defendants would resume legal proceedings. As for incompetent defendants, following a probable cause hearing to determine that the state has sufficient evidence in the criminal case, they would be subject to treatment. If a hearing found that a defendant might respond to treatment, either inpatient or outpatient treatment would be ordered for a period not to exceed 3 months.

For those defendants not likely to respond to treatment, or who did not respond during the 3-month period, Roesch and Golding propose that a provisional trial be held. This would be a full trial in which both prosecution and defense would present their cases. Such a trial has several advantages. It allows the defense to present evidence that might prove innocence and to respond to the prosecution's evidence. It also provides an opportunity for the continued observation and evaluation of a defendant who was presumed to be incompetent. This would be a real test of the validity of the initial decision. If at the end of the trial the defendant was found guilty, and it was clear that the defendant was incompetent, then the verdict would be set aside. These defendants could then be treated in the least restrictive setting and returned for trial at a later date, if competency was restored before the treatment limit had expired. However, if the defendant was seen to respond in a competent manner, the verdict would stand. The provisional trial would probably increase the understanding of the construct of competency and how it should be evaluated.

CRIMINAL RESPONSIBILITY
EXPERT TESTIMONY
FORENSIC PSYCHOLOGY
PSYCHOLOGICAL ASSESSMENT
PSYCHOLOGY AND THE COURTS
PSYCHOLOGY AND THE LAW

R. ROESCH

COMPLEXES

The concept of the "complex" has been used by a number of theorists associated with the psychoanalytic movement. It was introduced by Carl Jung, who is largely responsible for the development of the concept. Jung borrowed the term and the original formulation of the concept, however, from Theodor Ziehen. In studying word association, Ziehen observed that an individual's reaction time was often longer when a stimulus word relating to something unpleasant was presented. He reasoned that such a stimulus was associated with a feeling-toned complex of representations.

Jung went to work at the Burghölzli Hospital, where his chief, Eugen Bleuler, introduced the word association test and asked Jung to do research with it. Jung soon saw his task as the detection and study of complexes. He believed that complexes could be inferred not only from long reaction times but also from physiological reactions, such as the galvanic skin response and a change in respiratory pattern, to certain stimulus words. Jung regarded the complex as a constellation of associated ideas, affects, and images. The constellation can often be viewed as centering around an image corresponding to the idea or situation at the core of the complex. The idea or image central to the complex tends in some way to be incompatible with the habitual attitude of consciousness. Because the complex is relatively unconscious, and because some of the energy that would otherwise be available to consciousness is bound up in it, the complex acts as a somewhat autonomous part of the psyche.

Jung observed the interference of the complex with the performance of a task undertaken in consciousness. He conjectured that the complex could have similar effects on action and physiological processes in other situations. He viewed the complex as responsible for slips of the tongue, for gaps in our memory, for the forgetting of names, for accidents—in short, for the various phenomena that Sigmund Freud described in "Psychopathology of everyday life" as evidence for the operation of unconscious motives.

Jung believed that complexes could originate in several ways and that they took many forms. They could be produced by traumatic events or might arise as a result of moral conflict.

Jung regarded neurosis as a dissociation of the personality due to complexes and contended that the symptoms of the neurotic could be understood as the expression of complexes.

In the work of Freud the concept is assimilated to a theoretical system that emphasizes sexuality. In the work of Alfred Adler the concept is assimilated to a system that emphasizes the striving for power and the sense of inferiority that results from a lack of power. The one complex of importance to Adler was the inferiority complex, which he regarded as a characteristic feature of neurosis.

Jung developed the concept of the complex before his involvement in the psychoanalytic movement. After he became familiar with Freud's work and began an association of several years with Freud, he sought to relate his own ideas about the complexes to Freud's views of the unconscious.

ANALYTICAL PSYCHOLOGY
ARCHETYPES
WORD ASSOCIATION TESTS

R. W. COAN

COMPULSIVE PERSONALITY

The descriptive features of this personality include as prominent symptoms behavioral rigidity, emotional overcontrol, and a conscientious compliance with rules and authority. For this personality everyday relationships have a conventional, formal, and serious quality, and there is a conspicuous concern with matters of order, organization, and efficiency. This preoccupation with procedures and details interferes with the ability to view things from a broad perspective. The perfectionism, smallmindedness, and lack of spontaneity that characterize this disorder are manifest in cautiousness, indecisiveness, procrastination, and a tendency to be upset by deviations from daily habits and routines. Decision making is avoided or postponed, probably due to an inordinate fear of making mistakes. Considerable distress may be voiced concerning this indecisiveness and its consequent lack of efficiency. The characteristic air of austere and disciplined self-restraint precludes informality and the easy expression of feelings. Mindful of social hierarchies, these personalities tend to be authoritarian when directing subordinates and obsequious when reporting to superiors. In general, work and productivity take precedence over pleasure and informal relationships.

Theodore Millon outlines the following major diagnostic criteria for identifying this personality:

1. Restrained affectivity: is unrelaxed, tense, joyless, and grim; keeps emotional expression under tight control.

2. Conscientious self-image: sees self as industrious, dependable, and efficient; values self-discipline, prudence, and loyalty.

3. Interpersonal respectfulness: exhibits unusual adherence to social conventions and proprieties; prefers polite, formal, and correct personal relationships.

4. Cognitive constriction: constructs world in terms of rules, regulations, hierarchies; is unimaginative, indecisive, and upset by unfamiliar or novel ideas and customs.

5. Behavioral rigidity: keeps to a well-structured, highly regulated, and repetitive life pattern; prefers organized, methodical, meticulous work.

DIAGNOSTIC AND STATISTICAL MANUAL
PERSONALITY DISORDERS

T. MILLON

COMPUTED TOMOGRAPHY

Computed tomography (CT) scanning is a radiological technique that has revolutionized medical diagnostics. In particular, CT scanning of the head has eliminated the need for extensive use of more invasive neurodiagnostic techniques (e.g., angiography, pneumoencephalography) that involve risk of both morbidity and mortality. The technology of CT promises to alter the role of the clinical neuropsychologist, in that skills in lesion detection and localization will become increasingly devalued as CT scanning becomes almost universally available.

The CT technique, first introduced in Great Britain by European Musical Instruments (EMI) laboratories, offers a superb example of the application of computer technology to medical diagnosis. Computed tomography measures the attenuation of X rays passing through sections of the body from hundreds of different angles, and then combines this information to reconstruct pictures of the body's interior. With brain scanning, small differences in the density of cerebral structures can be measured and the basic anatomy of the brain can be viewed with startling clarity. Even more important, brain anomalies such as tumors or hemorrhages can be easily detected. The use of a contrast medium further enhances the images obtained. Multiple "slices" of the brain can be taken, permitting three-dimensional visualization of brain structure. Each slice can be photographed and stored in the patient's medical record; in addition, the data on each patient can be stored in the computer's memory and reconstructed at a later date. The use of serial CT scans enables the investigator to trace changes in brain morphology across time; this information may have both diagnostic and therapeutic implications.

Computed tomography holds great promise as a research tool as well as a diagnostic instrument. The technology can be used to assess structural brain changes associated with aging, dementia, alcoholism, and any number of neurological diseases. In addition, previously uncharted territory can be explored (e.g., recent studies have demonstrated increased ventricle size in disproportionate numbers of schizophrenics). Finally, CT scanning will permit precise correlations in those studies relating brain function to brain structure, leading eventually to a more adequate functional geography of the brain.

ALZHEIMER'S DISEASE
HALSTEAD-REITAN BATTERY
NEUROSURGERY

D. WEDDING

COMPUTER SOFTWARE

The term *computer hardware* refers to the configuration of electronic and electromechanical devices that make up a particular computer. *Computer software* refers to a program or sequence of logical commands that directs the computer hardware to perform a sequence of acts so that a particular task is accomplished. A compiler program allows the computer user to write a program in familiar terms that are then compiled into machine language, which in turn directs the computer to complete the required task. Perhaps the compiler programs best known to psychologists are FORTRAN and BASIC. A hybrid program is initially written in machine language and is loaded into the computer to perform a specific task. Thus a particular test program may direct the computer to present test items, store the testee's response, and, when the test is completed, total the score and print it out.

The most frequent use of computer software by psychologists is the use of specific sets of programs to perform statistical analyses. A second and perhaps more important involvement for psychologists is in the area of developing computer software to run psychological experiments. In simple terms, it is possible to use computers to present stimuli in particular orders and, if necessary, to transform and record responses to these stimuli. Another and potentially very fruitful area of computer software development is in cognitive psychology, where the concern is to develop programs (compilers) that perform cognitive tasks in the same way that individuals perform the same tasks. This area is important, because it may enable psychologists to understand both normal and abnormal cognitive processes.

COMPUTER-ASSISTED INSTRUCTION
INFORMATION PROCESSING

D. R. EVANS

COMPUTER-ASSISTED ASSESSMENT

Assessment is one of the most frequent and important functions of applied psychology. It involves the acquisition of behavioral and psychological data and the integration of that data to facilitate clinical decision making.

Problems with the traditional methods of clinical decision making have frequently been noted. These problems suggest that clinical decisions are frequently unreliable and invalid, and therefore of questionable utility.

One method of enhancing the reliability, validity, and utility of psychological assessment methods and, therefore, the decisions based on the derived data, is through computer-assisted assessment. Computer-assisted assessment can facilitate both the acquisition of data and the derivation of decisions based on that data. Computers can be used in the assessment process in several ways: (a) to present, score, and interpret psychological questionnaires; (b) to present items normally included in an interview and summarize responses to them; (c) to generate regression or Bayesian coefficients for diagnosis or other clinical decisions; and (d) to reduce and summarize observation-derived data.

Computers have been used to present, score, and interpret psychological tests, particularly the Minnesota Multiphasic Personality Inventory (MMPI). More recently, questionnaire items also have been presented on a video screen, with subjects indicating their responses on a keyboard.

The major advantages of computer-assisted questionnaire administration lies in increased and more reliable interpretive capabilities and speed. Computers can quickly score and provide interpretive summaries for a vast number of scales. They also can provide interpretations based on *profile analyses*—analyses derived from the relationships among scales, in addition to the absolute value of particular scales.

In computer-assisted interviews, patients are typically seated in front of a video console attached to a small computer. Interview items are presented on the screen and the patient indicates the response to each item (usually in a multiple-choice or true–false format) on a keyboard. The computer is programmed with interactive branching functions, so that the items presented are a function of prior responses by the patient.

Clinical decision making, such as psychiatric diagnosis, also can be facilitated by placing data acquired through traditional assessment methods into weighted regression or Bayesian equations. Instead of the typical clinical decision-making process involving subjectively based decisions, the values of preselected variables are entered into previously developed equations, and the resulting coefficients indicate probabilities of specific behaviors or diagnostic categories.

Computers also have been used to facilitate the reduction and analysis of observation data. Direct observation can result in a vast amount of data on the occurrence, duration, or conditional probability of many behaviors. However, observation data can be recorded directly through the use of automated data-recording systems. These are pocket-sized, battery-operated storage devices; the observer depresses particular keys when targeted behaviors occur. The data are stored in real time and can later be transferred directly to a computer for analysis. Although the automated data-recording technology has some idiosyncratic sources of error, it reduces observers' recording errors and enhances the speed and sophistication of analyses.

The benefits accruing to computer-assisted assessment are substantial. Compared to traditional methods of gathering and interpreting psychological data, computer-assisted assessment is faster, less costly in professional time, insensitive to interpersonal manipulations of clients, more consistent in presentation of stimuli to clients, less prone to recording errors, and more amenable to use by nonprofessionals. More important, although traditional clinical interpretation of questionnaire and interview data is limited to the knowledge and biases of the individual psychologist, computer-assisted interpretations can reflect the accumulated knowledge of a large number of psychologists, can encompass a greater number of variables, and can have a more substantive empirical foundation.

Several problems are associated with computer-assisted assessment. Perhaps the most significant is the issue of validity. Substantial efforts have been expended to develop standardized presentations of stimuli and output interpretations, such as interpretive statements based on MMPI profile analyses or etiological and treatment recommendations based on interactive interviewing.

CLINICAL JUDGMENT
COMPUTER SOFTWARE
COMPUTER-ASSISTED INSTRUCTION
DIAGNOSES

S. N. HAYNES

COMPUTER-ASSISTED INSTRUCTION

The development of personal computers that are small, powerful, and inexpensive has lead to increased interest in and accelerated use of computer-assisted instruction in the majority of educational institutions. These personal computers have the facility to control a number of external devices, such as audio- and videocassette recorders, and to handle a variety of input devices such as keyboard, light pen, and so forth. With this extensive range of options, the possibilities of computer-assisted instructional programs are no longer limited by the computer hardware itself, but by the ability of curriculum specialists and educators to configure and program the hardware.

Psychologists are involved in the development and evaluation of computer-assisted instruction programs at a number of levels that interact with one another. First, there is the interface between the learners' characteristics and the characteristics of the program. Questions concerning the impact of computer-assisted instruction on the users' level of anxiety, motivation, learning, performance, and recall are examples of these concerns. A second area of attention is curriculum development and programming. A variety of content areas and models of instruction have been developed and evaluated. These range through rote-practice, tutorial, simulation, and interactive models, with an extensive range of media. The third focus of attention of psychologists—particularly cognitive psychologists—has been toward the second goal. In short, the development of artificial intelligence models is extremely important in developing a fully interactional system, under which the computer reacts to the student's concerns, rather than the student's reacting to the limitations of the computer program. Many educational psychologists are examining the development and execution of evaluative paradigms to assess the cost-effectiveness of computer-assisted instruction.

COMPUTER SOFTWARE
INSTRUCTIONAL THEORY

D. R. EVANS

COMPUTERIZED ADAPTIVE TESTING

DEFINITION
Adaptive testing is defined in the *Standards for educational and psychological testing* as "a sequential form of testing in which successive items in the test are chosen based on the responses to previous items." Computerized adaptive testing (CAT), therefore, is adaptive testing facilitated by the use of computers. Strictly speaking, CAT is simply this procedure. However, the term *computerized adaptive testing* has been confused with other computer applications involving tests and testing procedures. Among these are computer-assisted testing, computer-based tests, computer-administered tests, and computer-generated test interpretation. What all of these procedures have in common is their basic reliance on computers. However, there are marked differences among them with respect to purpose and execution in the field of educational and psychological test-

ing. Although it may not be particularly germane to the specific topic of CAT, it may be worthwhile to review briefly the background that led to the current heavy use of and primary dependence on computers in testing.

ADAPTIVE TESTING

Adaptive testing is based on principles of sequential analysis first proposed by Wald. The primary objective of the technique is to produce a test, either in the cognitive or the affective domain, composed of items all within an individual's range of ability or the construct being measured, respectively. This is accomplished by first having a team of subject-matter experts or skilled item writers–test constructors develop a large pool of items relevant to the domain to be measured. The item in this pool should range from low difficulty level to high difficulty level in terms of proportion of testees answering the item correctly or proportion answering an item in a certain way. These procedures pioneered by Lord have since been modified and amended by him and other psychometricians.

COMPUTERIZED ADAPTIVE TESTING

As advances in computer hardware and software technology began to arise and as item response theory (IRT) as a method of item analysis began to be practiced, the stage was set for using computers in adaptive testing. The selection of which items to present to the testee and in which order are greatly facilitated by computer operations. Weiss, working at the University of Minnesota, is largely responsible for the initial developments in CAT. Recent developments and future proposals include the actual writing of the test items by the computer.

In its early applications, CAT was primarily limited to ability and achievement tests. Recent developments, however, have led to its application in noncognitive testing such as in the measurement of attitudes. In either case, the strategy is to present the testee with an item of moderate difficulty from the large pool to be followed in succession by an item selected by the computer from the same source, depending on the outcome of the previous answer. The items in the pool will have been calibrated through IRT methods, and the computer has been properly programmed. In this way the test can be said to "adapt itself" to the ability or the affective constructs of the testee, as the case may be. The desired outcome of CAT procedures is to develop a test that approaches equal validity and reliability throughout the range of content or constructs being measured.

ALGORITHMIC–HEURISTIC THEORY
EDUCATIONAL ASSESSMENT
HUMAN FACTORS
LIKERT SCALING
TEST STANDARDIZATION

P. F. MERENDA

COMREY PERSONALITY SCALES

The Comrey Personality Scales were developed to measure the following major personality characteristics, focusing on normal as opposed to pathological traits: trust vs. defensiveness; orderliness vs. lack of compulsion; social conformity vs. rebelliousness; activity vs. lack of energy; emotional stability vs. neuroticism; extraversion vs. introversion; masculinity vs. femininity; and empathy vs. egocentrism.

Other measures developed by Comrey as author or coauthor are the Achievement Motivation Scales, the Costello–Comrey Anxiety Scale, the Costello–Comrey Depression Scale, and a 35-variable, 216-item personality scale including neuroticism, dependence, compulsiveness, friend-

liness, and hostility. A "truth" scale was also included to indicate willingness of respondents to admit unflattering things about themselves.

MEASUREMENT
PSYCHOMETRICS

O. G. JOHNSON

CONCEPT LEARNING

A concept is a way of categorizing items and demonstrating which items are related to one another. In a concept learning task, certain attributes of the stimuli are related to one another according to a specified rule. Some concept learning tasks require subjects to discover the attributes, some require discovering the rule, and some require discovering both attributes and rule.

An attribute is a stimulus characteristic that can change from one presentation to the next. For example, a concept learning study may use stimuli that are either squares or circles, small or large, and pink or blue, thus varying the three attributes of shape, size, and color. In a concept learning task, at least one stimulus attribute is relevant. When an attribute is relevant, subjects must say "yes" when the attribute has one value (e.g., square) and "no" when the attribute has another value (e.g., circle). A concept learning task also may have a number of irrelevant attributes that are not related to a particular concept. If, for example, color and size are irrelevant attributes in a particular task, subjects must learn to ignore them in order to learn a concept.

A rule tells how the attributes must be combined. The two most common kinds of rules are called *conjunction* and *disjunction*. The conjunction rule uses the word *and*, as in "all figures that are square *and* pink." The disjunction rule uses the word *or*, as in, "all figures that are square *or* pink, or both."

From about 1930 to about 1970, concept learning research focused on identifying variables that affected the rate of concept learning. Some of these variables include type of rule (e.g., conjunction or disjunction), type of task (e.g., attribute discovery, rule discovery, or complete learning), number of relevant attributes, salience of the relevant attribute, and number of irrelevant attributes.

One finding that attracted particular attention is that subjects learn concepts faster when they are given positive examples (e.g., they are told that a pink square is an example of the concept) than when they are given negative examples (e.g., they are told that a blue circle is *not* an example of the concept).

THEORIES OF CONCEPT LEARNING

Many theories of concept learning are based on the idea that people try to solve concepts by making up hypotheses or tentative guesses and then testing these hypotheses.

NATURAL CATEGORIES

An important development in research on concepts involves natural categories or real-life concepts. Eleanor Rosch, whose work is summarized in Rosch and Lloyd's *Cognition and categorization*, pointed out that concept learning tasks use neatly defined, discrete attributes that are combined arbitrarily. In contrast, according to Rosch, real-life concepts are structured differently.

Rosch proposes that people decide whether an item belongs to a particular category by comparing that item with a prototype or best example for that category. For instance, a robin is highly prototypical of the category *bird*, whereas a penguin is a nonprototype.

Rosch and her colleagues discovered several characteristics of prototypes:

1. Prototypes are supplied more often than nonprototypes as examples of a category.

2. Prototypes can be substituted for a category name in a sentence, whereas nonprototypes cannot.

3. Prototypes serve as reference points to which other items are compared.

4. Prototypes are more likely to have attributes in common with other members of a family resemblance category. In a family resemblance category there is no single attribute that is shared by all members of a category, yet each member has at least one attribute in common with some other member of the category.

5. Categories organized on the basis of prototypes are learned more quickly than categories based on nonprototypes.

ABSTRACT INTELLIGENCE
COGNITIVE LEARNING STYLES
DISCOVERY LEARNING

M. W. MATLIN

CONCEPTUAL LEARNING AND DEVELOPMENT

A concept consists of an individual's organized information about one or more things—objects, events, ideas, processes, or relations—that enables the individual to discriminate a particular thing or class of things from other things or classes of things, and also to relate it to other things or classes of things. Concepts as mental constructs are the critical component of a maturing individual's continuously changing and enlarging cognitive structure. As a concept is learned at higher levels of understanding, it is used increasingly in four ways: (a) to identify newly encountered examples and nonexamples of the concept, (b) to understand principles involving the concept, (c) to understand taxonomic and other hierarchical relations of which the concept is a part, and (d) to solve problems requiring understanding of the concept.

The word *concept* not only designates mental constructs of individuals but also the meanings of words and other symbols accepted by social groups who speak the same language. J. B. Carroll related concepts, words, and word meanings this way: Words in a language can be thought of as a series of spoken or written entities. There are meanings for words that can be considered a standard of communicative behavior shared by those who speak a language. Finally, there are concepts—that is, classes of experiences formed in individuals either independently of language processes or in close dependence on language processes.

Knowledge regarding the learning of concepts, the course of conceptual development from infancy through adolescence, and individual differences has advanced rapidly. This has made possible the formulation of an integrated set of principles of conceptual learning, development, and individual differences.

1. *Four successively higher levels of the same concept are attained in an invariant sequence.* There are four levels of concept attainment, and certain mental operations are involved in learning each level. The four successively higher levels of understanding are *concrete, identity, classificatory,* and *formal.* A concept is learned at the concrete level when the individual first recognizes a particular example of a concept as being the same as one experienced earlier. For example, a young child attends to a clock on the wall, discriminates it from other objects in the environment,

represents the image of the clock internally, maintains the image, and after a period of time attends to the clock and recognizes it as the same thing attended to earlier. Attainment of a concept at the identity level is inferred by the individual's recognition of an object as the same one previously encountered when the object is observed in a different situational context or from a different spatiotemporal perspective, or when it is sensed in a different modality such as hearing or seeing. Generalizing the identity of objects and processes across environmental contexts is the new mental operation postulated to emerge as a result of learning and maturation that makes attainment at the identity level possible.

Attainment of a concept at the classificatory level is inferred when the individual recognizes two different examples of the same concept as being equivalent. Generalizing that at least two different things are equivalent is the new mental operation that makes attainment of the classificatory level possible.

Individuals demonstrate that they have attained a concept at the formal level when they can correctly identify examples and nonexamples of a concept, name the examples, discriminate and name the defining attributes of the concept, give a socially accepted definition of the word that represents the concept, and evaluate how examples of the concept differ from examples of other concepts.

Having the name of the concept and the names of the defining attributes promotes concept learning. The facilitative effects of being given the names of the concepts and the attributes have been interpreted as being due to mediating between the environmental input and the individual's responding, enhancing the distinctiveness of the concept examples, and enhancing the individual's sensitivity to the defining attributes of the concept. Although the preceding theorists do not agree regarding the internal mechanisms, it is clear that having the name of the concept and the names of the defining attributes aid the learner in perceiving intraclass similarity and discriminating interclass differences.

Providing the learner with a concept definition stated in terms of its defining attributes facilitates concept learning. When the learner also is presented with examples and nonexamples, the definition is more effective when given before the examples and nonexamples. The definition is necessarily stated in terminology that the learner comprehends. Having an appropriately stated definition reduces the number of examples and nonexamples required for learning the concept.

Experience with concept examples and nonexamples is essential for learning to classify correctly. The examples and nonexamples are most effective when they are presented simultaneously to the learner, when the examples differ from one another in their nondefining or variable attributes, and when the nonexamples differ from the examples in a minimum number of defining attributes of the concept. The examples are most facilitative when they range from easy to difficult and are matched to the nonexamples on the basis of having the same nondefining, or variable, attributes. The number of matched sets of examples and nonexamples, called *rational sets,* required for correct classification depends on the number of defining attributes the concept has, its abstractness, the ability of the learner, and the amount of other information presented. A probabilistic adaptive strategy for determining the number of examples and nonexamples that particular individuals need for learning particular concepts is less effective than advising learners regarding their learning needs, or enabling the learners to control the number of examples and nonexamples. Experiencing a proper number of rational sets of examples and nonexamples enables the learner to avoid errors of classification due to overgeneralization, undergeneralization, and misconception.

Enabling the learner to gain an overview of the organizational structure of a group of related concepts that are to be learned facilitates the subsequent learning of the individual concepts. Learners profit from recognizing that there are superordinate, subordinate, and coordinate concepts when learning the concepts that are parts of taxonomies, such as of the plant or animal kingdom. They also profit from recognizing that the concepts of other hierarchically organized groups, such as the basic process concepts of science, have dependency and parallel relationships.

Learning an algorithmic strategy for classifying instances as examples or nonexamples speeds concept learning. The algorithmic strategy calls for the learner to check whether the instance has each and all of the defining attributes of the particular concept. Arranging for the learner to gain feedback throughout the concept learning sequence is a final facilitative external condition of concept learning.

2. *Attainment of the four successive levels of the same concept continues for years, and any three successive levels develop concurrently for one or more years.*

3. *Attaining the successively higher levels of concepts is accompanied by increased understanding of principles and taxonomic relations and by more advanced problem-solving skills.*

As an indication of the different levels of concept understanding, students who have achieved mature functioning of the concrete or identity levels as their highest performance still are not able to understand related principles and taxonomic relations in which the concepts are embedded, or to solve problem-solving exercises requiring understanding of the concepts. Students who have achieved a mature classificatory level understand easy principles and taxonomic relations and also are able to solve simple problems. Mature functioning at the formal level, in comparison with the classificatory level, is accompanied by far greater understanding of principles, taxonomic relations, and problem-solving skills.

4. *Individuals of the same age vary in their levels of concept attainment.* Differences among individuals of the same age are large with respect to their attainment of concepts.

5. *Intraindividual variability in concept achievement becomes increasingly differentiated according to content fields during the elementary school years.*

Concepts are learned at a more rapid rate from age 6 to 9 than during later years, but from age 6 to 9 the various concepts are learned at different rates and with inconsistent gains from one year to the next. From age 10 to 12 there are more consistent gains from year to year, but the rate of learning concepts to successively higher levels decelerates. During years 13 throught 18 the rate of learning continues to decelerate, and some individuals achieve the formal level of many concepts, especially the concepts in subject fields in which they receive formal instruction in school.

Almost complete integration according to the academic subject fields taught in the intermediate grades occurs from age 10 to 12.

It is well to recognize that differences among individuals in their rate of concept development and intraindividual variability in concept achievement are so large that accurate predictions about a maturing individual's level of concept achievement cannot be made based on chronological age.

ABSTRACT INTELLIGENCE
CONCEPT LEARNING
DISCOVERY LEARNING
SCHOOL LEARNING
STIMULUS GENERALIZATION

H. J. KLAUSMEIER

CONDITIONED REFLEX THERAPY

Conditioned reflex therapy is based on the work of Ivan Pavlov, V. M. Bechterev, John B. Watson, and their followers. Neurotic behavior is seen as learned behavior. Insights, and interpretations of dreams, of symptoms, and of behaviors, are viewed as having no therapeutic utility. Treatment in conditioned reflex therapy is concerned only with the present behavior of the patient: Fix the now and we change the effects of the past.

Excessive inhibition is the basis of neurotic behavior. Although a certain amount of inhibition is necessary for living in society, modern training goes far past the necessary inhibitions in teaching children. These modes of behavior are learned through the threat of punishment, the denial of parental love, or the withdrawal of social approval—all fear-inducing stimuli. The result is the molding of inhibitory—and hence emotionally unhealthy—personalities. The problem of attaining emotional health is one of retraining—that is, of reconditioning—faulty emotional attitudes. The objective of treatment is the disinhibition of the patient.

Assertiveness training is helped considerably by six techniques:

1. Feeling talk; the deliberate utterance of spontaneously felt emotions. This includes emphatically expressing friendly feelings.
2. Facial talk; expressing and showing emotions.
3. Deliberately contradicting and attacking when one disagrees with others.
4. Using the word "I" deliberately and frequently.
5. Expressing agreement when you are praised.
6. Improvising more and planning less.

Conditioned reflex therapy has shown excellent results with a wide spectrum of neurotic disorders: anxiety, phobias, shyness, migraine, psychosomatic disorders, assertion difficulties, varied sexual dysfunctions, and work blocks of creativity.

COGNITIVE BEHAVIOR THERAPY
CONDITIONING
PSYCHOTHERAPY

A. SALTER

CONDITIONING OF COMPENSATORY REACTIONS

When the unconditioned stimulus (UCS) is a drug, the nature of the conditioned response (CR) is frequently opposite of that of the unconditioned response (UR). For example, epinephrine produces a decrease in gastric secretion as the UR, while the CR produces an increase in gastric secretion. Similar examples led to the idea that, following drug administration, a compensatory reaction occurs to counteract the physiological effect of the drug, as a sort of homeostatic adjustment. With repeated administrations, the compensatory mechanism is conditioned to attendant stimuli, but this conditioning holds only for certain drugs—for example, not for marijuana, but possibly for alcohol.

Research with rats suggests that classical conditioning plays an important role in drug addiction. According to Siegel, elated feelings or other positive effects of morphine are not conditioned to the cues of administration. Instead, a compensatory mechanism is conditioned to the cues present during injection. With repeated injections, the compensatory effects become stronger and occur earlier in time. Such conditioning counteracts the expected effects from taking the drug (conditioned tolerance), and the person must take larger and larger doses to achieve the expected effect.

Siegel's results with rats support the notion that drug tolerance is conditioned to the stimuli present during drug administration. In this research, analgesia to morphine is assessed by measuring the rat's latency to lick one of its paws that has been placed on a warm surface. Tolerance to morphine (increase in pain) is reflected in a reduction in latency with successive trials. That this is a conditioning effect is supported by the following findings of Siegel. The tolerance effect, like other conditioned responses, undergoes extinction if the drug (UCS) is omitted over trials by replacing it with placebo injections. A preconditioning exposure to the CS retards development of morphine tolerance just as it retards conditioning in general (latent inhibition). Partial reinforcement (presenting the CS without the UCS, say, on 50% of the trials) retards the growth of morphine tolerance just as it retards classical conditioning, even when the total number of drug trials is the same as for a 100% group. Conditioning of the compensatory mechanism has considerable generality, occurring with glucose, epinephrine, atropine, morphine, pentobarbital, and insulin. The immediate effect of insulin is to lower glucose levels in the blood, which causes the pancreas to release an enzyme that destroys insulin so that glucose can return to normal. Presumably, the pancreatic response is what becomes conditioned. In a series of experiments, Siegel ruled out possible alternative explanations of this conditioned insulin effect.

Hinson and Siegel have found inhibitory conditioning in rats in the development of tolerance to pentobarbital-induced hypothermia. During an initial discrimination phase, the positive conditioned stimulus (CS^+) was associated with the administration of pentobarbital and the negative stimulus (CS^-) with the administration of saline. Subsequently, half the rats received pentobarbital in the presence of CS^+ and half received it in the presence of CS^-. The CS^+ group showed the most tolerance (least drug effective), and the CS^- group showed the least tolerance (inhibitory conditioning) compared with appropriate controls. Nothing but a conditioning interpretation seems to fit these data.

The conditioning of drug tolerance can account for the development of drug addiction. When the compensatory mechanism is well conditioned to the cues associated with taking morphine and the cues are present but the morphine is not, then the compensatory reaction takes place with nothing to counteract its effects. Thus the compensatory effect makes the person sick (withdrawal symptoms), explaining the strong motivation to take the drug (addiction process).

The conditioning model of drug tolerance also provides an explanation of deaths among heroin addicts from an "overdose" even though they rarely take more heroin before they die than on other occasions. Addicts usually take the drug in the same place and around the same people so that the environmental conditioned stimuli come to elicit the compensatory physiological reaction that reduces the effect of the heroin. However, if the addict takes heroin at a different time and in a different place, there are no conditioned stimuli to elicit the compensatory response. Thus the regular dose of heroin has a much greater effect, and this could cause death.

The data for human beings seem to be consistent with the rat data and the preceding analysis. Drug addicts in the different environment of a hospital or prison find that in a week or two they can kick the habit. However, soon after they return to the old environment in which the habit was formed, at least 95% are back on the drug. In contrast, veterans who became drug addicts in Vietnam, and who were hospitalized for a short time in this country, returned to a different environment than the one in which the compensatory mechanism was conditioned. After many months only 7% of these veterans went back on the drug.

This analysis suggests that the way for a drug addict to go off drugs is to change the environment in which he or she lives as much as possible.

ANTOBUSE—CLASSICAL CONDITIONING
CHEMICAL BRAIN STIMULATION

CONTROLLED DRINKING
DRUG ADDICTION
DRUG USERS' TREATMENT
HABITUATION
REINFORCERS

M. R. DENNY

CONDUCT DISORDER

DEFINITION: ISSUES AND LIMITATIONS

The term *conduct disorder* (CD) has both descriptive and diagnostic meanings in psychology. At the descriptive level, the term is used, often loosely, to refer to a cluster of socially disruptive behaviors exhibited by children or adolescents. These behaviors, which are considered unacceptable in most social contexts, include noncompliance, defiance, verbal and physical aggression, overactivity, impulsivity, lying, stealing, truancy, vandalism, and substance abuse. At the diagnostic level, CD is used to refer to a specific psychiatric disorder that presupposes the presence of a set of fairly well defined behavioral symptoms and that can usually be made only if certain criteria are met (e.g., age and duration of symptoms). The fourth edition of the *Diagnostic and statistical manual (DSM-IV)* defines CD as "a persistent pattern of conduct in which the basic rights of others and major age-appropriate societal norms or rules are violated" and notes that this pattern is usually present in multiple settings.

There is strong empirical evidence for the validity of "conduct disorder" both as a descriptive and diagnostic label. Taxonomic studies of child and adolescent psychopathology have consistently isolated two core syndromes that are commonly referred to as aggression and delinquency. Although they generally apply to children ages 6 to 16 years, these syndromes are particularly reliable for boys. Taxonomic findings have their parallel in classification systems of childhood disorders. The *DSM-III-R* described aggressive antisocial behavior in children and adolescents under the broad diagnostic class of disruptive behavior disorders, a class that comprises attention deficit hyperactivity disorder (ADHD), oppositional defiant disorder (ODD), and CD. Oppositional defiant disorder is characterized by repeated disobedience, negativism, provocation, and opposition to authority. Conduct disorder is characterized by repeated violations of the basic rights of others and of major social rules. Conduct disorder often includes important features of ODD and ADHD but is a more severe disorder than ODD, in which most symptoms can have major legal repercussions. Empirical support for the *DSM-IV* distinction between ODD and CD also is available.

In spite of empirical support for its validity, it is still unclear whether *CD* refers to a single multifaceted disorder that changes in its manifestations as a function of development or to two or more distinct disorders with presumably different etiologies and developmental courses. Although taxonomic and diagnostic studies have long sought to describe specific subsets of CDs (e.g., the *DSM-IV* distinguishes between solitary aggressive, group, and undifferentiated CD), empirical support for such distinctions is weak. Recent evidence suggests that, in a majority of aggressive, antisocial children, conduct problems begin relatively early in life, manifest themselves in a variety of ways in childhood and adolescence, and often continue well into adulthood, although desistance can occur at any time along the path of development. Support for this unitary view comes from findings that ODD has an earlier age of onset than CD and that almost all youths with CD have a history of ODD, whereas only half of all children with ODD later manifest CD. Support also comes from the fact that reliable child predictors of adolescent or adult antisocial behavior have been difficult to find. Specific childhood behaviors are relatively poor predictors of later dysfunction. Rather, the number of antisocial problems exhibited in late adolescence or early adulthood is best predicted by the number of conduct problems exhibited in childhood.

DIMENSIONS OF CONDUCT DISORDER

Prevalence

Large-scale epidemiological studies conducted in several Western countries indicate that conduct problems in general have a prevalence rate that ranges from 8 to 12%, and that CD accounts for about 50% of that, with a prevalence rate of approximately 5%. Although very high, these figures are based on studies that relied on information provided by a single source to establish the presence of disorder. These figures do not imply that all children who meet statistical or diagnostic criteria for CD based on one source of information present severe problems in multiple settings, as evidence suggests that agreement between informants is usually low.

Gender Differences

Conduct disorder is more prevalent in boys, having a ratio of 3–4 : 1 in childhood and 2.5 : 1 in adolescence. This reduced ratio in adolescence reflects the fact that CD has a later age of onset in girls. The disorder appears around age 12 or 13 in girls, but around age 9 or 10 in boys. However, gender differences in prevalence may be diminishing, as recent evidence indicates that CD has dramatically increased in prevalence over the past decades in both genders.

Ethnic Differences

The prevalence of CD in childhood has not been found to be reliably associated to ethnicity. However, American and British studies indicate that serious CD is more prevalent in Black than in White adolescent males, even after controlling for group differences in socioeconomic conditions and police and court dispositions. More specifically, the association between CD and ethnicity becomes stronger as the seriousness of the offenses increases from minor delinquent acts to violent crimes and is generally stronger in studies that relied on official statistics rather than on self-report data. Blumstein et al. have shown that ethnic differences in prevalence rates reflect differences in participation in delinquent or criminal acts rather than frequencies of offending (i.e., larger percentages of the adolescent Black male population become offenders than of the White population). However, once they become offenders, Black males are not likely to commit a larger number of offenses per year than their White counterparts. The same is true of recidivism. A larger number of Black adolescents are arrested at least once, but rates of rearrest are comparable for Black and White offenders.

Stability, Chronicity

The majority of children with CD do not become high rate offenders in adolescence or criminals in adulthood. However, children, particularly boys, who present several behavior problems at an early age and in more than one setting often continue to manifest such problems over time. Conduct disorder shows little spontaneous remission. Rather, the disorder tends to remain stable or worsen over time and to show increased resistance to change with age, as illustrated in studies that have looked at continuities between childhood conduct problems and adolescent and adult adjustment.

Comorbidity

Most children with CD present additional psychosocial dysfunctions. The most common is ADHD. Shapiro and Garfinkel found that 45% of children in a sample of 7- to 13-year-old Americans who qualified for a diagnosis of ODD or CD also qualified for a diagnosis of ADHD. A comparable degree of comorbidity with ADHD has been reported by Offord and coworkers in a longitudinal study conducted in Canada: 59% for boys and 56% for girls ages 4 to 11, and 30% for boys and 37% for girls ages 12 to 16. ADHD is a comorbid characteristic that clearly adds to the severity of CD. Children who qualify for a dual diagnosis of CD and ADHD present aggressive, antisocial behaviors that are more numerous and severe and that are more likely to persist over time than children who receive a single diagnosis of CD. Recent evidence suggests that ADHD may exacerbate the behavioral problems of children with CD at least in part through its significant association with academic underachievement and failure.

Conduct disorder also has been found to be associated with diagnostic cofeatures such as depressive symptomatology and depression, social withdrawal, and somatization disorder. Although the degree of comorbidity of CD with these other disorders depends on the reference population, the level of symptomatology required to establish a dual diagnosis, and the age and gender of the child, Offord et al. noted that comorbidity affected the majority of CD cases in their longitudinal sample, with the exception of adolescent boys ages 12 to 16. Adolescent girls were particularly at risk, as more than 33% of them qualified for two diagnoses in addition to CD.

Costs

Conduct disorder gives rise to considerable psychological, social, and economic costs, such as those associated with mental health services; remedial education; law enforcement; harm to self, others, and property; substance abuse; and teen parenthood.

DEVELOPMENTAL TRAJECTORIES

Longitudinal studies indicate that a distinction should be made between adolescents with CD with early or late-onset histories of behavior problems. Early starters first present oppositional and aggressive problems between the ages of 4 and 8 in the context of the family. From this context, the developmental trajectory of early starters leads to the acquisition of coercive behavior patterns that become associated with interactional difficulties with teachers and peers and with academic problems in the early school years. The typical career of early starters is marked by high innovation and low remission rates. Over time, they tend to engage in novel and more serious antisocial acts and are slow to desist from their deviant path. In more extreme cases, early starters become chronic juvenile offenders (i.e., offenders involved in multiple police arrests and convictions). Although they only represent approximately 6% of the delinquent population, chronic offenders are responsible for 50% of all juvenile offenses. More generally, the early onset of behavior problems is the best predictor of aggression and antisocial conduct in later childhood, adolescence, and adulthood and of related problems such as violence, theft, and substance abuse.

Late starters, in contrast, do not present conduct problems before late childhood or early adolescence and do so usually in the context of a deviant peer group rather than of a dysfunctional family. They tend to limit themselves to generally nonaggressive antisocial acts, such as theft, truancy, and substance abuse and to have minimal academic skills, although poor academic achievement is commonly associated with CD in adolescence. Late starters have lower innovation and higher remission rates than early starters and, consequently, present problems that are usually more transient and somewhat less severe in nature.

FROM CONDUCT DISORDER TO ADULT DYSFUNCTION

Although research to date has not described anything that would amount to developmental trajectories from childhood or adolescent CD to adult criminality or psychopathology, there is clear evidence of continuities of dysfunction over time. The difficulties of children with CD not only remain evident over time, but also become compounded by additional problems in adolescence, such as school drop-out, substance abuse, and teenage parenthood, and in adulthood. In a large-scale epidemiological study, Robins et al. found that individuals who presented three or four symptoms of CD in childhood met criteria for a diagnosis of antisocial personality as adults in 1% of cases if symptoms began after age 12, and in 3% if they began before age 6. These figures increased considerably as the number of symptoms increased, so that individuals with eight or more CD symptoms in childhood received a diagnosis of antisocial personality as adults in 48% of cases if symptoms began after age 12, and in 71% if they began before age 6. These findings show clearly that not all children with CD grow up to be adults with antisocial personality disorder, but that the younger and the more aggressive and antisocial a child is, the less likely he or she is to revert to a pattern of nondeviant conduct.

This bleak picture is made bleaker by findings that childhood CD can have adult correlates other than antisocial behavior. Robins and Price reported that adults had a higher probability of meeting criteria for almost all adult psychiatric disorders if they presented CD symptoms before age 15. Besides antisocial personality, it would appear that childhood CD is reliably associated with substance abuse in adulthood as well as with mania, schizophrenia, and obsessive–compulsive disorder. Not surprisingly, CD also predicts unfavorable outcomes, such as unemployment, marital discord, and premature death.

Finally, the adverse consequences of childhood CD are dramatically emphasized by findings that the stability and chronicity of aggressive antisocial behavior can extend beyond individuals, as the disorder is often reproduced across generations. In a longitudinal study of aggression, Huesmann et al. found that a child's aggressive and antisocial behavior at age 8 was best predicted not by the aggressiveness of the child's parent in adulthood but by the aggressiveness of the child's parent when that parent was age 8. Although this study did not specifically investigate causal processes, this result suggests that more than modeling and reinforcement are involved in the transmission of CD across generations.

RISK FACTORS

Considerable research has shown that CD, especially of early onset, is associated with a host of risk factors ranging from biological to sociological characteristics. The available evidence must be interpreted with caution, however, as most studies have reported associations, rather than demonstrated causal relations.

Individual Characteristics

Genetic and temperamental differences have long been assumed to play a role in the development and maintenance of CD. Controversy surrounds the issue of genetic influences. Debate focuses on both conceptual and methodological issues and hinges on the nature of what may be inherited if there is genetic transmission of propensities to aggressive antisocial conduct and criminality. The debate aside, however, there is general agreement that many early starters present behavioral problems and excesses from a very early age. Studies of temperamental differences indicate that infants can be distinguished along behavioral dimensions such as difficultness, unadaptability, and resistance to control. Longitudinal work by Bates and his colleagues has shown that adverse temperamental characteristics predict negative control interactions with mothers at age 2, which in turn predict conduct problems in boys and girls at age 8. More generally, developmental evidence supports the contention that, in families marked by limited child-rearing skills and multiple stresses, such as parental psychopathology, marital discord, and socioeconomic disadvantage, adverse temperamental characteristics may become associated with early parent–child conflict, problems of discipline and features of inattentiveness–impulsivity by age 2 or 3, aggressive antisocial conduct by age 5, and the emergence of CD in later childhood.

Family Characteristics

The most reliable family correlates of CD include parental criminality, parental psychopathology, dysfunctional family interactions, and marital discord. Aggressive, antisocial children and delinquent adolescents are more likely to have criminal parents than their nondeviant peers. Factors accounting for this transmission are unclear, but unlikely to be mostly genetic. McCord found that sons of criminals were not more likely to become juvenile delinquents or adult criminals than were sons of noncriminals, unless one or both parents were aggressive during the child-rearing years and the parental relationship was marked by high conflict. McCord also reported that maternal affection, consistent discipline, and supervision acted as protective factors that significantly weakened the association between paternal criminality and son deviance.

If parental, especially maternal, competence can act as a protective factor in the development of CD, psychopathology may have the opposite effect. Maternal depression has often been found to be associated with aggressive, antisocial child behavior and to limit the effectiveness of psychological interventions aimed at modifying such behavior. Although parental psychopathology often precedes the emergence of child problems, it has not been established that maternal depression or other adult dysfunctions play a causal role in CD, as they may more simply reflect the main psychological and socioeconomic stresses mothers of deviant children and adolescents are often exposed to.

Families of aggressive, antisocial children often present chronic dysfunctional patterns of interaction. Specifically, a behavioral cluster characterized by child noncompliance on the one hand, and parental punitiveness and inconsistency on the other may be the core feature of the interactional style of early starters in early to middle childhood. In families that display high levels of aversive interactions and poor parental monitoring, overt child aggression is often accompanied by more covert antisocial problems, such as stealing, lying, cheating, and fire setting, that are predictive of conduct problems and delinquency in adolescence. Although dysfunctional family interactions clearly involve both parents and children, evidence suggests that they are usually present before the onset of conduct problems and may play a causal role in their development.

Marital discord has long been known to be associated with conduct problems. A review and metaanalysis confirm this association, showing that the relationship between discord and CD is particularly reliable for boys. In keeping with earlier evidence, recent work shows that CD is associated with open marital conflict more than with parental apathy or indifference toward each other. This last study found that interspousal aggression was a significant predictor of CD in 5- to 8-year-old children, even after controlling for overall levels of marital adjustment and intrafamily aggression. As in the case of dysfunctional family interactions, marital discord is often present before the onset of child conduct problems and may play a causal role in their development.

Socioeconomic Characteristics

Conduct order also is associated with demographic, social, and economic variables, such as area of residence, social isolation, and poverty, and their many correlates. Thus CD is more prevalent in poor inner-city areas than in suburban or rural areas, in children of families characterized by lack of positive social support, and in children of families marked by chronic disadvantage, as reflected by variables such as low income, unemployment, dependence on welfare and subsidized housing, and overcrowding.

TREATMENT

Reviews of intervention studies designed to modify the aggressive, antisocial behaviors of CD children indicate that, in spite of conceptual and methodological limitations, significant changes have been achieved. Although evidence shows that different forms of treatment may help children with CD and are preferable to no intervention, empirical support is strongest for treatment approaches that attempt to modify directly the behavioral excesses or social or cognitive skills deficits of disruptive children and adolescents, such as parent training, social skills training, and cognitive skills training.

Parent Training

Parent-training programs are designed to teach parents to deal effectively with their children's behavioral difficulties in the home. Most of these programs address the symptoms of ODD rather than CD and are, therefore, of greater relevance to children than adolescents. Evidence indicates that parent training offers a positive means of changing aggressive antisocial behavior in childhood, is generally more effective than traditional community-based clinical services, has favorable effects that are maintained for several years in as many as two-thirds of treated children and can be administered in cost-effective ways. However, evidence also indicates that approximately one-third of treated families do not benefit from parent training. Not surprisingly, many of these families present multiple problems, such as maternal depression, marital discord, social isolation, and socioeconomic disadvantage. Such findings have led to the development of procedures aimed at enhancing family-based interventions for CD, procedures that have met with varying degrees of success.

Social Skills Training

Social skills–training programs are designed to remedy the social skills deficits of children and adolescents with CD and generally rely on direct instruction, coaching, modeling, and reinforcement to teach the discrete behavioral components of specific skills. The bulk of the evidence is limited by the fact that most studies have not focused specifically on aggressive, antisocial behavior but on more loosely defined adjustment problems, such as disruptive problems, social skills deficits, and peer rejection. Carefully controlled programs can lead to improvements in overall adjustment or in specific targeted skills, but these programs often fail to bring about change in measures of direct relevance to CD, such as peer acceptance in childhood or rate of offending and recidivism in adolescence. In one of the few studies of direct relevance to CD, Hansen, St. Lawrence, and Christoff taught conversational skills to inpatient older children and adolescents with ODD or CD. The program was successful in that it led to the acquisition and generalization of the skills taught across time and settings, but the authors did not provide evidence that these positive changes were accompanied by corresponding reductions in CD symptoms.

Cognitive Skills Training

Relying on evidence that CD children and adolescents often interpret social reality in distorted ways, cognitive skills training programs seek to modify how participants process social information and solve social and interpersonal problems. Evidence indicates that this approach can effectively modify targeted cognitive processes and related task performance with impulsive, hyperactive, and aggressive antisocial samples.

PREVENTION

Conduct disorder has reached epidemic proportions in many Western countries. The scope of the problem, together with the knowledge that it is highly stable and chronic in nature and that available treatments are often limited, provide strong arguments for the development of preventive approaches. Evidence shows that primary prevention efforts may reduce early childhood aggression and result in improved social adjustment in late adolescence and early adulthood in samples that are clearly at risk for CD. In keeping with such evidence, large-scale, multisite preventive projects are being developed, implemented, and evaluated. These projects seek to identify children at risk for CD in the early school grades and

to provide multifaceted services aimed at the long-term prevention of the disorder. The challenge is great, but effective preventive interventions must be found if one is to reduce the scope and severity of CD to a level that will be significant and noticeable for society as a whole.

ADOLESCENT IDENTITY FORMATION
ADOLESCENT SEX OFFENDERS
MORAL BEHAVIOR
NEGLECTED CHILDREN
PARENT-CHILD RELATIONS
SCHOOL GANGS

J. E. DUMAS

CONFIDENCE LIMITS

Confidence limits pertain to interval estimation and are associated with the standard errors for statistics: sample means, correlation coefficients, predicted scores, and so forth. In interval estimation, attention is focused on determining the range of values, or the interval in which there is a high probability that the true parameter will lie. If one applies this concept to the statistic, the sample mean, it becomes obvious that no matter how carefully a sample is drawn or how large it is, there is no certainty that the sample mean is exactly equal to the population mean (parameter). This is due to the sampling errors prevalent in any sample because of chance factors causing fluctuations from sample to sample. Hence it becomes necessary to specify an estimated interval that is expected to include the true mean. This estimation is accomplished with a level of confidence analogous to that involved in hypothesis testing. The confidence limits are the complements of the levels of significance used in hypothesis testing. The sampling distribution of means assumes a normal shape about the mean of means ($\overline{\overline{X}}$) with the standard deviation (σ_m), the standard error of the mean. As the number of samples becomes infinitely large, the following conditions are true:

$$-1.96\sigma_m \leq \mu - \overline{X} \leq + 1.96\sigma_m \text{ (95\% confidence limits)}$$

$$-2.58\sigma_m \leq \mu - \overline{X} \leq + 2.58\sigma_m \text{ (99\% confidence limits)}$$

$$-3.29\sigma_m \leq \mu - \overline{X} \leq + 3.29\sigma_m \text{ (99.9\% confidence limits)}$$

The meaning of these statements is that at the specified level of confidence, the specified interval will include that percent of all possible means distributing themselves normally about the population mean, μ.

Confidence limits are useful in estimating the interval within which a "true" score is expected to lie at a specified level of confidence, given observed score. The sampling error of a reliability coefficient (r_{11}) is ($\sigma_e = \sigma_0\sqrt{1 - r_{11}}$). Hence, for example, the 95% confidence limits for a "true" IQ, given a deviation IQ of 110 on a test whose reliability is 0.84, are $98 - 122$ ($\sigma_e = 6$; $15\sqrt{0.16}$).

Confidence limits are also particularly useful ($\hat{X}$) in predictions based on measures of a known degree of validity. The standard error associated with a predicted score ($\hat{X}$) is the standard error of estimate ($\sigma_{y.x}$).

P. F. MERENDA

CONFLICT MEDIATION

Conflict mediation is defined as the efforts of a neutral third party who, at the request of the conflicting parties, assists them in establishing an acceptable resolution of their conflicts. Mediation differs from arbitration in that arbitration imposes a settlement on the parties after they have requested the intervention of the neutral judge. It differs from litigation in that in litigation the parties are represented by opposing council, each of whom seeks to establish a "victory" for his or her client. Mediation returns the opportunity and the responsibility for conflict resolution to the people directly involved in the conflict. The mediator assists the parties in finding their own way out of a dispute.

Mediation was first widely known during the period of the Italian city–states in the fourteenth and fifteenth centuries. Since then it has been expanding into interpersonal, interorganizational, and international affairs. The use of mediation ranges from marital dispute resolution to negotiations of out-of-court settlements.

The mediation process seeks to do the following:

1. Reduce the expense of litigation.
2. Ease the load on courts.
3. Lessen the degree of stress and tension experienced by the disputants.
4. Provide the possibility of a win/win outcome.
5. Provide a setting where the disputants can be authors of the settlement rather than victims of an imposed judgment.

The mediator is primarily a facilitator providing the parties with a joint examination of issues, a recognition of common objectives, and insights into opposing perspectives. The mediator performs as courier, interpreter, catalyst, and gentle persuader, making no judgments as to the merit of positions and rendering no decision as to who shall prevail.

The mediator helps the parties to do the following:

1. Communicate with each other.
2. Identify substantive issues and separate them from emotional issues.
3. Identify and clarify the issues causing the dispute.
4. Reassess their own positions.
5. Recognize superordinate goals.

The mediator should

1. Probe and ask direct questions to provide information and clarify misunderstanding.
2. Listen objectively to what the parties are really saying.
3. Observe what the disputants say and do. Body language and nonverbal behavior become an important source of information.
4. Maintain control of the hearing.

THE OPENING STATEMENT

The mediator's opening statement sets the basic procedural ground rules. These preliminaries are critical to successful negotiations. The presentation should put the disputants at ease and introduce a win/win problem-solving approach to the conflict. Points that should be covered include

1. A welcoming statement
2. An introduction of the mediator panel and participants
3. An explanation of the process
4. An explanation of the basic premises of confidentiality and impartiality
5. An explanation of ground rules:
   (a) Initial statements by complainant/respondant
   (b) Interruptions
   (c) Caucusing
   (d) Name calling
   (e) Written agreements

THE STAGES OF MEDIATION

The stages of mediation are comprised of ventilation, information gathering, problem solving, and bargaining.

If the parties have not developed the issues of the conflict in the initial joint exchange, the mediator must find a means to secure this information without either party losing face. The mediator must be flexible and able to cope with uncertainty and changing conditions. Essentially, during ventilation the mediator must listen actively to the disputants' issues and show concern for their feelings. This allows the mediator to gather as much information about the problem as possible, including those feelings that are central to the issues. Ventilation is often handled in private caucus.

After a hearing has reached the point where the disputants have drained at least a portion of their respective emotions, the parties can move toward problem solving and bargaining. It is important that the disputants now take an active role and directly communicate their needs and demands. This will create the psychological ownership that will make the final agreement work. The amount of commitment to resolving the dispute is proportional to their commitment to the outcome. During this phase the mediator channels the disputants toward the following:

1. Developing tradeoffs.
2. Establishing superordinate goals. If the disputants realize that only through a combined effort can the goals of both parties be achieved, then resolution becomes of utmost importance.
3. Creating a synthesis. The mediator may determine that the values in conflict are total opposites, and so may help foster a third view. This is not necessarily a compromise.
4. Allowing graceful retreat. The mediator must help parties in retreating without loss of face.
5. Identifying and suggesting possibilities not apparent to the disputants.
6. Narrowing the gap by pointing out similarities and minimizing differences.

When a hearing has reached an impasse, the mediator must take the time to work it through. This requires patience and skill. If the parties are not willing to negotiate, the mediator must look for motivating factors that can break the impasse. These factors have usually appeared during the initial stage, when needs and feelings were expressed. The mediator must refer back to this information and use it to reopen the negotiation.

To reach the agreement stage, the mediator must

1. Be positive.
2. Take control of the hearing.
3. Remain neutral.
4. Help the disputants see alternatives and options.
5. Be concrete.
6. Emphasize areas of agreement.
7. Narrow the impasse area.
8. Describe, not evaluate.
9. Check perceptions.
10. Test hypothetical alternatives.
11. Differentiate between needs and wants.
12. Be sensitive to feelings.

If the mediator performs the previously listed functions, most disputants will reach the agreement stage.

CONFLICT RESOLUTION
INTERVENER SURVIVAL

S. Leviton
J. L. Greenstone

CONFLICT RESOLUTION

Conflict refers to preferences for incompatible actions in a given situation. It may exist at the level of the individual, when a person is torn between different decision options such as entering law school versus taking a job. It also occurs among individuals when two or more parties in a social relationship have incompatible preferences for action. It can occur between groups, as in labor–management disputes over wages, as well as between organizations and between nations. Incompatible preferences within an individual form an intrapersonal conflict, while those between social entities such as individuals are termed social conflict. Social conflict assumes the interdependence of the parties: Neither can obtain its most desired outcomes independently of the other. Processes involved in the resolution of conflict are typically viewed as highly similar across all levels of social conflict.

Much psychological research on intrapersonal conflict resolution has focused on the ways in which people assemble information about decision alternatives and order their preferences. Although the resolution of social conflict involves similar information-processing considerations, it also includes various interpersonal strategies.

Distributive bargaining refers to the efforts exerted by parties to a conflict to alter each other's preferences and reach agreement. Such bargaining may involve verbal exchanges, when the parties attempt to reach a verbal agreement as to what each party will do, or it may involve actions. Nonverbal bargaining is illustrated by two automobile drivers who meet on a one-lane bridge, whereupon each attempts to intimidate the other by confidently entering the span. Bargaining that involves verbal exchange is often termed negotiation and typically includes the exchange of bids—proposals for resolution. It may also include the use of threats and the imposition of penalties.

Integrative bargaining refers to efforts parties in conflict make to develop new options not present in the set initially considered, but which offer both parties better outcomes than those of any possible agreement in the initial set.

Norm-following strategies involve the invocation of rules or precedents to resolve the conflict. In some cases these norms are simply precedents in the relationship between the conflicting parties themselves. In other cases norms are brought into the relationship from experience in other relationships or from knowledge of societal norms.

Third-party intervention as a means of conflict resolution may be sought by the parties when their independent efforts are ineffectual, or it may be imposed by the third parties or their constituents when continued conflict is seen as damaging to outsiders' interests.

The resolution of conflict at a given time may dispense with the issues permanently, if the parties believe the resolution is the best they can achieve, or it may be temporary, in which case a similar conflict may emerge between the parties at a later date.

CONFLICT MEDIATION
DISTRIBUTIVE JUSTICE
HOSTAGE NEGOTIATIONS
LABOR–MANAGEMENT RELATIONS

W. P. Smith

CONFLICT RESOLUTION THERAPY

Conflict may be hypothesized as underlying all psychopathology, leading to the assertion "no conflict, no psychopathology." Conflict is a recommended conceptual basis for understanding psychopathology, owing to its empirical nature, its salience in communicating to clients in distress, and its relevance to human clinical and social impasses.

Conflict theory is characterized by approach and avoidance gradients. In relation to the goal area, avoidance is steep and approach is gradual. Indecisiveness, vacillation, and the formation of persistent symptoms occur in relation to intense and lasting conflict.

It is hypothesized that all psychotherapy involves, directly or indirectly, the resolution of conflict. Conflict resolution can proceed by (a) increasing gradually the approach gradient toward a goal (getting over stage fright, approaching the admired one), or (b) reducing the avoidance gradient through catharsis or by exhuming the significant past. The latter route is more indirect, takes longer, and entails more uncertainty and less objectivity. The direct route by way of successive approximations to the goal may not give sufficient credence to the fearful and avoidance characteristics of the person's past and present behaviors. Ideally, the approach gradient route should meet the anxiety and avoidance characteristics of conflict by reinforced successive steps that will give rise to confidence and independence. Further, the avoidance reduction route is expected to make the person more willing to approach the formerly feared or avoided condition. The middle ground revolves around the great likelihood that both approach and avoidance work together, neither being wholly dominant, but each more salient at a given time.

CONFLICT MEDIATION
INNOVATIVE PSYCHOTHERAPIES
PSYCHOTHERAPY

E. L. Phillips

CONFORMING PERSONALITY

Laboratory research on conformity has followed two classic paradigms. In the one pioneered by Solomon Asch, a subject is given a perceptual problem that has an obvious correct answer, and the subject must respond publicly in the face of feedback that other group members have made an incorrect choice. Variations on this procedure sometimes substitute factual or attitudinal judgments for the perceptual problems. In the paradigm initiated by Muzafer Sherif, subjects are faced with a perceptual illusion and are asked to describe what they see, either alone or in a group.

Some studies have found reliable relationships between personality characteristics and a tendency to conform. Highly authoritarian individuals, for example, have been shown to be more likely to conform to an arbitrary perception of reality established by accomplices of the experimenter in a Sherif-type situation, and to be more inclined to obey an experimenter's orders to inflict extreme pain on another person, than were less authoritarian subjects. Other investigators have observed conformity to be associated with "field dependence," or a general tendency to be strongly influenced by external cues, as opposed to internal sensations and interpretations, in making perceptual judgments.

To the extent that laboratory research has sketched the outlines of a conforming personality, the picture is not very flattering. High conformers are relatively anxious, guilt-ridden, emotionally unstable, insecure in their self-concept, and at the same time somewhat authoritarian and obedient to the orders of a supervisor, even to the point of inflicting unjustified harm on another individual. As Hollander and Willis pointed out, however, tendencies toward conformity and obedience vary greatly in strength, depending on the nature of the task and the perceived legitimacy or expertise of others from whom influence is accepted. The opposite of conformity is not *anti*conformity but independence. The anticonformist is as much influenced by the group as the conformist, but reflexively says "no" when everyone else says "yes." The independent person accepts influence from the group when appropriate, but resists inappropriate or unreasonable attempts at influence.

ANXIETY
CENTRAL TRAITS
NONCONFORMING PERSONALITY
PERSONALITY TYPES

W. SAMUEL

CONFORMITY

Conformity is agreement on some trait, attitude, or behavior, based on common group membership. The empirical as well as conceptual problem involves the establishment of this agreement (which does not need to be perfect), and shows that it would not have occurred in the absence of the group. Conformity can be distinguished from other concepts by the absence of one of these conditions. If there is agreement on traits, but it is independent of group membership (e.g., if it is due to common circumstances), one speaks of *uniformity* of attitude or behavior. If agreement is obtained through force, promise of reward, or threat of punishment, one speaks of *compliance*. If uniformity has become so much a part of a person's self that it would persist in the absence of group membership, one speaks of *internalization;* the process by which this is accomplished during the life course is *socialization.* Conformity can be seen as an intermediate stage between superficial compliance and permanent internalization—as a conflict between what a person basically is and what group membership induces.

The interest in conformity as a topic in its own right is partly due to the social concerns of the second quarter of this century. Events in totalitarian countries, including extreme and virtually inhuman behavior on the one hand, and systematic enforcing of conformity on the other hand (e.g., "brainwashing"), prompted a need to distinguish between personal- and group-induced beliefs. In part, this was motivated by the hope that people's individual beliefs are good, and the fear that people's views could be swamped by a social juggernaut. Techniques to reproduce some of these influences in an isolated laboratory setting led to a detailed analysis of conformity and group influences and to a better understanding of the social process.

One of the earliest empirical studies of conformity was done by Floyd Allport. He proposed that conforming behavior can be recognized by its distribution, which follows an inverted J: Few people overconform (are to the left of the peak); the overwhelming majority are positioned exactly at the peak, accounting for the spike of the J; and a minority deviate from the norm, accounting for an elongated but low-level tail. He validated this hypothesis primarily by observation in field situations such as reporting to work, stopping at a stop sign, or using holy water in a Catholic church.

The classical experiments on conformity are those by Muzafer Sherif and Solomon Asch. Sherif's experiment was based on the phi phenomenon, an optical illusion in which a light point in a dark room seems to move in a straight line. Sherif showed that if a subject was paired with a confederate who judged the movement as larger than the subject did, the subject would increase his or her distance judgments gradually and correspondingly with a decrease of distance. Sherif thus established a common "frame of reference" for judging the size. Asch's study had the naive subjects give perceptual judgments in a group of confederates who agreed on the wrong answer; a considerable proportion of subjects gave the clearly wrong answer.

Critical analysis of the classical conformity experiments has shown that ostensibly conforming behavior can be derived from many different sources, not all of which have anything to do with social conformity.

Staying on a simplified empirical level, research needs to identify the instances that would confirm the presence of conformity in sense of the definition.

Most of these studies relate the desire to belong to a group to several expressions of conformity. These different processes define different conditions under which conformity occurs. One situation is that of extreme subjectivity of the issue, where only consent of a relevant group can assure belief of the individual; this is called the establishment of social reality through conformity. However, conforming may be individually advantageous. It might also be one way of obtaining some goal through cooperation, or might be an assertion of group membership, such as a uniform or sign. In each case a different set of issues will be a field for conformity, and different mechanisms will be used to achieve it, such as appeals to self-interest, reasoning based on social reality, or the threat of rejection for nonconformity.

The main contribution of the detailed experimental study of conformity consists in explicating the different conditions under which conformity occurs. This gives a better understanding of the social concerns from which this research originated. The fact that individuals can succumb to social pressure and act and even feel in a way that they would deny is their own, is undoubted; it can be reproduced under controlled conditions as well as observed under realistic conditions.

Conformity research has shown, however, that some of the mechanisms lead to intense conformity, which then becomes a part of the person's self. If effective, it is more properly called socialization; in fact, the development of a person is frequently seen as conformity behavior. However, historical experience has shown how outward conformity can be maintained for a long time, then dissolved when the pressure is removed.

Adherents to social reality construction insist that all attitudes and actions are constructed among individuals through negotiation. Division between personal and social aspects are conventions that in turn reflect the social arrangements of what is to be considered either.

AFFILIATION NEED
BYSTANDER INVOLVEMENT
CULTURAL DETERMINISM
DEVIANCE
FADS AND FASHIONS
GROUP COHESIVENESS
SCAPEGOATING

K. W. BACK

CONGENITAL INFECTIONS

A number of infections acquired by women before or during pregnancy may be transmitted to their offspring and have serious physical or behavioral teratogenic effects. These effects include prematurity, abnormalities in the infant, or even death, with consequent spontaneous abortion or stillbirth. Generally, this transmission is prenatal, but in some cases may be perinatal. Several of these infections have such similar clinical manifestations that they have been grouped as the TORCH complex, for toxoplasmosis, rubella, cytomegalovirus, and herpes, or the STORCH complex, which includes syphilis. Other infections such as varicella also may be transmitted prenatally with similar effects. Of particular concern, congenital human immunodeficiency virus (HIV) syndrome, leading to acquired immunodeficiency syndrome (AIDS), may have severe impact on the infant beyond transmission of the virus itself, adding one more element to an already tragic situation.

Effects these congenital infections have in common include intrauterine growth retardation; visual defects, including cataracts and microphthalmia; central nervous system defects, including microcephaly and cortical and cerebellar abnormalities, with consequent development delay, mental retardation, and seizures; and hearing loss. Infants without clinical signs may develop symptoms later.

Several factors increase concern about these infections. Some infections are difficult to differentiate on the basis of symptoms alone and may require cytologic testing for accurate diagnosis and subsequent appropriate treatment. Damage from some infections may occur to the fetus before the mother knows that she is pregnant and takes precautionary measures. Rubella, cytomegalovirus (CMV), and toxoplasmosis may go undected because affected children or adults often show only mild symptoms or are asymptomatic. Thus a pregnant woman may be unaware of an infection and its potential risk. Although knowledge of congential rubella is widespread, that of CMV and toxoplasmosis, now greater risk factors, is more limited. Because the brain is the organ most sensitive to teratogens during development, infections that produce limited visible effects on body structures may have more serious neurological and thus behavioral consequences.

SICKLE CELL DISEASE
SUBSTANCE ABUSE
TOXIC PSYCHOSES

R. T. BROWN

CONJOINT THERAPY

Conjoint therapy describes a treatment method simultaneously involving two or more members from a family or marital unit in a treatment session. The exact number of individuals present from the relational unit may vary. These individuals may come from a variety of settings in the patient's neighborhood, family kinship, or work environments.

Conjoint therapy did not evolve from a particular school of therapy, but rather was the somewhat simultaneous occurrence in the 1950s of a number of individuals across the United States. According to Jay Haley in his article "Family therapy," all persons who ventured into conjoint treatment methods had their original training in individually oriented psychotherapy. Many of the well-known therapists in this area acknowledge the influence of systems theory on their thinking. Essentially, systems theory emphasizes the interactive and interrelated nature of behavior. A person's behavior in this theory "does not occur in a vacuum" but rather is influenced by, and in turn influences, the environment in which it occurs. To fully understand a person's behavior, therefore, it is important to observe it within the context in which it occurs. The context of behavior in conjoint therapy is typically the relational unit—the marital partners or the family.

CHANGE INDUCTION GROUPS
MARRIAGE COUNSELING
SEX THERAPIES

R. P. KAPPENBERG

CONNECTIONISM

The basis of connectionism can be found in the writings of early philosophers. It is customary to point to Aristotle as the originator of associationistic principles, but credit for establishing connectionistic ideas as fertile explanatory concepts belongs more properly to the British empiricists of the seventeenth and eighteenth centuries. Thomas Hobbes, often regarded as a founder of the British tradition of empiricism, held that lawfulness in thought and action was produced by the connections of ideas through their occurrence in temporal proximity. An independent and more complete contiguity position was developed by John Locke,

who also accepted similarity of ideas as a basis for their association. Further refinements were made by British philosophers writing in the empiricist tradition. Although none were empiricists in a contemporary, scientific sense, their work and that of their successors helped lay the groundwork for the connectionism that developed throughout the nineteenth and twentieth centuries.

Although associationistic principles were subjected to rigorous scientific testing by the Russian physiologists I. P. Pavlov and V. M. Bekhterev, their theoretical efforts were sharply restricted to the problem of conditioning. It remained for Edward Lee Thorndike to develop a more comprehensive account of experience and behavior on the connectionistic principle.

Some idea of the thoroughness with which Thorndike adopted the connectionistic principle may be seen in these excerpts from his *Selected writings from a connectionist's psychology.*

> Connections lead from states of affairs within the brain as well as from external situations. They often occur in long series wherein the response to one situation becomes the situation producing the next response and so on. They may be from parts or elements or features of a situation as well as from the situation as a whole. . . . They lead to responses of readiness and unreadiness, awareness, attention, interest, welcoming and rejecting, emphasizing and restraining, differentiating and relating, directing and coordinating. The things connected may be subtle relations or elusive attitudes and intentions.

Thorndike's law of effect held that the positive or negative consequences of responses determined the degree to which they would be strengthened or weakened. Thorndike concluded that positive responses were more effective than negative and emphasized them in his theoretical writings. Thorndike later reported what he apparently regarded as an "independent proof" of the law of effect. The so-called spread of effect referred to the empirical strengthening of responses made in close contiguity to a reinforced response, even if they themselves were not directly rewarded. Although Thorndike's early postulation of a physiological "confirming reaction" as a basis of the law of effect was subsequently justified by the independent discovery of the reinforcing potency of intracranial self-stimulation, no such confirmation occurred for his spread-of-effect hypothesis. The law of effect and the spread of effect were vigorously criticized, on both theoretical and methodological grounds. Nevertheless, they represent a kind of culmination of the early philosophical ideas within a strictly scientific framework and so stand as one exemplification of the potential inherent in connectionistic thinking.

Other characteristics of Thorndikian connectionism were its elementarism, illustrated by his "identical-elements" theory of transfer of training and its stress on the automaticity of fundamental behavioral functions.

The learning theory of E. R. Guthrie also was based on strictly connectionistic, stimulus–response assumptions. Contiguity alone, without effect, was assumed to be responsible for learning. A similar but more sophisticated statistical learning theory was produced by W. K. Estes; it can be considered as a kind of springboard to the more recent surge of connectionistic theorizing.

CONTEMPORARY CONNECTIONISM

Given the fervor with which the so-called cognitive revolution of the 1960s strove to break with traditional, stimulus–response types of theoretical frameworks, it is all the more surprising to find connectionism playing a central role in so much cognitive theorizing of the 1990s. As suggested by the rather unusual heading ("Where Next? Connectionism Rides Again!") in Baddeley's book on memory, there has been an explosion of connectionistic, network-type theorizing applied to cognitive problems. The ready availability of such concepts as weighted nodes and the like in such network patterns as the increasingly popular "parallel distributed processing" proposal have made this kind of theoretical model attractive to researchers and theorists in a wide spectrum of problem areas. The common amenability to a network type of theoretical framing has probably been the factor most responsible for the synthesis of such seemingly diverse topics and functions as learning, language comprehension, artificial intelligence, computational science, and neuroscience. From neural networks in biology to knowledge representations in artificial intelligence, connections are now playing a key role in tying together many loose strands of data.

Serial processing, in which activation occurs in successive nodes along a chain of connections in a network, was initially a theoretically preferred concept. More recently, *parallel processing,* in which two or more independent lines of activation are assumed to occur, has become a more attractive alternative. A major advantage of this type of processing concept is that it more readily accommodates the simultaneous functioning of both conscious and nonconscious activations, thus taking into account the recently accelerated interest in nonconscious processes, such as those occurring in implicit learning and procedural tests of memory.

There have been some critics of this headlong rush to the bandwagon of connectionistic theorizing. For example, McCloskey has argued that in spite of their "explosion" into cognitive science with "conferences and symposia too numerous to count," connectionistic networks should be regarded more as theoretical tools than as theories themselves. McCloskey pointed to the need to understand how the networks operate before appropriate theoretical accounts can be developed from them. He analyzed the influential, much-cited connectionistic network, which Seidenberg and McClelland applied to the problems of word identification and lexical decision (deciding whether a presented string of letters is a word). His conclusion was that, in spite of the multiple, detailed weighing and such used in the network to account for experimental results, there was still a fundamental need for more verbal explanations before an adequate theoretical explanation could be achieved.

These cautions notwithstanding, the fact remains that connectionism has made a remarkable comeback since the mid-1980s and that its scientific future seems to be well assured, both as a theoretical tool and as a theoretical framework.

For balanced presentations of the details of this renaissance of connectionism, the books by Baddeley, Bechtel and Abrahamson, and Morris may be consulted.

ASSOCIATIONISM
LEARNING THEORIES
OPERANT CONDITIONING
PHILOSOPHY OF SCIENCE
THEORETICAL PSYCHOLOGY

M. H. MARX

CONSCIOUSNESS

Although consciousness is the most obvious and intimate feature of our being, philosophical as well as psychological discourse is replete with conceptual confusions and conflicting characterizations. R. B. Perry remarked, "How can a term mean anything when it is employed to connote anything and everything, including its own negation?" Most psychologists regard consciousness as awareness. Unfortunately, the concept of awareness is no less ambiguous. Awareness is used in almost every sense in which consciousness is employed. For example, awareness signifies perceptual awareness, introspective awareness, reflective awareness, subliminal awareness, self-awareness, awareness of awareness, and so on.

CONSCIOUSNESS AND THE UNCONSCIOUS

According to John Locke, consciousness is reflection, included in different mental acts such as perception, thinking, doubting, believing, willing, and so on. Consciousness is the essential transparent aspect of mind; nothing is hidden from it. The Lockian view of consciousness had such a pervasive influence that until the advent of Freudian psychoanalysis the notion of unconscious thought or perception was considered self-contradictory. Freud showed how complex thought processes can occur without awareness and how one's unconscious may contain beliefs, desires, and feelings of which one is unaware.

Freud saw meaning and purpose in unconscious material. Seemingly innocuous and unintentional acts such as slips of the tongue, forgetting, and misplacing of objects may be motivated at the unconscious level. That being so, the earlier characterization of consciousness as intentional, purposeful mental activity must be taken to apply to the unconscious as well.

Jung went further to blunt the distinction between consciousness and the unconscious. The unconscious, according to Jung, is the consummate source of our collectivity and creativity. The collective unconscious is "an image of the world which has taken aeons to form. . . . [It] consists of the sum of instincts and their correlates, the archetypes. Just as everybody possesses instincts, so he also possesses a stock of archetypal images."

Advances in cognitive psychology suggest that complex mental activity, including our ability to acquire, store, and retrieve information, is carried out by operations that are primarily unconscious and inaccessible to introspection.

The studies of "blindsight" and "memory without awareness" also show the contradictions involved in the conscious–unconscious dichotomy. Blindsight is the capacity among those with a damaged visual cortex to discriminate and respond to visual stimuli without being aware of them. Weiskrantz carried out a series of tests with a subject whose right visual cortex had been removed. As one would expect, the subject reported that he saw nothing when the stimuli were presented to his left hemifield. However, when he was asked to guess whether the stimulus was x or o, the subject guessed correctly in 27 of 30 trials, thus suggesting that he perceived the stimuli at some level.

The realization that thought processes such as perceiving, believing, willing, remembering, and so forth are also found at the unconscious level, though inaccessible to introspection, and that the line between consciousness and unconsciousness is not as sharp as it was once believed to be, renders the discussion of consciousness immediately complicated. The commonsense simplicity of conceiving consciousness as awareness becomes deceptive and sterile. If we can meaningfully refer to conscious as well as nonconscious awareness, the usefulness of awareness as a descriptor of consciousness becomes problematic. Consciousness as simple introspective awareness becomes a mere quality imposed on certain contents of experience. That quality may indeed be no more than certain cortical processes, because their destruction leads to loss of introspective awareness. Consciousness as a defining characteristic of mental phenomena is generally taken, however, to imply more than introspective awareness.

MANY SHADES OF CONSCIOUSNESS

The relationship of being to consciousness has been a perennial problem for philosophers. At the level of common sense, it generally is taken for granted that human beings are endowed with a body and a mind and that they interact to form functioning persons. In an attempt to provide a clear analysis of the mind and the body and their interaction, philosophers have arrived at a variety of views that give us the various perspectives we have of consciousness in scholarly discourse. These speculations fall broadly into two categories: (a) those that assert the reality of both the mind and the body and (b) those that deny the reality of one in favor of the other. The dualist theories build on the commonsense notion that the mind and the body are two different independent and interacting things. According to Descartes, for example, consciousness is the essence of mind and the mind is different from the body. There are in existence two radically different substances—the extended physical substance and the thinking, unextended mental substance. In principle, the latter is irreducible to the former.

The main problem with such dualism is the problem of interaction. How does the unextended mind interact with the extended body? Any kind of causal interaction between them, which is presumed by most dualist theories, comes into conflict with the physical theory that the universe is a closed system and that every physical event is linked with an antecedent physical event. This assumption preempts any possibility that a mental act can cause a physical event, unless the mental act itself is presumed in some sense to be physical. Parallelist theories attempt to circumvent this problem by assuming that physical and mental processes run parallel without influencing each other.

In contrast to dualistic theories, monistic theories postulate only one kind of substance: mind or matter. The subjective idealism of George Berkeley eliminated matter in favor of mind, and materialism denied mind in favor of matter.

Materialistic denial of mind–consciousness takes on several forms. Among these are: (a) outright denial of anything mental, including consciousness, that does not translate itself into objective behavior and performance; (b) acceptance of mental phenomena and denial that they have any causal efficacy because they are byproducts of physical processes in the brain; and (c) identification of mental phenomena with brain states.

J. B. Watson declared that there can be no such thing as consciousness. Contemporary resonance of such a radical view may be seen in the assertion of the futility of consciousness as a psychological concept. Stanovich writes: "Every issue in psychology that has touched 'consciousness' has become confused; and every bit of theoretical progress that has been attained has been utterly independent of any concept of 'consciousness.'" B. F. Skinner and those who followed believe that consciousness is an epiphenomenon of brain activity and has no causal efficacy; therefore, it can be denied any explanatory role in understanding behavior. The central-state materialism identifies consciousness with purely physical processes in the brain. Identity theorists like H. Feigl argue that consciousness is identifiable with the referents of neurophysiological concepts.

The newer materialism, unlike behaviorism, accepts the possibility of "inner" experience and its influence on the body and at the same time sees nothing in conscious experience that cannot be accounted for in strictly physical terms. The experience of consciousness, according to D. M. Armstrong, is no more than one part of the brain scanning another. "In perception," he says, "the brain scans the environment. In awareness of the perception another process in the brain scans that scanning." The inner sense that gives us introspective awareness is simply another brain process, and therefore, according to this view, there is no reason to hypostatize the existence of a process that can function independently of the brain.

There are well-known objections to all the previously mentioned renderings of consciousness entirely into behavioral, neural, or information-processing terms. As a fact of immediate experience, consciousness cannot be denied. The phenomenological experience of pain, for instance, is qualitatively different from neural excitations in the brain. The pain experience is homogeneous and continuous, whereas the neural events accompanying pain are heterogeneous, discontinuous, and spatially discrete events. In other words, unlike felt experience, brain activity is "grainy." Again, we know that our mental states may have profound effects on our body state. Placebos are known to have tangible effects. Psychosomatic illness is not delusional.

Phenomenologists like Husserl advance powerful arguments in support of consciousness as an essential aspect of our experience, without espousing a dualistic interactionism. Like Descartes, Husserl believed in the self-revealing character of consciousness, that consciousness cannot be denied without contradiction and that its nonbeing is utterly unimaginable. Consciousness is seen by Husserl as a function rather than an entity. Like Brentano before him, Husserl emphasized the intentional nature of consciousness. The external object, the content of consciousness, and our awareness of it are directly related by the intentionality of consciousness. Our knowledge of the world is not by way of sensations we receive, but is a consequence of the logical process of intention. The common world we share is not made possible by the sensations that tend to be discrete and private and cannot, therefore, reveal the universal and unitary character of their objects but by a "constitutive function" of consciousness that intuitively grasps their essence. The constitutive function of consciousness lies in the intuiting of the essence of objects so that we may understand their significance and meaningfulness to us. The unitary character that objects have as phenomena of our experience can only be understood in terms of their essences and not as a summation of their shifting qualities.

The centrality of consciousness in the human condition also is emphasized by Sartre in his existential philosophy. The very nature of consciousness, according to Sartre, is intentional and is always directed at something. Consciousness is not a container and not a stage on which objects are played. Its characteristic is the relevation of the thing to which it is directed. Its uniqueness consists in that it reveals itself while revealing the object. Thus for both Husserl and Sartre, consciousness is the principle of subjectivity that accounts for the manifest unity and significance of the phenomena of our experience.

CONSCIOUSNESS AND THE BRAIN

A. R. Luria, following Lev S. Vygotskii, held that consciousness is a complex structural system with semantic function. He rejected the dualistic postulation that consciousness–mind is fundamentally different in principle from material objects. At the same time, he viewed attempts to locate the mechanisms of consciousness inside the brain as misguided. Consciousness, according to Luria, is the ability "to assess sensory information, to respond to it with critical thoughts and actions, and to retain memory traces in order that past traces or actions may be used in the future." This ability is not a function of any one part of the brain. Rather, it "must be sought in the combined activity of discrete brain systems, each of which makes its own special contribution to the work of the functional system as a whole." Among the brain systems that are involved in conscious mental activity are: (a) the brain stem reticular formation, which controls the levels of wakefulness; (b) secondary zones of the posterior (afferent) cortical areas, which are involved in the recording of incoming information; and more important, (c) the medial zones of frontal lobes, which intimately participate in the formation of intentions and of action programs and play an essential role in the conscious regulation of goal-directed behavior.

John Searle asserts that mental states are real and have properties of their own. At the same time, these states are not dissociated from the brain. On the contrary, they are biologically based. Searle believes mental phenomena "are both caused by the operations of the brain and realized in the structure of the brain. On this view, consciousness and intentionality are as much a part of human biology as digestion or circulation of the blood. It is an objective fact about the world that it contains certain systems, viz. brains, with subjective mental states, and it is a physical fact about such systems that they have mental features."

Sperry regards consciousness as a primary source of causal influence. Consciousness is autonomous in its own right. It is not reducible to electrochemical processes. It is an "integral working component" in the brain. Sperry considers consciousness as a dynamic, emergent property resulting from the higher level functional organization of the cerebral cortex. As an emergent property, consciousness is in a sense determined by the neural infrastructures of the brain at the highest levels of its organizational hierarchy. However, at the same time, consciousness not only manifests characteristics not attributable to any of the constituent brain systems but also exerts regulatory control influence in brain processes. Thus mental phenomena are "causes rather than correlates" of neural events. "The brain physiology determines the mental effects and the mental phenomena in turn have causal influence on the neurophysiology." As emergent properties of cortical activity, conscious phenomena could functionally interact at their own level and also at the same time exert downward control over their constituent neural processes. Thus, according to Sperry, conscious states "supervene" rather than "intervene" in the physiological processes.

The attempts to grant reality and causal efficacy to conscious phenomena and yet regard them as manifestations of brain activity are criticized on the grounds that they are based on false analogies. It is difficult to conceive how a complex organization of neural processes gives us mental phenomena that are considered to be qualitatively different from physical phenomena.

Popper and Eccles, 1977, rejected the notion that consciousness is a function of complex neural organization. They found it difficult to account for the unity of conscious experience in terms of heterogeneous, discontinuous, and spatially discrete neural events. Similarly, self-consciousness and volition require for their explanation an agency independent of brain processes. Phenomena such as "antedating," by which conscious experience does not immediately follow stimulation but is referred backward in time, do not fit with the hypothesis of psychoneural identity. We do not know the precise physiological processes involved in the synthesis of perceptual experience. Eccles pointed out that the surface-negative potential in the cerebral cortex preceding simple voluntary moments, called readiness potential, takes considerable time to develop and is distributed widely over the cortex. This phenomenon, according to Eccles, suggests the action of the self-conscious mind on the specialized modules in the cortex that are critically poised at a special level of activity to produce consciously willed actions.

CONSCIOUSNESS AND PSYCHOLOGY

When psychology began as a separate discipline a little more than a century ago, it was defined as the science of consciousness. William James, for example, regarded psychology "as the description and explanation of states of consciousness-as-such." James's *The principles of psychology* profoundly influenced subsequent developments in Western psychology. Of the many different psychological doctrines of James contained in the *Principles,* none is more influential than his conception of the stream of consciousness. Affirming that consciousness is the "first and foremost concrete fact" of one's inner experience, he characterizes consciousness as an activity that is personal, selective, changing, and yet sensibly continuous. It has the function of choosing which objects to welcome and which to reject.

The changing, yet continuous, character of consciousness does not consist in any kind of linking discrete psychological events. One's mental life is not a "chain" or "train" of jointed bits of consciousness. Consciousness feels continuous because it "flows" like a river or a stream. Therefore, James calls it "the stream of thought, of consciousness, or of subjective life." The stream metaphor reflects the twin aspects of the continuous character of consciousness. First, when there is a time gap, the consciousness that follows relates itself to the one before it as if they belonged to one and the same self. Second, when there are shifts in the quality of consciousness from one moment to another they are never absolutely abrupt because no current psychological event takes place in a vacuum without some reference to the preceding events.

There are three distinctive strands in James's conception of consciousness, reflected in current discussions. The preceding account of consciousness contained in the *Principles* is generally accepted by cognitive psychologists concerned primarily with human information processing. In *The varieties of religious experience,* James expanded consciousness to include nonrational forms. He wrote, "It is that our normal waking consciousness, rational consciousness as we call it, is but one special type of consciousness, whilst all about it, parted from it by the filmiest of screens, there lie potential forms of consciousness entirely different." In his *Essays in radical empiricism,* however, we find: "For twenty years past I have mistrusted 'consciousness' as an entity; for seven or eight years past I have suggested its nonexistence to my students and tried to give them its pragmatic equivalent in realities of experience. It seems to me that the hour is ripe for it to be openly and universally discarded."

In the *Varieties* and the *Essays,* James abhorred intellectualism and defended experience against transempirical agencies, whether matter or mind. James's rejection of consciousness is methodologically akin to George Berkeley's rejection of matter. In rejecting dualism and its interactionist mode, James locates both mind and matter, the knower and the known in experience-as-such. What that experience is, however, remains as elusive as the interaction of mind and matter in dualistic postulations.

If there is any inconsistency in James, it is due to the two different senses in which he used consciousness, first in the sense of phenomenal awareness in the *Principles* and then in the sense of consciousness-as-such in the *Varieties.* The phenomenal and transcendental connotations continue to color much of the controversy surrounding the consciousness debate today. Some consider consciousness as a fact of its own, that it is autonomous and irreducible. It is the principle of subjectivity, whose reality is intuitively evident. Descartes' noncorporeal mind, Kant's noumenal self, Bergson's pure memory, Husserl's transcendental ego, and Sartre's nothingness seem to imply the existence of consciousness-as-such that, to use a term from quantum physics, seems to signify a nonlocal aspect of reality and the subjectivity in our being. Among contemporary schools of psychology, the transpersonal school holds such a view of consciousness. If we accept the reality of psi phenomena, it would be all the more compelling to consider the nonlocal aspects of consciousness.

The main stream of psychologists, however, limits consciousness to its restricted sense of phenomenal awareness. In that sense, consciousness is obviously localized and subject to space–time formulations. It is likely that the brain has much to contribute to our awareness of the world. Consequently, various sorts of mental phenomena may correlate with physiological processes in the brain and nervous system, and they could be investigated from a neurophysiological perspective. It does not follow, however, that all mental phenomena are ultimately reducible to brain states or that consciousness does not exist apart from these states. Some systems of Indian philosophy, notably the Sankhya school, consider mind to be essentially material while holding that consciousness-as-such is nonmaterial. Bergson also has insights as to the nature of the transition from the nonmaterial, pure memory to the material perceptions, that is, consciousness-as-such to conscious phenomena.

There is already an impressive scientific literature on meditation, even though much of it has suffered from conceptual confusion, methodological weaknesses, and some overgeneralizations. Future developments in the study of attention may hold the key for a more comprehensive understanding of consciousness.

AMNESIA
IMAGELESS THOUGHT
INTROSPECTION
MIND–BODY PROBLEM
SPLIT-BRAIN RESEARCH
STRUCTURALISM
UNCONSCIOUS INFERENCE
UNCONSCIOUS MATERIALISM

K. R. Rao

CONSEQUENCES, NATURAL AND LOGICAL

This concept contrasts with reward and punishment as a means of training children, and perhaps even more grandly, as a means of relating to others.

The simpler of the two divisions of this concept is natural consequences, which means the "trainer" essentially does nothing, letting the individual experience the consequences of his or her behavior, whether it be from the laws of nature or from the laws of other people. In applying this method of natural consequences to young children, two considerations apply: (a) Always inform the child of the probable consequences of the behavior, and (b) do not permit the child to experience these consequences if they are likely to be traumatic, dangerous, or possibly fatal. This method of training might well be called "learning from experience," because the parent-trainer believes that the best way of learning reality is to experience it.

Logical consequences is a concept more difficult to explain. It relates to the "trainer," using the term in a broad sense, as for example when an adult interacts with another to "teach him (or her) a lesson." The basic concept is a contract, expressed or implied, so that the object of the training will view the actions of the trainer as fair, and the behavior as logical.

The trainer either does or does not do something in terms of his or her perception of what is right. This is not to "punish" the child, but rather to "teach" the child the lesson.

This method of training is considered completely congruent with adult human relations: You pay a person only if he or she does the work promised; you avoid dealing with someone who is rude; you leave an appointed place after waiting a reasonable amount of time; you run from an impending accident; and so forth.

PARENTAL PERMISSIVENESS
PUNISHMENT
REWARDS
REWARDS AND INTRINSIC INTEREST

W. S. SUTTON

CONSERVATISM/LIBERALISM

Social science literature includes many discussions of ideology and specifically of sociopolitical liberalism and conservatism. Of particular interest is the notion of polarity in distinguishing conservatism from liberalism.

S. Tomkins offered a comprehensive set of assumptions of ideological polarity (with the liberal assumptions cited first): (a) Man is an end in himself versus man is not an end in himself; (b) Man is real versus man is unreal; (c) man should satisfy and maximize his drives and affects, versus man should be governed by norms, which in turn modulate his drives and affects; (d) values are what man wishes versus values exist independent of man; (e) man should minimize drive dissatisfaction and negative affects, versus man should maximize norm conformity and norm realization; (f) affect inhibition should be minimized versus affects should be controlled by norms; (g) power should be maximized in order to maximize positive affects and minimize negative affects, versus power should be maximized to maximize norm compliance and achievement; (h) conflict between affects within the individual and between individuals should be minimized, versus such conflicts should not be minimized; (i) conflict resolution of interests between individuals should be based on maximizing wish fulfillment and minimizing wish frustration, versus the resolution of conflicts of interest based on maximizing norm achievement or conformity; and (j) weakness should be tolerated and ameliorated versus weakness should not be tolerated and should be punished.

Therefore, according to Tomkins, the following questions differentiate the left-wing from the right-wing position: "Is man the measure, an end in himself, an active, creative, thinking, desiring, loving force in nature? Or must man realize himself, attain his full stature only through struggle toward, participation in, conformity to, a norm, a measure, an ideal essence basically independent of man?"

Offering a more politically focused description, C. Rossiter states that modern conservatism comprises nine core principles: (a) the existence of a universal moral order sanctioned and supported by organized religion; (b) the obstinately imperfect nature of humans, in which unreason and sinfulness always lurk behind the curtain of civilized behavior; (c) the natural inequality of humans in most qualities of mind, body, and character; (d) the necessity of social classes and orders, and the consequent folly of attempts at leveling by force of law; (e) the primary role of private property in the pursuit of personal liberty and defense of the social order; (f) the uncertainty of progress, and the recognition that prescription is the chief method of such progress as a society may achieve; (g) the need for a ruling and serving aristocracy; (h) the limited reach of human reason, and the consequent importance of traditions, institutions, symbols, rituals, and even prejudices; and (i) the fallibility and potential tyranny of majority rule, and the consequent desirability of diffusing, limiting, and balancing political power.

Conversely, D. Smith sees two primary themes underlying liberalism: (a) the dislike for arbitrary authority, complemented by the aim of replacing that authority by other forms of social practice; and (b) the free expression of individual personality.

Not all descriptions of liberalism and conservatism rely on a unidimensional conception, however. The most fundamental description of this polarity suggests that two dimensions discriminate between conservatism and liberalism, one describing the sacred and the profane, and the other describing the powerful and the weak. In this description liberalism would fall toward the end of the profane and weak dimensions, and conservatism toward the end of the sacred and powerful dimensions.

THEORIES

A number of theories have been advanced to account for the relationship between conservative–liberal attitudes and personality and cognitive styles. Hans Eysenck, for example, proposes a two-factor theory of personality and ideology with one factor, radicalism, dealing with the content of sociopolitical ideology, and the other factor, tough/tender-mindedness, dealing with cognitive style. On the content dimension, therefore, ideology ranges from radicalism to conservatism, and in the stylistic dimension, from the individual who is practical, materialistic, and extraverted, dealing with the environment by force or manipulation, to the individual who is theoretical, idealistic, and introverted, dealing with the environment by thinking or believing. One result of this conceptualization is that, for Eysenck, fascists and communists are quite similar in both their personalities and their cognitive styles.

In a comparable theory, Rokeach conceptualizes conservatives and liberals as being opinionated either to the left or right on issues, and at the same time, as being open- or closed-minded—that is, more or less dogmatic in their thinking. Thus for Rokeach, too, conservatism–liberalism is characterized by content and style dimensions, with open- and closed-minded conservatism being contrasted with open- and closed-minded liberalism.

Another psychological theory, originally discussed by T. W. Adorno and others and later modified by H. McClosky, is that of the authoritarian or conservative personality. This theory, basically psychodynamic in orientation, holds that the personality of the ideologue is projected onto the external world in such a manner that the individual creates a set of perceptions that express and agree with his or her fundamental psychological needs and impulses.

Finally, a fourth psychological theory accounts for conservative attitudes through genetic factors (anxiety proneness, stimulus aversion, low intelligence, unattractiveness, old age, and female sex) that combine with environmental factors (parental coldness, punitiveness, rigidity, inconsistency, and lower-class membership) to produce general feelings of insecurity and inferiority. These feelings of insecurity and inferiority then lead to a generalized fear of uncertainty, which produces an avoidance of stimulus uncertainty (dislike of innovation, novelty, and risk) and a response uncertainty (lack of self-reliance, and dislike of conflict and decision making), which ultimately results in a conservative attitude syndrome.

MASS-ELITE DIFFERENCES

Contrary to popular assumptions, conservatism is not necessarily related to upper-class membership. The relationship between socioeconomic status and political ideology is more complicated, with the poorly educated masses being more sociopolitically liberal on economic issues (favoring more welfare measures and more government intervention in economic life), but more conservative on noneconomic issues (emphasizing tradition, order, status hierarchy, duty, obligation, obedience, and authority).

Similarly, the sociopolitical elites exhibit greater liberalism and concern for the public welfare. The elites, for example, advocate using governmental power to improve the lives of the poor, the disadvantaged, and minorities by abolishing discrimination, poverty, and slums, ensuring employment, uplifting the poor, eliminating sickness, educating the masses, and instilling dominant culture values in all citizens.

IDEOLOGICAL TRENDS

Between 1939 and 1960 the general adult population tended to be evenly divided between self-declared liberals and conservatives, but more recently conservatives have come to outnumber liberals.

When self-identification is employed as a measure of ideological orientation, formal education level is directly associated with liberalism, the college-educated being the most liberal. Age also is related to liberalism, with the below-30 age group being considerably more prone to liberal identification then older age groups.

If attitudes are taken into account, individuals with lower income, formal education, and occupational status tend to be more liberal on social welfare issues but more conservative on civil rights, social issues (dissent and civil liberties), and foreign policy, whereas individuals with higher income, formal education, and occupational status are more conservative on social welfare issues but more liberal on civil rights, social issues, and foreign policy.

The political implications of liberalism–conservatism are especially important, because there has been a trend since 1960 for ideology to play an increasingly important role in electoral contests, particularly relative to political party identification and candidate evaluation.

AUTHORITARIAN PERSONALITY
NATIONAL CHARACTER
POLITICAL VALUES
SOCIAL CLASS

S. LONG

CONSTANCY

We perceive objects and events by their effects on our sense organs—the photic energy presented to the eye, the pressure waves that enter the ear, and so forth. Such physical attributes of an object itself as its size, its shape, and its reflectance are the *distal* stimuli in the world: properties that are relatively invariant for a given object and important in our dealings with the world. To perceive these properties, we must extract information about them from the patterns of stimulus energies at our sense organs—the *proximal* stimulation.

Proximal stimulation is generally in constant change: As we walk toward or away from any object, the size of the image that it projects on the eye's retina changes correspondingly (Figure 1A); the amount of light it provides the eye changes as the illumination on it changes (Figure 1B); and the location of its projection within the retinal image changes as the viewer's eye changes its direction of regard (Figure 1C).

From this flux of changing proximal stimulation we must derive our perceptions of the world, yet in general we do not see people change size as we approach them, nor do perceived objects change shape as we view them from a different angle, or change color and lightness when moved from light to shade, or move in space when we change our regard.

In short, the distal characteristics of objects appear to remain approximately constant, even though the proximal stimulation they present to the eye is in continual change. The major ways in which this is evident have been studied separately and given appropriate names: *size constancy, lightness constancy, shape constancy, loudness constancy, position constancy,* or generally *thing constancy.* As a more general principle, wherever the world presents constant and unchanging distal attributes and the sense organs receive changing proximal stimulation, we tend to perceive the constant distal attributes.

This is a restatement of a more general rule, formulated by Hermann von Helmholtz, that can be paraphrased as follows: *One perceives that state of affairs in the world that would, under normal conditions, have given rise to the pattern of proximal stimulation that affects the sense organs.*

THEORIES AND IMPLICATIONS OF CONSTANCY

The general problem is to explain how the perception of invariant distal attributes is achieved, given the changing proximal stimulation. There have been three general attempts at explanation, differing in power.

Classical Theory of Constancy

The first explanation, central to the classical theory of perception, states that the world is subject to physical regularities as illustrated for size and distance in Figure 1A, for reflectance and illumination in Figure 1B, and for eye movement and image movement in Figure 1C. As a result of having learned such regularities from our experiences with the world, we use them to solve the puzzles represented by proximal stimulation.

This general theory explains other phenomena as well, including the illusions and many of the Gestalt phenomena of organization. When spelled out, however, it has a long sequence of components that are unobservable and almost untestable as well, and for these it has drawn strong opposition. For example, size constancy would include these distinct stages: (a) sensing and interpreting the depth cues to obtain a percept of depth; (b) sensing the size of the retinal image; (c) evoking the relationship $S = k \times s \times D$ and solving for the apparent size.

Gestalt Theory of Constancy

Gestalt theory, the best-known opponent of the classical theory, assembled most of the indictments listed previously and, as an explanation of size and position constancy (Figure 1C), asserted that a form or shape is a stimulus to which the nervous system responds directly. A particular form has the same effect on the nervous system regardless of its particular place or size on the sensory surface, so that the perceived object remains invariant because its effective stimulus properties (its configuration) remains invariant. This explanation was never adequately worked out—particularly its applications to the many other kinds of constancy that must be explained—but it is clearly different from the classical explanation and contains an element that has had a great deal of influence.

Direct Theories of Constancy

The Gestalt explanation contained the notion that some aspect of proximal stimulation remains invariant inspite of its apparent flux, given an invariant distal stimulus; perceptual constancy then consists of the response to that invariant. The core of the notion was not new—it had been offered earlier by Ewald Hering and Ernst Mach, and has formed the core of two quite different kinds of direct theory of constancy.

The first of these are what can be termed *physiological theories of constancy*. Hering and Mach had proposed that innate networks of lateral connections exist between the receptors, as well as in the higher levels of the nervous system, that might account for at least some of the perceptual constancies.

Such networks are now known to exist, and they might indeed contribute to at least some forms of constancy. For example, an illuminated region in the retinal image reduces the response of an adjacent region of the retina through a process of *lateral inhibition*. When the illumination falling on an object and its surroundings increases, there is an increase in the light that the object provides to its image in the retina. However, the light reflected by the surround also increases, and so therefore does the inhibition by which its retinal image reduces the response to the object's image. The response to the object therefore would normally remain constant inspite of changes in the illumination, so long as the reflectances of the objects and surroundings is constant. (Moreover, several common illusions are covered by the same explanation, notably the facts of *contrast*, in which a bright surround is seen to make a gray object look darker.)

Considered by itself, this theory seems much more economical than the classical one. It would provide us with a sensory "channel" that responds directly to objects' reflectances under many conditions of viewing. However, there are all the other constancies to be explained and, until they are, the point about theoretical economy is moot. Neurological mechanisms and channels that would explain the constancies and other perceptual phenomena in a similar fashion are currently being proposed in abundance.

Constancy as Direct Response to Invariants

When the illumination changes, the light reaching the eye from an object and its surround both change, but the *ratio* of their intensities remains invariant (Figure lB). It has been recognized for many years that if sensed lightness were a response to that ratio, lightness constancy (and indeed lightness contrast) would then be a direct response to that variable of stimulation.

This helps explain a more general theory. In pursuit of his proposals about direct perception, J. J. Gibson has argued that we respond quite generally to the invariants underlying the transformations of the proximal stimulus pattern received by the normally moving perceiver, and that those invariants of course reflect the invariant structure of the physical world.

Although the proposal is an intriguing one, it should be noted that as yet no mechanisms have been suggested by which such invariants might be detected and used, nor is there any evidence that in fact they are used. Further, there exist demonstrations of precisely the kind of unconscious inference-like processes that lay at the heart of the classical theory; even if the direct theory is correct in major respects, therefore, it will not sweep away all the components of the classical explanation of constancy.

COGNITIVE COMPLEXITY
CONTEXTUAL ASSOCIATIONS
PERCEPTION

J. E. HOCHBERG

CONSTITUTIONAL TYPES

Constitutional perspective is a theoretical position that stresses the biological aspects of human behavior. William H. Sheldon is credited with pioneering work in contemporary constitutional psychology. Sheldon defined a discrete number of physical and temperamental variables that he asserted were of primary significance in understanding and explaining behavior patterns. The basic assumption underlying his somatotyping position is grounded in biological determinism.

Sheldon and his associates photographed and studied thousands of college students and found that they could be classified under three primary components of body build: endomorphy, mesomorphy, and ectomorphy. The *endomorph* is characterized by softness, roundness, and a large digestive system. Consistent with the softness and rounded quality is an underdevelopment of bone and muscle tissue. The *mesomorph* is characterized by strong bones and muscles. The mesomorphic physique is generally heavy, hard, and rectangular in outline. This person's body is strong, resistant to injury, and typically equipped for strenuous physical demands. The *ectomorph* is characterized by thinness and a large skin area and nervous system in proportion to size.

Each of the three body builds was considered to be a continuous variable that varied along a 7 point scale, and each person was given a set of numbers from 1 to 7. With such a system of measurement it was possible for Sheldon and his associates to obtain a more reliable and differentiated picture of a person's constitutional type than was the case with previous investigators.

After identifying the body types, Sheldon studied the basic components of temperament associated with various body structures. After examining evidence and correlating various clusters of temperamental traits, Sheldon concluded there were three basic dimensions of temperament: viscerotonia, somatotonia, and cerebrotonia. Individuals labeled *viscerotones* were characterized by relaxed posture, love of comfort, a need for approval and affection from others, and a high degree of sociability. Typical characteristics of *somatotones* included aggressiveness, love of physical adventure, risk taking, a need for and enjoyment of exercise, boldness of manner, love of dominating and lust for power, and psychological callousness. *Cerebrotones* were characterized by emotional restraint, tenseness, overly fast reactions, love of privacy, a degree of self-consciousness, a fear of people and social situations, and a basic need for solitude.

Calvin Hall and Gardner Lindzey propose four explanations for the association of types of physiques and basic temperaments: (a) the person's type of physique may determine his or her pattern of responses; (b) the relationship between body build and temperament may be mediated by certain stereotypes (with certain expected behaviors of persons with various types of physiques); (c) environmental influences may produce particular kinds of physique and also certain types of behaviors; and (d) both physique and behavioral tendencies may be largely determined by genetic factors.

Richard Ryckman assessed the theory in terms of six criteria: (a) in terms of *comprehensiveness*, the theory is inadequate, as it does not generate hypotheses outside its narrow province; (b) to Sheldon's credit, his approach contains *precision* and *testability*. With the use of a 7 point scale, Sheldon made it possible for other researchers to gauge with more accuracy the somatotypes and temperaments of people and to assess the relationship between these factors; (c) on the criterion of *simplicity*, Sheldon's theory has too few concepts and too few assumptions to account adequately for the range and diversity of phenomena involved in a theory of personality. (d) Although Sheldon has made serious efforts not to just illustrate but actually to prove his theory, the *empirical support* for his position is weak. (e) In terms of *heuristic value*, Sheldon's approach has not had a great impact in generating research efforts of other investigators. (f) As to *applied value*, Sheldon's theory has had very little practical value.

BEHAVIORAL GENETICS
IDENTITY FORMATION
PERSONALITY THEORIES

G. Corey

CONSUMER PSYCHOLOGY

There are two major aspects of consumer behavior: satisfaction of *needs* and the fulfillment of *wants*.

Consumer behavior that involves only needs requires relatively little explanation. It is sufficient to collect data on when, where, and what the consumer bought. When we want to understand the *why,* however, we are dealing with the more complex phenomenon of motivation.

Wants govern a large part of our consumer behavior. George Katona in *The powerful consumer* discusses the interaction between financial and psychological factors. Recession, affluence, and inflation are the results or the origin of consumer behavior and consumer psychology. Understanding the reason for attitudes, preferences, and expression of desires requires a combination of economics, anthropology, and psychology.

Although obtaining simple data about consumer behavior could be called "consumer psychology," this term applies more clearly to *why* consumers behave as they do. The answers to *why* questions concern *wants* more often than *needs*.

To bring about a deeper insight into consumer psychology, several factors have to be considered.

The Gestalt principle. Purchase of a particular product should be seen in its largest possible cultural framework. When wanting to find out why people buy a particular soap, it is more fruitful to study the more global Gestalt of bathing behavior. Thus many studies in consumer psychology start out with an analysis of basic questions.

The iceberg principle. The iceberg principle states that something is going on beneath the surface. When this notion is applied, it turns out that the majority of buying behavior—and also social behavior such as voting or giving up smoking—is governed by deep-seated reasons. If one accepts this principle, one avoids direct *why* questions in studying consumer motivation. If one uses why questions, the respondent is tempted to explain his or her motivations, which is often impossible.

The dynamic principle. Human motivations are not static. Social, economic, and psychological trends influence all forms of behavior. Questionnaire techniques that concentrate on present behavior often leave out all-important information. Asking people how much money they make leaves out the common sense recognition that whether someone has been increasing his or her income, standing still, or going down economically, is much more relevant than present income. Psychologically speaking, even though they may be earning the exact same amount, people who are moving up, standing still, or descending really belong to three entirely different categories.

Image and symbolism. Behind each product is an idea. What a consumer retains, after having been bombarded with advertising of a particular brand of a product, is the image of the product. It is the melody, the rhythm, the total configuration surrounding a product, a candidate, or a country. It is more than a nebulous phenomenon. Many research studies have shown that we immediately change our opinion and interpretation of a neutral statement, when we discover that a person we do or do not like is identified with it. We react to the signature rather than to the content of communication.

The application of these four principles—borrowed from anthropology, depth psychology, futurology, and symbolism—and their necessary translation into methodology, represent major innovations in consumer psychology. They are the framework for getting closer to consumer motivations. A distinction should be made between interpretive and descriptive research. Descriptive research *describes* consumer behavior. Such

information is of course highly important, but does not represent basic research. If we want to motivate and influence consumers, we need *interpretations* of consumer behavior. If we discount the deliberate lying of respondents queried, it is possible to develop statistically convincing descriptions and analyses of such behavior.

The method applied in modern consumer psychology research is to permit the respondent to describe his or her behavior in as many concrete details as possible without self-diagnosis. Instead of asking a person why he or she bought a particular car, the researcher gets the person to relate all the many details from the time when he or she first considered buying a new car to the final conclusion of the purchase; this permits an analysis by the researcher of the consumer's true buying motivations.

Good consumer psychology starts with the development of creative and intelligent hypotheses about consumer behavior. These hypotheses can stem from cultural frameworks, depth psychology, or futurology and symbolism. The question "Why do consumers buy a particular brand of soap?" can be a legitimate aspect of consumer psychology. By starting out with an analysis of bathing habits and rituals, the first principle is put to work. Soap may give consumers a feeling of more than physical cleansing. Baptism or ritual bathing washes one clean of sins and guilt (the iceberg principle).

The dynamic principle permits the researcher of consumer psychology to discover relative changes. These may concern income: Is it standing still, going up, or going down? The absolute amount may be the same, but consumer reactions may differ.

Symbolism is an important part of communication. Consumers understand nonverbal expressions often better than explicit ones. "Put a tiger in your tank" conveys a feeling of strength, although it sounds ridiculous when translated literally. Consumers often buy an image rather than the tangible advantage of a brand, or vote for an image rather than the promises of a political candidate.

Do we need new products? Consumer psychology invites moral dilemmas. As long as we are trying only to understand the consumer's behavior, everything is quietly accepted. The organizations interested in this behavior, however, are frequently involved in trying to motivate the consumer to buy a certain brand of product or to behave in a certain way.

Economists seem to be governed by a thought model concerning consumer wants and needs that resembles a pie. The more sections that have been cut out of this pie, the less that is left. They conceive of human needs and wants as being limited. Modern consumer psychology, however, shows that it is more accurate to describe these wants and needs as continuously expanding. The growth of the record industry started fairly soon after the emergence of radio. Being able, with the turn of a knob, to have many channels at the listener's disposal should have resulted in a smaller pie. What had been overlooked was that a more psychological law governs consumer needs: The more musical and acoustical entertainment consumers discovered, the more they wanted to have.

As consumer psychology becomes more recognized, it will help in influencing the often too rational and logical thinking of economists and market analysts. Thus during a recession, it is assumed, sales of luxury products should suffer, whereas in fact they usually increase. A purely logical explanation does not suffice. In times of insecurity we need symbols of quality and permanence, hence, whether we can afford to or not, we buy more expensive products such as a Mercedes Benz, jewelry, and cruises. In the future, we may have to speak more frequently of psychological economics as a new discipline.

ADVERTISING
APPLIED RESEARCH

CONSUMER RESEARCH
MOTIVATION

E. Dichter

CONSUMER RESEARCH

DEFINITION

Consumer research systematically studies the many aspects of human behavior related to the purchase and use of economic goods and services. The product-related focus includes research in advertising effectiveness, product features, and marketing techniques. Focus on the consumer has included the study of attitudes, feelings, and preferences, as well as an in-depth look at the many group influences on the decision-making process of the individual consumer. The field also studies the consumer as citizen and as a central figure in social/environmental problem solving. The scope and range of activity makes consumer research highly interdisciplinary. It integrates theoretical concepts and research approaches from social psychology, sociology, and economics. The applied orientation gives it a prominent family resemblance to engineering, medicine, and law.

In one sense consumer research is as old as the dawn of recorded human history, and in still another sense it is as young as the last few decades. Its longer history dates to the very beginnings of advertising, while its youthfulness dates from the point at which its own independence was formally established and recognized professionally.

Not until the 1920s did consumer research begin to focus on two-way communication: gathering information from consumers to prepare more effective advertisements. Still later, attention was given to consumer attitudes and opinions prior to product design. As this consumer focus steadily grew, it marked the appearance of a newly independent member of the advertising family—consumer psychology, which formally gained its own identity in 1960, when the Division of Consumer Psychology was formed within the American Psychological Association.

The most visible change that occurred with formal independence was a shift from looking strictly at the consumer's purchasing role to the more global perspective of the consumer. This perspective is clearly illustrated in the decision-process approach to consumer behavior. The purchase is considered to be but one stage in a purchase process; the approach considers it essential to analyze the events that precede and follow this act.

With the focus shift toward the consumer there has been prominent growth in attention to the consumer's thoughts, feelings, and perspectives. The question of what consumers want represented a significant step beyond the question of how to assure that consumers purchased what had already been produced. It also encompassed questions of consumer welfare, product safety, and the "truth-in-packaging" legislation of 1967, each representing central concerns within the consumerism movement of the 1960s.

A final focus shift observed by Jacoby is oriented toward the reciprocal nature of consumer behavior: (a) the responsibility of society toward the individual consumer, and (b) the responsibility of the individual consumer toward society. In this context, society's responsibility encompasses areas such as health care and delivery systems, and cultural and recreational facilities.

RESEARCH TECHNIQUES AND PROCEDURES

With its broad, interdisciplinary scope, consumer research taps an equally broad and diverse set of research tools and techniques. The more general the consumer research approach (e.g., consumer attitudes, thoughts, and feelings), the more likely that the research tool emphasis will be on scales or surveys.

Ad and Product Testing

Each of these constitutes a rather specific activity, and it is not surprising that the majority of techniques used has a correspondingly specific focus. In *ad testing* interest centers on the attention-getting capacities of different advertising features and their effectiveness in communicating the product or service message. Sophisticated laboratory techniques make it possible to *camera-monitor* and *computer-record* where an individual is looking on a page or screen. This videotaped record can then be carefully studied to determine whether the aspects considered important in basic ad design have had their desired attentional effect. Another technique utilized in settings ranging from ad design to the development of children's television programs is *binocular rivalry*. This technique simply places two ads in competition with each other by presenting them simultaneously. The test can vary several aspects of design to determine which is most effective in drawing viewer attention. Magazine-type formats can also be assembled that contain different versions of the target ad and test a variety of ad features while monitoring viewer attention.

Consumer Surveys

The goal of a consumer survey is to discern attitudes and opinions of the individual consumer. Opinion may be sought in relation to an existing product or service, or an approach may target general attitudes and personality characteristics that will enable the product or service designer to incorporate these findings into the planning of future approaches.

Market Segmentation

Once the consumer researcher has developed a profile of the individuals who constitute an existing or potential market, the next step is to reach those individuals with an effective message. This communication goal requires knowledge of reading, listening, and viewing patterns in terms of both specific programs and media. Commercial television relies heavily on the Nielsen ratings to provide viewing patterns and profiles. Radio has comparable ratings services (e.g., Arbitron), while general circulation data and readership surveys perform this research function in print media.

One aspect of this type of market analysis is seen within the "family life cycle" approach. The different stages of the adult life cycle are outlined and the characteristics of each are carefully studied for marketing implications.

Since consumer research established its own independent identity, it has grown dramatically. This growth parallels closely the expansion and diversification that have occurred in the entire field of applied research. With many academicians and professionals coming to it from several disciplines, the field lacks a uniformity of approach. Generalizations are difficult when the body of research comprises small "one-shot" studies rather than larger scale programs of research. As the field grows and matures, J. F. Engel and others see a need for more research programs in critical problem areas. Research priorities must be established and systematically pursued, while depth will come with more prominent utilization of theories and models. Continued rapid growth seems assured.

ADVERTISING
APPLIED PSYCHOLOGY

E. L. Palmer

CONTAMINATION (STATISTICAL)

Statistical contamination results from a failure to take into account major sources of variance that affect the relationship between research variables. Whenever two or more independent variables in combination affect a dependent variable differently than any of the independent variables would by itself, an interaction effect has occurred. If this interaction effect occurs as a result of the presence of an unintended independent variable, it is impossible to determine how much of the experimental results are due to the extraneous variable rather than to the independent variables specified by the researcher. To make this distinction, further research would be required. Statistical procedures can be performed on data with statistical contamination, but once it is recognized that the contamination is present, the findings are not interpretable. This source of error is difficult to correct, because the extraneous variable has not been recognized until after the fact, and the data needed to allow for this source of variance has usually not been collected. The best safeguard against this type of error is a thorough literature review prior to collecting data to ensure that the researcher is familiar with the major reported sources of variance.

Isaac and Michael list two types of statistical contamination that may result from unanticipated interaction effects. The first type is called *confounding*. This occurs when variance from an extraneous variable mixes with the variance of the independent variable.

The second type of statistical contamination is *cancellation of effects*. In this case an actual difference may be hidden from view by the presence of an extraneous variable that counteracts the effects of the independent variables.

ANALYSIS OF VARIANCE
DATA ANALYSIS
RESEARCH METHODOLOGY
STATISTICS IN PSYCHOLOGY

D. E. Bowen

CONTEXTUAL ASSOCIATION

Context has occupied an important but ambiguous position in psychological theory. Early treatments of the concept by English-speaking psychologists regarded context as background stimulation that sustained and supported behavior. One implication of giving context the same logical status as other sources of stimulation was that it could be treated as just another stimulus that could enter into association with other events. Used in this way, context enabled psychologists to account for how experience and, more specifically, learning could modify our perceptions.

E. B. Titchener, the leading proponent of structuralism in the United States, announced that sensations acquired their meanings from the context in which they occurred. Simple sensations have no meaning as such; meaning is present when other sensations or images accompany the original sensation. For Titchener, meaning was the totality of sensation conjured up whenever a particular sensation was experienced in a particular context. Even earlier, William James had discussed how initially confusable stimuli become more distinctive as a result of the addition of more distinctive cues, or associations, to each stimulus.

Why do such diverse traditions—Titchener's structuralism, James' functionalism, and the neobehaviorism of modern theorists—treat context in the same way? Inspite of their many differences, these traditions all have their roots in empiricism. They share empiricism's emphasis on the analysis of phenomena into basic elements, and its appeal to associationism to account for the unity of mental life.

Although context may function as a stimulus, entering into association with the events embedded within it, it is equally plausible that the context of a stimulus may serve as a metamessage that classifies the elementary stimulus (signal). The message conveyed by a signal may be determined by the context in which the message resides. In other words, the same stimulus may signal quite different messages in different contexts. Viewed in this light, context becomes a superordinate concept ordering and structuring behavior hierarchically.

PERCEPTION
STRUCTURALISM

E. J. RICKERT

CONTROL GROUPS

A control group is a group of subjects not subjected to the experimental treatment but like the experimental group or groups in every other way. The purpose of the control group is to provide a base against which to determine whether a change in the experimental group occurred, and to eliminate all explanations other than the treatment that differentiates the groups. Which group is experimental and which is the control would be determined by a coin flip, to avoid unconsciously giving the treatment to the group appearing more favorable. Because with random assignment every person has as much chance of being assigned to one group as another, differences between groups cancel out; on the average, one group will be like the other. If the groups are alike in every way except that only one receives the treatment, then behavioral differences between the children in the experimental and control groups may presumably be traced to the treatment. That is the logic of the method of differences expounded by John Stuart Mill.

However, even with large groups, where chance presumably evens things out, are the groups *exactly* alike? They cannot be, for each person is unique; it has been said no two persons have the same number of hairs on their heads. It is essential only that the groups be alike with respect to aspects related to that which is being studied. The problem, of course, is whether we know all those aspects. This is why random assignment is important; on the average, it not only evens out all characteristics—even the average number of hairs on the head—but also, and more significantly, unsuspected important variables. Indeed, Donald Campbell and Julian Stanley distinguish "true" experimental designs from "quasi-experimental" ones on the basis of whether subjects were randomly assigned to groups.

Differences between the groups that leave open alternative explanations of the results may result from (a) initial differences, (b) events occurring during treatment but unrelated to it, and (c) aspects of the treatment itself.

Initial group differences often appear where random assignment is not feasible—for instance, when one must use intact classrooms, or when characteristics of the experimental variable—length, complexity, unpleasantness—may require the use of volunteers.

Rival explanations may also result from events that occur during a study. For the control group to serve to eliminate such explanations, it must be exposed to the events as well. For example, a teacher might learn to more effectively prevent hyperactive outbursts, so that caffeine-treated students would appear less hyperactive. Unless *both* experimental *and* control group children were assigned to her class, or measures were taken to equate the way teachers of both groups learned to handle such incidents, this could become a rival explanation.

Finally, aspects of the intervention that are not part of the treatment being tested may produce differences. For example, the fact that one group knows they are being treated because they are given pills may itself produce an expectation of improved behavior. To eliminate this rival explanation, the control group must also be given a treatment indistinguishable by subjects, teachers, and researchers from the real treatment. In this instance a placebo—an inert pill—might be administered, with knowledge of who received it kept by a neutral party until after the results are in. This is known as a double-blind study.

DOUBLE-BLIND RESEARCH
MILL'S CANONS

RESEARCH METHODOLOGY
SAMPLING

D. R. KRATHWOHL

CONTROL OF BEHAVIOR

Within psychology there have been two very broad approaches to "controlling" behavior, based on quite different philosophical assumptions about the nature of human beings. The first, which might be termed *external causality*, is based on a set of assumptions labeled *mechanistic*, while the second, *internal causality*, is based on a set of assumptions labeled *organismic*. As outlined by Deci and Ryan in *Intrinsic motivation and human behavior*, the external approach assumes an empty, passive organism, while the internal approach assumes a structured, active organism. This assertion is something of an oversimplification, because many different theories are relevant to behavior control, but few represent pure forms of either the mechanistic or the organismic approach.

EXTERNAL APPROACH

Operant theory is an example of the mechanistic, external approach. Humans are assumed to be passive and reactive to environmental events, and behaviors are theorized to be a function of associations that have developed between stimuli and responses as a result of reinforcement processes.

With these assumptions and assertions, control systems are designed in terms of reinforcement processes. Four principles guide the design of such systems. The first, based on E. L. Thorndike's classic law of effect (*The psychology of learning*), states that behaviors that are followed by a reinforcement will be strengthened; that is, they will be more likely to recur. The second states that behaviors that are not followed by a reinforcement will be weakened and eventually extinguished. Third, punishments also tend to decrease the likelihood of a response recurring; however, they have the disadvantage of eliciting emotional reactions. Further, the response is more likely to spontaneously recur later following punishment than to do so following extinction. Still, punishments tend to produce quicker short-run termination of a response than does the mere withholding of reinforcements. Fourth and finally, the length of time until extinction (i.e., until the target response terminates), once reinforcements have been withheld, will depend on the schedule of reinforcement. If reinforcements had been given infrequently and unpredictably, responding will continue longer following the removal of reinforcements than if they had been given following each response.

In recent years there has been substantial modification of the behavioral position. Theorists such as Albert Bandura have asserted that people's cognitions mediate between stimuli and responses. The newer cognitive behaviorism adds two important principles to those already discussed. First, people can learn by observing others, so the procedure of modeling is used as a control technique. Second, self-administered reinforcements have been found to work more effectively than those administered by others, so self-reinforcement techniques have been developed. With self-reinforcement, the emphasis is still on reinforcements, but the administration procedures are different.

The most significant difference between behaviorism and cognitive behaviorism (i.e., social learning theory) is that the latter explains behavior in terms of people's expectations about future reinforcements, rather than in terms of past reinforcements and reinforcement contingencies. This change implies a somewhat more active organism, for it suggests that people will act on the environment to get desired outcomes. Still, this view runs into difficulties by focusing its analysis at the cognitive rather than the motivational level.

INTERNAL APPROACH

This approach asserts that the human organism is by nature active and that this activity is motivated by innate, intrinsic needs to be competent and self-determining. This has a number of implications. First, it implies that under certain circumstances people control themselves, because this can leave them feeling both competent and self-determining. Second, it implies—and research reported by Deci and Ryan confirms—that external reinforcements can actually undermine people's intrinsic motivation and control of themselves. Finally, as J. W. Brehm has demonstrated, it implies that when people are controlled externally, they may actually react against the controls and do just the opposite.

With the assumptions and findings of internal causality, control systems tend to be designed around the concept of intrinsic motivation. Because research has—shown that the conditions that promote intrinsic motivation are choice and positive competence feedback, control structures are designed to offer choice and provide feedback.

Choice and feedback enhance intrinsic motivation, yet they must be taken one step further to explain how people acquire behaviors that are deemed appropriate by superiors or society, but that they would not be likely to adopt on their own. Limits must be set for their behavior, but it must be done in a way that offers choice and feedback. This means setting limits as wide as possible, so that maximal choice will be available within the limits; further, when limits are established and consequences for transgression are set, it is preferable to let people choose whether to stay within the limits or to transgress them and endure the consequences.

To understand the types of control systems more fully, it is necessary to distinguish between two types of internal control of oneself. Deci and Ryan refer to these as *introjected* versus *integrated* internalization. Introjection refers to the process by which an external control has been internalized intact. It is, as it were, "swallowed whole." Integrated internalizations involve taking them on as one's own.

Deci and Ryan suggest that the integrated internalization results from limit setting that emphasizes choice and feedback, whereas introjection results from demands and sanctions. Cognitive behavioral theories, unlike the more orthodox behaviorism, emphasize the control of oneself, yet their cognitive analysis has not distinguished between the two types of self-control—introjected versus integrated.

FREE WILL
INDIVIDUALITY
INNER–OUTER DIRECTED BEHAVIOR
INTRINSIC MOTIVATION
LEVEL OF ASPIRATION
RESPONSIBILITY AND BEHAVIOR
SELF-DETERMINATION

E. L. DECI

CONTROL OF VARIABLES

Control is used in science in two somewhat related but basically different ways. In "popular" usage it refers to management. We say we want to control our tempers or to control inflation. This kind of control is a principal applied objective of science. The meaning is exemplified in the common statement that the objective of science is to describe, predict, and control.

The second usage refers to the elimination of selected variables in experiments, or experiment-like observations—thus "controlling" those variables. Eliminating the variation in controlled variables makes it possible to measure more effectively the influence of some other variable(s), called *independent*, on the measured, or *dependent*, variable(s). Such elimination of extraneous variation enables the researcher to reduce the natural ambiguity that clouds cause–effect relationships and so obtain more accurate data.

A variable can be controlled in two principal ways. The simplest way is making the variable exactly the same in all conditions or groups of subjects; for example, eliminating variation in sex of subjects by using only males or only females as subjects. The second way is to allow some operation of the controlled variable but to attempt to hold it at the same level in all conditions or groups of subjects; for example, by using equal numbers of males and females in each of the groups of subjects in the experiment.

Control of crucial variables is not always easy or even possible. The best example of this fact comes from astronomy. It is, of course, not possible to manipulate the action of stars and planets or other heavenly bodies so as to make controlled observations feasible. Nevertheless, it is possible to plan observations in advance so as to take advantage of the occurrence of certain natural events—in so-called natural experiments—and thereby achieve some degree of control in observations.

A similar situation exists in the field of neurophysiology, or neuropsychology, in which a scientist may wish to examine the effects of a certain kind of brain function and in so doing needs to eliminate the influence of (control) some other function. Although the scientist is not able to control the latter function by operating on the responsible brain part at some convenient time, this kind of operation may become necessary in certain patients as a result of disease or accidental injury, such as those occurring in automobile accidents or gunshot wounds.

The clinical psychologist who wishes to determine the relationship between a specified set of antecedent conditions in an individual's life history and a specified set of personality attributes or other behavioral measures must await the accumulation of enough cases with those conditions. Such an investigator does have an important advantage over the astronomer, however, in that he or she can make a more active effort to locate and study the kind of cases required. To use the control principle, cases that are otherwise equivalent but are without the particular set of prior conditions under investigation must also be examined as "controls." There are numerous ways in which this kind of passive control can be exercised.

ANALYSIS OF VARIANCE
ANALYSIS OF COVARIANCE
EXPERIMENTAL CONTROLS
EXPERIMENTAL DESIGNS
EXPERIMENTAL METHODS
EXPERIMENTAL PSYCHOLOGY
VARIABLES IN RESEARCH

M. H. Marx

CONTROL THEORY

"Control theory" is the most recent in a succession of names for the developing body of theory based on a feedback-system paradigm. Other names are "cybernetic-psychology," "general feedback theory of human behavior," or simply, "systems theory psychology."

Although self-regulatory (homeostatic) mechanisms came to be accepted as applying to the body, the idea that the same principles apply in the area of mind has gained ground more slowly. Beginning in the 1940s, a number of scientists began proposing that such principles could be seen underlying behavior. In spite of the growing conviction that cybernetic principles could be seen in many aspects of behavior, two unresolved issues continued to confound attempts to develop a more comprehensive and precise feedback model.

HOMEOSTASIS VERSUS ADAPTATION

How could behavior be controlled so as always to resist external disturbances to the steady state being maintained by the organism, and yet account for development and learning?

An equally difficult problem was accounting for the integration of behavior. Granted that some aspects of behavior showed the appearance of feedback control, did other principles apply to other aspects of behavior? How were the separate feedback systems in the organism tied together?

One team that continued to struggle with the questions of adaptation and integration published a coherent model back in 1960. They were William T. Powers, R. K. Clark, R. L. McFarland.

The most elementary concept of the new model is the negative-feedback control loop, closed through the environment and consisting conceptually of five elements:

1. The feedback function consists of a transducer sensitive to some particular, identifiable environmental variable, and a *feedback signal*, which relays a signal providing an analog of changes sensed by the transducer to the comparator function.

2. In the comparator function the *feedback signal* is compared with (a) a *reference signal*, giving rise to (b) an *error signal* whenever the comparator computes a discrepancy between the *feedback signal* and the *reference signal*.

3. The *reference signal* must be compatible with the *feedback signal*, so that comparison is possible, as for example when each is constituted by the flow of impulses along a nerve fiber.

4. The *error signal* is a function of any discrepancy between *feedback signal* and *reference signal*, representing the magnitude of the discrepancy.

5. The output function consists of any appropriate type of effector mechanism—that is, an effector capable of influencing the environmental variable monitored by the transducer mentioned in (1). The output exerts its effect on the environment in such a manner as to bring about a match between the *feedback signal* and the *reference signal*, which reduces the *error signal* to zero.

The significance of the basic control-loop concept is best mediated by translation into behavioral terms as follows. Consider the reference signal as representing the "desired state of affairs"; consider the feedback signal as representing the "existing state of affairs"; consider the error signal as representing the discrepancy, if any, between the existing and desired states; and consider the output function as the source of action on the environment capable of driving the existing state toward the desired state.

A profound consequence of this theory for psychology is the implication that living organisms do not control their environments by controlling their outputs. They control their inputs—their "perceptions,"—as Powers states in the title of his book, *Behavior: The control of perception.* Control over the environment results as a by-product of controlling one's perceptions when viewed from this perspective.

THE ORGANISM AS A HIERARCHY OF CONTROL SYSTEMS

The question of how the control hierarchy comes into existence is possibly the most speculative aspect of the model. Powers postulated an "intrinsic" system: a genetically determined, species-specific set of control circuits monitoring fundamental life-support variables such as oxygen-, temperature-, and other basic life-maintenance systems. This system exists apart from the learned hierarchy. An "organizing-reorganizing" system, activated by rising error signals within the intrinsic system, functions similarly to the random signal generator used by cybernetic engineers to inject miscellaneous neural impulses into the control hierarchy, thereby arbitrarily resetting reference signals and disrupting homeostasis. The resulting random action constitutes new learning, when the associated reference signals are stored in memory and become available for future implementation.

An intriguing implication of the above view is that, except for preprogrammed action patterns, no "behavior" can be performed intentionally until it has first been recorded as a result of "successful" random activity. The seemingly useless random flailings of infants take on a new significance in this light.

RESEARCH AND APPLICATIONS

Control theory research breaks with traditional approaches to research methodology in psychology. Most current research is based on a "causal model," in which influence is expected to flow in one direction. Cybernetic theory in general shows that "cause" is ambiguous when one examines variables under the control of negative feedback systems. Powers' book introduces a methodological approach taken from servo-engineering: "a test for the controlled variable." This consists of applying a disturbance to a variable suspected to be under feedback control and noting what happens. If, indeed, the variable is under feedback control, the system will resist the disturbance, the speed and magnitude of the resistance revealing the characteristics of the system.

EVALUATION

Although control theory provides the most natural theoretical basis for a major tenet of humanistic psychology—that behavior originates not in stimuli from the environment but within the organism—some humanistically inclined psychologists have viewed control theory as an attempt to model human behavior after machines.

Another critism made by some psychologists is that control theory fails to account for emotions. Little mention is made of emotion by Powers or other authors of feedback theories. The problem may be an ambiguity in the concept of "emotion" itself. Sometimes the word is used to refer to preprogrammed (i.e., unlearned) patterns of behavior. At other times it appears to convey observations about the energy with which some behavior is executed, without reference to either its objective or its manner of control. The major reason for the slow increase in adherents to control theory may be found in neither of the above types of objections but rather in the view put forward by T. S. Kuhn in *The structure of scientific revolutions,* which states that Powers' theory does not represent a logical development of the dominant paradigms in contemporary psychology, but rather constitutes a direct challenge to them. It reverses 300 years of perceiving behavior as under the control of stimuli from outside the organism.

BEHAVIORISM
GENERAL SYSTEMS
INDIVIDUALITY THEORY
PHYSICS AND BEHAVIORAL SCIENCE
TELEOLOGICAL PSYCHOLOGY

R. J. ROBERTSON

CONTROLLED DRINKING

Controlled drinking refers to the ability of an alcoholic who has exhibited out-of-control drinking patterns to return to normal, controlled alcohol consumption. The literature on this concept is complex and contradictory. It is coterminous with arguments concerning whether alcoholism is a unitary disease, with symptoms of increased severity that build on one another, finally producing a full-blown disease defined, in part, by loss of control over drinking.

THE DISEASE CONCEPT

The following assumptions represent the prodisease position. Alcoholism is a progressive, cumulative illness, with clear biological, psychological, and social causes. Similar to other diseases (e.g., cancer and diabetes), alcoholism is not caused by lack of willpower. Two essential features of this disease are *craving* and *loss of control.* Alcoholics exhibit a craving for alcohol that leads them, once the first drink is taken, to drink until intoxication. According to this position, alcoholics can never again drink successfully. Their disease is irreversible. They have lost the ability to control their drinking. Treatment requires abstinence and participation in a recovery program such as Alcoholics Anonymous (AA), which promotes abstinence and a commitment to the loss-of-control position ("once an alcoholic, always an alcoholic").

The antidisease perspective argues that alcoholism does not qualify as a disease. It is not an irreversible condition. There are no proven, invariant causes. It does not follow a predetermined path. The key conditions of craving and loss of control can be experimentally manipulated, suggesting that willpower is the key feature of the condition. Alcoholics can be taught to control their drinking; formerly heavy and problem drinkers can become successful social drinkers. They do not have to become abstainers. The nondisease position walks a fine line between the medical and moral positions.

The history of the concept *controlled drinking* has moved through five key phases, each phase being defined by conflicting arguments concerning whether alcoholism is a disease.

Phase One: 1935–1960

From 1935 (the creation of AA) to 1960, the unitary disease concept of alcoholism defined research, treatment, and public policy. Social scientists posited a progressive, four-stage medical model of alcoholism. Alcoholics, they argued, moved from the presymptomatic stage (drinking to reduce anxiety and stress), to the prodromal (onset of secret drinking and blackouts), crucial, and then chronic stages of addiction. In the crucial stage, the alcoholic loses control over alcohol consumption. Such individuals could never again go back to controlled, normal, social drinking.

This model defined four distinct types of alcoholics: (a) *alpha* alcoholics—those who are psychologically dependent on alcohol; (b) *beta* alcoholics—those who acquire a physical dependence on alcohol and develop physical complications caused by their drinking; (c) *gamma* alcoholics—those who have all the characteristics of alpha and beta alcoholics but in addition have lost control over their drinking; and (d) *delta* alcoholics—those who do not lose control but who cannot abstain from drinking.

According to Jellinek, the gamma alcoholic was the prevailing type of alcoholic in the United States and the one most likely to become a member of AA. This medical model held until the early 1960s. Many researchers have argued that it divided any population of drinkers into two categories: (a) a large group of harm-free, normal social drinkers and (b) a tragic minority of uncontrolled alcoholic drinkers.

Phase Two: 1960–1970

In 1962, D. L. Davies argued that many formerly heavy drinkers had become adjusted social drinkers, rather than abstainers. The Davies' report challenged the medical disease model and questioned the loss-of-control concept. This report was quickly supported by a series of national surveys indicating that individuals move in and out of problem drinking situations. At the same time, behavioral researchers, influenced by Albert Bandura's social learning theory, reported findings that indicated that the drinking patterns of gamma alcoholics, including loss of control and craving, could be manipulated in the laboratory.

In this new literature, alcoholism was transformed from a unitary disease into a multidimensional illness, with drinkers classified along a continuum from an occasional problem drinker, to a problem drinker, to a person in the acute stages of alcohol dependency. Abstinence now became only one among several treatment goals.

Phase Three: 1970–1980

Phase three was defined by controversy over the behavioral learning theory models. The mid-1970 Sobell and Sobell study of gamma alcoholics who were taught to drink socially aroused considerable controversy because many of their subjects in a follow-up study were found still to be drinking in an out-of-control manner.

During this decade, the Comprehensive Alcohol Abuse and Alcoholism Prevention, Treatment, and Rehabilitation Act was passed and revised. This act mandated federal support for the treatment of alcoholism and required that insurance companies be prepared to pay part of the cost of treatment for alcoholism. By 1980, there were more than 5000 alcoholism or substance abuse treatment centers in the United States, treating more than 1 million individuals a year at an annual cost of more than $15 billion. The prevailing form of treatment drew on the medical disease–AA concept of alcoholism. This was a paradox, for the dominant social science theories refuted the disease model.

Phase Four: 1980–1990

Community-based treatment methods developed in the United Kingdom, based on the behavioral, multidimensional views, gained favor. New treatment goals were developed in an attempt to match various degrees of harmful drinking with varying degrees of abstinence. The disease concept was called a myth (Fingarette) that not only supported the treatment industry but also prolonged the problem drinking careers of many, while absolving them of responsibility over their drinking. At the same time, it mandated a single treatment goal (abstinence), and one treatment modality (AA). Critics of the myth argued that no form of treatment was better than any other. Multivariant treatment models, rejecting the traditional concept of a unitary syndrome of alcoholism, were developed. Meanwhile, the federal Drug-Free Workplace Act was passed, giving employers the power to test their workers for drug use (including alcohol). The disease model underwrote this legislation.

Phase Five: Post–1990

This decade is defined by what David Pittman calls the new temperance movement, which builds on the "War on Drugs" of the 1980s. Various consumer and public interest groups attempted to reduce the per capita consumption of alcoholic beverages, arguing that there are enormous health risks associated with drinking alcohol. The medical disease model is alive in the publications of social groups like Co-Dependents Anonymous (CODA) and Adult Children of Alcoholics (ACOA) even as it continues to be attacked in the social science and public health literature.

Discourse in this field has nearly returned to where it was in 1935 when alcoholics were called weak-willed and alcoholism was defined as a moral illness or failure of self. Jellinek's attempts to formulate a multidimensional, progressive concept of the illness persists, even in the multivariant models of the behavioral researchers. The American population and the social science community persist in their debates concerning whether alcoholism is a disease defined by loss of control over drinking. The population is still divided into two groups, normal social drinkers and alcoholics, and AA remains the most popular form of treatment for this "disease."

ALCOHOLISM TREATMENT
ANTABUSE
DEPENDENCY
DRUG REHABILITATION
SELF-CONTROL
SUBSTANCE ABUSE

N. K. DENZIN

CONVERSION DISORDER

The term *conversion* derives from the Freudian concept of conversion hysteria, in which a psychosexual conflict was seen as being *converted* into a bodily disturbance. Today, conversion disorders represent a rather specific and rare clinical entity within the more general family of somatoform disorders. As such, one of the essential features is the presence of a physical complaint without demonstrable physiological or disease mechanisms to account for it. Specifically, according to the American Psychiatric Association's *Diagnostic and statistical manual of mental disorders, Fourth edition* (*DSM-IV*), conversion disorders present a "clinical picture in which the predominant disturbance is a loss of or alteration in physical functioning that suggests physical disorder but which instead is apparently an expression of a psychological conflict or need." Further, the symptoms are not under the person's voluntary control and they cannot be explained by pathophysiological processes. Symptoms restricted to pain or sexual functioning, or that are part of a more pervasive somatization disorder, are not classified as conversion.

CLINICAL PRESENTATION

Conversion symptoms tend to be fairly discrete and singular, with an abrupt onset during times of extreme psychological stress. In the most obvious or classic cases, the conversion symptoms involve pathological changes in sensory and motor functions, mimicking those found in neurological diseases. The most common symptoms cited in *DSM-IV* include paralysis, aphonia (disturbance of speech volume), blindness or tunnel vision, seizures, anesthesia (loss of sensation) or paresthesia (abnormal spontaneous sensation), and dyskinesia (disturbance of coordinated movements). In less common cases the conversion disorder may involve the endocrine or autonomic system, and result in such symptoms as false pregnancy (pseudocyesis) or vomiting.

ETIOLOGY

Prevailing social and cultural norms greatly influence the direct or indirect expression of various psychological impulses and needs, and determine the types of sick roles sanctioned or prohibited. The culture's exposure to various disease entities also affects the patient's choice of symptoms. Intrapsychic and secondary gain factors have long been cited in the etiology of conversion disorders.

Although once fairly common in both civilian and military life, conversion disorders—particularly the classical loss-of-function type—are now relatively rare, and occur primarily among rural and medically unsophisticated subgroups. Also undoubtedly adding to this decrease are the more stringent diagnostic criteria of *DSM-IV* and the separate categorization of such symptoms as psychogenic pain, psychosexual dysfunctions, and physical symptoms that are part of a more pervasive somatization disorder. Still, conversion disorders comprise about 5% of all neuroses treated.

COMPLEXES
HISTRIONIC PERSONALITIES
PERSONALITY DISORDERS

G. J. CHELUNE

CONVULSIVE SHOCK THERAPY

The modern practice of inducing convulsive seizures for psychotherapeutic purposes, either electrically or pharmacologically, stems from the observations of von Meduna in the early 1930s. According to L. B. Kalinowsky in *The convulsive therapies,* von Meduna observed that schizophrenia and epilepsy rarely occurred in the same patient and that mental patients frequently lost their symptoms after having spontaneous convulsions. Based on these observations, von Meduna reasoned that convulsions were somehow incompatible with schizophrenic symptoms, and introduced the use of Metrazol-induced convulsive seizures for the treatment of schizophrenia in 1934. Although the basic antagonism between epilepsy and schizophrenia has since been questioned, convulsive therapy continues to be widely used for a variety of severe psychiatric disorders, especially where drugs have proved ineffective.

A number of pharmacological agents (e.g., Metrazol, insulin, Indoklon) have been used to induce therapeutic seizures. However, these have been largely replaced by the use of electroconvulsive therapy (ECT), which was introduced by the Italian workers Cerletti and Bini in 1938. As outlined by the American Psychiatric Association's task force report, *Electroconvulsive therapy,* electroconvulsive therapy (ECT) is a relatively benign procedure if carried out in a highly controlled medical environment.

Although fractures, particularly of the dorsal spine, were once a major physical complication of ECT, the use of muscle relaxants has virtually eliminated this risk.

Neuroleptic drugs have largely replaced the use of ECT in the treatment of schizophrenia, although it is still occasionally used to treat acute schizophrenic breaks, especially if there is catatonic excitement. The most common use of ECT is in the treatment of endogenous depressions, where its effect can be dramatic.

BEHAVIORAL MEDICINE
DEPRESSION

G. J. CHELUNE

COOPERATION/COMPETITION

Although philosophers and theologians have long been interested in factors that foster cooperation or competition, usually viewing the former as a social virtue and the latter as selfishness and antisocial behavior, social scientists began to show serious interest in the empirical study of these concepts only in the late 1940s and early 1950s. This came about as conflict theorists came to view differences of interest, rather than anger or prejudice, as basic to the more serious forms of conflict. In a related development, researchers in social interaction turned toward theories based on the importance of the rewards and punishments that each person in an interaction can deliver to others, and away from viewpoints stressing the central importance of the attitudes and beliefs of individuals involved in an interaction.

The terms "cooperation" and "competition" refer essentially to collaborative effort and rivalry, respectively, with respect to either mutually desired goals or the means of achieving individual or mutual goals.

If the cooperation is pure, in the technical sense described by Morton Deutsch, the goal of one individual can be reached only if the other participants also attain their goals. In the case of pure competition, an individual's goals can be attained only if the others do not attain theirs, as for example in a game of poker. However, the extremes of pure cooperation and pure competition are rarely encountered; most situations are a blend of both.

A considerable amount of empirical psychological inquiry into factors that foster cooperation or competition was stimulated by theoretical developments in mathematics and economics, beginning with John von Neumann and Oskar Morgenstern's work, *Theory of games and economic behavior.* This mathematical game approach generated models that described the behavior of "rational" individuals in certain restricted situations of interdependence. A "rational" individual was taken to be fully knowledgeable about the nature of the interdependence and to be motivated by self-interest, seeking to maximize personal gain and minimize personal loss without regard for the gains and losses of the other parties. Psychologists developed laboratory analogies of these game situations in order to examine the extent to which "real" behavior approached "rational" behavior, and to study the influence of various situational variables (the nature of the interdependence, the presence or absence of communication, etc.) and predispositional variables (age, sex, cultural background, and motivational predispositions of the participants) on the course of the interaction.

Other approaches to the study of cooperation and competition also were developed, such as (a) laboratory interactions that mimicked real-life bargaining situations and that can be traced to the seminal work of economists S. Siegel and L. E. Fouraker, and (b) "locomotion games."

Psychologists interested in social interaction and the effects of group membership have also carried out empirical studies of cooperation and competition, but have generally avoided the laboratory game approach. The classic study in this domain is the Robber's Cave field experiment carried out by Muzafer Sherif and his colleagues, in which boys at a summer camp were divided into two groups that were then separated. In the first phase of the study, each group was put into situations designed to develop group solidarity and group identity. In the second phase, the two groups participated in a series of contests aimed at producing competitiveness and increased group solidarity. This led to considerable rivalry and even hostility between the groups. The last phase of the study addressed the question of how two hostile groups can be brought into harmony. Simply bringing the groups together for social events only increased hostility. However, when the experimenters created a series of "urgent" problems that required the collaborative efforts of the two groups to overcome—such as a breakdown in the camp water supply—intergroup hostility gradually decreased, new friendships developed across group lines, and a spirit of cooperativeness ensued.

In general, psychological research has shown that cooperative activity is most likely to emerge when the interacting parties share both a common goal and a common means of attaining that goal, while competition is most likely to occur when either the individual goals of the parties involved or the means of obtaining them are incompatible.

AFFILIATION NEED
ALTRUISM
BYSTANDER INVOLVEMENT
DEVELOPMENT OF HUMAN SOCIAL BEHAVIOR
FIELD DEPENDENCY
GROUP PROBLEM SOLVING
RIVALRY
SOCIAL CLIMATE EXPERIMENTS

J. E. ALCOCK

COPING

Coping has been widely and long regarded as having a central role in adaptation, yet it has defied universal agreement on definition and has been the object of little systematic research. Because coping has always been linked to the concept of stress, its recent popularization has been occasioned by a marked growth of interest in the stress concept. The links between stress, impaired functioning, and human misery on the negative side, and health, morale, and accomplishment on the positive side, have gradually led to the recognition that, although stress is an inevitable feature of the human condition, how people cope with stress is crucial in whether the adaptational outcome will be negative or positive.

Three approaches to coping can be distinguished. The first is a model derived from drive-reinforcement learning theory and is largely centered on animal experimentation. From this perspective, coping consists of acts, such as escape and avoidance, that successfully control aversive environmental conditions, thereby lowering the psychophysiological disturbance or degree of disequilibrium created by the aversive conditions. Among those using this model, primary theoretical and research interest is centered on a set of variables relevant to stress reduction, namely, the *predictability* and *controllability* of the environment, and *feedback* from the environment about the effects of coping.

The second model of coping is centered on psychoanalytic ego psychology concepts. Coping is understood as a set of ego processes that develop from infancy and are centered on ways of thinking about relationships between the self and the environment. The essential tasks of living are to survive and flourish in the human social environment, and this requires that instinctual drives be gratified while socially based dangers and constraints are managed realistically.

This model of coping is hierarchical. Coping is regarded as the most advanced or mature set of ego processes; events are handled realistically and flexibly in such a way as to maintain and promote mental and physical health. Defense mechanisms represent more primitive, neurotic processes characterized by greater rigidity and poorer reality testing.

Three shortcomings of these traditional models have been suggested. First and foremost, coping has been almost universally equated with adaptational success, as in the expression "I can cope with it" or "I learned how to cope." In the animal model, coping is defined as behavioral control over the environment through actions that prevent or turn off aversive conditions. Because, in the psychoanalytic ego psychology model, the most successful forms of coping are defined by a realistic or flexible rather than neurotic cognitive or ego process, the process of coping and its outcomes are confounded. That is, regardless of whether the person feels or functions better, coping adequacy is judged by the nature of the thought process itself. One could argue, however, that even so-called neurotic processes such as denial, cognitive avoidance, or intellectualized detachment can have optimal or at least favorable consequences under some conditions, as for example those in which nothing can be done to alter the situation. Indeed, this argument is supported by some research. By prejudging some ego processes as neurotic and others as mature or healthy, one can make a pejorative evaluation about many modes of coping that are both common and functional under certain conditions.

A second shortcoming of certain traditional approaches is that coping success is regarded exclusively in terms of the reduction of bodily disturbance. By definition, coping involves mobilization and effort. An interesting case in point is the Type A syndrome, which has as its cost the increased risk of heart attack. In tune with the physiological insights of W. B. Cannon and H. Selye, the animal model especially tends to treat stress and emotion solely in terms of increases or decreases of affective or bodily disturbances, thus omitting from concern diverse emotional qualities such as anger, fear, anxiety, guilt, relief, and happiness.

A third shortcoming is that research approaches arising from the above models—especially psychoanalytic ego psychology—have almost exclusively treated coping in research as a static trait or style when, in reality, coping is an active and complex process that changes with the phases of a stressful encounter and from one context to another. Field studies and clinical observation show that the thoughts, actions, and feelings involved in coping depend on the type of stressful encounter being experienced—for example, a work encounter versus a health encounter. The pattern of coping also depends on how the person appraises the situation, as for example whether it is judged as uncontrollable or as

open to ameliorative action. In the former instance, coping becomes more heavily oriented toward the regulation of emotion by avoidance, wishful thinking, or detachment, whereas in the latter, problem-focused modes predominate.

A third model of coping that emphasizes cognitive appraisal processes and a fluid, transactional, and process-centered approach to coping and its assessment. Coping is viewed as responsive to contextual variables, temporal factors, and feedback from the flow of events that affect adaptational outcomes. It is defined as efforts to manage demands that tax or exceed the person's resources. The word "manage" in this definition means that coping can include toleration of harm or threat, redefinition of past events, acceptance, and putting a positive light on the situation—a set of ways for managing oneself and one's thoughts and feelings—as well as mastery of the environment. By referring to demands that tax or exceed resources, coping is limited to conditions of stress in which one must mobilize to deal with new situations and draw on resources not typically used, and is distinguished from automatized adaptational behaviors that draw on readily available habits of response involving minimal effort. Two major functions of coping are delineated—problem-focused and emotion-focused—the latter representing cognitive forms of coping that include the traditional defenses.

It seems clear that denial/avoidant modes of coping have sometimes favorable and sometimes unfavorable outcomes. It is quite possible that what is most adaptive depends on when in the course of a threat such coping modes are activated; early denial and numbing may be useful, if ultimately abandoned for more realistic modes of coping. Also, the content and context of the threat itself—for example, the type of illness as a source of stress—may determine which mode of coping is more adaptive. The actual cognitive processes involved in a given form of coping could also be important. Perhaps denial of fact—for example, a diagnosis of cancer—puts the person at greater risk for damaging outcomes than denial of the implications of the fact. The latter process seems more refractory to being demolished by subsequent evidence, and may indeed be analogous to the illusions by which we all live.

HOW COPING MAY AFFECT HEALTH

To examine how coping might affect somatic health, one must first distinguish between short-term effects evident throughout a specific stressful encounter, and long-term effects.

With rare exceptions, the health consequences of coping are not influenced by the handling of a single encounter, but rather on the extent to which coping has been effective over the long run in many stressful encounters and arenas of living. To contribute to disease, coping ineptitude must occur repeatedly or chronically, as it were, and probably over a long period of time.

There are three main routes through which the coping process might adversely affect somatic health. First, it can influence the frequency, intensity, duration, and patterning of neurochemical stress reactions in one of three ways: (a) by failing to prevent or ameliorate environmentally noxious or damaging conditions; (b) by failing to regulate emotional distress in the face of uncontrollable harms or threats; or (c) by expressing a set of values and a corresponding lifestyle that are constantly mobilizing in a harmful way. However, we must recognize that diseases attendant on a specific coping pattern (for example, Type A and the increased risk of heart disease) may be the price paid for other, more salutary psychological outcomes, such as a high level of commitment and satisfaction in sustained effort or competition. Any mode of coping can have mixed outcomes, positive in some respects and negative in others; it is important for researchers to view the problem in its larger frame and to evaluate coping outcomes from the standpoint of multiple consequences and values and in diverse contexts.

Second, coping can affect health negatively, increasing the risk of mortality and morbidity, when it involves excessive use of injurious substances such as alcohol, tobacco, and other drugs, or when it involves the person in activities of high risk to life and limb.

Third, emotion-focused modes of coping can impair health by adversely affecting the management of stress. For example, denial or avoidance of thinking about a harm or threat can succeed in lowering emotional distress but simultaneously prevent the person from realistically addressing a problem that is responsive to suitable action.

Research and theory on the psychology of coping seems to have come of age. Along with the widespread public and professional intuition that coping is an essential ingredient of life, there is substantial evidence that the coping process does indeed affect adaptational outcomes for better or worse. What is lacking is specific information on which forms of coping have favorable and unfavorable consequences, in given types of persons and under specifiable conditions; also, there is little clarity about how coping produces the adaptational outcomes of interest.

STRESS CONSEQUENCES

R. S. LAZARUS

CORRECTIONAL INSTITUTIONS

The defining characteristics of correctional institutions are: (a) residential incarceration of legally adjudicated offenders; (b) the primary use of external and highly structured means to control behavior, that is frequently aversive in nature (e.g., solitary confinement, loss of privileges); (c) a sharp demarcation between staff and inmate roles; (d) usually an attempt to classify the offender according to personality characteristics, prior record, or rehabilitative potential; and (e) attempts to alter the course of the inmate's criminal career. Thus jails and similar holding facilities are not intended to be correctional institutions. Facilities that do meet the criteria include state and federal prisons, training schools for adolescent offenders, hospitals for the criminally insane, honor camps and work farms that are part of a penal system, and some transition houses for felons. In general, approximately a quarter of a million adult individuals enter prisons each year, and many thousands of adolescent offenders are committed to training schools. An unknown number of other individuals are incarcerated in other correctional institutions. Further, in addition to the approximately 10 million Americans arrested yearly, many others who are not arrested are nevertheless preventively detained in institutions, as for example in the forensic ward of a state hospital. In this regard, since the mid-1940s, an inverse relationship has been observed between individuals detained in correctional facilities administered by the criminal justice and mental health systems: As commitments of mentally ill offenders decrease in state prisons, for example, they tend to increase in state hospitals, and vice versa.

The historical view of the primary purpose of the correctional institution, based on the idea that evil-doing was voluntary, was to render *punishment.* When the particular form of revenge by society involved incarceration, society was protected by the isolation of the offender. Unfortunately, *protection of society,* a second purpose of punishment, is only for a limited time, during which the offender often becomes more entrenched in criminal behavior. This view is supported by perennially high recidivism rates, averaging about 66% nationwide. A third purpose of correctional institutions is *deterrence,* based on the notion that the offender who is punished will provide an example to be avoided by others, thus reducing the likelihood of similar acts being committed. Unfortunately, much uncertainty surrounds the outcome of criminal acts; it is unknown just how well deterrence works.

A final purpose of correctional institutions, only partially associated with the traditional concepts of vengeance, protection, and deterrence,

is *rehabilitation* of the offender. Massive rehabilitation efforts started in the 1930s and continue to this day, in spite of various estimates that less than 5% of correctional institutional staff are treatment personnel. As several reviews of the literature have suggested, rehabilitation has yielded disappointing or at best inconclusive results and has had no appreciable effect on recidivism. The same finding holds true for various psychological treatment approaches aimed at changing aspects of offenders' behavior or personality.

The *right to treatment* for psychological as well as physical disorders has been affirmed on a number of constitutional grounds. Generally, inmates are entitled to treatment if the symptoms are serious and curable, and bear the risk of harm if no intervention is provided. The *right to refuse treatment* has also been affirmed, particularly when treatment is seen as an instrument to enforce administration policy rather than to alleviate individual distress.

In general, in spite of attention given constitutional issues in correctional facilities, independent investigations suggest that massive constitutional infringements have been routinely experienced by the average inmate. Perhaps, as a number of psychological studies have suggested, this is due to the very nature of the correctional institution, with its total control over the individual and the dehumanizing effects on both staff and inmates. Other issues have concerned competence of treatment staff and administrators who may, for example, predict future violence by an inmate in spite of the low validity of such prognostications.

Points of agreement in regard to correctional institutions describe a cyclic effect over the last several decades. Areas of congruence among forensic professionals have included the following:

Large prisons and other correctional facilities should be phased out in favor of smaller, more versatile ones that are program-flexible and less dehumanizing.

The most effective way to change correctional institutions seems to be by legislative fiat rather than by working within the correctional system itself.

In spite of resistance to them, community programs have remained a viable force in the correctional institution program.

There is a trend to create specialized correctional institutions for offenders in such categories as the criminally insane, female offenders, adolescent offenders, retarded offenders, and those representing a low risk of escape.

Flat sentencing is in favor to fit the crime, with time off for good behavior. Indeterminate sentencing is currently seen as unjust and based on the unsubstantiated notion that criminal behavior can be predicted and that current intervention methods are effective.

Standards for correctional institutions should be formulated for each level of program involvement and be in tune with scientific and social advancements relevant to the criminal justice system.

CRIME
CRIMINAL RESPONSIBILITY
FORENSIC PSYCHOLOGY

H. V. HALL

CORRELATION AND REGRESSION

Issues in correlation and regression are related to the following major questions: (a) Is there some relationship between two variables X and Y such that, if we knew X, we could at least to some extent predict Y? (b) How strong is the relationship between X and Y? (c) Given the relationship between X and Y, what is the optimal rule for predicting Y

from X, and how good is this rule? When we are concerned with assessing the degree of relationship (strictly speaking, the degree of linear relationship), we are dealing with *correlation*. The term *regression* refers to issues related to the prediction of one variable from another.

THE CORRELATION COEFFICIENT

The Pearson product-moment correlation coefficient, r—usually just called the correlation coefficient—is an index of the strength of *linear* relationship between two variables and can range numerically from +1 to −1. A coefficient of 0 indicates that there is no linear relationship between X and Y. Positive values of the correlation coefficient indicate that there is a tendency for Y to increase as X increases, while negative values indicate that there is a tendency for Y to decrease as X increases.

A perfect correlation between X and Y would occur if Y could be predicted without error from X, using a prediction equation of the form $Y = aX + b$, where a and b are appropriately chosen constants. The correlation would be +1 if a was positive and −1 if a was negative. An equation of the form $Y = aX + b$ is referred to as a linear equation, because if Y was plotted against X, all points (X, Y) satisfying the equation would lie along a straight line.

The correlation coefficient is an index of the degree of *linear* relationship, and not of relationship in general. It is possible for two variables to vary systematically in a curvilinear fashion and still have a correlation of 0. Because of this fact, the correlation coefficient will tend to underestimate the degree of relationship.

Although there are a number of different but equivalent formulas for the Pearson correlation coefficient, a common computational formula is as follows:

$$r = \frac{N\Sigma XY - (\Sigma X)(\Sigma Y)}{\sqrt{[N\Sigma X^2 - (\Sigma Z)^2][N\Sigma Y^2 - (\Sigma Y)^2]}}$$

where N is the number of paired scores on X and Y.

Several cautions in dealing with the correlation coefficient should be noted. Just because X and Y may be correlated does not mean that there is a causal relationship. X may be correlated with Y because (a) changes in X cause changes in Y; (b) changes in Y; cause changes in X; and (c) changes in other variables cause changes in both X and Y. Among elementary school students, for example, vocabulary size is positively correlated with height, because both variables are related to age. In addition, the correlation coefficient will be reduced by "restriction of range."

CORRELATIONAL VERSUS EXPERIMENTAL RESEARCH

Experimental research involves the manipulation of one or more independent variables and often results in causal statements being made about the effect of the independent variables on the dependent variable. If the following three criteria are met, then it is a reasonable conclusion that changes in the independent variable caused the changes in the dependent variable: (a) a number of experimental groups are initially chosen not to differ systematically from one another; (b) the groups are treated identically except with respect to an independent variable; and (c) following the experimental manipulation, the groups differ reliably from one another.

Correlational research does not involve the manipulation of independent variables and in its simplest form consists of measuring a number of variables and determining the strengths of the relationships among them. Although such studies provide information about degree of relationship and even allow prediction of variables from what is known about one or more other variables, it is not possible to make causal statements. However, a variety of statistical analyses are becoming available that

allow the investigator to test whether a particular set of correlations is consistent with a given causal model.

The partial correlation coefficient $r_{XY.W}$ is an index of the strength of linear relationship between X and Y with the effects of W "partialed out." It is possible to partial out the effects of more than one variable.

MULTIPLE CORRELATION

Suppose we wish to arrive at the best prediction of variable Y (the criterion variable) on the basis of a number of other variables $X_1, X_2, X_3, \cdots, X_p$ (predictor variables). For example, we may wish to predict a measure of success in graduate school on the basis of undergraduate grades and verbal and quantitative Graduate Record Examination (GRE) scores. According to the procedures of multiple regression, we can derive an expression of the form

$$b_0 + b_1X_1 + \cdots + b_p X_p$$

(where the bs are appropriately chosen constants) that optimally predicts Y. The multiple correlation coefficient, r, is the Pearson product-moment correlation coefficient between the best prediction and the variable that is to be predicted, and as such is a measure of how good prediction is when multiple regression is employed.

CORRELATION METHODS
STATISTICS IN PSYCHOLOGY

A. D. WELL

CORRELATION METHODS

Correlation methods, which derive their name from the fact that they are based on the "co-relation" between or among variables, are statistical methods developed initially by Karl Pearson near the turn of the nineteenth century. They are closely related to, and in fact based on, the concept of regression developed earlier by Sir Francis Galton, who first began to study statistically the relationship between the heights of fathers and their sons. It was Galton who hired Pearson as a statistician to work with him and his father, who were influenced by their cousins, the Darwins, and were conducting a series of investigations involving the contributions of heredity to the development of human attributes. Because of this association between Galton and Pearson and the earlier discoveries by the former regarding regression, correlation methods have historically adopted the symbol "**r.**"

PRODUCT-MOMENT CORRELATION

Pearson defined the correlation coefficient as the "mean z-score product." Hence, r has become known as the product-moment coefficient:

$$r = (\Sigma Z_x Z_y)/N$$

Its legitimate calculation assumes that the two variables being correlated are continuous and normally distributed; that the lines of best fit for the joint bivariate distribution are straight; and that equal variability is present throughout the range of the joint distribution. In raw score form, a simple formula for calculating the Pearson product-moment correlation coefficient is

$$r = \frac{(\Sigma XY)/N - \overline{X}\,\overline{Y}}{\sigma_X \sigma_Y}$$

BISERIAL CORRELATION

A variation of the product-moment correlation coefficient also was developed by Pearson: the biserial correlation coefficient. If only one of the variables is continuous and reasonably normally distributed, whereas the other is artificially dichotomized—assumed to be continuous and normally distributed, but divided in two parts (e.g., pass/fail), the relationship between the two variables can also be expressed by r. In this case, the correlation coefficient is denoted by r_{bis}. Similar to the product-moment r, it ranges from +1.00 (perfect positive relationship) through 0.00 (no relationship) to −1.00 (perfect negative relationship). The biserial correlation method has proved very useful in item analysis procedures, because it measures the relationship between performance on each item on a test in terms of pass/fail and the total test score.

POINT BISERIAL CORRELATION

A further variation of the product-moment correlation coefficient is found in the point biserial r. This statistic shows the relationship between a variable that is assumed to be continuous and normally distributed and one that is truly discrete. This coefficient is denoted by r_{pbis}. Because in r_{pbis} the dichotomy is discrete rather than artificial, as in the case of r_{bis}, its sign is arbitrarily determined. Hence for all practical purposes, the range of r_{pbis} is 0.00 to +1.00.

The case also exists where both variables are considered to be continuous and normally distributed but are both artificially dichotomized, as in the biserial correlation method. This case, also developed by Pearson, is measured by the tetrachoric correlation coefficient, r_{tet}. The basic formulas and procedures for calculating r_{tet} are quite complex. Therefore, in practical applications of this method, approximations of r_{tet} derived from shortcut methods and tables are used.

RANK CORRELATION

A nonparametric analog to the parametric correlation methods exists in rank correlation, rho (ρ). It applies to the use of ranks rather than raw scores or standard scores in determining the degree of relationship between two variables. The rationale for the development of ρ does not require the adherence to any rigid set of assumptions, hence it is a nonparametric statistic. Its formula, derived from Pearson's product-moment formula by substituting ranked data for interval data, reduces to:

$$\rho = [1 - (6\Sigma d^2)/N(N^2 - 1)]$$

where d is the difference in rank between X and Y for individuals and N is the number of pairs.

MULTIPLE CORRELATION

The Pearson product-moment correlation methods and the Galton linear regression analysis methods were extended in 1897 by U. Yule to a multiple linear regression model involving the multivariate normal distribution. Multiple correlation methods measure the relationship between a *set* of continuous independent variables and a single dependent continuous variable. The multiple correlation coefficient is denoted by $R_{0.123\ldots p}$. Its calculation requires the solution of a set of simultaneous linear equations. The number of equations is equal to the number of independent variables.

It sometimes becomes necessary to eliminate the effect of a third variable in order to determine the real relationship between any pair of variables. The partial correlation coefficient expresses the relationship between two variables with the effect of one or more other variables eliminated. The partial correlation coefficent is calculated as a function of the bivariate product-moment correlations between Y, X, and X_2.

$$r_{y1.2} = \frac{r_{y1} - r_{y2}r_{12}}{\sqrt{1 - r_{y2}^2}\sqrt{1 - r_{12}^2}}$$

If one wishes to partial out two variables, say X_2 and X_3, the formula is:

$$r_{y1.23} = \frac{r_{y1.2} - r_{y3.2}r_{13.2}}{\sqrt{1 - r_{y3.2}^2}\sqrt{1 - r_{13.2}^2}}$$

CANONICAL CORRELATION

The general case for which multiple correlation represents the specific case in which the dependent set is a single variable, is the canonical correlation method. It was developed in 1935 by Harold Hotelling. The canonical correlation coefficients (R_{c_i}) are based on two sets of variables. In showing the relationships that exist between these two sets of continuous variables, several canonical coefficients are calculated; the number of R_cs being determined by and equal to the number of variables in the smaller set, if the number of variables in each set is not the same. In canonical correlation a linear combination of the variables in a set defines each dimension measured by the set. Each of these linear combinations is referred to as a canonical *variate*. They differ from one another in the weights they assign to the variables in the set. Canonical *correlations* are product-moment correlations between pairs of canonical variates, each pair consisting of one canonical variate from each set. Thus each canonical correlation is a measure of the degree of linear relationship between two dimensions, one measured by each set of variables. Canonical correlation is a method of multivariate statistical analysis.

CORRELATION AND REGRESSION STATISTICS IN PSYCHOLOGY

P. F. MERENDA

COUNSELING

COUNSELING AS EDUCATION

Counseling as education—or guidance, as it is often called—is related to the historical use of the term "counseling." Dictionary definitions emphasize giving advice and exchanging information.

Most historians of formal guidance view it as a twentieth-century phenomenon emerging as one of several reform movements to address the conditions resulting from the nineteenth century's Industrial Revolution. In addition to a humanitarian concern for the displaced, dislocated, and abused, the human resource needs of industrialization stimulated the emergence of guidance. A diversified and highly skilled work force was needed. For guidance pioneers, as for many other reformers and progressives, the public school was seen as a mechanism for social change. In terms of guidance, the school and its curriculum afforded opportunities for preparing individuals (including recent arrivals from foreign countries and persons from rural areas of America) for life in a highly industrialized democracy. It was the belief in utilitarian education that provided a fertile ground for the growth of vocational guidance.

The merger of vocational guidance and testing established it as an important foundation of counseling. Before the development of testing, vocational guidance relied on vocational education that stressed occupational information and advice. With the development of testing in the areas of ability, interests, occupations, and personality, vocational guidance obtained a scientific means to realize its commonsense notion of improving the worker–occupation relationship. This match was predicated on the ability to gather accurate information about the individual and his or her abilities and interests, and about the job. Testing and the later developments in trait and factor psychology provided the technologies that enabled guidance workers to conduct individual and job assessments.

The hallmark of the guidance model was the continued espousal of a scientific approach to counseling practice and research. In terms of counseling practice, the counselor was to use psychological methods such as psychological testing and valid scientific information in helping the client develop appropriate problem-solving skills and accurate self-understanding. In fact, counseling was seen as equiping the client with necessary skills and information to become a personal scientist. The same emphasis on the scientific method was adopted toward research in which a trait-and-factor methodology using psychological tests and correlational procedures was used.

COUNSELING AS PSYCHOTHERAPY

Around 1940 the dominance of the guidance model began to erode; by the end of the decade it was replaced by the psychotherapy model. A number of factors contributed to the decline. Part of the downfall coincided with social changes brought on by the end of the Depression and the beginning of World War II. These changes ushered in a new spirit of individualism against the perceived rigidities and authoritarianism of the past. Moreover, people were confronted with rapid social change that seemed to broadly affect their lives.

These effects went beyond educational or occupational problems as people sought help with all types of personal adjustment issues, especially in the areas of emotion and interpersonal relationships. In this "Age of Psychotherapy" the publication of *Counseling and psychotherapy* by Carl Rogers was important. This book challenged the guidance view of counseling as an adjunct tool in facilitating the gathering of accurate information and decision making. In the Rogerian model the focus is on individual problems, relatively independent of society. These problems are primarily emotional in nature, and the helper is concerned with establishing a therapeutic relationship and avoiding directive influences.

Although there have been changes and shifts of emphasis, the basic outlook has been a person-centered approach in which the self-determination capacities of the client are the focus of attention, concern, activity, and acceptance conveyed through a therapeutic relationship.

LATER DEVELOPMENTS

In the 1950s and 1960s, counseling as guidance—although less popular than psychotherapy—was stimulated by the development of professional organizations and the reemergence of the importance of schooling and work. As a result, there was a great demand for school counselors (the National Defense Act of 1958) and rehabilitation counselors.

However, the Division of Counseling Psychology competed with clinical psychology for psychological services. Such activities continue today (e.g., third-party payments). These activities have contributed to the further decline of the guidance tradition, and to a separation of counseling psychologists with doctoral-level training, from school and rehabilitation counselors with subdoctoral level training.

During this same time period, advances in social sciences brought significant conceptual developments (self-concept theory, stage theory) that transformed vocational guidance into career development. These advances also had an impact on the psychotherapy model. There were now numerous competing counseling models. It is important to stress that, from its history and theory, counseling represents a disciplined mode of action of working with people. Moreover, counseling is primarily associated with specific work settings and professional functions. Today, as in the past, counselors are primarily found in educational settings, most probably in an institution of higher education. They are most likely to engage in counseling or teaching, and to focus on the educational, vocational, and personal adjustment of the individual. In response to this traditional outlook, many have suggested the relevance of a counseling

perspective in industry and health. Some are moving into nontraditional counseling settings: private practice, general hospitals, corporations, and mass media. Others are recommending group work and consultation as primary activities.

Although a diversity of job-related activities is associated with counseling, certain emphases—some shared with other professions while others seem distinctive—form a counseling core.

1. As in many professions, a scientific approach to practice and research is adopted.

2. A focus on the individual is maintained with special attention given to nurturing the personal capacities of the person, as opposed to emphasizing pathology.

3. A concern for human development issues is emphasized, including educational decisions, occupational choice, and interpersonal adjustment.

4. Professional competencies include the skills and knowledge appropriate for establishing a therapeutic relationship, assessing the problem, initiating change, maintaining the change, and evaluating the outcome. Specialized competencies often associated with counseling would likely include interviewing, relationship enhancement, assessment, skill training, human relations, and career counseling.

COUNSELOR EDUCATION
DIRECTIVE COUNSELING

G. L. STONE

COUNSELING PSYCHOLOGY

Counseling psychology has undergone significant developments since its formal inception as a distinct helping profession in 1946. Originally devoted to assisting individuals in the search for appropriate occupations, it broadened into a profession that assists relatively intact persons in maximizing their developmental potential in all areas of their lives. In doing so, it makes use of a wide variety of sophisticated psychological interventions designed not only to assist people in adjusting to their environment, but also to modify environments to make them more suited to human needs.

DEFINITIONAL MODELS OF COUNSELING PSYCHOLOGY

The definition of counseling psychology has consisted of several emphases that distinguish it from related helping professions. First, counseling psychology has consistently followed an educational rather than a clinical, remedial, or medical model. Clients (not patients) are viewed as normal individuals who need assistance in coping with stresses and tasks of everyday life. The task of the counseling psychologist is to teach clients coping strategies and new behaviors that they can use in making maximum use of their already existing resources, or in developing more adequate resources.

Other methods may be used for reeducating clients besides the dyadic interview. Thus counseling psychologists may lead groups designed to enhance the lives of each of the members, or they may design and conduct workshops on various aspects of life planning, such as assertion skills or communications skills. The counseling psychologist may intervene in the client's immediate environment to facilitate client change and growth, and may relate to the client in real-life situations in addition to an office setting.

Counseling psychology's educational base is seen most clearly in public schools and in college and university counseling centers. There, however, the counselor's role has broadened from an almost exclusive concern with the vocational and educational guidance of youth to an increasing focus on the creation of a total educational environment conducive to learning. In the process, counselors find themselves doing not only vocational counseling, but also personal and emotional counseling in an attempt to maximize students' receptivity to education. Counselors may also act as consultants with faculty and administration to help create a total school environment that facilitates learning. School counselors generally are trained at the master's degree level, while college and university counseling psychologists typically possess a doctorate degree.

Counseling psychology stresses a developmental model. It attempts to assist clients in achieving their optimal development and in removing blocks to normal growth.

Counseling psychology has advocated preventive approaches to developmental problems in addition to, but not to the exclusion of, remedial approaches. The strategy in prevention is to identify individuals, groups, or settings that, according to theory and research, are seen as being particularly "at risk," and to intervene with appropriate individuals or in appropriate settings *before* a crisis occurs. This is analogous to public health measures designed to prevent the outbreak of disease rather than to cure it.

Counseling psychology, alone among the helping professions, pays particular attention to the role of occupation in the lives of people. Indeed, the profession derives much of its identity from the vocational guidance movement. With the post-World War II rise of affluence and the decline of the work ethic as a source of personal and societal values, counseling psychology broadened its aim to include personal development in areas other than work. The profession's methodology has likewise become more sophisticated, moving from a relatively straightforward one-time matching of persons and jobs to a consideration of psychological needs fulfilled by work, the selection of different occupations throughout the life span as a function of developmental stages, the differing career patterns of men and women, and an exploration of the meaning and value of work in relation to other activities such as leisure.

PROFESSIONAL IDENTITY OF COUNSELING PSYCHOLOGY

As counseling psychology evolved from its original base of vocational guidance, it overlapped with other helping professions. Thus as psychotherapy increasingly was practiced by counseling psychologists without reference to occupational selection, the overlap with clinical psychology grew. As counseling psychologists intervened in the client's network of social relations, their function overlapped with that of social workers. Meanwhile, clinical psychologists moved increasingly out of the mental hospitals, away from assessment of mental functioning as a primary activity, and toward a greater involvement with relatively intact individuals. Similarly, social workers moved away from case management and toward therapeutic counseling. There has thus been simultaneous movement of the three largest helping professions toward one another, resulting in a blurring of previously distinct role definitions and functions.

Exacerbating the identity problem is the historical linkage of counseling psychology with colleges of education, due in large part to the original mission of counseling departments to train school counselors. As, on the one hand, counselor education broadened in scope into counseling psychology and, on the other hand, vocational guidance became increasingly psychologically sophisticated, counseling psychology programs were often caught between education and psychology. The result is that the majority of counseling psychology programs approved by the American Psychological Association currently are located in colleges of education, rather than in departments of psychology. Although this makes sense in terms of the educational model of the profession, among counseling psychologists it has resulted in a split loyalty between the field of counselor education, which may not be psychologically oriented, and the field of applied psychology, which may follow a remedial, quasi-medical model. As the issues of licensing and credentialing, specialty guidelines, and

third-party payments become important, counseling psychologists are being forced to choose between education and psychology as their main knowledge base and source of professional identity. As a result, counseling psychology programs have taken on a greater emphasis on training in basic psychology, and the gulf between counseling psychology and counselor education appears to be growing.

THEORETICAL MODELS OF COUNSELING PSYCHOLOGY

The original Minnesota model of vocational counseling began during the 1930s with Edmund G. Williamson in the Student Counseling Bureau at the University of Minnesota and served as a model for most later university counseling centers. This was basically a rational decision-making process in which test interpretation figured prominently and that resulted in an educational or occupational selection. With the rise of the psychotherapy movement, counseling psychology models focused more on the *process* of the counseling relationship, rather than on the *outcome.*

Two theoretical models in particular—the decision-making and the counselor social influence models—warrant further discussion, as they represent a unique contribution of counseling psychology to applied psychology. Decision-making counseling involves the translation into the counseling process of the concepts and practices underlying decision theory, and in general attempts to teach clients, either individually or in groups, overt procedures and strategies for effective decision making. The decision-making model is especially suitable for vocational and career counseling, as illustrated by Mitchell, Jones, and Krumboltz in *Social learning and career decision making.* Counseling psychology's stress on prevention is nicely illustrated by the decision-making model; formal classes as well as other methods of teaching decision-making skills have been used to teach these skills to potentially high-risk populations *before* major decisions must be made.

Problem solving is closely related to decision making. In *Problem-solving counseling,* David Dixon and John Glover have integrated the pragmatic problem-solving methodology that characterizes a number of counseling psychology approaches with the research and conceptual literature on problem-solving. Both decision-making and problem-solving integrations represent a movement to include cognitive dimensions along with behavioral counseling.

The social influence model of the counseling process was originally proposed by Stanley R. Strong in the late 1960s. Strong drew on the interpersonal influence literature in social psychology to conceptualize the counselor's influence over the client as a result of the former's perceived expertness and credibility. Much research has since been done regarding the behaviors that contribute to counselor social influence; the conditions under which counselor social influence can be maximized; the relationship of social influence measures to other measures of counseling process and outcome; and social influence as a function of specific counselor and client attributes such as race, sex, and social class. Currently, social influence is one of the most influential models of the counseling process.

RESEARCH IN COUNSELING PSYCHOLOGY

Research in counseling psychology has changed over time. The largest change has been the ratio of empirical studies to conceptual or theoretical articles; in 1954, the ratio was 1 : 1, although in the 1980s there were more than nine empirical studies to one nonempirical study. Another change has been in the relative proportion of outcome research to process research, the former declining to a small proportion while the latter has risen to about 25% of the total. Process-outcome research has likewise shown a substantial increase, making the journal a major publication outlet for process-oriented research in applied psychology. Reflecting counseling psychology's deemphasis on vocational counseling, the percentage of research on vocational behavior has declined somewhat over the years, although this has been offset by the increase in research relating to counseling with special populations. Finally, social influence research has accounted for a significant portion of recent issues of the journal, thus emphasizing its prominent place as a process model in counseling psychology.

The quality and specificity of research in counseling psychology has likewise increased. Studies are much more likely now to use multifactorial designs, to make use of multivariate statistics, to provide tight experimental controls in order to eliminate extraneous sources of variance, and to investigate the effects of specific interventions on specific measures of change. There has been an increasing focus on what technique used by what counselor with what client results in what outcome under what conditions.

CAREER DEVELOPMENT
COUNSELING
HISTORY OF COUNSELING PSYCHOLOGY
OCCUPATIONAL COUNSELING

E. T. Dowd

COUNSELOR EDUCATION

Counselor Education is the term used to describe the academic and experiential training that leads to graduate degrees and professional certification in a wide variety of specialty areas involving the application of counseling techniques. A representative list of the specialty areas in Counselor Education include elementary and secondary school counselors, college counselors, group work counselors, marriage and family counselors, rehabilitation counselors, counselors for special groups, and counseling psychologists. Academic programs leading to training in Counselor Education include paraprofessional programs, baccalaureate programs, certification programs, master's programs, specialists (sixth-year) programs, and doctoral programs, depending on the level of training desired and/or needed.

Counselor Education programs tend to follow standards set forth by the professional organizations with which they affiliate. These organizations also serve as an outlet for reporting research through their various publications. The two professional organizations that counselors tend to affiliate with are the American Psychological Association (APA) and the American Association for Counseling and Development (AACD).

Counseling psychologists generally are concerned with mental health services as they relate to the educational and vocational problems of normal individuals. There is also a degree of overlap between counseling psychology and education, in that both counseling psychologists and educational counselors offer counseling functions and rely on psychological principles and techniques for appraisal, intervention, and therapeutic growth. In a study of characteristics of doctoral graduate counselors and counseling psychologists, C. Krauskopf, W. Thorenson, and C. McAleer concluded that there were three somewhat distinct groups of counseling psychology professionals: (a) a student personnel group that carried out educational/administrative functions, (b) a group that has assumed the traditional academic role of social and behavioral scientists, and (c) those counseling psychologists who have moved from the scientist/professional role to a practitioner's role.

Counselor education programs developed at institutions of higher education have used a wide variety of theoretical bases that provide underlying program philosophies. A partial list might include behavioral, cognitive, existential, field, phenomenological, rational-emotive, self-transactional analysis, psychosocial dynamics, and trait-factor theories. Current research indicates that no single theme tends to dominate schools of counseling and psychotherapy; D. Smith reported that eclecticism

appears to be the preference of the largest number of counseling psychologists. Concurrently, a steadily increasing experiential program is being used, which includes more time devoted to clinical activities, closer supervision of trainees, and an internship of at least 1 year at the doctoral level. Furthermore, these clinical activities are more often located in community agencies. Counselor Education programs that appear to be increasing in both size and scope include marriage and family counseling, gerontological counseling, substance abuse counseling, corrections counseling, developmental counseling, counseling for midlife change, and the wider use of counselor consultation.

COUNSELING
COUNSELING PSYCHOLOGY
HISTORY OF CLINICAL PSYCHOLOGY

F. P. Haehnlen

COUNTERCONDITIONING

In 1924, Mary Cover Jones, a student of John Watson, published a paper describing the successful treatment of a fear of rabbits in a 3-year-old boy named Peter.

Counterconditioning is a procedure in which a response to a stimulus is replaced or countered by pairing that stimulus with a new stimulus of differing valence. In the case of Peter, Jones presented the feared stimulus (the rabbit) in conjunction with a pleasant stimulus (food), with the result that the fear response was eliminated. It is important to note that the feared stimulus was introduced in a gradual fashion to ensure that at no time a fear response was elicited more powerful than the response of eating. Counterconditioning is somewhat similar to extinction in the classical (Pavlovian) conditioning paradigm. Both procedures result in the diminution or elimination of a response to a stimulus. In extinction, however, the conditioned stimulus is presented alone without the unconditioned stimulus, while in counterconditioning the conditioned stimulus is presented with a *different* unconditioned stimulus.

The term *counterconditioning* has been used in two ways that are often confused. Letting S stand for stimulus and R for response, consider two reflexes, $S_1 \rightarrow R_1$ and $S_2 \rightarrow R_2$, where it is impossible for R_1 and R_2 to occur together. In one use, counterconditioning is an experimental *procedure* involving the pairing of S_1 with S_2. The result of such a procedure is often the elimination of the weaker of the two reflexes. In the second use, counterconditioning is an inferred *process* that is offered as an explanation of this result. This process consists of the substitution of the stronger response for the weaker one. When the counterconditioning procedure is successful in eliminating a reflex, it does not necessarily follow that the process that produced this result is simple stimulus substitution. Other explanations advanced include the accumulation of conditioned inhibition, habituation under conditions of lowered arousal, and extinction.

Two types of counterconditioning have been widely used for therapeutic purposes with humans. These procedures are distinguished chiefly by whether the goal is to increase or decrease the attractiveness of a stimulus. In appetitive counterconditioning, the desired outcome is an increase in attractiveness, as in the case of Peter and the feared rabbit. Systematic desensitization is the most widely used technique based on this type of counterconditioning. Instead of using food as the positive countering stimulus, desensitization employs muscle relaxation. The goal is to reduce a fear response to a specific stimulus.

In aversive counterconditioning a stimulus becomes less attractive as a result of being paired with an aversive stimulus. An example is the use of electric shock paired with homosexual stimuli to try to reduce homosexual attraction.

BEHAVIOR THERAPY
CLASSICAL CONDITIONING
PSYCHOTHERAPY

S. G. FISHER

COVERT CONDITIONING

Covert conditioning is a process through which behavior changes occur, and is a set of behavior therapy procedures based on the covert conditioning model. This process involves the interaction of covert events such as imagery, thinking, and feeling. When covert conditioning is employed, the client is asked to imagine the target behavior and then to imagine a consequence that can change that target behavior.

Three basic assumptions underly covert conditioning: (a) the homogeneity assumption, (b) the interaction assumption, and (c) the learning assumption. The *homogeneity assumption* states that all categories of behavior, including overt and covert behaviors, obey the same laws. According to the *interaction assumption,* the various categories of behavior such as covert psychological behavior, physiological behavior, and overt behavior interact and influence one another in predictable ways. The *learning assumption* simply states that all behaviors are subject to the same laws of learning.

The behavior therapy procedures based on the covert conditioning process were developed by Joseph Cautela. In covert conditioning both the behavior to be changed and its consequence, which is responsible for changing the behavior, occur in the client's imagination according to the therapist's instructions. The first procedure developed was covert sensitization.

Covert sensitization has been used successfully with many behavior problems including obesity, drug abuse, self-injurious behavior, alcoholism, sexual disorders, smoking, and compulsive stealing. Several studies conducted by David Barlow and his colleagues have empirically demonstrated that covert sensitization is an effective treatment procedure with relatively long-lasting effects.

In 1970 Cautela described the development of covert positive reinforcement (CPR). Although covert sensitization was designed to decrease the frequency of inappropriate, unwanted target behaviors, CPR was intended to increase the likelihood of appropriate, wanted behaviors. The client employing CPR tries to experience, in his or her imagination, situations involving the target behavior. In CPR the image of the desired target behavior is immediately followed by the client's experiencing an image of a pleasant, hopefully reinforcing scene. CPR is therefore analogous to its operant counterpart, positive reinforcement. Covert positive reinforcement has been used to modify troublesome behaviors such as heroin addiction, phobias, and pain perception. In range of application, CPR may be the most useful of all the covert conditioning procedures.

There are some similarities between CPR and Joseph Wolpe's systematic desensitization: reliance on imagery, frequent use of relaxation training, and effectiveness in dealing with phobias. Because of these similarities, some psychologists mistakenly consider CPR to be a variant of desensitization. The applicability of CPR to a wider range of behaviors, including those without an affective component, and the results of experimental investigations into the mechanics of CPR have provided strong evidence in support of the operant theoretical bases of CPR.

Four more covert conditioning procedures have been developed: covert modeling (CM), covert negative reinforcement (CNR), covert extinction (CE), and covert response cost (CRC). In all cases, the covert conditioning procedure was based on its operant counterpart.

Covert modeling has been the most thoroughly investigated and widely used of these additional procedures. Alan Kazdin wrote a summary of CM research in Jerome Singer and Kenneth Pope's book, *The power of human imagination.* Covert modeling has been used in cases involving social skills training and motor behaviors, and is particularly helpful with clients who have difficulty imagining themselves in appropriate situations or performing certain behaviors. In CM the client imagines seeing a model performing the target behavior. Covert negative reinforcement can be an alternative to CPR with clients who have difficulty imagining something pleasurable happening to them. In CNR the client begins by visualizing an aversive scene, then switches to a scene of the behavior to be increased. Covert response cost is a useful adjunct to covert sensitization in which the client imagines the loss of a reinforcing stimulus contingent on the performance of a maladaptive behavior. Covert extinction is especially effective in modifying consummatory behaviors such as drug abuse and eating disorders: the client simply imagines performing the target behavior without the expected result.

Although covert conditioning procedures are usually first taught to clients by behavior therapists, the procedures are readily adaptable to self-control, thereby allowing the client to become more independent of the therapist. One such application that exemplifies the way individual procedures can be combined is the self-control triad (SCT). The SCT combines thought stopping, relaxation training, and CPR.

Other self-control uses of covert conditioning are tailor-made to meet the needs of individual clients and the behaviors they wish to modify.

BEHAVIOR THERAPY
COGNITIVE BEHAVIOR THERAPY
CONDITIONING
INNOVATIVE PSYCHOTHERAPIES
PSYCHOTHERAPY

J. R. CAUTELA
A. J. KEARNEY

CRANIAL NERVES

Cranial nerves differ from other nerves in that they emerge directly from the brain or cranium (more correctly, the brain stem). It is not uncommon for a person to manifest some behavioral aberration that might be diagnosed as psychological when, in fact, the abberration is a deficit due to cranial nerve impairment. Psychologists, therefore, need to be familiar with the basic anatomy and function of the cranial nerves.

In many of the cranial nerves, function can be classified in a manner similar to classification of spinal nerves, where each pair has a sensory (dorsal) root and a motor (ventral) root serving either a body wall (somatic function) or the viscera (visceral function). Although cranial nerves do not have separate roots, most have both afferent (sensory) and efferent (motor) capabilities. A few cranial nerves have specialized functions, such as the optic, olfactory, and auditory nerves.

The 12 cranial pairs are numbered in a sequence corresponding to where the nerve apparently attaches to the brain, going from anterior (olfactory, I) to posterior (hypoglossal, XII). A simplified summary of the nerves is portrayed in Table 1.

Strictly speaking, nerves I and II are not nerves at all, but rather evaginated extensions or protrusions of the brain. Also, unlike the spinal nerves, some cranial nerves have only efferent fibers and others only afferent.

BRAIN
CENTRAL NERVOUS SYSTEM

J. C. ROOK

Table 1   Cranial Nerves and Their Classification

Number	Name	Type	Function
I	Olfactory	Afferent	Sense of smell.
II	Optic	Afferent	Sense of vision.
III	Oculomotor	Basically efferent	Innervates all extrinsic eye muscles except the lateral rectus (see VI) and the superior oblique (see IV); parasympathetic innervation to ciliary muscle and to pupil.
IV	Trochlear	Basically efferent (Some afferent)	Serves the superior oblique muscle of eye (see III). (Proprioception).
V	Trigeminal (3 branches: opthalmic, maxillary, and mandibular)	Mixed: Afferent	In additional to proprioception, exteroceptive fibers serve the forehead, eyelid, cornea, iris, nose, nasal mucosa, most areas of face, teeth, lips, jaw, tongue, and external ear. Primarily tactile, but some evidence of pain and temperature also.
		Efferent	Innervates muscles of mastication such as chewing, biting, opening and closing of mouth, as well as movement of anterior $\frac{2}{3}$ of tongue (see VIII).
VI	Abducens	Basically efferent (Some afferent)	Innervates lateral rectus muscle of eye (see III & IV). (Proprioception).
VII	Facial	Mixed: Efferent	Two branches: the larger is the facial nerve as such and is basically motor. The minor nerve, referred to as the *intermediate* nerve, is complex. Facial efferent fibers supply the superficial musculature of face and scalp, glands and mucous membranes of pharynx, nasal cavity, and palate.
		Afferent	Conducts sense of taste from anterior $\frac{2}{3}$ of tongue (see IX) and innervates salivation. Also, some proprioceptive capacity for pressure and position sense from facial muscles.
VIII	Auditory or acoustic or vestibulocochlear	Two separate parts: Cohlear—afferent Vestibular—basically afferent	Transmits exteroceptive signals from Organ of Corti; fibers serve inner ear (semicircular canal, utricle, and saccule) for maintenance of equilibrium and position orientation.
		(Some efferent)	(Influences spinal cord, exerting facilatory action on extensor motor neurons, as well as on oculomotor movement [see III, IV, & VI).
IX	Glassopharyngeal	Mixed: Afferent	Conducts sense of taste from posterior $\frac{1}{3}$ of tongue (see VII); sensations from pharynx, eustachian tube, fauces, tonsils, and soft palate.
		Efferent	Innervates muscles of pharynx and stylopharyngeus muscle. Fibers of this and the next cranial nerve (X) serve the striated muscles of pharynx, larynx, and upper part of esophagus.
X	Vagus	Mixed: Afferent	Conduct exteroceptive sensation (pain and temperature) from auditory meatus and region of the ear. Sensory fibers serve pharynx, larynx, esophagus, trachea, thoracic and abdominal viscera (e.g., heart and intestines).
		Efferent	Fibers distributed to autonomic ganglia for innervation of abdominal and thoracic viscera (inhibit heart rate and stimulate gastric and pancreatic activity as well as gastrointestinal action). Serve base of tongue plus muscles mentioned in IX.
XI	Spinal accessory or accessory	Basically efferent	Innervates movement of pharynx, larynx, uvula, and palate, as well as to cardiac and laryngeal nerves. Another part serves the trapezius and sternocleidomastoid muscles.
		(Some afferent)	(Proprioception).
XII	Hypoglossal	Efferent	Serves muscle fibers of neck and tongue (for voluntary movements). Perhaps (along with V) involved in reflexes of sucking, chewing, and swallowing.

CREATIVITY

J. P. Guilford devoted his 1949 American Psychological Association presidential address to the topic of creativity, stating that only 186 out of some 121,000 entries in psychological abstracts had dealt with the topic. The situation has changed dramatically; an average of 250 dissertations, articles, and books have appeared each year since 1970. Several journals attest to the vigor of the field (e.g., *Gifted Child Quarterly, Imagination, Cognition and Personality, Journal of Creative Behavior,* and *Journal of Mental Imagery*). However, *creativity* lacks a precise definition in psychology, and attempts to measure creativity have encountered controversy.

Various societies have constructed an assortment of terms to describe activities that resemble what Western psychologists refer to as creativity. The first hexagram (or *kuan*) of the Chinese *Book of changes* (*I Jing*) is Ch'ien, the "Creative Principle." This hexagram expresses both the creative action of the Source of All, which causes "objects to flow into their respective form," and the Superior Person, who interacts with these forms when the time is ripe. This creative principle functions when superior persons harmonize their way of life with the universal flow. Confucius added, "Great indeed is the generating power of the Creative; all beings owe their beginnings to it; this power permeates all heaven."

Most Oriental, African, and Native American traditions used creative imagination to enrich and enhance everyday life; novel contributions were typically seen as gifts from deities or spirits who used humans as channels (a formulation not unlike Skinner's notion [1972] that the creator adds nothing to creation but is merely the locus through which environmental variables act). Yet, in some of these societies an individual who conceived or produced something unprecedented (e.g., a mask) would have been censured for breaking with tradition. In these societies, talented craftspeople were valued, but individuals with a flair for novelty were chastised. In Western civilization, not all individuals had equal opportunities for creative expression; for instance, women's creativity was not valued or encouraged and they were given few occasions to develop the skills (e.g., critical thinking) or life circumstances (e.g., solitude) on which creative productivity often depends.

The word *creativity* is linked with the concept of origin itself (consider the related term *originality*). Some psychologists require products to be of social value or to have attained some other type of consensual agreement if they are to be called creative, whereas other psychologists focus on the process by which these products come into being. Other attempts at definition conceptualize creativity as a unique achievement, ability, and/or attitude of a person or consortium of people. In each of these outlooks, there can be levels of accomplishment, utility, or originality, implying that some persons, groups, processes, or objects can be more or less creative than others.

Thus from the Western psychological perspective, *creativity* is a term that can be used to describe the process of bringing something new into being by becoming sensitive to gaps in human knowledge, identifying these deficiencies, searching for their solutions, making guesses as to a potential solution, testing one's hypotheses, and communicating the final product.

Attempts to measure degrees of creativeness have led to tests and rating scales of divergent thinking, of creative thinking, of creative perception, and of creative activity. Biographical inventories have been devised in an attempt to identify the creative person. Each of these attempts at assessment may be used for identifying highly creative individuals to offer them special instruction; entire programs in the United States—some of them statewide—have been based on these or similar assessments. However, these measures have been criticized on the basis of content validity, construct validity, reliability, clarity of instructions, relevance to different populations, and comprehensiveness, as well as the proclivity for their results to be influenced by situational or contextual factors. A number of promising outcomes have resulted from assessing level and/ or type of creativity through the use of such naturalistic assignments as writing poetry or short stories, assembling collages, or spontaneous problem solving.

In spite of their shortcomings, creativity tests have been used in many research projects. Barron and Harrington collated 70 studies in which positive and statistically significant relationships were observed "between various divergent thinking test scores and reasonably acceptable nontest indices of creative behavior or achievement." Even so, in some studies, creativity test scores failed to correlate significantly with creative behavior or achievement, suggesting the importance of identifying field-relevant thinking abilities in each professional area and selecting the test accordingly. Cognitive research has identified such qualities of creative thinking as the importance of extended work sessions, "playing" with ideas in various ways, using counterintuitive strategies, analyzing paradoxical elements of a problem, and shifting back and forth between the general and the specific.

When personality characteristics of people considered to be creative are identified, a common set of characteristics emerges, such as high valuation of aesthetic qualities in experience, broad interests, high energy, attraction to complexity, independence of judgment, autonomy, intuition, self-confidence, ability to resolve paradoxes or to accommodate apparently opposite or conflicting trains in one's self-concept, and a firm sense of one's self as creative. In addition, being first in the birth order appears to foster creativity as does early parental loss, perhaps because these occurrences lead to the "intensely experienced childhood" often related to later creative achievement. There are important differences among groups of creative people, such as the extensive degree of affective disorders found among writers and their close relatives, whereas research scientists grew up as "intellectual rebels" who tended to break their intimate family ties at adolescence.

Creativity training programs assume that creative behavior can be enhanced, an assumption that has not gained universal acceptance among psychologists who emphasize the importance of biological determinants and early learning. The authors of some approaches admit that important creativity-relevant skills cannot be influenced in a short span of time, because these components include such elements as knowledge of the topic, technical skills, and working and cognitive styles. As a result, these programs emphasize task motivation (through modeling, fantasy, emphasizing choice, deemphasizing evaluation, etc.) so that one's abilities are allowed expression rather than being undermined. Other programs take a more optimistic view regarding creativity enhancement, focusing on cognitive rather than social–psychological methods. For instance, programs in brainstorming accentuate deferment of judgment, synectics attempts to stimulate creativity through instruction in developing analogies, and creative problem solving teaches people how to generate unusual ideas, using such techniques as combining two or more disparate notions. Some programs for schoolchildren, such as the Purdue Creativity Training Program and the Productive Training Program, have been found effective in improving scores on standard creativity tests.

Future research studies need to identify the genetic markers for creative behavior, reconcile personality and cognitive research data in creativity, evaluate the part played by altered states of consciousness in creative ideation, determine the role of mental illness in blocking or facilitating creative expression, and specify what home and school variables are key factors in the development of highly creative individuals. The need for creative solutions to the world's many social, economic, and environmental problems reflects the importance of this field and of the psychologists who dedicate themselves to understanding the *I Jing's* creative principle as it manifests itself in human life.

ABSTRACT INTELLIGENCE
ARTISTIC MORPHOLOGY
HUMAN FACTORS
SOFT DETERMINISM
UNCONSCIOUS INFERENCES

S. KRIPPNER

CREATIVITY MEASURES

Creativity is an area of cognitive functioning important in a wide variety of tasks, including not only the arts, but also research and development engineering, scientific achievements, and other such endeavors.

Most creativity measures follow the work of J. P. Guilford's structure-of-intellect model. According to Guilford, a distinction can be drawn between convergent and divergent production as intellectual operations.

In convergent thinking, people are required to "narrow" their thoughts—to consider several options and choose the one best solution.

Such thinking is found in multiple-choice tests, as well as in most tests of general intelligence. In contrast, divergent production requires the ability to think in many different directions and come up with novel solutions to problems. It is divergent production that many creativity measures attempt to assess.

APTITUDE TESTING

P. G. BENSON

CREDENTIALING

Psychology is a tightly controlled profession. All jurisdictions in North America legislate the licensing, certification, or regulation of psychologists. Certification laws protect the use of the title "psychologist," while licensing laws, in addition to limiting the use of the title, also define the practice of psychology. In most states the minimum requirement for certification or licensing for those wishing to practice psychology is the doctorate degree. Most states also require supervised experience (often postdoctoral) in addition to the doctoral degree. Besides these educational and experience requirements, a formal examination is generally required. This is usually the Examination for Professional Practice in Psychology (EPPP).

There are an estimated 50,000 psychologists registered in the United States and about 5,000 in Canada. Each year, some 5,000 Americans take the examination for professional practice in psychology. This examination, required by most examining boards, is intended to verify knowledge in psychology.

Most states require that the earned doctoral degree be either in psychology or from a program that is primarily psychological in content. Furthermore, most states require that the doctoral degree be awarded from a regionally accredited institution. A number of regional accrediting agencies are recognized by the Council on Postsecondary Accreditation (COPA), which also recognizes a number of specialized accrediting agencies. The American Psychological Association is one of those specialized agencies; currently it accredits doctoral psychology programs in clinical, counseling, and school psychology.

To be eligible for accreditation by the American Psychological Association, programs must in regionally accredited institutions and be clearly identified and labeled as professional psychology programs. In addition, the faculty must have primary responsibility and authority for the program, and organizational responsibility for the program must be clearly defined. Also required are an organized plan of study providing the student with breadth of exposure to psychology, and supervised experience appropriate to the field. In addition, there must be an identifiable psychology faculty and an identifiable body of students in a given psychology program. Finally, the institution where the program is housed must demonstrate its support of the program by providing appropriate financial resources.

Most state laws have generic credentialing requirements applicable to all psychologists in public practice, regardless of specialty. The APA's *Ethical principles of psychologists* requires that psychologists accurately represent their competence, education, training, and experience.

A different type of credential is offered through the American Board of Professional Psychology (ABPP). Established in 1947 by the Council of Representatives of the American Psychological Association, ABPP awards diplomas in four fields of psychological specialization: clinical, counseling, industrial and organization, and school psychology. Applicants for the diploma must possess a doctorate in psychology from an accredited institution and have 5 years of qualifying experience in the field in which the diploma is sought. Four of the 5 years of qualifying experience must be postdoctoral. Currently, applicants for the ABPP

diploma must first file an application, including appropriate endorsements by other psychologists familiar with their work. Evaluation of the application is a requirement prior to admission as a candidate for the examination. Individuals admitted to candidacy are requested to present one or more work samples representative of that candidate's practice as a professional psychologist. Usually this consists of assessment and/or intervention activities typical of the applicant's practice. In addition, candidates are given an opportunity to be observed in their professional activities by the examining team. The examination itself consists of judgments concerning the effectiveness of the candidate's efforts toward constructive intervention, based on the candidate's assessment of the problems presented, awareness of the relevance of research and theory, and sensitivity to the ethical implications of professional practice. Successful candidates are awarded a diploma within their specialty and are also listed in the *Directory of the American Psychological Association.* More recently, other specialty boards have been or are in the process of being established.

Another organization that lists psychologists is the Council for the National Register of Health Service Providers in Psychology. Since 1975 this organization has published a list of psychologists who have applied voluntarily for inclusion and who meet the requirements for listing. The 1991 *Register* lists nearly 15,000 registrants. Current criteria for listing include current licensure or certification at the independent practice level by a state board of examiners of psychology, a doctorate degree in psychology from a regionally accredited institution, and 2 years' supervised experience in health service. One of those 2 years must be at the postdoctoral level, and one must be in an organized health service training program.

Passionate arguments have been raised for and against credentialing. The most vehement arguments have been heard with regard to the relationship between credentialing and competence as a professional psychologist. It has been pointed out that credentialing is important for the establishment of a profession and to protect the public. When one discusses providing competent psychological services to the public, however, one must recognize that psychologists are not the only ones to provide psychological or mental health services: The field is replete with provider groups.

In the same manner that psychiatry was once accused of trying to keep other professions out of its mental health "turf," so psychology is now accused of trying to keep other mental health professionals from qualifying for licensure. Given the success that psychology has had in passing licensure and certification laws in the various jurisdictions, more and more mental health professionals have either sought licensure as psychologists or statutory recognition of their own. Psychology has clearly moved from the emerging profession status of 30 years ago to the more firmly established "emerged profession" status of today. Yet it is still in the process of becoming fully established, and has been accused of undue concern for the establishment of the profession and not enough for matters of consumer protection, competence, and continuing education. Psychology is now devoting more energy to these concerns. In the process, the definition of what constitutes a psychologist and what constitutes a doctoral program in professional psychology are becoming more refined. There is always the danger that this may lead to exclusionism and elitism.

AMERICAN BOARD OF PROFESSIONAL PSYCHOLOGY
AMERICAN PSYCHOLOGICAL ASSOCIATION
COMPETENCY IN PSYCHOLOGY
PROFESSIONAL ETHICS

N. ABELES

CRESPI EFFECT

Named for its discoverer, Leo P. Crespi, the *Crespi effect* refers to an interesting phenomenon that occurs when, in learning experiments carried out with lower animals, the attractiveness of a reward is suddenly changed. Thus if a large amount of food provides the incentive, rats learning a maze run to the goal faster than if the amount of food is small.

Once these levels of performance are established, switching the amounts of food for the two groups has an immediate effect on performance. Rats that had received a large reward and now receive a small one run more slowly. Those that had received a small reward and now receive a large one show the opposite effect. Moreover, performance with the changed reward frequently overshoots the mark predicted from earlier performance. Those switched from a large reward to a small one run more slowly than expected, whereas those switched from small to large run faster. It is as if animals in the first group are "disappointed" or "depressed" by the sudden decrease in the attractiveness of the reward, while the others are "elated" by the sudden increase.

G. A. KIMBLE

CRIME

The study of crime has been of considerable public, political, and psychological concern. It has been the subject of great public controversy as well as major scientific activity. The earliest known philosophy concerning crime must date to the beginning of recorded history. Illegal and undesirable behavior are as old as the written history of humans. Early approaches to crime simply involved the concept of personal revenge or retaliation; justice was a matter for individual or family concern. As organized societies emerged, personal retribution gave way to collective and formalized responses in the form of decision-making groups or leaders.

Until the last 200 to 300 years, codification of criminal behaviors and appropriate punishments were a matter for church law. This state of affairs led to one of the early reform movements. During the eighteenth century, philosophers such as Voltaire and Rousseau began to question the domination of secular activities by the religious hierarchy. From this emerged a conceptualization of behavior as a result of rational choice rather than supernatural force. With the notion of individual free will and choice as its cornerstone, the classical approach to crime was conceived, which fostered points of view still prominent today. The widespread use of imprisonment, that sentences of varying length, stems from a classical view of punishment that fits the crime.

As the nineteenth century progressed, the classical assumptions of free will were challenged by a more positivist tradition, which argued that criminals were not wholly responsible for their actions. A point of view emerged that stressed individual and environmental causes of human behavior. If criminal acts were determined at least partially by factors beyond the control of individuals themselves, then disadvantageous environments, modes of upbringing, and characterological patterns were equally responsible for crime. With greater or lesser degrees of sophistication, these two schools of thought rule contemporary knowledge of the crime problem.

To further understand approaches to crime, it is necessary to grasp the varying definitions employed. The most prominent definition of crime, derived from official records, views crime as behavior that violates criminal law and is formally reported to law enforcement agencies. This definition is the basis of official tabulations concerning crime rates that are conspicuous in scientific study and the public media.

A second definition of crime derives from reports of victims. In periodic surveys conducted by public sector and private research organizations, citizens are surveyed concerning crimes of which they have been victims. Typically, survey data uncover considerably higher crime rates which present in the officially reported statistics. In addition, there are disproportional reporting rates by crime type.

A third aspect of the problem involves public perception. Periodic surveys indicate that crime is typically seen as one of the major problems facing organized society. Further, survey data indicate that a majority of citizens are fearful of becoming the victims of criminal acts themselves.

A further aspect of the study of crime involves the official mechanisms that society has organized in response to the crime problem. There are more than 3000 illegal acts codified in the federal criminal code, in addition to numerous others present in state and local criminal laws. There are three parallel criminal justice systems charged with responding to behaviors in violation of local, state, or federal law, and they share common components. There exist agencies charged with the observation and apprehension of reported criminals at the local level (city police departments, county sheriffs), at the state level (the state police), and at the federal level (the Federal Bureau of Investigation). Further, there are distinct entities charged with bringing alleged criminals to trial at the local level (the county prosecutor), the state level (the state's attorney), and at the federal level (the Attorney General). Finally, there are distinct systems components charged with the treatment, punishment, and rehabilitation of convicted criminals at the local level (county probation services, county jails), at the state level (state department of corrections, and parole and review boards), and at the federal level (federal parole officers, the Federal Bureau of Prisons).

Knowledge about crime can best be described in four traditions. Each tradition has its distinct historical roots and sets of knowledge relevant to crime. The first major approach to the study of crime, the *individual differences approach,* derived from positivist traditions. Knowledge in this area is based on such classic work as that carried out in the 1940s by the Gluecks. Physical, psychological, and social differences among 500 institutionalized criminals and 500 demographically matched noncriminals were observed. The essential conclusion was that crime was a result of various individual and social factors. This highly influential work resulted in an entire tradition of research. Consistent differences have been demonstrated between criminal and noncriminal populations using objective personality tests, cognitive performance measures, and projective personality measures. Representative work has found criminals to be less socialized, less intelligent, psychologically abnormal, morally immature, and victims of inappropriate upbringing and parenting styles.

The second major tradition of knowledge acquisition is based on the *social structural school of thought.* This tradition of research examines social structural and demographic differences among groups or subcultures in which crime rates are disproportionately high. Heavy emphasis is placed on environmental differences. The suggestion has emerged that crime is a result of differential access to legitimate and illegitimate means of attaining socially defined personal and material goals. Varieties of crime are explained by available alternatives for dealing with blocked opportunity structure, including gang delinquency, the importance of exposure to criminal peers and family members, schools as a primary source of blocked opportunity, and the criminal justice system itself as a perpetrator of continued crime. In addition, an entire tradition has arisen tracing the causes of crime to disorganized subsocieties in major urban areas.

A third major set of knowledge concerning crime has been entitled *labeling theory.* Deriving from the historical position of symbolic interactionism and an interpersonal view of human behavior championed by George Herbert Mead and Harry Stack Sullivan, the labeling position states that crime is a characteristic conferred on certain acts by influential audiences. Crime is used by society to specify the limits of acceptable behavior by selecting certain subgroups as criminal, identifying them formally in a variety of social ceremonies in courts of law, and relegating them to inferior social standing through incarceration and probation. From the labeling point of view, crime is not seen as a characteristic of an individual or a pathological-derived environment. Rather, crime is said to result from intricate social processes operative in the criminal justice system. Labeling theory derives considerable support from self-report studies of crime reporting widespread incidents of illegal activities. If most individuals drift in and out of illegal behavior patterns until either apprehended or left unnoticed, and if the conferring of the negative social label of criminal has adverse effects on future incidents of unlawful behavior, then the interaction between individuals and the criminal justice system is a major precursor of crime.

The fourth major source of knowledge derives from *learning theory.* From this point of view, criminal behavior exists because it is reinforced and differentially modeled in the society. Criminal behavior is not viewed as different from other forms of behavior, nor are individuals termed criminal viewed as abnormal, unusual, or otherwise different from the general population. From the learning theory point of view, crime is a function of criminal behavior being differentially modeled, performed, and reinforced. Socially acceptable forms of behavior are significantly lacking in the behavioral repertoire of the criminal.

Each of these major theoretical positions has had an impact on major approaches to the crime problem. Three major approaches prominently characterize treatment, rehabilitation, and corrective approaches. The first, the *deterrent approach,* involves the notion that punishment reduces crime. Yet there is great debate concerning the effectiveness of punishment as an approach to crime. Some studies conclude that swift and severe punishment acts to reduce criminal performance; others, that severe sanctions have no impact on criminal behavior.

A second major approach to crime involves treating noncriminal offenders. Various forms of individual therapy, group therapy, behavioral modification, educational programs, and vocational training and work programs all aim at ameliorating the individual and cultural deficits present in criminal populations. Research evidence concerning the effectiveness of treatment and rehabilitation approaches to crime is extremely mixed.

A final major approach to the crime problem has been through early detection and prevention. Drawing heavily on the individual differences approach mentioned previously, the prevention model seeks to identify potentially criminal individuals and apply early treatment procedures. Models of early intervention and prevention have met with little, if any, reliable success.

CRIMINAL RESPONSIBILITY
DEVIANCE
LABELING THEORY

W. S. Davidson II

CRIMINAL RESPONSIBILITY

Substantive criminal law delineates the types of activities that a person may perform that result in a criminal penalty. The act itself is called *actus reus,* and the necessary state of mind is called *mens rea,* or "evil mind." If persons do not have the requisite state of mind—*mens rea*—then they may not be held criminally responsible for the act. This assertion that the individual lacks the necessary state of mind is known as the insanity defense. This defense permits the trier of fact, judge or jury, to disregard the strict requirements of law where it finds that the person, as a result of mental illness, cannot be held responsible for his or her behavior.

Modern tests of criminal responsibility began with the M'Naughten case in 1843. This test is the sole rule applied in half the states, and at least one of the standards in all the states. The M'Naughten rule speaks to the issue of whether the defendant understood the nature and quality of his or her act and knew the difference between right and wrong with respect to it. The first American rule of criminal responsibility was set further in *State v. Pike,* based on forensic psychologist Isaac Ray's concept

of insanity. This decision and rule was known as the New Hampshire Doctrine. The charge to the court was that all symptoms and all tests of disease are purely matters of fact to be determined by the jury. This preserved the distinction between matters of law and matters of fact.

The second major test of criminal responsibility occurred in 1954 and is known as the Durham Rule, which holds that the accused is not criminally responsible if his or her unlawful act was the product of mental disease or defect. This rule relied primarily on expert medical testimony and created serious problems for the court in making proper decisions. It was overturned in *U.S. v. Brawnet 471,* in which the judge instructed the jury to acquit the defendant if at the time of his unlawful conduct his mental or emotional processes or behavior controls were impaired to such an extent that he could not be held justly responsible for his act.

A recent test of insanity is called the ALI test, which refers to the American Law Institute's model penal code. This test holds that a person is not criminally responsible for his or her act if at the time, as a result of a mental disease or defect, the person lacked the substantial capacity either to appreciate the criminality (wrongfulness) of his or her conduct or to conform that conduct to the requirement of the law. Excluded from this rule are abnormalities manifested only by repeated criminal or otherwise antisocial conduct. This test has gained increasing acceptance and is the law in many states and federal jurisdictions.

If a person is found to be not criminally responsible—that is, not guilty by reason of insanity–he or she may be detained in a hospital for the mentally ill. The person may be held until a court hearing determines that the individual does not suffer from a mental disease or defect that, as a result of release, would create a substantial risk of serious bodily harm to another person or serious damage to the property of another person.

Current proposals to abolish the insanity defense of criminal responsibility relate to a rule termed "guilty but mentally ill." This rule states that a person charged with a crime must be tried on the facts first, following which his or her mental state will determine the disposition. The concept is to hold all people responsible for their acts, but to treat rather than punish the mentally ill offenders.

COMPETENCY TO STAND TRIAL
CRIME
FORENSIC PSYCHOLOGY

R. C. Marvit

CRISIS INTERVENTION

Crisis intervention is an emerging discipline the major concern of which is providing immediate temporary emotional first aid to victims of psychological and physical trauma. Rape, child abuse, attempted suicide, spousal abuse, family disputes, assault, robbery, and burglary all have the potential for creating severe and unusual stress in a person's life. When such stresses occur and tax the coping skills of the individual to the point that effective and adaptive living is not possible, crisis occurs and the need for effective intervention is paramount. Without effective intervention, severe emotional disorganization often results and the physical as well as psychological well-being of the individual is threatened. With sensitive intervention, the likelihood of further injury is decreased, the possibility of resuming precrisis functioning is maximized, and the need for subsequent psychotherapy, counseling, or hospitalization is markedly reduced. Time is always a critical element. Because the ineffective or maladaptive behavior of the crisis victim must be interrupted, reduced, and redirected at the earliest possible moment after crisis onset, the intervener—unlike in other forms of individual care—must act with the greatest dispatch.

Little is known, and less is understood, about the effects of emotional stress on body and mind. For many relevant reasons, the study of crisis intervention is critical, regardless of academic or nonacademic background. Being a psychologist, psychiatrist, social worker, counselor, or other helping professional does not in itself ensure proper knowledge and skill training. Lack of professional training in no way precludes the potential for skillful and effective functioning during crisis situations. The necessary skills can be developed, refined, and utilized by any professional, paraprofessional, volunteer, lay person, law enforcement officer, attorney, minister, hot-line worker, teacher, or friend who cares about the mental well-being of those with whom they come into contact.

HISTORY OF THE CRISIS INTERVENTION MOVEMENT

The term *crisis intervention* has been equally overused and randomly applied, and has come to mean many different things. To the psychologist it may mean psychotherapy; to the counselor, short-term counseling; to the psychiatrist, perhaps hospitalization.

Crisis intervention theory is usually credited to Gerald Caplan and Erich Lindemann. Their studies of persons in actual crisis situations provided basic information in this area. Although their work was done subsequent to World War II, what would now be considered crisis intervention can be traced at least to the beginning of the twentieth century, to the help centers and settlement houses of the Northeast. Since that time agencies, hot lines, help houses, and the like have proliferated.

The National Institute for Training in Crisis Intervention brought together academics, professionals, paraprofessionals, lay volunteers, police officers, and others under one roof. Not only did crisis intervention theory begin to be further developed and standardized, but also many of the traditional barriers—especially between law enforcement officers and helping agency personnel—began to fall away. The result was better emotional first-aid care for crisis victims.

Various levels of training were developed and a plan proposed for the certification of interveners. In 1980 the American Board of Examiners in Crisis Intervention was founded, which certifies individual interveners from agencies and professions.

CRISIS INTERVENTION PROCEDURES

Crisis intervention is an immediate response to an immediate problem. The often disorganized, confused, and dangerous behavior of the crisis victim must be dealt with as quickly as possible by an intervener who can react immediately and skillfully. Such a response is designed to assist the victim to use personal and social supports and help him or her return to precrisis functioning levels.

To that end, a standard set of procedures is advocated. These instructions are not intended to concretize a set of rules or to obviate the need for personal style or creativity on the part of the intervener; to the contrary, they are designed to allow the maximum of both. Such a simplified format may be helpful, however, because of the many and varied behaviors and concerns with which an intervener must be concerned during high-stress encounters. Usually some stress and anxiety will also be present in the intervener as intervention is attempted. With simplified guidelines, the intervener can be sure that all areas are being covered, regardless of his or her own emotional state or the emotional state.

Immediacy

The crisis intervener must act to reduce the crisis level as soon as the victim is encountered. Act *now!* Crises may develop over time, and the results of intervention may be felt for a long time to come.

Control

Persons in crisis are often not in control of themselves or of their situation. For this reason and for reasons of safety, the crisis intervener must assume control of the situation and of the crisis victims. This is done quickly and maintained only as long as the victims are not able to maintain control

themselves. This may involve only seconds or minutes, or at times somewhat longer periods. A crutch is valuable when it is needed; a disability when it is not. Ways of gaining and maintaining control vary with the situation and with the creativity of the intervener. The physical presence of the intervener, having the victims seated, making unusual requests, lowering or raising the voice, a whistle or other loud noise, intervening with a partner, even the mannerisms of the intervener—all may contribute to the control exercised in a given situation. Without control, little else is possible that will help the victim, and the intervener may be in great danger.

Assessment

Why did the victim go into crisis at this particular time? What precipitating events led up to the crisis? What was tried by the victim or others to reduce the stressful situation? The crisis intervener must perform a quick and accurate assessment of the total situation and persons involved to determine how the crisis may be effectively handled. What is obtained must be accurate and usable. Concentrate on recent history only.

Disposition

What the intervener does will either help or hurt the victim. Therefore careful consideration must be given to the intervention "game plan." The more the victim or victims can be helped to work out by themselves with the intervener's assistance, the more substantial will be the results. The intervener's job is only to help the victim to return to a level of precrisis functioning. This is probably the major difference between crisis intervention and psychotherapy: intervention concerns itself with problem management, not problem resolution. If the intervention is done effectively, the probability of eventual problem resolution is greatly enhanced.

Referral

Critical, and yet often overlooked, in many crisis interventions is the referral of the victim, as needed, for additional or ongoing professional or community assistance. Many otherwise skillful interventions have failed because a referral either was not made or was made ineffectively by the intervener. Successful referrals are the result of careful planning and source investigation. Such information must be gathered by the intervener prior to intervention, so that referral can be done easily and provide the victim with all necessary information.

Follow-up

Follow-up is necessary to ensure the viability of the intervention. A call to a former victim may reveal new problems, lack of transportation to the referred-to agency, or a myriad of other occurrences that the intervener may correct, thereby saving an endangered but otherwise sound intervention.

INTERVENER SURVIVAL

J. L. Greenstone
S. Leviton

CRITERION IN EMPLOYMENT

The criterion is a measure (or estimate) of success on a job. Unless there is a good criterion of evaluating performance, one cannot take accurate aim in hiring, placement, training, merit rating, or promotion. In these days of strong unions, civil rights demands, and governmental intervention, absence of a good criterion can be disastrous. A mistake in hiring cannot be rectified by firing; in an extreme case, an employee must be promoted even when a supervisor would prefer a termination. Further, employment and guidance experts have trouble guiding a client into a given occupation or recommending the client to a potential employer if they cannot pin down with some certainty just what makes for success in specific vocations.

There are two principal difficulties in establishing a criterion: (a) *What actually does constitute success on the job?* and (b) *Even if accepted and statistically measurable criteria are present, how important is each?*

A criterion is a measure of performance level, expressed in quantitative terms, based on a complete job description. There are seven criteria of the criterion.

1. *A criterion should be quantitative.* Examples are dollar totals sold by a salesperson, units produced by a factory worker, or a time on the part of a track runner. Some data do not lie in continuous series from lowest to highest, but still can be treated statistically. They may lie in rank order.

2. *A criterion should parallel the actual job requirements.* If an individual is hired, the job description should tie in with successful performance on the job.

3. *A success criterion should depend on the worker's having control over performance.* Rating of quality of performance should take into consideration the complexities and difficulties of the assigned task.

4. *The criteria should present themselves in proper proportions.* There are major and minor requirements of any job. Each item should be considered, and in proper proportion. These proportions may be difficult to fractionate out. Relative time spent on each aspect of a job is a simple means of evaluating proportionate values, but is often an inadequate measure.

5. *A criterion should be measurable with some degree of consistency.* Efforts should be made to render the criterion of success as objective as possible, or to define it so that various raters can be reasonably uniform.

6. *The criterion should be expressed in comparable units.* Statistical devices such as percentiles, T-scores, and sigma (standard deviation) scores enable us to compare the degree of excellence of people in different occupations, or between levels.

7. *The criterion should be reduced, if at all possible, to a single figure.* In some instances the end product of the performance automatically takes care of this requirement. Often no single additive score appears, and total evaluation must be worked out either by some statistical technique like partial and multiple correlation, or by opinion.

Until recently, little attention was paid in the literature to defining the criteria of job success, or even thinking of what the criteria should actually be. The seven criteria suggested have limitations and/or situations in which they are only partially applicable, but the closer an organization can come to fulfilling these, the more satisfactory will be employment, rating, and promotion.

EMPLOYMENT PRACTICES
JOB EVALUATION

R. W. HUSBAND

CRITERION MEASURES

A criterion measure is a standard. In psychology, the criterion is usually a standard for judging the validity of a test. Sometimes it is also used to refer to the variable being predicted from other variables, as in a multiple correlation study.

When used to judge the validity of a test, the criterion measure is an accepted measure of the behavior under consideration. The higher the test correlates with that standard, the greater the criterion-related validity of the test. Criterion-related validity is divided into concurrent and predictive validities. Concurrent validity is found by correlating test scores with criterion measures taken at the same time. Predictive validity is found by correlating test scores with a criterion measure gathered at a later time.

The problem with criterion measures is to find measures that can be accepted as standards. This is less of a problem where it is possible to obtain work sample measures, as in the salesmanship example. Although there may be other important measures of good salesmanship—level of customer satisfaction, number and amount of repeat sales, and customer turnover—these are typically reflected in total sales. A composite criterion measure can also be prepared by weighting factors according to the average judgments of an appropriate sample of sales managers.

Standardization is more of a problem when the criterion represents a construct. The beginnings of that problem are hinted at in deciding what to include in "salesmanship." The more vague the construct, the greater the difficulty. One must define what to include in the construct, then find ways to estimate vague concepts such as "social success," then obtain agreement on how to weight these aspects in combination—a difficult task.

To be accepted as undisputed standards, criterion measures must be carefully analyzed to make sure they measure as intended. For example, Roy Goldman and Robert Slaughter point out that grade-point average is a poor measure of college success, because low ability students gravitate to easy courses where they can succeed, whereas higher ability students try courses that are more difficult and may receive a less than top grade.

Bogden and Taylor extensively discuss sources of criterion bias. They consider four types: (a) *criterion insufficiency,* or the omission of pertinent elements; (b) *criterion deficiency,* including extraneous elements; (c) *criterion scale unit bias,* or an inequality of scale units (e.g., the measure gives too many favorable ratings, instead of the few that would have resulted, had the scores yielded a bell-shaped distribution); and (d) *criterion distortion,* or the improper weighting in combining criterion elements.

The biasing factors that might appear include opportunity bias, halo effect, and experience contamination. *Opportunity bias* appears when some personnel have more opportunity to display the criterion behavior than others, so that the criterion is weighted in their favor even though, given equal opportunity, others might have done as well. *Halo effect* appears on rating scales when ratings of specific traits are influenced by the raters' general impression of the person being evaluated. *Experience contamination* occurs when the criterion behavior varies with the uncontrolled factor of experience.

APTITUDE TESTING
EMPIRICAL RESEARCH METHODS
MEASUREMENT

D. R. KRATHWOHL

CRITICAL INCIDENT TECHNIQUE

The critical incident technique is a job analysis method first described by John Flanagan in 1954. The method involves the collection of hundreds of anecdotal descriptions of effective and ineffective job behaviors that job incumbents, supervisors, and others have actually observed in the work setting. These anecdotes, called "critical incidents," must be specific behaviors that exemplify success or failure in some aspect of the job being analyzed. For example, a critical ineffective incident for a truck driver would be: "The driver failed to look in his rear-view mirror when backing up the truck and consequently hit a parked car." The observer reporting the critical incident is typically asked to describe: (a) what led up to the incident and the context in which it occurred, (b) exactly what the individual did that was effective or ineffective, (c) the apparent consequences of this behavior, and (d) whether the consequences were under the individual's control.

After several hundred critical incidents are collected, they are content analyzed and sorted by one or more judges into categories or "dimensions" of critical job behavior. These dimensions then serve as the basis for the identification or construction of job-related tests and other selection devices. They can also be used as a basis for the development of training programs.

A major advantage of the critical incident technique as a job analysis method is that it focuses on observable and measurable job behaviors. Disadvantages of the method include the considerable amount of time and effort required to implement it, as well as its neglect of average job performance.

The critical incident technique has been employed for several purposes other than job analysis.

INDUSTRIAL PSYCHOLOGY
JOB ANALYSIS
JOB EVALUATION
TASK ANALYSIS

W. I. SAUSER, JR.

CROSS-CULTURAL COUNSELING

The systematic study of culture and counseling is a phenomenon of the twentieth century. Initially the fields of psychoanalysis and anthropology were the focus of interest in studying cultures and mental health. The focus has since shifted from the anthropological study of remote cultures to the cultural variations in modern pluralistic and complex societies.

By viewing counseling and therapy in their cross-cultural context, several points become apparent: (a) counseling and therapy have spread rapidly to a complex social industry on a worldwide basis; (b) counseling and therapy are two of the many alternatives for intervention to influence mental health; (c) counseling and therapy as the *preferred* alternatives are based on assumptions generic to a small portion of the world's people; and (d) cross-culturally appropriate applications in counseling and therapy are necessarily responsive to the social context.

Wohl describes seven different operational contexts for crosscultural therapy. First, representatives of one culture study the therapeutic modes of another culture. This most obvious example emphasizes an anthropological or research interest, including studies of culture-bound disorders, traditional healers, folk treatment procedures, and topics of psychological anthropology.

A second category includes problems related to culturally different "minorities" within the larger cultural context—a concept enlarged to include special populations of age, lifestyle, sex role, and socioeconomic status as well as ethnic and nationality groups. Culturally differentiated groups have special and unique needs. Overemphasizing those demographic variables results in cultural stereotyping, just as underemphasizing them results in cultural insensitivity.

A third category comprises therapists working with culturally different clients through culturally different approaches. Work with immigrants, foreign students or sojourners, or a foreign medical resident coming to practice in the United States would be examples of this category.

A fourth category includes therapists applying their "back home" methods of therapy in a culturally foreign society, whether through research or service delivery.

A fifth category includes the exploration of a system of therapy independent of the person or persons transporting it. The basic premise of cross-cultural therapy is that a particular system of ideas and theories can be adapted to many culturally different societies.

A sixth category is exemplified by a therapist from one culture and a client from a second culture working in the context of a third culture.

Wohl's seventh category occurs when members of one culture have lived for a long period of time in another culture, borrowing elements from both their home and host culture. As a consequence, a "third culture" is developed to suit the special needs of the "bicultural" persons.

Pluralistic therapy recognizes a client's culturally based beliefs, values, and behaviors, and is sensitive to the cultural environment and to the network of interacting influences. Culturally effective counselors recognize their own values and assumptions in contrast with alternative assumptions, and translate those values and assumptions into action. Furthermore, they are aware of generic characteristics of counseling and any other contextual variables that influence the counseling process; they understand the sociopolitical forces that influence the attitudes of culturally different minorities or otherwise oppressed groups; they can share a client's worldview without negating its legitimacy or imposing cultural oppression on the client's viewpoint; and they are truly eclectic in their own counseling style, generating a variety of skills from a wide range of theoretical orientations.

Public policy statements clearly acknowledge the importance of the mental health consumer's cultural environment. The National Institute of Mental Health, the American Psychological Association, the American Psychological Association Council of Representatives, the American Psychiatric Association's Task Force on Ethnocentricity among Psychiatrists, and the President's Commission on Mental Health have all emphasized the ethical responsibility of counselors and therapists to know their clients' cultural values, and the public responsibility of professional organizations to meet the culturally different mental health needs in a pluralistic society.

Evidence came to light in the 1970s that mental health services were being underused by minority groups, and that behavior described as pathological in a minority culture—individualistic assertiveness, for instance—may be viewed as adaptive in a client from a majority culture.

Not all research supports the preference for matching clients and counselors from the same culture. The preference for counseling style seems more important than racial match among Black and White clients, Asian Americans, and lower class as compared with middle class people. Blacks use a counseling style with more active expression skills and fewer attending skills than White counselors. It appears that variables such as more active intervention styles for positive change through counseling are more important than racial similarity in building rapport. It is unwise to assume that membership in one particular ethnic or cultural group, class, or culture relegates a client to a particular racial type of therapist, even when the matching is done as a "culturally sensitive" intervention.

Cross-cultural practitioners have failed to develop grounded theory based on empirical data for several reasons. First, the emphasis has been on abnormal rather than normal behavior across cultures. Second, only in the 1970s did a pancultural core emerge for the more serious categories of disturbance such as schizophrenia and affective psychoses, so that they are recognizable according to uniform symptoms across cultures, even though tremendous cultural variations continue to exist. Third, the complexity of research on therapy across cultural lines is difficult to manage beyond prequantificated stages. Fourth, the research has lacked an applied emphasis related to practical concerns of program development, service delivery, and techniques of treatment. Fifth, there has been insufficient interdisciplinary collaboration from psychology, psychiatry, and anthropology, each approaching culture and mental health from different perspectives. Sixth, the emphasis of research has been on the symptom as a basic variable, to the neglect of the interaction of person, professional, institution, and community. Cultural differences introduce barriers to understanding in those very areas of interaction most crucial to the outcome of therapy, through discrepancies between counselor and client, experiences, beliefs, values, expectations, and goals.

The future requires advances in four areas: (a) conceptual and theoretical approaches beyond the diffuse and incomplete theoretical alternatives now available; (b) a sharpening of research efforts to identify those primary variables that explain what has happened, interpret what is happening, and perhaps predict what is going to happen in the migration of persons and ideas across cultures; (c) criteria of expertise for the education and training of professionals to work interculturally, adequately prepared to deal with the problems of a pluralistic society; and (d) revolutionary modes of providing services based on new theory, research, and training, so that mental health care is equitably and appropriately provided to members of a pluralistic society.

ACCULTURATION
CULTURAL DIFFERENCES
ETHNIC GROUPS

P. B. PEDERSEN

CROSS-CULTURAL PSYCHOLOGICAL ASSESSMENT

Psychological assessment relies on systematic reference to specific behavioral and physical variables. Behavioral variables may be divided into competencies and expectancies. Thus climbing coconut trees for food or driving an automobile might be indispensable activity in one culture and irrelevant in another. Physical findings tend to have greater cross-cultural reliability. The significance of physical findings such as the number of pounds an individual can lift is based on specific analyses of necessary competencies and expectancies for specific cultures.

According to David Wechsler, "Intelligence, operationally defined, is the aggregate or global capacity of the individual to act purposely, to think rationally, and to deal effectively with his environment." In deciding the cross-cultural applicability of measures of intelligence, analyses of the relevance of items or tasks are necessary. Suppose one asks, "What is the value of a free press in a society?" In one culture, this question might evoke various thoughtful concepts of the values of obtaining uncensored information. In another culture, the concept *free press* has no meaning. Verbal questions have limited cross-cultural utility. Still, assessment of vocabulary levels and degrees of verbal fluency might lead to meaningful information concerning language performance and thus intelligence. In intelligence testing, timed performance tasks such as arranging blocks to form an abstract design are considered culture-free measures of intelligence. However, examiners of Australian aboriginal children have discovered that, when presented with timed performance tasks, such children might be more interested in putting the examiner's stopwatch in their mouths than in constructing abstract designs. Lack of familiarity with the type of task and the objects used for its performance may pose a stumbling block for cross-cultural evaluation of intelligence. Culturally relevant task-oriented behaviors should be developed for within-cultural evaluation of intelligence. The degree of shared relevance of these tasks across cultures sets a limit on their cross-cultural utility.

The findings that various ethnic groups consistently differed in education achievement test scores have led to adjustments such as cutting scores for decision making. Thus a cut-off score for one individual might be based on membership in a particular ethnic–racial group. Advocates of altering cut-off scores argue that this renders decision making more culturally and ethnically unbiased. Opponents argue that differential setting of cutting scores is a political rather than an educational matter and that by such maneuvers educational instruments will lose their predictive validities.

Evaluation of emotional status and functioning in a cross-cultural context has been developed by the International Classification of Diseases–9, and its refinement in the International Classification of Diseases. There has been some success in defining and describing operationally pathological emotional states cross culturally.

Clinicians have often observed differential presenting patterns of symptoms among various cultural groups. To understand the significance of an Indian widow's intent to throw herself on the funeral pyre of her dead husband requires that the examiner understand not only the religious, but also the social and economic, context of such behavior. Such suicidal intent might be regarded in one society as being totally irrational; yet in another society it might be a reasonable act.

Psychological assessment of social functioning can be accomplished by interviewing subjects and others socially related to these subjects, by using objectively scored tests of personality as well as projective tests of personality, and by observing subjects in either natural or contrived situations.

Objectively scored tests of personality have enjoyed translation into other languages for purposes of assessment of social and emotional functioning. Translation difficulties occur even with objectively scored psychological tests. Forced-choice formats pose other difficulties. Adequacy of norms is still another problem. To assess cross-cultural validity of objectively scored tests of personality properly at least five important dimensions need to be addressed: (a) semantic, (b) technical, (c) content, (d) criterion, and (e) conceptual equivalence. Even the well-substantiated and cross-culturally validated statement that an individual tends to be suspicious of others must be understood in the cultural and microcultural environment in which an individual operates.

Some projective tests appear to have the promise of cross-cultural application. However, correlation of projective assessment results to measures of overt social behaviors have long been inconclusive.

Direct behavior observations in natural or contrived situations offer superior cross-cultural specificity and sensitivity. Yet these require time-consuming evaluator efforts and present difficulties in reliably assessing the meanings of a subject's performance.

The convergence hypothesis suggests that as societies tend to industrialize, they are inevitably pulled toward similarity.

CROSS-CULTURAL PSYCHOLOGY
CULTURAL DETERMINISM
CULTURAL DIFFERENCES
ETHNOCENTRISM
PERCEPTUAL DISTORTIONS

J. W. KOFF

CROSS-CULTURAL PSYCHOLOGY

The study of human behavior must include observations made all around the world, not just in the few highly industrialized nations where most research has historically been done. The concept of culture summarizes many of the major influences on human behavior and the bases for concepts of self- and group identity that people hold. Further, aspects of culture have major effects on the formulation, dissemination, and acceptance of programs designed to deliver psychological services or to use psychological principles. Cross-cultural research is also central to theory development and programs aimed at applying the lessons learned from research.

DEFINITIONS OF CULTURE

As with many complex concepts long studied by psychologists such as personality, intelligence, and abnormal behavior, no one definition of "culture" is widely accepted. Kroeber and Kluckhohn concluded by suggesting that many definitions contained "patterns, explicit and implicit, of or for behavior transmitted by symbols, constituting the distinctive achievements of human groups . . . [and] ideas and their attached values." Herskovits proposed the equally influential generalization that culture is "the man-made part of the human environment." Triandis made a distinction between physical and subjective culture. The former would include man-made objects such as houses and tools, while the latter comprises people's responses to those objects in the form of values, roles, and attitudes.

It is important to delimit the concept of culture, lest it be so all-encompassing as to explain little or nothing in particular.

Because much cross-cultural research has the goal of understanding concepts as seen by people in the culture under study, the influence of cognitive psychology has been strong. Much research has focused on people's knowledge about their world, their communication with one another given this shared knowledge, and the transmittal of this knowledge to the next generation. Given this emphasis, a third definition of culture suggested by Geertz captures the flavor of much cross-cultural research: "Culture denotes an historically transmitted pattern of meanings embodied in symbols, a system of inherited conceptions expressed in symbolic forms by means of which men communicate, perpetuate, and develop their knowledge about and attitudes toward life."

In research programs, many psychologists use aspects of all three definitions. In studies of ethnocentrism, for instance, the fact that ideas have "attached value"—suggested by Kroeber and Kluckhohn—should be added to the concept of "symbolic forms" that Geertz formulated. The fact that people's symbols are valued leads to ethnocentric thinking, especially concerning subjective elements such as ideology, religion, morality, or law. Ethnocentrism refers to the deeply held belief that one's own culture is the best (defined by that culture's own standards), and that others are inferior in many ways.

DEFINITION OF CROSS-CULTURAL PSYCHOLOGY
Cross-cultural psychology is the study of culture's effects on human behavior. More formally, cross-cultural psychology is the empirical study of members of various culture groups with identifiable experiences that lead to predictable and significant similarities and differences in behavior.

A term related to culture that has received a great deal of attention by psychologists is *subculture*. This term is frequently used when referring to groups of people who have had experiences (which can and do affect behavior) different from those of most people in a given country or society. People from the subculture live in the same country or society as another larger group, the latter group often being called the *majority culture*. Subculture is a flexible term and has been used to refer to deviant groups such as the drug subculture or the motorcycle gang subculture. Whenever a group of people develop their own norms, jargon, and means of communication, their actions become similar to that of various subcultures. Negative consequences, such as distrust of outsiders, also usually develop.

A person can belong to several subcultures as well as to a majority culture.

Some people might be considered members of a given culture, but explicitly reject certain values and prescribed behaviors of that culture. An example would be young, well-educated people who reject the work ethic and the accumulation of individual wealth, and instead prefer collective ownership of property. Several important points can be made in such cases, which are found in virtually all large and complex cultures. First, even though the people may reject the culture's values and behaviors, they are familiar with what they are rejecting, because the values and desirable behaviors were communicated to them and they had observed others who *did* accept the cultural norms.

A second point worth noting is that the entire span of individuals must be considered. People may rebel against convention in their youth, but as they become older acceptance of their culture's norms and values often proves functional. The responsibilities of parenthood often seem to conventionalize the most fiery radicals. Casino discusses the functional nature of people's identity in cross-cultural situations. People have a number of possible identities because of ethnic background (which often allows claims of *multiple* ethnic group memberships), religious affiliations, extensive travel to other cultures, education, job experiences, and so forth. People can then draw from this "smorgasbord" to meet the demands of various situations. If scholarships for advanced study become available to members of a certain ethnic group, then people may rediscover their link to that group through some long-forgotten relative. If entry into the workplace is desired, then the intercession of a friend (who has long accepted the work ethic) may be tapped.

WIDESPREAD USE OF "CULTURE" AS A THEORETICALLY IMPORTANT VARIABLE
Any definition is helpful insofar as it assists researchers in gathering better data. The concept of "culture" may run the danger of being so broad as to limit its usefulness. Reviewing research in developmental psychology, Harkness pointed to the "invisibility of the culture in psychological theory," arguing that the historical neglect of the concept led to an overemphasis on nativist theories of child development. Because so many aspects of culture are not assessed in the typical study *within* any one country, results are too often attributed to genetic factors or to the presence or absence of some supposed universal process. Similarly, Touhey pointed to the importance of culture in analyzing failures to replicate studies in social psychology: "A rapidly expanding body of research in cross-cultural psychology has alerted investigators to the possibility that many basic findings on personality and micro social processes will not generalize across cultures."

THE USES AND BENEFITS OF CROSS-CULTURAL RESEARCH
Although benefiting from the contributions of anthropologists in conceptualizing "culture," psychologists themselves have analyzed the uses and benefits that cross-cultural research can add to theory development.

Increasing Range of Variables
The most frequently cited use of cross-cultural research is to increase the range of independent variables, or a wider range of conceivable responses to dependent variables, in other cultures or in comparisons across cultures. The clearest example is undoubtedly the age at which babies are weaned. If researchers are interested in the relationship between the age of weaning and other parental decisions about child-rearing behavior, or between age of weaning and personality when the children reach adulthood, there is a restricted range within any one culture. In the United States and most countries in Western Europe, for instance, the age of weaning is 6 months to 1 year. However, because the accepted age is different in other cultures, ranging up to 5 years, researchers can relate the age-of-weaning variable to others if they compare samples across cultures. Information concerning many everyday behaviors of people around the world have been conveniently collected in the Human Relations Area Files (HRAF), a well-organized compilation of information concerning hundreds of cultures. The data contained there has been gathered largely by anthropologists, therefore topics of interest to them (e.g., kinship, land tenure, ritual) are emphasized. The data also center on directly observable behaviors such as age of weaning, parental disciplinary practices, and number of caretakers for children. More abstract questions of interest to psychologists, which could be gathered only by extensive questioning (e.g., people's connotations of intelligence, desirable person-

ality traits in children to help them meet future uncertainties) are only occasionally found in HRAF.

In one of the first large-scale research programs to investigate native versus learned theories, Segall and his colleagues attempted to relate features of the environment in which people are raised to independently assessed perceptual mechanisms. However, they could not do this research effectively in any one country because in any particular country the range of environmental features is relatively narrow. Instead, they studied a number of cultures with widely ranging features, especially the presence or absence of buildings built with tools, the number of 90° angles in the arrangement of the building materials, and the number of open vistas extending to the horizon. Data were gathered from 17 different samples in the United States, Africa, and the Philippines on people's reactions to a number of visual illusions that constituted the research project's test of perceptual tendencies. Because wide differences in susceptibility to visual illusions across cultures were found to be systematically related to environmental features, the existence of learned perceptual mechanisms was demonstrated. An important methodological feature of this study is worthy of note, being of potential usefulness in large numbers of cross-cultural studies. Segall and his colleagues found that people from cultures with many buildings constructed with 90° angles (called "carpentered environments"') were more susceptible to the Müller–Lyer illusion, while people from cultures with many open vistas were more susceptible to the horizontal–vertical illusion. For instance, United States subjects were more susceptible to the former, but less susceptible to the latter, than subjects in rural African villages. The interaction between sample and stimuli rules out many plausible alternative explanations, such as lack of familiarity with the task among one or more of the samples.

Unconfounding Variables

An intriguing possibility is that variables that occur together in one culture and hence are confounded in any statistical analysis can be studied separately in other cultures or if comparisons across cultures are made. The classic example is Branislaw Malinowski's analysis of the behaviors Sigmund Freud called the Oedipal complex. In cross-cultural analyses of the Oedipal complex, it appeared that Freud's observations were based on a limited set of conditions found in Vienna in the late 1800s.

In the Trobriand Islands, Malinowski observed that the father was not necessarily the object of a boy's hostility. Rather, ill feelings were directed toward his mother's brother, who is the family disciplinarian in that culture. A boy's tense relations with his uncle, then, could be predicted from knowledge that it is the source of discipline that is disliked. Malinowski suggested that the boy may indeed dislike his father, but because of the father's role as disciplinarian rather than as his mother's lover. Cross-cultural observations, then, unconfounded a situation found in Euro-American nations.

In many studies the "cross-cultural" or "culture" variables are simply labels for a package of confounded concepts. In analyzing intercultural marriages, Fontaine and Dorch worked with different categories of married couples so as to break down the overly general label of "cross-cultural." They gathered data from couples whose marriage was interethnic, involving different skin color; intercountry in origin, but not involving a skin color difference; and interreligious. They also gathered data from intracultural marriages so as to differentiate the issues faced by all married couples from those arising from the intercultural aspect. The researchers found that there were different dynamics in the marriages of interethnic couples, compared to intercountry couples. Interethnic couples reported more problems as, in their perceptions, being due to external factors in their communities, while the intercountry couples traced more problems to factors internal to the marriage partners or to the marriage itself. The authors interpreted these results as showing that differences in country of origin do not produce the same level of negative community response

as do differences in skin color. Thus interethnic couples indeed have external factors to which they must react, and that, understandably, are used as the explanation for many marriage problems. The intercountry differences are less visible to the community but are no less real to the partners, so intercountry couples attribute more problems to internal factors than do interethnic couples. The important procedural point is that Fontaine and Dorch could not have made the distinction in locus of attribution (i.e., internal v. external), if they had worked only with the broad category of "cross-cultural marriages." Instead, they unconfounded this packaged variable into the important component parts of interethnicity and intercountry of origin.

Study of Context in Which Behavior Occurs

The environment has been notoriously difficult to operationalize. The study of social context has been an active research focus for cross-cultural psychologists. In other cultures, because visiting investigators have not had as much experience with various everyday social contexts, they can more easily separate themselves from social situations and formulate hypotheses about the relative contributions of individual and contextual factors.

At times, psychologists interested in the applications of research knowledge can take advantage of knowledge about social context. Jordan and Tharp developed programs to teach Hawaiian and part-Hawaiian children to read. They had little success after importing methods. They did research, however, on children's everyday behavior in their homes and in their communities and found that the children spent large amounts of time sitting around telling stories to one another and listening to adults tell such stories. The researchers then used knowledge of this practice in the classroom. Reading skills improved dramatically.

So-called standardized tests are usually normed on children from the middle-class in the United States. The question arises: Are these tests fair for children from quite different cultures? This difficult question has been examined by some of the foremost scholars in test theory. The answer depends on the social context in which test scores are to be used. If used to make inferences about children's underlying competencies, about how they think, or their native ability compared to some other group, the tests would be used unfairly and would be inappropriate. However, if the purpose of testing is to assess the classroom progress of children from one cultural group in schools that are more familiar to children from another group, then the tests can be used fairly.

Maximization of Differences in Respondents' Attributes

If research hypotheses are supported in studies with different populations, the findings can be taken more seriously than hypotheses supported only by studies of homogeneous populations in one country. In cross-cultural studies, variances of respondents' attributes not directly related to the hypotheses are maximized, and these variances are often extremely difficult to obtain in any one research site. However, if research findings are supported in spite of the variance added from other cultures, then the hypotheses must be robust.

Social psychological research carried out in the United States has indicated that there is a strong relationship between perceived similarity among two or more people and the amount of positive attraction they have toward one another. Brewer was interested in determining the reasons for social distance among intact groups that have real differences, divergent goals, and (sometimes) a history of conflict. She tested the robustness of the similarity-attraction hypothesis by gathering data on intergroup perceptions from 30 tribal groups in East Africa.

The robustness of the similarity-attraction hypothesis could be tested in the presence of a great deal of additional variance brought on by a different research site (Africa), differences in economic-educational advancement, and differences in physical distance between tribes. The results showed that perceived similarity was the most powerful predictor of attraction as measured by the social distance scale.

CULTURE-UNIVERSAL AND CULTURE-SPECIFIC FRAMEWORKS: EMICS AND ETICS

Emics and *etics* refer to the two goals of cross-cultural research. One is to document valid principles in all cultures and to establish theoretical frameworks useful in comparing human behavior in various cultures. This is the "etic" goal. The other goal of cross-cultural research is to document valid principles of behavior in any one culture, with attention to what the people themselves value as important as well as what is familiar to them. Such an analysis has to reject the importation and imposition of frameworks from outside a culture because, by definition, a researcher cannot gain insight into emics by using foreign tools; the tools must be indigenous. This latter type is an "emic" analysis.

Cross-cultural researchers have attempted to deal with both etics and emics in their research. A system proposed by Brislin, drawing on earlier work by Przeworski and Teune, represents such an attempt. The researcher starts by examining concepts that may have cross-cultural validity, but keeps in mind that not all aspects of those concepts may be the same in all cultures under study. Aspects may be different both for cultures across nations as well as for various cultures or subcultures in a country.

EMICS AND ETICS IN PRACTICE: RESEARCH ON AUTHORITARIAN CONSERVATISM

Miller, Slomczynski, and Schoenberg were interested in studying the meaning of "authoritarian conservatism" in Poland and the United States. They attempted to find a core set of measurement items meaningful to respondents in both countries. These items would then measure the culture-common or shared meaning across respondents from the United States and Poland. In addition, the researchers sought to find items that measured culture specific aspects of the authoritarian-conservatism concept. One set of items were written so as to be successful in measuring additional aspects in Poland, and a different set of items were written so as to be successful in measuring additional aspects in the United States. The emic-etic approach, then, incorporates the strong possibility that concepts have different meanings across cultures. Rather than a throwing up of hands along with complaints about the difficulty of measurement across cultures, this approach takes as a starting point the need to look for both culture-general and culture-specific aspects of various concepts.

The emic items demand long labels. These are the aspects of a general concept somewhat unfamiliar to people from one country who are trying to understand another. Because Miller and her colleagues wanted to communicate their results to audiences in both Poland and the United States, the emics had to be interpreted. The core items are relatively easy to describe, because by definition they are aspects of the general concept in both countries. However, because one country's emic is less familiar to people from the other country, convoluted labels are sometimes necessary. Use of the emic–etic framework also has practical purposes, for instance, in preparing people who are about to live in a country other than their own. The etic aspects of a concept can be used to introduce material about life in another culture, because these aspects represent the shared meaning. The emic aspects can subsequently be introduced and receive special attention, because another country's emics may be unfamiliar and sometimes bizarre.

CROSS-CULTURAL RESEARCH EXAMPLES: LEARNING AND COGNITION

In much early cross-cultural research on learning and cognition, investigators have compared responses of various cultural groups in various parts of the world to responses from Euro-American groups. Inevitably, the researchers were struck by how slowly learning seemed to progress in the other cultures; how inefficient the people were in organizing material to be learned; how unsophisticated the explanations for their responses seemed to be; or how quiet and unresponsive people seemed to be in what—to the experimenters—was an interesting opportunity to learn new material and/or demonstrate learning prowess. Reacting against these interpretations, several more sophisticated cross-cultural researchers took a careful look at the results of such studies and recommended more caution and sensitivity in interpreting results. One of the major thrusts of this more recent research is the demonstration that learning is strongly affected by the social context in which people live and work.

For example, Labov analyzed the puzzling problem that young Black children in the United States are often termed "noncommunicative" and "nonfluent" by their White teachers in school. However, when these same children are among their peers outside of school, communication and fluency are striking; indeed, verbal repartee is a desirable, status-giving characteristic. In a similar analysis, a group led by Cole analyzed the difficulties encountered in schools by the Kpelle of Liberia, contrasting this with their skills at tasks outside of school. The verdict of "inadequacy in school" was often made by teachers, yet the skills that Cole tested outside of school (such as the estimation of volume) sometimes surpassed those of comparison groups in the United States.

Close examination of these and other learning situations prompted Cole to summarize a great deal of work in a short statement: "Culture differences in cognition reside more in the situation to which particular cognitive processes are applied than in the existence of a process in one cultural group and its absence in another." This summarizing principle has many implications. It means that people in all cultures have skills, but situational characteristics are important in allowing the skills to be easily used.

Another implication is that competence cannot necessarily be judged from performance. If a person cannot perform a task or do well on a test, this does *not* mean there is a deficiency in ability. This implication contrasts with the normal inference that if a person does not perform well, then there is no competence or ability. The preferred interpretation, supported vigorously by Cole, is that the task itself or the situational nature of the testing situation may well be causing the poor performance. These situational elements include uncommon materials involved in the task, unfamiliar time pressures to complete the task, the presence of a nervousness-producing, high-status "outsider" doing the testing, and so forth.

CROSS-CULTURAL RESEARCH METHODS: COMMUNICATING WITH SUBJECTS

Cross-cultural research methods have become a specialized study area and have been the focus of entire texts. A basic aspect of good methodology is communicating with subjects. Without clear understanding of instructions directed from the researcher to the participants, and without clear understanding of what responses mean, a research study may not only be misleading but may also possibly be damaging.

Various techniques have been devised to ensure good communication between researchers and participants. Irvine and Carroll suggest a number of steps in testing, such as separation of individual subtests to avoid confusion; oral instructions with visual aids; translation of instructions carried out by typical members of the respondent group; supervised practice on sample items; beginning any test session with items already familiar to respondents; and creation of an enjoyable atmosphere for testing. If the subject matter under study is a complex concept, such as the stage reached according to Piagetian theories of mental development, training studies can be introduced.

A little creativity may ensure researcher-participant communication. DeLacey made sure that Australian aboriginal children understood such terms as "red," "circle," and "round" by showing them wooden replicas and inviting them to handle the different shapes painted different colors. They were also asked to indicate examples of the terms before the actual experiment on classification ability began. In another study, Price-Williams tested the acquisition of various Piagetian concepts among the Tiv of Central Africa. In his experiment on the conservation of discontinuous qualities, the normal Piagetian method is to use beads in containers. Price-Williams tried his method but found communication difficulties were prevalent, so he changed the materials to nuts, far more familiar in the Tiv culture. Results showed a degree of conservation similar to acculturated European groups of children. In many cross-cultural studies of theoretical ideas where Euro-American children might be compared with children from other cultures, there is a factor that can be called "explicit attention to communication with subjects." When this factor is clearly present in a study, there is a greater probability of similar Euro-American and other-culture results. The standards for communication with subjects have become so high that when researchers report lower levels on a given measure among members of one culture as compared to another, sophisticated readers want assurances that the results are *not* due to the researcher's inability to encourage maximum performance.

Any definition of psychology must take into account observations made in various parts of the world, not just those few countries in which most psychological research has historically been done. Cross-cultural studies, then, are central to the development of psychology. Cross-cultural contributions should increase in the future, as more psychologists in various countries free themselves from the shackles of imposed theories from Euro-American sources. Psychologists in various countries can develop their own theories to explain research findings that differ from predictions based on Euro-American theories. Cross-cultural data can edit findings found in only a few countries, pointing to the specific limitations of theories. Further, cross-cultural data can provide a stimulus to new thinking, which in turn leads to new and more powerful theories.

ACCULTURATION
ATTRIBUTION THEORY
COMMUNICATION PROCESSES
CULTURAL DIFFERENCES
ETHNIC GROUPS
ETHNIC MINORITIES
ETHNOCENTRISM
FIELD DEPENDENCY
PIAGET'S THEORY
RESEARCH METHODOLOGIES
SCIENTIFIC METHOD
TASK ANALYSIS
TERRITORIALITY
WORK AND PLAY

R. W. BRISLIN

CROSS-CULTURAL TRAINING PROGRAMS

Cross-cultural training programs refer to formal efforts designed to prepare people to live and work in cultures other than their own. Ideally, such programs are structured, staffed by professionals with relevant training and experience, and take place in a setting designed to create an atmosphere conducive to learning. The nature of cross-cultural training is made clearer when its opposite is considered. Before going overseas on a business assignment, proper training can prepare people for the stresses of adjusting to another culture, differing ways of carrying out business negotiations in other cultures, and advice on accomplishing one's goals. The opposite is to simply send people abroad with no preparation and to let them succeed or fail on their own.

Most of the research concerning cross-cultural training has taken place since World War II. Reasons include the greater movement of students who take advantage of educational opportunities in countries other than their own, increases in technical assistance programs and of jet travel, the development of global marketplaces, increases in programs aimed at person-to-person contact across cultural boundaries (e.g., the Peace Corps, youth exchange programs), and increases in the number of independent countries, necessitating greater amounts of diplomatic contact. Cross-cultural training programs also are designed to help people work effectively with culturally different individuals within their own country. For example, programs have been designed for White social workers who are about to work with refugees from Southeast Asia and for Japanese-American teachers in Hawaii who have large numbers of students of Hawaiian ancestry. People skillful in designing and implementing cross-cultural training programs can be found in colleges and universities, the personnel departments of large businesses, government service, public school systems, churches, social welfare agencies, counseling centers, and in private consulting firms.

GOALS

Training programs are commonly designed with four goals in mind. For convenience, programs to prepare people for overseas assignments are discussed, although similar arguments can be made about programs to increase effective intercultural contact *within* any one large country. First, training programs (a) should prepare people to enjoy and to benefit from their overseas assignment, not simply to tolerate an unpleasant interruption in their lives. Because few can enjoy their assignments without cordial and effective interactions with others, programs should give guidance on developing relations with host country nationals, both in the workplace and during leisure time. One way of measuring progress is that people on overseas assignments should be able to list people with whom they work well, with whom they interact during their leisure time, and whom they can call on in times of need. Second, the host country point of view needs to be given attention. Good training increases the probability that *they* have positive attitudes about the sojourners in their country. By examining the first two goals, trainers can avoid the mistake of making conclusions based on people's *reports* of positive relations with hosts. In some cases, people can make a list of friends, but those "friends" might report that the people are insensitive, ethnocentric, and condescending.

Another goal is to provide guidance on how participants in training programs can accomplish their goals. Virtually all sojourners have concrete goals in addition to enjoying and personally benefiting from their assignments. Overseas students want to obtain university degrees within a reasonable amount of time; overseas businesspeople want to enter into trade agreements; diplomats want to develop treaties acceptable to all sides in a conflict; technical assistance advisers want to construct sanitation facilities, irrigation systems, or medical centers; cross-cultural researchers want to establish collegial relations so that information can be gathered and shared. Training can give people guidance on such topics as working through bureaucracies, negotiating with counterparts, keeping legal requirements in mind, identifying the resources needed for project completion, and so forth. Many times, training must be culturally specific, depending on the types of participants in programs. Foreign students working in the United States need to be prepared for the independence in scholarly inquiry that professors expect. American businesspeople working in Asia need to be more sensitive to the effects of their actions on the collective identity of their hosts. Diplomats need to be aware of the long history of animosities that various ethnic groups within a country may bring to the bargaining table.

The final goal is to assist program participants to deal with the stress that overseas assignments can bring. The most commonly used term associated with such stress is *culture shock,* or the set of strong emotions that result from having the familiar structures of one's own culture taken away. *People do not interact with each other in familiar ways! How they make decisions is a mystery! They are never clear when they try to communicate! They seem to talk about me all the time!* Cross-cultural trainers have adopted such stress-reduction methods as relaxation, cognitive restructuring, development and maintenance of valued leisure time activities, exercise, and the avoidance of health-threatening behaviors (e.g., increased alcohol use). Trainers frequently introduce the concept that program participants should not feel singled out for negative self-judgments. The feeling that "I am the only one who is having difficulties adjusting to the other culture" is common. If participants learn that most sojourners experience adjustment difficulties and feel the temptation to engage in negative self-thoughts, then the resulting stress is decreased.

APPROACHES

The various approaches to cross-cultural training can be examined by imagining a 3×3 matrix. The three columns have labels that refer to people's cognitions, emotions, and actual behavior. The three rows have labels that refer to low, moderate, and high amounts of trainee activity and involvement in the actual program. Such a matrix was examined by Brislin and Bhawuk, with the latter adding a dimension that referred to the amount of trainer involvement. For the present discussion, the differences between low and high trainee involvement on people's cognitions, emotions, and behavior are examined to highlight some key distinctions among choices of the content to be covered in programs.

In low trainee involvement aimed at cognitions, participants are placed in the role of audience members for various lectures, films, or carefully prepared demonstrations or they are given assigned readings. The content of such presentations and readings can include host customs, climate, day-to-day living arrangements, cultural differences that affect behavior in the workplace, advice on visas, and so forth. There are a number of risks in this approach to training. Trainees can become bored because of a lack of activity on their part and the many facts presented can be overwhelming and may fail to find a place in people's long-term memories. However, given the time constraints that most program developers face, there will always be a place for impactful and carefully prepared presentations about key facts that will affect people's adjustment to another culture. Furthermore, many of the more active training methods demand that people have a knowledge base that they can use in their group discussions, role-plays, simulations, and analyses of critical incidents. This knowledge base is often most efficiently presented in lectures, films, and assigned readings.

In high trainee involvement aimed at cognitions, program participants are challenged to think hard about their upcoming overseas assignments and to analyze their probable experiences using sophisticated concepts from research in the behavioral and social sciences. Some concepts have already been mentioned: stress and stress reduction, cognitive restructuring away from viewing oneself as the only one having problems, distinguishing self-reports about success from the reports of hosts, and so forth. Some of the most difficult concepts relate to behaviors that are perfectly appropriate and acceptable in one culture but that are boorish or even illegal in another. For example, teasing and mild sexual innuendo are acceptable behaviors for male–female workplace interactions in many countries. The same behaviors are considered examples of sexual harassment in other countries. One prediction for the future is that virtually all good cross-cultural trainers must cover male–female interactions in the workplace *and* keep current in research on gender issues in various countries.

In low involvement aimed at people's emotions, trainers move from coverage of just the facts about another culture and try to engage participants' affective reactions to their upcoming experiences. One method is for participants to hear presentations from either hosts or from "old hands" who have made successful adjustments. The advantage of employing such people is that they can answer questions from the point of view of people who have actually lived in the other culture. The disadvantage of this approach is that the hosts and old hands may tell a collection of interesting stories that add up to no clear set of conclusions. Program coordinators can avoid this problem through careful preparation and by guiding the guest presenters in what they will discuss. There are a number of topics hosts and old hands can cover that are almost sure to engage people's emotions. For example, the emotions of Americans are almost always aroused when they hear presentations about arranged marriages, suggested reasons for trade disputes with Asian nations, the quality of schools in Europe and Asia compared with the United States, differing views of what constitutes bribes, and the need to modify familiar behaviors to demonstrate cultural sensitivity as judged by hosts rather than by fellow sojourners.

In high trainee involvement aimed at emotions, participants may engage in role-playing exercises that force them to confront cultural differences. Often, members of the training staff role-play culturally different others, and program participants must achieve a goal (a visa extension or approval of a plan) by working with the staff. Role-plays can be emotional for participants because they must deal with ambiguity, unfamiliarity, and frustrations in their attempts to achieve their goals. Given the strong possibilities of intense emotional reactions, role-playing is not recommended as a training approach unless program developers have had a great deal of firsthand experience in its application. One approach has been developed that addresses people's emotions but decreases the chances of reactions being so intense that they bring the training program to a halt. This approach has trainees role-play a set of critical incidents that provide the outline of the script that trainees follow. Critical incidents are written to communicate a point about intercultural interaction, and they are written with characters, a plot line, and an end to the plot based on a misunderstanding between people from different cultures. For example, several of the 100 incidents describe people who confront behaviors that do not agree with their previous stereotype of how members of the other culture behave. This is a common experience that causes emotional reactions as people learn that their well-formed stereotypes simply do not give any guidance to effective behaviors. Trainees can read the incident, decide how it is to be role-played, and then perform it. Given that almost all the material in the incident will be familiar before its presentation, trainees will be less likely to have emotional reactions to the surprises that totally unscripted role-plays can cause. It is these surprises that lead to the risks associated with the use of role-playing as a training approach.

In low involvement aimed at behavior, trainees are introduced to the fact that behaviors different from the ones to which they are accustomed will lead to adjustment and goal achievement. This can be done through the use of modeling, in which members of the training staff demonstrate appropriate behaviors in important areas such as meeting others for the first time, ways of moving from small talk to discussions about important matters, ways of disagreeing without causing offense, and so forth. One way to approach the topic of behavior change is to list a set of social situations with which trainees are familiar in their own culture. Then, given their knowledge of other cultures, trainers can discuss or demonstrate behaviors that are appropriate for similar situations in the culture in which trainees will be living. For example, overseas students accustomed to taking lecture notes in a highly deferential manner will be exposed to behaviors that show how students in the United States can argue with their professors and put forward their own original thinking. Businesspeople accustomed to discussing the business at hand within 5 minutes of an initial meeting will be exposed to the importance of small talk and the importance of behaviors that build up trust between sojourners and hosts if the business dealings are in Asia or Latin America.

Technical assistance advisers accustomed to hiring employees on the basis of merit will learn, when working in some countries, that there will be pressures to consider the relatives of influential officials.

In high involvement aimed at behavior, trainees are put into social settings in which they have to change familiar behaviors to meet their goals. The difference between this approach and role-playing involves the extent and number of new behaviors that trainees are called on to perform. In this high involvement approach, the culture in which trainees are to live is simulated with as much fidelity as possible. When the training is "in country," this is relatively easy. Peace Corps training in Nepal, for example, calls for trainees to live with hosts for a significant period of time and later to attend sessions where their behaviors can be discussed and evaluated. In one of the most intense training programs that has been documented, participants about to live on remote Pacific islands lived in a simulated village set up in Hawaii. There they learned to behave in ways that contributed to adjustment and job effectiveness. They learned to gather their own food because there were few or no grocery stores. They learned to entertain themselves, because there were no televisions or movie houses. They learned to perform their jobs in the absence of technological aides to which they had become accustomed. They learned to deal with a lack of privacy. There were many drop-outs. One defense of this type of program, however, is that it is better to drop out during training in the presence of a supportive and sensitive staff. These supportive individuals will not be present if people decide to leave and return home after beginning their overseas assignments.

BENEFITS

Evaluation studies have demonstrated that well-designed training programs provide benefits to people's thinking, attitudes, and actual behaviors. People who have undergone training use fewer negative stereotypes, develop complex views about other cultures, and become more world minded in their thinking. They enjoy interacting with hosts and develop methods to cope with the inevitable stresses that even the most successful sojourn will bring. They have better interpersonal relations in multicultural work groups, interact effectively with others as reported by the hosts themselves, and can modify familiar behaviors to meet better the demands of the other culture. Given increases in the same factors that lead to the need for effective intercultural communication, such as immigration, global business, and the demands of various ethnic groups to be heard in the political arena, the future will undoubtedly see even more attention to cross-cultural training programs.

BEHAVIOR MODIFICATION
CROSS-CULTURAL PSYCHOLOGY
CULTURAL DIFFERENCES
INDUSTRIAL CONSULTANTS
ROLE-PLAYING

R. W. BRISLIN

CROSS-SECTIONAL RESEARCH

One can distinguish between studies in which subjects of different ages (born at different times) are compared—cross-sectional studies—and studies based on other methods of sampling. Most commonly, cross-sectional data-gathering—often referred to as *cross-sectional design*—is contrasted with what is called a *longitudinal design*, in which the across-age comparisons are for subjects who are regarded as born at the same time.

In development psychology, differences between subjects born in different years are often referred to as *cohort differences*. If there were a difference in the means for weight for the samples of 47-year-old men

in the longitudinal and cross-sectional studies of our example, this would often be a cohort difference.

In cross-sectional study (but not the longitudinal study), the age differences are also cohort differences: age and cohort differences are confounded. Age differences in longitudinal studies are confounded with time differences in history. This confounding does not obtain for the age differences in the cross-sectional study.

Cross-sectional and longitudinal studies thus differ in the kind of confound necesarily associated with age differences. However, the two kinds of studies differ notably in other ways as well. If the variables obtained for different age groupings are thought to be measures of the same attributes, calibrated in the same units, a longitudinal study can be said to involve repeated measures. Such data-gathering permits one to study the test–retest stability (within each person) of measures, an opportunity lacking in cross-sectional designs. However, if the aim of a study is to estimate effects associated with aging, these effects can be confounded in a repeated measures study with effects that result from measuring the same thing on more than one occasion. In developmental research this is an important difference: cross-sectional studies lack a firm basis on which to rest inferences concerning within-person development. This basis exists for longitudinal prediction analyses with either different measures or repeated measures.

Longitudinal follow-up can be added to a cross-sectional sampling. Also, one can draw entirely new samples of subjects in longitudinal follow-ups. When these two variations in subject-sampling are considered along with the possibilities mentioned earlier, a number of different sampling designs are generated. These too are useful in studies of development.

EMPIRICAL RESEARCH METHODS
EXPERIMENTAL CONTROLS
MEASUREMENT

J. L. HORN

CROWDING

Crowding is a syndrome of stress associated with high-density settings. It is a subjective, psychological state, usually negative in tone, based on appraisal of the impact of density.

Density and crowding are different, and their relationship has been the subject of much debate. Jonathan Freedman has argued that crowding and density are equivalent and there is no need to propose an intervening, subjective state. This is similar to the views guiding most animal and sociological/epidemiological research on the topic. However, data obtained in human field and laboratory studies are inconsistent with this notion, and Daniel Stokols has established the necessity of viewing density and crowding as different phenomena. Density is a physical variable, a ratio of group size (the number of people present) to spatial extent (the amount of space available). As either or both of these terms changes, density changes, and as density increases, the likelihood that people will feel crowded also increases. Crowding, then, is an experimental state based on appraisal of density and other factors that may make the effects of density more or less negative. Density is a necessary but insufficient condition for the experience of crowding.

However, people do not always feel crowded when density increases. High density at a sporting event, concert, or political rally is necessary to generate desired levels of excitement. In such cases, although density is fairly high, most people do not feel crowded. However, the same density can become aversive and be experienced as crowding under other circumstances, such as trying to get to one's car and leave the parking lot after the event is over.

Crowding, then, is a psychological variable that reflects the ways in which people expect or believe density will affect them. Research has indicated that several different kinds of other variables can affect this judgment. Men appear to be more negatively affected by small spaces than are women. In several studies, men in small groups who must interact in a small room became aggressive and negative about the experience. Women, placed in exactly the same situation, did not feel crowded, become aggressive, or feel negative. Something inherent in the socialization of men and women seems to predispose men to experience more stress than women under spatially limited conditions. Interestingly, men and women do not differ in their response to high density characterized by large numbers of people in less limited space

Cultural heritage can also influence judgments of crowding: What is crowded in one culture may not be experienced as crowding in another. The nature of the situation is also important. If high density facilitates the goals of a situation, it is unlikely that crowding will be experienced. If density is high enough to disrupt or interfere with these purposes, crowding is more likely. Thus high density at a party is less likely to be experienced as crowding than is high density in a grocery store.

Research with animals has suggested that high density can have serious consequences. For example, J. B. Calhoun observed reproductive failure, social withdrawal, and other forms of organic and social pathology in high-density rodent colonies. It is tempting to speculate that these effects generalize to human populations, but research indicates that they are milder for people. Because of the complexity of the processes by which people experience their environment, and the greater adaptive capabilities that people posses, these effects are somewhat different in human populations.

Crowding has consistently been linked to negative emotional tone. People feel worse when crowded than when not. This appears to be true whether crowding actually is experienced or is only expected; people who anticipate crowding also report more negative affect. Furthermore, research indicates that crowding results in physiological arousal: Several measures of sympathetic arousal, including heart rate, blood pressure, and skin conductance, have shown increases.

Some evidence of density-related health effects has also been reported. Most of this evidence reflects changes in the way people feel. Thus crowding is associated with more health complaints, visits to a clinic or dispensary, and so on. Additional research indicates higher blood pressures in crowded settings. One study reported a rather large correlation between density and death rate in a prison.

Crowding also affects a number of social behaviors. People tend to like people less when they are crowded than when they are not. In addition, people sometimes avoid other people when they are crowded. Baum and Valins reported a series of studies in college dormitories indicating that withdrawal was a primary response to crowding. Other studies have shown that people are less likely to initiate interactions with other people when crowded.

Research shows that people do offer help to others less often when crowded than when not. In addition, crowding has been associated with aggression. However, the measures of aggression used may be better explained as measures of emotional tone and interpersonal attraction. These measures include play in a bargaining game and judgments in a jury simulation. Few studies have demonstrated overt aggression as a result of crowding.

Crowding also appears to affect task performance. Complex task performance is more affected, with crowding causing poorer performance. This may be related to the arousal also associated with crowding, because arousal often causes decrements in complex task performance. Motivational problems may also influence performance. Several studies have found that prolonged crowding (e.g., in one's home) is associated with learned helplessness or helplessness-like decreases in apparent motivation. As a result, people may not try as hard to solve a problem or complete a task when experiencing crowding.

There are a number of ways to explain how these effects are caused. The first is the *overload* model, which borrows from computer systems concepts to describe how overstimulation can cause crowding. When the number of people in a setting becomes so large that people become overloaded with social inputs, they feel crowded. This model focuses on the frequency of social interaction and on withdrawal as a primary coping response. Another model concerned with *control* is a modification of the overload concept. It argues that social interaction during crowding is not only frequent but also often unwanted and unpredictable as well. When people can no longer regulate social experience and determine when, where, and with whom they interact, crowding is experienced.

Another model is based on *behavioral constraint,* or the degree to which one is free to behave as one wishes. Crowding occurs when density is sufficiently high that people get in one another's way and limit what each can do. Other models focus on resource availability and potential for involvement in the setting.

BYSTANDER INVOLVEMENT
ENVIRONMENTAL PSYCHOLOGY

A. S. BAUM

CRUCIAL EXPERIMENTS IN PSYCHOLOGY

The crucial experiment (*experimentum crucis*) has long played an important role in formal conceptions of progress and change in science. It is, in concept, the final arbiter between two competing theories.

Francis Bacon first formally described and named the crucial experiment concept, although it had been used long before. Bacon's original *instantia crucis* (instance of the fingerpost) was to be used when each of two rival explanations accounted equally well for all available empirical data, so that there was no basis for choosing one over the other. If conflicting predictions leading to mutually exclusive outcomes were derived from the two explanations, then a crucial experiment should be conducted such that the results would confirm one explanation and disconfirm the other.

THE DUHEM-QUINE THESIS

Pierre Duhem argued that crucial experiments simply are not feasible as classically conceptualized. Unambiguous falsification of a hypothesis is not possible. Any hypothesis may at some time be refuted, or a yet more satisfactory theory may be developed in the future. Later Quine stated that any one statement in a theory can be held true, regardless of evidence, if appropriate changes are made elsewhere in the theory.

Thomas Kuhn offered a view of crucial experiments similar to that of Duhem. According to Kuhn, most scientific work consists of "puzzle solving"—working out details within a particular paradigm. Experiments are not crucial because only one basic theory is being explored. Real change in science occurs during revolutions that involve a shift from one paradigm to another. Because, according to Kuhn, a paradigm determines how observations are to be made—in a sense, how the world is to be viewed—a theory cannot be refuted by experience. A theory is discarded when scientists come to see that it has so many problems that it is no longer useful, or less useful than another theory. Kuhn suggests that crucial experiments are more a part of science pedagogy—textbook science—than of science itself. Kuhn has further suggested that experiments frequently described as crucial in determining theory choice were performed long after the choice between theories had actually been made.

However, not all philosophers of science reject the value of crucial experiments. Most notably, Karl R. Popper has argued that, although theories can never be verified, "it must be possible for an empirical scientific system to be refuted by experience." Popper's falsificationist position runs counter to both Duhem and Kuhn.

The most direct attack on the Duhem-Quine thesis has come from Adolf Grünbaum, who argued that, first, crucial falsifying experiments are logically possible, and second, there have in fact been such experiments.

There is, then, no unitary or definitive philosophical position on crucial experiments. The variety of views can be seen in Harding, whose introductory chapter this article has followed in part. It is clear, however, that the absolutist confirmation–refutation view of Bacon has been discarded, along with linear views of scientific progress.

CHARACTERISTICS OF CRUCIAL EXPERIMENTS

True crucial experiments have one obvious characteristic: They must adequately test between two competing hypotheses. To do this, they clearly must be so well-designed that internal validity is assured.

A second characteristic of crucial experiments is that the designs are unusually creative. To test adequately between two competing theories, the experimenter must find a way to test conflicting hypotheses.

EXAMPLES OF CRUCIAL EXPERIMENTS

Some individual experiments or series of experiments appear to justify being called crucial. They have either clearly supported or refuted important aspects of theories. The studies conducted by Fred Sheffield and his students made the drive-reduction theory of reinforcement, if not actually untenable, at least unreasonable, and indicated that something akin to drive induction would need to be incorporated in accounts of reward. Two classic findings were that male rats learn a response that leads to mounting a female, but not ejaculation, and that nonnutritive saccharin is an effective reward. Harry F. Harlow's reports that infant monkeys formed strong attachments to nonnutritive cloth surrogate mothers, but virtually no attachments to wire surrogates that provided food, was virtually decisive evidence against traditional secondary-drive and psychoanalytic accounts of attachment.

Much of Edward C. Tolman's career was devoted to attempted crucial experiments confirming the role of expectancies, as opposed to stimulus–response (S–R) association, as the basic unit of learning. For example, research conducted by Tolman and his students on latent learning and spatial learning kept S–R theorists on the defensive for many years. Close analysis of the classic latent-learning experiment suggested that, although it provided considerable difficulties for S–R theories, it was not, in strong terms, a crucial experiment. Indeed, as would be expected by Duhem, Quine, and Kuhn, these experiments did not lead to an overthrow of S–R theories. However, modifications in, for example, Clark Hull's theory that enabled an S–R theory to account for some of the results made the theory more cognitive in character. Other findings presented persisting difficulties for S–R models.

Crucial experiments, at least in design, have played an important and continuing role in the development of several areas in psychology. One such area is the perception of space and objects in space, centering around the nativist-empiricist issues. Although such experiments seem conclusive, more recent research leads to questions about the original interpretation of the results. Further, other research on both nonhumans and humans suggests that aspects of depth perception are innate. Although none of the experiments resolved the initial issue, they have helped to clarify the area in crucial ways, and have largely transformed the original issues.

INFLUENCE OF EXPERIMENTS ON THEORETICAL CHANGES

Research has had considerable impact on theories in psychology. The examples given in the preceding section make clear that individual experiments have led to important modifications of some theories and virtual

abandonment of others. In that sense, certain experiments have been crucial.

EXPERIMENTAL METHODS
HYPOTHESIS TESTING
PHILOSOPHY OF SCIENCE
RESEARCH METHODOLOGY

R. T. Brown
C. R. Reynolds

CULTURAL BIAS IN TESTS

Various social class and racial groups show considerable mean differences in scores on a variety of standarized tests of mental ability widely used in schools, college admissions, the armed forces, and personnel selection in hiring. This is especially true of tests of "general ability," "intelligence" or IQ, and scholastic aptitude. One popular explanation for the observed social class and racial differences on such tests is the *cultural bias hypothesis,* which holds that (a) the typical experiences involving the acquisition of knowledge and skills are different for various subpopulations, and (b) the item contents of the tests are selected much more from the typical experiential background of certain groups (e.g., the White middle class) than from that of other groups (e.g., the poor and racial minorities), thereby favoring certain groups with higher average scores and disfavoring other groups with lower average scores on the test. Psychometrically, the problem is how to determine objectively whether the cultural bias hypothesis is a valid explanation of the observed mean difference between any two specific subpopulations on any specific test.

Before listing some of the valid methods for testing the cultural bias hypothesis, the three most common but wholly fallacious criteria of test bias should be discussed at the outset. The *egalitarian fallacy* is the scientifically unwarranted assumption that all subpopulations are equal in whatever ability or trait the test purports to measure, and that therefore any mean differences between groups indicates that the test is biased. The *culture-loaded fallacy* is the belief that because the item content of a test involves culturally specific knowledge or skills, it is necessarily biased against any particular group that scores lower than some other groups. The *standardization fallacy* is the notion that because a test was standardized for a particular population, it is necessarily biased against members of any other population.

The psychometric definition of bias is based on the statistical concept of bias: A measurement is biased if it systematically underestimates or overestimates the true value. A test is biased if an obtained score systematically underestimates or overestimates the true value of the trait it purports to measure in one group as compared with some other groups. More generally, a test is biased with respect to two (or more) groups if the scores for members of one group have a different meaning than they have for members of the other group. Objective statistical tests of bias, therefore, consist of a search for important psychometric features of a particular test that behave differently in the two or more subpopulations in question. The psychometric features of primary importance are those most relevant to the intended use of the test; predictive validity for a particular criterion, construct validity, reliability, and factor structure. Statistically significant differences large enough to be of consequence for the practical uses of the test scores, are indications of bias. These indicators may be classified as *external* (i.e., they rely on the correlation of the test scores with other variables that are independent of the test) and internal (i.e., they rely on internal psychometric characteristics of the test itself). Bias may also result from *situational* factors: the race, sex, dialect, attitude of the examiner, unequal exposure to previous similar tests, time pressure and anxiety in the test situation, and the like.

The preponderance of present evidence indicates that most current standardized tests of mental ability yield unbiased measures for all native-born English-speaking segments of American society today, regardless of sex or racial and social-class background. The observed mean differences in test scores among various groups are generally not an artifact of the tests themselves, but are attributable to factors that are causally independent of the tests.

CULTURE FAIR TESTS
PSYCHOMETRICS
RACE BIAS IN TESTING
RACIAL DIFFERENCES

A. R. JENSEN

CULTURAL DETERMINISM

Cultural determinism refers to the belief that culture controls an individual's destiny. Ruth Benedict in *Patterns of culture* asserted that children become a part of their culture with its perceived possibilities and impossibilities directing the course of their lives. This deterministic view of human development makes clear that, although individuals think they make a personal choice about a house, an article of clothing, or even food, actually their choice is determined by the culture: All that person does, eats, and feels is culturally determined. This powerful influence of culture has attained a maximum effect by the time a child is 5 years of age, so that the child sees no other way of behaving except that which is taught by the culture.

Frustrations and negative feelings often occur in children as they face cultural rules and expectations. Their resentment and hostility all too often accompany the process. In recent years resentment is seen in the conflict with and condemnation of the "establishment." Children strive for autonomy and expression of impulses, but such striving brings conflict with the cultural agents. The most important of these agents, of course, are the parents, especially the mother. Most children growing up in a family where cohesion and stability exist come to accept cultural rules as advocated by the parents. This acceptance is furthered by affectional bonds between parents and child. Through interdependence for emotional satisfaction, children conform to the teachings and wishes of the parents. In the acculturation process, children internalize cultural mandates so that the culturally valued ways of behaving become a part of personality.

The significance of the culture in determining behavior is seen in the concept of "social clocks": Not only is culturally determined behavior a reality in our lives, but also the expected and approved behavior must become a part of the individual by certain times. Bernice Neugarten and Gunhild O. Hagestad present this concept. Thus the age span is divided into periods of time through which we progress according to a timetable created by the culture in which we live; the life course must be run at certain speeds based on a predetermined schedule. In the time periods of childhood, adulthood, and old age, rewards and opportunities are given or withheld by the culture, depending on age and whether one's movement is in synchrony with the social clocks provided by the culture.

Cultural determinism, accordingly, means that in reality we have little choice about our life course, as Theron Alexander emphasized in "The life course issues." Cultural determinism leaves little opportunity for individual freedom or experimentation with other than culturally approved solutions to problems. Nor are individual differences based on genetic variation allowed free expression.

Conflict with cultural rules is particularly common in adolescents. The culture insists on conformity and age expectations, but adolescents are told sometimes they are not yet old enough for certain privileges, and at other times that they are too old. Misunderstandings result.

A considerable number of workers see the course of development as determined by biological factors as well as those existing in the culture. Jean Piaget, for example, in *The origins of intelligence*, took the position that stages of development are based on maturational factors. Seeing physical influences as factors of importance in determining behavior, therefore, in addition to culture, appeals to many.

ACCULTURATION

T. ALEXANDER

CULTURAL DIFFERENCES

Cultural, ways of believing and acting, vary over the world. Because of cultures' considerable influence, social scientists have been interested in their effect on human personality and behavior. Cultures differ not only in ways of making a living, but also in the possessions of people and in their ways of thinking.

Anthropologists and social psychologists have pointed out the benefits from studying simple societies in order to compare them with complex cultures such as that of the United States. By observing behavioral differences, they can gain ideas about which behavior varies with culture and which behavior is relatively innate and occurs in all cultures. Sometimes the results are astonishing and have considerable effect on social scientists' thinking about human behavior and development.

The classic example of such a change in view is one that resulted from Margaret Mead's work with Samoan culture reported in *From the south seas*. Early in the 1900s, G. Stanley Hall—especially in evidence in his two-volume work *Adolescence*—explained that adolescence is a stage created by physiological processes undergoing change based on programs in the genes. According to him, because the "storm and stress" result from changing physiological processes, the behavior was universal and found in all cultures. To investigate this idea, Mead went to Samoa to live among the people there. She found that in Samoa, parents' child-rearing techniques were quite different from that of the American culture. The parents of Samoan children strived to avoid conflict and did not restrict their children's play or coerce them into performing tasks. Because of this benign way of dealing with their children, conflict and emotional upset between parents and children seldom occurred. The children played in groups and only older children exercised any authority.

When the children reached adolescence they encountered the same conditions of child rearing as when younger: No rules or limits set by parents caused them upset, and no punishment brought hostility and resentment. The storm and stress so much a part of adolescence in advanced cultures did not occur. Still, the same physiological changes were a part of each child's life. Hall had attributed the emotional upsets so common in adolescents' behavior to body changes, but although the Samoans underwent the same changes, they did not have these emotional upsets.

As the result of Mead's work, generalizations were made and further questions were asked. How much of behavior is culturally determined and how much is based only on physical makeup? This question continues in controversy.

CROSS-CULTURAL PSYCHOLOGY
GROUP COHESIVENESS
ROLE EXPECTATIONS
SOCIAL PSYCHOLOGY

T. ALEXANDER

CULTURE AND PSYCHOTHERAPY

Culture can be viewed as both a source and a product of human behavior.

Each individual has a unique, specific biological endowment and is reared in a particular physical and cultural environment, sharing with others attitudes, ways of acting and communicating, modes of dress and types of food, a form of government, certain skills, a language, and religious practices. Many large, complex communities contain a variety of cultures.

Currently there is general agreement that major psychoses may appear in all cultures. The character of a psychosis, however, can be highly dependent on cultural patterning.

Different societies treat mental and physical illnesses differently. Illness may be cured or alleviated by sorcerers, shamans, medicine men, or *curanderos* (healers). Witchcraft or the evil eye has been thought, and is still believed in many areas of the world to cause various mental ills in the past. In some Native American groups certain forms of behavior, considered pathological in other societies, are acceptable.

Redlich, Hollingshead, and Bellis discussed the therapeutic treatment of individuals from five different socioeconomic groups. These investigators found that individuals from the lowest socioeconomic levels were least prone to seek treatment and least likely to change their attitudes toward therapy. Furthermore, people from these groups were more likely to be hospitalized than those from the two uppermost socioeconomic groups studied and were also likely to receive only medication and no psychotherapy at all. Carolyn B. Block, in "Black Americans and the cross-cultural counseling and psychotherapy experience," noted that Blacks are more often admitted to psychiatric hospitals and receive earlier discharge than Whites.

Freud was interested in cultures only in an intellectual way.

Roheim was the first psychoanalyst to do actual fieldwork and live in several preliterate societies. In *The origin and function of culture*, Roheim described how he saw firsthand that a variety of traumas never considered by Freud—especially those dealing with puberty rites—could bring about a variety of conflicts and complexes in a given society. He worked intensively with aborigines in Australia. Many anthropologists, psychologists, and psychoanalysts have since taken a similar psychodynamic view of individuals in various non-European cultures. However, others also have considered Freudian-based psychodynamic theory less generally applicable.

Cultural factors must be taken into account in the communication, verbal and nonverbal, between patient and therapist. In 1961, Jerome Frank, in *Persuasion and healing: A comparative study of psychotherapy*, showed that in spite of the goal of attaining emotional release, therapy requires intellectual communication and comprehension. However, this depends on common understanding of matters that may differ radically from culture to culture.

The kinds of questions to be asked, how they should be phrased, and what topics should be avoided in initial interviews are crucial matters in cross-cultural therapy. When doing fieldwork, the cultural anthropologist learns to structure interviews so that the questions asked are clearly understood. Carstairs, in "Cross-cultural psychiatric interviewing," pointed out that the language barrier can be a greater difficulty than anticipated in interviewing a patient from another culture. Carstairs found that, in India, patients would often pretend to understand more English than they actually did. This could lead to distortions interfering with the therapist's accurate evaluation of the patient's situation.

Hall coined the term *proxemics* for the study of the way human beings unconsciously structure space. He has described his work in "System of notation of proxemic behavior." In the United States two adults usually stand about 2 feet apart when talking to each other. To a Latin American or an Arab, to sit or stand so far as 2 feet apart seems rude. When the American therapist and patient sit several feet apart, this may be seen by the patient as aloofness and coldness on the part of the therapist.

Therapists are trained to understand their own feelings and those of the patient, and to deal with them appropriately. Sometimes, however, different customs of therapist and patient can cause a variety of unexpected feelings on the part of the therapist as well as the patient. A therapist must understand and appreciate different feelings and different problems related to the patient's own cultural patterns.

It has often been suggested that therapist and patient should come from the same culture (or from the same version of a culture) and be of the same sex. For example, a Japanese-American male therapist should work best with a Japanese-American male patient. However, many patients may want to work with a therapist from a different culture or a different version of their own culture. Patients may feel that a therapist from another or somewhat different culture will not condemn them as much as would a member of their own specific group. Successful therapy may depend more on the expertise of the therapist in understanding cultural differences and their associated values, attitudes, and behaviors than on the particular cultural group to which the therapist belongs.

CROSS-CULTURAL COUNSELING
CROSS-CULTURAL PSYCHOLOGY
CULTURE-BOUND DISORDERS

T. M. ABEL

CULTURE-BOUND DISORDERS

Culture-bound disorders refer to psychological disorders limited to members of distinct ethnocultural settings and traditions. Both the term and the concept are controversial and have been the topic of considerable debate, because they raise fundamental questions about the universality of psychological disorders. For some researchers, culture-bound disorders are simply variants of disorders found among Western people. For others, however, they represent disorders specific to non-Western people that cannot be classified among Western disorders.

A major part of the debate surrounds the question of cultural influences on psychopathology. Most psychiatric researchers have considered cultural variables unimportant. Thus if culture-bound disorders exist, culture must be assigned an important role. This poses problems for biological conceptions of mental disorders.

A number of terms have been used to describe culture-bound disorders: (a) exotic psychoses, (b) atypical psychoses, (c) esoteric disorders, (d) hysterical psychoses, (e) ethnic psychoses, (f) culture-bound reactive syndromes, and (g) culture-specific disorders. All these terms reflect the confusion regarding the nature of these disorders. Should they be considered psychotic or neurotic disorders? Do they have biogenic or psychogenic origins? Are they simply variants of mental disorders found in Western cultures, or are they culturally unique patterns of disorder? The answers are complex. For culture-bound disorders, case observations have been limited in number and quality. Often the research material is strong on opinion and weak on fact. Because many investigators have not even had access to cases, there has been a frequent reliance on secondary information from poorly trained informants.

TYPES OF CULTURE-BOUND DISORDERS

More than 30 culture-bound disorders have been reported in the clinical and research literature. However, among these disorders only a handful have received substantive attention, of which this article limits the discussion to *latah*, *amok*, *susto*, and *koro*.

Latah

Latah is found primarily among populations residing in Malaysia and Indonesia. It is present in both males and females, but is more frequent among the latter. Its two major components are a startle reaction and subsequent imitative behavior including echolalia (repeating what someone says), echopraxia (repeating what someone does), automatic obedience coprolalia (involuntary utterance of obscene words), altered consciousness, and fear. These can occur repeatedly. In most instances, the disorder is precipitated by a sudden stress.

H. B. M. Murphy, an anthropologist and transcultural psychiatrist, proposed a number of theories about the origins of *latah* and its relationship to cultural factors. He posits that certain Malaysian and Indonesian child-rearing practices predispose individuals toward hypersuggestibility, which then becomes linked to sexual functioning.

Researchers have speculated that *latah* is similar to hysterical disorders found in Southeast Asia, Siberia, and various parts of Japan. Pow Meng Yap, a transcultural psychiatrist who wrote extensively on culturebound disorders, noted that *latah* is similar to the following disorders: *miryachit, amurakh, olonism, imu, imubacco, young-dah-hte, bahtschi, yuan, malimali,* jumping, and Arctic hysteria. Of all culture-bound syndromes, *latah* has been the most popular subject among researchers.

Amok

According to Murphy, the term *amok* first appeared in the European literature in 1552 among accounts of Portuguese travelers to Southeast Asia who were describing religious zealots who had taken vows to sacrifice their lives in battle against the enemy. Over time, the term came to refer to individuals who emerge from periods of withdrawal and apathy with a sudden outburst of mania, agitation, and violent physical attacks on nearby people. Frequently, the attack ends when the *amok* individual is shot or killed by others in self-defense.

A number of theories of *amok* were advanced, variously attributing it to febrile diseases (e.g., malaria), nonfebrile diseases (e.g., syphilis), opium addiction, chronic disorders (e.g., brain damage), and sociopsychological distress. No theory has achieved lasting acceptance, and some researchers have come to conclude that *amok* does not represent a distinct disease syndrome, but rather an explosive dissociative state that can occur from a number of causes.

Pfeiffer noted that *amok* can be caused by a variety of factors including chronic illness, infections, sleep deprivation, sexual arousal, environmental stress, or heat. He claims it proceeds through three phases. In the first phase, the individual is withdrawn, passive, and neurasthenic. In the second phase, he (virtually all victims are male) experiences depersonalization, derealization, paranoia, rage, and somatic symptoms. In the third or *amok* phase, there is sudden violent behavior, amnesia, screaming, rage, and assault with a weapon (e.g., a machete). If the *amok*-runner is not killed, this phase is followed by exhaustion and a return to normal consciousness. Kiev observed that *amok* is similar to disorders encountered in other parts of the world, including malignant anxiety in Africa, *cathard* in Polynesia, *psuedonite* in the Sahara desert, and *negi-negi* in the New Guinea highlands.

Susto

Susto—also known as *espanto*—is found among Hispanic populations in Central and South America and also among Hispanic migrants in North America. It has been discussed by Rubel and by Gobeil. Although *susto* occurs across both sexes and all age groups, it is most common among children and young women. The term *susto* is applied to a wide array of phenomena.

In general, *susto* refers to "soul loss." It begins with a strong sense of fear and is followed by weight loss, appetite loss, skin pallor, fatigue, lethargy, untidiness, and excessive thirst.

Several theories of *susto* have been proposed. Kiev suggested *susto* is an anxiety disorder caused by unacceptable impulses that produce a reliance on projection, isolation, and displacement. In addition, he claims it provides a "sick" role that affords much secondary gain in the way of

attention and affection. He states: "Susto is . . . a culturally meaningful anxiety hysteria syndrome that affords the sick the opportunity of being recognized." Gobeil contends its occurrence in children may be due to insecurities and fears related to parental abandonment, especially under conditions of frequent mobility and migration.

Koro

Koro (sometimes known as *shook yong*) is found among Chinese populations in Southeast Asia and Hong Kong. In men, it is characterized by an intense fear that one's penis is withdrawing into the body. In women, it can be experienced as a fear breasts are shrinking or labia are withdrawing into the body. However, it is primarily a male disorder. It has been described by Yap and by Rin, who attribute it to beliefs about the balance of yin (female) and yang (male) forces related to sexual excesses. The intense fear takes the form of panic attacks or even a fear of death. In addition, there is sometimes shame over one's action, especially if there is frequent resort to prostitutes or masturbation.

CLASSIFICATION OF CULTURE-BOUND DISORDERS

Although some researchers believe culture-bound disorders represent dysfunctions specific to the ethnocultural settings and traditions in which they occur, others believe they are variants of disorders found in the Western world. The latter group have suggested several classification systems for the culture-bound disorders.

Kiev offered the following classification system for the culturebound disorders: (a) anxiety states: *koro, susto;* (b) phobic states: *mal ojo,* voodoo death; (c) depressive disorders: *hiwa-itchk, windigo* psychosis, malignant anxiety; (d) hysterical disorders: *latah;* (e) obsessional-compulsive neuroses: *shinkeishitsu,* frigophobia; (f) dissociative states: *amok, pibloktoq, hsieh ping,* spirit possession. For Kiev, the culture-bound disorders can be included among the subcategories of Western neurotic disorders.

Yap considered many culture-bound disorders to be variants of reactive psychoses. He suggested they constitute four basic patterns of psychopathology: (a) primary fear reactions : *susto,* magical death, *latah, malimali, imu, miryachit, young-dah-hte,* and magical fright; (b) hypereridic rage reactions: *amok; negi-negi;* (c) culturally imposed nosophobias: *koro;* and (d) trance dissociation states: *windigo* psychosis, *hsieh ping.* These patterns then can be placed among the three major categories of psychogenic or reactive psychoses suggested by K. Schneider (1959): emotional syndromes (*koro, susto*), paranoid syndromes, and disordered consciousness syndromes (*latah, amok, negi-negi, hsieh ping, windigo*).

The role of cultural factors in the etiology, onset, manifestation, course, and outcome of psychological disorders is well established (Marsella & White, 1982; Triandis & Draguns, 1981). Thus it should not be surprising that distinct cultural settings and traditions should be associated with specific disorders. A major problem for Western psychiatry has been its inability to accommodate its assumptions and knowledge to the finding that every culture fosters and maintains distinct disorders. There are disorders that are universal, but even they cannot escape cultural influences. Thus in this respect all psychological disorders are culture-bound. This is the case for schizophrenia and depression as much as it is for *koro, latah, amok,* and the other "culture-bound" disorders. Culturebound disorders call our attention to the ethnocentric biases of Western psychiatry and thereby provide us with the opportunity to clarify the puzzle of all psychological disorders.

CROSS-CULTURAL PSYCHOLOGY
CULTURAL DIFFERENCES
PERSONALITY DISORDERS

A. J. MARSELLA

CULTURE FAIR TESTS

The term *culture fair tests* refers to tests that are not biased toward a particular cultural group. Although it is technically impossible to develop a test that is completely free of cultural bias, there are many examples of tests that purport to be culture fair in nature. Cultural bias exists in a test when members from one culture are discriminated against in their ability to answer the questions solely on the basis of the culture in which they grew up. For example, if test items contain words or phrases that are common for middle class White Americans but are uncommon for lower class Black Americans, then the test is biased against the latter. According to W. James Popham in *Modern educational measurement,* test bias exists whenever members of a subgroup are unfairly penalized, or given an advantage, because of their membership in the subgroup. The bias may appear in (a) qualities of the test such as wording, (b) the way in which the test is administered, or (c) the manner in which the results are interpreted.

A test is considered culturally biased only if it measures something different in two or more subcultures, not because different cultural subgroups attain different scores on the tests. That is, a test is not necessarily culturally biased if minority children score lower as a group than majority children. Such a discrepancy may mean that minority children have not been taught information necessary to answer the item, and hence may be an indication of deficiencies in their instruction.

Although most test publishers make a conscious effort to reduce cultural bias in the items of a test, instructions, and interpretation of results, there have also been many attempts to develop "culture fair" tests specially designed to give equal score distributions for different subgroups. Most of these tests measure general nonverbal aptitude skills. One of the first systematic, large-scale attempts to construct a culture fair test was the Davis-Eells Test of General Intelligence. The Davis-Eells test assesses general reasoning ability by using cartoon pictures of persons in familiar situations, rather than relying on highly verbal or abstract content. The test was designed for ages 5 to 12. The examinees look at each picture and choose from three possible explanations of the situation read by the test examiner. However, research has shown that the test possesses questionable reliability and validity, and that it does not reduce the differences among subgroup performance on other intelligence tests.

A different approach to culture fair testing was developed by Lionel Penrose and J. C. Raven, who published the Raven Matrices Tests. These tests were devised to assess Charles E. Spearman's notion of a single general factor of intelligence common to all cognitive tests. There are three forms of the Raven Matrices Tests; the Standard Progressive Ma-

trices for ages 6 to adult, the Colored Progressive Matrices for ages 4 to 10, and the Advanced Progressive Matrices for "superior" adolescents and adults. The task of the examinee is to choose which of six alternatives fills the empty cell in a matrix to complete the matrix pattern (see Figure 1). The tests are administered individually or in groups and there is no time limit. The instructions are simple. The Colored Progressive Matrices are easier for young children than the Standard Matrices, and are particularly useful with children who are mentally retarded. All the tests are completed in 1 hour or less.

The Cattell Culture Fair Intelligence Tests are mostly nonpictorial and nonverbal and can be given individually or in groups, although the frequent and sometimes lengthy verbal instructions present difficulties for administration to large groups. Research with the Cattell tests shows that different cultural subgroups do not attain the same mean scores. These results, with other studies, indicate that subgroup differences are not attained primarily because of verbal content in the tests.

A different approach to culture fair testing is the *System of multicultural pluralistic assessment (SOMPA)* developed by Jane Mercer. Mercer's approach is to use a battery of instruments and to compare the scores attained not only against a national norm group, but also against scores of children from a similar background.

CULTURAL BIAS IN TESTS
INTELLIGENCE MEASURES
PSYCHOMETRICS
RACE BIAS IN TESTING

J. H. McMILLAN

CULTURE SHOCK

Kalvero Oberg is usually credited with inventing the term *culture shock* to describe the anxiety resulting from losing one's sense of when and how to do what in a new culture. A visitor to a foreign culture finds that familiar cues have been removed and strange or unfamiliar cues are substituted. The visitor is likely to respond with anything from a vague sense of discomfort to a profound disorientation, requiring a complete reorganization of thinking. Any new situation, such as a new job, new relationships, new lifestyle, or new neighborhood may involve some adjustment of role and change of identity resembling culture shock. Culture shock has come to mean the general condition in which any individual is forced to adjust to a new social system for which previously learned cultural values and behavior no longer apply.

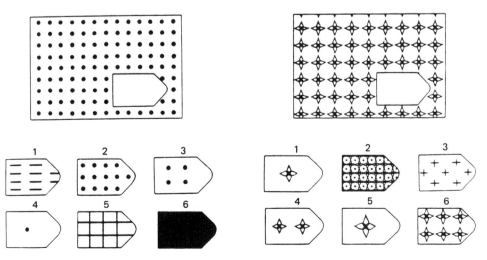

Figure 1. Examples of items from the Raven Matrices Tests.

The problems of culture shock can be identified by at least six characteristics. First, familiar cues about how the person is supposed to behave are missing or they now have different meanings. Second, values the person considered good, desirable, beautiful, and valuable may no longer be honored. Third, the disorientation of culture shock creates an emotional state of anxiety, depression, or even hostility, ranging from a mild uneasiness to the "white furies" of unreasonable and uncontrollable rage. Fourth, there is a dissatisfaction with the new ways and an idealization of the way things were. Fifth, recovery skills that used to work before do not seem to work any more. Sixth, there is a sense that this is a permanent condition that will never go away.

Experiencing the new culture often causes the individual to evaluate both the new and the old culture negatively. Until recently, culture shock has been assumed to be a consistently negative experience. Oberg mentioned at least six aspects of culture shock: (a) strain, resulting from the effort of psychological adaptation; (b) a sense of loss and deprivation, referring to former friends, status, profession, and possessions; (c) rejection by or of the new culture; (d) confusion, referring to role, role expectations, feelings, and self-identity; (e) surprise, anxiety, disgust, or indignation regarding the cultural differences between old and new ways; and (f) feelings of impotence as a result of the inability to cope in the new environment. Others have applied Oberg's term more widely to include "culture fatigue," "language shock," "role shock," and "pervasive ambiguity." Each definition has maintained the same meaning and applied it to different specific problem areas.

Peter Adler attempted to specify the process and sequence of stages in the culture shock experience. He used a five-stage sequence. (a) The initial contact, or the honeymoon stage, is when the newly arrived individual experiences the curiosity and excitement of a tourist, but the person's basic identity is rooted in the back-home setting. (b) The second stage is disintegration of old familiar cues and the individual is overwhelmed by the new culture's requirements. The individual typically experiences self-blame and a sense of personal inadequacy for difficulties encountered. (c) The third stage involves reintegration of new cues and an increased ability to function in the new culture. The emotions associated with this stage are typically anger and resentment toward the new culture as having caused difficulties and being less adequate than the old familiar ways. Because of this outward-directed anger, persons in this stage of culture shock are difficult to help. (d) The fourth stage continues the process of reintegration toward gradual autonomy and increased ability to see the bad and good elements in both the old and new culture. (e) The fifth stage is described as independence, in which the person has achieved "biculturality" and is able to function in both the old and new cultures.

This sequence of stages or steps has been referred to as a U-curve or, by including the re-entry back home, as a W-curve where the adjustment process is repeated in the back home setting. Church discusses 11 empirical studies in support of the U-curve hypothesis. These data support the general hypothesis but not full recovery to the original level of positive functioning. Five of the studies failed to confirm the U-curve hypothesis, indicating that there was no cross-sectional support for the basic thesis. In spite of the lack of empirical evidence, there is much heuristic support for the U-curve as a model of culture shock.

Furnham and Bochner discuss several problems in the U-curve hypothesis about culture shock. First, there are many dependent variables to consider as aspects of adjustment such as depression, loneliness, homesickness, and other attitudes. Second, the definition of a U shape is uneven in literature that tested the hypothesis with different persons who started out at different levels of adjustment, then changed at different rates. Furnham and Bochner suggest that research studying the process of culture shock should focus on interpersonal rather than intrapersonal variables.

Kealey found that in many cases staff of the Canadian International Development Agency who experienced intensive culture shock abroad were ultimately more productive than those who had experienced little or no culture shock. This is consistent with Adler's view that culture shock is a process of intercultural learning that leads to greater self-awareness and personal growth, which has become more favored than viewing culture shock as a disease. Ruben and Kealey found the intensity and directionality of culture shock unrelated to patterns of psychological adjustment. In some instances the degree of culture shock was positively related to ultimate professional effectiveness in the new environment.

Furnham reviewed the literature on sojourner adjustment, emphasizing the interpersonal rather than the intrapersonal aspect, in an attempt to classify the different kinds of culture shock. The first view of culture shock blames geographic movement, and a grieflike mourning reaction for lost relationships occurs. However, not all culture shock involves grieving, and there is no way to predict the severity of mourning.

The second view blames fatalism, pessimism, helplessness, and an external locus of control by the sojourner. However, this does not account for the different rates of distress and the assumption that most sojourners experience internal locus of control.

The third view suggests that culture shock is a process of natural selection or survival of the fittest by which only the best survive. However, because most research on culture shock is retrospective rather than predictive, this explanation oversimplifies the variables.

The fourth view blames culture shock on inappropriate expectations by the sojourner in the new setting. However, there is no proven relationship between unfulfilled expectations and poor adjustment.

The fifth view blames negative life events and daily routine interruption generally. However, it is difficult to measure life events and establish causality. Do distressed people cause negative events, or do negative events cause people to become distressed?

The sixth view blames a clash of values resulting in misunderstandings and conflict. However, some values are more adaptive than others and value conflict by itself is not a sufficient explanation.

The seventh explanation blames a social skills deficit, by which inadequate or unskilled individuals have a more difficult time adjusting. However, the role of personality and socialization is understated by this explanation, and there is an implicit ethnocentricism in the notion of adjustment.

The eighth view blames lack of social support, drawing on attachment theory, social network theory, and psychotherapy. However, it is difficult to quantify social support or develop the mechanism or process of social support to test this explanation.

Pedersen, expanding on work by Thomas Coffman, suggested several coping strategies for managing culture shock. First, the visitor needs to recognize that any important life transition is likely to result in stress and discomfort as a usual and normal consequence. The pain of culture shock may be seen as less of a deficit or disease by recognizing it as a normal response to change.

Second, the maintenance of personal integrity and self-esteem should become the primary goal of someone experiencing culture shock. Visitors often experience a loss of status in the new culture where language, customs, and procedures are unfamiliar. These visitors will need reassurance and support to maintain a healthy self-image and to restore their sense of self-efficacy.

Third, time must be allowed for the adjustment to take place without pressure or urgency. Persons adjust at their own rate, depending on the situation. Ultimate reconciliation of the new with the old may require a longer period of time than is convenient, but that time must nonetheless be taken.

Fourth, recognizing the patterns of adjustment will help the visitor develop new skills and insights. By charting the process of changes leading up to culture shock and predicting future stages in a logical sequence, the process may become more concrete and less ambiguous. Depression and a sense of failure should be recognized as one stage in the adjustment process and not as a permanent feature of the person's new identity.

Fifth, labeling the symptoms of culture shock will help the visitor interpret emotional responses to stress in adjustment. Knowing that others have experienced culture shock and have survived or even grown stronger from the experience can be comforting.

Sixth, being well adjusted at home does not ensure an easy adjustment in the foreign culture. In some cases, visitors may find themselves more homesick if they were much better off back home. It also is possible for people to carry their back-home problems into the new culture, resulting in maladjustment in both cultures while they seek to escape from old problems by going to new cultures.

Seventh, although culture shock cannot be prevented, it is possible to prepare persons for transition to new cultures and thereby ease the adjustment process. Preparation might include language study, learning about the host culture, simulating situations to be encountered and spending time with nationals from the home culture.

The current perspective of culture shock makes several generally accepted assumptions. First, culture shock is not a disease but a learning process, however uncomfortable or painful it might be. Culture shock may, however, be connected with pathological states or result in unhealthy reactions. Second, by metaphor, culture shock may relate beyond the situation of a visitor to another country. Persons experiencing any radical change in their life may experience a process of adaptation or accommodation resembling culture shock. Third, there is little if any measure of the culture shock process and/or proof for the U-curve or W-curve hypothesis, although the heuristic importance of culture shock as an explanatory model continues. Fourth, there are ways to prepare people for experiencing culture shock that will mediate the pain and discomfort resulting from that process. Finally, culture shock is a frequently experienced phenomenon that, to a greater or lesser extent, is familiar to most persons at one time or another.

BILINGUALISM
COPING
CULTURE BOUND DISORDER
GROUP PRESSURE
REACTANCE THEORY

P. B. PEDERSEN

CURRENT PSYCHOTHERAPIES

Several popular and largely different systems are outlined in this article, although for brevity's sake some important systems and techniques must be omitted.

PSYCHOANALYTIC PSYCHOTHERAPY

Classical psychoanalysis was originated by Sigmund Freud in the mid-1890s and has been modified—and often turned into analytically oriented psychotherapy—by many neo-Freudians.

According to psychoanalysis, emotional disturbances and behavioral dysfunctions mainly arise from: (a) antecedent—particularly early childhood experiences; (b) unconscious attitudes and experiences, often deeply repressed; (c) biologically based drives—especially erotic and aggressive drives—that create profound human conflicts; (d) fixations on early sexual stages of development such as oral, anal, genital, and latency stages; and (e) defensive maneuvers and avoidances that block people from changing.

To get at the main sources of the analysands' unconscious, repressed conflicts, and to undo their serious fixations, psychoanalysts use various therapeutic techniques: (a) free association; (b) dream analysis and interpretation; (c) the development of and working through of an intense transference relationship between the analyst and analysand; (d) a large number of sessions; (e) interpretation of the analysands' unconscious feelings and conflicts; and (f) revelation of the clients' defenses, and helping them to surrender the defenses.

ADLERIAN PSYCHOTHERAPY OR INDIVIDUAL PSYCHOLOGY

Individual psychology was originated by Alfred Adler. It has been followed fairly closely, but also significantly augmented, by many psychotherapists.

According to Adlerian theory, emotional disturbances are largely related to: (a) feelings of inferiority; (b) individuals' striving for their own greater glory rather than for social interest; (c) hesitancy to take risks and make full commitments to life; (d) refusal to give constructive meaning to one's existence; and (e) distorted perceptions and beliefs, leading to failure of learning.

Adlerian techniques of psychotherapy include: (a) clearly showing clients what their life goals are and how they can change their dysfunctional lifestyles; (b) confronting clients with their self-defeating ideas; (c) counter-propagandizing clients when their goals, purposes, and values are dysfunctional; (d) urging clients to take constructive actions that will change their self-sabotaging life goals; (e) constantly encouraging clients to assume responsibility for the directing their lives into more positive channels; (f) helping clients achieve the courage to be imperfect; and (g) showing clients how to develop their social interests.

ANALYTICAL (JUNGIAN) PSYCHOTHERAPY

Carl G. Jung broke with Freud around 1913. Jung viewed libido as general psychic energy instead of sexual energy and emphasized mythological and other symbols in the causation and treatment of emotional disturbance. Among Jung's followers, Gerhard Adler and E. L. Rossi have become fairly well known in their own right.

According to Jungian theory, emotional and behavioral disturbances largely stem from: (a) interference with the individual's strong instinct of individuation; (b) complexes springing from strong unconscious compulsions; (c) guiding symbolic messages from the unconscious that lead people astray; (d) inheritable predispositions that arise from the malfunctioning of the collective unconscious; and (e) the rise of sexual disturbances from general disturbances, rather than the latter from the former.

Jungian techniques of psychotherapy include: (a) showing clients that all suffering is a loss of meaning and that archetypes can provide healing powers; (b) helping clients symbolically understand the symptoms of their neuroses and, through this symbolism, showing them the way out of their underlying conflicts; (c) emphasizing the purposive, prospective functioning of the psyche; (d) revealing to clients the creative and healing powers of the unconscious; (e) making dream interpretations with emphasis on the symbolic meanings of the clients' dreams; (f) encouraging experiencing rather than mere intellectual understanding; and (g) gently but persistently encouraging clients to pay heed to and value their own inner world.

PERSON-CENTERED OR CLIENT-CENTERED THERAPY

Person-centered therapy (originally called client-centered therapy) was originated by Carl Rogers in the early 1940s. It has had several outstanding proponents, such as Victor Raimy (now a cognitive therapist) and Eugene Gendlin (now an experiential therapist). Although not practiced in any orthodox manner by many therapists today, it is incorporated in the theory and practice of innumerable theorists and therapists.

According to the Rogerian view, emotional disturbance largely arises from: (a) people's acquiring a negative self-concept because others, especially during their early years, do not sufficiently accept them and provide them with suitable conditions of growth; (b) a discrepancy between the self as perceived by people and their actual experience; (c) people's refusing to directly and freely admit to awareness aspects of themselves that are not consistent with their self-concepts; (d) people's tendency to overgeneralize, to be dominated by concept or belief, and to rely on abstractions rather than on reality testing; and (e) self-devaluation or feelings of worthlessness.

Rogerian or person-centered techniques of psychotherapy include: (a) engaging in a deep, intense caring relationship with the clients; (b) in the course of this relationship, consistently displaying genuineness, congruence, and empathic understanding of the clients and their problems; (c) nondirective and nonintrusive dialogue between therapist and client; (d) helping clients to exchange their conditions of lowered worth for a trust and valuing of the wisdom of their developing organisms; and (e) helping clients to achieve unconditional positive regard for themselves, largely through their experiencing the therapist's unconditional positive regard for them.

COGNITIVE BEHAVIOR THERAPY AND RATIONAL-EMOTIVE THERAPY

Modern cognitive behavior therapy originated in 1955 with Albert Ellis' rational-emotive therapy. Following the philosophical leads of Stoics, especially Epictetus and Marcus Aurelius, and borrowing some ideas from pioneers like Andrew Salter, Alexander Herzberg, and George Kelly, Ellis welded together some of the main elements of cognitive therapy as espoused by Alfred Adler, and of behavior therapy as espoused by John B. Watson and B. F. Skinner. A group of therapists have since arisen, all of whom do similar forms of therapy.

According to the theories of rational-emotive therapy (RET) and cognitive behavior therapy (CBT), the main contributions to emotional and behavioral disturbance include: (a) a strong tendency, both innate and acquired, for people to act both for and against their own and their social group's interest; (b) misperceptions and unrealistic observations and conclusions; (c) absolutist and irrational beliefs (1) that certain unpleasant conditions should not exist, (2) that it is terrible these conditions do exist, (3) that people displeased by such conditions absolutely cannot stand them, and (4) that people who bring about such conditions are worthless individuals; (d) the unreasonable escalation by people of their strong desires into godlike commands, demands, and insistences; and (e) intercorrelations and interactions among people's unrealistic and absolutistic thinking, their inappropriate emoting, and their self-defeating behaviors.

Techniques include: (a) showing clients how unfavorable conditions do not upset them, but the clients choose (consciously or unconsciously) to upset themselves; (b) teaching clients a number of cognitive, emotive, and behavioral methods to change their thinking, their inappropriate feelings, and their dysfunctional behaviors; (c) assigning clients homework; (d) *in vivo* desensitization and flooding as well as imaginal desensitization and gradual approaches to anxiety-producing situations; (e) behavioral reinforcement and penalties to encourage changes; (f) highly forceful methods such as strong self-statements and shame-attacking exercises; (g) semantic methods of therapy; (h) problem solving and applying the scientific method to personal and interpersonal difficulties; (i) a variety of psychoeducational techniques such as lectures, recordings, workshops, and bibliotherapy; (j) skill training to improve clients' abilities, interests, and achievements; (k) cognitive distraction, imaginal, and refocusing methods.

BEHAVIORAL PSYCHOTHERAPY

Behavioral methods in psychotherapy started with John B. Watson and Mary C. Jones in the 1920s and were popularized by Joseph Wolpe and B. F. Skinner and their followers in the 1950s.

According to behavior therapy theories, emotional problems largely arise from: (a) ineffective or maladaptive learning; (b) conditioning by others, particularly during early childhood; (c) self-conditioning and self-

practice of a dysfunctional thought, feeling, or action; (d) avoidance of situations that create anxiety; (e) lack of skills that lead to poor performances; and (f) misperceptions about reality.

The main techniques used in behavior therapy include: (a) focusing on changing the clients' present behavior; (b) actively and directively teaching clients how to change their dysfunctional thoughts, feelings, and behaviors and how to practice more functional ones; (c) imaginal systematic desensitization of anxieties and fears; (d) *in vivo* desensitization; (e) gradual desensitizing and flooding techniques; (f) showing clients how to use stimulus control and to change the situations that cause them problems; (g) correcting misperceptions and unrealistic beliefs; (h) skill training to improve clients' abilities, interests, and achievements; (i) contingencies of reinforcement for adaptive behaviors, and aversive conditioning for maladaptive behaviors; and (j) relaxation techniques.

GESTALT THERAPY

Gestalt therapy originated with the clinical work of Fritz Perls in the early 1940s. Perls' disciples include Joen Fagan, Walter Kempler, Abraham Levitsky, Laura Pels, Erving and Miriam Polster, Irma Lee Shepherd, James Simkin, and Joseph Zinker.

Gestalt therapy sees emotional disturbance as largely caused by: (a) a "shouldistic" attitude toward life; (b) obsession with thinking rather than doing; (c) refusing to live in the present, and centering oneself instead in the past or future; (d) reforming oneself or others instead of being oneself and accepting oneself as one is; and (e) refusing to accept responsibility for one's own decisions.

Main Gestalt therapy techniques include: (a) helping clients to be fully aware of their feelings in the here and now; (b) showing clients how to reject cognitive interpretations and explanations of their difficulties; (c) breathing and body work; and (d) helping clients achieve integration.

EXPERIENTIAL AND HUMANISTIC PSYCHOTHERAPY

Experiential, humanistic, and existential psychotherapy began with the work of philosophers such as Søren Kirkegaard, Edmund Husserl, Martin Heidegger, Martin Buber, and Jean-Paul Sartre, and with psychologists such as Wilhelm Dilthey, Abraham Maslow, and Wilhelm Reich. It covers a wide variety of theories and methods.

Experiential, humanistic, and existentialist therapists generally hold that emotional disturbance has these main roots: (a) refusal to take the risk of living fully and of accepting the inevitability of death; (b) inability to own one's own life and conduct, and to be fairly autonomous even though living comfortably in a community or social group; (c) overconformity, leading to continual pressure to ignore one's own experience; and (d) refusing to experiment with one's desires and wishes, instead forcing oneself into a narrow mode of experiencing.

Experiential, humanistic, and existential therapists use the following techniques: (a) emphasizing clients' felt senses and their inner processes of change and development; (b) helping clients to have a profound inner sense of truth; (c) using body work and physical methods of emotional release; (d) risk taking, so that clients change by forcing themselves to exist differently; (e) relating caringly and fully to clients, which encourages clients to relate caringly and fully to others; and (f) helping clients achieve unconditional positive regard or full self-acceptance, authenticity, self-honesty, and openness.

TRANSACTIONAL ANALYSIS

Transactional analysis (TA), originated by Eric Berne in the mid-1950s, originally was designed to supplement psychoanalysis.

According to TA theory, the main causes of emotional disturbance are: (a) children's receiving early messages or "tapes" from their "parent" ego states that encourage them to act in their "child" ego state instead of their more sensible and productive "adult" state; (b) the innate tendency of people to make the transactions among their ego states all-important and rigid; (c) resulting stereotyped habit patterns and lack of personal autonomy; (d) lack of early stroking or loving recognition by others; (e) retaining basic life decisions or scripts because they once had value during early childhood; and (f) the tendency to use defensive maneuvers or games to retain and reinforce early script decisions.

Transactional therapists use a variety of techniques, especially the following: (a) tracing clients' disturbed feelings back to their early decisive moments, then reeducating the clients to feel differently; (b) helping clients to achieve a balance of ego states; (c) showing clients how to reexperience decision moments and redecide important issues by self-confrontation; (d) giving clients an awareness of their self-power; (e) revealing and interrupting clients' defensive maneuvers or games; and (f) helping clients transfer ego state energies to lesser used ego states.

ADLERIAN PSYCHOTHERAPY
ANALYTICAL PSYCHOTHERAPY
BEHAVIOR THERAPY
CLIENT-CENTERED THERAPY
COGNITIVE BEHAVIORAL THERAPY
EXISTENTIAL PSYCHOTHERAPY
GESTALT THERAPY
PERSON-CENTERED THEORY FOUNDATIONS
PSYCHOANALYSIS
TRANSACTIONAL ANALYSIS

A. ELLIS

CURRICULUM DEVELOPMENT

It was recognized that structuring activities and attaining instructional goals were major components of curriculum, hence Johnson's definition, "a structured series of intended learning outcomes" became widely accepted. Later a distinction was made between *curriculum,* generally equated with content and materials, and *instruction,* generally equated with exposing students to the curriculum or the pupil–teacher interaction process.

Content-oriented curriculum has appeared in at least five varieties, the oldest being the *subject-area* curriculum, with roots in the seven liberal arts (i.e., grammar, rhetoric, dialectic, arithmetic, geometry, astronomy, and music). This tradition, originating with the Greeks and Romans, led to what is referred to as common, special, and elective courses. *Perennialist* curriculum stems from the philosophy that the primary purpose of education is cultivation of the intellect. It sees this end being best attained through the study of the three basic subjects of reading, writing, and arithmetic, as well as logic, Latin, and the classics. *Essentialist* curriculum, much like perennialism, emphasizes rigorous intellectual training, but acknowledges the importance of science, history, and foreign languages in addition to the three basics. *Subject structure* curriculum, developed in the 1950s and 1960s, was initiated in mathematics and science.

Ornstein also identified five varieties of the student-oriented curriculum that stress process and needs more than content. The oldest variety is traceable to Rousseau's publication of *Emile* in 1762, and became known as the *child-centered* curriculum. It stressed the needs and interests of the learner and was advocated by Johann Pestalozzi in Switzerland, Johann Froebel in Germany, Maria Montessori in Italy, and John Dewey in the United States. Summerhill, created by A. S. Neill in 1921, was also a part of this child-centered curriculum movement. *Activity-centered* curriculum, originating with W. H. Kilpatrick in 1918, advocated lifelike, purposeful activity, problem solving, and student participation.

Relevant curriculum, a third variety of student-oriented curriculum, was a product demanded by students and instructors in the late 1960s and early 1970s. It resulted in the introduction of courses such as environmental protection, women's studies, substance abuse, sexuality, and Afro-American literature. The *hidden* curriculum, which emerged in the late 1950s, focused attention on factors that interacted and at times conflicted with the formal curriculum. Efforts were made to minimize teacher authority, competition, and "right" answers while maximizing freedom, choice, and cooperation. This curriculum movement included a recognition and reduction of subtle forms of racial and cultural stereotyping in learning materials and educational practices. The fifth type of student-oriented curriculum identified by Ornstein is *humanitistic* curriculum, a product of the late 1950s and early 1960s. This movement emphasized the need for meaningful student–teacher relationships, student self-direction and independence, personal growth, and increased self-awareness.

The dichotomizing of curriculum as content-oriented or process- or student-oriented has conceptual and practical advantages. However, the distinction is somewhat artificial; content and process are seldom isolated in either the practical or theoretical study of curriculum. E. L. Thorndike provoked a major change in school curriculum with empirical studies that demolished the doctrine of formal discipline and led to the introduction of occupationally oriented courses. With a similar orientation toward and concern for curriculum and its usefulness, C. H. Judd and W. H. Winch emphasized ensuring that the school curriculum included the teaching of principles and strategies as well as practical skills. Throughout the twentieth century, psychologists have continued to provide theories and data relevant to the development of curriculum. The impact of these psychological contributions is difficult to assess.

The work of Benjamin Bloom and his followers accounts, to a great extent, for the mastery-learning movement as well as the printing of learning objectives now so prominent in instructional manuals and other curricular materials. R. M. Gagné's learning hierarchy and the research it generated help explain the increased emphasis on the sequencing of instructional units and their parts. Bruner's theory of instruction, with its emphasis on modes of learning, has provided an explanation and incentive for the integration of media and activities with lectures and readings. Jean Piaget's theory of cognitive development is used (and misused) to explain and justify much of the curriculum found in preschools, early childhood centers, and elementary schools.

Federal and state organizations combined with legislation have tended to play a more predominant and direct role in determining curriculum. The new science, the new math, and the back-to-basics movement are but a few of the recent curriculum-related movements traceable to the work of national and local organizations. The establishment and funding of research centers that develop curricula and examine curricula-related issues are further evidence of government's acknowledgment of the dependency of curriculum development on psychological research.

M. Fullan and A. Pomfret contend that curriculum evaluation consists not only of comparing and contrasting methods and content packages, but also of assessing and judging the implementation of curriculum innovations. It is in the process of implementation that changes in materials, structure, and student–teacher roles occur. Without a systematic assessment of such changes, learning outcomes may be misinterpreted and misattributed, implementation may be confused with or assumed to be the same as curriculum adoption, and the success or failure of curriculum innovations may be poorly understood.

ALTERNATIVE EDUCATIONAL SYSTEMS
INSTRUCTIONAL THEORY
SCHOOL LEARNING

M. M. CLIFFORD

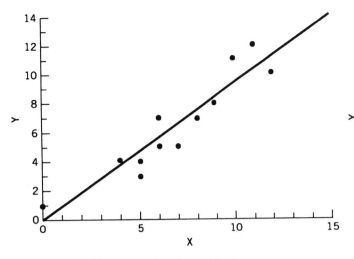

Figure 1. A positive linear relationship.

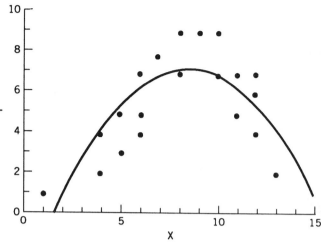

Figure 3. A curvilinear relationship.

CURVILINEAR RELATIONSHIP

The relationship between two variables (traditionally called X and Y) can be displayed on a scatterplot, with each subject's pair of scores represented by a point on the plot. X and Y are linearly related if the points on the scatterplot have a pattern that can be fit by a straight line. X and Y have a curvilinear relationship if the pattern can be fit by a curved line. Figures 1 and 2 are linear relationships, and Figures 3 and 4 are curvilinear relationships. The best fitting line is drawn through each figure.

Figure 1 illustrates two variables with a positive linear relationship. As X increases, Y tends to increase. Height and weight have a positive linear relationship: Taller people tend to weigh more than shorter people. Figure 2 illustrates two variables with a negative linear relationship. As X increases, Y tends to decrease. Age and errors on an arithmetic test have a negative linear relationship among children: Older children tend to make fewer arithmetic errors than younger children. In Figure 3, Y is highest for moderate levels of X. Anxiety and speed on a typing test have such a relationship: People low in anxiety are not motivated to go fast, and high anxiety interferes with performance. Figure 4 shows the opposite pattern. Y is lowest for moderate values of X. Physical attractiveness and how often one is noticed by other people may have such a relationship: Extremely attractive or unattractive people may be most likely to be noticed.

The most frequently used correlation coefficient, the Pearson product–moment correlation coefficient (r) tells the direction and strength of the *linear* relationship between two variables. Variables with a curvilinear relationship will have a low Pearson correlation. This low correlation suggests a weak relationship when a strong curvilinear relationship may exist. A special correlation, the eta coefficient, is used as an indicator of the strength of a curvilinear relationship. X can be used to predict Y using a regression equation. This regression equation will be a linear equation (the equation for a straight line) if the relationship between X and Y is linear. A linear equation will not fit a curvilinear relationship well, so it will not provide accurate predictions. The equations for the regression lines drawn in Figures 1 through 4 are as follows:

Figure 1: $Y = 0.94X - 0.08$

Figure 2: $Y = -0.91X + 13.98$

Figure 3: $Y = 2.56X - 0.15X^2 - 3.69$

Figure 4: $Y = -2.39X + 0.19X^2 + 13.10$

CORRELATION METHODS
STATISTICAL INFERENCE

M. J. Allen

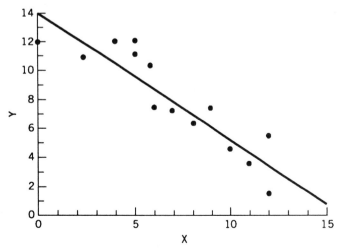

Figure 2. A negative linear relationship.

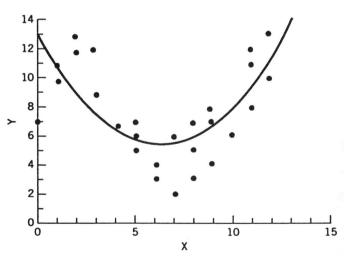

Figure 4. A curvilinear relationship.

CUTANEOUS SENSES

Cutaneous or skin senses are aspects of what is often referred to as the "sense of touch." Studies indicate that there are four different cutaneous senses; pressure (touch), pain, warm, and cold. It is thought that other cutaneous sensations, such as tickle and itch, are varieties of the four primary cutaneous senses.

Cutaneous *receptors* are not evenly distributed throughout the body in the dermis or inner layer of the skin. The nerve pathway to the brain from the cutaneous receptors is arranged in terms of areas of the body known as *dermatomes,* which are connected with the nerves to the spinal cord.

Local sign is a term that refers to the ability of an individual to localize, without looking, the portion of the body surface at which the skin has been stimulated.

The receptors for light touch are believed to comprise Meissner's corpuscles, hair follicle bulbs, and some free nerve endings. *Heavy pressure* is believed to have as its receptors the Pacinian corpuscles, which appear as onion-like bulbs, each with a central nerve fiber. Changes of pressure, rather than constant application of pressure, appear to lead to receptor function.

Two stimulated points on the skin cannot be distinguished from a single stimulated skin point when only one receptor or the same nerve serves the two stimulated points. The *two-point threshold* varies with the part of the body and is related to dermatome size, the largest being for the center of the back and the smallest for the tongue tip.

More remains to be learned about both reception of *pain* from the body and the site of reception of pain in the brain. Free nerve endings appear to be receptors for skin pain. Pain functions as a warning of injury to the body. A small amount of adaptation to slight skin pain has been observed.

Receptors remain to be identified for *warm* and *cold* stimuli, in spite of the fact that there are distinctly separate reception spots for such stimuli.

CENTRAL NERVOUS SYSTEM
PAIN
PSYCHOPHYSIOLOGY

B. B. MATES

CYBERNETICS

Cybernetics is concerned with recursive feedback loops or ongoing patterns that connect in a system. The focus is on the relationships between elements within the system. "Cybernetic systems are therefore patterns of organization that maintain stability through processes of change."

Cybernetic and cybernetic systems have similarities to and differences from general systems theory, viewing organisms as systems within systems (called subsystems, or "holons") or systems incorporating systems (called suprasystems). According to a general systems theoretical view, a system is a Gestalt with the whole being more than the sum of its parts, meanwhile maintaining a balanced, homeostatic steady state. Keeney refers to general systems theory as simple cybernetics or a lower level cybernetics.

When using a cybernetic systems perspective, it is necessary to make an epistemological shift, changing the way causality is viewed.

AN EPISTEMOLOGICAL SHIFT

An age-old question among philosophers refers to the causes of human behavior. When using concepts of systems theory, cybernetics, and cybernetic systems, one must shift to an unusual view of causality. A linear view states that A causes B, or one event causes another (e.g., as in the stimulus–response concept). Cybernetics and systems theory, however, are based on circular views of causality, reflected by mutually feeding patterns of behavior: A causes B and B causes A. Keeney, and Keeney and Ross, refer to circular causality as simple cybernetics.

KEY CONCEPTS

Cybernetic systems theory consists of several key dynamics: self-reference, feedback patterns, homeostasis, and self-autonomy.

Self-reference

Perception can be viewed in terms of relationships, that is, self-reference, or placing the perceiver in the observation. The relationship between the observer–perceiver and perceived reality can be analyzed in terms of patterns of relationships, because the observer is always part of the context by definition.

Feedback Patterns

Any living or mechanical system is organized by patterns connecting each element in the system. These patterns are referred to as feedback loops, or recursive communicative patterns of behavior. There are positive and negative feedback loops. Positive feedback loops initiate change by dumping new information into the system. Negative feedback loops are patterns that help maintain the system's status quo, or sameness. Balance or equilibrium can be restored through the calibration of feedback loops. At the highest level of a cybernetic system, equilibrium or homeostasis is continuously maintained through the complementary relationship between patterns of positive and negative feedback loops.

Homeostasis: A Dynamic Balance

Systems maintain a continuous ongoing dynamic balance referred to as *homeostasis*. Keeney emphasized that all living systems maintain a dynamic balance at their highest level, or else they would self-destruct and perish. According to the views postulated by early general systems theorists, change facilitates a state of disequilibrium, and then the organism returns to equilibrium. Change is encompassed by a recursive loop of stability. Change and stability are like two sides of the same coin; they cannot be separated. Negative and positive feedback loops also are complementary.

Self-autonomy

The cybernetic system is self-autonomous and self-maintained at the highest level of observation. It also is a closed system at the highest level. Self-autonomy is maintained through the processes of morphostasis. Paradoxically, a system's structure is maintained through calibrated patterns of change and stability.

CAUSAL REASONING
CODING
CONNECTIONISM
DEPROGRAMMING
EXCHANGE THEORY
FREE WILL
GENERAL SYSTEMS
PHILOSOPHY OF SCIENCE
REDUCTIONISM
SYSTEMS THEORY

M. S. CARICH

CYCLOTHYMIC PERSONALITY

The term *cyclothymic* was first coined by Kahlbaum in the mid-nineteenth century to describe what was then called "circular insanity." The symptoms represented a personality condition manifested by a chronic nonpsychotic disturbance of mood occurring episodically. The moods could be of mania, depression, or both. The intensity of these mood swings are not of sufficient intensity to meet diagnostic criteria of a manic-depressive (bipolar) disorder and the individual is not usually distressed by them.

The clinical features include intermittent biphasic but nonpsychotic changes of moods of elation and depression. The elation does not reach the level or duration of a full-blown manic episode; rather, the person experiences an elevated, expansive, or irritable mood. Accompanying phenomena include decreased need for sleep, increased productivity, a sense of enhanced capacity for attention, concentration, creative thinking, and self-imposed work habits. Social difficulties include buying sprees and financial extravagance. The depressive phase includes withdrawal, loss of interest or pleasure in usual activities, diminished productivity, reduced attention span, and excessive sleep. The mood changes may be separated by periods of normal behavior lasting as long as several months.

Onset is usually in mid- to late adolescence, with a noticeable change in moodiness. During adulthood, the elation phase may be adaptive and facilitate successful pursuits. When the mood swings are too severe, they are observably maladaptive. Diagnosis is readily obtained by the history of characteristic patterning of symptoms. Mood swings secondary to substance abuse must be ruled out. Onset over the age of 40 years may be of organic origin.

Occasionally the mood swings may progress into a full-blown manic or depressive psychotic episode. When this occurs there are the associated stigmata consistent with psychosis, including gross disorganization of thought, delusional thinking, and severely impaired life functioning.

DEPRESSION
DISPOSITIONAL SETS
MANIC-DEPRESSIVE PERSONALITY

R. C. MARVIT

D

DAY-CARE CENTERS

Day care, the day nursery, or crèche—defined as "an organized service for the care of children away from their homes during some part of the day"—originated in France.

Day-care centers in the United States, providing out-of-home rather than in-home care, were designed specifically to remedy economic difficulties by releasing women for employment, and flourished particularly during the Great Depression, World War II, and the War on Poverty. Besides working women, single parents, minorities, and poor and near poor families have used day-care centers more than other groups. However, care by a childsitter in one's own home or in someone else's home has been maintained as the dominant form of supplemental child care.

Most programs (a) are on a fixed schedule, 8 hours or more daily; (b) serve children younger than the age of 6; (c) are licensed; and (d) are run by professionals. The arguments in favor of day-care centers are several and generally rely on the assumption that such settings and programs provide certain quality advantages that home care cannot supply, including: (a) regulated standards for such factors as child : staff ratio, space, and equipment; (b) tailored services to meet the needs and interests of those served; and (c) more effectively delivered and efficiently monitored services (e.g., health and nutrition) because of a concentration of children in one location. However, there are three arguments against day-care centers: (a) the cost of the center care is higher than home care, (b) there is limited flexibility for change once the center becomes operational, and (c) not all locales have the numbers of children needed to justify a center.

DAY-CARE CENTER SETTINGS

The research literature has clustered around four primary situational dimensions: (a) the number of children, (b) physical size of the environment, (c) children : staff ratio, and (d) the characteristics of the children. For example, evidence suggests that when centers consist of fewer children (approximately 15 to 20), staff are more involved in praising, comforting, and questioning, and place less emphasis on rules and routines. As the number of children per square foot increases, negative behavior such as aggressiveness, destructiveness, and isolated behavior increase. Also, in age-segregated groups teachers are less affectionate and use less direct teaching, and children show more conflict and competition compared to age-integrated groups.

THE EFFECTS OF DAY-CARE CENTERS

Group care programs influence children's cognitive, emotional, and social development. It seems evident that 1 to 2 years of a quality program combined with an effective home program can make permanent positive changes in children's cognitive abilities, especially IQ. For youngsters growing up in economically disadvantaged environments, experience in center-based care appears to attenuate the declines in IQ often observed in children from similar situations of high risk or instability. With regard to emotional development, day care appears neither to harm the mother–child bond even when such care is initiated during the first year of life, nor to decrease the child's preference for mother compared to another caregiver. Children who spend some part of their day in a day-care center interact more with peers in both positive and negative ways.

Research is sparse and results are even more equivocal when the impact of day care on the family and other systems is considered. Mothers who participate in training programs form supportive networks by sharing information and assisting others in child care. Also, as parental satisfaction with child-care arrangements rises, employment and marital satisfaction increases as well.

Caution is warranted in interpreting these data. Continued research, both basic and applied, is needed to understand the potential optimizing influences of parents, families, child-service providers, and social networks on children.

EARLY CHILDHOOD EDUCATION
PRESCHOOL EDUCATION

F. DEUTSCH

DAY HOSPITALS

Day hospitals and day treatment centers also grew during the 1970s as a function of deinstitutionalization efforts. The day hospital prevents the individual from experiencing total isolation from family and community, while also requiring a smaller financial investment by both the state and client than does a fully staffed hospital providing care for all clients 24 hours per day. Clients of the day hospital are typically in transition from full-time hospital living to independent living, or arrive at the day hospital directly from the community in an effort to avoid total institutionalization. The transitional nature of the day hospital or day treatment center reduces the stigma and discourages the dependency that often accompany and follow long-term hospitalization. A primary focus of these facilities is to prepare clients for the tasks of daily living. Rehabilitation services usually combine individually tailored program groups with recreational, occupational, and milieu therapies, as well as vocational rehabilitation.

Given the diverse activities that take place in day hospitals and day treatment centers, they generally have multidisciplinary staff including psychiatrists, clinical psychologists, psychiatric social workers, psychiatric nurses, occupational and recreational therapists, and vocational counselors.

HALFWAY HOUSES
MENTAL HEALTH PROGRAMS

R. D. FELNER

DEATH ANXIETY

What might individuals mean when they say they are fearful of death? Some might express anxiety over the variety of losses thought to accompany *death,* whereas others may fear the loss of *contol* over their everyday lives that may come about as a function of dying.

Research suggests that both are multidimensional. Thus, concerns about death per se must be separated from those relating to the dying process, and also those about one's own death versus the death of significant others. Persons may or may not be consciously aware of their fears about death or dying, and not feeling particularly death anxious may simply reflect success at denial, in which case such fears may surface at a covert, unconscious level. The death-anxious individual may have physical complaints, have difficulty sleeping, change eating habits, have difficulty completing a task, or show an overconcern with the welfare of others. In such cases, individuals do not report being anxious or concerned about death or dying, but inexplicably experience a number of these difficulties. Relative to other conscious fears that may be repressed, anxiety over the deaths of others may be particularly difficult to deal with. Concerns over death also may be observed by simply noting a change in an individual's personality. In such cases, the individual may give away valued personal possessions or be excessively concerned over the welfare of others. Such feelings create inner turmoil and othen lead to behavior designed to finish "unfinished business."

Elderly persons do not report fearing death per se. They do, however, fear to a great degree the dying process—dying in pain, dying alone, or the loss of control over everyday events or bodily functions. Findings on the complex nature of death fear support the view that fear of death may reflect many concerns. Pinder, Hayslip, and Lumsden, and Fiefel and Nagy found that although older persons *and* younger persons do not differ in consciously expressed death fear, there are substantial age differences in covert (unconscious) death concerns, such as fears of losing others, pain and suffering, loss of goals and achievements, or loss of control; older persons experienced more covert death fear than did the young but reported less overt fear. Hayslip, Luhr, and Beyerlein found that while men with AIDS and healthy men expressed similar degrees

of conscious death fear, terminally ill men expreienced more covert death fears. It may be that in the face of imminent death, individuals need consciously to deny their fears about dying to continue functioning on a daily basis. Conte, Weiner, and Plutchik found no age differences using items that were straightforward in their intent (e.g., "Do you worry about dying?" "Do you worry that you may be alone when you are dying?").

Rather than age per se, factors such as health status and anxiety may play more important roles in explaining death concern in adults. While other factors interact with the age–death anxiety relationship, findings do not always present a consistent picture. Persons who are alone and/or institutionalized, who live in an urban setting, who have poor mental health, who are female, and who are poorly educated are all more likely to report fearing death. Many other studies, however, do not report a relationship between death fears and such factors as retirement, life satisfaction, religiosity, socioeconomic status, and sex. Moreover, ethnic variations in the expression of death fears have been found by Kalish and Reynolds and Bengtson, Cuellar, and Ragan.

It seems that interpreting self-reported fears of death is not as straightforward as it may seem at first. Much seems to depend on how death is interpreted. Fears about death must also be understood in light of life circumstances, value systems, and what it is about death and dying that the individual fears.

AGING: BEHAVIOR CHANGES
ANXIETY
FEAR
LOSS AND GRIEF
STRESS

B. HAYSLIP, JR.

DECEPTION

Deception refers to inducing a false belief in another. Often successful and rewarded when undetected, targets are subject to the influences of deception even when they know the message may be faked. False praise and adoration as well as concealing dislike and loathing allow smooth interaction with others—a social lubricant. Many who distort do not consider themselves to be faking.

Deception can occur anywhere within the context of the psychological evaluation. The two temporal foci of distortion are the times of the evaluation and of a previous relevant event. This means that deception for the present (i.e., the time of the evaluation) may be quite different from that presented for the past (e.g., clinical, criminal, or tort event). Patients sometimes deceive to get into treatment and deny psychopathology to leave it.

Simple response styles are used occasionally by the faker, denying or fabricating everything possible. Usually, however, mixed response styles are used, whereby people lie selectively in different ways about different things. An individual will sometimes change styles within one evaluation session, from denying problems to responding honestly as fatigue increases. This makes the assessment of deception more difficult, but not impossible, for the rigorous evaluator.

PROTOTHEORY AND EARLY WORK

Deception has traditionally been seen as ubiquitous and adaptive in nature. Some early conceptualizations viewed deception as originating in a universal instinct in the context of natural selection.

Principles of deception discussed by Hyman as having emerged from the early works include

1. All perceptions are inferred from sensory input and are, therefore, subject to distortion. People have perceptual guidelines as to what

constitutes reality, usually based on the most probable event, and these are capitalized on by deceivers.

2. Knowledge of deception does not equal action to escape, avoid, or expose falsehood. The early literature is replete with examples in which deception was seen as positive (e.g., white lies) or actually sought after (e.g., as in a magic show).

3. The notion of the *invited inference* has relevance. A deceiver should lead targets into the desired outcome rather than tell them what they should believe or what the result will be.

Relevant to a theory of deception as adaptation, Rogers stated the following:

> Inclusion criteria for the classification of malingering are shaped and largely predetermined by our explanatory theories. Current theories have postulated that the motivation to malinger is either the product of underlying psychopathology or criminal backgrounds. I have proposed a third model that malingering is typically an adaptive response to adverse circumstances that may best be understood in the context of decision theory. (p. 116)

CHILDREN AND DECEPTION

Developmentally, lying begins at a very early age, cuts across all socioeconomic statuses and educational groupings and continues unabated into adolescence and young adulthood. Children as duped parties show differential responses, depending on developmental and situational factors. As with adults, there is little connection between vulnerability to deception and ability to dupe others.

Jastrow explored the effects of conjuring and other forms of deception on children. Young children were seen as incapable of being fooled because they had an incomplete notion of causality. Jastrow erroneously believed that the spread of education would greatly reduce the chances for deception.

More recent data suggest that younger children view lying amorally, based on their inability to tell the difference between the internal (psychic) and external (environmental). The ability of children to deceive, because lying is one of the first interactive verbal behaviors to develop, seems to vary according to the sending capacity of the child and obtained feedback.

Leading into a thesis that deception is learned from early caretakers, studies show that deception and avoiding punishment are inversely related. Four-year-olds lie to avoid punishment (44% of entire sample) or for other self-centered reasons such as to have fun (10%) or for self-gain (14%). Teenagers view lying as a major social problem as seriously as adults do, in spite of near-universal deception in relationships among older teenagers and young adults. In general, as children get older, they, like adults, increasingly justify lying on altruistic grounds.

Deception is rampant in higher education and in those trained to be our leaders. Between 33 and 66% of high school and college students cheat, and the majority of college faculty has observed cheating at some time. More than 85% of college students were found to be deceptive to their partners, almost all in regard to other relationships, with the justification that they wanted to protect the duped party. Virtually all of the research with human subjects in educational settings incorporates misleading, incomplete, or blatantly false instructions, rationalized by the belief that knowledge of procedures would bias results.

DECEPTION IN THE MILITARY

A theory of deception is assisted by military studies, covering a wide range of war-related activities. Vast sums of money have been spent by the federal government in the systematic study of operational deception, much of it classified. The roots of current military thinking have their basis in the Old Testament, Carl von Clausewitz's *On war*, Chinese

philosophers such as Sun Tzu's *Art of war*, psychophysics and psychometrics, magic, and other sources.

Deception is viewed favorably by the military. An inverse relationship is usually found between the amount of deception employed and the strength of the military force. Deception is cheap in terms of labor and capital. Best of all, deception seems to work in most cases, given adequate planning, which accounts for its high favor and continued use.

VIOLENT CRIME AND DECEPTION

The National Institute of Justice (NIJ) estimates that about 83% of the American population will be victims of attempted or consummated violence during their lifetime.

Almost all violence involves deception. In burglary, concealment and blending into the environment are commonplace. Robbery often involves good faking, shown by innocuous approach behaviors, followed by bad faking, such as when the robber pretends to hold a pistol to the victim's back. Kidnapping also uses a combination of good and bad faking, as when the location of the victim is concealed, coupled with threats to harm the victim for noncompliance. Victims and their significant others can ill-afford to test whether the perpetrators are bluffing. Rape behaviors involve stalking, presenting verbiage designed to lull the victim into complacency, usually occurring at night or behind visual barriers. Date rape, in which the perpetrator is known to the victim, involves good faking.

Methods for evaluating violence-related deception are provided by Hall, and Hall and Pritchard. In general, a history of violence is the best predictor of further violence. The evaluative task becomes one of sifting through deception to uncover true basal violence.

WHITE-COLLAR CRIME

White-collar crimes include forgery, counterfeiting, fraud, embezzlement, bribery, theft of services and trade secrets or products, smuggling, tax evasion, and now, computer fraud. Always, the deceiver's position of trust, power, or influence has provided the opportunity for exploitation.

Works on how this type of deception operates are David Mauer's *The American confidence man*, Jay Robert Nash's *Hustlers and con men*, A. A. Leff's *Swindling and selling*, and Darwin Ortiz's *Gambling scams*.

The magnitude of the theft-at-work problem is reflected by base-rate studies that indicate that 26 to 42% of employees admit to stealing, depending on the work setting (covered in a 1990 review by Jones & Terris).

Attention has recently turned to paper-and-pencil tests of deception because the enactment of the Employee Polygraph Protection Act of 1988 severely delimited the use of the lie detector in private and most public settings (but not for federal law enforcement and private security positions). The traditional means of determining job applicant deception—credit and reference checks, employment interviews, and criminal background probes—are generally considered poor, at best. Kurke comments on tests designed to predict employee proneness to theft as follows:

> Although paper-and-pencil integrity and honesty tests can be criticized for accepting high false positive rates to ensure high true positives, there is evidence that the risk of reaching an erroneous selection decision on the basis of a paper-and-pencil honesty test is considerably less than if the decision were to be made on a random basis, on the basis of a traditional selection interview or on the basis of a weighted application blank.

In general, employees steal frequently, cause a huge financial loss, and are almost never caught. Integrity tests do seem to detect those who are more theft prone, with the overwhelming number of applicants not objecting to the testing in the first place.

Results of the testing can be considered, with proper safeguards, as part of the overall evaluation for job suitability. In practice, integrity tests are effective primarily because of people's ignorance of behavioral principles and inattention to long-term aversive consequences. As Kay stated, "One of the great wonders of psychology is that most people will make admissions on paper-and-pencil tests that they would probably never make in a face-to-face interview." The writer would add that assessees seem to operate on the same logic when audiotaped. After a few moments, interviewees behave as if the recording device were not there, incriminating themselves by revealing inconsistencies and admissions of various sorts.

EVALUATION FOR DECEPTION

The purposes of deception analysis within a psychological evaluation are as follows:

1. Examine the reliability and validity of database information.
2. Detect the possible existence of misrepresentation.
3. Determine the response style(s) used by the evaluatee.
4. Determine the magnitude of distortion.
5. Place symptoms, behaviors, or mental conditions associated with deception into clear perspective.
6. Generate hypotheses for further evaluation or investigation.
7. Communicate the decision path and the findings to the referral source.
8. Standardize eventually the deception analysis process.

In the clinical area, applications include selection for treatment, readiness for discharge, treatment motivation, transference and countertransference, and honesty of collaterals. In forensic applications, there is a wide relevance. Within the criminal area, these include: identification of perpetrators, competency to proceed, criminal responsibility, dangerousness prediction, and community monitoring of treatment. In the civil area, applications include evaluation for competency, witness credibility, child custody and divorce actions, personal injury and wrongful death, and employment screening and dishonesty.

PROFESSIONAL MISCONCEPTIONS REGARDING DECEPTION

Throughout the history of the mental health law disciplines, misbeliefs about deception have included the following:

1. *Most Spoken Words and Behavior Can Be Taken Literally.* Actually, most people distort, either unintentionally or intentionally. Popular surveys reveal that more than 90% of average Americans say that they lie regularly.

   Many forensic professionals believe that distortion does not occur in their evaluations. The frequency of deception in clinical settings and situations is unknown but is assumed to be high. In forensic settings, malingering has been confirmed or suspected in more than 20% of criminal defendants, with another 5% showing substantial unintentional distortion. The deception rates for litigants in civil actions may be even higher.

2. *The Evaluator Cannot Be Fooled (Other People Can).* In general, mental health professionals are not good at detecting faking. Worse yet, an inverse relationship is suggested: the greater the confidence, the lower the accuracy in detecting faking.

3. *Deception, When It Does Occur, Means That the Faker Is Mentally Sick.* Desperate people often resort to desperate measures to survive or adapt. A person who fakes insanity is not necessarily mentally ill but may want to avoid prison, a soul-destroying place under the best of conditions.

4. *DSM-III-R and DSM-IV Can and Will Allow for Deception Analysis.* *DSM-III-R* states that malingering should be suspected if (a) there is a forensic context to the evaluation, (b) a discrepancy between reported disability and "objective" findings exists, (c) there is lack of cooperation, or (d) the patient has an antisocial personality disorder.

   These criteria in *DSM-III-R* for detecting malingering are too limited, failing to take into account subclinical problems, extant methods of detection, and other population groups that fake. An explicit disclaimer to the use of the mental diagnoses in forensic contexts is presented in the manual. The reader is cautioned not to use the *DSM-III-R* guidelines for the detection of deception.

5. *Some Conditions, Such as Amnesia, Hallucinations, and Posttrauma Reactions Are Easily Faked and Nearly Impossible to Prove.* In Hall's studies, faked amnesia was detected with promising degrees of accuracy, hovering about 80 to 85% accuracy.

   Other conditions can be scrutinized for deception (e.g., Hall & Pritchard, in press). Hallucinations are hard to disprove, yet, base rates for comparison and decision criteria are available to assist the evaluator. Posttraumatic stress disorder (PTSD) can be assessed by psychometrics or arousal methods with built-in features to assess deception.

6. *Detecting Faking Is an Art and Cannot Be Taught.* Actually, the reverse appears to be true. Following a few simple rules increases the accuracy rate substantially above chance. Deception analysis is a trainable skill. The average mental health professional of any culture can be taught to detect faking adequately in a relatively short period of time.

7. *Near Absolute Accuracy of Detecting Faking Can Never Be Achieved.* It is a dangerous untruth to believe that near absolute accuracy of detecting faking can never be achieved. Saxe predicts, for example, that such development is a fantasy because honesty is situational and because "individuals have too many options available to encode their thoughts for us to be able to probe what they choose to hide." Recent technologies, such as DNA fingerprinting and P300 wave analysis, are nearly 100% accurate. The latter method is based on brain waves associated with stimulus familiarity rather than arousal (in contrast to polygraphy), voice stress analysis, and penile plethysmography.

Mental health practitioners and investigators face a moral dilemma much like those in the physical sciences in their development of harmful technologies. There appears to be an increased acceptance of deception as a means of exploiting others on the part of both institutions and individuals. This issue of too little versus too much accuracy in detecting deception suggests issues of balance and of ethical mandates. Promising degrees of accuracy have already been obtained in deception analysis. Resolution of moral issues now outweigh the benefits of continued technological improvements in deception analysis.

ADVERTISING
BARNUM EFFECT
COMPETENCY TO STAND TRIAL
FACTIOUS DISORDERS
FANTASY
ILLUSIONS
MALINGERING
MORAL DEVELOPMENT
PERCEPTUAL DISTORTIONS
SOCIAL DESIRABILITY

H. V. HALL

DECORTICATION

The term *cortex* refers to any outer layer of cells of the brain. Mammals have three kinds of cortex: pyriform cortex, which has olfactory functions;

archicortex, which comprises a large part of the limbic system or so-called "emotional brain"; and the neocortex, which is involved in most elaborate behaviors. Usually the term cortex refers to the neocortex or isocortex. The cortex has expanded most during evolution; virtually absent in fish, it comprises nearly 80% of the human brain. Decortications, or removal of the cortex, are performed on dead animals to analyze the anatomy of underlying structures, and on living animals to analyze the behavioral capacities of the residual brain. The latter procedure also tells something about the function of the cortex, because missing abilities can be presumed to be a property of the missing tissue.

The first decortications on living animals were performed for a rand purpose. In the early 1800s Pierre Flourens set out to prove that the mind was unitary and indivisible, as had been suggested by the philosopher René Descartes and was consistent with the religious beliefs of the era. The experiments were also designed to refute the theory, proposed by the phrenologists, that each part of the brain had a particular function. Flourens removed the cortex of chickens and pigeons and found that, irrespective of which part was removed, the animals showed behavioral impairments proportional to the amount, not the location, of the removed tissue. Flourens' experiments were sufficiently convincing to allow his view to dominate neurological theory for half a century. His experiments also began the field of psychology called physiological psychology. As it turned out, Flourens' choice of subject was unfortunate: Chickens and pigeons have virtually no neocortex. Many of the deficits the animals displayed may have been due to postsurgical shock.

The clinical observations of Marc Dax and Paul Broca had shown that speech in humans was located in the left frontal cortex, while the experiments on dogs by Gustav T. Fritsch and Eduard Hitzig in 1870 had demonstrated that electrical stimulation of restricted regions of the frontal neocortex produced movements of different body parts. Goltz removed the cortex of dogs and demonstrated that the neocortex alone was not essential for many movements. Goltz incorrectly interpreted his experiments to mean that function is not localized—that is, that every part of the brain participated in every function. Nevertheless, his experiments demonstrated that subcortical structures were capable of sustaining a wide repertoire of complex behaviors.

The procedure of decortication remains valuable for answering a number of questions. These concern the ability of subcortical structures to sustain behavior, the nature of neural organization underlying behavior, and the special nature of the contributions and organization imparted by the cortex and subcortex, respectively. The technique used to produce decortication is to open an aperture in the skull and remove the underlying tissue by aspiration. Animals, including humans, may also be born without the cortex because of genetic or other prenatal influences, but extensive damage may occur to the cortex because of postnatal injury. In experiments performed since 1900 it has been shown that decorticated animals are able to learn in both classical conditioning and operant conditioning paradigms, that they display most aspects of emotional and social behavior, and that they are capable of making most movements that normal animals make. They are deficient, however, in detecting patterns in sensory stimulation, in making complex patterns of movements, and in certain cognitive functions such as navigating through space using ambient configurations of sensory stimulation. In humans, reception and production of language are clearly "pattern" abilities that can be lost after cortex damage.

BRAIN

I. Q. Whishaw

DEFENSE MECHANISMS

Defense mechanisms are psychological strategies by which persons reduce or avoid negative states such as conflict, frustration, anxiety, and stress.

Because it is assumed that most people are motivated to reduce these negative states, theorists have devoted considerable attention to the identification of defense mechanisms, and a wide variety of mechanisms have been suggested. Most of the theorizing concerning the defense mechanisms has been provided by psychodynamically oriented individuals, primarily Sigmund Freud. More recently, however, alternative explanations for some of the behaviors in question have been offered by theorists with different perspectives.

Although the existence and effects of the various defense mechanisms are widely accepted, much of that acceptance is based only on case studies or anecdotal reports rather than on controlled scientific research.

Three points should be recognized concerning the defenses in general. First, defense mechanisms are used to *avoid or reduce negative emotional states.* Second, most defense mechanisms involve a *distortion of reality.* Third, persons are usually *not consciously aware of their use of most defense mechanisms.* If they were aware of their distortions, the distortions would not be effective for reducing the negative emotional states.

REPRESSION

Repression is the selective forgetting of material associated with conflict and stress. Repression serves as a defense because, if a person is not aware of the conflictive and stressful material, the conflict and stress will not exist for the person. There are three important things to note about repression. First, repression is *motivated selective forgetting*: It is a loss designed to selectively eliminate from consciousness the memories or related associations that cause the individual to experience conflict or stress. Second, repressed material is not lost but rather *stored in the unconscious.* If for some reason the negative feeling associated with the material is eliminated, the once repressed material can return to consciousness without having to be relearned. Third, Freud postulated two types of repression. The first type was *primal repression,* which involves a "denial of entry into consciousness" of threatening material. In this type of repression it appears as if the individual did not even perceive the material. Freud called the second type of repression *proper* or *afterexpulsion.* Once recognized, however, the material is repressed and the person is no longer aware of the material.

Repression is undoubtedly one of the most important concepts in the areas of personality and psychopathology. Indeed, the existence of repression is a prerequisite for the development of an unconscious because, apart from Carl Jung's concept of the *collective unconscious,* it is through repression that material supposedly enters the unconscious.

Primal repression was studied in the laboratory by flashing slides of stress-provoking and neutral words on a screen for very short periods of time and asking persons to read the words aloud if possible. It was found that the stress-provoking words had to be on the screen for longer periods of time than the neutral words before they could be read; from that it was concluded that the persons were not allowing the stress-provoking words to register in the consciousness. Subsequent research has indicated, however, that the difference in reading/recognition time between the stress-provoking and neutral words was due in large part to the fact that the persons were less familiar with the stress-provoking words and hence were less likely to recognize them when they were presented for only short periods of time. It was also found that persons were embarrassed by the stress-provoking words and therefore waited until they were sure that their reading was correct before saying the words. Empirically based alternative explanations such as these serve to weaken the research support for primal repression.

Research on proper repression mostly used some form of the following approach: Persons were first tested for their recall of a series of neutral stimuli, and then, for half the persons, stress was experimentally associated with the stimuli, whereas for the other persons stress was not associated with the stimuli. Following that, recall for the stimuli was tested again.

Next the stress was eliminated, and finally the persons were tested again for their recall of the stimuli. The results of these investigations generally indicated that when stress was associated with the stimuli, the stimuli were less likely to be recalled—an effect attributed to repression. It was also found that when the stress was removed, recall of the stimuli improved—a finding interpreted as evidence of a return of the repressed. Recently, however, it has been suggested that decreases in recall may have been due to interference caused by emotional arousal rather than repression. In this connection, it was found that associating very *positive* emotions with stimuli can also decrease the recall of the stimuli—an effect that could not be attributed to repression. Selective recall appears to occur, but the process may be somewhat different from what is implied by the term repression.

SUPPRESSION

In suppression, the person avoids stressful thoughts by not thinking about them. Because it is difficult not to think, suppression usually involves thinking about other nonstressful things that can replace the stressful thoughts, causing some writers to refer to this as *avoidant thinking* or *attentional diversion.* Suppression differs from repression in that with suppression the stress-provoking thought is available but is ignored and blocked by other thoughts, rather than being completely unavailable as is the case with repression. It is important to note that, unlike most other defenses, in some cases persons will *consciously* initiate suppression. If this is done repeatedly, the avoidance response may become habitual and may be used without awareness. There is a variety of evidence that persons do indeed use suppression and that it is effective in reducing stress.

DENIAL

In denial, a person does not attend to the threat-provoking aspects of a situation and changes the interpretation of the situation so as to perceive it as less threatening.

Denial differs from repression in that the person selectively attends and reinterprets, rather than obliterates, the experience from consciousness. Insofar as denial involves some selective attention, the process involves some amount of suppression. Because reinterpretation plays a major and unique role in denial, some investigators have used the terms *redefinition* and *reappraisal as* labels for this defensive strategy.

Laboratory research presents rather consistent evidence that persons spontaneously use this defense and that it is effective for reducing both subjective and physiological arousal in the face of threat.

PROJECTION

Projection involves the attribution of personality characteristics or motivations to other persons as a function of one's own personality characteristics and motivations. Three types of projection have been identified. In *attributive projection* a person is aware of possessing a particular trait and then attributes it to another individual. For example, a person who is aware of being afraid may project fear onto others. (It should be noted that the person using this type of projection is aware of the feeling but not of the use of projection.) There is ample research evidence for the existence of attributive projection. With regard to the defensive function of attributive projection, it has been theorized that if a person is stressed by the conscious possession of an undesirable personality trait, projecting that trait onto liked or respected individuals would enable the person to reevaluate the trait and thus make possessing it less stressful. Although there is some evidence that persons are more likely to project their trait onto liked or respected persons than onto other persons, there is as yet no consistent evidence that the projection reduces either subjective or physiological stress.

In *complementary projection* a person is aware of a particular characteristic or feeling and attributes the *cause* of it to another individual. For example, a person who is afraid might see others as frightening or hostile. There is substantial evidence documenting the existence of complementary projection. It is generally assumed that complementary projection serves a defensive function by enabling the person to see the world as consonant with and justifying his or her own feelings or activities. To this point, however, there is no consistent evidence that complementary projection is effective for reducing subjective or physiological stress. Finally, in *similarity* or *classical projection,* a person unaware of possessing a particular trait projects that trait onto other persons. Freud saw this type of projection as an aid to repression. The person not only repressed awareness of undesirable traits but also projected them outside to others. Although this type of response is probably the response most commonly implied by the use of the word projection, empirical research documenting its existence is wholly lacking.

DISPLACEMENT

Two types of displacement have been identified. The first, known as *object displacement,* occurs when a person expresses a feeling toward one person or object that in fact should be expressed toward another person or object. For example, a man who is angry at his boss may come home and agress against his wife, or a man who has lost his loved wife may lavish love on his children. Generally, object displacement is thought to occur when it is not possible to express the feeling toward the primary person or object, and thus it becomes necessary to express the feeling toward a secondary person or object. In the preceding examples, aggression could not be expressed against the boss because that would be dangerous, and love could not be expressed toward the wife because she was gone. There is ample research evidence that object displacement occurs, although in most cases the research is limited to the displacement of aggression.

The defensive function of object displacement can have two components. First, by not expressing the aggression against a dangerous primary target, the person avoids the threat of retaliation. Second, the expression of the feeling or drive is thought to result in a pleasurable cathartic effect. That is, in the case of the object displacement of aggression, danger is avoided and a drive is reduced. Experimental research provides some evidence for the cathartic effect. Specifically, object displacement appears to reduce subsequent aggression, but not to reduce physiological arousal.

In the second type of displacement, *drive displacement,* a person displaces the energy associated with one feeling into another feeling and thus expresses a feeling different from the one originally elicited. In contrast to object displacement, where the feeling remains the same but the target is changed, in drive displacement the target remains the same but the feeling is changed. The most commonly referred to instance of drive displacement occurs with sex and aggression. The energy associated with sexual arousal is often thought to be displaced and expressed as aggression, whereas the energy associated with the arousal of aggression is often thought to be displaced and expressed through sexual activity. The change of feeling enables the person to reduce the underlying drive, and to do so in an acceptable manner. The results of the experimental research on drive displacement are mixed, weak, and subject to alternative explanations, and thus do not provide much evidence for the phenomenon.

There are a number of explanations for changes in emotional targets or emotions other than displacement. For example, what appears to be object displacement may be a function of *stimulus generalization.* Specifically, a response that has been associated with a particular stimulus (person) may be elicited by a different but similar stimulus (person). It has also been suggested that arousal is nonspecific and becomes associated with specific drives as a function of the environmental cues available to provide labels for the arousal; thus if the cues change, the arousal will transfer. These explanations do not have the motivated defensive base inherent in the concept of displacement.

REGRESSION

The concept of regression suggests that when faced with conflict, stress, and particularly frustration, a person may return to an earlier stage of life in which the person was secure, and in doing so avoid the present conflict or stress. Freud identified two types of regression. In *object regression* a frustrated individual, attempting to obtain gratification from an object (or person), might go back to obtain gratification from an object (or person) from which gratification had been obtained previously. For example, an abandoned lover might seek attention from an earlier lover or even from his mother. In *drive regression* an individual frustrated in the attempt to satisfy one drive might obtain gratification by working to satisfy another drive.

Although regression is often cited as the explanation for much of the "immature" or "primitive" behavior seen in neurotic and psychotic persons, it does not appear that any empirical research has been published that documents the existence of effectiveness of regression.

IDENTIFICATION

When using identification, a person takes on the personal characteristics (behaviors, attitudes, etc.) of another person. Defensive identification can serve two purposes. On the one hand, if the satisfaction of some need is too threatening for a person to pursue, the person might identify with an individual able to pursue and satisfy the need, and thus can satisfy the need vicariously. On the other hand, by identifying with a feared or threatening individual, the person can take on the strength and threat of the feared individual and thus reduce feelings of vulnerability. The latter use of defensive identification is usually referred to as *identification with the aggressor*. Finally, it might be noted that through *imitation,* which could be considered as a superficial version of identification, one could model oneself after a successful person and thus avoid many problems and reduce stress.

COMPENSATION

When a person believes that he or she is inferior in some way, the person may attempt to overcome the feelings of inferiority and related anxiety by devoting additional effort to the area of the inferiority. Such behavior is referred to as *compensation,* and its defensive use was emphasized in the writings of Alfred Adler, who believed that much of our lifestyles are determined by our attempts to overcome real or imagined weaknesses. In Adler's case, he suggested that he had become a physician in an attempt to overcome his concerns about his physical/medical inferiority. Obviously, in many cases compensation would be an effective and appropriate response. The experimental research on compensation is limited but does support the existence of the phenomenon.

REACTION FORMATION

Freud suggested that if there was a possibility that threatening repressed material might return to consciousness, a person might attempt to reinforce the repression by using behaviors diametrically opposed to the kinds of behaviors that would result from the repressed material. For example, if a person found homosexuality threatening and had repressed homosexual tendencies, to reinforce the repression the person might engage in excessive heterosexual activities. Similarly, generosity is often interpreted as a defense against stinginess, and cleanliness as a defense against messiness. Such countermotive behavior is referred to as *reaction formation.*

Although some analogous research on animals has been reported, very little experimental research has tested the existence and effects of reaction formation in humans, and what little there is must be interpreted as weak and equivocal. Because the behaviors attributed to reaction formation are socially desirable behaviors, their use could simply be seen as attempts to gain reward/approval rather than as defensive attempts to avoid anxiety associated with unconscious material.

OTHER DEFENSE MECHANISMS

In addition to the defenses discussed thus far, others have been identified. Most of these other defenses have considerable overlap with those already discussed, or have not received much attention in the literature. *Rationalization* can be defined as the use of a "good" reason but not the real reason for behaving a particular way. With this strategy, a person can provide a rational explanation for the behavior, and in doing so conceal from him- or herself or others the less appropriate motivation. *Sublimation* occurs when a person converts the energy associated with an unacceptable impulse or drive into a socially acceptable activity. In many respects, sublimation is identical to drive displacement. In *isolation* a person separates the emotion from appropriate content and deals dispassionately with topics that would ordinarily be threatening or emotionally overwhelming. One technique of achieving isolation is to focus attention on the abstract, technical, or logical aspects of a threatening situation, rather than on the emotional components; this is called *intellectualization.* *Undoing* occurs when a person acts in an inappropriate way that elicits anxiety, then behaves in the opposite way so as to reverse or balance the original behavior and thus eliminate the anxiety that the first behavior engendered.

ANXIETY
PERSONALITY THEORIES
PSYCHOANALYSIS

D. S. HOLMES

DEINDIVIDUATION

Gustave Le Bon postulated the concept of a group mind. He suggested that in some circumstances persons lose their individuality and merge into the crowd. Such deindividuation was associated with a loss of inhibitions and the tendency of people to act in uncharacteristic and antinormative ways. From a historical perspective, persons have only slowly escaped from a deindividuated existence immersed in extended kinship relations, bonds, and tribes. Eric Fromm examined the emergence of individuality in human history and the sense of uniqueness and freedom that accompanied this development. According to Fromm, individuation is accompanied by a feeling of isolation, which often motivates people to join various groups.

Festinger, Pepitone, and Newcomb proposed that the person's focus on the group, which is associated with his or her attraction to the group, lessens the attention given to individuals. The focus on the group deindividuates its members, who are submerged and in a sense are morally hidden in the group. Deindividuation therefore lowers the person's inhibitions toward engaging in counternormative actions. Thus, according to this formulation, attraction to a group increases deindividuation, which in turn encourages behavior that is normally inhibited.

Ziller suggested that persons learn to associate individuation with rewarding situations and deindividuation with potentially punishing ones. A person learns to expect rewards for performing certain tasks well and wants to appear uniquely responsible for such actions. However, whenever the person expects punishment, there will be a tendency to hide or diffuse responsibility by submerging him- or herself into a group.

Zimbardo proposed that a large number of factors may lead to deindividuation, in addition to focus on the group or desire to avoid negative evaluation of moral responsibility. Among the deindividuating factors are anonymity (however created), the size of the group, level of emotional arousal, the novelty of ambiguity of the situation, altered time perspectives (e.g., when using drugs or alcohol), degree of involvement in group activities, and so on.

All these factors lead to a loss of identity or self-consciousness, which in turn causes the individual to become unresponsive to external stimuli and to lose cognitive control over emotions and motivations. The result is behavior that is usually under internal constraint, whether positive (love) or negative (aggression). The deindividuated person is less compliant to positive or negative sanctions from agents outside the group, hence behavior is less apt to conform to external rules and standards.

Diener offered a further theoretical modification by associating deindividuation with self-awareness. Persons who are deindividuated do not attend to their own behavior and lack awareness of themselves as distinct entities. The result is a failure to monitor or reflect upon one's own behavior, and a failure to retrieve appropriate norms of conduct from storage in long-term memory. Deindividuated persons also lack foresight and their behavior lacks premeditation or planning.

A rather wide scope of antinormative behaviors have been associated with individuation and deindividuation.

CONFORMING PERSONALITY
INDIVIDUALISM
NONCONFORMING PERSONALITY

J. T. TEDESCHI

DELIRIUM TREMENS

Delirium tremens (DTs) is an acute psychotic reaction associated with chronic alcohol abuse and characterized by a coarse tremor, acute anxiety, and agitation. It is a substance-induced disorder resulting from a disturbed metabolic state that causes an acute brain syndrome. It was once thought to be the result of alcohol withdrawal alone. However, delirium tremens may occur in a chronic alcoholic not only during withdrawal, but also following periods of prolonged heavy drinking or subsequent to a head injury or infection.

Typically, the delirium is preceded by a period of increasing restlessness, apprehension, irritability, and disturbed sleep. In its full-blown form, the person in DTs becomes confused and disoriented regarding time and place. Vivid visual and tactile hallucinations are common, particularly of small, threatening insects and animals. The patient's mood is one of fear and agitation, making sleep impossible. There are coarse tremors of the hands, lips, and tongue, from which the name delirium tremens derives. Physically, the person's speech is indistinct, heart rate is rapid and weak, he or she perspires freely, and epileptic seizures may occur.

Delirium tremens lasts from 3 to 10 days and represents a life-threatening condition. Without medical attention and proper precautions, the death rate from DTs as a result of heart failure, convulsions, hypoglycemic coma, and other complications may run as high as 15 to 25%. Minor tranquilizers such as Librium and Vistaril can significantly alleviate the agitation, anxiety, and gross, generalized tremors that accompany DTs.

Once the delirium resolves, the patient drifts into a prolonged, deep sleep. When the individual awakes, consciousness is clearer and there are few residual symptoms.

SUBSTANCE ABUSE

G. J. CHELUNE

DELUSIONAL DISORDERS

Delusions are generally regarded to be symptoms of disturbance of thought content. Kaplan and Sadock describe delusions as false beliefs that cannot be corrected by reasoning and that are not consistent with an individual's intelligence and cultural background. Historically, delusions are mentioned in ancient biblical texts and Chinese medical texts. In both instances, the contents of thoughts of individuals were considered as signals of mental disturbance. Delusions are distinguished from unconventional thinking, wishful thinking, or unpopular political beliefs. At various times, diagnosing delusion has been a political event wherein an individual expressing a culturally or politically deviant view has been considered delusional. Delusions as symptoms of mental disorder generally are based on peculiar logic, or clearly improbable sensory or somatic experiences. Faulty logic and lack of probability gives delusions their unique features.

A complete classification of delusions has not been formally attempted. However, many types of delusional thinking have been described and named as in the following listing (*DSM-IV*, 1994). There is the bizarre delusion that all people wearing red carry a certain secret message conveyed by some deity. There is the mood-congruent delusion, such as the untrue belief of a depressed person that he or she has committed a terrible crime. The nihilistic delusion is that the self, others, or the work is nonexistent. An erotomania delusion is the belief that a person, usually of higher status, is in love with the subject. Wealthy individuals may falsely believe in the disappearance of their possessions. Somatic delusions involve false beliefs about bodily functions—that one's brain is pulp, that one's lungs and stomach are gone, that one does not have a right or left side, and so forth. The well-known delusion of grandeur is an exaggerated conception of one's own importance or a self-identity as someone greater or more powerful—such as God or the president. Individuals suffering from delusions of persecution assume that outside forces persecute or injure them. A delusion of reference is the false belief that one is being talked about by others in a derogatory manner. There are delusions of remorse for imagined crimes, of being controlled by others, that one's lover or mate is unfaithful, and so on.

Arieti has pointed out that delusions may be fragmented or loosely organized or highly systematized and well developed. Loosely organized delusions may occur in recent onset conditions, associated with toxic or somatic disturbance, as well as in chronic deteriorating mental and physical illnesses. Systematized delusions may occur in paranoid patients, leaving the individual more cognitively intact in other areas.

The incidence of delusions is often difficult to assess because of reticence of clients to admit delusions in professional interviews. Examiners' tendencies to view people who reconstruct reality in the form of fiction as cranks also leads to a failure of delusional individuals to come to official attention, especially in rural communities. In a review by Morriss, Rovner, Folstein, and German of 125 patients newly admitted to nursing homes, 21% were assessed as delusional. Westermeyer, Lyfoung, Wahmenholm, and Westermeyer reported shared delusions of "fatal contagion" encountered in approximately 10% of refugee psychiatric patients belonging to the Hmong ethnic group from Southeast Asia.

According to the *DSM-IV*, delusions are the primary feature of a distinctively paranoid delusional disorder. Delusions may occur as secondary or associated features in major depression with psychotic features, bipolar disorder, brief reactive psychosis, cannabis delusional disorder, hallucinogen delusional disorder, induced psychotic disorder, inhalant intoxication, multiinfarct dementia with depression, narcissistic personality disorder, opioid intoxication, organic delusional syndrome, phencyclidine (PCP) delusional disorder, primary degenerative dementia of the Alzheimer type, schizoaffective disorders, schizophrenia, and schizophreniform disorder. The age of onset of the delusional paranoid disorder generally ranges from 35 to 45, and there are conflicting data on the sex ratio incidence. Both the onset and course are influenced by the overall course of the disorder in which they are embedded. There may be a higher rate of improvement in the relatively brief drug-induced syndromes but a lower rate of improvement in the chronic debilitating syndromes.

In Denmark, in one 4-year follow-up study of 88 first-admitted patients with delusional psychosis, only 25% of the patients remitted fully. In Norway, a sample of 72 first-admitted patients with delusional disorder who were followed for a mean of 10 years, showed that the duration of symptoms before admission was a significant predictor of outcome. A minimum duration of 6 months has been proposed for a diagnosis of persistent delusional disorder.

ETIOLOGY AND MECHANISMS OF ACTION

The etiology of delusional disorders is not precisely known. Psychological, psychobiological, and biologic theories have been offered to explain their origin. Day and Manchreck assert that many factors may form important roles in the development of the vulnerability to delusional disorders. Such factors as parental strife, frustrated instinctual needs, insufficient or excessive perceptual stimulation, and faulty intrapsychic maneuvers of the child to deal with stress predispose children to develop either positive or negative fantasies of omnipotence. Although Freud considered, denied, and projected homosexual fantasies of the paranoid delusional patient as causes, subsequent psychoanalytic thinkers have focused on a variety of Oedipal and pre-Oedipal stress-inducing experiences. Beck has identified severe cognitive misinterpretations in delusional disturbances of severely depressed patients. These misinterpretations were thought to fuel the depressive processes. In one study reported by Bental, Kaney, and Dewey, deluded depressed British patients were found to make excessively negative person attributions as the causes of negative events and were excessively certain about their judgments compared with depressed nondelusional controls.

According to psychobiological theory, delusions are the results of anomalous perceptual experience. The source of the difficulty may be the existing environment, the central nervous system, or the sensory apparatus. Delusions develop in response to changes in perception that demand explanation by the individual. Thus, delusions inform the patient about why things are happening, and the relief provided by these explanations fosters their perpetuation.

Physiological theory has drawn its impetus from the clinical findings of specific organic syndromes with associated delusions. Describing a case of pathological jealousy in a patient with Parkinson's disease, McNamara and Durso noted that symptom relief followed the discontinuation of amantadine, suggesting the link between this delusion and dopaminergic activity. Abruptly appearing and short-lasting delusions of substitution developed in a chronic paranoid schizophrenic with the acute onset of diabetes mellitus, suggesting the possibility of a known organic contributor. In 17 patients with Alzheimer's disease, the presence of delusions was associated with greater cerebral dysfunction and a focal neuropsychological defect as manifested in a significantly greater proportion of abnormal EEG patterns. Seizure disorder has been suggested as an associated physiological finding in a case of lycanthropy.

TREATMENT

Treatment of delusional disorders has spanned both the psychological and neurophysiological approaches. Psychoanalytic approaches tend to stress the unraveling of emotional issues and conflicts contributing to emotional impasses. One proposal is the analysis of the symbolic meaning of the delusion and its function in the conflicted psyche of the individual. Day and Manschreck stressed the importance of the therapist not becoming preoccupied with the details of the patient's delusional system, rather focusing more on interpersonal relationships and frustrations. Denial, projection, and contradiction are to be identified and faced by the patient

throughout the course of treatment. The client's misery is thereby exposed and fears of dread and loss and insult by the therapist are disclosed. Skillful timing of the therapist's interpretations is necessary for clients to either accept or critically evaluate the offered hypotheses without unproductive defensiveness. Patients must be encouraged to make amends with relatives or others whom they might have insulted or otherwise damaged by their false belief-induced behaviors.

Successful cognitive-behavioral treatment of delusions was accomplished in five out of six diagnosed schizophrenic patients by means of the specific interventions of a structured verbal challenge and by a "reality test" in which the beliefs were subject to an empirical test.

When the cause of the delusion was a reaction to a certain medication, successful treatment was accomplished by the withdrawal of the medication. Treatment of delusional patients with medications is sometimes difficult because patients may deny the psychological disorder. Furthermore, their sensitivity to side effects may block their compliance. Side effects should be explained to patients so as to minimize this difficulty. Delusional disorders are responsive to antipsychotic medications.

Frequently, delusional disorder patients can be effectively treated as outpatients. Nevertheless, hospitalization and even legal commitment may be required in cases of potentially suicidal or dangerous behavior.

ANTIANXIETY DRUGS
BRAIN INJURIES
COGNITIVE COMPLEXITY
DELIRIUM TREMENS
FUNDAMENTAL ATTRIBUTION ERROR
HALLUCINATIONS
HYPOTHETICODEDUCTIVE REASONING
MEMORY DISORDERS
MENTAL ILLNESS: EARLY HISTORY
PSEUDODEMENTIA
UNCONSCIOUS MOTIVATION

J. W. KOFF

DEMENTIA

Once considered an almost inevitable hallmark of normal aging, it is now recognized that senile dementia is an insidious disease process affecting memory, cognition, orientation, and eventually the ability for self-care. It is clear that normal aging does not necessarily result in senility. However, for individuals 65 and older, an estimated 5 to 10% of the population will demonstrate the irreversable symptoms of this primary degenerative disease of the brain.

There are many etiological factors associated with dementia. The most frequent include infections of the central nervous systems, brain trauma, various neurological diseases, cerebrovascular disease, and toxic-metabolic disorders. Although the symptoms are most common among the aged population, they can occur in children suffering from neurological disorders associated with dementia (e.g., Huntington's Chorea).

The two most common forms of dementia are related to Alzheimer's disease (AD) and cerebrovascular disease. The dementia associated with cerebrovascular disease is sometimes referred to as multiinfarct dementia. Both of these disease processes affect the cerebral cortex. Other dementing illnesses may be related to the degeneration of various subcortical structures. Clinically, the patient with dementia may first present marked behavioral changes that proceed the later manifestation of memory and intellectual deterioration. Joynt and Shoulson suggested three behavioral syndromes. First, normal behavioral traits may be accentuated to the point of eccentricity. Second, resistance may occur in response to novel social situations. Finally, mentally fatiguing operations may become impaired, resulting in more distractible behavior.

Intellectual changes and associated memory deterioration are characteristic of dementia. Memory for recent events or future appointments is generally one of the first areas in which problems are reported. Depression may complicate the difficulty in memory. Also, orientation may quickly become involved: It is not uncommon for the patient to become lost while walking around the block.

Although the intellectual deterioration over the typical 3- to 8-year course of the disease can be quite striking, automatic behavior such as walking, eating, and even smoking may not be affected until late in the disease process. In the final stages of the disease the patient may be mute, incapable of self-care, unable to recognize loved ones, and highly distractible. Death typically occurs from intercurrent illness.

Multiinfarct dementia is conceptualized as a distinctly different type of dementia according to the American Psychiatric Association, because its etiology is known to be due to cerebrovascular infarcts. The progression of the focal signs of the dementia is not slow as in AD, but manifests itself in a stepwise fashion. The onset of the symptoms may be abrupt, with focal neurological signs evident. Cerebrovascular disease is also present. The pattern of neuropsychological deficits is unique in each case because the dementia symptoms appear only as a result of each circumscribed infarct. Unlike AD or many of the subcortical dementing diseases, the course of multiinfarct dementia is erratic, depending on the cerebrovascular pathology.

Morphologically, dementia affecting the cortical structures is characterized by dilation of the ventricles as evidenced on computed tomography (CT) scans. Prominent cortical atrophy is most noticeable in the region of the temporal and frontal cortex. Senile plaques and neurofibrillary tangles are evident in the brain.

Dementia is often difficult to diagnose because of the insidious onset and relatively long-term course. Multiinfarct dementia is somewhat easier to identify, owing to its unique clinical and cerebrovascular pathology.

The most common and accurate means of clinical diagnosis remains based on data obtained from the neurological and neuropsychological examination. Francis Pirozzolo and Kathryn Lawson-Kerr suggested that, in addition to the traditional neurological examination incorporating a mental status assessment, the neuropsychological examination should include tests of intelligence, logical memory, paired associate learning, object naming, personality, visual discrimination, spatial reasoning and orientation, perceptual-cognitive speed, measures of right- versus left-sided performance, and language capabilities. Since symptoms associated with agnosia, apraxia, and aphasia will be evident in later stages of the disease, it is important to assess these functions so as to form a baseline against which to measure future performance.

Dementia due to cerebrovascular disease, normal pressure hydrocephalus, and psychogenic (pseudodementia) factors may be treatable. However, the medical treatment of most other dementias including AD, Pick's disease, progressive supranuclear palsy, and Parkinson's disease has not generally been successful in arresting the course of the disease. Pharmacological intervention has typically aimed at lessening the symptoms associated with progressive decline. Counseling and the development of support networks for the family are probably the most productive forms of intervention from a psychological standpoint.

AGING: BEHAVIOR CHANGES
ALZHEIMER'S DISEASE
BRAIN
COMPUTED TOMOGRAPHY
HUNTINGTON'S CHOREA
ORGANIC BRAIN SYNDROMES

G. W. HYND

DEPENDENCY

Dependency is the seeking of identity, support, security, and/or permission from outside the self. The dependency object may be another person; a social unit such as an extended family or a religious or fraternal order; an entity beyond the five senses such as a spirit guardian; or even a belief system in itself as for example nonviolence, to which the dependent is devoted and from which the dependent receives nurture in return.

By definition, dependency is reciprocal. The dependent seeks, expecting and receiving a dependency response: To give is to receive and to receive is to give. It is also obligatory: Dependents are *expected* to seek and receive return support. Failure to participate in this circle of obligation may result in a range of responses from verbal disapproval to ostracism.

Dependency differs from the related process of interdependence in which separate entities reciprocally seek identity, support, security, and/or permission from one another.

In "dependency societies," such as Japan, the fledgling ego is taught to defer inside a vertical authority system. The ideal of conformity is intended to strengthen the individual's sense of self-respect. In "independence societies" such as modern mainstream America, the fledgling ego is expected to move out of obligatory relationships in a horizontal authority system, rather than to defer. The ideal of self-focus is intended to strengthen the individual's sense of self-respect.

Key characteristics of dependency are bonding, obligation, reciprocity, trust, continuity, and involvement. Every culture or subculture defines "normal" dependency on the basis of its own value system.

While Western thought minimizes continuity between the living and ancestors, dependency cultures tend to consider discontinuity as threatening.

Even though there are cultural variations, there seem also to be certain universals in dependency. Key characteristics fall into three clusters.

The first cluster may be viewed as "negative" dependency, which hinders psychosexual development, crippling the ability to handle a variety of life situations. The second cluster can be considered "positive," enhancing the maturing process by aiding individuals and groups to function in ways that support their sense of well being. The third cluster relates to an absence or termination of dependency relationships, which may also cripple development.

It is useful to divide dependency theory into three "culture-time" phases: (a) preliterate, tribal, and folk (beginning to present); (b) modern colonial (1500–1945); and (c) postcolonial (1945 to present).

PRELITERATE, TRIBAL, AND FOLK STUDIES

Early ethnological studies tended to view dependency as structural networking based on tribal, village, folk, and extended family patterns that were seen, on the whole, as positive. They were thought to reflect security and other needs in a life setting severely limited by a prescientific world view and technical development.

In such a society individuals define themselves or are defined as they relate to others, rather than by how they fulfill or express themselves. Success in these interactions is considered the most important measure of mature self-expression.

MODERN COLONIAL

The interruption of traditional dependency patterns has been a major and often underestimated effect of colonial contact since the fifteenth century. As Mannoni has shown, a major factor in the conquest of native peoples was their own tendency to transfer dependency expectations from familiar authority figures to European authority substitutes.

Aggressive European cultures exploited native dependency while at the same time exporting values of independence, individualism, and progress, which did as much to weaken native resistance as the horses of

Cortez or the firearms of the British. With its emphasis on competition, the Protestant work ethic dealt a heavy psychological blow to traditional notions of reciprocity, obligation, and trust. Under long-term colonization the native personality is thought to have been severely stressed by the need to reconcile warring dependency belief systems.

During this same period in the Western world, dependency appears to have been systematically downgraded to "neurotic behavior." Sigmund Freud theorized that the helplessness of the infant was the source of life-long dependency bonds against which the maturing ego must implacably struggle.

Furthermore, Freud held that the psychological structures and functions of societies paralleled those of individuals. In modern thought—strongly influenced by Freudian theory—individuals must struggle to break free from dependence on groups as well as from a variety of others, beginning with Mother. What had earlier been seen as reciprocity came to be regarded as helplessness.

POSTCOLONIAL

In the Western world since about 1945, the belief has begun to emerge that undue stress on independence, change, and competition has contributed to massive alienation, anomie, and even morbidity rates. One response has been a trend toward the reinterpretation of dependency, as seen in a variety of recent developments. Carl Rogers, through his work on group dynamics, has encouraged a variety of lay and professional approaches that stress dependency interaction. More recently, "networking" has become a major drive among persons who recognize their need to relate to other individuals, especially in urban settings.

Another dependency development is affiliated families, in which non-blood kin members of two or three generations pool their needs and resources in a common dwelling or at least in the same community.

AFFILIATION NEED
ALIENATION (POLITICAL)
BONDING AND ATTACHMENT
CROSS-CULTURAL PSYCHOLOGY
PROSOCIAL BEHAVIOR

J. GURIAN

DEPENDENT PERSONALITY

Giving the disorder the status of a separate and major disorder, *DSM-IV* includes as its central feature behavior such as passively allowing others to take full responsibility for one's significant life activities, a characteristic traceable to the person's lack of self-confidence and to doubts concerning the ability to function independently.

Notable also is a willingness to subordinate one's needs to those of others on whom one is dependent, so as to avoid having to assume independent and self-reliant roles. Self-belittling and lacking in initiative, these patients hesitate to make direct demands of those on whom they depend, lest they jeopardize the security achieved. Many exhibit a social naiveté that is made tolerable, if not pleasing, by virtue of their genuinely obliging and friendly temperament. Appeasing and conciliatory submission to others is also a common trait, as is a conspicuous and often troublesome clinging to supportive persons.

Emil Kraepelin stressed the "irresoluteness of will" of these patients, and the ease with which they could be "seduced" by others. Psychoanalytic formulations of patients such as these were described in accord with psychosexual stage theory: They were identified as "oral" types.

Utilizing a biosocial-learning theory to deduce personality types, Theodore Millon lists the following diagnostic criteria for patients of this character.

1. Pacific temperament (e.g., is characteristically docile and noncompetitive; avoids social tension and interpersonal conflicts)

2. Interpersonal submissiveness (e.g., needs a stronger, nurturing figure, and without this one feels anxiously helpless; is often conciliatory, placating, and self-sacrificing)

3. Inadequate self-image (e.g., perceives self as weak, fragile, and ineffectual; exhibits lack of confidence by belittling own aptitudes and competencies)

4. Pollyanna cognitive style (e.g., reveals a naive or benign attitude toward interpersonal difficulties; smooths over troubling events)

5. Initiative deficit (e.g., prefers a subdued, uneventful, and passive lifestyle; avoids self-assertion and refuses autonomous responsibilities)

DEPENDENCY
PERSONALITY TYPES

T. MILLON

DEPENDENT VARIABLES

In research, the dependent variable is the attribute or performance being measured to determine the effect of manipulating an independent variable. The dependent variable may involve behavioral, physiological, or social characteristics depending on the nature of the study.

Selection of an appropriate dependent variable is vitally important to the outcome and interpretation of an investigation. Several matters should be considered in determining the appropriateness of the dependent variable selected. The first concern is that a dependent measure should reflect the construct being studied. Generally, a researcher will select the most sensitive and reliable dependent variable possible. The only circumstances when this rule of thumb is not appropriate is when such a measure is obtrusive, that is, when the act of obtaining the measure alters a subject's performance. Thus, the measure of choice is one that is maximally sensitive, reliable, and unobtrusive. Another consideration related to selection of a dependent variable involves avoiding ceiling or floor effects in the data. A ceiling effect occurs when the performance range of the task is limited so that subjects "top out." A floor effect reflects a task so difficult that many subjects cannot perform the task at all. Ceiling and floor effects provide artificial results and measure the limits of the task rather than subjects' ability to perform.

RESEARCH METHODOLOGY

C. J. DREW

DEPRESSION

THE CONCEPT OF DEPRESSION

Depression is a term used to describe a mood, a symptom, and syndromes of affective disorders. As a mood, it refers to a transient state of feeling sad, blue, forlorn, cheerless, unhappy, and/or down. As a symptom, it refers to a complaint that often accompanies a group of biopsychosocial problems. In contrast, the depressive syndromes include a wide spectrum of psychobiological dysfunctions that vary in frequency, severity, and duration. Normal depression is a transient period of sadness and fatigue that generally occurs in response to identifiable stressful life events. The moods associated with normal depression vary in length but generally do not exceed 7 to 10 days. If the problems continue for a longer period and if the symptoms grow in complexity and severity, clinical levels of depression may be present. Clinical depression generally involves sleep disorders, eating disorders, anergia, hopelessness, and despair. Sometimes problems assume psychotic proportions, and the depressed individual may attempt suicide and/or may experience hallucinations, delusions, and serious psychological and motor retardation.

CLASSIFICATION ALTERNATIVES

Through the years, a number of competing classification systems of depression have evolved based on the theoretical predilections and orientations of theorists and clinicians. These systems emphasize unitary, dualistic, and pluralistic classification and diagnostic assumptions. The unitary approach claims that there is basically one type of depression that varies in terms of severity. Within this framework, depression can be classified as mild, moderate, or severe. This viewpoint enjoys only limited popularity.

The dualistic approach assumes that there are two types of depression, including those that have clear psychological etiologies, short-term courses, and relatively benign outcomes and those with biological etiologies, long-term courses, and relatively poor outcomes. Among the dualistic patterns are reactive versus autonomous, neurotic versus psychotic, exogenous versus endogenous, and justified versus somatic depressions.

Pluralistic systems of classification include many types of depressive disorders. Grinker et al. proposed four types of depressive disorders based on a factor analysis of behaviors, moods, and responses to treatment. These types included angry depression, empty depression, anxious depression, and hypochondriacal depression. The American Psychiatric Association's *Diagnostic and statistical manual, fourth edition* (*DSM-IV*) (1994), also supports a pluralistic view of depressive disorders. As the official classification system for legal and medical purposes in the United States, the *DSM*-IV is an important system to understand.

EPIDEMIOLOGY OF DEPRESSION

There have been numerous epidemiologic studies of depression; however, differences in case definition, identification, and contact have resulted in considerable variations in the rates of reported depression. One study conducted on a sample of 18.5 million civilian noninstitutionalized people in the United States by the National Center for Health Statistics in 1981, using a 20-item depression symptom checklist, found that depression symptoms were higher among women, African-Americans, separated or divorced people, individuals with less than a high school education, and individuals earning less than $5000 per year. However, many of these statuses are correlated (i.e., there are more poor uneducated African-Americans). Nevertheless, the results point out the positive relationship between depression and certain social statuses exposed to higher life stresses.

EARLY DEVELOPMENTS

The history of depressive disorders can be traced to ancient Greece when Hippocrates (ca. 330 B.C.) distinguished among three types of disorders: mania, melancholia, and phrenitis (mental confusion and delirium). This was followed by the contributions of Aretaeus of Cappodocia who viewed melancholia and mania as expressions of one illness and as extensions of normal personality. He wrote extensively of the personalities of the manic and the melancholic. The latter term embraced many disorders in which depression was only one aspect. In 1621, Robert Burton, an Englishman, published a book on melancholia that has remained a classic on this topic: *The anatomy of melancholia*. In 1684, the French physician Theophile Bonet, proposed the term *folie maniaco-melancholique*. This was the first time someone coined a medical diagnosis for what today is called bipolar disease (manic–depressive disorder).

The pursuit of refinement in the diagnosis of depression was continued by Francois Bossier de Sauvage, who published a nosological system that included 14 subtypes of melancholy. Bonet's ideas were further developed

by Jean Pierre Falret. In 1854, he published a paper titled *De le folie circulaire* in which the separate experiences of mania and depression were acknowledged to be a single disease. At the same time, Jean Baillarger coined the term *folie a double forme* in 1853. Finally, Emil Kraepelin made a notable contribution by recommending the separation of dementia praecox from manic–depressive psychosis in 1899. In 1905, he suggested the term *involutional melancholia* as a diagnosis for a pattern of depression experienced during middle age. In subsequent years, there were many additional developments regarding the classification, etiology, and treatment of depressive disorders. However, the early history offers a context for understanding the extent to which this problem has been a topic of concern and debate throughout history.

THEORIES OF DEPRESSION

Biological Theories

Genetics. Largely because of diagnostic limitations, there has been little progress in the study of genetic contributions to depressive disorders. The inability to rigorously categorize the many forms of depressive experience have made it impossible to apply behavior genetic strategies (i.e., pedigree studies, twin studies, and adoption studies). However, research on bipolar disorders has been more successful because of the clarity of the diagnostic criteria. Twin studies and adoption indicate that genetics appears to be a major factor in the development of bipolar depressive disorders.

However, to date, there is little evidence to indicate whether the inheritance is based on a single gene (monogenic) or many genes (polygenic). One study of Amish people reported that a predisposition to bipolar affective disorders may be governed by a dominant gene at the tip of the short arm of chromosome 11. However, this study was criticized extensively, and a follow-up study by the same authors did not support this conclusion. Other researchers have suggested that single-gene views of affective disorder lack support. An evolving view on the genetics of depressive disorders, the stress diasthesis theory, assumes that a genetic predisposition may interact with stressful life events to produce depressive disorders.

Biochemistry

Neurotransmitter Theory. Many neurotransmitters have been implicated in the onset and course of depressive disorders. The largest group are the monoamines: epinephrine, norepinephrine, serotonin, dopamine, and acetylcholine.

At first it was believed that a deficit in norepinephrine (NE) was the primary cause of depressive disorders. This was supported by the findings that certain antidepressant medications (monoamine oxidase inhibitors and tricyclics) effected the levels of epinephrine in the neurosynapse. However, subsequent research indicated that although monoamine oxidase (MAO) inhibitors and tricyclics do increase NE and serotonin when first taken, the NE and serotonin levels return to previous levels within a few days. Because tricyclics and MAO inhibitors take 7 to 14 days to reduce depression, something else is operating. It has been suggested that antidepressants may alter sensitivity of postsynaptic neural receptors by reducing sensitivity of β-adrenergic receptors while increasing sensitivity of serotonin receptors. New antidepressant medications (e.g., Prozac, Zoloft) that function by increasing levels of serotonin in the neural synaptic cleft are proving effective for some types of depressive disorders. This view is consistent with the belief that serotonin deficits may be partially responsible for certain types of depressive disorders.

However, experiences with antidepressant medications generally point to the fact that different neurotransmitter deficits may be associated with different types of depression. Some depression may be caused by serotonin deficits and others by norepinephrine deficits. Indeed, it also may be that these deficits are associated with different stages in a depressive process.

Neuroenzyme, Endogenous Opiates, and Neuropeptide Theories. More recent biochemical theories of depression assume that neuroenzymes such as monoamine oxidase, acetylcholinesterase, and ATPase may be implicated. Still other theories emphasize the role of endogenous opiates and/or neuropeptides (chains of amino acids that include leuenkephalin, metenkephalin, and β-endorphins) and prostaglandins.

Electrolyte Metabolism Theories. One of the oldest biological theories of depressive disorders is that they are caused by disorders in the balance or concentration of certain electrolytes (i.e., electrically charged ions such as sodium, potassium, calcium, and chloride) in the cell. These ions play an important role in a cell's electrochemical transmission properties via the sodium–potassium pump.

In nerve cells, there is a higher concentration of potassium ions inside the cell and a higher concentration of sodium ions outside the cell. When these ions are in balance, the cell is at rest. However, when the cell is stimulated, the resting potential is altered as the neuron enters a state of excitability that requires changes in the ionization balance that lead to a nerve impulse. It has been suggested that in depressed people, there is more intracellular sodium. As a result, a smaller stimulus is required creating a chronic state of cellular activity that may be related to the fatigue and anergia associated with depression. In addition to possible dysfunctions with the sodium–potassium pump, research has also suggested that calcium, magnesium, and phosphate metabolism may be implicated in bipolar depression.

Neuroendocrinological Theories. Neuroendocrinological theories of depressive disorders are based on anatomic and physiological dysfunctions in the hypothalamic–pituitary–adrenal axis that is the basis of the human response to stress. For example, it is known that when an organism is under stress, the hypothalamus releases a corticotropic hormone (CRH) that controls the release of adrenocorticotropic hormone (ACTH) by the adrenal glands. ACTH stimulates the adrenal cortex to release two principal types of hormones or corticosteroids: mineralocorticoids and glucocorticoids. The principal mineralocorticoid is aldosterone, a substance that helps control electrolytes in extracellular fluids, while the principal glucocorticoid is cortisol (hydrocortisone), a substance that has an impact on the immune system. Cortisol chemistry may be related to depression. Recently, it has been learned that CRH secretion is responsive to serotonin and norepinephrine concentrations. Thus, there appears to be a complex linkage between neurotransmitters, neurohormones, and stressful life events that may lead to the onset and/or maintenance of depressive disorders.

Recent research has demonstrated adrenal gland hypertrophy (i.e., enlargement) in seriously depressed individuals. It is believed that the enlargement is a function of chronic corticotropin hypersecretion (i.e., hypercortisolemia) rather than adrenocortical sensitivity.

Light Cycles (The Pineal Body and Melatonin). A recent discovery has been that some people develop depressive disorders in response to exposure to seasonal variations in sunlight and darkness. This kind of depression has been termed seasonal affective disorder (SAD). Deprivation of sunlight among people in northern climates affects melatonin, a substance secreted by the pineal body. Researchers have found that if they expose some depressed people with SAD to bright light for extended periods of time during the winter seasons, the depression will disappear. The exact link between the melatonin secretion and the onset of SAD has not been identified.

Psychobehavioral Theories

Cognitive Behavioral Theories

Learned Helplessness. The idea of learned helplessness as an element of depression was advanced by Martin Seligman, based on his research on avoidance learning in animals. Seligman found that animals trapped in situations in which they can no longer escape harm or punishment become unresponsive or "helpless." Seligman found that this response pattern resembled depression in many respects and coined the term *learned helplessness* to describe the phenomenon. Learned helplessness may be more than an analogue for human beings, because it accurately describes what occurs when humans find themselves in circumstances in which their behavior cannot alter adverse environmental events, thus leading to resignation, hopelessness, and passivity. It is assumed that this pattern may eventfully lead to enduring deficits in neurotransmitters and hormones that are related to the onset and maintenance of depressive disorders.

Cognitive Construction of Self and Reality. The theory posited by psychiatrist Aaron Beck was based on his research on the relationship between thought and affect in human beings. Beck and co-workers suggested that errors in thinking cause depression. He noted that depressed people seem to hold a *negative triad* of beliefs that include (a) a view of self as unworthy and deficient, (b) a view of the world as cruel and aversive, and (c) a hopeless view of the future. This negative triad of beliefs lead to cognitive distortions in the depressed patient including problems such as (a) arbitrary influence, a conclusion drawn in absence of sufficient information; (b) selective abstraction, a conclusion drawn on the basis of but one of many elements; (c) overgeneralization, an overall sweeping conclusion, drawn on the basis of a single, perhaps trivial event; and (d) magnification and minimalization, or gross errors in evaluating performance.

For Beck, depression causes errors in thinking, and thinking can cause depression. The relationship is complex, and the causal directions are not clear. It may be that Beck's view describes what occurs once a person suffers from depression, but may not be the mechanism by which depression develops. However, it is conceivable that faulty thinking can shape behavior in such a way as to lead to certain types of depressive experiences. More research is needed on the role of faulty thinking in both the etiology and maintenance of depressive disorders.

Response Contingent Positive Reinforcement Theory. The response contingent positive reinforcement (RECONPOSRE) theory of depression was developed by Lewinsohn who theorized that individuals develop depression because they receive inadequate amounts of positive reinforcement. This may occur because (a) few events are potentially reinforcing for the individual, (b) there is little positive reinforcement available in the environment, and (c) the individual lacks the social skills necessary to elicit positive reinforcement. Research on normal people supports this position. However, RECONPOSRE theory has not accounted for more severe depression states and disorders. The issue is whether being depressed leads to these behaviors or whether these behaviors lead to depression.

Psychoanalytic Theories. There are many different psychoanalytic theories of depression, depending on the views and predilections of particular theorists. One theory posits that depression emerges when there is a loss of a significant other who has been both loved and hated. The hate or anger becomes denied, and guilt emerges, resulting in self-directed hostility. Other theories trace depression to oral fixation and dependency, regression to infantile states of helplessness and insecurity, a conforming personality structure, and so on.

CROSS-CULTURAL ASPECTS

Cross-cultural studies of depression have gained increased popularity in recent years, particularly in the areas of comparative epidemiology and symptomatic expression. Epidemiological studies have suggested that depression may not occur as frequently in non-Western countries as in Western countries. However, difficulties in case determination because of cultural assessment insensitivities and communication problems limit the accuracy of many studies. Cross-cultural research has indicated that many of the symptoms associated with depression in the Western world are not necessarily part of the depressive experience in non-Western cultures, especially the symptoms of guilt, existential despair, and negative self-esteem. In contrast, it appears that non-Western people may manifest their depression via somatization. Culture also plays an important role in the treatment of depression, as it influences the assessment and diagnostic process as well as therapist and client expectations, communications, and concepts of health and normality.

A serious source of depression among ethnic minority populations in Western cultures is racism and racial oppression. Because of racism, there is a denial of opportunity, a powerlessness, and a denigration of status to sizable sectors of ethnic minority populations. Ultimately, there is an absence of reward and reinforcement systems for ethnic minorities. All of these factors fit the learned helplessness, RECONPOSRE, and cognitive theories of depression. It is clear that many of the conceptions regarding the etiology, classification, and treatment of depression may be biased and ethnocentric

THE MEASUREMENT OF DEPRESSION

The need to assess depressive disorders for clinical and research purposes has led to the development of numerous psychological and biological measures. These measures have emphasized self-report, interviewer ratings, family evaluations, and indices of biological functioning (e.g., metabolites present in cerebral spinal fluid or urine). A detailed discussion of all these methods is available.

Psychological Measures

Depression can be assessed by such self-report scales as the Beck Depression Inventory (BDI), the Zung Depression Scale (ZDS), the Depression Adjective Checklist (DACL), and subscales from the Minnesota Multiphasic Personality Inventory (MMPI). Some clinicians prefer to use projective techniques such as the Rorschach (e.g., depression indexed by few responses and low color and motion determinants) and the Thermatic Apperception Test (TAT.) Rating scales, by which mental health professions evaluate patients on a series of behavioral and psychological scales and indices, such as the Hamilton Depression Scale, the Present State Examination, and the Structured Clinical Interview also have gained popularity in recent years.

Biological Measures

Biological measures of depression, including analyses of neurochemical metabolites in urine, blood, and cerebral spinal fluid, have not proved reliable or valid in spite of extensive efforts to develop them in recent years. The focus in these measures has been to use central nervous system (CNS) neurotransmitter metabolites as indices of levels of neurotransmitters. For example, 5-hydroxyindoleacetic acid (5-HIAA) is a metabolic by-product of CNS serotonin. By examining 5-HIAA levels in cerebral spinal fluid or blood, it is possible to obtain an index of serotonergic activity and concentrations in the brain. However, these tests have proved problematic and have yet to gain widespread acceptance.

One popular biological test of depression is the dexamethasone suppression test (DMST). Dexamethasone is a glucocorticoid that suppresses cortisol secretion, which is important in the functioning of the hypothalamic–pituitary–adrenal–cortical (HPAC). It has been found that levels of cortisol are often high in depressives. When given dexamethasone overnight, some depressives failed to show suppression of cortisol. It is believed that this reflects an overactivity of the HPAC axis, a problem associated with depression. Thus, the DMST has been used to index depression in some patients. However, this test has proven controversial because research has found that a variety of factors that affect the DMST test, including diet, fatigue, medications, sleep, and allergies. Because of reliability and validity problems among biological measures, the most popular measures of depression continue to be self-report instruments and clinical rating scales.

ANTIDEPRESSIVE DRUGS
BECK DEPRESSION INVENTORY
CONVULSIVE SHOCK THERAPY
CULTURE-BOUND DISORDERS
EPIDEMIOLOGY OF MENTAL DISORDERS
HUMORAL THEORY
LEARNED HELPLESSNESS
MANIC–DEPRESSIVE PERSONALITY
NEUROCHEMISTRY
PSYCHOENDOCRINOLOGY
PSYCHOPHARMACOLOGY
STRESS

A. J. MARSELLA

DEPRIVATION EFFECTS

A baby may be already deprived at the time of birth because of prenatal conditions that may have harmed the body and nervous system, and severely limited the expression of a genetic endowment that otherwise would have exerted influence on the kind of person the infant might have become.

Research evidence supports the notions that many babies are born already irritable, with hyperactive nervous symptoms; that some are born with mental retardation because of maternal malnourishment or alcoholism; that some have to cope with withdrawal symptoms because of maternal addiction to heroin, morphine, or methadone; that some are born with mongolism because of maternal age; that some are born with cleft palates because of medication prescribed for the mother during pregnancy; and that some are born grossly defective because the mother was exposed for diagnostic purposes to massive doses of X rays during the first 2 months of pregnancy. We are just beginning to comprehend the consequences to babies of nuclear accidents and nuclear tests.

During the first year of life the child's most urgent necessity is having a close, constant relationship to the mother or her ongoing substitute. Barring starvation, disease, or actual physical injury, no other factor is so influential in every aspect of the child's future development and well-being (Spitz, 1949). Failure to establish a continuing emotional contact during the first year results in general development regression to fetal-like functioning and death. Later, such failure results in a decline in developmental quotient; failure to develop control of bodily functions; lowered development of intelligence, memory, and ability to imitate; increase in general apathy; and for many, death. In his 5-year study of institution-raised children, 37% of Spitz's foundling-home children were dead before the second year of the study. One of the most profound impairments of children deprived of a close, continuing, interactive contact with their ongoing caretaker was in the social-emotional area, in their inability to form relationships with others. Their shallowness of feeling, their lack of emotional responsiveness, their impaired speech development, and their difficulty in obeying rules or making friends have been observed.

Many children are living with biological parents who fail to perform the mothering function. In Haimowitz's study of children brought to a hospital for a diagnosis known as failure-to-thrive syndrome, one third were diagnosed as having problems that were primarily emotional, caused by a subtle breakdown in the mothering function.

Harry Harlow's studies with infant macaque monkeys showed that presence and availability were the important features in maternal behavior. Harlow's baby monkeys, raised by inanimate, "surrogate mothers" made of terry cloth, appeared to be healthy and happy; however, when placed with other monkeys, they exhibited no normal social or sexual behavior. Those who were successfully impregnated, after great difficulty in mating, exhibited grossly abnormal maternal behavior ranging from indifference to the neonate to outright abuse.

Absence of maternal warmth brings serious consequences. Sears, Maccoby, and Levin reported that deprivation of maternal warmth was associated with the development of feeding problems or its alternative symptom, bed wetting.

People need contact and intimacy all through life. On the basis of peoples' need to be talked to, listened to, touched, and have their recognition hunger satisfied—Eric Berne developed his concept of *strokes*—"any act implying recognition of another's presence." Berne believed that to be ignored is to perish: Those who live stroke-starved lives will soon be crazy or dead.

Laboratory studies in which adults are deprived of all stimulation resulted in hallucinatory episodes. Furthermore, in instances of prolonged insufficient stimulation, degenerative changes in nerve cells follow inactivity of the reticular activating system of the brain. People need to be doing something. People need a sense of trust and safety, some of which is archaic, being established early in the first year of life. Where such a level of trust is impaired, the consequences are often naggingly persistent disruption of close and lasting relationships throughout one's life.

In the absence of self-esteem, the inevitable disappointments of life are interpreted as confirmation of inferiority and just punishment for inadequacy. The result may be violent antisocial behavior or what may be more common—an intense self-aggrandizing need for superiority and for accomplishments. Human infants, more helpless at birth and more physically underdeveloped than most other neonate mammals, are typically born as a litter of one depending on a caretaker for survival. Consequently, we experience a vulnerability that leaves its mark on the entire course of our lives.

AFFECTIVE DEVELOPMENT
MATERNAL DEPRIVATION

N. R. HAIMOWITZ

DEPROGRAMMING

J. Clark defined extremist religious cults as being characterized by the following: (a) wealthy living leaders who consider themselves to be messiahs or to possess special powers, (b) philosophies based on a system of dogmatic and absolutist beliefs, (c) a totalitarian system of governance, (d) requirements to obey group regulations without question, (e) a strong emphasis on acquiring wealth for the cult, and (f) little concern for the welfare of the individual cult member.

Potential converts are rarely made aware of these characteristics, but are usually given information quite different or even in direct opposition to what actually takes place. M. Singer and R. J. Lifton claim that once recruits are drawn far enough into a cult to be affected by group pressure, they are subjected to brainwashing strategies.

The end product of the indoctrination process is simplistic and stereotyped thought. As in hypnotic states, thought content is controlled largely from without rather than from within, resulting in blind obedience to the cult leader.

Comprehensive personality change can be effected by extremist religious cults within a few days to a few weeks, while J. Clark reported that after 4 to 7 years of cult life such changes may be irreversible.

Deprogramming consists of the facilitation of critical, flexible, creative, and independent thinking, and the correction of misconceptions about cult life. This is accomplished by encouraging the cult member to examine the cult ideology in the light of logic and empirical data. This examination can be catalyzed through a series of leading questions whereby the recruit is guided toward a systematic examination of issues on the basis of data available through his or her own life experience.

Straightforward filling of information gaps is also useful. For example, recruits may not know the true identity of the group they have joined; the fact that "creative community projects" give nothing to the community; that they will be expected to devote their life to the group; or that their marriage partner and the date of the marriage will be chosen for them. Of particular usefulness is a description and explanation of the indoctrination process.

Throughout the process the recruit's curiosity, questioning, and reasoning builds momentum until a point is reached that marks a change in the process. During this time the recruit may suddenly pause and become quiet and reflective, or express signs of shock. The recruit then usually "snaps." This moment is characterized by such sensations as tingling and shaking. Affectively, it may involve agonized crying and fear; cognitively, it is associated with a sudden change in worldview and a decision to leave the cult.

Treatment does not end with the "snapping" moment because for a period following it termed the "floating phase," a chance meeting, phone call, or even a word may result in the recruit snapping just as quickly back to the cult worldview. To prevent this, individuals usually require continued support and guidance until critical thought capacities are strengthened enough to be self-supportive.

GROUP PRESSURES
PERSUASIVE COMMUNICATION

G. K. LOCKWOOD

DEPTH PERCEPTION

Differential distance perception, known generally as depth perception, is primarily a result of the senses of vision and hearing. For vision there are two general classes of depth cues: monocular and binocular. Monocular depth cues are those that indicate distance through the use of one eye and include texture gradients, size, motion parallax, accommodation, linear perspective, interposition, shadow detail, and visual clarity. Binocular depth cues are convergence and retinal disparity. Several of these cues may be simultaneously operating, each one usually corroborating the others. It is difficult experimentally to identify which cues are operating at a given time.

Visual depth perception is studied in several ways. One approach is to have the subject (under binocular or monocular conditions) adjust a rod or needle such that it is equally distant relative to a standard. The visual cliff (with an apparent deep side and shallow side) can be used to test depth perception in human and nonhuman subjects by ascertaining the amount of preference for the shallow side. Three-dimensional perception can be provided by the stereoscope, which presents two nearly identical views separately to the two eyes. A later development has been the invention by Bela Julesz (*Foundations of cyclopean perception*) of random-dot stereograms: computer-generated patterns of random dots with pattern pairs that are identical except for a laterally displaced region. This region, when viewed with a stereoscope, appears to stand above or below the rest of the pattern.

Auditory depth cues are used by blind people who can approach and stop before a wall. Additional auditory cues for depth are amount of reverberation, spectral characteristics (atmospheric absorption is greater for higher frequencies), and relative loudness of known sounds.

EYE MOVEMENTS
VISION, THEORIES OF
VISUAL PERCEPTION

G. H. ROBINSON

DERMATITIS

Dermatitis is inflammation of the skin characterized by itching, redness, and sometimes oozing vesicular lesions. There are many skin diseases included in the dermatitis group, but two major ones are contact dermatitis and atopic dermatitis.

Contact dermatitis includes those inflammations due to external agents such as chemical allergens and toxins. The cause of a suspected contact dermatitis is determined by finding the sensitizer through a combination of patch tests. Once the sensitizer has been identified, it can be medically treated.

Also referred to as neurodermatitis, *atopic dermatitis* is an inflammation of the skin due to repeated scratching. The essential feature of atopic dermatitis is an intense itch. Although the cause of atopic dermatitis is unknown, its occurrence has been associated with personal or family history of allergic disorders such as asthma or hay fever, suggesting a hereditary predisposition. Psychological stresses and changes in climate seem to contribute to a flare-up of this dermatitis. Unlike contact dermatitis, atopic dermatitis is a chronic, recurring problem. Atopic dermatitis has been amenable to both medical and psychological treatment.

PSYCHOSOMATIC DISORDERS

T.-I. MOON

DESCRIPTIVE PSYCHOLOGY

The term "descriptive psychology" is historically related primarily to two German thinkers, Franz Brentano and Wilhelm Dilthey, and the meaning of the term evolved for both of them during their careers. After having fallen into oblivion for a while, description and qualitative analyses in psychology are arousing growing interest.

Descriptive psychology according to Brentano is limited to inner perceptions only. As Theo de Boer makes clear in his article "The descriptive method of Franz Brentano," early in his career Brentano considered descriptive psychology to be a mere preparatory phase of a total psychology that would simply discover and clarify what was in the psyche, so genetic psychology could establish the causal laws of simultaneity and succession. Later in his career descriptive psychology became an autonomous science that was intended to become the basis of normative sciences such as logic and ethics. It is in this sense that Brentano influenced Edmund Husserl, who also began with the idea of a descriptive psychology but later called it phenomenology, which he intended as a foundational science for philosophical knowledge.

Dilthey in his "Ideas concerning a descriptive and analytic psychology" traces the idea of a descriptive science back to Christian Wolff through Immanuel Kant, who emphasized the distinction between a descriptive and an explanatory method, then down to Theodore Waitz, who sketched out a complementary program of descriptive and explanatory psychology and whose ideas Dilthey transformed once again. Initially, for Dilthey, psychology was meant to be the foundational science for all the human sciences. But since the psychology prevalent during his lifetime—begun and developed by Herbart, Fechner, and Wundt—was

so limited in approach and content, Dilthey turned to the idea of a descriptive psychology that would present conscious facts exactly as it found them, rather than as a reconstruction of hypothesized elements such as explanatory psychology was attempting to do. Instead, descriptive psychology was to take as its object "the developed human, the completely evolved psychic life, and grasp, describe and analyze it in its wholeness." From this it can be seen that the meaning of descriptive psychology is not identical in Brentano and Dilthey, because for Brentano (early in his career) it is a necessary phase to be complemented by explanatory psychology, whereas for Dilthey it is in opposition to explanatory psychology. Brentano's later meaning of descriptive psychology is closer to Dilthey's intent (the idea of an autonomous science to found normative sciences), but differences in specific interpretations still exist owing to the different philosophical outlooks of the two men. Later in his career Dilthey was no longer sure that even descriptive psychology could serve as the foundational science for the human sciences.

"Descriptive psychology" is still an elastic term, but it is no longer limited to its historic meanings. Its core meaning is that psychical experiences must be described as they are experienced and rendered explicit. Phenomenological insights have extended it beyond the realm of inner perception (outer perceptions understood as "presences" can also be described), and the pressure of concrete problems has led to certain breakthroughs in methodology (purely qualitative and interpretive procedures have been developed).

HISTORY OF PSYCHOLOGY
OBJECTIVE PSYCHOLOGY
PHILOSOPHY OF SCIENCE

A. P. GIORGI

DETERMINISM/INDETERMINISM

The concept of determinism in philosophy has in it the element of necessity: Things must be just as they are because of antecedent causes. This notion is central to science, which maintains that, were one to know all factors involved in some forthcoming event, one could predict it exactly; or conversely, if an event occurs, that it is inevitable. Every thing and event in creation is the result, and will always be the result, of natural laws that can be determined by means of the scientific method.

When it comes to human behavior, an interesting set of alternative positions has been established that has real relevance outside psychology as a science or profession and that relates to general human behavior and institutions, including the laws of society and the dogmas of religion. What has occurred is an interesting set of contradictions. As noted, scientists view life as determined and generally believe in the inevitability of behavior: Were one to know everything about an individual, one could predict his or her every movement. However, throughout the history of society the common-sense view has been one of individual responsibility.

Indeterminism generally is taken to mean that the individual has freedom of choice, that people can predict the consequences of their actions and can decide how to operate, for example, in terms of their own selfish gain versus the good of the community. The purest example of indeterminism is the belief in free will, which holds that all conscious behavior is decided by responsible people. The laws of most societies and the dogma of many religions, especially the Judaeo-Christian ones, are based on the notion of individual responsibility: The consequences of punishment—whether in this world or in the next—are justified in terms of a person's moral judgments and behavior.

Psychologists take a variety of positions in this age-old controversy. Strict behaviorists tend to be strict determinists, while those with an existential bent tend to be indeterminists. However, perhaps in an illogical manner, most psychologists sit on both sides of this fence, asserting as part of the scientific method the necessity of determinism, but nevertheless operating in terms of indeterminism.

Fairly recent events in the world of physics cast doubt on the scientific legitimacy of determinism. Essentially, the issue has to do with the impossibility of determining at the same time the momentum of an electron particle as well as its position. Apparently, there will always be an area of uncertainty. Werner Heisenberg, who received the Nobel prize in 1932, developed from this observation what is generally known as the Heisenberg indeterminacy principle, demonstrating that Newtonian physics simply does not apply at the level of atoms. If we view the single human as the equivalent of an atom, we may now say that, while determinancy is true for the human species, leading to a deterministic nomothetic position, indeterminancy is also true for the human individual, whose behavior would be only partially explainable in terms of preceding events. In other words, the individual is impossible to predict with complete success.

EMPIRICISM
LOGICAL POSITIVISM
OBJECTIVE PSYCHOLOGY
PHYSICS AND THE BEHAVIORAL SCIENCES

W. S. SUTTON

DEVELOPMENT OF HUMAN SOCIAL BEHAVIOR

Social behavior occupies a place of paramount importance in the lives of human beings and its development therefore commands attention. Social behavior encompasses a human being's interaction not only with other persons but also with the world of things, which have acquired their meaning and status from the customs and practices of the culture.

The development of social behavior depends on and keeps pace with the development of such biological and psychological processes as maturation, perception, attention, memory, and learning, as these processes are modified by experience. Further, its development depends on the same processes of learning (taken in its broadest meaning) as the development of any other class of behavior, including trial-and-error learning, conditioning and the law of effect, social learning theory with its emphasis on imitation and modeling, and the comprehension of language. Thus, no child, no more than any human being, can behave socially in the absence of motor, cognitive, or linguistic skills.

Social behavior is by definition an interactive process; the behavior of any partner to the interaction modifies the behavior of the other person, even as it is being modified by the response of the other person. The interaction begins at birth, hence it may fairly be claimed that the human infant qualifies from birth as a social being.

Not only do human infants, requiring constant provision and care, depend for their survival on the ministrations of others, but they are in fact treated as social beings at birth. Mothers and fathers, for example, smile and vocalize to their newborn infants, and an analysis of the speech of hospital personnel to newborns provided ample evidence that even these unrelated persons viewed and treated newborns as fellow human beings.

From birth on, the uneven development of the human infants' sensory and motor systems, compared with the young of many other mammalian species, plays a special role in the development of their social behavior. In their ability to respond to visual, auditory, and tactile stimuli, they resemble precocial animals; in their inability to locomote and so secure nourishment or mingle with other members of their species by their own efforts, they resemble altricial animals. During the long period until effortless locomotion is achieved, what they see and hear, the objects

and persons with whom they have contact, as well as the routines of care, are provided by their parents. The gaze, speech, smiles, and other acts of caretakers not only evoke responses from the infants but just as often follow (are contingent on) the infants' looking at them, smiling, vocalizing, crying, and so on.

DEVELOPMENT DURING THE FIRST 6 MONTHS

Scales of infant development document many early social behaviors. Infants pay attention to people who approach them, show facial brightening and smiles in response to a person who smiles and talks to them, and are quiet when held. Even in the first month or so of life they vocalize in response to another's vocalizations. By 16 weeks of age they are already initiating social play. They have also learned that their crying brings people to their side, even as people learn what they should do to alleviate the cause.

During this early period, infants achieve the major accomplishment of learning to distinguish between the animate and the inanimate, between people and things. Although many objects in the world provide as varied visual and auditory stimulation as do people, people respond more often to the infant's behavior and, being human, their responses are more variable and less predictable. Especially the faces of people, on which infants fasten very early in life, not only present an ever-changing set of stimuli, but are almost always accompanied by speech appropriate to their own feelings and actions, as well as to those of the infants. It is people, finally, who minister to the infants' basic biological needs.

The infant's ability to distinguish between familiar and unfamiliar persons constitutes another major accomplishment of these early months. Although infants this young respond positively to all persons, the social responses to familiar persons are more expansive and come more readily.

These social accomplishments reveal the infants' growing perceptual abilities and the presence of a considerable memory.

THE SECOND 6 MONTHS

The social accomplishments of the infants' earliest days become richer and more varied as their perceptions deepen, their motor skills improve, and their knowledge increases. They repeat behaviors others laugh at, imitate sounds, and respond to their names. They learn the rules of the game of give-and-take and, whereas at 6 months of age they enjoy playing peek-a-boo, by 12 months of age they are already initiating a number of simple games.

About midway in this period infants begin to show distress when separated from their mothers and often from their fathers—a behavior that reaches prominence especially when they are ill or otherwise upset. The phenomenon was labeled separation anxiety by Spitz and described in hospitalized children by James Robertson and John Bowlby. These observations gave rise to the concept of attachment first sketched by Bowlby. Subsequently, attachment was studied empirically by Mary Ainsworth. Although Robert Cairns supplied a straightforward learning theory explanation of the disruption of behavior caused by the removal of familiar stimuli, the reliance of the concept of attachment on psychoanalytic and ethological theory remains strong.

As the concept evolved, component behaviors were delineated. The infant's seeking to maintain proximity to the mother, by staying close or by following her, was proposed as the primary indexing behavior. Then, as everyday observation showed that infants often wandered away at the beck and call of an enticing environment, such behavior was incorporated and labeled exploration from a secure base. The other component behaviors included the aforementioned distress at separation from the mother and the display of fear in the presence of strangers. In a later development, three types of attachment—secure, avoidant, and resistant—were proposed, based on differences in the infants' responses to the mothers' return after a series of experimentally manipulated events that ended in the infants being left alone in an unfamiliar environment. The nature of the infants' responses was attributed to differences in the mothers' sensitivity to the needs of their infants.

Attractive as the concept of attachment is, some qualifications are in order. The concept scants the differential contribution to the interaction made by different infants; infants vary as much as caretakers, and both contribute to the interaction. Also, infants are not always cared for exclusively by their mothers, and room must be allowed for attachment to other persons, as first proposed by Rudolph Schaffer and Peggy Emerson. Furthermore, infants not only crawl away from their parents, but do so in most unusual and hence unfamiliar settings (e.g., airports). Even when free to follow a parent, they often stop first to play with toys and on occasion will follow an unknown person. Thus, even for infants, a world of difference lies between a voluntary and a forced separation from loved ones. Finally, although infants may scrutinize unknown persons more intently and do not always smile at unsmiling persons, they do not show fear. Approached playfully or even normally, most infants respond positively. When fearful responses are reported, they have been experimentally produced by socially invasive procedures.

As children approach their first birthday, they show unmistakable signs that they are becoming aware of themselves as actors among other actors, signs that suggest the beginnings of a self-concept. Even when infants repeat an act the parents laughed at, a dawning sense of themselves as individuals can be surmised. A similar claim can be made for the behavior, common at about 10 months of age, of the infants' holding objects out to other persons with the apparent intent of drawing their attention to the object—a behavior followed sometimes now, but always in the second year, by actually giving them objects. Such behavior had long been practiced in the give-and-take game and is so well consolidated in the next few months as to qualify as a gesture of sharing one's possessions with another. Drawing other persons' attention to distant objects by pointing with the index finger is a related accomplishment. Now, when they themselves point to interesting spectacles, they also vocalize and look back at the person's face as though to check that the message is received. Infants, then, recognize other persons not only as separate from themselves, but also as persons with whom they can share an experience.

THE CHILD'S WIDER SOCIAL ENVIRONMENT

Even though fathers generally have spent less time with their infants than mothers and have been less responsible for meeting their moment-by-moment needs, what actually does occur during these intermittent interactions is especially highlighted. As actual studies of the nature of the interaction between fathers and infants now reveal, fathers are just as responsive to their newborn infants as mothers. Although fathers are as capable as mothers in ministering to the physical needs of their offspring, and often do so, their style undoubtedly differs from that of mothers. Certainly differences in how mothers and fathers play with their young children have been remarked: Fathers' play is more physical, including more rough-and-tumble, while mothers' is more vocal. Yet here as elsewhere, when engaging in comparisons, one fastens on differences and forgets the similarities that greatly outnumber them. Thus, the responses of children to their fathers resemble those to their mothers.

As soon as investigators turned their attention to fathers, the larger picture came into view: Members of the family—mother, father, and siblings if present—not only interact with the youngest member of the family in their own individual fashion, but each separate interaction is affected by all the others. The social behavior of the infant and young child develops and is refined in a complex and multifaceted web of social relations.

Interestingly, attendance in day-care or nursery school settings does not seem to result in the loss of the emotional bond between children and their parents, which supports the contention that what is important

is not the amount of time spent in interactions, but the nature of the interactions.

Interactions with Other Children

Even very young infants respond as socially to children as to their caretakers. It cannot be supposed that these very young children recognize other children as fellow creatures of their own small size and status. Rather, children being more lively than adults, they present more interesting stimuli, are more often playful, and may be more easily imitated.

Siblings, both older and younger, constitute a special class of children, distinguished by their familiarity and even more important by their contribution to the social web of the family. Although rivalry between siblings was vividly portrayed by David Levy in 1937, this does not tell the whole story. Naturalistic and laboratory studies, building on anecdotes, reveal many positive interactions. Older siblings entertain, talk to, and play with their infant siblings. As the infants become toddlers, their siblings help and comfort them, and in turn the younger siblings find their older brothers and sisters attractive models, following where they go and imitating what they do.

Unrelated children also engage in congenial social interactions. Even infants smile and reach out to other infants, and older, but still young, children play together, with and without toys, and engage each other in true conversations. Early experience with other children of their own age, as well as with those older and younger, is often considered as important for young children's social development as association with adults. They learn the rules of a more egalitarian interaction, and by comparing themselves with others of their own age acquire knowledge of their own capabilities—knowledge that contributes to their developing concept of self.

Aggressive Behavior

Although the play groups of little children conjure up images of a melee of squalling, fighting children, the truth is quite otherwise. Conflicts do occur, usually over the possession of toys, but these are few relative to more positive interactions and are more often resolved by sociable acts than by force.

DEVELOPMENT OF SPEECH

Of the many activities composing the category of social behavior, speech occupies a preeminent position. Not only are newborns spoken to, but throughout the children's lives almost every subsequent contact with the parents, as well as with all other persons, is accompanied by speech. Even within the first months of life they vocalize in turn, setting the stage for a dialogue, a term that can well stand as a metaphor for all social interactions. While children are very young, adults carry the main burden of the conversation, marking their speech by a lively intonation, many repetitions, and much asking of questions. In turn, the vocalizations of the infant come to resemble the sounds and especially the intonations they hear.

By the end of the first year infants have acquired a word or two, and soon thereafter many words, as attentive bystanders label not only the objects and events in the environment but also the infants' own behavior. The adults' labeling of the infants' gestures—in particular, the infants' pointing to objects—plays an important part in establishing the meaning of their first words.

In studies of the semantic and syntactic properties of the child's speech, its social origins and pragmatic properties tend to be overlooked. The *sine qua non* of social behavior is communicating with others, and the modes of communicating are many, nonverbal and vocal as well as verbal. The child's use of the verbal mode, as of the other modes, originates in social interaction and, once acquired, plays a role of increasing importance in all social encounters.

EARLY ACQUISITION OF PROSOCIAL BEHAVIOR

During the second year of the child's life a number of behaviors such as comforting, sharing, and helping make their appearance and, with appreciation and reinforcement, develop into socially valued behaviors. These positive behaviors, being common, low-key, and undemanding, tend to go unremarked, posing as they do no problems for parents and teachers.

From an early age little children become emotionally upset at the distress of others and offer them sympathy by word and deed. They often spontaneously share their toys and possessions, and the objects they find, with other people and children, both familiar and unfamiliar. In extending such nurturant acts to both animate and inanimate objects, they creatively reenact the care they themselves had experienced at the hands of their parents.

Among the prosocial behaviors, obedience to the words of the parents deserves separate attention. Although here, too, more attention has been paid by parents and investigators to incidents when children do not obey, complying with verbal requests is the more common response. In fact, complying begins early and appears to develop without coercion. By the middle of the second year little children carry out many simple commands not only readily but often with pleasure, stemming apparently from their newfound ability to fit their behavior to the words of others.

DIFFERENCES BETWEEN BOYS AND GIRLS

The sex of the child from birth is of paramount consequence to the beholder, if not yet to the child. No question is asked more consistently at the birth of a child than its sex.

Although many major attributes studies show no major differences in how parents rear their sons and daughters, nevertheless some do exist. For example, large differences fitting the culture's stereotypes were found in the type of toys parents provided for their young children. Parents of very young children profess to an intention to treat their children alike regardless of sex, they have been conditioned by a whole lifetime in a culture that has fairly definite ideas about sex-appropriate behavior. Furthermore, by 2 or 3 years of age children come to know, or at least to label, themselves as boys or girls, the first in a series of cognitive stages leading to gender identity sometime between 5 and 7 years of age.

Yet in the area of social behavior, no clear evidence has been presented of major differences in the interactions of boys and girls with parents, other adults, or children. Beyond infancy, as children come together in play groups and nursery schools, physical aggression, although on the whole infrequent relative to peaceable interchanges, is seen more often in boys than in girls.

AFFECTIVE DEVELOPMENT
BONDING AND ATTACHMENT
EARLY CHILDHOOD DEVELOPMENT
INFANCY
NORMAL DEVELOPMENT
PROSOCIAL BEHAVIOR

H. L. RHEINGOLD

DEVELOPMENTAL COUNSELING

In contrast to psychotherapy—which has been used most frequently in connection with a remedial orientation, looking at the individual's difficulties from the perspective of enduring deficits—developmental counseling has been used to emphasize the growth opportunities inherent in coping with personal decisions or difficulties. Developmental counseling seeks to ensure that individuals utilize transitional experiences to further

personal growth and soundness, including the heading off of enduring deficits and the chronic psychic pain that goes with these conditions.

The principal sources of this approach to human problems are the application of psychological perspectives to the efforts of adolescents to enter the world of work, and the struggles of economically and socially deprived individuals to get their lives on a socioeconomically stable and viable level. After starting at the beginning of the twentieth century in community-based programs for young people, vocational guidance was quickly taken up by the schools. Initially, it was directed toward making certain that the student looking forward to the world of work was sufficiently informed to make educational decisions. Broader educational and psychological perspectives, and progress in psychological knowledge and technical resources, first introduced the use of psychological tests, then broadened goals to include facilitating the development of cognitive skills needed for this and other effective decisions; firming up identity, which is embedded in choices of vocation; and fitting work into the psychological organization of the individual. This last concern, incorporating educational goals of preparing the individual for all phases of life—social and familial, as well as economic—led to the development of counseling and counseling centers that were concerned not only with students' educational and vocational decisions, but with their achieving emotional autonomy in their families and intimacy with peers without loss of autonomy, and with the reworking of family-based standards of conduct to fit students' circumstances as mature persons.

To understand the different ways in which developmental counselors approach their task, it is important to understand developmental counseling's roots in the family counseling of social casework. Early social workers represented society's response to conditions at the dawn of the twentieth century that had grown out of economic deprivation often wedded to ethnically based isolation giving rise to alienation. The populations served all suffered from undernourishment, disease, and crime, which increased the likelihood of malformed bodies and stunted emotional life. Beyond surface efforts to alleviate the immediate suffering, aid to such groups sought to develop ethnic pride and the educational and social skills needed for coping. Psychological and psychiatric concepts gradually turned attention to psychological and emotional strengths and weaknesses of families, to further help them face their difficulties and challenges. With the more recent renewed concern about institutional bias against minority ethnic groups and the impact of socially shared emotionally based prejudices, which has marked the 1960s and 1970s, much greater attention is being given to how organizational factors shape the psychological well-being of the individual and the resources developed.

BALANCING INDIVIDUAL AND SOCIAL PERSPECTIVES

The developmental counselor looks at the individual from three points of view: (a) one's evolving organization of motives directed toward self and others; (b) the behavioral and cognitive skills and other resources that surround and implement the goals that incorporate these motives; and (c) the social contexts that shape these organizations and interact with them.

The interventions of the developmental counselor are directed toward specific individuals or toward the social units of which each is a part. Thus, the developmental counselor may make his or her contribution by bringing to bear knowledge of psychological development in the role of consultant on curriculum or intimately related support systems.

DEVELOPMENTAL COUNSELING LIFE CYCLE AND LIFESTYLE

It is natural that concern with development should focus attention on children. But growth and change do not cease with entry into adulthood. Even the priority given to child development requires concern with adult development, because the vicissitudes of the development of parents, singly and as a couple, have an impact on their children. The rising divorce rates of the 1970s represent a very cogent illustration. But even apart from its bearing on children, one of the latent or manifest aspirations of any society, depending on its economic fortunes and development, is to maximize the opportunities for self-realization within a socially shared set of values.

Erik Erikson began filling a gap in psychodynamic theories of personality development, extended them to cover the full cycle from the cradle to the grave. His eight stages of the life cycle featured a series of crises each of which marked the attainment or mastery of an ingredient fundamental in further living, with failure in achievement representing a deficit that, unless overcome in later life, can keep one from living more fully. These psychological issues correspond to the largely age-related educational and social stages of life: entering formal schooling, the mastery of schooling, vocational decision making and entry into the world of work, marriage and family formation, retirement, and dealing with one's ultimate and inescapable fate.

Erikson's formulations provided a preliminary map to the developmental counselor in trying to understand the outcomes to be sought in helping the individual prepare for or cope with the strains of growing through a particular period of life. Counselors have devised programs to ease the transition for the preschool child, as well as the transition of a newly married couple into parenthood. Programs have been developed for those going through career changes, as well as for those preparing for retirement.

Rehabilitation counselors have had a well-established involvement with individuals' adaptation to illness and disability. The late 1970s were marked by an increasing interaction between psychologists and professionals concerned with physical health. This interaction has grown out of the increasing awareness that lifestyle is a major participating factor in vulnerability to cancer and heart disease.

ADOLESCENT DEVELOPMENT
ERIKSONIAN DEVELOPMENTAL STAGES
NORMAL DEVELOPMENT

E. S. BORDIN

DEVIANCE

The study of deviance is based on two different points of view. The first has viewed deviance as an exceptional, but consistent, variation from statistical norms. In other words consistent performance, behavior, or cognition, which is an unusual occurrence in relation to the overall population, is considered deviant. This definition has been prominently used in the psychological study of deviance.

The second prominent position has seen deviance as defined by the occurrence of single critical events. The occurrence of unusual and high-intensity behaviors characterized by mental illness and violence exemplify this point of view. The critical event view of deviance is the basis of legal definitions of deviance.

Deviance has been the thrust of major aspects of personality theory, clinical psychology, and social psychology. The study of deviance can be classified into four major positions. The first posits that deviance is a function of internal factors. Deviance is seen as *differences among individuals*. The individual differences point of view suggests that individuals or groups of individuals possessing certain levels of characteristics are more likely to become deviant. Individual differences are further posited to be causally related to deviance.

A second major explanation of deviance posits *social structural differences* as major precursors. Officially codified forms of deviance tend to be disproportionately represented among the lower socioeconomic strata

in our society. From a social structural point of view, it is suggested that differential access to legitimate opportunity, differential access to illegitimate opportunity, and alienation or enmity tend to be the critical ingredients causing deviance. From this point of view, deviance has both individual components, which are a result of differential social structures, and environmental aspects.

A third major explanation of deviance takes an *interactionist point of view*. Formally entitled "labeling theory," deviance is created by the reaction of critical individuals to a given act. Psychological disturbance, criminality, and underachievement are both formally and informally labeled as deviant. From the labeling perspective deviance is clearly an interaction between individual performances and society's reactions to those performances.

A fourth major point of view is that expressed by *learning theory*. Learning theory suggests that all actions, deviant and normal, are learned according to the laws of modeling, reinforcement, and punishment. Those individuals who display deviant behavioral patterns have received differential reward for such actions. From the learning theory point of view there is no inherent difference between deviant and normal behavior. Criminal behavior, abnormal behavior, and learning disabilities are learned.

ALIENATION (POLITICAL)
LABELING THEORY
PERSONALITY TYPES
REFERENCE GROUPS

W. S. DAVIDSON II

DEVIANT MATURATION

The average pubertal age for adolescents in the United States has undoubtedly declined during the twentieth century. Within any cohort generation, however, some adolescents mature earlier or later than normal. The psychological and behavioral effects associated with such deviant maturation have been the focus of considerable research. Because sex differences are typically found, males and females are discussed separately.

For boys during adolescence, early maturation is associated with decisive advantages. The boy maturing early is most likely to approximate the cultural expectations of masculinity—for instance, having an angular mesomorphic physique, being successful in athletics, and being perceived by adults and peers as attractive, capable, and mature. Studies reveal that peers, parents, and teachers ordinarily respond to early-maturing males with heightened expectations and positive feedback that, in turn, are reflected in the boys' own self-conceptions: They view themselves as being confident, mature, independent, and accepted by parents, peers, and other adults. In contrast, late maturers tend to have linear ectomorphic body types, are less successful in athletics, and are considered by peers and adults to be relatively less attractive, masculine, and mature. These negative expectations are reflected in the self-conceptions of late-maturing boys; they tend to feel inferior, helpless, inadequate, and rejected.

An investigation by Mussen and Jones found late maturers to be somewhat more imaginative, introspective, and expressive. Peskin revealed that this finding was pronounced when the time that had elapsed since the onset of puberty (pubertal age) was held constant for the two groups. Using existing longitudinal data, Peskin compared early and late maturers at various pubertal ages—for instance, at puberty (0), 2 years prior (−2), 2 years following (+2), and so on. Following puberty, the now chronologically older late maturer was found to be relatively more curious, exploratory, and intellectually inclined, while his early-maturing counterpart was more conventional and worried about social things such as acceptance, grades, making a good impression, and doing what was proper.

Several longitudinal studies have attempted to ascertain whether there may be long-term effects associated with differences in pubertal onset: Will early and late maturers continue to differ when they become adults? Differences in frequency of socialization have been found to persist into adulthood, the early maturer remaining relatively more socially involved and concerned with creating the proper impression. Mary Cover Jones found, however, that late-maturing males now in their late 30s tended to be relatively more insightful and adaptable than their earlier-maturing cohorts: The later maturers tended to be more tolerant of ambiguity, more selectively aware, more apt to achieve via independence rather than conformity, and less likely to be "moralistic" and "condescending."

With females the effects associated with early and late maturation tend to be somewhat opposite to those found with boys. Very early in adolescence, physically precocious girls have been found to enjoy less peer recognition, popularity, and social prestige than their physically delayed cohorts. While extremely late maturation can certainly be a liability, the slightly delayed girl is most apt to fit the stereotypic expectations of femininity: namely, having a petite ectomorphic physique, being reserved, quiet, and sensitive, and so on. Research has revealed that while the social evaluations of ectomorphic males tend to be consistently negative, ectomorphic females are evaluated favorably. Regarding self-conceptions, a study by Juan Cortés and Florence Gatti found that ectomorphic males and females both view themselves as being introverted, sensitive, considerate, gentle, reserved, and so on. However, sex-role judgments about the desirability of these characteristics vary by sex: A female who possesses these qualities is evaluated more positively than a male.

The relative advantages enjoyed by the physically delayed girl may not be a long-term phenomenon. For instance, comparisons of early- and late-maturing girls during middle and late adolescence have found few consistent differences. However, in a follow-up study of female adults, Harvey Peskin found that early-maturing females showed evidence of being comparatively more intellectual, responsible, open, and objective. In contrast, late maturers now in their 30s tended to have "brittle ego defenses" (were inflexible), felt victimized by life, gave up easily, tended to become disorganized by stress, and dealt maladaptively with frustration. As discussed previously, the opposite has been found with adult males.

In conclusion, some qualifications should be discussed. First, too much stress during adolescence can be debilitating. Second, factors other than nonstereotypic body types may trigger identity crises and personal development; simply fitting stereotypic expectations does not preclude personal development. Third, the longitudinal designs employed by the research reviewed previously have inherent limitations that must be considered. Finally, the available data base is limited and the samples have come from predominantly White middle class backgrounds.

ADOLESCENT DEVELOPMENT
ADOLESCENT IDENTITY FORMATION
HUMAN DEVELOPMENT
PRECOCIOUS DEVELOPMENT

M. D. Berzonsky

DIACHRONIC VERSUS SYNCHRONIC MODELS

Psychological theories vary with respect to the temporal duration of the activity to be explained. Theories confined to sequences of brief duration

are termed *synchronic;* their focus is on momentary actions at a given point in time. Theories concerned with sequences of activity extended in duration are termed *diachronic.* In a formal sense the distinction between theoretical types may be considered one of degree rather than kind. Because all human activity may be said to possess duration, theories vary with respect to the extension of the duration under question. There is no fixed point at which a theory can be said to be clearly synchronic or diachronic. However, because of the particular intellectual ethos in which the distinction has gained broad parlance in psychology, the terms have come to signify widely divergent orientations toward the nature of human activity and toward the science itself.

Traditional experimental psychology has generally employed theories of the more synchronic variety. That is, primary concern has been placed on phenomena of relatively brief duration. The reflex arc may be viewed as the most outstanding exemplar.

First, such study is generally although not exclusively committed to mechanistic explanatory concepts. That is, stabilized psychological structures (e.g., association networks, schemata, attitudes) or processes (e.g., assimilation and contrast, dissonance reduction, equilibrium seeking) are used to explain the relationship between the observed stimulus and response patterns. Second, the preferred methodology in traditional synchronic investigation is experimentation. The ideal methodological implement for tracing the precise connections between stimulus and response is said to be the controlled experiment. Finally, traditional synchronic inquiry tends to adopt a view of science in which human activity is to be explained by efficient causation. That is, human activity is said to be equivalent to the subject matter of any other science, and thus amenable to full explanation in terms of the necessary and sufficient conditions under which various activities occur.

The concept of diachronic theory has come to serve as a form of intellectual shibboleth. It first signals the investigator's concern with cross-time patterns of activity. However, this commitment is generally accompanied by a criticism of the traditional S-R and S-O-R orientations. As it is argued, the individual does not generally respond to stimuli temporally dissociated from their historical context, nor can the one's behavior be properly understood except by taking one's past history into account. That an individual responds to the stimulus of a smile with reciprocation cannot, on this account, be properly understood outside the cultural history in which such events are embedded. This form of criticism is frequently accompanied by a rejection of mechanistic forms of explanation, experimentation as the optimal methodology, and of the view that science should be based on a logic of efficient causation.

Among the strongest proponents of synchronic theory are developmental theorists—most particularly, those concerned with epigenetic sequence in cognitive development. To replace the mechanistic forms of explanation, Overton and Reese have originated the concept of *organismic* theory, which does not view developmental trajectories as a mere history of the stimulus conditions to which an individual has been exposed, but rather as a result of the individual's internal, genetically based developmental inclinations. Because changes across periods are likely to be qualitative, observational rather than experimental methods are preferred. A more radical view is favored by many social and life-span developmental psychologists. As K. J. Gergen has ventured in this case, most developmental trajectories are not fixed by genetics. Change across time generally depends on the rules and plans people follow, and such rules and plans may be abandoned at any time. This account thus restores voluntarist explanations to credibility.

K. J. Gergen

DIAGNOSES

Diagnosis, or more specifically, psychodiagnosis, refers to (a) the process of classifying information relevant to an individual's emotional and behavioral state, and (b) the name assigned the state, taken generally from a commonly accepted classification system.

The psychodiagnostic enterprise has been criticized because it tags a person with a label. Once an individual becomes identified as a patient, he or she may then feel the victim of an illness and may fail to take responsibility for resolving problems.

Some diagnostic categories may have a social stigma or even political implication. Diagnostic labels can cause social problems for the patient in part because they may imply a cause of the disorder and hence an implied judgment. Agreement about a diagnosis can be consistent across cultures, even though that same label may arouse quite different connotations regarding the distal etiology.

Erickson and Hyerstay observed that the history of human efforts to understand the mentally ill can be better understood as three separate histories: the history (a) of a naturalistic and empirical way of conceptualizing the cause of psychological disorders, (b) of how effectively problems are addressed, and (c) of how humanely the mentally ill are treated. Viewed in this way, the sometimes confusing history and cultural perspective of psychodiagnosis may be less troublesome.

DEVELOPMENT OF DIAGNOSTIC CATEGORIES

The comprehensive diagnostic system in use today had its modern beginning with the work of Emil Kraepelin, a German psychiatrist who made detailed observations of patients. He differentiated dementia praecox from dementia senilis and suggested four varieties of the former condition—simple, hebephrenic, catatonic, and paranoid. His nosological entity, dementia praecox, was severely criticized for nearly 50 years. Critics said that the alleged irreversible behavioral deterioration in this condition was reversible. Shortly thereafter, Eugen Bleuler accepted Kraepelin's four subtypes, but for dementia praecox he suggested the term "schizophrenia," which is now almost universally accepted. However, Kraepelin's (and Bleuler's) four subtypes came under criticism, and during World War II the U.S. Army Medical Department developed a revised classification system in which schizophrenic patients no longer had to be forced into a Kraepelinian "subtype."

Related work during World War II by William Menninger and others eventually led to the development of the *Diagnostic and statistical manual of mental disorders* (*DSM-I*), published by the American Psychiatric Association in 1952. This classification scheme was refined further and became *DSM-II*. After extensive field testing in a wide variety of clinical settings throughout the United States, *DSM-III* and *DSM-IV* were published that improved reliability of diagnosis through the use of operationally explicit criteria.

VALIDITY OF DIAGNOSIS

The validity of a diagnosis describes the extent to which a diagnosis is accurate, as judged by independent criteria.

Complex problems are raised in establishing the validity of a psychiatric diagnosis; for example, it is difficult to determine the "correct" criteria for schizophrenia against which a diagnostic accuracy will be judged. This may be solved in various ways. A common approach is to compare an admission diagnosis to the discharge diagnosis. But such a comparison is a doubtful criterion of validity. It constitutes inter-rater reliability measuring the agreement of opinions between two mental health professionals, albeit at different times and with presumably different information. Even if both raters agree on the label assigned, the larger issue still remains as to whether their diagnosis is correct (valid against external criteria).

Another way to estimate validity in diagnosis is to use operational definitions, such as assuming schizophrenia is properly defined by criteria in *DSM-IV*, or by other systems such as the Schneiderian first-rank symptoms; then, having established that schizophrenia is indeed the diagnosis

by these criteria, the second step is to evaluate the extent to which interviewers reach that same decision in their independent examination of the patient. Diagnoses can also be validated based on reference to different clinical courses and outcomes.

In constructing psychological tests, different types of validity are employed by test developers. However, in making a diagnosis based on an interview, predictive validity is most important (the prediction of different clinical courses, outcomes, and responses to therapeutic intervention).

An interview format was developed to structure the questions asked during the interview. The Renard Diagnostic Interview (RDI) and the Diagnostic Interview Schedule (DIS) are interview formats designed to be utilized by either a professional clinician or lay person, with diagnostic categories determined by subsequent clerical computation or computer scoring. Similarly, the Schedule of Affective Disorders and Schizophrenia (SADS) developed by Endicott and Spitzer was specifically designed for use by the clinician.

Standardized interview schedules are important for achieving increased rates of reliability and validity. They ensure that all important questions will be asked. The interview schedules provide well-tested phrasing for asking potentially confusing or embarrassing questions. The importance of a careful, thorough diagnostic interview of the type assured by a predetermined interview format cannot be overestimated.

The clinical diagnostic process generally begins in a two-person system—the doctor–patient relationship. The patient typically serves as the primary source of information. The clinical data available at this stage consists primarily of the patient's self-reported sensations, feelings, and thoughts. The target symptoms (behavioral or emotional) may not be immediately active at the moment of questioning; therefore, the reported sensations may be further mediated by memory.

Diagnostic judgments are often limited to the information obtained during the interview. There are many opportunities for error in this interview, both in the dyadic interaction and in the probability of misestimation of a diagnosis.

Unfortunately, many patients distort reality. Such distortions are obvious in the cases of the malingerer, the hypochondriac, and the Munchausen syndrome patient. However, a wide spectrum of other patients also deny or affirm illness.

Greater diagnostic validity can often be obtained by independently evaluating patients' self-reporting by interviewing informants, generally household family members. Gathering data from informants is frequently cost-effective because it leads to more congruent care for the needs of the patient.

The use of an informant for validating a diagnosis has its limitations. It is not always evident which person is the best judge, when there are disagreements about information.

CLASSIFICATION POSSIBILITIES

Zubin stated that the purpose of diagnosis is to communicate information about etiology (cause), prognosis (course and outcome), and therapy (treatment). Zubin's goals are difficult to attain. Adopting a system to make gains in one area generally leads to losses in another. There are problems at every turn. For example, consider the goal of communicating etiology. The etiologies of some disorders have been discovered, as in pellagra with psychoses, phenylketonuria (PKU), Down syndrome, and Parkinson's disease. However, our understanding of disorders may change. For this reason Asher suggested that diagnostic labels should be merely descriptive (like phobias) and not imply etiology or treatment.

Most conditions are more complex than once imagined. Single models are generally insufficient, and multiple etiologies are now believed to be responsible for most disorders. Because of the complexity of disorders, there has been the rise of the "biopsychosocial model" and of behavioral medicine and behavioral health.

Zubin, Blashfield and Draguns, and others have recommended attributes for an ideal psychodiagnostic system, but few have provided any viable options to our existing system.

Some behavior therapists have suggested that the diagnostic process should involve a thorough analysis of behavior and the environment in which it occurs. In such a system a traditional diagnostic label might not be necessary. An article by Kanfer and Saslow described how behavioral excesses and deficits, assets and liabilities are helpful in the clinical management of patients in the traditional psychiatric setting.

As research continues, many diagnostic categories will have more clearly defined parameters. This is illustrated by advances in neuropsychological assessment. Neuropsychological tests in the hands of a highly trained clinician can provide detailed and clinically useful descriptions of the assets and liabilities of the brain-injured patient.

Some psychologists have decried assessment, proclaiming there should be no differential diagnosis without differential treatment. Many different treatment methods are currently available, including effective psychoactive medications and psychotherapeutic treatments.

CLINICAL ASSESSMENT
CLINICAL JUDGMENT
RELIABILITY OF DIAGNOSES

J. D. MATARAZZO
L. D. PANKRATZ

DIAGNOSTIC AND STATISTICAL MANUAL OF MENTAL DISORDERS

The fourth edition of the *Diagnostic and statistical manual of mental disorders* (*DSM-IV*) was published in 1994 by the American Psychiatric Association, replacing prior revisions of the organization's official classification system. Despite misgivings concerning its orientation and scope by other mental health professions, as well as its divergence from the system promulgated by the World Health Organization in the 1977 ninth revision of its *Manual of the international statistical classification of diseases,* the *DSM-IV* is the standard handbook for psychodiagnosis employed by clinicians and researchers in the United States.

Substantially more comprehensive and systematically arranged than its predecessors, it includes detailed descriptions of major clinical and personality syndromes. To be exhaustive and inclusionary, information on each syndrome had to be ordered in a standard format.

PERSONALITY DISORDERS
TAXONOMIC SYSTEMS

T. MILLON

DIALECTIC

"Dialectic" is a generic term encompassing several different meanings, all relating to opposition, contradiction, and the duality of meaning.

Dialectic cannot be limited to either Socratic or Hegelian/Marxian terminology, for it has a long and complex history going far beyond this limited reference. As Freud noted in "The antithetical meaning of primal words," anthropological/philological study of ancient languages such as Egyptian reveals that many words in use bore *two* meanings, one the exact opposite of the other. Concept attainment seemed to have begun in human reason through the contrast of knowing at the same time what something both is and is not. Meanings are relational and in many instances this pattern is one of opposition. Another historical demonstration of the power of dialectical reasoning—reasoning based on dialectical

meanings—is the fact that Mo Ti (ca. 470–ca. 391 B.C.) founded a school of dialectical thought in ancient China. The dates of his life span are almost identical to those of Socrates (ca. 470–399 B.C.)—a remarkable parallel in the history of philosophy, since there was no possibility of cultural contact.

Although Eastern philosophies have been kind to dialectics, with such reasoning permeating Buddhistic thought, the fate of dialectics in Western thought has been decidedly negative. Dialectical machinations are at the root of sophistical dispute, an outcome that Socrates cautioned against as unnecessary and instead proposed that a *demonstrative* form of thought be used in coming to know truth. Demonstrative reasoning flows from premises that are "primary and true"—that is, not open to question via dialectical opposition.

Demonstrative reasoning has been furthered in Western thought, coming into psychology by way of British empiricism. Modern cybernetic or information-processing models of cognition rely exclusively on demonstrative conceptions of meaning and human reasoning. The rise of mathematical explanation did much to eclipse dialectic in modern times. Mathematics capitalizes on the singularity, linearity, unidirectionality, and noncontradiction that demonstrative reasoning promotes. Even so, continental philosophies such as those of Hegel and especially Kant have provided a continuing life for dialectical conceptions of reason. In Kantian philosophy the human being is said to be capable of reasoning to the opposite of certain givens, thereby achieving a transcendent capacity and a self-reflexive intelligence that brings agency to the behaving organism. In a sense, the person "resolves" the contradictions of life by affirming one meaning from among the many possibilities presenting themselves.

It is this latter style of explanation that psychoanalysis has relied on in framing its theories, even though Freud did not consider himself a dialectician. Jung *did* accept the validity of dialectics in understanding the human being. More recent theories in the existentialist tradition such as those advanced by Ludwig Binswanger and R. D. Laing are also heavily dialectical. In his later writings (e.g., *Structuralism*), Jean Piaget emphasized the importance of dialectic in his concept of formal operations.

Rychlak has argued that dialectic must be revived in modern psychological description, if a rounded picture of the human experience is to be achieved. Riegel relied heavily on dialectical conceptions in his theories of development. There is a rapidly growing body of research and sociohistorical analysis that relies on dialectical conceptions. Dialectical theories and the data they generate challenge psychologists to consider the basics of human nature.

CONCEPTUAL LEARNING AND DEVELOPMENT
EPISTEMOLOGY
GALILEAN–ARISTOTELIAN THINKING
INFORMATION PROCESSING

J. F. RYCHLAK

DICTIONARY OF OCCUPATIONAL TITLES

Produced by the U.S. Department of Labor's Employment Service in 1939, the *Dictionary of occupational titles* (*DOT*) provides standardized occupational information useful to individuals and professionals in the job-seeking process. The *DOT* represents an extremely wide variety of occupational activities related to the full range of service provided by the U.S. employment services.

Among the items included are descriptions of some 40,000 occupations, covering almost all jobs in the U.S. economy. Because it groups occupations into a systematic classification structure based on how jobs are related with respect to their tasks and requirements, it is extremely useful as a job placement tool. It enhances the ability of the personnel worker to match worker skills with job requirements.

The total system has many very useful features. The *DOT* can identify, for example, tasks that workers might have to perform in a particular occupation, the kinds of machines or tools that might be used, the amount of independent judgment that a worker might have to exercise in the performance of a job, and the setting in which the work might be done.

CAREER COUNSELING
JOB ANALYSIS

S. H. OSIPOW

DIFFERENTIAL APTITUDE TESTS

The Differential Aptitude Tests (DAT) are an integrated battery of eight tests designed for use in the educational and vocational guidance of junior and senior high school students. The tests in the battery are Verbal Reasoning, Numerical Ability, Abstract Reasoning, Clerical Speed and Accuracy, Mechanical Reasoning, Space Relations, Spelling, and Language Usage. A ninth score, a measure of scholastic aptitude, can be derived by combining scores on the Verbal Reasoning and Numerical Ability tests. An optional Career Planning Questionnaire is also included in the battery.

The current forms of the test (S and T) were standardized on a national sample of 60,000 students with normative data presented by grade and gender.

Validity data presented in the manual indicates that DAT scores predict grades in specific high school courses and differentiate students entering different careers. There is, however, little evidence to support the differential validity of patterns of scores on the various tests.

EDUCATIONAL ASSESSMENT
MEASUREMENT

F. G. BROWN

DIFFERENTIAL PSYCHOLOGY

This branch of psychology is concerned with the nature and origins of individual and group differences in behavior. Measurement of such differences has produced an extensive body of descriptive data of considerable scientific and practical interest in its own right. More basically, however, differential psychology represents one avenue to an understanding of behavior; its characteristic approach is through the comparative analysis of behavior under varying biological and environmental conditions. By relating observed behavioral differences to known concomitant circumstances, it is possible to investigate the relative contributions of different variables to behavior development.

As an organized field of scientific endeavor, differential psychology began to take shape during the last quarter of the nineteenth century. Francis Galton contributed significantly to the investigation of individual differences, devising tests for the measurement of sensorimotor and other simple functions, gathering data in a variety of settings, and developing appropriate statistical techniques for data analysis. James McKeen Cattell, an American student of Wilhelm Wundt, extended Galton's work in test development and incorporated this approach in the emerging field of experimental psychology.

The first systematic description of the aims, scope, and methods of a psychology of individual differences appeared in an 1895 article by Alfred Binet and Victor Henri, "La psychologie individuelle" (Individual psychology). A fuller development of relevant topics, together with summaries of available findings, was provided in 1900 by William Stern. The term *differential psychology*, first introduced in the subtitle of his book, was incorporated formally in the revised and enlarged later editions, whose title reads, *Die differentielle psychologie in ihren methodischen grundlagen* (*Methodological foundations of differential psychology*). Subsequent progress in the study of individual and group differences parallels closely the growth of psychological testing, as well as advances in related fields, notably genetics, developmental psychology, and cross-cultural psychology, all of which have made significant contributions to the methodology, data, and concepts of differential psychology.

SCOPE AND DISTRIBUTION OF INDIVIDUAL DIFFERENCES

Individual differences in behavioral characteristics are not limited to the human species, but occur throughout the animal scale. Investigations of animal behavior, from unicellular organisms to anthropoid apes, reveal wide individual differences in learning, motivation, emotionality, and other measurable traits. So large are these differences that the distributions of individual performance overlap even when widely separated species are compared.

Although in popular descriptions persons are often placed into distinct categories, such as bright or dull, and excitable or calm, actual measurement of any psychological trait shows individuals to vary in degree along a continuous scale. In most traits, the distributions approximate the bell-shaped normal probability curve, with the greatest clustering of cases near the center of the range and a gradual decrease in numbers as the extremes are approached. First derived by mathematicians in their study of probability, the normal curve is obtained whenever the measured variable depends on a very large number of independent and equally weighted factors. Because of the extremely large number of hereditary and environmental factors that contribute to the development of most psychological traits, the normal curve is generally accepted as the most appropriate model for trait distribution, and psychological tests are generally constructed so as to conform to this model.

HEREDITY AND ENVIRONMENT

Concepts

The origins of individual differences in behavioral characteristics are to be found in the innumerable interactions between heredity and environment that occur throughout one's life span. An individual's heredity consists of the genes received from each parent at conception. Genes are units of complex chemical substances transmitted on the chromosomes of the ovum and spermatozoon that unite to form the new organism. If there is a chemical deficiency or imbalance in one of these genes, a seriously defective organism may result, with physical pathology and severe mental retardation, as in phenylketonuria (PKU). Except for such pathological deviates, however, heredity sets broad limits to behavior development, and the limits are broader in the human than in lower species. Within these limits, what individuals actually become depends on their environment.

The environment comprises the sum total of stimuli to which the individual responds from conception to death. It covers a vast multiplicity of agents, ranging from air and food to the intellectual and emotional climate of home and community and the beliefs and attitudes of one's associates. Environmental influences begin to operate before birth. Nutritional deficiencies, toxins, and other chemical or physical conditions of the prenatal environment may have profound and lasting effects on both physical and mental development. Such terms as *inborn*, *innate*, and *congenital* are often misused with the false implication that all characteristics present at birth are hereditary. Another common confusion is the difference between organic and hereditary conditions. Mental retardation resulting from early brain injury, for instance, may be properly said to have an organic but not a hereditary origin.

Methodology

The many methods used to investigate the operation of hereditary and environmental influences in behavior development may be subsumed under three major approaches: *selective breeding, experiential control,* and *statistical studies of family resemblances.* Selective breeding for behavioral characteristics has been successfully applied to several species. From a single initial group of rats, for example, it proved possible to breed two strains comprising good and poor maze-learners, respectively. That the two strains did not differ in general learning capacity, however, was demonstrated by the finding that both strains performed equally well in other learning problems. Still another study of these selectively bred strains provided a clear example of the interaction of heredity and environment. When reared in restrictive environments, both strains performed almost as poorly as did the genetically "dull" rats reared in a natural environment. In contrast, an enriched environment, providing a variety of stimulation and opportunities for motor activity, improved the performance of the "dull" strain, both groups now performing at about the level of the "bright" rats in a natural environment.

Later selective breeding experiments extended these procedures to other species and other types of behavior. Of particular significance was the development of techniques for measuring individual differences in behavior among such organisms as the fruit fly *Drosophila.* It thus became possible to capitalize on the mass of available genetic knowledge regarding the morphology of *Drosophila,* as well as on such other advantages as the short time span between generations and the abundance of progeny. Through these procedures, a strain of fruit flies was bred that would fly *toward* a source of light and another that would fly *away* from it.

A second approach to the study of heredity and environment is concerned with the behavioral effects of systematic, controlled variations in experience. Experimental investigations of this question either provide special training or prevent the normal exercise of a particular function. This method has frequently been followed with animals to study a wide variety of activities, ranging from the swimming of tadpoles and the singing of birds to sexual behavior and care of the young. Significant effects of such experiential manipulations have been reported for nearly all types of behavior, including perceptual, motor, learning, emotional, and social reactions. Through such experiments, activities formerly regarded as completely unlearned or "instinctive," such as nest building and grooming of the young by rats, have been shown to depend on the animal's prior experiences. Even when the animal has no opportunity to learn the specific activity in question, its behavior may be influenced by the exercise of other related functions.

In studies of infants and young children, one group of experiments utilized the method of co-twin control, in which one identical twin is given intensive training in, for example, stair climbing, while the other serves as the control. The results generally show that, if training is introduced when the child is physically ready for it, progress will be faster than if training is given earlier. Other studies have compared the development of children reared in experientially restricted environments, such as orphanages, with that of children reared in more stimulating environments. Marked differences have been found as a function of the amount of adult contact, as well as the extent of physical stimulation and opportunities for motor activity. There is evidence, however, that appropriate educational programs, particularly when initiated in early childhood, may counteract the detrimental effects of such deprived environments on intellectual development.

The third major approach is based on statistical analyses of familial resemblance. Similarity of performance on both aptitude and personality tests have been investigated for parents and children, siblings, and both fraternal and identical twin pairs. In general, the closer the hereditary relation, the more similar were the test scores. On most intelligence tests, for instance, identical twin correlations are close to .90, being nearly as high as the correlations between test and retest scores of the same persons. Fraternal twin correlations cluster around .70; those between siblings cluster around .50, as do those between parents and children. It should be noted, however, that a family is a cultural as well as a biological unit. In general, the more closely two persons are related by heredity, the greater will be the similarity of their environments and the extent of their influence on each other. Special studies of foster children and identical twins reared apart permit some separation of hereditary and environmental contributions, but several uncontrolled conditions in these studies preclude definitive conclusions.

NATURE OF INTELLIGENCE

Composition

Intelligence has been commonly identified with the intelligence quotient (IQ) obtained on a standardized intelligence test. Such tests reflect at least partly the concept of intelligence prevalent in the culture in which they were developed. Modern intelligence testing originated with Alfred Binet's development of a test to assess intellectual retardation among schoolchildren. Intelligence tests have frequently been validated against such academic criteria as school grades, teachers' ratings of intelligence, promotion and graduation data, and amount of schooling completed. In content, most intelligence tests are predominantly verbal, with some coverage of arithmetic skills and quantitative reasoning. Different intelligent tests, however, may sample somewhat different combinations of abilities. Nonlanguage and performance tests, for instance, often make much heavier demands on spatial visualization, perceptual speed and accuracy, and nonverbal reasoning than do the usual verbal-type tests.

With the increasing participation of psychologists in vocational counseling and personnel selection came the realization that supplementary tests were needed to measure aptitudes not covered by traditional intelligence tests. As a result, so-called special aptitude tests were developed for mechanical, clerical, and other occupationally useful abilities. At the same time, basic research on the nature of intelligence was being conducted by the techniques of factor analysis. Essentially, these techniques involve statistical analyses of the intercorrelations among test scores in the effort to identify the smallest number of independent factors that can account for the intercorrelations. Among the aptitudes, or factors, thus identified are verbal comprehension, word fluency, arithmetic skills, quantitative reasoning, perceptual speed, spatial visualization, and mechanical comprehension. Through factor analysis, the functions measured by intelligence tests were themselves sorted into relatively independent verbal and numerical aptitudes. These aptitudes, in combination with those underlying special aptitude tests, now provide a more comprehensive picture of human abilities. Several of these abilities are incorporated in what are generally designated multiple-aptitude batteries.

From another angle, the increasing accumulation of data from cross-cultural research indicated that intelligence can have different meanings in different cultures. Both traits constitute intelligence, and the relative level of development of these traits reflects the demands and the contingent reinforcements provided by the cultures in which people function. Investigations in preliterate cultures show that those members who have been exposed to a substantial amount of Western-type schooling are more likely to respond in terms of abstract concepts and are less context-bound than are their more traditionally reared age peers. Within a cross-cultural frame of reference, available intelligence tests can be most appropriately described as measures of academic intelligence or scholastic aptitude. These skills represent a limited segment of intelligence, but a segment that is broadly applicable and widely demanded in modern, technologically advanced societies. Within such societies, academic intelligence correlates substantially, not only with school achievement, but also with achievement in most occupations and in other major societal activities.

The intellectual functions tapped by traditional intelligence tests have also been investigated by cognitive psychologists within the framework of information processing and computer simulation of human thinking. Although this area of research is still in its early stages, it is contributing to an understanding of what intelligence tests measure by focusing attention on processes rather than end-products in problem solving. *What* does the examinee do when responding to test items? Analyzing intelligence test performance in terms of elementary component processes may eventually help to identify each person's sources of strength and weakness. Such analysis should enhance the diagnostic use of tests and facilitate the tailoring of training programs to fit each individual's needs.

Life-Span Development

Longitudinal studies of age changes with respect to performance on traditional intelligence tests reveal a slow rise in infancy, followed by more rapid progress and eventual slowing down as maturity is approached. It should be noted, however, that the trait cluster measured by intelligence tests varies with age. In infancy, the IQ is based largely on sensorimotor development, while in childhood, it depends increasingly on verbal and other abstract functions. During the period of uniform formal schooling, the content of intelligence tests closely reflects what is learned in school. Later, changing patterns of intellectual development associated with progressive educational and occupational specialization may not be fully identified through available intelligence tests; they may require a broader spectrum of tests and other assessment procedures.

Average performance on traditional intelligence tests shows continuing improvement with age through the 20s. Among high-scoring groups, especially college graduates and those engaged in intellectually demanding occupations, such improvements may continue throughout life. In more nearly average samples, tested abilities tend to decline beyond the 30s, the drop being largest in tasks involving speed, visual perception, and abstract spatial relations. In cross-sectional studies, which use different samples at different age levels, age differences are likely to be confounded with cultural changes in the population because of lack of comparability of the different age groups in amount of education and other changing life conditions. Well-designed longitudinal studies of adults indicate that the decline attributable to age is much smaller than are the differences attributable to educational and cultural changes over time.

Intellectual Deviates

The mentally retarded and the gifted represent the lower and upper extremes of the distribution of intelligence. Because the distribution is continuous, there is no sharp separation between these groups and the normal. In terms of intelligence test performance, mental retardation is customarily identified with IQs below 70, representing about 2 to 3% of the general population. Decisions regarding the disposition and treatment of individual cases are based not only on the IQ but also on a comprehensive study of the individual's intellectual development, educational history, social competence, physical condition, and familial situation. Although a few rare forms of mental retardation result from defective genes, the large majority of cases can be traced to environmental conditions operating before or after birth and including both physical and psychological influences.

At the other end of the scale, the intellectually gifted have been investigated by various procedures and from several points of view. In a major, long-term project conducted by Lewis M. Terman and his associates at Stanford University, approximately 1000 children with Stanford–Binet IQs of 140 or higher were intensively examined and subsequently followed up at several life stages. IQs as high as these are found in slightly more than 1% of the general population. The results of the Stanford study, which have been corroborated in several investigations conducted elsewhere, revealed the gifted child as typically successful in school, healthy, emotionally stable, and having a wide range of interests. As they grew into maturity, these gifted children on the whole maintained their superiority in adult achievements.

The concept of intelligence was thereby broadened to include several creative abilities, such as ideational fluency and originality. Motivation, interests, and other personality variables were also found to play important parts in creative achievement, as did the psychological climate of the environment in which the individual was reared and in which he or she functioned as an adult.

GROUP DIFFERENCES

Sex Differences

The investigation of any group differences in behavioral characteristics presents several methodological and interpretive problems. In group comparisons, individual differences *within* each group have proved far greater than average differences *between* groups. The distributions of different groups overlap to a marked extent. Even when there are large, statistically significant differences between the mean scores of two groups, individuals can be found in the lower scoring group who excel individuals in the higher scoring group. It follows that one's group membership is not a dependable indicator of one's standing in psychological traits.

Another problem arises from the use of unrepresentative samples in which selective factors may have operated differentially for the populations under investigation. Insofar as more boys than girls may drop out of school, for example, a comparison of the intelligence test scores of high school boys and girls will show a mean difference in favor of boys. This difference would disappear if we were to include dropouts, who tend to score toward the low end of the distribution. A similar interpretive error in the opposite direction is illustrated by surveys of institutionalized mental retardates, which have generally shown an excess of males. Although once regarded as evidence for the higher incidence of mental retardation among males, these findings were later traced to selective admission policies. For various social and economic reasons, mentally retarded females were more likely to remain in the community than were males of the same intellectual levels.

The use of total scores on intelligence tests may also be misleading in group comparisons. In the construction of several intelligence tests, such as the Stanford–Binet, sex differences were ruled out by omitting or balancing out items that favored either sex. Even when this practice is not followed in selecting items, a composite score on a heterogeneous test may obscure existing group differences in specific abilities.

Psychological test surveys have demonstrated significant mean differences between the sexes in a number of aptitudes and personality traits. Females as a group excel in finger dexterity, perceptual speed and accuracy, verbal fluency and other tasks involving the mechanics of language, and rote memory for most types of content. Males excel in speed and coordination of gross bodily movements, spatial orientation, mechanical comprehension, and mathematical reasoning. Among personality differences, one of the best established is the greater aggression of the male. This difference is manifested early in life and is found consistently across cultural groups. It has also been observed in animals, notably subhuman primates and most other mammalian species. Several investigations indicated a stronger achievement drive in the male, but this difference was subsequently found to vary with the conditions under which it was assessed; the results may reflect in part the extent to which the context is task-oriented or person-oriented. There is considerable evidence that females exhibit a stronger social orientation and desire for social approval than do males, as well as less self-confidence and a higher level of anxiety in various situations.

Most investigations of sex differences yield only descriptive data about existing differences within a given culture. The origins of such differences must be sought in the complex interactions of biological and cultural factors. From a biological viewpoint, the different roles men and women play in the reproductive function undoubtedly contribute to sex differentiation in psychological development. The long period of childbearing and child rearing, which falls biologically on the female, has had far-reaching effects on sex differences in interests, attitudes, emotional traits, occupational goals, and achievement. Sex differences in aggression are associated with the greater body size, muscular strength, and physical endurance of the male. There is also considerable experimental evidence that aggressive behavior is related to the level of sex hormones. Another significant sex difference is to be found in the developmental acceleration of girls. Not only do girls reach puberty earlier than boys, but throughout childhood they are also further advanced toward their own adult status in all physical traits. In infancy, the developmental acceleration of girls may be an important factor in their more rapid acquisition of language and may give them a head start in verbal development as a whole.

The contributions of culture can be readily illustrated. Although living in the same homes, girls and boys in most societies are reared in different subcultures. In countless ways they receive differential treatment from parents, other adults, and age peers. The personalities of mother and father are themselves important factors in the child's developing concept of sex roles, providing models of what is expected of each sex in the particular culture. Sex-role stereotypes are likely to influence sex differentiation in motivation, interests, and attitudes. There is also some evidence that performance on cognitive tasks, such as problem-solving and achievement tests in reading and arithmetic, is significantly related to the degree of individuals' sex-role identification and their own evaluation of the sex-appropriateness of various activities. Most of the descriptive data regarding sex differences in psychological traits were gathered in the United States and other contemporary Western nations prior to the advent of the current feminist movement. The educational, occupational, and social changes promoted by that movement may be reflected in changes in the relative development of males and females in both cognitive and noncognitive areas.

Racial and Cultural Differences

Race is a biological concept referring to subdivisions of a species. It corresponds to such classifications as breed, stock, or strain in animals. Human races are formed when a group becomes relatively isolated, through either geographic or social barriers, so that mating among its members is more frequent than mating with outsiders. Over many generations, this process produces populations that differ in the relative frequency of certain genes. Because these differences are relative and not absolute, however, any racial group exhibits some variation in hereditary racial characteristics and overlaps with other populations in such characteristics. For this reason, the concept of race can be properly applied to populations, but not to individuals.

When persons are classified according to such categories as socioeconomic level, nationality, or ethnic identity, significant group differences are often found in child-rearing practices, sexual behavior, emotional responses, interests, and attitudes, as well as in performance on many aptitude tests. In all such comparisons, the direction and amount of group difference depend on the particular trait that is investigated. Because each culture or subculture fosters the development of its own characteristic pattern of aptitudes and personality traits, comparisons in terms of such global measures as IQ or general emotional adjustment can have little meaning.

Isolation of groups leads to cultural as well as racial differentiation. Hence, it is difficult to disentangle the contributions of biological and cultural factors to race differences in psychological traits. Test performance of hybrid, or racially mixed, groups has been investigated for this purpose. It has been argued that, if one race is intellectually superior to another because of genetic factors, the hybrid offspring of both races should be intermediate in intelligence. As commonly tested, this hypothesis is questionable because it assumes complete linkage between the genes determining skin color or other racial indexes and the genes determining intelligence. With incomplete linkage, the correlation between racial characteristics and intelligence would disappear within a few generations of cross-breeding. The results are further complicated by the fact that race mixture is usually selective within either or both races, as well as by the tendency toward greater cultural assimilation of hybrids into the majority population. In groups that were fairly homogeneous in their assimilation of the majority culture, and in which individuals were classified according to ancestry records rather than appearance, the correlation between test scores and extent of race mixture was negligible.

Another approach is concerned with changes in the comparative test performance of racial groups with age. Studies of Black infants and preschool children in the United States, for example, revealed little or no retardation in terms of White norms. Tests administered to schoolchildren in the same regions and time periods, however, showed significant mean retardation that increased with age. These findings are similar to those obtained with various other groups reared in educational and culturally restricted environments. The age decrement has been attributed to the cumulative effects of experiential limitations and to the increasing inadequacy of such environments to meet the expanding intellectual needs of the growing child. From a broader viewpoint, such an age decrement in relation to test norms may be said to occur when a test assesses cognitive functions not fostered in a particular culture or subculture.

A third approach compares samples of the same race reared in different environments. In general, such studies have yielded larger differences in test performance among subgroups of a single race living in different milieus than among different racial groups living under more nearly similar conditions. That the regional differences found within a racial population are associated with cultural differences rather than with selective migration has been demonstrated in several studies.

Studies of so-called equated groups of different races generally show substantial reduction in mean IQ differences, although some difference remains. Such studies are subject to several methodological difficulties. One is statistical regression toward the mean, which occurs whenever a matched-sample experimental design is employed with populations that differ in the equating variable, such as socioeconomic level. The effect of this procedure is to produce mean differences in, for example, IQ in the samples chosen, simply as a statistical artifact of the selection procedure. Another difficulty arises from the use of very broad categories for classifying such variables as socioeconomic and educational levels. With broad categories, it is likely that the individuals from one population cluster at the low end *within* each category, while those in the other population cluster at the high end, even though they were selected so that the total number within each category was the same.

A related difficulty pertains to the use of such traditional equating variables as parental occupation and education, whose relation to the child's psychological development may be too indirect and remote. There is an increasing tendency to construct home environment scales that are more detailed and more immediately relevant to the development of specified traits, such as scholastic aptitude. Use of such scales in comparative studies of Black and White preschool children and high school students yielded promising evidence of the dependence of group differences in intellectual development on the relevant characteristics of home environments.

In light of available knowledge, only a few conclusions can be drawn with confidence. First, no biological basis has as yet been clearly identified for any existing psychological race difference. Second, there is considerable evidence, from both racial studies and other types of investigations in differential psychology, showing the part played by cultural factors in producing the sort of behavioral differences commonly found among racial groups. Finally, in all psychological traits, the range of individual differences within each race is far larger than the mean difference between races.

With regard to group differences in general, we can say that empirically established *group differences* become *group stereotypes* when (a) mean differences are ascribed indiscriminately to all individuals within the group, and (b) the observed differences are assumed to be rigidly fixed, unchangeable, and hereditary.

ADOPTED CHILDREN
BEHAVIORAL GENETICS
GIFTED AND TALENTED CHILDREN
HERITABILITY
HUMAN INTELLIGENCE
INDIVIDUAL DIFFERENCES
PSYCHOLOGICAL ASSESSMENT
RACIAL DIFFERENCES
SEX DIFFERENCES

A. ANASTASI

DIGESTIVE SYSTEM

The digestive system refers to those organs involved in the process of breaking down ingested food into molecules that are used to nourish the body. The digestion system includes all the portions of the gastrointestinal tract—mouth, esophagus, stomach, small intestine, large intestine, rectum, and anus—and the organs that secrete chemical juices necessary for the digestive process: salivary glands, liver, gall bladder, and pancreas.

In the mouth the food is chewed into relatively small particles and mixed with saliva, which contains ptyalin, an enzyme that converts some starches to sugars. After the food passes through the esophagus and into the stomach, it is vigorously mixed with hydrochloric acid and the enzyme pepsin. This initiates the digestion of proteins. The food, which is now a thick liquid, is called chyme. When the particle size and chemical nature of the chyme is at the appropriate level, a sphincter opens, allowing the chyme to pass into the small intestine. In the small intestine pancreatic juice containing the enzymes trypsin, amylase, and lipase continue the breakdown of the partially digested food. The complete digestive process is aided by additional secretions in the small intestine including bile, which is produced in the liver and stored in the gall bladder.

When the food is completely digested it is absorbed in the walls of the small intestine and carried by the circulatory system to all parts of the body. The role of the large intestine is to store nondigestible waste products and to absorb small amounts of water and minerals.

R. M. STERN

DIRECTIVE COUNSELING

The primary focus in directive therapy lies on the intellectual abilities of the client. Cognitive skills are used to solve problems and improve mental health. Directive therapies are essentially rational in their approach. The counselor is viewed as a teacher, with the client as a learner. As such, the counselor assumes much more responsibility for the direction of therapy than in some of the more nondirective approaches.

Most directive theories follow an eclectic course stemming from a psychobiological model. In an eclectic approach to problem solving, the counselor must diagnose the problem and selectively choose the appropriate treatment plan based on elaborate background information. Rational/eclectic approaches draw heavily on a holistic medical model.

Frederick C. Thorne is credited with the most complete development of the eclectic, directive approach to therapy. He reacted against rigid schools of therapy, while believing that the therapist must be skilled in

all intervention strategies and able to employ all appropriate counseling methods and techniques.

Diagnostic procedures are crucial to this method. Clinical interviews, exhaustive case histories, and psychometric appraisal are all employed to develop an accurate clinical picture of the client. A psychodynamic assessment is also done that includes etiology, present clinical status, client personality strengths and weaknesses, and prognosis.

Taking the case history provides the basis for the therapeutic relationship between counselor and client. It also facilitates intellectual insight for the client and an opportunity for catharsis.

Evolving from a vocational adjustment base, the Minnesota point of view is largely associated with Edmund G. Williamson. This directive approach relies heavily on tests and primarily emphasizes educational or vocational problems.

The directive or instructional nature portrays the client as a person with potential who is underinformed and in need of additional information. An underlying assumption is that each individual needs to value the achievement of excellence as a human being.

E. G. Williamson presented five guidelines for the objective and scientific conduct of counseling: analysis, synthesis, diagnosis, counseling, and follow-up. Techniques include giving advice, suggestions, recommendations, and actively listening.

A more recent directive approach is the rational–emotive therapy (RET) developed by Albert Ellis. Viewing man as both uniquely rational and irrational, Ellis posited emotional disturbances as the result of illogical thinking. He identified 11 values or ideas that he said are superstitions—stupid, senseless, and irrational—and lead to widespread neurosis in Western culture. An RET therapist will use whatever techniques seem promising in an attempt to challenge and change the illogical thinking of the client.

COUNSELING
CURRENT PSYCHOTHERAPIES
RATIONAL–EMOTIVE THERAPY

R. C. BERG

DISASTER ANALYSIS

Disasters are catastrophic situations that are minor or major in severity, depending on the extent to which persons, goods, or property are affected. Every disaster has *psychological sequelae* in its impact. Although many events occur with tragic consequences for the victim or victims, such incidents are not considered disasters or catastrophic events unless many people are involved.

In this country each state has an emergency management agency. When the state resources are judged inadequate, the governor may request aid from the Federal Emergency Management Administration. Psychological assistance is supplied through the latter agency with the assistance of state mental health authorities and the National Institute of Mental Health.

Not until 1976 were rules and regulations printed in the Federal Register, recognizing the need to address mental and emotional problems resulting from disasters, although a few ad hoc government efforts to study such problems were made in the early 1970s. A legal precedent for the establishment of psychic impairment occurred when a class action suit was brought against the Pittston Mining Company as a result of the Buffalo Creek Dam disaster in West Virginia.

The third edition of the *Diagnostic and Statistical Manual* of the American Psychiatric Association (*DSM-III*) officially recognized post-traumatic stress disorders for the first time. These disorders are acute or chronic (delayed), depending on the time of onset; an acute disorder develops within and does not exceed 6 months, whereas the delayed types appear after or last more than 6 months. Such stress can be evoked in victims from a variety of situations—major disasters of either a natural or human-induced type, including torture, riots, and acts of terrorism, as well as industrial accidents and those events cited previously. Human-induced disasters can be either deliberate or fortuitous. Combat veterans and prisoners of war have experienced catastrophic situations that elicit post-traumatic stress disorders even many years after the precipitating events.

Post-traumatic stress disorders encompass the following essential criteria: (a) existence of a recognizable stressor that would elicit symptoms of distress in nearly anyone; (b) reexperiencing the trauma with symptoms not present prior to the trauma such as sleep disturbances, hyperexaggerated startle responses, or impairment in concentration; (c) psychic numbing or "emotional anesthesia"; (d) avoidance of situations that might be associated with the traumatic event.

Repeated analysis and study of disasters indicate that psychologically five phases are likely to occur: (a) an *initial impact* phase in which anxiety and specific fears are prominent; (b) a *heroic* phase where many persons may exhaust themselves physically and mentally in an effort to deal with the calamity and assist others; (c) *honeymoon* phase characterized by experiences of gratitude and joy at having survived and having received assistance from various private and government agencies; (d) a *disillusionment* phase manifested by resentment and frustration at officials and agencies for not doing more in a timely manner; and (e) a *reorganization* phase where a process of reconstruction occurs mentally and emotionally, as shown by realistic perceptions and acceptance of the need to take responsibility for personal solutions to the problems at hand.

Psychological treatment is clearly indicated for many victims of disastrous situations, particularly when the use of appropriate deconditioning and desensitization procedures can be employed. Without such intervention, in many cases the effects of the traumatic incident may persist for years.

STRESS

C. J. Frederick

DISCOVERY LEARNING

According to traditional views, learners acquire complex skills and concepts gradually, one step at a time, in logical progression. Gestalt psychologists challenged this notion, pointing out that learners often grasp complex skills or concepts inductively through a flash of insight—what they called the "aha!" phenomenon.

For insight or "discovery" insight to occur, learners must be motivated to attain a goal and must perceive their attainment of that goal as a solvable problem. So motivated, they cast about for techniques, tools, and approaches to enable them to reach the goal. The teacher who employs a Gestalt, inductive, or discovery-learning approach must therefore have some understanding of the perceptual field of the learner, and must create learning situations that foster proper motivation and leave the learner free to explore, experiment, and discover.

Educators who believe that educational programs should begin with the learner's view of the world also draw heavily on the theories of Jean Piaget, who maintained that children develop or "construct" symbolic concepts or "schemata" of their environment by interacting with it. J. S. Bruner said that a teacher should make learners as autonomous and "self-propelled" as possible, so they will continue to think and learn long after they have completed their formal schooling.

Students who are taught by this mode, he believed, are not "benchbound listeners"; they participate, evaluate and weigh evidence, consider alternatives, and arrive at conclusions that they may reexamine from time to time. Above all, they attempt to determine the principles that underlie the data they are considering. Bruner claimed that students who have practice in discovery learn to acquire information in ways that make it more useful in problem solving. Because their rewards are found within the context of self-initiated activity, they are aided in becoming free from external rewards and constraints. They are enabled to use heuristics—an approach to problem solving that employs intelligent guesses about probable solutions when only part of the necessary data is available.

Research comparing expository teaching methods with those designed to foster discovery learning has been inconclusive. B. Y. Kersh conducted experiments in which college students were taught mathematical principles by rote methods or were permitted to discover them heuristically. Students learned more under the rote-learning conditions, but motivation to learn more was stronger under discovery-learning conditions. Kersh noted, however, that motivation did not appear in sufficient strength unless students were willing to work intensively and without help for periods of 15 minutes or more. B. R. Worthen conducted a well-controlled study in which pupils in fifth- and sixth-grade classes were taught arithmetic by teachers who alternatively used discovery or expository methods for periods of 6 weeks. The expository method produced the best results as far as immediate recall was concerned, but retention 5 to 11 weeks later was better with material taught by the discovery method. The discovery method also facilitated greater transfer, as reflected in pupils' ability to use learned principles with other types of problems.

It may well be, as Lee Cronbach has suggested, that the cultural background of students has much to do with the way they respond to teaching methods; thus lower-class children learn best with traditional didactic or expository methods, especially when requirements are explicit and reinforcement comes rapidly. Problem-oriented methods (including discovery learning) seem better suited to middle-class children, according to Cronbach.

ALGORITHMIC–HEURISTIC THEORY
ALTERNATIVE EDUCATIONAL SYSTEMS
INSTRUCTIONAL THEORY
LEARNING THEORIES

H. C. Lindgren

DISJUNCTIVE PSYCHOTHERAPIES

Disjunctive therapies refers to systems of psychotherapy that employ various kinds of body treatments to generate desirable and favorable changes in thinking and behavior. Disjunctive therapy is a trivial aspect of the body–mind interaction but of theoretical and practical importance to traditionally and eclectically oriented professionals who practice the arcane art of psychotherapy.

One can imagine that in prehistoric times when people acted in ways displeasing or incomprehensible to others the viewers of such behavior communicated their displeasure by symbolic means, such as grunts and signals, as well as by physical violence. For example, there is evidence that some ancient people practiced trephination, possibly to release evil spirits from the brain. In the not so distant past, attempts were made to cure mental illnesses by tortures to drive the devil out of the body. Later, less painful body methods intended to scare the devil out of the mentally disordered person were used, such as lowering such a person into a pit filled with snakes. Even today restraints such as straightjackets and wet packs are employed, as well as therapies to the body that involve the use of water and electricity and an ever-increasing variety of drugs—all intended to have favorable behavioral effects on selected individuals through their physiological effects.

Many people deal on their own with psychological problems, such as anxieties, ruminations, post-traumatic flashbacks, and depression, by various self-assigned exercise tasks (e.g., running, swimming, weight lifting), hobbies (e.g., music, art), and active games (e.g., tennis, golf).

There are dozens of formal disjunctive therapies, some of which should not be called psychotherapy because they are of the physiological-physiological type, such as eye exercises intended to improve vision. There are, however, a good many disjunctive therapies of the physiological-psychological type. In every case, certain manipulations of the body, sometimes by the client and sometimes by the therapist are intended—and states—to have psychological benefits for clients.

A small number of principal disjunctive systems are summarized in this discussion. Instead of using evaluative words such as *claims, intends,* and *purports,* statements made in the literature as facts will be so stated (but with the reservation that all such statements are claims, not facts in reality).

ALEXANDER TECHNIQUE
Developed by an actor, Frederick Matthias Alexander, the Alexander technique improves the physical use of the body, enabling patients and students to obtain tension-free movement and well-coordinated musculature. Alexander found that if the neck muscles are allowed to be released during active movement, the head will balance up, "floating" off the spine instead of compressing it. The spine will lengthen, and the body will move in an integrated stress-free fashion. The approach is holistic, furthering positive change and self-awareness through mind–body integration. After faulty postural habits have been identified, the teacher uses his or her hands to shape and form the student to the improved kinesthetic positions through repeated guiding.

AQUA-ENERGETICS
Paul Bindrim, the developer of the aqua-energetics system, believes "that restricted breathing is the mechanism through which traumatized emotions are repressed and . . . reversal of this process leads to the spontaneous discharge of the repressed emotions and lessens the crippling effect of past traumatic episodes." Bindrim further states that "Aqua-Energetics increases the aliveness of the patient by opening neuromuscular blocks that inhibit the breathing process and impede the flow of life energy. With the increase of aliveness, symptoms are cured, realistic life adjustments are established, self-actualization and creativity displace dependency, and enlightenment reduces anxieties."

Central to this process is group therapy work in a body temperature-controlled pool; the clients are usually nude, a feature that facilitates the relaxation of chronic muscle tension (body armor). At that point, in the pool, Bindrim reports that "regression occurs, thereby releasing the repressed emotions and restoring the natural breathing process. Detached from past traumas, the patient's life energy is restored and his true identity then emerges."

Wilhelm Reich's character analysis included the therapeutic use of nudity. Abraham Maslow in *Eupsychian management: A journal* suggested that nudity might enhance sensitivity training groups. Landy initiated mixed male–female nude group therapy with the Peace Corps and in Job Corps staff training sessions.

CREATIVE AGGRESSION THERAPY
George Bach's creative aggression therapy focuses on all forms and manifestations of human aggression. The theory contends that aggression, whether seen, felt, or expressed is a naturally occurring energy created in the organism. Bach and Goldberg also assert that aggression is expressed privately in sexual and intimate relationships, as well as publicly in work and social situations. Sometimes it is expressed directly toward society at large.

Creative aggression therapy rejects the idea that aggression is primarily a defense mechanism against psychological stress factors and unresolved unconscious motivators. This method of therapy changes overt and covert aggressive feelings, attitudes, and actions by direct retraining methods. The principle method is "the fair fight system," which offers techniques of rituals and exercises to "fight for change" so that couples learn to channel their individual aggression in a constructive relationship direction.

DANCE THERAPY
All observable human behavior consists of body movement. Body movement as an expression of emotions dates back to prehistory. In ancient times, body movement was used in religious rituals to express celebrations, transitions, and hardships. Shamans danced to exorcise evil spirits. Over time, these ceremonial dances became ritualized, affirming identity and community, and still serve that purpose today.

When Isadora Duncan, whose style drew on inner feelings as expression, emerged barefoot and emotive on the stages of the West, modern dance was born and dance therapy began. Dance therapists believe that the body is the repository of memories of preverbal material and that it is directly available to the individual by movement, without first filtering it through language. E. D. Alperson points out that "the advantage of body movement is that it does not demand definition prior to expression, as verbalization would." The individual can explore the self directly from a state of flux. From this dynamic state emerge new ways of perceiving the self and, therefore, behaving. The insights resulting from the movement experience, are (only) then processed verbally. There is no basic difference between dance therapy and movement therapy with or without music: Both are holistic therapies.

Dance therapists work with all age ranges, all diagnostic categories of patients, and the physically disabled and deal with disturbances of emotional, cognitive, and physical origin through movement and dance intervention on a body level.

EYE MOVEMENT DESENSITIZATION
The eye movement desensitization and reprocessing (EMDR) procedure was introduced as a rapid treatment for anxiety and related traumas. Shapiro (1989) noted that lateral eye movements (saccades) produced decreases in post-traumatic stress disorder (PTSD) characterized by anxiety attacks, sleep disturbances, flashbacks, and intrusive thoughts.

The process calls for the therapist, after proper preparation of the client, to get the client to perform sets of rhythmic saccadic eye movements, while the patient holds in mind the most salient aspect of a traumatic memory. The procedure is generally effective in only one session. The results include (a) lasting reductions of anxiety; (b) changes in cognitive assessment of memory; and (c) cessations of flashbacks, intrusive thoughts, and sleep disturbances. This procedure is stated not to require systematic desensitization (SD) or flooding.

FELDENKRAIS PROCEDURE
Moshe Feldenkrais postulated that humans act in accordance with their self-image, which governs their every act, and is conditioned by three factors: (a) biological endowments; (b) education to their specific society; and (c) self-education, the independent element of social development. Because physical inheritance comes unsolicited and public education is forced on us, self-education alone is in our own hands. These three forces constitute self-image or individuality (personality). They also are the major determinants of the individual's success or failure in society and relationships. The individual forms the social mask worn throughout life

to display success or failure. Identification with the social mask causes one to lose touch with a sense of physical and organic drives (needs) and satisfaction. The private organic life and the gratification of internal organic drives are in conflict with the external social and financial existence of the mask. This is Feldenkrais' equivalent of emotional disorder.

Functional integration (muscle and breathing exercises) involves nonverbal manipulation of organic disabilities. Treatment is physically painful and psychologically profound because it is the immediate and direct (noncognitive) release of the stressed emotions that were psychologically invested in the maintenance of the social mask.

NEUROLINGUISTIC PROGRAMMING

Neurolinguistic programming (NLP) is a trademark and should not be confused with the scientific study of language and the brain called neurolinguistics. NLP is the study of the structure of subjective experience. NLP is not labeled as a psychotherapy; it is classified as a communication system. All external experience is represented internally in neurological channels that are psychoneurologically preprogrammed to correspond to major sensory channels: visual, kinesthetic, auditory, olfactory, and gustatory. NLP is used to make psychosocioneurological changes in the programming of human experience and activity.

One basic principle of NLP is reframing, which is used to communicate directly with parts of one's self-functioning outside of one's own awareness. Anchoring is another technique used to connect, noncognitively, a pleasant feeling from a past pleasant memory to a memory that has always elicited unpleasant feeling. Working together, reframing and anchoring can produce a current pleasant memory and feeling. When NLP is applied to psychotherapy, it purportedly provides a 5-minute cure for most phobias and irrational thoughts. It teaches people directly in a few sessions how to use their resources in more satisfying ways.

PRIMAL THERAPY

Primal therapy considers all mental disorders as neurosis and psychosis (except organic schizophrenia) caused by real or imagined painful experiences of childhood or infancy, including prenatal gestation. These painful experiences, beginning from the moment of conception, are the traumatic events and/or negative environmental influences that are the bases for the neuroses and psychoses stored physically in organisms. Because these traumatic experiences are nonverbal, they are hidden from the patient in later years and are experienced as maladaptive behavior. Janov contends that "pain is not learned as a cognitive idea but as a nonverbal experience and remembered nonverbally. Therefore, it cannot be changed or challenged if approached only with words." The patient must reexperience the primal trauma by following the nonverbal pain back to its origin. This process is reported to be as painful as the original trauma and is most often expressed in loud, vocal noncognitive sounds and noises, (i.e., screams), hence the term *primal scream*. Janov and Holden refer to this procedure as "neurosis in reverse" and note that "once the painful primary trauma has been reexperienced and therefore dealt with, the patient receives an immediate sense of euphoria, lucidity and profound calm." They also suggest that the maladaptive behavior will no longer be necessary and the patient will be cured.

REBIRTHING

Rebirthing is a regressive, holistic method that produces psychotherapeutic effects based on a simple breathing rhythm, executed without pauses between filling and emptying of the lungs. Breathing in this connected manner from a few minutes to hours, clients are able to focus and review events in their own individual past. Leonard Orr, the originator of rebirthing, established his theory entirely outside the framework of any current medical or psychological orientation. The theory postulates that thought

is creative and that because we are thinkers, the quality of our lives reflects the quality of our thoughts. These thoughts, which occur before, during, and after delivery, become our "personal laws" of life.

Personality results from the belief system or set of imprints that occur during the birth experience regarding self and reality. All problems that arise throughout the rest of life are related to the birth process and the established birth personal laws. Therefore, theoretically, there are no victims, because we have created all that has happened to us. By reexperiencing their birth in the course of rebirthing sessions, clients are able to examine their personal laws and either choose to let them go or amend them to be more realistic.

ROLFING

Established by Ida Rolf, a biochemist and physiologist, rolfing is a short-term therapy that calls for direct manipulation of connective tissues and muscles of the body. The primary goal is to generate structural change by adjusting the malleable elements of the body. During such manipulation, emotional discharges may occur, but the critical element is the physical readjustment. Rolfing is based on the concept of the unity of the mind and the body, and so it is a holistic theory. Rolf was influenced by the work of Wilhelm Reich who discussed character–muscular armoring that resulted in the blocking of natural energy, generating fearfulness, insecurity, and inability to be free and let go.

24-HOUR THERAPY

Devised by Eugene E. Landy, 24-hour therapy is for patients in extreme circumstances who would otherwise be treated in ICU or in controlled or locked wards of psychiatric hospitals. The procedure is to establish outside the locked ward the same hospital controls maintained in the locked ward. The essence of 24-hour therapy is that patients who are deemed self-destructive, nonproductive, and harmful to themselves or others and who have developed the ability to appear useless or incompetent as a manipulative maneuver are placed under the complete control of the therapist as if hospitalized. The therapist situates such a patient in the real-life and real-time environment at home, work, or play, with the same people and the same problems to solve as existed in his or her life before the need for treatment. The patient placed *in situ* has a therapeutic assistant(s) at all times, 24 hours a day. This assistant communicates regularly with the therapist and carries out the therapist's directions, based on hourly detailed reports that the assistant(s) makes to the therapist. As in the hospital, the therapist is in complete control of the patient and makes all decisions regarding activities and functions, applying natural and logical consequences in real-life, real-time situations. While in a locked ward situation, the therapist's decisions regarding the patient are expected and unquestioned, the same therapeutic decisions of the 24-hour therapist may appear to someone unfamiliar with the process as insensitive or inhumane. Some of these decisions include those regarding personal habits, lodging, freedom of movements, visitations, hygiene, food, transportation, and other personal desires. The therapist allows the patient to make decisions if they are congruent with the goals established before the start of the 24-hour therapy. As many times per day as necessary, the therapist and patient meet to assess the situations that have arisen and how the patient has or has not handled them. The therapist explains why he or she may have refused to allow the patient to handle situations in a certain way and changed or interceded in the patient's directions or behavior. Sometimes physical intervention may be necessary to prevent the patient from regressing to old, unsuccessful and destructive behavior that originally caused the patient to need treatment. The goal is to aid and assist the patient to grow and begin to operate in a self-sufficient responsible manner with awareness of the consequences of his or her actions. The patient's problems cannot be avoided, because the therapist, or assistant(s), is there to aid if an immediate rational change occurs; amelioration on the spot . . . 24 hours a day.

BEHAVIOR THERAPY
BEHAVIOR MODIFICATION
COGNITIVE THERAPIES
CURRENT PSYCHOTHERAPIES
INNOVATIVE PSYCHOTHERAPIES
PSYCHOTHERAPY

E. E. LANDY

DISPLACEMENT

Displacement of aggression refers to a redirection of harm-doing behavior from a primary to a secondary target or victim. An early theory of displacement was proposed by Sigmund Freud in *Beyond the pleasure principle.* Freud suggested that persons tend to attack the sources of frustration, but if an individual cannot attack such a source because the target is unavailable or too powerful, a substitute target may become the victim of the pent-up anger. This mechanism explained irrational behavior. Frustration cumulates as a buildup of inner tension and is expended when the individual expresses aggression toward a target. The amount of aggression is postulated to be directly related to the amount of cumulated inner energy. A sudden release of energy through aggressive action is referred to as catharsis.

According to Dollard and his colleagues, aggressive behavior should be considered—like all other kinds of behavior—to be subject to the laws of learning. When a person directs an aggressive response at a frustrating agent and the response is successful in removing the barrier to goal attainment, aggression is rewarded. A rewarded response is more likely to recur the next time the individual faces a similar situation. Thus, instead of producing catharsis and reducing the probability of aggression, success is apt to increase the likelihood of harm-doing.

The concept of displacement has been used to explain a wide variety of behavior. More positive and socially desirable behavior may also be interpreted in terms of displaced aggression.

The establishment of the frustration-aggression interpretation has been hindered by inadequate conceptual definitions of "frustration" and "aggression." Alternative theories are being developed, which rely on concepts drawn from factors related to interpersonal interactions rather than intrapsychic dynamics.

Displacement has played a central role in psychoanalytic theory. When, for internal or external reasons, the individual is inhibited from attacking the source of frustration, the energy (cathexis) is shifted to a substitute object or idea. This process represents a compromise by the person, who gives up a primary choice for a secondary or even a lower level alternative.

A displacement that is considered to be a positive cultural contribution is referred to as sublimation. According to Freud, the channeling of displaced energies into creative work was an important factor in the growth of civilization. Antinormative aggression could be minimized or curtailed by providing opportunities to people to vent hostilities in socially accepted ways.

PERSONALITY
PSYCHOANALYSIS

J. T. TEDESCHI

DISPOSITIONAL SETS

One can view people as having patterns of basic personality traits fitting into clusters that can be called "dispositional sets." In real-life characterizations of others we tend to typify people with a single term such as "friendly," "kind," "mean," "sociable," and so forth, and generally these single terms generate in the hearer a fairly good picture of the total person. Attempting a general pattern or conceptualization of personality using some sort of systematic position has been attempted by many people. There are two general ways of doing so: The first is clinical/intuitive/experiential and the second is mathematical, generally done by factor analysis.

An examination of mathematical attempts based on factor analytic studies shows very little agreement among investigators. J. W. French found in an analysis of 70 factor analytic investigations that no fewer than 450 factor names had been given to personality aspects; when he attempted to combine them, he ended up with 50 general factors, many more than any of the single investigators. E. F. Borgatta, attempting more or less the same thing, found only five: responsible, assertive, emotional, intelligent, and sociable. R. J. Corsini, who developed a personality measurement instrument—the "Chicago Q sort" came up with seven factors: lifestyle (introverted/extroverted), intelligence, emotional stability, dominance, activity, social sensitivity, and mood.

No matter how one looks at it, there is no reliability of factors based on the work either of single-factor analysts or those who develop tests. However, a somewhat different picture emerges when we examine the work of philosophers and clinicians; if we correct for differences in language, we find a remarkable degree of uniformity.

Using the typologies of Hippocrates, Alfred Adler, Karen Horney, Kurt Lewin, and William Sheldon, we note that Horney, Sheldon, and Lewin report three factors while the other two have four. It seems evident that these individuals have come to mutual agreement.

We can best demonstrate these positions by using the Horney triangle, since it appears that she most clearly delineated these personality aspects.

The top of the triangle is now called ACCORD and means an attempt by people to go along with others. A person at this corner may be very cooperative but may also be a dependent personality. The lower left-hand corner is labeled CONFLICT and represents people who go against others. The right-hand corner is called EVASION. The fourth term, which probably belongs best in the center of the triangle, is NEUTRAL. For example, if a person is neither in accord with others, nor in conflict, nor evading, then that person is neutral or perhaps indifferent.

ROLE TAKING
SELF-PERCEPTION

N. KEFIR

DISTRIBUTION OF PRACTICE

One of the most generally valid of all statements that can be made about human learning is that some forms of distributed practice are superior to massed practice. In this generalization, distributed practice refers to a situation where the subject rests between practice trials, whereas massed practice refers to the case where little or no rest is allowed. Experiments have shown that the amount of such rest between trials is an important determiner of the level of skill ultimately attained in a motor task. One of the most extensive studies of this variable was an early experiment by M. J. Kientzle, using an alphabet printing task. The subject was required to print the alphabet upside down and backward. Kientzle gave her subjects a series of 1-minute trials, separated by periods ranging from 3 seconds

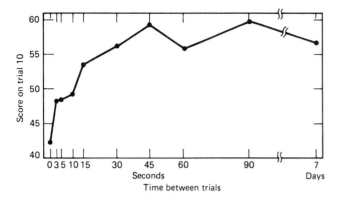

Figure 1. Performance as a function of distribution of practice in a motor learning task.

to 7 days, and obtained the results shown in Figure 1. It is clear that increasing the amount of rest between trials is beneficial up to at least 90 seconds. The slight decrease occurring with the very long rest periods probably resulted from forgetting.

**LAWS OF LEARNING
LEARNING CURVES**

G. A. KIMBLE

DISTRIBUTIVE JUSTICE

Distributive justice is one aspect of social justice. It refers to the extent to which social and personal norms of fairness are met in the shares of goods that members of a social grouping receive (e.g., in a business context, the share of a firm's profits that each member receives). It can also refer to the fairness of an individual's lot, without specific reference to the distribution of goods over persons—for example, whether a worker's wage is judged to be just. The term *absolute justice* is sometimes substituted for distributive justice in this latter sense. Norms of distributive justice are general, in the sense that they can in principle be applied in any situation involving any participants and any type of goods.

Early theoretical work on the social psychology of distributive justice identified one general norm, termed an *equity norm*. George C. Homans, who introduced the concept of justice to social psychology, saw it as a version of social reciprocity. He proposed that distributive justice norms prescribed that a person's share of desired goods be proportional to his or her contributions to the social relationship mediating these goods; thus, a worker's wages should be proportional to his or her efforts, skills, and other characteristics (e.g., age, seniority, ethnic background) valued in the society at large. Homans saw the distributive justice norm as internalized (in its general form) by most members of a society and as valued in itself. Part of the reward offered by a social exchange is the justice it embodies. Hence, according to Homans, people actively seek to create and maintain justice in their social relationships. Homans also proposed that people react to a failure of justice—injustice—in emotional terms, becoming angry if they are the disadvantaged partner, but guilty if they are unfairly advantaged.

The Homans views were and are widely accepted in social psychology, but there have been several elaborations of the concept. Some writers have noted that if the judged fairness of a distribution is the criterion for justice, there are, in addition to equity, two general distributive rules other than equity that qualify: equal distribution and distribution according to need. A considerable body of experimental laboratory research has clearly indicated that both equal and equitable distributions of goods are frequently made in groups, and both are seen as fair under some

circumstances. In general, young children (less than the age of 8) and people in long-standing personal relationships have been found to use equality norms more frequently than older children (especially older than the age of 11) and adults in momentary encounters or in formal organizational relationships, who more commonly use equity rules. The rule of distribution according to need has not been as clearly understood as the other two rules.

J. Stacey Adams elaborated the basic concept of equity as distributive justice through the use of a cognitive consistency theory developed by Leon Festinger. Adams suggested that the experience of inequity resulted in an uncomfortable state of psychological tension (or dissonance) in the perceiver, who then made efforts to reduce this tension. Adams suggested that these efforts might take the form of modifying the distribution either of goods or of contributions. For example, a worker who, given his or her qualifications, considers him- or herself underpaid, might reduce his or her effort or time on the job, while a worker believing him- or herself to be overpaid might increase his or her productivity. Both these efforts have been demonstrated in laboratory research. In addition, Adams pointed out that the perceiver might cognitively distort his or her contributions or share of goods in efforts to reduce the distress of perceived inequity, where actual manipulations of these factors were difficult or even impossible. For example, an underpaid worker might come to believe his or her contributions or qualifications were in fact not as valuable as he or she had thought. In the first decade of work on the concept of equity, most research was conducted in formal task or organizational settings, where contributions and goods (usually monetary outcomes) were easily identified and quantified.

Elaine Hatfield Walster, Ellen Berscheid, and G. William Walster broadened the scope of the concept of equity to also include intimate and informal relationships. This elaboration emphasized the role of purely cognitive operations in attempts to restore equity, and factors influencing a person's choice between objective and cognitive (or "psychological") strategies. For example, the phenomenon of blaming the victim was explicitly brought under the rubric of equity; where compensation is difficult or impossible, the perceiver can come to see the victim's fate as deserved and therefore as just.

**EQUITY THEORY
EXCHANGE THEORY
SOCIAL INFLUENCE THEORY**

W. P. SMITH

DIVORCE

Divorce is the legal dissolution of a marriage. There has been an increase in the incidence of divorce since the 1960s, with a corresponding increase in associated social and psychological problems.

Factors leading to divorce are many and change with time. "No-fault" divorce laws, which recognize such grounds as incompatibility and breakdown of the relationship, allow couples to dissolve marriages in an equitable, agreed-upon manner without an extended adversarial court proceeding. These laws also make it easier to obtain a divorce and may explain the increase in incidence.

Divorce has emotional implications for marital partners, children, and extended family members. Husband and wife often have feelings of loss of attachment with accompanying grief reactions and blame of the spouse, coupled with guilt feelings about their own failures, and general feelings of insecurity about social, emotional, and financial issues.

The effect of divorce on children varies with the age of the child, the process of resolving custody issues, and the parents' ability to cope with the problems of divorce. Young children are likely to blame themselves for the divorce, to worry about being abandoned, and to fantasize about parental reconciliation. Adolescents, despite initial anger and turmoil, have more independent resources for coping than do younger children. J. S. Wallerstein and J. B. Kelly have described the different responses of children of different ages to divorce. Parents have to deal with problems such as raising children without help, maintaining both personal and parental roles, and in the case of noncustodial parents, maintaining parental roles on a part-time basis. All family members face potential financial difficulties, as family income is divided between two residences.

Family members face additional social difficulties following divorce. Relationships with friends often change or end entirely. Divorced adults deal with issues of developing cross-gender relationships, often after years of not dating. Relationships with extended family often become strained as well, as parents of divorced adults deal with concern about their own responsibility for the breakup of the marriage.

The aftermath of divorce is usually quite difficult. Mavis Hetherington and her colleagues have found that boys from divorced families are often treated more negatively by others than are girls, that divorced parents are less affectionate with their children, that adolescent girls of divorced parents are more promiscuous, and that boys are more "feminized." However, there is also evidence that children in single-parent families function better than those in families with two parents in frequent conflict.

AFFILIATION NEED
BONDING AND ATTACHMENT
SINGLE PARENTHOOD

T. S. BENNETT

DOCTOR OF PSYCHOLOGY DEGREE

The doctor of psychology (Psy.D.) degree is awarded to psychologists whose education and training are designed to prepare them for careers of professional practice. With considerable variation in content and emphasis, the training programs that lead to the degree all include education in basic facts and principles of psychology, extensive supervised experience in application of procedures for the assessment and modification of psychological functioning, and an internship. Early proposals for Psy.D. programs did not include a dissertation requirement, but nearly all programs now in operation do so. Systematic inquiry is regarded as a form of practice rather than an end in itself, and the range of topics is broader than has traditionally characterized Ph.D. dissertations in psychology. Community-needs analyses, case studies, and theoretical inquiries, among other kinds of investigations, are all acceptable, so long as each inquiry contributes to improved understanding or constructive change in the way professional psychologists do their work. A typical program requires 5 years of graduate study beyond the baccalaureate degree.

The first formal proposal for a professional degree in psychology was advanced by Loyal Crane in 1925. He argued that education in the science of psychology was insufficient for the practice of psychology and that the Ph.D. degree was inappropriate as a professional credential. He urged development of programs expressly designed to prepare people for practice and the award of a professional doctorate analogous to the M.D., D.D.S., and other professional degrees, on completion of graduate studies. Crane's proposal was not cordially received in the academic community, and only two Psy.D. programs, both in Canada and both short lived, were attempted during the ensuing 40 years.

A conference on training in clinical psychology in Boulder, Colorado, in 1949 established the scientist–practitioner model as the dominant pattern for the education of professional psychologists, and the Ph.D. as the standard qualifying credential. In the Boulder model, as it came to be called, students were to be prepared as researchers, as well as clinicians, in the belief that each form of activity would enhance the other. The Boulder model was widely adopted in American universities and remains the most common design for the education of professional psychologists.

By the mid-1960s, however, expressions of discontent with prevailing Ph.D. programs were often heard. According to critics, most clinical programs in academic departments overemphasized research at the expense of training for practice, and psychologists entering professional careers, as more than half of them were doing by that time, were poorly prepared for the challenges they faced in their work. After lengthy deliberations, an American Psychological Association (APA) committee on the scientific and professional aims of psychology recommended the establishment of practitioner programs leading to the Psy.D. degree.

At another conference on training in professional psychology, held in Vail, Colorado, the concept of direct education for the practice of psychology was endorsed, as was the use of the Psy.D. degree to certify completion of graduate work in practitioner programs. In the years that followed, additional Psy.D. programs were developed in universities and professional schools throughout the United States, although the initial program at the University of Illinois was discontinued in 1980. By the early 1990s, more than 40 programs were in operation. Approximately half of these were in universities, half were in freestanding professional schools, and two thirds had been fully or provisionally approved by the APA Committee on Accreditation.

CLINICAL PSYCHOLOGY GRADUATE TRAINING
DOCTOR OF PSYCHOLOGY DEGREE
GRADUATE EDUCATION
SCHOOLS OF PROFESSIONAL PSYCHOLOGY

D. R. PETERSON

DOUBLE-ALTERNATION LEARNING

Double-alternation learning has been used to assess the contribution of the higher mental processes to learning. The earliest studies were done with mazes. Mazes are built in two general forms, spatial and temporal. Most mazes are spatial mazes in which the animal proceeds from one place to another as it goes from the starting point to the end box in the maze. Studies of double-alternation learning have used temporal mazes that require the learner to make different responses on different occasions in the same part of the maze. Figure 1 presents two mazes that have the

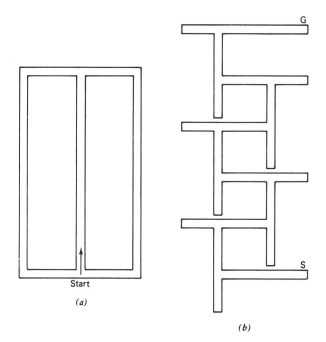

Figure 1. (*a*) Temporal and (*b*) spatial forms of the double-alternation maze.

same pattern. Both are double-alternation mazes, where the pattern is RRLL, and so forth, but one is a spatial maze and the other a temporal maze. In the temporal maze the starting point is the middle alley. To receive food, the animal must learn to run along this path and then turn, for example, to the left. When it returns to the central alley, it must enter it and then turn again to the left. After having completed two circuits of the left-hand portion of the maze, the animal returns again to the center alley; but this time the correct turn is to the right.

Rats are almost always unsuccessful in learning a double alternation in a temporal maze. One possible explanation is that mastery of the double-alternation maze depends on the intelligence of the subjects. There are two types of evidence that supports this interpretation. First, animals higher than the rat in the phylogenetic scale can learn the problem: Raccoons, dogs, monkeys, and children have all mastered it. Second, direct evidence comes from an experiment that used children as subjects, and a procedure where the child had to learn to find candy hidden in one of two boxes. Because the problem was a double-alternation one, the candy was hidden twice in the right-hand box, twice in the left-hand box, and so on. The children varied in chronological age (CA) from 2 years to 6 years, 9 months, and in mental age (MA) from 2 years, 3 months to 8 years. Both these variables were correlated between CA, and the speed of solving the problem was $+0.86$. The correlation with MA was $+0.81$. The youngest child to learn the double-alternation sequence was 3 years, 7 months. Unfortunately, intelligence test scores were not available for this child, but the remainder of the data suggest that the minimum MA necessary to solve the problem is about 4 years, 6 months.

Many of the children used verbalizations to aid in solving the problem.

ANIMAL INTELLIGENCE
EXPERIMENTAL DESIGNS

G. A. KIMBLE

DOUBLE BIND

Double bind is a concept characterizing an ongoing pattern of communication that imposes painful "no win" situations on its victim through two processes: first, through contradictory demands made at different levels of communication, and second, by preventing the victim from either discriminating and commenting on the bind or withdrawing from it. Originally studied in the relationships between schizophrenic adults and their families, the double bind was viewed as having causal relevance for their schizophrenia by having impaired their capacities to derive clear meaning from communications and to participate in normal social relationships.

Bateson and a group of clinicians and scholars collectively introduced a communication theory approach to the mental health field through pioneering contributions to the development of family therapy. Their work emphasized that there are, within families as within the individual's internal environment, homeostatic or stability-making processes that regulate their functioning and contribute to their survival. Within families, communication serves this function.

A single complex human communication can contain many messages of different *logical types* as defined by Bertrand Russell, often involving separate modalities that can contradict or reinforce one another. An aggressive utterance might, for example, be qualified by movements, postures, or voice tones conveying that "this is all in fun." Even the relationship of the message to surrounding events or shared past experience may contribute to its meaning.

The communicational approach holds that each transaction between the parties to a communication involves a relationship message proffering or affirming a relationship of a particular type, and a response that accepts, modifies, or negates the definition communicated. The angry transactions between adolescents and their parents may well have less to do with the apparent content of the quarrel than with the relationship changes being forged and contested.

Considerable learning, often nonverbal, is involved in the capacity to decode communications, particularly those involving apparent contradictions between levels, as with angry words said laughingly. When meaning is not apparent, people learn to shift to a more abstract level and to communicate about communication, thereby clarifying the meaning of ambiguous messages. Children initially lack this capacity; if they are blocked from learning how to learn about meaning, serious adulthood disorders may result.

The double bind involves a communication style that is pernicious in its reliance on internal contradictions and blocked learning. As studied in the families of schizophrenics, it appeared often in mother–child relationships in which the mothers seemed not to want to be understood: They could accept neither their children nor their rejection of those children. The double bind describes their covert pursuit of distant relationships disguised by reciprocal shows of loving behavior. Such parents appeared to invite closeness at one level while negating it at another.

COMMUNICATION PROCESSES
PARENT–CHILD RELATIONS
SCHIZOPHRENIA

R. E. ENFIELD

DOUBLE-BLIND RESEARCH

Double-blind research keeps both researchers and subjects "blind" to knowledge of the intervention or treatment. The importance of using double-blind procedures stems from the natural desire of researchers to find positive results for their hypotheses. Researchers or their assistants may inadvertently tip the scales in favor of an experimental treatment by cuing subjects, by deciding in favor of the experimental treatment in situations that are sufficiently ambiguous to be judged either way, or, where errors are made, by inadvertently making errors favoring the experimental treatment. Similarly, subjects aware that they are receiving an experimental treatment expect and accentuate positive changes, even though they are natural variations unrelated to the treatment. Especially if they anticipate further help from the researcher, some subjects try to respond as they think the researcher wants them to, regardless of their actual condition.

Under double-blind conditions researchers, assistants, subjects, and others involved in any way with a study are not allowed to know which subjects received the experimental treatment (experimental group) and which did not (control group). If identical-appearing treatments are used, but in a way that some neutral party can tell them apart, subjects in both groups might believe they are receiving the treatment. In a drug study the control group would receive an inert pill called a placebo that looks and tastes just like the drug treatment. Drug studies almost routinely use double-blind procedures, because expectations of efficacy can often be as effective as the drugs themselves.

Double-blind procedures cannot be used where (a) one's knowledge of treatment is part of the treatment itself; (b) it is obvious which treatment is to be favored from merely observing the treatment or being exposed to it; (c) the treatment can be readily identified from side effects; or (d) withholding a more favorable treatment would have ethical consequences.

The double-blind technique has the drawback of sacrificing therapeutic knowledge for methodological precision; one's clinical sensitivity is reduced because one is dealing with unknowns. Furthermore, treating subjects with unknowns can be demoralizing to both professional and subject. These objections can often be met, as William Guy and others suggest, through the use of an independent assessment team who are kept "blind" even though those who administer the treatment are not.

Research has shown that many steps in an experiment and many kinds of studies are vulnerable to knowledge of the desired result. Robert Rosenthal found that two thirds of observer errors favored this hypothesis. Although interpretation of effect sizes is still open to question, Rosenthal and Rubin's estimate of the *unintended* impact of expectancy effects suggests that it is as large as that of many treatments *intended* to have an effect.

CONTROL GROUPS
MILL'S CANONS
RESEARCH METHODOLOGY

D. R. KRATHWOHL

DOWN SYNDROME (MONGOLISM)

Down syndrome is the result of an extra chromosome, number 21. Thus, another name for the disorder is trisomy 21. The most common basis for the extra chromosome is called nondisjunction: In the formation of gametes from the parent cell of 46 chromosomes, instead of the two daughter cells each receiving 23 chromosomes, one cell receives 24 chromosomes and the other 22. The egg cell with 24 chromosomes is capable of being fertilized, producing a cell with 47 rather than 46 chromosomes and eventually a child with Down syndrome. The occurrence of nondisjunction increases steadily with the age of the mother. For mothers younger than 30, 1 child in 1500 has Down syndrome; for mothers older than 45, 1 in 65.

The main symptom of this chromosomal abnormality is low intelligence. Most people with Down syndrome are in the severely retarded range, with an IQ around 30. A few are only mildly retarded or even borderline.

There are numerous structural characteristics common to Down syndrome, many of which identify the disorder early in life: limpness in infancy; Oriental-like eyes from which the name mongolism was derived; a small skull, flattened in the back; a large, fissured, protruding tongue; short, heavy stature; short, stubby fingers; and the Simian line on the palms of the hands. In addition, many children born with Down syndrome have heart deformities and lowered resistance to respiratory infection (pneumonia), which meant, until the advent of antibiotics, that few Down syndrome children survived to adulthood.

In Down syndrome, development is generally slowed down, and mental age may not level off until an individual is 35 or 40. Although motor, speech, and sexual development are all slow, people with Down syndrome are often well developed socially, at least in comparison with other categories of mental retardation. They tend to be cheerful, cooperative, friendly, affectionate, and relaxed.

Although there is no treatment for Down syndrome, the new technique of amniocentesis permits examination of the fetus' chromosomes. If Down syndrome is detected, the parents can elect to have the child aborted.

CHROMOSOME DISORDERS
GENETIC DISORDERS
MENTAL RETARDATION

M. R. DENNY

DREAMS

Dreams have been the subject of scientific investigation since the mid-nineteenth century. Prior to that time, there was considerable speculation about where dreams came from and what they meant. A popular theory was that dreams were divine messages with prophetic intent. Because the messages were coded, they had to be decoded to understand them. This task was performed by persons with a gift for dream interpretation. Eventually, dream books were compiled that listed dream elements and their purported meanings. Dreams played a very important role in primitive and ancient societies and still do in many parts of the world. The history of the scientific investigation of dreams and dreaming may be divided into three periods: (a) 1861–1900, (b) 1900–1953, and (c) 1953 to the present.

1861–1900

In 1861, Alfred Maury, a French scientist, published his investigation of the effects of external stimuli on his dreams. The most famous example was Maury's guillotine dream: a long dream about the French Revolution culminating in Maury being sentenced to death. Just as the blade of the guillotine fell, he awoke to find that the headboard of the bed had fallen on his neck. The external stimulus had triggered a sequence of memories that constituted the dream. Other scientists of the period demonstrated the effects of organic conditions on the formation of dreams. There were also investigations of why dreams are forgotten, of the contents of dreams, of the relation of dreaming to thinking, and of the function of dreaming.

1900-1953

Sigmund Freud is the seminal figure of this period. The first edition of his *The interpretation of dreams* stimulated a period dominated by the clinical investigations of dreams.

Although Freud and his colleagues found that dream interpretation was an invaluable tool for uncovering the origins of patients' symptoms, Freud was also interested in dreams for what they revealed about unconscious mental processes. Dreams, Freud declared, are the royal road to the unconscious.

The dream is broken down into its elements and the dreamer is asked to free-associate to each element. From the free associations, the latent content or dream thoughts are determined. The manifest content is conscious, the latent content unconscious.

The motive for the formation of a dream is a *wish* repressed out of consciousness because it is intolerably painful. The most important of such wishes originate in early childhood and are sexual and aggressive in character. During sleep, the repressive agent—Freud called it the *censor*—is less vigilant, so that the unconscious wish can find expression in a dream. However, if the wish is expressed too openly, so much anxiety is generated that the person wakes. Consequently, in the construction of the dream the wish has to be disguised to get past the censor. The disguising of the wish constitutes what Freud called *dream work*. Dream work comprises four operations.

First is *condensation*. Freud observed that the dream as recalled is always much briefer than the latent content as determined by free association. This means that a number of dream thoughts have been condensed to form a single dream image. Second is *displacement*. The psychical values of the dream thoughts undergo displacement during the construction of the manifest dream. Vivid features of the manifest dream may represent relatively insignificant dream thoughts, and insignificant features of the manifest dream may represent dream thoughts of great importance. The third operation is *symbolization*. Repressed wishes are represented by innocuous symbols in order to evade the censor: The male genitals may be visualized as a fountain pen. The fourth operation, *secondary revision*, makes the dream more coherent and intelligible by interpolations and additions when a person is recalling a dream.

Probably even more than Freud, Jung valued dreams. He distinguished little dreams, which are merely a continuation during sleep of one's waking preoccupations, from big dreams with messages from the deepest layer of the unconscious. This layer Jung called the *collective unconscious* because it is the same in every person in every culture. The contents of the collective unconscious are mental structures, or *archetypes*, inherited from past generations.

To identify the expression of an archetype in a big dream, Jung devised the *method of amplification*. Dreamers are asked to say what each element in the dream reminds them of. They are instructed to keep the element in mind and not to let the mind follow whatever course it chooses as in free association. The element can be amplified not only by the dreamer but also by the analyst, and by references to mythology, art, religion, and literature.

The images in big dreams are symbols of the archetypes. These symbols are not disguises, but attempts on the part of the archetypes to express themselves. For Jung, symbols reveal rather than conceal.

Medard Boss, an existential psychotherapist, denies that dreams are symbolic, the product of the dream work acting on unconscious dream thoughts and repressed wishes, or that they are compensatory. A dream, should be taken at its face value. It illuminates the way in which the dreamer views existence.

1953 TO THE PRESENT

While watching sleeping subjects, Aserinsky observed that their eyes made rapid, conjugate movements periodically throughout the night. He and Kleitman believed that these rapid eye movements (REMs) might indicate that the person was dreaming. To test this hypothesis, they awakened subjects during periods when their eyes were moving and periods when their eyes were still. When asked if they had been dreaming, subjects recalled few dreams during non-REM (NREM) awakenings and a great many during REM awakenings. For the first time ever, it seemed, a physiological indicator of dreaming had been found. Subsequent investigations of REM periods showed that they had other distinctive characteristics. Brain waves are of high frequency and low amplitude, contrasted with waves of lower frequency and higher amplitude during NREM periods. There are irregularities of breathing, heart rate, and blood pressure during REM periods. There are also penile erections. For these reasons, REM periods are said to be states of psychophysiological activation.

Since there are four or five REM periods during a normal night's sleep, it was inferred that everyone has four or five dreams every night. By awakening persons during each REM period while they slept in a laboratory hooked up to an electroencephalograph, most of these dreams could be retrieved. Instead of depending on the relatively infrequent and possibly selective recall of dreams in the morning, a great many dreams that are supposedly more representative of one's total dream life could be obtained by awakenings in the laboratory.

A number of sleep–dream laboratories sprang up in the United States and Europe, and hundreds of investigations were performed. Unfortunately, the early findings were not substantiated. The greatest blow was the discovery—many times confirmed—that dreams are recalled on awakening from every sleep stage and not just from REM awakenings. All sleep, it appears, is dreaming sleep. Dreams recalled from NREM awakenings are somewhat more thoughtlike than dreams recalled from REM awakenings, but despite the overall difference a great many dreams from NREM awakenings are dreamlike. The obvious and disheartening conclusion is that there are no dependable physiological indicators or correlates of dreaming; at least, none have been discovered.

These negative findings, however, did not discourage all dream investigators. About the same time that Aserinsky, Kleitman, and Dement were making the first laboratory experiments, Calvin Hall began analyzing dream reports using the method of *content analysis.*

Hall and his colleagues devised categories for various elements in dream reports. Examples of these categories are (a) human characters classified by sex, age, family members, friends and acquaintances, and strangers; (b) animals; (c) interactions among characters, as for instance aggressive, friendly, or sexual; (d) misfortunes and good fortunes; (e) success and failure; (f) indoor and outdoor settings; (g) objects; and (h) emotions. Theoretical categories have also been formulated, as for example castration anxiety, orality, and regression. A number of other systems of content analysis have been devised by other dream investigators. Among them, the most sophisticated are those formulated by D. Foulkes. In an extensive laboratory investigation of children's dreams, cognitive development assessed by the analysis of dreams of children aged 3 to 15 appears to parallel their cognitive development in waking life.

One advantage of content analysis is that large numbers of dreams collected from males and females, children, adolescents, and adults, ethnic and nationality groups, people living at different time periods, and so forth, can be analyzed and quantified for differences and similarities. It has been found, for example, that women's dreams differ from men's in a number of ways. Men's dreams contain more male characters, strangers, physical aggression, sexuality, physical activities, tools and weapons, and outdoor settings than do women's dreams. Women's dreams contain more female characters, known characters, verbal activities, clothes, and indoor settings than do men's dreams. Hall and his colleagues have also studied dream diaries kept by individuals, often for years. One outstanding finding is that, in general, what an adult dreams about from one year to the next changes very little. Studies using content analysis indicate that there is considerable congruence between what we dream about and our preoccupations in waking life. This is known as the *continuity principle.*

FANTASY
IMAGERY
SLEEP

C. S. Hall

DRESS

Only since the turn of the present century have psychologists become interested in a scientific study of dress. For the most part, these early psychological studies were designed to determine what motivates people to dress as they do and why they choose the clothes they choose; their motives were tied to the fundamental human instincts.

Today, psychological studies of wearing apparel focus on the effects of dress on its wearers and on the judgments others make of them because of how dress affects their image. In other words, recent studies have concentrated on what dress can do *to* and *for* its wearers.

ROLE OF DRESS IN IMAGE BUILDING

The image a person presents to others is composed of many elements, each contributing to the general picture of the wearer. Of these elements, the most important are appearance, speech, and behavior. Although facial features, body size and build, and grooming are unquestionably important in determining a person's image, they are overshadowed by dress.

Appearance plays a dominant role in image because it is ever present and visible and tells certain things about a person that would not be communicated by speech and behavior. And in appearance, dress is the dominant element because it serves as a nonverbal form of communication, telling others, for example, what the sex of the wearers is, how sex-appropriate or sex-inappropriate they are, and what their ages and socioeconomic status are. Most important, dress gives a clue to the personality characteristics of the wearer, as for instance whether conservative or radical, poised and self-confident, or suffering from feelings of inferiority and inadequacy.

IMPORTANCE OF DRESS IN FIRST IMPRESSIONS

Psychological studies have reported that first impressions, once formed, not only persist but also have a profound influence on the treatment the person receives from others.

Laboratory studies of impression formation have given clues as to why dress plays a dominant role in first impressions. These studies reveal that people perceive others as wholes or "gestalts" before they begin to perceive them as parts. In looking at a man for the first time, for example, the observer gets an image of the total man, not of his face, hands, or ears. Then, after perceiving the man as a whole, the observer begins to perceive his different parts. What they will be and how long the observer's attention will be focused on them depends on two important factors: first, the attention value of a particular aspect of the person and second, the observer's personal interest or interests. Knowing the typical pattern of perception makes it possible to use dress effectively in influencing first impressions.

CONTRIBUTION OF DRESS TO ATTRACTIVENESS

Before their toddler days are over, children learn that those who are attractive get preferential treatment, while those who are homely or ugly are likely to be disciplined more strictly and harshly for misbehavior. As they grow older, the value of attractiveness becomes increasingly apparent to them.

In marriage, attractive men and women reportedly have a wider selection of potential mates; tend to marry those who are successful, both vocationally and socially; and separate and divorce less than those who are unattractive.

Throughout history, many techniques have been used to produce an attractive image, but at all times and in all cultures, dress and grooming have proved the most effective. This is because, first, they can add to the natural attractiveness of the individual and second, they can camouflage unattractive features.

CAMOUFLAGE VALUE OF DRESS

Laboratory studies of illusions have provided valuable suggestions for ways in which dress can camouflage unattractive physical features and thus create a more favorable image. Dress both covers up unattractive features and diverts attention from them so as to focus in on attractive features.

Five elements in dress have been used to play important camouflage roles. Dark *colors* distract viewers' attention from unattractive physical features such as overweight, while light colors attract attention. Plain *materials* have a far greater camouflage value than figured materials. An evening dress in material with an overall design creates the illusion of a large, heavyset woman, while the same dress in plain material will camouflage her weight. Plain materials have a greater camouflage value because there is nothing about them to attract and hold the viewer's attention.

Because the direction of *lines* serves to control eye movements, when a garment is designed in a style to direct the viewer's eye movements up and down the wearer's body, it creates the illusion that the wearer is tall. By contrast, horizontal lines in a garment direct eye movements across the wearer's body, and by doing so, create the illusion of a heavier person.

Decorations on garments also enhance attractiveness and provide camouflage. Ruffles, braids, buttons, or decorative designs not only heighten the attractiveness of a garment but also direct the viewer's attention to an attractive area of the body and away from an unattractive area.

While *padding* is a form of camouflage that goes back to the earliest days of dress, the reason for its camouflage value had to wait until laboratory studies of illusions provided the answer. These studies show that padding directs eye movements so that the viewer gets the illusion that some part of the body is larger than it actually is.

ROLE OF DRESS IN GROWING UP

In every culture, there are certain developmental tasks or learning experiences that all children and teenagers are expected to master. However, not all children or teenagers master these tasks at the ages when the cultural group expects them to do so.

To show the role played by dress in problems that complicate the adolescent years, several problems most common and most damaging to good personal and social adjustments will be used as illustrations. An attempt will also be made to show how dress can lessen or overcome these problems.

A major problem of childhood is becoming an accepted *member of a group*. This is essential if the child is to have playmates and learn to be a social person. Although many personality and behavioral traits contribute to group belonging, appearance is a dominant factor—above all, dressing like other group members quickly identifies the child as belonging. As a result, the child becomes an accepted member of the group and a participant in group activities.

Some children mature sexually earlier and more rapidly than others. This presents few serious problems for them. However, those who lag behind their age-mates—the late and slow maturers—continue to look like children while their age-mates look like adults or near adults. Because they look like children, adults treat them as such, denying them the privileges their more mature-looking age-mates are automaticaly given. Equally serious, former friends often break friendships and exclude them from their social activities.

The best way to cope with the problems the slow and late maturers face is to use dress to create the illusion that they are older and sexually more mature than they are.

APPERCEPTION
FADS AND FASHIONS
SOCIAL JUDGMENT THEORY
SPOUSE SELECTION

E. B. Hurlock

DRIVER'S LICENSE TESTING

In general, through the ages licenses have been used by the government for three main purposes—to grant special privileges, to establish control over certain behavior, and to raise revenue. Obviously a license is an asset, and the ability to grant or withhold one is an important power with social, economic, and political aspects.

In all nations where automobiles exist in significant numbers—which includes all the developed and developing countries of the world—there are now laws requiring a license to drive, and some testing of the applicant before a license is granted. At the same time there has been an increasing effort to standardize the requirements within and between nations.

In many ways this fact has placed a heavy burden on those who devise the tests and qualifications for original driver's licensure, and it may explain why psychometricians have become increasingly interested and involved in the development of appropriate tests for drivers. The testing procedure, as developed through the years, generally involves four major areas: vision, knowledge of the rules or laws, understanding of traffic signs, and ability to control the automobile. The latter three are of most interest to psychologists. Knowledge of rules and recognition of signs are usually combined into a paper-and-pencil objective test, while driving skill is typically judged individually, with the applicant driving an official observer through a set course of maneuvers.

From a psychometric standpoint, the problems in driver's license testing mostly involve establishing validity. As test methods became more sophisticated, and as governing authorities were more often challenged to justify the whole testing procedure, psychologists and statisticians were employed or contracted with to improve the driver's license tests. The knowledge tests (rules and signs) could easily be improved in reliability and internal consistency, but the politically desirable goal of validity for a criterion recognized as important by the public is difficult. Accident statistics, which are the negatively stated "bottom line" in driving-skill criteria, are hard to deal with because they are far from normally distributed. More and more there is an understanding that driving itself is a psychomotor skill, and that the knowledge considered fundamental by the licensing body represents a social and political fact that needs very little in the way of statistical support.

A crucial emerging concern in driver licensing, found internationally, involves the interrelated problems of alcohol consumption and traffic accidents. For many years there has been a public outcry against a situation that leads to more deaths than any war in history. There has been interest in developing personality profiles that would identify those prone to alcoholism, traffic accidents, or a combination of the two, with the intention of denying driver's licenses to those within the profile limits. Personality testing has usually been found too politically dangerous to implement widely, but research will probably continue. Another concern that overlaps this is a growing relationship between driving and ability to work, prompting occasional challenges to the idea of driving as a privilege that can be regulated by licensing, and an argument for the concept of driving as a right of citizenship that can be taken away only with just cause.

ACCIDENT PRONENESS AND PREVENTION
MEASUREMENT
TASK ANALYSIS

D. A. FRUCHTER

DRUG ADDICTION

NARCOTICS

There are a great many types of psychoactive drugs. Some of the main categories include (a) opiates, their derivates, and synthetic opiate drugs, which alleviate pain and anxiety; (b) sedatives, which induce relaxation and sleep; (c) stimulants, which increase the central nervous system's energy level; (d) tranquilizers, which lessen tension and anxiety; (e) analgesics, or pain killers; and (f) hallucinogens and psychedelics, which activate fantasy and imagination. These chemicals come in different forms: liquids, powders, capsules, and tablets. They can be ingested in many different ways, including intramuscular or intravenous injection, snorting (inhaling and sniffing), smoking, chewing, and oral consumption.

The choice of drug and the way it is used reflect the pattern and lifestyle of the drug user. The disorder—like all disorders—is a problem of the whole person.

Why do people take drugs, and why a particular drug? There are as many different reasons for using drugs as there are people who use them. Some reasons include the following: (a) escape and avoidance of problems; (b) conformity; (c) rebellion; (d) the desire for excitement and adventure; and (e) the need to lessen hurts.

The set of the user and the setting in which the drug is used affect the outcome of the drug experience. Neither the pharmacology of the drug used nor the personality traits of the user are the primary consider-

ation, but rather the purpose, goals, and aims for using a particular drug within a framework of personality and group dynamics.

Some drugs produce tolerance effects: Larger quantities of the drug are needed with continuing use to produce the same effects. Yet drugs *per se* have no real power over people. Drugs like heroin produce physical dependance and tolerance, but the more important consideration is the psychological dependency. It is relatively easy to deal with the physical problems of addiction, but much harder to cope with its psychological aspects.

Drug use and abuse are symptomatic of basic underlying problems. Drug usage indicates the alienation from the world felt by many young people. Drugs are to the real problem as a fever thermometer is to a fever. Addiction and drug use are only a side show activity—a way to evade the problems of everyday living.

ALCOHOL

Alcohol abuse is by far the most devastating world drug problem. Coleman, Butcher, and Carson claim that "alcohol has been associated with over half the deaths and major injuries suffered in automobile accidents each year, and with about 50 percent of all murders, 40 percent of all assaults, 35 percent or more of all rapes, and 30 percent of all suicides. About one out of every three arrests in the United States results from the abuse of alcohol."

Alcohol is a depressant, dulling the cortical functions of memory, learning, judgment, reasoning, comparison, and classification. It also overcomes repression and removes inhibitions.

ADDICTIVE PROCESSES
DRUG REHABILITATION
DRUG USERS' TREATMENT
HEROIN ADDICTION
SUBSTANCE ABUSE

D. N. LOMBARDI

DRUG REHABILITATION

In the late 1960s, narcotic addiction in the United States reached epidemic proportions with an estimated half million active heroin addicts. The federal strategy at that time was to combat the epidemic spread of heroin addiction and to control crime associated with narcotic addiction by prevention and treatment of addicts, while at the same time attempting to control the drug traffic and expand federal law enforcement.

Earlier treatment efforts had included psychiatric hospitals, heroin maintenance provided by physicians or clinics, and civil commitment. These were imperfectly evaluated, but the decision to fund community treatment programs was made under crisis conditions and did not consider evaluative data on earlier approaches. Beginning around 1969, the major modalities of treatment in federally supported, community-based treatment programs were methadone maintenance (MM) as an outpatient, therapeutic community (TC) with drug free as a resident, drug free (DF) as an outpatient, and detoxification (DT). Evaluation of outcome effectiveness was accomplished by collecting admission-background history data and bimonthly status evaluation forms up to termination of treatment from about 44,000 clients admitted to 52 programs, and by follow-up interviews with about 5000 samples approximately 5 years after admission.

During treatment, the most spectacular results were obtained in the MM programs, in which addicts stabilized on methadone used virtually no other opiates and engaged in very little criminal behavior. Compared with incarceration, this reflects a preferable and highly cost-effective approach. After treatment, between 25 and 50% of former addicts showed highly favorable outcomes on opiate use and criminality for up to at least 4 years. The performance of the treatment programs has reflected credit on the professional and paraprofessional staffs involved. It appears reasonable to conclude, however, that they do represent the interactions of clients motivated to engage in the treatment process and the staffs, environments, and regimens of the respective programs. Clients with negative attitudes toward treatment, such as the hard-core criminal addicts, for the most part have not responded favorably to treatment.

ALCOHOLISM TREATMENT
DRUG ADDICTION
DRUG USERS' TREATMENT
EFFECTIVENESS COMPONENTS OF PSYCHOTHERAPY

S. B. SELLS

DRUG USERS' TREATMENT

Programs designed to rehabilitate illicit drug users are found in a variety of settings in the United States. Counseling is provided to illicit drug users in state agencies such as a Division of Mental Health, a Division of Vocational Rehabilitation, or a Division of Offender Rehabilitation. In addition, many federal and private programs offer therapy to illicit drug users. The types of treatment offered include individual counseling, vocational counseling, group therapy, and family therapy. In addition, therapeutic communities offer an intense, although often criticized, treatment for illicit drug users.

INDIVIDUAL COUNSELING

Illicit drug users, especially when they no longer have ready access to illegal drugs, often want to receive individual counseling. Page and Sanders, in "Some characteristics of imprisoned, female drug abusers and implications for rehabilitation," found that almost half the female illicit drug users interviewed in a women's prison indicated that they wanted to receive confidential individual counseling to discuss issues such as their relationships with men and children, how they might avoid using illicit drugs, and similar topics. Unfortunately, in many agency settings certain factors compromise the quality of the individual counseling offered to illicit drug users. Ethical compromises are made by counselors working in the criminal justice system who attempt simultaneously to be a counselor and an authority figure with a client.

VOCATIONAL COUNSELING

It is unwise to separate the personal and vocational counseling needs of illicit drug users into distinct categories of counseling or therapy. The personal problems of many illicit drug users make it difficult for them to succeed vocationally, and their vocational failures compound their personal problems.

Many illicit drug users have worked only at unskilled jobs and have had unstable work histories. Page and Sanders reported that about half the female illicit drug users interviewed in a women's prison had no high school diploma or G.E.D. certificate. Even though most of these women had worked only at unskilled jobs, they still maintained high vocational aspirations. Vocational counseling and vocational and educational training form an integral part of the treatment services many illicit drug users need to receive.

GROUP THERAPY

Group therapy is one of the primary treatments employed with illicit drug users. One reason often cited for using it is the importance of the peer group to these clients. Illicit drug users often have experienced traumatic family relationships and leave home at early ages to become members of the drug culture. Peers in the drug culture often exert a powerful influence on the ways the illicit drug user thinks and feels. Group therapy attempts to foster a supportive atmosphere in which illicit drug users can help one another change in positive directions.

Many advocates of group therapy with illicit drug users recommend the use of highly structured and directive groups with these clients. W. Glasser stresses that therapy groups conducted with public offenders should focus on what these clients do to make themselves unhappy. Glasser thinks that counselors should emphasize the behavior rather than the feelings of public offenders to help these clients learn to act responsibly and effectively. L. Yablonsky advocates the use of Synanon groups to prompt illicit drug users to alter socially irresponsible behaviors. Synanon groups use strong confrontations as a means of forcing members to change antisocial behavior so as to conform to what is considered to be the behavior of a socially responsible peer group. Synanon groups usually are conducted in settings where it is possible for staff to exert a great deal of control over the lives of clients.

Other types of group therapy have been used with illicit drug users. The clients of these groups are encouraged to freely discuss feelings about a variety of subjects. The clients in these groups are regarded as being capable of finding solutions to the personal and interpersonal difficulties they face. Much research indicates that unstructured marathon group therapy can positively affect the attitudes of illicit drug users.

FAMILY THERAPY

Much has been written about the family backgrounds of illicit drug users, especially heroin addicts. Because many drug abusers have been exposed to unfavorable childhood experiences, family therapy methods are needed that help them either to resolve their contradictory feelings about families or to improve the ways they relate to families.

There is not much literature about family therapy with illicit drug users. Page and Powell advocate using preliminary individual and/or group counseling to help illicit drug users start to work through hostility toward family members before inviting these family members to participate in family counseling. Stanton and Todd advocate the use of a non-blaming approach of family therapy with illicit drug users.

THERAPEUTIC COMMUNITIES

Therapeutic communities are residential treatment programs to help residents resolve personal problems and teach them how to form and maintain responsible and caring interpersonal relationships. They are a type of milieu therapy in which everything that occurs in the lives of residents is examined in groups.

Many therapeutic communities for illicit drug users in the United States have been patterned after Synanon House. Yablonsky states that Synanon is an effective treatment for illegal drug users because the Synanon program controls the total lives of addicts. Dederich advocates using brain-washing techniques to change the ways addicts think and act. More recent research contradicts the earlier success rates cited by Dederich and shows that a majority of Synanon graduates resume abusing drugs or alcohol, or die, after reentering society.

A quite different approach to therapeutic communities is advocated by M. Jones. Jones states that social learning occurs in therapeutic communities when the residents resolve personal crises that occur with other residents in the program. As the residents resolve conflicts with other residents and with staff, they learn how to avoid similar conflicts in the future, and the interpersonal relationship styles of these residents change.

Staff members in this type of community are primarily responsible for helping residents learn about how they relate to others and for creating a nonauthoritarian, permissive group climate.

COUNSELING
DRUG ADDICTION
DRUG REHABILITATION
HEROIN ADDICTION
SUBSTANCE ABUSE

R. C. PAGE

DYNAMIC PSYCHOLOGY

The term "dynamic" relates to forces acting on a system. These forces include ongoing processes within the system as well as those external to the system. In psychology, *dynamics* relates to the interplay among motivating or driving forces that acts as a determinant of an organism's behavior. Thus, the term reflects a concern with the specification of motives and principles of motivated functioning. The term is also frequently associated with particular theories that emphasize the interplay among conscious and unconscious forces—drives, motives, needs, instincts, and wishes—in the direction of behavior. Such theories are known as psychoanalytic or psychodynamic theories of personality.

Theories of motivation are concerned, then, with specifying the motives characteristic of organisms and the principles of motive functioning that determine the initiation, maintenance, and termination of behavior.

Over the years a great variety of theories of motivation have been developed. These may be viewed as falling into three broad categories: (a) hedonic or pleasure theories; (b) cognitive or need-to-know theories; and (c) growth or actualization theories. A fourth category might also be noted that concerns the role of brain structures and neural mechanisms in motivated behavior. Research in this category typically is found in areas defined as psychobiology, biopsychology, or neurobiology.

HEDONIC OR PLEASURE THEORIES OF MOTIVATION

Hedonic or pleasure theories form the largest category of theories of motivation. In one form or another, theories in this group emphasize the guiding role of pleasure in the organization of activity. A number of subclassifications within this category are possible. Perhaps the largest subgroup of hedonic theories consists of those that emphasize the organism's efforts toward *tension reduction*. Such theories emphasize the disquieting state of affairs caused by internal tension, and the pleasure derived from the reduction of tension through the discharge of energy, expression of an instinct, or reduction in the level of a drive.

Woodworth took the concept of drive from the field of mechanics and viewed it as the source of motive power or force in organismic functioning. Thereafter, until the 1960s, this concept was used extensively by psychologists interested in human or animal behavior. Often distinctions were made between innate and acquired drives, primary and secondary drives, and viscerogenic and psychogenic drives.

In the area of animal behavior, the concept of drive played a major role in the learning theory of Clark L. Hull. According to Hull's stimulus–response (S–R) theory, learning involves motivational variables such as drives. The organism has primary or innate drives such as pain and hunger, as well as learned or secondary drives such as the desire for money and fears—both learned during the course of development. Although the concept of drive referred to an internal process, it could be used by behaviorist-oriented psychologists because it was tied to specific external conditions manipulated by the experimenter. Variations in drive level, manipulated by the experimenter, were then related to objectively defined and measured overt responses.

Hull's work was extended by Miller and Dollard, among others. They made a particular contribution in emphasizing the role of learned, secondary drives in human behavior. For example, anxiety was viewed as a secondary drive based on the primary drive of pain. The anxiety drive is important because it can be learned quickly, become a strong motivating force, and lead to a variety of behaviors relevant to normal and abnormal behavior. Considerable attention was directed by Miller and Dollard to the relation between frustration and aggression, as well as to the importance of drive conflicts in clinical phenomena. Thus, the approach–avoidance conflict between two drives was viewed as the basic ingredient for the development of neurotic behavior. Dollard and Miller attempted to integrate the achievements of learning theory as expressed in the works of Hull, with the achievements of psychoanalysis as expressed in the works of Freud.

A concept of motivation related to that of drive and used by many personality theorists is that of *need*. An important representative of such a view was Kurt Lewin, who viewed all behavior as driven by states of need or tension in the organism. As with Hull, needs could be primary and biologically determined, or secondary and acquired through experience. Lewin viewed the existence of a need as leading to tension; it was a force that pushed the organism into action. The organism was viewed as a dynamic system in that ordinarily multiple needs enter into action. The forces associated with these needs have the qualities of strength, direction, and point of application.

The operation of these forces, in Lewin's view, takes place in a dynamic field where the state of any part of the field depends on and influences other parts of the field. The valence of objects, in association with states of organismic need or tension, pulls the organism in various directions and sets the stage for gratification, frustration, or conflict. Where multiple needs and environmental objects exist, the organism may experience an approach–approach conflict, an avoidance–avoidance conflict, or an approach–avoidance conflict.

Another representative of the hedonic, tension-reduction view was Henry Murray. The basic motivational concept in Murray's system was that of need. Needs could be primary and viscerogenic, or secondary and psychogenic, and represented forces for action. Murray distinguished between needs and traits in that needs represented a potential for action, whereas traits were defined in terms of actual behavior. Murray also attended to the role of environmental objects, suggesting that the environment could be defined in terms of press or characteristics associated with the potential for need gratification.

The concept of *incentive* is important, yet independent of its relation to drive theory, and forms a second subcategory of hedonic theories of motivation. In the incentive theories there is an emphasis on the association of stimuli with pleasure or pain and the goal-directed striving of the organism to achieve various outcomes. Thus, these theories are hedonic, like drive theories, in their emphasis on pleasure, but, unlike most drive theories, they emphasize the orientation of the organism toward future goals or end points. McDougall rejected a mechanistic, reflex, stimulus-determined view of behavior in favor of an emphasis on active strivings toward anticipated goals associated with pleasure.

Theories of motivation emphasizing goals often are criticized as being teleological. However, goals operate in the present in terms of mental representations of desired outcomes or end points. Most recently, the concept of goals has returned to play an important role in cognitive, information-processing models of human behavior.

A third variant of the hedonic model of motivation is that based on *affect*. Here the emphasis is on the organism's efforts to maximize pleasurable affect and minimize unpleasant affect, although there is no necessary association of affect with physiological need or drive. One of the early significant theorists to emphasize the role of emotion in motivation was P. T. Young. According to Young, stimuli (internal and external) acquire incentive value through their association with affective arousal, which is experienced primarily as positive or negative in nature. Through the gradual accumulation of experience, involving the association of various stimuli with affective arousal, the person develops a value system. Affective processes play the central role in organizing, activating, regulating, and sustaining learned patterns of behavior.

It is important to recognize an overlap among groups. Thus, for example, many drive theorists have emphasized the importance of affect; McDougall emphasized the role of affect in goal development; and many affect theorists emphasize the importance of affects in the development and maintenance of goal system functioning.

COGNITIVE OR NEED-TO-KNOW THEORIES OF MOTIVATION

Indeed, by the 1950s, the concept of drive had almost been dropped entirely from the literature because of several reasons: problems in developing reliable measures of drives, particularly in humans; findings that did not support a tension-reduction point of view; and the growth of interest in information-processing theories associated with the cognitive revolution. In some ways, cognition replaced motivation as an important issue in the field. Some cognitive theories remained basically tension-reduction models.

Other cognitive theories, however, emphasized the motivation inherent in the information-processing activity of the organism. For example, J. M. Hunt, influenced by Jean Piaget, suggested that the organism always seeks to integrate new information with what is already known. Incoming information may be congruent or incongruent with what is known. Hunt cited evidence that incongruous or novel information instigates approach behavior but, when the disparity between incoming and already stored information becomes too great, withdrawal behavior may also occur. Hunt not only emphasized intrinsic motivation, but also suggested that differing degrees of incongruity between new and old information lead to various degrees of arousal and positive or negative hedonic tone. Thus, too little incongruity would be boring and too much would similarly lead to negative hedonic tone, whereas a moderate or optimum amount of incongruity would lead to a moderate degree of arousal, positive hedonic tone, and approach behavior. A cognitive model of motivation, then, was tied to a hedonic one.

George A. Kelly represents a theorist emphasizing a more purely cognitive theory of motivation. Kelly specifically rejected what he believed were the dominant "carrot and stick" theories of motivation—those emphasizing incentives that "pulled" the organism toward them, and those emphasizing drives that "pushed" the organism. Instead, Kelly suggested that every person is a scientist seeking to gain better predictability concerning events. According to him, people are always active, so a theory of motivation does not have to account for activity *per se*. In terms of direction of movement, people choose to act in ways that promise the greatest potential for elaboration of their construct system, thereby leading to enhanced prediction. People may experience negative affect in the sense of anxiety when they cannot predict events or experience threat when their entire construct (predictive) system is in danger. Furthermore, such negative affect will lead to corrective action.

The emphasis on cognition led many psychologists to be concerned with information processing in the absence of motivational considerations. To this day, work in the area of cognition for the most part remains disconnected from work in the areas of emotion and motivation.

GROWTH OR ACTUALIZATION THEORIES OF MOTIVATION

The third major theoretical approach emphasizes growth or actualization. Representative theorists include Andras Angyal, Kurt Goldstein, Abraham Maslow, and Carl Rogers. The common theme here is a rejection of the view that all human activity occurs in the service of tension reduction. Instead, there is an emphasis on activity stimulated by growth or self-

fulfilling tendencies, and that may at times involve increases in tension. These theorists, often linked together as part of the human potential movement, generally do not reject the idea that some activity may occur in the service of reducing tension. However, the most important and basic striving of the organism is seen as directed toward actualizing and enhancing the experiencing organism. Maslow, for example, suggested a hierarchy of needs involving both biological needs (hunger, sleep, thirst) and psychological needs (self-esteem, affection, belongingness). When biological needs are satisfied, psychological needs predominate. In fact, however, psychological needs may even override biological needs in importance. Thus, Rogers suggests that the basic actualizing tendency is the only motive that needs to be postulated and that people are most human when functioning in relation to this motive. Although theories that are part of the human potential movement have been important in personality and were quite popular during the 1960s and 1970s, the concept of actualization has proven to be highly abstract and difficult to measure in any systematic way.

PSYCHOANALYTIC THEORY

Finally, we can consider the specific theory most often linked with dynamic psychology—psychoanalytic theory. Psychoanalytic theory is dynamic in the sense that it emphasizes the importance of sexual and aggressive drives, and the derivatives from these drives, in human behavior. However, it also is a dynamic theory in its emphasis on the interplay among drives as expressed in concepts such as conflict, anxiety and the mechanisms of defense, cathexes and anticathexes, and compromise formations. According to such a view, the same phenomena may be the result of different combinations of forces, and a slight shift in energy may result in a dramatic alteration in the nature of the system.

Freud based his theory on the clinical phenomena presented to him by his patients and on the principles then current in biological science. Subsequent analytic theorists such as Alfred Adler and Carl Jung split with Freud over the nature of the fundamental motives in human behavior, although most held to a dynamic psychology in the sense of a system involving the interplay among motives or forces. Most recently there has been the beginning of an effort to focus on the clinical observations of Freud, and to reformulate the theory in terms that are less metatheoretical and less tied to what is now considered an outmoded energy point of view. Concepts such as cognitions, purposes, meaning, and action, rather than those of instinct, drive, force, and energy, are emphasized.

GENERAL SYSTEMS THEORY

Having considered various theories of motivation, we may turn to the broadest meaning of the term "dynamic" as found in general systems theory. Originally developed in biology and associated with Ludwig von Bertalanffy, general systems theory represents an effort to formulate principles of functioning that are characteristic of all biological systems. A system consists of interconnecting parts or units, the action of one having implications for the actions of others, while certain processes are characteristic of the whole. General systems theory distinguishes between open systems engaged in continuous exchanges with the environment, and closed systems unaffected by external forces. Also, a distinction is made between living systems, which are open systems capable of regeneration and growth, and nonliving systems, which may be either open or closed, but which are not capable of regeneration or growth.

Certain concepts and principles are seen as being useful in the understanding of all living systems. Such concepts and principles in particular relate to the dynamic aspects of organismic functioning. For example, the concept of *feedback* emphasizes the ability of the organism to make use of information resulting from its own actions. Associated with this is an emphasis on the purposive or goal-directed aspects of organismic functioning, in particular the process of *adaptation*.

Finally, in relation to the goal-directed quality of behavior, there is the concept of *equifinality*—the potential for the same goal or end point to be reached through multiple paths or means.

The dynamic aspects of general systems theory may be seen in its emphasis on ongoing processes within the organism and between the organism and its external environment. However, it does not tell us about the specific forces acting on the organism or the principles under which such forces operate. In terms of the more specific meaning of the term "dynamic," general systems theory tells us little about the motives that instigate and direct action.

CONCLUSION

The emphasis here has been on dynamic psychology as it relates to human behavior and in particular to personality theory. However, it is important to recognize that concern with problems of motivation exists in the areas of brain research, physiological psychology, and animal psychology (ethology) as well. Particularly in the latter, concern has increasingly focused on the interplay among motives rather than on the operation of single motives, and on the organization of behavioral processes over time rather than on the specific factors that determine behavior at a specific moment in time. It is processes such as these that general systems theory has tried to capture and that lie at the heart of a dynamic psychology.

GENERAL SYSTEMS
MOTIVATION
PERSONALITY THEORIES
PURPOSIVE BEHAVIOR
TELEOLOGICAL PSYCHOLOGY

L. A. PERVIN

E

EAR

The adequate stimulus for human hearing is defined conventionally as acoustic waves with a fundamental frequency between 20 and 20,000 hertz (Hz). However, Corso has shown that under specialized conditions young adults may hear tones at least as high as 23,000 Hz by air conduction or 95,000 Hz by bone conduction; at the lower end, auditory responses for air conduction may be obtained at least to 5 Hz.

ANATOMY AND PHYSIOLOGY OF THE AUDITORY SYSTEM

Figure 1 is a schematic drawing of the peripheral portion of the human auditory system divided into three major parts: outer ear, middle ear, and inner ear.

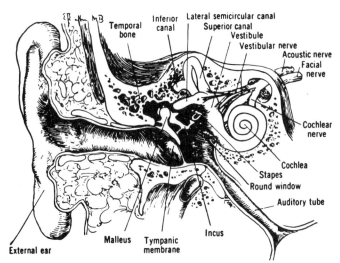

Figure 1. A semischematic drawing of the human ear.

Outer Ear

The pinna of the outer ear collects sound waves from the environment that are channeled into the external auditory meatus and arrive at the eardrum (tympanic membrane). The external meatus, approximately 2.5 cm in length and 7 mm in diameter, has a natural resonant frequency of about 3500 Hz. The tympanic membrane, a slightly oval structure with axes of approximately 9.2 and 8.5 mm, has an area of about 69 mm².

Middle Ear

The middle ear is an air-filled cavity that contains three tiny bones, which form the ossicular chain. In this chain the hammer (malleus) is attached to the inner side of the tympanic membrane, and the stirrup (stapes) is connected to the oval window; the anvil (incus) forms the link between the two. When acoustic waves strike the tympanic membrane, vibrations are transmitted across the ossicular chain to the oval window, which in turn sets up traveling waves in the fluids of the inner ear (cochlea). The ossicles act as a lever system with a mechanical advantage of approximately 1.3:1.0 and reduce the amplitude of vibration at the eardrum, while increasing the pressure at the footplate of the stapes. This mechanical advantage, multiplicatively combined with an effective ratio of approximately 14:1 for the area of the tympanic membrane to the oval window, produces a total transformer ratio of approximately 18.3:1.0.

Air pressure in the outer and middle ear cavities is equalized through the action of the Eustachian tube, approximately 1.5 inches in length, which connects the middle ear to the nasopharynx. The Eustachian tube is normally closed but opens upon swallowing so that equivalent air pressure is maintained between the two aural cavities. The middle ear also contains two intraaural muscles, tensor tympani and stapedius, which are respectively attached to the malleus and the stapes. These muscles provide a reflex response to intense sounds so that contraction serves as a protective mechanism for the inner ear.

Inner Ear

The inner ear consists of the cochlea, a coiled structure with approximately two and five-eighths turns, and its associated nerve network. It is divided longitudinally into three membranous ducts that are filled with fluids. Reissner's membrane separates the scala vestibuli and the scala media (cochlear duct), while the basilar membrane separates the scala media from the scala tympani. Rocking movement of the stapes against the oval window sets up traveling waves along the basilar membrane that serve, in turn, to activate the specialized receptor cells in the organ of Corti attached to the basilar membrane. The receptor cells along the basilar membrane are divided into two groups: approximately 4000 inner hair cells arranged in a single row and approximately 12,000 outer hair cells arranged usually in three (but occasionally up to five) rows. The hairs at the tips of the outer cells are embedded in the tectorial membrane so that during the transmission process the traveling wave induces a relative movement between the tectorial membrane and the basilar membrane. This movement creates a sheafing action on the cell that evokes a generator potential in the afferent nerve endings located at the base of the hair cells. If the potential reaches threshold, an action potential is elicited and a neural impulse is propagated along the auditory nerve. The transduction process of the inner hair cells is more speculative, but it appears that the action potential may be generated by the valving action of the flexible lip of the tectorial membrane.

Auditory Pathways

The human auditory system contains approximately 25,000 cochlear neurons; these afferent neurons synapse in the spiral ganglion with second order neurons that then collect to form the auditory portion of the eighth cranial nerve. The auditory pathways are shown in Figure 2.

Each cochlea is represented almost equally in both medial geniculate bodies, as well as in the auditory cortex of both temporal lobes of the brain. The efferent auditory system, also shown in Figure 2, descends from the cortex to the primary receptor cells in the cochlea. The pathways are less well established, but the efferent system appears to exert a monitoring function on the neural activity of the outer hair cells.

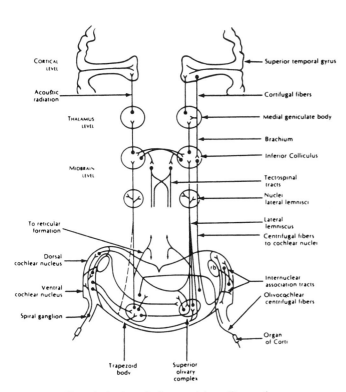

Figure 2. A schematic diagram of the auditory pathways.

AUDITORY DISCRIMINATION
AUDITORY DISORDERS
PERCEPTION

J. F. CORSO

EARLY CHILDHOOD DEVELOPMENT

Childhood is a culturally defined period in human development between infancy and adulthood, and, in historical perspective, a relatively recent social construction. Only in the past 400 years or so has the idea of childhood been a part of Western culture, with the recognition of this special class of people and special phase in the growth of each individual. The French historian Philippe Ariès analyzes the emergence of these ideas in *Centuries of childhood*. Early childhood, as a special and important subperiod of childhood, most often refers to the months and years between infancy and school age or middle childhood—ages 2 to 5 years. These *preschool* years are a time of significant and complex advances and reorganizations in behavior, and thus figure centrally in most theories of human development. Learning, perception, reasoning, memory, and social relations undergo important changes and progressions in early childhood.

Language is among the most impressive achievements in early childhood as the infant's babbling transforms itself into the very sophisticated language of the youngster at age 5, who is ready to enter the world beyond his or her family.

Psychoanalytic developmental psychology posits early childhood as the critical period in development during which major personality orientations emerge to continue into childhood, adolescence, and adulthood, forming boundaries and constraints on later modifications of intrapsychic organization, interpersonal relationships, and ego development. A person's sense of self as an individual and as a male or female is formed in important ways during this period of development. Sigmund Freud's theory of psychosexual development describing the oral, anal, and phallic/Oedipal phases of early childhood development, and Erik Erikson's theory of psychosocial development describing the tasks and crises of early childhood—trust versus mistrust, autonomy versus shame and doubt, initiative versus guilt, and industry versus inferiority—are among the most influential psychoanalytic contributions toward understanding early childhood development.

Cognitive developmental theories espoused by the Swiss psychologist Jean Piaget and his followers also emphasize early childhood development as a period of major steps in a child's construction of his reality and knowledge. The infant in the *sensorimotor* stage of intelligence develops knowledge of self and the world through a complex series of interactions with the environment that emphasize sensory and motor experience. In early childhood the child achieves *preoperational* and then *concrete operational* thinking, important levels of symbolic and representational thinking as a basis for classification and categorization of information, and for appreciation of important rules about the physical and interpersonal world.

Great teachers and theorists such as J. A. Comenius, Jean-Jacques Rousseau, J. H. Pestalozzi, Friedrich Froebel, John Dewey, Maria Montessori, and Anna Freud long ago recognized the importance of learning and development in early childhood. Nursery schools, kindergartens, and early intervention projects such as Operation Headstart are current manifestations of an appreciation of early childhood development not only in education and psychology, but also in social reform and public policy.

CHILD PSYCHOLOGY
INFANT DEVELOPMENT
NEONATAL DEVELOPMENT

D. L. Wertlieb

EARLY CHILDHOOD EDUCATION

Early childhood education, alternately referred to as nursery or preschool education, most frequently refers to programming for children of ages 3 through 5. However, infancy through kindergarten ages are included in some discussions as well. The program may be either home- or center-based, and the focus of intervention may be the child, the parent, or both. These educational programs may or may not be incorporated into a day-care context.

Early childhood education through the 1980s has broadened in scope and in choice of curriculum content. The content reflects the influences of such theorists and researchers as Sigmund Freud, Arnold Gesell, Jean Piaget, B. F. Skinner, and Maria Montessori, while the impetus for the increased existence and expansion of such programs can be attributed to the research of D. O. Hebb, J. M. Hunt, Benjamin Bloom, and Jerome Bruner, among others. However, there is no currently agreed-upon philosophy or curricular approach.

Bronfenbrenner concludes that active parental involvement is a critical ingredient for successful early intervention and recommends a sequence of five stages, the first four of which apply to early childhood education: (a) preparation for parenthood; (b) prior to childbirth, the assurance of an adequate physical environment; (c) ages 0 to 3 of the child: a focus on strengthening the parent–child bond and on parent involvement in a home-based program; (d) ages 4 through 6 of the child: a focus on the child's cognitive development in a center-based program, with continuing parental involvement.

There are a number of prevailing models of early childhood education. A selection of these includes the Engelmann–Becker model of the University of Oregon, emphasizing specific skill acquisition by means of an operant conditioning approach; the cognitive curriculum developed by Weikart in Ypsilanti, Michigan (High/Scope), based on Piaget's theories and research; the open education model developed in Newton, Massachusetts, by Heim, derived from the British infant schools; the Bank Street Model developed in New York City by Gilkeson, a broad and inclusive developmentally oriented approach; the Responsive model by Nimnicht at San Francisco's Far West Laboratory, which allows the child to explore freely at the child's own pace, with the staff providing responses to the child's initiatives; and Montessori's Italian-derived model, which offers a prepared environment emphasizing the values of care for oneself and one's property, includes materials to promote motor, sensory, and language education, and proceeds in strict sequence according to teacher demonstration.

The many models generally agree on the need for provision of some structure, the use of play as a primary tool of learning, low teacher–child ratio, and provision of ongoing teacher training and supervision. The models differ mainly in their views of the child as a learner, the role of the teacher, and the structure of the environment provided.

There is increasing evidence to support the effectiveness of an early education experience, particularly for children from a disadvantaged socioeconomic background; effectiveness has been demonstrated for short-term cognitive and social–emotional development, as well as for long-term decreases in academic and social problems. Caldwell reviews research that demonstrates that day care does not interfere with development of parent–child attachment; that it is positively associated with cognitive growth of disadvantaged children; and that it has no negative consequences for physical health.

The 1969 "Westinghouse study," which appeared to document negligible effects of even a full year of Head Start, has been criticized as inadequate in its methodology and incorrect in its conclusions by a number of investigators. It is a generally consistent finding that highly structured programs produce the most positive cognitive gains for children from disadvantaged socioeconomic backgrounds, regardless of the details of the particular curriculum, while middle-class children respond better on the whole to programs that encourage increased diversity and initiative. However, creativity and initiative appear associated with the more flexible programs for both economic groups.

Of particular interest, in view of criticisms that have stressed only short-term gains of programs for the disadvantaged, are the results of the Perry Preschool project and the report compiled by Lazar and others and Karnes and associates. The positive gains shown in these studies also support the need for well-monitored, tightly designed delivery systems, without which such results would be unlikely. Three specific characteristics of successful programs appear to be individualization of instruction, clear specification of goals/objects/procedures, and ongoing assessment of learner response and development.

ALTERNATIVE EDUCATIONAL SYSTEMS
MONTESSORI METHOD
OPEN CLASSROOM METHOD

C. S. Lidz

EARLY RECOLLECTIONS

DEFINITION
An early recollection (ER) is a memory of a specific incident of childhood. These memories stand out from the background of general memory as incidents that an individual can visualize through the "mind's eye" so that particular details, including the feeling and tone of the incident, can be recalled almost as though the person were reliving the experience. Generally, earlier memories are assigned greater significance because they occur closer to the development of the individual's basic attitudes and outlook.

HISTORY
Freud viewed ERs as having more significance than general memories. He reasoned that because they often seemed so trivial in content, ERs must serve the purpose of hiding more traumatic material related to infantile sexual development. Thus, these "screen memories" were to be examined in analysis in a similar manner to dreams so as to uncover and deal with the repressed traumatic material.

Alfred Adler also believed ERs were very significant. He agreed with Freud that it was immaterial whether these recollections corresponded to actual fact. However, Adler concentrated on analyzing the themes or movement presented in the actual manifest content. He viewed memory as a construction rather than a reproduction. In his view, memories were constructed to support an individual's existing attitudes and biases. ERs were seen to be the most significant memories because they lay close to the creation of an individual's frame of reference for organizing, interpreting, and acting in reference to the environment. Adler said that ERs reflected the perceptual framework within which individuals interpret their present experiences.

CLINICAL USE
In gathering ERs for interpretation, the usual procedure is to obtain a minimum of from three to six distinct memories so that common themes may be recognized. Subjects are usually asked to think back to the first incident they can remember in early childhood. Only those memories that form an individual incident are regarded as true ERs. It is important

to obtain the subject's feeling regarding the ER because this is thought to indicate their attitude toward the events in the recollection.

Interpretation of ERs requires training and experience, as does the use of any projective technique. This is characteristically accomplished in close cooperation with the subject, who confirms, denies, or alters the hypotheses generated. Each ER is studied in its totality for the characteristic cognitive and behavioral patterns, and a search is made for the broad themes that unify all ERs and reflect the individual's basic frame of reference.

RESEARCH

Research has failed to provide support for Freud's hypothesis that ERs serve as screens for traumatic material. There has, however, been promising support for Adler's view that ERs, as constructions, reflect an individual's frame of reference. Thus, they have promising potential as a tool in the analysis of personality.

Some differences have been found between the themes of ERs produced by individuals who are diagnosed as belonging to various neurotic and psychotic categories. There is no conclusive evidence, however, that psychologists can consistently and accurately predict diagnostic categories solely from ERs. There is evidence that ERs may serve as a method of gathering material similar to that revealed in some projective devices, with less investment of time. Psychologists trained in interpretation of ERs have discriminated homosexuals and predicted occupational choice and vocational preference. They have also distinguished personality correlates such as degree of activity and interest in others, anxiety, and locus of control. However, as Jane Taylor warns, research on recollections is at an early stage, and more must be conducted to check the optimistic claims generated from clinical experience with ERs.

DIRECTIONS

Early recollections have been used for many years as a projective technique in psychotherapy; indeed, Ruth Munroe calls it the first of the projective techniques. Only recently, however, has their value been recognized outside a relatively limited group of psychotherapists, most of whom have been followers of Alfred Adler. Many new techniques and applications of ERs have emerged from this widened interest. The next few years should provide more research and further developments in standardized interpretation procedures.

PERSONALITY ASSESSMENT
PROJECTIVE TECHNIQUES

R. B. Armstrong

EAST–WEST PSYCHOLOGY

East–West psychology is a term used to describe the integration of Eastern or Oriental religions, philosophical disciplines, and psychological practices with Western psychological theory and practice. Confucianism, Taoism, Hinduism, Buddhism, and Islam are among the approaches included in the Eastern tradition. The Western psychological tradition includes the major psychoanalytic, behavioral, and humanistic theories.

The inquiry includes some states that go beyond limits of the ego and personality levels as defined in traditional Western psychology, such as ordinary and altered states of consciousness, meta- or optimal health, self-actualization and human potential, and the full range of human existence and development.

BOUNDARIES OF WESTERN PSYCHOLOGY

The West has basically derived its understanding of phenomena from an intellectual and objective approach. In the classical Greek concept, the universe was viewed as comprehensible by reductionism, divisible, static, nonrelativistic, and atomistic. As defined in the philosophy of Descartes, matter and spirit are seen as being fundamentally different.

Roger Walsh and others ("Paradigms in collision") described the different levels and aims of psychotherapeutic intervention as (a) traditionally therapeutic—reducing pathology and enhancing adjustment; (b) existential—confronting the questions and problems or existence; and (c) soteriological—enlightenment, transcendence of the problems first confronted at the existential level. He said that Western psychologies and therapies focus on the first two levels, while the third is the chief goal of the consciousness disciplines that incorporate Eastern thought.

Western psychology recognized distortions of reality as pathological, but equated "reality" with the world as perceived in the waking state of awareness and perceived the self as separate from what is perceived. Daniel Goleman stated that this viewpoint denied access or credibility to reality as perceived in other states of consciousness.

Carl Jung, whose investigation of psychology included Eastern religions, began to widen understanding of the unconscious to incorporate a collective dimension common to all cultures and races. In asserting the existence of "impersonal" levels of consciousness, he took a step beyond former reductionistic and mechanistic theories. Jung commented on the boundaries of Western psychology when he said, "Western consciousness is by no means the only kind of consciousness there is; it is an historically conditioned and geographically limited factor, and representative of only one part of mankind."

THE EASTERN PERSPECTIVE

The Eastern worldview is dynamic and organic, seeing the cosmos as one inseparable reality, spirit and material at the same time.

According to the Eastern orientation, the usual state of consciousness is an illusory distortion of perception (maya) arising from a dualistic distinction between subject and object, between self and the other, and between the organism and the environment.

The aim of Eastern practices is to penetrate behind the veil of the accustomed reality into an awakened state or enlightenment. It is possible to transcend ego conflicts, view ego demands with detachment, and understand human experience in the light of an awakened state of mind.

Buddhist teachings indicate the necessity of freeing oneself from the analytic mind, from all conditioning and compulsive functioning of the mind and body, and from habitual emotional responses. The teachings discuss developing awareness in terms of fractions of a second, to awaken people to the fleeting glimpses of an open, precognitive spaciousness that occur before things are interpreted in a particular perspective. Gaps in the stream of thought permit a direct experience of pure awareness that, according to the Buddhist perspective, is the individual's true nature.

Eastern tradition has emphasized a personal, empirical approach to knowledge different from the Western path of scientific, impersonal, objective knowledge. As opposed to analytic and logical thinking, direct experiential knowledge is stressed.

In the Eastern tradition, the contemplative–meditative mode of knowing has been valued as accurate, whereas traditional Western science and philosophy have used only sensation–empirical and cognition–conceptual modes.

Meditation is one of the primary practices in the East for shifting away from the active, linear mode and toward the receptive and process-oriented mode. Meditation serves to dismantle the automatism and selectivity of ordinary awareness.

EMERGENCE OF EAST–WEST PSYCHOLOGY

As mental health professionals felt more and more limited by the theories of behaviorism and psychoanalysis, which were mainly derived from studies of psychopathology, and ignored certain areas—such as value, will, and consciousness—necessary for a full inquiry into human nature, humanistic psychology emerged in the 1960s as a model based on health and the whole person. Humanistic psychology recognized the individual's drive toward self-actualization and the ways in which this idea could be fostered in individuals, groups, and organizations.

Western science in the twentieth century found that the classical concept of reductionism and an atomistic divisible universe were inadequate as explanation. Modern theoretical physics has adopted a model of the universe that is holistic, indivisible, interconnected, and dynamic, unlike the former reductionistic and static view, and supports the findings of mystical insight. This view is consistent with and supportive of the emergence of East–West psychology.

Western psychology was compelled to encompass a broader scope by the development in the culture at large of the human potential movement, cross-cultural exposure, disillusionment with the materialistic dream and the use of psychedelic drugs and technologies for the induction of higher states of consciousness. This scope incorporated these experiences and values, which were domains already explored and described in Eastern thought.

Technological advances have permitted researchers to describe the physiological and biochemical correlates of altered states of consciousness. As mental health professionals have individually and collectively been influenced and affected by their contact with Eastern philosophy, they have synthesized this awareness into their own theory and practice of psychology.

The evidence of this synthesis was seen in the development of transpersonal psychology, documented by the publication of its first journal in 1969. A. Maslow foresaw as a fourth force of psychology a psychology that would be "transpersonal, transhuman, centered in the cosmos rather than in human needs and interest, going beyond humanness, identity, self-actualization, and the like." Transpersonal psychology is conceived of as promoting and facilitating growth and as expanding awareness beyond limits prescribed by most traditional Western models of mental health.

The transpersonal psychology movement brought together insights from other traditions and from modern depth psychology, and validated and influenced an emerging paradigm that incorporated a health- rather than disease-oriented model, transcendence rather than adjustment focus, and a transpersonal rather than a personality-level approach.

In the field of health care and health psychology, disciplines from the East have been incorporated into traditional Western medicine and health care delivery. Research in biofeedback has expanded the scope of behavioral and physiological psychology.

As a specific method of training the mind, increasing awareness, and directing human attention, meditation has gained widespread recognition in the areas of personal growth, health, and stress management. It is estimated that by 1980 more than 6 million people in the United States alone had learned some form of meditation. Clinically, meditation is being taught as a tool for stress reduction, control of addiction, and increased coping ability.

Educational psychology has been influenced by the awareness that both hemispheres of the brain must be stimulated, that the development of creativity, imagery, and fantasy through the receptive mode is as important as the development of logic and reasoning in the active mode.

HUMANISTIC PSYCHOLOGY
TRANSPERSONAL PSYCHOLOGY (I, II)
YOGA

S. F. WALLOCK

EATING DISORDERS

Several defined disorders in humans are related to eating behavior and to behavior immediately following eating. The most common of these, obesity, is discussed elsewhere.

Pica is the eating of substances that provide no nutrition by individuals older than 18 months of age. Although it is clearly most common in childhood, statistics concerning its prevalence tend to be unreliable because they are largely based on individuals seeking or being brought for treatment.

Rumination is chewing and swallowing food that was previously eaten and then regurgitated. The condition is rare, occurs mostly in infants, and affects both sexes equally. Some reports of success with behavioral treatments can be found in the literature, but no convincing outcome statistics are available.

ANOREXIA NERVOSA

Anorexia nervosa is characterized by the refusal to maintain a normal minimal weight in proportion to height, intense fear of obesity, and a distorted self-image (perceiving oneself as heavier than one really is). In women, the constellation of symptoms often includes amenorrhea. Much more common in females, who comprise 94 to 95% of those afflicted, it usually has its onset during the second or third decade of life. No longer considered rare, anorexia nervosa is more common in the middle and upper socioeconomic strata. Theories as to etiology vary from primarily psychological to essentially biological; none at this time finds universal acceptance.

Typically, the disorder's onset is abrupt and may coincide with a significant life change such as the beginning of menses or moving from one school to another. A key feature of the disorder is severe food restriction, often accompanied by bizarre patterns of food intake such as eating only alone, refusing all but a narrow range of foods, secretly throwing food away, squirreling away small amounts of food for later consumption, and compulsive ordering of food on the plate. There is an obsessive preoccupation with the exact quantity of food consumed and with its caloric value. Liquids too are often restricted. Diuretic and laxative abuse is common, as is forced vomiting. This vomiting may follow "binges" where a large amount of food is consumed within a brief period. Hunger is typically denied, although the patients' intense preoccupation with food—collecting recipes, cooking for others—tends to indicate that this is not so. Vigorous exercise is often part of the pattern.

The underlying personality structure is often compulsive, with patients tending toward perfectionism and rigidity. Suppression and denial of negative affect, especially anger, are frequently found. Typically, there is great fear of loss of control. In many cases there seems to be a rejection of adult heterosexuality coupled with a desire to remain prepubertal, protected, and unchallenged by the stresses of adult life. Depression is often apparent.

Symptoms are typically denied, and resistance to treatment is often powerful. Frequently the disorder is brought to the attention of the clinician only at the insistence of relatives or close friends. There is much debate concerning what constitutes effective treatment, with verbal psychotherapy and behavior therapy (operant conditioning) programs being the most popular.

Psychotherapy, usually conducted on an outpatient basis, risks allowing prolonged malnutrition. Behavioral methods are usually effective over the short term, but tend to be associated with high relapse rates. Drug therapies have also had some success, including tricyclic antidepressants and antipsychotics. Yet, none of the therapies mentioned has proven to be the answer; anorexia nervosa remains one of the few psychological disorders with a sometimes fatal outcome.

BULIMIA

Bulimia is an eating disorder characterized by rapid ingestion of large portions of food in a brief time span. This "binge" eating is usually done surreptitiously and is interrupted by self-induced vomiting, use of laxatives, abdominal distress, sleep, or by being "caught" by others. Binges are often followed by stringent dieting in an effort to keep weight within normal limits. Patients express fear of "losing control" and being unable to restrain themselves. "Bingeing" is often followed by guilt, shame, and depression.

Bulimia is more common in females and in higher socioeconomic classes. Unlike anorexics, however, bulimics are not usually emaciated, are not amenorrheic, and are overtly interested in sex. The age of onset tends to be higher—in the 20s. Etiology is unknown, but the disorder appears to be linked to depression.

Because this disorder is clearly associated with abnormal overt behavior, operant conditioning would appear to be applicable and has met with some success in the form of contingency contracting. All forms of psychotherapy, however, tend to be stormy and difficult.

Drug treatments have also been employed with varying success. Often recommended are diphenylhydantoin (Dilantin), an anticonvulsant, and tricyclic antidepressants. Drug treatments are best seen as adjuncts to psychotherapy or behavior therapy.

FOOD DEPRIVATION
OBESITY
OBSESSIVE–COMPULSIVE PERSONALITY

H. A. STORROW

ECLECTIC PSYCHOTHERAPY

Surveys of modern therapists have shown that the majority tend to be eclectic in their theories and techniques, rather than identifying with a single school or orientation. This trend represents a shift from the 1940s and 1950s, when most therapists identified with earlier pro- or antipsychoanalytic approaches. There are a great number of psychotherapists who call themselves "eclectics," ranging all the way from the pragmatic eclectic who simply uses anything that works, to the systematic eclectic who attempts to identify underlying principles and methods that all effective therapies have in common.

M. Goldfried asked leading representatives from different orientations (humanistic-existential, analytic, and behavioral) to respond in depth to clinical questions such as "What is the role played by new experiences in facilitating change?" and "In what way do you see the therapist–client relationship as contributing to the change process?" He found strong agreement on several points:

1. The importance of new experiences
2. The significance of the therapeutic interaction
3. The emphasis on a caring, trustworthy, and confident attitude by the therapist

Goldfried suggests that common principles relevant to all therapies can be found by focusing on strategies or principles of change that lie between the highest level of abstraction (the philosophy of each therapy) and the lowest level of abstraction (the particular techniques of each therapy). These strategies are said by Goldfried to function as "clinical heuristics that implicitly guide our efforts during the course of therapy." The task of systematic eclectic therapy could be described as making the implicit explicit.

FREDERICK THORNE'S SYSTEMATIC ECLECTIC THERAPY

One of the first modern efforts to formulate a systematic eclecticism was undertaken by Frederick Thorne, who spent his entire career developing, reformulating, and expostulating an eclectic approach to psychotherapy and counseling. He believed that psychotherapy should model itself after clinical medicine and "relate therapy to diagnosis with a clear statement of the indications and contraindications for use of all methods."

"Case handling" for Thorne was a broader term than "therapy." He defined "psychological case handling" as "a generic term referring to all the operations conducted by competent psychologically trained personnel in helping clients to get along better in life." Thorne recognized that psychotherapy was only one among several choices the therapist might use.

Although Thorne greatly admired the medical model, he broadened it far beyond the narrow objectivist forms it is sometimes given when applied to psychology. Thorne argued that personality growth must be a goal of all people and that psychologists need to develop skills and theories that promote psychological health. He proposed a very broad view of psychological health that "depends upon the degree to which any person succeeds in actualizing his potentials in learning to cope with all the standard situations of life, living actively and creatively, and acting out many roles well."

HISTORICAL BASIS OF SYSTEMATIC ECLECTICISM

Hart asserts that William James was the primary source for systematic eclectic therapy. James' special position in the history of psychology is due to his theory of consciousness, whch includes a concern about subconscious processes. Within the Jamesian formulation, psychotherapy becomes a practical search for the conditions that bring about individual changes in conscious functioning.

Functional eclectic therapy provides a theoretical connection between behavior therapy, humanistic–existential therapy, and analytic therapy. Hart sees all functional eclectic therapists as sharing seven points:

1. The immediate moment is the focus of clinical concern, with gaps in consciousness considered to be of special significance.
2. Feelings are regarded as conscious regulators of behavior; regulation is achieved through expression of feelings, not merely insight about feelings.
3. The self-concept and related self-images are always carefully examined.
4. Willful choices, plans of action, and philosophical and moral concerns are included within the purview of therapy.
5. Models of growth and health are given at least as much weight as models of psychopathology.
6. Conscious, subconscious, and unconscious processes are considered, but in that order.
7. A pragmatic attitude toward the tools of therapy is endorsed; a great variety of techniques and strategies are used.

EXAMPLES OF ECLECTIC APPROACHES

The social-skills training program developed at Livermore Hospital by P. Trower, B. Bryant, and M. Argyle combined ideas and methods from drama, social psychology, communication and linguistics, psychiatry, plus experimental and clinical psychology. They also cite the specific influence of Eric Berne, Carl Rogers, Carl Jung, Sigmund Freud, J. L. Moreno, cognitive behavior therapy, and milieu therapy in their program.

They used as their unifying model the image of the therapist as a teacher whose function is not mainly diagnosing, prescribing for, and curing abnormality, but identifying areas of life dissatisfaction, setting goals, and teaching skills.

A similar eclectic program of social-skills training, directed more to nonpatients, was described by Philip Zimbardo, who stressed the value of both understanding shyness and its causes and of undertaking specific, measurable, graded steps toward overcoming it. He made use of self-testing, journal keeping, relaxation, guided imagery, role playing, and mutual-help groups in guiding people to overcome unwanted shyness.

A different kind of eclectic approach, based on the medical model, is reported by George Everly and Robert Rosenfeld. These authors present both a multilevel analysis of the stress response that includes chemical, psychophysiological, and psychological measurements, and a multimodal treatment approach that includes client education in self-responsibility, various relaxation techniques, dietary recommendations, pharmacological treatment, biofeedback techniques, hypnosis, and physical exercise. Their stated goal is "to present a unique and clinically useful discussion of numerous and diverse treatment options."

Egan presents an eclectic developmental model for the counselor or trainer that covers specific techniques for responding to the clients' self-explorations, techniques for integrative self-understanding, and methods for facilitating actions. The basic contention of Egan's approach is that both clients and beginning counselors can learn from modeling and supervised practice.

What seems clear from these examples is that many different role models (educator, trainer, coach, clinician, and counselor) can be used to generate useful therapeutic programs.

COUNSELING
ECLECTICISM
FUNCTIONAL PSYCHOLOGY
PSYCHOTHERAPY

J. T. HART

ECLECTICISM

In common usage, eclecticism refers to the selection of the best features from a variety of sources and sometimes also to the correlated attempt to reconcile differences among those sources. In psychology the term has most often been used to refer to theoretical orientations, an eclectic position being one that either ignores or minimizes distinctions among theories while accepting what seem to be the most desirable aspects of each.

The psychological system most frequently labelled *eclectic* is functionalism. It has often been criticized on the grounds that insufficient attention is paid to critical theoretical differences—a criticism based on substantive rather than methodological arguments. An alternative interpretation is to emphasize *metatheoretical eclecticism*. Selection of the best methods from various sources is the objective of this form of eclecticism.

Extension of such an eclectic approach to interdisciplinary problems is a logical next step. This form of eclecticism may well be regarded as essential for scientific progress, particularly insofar as filling in the gaps between scientific disciplines is concerned. Even within a single discipline such as psychology, methodological eclecticism can be defended because few, if any, of the principles are so well established as to be immune from questioning.

The functionalist reply to the usual criticism would emphasize the need for breadth in problem selection and empirical technique, as well as tolerance in theoretical approach. Moreover, the opposition of various theoretical positions needs to be implemented in experimental designs so that adequate empirical bases for theoretical development can be provided.

It is important to recognized the temporary, yet recurrent, character of eclectism. Generally, it is a transient stage in the development of a maturing science. Thus, while some degree of eclecticism may be desirable, and perhaps even necessary, in the early stages of a new discipline or subdiscipline, it should gradually recede, only to reappear as new areas of research and theory are opened.

FUNCTIONALISM
PHILOSOPHY OF SCIENCE

M. H. MARX

ECOLOGICAL PSYCHOLOGY

The contribution of the ecological perspective to psychology has been to consider individual behavior as inseparable from its context, including the interpersonal, social, and physical aspects. The early classic work in ecological psychology was performed by Roger Barker and Herbert Wright.

For Barker and his followers the basic unit of analysis was the *behavior setting,* conceived as a bounded social and physical system that has a function or *program* to perform. Each behavior setting has its participants, its range of normative activities, and various physical artifacts that guide the flow of behavior.

Much of the work of Barker and his associates involved creating comprehensive baseline descriptions of behavior settings. In contrast to other branches of psychology, little use was made of measurement devices that could conceivably intrude on the setting, such as questionnaires, interview guides, and the like. The method was basically *ethnographic* in nature, involving laborious and lengthy direct observation of behavior settings and the compiling of *specimen records* of behavior. Measurement domains of interest have included the demographic mix of participants, the nature of the program or function being carried out, time and place boundaries, and what generic types of behavior occur. However, in the early work of Barker and associates there was very little attempt to aggregate descriptors on the basis of any *a priori* conceptual model.

From a conceptual perspective, the variables of interest to Barker-style ecological psychology are midrange between traditional psychology and sociology. The array of variables is obviously much wider than the discrete, single-stimulus orientation of psychology.

A recent development emanating from an ecological perspective has been the intentional manipulation of behavior settings. Another line of work in psychology from an ecological perspective has placed an even heavier emphasis on the experimental production and evaluation of social innovations and has virtually ignored the ethnographic method and conceptual nomenclature of Barker and his followers. The major importance of this work has been in extending experimental approaches to the field setting, as a way of systematically developing what are, in Barker's terminology, new behavior settings.

It should also be noted that other ecological perspectives on behavior can be found outside the psychology field. Some organizational researchers have concentrated on the physical and technological artifacts of work settings and attempted to intervene in both social and technical systems to produce desired behavioral outcomes. This field of *sociotechnical* design has many affinities with ecological psychology as described here, although most research has been conducted in industrial settings.

That behavior is a function of both intrapersonal and environmental factors has long been a premise presumably accepted by all psychologists, yet significant portions of the physical and social environment are ignored in traditional psychological research. The ecological perspective provides a way of maintaining a conceptual and empirical bridge to those important aspects of the environment.

COGNITIVE SOCIAL PSYCHOLOGY
CROSS-CULTURAL PSYCHOLOGY
SOCIAL CLASS

L. G. TORNATZKY

ECOLOGICAL VALIDITY

Ecological validity refers to the fact that an organism is genetically or environmentally prepared to exhibit different behaviors in different contexts or environments. The organism performs well at one time and place but not so well, or at all, in others.

By and large, ecological validity appears in the literature as a criticism of animal learning studies and comparative psychology because most animal behavior studies in the United States from 1930 through the 1970s were conducted in the laboratory with the white rat or pigeon as the usual subject. The whole approach was quite narrow; not only was the subject pool limited but the problems, situations, and responses were sorely circumscribed. There were clear exceptions, of course, with Schneirla's research in the field with army ants and other animals and Carpenter's work with nonhuman primates in Central America leading the way. A few isolated views of learning were aware of these strictures against the prevailing Zeitgeist quite early.

However, the bulk of the research published in the *Journal of comparative and physiological psychology* through the early 1970s was concerned with basic principles of learning from a standpoint that largely ignored the nature of the organism being studied. For the most part, the rat and pigeon were seen as animal models of human behavior. Later, psychological investigators emphasized ecological relevance and the importance of breadth in the study of behavior, as, for example, Kamil's study of foraging behavior and Barash's study of the social behavior of marmots. In fact, the range of behaviors studied subsequent to early experimenters attests to the ecological relevance of orientation, hoarding, nest building, exploration, ingestive behavior, play, tonic immobility, hibernation, predation, thermoregulation, elimination, care of body surfaces (grooming, dust bathing, etc.), dominance, social organization and facilitation, mimicry, aggression, cooperation, competition, avoidance, limitation, courtship and mating, parental behavior, tool use, and abnormal behavior. Timberlake's work represents an attempt to incorporate the ecological demands of different species into learning theory.

Boice has reviewed the literature on surplusage, a sidelight to the notion of ecological validity, surplusage notes that animals have evolved a greater ability to learn and remember than seems useful in the natural habitat. This is probably not too surprising and says little that contradicts ecological relevance.

An illustration of ecological validity is a study by Seyfarth and Cheney on vervets. These monkeys make different alarm calls for three different predators: leopards, eagles, and pythons. The monkeys decode the meaning of each signal to arrange their escape route to fit the predator. For example, they climb trees to leopard calls, search the sky or run into the bushes for eagle calls, and stand on their hind legs and search the grass for snake calls. Using recordings of the alarm types these investigators have demonstrated that the vervets respond selectively to the sound of the calls rather than to any visual cues.

In addition, Seyfarth and Cheney have determined that vervets are probably responding to the meaning of the calls not just the acoustic signals. The investigators exploited an habituation–dishabituation technique, and the monkeys made two quite different sounds to convey the same message: a loud trill, or *wrr*, and a harsh raspy chutter. Both *wrr* and chutter occurred when neighboring groups of vervets had been seen. They habituated monkeys to *wrr* and found chutter was also habituated and vice versa, but if the monkeys were responding to the sound of the call rather than its meaning, dishabituation should have occurred. With two different calls with different meanings habituation did not transfer from one to the other. Ecologically oriented research can alter our ideas about other animals' capabilities.

ANIMAL COMMUNICATION
AUDITORY DISCRIMINATION
AUDITORY PERCEPTION
BEHAVIORAL GENETICS
ECOLOGICAL PSYCHOLOGY
FIELD EXPERIMENTATION
HERITABILITY
INSTINCT
SPECIES-SPECIFIC BEHAVIOR

M. R. DENNY

EDUCATIONAL ASSESSMENT

Educational assessment refers to psychological (or psychoeducational) evaluation carried out with regard to decisions to be made in a school. The target may vary from the child in school to situational aspects of the educational setting, or program planning and evaluation. Most frequently, the focus is the individual learner, and the issue may be either the learning processes *per se* or the pupil's behavior in class. An assessment of the learner will consider the child's history and characteristics, the nature of the tasks with which the child must deal, and any relevant aspects of the home and school situation.

Educational assessment differs from other types of assessment not only in the focus on the school setting, but also in the assessment methodology. There may be more utilization of rating scales, observational approaches, criterion-referenced measures, and "dynamic" (test–teach–test) approaches than in traditional psychological assessment, which focuses on personality traits and dynamics.

Educational assessment, perhaps more than any other area of assessment, has been influenced by legal actions and court decisions reflecting current public sentiment and cultural mores. Current legislation requires that assessment instruments be administered in the child's native language, be valid for the specific purposes employed, be administered by trained professionals, and be applied in a manner that measures the aptitudes intended and not the obstructing handicaps. The law has also opened the records of assessors to the consumer, so that any information recorded on paper has potential exposure to parents, older children, or their counsel.

Controversies have arisen, on the one hand, over what intelligence is and whether current measures in fact assess it, and on the other hand, over whether it is sufficient to attempt to measure such a concept as intelligence—that is whether this is a relevant variable vis-à-vis education, in contrast to alternatives that propose to assess learning ability as a dynamic process. Another proposal is to assess competencies associated with specific predictive criteria such as job success.

McClelland described the redundancy of assessing learning ability with measures involving mastery of the abilities to be assessed. This is the dilemma of educational measurement in relation to populations whose experiences and opportunities are either more limited than or different from the majority culture as represented in the school system. Newland presented data suggesting that the IQ differences so frequently cited between advantaged and disadvantaged groups reflect performance on product-oriented measures, while such differences are considerably reduced on tests that tap conceptual processes. Such findings are expressed in increased concern with nondiscriminatory assessment—that is, in attempts to devise and determine approaches that on the one hand, do not obstruct individuals from minority groups from demonstrating inherent abilities, while, on the other hand, provide information meaningful for educational planning.

Program planning and evaluation is a relatively new and fast developing involvement for the educational assessor. As the psychologist's involvements within school systems broaden and increase in supervisory responsibilities, there is a corresponding increase in the need to become familiar with systems thinking and means of making large-scale decisions.

Finally, an area of research that promises eventual positive impingement on educational assessment is ecological psychology. Measures that express an ecological point of view include psychosituational assessment and the Assessment Procedure for Direct Application to the Classroom Instructional Strategy Sheet—both of them informal procedures—as well as the standardized coded approach of Wahler, House, and Stambaugh in *Ecological assessment of child problem behavior.* The hallmark of an ecological approach to assessment is the emphasis on naturalistic observation, where the assessor minimizes intervention and records events as they occur.

COLLEGE ACADEMIC PREDICTION
LEARNING OUTCOMES I AND II
SELECTION TESTS
TESTING AND LEGISLATION

C. S. LIDZ

EDUCATIONAL MAINSTREAMING

Mainstreaming in education refers to the integration of pupils with special needs into classes and programs of regular or "mainstream" education. This may involve the introduction of children with disabilities into a nonspecialized environment, or conversely may involve introduction of nondisabled students into a specialized educational setting; the latter process is referred to as reverse mainstreaming.

Mainstreaming has been given impetus by federal legislation for disabled persons, which prescribes the "least restrictive" placement of pupils with identified special needs along a continuum of full integration into a regular class (most desirable) through full-time placement in a specialized program (least desirable).

Mainstreaming is justified on several assumptions: (a) that children with disabilities will fare better socially and academically under the most normalized conditions possible; (b) that children without disabilities will be positively influenced and not hindered in their progress by association and interaction with disabled peers; (c) that the services necessary to support integration are identifiable and available.

Disabilities are not equal. Not only does each disability have idiosyncratic requirements for the achievement of increased normalization—for example, reduced architectural barriers for orthopedic disabilities, or sign language interpretors for the deaf—but teachers, pupils, and the general community have differing attitudes regarding the desirability of individuals with certain disabling conditions.

Mainstreaming program options include varying the daily proportion of regular classroom attendence of the disabled child; a "side-by-side" approach of dispersing specialized classrooms among regular classes within the same building; utilization of a resource room to provide specialized instruction for a pupil otherwise placed in a regular class; itinerant teachers offering direct instruction; the use of aides and volunteers; consultative support for regular classroom teachers; and referral to outside agencies for provision of specialized services.

Mere proximity of disabled and nondisabled children does not result in a successful mainstreaming experience. Children need to interact in order to modify their attitudes. Teachers need to intervene both personally and programmatically and, to do so effectively, require supportive consultative services and training experiences. There is evidence that the attitudes of teachers toward mainstreaming can be positively influenced by in-service training, but it is not clear that teachers are being given sufficient training and supportive experiences to enable them to accommodate exceptional children placed in their classrooms. For example, Best finds that only 54% of the teachers he surveyed had in-service education available to them, and, in the study by S. Graham and others,

the resource room teachers expressed satisfaction that they had good communication with regular classroom teachers, while the regular classroom teachers reported the opposite. The attitudes of teachers toward mainstreaming appear to reflect their feelings of ability to succeed with teaching special students, and success requires adequate supportive services.

Is mainstreaming an effective alternative to full-time special education for exceptional children? Any response must consider the continuum of mainstreaming strategies as well as the variety, nature, and degree of exceptionality. There is no simple positive or negative conclusion.

ACADEMIC ABILITY GROUPS
SCHOOL LEARNING

C. S. LIDZ

EDUCATIONAL PSYCHOLOGY

To understand educational psychology, one must recognize its origins. Educational philosophy and practice have served as its major foundations. In the first half of the nineteenth century, educational philosophers expressed increased concern for the quality of education as well as teacher preparation programs. In due time such concerns became a focal point for many educational psychologists. Johann Pestalozzi, the Swiss educator known as the "father of modern pedagogy," was among the first to emphasize the need for instructing teachers. His philosophical contributions, including the importance of stressing human emotion and kindness in the teaching of children, led to the establishment of normal schools to prepare teachers. Johann Herbart enunciated the doctrine of apperception and emphasized the need to relate new with old experiences and to attend to the sequencing of instructional units. A third educational philosopher, Friedrich Froebel, is credited with establishing the kindergarten movement in Germany in 1837, and with popularizing such concepts as self-activity, continuity, self-expression, creativity, and physical and mental growth and development. Although these three pioneers were at times criticized for the methods they used, they are given credit for stressing development as an essential part of the psychology of education.

The quality and theoretical bases of education continued to preoccupy educational leaders during the latter part of the nineteenth century. In 1899 William James emphasized the pragmatic aspects of psychology, while simultaneously cautioning teachers against expecting too much from this scientific discipline. James devoted much of his career to serving as an intermediary between psychology and education.

Early in the twentieth century Maria Montessori implemented her program of education, which combined work and play for young children. At approximately the same time John Dewey, at the University of Chicago, established his experimental school with its student-centered curriculum.

SCIENTIFIC AND APPLIED FOCUS

The scientific, experimental dimension characterizing educational psychology, although traceable to Wilhelm Wundt, is more traditionally and immediately attributed to Edward L. Thorndike, who earned the title "father of educational psychology." Thorndike, more than any other single individual, determined educational psychology's early development. He stated unambiguously that his objective was to apply "methods of exact science" to educational problems.

Charles Hubbard Judd (1873–1946), a contemporary of Thorndike, is also recognized as a chief contributor to the early development of educational psychology. A. A. Van Fleet (1976) points out that Judd, a student of Wundt, provided a marked contrast to Thorndike. While Thorndike and his students were preoccupied with learning theories, animal experiments, and the quantification of data, Judd and his students focused on transforming the educational scene—its content, organization, policies, and practices. This concern for school organization led to Judd's recommending the establishment of junior high schools, as well as junior colleges, and to his concentrating on ensuring smooth transitions between elementary school and secondary school, and between secondary school and college. Judd also stressed the need to democratize education: During his professional career, the percentage of youth attending secondary school increased from 7 to 75%. Judd focused both his experimental and theoretical work on school subjects and the best ways to teach them. He was highly critical of research not directly applicable to learning as it occurred in the school.

Thorndike and Judd provided a contrast that was to characterize subsequent movements and leaders of educational psychology. Thus, the measurement and learning theory movements with their laboratory origins, and the school and curriculum movements with their classroom orientation, moved forward with greater independence and less integration than desirable. Evidence of this independence was observed not only in publications and formal presentations, but also in relationships among schools of education, departments of psychology, and educational psychology units. Ironically, the discipline that professed to be concerned with the integration of psychology and education was often physically isolated from faculty in psychology and philosophically rejected by faculty in schools of education. The consequence for educational psychology tended to be a narrow concept of learning that was challenged, if not rejected, by educators and psychologists. The consequence for educational practice was a preoccupation with credentialing, professionalism, and curriculum development, with all too little concern for theoretical or psychological foundations.

The study of human development—today widely recognized as a major component of educational psychology—is most directly traceable to G. Stanley Hall, who focused his efforts on the study of adolescence, and Arnold Gesell, who explored and explained the early years of childhood. Their writings reflected a dependency on field observations, survey responses, and interpretations of nonexperimental data. Hall and Gesell were far more committed to gaining practical insights than to generating scientific theories. Because of the unscientific nature of their works and those of most of their colleagues, the field of child study was subject to much criticism.

RECURRING ISSUES: CONTENT AND NATURE

Debate regarding the proper content of courses and texts within the field of educational psychology began before Thorndike's edition was off the press. Over the years, numerous reviews and surveys have been conducted in an effort to identify the boundaries of this discipline.

The numerous studies designed to assess the content of courses and texts in educational psychology during the past 70 years all have revealed marked diversity within this discipline.

An issue related to diversity of content—and one just as old (and new)—is whether educational psychology is a discipline in its own right. Ausubel argued that, despite the fact and misfortune that many educational psychology textbooks contained little more than "watered-down miscellany of general psychology," educational psychology was indeed a discipline in its own right. He viewed it as "that special branch of psychology concerned with the nature, conditions, outcomes, and evaluation of school learning and retention," and included among the special subject matters of this discipline all cognitive, developmental, affective, motivational, personality, and social variables manipulable by educators and curriculum developers. He recognized educational psychology as an applied discipline and contended that it was distinct from psychology in terms of its specific school-classroom focus. Ausubel further argued that classroom learning problems could not be solved by merely extrapolating

from "basic-science laws that are derived from the laboratory study of . . . learning."

Others have contended that educational psychology amounts to little more than psychological theories placed in the context of education. The recency of such criticisms, coupled with the promptness and vehemency of the rebuttals elicited, is evidence that the validity of this discipline is not a settled matter. Issues associated with the measurement of learning are sure to keep the field of educational psychology alive and vibrant.

In 1982, nearly 14% of the members of the American Psychological Association identified themselves as educational psychologists and held membership in Division 15 (Educational Psychology) within the national association. The history of this division presents a picture of the struggle, controversy, and resiliency that has characterized educational psychology. While members of Division 15 are primarily affiliated with universities and research centers, a large group of educational psychologists is to be found in settings more directly related to the teaching and learning activities of schools.

INSTRUCTIONAL THEORY
LAWS OF LEARNING
LEARNING OUTCOMES I AND II

M. M. CLIFFORD

EDUCATIONAL TESTING SERVICE

In December 1947, the Educational Testing Service (ETS) was chartered by the New York State Board of Regents as a nonprofit corporation that would carry out the testing functions of the College Entrance Examination Board, the Carnegie Corporation, and the American Council on Education. Henry Chauncey, former dean at Harvard University and U. S. Navy examiner, and Devereux Josephs, former president of the Carnegie Corporation, were among the five founders of ETS. The new corporation dedicated itself to serving educational and government agencies, by providing tests and related services, and to expanding and improving testing theory and techniques through research.

Since its inception, ETS has grown tremendously and expanded from its main office in Princeton, New Jersey, to several regional offices in the United States and 5000 testing centers, of which 400 are in other countries. Ninety percent of the corporation's revenues stem from testing activities, which include academic testing programs at all educational levels from elementary and secondary schools to the graduate and professional school levels. By far the most voluminous of these activities are the Scholastic Aptitude Test (SAT) and the Preliminary SAT/National Merit Scholarship Qualifying Test programs, which handle a candidate volume of well more than 1 million students per year. ETS, together with the American College Testing Program—a similar, though smaller, organization—accounts for most of the screening of college applicants and selection of scholarship recipients in the United States. In addition, its Law School Admission Test, Graduate Management Admission Test, and Graduate Record Examination are widely used by graduate and professional schools for applicant selection. The Test of English as a Foreign Language helps colleges and universities determine if foreign students have sufficient proficiency in English to enter U.S. higher education institutions. ETS has also developed tests for specialty certification, such as the National Teacher Examination, and achievement tests in a variety of subjects through its Advanced Placement and College Level Examination programs.

Increasingly, since the 1960s, ETS came under attack from various sources for allegedly blocking the entrance to higher education for thousands of candidates through its admission testing programs. Criticism has centered on the presumptive lack of predictive validity of tests such as the SAT, on the purportedly excessive weight given to test score in admission decisions, and on the stringent security measures under which such tests are administered. One result of these criticisms was the enactment in the 1970s of state laws regulating the disclosure of testing information. ETS has vigorously defended its practices in a number of forums.

In addition to its academic testing activities, ETS provides a number of institutional services to educational centers. These include gathering information on financial aid needs for scholarship programs, locating minority graduate school applicants, developing instruments to evaluate college instructors and institutional functioning, and providing a broad range of consultative services aimed at improving assessment and instructional practices. In 1978 the ETS International Office was established to coordinate activities involving other nations.

Through its Center for Occupational and Professional Measurement Programs, ETS has also become heavily involved in developing and administering tests for licensing, certification, continuing education, and self-assessment in more than 50 occupations and professions. ETS also houses one of the largest open libraries of tests in the world, and the Educational Resources Information Center (ERIC) Clearinghouse for unpublished research and documents relating to testing, measurement, evaluation, learning theory, and human development.

Approximately 8% of ETS's budget is devoted to research activities through its research divisions. Funded by ETS, the federal government, and foundations, these divisions maintain a large staff of specialists who conduct basic and applied research in psychology and education.

ACADEMIC APTITUDE TESTING
PSYCHOMETRICS

S. P. Urbina

EDWARDS PERSONAL PREFERENCE SCHEDULE

The Edwards Personal Preference Schedule (EPPS) is a self-report personality inventory that measures 15 needs and motives: abasement, achievement, affiliation, aggression, autonomy, change, deference, dominance, endurance, exhibition, heterosexuality, intraception, nurturance, order, and succorance—all derived from Murray's theory of personality. The test is designed for college students and adults.

The EPPS consists of 210 items, each one containing two self-descriptive statements. Statements are matched on their social desirability but measure different needs. Test takers are to select the item in the pair that best describes them. This forced-choice format is used because Edwards found that the probability of endorsing statements was dependent on their social desirability scale value. By using a forced-choice format, test takers must respond on the basis of the item content (that is, the need or motive), rather than on the basis of the statement's social desirability.

The use of a forced-choice format results in ipsative scores—that is, scores indicating the relative strengths of the various needs within the individual. This presents some problems in interpretation of scores and in validity studies, as two test takers can obtain the same score on a test but differ in their absolute strength of the need or motive.

FORCED CHOICE
IPSATIVE SCALING
PERSONALITY ASSESSMENT
TESTING METHODS

F. G. Brown

EFFECTIVE COMPONENTS OF PSYCHOTHERAPY

All forms of psychotherapy, by and large, are followed by more benefit in more people than is informal help or the simple passage of time. This strongly suggests that, despite the clamor of conflicting claims by different schools and their doctrinal and procedural differences, all must share certain therapeutic features—features, moreover, that distinguish psychotherapies from other forms of help by friends, relatives, or others.

Three major distinguishing features can be noted: (a) the helper is a professional; (b) the proceedings are confidential; and (c) the therapy is grounded in a theory that "explains" the patient's distress and prescribes certain procedures for alleviating it. In addition, the therapeutic medium of all psychotherapies is symbolic communication, usually by words but sometimes by exercises and other bodily rituals that have a large symbolic component.

The forms of distress and disability assumed to be amenable to psychotherapy share significant psychological components. These range from emotional states exacerbating chronic illnesses to psychoses, but most patients in psychotherapy suffer primarily from so-called neurotic symptoms such as anxiety, depression, phobias, and obsessions. The specific aim of all forms of psychotherapy is to relieve symptoms, but this invariably includes implicitly strengthening patients' self-esteem, improving their coping strategies, and the like.

THE DEMORALIZATION HYPOTHESIS

Since all forms of psychotherapy are helpful, their shared features must counteract a type of distress and disability common to most seekers of psychotherapy. This condition may be termed *demoralization*—a sense of incompetence based on inability to solve some internal conflict or external problem, coupled with feelings of distress. Why some persons are more prone to demoralization than others is largely unknown. Inborn characteristics such as lack of stamina or hardihood probably have much to do with it, as does the extent of support from others.

An empirical definition of demoralization has been provided by the following list of complaints, scales of which a series of population surveys found to be as highly correlated as the probable error of each scale permitted: poor self-esteem, hopelessness–helplessness, dread (including fear of insanity), confused thinking, sadness, anxiety, psychophysiological symptoms, and perceived physical health. These include the most frequent complaints of patients in psychotherapy.

Except possibly for some phobias, some depressions, and obesity, no convincing evidence has emerged that one therapeutic approach is more successful overall than any other. A plausible hypothesis, then, is that patients seek therapy because of both demoralization and specific symptoms. Although both patients and therapists believe the aims of therapy to be relief of symptoms, successful therapy in fact counteracts the patient's demoralization, and this is the main source of benefit.

From the standpoint of the demoralization hypothesis, patients' complaints can be grouped into three classes. The first and most common are direct expressions of demoralization, notably anxiety and depression. They are also the most responsive to any therapeutic intervention. Second are symptoms related to pathologic organic processes such as cyclical depressions, hallucinations, delusions, and the like. Demoralization may often play an etiological role in these, because stressing the patient readily exacerbates them.

The final group includes so-called neurotic symptoms such as phobias, compulsions, obsessions, amnesias, and the like, currently believed to be symbolic self-perpetuating and self-defeating efforts to solve internal conflicts or persistent difficulties with others resulting from distorted perceptions of self and others. Their origin is customarily attributed to deficient or damaging learning experiences in early childhood.

SHARED FEATURES OF ALL PSYCHOTHERAPIES THAT COUNTERACT DEMORALIZATION

All therapies combat demoralization by seeking to counteract patients' feelings of discouragement, isolation, loss of self-confidence, and feelings of failure. Morale-enhancing features of all psychotherapies can be divided into those inherent in the therapist–patient relationship and the therapeutic setting, and those related to the processes of therapy.

Therapist–Patient Relationship

At the most general level, demoralization is combatted by the therapist's being a professional in the broadest sense of the term—the possessor of an expertise either recognized by society as a whole (as in the case of psychologists, psychiatrists, and social workers), or acknowledged by a group whose values are shared by the patient.

Furthermore, as a professional the therapist is expected to assume some responsibility for the patient's welfare, and the therapist's professional status reassures the patient that the therapist will not exploit the patient, and that the patient need not fear that what he or she says or does will disrupt the therapeutic relationship through angering, seducing, or otherwise causing the therapist to abandon the professional role. The therapist counteracts demoralization by conveying continuing willingness to listen to and respect the patient.

By accepting the patient for treatment, the therapist implies that the therapist believes the patient can be helped. This in itself inspires the patient's hope—an emotion that powerfully counteracts demoralization and is often probably healing in itself. Arousal of hope at the first therapeutic contact may account in large part for the large proportion of outpatients (60 to 80%) who improve significantly after one interview. The therapist also provides a consistent outlook, value system, and standards of behavior that help the patient to reduce confusion.

In addition to these general therapeutic features of the patient–therapist relationship, the therapist may influence the patient in specific ways through the therapeutic procedure. However "nondirective" the procedure may seem to be, patients tend to follow the therapists' leads, even when therapists are not aware of giving any. The influencing power of therapists rests on the patients' dependence on them for help, intensified by the patients' concern about the therapists' opinion of them. *Evaluation apprehension*, as it has been termed, has been shown to heighten a person's susceptibility to influence.

Therapeutic Setting

A private office or a clinic conveys the atmosphere of a place of healing. Because what occurs in therapy is confidential—that is, confined to the therapeutic setting—the patient is free to reveal thoughts, feelings, and attitudes, including shameful or repressed aspects of the self, without fear of consequences beyond the therapeutic situation. Thus, the setting in itself facilitates morale-enhancing experiences such as increased self-awareness and the relief following revelation of information or exploration of personal problems that the patient fears mentioning in settings of daily life.

MORALE-ENHANCING ASPECTS OF THE THERAPEUTIC PROCESS

Emotional Arousal

Although the reason is unclear, clinical experience indicates that beneficial change in the patient is facilitated by the emotional arousal accompanying therapy. This arousal may be caused by feelings toward the therapist; by reexperiencing repressed feelings toward self and family; in behavior therapies, by attempting to change habitual behaviors; by particular maneuvers to elicit strong emotions; or in other ways.

Cognitive and Experiential Learning

All therapies convey new information by helping patients to bring to awareness hitherto unavailable knowledge about themselves. To be most effective, these discoveries must provide a new emotional experience.

As models, guides, and advisors, all psychotherapists provide the patient with a variety of opportunities for learning better ways of coping with problems. By the type of questions asked, the therapist offers a model of rational decision making, including consideration of alternatives before acting.

Enhancement of the Sense of Self-Efficacy

Patients in psychotherapy typically believe themselves to be more or less at the mercy of inner feelings or external stresses. This state of mind is coupled with a sense of failure, as well as dysphoric emotions that further reduce the patient's coping capacity. Thus, strengthening the patient's sense of mastery or self-efficacy is probably the strongest morale-enhancing component of all psychotherapies. To this end, all therapies typically emphasize that therapeutic gains result primarily from the patient's own efforts.

IMPLICATIONS OF THE DEMORALIZATION HYPOTHESIS FOR TRAINING

The likelihood that all psychotherapeutic procedures are followed by essentially similar overall improvement rates should not be taken to imply that training of therapists is unnecessary. Therapeutic skill may be compared to musical talent: Not everyone can be a virtuoso, but—except for the few who are tone-deaf—anyone can learn to play an instrument and improve with practice. Similarly, mastery of one or more procedures maintains the therapist's own sense of competence, and thereby the patient's faith in the therapist—states of mind crucial for the success of all therapies. The feeling of competence also sustains the therapist's self-confidence in the face of the inevitable failures experienced by practitioners of all therapeutic schools. Finally, only through persistent, expert application of specific therapies can any hitherto undiscovered beneficial effects be discovered for different clinical conditions or personality types.

Ideally, then, training programs should teach several forms of therapy, so the student can pick those that are most congenial. The more a therapist can master, the better; but in any case the therapist can rest assured that, for most if not all patients, the chosen method will not be less effective than alternative approaches.

PSYCHOTHERAPY
PSYCHOTHERAPY RESEARCH

J. D. FRANK

EFFECTIVENESS OF PSYCHOTHERAPY

Evaluating the effectiveness of psychotherapy is clearly a matter of some importance and a topic of controversy since the 1950s. Before the 1950s, there had been little research to evaluate the effectiveness of psychotherapy. Many clinicians did not see the need to conduct such evaluations. To them, the effectiveness of psychotherapy was obvious even though there were occasional clinical reports of problematic cases. In 1952, Hans Eysenck, a British psychologist, reviewed 24 studies of psychotherapy and reached some startling conclusions. In essence, he concluded that psychoanalysis was decidedly less effective than no therapy and that so-called eclectic therapy was only slightly less effective than no therapy at all. Eysenck's article drew a number of angry and critical responses from psychologists, who found a number of serious faults with his analysis. Despite the defects in Eysenck's article, attention was drawn to the need for research to evaluate the efficacy of psychotherapy. Since then, there has been a steady increase in both the quality and quantity of research evaluating the outcome of psychotherapy, as well as a number of systematic reviews of this literature.

RESEARCH DATA ON OUTCOME

Eysenck contributed new and more comprehensive appraisals in 1961 and 1966 but reached conclusions similar to his earlier work. In 1970 Meltzoff and Kornreich reviewed 101 studies on the outcome of psychotherapy and noted that 80% of the studies reported positive outcomes. They also stated that the better the study, the more positive the outcome reported. This was followed by a review by Bergin that also concluded that psychotherapy on average secured modestly positive results. These reviews and appraisals have been followed by a number of others. Although most have tended to be positive, some critics, old and new, have made their views known. Of particular importance, however, was the appearance, first in 1977 and then more comprehensively in 1980, of a new statistical means of summarizing and evaluating a large number of studies. Instead of relying on individual reviewers, who conceivably might be biased in some ways when evaluating the results of numerous studies, the new procedure, called metaanalysis, reduced this potential source of bias. Essentially, in metaanalysis different research studies evaluated are treated similarly to the way subjects in a single study are treated. Subjects receiving psychotherapy are compared with subjects in control groups and an effect size (ES) is secured. The mean of the psychotherapy groups minus the mean of the control groups divided usually by the standard deviation of the control groups provides the ES. The larger the ES, the more positive the outcome of psychotherapy is considered to be.

The first published psychotherapy review using metaanalysis was completed by Smith and Glass in 1977 based on 375 studies. The obtained ES of 0.68 was interpreted as indicating that the average psychotherapy client exceeded 75% of the controls on the outcome measures used. In 1980, a more complete metaanalysis based on 475 published and unpublished studies was completed by Smith, Glass, and Miller. An ES of 0.85 was secured, indicating that 80% of the treated subjects exceeded the mean of the controls. These investigators concluded that psychotherapy was indeed effective.

These positive reports were responded to differently by different individuals. Clinicians practicing psychotherapy were quite pleased to accept these results. However, some psychologists such as Eysenck were quite critical. In particular, the lumping together of studies of both good and poor quality in the pool of studies evaluated was considered to be a weak aspect of metaanalyses. Smith, Glass, and Miller, in rebuttal, stated that most other reviews tended to be somewhat selective in a biased manner or did not specify clearly how the studies included were selected for review. One other finding in the large-scale metaanalysis by Smith et al. was that there were no really significant differences between the different forms of psychotherapy evaluated.

Since 1980, a number of additional reviews and metaanalyses were performed, and with few exceptions, the earlier results tended to be confirmed. Although not all reviews and metaanalyses obtain precisely the same quantitative results, as the research samples vary in size, composition, and outcome measures; nevertheless, the overall pattern is essentially similar and positive. Clients who receive psychotherapy show significantly better improvement at the end of therapy than do control subjects who do not receive treatment.

Some investigators emphasize that the results secured by means of psychotherapy are not limited or trivial. Although outcomes vary among clients, the majority are helped to some degree and many are helped to a clinically significant degree. Although some clients may show negative effects as a result of psychotherapy, this number is relatively small compared with those who demonstrate beneficial effects. One review on the effectiveness of psychotherapy concluded:

A large number of controlled studies reveal a positive therapeutic effect when compared with no treatment; and very few reviewers disagree with this basic overall observation.

ILLUSTRATIVE STUDIES AND RESEARCH ISSUES

Early studies of outcome had a number of deficiencies, including mixed groups of patients with unreliable diagnoses, variability and limitations in the criteria for appraising outcome, variability in the lengths of therapy, variability in the experience of the therapists, and inadequate statistical analyses. Sophistication of research in this area has increased noticeably since 1970. One of the first studies to be recognized as incorporating many improved features of research design in evaluating outcome in psychotherapy was conducted by Sloane, Staples, Cristol, Yorkston, and Whipple. The purpose was to compare the effectiveness of brief psychoanalytically oriented psychotherapy and behavior therapy. An unusual feature was the use of well-known and experienced therapists. Each of the three therapists in each group was to see 10 patients for a period of 4 months. The patients had been screened at the Temple University Outpatient Clinic and psychotherapy was considered to be a suitable treatment for their problems. In addition to two treatment groups, a "wait-list" control group of 30 patients also was used. These patients were promised they would receive therapy within a 4-month period. Patients were randomly assigned to treatment groups but were matched in terms of sex and "severity of neurosis." They were evaluated by a clinical assessor and the main focus of evaluation was on the three principal complaints agreed to by both patient and assessor.

To ensure that the two different forms of therapy were actually being conducted as prescribed by the respective theoretical orientations, the major features of each were listed, and tape-recorded sessions were made for purposes of appraisal. The two forms of therapy could be easily differentiated and were judged as complying with the basic tenets of each approach. The patients were evaluated at the beginning and at the end of therapy and also 1 year after beginning therapy. For ethical reasons, patients who had not made adequate progress at the end of the 4-month therapy period were continued in therapy. Thus, the 1-year evaluations were of limited value. The 4-month results at termination showed that the patients in the two therapy groups improved equally in all three of their target symptoms and significantly more than did the patients in the wait-list group.

Of particular interest in the National Institute of Mental Health (NIMH) study was the use of both general outcome measures of depression and psychological functioning as well as some specific measures to evaluate hypothesized differential outcomes for the two psychotherapies. On the general outcome measures, patients showed significant improvement at post-treatment, but no significant differences were found between the two forms of psychotherapy. More surprisingly, the two forms of therapy did not differ significantly on the more specialized measures of cognitive functioning and social adjustment that were hypothesized to favor the cognitive–behavioral and interpersonal theories, respectively.

In summary, a considerable amount of research has been conducted on psychotherapy, and generally the results have been positive. In most appraisals that compared different forms of psychotherapy, few differences have been secured, although cognitive–behavioral approaches have sometimes been found to be the most effective.

S. L. GARFIELD

EGO DEVELOPMENT

The term *ego development* is used in different ways by different authors. Most psychoanalysts use it in one of three ways: (a) to describe the period of formation of the self or ego in the first 2 or 3 years of life; (b) to describe the development of all ego functions, including what Heinz Hartmann called the "conflict-free ego sphere," that is, locomotion, speech, and so on; (c) to describe aspects of ego development such as those described by Erik Erikson as psychosocial tasks, entwined with psychosexual development (i.e., the development of drives and drive derivatives) and tied to age-specific life tasks. In clinical psychoanalytic use, disorders of ego development usually refer to problems arising in the period of ego formation; they are likely to lead to profound maladjustment or to "borderline" personality types.

Psychologists have delineated a different conception that has roots in Harry Stack Sullivan's *Interpersonal theory of psychiatry*. This conception, in addition to being a developmental sequence, is a dimension of individual differences that applies in principle at any age, although higher stages are never found in early childhood and the lowest stages are rare in maturity. Terms such as moral development, interpersonal reliability, and cognitive complexity have been used for aspects of the sequence.

STAGES

The earliest stage (or stages)—the *period of ego formation*—occurs in infancy. This stage is presocial, at first autistic, later symbiotic with the mother or mother figure. Acquisition of language is believed to be an important factor in bringing the period to an end.

The *impulsive stage* is next: The child confirms a separate existence from the mother by willfulness and is dependent on others for control of impulses. Persons at this stage are preoccupied with their own needs, often bodily ones, and see others as a source of supply. They live in a universe conceptually oversimplified, at least as to its interpersonal features. Rules are seen as specific prohibitions or as frustration of wishes rather than as a system of social regulation.

Growth at first is in terms of ensuring more certain gratification by tolerating some delay and detour, which leads to the *self-protective stage.* Children at this stage will often assert some degree of autonomy to free themselves from excessive dependence; however, their interpersonal relations remain exploitative. They are concerned with power and control, dominance and submission. In early childhood this period is normally negotiated with the help of rituals; when a person remains at this stage into adolescence and adult life, there may be a marked opportunism. Rules are understood, but are manipulated to the person's advantage.

Normally in late childhood there is a sea-change. One identifies oneself and one's own welfare with that of the group. Rules are partly internalized, are adhered to precisely because they are group-accepted and endorsed. This is the *conformist stage,* which has been widely recognized and described as a personality type. Conformity is valued for its own sake, and people tend to perceive others and themselves as conforming.

Many people seem to advance beyond the conformist stage by perceiving that they themselves do not always live up to the high standards of conduct that society endorses, and do not always have the approved emotions in some situations. This period is called the *conscientious-conformist level,* or the *self-aware level.* Whether it is a transition between the conformist stage and the conscientious stage or a true stage is an unsettled point. The person at this level sees multiple possibilities as appropriate.

At the *conscientious stage* rules are truly internalized. The person obeys rules not just because the group approves, but because they have been self-evaluated and accepted as personally valid. Interpersonal relations are understood in terms of feelings and motives rather than merely actions. The person has a richly differentiated inner life and—in place of stereotyped perceptions of others—a rich vocabulary of differentiated traits with which to describe people. Thus, their parents are described as real people with both virtues and failings, rather than as idealized portraits or as entirely hateful persons. Self-descriptions are also modulated; the person does not describe the self either as perfect or as worthless, but sees circumscribed faults that he or she aspires to improve. Achievement is valued, not purely as competitive or as social recognition, but as measured by the person's own standards. Persons at this stage may feel excessively responsible for shaping the lives of others.

In moving beyond the conscientious stage, the person begins to appreciate individuality for its own sake; thus this transitional level is called *individualistic.* It is characterized by increased conceptual complexity: Life is viewed in terms of many-faceted possibilities, instead of diametrically opposed dichotomies. There is spontaneous interest in human development and an appreciation of psychological causation.

At the *autonomous stage* the characteristics of the individualistic level are developed further. The name "autonomous" is somewhat arbitrary, as are all the stage names. No aspect of behavior arises suddenly in one era and perishes immediately on passage to the next. What characterizes this stage particularly is respect for the autonomy of others. A crucial case is the subject's own children, especially acknowledging their right to make their own mistakes. The person at this stage is often aware of functioning differently in different roles. One copes with inner conflict such as that between one's own needs and duties. Conflict is viewed as an inevitable part of the human condition rather than as a failing of self, other family members, or society.

Beginning at the conscientious stage and especially characteristic of higher stages is seeing oneself in a larger social context. This is particularly true of persons at the *integrated stage,* who are able to unite concern for society and for self in a single complex thought.

RELATED DOMAINS

Many authors have sketched stages of development closely related to the foregoing sequence. Clyde Sullivan, Marguerite Q. Grant, and J. Douglas Grant refer to their stages as "interpersonal integration." Their conception has been used in studies of differential treatment of different subtypes of delinquents.

Kohlberg has developed a system of stages for the development of moral judgment; his ideas have been widely applied. In schools they have been the basis for curricula to encourage moral development, including the forming of alternative schools on the model of "just communities."

Selman labels his stages "interpersonal perspective taking." He has studied school-age children, thus his work applies chiefly to early stages. He has also studied a small clinical sample.

Perry's sequence corresponds to some of the higher stages. John M. Broughton covered a wide age range. He was concerned with development of "natural epistemologies"—conceptions of mind, self, reality, and knowledge.

METHODS OF STUDY

Although the idea of character development goes back at least to Socrates, modern study begins with Jean Piaget. Kohlberg, Selman, and others have adapted Piaget's method of clinical interviewing. Kohlberg presents his subjects with an unfinished story ending in a moral dilemma. When the subject finishes the story, there follows a probing interview during which reasons for choices are explored; the stage assigned depends on the reasoning. Rest has evolved an objectively scored test that is an adaptation of Kohlberg's instrument. Broughton and Perry have worked out interviews beginning with broad, unstructured questions.

Loevinger, Wessler, and Redmore's scoring manual for a sentence completion test is sufficiently detailed as to be semi-objective and includes self-teaching exercises. Marguerite Warren (formerly Grant) and others working with the interpersonal integration system of C. Sullivan and colleagues have used a variety of instruments including interviews, sentence completion tests, and objective tests.

THEORIES

There are two major theoretical issues: Why is the ego (or self) as stable as it is? How and why does it manage to change at all?

The theories of ego stability are all variations of H. S. Sullivan's "anxiety-gating" theory. What Sullivan calls the "self-system" acts as a kind of filter or template or frame of reference for one's perception and conception of the interpersonal world. Any observations not consonant with one's current frame of reference cause anxiety. However, the main purpose of the self-system is to avoid or attenuate anxiety. Therefore, such perceptions are either distorted so as to fit the preexisting system, or—in Sullivan's phrase—they are "selectively inattended to." Thus, the theory states that because the self-system or ego is a structure, it is self-perpetuating.

Kohlberg has a structural theory of change. When a person at one stage repeatedly encounters and grapples with reasoning and arguments just one stage higher, conditions are optimal for assimilating the reasoning and hence advancing toward that stage.

Identification is the key to the current psychoanalytic theory of ego development. One moves ahead in part because one identifies with some admired model who is (or is perceived as being) at a slightly higher level. Although Kohlberg's theory is primarily cognitive and the psychoanalytic theory is affective, both imply a Piagetian model of equilibrium, disequilibration, and re-equilibration. Both are, in effect, "social learning" theories, though they differ radically from what is usually called social learning theory.

There is another element in the psychoanalytic theory that originates as social learning but becomes wholly internal to the individual. The ideal or model toward which the person strives or aspires need not be embodied in the environment. The capacity for constructing one's own model is what is called the "ego ideal."

Ausubel presents another theory of some aspects of ego development. Infants believe themselves to be omnipotent because their wishes are magically realized. (Here Ausubel is following Ferenczi's essay.) As children learn of their total dependence on their parents, they face a catastrophic loss of self-esteem. To escape that fate, they assign their former omnipotence to their parents and so become their satellites, shining in their reflected glory. In late childhood and early adolescence one should "desatellize," should learn to derive self-esteem from one's own achievements. Satellization and desatellization may miscarry at several points, resulting in various patterns of psychopathology.

Perry depicts many factors as contributing to both stability and change in the college years. His model of change has implications for a dynamic explanation. The student whose world view is, say, dualistic (right vs. wrong, us vs. them) at first, learns to perceive some special field as more complicated and multiplistic (many possibilities, everyone has a right to his or her own opinion). As the fields of application for the multiplistic view increase, those where the dualistic view apply correspondingly shrink, till the multiplistic view becomes the predominant one, with only isolated areas of life still seen in dualistic terms. The same paradigm applies for the transition from multiplistic to relativistic thinking (some views are better because they are grounded in better data or sounder reasoning). One of the generally accepted aims of a liberal education is to encourage acceptance of the relativistic nature of all knowledge. In Perry's view, relativism should be followed by acceptance of some commitments.

ERIKSONIAN DEVELOPMENTAL STAGES
IDENTITY FORMATION
SELF

J. Loevinger

EGO-STATE THEORY AND THERAPY

The term "ego state" was first coined by Paul Federn, a colleague of Freud, and the term has been used in several therapeutic approaches, although with differing meanings. The present system of ego-state therapy stems primarily from the personality theories and techniques developed by John and Helen Watkins. Their theory holds that dissociation is not an either/or, but like most other psychological processes is continuous. Their findings support the view that human personality is divided into organized systems of behavior and experience (cognitions, perceptions, affects, and motivations), that are partially dissociated from one another for purposes of adaptation and defense. These subsystems are called "ego states."

An *ego state* is an organized system of behavior and experience whose elements are bound together by some common principle, but are separated from one another by boundaries that are more or less permeable. Each ego state constitutes a kind of subself that has more or less individual autonomy in relation to other states and to the entire personality. Ego states at the lower end of the dissociative continuum are manifested by normal mood changes, and those at the upper end by overt, multiple personalities. In between these extremes they act like "covert" multiple personalities that influence the individual with relative degrees of autonomy, depending on their energy and the permeability of their boundaries.

When activated (usually through hypnosis), an ego state represents itself as subject ("I") and experiences other ego states and the entire individual as object ("he," "she," or "it"). The ego state that is primary at any given moment is said to be "executive." It is "the self" in the now.

When relatively less dissociated from one another, ego states function more or less cooperatively, even though inner conflict can occur. When more dissociated, they function with relative autonomy, and if highly dissonant and energized, they create severe inner conflict within the personality. Conflicts between ego states can be prominent factors in a number of maladaptive symptoms ranging from overeating, headaches, anxiety, and phobias to multiple personalities and psychotic reactions.

Ego-state therapy is the utilization of family and group treatment techniques for the resolution of conflicts among the different ego states that constitute a "family of self" within a single individual. It is a kind of internal diplomacy that may employ any of the directive, behavioral, analytic, or humanistic techniques of therapy. It is concerned with determining how each of the personality's subparts interacts with the others and what influence each has on the individual's behavior and experience.

In the practice of ego-state therapy, each state involved in a given problem is individually activated and studied to determine its needs, origin, function, objectives, and relative significance to the entire psychic economy of the patient. Needs are not dysfunctional in themselves, but the way in which they are manifested by an ego state can be self-defeating. For example, an achievement need may be expressed by an ego state through nagging. Such negative behavior will arouse another ego state to resist and initiate maladaptive conflict. The art of this therapy is to induce the stimulus ego state to change its behavior toward another state or toward the total personality, while still meeting its basic needs.

Ego states may develop in childhood through the introjection of parental figures, through traumatic events, or through normal growth and differentiation. The child introjects not only parent figures but often also the *drama* of their interaction within the family. The introjection always represents the child's *perception* of the external world, whether benevolent or malevolent. Therefore the introjected ego state thinks as a child, and the earlier the introjection, the more primitive the thinking.

Ego states can be activated nonhypnotically through certain special procedures, such as dividing the personality by chairs. However, an ego state can be best activated and assessed through hypnosis. Once it becomes executive, an ego state can be investigated by any of the usual methods of personality assessment (interview, psychological tests, etc.), but these are then applied to the subsystem (partial person) and not to the entire individual.

The therapist, in activating ego states, aims to elicit responses from already existing entities and not to create hypnotic artifacts. Accordingly, the therapist must take care not to suggestively influence a state's report about its origin, content, function, and needs. The ego state itself will report such data, including its name, if it has one.

Experience in therapy shows that the activation and study of individual states does not increase dissociation. The therapeutic goal is not "fusion."

As therapy proceeds, ego states move toward the less dissociated end of the continuum. They become more cognitively and affectively consonant. Their boundaries develop greater permeability, and within the "family of self" they become more socialized. The adult part of the personality is strengthened, and it functions as a dispatcher to determine when less mature parts are permitted to become executive.

When true overt multiple personalities are successfully integrated, the previous separate entities can still be hypnotically activated as covert ego states. J. R. Hilgard discovered covert, cognitive structural systems in normal personalities that he called "hidden observers." Hilgard's hidden observers appear to be the same phenomena as ego states.

CONSCIOUSNESS STATES
HYPNOSIS
MULTIPLE PERSONALITIES

H. H. WATKINS

EIDETIC PSYCHOTHERAPY

For Ahsen, personality is made up of a library of eidetic images, each having a visual core with somatic and meaning components. Because there are both innate and learned eidetic images, normal development is a product of the interaction of the two. A developmental eidetic image not only has a visual core, but also contains the individual's reactions to the original experience. Personality is not seen as a rational, organized whole but rather as a vast number of eidetic images derived from past experiences and heredity, some viewed by the self through the eyes of parents, other relatives, and even animals with whom one has associated.

Ahsen and his coworkers view symptoms as the product of distorted eidetic images. The aim of therapy is to bring about a reappraisal of the distortions by means of eidetic analysis. Such analysis may occur as the result of systematically reexperiencing the relevant images in one's history or the spontaneous development of significant images in the interview.

IMAGERY
INNOVATIVE PSYCHOTHERAPIES

V. RAIMY

ELECTRICAL NERVOUS SYSTEM STIMULATION

Stimulation of the nervous system is diagnostic and therapeutic. Wilder Penfield, surgically treating focal epilepsy, used electrical brain stimulation (EBS) in conscious patients to identify the epileptic focus. Noting the effect of EBS at numerous loci, Penfield labeled each site of stimulation and photographed the numbered brain, making a functional map of each patient's cortex. Therapeutic nervous system stimulation evolved from an "electronic shotgun assault on the entire brain" into implantation of multiple microelectrodes in peripheral nerves, spinal cord, or brain loci, computer-timed and sequenced, in an attempt to mimic neural firing patterns in a single functional system. Therapeutic stimulation, fairly successful in controlling specific capabilities, is far from the ability to control complex behavior patterns.

Attempts to stimulate the nervous system, dating from the late 1700s, did not gain access to deep brain structures until the invention of the stereotax in the early 1900s. Scientists have found that EBS can elicit numerous behaviors in animals (e.g., eating, drinking, hoarding, aggression, maternal, and sexual behaviors). A striking discovery was Olds and Milner's chance finding of "reward" circuits in the brain. Animals quickly learn to stimulate certain areas of their own brain mechanically.

Application of data on animal brain function to humans is difficult. Neurosurgeons have attempted to use EBS to overcome various behavioral problems in humans such as depression and aggressive outbursts, but methods for evaluating results are not adequately scientific to validate claims of success. Electrical stimulation of the human nervous system for circumscribed functions is better researched and more promising than attempts to control global emotional responsiveness or behavior.

AUTONOMOUS NERVOUS SYSTEM
BRAIN
CENTRAL NERVOUS SYSTEM
CRANIAL NERVES
ELECTROENCEPHALOGRAPHY
NEUROSURGERY

B. E. THORN

ELECTROCONVULSIVE THERAPY

Electroconvulsive shock therapy (ECT) is a controversial treatment applied to a small percentage of emotionally disturbed people, mostly those suffering from endogenous depression.

The treatment developed a bad reputation, partly because of people's associations with the terms "shock" and "convulsion," and partly because on occasion it was used carelessly or punitively. The treatment was sometimes repeated hundreds of times per patient. Side effects included a confused state, both retrograde and anterograde amnesia, cardiac complications, and even physical injury. With the advent of antidepressant and antipsychotic drugs, the use of ECT became much less common.

It can now be given only with the informed consent of the patient. The electrical intensity is lower than before, and the number of repetitions is ordinarily limited to six to eight, on alternate days. The ECT is preceded by muscle relaxants, such as methylscopolamine, or anesthetics, such as methohexital, to minimize discomfort and the threat of injury. Unilateral ECT, usually over the right hemisphere of the brain, can be therapeutically effective with a minimum of memory impairment and other side effects. Side effects are usually mild, unless ECT is combined with lithium.

In this modified form ECT has some demonstrable benefits for limited patient categories. It is strongly therapeutic for many endogenous depressed patients who fail to respond to antidepressive drugs. For depressed patients with psychotic thoughts, ECT is more effective than either antidepressive or antipsychotic drugs alone. Because ECT takes effect more rapidly than drugs, it is often recommended for depressed patients who are actively suicidal. For any application, the benefits of ECT are temporary. A relapse can be prevented by sustained use of antidepressant drugs.

The mechanism of ECT's therapeutic action is not known. The memory deficit that often occurs is not essential, and probably not even helpful, to the therapeutic effect. ECT has been found to increase norepinephrine turnover in the brain, to alter receptor sensitivity to monoamine synaptic transmitters, to increase the release of pituitary hormones, and to weaken the blood-brain barrier. Any or all of these effects may contribute to the antidepressant action.

Much interest has focused on the memory deficits that often result from ECT. Both anterograde and retrograde amnesia are demonstrable, to declining degrees, for about the first month after ECT. Patients continue to complain, however, about memory problems for another 6 months or so. It is possible that small but real deficits persist this long that do not show up in formal testing. It is also possible that the memory difficulty that patients experience soon after ECT sensitizes them to pay more attention to minor, normal episodes of forgetfulness.

DEPRESSION
ELECTRICAL NERVOUS SYSTEM STIMULATION
RIGHT TO REFUSE THERAPY

J. W. KALAT

ELECTRODERMAL ACTIVITY

Electrodermal activity (EDA) is a term used by psychophysiologists to refer to the electrical activity of the skin on the palms of the hand or on fingers. The first investigators to use this measure thought that it revealed the secrets of mental life. Today we think of EDA as a measure of the state of the organism's interaction with the environment.

The terms used to describe EDA have changed over the years. The term used at the turn of this century was *psychogalvanic reflex* (PGR). Later the term *galvanic skin response* (GSR) was used. The difficulty with this term was that it came to describe several different aspects of electrodermal activity (e.g., basal level and response amplitude). Most psychophysiologists have therefore dropped GSR in favor of *electrodermal activity* (EDA).

The electrical activity of the skin can be measured in two ways. First, a small current can be passed through the skin from an external source, following which the resistances to the passage of current are measured. This technique is the *exosomatic method*. The second or *endosomatic method* measures the electrical activity at the surface of the skin, with no externally imposed current. The exosomatic method has been modified today into the measurement of skin conductance (SC), the reciprocal of skin resistance. The endosomatic method is still used today to measure skin potential (SP).

EDA is recorded from electrodes placed on the palms of the hand or fingers, because these sites are rich in eccrine sweat glands, a special type of sweat gland. What makes them of particular interest to psychologists is that they respond primarily to "psychic" stimulation, whereas other sweat glands respond more to increases in temperature. The eccrine sweat glands are innervated by the sympathetic branch of the ANS, but the chemical transmitter at the postganglionic synapse is acetylcholine, not noradrenaline, as would be expected in the sympathetic nervous system.

The eccrine sweat glands, which can be thought of as tiny tubes with openings at the surface of the skin, act as variable resistors wired in parallel. Depending on the degree of sympathetic activation, sweat rises toward the surface of the skin in varying amounts through varying numbers of sweat glands. The higher the sweat rises in a given gland, the lower the resistance is in that variable resistor.

AUTONOMIC NERVOUS SYSTEM
CHEMICAL BRAIN STIMULATION
NEUROSURGERY

PSYCHOSOMATIC DISORDERS
SYMPATHETIC NERVOUS SYSTEM

R. M. STERN

ELECTROENCEPHALOGRAPHY

Many of the chemical events occurring in the individual neurons of the brain generate electrical signals. The record of these fluctuating electrical signals emanating from the brains of humans and other animals is called the electroencephalogram (EEG). Considerable technical advances have provided a technique for unobtrusively measuring brain activity for experiments on the relationship between brain and behavior, and for assessing various clinical conditions such as epilepsy and brain damage.

Nearly all EEG procedures involve electrodes—most commonly, metal discs pasted onto the scalp or wires placed in contact with the skull, or with the brain itself after a hole has been made through the skull. The EEG electrode can also be lowered into the brain to record the activity of deeper structures, although this is not a common clinical practice. The tiny electrical signals picked up by the electrodes must be amplified to be useful, and a trace of the fluctuations in voltage is recorded on paper using an ink-writing system or by using an oscilloscope and tape recorder.

The recorded EEG is actually a reflection of the activity of many millions of neurons located in a large volume of tissue in the brain. The major contributors to EEG are the excitatory and inhibitory electrical potentials generated at synapses between neurons. The electrical currents that are generated at synapses are conducted through a considerable volume of tissue, before being all summed together at the site of the recording electrode. This fact makes it difficult to locate specific generators of a particular electrical pattern.

EEG characteristically has a wavelike or rhythmical quality. The two basic dimensions for quantifying the EEG signal are the frequency of the waves (measured in cycles/second) and the size or amplitude of the waves (measured in millivolts or microvolts). The EEG observed in scalp recording from awake, alert subjects is typically composed of desynchronous, fast waves of low amplitude. Often when the subject is awake, but quite relaxed with eyes closed, a pronounced, relatively synchronized, 8 to 12 cycles/second rhythm is present, called the alpha rhythm. During normal sleep the EEG shows large, irregular, slow waves with occasional bursts of rapid, high-amplitude waves called "sleep spindles." Several clinical conditions such as coma, general anesthesia, and the period following an epileptic seizure are also associated with large, irregular, slow waves, reminiscent of "slow-wave" sleep. Periods of paradoxical or rapid-eye-movement sleep (dream sleep) are marked in the EEG by a pattern of activity that closely resembles the pattern observed in the awake, alert person.

Many studies have documented the correlation between EEG activity and states of "arousal," but more recently investigators have discovered correlations between EEG patterns and specific behaviors. Penfield and Jasper demonstrated relations between EEG and movement in humans.

Clinically, EEG recording is often useful in diagnosing certain pathological conditions involving the cerebral cortex, such as epilepsy, certain tumors, and strokes. Tumors composed of tissue that does not generate electrical activity, and cortical regions not functioning properly because of disruption of blood supply or some other trauma, can often be detected through scalp recordings. Pathology involving structures underneath the cortex is more difficult to detect by using scalp-recording techniques. However, depth EEG recordings obtained by lowering an electrode into the brain through a hole drilled in the skull can sometimes locate subcortical pathology.

Cortical EEG can also be recorded from fetuses in the uterus by means of electrodes on the surface of the mother's abdomen. However, studies of development of EEG have shown that the typical adult pattern does not fully appear until 11 to 14 years of age.

As a research tool, EEG has been used to assess the effects of a vast number of drugs. Many investigators have used EEG to discern specialization of behavioral functions within different parts of the cortex and subcortical structures. This has been accomplished by studying changes in EEG pattern during specific movements (movement-related potentials), or during presentation of specific sensory events (sensory-evoked potentials).

BRAIN
NEUROPSYCHOLOGY

R. J. SUTHERLAND
I. Q. WHISHAW

EMBRYO AND FETUS

The embryonic and fetal stages of human development are the shortest stages of development, lasting approximately 40 weeks. They are also the period of the most rapid qualitative and quantative change that the human organism undergoes. During the embryonic stage the organism develops from a single-cell fertilized ovum (0.14 millimeters in diameter) to a human embryo weighing .01 gram and measuring 3.2 centimeters in length, and the basis for the fully formed skeletal, muscular, circulatory, digestive, endocrine, nervous, and respiratory systems is established. This process takes approximately 8 weeks. This period of rapid growth and development is also the period of greatest vulnerability, morbidity, and mortality. While the embryo is protected within the amniotic sac and the uterus, these first 8 weeks of gestation are a critical period for damaging effects of outside agents that can cause abortion and/or structural and functional malformations. These agents are called teratogens. The most common categories of teratogens that specifically affect the embryo are drugs, radiation, and maternal infection.

The most dramatic example of the effects of drugs on the embryo is the thalidomide tragedy in Europe. Other types of drugs that have been linked to malformations during the embryonic period are some forms of tranquilizers, barbiturates, and synthetic hormones. Maternal exposure to radiation during the embryonic stage can lead to spontaneous abortion, still birth, chromosomal and genetic mutations, microcephaly, and mental and growth retardation. Forms of cancer such as leukemia that manifest themselves during childhood and adolescence are also linked to gestational radiation exposure.

Maternal infection can also have tragic consequences on the developing organism. The most damaging disease is rubella (German measles). When it is contracted by the mother during the first trimester, 50% of pregnancies are adversely affected and spontaneous abortion is common. Infants born with rubella syndrome are usually multiply impaired, the most common characteristics being blindness, deafness, heart malformations, intellectual impairment, and microcephaly.

Although the probability of structural and functional damage is greatest during the embryonic period, the fetal stage continues to be a period of vulnerability. This stage is defined as the period from the appearance of the first real bones through birth. Several maternal practices and characteristics can cause negative outcomes during this phase. Nicotine and alcohol have been demonstrated to affect embryonic growth. Mothers who smoke are at greater risk for giving birth to low-birth-weight and premature infants. Alcohol consumption has been linked to a number of malformations, including mental and growth retardation, facial and limb malformations, and heart defects. Narcotic addition by the mother will lead to narcotic addiction in the developing organism. More subtle long-term effects of these drugs during pregnancy, such as minimal brain damage and behavioral manifestations, are not fully known.

Maternal venereal diseases such as syphilis, gonorrhea, and herpes simplex can result in spontaneous abortion, stillbirth, and infection of the unborn child. Chronic maternal illnesses such as diabetes and anemia can also cause related malformations. Maternal malnutrition has been directly linked with prematurity, growth and intellectual retardation, sensory and neurological damage, and fetal death.

Although much is known about these influential factors, much remains as yet unknown about the potentially damaging effects of environmental pollutants, disease, and other factors that may cause physical and behavioral anomalies in the human organism.

BEHAVIORAL GENETICS
BIRTH INJURIES

K. A. McCLUSKEY

EMERGING PSYCHOTHERAPIES

The field of psychotherapy has undergone many changes over the years, most of which would have been difficult to predict. From a relatively slow development at the turn of the century, the pace has increased during the post-World War II years. From an activity that had little public recognition and visibility, psychotherapy has become a relatively popular treatment modality in the mental health area featured in popular magazines and television.

THE PROLIFERATION OF THE PSYCHOTHERAPIES

For a number of years, psychotherapy was dominated by Sigmund Freud and his disciples. Several prominent early analysts such as Alfred Adler and Carl Jung departed from the Freudian views to develop their own schools or forms of psychotherapy and this also was true of Otto Rank and Sandor Ferenczi. Later, in the 1930s and 1940s, Karen Horney and Harry Stack Sullivan produced additional approaches to psychotherapy that differed from traditional psychoanalysis. Although most of these variants would be classified as psychodynamic forms of therapy, a quite different form of psychotherapy was introduced in 1942 by Carl Rogers. First called nondirective therapy, it has been referred to as client-centered therapy since 1951 when Rogers published a book with that title and still later as person-centered therapy. Another new and distinctive form of psychotherapy, behavior therapy, also received recognition when Joseph Wolpe published *Psychotherapy by reciprocal inhibition.* Although earlier there were instances of the application of learning and behavior theories, such emphases received little attention from clinicians, and it was only after Wolpe's book was published that behavioral therapies began to be recognized as important therapeutic approaches.

The growth of psychotherapeutic approaches began to accelerate, with considerable speed. During the 1960s Sol Garfield listed more than 60 different varieties, which seemed at the time to be an astounding number. However, a *Report of the Research Task Force of the National Institute of Mental Health* referred to the existence of 130 different forms of psychotherapy. This rather surprising increase was followed in a few years by additional increases in the number of diverse approaches to psychotherapy. In 1980, Herink published *The psychotherapy handbook: The A to Z guide to more than 250 therapies in use today,* and in 1981, Corsini's *Handbook of innovative psychotherapies* listed 256 such therapies and summarized 66 principal variations. Kazdin cited more than 400 different forms of psychotherapy.

In a relatively short period of time, the dominant influence of psychoanalysis diminished and a large number of diverse new approaches and modifications made their appearance. This has certainly been an unexpected development and a difficult one to evaluate. Whether this represents unusual creativity on the part of psychotherapists, entrepreneurial zeal, or dissatisfaction with the previously existing forms of psychotherapy cannot be decided. However, some other developments paralleled this proliferation of the psychotherapies that had more unifying objectives. One was the increased popularity of eclecticism, particularly among clinical psychologists. The other was the efforts by some psychotherapists to integrate various features of two (or more) different forms of psychotherapy.

ECLECTICISM AND INTEGRATION IN PSYCHOTHERAPY

One finding reported repeatedly since the 1960s has been the popularity of an eclectic approach to psychotherapy among clinical psychologists. A survey of 855 members of the Division of Clinical Psychology of the American Psychological Association revealed that 55% of the sample followed an eclectic approach to psychotherapy. Although eclecticism does not provide psychotherapists with a specific unified schemata for working with patients, it allows therapists to have flexibility.

This is in contrast to what more traditional therapists may actually do, although they may not be fully aware of it. For example, although behavior therapists will describe their therapeutic efforts in terms of behavioral techniques, some actually use other techniques such as suggestion. In a similar fashion, psychodynamic therapists may be unaware when they are offering advice to the client.

An eclectic approach can be idiosyncratic. As a result, there can be great variability in terms of the therapeutic procedures used and applied by individual eclectics. Some may combine components of psychoanalytic and humanistic approaches; some may combine behavioral and Gestalt techniques. Many other combinations have been tried and applied in unique ways by individual therapists. On a more systematic level, a number of different kinds of eclectic schemes have been described in the literature, and even a *Handbook of eclectic psychotherapy* has made its appearance. Among the different approaches described in this book are multimodal therapy, systematic eclectic psychotherapy, functional eclectic therapy, a structural–phenomenological approach to eclectic psychotherapy, eclectic time-limited therapy, eclectic family therapy, and eclectic psychotherapy that emphasizes common factors among the psychotherapies. In practically all of these approaches, attempts have been made to select and combine techniques and procedures from any form of psychotherapy that has some empirical justification, makes sense to the therapist, or appears to meet the therapeutic needs of a given client.

Eclecticism was indicated as the preferred orientation or approach by Jensen, Bergin, and Greaves for clinical psychologists, psychiatrists, social workers, and marriage and family therapists. A related approach to psychotherapy, called integration, also made its appearance. Although there is some overlap between these two approaches, they can be differentiated in terms of their relative emphases or goals. Among eclectics there is a greater emphasis on the selection and use of therapeutic techniques and procedures from diverse schools of psychotherapy and less on any attempts at theoretical integration. The opposite would appear to be true of individuals identified with the movement toward integration. Although there also are differences among these latter individuals, there is a more serious attempt at some type of theoretical integration. A history of psychotherapy integration has been published by Goldfried and Newman.

If the different orientations or schools of psychotherapy can be viewed as providing different and specific emphases in psychotherapy that are distinctive for them, but lacking or incomplete in the other orientations, then it would appear plausible to hypothesize that some integration of therapies would provide a more comprehensive and effective approach to psychotherapy.

The different constructs, procedures, and views of the therapeutic process that constitute the different approaches to psychotherapy make the task of integration a difficult and complex one. Patients' resistance to therapy are acknowledged as important by most psychotherapists, regardless of orientation. The opportunity to confide in an understanding and empathic therapist, to be able to express one's innermost feelings

and emotions, to have one's distorted cognitions modified, to have explanations provided (regardless of theoretical orientation), to be encouraged to try out new and more successful behaviors, and to have hope replace demoralization are all important features of successful psychotherapy, regardless of the form of psychotherapy provided. One of the implications of this approach is that an attempt to delineate the basic variables responsible for change in psychotherapy would diminish the emphasis on the schools of psychotherapy and unify our therapeutic efforts with a more significant overarching conception of psychotherapy.

Eclectic and integrative emphases in the field of psychotherapy are receiving increasing recognition and are encouraging new developments and formulations within the field. The Society for the Exploration of Psychotherapy Integration is growing and publishes *The Journal of Eclectic and Integrative Psychotherapy*. The first international congress on eclectic and integrative psychotherapy was held in June, 1992.

ALTERNATIVE PSYCHOTHERAPIES
BRIEF PSYCHOTHERAPY
CULTURE AND ECLECTIC PSYCHOTHERAPY
GROUP PSYCHOTHERAPY
HISTORICAL ROOTS OF PSYCHOTHERAPY
INNOVATIVE PSYCHOTHERAPIES

S. L. GARFIELD

EMOTION AND MEMORY

Early memories have a strong emotional component. An autobiographical memory study by Wagegenaar and Groeneweg of concentration camp survivors indicates that events that happened 50 years ago are well remembered, but there also is evidence of repression of intensely emotional experiences unique to them, namely details related to witnessing torture and murder and being the victim of brutal maltreatment. In other words, intensity is not a safeguard against forgetting.

For the more ordinary levels of arousal, autobiographical data are in keeping with experimental studies in which emotional words and pictures of sufficient intensity are recalled better than nonemotional materials and with the theoretical suggestion by Posner that emotion increases the level of alertness as well as Walker's view that high arousal during the associative process produces greater permanent memory. Presumably, better retention can be due to better learning or better storage or both.

Walker's hypothesis includes the notion of temporary inhibition of recall right after high arousal, and Kleinsmith and Kaplan obtained results that support Walker's view. Eight words that produced different arousal levels as measured by skin resistance (GSR) (e.g., rape and vomit and dance and swim were used as stimuli for digit responses of two through nine). Low-arousal words were recalled better than high-arousal ones immediately following the study trial, but after 45 minutes and thereafter high-arousal words were recalled much better. Several similar studies confirmed better recall with high-arousal and long-retention intervals, but some did not find poorer recall with high-arousal and very short intervals. As with the life experiences mentioned earlier, the source of emotion or arousal was the stimulus to which something was being recalled. But much the same results were obtained by Weiner and Walker, using electric shock as a negative incentive or money as a positive incentive for correctly responding to a paired associates list. That is, retention was better with incentives than without incentives, increasing with incentive value and showing an even greater difference in favor of increased affect with a longer retention interval. Berlyne et al. also manipulated arousal with a completely independent agent by using white noise and found that white noise presented over ear phones during training improved recall, especially with longer retention intervals.

Bower and associates have studied the phenomenon of mood-dependent memory retrieval extensively. In essence, retrieval is supposed to be better if the subject's mood at retrieval matches his or her mood at learning. After conducting a few successful experiments in which subjects that felt happy at both learning and recall or felt sad both times recalled more than subjects tested in a mood opposite of the one of learning, they had a number of failures, which prompted Bower and Mayer to conclude that mood-dependent retrieval is an unreliable phenomenon, at least in the laboratory.

Blaney, in a review of affect and emotion distinguishes between mood-dependent memory and mood congruence, stating that material is better learned and retained if the material has emotional tone congruent with the subject's mood at acquisition and/or recall. The evidence for mood-congruent memory is much stronger than for mood-dependent memory, which is not too surprising theoretically because a cue that is clearly relevant for the material to be recalled is supplied by the congruent mood present at recall. In autobiographical memories, according to Blaney, these two effects are often confounded, which, in part, may account for the easy access to autobiographical memories. In general, the mood studies seem to work better if the induced moods are intense.

A clear example of an inhibitory effect of emotion on test performance is the phenomenon of test anxiety. For those who are most susceptible to worry and emotionality during a school test, the following seems to be true: The range of cues attended to is reduced, processing emphasizes the physical stimulus rather than semantic content; there is a slightly shorter digit span in high-anxious subjects, deficit is present for both recall and recognition tests, and the high anxious benefit more from relaxed retest conditions and memory supports like open-book tests than low-anxious subjects.

BLOCKING
DEFENSE MECHANISMS
EMOTIONS
MEMORY
PUNISHMENT

M. R. DENNY

EMOTIONAL CONTAGION

Emotional contagion is "The tendency to automatically mimic and synchronize expressions, vocalizations, postures, and movements with those of another person's and, consequently, to converge emotionally." Theoretically, emotions could be caught in several ways. Some researchers argued that conscious reasoning, analysis, and imagination can account for the phenomenon. Aronfreed argued that people must learn to share others' emotions, that contagion is a conditioned emotional response. Most, however, assume that emotional contagion is an even more primitive process that happens automatically, outside of conscious awareness. Hatfield et al. argued that the process of emotional contagion operates like this:

Proposition 1. In conversation, people automatically and continuously mimic and synchronize their movements with the facial expressions, voices, postures, movements, and instrumental behaviors of others.

Proposition 2. Subjective emotional experiences are affected, moment to moment, by the feedback from such mimicry. Theoretically, emotional experience could be influenced by (a) central nervous system commands that direct such mimicry–synchrony in the first place; (b) the afferent feedback from such facial, verbal, postural, or movement mimicry–synchrony; or (c) self-perception processes wherein individuals draw inferences about their own emotional states based on the emotional expressions and behaviors evoked in them by the emotional states of others.

Proposition 3. As a consequence, people tend to catch others' emotions moment to moment. Researchers have collected considerable evidence in support of these three propositions.

PROPOSITION 1

Researchers have found evidence that people do tend to imitate facial expressions, voices, postures, and instrumental behaviors of others. Facial mimicry is at times almost instantaneous. People seem able to track the most subtle of moment-to-moment changes. Haggard and Isaacs observed that emotional experiences and accompanying facial expressions may change with surprising speed—within a span of 125 to 200 ms. Social-psychophysiological investigations have found that emotional experiences and facial expressions, as measured by electromyographic (EMG) procedures, tend to mimic the changes in emotional expression of those they observe, and that this motor mimicry can occur at levels so subtle that they produce no observable facial expressions. When subjects observe happy facial expressions, they show increased muscular activity over the zygomaticus major (cheek) muscle region. When they observe angry facial expressions, they show increased muscular activity over the corrugator supercilli (brow) muscle region.

Such mimicry begins almost at birth. Haviland and Lelwica found that 10-week-old infants could and would imitate their mother's facial expressions of happiness, sadness, and anger. Mothers mimicked their infants' expressions of emotion as well. There also is voluminous evidence that people mimic and synchronize their vocal utterances.

PROPOSITION 2

Today, most theorists agree that emotions are tempered to some extent by skeletal feedback. Researchers have tested the facial feedback hypothesis in three types of experiments. In these experiments, they employed three different strategies for inducing subjects to adopt emotional expressions. Sometimes they simply ask subjects to exaggerate or to hide any emotional reactions they might have. Sometimes, they try to trick subjects into adopting various facial expressions. Sometimes, they try to arrange things so subjects will unconsciously mimic others' emotional and facial expressions. In all cases, scientists have found that the emotional experiences of subjects *are* affected by feedback from the facial expressions they adopt. There is an impressive array of evidence supporting the proposition that people's subjective emotional experience is affected, moment to moment, by feedback from facial, vocal, postural, and movement mimicry.

PROPOSITION 3

Researchers from a variety of disciplines provide evidence that emotional contagion exists. The majority of work has come from animal research, child psychologists who are interested in primitive emotional contagion, empathy, and sympathy, clinicians exploring the process of transference and countertransference, social psychologists, and historians.

BONDING AND ATTACHMENT
COGNITIVE PSYCHOPHYSIOLOGY
EMOTIONS
EMPATHY

E. HATFIELD

EMOTIONS

Emotions are generally thought of as strong mental states, usually involving excitement or high energy, that give rise to feelings and passions. There is also usually a valence or direction to this state: Emotions are generally positive or negative. Thus, surprise, euphoria, anger, or fear, while varying in how positive or negative they are, are strong, energetic feelings.

One of the most influential theories of emotion—developed independently by William James and Carl Lange—is usually referred to as the James–Lange theory of emotion. Basically, it postulated that emotions are made up of bodily changes (e.g., arousal) and a mental event or feeling. This in itself was not new. However, prevailing views of emotion at the time argued that an emotion-causing event was perceived, a feeling arose from that perception, and bodily expression of that feeling then followed from the feeling. In other words, the mental state involved in emotion was determined directly by the event; physiological aspects were secondary. But James and Lange disagreed. The mental state or feeling, which was the proper emotion, followed from bodily changes.

The James-Lange theories have generated a great deal of response. Research and theory followed the publication of their theories and have continued to the present. One of the more far-reaching of these responses was provided by Walter B. Cannon, who observed a weakness in the James–Lange formulation and proposed a theory of emotions based on their evolutionary value.

According to Cannon, events that caused emotions gave rise to arousal of the sympathetic nervous system. This arousal involved secretion of epinephrine by the adrenal glands and included changes such as increased heart rate, increased respiration, and increased muscle tone. Cannon argued that the function of this arousal was to prepare the organism to deal with the event—to fight or flee, for example. In other words, an event that could cause harm generated arousal—an "emergency response"—that prepared the organism to cope with the event. Increased heart rate, respiration, and so on, enabled the organism to respond more quickly, more alertly, and with greater strength, increasing its chances of survival.

Emotional states, Cannon argued, are related to this arousal, but they are not completely determined by one another. Bodily changes are constant; the same changes are involved in different emotional states. Feelings, in contrast, vary from situation to situation. He saw the hypothalamus as the seat of both arousal and feeling states, and emotion as the product of these states as integrated by the central nervous system.

Several theories or criticisms have appeared in response to this model. Some focused on the role of arousal in emotion. Others focused on the role of the central nervous system in emotion. Papez reported that specific areas of the brain were associated with emotion, and subsequent work has identified the reticular formation, extending from the thalamus to the brain stem, as the center of activation or arousal. Research also suggests that electrical stimulation of specific areas of the brain causes a general emotional pattern classifiable as rage or fear. However, despite the fact that areas of the brain are necessary for emotional expression, there do not appear to be specific locations in the brain for each emotion.

Much modern research on emotion has focused on the interplay between bodily changes and feeling states. Arnold argued that mental evaluations of events determine emotional response, including bodily changes and feelings. Part of this determination involves evaluation of sensations: Feelings are based partly on interpretation of events and partly on interpretation of bodily changes. Others have argued for more or less emphasis on evaluation of bodily changes, with the issue of primacy left unsettled.

Research supports both positions to some extent. Several studies have reported evidence suggesting that specific emotions can be reliably associated with specific patterns of physiological changes. Ax found that changes in blood pressure, heart rate, and skin conductance were some-what different when subjects were angry than when they were afraid. Other studies have found the same thing, but only a few emotions have been found to be associated with specific bodily changes. Consistent with Cannon's point that there were not enough different patterns of change to account for all emotions, research has identified only two or three different physiological precursors of emotion.

Like Cannon, Schachter and Singer believe that emotion is based on a physiological state of arousal. This arousal is the same for different emotions and serves primarily to motivate the individual to attempt to explain or label it. These labels are derived from the situation. In some cases they are fairly easy to derive. On confronting a bear, an individual experiences arousal and seeks to explain it. If the bear is wild, the arousal may be interpreted as fear, but if the bear is tame, arousal can be labeled excitement. The same cues in the situation are seen as the most important determinants of which emotion is experienced.

Some attention has been focused on understanding the dimensions of emotion. There are hundreds of different emotional states, many of which are subtle shades of others. To understand all these states, researchers have attempted to identify basic dimensions along which they can be placed.

COGNITIVE THEORIES OF EMOTION

A. S. Baum

EMPATHY

Empathy is generally understood to refer to one person's vicariously experiencing the feelings, perceptions, and thoughts of another. Some early European and American psychological and philosophical thinkers such as Max Scheller and William McDougall viewed empathy as the basis of all positive social relationships.

Within the context of this broad definition, various theorists and researchers have defined the term quite differently, each emphasizing different aspects or implications of this overall definition. Clinical psychologists and others doing research on therapeutic situations, such as Charles Truax, have tended to define the term most broadly, incorporating the therapist's intellectual understanding of the client, the therapist's sharing of the client's feeling, the ease and effectiveness of communication, and the therapist's positive attitude toward the patient. Such a broad definition of empathy is intuitively attractive, but the mélange of several aspects and implications of empathy leads to theoretical confusion because it is unclear which aspect is at the core, either definitionally or causally, with the other aspects being effects or derivatives.

Other psychologists such as Rosalyn Dymond have emphasized the cognitive aspects, focusing on the ability of one person to understand intellectually the inner experience of another. The significance of cognitive empathy appears to be the probable facilitation of communication between the two persons. Also implied is that the empathizer will tend to like, to help, and to accept the other more as a consequence of this empathy.

A third approach to empathy defines it as the empathizer's experiencing a given emotion because he or she perceives that the other is experiencing that emotion. Some developmentally oriented theorists maintain that such direct sharing of feelings between parent and infant is a key step in the maturation process. Empathetic emotional arousal has been reflected both in self-reports and physiological changes.

Stotland and his colleagues found, however, that the key antecedent condition for empathy appears to be the empathizer imagining himself or herself as having the same experience as the other—thus imaginatively *taking the role of the other*. This mental process contrasts with viewing the other in more *objectified* or *intellectualized* ways.

This approach to empathy overlaps with the cognitively oriented one described previously, to the extent that it is based on a cognitive or mental process of imagining. However, unlike the purely cognitively oriented approach, this cognitive process does not have to be veridical, so that the persons can empathize with an actor or a fictional character. Imagining the other person's experience appears to be based primarily on attributive projection because persons appear to empathize more with others who are in the same situation that the empathizer has experienced, observed closely, or previously imagined him- or herself experiencing.

The linkage between the process of imagining and the processes involved in physiologically or behaviorally manifest emotion may be complex. This linkage may occur as a result of direct, past association through a process involving subtle liminal or subliminal muscular movements, or it may occur in a direct neural fashion.

Philosophers and social theorists have long assumed that empathizing leads to greater helpfulness and even altruism. This simple relationship has been demonstrated empirically when empathy has been induced by instructions, as reported by Miho Toi and Daniel Batson. Stotland and his colleagues have shown that empathizing, when measured as an individual characteristic, also leads to altruism, especially when the helpful actions are easily taken. Hoffman and Herbert Saltzstein report that if parents have a warm relationship with their children and call their attention to the consequences of their behavior for the welfare of others, the children are more likely to treat others well than if these conditions are lacking.

In contrast, Stotland and his colleagues found that in situations in which help for a suffering other is not easy or even possible, the empathizer may attempt to escape the unpleasantness either physically or psychologically by "freezing" himself or herself. If the other's pain is extreme or manifest in great agony, an empathizing person may flee physically or psychologically from the situation. Batson and Coke report that this escape from unpleasant empathizing is less likely to occur if the person does not just empathize, but also sympathizes with the other—that is, reports feeling emotionally impelled to aid the other, feeling compassionate, sympathetic, and kind. Hoffman has shown that regardless of which approach has been taken to empathy, self-reports have shown higher scores among females than males.

EMOTIONS
IMAGERY
SOCIAL INTEREST

E. STOTLAND

EMPIRICAL RESEARCH METHODS

The word "empirical" means literally "that which is sensed." When associated with research methods, it refers to techniques and procedures involving sensory experiences. Empirical research methods, therefore, are said to be based on so-called "hard data." Furthermore, empirical research adheres to the *scientific method* as contrasted to other research methodologies such as naturalistic observation, library research, and the like. An important and necessary premise underlying empirical research methodology is that it provides for replication and confirmation/falsification. Empirical research's dependence on hard data requires high internal consistency and stability of the measures that represent the independent and dependent variables involved in its scientific investigations. Internal consistency is basic to stability; measures cannot be highly or even sufficiently reliable, unless the measures yielding the raw data to be analyzed are substantially intercorrelated. Failure to achieve this standard helps introduce error variance into the system and leads to ambiguous or misleading results.

SAMPLING PROCEDURES

Empirical research methods depend on appropriate and effective sampling procedures to produce reliable and valid data that may be legitimately and meaningfully generalized to populations of which the samples under investigation are truly representative or at least close approximations. Although most of the statistical methods applied to the analysis of empirical data assume, substantially, random selection and/or random assignment of subjects in research investigations, the critical issue does not lie with randomness *per se*. Rather, it rests primarily with avoiding the use of subjects, primarily or exclusively those who constitute highly restrictive or attenuated samples, as for instance college student volunteers, which is such a common and widespread practice in psychology and the other social and behavioral sciences. To do so counteracts the advantages of empirical research over other research methodologies.

PRECISION OF MEASUREMENT

Empirical research methods in general—and in psychology in particular—inevitably involve many measures. In psychology the measures are mainly of observed or perceived behaviors, self-reports, and other psychological phenomena. It becomes absolutely imperative that these measures be sufficiently precise to be both meaningful and valid. Otherwise, as in the case of improper sampling procedures, the advantages of empirical research methodologies are outweighed by faulty and/or misleading results. In using psychometrics, the researcher is faced with at least two serious problems: (a) the crudeness of even the most sophisticated and reliable instruments available for yielding measures on independent and dependent variables, and (b) the fact that all psychological measurement is indirect rather than direct. No psychological attribute can ever be measured directly; only its assumed manifestation in behavior is measured. For example, the attribute of "aggressiveness" can only be inferred as to degree possessed or displayed by a person on the basis of measurement on some scale or other psychometric device or technique designed to measure varying degrees of "aggressiveness" as defined and designed by the developers of the scale.

In psychological measurement, the measures that are entered into the data analysis are merely the observed scores (X_o). The "true" scores (X_t) are never known. They can only be estimated, and the estimate depends on the amount of error (X_e) determined to be present in any individual X_o. For all such measures, the observed score represents a range rather than a point (as may be the case, for example, in physics or thermodynamics). $X_o = X_t + X_e$. Hence, for empirical research to be meaningful, Xo values for all variables must be close approximations to Xt. This can only be accomplished by using highly reliable measurement instruments and techniques that are employed or administered by highly skilled and competent scientists or technicians.

EXPERIMENTAL CONTROL

In empirical research there are three kinds of variables that become involved in the experiments: (a) independent variables, (b) dependent variables, and (c) intervening or extraneous variables. The first two are introduced directly into the experimental design by the researcher; the third kind indirectly, but definitely, enter into the experiment and need to be controlled. Independent variables represent or are associated with environmental conditions that can be manipulated in the experiment; dependent variables represent or are associated with behavioral outcomes. In an experiment the objective is to vary the environmental conditions (independent variables) and observe the behavioral events (dependent variables) that occur, while at the same time controlling (eliminating the effect of) the influence of any other (extraneous) variables on the outcomes.

The experimental control of variables required in empirical research may be accomplished either through experimental design or through statistical methods.

EXPERIMENTAL DESIGNS

Basically, three major types of experimental designs are employed in empirical research: (a) hypothesis-testing designs, (b) estimation designs, and (c) quasi-experimental designs. *Hypothesis-testing designs* address the question of whether the independent variables influence the dependent variables. The statistical tests of significance utilized in these experiments are essentially two-tailed; conclusions are stated in terms of whether manipulation of environmental conditions either does or does not affect behavioral outcomes and produce changes in behavior.

Estimation designs proceed from hypothesis-testing designs in that they address themselves to quantitative descriptions of variables, but go further than merely testing the null hypothesis, largely through the application of two-tailed tests of statistical significance. They are employed to investigate the further question of *in what way* the independent variables affect outcomes. These experiments focus on quantitative and qualitative descriptions of the manner in which independent variables are related. Correlation methods are commonly utilized as statistical techniques for data analysis in these experiments. Great emphasis is placed on the setting of confidence limits and standard errors, and a main objective is to *estimate,* as accurately as possible, the true values of the dependent variables for all observed values of the independent variables.

Quasi-experimental designs are similar to hypothesis-testing designs, except that the independent variables are not manipulable or manipulated in the experiment. These types of designs are quite commonly employed in empirical research in psychology and the other social and behavioral sciences, primarily as a means of expediency. They represent research procedures that go beyond naturalistic observation, but do not reach the more sophisticated and valuable levels of the other two types of basic experimental designs.

ROLE OF STATISTICAL ANALYSES

Psychological research, whether empirical or not, is dependent mainly on data yielded by samples. Empirical research methods, therefore, are required to be further dependent on statistical analyses of these sample data in order to render tenable conclusions in the tests of hypotheses.

EMPIRICAL TESTING OF HYPOTHESES

The most highly valued experimental design in the conduct of empirical research in psychology and related sciences is the hypothesis-testing design. At this point a definition of a "hypothesis" as it relates to empirical research methodology is in order. An exceptionally concise and accurate definition is that given by Brown and Ghiselli:

A hypothesis is a proposition about factual and conceptual elements and their relationships that projects beyond known facts and experiences for the purpose of furthering understanding. It is a conjecture or best guess which involves a condition that has not yet been demonstrated in fact but that merits exploration.

Empirical confirmation of several interrelated hypotheses leads to the formulation of a theory. Theories that are constantly confirmed by empirical evidence on replication—especially if described precisely by mathematical equations—lead inevitably to the postulation of scientific law. In psychology, however, scientific law is an elusive concept. Psychological theories abound on the basis of empirical testing of hypotheses, but no psychological theory to date has attained the level of scientific law.

CONFIDENCE LIMITS
CONTROL GROUPS

P. F. Merenda

EMPIRICISM

Empiricism is the epistemological doctrine that knowledge arises from, and is grounded in, sense perception. It may be contrasted with two other frequently but not necessarily linked doctrines; nativism, holding that some knowledge is innate, and rationalism, holding that reason, not observation, provides the surest grounding of knowledge.

The roots of these disputes go back to the fifth century B.C. Empiricism arose as a response to the rationalism that began with Parmenides and was fully developed by Plato. Rationalists drew a sharp distinction between opinion, or fallible belief, and knowledge, or external and provable truth. They held that sensory experience yields only opinion about the changing world of appearance; because appearances can deceive, observation ought not to be relied on. Rationalists therefore advocate turning away from the senses altogether and searching for knowledge through reason. Opinion may or may not be true, depending on the fortuitous congruence of belief and observation; knowledge, in contrast, must be provably and externally true, and only logic—reason—can provide proof and certainty. Rationalists have also typically held that much if not all knowledge is innate; learning is the recovery of something latent in the soul or brain.

Beginning with Empedocles there arose a contrary philosophy, empiricism, distrusting reason's tendency to indulge in fanciful metaphysical speculation, and attempting to show that observation produces knowledge. In stronger forms, empiricism claims that observation is the *only* valid source of knowledge. Although the rationalist dismisses experience, the empiricist has to show that perception does in fact present truth; the empiricist must therefore study perception in order to justify it. This is the beginning of psychology. An empiricist such as Empedocles must tell us how perception works—clearly a psychological topic—in order to persuade us that his philosophy is correct. So theories of perception are the oldest theories in psychology, created to serve philosophical ends. Empiricists likewise distrust rationalists' nativist claims as appeals to the mysterious.

The empiricism versus rationalism–nativism debate began in modern form in the sixteenth century, when René Descartes reformulated rationalism and nativism, and John Locke reformulated empiricism. Within empiricism there are two schools—moderate and extreme. A moderate empiricist maintains that all ideas come from perception, but concedes that the machinery of the mind—faculties such as memory, imagination, and language—is innate. Extreme empiricists such as John Stuart Mill go further and claim that not only the content but also the processes of mind are learned.

Something of a synthesis of rationalism and empiricism was essayed by Immanuel Kant. Kant recognized science as the highest form of human knowledge and acknowledged that it begins with and systematizes experience. However, Kant held that human experience is necessarily shaped by innate characteristics of the human mind, which yield the orderly phenomena studied by science. Science therefore rests on a rationally provable foundation that is inherent in the mind and therefore prior to experience.

As scientists, psychologists are more likely to embrace empiricism than rationalism, a tendency greatly strengthened in the countries where psychology has most flourished, Britain and America, where empiricism is the dominant philosophy. Therefore, the empiricism–rationalism contrast has virtually disappeared, leaving the more familiar nativism–empiricism or nature–nurture debate. There have been exceptions to the dominance of empiricism. For example, Noam Chomsky challenged behaviorism's empiricism with his *Cartesian linguistics,* arguing that much of syntax is innate; he based linguistics on intuitions rather than behavior and regarded language as a logical system relatively unaffected by stimulus control.

LOGICAL POSITIVISM

T. H. LEAHEY

EMPLOYEE ATTITUDE SURVEYS

A consequence of sheer organizational size in large industrial corporations has been the tendency to depend on formal, bureaucratic organization and methods in the management of people in the work force. Such methods are generally impersonal and can contribute to erosion of trust and the alienation of employees in relation to company management. The development of trust often requires overcoming years of bad experience and beliefs among employees that management is exploiting them. To build loyalty and commitment essential to a motivated and productive work force is in many cases an uphill battle that requires at the outset an understanding of employee needs. Such understanding is fundamental to the development of a management philosophy that regards employees, including middle and lower levels of management, as participants in the achievement of corporate goals who expect career opportunities and personal growth in the accomplishment of their respective work; it is fundamental as well to a plan of organizational development action. Information about employees' work, jobs, and performance, and about company plans and outcomes, is essential in creating employee attitudes of job satisfaction and well being, and the belief that they are treated fairly and openly. Opportunities to express their ideas and participate in decisions related to their work and their jobs are important motivators.

Professionally designed, confidential attitude-survey questionnaires covering such important areas as conflict and ambiguity in roles and procedures, fairness of treatment, job challenge, supervisory conduct, opportunity for growth and advancement, cooperation, friendliness and warmth in the work place, and many other relevant factors can provide much needed information and at the same time open a direct and safe channel of communication from every employee to top management. By releasing the results freely and taking appropriate action to correct patent malpractice, management can demonstrate that it is listening to its employees and cares about them as stakeholders in the enterprise. Although the full cycle may in many cases involve years of dedicated effort, the results, reflecting a person-oriented philosophy, may be cost-effective in the extreme.

ATTITUDES
JOB EVALUATION

S. B. SELLS

EMPLOYEE PRODUCTIVITY

Employee productivity can be defined broadly as the amount of output per man-hour. Investment in technology establishes the productivity potential while human elements determine how closely a given plant will come to realizing that maximum potential.

Extensive research since the 1940s has shown that manipulating just one major human variable produces little or no gain in employee productivity. One of the more successful single variable manipulations, goal setting, produced an average gain in productivity of only 17%. One explanation for this lack of success with single variable research designs is that the impact of a single variable is overshadowed by a multiplicity of other variables that produce variability within each of the experimental and control groups. A second explanation might be that the experimental variable interacts with certain other variables in the experimental situation to produce unpredictable results.

Implicit in all three lists of variables are certain elements: mutual trust between management and labor, high job security, employee sharing in the productivity gains, emphasis on employee growth and development, goal setting, employee control over their own day-to-day activities, and the expectation that employees will develop new and better ways of doing their own jobs. Thus, the feasibility of this approach to high employee productivity has been demonstrated.

EMPLOYMENT PRACTICES
JOB EVALUATION

I. R. ANDREWS

EMPLOYMENT PRACTICES

Employment practices represents a vast number of methods used in the selection and appraisal of applicants or employees for positions in business and industry. These methods have received considerable attention because of the passage in 1964 of the Civil Rights Act, Title VII.

The regulation and control of how employers may select and appraise personnel stems from the original Title VII law, but has received increasing impetus from additional amendments and regulations. *Uniform guidelines on employee selection procedures (UGESP)* provide employers with guiding axioms for employee selection and appraisal. These guidelines are not the only forces affecting employers' personnel decisions: The Age Discrimination in Employment Act (ADEA) was followed by the Vocational Rehabilitation Act. In addition, the Equal Pay Act was passed in 1963, and in 1965 executive orders gave birth to the Office of Federal Contract Compliance Programs (OFCCP).

For all practical matters most employers are covered by one or another set of rules pertinent to personnel decisions. Complementing these rules are the guidelines applied by the OFCCP to federal contractors. Governed separately, the OFCCP takes an active stand in ensuring that federal contractors hire and make other employment decisions affirmatively—that is, it ensures that minorities and other groups in the work force are not underrepresented.

UNIFORM GUIDELINES ON EMPLOYEE SELECTION PROCEDURES

The *UGESP* is the most critical segment of the Civil Rights Act and pertains directly to the methods employers use in employment decisions. Specifically the law, as detailed in the *Guidelines,* forbids job discrimination on the basis of race, sex, color, religion, or national origin for employment decisions that are virtually all-encompassing. When the effects of this law are combined with the ADEA law, which protects groups ages 40 to 70, very few, if any, personnel decisions are exempted from regulation.

Adverse Impact Defined

The *Guidelines* specifically define adverse impact as "a selection rate for any race, sex or ethnic group that is less than four-fifths (4/5) (or eighty percent) of the rate for the group with the highest rate will generally be regarded by the federal enforcement agencies as evidence of adverse impact." The *Guidelines* further explain that selection rates greater than 80% will not be regarded as adverse; however, all rates are subject to some interpretation. From this general statement numerous methods for calculating adverse impact have been developed, including not only statistical methods, but also interpretations as to how to define the group for which the statistical methods will be applied.

Defining the group is generally done by examining either applicant flow or labor market groups. The applicant flow procedure entails an analysis of the hiring rate of the applicants for each job position, classifying the applicants and hires by race and sex. The labor market procedure entails comparing the hires to the number of people similarly qualified who are in the labor market for each position, by race or by sex. Although the former is subject to interpretations on defining an applicant, and the time period for which to use this method, it has a precision of measurement lacking in the labor market approach. The latter method uses broad classifications of employed persons by job categories and therefore reflects a lack of precision in measurement because it leaves open questions on geographic areas and the exactness of the requirements for the job—this latter a factor especially relevant for positions above general labor classifications.

Adverse impact is then used to establish the existence of a discriminatory employment practice. If this effect is demonstrated, a *prima facie* case is established, and the burden of showing the enforcement agency that the methods used in the personnel decisions were valid shifts to the employer. When this happens, the company is required to show that the method is valid, that incidental to its validity the method produced an adverse impact that cannot be overcome by the use of other employment procedures.

Validity Methods

The *UGESP* recognize the methods psychologists use in test validation, content, criterion, and construct validation. The focus in the *UGESP* is on all three types; however, the first two are methods typically encountered in court cases. When these validity studies are reviewed in court, equal emphasis is placed on the methods used to arrive at the conclusions of the study and on the study's practical impact. Methodologically, imperfections in the research design have been sufficient grounds for rejecting many a study. However, of more dramatic interest is the conclusion drawn from the study. In many cases these conclusions are translated into a utility rate that reflects the improvement in the employment decision from the existing methods. These comparisons are aimed at establishing a practical as well as statistically significant improvement in the employment decision-making process. Unless such a practical value can be established, moderate albeit significant findings may not be acceptable to the court.

There exists, however, an important consideration when calculating these adverse impact statistics. The consideration is the number of hires necessary to meaningfully calculate the impact ratios. When a percentage is calculated on a small number of cases, the margin of error is large, compared with the margin of error when the number of cases is large. The problem is further complicated when a comparison is made between two percentages that are either high or low. The magnitude of the differences between the two selection rates, combined with the problem of low numbers in some employment situations, argues for the application of two other statistical methods. These methods in some cases conflict with the four-fifths rate findings, strongly suggesting their application in most adverse impact analyses.

The two statistical procedures are the standard deviation rules as detailed by Grady and the test of differences between two independent proportions as detailed by Shoben. The standard deviation method involves comparing the observed number of hires with the expected rate of hires for a particular class. There is a serious problem regarding the magnitude of differences between the two percentages that warrants a more potent statistical method—the test of differences between two independent proportions.

The statistical method is a common test found in most statistics books. It involves the comparison between two selection rates, as does the four-fifths rate, but unlike that method it accounts for small sample size and percentage differences in selection rates by providing a standardization to the selection data.

The nature of the *Uniform guidelines* places an increased emphasis on the use of content validation strategies for determining the legality of a selection or appraisal instrument. Content validation methods may at times be confused with construct validation strategies.

Content validation is defined as an examination of a test to determine if the test item content mirrors the behaviors it purports to measure. A spelling test is a measure of spelling behavior in its simplest form. Construct validation is a strategy to define a broader set of behaviors through numerous measurement techniques. Constructs are broad traits such as intelligence, mathematical ability, and anxiety.

Content validation tends to be subjective, but may rely on statistical evidence to verify its findings. Construct validation requires sophisticated statistical techniques applied to large data bases to define a general trait. Subjective judgments tend to be applied after this analysis to interpret and refine empirical information.

These general remarks summarize an increasingly complex interface between psychology and the law. The issues of statistical tests applied to determine adverse impact and selection system validity will require the practitioner in this field both to be sensitive to the court's needs and to maintain an awareness of how courts have interpreted research results. The court cases cited in this article represent only a sample of critical incidents where the court's decisions have reflected an increase in its statistical sophistication. As additional and potentially more complex issues are tested, such as comparative worth, reverse discrimination, and the 80% rule, the court will look more and more to the psychologist and statistician for guidance and understanding.

CRITERION IN EMPLOYMENT
FORENSIC PSYCHOLOGY
INDUSTRIAL PSYCHOLOGY

R. S. ANDRULIS

EMPLOYMENT TESTS

Employment tests include all psychological assessment procedures used in selection and classification of personnel by employers. As such, nearly every type of psychological test can and has been used in making occupational decisions.

The most frequently used employment tests are now tests of aptitude, both general and specific. In the earlier stages of employment testing, general aptitude tests predominated the field, the most notable being the Army Alpha and the nonverbal Army Beta examinations. General aptitude measures continue to be used successfully as employment tests. General ability tests designed specifically for industrial settings such as the Wonderlic Personnel Test and the Thurstone Test of Mental Alertness remain in active use today, despite a strong push toward more specific tests of aptitude.

Tests of special aptitude are designed, as their name implies, to assess narrow slices of any individual's ability spectrum. Although a certain level of intelligence may be necessary to perform a given job, this may be insufficient in and of itself.

Until recently, conventional wisdom in employment testing held that the more specific the job, the more specific the test should be to predict performance on the job. Thus, task differences were believed to moderate the validity of employment tests. Recent work has generally refuted this doctrine, as considerably wider generalizability of validity across jobs and tests has been found than was previously believed to exist.

The validity of employment tests is a major issue in the field and not infrequently a bone of contention between management and employees and their representatives.

Employment tests can also be abused and misused. For these reasons the U.S. Equal Employment Opportunity Commission maintains a set of guidelines for employment testing. To promote the proper use of employment testing at a professional level, the Division of Industrial and Organizational Psychology of the American Psychological Association publishes a set of principles in personnel selection.

APTITUDE TESTING
EMPLOYMENT PRACTICES
SELECTION TESTS
TESTING AND LEGISLATION
WONDERLIC TESTS

C. R. REYNOLDS

ENCOPRESIS

Functional encopresis is generally considered a disorder of childhood. For the diagnosis of functional encopresis, feces must be inappropriately deposited at least once a month for 6 months. Clothing is the most likely inappropriate place for feces, but other locations such as the floor, a closet, or a cupboard may also be used.

In making a differential diagnosis it is important to distinguish functional encopresis from disorders caused by organic pathology. Hirschprung's disease is chief among the organic disorders that may be confused with functional encopresis.

Boys are three to four times more likely than girls to develop functional encopresis. Not surprisingly, the frequency of the disorder decreases with age. Between ages 4 and 5 years about 3.5 to 4% of boys and 1 to 1.5% of girls are encopretic, whereas by age 8, the frequency is about 2.3% in boys and 0.7% in girls. By age 12, the frequency of functional encopresis decreases to 1.3% in boys and 0.3% in girls. In rare cases, functional encopresis may continue into adulthood.

Although by definition functional encopresis is not the result of organic causes, many encopretics may experience ineffective gastrointestinal activity throughout their life span, but though this may be an important contributing variable, a definitive etiology for functional encopresis has not been forthcoming.

Encopresis may be associated with other neuropsychological disturbances of childhood such as attentional disorders, but more often the encopretic child has no other primary psychological problems and may be tractable and liked by adults. However, the nature of the disorder is especially odious within the context of Western culture and usually leads to significant disruption of relationships within the child's family and can disrupt formation of positive peer interactions. As a result the encopretic child will often have low self-esteem and withdraw from social contact.

Because encopresis is probably caused by the interaction of a number of variables, including physiological predisposition and difficulties in toilet training, treatment should be multifaceted. Both the child and the family should be involved in the treatment. Family counseling and therapy directed toward reducing conflict between the parents and the child is advised. One goal of family therapy should be to make the parents realize that the child is not being incontinent on purpose. Family therapy sessions also may be useful in identifying precipitating factors within the child's psychosocial milieu and changing attitudes toward toilet training, if the problem is primary functional encopresis and the child has not yet been continent for an extended period of time.

Although family counseling and therapy should be included, therapy for functional encopresis may be primarily medical in nature. Indeed, because the disorder can be associated with gastrointestinal difficulties, including constipation, it may increase the probability of a good outcome if medical care from a pediatrician is included in the program. Alternatively, functional encopresis may be viewed as a behavioral disorder of the individual patient. The emphasis of the therapy may thus best be placed on the behavior itself and behavioral modification techniques will often produce the best results. These may include such strategies as reinforcing each continent day with a star on a calendar belonging to the child. More technically complex biofeedback procedures also have been employed and are particularly successful in cases for which abnormal defecation dynamics occur. For example, Loening-Baucke has incorporated application of biofeedback into an integrated therapeutic approach that includes use of laxatives to overcome constipation and produce daily regularity, as well as family participation in record keeping and similar behaviorally relevant activities. The biofeedback procedures themselves involve insertion of an inflatable balloon approximately 11 cm into the rectum. The balloon is then inflated with 50 ml of air. Activity of the external anal sphincter muscle and the rectal motility are monitored. The patient is directed to attempt to excrete the balloon as if it were feces and is shown tracings of a normal child's external sphincter activity during defecation. Verbal and sound reinforcement (derived from the myographic recordings of external sphincter activity) serve as the biofeedback signals. Although complex and requiring specialized equipment and trained personnel, this biofeedback approach has been successful in treating encopresis, especially when constipation also is a significant complaint.

BEHAVIOR MODIFICATION
BIOFEEDBACK
DEVELOPMENTAL STAGES
ENEURESIS
FAMILY CRISES
INFANTILISM
IRRITABLE BOWEL SYNDROME
TOILET TRAINING

M. L. WOODRUFF

ENCOURAGEMENT

The concept of encouragement, stressed by Alfred Adler and Rudolf Dreikurs, refers to a basic attitude toward life believed necessary for successful living. All children are affected by the obvious fact of their relative inferiority relative to adults and are likely to develop attitudes of weakness and defeat unless someone in their environment encourages them—helps them to realize that their present inferiority is only temporary and that they have a chance to succeed in life. An optimistic attitude toward life is necessary for success; a pessimistic attitude guarantees failure. In the schools, the children who do not try to succeed are those who are discouraged and believe that nothing they can do will ever work out. Such profoundly discouraged children may well grow up to become psychotic because the psychotic may be defined as one who does not believe that he or she belongs in society: a person who is totally discouraged.

It is surprising, given the ultimate importance of this optimistic/pessimistic view of life people can take, that very little is known about the topic and that less has been done in the way of research. Only Adlerians, who believe in the principles of individual psychology, appear to stress the importance of encouragement.

Dreikurs stated, "Children need encouragement the same way that a plant needs water." However, even though parents and teachers may be aware of the importance of encouraging children, very often they do exactly the opposite in dealing with them, and in attempting to correct and improve them, succeed only in discouraging them. The key concept is criticism: Criticized children tend to direct the criticism at themselves rather than at the task; they tend to take it personally.

A number of suggestions can be given relative to criticism:

1. Avoid criticizing (or even praising) the person; relate to the task or the performance.
2. Even if something is poorly done, find something about it worthy of positive attention.
3. Stress the importance of having courage. When a child has failed, say, "You really tried hard." Thus, the emphasis will be on the effort rather than on the performance.
4. Avoid comparisons.

In verbally encouraging children, it is important not to build them up in one breath by appreciating them for dressing themselves, then deflate them in the next breath by commenting negatively on the color of the selected clothes. It is important to continually look at the children's individual strengths, rather than comparing them to other children's work and efforts. The emphasis should be on individual improvement, not on trying hard to be better than others.

It is necessary to develop as many alternatives as possible so as to create an encouraging atmosphere in the home, school, and community. Real opportunities must be created for children to contribute and develop a sense of belonging.

PARENT–CHILD RELATIONS
PYGMALION EFFECT

J. M. PLATT

ENDORPHINS/ENKEPHALINS

During the late 1970s and early 1980s, component parts of the polypeptide β-lipotropin began to receive a great deal of attention. Besides the adrenocorticotropic hormone (ACTH), which was already known as an adrenal gland stimulant involved with physiological arousal states, β-lipotropin includes a sequence of 30 amino acids called β-endorphin. Enkephalin is a small segment of this sequence. Endorphins are found in the pituitary gland and parts of the brain. Although animal studies have allowed direct access to brain tissue, human research has primarily been limited to the measurement of blood plasma endorphin levels.

Endorphins are similar to the opiate morphine in both chemical structure and effect. Hence, the contraction endogenous + orphine = endorphin. The primary effect of endorphins appears to be analgesic. Enkephalins also produce analgesic effects, but the effect is weaker and of shorter duration than that of endorphins. This, together with some evidence that the brain consumes endorphins in response to pain, has contributed to speculation that enkephalins may simply be by-products of incompletely consumed endorphins.

In addition to their analgesic properties, endorphins have been linked to thermoregulation, appetite, memory, lipolysis, reproduction, pleasure experiences, fat breakdown, antidiuresis, depression of the ventilatory response to carbon dioxide, and inhibition of thyrotropin and gonadotropin. There is also some evidence that endorphins are responsible for some of the pain relief attributed to the placebo effect. One theory holds that acupuncture stimulates endorphin secretion.

Stress—both physical (e.g., exercise, pain) and psychological (e.g., conditioned fear)—seems to stimulate endorphin secretion. One form of physical stress that has been linked to endorphins is aerobic exercise, particularly running. Several researchers have found increased endorphin levels in individuals who have recently exercised at what is considered an intense level, given their level of conditioning. Although plasma endorphin levels usually return to their baseline within 30 minutes of completing the exercise, Appenzeller suggested that endorphins are responsible for the "runner's high" and exercise addiction described by some frequent exercisers. Others have speculated that endorphins play a role in the lessened sensitivity to pain reported by many athletes who are injured while performing. There is further speculation that the successful use of exercise in treating some mildly depressed individuals may be related to abnormal endorphin levels sometimes found in psychiatric patients.

CENTRAL NERVOUS SYSTEM
NEUROCHEMISTRY

J. R. CAUTELA
A. J. KEARNEY

ENGINEERING PSYCHOLOGY

It is that branch of psychology that examines human behavior as it relates to the equipment, computer software, environments, and human—machine systems that characterize modern technology. Primarily, it has asked certain questions: What are the capabilities and limitations of human performance in using technology and its products? How should people and machines be shaped to fit each other? Here "machines" must be interpreted to include the creations not only of engineers but also of computer programmers and analysts, architects, training developers, and planners.

Clearly, engineering psychologists often find themselves closely associated with these other disciplines, as well as with physical anthropology and physiology. Within psychology, engineering psychologists border not only on experimental psychology, in which most early engineering psychologists were trained, but also on organizational and industrial, personnel, and operant subdisciplines. But they are distinguished by their emphasis on the physical features of technology as the sources of inputs to human behavior and the recipients of outputs. Because technology so greatly influences modern life, engineering psychology would seem to have considerable significance. Its growth is tied to that of the multidisciplinary field of human factors (overseas, ergonomics). Many, if not most, American engineering psychologists identify themselves also as human factors scientists, and some who engage in applications as human factors engineers.

HISTORY

Conventionally, the origin of engineering psychology is placed in World War II, with its major technological innovations in weaponry, aircraft, submarines, and radar. The demands these imposed on psychomotor skills and information processing seemed at times to exceed human capabilities. As a result, lives and battles might be lost. Things had to work right the first time; traditional trial-and-error development was not enough. With such a driving influence, military organizations began to foster engineering psychology to find out what operators of such new equipment could actually accomplish with it—where they might succeed and fail. Problems lay not only in the designs of displays and controls but in the workloads operators confronted and the environments in which they functioned. Tasks had to be accomplished within certain time limits and as free of error as possible. Past laboratory studies of psychophysics and psychomotor activity did not disclose enough about what people can and cannot do; investigations had to be directed toward special, more complex sensing, processing, and control activation, involving particular inputs from equipment to the operators and their outputs to manage it. Because some of the new technological marvels had to be operated in high-altitude and undersea environments hostile to human beings, it became necessary to find out how their performance was affected by increased or reduced atmospheric pressures, increased or reduced accelerations, noise, heat and cold, and vibration. The biological impacts of these conditions were studied by medical investigators and psychophysiologists.

Involvement in system design extended to other human–machine complexes, such as air-traffic control centers and power plants; the driving force behind the development was again life and death—as well as financial loss.

Military support continued for engineering psychology in numerous ways after World War II. For example, the Office of Naval Research funded a substantial research program led by Alphonse Chapanis at Johns Hopkins University, also an early one at New York University and later ones at many other universities and locations. The Army established a Human Engineering Laboratory that employed many engineering psychologists. The Air Force's Aerospace Medical Research Laboratory conducted extensive research itself and supported it elsewhere. When the Air Force began to require its contractors to conform to new requirements for human factors engineering in system and equipment design, contractors formed human factors groups in their engineering departments that included engineering psychologists. The first was at Hughes Aircraft under the aegis of Alexander Williams; other major aerospace concerns followed: Lockheed, Douglas, McDonnell (becoming McDonnell Douglas), Boeing, and Honeywell. The Navy and Army established similar requirements, which became consolidated in Department of Defense regulations and standards. Some engineering psychologists worked in laboratory research, some in development or applications, and some in both.

Some commercial support also developed early, first at the Bell Telephone Laboratories, then at International Business Machines and other large corporations. In subsequent years nonmilitary research, development, and applications increased, as evidenced in the number and size of in-house human factors groups as well as human factors consulting organizations, although often it was difficult to sort out what proportions could be claimed by engineering psychology. Product effectiveness for the user resulting from engineering psychology has seldom been an outstanding advertising feature in the competition for sales, although it might become so if prospective purchasers were more aware of it. However, product hazard has indeed become a "driver," and engineering psychologists have been testifying more and more as expert witnesses in product liability litigation.

Engineering psychology rarely penetrated factories in the early days. The work-related design of industrial machinery was preempted early by industrial engineers, while industrial psychologists concerned themselves with organizational and personnel problems. Eventually, however, engineering psychologists began to investigate robotics as a significant form of automation still requiring human involvement. They also studied quality control because human error is a major target of engineering psychology—and an important factor in productivity.

FOCAL POINTS IN REAL-WORLD APPLICATIONS
Outside academia, engineering psychology has concentrated on some particular aspects of human performance as dependent variables and on various categories of equipment, environments, and systems as independent variables affecting these. Its work has been applied to diverse human–machine aggregates. The dependent variables have largely though not exclusively consisted of the time needed and accuracy attained in a particular performance, components of human information processing, decision making, monitoring and vigilance, inspection and signal detection, accidents, auditory communication, psychomotor skills and skill acquisition, continuous manual control (tracking), reading, stress and fatigue, and various kinds of workload capacity. Categories of independent variables include systems, automation, tasks, controls and control devices, displays (including print), equipment and tool design, workload (mental and physical), work–rest cycles, procedures, maintenance activi-

ties, information feedback, training techniques, training devices, and ambient conditions (illumination, glare, noise, temperature, vibration, acceleration, and atmospheric pressure).

Among the human–machine aggregates have been aircraft (military and commercial), submarines, spacecraft, radar, sonar, undersea habitats, air-traffic control, highway transportation, automobiles, urban transportation, postal operations, residential environments, offices, telephonic and radio communications, nuclear power plants, mining, interactive computers, missile systems, command and control systems, health care delivery, and law enforcement.

UNIVERSITIES
A number of American universities have graduate curricula and give graduate degrees in engineering psychology, and some (e.g., the Air Force Academy) teaches it to undergraduates. However, the number has been shrinking for several reasons: (a) graduate work in human factors, including much of engineering psychology, has been shifting to engineering departments, notably industrial engineering; (b) employer needs have emphasized training in cross-disciplinary applications rather than in experimental research, although quite a few employers still regard the latter as an important qualification; and (c) psychology departments dominated by experimental psychologists tend to derogate engineering psychologists on the grounds that their research is too mundane—that is, insufficiently theoretical.

Most university research in engineering psychology tries to be "basic"—that is, abstract or highly generalizable—although some is applied: applicable to the processes and products of modern technology. Strong views have been expressed on behalf of each emphasis. A major research interest is human information processing, which largely originated in engineering psychology in the United States and Great Britain and in technological problems. But human information processing has become a major focus also of experimental psychology, which takes it as a virtual synonym for cognition.

With an increasing focus on computers, engineering psychology has been investigating language as an information-processing medium—but so has experimental psychology, or at least it has been investigating information processing with language as the medium. Thus, the difference between them has become blurred; inputs as well as outputs are much alike in each, in contrast to the marked differences when engineering psychology was oriented more toward psychomotor skills.

TECHNIQUES
Experimentation has been the primary investigative technique of both university and nonuniversity engineering psychology—one reason why academic training in experimental psychology has been useful. Experiments are conducted in laboratories, in field settings, and in mixes of the two. Some experiments outside academia are oriented toward general problems but most have some particular goal, such as to evaluate how well an operator performs with some specific equipment or to compare alternative displays or machines when operated by humans. The dependent variables are not necessarily the same in these two kinds of particular experiments. In the former, the time an individual takes or the errors the individual makes in reacting to a component can (but may not) be isolated, so only human performance is being measured—although, as an early engineering psychologist, Franklin Taylor pointed out, it is often difficult to exclude that of the machine component entirely. In the latter kind of experiments—the comparison of alternative devices—the investigator measures the joint output of the device and the operator. It has been questioned whether the study of such combinations constitutes "psychology." One reason justifying a psychologist's participation is the relative unfamiliarity of most engineers with experimental design, especially with respect to human variables.

When combinations of human operators and machines become large and complex, experiments evaluating them have been called "human–machine system experiments," and the investigators, "system psychologists." Such experiments are similarly large and complex, and experimental subjects function as teams or crews. Investigators have made comparisons between two designs for an operations center; have assessed system capabilities, as for example how many aircraft an air control center can bring into an airport in 1 hour; and have diagnosed problems, such as which system components or subsystems (including operators) should be held responsible for some particular level of system performance. In addition to design factors, such system experiments have investigated procedures, skill levels, and training methods. Generally, they simulate parts of the system or its environment.

Most nonacademic experimentation in engineering psychology takes place, however, on components within a system—on display design, maintenance procedure, skill requirement, or training device. Here, too, simulation is a principal tool, often created for the study. It consists, for example, of a mockup or of signals seen on a cathode ray tube. Some experimentation is exploration for discovery; some is verification for certainty.

Engineering psychology employs additional ways to gather data such as observations of real-world operations, examination of archival sources, and systematic querying of operators and maintainers to obtain their self-reports. Such self-report data from interviews or questionnaires are particularly useful in providing insights into problems that can then be studied more objectively.

Numerous analytic techniques are used by engineering psychologists. Foremost is task description and analysis. A related technique is computer modeling of human and machine performance. Data similar to those for task analysis are programmed into a computer, which can then be used to vary nontask factors such as workload, design changes, or procedural differences to determine how these alter the time and accuracy of a task.

Much of what engineering psychologists accomplish in the actual design of some equipment or system remains unknown to other psychologists and to the public. (In that sense they resemble clinical psychologists in private practice.) Furthermore, their contribution may not be apparent within a team effort. It is difficult to determine from the published word what engineering psychology has actually done to shape technology.

ORGANIZATIONS

The APA division of Applied Experimental and Engineering Psychology is an amalgam of varied professionals: some from universities, the government, and industry; some who concentrate on research, development, or applications; and some who identify more as experimental psychologists, or as human factors engineers.

Outside the United States, engineering psychology occupies a strong position in Russia and Great Britain and various continental nations have also produced distinguished engineering psychologists.

PROSPECTS

As long as technology continues to evolve and produce new processes in which humans participate or new products they use, there will be a continuing need for engineering psychology, or at least for psychologists concerned with the interactions between technology and people. The outstanding development in technology is automation—in the factory and office as well as in various products. Of increasing uncertainty is the extent to which something can or should be automated. Engineering psychologists can help resolve that issue by continuing to reveal human capabilities and limitations (especially cognitive) in technology-related performance, at the same time examining with some skepticism what intelligent machines can and cannot do.

But engineering psychology is also challenged to broaden its perspective. There is more to the impact of technology on human behavior than skilled performance. How people feel, why they act as they do, and their relationships with others—these emotional, motivational, and social variables are also influenced by technology, and in turn influence the shape it takes. Because these considerations demand systematic inquiry into the physical world of technology, virtually all psychologists have left them unattended, or attended only superficially. Engineering psychology—or psychology for modern technology—seems the logical candidate to fill this void.

APPLIED PSYCHOLOGY
HUMAN FACTORS
TASK DESIGN

H. M. Parsons

ENURESIS

Enuresis is involuntary urination beyond the age at which one is expected to have learned bladder control. Functional enuresis is the term applied when the disorder is presumed not to have a primary physical cause. Although enuresis can occur during waking hours, it is more common during sleep. Minimum numbers of episodes per month for different age groups have been established arbitrarily for the diagnosis to be made. The incidence of enuresis is higher among boys than girls.

There are multiple etiologies of enuresis. Factors that may contribute to the development of enuresis are genitourinary disorders, genetic or constitutional factors such as delays in maturation of bladder control or neurological sleep disturbances, failures in toilet training, disturbed intrafamily relationships, and acute stress of life changes such as the birth of a sibling or the loss of a parent. Most cases of functional enuresis spontaneously remit. The need for treatment typically results from the unpleasantness of the disorder and its implications for the child's interpersonal functioning.

Treatment of enuresis depends on the presumed etiology. The most common medication used is imipramine (Tofranil). After gradual withdrawal of imipramine, many children remain dry through the night, as reported by Judith Rapoport and her colleagues. Psychological approaches have included bladder control training by practicing the retention of fluids and increasing the child's sensitivity to changes in bladder distension; bell-and-pad devices for the bed that emit an auditory signal when moisture completes the circuit in an electrical grid; and awakening the child during the night to urinate.

TOILET TRAINING

T. S. Bennett

ENVIRONMENTAL MEASURES

Environmental measures are instruments utilized to identify the relationships that exist between persons and their environments, and thus provide information as to the degree of adjustment that an individual experiences in an environment. Although a large number of environmental measures exist, most follow approaches similar to those utilized by such investigators as R. G. Barker, who focused on specific environmental units that have both a space and time locus, or R. H. Moos, who focused on subenvironments or subunits in which individuals interact with one another on some regular and familiar basis. Moos and his associates, for example, utilized three major dimensions to measure environments and classify the similarities and differences among them: (a) relationship dimensions; (b) personal development dimensions; and (c) system maintenance and change dimensions.

Relationship dimensions were used to identify the nature and intensity of personal relationships within the environment. They assessed the extent to which individuals were involved in the environment and the extent to which they supported and helped one another. *Personal development dimensions* were used to consider the potential or opportunity in the environment for personal growth and the development of self-esteem. The precise nature of personal development dimensions varied somewhat among different environments and depended mainly on the goals of a particular environment. *System maintenance and change dimensions* were employed to assess the extent to which the environment was orderly and clear in its expectations, maintained control, and was responsive to change.

Various environmental measures, all based on the three major dimensions previously described, were developed to assess a number of environmental settings. The data derived from these and similar measures have been used primarily for research and applied purposes focusing on the design and ultimate improvement of various human environments by employing environmental assessment data to plan and implement environmental change.

ECOLOGICAL PSYCHOLOGY
ENVIRONMENTAL PSYCHOLOGY

C. H. HUBER

ENVIRONMENTAL PSYCHOLOGY

Environmental psychology is a specialized area that studies the relationships between behavior and the environmental context in which it occurs. Behavior here refers to both overt and covert acts and includes thoughts, emotions and so on. The environment refers to one's physical surroundings. Although environmental psychologists incorporate aspects of social environment in their work (e.g., family, reference groups), their primary focus is the influence of the physical environment. Thus, much of the research subsumed under environmental psychology deals with the influences of noise, air pollution, extreme temperatures, and the ways in which architectural designs structure space.

There has been some recognition of the importance of the environment in determining behavior for many years. The roots of experimental psychology were in controlled investigations of light, pressure, and other environmental events. Unfortunately, this interest was in discrete stimuli, so that studies of light were nothing like real-life exposure to varying intensities of light. Instead, they were studies of human sensation of isolated physical stimuli. Later, behavioral psychology recognized the importance of the environment in controlling behavior, but the environment as defined usually consisted of reinforcement schedules or isolated elements pulled out of an environmental setting.

The first approximation of this modern use of "environment" was provided by Kurt Lewin, who believed that behavior (B) is determined by personality (P) and environment (E). Hence, the equation B = f(P,E). Although Lewin's use of environment was largely social, it was a whole environment rather than a small piece of a setting pulled out of context and administered in controlled trials.

In the years between 1950 and 1970, the concept of environment grew slowly toward the rich contextual role in behavior that Lewin had envisioned. Festinger, Schachter, and Back conducted studies of friendship formation and group development in the physical context of a housing project. They reported clear influences of the layout of the project on these social processes. Subsequently, human factors researchers began considering technological environments, such as an airplane cockpit, and applied psychology toward determining how different designs influenced human response.

By 1970, there were researchers calling themselves environmental psychologists who studied environmental contexts and consequent behavior. However, environmental psychology views the environment as a whole rather than as a bundle of stimuli.

Glass and Singer conducted an extensive series of studies on the effects of urban stress. Subsequent research applied these laboratory findings to field settings. These studies provided information about naturalistic exposure to noise. The laboratory finding that having control over the environment reduces the impact of stressful events was extended to conditions other than noise. Control was found to reduce stress on crowded commuter trains and in high-pressure work settings.

Environmental psychologists generally prefer to move freely among several research approaches. Laboratory findings must also be studied under the harsh light of the real world. However, because it is often difficult to maintain good experimental procedures in the field, laboratory work is often needed to eliminate alternatives and refine concepts.

Another characteristic of environmental psychology is its emphasis on the interrelatedness of environment and behavior. The environment clearly constrains behavior, provides varying options in some instances, and influences behavior more subtly at other times. However, people also cope by changing their environments. Environment–behavior relationships are more or less in flux continuously.

Research in environmental psychology tends to be problem-oriented. Most work is directed toward solving problems, as for example ameliorating the effects of environmental stressors. Few, if any, theoretical orientations guide research across problem areas. Conceptual frameworks have been proposed for numerous problem areas, but they are secondary to work directly applied toward understanding or solving problems. Those theories that do exist are rarely used to explain more than one or two areas within environmental psychology.

There are, of course, exceptions. One is the stress model, which has been used to integrate research on a number of environmental stressors, including crowding, noise, and temperature.

The notion of nonspecific stress response—that people respond to all stressors in much the same way—is derived from the work of Hans Selye, who identified common responses to many different noxious agents and formulated a general adaptation syndrome to explain response to these agents.

Subsequent elaboration of the stress concept has identified appraisal as an important mechanism, explaining specific coping responses. In addition, differences in response to different stressors have been found. By and large, however, research has found that common responses to different stressors outweigh these differences, and at least two environmental events, noise and crowding, appear to influence behavior in a similar manner.

A more general orientation within environmental psychology is called *determinism*. Although not particularly popular, it has characterized a great deal of work on the effects of architecture on behavior. Its lack of popularity is due to its emphasis on environmental effects on behavior and its refusal to acknowledge the give-and-take between the two. In its most extreme form, this position argues that the environment causes certain behaviors, denying any interaction between environment and behavior. Architectural determinism poses the idea that people can adapt to any arrangement of space and that behavior in a given environment is caused entirely by the characteristics of the environment. Most theories of environment and behavior do not concur with this position.

Another perspective used by environmental psychologists is centered on the construct of arousal. Because arousal is one aspect of stress, this model is similar to the stress model. However, this one differs in that arousal, defined as increased brain activity and autonomic responding (e.g., heart rate, respiration), can be associated with events that do not cause stress. Pleasant stimuli as well as negative ones can elicit arousal, and research has suggested that any environment can be described in part in terms of its arousal-evoking properties.

Environmental load is yet another perspective used to study environment and behavior, focusing on attention as a key variable in the person–environment relationship. When the amount of information provided by an environment is greater than an individual's ability to process it, overload occurs. The converse, where there is too little information, results in underload. Overload has been used to explain problems of city life and crowding, while underload has been used to describe monotonous settings and the effects of isolation.

Another orientation toward environment–behavior relationships is R. G. Barker's ecological psychology. Barker was concerned primarily with the integrity of the context of behavior. Each instance of behavior has a spatial and temporal context, and this three-part unit, the behavior setting, is the proper level of analysis for environmental research. A number of processes operate to maintain these settings, and these can provide alternative perspectives on various environmental problems.

There are other theories and orientations in environmental psychology, but to a large extent the field remains relatively atheoretical. Theories that try to arch over all aspects of environment–behavior interchange become complex and burdensome. Instead, the field has evolved a set of smaller areas of investigation, each with models and literatures of its own.

The smaller areas within environmental psychology all have basic and applied aspects. Briefly, they include crowding, spatial behavior, architecture and behavior, environmental cognition, environmental education, environmental stress, and to a limited extent, technological environments.

APPLIED RESEARCH

A. S. BAUM

ENVIRONMENTAL STRESS

The concept of stress came from the field of engineering, in which an external event (stressor) caused a structural response (strain). The original research that utilized the term *stress* to explain organismic responses to environmental stimuli was conducted by Walter Cannon. Cannon noted that a "fight or flight" response could be detected in which animals responded to stressors by physiological arousal that prepared them to either fight or flee. This response also consisted of a homeostatic mechanism that returned the organism to its original physiological state shortly after the stressor was removed.

Hans Selye found that diverse environmental stressors resulted in a stereotyped organismic response. Although specific aspects of the organism's responses varied according to the natures of the stimulus and the organism, a generalized reaction was found to be superimposed on any specific physiological responses.

At this point, stress evolved into an interactional variable that encompassed both physiological and psychological processes. Selye termed this broad interaction of environment with physiological and psychological processes the "general adaptation syndrome." This syndrome encompassed changes in the hypothalamus, the pituitary, the thymus, the adrenal, and the gastrointestinal tract. The response encompassed an increase in physiological activity, a feedback mechanism that regulated the cessation of the response, and a return to homeostasis. Incidental or short-lived stressors caused little or no long-term organismic effect, while exposure to excess stress over time caused a state of physiological exhaustion. Selye found that each organism had an optimal stress level and that either overexposure or underexposure caused a deterioration in the level of functioning.

S. Levine found that rats not exposed to stressors during early life developed a later dysfunctional response to stress. It therefore seemed that some stress was necessary for optimal functioning. Kanner, Kafry, and Pines reported that, in their study of humans, the absence of positive conditions also caused dysfunctional responding. Even without specific environmental stressors, stress resulted from the absence of positive life and work factors.

Stressors can be either environmental or intraorganismic. Intraorganismic stressors can be physiological or cognitive, but would still have derived somehow from environmental stressors. Environmental stressors can be either noxious or pleasant, yet still elicit a stress response. The elicitation of a stress response in relation to a specific stimulus seems to be based on organismic perceptual processes in the reticular activating system of the brain.

Prolonged exposure to stressors results in diverse dysfunctions throughout the organism. All systems involved in the general adaptation response can experience a state of exhaustion. When continued for extended periods of time, this state contributes to numerous gastrointestinal, cerebrovascular, and respiratory disorders.

Another system impaired by extended exposure to stress is the immunological system. In their study of rats, G. F. Soloman, Amkraut, and Kasper found that both primary and secondary antibody responses were impaired by exposure to stress. Such an impact on the immunological system could contribute to added impairment of other organismic processes.

Environmental stimuli in themselves exist only as potential stressors until the organism perceives them as being stressful. The primary goal of research pertaining to environmental stress, therefore, is not to eliminate stressors, but to determine the optimal adaptational strategies for coping with specific stressors.

Ecological stressors are those external stimuli that exist in the physical environment. Two of the most commonly studied ecological stressors are heat and cold. Others that have received experimental attention are air pollution, sunlight exposure, fluorescent lighting, auditory stimuli, olfactory stimuli, gravitation, barometric pressure, and humidity. In all cases, these variables are elements of the physical environment that stimulate the organism to respond so as to retain homeostasis.

A second group of stressors may be termed "contingency stressors." These stressors are not normal aspects of the environment but exist as external events that affect the organism. Contingency stressors are accidents such as automobile crashes that induce some form of trauma. Much of the research pertaining to contingency stressors utilizes an approach that examines "stressful life events." This approach is based on the assumption that if major events, whether positive or negative, accumulate, they increase susceptibility to physical illness. Some contemporary researchers have criticized this approach on methodological grounds and suggested that everyday "hassles and uplifts" are more appropriate measures of contingency stressors. Other researchers have found that stressful life events are influenced by resources for coping with them. Coping, therefore, seems to be a central element in life events research.

Sociological stressors include such variables as socioeconomic status, malnutrition, workplace, educational level, and place of residence. This dimension pertains to the processes by which culture impinges on the individual. The design of the social system or organization presupposes certain forms of stress. The maintenance or change of such systems also generates certain stressors. Other sociological stressors would be processes such as prejudice.

The final general classification of stressors, self-induced stressors, include such variables as lifestyle stressors and voluntarily ingested stressors. Lifestyle stressors comprise such variables as the environmental consequences of maintaining a Type A behavior pattern, or those of a career choice, a personal value system, or an exercise program. Voluntarily ingested stressors include such variables as caffeine, nicotine, prescription and nonprescription drugs, and alcohol. Incidental to self-induced stressors may be side effects to prescription medication or allergens.

Stressors seldom act individually: People tend to be exposed to more than one at a time. The cumulative effect of stressors, therefore, is a relevant area of study.

BEHAVIORAL MEDICINE
ENVIRONMENTAL PSYCHOLOGY
GENERAL ADAPTATION SYNDROME
STRESS

R. H. STENSRUD

EPIDEMIOLOGY OF MENTAL DISORDERS

DEFINITION OF EPIDEMIOLOGY

Epidemiology is the health science that studies patterns of occurrence of disease and disorder, as well as causal factors that influence such patterns in human or animal populations.

PREVALENCE AND INCIDENCE

Two principal types of rates are employed by epidemiologists: prevalence and incidence.

Prevalence

Prevalence rate has been likened to a snapshot insofar as it describes the health of a group within a specified time interval. This interval can either be an instance in time, most typically a day (point prevalence), or an interval of months, years, or even decades (period prevalence). The time interval need not be a point or period in calendar time, but can refer to an event or events that happen to different individuals at different periods in calendar time. Within the designated time period, prevalence is defined as the number of individuals who are determined to have the disorder divided by the total number of individuals comprising the population of interest:

$$\text{Prevalence rate} = \frac{\text{Number of persons with the disorder during a specified time period}}{\text{Total number of persons in the population during a specified time period}}$$

One frequently reported rate, lifetime prevalence, refers to a measure of the proportion of persons who have had the disorder at any time during their lives. Lifetime prevalence rates are nearly always based on retrospective reports and are susceptible to the inaccuracies characteristic of such reports.

Incidence

Incidence describes the rate of development of a disorder within a group over a designated period of time. This time period is factored into the formula defining incidence as follows:

Incidence rate

$$= \frac{\text{Total number of new cases}}{\text{Total number in the population at risk}} \text{ per time interval}$$

In contrast to prevalence, which describes a proportion of *all* cases of the disorder in a designated population, incidence describes the continuing occurrence of *new* cases. Incidence is typically more difficult to determine than prevalence because persons who already have the disorder at the beginning of the study's time period must be identified and excluded from the incidence numerator. Because these individuals also are not at risk for developing the disease, they must also be excluded from the incidence denominator.

RISK FACTORS

It is possible to calculate the risk of developing a mental disorder on the basis of prevalence and incidence rates and a systematic account of other factors operating in the situation. Risk metrics indicate an associative or causal relationship between the presence of specific biological, environmental, or psychosocial factors and the occurrence of a disorder. Relative risk refers to the ratio of the incidence of a disorder among individuals known to have been exposed to a risk factor divided by the incidence among individuals known not to have been exposed to that risk factor. Attributable risk is the absolute incidence of the disorder that can be attributed to exposure to the risk factor. Attributable risk is typically calculated by subtracting the incidence of the disorder among an exposed group from its total incidence among an unexposed group. It is a useful indication of what might result were the risk factor(s) to be removed.

Risks vary in the degree to which they are associated with disorders and in the degree to which they cause disorders. Factor-related risks are risks that are frequently, though not always, observed in conjunction with a disorder. Factor-specific risks are necessary, although not sufficient, prerequisites to developing a disorder. Patterns that suggest a causal connection between a risk factor and a mental disorder include consistent association, precedence, and specificity of effect. In consistent association, a clear relationship is reported between the risk factor and the mental disorder over repeated studies. Elimination of the risk factor eliminates or markedly ameliorates the disorder. Introduction of the risk factor precipitates or exacerbates the disorder. In precedence, the risk factor is observed to be present before the disorder is observed. In specificity of effect, the effect of the risk factor is specific to the disorder under investigation. A major goal of the epidemiology of mental disorders is the identification of risk factors that contribute to, precipitate, or maintain mental disorders.

Comparing rates of disorder between various groups is considerably important. Such comparisons are frequently expressed as differences between rates, as ratios of one rate to another, or of many rates to a standard rate.

TYPES OF STUDIES

There are two fundamental types of epidemiological studies. Descriptive studies are undertaken to document the occurrence of disorders or disorder-related phenomena in a group. Descriptive studies generally measure the disorder and its related attributes in a somewhat diffuse or superficial manner. They provide observations concerning the relationship of disorders to such basic characteristics as age, gender, ethnic background, socioeconomic status, geographic location and distribution, time of occurrence, and so forth. Analytic studies are conducted to explain the observed pattern of the disorder within the group and thereby clarify the etiological factors involved in precipitating, maintaining, or alleviating the disorder. In contrast to descriptive studies, analytic studies tend to be more narrowly focused on a specific set of hypotheses and often require more rigorous study designs and more sophisticated quantitative analyses of findings. The three most basic types of analytic observational studies are prevalence studies, case-control studies, and cohort studies.

Prevalence studies investigate the relationship between disorders and other attributes of interest such as they exist in the population of interest during a particular time period. The presence, absence, or severity of the disorder are determined for each individual sampled, and the relationship between the attribute and the disease can be determined in either of two ways: (a) in terms of the presence, absence, or severity of the disorder in different population subgroups defined by the attribute, or (b) in terms of the presence, absence, or severity of symptoms for those determined to have the disorder versus those who were not.

Case-control studies are similar to prevalence studies in that they investigate the correlations between indicators of existing symptoms with other variables or attributes. The presence or absence of the disorder is determined for each member of the study and is systematically related to other factors or attributes. Typically, following an initial process of case determination, an appropriate control group of individuals without the disorder is identified. Correlations of other attributes to the disorder are determined by comparing the disordered group with controls for presence or severity of the attribute.

Cohort studies are undertaken to investigate more directly factors related to the development of the disorder. A group of individuals who are determined to be free of the disorder are identified at a particular time. Attributes of interest are measured in this cohort, then these individuals are followed up at various times to determine the development of the disorder(s) under study. The correlation of an attribute with the disorder is determined by splitting the population into subgroups according to the presence or level of the attribute initially and comparing the incidence of disorder among the various subgroups formed.

In actual practice, the neat distinction between descriptive and analytical studies is often blurred. A carefully designed and implemented descriptive study may provide a clear resolution of specific hypotheses. An analytic study, focused on a specific hypothesis, may coincidentally provide descriptive data of considerable interest.

SPECIAL ISSUES IN THE EPIDEMIOLOGY OF MENTAL DISORDERS

The difficulties inherent in the diagnosis of mental disorders within modern American society are compounded when individuals from various minority groups or from non-Western cultural backgrounds are studied. Psychiatric epidemiologists have long appreciated that many mental disorders manifest as patterns of thought, affect, or behavior that deviate from dominant cultural beliefs and expectations and are found to be disturbing by those who think, feel, or act them out or to others around them. Because different cultures have established different standards and upheld different expectations for their members, it follows that what might be considered disturbing or disordered in one culture may fall comfortably within the normal range of experience for another culture. Some of the most influential studies in the history of mental health epidemiology have addressed these issues.

THE VALUE OF EPIDEMIOLOGY TO THE MENTAL HEALTH COMMUNITY

The value of properly conducted epidemiological studies for theory building and for the therapeutic practice of psychology is unquestionable. Valid epidemiological rates are of fundamental importance in alerting the mental health community to those types of individuals most likely to be afflicted with a particular disorder, where the disorder is most likely to occur geographically, and when it is most likely to manifest for the individual case or come to the attention of the professional mental health care community. Thus, valid epidemiological information helps guide the individual diagnostic process and also may aid in the selection of appropriate and effective intervention strategies. Reliable epidemiological information also is obviously valuable for efficient planning of community mental health services and facilities. By providing information regarding the etiology of mental disorders and by raising new hypotheses regarding the nature of their antecedents, course, and consequents, epidemiological data make fundamental contributions to theory building for both fundamental understanding and treatment of mental disorders.

BACKGROUND CHARACTERISTICS
CONTROL OF VARIABLES

DIAGNOSES
ECOLOGICAL VALIDITY
EMPIRICAL RESEARCH METHODS
FIELD DEPENDENCY
SURVEYS
TAXOMETRIC METHODS

E. H. Spain

EPILEPSY

The term *epilepsy* comes from the Greek word meaning "to seize," hence the word seizure is used to describe an epileptic attack. A seizure is described by J. R. Hughes in "Epilepsy: A medical review" as an "excessive, disorderly, neuronal discharge, characterized by discrete attacks, tending to be recurrent, in which there is a disturbance of movement, sensation, perception, behavior, mood, or consciousness." Contrary to popular beliefs, epilepsy is a *symptom,* not a disease, and is best understood in terms of *seizure threshold*. We all probably inherit a certain seizure threshold, but if it is sufficiently high, our threshold for seizures will never be reached. However, for individuals with low thresholds or whose threshold has been lowered by a neurological disorder, a minimal amount of activation is needed to elicit an epileptic seizure. It is estimated that 1 to 4 million Americans fall into this latter category.

Epilepsy can develop at any age and may or may not be associated with a specific neurological disorder or identifiable precipitating factor. Those seizures that appear to be spontaneous and of unknown etiology are referred to as *idiopathic*—a term generally applied to seizures that appear to have an inherited basis, or for which the exact cause of the abnormal neural discharge eludes identification.

Seizures that develop secondary to known causes are called *symptomatic*. The most common causes of symptomatic seizures include head injuries, febrile seizures, brain tumors, encephalitis, cerebral vascular disease and malformations, hypoxia, drug and alcohol withdrawal, and metabolic disorders. While each of these etiologies affect the brain in its own unique way, the common denominator is that they all irritate or damage brain cells in such a way as to lower the individual's seizure threshold.

Since the causes, areas of brain involvement, and clinical symptomology of epilepsy are as varied and complex as the nervous system itself, the terminology and criteria for classifying seizures has varied widely. The International Classification of Epilepsy system lists four major classes of epilepsy: generalized, unilateral, partial (focal), and unclassified. These classes generally correspond to whether the whole brain (generalized), one hemisphere (unilateral), or a specific area within a hemisphere (partial) is involved. Specific types of seizures within each of these classifications have also been differentiated on the basis of clinical features and EEG characteristics.

The two most common types of generalized seizures are tonic-clonic (grand mal) and absence (petit mal) attacks. *Tonic-clonic attacks* occur in approximately 60% of epileptics and have distinctive stages. In the first or tonic stage, the muscles become rigid, consciousness is lost, and breathing stops. The tonic phase lasts for 10 to 15 seconds and gives way to the clonic stage, in which there are generalized muscle spasms and twitching, lasting another 45 to 50 seconds. After about 1 minute, the person relaxes and drifts into a deep sleep or comatose state called the postictal stage. Prior to these stages, but still part of the seizure itself, there may be a warning or aura stage in which the person experiences a strange sensation such as a peculiar noise, smell, or numbness.

The other common form of generalized seizure is the *absence attack*, which typically occurs in childhood and usually disappears by adulthood. The typical or simple absence attack involves only a diminution of consciousness rather than a complete loss, and muscle responses may consist of only slight facial twitching or rapid eye blinking. Ordinarily, the person is unaware that anything unusual has happened and resumes whatever he or she was doing prior to the attack. More complex absence attacks may involve what Hughes calls *automatisms*, "automatic kinds of movements, especially fingering of clothes, and various types of movement of the mouth, especially chewing." Other forms of generalized seizures include tonic and clonic seizures, infantile spasms, and myoclonic seizures.

Anticonvulsant medications have been found to be effective in reducing both the number and severity of epileptic seizures in most individuals. Other forms of treatment include cerebellar stimulation, surgery, biofeedback, and ketogenic diets. Based on the findings of the Epilepsy Foundation of America, it is estimated that with good medical care and appropriate drug therapy 50% of epileptics can live free of convulsions and another 30% can have their seizures reduced to a minimum. However, psychological and neuropsychological investigations have found that, while there is no "epileptic personality" or characteristic pattern of deficit, individuals with symptomatic epilepsy are generally more impaired than those with idiopathic seizures. Also, people with generalized tonic-clonic attacks fare less well than those with complex-partial seizures. Within a given seizure type, an early age of onset and higher frequency of seizures have been associated with increased mental impairment.

**BRAIN
CENTRAL NERVOUS SYSTEM DISORDERS
PSYCHOPHARMACOLOGY**

G. J. CHELUNE

EPISTEMOLOGY, PSYCHOLOGICAL

Psychological Epistemology is a new interdiscipline describing the psychological aspects of the knowing process. Its two major domains of investigation are the philosophical one of specifying the norms or criteria for justifying knowledge claims, and the psychological one of specifying the cognitive and other knowing processes.

Because of the enormous range and diversity of subject matter, contributions to the psychology of knowing have been essentially autonomous and isolated from one another. In short, psychological epistemology has been relatively unconscious and unconnected—a loose and uncoordinated collation of individual efforts. The most conscious and sustained attempt to provide a conceptual framework for this domain has come from Piaget's Institute in Geneva. However, Donald Campbell's evolutionary perspective and Royce's concept of epistemic styles also provide insightful conceptual frameworks.

Although all aspects of cognition are potentially relevant, the processes that have received the most attention are perception, thinking, intuition, symbolizing, and developmental.

Examples of important contributions in the perceptual area include James Gibson's arguments for naive realism, Egon Brunswik's plea for a probabilistic functionalism, the gestaltists' demonstrations of organizing principles, William O'Neill's review of perceptual theories, and the philosophical analyses of D. M. Armstrong and W. D. Hamlyn. Important contributions on the role of thinking include the research program of Herbert Simon and Alan Newell on problem solving, and the investigation of children's thought presented by Piaget and by Jerome Bruner.

The most thorough investigations of intuition are those reported by Malcolm Westcott and Kenneth Hammond, whereas the most insightful contemporary philosophical analysis of intuition is provided by Michael Polanyi, who views all epistemology as tacit or intuitive knowing. Although symbolizing has received less empirical investigation than the other cognitive processes, developments in psycholinguistics, as exemplified by the research of Charles Osgood, have included research on the symbolizing process. Important insights have also come from the psychoanalytic tradition, particularly Carl Jung, but the most important contributions to the understanding of symbolizing are the organismic theory of Heinz Werner and Bernard Kaplan, and the psychophilosophical analyses of Cassirer and Langer.

Finally, there is developmental psychology—in particular, the development of cognitive processes. Piaget's contributions have dominated thinking in this domain, especially his theory of stages in cognitive development and his hypothesis that these stages parallel the general development of knowledge.

**COGNITIVE COMPLEXITY
INFORMATION PROCESSING
PHILOSOPHICAL PSYCHOLOGY**

J. R. ROYCE

EQUITY

Equity theory is a strikingly simple theory. It is composed of four interlocking propositions:

> *Proposition I.* Individuals will try to maximize their outcomes (where outcomes equal rewards minus punishments).
>
> *Proposition IIA.* Groups (or rather, the individuals forming these groups) can maximize collective rewards by evolving accepted systems for equitably apportioning resources among members. Thus groups will evolve such systems of equity and will attempt to induce members to accept and adhere to these systems.
>
> *Proposition IIB.* Groups will generally reward members who treat others equitably and generally punish members who treat each other inequitably.
>
> *Proposition III.* When individuals find themselves participating in inequitable relationships, they become distressed. The more inequitable the relationship, the more distress they feel.
>
> *Proposition IV.* Individuals who discover they are in inequitable relationships will attempt to eliminate their distress by restoring equity. The greater the inequity, the more distress they will feel, and the harder they will try to restore equity.

Equity researchers find that men and women feel most content when engaged in equitable relationships. Both the overbenefited and the underbenefited feel intense distress after an inequitable exchange. The more inequitable the exchange, the more uncomfortable participants feel. Naturally, participants are less distressed by inequity when they gain from it than when they lose from it.

Researchers also find that people who discover they are in an inequitable relationship and become distressed try to reduce their distress by restoring either actual equity or psychological equity to their relationships. One can restore *actual equity* by actually altering one's own or one's partner's relative gains in appropriate ways.

Recent studies verify that the *overbenefited* often do voluntarily compensate the underbenefited.

Undoubtedly the underbenefited's first response to exploitation is to seek restitution.

People in unbalanced relationships can also restore equity in a second way by restoring psychological equity. They can destroy reality and convince themselves that the unjust relationship is perfectly fair.

Some distortions that harm-doers and victims have been found to use include blaming the victim, or denying responsibility for the victim's suffering.

E. HATFIELD

ERGOPSYCHOMETRY

Ergopsychometry is the testing of subjects under physiological or psychological load.

Persons who perform very well in neutral, stress-free situations, but who repeatedly fail in real "combat" situations—so-called "training champions"—are a well-known phenomena. Testing a subject in neutral situations may thus lead to faulty prognosis of that person's achievement behavior under load.

Some subjects show an unchanged or even increased performance level under load, whereas in other subjects the performance level decreases under load. When a group of top-level athletes and less successful controls were subdivided according to their success in competitions, an interesting result emerged: With the same amount of training, the less successful ones in most cases showed a marked performance decrease with regard to such factors as speed of optical information processing and decision-making speed, when tested under load. The successful athletes, in contrast, demonstrated a definite performance increase in the ergometer situation.

This strategy of testing is also being used in other areas where the prognosis of a person's performance under load is of decisive importance, as for example in the selection of aircraft pilots. In the first instance, of course, a choice of suitable tests is essential. Tests chosen on the basis of extensive preliminary studies are presented in a fully computerized experimental setup in a neutral situation and under physiological and psychological load, while simultaneously relevant physiological data are recorded. In this regard special emphasis is placed on the EEG and cortical DC potential shifts, which have been found to be a reliable indicator of arousal and capability. The reason for the differing influence of load on achievement behavior may possibly be found in different changes in the approach–avoidance motivation. By means of self-control techniques it may be possible to mitigate or eliminate such decreases in performance under load.

**APPLIED RESEARCH
HUMAN FACTORS
SPORTS PSYCHOLOGY**

G. GUTTMANN

ERIKSONIAN DEVELOPMENTAL STAGES

The developmental theory of Erik Erikson builds upon but extends Sigmund Freud's account of psychosexual development in significant ways. Erikson provides a life-span theory of psychosocial development and emphasizes the autonomous or conflict-free development of an adaptive ego. In addition to the gratification of instincts, human beings need to categorize and integrate their experience, according to Erikson. Therefore, a firm sense of ego identity—a perceived sense of personal wholeness and "continuity of experience"—must be achieved for optimal personal functioning.

The building and integrating of personality involves an eight-stage life-span sequence governed by what Erikson calls the epigenetic principle: "This principle states that anything that grows has a ground plan, and that out of this ground plan the parts arise, each part having its time of special ascendancy, until all parts have arisen to form a functioning whole." Each stage, from birth to old age, is marked by a normative crisis that must be confronted and negotiated. These crises may arise from intrapsychic conflicts (the first five parallel the Freudian psychosexual stages), but the quality of the social context in which resolution is attempted may vary; the crises are psychosocial in nature. Crisis "resolutions" leave their mark on the developing person, and each contributes to the totally formed personality. Ideally, however, a resolution should not be totally one-sided; too much trust or naiveté, for instance, can be maladaptive. A blend or positively balanced ratio of the two poles indicates optimal progress.

The stages are assumed to be interdependent and build upon one another in a cumulative manner. Also, each stage contributes a unique quality or virtue, such as hope or faith, to the evolving personality.

1. *Trust versus mistrust (infancy).* At birth, infants are dominated by biological needs and drives. The quality of their relationship with caregivers will influence the extent to which trust (or mistrust) in others and the world in general is sensed. The virtue of hope is associated with this stage.

2. *Autonomy versus doubt and shame (early childhood).* Social demands for self-control and bodily regulation (toilet training) influence feelings of self-efficacy versus self-doubt. The quality of will, the will to do what is expected and expectable, emerges at stage two.

3. *Initiative versus guilt (preschool age).* Here children begin actively to explore and intrude upon their environment. Will they sense guilt about these self-initiated activities, or will they feel justified in planning and asserting control over their activities? The virtue of purpose—the courage to pursue personally valued goals in spite of risks and possible failure—now ascends.

4. *Industry versus inferiority (school age).* The social context in which the first three crises are negotiated is predominantly the home and immediate family. In stage four, however, children begin formal instruction of some sort. Mastery of the tasks and skills valued by one's teachers and the larger society is now the focal concern. The quality of competence (with the tools and ways of the adult world) is said to develop.

5. *Identity versus diffusion (adolescence).* This is the pivotal step in Erikson's scheme, when adolescents actively attempt to synthesize their experiences in order to formulate a stable sense of personal identity. Although this process is psychosocial in nature—a social fit or "solidarity with group ideals" must occur—Erikson emphasizes the role of accurate self-knowledge and reality testing. Individuals come to view themselves as products of their previous experiences; a continuity of experience is sensed. Positive resolutions of prior crises—being trusting, autonomous, willful, and industrious—facilitate identity formation, whereas previous failures may lead to identity diffusion. Fidelity, the ability to maintain commitments in spite of contradictory value systems, is the virtue that emerges during adolescence.

In Erikson's theory, development continues throughout life. The three adult stages, however, are directly affected by the identity achieved during adolescence.

6. *Intimacy versus isolation (young adulthood).* In this stage one must be willing and able to unite one's own identity with another's. Because authentic disclosure and mutuality leave one vulnerable, a firm sense of identity is prerequisite. Love is the quality that ascends during this stage.

7. *Generativity versus stagnation (middle adulthood).* This is the time in the life span when one strives to actualize the identity that has been formed and shared with selected others. The virtue of care now emerges: Generative adults care for others through parenting, teaching, supervising, and so forth, whereas stagnating adults are absorbed in their own personal needs.

8. *Integrity versus despair (maturity).* The final Eriksonian stage focuses on the perceived completion or fulfillment of one's life cycle. When individuals become aware that death may be imminent, do they feel despair, either fearing or welcoming death, or do they perceive the order and meaningfulness of their one and only life within a larger perspective? Wisdom is the last virtue to emerge. The wise person understands the relativistic nature of knowledge and accepts that one's life had to be the way it was.

As a heuristic scheme, Erikson's theory has had a marked impact on contemporary developmental psychology, especially concerning adolescent development. Despite its popularity and apparent face validity, however, the empirical foundation for the theory is relatively weak. Erikson and others have provided a wealth of observational data.

ADOLESCENT IDENTITY FORMATION
BONDING AND ATTACHMENT

M. D. BERZONSKY

ERRORS (TYPE I AND II)

When statistical analyses are used to test hypotheses, experimenters typically set up a specific postulate, known as the *null hypothesis* (H_0), prior to collecting data. This predetermined postulation allows for an evaluation of research results on the basis of sampling distribution and normal curve probability theory. A null hypothesis deals with the relationship between variables and is posited so that either it or its negation will result in information that can be used to advance research hypotheses. After the data are collected and the actual statistics are derived, the researcher must decide whether or not to reject the null hypothesis.

This decision logically allows for the possibility of four outcomes, two of which are errors. A *Type I* error is made when the decision is to reject H_0 but H_0 is in fact true. A *Type II* error, however, consists of a decision not to reject H_0 when H_0 is in fact incorrect. The other two possible outcomes are a correct decision to reject H_0 or a correct decision not to reject it. The null hypothesis itself cannot be proved without knowing the "true" state of affairs, but it can be disproved if the obtained results are too unlikely to be compatible with it. Therefore, decisions based on statistical hypothesis testing are usually phrased in terms of levels of probability or levels of confidence in the correctness of various outcomes in light of H_0.

The probability of making a Type I error is labeled *alpha* (α) and is under the direct control of the experimenter. In setting alpha, the experimenter specifies the probability level associated with the decision to reject H_0 in terms of the proportion of times that this decision will be correct. The alpha level is also called the level of confidence or level of significance. In the social and behavioral sciences it is traditional to cast the null hypothesis in terms that negate the theoretically derived expectation of the experimenter or research hypothesis. If the alpha level is then set, as is typical, at 0.05 or 0.01, and the critical value of the statistics reaches or exceeds that level, it is possible to reject H_0 and to conclude that chances are 95 out of 100 or 99 out of 100, respectively, that the treatment does produce a measurable effect.

The probability of a Type II error is labeled *beta* (β) and cannot be directly controlled because it depends, among other things, on the size of the experimental effect or "true" state of affairs, which is unknown. Furthermore, setting a more stringent alpha level increases the chances of making a Type II error, because it makes it necessary for the experimental effect to be larger in size in order to be detected. In addition, whereas H_0 assumes only one sampling distribution, the alternative to H_0 is unspecified, and the value of beta will vary according to which alternative

sampling distribution, out of an almost infinite range, is correct. If one selects a specific alternate hypothesis, it is possible to calculate β and its inverse $1 - \beta$, which is called the *power of a test*. The only way the experimenter can increase the power of a test and reduce beta is to increase the number of cases sampled. As sample size increases, the standard error of a statistic—on which the critical value is based—decreases, and H_0 can be more readily rejected. The choices of the alpha level and of sample size are, therefore, of critical importance in statistical hypothesis testing and should be dictated by considering the relative seriousness of making a Type I versus a Type II error.

HYPOTHESIS TESTING
MEASUREMENT
RESEARCH METHODOLOGY

S. P. URBINA

ESCAPE–AVOIDANCE LEARNING

Avoidance learning and extinction are typically studied in the rat with electric foot shock as the aversive stimulus. In active avoidance, the rat is often placed in a runway, the floor of which is electrified at one end and is, at least temporarily, safe at the other end. The rat must move to the opposite end to escape or avoid shock. Before shock is delivered, the subject has several seconds in which to respond. A naive subject, however, fails to avoid and is shocked on at least one trial before escaping the shock chamber. Thus traditional avoidance learning always includes escape behavior and is appropriately called escape–avoidance learning.

When the situation is arranged so that the subject cannot avoid but can only escape shock, the termination of shock is considered reinforcing (termed negative reinforcement by Skinnerians), and learning to escape is usually measured by a reduction in latency with successive shocks (trials). In a one-way situation (see later), a series of, say, eight or ten escape trials also can mediate perfect avoidance learning when the opportunity to avoid is provided.

With a two-way, or shuttlebox, situation avoidance learning is slow, escape responses prevail, and perfect performance is rarely, if ever, attained. In a shuttle situation, the subject must learn to shuttle from one end of the alley to the other every time a warning signal (buzzer or light) is presented. This is difficult to do because no section of the alley is uniquely associated with either shock or safety. Thus fear is conditioned to the whole apparatus, engendering freezing; the rat has no distinguishable place to go to escape fear or relax, and after each escape trial it must learn to avoid by running right back into the region where it just got shocked.

In a one-way box, however, the rat is placed in a start chamber specifically associated with shock to which fear is conditioned, and the rat avoids by approaching a particular chamber that is consistently safe (i.e., where fear is clearly reduced or relaxation can occur). Some subjects in a one-way box learn to avoid in one trial, and learning to a 100% level in a mean of three or four trials is not unusual. Here the use of distinctive chambers and increasing the shock level up to a point facilitates learning. Presumably fear and safety are thereby segregated better, and reinforcement is enhanced (greater fear reduction), whereas the opposite is true in a shuttlebox where conditioned fear (competition from freezing and the like) is enhanced by these manipulations. The same manipulations that facilitate or hinder avoidance learning have been shown to have parallel effects in pure escape learning by Franchina and associates.

In passive avoidance, the subject avoids shock by not making a particular response. For example, the rat is placed on a small platform surrounded by an electrified grid. If it remains on the platform without stepping down, the rat avoids passively. Because it yields fast learning and is simple to use, many studies of amnesia and other behavioral effects of biological intervention use the passive technique for assessment purposes. Basically, the use of punishment, in which an aversive stimulus is contingent on a particular response, is the same as passive avoidance. Passive avoidance is impeded if an alternative safe place to approach actively is available after the rat has been shocked for stepping down and the more so the longer the rat remains in this safe place.

Mowrer's two-factor theory, or fear hypothesis, provides the main explanation of avoidance learning. Fear is conditioned to the shock area or warning signal, and escape from fear or the reduction of fear when the shock area or warning signal is removed is the reinforcement for the avoidance response (this is called secondary negative reinforcement by the Skinnerians, and the concept of fear is not invoked). Research by Denny and associates indicates that 2.5 min away from shock or fear-provoking stimuli on each trial provides a good opportunity to relax, confers optimal approach value to the nonshock or safe area, and yields optimal avoidance learning in one-way situations. Also the concept of relaxation in this context is especially valuable for explaining the extinction of fear-related behaviors such as escape and avoidance. Relaxation is directly incompatible with fear and presumably constitutes the competing response that extinguishes fear. In one-way situations, extinction appears to originate in the safe area where the longer the subject is confined, the more it relaxes, and the faster fear extinguishes, especially if the safe area is similar to the shock region.

Tortora, working with vicious dogs that had presumably learned to avoid punishment by being aggressive, trained them to avoid shock by promptly following 15 different commands (e.g., down, here, and heel). For many dogs a tone (safety signal) followed each correct response and was associated with a long shock-free, relaxation period. The safety tone clearly facilitated training, producing manageable, prosocial animals.

Results from a number of recent escape–avoidance studies indicate that without fear there is no tendency to avoid or to approach safety.

ANIMAL INTELLIGENCE
BEHAVIOR MODIFICATION
CLASSICAL CONDITIONING
CONCEPT LEARNING
INHIBITORY CONDITIONING
OPERANT BEHAVIOR
STRESS CONSEQUENCES

M. R. DENNY

THE ETHICAL PRINCIPLES OF PSYCHOLOGISTS AND CODE OF CONDUCT (1992 REVISION)

HISTORY

The 1953 ethics code of the American Psychological Association (APA) was one of the first such professional guidelines of conduct.

As it became increasingly important to develop a formal ethics code, Nicholas Hobbs assumed leadership of the Committee on Ethical Standards shortly after the end of World War II and spearheaded this project. The committee worked for 5 years, soliciting 1000 vignettes from the APA membership, describing ethical and unethical behavior. It ultimately developed a 171-page document, the *Ethical standards of psychologists*, a combined casebook and ethics code, consisting of 6 major sections and 28 subsections; the 6 sections were (a) competence, (b) integrity, (c) professional and scientific responsibility, (d) respect for people's rights and dignity, (e) concern for others' welfare, and (f) social responsibility. This was a quantum leap for an association that had been providing

research, teaching, and psychological services to the public for decades with little or no formal ethical guidance to its members.

Although the ethics code constituted a major advance and an excellent resource for the APA Ethics Committee, it did not provide specific guidance for the functioning of the committee or the rights of psychologists who had been complained about. These areas were described in *Rules and procedures*, an important companion piece to the code, and a document that, like the code, also was to be revised periodically. The first edition appeared in 1958, and it has been revised several times since then.

As the science and practice of psychology expanded over the years, there was a marked shift in the type and frequency of ethics complaints encountered by psychologists. This can be accounted for partly by the increasing numbers of APA members and affiliates, which approached the 100,000 mark in 1990, and the climate of American society, which was becoming more consumer-oriented, sophisticated, and litigious.

THE 1992 REVISION PROCESS

A major revision was needed, in part, many felt, due to the increasing risk of ethics complaints and malpractice lawsuits faced by psychologists in a litigious society.

In 1986, the APA Ethics Committee initiated a six-person subcommittee to begin the revision process. The original task force consisted of five senior psychologists, all of whom had served on the APA Ethics Committee and were experienced in using the ethics code regularly in adjudicating complaints.

The goals of the task force were to create a code that would be easily taught and easily learned, would contain one concept or idea in each standard instead of multiple ones, as in former revisions, and would address the broad variety of problems and dilemmas encountered by psychologists in various subspecialty areas. With these changes, the code would be easier to read and use for psychologists, consumers, and ethics committees.

The operating philosophy of the task force was teleological in nature, as was the first ethics code. A teleological process brings a focus to the outcome or results of an action; a choice is made because of the effects it has on others, not because it is "felt" or declared to be right or constructive. Such a pragmatic concept depends on perceivable consequences connecting a behavioral decision with its morality, in sharp distinction to the deontological approach, which holds that there are absolutes in morality that exist independently of the consequences of an act.

CHANGES IN STRUCTURE

In August 1992, after voting on a number of amendments, the council of the APA formally accepted the new document, the *Ethical principles of psychologists and code of conduct*. This version has done away with much ambiguity by dividing the document into two parts: general principles, aspirational in nature, and ethical standards, consisting of enforceable standards of behavior.

The six general principles form the guiding spirit of the document: competence, integrity, professional and scientific responsibility, respect for people's rights and dignity, concern for other's welfare, and social responsibility. Although the general principles are crafted in lofty and generic language, they are useful in helping psychologists to arrive at interpretations of the ethical standards.

The second section consists of the ethical standards; these are 102 principles divided into eight sections and listing specific, enforceable rules of conduct to which every psychologist as such must adhere. They are (a) general standards (potentially applicable to the professional and scientific activities of all psychologists; (b) evaluation, assessment, or intervention; (c) advertising and other public statements; (d) therapy; (e) privacy and confidentiality (again, potentially applicable to all psychologists);

(f) teaching, training supervision, research, and publishing; (g) forensic activities (a new section); and (h) resolving ethical issues.

Other structural changes included an innovative indexing system. For the first time each ethical standard had its own title and number, making it easy for anyone to locate a particular subject area. A table of contents and extensive cross-referencing within the document make the code user-friendly for psychologists and the general public.

SUMMARY

The new code represents a significant departure from every previous version; it remains to be seen how the new format and content will facilitate its application by consumers, psychologists, and ethics commit-tees alike. It may be a flawed document that will drift into obsolescence. But the structural changes may set a precedent that will be useful, it is hoped, for many years.

T. F. NAGY

ETHICAL PROBLEMS IN PSYCHOLOGY

The two major source documents with regard to ethical issues for psychol-ogists are the American Psychological Association's (APA's) *Ethical principles of psychologists* and *Ethical principles in the conduct of research with human participants.* In addition, the APA's *Criteria for accreditation of doctoral programs and internships in professional psychology* specifies that instruction in scientific and professional ethics and standards is re-quired for proper training in professional psychology.

Ethical principles involve value judgments that are often difficult to make; psychologists who do not spend enough time thinking of these issues are often confronted with ethical dilemmas. Three major ethical principles found in the APA's *Ethical principles of psychologists* will be explored: public statements, confidentiality, and competence.

PUBLIC STATEMENTS

This principle deals with activities of psychologists that help the public make more informed choices. Statements to the public should be based on the state of the art and science, recognizing that in any scientific endeavor there are limits and constraints to the available evidence. Fur-ther, the principle cautions psychologists to provide individual diagnostic and therapeutic services only within a professional psychological rela-tionship.

Two questions arise, however. First, will the advice be harmful to the individual concerned or to individuals participating vicariously? Second, what about the requirement that the advice be within the context of a professional relationship? The first question deals with a more general issue. What is the evidence that psychological help by trained profession-als is harmful? In *The benefits of psychotherapy,* M. L. Smith, G. V. Glass, and T. I. Miller point out that there is little evidence that psychotherapy is harmful and much evidence that it is beneficial. But one would still need to assess whether media advice is similar to psychotherapy as provided in a variety of professional settings. A related issue is whether the vicarious participants can be harmed by listening to others seeking help. So far, there is no evidence to that effect.

The second question, whether media help is within the context of a professional psychological relationship, presents a difficulty of definition. Most professional psychologists would agree (and case law concurs) that the professional relationship begins when the client makes contact (even by phone) with the professional and the professional agrees to continue to communicate with the client about the client's psychological concerns. This could be the paradigm for media communication. But not every psychologist is eager to provide psychological help through the media. One important question to be considered is whether the benefits of media communication on psychological issues outweigh the risks—an empirical as well as an ethical problem.

CONFIDENTIALITY

In the APA's preamble to this principle it is stated that confidential information obtained in one's work as a psychologist is not revealed unless clear danger could result either to that individual or to others. It is specified that this would be an unusual circumstance.

This issue presents two interesting ethical dilemmas. The first of these has to do with legal issues. Ziskin points out that a ruling of the California Supreme Court requires therapists to be reasonably careful in protecting intended victims from possible danger by their clients. This requires an assessment by the therapist of the likelihood that a given client will be dangerous. Such assessment should be pursuant to the standards of that therapist's profession. Thus the first dilemma for the psychologist is one between confidentiality and the requirement of the law. As it stands, the ethical principles do not require a conflictive choice between ethics and the law.

The more complex dilemma stems from the fact that the prediction of dangerousness by psychologists and other mental health professionals is generally not very accurate.

COMPETENCE

According to the ethical principles, psychologists are to provide only those services and techniques for which they are qualified by training and experience. Furthermore, they are to represent with accuracy their education, training, experience, and competence.

But professional competence is not an easy concept to identify. Spe-cifically, one needs to ask: competent with what problems and with what populations and in what instances? These are all difficult questions, many of which indeed raise ethical issues.

N. ABELES

ETHICAL TREATMENT OF ANIMALS

In *Animal liberation: A new ethics for our treatment of animals,* Peter Singer posed the following dilemma for the research scientist: "Either the animal is not like us, in which case there is no reason for performing the experiment; or else the animal is like us, in which case we ought not to perform an experiment on the animal which would be considered outrageous if performed on one of us."

In a speech to the psychology section of the British Association for the Advancement of Science, Alice Heim raised the following question: "With respect to animal experimentation . . . to what extent is it per-missible to use means which are intrinsically objectionable . . . ?" By "intrinsically objectionable" she referred to "experiments which de-mand the infliction of severe deprivation, or abject terror, or inescapable pain . . . on the animals being experimented upon."

In their development of the concept of "alternatives" to the use of animals in research, Russell and Burch defined alternative methods as those that either replace the use of laboratory animals altogether or reduce the numbers of animals used, or refine procedures to lessen their suffering.

These ideas mark a resurgence of concern in psychology over our relation to nonhuman animals and, in particular, to their treatment as research subjects. These concepts, and more generally the suggestion that psychology needed to reevaluate its position, issued largely from outside the United States with publications such as S. Godlovitch, and R. Godlovitch, and J. Harris' *Animals, men and morals,* Bernard Rollin's *Animal rights and human morality,* and Richard Ryder's *Victims of science.* Not until the late 1970s did American psychology begin to educate itself in the APA symposia "Present and Future Problems in Conducting Animal Research" and "Ethical Issues in Research with Animals."

Centered in England in the nineteenth century, an earlier humane movement was radically antivivisectionist, pressing for the abolition of all experiments involving surgical procedures and culminating in the Cruelty to Animals Act of 1876, which required the licensure of researchers utilizing living vertebrate animals. In the United States the first federal legislation addressing the conditions of laboratory animals did not pass until 1966. As amended, it defined humane standards for the transportation and maintenance of animals intended for research. However, it exempted the actual experiment from the requirement of humane standards. Even painful procedures were under no such requirements if, according to the researcher, they would interfere with the course of the experiment. Rodents, the most frequently used class of animals, as well as birds and farm animals, were completely exempted by the act.

Among the occasioning contexts of contemporary interest in animal welfare—or "animal rights," as they came to be called in the United States, given certain developments in moral philosophy—were the following: environmentalism; a broadening of the reformist impulse from racial and sexual discrimination to "speciesism"; a growing research literature in ethology and psychology evidencing a greater complexity, intelligence, and sensitivity in nonhuman animals than had previously been thought; and a remarkable increase in the numbers of animals being utilized in research.

Psychological research was singled out for criticism beyond its proportionate share of the combined research effort in catalogues of painful experiments with animals compiled by Dallas Pratt and Jeff Diner. Singer argued that the extrapolation of results to humans presented an ethical dilemma particular to psychology; Rollin referred to psychology as practicing "bad science" with "unnecessary cruelty." Within psychology, Ryder described the suffering of animals both in the experiment and during their "life in the laboratory"; Michael Fox questioned the validity of psychological research with animals kept under conditions of social and sensory deprivation, with resultant behavioral and physiological stress.

Yet psychologists have argued that the role of research animals has been and continues to be indispensable to the progress of scientific psychology. In his documentation of the contribution to society of psychological research, Perrie Adams listed learning theory and its application to biofeedback, programmed instruction, and behavior therapy, and the study of aggression, communication, memory, and brain development. While acknowledging these and many other contributions of useful knowledge, Ryder raised the question of whether this knowledge could have been acquired by other means. The spate of publications and symposia on the ethical treatment of animals that began in the late 1970s crystallized several issues:

1. An overriding question was the compatibility of such use of animals with "good science," (i.e., with the adherence to standard criteria of the experimental method). Does such adherence in and of itself constitute an adequate ethical position? If it does not, then on what grounds

could one be compromised for the sake of the other? Would compromise in either direction be a threat to psychology? Or again, as Fox argued, was the humane treatment of animals a prerequisite for good science, as it alone was likely to produce valid results?

2. Would a reevaluation of the ethics of our treatment of animals be consistent with the right of freedom of inquiry? Of course, in the right of consent there is precedent for accepting limits on experimentation, at least in the case of human subjects. Could a growing public demand for accountability extend to concern for the protection of animals, and would such accountability be consistent with the freedom of inquiry? A related question was raised in the political sphere: To what extent should psychology regulate itself, or should it accept or welcome externally applied constraints and monitoring? For example, should there be members from the public on animal care committees?

3. What is the proper attitude toward animals? Is an ethical attitude compatible with a scientifically based attitude? Dominant in contemporary science is the view that animals in research are tools or instruments to be controlled and measured. The animal exists for us. This attitude derives from scientific humanism, a prevailing ethos that holds that human welfare and human progress are the superordinate value. Given this value—albeit tempered by humane considerations whenever possible—any experimental procedure, no matter how painful to nonhuman subjects, is justifiable if the results are beneficial to human health or happiness. The primacy of humans, typically argued on the basis of their purportedly unique possession of rationality and/or language, implies that morality is fundamentally a human affair: Both moral agency and objects of moral concern are limited to the human sphere.

However, an attitude is emerging that is more life-centered than human-centered, accepting and valuing any animal for itself. This attitude is based on an ethic that argues that any animal has a certain way of living in its own natural setting—a set of preferred activities, certain social relations, and certain potentialities. This "way" constitutes the animal's interests. In turn, these interests constitute claims that compete with other beings' interests. As moral agents, then, we must give equal rather than secondary consideration to animals' interests.

ANIMAL COMMUNICATION
ETHICS OF PSYCHOLOGICAL RESEARCH

K. J. SHAPIRO

ETHICS OF PSYCHOLOGICAL RESEARCH

Throughout the social and biomedical sciences, there is interest in protecting the rights and well-being of human participants in research. The growth of such concern following World War II, which heightened during the 1960s and 1970s, probably reflects the memory of the Nazi medical experiments, certain abuses in North American medical experiments, disaffection with authority, increased professionalism, and increased commitment to social justice and civil rights. Most scientific and professional organizations have developed ethical codes. The U.S. Department of Health, Education, and Welfare (now the Department of Health and Human Services, or DHHS) developed regulations for protecting human subjects. Regulations provide that organizations set up an institutional review board (IRB), composed mainly of scientists and scholars, to judge the ethical adequacy of projects before they can be funded.

Most psychologists accept the necessity for such measures. Many, however, argue that the potential danger is small, whereas regulations constitute a threat to scientific freedom and creativity. Such controversy is a restatement of the age-old conflict between individual rights and social needs. For psychology, however, it can be argued that ethical and scientific considerations converge rather than conflict, because participants treated as partners are likely to give valid and usable information.

INFORMED CONSENT

Informed voluntary consent is the cardinal principle of ethical research. DHHS regulations note that this involves the knowing consent of an individual (or a legal representative) able to exert free choice without undue inducement or any element of "force, fraud, deceit, duress, or any form of constraint or coercion." To achieve these ends, it is suggested that investigators clearly communicate (a) what procedures are involved and their purposes, (b) any attendant discomforts or risks, (c) any benefits reasonably to be expected, (d) an offer to answer any questions, and (e) the person's right to withdraw consent at any time without prejudice. Application of the principle raises knotty questions, particularly in those studies in which subjects are kept ignorant or are purposely misinformed about the true purposes, procedures, or measures.

Research with Children and Psychiatric Patients

Research with children and patients limited in their ability to understand and decide has traditionally required the consent of the parent or legal guardian.

Research with People Less Free to Choose

Commonly, investigators are in a more powerful or prestigious position than their subjects, who therefore are not really free to decline. In the past, biomedical, behavioral, and social scientists have depended on populations less free to choose, precisely because of their availability and docility. Many critics have spoken out against the traditional practice of using the poor and powerless as subjects in medical research; extending the sample to include private as well as clinic patients would not only be more fair, but it would also serve the scientific end of having more representative data.

Uninformed Participants

Few ethical questions would be raised by a study involving open observation of, for example, children at play in a school yard, even though no one's consent was obtained. Similarly, studies based on archival data, such as school or medical records, seem morally justifiable, even though the students or patients did not give consent for these data to be used in research. Other studies, however, raise moral issues: A medical crisis is faked on the subway train to see how people react; a psychologist fakes symptoms and gets himself hospitalized in a psychiatric clinic; a sociologist volunteers to serve as a lookout to study homosexual activities in a public men's room; and a jury room is bugged with the judge's permission, but without the jurors' knowledge. All these actual research cases raise serious questions.

Misinformed Participants

Other research involves active deceit. To make important psychological phenomena more accessible for study, psychologists have attempted to create credible situations (fictional environments) in order to control the variables under study. Thus in an experimental stress study, individuals may be led to believe that they are intellectually inadequate or even that their lives are in danger. On topics such as cognitive dissonance or conformity, as many as 75% of the studies involve deception.

The basic argument for deception is that it brings important phenomena for study under controlled laboratory conditions. Such research is viewed as convenient, cheap, and valid. A second justification is that such research does little if any harm, and that any negative effects can be dissipated by "debriefing" the participants in a final interview.

Critics have responded with two types of arguments. The first asserts that deception is by its nature unethical, regardless of the potential gains

or minimal harms. The second includes a range of views that challenge the belief that laboratory controls somehow yield better data, question the claim that little harm is done, and present evidence that debriefing may not soften the impact of deception.

PRIVACY AND CONFIDENTIALITY

As with other freedoms, the right to privacy is not absolute, conflicting as it does with society's right to know. In considering privacy in psychological research, there are three major issues: (a) how sensitive the information is; (b) how the information is gathered (e.g., whether it involves unobtrusive measures with unwitting participants); and (c) whether the information, once collected, is treated as confidential.

Sensitivity of Information

Religious preferences, sexual practices, income, and other topics are clearly more sensitive than, say, food preferences or driving habits. Not only embarrassment but positive harm might result from some information being revealed.

Privacy Issues in Gathering Information

Studies based on observing subjects without their knowledge not only violate the principle of informed consent, but may be invasions of privacy as well. The more public the behavior and the setting, the less concern there need be with the invasion of privacy. However, the issue is more acute when there are intrusions into important and private parts of persons' lives or when basic values are involved.

Anonymity and Confidentiality

Participants are most protected if personal information is collected anonymously (e.g., on questionnaires filled out in a large auditorium and turned in unsigned). Anonymous or confidential material tends to be fuller and more accurate. Thus there is scientific as well as ethical gain in anonymity and confidentiality.

HARMS AND BENEFITS

Perhaps the most widely accepted principle of research ethics is that no harm should be done to participants and, if possible, that they should benefit from the experience. Psychological studies tend to be "low-risk research"; there is little documented evidence that participants have ever been harmed in it.

Where there is any possible risk, the investigator should do everything to minimize it. Possibly dangerous equipment should be carefully checked; drugs should be used only with medical safeguards. Vulnerable people should not be allowed to serve as subjects in possibly dangerous experiments. Should any distress become evident, the investigator should be prepared to give whatever clinical help is needed. Signs of potential harm should be monitored during the research session and for a reasonable period thereafter if there is the possibility of delayed effects. The possible risks in the experiment should be investigated in appropriate pilot experiments before any number of subjects are exposed.

Among the possible benefits to participants are (a) financial payments, which should not be so great as to be coercive and deprive people of necessary concern for their rights and well-being; (b) intrinsic enjoyment of the tasks involved; (c) clinical gains (even an interview intended for research may help persons understand their problems better; and (d) satisfaction in helping in the advancement of science.

Risk–Benefit Analysis

A basic tenet of most codes is that potential benefits should outweigh risks for a study to be ethically justifiable. When the risks are too high, a research study simply should not be done. In high-risk studies that *are* done, special precautions should be taken to protect the rights and welfare of the participants. It is important that these decisions be shared with colleagues.

In some cases both risks and benefits accrue to the participant. For example, in tests of an innovative therapy, the risks to the patient of departing from accepted practice may be more than offset by the potential gains. The risk–benefit ratio becomes a modern version of the principle that the end justifies the means. It also reflects the tension between individual rights and the common good.

The analysis of risks and benefits is difficult because they cannot be measured easily. Sometimes neither can be judged until the end of the study, but predictions can be made beforehand. Ultimately, deciding the risks and benefits has to include at least the investigators, colleagues, and participants. A risk–benefit analysis is a necessary step in deciding the ethical status of a study. It may not be sufficient to justify the research, but it may give sufficient grounds for abandoning it. However, a risk–benefit analysis has to be subordinated to a primary concern with individual human rights.

THE RISKS OF REGULATION

Concern with the rights and welfare of research participants, research review committees, and codes of ethics will surely remain a permanent part of the scientific scene, and, on the whole, to good ends. At the same time, regulation has its dangers. It is a costly, time-consuming process, using energies that might better be used in research itself.

Along with the administrative nuisance, there is the genuine question of whether regulation might not stifle scientific creativity.

Codes and regulatory procedures are probably necessary. Guideline and committee review can keep investigators sensitized to the inevitable moral dilemmas in human research. They can point to ways in which the interests of participants have been slighted and suggest alternative routes to research goals. The quest for principles, as well as efforts to test their applicability in particular cases, are necessary to keep us alert to human as well as scientific issues in psychology.

ETHICAL TREATMENT OF ANIMALS
PSYCHOLOGY AND THE LAW

S. J. KORCHIN

ETHNIC GROUPS

An ethnic group is usually considered to be a subculture within a larger society whose culture differs from it in important respects. The members of an ethnic group share, or are believed to share, a consciousness of their distinct identity as a group. This shared identity may be based on common religious beliefs, skin color, national origin, or other criteria. Typically, although not necessarily, an ethnic group will share certain informal rules of conduct that differ from those of the culture more generally. Certain rights and duties of membership, and often specialized linguistic patterns, are common to the membership. These patterns of interdependent behavior often distinguish members of an ethnic group from those falling within a social category. A social category is used to distinguish certain classes of people according to a set of characteristics (e.g., the infant population or the population of the state of Maine).

The description of patterns particular to a selected subculture no longer serves as an end in itself. Rather, such exploration usually serves as a vehicle to demonstrate the significance of a given theoretical perspective or to champion the cause of what is viewed as an oppressed or unfortunate group.

Ethnographic work within various subcultural groups may be contrasted with a second significant domain of research. Particularly within social psychology, investigators have been concerned with relationships among various ethnic groups. Typically, the concern is with traditions of

intergroup hostility, and with means of reducing existing tensions. Concern with characteristics of particular groups is limited in such cases to the ways in which these characteristics affect the relationships of the groups. Intragroup dynamics or characteristics are considered significant only to the extent that they affect intergroup relations.

A third and more recent line of inquiry draws from and contributes to each of these traditional endeavors. Sparked by the failure of the "melting pot myth" of ethnic integration and homogenization, and by the increasing pride displayed by many ethnic minorities in contemporary society, inquiry has been increasingly directed to processes and characteristics common across ethnic groups. Glazer and Moynihan's *Ethnicity* and Isaacs' *Idols of the tribe, group identity and political change* exemplify this orientation. The more general significance of ethnic identity, the process of cultural assimilation, and the transmission of ethnic practices across generations are of particular interest in this domain.

CROSS-CULTURAL PSYCHOLOGY
NATIONAL CHARACTER

K. J. GERGEN

ETHNIC MINORITIES

A variety of definitions exist regarding the term *ethnic minority*. The phrase typically denotes a nondominant group or groups in a population that possess or desire to preserve stable cultural, religious, and/or linguistic traditions, or characteristics significantly different from those of the population as a whole. Charles Wagley and Marvin Harris list five characteristics of ethnic minorities:

(1) minorities are subordinate segments of complex societies; (2) minorities have special physical or cultural traits that are held in low esteem by the dominant segments of the society; (3) minorities are self-conscious units bound together by the special traits that their members share and by the special disabilities which these bring; (4) membership in a minority is transmitted by a rule of descent which is capable of affiliating succeeding generations even in the absence of readily apparent special cultural or physical traits; (5) minority peoples, by choice or necessity, tend to marry within the group.

While such characteristics may provide some understanding of the similarities across ethnic groups, there is great variability within groups as well. As one way of capturing such intragroup heterogeneity, Louis Wirth outlined four types of minority groups based on their sociopolitical objectives:

1. *Pluralistic minorities.* Members desire peaceful coexistence with the majority culture and other ethnic groups.

2. *Assimilationist minorities.* Members desire amalgamation into the dominant society, often with a concomitant disuse or disowning of cultural, religious, and/or linguistic traditions.

3. *Secessionist minorities.* Members desire both cultural and political independence.

4. *Militant minorities.* Members desire domination over the larger society.

PSYCHOLOGY AND ETHNIC MINORITIES

Within the United States, emphasis has shifted from one ethnic minority group to another, depending on the social and political *Zeitgeist*. In the late 1800s and early 1900s, attention was focused on ethnic minorities originating in northern and southern Europe. After the 1920s, attention was focused on minorities immigrating from the Western Hemisphere and Asiatic countries.

Social and differential psychology have contributed much research to the study of these various ethnic groups. Cross-cultural, inter- and intragroup dynamics have been researched by social psychologists, whereas differential psychologists have assessed such concepts as individual intelligence, aptitude, and achievement. In the 1950s and 1960s, clinical and counseling psychology became increasingly interested in ethnic minorities, because of the community mental health movement emphasizing neighborhood-based treatment. Mental health practitioners were called on to provide culturally modulated services formulated according to the needs of local community groups.

In the early 1900s there was a distinction made between the "old" and the "new" immigrant. The former included those who came from Great Britain, Ireland, Germany, Holland, and the Scandinavian countries—a group of Anglo-Saxon and Germanic blood and Protestant in religion. Such characteristics were seen as related to the early tradition of American settlers. After 1882, and largely from 1890 to 1924, the geographic origin of the majority of immigrants shifted to the Mediterranean and Slavic nations: Russia, Poland, Austria, Hungary, Greece, Turkey, Italy, and the Balkan countries. From 1882 to 1890 there were almost 12 million "new" versus 7.5 million "old" immigrants.

Writers during this early period spearheaded the theory of racial superiority, asserting that the dominant Anglo-American population was threatened by the wave of southern European immigrants. Congress, influenced by these writings, asserted that assimilation of minorities was failing and was creating "racial indigestion." Racial purity was affirmed and the Immigration Act of 1924 was enacted, establishing a quota of 150,000 for European countries based on the number of foreign-born persons of each nationality in the United States as of 1890. Although this law imposed limits on immigration from Europe, it did not restrict migration from other Western Hemisphere countries or from the Philippines. With limitations imposed on European immigrants, demand for laborers increased, particularly in the southwestern states.

During this period psychologists studying individual differences were primarily concerned with assessing the factors contributing to the low scores on the (unknowingly inappropriate) intelligence tests administered to some immigrants.

Social psychologists and sociologists during the same period had three main points of interest: (a) studying the desirability of Mexican immigration from a social and economic standpoint; (b) examining the problems faced in attempting to assimilate Mexican immigrants into American ways of life; and (c) investigating the causes of high crime rates, poor health standards, high rates of dependency on public relief agencies, and erratic employment patterns.

This third point caused the greatest conflict. Two camps emerged, one arguing that the source of ills was the cultural characteristics inherited by Mexicans, and the other arguing that economic and political factors were paramount in producing such deplorable conditions.

Shortly after 1935 a third position arose known as *cultural determinism*, which maintained that values were the definers of culture and that problems would develop if these values were not congruent with those of the dominant culture. From 1950 to the 1970s, this position dominated the social sciences.

Then in the 1970s and early 1980s the position of cultural pluralism became increasingly popular in the study of Mexican Americans in particular and of other ethnic minorities in general. The pluralistic approach has influenced a number of psychological endeavors, chief among these being intelligence testing as evidenced by Jane Mercer's work.

The community psychology movement originating in the 1960s also helped promulgate this approach, with an emphasis on appreciating and accepting the diversity of ethnic cultures as represented in each community.

ACCULTURATION
ALIENATION

BILINGUALISM
CULTURAL DETERMINISM
ETHNOCENTRISM

A. Barón, Jr.

ETHNOCENTRISM

This term was initially introduced into the behavioral sciences by William Graham Sumner in 1906 in his volume *Folkways*. For Sumner the concept represented a conflation of two ideas: (a) the tendency for people to view their own group as the reference against which all other groups are judged, and (b) the tendency to view one's own group as superior to other groups. In its first usage the term bears a close resemblance to the concept of egocentrism; this tendency in itself does not imply the second. Although this conflation of components continues to prevail in some contemporary circles, ethnocentrism is more commonly tied today to the second of Sumner's tendencies, that of viewing one's own group—usually national or ethnic—as superior to other groups. Frequently the term is associated with the distinction, again traceable to Sumner, between the *in group,* that group to which one belongs, and the *out group,* any group other than that to which one belongs. Ethnocentrism in this sense is often used interchangeably with *out-group hostility,* or hostility directed to groups other than one's own.

Sumner initially proposed that the tendency toward ethnocentrism was universal. However, few investigators subscribe to this position today. Ethnocentrism is generally held to be not a "fact of human nature," but a result of particular conditions. Thus contemporary inquiry has been primarily directed to identifying (a) the underlying causes for ethnocentrism, its intensification, and its diminution, and (b) practical means of reducing ethnocentrism in society. Because of its many implications for society, the first of these concerns has occupied by far the greater share of attention.

Inquiry into the causes of ethnocentrism may be classified conveniently on the basis of the preferred explanatory locus. Thus theories vary with respect to whether the cause lies within the psychological, the interpersonal, or the sociostructural sphere.

Although each of these orientations furnishes, by implication, a variety of insights into the reduction of ethnocentrism, certain lines of investigation have been specifically concerned with this problem. As argued in this case, ethnocentrism may have a variety of differing roots. Often its origins cannot be dramatically altered (e.g., the kinship structure of society) or are no longer present (e.g., particular parent–child relations). Among the two most important concepts to emerge from inquiry of this variety are the *contact hypothesis* and the concept of *superordinate goals.* In the former, investigators such as M. Deutsch and M. Collins (*Interracial housing*) have found that by increasing contact between members of differing groups, intergroup hostilities can be reduced and positive relations promoted. However, as much subsequent investigation indicates, the conditions under which contact can engender such effects are circumscribed. For example, members of the differing groups must each have an equal voice in decision making, equal status in the group, and experience some degree of success rather than failure through their efforts. Other investigators such as the Sherifs have made a strong case for establishing common, superordinate goals for otherwise competing groups. It is argued that ethnocentrism is reduced when members of differing groups work together for goals that they share.

ETHNIC GROUPS
NATIONAL CHARACTER

K. J. Gergen
M. M. Gergen

ETHOLOGY

Ethology is the study of an organism's behavior in its natural environment, which encompasses not only the physical environment but also social interactions. Ethological study is also concerned with the role of natural selection in shaping animal behavior. This implies a basic assumption that the behavior is substantially determined by genotypes, which in turn are a product of the species' evolutionary history. This further implies that gene selection has been influenced by the consequences of the naturally occurring behaviors. Because such behaviors are the basic subject matter for ethology, ethologists have had little interest in traditional learning concepts or mental characteristics.

CONCEPTS IN CLASSIC ETHOLOGY

The usual starting point for ethological study has been ethograms, which are extensive, highly detailed descriptions of a species' behaviors in its natural environment. They originally emerged from the work of European naturalists such as O. Heinroth, J. H. Fabre, and D. Spalding during the latter nineteenth and early twentieth century. These early ethologists were impressed by the constant, stereotyped nature of many adaptive behaviors. Consequently, these stereotyped behaviors were often labeled as innate or instinctive. The ethological conceptualization of these behaviors was refined by Konrad Lorenz and Niko Tinbergen. Behaviors of this type were termed fixed-action patterns.

Fixed-action patterns are specific, stereotyped behaviors characteristic of a species and are assumed to be under strong genetic control. In fact, fixed-action patterns are so constant that they have sometimes been used as criteria for taxonomic classification of species. Furthermore, fixed-action patterns are usually elicited by specific stimuli (called releasers or sign stimuli) and are assumed to continue in the absence of the original releaser. Lorenz and Tinbergen assumed that for each fixed-action pattern, an animal had an innate neural program that responded only to stimuli resembling the usual sign stimulus found in its natural environment. This innate program was called an innate releasing mechanism (IRM). The releasing stimuli were thus likened to triggers that set off an IRM. A further important characteristic is that fixed-action patterns are highly specific behaviors; nest building, maternal behavior, and mating may include several fixed-action patterns, but are too global to be considered fixed-action patterns by themselves.

Later Developments in Ethology

Following Lorenz and Tinbergen's establishment of a basic theoretical foundation for ethology in the 1930s, many major changes occurred in the theoretical and empirical approaches of ethologists to animal behavior. The ethological theory, whereby action-specific energy accumulates until a sign stimulus releases a fixed-action pattern through operation of the IRM, is similar to other early drive-reduction theories ranging from Clark Hull's to Sigmund Freud's. Like these theories, the original IRM theory is deficient as an exploratory system because of an inherent circularity: The only way of measuring the action-specific energy is through the behavior that it was intended to explain. Furthermore, there is no evidence of a separate neurological subsystem corresponding to each presumed IRM of an animal.

The classic IRM theory does, however, have some value as a descriptive device. Many different behaviors are set off by relatively specific sign stimuli. Furthermore, many of these behaviors acquire lowered thresholds for elicitation with the passage of time.

A major change in ethological theory has been an increasing awareness of the strong influence of learning in animal behaviors, including that of fixed-action patterns. One example is imprinting, which was initially regarded by Lorenz as an innately released following behavior. Later research has amply demonstrated that a simple and rapidly formed conditioning probably underlies acquisition of imprinting. Although a specific releasing stimulus may initially elicit a fixed-action pattern, perceptual learning starts to occur immediately. Consequently, the fixed-action pattern becomes conditioned to whatever stimulus configuration is present as a releaser.

Another important modification in ethology has been the reduced scope of the theoretical explanations and behavior studied. Previously, theorizing was broad, encompassing large classes of naturally occurring behaviors, although research was often limited to observation of animals in naturalistic settings with little experimental intervention. Later ethological research has emphasized detailed experimental analysis of particular behaviors.

A field of molecular ethology has emerged that involves the study of the mechanisms by which a single gene affects behaviors.

Sociobiology is an approach to animal behavior that grew out of classic ethology. The origin of this approach is generally attributed to Edward Wilson. One basic assumption of sociobiology is that individual genes, not species, are the units of natural selection. A second assumption is that the genotype is correlated with different types of behaviors, including some highly complex social behaviors. Kin selection based on behavior is an important concept in sociobiology. It is a type of natural selection that occurs when (a) a behavior is correlated with genotype, and (b) that behavior increases the likelihood that others with the same genotype will reproduce, although the behavior may diminish the animal's own likelihood of reproduction. An example of such a behavior is alarm calling by ground squirrels. The alarm increases the caller's vulnerability to predators, but simultaneously decreases the vulnerability of nearby, related ground squirrels. Sociobiology has successfully predicted a number of animal behavior phenomena, especially in the eusocial insects.

ECOLOGICAL PSYCHOLOGY
INSTINCTIVE BEHAVIOR

J. E. King

EVOLUTION

Evolution is generally assumed to account for the variety of species on earth today. The changes that have taken place over millions of years are presumably due to (a) variation in the genes of a population, and (b) survival and transmission of certain variations by natural selection.

Variation in the genes may occur through mutation, but more often by genetic recombination through bisexual reproduction. According to Charles Darwin, natural selection interacts with genetic variation so that the fittest members of the population (those producing the most viable offspring) contribute most to the gene pool of subsequent generations. Chance is responsible for gene mutations and the juggling of genes in the population, but success in survival determines the perpetuation of genetic changes.

Evolution produces *speciation,* the origin of new species, when two or more populations of a species become insulated from each other in different environments. They evolve differently, and eventually these populations become different species. *Adaptation* occurs when the environment remains fairly constant and the entire species through natural selection becomes better suited to the environment. Behaviors, as well as anatomic structures, evolve through natural selection. Behavior can be adaptive or maladaptive in the evolutionary sense: Much of the study of comparative psychology, modern population ecology, and ethology consists of describing the adaptive value or origin of certain behavior patterns.

Presumably, evolutionary change does not have to be slow, gradual, and continuous. There are not necessarily any "missing links" in the fossil record of the evolution of *Homo sapiens*, and all aspects of an animal do not need to have evolutionary usefulness. Many changes may be accidentally linked to changes that are adaptive.

M. R. DENNY

EXCHANGE THEORY

Exchange theory is a body of theoretical work in sociology and social psychology that emphasizes the importance of the reward–cost interdependence of group members in shaping their social interaction patterns as well as their psychological responses to one another. Exchange theories assume that the basis of social life is found in the rewards and costs that people mediate for one another. Differences in the patterning of this interdependence are seen as responsible for such phenomena as social status, social power, group cohesiveness, competition and cooperation, and the development of social norms.

The most comprehensive theories of social exchanges are those of Thibaut and Kelley, Homans, and Blau. All social exchange theories involve an analogy between economic relationships and other kinds of social relationships. An exchange is assumed to occur when each of the parties involved controls goods valued by the others, and each party values at least some of the goods that others control more than at least some of the goods that he or she controls. Goods can be any commodity, act, or condition that people value. Hence people may exchange services for love, commodities for service, and so on. Indeed, in these theories the very basis of social life—its existence and patterning—is assumed to be found in such exchanges.

Homans' theory used the language of B. F. Skinner's behavioral psychology with terms such as frequency and value of reward, satiation, and extinction. However, the theory focuses on concepts of equilibration in exchange in attempting to explain social interaction in small groups. For example, the greater conformity of group members with middle status as compared to high status is explained in terms of conformity being provided by middle-status group members in return for the more valued expertise and material wealth of the high-status members. In addition, high status itself is conferred by lower status members upon higher status members as part of an exchange for the valued resources controlled by high-status members. Homans also used the concept of expectancy, and a particular normative form of it called the rule of distributive justice, as an important explanatory concept. The rule of distributive justice specifies that the parties to an exchange should receive rewards proportional to their costs and investments.

Blau's theory has much in common with Homans' theory. However, Blau makes more explicit use of economic concepts, such as indifference curves, than does Homans. Blau also placed much more explicit emphasis on the concept of power, defined as control over negative sanctions, including the withholding of reward. However, Blau saw social influence as additionally effected through normative obligation. Much of Blau's concern was with the roots of emergent social structure in social exchange in patterns in small groups.

Thibaut and Kelley used the language of group problem solving in their theoretical statements, although many of the assumptions are common to the reinforcement concepts of behavioral psychology. Their most comprehensive analysis was made of the two-person group or dyad. For this purpose they made extensive use of reward–cost matrices, which have their origin in game theory. Several indices of the parties' interdependence were developed.

Thibaut and Kelley defined a person's power in a relationship as the capacity to affect the other party's reward–cost outcomes by varying one's own behavior. They distinguished between two forms of power. Fate control was defined as a person's capacity to affect the outcomes of the other directly, through unilateral choice of his or her own behavior. A person who possesses a valuable commodity or service and can choose whether to present it to the other, possesses this type of power. When the two parties each possess this type of power, the conditions for social exchange exist. The second type of power, behavior control, does not in strict terms involve exchange. One has behavior control over another when one can alter the relative attractiveness of the other's behaviors for the other by varying one's own behavior. For example, if two people seek to pass through a narrow doorway in different directions simultaneously, each affects the desirability of the other's choice through his or her own choice: If one chooses to go on the right-hand side, one makes it more desirable for the other to choose his or her right-hand side (the first party's left-hand side). Many situations involving cooperation have this character, in which it is the particular combination of choices (i.e., coordinations) made by the parties that is important in determining the advantageousness of both parties' outcomes. In their later work, Kelley and Thibaut added the concept of reflexive control, which refers to the extent that a person can unilaterally affect his or her own outcomes in a relationship through the behavior chosen.

Any particular social relationship at any given point in time can include any or all of these forms of control. Through analyzing the particular combination of power in a given encounter, prediction (and prescription) can be made about the likely course of social interaction. A relationship characterized primarily by mutual fate control is likely to result in exchange; however, one characterized by mutual behavior control cannot be predicted without additional consideration of the degree of correspondence of outcomes in the matrix. Correspondence refers to the extent to which parties are in agreement in their preference ordering of the cells—the behavior combinations—in the matrix. To the extent that they agree, there is correspondence of outcomes (common interest), and coordination is likely to result. To the extent that they disagree, there is noncorrespondence of outcomes (conflict of interest), and social conflict is likely to result.

The basic analysis by Thibaut and Kelley was applied to dyadic relationships. However, the same principles were applied to larger groups, with implications for such phenomena as coalition formation, status, and role differentiation in groups. But the analysis was not applied to the larger societal structures of interest to Blau.

These theories assume the reducibility of all valued commodities, events, and situations to a single reward–cost scale of advantageousness of outcome. However, some other approaches to exchange argue that the concrete nature of the outcome sought will affect the nature of the exchange. U. G. Foa and E. B. Foa have argued for a classification of rewards according to their concreteness versus abstractness, and their situational specificity, with the assumption that outcomes that differ considerably on these dimensions will not be exchanged. For example, love will be exchanged for love, and not for money.

EQUITY THEORY
GROUP DYNAMICS

W. P. SMITH

EXECUTIVE SELECTION

There is a long history of efforts to select managers, and there are many studies on leadership. Being an executive involves a higher level of complexity and risk taking than does being a manager. Selecting executives, therefore, is an area unto itself.

There are no scientifically validated predictors of successful executive behavior. Different people succeed in different companies or leadership roles at different times under different circumstances.

Almost all the criteria for selection are derived from informed opinion. Authorities usually infer from the behavior of successful prominent executives the personal qualities that enabled those executives to succeed. To be successful usually means that the executive has strengthened the organization's capacity for perpetuation, while simultaneously sustaining its values and economic viability.

The characteristics of successful executives recur in many other reports. All writers recognize the strong need to achieve high goals that motivate the executive and his or her organization, as well as the need for dominance, power, and self-assertion, and the willingness to take risks. Successful executives must be flexible and able to change course readily when it becomes necessary to do so. They must face difficult situations, while simultaneously maintaining self-control under the most adverse circumstances, and must be able to integrate and use a great store of information, which is then translated into product or service. Executives must view the world broadly in economic and sociological terms, as well as with an understanding of historical and political forces and cultural and ethnic considerations.

To be an executive of a contemporary organization requires a high level of intelligence and a wide range of information from many different sources. Successful executives are well read and thoughtful, and as a consequence are sagacious. They have quick intellectual perceptions and can penetrate a mass of material to discern important issues. They are able to judge people and methods well.

Successful executives must have a sensitivity to their political and social environments, as well as to the natural environment, and have a social responsibility and social awareness. Increasingly, students of the subject agree on these issues. They agree also on the need for successful executives to motivate people, to capture their creative energies, and to direct those energies into problem-solving activity. The successful executive creates the conditions for identification with him- or herself, enhancing the capacity of subordinates as they work with the executive to master reality problems, to learn from those experiences, and thereby to increase their own adaptive capacities. Executives must accept the support of others in their role. To do that, however, means they must also be willing to risk losing the approval of others when disappointment or failure occurs. Also, they must receive ideas, analyze them, consolidate them into a position or stand, pursue them, enunciate them articulately, and support others in carrying them out.

A particular competence of the successful executive is the capacity to balance political forces both inside and outside the organization.

Psychologically speaking, successful executives are akin to parental figures in a given culture. People expect those who have executive power to behave toward them as parents in that culture ideally behave toward their children. This requires that executives be sensitive to others' feelings. Such sensitivity may also arouse feelings of guilt. Frequently, successful executives find it difficult to face up to the limitations and deficiencies of subordinates.

The best executives are mentors who develop successors who are better than they. They are held together by their integrity. They are significantly motivated by conscience and recognize the multiple obligations to a range of constituencies. The successful executive has a coherent and solid sense of self, good relationships with both subordinates and superiors as well as the external environment, and ability to manage stress well, which means flexibility and a sense of humor.

Summarizing the present characteristic behavior of executive candidates and juxtaposing it against the required behavior is as close as we can come to prediction. Although the approximation may be crude, it permits flexibility of thinking about the behavioral requirements of each situation at any given point in time, and lets us assess a range of candidates for the likelihood of success in that role at that time.

H. LEVINSON

EXHIBITIONISM

Exhibitionism means the deliberate exposure of the body, usually the genitalia, ordinarily to an unwitting and uncooperative individual. In most instances the exhibitionist becomes sexually aroused or derives some kind of sexual gratification from the behavior, although sexual motivation is sometimes denied.

Exhibitionism, in the form known to police and mental health professionals, is characteristically male and typically consists only of exposure of the genitalia. Exhibitionists constitute about one-third of all apprehended sex criminals, a definite plurality. This number unquestionably reflects the fact that most episodes take place in broad daylight in public places.

The exposure is almost always to females, about half under the age of 16, but patterns of exposure vary considerably. In some cases the behavior occurs aperiodically and/or only at times of great stress. There are also recorded cases in which the frequency was as high as 100 exposures per week. The penis may or may not be erect; spontaneous ejaculation may take place upon exposure; or the exhibitionist may masturbate to climax immediately thereafter. Occasionally there simply may be a feeling of diffuse, vague excitement.

The exhibitionist is more likely to be single than married, and a substantial minority have had no direct heterosexual experience. Most of those who are married have had poor sexual adjustments. About a quarter of exhibitionists perform under the influence of alcohol. The typical exhibitionist is an anxious, passive individual with strong feelings of masculine inadequacy.

It has been believed for many years that exhibitionism is a hostile rather than a sexual act and that the motivation of the exhibitionist is to shock or frighten his victim. However, recent clinical evaluations by Ruth Bray and Alex Gigeroff suggest that *some* reaction—regardless whether fear, disgust, or amusement—is more important to the exhibitionist than any *specific* reaction. Furthermore, it is probable that few exhibitionists clearly perceive the victim's reaction; fantasy may be more important than fact.

INADEQUATE PERSONALITIES
SEXUAL DEVIATIONS

E. E. LEVITT

EXISTENTIAL PSYCHOLOGY

Usually classified in the humanistic tradition, existential psychology nonetheless has independent distinctive features. Humanistic approaches take qualities of functioning that appear positive at face value, using them to understand life fulfillment through continual deepening of consciousness and development. Existential psychology also contains unique elements that can be illuminated by a finer classification between actualization and perfection fulfillment models.

Actualization theories assume that if unconditional positive regard is obtained consistently through the person's interaction with significant others, then already programmed inherent potentialities will be expressed in behavior, through built-in pressure toward actualization. The actualization of inherent potentialities leads to lifelong development, individuality, and fulfillment, and is an automatic, teleological, uncomplicated process, as long as there is support and appreciation from others. Developmental arrests and false directions occur only when significant others give conditional (self-interested) rather than unconditional positive regard.

In contrast, perfection theories (of which existential psychology is the paradigmatic example) make assumptions that set them apart from the actualization approach. In brief, perfection theories contend that lifelong development may take place regardless of whether others give unconditional support. For existentialists, development is more a matter of personal decision than of inherent potentiality. Although existentialists agree on the importance of a deepened consciousness and an emergent individuality, their understanding of the process whereby this comes about is different from that of actualization theorists.

Existential psychology assumes that the tendency to symbolize, imagine, and judge one's ongoing social, biological, and physical experiences is an inborn human capability. Exercising this cognitive capability lends individualized (subjective) meaning to experience and deepens awareness that life's patterns and directions are fashioned from the many decisions individuals make. Each decision leads toward either the future of new experience or the repetition of familiar experience marking the past. Nothing so teleologically specific and directional as inherent potentialities is emphasized. For existentialists, whatever consistent direction and development takes place in persons is fashioned on an ongoing basis from the accumulation of their discrete decisions.

Existential psychology considers it developmentally advantageous to choose the future rather than the past, because ensuing new experiences can lead to more deepening of meaning through stimulation of symbolization, imagination, and judgment than would be possible through a repetition of familiar experience. But to contemplate or actually to choose the future at a decision-making point will bring ontological anxiety of uncertainty as to what the unknown will bring. The alternative, choosing the past, also is emotionally painful, as it brings ontological guilt of missed experience. Persons falling into the habit of choosing the past must contend with an accumulation of ontological guilt in the form of the despair of meaninglessness. All this highlights how existentialists conceive development to be inherently more difficult and painful than do actualization theorists.

Existential psychology is somewhat vague concerning the concrete developmental steps leading to learned lifestyles. Nonetheless, one unusually concrete position discriminates early from later development. The principal task of early development is for the child to learn the self-perceptions marking hardiness (courage). To facilitate this learning, parents and significant others ideally should accept self-expression in the youngster and ensure an environment that affords variety, reinforcement, opportunities to succeed through effort, and limits. In such an environment, the youngster will develop the self-perceptions of commitment, control, and challenge, leading to the development of hardiness. Later development is more self-determined, as youngsters gradually leave the parental orbit, relying increasingly on their own decision making and interpretation of their resulting experiences. They pass through stages of aestheticism and idealism as they experience freedom from parental limits and struggle for values to provide their own structure. Fortified by hardiness, they are likely to be able to learn from failures, and this is the heart of ideal later development. Having learned the limitations of aesthetic and idealistic stances, they emerge into maturity, or the lifestyle of authenticity.

People in the authentic lifestyle show individualistic qualities in their definition of (a) self as persons who can, through decision making and interpretation, influence their social and biological experiences and (b) society as formed out of the actions of individuals and, therefore, changeable by them. The authentic lifestyle has unity and innovativeness. Biological and social experiencing show subtlety, taste, intimacy, and love. Because of hardiness, doubt is experienced as a natural concomitant of creating one's own meaning and does not undermine the decision-making process. Although authentic people can fall into self-deception,

they tend to correct this rapidly through their commitment to self-scrutiny and general reflectiveness. Hence there is not much accumulation of ontological guilt in the sense of missed opportunity or perceived personal superficiality.

In contrast, youngsters who do not encounter ideal conditions of early development never form hardiness and, in a real sense, remain dependent and unformed, whatever their chronological age. They are not able to rely on their own decision-making and cognitive capabilities to fashion authenticity from what they learn from experience. In particular, they cannot learn from failures, rushing to deny them instead of reflecting on what went wrong. Rather than entering into a genuine period of later development, they mimic people around them, displaying a conformist, immature lifestyle.

People in the conformist lifestyle define themselves as nothing more than players of social roles. Expressions of symbolization, imagination, and judgment are inhibited, leading to stereotyped, fragmentary functioning. Their biological and social experiencing is unsubtle and contractual, rather than discerning and intimate. Conformists feel worthless and insecure because of the buildup of ontological guilt through choosing the past rather than the future. Their worldview emphasizes materialism and pragmatism.

Existential psychologists have generally not done much systematic research. Most are psychotherapists who rely on the case study approach to communicate their ideas. Binswanger's case of Ellen West and many of Boss's (1963) cases have illustrated the existential approach to understanding human functioning.

Other bodies of research, although not undertaken with existential theorizing in mind, provide general empirical support for this approach. For example, Tyler has integrated a wide range of studies of individuality. Consistent with existential formulations, she found considerable evidence of possibility-processing cognitive structure in persons who underlie choice as a sign of individuality and creative living. Also relevant is the large body of research on internal versus external locus of control, initiated by Rotter, Seeman, and Liverant. Operating on the basis of locus of control and internal orientation leads to individualistic behaviors, whereas an external orientation leads to conformist behaviors. The accumulating research on the social desirability scale also lends general empirical support for the existential position. The emerging picture suggests that the greater the social desirability score, the more self-perceptions and behaviors show an interest in appearing attentive, consistent, and competent, whereas having a superficial interest shows lack of deep commitment to others and a general unwillingness to face facts about oneself. There is much here that confirms the existential formulation of the conformist lifestyle.

Existential psychology is emerging as a consistent, complete approach to understanding and influencing human functioning. Its many implications for education, treatment, and research are influencing psychologists in various ways.

S. MADDI

EXISTENTIAL PSYCHOTHERAPY

One of its chief exponents, Rollo May, has asserted that existential psychotherapy does not constitute a "school." It is marked rather by "an attitude toward human beings and a set of presuppositions about these human beings." Briefly, the attitude is one of accepting as real, meaningful, and legitimate the being-in-the-world of the client—the unique way in which the client experiences self and the world and gives direction to his or her life.

Existential psychotherapy is thus classified as one of the "third force" or humanistic psychotherapies—although early on it was called "existential psychoanalysis" and is still often referred to as "existential analysis."

Drawing from the work of philosophers such as Kierkegaard, Husserl, Heidegger, and Sartre, the theorizing and case study descriptions of existential therapists are often couched in idiosyncratic terminology. Hence they may speak of being-in-the-world as having three different patterns: *Umwelt, Mitwelt,* and *Eigenwelt. Umwelt* refers to behaviors grounded in human biology (sleeping, eating, excreting, copulating) and aimed at biological survival and satisfaction. *Mitwelt* refers to interpersonal relationships in which there is sharing or *encounter,* which seeks to prevent or alleviate feelings of loneliness or aloneness and to enrich life. *Eigenwelt* refers to behaviors of self-awareness, self- evaluation, and self-identity, which attempt to make one's life meaningful. Any behavior can be analyzed as revealing fundamentally unique relationships to one's natural world, social world, and self-world.

For existentialists, within biological, cultural, and historical limits, we are free to make of ourselves what we will, to choose who we are, what we become.

Freedom therefore carries a heavy—and potentially frightening—responsibility: the formation of our own destiny. But that is problematic only if one is aware of the freedom. In primitive and past societies, the consistency of cultural traditions provided a ready-made "meaning of life" that hid the extent of potential individual freedom. But with modern industrialism, urbanism, secularism, and scientism, old meanings and views of essential human nature were challenged and often found wanting. Hence for a variety of historical reasons, modern man—especially as the twentieth century proceeded—might experience life as meaningless and as lacking the interpersonal ties of earlier times. (In the terminology previously used, the *Eigenwelt* and *Mitwelt* suffered, and to live only in the *Umwelt* was felt to be clearly insufficient.) Existential psychotherapy is a response to those human beings who feel lonely, anxious, depersonalized, and alienated.

The actual practice of existential psychotherapy typically involves no technical jargon, even if its description sometimes does. The initial and ongoing task of the therapist is a phenomenological one: to understand as fully as possible the reality of the client—how that client experiences self, other people, and the natural world, and thus what meaning life has for the client (even if that meaning is outside of awareness). This understanding involves a high level of empathy. The therapist must "bracket" or set to one side his own values, perceptual patterns, and so forth as much as possible and imaginatively enter into the world of the other.

A number of conscious (although in practice automatic) presuppositions promote this process. Clients are worthy of respect. Each has a "lived reality" unlike that of any other person. Client behaviors—including so-called neurotic or psychotic ones—are attempts to cope successfully with the world as experienced (sometimes, simply attempts to reduce anxiety). The client is responsible for his or her behaviors. The therapist–client interaction provides the ground for understanding the client, for the client's self-understanding and self-acceptance, and for new client choices. The spatiotemporal focus in therapy is on here-and-now experiencing, not the past.

Through felt understanding and trust provided in the therapeutic relationship, and through intense exploration of present feelings, ideas, and inclinations, the client comes to understand the meaning he or she has given to life. The client is also enabled to recognize and imagine without fear the potentials for enriching existence with respect to natural processes, interpersonal relationships, and his or her relationship with the self. Ideally, the client becomes willing to take the necessary risks to try to actualize those potentials, and thus discovers or creates a more meaningful life.

Existential therapy has much in common with other humanistic and present-oriented therapies, and they are probably in its debt. Many principles of existential psychotherapy have become so much a part of other versions of humanistic therapy that its contributions largely go unrecognized.

Some criticisms of existential psychotherapy have been made: It is too heterogeneous to be considered a coherent theory; its terminology is opague or esoteric; its effectiveness is not scientifically verifiable; and data other than phenomenological data can be relevant in therapy. Given their phenomenological commitments, there may also be greater limits to understanding the "lived existence" of others than its theorists acknowledge.

EXISTENTIALISM
PHILOSOPHICAL PSYCHOLOGY

F. W. HANSEN

EXISTENTIALISM

Modern philosophy is said to have begun with René Descartes when, in attempting to find an absolute starting point for all knowledge, he described consciousness as a zone of indubitability that was radically different from matter, and so split humans into minds (consciousness) and bodies (matter), the former being the subject matter of philosophy, the latter of the sciences. Immanuel Kant furthered the split by distinguishing between knowable phenomena and unknowable noumena, and gave priority to the former and showed how consciousness and its *a priori* categories were the necessary conditions for the possibility of knowing anything. Hegel went on to build a system based on universal reason in which the absolute idea was most critical and the individual person played only a minor part. Scholastic philosophy, to the extent that it was still viable, was highly intellectualistic and progressed by making finer and finer distinctions. Thus when existentialism was born, philosophy was systematic, intellectualistic, absolutistic, impersonal, formal, abstract, and objective.

Kierkegaard thought that the truly important issues were overlooked by such philosophizing. Instead of systems, he claimed that truth was in the human subject. He asserted the priority of individuals over systems and emphasized the process of becoming rather than static essential insights into being. He emphasized the freedom of the individual as opposed to philosophical necessity, and had the audacity to challenge the supremacy of rationality in human affairs.

Kierkegaard was primarily a religious thinker, but Heidegger introduced the same themes into philosophy by combining Kierkegaardian insights with certain aspects of the phenomenological method introduced by Husserl; as a result, a genuine existential philosophy providing concrete analyses of significant philosophical themes emerged. While pure existentialism, true to its origins, is radically antisystematic and presents concrete analyses in terms of journals, diaries, and drama and literature, another stream of existentialism tries to be somewhat more systematic because of the influence of phenomenology, which has provided a method of generalizing concrete experience without formalizing it and thus creates the possibility of a science of concrete experience.

Because it can penetrate concrete experience, existentialism made an impact on psychiatry and psychology. It came into psychiatry because of Binswanger and Boss, who were both psychoanalytically trained and influenced by Heidegger.

From psychiatry, existentialism made its impact felt in psychology primarily through the efforts of May. In the existentialists' view, people were experiencing anxiety, meaninglessness, lack of caring, loneliness, and fear of death, whereas academic psychology was concerned with precision and measurement and the improvement of methods applied to problems defined largely outside the context of human experience. Thus the existential psychologists joined forces with the humanistic psychologists, as well as with some phenomenologically oriented psychologists, in order to create "third force psychology" as an alternative for those who found both behaviorism and psychoanalysis lacking.

Thus the essential project of existential psychology became one of establishing lived experience with all its complexities and concreteness as a legitimate subject matter for psychology. For most existential psychologists, coming to terms with the real problems of individuals and society far outweighs the *pro forma* criteria of science. Thus existentialists stress the pursuit of values, the problems of self-actualization and their obstacles, the development of personal freedom, the centrality of love and caring for others in human relationships, the concern for the ultimate meaning of life, and the ability to cope with the stresses and strains of everyday living in a harmonious way. Ultimately, existentialists say that these problems are more adequately understood within the context of a philosophy that speaks of humans as unfinished, with the clear implication that humans must respond to the possibilities that this incompleteness provides and freely choose to actualize them for the good of themselves and others.

FREE WILL
HUMANISTIC PSYCHOLOGY
PHENOMENOLOGICAL METHOD

A. P. GIORGI

EXIT INTERVIEWS

Exit interviews are used in employment settings, focusing on those employees who are leaving the organization. Two distinct purposes can be identified for such interviews: information gathering and information giving.

Information gathering is an attempt to curb financial losses associated with excessive turnover and to collect diagnostic information regarding organizational functioning. In contrast, information given to employees helps smooth their transition.

The value of exit interviews is open to question. Research by Joel Lefkowitz and Myron Katz showed that these interviews and a later follow-up questionnaire gave different reasons for leaving, with questionnaire results being more negative toward the company. The same general results were found by John Hinrichs in a study comparing exit interviews to results obtained by an interview with an outside consultant. In short, employees may be reluctant to give honest information directly to company officials.

INTERVIEWING
LABOR–MANAGEMENT RELATIONS
MORALE IN ORGANIZATIONS

P. G. BENSON

EXORCISM

An exorcism is a ritual, formalized by the Roman Catholic Church during the seventeenth century, performed on a person exhibiting signs of demonic possession. This ritual, described in the *Ritual romanum* in 1614 and still accepted as the official procedure, was directed at the Devil or "unclean spirit" assumed to inhabit the body of the possessed. Historically, demonic possession, one of the most engaging and dramatic explanations of disordered behavior, was mentioned only once in the Old Testament. Possession, however, is referred to frequently in the New Testament. Four complete cases of exorcism were performed by Christ. Tarugott Oesterreich, in his classic book *Possession and exorcism,* states that explanations relying on demonic possession have been reported in most countries at various times throughout history.

Signs of demonic possession may include the following: an offensive stench, tight lips, inability to pray, vomiting strange objects, rolling of the eyes, exhibiting powers beyond one's physical capacity, shouting obscenities, personality changes, prophetic wisdom, convulsions, and speaking or understanding a strange language. Most of those persons found to be possessed were women.

During the early Christian era, exorcistic skills were considered to be a special talent. Later, during the middle of the third century, the Church created the position of exorcist. The exorcist was typically a minor cleric. Exorcism consisted of two parts: First, the exorcist strengthened himself by praying; then the Devil—often named by the exorcist—was attacked, insulted, and commanded to leave the body of the possessed. Recovery was assumed to have occurred when the person returned to a prepossessed state. Contemporary Roman Catholic belief distinguishes between major and minor exorcisms, depending on the degree of possession. A brief exorcistic rite is often included in the baptismal ceremony of the Roman Catholic Church.

PSEUDOPSYCHOLOGY
RELIGION AND PSYCHOLOGY

C. H. FISCHER

EXPECTANCY THEORY

The concept of expectancy is central to much of mammalian and avian behavior. When a naive, hungry rat, for example, is first placed in the start box of a maze, it typically resists by spreading its legs so that one has to turn the rat on its side to get it through the opening. After a number of reinforced trials the rat eagerly leaps into the start box, may even try to claw open the start box door or take off over the top of the maze toward the goal box, if it is a complex maze. It makes sense to say that the rat now expects to find food, whereas at first it did not.

Tolman can probably be considered the main exponent of the expectancy theory, although the importance of expectation to behavior has several long-standing roots. For Tolman, cognitive expectation of a goal is established with experience and is one of the principal things learned by an animal in its habitat or in the laboratory. He called it a sign–Gestalt expectation or a "what-leads-to-what" sign–significate relation in which the sign is like a cue and the significate is usually some sort of goal. Tolman cited a number of experiments to support the notion of specific expectancies in rats and monkeys. For example, when a rat that has been running a complex maze under thirst motivation and water reward is made hungry, there is a momentary disruption of performance on the "shift" day, when it has no basis for expecting food. But on the next day with expectancy for the food reward established, the rat's performance is back to the previous level.

One of the more striking observations of expectancy behavior is reported by Tinklepaugh. In a delayed response situation, a piece of banana was hidden under one of two containers while a monkey watched. After a short delay, during which time a screen hid the containers, the screen was removed, and the monkey was allowed to choose and typically chose correctly. On a later trial, the experimenter substituted a less-preferred piece of lettuce for the banana. When the monkey turned over the correct container, revealing lettuce instead of banana, there was definite disruption of behavior. The monkey showed "surprise" and emotion, rejected the lettuce, and searched for the expected banana. Similar observations have been made (e.g., with rats when sunflower seeds were substituted for preferred bran mash and in recent experiments with chimpanzees). Animals other than humans clearly have some sort of expectancy for specific goal objects, but whether these expectancies are the sign-significate (S–S) type of Tolman, the fractional anticipatory goal response (R–S) of Hull, or something else is still a theoretical question. Human expectancies, of course, have a strong language component.

In one sense most classically conditioned responses qualify as expectancies, because the conditioned response (CR), when elicited by the conditioned stimulus (CS), comes forward in the behavior sequence and anticipates the unconditioned stimulus (US). Thus when a dog is conditioned to salivate to a bell, it can be said that the dog now expects food when the bell rings, and when a rat is shocked when a light goes on, the resulting conditioned fear means it expects shock or pain with light onset and behaves accordingly.

Bolles's expectancy theory of avoidance learning, with roots in Tolman's work, emphasizes the idea that learning involves the acquisition of information about the environment rather than the acquisition of S–R bonds. According to Bolles, there is no reinforcement or punishment mechanism operating in avoidance learning. The animal behaves appropriately (avoids) because it expects shock, say, in the shock chamber and expects safety elsewhere.

Expectancy is an integral part of instrumental appetitive learning, as illustrated by the differential outcome effect. In early DOE experiments, it was clearly demonstrated that expectancies based on different reinforcers (e.g., solid food versus liquid sucrose) have different stimulus consequences, to which different instrumental responses can be conditioned. This was shown (e.g., in a two-choice conditional discrimination study in which R_1 was reinforced to S_2 with food and R_2 was reinforced to S_2 with sucrose).

According to expectancy theory, the use of differential reinforcers should condition different expectancies to S_1 and S_2, whereas using the same reinforcer for both S_1–R_1 and S_2–R_2 would condition the same expectancy to S_1 and S_2. If the expectancies E_1 and E_2 for two different reinforcers have distinctive stimulus properties, then the unique interoceptive properties of E_1 and E_2 augment the exteroceptive differences between S_1 and S_2 and more precisely elicit the correct response (R_1 or R_2) In contrast, a single reinforcer would retard learning, because the same expectancy would be conditioned to both R_1 and R_2. Trapold not only demonstrated faster learning with different reinforcers (DOE), but also found that cue–reward pretraining that was the reverse of the pairings during training interfered with final learning. That is, incorrect expectancies had to be extinguished before the correct expectancies became operative.

DOE has been found by numerous investigators using a variety of different outcomes: food versus water, food of different quality or quantity, different delays of the same reinforcer, one a reinforcer and the other a neutral stimulus like a tone, and so forth. To the extent that there is a delay between S_1 or S_2 and the availability of R_1 and R_2, then E_1 and E_2 as intervening and long-lasting stimuli can mediate correct responding and enhance conditional discrimination learning even more than without such a delay.

Differential expectancies can probably be conceived of as images, emotional responses, or R_g–S_g and R_f–S_f in the Hull–Spence–Amsel tradition. The rather precise nature of two expectancies has been identified by Brodigan and Peterson in the pigeon in a conditional discrimination with three keys in an operant chamber. They found that the pigeon responds to the conditional cure (central key) with a response topography appropriate to the reinforcer that would be available for a correct re-

sponse on the subsequent choice trial (side keys). For example, in a food replacement trial, pigeons gave food-type pecks (i.e., sharp, open beak pecks to the central key); in a water reinforcement trial, pigeons gave a water-type peck to the key (i.e., slower, more sustained contact with the key).

The expectancy concept seems to relate to conditioning in another different but basic way. When Kamin discovered the phenomenon of blocking, he posited that a CS becomes strongly associated with a US only if the US is unexpected, or "surprising." Supposedly, surprising events are more likely to be rehearsed and retained than expected events. In the blocking experiment, stimulus A is the CS for a number of trials; then stimulus B is added so that the CS is an AB compound for many trials. Finally, when tested alone, B shows hardly any conditioning compared with A alone. Presumably, B is presented after the subject already expects the US, and without a surprising US, B is not well conditioned. To handle this aspect of conditioning, Rescorla and Wagner formulated an equation for Pavlovian conditioning in which they quantified and objectified surprisingness so successfully that it has flourished for 20 or more years.

Expectancy theory as explicitly applied to humans is best exemplified in the area of industrial-organizational behavior as a motivational manipulation. Here the important source of motivation is the specific expected outcome for the work effort expended. That is, a positively valued incentive or outcome functions selectively on actions that lead to it. This is in contrast to a drive notion in which energizing has a generalized effect. In brief, the theory has three parts: (a) an expectancy that work effort, including equipment, training, and skills, will accomplish the behavior (performance); (b) instrumentality, the means that connect behavior to outcomes such as recognition, awards, advancement, bonuses, co-worker involvement, and pay; and (c) valence, the attractiveness of a particular outcome. The worker's motivation to perform may not necessarily be fully conscious. For all practical purposes the theory predicts that the greater the value of the outcome and the higher the perceived probability that effort will lead to the reward, the greater the effort expended.

In the area of organizational psychology, expectancy theory engendered considerable research, but the results were only moderately supportive. Moreover, managers did not accept expectancy theory to any extent, because they had to do something that influenced many workers at once rather than one worker at a time. Goal-setting theory, which ignores individual differences in motives, has largely replaced expectancy theory for researchers of worker motivation.

ANIMAL INTELLIGENCE
BEHAVIORAL GENETICS
CONSEQUENCES
CREPI EFFECT
ECOLOGICAL VALIDITY
ETHOLOGY
EXPLORATORY BEHAVIOR
PURPOSIVE BEHAVIOR
REINFORCERS

M. R. DENNY

EXPERIENTIAL PSYCHOTHERAPY

Experiential therapy is a systematic way of performing therapy designed to make any theory of personality and therapy operational. Experiential therapy thus is a meta-theory, rather than one of the many personality theories.

In this way of practicing therapy, whatever intervention or response the therapist makes is considered in terms of its immediate, concrete change effect on the client's present bodily felt sense. If there is no immediate bodily felt change experienced by the client as valuable, the intervention is seen as failing to have an experiential effect and therefore as not to be therapeutically useful.

A variety of different theories have recognized this aspect of effective therapy.

EXISTENTIAL PSYCHOTHERAPY
FOCUSING
INNOVATIVE PSYCHOTHERAPIES

J. R. IBERG

EXPERIMENTAL AESTHETICS

Psychological approaches to aesthetics (Irvin L. Child, "Aesthetic theories") concentrate on ordinary observers (i.e., nonartists) and examine their response to art (or whatever has some claim to beauty) (e.g., the appreciation of the environment). The psychology of aesthetics, in contrast to the psychology of art and other approaches to the artist and creativity (e.g., psychoanalysis), also emphasizes cognitive and conscious phenomena such as perception. The aesthetic experience, and qualities such as harmony, goodness, taste, and the sublime, are also discussed by philosophers.

Experimental aesthetics has an obvious kinship with the psychology of art and aesthetics, but is distinguished by the rigor of its methodology. Although the term "experimental" usually implies laboratory study, its meaning in experimental aesthetics has been broadened somewhat to include the use of any highly controlled procedure, such as factor analysis. The rigor of experimental aesthetics has attracted both advocates and critics and has given it great influence.

Experimental aesthetics reflects the influence of its founder, Gustav T. Fechner (1897), a major figure in the early history of scientific psychology. Fechner's seminal research on preferences for shapes gave experimental aesthetics its reductionistic orientation. In order to investigate aesthetic phenomena scientifically, both the aesthetic stimulus and its response have to be simplified. This permits strict definitions, controlled manipulations, exact measurements, and statistical treatment. The key to these experimental strategies is the substitution of artificially constructed stimuli for the forms and colors of real art. Similarly, letters, vowels, and consonants are surrogates for poetry, and tones and chords are the building blocks for the musical experience. For the same reductionistic reasons, numerical ratings or rankings replace personal, intuitive, and metaphysical speculation. Aesthetic responses, taken from randomly chosen subjects with no special background in the arts, are pooled and expressed as group averages.

The search for an "aesthetic formula" is illustrative. In one well-known formulation, the aesthetic measure (M) of balance or unity (represented by the numerical value of "1") is defined as the ratio of order (O) to complexity (C). In the resulting formula $M = O/C$, the various components of a work of art can be physically specified, measured, and evaluated (the closer to "1," the more harmonious the object).

Two other features characterize the Fechnerian approach. The first is the priority given to the aesthetic stimulus, which initiates the aesthetic experience, feeling, and response. Experimental aesthetics has therefore been closely associated with the topics of sensation, perception, and cognition.

The second feature of experimental aesthetics is the broad definition given to aesthetics. The aesthetic stimulus can be anything that is pleasing, liked, admired, or pleasant; aesthetic experience can be initiated through any sensory mode; and the aesthetic response can be to any type of art, and even to some nonart. Thus, experimental aesthetics is applicable to the arts in general and to the relatively commonplace natural environment.

Experimental aesthetics was the first scientific approach to the arts, it has the longest continuing record of scientific research in the arts, and it is a staunch advocate of studying the arts scientifically. Experimental aesthetics reveals, in the starkest and clearest terms, the benefits and limitations of a science of art. It presents the case against the presumed arbitrariness, uniqueness, and subjectivity of the art world, qualities that allegedly make it immune to study.

Real art has been increasingly used. When it has been presented together with nonart, similarities between the two have been found. Both art and nonart can be shown (through statistical analysis) to have an underlying aesthetic factor; thus surrogates for art have validity. Another change has been the inclusion of personal variables. These, like introversion and extraversion, differentiate the aesthetic response.

Other directions characterize the extensive research of Daniel E. Berlyne. His research includes the subtle qualities of art, the so-called collative properties: complexity, novelty, surprise, and even mystery. Further, his research contributes to a general theory of stimulation, arousal, and affect. This theory holds that aesthetic objects (among other sources of stimulation, such as play and humor) initiate, sustain, and then satiate attention, feelings, and behavior. For example, as the complexity of art increases, preferences also increase; then they stabilize but ultimately decline. Optimum levels of stimulation—neither too low (boring) nor too high (overwhelming)—are preferred; input at either extreme is avoided, while the middle range of intensity is balanced. This hedonic relationship (described as an inverted U-shape) varies with the type of input; it can also differ among individuals (some prefer more stimulation, others less), perhaps because of their particular background or culture.

Experimental aesthetics has been criticized for its oversimplifications by aestheticians, art critics, and psychologists. The virtues of the experimental method have been judged as artificial, trivial, and irrelevant in addressing the important questions of aesthetics. Its overconcern with methodology, say its opponents, ignores substantive phenomena.

Defenders of experimental aesthetics insist that an elementary grasp of basic phenomena such as pleasantness, and their application to fundamental properties such as color, can be extended to real art, creating "aesthetics from above." Other criticisms of experimental aesthetics are unfair, as for instance attacks against the scientific method in psychology. But there are some major omissions. Several art forms (e.g., dance and literature) and most mediated phenomena (e.g., imagery) are neglected. The development of aesthetics in children has received little attention. Phenomenological accounts of the aesthetic experience are rare. Aesthetic persons have hardly been studied. Finally, the special status of the arts has been lost by treating nearly anything as aesthetic.

Experimental aesthetics has its shortcomings: concentration on vision, avoidance of the interview method, and a disinterest in individual differences. But the approach is flexible enough. No aspect of aesthetics need be omitted so long as the hallmark of experimental aesthetics—its methodological rigor—is retained.

The place of experimental aesthetics in the arts and general psychology seems assured. Less recognized is its relevance to a host of applied problems. These include decisions about the arts curriculum in education, and the use of color and music in business and industry. Other less familiar topics are the effectiveness of advertising, the ease with which instrument displays can be read, the determinants of residential choice, the changing fashions in dress and decoration, and factors in personal attractiveness. These areas and the more traditional ones reviewed earlier reveal the broad relevance of experimental aesthetics.

PSYCHOPHYSICS

M. S. Lindauer

EXPERIMENTAL CONTROLS

Edwin G. Boring developed three meanings in psychology for the word *control:* (a) a check, in the sense of verification; (b) a restraint, in the sense of maintaining constancy; and (c) a guide or direction. Controlled observations, and controls on experimental variables or checks on observations, are as old as science. The use in psychology, however, of an experimental control group as such—a separate group of individuals against which comparisons of the experimental group's observations are made—is encompassed within the twentieth century.

Because people who are not in psychological experiments do learn, mature, and change from experiences in daily living, experimental control groups for comparison purposes are valuable, almost necessary, in most of psychology, in order to have a context in which to interpret meaningful research findings. In addition, the almost inherent lack of ability to measure with precision in psychology has a decided influence on changes in observations over time. The research context in which the observations are made, the possible reaction of subjects in the somewhat unusual conditions of the psychological research study, and motivational differences between the experimental and control groups, can also reduce the quality of the comparisons needed for interpretation. These concerns are also the subject of experimental design and research methodology.

Attempts to develop experimental controls in psychological research include attempting to hold all variables constant except those being deliberately manipulated. This is difficult to do with human subjects, can be done only within rather broad limits, and often makes the experimental conditions so artificial that generalizations to the everyday psychological world are difficult.

Subjects in psychological research are sometimes used as their own experimental controls: They are observed; an experimental condition is applied; then they are observed again. This method is useful, if a large number of observations are made prior to the experimental condition. Such observations can be used to establish the stability of the subjects' behavior and its typical range. When the experimental treatment can be applied and withdrawn over time—again with many observations made in each interval between conditions—the experimental control is better. If a stable change can be observed after each of the conditions, then good comparisons and interpretations can be made.

In psychology, experimenters often match subjects on one or more variables, or group subjects by characteristics or prior conditions. If the matching or grouping can be followed by a chance allocation of subjects (i.e., at random) to experimental and control groups, the resulting experimental controls and comparisons are quite good. If not, there can be major errors.

Sometimes statistical adjustments are attempted as a control method in psychological research. Unless accompanied by the allocation of subjects to experimental and control groups by chance, these methods often are less than adequate to obtain good research comparisons.

CONTROL GROUPS
RESEARCH METHODOLOGY
SAMPLING

W. Asher

EXPERIMENTAL DESIGNS

Experimental designs guide researchers in performing an experiment. Experiments involve the planned introduction of a factor into a situation with the intent of associating it with a change in that situation. The introduced factor is usually called an intervention, treatment, or independent variable; the change is the measure of the dependent variable. Experimental designs are plans that detail what groups shall be established and how important plausible alternative explanations shall be eliminated. The linking of the intervention to effect and the elimination of all other explanations for the observed change are the major purposes of experimental design.

The simplest experimental designs involve an intervention given to a single subject or group of subjects with observations before and afterward to determine the change in their condition.

Experimental designs serve not only to relate variables to their effects, but also to rule out alternative explanations in which the variables are said to be confounded.

Only as we separate these effects can we attribute the change to the intervention; color in the display; or to the confounded alternate explanation, practice. In the language of experimental design, we would say we are controlling the confounded variable. How could we do so? There are four common control methods: (a) eliminating the confounded factor; (b) measuring the effect of the confounded factor and correcting for it; (c) comparing equivalent situations, one of which is affected by the confounded variable and treatment, whereas the other is affected only by the confounded variable; and (d) varying the treatment, but not the confounded variable, to see if effect follows the treatment pattern. Although there are other methods of control as well, these are the ones most in use.

THE LOGIC UNDERLYING DESIGNS

1. Hold a situation constant, introduce the treatment, and observe the change.

2. If a situation cannot be held constant but is changing, observe the pattern of change, introduce the treatment, and determine whether the pattern of change has been disturbed.

3. Hold two or more equivalent situations constant; keep one situation like the others in all ways but the treatment; introduce the treatment to the other (or its variations to still others), and observe the differences.

4. Relate the pattern of treatment application–withdrawal to the pattern of change; if there is a measure of treatment or intervention strength, relate the strength or intensity of the intervention to a relevant aspect, such as size or strength of change. (This works only if the change reverts back when the intervention is removed. It will not work with changes such as learning, which persist.)

Random assignment to experimental and control groups assures that the groups on the average "have every circumstance in common," both those suspected as being involved in the phenomenon as well as unsuspected variables, even irrelevant ones such as number of skin pores and length of finger nails. Indeed, Campbell and Stanley believe random assignment sufficiently important because of this protection for "hidden" variables that they label designs that *do not* use it "quasi-experimental designs," and those that *do,* "true experimental designs."

Factors such as level of education, learning ability, motivation, and socioeconomic status are often alternative explanations that we wish to rule out by assuring equivalence of groups. We do this by stratifying or blocking or matching on measures of these variables, and then randomly assigning subjects to experimental and control groups.

The logic of keeping all circumstances common save one is also employed in more complex designs such as factorial designs. These simultaneously examine the effect of several variables, yet there is always one or more groups of subjects that differ from another group or groups by only one circumstance or variable.

Mill noted that when one phenomenon varies as another does, then either one is cause and the other is effect or vice versa, or both are related to a common cause. Both the regression discontinuity design and the ABA or ABAB type of design depend on this logic, as do correlational studies that examine how closely the size of one variable (e.g., college grades) is related to the size of another.

Inference of causation from correlation is fraught with difficulty because the covariation may be due to a third variable.

CRITERIA OF GOOD DESIGN

A good design should reduce whatever uncertainty one has that the variables under study are related. In some studies, researchers may also intend that the results should generalize to other instances of the phenomenon. The design should do these things with the best use of one's resources, time, and energy, and within resource and time limits. It should fit an appropriate formulation of the problem rather than investigate the problem in too limited circumstances, cutting the problem to fit design requirements, or investigating a peculiar or atypical form of the question. Finally, the choices made in design formulation must be such that they build maximum confidence in the audience that the study was well done and that it was done with appropriate regard for ethical standards and institutional constraints. This is a large set of criteria, but to be realistic, this is what a researcher confronts.

The terms "internal validity" and "external validity" were used by Campbell and Stanley in 1963 to describe certain aspects of these criteria. These terms were later refined by Cook and Campbell in *Quasi-experimentation*. The capacity of a study to associate variables in the form in which they are represented in a study is referred to as the *internal validity* of a study. In particular, this refers to the capacity of the design to reject alternative explanations of the phenomena other than the intended one. *Construct validity* is the extent to which the form in which the variables are represented or measured in the study correspond to what was intended in the problem's original formulation. *Statistical conclusion validity* designates the proper use of statistics to infer that a relationship exists. *External validity* refers to the generalizability of the findings to other persons, settings, and times.

ALTERNATIVE EXPLANATIONS

A prime function of design is the elimination of alternative explanations that could otherwise explain the effect as readily as the presumed cause, the treatment. Each study probably has alternative explanations unique to its particular situation, but there are certain common ones that Cook and Campbell and Campbell and Stanley described. These they called "threats to validity," because they reduce internal or external validity. We can only discuss a few of them here.

History refers to events other than the treatment that occur during the study and might cause the effect.

Subjects may get older, wiser, or more experienced or skillful during the study, although this is not related to the treatment of interest—a development labeled "maturation."

Subjects do better the second time a test is administered because they are familiar with it, more relaxed, and so forth. Repeated testing lets factors affect the score that were not present at the first testing.

As a result of a pretest, a student may be forewarned as to what parts of an experimental curriculum he or she must study harder. The student's performance on the posttest is improved over what it would have been without the pretest; pretest and treatment interacted.

RELATIONSHIP OF DESIGN TO STATISTICS

There is some confusion about the role of design in relation to statistics, design often being seen as following whatever path statistics permit. Many designs—especially those involving analysis of variance—are popular because their relation to statistics has been so completely explored, and remedies for their contingencies and aberrations so well developed.

For most studies, statistics, besides describing the data, serve mainly to eliminate only one alternative explanation of the effect. In those instances in which the effect is very clear, inferential statistics become unimportant. But few psychological phenomena produce so strong an effect. If inferential statistics are to be used, there must be a working relationship between statistics and design, because it is quite possible to devise designs for which known statistical models are a poor fit. But the demands of the problem should be the determining factor in choosing a design. Only when no statistical model fits the design should trade-offs be explored to determine how much problem definition has to give to fit a statistical model.

In some studies with complex designs, statistics permit measurement and removal of the impact of one or more confounded variables that might otherwise provide alternative explanations of the effect. *But for all designs, the main protection against the whole range of possible alternative explanations must be provided by the design itself, rather than by statistics.*

DEVELOPMENT OF DESIGNS

The design for a simple study is primarily a matter of translating one's hypothesis or question into certain choices: (a) suitable *subjects;* (b) an appropriate *situation* or location; (c) the way the *treatment* variable will be administered; (d) how one *measures or observes* the effect; (e) the *basis of comparison*—how one assures that an effect occurred and that it was due to the treatment; and (f) the *procedure*—who gets what treatment and measures of effect, and when they get them.

SOME SAMPLE DESIGNS

The possible combinations of the preceding six characteristics are quite numerous. By concentrating on such general characteristics as when and to whom observations and treatments are given, we can describe some design patterns that are widely used and note some strengths and weaknesses. To do so, let us adopt the symbolism that "X" stands for treatment and "O" for an observation or measurement. Elapsed time during the study is portrayed from beginning to end by the distance of events from each other from left to right. "R" indicates that individuals were randomly assigned to groups.

Pretest–Posttest Design

Individuals randomly assigned to the experimental and control groups are tested before and after the treatment is administered:

$$R \quad O \quad X \quad O$$
$$R \quad O \qquad O$$

This widely used design controls for a large number of alternative explanations, including the repeated effect of testing, because both groups are tested twice. But treatment by testing interaction is an uncontrolled alternative explanation.

Posttest Only

The previous design, minus the pretest, controls for both testing and testing by treatment interaction. But one has to assume

$$R \quad X \quad O$$
$$R \qquad O$$

that the randomization has worked and the groups were equal at the beginning.

Solomon Four Group

Solomon and Lessac combined the features of the previous two designs so that comparisons permit assessment of testing by treatment interaction (OXO versus XO) and randomization is working (OXO versus O O), but this requires four groups and thus a larger number of subjects.

```
R   O   X   O
R   O       O
R       X   O
R           O
```

Designs Controlling Initial Levels of Groups

In a *matched pairs design,* one might use results of an intelligence test to match individuals in pairs, assigning a member of each pair at random to experimental or control group. This assumes considerable accuracy on the part of the test and, where individuals have nobody near them in score, can result in unmatched discarded cases. Such discarded cases might obviously limit the generality of the results, especially if, as is likely, scores at one or both extremes are underrepresented.

More common is the technique of blocking or stratifying, as in a *randomized block design.* Instead of subjects being paired, they are categorized (e.g., as high, middle, and low on an IQ test), and a randomly selected half of the individuals within each block are randomly assigned to experimental groups, and the rest are assigned to the control group.

Factorial Designs

Factorial designs permit consideration of the effects of two or more variables simultaneously. Groups are provided to measure the influence of all possible combinations of the variables.

Such designs are designated by the number of categories for each variable. The product of the number categories indicates the number of groups required. If a pretest as well as a posttest were given, this would be termed a *repeated measures* factorial design.

Factorial designs permit one to examine whether variables such as sex or body type alone have an effect on attending to radar patterns, whether any combination of these with the lower temperature have enhanced or reduced the effect, and whether all three together have an enhanced or reduced effect. The effects of combinations are called interaction effects.

Latin Square Design

A Latin square design, much like the factorial design, permits one to control for two or more variables. It trades off fewer groups for information that may not be needed. It takes its name from an ancient puzzle in which Latin letters were arranged in a table so that a given letter, which here represents a treatment or variable condition, appeared once in a row or column. In a 3 × 3 Latin square, each of three versions of a training program (A, B, C) might be assigned at random to a combination of ability level (high, middle, low) and motivation (high, middle, low), such that each training program is tried out once with each ability level and each motivation level.

This requires only nine groups in comparison to the 3 × 3 × 3 or 27 required by a factorial design. But it does not supply all the information that a factorial design would give regarding the possible heightening or depressive effect (interaction) of a particular level of ability or motivation with a particular training version.

Time-Series Designs

The ABA and ABAB experiments described earlier are time-series designs. Time-series designs follow an individual or group with repeated observations and repeated interventions or treatments. Sometimes the same treatment is used in the repetitions, sometimes different ones. A change should be observed following the intervention if it is effective, so that each person or group acts as its own control group. Where the effect of treatments persists, as in learning studies, subsequent interventions may be affected by the effects of earlier ones; therefore this "multiple treatment effect" needs to be anticipated as a possible confounding and contaminating factor. By contrast, certain tranquilizers that are excreted rapidly would show immediately in a set of time-series observations. Without further doses their effect would dissipate, but would reappear when dosage is resumed. Being able to show that the pattern of effect coincides with the pattern of times of intervention and its cessation is very convincing evidence that a cause–effect relationship exists.

Multiple Baseline Designs

These are time-series designs that measure one or more behaviors over time to establish baselines and then apply an intervention to one of the behaviors. If the intervention is effective, one notes a change in it, but not in the others. Allowing the pattern to return to stability, one then intervenes in a second baseline behavior, noting change in it but not in others, and so on.

CONTROL GROUPS
HYPOTHESIS TESTING
MULTIVARIATE ANALYSIS METHODS
RESEARCH METHODOLOGY
SCIENTIFIC METHOD
STATISTICS IN PSYCHOLOGY

D. R. KRATHWOHL

EXPERIMENTAL METHODS

Experimental methods are among the scientific methods used in psychological research. True experiments involve the careful observation of the effects of one or more variables (independent variables) on one or more outcome variables (dependent variables) under carefully controlled conditions with subjects randomly assigned to treatments.

The experiment could be made more complex by adding more independent or dependent variables. For example, time of day may be used as a second independent variable with three levels (morning, afternoon, evening), so that subjects might be randomly assigned to any of 12 different conditions (0 mg in the morning, 10 mg in the evening, etc.). It is clear that the number of subjects required for more complex designs would be greater than for simpler designs, because the number of subjects under each condition (e.g., 10 mg in the afternoon) must be sufficient to generalize about each event.

Although other scientific methods exist, the true experiment is the only method that allows researchers to make conclusions about cause–effect relationships. In the simple experiment having one independent variable (drug dosage) with two levels, if subjects in both the experimental and the control groups are treated in identical ways (except for the independent variable), and if subjects are randomly assigned to treatment conditions, then any differences between the activity level scores must be due to the independent variable.

Experimenter bias may create subtle differences between groups that confound the results of the experiment, making interpretations in terms of the independent variable less trustworthy.

Any differences between conditions can confound results. If different researchers handle the different stimuli, they, rather than the independent variable, may cause the results. Subjects may be more cooperative for an attractive researcher and less cooperative for an unattractive one, or possibly the different researchers score responses in different ways. Similarly, data-gathering locations may affect results.

The demand characteristics of the study's conditions—cues to the subjects about "appropriate" responses to the stimuli—can also confound results. For example, behaviors of other subjects in response to the stimuli may influence subjects who are tested in the same group, or unintentional smiles by the researcher may reinforce subjects who respond in the desired manner. One method to reduce experimenter and subject bias effects is to use "blind" research strategies in which subjects ("single blind"), or both subjects and researchers ("double blind"), do not know in which experimental condition each subject has been placed.

Sometimes independent variables cannot be manipulated by the researcher. For example, a study with gender, race, political party, frequency of marijuana use, or educational level as independent variables cannot randomly assign subjects to levels of the independent variables. Such variables sometimes are called nonmanipulated variables. The study of such variables cannot make use of a true experiment, but they are frequently studied in quasi-experiments. Interpretation of results for nonmanipulated variables is complicated, because various additional variables generally are confounded with them.

One way to facilitate interpretation of nonmanipulated independent variables is to match subjects on relevant confounding variables. For example, each high school graduate could be paired with a college graduate who matches in age, gender, social class, intelligence, and personality measures. The more complete the matching, the more comfortable the researcher can be in interpreting the effects of the independent variable. An alternative is to hold such variables constant (e.g., only do the research on middle-class male subjects of average intelligence and personality), so that the confounded variables cannot affect results. However, this would limit the researcher's ability to generalize results. A third alternative is to use a more complex design with gender, age, and so forth as additional independent variables.

Sometimes research strategies involve repeatedly testing the same subjects: A longitudinal study of human development may test the same group of children at ages 2, 5, 10, and 20, or a learning study may test subjects after every stimulus presentation. This introduces another complication that reflects an order effect: If level one of the independent variable always is tested before level two, differences may reflect the effect of the independent variable, but also may reflect practice, fatigue, or maturation. Thus if subjects are asked to rate the physical attractiveness of ten people, with slides showing the stimuli presented to all subjects in the same order, the rating of the third slide may reflect the stimulus, as well as an order effect. If the second slide, for example, is of a particularly attractive person, the third slide may be undervalued because of a contrast effect. If the third slide were in a different ordinal position, ratings would be different. Clearly, the solution to such problems involves manipulation of the order, so that different subjects receive the stimuli in randomly selected sequences. This is the technique of counterbalancing.

When more than one independent variable is studied, interpretation of the results may become complicated. Analysis of variance is the statistical technique most commonly used in the analysis of experimental studies. Key words in this analysis are *main effect* and *interaction*. A main effect occurs if, on the average, scores for the levels of the independent variable are significantly different from one another. If an independent variable has only two levels, a significant main effect indicates that the two levels led to significantly different scores on the dependent variable. However, if there are three or more levels, a main effect indicates that at least one pair of levels is significantly different, although it is possible that every pair of levels is significantly different (that is, A_1 and A_2 are different, A_1 and A_3 are different, and A_2 and A_3 are different, etc.). In such a case, appropriate post hoc analyses are used to interpret the main effect and discover which pairs or subsets of levels are or are not different from one another.

If more than one independent variable is examined, the independent variables may interact in such a way that the effect of one or more variables depends upon the level of one or more other variables.

Two major types of independent variables are *between-group* and *within-subject* variables. Between-group variables have different subjects for each level, so that comparisons of levels involve comparisons between independent groups of subjects. Within-subject variables have the same (or matched) subjects at more than one level, so that comparisons of levels involve comparisons of the same (or matched) subjects' performances.

Subjects can be assigned to experimental conditions in a number of different ways. For a one-way design, subjects can be randomly assigned to different levels (a between-group design) or can be tested at each level (a within-subject design). For a two-way design, either or both independent variables can be within-subject or between-group variables. The most simple two-way design is a completely randomized factorial design, with subjects randomly assigned to only one level for each variable, and with treatment conditions including all possible combinations of levels.

A design with at least one between-group and at least one within-subject variable is a mixed design. A subject (or set of matched subjects) generally is called a "block" (a term adopted from earlier agricultural work), and observations within a block are expected to be identical (within measurement error), unless the independent variables affect performance.

Campell and Stanley describe three *true experimental designs:* the pretest–posttest control-group design; the Solomon four-group design; and the posttest-only control-group design. Each of the three experiments requires the random assignment of subjects to conditions and has sufficient controls so that cause–effect inferences can be made with more confidence than in other designs. Multiple independent variables can be added through factorial methods.

Quasi-experimental designs involve variables that cannot be manipulated or controlled by the researcher, such as gender or block membership (without control groups). Such designs include the time-series experiment (a single subject or group of subjects is repeatedly measured, with one or more intervening conditions between measurements); the nonequivalent control-group, pretest–posttest design (like the pretest–posttest control group design, but without random assignment to conditions); and the multiple time-series design (a combination of the two preceding designs). Quasi-experimental designs are used when ethical or practical considerations preclude true experimental designs, and represent a compromise that allows some inferences about cause–effect relationships.

Correlational and ex post facto designs do not allow inferences about cause–effect relationships, but may have heuristic value (value in generating hypotheses for further research). Ex post facto designs compare preexisting groups, and may use retrospective data (data collected now, based on memories about the past) and match subjects on the basis of archival or retrospective variables. Retrospective data are open to serious validity problems, because people tend to recreate memories so that they are consistent with current views. Such designs are weaker than true experiments, but may be more ethical or practical.

All experimental methods must be used carefully and cautiously, with attention to ethical, practical, and statistical considerations. Scientific theory is built upon repeated, consistent research results; a single study represents only one piece of information for scientific evaluation.

ANALYSIS OF VARIANCE
CONTROL GROUPS
DOUBLE-BLIND RESEARCH
RESEARCH METHODOLOGY

M. J. ALLEN

EXPERIMENTAL NEUROSIS

This term refers to certain behavioral disturbances created in the laboratory in attempts to establish a model of naturally occurring human neurotic behavior. The two distinctive features of experimental neurosis are (a) the disruption of a previously established learned response, and (b) the appearance of severe agitation and aggressive behavior. The purpose of creating such a condition is to extend our knowledge about human psychopathology under conditions affording much greater experimental control than is possible in the natural environment. Typically, the subjects employed are animals, thus further increasing experimental control and eliminating certain ethical constraints.

Since Pavlov, two paradigms have been employed to produce experimental neurosis. The first is stimulus-discrimination conflict; the second is goal-orientation conflict, in which an aversive stimulus is used. Most investigators have chosen the latter paradigm, which was introduced by Jules Masserman in a series of experiments with cats. Masserman trained his cats to manipulate a device to obtain food when a signal consisting of a light and a bell was given. When this response was performed consistently, an aversive stimulus (electrical shock or a blast of air) was applied as the animal began to eat. The result was that the cats refused to eat and displayed fearful behavior such as trembling and attempting to escape from the cage; they also showed elevated blood pressure and heart rate. In some instances these responses persisted for months.

Masserman interpreted these results from a psychoanalytic perspective and regarded them as the outcome of a motivational conflict between hunger and fear. Joseph Wolpe questioned the necessity of conflict in creating experimental neurosis, arguing that the behavior of Masserman's cats was produced by the aversive stimulus alone. Using a procedure similar to that of Masserman, but omitting the presentation of food, Wolpe was able to produce the same behaviors. Other investigators have proposed that factors besides shock or conflict, such as frustration and confinement, are responsible for experimental neurosis. No one explanation has received general acceptance.

The classic neurotic symptom complex that most resembles the behavior of laboratory animals in experimental neurosis is phobia. According to the *Diagnostic and statistical manual, fourth edition* (DSM-IV), phobic disorders are characterized by "persistent and irrational fear of a specific object, activity, or situation that results in a compelling desire to avoid the dreaded object, activity, or situation." It is certainly debatable as to whether an animal's fear and avoidance of food in an experimental chamber in which it has previously been shocked qualifies as "irrational." With regard to etiology, there is little firm knowledge about how human neurotic symptoms develop. However, it is unlikely that trauma is at the root of very many such symptoms, as it is in all cases of experimental neurosis. Possibly the behavior observed in the laboratory is an adequate analog of a small subset of human phobic reactions.

Perhaps the strongest case for the usefulness of experimental neurosis as a model of human psychopathology can be made on the basis of comparable effective treatment techniques. Jules Masserman had some success in eliminating the symptoms of his cats by using treatments he regarded as analogs of psychoanalytic techniques, but these bore only superficial resemblance to such techniques. Joseph Wolpe devised a strategy that not only was successful with laboratory animals, but also led directly to the development of systematic desensitization, an effective treatment for anxiety in humans.

FIELD EXPERIMENTATION

S. G. FISHER

EXPERIMENTAL PSYCHOLOGY

Experimental psychology is psychology as a science, and thus is characterized by the way its content is obtained—namely, the manipulation of values in one domain to find how the values in another domain change. The object is, in general, to discover the relation between the response and the factor in the environment that is being manipulated. This factor is spoken of as the stimulus. Thus the content of experimental psychology is the result of studying cause and effect.

The factors involved are called *variables,* which can be dependent or independent. The event or response that is the object of study is the *dependent variable,* and the condition manipulated to bring about the result is the *independent variable.* The procedure implies prediction: If the independent variable is such and such, what is the chance that the dependent variable found in the experiment will be the value obtained in a future experiment? Mathematics are needed to indicate this. Statistical procedures have come to be required in the best experimentation.

Psychologists want to know about how the experiental world relates to the physical world, and how people relate to one another. Some independent variables are not physical, but are emergent phenomena. For example, psychologists may want to know why something they hear sounds "dark" or "pitiful" or some other specific experienced way. It is possible to make experimental manipulations of sound qualities to see where and when they sound a given way—pitiful, for example.

Although the experimental procedures just described have been applied in subhuman studies, experimental psychology has pertained largely to human studies of the sense modalities and to the studies of learning and the like. Psychologists have looked to those features of human activity to which they could apply experimental procedures.

Experimental psychologists characteristically give themselves to the study of specific problems in behavior, rather than to expressing the broad interrelations between the major aspects of behavior. In this, they differ from those psychologists who seek to assemble an overall picture of the human organism as a complex person, or who make a profession of helping people in their personal deficiencies or troubles.

There are five major problem areas in psychology: (a) action, its deviation, and goals—for the most part known as the study of motivation; (b) the relation or interaction between the organism and the environment; (c) forms of change that the organism manifests in overall behavior (maturation, learning, acclimatization, addiction, tolerance, development of physical fitness, and aging); (d) human internal disorganization and inner conflict; and (e) inability to meet demand (fatigue, tiredness, tissue impairment, work decrement, and boredom).

Not until the second half of the nineteenth century did psychology begin to be experimental. G. T. Fechner wrote *Elemente der Psychophysik* in 1860—a work credited with initiating experimental psychology. Wilhelm Wundt established the first laboratory of experimental psychology in Leipzig in 1879. Hermann Ebbinhaus made the first major study of *memory.* E. B. Titchener studied what he thought was *sensation,* the intended mental unit, to compare with the isolation of units in physics. Although he spent his life in this futile search, he became the arch example of an early experimental psychologist and trained many of the notable leaders in experimental psychology who immediately followed him.

In time, an important change occurred in the description of psychological subject matter—the distinction between consciousness and overt behavior. With this came the study of animal behavior and comparisons between humans and subhumans: comparative psychology. The technique of experimental psychology applied to subhuman subjects was called *behaviorism.* This, in the broadest sense, is a form of objective experimental psychology.

BEHAVIORISM
RESEARCH METHODOLOGY

S. H. BARTLEY

EXPERIMENTER EFFECTS

In conducting an experiment, investigators hypothesize, in essence, that one or several variables will have a particular outcome. Behavioral scientists plan their experiments to test the hypothesis under investigation and to eliminate as many rival explanations as possible. One rival explanation is experimenter effects, which are one category of extraneous factors that can shape the research results, obscuring the influence of the variable or variables being studied. Several important experimenter effects have been identified and investigated.

Sometimes experimenters—usually without attempting to—influence behavior in the direction of their expectations. This phenomenon is called experimenter bias. The case of clever Hans is an illustration. Hans was a horse that answered by stomping the correct number of times when asked addition, subtraction, multiplication, and spelling questions. Early in the nineteenth century the German psychologist, Oskar Pfungst, found that Hans responded to subtle, unintentional visual cues provided unknowingly by the horse's owner and trainer—especially imperceptible head movements.

Rosenthal's studies and those of others have shown that experimenter bias is often present in experiments. Their work suggests that researchers—like horse trainers—often cue subjects unintentionally through facial expressions and tones of voice. To minimize the impact of such bias, research psychologists try to reduce experimenter–participant interactions. Sometimes they present instructions over tape recorders. Sometimes they ask a person who does not know the hypotheses or the subjects' experimental condition, and who is not personally invested in the study's outcome, to conduct the research.

A second category of experimenter effects centers around attention—how much and what type of attention the experimenters pay to the groups in their research. F. J. Roethlisberger and William Dickson are credited with discovering that attention has important effects on the outcome of experiments. In the 1930s, they investigated ways to increase worker productivity in the Hawthorne plant of the Western Electric Company in Chicago. As part of the study, five women were isolated in a room while practices such as rest periods, working hours, and pay incentives were systematically changed. Roethlisberger and Dickson observed that the women's output increased overall—even when working conditions worsened substantially. The extra attention was presumed responsible for the outcome—an interpretation that is now controversial.

Most researchers try to shield their work from the effects of disproportionate attention to one group. They also attempt to give each group in their research the same sort of attention. Placebo conditions are often introduced to ensure that subjects in both experimental and control groups receive the same type of attention and consequently share common expectations.

EXPERIMENTAL CONTROLS
EXPERIMENTAL METHODS
HAWTHORNE EFFECT
RATER ERROR

L. L. DAVIDOFF

EXPERT TESTIMONY

In the early 1900s, lively debate began in scientific journals and law reviews all over the world on the psychology of testimony and the value of psychology to the judicial process.

Hugo Münsterberg brought together a number of essays on psychology and crime.

It was, unfortunately, somewhat premature, but it did not go unnoticed. John H. Wigmore, professor of the Law of Evidence at Northwestern University, wrote a scathing parody.

Wigmore's attack was telling: Few references to psychologists as expert witnesses appeared for a quarter of a century. Then in 1931, Lewis M. Terman, a professor of psychology at Stanford University, appeared before the Los Angeles Bar Association to present an address, "Psychology and the law." Terman took pains to refer to Münsterberg's *On the witness stand* and Wigmore's scathing response. He suggested that Münsterberg's error was in exaggerating the importance of psychology's contributions based on research then at hand. He went on to suggest that in light of significant scientific advances and potential, the ultimate significance of psychology for the legal profession could hardly be overstated. Terman emphasized the value of experimental psychology in clarifying errors of testimony. He ranged broadly in his presentation, suggesting that psychology might be helpful, among other things, in lie detection, evaluation of eyewitness accounts, clarification of the vagaries of the sanity pleading, and jury selection.

The role of the psychologist as expert witness in matters of mental disease or defect was spelled out in considerable detail in the landmark *Jenkins v. United States* in 1962. After indictment for housebreaking with intent to commit an assault, assault with intent to rape, and assault with a dangerous weapon, Jenkins was committed to a hospital in Washington, DC for a mental examination on September 4, 1959, to determine his competence to stand trial and his mental condition at the time of the alleged offense. Jenkins was given a series of psychological tests by staff psychologists under the supervision of Bernard I. Levy. Jenkins was also examined by several psychiatrists, who informed the District Court that he was incompetent. He was then committed to St. Elizabeth's Hospital until mentally competent to stand trial. At St. Elizabeth's he was tested extensively by Tirnauer, who concluded that Jenkins was schizophrenic. Two other psychiatrists found "no evidence of mental disease or defect." Ives administered additional tests and concluded that Tirnauer's diagnosis was correct. The trial court, *sua sponte* (on its own motion), instructed the jury to disregard the testimony of the three defense psychologists that the defendent had a mental disease when committing the crimes charged.

Judge Bazelon of the U.S. Court of Appeals held that the lower court erred on several points, including rejection of qualified psychologists as experts on the presence or absense of mental disease. This decision was rendered in spite of an *amicus curiae* brief submitted by the American Psychiatric Association, urging the court not to allow psychologists to qualify as experts. Bazelon's scholarly opinion defined the fully trained psychologist. In a rare concurrence, Judge Warren Burger (then Chief Justice of the U.S. Supreme Court) agreed with Bazelon. Since the Jenkins decision, the rejection of psychologists by the court as experts in their field of specialization has been considered a trial error.

It is important to understand that all psychologists are not likely to be accepted by the court as expert witnesses in all areas of psychology. The psychological expert must be qualified before the court in the matter about which he or she will testify. The rules of jurisprudence are specific:

> An expert is one who is so qualified by study or experience that he can form a definite opinion of his own respecting a division of science, branch of art, or department of trade concerning which persons having no particular training or special study are incapable of forming accurate opinions or of deducing correct conclusions.

As legal scholars have pointed out, the issue must be such that the expert may answer by giving an opinion that is a reasonable probability, rather than conjecture or speculation.

Most published reports of psychologists as expert witnesses have to do with competency evaluation and the sanity pleading. In this narrow area of expert testimony, psychologists have invaded the province of psychiatry. Although there is some tendency for psychologists to regard themselves as "second-rate" experts in these areas, the data suggests that psychologists as expert witnesses in matters of competence and sanity are successful and well regarded. Psychologists testify in civil matters involving personal injury, wrongful death, trademark infringement, product liability, and other matters. Psychologists have testified in criminal courts in matters of change of venue, death-qualified juries, prison conditions, and capacity to form criminal intent.

Judges are increasingly aware of the potential that psychologists have for the court.

Few graduate schools at this time prepare psychologists to function as expert witnesses in the courts. Psychologists who expect to function in this role must acquire education, training, and experience ad lib or from continuing education at the postdoctoral level. Interest in this area is burgeoning.

CRIMINAL RESPONSIBILITY
FORENSIC PSYCHOLOGY

T. H. BLAU

EXPLORATORY BEHAVIOR

Exploratory behavior is a set of behaviors whose function is to alter an organism's relationship to its environment by introducing additional information into the system. Although it does not have a clear biological function, it does affect the central nervous system directly and the physiological balance within the organism indirectly. Exploratory behavior can be divided into two types: specific and diversive.

Specific exploration is elicited in response to a situation of high curiosity induction. When a novel, complex, or incongruous stimulus or event introduces uncertainty, the organism becomes curious, a condition that is tense and uncomfortable. The organism responds to this aroused or tense state by exploring the specific stimulus or event that has induced the curiosity in order to identify and understand it clearly. The behavior serves to introduce new knowledge and alleviate the tension.

Forms of exploration include locomotion of the whole body, or its parts; investigatory, observing, and manipulatory responses; as well as more complex behaviors such as inquiry, reading, and listening. All these behaviors belong to the family of exploration because they are triggered by uncertainty and curiosity and serve to gain information from a specific source in the environment.

Epistemic responses are similar to exploratory responses, except that they are internal rather than external and serve to gain information and reduce epistemic curiosity by a process of directed thinking. Thus exploration proceeds within the cognitive rather than the perceptual system.

Diversive exploration is undertaken when, under conditions of boredom or diversive curiosity, an organism searches for stimulation.

Exploration may also be expressed in many other ways such as in play, recreation, creative production aesthetics, and humor. Thus a great deal of behavior that is not directed toward biological satisfaction is associated with exploratory behavior in its many forms.

INTRINSIC MOTIVATION
PLAY

H. I. DAY

EXPRESSIVE ARTS

Expressive arts are not often regarded as contributors to behavior change, although personality change has been attributed to expressive arts. As the data base for understanding behavior change is increased, the role of nontraditional and innovative therapies is enlarged. Expressive arts include poetry, music, writing, painting, dance, sculpture, and combinations of these arts. Often, expressive arts appear informally in therapy, are seldom researched, and usually are given only supportive roles. Nevertheless, the expressive arts offer challenges that command attention and call for research. The evidence suggests some heuristic leads.

1. Expressive arts allow for self-expression without the sometimes sizable confrontation found in talking therapies.

2. Expressive arts draw on personal experience and expressiveness common to all mankind. All societies produce examples of the expressive arts covered here and use them for emotional release and self-statements. Yet it is not assumed that the expressive arts reflect specific personal difficulties, social problems of the culture, or the like, but such results may appear. Expression does not necessarily imply an emotional catharsis, but may contribute to it.

3. The products of people in therapy utilizing the expressive arts appear to be less redundant than verbal descriptions of comparable behavior among psychotherapy clients. It is known that psychotherapy is characterized by high redundancy (rigidity, defensiveness, imperviousness to alternatives), and that overcoming redundancy is often a sign of progress.

4. The expressive arts are characterized by relatively more overt activity than is talking psychotherapy. This is especially true for dance and movement; somewhat true for painting, drawing, and sculpture; but less true for writing, whether it is prose or poetry. Yet the act of composing poetry or prose may put a responsibility on one that is more exacting than verbal reports.

5. Behavior and personality change do not seem to depend on a determination of the specifics of causality in the problem areas that one experiences. Expressive efforts can allow one to act on a problem without discerning its origin; it is the *effects* of the problem that are confronted by expressiveness, and this may be enough to promote change. Although there are more than 250 varieties of psychotherapy, there may be only two basic *types* of psychotherapy: those that locate the significant variables in the psyche and those that locate them in the person–environment exchange. If the latter conceptual position is the one under which expressive arts have their chief relevance (rather than revealing the "unconscious"), then those intercessions that promote change in the person–environment configuration may be all that is needed; nonspecific factors may be the most salient for many kinds of change. What may be more salient for change is *attribution* of cause by the client (or therapist), thus giving a handle on the matter that promotes action and change. Rather than seeking the "true" causal theory, the expressive arts help to mobilize the client for action (and possible problem solving), the exact nature of which is seldom specified, and may not need to be.

6. Conflict theory is offered as being a useful way to look at behavior change in general, and is offered as the most encouraging version of how the expressive arts promote change. Conflict is best understood in terms of approach and avoidance gradients with reference to goals. Avoidance shows a steepness in moving away from a goal area (to avoid danger), whereas approach to a goal is gradual. The point of intersection of the two gradients signals the area of highest anxiety and ambivalence or vacillation. Ordinarily psychotherapies based on uncovering the past, on emotional catharsis, tend to emphasize lowering the avoidance gradient; theoretically, positive and approaching behaviors result. Behavior therapies see incremental change in the approach direction as most heuristic. As a therapeutic approach moves slowly and unthreateningly toward goals, the anxiety aroused by treading on the avoidance tendencies may be lessened; approach can then proceed without first attending to avoidance as a prerequisite. Art expressiveness may be a subtle way of promoting approach behaviors without rapidly eliciting their avoidance counterparts. Fewer art therapy clients drop out of therapy as compared to talking therapy clients, and their ratings of success in therapy are uniformly higher than that reported by talking therapy clients.

7. Expressive arts therapy may allow the person to ride through the many emotional perturbations associated with verbal confrontation in therapy. Art simply does not ask the same questions about behavior change as talking therapy does and thereby escapes much minutiae. The many questions in traditional, verbal, uncovering therapy based on "Why?" and "Where did the problem come from?" and "What happened to me in the past?" simply do not occur *prima facie* in the art forms, although such questions may be asked by therapists steeped in the traditional past. Free of such constraints and assuming a relatively nonconfrontive posture toward the client, expressive arts engage the person with gentleness and openness in a way best described in terms of approach and avoidance conflict, and yield results not well explained by any traditional "depth" notions of therapy. The ready availability of most art forms to persons—whether patients or not—seeking personal expression, tension release, or the quieting of longer-range concerns is an encouraging one that should be pursued by researchers more fully.

LITERATURE AND PSYCHOLOGY
MUSIC THERAPY
POETRY THERAPY

E. L. Phillips

EXTRASENSORY PERCEPTION

Extrasensory perception (ESP) is an ambiguous term used to refer to many alleged esoteric phenomena such as clairvoyance, telepathy (mental communication), and precognition. Other associated terms—"psi" (for "psychokinesis") or "telekinesis"—have been coined to refer to alleged "mind over matter" operations such as moving objects about without touching them or bending spoons by sheer mental concentration. The basic idea summarized by the ESP label is that some people—perhaps only part of the time—may have knowledge of events obtained somehow without the use of the ordinary senses, or the power to move objects without physical contact.

To acquire acceptance by the scientific community, certain well-meaning and sincere believers conduct alleged experiments to obtain evidence or proof of the powers some people claim to possess. Thus blindfolded subjects will be asked to determine the colors of paper or cloth that they examine only with their fingers. Any success here would not be "extra" sensory, to be sure, but it would certainly be astonishing. So far, no acceptable demonstrations of such ability have ever been provided to the satisfaction of psychologists, although some physical scientists have been led to endorse certain demonstrations as inexplicable.

PARAPSYCHOLOGY
PSEUDOPSYCHOLOGY

B. R. Bugelski

EXTRAVERSION/INTROVERSION

The words *extraversion* and *introversion* have been in use for several centuries. Considered etymologically, they may be construed, respectively, as an "outward turning" and an "inward turning." They have long been used, in fact, with essentially those meanings, both in a physical and a psychological sense. The psychological usage can be found in writings dating as far back as the seventeenth century when extraversion referred to the turning of thoughts toward outer objects, and introversion

to the turning of thoughts inward to one's own mind or soul or the spiritual realm.

Carl Jung is largely responsible for directing the attention of psychologists to these concepts. Jung viewed extraversion versus introversion as the most basic dimension of human temperament, and believed that many major fluctuations and controversies in Western thought could be understood in terms of a clash between these opposing outlooks. He also believed that Western thought on the whole, in comparison with that of the Orient, stressed extraversion.

Jung defined *extraversion* as an outward turning of libido or psychic energy. This is equivalent to saying that extraversion means directing interest toward objects (other people or things) in the environment and functioning in relation to those objects. In an extraverted state one perceives, thinks, feels, and acts in relation to the object. *Introversion* was defined by Jung as an inward turning of libido. This implies a directing of interest away from the object toward the subject—toward the individual's own conscious experience. In an introverted state, perception, thinking, feeling, and action are determined more directly by subjective factors than by the object. The extravert—the individual habitually in an extraverted state—tends to respond immediately and directly to stimuli from without. Habitually in an introverted state, the introvert tends to withhold immediate responses and act on the basis of subjective considerations that follow the external stimulus.

The dimension of extraversion versus introversion has been subject to a variety of interpretations. Upon learning of Jung's use of these terms, Sigmund Freud concluded that extraversion was the healthy condition, whereas introversion constituted a predisposition to psychopathology. Jung, however, did not construe extraversion and introversion in quite this way and considered neither to be preferable to the other. The Freudian perspective tends to prevail in any society (e.g., the United States) that favors extraversion over introversion. There has been a tendency among American psychologists and educators to view extraversion as preferable and to reinterpret the dimension in terms of social behavior. Thus, extraversion has often been understood in terms of sociability, whereas introversion has been regarded as a tendency to withdraw from social contacts. Jung thought of the dimension primarily in terms of modes of experience or consciousness, and the behavioral definition itself reflects a more extraverted approach to psychology. Most efforts to construct questionnaire scales for the dimension reflect this shift in orientation, because the items have often contained extraversive scale content that pertains to sociability and introversive scale content that pertains to anxiety or neurotic symptoms. Strictly speaking, such scales cannot be regarded as measures of the Jungian dimension.

Murray contended that Jung's concepts encompassed a number of component variables that might be distinguished and assessed separately. He suggested novel terms for some of the components. One was the dimension of exocathection versus endocathection. This is concerned essentially with the value that an individual attaches either to the outer world (including practical action, social and political events, and the opinions of other people) or to the inner world (one's own feelings, fantasies, ideas, theories, images, etc.). Another such dimension was extraception versus intraception. This is concerned more with the determinants of perception, judgment, and action. *Extraception* refers to a tendency to be governed by concrete, clearly observable, physical conditions, whereas *intraception* refers to a tendency to be governed by more subjective factors: feelings, fantasies, speculations, and aspirations. The work of some of the major factor-analytic researchers—including Raymond B. Cattell, J. P. Guilford, and Hans Eysenck—also indicates the possibility of distinguishing some semi-independent components of the extraversion–introversion dimension. At the same time, their findings provide rather consistent evidence for a broad general dimension (perhaps represented by a higher-order factor) that corresponds rather well to Jung's concepts and enters into a large number of the specific individual differences that we find in human personality.

One factor-analytic theorist, Hans Eysenck, has devoted particular attention to this dimension and, in interpreting it, has borrowed a number of physiological concepts from Ivan Pavlov. According to Eysenck, introverts are characterized by very sensitive cortical excitation processes. They tend, therefore, to be intellectually and emotionally overwhelmed by moderate social and physical stimulation, and are relatively prone to anxiety and despair. As a consequence, they often resort to a self-protective retreat from their surroundings and may limit interaction by means of self-control or behavioral inhibition. Extraverts, in contrast, are characterized by less sensitive cortical processes or by a predominance of inhibitory cortical processes. Consequently, they require more stimulation from the social environment and may actively seek it to overcome their own cortical inertia.

CENTRAL TRAITS
CONSCIOUSNESS STATES
INNER/OUTER-DIRECTED BEHAVIOR
PERSONALITY

R. W. COAN

EYE

The protective tissue of the eye is composed of the lids, the transparent mucous membrane that lines the lids and continues over the eyeball (conjunctiva), the tear or lacrimal glands, and the fatty tissue of the orbit that acts to absorb shock.

The optical tissues of the eye include the cornea, the lens, the aqueous humor, and the vitreous humor or body. The cornea is the main structure responsible for refraction of light as it enters the eye. In addition to its refractive function, the cornea also acts to protect the eye and to give the eye its form and rigidity. Pertaining to these latter functions, it is appropriate to mention that the cornea is, in fact, continuous with the sclera, that tough white coat that forms the posterior four fifths of the eye and is primarily responsible for its form and rigidity.

The lens of the eye lies behind the cornea and the pigmented iris and is held in place by the zonular fibers, which are connected to the ciliary body containing the ciliary muscle. When the ciliary muscle contracts, the lens bulges, thereby increasing the refraction of light. This happens, along with pupilary constriction and convergence of the eyes, as part of the accommodation reflex that occurs when an object close to the eyes is viewed. The image focused on the retina by the cornea and lens is upside down and reversed right to left.

The uvea, composed of the iris, the ciliary body, and the choroid, controls the amount of light in the eye and also serves a nutritive function. The iris lies posterior to the cornea and anterior to the lens. It reacts to light with constriction and thus restricts the entry of light into the eye. It also constricts to enhance depth of focus when the eye focuses on a near object, and thus is associated with the accommodation reflex.

The retina is the photoreceptive and integrative portion of the eye. Embryologically, it is an outpouching of the surface of the brain. At the retina a light stimulus is converted into a neural code and transmitted over the optic nerve and tract to the brain. The neural organization of the retina is sufficiently complex to allow a fair amount of integration of visual information. The rods and cones are the photoreceptive cells of the retina, and are located in the retina's most posterior aspect. The cones function during daylight and are responsible for color vision. The rods function best in dim light and present the world in shades of gray. Rods are most numerous in the periphery of the retina, whereas cones become numerous toward the focal center. The fovea, or macula, is found in the focal center of the retina and contains only cones.

The process of visual perception is initiated when light is absorbed by the photopigments contained within the outer segment of the rods and cones. Rhodopsin (visual purple) is contained within rods. The cones appear to utilize at least three separate photopigments, which have peak absorptions at wavelengths of light corresponding to the colors blue, green, and yellow. There is, however, considerable overlap in absorption among these pigments. Chemical changes initiated in the photopigments of the rods and cones when light is absorbed produce the rod and cone generator potentials.

ACCOMMODATION
COLOR VISION
VISUAL PERCEPTION

M. L. WOODRUFF

EYE MOVEMENT DESENSITIZATION AND REPROCESSING

Eye movement desensitization and reprocessing (EMDR) is a rapid treatment methodology originated by Francine Shapiro for trauma-based symptoms such as nightmares, flashbacks, and intrusive thoughts. Shapiro observed rapid relief of distress in herself and in volunteers following multisaccadic lateral eye movements. She investigated the procedure in a controlled study of rape–molestation victims and Vietnam veterans and found large effects that were maintained at a 3-month follow-up.

PROCEDURE

The procedure begins with establishing rapport sufficiently, so that the patient will adequately self-report internal experiences. The patient is fully briefed about what to expect during and after the procedure, so that the profound affect to be experienced will not be overwhelming. Special effort goes to ruling out multiple personality disorder (MPD) using a screening device such as the Dissociative Experiences Scale. If the patient is a multiple, a special EMDR protocol applies. Using EMDR without the special protocol on an individual with undiagnosed MPD poses the risk of provoking an angry alternate personality to emerge during the procedure, thereby setting back therapeutic rapport considerably.

Before using EMDR, the therapist assesses the patient's memory of the target traumatic event for its visual, cognitive, and kinesthetic components. Distress levels are measured in subjective units of distress (SUDs). The patient also articulates desired cognitions about the event. Pretreatment confidence in those cognitions is assessed using a semantic differential scale.

EMDR proceeds as the patient is told to hold in awareness the distressing sensory aspects of the memory while the therapist moves a finger laterally to produce sets of eye movements in the client. After each set, the patient's experience is reassessed, variously producing reports of images, thoughts, or body sensations as the memory of the event is processed to completion. Often, an abreaction occurs in which the patient relives the event in multisensory detail. Immediately following this portion of the procedure is a period of heightened suggestibility in which the patient's desired cognitions may spontaneously emerge or may be installed with relative ease. This spontaneous shift or another closure procedure enables the SUD levels to reduce sufficiently to close the session comfortably. The patient is told to anticipate continued processing in the days following EMDR. Patient logs of such material are brought to the follow-up sessions, in which additional EMDR may be applied to emerging issues or memories.

THEORY

Theoretically, Shapiro postulated that a trauma produces an affective overload that upsets the excitatory–inhibitory balance of information processing. This causes processing of the trauma to be blocked and held in isolation in a neural network with its full charge of visual, cognitive, and affective meaning. This charge breaks through the dissociative barrier, separating the memory from normal awareness and is experienced as intrusive thoughts, nightmares, or flashbacks. EMDR penetrates the dissociative barrier in a way that reestablishes the balance and communication between neural networks. Properly conducted, EMDR processes traumatic material to completion, resulting in a cessation of intrusive symptomatology and a shift to more adaptive cognition. Following EMDR, patients describe shifts in their imagery, cognition, affect, and behavior, suggesting that the integration of material occurs on a basic schematic level. These shifts may generalize to related events that were not specifically targeted in the EMDR treatment.

PRECAUTIONS

The learning curve for the safe and effective use of the procedure is substantial. EMDR should not be attempted experimentally by clinicians not trained in its use. Risks to patients include ocular injury, retraumatization, and suicidal ideation.

ALTERNATIVE PSYCHOTHERAPIES
BRAIN
CANALIZATION
EFFECTIVENESS OF PSYCHOTHERAPY
IDIODYNAMICS
MENTAL IMAGERY
MULTIPLE PERSONALITY
STRESS CONSEQUENCES
VISUAL IMAGERY

S. PAULSEN

EYE MOVEMENTS

The eyes are rarely stationary. To the viewer, the world seems quite stable and the eyes are directed at will, but it is not so. Even when we intently view or fixate an object or scene, our eyes are free of large movements for only about 250 to 300 milliseconds, and fine movements are superimposed on even these seemingly stationary periods. Eye movements are generally functional in that they bring new information to central or foveal vision, and they change the scene so that receptors do not adapt and cease providing information to the visual cortex. Some eye movements such as fine tremors may be the result of muscle tension from the dense musculature servicing the visual system.

Each optical orbit is served by six muscles located in the medial aspect of the orbit. Anatomically they form three complement pairs. The medial rectus (nasal) and lateral rectus (temporal) allow for horizontal movement about the vertical axis. The superior rectus and inferior rectus provide practical complements for vertical movement, but also have horizontal and torsional components allowing for oblique movement as well. The inferior and superior obliques, located slightly diagonal to one another, control torsional movements along with the superior and inferior rectus. Not only do these muscle groups provide for a great deal of latitude in movement, but their density also provides a greater amount of musculature for the weight of movable organs than does any other structure in the body. Consequently, there result great speed and great resiliency to fatigue.

Generally, the eyes move conjugately or in parallel; one exception is the vergence movement system, where the eyes move in opposite directions toward or away from the nose. Movements of the eyes are classified as catching, holding, and fine.

The catching movements are stimulus bound movements. The principal catching eye movement is the *saccade*. Each day there are elicited approximately 230,000 saccadic eye movements. In general, the larger the eye movement, the greater the velocity: At 5° of visual angle or less, there is a velocity of approximately 200°/s, whereas larger saccades of more than 100° can obtain velocities in excess of 700°/s; however, 85% of saccadic eye movements are less than 15°. These eye movements are generally considered to be ballistic: Once initiated, they must reach the target before their course can be altered and another saccade initiated. Saccades seem susceptible and flexible to cognitive input and to target or scenic density. It is unlikely that successive saccades would occur in less than 150 ms, because it takes the visual system about 50 ms to program a saccade during a fixation, 20 to 30 ms to execute it, and 50 ms to regain clear perception. Saccades occur in a somewhat orderly sequence during reading, but appear to be more haphazard when one is searching or scanning a scene.

The quick phase of the *optokinetic nystagmus* is also a catching movement. When one is following a striped rotating drum or riding on a merry-go-round, at certain intervals a flick is made to direct the gaze to a new and usually backward feature of the drum or visual scene.

Holding movements hold the attended scene in central vision. Three kinds have been identified. *Vestibular movements* occur when the vestibular system of the inner ear provides feedback to the oculomotor system in order to keep the gaze on the target whenever there is movement of the head. *Smooth pursuit* or *tracking* or *slow phase nystagmus* is an example of holding movement in which the eyes follow a moving stimulus. If the moving stimulus accelerates at too fast a pace, corrective saccades are initiated, which accurately reacquire the moving stimulus until the next critical level for correction is reached. *Vergence movements* are also holding movements, but are nonconjugate (i.e., the eyes move in separate directions). The principal vergence movements are *conversions* and *diversions* and appear as a consequence of the overlap in a visual field. Vergence movements may be demonstrated by holding a pencil at arm's length and moving it toward the nose, which is convergence, and away from the nose, which is divergence. These movements are voluntary. They are slow responding and are generally small in angular extent.

A third set of extremely fine movements is collectively known as *physiological nystagmus*. These movements are superimposed on the larger movements and fixations discussed earlier and seem to have similar origins, but their purpose is poorly understood. *Fine tremors* have a median amplitude of approximately 17 s of arc, with frequencies ranging from about 25 to 125 cycles/s. *Slow drifts* occur with an amplitude of about 2 to 5 min of arc and an average velocity ranging from 1 to 5 min/s. This may be demonstrated by having a single source small red light in an otherwise dark room. Fixating the light for a brief time will provide evidence for the phenomenal movement of the light around the room. *Microsaccades* or *flicks* are another type of physiological nystagmus; they have an amplitude of from 1 to 20 min of arc, with a velocity peaking at about 10°/s. Rigorous experimentation has indicated that the very fine physiological nystagmus movements play no part in improving visual acuity.

Buswell and Tinker independently provided much of our understanding of reading behavior and picture viewing with their research from the 1920s into the 1940s. In short, they showed that saccade length and fixation duration were dependent on typographical features, context, and text difficulty. Emphasis shifted to greater specificity on the parts of words on which the eye movements landed, and on the flexibility of eye movements to change dynamics between sentences within passages, based on the reader's cognitive processing ability (i.e., the perceived importance of text selections). Measuring devices have become much more comfortable. Other devices are aimed at more natural viewing with no encumbrances or awareness by the viewer, in order to get more naturalistic estimates of behavior with slight trade-offs in precision. Driving behavior, pilot's view of the ground and instruments, learning disabilities, psychopathologies, and many other areas of research interest involve recording of eye movements.

For nearly a century, principal empirical emphasis has been directed at verifying one of four proposed purposes for the eye movement sequence. First, eye movements may maintain vision: Without them, receptors adapt, and scenes and pictures fade from view. Second, eye movements and their fixations may be responsible for perception: They seem to exhibit a psychomotor program directly related to a particular picture or scene that is viewed. Third, eye movements and their fixations may be directed by perception: Because fixations seem to fall in locations judged to contain high information such as contours, objects, and shadings, it is believed that some overall semantic content directs the eye movement pattern. Fourth, the eye movement sequence may provide a means for the encoding, storing, and subsequent reconstruction of the successive retinal images of the detail found in a scene or picture: Each individual provides an idiosyncratic eye movement pattern as a reflection of that individual's own viewing and interpretation of the scene. The possibility also exists that all these alternatives at one time or another are correct.

BIOLOGICAL RHYTHM

D. F. Fisher

EYEWITNESS TESTIMONY

Eyewitnesses to an event report what they were able to perceive; such reports also are limited to what the witnesses remember about the event. Hence both perception and memory are relevant in evaluating the completeness and veracity of testimony. Eyewitness testimony is highly persuasive for juries, more than other form of evidence.

MEMORY FOR FACES

Eyewitnesses are often called on to identify or to describe perpetrators, making face memory important for eyewitness research. In general, memory for faces is quite good, with accuracy high even at long retention intervals. However, large-scale errors have been documented. A number of factors can erode the accuracy of face memory, including such expected factors as brief exposure and long delay between the exposure and the subsequent identification. It also is well documented that individuals are far better in remembering faces from their own race than faces of other races.

In addition, subjects are much better at remembering that a face is familiar than they are at remembering why a face is familiar. For example, Brown, Deffenbacher, and Sturgill had subjects observe an event. Several days later, they showed the subjects mugshots of individuals who supposedly had participated in the event. The people in the photos were different from the people who had actually been on the scene. After some more days, subjects were shown a lineup of four individuals and were asked to select the individuals seen in the original event. Subjects often selected individuals who had been seen in the mugshots (i.e., they correctly realized that these individuals were familiar, but then misattributed this familiarity to the original event).

This experiment illustrates *photo-biased* identification. Related effects have been documented in which a person encountered in one circumstance is remembered as having been encountered in some other circumstance, a confusion often referred to as *unconscious transference.* In these cases, subjects are again correct in remembering that a face is familiar; their error arises when they attribute this familiarity to some specific prior episode.

Some strategies and some sorts of training can improve witness's memory for faces. Deep processing of faces leads to better memory. However, this is probably due to the number and variety of features attended to while one is doing deep processing. Thus face memory may be best if, when a face is being observed, one pays attention to many and diverse aspects of the face.

Eyewitness memory for individuals is often assessed via a lineup, in which the witness must select from a group of people the person observed during the original event. Many studies have examined the factors that influence lineup identifications and have sought ways to determine when a lineup identification should be trusted. For example, it appears that identification is equally accurate from a live or from a videotaped lineup, and the likelihood of correctly identifying a culprit also is largely unaffected by clothing or disguise. However, an *innocent* suspect is more likely to be misidentified as the culprit if the person is wearing clothes similar to those the witness remembers the suspect wearing.

The other individuals in the lineup are termed the foils or distractors. Lineups without foils entail considerable risk of misidentification. It also is crucial that the foils be of the same age, race, height, and weight as the suspect. If the eyewitness has verbalized other features of the culprit, the foils must be matched on these features as well. In fact, it seems more important that the foils resemble the witnesses' *description* of the culprit, rather than resembling the suspect.

Researchers have distinguished the functional, or effective, size of a lineup (i.e., the number of people among whom the witness is plausibly choosing) from the lineup's nominal size (the actual number of people). If several individuals in the lineup are rather dissimilar from the suspect, the functional size may be considerably smaller than the nominal size. In fact, the nominal size of the lineup plays only a small role in witnesses' identifications, but having an adequate functional size is crucial for identification accuracy. Consequently, researchers have developed a number of ways to quantify a lineup's functional size.

Lineup identifications are strongly influenced by the instructions given to the witness as well as the format of the lineup itself. Instructions explicitly acknowledging that the culprit may be absent from the lineup (making "none of these" a plausible response) tend to decrease the number of false identifications, while having little impact on the overall identification accuracy. Likewise, instructions can influence the likelihood of selecting any particular person from the lineup, emphasizing the importance of unbiased instructions. In addition, identifications seem more accurate when the members of the lineup are viewed one at a time, rather than simultaneously. Accuracy can also be improved by allowing witnesses to hear the suspects' voices, to view the suspects in their customary posture and gait, and it seems, to see them in three quarter profile.

EMOTION AND WEAPON FOCUS

Eyewitnesses are likely to be afraid or angry during the crime; this is particularly likely if the eyewitness is physically threatened at the time. In general, high levels of stress at the time of the event impair the accuracy of testimony. In contrast, low to moderate levels of stress may improve memory.

Research also has examined claims about *weapon focus,* a pattern alleged for eyewitnesses in which their attention is focused on the threatening weapon to the exclusion of all else. Consequently, the weapon (and perhaps details of the hand holding the weapon) will be well remembered, but little else. This is similar to a pattern resulting from emotional arousal, even in the absence of a weapon: According to the Easterbrook hypothesis, emotional arousal also narrows the focus of attention, so that one is less sensitive to many cues in the environment when one is emotionally aroused; as a result, one is likely to remember well the focus of one's attention during an emotional event while remembering other aspects of the event less well.

POSTEVENT LEADING AND MISLEADING QUESTIONS

Eyewitness accounts can be affected by the phrasing of questions. In one study, subjects were asked to estimate how quickly two cars were moving when they *hit* each other; other subjects were asked how quickly the cars were moving when they *smashed into* each other. Subjects in the "hit group" gave appreciably lower estimates than subjects in the "smashed group." In a different study, subjects were less likely to recall seeing a broken headlight if asked, "Did you see a broken headlight?" than if they were asked "Did you see the broken headlight?" This subtle change, from *a* to *the*, doubled the likelihood of a subject reporting the target object.

Leading questions also influence how an event is subsequently remembered. For example, in the hit versus smashed experiment, subjects also were asked 1 week later whether any broken glass was visible in the scene. (None was visible.) Subjects who had been asked the "smashed question" were far more likely to report (falsely) that they had seen glass, compared with subjects who had been asked the "hit question." In the same vein, subjects asked about a stop sign right after viewing an event are subsequently likely to report that they had, in fact, seen a stop sign, even though a yield sign was plainly visible.

Similar results are observed when postevent misinformation is delivered in narrative form rather than in questions. For example, subjects in many studies have witnessed an event, and then have read a description of the same event (analogous to reading a newspaper account or hearing reports from other witnesses). If this description contains false elements (e.g., mentions objects or actions that actually were not part of the original event), these false elements will often be reported subsequently by the eyewitness as part of the remembered sequence. Misinformation introduced in this fashion is capable of changing how people's appearances are remembered (in terms of their age, weight, or facial characteristics), what objects are remembered as being present in the scene, the colors of objects at the scene, and so on. In summary, a wide range of false memories can be planted in this fashion.

Related effects are observed if subjects are asked to recall an event soon after it occurs, and then to recall it again some time later. If errors occur in the initial recollection, they seem to become interwoven with the initial memory, so that subjects are likely to repeat the errors in subsequent testing. This resembles the postevent misinformation paradigm, except that in these studies the misinformation is provided by subjects' own initial recall.

MEMORY ACCURACY AND MEMORY CONFIDENCE

Eyewitnesses are more persuasive when their testimony is delivered with confidence than when their testimony is hedged with hesitation and expressed uncertainty (i.e., juries seem to assume a positive relationship between confidence and memory accuracy and therefore grant more credibility to confident witnesses). However, many studies have observed low or zero correlations between accuracy and confidence; some studies have documented negative correlations, with subjects more confident in their wrong answers than in their right ones. In contrast, some studies have observed positive correlations between confidence and accuracy, with more confident subjects being more accurate. This suggests that there are circumstances in which confidence is predictive of memory accuracy and other circumstances in which it is not. Specifically, confidence expressed after a lineup selection seems to be more closely associated with accuracy than confidence expressed before the lineup. Likewise, confidence is more closely associated with accuracy if the suspect is distinctive in appearance. Other related studies have been reported, each one asking what variables moderate the relation between accuracy and confidence.

The association between accuracy and confidence is never strong, and studies rarely document correlations greater than 0.30 or 0.40. Some studies have documented large errors, even in memories reported with total confidence; the rememberer is completely convinced of the veracity of a memory that happens to be false. Juries rely on confidence in evaluating a witness and therefore overuse confidence in assessing evidence.

OVERALL ACCURACY

Eyewitnesses may overlook many aspects of an event if a weapon is present or if the eyewitness is emotionally aroused. False memories can be planted after the event has occurred. Eyewitness confidence in a recollection is no guarantee of memory veracity. To what extent do these concerns undermine the credibility of eyewitness testimony?

A number of studies have assessed the overall accuracy of subjects' event memory, often focusing on flashbulb events: singular and surprising events that occur in one's life, often with considerable emotional impact. Subjects recall flashbulb events in considerable detail and with impressive confidence, but on close examination, many of these recollections turn out to be incorrect, often in important ways. This underscores the possibility of large-scale memory errors and the dissociation between confidence and memory accuracy.

Recall of flashbulb events is often rather accurate, overall, with subjects remembering many details even months after the event. Yuille and Cutshall examined memory for an actual crime witnessed by 13 bystanders, assessing eyewitnesses' memory 4 to 5 months after the event. In evaluating the memories, Yuille and Cutshall employed strict criteria (e.g., reported ages had to be within 2 years to be counted as correct and reported weights within 5 pounds). Even with these criteria, witnesses were correct in 83% of the details reported about the action itself, 76% correct in their descriptions of people, and 90% correct in their descriptions of objects at the scene.

CHILDREN AS EYEWITNESSES

Children's reports of an event are often incomplete; children also tend to have little idea about which aspects of the event are relevant to the courts. In addition, children's memory for events is often limited by their poor understanding of the event's causal structure or by their ignorance about various memory strategies. Despite these limitations, reasonably full and accurate reports can be elicited from children, even as young as 3 or 4 years of age. Children's recall, although sparse, tends to be accurate, and fuller reports can be obtained through the use of props and appropriate questioning. Special care must be taken, however, to minimize leading or misleading questions, because children seem at least as vulnerable as adults to the effects of postevent information. Finally, concern is often expressed that children's memories indiscriminately mix imagined and actual events. However, mixing is less common than is widely thought.

TECHNIQUES FOR IMPROVING EYEWITNESS RECOLLECTION

Police officers and other trained observers seem no more accurate than untrained individuals as eyewitnesses, although most people expect a memory advantage for law-enforcement professionals. Geiselman and colleagues have developed an approach for questioning eyewitness. Their cognitive interview employs several strategies to aid witnesses in retrieving information from memory. For example, witnesses are encouraged to recount the event in more than one sequence and from more than one perspective; witnesses also are led to reconstruct the environmental and personal context of the witnessed event. Evidence indicates that this technique is useful for improving both adult and child testimonies.

For many years, hypnosis was widely believed to enhance eyewitness testimony, according to the hypothesis that hypnotized witnesses would provide more complete accounts of the remembered event. Research has cast considerable doubt on this hypothesis. In general, hypnosis does not improve memory. Hypnosis does render the subject quite compliant and suggestible, leading hypnotized subjects to report more about the remembered event. However, in the absence of any memory facilitation, this report may include a certain amount of "confabulation" (i.e., sincere but false reconstruction of the target event, often incorporating details suggested by the questioner). Given this observation, most psychologists (and most courts) are skeptical about the value of hypnotically induced testimony.

CHILD PSYCHOLOGY
COGNITIVE ABILITIES

CRIME
CURVILINEAR RELATIONSHIP
EXPERT TESTIMONY
FORENSIC PSYCHOLOGY
IMPRESSION FORMATION
POLICE PSYCHOLOGY
SELECTIVE ATTENTION

D. REISBERG

F

FACE VALIDITY

Face validity can be defined as the degree to which a test respondent views the content of a test and its items as relevant for the situation being considered.

Face valid tests have content that is readily identifiable by test respondents and easily susceptible to faking, either consciously or unconsciously. Test developers who possess a theoretical orientation that assumes that individuals will not present themselves openly and honestly believe that face valid tests will result in inaccurate responses and, consequently, that such tests should be avoided. Alternatively, test constructors who adopt the theoretical perspective that people will present themselves openly and honestly believe that direct, transparent (i.e., face valid) tests are those of choice.

The research on technical validity has shown significant positive associations between face validity and accuracy. That is, test items having face validity, on the average, tend to be more technically valid or accurate (i.e., be better items because they tend to be more strongly associated with an appropriate criterion) than those items not possessing face validity. In addition, in situations where test respondents have been asked to fake their answers, face valid items (which are supposedly more susceptible to faking) were no less accurate than items that were not face valid.

The face validity of a test is an important factor for issues of public relations and litigation. Psychological testing should not be an antagonistic and irrelevant exercise for test respondents. Cooperation and good rapport between testers and testtakers is sound practice in all circumstances. The presence of face validity enhances the perceived relevance of a psychological test and reduces the likelihood of feelings of depersonalization and resentment in the individual being tested. A lack of face validity (regardless of technical validity or accuracy) may result in feelings of anger and frustration and of being cheated. Such feelings may well be acted upon, resulting in negative media publicity, public demands for the ending of assessment programs (e.g., in schools), labor–management confrontations, or even the initiation of legal proceedings.

COMPUTERIZED ADAPTIVE TESTING
CULTURE FAIR TESTS
TEST ANXIETY

R. R. HOLDEN

FACIAL EXPRESSIONS

Facial expressions communicate basic emotions: happiness, anger, disgust, sadness, and fear combined with surprise. People everywhere—including those in preliterate cultures—find it easy to identify the signs of these basic emotions. Moreover, such expressions occur spontaneously in young infants and in congenitally blind and deaf children.

Many psychologists interpret the universality of basic facial expressions as programmed by heredity. Alternatively, expressions may derive either from learning that is constant for the species or from the biologically adaptive responses of newborns.

Not all facial expressions carry universal messages. A likely possibility is that people pick up cultural display rules through observation.

Facial expressions play an important role in early human social relationships. From the first, they communicate vital information. The newborn's facial musculature is fully formed and functional at birth. The cry face—along with crying, the universal sign of distress—summons the caretaker to remedy problems. Social smiling, defined as smiling by an infant fixating on a caretaker, appears at around 3 to 4 weeks of age. Smiling is one of those infantile behaviors that seems to win caretakers over, stimulating the intense attachment feelings that bind adult and infant, increasing the baby's chances of receiving excellent care during its long developmental period.

Facial expressions after infancy provide accurate information to others about the occurrence of pleasant and unpleasant emotional states.

Facial expressions have other measurable effects on social behavior that psychologists have just begun to sample. In one study students learned more from teachers who showed positive rather than negative emotional expressions. In another study, the aggression of an instructor was affected by the learner's facial expression. Teachers were less likely to punish learners who looked angry and more likely to punish those who appeared happy.

EMOTIONS
GESTURES

L. L. DAVIDOFF

FACTITIOUS DISORDERS

A factitious disorder is characterized by symptoms "manufactured" by the patient that do not arise from the natural course of an illness. The person's goal is apparently to assume the "patient" role—in contrast to malingering, in which the goal and payoff are more directly observable.

Factitious *psychological* disorders include many patients who seek repeated psychiatric hospitalization by feigning hallucinations, delusions, and suicidal or violent ideation.

Patients with *medical* factitious disorders may have simulated, self-inflicted, or self-maintained symptoms. A patient may have a "fever" caused by manipulating a thermometer; however, a fever may exist secondary to self-injection of a harmful substance, or an existing fever may be maintained by surreptitiously rejecting prescribed medication. Patients with chronic factitious illness, sometimes called the Munchausen syndrome, travel from hospital to hospital presenting a medical emergency (generally with pain and bleeding) and providing a convoluted but believable history. They cannot easily be ignored because they may have serious medical problems or iatrogenic illnesses. Many of these patients use medical terminology with ease, are substance abusers, and may have a prison record.

MALINGERING
SOMATOPSYCHICS

L. PANKRATZ

FACTOR ANALYSIS

Factor analysis is a general label applied to a set of statistical procedures designed to identify basic dimensions or *factors* that underlie the relationships among a large number of variables.

Historically, factor analysis began with Francis Galton, who was concerned with the relationships between intelligence and anthropometric data, and Karl Pearson, who developed mathematical techniques for portraying points in space by lines and planes. The work of Galton suggested the concept of "latent factors" to account for the interrelated variables, whereas Pearson provided the earliest mathematical tools for constructing models to identify them.

The most recognized beginning of modern factor analytic techniques is the work of Charles Spearman, who attempted to account for the correlations among various aptitudes in the hope of measuring general intelligence. He proposed that those correlations could be generated by the combination of a single general-intelligence factor and secondary or "specific" factors that reflect the unique qualities of individual aptitude measures. Subsequent investigators enlarged Spearman's model of a general factor linearly combined with specific factors by adding the concept of "common" or "group" factors. L. L. Thurstone, in proposing his "centroid method," particularly championed extended factor models, which he referred to as "multiple factor analysis."

Over the years, investigators have developed a wide diversity of factor analytic techniques and mathematical models for factor analysis. Different approaches are currently valid for different research problems, depending on both the goal of the research and the underlying assumptions made by the researcher about the basic nature of human attributes. Computers have given the researcher a very rapid and efficient tool for greatly expanded multivariate approaches.

In conducting a factor analysis, variables such as scores on psychological tests, responses to questionnaire items, or quantified biographical data are correlated with one another. The resulting correlations are arrayed in an *intercorrelation matrix*, a chart displaying each of the correlation coefficients for every possible pair of variables being analyzed. Then, with one of a variety of specific factor analytic techniques, the relationships among the variables in the matrix are accounted for by mathematically reducing them to a number of basic dimensions or factors. If the correlations among the variables in the intercorrelation matrix are close to zero, then no factors will emerge from the factor analysis.

The term *factor structure* essentially refers to the set of factors derived from a factor analysis. Some of those factors are *common factors,* or factors that are shared to varying degrees among the variables, and *specific factors* unique to individual variables. Each variable in the analysis is accounted for by a linear combination of common and specific factors. In describing a factor analysis, each variable in the matrix is numerically expressed in terms of its *factor loading,* which refers to the extent to which that variable is "loaded onto" a given factor. Factor loadings vary between minus one and plus one because they are actually correlation coefficients between the factors mathematically derived in the analysis and the variables in standardized form. Thus, for example, if a particular intelligence test has a factor loading of 0.80 on a factor labeled as "verbal ability," the test is said to be highly loaded on verbal ability.

Many variables share something in common with one another. That "shared something" is the *commonality* of a given variable. It is expressed numerically, varying from zero to one, and represents the proportion of variability that a given variable shares, in one or more factors, with the other variables in the set analyzed.

The proportion of variability left over after the communality is called *specificity,* which reflects the uniqueness of a given variable.

Factors are actually hypothetical variables or "constructs" that portray the degree of interrelationships among the variables being analyzed. The meaning of a given factor is summarized from the attributes of those variables highly loaded on that factor. Thus, factor analysis enables the researcher to explore hypotheses regarding the basic dimensions underlying collections of related variables. It is an important technique for determining the minimum number of such dimensions needed to account for the variability among those variables.

CLUSTER ANALYSIS
EMPIRICAL RESEARCH METHODS
MULTIVARIATE ANALYSIS METHODS

A. E. DAHLKE

FACTOR-ANALYZED PERSONALITY QUESTIONNAIRES

In contrast to the subjective nature of psychoanalytic structures that dominated personality theory throughout the 1930s, psychometrically oriented psychologists embraced factor analysis as a means of bringing mathematical precision to the task of mapping the personality trait domain. However, the factor analytic approach has not paid off as fully as expected. There are many unresolved issues in personality measurement, and a wide gulf remains between the precision of the computational procedures and the deceptive lack of objectivity of the factor analytic methods.

Despite these problems, significant contributions have been made both in the delineation of trait taxonomies and in the development of factored personality inventories. R. B. Cattell, J. P. Guilford, and H. J. Eysenck have stood for many years as the major pioneering figures for factored trait theories of personality. Some methodological advances in their later work have incorporated progress in factor analytic and psychometric techniques, as well as the use of powerful computers that were not available for their principal developmental effort.

MULTITRAIT MEASUREMENTS

S. B. SELLS

FACTORIAL DESIGNS

A factorial design is one in which the effects of *two or more factors* on a dependent variable are studied simultaneously. Because the factors are dealt with in the same design, both their individual effects (main effects) and their joint effects (interactions) on the dependent variable can be assessed.

SINGLE-FACTOR DESIGNS

To make the preceding definition more understandable, first consider a design that is not factorial, namely, a single-factor design. Suppose an investigator wishes to assess the effects of fatigue on test performance by using three groups of subjects: a low fatigue group, a moderate fatigue group, and a high fatigue group. Because fatigue level is the variable manipulated or controlled by the investigator, it is referred to as the independent variable or *factor* in the design. In this example, the fatigue factor would be said to have three *levels,* one for each of the groups in the design. More generally, the single factor in this design may be referred to as A, and the levels of the factor as A_1, A_2, and A_3. (see Figure 1).

Test performance is measured for each subject and is referred to as the dependent variable. The goal of such a study would generally be to determine whether the dependent variable varied as a function of factor A. If, however, performance differed across levels of A by more than reasonably would be expected on the basis of random variability, we would say that the effect of factor A was statistically significant. A general statistical procedure for testing whether a factor has a significant effect is *analysis of variance*. Techniques also exist for testing more specific hypotheses (e.g., does performance at level A_3 differ significantly from that at A_1, and does performance at A_3 differ significantly from the average performance at A_1, and A_2?).

TWO-FACTOR DESIGNS

In a factorial design, more than one factor is employed. We can change the one-factor design into a factorial design by adding a second factor. Suppose that, along with the factor of fatigue, we have a second factor of test difficulty with two levels: easy and hard. More generally, we can say that a second factor B with levels B_1 and B_2 has been added to the design, so that the design is now as indicated in Figure 2.

In such a design—referred to as a 3×2 design because the first factor has three levels and the second factor has two—the effects of fatigue and test difficulty can be studied, as can their joint or combined effects. In the 3×2 design there are 3 times 2 or 6 groups, one for each combination of levels. Each group in the design is represented by one cell in Figure 2. For example, one group would be in the low fatigue condition and be given the easy test; another group would be in the high fatigue condition and be given the easy test, and so on.

At this point, matters can be clarified by using an *idealized* numerical example. We will assume (a) that there are equal numbers of subjects assigned to each group in the design, and (b) that there are no effects of random variability or measurement error, so that any differences obtained among groups will be due to *real* effects of the factors.

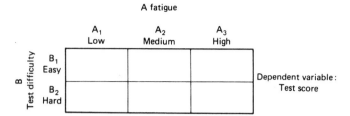

Figure 2. A 3×2 factorial design.

In Figure 3 the number in each cell represents mean test performance for subjects in the corresponding condition of the design. For example, subjects in the medium fatigue condition taking the hard test have a mean score of 50, whereas the subjects in the low fatigue condition taking the easy test have a mean score of 80. The numbers outside the table (called "marginals" because they are in the margins) represent the mean scores obtained at each level of each factor.

MAIN EFFECTS

A factor A is said to have a main effect if the mean scores on the dependent variable vary by virtue of being at different levels of the factor A. In our example there is a main effect of test difficulty because the mean score in the easy test condition (70) differs from the mean score in the difficult test condition (50). There is also a main effect of fatigue because the mean scores for the low, medium, and high fatigue conditions—70, 60, and 50, respectively—are not all the same (see Figure 4).

INTERACTIONS

It is also possible that there will be *joint effects* of these factors over and above the main effects. Such joint effects are referred to as *interactions*. An interaction between two factors A and B will be said to occur if the effect of one factor is *not* the same at every level of the other factor. In Figure 3, the main effect of test difficulty is 20 points. There is no interaction between test difficulty and fatigue because the effect of test difficulty is 20 points at each fatigue level. In this situation the factors A and B are said to be additive because the difference in mean scores between groups A_1B_1 (the group at level A_1 of A and at level B_1 of B) and A_2B_2 (i.e., $80 - 50 = 30$) can be obtained by adding the difference between A_1 and A_2 (10) to the difference between B_1 and B_2 (20). This holds for all combinations of A and B if there is no A X B interaction.

In Figure 5 the main effects are exactly the same as in Figure 3, but the B factor has different effects at the different levels of A. Test difficulty makes a difference of only 10 points for the low fatigue group, but a difference of 20 points for the medium fatigue group and 30 points for the high fatigue group. It can also be seen that the level of fatigue makes less difference in test performance for the easy test condition than it does for the difficult test. Finally, it can be seen that we do not have complete

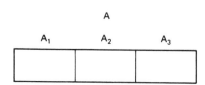

Figure 1. A single-factor design with three levels.

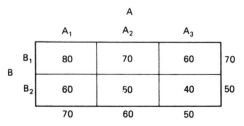

Figure 3. A 3×2 factorial design with no interaction.

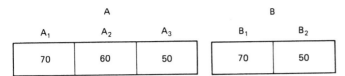

Figure 4. Main effect information available from Figure 3.

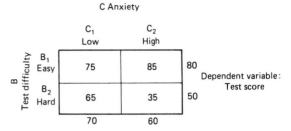

C Anxiety

Figure 6. A 2 × 2 design with an interaction.

additivity: The difference between the mean scores for cells A_1B_1 (75) and A_2B_2 (50) cannot be obtained by adding the differences between the mean scores for A_1 and A_2 (10) and B_1 and B_2 (20). In this case we would say that there is an A × B interaction, or an interaction between the factors of fatigue and test difficulty.

Interactions and main effects are logically independent. For example, consider the somewhat different design illustrated in Figure 6. The two factors are subject anxiety (with levels of low anxiety and high anxiety) and test difficulty (with levels of easy and hard).

In this case there is a very large interaction between anxiety and test difficulty. Test difficulty makes a mean difference of 10 points in test score for the low anxiety group, but a 50-point difference for the high anxiety group. In the easy test condition the high anxiety group actually does better than the low anxiety group, although increased anxiety hampers performance in the hard test condition. In this example there is a main effect of test difficulty because the mean test score in the easy test condition is 30 points greater than the mean test score in the hard test condition. This main effect is easy to interpret because increased test difficulty hampers performance at both levels of anxiety. There is also an overall main effect of anxiety, but this effect must be interpreted with great caution. Although low anxiety, when averaged over levels of test difficulty, resulted in higher test scores, low anxiety actually resulted in worse performance in the easy test condition.

There are certain advantages in dealing with a number of factors simultaneously in one design rather than dealing with the factors individually in a series of studies. The major advantage is that interactions between factors can be studied, which is not possible in single-factor designs. Moreover, main effects can be interpreted more appropriately. Low anxiety, when averaged over the two levels of test difficulty, results in better test performance than high anxiety, but this is not the case for the easy test condition.

Although each of our examples has employed only two factors, in principle any number of factors may be used. For each factor in the design, it may be determined whether or not there is a main effect. For each pair of factors, A and B, it may be determined whether or not there is an A times B interaction. An interaction between two variables is referred to as a first-order interaction. Higher order interactions involve more than two factors. For example, if A, B, and C are all factors in a design, there will be an A times B times C interaction if the A times B interaction is not the same at each level of C (or equivalently, if the A times C interaction is not the same at each level of B, or if the B times

C interaction is not the same at each level of A). Usually it is extremely difficult to interpret interactions involving more than two or three factors.

WITHIN- AND BETWEEN-SUBJECTS FACTORS

In working with factorial designs, a distinction must be drawn between factors for which repeated measures are made on the same subjects, and factors that do not use repeated measures. If a score is obtained for each subject at each of the levels of the factor A, the factor is called a *within-subjects factor*. If no subject has a score at more than one level of A, then A is called a *between-subjects factor*. Obviously, certain factors (e.g., sex) are inherently between-subjects factors. However, in many studies the investigator may choose whether a particular factor is to be a within-subjects or a between-subjects factor, and frequently the use of within-subjects factors results in greater efficiency.

In general, the interpretations of main effects and interactions are the same whether the factors are between-subjects or within-subjects factors. However, the assumptions necessary for statistical analysis and details of statistical analyses do vary, depending on whether the factors involved in the design are all between-subjects factors, all within-subjects factors, or some mixture of the two. In all cases, the statistical analyses can be thought of as trying to aid in the decision as to whether a particular effect (main effect or interaction) is "real," or whether the effect occurred only because of random variability and would not reliably occur if the study was repeated.

EXPERIMENTAL DESIGNS
RESEARCH METHODOLOGY
STATISTICS IN PSYCHOLOGY

A. D. WELL

FACULTY PSYCHOLOGY

The term *faculty psychology* applies to a large number of theories, all of which divided the mind into a collection of separate powers or faculties. The idea is ancient and appealing, and is well entrenched in everyday, common-sense psychology. When we say someone has "a good memory," we imply memory faculty. It is an easy and straightforward way of explaining behavior and personality.

Aristotle provided the basis for many later classical and medieval speculative psychologies. These frequently combined Aristotle's faculty psychology with primitive—and often fanciful—conceptions of the human brain, producing the earliest literature on localization of brain functions. The number of faculties and brain centers proposed varied, but that the brain was the seat of the mind was finally established.

Popular though it was with philosophers and physicians, faculty psychology did not escape criticism. William of Ockham (d. 1349) pointed out that, from the fact that the mind can perform a given function, one cannot conclude that it possesses a distinct and separate faculty for that

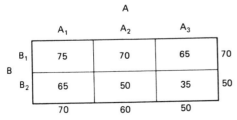

Figure 5. A 3 × 2 design with an interaction.

function. For example, people clearly remember things, but this does not mean that there is a mental power called "memory." Ockham proposed instead that the mind is unitary, but that it can do a number of things. Memory is simply the act of remembering; it does not need a special interior memory unit. Ockham's criticism anticipates later attacks on other faculty psychologies for falling into circular reasoning: The only evidence we have for the inferred memory faculty is that people can remember, and then we explain remembering by reference to the faculty of memory.

The idea of dividing the mind into faculties continued into the modern philosophical period. Although René Descartes said the soul was an undivided unity, he assigned it only one function—thinking. He retained other faculties, but assigned them to mechanical brain functioning, not to the free thought of the soul. John Locke also furnished the mind with a set of mental powers, and this became a commonplace of philosophical psychology; arguments centered, not on the existence of the faculties, but on how many there were and whether they were innate or learned.

In the late eighteenth and early nineteenth centuries, two especially important faculty systems were developed. The first was Scottish common-sense philosophy, founded by Thomas Reid. Reid divided the mind into 31 God-given powers, such as language, gratitude, duty, and memory. Reid's system was elaborated into a complete psychology by his student Dugald Steward, who proposed 48 powers, adding, for example, the sense of the ridiculous and moral taste. The Scottish system was enormously popular and widely taught, especially in the United States. When experimental psychology began in America, it had to contend with entrenched common-sense psychology for academic recognition.

The other new system of faculties that arose at this time was craniology, founded by Franz Joseph Gall, although Gall harshly criticized faculty psychologists. His system was tidied up into a philosophy named phrenology and popularized by Gall's erstwhile assistant, J. C. Spurzheim. Gall proposed that the mind and brain were divided into distinct and parallel organs. Unlike earlier faculty psychologists, Gall took a biological rather than a philosophical approach, and proposed faculties that showed individual differences among ordinary people and served biological ends of individuals and species such as love of offspring, self-preservation, and kindness. Unfortunately, Gall assumed that the contours of the skull revealed the power of underlying brain organs, and his followers' practice degenerated into pseudoscientific skull reading not too different from palm reading. Frequently condemned by the establishment, phrenology was nonetheless popular with the educated public, with artists such as Edgar Allen Poe, and with reformers such as the educator Horace Mann.

Strictly speaking, faculty psychology died in the twentieth century, at least as regards scientific psychology. Here and there, however, one can still detect the faculty idea at work in trait theories of personality and decompositions of intellect into subcomponents.

MEMORY
PHILOSOPHICAL PSYCHOLOGY
STRUCTURALISM

T. H. LEAHEY

FADS AND FASHIONS

Fads and fashions are highly visible changes in some aspect of social behavior, which may continue to be salient for varying periods of time and important to substantial proportions of the population.

Fads differ from fashions in several ways. Fad innovators may be found anywhere in the society, whereas fashions tend to originate in socioeconomic extremes and to support the established socioeconomic status system. Fads reflect the past hardly at all, whereas fashions are likely to reflect some periodicity. Fads may not appear for a period of time, but there is continuity in fashion.

FADS

A fad is a widespread preoccupation with an object of interest, a kind of behavior, or a point of view that is of limited duration and is indulged in immoderately. The preoccupation reaches a substantial proportion of the population, among whom it is conspicuous. The term "craze" is often used synonymously with fad.

Fads are particularly likely to be found in the area of recreation where there are relatively few deeply anchored attitudes that would have to be displaced.

In many cases, fads go through five phases. During the first, the idea is introduced and makes little progress. The notion catches on in the second phase and reaches peak momentum by the third. In the fourth phase, there is a drop in the number of new users and a decline in the enthusiasm of the older users. By the fifth and last phase, the fad has become a mere curiosity.

FASHION

Fashion is a relatively short-term change in style of appearance, clothing, furniture, or artifacts, which is almost compulsory and typically goes through four phases. When a fashion first appears, it may be greeted with derision but often catches on quickly and becomes dominant by its second phase. The fashion consolidates its gains in the third phase, becoming widely accepted. As part of the dominant culture in this third phase, it remains so until supplanted in the fourth phase.

Throughout the 1960s fashion could be explained by the trickle-down theory, according to which new approaches were first tried by an upper-class avant-garde, whose activities were widely reported in the mass media. Copies of the new fashion were then made for the middle classes. Subsequently, their peers tried the items, after which cheaper versions were made for the lower classes. Changes in the American social structure in the 1960s after the assassination of John F. Kennedy in 1963 led to a kind of "trickle-up" approach to fashion, with groups previously considered pariahs contributing new ideas that were then adopted by middle- and upper-class women, such as boots, colored stockings, miniskirts, and hot pants.

With the expansion of the women's liberation movement after 1968, society became less interested in women whose major activity was the wearing of expensive new clothing.

James Laver, with his *Style in costume,* has documented the operation of parallel forces regulating fashion in clothing, architecture, and furniture. Thus, during the 1920s the same straight-line shape could be found in skyscrapers, chairs, and the clothing worn by men and women. Charles Winick, in *The new people,* has related the prevalent silhouette of several epochs to the shape of their morality. Other interpretations of fashion have been economic, Marxist, psychoanalytic in terms of shifting erogenous zones, and anthropological in terms of cultural trends and predictable movements of style.

DRESS
INFLUENCE THEORY
PEER INFLUENCES
SOCIAL INFLUENCE THEORY

C. WINICK

FAMILY CRISES

One of the pioneering efforts in the study of family crises was by Ruben Hill, who evaluated the effects of stress related to family separation and reunion resulting from World War II. Hill derived the "ABC-X" formulation of crisis as well as the "roller coaster" adjustment course. The crisis formulation involves the event (potential stressor), termed A, interacting with the resources of the family in regard to the event, termed B, both of which interact with the definition of the event made by the family, termed C, all of which together produce X, the crisis. The course of recovery or adjustment involves initially a period of disorganization followed by an "angle" of recovery, leading to a new level of organization.

Thomas McMurrain described three categories of events that precipitate crisis: maturational events, exhaustion, and shock. *Maturational events* are transitional points that naturally occur as the family moves through its life cycle. Jay Haley stated that family stress peaks at transition points in the life cycle. Carter and McGoldrick divided life-cycle stressors into vertical and horizontal elements. Vertical stressors are passed to a family from a previous generation and include family patterns, myths, and issues. Horizontal stressors are what the family experiences as it transits from one stage of development to another.

Exhaustion results from an extended period of coping, which eventually produces a crisis arising from persistent stress. Some examples include long-term illness, marital incompatibility, and poverty-level existence over an extended period of time. The effects of exhaustion crisis are less dramatic in their precipitation. Because an exhaustion crisis may present with undramatic symptoms, it may be mistaken by those in the helping professions as unwillingness to cooperate or as irresponsibility to follow through, when the response may, in fact, result from the disorganization associated with exhaustion crisis.

Shock crisis is characterized by an event that occurs over a relatively short period of time and results in a sudden shock to the family, rendering it temporarily unable to cope. The crisis includes both profound and dramatic tragedies that occur unexpectedly, regardless of the mental health and stability of the family.

The problem-solving methods and coping strategies of the family are important in the family's response to crisis. David Reiss and his associates found that the family's method of problem solving could predict whether the family would become involved in a rehabilitation program for one of its members. Often the family with well-developed problem-solving abilities is able to handle a problem successfully, and in so doing precludes the occurrence of crisis.

Official support networks include neighborhood, family, kin, and mutual self-help groups. Neighborhoods that are cohesive and aware of crises among their members are more likely to respond in a helpful manner when a family is in crisis.

Kinship likewise can provide significant support in a crisis situation. However, the trend in the last few decades is toward the nuclear family. This cuts off kinship relationships that could otherwise reduce family stress in times of crisis. In response to this need for support, self-help groups are becoming more common. Such groups provide information and emotional support for specific types of crises.

Strengthening the individual or family unit may take many forms. Reestablishing ties with extended family members who have been out of contact due to distance or other reasons can provide external family support. Working with individual members of the family on stress reduction and coping techniques often provides a significant increase in the overall problem-solving abilities of the family unit. This approach is particularly effective in an exhaustion crisis.

Increasing adaptability in the family is especially appropriate when the family is limited by its perceptions of the event or handicapped by inadequate problem-solving skills. Redefining the perception of the problem can frequently be achieved by helping the family to more fully define the factors in the problem and their own emotional response to it. Increasing problem-solving skills may require nothing more than teaching some basic steps in problem solving, or it may range to full-fledged family therapy as a way of altering dysfunctional modes and approaches to problem definition and problem solving.

The extent and duration of the intervention will in large part be determined by the disruption caused by the crisis, the family's ability to adapt, and the resources available to the family. It is not unusual for a family to initially request external intervention in a crisis situation, then carry out the remainder of the crisis resolution independently as the family returns to self-sufficiency.

CRISIS INTERVENTION
FAMILY THERAPY
MULTIPLE FAMILY THERAPY

R. P. KAPPENBERG

FAMILY THERAPY

DESCRIPTION OF FAMILY THERAPY

Family therapy may be described as the attempt to modify relationships within the context of the family system. It views symptomatic behavior and problems as the result of faulty interactions, rather than as the property of a given family member. It is interpersonal rather than intrapsychic.

This theoretical framework leads therapeutically to a way of conceptualizing family process in which each member has a role in the maintenance of the system. The "identified patient" may be seen as the "problem," but the "cause" is the dysfunctional family system itself. It is the therapist's role to change the system by proper interventions. Various schools have arisen that differ on technique, but agree on the basic principle that the system—and not any individual—is the problem.

A system is made up of interdependent parts that have mutual causality, each part being related over a period of time so that there is some stability. Systems are either *open*—having a continuous flow or being subject to change—or *closed*. A family is an open system; a steam heating system is a closed system. An open system is characterized by three properties: wholeness, relationship, and equifinality.

Wholeness means that the system is constituted by its interaction and not just by the number of people present. *Relationship* refers to the interactions going on in the system—what is happening in the family among the members: their ongoing interactions and their repetitive patterns. *Equifinality* is the property of systems whereby they function independently of initial causes and can be changed by intervention in the here and now: They are not determined by their initial parameters.

FOUR HISTORICAL CONCEPTS

Some early concepts that form the roots of the four current major theories are as follows.

1. *Interlocking Pathologies.* Nathan Ackerman introduced the concept of interlocking pathologies, whereby the problems of one family member are tied up with interactions with other members. Ackerman saw these entangled roots in the family system and felt they were largely unconscious. The concept of interlocking, unconscious pathologies is endorsed by the school of Object Relations.

2. *Fusion.* Murray Bowen introduced the concept of fusion, originally noted in the families of schizophrenics, but present in so-called normal ones as well. Fusion means that various family members cannot act independently of one another and are stuck together, forming a vague, amorphous mass. Bowen therapy attempts to unhook family members from one another.

3. *Pseudomutuality.* Lyman Wynne and his associates observed a false kind of closeness or intimacy, which they labeled "pseudomutuality," characterized by a loss of boundaries among family members. As a way of coping with this pseudointimacy, Wynne suggested changing boundaries by breaking up existing alignments and splits to create new coalitions. Minuchin called this concept "enmeshment." The goal of structural family therapy is the creation of new alliances that seek to help "enmeshed" or "disengaged" family members become more independent. Structural family therapy is based largely on Wynne's thinking.

4. *The Double Bind.* "The double bind may be described briefly as an interaction pattern characterized by 'severe limitations' imposed by paradoxical communication in an 'intensely important relationship' that results in an 'untenable solution,' but one from which its participants are 'unable to extricate themselves' " (Abeles). Such processes are found in an extreme form in schizophrenic families, but also in a milder form in healthy ones. This discovery led investigators to look more closely at the rules governing communication. Bateson observed that every message has two aspects: a report and a command. The command aspect follows a series of rules, determined over a period of time, which tend to become self-perpetuating. This observation led to the notion that it is not necessary to delve into the origin of symptoms to produce change, but only to look at the behavior that perpetuates the system.

MAJOR SCHOOLS OF FAMILY THERAPY

There are presently four major schools in family therapy: Object Relations Theory, Bowen Theory, Structural Family Therapy, and Communication Theory.

Object Relations Theory

This approach traces its origin from Melanie Klein, who stated that interaction with others is not for the purpose of satisfying instinctual needs, but rather for the development of the self to differentiate between the self and objects.

A therapist working from this point of view will concentrate on unconscious denied projections, noting especially collusion—the cooperation of family members—in this process. Therapists from this school tend to spend more time on history and transgenerational issues than on symptoms, seeing the latter as caused by the former.

Bowen Theory

Bowen Theory has evolved into an integrated system. The system involves eight interlocking concepts: (a) triangles (under stress one person in a relationship fuses with a third party), (b) differentiation of self (the degree or extent of fusion), (c) a nuclear family emotional system (the patterns of functioning in one generation), (d) family projection process (the mechanism by which the nuclear family system produces impairment in a child), (e) emotional cutoff (the relationship with a family of origin), (f) multigenerational transmission (how pathology gets transmitted through the generations), (g) sibling position (determining how one views the world), and (h) societal regression (the problems of society are similar to those found in the family).

The goal of Bowen Theory is to help an individual become differentiated or unstuck from the family as the individual moves from a state of fusion to establish a "solid" self as opposed to a "pseudo" self in which one is still fused. The therapist is seen as a "coach" who teaches the family members to differentiate. Feelings are deemphasized and thinking is stressed. The process of differentiation is a lifetime task, as one struggles to stay in touch with the family system and still remain differentiated.

The triangle is "the basic building block of any emotional system" (Bowen). When the anxiety level rises between a couple, they involve a "third party" to maintain the balance of the system. This idea has proven fruitful in family therapy and has helped countless therapists to understand the role of symptoms, affairs, and psychosomatic illness in a way leading to new kinds of interventions.

Structural Family Therapy

Salvador Minuchin devised short-term methods aimed at rearranging family structures.

Minuchin's interventions derived from the ideas of realignment set forth by Lyman Wynne and the theories of H. S. Sullivan. Minuchin's goal is to change the structure of the alliances and coalitions of family members, and by so doing to change their experiences of one another.

Minuchin focuses on the ongoing interactions in the family that tend to reinforce existing behavior. He sees the family organization as posing the problem in family maladjustment, in that it needs the symptomatic member for its functioning. He aims at changing its present structure without a concern for origins. The family system is dysfunctional in the here and now because of its present organization, and not because of historical antecedents. The past does not concern the structural family therapist.

Communication Theory

This approach is a direct descendant of the Bateson theory of the double bind, which views pathology as a problem of communication. The emphasis here is totally on the current systemic interaction without any concern for the causes or origins of the problem.

The goal of this approach is to change the rules of the system. This may mean prescribing symptoms or using paradox as a way of changing the rules.

FAMILY CRISES
SYSTEMS THEORY

V. FOLEY

FANTASY

The word "fantasy" designates (a) the fantasizing ability as well as (b) the product of that function.

Fantasy holds a position between thinking and sensing or perceiving. When the mind actually produces fantasies, the fantasizer experiences that inflow on a receptive level. Although the output of fantasies can be elicited and their direction and content influenced by conscious intentions, usually fantasies emerge unconsciously, determined by memories, by past and primarily current emotional states, and by hopes and expectations for the future.

Fantasy produces what is not, what someday may or may not be, and what never has been. Fantasy also can merely distort reality. The production of the unreal generally takes place in the service of the ego. Whether fantasy as a creative function can produce anything authentically new that is not merely a new combination or a formulation of contents or content fragments of elements already available to knowledge and experiences has remained a philosophical question ever since Aristotle's *De anima*.

In its *primary* form a fantasy appears spontaneously from the unconscious to the receptive subject. *Secondary* fantasies are initiated and pursued from the conscious level, being evoked intentionally for a specific purpose. In the spontaneous fantasy the sense of the unreal is often missing while the fantasy is in progress. Normally, in retrospective analysis the nonreality status is readily assigned to a fantasy. Fantasies can be absorbing, rendering the fantasizing individual incapable of adequately attending to the demands of the environment. If a fantasy is assigned reality status, it stops being a fantasy and by definition enters the pathological realm, as in the cases of delusions, hallucinations, pseudologia fantastica, and paranoia.

Developmentally, fantasies precede the rise of logical thinking. Fantasy plays a considerable part in a child's life, especially as an important element in play. Consonant with the child's egocentric thinking, the fantasy–reality boundaries may be unclear; imaginary companions may be real and unreal at the same time, and children may perceive their fantasy lies as truth. Magical thinking is a realistic component of the fantasy world in which magical fantasies work. Only after the sense of reality has been clearly established can fantasy and delusional thinking in children be separated.

The primary intention of fantasy is to offer an alternative to reality. As such it serves two basic purposes: It stimulates creativity, which develops what is not (yet), and it acts as the psyche's balancing mechanism, offering the person a self-help tool to achieve emotional equilibrium (self-healing).

Nonreality offers humans a refuge from reality. Wish fulfillment, compensation, projection, and escape are among the prevalent mechanisms operating either like safety valves or like (re)vitalizers. For the timid individual, future projection and rehearsal of the not-yet-real act as track builders, making risk taking in reality and success possible.

The destructive use of fantasy exacerbates emotional problems. Seeking permanent refuge in the world of the unreal by assigning reality status to it amounts to sinking into self-deception and creating delusional worlds. Another form of negative outcome can arise when a fantasy used for abreactive purposes takes on the function of a rehearsal, especially if the content is a violent one such as suicide or murder.

Relatively little is known about the healthy, well-adjusted person's fantasy life, which seems to be related to the extent of unmet needs, fears, and desires. Death fantasies are known to be most prevalent in children, adolescents, and the elderly. They center on the person's own natural death, suicide, or murderous inclinations.

Fantasy is also employed for clinical purposes; psychological tests using projective techniques base their results on fantasy projections (as in the Thematic Apperception Test [TAT]). Various psychotherapeutic approaches employ fantasy as an exploratory or therapeutic agent.

CHILDREN'S FEARS
FEAR
ILLUSIONS

E. WICK

FATIGUE

A major problem area in understanding the human is *demand and the ability to meet it.* Demand from within may originate in local tissue or may be attributed to the individual as a person. External demands may be of two sorts—one social and the other purely physical, as when temperature makes demands on the thermoregulating mechanism of the body.

In everyday speech, fatigue is generally defined as inability to meet demand. But to be precise, only those cases in which the organism at the personal level is unable to meet demand should be called fatigue. The tissue changes themselves that reduce ability to function are more appropriately called *impairment.* When this impairment causes the organism at the personal level to become less able to function, the result is fatigue. If the impairment in any tissue is permanent, it is termed *injury.*

The term "fatigue" is commonly misused for cases in which *work decrement*—the slowing down of work—is in evidence, but the reason for work decrement often lies outside the workers themselves. To define fatigue, we can say that (a) something may happen to cells as cells, (b) something may happen to cell groups in some restricted parts of the body, and (c) something may happen whereby the organism as a person may not be able to function.

OCCUPATIONAL STRESS
WORK EFFICIENCY

S. H. BARTLEY

FEAR

Historically considered one of the primary emotions along with joy, anger, and grief, *fear* is the emotion of avoidance of a consciously recognized, usually external, eminent danger. *Anxiety,* in contrast, is the emotion of avoidance to perceived but largely unrecognized dangers, whereas *phobias* are irrational obsessions and intense avoidance of specific objects or situations. Fear, anxiety, and phobias are terms inappropriately used when they are interchanged. In some respects their confusion is understandable, because all three represent a state of arousal that results when an individual recognizes a lack of power or capability to handle some threatening situation, and all three have similar physiological states.

PHYSIOLOGICAL CHANGE

Concomitant aspects of fear are physiological changes primarily induced by the biochemical arouser, adrenaline. Adrenaline basically prepares the skeletal muscles for great strain as might occur in running to escape (flight) or in protecting self and property (fight). If the individual does not engage in vigorous physical activity of some sort following arousal, uncomfortable physiological changes occur such as trembling in arms and legs, general weakness, and heightened awareness of breathing and heart rate. Heart rate, systolic blood pressure, and respiration rate increase in the body's effort to divert blood flow from digestive areas, head, neck, and face to areas such as musculature that are in need of it. If the diversion from the cortex is too swift, there is inhibition of voluntary cortical function, and the individual faints into unconsciousness. This results in vastly reduced heart and breathing rates—not unlike the freezing posture witnessed in animals.

William James and Carl Lange independently arrived at the conclusion that the *experienced somatic state is the emotion:* In short, we are afraid because we tremble. Since the mid-1950s, cognitive theorists have challenged the James-Lange notion by demonstrating that thoughts can elicit the same physiological change as evidenced in an actual fear situation.

Confusion and loss of control such as that which occurs when an individual does not know how to ward off a life threat can lead to feelings of fear.

The notion that *fear is learned* is not new, but this does not detract from its popularity. Early in the twentieth century, John B. Watson provided demonstrations of the conditioning or learned aspects of fear. That is, a neutral or even previously pleasurable object would elicit a fear reaction after it was combined with a noxious conditioning stimulus. Although such learning may be more typical of phobic reactions, it is not unusual to witness similar associations in true fear.

Questions about whether the fear of death is natural as a preservation/reproduction force or whether it is unnatural and dependent on maternal attitudes, perceived security, or some irrational notion of the importance of each individual in society, will be argued for a long time. It is perhaps more important to raise the issue of the *utility* rather than the *innateness* of the fear of death.

The most common usefulness of the fear of death is the avoidance of life-threatening situations. Yet those who confront dangerous situations and attempt to save others are revered. Heroic gestures represent the first and foremost reflex to the terror of death. Christianity also utilized the fear of death as a means of encouraging commitment to correct present lifestyles with the promise of being born again, modeled after Christ's rising from the grave, and of receiving salvation and eternal life.

ANXIETY
CHILDREN'S FEARS
EMOTIONS
FEARS THROUGHOUT THE LIFE SPAN

D. F. FISHER

FEARS THROUGHOUT THE LIFE SPAN

Fears are a common discussion topic among those in the human services delivery fields as well as among the lay public. Some anxiety studies have actually dealt with fears, and some fear studies have investigated anxiety. Fear means that the threatening object, such as bugs, is clearly in focus, whereas with anxiety the threatening object, such as vague feelings of uneasiness, is not clearly in focus.

Measurement is difficult when studying fears. Open-ended interviews with individuals elicit more fears than checklist questionnaires. A confounding factor in the study of fears involves differentiating between just indicating that a fear is held and being really intensely fearful regarding a given item. Some may react with fear to given items, but this fear is not strongly felt. It is difficult to interpret the results of a survey if the researcher has not determined the strength of the indicated fears.

Despite the problems due to research design, it is still possible to offer a meaningful picture of commonly held fears. Younger children generally have more fears and hold them with greater intensity than do older children, adolescents, and adults. Regardless of age, people tend to see themselves as holding fewer fears in the present than in the past, and believe the future will see a further reduction in number. Females, blacks, and lower socioeconomic classes indicate a greater number of fears and more intense fears than do males, whites, and upper socioeconomic classes. Youngest and oldest siblings indicate more fears than those from a middle-born position.

FEARS OF CHILDREN

Without differentiating between number and intensity of fears, we can state that under the age of 4, children most often fear the unfamiliar: noise, objects, and persons. Boys ages 4 through 6 indicated personal safety as their greatest concern, whereas girls indicated noise and conditions associated with noise. At about the age of 8, children become more aware of their total environment and potential dangers; both boys and girls most commonly and intensely report fears of natural phenomena (tornados, hurricanes), ecological fears (polluted water and air), and fears of drugs (getting sick from, or dying from taking, drugs).

At about 11 years of age, ecological and natural phenomena fears continue. Yet there is an even greater concern, as indicated by popularity and intensity, for political items. This appears to reflect an increasing scope of environmental awareness, which now includes the world. By the fifth and sixth grades the majority of children view some of the news on television; viewers now see wars as they occurred that very day.

By age 11, children are more likely to actually have contact with drugs than are younger children, yet there is less indicated fear associated with the closer or actual contact than when the fear was remote, as in the case of younger children. There is evidence for a relationship between holding fears more often and intensely when there is little justification, and for a decreasing fear toward a menacing stimulus with increasing contact. By adolescence there is a clear movement toward adult-type fears that concern personal relations with family and friends.

School-related fears in the mid-1960s had diminished greatly. This decrease in fear by both children and adolescents may be the result of a new generation of parents who did not experience the economic depression of the 1930s.

FEARS OF ADULTS

The trend for educational fears to be secondary continues into the college years when personal relations, political items, and fears of growing old are most common for both sexes. Fears related to education are in reference to the expense involved rather than to achievement. College professors rank fears about the economic conditions in the country and political issues ahead of concerns about mediocre students, pressures to publish, gaining tenure, and lack of academic freedom. Lawyers also rank economic and political fears first, followed by too many immigrants and foreigners buying U.S. land. Physicians rank their fears similarly to lawyers, except that they rank fear of lawsuits first.

Among male blue-collar workers, the most common fears involve economics, personal happiness, and politics. Women—both of upper and lower socioeconomic status—report relationships with others, natural phenomena (thunderstorms, dark places), and political items most frequently, and economics often.

The concern for economic and political items continues into old age for both sexes. The fears of senior citizens are of physical and mental inadequacy, of getting old, and of losing loved ones.

CHILDREN'S FEARS
FEAR

J. W. CROAKE

FECHNER'S LAW

Gustav T. Fechner, professor of physics at the University of Leipzig, sought to measure the mind quantitatively. His interest was in ascertaining how sensations changed with changing stimulation. In his subsequent derivation of Fechner's law, he began with Weber's law—that the just noticeable difference in stimulation is a constant proportion of the stimulus magnitude, or $JND = kI$—and the assumption that the sensation (R) of a stimulus is the cumulative sum of equal sensation increments. Translating this into differential form, he started with $dR = a\, dI/I$ and integrated, under the assumption that R = 0 at the absolute threshold (I_o), to get the equation $R = c \log (I/I_o)$. This equation is Fechner's law, where R is the sensation magnitude, c is a constant (which depends on the logarithmic base and the Weber ratio), I is the stimulus intensity, and I_o is the absolute threshold intensity. The law states that sensations follow a negatively accelerated increasing (logarithmic) curve. For example, the increase in brightness experienced in going from 1 to 10 lamps would be the same as the increase in brightness in going from 10 to 100 lamps. Sensation increases arithmetically when stimulus magnitudes increase geometrically.

PSYCHOPHYSICS
WEBER'S LAW

G. H. ROBINSON

FEMALE SEXUAL DYSFUNCTION

Dysfunctions in female sexuality may occur in each phase of the sexual response cycle: desire, arousal, and orgasm or resolution. In addition, there may be pain or muscle spasm that prevents penile penetration or enjoyment of coitus. All can occur at random, during specific situations, or as a primary dysfunction in which the disorder has always been present.

Sexual dysfunctions in females, as in males, may stem from anxiety. Helen S. Kaplan described the causes as either current or remote. Current or ongoing causes occur during the sexual experience and create distraction, fear, anger, or other unpleasant emotional states; these interfere with the ability to relax and allow sexual arousal to build. Such immediate causes might include fear of failure, performance anxiety, lack of effective sexual technique, failure to communicate desires, or spectatoring—a term coined by William Masters and Virginia Johnson to describe conscious monitoring and judging of sexual behavior. Remote causes are derived from previous childhood experiences, intrapsychic conflict, and/or serious problems within the relationship between sexual partners. Guilt about past sexual experiences, extremely restrictive family and religious backgrounds, traumatic sexual experiences such as incest or sexual assault, or unconscious conflicts that evoke anxiety at the time of sexual encounters may result in maladaptive sexual functioning. Because sexual activities are more discouraged for females in Western cultures, there may be more difficulties in sexual functioning for adult women than for men. When the sexual disorder is absolute and arousal or orgasm has never occurred, remote causes are highly suspect in etiology. Current factors creating anxiety are more typically responsible for random or situational dysfunctions.

Relationship variables are frequent etiological factors. Communication problems, anger, lack of attraction to or love for the partner, power struggles, and lack of trust and respect create rejection, hostility, and distance between sexual partners. This impairs the woman's ability to abandon herself to sexual pleasure.

DISORDERS OF DESIRE

Disorders of desire were identified later than were other dysfunctions, when the scope of sexual performance was expanded to include the preliminary emotional and physical reactions of arousal and desire. Kaplan states that inhibited or hypoactive sexual desire may be the most common, sexual dysfunction.

Inhibited sexual desire (ISD) is referred to in the *Diagnostic and statistical manual, fourth edition* (DSM-IV) as a "persistent and pervasive inhibition of sexual desire" (i.e., the woman experiences low libido, lack of sexual response to genital stimulation, and lack of or very limited interest in and satisfaction with sexual activities). Women may react to this dysfunction with any of a wide range of emotions, from nonchalant acceptance to worry and acute distress. Sexual dysfunction is diagnosed when the individual experiences distress with the symptom. Absolute or primary inhibited desire is rare; situational ISD is more common.

ORGASMIC DYSFUNCTION

Orgasmic dysfunction is present when the female has great difficulty in experiencing orgasm, or is unable to do so with effective sexual stimulation. Adequate desire and physiological and emotional arousal may be present, but anxiety interrupts the arousal buildup prior to the orgasmic relief.

Controversy reigned for many years about the types of female orgasm and the desirability of each. Vaginal and clitoral orgasms were alleged before the work of Masters and Johnson in 1966. With laboratory data, they concluded that all orgasms are essentially similar and consist of sensory input from the clitoris and muscle contractions by the vagina. Conclusive data do not exist concerning the incidence of women who have orgasms during coitus without concurrent clitoral stimulation, although estimates range from 30 to 50%.

VAGINISMUS

Vaginismus is an involuntary spasm of the vaginal muscles that prevents penile penetration. Arousal and orgasm may be present, but penetration is impossible. This spasm is a conditioned response to the anticipation of pain with intercourse; phobic avoidance of intercourse is often present. Etiology may include incidents of rape, painful attempts at coitus, vaginal and pelvic conditions that engender pain with sexual contact (vaginal

infections, endometriosis, pelvic inflammatory disease), or misinformation or ignorance about sex. Vaginismus is a major factor in unconsummated marriages and is accompanied by fantasies of physical injury and pain. Gradual dilation of the vagina in a short time span (a few days) can often eliminate the muscle spasm and allow for penetration.

DYSPAREUNIA

Dyspareunia is similar to vaginismus in that there is pain associated with sexual intercourse; however, the involuntary vaginal muscle spasm is absent. Dyspareunia may be caused by insufficient vaginal lubrication due to lack of sexual arousal, senile vaginitis, or reactions to medication. It may also result from gynecological disorders such as herpes, vaginal infection, endometriosis, rigid hymen, or hymeneal tags. When pain accompanies intercourse, anxiety results, arousal diminishes, and there is avoidance of sexual encounter. Complete physical and pelvic examinations are required in the assessment and treatment of dyspareunia, because of the many physical factors that could contribute to the pain.

Sexual dysfunction typically is treated with some form of sex therapy. Often this is brief, behaviorally focused therapy that aims at symptom removal. Barriers to effective sexual functioning are identified, and a combination of communication and sensual touching assignments are given.

ANXIETY
MALE SEXUAL DYSFUNCTION
NYMPHOMANIA
SEX THERAPY

D. GERARD

FEMINIST THERAPY I

The feminist approach to psychotherapy has grown since about 1970, and incorporates understandings about women's development and mental health arising from the Women's Movement. It is eclectic with regard to techniques, using any that are consistent with a feminist understanding of the ways in which women's position in society influences their psychological development and is a source of distress.

The insight of the Women's Movement that "the personal is political" is the main underlying principle of feminist therapy. Seemingly individual problems are often the result of the social position of women as a group; this has implications for the kinds of therapeutic goals that feminist therapists are willing to undertake. Therapists help women to identify both social and personal sources of problems and to look for solutions that do not involve adjustment to oppressive situations.

A second principle of feminist therapy is that the relationship between client and therapist should be an equal one. The feminist therapist works to create a relationship of equal power and helps the client to examine objective power relationships in other areas of her life as well.

Feminist therapists pay particular attention to the potential for abuse of the power of expertise. They do not assume a superior status because of the expertise they bring to the therapeutic relationship, nor do they allow clients to treat them as superiors. The client is the real expert on herself and her experience. The therapist may suggest new ways of looking at and using that experience, but refrains from giving interpretations and diagnoses. Her task is to validate the client's experience, not to analyze it.

Third, therapy is seen as a value-laden enterprise. Therapists' values influence their work, and those who try to keep them from doing so confuse their clients and may manipulate them with personal beliefs and values presented as facts. The feminist therapist's solution to this problem is to make her values explicit and encourage her clients to do the same. Values that are likely to have a significant impact on the course of therapy (e.g., those having to do with sex-role expectations, sexual orientation and behavior, anger, and dependency) are clarified at the outset and throughout the course of therapy to reduce the likelihood of the client's being manipulated by the therapist.

While leaving the specific content of therapy sessions up to the client, feminist therapists pay particular attention to a cluster of emotional problems that arise because of the social position of women: awareness of anger and its direct expression, learned helplessness and depression, self-nurturance, dependency, and autonomy. More concrete issues frequently include financial independence, choices about sexuality, alternatives to sex roles in structuring relationships, work, and family choices. Feminist therapists support attempts to make life choices that may not be consistent with societal expectations (e.g., remaining child-free, choosing nontraditional work, living in a lesbian relationship) and challenge women's assumptions that they have no alternative but to fit into traditional sex roles. The feminist therapist values the client's assumption of personal power and her ability to make independent decisions, and encourages her to find support from other women in making changes that others around her may resist. Rawlings and Carter point out that it is not sufficient to simply encourage women to develop themselves; they also need support in overcoming the very real barriers to that development.

Feminist therapists are generally women. Male therapists, although they may practice nonsexist therapy in accordance with feminist principles, face two impediments to functioning fully as feminist therapists. First, most men are not able to overcome their own socialization enough to be able to enter into an equal relationship with a woman. Second, it can be argued that, in a sexist society, any relationship between a man and a woman is necessarily an unequal one, regardless of the goodwill of those involved. From this viewpoint, feminist therapy is intrinsically a woman-to-woman relationship.

ASSERTIVENESS TRAINING
PSYCHOTHERAPY
SELF-ACTUALIZATION

S. M. PARRY

FEMINIST THERAPY II

Feminist psychotherapy began to evolve during the late 1960s. It is based on the philosophical tenets of feminism, defined by Webster as "the theory of the political, economic, and social equality of the sexes." Feminist psychotherapy has no founder, no specific techniques, and no unified theoretical base. However, there is considerable agreement among feminist psychotherapists about the philosophical values and feminist principles that compose the underlying belief system.

Feminist psychotherapy is derived from political thought that identifies women as an oppressed group in Western culture. The feminist slogan, "The personal is political," describes an essential element of feminist psychotherapy, emphasizing the sociocultural basis for the development of women's sense of self and the psychological effects of devaluation, powerlessness, stereotyping, and patriarchy. To understand this movement, it is helpful to understand the principal feminist frameworks incorporated into the various forms of psychotherapy.

PRINCIPAL FEMINIST FRAMEWORKS

Feminist philosophies have been used to critique and revise the psychotherapeutic theories ascribed to by particular feminists. Jaggar and Rothenberg have identified three major feminist frameworks: liberal, socialist, and radical. Each framework differs in its conceptualization of women's oppression and methods for promoting equality. Although there are other ways of categorizing and describing the various forms of feminism, the following categorizations are drawn from the writings of Jaggar and Rothenberg.

Liberal feminism is often identified with Betty Friedan, author of *The feminine mystique,* who is credited with beginning the 1960s wave of the women's movement. Liberal feminism focuses on discriminatory legal and social policies that result in unequal civil rights and unequal educational and occupational opportunities. Liberal feminists, such as many members of the National Organization for Women (NOW), focus on eliminating economic and legal barriers to women's equality. They hold that there are minimal biological differences between the sexes and that sexism and the social construction of gender can account for apparent differences.

Socialist feminism draws on Marxist traditions and argues that sex and gender systems constitute the master class structuring of personal, social, and political realities. Women's oppression is not viewed only as the result of class oppression or capitalism. Socialist–Marxist feminists also identify the medical system as being a means of social control because it defines what is healthy or pathological and what is reasonable care. Social feminists expand Marxist theory to analyze how reproduction (not just production) is organized in society. Patriarchy and the nuclear family are seen as major factors in the oppression of women. Thus socialist–Marxist feminists focus on abolishing patriarchy and capitalism, seen as reciprocally mutually reinforcing systems.

In contrast to socialist feminists who believe that human nature is not biologically determined, radical feminists believe there are essential biological differences between the sexes. Within this framework, women are viewed as possessing a unique style, characteristically trusting and cooperative, whereas men are seen as adopting competitive, mistrustful styles. Proponents of the radical framework emphasize the importance of controlling reproduction and ownership of their bodies in eliminating the sexual class system. This perspective is based on the assumption that the oppression of women is the most fundamental form of oppression, and that it is woven into every aspect of life. Although this perspective recognizes the importance of economic equality for women, it argues that moving women into the work world will not eliminate the exploitation of women in family relationships.

According to Travis, the feminist frameworks have three basic points in common: (a) Women are oppressed; (b) the personal is political; and (c) process shares equal importance with outcome. Although these perspectives emphasize different sources of oppression, they all agree that women can best be understood in a broad social and political context.

DEVELOPMENT AND HISTORY
OF FEMINIST PSYCHOTHERAPY

Feminist therapy built on the achievements of early feminists of the mid-1800s and early 1900s, such as Susan B. Anthony, Elizabeth Stanton, and Margaret Sanger. Psychotherapists began to separate intrapsychic issues from the collective issues all women face in being a woman in a society that devalues their sex. This approach developed out of women's dissatisfaction with traditional models and theories of psychotherapy based on sexist assumptions. Such traditional models were seen to function "as a mechanism of social control, preserving the status quo and protecting the patriarchal structure of society by perpetuating sex-role stereotyping in both its theoretical stance and practical application."

Rosewater and Walker, and Dutton-Douglas and Walker, have documented the historical development of feminist therapy. Dutton-Douglas and Walker divided the development of feminist therapy into three phases. The initial phase began in the late 1960s and lasted about 10 years. During this phase, feminist therapists focused their attention on analyzing and critiquing the androcentric biases inherent in traditional therapies developed by males. About this time, psychology of women emerged as a field of study. The Association for Women in Psychology

(AWP) was formed in 1969 as was Division 35 of the American Psychological Association (Psychology of Women). As documented by O'Connell and Russo, the first peer-reviewed feminist psychological journals were published during this phase: *Sex Roles* appeared in 1975 and *The Psychology of Women Quarterly* in 1976.

During the second phase, feminist therapists incorporated feminism into the various therapy approaches by revising and/or eliminating the sexist parts. As a result, a number of feminist therapies were developed that shared core feminist values and precepts, yet varied in terms of their descriptions of pathology, human development, techniques, and interventions. The models were fragmented, however, and focused on a wide range of explanatory mechanisms ranging from the intrapsychic to the interpersonal to the sociopolitical. Feminists at the Stone Center at Wellesley College (e.g., Jean Baker Miller and colleagues) began to create a theory regarding women's development that emphasized the importance and centrality of relating and relationships to women's sense of self and identity. Other feminist therapists also developed theories that placed emphasis on women's greater relatedness. In addition, during this time period, the Committee on Women of the American Psychological Association's Division on Counseling Psychology developed a set of principles for responsible professional practice in counseling and therapy with women. In 1982 the First Annual Advanced Feminist Therapy Institute was held in Vail, Colorado, bringing together feminist therapists and thinkers in the first such formal convention of its kind.

Therapists in the third phase are developing a complete theory of feminist therapy. They recognized that theory is incomplete and is not clearly differentiated from other perspectives. Attempts are being made to expand on the applications of feminist practice by developing a comprehensive and coherent theory of feminist therapy. The theory integrates feminist thought with psychological models, and argues that personality and behaviors are not primarily intrapsychically based but are coping skills developed to survive in an oppressive world. This theoretical approach, in its attempt to be broad based and integrative, addresses the many oppressive conditions that women also may experience, such as ethnic, racial, and cultural problems.

Feminist therapists are explicitly *committed to feminist values* as a basis for conceptualizing therapy. This belief system affects ". . . the nature of women and mental illness, definitions, therapeutic interventions foci, therapist role, therapist–client relationship, and therapeutic goals." Feminist therapists recognize that much of women's emotional distress is the result of sociocultural factors; effective therapy, therefore, must involve external, societal changes in addition to internal changes. They assert that "much of women's pain is the result of circumstances external to them and that these circumstances must be changed" and that "women must be assisted to recover from the psychological damage that is so common to their experience."

Feminist therapy *rejects the adjustment, or medical model* of mental health that places the source of emotional problems within the individual, expecting women to conform to sexist social standards. It rejects therapeutic models that do not view women in relationship to the broader social context. Opposed, also, is the use of diagnostic labels that imply sickness and an internal locus. Studies by Chesler and Broverman et al. revealed how sexist standards of mental health placed women in impossible double binds, blaming the women victims by labeling them mentally ill. Feminist therapy is nonpathology oriented and nonvictim blaming; instead, it views behavior in terms of its coping or adaptation qualities.

Feminist therapists are *committed to political advocacy* and emphasize political consciousness both within therapy and in their communities. The feminist slogan, "The personal is political," describes the feminist perspective regarding the essential interrelatedness of the experiences and psychological problems of individual women and the societal oppression of all women. Consciousness raising is often an element of therapy. Feminist therapists educate their clients about gender stereotyping and

how their particular problems are related to the powerlessness of women as a group. They focus on how their clients are understanding gender and how this limits their ability to live life fully. They highlight gender issues and interact with their clients in ways that encourage them to behave nonstereotypically. In addition to acting as client advocates, feminist therapists often advocate on behalf of all women by educating their communities about women's experiences and issues. Their varied activities demonstrate their commitment to a perspective that acknowledges the reciprocal nature of psychological healing and the liberation and empowerment of all women.

The *empowerment of clients* involves redefining power so that women can affirm the strategies they use to survive in a system that denies them overt power. In other words, women are helped to recognize the power they possess, to value "woman power," and to become more aware of their own strengths. Clients are encouraged to become more personally powerful, to take greater control of their lives, and to be more autonomous and self-directed. Through therapy, women are helped to recognize and validate their needs, perceptions, and behavior as appropriate, given their situation—to understand how best to survive given their circumstances. Women are assisted in learning new modes of power through the therapeutic relationship itself, which models an egalitarian relationship.

One of the most fundamental aspects involves the *egalitarian nature of the therapist–client relationship*. The therapist assumes equality and views the client as a partner in therapy worthy of value and respect. Such an approach demystifies the power relationship and creates a climate that encourages client empowerment. This requires the therapist to reject authoritarian, hierarchical power relationships and to develop an open, genuine, and appropriately self-disclosing interactional style, thereby communicating respect for the client's capacity for nurturance and self-healing. Feminist therapists reject the role of an expert and assume the role of a facilitator, guide, or companion encouraging questions about the client's own values and approaches. They assist the client in recognizing how she is an expert about her own experience and in discovering and valuing her own inner voice.

In approaching the relationship on an equal basis, the therapist does not consider the client as having the same skills as the therapist. Rather, therapists place equal importance and value on the client's knowledge of herself and the therapist's skills, emphasizing that both are needed for successful therapy. According to Malmo and Laidlaw,

> Equality in this context does not mean sameness, nor does it mean reciprocity in the relationship. What it does mean is a valuing of individual worth and a mutual respect for the differing expertise of each person. . . . Further because the therapist enters the therapeutic relationship as herself and not as a detached authority, the relationship resonates with genuineness, openness, mutual respect, and warmth.

PROCESS OF FEMINIST PSYCHOTHERAPY

The actual process of feminist therapy varies according to the therapeutic orientation of the therapist. Generally, however, Smith and Siegel conceptualized the process of feminist therapy as consisting of three stages. During the first stage, the client is helped to understand how her personal problems have a social etiology: how the personal is political. In the second stage, power is redefined, an egalitarian relationship with the therapist is modeled, and the woman learns to recognize her own strengths. During the third stage, the therapist supports the client in her growth and as she tries out new ways of being. The process of feminist therapy is described in Chaplin, Gilbert, Greenspan, Sturdivant, and Russell.

Feminist psychotherapists have increased knowledge about the various problems commonly experienced by women. Such involvement in women's issues has increased an awareness of the preponderance of child abuse, spouse battering, sexual assault, and incest. They have focused attention on issues involving women's anger, body image and compulsive eating, assertiveness, personal boundaries, depression, infertility, female sexual dysfunction, lesbianism and bisexuality, and pornography, among other topics. Maracek and Hare-Mustin in their review of the history of feminism and clinical psychology concluded that feminists have called attention to the sexist use of concepts and psychiatric diagnoses, misuse of medication, sexual misconduct in therapy, and psychological problems arising from gender inequality in everyday life. O'Connell and Russo similarly reviewed women's heritage in psychology and illustrated how "feminists have gone beyond reactive critique to develop new theories, methods, and techniques." They documented how feminist critiques have transformed psychology as a discipline, including the subfield of psychotherapy.

CRITICISMS AND CRITIQUES

Feminist psychotherapy has been criticized on a number of counts. Most notably, it has been criticized for the lack of agreement on the theory and practice of therapy. Merely modifying traditional theories according to feminist or nonsexist principles is difficult in that many such theories are incompatible with the feminist perspective due to their intrapsychic focus and inattention to societal and political factors. Second, it has been criticized for being racist or at least overly biased in favor of Whites in that it was "developed by and for white women. . . . Currently, feminist therapy theory is neither diverse nor complex in the reality it reflects." Kanuha argued that feminist therapy will become yet another White exclusionary system unless it incorporates racial and cultural elements from numerous cultures into the theory. Some radical feminists view all forms of institutionalized therapy as being sexist and yet another form of oppression.

Feminist psychotherapy has grown tremendously since its inception. However, Brown and Brodsky noted that "feminist therapy has always suffered from the stereotype that it is for women only." Although they acknowledged that adult women were the primary focus initially, feminist therapists have always dealt with a variety of populations and are expanding their practice to "more fully address the needs, concerns, and realities of men, children, families, elders, and people with disabilities." It has also suffered from the stereotype that it devalued the contribution of men and assumed that men are not feminists.

Finally, feminist therapy lacks formal standards and established training centers, although the beginnings of such training opportunities are available at the Stone Center at Wellesley College, the Women's Therapy Centre Institute in New York, and the Psychology of Women Institute of APA's Division 35.

ASSERTIVENESS TRAINING
COHORT DIFFERENCES
EQUITY
FEMINIST THERAPY
MASCULINE PROTEST
PSYCHOTHERAPY
SELF-DETERMINATION
SEX ROLES
SEXISM

T. L. NEEDELS

FETAL ALCOHOL SYNDROME

Fetal alcohol syndrome (FAS) is a complex of physical anomalies and neurobehavioral deficits that may severely affect offspring of heavy-drinking mothers. Less serious sequelae of heavy maternal drinking are commonly termed fetal alcohol effects (FAE). FAS is associated with three effects or "the triad of the FAS": (a) growth retardation of prenatal origin, (b) characteristic facial anomalies, and (c) central nervous system dysfunction. First described in 1973, FAS has since been the subject of more than 2000 scientific reports. Incidence estimates suggest that FAS may be the leading cause, ahead of Down syndrome and fragile X syndrome, of mental retardation in the Western world. It is certainly the most prevalent, known, environmental, and preventable cause of mental retardation. In 1987, Abel and Sokol estimated that as much as 11% of the annual cost of mental retardation in the United States might be devoted to FAS cases, and that the annual cost of treatment of all FAS-related effects was $321 million. Follow-up studies, described next, confirm that alcohol is a teratogen that produces lifelong impairments.

DIAGNOSTIC CRITERIA AND COMMON CHARACTERISTICS

The Fetal Alcohol Study Group of the Research Society on Alcoholism established minimal criteria for diagnosis of FAS, based largely on Clarren and Smith's summary of 245 cases. FAS should be diagnosed only when all three of these criteria are met:

1. Prenatal and/or postnatal growth retardation (below 10th percentile for body weight, length, and/or head circumference when corrected for gestational age).

2. Central nervous system dysfunction (neurological abnormality, developmental delay, or mental impairment less than 10th percentile).

3. Characteristic facies (at least two of the following three facial dysmorphologies: (a) microcephaly, head circumference less than 3rd percentile; (b) microphthalmia and/or short palpebral fissures; and/or (c) poorly developed philtrum, thin upper lip, and flattening of the maxillary area).

A more extensive set of features associated with FAS in Clarren and Smith's cases is shown in Table 1. In addition to the three criteria, a history of drinking during pregnancy should be present for confident diagnosis, because no individual feature is specific to prenatal exposure to alcohol. However, Streissguth, Sampson, Barr, Clarren, and Martin have suggested that "FAS and alcohol teratogenicity are reciprocal terms. . . . Identifying a child with all the features of FAS strongly suggests that the child was affected by alcohol *in utero*." Of importance, they also stated that although alcohol teratogenicity may cause a "milder" FAS or FAE phenotype, such milder phenotypes should not be inferred to result necessarily from alcohol: "Other environmental or genetic problems could produce similar manifestations. . . . When examining the individual patient, the examiner cannot be sure that alcohol produced a 'possible' fetal alcohol effect, even when a maternal history is positive for alcohol." An important attributional implication, as Brown suggested, is that women who have occasionally consumed small amounts of alcohol during pregnancy and have slightly deformed infants should not be made to feel guilty or told that alcohol caused the deformities. Women should certainly take precautions during their pregnancy, but do not have control over everything that may affect their babies.

Growth retardation is the most common characteristic of FAS. Although low birth weight is associated with other maternal factors, several of which, including smoking, malnutrition, and drug abuse, also are associated with alcohol abuse, two lines of evidence suggest that alcohol induces prenatal growth retardation: (a) The other maternal factors are rarely associated with other defining features of FAS, and (b) offspring of pregnant animals given alcohol show both growth retardation and virtually all other physical and neurobehavioral features of FAS. One unusual characteristic of FAS-induced growth retardation is that it is not followed by catch-up growth in infancy or childhood.

As West has observed, "Central nervous system dysfunction is the most devastating and one of the more consistently observed clinical abnormalities in surviving offspring of mothers known to have consumed large

Table 1   Principle Features of Fetal Alcohol Syndrome Described by Clarren and Smith (1987)[a]

Feature	Manifestation
Growth deficiency	
Prenatal	Height and weight at least 2 SD below the mean[b]
Postnatal	Height and weight at least 2 SD below the mean;[b] disproportionately diminished adipose tissue[c]
Central nervous system dysfunction	
Intellectual	Mild to moderate mental retardation[b]
Neurologic	Microcephaly;[b] poor coordination;[c] hypotonia[c]
Behavioral	Infancy: irritability;[b] Childhood: attention deficit hyperactivity disorder[c]
Facial anomalies	
Eyes	Short palpebral fissures[b]
Nose	Short, upturned;[c] hypoplastic philtrum[b]
Maxilla	Hypoplastic[c]
Mouth	Thinned upper vermillion;[b] Infancy: retrognathia;[b] adolescence: micrognathia or relative prognathia[c]

[a]Modified after Clarren and Smith (1978).
[b]Seen in >80% of cases.
[c]Seen in >50% of cases.

amounts of alcohol during pregnancy." Mental retardation or subnormality is the most common central nervous system (CNS) indicator associated with FAS. Average IQ of affected children is about 65 to 70, which is in the mild mentally retarded range, but variability is high. Children with the most severe morphology and growth indicators have the most severe intellectual and other CNS deficits. Affected infants and children may also show failure to thrive, poor sucking, retarded speech and motor development, fine-motor dysfunction, repetitive self-stimulating behaviors such as head rolling or head banging, auditory deficits, and seizures. Symptoms of attention deficit hyperactivity disorder (ADHD) are common and associated with school problems. Seizures occur in about 20% of cases but are not considered characteristic of FAS. Prenatal alcohol has a variety of adverse effects on the developing CNS.

Difficulty of diagnosing FAS should not be minimized and leads to failures in diagnosis. As one indication of the problem, Little, Snell, Rosenfeld, Gilstrap, and Gant examined the medical records of infants born to women who had reported alcohol abuse during pregnancy. Medical records indicated that 6 of 40 infants had distinct FAS characteristics, including facial dysmorphologies, microcephaly, and fetal growth retardation. Regardless of their characteristics and the alcohol abuse reported in the mothers' obstetric records, none of the infants had been diagnosed as FAS or FAE. Failure to diagnose may result from several factors. As indicated previously, physical characteristics of FAS overlap with other syndromes and may be difficult to detect in some ethnic groups. Furthermore, some neurobehavioral effects will only become apparent during development.

HISTORICAL BACKGROUND

Although a number of authors have claimed to find ancient reference to damaging effects of maternal alcohol consumption, Abel, after a thorough review, suggested that those claims rest on erroneous secondary sources or mistranslations. Abel did report suggestions of adverse effects of maternal drinking in seventeenth-century England and that several writers observed during the "gin epidemic" in the early eighteenth century that children of mothers who drank heavily were small, sickly, and mentally slow. Furthermore, a number of nineteenth-century reports linked stillbirth, infant mortality, and mental retardation to maternal drinking during pregnancy.

However, studies in the early twentieth century failed to find a link between maternal drinking and adverse effects on offspring. Elderton and Pearson reported no relationship between parental drinking and intelligence or appearance of children and suggested that children of

alcoholics might have problems because parents and children shared "defective germ plasm" or because the parents provided a poor home environment. Although their claim was much criticized, it was later supported by Haggard and Jellinek, who denied that prenatal alcohol produced malformations. Thus, however inaccurate from the perspective, Montagu's conclusion was apparently well founded: "Unexpectedly, alcohol in the form of beverages, even in immoderate amounts, has no apparent effect on a child before birth. . . . It now can be stated categorically . . . that no matter how great the amount of alcohol taken by the mother—or the father, for that matter—neither the germ cells nor the development of the child will be affected." As Brown suggested, the timing of Montagu's publication has a certain irony, appearing at about the time Lemoine, Harousseau, Borteryu, and Menuet began their study of the offspring of 127 alcoholic parents. In 1968, they reported that several of the children had such characteristic anomalies that maternal alcoholism could be inferred from them. The abnormalities were in the three areas now associated with FAS: growth retardation, low intelligence, and facial anomalies. Their paper, published in French, although with an English abstract, had little impact and was unknown to Jones and Smith and their colleagues at the time of their initial reports in 1973. Those reports brought the effects of maternal alcoholism to international attention, in part by providing a name, fetal alcohol syndrome, that "dramatically refocused interest on an important perinatal risk."

INCIDENCE AND RISK FACTORS

Worldwide incidence of FAS is estimated as approximately 1.9 per 1000 live births, although estimates vary widely across study and country. Given that FAS may be undiagnosed in infancy, actual incidence may be higher. The varying estimates may reflect sampling error and use of different diagnostic criteria as well as actual national or regional differences. A further general and important complication is that degree of maternal drinking virtually always rests on retrospective self-reports. The reliability of such reports is highly uncertain, and both incidence estimates and some apparent correlates of FAS may be affected by this measurement problem. As would be expected, incidence varies most with degree of prenatal maternal drinking. Full-blown FAS appears to be associated only with heavy maternal drinking; no cases have been reported among moderate drinkers. FAS may occur in 30 to 50% and FAE in 50 to 70% of offspring of truly alcoholic women who consume eight or more drinks daily. Some studies report incidence as high as 80% in low socioeconomic samples (SES).

Incidence of human newborns with some features of FAS also increases with the amount of prenatal maternal alcohol consumption. Degree of physical growth retardation also is dose related. A dose-response curve is found in virtually all animal studies: Number and severity of offspring anomalies increase with amount of prenatal exposure to alcohol. Well-controlled animal studies have confirmed that the damage is from prenatal alcohol and not secondary to some other effect.

Some effects of prenatal alcohol appear to occur only above a certain threshold level of exposure (e.g., Ernhart et al. reported that women who drank small amounts of alcohol early in pregnancy had children with no incidence of FAS-related neonatal physical anomalies above that of a control group). However, teratogens typically have neurobehavioral effects at levels below those at which physical defects are shown. Owing to, among other things, the subtlety of neurobehavioral effects of alcohol and unknown factors contributing to individual differences in susceptibility to alcohol, no safe level of alcohol consumption by pregnant women can be given.

FAS is seen more commonly in offspring from lower socioeconomic status (SES) mothers. A variety of possible reasons exist for this relationship, including the fact that alcoholism is inversely related to SES. Even when alcohol intake was equated, however, Bingol et al. found that incidence of FAS and FAE was 71% in offspring of heavy drinking, low SES mothers and only 4.6% in offspring of heavy drinking, middle- to upper-SES mothers. However, SES was confounded with ethnicity, complicating interpretation. Sokol et al. have identified several specific risk factors in a study comparing FAS infants with a control group of nonaffected infants. Using discriminant analyses, they identified four significant prenatal maternal risk factors: (a) percentage of drinking days during pregnancy, (b) positive score on the Michigan Alcoholism Screening Test (MAST), (c) high parity, and (d) African American background. These four factors together explained 63.6% of the variance in FAS versus non-FAS outcomes. The authors estimated that in the absence of these four factors, the likelihood of an offspring being affected with FAS is less than 2%, whereas in the presence of all four factors, the probability jumps to 85.2%.

Research conducted with human and nonhuman subjects suggests that some of the variability in incidence of FAS–FAE stems from genetic factors. Clinical reports indicate that dizygotic (fraternal) twins of alcoholic mothers show differential development and performance. Maternal factors are implicated in research by Chernoff: Pregnant mice from two different strains given comparable doses of alcohol had different blood alcohol levels, and the strain with higher levels had offspring with higher incidence of anomalies.

FAS IN ADOLESCENTS AND ADULTS

FAS has effects, although in somewhat modified form, that last into adulthood. According to longitudinal studies, FAS–FAE adolescents and adults were about 2 standard deviations (SD) below the mean in height and head circumference, although variability was high; little overall catch-up growth had occurred. The characteristic low weight of FAS–FAE children had largely disappeared, although weight-to-height ratios were even more variable than other measures.

The facial dysmorphologies characteristic of FAS children became less distinctive with age. Although some features (such as short palpebral fissure length) remained, growth in a number of facial areas reduced the extent of the overall abnormal appearance.

The average IQ of the 61 FAS–FAE adolescents and adults reported by Streissguth et al. was 68, just into the mild retardation level. The FAS mean was 66 and the FAE was 73. Variability was again high, with IQ ranging from 20 to 105; no FAS individual's IQ was above the low 90s. Those with the most severe growth retardation and facial dysmorphologies in childhood continued to have the lowest later IQ scores. Only 6%

of the 61 were in regular classes and not receiving special help; 28% were in self-contained special education classes, 15% were neither in school nor working, and 9% were in sheltered workshops. Although academic deficits were broad, arithmetic deficits were particularly large. Academic performance had not improved since childhood. Even FAS–FAE individuals who were not mentally retarded showed poor socialization scores and an unusually high level of maladaptive behaviors, including poor concentration and attention, sullenness, impulsivity, lying, and cheating. However, their family environments were highly unstable, making it difficult to determine whether many of these effects were owed to prenatal alcohol exposure, or to postnatal environment, or an interaction between difficult infants and inadequate parenting. Only 9% were still living with both parents; the mothers of 66% had died, many from alcohol-related causes.

PREVENTION

Although 100% preventable theoretically, FAS may prove resistant to reduction efforts in practice. Alcohol abuse is notably resistant to treatment, and relapse rates are as high as 75% 12 months after treatment. Thus education programs on the adverse effects of prenatal alcohol may lower alcohol consumption of moderately drinking women during pregnancy but are unlikely to affect alcohol-abusing or alcoholic women whose infants are most at risk. Although a variety of general approaches are available, treatment and prevention programs targeted specifically at women may be necessary to decrease the incidence of this tragic condition.

ALCOHOLISM TREATMENT
BIRTH INJURIES
CHILD NEGLECT
DEPRIVATION EFFECTS
EMBRYO AND FETUS
INFANT DEVELOPMENT
MINIMAL BRAIN DYSFUNCTION (DIAGNOSIS)
MINIMAL BRAIN DYSFUNCTION (INTERVENTION)
NEUROTOXIC SUBSTANCES
SUBSTANCE ABUSE

R. T. BROWN

FIDUCIAL LIMITS

Fiducial limits are the boundaries of the *fiducial interval*. The term "fiducial interval" was introduced by Sir Ronald Fisher, who argued in favor of fiducial probability as the basis of all statistical inferences. The term "fiducial" comes from the Latin *fiducialis*, meaning "trust." The method of fiducial probability is based on the premise that the distribution of a statistic or of an estimated parameter should not be assumed a priori. Rather, all inferences should be based on the sample observed. We should "trust" only those predictions based on observed and observable data.

In seeking an estimate of μ, we wish to know the degree of accuracy that can be attributed to our estimate. Typically we seek to establish a range of possible values of μ such that there is a 95% chance that the interval contains the true value of μ. This range of values is the *fiducial interval,* and its boundaries, the *fiducial limits*.

According to Fisher, the appropriate way to construct this interval is by calculating the probability distribution of possible values of μ. This may be done by first solving for μ in the equation of t, a statistic with known probability distributions. By substituting values of t, we obtain the fiducial distribution of values associated with μ. The probabilities associated with the t distribution are applicable to this derived fiducial distribution, and to statements regarding μ. "We may then state the probability that μ is less than any assigned value, or the probability that it lies between any assigned values, or, in short, its probability distribution, in light of the sample observed."

Fiducial limits can be constructed for any known distributions such as the normal curve, and for distributions belonging to the test statistics *t* and *F*. In psychology it is customary to retain the null hypothesis (and to reject the alternative research hypothesis of a treatment effect) if the computed test statistic falls within a chosen fiducial interval containing the most likely 95% of the distribution. Values more extreme than the fiducial limits result in rejection of the null hypothesis and confirmation of the research hypothesis.

In *Statistics: An introduction*, D. A. S. Fraser noted, "Many statisticians have attempted to interpret Fisher's method, few to Fisher's satisfaction." The attempts center around the use of procedures to construct *confidence intervals* and corresponding *confidence limits*. Fisher objected to such procedures because they involve a priori assumptions about the characteristics of the distribution sampled. According to Fraser, when only one parameter is involved, fiducial methods and confidence methods actually yield the same result; when more than one parameter is involved, the results are sometimes different. However, the terms "fiducial interval" and "fiducial limits" have come to be used almost interchangeably with "confidence intervals" and "confidence limits," respectively. In *Psychological statistics*, Quinn McNemar summarized a widespread view of the subject: "The limits set by the confidence interval method are so very similar to *fiducial limits*, and the level of confidence, sometimes referred to as the *confidence coefficient*, is so much like fiducial probability that the beginning student can well let the mathematical statistician worry about the theoretical difference between what seems to be two ways of doing the same thing."

CONFIDENCE LIMITS
HYPOTHESIS TESTING
STATISTICAL INFERENCES
STATISTICS IN PSYCHOLOGY

A. MYERS

FIELD DEPENDENCY

Field dependence–field independence (FD–FI) is the name given to a particular cognitive style defined and promulgated by Herman Witkin as an integral part of his broader concept *of psychological differentiation*. The latter is a term for a developmental process characteristic of all organisms, and implies specialization of function at both the physiological and psychological levels.

An individual's degree of psychological differentiation reflects the extent to which the person can separate perception of self from that of nonself and/or recognize the boundaries thereof. It also implies the degree to which such psychological activities as remembering, thinking, and acting can be segregated from one another. As this process of psychological differentiation develops within an organism, the person develops consistent patterns of controls over various psychological activities—patterns that are labeled *cognitive style*. Because psychological differentiation as a process affects a number of domains of psychological activity, there are a number of possible cognitive styles, among which is that of field dependence–field independence, which Witkin and his colleagues and students made the focal point of their research and theory.

FD–FI is a bipolar dimension reflecting characteristic styles of intellectual functioning. The emphasis in the delineation of this concept has been on FI. FD (with a few exceptions) tends to be described as either the "opposite" or "absence" of FI, depending on the behavioral domain.

The extreme FI individual would be one whose cognitive style reflects an extreme degree of psychological differentiation. Thus the FI person

can readily restructure a perceptual situation or impose a structure where one is absent or minimal. There is a strong sense of identity of self as separate from others. The individual thus has a clean delineation of the separation of self, needs, and values from those of others.

The polarity of FD–FI does not extend to overall social desirability of a particular cognitive style. FI individuals tend to detach themselves from others and behave in a relatively impersonal manner. Rather than interact with their environment, they are more prone to analyze it. FD people, in contrast, interact with others in the environment and tend to develop sensitivity to what others are thinking or feeling. Thus they build an information and skills bank from their relationships with others. This, in turn, may enable them to cope with everyday problems at a level equal or superior to that of the FI person.

The theoretical framework for the FD–FI concept had its origins in early work of Witkin, his colleagues, and his students, who were deeply interested in the patterns of individual differences in perception—particularly, perception of the upright with respect to the pull of gravity. This work led to the widespread recognition of particular procedures that have come to serve as definitive operational delineators of FD–FI: the Rod and Frame Test (RFT), the Body Adjustment Test (BAT), the Rotating Room Test (RRT), and the Embedded Figures Test (EFT). Each of these was considered by Witkin to reflect related pattern characteristics of FD–FI. Although these tests may be intercorrelated, they need not necessarily be so.

The RFT consists of a large square frame attached to a holder and stand that permits it to be rotated 360°. At the center of the frame is attached a movable rod that bisects the frame in any position. Both rod and frame are painted with luminous paint, so as to be visible in the dark under black light. With the initial presentation position of the rod and the frame varied, the subject's task, while sitting in the dark, is to adjust the rod to a position truly vertical with respect to the pull of gravity. A large discrepancy presumably reflects the lack of the visual field (the dark) and thus a person prone to FD. A small RFT discrepancy indicates FI.

The BAT is a small room so constructed that it can be tilted clockwise or counterclockwise. Within this room is a chair for the subject that the experimenter can also tilt. The subject, when placed in a tilted chair in the tilted room, is requested to adjust the chair to be upright with respect to gravity. Those who adjust the chair to the tilt of the room, rather than to gravity, are deemed FD.

In the RRT, the visual field remains upright while gravitional force on the body is changed. Thus an upright room is attached to a track so that it can be moved in a circle, thereby producing an outward-directed centrifugal force. The subject is seated in a tiltable chair, which is adjusted by the experimenter so that it is at an angle to the room. The task is to adjust the chair so that one's body is "straight." An FD person is likely to adjust the chair to "straight" in terms of the room, whereas the FI individual adjusts more in terms of the angle of centrifugal force, thereby having a score with a greater discrepancy from the gravitational upright.

The EFT consists of an adaptation of the classic "Gottschaldt Figures." The subject is presented with a series of figure diagrams of various colored patterns, within which are contained the outlines of a single, simpler figure. The boundaries of the embedded figure often cross the color and design boundaries of the larger figure. The test is scored in terms of the mean number of seconds (up to a maximum of five minutes) that a person requires for finding the simple figure within the complex one. Again, an FD person, caught up in the complexities of the visual field, would take longer than an FI person.

Performance on one or more of the above tests has served as the anchor for a body of literature on FD–FI, which began in the late 1940s and continues to grow, evolve, and develop. Performance on RFT, BAT, and RRT presumably reflects the degree to which one relies on impressions from one's body in making the judgments (FI), as contrasted with reliance on the visual field (from which the concept of field dependency presumably got its name). The EFT samples a different aspect of differentiation: the ability to break up or restructure the overall larger figure in order to perceptually isolate the smaller figure. This, in turn, reflects a perceptual analytic ability to impose structural reorganization on any given setting, as well as to abstract elements from that setting. It is also highly correlated with what is traditionally known as spatial relations ability.

CONTEXTUAL ASSOCIATIONS
FIGURE/GROUND
PERCEPTUAL ORGANIZATION

M. E. REUDER

FIELD EXPERIMENTATION

Up until the 1940s, most psychological experimentation had been conducted in controlled laboratory settings. Since then, a small but growing body of research has involved experimentation in nonlaboratory field settings.

The conceptual and methodological rationale for field *in vivo* experimentation has been twofold. The growth of research on social psychological issues (e.g., attitude formation, prejudice, group processes, conformity) led many investigators to question whether the variables of importance in such phenomena are not fundamentally distorted in an artificial laboratory setting. One result has been to advance laboratory deception and "staging" to a high art form, but another has been to increase the use of field investigation. In a parallel development, field experimental techniques began to be used to study the effects of large social programs, which could in no way be tested by a laboratory proxy.

Social psychology has always been in conflict about the extent to which variables of interest can be studied in the laboratory as opposed to real life. The social psychological tradition of field experimentation was heavily influenced by several "group dynamics" studies conducted in the 1940s.

The other major tradition of field experimentation heavily involving psychologists has been the evaluation and development of social programs and government policies. Much of this development occurred during the 1960s, paralleling massive increases in federal social welfare spending. In field experiments of this genre the "independent variable" has often been a large and complex social program that may serve many clients ("subjects," in terms of the experiment) for months or years. The experimental design usually involves random assignment of individuals, groups, or organizations to one of several alternative remedial social programs.

The expansion of experimentation into field program evaluation has been accompanied by the growth of a large methodological and conceptual literature. Because the independent variable in a program evaluation field experiment is itself a large social system, a great deal of this "methodological" literature has actually been concerned with management and logistical issues. For example, in order to infer effects from experimental social programs, the treatment (program) must be maintained constant over the course of the study, and must be fully implemented at the start. The management task to accomplish that is considerable, and there is mounting evidence that attenuated treatment effects in field experiments may merely be the result of attenuated treatments. To successfully conduct field experiments, psychologists need skills in addition to methodology *qua* methodology.

Field experiments will continue to occupy a place in traditional psychological research and a growing role in the development and evaluation of government programs. Despite logistical and management problems, the field experiment remains a powerful methodological tool for discovering the effects of social variables in real settings.

EXPERIMENTAL DESIGNS
FIELD RESEARCH
RESEARCH METHODOLOGY

L. G. TORNATZKY

FIELD RESEARCH

The purpose of field research in the most general sense is to apply scientific method to practical human problems in organizational contexts. Field research overlaps with program/product development and formative evaluation. The field research movement in education was stimulated by the perceived gap between educational research findings and educational practice, and attempted to bring about a closer cooperative interaction between researchers and practitioners.

The purpose and sequence of steps of field research in business and industrial organizations are similar to those in educational contexts. Research data pertaining to a system problem are collected; changes are made in the system based on the data; and the consequences of these changes are evaluated by the collection of more data. Thus the field research model is a dynamic, informational feedback procedure based on an immediate practical concern in a system or organization.

Critics of the field research model point out that scientists do not subscribe to a naive here-and-now empiricism, but rather base their efforts on a knowledge of previous research and some kind of theoretical framework. Field research is also said to suffer from problems of control over extraneous variables and from a lack of generalizability of the findings. On the positive side, although a quarter century of field research in the schools has not completely closed the gap between research and practice, it has made educational practitioners more aware of and knowledgeable about research methods and findings. More teachers and other practitioners in education and other organizations are doing field research, although such research is usually of the survey or quasi-experimental type rather than controlled experimentation.

ACTION RESEARCH
FIELD EXPERIMENTATION
RESEARCH METHODOLOGY

L. R. AIKEN

FIELD THEORY

Field theory was developed by Kurt Lewin out of the orientation that to understand behavior, the Gestalt or total situation had to be considered. Lewin carried this orientation into new areas, using as his model the thinking patterns of topological mathematics and the field theory of physics. His viewpoint is often labeled "neo-Gestalt."

The theory is based on a number of assumptions that make both its terminology and its dynamics difficult to follow, unless one becomes fully immersed in its philosophic terms and special concepts. Lewin totally rejected the Aristotelian approach to science, including any emphasis on past or future, cause or effect. For him, psychology was a realm of scientific investigation totally different from biology, physics, or other natural sciences. The concepts, objects, and events of the latter may have some relevance for behavior, but only in terms of *psychological* relevance. Even if the behaving individual is remembering the past or projecting into the future, he or she is doing this in the immediate present. Thus only those aspects of the past (or future) that are currently part of the immediate situation have relevance.

Unlike many theories that tend to ignore individual differences, field theory focuses on them. Lewin maintained that the person's perception of the environment is affected by the impact of the environment and such impact, in turn, alters subsequent perception. The environment surrounds the person. Yet the person (P) is never part of the environment (E), nor is the latter part of the person. There are, however, permeable psychological boundaries by which changes in the one can effect changes in the other.

Within the person there are two major regions, an inner core (analogous to a nucleus) and a surrounding area. The inner core is further subdivided into its own regions, which correspond to various needs, cognitive structures, and so forth. The area surrounding this core is the motor-perceptual area. This latter relatively undifferentiated area presumably provides the avenue by which the incoming events of the psychological environment (perceptual) reach the core, and also provides the outgoing (motor) avenue for needs to impact on the environment.

The psychological environment is also subdivided into a variety of regions having more or less permeable boundaries. These regions constitute the "valences" (attractions or repellants of their environmental contents, e.g., goals or goal objects). The particular valence of a region is developed (differentiated) across time as the developing person and the environment continue to grow and change.

Field theory provides a means for describing, analyzing, and predicting behavior primarily by determining the components of the vector field in a particular situation and ascertaining the direction and intensity of the movement to be expected. However, it also predicts changes in the person that may ensue from the person's having engaged in a behavior, as well as from changes in the environment that may gain or lose salience in and/or for subsequent behavior.

GENERAL SYSTEMS
GESTALT PSYCHOLOGY
PHYSICS AND THE BEHAVIORAL SCIENCES

M. E. REUDER

FIGHT/FLIGHT REACTION

Fighting and fleeing are the two basic responses available to most animals, including humans, when dealing with danger. A threat to the survival of an organism will be met with one or both of these behaviors. The threat may be real or perceived, and the response may be physical or, in the case of humans, abstract or intellectual. Further, the fight/flight response may be by an individual alone or by a group acting together.

A genetic basis for fight/flight behaviors shares an argument for the more general topic of aggression. That is, these behaviors have been prevalent throughout history; they are shown by almost all species of animals; they appear early in childhood; and they appear to be of some survival value. In contrast, learning is an important factor influencing aggressive acts.

W. R. Bion incorporated fight/flight behavior into an elaborate theory of human behavior. This theory has had great impact on the understanding of individuals' actions, especially as they occur in a social context. W. R. Bion and others such as Henry Ezriel brought greatly increased understanding of the relationship that exists between the basic biological drives in man, such as fear and anxiety, and other observed behaviors, both abnormal and normal.

CENTRAL TRAITS
DEFENSE MECHANISMS
LEARNED HELPLESSNESS

S. BERENT

FIGURE/GROUND

The figure–ground relationship refers to an organizational tendency in perception. When two regions share a mutual boundary, the figure appears to have a distinct shape. In contrast, the ground appears to be "left over," merely constituting a background. The figure–ground relationship was first described by the Danish Gestalt psychologist, Edgar Rubin.

Several factors distinguish the figure from the ground:

1. The figure has a well-defined shape, whereas the ground seems to have no shape.
2. The ground appears to continue in back of the figure.
3. The figure appears closer to the viewer and seems to have a definite position in space; the ground seems farther away at some unspecified location in the background.
4. The figure is more impressive and memorable than the ground.
5. The figure looks brighter than the ground.

In most cases in everyday perception, figure–ground relationships are unambiguous. Areas that are familiar, relatively small, enclosed, symmetrical, and vertically or horizontally oriented tend to be perceived as the figure. However, some stimuli demonstrate ambiguous figure–ground relationships. In these situations, one region is initially perceived to be the figure and the other area, the ground; however, figure and ground reverse periodically.

GESTALT PSYCHOLOGY
PERCEPTION

MARGARET W. MATLIN

FIXED-ROLE THERAPY

This approach to psychotherapy—developed by George A. Kelly—is used to explore personal lifestyle problems as well as to effect therapeutic changes. The theory of fixed-role therapy (FRT) is based on Kelly's assumption that each person develops a unique, hierarchical organized system of personal constructs that guides one's behavior by the anticipation of events. In FRT, clients, with help from their therapists, experiment actively by playing the roles of hypothetical characters for one to several weeks. In short, in real life they role-play being someone else.

The method starts with the clients writing brief self-characterizations that lead to conclusions about their use of personal constructs to structure their behavior. "Enactment sketches" are then prepared to portray contrasting roles. These are to portray someone who acts from a different point of view and are to contain at least one contrasting construct: Thus if the self-characterization includes submissiveness as a central construct, the enactment sketch may call for the client to be aggressive.

The client and therapist usually meet every other day to evaluate and to make further plans. After the enactment period of 1 or more weeks, clients are to resume their original roles, but with the expectation that this period of fixed role-playing will have facilitated the creation of more adaptive personal constructs. Kelly reported that this system of therapy was appropriate for only a small percentage of clients, but also that he had used it successfully with psychotics and neurotics.

INNOVATIVE PSYCHOTHERAPIES
PERSONAL CONSTRUCT THEORY

V. RAIMY

FLESCH FORMULAS

The Flesch Readability Formula, developed by Rudolph Flesch, predicts the reading ease and human interest of written material. The formula for reading ease (RE) is RE = 206.835 − 0.846 *wl* − 1.015 *sl,* where *wl* is the average word length in syllables, and *sl* is the average sentence length in words. The formula is calculated from the entirety of a short piece of writing or from 3 to 5 random 100-word samples from an article (up to 25 to 30 samples from a book).

A "word" is any combination of letters or numbers surrounded by white space, including such items as *don't, ASAP, 1984, $82,354,* and *full-length.* To count the number of syllables in a word, one simply pronounces the word, phrase, or symbols and tallies the syllables. Thus average word length in syllables is the number of syllables per 100 words; *C. O. D.* has three, whereas *1984* has five, as does *hippopotamus.* To determine average sentence length, one counts the number of sentences in the sample, including the last sentence if the 100th word is beyond the middle of that sentence. A "sentence" is considered to be a complete thought; in this sentence, the words since the last period would qualify as *two* sentences. Incomplete sentences and sentence fragments are counted as complete sentences.

Inserting these two values into the formula will typically yield a rating ranging from 0 to 100. An RE score of 90 to 100 identifies very easy reading (such as one would find in comic books), with approximately 123 syllables per 100 words and including 12 to 13 sentences. Anyone who has completed fourth grade (i.e., is functionally literate) should be able to answer 75% of the questions about such reading. A reading score of 0 to 30 means the reading is very difficult, such as would be found in scientific or professional writings. Such reading has an average of 192 syllables per 100 words, includes only 3 to 4 sentences, and is suited for college graduates.

Flesch also developed a Human Interest (HI) score: HI = 3.635 *pw* + 0.314 *ps,* where *pw* is the average percentage of "personal words" and *ps* is the average percentage of "personal sentences." Personal words include all nouns that have a natural gender, all pronouns except neuter pronouns (e.g., *it, their, and themselves,* unless they refer to people rather than things), and the words *people* (if used with a plural verb) and *folks.* Personal sentences include spoken sentences (marked by quotation marks or otherwise, but not quotes within quotes or indirect quotations), questions, commands, sentences aimed directly at the reader, exclamations, and grammatically incomplete sentences or fragments whose meaning must be inferred from the context.

The HI score will also typically fall between 0 and 100, where 0 to 10 means "dull" writing as found in scientific and professional journals. Averaging 2% "personal words," such writing typically has no "personal sentences." A score of 60 to 600 identifies dramatic writing as found in fiction writing, which averages 17% personal words and 58% personal sentences.

The RE formula doubtless overestimates the difficulty of reading. Clearly, it is not sensitive to the use of metaphor; it makes no adjustment for long words with which a reader may be quite familiar (e.g., Massachusetts); it can be "tricked" into rating a multisentence, short-word piece of writing as unduly easy; and it ignores both the semantics and the syntactical structure of sentences. However, applied with common sense, the Flesch formulas permit a wide variety of typical reading matter to be compared against a common scale for both reading ease (because this relates to standard reading tests) and human interest.

MEASUREMENT
PSYCHOLINGUISTICS
READING DISABILITIES

R. A. KASSCHAU

FLOODING

Flooding is a behavior therapy procedure employed primarily for eliminating fears and phobias. The most common usage is characterized in a paper by Marshall, Gauthier, and Gordon: "Flooding is a generic term for procedures that have as their goal the extinction of classes of maladaptive responses to aversive stimuli for prolonged periods in the absence of actual physically injurious consequences." As reflected in this definition, flooding has two central features. First, the patient is somehow *exposed* to the feared or aversive stimulus. Second, the person is confronted with intense or highly aversive versions of the stimulus, usually for extended periods of time.

Flooding has been shown to be highly effective for the treatment of agoraphobia. Combined with response prevention, it is also useful for treating obsessive-compulsive disorders. There are two common strategies for exposing the patient to the aversive stimuli. *In vivo* flooding involves exposure to the real stimuli, often in the natural environment. The therapist may accompany the patient or direct the patient to engage in the activity alone. In *imaginal flooding,* the stimuli are presented in the imagination: The patient simply visualizes the critical items as vividly as possible. Generally, *in vivo* exposure tends to be more effective.

INNOVATIVE PSYCHOTHERAPIES
PSYCHOTHERAPY

A. S. BELLACK

FOCUSING

Focusing is a psychotherapeutic technique developed by E. T. Gendlin that emphasizes direct inward attention to a bodily sensed, unclear "edge" (i.e., to the bodily discomfort specifically connected to a given whole problem or situation). At first fuzzy, such a *"felt sense"* then *"shifts"* in the body and comes into focus. New specific steps toward problem-resolution arise with such a "shift," but its main purpose is the physical change itself.

The bodily felt sense is usually not already there, but must first form. At the outset there may be nothing at all, or a very slight bodily discomfort directly connected with the problem. Compared with one's familiar feelings, this bodily sense seems slight, vague, and closed.

The next step is to sense the *quality* of this bodily sense by using an appropriate word or image. The patient "resonates" the word or image actively with the bodily sense, testing and confirming their suitability. Successful resonating should bring some physical relief.

Successful psychotherapy cases have differed significantly from failures, showing more attention to the directly sensed unclear "edge." Therefore, it was concluded that people should not be allowed to continue indefinitely in such failure-predicted therapy. Instead, this crucial mode of attention should be directly taught.

Aside from its use in psychotherapy and with personal problems, focusing is being used in the teaching of creative writing, in stress reduction, healing, business, education, spirituality, and other domains.

EXPERIENTIAL PSYCHOTHERAPY
INNOVATIVE PSYCHOTHERAPIES
PSYCHOTHERAPY

E. T. GENDLIN

FOOD DEPRIVATION

Reducing the nutritional intake of an organism has been employed in a variety of contexts by psychologists and by researchers of interest to psychologists. Clinical studies of human malnutrition or undernutrition are also relevant to a consideration of the psychological effects of food deprivation.

One complication in studies of food deprivation effects on behavior is that lack of food frequently results in voluntary restriction of water intake. Among rats, some strains decrease water intake much more than others after food deprivation. In one study in which a large number of strains were compared, water intake after food deprivation varied from 17 to 95% of undeprived intake.

In general, food intake increases with increases in food deprivation, but there are complications. In one study rats maintained on a 23-hour food deprivation schedule ate significantly less food with longer deprivation times. However, this result may have been a function of adaptation to a particular feeding schedule. There is an inverse relationship between latency to eat and length of food deprivation.

There is an interaction between taste and food deprivation (e.g., more saccharin is eaten by food-deprived than by nondeprived animals). In addition, increasing food deprivation in rats results in greater tolerance for food adulterated with quinine.

Suppression of a punished response for food reward is decreased by increases in food deprivation. At low levels of deprivation the punished response is almost completely suppressed, but there is very little suppression at higher levels.

The EEG during food deprivation is characterized by an activation pattern of low voltage and fast activity. Greater amounts of slow wave activity are seen in sated animals. Also, it was found that the heart rate increased monotonically during bar pressing for food on a CRF (continuous reinforcement) schedule with increasing food deprivation up to 48 hours.

FOOD DEPRIVATION AND LONGEVITY

Some of the variables investigated in studies of food deprivation effects on longevity are the age at initiation of the diet, the effect of the restricted diet on the occurrence of life-span limiting diseases (particularly cancer), and biochemical and physiological mechanisms that might play a role in the increased longevity. Neural changes after dietary restriction have been observed. In one study it was found that restricted-diet rats did not show age-related decreases in striatal dopamine receptors exhibited by ad-lib-fed animals.

EFFECTS OF EARLY MALNUTRITION

In animal studies, undernutrition has usually been imposed by separating the young from the mother for some period each day, giving an excessive number of young to each mother, or by underfeeding the nursing mother. Despite the variations in methodology, some conclusions can be made: (a) The growth of the developing brain is stunted by undernutrition, but to a slight degree relative to body size stunting (e.g., when body weight was reduced by 50%, reductions in brain weight of 8 to 20% were seen); (b) the brain stains less well for myelin; (c) the brains of rats subjected to postweaning undernutrition have minimum changes in size and composition (a variety of animal studies have reported that the most affected brain area is the cerebellum); and (d) brain cell number, as measured by changes in DNA, is reduced in animals subjected to protein–calorie malnutrition early in life.

The response to nutritional rehabilitation in animal research depends on the developmental stage during which the nutritional insult occurs. The evidence suggests that sufficient rehabilitation can alleviate any alteration of brain size and body weight if undernutrition was imposed on mature or nearly mature animals. By contrast, undernutrition during certain "critical periods" in early development limits the ability of the animal to profit from nutritional rehabilitation. The result is a permanent deficit in body weight and brain size, in cell numbers and composition, and in neural myelination.

Critical periods for the effects of undernutrition vary across species, primarily because of species differences in the timing of neural development.

Because of motivational and emotional changes in animals subjected to early malnutrition, it is not known whether the impairment in learning typically seen reflects diminished capacity or merely performance changes.

Previously malnourished animals are overreactive to both food and stressors other than food. In rats, for example, reduced movement in an open field has been reported following a loud noise. Electric shocks inhibited behavior or resulted in greater avoidance in comparison with control animals. Overreactive behavior has also been seen in previously undernourished pigs and rhesus monkeys.

In humans, at least two conditions have been reported to result from food deprivation. Nutritional marasmus has been known for centuries and results from chronic deficient caloric intake. Marasmus may affect people of any age, although the effects on growth—either somatic or neural—are much greater if the condition exists during the first years of life.

Kwashiorkor, first recognized in this century, is a disorder caused by protein malnutrition. The age of onset is from 1 to 3 years. The psychological changes in the child with kwashiorkor include apathy and irritability. The affected children are somnolent, with periods of monotonous crying or echolalia. There may be stereotypy, tearing and eating of clothing, and coprophagia. Anorexia, nausea, vomiting, and diarrhea are seen in almost all patients. There is a high mortality rate (30 to 50%).

It is impossible to conclude that early malnutrition is responsible for the reduced intellectual performance in studies in which it has been seen. Some other factors that undoubtedly contribute to reduced performance are poor hygiene and medical care both pre- and postnatally, limited vocabulary of the parents, and child abuse.

In a study of starvation effects on adults, no changes were noted in performance on IQ tests or tests of sensory discrimination. There were adverse effects on attitude and initiative, and there was a reduction in voluntary intellectual activity. Subjects complained of dullness, poor concentration, and lack of comprehension.

EATING DISORDERS
MALNUTRITION

B. M. THORNE

FORCED-CHOICE TESTING

Forced-choice testing involves comparative, as opposed to absolute, rating of items. The forced-choice technique is usually employed in self-inventories such as interest inventories or rating scales. The person responding to the items is presented with pairs or triads or as many as five or six characteristics, activities, or other descriptions related to the quality being measured and equally matched in desirability or undesirability. The respondent must rank these by indicating which is most and which is least preferred (or most descriptive and least descriptive), and which fall at each point between the two extremes.

In contrast, "absolute measurement" is often accomplished by rating scales that employ an agree/uncertain/disagree, or a like/indifferent/dislike format, sometimes with added degrees of intensity between the two extremes: like intensely, like somewhat, neither like nor dislike, dislike somewhat, or dislike intensely. Proponents of absolute scaling are critical of the forced-choice format because it does not permit expression of the degree to which one likes an activity or quality, or thinks it important or descriptive. Proponents of the forced-choice format, however, argue that it counters the tendency to rate most things somewhere between the two extremes, or to mark choices on the basis of their perceived social desirability. Another argument is that the forced-choice item represents a real-life situation: One cannot do three equally attractive things at precisely the same time, and often one has to choose among three equally unpleasant activities.

PSYCHOLOGICAL ASSESSMENT
SCALING
TEST CONSTRUCTION

E. E. DIAMOND

FOREIGN LANGUAGE APTITUDE

Some individuals appear to have a "knack" for learning foreign languages, whereas others report great difficulty even when well motivated. This suggests that individuals differ in foreign language aptitude. From early in the twentieth century there have been attempts to devise tests or other procedures that would forecast an individual's success in learning a foreign language.

Foreign language aptitude is to be sharply distinguished from aptitude for *native* language learning. The ability to learn the first language—the "mother tongue"—appears to be a virtually universal characteristic of the human species, although individuals may differ in the rate and quality of first-language learning. The capacity to learn a first language seems also to extend to the simultaneous learning of two or more languages, as in bilingual and multilingual communities and settings. Strictly speaking, foreign language aptitude pertains to the capacity to learn a second language *after* the individual has already learned a first language and has passed beyond the age (about 5 to 7 years) when first-language aptitude is no longer operative in learning a second language.

The idea that individuals differ in foreign language aptitude appears to be confirmed by the finding that certain measurements taken prior to a period of foreign language study correlate substantially, and sometimes quite highly, with success gauged at the end of that period. An interpretation of this finding is that individuals differ in their maximum or optimum *rate of learning* a foreign language (i.e., individuals with high aptitude can attain a satisfactory level of mastery in a relatively shorter time than individuals with low aptitude, and instruction can be geared to their higher potential). This interpretation does not imply that low-aptitude individuals are unable to learn a foreign language, only that they are expected to take much longer to attain a given level of mastery than individuals of high aptitude.

As in any effort to construct aptitude tests, researchers have begun their work by making an analysis of the task of foreign language learning as it presents itself in typical learning situations, seeking to determine what individual characteristics might interact with the learning task. A language consists of several interrelated systems that must be learned: its phonology (the system of sound units and relationships out of which its words and expressions are constituted), its grammar and syntax (the system of rules by which meaningful utterances and written sentences are generated), and its lexicon (the extensive repertoire of meaningful words and idioms that is drawn on in the composition of utterances and written discourse). In addition, a foreign language usually has a writing and spelling system that must be learned if the individual is to read and compose written materials in the language.

It might be supposed that cognitive abilities interact differently with these aspects of the foreign language system, and this in fact appears to be the case. Foreign language aptitude is not a unitary entity, but rather a collection of abilities that operate to make an individual able to handle different aspects of the learning task.

Several successful batteries of foreign language aptitude tests have been constructed. These tests measure approximately the same set of cognitive abilities predictive of success in foreign language learning.

COGNITIVE ABILITIES UNDERLYING FOREIGN LANGUAGE APTITUDE

Research has suggested that at least four types of special cognitive abilities underlie talent for learning foreign languages in typical courses of training, especially those placing emphasis on the spoken language.

Phonetic coding ability is a type of memory capacity whereby the individual has the ability to perceive the sounds of a foreign language and the sound shapes of words and expressions, and mentally "code" them for memory storage and later retrieval. It appears *not* to involve the ability to discriminate between foreign sounds; most learners have the capacity to learn phoneme discrimination under proper instructional conditions. Rather, it involves the ability to attend to the precise phonetic shapes of foreign sounds and words and to remember these shapes, especially when they utilize phonetic features not found in the learner's native language. This ability can be tested in a number of ways, informally by presenting foreign sounds and words and eliciting imitations of them after a few seconds of interfering activity, but more formally (e.g., by requiring the examinee to learn associations between sounds and phonetic symbols).

Grammatical sensitivity is the ability to perceive grammatical relations in a foreign language and to understand the role of grammar in the generation and interpretation of utterances and sentences. One form of test is to require the examinee to perceive grammatical relationships in the native language.

Rote associational memory has long been recognized in factor-analytic studies of cognitive abilities; it is evidently operative in the acquisition of the large repertoire of essentially arbitrary associations between words and meanings that must be learned in a foreign language. It can be tested by a work-sample approach requiring the examinee to learn and then show knowledge of a small sample of such arbitrary associations (e.g., in a made-up language).

Inductive ability is a general cognitive capacity that is measured in many batteries of cognitive ability tests—the ability to see and infer rules governing patterns of stimuli. In foreign language aptitude tests, it is assessed by ascertaining how well the examinee can induce and apply relevant rules and relationships in sample materials in a real or made-up foreign language.

Scores on foreign language aptitude tests are substantially correlated with scores on general intelligence tests, but this correlation probably arises from the fact that some of the special aptitudes required in successful foreign language learning are also factors measured in intelligence tests. This is true of inductive ability, but less true of the other abilities mentioned previously. Foreign language aptitude tests usually yield higher correlations with measures of foreign language learning success than general intelligence tests do, by virtue of the fact that they include measures of the special aptitudes required.

THE PREDICTIVE VALIDITY OF FOREIGN LANGUAGE APTITUDE TESTS

The average validity coefficients obtained with foreign language aptitude tests are among the highest in the field of applied psychology. For a number of years foreign language aptitude measures were important criteria for selection of volunteers in the U.S. Peace Corps because most of these trainees were required to learn a foreign language for their work in host countries. Validity coefficients averaging about 0.5 to 0.6 were regularly found. Candidate Peace Corps volunteers were well motivated both in taking the tests and in pursuing the highly intensive foreign language courses they were given.

Many variables can influence the degree of predictive validity shown by an aptitude test. Motivation in test taking and language learning is only one of these. The type of instruction—intensive, systematic, and stressful versus spaced-out, relatively unsystematic, and tolerant of student errors and failures—is another.

The most successful foreign language learners are likely to be those who are above average or superior in all or nearly all the special aptitudes required for success.

**APTITUDE TESTING
COGNITIVE ABILITIES
PSYCHOLINGUISTICS**

J. B. CARROLL

FORENSIC PSYCHOLOGY

Forensic psychology deals with the interface of psychology and the law, and with the application of psychology to legal issues. This specialty includes a wide range of clients and settings, including individuals of all ages, couples, groups, organizations, industry, government agencies, schools, universities, inpatient and outpatient mental health settings, and correctional institutions. Forensic psychologists may become involved in such diverse areas as criminal competency and responsibility, tort liability and/or damages, products liability, mental hospital commitment and treatment, divorce and custody litigation, treatment of offenders, rights of patients and offenders, special education, eyewitness identification, jury selection, police selection and training, employment practices, workers' compensation, and professional liability.

Although psychiatry has had a role within the legal system for many years, it was not until Judge Bazelon's decision in *Jenkins v. United States* in 1962 that psychology obtained firm legal status. In Jenkins, a criminal case, the trial judge had ordered the jury to disregard the psychologist's testimony regarding mental disease. He did so on the basis that a psychologist is not qualified to give a medical opinion. The Court of Appeals ruled that the judge was in error and stated that "some psychologists are qualified to render expert testimony in the field of mental disorder." The court went on to suggest criteria for qualifying a psychologist as an expert. In the years since that decision, other cases have substantially broadened the issues included within the psychologists' legally defined expertise. Today, although there are some differences among states and between the state and federal governments, psychologists are regularly accorded expert status in practically every appropriate area of criminal, civil, family, and administrative law.

The growth of forensic psychology has been manifested in a variety of other ways. Some interdisciplinary programming between law schools and psychology departments began in the 1960s. The early 1970s witnessed the development of joint Ph.D.–J.D. degree programs and psychology Ph.D. programs with a specialty in forensic or correctional psychology. Today there are a substantial number of such programs, and also a growing trend within psychology graduate schools to include law-related courses in the curriculum.

A number of professional organizations have also emerged. These include the American Association of Correctional Psychology and the American Psychology–Law Society. In 1980 the American Psychological Association membership approved the creation of a Division of Psychology and Law (Division 41). The APA has also appointed a Committee on Legal Issues (COLI). The American Board of Forensic Psychology was established in 1978. Its purpose is to identify qualified practitioners to the public and to promote forensic psychology as a recognized discipline.

Another manifestation of growth is the publication of journals and books specific to the field. Among the important journals are *Law and Human Behavior* and *Criminal Justice and Behavior,* although many other journals also publish relevant articles. Among books that provide an overview of the field are Lipsitt and Sales, *New directions in psycholegal research;* G. Cooke, *The role of the forensic psychologist;* and Schwitzgebel and Schwitzgebel, *Law and psychological practice.*

SPECIFIC ISSUES ADDRESSED BY FORENSIC PSYCHOLOGISTS

In most forensic cases the questions that the psychologist is called upon to answer fall into three categories: (a) diagnostic questions concerning personality dynamics, presence of psychosis or organicity, evidence of malingering, and so on; (b) questions involving inference from the diagnostic level to opinions regarding specific legal questions, competency to stand trial, the relationship of a psychological disorder to an accident, the best interests of the child, and so forth; and (c) questions regarding disposition—need for treatment and prognosis, potential for future dangerous behavior, and the like. To address these questions, the forensic psychologist must not only possess the usual evaluation skills, but must also be aware of special screening instruments and relevant case law. Also, there will be important confidentiality issues that will vary from situation to situation.

The psychologist must also work with attorneys prior to the evaluation to determine the questions to be addressed and to help them understand what the evaluation can and cannot do. The attorney must also understand that the payment of a fee is for the evaluation only, and that there is no commitment on the part of the psychologist to testify on behalf of the client. Whether testimony occurs will depend on the findings of the evaluation.

It is also necessary for the psychologist to take a "forensic history," which is more comprehensive than the usual one and is likely to include such information as hospital records, police reports, and statements of witnesses. These sources of information will then be referenced in the report based on the evaluation.

TESTIFYING IN COURT

In some cases the report of the forensic psychologist will be accepted without an appearance in court. But at other times the psychologist may be called to testify. Giving testimony can be a traumatic experience: The key to minimizing difficulties is thorough preparation. This preparation takes place on several levels. The first level involves a thorough knowledge of the relevant law, the tests used, and the test findings. The psychologist must also be able to express the test findings without using excessive jargon and by utilizing behavioral examples that will illustrate the statements made. The second level of preparation involves meeting with the attorney. The forensic psychologist must abide by ethical principles and must retain personal integrity. However, the psychologist also has the responsibility to present the findings as effectively as possible. The attorney, in contrast, is required to advance the client's interests. The attorney has been taught never to ask a witness a question to which the attorney does not already know the answer. Preparation, therefore, includes an agreement between the psychologist and the attorney on the order in which the findings will be presented, on what questions will be asked, and on what the psychologist's answers will be. It is also helpful to review likely cross-examination questions for the psychologist to indicate what the answers would be.

The credibility of the psychologist in the courtroom will depend on several factors. The first of these is credentials: The psychologist should provide the attorney with a curriculum vitae, which the attorney can use when presenting the psychologist's qualifications. The credibility of the psychologist will also depend on courtroom demeanor. The psychologist on the witness stand must remember that the cross-examining attorney is only doing a job when questioning the credibility of the psychologist and of the findings. Also, the courtroom situation often is not as formal as expected, and the judge is usually helpful to an expert witness. In giving testimony, the psychologist should not hesitate to say that he or she did not understand the question or does not know the answer, or that there is insufficient information to answer the question.

FORENSIC TREATMENT

Forensic treatment covers as wide a range of cases as forensic evaluation. In criminal cases, treatment may consist of therapy focused on returning an incompetent individual to competency, or it may provide emotional support to the person who must face imprisonment. Treatment in criminal cases sometimes includes therapy focused on personality problems, or on aggressive or sexual behavior of the individual while incarcerated or in outpatient therapy as a condition of probation or parole. Treatment of offenders requires special knowledge about the criminal justice system, the nature and effects of the prison environment, the probation–parole system, and the personality characteristics and/or behavior frequently observed in offenders. Group therapy or behavioral therapy techniques are often valuable in treating sexual offenders, offenders with alcohol problems, and others.

In a civil damage situation, treatment may consist of insight-oriented or supportive psychotherapy. In addition, special methods such as behavior therapy, cognitive therapy, or biofeedback may be used to treat anxieties, phobias, or depression. The therapist must be aware that testimony may be required in court, and this may at times influence both the mental status of the client and the course of the therapy. Often in such cases the therapist may find the legal situation to be at odds with the therapeutic situation. In such cases, the therapist has a responsibility to make the patient and the attorney aware of the recommendations, but the final decision as to whether to proceed on those recommendations lies with the patient.

In the child custody situation, treatment is often ordered by the court either to avoid a full custody litigation or as part of the resolution of the conflict. The focus of treatment is to help the child to make a positive adjustment, and this of course requires treatment of the child. However, treatment of the parents is almost always required as well. The treatment of the parents focuses on such issues as communication processes in dealing with the child, unconscious or conscious derogation of the other parent to the child, and resolution of conflicts between the parents.

RESEARCH IN FORENSIC PSYCHOLOGY

Many of the questions asked of the forensic psychologist require only description of the present status of an individual. But many other questions make an explicit or implicit request for a prediction of future behavior. The answers to such questions as the probability of future dangerous behavior, response to treatment, or the adjustment of a child under various possible alternative living situations require not only thorough clinical evaluation, but a knowledge of relevant research. The research may often reveal that clinical lore is incorrect. A recent example of this involves the findings regarding children's adjustment to the trauma of divorce. The state of the art is such that it is often difficult to support a clinical opinion within the framework of available research findings. It is, therefore, incumbent on the forensic psychologist to be both the recipient and the provider of research on these questions. In other types of cases, such as those involving eyewitness identification, the primary basis on which opinions are offered is the research.

The forensic psychologist must keep abreast of new information that emerges from research. Such effort, along with up-to-date knowledge of the law and modifications of the law by new cases, provides a perspective that, when combined with a thorough clinical approach, allows the forensic psychologist to be of greatest service to the legal system.

CRIMINAL RESPONSIBILITY
EXPERT TESTIMONY
JURY PSYCHOLOGY
PSYCHOLOGY AND THE LAW

G. COOKE

FORGETTING

Forgetting is the loss of information from any point in the memory process or memory system. William James suggested that in real life, in spite of occasional surprises, most of what happens is actually forgotten. Sir Frederic Bartlett indicated that memory was hardly ever exact.

Hermann Ebbinghaus in *Memory* described three major theories of forgetting: one in which the earlier images are overlaid and covered by later ones; a second in which the persisting images suffer changes; and a third in which the images crumble into parts, with a resultant loss of separate components instead of general obscuration.

Different methods of learning and memory measurement have been used to evaluate the amount and/or rate of forgetting. Ebbinghaus used the number of trials to relearn items as a percentage of the number of trials required to learn the material originally. The difference between this percentage and 100% was called the rate of forgetting. Forgetting is the rule, not the exception. Theoretical approaches have produced research results that only in part explain the losses from memory.

MEMORY
SHORT-TERM MEMORY

N. S. ANDERSON

FORM/SHAPE PERCEPTION

Perception of a form or shape, including figural detail and pattern, is generally accomplished by organisms through analysis of stimulus features from the sensory input. There is not a lot of agreement about what constitutes form/shape. Because contour and edge perceptions are hypothesized to be done at the retinal level, there are vision experts who propose that contour and edges are the basis of complex form perception. The constructs of visual perception allow coding at the retinal and other neural centers. An information-processing analysis of vision requires a first stage of figural synthesis, as described by Ulric Neisser in *Cognitive psychology*. The figural synthesis is the manner in which stimulus information is transferred from the icon and synthesized into a form. For pattern or shape recognition to occur, the synthesized information is then transferred to memory to produce a unique response. One of the major problems for pattern recognition or perception theorists is to discover how the organism consistently responds or recognizes forms or shapes when they are presented in different sizes and retinal locations, are degraded by poor or noisy environmental conditions, or are partially outlined or in cartoon or picturelike formats.

Two general approaches in the theories are the feature extraction or template-matching approach. Most vision researchers agree that organisms respond to organization of the different features as demonstrated by William Uttal in his experiments on humans in identifying degraded letters, described by him in *The psychology of sensory coding*.

Clarence Graham in *Vision and visual perception* indicated that research on form perception includes the "identification and specification of conditions necessary for naming, recognizing, denoting or discriminating forms or aspects of forms." The first aspect of form perception he discussed was that of contour perception. Most research in form/shape perception is based on basic visual aspects regarding the characteristics of luminance distribution that produce lines or Mach bands, discriminable differences in forms, figural aftereffects (including influences of distance and temporal factors, displacement, and tilted line effects), visual illusion changes due to unspecified cues, and estimation of the vertical.

In considering three-dimensional perception, James J. Gibson indicated in *The ecological approach to visual perception* that object perception can be based only on form perception. Gibson suggests that features are important in that "what counts is not the form as such but the dimensions of variation of form."

Although form and shape are frequently used interchangeably, Leonard Zusne wrote in *Visual perception of form* that "form" is the more general term and "shape" the more specific. He also indicated that there is not much agreement on what is meant by "form," but that specific operations led investigators to use the term. These operations include "the corporeal quality of an object in three dimensional space, the projection of such an object on a two dimensional surface, a flat two-dimensional pictorial representation, a nonrepresentational distribution of contours in a plane, or the values of coordinates in Euclidean space."

APPERCEPTION
CONSTANCY
PERCEPTION

N. S. ANDERSON

FORMATIVE THEORY OF PERSONALITY

This theory started in the late 1960s at Duquesne University with the pioneering work of Adrian van Kaam in contemporary physics. Formation is defined as the basic evolutionary process of the universe perceived as an energy field of constantly rising and falling forms. Each element in the universe tends to realize and maintain its unique form potential in dialetical interaction with its formation field. Subhuman life forms give form in accordance with instinctual form directives, whereas the human life form must disclose and implement its own. In this process, personality is born. Personality is seen as a unique movement of disclosure and tentative implementation of receptive and creative directives within their corresponding formation fields. Foundational personality theorists are in search of form directives that can be scientifically appraised as foundational or universal.

STRUCTURAL EFFECTS OF PERSONALITY FORMATION

The primary personality structures effected by formation are the foundational, core, current, and apparent forms of life. The potential form of the human personality is the effect of biogenetic preformation. It concretizes itself in the emergent core of the personality via its provisional, current, latent, and manifest or apparent forms.

The core of the personality is relatively enduring. It forms itself mainly between birth and early adulthood. In later life it is usually not changed fundamentally. The core may be modulated by the current apparent and actual forms the personality assumes. The core functions, among other things, as an integrative center of global formative effects. As such, it gives a unique vibrancy and color to the personality when it tries to express concretely the foundational potential life form with which it is endowed by biogenetic preformation. The core form, in turn, further concretizes its forming tendencies in the more specified motions of the current and apparent forms of the emergent personality. The core form of the personality functions ideally as the guardian of the consonance between current and apparent personality aspects and the foundational potential life form, which is the biogenetic ground of the personality.

The transconscious dimension contains the aspirations typical of a particular personality. Like the unacknowledged tendencies of the infra-conscious dimension, they may at times penetrate the barriers that sepa-

rate the preconscious dimension from the infra- and transconscious dimensions that surround it. Once they penetrate this barrier, they interact with all the other formative forces that are constantly interacting with one another within the field of preconscious energy.

In relation to these dimensions of consciousness, the theory speaks about *formation conscientization:* the act of bringing to focal awareness, at the appropriate moment, the directives that actually in some measure give form to the personality, be it on a pre-, inter-, infra-, or transconscious level.

PERSONALITY THEORIES
PHILOSOPHICAL PSYCHOLOGY
RELIGION AND PSYCHOLOGY

A. VAN KAAM

FRAGILE X SYNDROME

Little known until the 1980s, fragile X (fra[X]) is a chromosomal abnormality now seen to be the most common heritable cause of mental retardation. Down syndrome, the primary genetically based cause of mental retardation, arises through the nondisjunction of chromosome pair 21 during meiosis; it is genetic but not inherited. Based in a weak or fragile site on the X chromosome, fra(X) is sex linked and thus expressed more frequently in males. It is the only one of the more than 50 X-linked disorders associated with mental retardation that is of frequent occurrence. Although estimates vary across studies, incidence is about 1 in 1500 in males and 1 in 2000 in females. Fragile X may account for 2 to 7% of retarded males. It has two unusual genetic characteristics: (a) Heterozygotic (carrier) females, who have one normal X chromosome and one with the fragile site, may show impaired intelligence and specific learning disabilities; and (b) about 20% of males who inherit the fragile site are nonpenetrant, showing no apparent physical or psychological effects and no evidence of fragility on cytogenetic analysis. They do, however, pass the X chromosome on to their daughters who may have affected sons. As a further complication, repeated cytogenetic testing fails to reveal the fragile site in more than 50% of unaffected carrier females.

HISTORY

From the beginning of the twentieth century, researchers have noted a considerable excess of males, frequently about 25%, with mental retardation. Martin and Bell in 1943 and others thereafter described families in which mental retardation was inherited in an X-linked pattern. Although Lubs first described the fragile X site in 1969, his description drew little interest until Sutherland reported that some fragile sites were expressed only if lymphocytes were grown in a culture medium that lacked folic acid. The discovery of folic-acid sensitivity of fra(X) and some other fragile sites led to more accurate diagnosis, which in turn led to the discovery of the high incidence of fra(X) and an exponential growth of interest generally in X-linked mental retardation. Retesting has indicated a fra(X) basis for the retardation in the family studied by Martin and Bell.

CHARACTERISTICS

About 66% of affected adult males show a "clinical triad": (a) moderate to severe mental retardation; (b) characteristic craniofacial features, including large forehead, protruding chin, and elongated ears; and (c) large testes (macroorchidism). However, affected individuals show such a variety of characteristics that diagnosis can firmly be based only on cytogenetic analysis. Females and prepubertal males are even more variable. Although most males show an "overgrowth syndrome" from birth, with head size, fontanel, and body measurements exceeding the 97th percentile, macroorchidism and craniofacial features are much less distinct in prepubertal boys. The following summary of characteristics of affected individuals is based on information in Bregman, Dykens, Watson, Ort, and Leckman; Brown et al.; Curfs et al.; Dykens & Leckman; Fryns; and Hagerman.

Physical Features

In addition to the characteristic craniofacial features, macroorchidism, and overgrowth, males with fra(X) may show a variety of other features, such as hyperextensible joints, high arched palate, mitral valve prolapse (a form of heart murmur), flat feet, and low muscle tonus. Female carriers, particularly those with subnormal intelligence, may also show facial features, including high broad forehead and long face, and hyperextensibility.

Cognitive Features

Approximately 70% of affected males have moderate to severe mental retardation, but the degree of retardation varies from mild to profound, with a small percentage of cases in the low normal range of intelligence. Males frequently show a decline in IQ, but not absolute intelligence, with age. Affected males have particular difficulty with sequential processing and short-term memory for information presented serially, performing poorly on tasks requiring recall of series of items or imitation of a series of motor movements. This deficit in sequential processing differentiates fra(X) individuals from those with other forms of mental retardation. Affected males perform relatively well on tasks requiring simultaneous processing and integration, such as block design.

Although most carrier females have intelligence in the normal range, about 30% test in the retarded range. Furthermore, an unusually high number of those with at least average intelligence show learning disabilities. Females also show deficits in sequential processing and visual spatial skills, performing poorly on digit span, block design, and arithmetic tests. Some evidence suggests that, unlike males, the IQ of affected carrier females increases with age.

Language

In affected males, language development in general is delayed. In addition, specific problems such as perseverations, repetitions, echolalia, and dysfluencies are often shown, some of which may stem from general deficits in sequential processing.

Behavioral Characteristics

Hyperactivity and attention deficits are particularly common sequelae of fra(X), particularly in males. Many affected individuals also are socially withdrawn, show gaze aversion, and engage in self-injurious behavior, particularly self-biting.

Relation to Other Disorders

Affected males also may have seizure disorders. Furthermore, fra(X) appears to coexist with autism: Many fra(X) males show characteristics of autism and a percentage of diagnosed autistic males test positive for fra(X). The degree of overlap varies greatly across studies, presumably in part owing to differing criteria for autism, but it is sufficient to suggest that autistic males routinely be screened for fra(X).

FOLIC ACID TREATMENT

Folic acid has often been used in attempts to reduce symptoms associated with fra(X). Double-blind studies indicate that such treatment does not affect scores on intelligence tests, but may reduce hyperactivity and increase attention span. However, questions exist as to whether folic acid treatment is as effective as traditional treatment for attention deficit hyperactivity disorder (ADHD) with stimulant medication.

IMPLICATIONS

Psychological approaches are of importance in dealing with fra(X) for at least two reasons: (a) The diffuse and variable physical effects of fra(X) in children place additional significance on the role of psychological assessment in identifying potentially fra(X) children for cytogenetic analysis, and (b) cognitive characteristics of those with fra(X) have important implications for treatment and educational programs. Owing to the variety and variation in problems exhibited by those with fra(X), a team approach is recommended for treatment. Furthermore, the clear distinction between characteristics of those with fra(X) and those with Down syndrome indicates heterogeneity among groups with organic retardation, which may have theoretical implications. Fra(X) can be identified antenatally with a special test, but the incomplete penetrance in males, phenotypic effects in a significant number of carrier females, and difficulty of diagnosis in unaffected females all complicate genetic counseling. Finally, although much has been learned about fra(X), Wells and Brown's suggestion that "subsequent data may modify or change existing knowledge regarding fragile-X" remains as a useful caution.

CHROMOSOME DISORDERS
EMBRYO AND FETUS
INBREEDING AND HUMAN FACTORS
MENTAL RETARDATION
MINIMAL BRAIN DYSFUNCTION

R. T. BROWN

FREE RECALL

Free recall is widely used to study memory and learning. Typically, a person is given information to learn and then is later asked to recall the information in any order he or she wishes. Information can vary from lists of unrelated words or digits to complex prose.

The free-recall paradigm has contributed to the development of cognitive psychology. For example, the free recall paradigm has helped to explain the primacy and recency components of the serial position curve. The primacy effect has been attributed to increased rehearsal and entry of those items into long-term memory (LTM), whereas the recency effect has been explained by the entry of the last items into short-term memory (STM). Because items at the end of the list are not rehearsed and consequently are not in LTM, they are lost if the subject is given a distractor task immediately after the list is presented.

Early research suggested that the most important aspect of free recall is in the learner rather than in the stimulus material he or she is given. That is, there is a tendency for people to recall items together that are objectively or subjectively related to one another, even though they were separated during presentation. A report by Bousfield gave impetus to the study of the learner's internal organizational processes. Participants were given a randomized list of 60 words consisting of four 15-word categories. Immediately after presentation, subjects were given 10 min to write down all the words they could remember in any order they wished. People tended to recall and cluster the words into the inherent categories rather than in the order that the words were presented.

A disadvantage of typical clustering studies is that they only tap the type of organization for which the experimenter is looking. The relations among items in the list are defined by the experimenter, and the obtained measures of organization depend on how well the participant's recall matches the experimenter's list categories or associations. Tulving argued that subjects not only use the experimenter's inherent list structure, but also tend to find their own idiosyncratic relations among the words in the list. Thus clustering experiments tend to underestimate the extent of the total organization a subject imposes on the list during learning and uses during recall. By having subjects repeatedly learn and recall the same lists of unrelated words presented in a different random order each time, Tulving was able to demonstrate idiosyncratic subjective organization on the part of the learner.

Free recall also has been used to study prose comprehension and recall of both expository and descriptive texts as well as narratives. Although early research suggested that people tend cognitively to organize text into a hierarchical or logical pattern of meaning for later recall, subsequent research showed that there are individual differences in recall and inferred organizational patterns as a function of age and reading ability. In fact, free recall methods are currently being used to find learning strategy differences among people postulated to have differing learning styles.

The use of free recall methods to illustrate the tendency of people to reorganize material continues to be used as evidence for inferring organizational processes on the part of the learner. Thus free recall research is used to support the major tenet of cognitive psychology (i.e., that the learner is not a passive recipient of information from the environment; rather, he or she actively organizes information into his or her knowledge memory structures).

COGNITIVE LEARNING STYLES
FORGETTING
MEMORY RETRIEVAL PROCESSES

B. R. DUNN

FREE WILL

In psychology and in psychologically oriented philosophy two extreme positions have been taken on the question of free will. One—widely associated at present with psychology and often presented as a basic assumption in introductory textbooks of general psychology—is that free will is entirely illusory, that in order to be scientific, psychologists must believe that all human behavior or experience is absolutely determined by causal processes that are in principle knowable. The other extreme, especially associated in this century with the existentialist movement in philosophy, is that human free will is real and ubiquitous in the sense that all experience and action involve some element of free choice, that with no change in the antecedent conditions, one could always have experienced or acted somewhat differently from the way one did.

Among psychologists, the extreme deterministic position often seems to be based on the belief that it is taken by, and is somehow essential to, the physical sciences, and that it must be a basic assumption of any genuinely scientific enterprise. Quantum physics has accepted some degree of indeterminacy as an inevitable principle. Conditions, the knowledge of which would be needed for perfect predictability in psychology, would often include internal processes that could not be accurately known without interventions that would change them and hence the outcome; this seems sufficiently analogous to the basis for indeterminacy in quantum physics to argue for extension of the principle to psychology. Once indeterminacy is granted to be inevitable, a distinction between free will and a determinism that cannot possibly be verified may become scientifically meaningless.

The argument for free will is most often empirical. Having acted, a person often feels certain that he or she could have acted differently, could have made a different choice; free will, it is argued, is thus a basic fact of experience. This argument cannot escape the objection that causal determinants may simply not yet be sufficiently identified and understood.

Another pragmatic basis for a choice of positions on the issue of free will is the effect of various positions on general human welfare. Advocates of rigid determinism sometimes consider acceptance of their position necessary for convincing people that human behavior can be predicted and controlled, so that the future of humanity can be influenced by "human engineering" just as physical events can be influenced by engineering based on the physical sciences. Opponents of rigid determinism

argue that acceptance of that position eliminates hope of deliberate change and thus has a detrimental influence.

BEHAVIORISM

I. L. CHILD

FREEDOM

The predominantly deterministic strategy adopted very early in the development of psychology as behavioral science appeared to make explicit recognition of freedom inconsistent. Considering behavior as lawful within a deterministic lawful natural system seemed to allow no place for the notion of freedom in a scientific psychology. Occasionally there have been psychologists somewhat outside the main stream of behavioral psychology who dealt with freedom as a real and central psychological issue. It has been primarily the business of legal scholars and social and political philosophers such as J. S. Mill and Isaiah Berlin to examine the issues of human freedom.

The concept of and belief in freedom play a very significant role in regulating individual behavior, social organization, and politics. Recently, psychologists have become involved, in spite of B. F. Skinner's reassertion that the concept of freedom is alien to lawful natural systems, including human behavior, and does nothing but confuse our understanding.

Within the growing literature of humanistic psychology, or a human science approach to the study of human behavior, freedom is a significant theme. The human science point of view takes consciousness, self-awareness, agency, and choice as patent givens of human behavior. Although the impact on present behavior of both recognized and unrecognized historical determinants is acknowledged, there remains a zone of action. Even when behavior seems totally circumscribed or coerced, there remains a realm of attitudinal freedom (i.e., the point of view one takes toward one's circumstances).

Empirical research directed specifically at the study of human freedom has been conducted primarily within more traditional frameworks. Social psychologists have approached the study of human freedom through three distinct routes: attribution theory, reactance theory, and experiential studies.

THE ATTRIBUTION APPROACH

The attribution approach to human freedom is concerned with the conditions under which freedom is attributed to (or perceived in) the behaviors of others or the self. *Decision freedom* is a function of the magnitude of the discrepancy in expected gains from alternative courses of action. When the expected gains are approximately equal, decision freedom is high because the choice is not coerced by discrepant expected gains. The decision is seen to be controlled by the decision maker rather than by the options. *Outcome freedom* is a function of the estimated probability of actually obtaining the expected gains. Thus if an individual is seen to be making a choice between alternatives that are about equal in expected gains and about equally available, a choice between them is seen as a free choice, uncoerced by either discrepant gains or discrepant availability.

If behavior is perceived as a consequence of coercion, observers do not believe the behavior tells them very much about an actor. Although decisions or choices between alternatives are perceived as freer when the valences become more alike, the effect is much more pronounced in choices between positive than between negative alternatives. Freedom is more strongly attributed to choices when the choices are among a moderate number of alternatives as contrasted to a very small or very large number, and when the behavior observed is concordant with what the observer believes to be a predisposition of the actor.

THE REACTANCE APPROACH

A second line of study is based on Jack Brehm's *A theory of psychological reactance*. Reactance is conceived as a motivational state aroused when behavioral freedoms are eliminated or threatened with elimination, and this motivational state organizes behavior toward restoring behavioral freedoms. Behavioral freedoms are specific to situations, and are defined as knowing (believing) that several courses of action are open to one, and knowing (believing) that one has the requisite skills and resources to pursue any of the recognized options. In a wide variety of settings, the research indicates that people do operate so as to restore specific behavioral freedoms that are removed or threatened with removal, and that options under threat gain in attractiveness. The bestowing of a favor on someone, which implies a reciprocal obligation, can arouse reactance; so too can the act of making a decision, in that, as one approaches a choice, the availability of a less-favored option comes under threat, and this option increases in attractiveness. Reactance studies suggest many implications for social influence processes, consumer psychology, advertising, public relations, and decision making.

THE EXPERIENTIAL APPROACH

A third approach has been employed by Malcolm Westcott, who has studied human freedom primarily as an experience and distinguishes this sharply from freedom as an attribution or an ontological state. He has been concerned with the extent to which people report that they feel free under a variety of theoretically important conditions. Drawing on both the reactance literature and the attribution literature, as well as on philosophical and interview sources, he derived seven kinds of situations purported to contribute to human freedom. Using several concrete examples of each type of situation in a questionnaire format, he asked respondents to indicate how free they felt in each. People reported that they felt most free when they were released from unpleasant conditions, including both physical pain and social frustration, and when they were engaged in performing skilled behaviors. These contrasting conditions leading to high degrees of feeling free paralleled the widespread philosophical distinction between negative liberty or "freedom from" and positive liberty or "freedom to." People reported feeling least free when they were obliged to recognize limits on what they could do—even realistic limits—and when they were making difficult decisions.

In addition, when respondents were queried about opposites to feeling free, the opposition to such feeling varied systematically from situation to situation. In some situations, external blockage was the primary erosion to feeling free; in others, conflict and indecision or vague unpleasant affect were the principal opponents. Therefore, from a dialectical point of view, feeling free is not the same experience in all situations.

CONCLUSION

The differences among these three approaches to the psychological study of human freedom are primarily in their orientations: freedom as attributed to one's own acts or the acts of others; freedom as a belief that one has behavioral options and can exercise them; freedom as an experience arising to different degrees under different conditions, such as release from pain or frustration, or engagement in skillful behavior or decision making. The findings from these three perspectives sometimes complement one another and at other times conflict.

PHILOSOPHICAL PSYCHOLOGY
REACTANCE THEORY

M. R. WESTCOTT

FREQUENCY JUDGMENT

Among the cognitive functions that have been most intensively studied, judgment of the frequency of stimulus or event occurrence seems to have some unique properties. In contrast to other cognitive functions, frequency judgment appears to be essentially age invariant. As Hasher and Zacks have argued in two provocative articles, sensitivity to the frequency of stimulus occurrence does not improve very much with age from kindergarten into and even perhaps through the adult years. The other cognitive functions, notably free recall and recognition, generally show large and regular increments over the developmental years.

AUTOMATICITY

The principal theoretical interest in the Hasher and Zacks proposition attaches to the alleged automaticity with which frequency information is encoded. Frequency information seems to be encoded without any intention on the part of the subject to do so. Although there have been disagreements on this issue, the basic position remains essentially intact. Children of different ages, intellectual status, and educational background appear to be equally likely to encode and retrieve fundamental frequency information; on frequency judgment tests they perform substantially as effectively as college students and mature adults.

The automaticity argument is strengthened by the fact that in the experiments reported, little if any improvement has been found in the frequency judgment performance of subjects fully instructed in advance as to the nature of the task and encouraged to attend to and remember stimulus frequency during the study session; experimentally naive subjects, whose encoding of frequency information is "incidental," do just as well. The preinstructed subjects often report that they just get more confused from their conscious efforts to keep track of the frequencies of the numerous stimuli typically presented in the study session. Furthermore, in support of the automaticity argument, practice, which can be a powerful determinant of improvement in performance in such cognitive processes as recall, has not been shown to be effective in frequency judgment performance.

Hasher and Zacks postulate that spatial location and temporal order are automatically (i.e., effortlessly) encoded. The evidence for automaticity seems to be better for spatial location (e.g., Ellis concluded that the "main thrust" of the Hasher and Zacks argument was supported for spatial location by his results).

STRATEGIES

Although the fundamental frequency information may be equally well encoded over development, its retrieval may vary with age and educational achievement to some extent. If so, any important differences in retrieval performance may be primarily attributed to different strategies that are used. Older children, for example, have been found to be more likely than younger children to report that they used estimates of stimulus familiarity (or strength) in their attempts to retrieve frequency information; the younger children were more likely to report that they tried to count separate occurrences of the stimuli.

MEASURES

There are two principal ways in which judgment of stimulus or event frequency can be measured: (a) the absolute method, in which the subject is asked to make an exact numerical estimate of frequency for each stimulus; and (b) the relative method, in which two of the stimuli are presented together and the subject's task is to select the one that he or she thinks was the more frequent.

A major advantage of the absolute method is that the numerical estimates thereby made available are amenable to a large number of quantitative treatments. These include product-moment correlations with actual frequencies and various other statistical treatments such as *t*-tests and analyses of variance of the absolute estimates or number of correct responses, of deviations of subject-generated estimates from actual frequencies, and of the numerical estimates sorted out in terms of the actual frequencies. All of these and more have been used in research on this problem.

The major advantages of the relative, or paired-comparison, method are that it is simpler and, therefore, probably easier to use with younger and intellectually impaired subjects and that it may be a more sensitive measure. With a balanced set of close item frequencies (e.g., 1 and 2, 2 and 3) and more remote item frequencies (e.g., 1 and 4, 2 and 5), the mean proportion of correct responses usually approximates 75%; as indicated earlier, there is typically little variation with such variables as age, intelligence rating, educational achievement, and the like—all variables that generally affect recall and recognition of studied items.

THEORY

Although there is no agreement on a theoretical interpretation of how frequency judgments are made, the most generally accepted interpretation is by Hintzman. It is based on the presumption that when asked to estimate frequency, a subject recalls and counts the separate earlier-experienced occasions in which the target stimulus occurred (e.g., the particular sentences in which the word had been included, or more often simply its occurrences in the word list that had been studied). This interpretation replaced the more traditional view that it is the "strength" of the more frequently occurring stimuli that determines the frequency judgments.

The counting or multiple traces interpretation is more credible for the lower item frequencies. Hintzman recognized that some other interpretation might be necessary for the higher frequencies. The item-frequency variable has been inadequately analyzed in research on the problem. Still unsettled, with conflicting empirical results, is the issue of the relationship between frequency judgment and recognition memory (i.e., when low frequencies are involved, does the subject simply decide whether the target word is "old," thus deserving of some positive numerical estimate, such as 1 or 2 or "new" (not in the study list), thus rating only a 0 frequency estimate?).

Whatever the ultimate theoretical interpretation of frequency judgment, a more adequate account of the role of the item-frequency variable is almost certain to be involved.

ANIMAL FORAGING

Some kind of frequency judgment seems to be involved in animal foraging (as well as in other less-studied forms of animal learning). In foraging, deciding when to leave and when to return to particular feeding areas is related to the number of successes (finding food) as well as to the number of failures the animal associates with each examined patch. Although animals can somehow take such frequency information into account, exactly how they do so remains to be explained. It would seem that a "counting" hypothesis would be less applicable to the foraging animal than to the human. Some kind of generalized "strength" factor, similar perhaps to the "feeling of familiarity" that was often mentioned by older children in their retrospective reports on the frequency judgments they had made, would seem to be, again intuitively, more probable for the foraging animals.

ANIMAL SOCIOBIOLOGY
JUDGMENT AND DECISION MAKING
SPECIES-SPECIFIC BEHAVIOR

M. H. MARX

FROMM'S THEORY

Eric Fromm was concerned about a diversity of topics related to his search for the essence of human nature. He converged several humanist approaches to define human nature as essentially dynamic and dialectic. The essential in man is his capacity to act with freedom and to understand love as an objective communion. People are considered essentially equal, without sexual or status differences.

Self-awareness, reason, and imagination disrupt the harmony that characterizes animal existence. The emergence of these traits made humankind into an anomaly, a freak of the universe. Part of nature, subject to physical laws and unable to change them, humans transcend the rest of nature. Being aware of ourselves, we realize our powerlessness and the limitations of our existence. We visualize our own end—death.

Fromm referred to needs rooted in the peculiarity of human existence. These include the need for relationship, because feeling isolated leads to disintegration just as inanition leads to death. Also, there is the need to transcend, to rise above the possivity and accidentality of our existence; this need makes us become original and look for freedom. The need to transcend offers us the option to create or to destroy, to love or to hate. The satisfaction of the need to create induces us to happiness, destruction, or suffering. A third need is rootedness, that leads us to security and helps us to avoid anxiety and loneliness. A fourth need, identification, gives us a concept of self since we need to feel and say, "I am myself." A fifth need, orientation, is a peculiar need based on our existential situation, our humanity, imagination, and reason; it refers to the purpose of finding a sense for or a value to existence.

For Fromm, social character implied the adaptation of free individuals to social conditions that develop the character traits inducing them to behave in the same way that, within their culture, most people do. Social character internalizes the external needs, orienting individuals toward tasks required by the socioeconomic system.

EXISTENTIALISM

R. NUÑEZ

FRUSTRATION–AGGRESSION HYPOTHESIS

The frustration–aggression hypothesis is a model originally proposed by Dollard, Doob, Miller, Mowrer, and Sears in their classic book *Frustration and aggression,* which attempted to explain human aggression in terms of a few basic concepts. While rejecting the Freudian notion of innate and accumulating aggressive energy, the model proposed that there is an inborn tendency to respond aggressively after being frustrated. Frustration always leads to aggression and aggression is always caused by frustration. Frustration is defined as interference with behavior directed toward a particular goal, and it leads to a latent aggressive state, which they referred to as *instigation*. The degree of frustration and the strength of the instigation depend on the strength of the goal-seeking behavior (how strongly motivated the individual is to achieve the goal), the extent of the interference (whether goal seeking is merely delayed or completely blocked), and the number of goal-directed behaviors subjected to interference (aggressive inclinations that will be summated over repeated frustrations).

This model incorporates the concept of inhibition. Inhibition is proportionate to the anticipated likelihood and severity of punishment for aggressive behavior. When the instigation is greater than the inhibition, then aggressive behavior toward the frustrating agent is produced. If the inhibition is greater than the instigation, then aggression will be displaced to alternative targets. If frustration is ongoing, eventually instigation will exceed inhibition, and aggression toward the frustrating agent will occur.

This classic version of the frustration–aggression hypothesis has not been substantiated by empirical research, although in some circumstances frustration does lead to aggression. However, laboratory and field studies have demonstrated that although frustration may lead to aggression, it does not do so invariably, and it can also produce withdrawal and other behaviors. Moreover, not all aggression is preceded by frustration, because it is often used instrumentally to obtain a goal.

Although the failure to produce adequate empirical support for the frustration–aggression hypothesis led many psychologists to abandon it, Leonard Berkowitz reformulated the hypothesis in a way that accounted for the finding that frustration does not always lead to aggression while also acknowledging the important role played by situational factors. He proposed that frustration produces only a *readiness* to act aggressively, but to produce aggression, appropriate environmental cues or "releasers" are usually necessary to trigger it or to indicate that it is allowable or appropriate.

Berkowitz has proposed a further reformulation of the frustration-aggression hypothesis in terms of aversively stimulated aggression. (Instrumental aggression, which is deliberately directed at attaining some goal, is excluded from the realm to which this hypothesis applies.) He argues that the reason that frustrations give rise to aggressive tendencies is because they are aversive to the individual, producing negative affect, and it is this negative affect that produces aggressive tendencies. Thus frustration is not a necessary condition for aggression to occur, because other aversive events also can produce negative affect, which in turn can produce aggressive tendencies.

Aversive events can be of either a physical nature (e.g., pain and excessive heat) or a psychological nature (e.g., frightening information). Although there is a defensive component to the resultant aggressiveness, insofar as the individual attempts to remove the source of the unpleasantness, there also is an active inclination to harm available targets. Social learning factors, based on reinforcement history, will either increase or decrease the likelihood of aggression as well as determine the target and form of the aggression.

Cognitive factors play an important role as well according to this revised model. Cognitive appraisal of a situation will influence the extent to which frustrations elicit negative feelings—be they annoyance, sadness, pain, or other unpleasantness. Once such negative affect is stimulated, it elicits an experience of anger. Subsequent cognitive activity will either lead to the expression of that anger through aggressive behavior or nullify its effects altogether. For example, anticipated failure to attain a goal will be less unpleasant than unanticipated failure. People also are more likely to be upset and to attack their frustrators if they believe that the frustration was deliberate and directed at them.

Social learning theorists dispute the frustration–aggression hypothesis and argue that frustration (and aversive stimulation in general) only produces generalized arousal and that social learning determines how this arousal will influence behavior. According to this view, aggressive responses are acquired because they are effective. Thus people learn to perform aggressive actions and learn the circumstances under which aggressive behavior is likely to be rewarded.

AGGRESSION
COOPERATION–COMPETITION
CROWDING
OBEDIENCE
PUNISHMENT
REWARDS
SADOMASOCHISM
SELF-CONTROL
SOCIAL EXCHANGE THEORY

J. E. ALCOCK

FUNCTIONAL ANALYSIS

Behavioral assessment emphasizes the use of empirical methodologies to quantify target behaviors and the many factors that control them. The term *functional analysis* has historically characterized a wide array of behavioral assessment activities and has been defined as "the identification of important, controllable, causal functional relationships applicable to a specified set of target behaviors for an individual client."

This definition carries with it several explicit and implied characteristics. Causal functional relationships are a key component of the functional analysis. By itself, a functional relationship implies only covariation between two variables. Some functional relationships are causal, whereas others are strictly correlational. Because the information contained in a functional analysis is primarily used for intervention design, the behavioral assessor is most interested in isolating and quantifying *causal* functional relationships.

Causal functional relationships can be mathematically described as elevated conditional probabilities, which state that the probability of observing a topographical change in a target behavior, given that some hypothesized causal event has occurred (its conditional probability), is greater than the probability of observing a topographical change in a target behavior without prior occurrence of the hypothesized causal event (its base rate or unconditional probability). To illustrate, let A be a change in blood pressure level (the target behavior); B, a change in daily stressors (hypothesized causal event); and P, probability. A causal functional relationship would be tentatively inferred if the probability of blood pressure change subsequent to daily stress change ($P[A/B]$) is greater than the base rate probability of blood pressure change ($P[A]$).

Many variables may have causal functional relationships with a particular target behavior. For example, dysregulation of central nervous system neurotransmitter systems, loss of response–contingent reinforcement, increased levels of aversive consequences, negative self-statements, and seasonal changes in sunlight may all exert a causal influence on the depressed mood of a particular client. The subset of variables that have nontrivial causal effects on a target behavior are most relevant to the design of behavioral interventions. Therefore, a second characteristic of the functional analysis is an emphasis on identifying important causal functional relationships.

Important causal functional relationships are sometimes uncontrollable. Significant historical events (e.g., a traumatic experience) and biological attributes (e.g., genetic heritage) are two sets of important causal factors that cannot be modified. Because behavioral interventions are designed to bring about change in target behaviors, a functional analysis will typically be restricted to identifying controllable (and often current) causal functional relationships.

A further characteristic of functional analysis is a focus on identifying causal functional relationships applicable to specific target behaviors for an individual client. This idiographic emphasis is consistent with the behavioral axiom that important within- and between-person differences exist in the causes of behavior.

Finally, because the functional analysis is defined in terms of the target behavior, a wide range of causal relationships are examined in the assessment process. Thus complex permutations of the antecedent-response, response–response, response–consequence, and antecedent-response–consequence interactions must be carefully considered.

IDENTIFYING CAUSAL FUNCTIONAL RELATIONSHIPS

Educing that a causal functional relationship is present between a controlling variable and the target behavior requires the presence of (a) "cues to causality" such as elevated conditional probabilities and/or reliable covariation, (b) temporal precedence (i.e., the hypothesized causal variable precedes the observed effect on the target behavior), and (c) the exclusion of plausible alternative explanations for the observed relationship.

Several assessment methods can be used to determine whether a causal functional relationship exists between a controlling event and the target behavior. Time series analysis and single-subject designs can be used to evaluate empirically the strength and reliability of causal functional relationships. These methodologies, however, can be problematic because they require multiple points of measurement and considerable effort from the client and can typically only evaluate the interactions among a few variables.

Contemporaneous administration of different behavioral assessment devices (e.g., self-report inventories, observational measures, behavioral interviews, self-monitoring, and psychophysiological measures) also can provide information about causal functional relationships. For example, a client may report high levels of social anxiety on a self-report inventory, demonstrate high levels of heart rate reactivity during role-playing exercises in the psychophysiology laboratory, and be observed to have poor social interaction skills during a behavioral interview. Given these data, it may be plausible to hypothesize that the client's social anxiety is caused by excessive sympathetic nervous system activation combined with social skills deficits. These causal speculations are susceptible to alternative explanations, however, due to the inability of the assessor to establish temporal precedence. In the example just cited, it may be equally plausible to hypothesize that social anxiety and excessive sympathetic activation cause social skills deficits.

The use of marker variables is a third way to identify causal functional relationships. A marker variable is a conveniently obtained measure reliably associated with the strength of a causal functional relationship. An example of an empirically validated marker variable would be the carbon dioxide inhalation challenge. Panic disordered patients, relative to nondisordered controls, are significantly more likely to experience acute panic symptoms when induced to repeatedly inhale air with high concentrations of carbon dioxide. Thus responses to this easily administered test can be used as a marker for observing whether the complex biobehavioral relationships that characterize panic disorder are operational for a particular client.

Although the marker variable strategy can provide important information about causal functional relationships, few empirically validated marker variables have, as yet, been identified in the behavioral literature. As a result, behavioral assessors have tended to rely on unvalidated marker variables, such as client reports, to identify causal functional relationships (e.g., a client diagnosed with posttraumatic stress disorder may report that increased flashback frequency is caused by increased marital stress). The extent to which these client reports accurately reflect the presence and strength of causal functional relationships is a matter of continuing debate.

SUMMARY AND FUTURE DIRECTIONS

The functional analysis emphasizes the identification and quantification of important, controllable causal functional relationships for the purposes of intervention design. Establishing causal functional relationships by using rigorous empirical procedures, however, remains a formidable task for most behavioral assessors. Indeed, one review of the behavioral literature found that pretreatment functional analyses were conducted in only 20% percent of the 156 cause studies published between 1985 and 1988.

Use of functional analytic procedures may increase when additional empirically validated marker variables are made available to the behavioral assessor and when the following important questions are addressed. First, do pretreatment functional analyses of problem behavior lead to significantly more effective interventions? Second, can properly trained behavioral assessors reliably identify causal functional relationships?

Third, how generalizable are functional analyses across persons, behaviors, and settings? Fourth, what are the decisional processes that govern the generation of a functional analysis among behavioral assessors?

ACTION RESEARCH
CAUSAL REASONING
CLINICAL ASSESSMENT
DEPENDENT VARIABLES
IDIODYNAMICS

W. H. O'BRIEN

FUNCTIONAL AUTONOMY

Gordon W. Allport coined the term *functional autonomy* to refer to motives that have become independent of the needs on which they were originally based.

When first introduced, this concept of functional autonomy was both radical and controversial. The motivational theories prevailing in North American psychology focused almost exclusively on mechanisms directly linked to basic physiological needs. In contrast, Allport's functional autonomy raised the possibility that motives could function quite independently of any physiological need or drive. This liberalized conceptualization of motivation had important implications for several key issues in psychology. It provided an image of the individual as an active agent rather than a passive entity entirely under the control of biological needs and immediate stimuli. It allowed for explanations of behavior that emphasized the present and the future rather than the past. It also pointed to the role of complex and unique patterns of motives in shaping and defining individual personality.

In contemporary psychology, the idea of functionally autonomous motives has been accepted into the mainstream of psychology.

INTRINSIC MOTIVATION
MOTIVATION

R. E. GORANSON

FUNCTIONAL PSYCHOLOGY

The signal event in the formulation of functional psychology was the publication of William James's work, *The principles of psychology*. The Jamesian definition of psychology as the study of the functions of consciousness (including subconscious processes) quickly became the dominant approach to academic and professional psychology. The American functional school of psychology displaced the European introspectionist school which had more narrowly defined psychology as the study of mental contents.

The functional approach supplemented introspection with descriptions of behavior, questionnaires, mental tests, and physiological experiments, and included the study of children, comparative studies of animals, studies of the insane and the mentally disabled, and field reports on preliterate peoples. Functional psychology broadened the scope of psychology to include most of the major topics and methods of investigation used in contemporary psychology.

J. T. HART

FUNCTIONALISM

As a school or system of psychology, functionalism had its roots in Darwin's theory of evolution as well as in the psychology of William James. Darwin's doctrine of natural selection stated that those variations of a particular species best able to adapt to a particular environment would survive and perpetuate themselves, whereas those variations less able to adapt would die off. Darwin also believed that the mind evolved along with the body; therefore, the whole process of adaptation could apply to the mental as well as to the physical.

The ideas set forth in the psychology of William James constituted a more immediate influence on functionalism. James stressed psychological adaptation and adjustment. Sometimes the mind aided the body in its survival. In the case of reason and problem solving, mental activity was preeminent and promoted survival. Yet reason had its seat in the machinery of the brain and operated, in part, to help fulfill bodily needs. At other times, as in the case of habit, traces left in the brain governed the habit, leaving the mind free for more useful endeavors.

A second aspect of James's psychology that influenced functionalism was his pragmatism. Ideas had value only if they were useful. The pragmatism that James fostered was taken up by John Dewey, the first of the functionalists to apply it to social problems and education.

Functionalism arose as a protest against existing systems. Its main protest was against structuralism. For the functionalists, the subject matter of psychology was mental processes or functions and *not* the study of the contents of consciousness as the structuralists had stated. Furthermore, functionalism was concerned with utilitarian, common-sense issues in psychology. Finally, the structuralists had maintained that mental functions were not subject to introspective analysis; it was the *contents* of the mind that could be analyzed. The functionalists disagreed, believing they could study mental functions if the proper methods were applied.

Although functionalism was less organized and less closely knit than structuralism, certain tenets characterized the system: (a) Psychology should deal with mental functions rather than contents. (b) Pschological functions were adjustments to the environment. (c) Psychology should be utilitarian, allowing for practical applications. (d) Mental functions were a part of the whole world of activity that included the mental and the physical. (e) Psychology was very closely related to biology; therefore, an understanding of anatomy and physiology would help in the understanding of mental activity.

The development of functionalism as a school of thought was the result primarily of three men: John Dewey, James Angell, and Harvey Carr.

Harvey Carr organized functionalist ideas in the most coherent fashion. The core of Carr's psychology was to be found in his description of the "adaptive act," which had three separate but interrelated aspects. First, there was a motivating stimulus, which remained relatively persistent until the organism acted in such a way as to satisfy it. The motive aroused and directed the activity. Second, there was the sensory stimulus, which acted as an incentive or goal. Finally, there was the activity or responding, which continued until the motivating stimulus was satisfied. It should be noted that the adaptive act was a function of the whole situation.

The adaptive act obviously involved learning. Association was extremely important. Carr distinguished between descriptive and explanatory laws of association. Association by similarity fell under the descriptive laws. Explanatory laws included association by contiguity (a coming together in space and time), which explained the origin of the association. Strength resulted from continued repetition. The law of frequency applied here: The more often an act was performed, the stronger it would become.

Carr interpreted emotions as organic adjustments or readjustments. In anger, persons exhibited an increase of energy, allowing them to overcome obstacles. The energy came from internal physiological processes. In fear, likewise, a person was energized to flee from enemies. These emotions were biologically useful. But other emotions such as sorrow or envy did not seem to have utilitarian value. Emotions arose when other avenues or adaptation seemed to be lacking. Carr supported the more classical theory of emotions in which a person saw a dangerous object, became afraid, and consequently ran. The fear energized the

biological functions allowing him to run. This was in opposition to the James–Lange theory of emotion.

Like structuralism, functionalism no longer exists as a distinct psychological system. Some psychologists maintain a kind of functionalist position in stressing adaptation of an organism to its environment. Generally speaking, functionalism has fallen into the mainstream of psychology.

HISTORY OF PSYCHOLOGY STRUCTURALISM

R. W. LUNDIN

FUNDAMENTAL ATTRIBUTION ERROR

Fundamental attribution error (FAE) is part of attribution theory dealing with the processes people use to explain behavior. Inferences about causation of a person's actions fall into two categories: internal (or characteristics of the person) and external (or characteristics of the social or physical environment). Fundamental attribution error, sometimes called overattribution, is the general tendency of an observer to perceive another person's behavior as caused by internal, personal characteristics or dispositions rather than external, situational influences. Conversely, the behaving person (the actor) tends to see his or her own behavior as caused by the situation. The concept of FAE grew out of an extensive body of research on social perception and cognition, and in turn, the concept has stimulated much research. The well-established observer overemphasis on personal traits and underemphasis on context raise serious questions about bias in many situations in which people judge other people, such as in clinical assessment or treatment, voting for political candidates, and jury decisions.

Weary, Stanley and Harvey note that this prominent tendency to overattribute internal causes had been recognized by early social psychologists such as Fritz Heider. Edward Jones and Richard Nisbett described this as the actor–observer effect, and in further research Lee Ross gave FAE its name. Typical experiments might involve judging statements allegedly made by persons under various conditions or comparing subjects' reasons for their own choices and the choices by others. Subjects might report causes of actions while viewing themselves or another person on videotapes. The FAE process is so strong that even when the observer is told something about the situational conditions of other actors, there is a tendency to attribute their actions to personal traits. In daily life, this seems related to blaming the victim of rape, poverty, and other social problems. There is a widespread likelihood that psychologists will overattribute observed results to individual dispositions.

There are several approaches to explaining FAE. Baron and Graziano state, "The best current explanation involves differences in the amount and type of information most available to actors and observers. . . . When people inspect their own behavior as actors, they have a lifetime of previous behavior against which to compare it. When they make attributions to others, however, they almost never have the same amount or quality of information available." Also, actors and observers differ in information that is salient or striking to them: What is figure and what is ground?

The application of attribution theory to clinical work is of considerable importance. Some studies have shown that a dispositional bias may exist among professional helpers, but this bias has not been clearly proven. Because the tendency to overattribute problems to personal characteristics is common in the general population, it would seem important in clinical training to help students examine their explanations of clients' feelings and behaviors. Counselors and clinicians also may use FAE as part of attribution therapy helping the client to reframe self-attributions. Depressed patients tend to use self-blame much more than others do.

Some studies have shown that cognitive therapy or instructions to decrease the tendency to attribute negative events to global, stable, and internal attributions may help reduce depression or immunize people against a sense of helplessness. The Attributional Style Questionnaire is one method used to explore individual differences among clinicians and others.

Other areas of application of the FAE principle are in legal and international situations. FAE questions, for instance, may be decisions about the intent of an individual alleged to have committed a crime. Tetlock, McGuire, and Mitchell, in discussing the security problems of nations, point out that FAE exacerbates tendencies to attribute hostile intentions to others and leads even peaceful states to arm excessively. Policymakers see arming themselves as defensive and assume that others' military buildups are aggressive.

There are several cautions and limitations about the FAE bias. It is important to note that FAE refers to a relative tendency of observers to attribute to the actor more responsibility for behavior than does the actor; it does not say anything about the accuracy of causal claims. There are few research attempts to determine the reality or truth of attributions; questions may be raised about the accuracies of the observer, the actor, or both. Another caution is that observers often make personal attributions because of efficiency; if information about the actor's situation is not available, it may not be possible or practical to take the complexity of the actor's view into account. Attitudes in the attributional process also are important; the actor–observer differences may be diminished by an observer having an empathic attitude or being personally involved with the actor. There seem to be cultural differences in the FAE tendency; North Americans may have a bias toward blaming the individual in contrast to people in India or other collectivist cultures. Considerable work needs to be done to clear up the theoretical confusions about how FAE relates to similar concepts such as self-efficacy and internal and external loci of control.

COGNITIVE DETERMINANTS OF BEHAVIOR
HUMAN FACTORS
INTERNALIZATION
INTROSPECTION
LIFE EVENTS
LOCUS OF CONTROL
SCAPEGOATING

N. D. SUNDBERG

G

GALILEAN/ARISTOTELIAN THINKING

Two contrasting modes of scientific thought or logic have characterized the development of science since ancient times—Aristotelian and Galilean. The first of these, the Aristotelian mode of reasoning, is generally considered to have retarded the growth of modern science. Only after the appearance of the Galilean mode of logic were significant advances made in physics, biology and, more recently, psychology.

ARISTOTELIAN MODE OF SCIENTIFIC REASONING

Aristotelian reasoning emphasizes "local determination." Causality lies in the essential nature of the object rather than in the environment. The role of the environment is limited to "disturbances" that occasionally modify the object's behavior. Further, Aristotelian logic emphasizes dichotomies, as in the distinction between heavenly and earthly process employed by Aristotelian physicists. The psychological counterpart to such reasoning is the tendency to view people as either normal or abnormal, intelligent or unintelligent. Another feature of this mode of reasoning is its emphasis on valuative concepts: Certain forms of motion such as circular and rectilinear motions were judged to be "good" or "higher." The modern counterpart in psychology is the tendency to distinguish between normal and pathological behavior.

GALILEAN MODE OF SCIENTIFIC REASONING

In contrast, Galilean scientific logic emphasizes the interactive nature of the object and its environment. For Galilean physicists, the cause of an object's behavior does not inhere in the propensities of the object, but in the functional relationship between such propensities and the environment. Galilean logic views the behavior of objects and people as situation-specific. According to this mode of logic, the primary task is one of studying the conditions under which particular events or actions occur. In addition, this form of logic emphasizes the continuous nature of variables and is nonvaluative. People are neither normal nor abnormal; rather, there are degrees of normality, just as there are degrees of intelligence.

PHILOSOPHY OF SCIENCE

M. S. GREENBERG

GAMBLER'S FALLACY

The gambler's fallacy or the Monte Carlo fallacy, reflects a common misconception of chance events. Suppose that a coin is tossed a number of times in succession. If a string of ten heads is produced and if the coin can be presumed to be fair, it would seem intuitively likely to most people that a tail is overdue. However, that inference is false.

This fallacy is technically referred to as a *negative recency effect:* The tendency is to predict that the event that has recently been occurring with the greatest frequency will soon stop occurring. It is based in a belief in local representativeness (i.e., that a sequence of randomly produced events will represent the characteristics of the random process even when the sequence is short). Thus a random generator such as a coin toss should, according to this misconception, produce outcomes that appear— even over the short run—to give no particular preference to one or the other of the possible outcomes. If a string of a particular outcome is produced, then it is expected that the chance sequence must correct itself in the near future, and a deviation in one direction thus needs to be balanced by a deviation in the other. Randomly generated strings, however, especially if they are relatively short, often appear quite unrepresentative of the random process producing them.

The gambler's fallacy is more than a reflection of the statistical ignorance of laypeople, because it can be observed even in the private lives of the statistically sophisticated. It reflects two aspects of human cognitive function: (a) the strong and automatic motivation that people have to find order in what they observe around them, even should it happen to be a series of outcomes from a random process, and (b) the all-too-human predilection to ignore base-rate probabilities while giving in to intuition. Although logic may persuade us that a chance process does not keep track of its outcomes, our intuitive reaction can be powerful and can sometimes overwhelm logic. Reed examined the relative impacts of logical and intuitive thought and argued that the latter often seems more compelling than the former, probably because such inferences simply spring to mind, therefore defying logical analysis, and are often accompanied by a strong feeling of being correct. Although it is not possible to see the process by which such intuitive "conclusions" are found, the process of logical reasoning is open for examination and critique. People are thus in control of logical thought, whereas they merely receive the outcomes of intuitive thought, which imbues the latter with a powerful sense of feeling right.

The gambler's fallacy is most likely to occur when chance alone produces the outcomes. When some skill is involved, a positive recency effect is more often observed. The observer is likely to see a string of successes (e.g., by a billiards player) as indicative of a hot streak and will bias his or her predictions of the next outcome in a positive rather than a negative direction. Even the tossing of dice can lead to a positive recency effect to the extent that the individual believes that the outcome is in some manner influenced by the thrower's "skill."

BARNUM EFFECT
GAMBLING BEHAVIOR
STATISTICAL INFERENCE

J. E. ALCOCK

GAMBLING BEHAVIOR

Gambling, a redistribution of wealth on the basis of chance and risk, is an event that always involves loss to one party and gain to another. In some gambling games, such as poker and blackjack, elements of skill combine with chance to influence the outcome. Whether participation in events involving chance outcomes is simple recreation, reasonable risk taking, or irrational gambling seems to depend not so much on the nature of the game or transaction itself as upon the motivations and personality characteristics of the participant.

HISTORICAL AND SOCIAL ASPECTS

Clemens France noted a tendency for gambling to wax and wane in popularity over the centuries, with periods of excess alternating with periods of suppression. France suggested that gambling might be a healthy release for pent-up forces within the personality.

The Commission on the Review of the National Policy Toward Gambling reported that 61% of the population engaged in some kind of gambling and that 80% of Americans approved of gambling in some form. The report also included an estimate that there were approximately 1.1 million compulsive gamblers in the country and that the increasing availability of gambling might pose significant problems. The Commission also concluded that many antigambling laws were simply impossible to enforce.

RECREATIONAL GAMBLING

Although gambling is a problem for some, it is often viewed as a normal, natural, and healthy recreation for the majority. With widespread legalization of various forms of gambling in many states, gambling has become a readily available recreation for Americans, as it has long been in many other countries.

RISK TAKING AND UTILITY THEORY

Apart from psychoanalytic theories of gambling behavior, there has been relatively little psychological theory building to explain the attractiveness of gambling. Several attempts have been made to include gambling in a general theory of risk taking. Daryl Bem wrote that willingness to take reasonable risk is a valuable characteristic. The motivation to achieve, he said, is positively correlated with realistic risk taking, whereas fear of failure may be associated with foolish or excessive risk taking. Eric Knowles pointed out that there is great difficulty in defining risk taking as a specific class of behaviors, and that there are few common elements in different situations. To explain gambling by saying that it is a special case of risk taking is therefore difficult.

Economic utility theory attempted to explain how the subjective value of a given risk to an individual could outweigh the objective value of a possible payoff. The willingness to assume gambling risks varies, depending on the relative wealth of the individual, psychological factors, and the hope of gaining an otherwise impossible financial goal.

THE GAMBLING LIFESTYLE

For some individuals gambling has become the central organizing theme in life. Jay Livingston traced the development of gambling from its first challenge as an adventure to its final compulsive stage in which borrowing, stealing, and lying inevitably led to alienation and desperate attempts to stop. Henry R. Lesieur described how gamblers acquire a chase philosophy in which they endlessly try to "win back" what was lost in defiance of laws of probability, thinking that gambling, which caused their problems in the first place, is the only solution; thus the alternatives to gambling are limited by gambling itself. This is not to say that all frequent gamblers are compulsive; the majority probably are not.

THE PSYCHOANALYTIC APPROACH

In "Dostoevsky and parricide" Sigmund Freud used the life of Fyodor Dostoevsky to illustrate how the psychodynamic view might explain adult addiction to gambling in terms of childhood sexual conflicts. Robert Lindner pointed up the gambler's dilemma: Winning is desirable because it fulfills the childish wish for omnipotence and is a symbolic approval of incestuous urges, but losing is also desirable because it provides punishment for forbidden incestuous acts and thus removes the pain of guilt. Because winning produces intolerable guilt, whereas losing proves the lack of omnipotence, the gambler is caught in an endless repetitive search for a solution. Edmond Bergler traces the roots of gambling to childhood rebellion, oral and anal sexual investment, and the forbidden act of masturbation. Because there were symbolic thematic elements in common in both childish sex play and gambling, these theorists assumed a causal relationship. But convincing objective evidence is scarce; the burden of proof lies on the interpretation of case histories.

THE MEDICAL MODEL OF PATHOLOGICAL GAMBLING

Many psychoanalytic theorists were psychiatrists trained initially in medicine, so it is understandable that they came to accept compulsive gambling as a disease or sickness of the mind. Bolen and Boyd used the term "pathological gambling" to describe cases they had seen in psychiatric practice, but held that gambling was symptomatic of a wide variety of specific mental disorders and not an illness in its own right. Moran argued convincingly that gambling could be a primary diagnostic entity and gave a detailed, objective description of the syndrome. Symptoms included preoccupation with gambling, an overpowering urge to gamble, tension, inability to control gambling, chronic shortage of money, family conflict, and loss of employment due to gambling.

Robert Custer, the first to treat gamblers in a hospital program, further refined the diagnostic criteria for pathological gambling and was primarily responsible for the inclusion of the illness in the 1980 edition of the American Psychiatric Association's *Diagnostic and statistical manual of mental disorders* (DSM-III).

By no means has the medical model of pathological gambling gone unchallenged. Behaviorists saw gambling, not as sickness, but as a simple behavioral phenomenon resulting from conditions of learning. Hankoff argued that the idea of gambling as a disease is circular reasoning because the presence of the symptom of gambling is the only proof that the disease exists. Hankoff argued that the disease model might absolve the gambler from responsibility for doing something about the problem. Robert Herman also examined and rejected a medical model, saying that assigning labels to people might actually make the problem worse.

THE BEHAVIORAL VIEW
Terry J. Knapp employed basic principles of operant behavior to explain persistent gambling, saying for example that since betting is only occasionally reinforced by winning, gambling represents the result of intermittent or partial schedules of reinforcement. Such schedules are known to produce behaviors that are extremely resistant to extinction.

Behavioral psychologists have sometimes settled on an "addictive behavior" model in which gambling is seen as one of many similar dependencies or abuse patterns. Ralph G. Victor argued that addictive gambling resulted from an interaction between certain personality characteristics and contingencies of reinforcement, thus suggesting the possibility of compromise between medical and behavioral views.

THE TREATMENT OF PATHOLOGICAL GAMBLING
Modern treatment techniques include heavy emphasis on group psychotherapy, education, activities therapy, and plans for restitution of money owed because of gambling. David Lester reviewed other behavioral treatments such as pain aversion, in which electric shock is associated with betting and paradoxical intention in which the therapist orders the patient to gamble according to a strict schedule that the therapist devises. But pathological gambling is often highly resistant to all forms of treatment.

ADDICTIVE PROCESS
ALCOHOLISM TREATMENT

J. I. TABER

GEISTESWISSENSCHAFTLICHE PSYCHOLOGIE
There is no exact equivalent in English for *Geisteswissenschaften*, which is sometimes translated as "human studies" but more recently as "human sciences," and is contrasted with *Naturwissenschaften* (natural sciences) and differentiated from *Kulturwissenschaften* (cultural sciences). In general, human sciences refer to those sciences that theoretically take into account distinctively human activities. William Dilthey's essential project was to provide an epistemological grounding for all these sciences that would be equal to, but different from, the grounding that the natural sciences enjoyed. Because all the human sciences share a concern for how humans relate to aspects of their world or fellow humans, despite diverse other differences, William Dilthey tried to make explicit the theoretical structure of this common ground in order to make manifest

its difference from natural scientific grounding, lest the human sciences continue their erroneous imitation of the natural sciences. Dilthey bases his distinction between human sciences and natural sciences on two different kinds of experience: The former depends on "inner lived experience" and the latter on "outer sensory experience," and because the two types of experience differ, knowledge based upon them also will differ.

HISTORY OF PSYCHOLOGY
NATURWISSENSCHAFTLICHE PSYCHOLOGIE
PHILOSOPHY OF SCIENCE

A. P. GIORGI

GENDER ROLE STRESS
The term *gender* is being reexamined in the literature; the term *role* does not distinguish between multiplicity of expectations, and *stress* is a concept ambiguous enough that some psychologists avoid using the term altogether. The use of *gender* was introduced in behavioral and social sciences to distinguish it from the concept of sex. Gender was distinguished from sex in feminist literature to emphasize that anatomy is not destiny because sex is biologically defined and gender is culturally constructed. Male and female are examples of a sexual distinction, whereas masculine and feminine are examples of gender description. The term *sex role* is still occasionally used synonymously with *gender role* in the psychological literature because of past practices.

Multiple expectations are associated with roles often in conflict with one another. Anthropologists have dichotomized these traditional gender roles as roles aligned with nature for women and culture for men or encompassing private and domestic domain roles for women versus public and political domain roles for men.

Studies of stress usually include (a) stressors, (b) stress process such as perception and feeling of danger or loss of control, and (c) stress responses such as psychosomatic illnesses. The sources of stressors are usually external; they also can be self-imposed. Women in executive positions may think they must perform much better than their male counterparts. Individual predisposition and cognitive appraisal are important in defining the degree of stress of a situation. What is considered to be a potentially stressful situation by some, may be perceived favorably by others. Not all stress is dysfunctional. Some individuals seek stressful situations such as ice climbing and skydiving. Stress also can be hidden and not be apparent to an observer or even to the stressed person.

Gender role stress is primarily induced in three ways. First, stress can result from socially defined gender roles and gender-related attitudes and practices (e.g., a deserving and qualified female employee being passed for promotion contrary to stated policies). Second, stress may arise because of violations of socially defined gender roles. Traditional sex and gender differences are based on a dichotomy of men and women in typical relationships as the only acceptable social norm. Negative sanctions are attached to violations of this norm. Traditional concepts of gender roles are rigid and constricting, given the many possible variations in human relationships. For example, lesbian youth in this country have high suicide and suicide attempt rates, probably due to their inability to cope with negative attitudes and feelings of desperation. The third cause of stress results from the ambiguities found in the definition of gender roles, which are not static. The concept of a gay or lesbian family is problematic to many, because of a social predisposition to view family relationships in terms of procreation, sex, and power.

Role stress analysis may be focused on one or more sets of variables and conducted in the context of three parallel but interrelated systems: (a) physiological, (b) psychological, and (c) social. Of the many possible components and subcomponents of the social system, only five are partially and briefly addressed here: (a) social institutions (work and employment, and family), (b) social relations, (c) social stages or life cycle, (d) social images and identity, and (e) social change.

GENDER ROLE STRESS IN WOMEN

Physiological and Psychological Systems

Stress affects men and women differently physiologically and psychologically. Although there are no major differences in the rate of psychiatric disorders among men and women, there are significant gender differences in types of disorders. Women have higher rates of depressive episodes, phobias, and obsessive and compulsive disorders. Different life situations faced by women, diagnoses of disorders by male physicians, and willingness of women to express problems they are facing and seek help are some explanations.

Social Systems

Work and family are the two principal spheres of activity for all men and women. Historically, a large segment of women were forced to enter gender-appropriate, female-dominated occupations, except during World War II. Women earn less than men and also face the glass ceiling. Work done by women is often devalued. Historically, the contributions of women from art to zoology have often been ignored or misappropriated.

Sexual discrimination is deeply embedded in the world of work, from advertisements for work to retirement provisions. Sexual harassment is a common occurrence for women.

Home and place of employment have remained separate since the Industrial Revolution. Men moved from homes to factories, mines, and offices for employment while women stayed at home. Even with increasing numbers of women entering the labor force, domestic work is still primarily a woman's responsibility. Women who try to straddle both family and employment spheres are faced with inadequate child-care facilities and maternity leaves.

Inequality in marriage and after divorce is another source of stress. Divorce is a principal traumatic event in women's lives and a major factor in the feminization of poverty. Women face a number of burdens and handicaps as single parents. They experience stress in other areas as well, such as education, religion, law, and politics because of prejudice and discrimination.

The threat of violence means that women must restrict their activities and participation in social activities. Date rape, marital rape, sexual abuse of female children, sexual harassment, obscene phone calls, spouse abuse, and other forms of violence are some problems faced by women.

Stress is experienced by women throughout their life cycle. Stress associated with menstruation and menopause varies considerably for different individuals and cultures. Women face additional sources of stress during their adult life, including pregnancy, childbirth, motherhood, and the empty-nest syndrome.

Although the identity of a man is established through his social or job status, the identity of a woman is most commonly established through her relational status with men or her familial roles. Feminist scholars have pointed out that the identity of a woman is best described as "other" and as an outsider. In a man-made language, a woman is often subsumed under the term *man,* which denies a woman her special identity.

Women's bodies are used as sex objects and to sell consumer goods and produce pornography. Many acts are committed against women's bodies, such as binding the feet of female children in China.

Major social changes have created ambiguity and uncertainty about gender roles and different types of stress. For example, women's entry into the professional career pool has highlighted the need for child-care facilities. Many mothers feel guilty about leaving a child under the care and supervision of someone else. Entry into a profession has introduced for many women the dilemma of having children before their biological clocks run out and the desire to enhance their careers. Backlash has ensued against demands by women for equality and equal opportunity.

The issue of abortion is extremely stress producing because of concerns about women's civil rights, rights over one's body, and other ethical issues pertaining to human life and human rights. The "abortion" pill (RU 486) has injected more sexual politics into the abortion issue on an international scale.

GENDER ROLE STRESS IN MEN

Physiological and Psychological Systems

Men are more prone to suffer from stress-related cardiovascular diseases. They have a higher rate of alcohol and other drug dependencies and abuse than women. Although women are more likely to seek help during times of stress, men try to deal with their stress by themselves or not at all.

Social Systems

An occupation is generally the center of men's work activities, holding primacy over other roles. Employment roles and family roles of men are so widely separated that there are no corresponding figures in the census data for "working fathers" comparable with those for "working mothers." Because of the centrality of occupations in men's lives, employment-related roles constitute the principal source of stress for men.

Family roles are important to men, who are traditionally expected to be the primary breadwinners, and often are the sole source of monetary support for the family. Marriage and divorce create different types of stress for men than for women. After a divorce men face problems such as lack of a social network of friends, the visitation of children, and the necessity for providing monetary support for their children. Because women usually have custody of children, divorced men often feel like outsiders or strangers to their children.

Social contacts and networks of friends for men tend to be related to their work, sports, and hobbies. As a result, men usually have few intimate friends, and more men count their spouses as close friends than do women. Men are expected to take an active or aggressive role in relationships with women, which carries with it the risk of rejection and failure. Men are often reluctant to communicate effectively about their personal lives, thereby limiting their range of stress-coping strategies. Socialized to be competitive from childhood, men reflect this in many areas of their lives. Competition takes several forms, and winning may become everything. In the past, men competed with other men for jobs. Now women also are competitors for jobs held by men.

Men do not undergo as many clear-cut stages of biological and developmental changes as women do. Yet they undergo stages of stress in adolescence, marriage, fatherhood, and retirement. Men fantasize about retirement, but many men feel worthless if not gainfully employed.

Images of men depict them as strong, silent, macho, competitive, and in control of their emotions. Men also are criticized for being aggressive, violent, uncommunicative, insensitive, unable to express themselves, and not being compassionate enough. Such conflicting expectations constitute a source of stress for men.

Social changes introduce ambiguities and uncertainties into social roles, especially gender roles. A crisis of masculinity exists due to an inability of men to redefine masculinity in terms acceptable to both men and women. Men feel threatened and inadequate as the norms of sexuality change. However, all changes are not necessarily stress producing. For example, organizations such as the National Organization for Men Against Sexism indicate a positive response to the feminist movement and acceptance of a need for change.

S. R. SONNAD

GENERAL ADAPTATION SYNDROME

Hans Selye proposed that all humans show the same general bodily response to stress. He labeled these reactions the general adaptation syndrome (GAS). According to Selye, no matter what the stress is, the general reaction of the body is similar, although the specific organs that eventually break down may differ, depending on individual predisposition. He maintains that the underlying mechanism for breakdown is a prolonged overall increase in the activity of the sympathetic nervous system. The sequence of events that follow prolonged stress, according to Selye, are alarm, resistance, exhaustion, and death.

During the *alarm stage* all the physiological responses involved in maximizing energy production are activated, including the release of epinephrine by the adrenal medulla and adrenocorticotropic hormone (ACTH) by the anterior pituitary, thus increasing glucose levels in the blood. Breathing rate and heart rate both accelerate.

If stress continues, the body enters the *resistance stage* and appears to have returned to normal. For example, breathing rate and heart rate return to their prestress levels. However, the elevated level of ACTH continues; this maintains a high level of glucose, but on the negative side in terms of the organism's health, it makes the body vulnerable to infection.

Selye maintains that, if the stress continues, bodily processes start to break down in the *exhaustion stage.* The glands cannot continue their elevated levels of secretion; the raw materials required for energy are depleted; and the body exhausts itself. The stage of *death* may follow.

Selye has observed this three-stage reaction to prolonged stress–alarm, resistance, exhaustion—in a variety of laboratory animals. The extent to which the GAS is applicable to humans has yet to be determined.

R. M. STERN

GENERAL APTITUDE TEST BATTERY

The General Aptitude Test Battery (GATB) was developed by the U.S. Department of Labor's Employment Service as a tool for counseling in various state employment offices. For such counseling purposes, many specific occupations have been grouped on the basis of similarity of aptitude requirements. The profile of test scores associated with each job family is called an occupational ability pattern (OAP).

The GATB was developed with the intent of broad applicability to widely divergent occupations. It can be used in connection with the Department of Labor's *Dictionary of occupational titles.*

One criticism of the GATB centers around the use of OAPs. Specifically, for each group of occupations, three test scores are used to predict success, based on empirical validities. The difficulty with this approach is that it represents a multiple-cutoff strategy, yet for some occupations it may be possible to compensate for low abilities with other, very strong abilities.

P. G. BENSON

GENERAL INTELLIGENCE FACTOR

A general factor common to all cognitive abilities was originally hypothesized by Sir Francis Galton, but Charles E. Spearman made the first objective empirical test of the hypothesis. The general factor, which Spearman signified as *g,* was the basis of his two-factor theory—that every mental test measures only two factors: a general factor *g,* common to all tests, and a specific factor *s,* peculiar to each test. The method of factor analysis developed by Spearman made it possible to show precisely the degree to which each test among a battery of diverse tests measures the *g* factor common to all the tests in the battery. This is a test's factor loading on *g,* or simply its *g* loading; it can be thought of as the correlation between scores on the particular test and the *g* factor if a hypothetical test could measure *g* and nothing else. Spearman's principle of "the indifference of the indicator" meant that *g* could be measured by an infinite variety of possible tests, regardless of the sensory modality, specific knowledge content, or particular skills required to perform the test. Because tests that involve seeing relationships and grasping concepts, reasoning in the abstract, and solving novel problems are the most highly *g*-loaded and discriminate most clearly between persons ordinarily judged to be of high or low intelligence, *g* is considered practically synonymous with general intelligence.

At the level of analysis represented by factor analysis, there is no doubt about the existence of *g* in the cognitive abilities domain. The demonstration of a large *g* factor is merely a consequence of the more fundamental fact that all cognitive tests, however diverse, show positive intercorrelations in representative samples of the general population. But it became apparent that other factors besides *g* are necessary to account for all the intercorrelations among tests. These additional factors—common only to certain groups of tests—are termed *group factors.*

The method of multiple factor analysis with rotation (transformation) of the factors to approximate a criterion of "simple structure," most clearly revealed the group factors, which Thurstone termed *primary mental abilities.* The most clearly established primary factors are reasoning, verbal comprehension, verbal fluency, number, spatial visualization, perceptual speed, and associative memory. But the mathematical nature of Thurstone's method of factor analysis precluded the emergence of Spearman's *g* factor, which becomes submerged among the primary factors. This seeming disappearance of Spearman's *g* in the work of Thurstone and his followers was a point of great theoretical dispute until it became apparent that it was a mathematical artifact of the particular method of factor analysis. Thurstone himself finally pointed out that if the primary factor axes are rotated to the best possible simple structure solution, they are oblique (correlated), and a factor analysis of the intercorrelations among the primary factors yields a *second-order factor* that is the same as Spearman's *g.* This type of *hierarchical* factor analysis, in which *g* emerges as a second-order (or higher-order) factor, is now the most generally preferred method for extracting the *g* factor.

It has proved impossible to devise tests that are factor-pure measures of the primary mental abilities. Tests of primary mental abilities are always substantially intercorrelated, a fact accounted for by the *g* factor in all cognitive tests. Thus the "purest" tests that can be devised measure a single primary ability plus *g,* with *g* usually accounting for the larger proportion of the total variance (individual differences) in the test scores.

There is as yet no generally accepted theory of the fundamental nature of *g,* and we are still far from understanding the brain mechanisms that would explain *g.*

Although *g* may not be well understood theoretically, it is unquestionably the single largest source of individual differences in all cognitive activities that involve some degree of mental complexity, and that eventuate in some form of behavior assessable in terms of an objective standard of performance.

HUMAN INTELLIGENCE

A. R. JENSEN

GENERAL SYSTEMS

General systems theory attempts to find models applicable across disciplines. If the same model (or analogy) can be applied to metallurgy, agriculture, business, and music, we have a "general system." Mathematical operations are the most obvious of such systems, but other models are equally significant. A very frequently used model is the "open" as against the "closed" system. Every system can be described in terms of "openness" and "closedness," meaning that almost any conceivable system can be described in terms of how self-sufficient it is, how subject it is to influence from outside.

Learning theory assumes a limited sort of system. Behaviors that are regularly rewarded tend to become a persistent system wherein a given range of stimuli provoke a given range of responses. Personality psychology, however, tends to put strong emphasis upon systems. Many personality psychologists assume that all the behavior of a personality belongs to one system (with the exception of "multiple personalities"). The urge toward "self-consistency" is one of the strongest features of "personality." Trait theories assume a more limited concept of system, as do stimulus–response theories.

However, other models have wide application in psychology and in other disciplines. Homeostasis is an excellent example. Originally a physiological model to explain the reciprocal relations between different parts of the organism in maintaining a "constant state" of "internal environment," it was used to explain the stability of the personality—preservation of the self-image. But probably the best illustration in psychology of a general systems concept is that of stress. Hans Selye's research indicated definite change in physiological structure as a consequence of biological stress. Psychological stress would be that which causes permanent change in the personality.

Stress would be that which fundamentally alters the observed pattern. Stress, then, would be a model that fits the observed data of an event followed by a fundamental change in the behavior of the organism. Both personality and stress are, therefore, constructs or systems.

"General systems" are apt to be confused with "systems" and with "systems analysis," but these are different concepts. The term *system* applies to a model within a discipline such as a communication system, an administrative system, or a governmental system. It becomes a *general system* only when it is applicable to two or more fields, and *systems analysis* is more concerned with analyzing the makeup of specific systems than with giving overall descriptions or building generalized models.

Ludwig von Bertalanffy is usually considered the founder of the general systems school of thought. He saw it as "a science of science." Anatol Rapoport, a philosopher and mathematician, established a strong mathematical coloration of the discipline.

The general systems movement has in some cases been merged with cybernetics. This was a term popularized by the mathematician Norbert Wiener to cover the field of automatic controls, servomechanisms, thermostats, and such. It was basically concerned with automatic (or "programmed") control.

Kurt Lewin adapted his concepts to psychology with his "field theory." Ecology may be regarded as a biological field theory. In psychology almost all holistic or organismic theories have some of the characteristics of fields. Reductionism (or elementalism) in science tends to ignore systems or wholes. General systems theory tends to play down elementalism and reductionism. Each entity is seen as functioning in context, although there may be different levels of systems. Systems can be arranged hierarchically, with each included in a more inclusive system, and each made up of less inclusive ones. The same general system is not necessarily applicable at all levels, but they are all systems, nevertheless.

There have been many forerunners of general systems theory, but two have had unusual impact on scientific thought: Gestalt psychology and holism or the emergent evolution approach. This was the observation that many "emergents" could not be predicted from their elements. Emergents are something other than the sum of their parts. The holists failed to specify in what way these emergents were different from their elements; they simply noted the difference.

Gestalt psychologists went a step further, suggesting that it was the configuration or pattern of the parts that was the new element. To the Gestalt psychologists (and most cognitive psychologists), the configuration or pattern of events is more important than the elementary events themselves. The elementary events achieve meaning through their relationships. General systems theory avoids this controversy (elementalism vs. holism) by simply insisting that the study of the system is important, particularly when one is able to compare it with other systems at other levels.

FIELD THEORY
SYSTEMS THEORY
THEORETICAL PSYCHOLOGY

W. E. GREGORY

GENETIC DISORDERS

As the result of genealogical research, a number of disorders are known to be inherited. If a disease is genetic, some protein or enzyme is abnormal or missing in the afflicted individuals. The best-known heritable diseases will be discussed here alphabetically.

ACHONDROPLASIA (DWARFISM)

Dwarfism is caused by an *autosomal dominant mutated gene.* (An autosomal gene is one on a chromosome other than the X chromosome.) The dwarfed parent has a 50% risk of producing a dwarfed child. If both parents have the problem, the risk for each child increases to 75%.

AMYOTROPHIC LATERAL SCLEROSIS (ALS)

ALS is caused in 10% of cases by an *autosomal dominant* gene, although there is a variant in some children caused by an *autosomal recessive*. If a parent with ALS has no family history of the condition, the children probably will be spared. ALS affects twice as many males as females. ALS affects the motor neurons in the brain and spinal cord, causing muscle atrophy and spasticity.

ATAXIA

Friedreich's ataxia is caused by an *autosomal recessive gene,* Marie's ataxia by an *autosomal dominant.* Two recessive genes, one from each carrier parent, are necessary for a child to have Friedreich's ataxia. If both parents are carriers, the child has a 25% chance of developing the disease. In Marie's ataxia, if one parent has the dominant gene, each child has a 50% chance of contracting the disease.

CLEFT PALATE

Cleft palate is due to *recessive* inheritance, possibly related to more than one gene. There is a separation of the bones in the roof of the mouth, which are normally united in early development. In *cleft lip* a separation of the bones of the upper jaw and/or upper gum ridge and lip occurs. These abnormalities form in the first trimester of pregnancy.

COOLEY'S ANEMIA

Cooley's anemia is caused by an *autosomal recessive gene* appearing in Italians and Greeks, and less frequently in children of Mediterranean American parents and those of Syrian, Israeli, and other ancestry. If both parents are carriers (with the defective recessive gene), there is a 25% chance of each child having the disease.

CYSTIC FIBROSIS (CF)

CF is caused by an *autosomal recessive gene*. If both parents carry the gene (as carriers), each child has a 25% chance of having CF, and a 50% chance of being a carrier like the parents. If both parents have CF (i.e., *both* CF genes), *all* their children will have the disease.

DIABETES MELLITUS ("SUGAR DIABETES")

Diabetes mellitus is caused by an *autosomal recessive gene*. If both parents are diabetic, *all* their children will have the disease. If a diabetic marries a nondiabetic whose family history includes diabetics, the nondiabetic may be a carrier, so that each child has a 50% chance of having the disease. If two carriers marry, each child has a 25% chance of succumbing to the disturbance of digestion.

There are two types of diabetics. *Blameless diabetics* are children under 10 who develop the disease because of heredity and through no fault of their own. They are overheight but not overweight. *Blamable diabetics* allow themselves to get overweight, increasing their chance of becoming diabetic. A sedentary life and lack of sufficient exercise cause them to get fat. The tendency to diabetes is greatest in women at menopause and especially following a hysterectomy.

DOWN SYNDROME ("MONGOLISM")

A small percentage of Down syndrome births are caused by an *extra autosomal chromosome, #21,* causing the affected child to be smaller and its mental and physical development to be slower. It appears in all races and nationalities. Amniocentesis can reveal the extra chromosome in the mother's intrauterine fluid.

DYSAUTONOMIA

This disease appears mostly in Jewish children and is caused by an *autosomal recessive gene*, so that two carriers will produce children with a 25% chance of having the problem and a 50% chance of being carriers. Dysautonornia is apparent at birth because the baby has a fixed, vacant stare and has difficulty sucking and swallowing.

DYSTROPHIC EPIDERMOLYSIS BULLOSA (DEB)

Dystrophy refers to deterioration. DEB is caused by a *dominant autosomal* or *recessive autosomal gene*. In the dominant form, a parent with DEB provides a 50% chance that each child will contract the disease. In the recessive form, a DEB parent has children who are all carriers without the disease. When two carriers have children, there is a 25% risk of each child having the disturbance.

HUNTINGTON'S DISEASE (HD)

HD is caused by an *autosomal dominant gene*. If one parent has this disease, each child has a 50% chance of developing it. HD is a neurological disorder reported at all ages. Chorea—fast, irregular, involuntary, uncontrollable movements of the face and extremities, once called St. Vitus Dance—occurs in families characterized by a nervous temperament.

HEMOPHILIA

Hemophilia is caused by a *sex-linked recessive gene in the X chromosome of the mother*. A woman must have the recessive gene in both X chromosomes to have the bleeding problem herself because the normal allele would overrule the abnormal gene. The male, only having one X chromosome, will have the disease if his X from the carrier mother bears the defective gene. An affected male cannot have hemophilic sons because his X chromosome, combined with a normal X in his wife's ovum, will produce only a female carrier. But if a carrier female has children, each son has a 50% chance of being hemophilic, and each daughter a 50% chance of being a carrier.

MUSCULAR DYSTROPHY (MD)

MD refers to a group of chronic hereditary diseases characterized by progressive degeneration and weakness of voluntary muscles. MD is usually caused by a *sex-linked recessive gene on the X chromosome*, inheritance being similar to that of hemophilia. It may occur at any age, but its most common form strikes children between 2 and 6. The child seems normal at birth, but at from 4 to 5 years of age can no longer use the legs properly. When the back muscles weaken, the child cannot sit erect, and the stronger muscles pull against the weaker ones until the body becomes twisted. The deterioration progresses until all the voluntary muscles degenerate.

OSTEOGENESIS IMPERFECTA (OI)

OI can be caused by a *dominant autosomal* or *recessive autosomal gene*. This "brittle bones disease" causes easy fractures plus severe pain, limited activity, and stunted growth. Other signs are loose joints, excessive sweating, poor teeth, deafness, and often blue corneas. The most severe form is *OI congenita,* involving multiple fractures at birth, some even in the womb. Many deformities keep the child in a wheelchair or bed.

PHENYLKETONURIA (PKU)

This dietary problem results from an *autosomal recessive gene* causing a protein metabolism disturbance and ends in severe mental retardation unless alleviated by a special diet. If two carriers of the defective gene have children, each child has a 25% chance of developing the protein defect.

RETINITIS PIGMENTOSA (RP)

RP results from the action of an *autosomal recessive gene,* so that children of two carriers have a 25% chance of developing the disease. If one parent has the problem (i.e., *both* defective genes), all of the children will be carriers, but none will have the disease. In contrast, all the children of two affected parents (each having the defective recessives on *both* chromosomes) will have the affliction. RP occasionally is caused by a *sex-linked dominant gene in the mother's X chromosome,* so that if the mother has the disease, each child of either sex has a 50% chance of showing the symptoms, and 50% of the daughters will be carriers.

SICKLE CELL ANEMIA (SCA)

SCA is found mostly in Blacks, but also occasionally in Italians, Sicilians, Turks, and East Indians. It is caused by an *autosomal recessive gene,* so that two carriers will have children that have a 25% chance of getting the anemic condition. One parent with SCA married to a normal person will have children without the disease, but all will be carriers. If both parents have SCA, all their children will contract the condition.

SPINA BIFIDA (SB)

SB is caused by an *autosomal recessive gene* with irregular heredity due to the influence of other genes. Once parents have one SB child, the odds of a second such child increase from 2 per 1000 to 1 in 20. SB involves a cleft spine, because the vertebrae fail to come together in the first trimester of pregnancy. Victims are more often girls than boys.

TAY-SACHS DISEASE (TS)

TS is caused by an *autosomal recessive gene,* such that two carriers will have children with a 25% chance of developing the disease. TS is a fatal neurodegenerative disorder that occurs mostly in Ashkenazi Jews of central and eastern European ancestry. Infants appear normal at first, but before they reach 2 years of age, they become inactive, bedridden, blind, and unresponsive, having seizures, infections, and feeding problems.

TOURETTE SYNDROME

Tourette syndrome is caused by an *autosomal dominant gene* with "reduced penetrance and variable expression." A person may inherit a dominant gene but show no signs of the disease. This is called "nonpenetrance," displayed more often by dominant than by recessive genes. If the disease is severe, it is "fully expressed."

TURNER'S SYNDROME

Turner's syndrome is caused by a *sex-linked gene in a missing or distorted X chromosome of females only,* resulting in undeveloped ovaries and poor bone growth in the female victims. The defective X chromosome causes short stature; victims are midgets with normal body proportions. Sexual maturation is inadequate.

GENETIC DOMINANCE AND RECESSIVENESS
HERITABILITY

H. K. FINK

GENETIC DOMINANCE AND RECESSIVENESS

Ironically, we know a good deal more about the inheritance of animals than we do about humans.

Inheritance results from gene combinations. Genes are biochemical entities in chromosomes that determine the potential for sex and other characteristics at conception. Chromosomes come in pairs in the nucleus of the sperm and the nucleus of the egg. There are 23 pairs or 46 chromosomes in human beings, of which one pair is called the sex chromosomes because they determine the sex of the future organism. Females bear two X chromosomes, whereas males possess an X and a Y. The Y chromosome is smaller and contains fewer genes along its surface.

As a result of ovarian cell division, all eggs contain one X chromosome, whereas the sperm cells from the male testes contain either an X or a Y. Thus there is a 50% chance of a human ovum being fertilized by either an X- or a Y-bearing sperm, so that the babies born in the population should be 50% female and 50% male. (Slightly more male infants appear, but they die more readily, so that the ratio of male to female becomes equalized; then, as children grow older, the ratio changes to favor female survivors, because of women's greater resistance to disease.)

Although little is known about gene location along the sex (X and Y) chromosomes and along the autosomal (body characteristics, exclusive of sex) chromosomes, there must be *innumerable* genes along each chromosome, given the complexity of the makeup of humans and what is known about inheritance in other animals. A gene is the biochemical location of an influential determinant that causes a particular trait or condition (such as blue eyes or hemophilia) or a part of the body (e.g., the thumb epidermis) to develop.

The map of the genes along the chromosomes is called the individual's *genotype,* whereas the *phenotype* is the expression of these genes in the flesh of the body. A "dominant" gene can cause its effect in haploid (single) number, because it is stronger than a recessive allele (the gene on the same location on the opposite chromosome of a pair). When a trait comes from a recessive gene, the diploid number (both alleles or genes at the same locus on a pair of chromosomes) is necessary to create the trait or defect in the phenotype. A person having the recessive gene for some inherited deficiency or disease on one chromosome, but having the normal allele on the other chromosome, is called a "carrier," because this potential parent carries the defective gene in haploid form but cannot give expression to it unless it joins with another defective recessive in the other parent to produce an affected infant. The exception to this rule is a sex-linked recessive gene on the X chromosome of a female carrier. When this recessive gene joins with the husband's Y chromosome, the XY son will exhibit the disease as if the Y chromosome did not exist.

A dominant gene always overrules a recessive gene, but two recessives at the same locus on a pair of chromosomes are strong enough to allow the trait or defect to show in the phenotype, and a recessive on the X chromosome of a male will also usually show up in the phenotype or body of the child.

Dominant traits in humans include dark and curly hair; white hair patch; male baldness; brown, hazel, or green eyes; normal pigmented skin; fused fingers or toes or extra digits; shorter fingers (because of a missing finger joint); dwarfed limbs; double-jointed body; poison ivy immunity; Rh positive factor; normal blood-clotting factors; and blood types A, B, and AB. *Recessive traits* include straight, light, or red hair; female baldness; blue or gray eyes; lack of skin pigment (albinism); normal digits; susceptibility to poison ivy; night- and color-blindness; deaf-mutism; Rh negative factor; hemophilia; and blood type O.

GENETIC DISORDERS
HERITABILITY

H. K. FINK

GENETIC FITNESS

There is good evidence that behavioral patterns evolve just as do other characteristics of animals. For behavioral evolution to occur, there must be some genetic influence on behavior; evolution cannot occur unless behavior reflects the genotype to some degree. (It must be emphasized, however, that this does not imply that genes "determine" behavior, that the environment is unimportant, or that such behavior is unmodifiable.) The primary driving force of evolutionary change is natural selection. At the heart of natural selection is the concept of genetic fitness. Genetic fitness, then, is a key concept in understanding the evolution of behavior and how behavior affects subsequent evolutionary change.

Although it will be necessary to qualify some aspects of a first definition, genetic fitness can be viewed as the relative contribution of an allele to the gene pools of future generations by different individuals. Usually, the consequences are examined only in regard to the subsequent generation; however, long-term, multigenerational consequences are of special interest and merit consideration. It should be noted that including the concept of fitness in a definition is somewhat tautological. An animal that leaves a greater number of viable, fertile offspring than do others is, by definition, more fit. This says nothing about physical "fitness," skills, or desirability; it refers simply to the relative number of viable, fertile offspring left behind. One escapes the tautology by demonstrating what factors affect fitness.

LEVEL OF SELECTION

Much writing in recent decades has been directed at the question of the level at which natural selection acts, and thus the level at which the concept of fitness might be applied. It is commonly believed that animals reproduce "to perpetuate the species." Behavior often is viewed as occurring for the good of the group, or species, rather than for the benefit of the individual. Wynne-Edwards, for example, spelled out an elaborate theory based on the view that animals regulate their population sizes for the good of the group, so that they do not produce more individuals than the environment can support.

The view that selection often works at the level of the group has been generally discredited. It may be more useful to study selection at the level of the gene rather than the population or species. This leads to the idea of the selfish gene. The concept of fitness, however, generally is applied at the level of the individual or, more precisely, the genotype of the individual. The first problem with the proposal that selection works at the level of the group concerns the relative rate at which effects could occur. Mathematical models reveal that populations would have to form and become extinct at unrealistically rapid rates for the consequences of individual behavior for the group to be more important than those for the individual. Thus, although "selfish" behavior may generally be to the detriment of the group, under most conditions these detrimental conditions are outweighed by the benefits to the individual relative to other individuals in the group.

A related problem with group selectionist thinking can be seen by examining the action of selection in population regulation. Suppose, as Wynne-Edwards proposes, that as a population grows, some individuals curtail reproduction for the good of the group. The genes associated with traits leading the animal to curtail reproduction will be less frequent in the next generation. It is the genes of those individuals that continue to reproduce that will be most common. Natural selection will thus act against those altruistic individuals who act for the good of the group to their own detriment in fitness unless the rate of disappearance of groups is rapid. Individuals may curtail reproduction temporarily, but such behavior generally appears to maximize the production of viable offspring by the individual in the long run.

Much behavior can be understood in this context. A male langur monkey who takes over a troop from another male often kills all of the young in that troop. Siblicide, the killing of one's sibling, is very common among many species of birds. In colonial breeding gulls, unguarded eggs often are eaten by neighboring gulls. Such behavioral patterns would be difficult to understand if one believed in good-of-the-group arguments, but they make perfect sense, however much we may deplore them, in the context of the maximization of individual fitness levels.

DIRECT AND INDIRECT FITNESS

The operation of selection is more complicated than implied thus far. The bottom line for fitness concerns gaining representation for copies of one's genes in future generations. However, copies of one's genes reside not only in one's body, but in the bodies of close relatives. The coefficient of relationship refers to the proportion of genes that two individuals share by descent. Individuals of most species share 50% of their genes with each parent and with their offspring. On the average, they share 50% of their genes with their siblings and 25% of their genes with their first cousins. An individual can secure representation of his or her genes in future generations by enhancing the production of those copies of the genes that reside in the bodies of close relatives. Fitness gained by one's own reproductive activity in producing direct descendants is called direct fitness. Fitness gained by facilitating the survival and reproduction of close relatives (excluding direct descendants) is called indirect fitness. The sum of an organism's direct fitness plus its indirect fitness, the increment in the fitness levels of its kin for which it is responsible, is its inclusive fitness. It is inclusive fitness, viewed from the perspective of an animal's lifetime, that is the true bottom line in the currency of natural selection.

ALTRUISM

The operation of indirect fitness often is referred to as reflecting kin selection. Inclusive fitness levels sometimes can be increased when the individual engages in acts that decrease its own direct or personal fitness if the act increases its indirect fitness by an amount sufficient to more than offset the loss. Such acts are referred to as altruistic. Altruistic behavior produces an increase in the direct fitness of one or more close relatives at a cost to the direct fitness level of the individual displaying the act. Much solicitous behavior toward other individuals and many behavioral patterns such as signals warning of the approach of predators can be viewed as altruistic and understood as reflecting the action of indirect selection. Perhaps the ultimate example is of sterile castes of some species of insects, which appear to gain fitness by helping kin.

Because indirect selection works only for close relatives, it would be important that the animal be able to direct its behavior selectively at kin. This often necessitates some mechanism of discriminating kin from nonkin. Many such mechanisms have been revealed in recent years.

Even altruistic behavior produces an increase in inclusive fitness because the loss in direct fitness is more than compensated for by the gain in indirect fitness. The saying goes: "scratch an altruist and watch a hypocrite bleed." Behavior that produces a decrease in the inclusive fitness of an individual ought never to evolve.

RECIPROCAL ALTRUISM

Another way in which altruistic behavior can evolve is when two unrelated individuals behave as if they have formed a pact ensuring mutual aid; this is referred to as reciprocal altruism. Reciprocal altruism is behavior displayed between unrelated individuals and conducted according to the rule that an individual who is helped in a certain situation by a particular other individual will reciprocate and help the other individual when a similar situation arises. The altruistic act should entail some immediate cost, but the reciprocity should produce a long-term benefit that outweighs the short-term cost, with costs and benefits always calculated in regard to inclusive fitness. Generally, behavioral patterns evolving via reciprocal altruism will be expected to have relatively low costs relative to benefits.

The major risk in the evolution of behavior via reciprocal altruism is that "cheaters," individuals who reap the benefits of altruistic acts without reciprocating and hence incurring the costs, will appear. For these reasons, it is generally believed that behavior can evolve only in species that are relatively long-lived and have individual recognition. In that way, they can enforce rules of reciprocation and discriminate against individuals who do not reciprocate.

An example of this kind of behavior is provided by male baboons that live in a hierarchical social structure. A pair of unrelated males may consistently help each other out in dominance struggles and thus the coalition may do better in the struggle for resources than either could do alone.

ENVIRONMENTS

It may appear as though a single alternative may always be the most adaptive in the sense that it leads to the highest levels of inclusive fitness. This is an oversimplification. Different alternatives may lead to maximization of fitness in different environments. What is an effective strategy in one environment may not be so in another.

The environment includes not only inanimate objects and members of other species, but members of one's own species as well. The best strategy may depend on what others in the population are doing. This leads to the concept of the evolutionarily stable strategy (ESS). Technically, an ESS is that strategy from a set of alternative strategies that, if adopted by most members of a population, cannot be bettered in the sense of an alternative strategy leading to higher fitness levels. ESS implies that what is the optimal alternative will vary with the alternatives adopted by others in the population. An example can be found with sex ratios. Because each individual has one mother and one father, the total fitness of males and females in a population must be equal. Thus if others in the population are producing more males than females, it would be beneficial to invest more in females; the reverse would be the case if males were in short supply. There is no one best alternative; the alternative leading to greatest fitness levels depends on what others are doing.

The concept of genetic fitness lies at the heart of all considerations of the evolution of behavior and the adaptive consequences of alternative behavioral patterns. All behavior can be viewed in relation to its consequences for effectively getting the genes of the organism's genotype into the gene pools of future generations. Although hard to measure, considerations of fitness are thus pivotal in the study of behavior.

ADAPTATION
NATURAL SELECTION
SPECIES-SPECIFIC BEHAVIOR
SURVIVAL ANALYSIS

D. A. DEWSBURY

GENIUS

As a concept, genius is closely related to *giftedness, creativity,* and *precocity.* From F. Galton's 1869 study of eminent men onward, definitions have been problematic. Although *genius* and *giftedness* are sometimes seen as synonyms, genius connotes exceptionally rare and prodigious achievement, whereas giftedness, especially in the context of identifying and encouraging academic or creative talent, has been defined in less restrictive ways. Albert's productivity-based definition of genius referred to the person who "produces, over a long period . . . a large body of work that has significant influence on many [others] for many years"—work creating a "major shift" in perceptions or ideas.

Biographical studies from 1869 to the 1940s focused on historically eminent persons, reporting that they tended to come from families of high occupational level and had histories of good health and character. Little support for a link between genius and either pathology or physical frailty was found, challenging long-held notions.

Intensive studies were undertaken of living scientists, artists, and professionals recognized as unusually productive or creative. Other than high intelligence, some common features of personality, work motivation, and perceptual style characterized these subjects. This work overlapped research on creativity, expanding the concept of giftedness beyond traditional IQ-based definitions to include originality and imaginativeness. Various measures of creative ability were designed and investigated.

GIFTED AND TALENTED CHILDREN
HUMAN INTELLIGENCE

A. B. PRATT

GERIATRIC PSYCHOLOGY

Interdisciplinary in nature and process, geriatric psychology is the science of the behavior of the aged. Geriatric psychology, with its medical, neurological, psychiatric, and physiological emphases, involves the behavioral, biological, and social sciences. The importance of cross-cultural and cross-national studies in geriatric psychology is increasingly patent in research.

Geriatric psychology is a rather new area of interest: Experimental studies of aging became a matter of concern only in the last 50 years. Geriatric psychology must be concerned with the terrors of loneliness in old age, worry about illness or shelter, anxiety over finances, or the unhappiness that results when one generation infringes on the life of another. Geriatric psychology must deal with the fact that aging is not synonymous with disease; that aging is not a state of ill health; and that a disabling, lengthy sickness is not an inevitable part of growing old. It must, however, promote understanding of the mental and emotional problems of the later years of life, because accumulated physical handicaps plus a general deterioration in bodily functions superimpose a heavier burden on whatever emotional traumata may have developed earlier within the individual.

The "graying" of America is a major demographic trend. The total number of older Americans is expected to increase from some 30 million to 55 million by the year 2030. The 75-plus age group is the fastest growing segment of the population.

Mental illness is more prevalent in the elderly than in younger adults. An estimated 15 to 25% of older persons have significant mental health problems. Psychosis increases after age 65, and even more so beyond age 75. Twenty-five percent of all reported suicides in this country are committed by elderly persons. The chronic health problems that afflict 86% of the elderly and the financial difficulties faced by many clearly contribute to increasing stress. The stresses affecting the mental health of the elderly are multiple and pervasive.

A basic geriatric problem of a psychological nature concerns elderly individuals who share households with kin. Although there has been a definite decline in the number and proportion of multigenerational households, the decline has been greater for the "young-old" (65 to 74) than for the "old-old" (75+), with only slight differences in the proportion of "single" elderly males and "single" elderly females living in multigenerational families. In spite of the decline, the multigenerational household is still viable for approximately 2 million elderly persons.

The principal reason for institutionalizing cognitively impaired older persons is the caregivers' inability to continue providing help and not the severity of deficits. Feelings of burden were significantly correlated with the frequency of visits made by others, but not with other variables such as the severity of cognitive impairment and frequency of memory and behavior problems. These findings suggest the importance of facilitating natural support systems as an essential part of providing services to the families of the impaired elderly. To be sure, the physical manifestations of aging are only a small part of the process of growing old. Changing attitudes, behavior, and overall personality—often the results of societal pressure—are now recognized as equally important considerations in the study of geriatric psychology.

Birren and Sloane wrote: "A national health problem which is most severe in terms of its prevalence and cost is a group of mental disorders and dysfunctions which are associated with aging. . . . More important, perhaps, is a cost that cannot be measured or tabulated: the loss of human potential and of the affected person's capacity for adaptation and ability to contribute to human welfare."

Geriatric psychology also concerns itself experimentally and theoretically with the signs and symptoms of disease processes. Widespread inflammation, muscular rigidity, cough, pain, and fever in the elderly are not minor but acute processes. Senile persons cannot easily withstand extremes such as heat, cold, overeating, starvation, and dehydration. The older individual has accumulated many scars from the hazards of life: injurious habits, poor nutrition, intoxications, infections, and actual injuries, including the psychological traumata incident to a long life.

Another important aspect of geriatric psychology is the sexuality of the older person. Men and women continue to be physiologically capable of sexual functioning, although in most older persons interest in sexual activity and actual performance decline with age. Older men are more interested in sex and more active sexually than older women.

Parron, Solomon, and Rodin emphasize the need to direct the behavioral sciences toward a wider range of health problems than the mental health issues with which they have traditionally been concerned, to link the biomedical and behavioral sciences, and to stimulate interdisciplinary clinical and basic research. They point out that new research initiatives should be undertaken with respect to the changing vulnerabilities of the elderly to disease, the relationship of attitudes and beliefs regarding health and illness that influence the health behavior of the elderly, and the relationships of the health care provider to the elderly patient.

No less should appropriate attention be given by mental health practitioners to the immunologic status of the elderly (e.g., the impact of behavioral processes of adaptation on immune function, the impact of age-related changes in immunologic competence on behavior, and the role of the immune system in mediating relationships between behavioral processes of adaptation and the maintenance of health and the development of disease).

One of the major problems in the work of the geriatric psychologist is that of chronic, "degenerative" diseases. Most of the disorders of old age are of doubtful etiology. They usually arise from factors within the patient, are highly variable, and are in operation years before they are overtly manifested. Unless and until the causative factors are unequivocally established, geriatric psychology must aim at control rather than cure, and at *prevention* through better supervision and living.

The keynote in geriatric psychology is *individualization*. Each elderly person must be separately assessed and inventoried. The psychological changes produced by old age are many. In fact, recognition of "abnormal" mental and emotional features in persons of advanced years still remains one of the real perplexities of medical practice. Nowhere in the fields of psychiatry, neurology, and geriatric psychology are holistic principles of practice more meaningful than in treating geriatric individuals because the aged person's mental condition will always be complicated by organic disorders of some kind.

Studies of health behavior in the elderly must take into account the social conditions as well as the underlying physical and psychological changes that occur with age. These changes function as a substrate for the influence of age and the presentation of disease, the response to treatment, and the complications that ensue. Of particular interest in both domains is the variability of physiological changes within and among individuals. Understanding the relationship among central nervous system, endocrine, and immune functions may help in identifying one of the bases for this variability.

AGING AND BEHAVIORAL CHANGES
GERONTOLOGY
LIFE-SPAN DEVELOPMENT

H. L. SILVERMAN

GERONTOLOGY

Gerontology is the science of aging. It is distinguished from geriatrics, the science of the medical and hygienic care of diseases of the aged. Gerontology overlaps geriatrics and is far broader in scope. As a science, it studies the processes of aging as well as the statuses of the aged. Therefore, there are gerontologists involved in basic research and academic study of aging and the aged, and applied gerontologists who administer to the aged directly as well as indirectly through evaluation research, policy development and implementation, and administration and organization of programs for the health and welfare of the aged.

The study of gerontology is necessarily interdisciplinary. All the disciplines of the social and behavioral sciences and many of the fields within the biological sciences bear on aging and the aged.

Aging involves biological change. Some change with age is clearly the result of biological influence—most undeniably in certain diseases. Some change with age may be due either to biological change or to change in the individual's situation, which in turn prompts biological change. Situational changes can range from international economic and political events to personal events such as retirement, loss of spouse, and intrapsychic developments. In the biological sciences the primary fields of interest for gerontology are cell biology, endocrinology/pharmacology, genetics/longevity, immunology, molecular biology/biochemistry, morphology, neurobiology, nutrition, and physiology.

Gerontology in clinical medicine involves all medical health professionals. Subject fields in clinical medicine of especial interest to gerontology include cardiology, dermatology, endocrinology, gastroenterology, gynecology, hematology, rheumatology, nephrology, neurology, oncology, ophthalmology, orthopedics, otolaryngology, pharmacology, psychopharmacology, and urology.

An example of an area within gerontology in which psychologists are active, and in which psychological, social scientific, and/or social research investigations may be conducted, is retirement.

Any area or subject of interest in psychology, the behavioral and social sciences, and the life and health sciences that is not particular or exclusive to another age group is an appropriate subject for study in gerontology. The crucial and most difficult point in all pure gerontological research is the determination of change due to age or aging itself—change that is universal and exclusive to aging, and not the result of social or cultural factors that might differ among populations. In an attempt to focus on this issue, as well as to explore efficacy of differing approaches and treatments in different cultures, the importance of cross-cultural and cross-national studies is increasingly acknowledged in gerontology.

AGING AND BEHAVIORAL CHANGES
CROSS-CULTURAL PSYCHOLOGY
GERIATRIC PSYCHOLOGY
RETIREMENT

G. J. MANASTER

GESTALT PSYCHOLOGY

Early in the twentieth century, Gestalt psychology came about as an amendment to the traditional method of scientific analysis. The accepted way of analyzing a complex phenomenon scientifically had been that of describing the parts and arriving at the whole by adding up the descriptions thus obtained. Recent developments in biology, psychology, and sociology had begun to suggest, however, that such a procedure could not do justice to phenomena that are field processes—entities made up of interacting forces. The need for a revision was felt first in the life sciences, but inevitably extended to the physical sciences as well. Gestalt psychology thus became a component of a more broadly conceived Gestalt theory concerning scientific method in general.

This extension into the physical sciences became an integral aspect of the Gestalt approach for two reasons. First, many psychological phenomena, especially those in perception, could be described but not explained by what was observable at the level of conscious experience. It was possible to determine by laws or rules which conditions led to which consequences, but the only way to indicate the causes of such happenings was by reference to the physiological counterpart of the observed phenomena.

This procedure, then, implied a parallelism between psychological experience and correlated processes in the nervous system. The laws governing the functioning of the brain and, by extension, the physical universe in general, were assumed to be reflected in mental activity as well. Such a view—a second reason for Gestalt psychologists to stress the link with the physical sciences—made it possible to coordinate the functioning of the mind with the organic and inorganic world as a whole.

In textbooks of psychology the Gestalt approach is often exemplified by the "rules of grouping." Although easily reconciled with traditional analysis, these rules were presented by Wertheimer in preparation of what might be called a Copernican switch from a mere linking of elements "from below" to a primary concern "from above" with the total structure of the phenomenon.

In his paper "Laws of organization in perceptual forms," Wertheimer showed that the formation of Gestalt patterns is governed by a supreme principle which he referred to as the tendency toward the "good Gestalt" or the *Prägnanz* principle meant to describe a strictly objective tendency toward the greatest simplicity and regularity.

This tendency toward the simplest structure available under given circumstances or, to use a related criterion, toward the lowest available level of tension, has been of great explanatory value, especially in the exploration of sensory perception. Nevertheless, the simplicity principle alone was insufficient to account for perceptual Gestalten. If it ruled unopposed, it would reduce percepts to an amorphous homogeneity, to the limiting case of structure. What was needed was a counteragent, an anabolic tendency that offered constraints to the organizing forces in the field. In perception, the principal supplier of such constraints was the world of stimuli impinging on the receptor organs of the senses, especially those of vision, hearing, and touch.

At the retinal level, little if any of the Gestalt organization takes place. (The more recently discovered receptive fields in the retinae or the cerebral cortex of animals do not activate Gestalt processes.) At the higher levels of the visual apparatus, the stimulus configuration constrains the physiological field process, which is determined first of all by the tendency toward simplest structure (i.e., the physiological counterpart of the percept assumes the simplest structure compatible with the stimulus situation). A Gestalt has come about through the interaction between the stimulus configuration and the organizing powers of the visual field.

It is this interaction between tension-enhancing and tension-reducing forces that brings about the state of what Wertheimer called *Prägnanz*.

Gestalt structures vary all the way on a scale extending between two hypothetical poles. At the one extreme, there would be the state of total interaction. At the other extreme, the parts of a whole would be totally independent of one another, so that what happened at one place in the constellation would have no effect on the remainder.

Interaction in a Gestalt context is the very opposite of the functioning of machines, in which, in Köhler's formulation, the form of action in the system is entirely prescribed by the constraint. All action takes place along preordained channels. Machines can serve also as illustrative models for the networks of defined concepts that constitute intellectual reasoning, such as scientific theories. It must be made clear that although field processes in psychology and elsewhere must be understood as Gestalten, a scientific statement itself, by its very nature, can never be a Gestalt. Gestalten exist in perception, in mental imagery, in the dynamics of the human personality, in physiological and physical states of interaction, but they can be conceptualized only through networks of relations. The validity of the scientific description depends on how faithful an equivalent it offers, with its own means, of the Gestalt structures it undertakes to match.

The Gestalt approach requires that the subdivision of a whole into its components be effected in strict obedience to the cleavings inherent in the given structure itself. As a practical consequence, the range of a problem singled out for investigation cannot be arbitrarily staked out, but depends strictly on what is relevant for the processes under scrutiny. To discover the proper range of a problem is nearly tantamount to finding its solution.

Gestalt structure extends in the time dimension as readily as in the space dimensions, and the principles governing time and space are similar. The Gestalt analyses of spatial relations have had very little competition, but when it came to sequences in time, Gestalt psychology had to cope with a powerful tradition that explained all temporal connections by the laws of association. In its original form—in Aristotle—associative connections were based on something either similar or contrary to what we seek, or else on that which was contiguous with it. Such criteria were compatible with the Gestalt effort to derive connection from structural organization. When, however, it was asserted that associations come about by mere frequency of occurrence, Gestalt psychologists raised objections. A doctrine according to which anything could become associated with anything if it had been its neighbor often enough replaced meaningful belonging with a whimsical subjectivity.

Gestalt psychologists denounced conditioning by mere repetition as the lowest form of learning and opposed it with learning through understanding. Productive learning was now asserted to occur when a person or animal acted according to the demands of a given structure. Effective learning could come about only when the learner perceived the connections among the decisive elements of a given situation by what was called "insight."

A decisive difference between the purely perceptual grasp of a given structure and a "problem situation" in the more particular sense of the term should be mentioned here. In simple perception, problem solving is limited to finding the structure inherent in the stimulus data. A harder task challenges the observer when a situation presents itself as organized in a way that conceals the connections needed for a solution. Restructuring may consist in merely looking at the situation differently or may require an actual rearrangement of the components.

The restructuring of a Gestalt is an eminently dynamic activity of field forces, but so is all structuring in the first place. In fact, a structure by definition never ceases to be a constellation of forces. Just as an apparently stable social pattern such as a family group never ceases to be a more or less balanced arrangement of various motivational tendencies, so a visual pattern presents to the sensitive eye a system of variously directed vectors that keep one another in balance. This reflection of the corresponding physiological field forces in experience is what Gestalt psychologists describe as perceptual expression. Expressive qualities are authentic and objective properties of all percepts. They can even be called the primary qualities conveyed by perceptual shape, size, movement, intensity, timbre, and so on.

Perhaps the most characteristic aspect of the Gestalt view is its profound respect for the "givenness" of the world as an objectively existing cosmos held together by law and order. It is a view that leads to a theory of value based on the criterion of objective requirement. Whether it be the irrational pressure of an instinct or the demands of the categorical imperative, value in Gestalt psychology is considered a field force—one that by no means issues always from the ego needs of the person who is doing the valuing. Gestalt psychology is therefore in strong philosophical opposition to a worldview that describes values as purely subjective and arbitrary, and therefore as idiosyncrasies to be excluded from the scientific image of the world.

FIELD THEORY
PERCEPTION
SYSTEMS THEORY

R. ARNHEIM

GESTALT THERAPY

Gestalt therapy is an existential and phenomenological approach emphasizing the principles of present-centered awareness and immediate experience. To discover how one blocks one's flow of awareness and aliveness, the individual in therapy is directed to fully experience current thoughts, feelings, and body sensations. By assuming greater responsibility for experience, one learns to trust one's own resources and become less dependent and manipulative in relating to others. Gestalt therapy is nonanalytical and noninterpretive, encouraging patients to find their own meanings, set their own goals, and make their own choices.

ORIGINS

Gestalt therapy was developed by Frederick S. (Fritz) Perls. Perls' broad interests in existentialism, Eastern religions, and Gestalt psychology led him away from the Freudian viewpoint toward his own theory and method of therapy. Perls saw the human being as a unified organism, an integration of mental, physical, emotional, and sensory processes expressed in the present moment.

MAJOR THEORETICAL CONCEPTS

Gestalt theory suggests that the natural tendency of the organism is toward growth and satisfaction of basic needs. The healthy individual is responsive to inner urges and trusts them as a basis for choices and decisions. If one denies aspects of one's being by blocking awareness or attempting to live up to a rigid set of "shoulds," one loses the capacity to support oneself adequately and becomes alienated from inner strivings and resources. A continuing flow of needs and wishes come into awareness, each of which can be thought of as a Gestalt, a figure or focus that emerges out of an undifferentiated background of experience. In healthy functioning, the organism mobilizes to meet each need, making contact with aspects of the environment appropriate to need satisfaction. In this manner the equilibrium of the organism is restored.

For this self-regulating process to function, it is essential that the organism have sufficient *awareness* (i.e., be in touch with thoughts, feelings, and sensations as they occur from moment to moment). Because awareness can be focused only on one place at a time, the person occupied with either the past or the future is not aware of what is happening in the present.

Perls emphasized the importance of accepting responsibility for one's own behavior. Instead of denying, blaming, projecting, and displacing responsibility for one's experience, the individual is encouraged to accept thoughts, feelings, and actions as parts of the self. Instead of blaming the environment for what we imagine we cannot do for ourselves, we must each do our own work, take our own risks, and thereby discover who we are and of what we are capable.

In Gestalt theory a key concept is *unfinished business:* uncompleted situations from the past accompanied by unexpressed feelings never fully experienced or discharged. Carried into present life, these incomplete experiences interfere with present-centered awareness and authentic contact with others. Perls believed that unexpressed resentments were the most frequent source of unfinished business. Unfinished business can be resolved by reenacting (either directly or in fantasy) the original situation and allowing the associated affect to be experienced and expressed. In this way completion is achieved, preoccupations with the past dissipate, and the individual can redirect attention and energy to new possibilities.

THERAPEUTIC GOALS AND ROLE OF THE THERAPIST

In Gestalt therapy the goal is not mere symptom relief but rather personal growth. The therapist assists the patient to achieve greater self-acceptance, to assume more personal responsibility, to reintegrate disowned or split-off aspects of personality, and to be more authentic and less manipulative in relating to others. Noting discrepancies between what the patient is saying and doing, the therapist makes interventions based on the patient's present behavior. Interventions tend to be descriptive rather than interpretive.

The therapist not only observes the patient's process but also brings his or her own individuality into the encounter. The Gestalt therapist believes that she or he is as much a part of the therapeutic interaction as the patient and takes responsibility for being present in a direct, spontaneous, and self-disclosing manner.

TECHNIQUES OF GESTALT THERAPY

Gestalt therapists have described a variety of techniques—some of them powerful and dramatic—that they use to sharpen direct experience, heighten conflicts and polarities, foster freer expression, or to bring into awareness blocks and avoidance mechanisms. Perls cautioned therapists, however, not to become technicians depending on a bag of tricks or "gimmicks."

In Gestalt therapy as practiced by Fritz Perls, *taking the "hot seat"* indicated a person's willingness to engage with the therapist. In this case the hot seat was a chair facing the therapist. An additional "empty chair" next to the patient might be used to imagine the presence of a significant other or disowned part of self for the purpose of initiating a dialogue. The technique of *dialogues* is helpful in identifying projected and denied parts of the personality. By using two chairs and moving back and forth between them, the patient carries out a "conversation" by speaking alternately from each position. As the interplay between these polar opposites is heightened and more fully experienced, integration through greater self-acceptance becomes possible.

The Gestalt therapist attends to the full range of a patient's expression, not just words. *Nonverbal cues* such as body posture, gestures, or tone of voice often reflect an aspect of functioning outside the patient's awareness. The therapist may ask a patient to exaggerate or repeat a gesture, for example, and through this intensification allow the patient to discover its function or significance.

The Gestalt method of *dream work* grew out of Perls' belief that dreams are among our most spontaneous productions. Each dream is thought to contain an existential message—an expression of aspects of the dreamer's present state of being. By becoming every object and character in the dream (both animate and inanimate), the dreamer can identify with and thereby reown projections, conflicts, and unfinished situations reflected in the dream.

APPLICATIONS OF GESTALT THERAPY

As originally practiced by Fritz Perls, Gestalt therapy was primarily an individual form of treatment carried out privately or in the presence of others in workshops or training groups. Other Gestaltists have applied the principles to group therapy in a way that encourages more interaction among group members. They have extended the work to a broad spectrum of client populations and settings.

EVALUATION AND CURRENT STATUS

Gestalt therapy at its best can be energizing and enlivening through its emphasis on direct contact, expressiveness, focus on feelings and body experience, and minimal theorizing and interpreting. Critics, however, have pointed out that this approach can be anti-intellectual, technique-dependent, overly confrontive, and suitable only to well-motivated, verbal clients. Because Gestalt techniques can release intensive affect, Irma Lee Shepherd expressed concern about the appropriateness of their use with severely disturbed patients and those who lack impulse control. There is general agreement that negative consequences can be minimized by the mature, well-trained therapist adequately grounded in the conceptual framework of Gestalt therapy, who works with a client population with which he or she is experienced and comfortable.

GESTALT PSYCHOLOGY
PSYCHOTHERAPY
PSYCHOTHERAPY TECHNIQUES

T. A. GLASS

GESTURES

Gestures are an integral part of the system of communication, and are part of a "language" when language is broadly defined as the expression and reception of ideas and feelings. Gestural language, which contains hundreds of thousands of different signals, is thought to have preceded oral communication by almost a million years.

To become a gesture, an act must be seen by someone else and must communicate some piece of information to that person. The scope of nonverbal movements encompassed in the term "gesture" has long been debated.

Similarly, the question has been raised regarding the intentionality of the nonverbal movement or gesture. Those who perceive gestures from a "receiver-oriented perspective" choose to include unintentional behaviors within the definition of a gesture because they may be interpreted as intentional by the receiver and thus are a "communication."

Besides the incidental, nonsocial gestures that transmit secondary messages, gestures can be placed in three general categories. *Symbolic gestures* such as crossing oneself or saluting the flag stand for a customary event or idea. *Iconic gestures* look like the thing they are meant to represent, such as the shape of a bowl made with the hands. *Expressive gestures* include such behaviors as smiling, sneering, and grumbling. Symbolic gestures, which often replace language, are usually consciously known by their users and have significance to a particular group. The North American Indians are among those groups that developed a systematic sign language of their own. Gestures, besides replacing speech, can qualify the meaning of speech and thus are metacommunicative. For example, placing one's right palm over the heart indicates sincerity and affirms the gesturer's veracity.

The investigation of gestures overlaps with the study of nonverbal behavior and communication. Modern scientific study of movement behavior began with Darwin's treatise on the origins and functions of facial and bodily expressions based on the author's observations. Although stating that certain gestures were learned, Darwin argued that most bodily expression is innate or inherited rather than learned.

Weston La Barre, in contrast, explored the cultural dimension of gesture and said that the anthropologist must be wary of those who speak of an "instinctive" gesture on the part of the human being. For example, nodding the head as an indication of affirmation and the rotation of the head on the axis vertebra for negation had been accepted as "instinctive" gestures based on the infant's rooting response and then its refusal of the mother's breast. However, La Barre offered many alternatives from other cultures: For example, among the Ainu of northern Japan, the hands rather than the head are used to gesture affirmation or negation, whereas the Abyssinians say "no" by jerking the head to the right shoulder and "yes" by throwing the head back and raising the eyebrows.

Hewes analyzed "postural habits" cross-culturally, and Hall wrote about cultural differences in proximity and touch in research that he called "proxemics." Lomax and others developed a system called choreometrics, showing how movement styles related to the socioeconomic subsistence activity levels of a culture. Studying pancultural aspects of body movement, Eibl-Eibesfeldt found that eyebrow flashes and smiles occurred in greetings of diverse cultures, and Ekman and Friesen found that certain facial expressions were universal. Darwin found that specific fixed expressions characterized some mental disorders.

Wilhelm Reich noted frequent contradictions between verbal content and affective behavior. He considered the patient's mode of behavior to be as important as what the patient said.

Freud considered many "chance acts" to be analogous to unconscious attitudes. Maurice Krout studied the incidence and significance of various "autistic" gestures (e.g., scratching or twisting a lock of hair), suggesting that those gestures might be unconsciously produced in relation to an intrapsychic conflict; he associated fist gestures with aggression and certain finger gestures with shame or conflicts over achievement or affection. He also found individual and sex differences in the performance of specific gestures.

Ray L. Birdwhistell, an anthropologist, argued that body movement, rather than reflecting individual inner states of emotion or attitude, was simply one culturally determined channel of communication, and that movement patterns were learned through sociocultural experience. He coined the term "kinesics" for a methodology concerned with the communication aspects of learned body motion behavior. The analog of kinesics is descriptive linguistics. Birdwhistell saw communication as a multichannel system of which movement patterns were one part. He rejected the study of isolated examples of vocalic variation or gesture and posture, and focused on an interactional approach. Birdwhistell and Scheflen developed a naturalistic observation procedure, which Scheflen called "context analysis," to study the detection and isolation of units of behavior within a communication system.

Condon and Ogston, using this interactional or contextual approach, have shown how body movement among individuals, or between an individual and his or her own speech, may be synchronous at the "micro" level.

The emphasis on group and family therapy with increased use of videotape and film has popularized the study of the interactional and communicative aspects of body motion along with the study of the relationship between individual and cultural differences and the intrapsychic level in movement.

E. Sapir wrote: "We respond to gestures with an extreme alertness and, one might almost say, in accordance with an elaborate and secret code that is written nowhere, known by none, and understood by all." The analysis of gestures has offered valuable information about this silent language. Gestures, whether studied from a psychological or cultural point of view, offer revealing insights into the "language" of communication with regard to both meaning and style.

COMMUNICATION PROCESSES
CROSS-CULTURAL PSYCHOLOGY
FACIAL EXPRESSIONS
SYMBOLIC INTERACTION

S. F. WALLOCK

GIFTED AND TALENTED CHILDREN

Of the various definitions of the gifted and talented, one used by the U.S. government is comprehensive and infers a movement in support of special educational opportunities for the gifted and talented. It reads: "Gifted and talented children means children, and whenever applicable, youth, who are identified at the preschool, elementary, or secondary level as possessing demonstrated or potential abilities that give evidence of high performance capability in areas such as intellectual, creative, specific academic, or leadership ability, or in the performing and visual arts, and who by reason thereof require services or activities not ordinarily provided by the school."

This definition constitutes a greatly expanded notion of the concept of giftedness and would include within the gifted and talented category students seen as performing, or able to perform, in the top 3 to 5% of all students. Systematic attempts to categorize these people began with Francis Galton. The advent of intelligence testing provided an objective measure by means of which one could identify, within broad statistical limits, children with the highest potential—the intellectually gifted. L. M. Terman had a lifelong interest in genius and the gifted. Terman conducted a longitudinal study of 1500 gifted individuals that continued after his death.

These developments had a positive effect on identification of the gifted, but they also had negative effects because the gifted were noted only on the basis of IQ. Reliance on IQ alone to identify the gifted eliminated many culturally different students from consideration. Efforts were made to find the means for identifying gifted and talented children in different cultures.

Although the gifted and talented may be found in all walks of life, more stable homes and above average socioeconomic statuses prevail. They tend to be successful in school socially as well as academically, and to be healthy physically and emotionally. These same positive characteristics are related to the family situation and socioeconomic groups from which gifted and talented students tend to come.

Gifted children are not immune to the problems faced by all children as they grow up and are open to additional problems related to their giftedness. Additional problems may come from the pressure of expectations that others have for them or that they have for themselves. Problems may arise through lack of match of social and scholastic levels. Problems may also arise with peers as well as adults as their strengths become social or behavioral liabilities.

The general thrust of the movement urging education for the gifted and talented appears to have two goals: to realize the potential of these children for the good of society, and to realize their potential for their own success and happiness. The types of programs suggested include early school admission, acceleration and grade skipping, advanced study, independent study, the mentor approach, special resource room programs, and special classes.

CHILD PSYCHOLOGY
HUMAN ABILITIES
INDIVIDUAL DIFFERENCES

G. J. Manaster

GLANDS AND BEHAVIOR

Glands may be classified as either exocrine or endocrine. Exocrine glands have ducts. Their products perform their functions in the immediate vicinity of the secreting gland, but outside the tissues of the body, although this may mean within the mouth or gastrointestinal tract. Sweat glands, salivary glands, and the exocrine pancreas, which secretes peptides involved in digestion, are examples. They have little direct influence on behavior. Endocrine, or ductless, glands secrete their products into the bloodstream and exert their effect on organs distant from the secreting gland. Several can produce profound direct effects on (a) maintenance of homeostasis; (b) modulation of emotional behaviors, especially those related to stress; and (c) sexual and gender-related behaviors.

There are six endocrine glands, and two of them have structurally and functionally distinct divisions. The pituitary, one of these latter two glands also known as the hypophysis, lies at the base of the brain and is connected to the hypothalamus by the infundibular or pituitary stalk. The anterior division of the pituitary is significantly larger than the posterior division and is called the adenohypophysis. The adenohypophysis is truly a gland and secretes growth hormone, adrenocorticotropic hormone, thyroid-stimulating hormone, prolactin, and the gonadotropins. Levels of hormones secreted by the adenohypophysis are controlled by the hypothalamus through its connections to the median eminence where axons from the cells of the parvicellular system of the hypothalamus release factors that either stimulate or inhibit release of anterior pituitary hormones.

The posterior division of the pituitary, the neurohypophysis, receives direct innervation from the hypothalamic magnocellular neurosecretory system. The cells of origin of the magnocellular neurosecretory system are located in the supraoptic and paraventricular nuclei of the hypothalamus, and they send axons to the neurohypophysis. The terminals of these axons release oxytocin and vasopressin that enter the bloodstream.

The adrenal gland also has two parts. Its outside is the cortex. Releasing hormones from the pituitary stimulate cells of the adrenal cortex to release either mineralocorticoids or glucocorticoids. Mineralocorticoids such as aldosterone work on the kidney to enable conservation of salt and water. Glucocorticoids are involved in the body's response to stress. The inside of the adrenal gland is the medulla. Its cells are the target of preganglionic sympathetic axons from the spinal cord and release adrenalin and noradrenalin into the bloodstream.

The testis of the male and the ovaries of the female comprise the gonads. Both the female and male gonads secrete estrogen, progesterone, and testosterone. The relative amounts of these hormones determine the sexual characteristics that distinguish the two genders.

The remaining endocrine glands are the pancreas, thyroid, and parathyroid. The endocrine pancreas secretes insulin necessary for glucose and fats to enter cells so that the cells can use them for energy or, in the case of fat cells, store them. The thyroid gland secretes thyroxin, which regulates metabolic rate and protein synthesis by cells throughout the body. The parathyroid secretes a hormone involved in the regulation of calcium concentration in blood. This gland has little direct influence on behavior.

The activity of virtually all endocrine glands, with the exception of the adrenal medulla, is directly modulated by hormones released from the pituitary, whereas the pituitary is regulated by the hypothalamus. Although the adrenal medulla receives direct input from the sympathetic division of the autonomic nervous system, even the release of adrenalin and noradrenalin by this gland is influenced by the hypothalamus, because of its ability to control the autonomic nervous system. Any discussion of the role of glands in the regulation of behavior must include the hypothalamus.

HORMONAL INFLUENCES ON HOMEOSTATIC MECHANISMS

The concept of homeostatic mechanism refers to any activity or group of activities designed to maintain a cell, an organ, or an entire organism in a steady state optimal for survival known as homeostasis. At the cellular level, an example of such an activity would be activation of the sodium–potassium pump to regain intracellular and extracellular concentrations of these two ions appropriate for the resting membrane. Eating and drinking behaviors are examples of homeostatic mechanisms at the level of the whole organism. Neural and hormonal systems are involved in maintaining organism homeostasis in mammals.

To maintain homeostasis, the body requires a variety of substances such as vitamins, minerals, trace elements, fats, carbohydrates, and proteins. If excess amounts of any of these substances are present in the circulation, they may be either excreted or stored. If too small an amount is present, it is necessary, in most cases, to ingest the missing substance. However, inadequate levels of vitamins, minerals, and trace elements (with the possible exception of salt) do not induce hunger. Hunger and consequent behaviors related to finding food and eating are induced by low levels of carbohydrates, fats, and possibly proteins.

The endocrine pancreas is the gland involved in the modulation of feeding. The islands of Langerhans scattered throughout the pancreas compose its endocrine division. Three different cell types within the islands of Langerhans secrete three hormones involved in regulating the availability of glucose to cells. These are glucagon, which raises blood glucose; insulin, which lowers the level of blood glucose by binding with cell membranes throughout the body and brain to permit entry of glucose into the cell; and somatostatin, which appears to regulate the release of glucagon and insulin. Insulin is the hormone of the endocrine pancreas most directly related to eating behavior.

Insulin is secreted in response to increased levels of blood glucose. This may occur after a meal or if glucagon is released and circulating glucose increases. Increased insulin levels cause glucose to enter cells more quickly where it is either used for fuel or, in the case of fat cells, is converted to triglycerides and stored. Blood glucose levels then drop. Data support the contention that hunger and eating are initiated when nutrient levels, especially glucose levels, decrease in the blood. Thus a high insulin level could lead to hunger because it decreases blood glucose. Furthermore, insulin levels can be influenced by the hypothalamus, and disruption of this control by hypothalamic lesions may explain some of the effects of such lesions on eating behavior and body weight.

The dorsal motor nucleus of the vagus nerve provides input from the brain to the pancreas. Neurons of the lateral hypothalamus send input to the dorsal motor nucleus, and stimulation of the lateral hypothalamus increases circulating insulin levels. Neurons in the lateral hypothalamus appear to be sensitive to changes in blood glucose use, either because they have glucoreceptors themselves or receive neural feedback from liver glucoreceptors. Bilateral destruction of the lateral hypothalamus produces an animal that will not eat and will starve unless it is carefully nursed back to health. It has been suggested that this effect is due to loss of lateral hypothalamic stimulation of the vagal nucleus, which leads to increased levels of insulin. Thus an animal without its lateral hypothalamus has continued levels of low insulin and low rates of glucose utilization. Therefore, its brain does not sense that it is hungry, and eating is not initiated. This is, of course, not a complete account of the neural control of hunger and eating, nor is it the only mechanism by which the lateral hypothalamus influences eating, but it does provide the first example of how the hypothalamus and a product of an endocrine gland interact to modify homeostatic behavior.

A second example is provided by drinking, which is part of a homeostatic mechanism designed to regulate body water content, salt concentration, and blood pressure. When blood volume decreases as a consequence of water loss, as might occur during heavy exercise that results in excessive sweating, blood volume drops, and blood flow slows down. This decrease in blood flow is sensed by the kidney, which responds by releasing renin, which in turn is converted to angiotensin in the bloodstream. Angiotensin does two things: It stimulates the adrenal cortex to release the hormone aldosterone, which stimulates the kidney to return sodium to the bloodstream. As the sodium is returned to the bloodstream, water is carried with it, and blood volume is partially restored by this mechanism. Angiotensin also stimulates the subfornical organ in the brain. Neurons in the subfornical organ in turn stimulate the circuitry in the medial preoptic area that mediates drinking behavior via connections to the midbrain. In addition, loss of extracellular water stimulates osmoreceptive neurons in the nucleus circularis of the hypothalamus that stimulate the supraoptic nucleus. This causes antidiuretic hormone (ADH) to be released from the posterior pituitary. ADH causes the kidney to concentrate urine and return water to the bloodstream. Therefore, thirst and drinking are also homeostatic mechanisms greatly influenced by glands.

HORMONAL RESPONSES TO EMOTIONAL STRESS

The two principal kinds of emotional behavior influenced by endocrine glands are those related to stress and those related to gender-specific sexual behavior. Gender-specific behaviors are not only those behavioral patterns involved in mating and care of the young, but also acts such as intermale aggression not directly involved in reproduction of the species. Certain of the gonadotropins are necessary to organize the development of the neuronal circuits that underlie these behaviors.

Terms used to classify emotions generally include happiness, love, grief, guilt, and joy. However, most of these are impossible to define with sufficient operational rigor to permit scientific study, especially when animal models are used to unravel the neural and endocrine contributions to the emotional state and accompanying behavior. This is because these categories of emotion have not been constructed and refined from empirical observation. Rather, they are words taken from everyday language that describe either the speaker's introspective state or the internal state of another individual inferred from that individual's behavior. Therefore, the contribution of the neuroendocrine systems to many emotional states commonly described in everyday terms is not known. However, the relationship between stress and the neuroendocrine system is well established, and this relationship may be extended to the states of fear and anxiety.

Fear may be usefully regarded as a response to a specific stimulus present in the environment, whereas anxiety is an anticipatory response to a possible threatening event. Fear, then, is generally a shorter-lived state, whereas anxiety may be chronic and generalize to the degree to which it is not bound to a specific stimulus. However, both of these states produce similar endocrine responses. The simplest of these responses involves discharge from the sympathetic neurons located in the spinal cord. The axons of the sympathetic neurons terminate on visceral organs, including arteries. Their activity during periods of stress increases blood pressure, heart and respiratory rates, and the release of liver glucose stores, while gastrointestinal motility is decreased. In addition, sympathetic activation of the adrenal medulla increases the release of adrenalin and noradrenalin into the bloodstream.

The adrenal cortex also is involved in response to either acute (fear) or chronic (anxiety) stress. However, the adrenal cortex is not directly activated by the sympathetic nervous system. As noted earlier, the adrenal cortex is activated by adrenocorticotropic hormone (ACTH). ACTH is released from the adenohypophysis (anterior pituitary) and stimulates the adrenal cortex to release glucocorticoids (cortisol, cortisone, and corticosterone). The glucocorticoids increase cardiac and vascular muscle tone, enhance the release of nutrients into the blood, decrease inflammation, and inhibit protein synthesis. The release of ACTH by the anterior pituitary is controlled by the hypothalamic hormone, corticotropin-releasing factor (CRF). CRF is manufactured by neurons in the paraventricular nucleus of the hypothalamus and is transported down the axons of these neurons and released into the portal circulation of the adenohypophysis where it stimulates release of ACTH. The paraventricular nucleus is strongly influenced by structures in the limbic system, such as the amygdala, that are involved in modulation of fear responses. The secretion of glucocorticoids by the adrenal cortex is closely linked to parts of the brain involved in elaboration of fear states and intensification of behaviors that accompany them.

Activation of both the sympathetic-adrenal medullary response and the hypothalamic-pituitary-adrenal cortical response are obviously adaptive in the face of immediate, comparatively short-term threat. These responses help the organism to fight or flee. However, as described by Selye, continual activation of these systems by chronic stress can lead to serious consequences for health. Selye referred to the changes produced by long-term stress as the general adaptation syndrome (GAS) and divided it into three stages. The first stage is the alarm reaction during which the body significantly increases the production and release of the stress hormones. This first stage lasts only a few hours, but the second stage, resistance, may continue for days or weeks. During this stage, blood levels of adrenalin, noradrenalin, and the glucocorticoids remain high. The final stage is exhaustion when the body can no longer respond to the stress.

GAS may be brought about by any stressful situation, including chronic physical stress (e.g., from exposure to extreme cold or in times of real physical danger), but it also may occur as a result of continual psychological stress. As originally described by Selye, the physical correlates of GAS include enlarged adrenal glands, with a marked increased in size of the adrenal cortex as its cells respond to the actions of ACTH and attempt to produce ever larger quantities of the glucocorticoids, as well as a shrunken thymus, weight loss, and gastric ulcers. Gastric ulcers are caused by chronic decrease in blood flow to the gut. Substantial rates of blood flow are necessary for maintenance of the mucosal lining that protects the stomach from the digestive acids. As a consequence of chronic activation of the body's stress response, the gut's blood flow is so decreased that its mucosal lining deteriorates, and the stomach's hydrochloric acid produces ulcers.

The cause of the shrinkage of the thymus noted in GAS is not known. The thymus is responsible for producing many of the lymphocytes (key cells in the immunologic defense of the body from infection), and chronic stress decreases the ability of the immune system to respond. The mechanism for stress-induced reduction in immune responsiveness is known and involves the increased amounts of circulating glucocorticoids present during stress.

Enhanced levels of glucocorticoids decrease protein synthesis. As a short-term part of a response to threat this is useful because it conserves metabolic energy. However, the decreased protein synthesis extends to those proteins that form the receptors on cells that recognize foreign elements in the blood. These receptors constitute antibodies, and the cells are the white blood cells (leukocytes), including the lymphocytes. During stress, production of both the antibody receptors and the cells that carry these receptors decreases. Prolonged periods of stress results in immunosuppression and increased susceptibility to infectious disease and the development of cancer.

Abnormally high levels of the glucocorticoid cortisol also have been found in 40 to 60% of depressed patients and is known to be caused by enhanced secretion of CRF by the hypothalamus. The hypersecretion of CRF by the hypothalamus is probably a specific effect of the general dysfunction of the ascending aminergic neurotransmitter systems (dopamine, norepinephrine, and serotonin) thought to be the biological cause of depression.

The overall effect of activation of the neuroendocrine systems involved in response to stress is to produce a state of enhanced readiness for physical action without necessarily activating specific neural circuits that produce directed behaviors. Although such activation may be beneficial for survival in the face of real threat, prolonged activation of these systems is detrimental to health.

GENDER-SPECIFIC BEHAVIOR

Gonadal hormones exert effects on the nervous system and consequently on behavior that depend on the stage of development of the organism. During critical developmental periods, gonadal hormones produce permanent changes in the organization of neuronal circuitry, which results in sexual differentiation of behavior. In the adult, gonadal hormones can activate gender-typical behaviors, but the behaviors do not persist in the absence of the hormone, and structural changes in the brain are not produced.

One gene determines whether the fetal animal or human will differentiate into a male or a female adult. Sexual dimorphism includes obvious body characteristics such as the form of the external genitalia as well as the organization of various neural systems and is determined by whether or not the sperm contributes an X or a Y sex chromosome when it fertilizes the egg. If the sperm contains an X chromosome, the resulting XX mix causes the fetus to develop as a phenotypic female. When the ovaries begin to secrete gonadotropins, the secondary sex characteristics and the brain will be feminine. If the sex chromosomes are XY, testis

will develop, and the secondary sex characteristics and the brain will be masculine.

The critical gene that determines whether or not the gonads will become either ovaries or testes is located in the middle of the short arm of the Y chromosome. The gene is called the sex-determining region of Y and encodes for production of testes-determining factor (TDF). The presence of TDF causes the testes to develop. The testes in turn secrete two hormones that are responsible for the phenotypic development of the fetus as a male. If these hormones are lacking, no signals are sent to alter the intrinsic default developmental sequence, and the fetus develops as a female. Testosterone, secreted by the Leydig cells of the testes, changes the sex organs, mammary gland anlage, and nervous system into the male pattern. The second hormone is secreted by the Sertoli cells of the testes and is called Müllerian duct-inhibiting hormone (MIS). MIS causes the tissues that would become the oviducts, uterus, cervix, and vagina to be resorbed.

Although conducted before the discovery of MIS, an early experiment by Phoenix, Goy, Gerall, and Young serves to distinguish the roles of these two hormones and demonstrates the importance of testosterone for masculization of adult behavior. Fetuses of both sexes are exposed to high estrogen levels from the mother's circulation. Thus the primary secretion of the fetal ovaries is reinforced by estrogen from the mother. Phoenix et al. wondered what would happen if female fetuses were exposed to higher than normal levels of testosterone. To answer this question, they injected large amounts of testosterone into pregnant guinea pigs. The external genitalia were unequivocally male, but the internal genitalia were female. These animals were now pseudohermaphroditic. The explanation of this phenomenon is that the external genitalia were shaped as male by the influence of the testosterone; however, the oviducts, uterus, cervix, and vagina existed because these guinea pigs were not exposed to the second testicular hormone, MIS, so development of the internal genitalia proceeded according to the default female plan.

The second observation was more important. In normal adult female guinea pigs, administration of estrogen and progesterone produces strong lordosis when the female is mounted by the male. Lordosis is a gender-specific behavior activated in the adult female by the presence of estrogens in the circulation. Phoenix et al. found that the female guinea pigs exposed to testosterone in utero demonstrated little lordotic behavior when injected with estrogen and progesterone as adults. However, although they had functioning ovaries, they displayed as much mounting behavior as male litter mates when injected with testosterone. Mounting behavior is often used as an experimental index of the male behavior pattern and is seldom seen in normal adult females, even with testosterone injections. Prenatal exposure to testosterone may have not only produced masculine external genitalia but may also have changed parts of the circuitry of the brain to the masculine pattern.

There are relatively short critical periods in the development of the animal when manipulation of levels of sex steroids makes a difference in development of adult patterns of sexual behavior. Rats have a 21-day gestation period. The testes appear on the 13th day of embryonic life and secrete androgens until the 10th day after birth. Androgen secretion then virtually ceases until puberty. Castration at the day of birth causes male rats to display female sexual behavior as adults when injected with estrogen and progesterone and mounted by normal males. Male rat pups castrated after postnatal day 10 will not display lordosis as adults. This suggests that there is a short critical period when the brain is influenced by testosterone to develop circuitry for male sexual behavior.

Furthermore, the anterior pituitary of both males and females secretes luteinizing hormone (LH) and follicle-stimulating hormone (FSH). As noted previously, release of hormones from the anterior pituitary is under control of the hypothalamus. In males, LH and FSH are released at a steady rate, but in females, the release of these hormones is cyclical, and their levels are related to the cyclical activation of the reproductive organs. If male rats are castrated shortly after birth, cyclical release of LH and

FSH will occur. If ovaries are implanted into adult genetic males that were castrated within 1 day of birth, these ovaries can cyclically ovulate, and the host male rats demonstrate behavior normally shown by females in estrus.

Exposure to higher-than-normal levels of androgens at critical periods clearly can produce male behavior in genetic females, and lack of exposure to these hormones can feminize genetic males. Thus females exposed to high levels of testosterone during the critical developmental periods will exhibit mounting behavior at a rate similar to that of genetic males, and males lacking testosterone during the critical period will fail to exhibit mounting behavior, but will exhibit lordosis when exposed as adults to estrogen. A correlated observation to the results of these experimental manipulations is that in normal males and females, exposure to homotypic hormones (i.e., hormones appropriate to the sex of the animal) can trigger sex-specific behaviors (e.g., lordosis on exposure of a normal female to estrogen and progesterone). These observations suggest that the brain (a) must be responsive to sex steroids and (b) there should be differences in organization of at least some parts of the brain between males and females.

For the central nervous system to respond to gonadal hormones, receptors for androgens, estrogen, and progesterone must exist in neural tissue. Such receptors are located in neurons found in several regions of the central nervous system of the rat and monkey. These areas include not only the hypothalamus, but also the frontal and cingulate cortex, amygdala, hippocampus, midbrain, and spinal cord. Unlike receptors for neurotransmitters, receptors for sex steroids are typically found in the cell nucleus, not in the cell-limiting membrane. Therefore, rather than changing plasma membrane properties, gonadal hormones influence DNA and the transcription of genes. This action permits these hormones potentially to exert influence over many functions of the cell.

The presence of receptors for the different gonadal hormones in the brain differs between the sexes. For example, it was noted previously that in females LH is released in relationship to the cyclical activation of the reproductive organs, whereas in males LH release is continuous at a steady level. Release of LH is regulated by neurosecretory cells of the anterior pituitary that secrete LH-releasing hormone (LHRH). The LHRH neurosecretory cells do not have sex-steroid receptors. These cells, however, receive neural input from neurons in the preoptic area of the hypothalamus. These preoptic neurons do have receptors for estrogen. Thus in normal females, as the ovarian follicles grow, the secreted estrogen stimulates neurons in the preoptic hypothalamus, which in turn stimulate LHRH neurosecretory cells to produce LH. In the brains of genetic females that have been exposed to high levels of androgens either prenatally or immediately postnatally, the preoptic cells do not express estrogen receptors and do not respond to estrogen activation. Therefore, the male pattern of LH secretion ensues.

The structure of the brain differs between males and females. The most obvious example is the sexually dimorphic nucleus located in the preoptic area of the hypothalamus. This nucleus is much larger in males. Unfortunately, its function is not known. Raisman and Field observed differences in organization of input to the preoptic area of the hypothalamus.

In addition to their influence on reproductive behaviors, the gonadal hormones also may have organizing and triggering effects on other types of behavior. For example, aggression between males is positively related to testosterone levels, whether or not the males are competing for a female. These effects may be related to neural events taking place in the medial and preoptic hypothalamus. Aggressive play is much more prevalent in male animals, and the incidence of this form of play is sharply reduced in male rats if they are castrated before postnatal day 6, but not if they are castrated later in life. Conversely, female rats given large doses of testosterone within the first 6 days of life exhibit as much aggressive play as males when this activity develops several weeks later. Similar findings have been reported for monkeys, but the manipulations must be made prenatally.

In summary, gonadal hormones have the capability of organizing behaviors if administered during certain critical periods of development of the organism. Presumably, this organization is due to the influence of these hormones on the developing brain circuitry, but the exact causal sequence between hormonal release and final brain circuit is not known. The exact timing of the critical periods when gonadal hormones can permanently influence behavior varies according to species, but critical periods occur either late during gestation or immediately after birth. The behaviors organized are those related to sexual activity but also include other behavioral patterns, particularly those reflecting aggression. Exposure to gonadal hormones also can activate behaviors such as mounting or lordosis in adults if appropriate sensory events, such as a receptive female in the case of male mounting behavior, are present. Gonadal hormones also influence the actual morphology of the sexual organs and secondary sex characteristics. Alterations in external sex characteristics might also influence behavioral expression, particularly in humans for whom sex roles are heavily influenced by gender assignment based on external appearance and consequent social learning.

ADRENAL GLANDS
ANIMAL AGGRESSIVE BEHAVIORS
ANIMAL SEXUAL BEHAVIORS
BEHAVIORAL GENETICS
BIOLOGICAL RHYTHMS
EMBRYO AND FETUS
ENDORPHINS–ENKEPHALINS
FATIGUE
GENERAL ADAPTATION SYNDROME
GENETIC DOMINANCE AND RECESSIVENESS
GENETICS AND PERSONALITY TRAITS
HOLISTIC HEALTH
HOMEOSTASIS
HORMONES AND BEHAVIOR
HUMAN SEXUALITY
HYPOTHALAMUS
MALNUTRITION AND HUMAN BEHAVIOR
NEUROCHEMISTRY
OBESITY
PITUITARY
SEXUAL DEVELOPMENT
STRESS
STRESS CONSEQUENCES
TRANSSEXUALISM
WEIGHT CONTROL

M. L. WOODRUFF

GLOBAL CRISES

In the last decade of the twentieth century, 15 to 20 million people died annually of malnutrition-related causes. The situation was exacerbated by an explosive population growth, with the world population doubling every 40 years, affecting "virtually every aspect of the earth's ecosystems [including] . . . an accelerating deterioration and loss of the resources essential for agriculture." Ecological problems include pollution, acid rain, desertification, forest clearing, topsoil loss, ozone depletion, carbon dioxide buildup, greenhouse effect warming, and the extinction of many species of animal and plant life.

PSYCHOLOGICAL ROOTS
Our contemporary crises are caused by beliefs about ourselves, others, and the world. Beliefs include self-limiting assumptions such as "There's nothing I can do." Beliefs about others include "It's their fault, not ours, that they're hungry." This can result in what Erik Erickson calls pseudospeciation.

Zero-sum us-versus-them beliefs create a worldview in which the world is regarded as a battlefield on which the forces of light (us) must combat the forces of darkness (others). Such beliefs are both cause and effect of a belief that solutions can be obtained only by domination.

Numerous questionable beliefs underlie military strategies, including "Increased numbers of weapons mean increased security" and "Nuclear war is winnable." Questionable beliefs about the world such as "It's hopeless" and "There's nothing that can be done" exacerbate feelings of apathy and despair and may prove self-fulfilling. Beliefs that the earth and all life exist primarily as human resources, rather than having intrinsic value in themselves, may foster plunder and ecological insensitivity. Statements such as "I'd rather not think about it" sap motivation to respond in appropriate ways.

PSYCHODYNAMICS
Projection fosters blame by attributing unacknowledged shadow facets of self-image and motives to others, thus creating what Jerome Frank calls "the image of the enemy." Even hostility-reducing overtures by the enemy are viewed as signs of deceit. Such psychological mechanisms, once set in motion, can assume a deadly momentum.

The emotional impact of others' suffering can be reduced by intellectualization. For example, "nuke speak" is "a strange and bloodless language by which the planners of nuclear war drain the reality from their actions." The result of these defense mechanisms is what Robert Lifton calls psychic numbing: a narcotizing of awareness.

BEHAVIORAL PERSPECTIVES
Environmental consequences often involve long lag periods before problems are identified (e.g., fluorocarbon destruction of the ozone layer). Yet the electorate usually reelects political leaders who promise short-term gratification: *après moi la déluge* views. Decision makers are often far removed from the consequences of their decisions. They can direct distant wars, allow millions to starve, or pass legislation allowing pollution, without ever seeing the results of their decisions.

SOCIAL LEARNING PERSPECTIVES
Reviews of more than 3000 research studies show that the media, especially television, exert enormous psychological and social influence. Given the experimentally demonstrated power of television modeling, there is cause for concern about the media's preoccupation with violence and warfare, glorification of aggressive and consumptive lifestyles, reliance on sensationalism and emotionalism, and avoidance of analyses of complex global issues.

Non-Western Psychologies
Buddhist psychology offers sophisticated analyses of individual and social pathology, claiming that all pathologies can be traced to three root causes: the "three poisons" of addiction, aversion, and delusion. Other Asian psychologies say that addiction fuels greed, possessiveness, and frustration and reduces flexibility and choices. Aversion, the desire to avoid or attack unpleasant stimuli, is addiction's mirror image and a source of anger, attack, fear, and defensiveness. Yet as both Eastern and Western psychologists know well, such "poisoned" behavior results only in transient satisfaction. Delusion of mind, say Asian psychologies, is neither clear, optimal, nor wholly rational. Faulty beliefs filter and distort perception,

motivation, and one's sense of identity in powerful yet unrecognized ways, but are rarely recognized because they are culturally shared.

Much in the world and our collective behavior can be regarded only as insanity. "World is said to totter on 'brink of madness'," claimed the headline of an American Psychological Association publication reporting the conclusions of the 1983 World Congress on Mental Health. Recognition of this insanity is necessary for alleviating it and its life-threatening global complications.

PSYCHOLOGICAL PRINCIPLES OF HELPFUL RESPONSES
The following are hypothesized principles for effective responses intended to address causes identified in the previous section.

Beliefs
"The underlying images held by a culture or person have an enormous influence on the fate of the holder." When traditional images lag behind cultural progress and fail adequately to address novel situations, then periods of social turmoil and even crisis develop. Our culture may be at such a stage. In choosing our beliefs we are, therefore, also choosing the images that will guide our culture into the future because, as Gregory Bateson said, "the world partly becomes-comes to be-how it is imagined." The following are selected hypothesized beliefs that may be helpful for us to adopt.

> *Belief about Ourselves.* I personally can make a useful and unique contribution.
>
> *Belief about Others.* Despite diverse cultural and ideological backgrounds, all people share a common humanity with similar existential givens, fears, defenses, and aspirations.
>
> *Belief about the World.* The threats to human survival and ecological sustainability may be solvable.

These, then, are some of the beliefs that may provide a basis for a psychology of survival. Together they may encourage a cautious, partly self-fulfilling realism and optimism toward the world; responsibility, self-efficacy, and conscious choice in individuals; and empathy and universality with others.

Education
Because many faulty beliefs and behaviors can be traced to ignorance, it follows that corrective education is essential. "Human history becomes more and more a race between education and catastrophe," H. G. Wells said. Few schools and universities offer adequate courses on global problems, and few psychology or psychiatry departments offer courses on their psychological dimensions. Here is a vital role for mental health professionals.

Social Learning Theory and the Media
Given the media's psychological and social power, it may be crucial to encourage more socially relevant programming. Mental health professionals have demonstrated the deleterious effects of current media programming. These contributions can be expanded by extending research and educating the public, the media, and legislators about the implications of media content.

Commonality, Shared Purpose, and Universality
Recognition of commonalities is important because so many contemporary difficulties are no respecters of traditional boundaries. Ecological imbalances, pollution, and radioactive contamination do not halt politely at international borders. As Jerome Frank put it, "The psychological problem is how to make all people aware that whether they like it or not, the earth is becoming a single community." The problem also is how

to make people aware of the necessity of cooperation if these problems are to be solved. This holds, not only because the problems are more than any one nation can handle, but also because experiments suggest that cooperation on desired goals that no one group can accomplish alone may be one of the most effective ways of resolving mutual hostility.

Thus the task is to work to shift perception from a focus on differences to a focus on similarities, from a dualistic emphasis on conflicting groups and cultures to a unitive appreciation of shared humanity, from a fragmentary view that sees humans apart from nature (and nature itself in parts) to a holistic vision that recognizes the unity and interconnection of all parts.

MENTAL HEALTH PROFESSIONALS AND THE GLOBAL CRISES

Mental health professionals can make significant contributions. Individuals can provide public and professional education through lecturing, writing, and media; establish relevant courses; offer consultation to individuals, groups, and legislators working on these issues; and do background research.

ALTRUISM
CONFLICT MEDIATION
DISTRIBUTIVE JUSTICE
ETHICAL PROBLEMS IN PSYCHOLOGY
GEMEINSCHAFTSGEFÜHL
LOCUS OF CONTROL
POWER
PUBLIC POLICY
SOCIAL INTERVENTIONS
SOCIOPSYCHOLOGICAL DETERMINANTS OF WAR AND PEACE
ZEN BUDDHISM

R. WALSH

GRADING IN EDUCATION

Grading or marking is a summary evaluation of a student's performance or progress at the end of a specified period of instruction. Grades communicate to students and parents relative strengths and weaknesses in learning; help teachers and counselors develop appropriate instruction and guidance; provide administrators with a means to determine promotion, graduation, honors, athletic eligibility, and other reporting needs; and help prospective employers and colleges to evaluate applicants.

In many elementary schools a two-category marking system is used. A list of skills or knowledge areas is developed for the period of time covered, and the teacher indicates one of two choices to communicate student progress. The categories are typically pass/fail or satisfactory/unsatisfactory. Although the two-category system is also used for higher grade levels, most junior and senior high schools and colleges use a greater number of choices. The most widely used method is to assign a single letter (A, B, C, D, F) or number (5, 4, 3, 2, 1, or 60, 70, 80, 90, 100) to represent performance in each area. Pluses and minuses (B+, C−, A−) are sometimes added to provide more than five choices.

Whenever numbers or letters are used in grading, it is necessary to clearly define what each letter or number means. One approach to establish meaning is norm referenced. The use of norm-referenced grading involves ranking all students in order of performance and assigning numbers or letters on the basis of each student's position within the entire group. In this system students are compared to one another, and teachers may designate the top 15% as As, the next 25% as Bs, 40% as Cs, 15% as Ds, and the bottom 5% as Fs. This results in "grading on the curve," because the grade depends on the individual's relationship to others in the distribution. This type of grading is independent of the number of questions answered correctly. A second way to convey meaning is to use absolute standards, or a criterion-referenced method. Most grading practices utilize a combination of norm- and criterion-referenced methods. Norm-referenced approaches are most useful in sorting students and assigning honors, whereas criterion-referenced approaches best represent the degree to which school and classroom objectives have been achieved.

ACADEMIC ACHIEVEMENT TESTS READING MEASURES

J. H. McMILLAN

GRADUATE EDUCATION

Historically, the nature and scope of graduate education in the United States can be traced to higher education pioneers such as Daniel Gilman of Johns Hopkins University, G. Stanley Hall of Clark University, and William Rainey Harper of the University of Chicago. They envisioned a school for research and instruction of the highest degree without the burdens of undergraduate education. This was based on the German concept of graduate education, which emphasized original research initiated by the academicians of the university.

Official recognition of graduate education occurred in 1876 with the founding of Johns Hopkins University. Shortly after its opening, other graduate schools or departments were established in America. Today more than 700 institutions offer the doctoral degree.

MASTER'S DEGREE

The master's degree—notably the master of arts (M.A.) and the master of science (M.S.)—is the first graduate degree one can earn. Currently more than 400 different master's degrees exist in such diverse areas as business administration (M.B.A.), fine arts (M.F.A.), education (M.Ed.), theology (M.Th.), and master of applied science (M.A.Sc.).

DOCTORAL PROGRAMS

The Ph.D. most notably symbolizes the nature and purpose of doctoral work. It is a research degree and the highest academic degree awarded. Historically, it has symbolized original contributions to knowledge. To meet the needs of professional areas in which a Ph.D. would be inappropriate, universities have introduced doctoral programs in numerous other areas such as business administration (D.B.A.), education (Ed.D.), psychology (Psy.D.), and Social Work (D.S.W.).

Differences among doctoral programs reflect major curriculum requirements for the nature and scope of study, research, and/or practice. However, in some cases there is little or no distinction among degrees.

A relatively new development in graduate education since the mid-twentieth century has been postdoctoral education. Essentially, it allows individuals who possess a doctoral degree to further their study and perhaps do research in a wide variety of fields. Many universities as well as institutes and agencies provide postdoctoral fellowships, programs, and internships allowing advanced study and technical experience beyond the doctoral degree.

Several professional organizations exist whose main focus is concerned with the development of graduate education.

GRADUATE TRAINING IN PSYCHOLOGY

L. V. PARADISE

GRADUATE RECORD EXAMINATIONS (GREs)

The graduate record examinations (GREs) are graduate-school aptitude and achievement tests and the associated testing program, conducted by the Educational Testing Service (ETS) for the Graduate Record Examinations Board. Originated in 1939 by the Carnegie Foundation for the Advancement of Teaching and several Eastern universities, and since expanded and revised, the program is widely used by graduate institutions, and respected among psychometricians for its technical quality. An applicant takes the aptitude test and an advanced test in the field of the undergraduate major. All scores are reported on a 500 ± 100 standard-score scale. A composite score is based on the aptitude and advanced score.

The *aptitude test* includes items on verbal reasoning, verbal comprehension, mathematical reasoning, and data interpretation that are suited to advanced undergraduates; it yields verbal (V) and quantitative (Q) scores. A new section added in 1977 and revised by 1981 gives an analytical (A) score based on analytical-reasoning items and logical-reasoning items (revised version).

The *advanced tests* are available in 20 fields: biology, chemistry, computer science, economics, education, engineering, English literature, French, geography, geology, German, history, mathematics, music, philosophy, physics, political science, psychology, Spanish, and sociology. Some tests yield a total score; others include part scores for subdivisions of the field as well.

V, Q, and A aptitude scores and all total scores for advanced tests have consistently met professional standards for reliability. Among criterion measures used in predictive validity studies have been graduate-school grade point averages, attainment versus nonattainment of the Ph.D. within 10 years, and performance on departmental comprehensive exams. In general, combining undergraduate grade point averages with GRE scores has given the highest validities, and the GRE composite score alone has predicted criterion better than undergraduate GPA alone.

APTITUDE TESTING
COLLEGE ACADEMIC PREDICTION
INTELLIGENCE MEASURES
PSYCHOMETRICS
SELECTION TESTS

A. B. Pratt

GRADUATE TRAINING IN PSYCHOLOGY

The first person to enroll for a graduate degree in psychology was Joseph Jastrow, who received his doctorate from Johns Hopkins University under Hall in 1886.

Graduate training at that time was laboratory based and experimental. Although administratively included as a part of the Department of Philosophy in most universities, psychology was clearly a science. The early psychologists viewed psychology as an experimental science allied to, but not a part of, physiology.

There was not much discussion about the nature of graduate training in psychology until after World War II. Graduate students simply were trained in the mold of their mentors. Upon receiving their doctorates, they were expected to take a university appointment and teach and research in the manner of their graduate professors.

Immediate postwar pressures on professors to train their students in other than their own images and for roles other than academic resulted in a series of conferences on graduate training: the 1949 Boulder conference on "Training in Clinical Psychology"; the 1951 Northwestern confer-

ence on "Recommended Standards for Training Counseling Psychologists at the Doctorate Level"; the 1955 Thayer conference on "School Psychologists at Mid-Century"; the 1955 Stanford Institute conference on "Psychology and Mental Health"; the 1958 Miami Beach conference on "Graduate Education in Psychology"; the 1965 Chicago conference on "Professional Preparation of Clinical Psychologists"; and the 1973 Vail conference on "Levels and Patterns of Professional Training in Psychology."

The first four of these conferences all dealt with some aspect of the curricular issues associated with training particular professional, as distinguished from academic, psychologists. The Boulder conference set the mold. The conference concluded that psychology was a science, that clinical psychology was an application of that science, and that a clinical psychologist was expected to know the science of psychology the same as any other psychologist. The clinicians' clinical skills and knowledge were to be added to their skills as research scientists. The conference then specified 12 basic areas of study to be included in the clinical training program, among them human physiology, personality theory, developmental psychology, psychopathology, psychotherapy, and practicum and internship experiences.

The Northwestern conference and the Thayer conference followed suit for the specialties of counseling and school psychology, respectively. Stanford reviewed the training scene in the mental health field 6 years after Boulder. The participants noted problems in certain areas: training for community mental health, clinical specialization, practicum training and facilities, mental health research, and departmental organization.

The Miami Beach conference was concerned with graduate training for all subareas of psychology. The report noted that there was strong acceptance of the idea that the defining characteristic of the Ph.D. psychologist was research training. Professional abilities, thus, still were to be added to the skills and knowledge of the research scientist.

The Chicago conference encouraged exploration of new professional training procedures. By 1980 there were 37 professionally oriented training programs both inside and outside the university structure in the United States.

In 1973, 153 people, representing a variety of psychological interests, met in Vail, Colorado. Eight recommendations were specifically concerned with doctoral training. The tenor of those eight recommendations was shown by their general introductory statement "that doctoral training programs [should] broaden the range and nature of core academic courses and professional training requirements. These modifications can and should be accomplished without sacrificing standards for educating students in the fundamentals of behavioral science." Lowell Kelly and Lewis Goldberg's 1959 conclusion still seemed valid: the " 'PhD in Psychology,' while an objective criterion, has surprisingly little uniformity of meaning from university to university and from specialty to specialty." Unlike medicine and law, graduate training in psychology had not been codified.

CAREERS IN PSYCHOLOGY
CLINICAL PSYCHOLOGY
GRADUATE EDUCATION

R. S. Harper

GRAPHOLOGY

Graphology is the practice of evaluating personality and/or character from a sample of a person's handwriting. Some graphologists use the analytic approach, in which relatively isolated aspects of the script are allegedly indicative of specific personality traits of the writer. Other graphologists argue that personality characteristics are related only to the *patterns* of such isolated elements of the writer's script. Although it is clear that a person's handwriting is affected by marked physiological changes produced by disease, alcohol and certain other drugs, and by aging, research to date does not support any definitive conclusions regarding the correspondence of either the elements of an individual's handwriting or patterns of these elements and the individual's personality or character.

Although most scientists regard graphology as a pseudoscience, some American business firms routinely utilize the services of graphologists in the selection of their personnel.

PERSONALITY ASSESSMENT
PROJECTIVE TECHNIQUES

E. LOWELL KELLY

GRIT

GRIT—Graduated and Reciprocated Initiatives in Tension reduction—is a proposed strategy for avoiding nuclear escalation and war. *"Calculated"* escalation is designed to push the villainous *theys* beyond their risk ceiling before the heroic *wes* reach ours. This strategy has four salient features: (a) the steps *are unilaterally initiated;* (b) each step propels the enemy into *reciprocating,* if they can, with more aggressive steps of their own; (c) such steps are necessarily *graduated* in nature, because of the unpredictability of technological break throughs, the limitations imposed by logistics, and the oscillating level of perceived threat; (d) calculated escalation is obviously a *tension-increasing* process, the termination of which is a military resolution leading to victory, defeat, or (in our time) possibly even mutual annihilation.

APPLICATIONS OF GRIT STRATEGY

There has been considerable experimentation with the GRIT strategy, but mostly in the psychological laboratory. There have been sporadic GRIT-like moves in the real world, but for the most part, these have been one-shot affairs, always tentatively made, and never reflecting any genuine change in basic strategy.

The one exception was the "Kennedy Experiment," in which he outlined "a strategy of peace," praised the Russians for their accomplishments, and announced the first unilateral initiative: The United States was stopping all nuclear tests in the atmosphere.

Khrushchev reciprocated with a speech welcoming the U.S. initiative, in which he announced that he had halted production of strategic bombers in Russia. Conclusion of a test ban treaty, long stalled, was achieved.

What was the psychological impact of this GRIT experiment? Few people who lived through that period would deny that there was a definite warming of American attitudes toward Russians, and the same is reported for Russian attitudes toward Americans.

Escalating conflicts that involve another nuclear power unquestionably carry the greatest risk. Simply doing nothing—remaining frozen in a status quo that is already at much too high a level of force and tension—is certainly not without risk over the long run.

POLITICAL VALUES
SOCIOPSYCHOLOGICAL DETERMINANTS OF WAR & PEACE

C. E. OSGOOD

GROSS MOTOR SKILL LEARNING

The acquisition of motor skill, sometimes referred to as motor learning, has been the object of a great deal of experimental work. By far the most popular apparatus for such study has been the pursuit rotor or rotary pursuit test.

The most important variable affecting performance during the acquisition of skill is *distribution of practice*. Typically, performance is very much better with spaced practice than with massed practice. Special procedures employed along with distribution of practice reveal certain other important phenomena. For example, a rest of 10 minutes or more following a series of massed practice trials produces an increase in performance called *reminiscence*. This spontaneous improvement means that the reduced performance under massed practice is an effect on performance exclusively; massed practice subjects have learned just as much as distributed practice subjects.

Sometimes this last fact is partially obscured by the subjects' need to warm up after the rest following massed practice. The theory that the effects of distribution are on performance rather than on learning is further supported by the data obtained following a test for reminiscence. If the subjects are returned to a massed-practice schedule of trials, their performance decreases. Somewhat surprising, this decrease typically continues until the learning curve has returned approximately to the level where it would have been if no rest period had been introduced; then performance begins to increase. If subjects switch to distributed practice following the rest, their performance shows no trace of the previous experience on massed practice after the necessary warmup.

DISTRIBUTION OF PRACTICE

G. A. KIMBLE

GROUP COHESIVENESS

Group cohesiveness has been defined in many ways. Leon Festinger defined the concept in terms of forces that lead an individual to remain in or leave a given group. One way to understand group cohesiveness rests on the idea of "task." Implicitly or explicitly, every group has a task or tasks it must accomplish. Many schemes have been presented for categorizing group tasks. Some approaches have emphasized the unconscious motives harbored by group members. Others have specified aspects of communication among group members. Still others have focused on the content of observed aspects of the work of the group. The extent to which members of a group identify with and work toward a common task is a measure of group cohesiveness.

What influences group cohesiveness? Although Rabbie and colleagues have suggested that competition between groups has no more effect on ingroup cohesion than does intergroup cooperation, the majority of writers over the years have agreed that hostility toward an outside person or persons serves to strengthen cohesiveness within a group.

Bion suggested that group tasks often derive from members' unconscious and primitive needs and expectations. He classified these activities as "dependence," "fight–flight," and "pairing." These activities reflect assumptions shared by all in the group. The task or purpose of the *dependent group* is to be sustained by a leader. In the *fight–flight group* the purpose is simply to defend against some threat, either by fighting someone or something or by running away. In the *pairing group* the members act as if their purpose is union and some new entity will derive from that unity. Bion believed that it was necessary to attend to both work and basic aspects of group activity to fully comprehend a given group and such group considerations as cohesiveness.

To explain how individuals in a group come together to behave toward some common end, Thomas French developed the concept of "focal conflict." Similar ideas have been postulated by other writers as well. In general, such notions refer to a tendency for groups to attend to topics that have relevance, often by reducing anxiety for all members. Many specialties have concerned themselves with group phenomena. Personality and psychotherapy theorists, social and organizational psychologists, anthropologists, and educational specialists are but a number of professions interested in this topic. Diverse methods and emphases have influenced conclusions. An integration of findings about group cohesiveness has not yet been achieved.

COOPERATION/COMPETITION
DEVELOPMENT OF HUMAN SOCIAL BEHAVIOR
INTERACTIONAL PSYCHOLOGY

S. BERENT

GROUP COUNSELING

Group counseling is typically conducted with a small number of people, usually seven to ten. The individuals in the group provide the subject matter for discussion by sharing their personal thoughts, feelings, and behavior. Group members are expected to be involved in the process by reacting to other members through feedback, support, and problem solving.

The leader usually has had special training in group counseling techniques and strives to create an atmosphere of trust, openness, responsibility, and interdependency. The leader typically models his or her behavior and guides group members through the processes of understanding, caring, and conflict management.

Differences between group counseling and group psychotherapy center on the composition of group membership, the degree of personality change expected, and the nature of the group leader's training. Methods and procedures used in counseling and therapy groups are quite similar.

Members of a counseling group can come from virtually any walk of life and typically fall within the normal ranges of adjustment and ability to cope with life situations. They join counseling groups to gain deeper personal insights and to develop their personal potentials. Therapy group members bring more severe personality problems to the group and may be mildly to chronically neurotic, with limited ability to deal with life problems. They usually require more intensive personal work in restructuring basic personality patterns.

Both counseling and therapy group leaders require special training in the conduct of groups. Counselors typically focus their training on normal life-span development. Psychotherapists usually spend more training time with abnormal populations and in the study of psychopathology.

Groups are a natural phenomenon in human history. Forerunners of organized groups include various religious movements, drama, and morality plays. Some historians cite Mesmer's work as a precursor of group treatment.

Most, however, note the "class method" work of J. H. Pratt as the beginning of scientific group treatment in the United States. Pratt used a directive-teaching methodology with his tubercular patients as he instructed them in hygiene. His original intention was to boost their morale through more effective cleanliness. The method more closely resembled what we think of as guidance today. It soon became clear that his patients were deriving more benefit from the supportive atmosphere of the group than from the information imparted in the lectures.

Alfred Adler and J. L. Moreno began using group methods in Europe. Adler would counsel children in front of a group, with the primary purpose of instructing other professionals in individual counseling. Again, the observation was made that the group or audience, as they asked questions and interacted, had a positive impact on the counseling. This methodology continues to be used by present-day Adlerians with the dual purpose of teaching and counseling.

Moreno used group techniques with the street people of Vienna. He worked with children, displaced persons, and prostitutes as he found them in their environments. Moreno introduced psychodrama into the United States; he coined the terms *group therapy* and *group psychotherapy*.

Others who have had great influence on group therapy in the United States include S. R. Slavson, who introduced methods known as activity group therapy. His methods were developed with socially maladjusted children. Rudolf Dreikurs applied Adlerian principles in his work with family groups and children in Chicago. Carl Rogers and his client-centered or phenomenological approach helped popularize group work. A shortage of adequately trained personnel and a great need for reconstructive and supportive therapy accelerated the adaptation of Rogerian principles to group work with veterans.

Although practitioners attempted to clarify the terms "group guidance" and "group counseling," considerable controversy raged because writers continued to argue that counseling was intimate and personal and should be done individually. The professionalization of school counselors and counselors in public agencies and private practice has added credibility and acceptability to group counseling procedures.

Other influences in the acceptance of group counseling as a viable treatment include the Human Potential Movement and professional counselor organizations such as the American Personnel and Guidance Association and the American Psychological Association. Each of these major organizations has ethics codes that specifically address the area of group work.

Gazda, Duncan, and Sisson clarify the distinctions among various group procedures:

Group guidance and certain human potential-type groups are described as primarily preventive in purpose; group counseling, T-groups, sensitivity groups, encounter groups . . . are described as partially preventive, growth engendering, and remedial in purpose; group psychotherapy is described as remedial in purpose. The clientele served, degree of disturbance of the clientele, setting of the treatment, goals of treatment, size of group, and length and duration of treatment are, accordingly, reflected in the emphasis or purpose of each of these three distinctly different groupings.

Corey and Corey offer an explanation of group counseling that characterizes it as generally practiced at present:

Group counseling often focuses on a particular kind of problem—educational, vocational, social or personal—and is often carried out in institutional settings, such as schools, community mental-health clinics, and other human-service agencies. The counseling group generally differs from the therapy group in that it deals with conscious problems, is not aimed at major personality changes, and is frequently oriented toward the resolution of specific and short-term issues, and is not concerned with treatment of neurotic or psychotic disorders.

Yalom addresses what he terms curative factors that operate in every type of therapy group. Historical influences from group guidance, dynamics, and psychotherapy can be observed in the various factors.

Imparting of information. Included in this function is didactic instruction by the counselor, as well as advice, suggestions, or direct guidance about life problems offered by either the counselor or other group members.

Instillation of hope. Pregroup high expectations for success and hope and faith in the treatment mode have been demonstrated to be related to positive outcomes in groups.

Universality. The participation in a group experience often teaches people that they are not alone or isolated with the "uniqueness" of their problems, which are shared by others. This knowledge frequently produces a sense of relief.

Altruism. Group members help one another by offering support, suggestions, reassurance, and insights, and by sharing similar problems with one another. It is often important to group members' self-image that they begin to see themselves as capable of mutual help.

The corrective recapitulation of the primary family group. Groups resemble families in several significant ways. Many group members have had unsatisfactory experiences in their original families; the group offers an opportunity to work through and restructure important family relationships in a more encouraging environment.

Development of socializing techniques. Although methods may vary greatly with the type of group, from direct skill practice to incidental acquisition, social learning takes place in all groups. The development of basic social or interpersonal skills is a product of the group counseling process that is encouraged by member-to-member feedback.

Initiative behavior. A group member often observes the work of another member with similar problems. Through "vicarious" therapy the group member can incorporate or try out new behaviors suggested or modeled by the group leader or other members.

Interpersonal learning. The group functions as a social microcosm providing the necessary therapeutic factors to allow corrective emotional experiences. Group members, through validation and self-observation, become aware of their interpersonal behavior. The group, through feedback and encouragement, helps the member see maladaptive social/interpersonal behavior and provides the primary supportive environment for change.

Group cohesiveness. Cohesiveness is defined as the attractiveness a group has for its members. More simply it is "we-ness," "group-ness," or "togetherness." Cohesiveness in a group is analogous to the rapport or relationship between individual counselor and client. The acceptance and support demonstrated by the group, after a member has shared significant emotional experiences can be a potent healing force.

Catharsis. The group provides members with a safe place to ventilate their feelings rather than hold them inside. The process encourages learning how to express feelings in general and to express negative and/or positive feelings toward the leader and other group members.

Although these curative factors are cited by most authors as advantages for the use of groups as a treatment method, there are also several risks and limitations. Corey and Corey caution that groups are not "cure-alls" and that not all people are suited for groups. Some potential members may be too suspicious, hostile, or fragile to gain benefits from a group experience. Additionally, there is often a subtle pressure to conform to group norms.

When a group member accepts the process of the group, there is the possibility of some psychological hazard. As members open up, they may become vulnerable. As this vulnerability is carried back to the significant people in their lives, there must be adequate support resources to cope effectively.

Absolute confidentiality is difficult to ensure: Some members may talk outside the group about what they have heard. Also, scapegoating may occur, especially if the group leader is not effective in intervening when several members attack a particular person. Any intervention system as potent as a group can cause a major disruption in one's life. Changes can occur in lifestyle and values, and in loss of security. Potential group members should be aware of these risks and limitations.

CLIENT-CENTERED MODEL

This group model developed by Carl Rogers and his proponents is based on the assumption that human beings have an innate ability to reach their full potential. This includes the potential to solve their own problems, given a free and permissive atmosphere. The group leader is seen as a facilitator who is unconditional and genuine in his relationship with group members.

THE GESTALT MODEL

Frederick S. Perls and his followers are responsible for the development of Gestalt therapy in groups. The group experience focuses on an intensive here-and-now orientation. The experiencing of the present moment provides insight into personal behavior and creates the insight upon which new decisions for behavior change can be made. Group members are taught to take personal responsibility for all of their feelings and behavior.

TRANSACTIONAL ANALYSIS

Eric Berne developed the conception of ego states, which he termed the Parent, the Adult, and the Child. In groups, the goal is for members to become aware of the ego state within which they most usually function. To develop this awareness, members will examine their early programming, the messages they received from their parents, and their early decisions as to their personal worth and position in life.

THE RATIONAL-EMOTIVE THERAPY MODEL

The RET approach developed by Albert Ellis basically uses an educational rather than a medical or psychodynamic model. Direct behavioral action taken upon one's belief in irrational ideas that result from verbal self-indoctrination form the bases for behavioral change.

The goal of therapy is to assist group members in internalizing a more rational philosophy of life and thus to behave and live life more fully. A major feature of an RET group is the use of homework to be done outside the group, ensuring that members keep their progress moving. There is also a heavy use of behavior therapy techniques.

Other theoretical approaches that have gained some measure of acceptance, but that may be limited to certain distinct settings, include the psychoanalytical model, the reality therapy model, the behavior therapy model, the development approach, and an eclectic human resource development model.

COUNSELING
GROUP DYNAMICS
GROUP PSYCHOTHERAPY

R. C. Berg

GROUP DYNAMICS

The importance of groups has long been recognized by students of society, but the study of groups as a special topic began only in the 1930s and 1940s. Three sources—social importance, practical use, and scientific understanding—have been the joint foundation of group dynamics; they have also contributed to a fragmentation of interests up to the present time.

BACKGROUND

The definite establishment and naming of the field of group dynamics is due to Kurt Lewin. Lewin had established a psychology of personality using geometric forms that employed such social concepts as boundaries, specialization, direction, and planning to explain the actions of the person (topological psychology). This theory could then be transformed back to an interpretation of groups; for instance, one could give the different subfields of a person a natural interpretation of roles and statuses, and view the boundaries between them—as well as their strengths—as obstacles to social mobility.

This theoretical model turned out to be applicable to a set of experiments that had already been performed on groups. These included Lewin's own—particularly those with Lippitt on autocratic and democratic group atmosphere—as well as Mayo and Roethlisberger's experiments on groups in a factory, Sherif's on group conflicts in a camp group and on the development of group standards, and Moreno's on sociometric study in residential groups. These forerunners showed different techniques and possible sites for group experiments. An additional feature was that they could be performed under the abstract conditions of laboratory experiments as well as in actual life situations or field experiments.

The question of applicability relates to the social context in which group dynamics arose: the heightened mobility and weakening of established social structure in the wake of the Depression and World War II. The common theme of beneficial action of the group could be recognized; it was taken as an established dimension for the study of groups, investing it with a kind of messianic flavor. This interest led to a split in the meaning of group dynamics as a science of groups and as a program on the value of groups. All these trends combined in the formulation of group dynamics. Lewin's relevant theoretical and practical works are collected in *Field theory in social science* and *Resolving social conflicts.*

THE NATURE OF GROUP DYNAMICS

Theory

The theory of group dynamics looks at a small person-to-person group as a unit. A group can be defined as an association of persons small enough that all can stay in personal contact with one another.

In common with Lewin's general program of science, the concepts of group dynamics represent structural and dynamic aspects. The structural aspects were represented by simple graphic representations of an oval divided into subregions. They exhibit simple relationships such as adjacency of subregions, the shortest path from one to another, accessibility from outside, and centrality. The strength of a boundary can be represented by weaker and heavier lines. Inspection can describe all the structural effects within a group, which can be interpreted as stratification, articulation, peripheral and central positions, and the features of groups.

Parts of the group picture can be seen as individuals, but these parts can also be defined as functions or roles within the group, as possible places for individuals that may stay unfilled at any time. The nature of this subdivision is not given, but depends on the particular use to which the parts are put. Roles may be defined by the nature of the task, by conditions of group functioning, or by a theoretical scheme imposed by a leader, resource person, or opposition. The spatial arrangement of the roles can indicate mobility, communication or other interactions.

The dynamic concepts have a rough analogy to mathematical concepts, principally with those of applied mechanics. They include locomotion, vectors, forces, tension, goals, power, and power fields. All these concepts invest the group with change or at least the possibility of change. Change may involve the whole group, in which case the group is seen as embedded in some other structure through which it is traveling. If the group is trying to complete some task, the field is the steps leading to this completion. Forces are then inferred as directing the group toward the goal region, which represents completion of the task; this region is then said to have valence for the group. However, the group may have an additional goal, be able to use different paths to complete the goal, or have a negative valence (or abhorrence) of a region that has been crossed in search of the goal, in which case conflicts will be created. The path indicated by the resultant of the forces will then be the preferred path to be taken by the group.

The intent to reach a group goal is also seen as a tension within the group that is relieved by the attainment of the goal. Tensions are generalizations of drives, but they can be set up simply by a wish or instruction to attain a certain goal. Thus interruption of a task can lead to an increase in tension; attempts to release this tension will result in appropriate actions, either in reality by trying to complete the task, or in fantasy as seen in group discussions or imagination productions of the group.

While the dynamic concepts discussed up to now refer to action of the group in its environment, power and its associated concepts link the group to its members. Power differentiates the subregions or individuals within the group: One region has power if its movements or changes will result in corresponding changes in other regions. One can assign a certain degree of power to each region and in this way describe a power field for the whole group.

In addition to power exerted by individuals, the group as a unit is capable of exerting power itself. In fact, investigations of the power of the group over its members have realized some of the most important research and applied achievements in the field. Multiple membership will lead to conflicts within individuals correlated with the variations in power; these may lead to stress as well as changes in group membership if the stress becomes intolerable.

Research

The reputation of group dynamics rests particularly on its creation of new research traditions in experimental social psychology: groups and group membership, pressure for conformity, power and influence, leadership and performance, motivational processes, and structural processes. Each of these topics depends on some combination of the theoretical concepts and represents innovative research.

The study of *group membership* deals with the creation of group boundaries and the bases of the power of the group over its members. The empirical question, then, is to define the boundaries and strengths of the group in terms of membership and cohesion.

Pressure for conformity represents the power of the group over its members. In translating the abstract concept of power into the operation of creating conformity, a variety of factors had to be considered in experimental as well as field studies. The stress toward conformity is not equal in all members, nor is it expressed equally for all attitudes and behaviors. Thus leaders are given leeway to break rules and are even required to be innovative, and a long-established group will attain power over its members and tolerate diversity over many issues as long as crucial issues are accepted. In the main, though, adherence to group standards is a function of the cohesion of groups.

Under the heading of *power and influence* the dynamic relationships of group members have been explored. These studies have usually specified the techniques used to increase compliance with influence. Techniques can be identified that rely on general social conditions such as appeals to legitimacy or expertise, or that use purely interpersonal processes such as flattery, or that are based on exchange or possible future interaction. Thus experiments on the manifestation of social power can show how leadership positions are maintained, but also can treat mechanisms that maintain a group by mutual influences of members, including the establishment of trust.

Tension within the group, just as in the individual, can be identified with *motivation*. In groups we sometimes find formal records of goal setting and of efforts to reach those goals. Observation of groups in action would measure the creation of the tension and differentiation of tension within the group.

Group structure and its effects represent the topological aspect of the theory. The study of communication and control in task-oriented groups, and of sociometric patterns in existing groups, is one of the most intensive research areas in the field.

Practice

Applications of group dynamics had a distinctive development. Lewin and his associates created workshops in which participants learned skills in working with groups, and in which the teaching technique used an application of group dynamics in inducing influence, assigning roles, and establishing group goals. The basic format of the workshop, which would be called sensitivity training, was established. The content was mainly concerned with group process and involved the following: examples taken widely from current interaction and participants' backgrounds, observation of the process and "feedback," use of both positive and negative affect to create an intensive emotional atmosphere, and emphasis on the value of personal and organizational change.

Group training proper was partly superseded by the "human potential" movement. Here the emphasis was on the individual and personal growth. The basic techniques were the same, but the emphasis changed subtly toward self-expression, physical manipulation, and even more intense emotional experience; the groups were now called encounter groups.

GROUP COHESIVENESS
GROUP STRUCTURE
SMALL GROUPS

K. W. BACK

GROUP PRESSURE

It is not possible for a person within range of a group to be free of its effects. The group has been viewed as a major factor in determining the behavior of individual members.

As pointed out by W. R. Bion, every group exists only in the service of some purpose. This implies a relationship between unity of purpose within the group and successful task completion. Worchel and Cooper summarized the research in this area by stating that high cohesiveness does aid groups in task attainment.

Thomas French developed the concept of "focal conflict" to explain how individuals in a group come to "cooperate" toward attainment of a common goal. Members, either individually or collectively, may work to exert pressure on others in the group to conform to their immediate task needs.

Such pressures can be enormously effective, influencing not only task selection but individual beliefs, attitudes, and even perceptions of reality. M. Sherif, using the "autokinetic phenomenon," demonstrated that an individual group member's perception of such characteristics as direction,

amount, and speed of the light's "movement" could be greatly influenced by the verbal statement of judgments of other group members. S. E. Asch showed that individuals could be greatly influenced in a variety of perceptual judgments.

The desire for social approval is so deeply ingrained in most people that they will readily conform to the expectations of others rather than risk disapproval. An individual's need for acceptance by others in a group may be so strong, in fact, that it generalizes to complete strangers.

The threat of social rejection or other punishment can serve as a powerful reinforcer for conforming behavior.

Henry Ezriel elucidated mechanisms through which individuals pressure others and are influenced by them in turn. Individuals have three basic ways of relating to one another: the "required relationship," the "avoided relationship," and the "catastrophic relationship." In the required relationship, individuals interact in ways that they believe meet others' expectations. In return, a given individual wants others to meet his or her expectations. Individuals avoid behaving in ways that might fail to meet expectations of others and pressure others to reciprocate. The required relationship exists because of a belief that catastrophe might follow direct expression of the "avoided" thoughts or feelings. Such thinking permeates group interactions, fostering collusive rather than cooperative relationships and militating against honesty and sincerity in human interactions.

AFFILIATION NEED
CONFORMING PERSONALITY

S. BERENT

GROUP PROBLEM SOLVING

The comparison of group versus individual problem solving represents a central question for the field of group dynamics, and most work in group problem solving has focused on this issue. By contrasting the problem solving of individuals working alone with individuals working in groups, the psychologist can shed much light on conceptual models of group functioning. Furthermore, a great deal of the world's work is accomplished in group settings. Thus educational, organizational, and social psychologists, among others, must wrestle with the relative efficacy of group or individual problem-solving modes, and if groups are used, they must devise ways to maximize the group's productivity.

If the sheer problem-solving productivity of groups compared to individuals working alone is examined, the groups almost always show superiority. However, if the total effort of the group is measured by using such techniques as comparing person hours expended, the picture is much more complex. In some instances the group expends more total effort than an individual working alone, and in some instances, less. When monetary or personnel resource considerations are important, it becomes crucial to designate those circumstances in which the group process facilitates individual effort and those in which the group process hinders it.

The question of the superiority of group or individual problem solving can be put in the context of the opposing forces of "process loss" and "process gain" that occur in groups. Ivan Steiner has defined "process loss" in terms of the difference between potential group productivity and the actual group productivity resulting from faulty group process.

There are characteristics of the group that hinder efficiency. Process loss factors include the time wasted when the group fails to recognize the solution when it is offered, the reluctance of given members to participate fully in the group, and the reduction of member effort as a result of group experience. Although a large number of social psychologists have noted process loss to be common, there are studies that indicate a "process gain" as a result of the group experience. Group interaction can improve the efficiency of group productivity with the proper group composition, group norms, and group task design. Hill pointed out that "process gain" and "process loss" are both probably present in the group problem-solving situation. Laughlin and Adamopoulous indicated that group members not only teach each other within the group, but also that this learning carries over after the group sessions to subsequent individual problem-solving behavior. Thus the long-term view often dictates that, regardless of short-term process loss, group problem-solving sessions are important learning experiences.

One of the major factors associated with the relative effectiveness of groups in problem solving is the role of the "best individual" in the group. Often the "best individual" in effect solves the problem and other members are just spectators. If the best individual can be identified, it may be wise to minimize the distraction of that individual by eliminating the group situation and putting the talents of the remaining group members to other uses.

There are situations in which group performance is below that of the best individual. These are tasks in which the problem requires that group members combine several steps toward the solution and in which the solution is not easily perceived. Strategies in which group members perceive and support the correct solution are characterized by "disjunctive" or eureka problems. In contrast, when tasks are conjunctive and require that the best individual persuade other group members of the validity of the solution, the group severely hinders the individual.

According to Kelley and Thibaut, situations in which the group is better than the best individual seem to include tasks that are easily divisible and members that possess heterogeneous abilities. However, this type of situation might not be considered a true group problem-solving task, but simply a setting for the coordination of division of labor.

Programs have been proposed to maximize process gain and minimize process loss. The development of techniques that train group members to manage their own group more effectively could be accomplished by teaching groups about the processes that hinder optimal performance. Janis and Mann recommended that groups be counseled to look for a variety of decision alternatives, be trained in techniques that reduce defensiveness within the group, and that structured techniques be used.

Other behavioral scientists have developed a structured system of group communication processes to allow a group to most efficiently deal with a problem. The *Delphi method* allows for the collection, combination, and feedback of individual solutions, and decision making by a group of individuals. This technique has the advantages of group problem solving without face-to-face interaction process loss. It has been widely applied in a variety of government and industrial planning groups. These approaches point out the need to keep the group from distracting individuals, and to develop environments that prevent the group from narrowing its members' thinking about alternative problem solutions.

It should be recognized that group problem-solving situations have another purpose in their ability to increase the participants' commitment to implementing the solution when formulated. A variety of management approaches, particularly as practiced in Japan, have emphasized group participation. Thus, even in those cases in which short-run efficiency concerns might dictate individual problem solving, the group method might be preferable for the sake of increasing long-term member acceptance of the solution. Decisions on problems can be made by the leader alone (autocratic), in consultation with the group, or in a face-to-face group meeting. The optimal problem-solving decision method depends on the decision quality demands, the importance of group acceptance of the decision, and various factors of group dynamics in the decision-making group.

The classic model of group creative problem solving as designed by Osborne begins with problem definition and clarification. Next comes further fact finding to gather information about forces impinging on the problem and about the nature of the problem itself. This is followed by a group process known as brainstorming wherein, in an atmosphere of deferred judgment, the group produces as many divergent responses as possible. Convergent thinking is antithetical to a solution in this stage of the process, as is critical evaluation of suggested solutions. After a successful brainstorming session, the group begins to evaluate and criticize the different alternative solutions, ultimately choosing the strategy to be implemented. The next stage is the actual implementation of the solution, followed by its evaluation for effectiveness. As with other group procedures to problem solving, creative problem-solving approaches do not work better than individual approaches in all instances. Group creative problem solving is most effective when the information needed to solve the problem is scattered among several individuals, when implementation rests with many individuals, when individuals have been trained in the process of creative problem solving, when the problem is a "real" one with a definite payoff for a solution, and when there exists good interpersonal effectiveness among the group members.

COMMUNICATION SKILLS TRAINING
GROUP DYNAMICS
PRODUCTIVITY

L. A. JACKSON, JR.
C. R. REYNOLDS

GROUP PSYCHOTHERAPY

The application of psychotherapeutic principles with a group of people simultaneously is called group psychotherapy. Most commonly, group therapy involves a small number of participants (often six to ten) and one or two group therapists. Most approaches used with individuals—and many that are not—are applied to group therapy.

There are both economic and therapeutic advantages to group treatment. Economically, therapist time spent and the cost of treatment can be reduced by group approaches. Therapeutic advantages lie in the possibilities that group therapy offers for personality change. Yalom identified ten categories of curative factors present in group therapy: (a) imparting information, or communication of instructions or advice by therapists or group members; (b) instillation of hope, which is especially powerful in group therapy, as each member can see the treatment progress made by every other member; (c) universality, or the discovery by each member that other members have similar feelings or problems; (d) altruism, or the feeling of being helpful or of being needed by other group members; (e) the corrective recapitulation of the primary family group, the experience of interacting in a therapeutic manner with a group similar in some ways to the structure of a family; (f) the development of socializing techniques, or improving interpersonal skills through interaction and feedback; (g) imitative behavior, or the opportunity for group members to observe and copy several models of appropriate behavior of others; (h) interpersonal learning, or the opportunity for testing a variety of behaviors with others; (i) group cohesiveness, or the solidarity and attractiveness of a group for its members; and (j) catharsis, or the ventilation of feelings with others in a safe environment.

Despite its advantages, group therapy has limitations. First, some members may be reluctant to air intimate emotional issues. Doing so may put those members at risk for receiving feedback that exacerbates their problems, particularly when the issues discussed are those against which there are strong social proscriptions. Second, the process of group interaction may become so time-consuming that individual concerns of group members are not dealt with, which complicates the therapist's role. Finally, the behaviors and mores appropriate to the protected, supervised group setting may not be appropriate in more natural settings; some group members may have trouble applying them in their own life situations. There is still disagreement about which problems can be better dealt with in group than in individual therapy.

Therapy groups differ in goals, composition, and techniques used. Some groups have specific goals, themes, or tasks (e.g., groups formed to teach a certain skill or to resolve a certain type of problem). Other groups have less-stated structure and no established theme.

Some therapy groups are composed of specific types of individuals. Some, in contrast, are more heterogeneous, with a wide range of problems to be dealt with therapeutically. Most groups have some degree of homogeneity. Group therapy can be time-limited or open-ended, open or closed in accepting new members after the first meeting, and may vary in other ways. The widest variation among groups is in therapeutic techniques used. Some group therapists work with one group member at a time, whereas others work toward facilitating the interaction among the members.

One of the earliest schools of individual psychotherapy to be applied to groups was the psychoanalytic model. Another early group technique was Moreno's psychodrama approach, a therapeutic approach in which group members actually act out problems to gain new insights and awareness. Behavioral approaches to therapy have also been extended to groups. The group setting provides more opportunities for learning positive behavior and unlearning dysfunctional behavior than one therapist can provide in individual therapy.

The Gestalt and transactional analysis approaches to therapy have been extremely popular in group therapy. Fritz Perls applied his approach to groups, usually by working with one group member at a time. Gestalt group therapists seek to integrate all aspects of the individual into a unified whole. This integration provides observing members the opportunity to learn by identifying the conflicts of the other members with their own. Berne advocated a group approach as the most efficient use of transactional analysis because it allows transactions to be examined as they occur in the interpersonal context.

T-groups (training groups) were established to study and teach the effects of the group's experiences on its members. Aronson described the main goals of T-groups as developing a willingness to examine one's behavior, learning more about people, becoming more interpersonally honest, working cooperatively, and solving conflicts logically and rationally. Encounter groups and sensitivity-training groups are similar approaches with less structure and an emphasis on increasing self-awareness and personal growth. Rogers has applied his client-centered approach to the context of encounter groups. Some encounter group leaders use a variety of planned exercises to mobilize the group process.

Other approaches to group therapy include art and dance therapy, body therapy groups, theme-centered interaction, and groups aimed at developing a variety of specific skills. There are a variety of self-help groups that serve a therapeutic function in addition to more traditional therapy groups.

One application popular in recent years is the marathon group. Marathons are groups that last for extended periods of time, leading to fatigue, breakdown of psychological defenses, and intense interpersonal interaction.

Functions of the therapist in a group may involve facilitating member participation, interaction and problem solving, focusing conversation, supporting upset members, mediating among members in conflict, and assuring that group rules are established and adhered to. The difficulty involved in understanding and managing group process issues, in addition to the emotional issues of each member, means that group leaders must be particularly well trained, sensitive, and competent.

There are ethical issues unique to group therapy. Group members are not bound by the same ethical constraints as are professionals. Group therapists must therefore be particularly sensitive to establishing clear standards for confidentiality among group members.

GROUP COUNSELING
HUMAN POTENTIAL
MECHANISMS OF GROUP PSYCHOTHERAPY

T. S. BENNETT

GROW

GROW is an international community mental health movement of more than 500 self-help groups that originated in Australia. The movement has spread to five other countries. GROW provides a round-the-clock caring and sharing community to rehabilitate those who have experienced serious mental disorders. The groups also assist others in preventing emotional maladjustment.

Typically, the groups are administered by a trained GROW organizer. This person entrusts the chairing of the structured $1\frac{1}{2}$- to 2-hour weekly meeting to a group member who is demonstrating progress in working toward maturity.

GROW'S formula for mental health and happiness is expressed in the statement: "Settle for disorder in lesser things for the sake of order in greater things; and therefore be content to be discontent in many things." GROW's effectiveness has been investigated by a pioneering 3-year study supported by the National Institute of Mental Health.

A. J. VATTANO

GUTTMAN SCALE

The notion of "cumulativeness" as a desirable property of a scale was introduced by Louis Guttman. In several contributions Guttman developed the ideas and techniques of scale analysis to the point where cumulative scaling considerations are regarded as mandatory.

Generally, any set of items such as questions on a questionnaire are cumulative when they can be ordered so that respondents answering *yes* to any item will answer *yes* to all items lower (or higher) in the order, and will answer *no* to all items higher (or lower) in the order.

The question, "Do the items form a unidimensional scale?" was replaced by the question, "How many dimensions does it take to represent a given body of data?" This new question recognizes that a set of items may exhibit a number of different dimensions. The general technique is called *multidimensional scalogram analysis* (MSA).

MSA-1 is a method of data analysis not constrained by level of measurement or other special assumptions. Each observation or case is geometrically represented by a point in an *m*-dimensional space; variables are represented by partitions, and variable subclasses by regions defined by the partitions. A solution in a given number of dimensions consists in finding a configuration of points falling in multi-item regions such that the original set of observations assembled in the form of a data matrix may be reproduced within acceptable limits. A *coefficient of contiguity* measures the extent to which the input may be accurately reproduced from the output.

In general, the number of dimensions required to represent a body of data decreases when the number of empirically occurring distinct case profiles is fewer than the logical possibilities.

RATING SCALES
SCALING

M. S. BLOOMBAUM

H

HABITUATION

Habituation is a relatively persistent waning of a response following continuous or (usually) repeated stimulation that is not followed by reinforcement. For some investigations it is an empirical result, whereas for others it is a hypothetical construct, depending on the depth and character of its study. Fatigue, drugs, adaptation, and injury, although they produce response decline, are not included under this term and are quite separate. Other terms are used in other contexts, however, for probably related phenomena.

The orienting reaction exhibits habituation's typical characteristics. When a strange, unidentified noise alarms a wild animal, it usually stops whatever it is doing, becomes motionless, and scans its surroundings in search of the sound source in preparation for flight. If only the usual rustling ensues, it is interpreted as absence of danger and the animal shortly resumes its original activity. Subsequent similar noises, if uneventful, call forth similar but progressively weaker and shorter alerting responses, perhaps to finally eventuate in no outward sign of disturbance. The basic response or its rudiments can be seen in most species down to flatworms, and some investigators claim habituation in coelenterates and even protozoa. Different mechanisms are likely to be required to explain the similarity in results.

A second example, although considerably different in some respects, is essentially similar in others. Repeated severe coolings of a particular finger result in a progressive reduction of the associated cold pain. To the environmental physiologist this phenomenon is known as *specific habituation* when the response is restricted to the finger involved. *General habituation* is a change in the psychological "set" that results in a generalized diminution in response to the repeated stimulus. *Acclimatization* refers to the functional compensation that occurs over a period of days or weeks in response to a complex of environmental factors, as in seasonal or climatic changes. *Acclimation* refers to the same type of adjustment to a single environmental condition, as in controlled experiments.

Habituation of the orienting response, the type most extensively studied, is of theoretical interest because it represents one of the most primitive types of learning: a persistent change in behavior in response to experience.

Among habituation's main characteristics are the following: (a) After a long enough absence of stimulation, the originally strong but now diminished response will reappear at full strength (spontaneous recovery); (b) the more frequent and regular the eliciting stimulation, the faster the habituation; (c) the stronger the stimulation, the slower the habituation, although some near-threshold stimuli may not habituate, and very strong stimuli may elicit defensive responses that differ in characteristics from orienting responses; (d) additional stimulation beyond that which "completely" abolishes the original response (below-zero habituation) further prolongs habituation and delays spontaneous recovery; (e) habituation may generalize to other similar stimuli; (f) but presentation of another usually stronger—but sometimes much weaker—stimulus than is customary may restore the original response (i.e., cause "dishabituation").

Several approaches have been taken to elucidate the nature of the neural mechanisms involved in short-term habituation. According to the *synaptic depression* model, sensory input activates small interneurons in the periphery of the reticular formation. They in turn activate those neurons at the reticular formation's core that evoke cortical arousal in higher mammals. But it is necessary to first demonstrate that synaptic depression is possible, and to this end a simpler animal model has been useful. The sea hare (*aplysia*) possesses only a few easily identified ganglia.

Habituation studies show that repeated stimulation of a single sensory neuron evokes progressively smaller excitation potentials in the postsynaptic membrane. No change occurs in the postsynaptic membrane itself. The decrease in the postsynaptic response occurs because progressively fewer quanta of the neurotransmitter acetylcholine are released into the synaptic cleft. It is presumed that something like the sea hare's synaptic depression also occurs in the reticular formation.

Sokolov proposed a *match–mismatch* model to explain habituation, assuming that in higher mammals a stimulus elicits a neural representation of itself that is relatively permanent (engram). The neural consequences of subsequent stimuli are compared with the engram of the originally alerting stimulus; if the later stimulus matches the former, no reticular arousal occurs and habituation ensues.

One frequently finds in experimental work that the first response to the alerting stimulus is not the strongest; the magnitude of the next few responses may exceed that of the first, and only in subsequent trials does response strength diminish. One also finds that a habituated response can be rejuvenated (*dishabituated*) by a different, usually strong stimulus. Originally this dishabituation was thought to be merely a release of habituation, but it is now believed that another process, *sensitization*, underlies the augmented responding. Accordingly, the curve of responding usually seen is complex, having an initial rise and subsequent decline. Its shape is the result of the combined action of sensitization and habituation. Habituation becomes dominant after repeated stimulations, whereas sensitization remains at a constant level or declines. Some evidence points to the existence of neurons that only habituate and—in the opinion of some—markedly sensitize.

ACCOMMODATION
ADAPTATION
FATIGUE

A. J. RIOPELLE

HALFWAY HOUSES

Halfway houses are small group homes designed to aid institutionalized patients in their transition to independent life in the community. Halfway houses vary in their location, size, purpose, and patient population. However, most are located in the community, house 15 to 30 residents, serve as a transition facility between an inpatient institution and the community, and function as the primary but temporary residence of patients. Most halfway houses admit patients with substance abuse, psychiatric, or antisocial behavioral problems. Although halfway houses were originally intended to bridge the gap between institutionalization and community life, many now serve as initial referral sources.

Several factors contributed to the halfway house movement. There was a deemphasis on long-term institutionalization and an increased emphasis on placing psychiatric and other patients in a minimally restrictive treatment environment. In addition, certain social and legal actions promoted the release of many institutionalized individuals. Concurrently, advances in psychopharmacology reduced the symptomatology of many patients and facilitated their release from institutions. Parallel developments in the criminal justice system stressed the need for transition facilities to help convicts adjust to independent community life after long periods of incarceration.

The primary goal of halfway houses is to assist residents in developing the skills necessary for successful life in the community. Specific aims include helping the resident gain control over problem behaviors, the development of better social skills and social relationships, the acquisition of employment in the community, the acquisition of financial skills, and the development of self-help skills.

The goals of halfway houses also involve philosophical, social, and educational functions, including an avoidance or decrease in the length of institutionalization, reduced treatment cost, the use of a minimally restrictive therapeutic environment, and minimizing community disruption accompanying the admission and discharge of individuals in an institution. Halfway houses also perform an educational function by acquainting the community with the characteristics, special problems, and needs of the resident.

Most halfway houses rely on nonprofessional staff and attempt to provide a supportive environment for residents. Specific programs often include planned recreational and social activities, house meetings, group therapy, assigned household responsibilities, and personal counseling. Most houses have strict rules concerning appropriate behavior, and residents frequently participate in halfway house government.

Many halfway houses employ some type of contingency program to encourage and reward responsible behavior. Administratively, halfway houses are most often affiliated with or sponsored by churches, private institutions, hospitals, or mental health centers.

Halfway houses seek to gradually "shape" residents into acquiring the skills necessary for successful community living while they are gradually reintegrated into the community. The emphasis on successive approximation to independent community life is based on the finding that the first few months following release from an institution are associated with the greatest stress and risk of recidivism.

Although the rationale and goals of halfway houses are appealing and have substantial face validity, there is little empirical support for their effectiveness. Most of the research has involved uncontrolled outcome studies or has sought to establish predictors of successful outcome. The predictors most frequently associated with outcome are indices of alcoholism, prior hospitalization, employment while at the halfway house, community ties, and age. Because of methodological deficiencies and the inconsistent outcome of published studies, the efficacy of halfway houses remains to be demonstrated.

One impediment to conducting research is that the houses are conceptually and operationally diverse. Halfway houses would be expected to vary in their effectiveness as a function of their theoretical rationale, specific programs, staff training and characteristics, degree of community support, and type of patients admitted.

There is a striking lack of empirical basis for the specific programs used in halfway houses. For example, there is a substantial and growing research literature on methods of teaching individuals social skills, marital skills, and methods of securing employment. However, most halfway house programs continue to use outmoded and intuitively based methods to achieve these goals.

A halfway house is primarily a *concept* of treatment and need not involve a physical facility. Successful reintegration of institutionalized individuals into the community can be facilitated through shaping, education, training, and gradual approximation to community life without a specific physical facility devoted to such an enterprise.

S. N. Haynes

HALLUCINATIONS

An hallucination is typically defined as a false sensory impression. The "false" part of this definition refers to the lack of an external set of referents that, to the evaluator, would explain and support the individual's description of the event. Dreaming is considered by some to be a common example of a hallucinatory experience, surrounded at the onset of sleep in some people by hypnogogic hallucinations and by hypnopomic hallucinations upon waking.

Various estimates place between one eighth and two thirds of the normal population as having had hallucinations while awake. The phenomenon appears more frequent the more it is investigated, with tactile then auditory hallucinations as the most common. The occurrence of hallucinations may not necessarily be related to psychopathology. Posey and Losch found confirmatory evidence for this from their 375 college students, based on interviews and Minnesota Multiphasic Personality Inventory (MMPI) results. These authors found that the most common auditory hallucinations involved hearing a voice calling one's name aloud when alone (36%) and hearing one's own thoughts as if they were spoken aloud (39%).

Preschool children may experience hallucinations as part of their normal development. Schreier and Libow found that those 2- to 5-year-old children experiencing phobic hallucinations were uniformly bright and independent.

For both normal and psychiatric persons, the typical phasing of hallucinations consists of the (a) startle reaction when confronted with the sensory impression, (b) organization (coping), and (c) stabilization.

Culture appears to moderate the occurrence, quality, and frequency of hallucinations. Third World cultural groups—particularly Africans, West Indians, and South Asians—hallucinate more often than those in industrialized societies. Within the United States, Blacks and Hispanics report more auditory hallucinations than Whites, which tends to lead to a higher risk of misdiagnosis in the direction of psychopathology. Gender differences are not apparent from the literature.

In nonpsychiatric populations, hallucinations have been known to be caused by (a) exhaustion, as in the last stage of the GAS cycle; (b) sleep deprivation; (c) social isolation and rejection; (d) a severe reactive depression; (e) amputation of limbs, as in the phantom limb experience with kinesthetic sensations; (f) prescribed medication; and (g) a secondary outcome of substance intoxication by the hallucinogens (e.g., LSD, mescaline, psilocybin) and other drugs (e.g., morphine, heroin, cocaine). Formication, a tactile hallucination, is a creeping sensation under the skin and may be experienced by, for example, persons who use cocaine.

In the organic brain syndromes, hallucinations may be caused by a variety of events, including (a) delirium; (b) tumors associated with increasing intracranial pressure; (c) temporal lobe lesions; (d) seizures of several types; (e) alcohol-related encephalopathy; (f) head injury, as in postcoma experiences and disorientation; and (g) irritation of various sensory pathways, such as the visual pathways transversing the temporal lobes causing Lilliputian hallucinations or the olfactory pathways causing hallucinations of distinctive odors such as burnt rubber.

Not all organic brain-induced hallucinations involve the perception of a separate reality. In organic hallucinosis, for example, the (usually auditory) hallucinations may arise within a full state of alertness and orientation. In Lilliputian hallucinations, the affected person knows the small figures are not real; they are not associated with delusions.

Support for cerebral insult as the cause of some hallucinations stems from lateralization data. Chamorro et al. described the case of a 41-year-old woman with a subcortical CVA in alcohol withdrawal with visual hallucinations confined to the right side of space. DeMorsier reported a case of visual hallucinations localized in the left half of the visual field associated with sensory-motor hemiparesis. Khan, Clark, and & Oyebode reported on a 72-year-old female with unilateral auditory hallucinations related to deafness on the same side, which disappeared with a hearing aid. Tanabe et al. described a case of verbal hallucinations lateralized to the right ear, associated with fluent aphasia and a CVA in the left superior temporal gyrus. Other studies that support a cerebral insult interpretation of hallucinations are presented in Table 1.

The major psychotic disorders are often associated with hallucinations. Vivid hallucinations can be seen in all the schizophrenic subtypes. Halluci-

Table 1   Hallucinations Correlated with Cerebral Insult

Auditory Hallucinations

Reduced platelet MAO activity (Schildkraut et al., 1980)

Hypothyroidism (Pearce & Walbridge, 1991)

Alzheimer's disease (Burns, Jacoby, & Levy, 1990)

Atrophy of left superior temporal gyros (Barta et al., 1990)

Visual Hallucinations

Vascular insufficiency of temporo-parieto-occipital regions (Schneider & Crosby, 1980)

Lesion of right diencephalon (DeMorsier, 1969)

Subcortical infarct interrupting striatocortical pathways (Chamorro et al., 1990)

Anterior cerebral artery occlusion (Nakajima, 1991)

Tactile and Other Hallucinations

Peduncular hallucinosis associated with paramedian thalamic infarction (Feinberg & Rapcsak, 1989)

Stereognostic hallucinations and haptic sensations associated with biparietal lesions (Stacy, 1987)

---

nations are encountered within the affective disorders. In major depression, for example, the examiner using the *Diagnostic and statistical manual of mental disorders* criteria is asked to determine whether or not reported hallucinations are mood congruent or mood incongruent. Schizoaffective psychosis, a combination of thought disorder and affective psychosis, often has hallucinations as an associated feature.

Early work suggesting that different mental conditions involve different types of hallucinations is illustrated by Alpert and Silvers. A total of 80 adult hallucinating inpatients who were either alcoholics or schizophrenics were studied. The differences in hallucinations between the two groups were as follows. In alcoholics, (a) the onset of the hallucinations in their illness was early; (b) the type of sound was nonverbal or consisted of unintelligible voices; (c) the perceived source was outside the body; (d) patterned visual stimulation decreased the frequency of hallucinations; (e) arousal increased the frequency; (f) delusions accompanied the hallucinations infrequently; and (g) patients were often eager to discuss the experiences. In contrast, in schizophrenics (a) the onset was later; (b) voices were usually clear; (c) hallucinations were perceived to originate inside the body; (d and e) patterned visual stimulation and arousal created no change in frequency; (f) delusions were more frequent; and (g) patients were reluctant to share their hallucinatory experiences.

Hallucinations can be set off by multiple or indirectly combining events. Tactile (haptic) hallucinations can be secondary to schizophrenia, withdrawal from alcohol, or drug intoxication. Olfactory hallucinations (the false perception of smell) and gustatory hallucinations (the false perception of taste) are often experienced together in such conditions as temporal lobe epilepsy and schizophrenia. Reflex hallucinations involve irritation in one sense, creating an hallucination in another (e.g., a toothache setting off an auditory hallucination in a schizophrenic). Finally, kinesthetic hallucinations involve the sensation of altered states of body organs for which no receptor apparatus could explain the experience. This is found in psychotics and also in organics (e.g., a burning sensation in the brain caused by schizophrenia or a severe depression). The thalamic pain syndrome also can account for the perception.

For both normal and psychiatric populations, hallucinations may serve an adaptive function. Benjamin's 30 individuals with mental illness reported an integrated, interpersonally coherent and complementary relationship with their auditory hallucinations.

Hallucinations are ubiquitous and adaptive, occurring in persons who are considered normal and all the major psychiatric diagnostic categories. Speculation continues regarding etiology (e.g., whether hallucinations associated with cerebral insult represent a release from inhibitory neural

mechanisms). Psychological explanations are just as valid (e.g., that hallucinations represent intrapersonal and/or interpersonal dynamics that help the individual adjust to a changing and often threatening environment). Both neurological and psychological theories are plagued with the lack of a direct method to measure hallucinations.

Interventions for hallucinations vary widely from spontaneous recovery to invasive drug procedures, which frequently cause hallucinations themselves as a toxic side effect. Cognitive behavioral methods have generated some interest (Table 2). Investigation into this fascinating domain of human behavior is projected to continue as part of a heightened interest in altered states of consciousness.

H. V. HALL

HALLUCINOGENIC DRUGS

Drugs producing hallucinogenic effects have been known to humanity for centuries. Most of these drugs have been used in conjunction with religious ceremonies or specific cultural events, their abuse not being tolerated. Hallucinogens by definition have the capability of producing hallucinations (sensory experience in the absence of external stimuli). However, most hallucinogenic drugs will produce such an effect only at quite high doses, which in turn produce unpleasant physical and emotional side effects such as nausea and panic. Consequently, some authors argue that a more descriptive name for this class of drugs is psychotomimetic (literally, mimicking psychosis) because of the behavioral and emotional changes that occur.

While it is true that significant behavioral and emotional changes can take place, it is also well recognized that one major difference between a true psychotic experience and a drug-induced one is the ability of the individual in the drug-induced state to differentiate between what is real and what is not. In addition, most drugs in this category will produce some, but not all, of the cognitive, emotional, personality, and perceptual changes associated with psychotic experiences. Consequently, a third group of experts argues that the term "psychedelic" or "mind-expanding" drugs should be used. These authorities argue that most individuals take such drugs neither for their hallucinatory effect, nor certainly for their ability to induce a psychotic state, but to induce an expanded perceptual state in which they are able to perceive objects from a different perspective, or to experience nuances of perception previously unrecognized by the individual. In this article, the terms hallucinogenic, psychotomimetic, and psychedelic are used interchangeably in identifying this class of drugs.

The chemical and pharmacological classifications of hallucinogenic drugs are also open to argument among authorities in the field. Robert Julien provides a breakdown of the drugs based on the neurochemical system that each one most affects: acetylcholine psychedelics (e.g., atropine, scopolamine, malathion), norepinephrine psychedelics (e.g., mescaline, STP), and serotonin psychedelics (e.g., LSD, dimethyltryptamine, psilocybin).

Some authorities also include the amphetamines in the general category of psychotomimetic drugs. This classification of a drug otherwise considered a central nervous system stimulant is due to its ability to produce responses that closely match that of florid paranoid psychosis when the drug is used in higher doses over a period of time.

Finally, marijuana is classified in various ways owing to its differential effect. Depending on dosage, marijuana is a mild hypnotic or a sedative. At higher doses the active ingredient, tetrahydrocannabinol (TCH) is capable of producing psychedelic effects similar to those of LSD. Hashish, a concentration of the marijuana plant's resin, is particularly capable of producing these psychedelic effects. At present, the exact site and method of action of THC are not known.

Authorities in the field generally agree that the effects of these drugs vary considerably, based on the type and amount of drug used. However,

Table 2   Diminishing Auditory Hallucinations

Method	Condition	Reference
Relaxation tapes	Schizophrenics	Hustig et al. (1990)
Stimulating tapes	Schizophrenics	Hustig et al. (1990)
Increasing ambient noise levels (via hearing aid)	Anxiety and depression	Fenton and McRae (1989)
Stop-and-name technique (with occluded auditory input to ear)	Schizophrenics	Birchwood (1986)
Switching (concentration on visual stimulus)	Process schizophrenics	Heilbron et al. (1986)
Holding (repeating words to ignore later words)	Reactive schizophrenics	Heilbron et al. (1986)
Diversion strategies	Schizophrenics	Allen et al. (1985)
Satiation therapy (prolonged exposure to voice)	Obsessional thoughts	Glaister (1985)

significant variation will also occur depending on the attitude (feeling state) of the individual at the time of taking the drug, the individual's knowledge and familiarity with the particular drug and other similar drugs, as well as factors in the drug taker's immediate environment. With so many variations of these factors possible, it is difficult to predict what response any one individual will have at a particular time to the various drugs of this type.

Hallucinogenic drugs are most commonly taken into the body by oral ingestion; they are rarely injected. Cannabis is most commonly smoked, leading to rapid absorption through the lungs and into the bloodstream. Normally, the effects can be felt within 5 minutes. Oral ingestion of cannabis or of the other psychedelics typically takes approximately 30 minutes before an effect is felt. Duration of drug effect varies by dosage and drug type, with drugs such as cannabis being somewhat shorter acting (approximately 3 hours), whereas drugs such as LSD will typically last 12 hours or more.

Psychotic reactions are but one concern about the group of stronger hallucinogenic drugs. Flashbacks have been reported by a number of drug users, mostly from LSD. The precipitator for the flashbacks can be use of other drugs, alcohol, or stressful situations, but in some cases they occur with no apparent cause.

A final reason for caution derives from the combination of sensory distortion and emotional alteration caused by this group of drugs. Individuals may experience a "bad trip" and, through panic and distortion, engage in behavior resulting in death.

It is in large part these various adverse reactions to hallucinogenic drugs that have caused their demise as psychotherapeutic agents.

AMPHETAMINE EFFECTS
CHEMICAL BRAIN STIMULATION
MARIJUANA
NEUROCHEMISTRY
PSYCHOPHARMACOLOGY
STIMULANTS

R. P. KAPPENBERG

HALO EFFECT

The halo effect is the tendency of a rater to evaluate an individual high on many traits because of a belief that the individual is high on one trait: The rated trait seems to have a spillover effect on other traits. The halo effect was first empirically supported by E. L. Thorndike.

The halo effect is detrimental to rating systems because it masks the presence of individual variability across different rating scales. Many suggestions have been made for coping with it, as for instance rating all people on one trait before going to the next, varying the anchors of the scale, pooling raters with equal knowledge, and giving intensive training to the raters. The latter technique seems to be the most effective and frequently used approach to counter this effect.

Closely related to the halo effect is the "devil effect," whereby a rater evaluates an individual low on many traits because of a belief that the individual is low on one trait assumed to be critical. The halo (or devil) effect usually increases to the extent that the rated trait is vague, difficult to measure, or seen as a subset of another rated trait.

RATER ERRORS
RATING SCALES
SCALING

L. BERGER

HALSTEAD–REITAN BATTERY

The Halstead–Reitan Battery consists of a series of individual neuropsychological measures, which in combination permit the skilled examiner to make rather detailed inferences about the integrity of the cerebral hemispheres. Because the brain is the organ of adaptive behavior, brain dysfunction is typically observable in some behavioral aberration. The tests included in the Halstead–Reitan Battery are designed to sample behavior across every possible sphere and assess all major cognitive, sensory, expressive, and motor functions.

Many of the subtests included in the Halstead–Reitan Battery are well known and are widely used by nonneuropsychologists. These include the Wechsler Adult Intelligence Scale (WAIS) and the Minnesota Multiphasic Personality Inventory (MMPI). Other tests were developed or adapted specifically for the battery. The Category Test is regarded as one of the most sensitive measures of cerebral impairment.

Another excellent general measure of cortical function is the Tactual Performance Test. Other Halstead–Reitan tests include the Speech-Sounds Perception Test, the Rhythm Test, the Finger-Oscillation Test, and Trails A and B. In addition, sensory-perceptual, lateral dominance, and aphasia examinations are included as part of the battery. Cutoff scores suggestive of brain impairment are provided for most tests, and the most sensitive tests are included in the calculation of the Impairment Index, a general measure of cortical dysfunction.

Somewhat different tests are included in two other versions of the Halstead–Reitan Battery developed for assessing younger and older children. The children's versions of the battery have not been as well validated as the adult battery.

BRAIN

D. WEDDING

HAND TEST

The Hand Test, a projective technique, was first published in 1962 and in the intervening years has been extensively normed and validated. Boden commented on the "impressive array of research studies," concluding that "on balance the validity data seem to indicate that the Hand Test stacks up well against other commonly used projective techniques."

The Hand Test was originally developed to mirror the presence or absence of prototypal action tendencies to blunt the accusation that projective techniques cannot predict behavior.

The stimuli consist of ten cards, $4\frac{3}{8}'' \times 3\frac{3}{8}''$ in size. The first nine cards portray simple line drawings of hands and the last card is blank. The subject is requested to "tell me what it looks like the hands might be doing" and, on the last card, to "imagine a hand, and tell me what it might be doing." Responses are scored and categorized along four major dimensions, according to whether the projection involves other people (interpersonal), the impersonal world (environmental), difficulties in relating to people or things (maladjustive), or an inability to develop a meaningful action tendency (withdrawal). These major quantitative modalities are further broken down into more individualized scores that help to describe the subject's personality. For example, "interpersonal" consists of six separate scores, depending on whether the response entails relations with others that are affectionate (AFF), dependent (DEP), communicative (COM), exhibitionistic (EXH), directive (DIR), or aggressive (AGG).

In addition to the stimulus cards, the test kit includes a scoring booklet, a revised adult manual, a children's manual, and two monographs. Although scoring and interpretation are relatively straightforward compared with other more complex projective techniques such as the Rorschach, proper use requires clinical training and experience, and the test is intended for graduate-level students and professionals.

Although the assumptions of the Hand Test were rationally derived, its validity is empirical and was established mainly by comparing normal samples with various known clinical groups, obtaining differences in expected directions. For example, as anticipated, psychotic individuals tend to score high on the "withdrawal" score, whereas neurotics produce a buildup on "maladjustive." Ongoing clinical use suggested additional scoring nuances of diagnostic significance, and these were eventually incorporated into the overall scoring scheme as parenthisized or qualitative scores. For instance, a response that is given more than once would also receive a parenthisized repetition (REP) score.

Initially, because of its purported ability to disclose behavior, the Hand Test was represented as an instrument primarily of value for predicting aggressive, acting out tendencies. Since then, the test has become a more general clinical tool, useful for formulating diagnoses and psychodynamics with a variety of populations. It can sometimes be helpful in determining the risk of antisocial behavior but should be used cautiously in this respect. The so-called acting-out ratio (AOR) that compares positive interpersonal relationships (i.e., AFF, DEP, and COM) with negative ones (i.e., DIR and AGG) has been touted as a predictor of aggressive tendencies, but its usefulness is circumscribed, and as is true for any projective test, the Hand Test works best when viewed holistically (i.e., it is unwise to rely on just one or two indices in drawing diagnostic conclusions).

The Hand Test does not require literacy, can be administered to anyone 7 years of age or older, takes only about 10 minutes to administer, is readily integrated into a test battery, is relatively easy to learn, and can be used for screening purposes. Interpretively, however, it is limited by the fact that it tends to measure the facade or behavioral overlay and, therefore, does not reveal a complete picture of the personality. Also, the test is deceptively simple, and one of its putative advantages, facile assimilation, can be a trap for the unwary. The instrument requires a clinical background and some study and experience to be used effectively.

Because of its brevity and ease of administration the Hand Test has also proven useful for research. Past research has centered mainly on establishing meaningful differences among clinical samples and predicting antisocial behavior, but the test has also been employed to establish a theoretical underpinning for Structural Analysis, to investigate cultural differences, and to gain insight into various psychopathological syndromes such as multiple personality, anorexia nervosa, and the "compulsive facade," a compensatory reaction to brain damage.

CLINICAL ASSESSMENT
PROJECTIVE TECHNIQUES
RORSCHACH TECHNIQUE
THEMATIC APPERCEPTION TEST

E. E. WAGNER

HANDEDNESS

Handedness refers to the dominance of one hand over the other for writing, manual skills, and activities. Hand preference also involves the eyes and speech. The left cerebral hemisphere of the brain controls the operation of the right hand, rightward eye turning, and speech, whereas the right hemisphere monitors the left hand, leftward eye turning, and spatial and temporal tasks.

It is estimated that 90% of the world's population prefers to use the right hand. The mystery of universal right-hand preference prompts many theoretical explanations.

Right-hand dominance may be traced back to the cave dwellers. Precursors to humans were left-handed, according to anthropological evidence. There is conjecture that the evolutionary change from left- to right-hand dominance evolved when tools were invented.

The operating hand that eventually will be preferred may be discovered as early as 4 weeks of age when the infant lying on the back assumes a fencing-like position. The head is turned to the preferred side, toward which the hand and arm are extended while the opposite arm is crooked. Gesell spoke of this fencing position as fundamental to eye–hand coordination.

Gesell referred to an active eye and a subordinate eye. The right eye is usually dominant, and the visual stimuli in the right field of vision, including the right hand, are projected onto the left hemisphere of the brain. In other words, the right eye and right hand work together.

However, cooperation does not always exist. Several competing activities originating in the same hemisphere may interfere with one another: For example, speaking can interfere while one is simultaneously writing with the right hand. When we speak (using the left brain), we detect things in our right field of vision, but may miss something in the left field.

The brain's left hemisphere also controls the movements of the right hand and is the speech center of approximately 98% of right-handers and more than 50% of left-handers. The left brain then controls both written and spoken language. The preeminence of the left hemisphere for speech—a peculiarly human activity—is necessary for communication and ultimately for the survival of the human species. Specialization of the left brain for speech occurs as early as the fetal stage, and speech registers in the newborn just 12 hours after birth. These findings suggest that there is an inborn biological tendency for speech.

There is the possibility that right-handedness is either genetic in origin or a product of learning. Instead of either extreme, handedness may be a combination of hereditary potential coupled with environmental stimulation that accounts for handedness, although the question of how much each factor contributes remains unanswered.

One can tell that a person is employing the left hemisphere by watching to see if the eyes move rightward when that person is talking. It is possible to discover the left-hander who is using the language center in the left brain when he or she writes holding the left hand in a hooked or inverted position (i.e., when the left-hander thinks like a right-hander). The left-hander who speaks and moves the eyes leftward or who writes in a noninverted fashion is employing the right brain for both written and spoken language.

Because approximately 40% of left-handers have speech centers in their right brains, it is suggested that left- and right-handers perceive their respective environments differently. A small proportion of left-handers have speech centers in both sides of the brain. The bilateral distribution of speech in the brain may result in superior abilities for those left-handers. The close connection between intellectual and verbal abilities has been long established. Left-handers who have made their mark in history include Leonardo da Vinci, Michelangelo, Benjamin Franklin, Babe Ruth, and Harry Truman. Left-handers comprise about 10% of the world's population and are growing in number. The growth may be due, in part, to the elimination of prejudices against left-handers and diminished attempts to change left-handedness by force.

If left-handedness is a puzzle, ambidextrousness is a bigger riddle. Are there people who skillfully employ both hands equally well in all tasks? It would appear that, even among the ambidextrous, one hand still prevails in certain tasks.

Instead of viewing people as strictly right- or left-handed, contemporary researchers view them as using predominantly the lead hand in certain activities and the opposite hand in others. Brown refers to 10 tests to determine which hand is the lead hand: writing; striking a match; sweeping a broom; drawing; taking a lid off a box; using a spoon, a knife, and scissors; throwing; and brushing the teeth.

BRAIN LATERALITY
HUMAN DEVELOPMENT

S. S. BROWN

HANDICAPPED (ATTITUDES TOWARD)

Federal legislation regarding the rights of the handicapped has resulted in parallel societal and individual attitude changes toward individuals with handicaps, as similarly occurred with other civil rights legislation involving minority groups.

Medical advances in surgery, biochemistry, artificial organs, and amniocentesis, among others, have resulted in persons with handicaps living longer. Technological advances enable many such individuals to be more mobile. Innovative prosthetic devices, often in concert with computer technology, have fostered lessened dependency on others and increased integration into the mainstream.

Public buildings and sidewalks are required to be barrier-free, and architectural standards for new public construction include provisions for access and mobility within all areas. Consequently, individuals with handicaps are more often seen within community settings.

Public schools must provide all children, regardless of the severity of handicap, with a free and appropriate educational program in the least restrictive environment. Many children who were formerly educated in separate schools or in institutions are now attending public school. All children with handicaps, to the maximum extent possible, must be educated with their nonhandicapped peers. Mainstreaming students with disabilities has provided the opportunity for most school-age children to have classmates with mental retardation, sensory loss, emotional disorder, or orthopedic disability. Numerous support and self-help groups have been formed for the disabled and their families. Public awareness and knowledge is further heightened by television portrayals and other media coverage of individuals with various handicapping conditions, who are

often seen as overcoming incredible odds through grit and determination in order to lead full and wholesome lives.

Research studies indicate that the nonhandicapped's discomfort or stereotypic attitudes can be modified through planned experiences. Methods that have met some success include visits to schools or institutions, personal or media presentations about handicapping conditions, group discussions to analyze the dynamics of prejudice, and activities designed to simulate a handicapping condition.

Experimental studies demonstrate that contact between disabled and nondisabled can effectively increase positive attitudes if both parties are of comparable socioeconomic status. Simulation activities can also cause a positive shift in attitudes, particularly if a component of these activities includes observations by the nondisabled of the social reaction of others toward the handicap they are simulating. But even though legal, medical, technological, and architectural changes have increased the visibility and acceptance of persons with handicaps, increased interaction does not automatically promote the development of more positive attitudes or lead to a corresponding decrease in negative or stereotypic reactions.

HANDICAPS

A. THOMAS

HANDICAPS

A handicap is a constellation of physical, mental, psychological, and/or social properties or processes that complicate or compromise a person's adaptation such that optimal development and functioning are not achieved. It is useful to distinguish *disability,* a physical or mental impairment or defect that affects a person's functioning, from *handicap,* a particular set of social and psychological reactions to these effects. Unfortunately, there exist in the literature numerous instances in which this useful distinction is employed, but interchanged. The former distinction will be maintained here, with emphasis that a disability does not necessarily imply a handicap.

Two major approaches to conceptualizing handicaps will illustrate the complexity of the transformation of a disability into a handicap. The dominant approach uses disease and illness metaphors to account for the individual differences or deviance represented by the disability. The disability is a negative property that sets the individual apart from "normal" people and requires medically oriented interventions such as diagnosis and treatment.

This medical orientation predominates in current professional practice and public policy. Other dimensions critical to the classification of handicapping conditions are indications of severity, as well as acknowledgement of common overlapping or coexisting disabilities, as implied in notions of the multiply handicapped individual. Further, the particular domain in which the handicap presents or intrudes can be indicated in a classification schema, as in the notion of educational handicaps—conditions that interfere with a child's school achievement. Each of these conditions affects or limits a person's functioning and potentially compromises a person's development and adaptation.

An alternative approach to conceptualizing handicaps considers the handicap a social construction rather than an inherent property or trait of the disabled individual. Nettie Bartel and Samuel Guskin articulate this approach:

A handicap is a social condition, a condition created by society. A person's bodily or behavioral condition becomes a handicap only to the extent that society, other people, or the person himself define his condition, as distinctive and undesirable. . . . The result of this social definition is to create distinctive environments and behaviors, which sequentially remove the person further and further from normal life patterns and, in time, convince all concerned that the person truly is handicapped.

Approaching handicaps as social constructions leads quickly to drawing parallels between handicapped persons and other minority or disadvantaged groups. *Handicapism*—prejudice against disabled or deviant individuals—thus becomes a counterpart to racism and sexism as a powerful force in our society, whether in its individual, institutional, explicit, or implicit forms.

The civil rights movement made headway in increasing awareness of and responsiveness to people with challenges. A variety of legislation and court decisions have moved our society in the direction of more humanitarian and pluralistic approaches to them. The Rehabilitation Act of 1973, and the Education for All Handicapped Children Act represent this major thrust toward guaranteeing educational, civil, and human rights for individuals with challenges and specifying governmental obligations for ensuring advantages for their psychological and physical well-being. In particular, concepts and policies such as *deinstitutionalization, mainstreaming,* and *normalization* form the basis of these approaches. Deinstitutionalization refers to efforts to remove the handicapped from institutional and segregated settings and provide for their special needs in the community. This involves mainstreaming individuals into the least restrictive settings, thereby increasing their opportunity for optimal and normalized development.

D. L. WERTLIEB

HAWTHORNE EFFECT

The Hawthorne effect is named for a series of studies conducted from the late 1920s through the 1930s at the Western Electric Company's Hawthorne Works near Chicago. Many textbooks cite these studies as central in the historical development of industrial/organizational psychology. Stated in its simplest form, the Hawthorne effect suggests that any workplace change, such as a research study, makes people feel important and thereby improves their performance.

The Hawthorne studies had five distinct research phases: the illumination experiments, the relay assembly testroom experiments, the mass interviewing program, the bank wiring observation room experiments, and the program of personnel counseling.

The illumination experiments had the purpose of relating levels of lighting to worker productivity but no clear functional relationship could be found.

The second major phase of the Hawthorne studies was an attempt at studying workers' performance under carefully controlled conditions. For this reason, five employees were isolated in a separate room, along with a person who assigns work and a research observer. Although it is often reported that all experimental conditions in the relay assembly testroom led to improved production, the overall trend for improved production did not necessarily apply to individual workers.

It was apparent that the social impact of the research was far greater than the impact of changes in lighting or rest breaks. To clarify this issue, the mass interviewing program was begun. In the third phase more than 20,000 employees were interviewed.

The fourth phase grew out of the mass interviewing program. Given the importance of social groups in the workplace, the bank wiring observation room studies were designed as an intensive investigation of such groups. For this, 14 men were observed and interviewed for over 6 months, which produced a wealth of data on work groups.

Finally, the fifth phase involved an extensive program of personnel counseling. Counselors were employed who could be approached by employees and confided in as impartial agents. With the opening of such communication channels, supervisors could be assisted in improving their behavior. In general, the researchers reported a number of improvements in intraorganizational communication.

Kahn pointed out that the Hawthorne effect cannot be counted on to emerge from all research studies. His analysis suggests that worker participation in important decisions plays a major role in eliciting the effect.

EMPLOYEE ATTITUDE SURVEYS
FIELD EXPERIMENTATION
INDUSTRIAL PSYCHOLOGY
INDUSTRIAL/ORGANIZATIONAL PSYCHOLOGY

P. G. BENSON

HEALTH CARE SERVICES

The U.S. health care system is a complex mixture of separate subsystems of care, each of which has developed separately and serves specific segments of the population.

The modern U.S. health care system has had three important periods of development. The first period began in the mid-nineteenth century when large hospitals began to flourish. The development of hospitals symbolized the institutionalization of health care for the first time in this country.

The second period began around the turn of the century with the introduction of the scientific method into medicine. Prior to this time, medicine had been an informal collection of unproven generalities and good intentions.

Prior to World War II, this country underwent a major social, political, and technological upheaval that ended the second period of health care development. The scientific advances continued, paralleled by an increasing interest in the social and organizational structure of health care. During this period, attention was first directed toward the financing of health care, with the resultant formation of health insurance plans. Increasing concentration of power in the federal government was witnessed by the Hospital Survey and Construction Act, by the huge research budgets of the National Institute of Health, and by the passage of Medicare.

Many types of services are part of a total system of health care. Every individual system of health care provides different services with varying levels of intensity. The systems providing these elements may be either formally or informally organized. Whatever the type of system or the type of financing that pays for the care, some basic range of services as listed next are necessary if the people served are to reach their fullest human potential.

Public health services and preventive medicine aim at protecting food and water, air, roads traveled, and the environment. A specific personal function is the prevention of certain illnesses, including vaccination against poliomyelitis and various childhood illnesses. There is also the general function of educating the public regarding matters of health.

Emergency medical care must be provided for acute emergency health problems, whether simple or serious. This includes emergency transportation, trained paramedic personnel, hospital emergency rooms, and a variety of other personnel and facilities.

Nonemergency ambulatory services are for problems requiring simple ambulatory patient care. The services required are usually rudimentary diagnosis and early treatment, along with general guidance on how to use the health care system further if the problem persists.

Complex ambulatory patient care services provide for those patients whose complaints require considerably more professional training and judgment. The skills involved are diagnosis, medical treatment and a detailed knowledge of diagnostic tests and medications.

Simple inpatient hospital care provides short-term, institutional care that focuses highly technical resources and personnel on a patient's problem for a short period.

Complex inpatient hospital care treats illnesses requiring much more complex, more serious, and more prolonged hospital care. The services are more complex, elaborate, and expensive. They require many highly trained professionals of different kinds.

Long-term continuing care and rehabilitation are necessary for some illnesses once the acute intensive phase of treatment is completed. This care may last for a few weeks or for years, begins in the hospital and is continued in a long-term facility. The services are related to nursing; physical activity; emotional support; and social problems of income, housing, and family relationships.

Care for social, emotional, and developmental problems usually require a wide range of services. These services provide more total long-term life support than the usual physician or hospital service for acute physical illness.

Transportation must be available for emergency care for incapacitated patients, or for socially disadvantaged patients who cannot take advantage of the system's resources without transportation assistance.

Financial compensation for disability is also needed. Total recovery from illness involves much more than technical health care. Recovering patients may require financial assistance to renew their former life patterns.

PRIMARY PREVENTION OF PSYCHOPATHOLOGY RIGHT TO TREATMENT

R. T. GIUBILATO

HEALTH PSYCHOLOGY

"Health psychology is the aggregate of the specific educational, scientific and professional contributions of the discipline of psychology to the promotion and maintenance of health, the treatment and prevention of illness, and the identification of etiologic and diagnostic correlates of health, illness and related dysfunction" and to the analysis and improvement of the health care system and health policy formation. Health psychology draws on virtually every core field within psychology and thus links psychology to *behavioral medicine.*

Although health psychology is a relatively new field, its roots are as old and as varied as psychology itself. John B. Watson wrote: "The medical student must be taught that no matter whether he is specializing in surgery, obstetrics, or psychiatry, his subjects are human beings and not merely objects on which he may demonstrate his skill." A major focus of health psychology is upon the training of health care personnel, accounting in part for the growth of behavioral science curricula and appointments of psychologists in medical schools and related settings.

Medical psychology, a subspeciality of clinical psychology, emphasizes professional practice and service delivery to patients with physical illness, often in hospitals and usually as part of a consultation–liaison psychiatry service. The clinical orientation emphasizes mental health concerns, although the influence of psychotherapeutic intervention on the course, outcome, and costs of a variety of physical illness is well documented. A related emphasis is on so-called *psychosomatic illness*—diseases presumed or demonstrated to be caused or complicated by emotional or psychological factors. More recently, in psychosomatic medicine as well as in medicine more generally, the movement is toward more holistic

and comprehensive biopsychosocial conceptualizations of health and illness that give proper consideration to emotional or psychological factors in virtually all illness or health.

Pediatric psychology represents a "new marriage" between pediatricians and psychologists with collaboration around meeting the developmental and health needs of children and their families in service delivery, training, and research.

Shifting priorities are evident in the focus of health care professionals upon what is termed the "new morbidity"—problems presented for medical care that are heavily or primarily psychosocial in origin, such as child abuse, learning disorders, "problems in living," and stress disorders.

Rehabilitation psychology is most often involved in assessing, counseling, or treating patients with chronic disorders or physical disabilities. Collaboration with professionals in rehabilitation medicine and allied health services represents one of the major interdisciplinary linkages basic to the field.

Among the major issues faced by health psychology is training. Relatively few psychologists have been trained explicitly as health psychologists. A small number of predoctoral and postdoctoral training programs have been established specializing in health psychology.

BEHAVIORAL MEDICINE HEALTH CARE SERVICES HOLISTIC HEALTH PRIMARY PREVENTION OF PSYCHOPATHOLOGY

D. L. WERTLIEB

HEALTHY PERSONALITY

A striking gap in systematic psychology is the lack of an explicit theory of healthy personality. This is partly because society has not required that research focus on health: People who function constructively and productively do not jeopardize civilization, whereas criminals and emotionally disturbed, defective, or helpless individuals do.

Another reason is that it is easy to identify the phenomena of abnormality and bring them under the control of the investigator. "Symptoms" are aspects of behavior that lie outside the preferred or established social system. As a consequence, we have laws and modes of social regulation that bring such persons together in settings readily amenable to investigation—hospitals, prisons, and other institutions.

Furthermore, there exists an implicit belief that people who are "normal" have a right to privacy, to conduct their lives in their own way.

For all these and other reasons, we have a far more highly developed psychology of the abnormal than of the healthy. Theories of healthy personality are mostly derived by implication from theories of disordered personality. But healthy personality is just as distinctive a "diagnostic category" as any other kind of personality.

WHAT IS PSYCHOLOGICAL HEALTH?

Personality theory attempts to describe and/or explain the *intrinsic* properties of the person and their relation to behavior. Because every act is always determined both by characteristics of the person and by characteristics of the situation, a further problem concerns how interaction between intrinsic properties and *extrinsic* conditions in the environment influence behavior.

All theories of personality deal with one or more of four basic functions of intrinsic properties.

Instigation. Persons have characteristics that impel them to move and act: Some general internal force changes in intensity, with a resulting change in behavior.

Regulation. When arousal varies, some pattern of acts occurs that serves to express or gratify the arousal state. Such a pattern selects one among alternative modes of acting. A given alternative is determined by intrinsic regulative systems, or *attitudes* (as they interact with the environment).

Experience and meaning. Complementary to regulation is the processing of information by which present stimuli and feedback from ongoing behavior are related to—and integrated with—present acts. Sensory data and associated feelings are stored and retrieved by conceptual processes, yielding *concepts* or meanings. This continuous organization works in partnership with the selective regulating process to determine the patterns and sequences of behavior that actually occur.

Style. Finally, each person displays distinctive personal characteristics. Even if two persons are similar in instigation, regulative mode, and conceptual properties, they still differ in how behavior is manifested. Most personality tests have been constructed to yield more information about style than about the other three functions.

One could, then, examine psychological health from the standpoint of these functions. Thus we might identify structures and dynamic processes that especially characterize healthy personality.

THE COMMON-SENSE INTUITIVE VIEW

Psychologists who emphasize the need to study healthy personality have mainly pointed to traits that differentiate health from mere "normality" or from the absence of significant psychopathological symptoms. Shoben suggested that healthy people are characterized by self-control, personal responsibility, democratic self-interest, and ideals.

Jourard provides a particularly sensitive and thoroughgoing description. Healthy people continuously expand their consciousness of themselves, other people, and the world; increase in their competence to fulfill basic needs, grow in response to threat; and develop realistic and satisfying roles and interpersonal relationships.

PSYCHOANALYTIC THEORY: THE NEUROTIC MODEL

Psychoanalytic theory has been a major influence in the development of personality theory. Therefore, it is worth considering its special perspective on psychological health.

The neurotic person has a great weight of unconscious conflict, suffers from a burden of anxiety, and ties up a great amount of energy in defensive patterns of behavior. Consequently, a neurotic person has difficulty in satisfying instinctive impulses and engages in much futile, wasted, and unproductive activity. Psychoanalytic theory has no really meaningful conception of healthy personality. Rather, it presents everyone as basically neurotic, but some people as less than others. This "ideal or normal neurotic" differs from the neurotic in two ways: balance and sublimation.

Balance. The structural systems in personality are better balanced in the normal person. The energies of the organism are so distributed among the three systems that each has an amount appropriate to its special functions. Thus the ego has sufficient energy to perceive reality and to accommodate the superego, while finding the means to gratify the id.

Sublimation. Defensive tactics differ between neurotic and normal people. Literally, sublimation signifies the deenergizing of instincts by the ego, which then takes over their energy and employs it for its own ends. In this way the ego can engage in socially desirable (civilized) behavior. From the standpoint of society, sublimation is a "successful" defense because it avoids conflict and anxiety and accomplishes what the socialization process intends. Clearly, a normal person might be viewed merely as someone whose ego, having a greater store of sublimated energy than that of the neurotic, therefore has a larger number of socially approved patterns of behavior.

The concept of sublimation, however, is ambiguous. It is hard to separate it from other defensive mechanisms. It appears that repression is still necessary, after which the ego simply directs libido to a new channel. This process is fundamentally no different in principle from any activity of the ego. Therefore, the normal person simply uses more of a different defense.

The sublimation principle is also unclear about the character of instigation in the neurotic and the normal. This is perhaps the most difficult point in all of psychology. Sublimation implies that civilized behavior is motivated by the same instincts as neurotic behavior, but merely in changed form. Still, we must consider the possibility that acquired patterns of behavior may be motivated *in their own right*, without repression or defense (even "successful" defense). Surely one contribution—perhaps the major one—of modern psychology is the recognition that learning is just as powerful a determinant of human behavior as biological forces.

Beyond psychoanalysis lie theories that directly address the issue of actual structural and dynamic properties of healthy personality. On the first score we may invoke a principle of *integration* among structures, and on the second, one of *progression* in the development of dynamic systems.

Various theorists in the psychoanalytic tradition have criticized Freudian propositions and reached positions at least to some degree in line with these two principles. They question the strictly biological determinism of Freud by pointing to the role of socialization as a function of sociocultural conditions, enlarge on the autonomous role of the ego in controlling and integrating behavior, view the superego in positive as well as negative terms and allow for changes that occur at mature stages of development. However, for the most part these critics still focus primarily on neurosis, with principles pertaining to health resting on inference.

Both principles are clearly evident in the efforts of theorists such as Alfred Adler and C. G. Jung to revise and go beyond psychoanalysis, and are especially visible in the emergence of humanistic theorists.

BEYOND PSYCHOANALYTIC THEORY

Humanistic theorists identify forces in human instigation fundamentally different from those in lower animals. These impulses have been variously called striving for superiority (Adler), wholeness or selfhood (Jung), and self-actualization (Rogers, Maslow).

Whereas some theorists posit a single, universal force (e.g., Rogers), others treat such instigation as one among many motives (e.g., Maslow). Most humanistic theorists maintain that self-actualizing instigations are instinctive, but others have realized that they may be acquired through learning. Regardless of such differences, instigations such as seeking spiritual expression, aesthetic impulses, the search for truth or meaning, altruism, and the like are viewed as universal in human beings.

Self-actualization implies that the sources of developmental progress lie inside the person. The dominant trend in life is the discovery and release of these potentials.

Viktor Frankl criticized this conception of self-actualization. The process is actually a search for meaning. Behavior has a significance, a meaning, toward which we grope. Self-actualization is merely an extra bonus that we may gain. The central characteristic of truly human striving becomes *self-transcendence,* rather than self-actualization.

Progress toward self-transcendence depends on gaining greater control over our lives. There is never a situation in which there is no choice between alternatives, no matter how caught one may seem to be in some uncontrollable bind. The identification of alternatives is a first step toward freedom. Attempting to choose between them is the next step. In successive steps the more the process of choosing continues, the greater the potential advance toward freedom. No person can ever be completely free, but everyone can become *freer.*

Humanistic theories stress that intrinsic properties undergo continuous change over the life cycle. For Carl Rogers, the self serves as the focus, with reference to which perceptions are organized and rendered consistent. Experiences are progressively assimilated into this system, which becomes potentially better and better integrated, moving away from a purely personal value system toward "a continuing organismic valuing *process.*" A similar theme runs through Maslow's views: Self-actualizing people achieve a harmoniously functioning hierarchy of motives without conflict, in which the higher motives are no longer blocked by demands at a lower level.

Erikson treated successive periods in the life cycle as existential nuclear conflicts. Experiences in one phase influence later stages. Unless the conflict is successfully resolved, a person cannot successfully cope with later conflicts.

Psychological health, then, appears as a progressive integration of fundamental kinds of experience into an inclusive system. The healthy person at a given point in life has resolved previous nuclear conflicts and is therefore capable of dealing constructively with the basic problem of the current stage.

Jung discussed integrative progression in the development of personality. Jung recognized that the unconscious has a two-fold character: personal and collective. The former is the great body of complexes and conflicts, held in check by the ego's repressive function, which arise from the events of one's special kinds of experience during the socialization process. But this conceals the potential experiences of all human beings, namely, the *archetypes:* the common denominators of the human condition.

There are two reasons why archetypes are considered by Jungians to be universal in human experience and hence to recur in every successive generation. First, all human beings inevitably have similar experiences. Second, all human beings possess large and complex brains, an inevitable function of which is to identify, interpret, and manipulate one's experience symbolically. Thus whenever one starts to examine one's own experience and search for an understanding, one begins to discover archetypes.

The personal unconscious stands in the way of apprehending archetypes. Ego defensiveness in all its aspects stultifies progress toward humanness. These "hangups" characterize the neurotic.

The aim of development is to release the potentials of the collective unconscious and assimilate them to the self, a kind of mystic center in personality. The self is the realization of whatever wholeness or perfection one may achieve. Progress involves a process of individuation by which one becomes aware of the differences between conscious and unconscious and begins to recognize both one's own individuality and also one's membership in the human race. By bringing these awarenesses into consciousness, one discovers all the conflicting opposites in the human condition.

From this analysis emerges a view of healthy personality as a progression toward reconciling one's personal experience with universal humanness. One can think, feel, and act to a greater degree at a human, rather than a personal (ego-defensive), level.

PSYCHOLOGICAL HEALTH

In sum, psychological health is just as much a matter of the structure and dynamics of personality as is neurosis or any other developmental pathway.

Diverse though personality theories may appear, they are all concerned with some combination of instigation, regulation, meaning, and style. By examining the development, properties, and interrelationships among these functions, certain themes emerge that go beyond a mere listing of traits or the invoking of a few behavioral criteria such as "adjustment," "stability," "productivity," or "conformity."

With respect to structure, healthy personality can be seen as continuous change rather than as the establishment of fixed systems. In general, personality structures achieve an increasing harmony in which instigative,

regulative, conceptual, and stylistic functions merge into an inclusive whole.

ERIKSONIAN DEVELOPMENTAL STAGES
PERSONALITY
TRANSPERSONAL PSYCHOLOGY I, II

W. E. VINACKE

HELPING BEHAVIOR

Helping behavior is defined as an act that benefits others and for which no external rewards were promised. It is a category of prosocial behavior that encompasses all the positive forms of social behaviors that aim to benefit others. Helping behavior includes sharing, giving, aiding, and comforting.

Helping can result from numerous motives such as feelings of obligation, compliance with a request or threat, expectation of rewards, indebtedness, or compensation. The motives for helping behavior can be classified by moral quality. An altruistic motive is the highest moral level helping behavior. An altruistic act is defined as voluntary and intentional behavior carried out for its own end to benefit a person.

Directing psychologists' attention to this study were a number of influences: a social zeitgeist characterized by preoccupation with the improvement of the quality of life in the 1960s and early 1970s; the theorizing about moral judgment development by Piaget and Kohlberg; the pioneering studies of Berkowitz on socially responsible behavior of individuals toward others dependent on them for their goal attainment; and the studies of Darley and Latané about bystanders' intervention in emergency situations.

The majority of helping behavior studies investigated the conditions under which specific situational and personal variables facilitate or inhibit helping acts. It has become obvious that helping behavior is multidetermined and that the determinants relate in different ways, contingent on the specific situation and the specific personality tendencies.

Latané and Darley proposed a decision-making model of helping process specifically for emergency situations. Their model consists of five sequential decisions. First, the bystander has to notice that something is happening. Then, once the person is aware of the event, the event must be interpreted as an emergency. The person must next decide whether it is his or her personal responsibility to act. Once that decision is made, the person must decide what form of assistance can be given. Finally, the person must decide how to implement the decision to help. Piliavin and others suggested that the decision whether to help or not depends on several mediating variables: the extent of feeling of "we-ness" between the recipient and the potential helper as perceived by the latter, arousal, attribution of arousal, and the perceived costs and rewards for direct helping. These mediating variables, it was suggested, were influenced by situational characteristics, the potential helper's traits and state, and victim characteristics.

Bar-Tal suggested that two judgments—cost–reward calculation and the consideration of attribution of responsibility (the decision as to why the other person is in need)—determine the decision whether to perform any helping act. In addition, four types of variables appear to affect the judgmental process: personal, situational, cultural, and variables related to the characteristics of the person in need. Staub proposed a general model that specifies the manner in which situational and personality factors jointly affect helping behavior. Helping behavior occurs as a function of personal goals (motives); however, the activation of the behavior depends on the importance of the goal relative to other goals and the characteristics of the situation. Finally, Schwartz and Howard presented a five-step sequential model that involves (a) the perception of someone in need, as well as identification of potential helpful actions and recognition of one's own ability to engage in these actions; (b) generation of feelings of moral obligation; (c) assessment of the costs and benefits of potential actions; (d) evaluation and reassessment of potential responses; and (e) selection of an action.

Four major approaches have addressed the development of helping behavior, especially that of high moral quality: evolutionary, psychoanalytic, social learning, and cognitive developmental. The *evolutionary approach* looks for the biological and social conditions that may facilitate the development of altruistic behavior. Two views are presented. The first view holds that altruistic behavior is functional for human survival; therefore, genes for altruistic behavior were favored and multiplied in the population. The second view postulates that altruistic behavior has been developed through sociocultural evolution: that human beings are innately selfish, but that social evolution through cultural indoctrination countered the individual's selfish tendencies in order to promote altruistic behavior, which has a survival value for a group or society.

The *psychoanalytic approach* emphasizes the lasting effects of early experiences.

The *social learning approach* suggests that helping behavior is learned via interaction with the social environment. This approach emphasizes mainly reinforcement and modeling, but also induction and role playing as conditions that foster the acquisition of helping behavior. The *cognitive developmental approach* stresses the qualitative changes resulting from cognitive, social perspective, and moral judgment developments as necessary conditions for the development of high quality prosocial helping behavior.

An integration of the two latter approaches was proposed within a cognitive learning framework. This approach, while recognizing the influences of the cognitive, social perspective, and moral judgment development on helping behavior development, also emphasized the development of a self-regulatory system as a determinant of the development of altruistic behavior. According to this approach, it is the self-regulatory system that produces self-control—the ability to perform sacrificing behavior without expecting external rewards.

COOPERATION/COMPETITION

D. BAR-TAL

HEREDITY AND INTELLIGENCE

The respective contributions of heredity and environment to the development of human intelligence have been debated by philosophers as well as the general public for centuries. The position taken is often more determined by the participants' social-political-economic philosophy than by the evidence. The debate goes on even when the participants disagree concerning the definition and measurement of the trait that heredity and environment are supposed to influence. Most of the data related to the nature–nurture question are test data. This discussion focuses on the scores made on standard tests of intelligence.

Fundamental Difficulties

Because controlled experimentation is barred by our moral code, we are forced to turn to data that are difficult to interpret. The investigator is handicapped by several factors. In the first place, biological and cultural inheritance co-vary. Genetics is also a stochastic mechanism. Hypotheses must be tested probabilistically, but humans have relatively few offspring, and there is a long time span between generations. Pedigree analysis is difficult, at best, for traits determined by a single pair of genes, but most important human traits are polygenic in origin, rendering pedigree analysis hopeless.

As a result, the data concerning the broad heritability of human intelligence are based on comparisons of the size of correlations between various members of a family for scores on an intelligence test. These are called family resemblance coefficients.

The Concept of Heritability

Broad heritability, symbolized as h^2, is the contribution to the total variance of the phenotypic expression of a trait of genetic factors in a specific population. Theoretically, this variance can be broken down into the following components: additive genetic, assortative mating, dominance deviation, epistatic interactions, environmental, covariance of genetic and environmental, interaction of genetic and environmental, and measurement error.

Measurement Requirements

Correlational data for heritability estimates must meet certain measurement requirements, but the correlations in the literature involving the heritability of human intelligence are defective on almost every count. A listing of the essentials follows.

1. The population sampled must be carefully specified. Heritability is tied to a biological population developing in a particular environment.

2. The biological relationship must be carefully and accurately determined. The zygosity of twins in several studies, perhaps most, has been determined on the basis of inadequate criteria.

3. The sample studied must be representative of the specified population. It is difficult to justify anything other than a standard sampling design.

4. The sample size must be sufficiently large to permit determination of a small confidence interval about the sample correlation. Most investigators overinterpret correlations based on small samples.

5. In the optimum design, only one form of the test should be administered to the members of each kinship group. Two forms should be as nearly parallel as possible in spite of wide differences in ages of those tested. If multiple forms are used, the several forms must be parallel and accurately calibrated to each other.

6. The reliability of the tests must be determined by an adequate methodology, and in the sample to whom the test has been administered. The reported reliability in the test manual is inadequate.

7. The validity of the tests must be established. Standard tests of intelligence such as the Stanford–Binet or the Wechsler tests contain many components. The estimate of h^2 obtained from correlations involving the total score can be greater than that obtained from any one of the components.

8. Use of a surrogate for a standard test is unsatisfactory. Both years of education and occupation have at best only moderate validity.

9. The intercorrelations of estimated true scores over n occasions on standard tests of intelligence—or for that matter on standard measures of physique—during the first 18 years or so of development form a clearly delineated simplex matrix. Correlations between adjacent occasions are less than the reliabilities on each occasion and become progressively smaller, the larger the number of occasions intervening between the two test administrations. Intercorrelations over occasions for adults undoubtedly follow the simplex pattern also, but with slower rates of change there is less of a problem. There are at least two corollaries of this phenomenon.

(a) One cannot assume that heritability estimates obtained at one age are estimates of heritability at any age. This holds for both physical and psychological traits.

(b) Family resemblance coefficients must be obtained for populations controlled for age. One cannot assume, for example, that parent–child or sib–sib correlations are independent of age.

10. Comparison of heritability estimates obtained from different populations is hazardous at best. It is essential that means and variances of the phenotypic measures be reported and attention called to any evidence for differences in the range of talent in the two populations.

11. Adoption studies, including studies of twins separated at or soon after birth, require random assignment of children to available foster parents. In the strict sense, random assignment is always lacking. Evidence concerning the degree of selectivity along several possible dimensions must be obtained.

Missing Data

Future research can improve substantially on the data used to make estimates of h^2 by attending to the preceding standards. The data can also be expanded. Among the missing family resemblance coefficients are those involving half-sibs. These individuals should be separately categorized as to whether the relationship is through the mother or the father in order to control partially for prenatal influences. There are also no correlations currently in the literature for double first cousins or grandparents. Data are almost nonexistent for relatives outside the child's immediate family. There are also few data for American minority groups.

Precision of Heritability Estimates

For the present, about the most one can conclude from the family resemblance literature is that the correlations can be rank-ordered in the size expected from the genetic model, but one can draw the same conclusion from an environmental model. The more precise predictions from the genetic model, as compared to any current environmental one, are indeed an asset from the scientific point of view, but the advantage cannot be realized without having high confidence in the data.

Any precise estimate is suspect. A range of 0.20 to 0.80 for the heritability of intelligence in the American White majority represents a reasonable view of the matter. This wide range of uncertainty is disquieting for many, but it reflects the quality of evidence. When tied to a belief that there is an inadequate basis for the interpretation of test scores, or that data from tests can have no relevance for issues of social policy, the disquiet is unjustified.

IRRELEVANCE OF HERITABILITY ESTIMATES

Although family resemblance coefficients do fit approximately the genetic model—and might or might not fit more accurately, given better data—empirical observations, not theories, are the dependable bases for test use and interpretation. These observations are the relevant considerations for the determination of social policies. Empirical data do not control the formation of social policy, but social policies based on incorrect assumptions about the nature of the data are highly suspect.

Misunderstandings of the Concept of Heritability

The concept of heritability is widely misunderstood, and its implications are contraintuitive. If h^2 were to equal unity, let alone 0.80, it might still be possible to increase the mean level of intelligence in a population by the discovery of an environmental manipulation that is currently inoperative in that population. If the gain were constant, h^2 would still equal unity. If h^2 were less than unity, the use among the lower 25% of an environmental manipulation currently operative in the upper 25% of the population would increase the intelligence of the lower 25%, reduce the total variance, and increase the estimate of h^2. A high value of h^2 in a highly fluid, democratic society could mean that opportunity had been well equalized. High heritability does not inevitably lead to a highly stratified, static society. Disregarding the effects of assortative mating and given high h^2, the correlation expected between parent and child is only 0.50. Knowing the intelligence of the parent, we can place the expected value of the child halfway back to the population mean of the

parents. The genetic mechanism is a producer par excellence of individual differences. The expected variance about the regressed scores for children and parents, respectively, is 75% of the total phenotypic variance. Many liberals have feared high heritability erroneously and, in consequence, have rejected the possibility on grounds of their personal values.

Predictive Validities

There are many correlations between scores on intelligence tests and important social criterion measures showing that the test is measuring something important about people. Being able to estimate an individual's genotype as an intermediate step before the estimation of criterion performance adds nothing to the accuracy of the latter.

Intelligence and College Attendance

In a wide range of talent, the correlation between measures of parental socioeconomic status and a child's intelligence is about 0.40. This may or may not be environmentally determined, but the below population proportions of middle- and low-status students in high-status colleges, graduate schools, and professional schools—and thus in high-status occupations as well—is not by any means due solely to this relationship. An important determiner is the relationship between family status and college attendance. This correlation is higher than it ought to be in a country dedicated to equal opportunity and to the worth of the individual. The correlation between family status and intelligence of the student accounts for only a small part of the relationship with college attendance.

Inheritance of Privilege

Reported correlations between parent and child differ rather widely. A reasonable value for purposes of discussion is 0.50. On either environmental or genetic grounds, the correlation between grandparent and grandchild should be considerably lower. A value of 0.25 is reasonable. Therefore, it is highly predictable that high ability generally tends to dissipate over several generations more rapidly than high status or large fortunes. Social mechanisms protect low-ability offspring.

Education and Intelligence

Mean scores on intelligence tests with implications for increased criterion performance have shown marked increases in the United States, probably as a result of social action. One's best guess is that it was the result of the massive national effort required to produce an increase of about two and one-half years of additional schooling for the two age groups tested in 1917 and 1942. Between 1942 and 1960 the gain in mean years of formal schooling was little more than one year. Although there have been gains in this dimension since 1960, the gains in intelligence have leveled off or perhaps slightly reversed. Continuation of this effort shows little promise.

If the point of zero returns on number of years of formal education has been reached, is there a realistic prospect that additional returns could be gained by increasing the quality of formal education? The answer must be "maybe." The new and relatively firm finding that rules out "no" is the gain in reading comprehension of low-scoring 9-year-olds. One's best guess concerning the causes for the gains is the massive national effort to provide compensatory educational programs. There are no cheap or easy gains.

Modification of Fertility

When one looks dispassionately at the intelligence or status of persons at the low ends of these scales, one can support a policy to encourage those parents least likely to provide desirable biological or social inheritance for their children to have fewer children. The average child of such parents is below average in ability, although not as low as the parents. The environmental basis for a policy designed to accomplish a reduction in family size is at least as strong as the genetic one. Modification of birth rates as a function of either parental intelligence or status will produce a change in the mean intelligence of the children, no matter what the causes may be for their phenotypic level. This conclusion is completely independent of whether the mechanism is genetic or environmental.

COGNITIVE ABILITIES
HEREDITY
HERITABILITY
INTELLIGENCE MEASURES
NATURE–NURTURE CONTROVERSY

L. G. HUMPHREYS

HERITABILITY

Heritability can be thought of as the squared correlation between the phenotypic and genotypic values on a trait in the population. The heritability of a trait cannot be estimated from study of an individual, because h^2 expresses a proportion of the total variance in some phenotype, and variance depends on differences among individuals. Because h^2 is estimated in a sample of the population, it is subject, like any other sample statistic, to sampling error, the magnitude of which is inversely related to the square root of the sample size. Estimates of h^2 are also influenced by the amounts of genetic and environmental variability in the population sampled, and by the nature and reliability of the trait measurements. Thus h^2 for a given trait is clearly not a constant like π or the speed of light. It is more akin to a population statistic such as the infant mortality rate in a given population at a given time and in a given place under a given criterion for tabulating infant deaths.

Heritability can be most clearly understood in terms of the components of variance making up the total phenotypic variance of the trait in question. The total phenotypic variance V_p can be expressed as the sum of the following components of variance:

$$V_p = V_G + V_E + V_{GE} + 2\text{Cov}GE + V_e,$$

where V_G = genetic variance
  V_E = environmental variance
  V_{GE} = statistical interaction of genetic and environmental factors
  $\text{Cov}GE$ = covariance of genetic and environmental factors
  V_e = error variance due to unreliability of measurements.
The genetic variance, V_G, can itself be divided into four components:

$$V_G = V_A + V_D + V_{Ep} + V_{AM},$$

where V_A = additive genetic variance,
  V_D = nonadditive genetic variance due to dominance (interaction of alleles at the same chromosomal loci),
  V_{Ep} = nonadditive genetic variance due to interaction among genes at different loci, termed *epistasis,* and
  V_{AM} = genetic variance due to assortative mating (i.e., the increment in genetic variance attributable to the degree of genetic resemblance between mates on the characteristic in question).

Given all the above components of variance, one can precisely define heritability. There are two definitions, narrow and broad heritability, signified h_N^2 and h_B^2, respectively:

$$h_N^2 = V_A/V_p \text{ and } h_B^2 = V_G/V_p.$$

Estimates of h_B^2 sometimes include other components in the numerator:

$$h_B^2 = (V_G + V_{GE} + 2\text{ Cov}GE)/V_p.$$

In quantitative genetics, h^2 without subscript usually means heritability in the narrow sense, h_N^2; in behavioral genetics it usually means heritability in the broad sense, h_B^2.

The heritability (h_N^2 or h_B^2) of a trait is estimated from various kinship correlations, from which the various components of phenotypic variance can be estimated. The correlation between monozygotic twins separated at birth and reared apart in uncorrelated environments is itself an estimate of h_B^2. The regression of single offspring on midparent (the average of both parents) is an estimate of h_N^2 only, provided the offsprings and parents have not shared a common environment. (Hence the importance of adoption studies for the estimation of heritability.) The use of other kinship correlations involves much more complex formulas for estimating variance components and heritability.

Heritability is an important theoretical concept for understanding the sources of individual differences in behavioral traits: abilities, personality factors, and mental illness. However, three popular misconceptions about heritability should be dispelled: (a) It does not refer to the absolute amount or value of a trait or characteristic in an individual, but to the proportion of *variance* in the trait conditioned by genetic factors; (b) there is no necessary relationship between the heritability of a trait and its psychological or social importance; and (c) there is no necessary or absolute relationship between the heritability of a trait and its mutability in potential response to all possible environmental factors. That is to say, the proportion of trait variance attributable to nongenetic or environment factors (i.e., $1h_B^2$) refers only to variation in the environmental factors that are actually contributing to phenotypic variance in the population at the time h^2 has estimated. Such an estimate does not, and logically cannot, take into account the possible effects of environmental factors (or novel combinations of factors) that are not currently present in the population.

BEHAVIORAL GENETICS

A. R. JENSEN

HERITABILITY OF PERSONALITY

Heritability of personality traits is one of the oldest, as well as one of the most hotly debated, topics of modern psychology. The roots of such theorizing can probably be traced back several thousand years to Plato, who presupposed genetic determinants of ability.

It was the ardent belief during the eighteenth and nineteenth centuries that people were born as "blank slates" (*tabula rasa*) on which the environment inscribed the elaborate and detailed architectural plans for the developing personality.

One of the derivatives of the tumultuous sociopolitical and cultural changes during the early decades of the twentieth century was a need to look "inward" for answers to the baffling riddles of human behavior.

The pioneer in this area was Galton, who posed the simple, straightforward prediction that any differences between identical twins must be attributable to environment because genetic contribution had presumably been held constant. He further argued that differences between fraternal twins could be due to either heredity or environment. Galton's assumptions, although insightful, were not entirely correct.

Gottesman concluded that the component of variance attributable to genetics in social introversion was highly significant. Similarly, Scarr found that more than half of the within-family variance on social introversion–hextroversion in a large sample of twin girls was accounted for by genetics. There is substantial evidence to support Scarr's conclusion that "social introversion–extraversion is a basic dimension of responsiveness to the environment. . . . Twin studies find significant genetic contributions to it."

A longitudinal study examined the stability from adolescence into adulthood of personality traits with significant heritability. For the adolescent subsample, the depression, psychopathic deviate, paranoia, and schizophrenia scales of the Minnesota Multiphasic Personality Inventory (MMPI) evidenced significant heritability. This pattern did not carry over into adulthood where hypomania, the K scale, and ego strength showed significant heritability. Only anxiety and dependency demonstrated evidence of significant heritability at both ages. It is apparent that, although there is a significant component of heritability in the fashioning of personality, there are also considerable changes with age in which specific traits manifest signs of heritability. Investigators posited several explanations for age effects in the heritability of personality traits, one of which is that changes in genetic variance are a function of gene regulation and genotype—environment interaction and correlation. It is also possible that development is inversely correlated with genetic influence on a trait. That is, since development is most accelerated during adolescence, more traits would be under genetic control during this period. It is also apparent that the potential influence of the environment on personality is, at least in part, a function of time: the longer the exposure to prepotent events, the greater the probability of influence by those events.

At least one longitudinal study did find stability in the dimension of introversion–extraversion. Investigators followed children from birth to adulthood, discovering that the tendency to be socially inhibited was quite stable from age 10 to adulthood. In fact, there was even evidence for stability in this dimension from age 3 onward.

There are several other sources of data suggesting a heritable component in a general personality dimension of introversion–extraversion. An attempt to examine genetic contributions to personality was made by Claridge, Canter, and Hume. The sample of 44 pairs of MZ twins and 51 pairs of DZ twins was subjected to an extensive battery of personality, cognitive, and psychophysiological tests. According to the personality questionnaires, MZ twins were significantly more alike on sociability, self-criticism, and intropunitiveness, the last two traits being attributable to variations in anxiety and extroversion.

Another study examined the genetic and environmental contributions to sensation seeking in a sample of 422 pairs of twins. The investigators found that 58% of the variance in the overall sensation-seeking score, and 69% of the reliable variance (after correcting for test unreliability) was attributable to heredity. This heritable component is quite high for a personality trait and compares favorably with the research of Eaves and Eysenck, who reported that 42% of the uncorrected and 60 to 70% of the reliable variation in extroversion in 837 pairs of adult twins was attributable to genetics. Eaves and Eysenck found that the unitary trait of extroversion provided more powerful discrimination with respect to genetic and environmental determinants than either of its components—sociability and impulsivity—taken separately. Whatever gene action does control the general trait of extraversion, it appears to be primarily additive.

If we assume that introversion–extroversion is influenced by some genetic factor, that factor could be specific or polygenic. Most gene-determined human variability derives from polygenic effects. This amounts to the simultaneous occurrence of numerous minor aberrations which, when all lumped together, are not individually detectable. They blend into a Gaussian distribution for that trait. A polygene is something like a Mendelian major gene; it has a small multiply mediated effect on trait variation relative to all the variation observed in that trait. The expression of certain traits depends much more on the cumulative pulling power of all genes concerned than on a few nonspecific genes. Hence polygenes tend to be very sensitive to environmental factors. The principal alternative to polygenes are those disorders with specific gene etiologies. Huntington's chorea, for instance, is caused by one dominant gene, although as yet we are unable to trace the pathway from the gene to its behavioral expression. Phenylketonuria (PKU) is caused by two recessive alleles wherein a specific congenital metabolic error exists.

The cases of single-gene substitution are relatively straightforward. It sometimes happens, however, that a continuous distribution of genotypes results in discrete phenotypes for certain disorders. The disorder would appear to have a continuously distributed liability, and would be manifested when some variable exceeds a threshold. The phenotypic discontinuity is not genetic, arising only when the threshold is exceeded. There are many assorted quasi-continuous disorders such as diabetes mellitus, ulcers, and cleft palate. Some theorize that schizophrenia falls in this category.

If we wish to maintain that a personality dimension such as introversion–extroversion has a genetic component, we are in effect saying that a specific genetically coded biochemical error exists, which results in the behavior labeled as introversion or extroversion. The trait itself *cannot* be inherited. There must be some intermediary effect, such as a genetic code, which results in a biochemical error. Given what is known about the behavioral manifestations of introversion and extroversion, it is highly unlikely that it could be tied to a specific gene or, for that matter, exclusively to heredity without regard to the environment.

Although research on the heritable nature of certain personality traits has yielded highly interesting and encouraging results, these data should not be misinterpreted nor alternative explanations overlooked. It was noted at the beginning that Francis Galton made a fair assumption that MZ twins are genetically identical. This assumption is less a postulate of the laws of inheritance than a hypothesis. Darlington pointed out that intrachromosomal genetic changes (gene mutations or chromosomal errors at mitosis) may result in asymmetry. Indeed, it is even possible for two sperms to fertilize the halves of one egg.

A related issue is the determination of zygosity. The similarity method is the one typically used. This method includes several possible comparisons. Objective single-gene traits such as blood type and serum protein can be used. Morphologic features such as eye color, ear shape, and nose shape can be used, although these are less reliable. Ridge counts from fingerprints have also been used to determine zygosity. The ultimate test for zygosity is skin grafting, although this is obviously impractical for research purposes. In any event, monozygosity can be determined only with a specifiable probability, never with absolute certainty.

A cogent criticism of the twin research concerns the evidence that MZ twins are reared in a more homogeneous environment than DZ twins. That is, some of the variance in high MZ intragroup correlations may be accounted for by highly similar environments rather than genetics.

Finally, the relative contribution of genetic control over personality traits may well depend on the specificity of the traits or behaviors examined. Matheny and Dolan reported that "sociability was found to be an isolable and genetically influenced factor, but its relations with other factors of a social nature did not produce any evidence for a strong link between actions toward others and actions taken to be with others, a distinction between the quality and quantity of social interactions." Horn, Plomin, and Rosenman found certain aspects of sociability to be genetically influenced (conversational poise, compulsiveness, and social ease), whereas other aspects were more environmentally influenced (leadership confidence, impulse control, and social exhibitionism). The investigators concluded that although most definitions of sociability imply gregariousness or the need to be with people, their factor derived from "genetic items" was quite specific and limited to talking with strangers.

The question raised here boils down to what aspect of the organization of personality or of a particular trait of personality is genetically controlled. The problem we face is explored by Dobzhansky, namely, separating genetic fixity from phenotypic plasticity. Dobzhansky maintained "that an essential feature of human evolution which has made our species unique has been the establishment of a genetically controlled plasticity of personality traits. This plasticity has made man educable and has made human culture and society possible." Were we able to hold development constant, observed variance in personality traits would reflect genotypic variability. In reality, development is unique for every individual. Hence, variance in personality traits unequivocally reflects environmental factors. The question, then, is to what extent we inherit constitutional factors that influence the acquisition of certain personality traits. If something akin to "parasympathetic dominance" is inherited, then there is, in effect, a predisposition to behavior patterns that are labeled extraversion" (and the panoply of traits associated with it)!

BEHAVIORAL GENETICS
HEREDITY
HEREDITY AND INTELLIGENCE
HERITABILITY

R. A. PRENTKY

HEROIN ADDICTION

DERIVATION AND INTAKE
Heroin (diacetylmorphine), a derivative of opium, is a resinous mixture of 18 alkaloids obtained from the opium poppy (*Papaver somniferum*). The alkaloid of greatest concentration in opium is morphine, composing about 10 to 15% of the mixture.

Heroin is sold on the street as a powder, usually mixed with sugar or quinine in a typical ratio of one part heroin and nine parts adulterants. Heroin can be smoked, inhaled, or injected subcutaneously (skin popping). However, most addicts "mainline" by injecting heroin directly into veins of the arms or legs, or under the tongue.

During the nineteenth century, opiates, including morphine and heroin, were commonly used in a variety of medicines and were readily available to consumers. Concern over their addictive properties resulted in federal regulation. Initial regulations were generally ignored, but opiate use decreased with the enactment of stricter laws during the 1920s.

PHYSIOLOGICAL AND BEHAVIORAL EFFECTS
Heroin, in a fat insoluble form, enters the brain through the blood–brain barrier and binds readily to specialized receptors in the central nervous system. Two or more receptor sites appear to separately mediate the euphoric and painkilling actions of heroin. These receptors also bind endogenous opiates (enkephalins and endorphins), which have effects similar to some of those of the exogenous opiates. Heroin is completely metabolized by the liver within 4 to 5 hours after intake.

The behavioral and systemic effects of heroin vary among users but can be divided into two stages: a "rush," followed by a sustained feeling of euphoria. The rush has been characterized as an extremely pleasant whole-body orgasm which lasts 1 to 15 minutes; the euphoric phase lasts 3 to 5 hours. During this latter phase, aversive feelings and perceptions such as fear, anxiety, worry, and pain are dramatically reduced. Appetitive drives such as hunger, thirst, and sex are also reduced. Physiological signs of heroin intake include pupil constriction, increased skeletal muscle tension, respiratory depression, reduced gastrointestinal peristalsis, rapid eye movement (REM) suppression, and electroencephalogram (EEG) characteristics of a drowsy state.

DEVELOPMENT OF TOLERANCE, WITHDRAWAL EFFECTS, AND ADDICTION
With continued and frequent use, individuals develop a tolerance for opiates (i.e., increasingly larger amounts are required to produce the same effects). The degree of tolerance varies with the specific response and is directly related to the dose and frequency of intake. Cross tolerance among opiates also develops.

Withdrawal effects occur after heroin has been metabolized, and the severity of withdrawal symptoms is directly related to the frequency of use, typical dose level, and duration of use. Withdrawal effects appear also to be influenced by behavior patterns of the user and the social environment in which withdrawal occurs. Withdrawal symptoms for frequent users include anxiety, hot and cold flashes, yawning, runny nose, watery eyes, increased respiration and heart rate, sweating, diarrhea and vomiting, abdominal cramps, restlessness, back and extremity pains, dehydration, weight loss, and an intense craving for heroin. These symptoms frequently reach their peak in 30 to 40 hours and may last 3 to 5 days. They are relieved within 3 to 5 minutes following the administration of opiates.

There are significant differences in withdrawal symptoms among heroin users. Some experience only mild, brief symptoms, whereas the symptoms experienced by others are intense and last for days. Many heroin users withdraw periodically to reduce their tolerance levels, so that euphoric effects can be obtained with a smaller amount of heroin. Unlike withdrawal from some other drugs such as barbiturates, opiate withdrawal is seldom life-threatening.

Withdrawal symptoms are the primary defining characteristic of dependence or addiction. Dependence occurs when normal functioning cannot be maintained in the absence of a drug and is usually observed with the regular use of heroin over a 30-day period. Addiction can be situation-specific and time-limited.

The number of heroin addicts in the United States is difficult to estimate, but most authorities quote figures close to 750,000. Most addicts are found in large urban environments, but an increasing number have been reported in suburban areas and smaller cities. The incidence of heroin addiction is significantly higher in minority cultures. Although addiction has been observed in individuals as young as 12 years old, heroin use beginning in late adolescence is a more typical pattern.

DETERMINANTS OF USE
A number of studies have attempted to identify personality or behavioral patterns associated with heroin use. The greatest proportion of addicts do not fit into a single personality category, but vary greatly in behavior and personality.

PERSONAL AND SOCIAL RAMIFICATIONS
Frequent and continued use of heroin can cause significant impairment of daily functioning, which may result in loss of job and family. In addition, because of their lifestyle and methods of heroin intake, addicts frequently suffer from malnutrition, a variety of respiratory and circulatory disorders, and a reduced resistance to infection. However, most of the negative ramifications from heroin use are a result of its illegality. Because heroin is illegal, it may cost an addict as much as several hundred dollars a day to support the habit, causing many addicts to engage in criminal activity to pay for heroin.

TREATMENT
Traditional treatment programs for heroin addicts involve initial withdrawal from the drug followed by personal counseling, group therapy, and learning occupational and personal management skills. These programs focus on building new social and occupational repertoires, helping addicts achieve insight into their motivations for drug use, and attempting to alleviate some of the addicts' feelings of inadequacy and helplessness. The effectiveness of these programs has been quite disappointing. The proportion of treated addicts who do not resume their addictions following treatment ranges from 10 to 25%.

A more promising treatment involves the augmentation of skills training with the use of an opiate receptor agonist, a substance such as methadone (methadone hydrochloride), that binds to the same receptor site. Methadone is a highly addictive but synthetically produced heroin agonist narcotic that minimizes one of the primary incentives for heroin use—the heroin-induced rush and euphoria. Methadone does not produce the same degree of tolerance as heroin, and withdrawal effects tend to be milder. Methadone can be prescribed by certain physicians and, being legal, is inexpensive.

Legalization has also been suggested as a method of reducing the negative social impact of heroin use. The illegality of the drug makes it very expensive, encourages criminal control of supplies, reduces attempts by addicts to seek help, increases the rate of crimes by addicts attempting to support their habit, and requires substantial police time in enforcement. Legalization of heroin in Great Britain has not solved all heroin-related problems, but has successfully addressed many of them.

AMPHETAMINE EFFECTS
CHEMICAL BRAIN STIMULATION
ENDORPHINS/ENKEPHALINS
NEUROCHEMISTRY
PSYCHOPHARMACOLOGY
SUBSTANCE ABUSE

S. N. HAYNES

HETEROSYNAPTIC FACILITATION

Heterosynaptic facilitation (HF) refers to a basic mechanism for changed functioning in the central nervous system and is assumed to be involved in both nonassociative learning (sensitization) and associative learning (classical conditioning). Heterosynaptic facilitation is the effect of stimulation of one nerve that extends to afferent nerves not stimulated at that time. HF is a persistent phenomenon of increased synaptic transmission in convergent neuronal pathways. One brief stimulation may produce facilitated transmission lasting from several minutes to hours (short-term facilitation), whereas series of stimulations repeated over several days may produce facilitated transmission lasting for weeks (long-term facilitation). Neuronally, short-term facilitation is characterized by a broadening of the presynaptic action potential, and long-term facilitation is characterized by neuronal growth with an increase in the number of varicosities and in the number of active zones in the terminals.

HF was first analyzed by Kandel and Tauc and has since been extensively investigated in the "gill-withdrawal-reflex circuit" of the marine snail *Aplysia* because of this animal's relatively simple neuronal system with large identifiable neurons. If either the siphon or the mantle shelf of the *Aplysia* is touched, the siphon, mantle shelf, and gill are all withdrawn. Sensitization of this reflex takes place if a noxious stimulus is applied to the tail of the snail. The tail sensory neurons activate facilitatory interneurons that end on the synaptic terminals of the sensory neurons from the siphon or the mantle of the *Aplysia*. This axo-axonic activation of the sensory siphon neurons leads to a change in their terminals.

In the *Aplysia,* heterosynaptic facilitation also has been demonstrated to be involved in both simple classical conditioning and discriminative classical conditioning. If a light touch of the animal's siphon (conditioned stimulus) is immediately followed by a strong shock to the tail (unconditioned stimulus), and if this sequential pairing of stimuli is repeated every second minute for several trials, the conditioned stimulus alone will, in the end, be sufficient to elicit a strengthened withdrawal response.

Associative learning requires both temporal contiguity and contingency of the conditioned stimulus (CS) and the unconditioned stimulus (US). In *Aplysia*, CS must always precede the US within a time interval of about 1 second. Hawkins, Carew, and Kandel demonstrated that the spike activity in the sensory neurons of the siphon was most effective if

CS preceded the US by 0.5 seconds. A delay of 2 seconds prevented CS–US associative learning. In discriminative conditioning, the extracellular postsynaptic potential (EPSP) has been demonstrated to be activity dependent. This means that the EPSP in the neuron of the paired pathway is much greater than that of the neuron in the unpaired pathway (probably due to habituation in the unpaired pathway).

The intraneural mechanisms of HF are of special interest. At least some of the facilitatory interneurons are serotonergic. Serotonin release enhances transmitter release from the sensory neurons by activating adenylate cyclase, which leads to an intracellular increase in cyclic AMP. The result is a reduction in the outward K^+ current that prolongs the action potential and thereby allows for a longer period of Ca^{2+} influx. Similar to sensitization, classical conditioning also has been shown to depend on an increased cyclic AMP synthesis. Thus the molecular mechanisms responsible for the increase in spike duration during sensitization and classical conditioning seem to be similar. Abrams has demonstrated that Ca^{2+} influx is critical as an intracellular analogue of the conditioned stimulus. Abrams, Karl, and Kandel have explained on the basis of molecular mechanisms the temporal requirements in classical conditioning. Optimal conditioning required that a pulse of Ca^{2+} temporally overlap the addition of the facilitatory transmitter serotonin. The results indicated that Ca^{2+} calmodulin may serve to prime adenylate cyclase for optimal stimulation by the facilitatory transmitter. However, these details may vary with species.

In the *Aplysia*, spike activity in the postsynaptic neuron is not necessary or sufficient for eliciting HF and does not seem to be involved in conditioning of the gill-withdrawal reflex. However, in other species, such as rats, cats, and humans, activity-dependent synaptic changes do require postsynaptic activity in agreement with the Hebb model. Moreover, these changes have been directly linked to mammalian learning and memory. A mammalian analogue of heterosynaptic facilitation is long-term potentiation. LTP has been documented in several brain areas, including the hippocampus, visual cortex, prefrontal cortex, and frontal cortex.

ANIMAL MODELS
BEHAVIORAL GENETICS
ELECTRODERMAL ACTIVITY
NEURAL MECHANISMS OF LEARNING
NEURAL NETWORK MODELS
SENSORIMOTOR PROCESSES

F. K. JELLESTAD

HIDDEN FIGURES TEST

The Hidden Figures Test measures the cognitive style of field dependence and field independence. It was derived from the Embedded Figures Test used by Witkin and his associates. The Embedded Figures Test had two sets of 12 cards with multicolored shapes. The object of the test was to identify the simpler shapes within the more complex ones. The Hidden Figures Test uses a multiple-choice format for 32 items presented in black and white. The testee is asked to identify from five alternative shapes the one simple shape present in the more complex shape. The testee has 10 minutes to respond to all items. The score is the number right minus a correction factor.

FIELD DEPENDENCY
MEASUREMENT

R. S. ANDRULIS

HIGHER-ORDER CONDITIONING

Higher-order conditioning refers to the use of the conditioned stimulus from one phase of an experiment (CS-1) as the unconditioned stimulus (US) for further conditioning. In one demonstration reported by Pavlov, CS-1 was an auditory stimulus, whereas the original US was food, and the conditioned response (CR) and unconditioned response (UR) were both salivation. When the CR to CS-1 had been firmly established, a black square (CS-2) was presented briefly before CS-1. On the tenth pairing of the black square and the auditory stimulus, a salivary response—about half as strong as the response to the auditory stimulus—occurred to the square. This is an example of higher-order conditioning—specifically, a conditioned reflex of the second order. Pavlov found third-order conditioning possible, but only with defense reflexes such as those in response to shock. Fourth-order reflexes could not be established in dogs.

Typically the higher-order CRs were small in amplitude and long in latency and had only a short life span. This last fact follows from the consideration that the higher-order conditioning procedure is one in which the first-order CR is subjected to extinction: CS-1, now functioning as a US, occurs without reinforcement. Because of this, trials with the paired stimuli, following an early establishment of the secondary reflex, lead to its gradual disappearance.

The fact that higher-order conditioning is a somewhat evanescent phenomenon does not diminish its theoretical importance, which is that the reinforcement (US) in the higher-order conditioning procedure obtains its reinforcing power as a result of learning. In modern terminology, the secondary conditioned reflex is established on the basis of a secondary reinforcement. The process of secondary reinforcement has been of much greater interest in the field of operant learning than in classical conditioning.

CLASSICAL CONDITIONING
CONDITIONING
LEARNING THEORIES

G. A. KIMBLE

HISTRIONIC PERSONALITY

The label "histrionic" in the *Diagnostic and statistical manual of mental disorders* (*DSM-IV*) is relatively new, replacing the term "hysterical." As a concept, the classification of hysteria can be traced back to the early Greeks and Romans. In the mid-1840s, the symptom picture of clinical hysteria was broadened to encompass a personality type—one especially prevalent, if not exclusively found, among women. Theodore Millon listed the prime criteria for diagnosing the histrionic personality as follows:

1. *Fickle Affectivity:* displays short-lived, dramatic and superficial affects; reports tendency to be easily excited and as easily bored.

2. *Sociable Self-Image:* perceives self as gregarious, stimulating and charming; attracts fleeting acquaintances and enjoys rapidly-paced social life.

3. *Interpersonal Seductiveness:* actively solicits praise and manipulates others to gain attention and approval; exhibits self-dramatizing and childishly exhibitionistic behaviors.

4. *Cognitive Dissociation:* integrates experiences poorly, which results in scattered learning and unexamined thought; reveals undependable, erratic, and flighty judgment.

5. *Immature Stimulus-Seeking Behavior:* is intolerant of inactivity, leading to unreflected and impulsive responsiveness; describes penchant for momentary excitements, fleeting adventures, and short-sighted hedonism.

DIAGNOSTIC AND STATISTICAL MANUAL OF MENTAL DISORDERS
PERSONALITY DISORDERS
PERSONALITY TYPES

T. MILLON

HOLISTIC HEALTH

Holistic health addresses itself to the whole person. The first record of a holistic approach to health can be traced to China during the reign of the Yellow Emperor, Huang-Ti, almost 4000 years ago. This system of medicine, designed for the treatment and prevention of disease, was based on the use of herbs, acupuncture, and massage. A central element of the approach was *Ch'i Kung,* a body–mind discipline of breath control, physical exercise, proper diet, and mental discipline. The overall goal of *Ch'i* Kung was to enhance health, disease being considered an unnecessary accident resulting from loss of internal harmony and spiritual balance.

In the West, the two most influential approaches to health were systematized in Greece. Hippocrates (ca.460 to ca.377 B.C.) is considered by many to be the father of medicine. The Hippocratic method was strikingly similar to that of the Chinese, in that individuals were guided by physicians toward recognizing the natural state of health that accompanied living in harmony with themselves and nature. The roots of psychosomatic medicine and holistic health as practiced in contemporary Western cultures derived from the Hippocratic school, which treated the whole person in interaction with his or her world.

Galen (129 to 199 B.C.) provided an alternative form of treatment. While still treating the whole person, Galen suggested that pathology resulted from impaired parts, and that the diagnosis and treatment of organ-specific disorders were central to medicine.

Because of the overwhelming influence of the Christian Church, Galen's suggestions were subsequently repressed, whereas those of Hippocrates were followed. Hippocrates' work was treated as an affirmation of the Church contention that disease was a punishment from God. Not until the Renaissance did the open spirit of inquiry permit researchers to question the Hippocratic method and return to Galen's approach. The scientific method that evolved from this spirit of inquiry led to a deeper understanding of the human body and its functions.

Harvey's empirical studies corresponded well with the philosophizing of his contemporary, René Descartes, creating an attitude toward phenomena that led to the discovery of bacteria, antibodies, and most contemporary medical data. The goal of this medical tradition was to reduce treatment to the lowest common denominator, treat the malfunctioning part, and expect the human mechanism to return to normal functioning.

Such an approach attained tremendous success. With the findings of Pasteur and Koch that microorganisms caused disease, the Hippocratic tradition seemed to have been replaced by a physicalistic medicine.

By the 1930s, holistic medicine had emerged as a "new" psychosomatic medicine. This was in part due to the phenomenal success of physicalistic medicine. Many contagious diseases were now so controlled in the developed countries of the western hemisphere that new disorders became prevalent. Although it was not recognized at the time, these new diseases were lifestyle disorders. Coronary heart disease, cancer, and other illnesses resulted from prolonged exposure to certain personological or environmental contingencies and not from microorganisms. The physicalistic tradition evolved the only treatment its paradigm could comprehend: surgery. Hospitals grew larger and physicians became more specialized. As late as the 1970s, only 0.5% of our national health budget was spent on prevention, and only 2.5% on health education and health promotion. Yet more than 50% of the deaths in the United States were due to preventable disorders.

As physicalistic medicine continued its attempts to cure these new disorders, two major problems arose: the increased cost of health care delivery systems and the emergence of iatrogenic disorders. The cost of health care rose from 4% of the gross national product in 1950 to 7% of the gross national product in 1970. For every five people admitted to a research hospital, one acquired an iatrogenic disease. This meant that 20% of the patient population acquired a disorder caused by the medical treatment they had received. With increased specialization, the cost and hazard to patients increased.

Another reason for the trend toward a more holistic medicine was the increasing realization on the part of prominent researchers that health could not be maintained through a solely physicalistic approach. The person most responsible for this awareness was Hans Selye with his conceptualization of a general stress response emphasizing the interaction of individual and environment. Stress was a holistic concept intended to account for the failure of specific organs and the emergence of specific disorders through a description of a generalized adaptational organismic response to environmental stimuli. When prominent microbiologists such as René Dubos began suggesting that socioeconomic factors played more of a role in personal health than did antibiotics, holistic health gained additional prominence.

Other factors such as the nature of one's diet, cigarette consumption, alcohol consumption, substance abuse, and exercise habits also have been found to contribute to health or illness. These "lifestyle factors" pertain to the psychoeducational experiences from which people develop long-term behavioral patterns.

A third set of factors, related to personality, correspond closely with lifestyle patterns. One of the most popular and widely recognized elements within this dimension is the A-type personality. Two physicians, Meyer Friedman and Ray Rosenman, were the first to recognize and begin treating the A-type personality pattern.

It required the political and social environment of the 1960s to make holistic health a dominant force in U.S. health care services. People sought to participate in their health maintenance. Sports such as jogging became popular during the 1970s, as increasing numbers of people sought to "get in shape." The emergent concept of "wellness" drew professionals and charlatans alike to the booming business of holistic health.

In the 1980s holistic health became more respected. Empirical studies have demonstrated its efficacy, many charlatans have been exposed, and holistic practices have been integrated into medical settings. Scientific theory has not yet encompassed the ramifications of a truly holistic paradigmatic shift, and doing so may be difficult.

In pragmatic ways, holistic health has created a revolution in the health care delivery system. This is largely due to the financial constraints under which hospitals and insurance agencies have worked since the early 1970s. Only recently has preventive medicine become cost-effective for sectors of the health care delivery system. "Wellness" programs have been developed, while insurance companies have begun to encourage their clients to develop health maintenance programs to keep down medical costs.

As this process spread, this country's conceptualization of health was both broadened and clarified.

Holistic health is concerned with the physical, interpersonal, psychological, vocational, and spiritual dimensions of each service recipient. It is interdisciplinary in that dentists, physicians, clergy, sociologists, psychologists, counselors, educators, and business leaders are among the many professionals working together to create health-enhancing environments.

Holistic health is concerned with the enhancement of positive health as well as with the treatment and prevention of disease. Empirical data are derived from phenomenologically designed studies. Historical religious teachings are utilized as sources of data for such health strategies as yoga, meditation, herbalistic treatment, and acupuncture.

Holistic health is phenomenological in that it is based on the assumption that people are best treated within the context of their own lived worlds. People are best helped by services that are nonintrusive and that permit them to remain within their own home, family, and community. Services are most effective when they respect the health belief system of the person rather than imposing the service providers' belief system.

Holistic health is a cooperative venture. Authority and control are minimized as service providers move from the model of physician, patient, and prescription to the model of counselor, client, and contract. The self-responsibility for one's health becomes a central element to any health services provided. Self-responsibility implies the willingness and capacity of the individual to implement and maintain patterns of behavior that are health-enhancing. Often this requires the termination of a behavior pattern that is dysfunctional (e.g., cigarette smoking).

The process requires a strong sense of self-responsibility. Research on compliance to medical regimes suggests how difficult such a process may be. In many studies of patient compliance to physicians' prescriptions, noncompliance rates as high as 60% are found. The rate of failure to appear for scheduled appointments ranges from 20 to 50%.

Compliance to lifestyle modification programs fare even less well. In research conducted on weight-control programs, 90 to 95% of patients fail to achieve a desirable weight. Of people who quit smoking, up to 75% report resuming smoking within six months.

Noncompliance, a major problem for physicalistic medicine, becomes an even more serious issue for holistic health. Service recipients must be motivated to adopt and maintain positive behavioral lifestyles, which can be done best through enhancing their sense of self-responsibility and internal control.

If holistic health is successful in enhancing people's sense of personal empowerment and internal control, holistic health may make strides toward guaranteeing higher rates of disease prevention, voluntary compliance, and health enhancement.

Health services that use authority and control to coerce compliance may ensure short-term adherence to therapeutic regimes, but may not ensure the long-term maintenance of positive lifestyle behaviors.

The movement in holistic health toward the enhancement of an internal locus of control therefore offers the entire health care delivery system an opportunity to address the multidimensional nature of self-responsibility and its impact on personal lifestyles. It is hoped that the sense of personal power will generalize to other aspects of people's lives such as interpersonal relationships, work productivity, and family relationships.

To create voluntary change that is self-perpetuating, to move from a lifestyle oriented toward short-term rewards to one of long-term rewards, and to deinstitutionalize some medical services are no small tasks. Knowing what is best for one's health and practicing positive health habits often do not coincide.

Knowles speculated that personal inability to implement and maintain a health-enhancing lifestyle may relate to five factors: a denial of death and disease while maintaining a strong orientation toward short-term rewards; the belief that nature, death, and disease will be conquered through science; not wishing to live under certain socioeconomic or interpersonal constraints; depression; and lack of interest in following physicians' orders. These factors must be addressed if holistic health is to provide concrete gains in America's health.

The U.S. health care delivery system has experienced much recent change. Services that diagnose and treat disease remain important while health maintenance, health empowerment, and motivation become increasingly central to services.

The advances of modern physicalistic medicine are not ignored, but prevention is accentuated, and living in harmony with nature becomes central to positive health.

R. H. STENSRUD

HOLTZMAN INKBLOT TECHNIQUE

The Holtzman Inkblot Technique (HIT) was designed by Wayne Holtzman and others in 1961 to overcome the psychometric weaknesses of the Rorschach Inkblot Test. It contains the following features:

Test Material. A set of new blots was designed and the number increased to 45 to replace Rorschach's 10. A parallel set was also constructed. High equivalent reliability has been established between the two forms.

Procedure. The task assigned the testee is radically changed. The testee is limited to only one response for each blot.

Scoring. Twenty-two response variables are scored, and a weighted system of scoring yields a single numerical score for each of these variables.

Interpretation. Holtzman and his colleagues provided extensive data on the intercorrelations and factor analyses of the inkblot variables, as well as their correlations with personality inventories.

There is research evidence that the movement score measures imaginative capacity and ideational maturity, and that HIT differentiates between diagnostic categories such as schizophrenia and depression. Gamble summarizes the research in the following areas: examiner and set influences; developmental changes; cross-cultural studies; and the relation of HIT scores to cognitive processes, aggression, body image, and diagnostic categories.

Holtzman has shown little concern for the conceptual validity of HIT. The research has focused on relating separate inkblot variables to traits or diagnostic categories. The principal clinical use of an inkblot technique—that of describing the individual's personality—has been lost.

E. M. SIIPOLA

HOMELESSNESS

Even though homelessness is an age-old problem, its empirical investigation is only a decade old. More than 50 scientific studies of homelessness were conducted in the 1980s. As far as the problem proliferated, so did the research. More than 800 articles relative to homelessness were published in 1988, whereas only 30 had appeared in 1980. Special issues on homelessness have been published in the *Journal of Social Issues* and the *American Psychologist.*

Research on homelessness is fraught with controversy. There is lack of agreement about such fundamental matters as the following: What is homelessness? Who are homeless? What are the causes? How many homeless people are there? What are the consequences of homelessness? What are the solutions to the problem?

WHAT IS HOMELESSNESS?

Homelessness is more than the absence of a permanent address. It is a condition in which a very large and growing portion of people in the United States and most likely the rest of the world find themselves. It means being cut off from relatives, social groups, and community organizations and losing a sense of belonging to society. The psychological impact of homelessness can be as detrimental to one's self-esteem and well-being as the physical loss of a shelter.

WHO ARE THE HOMELESS?

Before the 1980s, homeless people found temporary lodging in such places as missions, flop houses, and skid row, but they were seldom without shelters. They were mainly older, unmarried, white men who had high levels of alcoholism, mental disorders, poverty, and social isolation. They were labeled bums, derelicts, winos, and psychos.

The new homeless include the working poor as well as women and children. They are relatively young and disproportionately from minorities (i.e., Blacks, Hispanics) and die at an average age of 50. Rapidly growing newcomers to homelessness are single women, adolescents, and families with children. About one third of the homeless in U.S. cities are entire families.

CAUSES

Research relative to homelessness pursues two separate causes. Some blame the homeless, who are viewed as troublesome misfits. Homelessness is thus thought of as situations composed of deviant persons who bring their condition on themselves. They are identified as primarily having alcohol, drug, and mental (ADM) disorders.

About 30 to 40% of the homeless population is affected by alcohol abuse and approximately 10 to 15% are drug abusers. About 10% have serious mental disorders, and some are multiply impaired. The statistics do not reveal whether these problems have come about before, during, or after homelessness. Substance abuse is not considered to be either the cause or the consequence of homelessness, but rather to be a preexisting condition aggravated by loss of housing. The proportion of mental disorders among the new homeless has not changed from that of the old homeless, even with the advent of deinstitutionalization.

There have been ten articles written on the mental health of the homeless for every article dealing with poverty, unemployment, or other economic causes leading to homelessness.

The second causation considered by researchers is the environment. Research frequently cites the underlying causes of homelessness to be extreme poverty and a dearth of affordable housing. In 1989, there were nearly 205 times as many low-income households as available low-income housing units. Among those who do have permanent homes as of 1992, close to 10 million have an income level so low that they are in danger of being added to the growing rolls of the homeless.

According to the *single calamity hypothesis,* homelessness grows out of a single crisis. Consequently, it would be difficult to predict which individual characteristics, experiences, and behaviors lead to homelessness. An individual crisis that occurs often to the homeless is a major illness. Thus the onset of poor health may lead to homelessness and at the same time also be a consequence of it. Another crisis is the loss of a job followed by a lapse into unemployment. Racism, particularly against Blacks, has played a powerful role in bringing about and perpetuating homelessness.

HOW MANY PEOPLE ARE HOMELESS?

As of 1992, more Americans were homeless than at any time since the Great Depression of 1929. The actual number of new homeless is uncertain, and the number cited largely depends on the study used. There are countless people unaccounted for who manage to live in temporary locations such as subway caves, empty buildings, airports, parks, jails, hospitals, clinics, single-room occupancy hotels, and treatment programs, doubling and tripling up with others, Cross-sectional studies have limitations, and the research is unsophisticated. There also is an apparent lack of longitudinal studies to trace individuals from entry into homelessness until they exit.

The ranks of the homeless have been swelling each year by 25%. There are more than 700,000 homeless on any given night as of 1992 in the United States. Other estimates of the homeless approach 7 million.

CONSEQUENCES

Homelessness often leads to stress, psychiatric disorders, and substance abuse; alcohol abuse is the most prevalent health problem. The cases of tuberculosis among the homeless is at least 25 times the rate among the urban population generally. Also among those homeless are AIDS victims, who are ten times more likely to be infected than members of the urban population in general. In addition, the homeless typically lack adequate medical care or access to treatment. Medicaid as well as other welfare benefits are often unattainable to the homeless.

Children

Children are at greatest risk for the detrimental effects of homelessness. Their number is growing faster than any other segment of the homeless population. Approximately 750,000 school-age children are homeless, and most suffer physical, psychological, and emotional damage. Approximately half of the homeless children studied had symptoms that called for psychiatric referrals. Their physical development may be delayed. Child care is difficult to find. In addition, children are susceptible to infectious and communicable diseases due to malnutrition, vitamin and mineral deficiency, unsanitary and overcrowded living conditions, and lack of immunization.

Among the homeless 3- to 5-year-olds, various behavioral problems have been observed, including difficulties in sleep, attention, aggression, speech, shyness, dependency, coordination, and toilet training. Children older than age 5 frequently act out their anxieties. The foreboding danger for children is the inevitability that they are virtually trapped into poverty with no escape from homelessness. Thus poverty and homelessness may become a self-fulfilling prophecy passed on through the generations.

Bonds between the homeless parent and children weaken, because parents are likely to assume a diminished role as disciplinarians and nurturers. Potential for child abuse is ripe when the frustrations of homelessness exceed parental self-control.

Far too many homeless children skip school, fail and repeat grades, perform below the average, test poorly in reading and math, and are functionally illiterate.

Adolescents

Each year about 1.5 million youths aged 10 to 17 are homeless. They are described as street kids, runaways, throwaways, and system youth who leave social service placements. Frequently, adolescents come from dysfunctional families in which they are physically and sexually abused.

Health and substance abuse problems are common as well as sexual experiences, which make adolescents vulnerable to hepatitis and AIDS. Approximately 60,000 homeless adolescents are infected with HIV.

Lack of supportive and functional families is cited as the key factor associated with homeless adolescents. Large numbers of homeless youth are depressed and at risk for suicide.

Psychological Trauma

Homeless people may suffer from extraordinary stresses (i.e., psychological trauma resulting from loss of housing, living in a shelter, or victimization). A symptom of psychological trauma is social disaffiliation (anomie), breaking the bonds of attachment to significant others and to social institutions. Homelessness leads to distrust of others and isolation.

A second symptom is learned helplessness. Traumatized homeless individuals come to believe that they have no control over their lives and that they must depend on others to fulfill their basic needs. Among the homeless who suffer from traumatic victimization are battered women, some of whom report having been abused in childhood. In addition to social disaffiliation and learned helplessness, traumatized women also may display other dysfunctional symptoms, and many are abusive parents.

SOLUTIONS

Homelessness impinges on everyone in some way. When food and shelter are lacking, individuals cannot reach their need of personal fulfillment or self-actualization. Human resources that could be applied to improve the quality of their lives remains untapped.

In our society, because homelessness results from poverty, the first priorities for helping the homeless include building affordable housing, providing income enhancement, and expanding health care.

The magnitude of the problem is so great that many believe only a federal effort to finance and administer such a project could eventually bring its resolution. Failure to act eventually will be costly to the public and in terms of human suffering. Temporary shelters will become a permanent feature of the American landscape, and the homeless will continue to multiply at an uncontrollable and unprecedented rate at home and abroad. The projected number of homeless in the United States could reach 18 million by the year 2000. About 7 out of 100 persons could be homeless in the future.

S. S. BROWN

HOMEOSTASIS

Complex organisms must maintain relatively stable internal environments to survive and move freely through the changing and often adverse conditions that surround them. "Homeostasis" is the name given to this constancy by Walter B. Cannon.

Cannon described his findings as instances of the maintenance of steady states in open systems. In 1926, he named this steady condition "homeostasis" and offered a set of postulates regarding its nature, upon which he later expanded, publishing an overview of homeostasis and the regulatory mechanisms identified up to that point. The body, he asserted, was able through homeostatic reactions to maintain stability in the fluid matrix surrounding the body cells, thus controlling body temperature, blood pressure, and other aspects of the internal environment necessary for life. Homeostasis was also maintained in the levels of supplies needed directly for cellular activities.

Cannon's concept of homeostasis emerged as a complex statement regarding the existence, nature, and principles of self-regulating systems. He emphasized that complex living beings are open systems made up of changing and unstable components subjected continually to disturbing conditions precisely because they are open to their surroundings in so many ways. Thus, while continuously tending toward change, they nevertheless must also maintain constancy with regard to the environment in order to preserve circumstances favorable to life. Adjustments within such systems must be continuous. Homeostasis therefore describes a state that is relatively, rather than absolutely, stable.

The concept of the open system challenged all conventional views regarding the appropriate unit of analysis of an entity. If the heart, lungs, kidneys, and blood, for example, are parts of a self-regulating system, then their actions or functions cannot be understood by studying each alone. Full understanding comes only from knowledge of how each acts with reference to the others. The concept of the open system also challenged all conventional views of causality, substituting complex reciprocal determination for any notion of simple serial or linear causality. Homeostasis therefore offered a new perspective both for viewing the behavior of systems of many sorts and for understanding people as members of open systems.

ADAPTATION
GENERAL ADAPTATION SYNDROME
GENERAL SYSTEMS
LENS MODEL
MIND/BODY PROBLEM

R. E. ENFIELD

HOMOSEXUALITY

Homosexuality refers to sexual behaviors, desires, attractions, and relationships among people of the same sex as well as to the culture, identities, and communities associated with them.

For conceptual clarity, it is important to distinguish among four different phenomena commonly included under the rubric of homosexuality.

First, the term is used to describe specific sexual acts. A second use of the term refers to enduring patterns of sexual or romantic attraction for partners of one's own gender. A third aspect of homosexuality is psychological identity, a sense of self defined in terms of one's attractions. In the United States, people who have developed an identity as a homosexual person typically refer to themselves as *gay,* with many women preferring the term *lesbian* for their sexuality. A final use of the term refers to a minority group membership.

Homosexual behavior does not appear to be limited to any particular era of human history. Our contemporary understanding of such behavior and its relationship to a larger cosmology, however, have evolved fairly recently. Modern attitudes toward homosexuality have religious, legal, and medical underpinnings. Before the High Middle Ages, homosexual acts appear to have been widely tolerated or ignored by the Christian church. Beginning in the latter twelfth century, however, hostility toward homosexuality began to take root and eventually spread throughout European religious and secular institutions. Condemnation of homosexual behavior as "unnatural," which received official expression in the writings of Thomas Aquinas and others, became widespread and has continued to the present day.

Many early American colonies enacted criminal penalties for sodomy. In some places, such as the New Haven colony, male and female homosexual acts were punishable by death.

By the end of the nineteenth century, medicine and psychiatry were competing with religion and the law for jurisdiction over sexuality. Discourse about homosexuality expanded from the realms of sin and crime to include pathology. This historical shift was generally considered progressive, because a sick person was less blameful than a sinner or criminal.

However, homosexuality was not universally viewed as a pathology. Whereas Richard von Kraft-Ebing described it as a degenerative sickness in his *Psychopathia sexualis,* Sigmund Freud and Havelock Ellis both adopted more accepting stances. Ellis urged that homosexuality be treated as a normal variant of human behavior such as left-handedness. Although Freud believed that homosexuality represented a less than optimal outcome for psychosexual development, he nevertheless asserted in a 1935 letter that "it is nothing to be ashamed of, no vice, no degradation, it cannot be classified as an illness."

The religious and legal perspectives nevertheless remained influential. Homosexual relations continued to be condemned by most major religions and were illegal in the United States and most other countries.

American psychoanalysis, psychiatry, and psychology treated homosexuality as a form of psychopathology during much of the twentieth century. This view became wedded to official government policies during World War II. Although homosexual recruits were often accepted during the early years of the war when the need for personnel was greatest, they were later expelled in a series of witch-hunts during the war's waning years.

Ironically, the mass courts-martial and discharges provided a major impetus for the development of lesbian and gay communities and the modern movement for gay rights. Men and women discharged from the military for homosexuality were ineligible for benefits under the GI Bill because of their undesirable discharge as a "sexual psychopath." Because the reason for their discharge was made known to their local draft board (which was not required to maintain confidentiality), they often were socially ostracized and unable to secure employment or attend college. Consequently, many gay people chose not to return to their hometowns and instead settled in large cities. There they developed social networks and a community, including bars and private clubs, in which they might meet discreetly to socialize and relax.

In the 1970s, these small-scale efforts developed into a movement for gay and lesbian rights. The signal event occurred on June 27, 1969, when the police raided the Stonewall Inn, a gay bar in New York City. Although such harassment was fairly routine, the patrons on that night did not acquiesce as usual. Instead, they attacked the police, and the ensuing confrontation erupted into a riot that lasted for 3 nights. In the months and years immediately following the Stonewall rebellion, the gay liberation movement flourished, influenced by campaigns for racial, ethnic, and gender equality that had matured during the 1960s.

One of the early targets of the new movement was the psychiatric establishment. Homosexuality had been included in the first *Diagnostic and statistical manual (DSM)* of the American Psychiatric Association, published in 1952.

The first published study comparing the psychological functioning of a nonclinical sample of homosexuals with comparable heterosexuals was conducted by Evelyn Hooker. She administered projective tests to gay men and to a sample of heterosexual men matched for age, education, and IQ. A panel of experts, unaware of each participant's sexual orientation, judged most of the men in both groups to be free from psychopathology. Furthermore, they could not differentiate the homosexual men from the heterosexuals at a level better than chance. Hooker concluded that homosexuality did not constitute a clinical entity and was not inherently associated with pathology.

Hooker's results subsequently were replicated in numerous empirical studies. In 1973, the weight of empirical data coupled with changing social norms and the development of a politically active gay community in the United States led the board of directors of the American Psychiatric Association (APA) to remove homosexuality from the *DSM.* Their decision was supported in 1974 by a vote of the membership.

The movement to declassify homosexuality as a diagnosis has been strongly supported by the APA since 1974. The APA has passed numerous resolutions supporting equal rights for lesbians and gay men in employment (including teaching and military service), child custody, and access to services. Similar moves have been taken by other professional and academic groups.

PREVALENCE OF HOMOSEXUALITY

Because of the stigma that continues to be attached to homosexuality as well as the difficulties of defining exactly who should be considered gay or homosexual, no accurate estimate exists for the number of gay people in the United States today. The figure of 10% is widely quoted, based on studies conducted by Alfred Kinsey and colleagues in the 1940s and 1950s. Kinsey, however, never assessed whether his respondents were gay. Rather, he asked them about their sexual behavior and fantasies and found that 10% of the males in his sample were more or less exclusively homosexual for at least 3 years between the ages of 16 and 55. For women, the corresponding figure was between 2% and 6%, depending on their marital status.

Unfortunately, no studies comparable to Kinsey's have since been conducted in the United States. Current data about human sexual behavior in general, including homosexual behavior and identity, are lacking. A review of five surveys with probability samples conducted between 1970 and 1990 concluded that the proportion of U. S. adult males who *report* homosexual behavior in adulthood is roughly 5 to 7%. These studies focused on men and addressed sexual behavior, not sexual attraction or orientation. A national telephone survey commissioned by the San Francisco *Examiner* in 1989 found that 6.2% of respondents described themselves as lesbian, gay, or bisexual. Because the considerable stigma attached to homosexuality deters many respondents from reporting it, and because not all individuals (heterosexual or homosexual) are sexually active, these estimates must be assumed to represent a lower bound.

BEHAVIORAL AND SOCIAL RESEARCH

Before the 1970s, the bulk of scientific research on homosexuality was directed at discovering its etiology. More recently, many researchers have recognized that the causes of heterosexuality are equally puzzling. Consequently, scientific inquiry now focuses on the broad question of the beginnings of sexual orientation.

Three competing perspectives can be identified within this area of research. Many researchers have assumed that homosexuality and heterosexuality are universal characteristics of human beings (some also have extended the concepts to other species) and have sought biological or environmental sources for sexual orientation. Biological explanations have focused on genetic or prenatal hormonal factors, whereas environmental explanations have considered early family relationships, classical conditioning, social learning throughout the life span, and other factors. Theorists favoring each of these variables have usually been able to find at least some empirical support for their theories and some empirical disconfirmation for competing views. Although the two general approaches were once pitted against each other in a nature–nurture debate, most researchers in this tradition now assume that biological and environmental variables both are important; their relative contribution to adult sexual orientation, however, remains unknown.

The second broad perspective on the origins of sexual orientation views sexual orientation as a phenomenon specific to particular cultures. According to this social constructionist paradigm, different societies organize human sexual relations in a variety of ways. Although female–male, female–female, and male–male sexual *acts* occur in all societies, they do not necessarily endow the actors with an identity or social role that corresponds to Western notions of heterosexuality and homosexuality. Consequently, any attempt to identify biological roots for sexual orientation is fundamentally misguided, because this involves seeking a biological explanation for a cultural phenomenon.

Striving for a middle ground between these two perspectives, some scientists have proposed a third approach. Although this interactionist perspective has not yet been stated in a definitive form, its general assumption is that commonalities exist among cultures in patterns of sexual behavior and attraction; these commonalities have a biological basis to some extent.

One benefit of the debate about sexual orientation has been concerning a pluralistic view of human sexuality. Scientists increasingly have come to appreciate that homosexuality and heterosexuality are not unitary phenomena, that even in our own culture different people develop and express their sexual orientations in different ways. Consequently, scientists increasingly believe that no single theory will explain the development of heterosexuality or homosexuality in all people. Indeed, some researchers have emphasized this view by framing their work in terms of heterosexuali*ties* and homosexuali*ties*.

Whether or not it is a universal human phenomenon, sexual orientation is experienced by most people in the United States and other Western industrialized societies as a deeply rooted and unchangeable part of themselves. Many adults report that they never made a conscious choice about their sexual orientation and that they have always felt the same type of sexual attractions and desires. Nevertheless, when homosexuality was assumed to be a form of psychopathology, psychiatrists and psychologists often attempted to "cure" it (i.e., to change homosexual people into heterosexuals). Even today, some psychotherapists and religious counselors try to change people in this way. The "success" of their techniques, however, is highly doubtful, and the ethics of their therapies have been challenged by many mental health professionals and human rights advocates. The majority of therapists now attempt to help lesbian and gay clients to adjust successfully to their sexual orientation, to develop meaningful intimate relationships, and to cope with societal stigma.

Many gay men and lesbians seek a therapist's help in acknowledging their homosexual orientation and disclosing it to others. "Coming out" can be especially difficult for people who have internalized society's negative attitudes toward homosexuality, and who believe negative stereotypes about people who are gay. Many psychotherapists devote special attention to helping their gay clients to overcome this internalized homophobia. Self-help groups now exist in most cities and on many college campuses through which gay men and lesbians share their coming out experiences and develop positive feelings toward their sexuality.

Just as the focus of psychotherapy with gay men and lesbians has changed in recent years, so too has the emphasis shifted in empirical research. Increasingly, studies of homosexuality address the problems and challenges faced by lesbians and gay men as a result of societal prejudice and discrimination. Perhaps the most important overall insight provided by such research is the realization that gay men and lesbians are no more homogeneous than the heterosexual population.

HOMOSEXUALITY AND STIGMA

Although antigay prejudice remains widespread in the United States, heterosexuals' attitudes toward lesbians and gay men appear to have become somewhat more accepting since the Stonewall rebellion. Numerous public opinion polls show that the majority of respondents continue to regard homosexual behavior as immoral. Growing numbers, however, oppose discrimination in employment on the basis of sexual orientation. Gallup polls between 1977 and 1992 documented a gradual increase in support for gay men and women to work in the armed forces, as members of the clergy, and as elementary school teachers.

The American public also has grown more supportive of efforts to repeal state sodomy laws. In 1977, equal numbers of Gallup respondents (43%) agreed and disagreed that homosexual relations between consenting adults should be legalized. The trend appeared to be toward greater support for legalization. In the mid-1980s, however, this trend sharply reversed, probably due in part to public concerns about the new epidemic of acquired immunodeficiency syndrome (AIDS) that, in the United States, disproportionately affected gay and bisexual men (most of the AIDS cases reported worldwide, however, were traced to heterosexual intercourse). In 1986, only 32% supported legalizing homosexual relations, whereas 57% opposed it. This also was the year in which the U.S. Supreme Court, in *Bowers v. Hardwick,* upheld the right of states to enact sodomy laws, despite an amicus brief opposing such laws filed jointly by the American Psychological Association, American Psychiatric Association, and American Public Health Association. By 1989, however, as the public learned more about AIDS, the trend had reversed again. In 1992, a plurality of Americans supported legalization (48 to 44%).

Despite these shifts in public opinion, sodomy laws still exist in nearly half of the states. In addition, discrimination in employment and housing on the basis of sexual orientation is not prohibited by federal law. Laws prohibiting such discrimination have been enacted in most major U.S. cities and in several states, however.

Prejudice against lesbians and gay men because of their sexual orientation has been called by several names. Most popular among them has been *homophobia*. This term suggests that hostility toward gay men and lesbians represents a clinical pathology rather than a social phenomenon similar to racism and anti-Semitism. Other terms such as *heterosexism* may better describe these attitudes.

Empirical research has identified several consistent correlates of heterosexuals' prejudice against lesbians and gay men. Individuals with more negative feelings are likely to be older, less educated, male, rural, and residents of the U.S. Midwest or South. They are more likely to attend religious services frequently and to hold traditional beliefs about the social roles of men and women as well as restrictive views about sexual behavior. They also are less likely to have had a close relationship with an openly gay person.

During the 1980s, public recognition of the problem of violence against lesbians and gay men grew. Reports of beatings, sexual assaults, and murders became more common. Small-scale surveys with samples of convenience indicated that a significant number of lesbians and gay men had experienced physical assault because of their sexual orientation.

In response to the violence, lesbians and gay men organized neighborhood patrols and service agencies in cities such as San Francisco and New York. In concert with members of racial and religious minorities, who also experienced an apparent upsurge in what have come to be called hate crimes, members of the gay community lobbied state and congressional representatives to enact legislation in response to the violence. Many states adopted laws that imposed severe penalties on hate crimes. In 1990, the Hate Crimes Statistics Act became federal law. It required that the government collect data concerning the prevalence and nature of such crimes to develop effective policies for combating them. The act was historic in part because it included antigay hate crimes in its purview and represented the first federal legislation to address explicitly the needs of lesbians and gay men.

In summary, views of homosexuality changed dramatically during the 1970s and 1980s. Generally, psychology now regards homosexuality as a different rather than pathological form of sexuality, recognizes the considerable diversity that exists among gay men and lesbians, and seeks to address the problems faced by lesbians and gay men as a result of the stigma historically associated with homosexuality in the United States.

ADOLESCENT DEVELOPMENT
AMERICAN PSYCHIATRIC ASSOCIATION
BISEXUALITY
DIAGNOSES
HUMAN SEXUALITY
PARENT-CHILD RELATIONS
PREJUDICE AND DISCRIMINATION
VIOLENCE

G. M. HEREK

HONESTY TESTS

The early classical research on honesty in the late 1920s led to a pessimistic view of the possibility of predicting honesty from paper-and-pencil instruments and suggested that honesty and dishonesty differed for the individual from situation to situation.

Business, industry, and government, faced with staggering losses attributable to employee theft, have attempted to deal with the problem of dishonesty in a variety of ways. The least standardized and usually least successful method has been the use of background investigations

and reference checks. Skilled field investigations by such organizations as the FBI, other federal police agencies, and some police departments have been fairly successful in identifying individuals with "bad records"; but many investigation programs are routine, limited, and very *likely* to miss critical relevant information.

A second method, widely used by government agencies and private employers, is the polygraph or lie detector preemployment interview. The polygraph is of use in identifying those who have committed past indiscretions, but probably not in predicting who are *likely* to commit defalcations.

The prediction of future behavior has been attempted by means of three main paper-and-pencil approaches: biographical data, standard personality tests, and more recently, tests designed specifically to elicit low-integrity attitudes.

The majority of psychologists involved in predicting lack of integrity or proneness to delinquency have used standardized personality measures under the assumption that future delinquency is predictable on the basis of indications of personality deviance such as antisocial personality, sociopathic personality, and psychopathic deviation.

Significant predictions of proneness to delinquency have been claimed for a number of measuring instruments. Among them are the Minnesota Multiphasic Personality Inventory (MMPI), the California Personality Inventory, the Id–Ego–Superego Test, the K D Scale and Checklist, and the Activity Vector Analysis. These are "objective" personality tests in which the examinees check "yes" or "no" to indicate that the statements included (e.g., "People are against me") do or do not describe them.

Other psychological tests and questionnaires share one important characteristic: From the point of view of the person taking the test or questionnaire, their intended function is *disguised*. The subject is generally aware that the test measures some aspect of personality, but the subject is generally not aware that the test is supposed to yield a measure of honesty or proneness to delinquency.

A number of tests were subsequently developed that are more direct in approach. In them, the applicant cannot help but be aware that honesty and integrity are at issue.

APPLIED RESEARCH
INDUSTRIAL PSYCHOLOGY
JOB SATISFACTION
LIE DETECTION

P. ASH

HOPELESSNESS

Hopelessness refers to a psychological characteristic defined by pessimism or negative expectancies. Within cognitive therapeutic approaches, hopelessness is viewed as a set of negative cognitions about the future. These cognitions have been implicated as relevant for understanding a variety of psychological problems such as depression, suicide, schizophrenia, alcoholism, sociopathy, and physical illness.

Although hopelessness historically had been linked clinically to affective problems, it was the work of Aaron T. Beck that resulted in the recent upsurge of interest in the concept. Before Beck's involvement, the supposed nebulosity of the concept of hopelessness had deterred attempts at its objective measurement, thus limiting clinical research and applications. As a result of clinical observations and on research demonstrating associations between pessimism and self-harm, hopelessness has now been quantified by the use of various specifically defined psychological tests. Hopelessness may be composed of interrelated facets representing negative feelings about the future, loss of motivation, and negative future expectancies.

Hopelessness is now regarded as the preeminent psychological predictor of suicide and its accompaniments, being linked in psychiatric patients to the presence of suicidal intent and suicidal ideation, and to subsequently completed suicides. Hopelessness, in fact, may be a more important predictor of suicidal intent than depression. When hopelessness is statistically controlled, previously significant associations between depression and suicidal measures become nonsignificant. However, when depression is statistically held constant, previously significant associations between hopelessness and suicidal measures remain significant. Thus emerges the suggestion that hopelessness mediates the association of depression to suicide:

$$Depression \rightarrow Hopelessness \rightarrow Suicide$$

Although the relationship between hopelessness and suicide measures is significant, the association is far from perfect. Not all extremely hopeless people are suicidal, nor are all suicidal persons necessarily hopeless. Nevertheless, hopelessness represents an important clinical sign of suicidal potential.

DEPRESSION
LEARNED HELPLESSNESS
SUICIDE

R. R. HOLDEN

HORMIC PSYCHOLOGY

Hormic psychology is primarily the result of the work of William McDougall.

McDougall defined psychology "as the positive science of the conduct of living creatures," equating the term "conduct" with behavior.

The term "hormic" comes from the Greek ὁρμή, meaning "urge." An urge seeks a goal. For McDougall, goal-seeking behavior became the core of a psychology of all living organisms. He described what constituted purposive or goal-seeking behavior: (a) The behavior was spontaneous; (b) it persisted until the goal was fulfilled; (c) it could be variable, so if a goal was not achieved in one way, the organism could try another; (d) a particular act was completed when the goal was achieved, but other acts would follow to achieve other goals; and (e) there was improvement with repetition. Although McDougall stressed the instinctive nature of goal seeking, some learning could occur.

McDougall set forth a theory of instincts that became an integral part of his system. An instinct had three aspects. First, for any particular instinct there was a perceptual predisposition to notice certain stimuli and not others. Second, there was also a predisposition to make movements that would lead to the goal. Third, in between the perception and the movements to the goal lay an emotional core that constituted the energy or driving force of the instinct.

McDougall listed 12 major instincts in humans. Subsequently, he added to the list, so that by 1932 it had grown to 17. At the same time the term "instinct," as applied to human behavior, was falling into disfavor among psychologists, so he changed the term to "propensity," although the basic concept remained unchanged. McDougall's original list contained the following instincts: hunger, rejection of certain substances, curiosity, escape, pugnacity, sex, maternal or paternal instinct, gregariousness, self-assertion, submission, construction, and acquisition. All instincts had an emotional core. For some of the instincts, McDougall could not identify the emotional core; nevertheless, he insisted it was there. The 5 instincts later added to the original 12 were appeal (crying out), laughter, comfort, rest or sleep, and migration.

Some more complex human behavior involved a combination of two or more instincts. These combinations were identified as "sentiments" when directed toward the same object. For example, a man's love for his wife involved both the sex and maternal instincts. McDougall believed that much of our social behavior involved the combination of instincts, but there was no single "social instinct" as such. As a result of these combinations, our social behavior could be accounted for.

The fulfillment of an instinct improved with repetition. Both the perceptual and movement predispositions could be modified. As a person grew from infancy to adulthood, the pugnacity instinct could change from early aggression toward the parents to later aggression toward a variety of other people who might constitute a threat, whether other individuals in the immediate environment or the enemy in time of war. These modifications were the ways in which McDougall explained learning.

McDougall accepted the doctrine that man was endowed with certain native capacities such as intelligence, musical or artistic talent, or an aptitude for certain mechanical or athletic activities. However, for the native capacities to become actualized, some instinct had to operate as a push toward their fulfillment. If no instinct operated, the potential would never be fulfilled.

McDougall remained the champion of a number of unpopular causes. He adopted an animistic doctrine of "soul," arguing for a bit of "soul" even in inorganic matter. He also believed in psychic phenomena.

Perhaps the most unpopular of his causes was the belief in the Larnarckian theory of evolution, which stated that characteristics acquired by the parents could be passed on to their offspring.

McDougall engaged in a debate with John Watson, the founder of behaviorism. In the debate Watson attacked the notion of human instincts in favor of learned behavior. McDougall retorted that Watson's denial of the concepts of mind or consciousness, which McDougall had accepted in his doctrine of "soul," eliminated a good deal from the legitimate subject matter of psychology.

R. W. LUNDIN

HORMONES AND BEHAVIOR

Hormones are chemical substances synthesized and secreted by the endocrine glands. The hormones are transported by the blood supply until they reach a target organ and regulate its activity. Hormones function in communication within the body, integrating and regulating bodily activities and responses. Thus they have important effects on behavior in human and nonhuman animals.

THE HORMONES AND ENDOCRINE GLANDS

There are three principal types of hormones. Peptide hormones are chains of amino acids of varying lengths. Steroid hormones are built about a particular structure based on a four-ring, 17-carbon aromatic nucleus. Biogenic amines are amino acid derivatives of tyrosine that also can function as neurotransmitters.

The master control gland of the endocrine system is the pituitary gland situated at the base of the brain just beneath the hypothalamus. The anterior pituitary secretes at least seven different peptide hormones. Adrenocorticotropin (ACTH) stimulates the secretion of steroid hormones by the adrenal cortex. Follicle-stimulating hormone (FSH) is a gonadotropin that promotes the growth of ovarian follicles and the secretion of estrogens in females and stimulates the formation of sperm in the male testis. Luteinizing hormone (LH) triggers ovulation and the formation of corpora lutea, modulates progesterone formation in females, and promotes the secretion of androgens in males. Prolactin functions in the mammary gland to initiate the secretion of milk and in the ovary in the maintenance of the corpora lutea and the regulation of progesterone secretion. The other anterior pituitary hormones are somatotropin or growth hormone, thyroid-stimulating hormone, and melanocyte-stimulating hormone. The posterior pituitary secretes vasopressin or antidiuretic hormone, which elevates blood pressure and promotes the reabsorption of water and oxytocin, which stimulates smooth muscle contraction as in the mammary glands and the female reproductive tract. Both are synthesized in the hypothalamus.

The pituitary gland is regulated by hormones from the hypothalamus. These are peptides that function to increase or decrease the secretion of pituitary hormones. The hypothalamic hormones include somatostatin, thyrotropin-releasing hormone, luteinizing-hormone–releasing hormone, corticotropin-releasing hormone, growth hormone–releasing hormone, and prolactin-inhibiting hormone.

A variety of hormones are produced by the gonads and placenta. Estrogens, such as estradiol, function in the development and maintenance of the female reproductive tract, in the stimulation of the mammary glands, in the development of secondary sex characteristics, and in the regulation of behavior. Progestins such as progesterone often work in synergy with estrogens in affecting the female reproductive tract, mammary glands, and behavior. Androgens, such as testosterone, influence the development and maintenance of the male reproductive tract, secondary sex characters, and behavior.

The central part of the adrenal gland, the adrenal medulla, secretes epinephrine (adrenaline) and norepinephrine (noradrenaline), which function to mobilize bodily functions in times of emergency. The outer covering of the adrenal gland, the cortex, secretes at least 28 different steroids related to metabolism and resistance to infection. Other hormones are secreted in the thyroid gland, the parathyroid gland, and the pancreas.

PHYSIOLOGICAL CONTROL AND EFFECTS OF HORMONES

The body possesses exquisite mechanisms for the regulation of the formation and secretion of hormones. In a typical system, a hypothalamic-releasing hormone acts on the pituitary gland to stimulate the secretion of a peptide. The peptide travels via the bloodstream to increase the secretion of a hormone by the target gland. This hormone has at least two effects. One is the primary function for which it has evolved. The other is to feed back to the hypothalamus and/or pituitary to decrease the secretion of the hormones that started the process. Thus in the pituitary–adrenocortical system, for example, the hypothalamus secretes corticotropin-releasing hormone, which travels to the pituitary to stimulate the secretion of ACTH, which stimulates the secretion of cortisol by the adrenal cortex. The cortisol has its effects on target tissues and the liver and feeds back to decrease the secretion of corticotropin-releasing hormone and ACTH. The system works in a manner similar to that of the thermostat found in many homes. Cold temperatures cause movement in the thermostat, which turns on the heat; the heat warms the house but also feeds back on the thermostat to turn it off. For this reason, the hypothalamic–pituitary–target organ system sometimes is called a *hormonostat*.

Hormones are believed to have their effects at the level of the cell by affecting the formation of specific proteins. The hormone enters the cell and binds to a specific receptor molecule to form a hormone-receptor complex. The complex is then altered in such a way that it can enter the cell nucleus and bind to nuclear components to promote the transcription of specific messenger RNA (mRNA); the mRNA is translated into specific proteins, which have physiological effects.

METHODS

Two methods for determining the amount of hormone present in a system have been in common use. Bioassays are based on the assessment of the effects of the hormone in a physiological system in the body of an animal, the biochemistry of which has been determined, so that the amount of hormone present can be estimated from the response in the system rela-

tive to a known standard. Most assays are now done using laboratory methods of radioimmunoassay (RIA). The amount of hormone present can be determined by incubating radiolabeled hormone, the unlabeled sample, and specific antibodies to the hormone. These are more sensitive and accurate than bioassays.

Many methods have been used in relating hormones to behavior: Correlational and experimental methods are the most common. With correlational methods, the natural variation in the amount of hormone present is correlated with variation in behavior. This method has been commonly used in determining correlates of the estrous cycles of mammals. Laboratory rats have 4-day estrous cycles in which the unmated female ovulates once every 4 days. This cycle is regulated by fluctuating levels of hormones in the female's body. On the day of estrus, the female shows a decrease in body temperature, food and water intake, and body weight, but an increase in running activity, and she becomes sexually receptive. With the advent of RIA assays it has become possible to conduct correlational analyses with respect to specific hormones in a variety of systems with much greater sensitivity than previously was possible.

EFFECTS OF HORMONES IN ADULTS

The examples discussed previously reveal the ways in which hormones act in adults to activate potential behavioral patterns. When the hormones are present, the behavior is displayed; when the hormones disappear, the behavior disappears. This reversibility of effect is characteristic of hormonal action in adults. The other element in this aspect of the system is the stimulus. The hormone does not trigger the behavior directly but sensitizes the animal to respond in the presence of specific stimuli. Thus presentation of a female to an intact male animal may produce mating behavior, whereas presentation of a male may produce aggression; both are influenced by the same hormones.

As noted previously, hormones may affect behavior by acting either on peripheral targets, such as the scent glands of gerbils or the antlers of deer, or directly on neural mechanisms. Alternatively, hormones may alter sensitivity in sensory-perceptual systems. For example, the receptive field of the pudendal nerve of female rats, which lies in the genital region, changes in relation to estrogen levels so that the female is sensitive to tactile stimulation over a larger bodily region when she is in estrus.

EARLY HORMONE EFFECTS IN HUMANS

Effects of early hormones in humans have been studied in relation to three syndromes. With progestin-induced hermaphroditism, female babies born to women who were administered progestins to maintain their pregnancies were masculinized. Congenital adrenal hyperplasia (CAH), also called the adrenogenital syndrome, is a hereditary disease caused by an enzyme deficit in the adrenal gland so that a genetic female produces androgen instead of cortisone. With androgen insensitivity or testicular feminization, a genetic male secretes testosterone but, because of an enzyme deficiency, the target cells do not respond to it.

In all three cases, there is an ambiguity of gender, and the individual may be assigned as either male or female. However, humans are quite different from other animals in various respects. In general, humans of ambiguous gender adopt the gender identity of the sex to which they are assigned and in which they are reared. Thus environmental effects are quite important.

Although individuals of ambiguous gender resulting from these three syndromes generally accept the gender to which they are assigned, various subtle effects of the early hormone abnormalities have been detected. In studies of the 1960s, the hormone-exposed females appeared more likely than other genetic females to prefer jeans to dresses and professional careers to homemaking. However, the culture has changed. In one study progestin-exposed women given personality tests were more found to be more independent, sensitive, self-assured, individualistic, and self-sufficient than other women. Subjects exposed to estrogen were more group oriented and group dependent. In another study, Ehrhardt et al. found rather minimal effects of exposure to diethylsilbestrol (DES); however, DES-exposed women showed less orientation toward parenting than did controls.

OTHER EFFECTS OF HORMONES IN HUMANS

Many other effects of hormones on human behavior have been reported. An important distinction in studies of human males, in parallel with that in other animals, is between motivation, desire, or libido, on the one hand, and capacity or performance on the other hand. Thus, in rats, estradiol benzoate (a form of estrogen) produces no facilitation of performance, as determined by penile reflexes measured in an "ex-copula" reflex testing apparatus, but some facilitation of copulatory behavior as displayed with a female, a procedure that includes motivational effects. By contrast, dihydrotestosterone facilitates ex-copula reflexes, but not copulation. Analogously, castrated and hypogonadal men show good erection to stimuli, but few spontaneous erections during the day. Thus castration decreases libido. With aging, by contrast, desire remains but capacity deteriorates. Castration has been used as a treatment of sex offenders, but its effects do not justify such treatment.

During the seventeenth and eighteenth centuries, castrati, men who had been castrated before puberty to preserve their high-pitched voices, played an important role in opera. However, many psychological and physiological abnormalities were caused by this treatment, including abnormal fat deposition, abnormally long arms and legs, and probably disturbances in psychosexual orientation.

In other studies, men who were winners of doubles tennis matches had higher testosterone levels than did losers. There was no such difference when prizes were awarded by lottery. Recipients of medical degrees showed increases in testosterone several days later. In another study, testosterone was found to rise just before most matches; players with higher testosterone levels generally did better. After matches, the testosterone levels of the winners rose relative to those of the losers. There is some suggestion of a relationship between androgens and dominance-related behavior that may apply to such situations.

Studies of hormonal effects in human females have been especially controversial because of possible implications for gender issues. There have been many reports of changing mood, performance in cognitive tasks, sensory sensitivity, sexual activity, performance of tongue twisters, and making precise hand movements during different phases of the menstrual cycle. Although there have been many negative results, there is a sufficient number of studies with positive results to suggest that at least some of these effects are real and reliable.

Even more controversial has been research suggesting a hormonal basis for sexual orientation, including homosexuality. The results are not conclusive, but it is clear that if there is an important endocrine effect, it is embedded within a complex web of dynamic interactions among genetic, hormonal, environmental, and social factors.

Hormones play a pivotal role in the integration and control of behavior in a wide range of species and situations. However, they do so only as part of very complex interactive systems, and thus simplistic interpretations of hormone effects are to be discouraged.

ACQUIRED DRIVES
ADOLESCENT DEVELOPMENT
ADRENAL GLANDS
ANIMAL PARENTAL BEHAVIOR
BIOLOGICAL RHYTHMS
ETHOLOGY
FIELD DEPENDENCY

HERITABILITY
SOCIOBIOLOGY
SOMATOPSYCHICS

D. A. DEWSBURY

HORNEY'S THEORY

In essence, Horney's theory involves a unique synthesis of Freudian and Adlerian ideas. Like Freud, she stresses the importance of powerful unconscious intrapsychic conflicts—a conception that Adler's holistic model specifically rejects. Yet she differs markedly from orthodox psychoanalysis in several respects: by dispensing with the construct of libido; by rejecting the assumption that all human beings are motivated by inborn illicit instincts such as incest and destructiveness; and by emphasizing the social, rather than the biological, determinants of personality.

CAUSES OF NEUROSIS

Every individual has the capacity and desire to develop individual potentialities in constructive ways and to become a decent human being. Psychopathology occurs only if this innate force toward positive growth and self-realization is blocked by external social influences.

Whereas the healthy child develops a sense of belonging to a safe and nurturing family, the child reared by neurotic parents becomes profoundly insecure and apprehensive and views the world as unfriendly and frightening. Alleviating this intense *basic anxiety* now becomes the child's primary goal, one that overrides its innate healthy desires and needs. To this end, the child rejects warm and spontaneous dealings with other people in favor of manipulating them to his or her own advantage. Thus the healthy quest for self-realization is replaced by an all-out drive for safety—the hallmark of neurosis.

MOVING TOWARD, AGAINST, AND AWAY FROM PEOPLE

The neurotic striving for safety is accomplished by exaggerating one of the three main characteristics of basic anxiety: helplessness, aggressiveness, and detachment.

The neurotic solution for *helplessness* is typified by excessive desires for protection and exaggerated, hypocritical compliance with the wishes of others (*moving toward people*).

The neurotic solution of *aggressiveness* is typified by the belief that life is a Darwinian jungle in which only the fittest survive (*moving against people*). Those who emphasize this orientation regard most other people as hostile and hypocritical, and are likely to conclude that genuine affection is unattainable or even nonexistent.

The neurotic solution of *detachment* is typified by avoiding intimate or even casual contacts with others (*moving away from people*).

Whereas the healthy person is free to move toward, against, or away from people as circumstances dictate, the three neurotic solutions are compulsive and inflexible. However, they are not mutually exclusive. In each instance, the two orientations that are consciously deemphasized remain powerful at an unconscious level and conflict with the dominant orientation.

THE IDEALIZED IMAGE

Those who suffer from neurosis repress not only their painful inner conflicts, but also the faults and weaknesses that they perceive—and despise—in themselves. Instead they form a conscious self-image that is exaggeratedly positive, and which reinforces the dominant neurotic solution.

This grandiose *idealized image* seems quite normal and realistic to its creator. The result is a vicious circle: The idealized image drives the individual to establish unattainable standards and goals that make ultimate defeat a certainty; this in turn increases the sufferer's self-contempt, intensifies the inner conflict between the fallible true self and the idealized image, increases the dependence on the idealized image; and furthers a compulsive and insatiable striving to bolster this unrealistic image by achieving glorious triumphs.

THE TYRANNY OF THE "SHOULD"

The relentless inner demands that aim toward the actualization of the idealized image resemble the workings of a totalitarian police state, a quality that Horney characterizes as "the tyranny of the should." These "shoulds" so dominate conscious thought, and so obscure the repressed innate healthy drives, that the sufferer no longer is able to recognize what he or she truly needs and desires. To liberate drives toward self-realization that have been so thoroughly blocked and to enable the sufferer to replace the compulsive and painful striving toward unreachable goals with activities that are enjoyable and rewarding typically requires formal psychotherapy.

R. B. EWEN

HOSPICE

The first American hospice was established in New Haven, Connecticut, in 1974. As of 1993, there were more than 150 operational hospices in the United States. A hospice strives for a holistic approach to the terminally ill, offering medical care as well as attention to the spiritual, emotional, and social needs of dying patients and their families. All hospices exist to enhance the quality of remaining life for those they serve. The particular and highly personal needs of dying patients are believed not to be adequately addressed or met by acute care facilities.

A holistic perspective on terminal illness implies utilizing the expertise and services of many people. These team members attempt to provide a maximally supportive, individualized treatment program for dying patients and their families. A team approach affords the best assurance of avoiding duplication of effort and service delivery gaps.

A major objective of a hospice program is to make it possible for patients to die at home in familiar surroundings with loved ones close by. A home care team is therefore essential to any hospice effort. The home care team usually consists principally of trained hospice volunteers who perform nonmedical functions. They are trained to be supportive and to communicate with the families about any issues and concerns regarding the approach of death.

Terminal illness often requires temporary hospitalization. The manner in which home care is interfaced with inpatient care results in three models of hospice programming. Each of these models has been used successfully by hospice organizations, frequently with modifications to fit the needs of a given community.

HOME CARE UNIT

Often organized as a church or service club project, the home care unit model is generally used by groups just beginning operations or in smaller communities. Advantages are organizational simplicity and economy. A disadvantage is that success depends upon how well the home care project can cooperate with already existing health care deliverers. Persons unconnected with the hospice have to be educated into an acceptance of the hospice approach to terminal care.

HOSPITAL-BASED UNIT

Hospital-based hospice operations are commonly found in large communities with a teaching hospital. One advantage of this model is that it makes use of an already well-coordinated health care delivery system and becomes an extension of existing services. The usual form of implementation is the creation, within the hospital, of a palliative care unit in which the special needs of dying patients are given priority. The home care team in this model operates under the direction of the palliative care unit staff. Continuity for the patient between inpatient and outpatient care is thus assured.

FREE-STANDING UNIT

The free-standing unit model, or full-service hospice, is the only model in which the hospice staff have control of all aspects of terminal care. A disadvantage of this model is that such a unit risks being viewed as competitive with other local health care facilities.

In each of the three models of hospice care, some general principles are apparent: (a) skilled pain control and symptom management, (b) physician-directed admission and treatment, (c) multidisciplinary care, (d) 24-hour, 7-day service, (e) consideration of patient and family together as a unit of care, (f) at least 1 year of bereavement follow-up for the family, (g) use of trained volunteers in all nonmedical aspects of care, (h) structured communication among multidisciplinary team members, (i) consultation or use of available community resources, and (j) provision of community education about death and dying.

LOSS AND GRIEF
TERMINALLY ILL PEOPLE

D. L. KITCH

HOSTAGE NEGOTIATIONS

The *contain and negotiate method* of hostage recovery is a technique of crisis intervention used to defuse and resolve situations in which a perpetrator holds a person's life as surety to barter for a goal. This method was formalized by Harvey Schlossberg, a psychologist for the New York police.

Prior to the refinement of the contain and negotiate method, traditional police response to hostage taking allowed three alternatives: (a) direct assault, in which police assembled an armed force with superior firepower and attacked the perpetrator's position; (b) the use of chemical agents to deliver tear gas or noxious smoke so as to force the perpetrator from cover and concealment; and (c) selected sniper fire, whereby a marksman was directed to sight and shoot the perpetrator. These techniques frequently resulted in injury or death to the perpetrators, police personnel, and hostages.

Alarmed by the killing of Israeli athletes in a hostage situation at the 1972 Olympics, New York Police Department authorities directed Schlossberg to research and design an intervention technique that would protect the lives of all involved in hostage incidents. The innovation uses personnel specially trained in psychological techniques for negotiating the release of the captives and the surrender of the captor.

The police negotiator must remain flexible in assessing and planning the operation, working within perimeters established by tactical police units to contain captor and captives in the smallest possible area and, by a sagacious show of force, to emphasize to the perpetrator that imminent escape is impossible. Hostage negotiators must propound each decision on the philosophy that the lives of all involved in the situation are sacred. Their main objectives are to protect those lives while using time and transference to negotiate a resolution that will allow each principal in the process to save face with his or her own constituency.

Effective use of basic interpersonal communication skills is primary and is supplemented by environmental manipulations that involve (a) the use of special lighting equipment; (b) music and sound; (c) the control of utilities such as heat, air-conditioning, electricity, gas, and water; and (d) food and potable beverages. Hostage takers are encouraged to verbally ventilate their frustration and anxieties to the negotiator, who is constantly striving to establish an "I-thou" relationship with the captor. The negotiator wishes to be seen as a "middleman" who eventually cooperates with the abductor to negotiate a safe, sane settlement to the situation.

Practically all demands made by the hostage taker are negotiable, with two exceptions: (a) supplying weapons or ammunition and (b) exchanging or providing additional hostages. Since its inception, the contain and negotiate method has been eminently successful in safely resolving the majority of steadily escalating hostage situations in the United States.

NEGOTIATION

W. R. FOWLER
J. L. GREENSTONE

HOT LINE SERVICES

The telephone hot line offers members of a selected community free, immediate, and anonymous access to a counseling service, typically provided by a trained volunteer worker or paraprofessional. The original purpose of these telephone-based counseling services was to give help in emergency situations. Subsequently, their function and setting broadened to include the provision of information, referral, and empathic listening for even minor problems in community mental health and college counseling centers.

The hot line has been understood as an application of technology that offsets the complexity and impersonality so common in a technological society. In particular, the telephone may offer certain unique features to a counseling process such as caller and counselor anonymity and caller control.

Historically, the hot line emphasized more effective employment of professionals in consultative and supervisory roles, together with the use for direct service of paraprofessionals indigenous to a target community. It also shifted to an active public health model aimed at reducing incidence, in part by teaching social competence and coping skills to populations at risk.

COUNSELING
SUICIDE PREVENTION
TIME-LIMITED PSYCHOTHERAPY

K. J. SHAPIRO

HOUSE–TREE–PERSON TEST

The House–Tree–Person test (H–T–P) is a popular projective test in which the testee is asked to draw three separate objects: a house, a tree, and a person. The testee is then asked approximately 20 intrusive questions about each drawing, including descriptions, interpretations, and associations.

The purpose of the H–T–P is to assess the personality and provide a measure of adult intelligence. The interpretation is based on two assumptions. First, the drawings are regarded as perceptions of oneself and one's environment: The Person represents the self, the House one's home, and the Tree one's larger environment. Second, through the drawings and verbal material, the testee provides clues to the details that have a special personal significance.

PERSONALITY ASSESSMENT
PROJECTIVE TECHNIQUES

E. M. SIIPOLA

HUMAN BEHAVIORAL RHYTHMS

The performance capabilities of a human adult vary considerably as a function of time, and some fluctuations are regular enough to be described as rhythmical. The most obvious behavioral rhythms are the daily or circadian, clearly illustrated by the many differences between the sleeping and waking states. But reference to the sleep cycle provides an incomplete account of the 24-hour rhythm. If wakefulness is artificially imposed at night, vigilance, pattern recognition, reaction time, coordination, and problem solving are significantly poorer around 0300-0400 hr than during the usual hours of activity. This accounts at least in part for the lower production and higher accident rate typically found in night shift industrial work compared to the day shift. Further, when repeated tests are given in a temporally balanced sequence during the usual time of wakefulness, mean performance on relatively simple tasks is generally better at the later testing hours than the earlier, by as much as 20%.

Attempts have been made to relate these behavioral cycles to such biological cycles as adrenal corticosterone production and body temperature.

Not all performances improve throughout the day. The increase in digit span from 0800 to 1030 is followed by a steady decline, in spite of the continuing rise in body temperature, and on more intellectually demanding tasks the highest score is likely to be made on the first morning test. It has been suggested as a working hypothesis that when memory load is low, the relation between temperature and performance is direct, but with high memory load the relationship becomes inverse.

Under normal conditions the individual's various functions maintain relatively fixed time relations to one another and to the sleep/wake cycle. When a change is made in the socially imposed living schedule, for example by transferring from day shift to night shift work or by traveling rapidly to a distant time zone, adjustment to the new regimen will occur almost immediately for some functions, but for others the process may require several days. During this transition period the usual temporal relations among the functions are necessarily lost—that is, there will be a state of so-called internal desynchronization, which may result in a variety of physical and psychological disturbances.

Less is known of behavior cycles shorter than and superimposed upon circadian rhythms. A basic rest/activity cycle (BRAC) of 90 to 100 minutes has been postulated, reflected not only in the rhythmic occurrence of rapid eye movement episodes during sleep, but also in changes in a variety of performance measures during wakefulness.

In many laboratory animals, rhythms approximating the periodicity of tidal, lunar, and annual environmental events have been clearly charted. In humans, the analysis of population data reveals systematic seasonal variations in birth rate, general mortality, and suicide. For some values there seems to be a significant relation to latitude, and in certain countries there has been remarkable consistency over the decades. The nature of the environmental factors that produce such regularities and the basis for the organism's responsiveness to them have yet to be ascertained.

ACCIDENT PRONENESS AND PREVENTION
CIRCADIAN RHYTHM
EMPLOYEE PRODUCTIVITY
RHYTHM

F. W. FINGER

HUMAN COURTSHIP PATTERNS

Courtship is an institution through which unmarried people and/or their kin interact to obtain a commitment to marriage. Societies differ in the extent to which courtship is parentally dominant or participant-run. Parents can exercise influence directly by arranging marriages or through threats of withholding needed material goods. They can exert control indirectly through choice of residence or school, or by inculcating values that will later guide their children's choices of mates.

In colonial America, the presence of a strong individualistic tradition and the absence of an entrenched kin network both conspired to weaken parental control, even though parents in this country were at the height of their influence during that time. Courting couples had relatively little contact with one another outside the parental home, reinforcing parental dominance. When dating began to develop during the nineteenth century, young men and women saw each other exclusively, but they were able to venture beyond their parents' view.

Recreational dating, in which each eligible adult had contact with several partners simultaneously and was under no obligation to pursue marriage with any one of them, was an outgrowth of twentieth-century social change. Whatever its form and function, dating as it was known through the first half of this century has waned dramatically. Single men and women are more likely to have group-oriented contact aimed at getting to know one another as companions rather than pairing off.

It has been hypothesized that couples pass through five successive stages in moving from initial contact to matrimony. During an initial contact stage, strangers communicate enough about themselves to allow each other to determine whether interest is sufficient to justify further contact. During the second stage they establish a linkage based on knowledge of each other as unique people rather than as stereotypes. They move to the third stage of friendship as they begin to develop a strong sense of liking for each other, and then to the fourth stage of close association as they reveal enough about themselves to become each other's confidant. Finally, they achieve a state of bonding premised on a relatively complete knowledge and acceptance of each other. Although societies or individual couples may truncate these stages, they represent stages of mate selection, attraction, and commitment that are virtually universal.

Studies of the sexual side of courtship have revealed that even during times of comparatively greater parental control, marriage-bound colonial men and women achieved a significant level of intimate contact. Although some differences in attitude persist between men and women, the majority of youth view sexuality as an expression of intimacy in relationships and value it as an opportunity for human contact as opposed to exploitation.

Cohabitation too has become a prevalent dimension of courtship. Researchers have defined cohabitation in a variety of ways, the common denominators being a couple committing to a shared living situation without legal or religious sanctions prior to separation or marriage.

Cohabitors tend to be bimodally distributed, the bulk being young adults, but with an increasing number of older persons opting for this lifestyle. Perhaps because of their youth, cohabitors tend to have lower annual incomes than their married counterparts. In addition, cohabiting couples tend to be less religious, urban, and more likely to have been married before than those who date or are married.

An expected higher rate of matrimony for couples who live together, as opposed to those who do not, has not been found. Nor has cohabitation been found to increase the likelihood of marital success, as contrasted with the experience of those who merely dated premaritally. For example, when contrasted with premarital daters, cohabitors were no less likely to experience infidelity in marriage. Further, they experienced roughly the same number of problems and were no more likely to have nontraditional sex roles with higher egalitarianism after marriage.

Although some two thirds or more of cohabiting couples will probably not marry, the vast majority of such couples express a desire to marry someone, if not their current partner, sometime in the future. Therefore, premarital household formation should be viewed as one variant of courtship rather than as an alternative to marriage for all groups other than the elderly, who may cohabitate rather than marry for economic, among other, reasons.

CULTURAL DIFFERENCES
RITES DE PASSAGE

R. B. STUART

HUMAN DEVELOPMENT

Life-span human development is the newest and most complex area of human research and theory. It includes the study of (a) the full breadth of life from conception until death; (b) the full depth of life from its changing biological, psychological, and sociological foundations to its dynamic expressions in feelings, thoughts, and actions in a wide variety of cultural and historical settings; (c) the investigation and development of life-span theories and methodologies for describing, explaining, and predicting developmental changes; and (d) the search for new means for optimizing the entire course of development.

The major advantage of a life-span perspective is that it creates a meaningful framework for relating and integrating separate age-related phases of life and significant life events to the entire sequence of human life.

THE BREADTH OF HUMAN DEVELOPMENT

The bulk of scientific publications on the human life span has appeared since the 1970s. Such records reveal that the three phases of human life needing the most exploration are adulthood (about two thirds of the life span), old age or gerontology, and death and dying or thanatology. For life-span developmentalists the study of aging and dying is as important as the study of infancy and birth, because (a) there is a need to establish the end point of life as well as the beginning in order to anchor and give direction to the rest of the life course, and (b) today more people in highly developed nations can expect to live happy and healthy lives well into their 80s, and perhaps enter into their second century of life. Predictors of successful aging, defined as survival until age 75 with good health and happiness, include being happy and healthy prior to old age, higher income and education, social activity (especially organizational membership), and a continued state of being single or married, as opposed to widowhood, separation, or divorce.

The modern study of adulthood is a growing but still developing discipline. The study of adult development will begin to become life-span–oriented as longitudinal studies explore the influences of infancy and childhood into later life. At the same time, research on the aging population characteristics will be pushed backward in time in the search for predictors of successful and unsuccessful aging. The life-span perspective views adulthood as a time of enormous growth and change.

The least explored territory of human experience is dying and death. Historically there has been a state of mutual and comfortable coexistence between the living, the dying, and the dead. According to Aries, during the Middle Ages (fifth to the twelfth century) the dead were buried in church courtyards, which were also public meeting places and playgrounds. Dying was gentle and expected; loved ones—even the children—gathered to witness it. The second period (twelfth to the nineteenth century) witnessed the gradual separation of the living from the dead. With the new Christian belief that the Last Judgment did not come at the moment of death but at the Second Coming of Christ, cemeteries were removed from church grounds, individual tombs were constructed with personalized inscriptions, and open mourning for the deceased began. The third view, which separated the living from the dead, started about 1930 (especially in the United States) and continued with little change until the 1970s. Most people would go quietly to hospitals for the special purpose of dying alone, surrounded by strangers and electronic gadgets and away from loved ones. Perhaps in sympathetic reaction to the cruelties of solitary dying, there has been an upsurge of interest in the dying process. Few have captured the essence of the final significance of dying better than Elizabeth Kübler-Ross. Her five stages of dying—denial, anger, bargaining, depression, and acceptance—may be viewed also as stages of living common to major crises throughout life: stepping-stones for learning to live, love, and create again.

THE DEPTH OF HUMAN DEVELOPMENT

Within the major discipline of life-span human development, the subdiscipline of *life-span developmental psychology* provides the greatest depth and breadth. It covers cognitive (learning, thinking, language, and intelligence) development, emotional development, and social development, while paying "lip service" to biological, historical, and cross-cultural determinants. The recent emergence of a life-span orientation in the sociocultural disciplines is reflected in sociology, cultural anthropology, and cross-cultural psychology. Historically related determinants of human development are finally being analyzed by psychoanalysts employing the same archives as the historians. They ask how each generation of parents and children created those issues that are later acted out in the drama of private and public lives. For example, L. de Manse proposes the following six major changes in parent–child relations during the past 2400 years. Each stage represents a significant improvement in child rearing:

1. *Infanticidal mode* (antiquity to fourth century A.D.). In this stage, parents routinely resolved their concerns over unwanted infants by killing through starvation, exposure, strangulation, smothering, or other means.

2. *Abandonment mode* (fourth to thirteenth century). It was now believed that infants had souls and therefore could not be killed. Children were now abandoned to the wet nurse, to the monastery or nunnery, to the foster home, or to the homes of the wealthy as servants. There was severe emotional isolation and physical abuse in the home.

3. *Ambivalent mode* (fourteenth to seventeenth century). Ambivalence, or simultaneous attraction and dislike, toward their own children resulted when parents permitted children to enter into the parent's emotional life. Because children now formed an integral part of the parent's own existence, the children had to be molded or beaten into the shape that matched parental self-images.

4. *Intrusive mode* (eighteenth century). Children were now viewed more objectively because they were less dangerous, since the parents had fewer negative feelings to project onto them. Parents could love their children more, which led to the birth of pediatric and public education.

5. *Socialization mode* (nineteenth to mid-twentieth century). The popular conception of modern childhood becomes fully developed. The special and prolonged needs of children are now honored by parents and society. Child labor and protection laws are enacted, and fathers begin to participate in child-care chores.

6. *Helping mode* (mid-twentieth century on). With the guiding assistance of loving and knowledgeable parents, children become active directors or full participants in their own development.

Optimally, the study of life-span human development seeks to integrate all significant determinants of human development.

LIFE-SPAN THEORIES AND METHODOLOGIES

There are no adequate theories or methodologies for life-span human development. Existing theories with life-span potential can be classified into two broad categories: the mechanical and the organismic. The three assumptions of the mechanical view are: (a) Development is due essentially either to genetic inheritance with "lip service" given to life's experiences or to life's experiences with "lip service" given to genetic determinants; (b) the person plays an essentially passive or reactive role; (c) development consists of sequences of small measurable increments or decrements. The three assumptions of the opposing organismic view are: (a) Development results from the interaction of both experience and genetic factors; (b) the developing person is the most important producer of his or her development; and (c) development consists of predictable, invariant, and qualitatively different stages. Perhaps the growing awareness that humans are both active and reactive is leading to a gradual integration of divergent views into more powerful combinatorial theories such as those of John Bowlby, who combined psychoanalysis and ethological evolutionary theory (based on animal research) and Albert Bandura, who combined learning and cognitive theories.

Life-span research is constantly seeking ways to extend its time limits. The standard cross-sectional research method measures different age groups (thus representing the life span) only once and all at the same time. The essential problem is that development varies both as a function of age and of historical life experiences. The standard longitudinal method measures the same age group repeatedly as they mature over the life cycle. The major problem here is to determine if the changes were developmental or due to increased skill in taking the same tests over and over again. These sources of errors can be significantly reduced by combining both designs into a more comprehensive cross-sequential analysis. In essence, fresh participants representing the various age groups continuously join the original research group over time.

ADOLESCENT DEVELOPMENT
ADULT DEVELOPMENT
INFANT DEVELOPMENT
LIFE-SPAN DEVELOPMENT
MIDDLE AGE
NEONATAL DEVELOPMENT
THANATOLOGY

J. O. Lugo

HUMAN FACTORS

These two words have come to designate a multidisciplinary applied science and a practitioner field centering on human considerations in modern technology: relationships between technological processes and products (systems, environments, machines) on the one hand, and their users (operators, decision makers, maintainers) on the other hand. Although the preponderant discipline is psychology, others include engineering (mostly industrial, electronic, and mechanical), computer science/programming, physical anthropology, physiology and medicine, industrial design, and education and training. Human factors scientists conduct experiments, surveys, and analyses to generate technology-related knowledge or solve applied problems; practitioners apply knowledge to technology development and use, working with developers and designers. The principal target has been the combined performance of humans and machines or the skilled performance or work of humans operating machines. "Ergonomics" (study of work) is the European and Asian counterpart of "human factors," emphasizing physiological effects as well as performance.

Human factors tries to improve human–machine–environment performance either by adapting the machine or the environment to human capabilities and limitations, or by adapting humans to machine requirements through training and selection. Machine–environment adaptations make up that portion of human factors called "human factors engineering."

Although some human factors research in printing and in vehicles and highways occurred earlier, World War II showed the need for studying and optimizing human factors in complex military systems such as aircraft, submarines, and radar. Courses and graduate programs in human factors were eventually established in about 50 universities in the United States and elsewhere. Initially these were found mostly in psychology departments, but the main locus shifted to industrial engineering. Nonmilitary human factors work in industry began at the Bell Telephone Laboratories but extended to many other major corporations.

For military users a weapon or vehicle had to perform as effectively as possible the first time it was operated in combat, and human factors science and applications could help. Some manufacturers began to incorporate human factors knowledge into their products because they were sued if they failed to do so and users were injured. Competition among interactive computer systems invigorated human factors, which investigated and improved the contents and formats of displays under software control. Many new forms of automation, both military and industrial (e.g., robots) also called for human factors support. One of the initial steps in a human factors analysis is to identify the tasks that should be automated and those that should be performed by humans, and then to devise the best combinations.

When human factors research and application began, they were focused on relatively simple problems. Displays and controls have continued to occupy human factors attention because they constitute the interface between person and machine, but larger assemblages—consoles and panels—came under scrutiny, and then entire systems or subsystems. Complex multivariable experiments were conducted to probe work-load capacity, procedures, and training techniques.

ENGINEERING PSYCHOLOGY
INDUSTRIAL/ORGANIZATIONAL PSYCHOLOGY

H. M. PARSONS

HUMAN INTELLIGENCE

The major, compelling issue is whether intelligence is one unified, comprehensive ability or a collection of different specialized abilities. Another issue is the nature–nurture controversy—the extent to which an individual's intellectual level is determined either by inborn genes or by the environment.

TESTS FROM NATIONAL SOURCES

Because of his interest in eugenics and his concern for perpetuating good human qualities, Sir Francis Galton in England assembled a list of sensory and motor tests in the belief that sensory and motor functioning was basic to mental capability.

There were also several sources of test development in Germany. Emil Kraepelin was concerned about assessing deficits in mental functioning in his patients. Hugo Münsterberg, an industrial psychologist, was concerned with assessing talents of employees. The Würzburg psychologists were using test items in laboratory studies of thinking processes, and Hermann Ebbinghaus was deriving methods of measuring the effectiveness of memory at different stages of memorizing.

The real breakthrough in test development came with Alfred Binet in France. He devised the first Binet Intelligence Scale in 1905. Binet rejected the simple "less mental" Galton type of tests in favor of items of the German type that emphasized understanding, memory, and thinking.

Binet took advantage of the known fact that the older the child, the greater the chances that an item would be answered satisfactorily. Every item could therefore be given a mental-age value.

These procedures implied that all items measure the same ability; they were all related to age. Binet, however, believed that different kinds of items measure different abilities. He even believed that there are several different memory abilities. But Binet's scale was meant to help make a single administrative decision, the identification of slow learners, by comparing mental with chronological age. Binet revised his scale in 1908 and 1911.

The most noteworthy initial use of intelligence tests in the United States was that of James McKeen Cattell in the late 1890s. After some study with Sir Francis Galton, Cattell brought Galton's tests across the Atlantic and put them to use with students at Columbia University. It was very disappointing, however, to find that the test scores correlated poorly to grades earned by students in many kinds of courses.

While Binet was developing his scale in France, Lewis M. Terman was experimenting with test items of the Binet type in America. Terman's eventual Stanford–Binet Scale was first published in 1916, with revisions in 1937 and in 1960. Advances beyond the Binet scale included the use of the intelligence quotient (IQ) instead of the mental age. The IQ was derived by dividing the mental age by the chronological age and multiplying by 100. Another advance extended the Binet scale to the superior adult level.

It became apparent, however, that the single IQ score provided by the Stanford–Binet was not equally predictive of success in various kinds of human activities. The most obvious gap was between verbal and nonverbal activities. One outcome was the development of David Wechsler's two scales: the Wechsler Intelligence Scale for Children (WISC) and the Wechsler Intelligence Scale for Adults (WAIS). In each case, from 11 scores on different kinds of tests two IQs, one verbal and one nonverbal, can be derived. From a combination of all 11 tests, a global IQ can be obtained.

SPECIAL KINDS OF TESTS

Group Intelligence Tests
During World War I the need to determine the intellectual status of military personnel called for a mass-production approach to replace the individual administration of tests such as the Binet type. Therefore, the Army Alpha Examination was developed and administered to thousands of servicemen. An Army Beta Examination was designed for the illiterate men. Group tests were also later produced for civilian use.

Primary Mental Ability Tests
Further distinctions in measurement were introduced by L. L. Thurstone after his landmark factor analysis. His Primary Mental Abilities (PMA) tests provided scores for seven different abilities. Showing the Thurstone influence, the U. S. Government's General Aptitude Test Battery (GATB) was soon developed. Aptitudes for numerous lines of work were covered by this set of tests. More recently the Educational Testing Service has prepared a larger collection of factor tests.

Test Batteries
During World War II, the U.S. Army Air Forces employed psychologists to improve methods for classifying its recruits for flight training. For measuring intellectual status, the multivariate approach was adopted. Further factor analyses were done, adding more new factors to the list of primary mental abilities to determine which group of factor tests would predict success in each assignment; various weights were given to different tests to maximize accuracy of prediction.

Different kinds of tests with different weights were predictive of success in different lines of training, as is also true in higher education.

There have been many other experiences showing the benefits of employing weighted batteries of tests for predicting success in different educational and vocational assignments of individuals.

Tests of Infant Intelligence
Even in a very brief history of intelligence tests, those made for infants should not be overlooked. A surprising and somewhat disturbing finding was that an IQ obtained for an infant with such tests did not correlate well with the IQ found in later years, perhaps because infants were showing different abilities than the ones presumably measured by the test.

THE NATURE OF HUMAN INTELLIGENCE
Apart from Binet, those who developed tests in the early part of the twentieth century showed little concern about the nature of intelligence, their main concern being whether the tests gave them practical information. Some psychologists, however, did ask, "What is this thing called 'intelligence'?" The quest for a definition was more or less brought to a halt when E. G. Boring somewhat facetiously remarked that intelligence is whatever the tests measure. This suggestion challenged those concerned to take a closer look at the tests themselves to see what they actually required the examinee to do in the way of mental operations to make a good score.

Intelligence as Learning Ability
Naturalists had thought of intelligence as ability to learn because it involves the individual's capacity for inventing new ways to cope with the environment. Binet and others had tied intelligence to the distinction between slow and normal learners in school. The net result of these experiments was the discovery that there is little relation between IQ and *rates* of learning in different tasks, and that the strength of the relationship varies from one task to another. The conclusion had to be that there is no one ability to learn. Furthermore, later experiments showed that *different* abilities are related to effective performance on the same task during learning, and that the importance of the different abilities changes as learning proceeds.

The Correlation Coefficient: Factor Analysis
The approach most often taken utilized the coefficient of correlation between pairs of tests.

Two tests that correlate positively are assumed to measure one, or perhaps more than one, underlying ability or abilities in common. If two tests correlate zero, they have nothing in common: They measure independent abilities or factors. If two or more tests have a factor in common, the nature of the ability indicated is decided by observing that those tests require the same kind of mental process from those who take the test. The underlying ability in common to two or more tests is known as a "factor." The procedure for finding factors from intercorrelations is known as "factor analysis."

HISTORICAL MODELS OF INTELLIGENCE
Over the years several types of models have been suggested for intelligence based on information from factor analysis. The models feature logical relationships among the factors.

Spearman's One-Common-Factor Model
The first model was suggested by Charles Spearman, the father of factor analysis. Spearman was convinced that intelligence has a unitary, comprehensive ability common to all tests of an intellectual nature. Each test has in addition, its own "specific" factor. The universal factor he called *g* for "general." Specific factors were labeled *s*.

Spearman finally admitted that there are limited sets of tests, each of which has something in common in addition to *g*. He therefore recognized what he called "group factors." He identified three of these factors as *verbal*, *visual*, and *numerical* abilities. He thought that there should also be a group factor for understanding the psychological events occurring in other persons, but he did not investigate the idea. Much later, four such broad abilities were identified by factor analysis.

Other Models of Intelligence
Followers of Spearman have held tenaciously to belief in a general *g* factor, but they have recognized a larger number of group factors of different breadth or generality. Cyril Burt and Philip E. Vernon suggested models that are alike in having a universal ability at the apex, with broader group factors under it at the second level, narrower factors at the third level, and so on.

The evidence for a universal ability *g* is questionable. The existence of *g* calls for positive correlations among all tests of an intellectual nature. In a collection of some 48,000 coefficients of correlation among such tests, it was found that 17% of them were below 0.10, with some of them zero and some even negative. The structure-of-intellect or SOI model developed by J. P. Guilford is the most comprehensive and detailed. It calls for 150 different abilities, of which 105 have been demonstrated, some of them several times and by other investigators. The remaining factors have not yet been demonstrated but are predicted by the nature of the SOI model because the model is systematic. In simplest terms the model is a cross-classification of basic SOI abilities in three dimensions: (a) kind of mental *operation* or process involved (such as memory or judgment), (b) kind of informational *content* (such as visual or verbal), and (c) kind of informational *product* (such as class or relation).

DETERMINERS OF INTELLECTUAL STATUS

Heredity
Of all issues holding the attention of psychologists and educators, probably none has generated as much heat as that regarding the extent to which individuals' intellectual development is determined by hereditary genes compared to environmental influences. The issue has importance also in social and political affairs.

Investigators of this problem have naturally used measures of status, and this has usually been in terms of IQ.

Erlenmeyer-Kimling and Jarvik have assembled data from numerous studies of similarities in IQs between pairs of individuals with different degrees of similarity in IQ and in home environment. From such data we can extract information as to how similar such pairs of persons turn out to be.

Identical twins reared together have a similarity index of 77%. (The index of similarity used here is the square of the coefficient of correlation, which indicates the extent of overlapping of two sets of things correlated.) This high rating is due to identity of heredity and a high degree of similarity in environment. Identical twins reared apart have a similarity in IQs of 56%. The difference between the two indices is 21, which reflects the difference in environmental conditions. On the whole, heredity seems to be far more important than environment. But the influences of the two determiners are not completely separable. To some extent they vary together, as when identical twins are likely to be assigned to homes with similar environments, and when parent and child have similar educational advantages.

Vernon concluded that we may attribute 60% of the determination of IQ status to heredity, 30% to environment, and 10% to combined effects of the two. This conclusion applies under the general run of conditions. Where there are special interventions from enriched environments, the balance goes more toward environmental determination.

The multivariate approach treating special abilities separately calls for more detailed information on the effects of heredity. It could well be that some abilities are affected by heredity more and some less.

Environment

There is a multitude of environmental influences that may aid or hinder development of intelligence in individuals.

Effects of sensory deprivation or of enrichment have been studied both in young children and in young animals. With the latter, the deprivation has involved keeping the experimental animal in a cage with uniform gray walls during the early days. With children, subjects have been chosen who had very poor vision or hearing during infancy. In both kinds of subjects, a common finding is subnormal development of brain cells and poorer performances. Sensory enhancement has involved environments rich with variations in lights and sounds and various objects to be encountered. The common effect on both kinds of subjects has been superior performances in psychological tests. Even handling lower animals produces improvement in behavior.

Orphanage life is another kind of environmental deprivation because the children lack the personal attention that would occur in normal families. These children generally show slower intellectual development.

IQs have been correlated with various *parental conditions* that might be expected to influence child development. Unfortunately, some such influences are also related to the parents' IQs, which contain hereditary contributions. Havighurst and Breese found that kinds of tests related to academic aptitude correlated higher with amount of parent education than did tests of nonacademic aptitudes.

In a study of environmental effects on intelligence it is pertinent to look into the amount and *kind of education* children receive. In England a study of canalboat children who attended school only 5% of the time showed their average IQ to be 70. The longer children live under this condition, the lower their IQs become. The average IQ was 90 at the age of 4, but dropped to 60 by the age of 12. Similar findings have been found in the United States. Vernon cited results in which children with poor educational advantages sometimes show marked increases in IQ when education is improved. Decrements in IQ with poor education are greater for verbal than for nonverbal tests, as one would expect.

Some studies of educational effects have considered the kinds of education rather than the amounts, as well as effects on different kinds of tests. One large study was done by Broyler, Thorndike, and Woolyard. Tests were given at the beginning and at the end of the school year to about 13,000 high school students; in between, the students took different kinds of courses. The greatest gains in IQ were found for students taking courses in science, mathematics, and languages; the smallest, for students taking dramatics and domestic science.

Nursery school attendance often results in increased IQs, but not always, depending on what kind of treatment is applied to the children. The same is true of effects of Head Start programs of recent years. The longer a child remains in such programs, the greater the benefits when they do occur. The best results are obtained by involving the mothers of the children in the program—in "selling" the idea of its importance so as to gain her cooperation—and by teaching the mother how to teach the child. Typical improvements in IQ under these conditions have been about 15 points.

Among the environmental effects on development of intelligence we may also consider *physiological* conditions. Some of these conditions occur before birth, some at the time of birth, and some after. The mother's blood is also the blood of the fetus. Consequently the mother's diet, the drugs she takes, and her habits of smoking or taking alcohol can affect the child's intelligence, as can even her mental condition such as stress. The birth itself may be particularly difficult, with possible brain injuries.

SEX DIFFERENCES

To what extent is intelligence related to the sex of individuals? This question has usually called for an answer in terms of one value, but it is much more meaningfully answered in terms of special abilities, for if there are differences in opposite directions for component tests, in a composite score those differences would tend to cancel out.

Differences in IQ sometimes favor males and sometimes females, depending on the age level and also upon the component tests. In the Wechsler Adult Intelligence Scale, for example, the averages favor males in five tests, females in four, and neither in two. The total score gives a slight edge to males.

Differences in Special Abilities

In other studies of sex differences using other special tests, the sex differences are also in both directions. In terms of the kinds of mental operations involved, males tend to excel in tests of cognition, whereas females show greater fluency of ideas. In terms of the major kinds of information, males excel in using visual information, and females in dealing with word meanings. These two differences seem to suggest that females have better left-brain development and males have better right-brain development (in right-handed individuals). With respect to kinds of items of information, females tend to excel when the abilities deal with units (words, for example), whereas males are more often ready to revise items of information.

RACIAL AND ETHNIC DIFFERENCES

General interests in peoples and in comparisons between them naturally involve questions about racial and ethnic differences in intelligence. Unfortunately we are not able to make any very positive statements regarding such differences. Good sampling of ethnic groups is difficult to achieve because both racial and ethnic groups appear in subgroups. There is also the question of what tests to use. Tests are developed and standardized within one culture. From an experimental point of view, test results are accurate for comparative purposes only within the same culture. There are no truly culture-free tests. Attempts to develop "culture-fair" tests have resulted in tests confined to visual content. All they can tell us is that different groups are nearly equivalent in visual abilities, other abilities remaining largely untouched.

One thing learned by factor analysis studies is that within groups that have had European-type education, tests have tended to measure the same factorial abilities in different racial and ethnic groups. With further efforts to achieve equivalent cultures, perhaps some desired comparisons can be made.

One or two somewhat consistent differences can be mentioned. Comparisons of Black and White samples in the United States show typical IQ differences of nearly 15 points in favor of Whites. The ranges of IQs for the two groups overlap considerably, with some Black children at the higher IQ levels. The Black–White difference depends somewhat on sex membership and upon what special ability is measured. The differences in IQ and in school achievement are smaller for Black females. Blacks do relatively better in rote memory tests and relatively poorer in visual tests. For other special groups, Jews tend to score higher than other White ethnic groups; Japanese and Chinese tend also to score higher.

GROWTH AND DECLINE

The story of intelligence is not complete without an account of how it develops and declines in typical individuals. The subject of intellectual growth may be considered along two lines. One may be called "quantitative" and the other, "qualitative."

Intellectual Growth

In studies of the quantitative approach, the question naturally arises as to whether the same abilities are being measured at different age levels.

The solution would be to determine by factor analysis the kinds of tests that measure the same factorial abilities at different age levels, but little of this has been done. There is already evidence that some of the factors do appear at widely different age levels.

A Growth Curve for an IQ Scale

Using mental-age levels obtained from the Stanford–Binet Scale, Thurstone and Ackerson plotted a curve relating mental age to chronological age. Mental-age values were transformed into values on an absolute scale of equal units and an absolute zero point. In the early years there is an increasing rate of growth, then after about 10 years a decreasing rate in an S-shaped relationship. The curve levels off somewhere after age 17.

Growth Curves for Special Abilities

Thurstone also produced S-shaped growth curves for some special abilities. All of them differ in the age level of the inflection point and in the age of reaching maturity.

There has been unusual interest in the development and the age of maturity of abilities that contribute to creative thinking. In tests of this kind, Torrance found what he called a "fourth-grade slump" for boys in various countries and cultures. There is recovery and renewed progress later. Other studies with similar tests show scores reaching maturity between ages 20 and 25.

Other studies have dealt with actual creative productions of outstanding quality by recognized creative people. Lehman and Rossman were leaders in this direction. The years of highest *quality* of productions, as rated by experts, varied for different fields (inventors, scientists, writers, etc.) but were generally in ages 25 to 30, or a bit later than occurred with *tests* of creative qualities. *Quantity* of production remains fairly constant, even into old age.

Qualitative Description of Growth

The most detailed descriptions of how intellectual functions grow have come from Jean Piaget. His chief motive was to learn how individuals acquire knowledge and use it.

What Piaget regarded as well-marked stages and substages begin with the infant and his stimulus–response "schemas." The infant observes the environment, but also observes the consequences of his or her actions and makes revisions if needed. Piaget's first two stages are *(a) psychomotor activity,* lasting from birth to the age of 2; and (b) *concrete operations,* lasting from 2 to 11, during which there is a stockpiling of items of concrete information that relate closely to the environment. The third stage, from 11 to 15, involves formal *operations.* This involves abstract ideas with the use of propositions and logical reasoning. Many individuals barely reach this level because they have lived in simple environments.

Intellectual Decline

One good source on the subject of decline in IQ is Wechsler. His curve of relationship between IQ and age after maturity of IQ shows a peak between 20 and 25, a slight decline to age 50, and a slightly increasing decline to age 75, which is as far as his curve goes.

When Wechsler considered declines for the special abilities measured by his 11 component tests, there were quite varied results. For example, the decline for his Information test shows very little loss even to the age of 75. On the other hand, the Digit Symbol test shows an unusually rapid decline after age 25.

There is additional information regarding declines of special abilities. From observations in daily life, loss of memory is a common failing in the elderly. Other abilities may have held up much better.

When abilities are distinguished as to kinds of items of information, the most notable loss is in dealing with systems such as series or sequences, and other patterns. This defect shows up when an elderly person shows difficulty in understanding complicated instructions and in remembering them when taking a test. It also shows up in failure to grasp the nature of a complex problem and in failing to solve it. There is a notable loss in flexibility, as shown in hesitation to change an item from one class to another, or to make changes in an item of information.

In considering declines in mental abilities, one must remember that the conclusions just mentioned pertain to the normal aging person. Owing to some conditions of health—hardening of the arteries, for example, with poor supply of blood to the brain—more drastic declines may occur. It should also be noted that such effects tend to break down the distinctions among special abilities, increasing intercorrelations among them because of the brain condition that affects abilities in common. On the brighter side, it should be remembered that abilities improve with exercise even in old age; continued intellectual activities could be applied to retard decline.

CONCLUDING REMARKS

A formal definition may now be stated: *Intelligence is a systematic collection of abilities or functions for processing different kinds of information in various ways.*

Although a single score such as an IQ is very useful for many purposes, the most meaningful and predictive testing is done in terms of unique mental qualities unambiguously defined. The story is by no means complete, but future directions are clear for the search for further information. The human family may thus be in a much better position to develop, control, and use its most unique resource: intelligence.

COGNITIVE ABILITIES
CREATIVITY MEASURES
FACTOR ANALYSIS
GENERAL INTELLECTUAL FACTORS
HEREDITY AND INTELLIGENCE
INTELLIGENCE MEASURES
STANFORD–BINET SCALE
STRUCTURE OF INTELLECT MODEL
WECHSLER INTELLIGENCE TESTS

J. P. Guilford

HUMAN POTENTIAL

Human potential (HP) has taken on a specialized meaning: the conviction, held by a widely varying group of practitioners, that normal human beings utilize only a small percentage of their positive potential. Further, these practitioners—representing many schools of thought and diverse training experiences—have spontaneously agreed to pool their varied approaches toward the general goal of fulfilling this potential. This development has gradually been recognized as the human potential movement.

As a development in the social and behavioral sciences, human potential has a number of distinguishing characteristics. First, it starts where psychotherapy concludes, with a normally functioning human being.

Second, the complexity of HP approaches makes it different from other forms of psychotherapy. HP is definitely a multimethod orientation based on the conception that each individual represents a unique configuration of abilities. By providing many different avenues of approach, the likelihood of utilizing some that are keyed to each individual is increased.

The contemporary roots of the human potential movement can be traced to the first decade of the twentieth century. The earliest principal figure was William James, who was clearly a precursor in three areas of human potential. First, as early as 1901 he was supporting the study of paranormal psychology as containing the possibility of a great breakthrough. Second, he conceived of the area of alternate states of consciousness and emphasized its importance. Third and most central, he described a program of investigation of human potentialities emphasizing the two major issues in the field: (a) documenting instances of individual high-level functioning, and (b) studying methods designed to produce such functioning. A second major figure in the development of this area is Dr. J. L. Moreno, generally associated with psychodrama, role playing, and sociometry. In both philosophy and technical innovations he provided the background for the development of many of the methods more recently evolved by HP practitioners. A third and more recent figure—generally credited as the immediate father of the HP movement—is the American psychologist Abraham Maslow, who defined the concept of "peak experience," collected instances of such experiences, and studied the conditions that fostered their development.

The current status of the HP movement is difficult to describe. In the 1960s and early 1970s, it was something of a fad. This aspect has faded, and something less well defined but probably more enduring has emerged.

Although the human potential orientation bears some resemblance to other forms of psychotherapy such as the client-centered approach with its emphasis on positive human functioning, its contrasts are more striking than its similarities. For example, all systems of psychotherapy tend to assume that their approach is better than any other. But because of the diversity of HP approaches, it is hard for its practitioners to be so ethnocentric.

A parallel concern for most psychotherapists is the issue of training criteria for practitioners. The more specific the therapy, the easier it is to establish guidelines and enforce them. But because of the multiplicity of HP methods, it is much harder to establish training criteria. The result is a wider diversity of backgrounds among practitioners.

Every psychological innovation is accompanied by a parallel social structure that provides the setting for the activity. In the HP movement this structure is the growth center. The original growth center, Esalen, on which all others were modeled, was developed in the early 1960s at Big Sur in California. The purpose of Esalen was to provide a setting for workshops on human potential topics. Unlike almost any parallel social institution, it had no connections with either the government, big business, or universities. Further, Esalen and the many other growth centers that it inspired were often located off the beaten track. Consequently, they were relatively free to experiment and offer any program that they wished, with only one basic limitation: People had to be willing to pay for the experience. Finally, because the centers were not identified with any particular method or school of thought, they did not get caught in the familiar bind of having to claim that the approach they offered was better than any other.

The growth center became the living expression of the human potential movement. It was the place where the methods were practiced and the people most interested in experiencing them could be found. Although it is difficult to establish a precise figure, W. C. Schutz estimated that in the early 1970s there were from 150 to 200 growth centers active in the United States. Although growth centers continued to function in the early 1980s, they have been supplemented and to some extent supplanted by more specialized organizations devoted to particular methods of inner work.

Because of the variety and complexity of HP approaches, it is extremely difficult to describe precisely what occurs, but a limited number of recurrent themes prove helpful. Perhaps the most familiar is the "peak experience." Without the recognition of this possibility of high-level functioning, the various methods employed by HP practitioners would have little meaning.

A second common theme, expressed in varying terminology, is that of "life force," viewed as a positive creative expression. The methods employed are designed to either increase the flow or remove the block of psychic, emotional, and physical tension inhibiting such flow. Health and growth are generally viewed as the expression and byproduct of this activity.

Third, it is generally assumed that people are quite similar on deeper levels of their experience, so that differential diagnosis as a criterion for group membership is underplayed.

Finally, there is a willingness to remove methods from the context in which they were developed and still find them useful. Thus a Zen breath meditation may be used in conjunction with a creative brainstorming exercise, although they come from totally different types of social and cultural developments. This may do some violence to the subtleties involved in each experience, but it facilitates effective combinations that might not otherwise occur. This possibility is a hallmark both of the HP movement and to some extent of the times.

HUMANISTIC PSYCHOLOGY
MEDITATION
PSYCHOTHERAPY

J. H. MANN

HUMAN RELATIONS TRAINING

There are two central thrusts to human relations training: (a) self-awareness, especially awareness of the impact of the self on others in the group; and (b) group dynamics, including the processes of group development, group roles, task versus maintenance functions in groups, and issues involved in intergroup relations. When human relations training focuses on the individual manager and the enhancement of his or her individual management style, with only secondary attention to the organizational context in which these skills are to be applied, such training is one kind of *management development*. When, in contrast, human relations training is conducted in the workplace with intact work teams, the process is called team building, a strategy used in *organization development*. The following discussion deals only with human relations training in the first context, management development.

In human relations training for self-awareness, one useful concept is the "Johari Window." In the Johari Window, Quadrant 1, the open or public quadrant, represents the behaviors known to the self and to others. Quadrant 2, the blind quadrant, represents behaviors known to others but not to the self, while Quadrant 3, the hidden area, refers to behaviors known to the self but not to others. The unknown quadrant, Quadrant 4, represents behaviors known by neither self nor others. One important goal of human relations training is to increase the size of the public area (Quadrant 1) and to reduce the blind and hidden areas (Quadrants 2 and 3).

The enlarged public area with its heightened self-awareness leads to greater interpersonal competence, especially in group settings. Such personal development is typically accomplished by participation in a training or T-group, sometimes also called a sensitivity training group. There, in a relatively unstructured fashion, a group of 10 to 12 strangers plus one or two facilitators create a laboratory environment in an atmosphere of trust, nondefensiveness, and warmth in order to pursue heightened self-awareness. Such programs typically last from 2 to 6 days.

The research evidence on the effectiveness of human relations training suggests that, although such training does produce clearly discernible positive changes in behavior, there is little evidence that the effects of training transfer to the participant's home situation.

HAWTHORNE EFFECT
T-GROUPS

L. D. GOODSTEIN

HUMAN SERVICES

The field of human services, an applied social science, is ever expanding and constantly changing. Included under the rubric of human services are physicians, psychiatrists, psychologists, counselors, social workers, rehabilitation and correctional workers, vocational specialists, and the like, plus aides, paraprofessionals, and laymen with special skills.

Human services are historically related to the field of mental health. Progress has been made in fostering a scientific approach to mental illness, leading to the expansion of the human services field.

Through the course of history some philosophers and healers maintained an enlightened point of view with regard to mental afflictions. The first revolutionary period in mental health, the moral revolution, occurred in the eighteenth century with the work of Philippe Pinel, a French physician. He urged a more humane treatment of the mentally ill. In addition to the unshackling of patients, he believed in kindness, fresh air, and consideration of the role of the emotions in mental and physical disturbances.

The second revolutionary period in mental health stressed dynamic psychiatry and psychology as vital forces in the understanding and treatment of emotionally disturbed individuals. This period began in the latter half of the nineteenth century with the advent of psychoanalysis and the contribution of its founder, Sigmund Freud. Adolf Meyer believed strongly that mental illness is a result of learned inappropriate behavior patterns: Hence psychotherapy was essentially a process of reeducation in which healthy patterns of behavior were to replace the old ones. Significant too was the establishment of the National Association for Mental Health.

The third revolutionary advance in mental health came about in the 1950s with the introduction of psychopharmacological agents that proved helpful in decreasing destructive and bizarre behavior. The resultant improvement in patient self-management was followed by a fourth revolutionary approach wherein hospitalized and institutionalized patients were released from confinement and then treated within their own community. This change has had a great effect on the development of the human services field.

The experience of men under arms during World Wars I and II underlined the need for improvement in mental health care. The public was forced to recognize the nature of mental illness, and the shortage of personnel needed to deal with the problem was pinpointed.

Congress responded by passing the Mental Health Act of 1946. States were to be helped through the National Institute of Mental Health in developing programs for increased training and research. In 1955, the Mental Health Act was passed. Funding was provided for a Joint Commission on Mental Illness and Health. In 1959, George Albee pointed out in a study for this commission that the professional sector alone could never meet the health care needs for a majority of people.

The result of these reports led to recommendations for training, research, the establishment of aftercare and mental health clinics, new programs for the acutely and chronically ill, and residential facilities, together with enabling legislation for funding. The impetus resulting from these recommendations and the efforts of President John Kennedy eventually led to the Community Mental Health Centers Act of 1963. This act called on the National Institute of Mental Health to set up requirements and regulations for the establishment of community mental health centers. Multipurpose and diverse services were to be made available to the general public.

Within this framework the contemporary human services movement has flourished. Short-term treatment, crisis intervention, creative therapies, group orientation, and the like are all part of the human services movement. Improvements grew steadily after the enactment of the 1963 law, until reductions in funding in the mid-1990s.

The human services model is best understood when compared with the medical model. Specifically, the medical model regards the individual coming for help as a person whose problem is categorized as a disease. By comparison, the human services model includes—but is not limited to—the individual seeking help whose behavior poses a maladaptation problem that needs to be replaced with a more appropriate and positive approach. The individual is expected to take an active part in ongoing therapy with a view to changing self-perception. As a profession traditionally dedicated to the welfare of the patient, the medical field could not ignore the goals of the human services field. Psychiatrists, general practitioners, and surgeons have stressed patients' responsibility for their welfare in matters of diet, exercise, recreation, and rest.

The contemporary human services movement includes a trend toward the holistic approach to therapy. Another trend is the utilization of volunteers from all walks of life. Interviewing, referral, consultation, crisis hot lines, and recruitment are only a few of the vital services of the present volunteer movement.

The human services movement has also been effective in such areas as police work, legal service, corrections, education, health, social work, medicine, psychiatry, and psychology. The result has been the proliferation of training and educational programs with a positive use of human resources.

The logistics of treating individuals in their communities has stimulated a series of new careers and roles in the human services field. Career ladders have become available, and personnel with less training serve as vital components in community mental health services that were previously lacking. The influx of large numbers of human services workers into a field normally considered the domain of the professions has met with some opposition from those who hold a traditional point of view in the helping professions. The future of human services will be determined by financial and ethical considerations and by the perceived need for trained and experienced personnel.

COMMUNITY PSYCHOLOGY
PRIMARY PREVENTION OF PSYCHOPATHOLOGY

A. LERNER

HUMAN SEXUALITY

Sexuality in humans describes the breadth of functioning from basic physiological differences between males and females, to traits that characterize masculinity and femininity, to covert and overt sexual behavior.

Often the word "sex" connotes sexual acts: sexual intercourse, kissing, and petting. Yet sex is more than what human beings do behaviorally: It is what they are as well. Harold Lief, John Money and Anke Ehrhardt, Robert Stoller, and others have identified various components of sexuality: biological sex, gender identity (also called sexual identity), and sex role behavior.

BIOLOGICAL SEX

Biological sex refers to the chromosomes (XX or XY) that make humans female or male and the hormones that enable bodies to develop secondary sexual characteristics such as pubic hair. The hormones that create bodily changes are secreted prior to birth, at puberty, and into adulthood. The role of fetally secreted hormones is to translate the message of the chromosomes (male or female) to the brain and genitals, so that at birth there is usually either a well-defined penis and testes or vulva, vagina, uterus, and ovaries. Without fetal androgen, the fetus develops as a female. Genetic mistakes do occur due to chromosomal oddities or insufficient or excessive androgen production during critical periods. Fetal hormones have a vital role.

GENDER IDENTITY

John Money and Anke Ehrhardt define gender identity as the "sameness, unity, and persistence of one's individuality as male, female or ambivalent." Thus the sense of being male or female is due to the interplay between the labeling of the baby as one sex or the other (a result of genetic makeup and hormonal influence) and the reactions of the society around the infant to that maleness or femaleness. Gender identity is believed to be established by 18 months to 3 years of age.

Gender identity also refers to the sense the individual has of masculinity or femininity; it is the public expression of gender as well as of biological and environmental influences on the developing child. From the moment of birth there is assignment to one sex or the other, and treatment by family and culture differ depending on the label—female or male. Those differences in treatment shape basic perceptions of self. Human beings are continuously bombarded with messages of how to be appropriately masculine or feminine—messages that vary widely among cultures and races. Parents are especially important in this process. Parental instructions are strong enough to override genetic and physical gender assignments.

Transsexualism is the most extreme form of gender confusion: The person from early childhood believes himself (these are more often genetic males than females) to be female. The male experiences himself as being in the wrong body and may dress, behave, and pass as a female, and even seek sex reassignment surgery.

SEX ROLE BEHAVIOR

Sex role behavior refers to sexual behavior as well as to masculine or feminine behavior. Despite attempts by some to avoid labeling personality traits as masculine or feminine, males are still typically viewed as more aggressive and less aware of feelings, whereas females are viewed as nurturing and emotional. Sex-typing is stronger in some cultures and social classes than in others; however, the male role is usually instrumental: He attempts to control the environment. The female role is expressive: She is encouraged to be aware of and responsive to others. In addition to the influence of social conditioning, there are indications that boys and girls basically tend to prefer different types of activities from early childhood. Although these desires are strongly influenced by the environment and the available role models, they also show consistency across cultures.

SEXUAL BEHAVIOR

Sexual behavior is present from early infancy: Male and female babies enjoy genital stimulation, however discouraged this may be by their caretakers. At birth there is capacity for either penile erections or vaginal lubrication. Humans learn from the environment how to express sexual feelings. A major theoretical controversy exists in explaining the impetus for sexual behavior. Followers of Sigmund Freud subscribe to an innate drive theory. Another view postulates that sexual feelings and behaviors are learned responses to social expectations. Probably neither view is totally true in itself; rather, sexual drive and its behavioral expression stem both from internal states and from external influences.

Surely there is a strong environmental influence, given the incredible range of sexual expression and the various differences across cultures. Yet it has also become evident that there are internal neural responses in the brain that correspond to emotional sensations of sexual interest or drive. William Masters and Virginia Johnson equated the sexual drive with other "natural" drives such as hunger, breathing, and the need for sleep. Each of these drives is modified and shaped by the environment. Sex, though, is the only one that can be denied for extended periods of time without apparent detrimental effect.

Much of the sexuality literature as well as public attitude toward sexual behavior centers around morality and control. What is appropriate sexual behavior? Each culture delineates the rules, and there are tremendous differences among cultures. Meanings are ascribed to physical sensations based on the social context in which they occur. C. S. Ford and F. A. Beach take a cross-cultural perspective in addition to an evolutionary or transtemporal approach; they assert that the cultural context must be known in order to give meaning to acts. Only by examining the social context can any sexual practice or prohibition become understandable. What is defined as moral and/or normal in a society is linked with rules of economics, inheritance, and ownership.

Lief, in a review of sexual standards across cultures, makes several generalizations:

1. Unlimited sexual access to all people does not exist in any culture; therefore, some restrictions-based on age, consent, familial relationship, and laws-exist in all societies.

2. Some form of incest taboo is always found, although the definitions of incestuous partners vary greatly.

3. Heterosexual intercourse is the preferred and predominant pattern of sexual behavior in all cultures.

How does the majority culture of the United States view sexual behavior? On the surface there are conflicting messages. Sex is used in advertising to sell products and is shown on television and movies in increasing explicitness. Yet there remain strong taboos about sexual expression outside of marriage. Such views are promulgated largely by religious organizations and are backed by the legal system, yet are ignored or violated by many within the culture. This is in part because the society is in flux. There is movement from procreation as the defined purpose of sexual behavior toward intimacy and increasingly toward recreation. Sexual behaviors are becoming separated from the emotions of love and commitment.

Sexual behavior may express the entire range of emotions—not simply love, lust, or wish for intimacy, but also anger, sadness, nurturance, or brutality. The rules of the culture define what is allowable in order to control the populace—the result of a collective notion that sexual desire is "inherently unstable and anarchic."

As the role of sex in the United States has been given greater prominence, a new role has emerged—sex as a measure of interpersonal competence. Skill as a sexual partner and performer is now of higher concern than ever before. Especially for females has there been a change. Earlier in the century women were supposed to engage in sexual intercourse as a condition of marriage. Today they are expected to be active partners who are efficiently orgasmic.

SEXUAL VARIATIONS AND DIFFICULTIES

An overview of human sexuality would be incomplete without addressing the problems and variations in the expression of sexuality. More than most issues, sexuality has been removed from the realm of the natural and distorted by connotations of evil, sin, and perversion. Rather than being an area of life that is considered mundane, it has been both diminished to the unspeakable and elevated to a place of central importance.

In 1886, Krafft-Ebing published an influential book that implied that sex is perverted and disgusting. Krafft-Ebing, a forensic psychiatrist, wrote of sex crimes in detail and extended the book to include descriptions of sexual variations such as homosexuality, masturbation, and fetishism. Sex was viewed as highly dangerous, requiring shame and social sanctions for its control.

Since Krafft-Ebing, the image of sexuality as perversion has lessened considerably, yet there exist various forms of sexual expression still viewed commonly as perversions. These acts are considered to be perversions because they are substitutes for penile-vaginal intercourse, which the American culture (and most others) considers to be the normal way of expressing sexual desire.

Various theories exist to explain these deviations. Robert Stoller believes that hostility underlies all perversions. Psychoanalytic theory postulates that fixation or regression to prior psychosexual stages of development underlies deviations and that castration anxiety is a central component.

Sexual acts considered to be deviant and harmful to others are against the law, and legal consequences or imprisonment may result, although in recent years the legal consequences have lessened.

SEXUAL ORIENTATION

Homosexual orientation (erotic attraction to members of the same sex) is still generally considered a perversion. However, homosexuality and bisexuality are gaining increasing acceptance as normal variations within the spectrum of sexual expression. Kinsey and associates created the concept of a seven-point continuum of sexual expression from "exclusively heterosexual" to "exclusively homosexual." Sexual behaviors as well as psychological reactions (feelings, desires) were included in this scale. More recently a third dimension has often been included to describe sexual orientation: sexual fantasies. Human beings vary in the consistency among the components—behavior, fantasy, and desire/love—which complicates the tendency to label in an either/or fashion.

What is the incidence of homosexuality? The Kinsey reports provide important basic data, although they suffer serious sampling biases in that the respondents were all Caucasians and the information was gathered by self-report exclusively. Despite these weaknesses, the studies provide estimates of the incidence of homosexual behavior. Thirty-seven percent of the 5000 men in the sample had had at least one homosexual contact leading to orgasm, and 10% had had periods of exclusive homosexual behavior for 3 years or more. For females, the percentages are lower: 13% had had at least one homosexual contact leading to orgasm (whereas 28% reported homosexual arousal), and between 2 and 6% of unmarried women (1% of married women) had been exclusively homosexual.

SEXUAL DYSFUNCTIONS AND SEX THERAPY

Sexual dysfunctions occur in many people over the course of their lives; frequently they are transient and are caused by specific stresses within the relationship between the partners. These dysfunctions are most easily treated. The factors that lead to anxiety (cognitive, behavioral, and emotional) are identified, and couples are typically assigned behavioral tasks designed to reduce the anxiety associated with sexual intimacy, thus eliminating the symptoms. In some cases of sexual dysfunction, though, there are more intractable underlying psychological causes.

Sex therapy as a behavioral treatment was developed primarily by Masters and Johnson. They invented the now familiar techniques of sensate focus, genital pleasuring, and nondemand coitus used in most treatment regimens for sexual dysfunctions. Sensate focus involves gentle caressing of the body without touching breasts or genitals and without leading to intercourse. Genital pleasuring is a continuation of sensate focus with the addition of erotically teasing genital touch. Nondemand coitus is intercourse slowed down to enable the partners to better focus on the pleasures felt rather than the pressure to "perform."

Sex therapy techniques are most successful when used with loving, committed couples who do not have serious psychopathology or marital dysfunctions. Helen Kaplan adds the factors of drug or alcohol addiction, severe depression or anxiety, and lack of motivation and commitment as predictors of poorer prognosis for sex therapy. Without these factors, up to 80% of sexual dysfunction cases can be successfully treated with short-term behavioral methods.

HOMOSEXUALITY
INCEST

SEX DIFFERENCES (DEVELOPMENTAL)
SEXUAL DEVIATIONS
SEXUAL DYSFUNCTIONS
SEXUAL INTERCOURSE

D. Gerard

HUMANISTIC PSYCHOLOGY

Humanistic psychology is both a social movement within psychology and an enduring perspective. Both aspects require attention and analysis. The concept of humanistic psychology implies a contrast with scientific psychology. Humanistic psychology in most of its manifestations gives priority to human experience, the meaningful life of the common-sense world that makes contact with its embodiments in works of art and documents of the "humanities." Most of the proponents of humanistic psychology have been engaged in psychotherapy as a privileged window on human experience, and the humanistic movement has been heavily involved in the applied psychology of personal growth and change.

ANTECEDENTS

During the 1920s and 1930s, American psychology was dominated in its mainstream by dogmatic behaviorism, a positivistic view that regarded conscious human experience as out of bounds scientifically. In this unfriendly setting, a psychology of personality emerged in the late 1930's. With exposure to phenomenological and preexistential European models, Gordon Allport provided a broadly based framework for studying the mature ego and how it develops; Henry Murray brought a Freudian–Jungian orientation to bear on personality from a point of view that paid special attention to depths inaccessible to consciousness from which both creativity and neurosis might erupt. Immediately after World War II, two other major theorists of personality issued important systematic books: Gardner Murphy and George Kelly.

Meanwhile mainstream behaviorism, in the later sophisticated version represented by John Dollard and Neal Miller, tended to find common cause with psychoanalysis (the fortunes of which were then riding high), but was inherently in opposition to views of personality such as Allport and Kelly's, which rejected both the mechanistic premises of behaviorism and the biological reductionism of classical psychoanalysis. Personality psychology as it took shape after World War II was the base from which humanistic psychology emerged.

THE FOUNDING OF HUMANISTIC PSYCHOLOGY

In 1964, a conference at Old Saybrook, Connecticut, launched humanistic psychology as a social movement within psychology. Leading figures in the psychology of personality and in the humanistic disciplines participated: Gordon Allport, Henry Murray, Gardner Murphy, and George Kelly of the founding generation; Charlotte Bühler, representing a European tradition of research that was subsequently labeled "life-span development"; Jacques Barzun and René Dubos as humanists from literature and biological science; and Carl Rogers, Abraham Maslow, and Rollo May, who became the intellectual leaders of the movement.

Rogers, Maslow, and May established the initial character of humanistic psychology and remained its most respected figures. The view of human functioning that Rogers developed assumed intrinsic tendencies toward self-actualization which the vicissitudes of socialization could block, but which would predictably be released by the therapeutic relationship of unconditional positive regard, accurate empathic understanding, and honesty and integrity. Abraham Maslow came from a background in the experimental study of primate behavior. Under the influence of Kurt Goldstein, Maslow developed a hierarchical theory of human motivation. Physiological needs call preemptively for satisfaction; then follow needs for safety, for love and belonging, and for esteem. Both Rogers and Maslow, then, embraced self-actualization as an empirical principle and as an ethical ideal. They aligned themselves with Jean-Jacques Rousseau's romantic view of human nature as intrinsically good but corrupted by society, as distinguished from Freud's Hobbesian view of human nature as problematic, tinged with intrinsic evil, and from the behaviorists' Lockean assumption of human plasticity under environmental programming.

Strongly influenced by the existential theologian Paul Tillich, Rollo May brought the European current of existentialism and phenomenology into humanistic psychology. His books introduced American psychologists to ideas stemming from Kierkegaard and Heidegger, whereas in later popular works he emphasized the inherently tragic aspects of the human condition. Rogers' emphasis on empathic understanding of the person's experiential world had been tagged as "phenomenological."

IMPACT OF THE COUNTERCULTURE

The founding of humanistic psychology as a Third Force essentially coincided with the emergence of the counterculture of the "flower children" and drug-oriented "hippies" as a phenomenon of the 1960s.

In its psychological aspect, the counterculture had a number of features that established resonance with humanistic psychology. There was its *individualism:* the fulfillment of the individual as the center of value, virtually stripped of concern with interdependence and commitments to the lives of others. There was its sentimental belief in *human perfectibility,* neglecting political and ethical modes of enhancing actual life among imperfect creatures at cross-purposes with themselves and others. There was its stress on the value of *self-disclosure.* Easy but superficial intimacy was sought in attempts to bypass the work required to develop and maintain caring personal relationships. There was emphasis on the *here and now—*a fecklessness about past and future that ill accords with self-control and the commitments to self and others. There was *hedonism,* which is implied in life in the here and now with minimal baggage of moral commitments. Finally, there was *irrationalism,* manifested in disparagement of science and of rational problem solving, in reliance on intuition over evidence, in uncritical affinity with the occult, and in the celebration of drug-induced "highs."

The founders of humanistic psychology were not antiscientific. They sought rather to correct the biases of behaviorism and psychoanalysis so as to produce a psychology truer to human life and more useful for its improvement.

THE ENCOUNTER GROUP MOVEMENT

The focus of humanistic psychology during the 1960s and 1970s, the encounter group movement had several roots. One was the work of J. L. Moreno, a messianic Austrian psychiatrist, who before 1920 was writing about psychological encounter and using the spontaneous theater of psychodrama (his term), which he subsequently promoted in America as a psychotherapeutic technique. Another was the sensitivity training originated by Kurt Lewin and his students. Lewin was an exponent of "field theory" in psychology. He was virtually the father of modern American social psychology and developed the self-studying group, professionally "facilitated" but not "led," as a technique for training people in human relations skills. Sensitivity training became a movement in its own right, isolated from academic social psychology and more closely linked to industrial-organizational psychology as it developed. Aspects of this tradition got absorbed in the encounter group movement. A third influence was Gestalt therapy, represented at Esalen by its principal developer Fritz Perls: a group approach in which the therapist plays a very active part, using a variety of techniques including role playing to focus participants on holistic emotional experience of the here and now. At Esalen the "intensive group experiences" orchestrated under these influences—typically, weekend "marathon" occurrences—also kept company with body-oriented techniques influenced by Wilhelm Reich, forms of massage, and meditational techniques and yogic exercises influenced by Eastern religion. Alan Watts had sponsored Eastern religion as an ideology for psychotherapists, and it foreshadowed the mystical side of the humanistic movement.

TRANSPERSONAL PSYCHOLOGY

The irrationalist, mystical tendencies pressing from the counterculture found the boundaries of humanistic psychology confining. Within the humanistic movement, and not rejecting it, a conception of "transpersonal psychology" was developed that frankly avowed its affinity to Sufi and other forms of mysticism and focused on supposed processes connecting individual consciousnesses to a larger spiritual ocean in which they participate, here echoing ideas suggested by Carl Jung. Humanistic psychology as a social movement was responding to the cultural lack of faith, hope, and charity, but in so responding, it was presenting itself as a religion and losing touch with the science of psychology.

OTHER FACETS OF HUMANISTIC PSYCHOLOGY

The humanistic movement was not entirely absorbed in Esalen and encounter groups; other contemporary aspects should be noted. Among them was Viktor Frankl's logotherapy, a religiously existentialist version of psychoanalysis rather similar to the approach taken by Rollo May—an account of the human predicament that emphasizes the human need to place death and suffering in a context of human meaning that can be lived with. Another was Amadeo Giorgi's interpretation of the phenomenological philosophy of Merleau-Ponty: a philosophical humanistic psychology not caught up in the "touchy-feely" aspects of the movement. Still another was David Bakan's scholarly vision, an interpretation of dialectically related principles of agency and communion.

The movement produced its own critics. Particularly Richard Farson, a former student and close colleague of Carl Rogers, objected to the mindless fascination with therapeutic gimmickry that he saw as corrupting humanistic psychology. There were also attempts to domesticate the movement and bring it into the fold of academic scientific psychology, while at the same time reforming academic psychology in a humanistic direction. Psychologists tried, also, to negotiate the conflicts between mechanistic behavioristic psychology and humanistic psychology. But practical rapprochement did not resolve the underlying philosophical issues. On the behavioristic side, Albert Bandura stretched his social learning theory to accommodate central humanistic concerns in developing a theory of reciprocal determinism in which he managed to take into account self-control and personal initiatives in constituting one's environment.

SECULAR HUMANISM: A NEGLECTED VERSION OF HUMANISTIC PSYCHOLOGY

Humanistic psychology as a social movement systematically ignored a major strand of psychological thought with excellent humanistic credentials: the psychology of "secular humanism." The concept of secular humanism is best understood within the existentialist tradition of humanistic thought. Humankind is a "thinking reed," as Pascal put it, vulnerable, incomplete, needing God's validation. In the contrasting secular humanist spirit of Shakespeare and Montaigne, Nietzsche in the nineteenth century and Sartre in the twentieth proposed a mundane, godless humanism, also existentialist in its concern with the responsibility entailed by human self-consciousness.

For the religious existentialist, an authentic appreciation of the human situation leads to acknowledgment of human insufficiency in the face of both death and life, alleviated only by willing submission to God. For the atheistic existentialist, in contrast, reliance on God means regression to childish dependence; human dignity requires the clear-headed acceptance of self-choosing existence in a neutral world. Human meaning is a human creation. The religious and the secular views cannot be reconciled, although both presuppose attentiveness to tragic ingredients of human existence ignored by mainstream humanistic psychology.

HUMANISM AND SCIENCE IN PSYCHOLOGY

Since the beginning of the twentieth century, a distinction introduced by the German philosopher Dilthey has echoed in various versions through modern social thought: the distinction between the natural and the mental or cultural sciences. Perhaps the clearest phrasing of the distinction contrasts the perspective of *causal* understanding, traditionally from a standpoint external to the behaving person, with *interpretive* understanding, usually within the person's own perspective—a realm of feelings, meanings, intentions, and values.

The causal perspective, as it applies to human beings, finds continuity with the natural sciences of the physical and biological world. The interpretive perspective emphasizes the uniqueness of human beings as symbolizing, culture-bearing creatures who act in a frame of past and future, who can make sense or nonsense to themselves, who are capable of deceiving themselves and others and of seeing through one another's deceptions. Both perspectives obviously apply to human beings.

When these perspectives are clearly drawn, they define a sharp polarity, both necessary, yet incapable of synthesis into an integrated theory. This may be the best our theorizing can do, but it is not only dissatisfying: It also gives us no help with the fact that in the phenomena of selfhood, the meanings or interpretations that we ascribe to our characteristics and actions are empirically important causal factors in what we do. To the extent that this is the case, it can be argued that for the distinctively human world, interpretation and causal explanation must somehow be joined; that, indeed, the only satisfactory *science* of human experience and action must be one in which hermeneutic interpretation plays a central part conjoined with causal explanation.

DISTINCTIVE TASKS FOR HUMANISTIC PSYCHOLOGY

Scientific psychology has changed since the founding of the humanistic movement as a "Third Force." As the movement falters—partly through its own countercultural excesses, and partly in response to the changed situation in psychology—one may appropriately ask what special foci of attention continue to hold promise from a humanistic perspective.

In the first place, a humanistic psychology has special responsibility to keep windows open on actual human experience. As psychotherapy becomes more technological and the new cognitive psychology occupies itself with flow charts of information processing, the need continues for close attention to human experience in the psychological studies.

Second, the attempt to understand the reflexive aspects of selfhood poses a major challenge. If indeed the reflexiveness of selfhood implies that personality is substantially constituted by the symbolic-cultural content of our self-construals, then our theories of personality will have to be cast with more explicit attention to the historical and cultural context if they are to be scientifically valid.

Two developments in psychological studies may especially inherit the mantle of humanistic psychology in the spirit of humanistic science that characterized the founding generation. One is the resurrection of holistic personality study. The other development is the interdisciplinary movement—in which psychology participates centrally—of life-span human development. As the movement has developed, the lifespan approach has been explicitly concerned with the dialectical interplay between human lives in their social context and historical change. It has also called into question earlier assumptions about the stability of psychological characteristics and the determinative impact of early experience.

BEHAVIORISM
EXISTENTIALISM
RELIGION AND PSYCHOLOGY

M. B. SMITH

HUMOR

Few concepts in psychology can match the complexity of humor. The subject has been approached from its stimulus structure. Is humor simply one response and, if so, is it measured by inner or outer changes? What are the relationships between physiological responses, comprehension, production, and simple appreciation? Can humor be analyzed into different types motivated by different purposes and therefore reflective of varying degrees of maturity and pathology? If a response is to be judged, how should this be done, and who is to make the judgment: oneself, impartial observers, peers, or friends? How do physiological responses with their differing latencies, frequencies, and amplitudes relate to social judgments under varying degrees of stress?

What little speculative knowledge is available proceeds from trying to test in the lab what can hardly be measured anywhere. The clinician, more often than not a psychotherapist, constructs an intellectual map by looking for similarities and differences in treatment outcomes of patients with varying amounts of infrequent humor.

The writings of the most influential therapists have abundant references to the healing qualities of humor and often have made that process the assumed goal of treatment. However, explicit references to that state are rare in their case histories and theorizing.

Three psychologists who have been most vocal about the tactics and goals of humor are Albert Ellis, Harold Greenwald, and Walter O'Connell. Ellis uses self-contradiction, incongruity, and exaggeration to challenge negative assumptions of the patient as they unfold. Greenwald views therapy as an opportunity for playing with events formerly regarded as "traumatic," to find ways of using the painful past for the enhancement of future enjoyment. The humorous attitude is the criterion of maturity in O'Connell's natural high therapy in which clients' well-practiced attempts to cling to guilt and discouragement for useless social influence (power) are subjected to the therapist's jocular dismay and comic over- and understatements of the patients' mistaken certainties.

Humorists-as-therapists, as a rule, see themselves as active guides, demolishing by words and action an often cherished "reality" of patients who see themselves as worthless, isolated, and of no positive value in universal evolution. Humorous psychotherapy is conducted with respect for the patient's person, in spite of the therapist's disdain for the painful and paradoxical power of the patient's current discouragement. Psychotherapy is seen as a game in which an encouraging therapist vies with a discouraged client. The creativity involved in all ploys, even those that are subject to laughter, is the action of the game. In humorous psychotherapy there are no passive victims in the serious (but not grave) interactions. It concurs with holistic medicine in which so-called patients become pupils, learning the theory and practice of self-control and self-enhancement while contributing to the development of similar states for others.

There are few source books for the curious to get an intellectual grip on the study of humor. Sigmund Freud's two studies—*Jokes and their relation to the unconscious* and *Humor*—set the theme for future scholars to follow. Unfortunately, most researchers overlooked Freud's distinction between humor as the mature ability to repudiate one's suffering and wit as the release of repressed drives or possible aimless play. Humor is not mentioned in personality theories, as a rule. Daniel Berlyne has studied the effects of arousal, curiosity, and exploratory behaviors on humor appreciation. Paul McGhee extended the study of humor to the relationship between cognition and behavior, especially with children.

Jerry Suls researched the relationships of the perception and resolution of incongruity and humor responses. Social functions of humor have been interests of William Martineau, Jacqueline Goodchilds, and Lawrence LaFave. Jeffrey Goldstein has studied the saliency of the stimuli involved in "humor" as being of more importance than the repressed drives. Here we see one example of the general trend of confusing Freud's ideas of humor with those of wit and then finding wit to be far more complex than a mere signpost to the repressed. Once again, one must be wary of generalizations across researchers' work because of different definitions of humor and the measurements thereof.

Walter O'Connell has made the distinction between measures of wit and those of humor and has researched stimulus, mediational state, and social setting variables. O'Connell found evidence of personality differences between the aggressive and competitive wit and the nonjudgmental optimistic humorist. He then turned to clinical inferences about the growth of humor. O'Connell believes that the sense of humor consists of the conviction of one's unconditional worth as a person. In addition, the humorist feels like a universal, irreplaceable force in life sharing similarities with others.

Professional interest is accelerating rapidly. The well-circulated account of Norman Cousins' self-healing of a near fatal illness through massive doses of humor (and vitamin C) has called attention to the neglected dynamics of humor as a therapeutic agent. Freud's clinical insight into humor is receiving new life by being assimilated into new theories.

Humor as a stimulus for growth of self-esteem and optimistic belonging, as well as a reflection of those inner qualities, has a fruitful future. Pain reduction and prevention of violence toward self and others through humor raises questions about the mutual interplay of endorphins, immunology, and humor. Accounts of the success of humor in the rearing and treating of children and in the social defusing of riotous conditions opens the issues of humor interventions for the optimal functioning of homes, schools, churches, and all other facets of institutional living.

W. E. O'CONNELL

HUMORAL THEORY

The doctrine of bodily humors was first set forth by Hippocrates. In developing the idea he borrowed from the philosophy of Empedocles, who held that the universe was made up of four basic elements: earth, air, fire, and water; when these were combined in one way or another, all known substances could be explained. Corresponding to the four elements were the four qualities: warm and moist (air), cold and dry (earth), warm and dry (fire), and cold and moist (water). When applied to the human body, they assumed the form of the four humors: blood, black bile, yellow bile, and phlegm. These humors, for Hippocrates, constituted the body and could cause both disease and health, depending on their balance, excess, or deficiency.

It was left for Galen, an eminent Greek physician, to formulate the doctrine of the four temperaments and relate them to Hippocrates' theory of the humors so that individual differences in behavior and emotion could be explained. A preponderance of blood led to a sanguine or cheerful personality, whereas an excess of black bile resulted in a melancholic temperament. An excess of yellow bile led to the choleric temperament (fiery, quick to anger), and a preponderance of phlegm led to the phlegmatic temperament.

The doctrine of the four humors and their accompanying temperaments remained until about A.D. 1400 and the coming of the Renaissance and the rebirth of medicine. Although the doctrine has now faded, vestiges remain in such expressions as "good humor," "bad humor," and "humorous." There is also some survival in theories of personality types in which people are described by the dominance of a particular temperament.

PERSONALITY THEORIES
TEMPERAMENTS

R. W. LUNDIN

HUNGER

Hunger and satiety are curious phenomena. All of us point to our stomachs when asked where we experience hunger or satiety, yet hunger is not simply the result of the absence of food in the stomach. Satiety similarly does not require that it be full (extreme stomach distension can, in fact, be quite unpleasant). As scientific methods became more sophisticated, physiologists demonstrated that rhythmic contractions of the stomach were correlated with hunger. Denervation of the stomach, which abolished all sensations that arise from it, did not abolish hunger, demonstrating that correlation is not necessarily causation. That the stomach is not the source of sensations essential for the experience of hunger has been demonstrated still more convincingly. Modern surgical techniques have made it possible to remove the stomach from experimental animals as well as from some unfortunate human patients. The procedure alters the pattern of food ingestion because there is no substantial storage available, but hunger as well as satiety continue to be perceived, and daily food intake soon returns to normal levels.

The experience of hunger presumably arises when brain mechanisms receive neural and/or hormonal signals that reflect the depletion or repletion of metabolic fuels. This conclusion is supported by the results of recent experiments demonstrating that laboratory animals can learn to feed themselves by emitting a behavior (such as lever pressing) that results in an intravenous injection of a liquid diet. Well-trained animals self-administer essentially normal quantities of food and adjust their rate of injection-reinforced behavior in response to changes in the size or caloric density of the injection. Hunger as well as satiety appear to be experienced even though no food enters the stomach or the upper gastrointestinal tract from which it is normally absorbed.

Animals have evolved elaborate neural and endocrine mechanisms to ensure a steady resupply of the nutrients that provide the basic fuels for metabolism. The system is complex because it is not a simple depletion–repletion mechanism. Energy intake must match energy expenditure, but the equation need not be balanced in the short term because energy can be stored (as fat) and recalled in times of need.

Humans and other complex animals have evolved multiple control mechanisms. Animals become hungry and eat discrete meals at intervals related to the depletion of readily available nutrients from the body. Most humans also manage to keep their body weight within some acceptable limits over the long term.

Errors do creep into this system of regulatory influences, because food intake is not entirely determined by need. Humans often eat, not because the energy stores are depleted, but for a variety of other reasons. To mention just a few, (a) it is lunch or dinnertime—hunger may be classically conditioned; (b) one passes by a stand—the sight and smell of food can induce complex cephalic (i.e., conditioned) reflexes that result in hormonal as well as neural changes similar to those occurring during a meal; (c) one is offered tempting snacks at a party—incentive motivation can be a powerful determinant of eating; and (d) one experiences stress or other emotional upheavals—such compensatory eating is a principal problem in many cases of dietary obesity.

The major influence of taste on what and how much we eat is readily demonstrated when one offers any novel appetizing food to a person who just seconds ago refused to eat another bite of anything. This is an example of sensory-specific satiety, which is a frequent cause of overeating and obesity in modern society.

Human subjects fed intragastrically (and thus not allowed to taste their food) do not report normal satiety even though they receive adequate nutrition. When permitted to drink the same liquid diet that was just injected into their stomachs, they consume nearly as much again, another demonstration of the importance of sensory influences.

This points to another eccentricity of the phenomenon. Although hunger is the psychologist's favorite example of the tight interaction of biological need and motivated behavior, humans as well as other species accumulate an often embarrassing surplus when a varied, tasty, and nutritious diet is freely available. Many individuals could easily survive for weeks and even months without eating, yet they stick to a pattern of three or more meals (plus assorted snacks) per day, claiming to be hungry. Although overweight, some people find it extremely painful to reduce the size of their meals because they are certain that smaller meals do not result in the desired degree of satiety.

Laboratory animals also eat discrete meals on a regular schedule when food is freely available. The periodicity of meals implies an awareness of energy depletion, and the equally tight control over meal size implies awareness of repletion. Animals work harder for food rewards following longer periods of deprivation. However, psychologists have learned that the secret of stable instrumental behavior is starvation to a body weight significantly below the normal level so that "need" may well become a factor in the animal's motivation. Laboratory animals also overeat when offered a tasty, varied, and nutritious diet, but quickly shed the excess pounds when returned to their standard monotonous fare.

Just why individuals experience hunger on a quite regular schedule even when there are ample energy reserves has remained something of a mystery. Because humans do not appear to be responsive to the state of their energy (i.e., fat) reserves, hunger must reflect the short-term depletion of some readily available source of energy.

Glucose is the only metabolic fuel that can readily be used by all tissues and is an essential brain fuel even though brain cells can use ketone bodies for as much as two thirds of their metabolic needs during periods of prolonged starvation. Jean Mayer, therefore, proposed that hunger might be due to the activation of a "glucostatic" mechanism that senses the cellular use of glucose. The glucostatic theory of hunger is supported by the fact that systemic injections of the pancreatic hormone insulin elicit hunger in humans and food intake in many other species. Insulin increases cellular uptake of glucose, and this results in hypoglycemia (low blood sugar). This, in turn, causes cellular glucoprivation (lack of glucose). The proverbial fly in this particular ointment is the fact that insulin increases hunger only when large doses are administered that produce blood levels of the hormone far in excess of any normally occurring concentration.

Nerve cells that appear to be selectively sensitive to glucose and/or insulin have been found in regions of the brain believed to be concerned with hunger. Interest in the glucostatic hypothesis nonetheless has declined in recent years, largely because the connection between glucose utilization and hunger has not been more firmly established in spite of intense scientific investigation. In 1980, LeMagnen demonstrated that blood glucose levels do in fact decline a few minutes before a meal is begun (and an even sharper drop occurs when food is not available at the time the meal would have begun). Once again, correlation does not prove causation, but the fact that it was established after decades of failure gives the glucostatic theory a new lease on life.

All cells of the body use proteins and fats, either directly or after conversion to glucose. Many contemporary investigators, therefore, argue that hunger may not be related to one specific nutrient or its metabolites but, instead, to the rate of energy expenditure. Energy is used for two main purposes: (a) basal metabolism, the cellular processes that generate heat, and (b) motion of the body. Most energy is used to sustain basal metabolism. Basal metabolic rate (BMR) is influenced by many variables, including genetics and the availability of nutrients. A high BMR requires more energy. Conversely, a decrease in caloric intake reduces BMR. This

is the principal reason why individuals on reducing diets lose less and less weight as time goes on.

Contemporary "energostatic" theories of hunger have their roots in the thermoregulatory theories of the 1940s. Early versions suggested that animals eat to keep warm and stop eating to avoid overheating. More recent models do not require conscious appreciation of body temperature changes. Instead, they propose that changes in the availability of nutrients might be sensed by brain mechanisms that regulate body temperature. An association between hunger and temperature regulation is suggested by many observations. To mention just a few examples, humans as well as other animals eat more in cold environments than in hot climates. Furthermore, heat production increases during the metabolism of food, and the magnitude of this effect varies for different components of the diet. Moreover, the satiety value of a food varies as a function of its effect on body temperature. There also is some evidence that certain animals modify their intake of different diets so as to maintain constant heat production rather than constant energy intake.

Until recently, attempts to relate the onset and/or termination of meals directly to basal metabolic rate were not successful. This was true, at least in part, because eating is preceded and accompanied by increased locomotor activity, whereas the cessation of eating typically coincides with rest and even sleep. Traditional measures of BMR (such as oxygen consumption) cannot distinguish between basal metabolic rate and energy expenditure due to activity. In recent years, the availability of computers and sophisticated devices for the continuous assessment of locomotor activity have overcome these problems. It is now known that there is a close correlation between BMR and food intake (and presumably hunger) in the rat. The basal metabolic rate declines just before a meal and rises sharply during it, before leveling off when the animal stops eating. These observations provide strong correlational support for an energostatic theory of hunger. They do not, of course, prove that changes in BMR itself are, in fact, the proximal cause of hunger or satiety.

BRAIN MECHANISMS

The development of stereotaxic instruments around 1920 allowed investigators to stimulate or destroy small portions of the brain without significantly damaging surrounding tissue. The result was an explosion of information about the functions of subcortical structures that had been largely immune to study. Within a few years, it was known that damage to the ventromedial nucleus (VMN) of the hypothalamus at the base of the brain resulted in excessive eating and weight gain. Electrical stimulation of the region was reported to stop eating. Damage to the adjacent lateral hypothalamus (LH) abolished eating and led to death unless special nursing care, including intragastric infusions of fluids and nutrients, was applied. Voluntary ingestive behavior eventually returned, but pronounced deficits in energy (as well as fluid) regulation persisted often indefinitely. Electrical stimulation of the LH elicited eating and resulted in obesity if applied chronically. The ventromedial hypothalamus does appear to exert major influences on metabolic and hormonal mechanisms closely related to the regulation of energy metabolism and hunger, but its role is certainly far more complicated than the original satiety center notion suggested. Among its multifaceted functions is the regulation of pancreatic insulin release, which in turn governs glucose utilization throughout most of the body. The lateral hypothalamus may influence hunger by influencing reactivity to internal and/or external sensory inputs and perhaps by participating in the direction of responses to them. Whether these functions are attributable to nerve cells indigenous to the region (rather than fibers of passage) is the subject of considerable contemporary discussion.

The hypothalamocentric theory of hunger is tolerated by most investigators in the field largely because no viable alternatives have been offered. Other regions of the brain have been shown to modulate hunger, satiety, and energy metabolism, but their influence is typically minor, indirect, and in most cases, poorly understood. What was once thought to be a model system relating motivation to brain activity has become the object of neglect and disregard.

APPETITE DISORDERS
CAFETERIA FEEDING
DEPRIVATION EFFECTS
EATING DISORDERS
FOOD DEPRIVATION
MALNUTRITION AND HUMAN BEHAVIOR
OBESITY
WEIGHT CONTROL

S. P. GROSSMAN

HUNTINGTON'S CHOREA

Huntington's chorea, also known as Huntington's disease, is a genetically determined disorder of the central nervous system first described by George Huntington in 1872. Reliable estimates of its prevalence are not available because of the frequency with which it is misdiagnosed or concealed.

The first observable symptom is often a facial twitch, which gradually spreads to tremors and loss of voluntary control elsewhere. Locomotion, speech, and swallowing become more impaired and eventually impossible. Mood becomes depressed. Hallucinations, delusions, and other common symptoms may closely resemble schizophrenia, and many Huntington's patients are misdiagnosed as having schizophrenia, especially in the early stages. In the later stages, however, the intellectual, memory, and movement disorders become much more severe than in schizophrenia.

The usual age of onset is 30 to 40, with some cases originating as early as 20 or as late as 60. The disease is progressive, with the expected result being death about 15 years after onset. The cause of death is usually heart failure, inability to breathe, or pneumonia.

These behavioral symptoms are related to a progressive loss of cells in the basal ganglia of the brain. There is also an associated decrease in the brain concentrations of the synaptic transmitters acetylcholine, gamma-aminobutyric acid (GABA, or L-dopa), serotonin, and glutamine, especially in the basal ganglia. The decline in these transmitters may lead to excessive activity of catecholamine synapses through a loss of inhibition. Treatment often includes major tranquilizers (neuroleptics) or other drugs. However, none of the drugs yet tested retards the deteriorating course; at best they reduce the twitches and some other problems.

Males and females are equally affected, and anybody with one affected parent has a 50% chance of developing the disorder. However, genetic counseling is complicated by the late age of onset.

There has been some interest in finding a way to detect Huntington's disease before it becomes symptomatic, largely for genetic counseling purposes. Klawans, Paulson, Riegel, and Barbeau administered L-dopa to 30 young adults at risk for Huntington's disease. (L-dopa aggravates symptoms once they become apparent.) Under the influence of L-dopa, 10 of the 30 developed temporary tremors resembling Huntington's disease. In an 8-year follow-up study, 5 of these 10 had developed the disease, whereas only 1 of the other 20 had done so. Thus this test shows promise of providing presymptomatic detection. However, some have questioned the ethics of the test because it may lead to hopeless despair if it indicates the presence of the condition, and because of the hypothetical possibility that the L-dopa test might actually accelerate the course of the disease.

CENTRAL NERVOUS SYSTEM ORGANIC BRAIN SYNDROMES

J. W. KALAT

HYPERACTIVITY

Hyperactivity refers to a qualitative and quantitative description of motoric behavior or motility, a nonspecific symptom of a variety of medical and behavioral disorders, and a common syndrome of childhood psychopathology first identified more than 100 years ago. Given this range of referents, it is not surprising that there is considerable debate over appropriate use of the word, and also a range of related terms and concepts often treated synonymously or interchangeably.

"Activity level" is one of several categories of temperament—constitutionally based qualities of responsiveness that are evident in observable, fairly reliable and stable form from birth (and perhaps before) on. As such, activity level is a dimension of individual difference among human beings that has significant implications for development and adaptation. Hyperactivity, as a statistical or clinical extreme, then has particular implications for problems in development and adaptation. When there is a less than optimal goodness-of-fit or a mismatch between the child and the environment, a high activity level or hyperactivity can be identified or perceived as a behavior problem or symptom.

Despite wide usage to the contrary, hyperactivity does not actually constitute a syndrome in the technical sense of the word. Neither do the particular patterns or constellations of factors form a unitary cluster, nor is there adequate evidence of common causation or etiology, both the *sine qua non* of a "syndrome." Rather, on the one hand, hyperactivity as a symptom is part of a number of syndromes, whereas on the other hand, it is likely that what is today considered the hyperactivity syndrome while eventually be understood as several different syndromes.

Current prevalence estimates for the syndrome generally range from 0.01 to 3%, although some estimates as high as 22% have been reported. Many more boys than girls are affected, perhaps in a ratio of 10 to 1. Differences in diagnostic criteria and problems in diagnostic reliability account for some of the variation in prevalence reports. Recent research has shown that the disorder appears earlier than school age, with some suggestion that a hyperactivity syndrome can be identified late in pregnancy. The persistence of the disorder beyond early adolescence is better substantiated with evidence of long-term symptoms, especially problems with attention and impulsivity.

Etiology of the disorder remains unknown, with a variety of hypotheses supported by a range of clinical and empirical evidence. Genetic, organic, psychological, and environmental explanations have all garnered some support. Psychological hypotheses have included reference to particular child-rearing patterns as well as learning patterns. Environmental factors may include toxins such as lead, radiation stress associated with conventional fluorescent lighting, food additives, and maternal smoking and drinking effects on the fetus. It is likely that the actual etiology is multifactorial.

Consistent with the variation in etiological hypotheses, assessment and treatment of the disorder is wide-ranging. Neurodevelopmental, psychological, and psychoeducational evaluations are typically able to identify the disorders from the particular perspective of each approach. A variety of electroencephalographic, telemetric, and electrophysiological measures more closely associated with attentional and central nervous system arousal indices of the disorder appear in clinical research. Comprehensive multidisciplinary assessment is particularly desirable in diagnosing an attention deficit disorder.

Psychopharmacological treatment with stimulant medications such as methylphenidate or dextroamphetamine is the most common, effective, and yet controversial approach. Again, consistent with the earlier notion of multiple syndromes, some children respond quite well to medication. It is generally recognized that medication alone, even for these subjects, may not be enough to address either the primary disorders or the secondary reactions of the child and those significant people around the child. Therefore a variety of counseling, guidance, behavior-modification, and psychoeducational interventions must be considered as necessary adjuncts to medication.

ORGANIC BRAIN SYNDROMES
SCHOOL ADJUSTMENT

D. L. Wertlieb

HYPERTENSION

Hypertension, a disorder affecting the cardiovascular system and commonly known as high blood pressure, is a major health problem. It is characterized by chronic elevation of diastolic and, typically, systolic blood pressure without demonstrable pathology of either the blood vessels or the heart. Hypertension is a primary cause of adult sickness, disability, and death in the United States, afflicting approximately 20 to 35 million persons. In addition, it is one of the most important risk factors in the promotion of atherosclerotic diseases, kidney failure, congestive heart failure, coronary heart disease, heart attack, and stroke.

Blood pressure occurs on a continuum with no clear division between normal and elevated pressure. Furthermore, the blood pressure values of concern to a practitioner vary as a function of a patient's age, sex, and environment. In general, longevity in adults is progressively shortened as blood pressure chronically exceeds 100 mm of mercury systolic and/or 60 mm of mercury diastolic, and a diagnosis of hypertension is usually provided when a patient's blood pressure is 160/95 mm Hg or above. Hypertension may readily be ascertained through indirect measurement with a sphygmomanometer. The treatment strategy depends on the etiology of the malady. Primary or essential hypertension refers to an instance in which the cause is unknown, whereas secondary hypertension is the result of an identifiable antecedent such as malfunction of particular endocrine organs, coarctation of the aorta, pregnancy, or oral contraceptives. Although secondary hypertension may be ameliorated via surgery or chemotherapy, this category accounts for a relatively small percentage of the cases.

In contrast to the low incidence of secondary hypertension, in about 80% of the patients evidencing hypertension there is no clear cause for the disease. Even though this type of hypertension is of unspecified etiology, it has been recognized for a long time that emotional factors, stress, and a high-paced lifestyle have an elevating effect on blood pressure. Within this context, much research has been directed toward establishing effective behavioral treatments.

Treatment consists of varied combinations of antihypertensive pharmaceuticals, progressive muscle relaxation, meditation, yoga exercises, autogenic training, biofeedback-assisted relaxation, and blood pressure biofeedback.

BIOFEEDBACK
MEDITATION
MUSCLE RELAXATION
STRESS

W. W. Wenrich

HYPNOSIS

It is difficult to give a satisfactory definition of hypnosis. Most authorities would agree that hypnosis occurs (a) within the context of a special hypnotist/subject relationship during which (b) suggestions of distortions of cognition, perception, memory, and affect can be responded to by (c) some individuals. Many of the arguments about the nature of hypnosis depend on which of these three aspects is the focus of theory and research. Thus hypnosis appears to be characterized by the subject's ability to temporarily accept as reality suggested distortions of perception, cognition, and affect.

A BRIEF HISTORY

The modern history of hypnosis begins with Franz Anton Mesmer, who, like others before and since, tried to apply discoveries in physics—in this case, the principles of magnetism—to mental health. Several ingenious experiments conducted by a royal commission headed by Benjamin Franklin led to the rejection of Mesmer's animal magnetism theory. The alleged therapeutic cures were dismissed as due to "mere imagination."

James Braid in 1852 first introduced the term "hypnosis" from the Greek *hypnos* (to sleep). Jean Charcot considered hypnosis a manifestation of hysteria. Sigmund Freud was influenced by Charcot; his observations of the hypnotic abreaction in his famous case with Breuer were influential in his development of the concept of unconscious motivation. Hippolyte Bernheim saw hypnosis as a manifestation of suggestibility—a view carried forward by the first major research program in hypnosis conducted by Clark Hull.

MEASUREMENT OF HYPNOSIS

A number of standardized scales have been developed testing response to suggestions chosen by a consensus of experts, which have made it possible to measure hypnotic states. The scales are based mainly on objective behavioral ratings of responses to suggestions graded in difficulty, which cover a gamut of suggested subjective experiences during hypnosis. About 30% of normal subjects and hospitalized psychiatric patients will score in the high range of hypnotizability, while another 10 to 25% will have very limited capacity to experience hypnosis.

CHARACTERISTICS OF HYPNOSIS

The methodological sophistication of contemporary hypnosis research is considerable and contributes to general psychological theory. Hypnosis research has made contributions to the evaluation of various phenomena: subjective experience, verbal reports, the limits of human performance, attention and consciousness, factors involved in the social psychology of the psychological experiment, and clinical applications.

One unique characteristic typically not found in unhypnotizable subjects who are asked to fake hypnosis is trance logic or the ability to tolerate logical incongruities. For example, a hypnotized person is asked to hallucinate his friend Joe sitting in a chair on his left when Joe is really sitting off to the right. The hypnotized individual will converse with the hallucination in a realistic way. When pushed by the experimenter who points to the real Joe, the hypnotized subject will remain quite comfortable in maintaining the duality of the real and hallucinated person. If prompted, he can easily determine which is the hallucination—even while calmly maintaining the hallucination. Simulators will deny that the real Joe exists or the "hallucination" will disappear. At one level the person knows reality exists, but at another level it can be suspended in an effortless absorption in a fantasy world. Although the distorted and confabulated material may be important therapeutically, there is a disturbing tendency for hypnosis to be used in forensic applications based on the faulty premise of accurate recall. Hypnotized subjects can lie under hypnosis just as easily as in the waking state. Hypnosis can play an important role in pain control. Hypnotic analgesia can best be understood in terms of at least two distinct processes: (a) the direct effect of hypnosis on changing pain, whether this be at a sensory, physiological, or primary level (some recent evidence suggests that endorphins are not involved, as they are in other methods of pain control, including acupuncture); (b) placebo-like effects that occur because of the special context in which hypnosis is induced, regardless of how hypnotizable the person is.

These characteristics of hypnosis whereby the hypnotized subject seems tuned to multiple cognitive pathways and able to easily distort reality while remaining aware of its existence at other levels of awareness—coupled with the extreme stability of hypnotic performance even over several years—have led many investigators to speculate that particular people must be prone to experience hypnosis. The typical hypnotizable person has the capacity to become totally absorbed in ongoing experiences (e.g., becoming lost in fantasy or empathetically identifying with the emotions of a character in a play or movie). He or she reports imaginary playmates as a youngster.

Hypnotizable subjects are able to manipulate memory at will. Good hypnotic subjects have superior memories, particularly for events of many years before. The hypnotizable person falls asleep quickly at night and has other characteristics that cluster together to define an individual difference dimension of the "control of consciousness" or a basic individual difference in cognitive flexibility. This flexibility dimension suggests that the hypnotizable person should have an advantage in the treatment of habit disorders and specific symptoms. Hypnotizability is a significant prognostic index of recovery from psychiatric illness and of the ability to give up symptoms.

CLINICAL HYPNOSIS

The use of hypnosis as an adjunctive treatment modality has been increasing rapidly as it becomes more accepted and as training facilities improve. Hypnosis is a technique and not a science or a treatment. Its use must be integrated into the specialized skills of the professional in his or her own area of competence. Like any adjunctive method, it is the skill of the therapist—knowing what to treat, when not to treat, possible side effects and complications—that define the safety and efficacy of the technique.

Clinical Applications

Hypnosis has been used in the treatment of a wide variety of medical, psychological, and behavioral problems. Claims of dramatic results are usually not documented by careful studies. Hypnosis tends to be more effective in those conditions that have a clear-cut etiology and is relatively less effective where there are issues of psychodynamics or behavioral control. Similarly, it is difficult to treat habit disorders, particularly those that are easily partially reinforced (e.g., eating and weight disorders). However, hypnosis is especially useful in habit control in which, for whatever reason, the patient is ready to give up a symptom but needs legitimization and often a dramatic intervention to justify change.

Hypnosis is useful in establishing whether patients have the resources to develop some kind of meaningful self-control and cognitive mastery over their symptoms.

Finally, hypnosis is a useful adjunct in behavioral interventions, particularly because fantasy and cognitive distortions can be produced quite readily during hypnosis as an adjunct to behavioral and cognitive therapies.

The clinical application of hypnosis as a specialized technique runs far ahead of our basic understanding of the nature of the hypnotic phenomena. Indeed, the role of social psychological variables and the interaction of the hypnotist/subject makes it difficult to study hypnosis in its own right.

HYPNOSIS AS A RESEARCH TOOL
HYPNOTHERAPY

SUBLIMINAL PERCEPTIONS
SUGGESTION THERAPY

F. J. EVANS

HYPNOSIS AS A RESEARCH TOOL

Traditionally, scientific investigations involving hypnosis have concentrated on attempts to clarify the nature of hypnotic phenomena, measurement of individual differences in hypnotic susceptibility, and clinical applications of hypnotic techniques to such fields as psychotherapy, treatment of symptoms, and alleviation of pain accompanying severe illness. In the mid-1950s, another use for hypnosis began to claim systematic attention, namely, it use as a tool for exploring psychological processes in a variety of areas including emotions, experimental psychopathology and psychodynamics, memory, motivation, and perceptual experience.

Manipulations of emotion have been accomplished by several approaches. One of the earliest and most common was suggesting directly under hypnosis that the individual will feel happy, sad, angry, or upset upon awakening, with amnesia for the prior hypnotic instruction. A second technique implants false memories, labeled paramnesias, under hypnosis (e.g., stealing money from a friend's wallet), and thereby creates emotionally loaded conflict. Another procedure requires subjects under hypnosis to narrate personal experiences in which they felt a particular emotion such as anxiety or pleasure. The most pertinent episode for each affect is then "relived"; the emotion is subsequently dissociated from its originating content; and finally the "free floating" emotion is varied in intensity, each degree being assigned a posthypnotic cue to which the subject responds in the waking state while amnesic for the hypnotic programming.

Although most of the hypnosis research involving memory has concerned attempts to clarify the nature of posthypnotic amnesia by applying concepts from cognitive psychology, some investigations have utilized hypnotic techniques to study normal memory processes. For example, content registered in distinctive mental contexts created under hypnosis has been shown to have a remarkable capacity for retrieval in both short-term memory and long-term memory. Another line of research has used brief excursions into deep hypnosis as a tool for exploring memory consolidation or the "reverberation" of stimulus material during the interval between its initial registration and subsequent report. In addition, hypnotically programmed degrees of cognitive arousal ranging from peak alertness and concentration down to near stupor, when inserted into the consolidation period, also proved to have systematic effects on retention.

In the realm of perceptual experience, much hypnosis research has investigated negative visual hallucination, the process whereby stimuli present in the visual field are somehow prevented from reaching conscious awareness. In addition, this technique has been used as a tool to create analogues of hysterical conversion reactions. Extensive work by E. R. Hilgard and his associates on hypnotic analgesia, which can be considered negative hallucination applied to the conscious perception of pain, has led to the formulation of a theory of divided consciousness. This line of research bears directly on central issues in cognitive psychology (e.g., parallel versus serial processing of information).

Hypnotic training can thus be utilized to shape variables such as free-floating anxiety, into pure form, and manipulate their intensity to a systematic degree. Their onset and offset can thus be regulated with greater precision. Fatigue and monotony effects can be minimized by hypnotic instruction. Powerful associations such as the attachment of a particular type and degree of emotion to verbal stimuli can be formed more expeditiously than otherwise. Furthermore, complex states can be isolated into component parts for purposes of experimental analysis (e.g., the separation of cognitive from somatic aspects of arousal). Because hypnotically programmed variables are typically activated in the waking state by means of posthypnotic cues, with amnesia for the prior training, the opportunity for experimental data to be confounded by spontaneous conscious thought is lessened. Subjects are specifically instructed under hypnosis not to be self-conscious later when performing programmed behavior. Conversely, postexperimental inquiries conducted under hypnosis, in which amnesia no longer applies, often provide a wealth of otherwise unattainable information about the waking experimental performance.

These advantages of hypnosis as a research tool are accompanied by certain limitations that must be recognized. One obvious concern is deliberate deception or faking on the part of a subject who merely pretends to execute hypnotic instructions. A more insidious objection is that hypnotized individuals are even more susceptible than other subjects to the demand characteristics of the experimental setting.

Another limitation resides in the fact that hypnosis research, for reasons of expediency, typically involves the selection of those individuals as subjects who score highly on standard tests of hypnotic susceptibility. This raises the question, perhaps in stronger form than usual, of the generalizability of obtained results. A related objection is that the number of subjects employed in studies involving hypnosis is often small. The other side of the argument holds that the hypnotically trained individual serves as an ideal "preparation" for experimental analysis, and also that the statistical application of within-subject rather than between-subject designs in this research genre itself provides an especially powerful tool for isolating experimental effects.

RESEARCH METHODOLOGY

G. S. BLUM

HYPNOTHERAPY

Hypnotherapy is not only treatment by hypnosis; it is any form of psychotherapy practiced in conjunction with the hypnotic modality, within that altered state of consciousness called a hypnotic trance. Hypnotherapy also includes a number of specific suggestive and analytic techniques not normally practiced when patients are in the fully conscious, nonhypnotic condition.

HISTORY

Treatment of human ills involving suggestions administered to patients in trance states has probably been practiced throughout human history. However, Anton Mesmer is generally recognized as the first modern hypnotherapist.

In the 1840s, James Esdaile in India performed more than 1000 operations using hypnosis as his only anesthesia. John Elliotson and James Braid in England employed hypnosis in the treatment of a wide variety of medical disorders. In France, A. A. Liébeault, Hippolite Bernheim, and J. M. Charcot experimented and published on the values of hypnosis in therapy. Their work served as a stimulus for Sigmund Freud.

During World War I hypnotherapy was employed by Georg Simmel in Germany and J. A. Hadfield in England to treat war neuroses, and during World War II John Watkins extended these approaches further in the treating of battle casualties. Milton Erickson developed many complex ways of employing hypnotic suggestion for approaching a variety of disorders.

DISORDERS TREATED BY HYPNOTHERAPY

A wide variety of conditions are amenable to hypnotic influence. Surgeons and anesthesiologists often have found it useful in controlling pain, relaxing the anxious patient, relieving postsurgical depression, and controlling nausea. Hypnotized patients more readily accept unpleasant diagnostic procedures with instruments such as bronchoscope, gastroscope, or proctoscope.

The skin is especially susceptible to emotional and suggestive influence, and hypnosis has been found helpful in treating warts and neurodermatitis. Sexual disorders such as impotence and frigidity often respond favorably to suggestive or hypnoanalytic procedures. Neurotic and psychosomatic disorders have been successfully treated by hypnosis. Obstetricians have found hypnosis of benefit in handling the pain and anxiety problems of gravid patients and in ameliorating the stress of delivery. Because hypnotizability seems to peak between the ages of 10 to 12, numerous uses for hypnosis have been found by pediatricians and child psychologists.

Many clinical articles have been published reporting success in the hypnotherapeutic treatment of habit disorders such as enuresis, nailbiting, stuttering, smoking, bulimia, and obesity. Hypnosis, combined with behavior therapy techniques, has been reported as superior to behavioral modification or suggestion alone.

Personality disorders such as sociopathy and drug or alcohol addictions have generally been found refractory to hypnotic treatment. Hypnosis is especially indicated in the treatment of amnesia and multiple personality. However, it is seldom used with psychotics, although some practitioners have reported success with this condition.

In general, any condition that can be approached psychotherapeutically may be treated with hypnotherapy in hypnotizable patients. Hypnotizability can be measured informally and by standardized tests. The more fragile the personality integration and the greater the strength of violent unconscious tendencies, the greater the sensitivity and skill required of the hypnotherapist. Careless hypnotic intervention "in depth" into such personalities may initiate maladaptive or psychotic behavior and leave the patient in a worse condition.

TECHNIQUES OF HYPNOTHERAPY

An "induction" and some type of "deepening" usually precedes actual therapy. Hypnotic "trance" is not either/or but lies on a continuum ranging from hypnoidal relaxation to "deep" states of involvement. Although many patients make favorable response to suggestions when lightly hypnotized, for best results it is usually considered wise to induce as deep a state as possible before beginning treatment. The techniques of hypnotic induction are many, but most include suggestions of relaxation, monotonous stimulation, involvement in fantasy, activation of unconscious motives, and initiation of regressive behavior.

The skill of the hypnotherapist inheres in an ability to phrase suggestions in line with the motivational needs, both conscious and unconscious, of the patient. Suggestions may be simple and direct or complex.

Suggestions may be timed for immediate effect or aimed at gradual improvement posthypnotically.

COMPLEX TECHNIQUES OF HYPNOTHERAPY (HYPNOANALYSIS)

Sometimes the supportive and directive methods of suggestive hypnotherapy are insufficient to resolve a condition. Unconscious conflicts continue to maintain the symptom, and deeper methods of personality intervention are required. The practitioner then turns to hypnoanalytic procedures.

An interview conducted with the subject in a hypnotic state is usually richer in details than one done in the conscious state. Differences between what is reported under hypnosis (where criticality is lower) and what is said outside it may be quite significant. Controversy exists among researchers as to the extent that such memories are correct and accurate for the regressed age.

Relived emotional experiences (abreactions) are induced by regressing the patient back to traumatic episodes and then having the patient experience them to the point of physical and emotional exhaustion.

Under hypnosis patients often report dreams apparently forgotten in the conscious state. They also offer more details to dreams only minimally remembered consciously.

Dreams can be initiated under hypnosis. Such experiences are in line with the findings of Josephine Hilgard that hypnotizability is significantly related to the ability to fantasize.

Dissociation may be specifically used to construct a "revealing defense," hence to place distance between an unacceptable impulse and an overt response. Such techniques need to be followed by "working through" and ego integration just as in other analytic therapies if the individual is to achieve genuine insight and behavioral change. The same transference reactions that characterize other analytic therapies appear during hypnoanalysis, often earlier and stronger, and the hypnoanalyst must be prepared to deal with these constructively.

Hypnoanalytic ego-state therapy is a recent therapeutic approach based on the finding that dissociation lies on a continuum. Ego states are covert patterns of behavior and experience that under hypnosis act like separate personality identities or unconscious multiple personalities. However, internal conflict between them may induce anxiety, neurotic symptoms, or maladaptive behaviors.

Under hypnosis the therapist activates each state separately and studies its origins, needs, feelings, and relationships with other such states and with the entire personality. A kind of internal diplomacy is then practiced, which is like group or family therapy, except that the "family" of ego states exist within a single person.

Hypnotherapy does not supplant any of the other psychotherapies, but by its ability to potentiate suggestions, create or undo dissociations, initiate fantasies, stimulate memories, and induce relivings it offers therapists (psychoanalytic, behavioral, cognitive, and humanistic) greater flexibility in achieving treatment goals.

FORENSIC HYPNOSIS

There is recurring legal and psychological interest in the use of hypnosis to break down amnesias and enhance the memories of witnesses. Because of the possibility of eliciting false memories, Orne has suggested safeguards aimed at minimizing contamination. Of considerable concern also is the question of whether such hypnosis should be practiced only by qualified mental health personnel (physicians and psychologists) or whether it is appropriate for use by police interrogators.

HYPNOSIS
HYPNOSIS AS A RESEARCH TOOL

J. G. Watkins

HYPNOTIC AGE REGRESSION

Hypnotic age regression, the reinstatement of previously acquired but subsequently forgotten or extinguished responses, feelings, and/or memories during hypnosis, was first reported in the literature by Robert von Krafft-Ebing in 1889.

The underlying cause for such behavior has not been clarified. Two theories to explain casual observations of individuals during age regression are functional ablation and role taking. According to the former, learned and maturational behaviors that appeared after the age to which the individual has regressed are said to be functionally ablated by the suggestions of hypnotic age regression, and no longer accessible as part of the person's response repertory. The role-taking explanation holds that the individual plays the role of an age-regressed person as perceived,

acting out what is thought to be expected by the hypnotist. Neither theory has been established as totally correct. The responses of hypnotically age-regressed individuals are a mixture of age-appropriate responses and responses more appropriate to actual chronological age. Age-regressed responses are colored by experiences obtained after the suggested age; complete functional ablation does not occur, nor are the responses totally role-enacted.

Hypnotic age regression is used clinically in the context of ongoing psycho- and hypnotherapies, primarily as a method for enhancing recall or for otherwise making conscious and available the events, feelings, memories, and emotions from the past.

Experimental investigations of hypnotic age regression have attempted to reestablish infantile and neonatal reflexes, childhood illusion patterns, childhood moral development stages, conditioned responses subsequently extinguished, alterations in the brain wave (EEG) and pulse rates, childhood behaviors as measured on Piagetian-like tasks, reduced mental age as measured by intelligence tests, and childlike responses on projective tests. Such investigations have also undertaken to enhance memory recall (e.g., of exact days of the week of special events, previously learned nonsense syllables, and poetry). For each positive finding, negative findings also have been reported; the degree to which hypnotic age regression enhances the reestablishment of previous behavior over other therapeutic and experimental maneuvers requires continuing investigation.

HYPNOSIS
MULTIPLE PERSONALITIES
PERSONALITY INTEGRATION

W. E. Edmonston Jr.

HYPOTHALAMUS

The hypothalamus is a cluster of nuclei (or centers) in the brain that participates in the initiation and/or control of autonomic responses such as temperature regulation, increased blood pressure, sweating, and dilation of the pupils of the eyes.

The hypothalamus exerts this control by two separate mechanisms: (a) It influences the activity of other groups of cells, both autonomic and somatic, that lie in the brain stem and other portions of the central nervous system; (b) it acts as the major nervous control center for the endocrine glands.

P. A. Bard showed that, even with all brain tissue above the hypothalamus removed, cats could manifest full-fledged rage. But if the hypothalamus, along with the brain tissue above it, were removed, only incomplete components of rage could be evoked.

The hypothalamus takes part in the control of sexual behavior—a participation both neural and endocrine.

The hypothalamus plays a crucial role in the body's temperature regulation and in the activity of the pituitary gland, sometimes called the "master gland" because it plays a role in controlling other glands.

BRAIN
LIMBIC SYSTEM

S. H. Bartley

HYPOTHESIS TESTING

Research hypotheses are predictions based on reasoning from a theory or past findings about the results of a study. Ideally, hypotheses are specific and concrete so that they indicate specific criteria needed to test them and can be proven or disproven unambiguously. The criteria used to test hypotheses are called dependent variables. The process of generating testable hypotheses serves to clarify the questions being asked about a particular research problem. It forces the researcher to specify the concrete data needed to come to a conclusion about the hypothesis as well as how the data will need to be analyzed.

The statistical procedures used to test a hypothesis have, by convention, been set up on the assumption that any differences in the dependent variables are due to chance. The procedures ascertain the probability that any apparent difference is not an actual difference. Consequently, when hypotheses are examined statistically, they must be represented in the null form (i.e., predict no difference). When the statistical analysis indicates that there is a high probability of there being no actual difference among the dependent variables, the null hypothesis is accepted. When the probability of there being no actual difference is low, the null hypothesis is rejected.

When a research hypothesis is supported, it means that the changes in the data cannot be attributed to chance. It also means that causal factors stated in the hypothesis may explain the changes, but does not prove that they do as long as there are alternative hypotheses. As a result, the process of theory building is not a matter of proving a hypothesis, but rather of eliminating inadequate hypotheses until one continues to survive attempts at disconfirmation.

If a research hypothesis predicts that the dependent variable will change in a particular direction (e.g., become larger or smaller), then the corresponding statistical hypothesis is analyzed by using what is termed a *one-tailed test,* which focuses on only one end of the sampling distribution and analyzes changes in the hypothesized direction. If it is hypothesized that change could occur in either direction, a *two-tailed test* is used.

When deciding whether to reject or accept a statistical hypothesis, two types of error are possible. A *Type I* or *alpha error* occurs when the hypothesis of no difference is rejected, when in fact there was no real change in the dependent variable. Prior to an experiment, a researcher decides how much he or she is willing to risk a Type I error by choosing a level of significance. The level of significance, or alpha, is the probability of a given change in the dependent variable occurring by chance. The typical level of significance used for rejecting the null hypothesis is $p = 0.05$ or 0.01.

A *Type II* or *beta error* occurs when a hypothesis of no change is accepted, when in fact there has been a change. The chances of making this error decrease if alpha (the level of significance) is increased or if the sample size is increased. Reducing the variance within the sample or increasing the magnitude of the experimental effect can also reduce the chances of a Type II error.

Because the probability of one type of error decreases as the probability of the other increases, a researcher must decide which is preferable in a given situation. In instances in which labeling a chance difference as a genuine difference is costly, a conservative approach can be taken by setting the level of significance low. Alternatively, in instances in which it would be costly to overlook any promising leads, a higher level of significance can be set, thus reducing the chances of a Type II error.

The power of a statistical test is the probability of correctly rejecting the hypothesis of no difference. It is equivalent to 1 minus the probability of a Type II error. The power of a statistical test can be increased by using the methods for decreasing the chances of a Type II error mentioned previously.

Statistical significance is not synonymous with practical significance. A decision about practical significance is made independently of statistical procedures and can only be arrived at by individuals who are aware of the specific situation in which the research findings might be applied.

RESEARCH METHODOLOGY
STATISTICAL INFERENCE

G. K. Lockwood

HYPOTHETICAL-DEDUCTIVE REASONING

This model of psychological inquiry is more exactly called the *hypothetico-deductive method* and is associated with C. L. Hull. The method blends the formulation of hypotheses from observation or experiment (induction) with the generation of larger-scale postulates from which new predictions can be extracted (deduction). The predictions can then be tested, anchoring the effort again to an empirical base. Hull's principal books revealed his conviction that the method was a powerful tool for a naturalistic psychology: Predictions confirmed by test would strengthen a theory; those not confirmed would signal the need to revise the theory. Noted uses of the hypothetico-deductive method were seen in Hull's own work on animal learning and in K. W. Spence's elaborations of Hullian theory.

In Hull's day certain philosophers of science, especially those known as *logical empiricists,* had developed conceptions of how science is done that centered on the logic of scientific work—a logic that had much in common with Hull's method. As this philosophy was challenged by later approaches that put more stress on the sociology of scientific discovery, the underpinnings of Hullian scientific procedures seemed less secure than before. Many humanistic psychologists ridiculed Hullian psychology as a rigid little science irrelevant to the interesting questions about human beings.

HUMANISTIC PSYCHOLOGY
HYPOTHESIS TESTING

A. B. Pratt

HYSTERIA

The term *hysteria* has been used to describe a variety of maladaptive behavior patterns that have ranged in severity from a type of personality disorder (hysterical personality) to a form of psychosis (hysterical or factitious psychosis). However, hysteria has most frequently referred to a neurotic form of psychopathology. Although it can be said that hysterical symptoms allow individuals to avoid unpleasant situations without assuming responsibility for their behavior, this hardly distinguishes them from other neurotic behavior patterns that serve the same purpose. Because the term "hysteria" refers to a heterogeneous group of symptom patterns and adds little discriminatory power to the diagnostic process, it has been essentially eliminated from the current classification system of psychiatric disorders.

NOSOLOGY OF "HYSTERICAL-TYPE" DISORDERS

The major types of hysteria have been broken down into more discrete and homogeneous groupings, each constituting an individual disorder. *Somatoform* refers to those disorders in which physical symptoms are the chief complaint, yet no demonstrable physiological or disease mechanisms account for the symptoms. Three discrete disorders that had previously been labeled hysterical in nature have been identified: somatization disorder, conversion disorder (hysteria of the conversion type), and psychogenic pain disorder.

Somatization disorder is marked by recurrent, multiple, and persistant somatic ills with no evident cause, often starting in the early years.

In *conversion disorders* the symptom picture is much less varied and usually involves a single, predominant loss or alteration of physical functioning (paralysis, blindness, seizures, etc.) that is not under the person's voluntary control but also cannot be explained by pathophysiological processes. Typically, there is a temporal relationship between some environmental event and the abrupt appearance of the conversion symptom, which allows the individual to achieve both primary and secondary gain from the symptom. *Primary gain* is achieved when the symptom allows the person to temporarily avoid an unpleasant emotional conflict, whereas *secondary gain* is achieved through the symptom by gaining others' attention and support for being incapacitated and/or by allowing the person to avoid an aversive activity. Although conversion disorders were fairly common around the beginning of the twentieth century and provided the cornerstone for Freud's theory of psychopathology, they are now relatively uncommon and occur primarily among medically unsophisticated populations.

The psychological factors in *psychogenic pain disorder* are similar to those found in conversion disorders, but psychogenic pain is treated separately because it usually runs a much longer course than conversion symptoms and has different treatment implications. Behavioral approaches have proven quite effective in dealing with psychogenic pain disorders.

Classification of hysteria of the dissociative type has been refined to include separate categories for psychogenic amnesia, psychogenic fugue, multiple personality, and sleepwalking.

The disturbance in recall is usually for a circumscribed period of time in which there is either a total or selective failure of recall for events that occurred during that period. It is believed that these forms of amnesia allow the person to avoid consciously acknowledging highly charged, emotionally painful events.

The essential feature of *psychogenic fugue* is a traveling "away from one's home or usual locale with assumption of a new identity and an inability to recall one's previous identity." In fugue states there is an alteration of both motor behavior and identity. Such instances are quite rare except in times of war or natural disaster, and heavy alcohol use may be a predisposing factor. Usually the symptoms are of brief duration and recovery is rapid.

Although rare, *multiple personality* is perhaps the best known of the dissociative disorders, entailing the existence of two or more distinct personalities, each having its own complex makeup and social relationships. The individual's behavior is determined by the personality that is dominant at that particular moment. The clinical course of multiple personality tends to be more chronic than other dissociative disorders; childhood trauma and abuse appear to be the main predisposing factors.

The last form of dissociative disorder to be considered here is sleepwalking. *Sleepwalking disorder* is typically a disturbance of childhood that involves repeated episodes of getting out of bed and walking about without full awareness or later recall. The episodes are usually brief, lasting a few minutes to a half hour, and seem to occur during periods of nondream sleep. The major differential diagnosis is complex-partial seizures (psychomotor epilepsy), which can also occur during sleep but which have evidence of abnormal brain wave (EEG) activity.

CONVERSION DISORDER
MULTIPLE PERSONALITIES

G. J. CHELUNE

I

IDENTITY CRISIS

Erik Erikson describes the eight-stage process of ego development characterized by a series of psychosocial crises. In adolescence, the main task is that of solving the identity versus role diffusion conflict. During this process, an identity crisis (IC) may occur.

Because identity is considered by psychoanalytically oriented theorists to be one of the most important aspects of ego strength and ego development, the identity crisis is emphasized.

Erikson explains identity as an integration of all previous identifications and self-images. Identity formation is a restructuring of all previous identifications in the light of the anticipated future. Although identity development attains a crisis potential only in adolescence, it starts in infancy. In highly structured societies with puberty rites or externally defined roles for adolescents, the IC is less pronounced than in democratic societies.

Trying to escape the crisis, some adolescents experience a premature foreclosure and so fail to develop their full potential; others extend the crisis and the identity confusion indefinitely, thus diffusing their energy in a prolonged conflict and doubt about choice of identity. Sometimes the identity confusion finds expression in a "negative identity" in which a dangerous or socially undesirable role is adopted. Fortunately, without any major crisis, the majority develop one of the several positive potential selves.

Severe IC may be prevented in different ways. Parents and significant adults should avoid excessive demands and overly ambitious goals for their children. Adults should also encourage children to pursue their interests by praising their efforts, by encouraging them when they encounter difficulties, by helping them to explore and develop their resources, by teaching them responsibility by letting them face the consequences of their actions unless too dangerous, by respecting them as persons and not humiliating them when they fail to live up to the adults' expectations, and by helping them increase the responsiveness toward others that leads to the development of identities conducive to good adjustment to society. Adolescents should also be provided with a variety of positive live or fictional models to emulate, with opportunities for testing several acceptable roles, and with knowledge about themselves and about the resources and choices offered by the culture in which they develop.

Faulty handling of the IC has been found to be correlated with a variety of problems, from psychological development difficulties to pathology. The severe, acute identity diffusion is linked with the inability to make decisions, confusion, loss of identity in a crowd, difficulty in establishing satisfying relationships with a tendency toward isolation, difficulty in work, and poor concentration. Because identity is considered to be one of the basic elements of ego strength and development, the unsatisfactory resolution of the IC leaves the individual less equipped to cope with the adjustment demands.

Although the most profound IC is likely to occur during the adolescent years, it can be experienced at any age. Erikson initially applied the term IC to the experience of World War II veterans. Later, he observed a similar confusion in disturbed adolescents and concluded that an IC is part of the normal adolescent development. His experience as an immigrant let him also understand that even though one may have resolved the adolescence IC, later dramatic changes in life can produce a renewal of crisis. In addition to immigrants, many other categories of people may experience IC: discharged military who previously had a position of glamour and status, retired people whose identity was almost exclusively based on their work, welfare recipients who may feel like "nobodies" because in our society identity is frequently defined by occupation, mothers whose children have grown up and left home (the empty nest syndrome), people who find themselves having to change their future plans because of an unexpected disability, and so on.

Other studies dealt with the crisis experienced by the dying person. The loss of human contact, family, friends, body function, and consciousness threatens the person's sense of identity.

Although there are justifications for extending the concept of IC to events in adult life, the tendency to apply it to institutions and countries (e.g., Company X suffers from an identity crisis) is an overextension and tends to distort the concept.

ERIKSONIAN DEVELOPMENTAL STAGES
IDENTITY FORMATION

D. MOTET

IDENTITY FORMATION

Personal identity refers to a sense of sameness or continuity of the self despite environmental changes and individual growth. Personal memories of the past as well as hopes and aspirations for the future provide evidence in the present of this sense of identity.

Identity versus identity diffusion is the interactive conflict that Erikson posits as the main dilemma of adolescence. Sudden growth, development of the genitals, and the onset of sexual urges all create a discontinuity with the individual's previous experience. The question "Who am I?" takes on a new urgency as the pubescent youngster struggles with maintaining self-esteem and personal continuity. Adolescents do not all resolve the identity dilemma with an affirmative conclusion. Some choose a negative identity, a rejection of previous identification, whether of race, sex role, religion, or socioeconomic position.

The resolution of the identity–identity diffusion dilemma requires both a crisis and a commitment. By "crisis" is meant youth's confrontation and struggle with alternatives among potential personal choices (e.g., choosing a future occupation or religious affiliation). Commitment refers to a strongly held personal choice after one has struggled with alternatives. A committed individual can be said to have achieved a certain level of identity.

Aside from *identity achievement*, other statuses are possible. *Identity diffusion* implies a lack of commitment regardless of whether there has been a crisis. *Identity foreclosure* is the status of a person who is firmly committed without ever having considered alternatives: In other words, there has never been a crisis, and the identity choice may be as much the parents' as it is the individual's. *Moratorium* refers to an ongoing crisis that as yet shows no clear commitment.

ERIKSONIAN DEVELOPMENTAL STAGES
IDENTITY CRISIS

J. P. MCKINNEY

IDIODYNAMICS

A conceptualization of human behavior and/or experience dating from 1950 to 1951 in which the *event* is the irreducible entity and the *idioverse* replaces the concept of *personality*. The ultimate aim of general psychology, personality theory, and clinical psychology is to achieve an understanding of the particular individual and, if possible, predict and control his or her behavior. Up to now, however, this objective has been an unrealized ideal. The recent ascendance of cognitive psychology, which is largely a protest against the narrowness of neobehaviorism, represents an effort to include more than overt, segmental responses as a basis for generalization and to admit intervening variables not unlike those that abound in theoretical physics. In psychology, competing approaches (usually designated as schools) illustrate the continuing quest. If one now adds an emphasis on the uniqueness of individuals, the goal seems even more remote.

Idiodynamics is a conceptualization in which the events of individual experience are employed at the very outset as the building blocks of behavioral science. In the collection of such data, however, whether by naturalistic observation or experiment, certain guiding principles are essential. These are the fundamental postulates of idiodynamics: (a) *Response dominance.* Unlike both general psychology and most approaches in clinical psychology, all of which adopt stimulus–response relationships as the starting point for observation, idiodynamics concentrates on response–response relationships. These latter, although publicly observed, allow for inferred intervening variables. (b) *Configuration dominance.* This complements the subordination of the stimulus by the subordination of the part to the whole. The *idioverse*—the universe of events that replaces the subject or person—by its wholeness makes stimuli and responses mutually definitive. The response often defines or helps to define the stimulus in the total pattern. Each idioverse is unique by genetic endowment and by particular subsequent experiences. The idioverse thus constitutes the particular individual.

Idiodynamics had its origin largely in three areas of empirical investigation: (a) the experimental redefinition of clinically derived psychoanalytic concepts, (b) the intensive study of individual mental patients by supplementing anamnesis with projective and psychometric methods, (c) the reconstruction of the life and work of creative individuals by an approach designated as "psychoarchaeology."

One early result of this program of research was a formulation by Rosenzweig, "The experimental situation as a psychological problem." It exhaustively examined the earlier methodological literature of experimental psychology vis-à-vis the evidence of the current research program from the standpoint of which the reciprocal interactions between the observer and the subject were schematically classified. In regard to this reciprocity, the terms *subject* and *observer* were preferentially replaced by the terms *experimentee* and *experimenter*. It was shown that in the early German literature just such a reciprocal terminology was employed in *Versuchsperson* and *Versuchsleiter*. The chief contribution of Rosenzweig's paper was a schematic classification of the various typical interactions encountered in previous and current investigations. This advance in experimental social psychology and psychodynamics made no impact until more than 20 years later when, in the mid-1950s, Robert Rosenthal and others began to publish their independent findings on such phenomena as "experimenter bias."

The first formulation of the complementarity between experimenter and experimentee was followed by three other similar contributions: "Some implicit common factors in psychotherapy," in which C. S. Sherrington's neurological principle of the "final common pathway" was, without deliberate intent, applied to the very different field of psychological therapy; "Schools of psychology: a complementary pattern," in which the natural division of labor among the five then current schools was shown to represent a complementary pattern in which a selected type of problem achieved acceptable resolution by methods and concepts appropriate to the preferred emphasis; and "Converging approaches to personality: Murray, Allport, Lewin." Each of these contributions stressed a different kind of complementarity although all were guided, implicitly, if not explicitly, by an overriding principle.

Later it became evident that the principle of complementarity that seemed so apt for the solution of the contending purviews in psychology had become a key to seemingly irreconcilable theories in physics. In 1927, the principle of complementarity was offered by Niels Bohr as an alternative to Heisenberg's "indeterminacy" and as a new way of reconciling the conflicting conceptions of light as consisting of waves, on the one hand, and particles, on the other hand. To Bohr, both formulations were justified and equally true once it was recognized that each formulation required and was served by a different observational approach. Not all physicists were ready to embrace this solution of contradictory formulations that Bohr applied, not only to the theory of light, but to other problems in physics. By 1937, when Rosenzweig's paper on schools of psychology appeared, Bohr was simultaneously recommending that complementarity be extended beyond the physical to the natural sciences, including biology and psychology. However, none of Bohr's papers were known to the writer when the latter's contributions were made between 1933 and 1944.

Another basis for idiodynamics is illustrated by Figure 1. It highlights the fact that psychology tends to have developed historically and exists today as a coordinate composite of the cognate sciences. These sciences may be arranged, not only in the traditional vertical hierarchy, but also horizontally, with the implication that each discipline is autonomous. It is not necessary to reduce one discipline to a lower and more fundamental one that is supposed to have greater dignity or explanatory power.

During the twentieth century, psychology has marshaled its forces in relation to physics as psychophysics, to physiology as psychophysiology, to biology as psychobiology (one may skip psychodynamics for the moment), and, quite recently, to sociology and anthropology as aspects of what may be called the psychosocial sciences. The term *social psychology* has, of course, been used in this context as has *cultural anthropology*.

One may now return to psychodynamics in Figure 1. As is apparent, *idiodynamics* has been inserted to supersede *psychodynamics*. There is here a unique self-consistency: Idiodynamics is psychology sui generis; one might almost call it "psychopsychology." After all, psychodynamics— and, even more completely, idiodynamics—insists on remaining in its own (experiential) universe of discourse. Although from certain unsympathetic standpoints this insistence would, of course, be condemned as subjective, from the present one it is both natural and proper. In the broadest sense of the term *behavioral* (e.g., the usage of R. S. Woodworth), idiodynamics is phenomenologically behavioral.

The designation *humanics* at the apex of Figure 1 is a synonym for the more familiar *psychology*, but it even more clearly bespeaks "the behavioral sciences." It recognizes in one word that psychology is, in fact, although implicitly, a composite discipline of coordinate members.

If a complete picture of so-called psychology is to be rendered, all the coordinates need to be engaged.

A crucial distinction in idiodynamics is the threefold complementary way in which behavior may be alternatively explained: nomothetic, demographic, and idiodynamic (Table 1). These three modes are known as "norms". They were first designated as universal, group, and individual, and illustrated by reviewing the role of association in the history of psychology. The principles of association were first described by the early Greek thinkers by reference to similarity, contiguity, and so forth, and even in present-day theories of learning such principles are represented. These appear to be universally valid norms. After Francis Galton, these formed the basis for experimental studies of word association conducted in Wundt's laboratory of experimental psychology in Leipzig. But even there it was soon recognized that certain groups of individuals, including mental patients of a given diagnosis, produced associations peculiar to or characteristic of the groups. In these terms certain kinds of associations consistently produced by an individual helped to classify him or her as belonging to a given group (e.g., the clang associations of the manic patient). Finally, in Jung's research on complexes, the individual or individualized potential of certain word associations were seen as pointing to a unique organization or constellation of thoughts, images, and feelings in one particular person. This insight adumbrated the idiodynamic orientation. The association of ideas could be alternatively accounted for in one or another of these modes according to the objective of the study.

These three explanatory modes are now more appropriately designated *nomothetic, demographic,* and *idiodynamic* to avoid the quantitative reference misleadingly emphasized by the earlier terminology. The confusion is evident in the writing of Gordon Allport who commended the formulation of typical norms but then erroneously equated each type with the size of the population in question. In this way he tended to confound the *idiodynamic* with the *idiographic*.

From Figure 1 and Table 1 arises Figure 2, which portrays the parameters of the idioverse. The coordinates of the composite in Figure 1 have been reassembled factor-wise, and the idioverse is conceptualized as a universe of experiential events, representing a given person at a particular time. Figure 2 includes three milieus—two that persist through time and a third that is more transitory and fluid but represents the phenomenal personality at a given moment. From the one side, an organic (and genetic) milieu affects the idioverse biogenically; from the other, a cultural (and social) milieu contributes sociogenically, and both of these relatively permanent transmitters overlap and coalesce in the transitory matrix of the idioverse. In that matrix, determinants from the two persisting milieus flow through continuously, are generatively transformed, and provide the idiodynamic signals for a complete understanding of a given human event. While it endures, this vehicle—the matrix of the idioverse—is psychologically paramount, and its norms make intelligible to the prepared observer the person who feels, thinks, and acts.

The three types of norms represented in Table 1 are to a large extent coordinate with the three milieus shown in Figure 2: The *biogenic* tends to be used nomothetically; the *sociogenic* is used demographically; and the matrix of the idioverse is closely allied with *idiodynamic* norms *per se*.

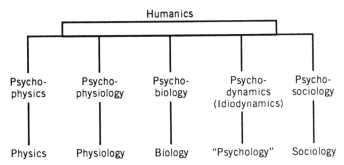

Figure 1. Psychology as a coordinate composite.

Table 1   Three Types of Explanatory and Predictive Norms

Nomothetic (universal)	Functional principles of general psychology considered valid by and large
Demographic (group)	Statistical generalizations derived from particular cultures or classes of individuals
Idiodynamic (individual)	Distinctive markers recurring in a given, single population of events (idioverse)

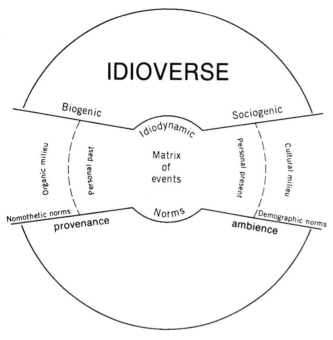

Figure 2. Dimensions of the idioverse.

The temporal aspect of experience is crucial in idiodynamics. Although in the matrix of the idioverse everything is of the present tense, the biogenic milieu tends to stress derivation from the organic past. These inputs interact with those from the cultural past, and all of these inputs converge in the adaptively creative and future-oriented matrix of events. In that matrix, the personal present and personal past mingle as do perception and memory.

There are three empirical ways in which idiodynamics has been and can be further implemented. The one that initiated the approach, as already mentioned, appeared as a systematic survey of the experimenter–experimentee interaction. It demonstrated that, in contrast to the situation in the impersonal sciences (physics and chemistry), the situation in the psychological laboratory involves at least two interacting human individuals. The specific characteristics and expectations of each person must be taken into account. This caution applies to both the design of the experiment and the interpretation of results. Implicit here is a form of relativity, not of space–time, to be sure, but an interpersonal reciprocity that affects the process of observation. From subsequent work by many other investigators, it is now clear that the interactive reorientation was a first step toward idiodynamics as shown by Adair. But its possibilities are only beginning to be exploited.

The second way in which idiodynamics expresses itself in experimental methodology is through the use of quantitative measures evolved by self-reference (e.g., the use of the experimentee's modal reaction times as a basis for clinically and experimentally evaluating his or her other responses). An early example appeared in the complex indicators of the word-association method. A second example is found in Rosenzweig's "The investigation of repression as an instance of experimental idiodynamics" in which memory as related to affect was analyzed.

The third empirical methodology is not in the strict sense experimental, but it can be as objectively valid as field studies in biology. The method exploits the linguistic aspects of the idioverse, which are the most accessible and most characteristic of *Homo sapiens*. One may employ the various techniques available in clinical and other areas of applied psychology, but it requires hermeneutic methods of analysis that stress operative levels of communication to reveal the meanings that inhabit the idioverse. These levels are the *immediate* or literal level, the *intermedi-*

ate or allusive, and the *inframediate* or the most intimate and often recondite. This last level is usually the most intimate because the individual often harbors secrets there. The methodology by which these layers are unraveled has been called "psychoarchaeology." All the levels are studied concurrently, with the assumption that they will not necessarily be represented with equal force or frequency in every production.

This method can be employed with documents such as psychotherapy transcripts, diaries, letters, and the data yielded by projective psychological techniques. However, the most rewarding data are available in the imaginative productions of creative writers, the elite of whom are almost compulsively involved in veiled self-exploitation and self-exposure. These individuals employ the levels intuitively as endogenous to their artistry. In conducting research with such data, it is crucial to take into account, not only the artistic productions, but also the other available biographical evidence from the entire life span. Peculiar sensitivities of the organic milieu as well as insistently recurrent modes of response to social encounters must be considered because the levels express, not only the coalescence of the three milieus of one idioverse, but also their interpenetration with other idioverses.

FORMATIVE THEORY OF PERSONALITY
GENERAL SYSTEMS
HERITABILITY
PERSONAL DOCUMENTS
PERSONOLOGY
THEORETICAL PSYCHOLOGY

S. ROSENZWEIG

IDIOGRAPHIC–NOMOTHETIC PSYCHOLOGY

Social scientists may choose to formulate either idiographic or nomothetic interpretations of phenomenona. These terms were coined by Wilhelm Windelbrand to describe the work of the natural sciences on the one hand, and, on the other hand, the cultural or human sciences, in which individual cases were studied. An essential conflict defines the two points of view. Scientific generalizations are assumed to be nomothetic or law-like. But for these predictions to be used, they must be applied to particular cases, and individual cases (idiographic analysis) may not conform to general laws.

Idiographic science involves the intensive analysis of single cases, with the attempt to formulate interpretive statements pertaining only to the case or to the class of phenomena that the case represents. Idiographic interpretations are based on the particularities of a given case. Their claim to validity rests on the power of the descriptions produced by the researcher. These descriptions attempt to capture the perspectives of those studied. It is assumed that different interpretations are likely to be meaningful in different realities. Any interpretation will be shaped by local particulars and interactions between the researcher and those studied.

Nomothetics rests on the claim that scientific laws can be formulated only statistically through the study and analysis of a large number of randomly selected cases. Nomothetic generalizations are assumed to be time and context free. They do not depend on the specifics of a particular context or case.

The conflict over idiographic and nomothetic models of science and inquiry has plagued the social sciences in general and psychology in particular since the beginning of the twentieth century, although the origins of the debate can be traced to the rise of the human disciplines in the eighteenth and nineteenth centuries.

Fundamental assumptions regarding the nature of inquiry, philosophies of science, and the purposes of the social and psychological sciences are involved in the idiographic–nomothetic debate. Arguments by feminist scholars and scholars of color have sharpened this debate. Such individuals believe that the methods of nomothetic science have often been used as tools of oppression, producing knowledge that is biased in the direction of a male-dominated science. Postpositivist, critical theorists and postmodernists also have criticized nomothetic science and its assumption that knowledge is free of bias, personal values, and political ideology. These theorists argue that nomothetic science is often used as a form of political control.

Stated most succinctly, the issue revolves around whether psychology will be a causal science seeking general laws of human behavior or an interpretive, praxis-based discipline seeking greater and deeper understanding of social and psychological processes..

Nomothetic investigators reject idiographic interpretations. They regard them as being unscientific or journalistic. Conversely, ideographic researchers argue that nomothetic studies are of little value because all interpretations are assumed to be contextual and specific to given cases.

NOMOTHETIC PSYCHOLOGY

Nomothetic psychology seeks the discovery of scientific, statistically valid, generalizable laws regarding human behavior. Certain assumptions underlie this point of view. First, causal explanations of social phenomena are sought. A variable-analytic language that rests on the operationalization of variables and concepts is employed, and strict cause–effect models of inference are used. Second, the quantification of mental and behavioral processes is pursued. Third, it is assumed that causal propositions formulated on the basis of the careful study of randomly selected subjects can be generalized to nonobserved populations. Fourth, the nomothetic scientist endeavors to construct (typically) nonnaturalistic experimental laboratory settings in which scientific observations are gathered. Fifth, to the degree that the findings from idiographic methods are used in nomothetic science, they are frequently regarded as useful only for explanatory, descriptive, or illustrative purposes (e.g., pretesting). Sixth, nomothetic theories are deductive and probabilistic and offer functional explanations of phenomena. Idiographic psychology and its methods are regarded as useful only to the extent that they contribute to the construction of scientific theories that meet the foregoing criteria.

IDIOGRAPHIC PSYCHOLOGY

In twentieth-century psychology, the work of Gordon Allport is most commonly associated with idiographic psychology, which rests on certain assumptions and methods. In the words of Allport, it is assumed that "psychology will become *more* scientific (i.e., better able to make predictions) when it has learned to evaluate single trends in all their intrinsic complexity, when it has learned how to tell what will happen to *this* child's IQ if we change his environment in a certain way." Allport's assumption requires a deep and sustained interest in the study and analysis of a single case over a long period of time; longitudinal studies are required.

Specifics, not universals, are explored by the idiographic psychologist. Because each individual is assumed to be unique, the psychologist must work with a theory and a set of methods that retain and reveal individual differences. Then, there is an attempt to permit the individual subject to speak in his or her own language, to secure the meanings that hold for persons in their life world, and to capture those meanings and experiences with methods that are relatively unstructured, open-ended, projective, and interpretive. Personal documents and life histories are used, as are unobtrusive and indirect measures of personality, in combination with other methods and techniques in a triangulated fashion. Naturalistic research conducted in the everyday situations of individuals is favored by the idiographic psychologist.

ETIC AND EMIC INVESTIGATIONS

The contrast between nomothetic and idiographic psychologies may be compared with the *etic* and *emic* controversy in recent anthropological theory. Etic investigations are external, comparative, and cross-cultural. Distance from particular cultures is sought so that general patterns can be discovered. The specific, unique configurations of meaning that pertain within a single culture are set aside in an effort to discover cross-cultural universals. Emic investigations study cultural meanings from the inside, seeking to uncover the cognitive categories and classification systems that members of particular cultures and cultural groupings use. Emic investigations are particularizing; etic investigations are generalizing. Furthermore, emic investigations are framed from the insider's point of view. Emic studies implement the idiographic approach to science, whereas etic studies are committed (usually) to the nomothetic approach.

THICK VERSUS THIN DESCRIPTIONS

Thick, as opposed to thin, descriptions go beyond the mere reporting of fact, correlational coefficients, or significance tests to the level of detail, emotion, meaning, nuance, relationship, and interaction. Thick descriptions are emic and idiographic. If combined with the traditional methods of the idiographic psychologist, thick descriptions would permit a deeper probing of the underlying personality and interaction patterns that idiographic psychologists endeavor to discover and understand. Nomothetic psychology primarily rests on thin descriptions, etically discovered.

PROGRESSIVE–REGRESSIVE METHOD OF SARTRE

Jean-Paul Sartre proposed a method of inquiry that, in many significant respects, synthesizes the above discussion. The progressive–regressive method of investigation seeks to situate and understand a particular subject or class of subjects within a given historical moment. Progressively, the method looks forward to the conclusion of a set of acts or projects undertaken by the subject (e.g., the production of a novel). Regressively, the method looks backward to the conditions that embed and embody the projects and practices of the subject. By moving forward and backward in time, the subject and his or her projects are situated in time and space. The unique differences in the person's life are revealed while the commonalities and similarities shared with others are likewise revealed. The method also is analytic and synthetic, in that analysis is woven through the main threads of the subject's life in a synthesizing, interpretive fashion.

FEMINIST INQUIRY

Recent developments in feminist scholarship expand the idiographic–emic approaches in new directions. More reflexive epistemologies that place the investigator in the center of the research process are being developed. African American, Hispanic, and Third World feminists are studying how colonial (positivist–nomothetic) discourses misrepresent the lives of women in diverse contexts. Other scholars are challenging the objective biases of the nomothetic approach. This perspective, they assert, assumes that a static world of objects can be studied (not created) by the methods of objective science. They contend that the scientist creates the world that is studied. These researchers note that studies of women have traditionally treated females as static objects to be viewed through the lens of an objective (male-dominated) science. Other feminist scholars are experimenting with new writing forms, including autoethnographies, performance texts, and poetry.

CROSS-SECTIONAL RESEARCH
EMPIRICAL RESEARCH METHODS
FEMINIST PSYCHOTHERAPY
IDIODYNAMICS
LIFE EVENTS

N. K. Denzin

IDIOT SAVANT

Bernard Rimland, who coined the term "autistic savant," describes an idiot savant or autistic savant as "an individual who can perform various mental feats at a level far beyond the capacity of any normal person, but whose general intellectual level is very low."

Those believing that subnormal intelligence is due to mental retardation have traditionally referred to such an individual as an "idiot savant." Those who believe, as Rimland does, that subnormal intellectual functioning results from autism, refer to the individual as an "autistic savant."

D. L. Holmes

ILLUSIONS

Illusions are misperceptions of the environment. The essential notion of an illusion is that it leads the perceiver to misjudge the stimulus, to have a nonveridical perception. The Müller–Lyer illusion is a visual illusion, probably the most studied of all visual illusions, in which the perceiver misjudges the length of lines. The lines are equal in length, yet the one on the left in Figure 1 is judged to be approximately 25% longer than the other. The illusion has been used to illustrate the unreliability of the senses. Stage lighting, makeup, dress fashions—our visual world is full of the practical application of illusionistic principles.

Illusions are an important part of survival for many species. *Protective coloration* means that an animal takes on coloration similar to that of the environment for protection. Some species have ways to hide in shadows by shading that makes it hard to localize the object and dark streaks that camouflage a conspicuous eye (e.g., the raccoon). Blending in with the background indeed creates a misperception, but not a significant distortion, as when one attributes distance to a physically near object.

We have no systematic ecological classification of all the illusions in nature and in daily life. Illusions occur in all sense modalities. Best studied are the visual illusions. The Müller–Lyer visual illusion already mentioned is also a tactual illusion. In the horizontal–vertical illusion, a horizontal line is bisected by a vertical one of equal length, but, the vertical line appears longer. The Poggendorf illusion has an oblique line that intersects two parallel lines. The portion between the parallel lines is blank, and the oblique line appears to exit somewhat below the point where one would infer that it should. The Ponzo illusion has two approaching lines, as in the linear projection of a road in a picture, in which the distant

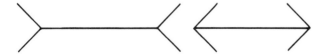

Figure 1. The Müller-Lyer illusion. The two horizontal lines are of equal length, but the line on the left appears to be much longer. To make the lines appear subjectively equal, the line on the right must be approximately 25% longer than the one on the left.

part seems to converge. Two equal lines between the converging lines, one near the front and the other one near the back of the two lines, seem to be of unequal length, the farther line appearing longer.

The ambiguity of empty visual fields and unusual contexts is responsible for many illusions. A fixed dim light in the dark seems to move—an illusion known as the *autokinetic effect,* exhibited by dim stars on a summer night.

The proprioceptive system is responsible for many illusions, one being the drunken walk of the experienced sailor who feels the ship as steady and the dry land as heaving. The aircraft pilot catapulted from a carrier sees objects appear to rise (the oculographic illusion) while the pilot's body feels tilted backward (the oculogravic illusion). The airplane may seem to be climbing too fast, but corrective action—putting the nose of the aircraft down—may result in a crash into the sea. The illusion is particularly compelling at night when visual references are lacking.

Sound localization is ambiguous and is helped by a visual reference. Thus sound is ascribed to the dummy, not to the ventriloquist (the ventriloquist effect). High-pitched sounds, particularly continuous sounds of a single note, are difficult to localize.

The cutaneous "rabbit" is an illusion of localization, of knowing precisely *where* taps are felt on the skin. If one has three contactors four inches apart on the forearm and gives the lower one five separate taps, then the middle one 5 taps and the last one 5 taps, the feeling is not of bursts of pulses at 3 different places, which is what actually happens, but rather of 15 pulses spread out over the forearm, like a "rabbit" running up the arm. This is because localization on the skin is very imprecise. Similarly with hearing: If seven successive sounds are spread over three speakers, a person hears seven sounds in different places—an auditory "rabbit." The visual fovea is very accurate for spatial localization, but successive lights in the periphery of the eye can also give the illusion of coming from more places than are actually in the source. The "rabbit" is multisensory.

Taste illusions are illusions in which the taste of one substance influences the subsequent taste of another. Salt can make water taste sour, and sucrose can make water taste bitter.

R. D. Walk

IMAGELESS THOUGHT:
THE WÜRZBURG SCHOOL

Wundt had originally postulated that consciousness was made up of only three elements: sensations, images, and feelings. Titchener had placed primary emphasis on images as the "vehicles of thought." The Würzburg psychologists, M. M. Meyer, J. Orth, H. J. Watt, and N. Ach, under the leadership of Oswald Kulpe, challenged the Wundtian system by arguing that in their "systematic experimental introspection" studies they found no evidence that imagery was important or even present in certain tasks (*Aufgaben*) in which thinking or judgment was assumed to be required. Thus Meyer and Orth found that a correct judgment of difference or equality of weights could be made in the absence of imagery. They concluded that additional conscious content in the form of conscious attitudes (*Bewusstseinslagen*) could be detected as functional in determining judgments.

Wundt and Titchener dismissed these criticisms as irrelevant in that, according to them, the Würzburgians were not studying thinking so much as the effects of previous experience in which no thinking was actually occurring. At the present time the Würzburg school, although primarily of historical interest, is represented by numerous cognitive psychologists who have revived the reaction-time experiment as a powerful tool in analyzing the factors that determine judgments of similarity and difference in situations in which a subject responds as quickly as possible after seeing two stimuli or sets of stimuli in rapid succession. Such experiments have led to many new insights into the breadth and limits of human perceptual and retentive capacities.

HISTORY OF PSYCHOLOGY

B. R. BUGELSKI

IMAGERY

In everyday conversation an image is supposed to be some kind of mental experience, a picture in the "mind's eye." Such a description is referred to as the "picture metaphor," but imagery also refers to experiences in other perceptual areas such as hearing, tasting, and kinesthesis. When people claim that they actually see nonpresent objects, they are said to be hallucinating. If present objects are misinterpreted, we refer to illusions.

Images are commonly described as faint and fleeting, undetailed, and partial, but some people report having vivid, detailed images. Presumably people differ in the strength of their imagery, and certainly they differ in scores attained on various tests of imagery designed to measure the vividness or clarity of images in various sense areas. The tests are reasonably reliable in that the scores are stable enough, but what validity they may have is difficult to establish because no one can share any other person's imagery.

In the early history of psychology Wilhelm Wundt considered images as one of the three basic elements of consciousness, along with sensations and feelings. Images were regarded as revived former sensory-perceptual experiences. They were commonly accepted as fundamental psychological phenomena whose reality could hardly be questioned.

Because of the personal, subjective, nature of reported imagery, John B. Watson described images as "the ghosts of sensation." Images lost favor as objects of study as long as behaviorism held sway, but began to enjoy a recovery of interest in the 1960s and 1970s as what has come to be called cognitive psychology began to capture the interest of psychologists. Imagery again began to play a role in the areas of learning, perception, thinking, and meaning.

One important cause of the revival of interest in imagery was the publication of Frances Yates' *The art of memory.* Yates described how the early Greeks and Romans practiced various mnemonic skills based on images of already known frames of reference such as the structure of one's house. One could remember long lists of items by imaging each item in one room after another. Following Yates' book, a large number of studies of mnemonics appeared. The only limit to the mnemonic procedure appears to be that of allowing enough time for two images to be associated, which usually takes about 5 seconds.

Other investigators asked subjects to rate long lists of words for their imagery value on a scale from 1 to 7. It was found that high-imagery words could be learned very quickly, in contrast to low-imagery words. More important, it was found that high-imagery words could be learned more quickly than high-meaning words. It could then be argued that imagery was more important than meaningfulness and that, indeed, it was a better index of *meaning* than the so-called meaningfulness measures.

In the area of perception, studies led to identifying imagery with brain centers involved in processing perceptual discrimination for different sensory inputs. In split-brain research it was discovered that the right hemisphere appears to be strongly involved in processing visual forms and structures as compared with the well-known involvement of the left-

brain with linguistic concerns. It was discovered that mental rotation took approximately the same time as a physical rotation of a figure would take, and the subjects were then judged to have been rotating the figure imaginally or mentally.

All imagery is difficult to describe in crisp, neat communication, just as are all internal reactions. We do learn to describe some of our internal reactions such as hunger and thirst, but to actually describe how hungry one might be is probably impossible. To describe an apple seen in imagination is equally impossible if any strict criteria are applied. The fact that we have trouble describing our images does not make them any less real than toothaches or other pains. But however real they may be, we must recognize that images are not likely to be good guides for all decisions.

In studies of so-called eidetic imagery it was once believed that children—or at least some children—enjoyed remarkable imagery that practically amounted to looking at the real thing. Ralph Haber has demonstrated, however, that children alleged to be "eidetic" were no more accurate than other children in describing previously viewed pictures. The verity value of imagery is still highly questionable. Conditioned responses have long been recognized as varying from the unconditioned response. There is no reason why images should be any more precise as reproductions of a prior response. After all, the stimulus for the actual reaction is not present.

The practical value of imagery has been exploited in a number of ways in the last two decades. Perhaps the greatest exploitation has been in the area of behavioral therapy in which clinical psychologists ask patients to imagine the kinds of things that give them anxiety or create problems for them, then teach them to relax while imaging their (formerly) distressing situations. With care and patience, such patients can be brought to relax in the presence of the real situations after having the appropriate practice with imaginary threats. Transfer from the clinical office to the real world cannot be assumed, however, and practice in actual anxiety-provoking situations must be introduced.

Another interesting application of imagery has been in sports and skills such as dart-throwing, gymnastics, and basketball free throws. People who spend some time imagining going through successful motions apparently can improve their scores more than control groups who do not engage in "mental practice." Should such an advantage from mere imagining prove reliable, many additional areas could probably benefit. It remains for the details of the imaging sessions that are actually beneficial to be spelled out.

EIDETIC PSYCHOTHERAPY
IMAGELESS THOUGHT

B. R. BUGELSKI

IMAGINARY COMPANIONS

During early childhood (ages 2 to 6), many children have imaginary friends who are alive only in their imaginations. Strictly speaking, imaginary companions are invisible, so a stuffed animal or doll that a child believes to be alive does not qualify.

Because fantasy and magical thinking are characteristic of the thought processes of children at this age, the fact that a child seems to be talking to thin air or insists that an invisible friend is truly alive is not a sign of pathology. In fact, imaginary companions may be a sign of mental health because they often help a child to cope with loneliness, fear, or other problems.

There is some evidence that children who have imaginary companions are not only more creative, but also more intelligent than peers who do not have them. Only if a child seems to live entirely in a fantasy world, unable to relate to real people, should adults become concerned.

EARLY CHILDHOOD DEVELOPMENT
FANTASY

K. S. BERGER

IMITATIVE LEARNING

Imitation is commonly accepted as an innate tendency to mimic or copy others. The fact that there is a name for some alleged phenomenon does not prove its existence, and there may be more appropriate explanations for "imitative" behavior. Imitation not only is alleged to cover routine activities as in children's play, but also is supposed to play a role in learning. O. H. Mowrer has provided a suitable explanation of such modeling behavior. The model, if admired by the observer, engages in some behavior such as kicking a "Bobo" doll. Later the observer, given the opportunity, also kicks the doll. According to Mowrer, watching the model is accompanied by positive emotional reactions that become conditioned to the features of the situation. When the doll is available, the positive emotional reactions are revived, and the kicking behavior may ensue, enhancing the positive emotional reaction. The kicking is probably not a precise replication of how the model kicked. It is not necessarily the specific response, but the more general destructive pattern, that is "aped."

In new learning situations it is an age-old practice for teachers to say, "Let me show you." They then perform some operation that the learner observes and tries to duplicate. It is learning by observations—a factor in all learning. Whether there is a teacher or model or not, learning requires observation of the factors in a situation, and response to such factors. Without a teacher, a learner may waste a lot of time observing wrong or irrelevant features. A teacher or model saves this time by pointing out or illustrating specific factors that must be observed and responded to.

Imitation is not a special force or tool that operates independently to produce learning. We tend to do what we see others doing if we also observe the satisfactory outcomes of their behavior. If we do not observe completely and carefully enough, all our efforts at imitation will be useless. Learning requires the association of relevant stimuli with other stimuli or responses.

CONTEXTUAL ASSOCIATIONS
LEARNING THEORIES
SELECTIVE ATTENTION

B. R. BUGELSKI

IMMATURE PERSONALITY

Immature personality, a generic term, subsumes several related but distinguishable personality features. Central to its meaning is the concept of psychological maturity. Psychological maturation can be characterized as a stage of mental and emotional equilibrium that allows one to pursue the life one chooses without undue stress or strain, and allows one to cope with inevitable frustrations and conflicts with a minimum of infantile behavior and experience. Thus the immature personality is lacking in emotional equilibrium, so that even minor stress precipitates disturbances in emotional tone.

There has been little empirical research on the immature personality; however, clinical speculation on the etiologic nature of this disorder is sometimes offered. Individuals of this type often reveal a history extending back to childhood of emotional instability, difficulty in tolerating frustrations, and a strong persistence of very early childish traits. Many are believed to have never been exposed to a mature, stable, consistent

environment. Hereditary or congenital explanations have also been offered, but documentation for these is generally lacking.

The immature personality as a diagnostic entity is virtually absent from American nosological systems and has not been used in European circles for several years.

In the 1952 edition of the *Diagnostic and statistical manual of mental disorders (DSM)* the emotionally unstable personality was offered as a personality trait disturbance and described as including excitability, ineffectiveness when confronted with minor stress, undependable judgment, and fluctuating emotional attitudes toward others because of strong and poorly controlled hostility, guilt, and anxiety. The emotionally unstable personality is extremely difficult to treat because they rarely seek treatment of their own volition and frequently terminate treatment prematurely.

The passive-aggressive personality with three subtypes—passive-dependent, passive-aggressive, and aggressive—was listed in the 1952 edition of the *DSM* and parallels the passive dependency and aggressiveness subcategories of the immature personality. The passive-dependent type was characterized by helplessness, indecisiveness, and a tendency to cling to others and establish dependent relationships. The parasitic aspects of their relationships with others make them appear like young children, always looking to others to meet their own needs.

The passive-aggressive type is prone to conflicts with authority and expresses aggression through obstructionism, inefficiency, obstinacy, hostility, manipulation, and covert defiance. They are childish in the sense that a young child might not have the strength, courage, or ability to rebel openly, yet may be slow, inefficient, obstinate, and pouting in accomplishing a requested task. Treatment prognosis is good if the individual recognizes the self-defeating nature of the behavior.

The aggressive type was viewed as having a persistent reaction to frustration with irritability, temper tantrums, and destructive behavior, along with pronounced dependency on others. Such individuals may at one moment display unprovoked and unreasonable anger, then soon become sullen, tearful, or guilty with no clear precipitant. They rarely achieve beyond a restricted level of social or occupational functioning because of their childishness and extreme emotional instability. The similarity of these subcategory types is evident; it is not unusual for them to occur together.

NONCONFORMING PERSONALITY
PASSIVE-AGGRESSIVE PERSONALITY
PERSONALITY DISORDERS
PERSONALITY TYPES

P. A. MAGARO
R. M. ASHBROOK

IMMUNOLOGICAL FUNCTIONING

The immune system represents a complex series of mechanisms whose principal function is to protect the organism from foreign substances that lead to disease; it may also be essential as a defense against cells that have undergone neoplastic transformation. The immune system comprises two major categories, the cellular and the humoral immune systems, both of which involve the action of lymphocyte cells.

The principal components of the cellular system are macrophages and T-lymphocytes, the latter being thymus-derived or thymus-influenced. It is thought that the main function of T-cells is defense against certain microorganisms, intracellular bacterial pathogens, and viruses, and that they are responsible for delayed skin hypersensitivity, rejection of allografts, and antitumor actions. The T-lymphocytes can be subdivided into specific classes: regulatory and effector T-cells. The regulatory cells may be either helper or suppressor cells, whereas effector cells are responsible for the immune reactions. Macrophages are responsible for presenting the foreign particle (antigen) to the T-cell, and may determine which cells will be stimulated by particular antigens. Moreover, macrophages may regulate the magnitude of the T-cell response by influencing cell division or differentiation. The major component of the humoral immune system is the B-cell. The immunological function of the B-lymphocytes is expressed through the production of antibodies or immunoglobulins (IgM, IgG, IgA, and IgE).

Once the individual is exposed to a particular antigen, increased resistance to infection is exhibited upon reexposure to that antigen. In effect, having been exposed to an antigen, both T- and B-cells have a "memory" for that antigen, resulting in a relatively rapid and pronounced reaction to it. The memory appears to be specific and long-lasting and is associated with an increased number of specifically reactive T- and B-cells.

The occurrence of tolerance, essentially the opposite of the sensitization or memory effect, has also been noted in response to antigens. (i.e., with repeated exposure to a particular antigen, immune responsivity may decline). The fact that an animal's immune system does not react against its own tissue may be an instance of tolerance. Under some conditions this resistance fails, resulting in autoimmune diseases such as rheumatoid arthritis, myasthenia gravis, or systemic lupus erythematosus. In addition to a role for T-cells in immunosurveillance against cancer, it has been suggested that other effector cells, termed natural killer cells, may be fundamental to immune surveillance. It is thought that natural killer cells may react within a few hours to foreign substances, as opposed to the 5-to-7-day period for the primary response of T-cells and the 2-to-5-day response of sensitized T-cells. Accordingly, this type of broad-range defense may act as a temporary measure until the more potent and specific immune response is sufficiently potent.

Increasingly greater attention has been devoted to the possibility that immunological changes, and hence susceptibility to disease, may be influenced by psychological factors. Indeed, it has been demonstrated that stressful situations may alter immunological activity and increase susceptibility to some immunologically related diseases. It seems, however, that a variety of factors will determine the immunological changes observed. Moreover, the immune response may be subject to conditioning processes, such that the immunosuppressive effects of agents such as cyclophosphamide can be induced with cues that had been paired with the drug.

Although immunological functioning was traditionally considered to be independent of central nervous system activity, it has been shown that manipulations that alter central nervous system functioning (e.g., lesion of the anterior hypothalamus) will affect immune responsivity. Conversely, antigen administration appears to alter activity of neurons in some brain regions. Extensive documentation is also available, indicating that hormonal changes have profound influences on immunological functioning. Accordingly, it is certainly possible that the central nervous system manipulations influence immunological activity via alterations of hormonal secretion.

PHYSIOLOGICAL PSYCHOLOGY
PSYCHOPHYSIOLOGY
STRESS CONSEQUENCES

H. ANISMAN

IMPASSE/PRIORITY THERAPY

Impasse/priority therapy (IPT) is a four-part therapeutic structure intended to lead people from a minus to a plus situation. Theoretically, all people are seen as moving toward goals, but in some cases the goals are of the "useless" rather than the "useful" type. The intention of this therapy is to change participants' direction toward usefulness in terms of social interest.

This therapy involves four stages. First there is *individual therapy* following an intake interview; this stage lasts for about 20 individual sessions. Second is the *marathon,* which runs for 5 consecutive days, 8 hours daily. Third is the *workshop,* which takes about a year, in which groups meet for 40 sessions. Every other week, members attend a 5-hour session. Fourth *is advanced study and community work.* Participants are now seen as "students"; it is recommended that they begin advanced courses and volunteer for hot-line work and other social interest activities, on the theory that only doing things for others guarantees good mental health.

GROUP PSYCHOTHERAPY
INNOVATIVE PSYCHOTHERAPIES

N. KEFIR

IMPLICIT LEARNING AND MEMORY

Implicit learning and implicit memory are characterized by an improvement in task efficiency that does not seem to depend on conscious effort and is not accompanied by any form of conscious experience directly related to that improvement. Although this kind of nonconscious behavioral function has been known for at least a century, it is only within the decade of the 1980s that its full theoretical significance has been recognized.

Because a demonstration of learning necessarily depends on some kind of memory of past experience, learning and memory are so intimately interdependent as to make clear-cut distinctions difficult. Nevertheless, a relative distinction can be made. Here the usual distinction is adopted; learning is defined as a process by which a change in behavior in some problem situation, usually in the direction of improved efficiency, is attained, and memory is defined as the subsequent demonstration of the retention of the effects of experience.

IMPLICIT LEARNING

Implicit learning is best described by example. Two contemporary research programs are nicely illustrative.

Reber's Artificial-Grammar Task

Reber's use of artificial grammar as an experimental task has yielded a continuing wealth of results that bear directly on the role that nonconscious processes can have in learning. In Reber's first report, a large number of letter strings, each containing a small number of consonants, were presented in an order determined by a set of rules so complex as to be virtually undetectable by subjects. Nevertheless, the subjects showed a progressive improvement in their ability to differentiate between grammatical (i.e., according to rule) and nongrammatical strings. In a later, especially persuasive study, subjects specifically instructed to search for the rules so that they could verbalize them not only failed to find any, but also did more poorly in differentiating grammatical and nongrammatical letter strings. Reber described his work in detail in a review article.

Lewicki and Hill's Pattern Learning

Pawel Lewicki and Thomas Hill have developed a number of perceptual learning tasks that show a surprisingly high amount of nonconscious acquisition of cognitive information. Their earlier work dealt with the ability of subjects to detect and use covariations in stimulus patterns. For example, when there was a nonsalient covariation of distractor features and target location (such as of a numeral) in a matrix pattern, subjects in several experiments were able to locate the targets with increasing efficiency, even though they were unable to verbalize the basis of their success. The same pattern of results occurred even when the subjects were faculty members of the psychology department who were familiar with the purpose of the experiment; in postexperimental debriefing they could provide no evidence that they had discovered any basis for their improvement in efficiency. In later research, it was found that perceptual biases established in early responses to ambiguous stimulus patterns would often not only persist but actually increase (in their terminology, "self-perpetuate") over later, extended trials—again, in the absence of any verbally available cognitive information.

IMPLICIT MEMORY

Ebbinghaus's Savings Method

As Roediger noted, pioneer experimental psychologist Hermann Ebbinghaus deserves credit for an early systematic demonstration of implicit memory. In his monograph, he not only clearly distinguished between voluntary and involuntary recollection, but also included a "third and large group of cases" in which prior experiences exert an influence without any trace of conscious recollection: "Most of these experiences remain concealed from consciousness and yet produce an effect which is significant and which authenticates their previous experience."

Ebbinghaus invented the savings method to measure this third class of cases for which the currently popular introspective approach was not feasible. After a subject had learned some material, say a set of nonsense syllables, to a criterion of mastery such as one perfect recitation, the subject was at some later time given exactly the same task again, and the number of trials required to meet the same criterion was recorded. The difference between the two measures (learning and relearning) was a savings because the second task was normally mastered more quickly than the first task, and was interpreted as reflecting the retention of some kind of knowledge, even if no conscious cues as to its nature were present.

Evidence from Amnesia

Long regarded as incapable of retaining new experiences, even while still perfectly capable in other perceptual and cognitive functions, the type of brain-damaged patient diagnosed as amnesic was found to be essentially normal in what we now called implicit, indirect, or procedural memory tests. In one much-cited early study Warrington and Weiskrantz found that their amnesic subjects were just as capable as normal control subjects in completing word stems (e.g., responding "marble" to the stimulus *mar*___after being first shown, or primed by, a list of words including *marble*), even while remaining markedly deficient in remembering those words in the study list when given a free-recall (explicit or declarative) test. The instructions in the implicit or procedural test simply ask the subject to find a word to complete the stem; in contrast, the explicit test calls for a declaration of studied words.

A review by Shimamura contains a number of replications of the Warrington and Weiskrantz results, including a total of eight implicit tests that gave the same results as the word-stem test. In a more recent report amnesic patients were again found to perform as well as normal subjects on an artificial grammar task, but showed the usual inferiority when asked to select in a recognition test the examplars that had been used in setting up the artificial grammar task.

Normal Subjects

Although less dramatic than the data collected from amnesiacs, the results of experiments with normal subjects have shown the same kind of dissociations between explicit and implicit memory tests. Jacoby found a complete reversal of results in the implicit compared with the explicit test. Subjects first read words out of context (e.g., *cold*), in context (e.g., *hot–cold*), or to be filled in or generated (e.g., *hot–????*). They were then given either an explicit (recognition) test or an implicit (perceptual-identification) test. In the explicit test, the well-established generation effect was confirmed (i.e., generated words were most often recognized). Also, out-of-context words were least often recognized. Exactly the opposite pattern of results occurred in the implicit test.

Numerous other dissociations between explicit and implicit memory tests were reported throughout the decade of the 1980s. This surge of results with so many counterintuitive results made implicit memory the hottest topic in memory research.

Theoretical Issues

A fundamental theoretical question raised by the research showing so many dissociations between explicit and implicit tests was whether the results require the assumption of more than one memory system. One strongly advanced position was that the results did constitute evidence for separate underlying brain systems. However, an opposing view held that they could be equally well explained in terms of the different relationships between processing and encoding operations at study and test. Schachter provides both a detailed summary of the alternative positions on the problem and a suggested resolution by means of a "cognitive neuroscience" approach.

Evaluation of Nonconscious Cognition

Finally, one can ask about the importance of the various nonconscious cognitive processes considered as factors in implicit memory. Such a question ("Is the unconscious smart or dumb?") was asked by Loftus and Klinger in their introduction to a set of articles on nonconscious processes; the various contributors were invited to answer this interesting, albeit premature, question. Lining up on the "dumb" side were Greenwald, "well-established phenomena . . . are limited to relatively minor cognitive feats," and Bruner, "not very smart but a big help anyway." Clearly on the "smart" side were Erdelyi, "The phenomena that the *unconscious* sloppily subsumes are not stupid or dumb," and Lewicki, Hill, and Cyzyewski, "data indicate that as compared with consciously controlled cognition, the nonconscious information acquisition processes are not only much faster but are also structurally more sophisticated."

Sitting more or less on the fence and preferring to await further developments before answering the question were Kuhlstrom, Barnhardt and Tataryn, Merikle, and Jacoby, Lindsay, and Toth, although the latter did acknowledge concerns that "suggest that the power of unconscious processes may be badly underestimated by experiments that present single word or phrases out of context."

INFORMATION PROCESSING
INFORMATION PROCESSING (UNCONSCIOUS)
INFORMATION PROCESSING THEORY
MEMORY EXPERIMENTS
MEMORY RETRIEVAL PROCESSES

M. H. MARX

IMPLOSIVE THERAPY

A form of behavior therapy developed by Thomas Stampfl in the late 1950s, implosive therapy is based on the hypothesis that neurotic behavior—notably intense anxiety—develops as an avoidance mechanism for coping with a repressed traumatic experience, and that the relative success of avoidance enables the anxiety to persist. In treatment the patient's anxiety is increased and maintained at an almost intolerable level by imagining a series of provoking cues, described either by the therapist or by the patient with the therapist's assistance, until the anxiety dissipates.

Proponents believe that the technique reinforces anxiety control and extinguishes related public responses by depriving the anxiety of its avoidance function.

ANXIETY

F. W. Hansen

IMPRESSION FORMATION

The origins of research on impression formation can be traced to an influential paper by Solomon Asch, "Forming impressions of personality." Two major issues were addressed in the paper. First, when forming an impression, the perceiver must somehow cope with what is often a heterogeneous set of facts about the other person. The second problem was in knowing exactly what the perceiver's impression is. How does a researcher go about measuring something as intricate—and yet amorphous—as an impression?

The main substantive concern raised by Asch was the importance of understanding how people cope with the diverse information items they receive about another person. This is sometimes referred to as the "information integration" problem. Two distinct theoretical perspectives have been advanced. The *Gestalt approach* argues that people adopt a configural strategy. They appraise the entire information array and arrive at a thematic interpretation that integrates all the disparate items into a coherent whole. This process often involves reinterpretation of some information items and the discounting of others.

The *cognitive algebra approach* argues that each item of information contributes independently to the overall impression. Unlike the Gestalt approach, this view assumes that the information items are not actively interrelated into a single meaningful configuration. Rather, the evaluative implications of each item are extracted at the time the item is first received and are combined with any preexisting evaluative response to yield the present evaluative impression of the other person. It is referred to as the cognitive algebra approach because information items can be combined through such algebraic rules as "averaging," "adding," or "multiplying." Although these two theoretical perspectives are very different in their conceptual assumptions, they have proven equally adept at accounting for the primary empirical findings in the field.

Most research in the area of impression formation has focused on first impressions. Subjects participating in the research are given a list of personality-trait adjectives and asked to form an impression of a hypothetical person who possesses that particular set of traits. The resulting impressions are found to be affected by a variety of characteristics of the information items.

When information items are presented sequentially, both *primacy and recency effects* have been observed.

After an overall impression is formed, subjects are sometimes asked to give a separate rating to one of the items in the set. In this case, *meaning shift effects* are reliably obtained. A particular trait such as "cooperative" is evaluated more positively (e.g., similar to "selfless") when the other traits in the set are positive. It receives a less favorable interpretation (e.g., similar to "compliant") when the remaining information is negative.

The number of items in the information set can be large in some cases and small in others. Substantial *set size effects* have been obtained in impression formation research. As the number of positive items increases, impressions become more favorable; as the number of negative items increases, impressions become more unfavorable.

Most studies in this area have used traits exclusively as the stimulus information provided the subject. It is possible that the findings would be very different if other kinds of person information were used (e.g.,

behaviors, social affiliations, physical appearance, and demographic features). However, the little research that has been conducted with nontrait stimuli suggests that this problem may not be a major concern.

In this research area, the subjects are usually forewarned that they are to provide an impression rating after seeing the trait set. Consequently, they undoubtedly are actively developing their impression responses during the time they encounter the information items. Thus there is little or no role for memory in this impression formation task. In contrast, the development of impressions (even first impressions) in our everyday social encounters necessarily involves memory processes. It is presently unclear what changes in the Gestalt and cognitive algebra formulations would be required to accommodate memory for previous information.

ATTITUDE MEASUREMENT
SOCIAL COGNITION

T. Ostrom

IMPRINTING

First used by Konrad Lorenz, the term *imprinting* designates the process of rapid development of social attachments by young animals toward their mothers. The social attachments are directed and confined to stimuli with which the young have specific appropriate experience at an appropriate time. The exact stimulus object to which the birds respond in this way maintains its capability of evoking the adient response (attachment) through much of the young animal's life. The originally great diversity of objects capable of eliciting attachment becomes restricted to only the class or classes of objects encountered during the limited acquisition period.

D. A. Spaulding, the first to describe the phenomenon, showed that the attachment need not be restricted to the mother, although it normally is. He noted that as soon as newly hatched chickens could walk, they would follow any moving stimulus. This promiscuity of following could be observed in visually naive chicks only during the first few days.

The strength of the attachment can be seen in one or more of the following tests: (a) *recognition at reunion*, in which, after separation, more imprinted birds return to the imprinting stimulus than do control chicks; (b) *choice*, in which experimental and control birds are presented with a training and a control stimulus; (c) *distress at separation*; (d) *run to mother*, in which somewhat dispersed chicks are exposed to a novel, frightening stimulus, whereupon the imprinted but not the control chicks are expected to retreat to the training stimulus; and (e) *work for reunion*, in which the birds must perform an arbitrary response such as a bar press to obtain access to the training stimulus.

Lorenz and others distinguished imprinting from ordinary learning because (a) imprinting can take place only during a limited critical period; (b) once imprinting is accomplished, forgetting does not occur; (c) conventional rewards are not necessary to imprinting; (d) certain responses to the imprinted stimulus may not appear until late in life, long after the imprinting took place; (e) imprinting occurs more readily, when trials follow each other quickly than when they are widely spaced, contrary to most associative-learning experience; and (f) painful stimuli strengthen imprinting, whereas punishment usually results in the avoidance of the associated stimulus.

The term "critical period" has been weakened somewhat into "sensitive period" because the all-or-nothing character of the former term does not stand up to fact. Instead, there seems to be a quantitative rise and fall in the ease or strength of imprinting. Moreover, additional experiences may interfere with imprinting.

The belief that imprinting is irreversible is no longer widely held. It has been shown that attachment can be transferred to new stimuli. In addition, a number of species do not direct their adult social attachments strictly to the parental figure or to its species.

Although much of the research on imprinting has been done with birds, a few observations suggest that similar processes occur in mammals. Sheep, horses, and other hoofed animals can be imprinted to humans if a person assumes the parental role shortly after birth. Dogs are known to form close attachments to persons who care for them between the fourth and sixth weeks of life. The pattern of treatment, nurturant or punishing, seems to be of little importance.

ETHOLOGY
INSTINCTIVE BEHAVIOR

A. J. RIOPELLE

INBORN ERRORS OF METABOLISM

Inborn errors of metabolism (IEM) are inherited single-gene–based disorders of intermediary metabolism. Arising initially through mutation (i.e., alteration of DNA), they are transmitted across generations according to classic Mendelian principles.

Phenylketonuria (PKU) is best known, but many other IEM have important psychological sequelae. More than 300 IEM are listed in McKusick's *Mendelian inheritance in man;* more are discovered regularly. Of the approximately 200 enzyme defects, some 80% are autosomal recessive; the rest are autosomal dominant or X-linked. Of the additional about 100 nonenzyme protein defects, roughly 90% are more or less evenly divided into autosomal dominant or recessive, and the remainder are X-linked recessive. Although individually low in incidence, in combination, IEM affect about 1 in 1000 newborns.

GENERAL CONCERNS

IEM are of interest for at least seven interdependent reasons. (a) Many have severe adverse psychological and behavioral effects, including mental retardation, seizures, and motor dysfunction, stemming from interference with normal central nervous system (CNS) development. Indeed, some 30% of individuals affected by an IEM are at risk for CNS damage. IEM with such effects include PKU, maple syrup urine disease, galactosemia, and the mucopolysaccharidoses (e.g., Hurler's syndrome, Scheie's syndrome, and X-linked Hunter's syndrome). In addition to mental retardation, the X-linked Lesch-Nyhan syndrome is associated with persistent and severe self-mutilation through self-biting. (b) The dietary treatment available for several IEM may present management and family interaction problems during the developmental period. (c) Dietary treatment for some IEM is only partially effective, leading treated individuals to have subnormal intelligence and/or specific learning disabilities. (d) Women given dietary treatment for IEM are still unable to metabolize a particular substance. Consumption of normal foods during pregnancy may produce serious damage in their fetuses. (e) A number of IEM are invariably fatal, leading parents to be in severe distress and frequently in need of counseling. (f) Owing to the Mendelian characteristics of the disorders, affected individuals, their parents, and other relatives may require genetic counseling. (g) Recent advances in techniques for investigating these disorders has led to an "avalanche of new information" on the metabolic, molecular, and genetic details of many IEM. With that knowledge have come new methods of detection and treatment.

GENETICS: BASIC OUTLINE

Normally, humans have 23 pairs of chromosomes, 22 pairs of autosomes, and 1 pair of sex chromosomes. During meiosis (process of formation of germ cells, the sperm and egg), each pair splits such that sperm are 23X or 23Y and eggs are 23X. During sexual recombination, when a sperm and egg unite, a total of 46XX (female) or 46XY (male) is reconstituted. A number of traits, including IEM, are determined by single genes; different forms of genes (alleles) allow for variations in those traits. An individual who has inherited the same allele on both chromosomes is homozygotic; one who has inherited two different alleles is heterozygotic. For some traits, one gene for a given trait will be dominant and expressed regardless of the contribution of the other gene. In such cases, individuals who are either homozygotic for the dominant gene or heterozygotic will express the same form of the trait; the alternative form will be expressed only in individuals who are homozygotic for the recessive trait. X-linked recessive traits, for which genes are located on the sex chromosomes, may be expressed more frequently, or even exclusively, in males. Heterozygotic females have a dominant gene on one X chromosome that will suppress a recessive gene on the other X chromosome; males may have no counterpart gene on the Y chromosome, allowing expression of the recessive gene on the single X chromosome.

In terms of disorders such as IEM, those determined by a dominant gene on an autosome are referred to as autosomal dominant (AD); those determined by a pair of recessive autosomal genes are termed autosomal recessive (AR); and those determined by a recessive gene on the X chromosome and expressed largely in males are termed X-linked recessive (XR). In terms of inheritance, an AD trait will be expressed regardless of the counterpart gene. Thus a heterozygotic individual affected by an AD disorder has a 50% chance of transmitting the disorder to offspring. A woman who is a heterozygotic carrier of an XR disorder has a similar 50% chance of passing the disorder to her sons. An AR disorder typically appears in a family line in offspring of two heterozygotic carriers who have a 25% chance of having a child who is homozygous for the recessive trait.

A number of factors beyond the scope of this review, including codominance, penetrance, and variable expressivity, complicate the genetics of single-gene traits. Furthermore, through mutation of a gene, a disorder, particularly a dominant one, may appear suddenly in a family line. Finally, molecular genetic research has demonstrated that apparently single disease entities may arise from the action of different mutations at a single locus or at different loci, a phenomenon called genetic heterogeneity. Indeed, several disorders have AR, AD, and XR forms. In some cases, individuals who appear homozygous for an AR disorder may actually have inherited different abnormal alleles from each parent leading to genetic compounds. Such compounds are known to occur in a number of IEM, including phenylketonuria, galactosemia, and Scheie's syndrome. Finally, individuals who are heterozygotic for some autosomal recessive IEM may show symptoms, particularly under certain environmental conditions. These and other factors indicate that dominant and recessive disorders are best seen as extremes on a continuum rather than as distinct entities. Further information on genetic effects is provided by Beaudet et al. or medical genetics textbooks.

DETECTION AND DIAGNOSIS

Newborn screening tests are available for several IEM. Most states require tests for hyperphenylalemias (PKU and related disorders), maple syrup urine disease, and galactosemia, among others. Screening tests for a number of others, including Lesch-Nyhan syndrome and tyrosinemia, are available but not widely used.

Many IEM present acute life-threatening symptoms during the newborn period. These include vomiting, diarrhea, jaundice, lethargy and coma, seizures, and unusual body or body fluid odor. Other IEM may have a more gradual onset with symptoms that gradually appear during infancy. Common symptoms include developmental delay, enlarged spleen or liver, coarse faces, failure to thrive, and unusual body odor. Many of these symptoms, both acute and gradual, are common to other disorders, complicating diagnosis. Their presence suggests the need for the metabolic and various quantitative tests that lead to specific identification of IEM.

TREATMENT

Effective treatment involves extraordinary measures that shift development from its predicted abnormal pathway. Traditional treatments have included dietary modification and replacement of an end product that is deficient owing to impaired metabolism. However, increased understanding of the pathophysiology of many IEM and advances in molecular genetics are leading to other treatments. Detailed descriptions are available.

Treatment at the Metabolite Level

A variety of approaches attempt to avoid the effects of the impaired enzyme through dietary or pharmacologic treatment. Dietary restriction of the substrate reduces the substance that cannot be metabolized and that accumulates behind the metabolic block. For example, treatment of PKU involves a diet low in phenylananine that reduces accumulation of toxic phenylketones. The treatment is a classic example of a genetic–environment interaction and modification of range of reaction owing to a new environmental circumstance, the special diet. Some IEM can be successfully treated by removing a particular type of food from the diet. Thus a diet free of galactose, including use of lactose-free formulas, prevents the mental retardation and cataracts associated with galactosemia.

Dietary modifications do not cure the disorder; affected individuals still cannot metabolize a substance. Traditionally, such individuals have been taken off the special diet and have begun eating normal food at the end of the developmental period. This has led to severe adverse prenatal effects on the offspring of affected women. Because the women are eating normal food, which they are unable to metabolize appropriately during pregnancy, a toxic substance is produced and circulates to the developing embryo–fetus, causing prenatal death or mental retardation and other severe CNS abnormalities. Thus a genetic disorder in the mother leads to an adverse prenatal environmental effect in the offspring. Although maternal phenylketonuria is the best-known example of this effect, it occurs in galactosemia and may be expected in other IEM treated by diet during the developmental period. The extent to which an affected woman's return to the diet reduces adverse prenatal effects varies with the disorder and the time of return to the diet.

In replacement of the deficient end product, a needed metabolic product that is deficient owing to the metabolic block is provided pharmacologically. Cretinism, resulting from a block in thyroxine production, can be prevented by thyroid hormone replacement. Other approaches involve depletion of storage substances and use of metabolic inhibitors.

Treatment at the Level of the Dysfunctional Protein

In amplification of enzyme activity, a required cofactor is provided that facilitates the activity of the deficient enzyme. For some IEM based on a nonenzymic protein deficiency, direct replacement of the mutant protein is effective; attempts at direct replacement in enzyme-based disorders such as Tay-Sachs disease have been much less successful. Modifying the mutant protein by adding subgroups may in some cases enable normal functioning.

Organ Transplantation

Organ transplants offer the possibility of replacing the organ that is not providing a required protein with a normal organ that does.

Genetic Engineering

Recombinant DNA technology and increasing knowledge of the specific location of genes for various traits through the Human Genome Project present the possibility of actual removal of the defective gene replacement with a normal one.

BEHAVIORAL GENETICS
DEVIANT MATURATION
GENETIC DISORDERS
GENETIC DOMINANCE AND RECESSIVENESS
HERITABILITY

R. T. BROWN

INBREEDING AND HUMAN FACTORS

Inbreeding is mating between genetically related persons, that is, persons who share genes derived from a common ancestor. The degree of inbreeding is a function of the number of common ancestors and the number of generations they are removed. Specifically, degree of inbreeding is expressed quantitatively as the average probability that the offspring will receive two of the same alleles (alternate forms of a gene) from the same ancestor. Brother–sister and parent–offspring matings are the highest degree of inbreeding found in humans. Incestuous matings have been taboo in all human societies throughout history, probably because of the high frequency of genetically undesirable effects, both physical and mental, on the inbred offspring. Mating of first or second cousins, however, is still relatively common in some societies; the adverse effects on the offspring are much more subtle than in the offspring of incestuous matings, but are nevertheless clearly detectable. For individuals born with rare genetic defects—particularly various forms of severe mental deficiency—the percentage of their parents who are first cousins is some 20 to 40 times as great as the percentage of first-cousin matings in the general population.

The effects of inbreeding are understandable in terms of genetic theory. Inbreeding simultaneously affects all traits, physical and mental, that are conditioned to any degree by genetic factors. Inbreeding does not alter gene frequencies, but changes the frequencies of various genotypes (i.e., specific combinations of genes). Inbreeding always increases the amount of homozygosity and decreases heterozygosity. A general consequence of this relative increase in homozygosity is an increase in trait variance; inbred offspring are more variable in every trait influenced by segregating genes (i.e., genes with two or more allelic forms).

The one other effect of inbreeding—probably the most important—occurs when a trait involves dominant and recessive alleles. If, as is usually the case, the dominant alleles enhance the phenotypic expression of the trait and the recessive alleles diminish the trait, the overall effect of inbreeding is to diminish the expression of the trait in the inbred individual. The reason, essentially, is that inbreeding increases the chances that the recessive alleles will be paired with other recessives, thereby depressing the trait—an effect known as *inbreeding depression*. The probability of recessive mutant or deleterious alleles coming together is much greater in inbred persons. Because most deleterious characteristics are recessive, inbreeding increases the risk of genetic defects in the progeny.

However, even a nonpathological trait variation that involves some degree of directional dominance, as do height and intelligence, will show inbreeding depression. A number of studies of the offspring of incestuous matings show that this high degree of inbreeding is correlated with lowered IQ; about one third of such children show marked defects and are placed in institutions for the retarded.

BEHAVIORAL GENETICS
HERITABILITY

A. R. JENSEN

INCENTIVES

A *positive reinforcer* or a *negative reinforcer* serves two quite different functions in the control of behavior. On the one hand, such events are critical to learning, although the mechanism of this influence remains controversial. On the other hand, they are motivators. This latter role identifies the concept of *incentive,* the motivational value of a reinforcer. The *Crespi effect* provides a demonstration of the operation of an incentive at the level of the laboratory rat. At the human level, approval, reproof, and money are examples.

CLASSICAL CONDITIONING
CRESPI EFFECT
REWARDS

G. A. KIMBLE

INCEST

The term *incest* is broadly construed to refer to sexual behavior between individuals who are related in any fashion except directly by marriage. Beyond this consensus, definitions found in various state laws and those proposed by experts differ along two dimensions: specific behaviors involved and specific relations of participants.

Some definitions list only vaginal and anal coitus as behaviors involved in incest, whereas others include oral-genital behaviors and even fondling or mutual exhibition of the genitalia. These differences, especially among surveys and other research reports, make it difficult to estimate the incidence of various types of incest, however defined. Furthermore, any collation of data is bound to be attenuated by a significant failure to report on the part of victims—a tendency that incest shares with rape. A comparison of recent surveys suggests that if incest is broadly defined to include casual types of sexual contact, and if a large unselected sample is surveyed, then sibling incest will be the most common with a reported incidence of 10 to 15%.

In contrast, if the researcher seeks out individuals who have already reported incest, then the father–daughter form is the most common. Proportionately, coitus appears to occur more often in the father–daughter dyads than among siblings. The perennial belief that incest occurs primarily in lower-class and rural communities is not supported by recent data. The fact that the lower-class offender is more likely to come in contact with law enforcement agencies has distorted the overall picture.

The impact of incest, especially its long-term effects, has been generally thought to be malignant, although some data indicate that the effect of incest is not that simple. For example, Joan Nelson found that the long-term reaction was more likely to be untoward if the incest occurred prior to age 10. Nelson also reported that a negative effect was more likely if coitus had occurred, as opposed to other, more superficial forms of sexual contact. Mavis Tsai and others found that a malignant outcome was more likely when the incestuous relationship lasted for a number of years, as opposed to relationships of relatively short duration.

Almost every society regards incest, defined as sexual activity between members of the nuclear family, as taboo. Every state in this country has a statute punishing incest. In those states that have recently recodified laws dealing with sexual behavior, the victim must be a minor. However, incest in which the victim is an adult is extremely rare.

CHILD ABUSE
SEXUAL DEVIATIONS

E. E. LEVITT

INCOMPLETE SENTENCES

The incomplete sentences method is a technique of psychological assessment. Typically, the first word or words are presented by the examiner and are referred to as "stems." Some examples of stems would be: I like . . . ; What annoys me . . . ; I wish . . . ; Most girls . . . The method has been used for many specific purposes such as the examination of personality, the assessment of attitudes, the prediction of achievement, and the identification of contrasts between groups.

Perhaps its most visible role has been in clinical assessment. In this context, the incomplete sentences method is often regarded as a kind of projective test. In the process, individuals reveal a good deal of their personality. At the same time, incomplete sentences are not as ambiguous as other projective tests and therefore might better be regarded as "semiprojective" devices. Their best use is usually to provide clues as to how the individual generally behaves or what impression he or she wishes to convey. Incomplete sentences may be administered in group settings and thus are relatively economical to use. Although they cannot be computer-scored, nonprofessionals can be trained rather easily to score them for specific purposes.

Over the years, a host of specific forms of sentence completion tests have been devised. The best-known and most widely used device is the Rotter Incomplete Sentences Blank (ISB) developed by Julian Rotter and his colleagues. The ISB contains 40 stems of the kind noted earlier. Its principal use initially was in the assessment of general adjustment. Each response is scored on a seven-point scale for degree of conflict. These separate item scores are then summed to provide an overall adjustment score. Considerable reliability and validity data exist for this use of the ISB. The ISB can, however, be used for purposes other than measuring simple adjustment.

PERSONALITY ASSESSMENT
PROJECTIVE TECHNIQUES
SENTENCE COMPLETION TESTS

E. J. PHARES

INDEPENDENT PERSONALITIES

"Independence" is a concept that has received varied treatment in psychology. In general, it is defined as acting more in accordance with one's own needs, perceptions, or judgments than in response to the demands of the environment or the influence of other persons. Although it is not difficult to identify instances of independent behavior, it is quite difficult to explain them systematically.

An independent personality may be viewed in terms of either motivation or mode of self-regulation. In the former case one would expect to see a pattern of striving that cuts across or integrates many kinds of acts. In the latter case, one would expect to see a kind of strategy that governs how a person acts in striving for many different kinds of goals. In a common-sense way, then, independence as a motive is associated with seeking the rewards of the freedom to act without interference from others (or the environment), while as a regulator it is expressed by individualism and involvement of the self in decisions. Either as a motive or as an attitude, situational conditions influence what behavior actually occurs.

SOCIAL INFLUENCE AND INDEPENDENCE

One line of investigation regarding independence concerns response to the opinions of other persons, as initiated by S. E. Asch's now-classic experiments on the effect of unanimous opinions. Independents typically were convinced that they were right in spite of opposition and maintained their confidence as trials proceeded.

Asch's findings prompted a good deal of research concerned with other majority conditions. Of special interest here are studies that sought to clarify the personality determinants of independence. Much in line with Asch's findings, they found that independents tend to be self-reliant, persuasive, expressive, unconventional, and able to think for themselves; conformists tend to be submissive, conventional, easily upset by stress, and suggestible, and lack insight into their own motives and attitudes.

Other investigators have elaborated this distinction to allow for other kinds of response to influence. Thus we can recognize cases where a person actually opposes authority and responds antithetically to it ("anti-conformity"), as well as the cool and objective independence just described. Yielding is not always simple compliance, but may result from a positive evaluation of evidence followed by a decision to agree with the source (a kind of "rational conformity").

FIELD INDEPENDENCE

A series of studies by Witkin and his associates led to the delineation of the perceptual styles of field dependence and field independence.

Subjects vary widely in their ability to separate the characteristics of the perceived field from their own place in it, leading to a distinction between independence and dependence. The former, marked by accuracy of perception, is the ability to deal in an analytical fashion with the field, but the latter, involving less ability to do so, shows confusion about the cues present in the environmental field.

The investigators found a good deal of consistency in these styles across tests, and noted that they become more general and stable with age into adulthood. Data from personality tests yielded contrasting patterns. Thus the field-independent person appears as active, self-aware, adept at expressing and controlling emotional impulses directly, self-assured, and able to compensate for inferiority feelings. The field-dependent person emerges as passive, lacking in self-awareness, repressing impulses, utilizing infantile defenses against anxiety, lacking in self-assurance, and yielding to inferiority feelings. In addition, field dependence especially characterized the female subjects in these experiments. However, recent clarification of sex differences indicates that this pattern is probably a function of the traditional sex role rather than of biological gender. The "independents" of Asch's study and the "field independents" of Witkin's are generally similar in traits.

PSYCHOLOGICAL DIFFERENTIATION

Witkin and Goodenough elaborated a more general theory. Psychological differentiation entails the segregation of self from nonself. The field-independent person relies on self-reference, whereas the field-dependent person relies on the environmental context as perceived.

Witkin and Goodenough apply this view to interpersonal behavior. Here, field-dependent persons possess social skills that enable them to interact more effectively with other people. This contrasts with the impersonal orientation of field-independent people.

AUTONOMY

H. A. Murray used the term *autonomy* for an acquired or psychogenic motive embodying the notion of independence as an instigating force. It is one of several motives that "have to do with human power exerted, resisted, or yielded to." He defined autonomy as follows: "To resist influence or coercion. To defy an authority or seek freedom in a new place. To strive for independence."

Certainly it is intuitively appealing to recognize that a striving for freedom and control over one's behavioral outcomes may in some persons be a functionally autonomous motivational force. Indeed, it is surely as distinctively human a motive as any other. At present, however, we have little systematic theorizing or research pertinent to it. The identification

of cognitive styles or attitudes, as in the work of Witkin, is not sufficient for an understanding of the deeper and more general determinants of behavior that we label "independent."

To understand behavior that can be called "independent," then, it is necessary to clarify the factors that determine it. One should distinguish among several kinds of determinants, each representing a different emphasis. A review of approaches to the problem of independence would include the following: authoritarian personality, internal and external loci of control, moral development, ego functioning, and deindividuation. Also relevant are investigations of personal control, choice, and freedom.

AUTHORITARIAN PERSONALITY
CONFORMING PERSONALITY
INDIVIDUALISM
LOCUS OF CONTROL

W. E. VINACKE

INDEPENDENT PRACTICE

Whereas psychologists are trained to conduct a wide variety of psycho-therapeutic interventions of various styles and approaches, and to assess intellect, aptitude, personality, neuropsychological functioning, and marital adjustment, agency or institutional practice generally restricts the psychologist's practice to those elements required by the institution for which the psychologist works. In the independent practice setting, clinical psychologists tend to work autonomously. They have the opportunity to decide on the best utilization of their own skills and tools.

During the 1950s, there were perhaps 50 psychologists in full-time independent practice in the United States. As of 1995, at least 10,000 psychologists were in full time independent practice. It is generally agreed that those who enter independent practice in clinical psychology should have the doctorate from an approved training institution, as well as 2 years of postdoctoral supervised experience in clinical psychology. Various states have licensing or certification requirements that represent the journeyman level of competence for independent practice.

Most psychologists committed to independent practice have found that there are considerable advantages to this role model. These include:

1. The opportunity to offer a broad spectrum of psychological services.

2. The opportunity to develop services that the practitioner knows best, enjoys most, and delivers effectively.

3. The free choice and opportunity to avoid rendering partial, long-delayed, or inappropriate services.

4. Relative freedom from political and bureaucratic constraints and demands.

5. Fair compensation for extra skill, effort, or commitment.

6. The opportunity to become an experienced practicing clinician without loss of status or income.

7. The opportunity to pursue a broadening of skills and training without the constraints of institutional budgets.

8. The option of offering services to anyone without regard to eligibility.

9. The opportunity to make oneself available as a trainer of skill and experience.

10. The option of selecting surroundings, equipment, supporting staff, and the style of service delivery. Excellence and its pursuit is limited only by the practitioner's education, training, ethical constraints, and goodwill.

11. A clearer attribution of success or failure to the practitioner.

12. The opportunity to be the first and last person to see the consumer. Direct access increases the probability of delivery of competent service, more personal involvement, early resolution of misunderstandings, and better evaluation of benefit.

13. The freedom to adjust fees to the consumer's income.

14. Freedom from institutional constraints—real or symbolic.

15. Variety of activity and scheduling flexibility, which are likely to increase the quality of life of practicing professionals.

Surveys indicate that in American communities the range of saturation for full-time independent practitioners of psychology is from 1 per 2500 population to 1 per 135,000. Thus this particular role model for clinical psychologists offering direct consumer service may be the model of the future.

CLINICAL PSYCHOLOGY CREDENTIALING

T. H. Blau

INDIVIDUAL DIFFERENCES

The communication system developed by humans not only makes them unique in regard to other animals, but also makes individuals unique in regard to one another. Speech and language require adequate physical and neural development and similar sensory experiences for humans to develop the basic skills required in communication. Genetic or physical damage to all or part of the nervous system or inadequate sensory development or inadequate learning experiences, can make individuals different. The age at which experiences occur, as well as emotional factors and opportunities, can contribute to individual uniquenesses.

As a result of human uniqueness, psychology has had to turn to more general and less effective group approaches to try to gain information about the individual. Methods of evaluation and statistical techniques had to be developed to make the evaluation results useful. This has taken a great deal of time; as a result the scientific investigation of individual differences, along with the special factors that exist in each case, is of relatively recent origin. It has become a specialized area within the general field of psychology known as differential psychology.

A major problem in differential psychology is the kind and number of ways an individual can be different. Differences start at conception as a result of the great differences in the chromosomes and genes available in each parent. There are the effects of environment on the selection of chromosomes and genes plus the physical, mental, and emotional state of the mother who carries the child to be. Other factors include the nutrition available during the developmental period and after birth, the amount of stimulation available after birth, the type and kind of traumatic experiences that may occur, the others in the individuals' environment, and the type and kind of educational experiences available.

The particular genes supplied by the parents are the determiners of the basic physical, mental, and emotional development of the individual. Each set of genes is unique, even in the case of identical twins. Recent studies have found maternal environmental differences that can affect the development of one twin more than they affect the other.

The environment can only modify what is already present. For example, failure to supply something that is needed such as vitamins or proteins, or the presence of harmful physical or chemical factors can make dramatic changes.

Stimulation is necessary for the normal development of an individual. Sensory deprivation can lead to retardation in motor and mental development.

Traumatic experiences in the form of shocks or insults can create individual differences. A fall in which the head or neck are damaged can affect physical, mental, and emotional development. Emotional experiences of a traumatic nature can have a short-term or long-term effect on intellectual development. A devastating illness can leave physical, mental, and emotional damage in its wake.

Sexual differences are observable after birth. A girl tends to develop faster than a boy, and this will affect brain development. Early developers have better verbal than spatial abilities, whereas late developers perform better on spatial than on verbal tasks.

In the area of physical growth a relatively orderly sequence of development exists, primarily based on inheritance. Although the order is relatively the same from child to child, the rate of development can vary tremendously, with some infants reaching the stage of standing or walking months ahead of others. Sex differences play a primary role here: By 5 years of age, girls tend to be 4 months or more ahead of boys. Major differences between the sexes can be seen in the preadolescent growth spurt that occurs toward the end of the childhood period, beginning 2 years before adolescence. The average girl begins her growth spurt shortly after age 10 and achieves adolescence by approximately 12.5 years, with a deceleration of growth by age 14. The average boy begins his growth spurt at about 13 years and achieves adolescence around age 15, with a deceleration of growth after 16.

Learning experiences play such an important part in emotional development that no clear-cut differences in emotional behavior have been found for the two sexes. As a child matures, the emotional characteristics undergo major changes and the type of experiences that generate emotional reactions also changes. Parental attitudes and behavior, the culture, and the environment are all important factors in an individual's emotional development, but so are the individual's own characteristics.

Francis Galton is given credit for the first systematic investigation of individual differences. Convinced that heredity was the major factor in differences among people, he devised a sensory-motor test that discriminated among stimuli. This test has been called the first measure of intellectual potential.

James M. Cattell was interested in the difference between individuals in several areas including academic success. He is said to have used the term "mental test" as early as 1890.

Alfred Binet became interested in individual differences as a result of his work with hypnosis and his observations of the different ways his daughters solved problems. Working with Theodore Simon, he developed the first real intelligence scale in 1905 when he assembled a group of cognitive and sensory tasks in an attempt to identify retarded children in the French school system.

Testing materials and approaches have greatly improved. New techniques for evaluating testing materials and their results have increased the usefulness of these devices. As a result, it is easier today to determine an individual's strengths and weaknesses and then to place that individual in the best existing educational or training program designed to meet his or her needs.

Measurement is the only way that has been found to determine how one person will differ from another in ways that cannot be directly observed.

Intellectual functioning is the area most frequently involved in controversy over devices used for measuring individual differences. An individual's intellectual functioning depends on the inherited potential plus an environment that permits the development of that potential. But IQ is not a constant characteristics such as eye color. If IQ scores are accumulated on the same individual over a period of time, there is an increase in the constancy of the scores. This improvement in constancy can be related to the changes that occur as the result of maturation, plus the experiences that improve the individual's ability to deal with information in the nervous system. There are also the learning experiences that over a period of time fill in some of the earlier gaps in knowledge until some degree of balance is reached and the scores become more and more alike.

There are many aspects of intelligence not adequately dealt with on an IQ test, which tends to concentrate on abilities most relevant to school learning.

An accurate picture of intelligence requires the sampling of performance in a broad range of abilities. The scores obtained reflect experiences that have taken place in and out of educational institutions interwoven with psychological factors pertinent to the particular individual.

No matter what test is used to measure individual differences, there are always additional factors to be considered such as the individual's physical, mental, and emotional state at the time of the examination; the ability of the individual to understand the directions or to use the materials effectively; the time of day, week, or month; the area used for testing, the temperature, the amount of light available, and the amount of noise in the background. Any one of these things and many more can affect the score of a particular individual on a particular day.

CHROMOSOME DISORDERS
DEVELOPMENTAL DIFFERENCES
DIFFERENTIAL PSYCHOLOGY
LIFE-SPAN DEVELOPMENT

F. D. BRESLIN

INDIVIDUAL EDUCATION

Individual education is a system of general education based on the humanistic personality theory of Alfred Adler, but consistent with other Third Force theories such as those of Carl Rogers, Albert Ellis, Abraham Maslow, and James Bugenthal.

Individual education operates on certain specific hypotheses. First, children are ambitious and will attempt to learn as much as possible in as quick a manner as possible if the subject to be learned seems meaningful to them and they are permitted to find their own way to learn the subject. Second, children want to belong and adjust; school friction is a function either of the basic maladjustment of the child to any school or of the school not operating properly according to a basic psychology of children. Third, the purpose of a school is to inculcate not the relatively trivial three Rs of reading, 'riting, and 'rithmetic, but rather the important four Rs of Responsibility, Respect, Resourcefulness, and Responsiveness (social interest).

An individual education school has only three rules: (a) Do nothing that could be dangerous to yourself or others or damaging to property; (b) always be under supervision or en route from one supervised place to another; and (c) leave the room immediately and in silence if a teacher points at you. The latter is the only order a teacher can give.

In individual education every child has the right to petition any faculty member to be his or her teacher adviser; there is no assigned homework; subjects are taught in terms of weekly units and evaluated by short objective tests whose results are indicated on the child's progress chart; there are no report cards; the faculty is not permitted to communicate with parents unless the child is willingly present; and children need not go to classes, but may go to the library or the study hall instead. In addition to a normal academic program, there is also a creative program that consists of teaching whatever children want to learn, whatever faculty or others wish to teach, and whatever of these the principal will permit to be taught.

Evidence indicates that children actually learn more academics in less time compared with traditional schools; that disciplinary incidents are reduced to practically zero; that children learn social and prevocational skills; and that parents, faculty and children prefer individual education to the traditional system. According to Edward Ignas, individual education is theoretically consistent with the values of American political philosophy.

ALTERNATIVE EDUCATIONAL SYSTEMS
APPROACHES TO LEARNING
LEARNING OUTCOMES

B. OZAKI-JAMES

INDIVIDUALISM

In common usage, *individualism* is defined as leading one's life in one's own way without regard for others. Individualism may be separated from *individuality,* which is the sum of the qualities that set one person apart from others. To *individualize* is to distinguish a person as different from others, whereas to *individuate* is to make a person individual or distinct. Individualism is also distinct from *autonomy,* which is the ability to understand what others expect in any given situation and what one's values are, and to be free to choose how to behave based on either or both. Whereas individuality and autonomy are important aspects of healthy psychological development and health, individualism is not.

Based on the theorizing of Morton Deutsch and David Johnson and Roger Johnson, *individualism* may be defined as believing and behaving as if one's efforts and goal attainments are unrelated to or independent from the efforts of others toward goal attainment.

There is considerable research comparing the relative effects of individualism, cooperativeness, and competitiveness. Individualism, compared with cooperativeness, tends to be related to (a) lower beliefs that one is liked, accepted, supported, and assisted by others; (b) less seeking of information from others and utilizing it for one's own benefit; (c) lower achievement, intrinsic, and continuing motivation, and greater orientation toward extrinsic rewards; (d) less emotional involvement in efforts to achieve one's goals; (e) lower achievement; (f) lower ability to take the cognitive and less healthy processes for deriving conclusions about one's self-worth; (g) lower psychological health as reflected in greater psychological pathology, delinquency, emotional immaturity, social maladjustment, self-alienation, self-rejection, lack of social participation, basic distrust of other people, pessimism, and inability to resolve conflicts between self-perceptions and adverse information about oneself; and (h) less liking for others and more negative interpersonal relationships.

If the direct evidence is not very favorable toward individualism, the writings in personality and clinical psychology are even less so. Effective socialization brings with it an awareness that one cannot achieve one's life goals alone; one needs other people's help and resources. Psychological health requires a realization that one's goals and the goals of others, one's efforts and the efforts of others, and one's success and the success of many different people are all related and interdependent. Individuals high on individualism do not have a high degree of such awareness. Individualism often brings with it the following: (a) feelings of alienation, loneliness, isolation, inferiority, worthlessness, depression, and defeat; (b) attitudes reflecting low self-esteem, an emphasis on short-term gratification, and the conviction that no one cares about oneself or one's capabilities; and (c) relationships characterized by impulsiveness, fragmentation, withdrawal, and insensitivity to one's own and others' needs.

AFFILIATION NEED
AVOIDANT PERSONALITY
COOPERATION/COMPETITION
INDEPENDENT PERSONALITIES

INTERPERSONAL RELATIONS
SOCIAL ISOLATION

D. W. JOHNSON
R. T. JOHNSON

INDIVIDUALITY THEORY

Individuality theory refers to that class of theory that attempts to account for individual differences. Although individual differences have been reported for every psychological process investigated, from reaction time to values, the areas of intelligence and personality have been the most thoroughly researched. Moreover, the most important theories of individual differences in intelligence and personality have been cast in terms of factor analysis.

The basic idea behind the factor model is that complex behavioral phenomena such as intelligence can be decomposed into simpler components known as factors. However, if these primary components are correlated, then one can also identify higher order components as the determiners of lower-order factors. The uniqueness or individuality of each person is identified by the person's multidimensional profile.

Subsequent research has revealed three classes of factors: (a) general: those components common to a very large set of tests; (b) group: those components common to a relatively small set of tests (i.e., at least three, but not all tests of the battery); and (c) specific: those components unique to each test.

The many substantive factor theories are variations in the way these three classes of factors have been combined. For example, Charles Spearman's two-factor theory of intelligence postulates one superfactor, g, plus a specific factor for each test. L. L. Thurstone's theory of primary mental abilities, in contrast, focuses on the identification of a large number of group factors such as space, memory, induction, deduction, number, and verbal comprehension. Subsequent factor theories of intelligence constitute various syntheses of the Spearman and Thurstone theories.

The most influential of these is J. P. Guilford's structure of intellect model. In its original form, Guilford postulated the existence of 120 orthogonal factors, 100 of which have been empirically confirmed.

In later revisions Guilford added a fifth content category, thereby increasing the number of possible primaries to 150. He has also hypothesized that the interactions between the three facets of Operations, Product, and Content should give rise to 101 higher-order factors, 85 at the second order, and 16 at the third order.

A major criticism of the factor approach is that it fails to get at the process aspect of psychological phenomena. Hans Eysenck has overcome this shortcoming by interweaving the findings of experimental psychology and biopsychology with factor analytic findings. However, in accomplishing this, Eysenck fails to do justice to the multidimensionality of factor analysis. In fact, he limits himself to only three higher-order factors: introversion–extraversion, emotional stability–instability (i.e., neuroticism), and psychoticism.

A second objection to extant factor approaches to individuality is that any one of them accounts for only a relatively small segment of the total domain. This suggests that a synthesis of such partial approaches will provide a more adequate theory. One such synthesis has been provided by Joseph Royce and his associates. Their approach includes the following three major syntheses: (a) *methodological:* a synthesis of psychology's two sciences (i.e., the experimental and correlational approaches); (b) *conceptual:* the integration of concepts from factor theory, systems theory, and information processing theory; and (c) *empirical:* the relevant empirical findings from all sources. In this theory, personality, or the total psychological system, is conceived as a hierarchically organized composite of six interacting systems: sensory, motor, cognition, affect, style, and value. Each of the six systems is also analyzed as a multidimen-

sional hierarchy of subsystems. Thus complex molar phenomena such as emotion, world view, and lifestyle are explained as the outcome of interactions between both factors and systems.

FACTOR ANALYSIS
GENERAL SYSTEMS
STRUCTURE OF INTELLECT MODEL

J. R. ROYCE

INDUSTRIAL CONSULTANTS

An industrial or management consultant provides an organization an independent, advisory service based on professional knowledge and skills relevant to solving the organization's practical management problems. *External consultants* are not part of the organization to which the service is provided; *internal consultants* are typically part of a corporate or headquarters human resource development staff who may provide consulting assistance to other parts of the organization.

Several aspects of this definition require explication. First and most important, external consulting is an independent service characterized by the detachment of the consultant. Thus the consultant comes to the client organization with a fresh perspective, an impartial, external point of view, and no commitment to the organization other than to be helpful.

Second, the external consultant has no direct authority to make any changes in the organization; thus the consultant's role is always advisory. Most consultants recognize the need for client involvement in the earliest possible stages of the consultancy.

Third, consultation is built on the professional knowledge and skill of the consultant. A psychologist becomes an industrial consultant by developing a considerable awareness and understanding of a broad range of industrial management processes and problems. In this context, consulting is not providing a set of preprogrammed solutions to management problems; rather, it is working with the client to develop innovative but feasible solutions based on a thorough analysis of data.

In general there are two types of industrial consultants—expert and process. An *expert consultant* has an extremely high degree of competence in a subject area directly relevant to the problems faced by the client. Expert consultants listen to the client's request for information, attempt to clarify the need, and then provide the information along with suggestions for implementation.

A *process consultant* typically is brought in to help diagnose problems in the human relations area. The initial focus of a process consultant is on assessment and diagnosis—on the collection of data and on integrating these data into a coherent pattern. Once the client and consultant agree on the diagnosis, they make a joint effort to consider alternative solutions to remedy the problem. The choice of the solution is always the client's, as is the implementation, although the consultant is actually engaged in facilitating the client's solution.

Process consultation is the primary strategy of organization development (OD). Organization development has been defined as a planned, organization-wide effort, managed from the top, to increase organizational effectiveness and health through planned interventions in the organization's processes by using behavioral science. Among the several strategies of OD are team building, management of intergroup relationships, survey-guided development, transition meetings, confrontation meetings, and coaching.

HUMAN FACTORS
ORGANIZATIONAL DIAGNOSIS

L. D. GOODSTEIN

INDUSTRIAL PSYCHOLOGY

That branch of psychology concerned with the scientific study of behavior in the workplace and/or the application of psychological knowledge to that setting is known as industrial psychology. The field stresses both the need to increase the knowledge base related to how and why people behave as they do at work and the need to apply what is known about human behavior to better meet the needs of employees and employers.

Industrial psychology represents the merging of two disciplines from within psychology. The first is the study of individual differences. Psychologists well grounded in the understanding of human abilities brought this knowledge to the workplace and focused upon the match of job demands with individual skills and abilities. The second focus of industrial psychology came from the social psychological tradition of field theory. This focus, best expressed by Kurt Lewin, was concerned with the attitudes and behaviors of people in social settings when those settings were the interpersonal ones of the workplace.

SELECTION AND PLACEMENT

One of the most important concerns of an industrial psychologist is that of selecting individuals to fill the various work roles in an organization and of distributing the employees hired by the organization so as to match persons to jobs. Lee Cronbach and Goldine Gleser pointed out that *selection* occurs when there are more individuals than there are jobs; thus one of the decisions made is to assign some persons to the group that are not placed on jobs (not hired); *placement* occurs when the number of persons equals exactly the number of positions to which they are to be assigned.

Job Analysis

A job analysis is the study of the job requirements. This first involves a description of the duties and responsibilities of the person who holds the job. In addition, the job analysis goes beyond the simple description of what must be done to suggest the human characteristics necessary to accomplish the job successfully.

The importance of the job analysis cannot be overemphasized. It is absolutely necessary that the nature of the job be understood before any attempt is made to select or place persons in the job. For organizations to justify selection decisions, it must be demonstrated that an appropriate job analysis has been conducted. Job analyses are also essential for developing compensation systems and guiding career development and training programs.

Personnel Testing

Once the job characteristics have been assessed, it is necessary to assess the attributes of individuals so as to match persons with jobs. The industrial psychologist must choose methods for assessing the job-relevant individual characteristics that (a) are appropriate for the job characteristic being assessed, and (b) possess acceptable psychometric properties of reliability and validity. Because standardized tests of skills and abilities, aptitudes, and/or interests often provide the best means of accomplishing these two objectives, the industrial psychologist must have a thorough knowledge of the standardized tests available and how to construct and evaluate tests.

It is the professional, ethical, and legal responsibility of the industrial psychologist to develop assessment procedures that are reliable and valid and do not discriminate unfairly against any group.

Criterion Development

Once employees are on the job, ways of assessing their effectiveness must be developed. This task encompasses the classical criterion problem that has received considerable attention from industrial psychologists. The development of criteria first involves the identification of those job behaviors or outcomes relevant to effective job–role accomplishment, and then developing ways to assess validly and reliably the dimensions identified. The criteria often are based on ratings of employees provided by others who can observe the employees' behavior. Ratings obtained in this fashion make up what are called performance appraisal systems.

Validation

The final step in the selection and placement process is to evaluate the fit between individual characteristics used for selection and the effectiveness of these individuals on the job. This complex process is referred to as the validation process or the validity study.

PERFORMANCE APPRAISAL

Judgments about the effectiveness of employees' job performance often must be based on subjective evaluations obtained from other individuals. Although these judgments can be made by any of a number of individuals on the job, the task of judging employees' performance is usually accomplished by their immediate supervisors. These evaluations serve a wide variety of functions. Performance evaluations can be used as criteria for validating selection systems. They are also used for determining raises, promotions, and assignment to training programs, and for counseling employees about their performance on the job or their long-term career goals. In organizations too large for everyone to know everyone else, such systems are necessary for aiding decisions.

For the industrial psychologist, the establishment of such a system requires that rating scales and procedures for using them be developed so that the rater provides as unbiased and accurate ratings of employees as possible. To accomplish this, one is faced with complex issues of scale development and policies for conducting such ratings.

Industrial psychologists have devoted most of their efforts to the development of valid rating scales to minimize rating errors. Some major advances have been made in this area. Perhaps the most important is the use of critical incidents: specific descriptions of important behaviors obtained from job incumbents about their own jobs and in their own words.

TRAINING

When employees or potential employees do not possess the knowledge, skills, or abilities needed to perform their jobs, it often is decided to obtain these through training rather than through employee selection. Industrial psychologists are involved in all four of the major phases of training. The first phase is a needs analysis, which considers the present and near-future demands of the jobs in the organization and then, in a very real sense, inventories the extent to which the work force possesses what is and will be needed. This analysis considers not only the present employees, but also estimates the losses of personnel through retirement and other forms of turnover during the time period of interest. Once the needs analysis is complete, the industrial psychologist plans the training programs to meet these needs. During this second phase, he or she applies what is known about human learning and the knowledge available about training methods to best facilitate the development of the knowledge and skills needed.

The third phase of the training process is the actual training. Industrial psychologists frequently are involved with conducting training sessions. Finally, the effectiveness of the training should be assessed. It is the responsibility of industrial psychologists to attempt, as much as possible, to build into the conduct of training programs ways to assess their effectiveness.

WORK MOTIVATION

Ernest J. McCormick and Daniel R. Ilgen point out that the industrial psychologist deals with motivation at three different levels. First of all, he or she must have a thorough knowledge of human motivation in general.

At a second more work-related level, at least four general motivationally oriented processes are applied by the industrial psychologist: incentive systems, goal setting, participation in decision making, and job design. *Incentive systems* development involves the association of valued rewards with behaviors that the employer wants to encourage. To use incentives effectively requires a thorough knowledge of what is valued by employees and the likely behavioral effects of making valued outcomes contingent upon performance. In addition, one must be aware of the relative value of the incentives in the marketplace.

Goal setting involves the establishment of standards for performance and feedback with respect to those standards.

Participation in *decision making* is predicated on the assumption that employees desire to have more say in what goes on at work. Industrial psychologists often have attempted to build participation into managerial/leadership training, performance appraisal, and other processes in work settings. The success of these procedures is mixed and to a large extent depends on whether one is interested in increasing performance or employee satisfaction.

Finally, within the workplace industrial psychologists attempt to influence the motivation of employees through *job design*. In this case the goal is to design jobs so that job incumbents will believe that their needs can be met best by behaving in a way that meets the organization's goals. The final step in the design of motivationally oriented systems is to tailor the general motivational strategies to the particular organization.

JOB SATISFACTION

A great deal of effort has been expended by industrial psychologists to assess work attitudes. In particular, there is considerable interest in measuring employees' satisfaction with their jobs. Much of the earlier work was motivated by the assumption that the more satisfied people were with their work, the more productive they would be. In the face of repeated failures to show that this is true, later work with job satisfaction has stressed the value of a satisfied work force as an end in itself. Also, information about satisfaction has a great deal of diagnostic potential for the organization.

Two classes of job satisfaction scales have been developed: tailor-made scales adapted specifically for a particular organization and standardized scales researched and validated in a variety of organizations. The advantage of the latter is that they have been shown to have high levels of validity and reliability; also, they have norm data to which to compare the responses of any particular work group. The two most popular standardized scales are the Job Descriptive Index and the Minnesota Satisfaction Questionnaire.

Job satisfaction measures are perhaps most useful when they are a part of a regularly scheduled attitude survey repeated over time in the same organization. If the survey is repeated over time it can serve as an excellent vehicle for providing feedback to employees on a regular basis, for spotting trends in changes in attitudes, and for training supervisors about the feelings of the people who work for them.

JOB DESIGN

In particular, jobs must be designed to fit the abilities of the individuals who hold the jobs, as well as their motivation. Therefore, industrial psychologists tend to take one of two general approaches to job design. One is a motivational approach. Recent motivational emphasis has been on changing jobs so that they allow job incumbents more control, autonomy, feedback, and opportunity to be involved in their work. This point of view underlies the area known as job enrichment.

The other orientation toward job design concentrates on individual abilities and attempts to design tasks in jobs to match, as closely as possible, the abilities of the jobholders. This field is known as human factors engineering or ergonomics. Human factors has been strongly

influenced by the information-processing capabilities of human beings and machines with respect to the interface between people and computers, and also by the technological advances in robotics.

D. R. ILGEN

INDUSTRIAL/ORGANIZATIONAL PSYCHOLOGY

Industrial/organizational (I/O) psychology deals with people in the workplace. It looks at how individuals are affected by the structure and practices of the work organization, by co-workers and managers, and by the physical and social environment of the workplace. A multidisciplinary subject, I/O psychology has diverse branches. The main two are *personnel* psychology, which deals with recruiting, selecting, training, evaluating, and helping employees in the context of the organization's present and future needs, and *organizational* psychology, which looks at how people relate to each other and with the organization, and how their emotional and social needs are to be respected. *Ergonomics* covers the modification of tools and other aspects of the physical environment so that the job can be performed easily, effectively, and safely, and *consumer* psychology studies how the products or services provided by the organization can be tailored to customers' needs and wants, and effectively promoted.

IMPORTANCE OF I/O PSYCHOLOGY

Although this mainly applied branch of psychology focuses on people at work, many aspects of daily living are touched by the problems studied and solutions found in this engaging topic. Many people devote more of their waking hours to working than to any other activity, and they achieve much of their self-esteem and social prestige through their occupational identification. If their work goes well, they have a good chance of being generally content; dissatisfaction on the job is likely to make them unhappy people. Virtually everything that clothes, houses, transports, cures, educates, or entertains people is the product of industry, and the means to acquire these goods and services stem from all members of industry, from owners and managers to newly hired employees.

Whether an entire nation rises or falls depends not so much on its natural resources, location, or sociopolitical history as on its workforce. Some countries, although hampered by ill fortunes of geography and history, have achieved a level of success envied by most other nations. This success can be attributed to the hands and the attitudes of the people of these countries. So in terms of the individual, the corporation, or the nation, few topics are as central as personnel psychology.

Without the discipline of ergonomics, cars, furniture, appliances, and surgical instruments would be less well designed for efficient use. Technology such as air transportation or robotics would be restricted, and space exploration and nuclear power generation would be virtually impossible. Finally, consumer psychology touches everyone's life daily; that is, almost everything people own came, indirectly or directly, through a purchase decision.

HISTORY OF I/O PSYCHOLOGY

I/O psychology is a recent specialty of psychology. As an applied area, it has a problem-solving orientation, and its two spurts of growth were associated with World War I and World War II.

The Early Years

As an art, I/O psychology reaches back to the beginning of civilization, but as a formal science, it began in the early 1900s. Until 1915, only two people in North America could be termed industrial psychologists, Hugo Münsterberg and Walter Dill Scott, both of whom had received their experimental psychology doctorates in Germany under Wilhelm Wundt. The role of the founder of industrial psychology is generally accorded to Scott on the basis of his early-1900s advertising books. These books set the tone for psychology's becoming not only an academic, but also an applied, discipline. In 1919, Scott founded the first consulting firm to specialize in personnel problems.

The early practitioners, influenced also by Münsterberg's 1913 book *The psychology of industrial efficiency,* focused on personnel selection and placement, work safety, and advertising. Münsterberg was a charismatic German psychologist who taught testing at Harvard, was the first personnel consultant (for the Boston Street Railway Co.), and became president of the American Psychological Association (APA). His influence was curtailed when the United States declared war on Germany in 1917, the year after his death.

Another dominant force was Frederick Winslow Taylor. As an industrial engineer for a large American steel mill in the late 1800s, Taylor devised workplace strategies that are felt to this day. In his 1911 book *Principles of scientific management,* Taylor contended that each task should be simplified so that each worker would do the minimum, but do it repetitively and efficiently, using tools fitted to the task. The best worker was to be scientifically studied in terms of time taken and techniques used; this exemplary performance was to be the criterion against which other workers would be measured and paid. (Taylor's "time-and-motion" study was paralleled by Frank Gilbreth, an engineer, and his wife Lillian, a pioneer female psychologist, both of whom studied the reduction of unnecessary motion with motion pictures.)

Taylor recommended that all planning, pacing, maintenance, and other decisions were to be made by management. Feeling that motivation and work productivity are determined by economic rewards, he recommended piece-rate pay, thus originating incentive plans and performance-based pay. His supporters believed that workers were inherently lazy and needed to be continuously watched and measured, sparking the rapid growth of unionism. However, Taylor was concerned with the human aspects of fitting the best employee to a given job and he denounced the exploitation of workers. His research on efficiency led to increased productivity for the company and increased pay with less fatigue for the employee.

World War I

Despite the work of the pioneers, the psychology of work did not make a conspicuous mark as an academic discipline or as a profession until after the beginning of World War I. The flagship journal of the field, *Journal of Applied Psychology,* began in 1917, which was 25 years after the founding of the APA.

Previous modern wars had been fought mainly with single-shot, muzzle-loading firearms that had about the same effect—in accuracy, rapidity of fire and penetration—as the medieval longbow or the Roman catapult. Because this new war was fought with breech-loading weapons instead of muskets or cannons that shot a ball inaccurately over short distances, soldiers could shoot long-distance projectiles accurately, repeatedly, and far. Hence, the projectiles, instead of being fabricated individually by the soldiers in the midst of battle, were factory produced by the billions. Now survival depended on mass production at home as much as on soldiers in the field.

Military recruiters had more candidates than needed. When the world's most industrially powerful country suddenly mobilized for war, millions of men were available along with the communication and transportation systems to move tens of thousands of them as needed. How were they to be selected and assigned? At the outset of the war, the U.S. Army commissioned the development of a written test to screen unsuitable recruits from training programs.

The groundwork had been laid by Wundt, who developed tests designed to predict learning ability as early as 1879. A decade prior to World War I, Alfred Binet had been commissioned by French educational authorities to devise a test to predict how certain children would fare at school. When the war was starting, Lewis Terman at Stanford University adapted Binet's concepts into a test that allowed an Americanized Stanford–Binet test, which allowed a child's overall mental ability to be expressed by a single "IQ" number. Consequently, psychologists could adapt the new IQ test into a military version, and the APA urged its members to lend professional assistance to the war effort.

Arthur Otis had already designed intelligence tests for mass administration in industry. Borrowing Otis's strategy, the versatile psychologist Robert Yerkes designed a group intelligence test for general military use. It was suitable for a wide range of young adults, brief and simple to administer, and easy to score in vast numbers. The Army Alpha was for literate recruits; the Army Beta was administered to the 30% who could not read or speak English.

Further development of tests, including selection interviews, followed. Job specifications were formalized, job knowledge (trade) tests were devised, predictors to select officer- and pilot-training candidates were prepared, and counseling programs were instituted. The testing program was eventually used to classify all recruits in all branches of military service; in a 2-year period almost 2 million men were classified on the basis of their test results.

Between the Wars: The Hawthorne Research

World War I brought not only political and economic changes, but sociological changes as well. Rural lads who had been promoted to positions of responsibility were not likely to go back to the farm. A large group of psychologists who had learned how to use tests to predict job performance applied the techniques developed for the military to select personnel in industry and education after the war. At the same time, universities began to offer courses in applied psychology. Now personnel psychology was both an academic discipline and an applied profession.

Sparked by the work of Taylor, in 1924, a telephone assembly plant in Hawthorne, Illinois, began routine "scientific management" research on variables such as the effects of workplace illumination on productivity. The lighting intensity in one room was left as is and varied in another. After almost every increase or decrease, the women in both rooms increased their production!

The puzzled management hired Harvard Business School professor Elton Mayo as a consultant. Still following the ideas of Taylor, Mayo began what seemed at the time to be minor follow-up research on the effects of lighting and a dozen other variables on productivity. Again, Mayo concluded that no matter what changes were made, productivity undoubtedly rose due to the simple act of paying attention to the assemblers. This finding began a series of four major studies during the next 12 years. Mayo brought into the project W. Lloyd Warner, a young anthropologist who had studied isolated natives in Australia and urban residents in Massachusetts, permitting the incorporation of anthropological field methods into the study.

One study by Mayo and Warner on male assemblers whose work environment was not being altered suggested that they were all restricting their output to some unwritten standard. The researchers gradually switched their attention from the job situation (e.g., illumination levels and work schedules) to the attitudes, morale, and the social and status relations of the employees, that is, to *human relations.* Careful 90-minute interviews conducted with more than 20,000 employees disclosed the importance of the *informal social structure,* the formation of work groups that established their own views of productivity norms.

By modern standards the research was poorly controlled, but one discovery, the energizing response to the simple act of "paying attention," has become entrenched as the *Hawthorne effect.* The other discovery is the way in which social influence can affect output. These two findings led to continued study not just of selection and placement, but also of the *social* aspects of work that influence both morale and motivation.

The Hawthorne studies began a collaboration between social psychologists and industrial psychologists, but this partnership was not to be smooth. Social psychologists believed that they were the true academics and that the industrial psychologists, with their applied and profit-making orientation, belonged in a school of business rather than in a psychology department. Industrial psychologists believed that their cut-and-dried approach to studying "job analysis" and "time and motion" was not applicable to investigating social dynamics. Gradually, the two views merged; now, most I/O psychologists have studies social psychology, and most social psychologists can apply social psychology theory to the workplace.

World War II

World War II brought a surging need for more of the same type of personnel related studies that had been innovated in the earlier war. A generation had passed, and graduates of the industrial psychology graduate programs that were started after World War I answered the call. Between the start and the end of the war, membership in the APA reportedly rose from 2600 to more than 4000. More than 2000 of these psychologists had responded to the needs of the U.S. military, with 1250 working full time on war issues.

The work of these pioneers was varied. Edwin Boring, an early historian of psychology, edited a 1943 book *Psychology for the fighting man,* and later wrote a textbook on military psychology. A few worked on psychological warfare and equipment design, but the primary task was again to classify recruits. The main instrument was the new Army General Classification Test, which separated the recruits into general categories dealing with their abilities to serve as a soldier. Instead of measuring a single global attribute called intelligence, a number of specific aptitudes were assessed, leading to officer or trade training. More sophisticated tests were added for specialized applications as needed.

There were some spillovers from military psychology to civilian applications during this period. Because factories were hard pressed to keep up with the production demands of the military, psychologists in the U.S. and England studied productivity, absenteeism, work schedules, and equipment design. Most American military psychologists had been testing, interviewing, classifying, and counseling. Some also worked at analyzing data and developing training programs; a few dealt with psychological warfare, military task performance, and equipment design. These areas have been part of I/O psychology ever since. Canadian psychologists studied the effects of fatigue and sensory deprivation on the performance of tasks requiring constant alertness, and they also researched pilot training and morale.

No matter how well the military personnel were selected, trained, and motivated, some of the powerful new equipment of war was beyond human ability to operate as effectively as expected. This led to the rapid rise of *ergonomics,* which examined ways of designing equipment. Ergonomics (also known by its original name of *human factors engineering*) had dealt with improving industrial efficiency, but now was called on to save lives and win battles. It rapidly spread to civilian applications after the *Journal of Applied Psychology*'s first paper on human engineering in 1947.

Post-World War II

After World War I, the contributions of the first industrial psychologists had been applied in modest measure to civilian life. After World War II, it was as if the profession had learned from the earlier experience how to apply war-related advances to the post-war world.

In the 1950s, especially in the United States, industrial psychology achieved considerable stature and respectability, especially after the inception of the journal *Personnel Psychology* in 1948. Academically, its research and statistical rigor brought industrial psychology respect as the most scientific of the applied areas of psychology. In the field, industrial psychologists established private and consultancy practices, and many were hired as full-time employees of major corporations. The discipline became a major force in shaping industrial efficiency, mainly finding technical solutions to problems raised by clients.

The APA continuously responded to the increasing contributions of applied psychology, first publishing its *Technical recommendations for psychological tests and diagnostic techniques* in 1954. Its divisions include the Society for Industrial and Organizational Psychology (SIOP), as well as Applied Psychology, Military Psychology, Engineering Psychologists, and Consumer Behavior.

By 1970, the name of the discipline was changing from *industrial psychology* to *industrial and organizational psychology,* reflecting first the increasing integration of social psychology concepts and then the development of a separate theory and literature in organizational behavior. These changes moved the focus from the individual employee to the overall organization, from a micro to a macro perspective. The first major textbook to reflect this change was published in 1969.

Organizational pychology, which has been displacing ergonomics and consumer psychology as focal points, examines variables such as communication; leadership; group decision making; conflict management; organizational power, politics, social influence, and structure; team building; the impact of new technology on the organization; and organizational analysis and development. Some university courses titled "Organizational Psychology" cover the microtopics under "Human Resource Management."

Advances in I/O psychology have stemmed more from without than within, as is often the case with applied disciplines. The major recent external influence has been the massive sociolegal change, which applied strong principles of human rights to many aspects of life, including the workplace. This change, led by Scandinavia and the United States, prohibits workplace discrimination based on sex, race, origins, and beliefs. Now, legislation in many jurisdictions prohibits the practice of personnel discrimination that violates public policy. Another influence that affected I/O psychology is the conviction that the greater the power the more the responsibility. Thus, major employers are seen as somewhat responsible for the quality of life of the employee and the community.

The relationship between employer and employee, and between employer and society in general, has changed markedly. In the past, employers had total control over employees during work hours and no responsibility thereafter. Now, we accept the notions of social responsibility, corporate ethics, and public accountability. The social conscience in the workplace is seen in remedial and catch-up programs for the disadvantaged; better health, day-care, and retirement programs; and attention to the quality of work life.

Current Problems and Issues

Many traditional workplace problems have persisted. For the employer, there is absenteeism, turnover, indifference, and disloyalty, as well as employee recruitment, selection, training, and evaluation. Long-lived problems for employees include poor communication with management and inadequate recognition. Following are recent problems that add to the pressure:

The Changing Job. New jobs, once abundant in manufacturing, are becoming scarce. Most openings are for low-skill, dead-end positions in service industries. What jobs there are offer less security than formerly. Employees are still being replaced by machinery and as a result of "restructuring," in which companies close or relocate, or use microelectronic and satellite technology to transfer work such as programming and routine data entry to workers elsewhere. Just as some factories are relying on "just-in-time" delivery of components, they hire temporary or contract workers ("just-in-time personnel") where they can.

The Changing Union. Unions are losing power, as governments give all employees many rights that unions innovated. Because unions once controlled job classification, seniority brought relief from physically demanding, repetitive work, which would be turned over to young newcomers. Now employees are expected to work harder and longer at the same jobs they were hired for decades earlier. The duration of the work week is now defined by law, but employers, faced with expensive fringe benefits and training costs, would rather induce an existing employee to work overtime than to hire and train an additional staff member.

The Changing Equipment. There has long been tension between workers and their workplace machinery, but it has taken a new face. Computers do not work intuitively, and workers may feel the machines control them rather than vice versa. Jobs that were once described in terms of the skills or knowledge required became defined in terms of the equipment to be operated. "Labor-saving" machinery has not reduced workers' labor as much as it has lessened employers' costs. The employer who has replaced several workers with a costly machine wants it to be run efficiently and continuously, preferably while reporting to management how it is being operated. The stagecoach driver of old has become a jet transport pilot, the lamplighter a nuclear power plant technician. With less margin for operational errors, the cost of which can be enormous, machines are still driving the operators.

The Changing Marketplace. With the reduction of political trade barriers and more efficient transportation, the marketplace is increasingly global. This justifies investing huge sums of development resources and also makes it harder to predict demand and to serve consumers. Decision makers must be fast and accurate to avoid disastrous errors. Retailing is also changing, with specialized catalogues and huge warehouse stores. Advertisers are targeting more specific types of prospects, and there are new forms of marketing and more sophisticated approaches to customer service.

The Changing Employee. The North American employee is no longer the White male breadwinner with a job that pays enough to maintain his family in which the wife stays home. Current job applicants represent more diversity in education, work experience, ethnicity, disability, sex, and life-style, and they are becoming older. Employees are also consumers, and it is the employment that permits the purchase of goods. In the past, peoples' needs were simple and there were few goods for sale. Now there is a vast range of goods that people want, and both domestic partners may have to work in order to pay for them.

The Changing Management. Management is trying to humanize the workplace and improve the quality of work life. But sophisticated machinery and surveillance technology gives more information about and control over the employees, who are vigilant about their entitlements.

The Changing Organization. Jobs were once rigidly classified by training, formal designations, the apprenticeship system, custom, and union contract. Now employers are gaining the right to move workers where needed and to have them do whatever is assigned to them. This removes the job classification barriers and the opportunities for downtime. Workers are being trained to think of themselves as part of a large team and to focus on ways of improving productivity and quality. But many workers are finding that this reduces the number of jobs, that they are acquiring multitasking rather than multiskilling, and that they are being made to work harder rather than smarter.

Status

The center for I/O psychology is the United States, where there are approximately 90 universities offering graduate programs, mostly at the doctoral level, and some 5000 professionals. Almost all new graduates, around half of whom are women, find professional employment. Most senior I/O psychologists have a doctorate; one third of them work in colleges or universities, one quarter each in industry and consulting work, and most of the remaining work for the government and the military. Two thirds of American graduate degrees are at the master's level; two thirds of these graduates work in industry. Other countries where graduate training in I/O psychology is offered in at least two institutions include Canada, Germany, England (where the discipline is "Occupational Psychology"), New Zealand, South Africa, Australia, and Israel. As an undergraduate course, I/O psychology has become increasingly popular since the 1970s, whether as part of a psychology major or a business program, or as an elective.

The most important English-language journals in I/O psychology are: *Journal of Applied Psychology, Personnel Psychology, The Industrial-Organizational Psychologist* (SIOP's quarterly newsletter), *Organizational Behavior and Human Decision Processes, Academy of Management Journal,* and *Academy of Management Review.* These American serials are increasingly publishing papers from researchers in other countries.

As a profession, I/O psychology is vibrant and valuable. Many major American firms employ a staff I/O psychologist, although the job title may be Manager of Employee Relations, Director of Management Development, Senior Staff Specialist, Head of Organizational Planning, or even Director of Advertising, Business Systems Supervisor or Manager of Consumer Research. One review of more than 200 studies in which psychological theory was used to increase industrial output reported that nine tenths of them showed higher productivity on at least one concrete measure. Since then, theory and research have grown considerably more sophisticated; for example, analyzing work in terms of its cognitive and social, as well as physical, aspects.

I/O practitioners can save not just money for the company, but also the firm itself. As corporations are harried by global competition, legislative restraints, a demanding workforce, critical customers, and nontraditional employees and clients, managers need to be professional, responsible, and responsive. Organizations that must change in order to survive may well benefit from consultations with organizational development practitioners. As an academic discipline, I/O psychology continues to make solid contributions to the fund of knowledge in the social sciences and business.

A. AUERBACH

INFANT DEVELOPMENT

Infant development is the study of infancy from the framework of the rest of the life course. This broad approach investigates (a) prenatal influences, (b) infant development as such, (c) infant influences on the rest of human life, and (d) the search for means for optimizing both infant and human development. Placing infancy in a life-span perspective converts it into an interdisciplinary field covering psychological, biological, and sociological developments in different cultures and over historical time.

INFLUENCE OF INFANT DEVELOPMENT ON LATER LIFE

Students of personality, beginning with Sigmund Freud and others such as A. Adler, present the major case for the occurrence of significant continuities from early to later life. In general, however, published observations have seriously questioned the psychoanalytic life-span predictions. Nevertheless, modern psychoanalysts such as E. H. Erikson and J. Bowlby continue to present long-term evidence that certain infant experiences such as love and trust have effects that significantly alter the course of human life. Psychohistorians such as L. DeMause provide historical support, dating back hundreds of years, that early infant experiences powerfully influence later adult personality and child-rearing practices.

The major evidence for diminishing the importance of early infant experiences in later life comes from research studies comparing the effects of early deprivation and later growth-promoting and enriching life experiences. These studies indicate that early deficits remain as defects only as long as the defective conditions continue to exert their detrimental influences on the growing person.

In contrast, although the influence of early infancy on later life may be modified, these findings do not mean that the importance of infancy for later optimal development has been significantly diminished. It does indicate, however, the positive value that infant development has much more plasticity or openness to change than had been previously realized. Early efforts toward optimizing the course of infant development may improve the quality of life during both infancy and the rest of the life span.

IMPROVEMENTS IN LIFE-SPAN RESEARCH

The acceptance of a life-span perspective has encouraged the expansion of infant influences into later development. New longitudinal research designs permit the more accurate tracking of those developmental processes suspected of influencing both early and later development.

Research is now also evaluating the effects on infant development of cultural and parental values. Once it is appreciated that much of current development is a matter of social selection from a much broader horizon of human experiences, the awareness and potentialities for optimizing development across the entire course of life are greatly enhanced.

Life-span research is also increasingly studying multiple and interacting sets of related variables in a more realistic attempt to understand the enormous complexities of human development. Nearly all previous longitudinal research was limited to the effects of single variables such as infant activity level, attachment of infant to caretaker, and infant maturational schedules. Although there is value in such specificity, it fails to do justice to the complex origins of human development and the changing nature of its environment.

LIFE-SPAN INFANT INFLUENCES

During infancy the human being progresses from a primarily reflexive and predictable existence to a socially organized, emotionally expressive, and intellectually competent organism able to find solutions to simple problems prior to acting on them.

Two prenatal factors most likely to have a life-span impact are genetic and nutritional influences. The overall incidence of recognized genetic diseases is about 5% of all live births, and about 7 to 8% of the total U.S. population according to the National Institute of General Medical Sciences. Furthermore, each human being carries five to eight recessive genes capable of producing genetic defects, in addition to possibly carrying late-appearing dominant genetic defects such as Huntington's chorea, Wilson's disease, and late-type diabetes mellitus.

Proper maternal nutrition before and after conception is the single most important factor in ensuring a healthy baby at birth and, possibly, throughout life itself. Furthermore, there is mounting evidence that the earlier the malnutrition, the more severe the resultant brain retardation and the more likely the occurrence of reduced intellectual functioning

throughout the entire life span. The reason for lowered mental abilities becomes clear with the findings that prenatal malnutrition results in a 15 to 20% reduction in total brain cells found at birth, and that 25% of the total adult number of brain cells are present at birth. Furthermore, if there is malnutrition both in the uterus and during the first 6 months after birth, there is an incredible 60% reduction in total brain cells. Because virtually all brain cell production ceases between 12 to 15 months of life, there is little time for the poorly developed brain to normalize.

The search for optimal infant development goes on in biological, social, and psychological domains. Optimal nutrition during pregnancy and infancy is a necessary but not sufficient condition for optimal brain development (optimal environmental stimulation is also needed), and optimal brain development is a necessary but not sufficient condition for optimal social and psychological development (optimal psychosocial interactions are also needed).

No one questions any longer the overwhelming power of experience on all domains of development: Without stimulation, the infant becomes sick and dies; with stimulation, the infant survives and develops; with optimal stimulation (a process as yet not adequately defined), the infant flourishes. Infant psychological development—the most researched of all domains—offers a rich reservoir of growth-enhancing developments that may form the much-needed matrix for life-span development. One candidate for consideration as an essential lifelong development is the development of love from its symbiotic (parasitic) beginnings to self-love, to parent–child love, and to brotherly love.

Another possible lifelong development is the development of intelligence as analyzed by J. Piaget from infancy through adulthood. His work on the development of human abilities remains incomplete because he believed that human intelligence existed beyond those forms of it being measured today. A third lifelong development might be that of perception, from the newborn's readiness to respond to gross changes in taste, temperature, loudness, color hues, pressure, pain, odors, rhythms, movements, and location in space through its development and gradual decline beginning during the third decade of life. A fourth lifelong development might be social development from the first social recognition (a newborn, when held up and talked to, will gradually—with effort—establish human contact) to the socialization process that enables the infant to learn how to become human.

BEHAVIORAL GENETICS
DEVELOPMENTAL PSYCHOLOGY
EARLY CHILDHOOD DEVELOPMENT

J. O. LUGO

INFANT PERCEPTUAL ABILITIES

Characteristics of Infant Perception

In his *Principles of psychology,* William James described the perceptual world of the infant: "The baby, assailed by eyes, ears, nose, skin, and entrails at once, feels it all as one great blooming, buzzing confusion." This view of infant perception as confused and undifferentiated has been a persistent one. In the 1960s, it was still believed by some that the newborn could not focus its eyes or respond to sounds. However, views of infant perceptual skills began to change drastically with the invention of a number of ingenious techniques for studying the infant's perceptual world. The goal of these methods has been to use existing behaviors of the infant to discern those stimuli to which the infant is attending.

INFANT VISUAL SKILLS

Numerous studies have indicated that the infant has remarkable visual skills. Among the most influential studies have been those that explore infant perception of depth and pattern.

The Perception of Depth

Although Berkeley proposed that the perception of depth and distance is acquired rather than innate, this remained a philosophical issue until research techniques were developed that enabled it to be systematically explored in research with actual infants.

One of the most important techniques developed to study infant perceptual skills has been the visual cliff, which was designed to investigate depth perception by providing contrasting surfaces designed to appear either shallow or clifflike. While the entire surface of the device was solid to the touch, patterned material flush against the glass on one side created a surface that also appeared solid. However, on the other side, the patterned material hung down to and covered the floor. Viewed through the clear glass, the patterned material some distance away created a visual drop-off or cliff. Infants from 6 to 14 months in age were placed in the center, and the child's mother called to the child to crawl to her. The infants overwhelmingly preferred the shallow side to the cliff side, indicating that they discriminated depth at least as soon as they could crawl.

When the visual cliff was employed in conjunction with devices to measure the rate of infant heartbeats, it was found that infants as young as 2 months can distinguish between the shallow and deep sides. However, although these results demonstrate very early depth perception, they do not conclusively indicate that such perception is innate in human infants. Still, when an animal such as a baby goat demonstrates depth perception at the age of only 1 day, this supports the conclusion that such perception is innate in humans as well.

Perception of Patterns

The visual preference technique has been used to determine whether infants can distinguish between patterns. This method involves presenting infants with two different patterned surfaces. By observing the infant through a peephole and recording where the infant is looking, the experimenter can determine whether the infant looks more at one pattern or the other. A preference for one pattern rather than the other indicates that the infant can visually discriminate between the patterns.

Pioneering studies by Fantz studied visual preferences in infants as young as a few days old and found that infants demonstrated a considerable degree of visual acuity or the ability to discriminate precise details. Of special interest was the ability of infants to discriminate a facelike pattern from a nonface pattern. These results suggested that faces convey an unlearned, primitive meaning to infants as soon as a few days after birth. By the age of 2 months, infants demonstrate a clear preference for a facelike pattern in contrast to a pattern having scrambled features or equivalent stimulus energy in a nonface pattern. Other research has shown that an infant as young as 3 months can recognize a photographed representation of his or her mother's face.

Detection of Novel Stimuli

Habituation occurs when a repeated stimulus becomes familiar and no longer elicits a response. A change in responsiveness when a different stimulus is provided indicates that the distinction between familiar and novel stimuli has been detected. Comparison of responses to familiar and novel stimuli thus provides another approach for exploring the perceptual world of the infant. From the many studies that have used this technique, it is apparent that the change from an old to a new stimulus can be used to recapture the infant's interest almost from birth. Thus infants are by no means passive recipients of environmental stimulation; they respond to novelty and change.

Among the many perceptual processes that the habituation method has been used to investigate is the perception of color. When 4-month-old infants were habituated to a particular wavelength of light, they exhibited interest when the wavelength was shifted to one perceived by adults as a different color, suggesting that infants have color vision similar to that of adults.

Active Search for Visual Stimulation

The investigation of the active involvement of infants in seeking visual stimulation has used research techniques that capitalize on the tendency of infants to suck on an object placed in the mouth. In such studies, a particular sight could be presented to reward an infant for sucking more strongly or more frequently on an artificial nipple designed to be sensitive to such changes. Infants have been found to suck more forcefully to view visual images on projected slides. Another study found that infants would modify their sucking behavior to be able to look at clear rather than blurred images. These and other studies have indicated that infants have highly developed visual skills at birth or shortly thereafter. Is this also true for the world that the infant hears?

INFANT LISTENING SKILLS

Just as infants can see at birth, they can also hear. Not surprisingly, much of the research on infant hearing has been concerned with the perception of language. It is of interest to note that just as infants respond at an early age to human faces infants also seem particularly attuned to language and the human voice.

Rather than being passive listeners, infants actively respond to adult speech. One study found that infants' movements appear to be synchronized or in time with adult speech from birth or soon after. Infants responded to human speech in English and Chinese but not to such sounds as disconnected vowels or tapping sounds. Such responsiveness to language patterns may play a role in preparing the infant for the later acquisition of language.

A number of studies have indicated that an infant as young as a few days to 1 month in age can discriminate his or her mother's voice from the voices of other females and can even respond to his or her own name when pronounced by the mother. Such auditory recognition of the mother precedes the development of visual recognition and is likely of importance in the infant's formation of an attachment bond to its mother.

Discrimination of Speech Sounds

By the age of 6 months, infants can discriminate between any two of the basic sounds (phonemes) that make up language.

Response to Emotion in Speech

By the age of 7 months, infants are able to relate voices and faces that communicate similar emotions. Babies expect a happy voice to come from a happy face and an angry voice to come from an angry-looking face.

Prenatal Listening

When mothers-to-be read stories aloud during the last 2 months of pregnancy, infants tested 1 or 2 days after birth preferred to hear the same stories read during pregnancy rather than new stories. Thus the development of listening skills begins even before birth.

PERCEPTUAL SKILLS IN OTHER SENSES

Touch

An infant's sense of touch, as demonstrated in the rooting reflex, makes an important contribution to early feeding behavior. When a baby's cheek is touched, the baby will open its mouth and turn its head to search vigorously or to root for a nipple. When a nipple is encountered, the baby will automatically begin sucking on it.

Taste

Infants as young as 1 day old are sensitive to taste and prefer sweet liquids to nonflavored ones. However, it is not entirely clear whether this is due to nature or nurture. Research with rats indicates that the mother's diet when she was pregnant strongly influenced newborn rats' taste preferences.

Smell

An infant can smell the difference between its mother and a stranger, an ability that is present by about 6 weeks of age. Thus together with the sight and sound of the mother smell may play a role in the infant's attachment to its caretaker.

INFANT PERCEPTUAL SKILLS RECONSIDERED

The infant's perceptual world is emphatically *not* the "blooming, buzzing confusion" proposed by William James.

Far less clear are conclusions in regard to the nature–nurture issue. As Gibson has proposed, it may well be that this is a false issue and that research energies should be directed instead toward clarifying how nature and nurture interact. Another trend concerns determining exactly what sort of environmental sensory information infants pick up and its role in cognitive development. The continuing ingenuity of researchers to find ever more revealing ways to explore the infant's perceptual world will ensure that infant perceptual skills will continue to be a thriving focus of research.

BONDING AND ATTACHMENT
COGNITIVE ABILITIES
EARLY CHILDHOOD DEVELOPMENT
INFANT DEVELOPMENT
PERCEPTUAL DEVELOPMENT

F. M. CAUDLE

INFANT PLAY BEHAVIOR

Research in the 1930s on social participation of young children revealed that play activities become increasingly social from the first few months of age through early childhood. M. B. Parten's classic study of preschoolers between 2 and 5 years of age led to the traditionally held view that social interaction develops through a sequence of stages. In the earliest stage, children show relatively little interaction when among peers, and their play is chiefly *solitary*. The next stage, *parallel* play, involves more socialized activity because children play beside one another with similar materials, but do not interact substantially. After children reach 3 years of age, the most advanced stages of social participation begin to dominate. In *associative* play there is some sharing of materials and interaction, but play activities are not coordinated, whereas in *cooperative* play children act together in tasks that involve shared goals and rules.

A post-1970 resurgence of research attention to infant–infant encounters has revealed infants to be far more interested in and competent at social interaction with agemates than the traditional view describes and has also discovered that children's social interactions become increasingly frequent and complex throughout the first 2 years. The present discussion focuses on the development of infant and toddler play between the approximate ages of 6 months and 3 years.

When studied in a social situation with agemates and/or adults (usually the mother, who is instructed not to initiate interaction), infants and toddlers engage in substantial amounts of nonsocial activity (solitary play and irrelevant behaviors) and parallel play that may be regarded as "marginally social." Although the occurrence of nonsocial activity does not decline appreciably during the second and third years, the incidence of social play increases and becomes the most frequent type of activity by about 24 months of age. Recent research has led to a reinterpretation of the role of nonsocial and marginally social behavior in children's play. The results of these studies suggest that (a) social participation develops gradually, beginning in infancy, and does not show a stage-wise progression in which play shifts with age from being chiefly solitary to being mainly parallel and then social; (b) parallel play functions in the stream of children's activities as a bridge from nonsocial to social behavior; and (c) after the age of 18 months or so, nonsocial behavior does not necessarily reflect an immature level of play in normal children.

FACTORS IN PLAY DEVELOPMENT

Research has identified several influential factors in infant and toddler social play.

Toys and Other Objects

The role of objects in social play seems to change with development. Studies with infants between 6 and 14 months have found that peer interaction does not depend on, and may be reduced by, the presence of toys. In the second year, however, toys appear to promote interaction.

Peer–Peer Familiarity

Unfamiliar peers attract a considerable amount of social attention, particularly in infancy. But familiarity appears to affect the specific social activities that occur among infant peers: Familiar infants are more likely than unfamiliar infants to seek close proximity, touch one another, and show positive rather than negative affect, such as by smiling or laughing. Social participation by 3-year-olds also manifests an effect of familiarity, such that familiar peers show more associative and cooperative play and less onlooker behavior (watching but not interacting) than do unfamiliar peers.

Social Experience

Most American infants receive very little opportunity for social contact with peers, but when they do—even for just a few hours per week—their social competence is enhanced. Vlietstra compared the behavior of children who attended half-day versus full-day preschool and found that the full-day children showed more positive social interaction with peers.

Individual Differences

Substantial differences have been observed between individuals in their social activity with infant and toddler peers. Some infants tend to be more socially active than others, and these individual differences tend to persist into toddlerhood. However, children under 3 years of age generally show no gender differences in social activity.

Parents and Teachers

When infants and toddlers are given the choice of interacting with a peer or their own mother in a free-play situation, the children tend to direct more social attention toward the peer. Eckerman and colleagues found that in infancy the social acts toward the peer tend to be distal behaviors such as looking or vocalizing. Then, during the second year of life, activities with peers increasingly involve play materials, whereas contact with the mother by proximity seeking and touching declines.

In day-care settings, teacher–child and child–child interactions occur frequently. Holmberg found that infants engage in far more interactions with teachers than with peers, chiefly because the teachers do most of the initiating. The number of interactions among peers equals the number involving teachers by about 3 years of age.

INFANT DEVELOPMENT
INFANT SOCIALIZATION

E. P. SARAFINO

INFANT SOCIALIZATION

The term infant, meaning "without language" in Latin, generally includes children from birth to 2 or $2\frac{1}{2}$ years. Socialization is the process by which the individual becomes a member of the family, culture, and society—a process that begins at birth and continues throughout the life cycle, involving a complex of formal and informal institutions. During infancy the baby's most immediate contacts translate and mediate the strictures of the society.

The infant as a particular object of socialization is important for several reasons. During the life span the first 18 months of life is the period of most rapid growth. Accordingly, environmental insults such as malnutrition and physical or emotional abuse are thought to have a more deleterious effect on the developing child then than later in life, whereas according to many authorities, environmental enrichment during infancy may have equally long-lasting effects. Because at birth the infant has no prior experience with culture, one may attempt to assess the relative contribution of the environment to development.

Notions about the basic nature of the infant are implicit in all studies of socialization. The infant has frequently been portrayed as an asocial barbarian at birth who needs to be civilized, and has also been described as satanic needing to have the devil exorcised. Aristotle and Locke attributed to the infant a tabula rasa on which the influence of environment is imprinted. More recently the infant has been characterized as being born with specific social attributes and is conceived as an active participant in the socialization process.

BACKGROUND

Research in socialization was spearheaded by social anthropologists interested in the relationship between culture and personality. In the early 1930s, under the aegis of Edward Sapir and John Dollard, a group of scholars from various disciplines began to focus on childrearing as a crucial element in the understanding of cultural transmission. A major impetus came with the publication of Freud's *Totem and taboo*, and psychoanalysis joined hands with cultural anthropology.

Because the cornerstone of psychoanalytic theory rests on the outcome of the environmental mediation between the asocial drives of the infant and the demands of society, how an infant was fed, weaned, and toilet-trained became critical issues for study. Psychologists added their brand of behaviorism, and a complex network of cross-cultural studies of socialization was launched.

Within the normal limits of any culture, given that the infant is healthy, socialization of the infant will not alter major transitions that occur in its growth toward becoming a fully functioning member of society.

All cultures tend to the basic needs of the infant because all infants are helpless at birth and cannot survive without nurturance. All cultures have prescriptions and proscriptions for the care and feeding of infants. According to Margaret Mead, any infant will become a member of the culture in which it is reared.

INVARIANT INFANT CHARACTERISTICS

Gender

One of the most salient characteristics determining the socialization of the infant in any culture is sex. From the moment of birth this will influence how it is treated by others, impose basic behavioral differences, and identify its self-concept and later role determination. As early as 1 year, however, it is impossible to determine the relative contribution of socialization to the differences between the sexes.

The foundations for socialization of sex-typed behavior are firmly entrenched even before birth. It is a common finding in the United States and other countries as well that male infants are preferred to female, particularly in the case of a firstborn. Studies have demonstrated clearly that in U.S. culture, at least, we begin early to differentiate appropriate behavior on the basis of gender. Overall, the adult male behaves in a more stereotypic way toward infants, depending on the sex of the child, whereas the adult female's behavior is similar in most aspects toward both male and female infants.

One's gender identity is inseparable from one's self-concept. John Money postulates that this identity is acquired between 2 and 3 years of age, and that any attempt to alter this identity after this time will meet with resistance and result in psychological stress. By the age of $2\frac{1}{2}$, infants know their own sex quite clearly and discriminate between male and female adults as well as peers.

Development

One obvious aspect of infant socialization that differs from that of the older child and young adult is a rapidly changing behavior. Socially, emotionally, cognitively, structurally, and in motor skills the older toddler barely resembles the newborn.

Newborns arrive with a set of preprogrammed reflexes that during the course of the first year remain as the foundation for intentional skills such as holding and releasing, sitting, walking, smiling, and talking. These motor skills are considered to be specific, hereditary equipment, but any given culture imposes different restraints on their evolution in the newborn.

Large numbers of infants are swaddled; some infants are "taught" to sit; others are never allowed to crawl. In some cultures the infant is covered with a blanket and kept in a dark room for the first 3 months. Yet despite all these disparate practices the infant emerges from infancy as a competent, accomplished child ready to sally forth into the next stage.

Language

Language is so embedded in culture that becoming a member of a language community is tantamount to socialization, but for the infant such socialization also involves the precursors of language. Data indicate that the infant is an active participant in its linguistic environment from birth. The infant demonstrates a fine ability to discriminate between language sounds.

Language involves a sound system, and the newborn infant comes into the world elegantly equipped to produce arresting noises. The infant's first communication, reflexive in nature, is the cry. The cry is universally aversive; adults learn quickly to facilitate the cessation of this aversive stimulus.

In addition to the phonological aspects of language, language includes a system of semiotics as well as syntax. Semiotics refers to that aspect of language that conveys meaning to the sound system; syntax refers to the principles of combining words into grammatical sentences.

Language is a major vehicle through which the actor becomes aware of how significantly he or she is viewed by others and provides a basis for individuation, a cornerstone of socialization.

The infant cannot be taught language until there is sufficient and necessary development of the central nervous system. The ability to develop a symbol system will parallel the infant's mastery in the process of becoming unembedded and its knowledge that objects exist apart from itself.

In different cultures different aspects of language may be stressed. The Baganda, Mixtec, and Japanese stress that the infant should understand what it is told but not answer back to elders, whereas the Italians and Americans coach their infants to speak. In spite of these differences, this interaction between the maturing organism now capable of language and its language environment produces a language-competent child between 3 and 4 years of age.

Current evidence suggests that all individuals acquire language in much the same fashion despite the vast variety and complexity of languages. Language is a part of one's culture and, much like the infant itself, it is both a product of socialization and an agent of the process.

AGENTS OF SOCIALIZATION

Father and Family
Margaret Mead suggested that fathers were a biological necessity but a social accident. Sociologists refer to the family as a system that of course includes the father as a major component, but regarding socialization of the infant, the father's role is to support the mother.

M. Lamb has suggested that fathers play a different but equally important role in the socialization of the infant. Lamb poses that the mother serves as an all-important source of security for the infant, whereas the father provides an exciting and challenging stimulus and serves to buttress the infant's burgeoning cognitive capacities. Cross-cultural data reveal father involvement with the infant to be limited, if not nonexistent, in many cultures. If fathers participate, they are more active participants in the rearing of their infant sons than of their daughters.

Mother
The major portion of infant socialization involves the mother–infant dyad. Under usual circumstances the mother assumes primary care for the infant during the newborn period.

The mother's relationship with the infant is determined by economic factors that impinge on her time, as well as the space for family living and the number of others in the household.

L. Minturn and W. Lambert reported that U.S. mothers had more exclusive care of their infants than mothers in six other cultures studied. Mothers in the United States also had more time and space available for the care of infants and had fewer children in the family.

In a culture that values independence, individuality, and self-reliance the mother is more likely to foster behavior in her infant that reflects these values: exploration, self-help skills, and early motor skills. Infant stimulation or education is considered important for later development.

There has been a tacit assumption that during infancy the mother is the person responsible for socialization. Maternal deprivation has been thought of as detrimental to the infant's mental health, and "multiple mothering" has been questioned. Despite the extensive studies of Casler, Rutter and Yarrow that have demonstrated that the purported ill effects of multiple mothering or other than mother care during infancy cannot be substantiated, there are still those professionals who question this data.

Peers
We know much less about the influence of an infant's peers as agents of socialization than about other persons in the infant's environment. Anthropological studies document the use of other children to augment infant care, but little systematic review is available. Weisner and Gallimore ascertained from cross-cultural data that nonparental care-giving is either the norm or a significant factor in infant socialization. They found young female caretakers to be largely responsible for other-than-mother care, and from what we know about the development of the young child, being cared for by a child is likely to have different consequences than primary care by an adult.

We also know little about social interaction between infants and how this affects the developing child. Recently, there has been a resurgence of interest in peer relationships between infants, and we have data to support that infants do engage in social exchange. We know that relationship with agemates undergoes a predictable alteration. Adult behavior may be more predictable than infant behavior, but given the opportunity, the infant does develop playmates. As yet we know little concerning how these relationships alter the developing child's world.

Infant
Traditionally, socialization studies have been limited to those conspicuous features of a child's environment considered to be the source of the child's current behavior and/or the cause of later personality structure. Richard Bell questioned the naiveté of the notion that socialization is a process that happens only to the developing infant and stressed the importance of the infant's own contribution to the caretaking. Newborn infants are preadapted for social exchange. Their behaviors are truly social from the very beginning. The newborn teaches new parents how to parent; in the apt words of one authority, "of men and women he makes fathers and mothers."

According to ethologists, the infant of any species that depends on adult care for survival possesses features that release parental behavior and assure care.

During the course of maturation the infant produces responses that universally promote a parental–filial bond. John Bowlby lists these action patterns as crying, smiling, sucking, clinging, vocalizing, looking, and following. The baby does give the mother cues regarding her social interaction. Brightening, smiling, and laughing indicate to responsive adults that the infant enjoys their company.

Older infants may in fact take the lead in prosocial behavior. Their first games involve sharing toys, give-and-take; they share their world by pointing with the index finger and will spontaneously imitate the parental behavior of adults. This is apparently universal behavior and has been repeatedly reported by almost all child watchers.

Other-than-Mother Care
There is a natural relationship between the type of care given to infants and a culture's economic structure. In those cultures dependent on the labor of women outside the home, alternative forms of care—other-than-mother care—become a necessity. In many cultures the infant is cared for by the mother until weaned. Until weaning, the relationships may be extraordinarily intimate. In many of these cultures child nurses, usually elder siblings or cousins, may have certain charge of the infant and weaning. In cultures in which women of the same family or clan share a common courtyard, it is not uncommon for many to be responsible for the care of the infant.

Care for the infant outside the home is not uncommon in many industrial nations. France, Sweden, Belgium, and Italy all provide government-sponsored infant care. Both Russia and China furnish extensive government-supported care and education for the infant. Israel's kibbutzim provide an excellent example of other-than-mother care for the infant, sometimes with the intent to alter traditional Western European socialization practices.

In both the United States and Great Britain infants are cared for in their own homes with "minders" or babysitters, or formal or informal arrangements are made for infants to be cared for in another's home. This care provides surcease from the constant demands of infant care for the mother or allows her to obtain employment. The mother selects care she deems appropriate, and there is no programmatic socialization as found in other countries.

BONDING AND ATTACHMENT
DAY-CARE CENTERS
EARLY CHILDHOOD DEVELOPMENT

INFANT DEVELOPMENT
PARENT–CHILD RELATIONSHIPS

H. W. ROSS

INFANTILISM

Introduced by Lasequie in 1864 as a term referring to behaviors of adults that mimic infants, the term "infantilism" has undergone some changes. The concept refers to behaviors, physical status, or emotional states that display behavior characteristic of infancy.

Wilhelm Stekel used the term to refer to "conditions which are of psychic origin, pertain primarily to the sexual sphere and represent effects of fixation on or regression to infantile levels of emotional development." The behavior is a manifestation of an unconscious return (or a desire for a return) to prior levels of functioning aimed at reducing anxiety and insecurity. Such behaviors typically have sensual overtones in that there is a gratification derived from the reduction of unpleasantness similar to that of infants. In psychoanalytic theory, this is accompanied by self-centered associations of being the center of attention and pleasure.

This concept is involved in the interpretation that partial infantilism is responsible for the enuresis and encopresis sometimes found in emotionally disturbed individuals.

ANXIETY
IMMATURE PERSONALITY

R. A. LEARK

INFECTION THEORY

Infection theory is the view that theories in psychology generally cluster around a fundamental concept disseminated by professionals in centers of learning and research, particularly in prestigious graduate schools when a professor shares his or her ideas with students of high potential or with professional colleagues. Promising students research their professors' ideas, perpetuate them throughout their careers, and enhance and strengthen them through experimental research. When these former students begin to publish, their mentors gain an increasingly wider audience and thereby enhance their reputations. Once these disciples become influential, the hypotheses of their mentors are reviewed in publications, supported orally and verbally, and circulated in classrooms and elsewhere.

One consequence of the infection effect is the inbreeding of ideas. Instead of a free and open exchange of theories, hypotheses of authors with fewer personal contacts tend to be muted.

SOCIAL INFLUENCE THEORY

W. S. SAHAKIAN

INFERENTIAL BIAS IN MEMORY

INFERENCE

An inference is based on at least tentative acceptance of implications provided in the presented information and various contextual conditions, such as a speaker's tone of voice and facial expression, so that a conclusion is suggested.

However defined, inference is a subtle concept that has a role in an exceptionally wide range of cognitive phenomena. Four major areas may be distinguished: (a) logical processes, inductive, and deductive; (b) cognitive psychology, in which the emphasis is usually on how categories are inferentially accessed; (c) social cognition, in which the emphasis is on how inferences are drawn from categorizations that have been accessed; and (d) comprehension of discourse, on which this article focuses. Barsalou has reviewed the unconnected way in which related research in areas b and c is typically performed.

INFERENCES IN DISCOURSE

In linguistics, the essential role of inferences in facilitating comprehension of discourse has long been recognized. Gaps in information specifically provided are so common and so wide that comprehension would be incomplete without the making of inferences. The different types of inferences thus used have been described by Singer and Thorndyke.

INFERENTIAL BIAS

Within psychology, early research on inferences as factors in discourse, dating from the 1970s, was carried out within the linguistic tradition. Much of this research was with children as subjects and involved the identification of sentences as having been or having not been presented earlier in a study session. One of the more common independent variables in this research was the explicit or implicit use of an instrument. For example, compare these sentences: "The truck driver stirred the coffee in his cup with a spoon" and "The truck driver stirred the coffee in his cup." The latter sentence obviously implies that a spoon was used (although that inference is not logically required—some other instrument like a wooden rod or a finger could have been used).

In one early developmental study, older children recalled as many studied sentences when only an implicit instrument (e.g., *spoon*) was provided in the test about as well as when the cue had been explicit in the sentence; younger children, in contrast, recalled more of the sentences with an explicit instrument as a cue, indicating a lesser tendency to make inferences.

More traditional types of memory tests have been used. For example, both the recall of implicit words (e.g., *bird* from the study sentence "All the seeds in the feeder had been eaten") and the use of such implicit words as associates in a word-association test were found to increase over the elementary school grades.

Susceptibility to inferential bias in memory has been demonstrated in both regular and gifted elementary school students. "Forward-consequence" inferences were used in one study. Some action or event is implied but not logically required; for example, consider this story: "A lioness woke up hungry after a long sleep. She went hunting and found a small herd of antelopes. They were feeding in some very tall grass." Regular students showed a strong tendency (50% or more errors) to answer *true* to false test items designed to measure inferential bias (e.g., "The lioness killed and ate an antelope"). They showed no improvement over the second to the sixth grade. Gifted students showed some improvement (reduced error scores) but only at the sixth-grade level.

The results contrasted sharply with the predictably steady improvement in error rates found over grades for factual test items. Examples of the latter type were "The lioness woke up hungry and went hunting," which was, of course, true, and "The lioness woke up her mate to go hunting," which was false. Both types of student showed this kind of improvement over the grades, and the expected superiority of the gifted children on these items also was clearly demonstrated.

In the experiment just described, all of the inferential-bias test statements were considered to be false because the subjects were specifically instructed to answer in accordance with the way the story had been told. The extent to which susceptibility to inferential bias was nonetheless evidenced (only the gifted sixth graders showing any appreciable resistance to it by predominantly answering inferential-bias test items correctly as false) suggests that this kind of memory determinant is indeed widespread. These results also suggest the need for new instructional techniques to curb it or, more broadly construed, to encourage in schoolchildren the proper identification of it and other types of inference by appropriate description, explanation, and practice.

EXCEPTIONAL MEMORY
FORGETTING
MEMORY
MILL'S CANONS
SELECTIVE ATTENTION

M. H. MARX

INFERIORITY FEELINGS

Alfred Adler distinguished between inferiority feelings and inferiority complex. Adler assumed a feeling of inferiority on the part of everyone. He pointed out that to be human means to feel inferior. Inferiority feelings were traced to the child's smallness and dependence in a world of adults, and later to the pursuit of perfection.

Feelings of inferiority may serve as a stimulant to healthy, normal striving and development. They become a pathological condition only when the individual is overwhelmed and becomes depressed and incapable of development. Orgler states that Adler found that inferiority complexes can develop from three sources: organ inferiority, spoiling, and neglect. When feelings of inferiority result in avoiding participation in the community, they become a complex.

Whenever a person feels inferior, it implies comparison with another person or some standard or norm. Such comparisons are the starting point of much human misery. The word inferiority is derived from the Latin *inferus*, meaning "below" or "under." Next, a host of other negative factors occur, including anger, competitiveness, and a consequent loss of initiative because competition, by focusing one's efforts on a rival, precludes spontaneity. Furthermore, one may act in a superior manner: A superiority complex can compensate for an inferiority complex.

To conquer the feeling of inferiority, two things must be done. First, one must stop comparing oneself to another so as to give full and undivided attention to the problem or task at hand. Second, one must surrender the need to be superior. Renouncing the need for superiority and privilege, one finds one's balance, gains momentum, and ceases to feel inferior.

Inferior self-assessment is always a negative thing, yet sometimes it serves as a stimulus for constructive and useful compensation. Out of weakness and deficiency can grow strength. In such a situation it is not inferiority itself that is of advantage, but the constructive overcoming of weakness and deficiency.

Related to inferiority feelings are feelings of inadequacy. Whereas inferiority implies feeling not as good as someone else, the inadequate person feels unable to cope with tasks. The frame of reference is not another person but the task one cannot handle. Just as, according to Adler, one overcomes inferiority feelings by giving up comparisons and the desire to be superior, so, to overcome inadequacy, one must focus on the task at hand and have the courage to be imperfect.

INADEQUATE PERSONALITY
PERSONALITY DISORDERS

D. N. LOMBARDI

INFORMATION PROCESSING

Several crucial assumptions are shared by researchers who adopt the information-processing approach to the study of human behavior. The most important assumption is that behavior is determined by the internal flow of information within a person. Because this information flow is internal and invisible, special techniques and methodologies are used to allow inferences about this postulated flow. But all these techniques share the basic goal of information-processing research, which is to map internal information pathways.

The information-processing approach uses techniques in many ways similar to those used by engineers designing large systems. The human is regarded as a complex system, and experimental psychologists try to discover what happens inside the "black box." The effort to understand internal information flow proceeds primarily by testing alternate representations based on different arrangements of subsystems with different properties. It is not sufficient to create a model that will duplicate the behavior of humans, although this is of course a necessary requirement for any information-processing model. Thus the information-processing theorist must duplicate, not only behavior, but also the internal patterns of information flow before an acceptable explanation of human thought and action can be found.

Information-processing models differ in the number and arrangement of subsystems. Many possible arrangements are reasonable, so that theorists must try to show how their model is superior to other competing models. There is seldom complete agreement about which model is best; this can confuse the nonspecialist wishing to learn only a little about information-processing models. Even extremely good models are eventually replaced by newer theories, or even by older theories that are reborn because of new data or new techniques.

The typical information-processing model represents the human cognitive system as a series of boxes connected by an assortment of arrows. The boxes represent subsystems that perform different functions and processes that route information to and from the various boxes. Each box represents a generalized kind of information transformation that goes on inside one's head. As the models become more refined, the level of detail represented by a box becomes finer. A box that represents a relatively fine level of detail is often called a stage of information processing or an isolable subsystem. The precise definition of a stage is mathematically sophisticated, but we will not be far off if we think of it as corresponding to a single transformation of information. In general, the output of a stage will not match its input. For example, one common model of memory assumes that printed words received through the eyes get recoded into a format that is related to how the words sound when read aloud. This transformation occurs even though people were not asked to pronounce the words. Therefore, a visual input has been transformed into an auditory (i.e., acoustic or phonological) output. This kind of transformation is common in machines.

Different arrangements of stages are required to model the flexibility of the human information processor. The simplest arrangement occurs when several stages are linked in a straight line with the output of one that then becomes the input of the succeeding stage. This is called serial processing because no stage can perform its own transformation of information until it receives the output of the preceding stage in the chain. This, of course, will not happen until that stage has received information from its preceding stage. Similarly, serial processing models require each stage to wait its turn before producing an output.

If a stage need not wait for other stages to finish, the arrangement is called parallel processing. In parallel processing several stages can access the same output simultaneously. An arrangement with both serial and parallel components is called hybrid processing. Hybrid processors are often more powerful than serial or parallel processors, but this extra power is gained by making the model more difficult to understand and analyze. Because many people find serial models easier to understand, most information-processing models are serial.

Although we now have an excellent scheme for classifying the structure of a model into three categories—serial, parallel, and hybrid—

structure alone cannot determine the predictions a model will generate. We must also know the "price" that each stage demands for performing its transformation of information. This is called resource allocation or capacity. Capacity is a hypothetical construct that controls how efficiently a stage operates. In some models it is assumed that each stage has adequate capacity to do its own thing, regardless of how many other stages are operating and how complex these operations might be. Other models assume that capacity is limited, so that stages must compete for available processing resources. In these models a stage cannot always operate as efficiently as if it were the only stage in the system. Thus, to generate predictions for a model, we must specify both the structure of the model and its capacity assumptions. The best models of human information processing specify (a) the number and configuration of internal processing stages, (b) the capacity requirements of individual stages, and (c) the total availability of capacity and rules that govern distribution of capacity to individual stages.

INFORMATION-PROCESSING THEORY

B. H. KANTOWITZ

INFORMATION PROCESSING (UNCONSCIOUS)

The role of consciousness in the processing of sensory information has been a difficult and surprisingly ignored problem. With the return of "mind" to a central place in American psychology, however, increasing amounts of attention have been paid to it. Nevertheless, the problem remains essentially unsolved and merits continuing examination.

EXPERIMENTAL EVIDENCE

Some of the clearest support for unconscious monitoring and semantic analysis of ongoing flows of information comes from auditory research. For example, Corteen and Wood had subjects shadow (repeat verbatim) prose presented to one ear, apparently oblivious of the words simultaneously being presented to the other ear. Nevertheless, both words that had themselves been previously associated with electric shock *and* their semantic associates produced significant galvanic skin responses when presented to the second ear without disturbing the shadowing performance.

More recently, positive evidence for unconscious processing has accumulated from studies of visual perception. Some especially striking results were reported by Marcel. First, Marcel used brief tachistoscopic presentations followed immediately by a visual pattern mask. The role of the pattern mask in this and related research is crucial. Such "backward masking" apparently blocks out the neurophysiological basis of the percept (sometimes called the "icon") and thereby prevents consciousness of it. At the same time, however, processing of the briefly perceived cue along various dimensions has started and is not blocked out by the mask. In this connection, it should be noted that the heart of the notion of unconscious processing is the assumption that consciousness depends upon a different neurophysiological processing system than the classical systems that transmit sensory information from receptors to cortical centers.

In Marcel's first procedure, either a word or a blank card was presented, followed by the mask. The subject was then asked three questions: (a) Was anything shown before the mask? (b) Which of the two words now shown (in a supraliminal test) is visually more similar to the cue? (c) Which of the two words next shown is more similar in meaning to the cue?

Marcel's procedure was to lower the presentation time for the target gradually, beginning with fairly long intervals for which the subjects were able to make fairly accurate present/absent judgments. He found that even after that judgment reached a chance level so that it could be assumed that the cues were no longer detected, all the subjects were still making clearly suprachance decisions on the visual similarity and the meaning questions. When they reached a chance level on the visual similarity decision, they were still able to respond above chance on the meaning question. This effect Marcel labeled "unconscious reading," on the assumption that effective lexical functions were occurring in the absence of consciousness.

Marcel's second design also utilized the *associative priming* phenomenon in which prior presentation of a verbal associate (e.g., *horse*) as a cue immediately preceding the target string of letters (e.g., *pony*) facilitates positive lexical decisions—that is, responses to the targets are reliably faster than in control cases (e.g., the unrelated cue *rifle* preceding *pony*).

Marcel's results were, in brief, that typical associative priming occurred when the associative cue was pattern-masked (i.e., presented subliminally) and the subject, therefore, could not respond consciously to it.

As a final illustration of the way in which unconscious processing occurs consider Kunst-Wilson and Zajonc's demonstration of affective discrimination in the absence of recognition of the same cues. Extremely short tachistoscopic presentations (1 ms) that precluded conscious identification were used without masking. Subjects were first given 5 such showings of ten irregular, randomly constructed octagons. They were then asked to select one member from each of 10 pairs of octagons on the basis of (a) which had been shown previously under the degraded condition, and (b) which they liked better. Each pair, shown for 1 s, consisted of a previously shown octagon and a control figure, independently matched for affective value. The results, which were consistent with Zajonc's assumption of the primacy of affective reactions, showed clearly that the "familiar" figures were preferred, but that they could not be discriminated from the controls in terms of recognition memory.

The perceptual researches just described complement the somewhat more complex and even more controversial psychodynamic research that also supports the unconscious processing principle. These many diverse lines of inquiry converge to suggest that unconscious processing of information needs to be considered in any complete picture of mental functioning.

CONTEXTUAL ASSOCIATIONS
INFORMATION-PROCESSING THEORY
PERCEPTION
SELECTIVE ATTENTION
UNCONSCIOUS INFERENCES

M. H. MARX

INFORMATION-PROCESSING THEORY

Information-processing theory concerns how people attend to, select, and internalize information, and how they later use it to make decisions and guide their behavior. Information-processing psychologists theorize about human cognitive capacities and behavior, using computational, linguistic, and information theory concepts. This has stimulated the development of viable theory and significant research in various areas of psychology, especially perception, memory, attention, language, thinking, and problem solving. Information processing is currently a leading orientation in experimental psychology.

The information-processing perspective is a family of loosely related theoretical and research programs. As is true of any scientific subgroup, the presuppositions, theory, and research methodology are all only partially shared. There is, however, sufficient overlap to describe them as a paradigmatic subgroup clearly distinguishable from others such as transformational linguistics, Piagetian psychology, or more remote approaches such as radical behaviorism.

Information-processing psychology can be divided into elements originating within experimental psychology and elements imported from external sciences. The contributions from within psychology come primarily from midcentury behaviorism, verbal learning functionalism, British experimental psychology, and theories of human engineering and performance. Extrapsychological contributors include mathematical logic, communication engineering and information theory, transformational linguistics, and computer science. Some of these antecedents were affirmatively adopted in whole or in part.

INFLUENCE OF MID-CENTURY BEHAVIORISM

Behaviorism was basically antimentalistic, concerned with animal behavior, and committed to extending conditioning principles to all areas of psychology. Difficulties encountered in attempting to extend behaviorist theory and method to human symbolic processes—in particular to language capacities—was one of the principal factors leading to the rise of the information-processing paradigm. As disillusionment became widespread, psychologists turned to external theories to guide their research programs. The result was a massive paradigmatic shift away from behaviorism.

Yet information-processing psychologists shared with their behaviorist predecessors a firm belief in empiricism, operationism, and the nomothetic ideal. General methodological and statistical preferences, therefore, persisted through the paradigmatic shift. They adopted new ways of looking at familiar questions and redesigned their experiments.

The new view rejected certain parts of the behaviorist tradition: general extrapolation from a small set of learning principles, animal data as a source of basic principles, and conditioning as the fundamental form of learning. Perhaps most important, information-processing psychologists scuttled the antimentalist emphasis of behaviorism, along with its extreme environmentalism and its exclusive emphasis on the external causes of behavior. Innate capacities were reintroduced, and internal processes such as plans, strategies, images, and decisions were proposed. Experiments using human subjects replaced animal experimentation, and internal processes were coupled with external determinants of behavior. Eventually, most researchers concerned with higher mental processes found internal processes and structural components to be acceptable theoretical elements. The reorientation was greatly facilitated by analogies, facts, methods, and theories from sister sciences that dealt in one way or other with symbols and symbol manipulation.

INFLUENCE OF INFORMATION THEORY

The stunning development of twentieth-century communication technology such as the telephone, radio, and television has occurred because much is known about the abstract nature of communication systems. Communication scientists have formulated and tested general laws describing generalized operating modes of communication systems, both ideal and real. Concepts and laws appropriate to communication systems were applied to biological and physical systems not normally viewed as communication channels.

Early information-processing psychologists were struck by the potential analogy of the human information processor and the theoretical information channel. Certain human abilities were conceived as part of an information-handling channel with built-in states and limitations. Research was designed to determine the channel's properties and capacities for transmitting different types of information. A number of technical concepts such as uncertainty, information, bit, source, message, destination, and encoding were borrowed from communication theory. A major impetus for this technological and conceptual transfer to experimental psychology was the work of Claude Shannon. Shannon's mathematical

theory of information applied to any message from any source transmitted by any means to any receiver. Shannon's theory no longer influences psychological research to any great extent. However, many concepts derived from his work remain an important part of information-processing psychology.

INFLUENCE OF TRANSFORMATIONAL LINGUISTICS

Noam Chomsky argued that language could never be scientifically explained or understood in behaviorist terms. These approaches, he insisted, fundamentally misconceived the nature of language by ignoring its most essential properties: structure, rules, and grammar. In his view, language must be explained by reference to rules in the head that enable one to deal with structure (i.e., the systematic relationship between the parts of a sentence such as phrases and clauses). Mastering a language, to a linguist, involved internalizing the system of rules governing those relationships. Structure is a concept that ill fits behavioristic science; it is impossible to cast the internalization of structure as the learning of physical stimuli and responses. The importance of rules in the head was explicitly formulated by linguists in the "competence-performance" distinction. Competence is the knowledge of language that a speaker carries around and uses to produce and understand utterances; performance is actual speaking and listening. Linguists and psycholinguists argued for the development of theories of competence and had to postulate that innate capacities to understand and generate language existed. The child was viewed as a "language acquisition device," preprogrammed by nature to extract from its environment the information needed to acquire a linguistic system. While linguists attacked behavioristic psychology as anachronistic and witless, the behaviorists counterattacked, declaring linguistics to be antiscientific and muddled.

Discouraged by the poor success of behaviorism in constructing theories of language behavior, the nascent information-processing paradigm looked increasingly to linguistics for ideas. Chomsky's paradigm and theories were initially borrowed in their entirety. However, information processing is now less dependent on linguistics than it once was, having identified a number of linguistic concepts that are psychologically useless. Moreover, linguistics continued to evolve. Considerable work in psychology and linguistics now focuses on semantics, easily the weakest spot in Chomsky's theoretical system. Nevertheless, much remains from the early interaction of information-processing psychology and linguistics. The competence-performance distinction appears to be accepted implicitly. Current research seeks to discover the psychological processes or mental operations that underlie linguistic performance. The productivity and creativity first identified with language are now attributed to other cognitive activities as well, including perception, memory, thinking, and understanding.

INFLUENCE OF COMPUTER SCIENCE

Computer science is a family of loosely related subspecialties, including algorithm theory, numerical methods, automata theory, programming languages, and artificial intelligence. Computer science and information-processing psychology evolved in tandem; both are derived from seminal work in mathematical logic, and both are concerned with the nature of intelligent behavior. The appearance of computing machinery and the conceptual foundations on which it rested contributed an alternative metaphor for human mental and intellectual capacities, a theoretical framework, and a representational language in which behavioral theories could be expressed.

A number of theories of cognitive processes have been cast in the form of computer simulations. Theories of thinking and problem solving, in particular, have benefited from this formalism, possibly because human thought appears to be serial in nature.

The most pervasive contribution of computer science was an alternative metaphor for mental processes. Such analogies are enormously important in scientific inquiry, exerting a powerful influence on the selection of research questions, the structure and interpretation of experiments, and the construction of theory. The computer is an artifact whose properties are relatively well understood, and the analogy is compelling. Computers take in symbolic input, recode it, match it to internally stored patterns, make decisions about it, generate some new expressions from it, store some or all of it, and give back symbolic output. By analogy, that is most of what information-processing psychology is about: how people take in information, recode and remember it, and use it to make decisions and guide observable behavior. With their knowledge of computer science, information-processing psychologists theorize about human capacities and behavior, using such computational concepts as buffer, executive processor, compiler, and system architecture.

At the beginning of the twentieth century David Hilbert challenged his colleagues to formalize the intuitive concepts of proof, computability, completeness, and consistency. Alan Turing described the "universal machine" in a 1936 paper on completeness and computability.

The "universal machine" may be thought of as a hypothetical system having a small set of primitive operations with which it can solve a formidable range of mathematical problems. The ideas in Turing's paper foreshadowed the invention of the modern digital computer; in fact, everything actual computers can do is reducible to the fundamental capabilities of Turing's universal machine. The importance of Turing's discovery to cognitive psychology lies in the fact that the universal machine effectively concretizes the abstract processes involved in symbol manipulation. The abstract symbols of formal logic could be copied, transformed, rearranged, and concatenated in much the same way as physical objects. Symbols and symbol-manipulating processes thus became tangible objects of study. This insight opened the way to showing that at least some human ideas, mental capacities, and brain processes could be identified with physical symbol systems, containing symbolic representations that are altered by precisely defined symbol-manipulating processes. "Mental events" could thus be described in a theoretical system that also applies to concrete, physical things.

A precise formulation of this bridge between the abstract and the concrete was the achievement of Alan Newell and Herbert Simon. Newell and Simon's "physical symbol system" hypothesis presupposes that important aspects of the human mind, the brain, and the computer are separate instances of the same kind of system. The physical symbol system hypothesis, whether or not explicitly expressed, underlies much of the research and theory in information-processing psychology, and therefore must be tested and refined by experimentation. At its core, the concept may define the presence of intelligence in a system and explain how an intelligent system—human or artificial—creates new knowledge.

ALGORITHMIC–HEURISTIC THEORY
CLASSICAL CONDITIONING
COGNITIVE COMPLEXITY
EPISTEMOLOGY
INFORMATION PROCESSING (UNCONSCIOUS)
LANGUAGE DEVELOPMENT

R. LACHMAN

INGROUPS/OUTGROUPS

In his *Folkways* of 1906, the sociologist William Graham Sumner was able to consolidate a substantial ethnographic literature on group self-images and attitudes toward neighboring groups under the terms "ethnocentrism," "in-group," and "out-group."

In introducing the concept of ingroup–outgroup differentiation to the social sciences, Sumner set the stage for a long line of research on how group identification affects an individual's perceptions of as well as attitudes and behavior toward other persons and groups. An ingroup is generally defined as any social group or category of which an individual is identifiably a member. Technically, outgroups are any social groups to which the individual does *not* belong, but in practice particular outgroups are usually identified with reference to any specified ingroup (males–females, neighboring ethnic groups, competing nations, etc.). Attitudes and behaviors are biased in favor of ingroup members over outgroup members. The preponderance of research evidence supports this proposition, although some important moderating variables have also been identified.

RESEARCH APPROACHES

The study of ingroup–outgroup attitudes and behavior has been the subject of multiple methodological approaches. Most of the systematic research in the area can be classified into three types—attitude surveys, field studies, and laboratory experiments—each of which has contributed somewhat differently to the understanding of ingroup biases.

Attitude Surveys

Much of the empirical data on intergroup attitudes and behaviors are based on surveys or opinion polls in which the unit is the modern nation state or racial or ethnic subgroups within a state. By examining the differences between respondents' evaluations of their own and other groups, these studies have documented pervasive tendencies toward ingroup favoritism on a number of dimensions. Evaluative bias in favor of ingroups is not totally indiscriminate, however. It is obtained most consistently in attributions of positive character traits such as "moral," "peace-loving," "trustworthy," and "cooperative," but on other evaluative dimensions ingroups are not always rated as higher than outgroups. There is also some evidence that groups occupying a minority status within a society adopt some (though not all) of the majority group's derogatory stereotypes in their self-image.

Field Studies

In 1954 Muzafer Sherif and his colleagues undertook one of the first studies of the induction and reduction of ingroup–outgroup bias in the context of a boys' summer camp. In general, ingroup solidarity was enhanced in the presence of conflict with an outgroup. Reductions in these biases were achieved when the nature of the relationship between the two groups was altered by the systematic introduction of superordinate (shared) goals that required cooperative interaction.

Since the Sherif study, most of the field experiments on ingroup–outgroup attitudes have been conducted in contexts involving preexisting social groups such as racial and ethnic groups in desegregated settings. Empirical evidence indicates that contact *per se* is not sufficient to reduce awareness of ingroup–outgroup differentiation and attendant preferential biases. Consistent with Sherif's findings, significant changes in intergroup acceptance are obtained only under conditions that promote extensive cooperative interaction between members of the different groups. Even when cooperative acceptance is achieved, it is not clear whether its effects on attitudes toward outgroup members are limited to the immediate setting or whether they will generalize to other members of the outgroup and other situations.

Laboratory Experiments

Whereas field research on ingroup–outgroup attitudes has focused on documenting the presence and extent of evaluative biases in favor of ingroups, laboratory research has been conducted to identify the minimal conditions under which ingroup–outgroup differentiation can be developed and lead to preferential biases. Much of this research has employed a paradigm developed by Henri Tajfel and his colleagues at the University of Bristol to study ingroup–outgroup discrimination in a situation involving no face-to-face interaction among group members, anonymity of group membership, and an arbitrary basis for group differentiation. Apparently any form of categorization into groups, even in the absence of information about similarity–dissimilarity among group members or any direct conflict between groups, is sufficient to generate ingroup favoritism. In general, any factors that serve to enhance the salience of category distinctions (such as minority status, differential treatment or status, or the presence of intergroup competition) tend to increase the degree of bias exhibited on both behavioral and attitudinal measures.

Because it concerns the relationship between intergroup behavior at the societal level and attitudes and perceptions at the individual level, the concept of ethnocentrism or ingroup bias provides a link between sociological theories of group relations and psychological theories of interpersonal attraction.

Realistic Group Conflict Theory

Sumner's thesis on the origin of ethnocentrism and intergroup hostility explicitly recognized the role of competition over scarce resources in the initiation and perpetuation of group differentiation and conflict. The Sherif study is regarded as a major source of support for realistic group conflict theory predictions. The study was not, however, a complete experimental test of the theory, because no assessments of attitudes toward ingroup and outgroup were made prior to the introduction of intergroup competition. Thus the results of the study do not indicate clearly whether the presence of conflict or competition between groups is a *necessary* condition for the emergence of ingroup favoritism and outgroup hostility.

Psychoanalytic Theory

Whereas realistic group conflict theory places the origin of ingroup–outgroup discrimination in processes operating at the group level, psychoanalytically oriented theorists trace such biases to the needs and motives of individuals. Probably the most extensive treatment of the subject from a psychoanalytic perspective is represented in the *The authoritarian personality* by T. W. Adorno, Else Frankel-Brunswik, Daniel Levinson, and R. Nevitt Sanford. According to the theory behind the authoritarianism concept, generalized hatred and distrust toward outgroups—particularly prejudice against racial and religious minorities—derives from projection of repressed hostilities originating in childhood experiences with parental authority. In this view, then, derogation of outgroups relative to ingroups develops in the service of maintaining the individual ego or self-esteem.

Categorization Theory

A number of theorists have sought to explain ingroup–outgroup biases in terms of the general cognitive processes by which human beings structure, simplify, and give meaning to their physical and social environments. In this view, intergroup perceptions derive from the same processes of classification and categorization that apply to the perception of physical objects. One perceptual phenomenon associated with category differentiation is the *assimilation–contrast* effect: There is a strong tendency to accentuate intercategory differences and intracategory similarities on that dimension. When extrapolated to social differentiation, this implies that members of the same social group will be seen as more similar to one another and more different from members of other groups than they actually are. However, there is a general tendency for ingroup bias to be more selective than would be expected based on categorization alone. Accentuation of differences in favor of the ingroup occurs readily for groups who occupy a superior position on the dimension of evaluation, but convergence or perceptual reduction of differences is often found for groups who hold an inferior position.

Social Identity Theory

A theory that combines the basic features of categorization theory with some aspects of motivational theories was developed by Henri Tajfel and John Turner. In this perspective, the perceptual effects of category differentiation are coupled with a posited drive for "positive self-identity" and social comparison. An individual's social identity is presumed to be highly differentiated, based in part on membership in multiple significant social categories. When a particular category distinction is highly relevant or salient, the individual responds with respect to that aspect of social identity, acting toward others in terms of their group membership rather than their personal identities. At this level, the motivation for positive self-identity takes the form of a desire to differentiate the ingroup from the outgroup to the extent that favorable comparisons are available on dimensions relevant to the ingroup–outgroup distinction. Social competition is generated by group differentiation. Ingroup–outgroup differences provide the basis for accentuating social comparisons that favor the ingroup in the service of positive self-identity.

AFFILIATION NEED
CROSS-CULTURAL PSYCHOLOGY
ETHNIC GROUPS
GROUP COHESIVENESS

M. B. BREWER

INHIBITORY CONDITIONING

The study of conditioned inhibition was significantly advanced when Robert Rescorla published an article in which he argued that a conditioned stimulus (CS) must pass not just one but two separate tests before it could be declared inhibitory. First, when presented together with a known excitatory CS, it must reduce the level of responding to that excitor. Second, if paired with an unconditioned stimulus (US), it must acquire excitatory strength more slowly than would a neutral or novel stimulus paired with the same US. The first of these tests is called a "summation test" because it presumably involves the algebraic summation of conditioned excitation and inhibition. The second test is called a "retardation test" because excitatory conditioning to the presumed inhibitor is expected to be retarded. If the alleged inhibitor passes only one of these tests, then its effects need not be attributed to conditioned inhibition. Instead its effects could be attributed to distraction in the summation test and to inattention in the retardation test. However, if it passes both tests, then it cannot possibly be a stimulus that is simultaneously distracting and ignored. It must have acquired the ability to oppose excitatory conditioning.

Charles Zimmer-Hart and Robert Rescorla suggest that conditioned inhibition is not weakened (extinguished) by the CS-alone procedure typically used to extinguish conditioned excitation. Robert Hendersen and David A. Thomas suggest that, unlike conditioned excitation, conditioned inhibition is forgotten over a retention interval. Paul Brown and Herbert Jenkins present data obtained in an operant conditioning setting that seem to overcome the reservations that B. F. Skinner voiced about the need for the concept of conditioned inhibition.

CLASSICAL CONDITIONING
OPERANT CONDITIONING

J. J. B. AYRES

INNER/OUTER-DIRECTED BEHAVIOR

The problem of internal as compared to external control concerns, first, the circumstances under which one perceives one's own behavior to be determined by forces in the environment or by oneself. Second, it concerns the possibility that even in the same situation, people differ in the processes that govern their own behavior.

Almost any line of research points to the influence of cognitive factors in the selection and control of response. The Würzburg school showed how instructions or task conditions induce in the subject a *set* or particular kind of readiness to respond, which then determines subsequent responses. Following the lead of E. C. Tolman, many psychologists employ the term *expectancy* for this phenomenon. Even more generally, the term *attitude* refers to the regulative function in personality.

A set is essentially defined by experimental conditions and is inferred by effects associated with variations in those conditions. But an attitude requires measurement independent of the situation, such as by a personality test. When differences appear in performance, then, we would link them with intrinsic variations in cognitive structure.

It is usually not sufficient just to assess a personality variable. Its mere presence in the subject does not guarantee that it will influence response. For this reason, an experimenter needs to include conditions that maximize its operation. These conditions include *arousal* or *induction* aimed at the variable in question, and a task that engages the subject's *interest* or commitment enough to involve his or her resources.

Research on internal—as compared to external—control of behavior has employed strategies, on the one hand, of manipulating cognition by extrinsically imposed conditions, and on the other hand, by identifying groups who differ in antecedent assessment of these inferred characteristics. The former approach has to do with sets or expectancies, the latter with attitudes. In neither strategy has the requisite conditions just mentioned always been fully recognized.

EXPECTANCIES OF CONTROL

Interest in the problem of personal control owes much to research on frustration and its effects—situations in which a person is blocked in attempting to attain a goal. Emotional arousal and aggression may thereby be elicited (although negative effects are typically emphasized, constructive or coping efforts may also be evident). Such reactions vary with the degree of control one has over the threatening conditions. For example, with a threat of electric shock, subjects prefer certainty that the shock will occur to uncertainty or inconsistency, and report less anxiety when they control the shock lever. Other studies bear out the fact that perception of control of aversive stimuli significantly reduces subjective discomfort.

Even an "illusion of control" influences one's reactions to a situation.

The "self-fulfilling prophecy" is another interesting phenomenon. An expectation about what will happen influences one's behavior.

Archibald has reviewed possible interpretations of such effects. An expectation of failure may arouse anxiety so that a person tries to alleviate such feelings, or the aroused state may produce inappropriate effort (trying too hard or paying attention to the wrong cues). Alternatively, an expectation of a favorable outcome may simply increase effort and thereby facilitate performance. A person highly involved in a task may be oriented primarily to preserve self-esteem or some important value. Therefore, the task or goal may be redefined to avoid disconfirmation of the expectation. Thus if one expects to fail, the task may be perceived as too difficult, with an adverse effect on performance. Clearly, no explanation fits all cases.

REACTANCE

Brehm and others presented a systematic analysis of what occurs when the environment imposes restrictions on a person's freedom to act. Such conditions, Brehm argued, induce arousal, which makes a person act to prevent a further loss of freedom and to reestablish the diminished or threatened freedom. This counterforce he calls "reactance."

Experiments have confirmed predictions from the theory.

ORIGIN–PAWN ORIENTATIONS

De Charms extended Heider's causality proposition. An Origin feels that environmental effects are produced by oneself and thus has a sense of competence and control. A Pawn perceives that events are caused independently of one's actions and thus feels powerless or ineffectual.

LOCUS OF CONTROL

Rotter devised a test for a related attitude. It is conceptualized as general beliefs concerning the relation between one's own actions and events. *Internal control* is the belief that an event is contingent on one's own characteristics or acts. *External control* is the perception that one's behavior is controlled by forces beyond (or mostly beyond) one's control, such as fate or luck. This distinction has been made by other social scientists as well, such as Fromm and Riesman.

The Internal–External Control Scale gets at one aspect of the expectancy component. The subject is asked to choose between pairs of statements, and the score is the number of "external control" alternatives chosen (thus a low score reflects internal control). For example, in one item there is a choice between making plans confidently and reluctance to do so for fear that bad luck may foil them.

This scale has prompted a great deal of research as well as the development of new measures. Several investigators have employed factor analysis to clarify the components of the scale. In particular one needs to distinguish, as aspects of the external locus, between control by powerful others and control by chance, and between defensive and nondefensive externals. Nondefensive externals assume more personal responsibility for their actions than do the former.

Research shows that internals tend to perceive themselves as capable of controlling events, whereas externals tend to attribute outcomes to luck, chance, or other forces that control them. In general, internals are more confident than externals.

LEARNED HELPLESSNESS

Seligman developed the notion of learned helplessness, which may ensue when one experiences outcomes that occur independently of one's activity (i.e., are uncontrollable). Hiroto and Seligman exposed subjects to an aversive noise or to a concept task. Some of them could "escape" the noise by pressing a button that terminated it. For some subjects the concept problems were unsolvable, whereas for others they were solvable. Control subjects merely listened to the noise or inspected the problems. Next, the subjects either experienced the same conditions again (albeit with instructions that they could do something to escape) or received anagrams to solve the problem. The subjects who received "helplessness training" (inescapable noise or unsolvable problems) displayed learned helplessness because they were impaired in learning how to escape the noise or in solving the anagrams (depending on which sequence they encountered).

Clearly, the attitude of the person ought to influence how a task is treated. Hiroto utilized a test derived from the Rotter scale in an experiment on learned helplessness. One set of instructions emphasized skill; the other emphasized chance. The "no escape" pretreatment produced helplessness effects. But externals were adversely affected regardless of pretreatment or instructions; in fact, internals performed very much like the control subjects. In the helplessness training pretreatment, internals tried more often to escape than did externals. Zuroff has also shown that the effects of helplessness training are to be understood as a function of the subject's expectancies, whether sets or attitudes. In addition, as Koller and Kaplan, and Gregory and colleagues show, it is the lack of explicit cues that adversely affects the performance of externals, in keeping with their greater influence by environmental conditions.

LOCUS OF CONTROL AND REACTANCE

Thus the effects of extrinsically imposed conditions vary as a function of personality characteristics. The interaction between internal–external control and the induction of reactance appears in a study by Cherulnik and Citrin. Subjects rated four attractive posters and were promised a choice of one of them as a reward. However, in a second session, when new ratings were obtained, the poster rated as third highest (identified separately for each subject) was not available. Some students were given *impersonal* instructions (that the shipment of posters inadvertently failed to include that poster); others were given *personal* instructions (that the experimenters had excluded one because evidence indicated that it would not be "meaningful for that student"). A control group merely made the two ratings. When freedom was limited, internals rated the eliminated option much more attractive under *personal* conditions, whereas the externals displayed this effect under *impersonal* conditions. Although restrictions on freedom may have general effects, they are contingent on relevant personality variables.

PERCEPTIONS OF CAUSALITY

Research on attribution processes stemming from conceptualizing by Heider, and on expectancies associated with achievement motivation converge on the locus of the control variable. Theories of achievement motivation and internal–external control share some common features.

Accordingly, Weiner and associates have presented a systematic picture of how internals and externals perceive their performance. Internals tend to attribute their success or failure to their own characteristics—ability and effort, whereas externals attribute their outcomes to factors outside themselves—difficulty or luck. Several studies support this distinction.

Persons high in achievement are especially likely to attribute success to ability and effort, which increases feelings of accomplishment. When failure occurs, the outcome is attributed to lack of effort, which, as an unstable condition, can be increased. These persons prefer tasks of intermediate difficulty in which difficulty can be countered by increased effort to enhance the likelihood of success. They act vigorously because they believe that effort leads to success, and tasks of intermediate difficulty are most likely to benefit from effort.

In contrast, persons low in achievement avoid achievement-related activities because they attribute success to external factors, and effort is not considered to affect the outcome significantly. They give up when failure threatens because they believe that it results from a lack of ability (a stable and uncontrollable factor). These persons prefer easy or difficult tasks, which minimize self-evaluation.

DISPOSITIONAL SETS
LOCUS OF CONTROL
PERSONALITY

W. E. VINACKE

INNOVATION PROCESSES

The study of innovation describes the process by which ideas are transformed into new products, physical or social processes, or technologies, and are ultimately brought into widespread use. As a field of inquiry, research on innovation has a strong multidisciplinary tradition, but also a confusing array of units of analysis and only a limited number of integrating concepts. This is partly understandable because the phenomenon of innovation occurs in both private and public organizations, is longitudinal to the extent of years, involves innovations that can be either hardware technology or social systems, and can encompass activity at individual, group, or organizational levels of aggregation.

One concept that has been quite persuasive concerning innovation is that the process moves in a generally linear path of various stages: (a) acquisition of initial *knowledge* about an innovation, (b) *persuasion* about its benefits, (c) a *decision* about adoption, and (d) *confirmation* of the decision. This particular stage model is only illustrative; many others have been proposed.

One major addition has been to longitudinally extend analysis of innovation processes in order to consider postadoption behavior more closely. Much of the early research on innovation was conducted in agricultural settings in which a single individual could either adopt or not adopt a new product in a fairly straightforward manner. When the field became involved in studying more complex innovations in organizational settings, it also became clear that the *implementation* of innovation was a crucial issue. It has been found that despite positive decisions to adopt innovations, they may often be discontinued, not fully deployed, or significantly altered or adapted in dysfunctional ways.

Congruent with the above lines of inquiry, there has been an increasing awareness that innovation is an *organizational* phenomenon. This has had two important ramifications: (a) an increased interest in organizational and contextual variables that influence innovation, and (b) an expansion of the breadth of inquiry beyond looking at dissemination of innovation to *users* to also consider how innovations get developed by *producers*.

An important set of findings concerning private firm innovation has been that small firms tend to be disproportionately more innovative in the creation and development of new products and processes. Congruent with these findings has been work on the management of research and development itself. It appears that flexible social structures and unhampered information flow are also crucial in successful research and development.

The focus on organizations as the locus of innovation phenomena has also highlighted the role of factors that impinge on organizations from without. In the terminology of economics, these contextual or "exogenous" variables are often the result of government policy or practice. Obviously the particular external or policy factors that are important in innovation differ significantly between public and private sector organizations. The incentives operating within public organizations have in fact been held to be disincentives for innovation.

Innovation processes, both as a set of phenomena and as a field of inquiry, are frustratingly complex. Innovation, as a generic process, can be used to conceptualize virtually all changes in our social environment. As researchers develop a more manageable set of descriptive models and agreed upon paradigms of research, the importance of inquiry into innovation processes will become more apparent.

GENIUS
INDIVIDUALITY THEORY

L. G. TORNATZKY

INNOVATIVE PSYCHOTHERAPIES

In this encyclopedia, a number of major innovative psychotherapies are summarized separately. This formidable group of therapies is still only a relatively small percentage of the total number of current psychotherapies. Corsini's *Handbook of innovative psychotherapies* lists approximately 250 such therapies, and Richie Herink's *Psychotherapy handbook* summarizes approximately as many.

There are probably more than 500 different systems of psychotherapy in use today—some such as Daniel Motet's allocentric psychotherapy have a specific theory but no literature and are probably used by no one except its developer; some, like Erhard Sensitivity Training (est), have no theory but have been used by tens and perhaps even hundreds of thousands of individuals; and some like Aikido (listed by Herink as a psychotherapy) have few people who might even view them as psychotherapy. This article summarizes certain other innovative systems of psychotherapy.

AESTHETIC REALISM

The most unusual part of the aesthetic realism system is probably the use of a troika-type of counselor therapy. According to Martha Baird and Ellen Reiss, who in turn quote Rebecca Thompson: "A consultee speaks for an hour with three consultants, in an atmosphere at once formal and casual. Our method is one of critical questions and answers. The purpose is to have a person see his or her questions and feelings, however intricate, as objects that can be studied." The theory and philosophy of aesthetic realism comes from the work of Eli Siegel, who believed that the single major cause of all human psychological problems was contempt for the world.

COVERT CONDITIONING

Developed by Joseph R. Cautela, covert conditioning has elements of eidetic therapy and other procedures that call for psychoimagination. The individual in treatment imagines performing undesirable behavior, mostly for the purpose of changing undesired habits. The procedures involve relaxing the patient, making the patient aware of the undesired behavior, and then getting him or her to imagine various consequences of the undesired behavior.

CREATIVE AGGRESSION

Developed by George R. Bach, creative aggression is described as a form of therapy that changes thoughts, feelings, and behavior through direct retraining methods that involve overt expression of aggression under controlled conditions known as exercises. Bach attempts to teach people how to fight fair. The most unusual aspect of his method is the use of *batacas,* soft rubber bats that can be used to strike others but that will not result in anyone getting really hurt.

DIRECT DECISION THERAPY

Direct decision therapy, developed by Harold Greenwald, is a good example of an eclectic system. Built up by Greenwald from his own training as a psychoanalyst and influenced by a number of other theorists, especially Alfred Adler and Albert Ellis, it also contains Greenwald's own unique contributions. The system has six principal steps: (a) a clear-cut statement of the problem or problems by the patient, (b) an examination of the patient's history to find out the origin of the problem (i.e., to locate the first time that the particular decision was made to operate in a particular nonfunctional manner), (c) an examination of the rewards or payoffs that are achieved by operating in this manner, (d) an understanding of the context of the original poor decision to learn the reason why the person deviated from normal behavior, (e) an examination of options such as whether to keep going in the direction of the original mistake or to take another path, and (f) coming to new decisions about which direction to go in with the help of a therapist who oversees the patient's progress.

DIRECT PSYCHOANALYSIS

Direct psychoanalysis, a method of treating seriously disturbed people, was developed by psychiatrist John Rosen in the 1940s. In 1945, he published *The treatment of schizophrenic psychosis by direct analytic therapy* to explain his theory and methodology. His procedure involves close supervision of patients, stressing verbal interactions with patients that can last for hours. The main effort of the therapist is to be active in interpreting the patient's verbal and physical behavior, providing insight. No drugs or shock therapy is permitted. Rosen's theory is that severe mental problems start at birth, depending on mothers' rejection of children, and that vulnerable individuals regress to infancy in later life.

INTENSIVE JOURNAL THERAPY

In intensive journal therapy (IJT) the participant takes a basic workshop in the principles of the therapy, then creates an intensive journal workbook. One then works on one's own, supplementing the therapy with periodic readings of material or attending new workshops. Intensive journal therapy is the development of Ira Progoff, who in turn was affected by the theories of Sigmund Freud, Carl Jung, Alfred Adler, and Otto Rank. As is true of a number of innovators in this field, Progoff added what appeared to him to be needed. The important difference in this system is the unique use of personal workbooks, the equivalent of diaries. The workbook represents a kind of directive diary in which one writes out various aspects of life in terms of some 20 different sets of directions. Consequently, IJT represents a kind of self-analysis and has interesting connections with meditation and person-centered therapy in terms of putting the burden of the treatment on the client.

INTERPERSONAL PROCESS RECALL

The most innovative aspect of interpersonal process recall is the use of audiovisual playback of a therapeutic session in which both therapist and client are interviewed by a third person during observation of the played-back session. Developed by Norman J. Kagan, this technique is stated to be a powerful method for stimulating recall and in fostering growth and behavior change. It does not evolve from any specific personality theory, but has been synthetically developed on the basis of experience with the process.

MULTIPLE IMPACT TRAINING

Multiple impact training is a commonsense system of training people to be more competent. Developed by George M. Gazda (1981), it consists of a method for first evaluating people in terms of their basic developmental modalities and life skills, seen as five in number: (a) cognitive (problem-solving skills, etc.), (b) physical–sexual (family relationships, etc.), (c) moral (personal values), (d) vocational (career aims), and (e) psychosocial (communication skills, etc.). The trainee is evaluated in terms of these five areas—usually by consensus of a committee—then a specific pattern of training is suggested related to the noted deficiencies, following which a reevaluation measures any degree of improvement.

ORGONE THERAPY

Developed by Wilhelm Reich, orgone therapy is based on the concept of a source of biological energy that when blocked results in physical and mental pathology. The blocking of orgone is released by a variety of psychological and physiological procedures. The psychological procedures are the usual ones calling for the expression of repressed emotions. The physiological ones call for attacking what Reich termed the body armor, physiological rigidity, through various procedures, including changes in body posture. The result is a person who is orgastically potent (i.e., among other desirable changes the individual can have a satisfactory orgasm).

POETRY THERAPY

Like free association, psychodrama, and hypnosis, poetry therapy is a procedure—called by Arthur Lerner, a prime exponent of this method—a tool to be used by psychotherapists. Poetry can be valuable in a variety of ways (e.g., in expressing one's self through writings, through silent readings, and through readings to an audience). Poetry, as with music, can evoke memories, which in turn can affect feelings and change attitudes.

PRIMARY RELATIONSHIP THERAPY

Developed by Robert Postel, who never wrote on the subject, primary relationship therapy (PRT) is a system of reparenting for people who were—or believe they were—rejected by their parents. Probably the sole publication on this method is by Genevieve Painter and Sally Vernon. PRT involves the client in an open, close, personal relation with the therapists, one of whom plays the mother and the other, the father. The therapists will treat the patients as young children, cuddling them, feeding them, playing with them, and in other ways acting as ideal parents for infants and young children. As the therapy continues and as the patient begins to grow emotionally, the system begins to modify, generally ending in group therapy.

PROVOCATIVE THERAPY

Provocative therapy apparently violates a good many of the usual concepts maintaining that people in therapy should be treated with kindness, consideration, and respect. Developed by Frank Farrelley, the system has some elements in common with Albert Ellis's rational–emotive therapy in that it attempts to change false ideas and erroneous assumptions. A strong affective experience is established by the therapist, who then uses nonpredictable behavior, especially humor, to promote growth. The therapist uses direct confrontive communication, including sarcasm and ridicule, to make points directed at getting the patient back on the track of reality. This is a serious procedure that employs humor as an essential part of the whole therapeutic process.

RADICAL PSYCHOTHERAPY

The term *radical* is used here in the political as well as the theoretical sense. Developed by Claude Steiner, radical psychotherapy holds that all psychiatric difficulties are forms of alienation, resulting from oppression of people who are isolated from one another. The proper solution is a political theory of cause and a political system of cure. In contrast to the style of life found in current societies, it proposes a cooperative style of life and recommends coalitions by the oppressed against the powers-that-be. Alienation is seen always as a function of oppression. Steiner offers the formula:

$$\text{Alienation} = \text{oppression} + \text{mystification} + \text{isolation}$$

Direct social action to fight oppression, mystification, and isolation are the recommended methods of treatment.

AUTOGENIC TRAINING
BIOFEEDBACK
BRIEF THERAPY
COGNITIVE THERAPY
CONDITIONED REFLEX THERAPY
CONJOINT THERAPY
COVERT CONDITIONING
EGO-STATE THEORY AND THERAPY
EIDETIC PSYCHOTHERAPY
FEMINIST THERAPY

FORMATIVE THEORY OF PERSONALITY
IMPASSE/PRIORITY THERAPY

R. J. Corsini

INSIGHT LEARNING

According to many traditional learning theories, such as that of Edward L. Thorndike, learning takes place as the result of a gradual process involving trial and error. An alternative view, promulgated especially by the Gestalt psychologists, is that in some situations animals display insight learning, believed to entail a fundamental perceptual restructuring of the objects and events in the environment. Psychologists disagree as to whether insight learning truly represents a fundamentally different process or whether a single process might be involved in all learning and problem solving.

In an *Umweg*, or detour, problem an animal is placed near a goal object but separated from it by a barrier such as a set of bars or a mesh screen. Two kinds of behavior may be observed in such situations. First, animals may engage in trial-and-error behavior, in which they fixate on the object and make various movements directed toward it; these may eventually lead the animal around the barrier to the object, apparently by trial and error. Alternatively, they may pause and then suddenly move in a smooth and continuous manner around the barrier to the goal object. Advocates contend that the latter pattern would be an instance of insight learning. It is differentiated from trial-and-error learning. First, the change in behavior often appears sudden and complete; this contrasts with the gradual changes characteristic of trial-and-error learning. Such transitions generally are preceded by a pause and then are smooth and error free. The change in behavior is not a consequence of reinforcement; indeed, the change in behavior usually occurs before the delivery of the incentive. Such solutions to problems generally transfer to a wide range of situations and are retained for considerable periods of time. It is generally assumed that they result from a perceptual restructuring of the environment.

The classic work on insight learning was conducted with chimpanzees by Wolfgang Köhler during World War I. Bananas were suspended from the ceiling, and the chimpanzee could reach them only by moving a box underneath the bananas or by stacking boxes under them, so that it could climb up to reach the bananas. In other experiments, a chimp had to use a rake or a stick to pull in objects placed outside of its cage. The animal might have to use a short stick to rake in a long stick, which could then be used to get the bananas, or to put two short sticks together. The object was to investigate the processes used in solving problems and to show that the elementistic, associationistic, and reductionistic explanations of more behavioristic approaches were inadequate. Köhler believed that the tasks used by the associationists did not permit the animal to display the perceptual reshaping characteristic of true insight learning. The chimps appeared to gain insight, as suggested by the indications just described.

Some psychologists contend that the behavioral patterns displayed by the chimpanzees in Köhler's situations were not as novel as he thought them to be and that their occurrence could be explained with more elementistic principles. In the view of Paul Schiller, for example, the responses in the stick-joining problem represent a set of innate motor patterns triggered by the appearance of the appropriate stimuli. According to Schiller, the provision of an incentive slows, rather than hastens, the animal's joining of sticks. Mature animals given two sticks with no food present typically fit the sticks together in less than an hour. Furthermore, some of the animals that joined sticks in play were unable to solve problems by joining the two sticks. Similarly, when tested with boxes and no suspended bananas, chimps often stacked the boxes, climbed onto them, and reached toward the ceiling. "For the human observer it was hard to believe that there was no food above them to be reached." Such motor patterns are natural, and the distraction created by incentives such as bananas interferes with the normal manipulative habits of the chimpanzees. Furthermore, there is a strong maturational component, so that older animals have at their disposal more comprehensive motor complexes that can be triggered in problem-solving situations. Prior experience is important in the development of these more comprehensive motor complexes. For Schiller, smooth solution in the *Umweg* situation reflects not a novel behavioral pattern nor the result of insight, but a change in speed in the serial elicitation of previously determined responses. The solving of these problems is, for Schiller, a serialization and condensation of innate motor patterns.

Epstein, Kirshnit, Lanza, & Rubin, used operant procedures to shape pigeons so that they learned (a) to push a small box toward a small green spot located at various places on the floor in their chamber, (b) to climb onto a box and peck at a small facsimile of a banana that was suspended overhead, and (c) not to move directly toward the facsimile when it was suspended overhead. The reward was access to grain from a standard dispenser. When tested for the first time in a situation in which they had to combine these behavioral patterns to move the box to reach the facsimile bananas, the pigeons behaved remarkably like Köhler's chimpanzees. The interesting question about these experiments is whether they reflect the same underlying processes as used by Köhler's chimps or whether they might merely entail superficially similar behavior with very different underlying processes, what one might call a behavioral phenocopy. One might teach a pigeon to peck at correct answers on a Graduate Record Examination so that it could achieve a score of 1500, but the process would be very different from those used by humans, and the pigeons would be unlikely to succeed in graduate school.

Animals in problem-solving situations frequently show a delay followed by a sudden correct solution to the problem. In at least some situations, these solutions represent the serial display of previously established learned and innate behavioral patterns. It remains an open question as to whether in some of these situations there is a fundamentally different restructuring of the perceptual environment of the sort that Köhler believed to characterize true insight learning.

**ANIMAL INTELLIGENCE
GESTALT PSYCHOLOGY
LEARNING THEORIES**

D. A. DEWSBURY

INSTINCT

"Instinct" and its often used (if somewhat sanitized) synonym, "innate behavior," do not have a single widely accepted meaning. Instinct's usefulness as an explanatory or descriptive concept is suspect in the minds of many, and its usage has varied from period to period in the history of psychology. Because of its dubious virtues and ambiguity as well as the changing philosophy of science, some scientists have rejected the concept outright, whereas others have vigorously maintained its obvious utility. Most of the stoutest opponents have somehow changed their definitions of the substrates of behavior to accommodate aspects of the concept.

Innate or species-typical behavior is prominent in ethology texts. The behaviors subsumed under this term share several—but often not all—of the following characteristics: (a) they are goal-directed and terminate in specific consequences such as food, water, or sexual partner; (b) they provide benefits to both the individual and the species; (c) they are suitably adapted to and congruent with the normal environmental circumstances (although often maladapted to unusual conditions); (d) they are common to most if not all the individual members of the species (although

their particular manifestations may vary from individual to individual); (e) they develop or appear in a definite order and regularity in the life of the individual in accordance with the processes of growth and maturation; and (f) they are not learned on the basis of individual experience (although they may emerge in the context of learning, and learning may take place in relation to them).

Essential to the concept of innate behavior are the adaptedness of the behavior and the genetic causal organization of behavior. Instinctive behavior is usually contrasted with "learned" behavior, which emerges gradually or abruptly, is highly variable among the individuals of a species, differs greatly in its motor pattern, and depends on a multiplicity and diversity of cues.

Daniel Lehrman challenged the proposition that "instinct" and "innate" are meaningful concepts, because no list of behavior is totally uninfluenced by learning, which can take place *in utero* or, as with birds, in the egg. Niko Tinbergen recognized that the two processes—intergeneration phylogeny and intraindividual learning—are quite distinct, but asserted that virtually all behavior is a product of both, and that to make a sharp distinction between them leads to a false dichotomy.

Konrad Lorenz suggested that internal drives affect the activation of genetically derived fixed action patterns (FAPs).

These FAPs are normally not actualized because the internal drive to express them is usually below activation threshold. The reaction-specific drive that regulates the release of FAPs was called specific action potential (SAP). It can be triggered into action by a sign stimulus that is appropriate for the innate releaser mechanism (IRM). Although the particular theoretical IRM concepts have been challenged, they demonstrated that purposeful intentions were not needed as explanations of animal behavior.

Tinbergen suggested an alternative hypothesis: that behavior is hierarchically organized, with broad motivational centers dominant over multiple branching specific levels, each of which terminates in specific FAPs. The IRMs thus become transformed into regulators for pathways, so that the animal proceeds from a very generalized appetitive pattern through progressively more predictable and specialized responses until a final consummatory act is attained in the presence of appropriate releasers.

Most observers of animal behavior are of the opinion that much of the behavior of lower organisms is predominantly instinctive, whereas that of higher organisms is richly elaborated by learning, with characteristically great individual differences in the expression of the behavior. Nevertheless, Sigmund Freud asserted that human behavior grows out of the expression of two contrary sets of instincts: the life instincts that enhance life and growth, and the death instincts that propel us toward destruction. Abraham Maslow too has elaborated a hierarchial structure of motives extending from simple physiological needs of hunger, thirst, and so forth to self-actualization.

**COMPARATIVE PSYCHOLOGY
EVOLUTION
INSTINCTIVE BEHAVIOR**

A. J. RIOPELLE

INSTINCTIVE BEHAVIOR

Most psychologists would agree with the following definition: Instinct is a more or less complex pattern of behavior elicited by a more or less specific pattern of stimuli (internal or external) without the benefit of any opportunity for this sequence to be learned. In addition, the term instinct usually includes the ideas that (a) the sequence ends with some form of consummatory behavior or is peculiarly adaptive; (b) the behavior is specific to and occurs universally within like-sexed individuals of a species; and (c) the behavior is stereotyped and rigid, although modifiable to some degree in certain individuals and species.

The concept of instinct fell into disrepute in the 1920s when several thousand instincts were variously proposed to account for behavior in general. This abuse of the concept led to its demise. Nonprofessionals continue to misuse the concept even more by equating instinct with well-established habit. The technical term was revived by ethologists K. Lorenz and N. Tinbergen and was assigned a meaning similar to, but decidedly more theoretical than, the definition given above.

The ethologists developed a special terminology and described instinctive, or genetically preprogrammed, behavior patterns as a sequence of events: sign stimulus ("releaser") → innate releasing mechanism (IRM) → fixed action pattern (FAP). The IRM, a neural process, is triggered by the sign stimulus and mediates the FAP—innate, stereotyped responses.

An ethological analysis describes consummatory acts such as nest building and copulating without reference to an animal's working toward a goal of having a nest or producing young. Instead, it assumes that a response is elicited when an appropriate releaser is present. The releaser-response sequence means that a response typically brings about a releaser, which elicits the next response in the sequence, which leads to the next releaser, and so forth throughout the chain. In such instances, the chain of stimulus–response (S–R) units is not learned but instinctual. However, just because a behavior chain is an instinct does not mean that the analysis of the behavior stops there. One must still determine the conditions under which the chain occurs, identifying, for example, the sign stimuli or releasers. Instincts are not disembodied responses that occur in a vacuum. They are tied to stimuli; only very rarely are internal stimuli powerful enough to evoke an instinct without external stimulus support (in a vacuum).

Ethologists tend to see behavior as either innate or acquired, but this is probably not accurate. Most psychologists view the nature–nurture problem as a pseudoproblem. Behavior is always jointly determined by heredity and environment, and trying to determine proportional influence is often unprofitable. Early environment can influence development and resulting gene-based behaviors, and learning always involves the modification of given innate behaviors. Learning simply means that behaviors *already* in an organism's repertoire are increased in frequency or accuracy, hooked up to new stimuli, specified to certain stimuli rather than others, or organized in a particular sequence.

COMPARATIVE PSYCHOLOGY

M. R. Denny

INSTRUCTIONAL SYSTEMS DEVELOPMENT

Instructional systems development (ISD) is a methodic, systematic approach to the design, implementation, and evaluation of instruction. The ISD methodology is the approved set of procedures adopted by the U.S. military services for developing military training. The principles and procedures of the ISD methodology are not exclusive to the military services.

In the early 1970s, the Interservice Committee for Instructional Systems Development was established by the four U.S. military services to oversee the development of documentation prescribing state-of-the-art procedures for designing military training. In 1975 the Interservice Committee published *Interservice procedures for instructional systems development.* The document was significant in three respects. First, it integrated (from the military services and selected disciplines) state-of-the-art procedures and techniques for systematically developing instruction. Second, the ISD methodology provided the military services with a uniform approach to developing training. Third, it provided a common framework for comparing military training requirements, products, and research. The various military services have tailored the ISD methodology to match their respective training contexts, and the core procedures of the methodology are presently used by all the U.S. military services.

ISD is implemented in five distinct phases, beginning with the analysis of trainee performance requirements and concluding with an evaluation of the program of instruction. A brief description of the five ISD procedural phases follows.

> *Phase I: Analyze.* Phase I activities analyze the job requirements and work setting to produce an operational description of the job tasks, working conditions, and indicators of acceptable job performance.
>
> *Phase II: Design.* The second phase identifies the specific objectives of training and designs a program of instruction based on them. A testing strategy is then developed to assess student achievement of the training objectives.
>
> *Phase III: Develop.* The third phase develops the actual program of instruction, including lesson plans, courseware and media, testing materials, and a management plan for implementing the instruction. For each training objective identified in Phase II, specific learning events and corresponding materials are developed to form the training-delivery system. The program of instruction is then field tested on a sample of trainees by the course designers. Subsequent to the field test, any necessary adjustments to the instructional program are made before formally implementing it.
>
> *Phase IV: Implementation.* The fourth phase involves three major activities. First, a staff of instructors is trained to formally implement the instructional program. Second, the program is implemented for the actual trainee population (i.e., an initial, complete cycle of instruction is accomplished). Third, program evaluation data are obtained from the first completed cycle to provide the information necessary to improve succeeding cycles of training.
>
> *Phase V: Evaluate.* The fifth and final phase of the methodology assesses the effectiveness of training. First, the students' performance in the training program is assessed to determine the degree to which new learning occurred. Second, their performance on the job (i.e., posttraining transfer of learning) is assessed to determine how well the learning was retained and applied to the real-world setting. The evaluation phase thus provides a quality control check on instruction and guides any necessary revisions to the training program before it is reimplemented.

The ISD methodology is rich with procedures and techniques for effecting its five phases.

INSTRUCTIONAL THEORY

D. G. Faust

INSTRUCTIONAL THEORY

Any viable theory of teaching and learning must first include some way of specifying what must be learned, or equivalently, some way to represent competence. Second, it must elucidate the processes by which people use, acquire, and modify their existing knowledge. Third, there must be some way to find out what individuals know at any given stage of learning, including a way to determine their initial knowledge. Fourth, a fully adequate theory of teaching and learning must allow for the growth of knowledge over time as learners interact dynamically with a changing teaching environment. Finally, the theory must work: To cite Kurt Lewin's dictum, "there is nothing so practical as a good theory."

The essential first step in designing instruction is to identify (a) the educational goals: what the learner is to be able to do after instruction, and (b) prototypic cognitive processes or rules: what the learner must learn so as to perform successfully on tasks associated with the educational goals.

In structural learning theories, what must be learned is one or more rules. In such theories, rules are theoretical constructs used to represent all kinds of human knowledge. A rule consists of a domain or set of encoded inputs to which it applies, a range or set of undecoded outputs that it is expected to generate, and a restricted type of procedure that applies to elements in the domain.

Structural learning theory provides a general method of analysis, called *structural analysis,* by which the rules to be learned can be derived from suitably operationalized educational goals. The first step involves selecting a representative sample of problems associated with the educational goal in question.

The second step involves determining the scope of each selected problem and identifying rules for solving each type. Identifying such rules involves several identifiable substeps.

1. Assumptions must be made regarding the minimal encoding and decoding capabilities of the students in the target population. The remainder of any analysis will be adequate just to the extent that these assumptions are applicable to individual students in any given target population.

2. The analyst must decide the scope of each sample (prototypic) problem. This scope effectively defines the domain of the rule associated with each prototype.

3. Next, the analyst must identify the cognitive steps (operations and decisions) involved in solving each of the representative problems. These operations and decisions must be sufficiently simple that using them refers only to encoding/decoding abilities that are assumed to be available to all in the target population. The operations also must be atomic in the sense that, for each student in the target population, correct use of an operation once is indicative of uniform success, and incorrect use, of failure.

Much more can be said about the actual processes by which rules are constructed. The essential is that the use of structural learning theories for purposes of designing instruction necessarily begins with a structural analysis of the subject matter in question. Notice, in particular, that nothing is said about a taxonomy of subject matter content; unlike taxonomic approaches to instructional design, *all* content according to the structural learning perspective must be analyzed.

Once a structural analysis has been completed, designing an effective instructional strategy follows directly and precisely from the theory. Specifically, once an analysis has been completed, one knows (a) what the student is to be able to do upon achieving the educational objectives, and (b) what the student must consequently learn.

By testing on a small, finite set of problems, it is possible to identify precisely and unambiguously which parts of the rule any given individual knows and which parts he or she does not know. Such testing, in effect, defines the student's entering level. It is sufficient for this purpose to test each subject on one randomly selected item from each equivalence class, because according to the atomicity assumptions, success on any item implies potential success on all other items from the same equivalence class. By capitalizing on hierarchical relationships, conditional testing may require even fewer test items.

Prescribing instruction, then, follows directly from what the student knows. All one need do is identify the missing portions of the desired rule and present them to the student. Existing theory provides a far more generalized basis for instructional prescription that in principle may be used with any subject matter that might be of interest—no matter how complex that subject matter and, if improving instructional efficiency rather than theoretical completeness is the goal, no matter how unstructured.

ALGORITHMIC–HEURISTIC THEORY
LEARNING THEORIES

J. M. SCANDURA

INSTRUMENT DESIGN

When used in the context of the social sciences, the word "instrument" can refer to anything that provides a measurement. For example, an IQ test is an instrument designed to measure intelligence. Other types of commonly used instruments include questionnaires, personality tests, rating scales, and surveys. In general, instruments include some means for quantifying their results in a numerical form that can be readily used for comparisons. Instrument design is "the process of selecting or developing measuring devices and methods appropriate to a given evaluation problem." The individual items of an instrument are usually first selected either on a theoretical basis or as a result of the experience of the person designing the instrument. In designing an instrument, two critical questions must be addressed: (a) Is the instrument reliable? (b) Is it valid?

Reliability is the consistency with which an instrument measures something across time. The concept of reliability is also used in the physical sciences. There are basically three methods for testing reliability. The first is the test–retest method in which an individual takes a test twice with some time interval occurring between the two administrations of the instrument. The second is the split-half method in which an individual's scores on half the items of an instrument are compared with the individual's scores on the other half. The third is the alternate form method in which two parallel forms of an instrument are administered to an individual, and the results are compared. Each of these methods has relative strengths and weaknesses; which method is employed depends on which weaknesses are most tolerable for a particular instrument.

Validity is the extent to which an instrument measures what it is supposed to measure. *Content validity* states how well the items on the instrument reflect a representative sample of all possible facets of the theoretical characteristic that are supposed to be represented by the instrument. This is usually accomplished by reflecting logically on the items of the instrument and choosing the items that seem to best represent the desired characteristic. *Criterion-related validity* states how well the test instrument compares with other measures of the theoretical characteristic that the test instrument is designed to measure. When a new instrument is first designed, other criteria must be identified against which the instrument can be compared to give an estimation of its criterion-related validity. Finally, *construct validity* states to what extent performance on the test fits a theoretical scheme or construct regarding the attribute the test purports to measure. In other words, it states how well test performance can be predicted by knowledge of the theoretical model upon which the test is based. As with the first type of validity, this is accomplished by rational analysis. Although some instruments that measure traits thought to be in constant flux may be useful even though they have poor reliability, no instrument can remain useful if it is found to have poor validity.

INTELLIGENCE MEASURES
PSYCHOMETRICS
RATING SCALES

D. E. BOWEN

INTEGRITY GROUPS

Integrity groups (IGs) are a community mental health resource for assisting people in coping with problems of living through self-change. These self-help groups were developed by O. Hobart Mowrer. Integrity groups are based on Mowrer's view that many psychosocial disorders are a consequence of individuals breaking commitments and contracts with significant others in their lives. The indicated remedy for helping someone deal with these concerns is to involve the person in a support group of about eight other similarly engaged individuals.

The social learning approach that characterizes these groups consists of a particular constellation of structure, goals, and shared leadership; group intake in which experienced members model appropriate group behavior; behavioral guidelines and ground rules for conducting weekly meetings; a contractual agreement to practice honesty, responsibility, and involvement inside and outside the group; individual commitments for specific behavior change; an expectation that verbal intentions will be translated into actions; and a considerable amount of group support and reinforcement for behavior change. Group members are available to assist one another as needed during the intervals between the weekly 3-hour meetings. The emphasis on self-responsibility and mutual support is expressed in the IG motto: "You alone can do it, but you can't do it alone."

GROUP THERAPY
PEER GROUP THERAPY

A. J. VATTANO

INTELLIGENCE MEASURES

Intelligence is a broad term referring to complex mental abilities of the individual. Psychologists who measure intelligence have variously employed the term to indicate the amount of knowledge available and the rapidity with which new knowledge is acquired; the ability to adapt to new situations and to handle concepts, relationships, and abstract symbols; and even simply that phenomenon that intelligence tests measure. IQ scores derived from clinically administered individual intelligence tests can predict academic achievement for the top 90% of the general population who proceed through school in regular classes, whereas identifying individuals in the bottom 10% with IQs below 80 who may require specialized educational, psychological, or medical assistance.

An IQ score is *not* the only measure of intelligence. It is merely the score earned by a person on a particular set of tasks or subtests on a test of *measured* intelligence compared to the scores of those upon whom the test was normed (or standardized). Intelligence as the lay person understands it is more than the sum of the measured psychometric abilities tested by an IQ test. Intelligence also includes level of *adaptive ability* in such hard-to-measure but critically important characteristics as grades in school, performance at work, and success as a parent and as a citizen more generally. This section uses the term intelligence as a human characteristic best assessed by an index of the individual's *measured intelligence* (namely, an IQ score) plus an index of that same individual's *adaptive success* in everyday life (grades in school, standing on the occupational ladder, community achievement, and so on).

NONINTELLECTIVE FACTORS IN MEASURED INTELLIGENCE

The English psychologist C. E. Spearman demonstrated the presence of at least one *general factor* (*g*) in the degree of success demonstrated in classroom tests and tests of achievement requiring intellectual ability. He also demonstrated the existence of *specific factors* (*s*) by showing that, despite this trend to perform at the same level on most tests, some individuals appeared to do exceptionally well in specific areas. Whether

intelligence is basically a single ability (*g*) or an aggregate of numerous specific and different intellectual abilities (*s*) was debated by psychologists for three generations and still remains unresolved.

Beginning in 1930 a third dimension of human intelligence was identified: qualities of a person's individual level of intelligence reflected in his or her observed "personality" or "temperament" that are unique to that individual and as important as the measurable elements for understanding the person's level of adaptive success in everyday living. Subsequently, Wechsler termed these components *nonintellective factors* in general intelligence. Even when dealing exclusively with measured intelligence, 30 to 50% of the total factor variance in individual differences in measured intelligence was unaccounted for. This meant that the remaining variance involved nonintellective factors and consisted of such components as drive, energy, impulsiveness, and so on. Since that time, a number of other nonintellective factors have been identified as crucial to the full assessment of an individual's intelligence, including (a) motivation, (b) physical health, (c) level of aspiration, (d) anxiety, (e) level of maturation and personality integration, and (f) life history.

Binet's main hope for the first successful test developed by him and Simon in 1905 was that it would serve as an *objective* yardstick for ascertaining which children were educable in the public schools, which ones needed extra or special education classes, and which were too intellectually retarded to benefit from regular schooling and therefore needed institutionalization. Not only did his test differentiate the educational approach needed by these three broad groups of children (regular classes, special education classes, and institutionalization), but also in time his test proved capable of differentiating within each of these broad groupings.

First Binet and later the Wechslers concluded that intelligence is a quality of the total person and not a separate component that can be measured by IQ tests in isolation. A judgment of one's intelligence level requires the assessment of current adaptive performance in everyday living ascertained from a clinical history, existing environmental circumstances, and current behavior, as well as performance on a test of measurable intelligence. Because one's level of accomplishment is the result of both past and current experiences and abilities, it is susceptible to change when conditions in the individual or environment change. Such changes may result in a change (modest or major) in the individual's functional level of adaptive intelligence.

INTELLIGENCE TESTS

Arithmetic skills, information, reasoning, manipulation of objects, vocabulary, and memory functions constitute some of the tasks employed in tests of measured intelligence, whether they are called primary grade achievement tests, Scholastic Aptitude Tests (SATs), or intelligence tests. The objective of each of these types of tests is to appraise overall performance so as to obtain an estimate of general intellectual potential. Numerous tests of these types can be combined to furnish a single measure of intelligence because of their functional equivalence. To obtain a person's IQ or relative standing, one can add together the results obtained from tests of apparently disparate abilities because scores on such tests are known to be related (correlated), thus providing a measure of global intelligence.

The Stanford–Binet and the Wechsler scales are individually administered tests widely used today by educational psychologists, industrial psychologists, and clinical psychologists whose day-to-day work involves an intensive clinical, school, or job-related investigation of a person's intellectual functioning. *Group* intelligence tests such as the Scholastic Achievement Test provide the advantage of administration to many persons at the same time. However, such tests are used primarily for purposes of classification and screening in schools, the military, employment settings, and hospitals and clinics that process large numbers of patients.

Prerequisite to a correct interpretation of an individual's IQ test score as one of the two components of intelligence is a knowledge of some basic characteristics of such IQ scores—specifically, knowledge of their norms, reliability, and validity.

Norms are the scores obtained from a large number of subjects during the process of standardizing a test. These multiple person-derived scores serve as a standard for comparison against which a single individual may be evaluated. If such a client differs in sex, race, or socioeconomic status from the group upon whom a test's norms were derived, then the test is not valid for this individual. Test norms are generally reported as mental ages, standard scores, or percentiles. A child's mental age (MA) is the age of all other children whose test performance he or she equals.

The measurement of intelligence as reflected by IQ test scores reveals that individuals vary by degrees along a continuous scale. A percentile is a score that divides the sample population into 100 parts. It tells the percentage of individuals found below a given score. Standard scores show an individual's distance from the mean in standard deviation units. The mean IQ is arbitrarily set at 100. That number is merely a convention. The standard deviation (SD) is a measure of the variability of the IQ scores of many individuals around that mean. Ordinarily, 50% of all persons earn an IQ score between 90 and 110, with 25% obtaining IQs below 90 and the remaining 25% earning scores above 110. The 25% of the population scoring below 90 has been classified progressively by psychologists as dull normal, borderline, and retarded, respectively. For better treatment and education of such individuals, the retarded classification was subsequently divided into subcategories of mild, moderate, severe, and profound retardation. The remaining 25% of the population scoring above 110 is classed as bright normal, superior, and very superior as measured on the Wechsler scales. Approximately 2% of the population is found in each of the extreme categories of very superior or retarded.

Reliability refers to the consistency of a person's test score. It is usually obtained by comparing (correlating) the individual's test score with a second score obtained by readministering the same test to that person or with the score from an alternate form of the same test. *Validity* refers to whether the test used actually measures what it purports to measure: Namely, what can be inferred from the test score by reference of it to something outside the test. Thus validity is commonly employed to describe the extent to which IQ test scores correlate with past or future measures of the individual's performance such as scholastic achievement or success on a job.

Some objective measures of an individual's level of adaptive success have been developed (especially for children's levels of success in day-to-day living). Correlations ranging from 0.58 to 0.95 have been reported between the score obtained from such adaptive behavior scales and an intelligence test on the same child, indicating that adaptive behavior and measured intelligence are correlated but not identical. Experts agree that in the field of mental retardation, the use by a skilled professional of a client's IQ score, indications of socioadaptive behavior, and clinical history has improved the diagnosis of mental retardation to a level of validity more accurate than that of any other diagnosis in the field of psychopathology.

Like most tools, psychological assessment techniques can be used for a diversity of purposes, some destructive and some constructive, and their use cannot be separated from the training, competence, and ethical values of the psychologist. Most intelligence test users employ them wisely and humanely and—in conjunction with measures of adaptive success—in a manner that maximizes the potential of each individual taking the examination.

HUMAN INTELLIGENCE
MEASUREMENT
STANFORD–BINET INTELLIGENCE SCALE
STRUCTURE OF INTELLECT MODEL
WECHSLER INTELLIGENCE TESTS

J. D. Matarazzo
D. R. Denver

INTERACTIONISM

Interactionism—or interactional psychology—in its most general sense, considers behavior to be jointly determined by personal and situational factors. A second meaning is that persons and situations are seen as exerting a reciprocal influence on each other. Not only can situations affect persons' behavior, but people can also actively exert their influence over situations by the meanings they ascribe to them and by their choice of which situations to enter or not.

Probably the best known of the earlier interactionist positions is that of Kurt Lewin as expressed in his equation, $B = f (P E)$ (i.e., behavior is a function of the person and the aspects of the environment that have contemporaneous relevance for him).

Another historical example of interactionist thinking comes from the writings of the personologist, Henry Murray.

There is consensus among researchers of various theoretical persuasions about the desirability of an interactionist approach, although the appropriate interpretation of person–situation interactions is a source of disagreement. For social behaviorists, the existence of interactions points up just how idiosyncratically behavior is organized within each person and hence how hard it is to predict. Trait theorists, however, draw quite different conclusions. Eysenck and Eysenck, for example, point out that replications of theoretically based personality-by-situation interactions are quite frequently found, and that such replications argue against behavior being idiosyncratically organized within each person. Thus for trait theorists, replicated interactions between a personality measure and a situational variable demonstrate just how refined predictions from personality measures can be.

A number of developments can be identified as signposts pointing toward the current popularity of interactionism. Undoubtedly the adoption of an interactional perspective was contingent upon the more general institutionalization by the 1950s of research designs with multiple independent variables and the use of analysis of variance techniques. Cronbach's presidential address at the annual convention of the American Psychological Association calling for the study of aptitude-by-treatment interactions to close the historical gap between the experimental and correlational traditions in psychology was widely noted. In 1968, W. Mischel presented a wide-ranging attack on the concept and measurement of personality traits, claiming, among other things, that situational determinants account for much more of the variance in behavior than do individual differences. In the ensuing controversy between situationists and advocates of a trait approach, it evolved that the "amount of variance" question was a pseudoissue, with many of the protagonists in the debate reaching conciliatory agreement around an interactionist position. In fact, Mischel himself in a later presentation softened his earlier position and noted that "it would be wasteful to create pseudocontroversies that pit person against situation in order to see which is more important. The answer must always depend on the particular situations and persons sampled."

SOCIAL PSYCHOLOGY

T. Blass

INTERBEHAVIORAL PSYCHOLOGY

Interbehavioral psychology stands in sharp contrast to traditional ways of understanding psychological events. Traditionally, the prevailing dualistic view holds that a person consists of two irreducible entities: a visible portion, the body, and an invisible portion, the mind. Another more materialistic view, known as classical behaviorism, rejects the notion of mind and attributes psychological activity to the brain.

According to popular as well as mainstream psychology based on the dualistic approach, all psychological occurrences emanate from the brain, the mind or both. Often the terms brain and mind are used interchangeably. Regardless of which one is stressed, either is believed to (a) initiate action or (b) act at the instigation of factors outside the organism. Also, according to the traditional view, besides acting as a "storage house" of memories, either the brain or mind is an executive controlling and coordinating center.

Interbehavioral psychology, first formulated by J. R. Kantor, starts with a complete rejection of all the hypothetical entities so prominent in much of mainstream and popular psychology. It holds that there is no scientific basis for imaginary "storage" and "executive" centers, whether imputed to the brain or the mind.

In his approach to psychological events, Kantor started with the assumption that psychological events are considered to be a part of nature, not apart from nature. Embarking on psychological inquiry with a naturalistic approach, Kantor stated that one never finds an organism performing solo as if in a vacuum. Always the organism is confronted by a stimulus object—another organism, thing, or event. Both factors must be taken into account in attempting to understand the learning event. If either variable is missing, that event cannot occur.

Prior to Kantor, an organism-centered approach focused on living things as the source of psychological happenings. Under Kantor's approach, the organism is demoted to a status comparable to that of the stimulus object because stress is on the *interaction* of the two chief variables. The action of each is considered to be mutual, coordinate, joint, and reciprocal.

Although organism and stimulus object hold a nuclear position in a psychological event, Kantor included still other variables. For example, seeing can only occur where light is a medium of contact. Light must therefore be acknowledged as a medium of contact for visual interactions. Among other media of contact, air permits auditory interactions.

The interbehaviorist makes use of a field approach similar to that of the ecologist in biological inquiry. Ecology may be defined as the study of the relationship of organisms to their environment and to one another—not organisms alone or environments alone, but their reciprocal, mutual, and joint activity as a *system*. The ecologist does not really study organisms at all, but *what occurs* between organisms and their surroundings.

The interbehaviorist defines *field* as the interaction of the complex or totality of interdependent factors that make up a psychological event. The organism–stimulus object, media of contact, and setting factors are the analyzable constituents of a psychological field.

However, our analysis is not yet complete because, according to the interbehaviorist, we cannot "make sense" of a single event torn asunder from its continuity. Our proper understanding comes from viewing this fragment within its context or continuum because we discover that events are also related to one another. The interbehaviorist relies heavily upon the principle: *present events are a function of antecedent events*. Therefore, we arrive at Kantor's fundamental conception of reactional biography. We can now view a single event as a field, or we can expand our notion of field to embrace a large enough flow of behavioral events—large enough to yield understanding. But note two points: (a) There is a difference between the larger framework of the interbehaviorist, and the traditional view of behavior as occurring as an imaginary, shrunken encapsulation somewhere within the organism's head (i.e., its brain or mind); and (b) the interbehaviorist deals only with observables because even though past events cannot *now* be observed, they were observable and not imaginary.

PHYSIOLOGY AND PSYCHOLOGY

How does the subject matter of psychology differ from that of physiology? On logical grounds, it would seem that the more clean-cut the segregation of data, the more refined will be the results of our study. It is just such a supposition that encouraged Kantor to isolate psychological data from the data that interest the physiologist.

Insisting on a clear separation between the two fields, Kantor has achieved such a delineation, not on the basis of some arbitrary or *a priori* basis, but empirically as the result of a first-hand inspection of the data. As a consequence, we can identify the subject matter of psychology by applying the following criteria without resorting to brain or mind concepts.

1. *Psychological events are historical.*   One must learn how to hate, love, speak, vote, and pray, but not how to sneeze, breathe, or digest. The former must be studied in a different dimension—the reactional biography or interactional history, and not the space–time framework involving organ functioning or the growth and decline of the biological organism.

2. *Psychological events show a greater specificity than biological events.*   You can elicit a knee jerk with a cardboard, reflex hammer, knife handle, board, and so on, but ask a person to name those objects, and you are certain to witness specificity of response with a different name for each object.

3. *Psychological events show integration.*   Reactions that were once separate can be combined into integrated unified activities.

4. *Psychological events show variability.*   Even over a long period of time under normal conditions reflexes show a deadly monotony. Trial-and-error behavior belongs here.

5. *Psychological events are modifiable.*   Psychological life is replete with learning. Today we realize that even the severely mentally retarded can demonstrate learning or modifiability.

6. *Psychological events show inhibition.*   Children must be "civilized" to inhibit certain reactions (e.g., in visits to the homes of others). Human behavior is hemmed in by ethical, moral, and religious precepts and is thereby more inhibited than that of other species.

7. *Psychological events show delayability.*   This greater flexibility of the time dimension permits more detachment from the immediate present and tends to segregate the psychological events.

Although there are no absolutes, we may be sure that when an event in which a living organism in contact with stimulus objects shows several of the foregoing characteristics, we are observing a psychological event. By this procedure, we have isolated a fairly distinct set of data for further analysis.

THE UNIT OF BEHAVIOR STUDY

Having isolated a distinctive subject matter for psychological investigation, we now proceed to the next problem posed by the uninterrupted flow of behavior that we must somehow grasp. How can we circumscribe a convenient unit of study out of this dynamic complexity? Just as one can "freeze" the action of a motion picture film at a single frame, so also the interbehaviorist can isolate the irreducible unit or slice of psychological happening that he or she designates as the behavior segment. More particularly, the behavior segment is defined as a single stimulus and its correlated response within the context of the medium of contact and setting factors as described earlier.

Coordinate with stimulus function, the interbehaviorist connects the notion of response function. Here we note that the physical movement *per se* in its particular configuration cannot be taken at face value. Things are relative here, too. The topography of the response is not significant because any one of the response configurations serves an equivalent response function. It should be apparent that the interbehaviorist parts company with the traditional psychologist, who treats responses in a more rigid, physicalistic manner.

In brief restatement, interbehavioral psychology is distinguished by the following features: abandonment of dualism; adoption of a naturalistic approach; the espousing of a field paradigm that demands minute analysis and specification of the variables involved in that field; differentiation of psychological data from physiological data; and strict reliance on the principle that present events are a function of antecedent events.

MIND/BODY PROBLEM
MONISM/DUALISM
THEORETICAL PSYCHOLOGY

N. H. PRONKO

INTERDISCIPLINARY TREATMENT

An interdisciplinary team approach enlists the aid of two or more individuals trained in different disciplines. Its goal is to increase the quality of care through the integration of the diverse knowledge provided by the various disciplines. Although interdisciplinary approaches are frequently extolled in the literature, little research has been done to evaluate the effectiveness of an interdisciplinary approach.

Despite this lack of research evidence, A. J. Ducanis and A. K. Golin believe interdisciplinary treatment teams have become commonplace because of (a) the concept of the whole client, (b) the needs of the organization, and (c) external mandates. The concept of the whole client emphasizes the importance of viewing the client or patient as a total entity with interrelated parts. Consequently, when one chooses a treatment, one must be aware not only of the effects upon the identified parts, but also of possible secondary effects upon other parts of the system. When a number of disciplines are involved in a treatment approach, the effect of each discipline's treatment strategy is known to the others and can be evaluated as to its secondary effects.

The increasing complexity of organizations has also provided impetus for using an interdisciplinary approach. In complex organizations, an interdisciplinary team approach is used to increase the quality of communication and to clarify lines of authority within an organization. To counteract fragmentation, organizations have responded by integrating the diverse disciplines into functional units that subsequently must learn to cooperate with one another.

Requirements from state, federal, and other funding sources are likewise increasing the frequency of interdisciplinary approaches as they externally mandate the formation of interdisciplinary teams as a requirement for funding. These mandates are made under the rationale of improved quality of care, as well as increased professional accountability resulting from interdisciplinary teams.

The development of the interdisciplinary approach is the direct outcome of the development of professional groups and their subsequent specialization and stratification. Ducanis and Golin cited the development of professional status as a process requiring (a) a need to be filled, (b) individuals who develop the knowledge and skills required to fill that need, and (c) the formation of those individuals into an identified group perceived by others to possess specialized knowledge and training. The movement through these steps has occurred for a number of groups in the health and mental health professions. The first group to move through these steps in both the health and mental health areas was the physicians.

Gradually, however, the simpler duties done by the physician were delegated to assistants, so as to provide the physician more freedom in treating complex cases in which the full range of the physician's knowledge and skill would be needed. Over time, these groups have developed their own bodies of knowledge and sets of skills, becoming recognized by others as having specialized knowledge and training. Simultaneously, this has created a knowledge explosion such that one individual can no longer be expected to have all the knowledge found in the various "allied health" disciplines.

The operation of a fully functioning interdisciplinary treatment team approach differs little from that of a well-functioning team in any other area of endeavor. The goal of the group is the first and most critical aspect of a functioning team. Irwin Ruben and his associates emphasize that a clear-cut understanding of the purpose of the group is required of all group members for the group's knowledge and skills to be focused appropriately on the task at hand. Vailetutti and Christoplos state that the general purpose of the interdisciplinary team is either to diagnose (evaluate) and treat the identified problems or to diagnose and then refer to another setting for treatment.

Membership in the group is determined by the contribution that each prospective group member can make to the overall goal of the group. The composition of the team will depend on the type of problem presented by the patient/client, the organizational setting, and the availability of various disciplines for participation. The most common professions with which the psychologist works in interdisciplinary treatment include psychiatry, neurology, plastic surgery, internal medicine, allergy, and physiatry in medicine and nursing, social work, physical therapy, and occupational therapy in allied fields. Some of the settings include schools, mental health centers, hospitals, government and private rehabilitation agencies, and alcohol and drug treatment centers.

A final aspect of team composition involves the decision to include or exclude the patient/client from the team decisions. There is a trend toward inclusion of the patient in health care decisions, but there has not been sufficient research to evaluate the effectiveness of this approach.

A functioning team is interactive in nature, and the solutions arrived at are the product of the entire group. The particular process of decision making may vary from autocratic to democratic, depending on the type of problem to be handled by the group, the patient population, and the knowledge and skill of the group leader, as well as the knowledge and skill of the membership.

Whereas the more autocratic procedure requires greater knowledge and skills on the part of the leader, the more democratic approach requires knowledge and skills on the part of both leader and group members. The knowledge and skills required include not only the individual's discipline specialty training, but also training in the area of group function. The more democratic interdisciplinary team approach should occur more frequently hereafter as the allied health disciplines become more recognized and accepted.

Regardless of whether autocratic or democratic leadership styles are used, a number of difficulties arise with an interdisciplinary treatment approach. The most apparent problem in interdisciplinary treatment is shared terminology. As each discipline evolves, it tends to develop specialized terminology. Although this specialized vocabulary is frequently a requisite part of increased knowledge, it can cause difficulties in interdisciplinary group operation owing to the unfamiliarity of others with the terms used or the use of the same term to mean slightly different things for different disciplines.

Perhaps less observable but certainly as problematic is the difficulty arising from the various ways in which disciplines conceptualize problems. Physicians, for instance, are said to think in terms of a "medical model" or "disease model." This model has been challenged as too restrictive by some who suggest substituting "health models" or "behavioral models" in its place.

The difficulties in the interdisciplinary treatment approach may extend to professional identity. Whether to accept suggestions as to a treatment approach recommended by another discipline can have implications concerning the relative importance of that discipline vis-à-vis one's own.

Finally, interdisciplinary treatment teams—like any team approach—can be quite costly in that a number of highly paid professionals are brought together to arrive at decisions. Someone must pay for the professionals' time while in the meeting, and eventually the cost is borne by the patient/client.

In spite of the difficulties present in an interdisciplinary treatment approach, there are significant advantages that lend support to its continuation as a treatment method. It is to the benefit of the patient or client to have a well-functioning interdisciplinary team because the individual members of the team are thereby able to have a broader (whole person) percept of the patient/client rather than a more restricted single disciplinary view.

Often the variations in problem identification and treatment approaches benefit the patient and the treatment team in expanding options for both. This lends to both breadth of approach as well as specialization within each aspect of treatment. In this way the patient benefits directly from the increased quality of care while the team members benefit by the increased knowledge and skill arising from shared perceptions.

BEHAVIORAL MEDICINE
HOLISTIC HEALTH
MENTAL HEALTH CONSULTATION TEAMS
TEAM PERFORMANCE

R. P. KAPPENBERG

INTEREST INVENTORIES

Various methods for determining an individual's preferences for specific topics or activities are available, including direct observations of behavior, performance on ability tests, responses to projective test items, and self-report inventories. The last of these—inventories of interests in educational, social, recreational, and vocational activities—has stimulated a great amount of research and development.

Two landmarks in the history of interest measurement were the Strong Vocational Interest Blank for Men and the Kuder Preference Record. These instruments and their successors have helped two generations of high school and college students become acquainted with career options and aware of their vocational interests. Such tests have also played a role, to some extent, in employee selection and classification in occupational contexts.

Publication of the first Strong Vocational Interest Blank for Men in 1927 and one for women in 1933 was followed by various revisions of each; in 1974, they were merged into the Strong–Campbell Interest Inventory, a restandardization of which was published in 1981. Further development of Frederic Kuder's inventories also occurred, represented by the publication of the Kuder Form A: Personal Preference Survey; Kuder Form C: Vocational Preference Record; Kuder Form DD: Occupational Interest Survey; and Kuder Form E: General Interest Survey.

The item format on the Strong–Campbell Interest Inventory requires examinees to indicate whether they like, dislike, or are indifferent to a list of occupations, school subjects, activities, amusements, and types of people. There is also a section on which examinees are asked to choose between two activities, and another section on which they indicate whether each of 14 characteristics describes them. In contrast, the Kuder items are forced-choice triads on which examinees indicate which of the three things they would most like and least like to do.

The Strong inventories were originally scored by the empirical procedure of comparing the examinee's item responses with the responses of specific occupational groups of people. Thus scoring of the Strong inventories was *normative*, in contrast to the *ipsative* scoring of the original Kuder inventories. The Kuder Preference Record is scored on ten interest scales, consisting of items having high correlations with one another but low correlations with the other scales. The forced choice format of the Kuder inventories makes it impossible to score high or low on all scales. A typical score profile on the Kuder Preference Record consists of one or more high scores and one or more low scores, but mostly average scores.

The Strong–Campbell Interest Inventory is scored both in the traditional empirical manner (162 "occupational scales") and the Kuder "interest cluster" way (23 "basic interest scales"). By employing J. L. Holland's interest classification scheme, the Strong–Campbell Interest Inventory is also scored on six "general occupational themes." A further indication of the rapprochement between the methods of scoring the Strong and Kuder inventories is seen in the fact that the Kuder Form DD: Occupational Interest Survey is scored empirically by comparing the responses of examinees with those of specified occupational groups.

Like most inventories of interests and personality, the Strong–Campbell and Kuder instruments can be faked. It seems reasonable that they are more likely to be answered honestly in vocational counseling situations than when used for applicant selection.

Although the Strong–Campbell and Kuder inventories dominate the field of interest measurement, there are many other entries. Noteworthy among these are factor-analyzed instruments such as the Guilford–Zimmerman Interest Inventory and the G-S-Z Interest Survey, as well as general interest surveys such as the California Occupational Preference Survey, the Jackson Vocational Interest Survey, and the Ohio Vocational Interest Survey. In addition, there are special inventories for children ("What I Like to Do," Career Awareness Inventory), for the disadvantaged (Geist Picture Interest Inventory), and for assessing interests in skilled trades (Minnesota Vocational Interest Inventory). Following J. L. Holland's theory of the relationships of interests to personality is the Vocational Preference Inventory. Also developed with reference to a specific theory of personality is the Hall Occupational Orientation Inventory.

Interest inventories have found their greatest use in vocational counseling. The modern approach is to use inventories in conjunction with other kinds of career educational materials to introduce young people to the world of work. One distinction to be made clear to counselees is that interest is not the same as ability; a high score on an interest inventory scale should not be interpreted as indicating an ability to pursue related occupations. To minimize the tendency to overinterpret scores on interest inventories, such scores should be interpreted only in the light of other supporting and clarifying information about counselees. Thus vocational counseling is most effective when scores on ability tests and interest inventories, as well as school grades and information on out-of-school activities, are available to counselors.

CAREER COUNSELING
COUNSELING
JOB SATISFACTION
OCCUPATIONAL SUCCESS PREDICTION

L. R. AIKEN

INTERNAL VALIDITY

Internal validity pertains to the degree of assurance that can be attributed to a suspected causal relationship between variables. An experiment has internal validity to the extent that observed effects can be attributed to independent variables and not some other extraneous factors.

An imputation of causality generally assumes that two variables—the cause and the effect—will covary, but before internal validity can be inferred, it must be demonstrated that A does indeed *cause* B (i.e., that the occurrence of A alone produces B). One could, for example, erroneously assume that home instruction in the performance of perceptual–motor tasks (a) causes children to earn better grades in school (b) when, in fact, it is parental concern and attention (c) rather than the perceptual–motor training per se that produce the desired result.

Psychological experiments are particularly vulnerable to the misleading and unintended effects of adventitious variables because they can rarely be performed within pristine confines such as a physics laboratory. Therefore, designing an experiment in such a way that when positive results ensue causality can be inferred has become a preoccupation of thoughtful researchers in psychology.

Internal validity can be contrasted with external validity, which refers to the generalizability of results beyond the specific context in which internal validity was obtained. For example, if it could be shown, under carefully controlled conditions, that overcrowding in cages causes aggressive behavior in white rats (internal validity), would this also hold true for humans living in a ghetto (external validity)?

Internal validity should be differentiated from construct validity, which is a theoretical explanation of a hypothesized cause–effect relationship. In most cases, however, if internal validity seems reasonably established, a researcher would want to formulate a conceptual framework or construct to account for the relationships. Also, internal validity should not be confused with internal consistency, which is a testing term relating to intercorrelations among a set of items.

In attempting to establish internal validity, it is necessary to verify the sequence of events. Obviously, if there is a relationship between A and B and A always precedes B, it is logical to assume that A causes B and not the reverse. Along with instituting as much environmental and situational control as possible, psychologists conducting research are concerned with selecting subjects in such a way as not to bias assignment to experimental and control groups. They also resort to sophisticated experimental designs such as covariance and counterbalancing to exert statistical controls over variable effects so that informed judgments about causal relationships can be made.

The following, in abbreviated form, is an analysis taken from Cook and Campbell of problems that can arise in conducting quasi-experimental or field research in psychology, all of which pose potential threats to internal validity.

1. Events can transpire during the time that has elapsed between two evaluations that can alter the subjects' reactions. For example, if the effect of a new drug on reducing anxiety is being tested but a tornado hits the locale during the interim between evaluations, measures of anxiety may be unduly influenced by the fear-inducing catastrophe.

2. By the same token, naturally occurring maturational changes over time also can produce effects that contaminate the experiment (i.e., improvement in perceptual–motor skills in children could be due to simple aging rather than training).

3. In research involving repeated testings, many exposures to the same instrument can produce a cumulative effect that contaminates the treatment being investigated (e.g., improvement in IQ due to an "enriched" environment could be a result of familiarity with the intelligence test).

4. Changes in the instruments used to make evaluations, whether they be mechanical or human, can produce effects other than the treatments being investigated: A spring can lose its elasticity and a rater can alter his or her orientation over time.

5. If the phenomenon of statistical regression (the tendency for higher and lower scores to revert toward the average on retesting) is ignored, an overly positive and misleading estimate of a relationship can be obtained, and consequently, erroneous conclusions about causality drawn.

6. An unintentional bias in allocating subjects to control and/or experimental groups can produce results related to these unsuspected but nonrandom assignments of cases. Differences among the groups due to selectivity rather than the treatments being investigated can then lead to unwarranted conclusions.

7. Any loss of cases during the conduct of an experiment as a result of dropout, illness, or even death can bias the results of an experiment if the attrition turns out to be nonrandom.

8. Uncertainty about whether A is caused by or is a result of B has an obvious bearing on internal validity. Does the football team play better because of larger crowds, or do larger crowds come to the game because the team plays better?

9. Accidental and unwanted communication among treatment groups destroys the experimental naïveté of the subjects and can induce attitudes and expectations unrelated to the purpose of the research. Along the same lines, the experiment itself could generate compensatory rivalry, resentment, and demoralization in participant subjects and/or groups, all of which are not germane and could differentially affect the results.

10. Because experimenters do not operate in a vacuum, it sometimes happens that, for administrative or social reasons, groups receive compensatory treatment that tends to equalize effects and work against the achievement of valid results. For example, giving at least minimal therapy to a control group of patients who were to receive no therapy at all could be justified for humanitarian reasons but patently defeats the intent of the experiment.

There is no way to conduct a perfect experiment (i.e., one in which control is so complete that it would be impossible to explain away an effect or relationship as artifactual). Furthermore, the context in which psychological experiments are usually conducted makes them especially vulnerable to interpretive ambiguity and the drawing of erroneous conclusions. An intimate knowledge of the field and cognizance of the many pitfalls involved in quasi-experimental research can, however, help the psychologist to design an experiment that is more likely to permit genuine inferences about internal validity.

CONFIDENCE LIMITS
EXPERIMENTAL DESIGNS
HYPOTHESIS TESTING
MILL'S CANONS
PROBABILITY
STATISTICAL SIGNIFICANCE

E. E. WAGNER

INTERNALIZATION

Internalization involves bringing some aspect of the external world into one's private mental life and having that internal representation of the external world exert an influence over one's thoughts and behavior. Schafer distinguishes three varieties of internalization: introjection, identification, and incorporation.

Introjection establishes an "inner presence" that is not perceived as being an integral part of oneself. A person carries on an internal relationship with his or her introjects in much the same way as such relationships would be carried on with other people (or with particular features of other people) in the external world. These internal relationships may be either pleasant and comforting or unpleasant and disturbing.

Identification refers to a modification in various aspects of one's subjective self so as to increase one's resemblance to another person taken as a model. It is possible to identify with animals or machines, but the term is usually applied to situations in which one individual's beliefs, values, and behavioral style are adopted by another. Identifications may be either total or partial. Even when it is only partial, however, an identification makes a significant change in a person's self-concept, and this distinguishes identification from introjection. According to psychoanalytic theory, identification is the mechanism by which the superego or self-regulating moral code is initially established in the child, although new identifications may be made at any time in a person's life.

Finally, *incorporation* is a very specialized form of internalization in which one person perceives all or part of another individual as constituting all or part of him- or herself. Because it is practically impossible for one person to be the same as another, incorporation is a less realistic and more primitive process of internalization than is identification.

IMITATION LEARNING
PERSONALITY

W. Samuel

INTERNATIONAL CONFERENCES

International conferences have emerged as a new education industry competing with formal educational institutions for the transfer of knowledge internationally.

International conferences are separated into those whose purpose is to exchange information, such as scientific congresses and seminars, and those expected to arrive at some decision or recommendation, such as professional associations, trade unions, or intergovernmental meetings, where there is greater need for procedural control.

The complex psychological, cultural, ideological, and semantic factors affecting the success of some international conferences and the failure of others presents a challenge to international social scientists. Social science research on international conferences has attempted to articulate the complexity of variables regarding international conferences through a variety of research studies. Most research evaluating conferences measures *participant satisfaction* as the criterion of success. A second cluster of research measures *process variables* such as reaching agreement, resistance by participants, and the role of the chairperson in defining issues as the relevant criteria of success. A third cluster of research is focused on how a conference avoids or copes with *problems* that arise during the conference. A fourth group of researchers emphasize *planning* variables such as selecting the participants and defining their roles in the conference as most significant in contributing to success or failure. A fifth group of researchers emphasize the *structure*—size, duration, and other arrangements that contribute to the success or failure of the conference.

Research indicates that small conferences have many advantages over larger ones. In fact, the number of smaller conferences is increasing rapidly. Small conferences are more cost-effective, encourage a more intensive participatory role for participants, do not exclude the nonelite organizational members, facilitate professional communication and feedback, and result in collaborative projects more frequently. Collegial contact for peer support and reaffirmation is probably the most important function of international conferences; it is achieved through opportunities to reaffirm professional solidarity by formal and informal communication among seniors and peers.

Sharp provided a comprehensive framework for studying international conferences. Included among other topical clusters of variables are the physical and social environment, the internal structure, the substantive preparation, conference leadership, language and semantic variables, nonverbal communication processes, drafting of documentation, impact of differences in ideology, patterns of participation, and the levels of official representation.

INTERNATIONAL PSYCHOLOGY

P. B. Pedersen

INTERNATIONAL ORGANIZATIONS OF PSYCHOLOGY

The establishment and growth of psychological organizations whose jurisdiction transcends the geographic boundaries of individual nations afford members of the world psychological community numerous and diverse opportunities to meet with one another, to engage in an active exchange of opinions and ideas, to advise and counsel one another on questions of psychological theory and practice within a cross-cultural framework, and to advance common scientific objectives.

In terms of international endeavors in psychology, attention is turned to the International Congress of Psychology, which first convened in Paris in 1889. International congresses have been held at roughly regular intervals ever since (they now occur once every 3 years). The intent of such congresses is to provide periodic forums for the exchange of ideas and information.

Since 1951, when it was founded in Stockholm, responsibility for the organization of these international congresses has rested with the International Union of Psychological Science, the general international body in psychology. In its statutes, the International Union is described as "an organization uniting those National Societies and Associations whose aim is the development of scientific psychology, whether biological or social, normal or abnormal, pure or applied." The International Union has a consultative status with UNESCO, and numbers among its various affiliates the Interamerican Society of Psychology, the International Association of Applied Psychology, and the International Council of Psychologists.

The Interamerican Society of Psychology, established in 1951 in Mexico City, is dedicated to improving and fostering communication among psychologists in North and South America. It has been responsible for organizing annual or biennial congresses situated by and large in Latin America, and has initiated a number of projects aimed at improving relations between the Latin American countries and the United States.

The International Association of Applied Psychology was founded in 1970. This organization sponsors international congresses dealing with applied psychology.

Other psychological organizations meeting on an international scale fall into the special interest category.

The Committee on International Relations, under the aegis of the American Psychological Association, is dedicated to the promotion and coordination of international contacts between American psychologists and those from other nations.

HISTORY OF PROFESSIONAL PSYCHOLOGY
INTERNATIONAL CONFERENCES

F. L. Denmark

INTERNATIONAL PSYCHOLOGY

Psychology has been an international enterprise since its beginning as a modern science in the late nineteenth century. When most psychologists use the term "international psychology," they are referring to various forms of organized psychology at the international level. Sometimes the term also designates the social psychology of international relations or the comparative study of psychological processes across different nations and cultures, as in cross-cultural psychology.

SOCIAL PSYCHOLOGY OF INTERNATIONAL RELATIONS

The systematic use of psychological concepts and methods for the development of theory, research, and policy studies in international relations is a relatively new area of specialization within social psychology. Generally interdisciplinary in character, these social-psychological approaches deal with the problems of interaction among nations, often with a goal of reducing tension and promoting international cooperation. Among the kinds of research that deal specifically with the international behavior of individuals are studies of national stereotypes or images, studies of attitudes toward international affairs, of national ideology and how it is communicated, and of the effects of cross-national contacts on individual or group behavior.

INTERNATIONAL STUDY OF PSYCHOLOGICAL PROCESSES

Cross-cultural psychology expanded greatly in the last quarter of the twentieth century. Cross-cultural, comparative approaches are particularly appealing for the study of sociocultural factors in any aspect of human development.

The most common type of cross-national or cross-cultural study involves only two cultures. Comparisons between two nations are generally very difficult to interpret because many cultural differences are operating that might provide alternate explanations of the findings that cannot be ruled out. The inclusion of subcultural variation and social factors within each nation enhances the likelihood that interpretable results can be obtained.

International psychology is only one aspect of cross-cultural psychology, the latter encompassing a much wider range of comparative studies. The search for cultural variation and its consequences for psychological functioning may be limited to a study of cultures within one large multicultural nation rather than international differences in culture.

ORGANIZED PSYCHOLOGY AT THE INTERNATIONAL LEVEL

The first International Congress of Psychology was held in 1889, less than 10 years after the founding of the first laboratory of experimental psychology. The rapid exchange of new ideas and methods of research across the different countries of Europe and the Americas produced a truly international psychology with a predominantly Western orientation. Most of the early leading academicians received much of their training in Germany or Great Britain.

At the 13th International Congress of Psychology held in Stockholm in July 1951, the International Union of Psychological Science (IUPsyS) was formally established. The IUPsyS is the only international organization that has as its members national psychological societies rather than individuals.

The major aims and objectives of the IUPsyS are to promote the exchange of ideas and scientific information among psychologists of different countries, to foster international exchange of scholars and students, to collaborate with other international and national organizations in promoting psychology as a science and profession, and to encourage international projects that will further the development of psychology.

Most international organizations in psychology have individuals rather than societies as members. The oldest is the International Association of Applied Psychology founded in 1920 by Edouard Claparéde. As in the case of IUPsyS, the International Association of Applied Psychology sponsors a world congress every four years. Between congresses, the Association sponsors international projects and exchanges such as the International Test Commission. A number of special interest divisions within the Association deal with more narrowly defined international issues in applied psychology.

Smaller international organizations also exist to meet the specialized international interests of psychologists. Illustrative of such organizations are the International Council of Psychology, the International Association for Cross-Cultural Psychology, the Interamerican Society of Psychology, the European Association of Experimental Social Psychologists, the International Association of French-speaking Psychologists, and the International School Psychology Association.

These associations are comprised almost entirely of psychologists. Some interdisciplinary associations have large numbers of psychologists as members. Leading examples of such associations are the International Brain Research Organization and the International Society for the Study of Behavioral Development.

The development and status of psychology in different countries and regions of the world vary considerably. As one would expect, the most highly developed scientific psychology exists in North America, Europe, and Japan. Rapid growth in the late twentieth century has also occurred in Australia, Brazil, and Mexico, with several other countries of Latin America and Asia close behind. In a major survey of trends in development and status of psychology throughout the world, Mark Rosenzweig estimated that there are over a quarter million recognized psychologists throughout the world. The greatest concentration exists in the United States and Canada, followed closely by Western Europe.

Although the scientific principles of psychology are valid regardless of cultural boundaries and politics, the scientific status of psychology and its social relevance vary greatly throughout the world. No doubt the greatest changes in the next several decades will occur within the more rapidly developing countries of Latin America, Africa, and Asia.

INTERNATIONAL CONFERENCES
PSYCHOLOGY AS A PROFESSION

W. H. HOLTZMAN

INTERPERSONAL ATTRACTION

As defined by social psychologists, interpersonal attraction refers to a favorable attitude toward or feeling of liking for another person. Most empirical research has focused on first impressions and initial encounters, although attraction between individuals in ongoing relationships is drawing increased attention. Initial impressions are found to guide a person's behavior toward another individual and may elicit from the other responses that are consistent with, and thus reinforce, the initial impression. As a general rule, we are attracted to individuals who, we believe, possess favorable characteristics or qualities, and we dislike individuals to the extent that we perceive them to have unfavorable attributes.

Physical appearance. People of all ages tend to prefer physically attractive to physically unattractive individuals. Within a given culture or subculture there is considerable agreement in judgments of a person's physical attractiveness, but little is known about the particular attributes or combinations of attributes that define beauty. The physically attractive are perceived as likely to possess such socially desirable personality traits as sensitivity, kindness, modesty, intelligence, and sociability, and consistent with these stereotyped beliefs, physically attractive individuals are liked better than the physically unattractive. There is evidence, however, that physical appearance has a greater influence on the attraction of males to females than vice versa.

Behavior. Impressions are often based on observation of overt behavior in combination with the context in which the behavior occurs. Research on causal attribution has shown that the behavior of another person is frequently explained by attributing corresponding personality dispositions to the person. These inferences are later reflected in liking or disliking for the person.

There is some evidence that liking is influenced by such nonverbal behaviors as smiling, eye contact, physical touch, and body posture. The effects of self-disclosure appear to depend on the circumstances under which the information is disclosed and, most important, on whether the information disclosed is socially desirable or undesirable.

Similarity. Our attraction to other people increases as a direct function of the extent to which we perceive them to be similar to us in their opinions, interests, and personality characteristics. Numerous laboratory and field experiments have provided strong evidence in support of this conclusion.

Consequences of attraction. The consequences of interpersonal attraction have received much less scrutiny than have its antecedents. Of course, in the context of ongoing relationships, antecedents and consequences cannot be easily separated. Thus interaction between individuals may increase the similarity of their opinions and interests, which in turn may affect liking and further interaction, and so on.

Many reactions to another person appear to be largely unaffected by the person's attractiveness. In contrast, attraction to another person generally produces a tendency to approach and affiliate with that person. To be sure, situational and personality factors greatly influence the forms this approach tendency will take.

ATTITUDES
FACIAL EXPRESSIONS

I. AJZEN

INTERPERSONAL COMMUNICATION

Interpersonal communication refers to the transfer of information by a source to a specific other target or identifiable group members. These communications typically occur in face-to-face interactions, although they may also occur by mail, telephone, or other electronic means. H. D. Lasswell captured in one sentence much of the subject matter of human communications: "Who says what in what channel to whom with what effect?"

Electrical engineering principles were applied by Shannon and Weaver to human communications. The mind of the communicator may be considered the source of the communications. Presumably, messages originate in the brain and are encoded for transmission to other people. The source must have a means of transmitting information, such as speech, gestures, or writing. The message is encoded and sent as a signal to a receiver, who must decode the message. Thus the destination of a message is the mind of a target or receiver person.

This information model is helpful in examining some of the more important questions regarding interpersonal communications. It should be noted that the source may unintentionally communicate to others, as when nonverbal cues betray a liar. Of course, the source may not even be aware of a communication.

Intentional communications may be examined in terms of the degree to which the interpretations of the source are accurately received by the target. For some communication theorists it is the sharing of interpretations and not just the exchange of information that lies at the heart of the communication process. Any interference with accurate transfer of information is referred to as noise in the system. Noise may be due to ambiguous encodings, problems with channels through which signals are transmitted, or faulty decoding by the target.

One should not construe disagreement between two persons as necessarily caused by noise. A target may be able to take the viewpoint of the source and fully understand the interpretation communicated, but nevertheless disagree with it. Often persons believe they have not been understood, when in reality the target persons disagree with them.

There has often been confusion even among scientists in distinguishing between language and communication. To make the distinction, one must understand the differences between signs, signals, and symbols. Signs are environmental stimuli that the organism has associated with other events. Signs are inflexibly and directly related to their associated events.

Signals are signs produced by living organisms. Most animals can use signals in their interaction with other animals. Thus birds may emit love calls, insects may transmit odors, and monkeys may manifest threat gestures.

A symbol, like a signal, has a referent. However, symbols do not necessarily refer to physical reality and may not have space–time relationships to their referents. Symbols derive their meaning from a community of users and not through a connection with a referent. The use of symbols allows the development of various abstract areas of knowledge such as history, literature, religion, art, and science. Furthermore, it provides the basis for the individual's construction of social reality, including a self-concept.

The available evidence indicates that only humans use symbols. Thus it appears that the symbol represents an important discontinuity in phylogenetic development between humans and all other forms of life.

Language is a means of information processing and is used to store, manipulate, create, and transmit information. No analysis of interpersonal communication among humans would be complete without a consideration of the symbolic aspects of language. One important property of symbols is that they may refer to classes of things, and they may have multiple meanings. Thus error in communications is both frequent and inevitable. That is, noise tends to be an inevitable feature of interpersonal communications.

Situations and relationships with others provide a context within which persons can share interpretations of communications and hence reduce noise. The individual's definition of the social situation typically involves certain expectations about the behaviors of others, the rules that define and regulate interactions and guide to conduct. These expectations provide a frame of reference within which the person encodes and decodes information.

Communications have a number of functions. They allow the coordination of behaviors of individuals in a group. Interpersonal communication also allows for instruction in which one individual helps another to learn skills or develop new frames of reference. Perhaps most important of all, communications function as means to influence others. Messages used for purposes of power and influence may be considered actions with as much impact as skeletal behaviors. Thus communicative actions are sometimes referred to as speech acts.

Speech acts that serve to control reinforcements may take the form of threats or promises, which may be contingent or noncontingent in form. Promises, unlike threats, carry a moral obligation of fulfillment by the source.

There are several speech acts that may be classified as means of information control. Persuasion represents a source's attempt to influence a target's decisions. Among the types of persuasive communications are warnings, mendations, and activation of commitments.

Another classification of speech acts refers to their function as self-presentational. Actors project certain identities to others and engage in various tactics to foster desired identities in the eyes of others. Among the more prominent speech acts devoted to impression management are accounts, entitlements, enhancements, and ingratiation.

Gestures, visual contact, body orientation, and the use of interpersonal space may substitute for verbal communications or may serve as a context within which to interpret verbal communications. In many instances nonverbal responses act as signals and do not convey symbolic forms of information.

INTERPERSONAL PERCEPTION
LANGUAGE IN GREAT APES

J. T. TEDESCHI

INTERPERSONAL PERCEPTION

The impressions we form of other people serve as an important basis for interpersonal interactions. Person perception is a complex topic and clearly different from space perception. In person perception the observer is concerned with the interior psychological processes of the stimulus person. These have little to do with sensory mechanisms, but instead are answered by inferences or attributions made by the observer. In a way, "person perception" is a misnomer that perhaps would be better expressed as "person inferences." Much of the topic is currently referred to as attribution theory.

Fritz Heider noted that there are three differences between the perceptions of objects and persons. First, persons are assumed to experience an interior life and objects are not. Each person experiences thoughts and emotions, and assumes that others do also. Second, objects are not perceived as causes of their own actions, whereas persons are often viewed as first causes. The concept of responsibility is inextricably interwoven with the notion that one acts for one's own interior reasons rather than in response to the inexorable forces of the environment. Third, persons can deliberately manipulate and exploit the perceiver, whereas inanimate objects do not. One purpose of person perception is to allow the observer to predict the probable actions of the stimulus person, so as to anticipate in planning his or her own actions.

The study of person perception is essentially an attempt to reconstruct the way the average person on the street processes information about other people and the self. The observer is interested in answering the question of why the stimulus person acted as he or she did. According to Heider, causes for behavior are attributed to either the environment or the person. When the action can be attributed to environmental causes, the actor is not held responsible for the positive or negative effects of his or her behavior, but when factors inside the actor are perceived as the origins, the actor is held accountable for the effects.

Much of the work done in the area of attributions is concerned with the rules that observers use in attributing cause to the environment or the person. Heider believed the interpersonal function of person perception is to allow the observer to predict and control the behavior of others.

The tendency of observers is to accept the first sufficient cause as the reason for behavior. The impact of any particular cause in producing an effect is discounted, however, if other plausible causes are present. This discounting principle may lead to attributions to both environmental and person causes of behavior. Furthermore, the more effects the observer believes are associated with the actor's behavior, the more plausible causes there can be. Harold H. Kelley, who proposed the discounting principle, also suggested an augmentation principle: The more costs the actor risks in order to act as he or she does, the more likely the observer is to attribute the behavior to person causes. The rule of thumb is that the more the actor's behavior deviates from what the observer believes most people would do, the more likely the action is associated with something peculiar about this actor.

An observer may observe an actor only once or may have multiple opportunities to witness behavior. Most attributional rules can be categorized as based on either a single observation or on multiple observations. Among the former are the following.

1. *Out-of-role behavior.* Out-of-role behavior can be construed as derivative from the augmentation principle. The person who is out of role has given up customary rewards and is apparently willing to accept negative reactions from others. The action must stem, therefore, from some inner personal factors.

2. *Noncommon effects.* An observer may mentally reconstruct the decision making of the actor in order to understand the choices made. It may be assumed that the chosen alternative is preferred because it maximizes some value for the actor, at least as compared to the other alternatives. That is, some effect that is noncommon to the decision alternatives is the basis for the decision that is made, and that effect reveals something about the decision maker.

3. *Hedonic relevance.* When the actions of another person have some positive or negative impact on the observer, the latter has a stronger tendency to attribute the behavior to personal causes.

4. *Personalism.* When the observer experiences positive or negative effects from the actor's behavior, consideration will be given to whether those effects were specifically aimed at the observer. When the observer believes the behavior was directed at him or her (personally), the observer more confidently makes a person attribution.

Harold H. Kelley has provided a model of the rules used by naive observers in making attributions after multiple observations of an actor. If the observer does not have a ready causal schema within which particular actions are analyzed, causes attributed, and responsibility assigned, he or she will rationally process the data available, much as a scientist would. According to Kelley, the following principles will allow the observer to make attributions to the person, the environment, or both:

1. *Consistency.* Consistency of reaction suggests a stable environmental cause, whereas inconsistent reactions suggest fluctuating personal causes.

2. *Distinctiveness.* Generally speaking, the more distinctive the person's response, the more apt an observer is to make an environmental attribution, and the less distinctive the response, the more likely it is that a personal attribution will be made.

3. *Consensus.* If a large number of people react in the same way to a situation, an environmental attribution will be made. But if the person reacts in a manner different from that of most other people, a personal attribution is more likely.

There is a tendency for divergences in attributions between actors and observers. Actors tend to see their own actions as strongly constrained by the environment. In contrast, as Heider has noted, the behavior of the actor tends to engulf the perceptual field of the observer. This focus on the actor to the exclusion of the environment is referred to as the fundamental attribution error and leads observers to make stronger personal attributions than do actors. Also, of course, actors have more information about themselves and a wider context of attribution than do observers.

E. E. Jones and K. E. Davis have argued that once an observer makes an attribution to personal causes, a correspondent inference will be made from the characterization of the observed behavior and the motive inferred as underlying that behavior. The observer notes effects that occur in the environment and traces these back to the behavior of an actor. If the behavior is attributed to environmental factors, the information processing ceases. However, if a personal attribution is made, the observer assumes the actor intended the effects observed. Intent implies that the actor has foreknowledge of the effects and the ability to produce them. Intent refers to the effects and not to the behavior in question. If intent is attributed to the actor, a motive for the intention is inferred.

Correspondent inference assumes a commonality between the nature of a response and the motive attributed for it. This theory assumes that whenever an observer makes an attribution of cause to the person, a correspondent inference will be made. It must be further assumed that the identification and labeling of responses is unproblematic and is a given, much like the proximal energies of space perception. It can be argued that an action cannot be identified apart from the goals assumed as guiding the actor.

Clearly, observers do form overall impressions of other people. Information is gathered from direct observations and from reports by other observers. Some kinds of information are more central in forming overall impressions, and other information is more peripheral or unimportant.

Norman Anderson has proposed mathematical models of how observers process and weigh information provided (in adjectival form) about actors. How likable a person is may be more heavily weighted by some traits than others, and earlier information may be given more weight than later information. The primacy effect may be due to discounting of later information or may occur by inattention after an early impression is formed. These ideas can be presented in the form of an algebraic weighted averaging model, which has received rather impressive support from empirical studies.

Social psychologists have had a traditional concern with the accuracy with which observers attribute emotional states and personality traits to actors. Observers are fairly accurate in identifying emotions from viewing only facial expression, hand movements, still photographs, and voice inflections. Furthermore, there is rather good agreement across very different cultures in making these attributions to identical stimuli. The latter finding has provided some support for the Darwinian belief that cultural expressions have evolved through the phyla. Viewing cues in social context allows observers in all cultures to provide more "accurate" labels of emotional states.

Each person tends to develop an implicit theory of personality in which certain kinds of traits and dispositions are viewed as being mutually associated or dissociated. For example, an observer who makes a correspondent inference that another person has a power motive may then construct through a chain of inferences that the stimulus person has a series of other traits (strong, exploitative, aggressive, cold, impolite, etc.).

Observers tend to assume that other people will behave consistently over time. To attain a view of the world as orderly and predictable, the observer tries to maintain organized and meaningful impressions of other people.

Observers will often cluster traits together as descriptive of a particular category of people. This picture in our heads is referred to as a stereotype. A social stereotype exists when a sizable group of people agree on the category-based cluster. In this sense stereotypes help to organize perceptions of people and to provide a basis for predicting what strangers are likely to do. Although there may be a grain of truth in some stereotypes, at least as they apply to entire groups of people, they tend to present an impoverished and inadequate basis for understanding and interacting with individuals.

An important stereotype recently investigated by social psychologists refers to beautiful women. It is generally believed that beautiful women have more dating opportunities and more socially desirable personalities, and are happier and more intelligent. Beautiful women may also have an advantage in job interviews and in ratings of performance. However, there is evidence that at higher levels of management, physical attractiveness is an asset for men but a handicap for women.

It can be seen that most of the literature on interpersonal perception assumes that a stimulus person is inert and merely stands (as for a portrait), whereas the observer draws inferences from the behavior performed. However, the actor may have much to gain or lose by the impressions given off by behavior and hence is motivated to effect them in some way. Thus the actor may engage in one or more of a numerous assortment of possible impression management strategies to negotiate an identity in the eyes of the observer.

Impression management may be defensive in remedying a spoiled identity resulting from negative behaviors or in warding off negative impressions in advance of behavior.

Impression management behaviors may also be assertive in the sense that the actor tries to establish a preplanned identity in the eyes of the observer. If a personal attribution is made, the actor will gain responsibility and credit for the positive effects and is apt to gain approbation or other rewards for so doing.

The study of interpersonal perception has not yet incorporated the dynamic interaction proposed by impression management theory. The attribution process appears to be static and perhaps relies too much on rational models of information processing. Future focus is likely to examine strategies of impression management and how observers penetrate attempts to control their impressions in forming judgments of actors.

FACIAL EXPRESSIONS
INTERPERSONAL ATTRACTION
SOCIAL COGNITION
STEREOTYPING

J. T. TEDESCHI

INTERPERSONAL SKILLS DEVELOPMENT

Interpersonal skills are constellations of behaviors that define and may circumscribe the quality of person-to-person relationships. The concept of looking carefully at how people behave with one another qualitatively is a relatively new dimension in psychology. Most often, interpersonal skills are defined as communication skills, and most systematic study has been devoted to the verbal and nonverbal communication transactions.

The concept of interpersonal skills development and subsequent training implies that these skills are acquired rather than latent. Because of this focus on learning, the impact of culture, environment, social expectations, and societal and personal values are of interest to the therapist and communication theorist.

Alfred Adler, a social democrat, was the first to view humans as essentially social beings whose behavior is purposive and goal-directed. The later work of Karen Horney, with her emphasis on the cultural impact in the formation of neurotic conceptions of self, and—most important—the interpersonal theory of Harry Stack Sullivan, provided pathways for future theoreticians to follow in exploring the more subjective worlds of their patients.

In addition to his concern with a client as a "whole person," Rogers gave impetus to the concept that there is a central core of "facilitative" conditions crucial in developing a constructive relationship between therapist and client. He identified these conditions as therapist-offered empathy, warmth, and genuineness.

Charles B. Truax and Robert T. Carkhuff focused intensive research efforts toward identifying new knowledge of the ingredients of effective counseling and psychotherapy that result in client benefit. The primary methodological breakthrough from this impressive volume of research was the development of a reliable series of scales for the measurement of the identified interpersonal conditions of accuracy, empathy, nonpossessive warmth, and the therapist's self-congruence.

Samovar and Rintye emphasized that human speech exhibits common elements and that human attention is highly selective. They posited that humans actively seek consistency between their self-image, behavior, and perceived information, and that they maintain perceptual consistency by distorting information or avoiding data they cannot change.

They contended that active listening on the part of the receiver of information produces better retention. Social roles and statuses influence communication in organizations, and no symbol or word has a fixed referent (i.e., the "meaning" of the word is attached to the sender or receiver rather than to the word itself). They also addressed the issue of how nonverbal language contributes to human communication.

Carkhuff and his associates developed an interpersonal helping model primarily for use in therapeutic settings. Their model, which is essentially training- and learning-oriented, focuses initially on the skill of discrimination or the ability of the person to fully understand the message sent both in content and process. The ability to receive a message fully depends on the receiver's level of attention.

How a person responds to a message is critical to the continuance of constructive communication and lays the foundation for initiative action. Six interpersonal conditions have an impact on the effectiveness of communication: three facilitative and three action conditions.

Facilitative conditions. When these conditions are offered in communication at observably high levels, they tend to facilitate one's effort to explore and understand oneself.

1. *Empathy.* This is the ability to merge temporarily with another person and see the world through that person's eyes. It is the ability to understand the experiences and feelings of the other person.
2. *Respect.* This is the ability to communicate caring for and belief in the potentials of another person.
3. *Concreteness.* This is the ability to assist another person to be specific about the feelings and experiences that person is talking about.

Action conditions. When these conditions are offered in communication at observably high levels, they tend to lead one to initiate and take action upon one's own ideas.

4. *Genuineness.* This is the ability to be one's real self in a relationship with another person.
5. *Confrontation.* This is the ability to tell the other just the way it is and to point out discrepancies between words and action and perceived realities.
6. *Immediacy.* This is the ability to understand the feelings and experiences that are going on between oneself and another person.

**GROUP PSYCHOTHERAPY
SOCIAL SKILLS TRAINING**

R. C. BERG

INTERVENER SURVIVAL

Intervener survival addresses the needs and concerns of interveners who perform interventions in crisis situations. It is not sufficient to learn crisis management procedures without also attending to the stresses and tensions that impinge on the intervener and thereby affect his or her ability to perform the intervention effectively and efficiently. The intervener who experiences personal crises while attempting to assist others is of no help to anyone. Sometimes it is assumed that trained professionals somehow have mastered the areas of concern that plague less trained nonprofessionals, but this does not seem to be the case.

While involved in the crises of others, interveners may neglect their own needs, health and nutrition, and safety. If interveners fail to place the same value on themselves as placed on those they help, they may soon lose their effectiveness and cause physical and emotional damage to themselves. Conversely, if they are aware of these areas, have spent the appropriate time and energy attending to them, and have taken the prescribed steps to reduce the intensity of problems in their own lives, they are better prepared to focus attention on the crises of others.

The intervener must maintain a personal sense of security and thereby avoid a personal crisis while attempting to assist someone else.

Effective intervention into crisis situations requires that interveners consider their emotional and physical preparedness to intervene in the particular situation at hand. Interveners should consider the following:

1. Is this an intervention that I can physically and emotionally handle?
2. Will personal, unresolved biases or prejudices interfere with my ability to be effective?
3. Is my physical safety in jeopardy if I intervene in this situation?
4. Is the line of communication between my partner and me fail-safe? Have our roles been clearly defined and accepted so as to avoid confusion and conflict?

If the intervener is clear about the goal, reasonably certain of personal safety, in agreement with the team partner on procedure, and prepared to intervene regardless of the situation, then he or she will survive emotionally and physically.

OCCUPATIONAL STRESS

S. LEVITON
J. L. GREENSTONE

INTERVENING VARIABLE

An intervening variable is an unobservable link between two observed variables. Many of our assumptions about the causes of human behavior postulate an intervening psychological variable that mediates between the stimulus and response. For example, imagine two children on the playground. George bumps Sam, then Sam hits George. The stimulus (being bumped) presumably caused Sam's response (hitting George). However, in order to understand the causal link, we need to postulate an intervening variable. Sam is bumped (the stimulus); Sam thinks, "George hurt me, so it's fair to hurt him back" (the intervening variable); then Sam hits George (the response). The introduction of an intervening variable allows us to understand why people react differently to the same stimulus. For example, William runs away when George bumps him, but David laughs when George bumps him. Perhaps the intervening variable for William is his thought, "George is stronger than I am. If I don't run, he'll hit me again." When George bumps David, David laughs, perhaps because he interprets the bump as another example of George's playfulness or clumsiness.

The intervening variable is not observable. We observe two things: the stimulus (getting bumped by George) and the response (hitting George, running away, or laughing). Psychotherapists work with clients to understand the intervening variables that lead to maladaptive responses. Psychoanalysts may look for intervening variables related to early life experiences. Cognitive therapists may help people replace unacceptable intervening variables (negative self-talk) with more adaptive ones (positive self-talk). For example, a client who is afraid of the dark may be taught to redefine darkness as relaxing and nonthreatening.

Psychologists explain consistencies in human behavior by postulating intervening variables that are relatively stable characteristics of individuals, such as personality traits or abilities. It might be postulated that Sam is pugnacious, William has low self-esteem, and David has a good sense of humor.

The interpretation of a response depends on what intervening variable is applied. Imagine that a child has just failed an exam. It can be postulated that the intervening variable is competence, the motivation to study hard, or the support of caring parents. Did the student fail because of ability, motivation, or parental assistance? How the intervening variable is interpreted affects how a therapist responds to help the child improve. Should the child be moved to a lower-level class or be provided with better motivation, or should the therapist work with the parents? If the wrong intervening variable is selected, the remediation may be ineffective. Psychologists use interviews and tests to assess intervening variables.

Psychological theories postulate intervening variables such as ego strength, locus of control, and cognitive dissonance. These unobservable variables provide theoretical links between stimuli and responses. An effective intervening variable allows better understanding and prediction of behavior. Albert Ellis's rational–emotive psychotherapy is based on the concept that cognitive intervening variables can be changed.

INDIVIDUAL DIFFERENCES
RATIONAL–EMOTIVE THERAPY

M. J. ALLEN

INTERVIEWING (SELECTION)

Organizations rarely select members at random. Opportunities for employment or educational programs are typically given to those judged to merit them. Many procedures are used to assess merit, but few are used as widely as the selection interview.

An interview is a conversation between a candidate and a person (or group) who makes or influences the selection decision. As a selection tool, its primary purpose is the assessment of candidate merit (either an overall assessment or the assessment of specified characteristics); however, it also serves other purposes. It is a forum in which the employing organization or school can explain the nature of the organization, the details of the job or program, and what it expects of successful candidates. It also serves a public relations function, even for those ultimately rejected; an interviewer who gives an impression of fairness and consideration can create or preserve a favorable organizational image.

Selection interviews are notoriously unreliable and invalid. Reviews of interview research have consistently confirmed the findings that reliabilities are poor and that interviewers' judgments do not generally predict future performance.

Nevertheless, because interviews continue to be used widely, substantial research efforts have been directed toward finding principles for their improvement. Unfortunately, most of the research has used simulated research, the simulations usually consisting of pieces of paper giving the "interviewer" information about candidates or candidate responses to questions. Without interaction, the applicability of the research to real interviews must be seriously questioned. Two studies reported by Douglas Gorman, William Clover, and Michael Doherty demonstrated clearly that the judgments interviewers make on the basis of paper information are quite different from those made when the same information is accompanied by face-to-face interaction.

Despite a generally gloomy picture of the value of selection interviews, there are some positive research findings. Valid predictions were reported in selecting stockbrokers; in managerial assessment centers; and in group interviews. Because interviews are sometimes valid, perhaps the emphasis in research should first be directed toward the identification of interviewers who make valid judgments and toward finding out what cues they observe (or overlook) in making their judgments.

However, people who must conduct interviews cannot wait for such research results. Some suggestions seem appropriate, even without firm research foundations.

1. Use a structured interview specifically designed for the selection problem at hand. Thorough knowledge of the job or educational program permits planning an agenda explicitly directed toward relevant information.

2. Listen; don't talk too much. To obtain relevant information, the interviewer must allow the candidate to do most of the talking. Paradoxi-

cally, the greater the proportion of time the interviewer talks, the more favorably the interviewee is evaluated.

3. Avoid premature judgments. Regardless of interview length, judgments are often formed very quickly. It may be helpful to continue to seek new information by allowing the candidate to keep talking; it may also help to divide the interview into segments, each with its own task according to objective and evaluation.

4. Avoid prejudicial questions. Some questions, whether intentionally or not, foster or imply prejudice—especially if used inconsistently.

Most legal and technical problems surrounding selection interviews can be avoided by using the standardized interviews tailored to the specific jobs or academic settings involved. Unfortunately, such standardization is not a common practice.

R. M. GULON

INTRINSIC MOTIVATION

Throughout the history of psychology, theories of motivation have attempted to provide accounts of *why* people behave as they do. Although innumerable theories have addressed questions of motivation, until recently there have been only two major systems for the study of motivation. The first, developed by Sigmund Freud as an integral part of his psychoanalytic psychology was based largely on the systematic study of his psychiatric patients; while the second, developed by C. L. Hull as an integral part of his drive theory of learning, was based largely on the experimental study of rats running mazes. Although these two systems are radically different in many respects, both assert that all motivation is reducible to a small number of biological drives or instincts: sex and aggression for Freud, and hunger, thirst, sex, and the avoidance of pain for Hull.

Although many behaviors such as eating are related directly to drives, organisms also engage in a wide variety of behaviors not immediately instrumental to the satisfaction of drives. In psychoanalytic theory, sublimation refers to the transformation of sexual energy into an energy available for the pursuit of "higher" goals. This transformation results from internal conflicts between the basic drive and one's perception of the demands of the environment. In drive theory, secondary drive refers to any apparent need for reinforcements that do not satisfy basic drives. These apparent needs for secondary reinforcers develop through the process of pairing what was an originally neutral stimulus (e.g., a puzzle solution) with a primary reinforcer (e.g., food). Thus, according to the theory, solving puzzles becomes reinforcing, and people appear to have a drive for solving puzzles, not because puzzle solving is inherently satisfying but because it was previously paired with a primary reinforcer.

Increasingly, in both realms of inquiry these concepts were seen to be inadequate. H. Hartmann pointed out that young children display a variety of behaviors that seem to be free of conflict (i.e., not the result of sublimation), and Berlyne noted that various activities such as exploration occur so avidly and so soon after birth that secondary reinforcement could not possibly account for them. In response to these inadequacies, Robert White suggested that there is an innate, intrinsic motivation for interacting effectively with the environment.

Reflecting the fact that the concept of intrinsic motivation was introduced to account for behaviors that could not be explained in terms of drives and reinforcements, the most frequently used definition of intrinsically motivated behavior states that it is behavior occurring in the absence of any apparent external reward. Deci defined intrinsic motivation in terms of the innate needs to be *competent* and *self-determining* in relation to one's environment. These needs underlie a wide variety of behaviors including exploration, play, and learning, and motivate people to seek and attempt to conquer an ongoing series of challenges that are optimal or appropriate for their capacities. Whereas drive theories imply that humans prefer quiescence and minimal stimulation, intrinsic motivation theory suggests that they desire optimal stimulation as well as quiescence.

Deci and Ryan have summarized the various experiments and organized them into a theoretical framework. They suggested that every environmental event has two functional aspects, a *controlling* aspect (to bring about a specific behavioral outcome) and an *informational* aspect (to inform people about such things as their effectiveness at some activity). If the controlling aspect is so salient as to pressure people toward specified outcomes, intrinsic motivation will be undermined, but if it implies the inverse of control, namely choice, intrinsic motivation will be enhanced. This implies, that the impact of external events depends on the way they are perceived and interpreted by the recipient.

ACQUIRED DRIVES
CONTROL SYSTEMS
SELF-DETERMINATION

E. L. Deci

INTROSPECTION

Introspection (literally, looking inward), a popular methodology of psychologists toward the end of the nineteenth and in the early decades of the twentieth century, is a method of inquiry in psychology in which subjects attempt to examine the contents and processes of their consciousness. Introspection was used in the study of a range of psychological processes including memory, learning, thinking, problem solving, dream analysis, and perception.

The method of introspection was not a simple reflection on experience. Subjects were rigorously trained in the process of examining, describing, and reporting immediate sensory experience in response to systematic questioning. Edward Bradford Titchener defined the conditions for optimum introspective observation: Subjects should be unbiased and should prevent other associations from influencing the report of the immediate experience. In addition, subjects should be alert, free from distractions, healthy, fresh and free from fatigue, and interested in the experience under study.

Introspection was the principal method of the structuralist schools, led by Wilhelm Wundt in Germany and Titchener in America, that defined psychology as the study of conscious experience. Structuralists sought to break down experience into its component parts or elementary sensations. Sensation was considered primary with perceptual processes being viewed as secondary organizing activities. A subjective understanding of consciousness and the contents of mind was the goal of structuralist psychology.

This view was opposed by the members of the Gestalt school who rejected the assumption of primary elements of experience in favor of innate organizational propensities and a holistic view of perception. The functionalist school represented by John Dewey also opposed the subjective introspective approach, emphasizing instead the importance of systematic, objective demonstration and experimental testing of theory. The behaviorists such as J. B. Watson condemned introspection as qualitative and unreliable, and opposed the consideration of all notions of subjective experience and questions of consciousness, emphasizing only observable behavior analyzed in terms of measurable stimuli and responses.

GESTALT PSYCHOLOGY

R. C. Adams-Terem

INTROVERSION–EXTRAVERSION

In 1921, Carl Jung coined the terms *introversion* and *extraversion* in *Psychologische typen* (*Psychological types*). For Jung, introversion meant a turning inward of the libido, whereas extraversion referred to a directing outward of the libido. Either term can be spelled with an *o* or an *a,* that is, *intraversion* and *extroversion.* Although it is inconsistent, the terms as used in the Myers–Briggs Type Indicator (MBTI), a popular personality test based on Jung's type theory, are *introversion* and *extraversion.*

An introvert is a person whose mind and emotions are turned inward (i.e., have strong references to self). Jung believed that the introvert directs the libido inward because of feelings of inferiority, an idea reminiscent of Alfred Adler. Especially in times of stress, introverts tend to withdraw into themselves, to avoid other people, and to be primarily interested in themselves. The introvert leans toward self-sufficiency. An introvert's essential stimulation is from within, from one's inner world of thoughts and reflections. Introverts are often reserved and hard to get to know; they tend to bottle up their emotions and need privacy.

By contrast, extraverts are oriented primarily to the outer world, tending to focus their judgments and perceptions of people and things. Extraverts are energized by other people and external experiences, they tend to express their emotions, need relationships more than privacy, and are usually friendly, talkative, and easy to get to know. Although extraverts may seem shallow to introverts, introverts may seem withdrawn to extraverts.

The extraversion–introversion (E–I) index is one of four dichotomous scales on the MBTI. The other scales are sensing–intuition (S–N), thinking–feeling (T–F), and judgment–perception (J–P).

AFFILIATION NEED
INDIVIDUAL DIFFERENCES
LIFESTYLE ASSESSMENT
PERSONALITY TYPES

B. M. Thorne

INTUITION

The term *intuition* has been applied to a great variety of events and processes, some of which clearly occur and some of which are far from clearly demonstrated.

Conceptions of intuition within philosophy range from the most primitive of mental functions to the most sublime: from simple awareness of existence to the apprehension of ultimate truths. But Mario Bunge denounces all notions of intuition. For him, the phenomenon in question is rapid inference. So there is no unanimity in philosophical circles concerning the nature of intuition or the legitimacy of a process or phenomenon so named.

PSYCHOLOGICAL CONCEPTIONS OF INTUITION

Psychologists too have a wide range of uses for the term, many of which reflect philosophical contentions. In discussing the intuition of self-evident truths, Hermann Helmholtz argued that intuitions were rapid unconscious inferences developed from common experience. The idea of apprehending events as totalities through intuition, as in the Gestalt position, was opposed by the associationist position, which argued that totalities were built up as inferences from separate sensory events.

Early in the controversy, the opposing viewpoints were quite clear: The intuitionists were striving for comprehension, understanding, and the grasping of a totality, while the psychometrists were striving for successful predictions. The former was a scholarly, aesthetic appreciation of individuality, while the latter was a practical aim, rooted in the mental testing movement and the study of individual differences. In effect, the two viewpoints could be seen as having nothing to do with each other. But these distinctions have been blurred, and clinical (intuitive) methods have been pitted against statistical (psychometric) methods in the task of prediction. Almost without fail, the statistical method has been found to be equal or superior to the clinical method in this task. But there has been no appraisal (perhaps there cannot be any) of a global understanding or grasping of the totality of a personality. If the aims of the two methods had been kept as distinct as they were originally, perhaps no controversy would have developed.

MAJOR THEORIES

Carl Jung presented intuition as one of four mental functions—the others being sensation, thinking, and feeling—possessed by all people but developed to greater or lesser degrees in different individuals. Intuition focuses on a nonjudgmental perception of possibilities, implications, and principles, at the expense of details. Intuition may exist in the introverted or extroverted mode, leading the introverted intuitive to be in especially intimate touch with archetypes, and the extroverted intuitive to be especially understanding of external events such as politics, business, or social relations.

The most recent work in the area is the most comprehensive. Bastick reviewed a great variety of definitions and descriptions of intuition from diverse fields, and derived 20 different properties said to be characteristic of the process, such as emotional involvement, speed, empathy, and subjective certainty. He suggests that in these properties intuition contrasts with logic that involves conscious step-by-step analysis independent of the emotions and past experience of the thinker. But Bastick argues that thinking, which is ordinarily termed *logical* or *analytic,* is interwoven with intuitive processes and cannot exist independently.

It appears that there are two broad notions of intuition among psychologists. First, intuition is conceived as solving problems or making judgments by means of information and/or processes that are informal, inexplicit, or obscure. The criterion of accuracy, plausibility, or value is generally implied and sometimes made explicit; a simple bad guess does not generally qualify as intuition. Second, intuition is conceived as a cognitive/emotional step that goes beyond judgment, decision making, or learning to reach a full comprehension and appreciation of a personality, situation, or subject matter, sometimes with an aesthetic component, and often significantly modifying one's phenomenal field.

EMPIRICAL RESEARCH ON INTUITION

Most empirical studies involving intuition as a concept have been more concerned with the outcome of decision making or judgment than with the intuitive process itself. There have, however, been lines of research that take the process, or some aspect or correlates of it, as their central concern.

One line of research, beginning more than 50 years ago, has been concerned with "the good judge of personality" and has focused on the characteristics of persons who displayed special accuracy in judging others. These studies of social judgment have culminated in the work of Nisbett and Ross concerning the successes and failures of intuitive social judgment in a wide variety of situations. Nisbett and Ross argue that most humans generally operate as intuitive scientists, employing knowledge structures and judgmental heuristics that bring past experience, expectations, informal theories, and beliefs to bear on the situation and reduce complex inferential tasks to a few judgmental operations. The estimates of the parameters of a situation, probabilities, causal efficacy, relevance, and so on may be accurate or inaccurate. Nisbett and Ross contrast the judgments made by subjects operating as intuitive scientists with judgments made by scientists employing explicit methods. Generally, the intuitive scientists' judgments are less accurate than those of the formal scientists.

Most often, this lack of accuracy does not matter very much, although at times it can be disastrous. Furthermore, having made predictions in social situations, people are prone to act in such a way as to make them come true, thus confirming their judgments.

Nisbett and Ross analyzed in detail the bases for the intuitive judgments that are made by everyone all the time and proposed methods by which people could become more skilled and accurate in their inferential behavior. For these authors, then, it is evident that intuition or intuitive behavior is a natural human propensity to make inferences on the basis of deficient information and deficient operations. Unfortunately, there are no data reported concerning individual differences, that is, whether some persons are consistently more successful than others, or even more successful than the explicit scientist.

In contrast, Malcolm Westcott conducted research focused explicitly on individual differences and worked from the definition of intuitive thinking noted earlier as "reaching conclusions on the basis of little information that are ordinarily reached on the basis of significantly more information." This definition makes clear the minimal explicit data base as well as the accuracy of conclusions as confirmed by subsequent consensus.

Over a large number of samples of university-level subjects, there was consistent evidence that different individuals required different amounts of information before they were willing to offer solutions, and that different individuals consistently had greater or less success in solving the problems. Most important, these two features of behavior were consistently uncorrelated. Thus, persons who met the definition of "intuitive" could be identified as those who consistently solved problems accurately while requiring significantly less information than was required by others. It was also possible to identify three other groups of subjects: those who took little information and were consistently wrong in their solutions; those who required significantly more information than others and were consistently successful; and those who required excessive information but were still typically wrong.

Finally, an empirical phenomenological description of intuition as experience was attempted by Margaret Denis. She employed a notion of intuition as "an integrative and holistic cognition beyond reason."

Through interviews with adult learners, Denis derived a nonexhaustive set of 18 characteristics of intuitive learning that can interact with each other in the learning process and produce experience that goes beyond the more traditional notions of learning. The experience of intuition, reaching this holistic cognition, was described by different interviewees in cognitive terms, in physiological terms, as centered on self-awareness, as involving an expression of the unconscious, and so forth.

SUMMARY

The term *intuition* has a great many different meanings and a very long history of investigation in both philosophy and psychology. The dimensions below capture the space within which conceptions of intuition lie.

1. Intuition as nonsensory knowing of nonempirical truth, as in an intuition of God (Spinoza)
2. Intuition as nonsensory knowing of empirical truth, as in the perception of possibilities (Jung)
3. Intuition as inference or judgment based on partial or inexplicit information or processes (Nisbett and Ross, Westcott)
4. Intuition as a step beyond reason and inference to a full apprehension or comprehension (Allport, Bastick, Denis)
5. Intuition as revealing truth, by definition (Spinoza)
6. Intuition as a process open to error (Nisbett and Ross)

It should also be noted that cutting across all the above conceptions of intuition is another dimension. There are conceptions of intuition that see a discontinuity between intuition and reason, and place the two as complementary, antagonistic, or alien to each other. Other conceptions of intuition see a continuity from reason to intuition, based on a dimension of implicitness–explicitness of cues and evidence, or a dimension of informal–formal use of inference strategies.

ABSTRACT INTELLIGENCE
CONTEXTUAL ASSOCIATIONS
PHILOSOPHICAL PSYCHOLOGY

M. R. WESTCOTT

IPSATIVE SCALING

The word *ipse,* meaning truly oneself, has been passed down to us from Latin. The word *ipsative* means that the person is the standard. Raymond B. Cattell introduced the idea of ipsative scaling to psychology to distinguish between subjective and objective standards in respect to which psychometric devices can be calibrated.

To measure is to record differences and express these as numbers in terms of magnitudes of deviation from an origin. The magnitudes and the origin must be defined relative to a standard. The question Cattell addressed in distinguishing ipsative scaling from other forms of scaling—namely, normative and interactive—is "What standards can be used to achieve psychological measurement?"

Normative and interactive scales are objective, or indifferent to standards within individuals, whereas ipsative scales are subjective, or expressed in terms of the standards of individuals. In ipsative scaling the payoff units, performance units or norm units, are determined with reference to one's own values, one's own grading of performances, and one's own samples of one's own behavior.

It is difficult to define a person's own standards, of course. To accomplish this for purposes of ipsative measurement, the psychologist attempts to specify a response domain—of values, performances, or the like—wherein respondents can meaningfully choose between, or order, different areas of the domain. Of course, we still must ask "Motivation to what—to understand music, to be recognized, to meet the opposite sex?" The psychologist deals with this question by obtaining several different ipsative indicators of that which is being measured. If the aim were to measure motivation to understand music, the respondent might be asked to indicate the proportion of money (a limited resource for most people) spent on records, concerts, sheet music, and the like.

These examples indicate what is called self-ipsative scaling, in which the response format in one way or another requires the respondent to allocate a resource represented by a set of items. In the Allport–Vernon Scale of Values, each item requires a respondent to indicate which of several pursuits—intellectual, aesthetic, religious, business, and so on—the subject values most. The measure of a particular value (e.g., aesthetic orientation) is the sum of responses indicating that the respondent puts the pursuits associated with that value ahead of the other pursuits.

This kind of scoring means that, to the extent that one obtains a high score on one ipsative variable, one must obtain correspondingly lowered scores on the other ipsative variables. This pushes the intercorrelations among ipsative variables toward the negative.

Self-ipsative scores are thus operationally (i.e., experimentally) dependent. It is important to realize this when planning data analyses for ipsative variables. The matrix of intercorrelations among ipsative variables is singular, for example, which means that one should not try to invert it to obtain multiple regression weights. Factors derived from such a matrix have anomalous qualities that make them difficult to interpret in a sensible way.

Ipsatization is sometimes imposed by the test scorer. Ipsative scaling is realized by applying a scoring formula to scores that otherwise are normative or interactive. For example, a respondent's knowledge about the graphic arts might be regarded as an indication of that person's evaluation of aesthetic pursuits.

MEASUREMENT
PERSONALITY ASSESSMENT
SCALING

J. L. HORN

IRRITABLE BOWEL SYNDROME

Irritable bowel syndrome (IBS) is a chronic psychophysiological gastrointestinal disorder that involves a cluster of physical symptoms—among them chronic abdominal pain and changes in bowel movement routines—in the absence of any known physiological abnormality that could account for them. Because there is no known physiological basis, the definition of the disorder is simply descriptive, a collection of associated symptoms. It was first described in the early nineteenth century, but was only identified as a psychophysiological disorder well into the twentieth century.

In the most common form, often referred to as spastic colon, the primary symptom is abdominal pain, usually accompanied by alternating constipation and diarrhea. The pain is generally relieved by a bowel movement, or sometimes by passing gas, and is described variously by sufferers as being dull, cramplike, burning, aching, or sharp, with intensity varying from mild to severe. A second form of IBS involves painless diarrhea as the major symptom.

Other symptoms may include the feeling that despite bowel movement, evacuation has been incomplete; the presence of mucous in the stools; a feeling of distension in the abdomen; and changes in bowel habits—looser stools or more frequent bowel movements with the onset of the abdominal pain. Heartburn, nausea, and vomiting may also be present. Indeed, any autonomic reaction associated with emotional arousal, including palpitations, cold hands and feet, clamminess of the skin, fatigue, a lump in the throat, dizziness, numbness and tingling in the hands, spots before the eyes, and trembling, also may accompany the syndrome.

It is a distressing syndrome and the most common disorder of the digestive tract, occurring in 10 to 15% of adults; it has been variously estimated to be responsible for between 40 and 70% of all referrals to gastroenterologists. It is the second most common cause of industrial absenteeism due to illness, and in the UK, IBS is cited as the tenth most common cause of hospital admission for women and the sixth for men. Between 50 and 65% of untreated patients with this problem improve spontaneously over a period of several months. However, most of these untreated cases ultimately will suffer relapses, for the disorder is generally chronic and periodic in nature.

Although the physical aspect of this psychophysiological disorder is not well understood, the abdominal pain is most likely caused by spastic colonic contractions as well as excessive stretching and distention from gas and stool in the colon. Physiological investigations indicate that, compared with persons who are considered normal, colonic contractions in the IBS sufferer tend to be more active; the pressure in the colon is generally higher; and the colon is more sensitive to physiological stimulation (such as food intake) and emotional stress. However, apart from these differences in degree, there is no pattern of colonic motility that differentiates the IBS sufferer from normal persons. Emotional arousal normally affects the intestines, and the colonic movements in IBS seem to be indistinguishable from those associated with normal emotional arousal but may be more prevalent in the IBS sufferer because of chronic emotional tension.

Psychological factors appear to play a significant role in this disorder. Chronic emotional stress accompanies the onset or worsening of symptoms in most sufferers. Psychological symptoms that commonly accompany this disorder include depression, anxiety, irritability, and somatic preoccupation. Certain people are more prone to develop this syndrome: IBS sufferers have been described as typically rigid, overconscientious, compulsive, prone to guilt feelings, dependent, oversensitive, subject to worry, underassertive, perfectionistic, and possessing a high need for approval.

Medical attempts to eliminate IBS symptoms are rarely successful, and, given the large involvement of psychological factors, psychological treatment is more and more being recognized as essential. A psychological approach to this disorder is usually focused on (a) teaching the sufferer how to relax deeply, especially in stressful situations; (b) guiding the individual to deal with stress, anxiety, and hostility in an appropriate manner so as to minimize the emotional reaction; and (c) assisting the individual to reduce emotional rigidity, anxiety, dependency, and guilt proneness.

A-TYPE PERSONALITY
BIOFEEDBACK
CONVERSION DISORDER
ENURESIS
MUSCLE RELAXATION
NEUROPSYCHOLOGY
PSYCHOSOMATICS
TOILET TRAINING

J. E. Alcock

ISOMORPHISM

In psychology, the term *isomorphism* is identified with the classical Berlin school of Gestalt psychology. The concept was used by Gestalt theorists to characterize their particular approach to the mind-brain problem; they argued that objective brain processes underlying and correlated with particular phenomenological experiences are isomorphic with (i.e., have functionally the same form and structure as) subjective experiences.

The etymology of *isomorphism* makes the term appropriate for such a theory. The Greek root *iso-* means "same, equal, or identical," and *morph-* means "form, shape, organization, or structure." What the Gestalt psychologists intended to convey with their idea of isomorphism is that the Gestalt properties—the form, shape, organization, and structure—of biophysical, electrochemical processes in the brain that underlie subjective cognitive experiences are identical to the Gestalt properties---the form, shape, organization, and structure—of the experiences themselves. This proposal contrasted sharply with the relatively inert connectionistic mind-brain theories that prevailed during the first half of the twentieth century, which viewed the brain more as a giant switchboard of interconnected insulated switches and wires than as a dynamic system of interdependent electrochemical biological processes constituting a complex interactive field.

Because such a dynamic, interactive field conception of brain function and activity was radically different from the much more static and mechanistic view of the brain implicitly taken for granted by the majority of psychologists of the time, the Gestalt idea of isomorphism was generally not well understood. Gestalt theorist Mary Henle wrote, "I know of no concept in psychology that has been more misunderstood, indeed more distorted, than isomorphism."

One reason for such distortion or misunderstanding is that the term had been used, long before the Gestalt psychologists adopted it, in such fields as chemistry, crystallography, and mathematics in a way that typically implied a piecemeal orientation totally foreign to the Gestalt conception. In mathematical set theory, for example, two groups of items are isomorphic if there is a perfect correspondence between the two sets, such that there is a one-to-one identity between them, that is, that each item in the first set can be paired one for one with an item in the second set.

Such one-to-one correspondence between two isomorphic processes or phenomena is contrary to the Gestalt approach. For example, two dotted circles, one composed of 20 dots along its circumference and another of 22 dots, are isomorphic in the Gestalt sense of having the identical functional form; the number of dots composing each circle is immaterial as long as there are enough of them to specify the shape reasonably clearly. What is crucial is precisely the form, shape, or structure itself, not the number of elements that happen to make up its "parts." Thinking in terms of one-to-one correspondence of dots on the circumference of the two circles is a piecemeal, disconnected caricature that ignores the dynamic characteristics of the continuity of the trajectory of the circumference of a circle, of the equidistance of each part of the circumference from the center, and so forth, that make up the essential Gestalt or configuration of a circle. Two circles, whatever the number of "elements" composing them and irrespective of their color or size, are isomorphic simply because they both are circles (i.e., both display the circular shape). Comparably, two squares are isomorphic even if they are made up of different "elements," or are of different sizes, brightnesses, or colors. Furthermore, although the notes of a particular melody are totally different when that melody is played in different keys, the sequences of notes are isomorphic; that is, they are still the same melody—and variations on the melody remain isomorphic as long as the basic melody is still recognizable (even if some variations might contain many more notes than others).

The first reference to isomorphic brain processes in the Gestalt sense to perceptual processes is in a 1912 paper on apparent motion by Max Wertheimer that is generally considered to have launched the Gestalt school. The reference concerns processes in the brain presumed to correspond to one version of the phi phenomenon or the perception of motion when there is in fact no motion in the physical stimulus. Assume, say, two short vertical lines, *x* and *y*, each about 1 inch long, separated horizontally by about 1 inch. If line *x* is exposed for a few seconds, then disappears, and a brief fraction of a second later line *y* is exposed, it may appear to the observer that what was shown was not two different lines successively exposed, but a single line that moved from location *x* to location *y*. If the sequence is continued, so that a very short time after line *y* disappears line *x* is exposed again, then line *y* reappears almost immediately after line x goes off, and so on, as long as the distance and time relations are appropriate, then the result is that a single line is seen as moving consistently back and forth. If the time between the removal of one line and the appearance of the other is too long, the observer experiences two stationary lines in two different places being successively exposed; if the time interval is too short (or if there is overlap in the time that both lines are exposed), the observer reports two stationary lines being exposed in two different places.

What happens in the brain under the conditions in which a single moving line is seen in such an experiment? Wertheimer argued that virtually every mind-brain theory assumes that there must be excitation of particular parts of the visual cortex when the observer sees the lines, one area of excitation that corresponds to line *x*, and another nearby that corresponds to line *y*. Furthermore—and here is where Gestalt theory deviates from other mind-brain theories—when motion is perceived, *there must be some kind of a short circuit* between the brain area corresponding to line *x* and the nearby area corresponding to line *y;* this *short circuit is the brain process that is isomorphic* with the experience of a single moving line. The Gestalt properties of the process in the brain must somehow correspond to the Gestalt properties of seeing a single moving line rather than two separated, stationary isolated lines.

Wertheimer's fairly rudimentary theoretical conception was elaborated in much greater detail by two of Wertheimer's Gestalt colleagues, Kurt Koffka and especially Wolfgang Köhler (in extensive biopsychological and perceptual experiments). Köhler and collaborators generated some rather surprising predictions from the theory and managed to validate these predictions experimentally. An entire monograph was devoted to what Köhler and Hans Wallach called figural aftereffects, a set of perceived distortions of figures that are generated by prolonged prior observation of other figures.

Assume, for example, that the perceived distance between two points in the visual field, x and y, is isomorphic with the electrical resistance between their corresponding locations in the visual cortex, X and Y. If the resistance is greater, then the brain processes X and Y are functionally far apart and the perceived distance between the corresponding points in the visual field, x and y, should be greater; if the functional distance, (i.e., the electrical resistance) between the two brain processes X and Y is small, then the perceived distance between their experienced isomorphic counterparts, x and y, should also be small.

Now if some way can be found to change the resistance between two points in the visual cortex, then such a change should result in a corresponding change in the isomorphic visual experience. It is well known that any excitatory process that continues for some time in neural tissue will generate a process that inhibits the continuation of that excitatory process; every continuing excitation generates its own inhibition. According to the theory of isomorphism, this inhibition is satiation, or an increase in electrochemical resistance. One way to generate enhanced resistance between two points in the visual cortex, therefore, is to excite it with an appropriate visual stimulus. If the brain area corresponding to the space between two points in the visual field is stimulated for some time by a figure exposed visually in that space, this should increase the satiation, or resistance, in the space and the same two points in the visual field should, therefore, appear farther apart than before. A wide variety of experiments testing this kind of prediction were performed by Köhler and Wallach, and such distortions were indeed corroborated.

A large number of experiments made the theory of isomorphism widely discussed by the middle of the twentieth century. In the early 1950s, two prominent neuroscientists, Karl Lashley and Roger Sperry, performed some radical animal experiments in an effort to disprove the theory. They experimentally altered the electrical properties of the visual cortex of cats and monkeys by making incisions in their brains and inserting insulating material into the cuts or by placing gold foil or tantalum wire (excellent electrical conductors) directly on the surface or into the substance of the animals' visual cortices. Such disturbance in the electrochemical, biophysical characteristics of the brain, they argued, should interfere profoundly with the continued performance of visual discriminations that the animals had learned previously, if Köhler's specific theory of isomorphism is indeed correct. But none of these massive alterations in the visual brain medium produced any change in the animals' ability to make the visual discriminations they had learned before the surgical insults were made.

Köhler responded by pointing out various technical flaws in these experiments and arguing that the local changes in the electrical characteristics of the altered brains should redistribute and reorganize their field properties almost instantaneously, hence no disturbance in visually guided performance would be expected. Neither Lashley nor Sperry rebutted these arguments, but Karl Pribram, another prominent neuropsychologist, performed a variant on the Lashley–Sperry studies late in the 1950s. He altered the electrical activity of some monkeys' visual brains by irritating them with a cream of aluminum hydroxide; once again, there was no interference with the retention of previously learned visual discriminations, but Köhler's point that natural physical field processes would almost immediately redistribute the change produced by local irritation was not addressed by Pribram's experiment either.

Interest in the Gestalt isomorphism hypothesis waned during the 1960s and 1970s; discussions of it in books about perception and physiological psychology became rare by the 1980s. The predominant view by the late 1980s and early 1990s among neuroscientists about how the brain functions left no room for processes as dynamic, interactive, field-theoretical and systems-oriented as the Gestalt view of isomorphism.

BRAIN
CRANIAL NERVES
FORM–SHAPE PERCEPTION
GESTALT PSYCHOLOGY
ILLUSIONS
IMAGERY
MIND–BODY PROBLEM
MOLAR–MOLECULAR CONSTRUCTS
PERCEPTUAL ORGANIZATION
SPLIT-BRAIN RESEARCH
VISUAL IMAGERY

M. WERTHEIMER

ITEM ANALYSIS

The major purpose of item analysis is to provide information on the extent to which the individual items making up a test are functioning in a desired manner. This information can then be used to improve the reliability and validity of the test by editing or discarding poor items. An item analysis of an achievement test may also provide diagnostic information on what examinees know and do not know, serving as a basis for instructional planning and curriculum revision.

Item analysis information may be either rational (judgmental) or empirical (statistical). A rational item analysis entails careful inspection of each item to determine whether its content is accurate, congruent with the test specifications, free of cultural or other bias, and not contrary to standard item-writing guidelines. This approach is characteristic of item analyses of criterion-referenced achievement tests, but it can also be applied to norm-referenced tests.

Empirical item analysis involves the calculation of one or more statistical measures of item functioning, including an item difficulty index, an item discrimination (validity) index, and some measure of the functioning of distracters. The difficulty index (p) of an item is computed quite simply as the proportion of people tested who answer the item correctly. The optimum difficulty index varies with the purpose of the test and the type of item.

The procedure for determining an index of the ability of an item to discriminate among examinees attaining different scores on the criterion variable depends on the nature of the criterion and the type of test. The usual internal criteria for an achievement test are the total scores on the test itself, which are rank-ordered and divided into upper (U) and lower (L) groups. In the case of a norm-referenced test, these two groups usually consist of examinees in the top 27% and the bottom 27% of the distribution of total test scores. Then the discrimination index (D) for each item is computed as $D = p_u$, where pu and p_L are the proportions of examinees in the top and bottom groups, respectively, who answer the item correctly. With an external criterion such as performance ratings or school marks, the item discrimination index is computed as the point-biserial correlation (r_{pb}) between item score (0 or 1) and scores on the criterion continuum. Obviously, the closer either D or r_{pb} is to 1.00, the more valid is the item as a discriminator between high and low scorers on the criterion. Depending on the size of the group of examinees on whom the indexes are computed, D or r_{pb} values as low as 0.20 may prove sufficient for retaining items. It should be noted, however, that selecting items on the basis of D will tend to yield an internally consistent, homogeneous test. In contrast, selecting items on the basis of r_{pb} will usually produce a less homogeneous test, but one with greater validity for predicting an external criterion.

Determination of the discriminative power of items on a criterion-referenced test involves a bit more work than was previously mentioned. W. J. Popham describes two procedures: (a) pretest–posttest differences and (b) uninstructed versus instructed group differences.

Although an item analysis of a multiple-choice test focuses on the difficulty and discrimination indexes of individual items, responses to the incorrect options (distracters) may also be examined. In general, each distracter should be equally attractive to examinees who do not know the answer to an item. Furthermore, the ratio of the number of examinees in the upper group (on the criterion) to the number of examinees in the lower group should be approximately equal for all distracters.

EMPIRICAL RESEARCH METHODS
TEST CONSTRUCTION

L. R. AIKEN

J

JAMES–LANGE THEORY OF EMOTIONS

The James–Lange theory of emotions has been the subject of considerable scientific debate since its publication by William James in *Principles of psychology*. Portions of James' theory had been formulated by the Danish physiologist Carl Georg Lange in 1885. James combined his views with those of Lange, hence the name the *James–Lange theory of emotions*. The theory offers a physiological explanation of the constitution, organization, and conditioning of the coarser emotions such as grief, fear, rage, and love and the *subtler* ones such as moral, intellectual, and aesthetic feelings.

The general causes of the emotions are assumed to be internal, physiological, nervous processes *and not* mental or psychological processes. The emotions are the result of organic changes that occur in the body as a reflex effect of an exciting object or fact confronted by the person.

There are three factors in the sequence of an emotional experience: (a) the perception of an exciting fact or object by the person; (b) a bodily expression such as weeping, striking out, or fleeing; and (c) a mental affection or emotion, such as feeling afraid or angry. Many theories of emotion, as well as common sense, place the bodily expressions of weeping, striking out, or fleeing *after* the emotion of anger or fear. The James–Lange theory alters this sequence, placing bodily expressions *between* the perception of the exciting fact and the emotion.

The debate that has surrounded the theory involves the relative importance of central nervous system processes and social environmental factors in the production of emotion. Centralists (including James and Lange) have argued that there are discrete physiological changes for each emotion. Peripheralists argue that there is no discrete physiological change for each emotion; rather, there is only a bodily state of arousal modified by factors in the social environment. The experimental evidence is inconclusive.

Jean-Paul Sartre critically evaluated the James–Lange theory from a phenomenological perspective and rejected it on the following grounds. First, behavior, physiological or expressive, is not emotion, nor is the awareness of that behavior emotion. Second, the body does not call out its own interpretations; they are given in the field of consciousness of the person. Third, the bodily disturbances present in emotion are disorders of the most ordinary kind and are not the causes of emotion. They ratify emotion's existence for the person and give emotion its believability, but are not its causes. Fourth, to have considered only the biological body—independent of the lived body—and the person's consciousness of the body as the source of emotion was to treat the body as a thing and to locate emotion in disorders of the body.

The James–Lange theory of emotions remains a viable theory today. The factors isolated by the theory are not disputed. Controversy remains, however, over the ordering of the sequence of the factors, and on the emphasis to be given to strictly physiological—as opposed to social and psychological—factors and processes.

COGNITIVE THEORIES OF EMOTIONS
EMOTIONS, THEORIES OF

N. K. DENZIN

JOB ANALYSIS

The design of research and psychological programs in organizations often requires knowledge of aspects of the jobs people do. The process by which this knowledge is acquired is *job analysis;* a *job description* is the record of the results of the analysis. Sometimes these terms are used interchangeably.

Fundamentally, jobs are analyzed to answer two kinds of questions: (a) what is done on the job? and (b) what resources are needed to do it? Answers to the first question may describe work outcomes or accomplishments, tasks or responsibilities, work methods and procedures, and other job-related behavior common to all the people who do the job. A comprehensive study of a job may also provide information about diversity in the procedures followed or about possible but unexpected and even undesirable consequences of actions at work. Answers to the second question may describe physical resources (e.g., tools, equipment, or materials), social or organizational resources (e.g., supervisory or co-worker interactions and staff services), or the personal resources of the worker (e.g., skills, knowledge areas, abilities, or other personal characteristics needed for effective performance).

Job descriptions provide the basis for many kinds of research and practical program planning. Examples of their use are found in job design, development of training programs, career counseling, job evaluation, and identification of job knowledge or skill or of more abstract constructs to be assessed in personnel selection.

The number of distinguishable methods of job analysis is large; however, most methods can be subsumed under five broad categories.

Self-Report

The incumbent is the basic source—often the only source—of job information; some job descriptions are no more than the incumbent's report based on a somewhat introspective look at what is done.

Direct Observation

Some jobs can be studied by watching the incumbents do their work. Observational aids such as cameras or stop watches may be used, and the observations may be taken in planned time samples. This method is informative for jobs consisting of easily observed physical activity and short work cycles, but is not very helpful for jobs that are basically cognitive in nature.

Document Searches

Peace officers file reports of incidents in which they are involved. Complaint registers may be available for them and for people in other service occupations. Memoranda may report on unusual but important activities and achievements. Medical records may identify health or safety hazards in the work environment or in work methods. Prior job descriptions may exist.

Interviews

Incumbents, supervisors, or other workers with related activities can be interviewed, singly or in groups, to identify broad categories of job characteristics and details within the categories. Interviews in the early stages of analysis may be open and unstructured; if the analysis is to include several different jobs, standard interview forms may be needed.

One special approach that works well in group interviews was developed by John Flanagan. Employees or others can be asked to identify critical incidents–examples of particularly effective or ineffective performance. The description includes the chain of events leading up to the incident and the subsequent effects. From a collection of incidents, much can be learned about safety hazards, influences on judgments, or personal characteristics related to the quality of performance. The technique is particularly well adapted to jobs where much that is important about the job is not readily apparent to others.

Survey Methods

Where many jobs are to be studied, or where many people working under the same job title may have variations of the basic job, questionnaires and job inventories can be used to collect information ordinarily developed by the other methods. The development of an inventory may require observation and interviewing; if it is to be widely or frequently used, it may also require a trial and revision before undertaking the full-scale survey.

APPLIED RESEARCH
INDUSTRIAL PSYCHOLOGY
JOB EVALUATION

R. M. GUION

JOB EVALUATION

People with different jobs receive different pay. The fact of pay differentials is usually accepted as fair, although different justifications for them may sometimes be based on contradictory values. In most organizations in industrial societies, relative pay differences are usually considered equitable if they reflect relative differences in relative worth to the organization. The process of measuring differences in the relative worth of jobs is called job evaluation.

There are many different methods of job evaluation. A common approach can be described in five steps: (a) job descriptions are provided to members of a job evaluation committee; (b) a set of characteristics or dimensions along which jobs differ, the so-called compensable factors, are developed by or presented to the committee; (c) on the basis of the job descriptions, committee members rate or otherwise evaluate each job on each dimension and reach a consensus on the ratings; (d) all ratings for a job are summed, and weighted according to an accepted formula,

to provide a measure of job worth; and (e) the sums are translated into pay rates. The basic value judgments are identified in the second and fourth steps: the designation of the compensable factors and the relative weights assigned to them.

BASIC JUDGMENTS

Someone, or some group, must decide which job characteristics should be used as a basis for compensation. Definitions of factors may be broad in some programs and narrowly precise in others. Whatever the nature of the final list of compensable factors, it must be established, and there must be consensus on the relative weights. Without consensus, acceptance of the resulting pay plan is not likely. It follows that these judgments should be reached collaboratively by people representing different levels and functions in the organization. If there is a union, there should be union representation. If there is no union, the principle of worker representation or participation is still important.

WAGE SETTING

Job evaluation as such identifies the relative worth of jobs within a set studied. The translation of abstract indices of relative worth into actual pay scales ordinarily requires the use of "key jobs"—jobs found throughout a community or industry with reasonably uniform pay scales. Uniformity exists because the market forces of labor supply and demand have stabilized. For such jobs, a curve can be statistically established to show how relative worth measures are related to the pay rates for the key jobs. The same curve can then be used for other jobs to establish pay rates that will be seen as equitable.

COMPARABLE WORTH

Law in the United States has established that men and women performing the same jobs should have the same pay. An extension of the principle is that people doing work of comparable worth should receive equal (or comparable) pay. Robert Livernash stressed that job evaluation systems must be used or developed to handle this issue of equity. However, Ruth Blumrosen argued that, historically, women have been segregated in a small number of occupations and that the oversupply in such jobs has depressed their wages. If such jobs are included among the "key jobs," traditional job evaluation perpetuates the effects of prior wage discrimination.

INDUSTRIAL/ORGANIZATIONAL PSYCHOLOGY
INDUSTRIAL PSYCHOLOGY
JOB ANALYSIS

R. M. GUION

JOB SATISFACTION

Over the years, beginning in the early 1930s, psychologists have endeavored to determine the components of job satisfaction—that quality or combination of qualities that has escaped precise definition because it has many different points of reference, and few workers are satisfied with all aspects of their jobs.

Donald Super described satisfaction with one's work as the most important outcome of successful vocational planning. He found job satisfaction to be a function of occupational level within broad classes of occupations—for example, manual and nonmanual. Within each class, workers at the higher levels expressed greater satisfaction with their work than did workers at the lower levels. Super's work also indicated that satisfaction shows cyclical changes with age; workers were less satisfied at ages 25 to 34 and 45 to 54 than at other ages. These differences might be related to the different stages of vocational development described by Super.

Robert Hoppock recently pointed out that there is now a great deal of evidence that satisfied workers are found in all occupations and that some workers in repetitive and manual jobs are better satisfied than those in more creative occupations.

With the social unrest and changing mores of the 1960s and early 1970s, the theme of "worker alienation" became widespread. Poor morale, especially among blue-collar workers, was said to be rampant in the American workplace, accompanied by apathy, absenteeism, and even industrial sabotage. The U.S. Department of Health, Education, and Welfare appointed a special task force to investigate and report on the situation. The report immediately became the object of both praise and criticism. Among the critics was Harold Wool, a senior economist. He contended that a review of available research—some 2000 surveys of job satisfaction conducted in the United States over a period of several decades—revealed that few people expressed extreme satisfaction with their jobs; but still fewer reported extreme dissatisfaction, while the greatest number described themselves as "pretty satisfied." Phyllis Stewart and Muriel Cantor related problems of alienation and loss of job satisfaction to workers' lack of control over their product in both industrial and bureaucratic settings.

The status of job satisfaction in America was brought into focus again as the result of a survey conducted by Graham Staines and Robert Quinn that showed an appreciable drop in overall satisfaction between 1973 and 1977, although there had been no change between comparable surveys in 1969 and 1973. The general index showed a slight but significant decline, and the specific index showed a marked decline for five of six areas—comfort, challenge, financial rewards, resource adequacy, and promotions; only relations with coworkers showed no decline. Although the decline affected all demographic and occupational classes, there were some differences. Thus, men showed a greater decline than did women, and older workers also showed a decline. The decline was about the same for White and Black workers, but Black workers remained less satisfied than Whites. Satisfaction was down in all educational categories, but more so among workers with college degrees. Those in the lower skilled occupations showed more decline than those in the higher skilled occupations, as Super had found years earlier.

A number of investigators have speculated that declining job satisfaction can be traced to a growing gap between job expectations and the realities of the job situation. Others have questioned whether more satisfied workers are also more productive workers. Opinion remains divided, as do the results of research.

MORALE IN ORGANIZATIONS

E. E. DIAMOND

JOB SECURITY

Theorists such as A. H. Maslow have identified job security as one of the main components of workers' job attitudes and interests. Threats to job security can arise from either economic forces that lead to a reduction in the demand for labor, or from an employer decision to discharge a worker for poor work performance, nonperformance, or other related reasons. Various protections exist against each of these threats. Unions have led the way in the development of grievance procedures and third-party arbitration to protect workers against discharge for reasons other than "just cause"—that is, arbitrary discharges not caused by either economic or work performance reasons. Tenure rules, individual employment contracts, civil service statutes, and various laws prohibiting discrimination on the basis of race, age, sex, religion, national origin, union

membership, and so on, also limit the rights of employers to arbitrarily discharge workers.

Economic threats to job security can lead to either temporary job loss or layoff because of a downturn in the business cycle, or to a permanent or indefinite job loss. Providing protection against economically caused job loss is more difficult than protecting against arbitrary discharge. Among the most common protections is the accumulation of seniority on the job. Some companies and unions have negotiated or administratively developed work-sharing practices whereby they cut work hours rather than laying off workers during temporary downturns. Other employers engage in human resource planning efforts to plan their work and its allocation so as to minimize employment disruptions.

Finally, a number of compensation programs have been developed to reduce the financial losses associated with job loss. Still, the threat of job loss imposes significant economic costs and can produce significant social and psychological damage to workers and their families in the form of mental stress, loss of self-esteem, and increased family and community tensions. It therefore remains one of the most important social and economic problems of industrial society.

EMPLOYEE TURNOVER
EMPLOYMENT PRACTICES

T. A. KOCHAN

JOB STATUS

The work that people do serves many functions, one of which is to act as an identifier, to locate individuals socially vis-à-vis other people. Generally, power and privilege rest with individuals who possess (a) knowledge and skills to perform valued tasks; (b) control over economic resources; and (c) authority over others. Therefore, it is not surprising to find professionals and higher managers consistently ranked at the top of the status scale, followed by technicians, semiprofessionals, and lower managers, then by white- and blue-collar workers, and at the end of the scale, unskilled service providers and laborers.

Jobs differ in the way they are socially stratified. There is agreement, shared by men and women, persons of different ethnic groups, and members of past and present societies, regarding the location of occupations on a hierarchy of prestige. Work that requires specialized skills or has authority or control over valued resources is generally the most highly regarded.

JOB EVALUATION
LABELING THEORY

S. YUEN

JUDGMENT AND DECISION MAKING

Studies on judgment and decision making can be divided into four decision categories: the behavioral, the cognitive, the organizational, and the decision support systems. Each has its own theoretical perspective and methodology for analyzing decision-making behaviors and building its models.

BEHAVIORAL DECISION APPROACH: UTILITY AND PROBABILITY

Although the idea of utility and probability has a long history, dating back about 400 or more years, the modern history of decision analysis theories started with von Neumann and Morgenstern who published *Theory of games and economic behavior*, establishing risky choice as a topic of psychological study. Savage provided a set of axioms, with the simultaneous measurement of both the utility and the probability of an outcome, that expanded the utility theory. In the meantime, Edwards introduced the Bayesian approach to psychological studies on judgment and decision making, which takes base rate, prior odds, posterior odds, and the likelihood ratio into consideration and is a normative model based on probability theory. Edwards also introduced the idea of subjective probabilities and the maximization of subjective expected utility that had become a descriptive model of decision-making psychology. Some static models are founded on the assumption that people choose among courses of action on the basis of two variables: the value associated with action outcomes and the likelihood that certain actions will lead to the valued outcomes. von Winterfeldt and Edwards argued that people faced with complex tasks involving multiple value dimensions need a multiattribute utility theory to break down the evaluation task into attributes to make single-attribute evaluations. The trade-offs among attributes are then quantified as importance weights for attributes to reaggregate into an overall task evaluation in decision making. Three classes of techniques have proven to be effective for multiattribute utility analysis: the simple multiattribute rating technique for value measurement, the indifference methods for value measurement, and the lottery-based methods for utility measurement.

COGNITIVE AND DECISION PROCESS APPROACH

Because many decisions involve uncertainty, numerous studies have focused on the assessment of probabilities under various situations. The probabilities for some events should be interpreted as degrees of confidence. For a large set of probability assessments, a kind of validity can be examined (i.e., calibration) in terms of the real probability that certain events occur. A general finding is that people often assess the probability with overconfidence, which is related to the difficulty of the task, especially in general knowledge tasks. Some other experiments have been devoted to the conservatism in information processing in decision making and showed that conservatism could be attributed to either the failure in perceiving the data-gathering process accurately or the failure in combining information properly. Some diagnostic systems were designed to overcome the deficiency of the conservatism in decision making.

In addition to overconfidence and conservatism, cognitive bias and heuristics are widely noted in a number of studies. Typical bias and heuristics include representativeness (insensitivity to prior probability of outcomes, sample size, predictability, and statistical misconceptions), availability (biases due to the retrievability of instances, the effectiveness of a search set, the imaginability, and illusory correlation), and anchoring (insufficient adjustment and biases in evaluating conjunctive and disjunctive events and in assessing subjective probability distributions).

The decision-making process is characterized largely by the heuristics and cognitive strategies the decision maker adopted. Various kinds of cognitive strategies are classified in decision-making studies, depending on people's knowledge structure and the information structure of decisions. People use the additive difference model, the elimination-by-aspects model, and intuitive and analytic strategies. To elicit cognitive strategies in the decision process, process-tracing techniques were developed, including simultaneous verbal protocols and information search measurement. Both reliability and validity of the process-tracing techniques in understanding human information processing are demonstrated in many studies.

ORGANIZATIONAL APPROACH

Judgment and decision making also are extensively studied in the organizational context. In a study on decision making and administrative organizations, Simon emphasized the importance of fact and value premises in decision making and defined the notion of bounded rationality in relation to the choice behavior in organizations. This has had a significant impact on the thinking of organizational decision making. Another area in the organizational approach to judgment and decision making is group decision making. The two popular topics in group decision making are groupthink and group risk taking in decision making. Janis defined groupthink as a collective pattern of defensive avoidance in which the members use their collective cognitive resources to develop rationalizations supporting shared illusions in decision making. At the organizational level, much attention has been paid to participation and influence-power-sharing in decision making. In a 3-year field study of 129 large companies in eight countries, Heller and Wilpert developed a model of influence-power-sharing and skill used in organizational decision making and the method of group feedback analysis. Wang further proposed a process model of organizational decision making, illustrating the effects of influence-power-sharing on both competence use and managerial transparency (two-way communication and sound psychological climate for goal pursuing), which in turn lead to changes in decision effectiveness.

DECISION SUPPORT SYSTEMS APPROACH

In the areas of decision aid and decision support, various kinds of decision support systems have been developed for unstructured decision tasks. To support decisions, the decision problems must be structured, which includes identifying the problem, developing an overall analytic structure, and structuring value trees. An important task in designing decision support systems is to develop decision modeling and decision support information. Some useful types of decision modeling include (a) causal models focusing on the causal relationships among different decision factors; (b) mathematical models developing some mathematical formulas for the quantitative relations of key indicators for decisions; (c) operational research models producing powerful standard models for management decisions (e.g., allocation, queuing, and competitive models); and (d) heuristic models attempting to derive suboptimal solutions, a satisfying approach. In a series of experiments on the effects of decision support information, Wang and Zhong demonstrated that type of decision support information greatly affected subjects' information search patterns and modified their cognitive strategies during the decision-making process. A multilevel decision support model was proposed with the compatibility between types of user knowledge networks and levels of decision support as its key concept.

ALGORITHMIC–HEURISTIC THEORY
CLUSTER ANALYSIS
CURVILINEAR RELATIONSHIP
ECOLOGICAL VALIDITY
NONPARAMETRIC STATISTICAL TESTS
PARAMETRIC STATISTICAL TESTS
PHILOSOPHY OF SCIENCE

Z.-M. WANG

JURY PSYCHOLOGY

The right of an accused person to a trial by jury was first announced more than 750 years ago in the declaration of English liberties known as the Magna Carta. Since then, trial by jury has been a cornerstone of Anglo-American jurisprudence. This right affords to the defendant in a criminal case, and in some instances to litigants in a civil matter, the opportunity to have the facts determined by a group of ordinary citizens. This group, the jury, generally consists of 12 persons, although the number may vary in certain jurisdictions.

Prospective jurors are summoned to serve from the community in which the trial will take place. The group so summoned is commonly known as the jury pool. At the commencement of the trial, prospective jurors are called at random from the pool and are subject to interrogation by the attorneys for the parties and/or by the judge in a process known as *voir dire examination.* The purpose of voir dire is to attempt to determine bias for or against the litigants or defendant. Allowing actual bias as a ground for challenge is judicial recognition of the effect that conscious or unconscious preconceptions may have on a juror's verdict. In addition to numerically unlimited "for cause" challenges, the respective attorneys are afforded a limited number of peremptory challenges ranging from a low of 3 to a high of 20, depending on the jurisdiction and the nature of the case.

From a psychological standpoint, no phase of a trial is more important than the voir dire examination of prospective jurors. Jurors often find the beginning of the trial new and exciting. They are stimulated and their awareness is at a high point. Since the voir dire precedes the opening statements of counsel and the submission of evidence, at this point the jury is most perceptive and attentive. First impressions can and often do color the subsequent attitudes and receptivity of jurors. In the process of selecting the jury, counsel are also establishing their own essential credibility.

Investigations are available on the effect on jury behavior of nationality, sex, social status, occupation, family status, the role of the foreman, education, prior jury experience, and other socioeconomic factors. In addition, studies are available on how the credibility of a witness is affected by his or her physical appearance, likability, eye contact, clothing, and "body language."

In the 1950s, psychological researchers Adorno, Frenkel-Brunswik, Levinson, and Sanford developed a personality theory designed to measure what was termed "prefascistic" or antidemocratic trends in individuals. Further studies demonstrated that authoritarians are favorably inclined to the prosecution in criminal cases on the issues both of guilt and punishment. However, egalitarians tend to side with the defendant in criminal cases and are less punitive than authoritarians. To a lesser extent, in civil cases involving liability for money damages, egalitarians often side with the plaintiff and authoritarians with the defense.

Another personality construct relating to jury behavior concerns the belief in the internal–external locus of control of events. "Internals" believe that they have significant control over events that happen to them. "Externals" are more inclined to believe that outcomes are determined by factors external or extrinsic to themselves. Studies indicate that "internals" are more likely to attribute responsibility for the crime to the defendant and to render harsher sentences.

The direct entry of social science techniques into jury selection is generally considered to have first occurred in the trial of eight antiwar activists in Harrisburg, Pennsylvania in 1971. During the course of voir dire, in what has been referred to as the "Harrisburg Eight" trial, the team of sociologist Jay Schulman and psychologist Richard Christie introduced "statistical modeling" into jury selection procedures. Statistical modeling involves extensive survey work in the community from which the jury pool will be selected. Field workers attempt to gather, by interview, demographic and socioeconomic background information such as religion, age, sex, occupation, and the like, and to correlate such backgrounds with preconceptions and predispositions bearing on the trial issues. This information is cross-tabulated and fed into a computer. The readout is programmed to identify the "ideal" juror as well as acceptable and unacceptable profiles.

Critics have compared the juries so chosen to "sociologically loaded dice" and a scheme of "social science jury stacking." Defenders of the techniques point out that even the researchers themselves are aware that people do not always act according to their dispositions.

CLINICAL VERSUS STATISTICAL PREDICTION
PSYCHOLOGY AND THE LAW
STEREOTYPING

E. L. HUDSON

JUVENILE DELINQUENCY

Juvenile delinquency is defined usually as legally prohibited behavior committed by a juvenile. The exact age at which delinquency applies depends on state law. Children under 8 are usually not remanded to a detention home or youth house, but ordinarily are placed in a shelter facility. Depending on the severity of the delinquent behavior, a youngster might be considered either a juvenile delinquent or a JINS (juvenile in need of supervision). Behavior of the latter category-such as loitering, truancy, running away, trespassing, and incorrigibility—would not be considered criminal if committed by an adult. Juvenile delinquency includes criminal offenses such as breaking and entering, burglary, shoplifting, arson, rape, and homicide.

A special report in 1981 noted that one third of all major crimes are committed by people younger than 20 years of age. No ethnic, religious, racial groups, or socioeconomic levels are free from the apparently rapidly rising tide of juvenile problems.

CRIME
DEVIANCE

D. N. LOMBARDI

KUDER OCCUPATIONAL INTEREST SURVEY

The Kuder Occupational Interest Survey was developed in 1966 by Frederic Kuder. It consists of 300 occupationally relevant activities arranged in triad form. Persons taking the survey mark one most-preferred and one least-preferred activity for each of the 100 triads. These responses are then compared with those of representative members of 126 occupational groups and 48 college-major groups. Occupational scales are representative of the range of occupations described in various U.S. Department of Labor publications and of the occupational hierarchy from professional to skilled trades occupations. College-major scales are representative of majors offered in colleges throughout the United States.

Results are reported in rank order of similarity of responses to those of the criterion groups, separately for occupations and college majors. (For 39 of the occupations and college majors, "twin scales"—separate scales representing men and women in the same occupation or college major—have been developed. The reason for separate development by gender is that women and men—even those in the same occupation or college major—differ significantly in their responses to a number of the survey items.) Results on all scales are reported to all respondents, regardless of gender. Respondents are advised to consider their ranks on all scales in making occupational and educational plans and decisions. Comparisons are also given for ten broad vocational areas. It should be noted that, although the original scales were developed in 1966, new scales are developed periodically.

APTITUDE MEASUREMENT
FORCED CHOICE TESTING
VOCATIONAL INTEREST MEASUREMENT

E. E. DIAMOND

L

LABELING THEORY

In contrast to other prominent theoretical positions that may place the source of deviance solely within the individual or solely within society, the interaction that results from societal reaction to individual behavior is the central thrust of labeling theory.

Therefore, deviance is created by other individuals' reactions to a given act. K. T. Erickson called those groups or individuals with the ability to label the "influential audience." Certain behaviors become designated as deviant, illegal, or indicants of mental illness when they have been sufficiently codified *and* when a group has sufficient power to impose codified standards. Both the behavior and the individual displaying the behavior become labeled as deviant.

Many critics of formal labeling processes (e.g., courts) suggest that the labeling of deviance is an irrational and unjust process. Research indicates that the extent to which deviance is attributed to an act depends on how widely that act varies from the experience of the audience, the location of the act and its observability, and the implied motivation. It is further the case that deviants of any group are considered to be members of a homogeneous class once the label of deviance has been attached.

DEVIANCE

W. S. DAVIDSON II

LABOR–MANAGEMENT RELATIONS

Labor–management relations is the study of the interactions among workers and employers in industrial societies and the rules and procedures that govern employment relationships. It is one of several subfields within the broader field of industrial relations. Management relations concentrates on the roles played by individual workers, labor organizations, employers, and government agencies in establishing and administering employment relationships.

At least three different philosophical or ideological perspectives have provided normative foundations for research on labor–management relations; the Marxist, pluralist, and consensus-based behavioral models of organizations.

Marxists see labor and management as separated by a fundamental conflict of interests derived from the larger class struggle in capitalist society. Research adopting this perspective, therefore, has focused on the strategies used by the state and by employers to control worker behavior and to extract surplus value, and on the responses of workers and labor organizations.

Pluralists share the Marxist view that there is an inherent conflict of interests between workers and employers; however, they view the conflict neither as all-encompassing nor as limited to employment relationships in a capitalist society. Instead, employment relationships are inherently mixed-motive in nature: Workers and employers have both conflicting and common interests. These differences are expected to exist under all social and political/economic systems. The task of research adopting the pluralist perspective is therefore to identify effective strategies for negotiating or accommodating the conflicting interests, while at the same time searching for ways the parties can more effectively pursue their shared interests.

The pluralist school is the dominant approach of most North American and Western European scholars and provides the normative foundation for most labor legislation in Europe and North America. Therefore, most research on labor–management relations has focused on procedures such as collective bargaining, plant level workers' councils, and alternative systems of worker participation and representation in management as strategies for achieving effective accommodation among labor and management interests. An equally important body of research has examined the effectiveness of labor legislation and the role of national governments in regulating labor–management relationships.

Since the founders of the pluralist view were institutional labor economists, there is a strong institutional research tradition that remains popular today. The growth of the quantitative social sciences, however, has also produced an increase in the use of econometric and psychometric research on labor–management relations policies and practices.

Adherents to the *consensus-based paradigm* do not see inherent economic, class, or structural conflicts of interests separating workers and managers. Although conflicts can develop in work organizations, effective management of structural and interpersonal relations should be able to integrate the goals of individuals and organizations.

Although the range of policies covered in a typical labor–management relationship varies across settings and over time, it typically would include wages and other forms of compensation, hours of work, working conditions, rights to participate in decisions, and rights protecting individuals from arbitrary or discriminatory treatment or actions.

ARBITRATION
EMPLOYMENT PRACTICES
INDUSTRIAL/OPERATIONAL PSYCHOLOGY

T. A. KOCHAN

LANGUAGE DEVELOPMENT

Learning language is a lifelong process, beginning in the first months of life and continuing throughout adulthood. The most rapid learning occurs during early childhood, as by age 6 children have mastered the basic pronunciation, grammar, and more than 90% of the basic vocabulary of their native language.

THEORIES OF LANGUAGE DEVELOPMENT

Two quite different theories have been proposed to explain the human ability to learn language. One, originally proposed by B. F. Skinner in *Verbal behavior,* suggests that children learn to talk through classical and operant conditioning.

The second theory, proposed by Noam Chomsky and by David Mc-Neill argues that language learning is largely innate. It is as if there were a "language acquisition device" (LAD) in the mind already programmed with the underlying linguistic rules. Only a minimal amount of specific language information is needed to learn whatever language the child's parents speak.

Although both theories have their adherents, a third perspective on language development seems more firmly grounded in research. This theory holds that the *interaction* between infant and caregiver, and between one person and another, is the heart of language learning. That humans are innately sensitized to learn language is shown by evidence from deaf as well as hearing infants.

ASPECTS OF LANGUAGE

Four separate aspects of language development have been studied: phonology (the sounds), syntax (the underlying structure), semantics (the meanings of words and phrases), and pragmatics (the practical communication skills).

Phonology

From the moment of birth, infants communicate with various cries, indicating hunger, pain, need for attention, and so forth. By 3 months, infants laugh and "coo," emitting vowel-like sounds of pleasure, and from 6 to 12 months they babble a variety of sounds. Infants gradually become more intentional and responsive in their noisemaking. They babble in response to talk and then wait for a reply long before the content of the reply is understood. At about 12 months they are speaking their first words. From this point on, the sounds they produce come closer to standard speech, although many 5-year-olds still have some articulation problems. After puberty, it becomes much more difficult for people to learn to produce sounds they have not practiced in childhood.

Semantics

Even before they begin to speak, infants understand the meanings of words. By 18 months, most children have a speaking vocabulary of a dozen or more words and seem to comprehend far more. At about age 2, many children undergo a "language explosion" as new words and phrases enter the vocabulary rapidly.

Although semantic understanding proceeds rapidly in early childhood, certain common words are troublesome because they demand more cognitive sophistication than young children possess. In our culture, at almost every age, the complexity and precision of a person's vocabulary is probably the best single indicator of intellectual ability and education.

Syntax

Children demonstrate some understanding of the structure of language when they first put two words together to make a sentence, an event that usually occurs between 18 months and 2 years. Syntactical understanding improves with age in a regular sequence. Preschoolers show an impressive grasp of much of the syntax of their mother tongue, but during middle childhood, adolescence, and adulthood people become progressively better at understanding and applying the formal rules of syntax.

Pragmatics

A person's ability to communicate with language involves far more than acceptable phonology, semantics, and syntax: It involves tailoring the form of the message to fit the needs of the audience. Pragmatics is the study of these differences.

Gestures and body language play a large role in pragmatics and are evident in the first months of life as infants wave their arms in excitement or avert their gaze to indicate that they do not want to play. It is hard to know how much of this is intentional, but when a 1-year-old raises her arms to be picked up or points his or her finger at a desired toy—especially when either gesture is accompanied by an insistent grunt—the message is clear.

CHILDREN'S BEHAVIORAL STAGES
SPEECH DEVELOPMENT

K. S. BERGER

LANGUAGE IN GREAT APES

The issue of mental continuity is a major one stimulating research investigating language in great apes. In what does the uniqueness of *homo sapiens* lie? Many argue that to have a mind or to be capable of thought depends on language; for some philosophers, mind is identical to the ability to use language.

There were early attempts to teach apes to produce words vocally. Subsequent research indicated that apes may lack the necessary physiologic machinery to produce something akin to human speech.

The pioneering work of Beatrice T. and R. Allen Gardner took advantage of the apes' natural tendencies to use manual gestures. Francine Patterson has taught gorillas to produce hand signs as well as to understand spoken English. Herbert Terrace and his associates have used videotape extensively in the data collection process and have gathered a large corpus of the hand signs of the chimpanzee Nim. There are also two nonsigning projects using artificial visual designs: Sue Savage-Rumbaugh and Duane Rumbaugh have used a computer-based lexigram system, while David Premack has taught chimpanzees to use haphazardly shaped plastic chips that are wordlike in function. The importance of a strong positive social relationship between the ape and the trainer is emphasized in most projects, because such bonds obviously exist for humans in the initial acquisition of language.

From all these studies one can conclude that signs and items in the artificial lexicons occasionally operate as if they represent objects or events in the real world. Yet there is no convincing evidence that apes' utterances are grammatical. Furthermore, the rate of acquisition for the apes is dramatically lower than that of human children; the average length of utterance is short; and the apes seem to repeat much and not add to what has just been communicated to them. It is thus difficult to conclude that the apes' productions bear more than a rudimentary similarity to human language. However, one would probably find it difficult to describe the production of young children as linguistic if we did not know that these children will grow into language-using adults. The ape language projects do indicate cognitive abilities and possible mental states in the apes.

ANIMAL COMMUNICATION
ANIMAL INTELLIGENCE
SIGNS AND SYMBOLS

D. ROBBINS

LATE-LIFE FORGETTING

There is public concern that memory loss signals the beginning of Alzheimer's disease or senility. Early diagnosis combined with intervention and family support can assist older adults with memory loss to function and to manage life on a daily basis in the least restrictive setting.

The first task for the health professional faced by a patient concerned about memory loss is to ascertain whether the symptoms are indicative of dementia or whether they are the result of normal decline in cognitive abilities associated with the aging process. Even if there is a diagnosis of dementia (defined by the American Psychiatric Association as a loss of intellectual abilities of sufficient severity to interfere with social or occupational functioning), it is important to determine whether the dementia is reversible or not. If the cause is determined promptly, some dementias are reversible because an almost limitless array of diseases and behavioral disorders can result in a dementing process. Muriel Lezak points out that memory loss serves as a starting point for differentiating individuals with normal forgetting from those who do not warrant a diagnosis of dementia.

Two types of memory impairment are described by Asenath La Rue to distinguish between normal and abnormal forgetting. Originally these were labeled benign senescent forgetfulness and malignant senescent forgetfulness. Benign forgetfulness was characterized by memory failures limited to relatively unimportant facts but included the ability to recall these at a later time. Most of the forgotten aspects were part of the remote, rather than recent, past, and the individual was usually aware of the memory loss and could compensate for it. In some ways, this type of forgetting is not unlike the absent-minded professor stereotype. In contrast, malignant forgetfulness of old age included distortion of memories, reduced retention time, and difficulties in remembering recent events and experience. In addition, disorientation to place, time, and eventually person also occurred. On the surface, this seemed to be a straightforward distinction between types of forgetfulness. Critics have speculated whether benign and malignant senescent forgetfulness are points on a continuum rather than separate conditions.

There have been attempts to define changes in memory associated with normal aging. A National Institute of Mental Health work group was established in 1986 to study and encourage research and communication in this area. This work group published diagnostic criteria for what they termed age-associated memory impairment (AAMI). The criteria for AAMI required the presence of memory complaints based on a gradual onset of memory loss in adults 50 years and older functioning within an acceptable intellectual level (specifically defined by the criteria). To meet the criteria of AAMI, individuals must perform one standard deviation (SD) below the average established for younger adults on tests of recent memory. In addition, a number of criteria exclude an individual from meeting the AAMI category. These include the presence of dementia, alcohol dependence, depression, certain neurological disorders, and/or other medical disorders. Current use of psychotropic drugs also would disqualify an individual from meeting the diagnostic criteria. AAMI, it was argued, was designed to describe older adults who have memory problems but do not suffer from a neurological impairment. It was assumed that AAMI is a normal consequence of aging in a proportion of older individuals.

Richard C. Blackford and Asenath La Rue take some issue with the measurement aspects of AAMI. They recommended that there should be two categories within AAMI: age-consistent memory impairment and late-life forgetfulness. The criteria for age-consistent memory impairment include performance on 75% of memory tests used that are within +1 SD of the mean established for that participant's age.

The criteria for late-life forgetting requires performance on 50% or more of tests given that are within one to two SD below the mean established for that age. The exclusion criteria for each of these subcategories is somewhat similar to those stated previously for age-associated memory impairments. All these categories apply to individuals between the ages of 50 and 79 so that individuals 80 and older are excluded.

ALZHEIMER'S DISEASE
MEMORY DISORDERS

N. Abeles

LATERAL DOMINANCE

Lateral dominance is the use of one side of the body more often or more skillfully than the other in unilateral activities. The most obvious example of lateral dominance is more frequent or skillful use of one hand over the other. Lateral dominance is associated with asymmetrical organization of the functions of the two cerebral hemispheres, although the relationship is not exact.

The majority of people are right-handed, although there is considerable variation in the discrepancy between the efficiency, force, and frequency of use of the right hand as opposed to the left.

The preference for the use of one foot or one eye over the other, while not as frequently studied as handedness, is as important a part of lateral dominance. Although most right-handed people are also right-footed and right-eyed, there are many whose eye/hand/foot lateral dominance is mixed. Although environmental factors probably play a large part in determining lateral dominance, some studies suggest that there may be hereditary influences as well.

BRAIN LATERALITY
NEUROPSYCHOLOGY
PSYCHOPHYSIOLOGY

T. S. Bennett

LAW OF FILIAL REGRESSION

For many continuous traits such as stature and intelligence, it is generally found that the adult offspring of a given parent deviates to a lesser degree from the mean of the population than does the parent. That is, the offspring "regresses" toward the population mean. Sir Francis Galton termed this observation "the law of filial regression to mediocrity." He conceived of it as a fundamental law of heredity. But he probably overestimated its fundamental significance, and we now know his theoretical explanation of the phenomenon to be incorrect.

The importance of Galton's law of regression for psychology arises from his argument that general mental ability, which he believed to be largely inherited, manifests filial regression in the same way as stature and other hereditary physical traits. Indeed, empirical evidence from mental tests obtained on parents and children has borne out Galton's argument: The offspring of exceptional parents (in either direction of deviation from the population mean) are less exceptional than their parents, and by a constant fraction of the parents' deviation from the mean.

To correctly understand the phenomenon of regression requires that one distinguish clearly between the statistical (descriptive) and the substantive (causal) aspects of the phenomenon. The regression coefficient (i.e., the slope of the regression line) merely *describes* the raw fact of regression quantitatively; it does not *explain* anything. Because the regression coefficient, when based on standardized scores in both variables, is the correlation coefficient r, it is a mere tautology to say that when any two correlated variables, x and y, are less than perfectly correlated (i.e., $r_{xy} < 1$), the standardized regression slope will be less than 1, and the corresponding value of y for any given value of x will deviate less from the population mean of y than x deviates from the mean of x, and vice versa. Statistically, regression and correlation essentially describe or quantify the same phenomenon, which is most simply thought of as imperfect correlation between two variables. Hence, the theoretical explanation of regression is essentially the explanation of why the two variables in question (e.g., fathers' and sons' heights) are not perfectly correlated. For any particular trait, genetic factors may or may not be a part of the explanation. It is a question that can be answered only by empirical investigations expressly designed to test an explicit genetic model.

The possible causes of regression among parents and offspring (or any other kinships) can be classified into three main categories: (a) errors of measurement, (b) genetic factors, and (c) environmental factors.

1. Unreliability or measurement error attenuates correlation and thus contributes to decreasing the slope of the regression line. The effect of attenuation can be corrected, provided we know the reliability of the measurements.

2. The genetic aspect of regression, assuming trait variation involves hereditary factors, results from the fact that each offspring inherits only a random half of each parent's genes. The more deviant the parent, the more likely the deviation is caused by relatively rare nonadditive combinations of genes, such as dominance and recessiveness and epistasis. Rarer combinations of the parental genes are less likely to be passed on to the offspring, who therefore will generally differ from the parents in the direction of less deviance from the population mean. A well-known method in genetics for estimating the "narrow heritability" of a trait (i.e., the proportion of trait variance attributable to additive gene effects) is the regression of the offspring on the midparent. But this method is strictly valid only if parents and offspring have not shared the same environment; it is necessary that the offspring have been reared in environments selected at random in the population.

3. Because individual differences in the development of a trait may be affected by environmental factors, and because parents and their offspring (or siblings, twins, or other kinships) do not share identical environments, the correlation between relatives may be decreased because of differences between their environments. The more deviant parents, for example, may have had more rare and unusual environments than the environments they provided for their own children, hence the children will be less deviant than their parents. There is nothing in the phenomenon of regression *per se* that proves either genetic or environmental causes or some combination of these.

HEREDITY AND INTELLIGENCE
HERITABILITY
STATISTICS IN PSYCHOLOGY

A. R. JENSEN

LAW OF PARSIMONY

The law or principle of parsimony of holds that the simplest of alternative theoretical accounts is to be accepted whenever the alternatives are equally consistent with empirical data.

Complicated theoretical explanations are more likely to be erroneous than simpler ones.

HISTORY

Adaptation of the principle of parsimony to psychological problems was accomplished by the British comparative psychologist C. Lloyd Morgan. Morgan's position is usually represented by the following widely quoted statement: "In no case may we interpret an action as the outcome of the

exercise of a higher psychical faculty, if it can be interpreted as the outcome of the exercise of one which stands lower in the psychological scale." This position has come to be known as *Lloyd Morgan's canon;* an earlier, more general, and much more picturesque name for the law of parsimony is *Occam's razor*. The operational use to which such a razor is put should be self-evident.

Lloyd Morgan's canon was intended to refer to explanatory accounts of animal behavior, especially unusual feats of animals too often attributed to humanlike capabilities. Newbury provided an early extensive treatment of the many ramifications of Lloyd Morgan's canon as a methodological principle within psychology.

APPLICABILITY

It is important to recognize the wide range of conditions under which the parsimony principle can be applied. Perhaps the most significant dimension here is that of theoretical versus real-life setting. In the former case, little damage of a practical sort is likely to be suffered if a serious error is made, that is, if the more complex theoretical account is erroneously accepted. As a matter of fact, it is just such active seeking of error in the testing of hypotheses that is the hallmark of the experimental method. Not so in the latter case, unfortunately. Here life-and-death decisions may well be involved (e.g., in the realm of military affairs), and a great many lives may be needlessly sacrificed when some more complex account is mistakenly accepted and acted on. Less dramatically, but in an essentially similar manner, crucial social, political, and economic decisions often revolve around the acceptance or rejection of differentially complex theoretical accounts relating directly to social policies (e.g., early interventions such as the Head Start program). Acceptance of complex but faulty hypotheses can have drastic consequences. It is thus crucial that parsimonious theoretical filters be carefully applied to alternative interpretations of fundamental issues. Unfortunately, it is in these areas rather than in the strictly theoretical (academic) ones that decision makers are least likely to be knowledgeable and experienced with respect to application of the parsimony principle. Hence, it is important for those who are so experienced (scientists and academicians) to contribute as much as possible to the decision making, as is regularly done, for example, by forming special committees of the National Research Council (NRC).

NRC COMMITTEE ON ENHANCEMENT OF HUMAN PERFORMANCE

An especially good example of how the principle of parsimony operates in the evaluation of complex theoretical propositions is afforded by the functioning of one such NRC committee. As the world's largest training institution, the U.S. Army has been necessarily sensitive to claims for enhancement of human performance made for many diverse instructional programs. Such proposals range from the use of meditation and altered mental states to sports psychology techniques intended to prepare one for performance under intense pressure. They have all had strong advocacy of one kind or another within the military community. However, most of them did not originate within the scientific community, so that the usual testing and evaluation techniques were not readily applied.

Besieged by such a variety of highly touted programs that obviously needed thorough scientific evaluation, the army recognized the need for behavioral as well as the traditional engineering (hardware) evaluations and in 1984 formally asked the National Academy of Sciences for help. A special committee of 13 psychologists was established under the auspices of the NRC. In its first phase, the committee analyzed the degree of scientific support for a number of unconventional, New Age techniques; its initial report was published by the National Academy Press in 1988 and proved to be a best-seller.

In the second phase of its work the committee proceeded to investigate more basic issues of performance enhancement. Numerous unsuspected relationships were uncovered; for example, it was shown that certain factors associated with relatively poor training performance, such as distributed rather than massed practice and the use of irregular conditions in training, were nonetheless associated with *superior* subsequent (after training) performance. Little positive support was found for several popular techniques such as meditation (beyond the conventional effects of relaxation) or subliminal tapes.

These bits and pieces selected from a wide-scale attack on the performance problem can do little more than suggest the no-nonsense flavor of what was, in effect, a far-reaching application of the parsimony principle to a set of important behavioral problems, but they do appear to constitute deep-seated support for the scientific use of the parsimony principle. Details of the second phase of the NRC committee work are available in an interim report as well as the report itself.

CAUSAL REASONING
INFERENCES
MILL'S CANON
OPERATIONAL DEFINITION
REDUCTIONISM

M. H. MARX

LEADERSHIP AND SUPERVISION

Leaders manage and managers lead, but the two are not the same. Leaders and supervisors both may play interpersonal, informational, and decisional roles, but supervisors also engage in nonleadership activities such as checking, planning, investigating, coordinating, evaluating, supervising, staffing, negotiating, and representing.

Skill as a leader and in relating to others is a most important requirement at all levels of management. Human relations skills are seen as most important to middle managers relative to technical skills. The single most important function of first-line managers is that of supervising and leading others. Two factors that account for much of the individual differences in supervisors' behavior have been termed *initiation of structure,* instrumental in planning and organization, and *consideration,* showing concern for subordinates' needs.

The intangibles of leadership are seen among managers to the degree that they remain far from fully programmed robotic decision makers. Oriented toward action, not reflection, managers rely on judgment and intuition rather than on formal analysis, making it difficult to clearly observe their decision-making processes. Because interpersonal communication is favored over written documents, managers spend a good deal of time on the telephone or in meetings, where leadership and interpersonal performance count heavily.

Effective leadership relate strongly to supervision and management among several factored dimensions isolated by Morse and Wagner. Multiple regression analyses suggested that, overall, the managerial activities of most consequence-to-end results were managing the organization's environment.

The initiative, risk-taking, path-finding behavior of the outstanding leader may conflict with the demands for reliability and conformance to organizational rules and constraints displayed by the effective administrator. Clearly needed is a contingent approach to understanding the relative importance of the leadership and nonleadership aspects of supervision and management.

LEADERSHIP EFFECTIVENESS
LEADERSHIP STYLES

B. M. BASS

LEADERSHIP EFFECTIVENESS

By "leadership" is meant the direction, supervision, or management of a group or organization. The leader may be "emergent"—that is, either informally acknowledged, elected by the group, or appointed by the organization of which the group is a part.

In its short history, empirical research on leadership has evolved from a simplistic search for the magic leadership trait or the best way to behave toward group members, to the more complex view that different situations call for different types of leader behaviors or leader personalities.

With the demise of leadership traits, researchers turned their attention to the behaviors and management styles that might differentiate effective from less effective leaders. A highly original and widely publicized study by Lewin, Lippitt, and White first brought leadership research into the laboratory to investigate the effect of different leader behaviors on leader–member relations and follower involvement. They found that a democratic, participative leadership style produced more involved and satisfied group members than did autocratic or laissez-faire leadership.

The dominant theories and related research of the 1940–1960 period had three main characteristics: (a) These theories ushered in the belief that the best method of leadership is based on an employee-centered or human relations-oriented approach; (b) they concentrated their research efforts on such interpersonal variables as leader attitudes, behaviors, and motivation; and (c) they relegated such cognitive variables as the leader's intelligence, task ability, and job knowledge to obscurity. This latter view, that cognitive variables were of little importance, was not shared by practitioners who had to predict future managerial performance or make recommendations on promotion and placement of executives.

During this period, investigators began the systematic study of behaviors associated with effective leadership. This research led to two important "behavior factors." One factor, labeled "consideration," included socioemotional, expressive behaviors indicating concern for the opinions, feelings, and welfare of subordinates. The other factor, "structuring," involved assigning roles and tasks to group members, setting standards, evaluating performance, and focusing on the task.

The Contingency Model

This theory classifies leaders as motivated primarily either by the need to accomplish assigned tasks or by close and supportive relations with members of their group. The leadership situation is classified as giving a high, moderate, or low degree of power, influence, and control to the leader. Situational control indicates, in essence, the probability of being able to accomplish the task. Situational control depends on the degree to which (a) the group is dependable and supportive, (b) the task is structured and clear as to goals and method, and (c) the organization gives the leader position power—legitimate power to reward and punish.

The effectiveness of leaders is dependent (or contingent) on both the leader's personality and the characteristics of the leadership situation. Task-motivated leaders perform best in high-control and low-control situations; relationship motivated leaders perform best in moderate-control situations.

The contingency model has generated considerable controversy. However, a comprehensive review and meta-analysis of 127 published tests supported the model beyond reasonable doubt. The theory has led to a number of nonobvious hypotheses.

The leadership training method, "leader match," that is based on the contingency model teaches leaders to modify critical aspects of the leadership situation (e.g., leader—member relations, task structure, and position power), so that it will match their personality, rather than trying to change their personality or core behaviors. A number of well-controlled field experiments have shown that this training method improves rated leadership performance.

Path–Goal Theory

A theory involving the interaction of behavior and leadership situation was developed by House. It states that the leader must motivate the subordinate by (a) emphasizing the relationship between the subordinate's own needs and the organizational goals and (b) clarifying and facilitating the path subordinates must take to fulfill their own needs as well as the organization's goals. The theory predicts that structuring behavior (i.e., coaching, direction, specifying goals) will have positive effects when the job is unclear, but negative effects when duties are clearly specified. Considerate behavior (support, warmth, concern) will have beneficial effects when the job is boring or aversive. Research supports the theory's prediction relating to employee job satisfaction and subordinate motivation; predictions on performance have not been well supported.

Normative Decision Theory

Vroom and Yetton's model prescribes the conditions under which leaders should make decisions autocratically, in consultation with group members, or with group members fully participating in the decisions. The theory assumes the following: (a) individual decisions are more time-effective than group decisions, (b) subordinates are more committed to a decision if they participate in its formulation, and (c) complex and ambiguous tasks require more information and consultation for reaching high-quality decisions. Tests of this theory have been based on retrospective reports; further research is required to evaluate the predictive validity of the theory.

Transactional theories deal with the way in which leader style and behavior interact with subordinate behavior and performance. Hollander showed, for example, that the leaders' status increases in proportion to their contribution to the group goal. Leaders must prove their worth by competence and commitment to group values, for which they then receive "idiosyncrasy credits." These credits allow the leader to diverge from accepted group norms and standards, to strike out in new directions, or to be forgiven for minor transgressions. Graen's model shows that a leader will develop different role relations with various members of the group, and that satisfying leader-member exchanges improve leader relations and job satisfaction while dissatisfying exchanges do not.

Leadership theorists have returned increasingly to the study of cognitive processes. In studies of leader judgments, Green and Mitchell found that leaders were more critical of their subordinates if their behavior had very adverse consequences than if the *same* behavior had no negative consequences.

The contribution of the leader's intellectual abilities and job relevant experience to performance was reexamined by Fiedler, Potter, Zais, and Knowlton. Their series of studies suggests that intelligence and job knowledge were prematurely abandoned by leadership researchers and that these important variables need to be reintroduced into leadership theory.

Another important development in the area has been research on the effects of critical job characteristics and task components on leader and group member behavior and performance.

LEADERSHIP AND SUPERVISION
LEADERSHIP STYLES
LEADERSHIP TRAINING

F. E. Fiedler
M. M. Chemers

LEADERSHIP STYLES

Although the classic leadership style experiment of Lewin, Lippitt, and White was reported in 1939, most of the leadership research during the 1940s centered around the identification of individual traits that differentiate leaders from nonleaders or effective from ineffective leaders. In the 1950s and 1960s, this trait approach was displaced by the attempt to identify observable effective leader behaviors. Within that general research focus, attempts to identify such behaviors were usually discussed under the heading of leadership style and/or leader behavior.

The early 1950s studies sought to establish measures of leadership style. It became clear by the 1960s that situational factors had a strong impact on the appropriateness of a given leadership style. This realization gave rise in the late 1960s to situational theories that attempted to specify the conditions under which a particular leadership style was apt to be effective. Several situational theories introduced intervening variables to help explain why a given leadership style works better in some situations than in others.

TAXONOMIES

In one of the earliest leadership style experiments Lewin, Lippitt, and White found that democratic leaders were more effective than authoritarian leaders who overcontrolled events or laissez-faire leaders who undercontrolled events. This early beginning was followed by two major research programs: one by D. Katz and others, and one by Fleishman. Although their methods for creating measures of leader behavior were quite different, each program eventually settled on a two-variable taxonomy. Each taxonomy had one production-oriented dimension and one employee-oriented dimension. The most effective leaders tended to be high on both variables. Most of the studies were correlational, so the direction of causality was uncertain. Attempts to corroborate the results with field research studies were only partially successful. It was discovered that the leadership style that was best in one situation was not necessarily best in another.

A counterpart to the global dimensions used in early studies is found in the Hersey and Blanchard model. As true for earlier formulations, their "task behavior emphasis" and "relationship behavior emphasis" categories are broadly defined and are assumed to be independent. At the opposite extreme among the current theories is Gary Yukl's 19-category taxonomy of leader behaviors. This taxonomy was developed through a 4-year research program and the behavior categories are intuitively attractive for describing a leader's behavior.

Modern theorists generally have believed that two broadly defined categories are not sufficient. Unfortunately, when theorists venture beyond the two basic categories, they disagree as to which variables are most essential and how many variables are needed. Attempts to resolve this issue are complicated by the fact that leadership style refers to the pattern of scores across whatever leader behavior categories are used.

Currently available taxonomies ignore or play down the question of *how* leaders do what they do. Yet the definition and measurement of leadership style seems incomplete without a description of how a leader exercises influence over subordinates. One might also ask if leadership style can be described adequately without considering other aspects of a leader's interpersonal style.

SITUATIONAL VARIABLES

As was true for leadership style taxonomies, there is no consensus about situational variables. Theorists are united only in their agreement that situational variables are essential for finding systematic relationships between leadership style and leader effectiveness criteria. This unanimity occurred because research results from a wide variety of settings have shown that no one leadership style is optimal for all situations.

The central situational variables theorist has been Fred Fiedler. In his theory the appropriateness of a given leadership style varies as a function of situational variables. To summarize his research findings, Fiedler collapses eight situational patterns into a single dimension: How favorable the situation is for the leader. The situation is most favorable when leader–member relationships are good, when the leader has a substantial amount of position power, and when the task is highly structured. The situation is least favorable when the leader–member relationships are poor, position power is low, and the situation is unstructured. At either of these extremes the more successful leaders are those oriented toward successful task completion. In the center range of the favorability scale, the more successful leaders are those oriented toward successful interpersonal relationships. Although this general finding is based on extensive research in a variety of settings, its value is limited by confusion surrounding the construct validity of Fiedler's measure of leadership style. Even with this limitation, however, most critics concede that Fiedler's research program has demonstrated the viability of the situational approach for the study of leadership style.

In the House and Dessler model we find that Fiedler's three variables have been gathered under one heading, "task/environment characteristics," and that the Hersey and Blanchard variable has been expanded under the heading of "subordinate characteristics" to include a more diverse set of elements. An adequate description of the leader's situation must consider both the characteristics of the subordinates and the nature of the task and the organizational environment.

The situational model suggested by Vroom and Yetton has a more limited intent: the specification of the conditions under which a leader should use five different kinds of decision-making procedures. At one extreme the decision is done autocratically by the leader, while at the opposite extreme the leader presents the problem to the group, acts as a discussion group moderator, and goes along with whatever solution the group recommends. In choosing a decision-making style for a particular decision, the leader must consider situational factors that affect the quality of the decision and situational factors that affect subordinate implementation of the decision.

A different approach to the use of situational variables is one that treats situational characteristics as the independent variables and leadership style as the dependent variable. Within this perspective the leader's behavior is partly *caused* by lateral interdependence with other work units, size of unit, technology, and so forth. In effect, there are situational demands and constraints that limit the leader's choice of behaviors. To the extent that these limitations can be understood, it might be wise to assign persons to situations in which their natural leadership style predispositions are appropriate.

Another major change in leadership-style theory building is the introduction of intervening variables to help understand why a given leadership style might be advantageous in one situation but not in another. Within this framework, leadership styles have an impact on intervening variables that in turn have an impact on effectiveness criteria. This refinement in theory is attractive on at least two counts. First, a leader has more control over an intervening variable such as "subordinate work effort" than on an effectiveness criterion such as "productivity." Second, using intervening variables should help one understand the empirical data generated and, in the absence of empirical results, should offer guidelines for the manager whose behavioral choices cannot be postponed until the research study has finally been tallied.

SUMMARY

From a strictly scientific perspective, the last 50 years of leadership style research have neither produced an abundance of well-established empirical facts nor produced widely accepted leadership style taxonomies or lists of situational variables. From a strictly practical viewpoint, in contrast, a number of perspectives in recent theories have potential value for leaders. If not definite answers, they at least provide constructive ways of thinking about leadership style choices.

LEADERSHIP EFFECTIVENESS
LEADERSHIP SUPERVISION
ORGANIZATIONAL CLIMATE

I. R. ANDREWS

LEADERSHIP TRAINING

Ideally, the training approach begins with a training needs analysis to determine which persons in the organization need to learn what about leadership. This is followed by the design and execution of training programs that fulfill one or more of the identified training needs. Finally, there should be an evaluation of the training programs to see if stated training objectives were achieved. These three steps in leadership training are discussed in turn. At the simplest possible level, training needs analysis is the process of pinpointing the weak areas in the leadership practices of any one individual that might be corrected through training.

To supplement the analysis of behaviors and activities, a variety of situational factors should be studied to determine the kinds of leadership styles appropriate to the leader's current position and probable future positions. Of critical importance in this analysis would be situational factors that affect the kinds of influence styles and the kinds of interpersonal styles that are most appropriate. The person's current capabilities would be compared against position demands to determine training needs. Then, as a final stage in the individual needs analysis, the weak points identified in the preceding steps could be cross-referenced against a checklist of leadership skills, knowledge, and attitudes.

A second approach to leadership training needs analysis begins with the identification of leadership problem areas found in the performance records of the leader population.

The third approach to training needs analysis begins with personnel planning to estimate what kinds of leaders will be needed when and in what quantities. Coupled with that is an assessment of future organizational goals and strategies that affect the kinds of leadership required. Critical here is the anticipation of environmental and technological pressures that could create a need for changes in existing leadership practices.

Once the training needs and priorities have been established, the next step is the design and execution of training programs. What instructional content should be included and what type of learning processes would be optimal for producing the kinds of changes that were defined in the training needs analysis? At present there are no scientific ways to answer either of these two basic questions.

From an academic perspective, training program evaluation surged ahead during the 1970s, possibly as a direct spinoff from a more general interest in all kinds of program-evaluation research. Unfortunately, this rapid progress on the academic side of training evaluation has not been paralleled by changes in what training practitioners do. In surveys of actual practice in industry only 2.5% of the firms consistently attempted to assess the impact of training at the "ultimate objectives" level. Only 6.4% of the firms said that they always attempted to measure behavior changes on the job. Even more remarkable, only 13.4% reported that they always attempted to assess learning at the end of the training period, while 6% reported that they never made any attempt to evaluate training, even at the level of participant reaction to the training.

LEADERSHIP EFFECTIVENESS

I. R. ANDREWS

LEARNED HELPLESSNESS

Learned helplessness is a phenomenon in the area of reactive depression and human task performance, although it was first investigated in research on animals. The term was coined by Martin Seligman and his coworkers. A typical study included two groups of animals, usually dogs. The experimental group was given a series of painful electric shocks while being constrained in a Pavlovian harness; a control group was not shocked. On an ensuing shock-avoidance task, which demanded leaping over a low barrier in a shuttlebox, the control group was found to learn the avoidance response readily, while the experimental group tended simply to endure the pain without trying to escape. This experience left them in a state of learned helplessness: unmotivated to respond in a situation where escape was in fact possible.

The crucial factor in the development of the helpless state seemed to be that the animal's very first experience in the research involved *inescapable* shocks. Seligman viewed the helplessness syndrome as an analogue to the etiology of chronic failure and reactive depression in humans.

Several studies have attempted to apply analogous experimental procedures to human subjects, using much milder aversive stimuli. The typical results of such studies were that the group exposed to the inescapable pretreatment had greater difficulty learning the appropriate avoidance response on the test task (as indicated by more errors and longer response latencies) than did the groups receiving the escapable or control pretreatments.

Other studies have utilized a cognitive test task to demonstrate that helplessness will generalize from one type of situation to another. It has usually been found, as would be predicted from Seligman's notion of a generalized motivational deficit, that subjects pretreated with inescapable shock or loud noise show impaired performance in solving anagram and concept formation problems, in comparison to subjects exposed to escapable or control pretreatments.

Yet another set of investigations has employed cognitive tasks in both the induction and the test phases of the learned helplessness paradigm. Typically, helplessness is induced by providing noncontingent feedback on a concept formation problem, thereby making the problem insoluble. Relative to people receiving pretreatment with soluble problems or to untreated controls, those in the helpless group showed performance deficits on an anagrams test task. The majority of studies of this type, however, have obtained results that deviate to a greater or lesser degree from Seligman's original model for learned helplessness.

Wortman and Brehm argued that helplessness pretreatments, if relatively mild, induce a state of psychological reactance in subjects that motivates efforts at resisting any threat to their control of their environment and so produces a facilitation effect. If the pretreatment is more prolonged or severe, however, control will be perceived as hopelessly lost and coping efforts will be undermined.

Seligman and his associates reformulated the original animal-based model for learned helplessness. Adopting some concepts from attribution theory, the reformulated model notes that a failure to avoid aversive stimuli or to solve concept formation problems on a helplessness-inducing pretest may be attributed to either internal or external factors that, in turn, are anticipated to be either stable or unstable from one situation to the next.

When attributions for failure on a helplessness-inducing pretest are made to unstable factors, one is likely to see renewed efforts at coping on a subsequent task and, very possibly, a facilitation effect rather than learned helplessness. When, in contrast, attributions for failure are made to stable factors, subjects are likely to show the performance deficits on subsequent tasks that are characteristic of learned helplessness. An important distinction remains, however, between helplessness arising from attributions to internal factors and helplessness arising from attributions to external factors: internal attributions for failure are much more likely to lower self-esteem. It is when self-esteem has been lowered by a helplessness-inducing pretreatment that one is particularly likely to observe subsequent deficits in problem solving and effective coping.

Finally, Abramson, Seligman, and Teasdale draw a further distinction between attributions for failure that are "global" versus "specific." A global attribution implies a highly generalized sense of helplessness such that the subject will show impaired coping on tasks and in situations very different from the one that has just produced a failure experience. By contrast, someone making a specific attribution for a failure experience will probably feel helpless only on tasks quite similar to the pretreatment.

The reformulated model has been criticized by Wortman and Dintzer, who noted that it "provides no clear basis for predicting when facilitation effects will occur." Furthermore, two experiments found facilitation effects in conditions predicted to produce the strongest deficits.

Some investigators have suggested that the physiology arousing properties of helplessness-inducing pretreatments may provide yet another theoretical avenue toward resolving contradictions in both the animal and human literature on this topic. Researchers have verified that subjects exposed to uncontrollable, as opposed to controllable, aversive stimulation show evidence of greater arousal on both physiological and self-report measures.

Two personality characteristics have been studied extensively as factors that may contribute to someone's susceptibility to learned helplessness. One of these is generalized expectancies for internal versus external control of reinforcement. Hiroto reported that externals showed a greater impairment of performance following a helplessness-inducing pretreatment than did internals. Gregory and others reasoned that internals, because of their strong need to control their environment, are quite disturbed by feedback indicating a lack of control, whereas externals, who do not believe they have much influence over events in the first place, are better able to tolerate failure feedback with equanimity.

The other personality characteristic that has received a great deal of attention in the learned helplessness literature is depression, typically measured by using a paper-and-pencil scale devised by A. T. Beck. Seligman and his associates have demonstrated that chronically depressed individuals show performance deficits in laboratory settings comparable to those shown by normally nondepressed subjects in a temporary state of learned helplessness. From these and other observations, Seligman concluded that depressed patients believe or have learned that they cannot control those elements of their lives that relieve suffering, bring gratification, or provide nurture—in short, they believe that they are helpless.

ANXIETY
DEPRESSION

W. SAMUEL

LEARNING CURVES

Progress in learning reflects itself in a number of different ways: increases in the rate, probability of occurrence, speed and vigor of responding, decreases in latency (time required to initiate a response), time required to complete a task, and number of errors committed in doing so. These changes in performance are frequently presented in one of a variety of forms called *learning curves,* in which the baseline is most often the number of practice trials but occasionally is time. The vertical axis represents one of the measures just mentioned.

The different measures of learning behave in different ways if the learning involves practice. Amplitude, probability of occurrence, speed of responding, and rate curves show an increase; latencies and other time measures decrease. Probability and percentage of response curves often show a double inflection. Because conditioned responses sometimes do not appear until after several reinforcements, the first portion of the curve may be flat. This portion is followed by a positively accelerated increase, which is soon replaced by a negatively accelerated one, as a maximum is approached.

Most learning curves are for groups of subjects, rather than for individuals. For many purposes this creates a problem, especially in experiments where subjects are run to some criterion such as 100% conditioning in a block of trials. Different subjects will take different numbers of trials to reach the criterion, and it becomes difficult to find a baseline against which to plot the response measures to represent the course of acquisition. One solution to this problem is in the use of the *Vincent curve*. The total number of trials required for each subject to reach the criterion is divided into fractional parts such as tenths, and measures are plotted for these portions. This method makes it possible to combine data for subjects whose performances differ widely.

Unfortunately, this and other procedures for combining data may distort the picture of acquisition presented by the learning curve. For one thing, the typical performance of individual subjects in a learning experiment is irregular, showing chance upward and downward excursions. To select the first point at which a subject reaches some arbitrary level as the criterion of learning is very often to stop the learning session at a point that is accidentally high. This fact accounts for at least some of the end spurts obtained in Vincentized data. These appear as rather sudden increases in the final segment of practice. It now seems that they often occur as *criterion artifacts*, because the experiment is terminated after a series of unusually good performances.

CLASSICAL CONDITIONING
OPERANT CONDITIONING

G. A. KIMBLE

LEARNING DISABILITIES

If an individual does not benefit from a regular education program and is not socially disadvantaged, intellectually limited, or pedagogically deprived, and shows no evidence for hard sign neurophysiological dysfunction, that individual is characterized as learning disabled. If an individual has difficulty communicating either expressively or receptively, and cannot read or do mathematics within the criterion range established by the school district, that individual is similarly considered to be learning disabled.

The lack of precision in evidence for this characterization of the learning disabled reflects the confusion found in clinical and educational settings. Concern over learning disabilities is widespread and has become a major field of interest in neurology, education, psychology, and medicine. The disability may be specific to reading or generalized to all cognitive areas. It may be present with or without behavioral, social, or motor problems. In short, learning disabilities are idiosyncratic: Each case is symptom-specific. Major concerns for any professional are the appropriate diagnostic and remedial/compensatory programs.

Estimates of the frequency of learning disabilities vary dramatically because of the lack of precise definition, but the following guidelines seem to hold internationally for the literate population: 2 to 4% show signs of severe disability in interpreting text, communicating verbally, and writing, while another 3 to 5% show substantial difficulty with specific areas such as reading (dyslexia), writing (dysgraphia), and math (dyscalculia). In contrast, readers who do poorly because of intellectual limitations or poor skill acquisition can account for as much as 15% of the population; although candidates for remedial aid, they are not considered to be learning disabled. Loose criteria also hinder the accumulations of more accurate statistics on frequency. Learning disabilities are known to be distributed equally across age, socioeconomic status, intellectual levels, and throughout all literate cultures.

In line with the limits of specifying the disability as expressed previously, the following characteristics may or may not be present in any one individual. First, there may be difficulties with receptive or expressive language. There may also be verbal and nonverbal thought disruption (nonpsychopathological).

Memory deficits, especially in short-term memory, can be found in many learning disabled persons. *Perceptual* and *cognitive deficits,* such as reversal and poor discrimination of letters, failure to group and categorize similar items, and poor problem-solving skills are common. When perceptual or cognitive deficits are identified, they should be separated from attentional deficits or the failure to stay on tasks to completion. Although the latter deficits are susceptible to behavioral change, the former are not, but the perceptual and cognitive deficits may be eliminated as the attentional deficits are remediated.

In addition to the frequently occurring perceptual, cognitive, linguistic, and neurological dysfunctions, the learning disabled also frequently show signs of social and emotional disorders. Because most of these children become separated in some way for at least some time during each day from their regular classroom activity, they begin to feel "different." It is not unusual for the learning disabled adult or child to have a poor self-image, self-concept, and self-esteem; to lack the will to pursue tasks because of the difficulties present; to show numerous psychosomatic disorders; and to withdraw from social contact. Others may overcompensate by becoming disruptive in whatever class they are in, being quarrelsome toward peers or classmates and delinquent toward society. Hyperactivity is frequent among the learning disabled and also proves disruptive to staying on task. Behavior training has been found to be effective if the hyperactive behavior is nonorganic, otherwise both Ritalin and Pemoline (Cylert) prove effective and do not interfere intellectually.

Because of the complexity of the syndromes evidenced in learning disorders, it is especially important to remove professional isolation. An interprofessional assessment would include a history of the individual and family; a physical and neurological exam; a psychological assessment including an intellectual, perceptual, and personality profile; and an educational program development.

In 1977, Public Law 94-142 was put into effect. A landmark event, it guaranteed equal educational opportunity to all disabled persons ages 0 to 21 years. The law also defined learning disabilities as a handicap and mandated that the states and their subdivisions provide the necessary services. Although implementation was a slow process owing to politics, economics, and redefining issues, more learning disabled persons are being identified and are receiving necessary services than ever before.

Because of the law, early detection of "high-risk" children is enhancing knowledge of remediation and compensation; new directions are being taken toward implosive verbal exposure; and alternate means of communication such as oral reports are being encouraged. Similarly, counseling toward appropriate career goals and college curricula aimed at the learning disabled student are becoming more frequent.

EDUCATIONAL ASSESSMENT
MINIMAL BRAIN DYSFUNCTION
SCHOOL LEARNING

D. F. FISHER

LEARNING OUTCOMES: AN EDITORIAL NOTE

As is the case with *transpersonal psychology,* this subject is in our judgment so important and has so wide a scope that two different treatments are indicated. There is relatively little overlap in the two versions. We believe that the reader, by reading and contrasting both, will obtain a much fuller and more accurate understanding of this topic.

R. J. CORSINI
A. AUERBACH

LEARNING OUTCOMES, I

The primary means of indicating that learning has occurred is to show that some newly appearing human performances are possible, when required by appropriate circumstances. The inferences that can be made from these changes in performance are to the effect that individuals have acquired some new entities in their long-term memory store—entities not present before the learning occurred. The outcomes of learning, then, are neural states that persist over considerable periods of time, as shown by tests of retention. Because the effects of these states are to make individuals persistently capable of exhibiting particular kinds of performance, it is reasonable to think of them as *learned capabilities*.

DIFFERENCES IN LEARNED CAPABILITIES

From a broad and practical view, it is of considerable help in defining the boundaries of knowledge in the field of human learning to distinguish some principal types of learning outcomes. The latter clearly differ from one another in the performances they make possible. They differ too in important respects in the specific conditions optimal for their learning. Presumably, they also differ in the nature of the cognitive structures that represent them in long-term memory.

VARIETIES OF LEARNING OUTCOMES

On the basis of the criteria previously described, five kinds of learned capabilities may be distinguished.

1. *Verbal knowledge (declarative knowledge).* This kind of knowledge ranges from single names and labels through isolated "facts" to bodies of organized information. The kind of performance made possible by such knowledge *is stating* (declaring) orally, in writing, or in some other medium.

2. *Intellectual skills (procedural knowledge).* These capabilities enable the individual, by manipulation of symbols, to demonstrate the application of concepts and rules to specific instances. The distinction between "knowing that" (declarative knowledge) and "knowing how" (procedural knowledge) was given prominence by the philosopher Gilbert Ryle.

3. *Cognitive strategies.* These are skills used to direct and influence cognitive processes such as attending, perceiving, encoding, retrieving, and thinking. Cognitive strategies of problem solving were studied in concept-identification tasks by Bruner, Goodnow, and Austin. More recently, the effects of cognitive strategies in controlling or modifying other cognitive processes of learning and memory, such as attention, encoding, and retrieval, have been studied extensively. When taught to and deliberately employed by learners, such strategies constitute a major aspect of what is called *metacognition*.

4. *Attitudes.* This fourth kind of learning outcome is generally considered to possess affective as well as cognitive memory components. Attitudes are learned states that influence the choices of personal action the individual makes toward persons, objects, or events.

5. *Motor skills.* Learning outcomes sometimes consist of actions accomplished by smoothly timed muscular movements called motor skills. Most motor skills involve performing procedures, sometimes lengthy ones. The procedure itself may be simple or complex and has been called the *executive subroutine.* This procedure may be learned separately or as an early stage of acquiring the motor skill. Learning the motor skill itself is a matter of acquiring increasing smoothness and precise timing of muscular movement. Often, the executive subroutine has the function of molding part skills into a total skill.

RELATION OF LEARNING OUTCOMES TO THE SCHOOL CURRICULUM

The outcomes of school learning are usually stated as curricula, composed of subject-matter contents such as reading, writing, mathematics, science, history, and so forth. Each of these subjects usually includes more than one category of learning outcome. Thus, arithmetic is made up largely of intellectual skills, but includes also some essential verbal knowledge about situations in which quantitative concepts are applicable.

Clearly, the five kinds of learning outcomes—verbal knowledge, intellectual skills, cognitive strategies, attitudes, and motor skills—cut across the traditional subject matters of the school curriculum. Each content subject typically seeks to establish more than one kind of capability in students. To achieve optimally effective learning, as well as optimally efficient management of learning, the design of instruction in each subject-matter field must take into account the different requirements of each type of learning outcome.

RELATION TO OTHER TAXONOMIES

Perhaps the best-known taxonomy of learning objectives is that proposed by Bloom and his coworkers. Although the categories described in this article have been independently derived from a different theoretical base, they show great similarity to Bloom's topics and are in most respects compatible. The three major strands of the Bloom taxonomy are the *cognitive domain,* the *affective domain,* and the *psychomotor domain.*

CONDITIONS OF LEARNING FAVORABLE FOR EACH OUTCOME

From learning research and theory, it is possible to specify with reasonable assurance the conditions favorable to the learning that lead to each outcome. These conditions differ somewhat in each case, and the existence of these differences provides a major reason for distinguishing among learning outcomes in designing instruction.

Verbal Knowledge

A number of lines of evidence support the theoretical contention that *prior knowledge* is of great assistance to the learning of new knowledge. The precise nature of the relation between old knowledge and new—in the sense that the former aids the learning and retention of the latter—is presently a matter of active investigation. A second factor of importance for optimal learning is the *organization* of the instructional communication (or other stimulus), which affects the process of encoding. The inclusion of *contextual* cues at the time new knowledge is learned is another condition favoring retention of that knowledge.

Intellectual Skill

The primary condition affecting the learning of intellectual skills is the *accessibility of prerequisite skills.* In contrast to the case of verbal knowledge, these subordinate skills are related to the new skill to be learned as components. The implication is that instruction for optimal learning requires the precise identification of these prerequisite skills, by methods of task analysis. A second condition affecting the retention of intellectual skills is *spaced review* and *practice.* Many basic skills prerequisite to skilled performance in reading, writing, and arithmetic, apparently need to be practiced to the level of automaticity.

Cognitive Strategies

Because cognitive strategies are a type of skill, one might expect optimal conditions for learning to be similar to those for intellectual skills. In a sense this is the case: Prerequisite skills must be mastered for cognitive strategies to be learned. However, the prerequisite skills of strategies are often extremely simple, well practiced, and readily accessible. Many strategies of attending, learning, retrieving, and problem solving can be conveyed (or retrieved) by means of a *brief verbal communication.* Some strategies of problem solving, however, do not appear to persist unless *practiced in a variety of contexts.* Recognition of this fact leads the designers of instruction to suggest that students be given frequent opportunities to solve novel problems.

Attitudes

Although attitudes may be acquired in numerous ways from the experiences of living, it appears that the most dependable deliberate arrangement of conditions for optimal learning involves the technique of *human modeling.* The human model can be an actual human being, a pictured person, or even a printed description. It is most desirable for the model to be perceived by the learners as admirable, credible, and powerful. The procedure leading to attitude learning or modification, according to Bandura, includes two steps: The model (a) communicates or demonstrates the choice of action reflecting the target attitude and (b) is seen to experience satisfaction and be rewarded for this action choice (vicarious reinforcement). Subsequently, additional strength of attitude can presumably be attained when the learners themselves are reinforced for their choices of personal action.

Motor Skills

The learning of a motor skill often begins, as Fitts and Posner point out, with the acquisition of a cognitive component (actually, an intellectual skill) called the *executive subroutine.* This is the procedural part of the skill. Sometimes separate practice is undertaken of *part skills.* The various components of a complex motor skill come together in *practice of the total skill.* Indeed, it is practice and practice alone that brings attainment of the smoothly timed action that is recognized as a motor skill.

DISCOVERY LEARNING
EPISTEMOLOGY
LEARNING THEORIES

R. M. GAGNÉ

LEARNING OUTCOMES, II

The term *outcome* broadly refers to what an individual has learned as a result of having been engaged in a learning activity of some kind. Within different research perspectives, however, the term takes on a more precise meaning that varies in crucial ways from one perspective to another. These variations, and the assumptions that underlie them, can be examined in relation to *traditional, neo-Piagetian,* and *phenomenographic* research perspectives.

THE TRADITIONAL PERSPECTIVE AND ITS SHORTCOMINGS

Within traditional research on learning the outcome of learning is neutral in content and quantitative in character. The experimental procedure commonly followed is to investigate the effect of one or more independent variables on a dependent variable specified in advance. If the resultant findings are in accord with hypotheses derived from a theory, the validity of that theory has been supported.

In all these experiments the dependent variable is in a quantitative form that makes the content of learning invisible; of no interest in itself, it is there simply because there cannot be any learning without a content of some kind. These two aspects of the conventional paradigm of research on learning—the quantitative nature of the dependent variable and the

instrumental character of the content of learning—are logically related to a third and superordinate aspect: the aim of arriving at general (and content-neutral) statements about learning, applicable to any kind of subject matter.

Whether this approach is a reasonable basis for psychological research on learning, its relevance to the educational context is questionable. A school is not concerned only with students' acquisition of information and skills: One of its *main* tasks—indeed, many would argue, the main task—is to shape and change pupils' ways of thinking. Thus, schooling should facilitate a transition from common-sense notions of the surrounding world to conceptions more in line with scientific ways of thinking.

The history of science clearly shows that the conceptual frameworks of every scientific discipline have repeatedly gone through radical qualitative shifts, while research on cognitive development points to restructurings of the maturing child's reality that are similar, even if less obvious in their everyday context. To describe outcomes of learning in this particular sense, it is necessary to discover what qualitatively different conceptions of the content of learning are apparent after the teaching/learning process has occurred. To describe the preconditions of learning, it is necessary to find out what qualitatively different preconceived ideas the learners have about the content they will encounter.

In this alternative interpretation, then, *outcomes of learning* are defined as the qualitatively different ways of understanding the content of learning. In what follows, two alternative approaches to this problem will first be examined in turn and then discussed in relation to each other.

A NEO-PIAGETIAN APPROACH

If learning is conceptualized as was previously described, the distinction commonly made between learning and development becomes somewhat difficult to maintain. Transitions between qualitatively different ways of thinking represent the well-known Piagetian view of cognitive development. It seems easy to understand that the most widespread approach to the description of outcomes of learning has been based on the extension of Piagetian thinking into various subject-matter domains.

It is important to note that these researchers consider their work as studies less of learning than of development. Levels of thinking in different content areas were conceptualized as resulting from the application of general operatory structures to those domains. This was held to be true in both an epistemological and an ontological sense. The former refers to the expectation that the researcher will be able to discern the levels of thinking in a particular content domain by applying the description of the general Piagetian stages to that domain. In contrast, if students exhibit a certain level of thinking in relation to a particular content, they are interpreted as having applied the general operatory structures characteristic for the corresponding stage of development to that particular content.

Research has, however, cast doubt on the validity of this line of reasoning. Flavell and Hundeide among others have summarized many investigations challenging the notion of stages and content-free mental structures.

It is nonetheless important to acknowledge what has been achieved. The assumption of stage-related mental structures may not be warranted, in light of the empirical evidence now available of variation in performance on tasks that differ in content and context but are structurally similar. Yet the differences in thinking described are of great interest in themselves, whether the differences are stable across varying contexts and subject matter or not.

Biggs and Collis consider the different levels of thinking identified in these domains as outcomes of learning rather than development-related phenomena. The name they gave to their model of description—SOLO (Structure of the Observed Learning Outcomes)—reflects this. According to these authors, mastering a skill or a knowledge domain can be viewed as a miniature development that can be described in terms of transitions between qualitatively different levels of thinking.

If a group of students who have been dealing with a certain content is observed, it is likely that different students will have advanced to different points. The qualitatively different levels of thinking observed will then appear as qualitative differences (between individuals) in the outcome of learning.

The five general levels of thinking described by Biggs and Collis are as follows:

1. *Prestructural.* A nonexistent, irrelevant, or otherwise inadequate attempt to learn a component is made.

2. *Unistructural.* One relevant component is acquired.

3. *Multistructural.* Several relevant components are acquired, but additively and independently of each other.

4. *Relational.* The components become functionally or conceptually interdependent.

5. *Extended abstract.* The integrated components become part of a more general case, which in fact forms a new mode.

These five levels of thinking correspond to Collis' modification of Piaget's stages: preoperational, early concrete, middle concrete, concrete generalization (originally, early formal), and formal. Biggs and Collis argue that the characteristics that a certain individual's thinking exhibits on various tasks may vary widely, but that the characteristics themselves (in the sense of categories of description) are applicable to the various tasks regardless of content.

A PHENOMENOGRAPHIC APPROACH

The third perspective originates mainly from the work of a Swedish research group. Marton has argued that description of the qualitatively different ways in which people experience, conceptualize, perceive, and understand various aspects of the world around them should be considered as an autonomous scientific specialization, termed *phenomenography.* The arguments for seeing this as an autonomous field of concern are twofold. First, categories of description that characterize people's notions about reality are considered to be of interest in themselves—not the least in educational contexts. Second, such categories cannot be derived from more general properties of the human mind, but must be investigated in their own right.

The relevance of phenomenography to research on learning stems from the conceptualization of learning as a change between qualitatively different ways of understanding a phenomenon or an aspect of reality as contrasted with, for instance, a conceptualization of learning as a memorization of something read or as an acquisition of facts, details, and so on. Because phenomenography is concerned with discerning the different ways in which we understand aspects of the world around us, learning is seen as a transition between phenomenographic categories.

In general, phenomenography offers an alternative way of describing both effects and preconditions of learning and teaching. It aims at making explicit *what* (conception) is changed to *what* (conception). By pinpointing levels of conceptions of fundamental aspects of reality, it identifies a possible dimension of change, and by revealing the everyday ideas about the content of learning and teaching that the students bring with them to the school situation, it increases the likelihood of change.

SIMILARITIES AND DIFFERENCES BETWEEN THE TWO ALTERNATIVE APPROACHES

As pointed out earlier, within both a neo-Piagetian and a phenomenographic approach, learning is conceptualized as a transition between qualitatively different forms of thought and is thus seen as a miniature develop-

ment. In a normal school situation it seems quite reasonable to expect that, at the time of a particular observation, different students have advanced to different levels. The outcome of learning will thus be described in terms of qualitative differences. Furthermore, in relation to both ways of describing qualitative differences in the outcome of learning, some correlates have been found in the differing ways in which students set about the learning tasks that account for those differences. Biggs has identified three independent dimensions in study process: utilizing, internalizing, and achieving. The students' ways of studying were found to be highly correlated with learning outcomes.

In spite of these obvious similarities, there is an important difference between the two sets of studies that has to do with the role of content. Biggs and Collis use a general structural model as a point of departure. As the actual content varies in different instances, the realization of categories also will, of course, vary on a concrete level. The structural properties are considered to remain the same, however. Furthermore, they form an explicit hierarchy, as the notion of levels would suggest.

The phenomenographic approach is radically content-oriented because deriving categories of description in relation to various contents of learning is considered to be the main task. The different categories may or may not form a hierarchy in a particular case (of content).

In the SOLO-model the description of outcomes of learning takes the form of the application of the general model to new content domains, while in phenomenography each new phenomenon, concept, or principle studied requires the discovery of the qualitatively different ways in which that particular phenomenon, concept, or principle is thought about, experienced, or "lived."

EPISTEMOLOGY
LEARNING STYLES
STRUCTURAL LEARNING THEORY

F. I. MARTON

LEARNING STRATEGIES

Learning strategies are methods people use to learn and retain information. They are usually effortful and under the learner's cognitive or conscious control.

MNEMONICS

Mnemonics facilitate the learning and recall of difficult material. Several of these are based on verbal mediation strategies in which two words or ideas are associated by a word or a phrase (the verbal mediator) that links them. For example, assume one is attempting to learn the German word *Handschuh,* which means "glove." A useful verbal mediator might be to think of glove as a "shoe for the hand."

Other useful mnemonic strategies use visual imagery to some degree. The best known is the method of loci. This strategy was developed by the ancient Greeks and consists of (a) identification of familiar places (e.g., rooms in a house) sequentially arranged, (b) generation of images of the item to be remembered that are then associated with the places, and (c) recall of the items by revisiting the places (e.g., the great room). Other useful image-based mnemonics are the pegword system and the keyword method.

REHEARSAL

Rehearsal is the extended repetition of information after it has been presented (e.g., the telephone number to call for a tow truck). Early stage theories of memory assumed that the more an item is rehearsed in short-term memory (STM) the more likely it will be transferred into

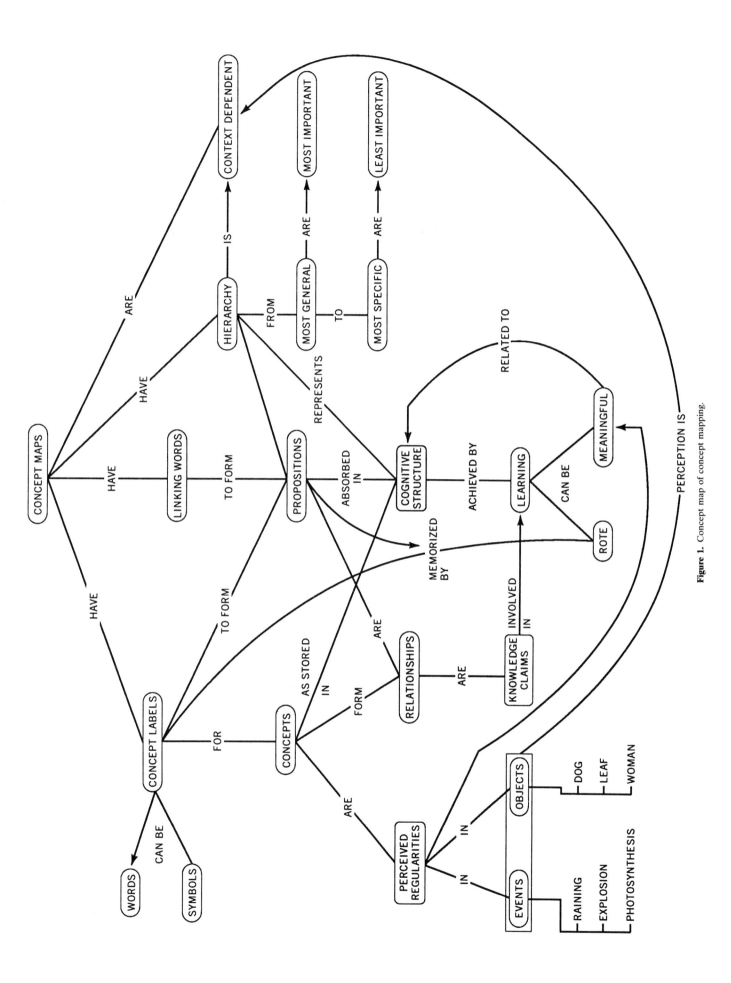

Figure 1. Concept map of concept mapping.

long-term memory (LTM). If a person holds the information in STM but does little more, it is called maintenance rehearsal. This is not effective in the long run. If an individual's car is broken down on the highway, the owner uses maintenance rehearsal just long enough to call the telephone number of a garage given to him or her by Information. For long-term retention of material, a person must engage in elaborative rehearsal strategies in which material is actively reorganized in STM in relation to material stored in LTM. Although the next two topics, internal organization and semantic elaboration, could be viewed as types of elaborative rehearsal, they are discussed separately.

INTERNAL ORGANIZATION

Organizational strategies are effective schemes that can be used to improve LTM. Typically, they involve the tendency to group material into categories or chunks for later recall. In a classic study, Bower, Clark, Lesgold, and Winzenz gave college students 112 words to learn. The words fell into four categories (plants, minerals, etc.) and the students were given four trials to learn them. For some students, the words were presented in random order, while for others, the words were arranged in the four conceptual hierarchies (i.e., a separate hierarchy for each category). The students presented with hierarchically organized lists remembered all 112 items whereas those who received no organization only remembered 70 items.

SEMANTIC ELABORATION

Semantic elaboration can be seen as a form of cognitive construction. It is a process of creating meaning by using new information and a person's existing knowledge base to construct a meaningful interpretation of that new information. Many theorists believe that information is organized based on schemata that are generalized knowledge structures used for understanding and learning information. A special type of schema called a script is an organized behavioral scenario used in particular contexts (e.g., a restaurant script whose sequence can include being seated, looking at a menu, ordering a meal, paying the bill, and leaving a tip). When an individual eats at a Japanese restaurant for the first time, the restaurant script can be called up to let him or her understand the context, although modifications of the script (e.g., sitting on the floor) have to be made.

Although schemata and/or scripts are developed from experience, recent methods have been developed that help people develop complex knowledge structures by externalizing them. One of these methods is concept mapping. Basically, a concept map is a graphic representation of the relationships between concepts held by an individual, materials of a lecture, textbook, and so forth. These concepts are linked together in a hierarchical system of propositions (concepts linked together by words that relate them). Figure 1 shows a concept map on concept maps. Concept maps help the student identify, understand, and organize the concepts to be learned.

Maps can be used to help learners comprehend their existing knowledge and help them relate new concepts to those they already know. As new learning continues to occur, it is strengthened because it is incorporated into the existing framework, which changes over time with the incorporation of new concepts and relations.

If the material has little meaning but is necessary or difficult to remember (e.g., an address), then rote rehearsal is useful. Different mnemonic techniques work well for some types of material, whereas other mnemonic methods work well for other material. For example, for serial learning, the method of loci works well, whereas for paired-associate learning, imagery mediation appears to be superior. For more meaningful material that will be used in the future, some type of semantic elaboration should be used.

B. R. DUNN

LEARNING THEORIES

Learning theories seek to organize existing findings about learning in an elegant manner and guide the search for new and important findings. In the case of learning theories, the findings on which the theories are based concern the conditions that bring about and maintain behavioral change as a result of the experience of the individual organism.

Although some differences among learning theories arise from variations in the emphasis given different findings, most of the differences originate in disagreements about how best to interpret a common set of findings. The theoretical approach self-described as the experimental analysis of behavior attempts to organize findings on the behavioral level without appeal to either hypothetical processes or physiological events. However, many learning theorists take exception to an account of learning that confines itself to the behavioral level. Three circumstances are often cited as problematic. First, the time interval between behavior and its antecedents may be quite large. To span this gap, some theorists hypothesize enduring entities such as habits or memories that intervene between the observable antecedent of the appointment and the subsequent action. Second, we often behave differently in what appears to be the same environment. Unobserved states of the organism, often called motivations, are hypothesized to account for the observed behavioral differences. Lastly, complex evolutionary and individual environmental histories permit highly skilled responses in the absence of observable behavioral intermediaries. In such circumstances, the prior environments necessary for the skill and the events that intervene between the problem and its answer are largely unobserved. Confronted with limited knowledge of the events that predate the observed behavior and ignorance of the intervening neural events, unobserved cognitive processes are hypothesized to account for the behavior.

Because of these three circumstances, most theories of learning propose hypothetical processes—usually called intervening variables—that intervene between observable environmental and behavioral events. The theories differ among themselves, however, in the precise nature of these intervening variables. Although learning theories deal with a number of issues, the present discussion focuses on one topic: the nature of reinforcement.

EXPERIMENTAL ANALYSIS OF BEHAVIOR

Two procedures whereby behavioral change may be brought about are recognized in the experimental analysis of behavior: respondent conditioning and operant conditioning. In respondent conditioning—more commonly referred to by other theoretical perspectives as classical or Pavlovian conditioning—a neutral stimulus is regularly followed by another stimulus that already elicits a response. As a result of this sequence of events, the formerly ineffective stimulus comes to evoke a response that may closely resemble the elicited response. Although respondent conditioning plays an important role in learning, particularly of emotional responses, most learning involves operant conditioning.

In operant conditioning the reinforcer occurs following a response. The response on which the reinforcer is dependent (technically, contingent) is called an operant, because it operates on the environment to produce the reinforcer. Operant conditioning is thought to play the more important role in human behavior because, by progressively altering the response on which the reinforcer is contingent, it is possible to develop new and more complex operants. This process is called shaping the operant.

For the experimental analysis of behavior as it was developed by B. F. Skinner, a reinforcer was simply a stimulus that, when placed into the relationships specified by respondent and operant conditioning procedures, increased the subsequent likelihood of behavior.

Skinner explored the implications of reinforcement for human behavior more systematically than any other theorist. In this pursuit he tried to avoid the introduction of new processes not potentially observable in some form in conditioning experiments from the animal learning laboratory. His accounts of complex behavior assume that the often incompletely observed and subtle behavior of humans conforms to the same principles as do fully observable behaviors.

INTERVENING VARIABLE THEORIES

Because of the three problems of memory, motivation, and cognition, most learning theorists have supplemented Skinner's experimental analysis of environmental and behavioral variables with intervening variables. Intervening variables are conceptual constructs whose meaning is defined by their relationship to many environmental variables whose common effects they are intended to summarize.

Tolman's Expectancy Theory

Thorndike, influenced by Darwin's evolutionary premise of continuity among the species, began the transition to a less mentalistic psychology. Finally, John B. Watson urged the elimination of mentalistic concepts altogether. Under the influence of this thinking, Tolman substituted logically defined intervening variables for the earlier philosophical mentalisms.

Regarding the focus of this discussion (reinforcement), Tolman did not follow E. L. Thorndike's lead. Thorndike had viewed the consequences of responding as essential to strengthening the associative bond between stimulus and response. He called this forerunner of modern reinforcement theory the law of effect. Tolman believed that the consequences of a response did not affect learning *per se,* but only the overt expression of the underlying learning processes. The distinction between learning and performance arose as an interpretation of latent learning experiments. The intervening variable reflecting learning was variously labeled as the theory developed, but may be termed an *expectancy.* The expectancy was dependent solely on the temporal succession—or contiguity—of environmental events, and not on the consequences of responding.

Pavlov's Physiological Theory

For Pavlov, as for Tolman, contiguity between events was sufficient for learning. The events were inferred processes in the brain corresponding to the areas activated by the neutral stimulus and the eliciting stimulus. The evolutionary consequences of the learned response were acknowledged, but were not experimentally manipulated, hence their role in learning was unclear.

Guthrie's Molecular Theory

Like Tolman and Pavlov, and unlike Thorndike, Edwin R. Guthrie viewed contiguity as sufficient for learning. However, the temporally contiguous events were not broadly defined (i.e., molar) environmental events as Tolman had held. Each molar environmental event was assumed to be composed of many molecular stimulus elements that Guthrie called "cues." Each molar behavior, which Guthrie called an "act," was composed of many molecular responses called "movements." When a cue was contiguously paired with a movement, the movement became completely conditioned to that cue. The learning of a behavioral act developed slowly only because most acts required the learning of many constituent movements in the presence of many specific cues.

Hull's Drive-Reduction Theory

The use of intervening variables in learning theory reached its most extensive development in the work of Clark L. Hull. Like Guthrie, Hull attempted to provide a common interpretation of the behavioral changes produced by both the classical and operant procedures. Both stimulus–response contiguity and drive reduction were necessary components of Hull's concept of reinforcement.

When the conditions for learning were met, the intervening variable—habit—was affected. Habit was a logically defined construct that summarized the common effect of several environmental variables on several behavioral variables. The relationships between the environmental variables and the intervening variable of habit, and then between habit and behavior, were both expressed by algebraic equations. Although some of his intervening variables employed physiological terms in their statement, Hull's experimental work and theorizing were almost exclusively at the behavioral level. Kenneth W. Spence, his collaborator in much of his theory construction, was especially careful to define intervening variables in purely logical terms.

SUBSEQUENT DEVELOPMENTS

Although none of the intervening variable theories emerged unchanged into the latter half of the century, two of their characteristics influenced subsequent theorizing: The subsequent theories are typically quantitative and they deal with a circumscribed range of content—that is, they are "miniature" theories.

Hull's theory was a first step toward a quantitative theory of behavior, but its algebraic equations did little more than state the concepts concisely. Estes developed the first truly mathematical learning theories. Other quantitative theories, instead of drawing on probability theory and mathematical statistics, were informed primarily by information processing or computer models.

Within intervening variable theories, the most significant contribution to a reinforcement principle has come from the empirical work of Leon J. Karnin and the related theoretical work of Robert A. Rescorla and Alan R. Wagner. Using a classical conditioning procedure, a neutral stimulus contiguous with an otherwise effective reinforcer does not acquire control over a response if the neutral stimulus is accompanied by another stimulus that already evokes the response. On the behavioral level, some discrepancy between the response elicited by the reinforcer and the response occurring during the neutral stimulus must supplement contiguity if learning is to occur. The precise nature of the discrepant event has yet to be identified.

Within the experimental analysis of behavior, theoretical work has also become more quantitative, although it uses primarily deterministic rather than probabilistic systems. Following work with a single reinforced response, the theory has been extended to more than one reinforced response and to interactions of reinforced responses with other responses. Stated most broadly, these theories depict reinforcers as causing a reallocation of the organism's responses among the possible behavioral alternatives. The resulting reallocation minimizes the change from the allocation prior to the institution of the operant contingency and is sensitive to the momentary probability of reinforcement for each response. There is reason to believe that the work by intervening variable theorists on classical conditioning and by experimental analysts on operant conditioning is converging on a common understanding of reinforcement in which behavior changes so as to minimize the net discrepancies associated with all eliciting stimuli present in the environment.

CLASSICAL CONDITIONING
LEARNING OUTCOMES I, II
LEAST PREFERRED COWORKER SCALE
OPERANT CONDITIONING
REINFORCEMENT SCHEDULES
THORNDIKE'S LAWS OF LEARNING
TWO-PROCESS LEARNING THEORY

J. W. DONAHOE

LEARY INTERPERSONAL CHECKLIST

Timothy Leary discussed the development of a classification system of interpersonal behavior that consisted of a circular array of 16 variables demarcated by two perpendicular axes termed *affiliation* and *power*. One end of the affiliation axis was labeled hostility and the opposite end, affection. The opposing ends of the power axis were labeled dominance and submission. These two divided the circle into quadrants that in turn, were divided into octants, labeled as follows: Aggressive–Sadistic, Competitive–Narcissistic, Managerial–Autocratic, Responsible–Hypernormal, Overconventional–Cooperative, Dependent–Docile, Masochistic–Self-Effacing, and Distrustful–Rebellious. The circular array was further differentiated by developing four levels of intensity for each variable. For instance, the hostility end of the affiliation axis was viewed in terms of the critical, angry, furious, and enraged levels.

An average test–retest reliability for each octant was reported as 0.78, which suggests an adequate degree of internal consistency for personality research. Intervariable correlations have also been examined to determine whether the relationships among the 16 variables can be described in terms of a circle. It was found that the correlation between variables decreased as variables that are farther from each other with respect to their placement on the circle are correlated. This finding supported the hypothesized circular arrangement.

PERSONALITY ASSESSMENT

G. K. LOCKWOOD

LEAST PREFERRED COWORKER SCALE

The least preferred coworker (LPC) scale is a self-report questionnaire made up of a series of semantic differential items such as pleasant/unpleasant, friendly/unfriendly, and rejecting/accepting. The respondent uses the scale to describe the coworker with whom "you can work least well."

The high LPC leader uses positive adjectives to describe the least preferred coworker, while the low LPC leader uses the low end. In comparison, the high LPC leader separates the personality of the individual from task performance, while the low LPC leader does not.

Fiedler designed and uses the LPC score to predict whether a leader will be effective in a work environment. Fiedler predicts that low LPC leaders will be most effective in strongly favorable and strongly unfavorable environments. The high LPC individual is predicted to be a more effective leader in moderate environments.

The LPC scale has been criticized for being unreliable and situationally dependent. Answers on the scale are strongly affected by one's present leadership situation.

EMPLOYEE ATTITUDE SURVEYS

L. BERGER

LEISURE COUNSELING

Leisure counseling emerged as a specialty within the counseling profession only during the 1970s, with its own literature, professional journals, and practitioners. It as yet lacks a substantive theoretical base and solid research support for its concepts, although these are beginning to appear. Leisure counseling has been the province of two professional groups, those concerned with leisure studies (including therapeutic recreation) and those concerned with counseling. There has been a tendency to perceive leisure behavior as a matter of choosing activities, rather than looking at leisure from the point of view of the psychological *meaning* of these activities for the individual.

The recent interest in leisure counseling can in part be traced to increasing affluence in Western Europe and North America, and the decline of the Protestant Ethic as a source of individual and societal values. Whereas in previous times of scarcity, work was extolled and leisure denigrated, we are now increasingly turning to leisure as a major source of life satisfaction and meaning. This is especially true for those individuals whose work often lacks meaning and intrinsic interest. Unfortunately, it is precisely those people whose leisure activities are often lacking in variety, challenge, and meaning.

DEFINITIONS OF LEISURE

At least four categories of leisure definitions have appeared in the literature, although they overlap conceptually. *Residual definitions* view leisure as what one does in the time left over after the necessary activities of life have been accomplished. *Activity-related definitions* define leisure by the type of activity in which one engages. Certain activities are considered to be leisure and others defined as work, regardless of the context in which they occur.

Work-related definitions of leisure reflect the value structure of the Protestant Work Ethic. The first has been called *complementary*, or *spillover*, in which the nature of one's leisure activities is similar to one's work activities. The second type has been called *supplemental* and refers to leisure activities intentionally chosen to be quite different from those typically engaged in while at work. *Compensatory* leisure refers to activities that are designed to reduce or eliminate stresses or tensions that the individual experiences in daily life.

Psychological definitions of leisure tend to stress the *meaning* of the leisure experience for the individual, rather than the type of activity engaged in or its relation to some other activity. J. Neulinger defines leisure as a state of mind—being at peace with oneself and what one is doing. His concept of leisure revolves around two bipolar constructs: freedom versus constraint and intrinsic versus extrinsic motivation.

NEEDS AND MOTIVES FOR LEISURE

Many personality theorists of diverse orientations note that a basic human task is the development of a sense of competence, mastery, or self-efficacy. It has been found that individuals choose those activities in which they perceive themselves to be competent because participation in such activities elevates one's sense of competence and enhances one's sense of freedom. Furthermore, learning *new* leisure skills (assuming minimal and increasing competency) enhances one's self-concept, whereas practicing already learned skills only maintains one's existing self-concept.

Other needs and motives for leisure have also been found. People appear to be motivated by a need for optimal arousal and incongruity, or what one might call "novelty value." The level of optimal arousal will of course differ from individual to individual, but participation in leisure activities can help satisfy this need for everyone. In addition, leisure is valued to the extent that it provides positive interpersonal involvement.

EMERGING LEISURE PARADIGMS

Several comprehensive treatments of the psychological nature of leisure have recently appeared. McDowell has argued that the leisure experience is characteristic of "right-brain thinking," while work consciousness is characteristic of "left-brain thinking." In addition, he has developed the concept of leisure well-being, which he defines as "an esthetic, enjoyable, satisfying, healthful and dynamic leisure-style." McDowell suggests that leisure well-being involves four key components of self-care: coping, awareness–understanding, knowledge, and assertion.

Seppo E. Iso-Ahola considers the four most important determinants of the perception of an experience as leisure to be (in order of importance) (a) perceived freedom to engage in the activity, (b) intrinsic motivation to engage in the activity, (c) whether the activity is related to daily work, and (d) whether the activity is oriented toward final goals or instrumental goals. There is some evidence that, given an already high level of interest in an activity, expected external rewards for engaging in that activity can actually *reduce* the individual's later engagement in it.

The phenomenon of leisure has also been examined from an attributional point of view. Attribution refers to the process by which a person assigns causes to events, behaviors, and outcomes, in an attempt to construct causal meaning out of situations. Attributions have been found to have three dimensions: internality–externality (whether the cause resides within or outside the individual); stability–instability (whether the cause is stable over time); and globality–specificity (whether the cause is common to many situations). The positive relationship between perceived freedom and internal causality is quite high, therefore individuals tend to define leisure as those activities attributed to internal stable causes.

An internal-unstable attribution for the leisure activity would be made when the individual is engaging in new activities in which competence is sporadic. It would be especially useful in this situation to assist the person in attributing success to internal factors, rather than external factors, so that participation in the activity is maintained and is not labeled as "work."

The global-specific dimension refers to attributions of leisure competence (or incompetence) of oneself in relation to perceived competence of others.

MODELS OF LEISURE COUNSELING

Numerous models of leisure counseling have been proposed in the last few years, organized by Tinsley and Tinsley into three categories: (a) leisure guidance, (b) leisure decision making, and (c) leisure counseling. Leisure guidance models stress information-giving techniques that focus on assisting clients in choosing appropriate leisure activities that are interesting to them. In leisure decision-making models, the focus is still on assisting the client in choosing appropriate leisure activities, but there is a greater use of the client–counselor relationship as part of the leisure-counseling interaction, as well as a greater awareness and use of the decision-making process. Leisure counseling involves a holistic focus on the total individual and the establishment of a facilitative counseling relationship.

GOALS OF LEISURE COUNSELING

A primary goal of leisure counseling is to provide for an increase in the clients' perceived competence by engaging in activities at which they can succeed. A second goal is to provide for the clients' increased sense of freedom by engaging in freely chosen, competence-enhancing activities.

Another goal of leisure counseling is to increase an individual's level of optimal arousal and incongruity, an area in which many people are sorely lacking. In principle, this can be accomplished by increasing the variety, challenge, and complexity in one's leisure experience.

Leisure activities can also serve as a trial preparation for subsequent activities: Numerous people have turned hobbies into satisfying occupa-

tions. Leisure activities can also satisfy needs that cannot be met through other activities (e.g., work).

FREEDOM
STRESS

E. T. DOWD

LEITER INTERNATIONAL PERFORMANCE SCALE

The Leiter International Performance Scale (LIPS) is an individually administered intelligence test that is being increasingly used as a general measure of intelligence in situations where a "culture fair" test is needed.

The LIPS is completely nonlanguage and instructions are given in pantomime. The test consists of problems in matching colors, duplicating designs, matching shades of gray, estimating the number of dots in a given area, recognizing form, numerical reasoning problems, and so forth. It also uses number, perceptual, and abstract reasoning tasks.

The basic version of the LIPS is suitable for testing persons from 2 through 18 years of mental age. A later version of the test—the "Arthur Adaptation of the Leiter"—is considered suitable for testing children between the ages of 3 and 8

The reliability coefficients of the LIPS range in the low 90s. Relatively little data are available regarding validity. Despite its popular use as a culture fair test, some studies indicate that so-called culturally deprived persons may actually have more difficulty on this type of test than they might on a Wechsler Intelligence Scale. As with all psychological tests, caution should be used in interpreting test results.

CULTURAL BIASES IN TESTING
INTELLIGENCE MEASURES
NONVERBAL INTELLIGENCE TESTS

M. P. MALONEY

LENS MODEL (BRUNSWIK)

Egon Brunswik was one of the first psychologists to attempt to deal with the fact that we live in an environment that is, to an important degree, unpredictable. He considered that even seemingly lawful relationships, such as the apparent correspondence between the perception of an object, its size, distance, or identity, and the actual physical reality that we measure with instruments, is really the result of a complex *behavioral achievement* involving judgmental processes based on the lifelong experience of the observer. To describe the process by which perception occurs, he invented the *lens model* as a heuristic to demonstrate the various stages involved.

To begin with, there is the *distal stimulus,* which is the actual object or relationship in the external environment, that the individual is trying to perceive. Unfortunately, the pattern of proximal stimulation does not unambiguously allow one to reconstruct the distal stimulus.

Typically, we are presented with a number of *cues,* some of which are more reliable predictors of the distal stimulus than others. Brunswik would say that they differ in terms of their *ecological validity.* Through experience, we begin to assess the validity of various cues, using an internal set of learned probabilities. The final *behavioral achievement* involves an attempt to reconstruct the distal stimulus—or, more precisely, to construct a percept based on the available proximal stimuli and our assessment of the validity of cues and how they should be combined. Because there are often only probabilistic relationships between the proximal cues and the actual stimulus in the environment, our final percept may be in error, and it will certainly change with experience.

This theoretical position is sometimes called *probabilistic functionalism*. The general ideas that it embodies have found application in explaining numerous perceptual processes, including constancies and visual illusions.

APPARENT SIZE PERCEPTION
PERCEPTUAL DISTORTION

S. COREN

LESCH–NYHAN SYNDROME

Lesch–Nyhan syndrome (or HPRT syndrome) is a rare X-linked inborn error of purine metabolism expressed only in males. Its most distinctive and horrific feature is severe and chronic self-mutilation, particularly self-biting of fingers and mouth areas, that may lead to considerable tissue destruction and loss. Because pain perception is normal, affected children may actually beg to be physically restrained. Other features include mental retardation, choreoathetosis, spasticity, hyperuricemia, and in later life, gout.

DEVELOPMENT AND DIAGNOSIS

Lesch–Nyhan males are normal at birth. Delay in motor development begins at 3 to 4 months of age, choreoathetosis and other motor dysfunctions appear at about 1 year, and self-mutilation develops during childhood or adolescence. Frequently, the disorder is differentiated from cerebral palsy only with the onset of self-mutilation. Diagnosis can be confirmed through testing for HPRT activity in tissue samples.

METABOLIC AND BIOCHEMICAL BASIS

A combination of metabolic abnormalities increases uric acid production and hyperuricemia, which predisposes to later gout. The neurologic abnormalities appear to be unrelated to hyperuricemia. Research suggests that self-mutilation is based in reduced dopamine neuron function and norepinephrine turnover.

TREATMENT

Behavior modification may reduce self-mutilation, but continuous monitoring is necessary. Physical restraint or even removal of teeth may be needed to control damage from self-biting.

Allopurinol effectively reduces HPRT-based hyperuricemia and its various renal effects and gout, but has no effects on the neurologic abnormalities. Although treatment with a variety of biochemical agents has produced no lasting reduction in self-mutilation, pharmacological manipulation of dopamine transmission offers the possibility of effective control. Stout and Caskey have suggested that "the devastating nature of the Lesch–Nyhan syndrome, the lack of therapeutic alternatives, and the development of efficient gene transfer techniques have made this disease a prototype for the study of gene replacement therapy."

BEHAVIORAL GENETICS
DEVIANT MATURATION
GENETIC DISORDERS
INBORN ERRORS OF METABOLISM
SEX CHROMOSOME DISORDERS

R. T. BROWN

LEVEL OF ASPIRATIONS

Psychologists have classified people according to their goals in life. Some believe that these goals or aspirations are determined by basic personality traits formed early in life. Aggressive/submissive, inner-directed/outer-directed, and active/passive are among such attempted groupings.

Aspirations are the driving forces in personalities. They are more important than the abilities which one is born with or acquires through environment and education because what really matters is what one does with these character and personality traits.

By measuring the distance between a desired level of aspiration and the level reached up to now, a "motivational differential" can be established. By then tracing the various points on the scale and combining them, an aspiration profile can be established. Thus, one can discover whatever gap exists.

Levels of aspirations may be too high or too low. In both cases adjustments are necessary. A management problem encountered frequently is that a person feels overqualified for a job. Sometimes setting levels too high can serve as an excuse for not trying harder.

Different societies distinguish themselves by the limits they set to aspirations. For hundreds of years ordinary citizens were told that limits to their growth were established by their social standing and class, by law or established rules, and by predestined and ordained possibilities.

In most Western democracies there is a growing recognition that human potentialities are almost limitless. Not even the IQ represents a hurdle.

INDIVIDUALISM
OPTIMAL FUNCTIONING

E. DICHTER

LIBIDO

Libido theory is among the most far-reaching and controversial notions in psychoanalysis. Libido refers to the sexual biological instinct, drive, or psychic energy. The metapsychology of its vicissitudes and reorganizations over the course of development through the psychosexual stages—oral, anal, phallic, latency, and genital—formed the core of early psychoanalytic theories of developmental psychology, psychopathology, and clinical practice.

Freud himself had strong allegiance and high hopes for biological causation and explanation, but still broadened his notion of libido to include the sensual as well as the more basic sexual aspects of life. As early as 1916, Carl Jung attacked Freud's theory of libido, arguing that sexuality was only a variant of a more primal, undifferentiated form of psychic energy or life force. David Rapaport replaced the libido concept with a general, nonspecific drive energy as he cast traditional instinct and id-oriented psychoanalysis into a more comprehensive ego psychology. The growing concern with the bankruptcy of hydraulic, thermodynamic, and drive discharge models led to the elimination or deemphasis of libido theory in many recent psychoanalytic reformulations.

Aside from the ongoing controversy over what role, if any, libido plays in a psychoanalytic psychology or any other theory of behavior or pathology, two abiding domains of concepts derived from libido theory remain useful, especially when their metapsychological nature is appreciated and respected. One domain is the qualitative properties of libido—or any instinctual energy—that serve as the structure, process, and organization for the so-called drive.

The second useful domain of concepts derived from libido theory are those of the developmental progressions of psychosexuality and object relations. Libidinal gratification was associated with sensuality or activity focused about each of the so-called erotogenic body zones implied in the stage sequence. Particular qualities of character and/or pathology were associated with the successes, failures, and compromises at each mutually influential step of the developmental process. A related progression of libido from autoeroticism (gratification through one's own body) to narcissism (love of one's self) and object love (gratification through investment and involvement with other people) complements the psychosexual progression, contributing yet another of the major developmental lines that form the framework for psychoanalytic diagnostic classification.

HUMAN SEXUALITY
PSYCHOANALYSIS

D. L. WERTLIEB

LIE DETECTION

An instrument that monitors one or more involuntary physiological variables from a person under interrogation is popularly called a lie detector. The most common instrument for this purpose, the *polygraph,* normally monitors breathing movements, relative blood pressure, and electrodermal responses (which are related to the sweating of the palms). Many examiners now use some form of *voice stress analyzer,* the most common of which measures the amount of low-frequency (10 Hz) warble present in the speaking voice. Voice analyzers do not require attachments to the subject and therefore can be used covertly, even over the telephone.

It is popularly believed that these or other instruments can identify lying by detecting some response or pattern of responses specific to deception. Although such claims have been made from time to time, no specific lie response has ever been objectively demonstrated. All one can determine from the polygraph chart is that the subject was relatively more disturbed or aroused by one question than by another; one cannot determine *why* the subject was aroused, whether, for instance, the question elicited guilt, fear, or anger.

The examiner must therefore try to infer deception from the difference in reaction elicited by different types of questions. For many years the standard question format was that of the *relevant/irrelevant* (R/I) test. Relevant questions (e.g., "Did you take the $1000 from the safe?") were intermixed with irrelevant questions (e.g., "Did you eat breakfast this morning?"). If the subject appeared to be more disturbed by the relevant than by the irrelevant questions, he was vigorously interrogated. Many innocent persons are likely to be disturbed by the accusatory relevant questions, however, so that the R/I test produced a high rate of false-positive errors.

Since the 1950s, most examiners have come to use some form of *control question format,* in which a third type of question is added to the list. Control questions refer in a general way to prior misdeeds of the subject. The theory of the control question test is that an innocent person, able to answer the relevant questions truthfully, will be most disturbed by these control questions and show stronger physiological reactions to them, whereas the guilty person will react most strongly to the relevant questions.

Most of these tests were administered for employers in the private sector. Most city police departments employed polygraph or voice stress tests as an aid in deciding which criminal suspects should be released and which prosecuted. In perhaps 17 states polygraph evidence was admissible in criminal trials when both sides had so stipulated prior to testing. In 1981, however, the supreme courts of Colorado, Illinois, and Wisconsin reversed prior decisions and ruled that polygraph evidence would no longer be admissible even under stipulation. At least 15 states prohibited employers from requiring employees or job applicants to submit to lie detector testing, and similar statutes had been introduced in other legislatures.

Polygraph and voice stress examiners claim very high rates of accuracy, ranging typically from 95 to 99%, but these claims have not been supported by credible research.

It is important to examine the fate of the truthful or innocent subjects separately because the consequences of "failing" a lie detector test in real life can be very serious. In three studies, the charts of the innocent suspects were scored as "deceptive" in 55%, 39%, and 49% of the cases respectively, indicating that the polygraph test is biased against the truthful person.

ANXIETY
EMPLOYMENT PRACTICES
FORENSIC PSYCHOLOGY

D. T. LYKKEN

LIFE EVENTS

Researchers have long been interested in understanding how individuals and environments affect each other, primarily so as to describe and explain age-related behavior and individual differences. One focus has been to study life events. A life event is indicative of, or requires a significant change in, the ongoing life patterns of the individual. These events can occur in a variety of domains (family, health, and work) and may be age-graded (school, marriage, and retirement), history graded (war and depression), or nonnormative (illness and divorce). Most of the adolescent and adult literature reflects a sociological tradition of assessing the impact of life events as transitions between major roles, age grades, status gains and losses, and so forth.

When an event is shared by many people of the same age, the probability of its occurrence is high, and the stage for anticipatory socialization is set. These normative events have been classified by some researchers as biological, social, or physical, referring to the environs. Others have preferred to apply models of stress to classify life events and speak of social, psychological, and physiological reactions to harmful, threatening, or challenging phenomena. Individuals usually are asked to rate the amount of stress or behavioral change associated with lists of life events, which are then analyzed to determine their timing, sequencing, and clustering.

Several theorists have suggested that there is an underlying structure to adult life. D. J. Levinson has proposed a universal sequence of periods and transitions in human development within which life events have their impact. The primary task of stable periods is to build a life structure by making certain choices and striving to attain certain goals. The primary tasks of the transition periods are to terminate the existing life structure and initiate a new one by reappraising old choices and goals and moving toward new ones.

It appears that there may be a relationship between affective positivity and control over life events. When events are regarded positively, people tend to assume they had influence or control over those events. Others have suggested that generating positive feeling states may enhance an individual's capacity to adapt to stress. Also, the absence of negatively related events is correlated with adjustment.

Research on children's reactions to life events is sparse, so normative patterns are not yet known. However, three stressful life events—changing residence, changing schools, and family crises such as divorce and the death of a parent—have been studied consistently, producing equivocal findings. Data also show that, for children, stresses experienced singly or even in sequence are not as problematic as those experienced in combination; furthermore, boys more than girls are damaged by family disruption and discord. Negative emotional reactions have been found to increase with age, especially in the areas of health and family, while positive emotional reactions were reported to be associated with life events reflecting interactions with parents and peers.

CAREER CHOICES
DEVELOPMENT OF HUMAN SOCIAL BEHAVIOR

F. DEUTSCH

LIFE-SPAN DEVELOPMENT

The point where change occurs throughout the life cycle is critical. Traditional approaches to human development have emphasized change from birth to adolescence, stability in adulthood, and decline in old age. Sears and Feldman have captured the flavor of some of the most important adult changes. The changes in body, personality, and abilities may be great during these later decades. Strong developmental tasks are imposed by marriage and parenthood, by the waxing and waning of physical prowess and of some intellectual capacities, by the children's exit from the nest, by the achievement of an occupational plateau, and by retirement and the prospect of death.

A number of stage-crisis theories have been developed to explain the change adults undergo, the best-known being Erikson's theory, and in the popular literature, Gail Sheehy's *Passages.* Many theorists and researchers, however, have not been satisfied with the stage-crisis approaches to adult development. To obtain a more accurate view of adult development, many experts believe that the study of life events adds valuable information. Hultsch and Deutsch point out that our lives are punctuated by transitions defined by various events. Particular emphasis is placed on the stressful nature of these events. Events typically thought of as positive (marriage or being promoted at work), as well as events usually perceived as negative (death of spouse, being fired from work), are potentially stressful. Factors that can mediate such stressful life events include internal resources (physical health, intellectual abilities) and external resources (income, social supports). Adaptation involves the use of coping strategies that result in behavioral change.

Broadly speaking, there are two theoretical approaches to the study of personality development, one focusing on similarities and the other on differences. The stage theories all attempt to describe the universals—not the individual variation—in development. Farrell and Rosenberg suggest a more complex model, one anchored in the idea that individuals are active agents in interpreting, shaping, and altering their own reality.

In a recent discussion of life stress, I. G. Sarason has called attention to the wide array of individual differences in the frequency and preoccupying characteristics of stress-related cognitions. Although the most adaptive response to stress is a task orientation that directs a person's attention to the task at hand rather than to emotional reactions, some individuals are task-oriented while others are not.

Sarason emphasizes that the ability to set aside unproductive worries and preoccupations is crucial to functioning under stress. At least five factors influence how an individual will respond to life stress, according to Sarason:

1. The nature of the task or stress
2. The skills available to perform the task or handle the stress
3. Personality characteristics
4. Social supports available to the person experiencing stress
5. The person's history of stress-arousing experiences and events

But while adults are likely to experience one or more highly stressful events during their lives, an increasing number of individuals are reaching late adulthood in a healthier manner than in the past.

ADULT DEVELOPMENT
AGING: BEHAVIORAL CHANGES
HUMAN DEVELOPMENT

J. W. SANTROCK

LIFESTYLE ASSESSMENT

A significant contribution to understanding human behavior was Alfred Adler's concept of lifestyle. Adler believed that understanding the human personality involves recognizing that each individual's behavior has social meaning, is unified, and contains definite patterns (a lifestyle) is based on subjective perception, is purposeful and goal-directed, and is motivated by a desire to overcome feelings of inadequacy coupled with an urge to succeed.

DEVELOPMENTAL PHASES

Four developmental phases characterize Adlerian counseling.

1. *Rapport and mutual trust* between counselor and client are established. Understanding another person's lifestyle is the highest form of counselor empathy, according to Adler. People who are experiencing interpersonal conflicts may have difficulty in forming close relationships. This makes the counseling process an important first step for the client toward social living.

2. *A psychological investigation* focuses on a systematic lifestyle interview plus other relevant psychometric instruments. Rudolf Dreikurs suggested that a lifestyle investigation begin with a "subjective" and an "objective" exploration. The former includes all a person's concerns, problems, and symptoms, while the latter assesses how the client is functioning in the five general life tasks of work, friendship, love, self-esteem, and moral–ethical beliefs.

3. *Interpretation* seeks to add insight and understanding to the basic existential questions of life, self, and others. Confrontation concerning discrepancies between actions and words, or between ideal and real goals, is employed.

4. *Reorientation* utilizes encouragement as a major therapeutic tool in creating changes in attitude and/or behavior. In the final phase of counseling, the counselor and client work together to consider alternative beliefs, behaviors, and attitudes—a change in the client's lifestyle. Specific reference is made to "subjective" concerns stated by the client during the lifestyle investigation. The counselor uses the lifestyle summary to reveal the individual's faulty beliefs and self-defeating behavior. Once these are acknowledged in the counseling dialog, the client is consciously aware of them.

LIFESTYLE THEORY

A systematic lifestyle investigation involves regression to formative childhood influences to determine existential decisions regarding life, self, and others that affect present behavior and may affect future behavior. Thus, although the time reference is early childhood, determination of implications for the present and future is the goal of the assessment. An investigation of this type focuses on such familial concerns as birth order, interpersonal relationships among family members, the siblings' main competitors, family values, and the individual's early recollections of formative experiences by means of a structured interview format.

Such a position is similar to Gordon Allport's "mode of being in the world" and Adrian Van Kaam's "mode of existence." The optimistic philosophies of all such theorists include the belief that an individual's past decisions and patterns can be continually reviewed, modified, and/or changed. Thus, an understanding of one's style is the first step to behavior and/or attitude change.

By exploring and assessing an individual's lifestyle, it is possible to develop an understanding of that person as a self-consistent and self-directed entity whose central theme is reflected in all personal actions as forward-oriented, purposive, and determined by individual values, rather than by simple physiological responses to the environment.

INTERPRETATIVE STRATEGIES

According to Dinkmeyer, Pew, and Dinkmeyer, an Adlerian systematic lifestyle summary includes identification of the following:

1. The individual's problems and feelings of deficiency
2. Directions taken by the individual to overcome the perceived deficiency
3. The relationship between such direction and cooperative social interest
4. Specific areas of difficulty the individual experiences with life tasks
5. How the individual is avoiding the resolution of problems
6. How the individual manages to feel superior while avoiding confrontation of problems
7. Contributing influences from the individual's past history

Daniel Eckstein notes that such an interpretive summary should also use support and encouragement to identify the individual's strengths and assets.

The following three general lifestyle typologies can be of assistance as a starting summarization.

1. *Number-one priorities.* Adler noted that early in life individuals select a number-one priority as a means of answering the basic existential question of "What is most important in my belonging with the group?" These include superiority, control, pleasing, and comfort. The "fears to be avoided" of such priorities include meaninglessness, humiliation, rejection, and stress respectfully.

2. *Fourteen general lifestyle themes.* Harold Mosak identified the following general lifestyle types: the getter, driver, controller, right, superior, liked, good, opposed, victim, martyr, baby, inadequate, avoid-feelings, and excitement-seeker personalities.

3. *Styles of living questionnaire.* Robert Driscoll and Daniel Eckstein modified Frank Thorne's lifestyle categories—aggressive, confronting, defensive, individualistic, and resistive—to the following five descriptive animal labels:

a. *Tigers* are generally aggressive. They enjoy exercising authority, like to be the center of attention, and may insist on having their own way.

b. *Chameleons* are generally seen as conforming. Flexible, they are more likely to face problems directly.

c. *Turtles* are generally defensive. They are earnest and resourceful and lead self-controlled, stable lives.

d. *Eagles* tend to be seen as individualistic. They are not concerned with public opinion and may be egoistic and infringe on the rights of others so as to get their own way.

e. *Salmon* usually are resistive. They prefer to "swim against the current" rather than support "establishment" values.

ADLERIAN PSYCHOTHERAPY
CLINICAL ASSESSMENT

D. G. ECKSTEIN

LIKERT SCALING

Likert scaling derives its name from its inventor, Rensis Likert, who first developed this approach to attitude surveys. The prime advantages of his technique were that it was much quicker to develop and adopt than the previously used Thurstone technique, which required the use of judges and extensive item evaluation. Furthermore, the Likert scaling approach does not necessitate the use of negative items, a benefit that explains its widespread industrial applications.

The Likert technique consists of a series of statements to which one responds using a scale of possible answers: Strongly Agree (5), Agree (4), Neither Agree nor Disagree (3), Disagree (2), and Strongly Disagree (1). This five-point Likert Scale can be expanded to seven or more steps with a modification of the adverbs (Strongly, Moderately, and Mildly). The five- and seven-point scales are the most common forms in use.

Modifications of the Likert Scale include the forced-choice Likert approach (no neutral category), and the Faces approach, which uses faces scaled from a smile to a frown for illiterate respondents. The reliability of the Likert Scales are in the 0.90 range, and the scales' results correlate approximately 0.80 with the Thurstone technique.

RATING SCALES
SCALING
THURSTONE SCALING

L. BERGER

LIMBIC SYSTEM

The limbic system includes the septal area (subcallosal area and associated subcortical nuclei), the cingulate gyrus, the hippocampus, the amygdala, portions of the hypothalamus, especially the mammillary bodies, the anterior thalamic nucleus, the habenula, and parts of the midbrain. These brain areas are reciprocally interconnected through many axonal pathways including the fornix, cingulum, stria terminalis, stria medullaris, mammillothalamic tract, medial forebrain bundle, and habenulointerpeduncular tract.

The limbic system can be considered a system because of the significant anatomic relationship of its structures to one another and to the hypothalamus, not because these structures are necessarily homogeneous in function. Indeed, limbic structures have been associated with a variety of functions. For example, the hippocampus is important in the formation of memories in both humans and animals; the septal area appears to be involved in species-typical emotional responses; and the amygdala may be involved in learned responses to aversive stimuli. The cingulate cortex may be involved in the appreciation of pain in humans and in acquisition of conditioned avoidance responses in animals. In addition to the behavioral categories previously listed, these limbic areas, as well as the other structures within the system, have been associated with the modulation of many other behaviors. Moreover, the hippocampus, septal nuclei, and amygdala may also influence the release of pituitary hormones. As a generalization it can be stated that the limbic structures participate in the operation of mnemonic, emotional, and motivational processes by means of their relationships with one another, the neocortex, hypothalamus, endocrine, and autonomic nervous systems.

BRAIN
CENTRAL NERVOUS SYSTEM

M. L. WOODRUFF

LIMEN

In psychophysics a limen or threshold has two meanings: For any sensory modality, (a) the *absolute limen* is the weakest stimulus that can be detected, while (b) the *difference threshold* is the smallest difference in stimulation that can be detected. These concepts have been generalized to other psychological subject matters, including the field of learning.

A similar use of the concept of threshold has appeared in applications of the theory of signal delectability to recognition memory. In this case, the threshold corresponds to the subject's *criterion* for responding positively, when asked to say whether a particular item in a list of materials is recognizable as one experienced earlier. In this case the subject sets a criterion (threshold) and responds "yes" if the feeling of familiarity exceeds this criterion or "no" if the feeling of familiarity falls below it. These data are used to calculate measures of memorability.

PSYCHOPHYSICAL METHODS
PSYCHOPHYSICS

G. A. KIMBLE

LITERATURE AND PSYCHOLOGY

The emergence of psychology as a separate discipline in the late nineteenth century brought to the forefront the relation of this new science to the humanities. Two great figures of that time, William James and Sigmund Freud, loomed large in this issue. Both were trained in medicine and psychology, but viewed themselves as psychologists; both were attracted to philosophy; and both were to receive renown as writers. William James' duality was mirrored in his younger brother Henry, whose reputation as a writer is based importantly on his psychological insights and understanding.

It is fitting that Freud should have met William James in 1909 on his only visit to America. As he evolved psychoanalysis, he always understood that humanistic studies were vital to his thinking, and he criticized the lack of such studies in the medical curriculum, especially for the training of someone who was to become a psychoanalyst. The cornerstone of his clinical theory was the Oedipus complex, influenced not only by his clinical observations and his self-analysis, but also by his familiarity with Sophocles' tragedy, which he had translated as a youth. The specific writers who influenced him were many, including Shakespeare, whose works he had read in English as a youth; Goethe, whom he was fond of quoting; and Dostoevski, whose psychological acumen he so admired. Freud created not just a theory of the human mind, but works of great literary merit. He wrote psychology as literature on a level that has not been equaled since.

Man is a linguistic beast, and Freud recognized that any comprehensive theory of human behavior must come to grips with this simple fact. Freud used the analysis of language as the foundation on which he erected his theoretical edifice. Freud's analysis of dreaming provided him with his basic concepts concerning the operation of the human mind and its cognitive processes. Concepts with linguistic referents inform his analysis of dreamwork, including censorship, condensation, displacement, secondary revision, and symbolization.

The importance Freud gave to language is reflected in all areas of his thought. He began with an analysis of slips of the tongue and other verbal parapraxes. Similarly, he elaborated how wit and joking are forms of language that reveal the complex workings of the mind. Then too, Freud evolved a "talking cure," the technique of psychoanalytic therapy in which two people converse as a means of alleviating neurotic suffering.

The concern with transformational processes provides a fundamental meeting ground for psychology and literature. We interpret literature and we interpret dreams, and in this way recognize that hermeneutics, the study of the interpretive process, is central to psychology and literature. Freud was preoccupied with these transformational processes in his theory not only in cognition—as in the distinctions of unconscious versus conscious, primary process versus secondary process, repressed versus

return of the repressed, and manifest dream versus latent dream—but also in transformation or vicissitudes of instincts, as in love versus hate.

This transformational or two-language nature of psychoanalysis brings it into congruence with a number of contemporary approaches to language, including the structuralist approach of the French psychoanalyst Jacques Lacan and the deconstructionist approach of Jacques Derrida. However, it is in the transformational–generative theory of language that we find striking similarities to the nature of Freud's thought. The parallel between Freud and Chomsky has been amplified by M. Edelson, who notes that both men posit the presence of deeper structures forming the basis of surface structures, as well as stress the importance of transformational operations by which the language of the deep structure is represented in the language of the surface structure. Echoing Freud's basic distinction between primary process thought and secondary process thought, Fodor assumes a private language that is the precursor of the public language. In consonance with Chomsky's idea of "language and unconscious knowledge," he holds that to learn a language we must have available another private language. Fodor is led to speculate on the "vocabulary" of the code by which the private language is transformed into the public language.

Literature of the late nineteenth and early twentieth centuries, as in the works of Proust and Joyce, exemplifies the concern with levels of language. Joyce's novels can be considered as progressive movements from the public language of the conscious to a predominant emphasis on the private language of the unconscious. It is as if Joyce wished to write in the private language that forms the substrate of all literary works. It is poetry, however, that reveals most directly the transformation process from the private to the public language. The poet's language bridges primary and secondary processes and focuses on the transition from one to the other. Early in this century F. C. Prescott recognized the parallel between such poetic tropes and the process of dreamwork developed by Freud, a parallel subsequently elaborated by the psychoanalyst E. F. Sharpe. Thus, psychoanalysis, literature, and linguistics converge upon transformational operations, and the problem of interpretation of the text, or hermeneutics, becomes a central issue.

Because psychoanalytic interpretations of literature initially emphasized the major developmental themes explicated by Freud, there has been continuing interest in the oral, anal, and phallic aspects of literature, often with predominant emphasis on the Oedipal state of development. With the development of ego psychology within psychoanalysis, psychoanalytic literary criticism took a turn toward emphasizing the more adaptive, synthesizing aspects of literary productivity. The emphasis of ego psychology was to construe literary effort as positive, coping behavior in which the regression was purposive and controlled, otherwise the fantasy emanating from the primary process would become too private and preclude artistic communication with the reader. Erikson's work gave psychoanalytic interpretations of literature a firmer foothold by emphasizing the cohesive, integrative role of the writer's ego identity on the one hand, and his or her place within the context of the social, cultural, and historical forces on the other hand.

Freud turned more to pre-Oedipal issues late in his life, as he distinguished between the psychological development of the male and female child, and recent feminist literary criticism has moved in this direction. Freud maintained that the pre-Oedipal relationship with the mother was of more basic significance for the development of the female child than was the Oedipal period. Such a formulation is central in the feminist approach to problems of female identity formation. The intense interest women critics are displaying in this issue of female identity formation in relation to writing is one example of the mutual contribution of literature and psychology in the development of both.

Using a paradigm centering on Oedipal issues, the literary critic Harold Bloom has made bold forays into psychoanalytic concepts in advancing a theory of literature. Bloom emphasizes rhetorical tropes in poetry as manifestations of mechanisms of defense. More generally, Bloom is concerned with the thesis that repression as a defense operates importantly in how writers deal with their literary precursors. Repression operates by causing writers to misread their important precursors, and by otherwise distorting their influence.

Because Bloom's thesis implies that all reading of prior texts is a misreading of these texts, it broaches the important problem of the psychological bases of the reader's response to literature. The foremost theoretician of this issue has been N. N. Holland. It is apparent that every reader of a text responds to the text with some interpretive schema that reflects her or his personality.

Another promising approach is to consider different analyses of the same text by a group of literary critics, in an effort to identify common interpretational structures irrespective of each critic's idiosyncratic interpretation of the text. Such metaanalyses of interpretations of literature bear important similarities to the need in clinical psychology to identify common elements and structures in the interpretive diagnostic and psychotherapeutic efforts of clinicians.

The structuralist view rejects the idea that texts exist to be interpreted, or that they contain truth or meaning. Structuralists seek a systematic "scientific" framework that allows them to reduce texts to basic semiotic categories, such that the experience of the reader is nullified. The text reads itself.

Lacan, influenced by the structural linguistics of Saussure and the structural anthropology of Levi-Strauss, has as a central tenet: the idea that the unconscious is structured like a language. Lacan rejects American psychoanalytic ego psychology and its emphasis on the adaptive, synthesizing, and integrative aspects of the ego in literary creativity. In contrast, Lacan stresses the alienated otherness of the ego and self, which he considered central to Freud's concepts of narcissism and identification. The infant first begins to develop its alienated self in what Lacan calls the "mirror stage" of development, such that the mother as a mirror is the basis of the infant's self as the other. Lacan's idea of the mirror stage allows the reintroduction of the concept of *imago* into literary analysis and provides a link between psychoanalytic conceptions and the archetype of Jung.

The deconstructionist program has been strongly influenced by Heidegger, Freud, and Lacan. More severely than Lacan, Derrida wishes to establish the text as both a presence and an absence, such that the text is ultimately effaced. The text of Freud or any writer is erased, deconstructed, or dismantled, in order that it can be reconstructed or rewritten so as to show the text what it "does not know." The ultimate effect of Derrida's criticism is to render texts, Freudian or otherwise, open-ended, without closure, never fully fathomed, never fully constructed, or deconstructed. As in Freud's final commentary on psychoanalytic therapy, the text becomes both terminable and interminable.

What might the psychologist learn from literature? Perhaps the most psychologically astute of these poets was William Blake, whose startlingly acute and direct penetrations of the human psyche have yet to be adequately recognized and studied. Not only were his ideas precursors of both Freud and Jung, but the entire corpus of his work, both literary and artistic, also demands an exegesis in its own psychological terms that could yield important conceptualizations of the human personality.

The Romantic turn toward the self is strongly exemplified in Wordsworth, whose poetic texts contain some of the most vivid recapitulations of early childhood experience, including infancy. The complex ideas of Coleridge speak to many contemporary psychological issues, including his concepts concerning imagination and fantasy. The contributions of Keats to psychological understanding have been more generally recognized, including his emphasis on identity as a crucial element in personality formation, and his ideas about the creative process, including negative capability, his oxymoron for a process reaching into issues central to Freud's theory of dreams.

Psychology, in seeking a systematic understanding of the human personality, needs to be reminded by literature where its conceptions fall short of the depth, complexity, and richness that characterize the human being.

J. BIERI

LOBOTOMY

A lobotomy is a specific type of psychosurgery in which a lobe of the brain (frontal, parietal, temporal, or occipital) is cut into or disconnected from other brain areas. The *prefrontal lobotomy* is a specific type of lobotomy involving a portion of the frontal lobes.

In 1935, Egas Moniz heard a paper on the effects of prefrontal damage in chimpanzees. Although the emphasis of the report was on the learning deficits caused by the damage, Moniz was particularly intrigued by the comment that one chimpanzee was much more manageable postoperatively.

Shortly after the conference, Moniz and Almeida Lima performed the first prefrontal operations. In 1936, Moniz published the results from his initial 20 patients. Of the 20, Moniz claimed that 7 were cured, 7 had improved, and 6 had not improved. From this somewhat less than auspicious beginning, lobotomy became a widely adopted method of treatment for the severely ill mental patient.

Lobotomy in particular, and psychosurgery in general, reached a peak in the late 1940s and declined rather precipitously in the mid-1950s. Evaluation of the effects of the prefrontal lobotomy is quite difficult. Operations were performed by a bewildering variety of methods on a variety of patients with different diagnoses. Recovery or lack of recovery was often assayed mainly in terms of the patient's manageability.

Standard intelligence tests were frequently employed in patient evaluation, and the results generally did not reveal intellectual deficits. However, more subtle changes were often reported, including lack of initiative, apathy, inability to maintain directed activity, tactlessness, and increased distractibility.

In addition to changes in brain areas selected for removal, there have been changes in the techniques employed to produce the damage. In the early days of psychosurgery, almost all were performed with knives of different shapes and sizes. With the advent of stereotaxic surgery, brain areas began to be destroyed with electric current, radiofrequency waves, freezing probes (cryogenic surgery), ultrasound, compression, and heat.

In summary, psychosurgery is an attempt to alter behavior beneficially in psychiatric patients by neurosurgery. The rationale for particular operations has come rather loosely from neuropsychological animal research. The lobotomy was most used at a time prior to the introduction of effective pharmacological agents.

**BRAIN
PSYCHOSURGERY**

B. M. THORNE

LOCUS OF CONTROL

Locus of control refers to a set of beliefs about the relationship between behavior and the subsequent occurrence of rewards and punishments. The more precise phrase for these beliefs about locus of control is *internal versus external control of reinforcement (I-E)*. Reinforcements (either positive or negative) perceived by the individual as being the result of his or her own behavior, efforts, or relatively permanent characteristics are examples of *internal* beliefs. *External* beliefs, in contrast, involve perceptions that reinforcements occur as the result of luck, chance, fate, or the interventions of powerful others, or else are simply unpredictable because of the complexity of events. Beliefs about locus of control or I-E are not either/or but can fall anywhere along a dimension marked by external beliefs at the one extreme and internal ones at the other.

The I-E concept was first outlined by Julian Rotter. He not only defined the concept but also described a social learning theory framework in which it could be incorporated. In addition he reported a considerable amount of psychometric data and construct validity studies on a personality inventory, the *I-E Scale,* designed to measure the concept.

THEORETICAL BACKGROUND

Many who employ the locus of control concept do so without considering how the concept fits into a larger scheme of factors that affect behavior. Such a simplistic use has sometimes led to failures in prediction, frustration over the small amount of variance accounted for by I-E, or difficulty in generalizing from one study to the next. But I-E was originally conceptualized as only one variable in a larger social learning theory scheme. This theory described several variables that act in concert to produce a behavior in a given situation: (a) expectancies; (b) reinforcement values; and (c) the psychological situation.

I-E is regarded as a generalized expectancy regarding how best to categorize situations that present the individual with a problem to be solved. Locus of control, then, is a generalized expectancy or belief as to the optimum way in which the relationship between one's behavior and the subsequent occurrence of reward and punishment should be viewed.

In any given situation the expectancy that a specific behavior will lead to a particular outcome is determined by three variables. First, there are specific expectancies for the success of a given behavior based on previous experience in the same situation. Second, there are generalized expectancies for success based on experience generalized from related situations. Third, there are numerous problem-solving generalized expectancies, of which I-E is but one example. These three variables all interact to determine one's expectancy for the success of the behavior in question. The amount of previous experience in the situation determines the relative influence of each variable.

MEASURING I-E

The most widely used device to measure locus of control as a generalized personality characteristic is the *I-E Scale.* The scale consists of 23 forced-choice items along with 6 filler items to help disguise the purpose of the test.

Rotter's original data showed little evidence that the scale was anything but unidimensional. Since then, however, considerable evidence has begun to accumulate about the multidimensional nature of I-E. Furthermore, a variety of additional scales have been developed to measure specific areas of I-E beliefs (health care, politics, etc.). Many of these are adult scales, but children's scales have also appeared.

RELATIONSHIPS BETWEEN I-E AND PERSONAL CONTROL

An internal belief orientation would seem to imply that an individual would adopt a more active and controlling posture toward the environment. In fact, a great deal of evidence exists to support this observation. The existence of this evidence speaks as much as anything else to the validity of the I-E Scale because the bulk of the research has employed that scale.

In the realm of health and body care, a variety of evidence supports the foregoing notion. One of the earliest pieces of I-E research demonstrated that internal tuberculosis patients possessed more information about their physical condition and sought more such information from physicians and nurses than did their external counterparts. It has also been noted that internal smokers are somewhat more likely to heed warnings to give up the habit as compared to external smokers. Similarly,

there tends to be a relationship between internal beliefs and prophylactic dental behavior, effective involvement in weight reduction programs, acceptance of preventive medical shots, participation in physical fitness activities, and cooperation with a variety of medically advised regimens. Even the use of seat belts in automobiles is more typical of internals. Given the complex, multidetermined nature of the foregoing behavior, it is impressive that a general, nonspecific personality variable can show such relationships.

In many ways, internals seem more competent than externals. Perhaps this stems from their more active efforts to acquire information that will enable them to have the effects on their environment that they believe they can have.

When others seek to exercise interpersonal influence, internals would be expected to be more resisting than externals; at least an internal's acceptance should be more thoughtful and analytical rather than simply reflexive. A variety of studies have supported this expectation. The evidence comes from conformity situations, subtle influence conditions, and others. To the extent that verbal conditioning represents an influence situation, the evidence is supportive here too, as we find that externals are more readily conditioned, whereas internals are more resistant to this kind of subtle influence. Similar results emerge when considering attitude change. Externals seem unusually susceptible, especially when confronted with sources of high prestige.

When achievement is studied, the results are highly complex. In children academic success is related to internal beliefs, but in college students the relationship wanes or else becomes inconsistent. Similarly, in the case of need for achievement, relationships are quite inconsistent and often clouded by sex differences. In a related area, it has been found that internal children are more able to defer immediate gratification in favor of delayed rewards. Similarly, because externals more often attribute their performance to "other" factors, they cannot fully experience the sense of pride and satisfaction that stems from achievement and is such an integral part of the achievement syndrome.

More recent work has been directed toward the possibility that some externals adopt their beliefs as a defensive response. That is, they do not "really" believe the world is organized in an external fashion. Rather, their external beliefs represent a kind of defensive rationalization to account for their failures or anticipated lack of success. What this line of research suggests is that the beliefs of some externals are "congruent" with their previous experience or history of reinforcement, while the beliefs of others are "defensive" attempts to minimize the debilitating effects that failure otherwise would.

ANTECEDENTS OF I-E

Perhaps the most serious gap in the locus of control literature is the systematic study of how I-E beliefs develop. However, some relationships have been noted in a broad fashion. For example, parents who are warm, protective, positive, and nurturant in their child-rearing practices tend to produce internally oriented children. Consistency of parental reinforcement, discipline, and standards are also linked to the development of internality. Research also suggests that lower socioeconomic status is associated with external beliefs. Racial and ethnic groups that have little access to power and mobility likewise show more external belief systems. Some evidence also suggests that certain cultures may more or less directly teach external beliefs.

FIELD DEPENDENCY
INNER/OUTER-DIRECTED BEHAVIOR
OBEDIENCE

E. J. PHARES

LOGICAL POSITIVISM

Despite its rather quick fadeout from the philosophical scene, logical positivism exercised an influence over psychology and related fields that can be detected today and will probably be felt in the future as well.

The central themes of logical positivism grew out of a series of dialogues during the 1920s by a group of philosophers and scientists who became known collectively as the Vienna Circle. They were attempting to build on a foundation established by the physicist Ernst Mach, who advocated a new philosophy of science—indeed, of all sciences. The term *logical positivism* itself was introduced by Feigl and A. E. Blumberg to summarize the general set of conceptions.

Logical positivism spearheaded a crusade against much of the philosophical establishment, especially *metaphysics.* The action soon involved other targets as well, including the much newer field of psychology, then beginning its period of rapid growth. The general aim was positive: to prepare the way for a unification of all the sciences based on empirical facts and a lucid set of theoretical propositions. Logical positivists asserted, "We will never arrive at the right answers, if we spend much of our effort on the wrong questions."

The *principle of verification* became perhaps the most effective weapon in this attempt to overturn pseudoquestions and pseudopropositions. Ayers describes this principle as follows: "The principle of verification is supposed to furnish a criterion by which it can be determined whether or not a sentence is literally meaningful. A simple way to formulate it would be to say that a sentence had literal meaning if and only if the proposition it expressed was either analytic or empirically verifiable." It is essential to note that the principle is applied not to external reality (about which the positivists had their doubts), but to the form of the sentences we construct. Attention was directed to the logical structure of verbal (or mathematical/symbolic) formulations. What, for example, is to be made of the sentence, "It is either raining here or it is not"? This particular sentence is not "wrong" or "false": It is the *inability* of this sentence to be proven true or false that reveals its uselessness.

Actual examples in philosophy and science seldom come in so simple a form, and therefore considerable work is required to determine if one is dealing with an *authentic proposition* (one that could be proven or disproven) or with a fancy linguistic masquerade. Logical positivists differed among themselves in their response to statements hopeful of passing the verifiability test. Most took the moderate view that a statement is authentic if it can be verified in principle.

Gradually, the principle of verifiability was transformed into the concept of "testability" or "confirmability." The original principle had proven perhaps just a little too successful: It was making demands that even propositions in the "hard sciences" had difficulty meeting.

Psychology has been influenced by logical positivism and analytic philosophy more than generally realized. These critical philosophies, directing attention to the structure of questions and answers, were most evident at the very time when the generations who created contemporary psychology were appearing. What might be called "micromodels" have proliferated in psychology: small, tightly focused systems of propositions about highly specific phenomena, usually related to a limited set of empirical procedures. The taste for large-scale theories may have been diminished by knowledge of the many ways in which complex propositions can go awry. The field of psycholinguistics continues to express and build on a consciousness stimulated, in part, by logical positivism.

Finally, one should not confuse logical positivism with an earlier philosophical approach that also made use of this key term. Auguste Comte offered a comprehensive system known as "positive philosophy." This was also a prescience, antimetaphysics approach, motivated by strong concerns for the future of humanity in an increasingly technical and fragmented world, but historically it was quite distinct from the Vienna Circle.

**EMPIRICISM
PHILOSOPHICAL PSYCHOLOGY**

R. KASTENBAUM

LOGOTHERAPY

The Greek word *logos* denotes meaning, and logotherapy can be defined as a meaning-centered psychotherapy. It was founded by Viktor E. Frankl. The motivational theory underlying Frankl's approach focuses on what he calls "the will to meaning" in counterdistinction to "the will to power" and the "will to pleasure" (the pleasure principle). Today more and more patients complain of a feeling of meaninglessness, and much of the ills and ailments of our time, according to Frankl, can be traced back to this frustration in a "search for meaning." The result of this state of affairs is the neurotic triad: depression, aggression, and addiction. Empirical evidence has been furnished by logotherapists that the feeling of meaninglessness is at the root of the neurotic triad.

No logotherapist can hand out or "prescribe" meanings. It is the objective of logotherapy to *describe* the process of meaning perception by way of a phenomenological analysis, so as to find out how normal people arrive at meaning and consequently at a sense of fulfillment.

From such analysis Frankl has distilled his "logo theory" according to which meaning can be found in doing a deed, creating a work, or in experiencing something (art, nature, culture, etc.). Logotherapy also offers a special technique for the treatment of obsessive–compulsive and phobic neuroses. This technique is called *paradoxical intention* and can be defined as having the patient try to do, or wish to have happen, precisely that which he or she fears. The effect is to disarm that anticipatory anxiety that accounts for much of the feedback mechanisms that initiate and perpetuate the neurotic condition. Another logotherapeutic technique called dereflection is designed to counteract sexual neuroses such as frigidity and impotence.

**EXISTENTIAL PSYCHOTHERAPY
PSYCHOTHERAPY**

V. E. FRANKL

LONELINESS

Loneliness constitutes a destructive form of self-perception. The lonely feel left out, forgotten, unneeded, and ignored. It seems likely that thoughts concerning the loss of the past and those in it, and the high regard for others as shown by illogical beliefs impose unreasonable demands on the individual. Such demands usually go unfulfilled, causing individuals to feel more isolated because of themselves and to interpret their present condition as catastrophic.

ORIGINS OF LONELINESS: THE IMPERATIVES

The *neurological imperative* dictates an optimal range of stimulation in the physical, cultural, and interpersonal environments. There are also qualitative constraints: There must be meaningful human interaction, the lack of which accounts for feelings of loneliness in a crowd. The *psychological imperative* cautions against being rejected or left out, which will lead to feelings of being unloved and rejected. The *social imperative* dictates that if we are excluded from the group, we will not get what we need and what we want out of life. Such exclusion is viewed as a challenge to basic motives seeking safety and the satisfaction of physical and reproductive needs. The *cognitive imperative* mandates that we be able to send and receive messages so as to survive in society. Barriers to communication, such as a foreign language, lead to feelings of isolation.

Illness and death rates are higher for the single, widowed, and divorced. These higher rates may result from reduced endorphin, the body's natural immunizers. Alternatively, the higher illness and death rates could be due to some illogical, self-fulfilling expectation of members of these groups based on a perceived lack of deserving happiness, of deserving only loneliness. Whatever the cause, an important contributor to loneliness is a sense of *loss* or *separation* from someone or something in the past once viewed as the essence for survival.

Another component of loneliness is *control*. Having control over any given social situation decides the difference between feeling lonely and being alone.

COUNTERING LONELINESS

Loneliness provokes a broad spectrum of reactions. Productive ways of countering feelings of loneliness are highly individualistic, but may be placed in the following framework. First, attempt to reduce the irrational beliefs that tend to accumulate regarding the catastrophe, unfairness, and self-depreciating aspects of being alone. Second, assume a personal motivation for the feeling; then, by acting instead of obsessing, one can dissipate the feelings. Third, substitute reliance on oneself for reliance and support provided by the consensus of others. Fourth, work to believe that the lonely condition will probably not last forever.

AFFILIATION NEED
INTERPERSONAL ATTRACTION
LOVE
NEGLECTED CHILDREN

D. F. Fisher

LONGITUDINAL STUDIES

Longitudinal studies involve the observation of individuals or groups over time in order to assess change. The longitudinal study is an important research method in developmental psychology, where time-related phenomena are under investigation. Often the intent is to study behavioral or physiological changes that may occur as one grows older. Two major approaches have been employed to investigate the time-related trajectory of change: cross-sectional and longitudinal designs. *Cross-sectional* studies measure a given dependent variable (e.g., IQ) on several different age cohorts. In this type of study one may measure IQ on groups that were, say, 4, 7, 10, and 12 years old. *Longitudinal* investigations record the dependent variable on the same cohort of subjects over time (e.g., when they are 4, 7, 10, and 12 years of age).

A major strength of longitudinal designs is that researchers are able to follow the same subjects over the period of the study. This permits examination of change in the same individuals as they develop or decline. Consequently, longitudinal investigations permit more direct inferences regarding development than cross-sectional studies. Longitudinal designs also present certain difficulties. Because the subjects are measured repeatedly, it may be possible to observe changes that are partially due to the effects of repeated assessment. Another potential problem is subject attrition: Because longitudinal studies often continue for a long period of time, a certain number of subjects may be lost for a variety of reasons

(death, moving, or refusal to continue). Such studies remain an important research method in psychology, but are seldomly undertaken because of the time and expense involved.

CROSS-SECTIONAL RESEARCH
EMPIRICAL RESEARCH METHODS
EXPERIMENTAL DESIGNS

C. J. Drew

LOSS AND GRIEF

Loss may be defined as being deprived of or being without something one has had and valued. Grief is the emotional suffering caused by loss. Mourning is viewed as the conventional behavior determined by the mores and customs of a given society dictating the ways in which individuals should conduct themselves following a loss. Grief reactions are physiological and psychological rather than cultural.

Loss itself may occur in a variety of forms. Four major categories are discussed by David Peretz: (a) loss of a significant loved or valued person, (b) loss of a part of the self, (c) loss of external objects, and (d) developmental loss.

Developmental loss refers to the various transitions human beings encounter as they mature from infancy to old age. These include the maturational tasks of infancy, puberty, adolescence, midlife, and retirement.

Although loss and grief were discussed by such writers as Sigmund Freud, Karl Abraham, and Melanie Klein early in the twentieth century, elaboration of these concepts began only in the 1940s. In 1944, Erich Lindemann explored the emotional reactions and adjustment patterns of the survivors and relatives of victims of the Coconut Grove Nightclub fire in Boston. A major conclusion of his study was that grief is not only a natural but also a necessary reaction after loss for healthy adjustment and resolution to occur. Lindemann's article ignited the crisis intervention movement in America.

Not until the publication in 1969 of Elizabeth Kübler–Ross's *On death and dying* was specific attention placed on the dynamics of grieving. Kübler–Ross examined various reactions by terminal patients to their impending deaths. She delineated several stages that have formed the basis for further elaboration and discussion by subsequent researchers.

Kübler–Ross' stages refer to anticipatory grief, which is grief expressed in advance of loss when the loss is perceived as inevitable.

1. *Denial and shock.* The person denies that the loss is inevitable.
2. *Anger and irritability.* The person questions why the loss should be happening and feels resentful.
3. *Bargaining.* The person attempts to postpone the inevitable through magical thinking.
4. *Depression and beginning acceptance.* A period of hopelessness results in which the person recognizes that, in fact, the loss is inevitable.
5. *Acceptance.* This signifies a point of change toward a more positive attitude regarding the loss. Death is seen as a fulfillment of life.

Simos presents a three-phase outline for conceptualizing the phases of grief *after* a loss has occurred rather than in anticipation of it:

Phase 1. Shock, alarm, and denial.

Phase 2. Acute grief consisting of continuing, though intermittent and lessening, presence of denial; physical and psychological pain and distress; contradictory emotions and impulses; and "searching behavior" involving preoccupation with thoughts of the loss, compulsion to speak about the loss, disorientation, aimless wandering and restlessness, and lethargy, demonstrated by (a) crying, anger, guilt, and shame; (b) helplessness, depression, and hopelessness; (c) decrease in pain and increasing capacity to cope over time; (d) a compulsion to find meaning in the loss; and (e) beginning thoughts of a new life without that which has been lost.

Phase 3. Integration of the loss and grief. If the outcome *is favorable*, there is an acceptance of the reality of the loss and a return to physical and psychological well-being. If the outcome is *unfavorable*, the reality of the loss is accepted with a lingering sense of depression.

The stage or phase method of conceptualizing grief processes has proved quite popular and has been applied in a variety of forms to other losses as well, including divorce, homosexual identity formation, and spinal cord injury. There is a good deal of overlap and the progression involves recycling from one stage or phase to another. Furthermore, no two people will react alike to the same loss, and the same person may not react in the same way to every loss. Still, these conceptualizations provide guidance in understanding the varieties of losses and grief reactions experienced by human beings and point toward hopeful and healthy patterns of recovery.

CRISIS INTERVENTION
SUICIDE

A. BARÓN, JR.

LOVE

WHAT IS LOVE?

Most researchers agree that "love" comes in different forms. Zick Rubin distinguishes between *liking* and *loving*. Romantic love comprises such elements as responsibility for the other, tenderness, self-disclosure, and exclusivity. In contrast, liking is an attraction for the other that includes respect and the perception that the other is similar to oneself.

Hatfield and Walster distinguished between *passionate love* and *companionate love*. Passionate love is an intensely emotional state and a confusion of feelings: tenderness and sexuality, elation and pain, anxiety and relief, altruism and jealousy.

Companionate love, in contrast, is a less intense emotion, combining feelings of friendly affection and deep attachment. It is characterized by friendship, understanding, and a concern for the welfare of the other.

John Lee distinguishes between six types of love. *Eros* is a romantic and sexual love, a need to know everything about the loved one and experience her or him fully. *Mania* is an obsessive and demanding love, often accompanied by pain and anxiety because the need for attention from the other is insatiable. *Ludis* is a self-centered, playful love; love is treated as a game to be won. *Storge* is a compassionate love, a solid peaceful love between close friends. *Agape* is a saintly "thou"-centered love, always patient, forgiving, and kind. *Pragma* is practical and logical love, given only after one has determined whether or not the partner is a "good catch."

WHOM IS ONE MOST LIKELY TO FALL IN LOVE WITH?

Proximity is perhaps the most important determinant of who people end up choosing as friends, lovers, and spouses. In general, the closer in distance people are to others, the more chances they have of becoming familiar with them; knowledge quite often leads to attraction and love. In addition, when people are in close proximity to others, there are more chances to be in rewarding situations with them.

Not surprisingly, *physical attractiveness* is another major determinant. There are probably three reasons why people are attracted to good-looking people: (a) good looks are in and of themselves aesthetically pleasing; (b) there is prestigious value associated with merely being *seen* with a good-looking partner; and (c) in accordance with the "beautiful is good" stereotype, most people assume that the beautiful possess socially desirable personality traits and lead happier and more successful lives than do unattractive persons.

Similarity is also important. People tend to fall in love with those who are similar to themselves in background and social characteristics, values and interests, and attitudes. The lion's share of researchers' attention has focused on the relationship between the similarity of attitudes and people's attraction toward one another.

There are several possible explanations for why people come to like and love similar others. First, people are more likely to encounter similar than dissimilar others. Second, there are social pressures to interact with similar others. Finally, in cost/benefit terms, it is more rewarding (and less costly) to interact with similar others, who generally confirm our beliefs about reality.

There is some suggestive evidence that, paradoxically, we fall in love with those who complement us in certain ways, as suggested by the old cliché, "Opposites attract." Robert Winch argued that people fall in love with those who complete and/or complement their own personalities and needs. Unfortunately, other researchers have been unable to replicate the Winch findings. All in all, the data indicate that people tend to select mates who possess similar, rather than complementary, personalities and needs.

WHAT IS PASSIONATE LOVE?

For centuries, theorists have bitterly disagreed over what passionate love really is. Kendrick and Cialdini argued that, in general, passionate love is explained by the same "reinforcement" principles that explain "interpersonal attraction." They argued that the more potent the reinforcements people receive from others, the more they will like and love the others. Thus, they insist that passionate love is stimulated by intensely positive experiences and dampened by intensely negative ones.

However, a minority of theorists take the opposite tack. The evidence suggests that for most people love is associated with both pleasure and pain, and may be stimulated by either.

There are physiological reasons why love might be linked to both pleasure and pain. Physiologically love, delight, and pain have one thing in common—they are intensely arousing. Joy, passion, and excitement, as well as anger, envy, and hate, all produce a "sympathetic" response in the nervous system. This is evidenced by the "symptoms" associated with all these emotions: a flushed face, sweaty palms, weak knees, butterflies in the stomach, dizziness, a pounding heart, trembling hands, and accelerated breathing.

An abundance of evidence supports the common-sense contention that, under the right conditions, intensely positive experiences such as euphoria, sexual fantasizing, an understanding partner, or general excitement can fuel passion. But there is also some evidence for the more intriguing contention that, under the right conditions, anxiety and fear, jealousy, loneliness, anger, or even grief can also fuel passion.

Recently, more laboratory research indicates that under the right conditions any state of intense arousal can be interpreted as the stirrings of desire—even if it is the result of an irrelevant experience such as listening to a comedy routine, jogging, or listening to a description of a mob mutilating and killing a missionary. Strange as it sounds, then, evidence suggests that adrenaline makes the heart grow fonder. Delight is surely the most common stimulant of passionate love, yet anxiety and fear can sometimes play a part.

DO MEN AND WOMEN EXPERIENCE LOVE IN THE SAME WAY?

Men and women share most feelings and experiences. However, evidence suggests that there are subtle differences in how concerned men and women are about love and in how they react in their relationships. Some of the following differences have been found:

1. Men tend to be more "romantic" than women.
2. Men seem to fall in love faster than women. Men also tend to be slower to fall out of love, and are likely to suffer more from a breakup, possibly because they have no one but their mate in whom to confide.
3. Women are more likely than men to experience the agony and ecstasy of love.
4. In casual relationships, women are more likely to disclose their feelings—both positive and negative.

In a deeply intimate relationship, men and women differ little, if at all, in how much they are willing to reveal to each other. They differ, however, in the *kind* of things they are willing to share. Men are more willing to share their views on politics and their strengths; women, their feelings about other people and their fears.

HOW CAN PEOPLE TELL THAT SOMEONE LOVES THEM?

There are several tell-tale body signs. Lovers give away their feelings by several body signs, including special attention to physical appearance (preening gestures). People who love each other tend to spend a great deal of time gazing into each other's eyes. They also want to touch each other and tend to stand close. Perhaps most obvious of all, when people love someone, they want to spend a great deal of time with the other and want to do things for that other person.

INTERPERSONAL ATTRACTION
SPOUSE SELECTION

E. HATFIELD

LURIA–NEBRASKA NEUROPSYCHOLOGICAL BATTERY

The Luria–Nebraska Neuropsychological Battery is the standardized version of the psychological procedures originated by the Russian neuropsychologist Alexander R. Luria, and subsequently reorganized by Charles J. Golden and his associates, into a standardized battery for the purpose of clinical neurodiagnosis. Luria conceived of behavior as the result of the interactions between all areas of the brain and favored the use of simple test procedures that reflected relatively noncomplicated patterns of brain interactions, so that functional systems of the brain could be more precisely investigated.

Luria's testing methods were not immediately accepted by American clinical neuropsychologists because of the absence of a standardized, quantitative scoring system and of experimental evidence supporting the validity of the test procedures. To alleviate the psychometric deficits of the Luria techniques, Golden and his colleagues transformed Luria's test items into standardized test procedures and objective scoring systems, with a battery that allowed a clinical evaluation on a quantitative level, as well as a qualitative level. The standardized version assesses major areas of neuropsychological performance, including motor, tactile, and visual skills; auditory abilities; expressive and receptive speech functions; reading, writing, and arithmetic abilities; spatial skills; and memory and intelligence.

DESCRIPTION OF THE BATTERY

The names of the scales of the Luria–Nebraska Neuropsychological Battery are as follows:

1. Motor functions
2. Rhythm (acoustico–motor) functions
3. Tactile (higher cutaneous and kinesthetic) functions
4. Visual (spatial) functions
5. Receptive speech
6. Expressive speech
7. Writing functions
8. Reading skills
9. Arithmetical skills
10. Memory
11. Intellectual processes

There are three additional scales, based on some of the previous items.

12. Pathognomonic scales. This scale consists of simple items rarely missed by normals and is highly indicative of brain dysfunction.
13. Right hemisphere. This scale measures the motor and tactile functioning of the left side of the body.
14. Left hemisphere. This scale measures the motor and tactile functioning of the right side of the body.

VALIDITY STUDIES

The Luria–Nebraska has been found to be useful in determining lateralization and localization of brain disorders. The effectiveness of the Luria–Nebraska was compared with that of the Halstead–Reitan Neuropsychological Battery. Both test batteries were administered to 48 brain-damaged and 60 normal patients. The results showed a high degree of relationship. Discriminant analysis found both batteries equally effective in identifying the brain-damaged patients, with hit rates of more than 85%.

Research on the Luria–Nebraska suggests that it can be an effective instrument for the diagnosis, lateralization, and localization of brain damage. The Luria test data also appear highly applicable to rehabilitation planning for brain-injured patients.

BRAIN
CLINICAL ASSESSMENT
CLINICAL EVALUATION TECHNIQUES
HALSTEAD–REITAN BATTERY
MINIMAL BRAIN DYSFUNCTIONS: DIAGNOSIS
TESTING METHODS

W. T. TSUSHIMA

M

MAGICAL NUMBER SEVEN

The phrase *magical number seven* became part of the language of psychology through an influential article titled "The magical number seven, plus or minus two: Some limits on our capacity for processing information." This article identified characteristics of human judgment and memory that would eventually become central research topics in the then-emerging theoretical perspective that has come to be known as cognitive psychology.

SPAN OF ABSOLUTE JUDGMENT

One characteristic of human information processing that Miller singled out for attention is the span of absolute judgment, or the maximum number of separate items for which amount or magnitude could be estimated at any given time. Miller reviewed numerous studies to demonstrate that the average number of stimulus categories that could be distinguished at one time fell within a narrow range on either side of the number 7. This was true for a wide variety of tasks, including identifying the pitch of auditory tones, judging the loudness of sounds, or identifying the saltiness of salt solutions.

When identifying or judging the magnitudes of individual stimuli, subjects would make few or no errors up to the "magical number seven, plus or minus two." However, when confronted with a larger number of stimuli, the error rate increased. Miller referred to this limitation in the number of items that could be judged without error at any one time as the channel capacity. The wide variety of contexts for which it holds led Miller to propose that it might result from inherent characteristics of the nervous system.

SPAN OF IMMEDIATE MEMORY

The span of absolute judgment bears certain similarities to the span of immediate memory, which consists of the number of items that can be remembered on a memory task when memory is tested immediately. It seems that the immediate memory span can encompass about seven items as well, one observation that led to Miller's use of the label *magical* for the number seven.

One demonstration of this seven-item bottleneck can be found in an experiment by the pioneer memory researcher, Hermann Ebbinghaus. One of his many memory studies investigated the relationship between the length of a list of nonsense syllables and the number of repetitions needed to be able to recite the list once without error. Ebbinghaus found that he could remember a list of 7 syllables after only one repetition. However, for a list of 12 syllables, he found that more than 16 repetitions were needed. Insights gleaned from contemporary discussions of the magical number seven enable more complete understanding of these experimental results obtained over a century ago. Clearly, the seven-item list was within the span of immediate memory, but the longer list was not.

CHUNKING

When one attempts to force more than seven items into the memory at once, earlier items are usually displaced so that more recent ones can be included. However, there are ways to get around this bottleneck. Perhaps the least efficient way is the rote rehearsal that Ebbinghaus deliberately employed.

The far more effective strategy is *chunking,* the process of grouping single items on the basis of some organizing principle. Or items may be combined into larger patterns based on information already stored in long-term memory. Thus, although the immediate memory span is limited to seven items, the amount of information in each item can be increased by building larger chunks. For example, consider this series of numbers: 1 4 9 2 1 7 7 6 1 9 4 1. If these numbers were pronounced individually and you were asked to remember them, you would find them to be beyond the limitations of your immediate memory span. However, when organized into three chunks—1492 1776 1941—the 12 separate digits now represent significant dates in U.S. history, information already stored in long-term memory.

The success of many mnemonic devices (memory aids) results from the fact that their deliberate use results in transforming material to be learned into a manageable number of chunks.

IS THE NUMBER SEVEN STILL MAGICAL?

Recent research has suggested several refinements to the earlier view of the magical number seven, which proposed that the memory span is about the same size, regardless of whatever types of items are to be stored. It now appears that the size of the memory span does depend somewhat on the nature of the material to be stored. For example, the memory span can hold more numbers than words. Also, the way that items are encoded affects the size of the memory span. People can hold more items that have been encoded acoustically (according to the way they sound) rather than visually (by looking at them). Nevertheless, the number seven does seem to retain its omnipresent quality.

ATTENTION SPAN
MEMORY
MEMORY SPAN

F. M. CAUDLE

MAGNITUDE ESTIMATION

This psychophysical method was invented by S. S. Stevens in order to investigate sensation magnitudes. Procedurally, magnitude estimation has the observer assign numbers to represent proportionally the magnitude of each stimulus in a series of stimulus presentations. The observer may be given a standard stimulus and be told to call the standard 10 units. The number assigned to the standard is called the modulus. Comparison stimuli are then assigned numbers in relationship to the standard and proportional to the modulus. The modulus is usually assigned to a stimulus intermediate in magnitude to other stimuli. In some investigations no specified modulus (and no standard) is given.

The magnitude estimation procedure has been used extensively in studies of how numerical estimates of stimuli vary with the stimulus magnitudes. Much of this work confirms Stevens' psychophysical power law, $R = cI_n$, where R represents the numerical estimate, I is the intensity of the stimulus, c is an empirical constant, and n is an exponent characteristic of the sense organ. Tabulated values of n exist for dozens of perceptual continua.

Magnitude estimation has also been used in the evaluation of stimuli that are not physically quantifiable. In some cases (e.g., seriousness of theft as a function of amount taken), an exponent can be determined for the power law; in others, scales similar to those constructed from paired comparisons are produced more quickly by magnitude estimation.

PSYCHOPHYSICS

G. H. ROBINSON

MAINSTREAMING (PSYCHOTICS)

Mainstreaming is employed in the community as an alternative to hospitalization and the usual community mental health system. Patients with chronic schizophrenia or other chronic mental illnesses are helped to function through use of support systems available to the average person in the community.

Interventions are structured within the rehabilitation model. Severely ill mental patients are encouraged to model themselves after healthy normals rather than after other patients. The final goal is for each patient to obtain as much support as necessary from the usual community resources.

Mainstreaming takes persons who are ordinarily unable to live in the community, because they are sick and disorganized, and helps them to develop techniques to enter the normal world. They can often live independently, sometimes support themselves, and take a more useful role in society. The illnesses are not cured, but the patients are enabled to function much better.

DAY HOSPITALS
HALFWAY HOUSES
REHABILITATION

V. RAIMY

MAKE-A-PICTURE-STORY TEST

The Make-A-Picture-Story (MAPS) test, a picture thematic projective technique devised by Edwin S. Shneidman, has been called a "cousin" of the Thematic Apperception Test (TAT). It consists of achromatic background pictures: A living room, street, bedroom, bridge, and so on. There are also 67 separate human and animal cutout figures. The subject's task is to take one or more of the figures, place them on a background picture, then tell a story about that situation.

CLINICAL ASSESSMENT
PERSONALITY ASSESSMENT

E. S. SHNEIDMAN

MALE SEXUAL DYSFUNCTION

There are various schema for clarifying sexual dysfunctions in men, but the most widely accepted is that proposed by William Masters and Virginia Johnson. The classification is fourfold: (a) primary impotence, (b) secondary impotence, (c) premature ejaculation, and (d) retarded ejaculation.

Impotence, in general, means the incapacity for the penis to become or remain sufficiently erect to engage in sexual intercourse. Ejaculation is the expulsion of seminal fluid from the penis during orgasm. The modifying terms primary, secondary, premature, and retarded require more careful definition. Primary impotence is the easiest to define because it lacks a frequency factor. The man who has primary impotence is an adult who has never been able to obtain or maintain an erection so as to engage in sexual intercourse.

Secondary impotence is diagnosed when a man has been unable to obtain an erection in at least 25% of sexual encounters. The period of time over which this percentage is applied is not noted. Premature ejaculation is diagnosed when the man has been unable to maintain an erection long enough to produce an orgasm in his partner in as many as 50% of sexual encounters. Masters and Johnson note that this definition, of course, does not apply if the female partner is herself orgasmically dysfunctional. Helen Singer Kaplan suggests that the significant characteristic defining premature ejaculation is not ejaculation latency or number

of thrusts, but the fact that the man is unable to exercise voluntary control over ejaculation. The definition problems can be resolved if we abandon the notion of absolute or ideal standards of performance and add a motivating unhappiness as a crucial factor.

Secondary impotence and premature ejaculation are the most common male dysfunctions. Primary impotence and retarded ejaculation are relatively rare. Secondary impotence and retarded ejaculation both increase in frequency among aging men. Much of the incidence of impotence among the elderly may be due simply to absence of a partner.

A wide variety of diseases and physical damage can cause dysfunction in men, especially impotence. The usual estimate is that one out of every two men with chronic diabetes mellitus will eventually become impotent. Chronic drug use—especially drugs commonly prescribed for the control of hypertension—may also result in impotence or retarded ejaculation. Nevertheless, the perennial belief among experts in this area is that 90 to 95% of all cases of male sexual dysfunction are caused by psychological and emotional difficulties. Recent data suggest that this estimate may be questionable for impotence, and that organic and physical factors play a more important role in the etiology of this condition than has been previously believed. Sallie Schumacher and Charles Lloyd report that 72% of 102 impotent men had some serious organic illness, primarily cardiovascular and respiratory.

Treatment of secondary impotence and premature ejaculation is frequently successful when the primary cause is not physical. Primary impotence and retarded ejaculation are also successfully treated, but somewhat less often. Treatment outcome when the primary etiology is physical varies, depending on a complex of factors. Impotence or retarded ejaculation as a function of diabetes or central nervous system damage cannot be reversed. For such patients, various penile prostheses have been developed. The overall report on their use is that sexual intercourse is satisfactory for the impotent man's partner but not for him.

FEMALE SEXUAL DYSFUNCTION
HUMAN SEXUALITY
SEX THERAPY
SEXUAL DYSFUNCTIONS

E. E. LEVITT

MALINGERING

The *Diagnostic and statistical manual of mental disorders (DSM-IV)* states that the essential feature in malingering is the *voluntary* production and presentation of false or grossly exaggerated physical or psychological symptoms. These symptoms are produced for an obviously recognizable goal. The goal relates to the person's situational or circumstantial factors and is not a psychological or "dynamic" goal.

Although numerous articles have been published on the general topic of malingering, few specific conclusions can be made. Research and publications in this area can be loosely organized into several different topic areas: military studies, simulation of psychosis, psychological tests in malingering, general simulation of medical disorders, and compensation cases.

The simulation of psychosis studies are a group of primarily anecdotal and case studies. In case study articles, there has been little systematic research effort in this area. The majority of the studies were published by psychiatric centers or in cases relating to persons feigning psychosis to avoid criminal responsibility.

Malingering has been investigated in research studies with nearly all the major psychological tests. However, the total number of studies is relatively small; often, only five or six studies with a given test have been reported over several decades. The literature can be organized into three issues: (a) intellectual incompetency, (b) organic impairment, and (c) psychological maladjustment. It does appear, however, that psychological tests can be useful in determining malingering on a case-by-case basis.

Studies related to the general simulation of medical disorders are probably more numerous than in any other subarea of malingering. The studies, however, are extremely varied, and hard empirical data are lacking. Most of these studies are case reports of attempts to detect the feigning of an illness by conducting certain types of medical examinations.

Increasing concern over the last few decades has focused on malingering in compensation cases. Compensation cases refer primarily to Workers' Compensation claims and personal injury claims. In both of these types of cases, an individual is alleging some type of physical or psychological impairment and is attempting to gain monetary compensation. As in all areas of malingering, there is an urgent need for more exacting, better-designed research.

FACTITIOUS DISORDERS

M. P. MALONEY

MALNUTRITION AND HUMAN BEHAVIOR

Famines and their disastrous consequences have been a specter haunting humankind for millennia. A variety of behavioral alterations have dietary origins.

There are two basic *types of malnutrition:* (a) deficiencies of food intake in general and (b) lack of essential specific nutrients such as amino acids, vitamins, and minerals. Generalized malnutrition has two forms: clinical (acute) and subclinical (chronic). In the clinical category three subgroups may be identified: *kwashiorkor,* characterized by edema and moderate underweight; *nutritional marasmus,* with marked underweight and no edema; and *marasmic kwashiorkor,* with marked underweight and edema.

In the acute phase of clinical malnutrition, *children* show profound apathy, irritability, and marked reduction of voluntary movements. A study in Jamaica showed that episodes of clinical malnutrition in infancy may have a profound effect on subsequent mental development. In a population in which generalized malnutrition was endemic, Singh and others found that the lower the relative body weight (a measure of nutritional status), the lower was the child's IQ.

Graves compared better-nourished and less-well-nourished *infants.* The latter group showed a reduction of exploratory behavior as well as fewer interactions between the infant and the mother, such as smiles and babbling.

MARASMUS

J. BROŽEK

MANAGED MENTAL HEALTH CARE

Managed health care has evolved so swiftly from the 1980s to the 1990s that its definition must remain fluid. Based on the premise that providers will alter their use of services in response to financial incentives, it includes a wide variety of techniques that integrate the financing and delivery of health care services to covered individuals. Broadly interpreted, the term is applied to many products and services that range along a continuum from simple preauthorization to provider-negotiated delivery systems. Managed care was created to control the costs, use, and quality of health care, but much controversy exists and many criticisms have been launched against its ability to fulfill these goals. Managed mental health services can coexist with or be delivered within general managed health care systems, or they can be separated ("carved out") from general health care plans and contracted to specialized providers who are responsible for utilization control, provider selection, finances, and quality assurance.

HISTORY

The history of managed mental health care is intertwined with the history of managed health care. Initially, the intent was to deliver affordable and accessible care to poor and middle-class laborers and farmers who wanted to eliminate the threat of sudden, unexpected medical bills. In 1929, Michael Shadid arranged with farmers in Oklahoma to provide and receive comprehensive health care for a fixed monthly fee. Despite resistance and opposition from the traditional medical community, prepaid health care survived and evolved. First-generation health maintenance organizations (HMOs) formed in various locations with the help of industry, city government, organized labor, and philanthropic organizations. The federal government became actively involved during the Nixon administration when Paul Ellwood advocated changing the incentives in the American health care system by supporting the growth of HMOs. The HMO Act of 1973 (Public Law 97-222) and its consequent amendments gave governmental support for this alternative form of health care delivery in the form of loans and grants to organizations willing to provide or arrange for comprehensive, specified inpatient or outpatient services; to serve a voluntarily enrolled population; to charge a fixed per capita fee that was not related to how much service would actually be used; and to assume some financial risk. Although initial legislation provided that HMOs be organized according to one of three models—staff, group, or independent practice association—later legislation allowed providers to combine elements of these models. Variant models continue to emerge. In 1981, federal funding for HMOs stopped, and the involvement of the private for-profit sector grew.

Mental health care became an integral part of the benefit package in managed care only with the passage of the HMO Act of 1973. To be federally qualified, an HMO had to provide mental health–substance abuse treatment in the form of short-term, outpatient mental health evaluation and crisis intervention services, as well as 60 days of inpatient services. The mental health component of health care became a matter of concern to payers when costs started rising at a rate greater than that of other health care services. Mandating mental health benefits into managed care has been accompanied by reluctance on the part of payers because of the fear that if people are allowed free use of mental health services, overuse will cause out-of-control costs. Arguments against the concern of overuse have been based on the "medical offset effect" research that showed that the use of mental health services leads to an eventual reduction in general medical health services.

Managed mental health care companies who subcontract the delivery of mental health care for a given population have increased. The advent of managed mental health care raises a number of issues reflective of the current state of the American health care system.

FORMS OF MANAGED HEALTH CARE

Forms of managed health care can be defined according to structural characteristics, relationship of provider and patients to systems, and financial arrangements. The lines between types of organizations are blurred. Many mixed models, or hybrids, that blend the characteristics of more than one model have emerged. Variation came from diverse sets of local and regional requirements.

The principal types of managed health care are as follows:

1. The staff model health maintenance organization offers necessary health services to a defined population for a fixed price. This method of financing is called capitation. Providers are salaried employees or contractors who usually work in specific locations and are expected to deliver cost-effective care and keep hospitalizations to a minimum. Patient freedom of choice of provider is limited to the staff of the HMO.

2. In an independent practice association (IPA), individual providers contract with an HMO to provide care in their own offices to HMO subscribers. Reimbursement can be fee-for-service on a prearranged fee schedule, capitated, or a percentage of the subscriber's premium. Contracts can be made between the provider and the IPA (direct contract model) or between the HMO and the IPA. When the contract is between the provider and the IPA, a risk pool is established into which each provider contributes, putting the provider at risk to cover excess expenses through a percentage holdback. When the contract is between the HMO and the IPA, the HMO establishes a risk pool into which each provider contributes, putting the HMO at risk to cover excess expenses through a percentage holdback. IPA incentives to control use are diluted because cost sharing is diffuse. When retaining fee for service payment, cost sharing is spread across all providers involved.

3. Group model HMOs contract with groups of providers to provide services and devote a specified percentage of their practice time to HMO subscribers on a salaried or fixed capitated basis. Providers usually practice in a group in a central location. In cost-sharing HMOs, there are financial incentives for providers to deliver cost-effective care because they share in the group's profit or loss. Individual providers are usually at risk for overruns or can share savings at the end of a fiscal period.

4. In a preferred provider organization (PPO), caregivers are theoretically selected because their treatment patterns are consistent with cost-effective care. PPOs do not offer comprehensive health services. Providers are not at risk. They maintain an exclusive fee-for-service billing arrangement with a predetermined subscriber group. Payment for services is negotiated and includes discounted rates or a schedule of maximum payments in return for a certain volume of referrals. Although consumers may be able to use nonparticipating providers, they are encouraged to use the PPO provider by being given greater financial incentives in the form of reduced copayments or deductibles. The purchaser buys services at a lower cost, the consumer pays less or sometimes nothing if a PPO provider is used, and the provider receives an increased flow of referrals. PPOs often use some form of review procedure to control use.

5. An exclusive provider organization is a form of PPO that pays only for services to participating providers.

6. In a broker model, independent brokers in specific geographic areas serve as liaisons between providers who want to sell and buyers who want to purchase services. The broker helps to establish and/or arrange a network of providers and sells the services to groups of individuals (small businesses, self-insured companies, guilds, etc.) who group together to purchase the services for specific, discounted rates.

7. A network model is a hybrid plan that combines features of the IPA and group and staff models and contracts with an HMO to provide services.

8. In a point-of-service or open-ended plan, reduced fees or increased benefits are offered to consumers to encourage the use of specific network providers. Increased charges, copays, or deductibles may be charged if the patient uses out-of-network providers. This arrangement allows the consumer to have the comprehensive benefits of an HMO while still being able to use nonsystem providers of their own choice even though there is a financial disincentive to do so. This plan replaces the unrestricted choice plan with the opportunity to use a managed care network.

9. In an employee assistant program (EAP), mental health and other services are provided to the employee in the workplace or off-site. The hope is that early intervention may help an employee to solve mental health or substance abuse problems that are diminishing the quality of his or her work performance. EAPs employ personnel from the company to provide service, contract with outside providers, or do both. Some EAPs add managed mental health programs so they can offer comprehensive mental health services.

10. In a social HMO, the range of services are extended to include not only comprehensive health services but also social services such as assistance for shut-in elderly. Although a few demonstration projects were run in the 1970s, little research or work is currently being done on developing this form of health care system.

Utilization review and management are the simplest managed care methods devised to evaluate the medical necessity and appropriateness of mental health services before, during, or after they are rendered. In prospective management, the necessity for inpatient or outpatient services is determined before the service is rendered (e.g., precertification and second-opinion programs). In concurrent review, treatment is monitored to ensure that services continue to be appropriate. In retrospective review services are evaluated to see whether treatment provided in the past was appropriate.

HEALTH CARE SERVICES
MENTAL HEALTH PROGRAMS
MENTAL HEALTH TEAMS

C. S. AUSTAD

MANAGEMENT DECISION MAKING

Various approaches have been proposed to understand and improve management decision making. These approaches generally make use of a "divide-and-conquer" strategy, whereby a large decision problem is divided into smaller parts.

There basically have been two types of research on decision making. The first is concerned with the development and application of normative decision rules based on formal, logical analyses derived from economic or statistical considerations. The second involves a descriptive analysis of how people actually go about making judgments and decisions.

NORMATIVE ANALYSES

As initially outlined in 1947 by John von Neumann and Oskar Morgenstern, a variety of techniques have been proposed for making optimal decisions. A distinction usually is drawn between normative analyses under riskless (or certain) conditions and risky (or uncertain) conditions. An application of each type of analysis is outlined here.

Multiattribute Utility Analysis

This approach, generally labeled MAU, applies to decisions made under riskless conditions. This approach involves obtaining an overall utility value for each decision alternative and then selecting the alternative with the highest utility. There have been a variety of applications of MAU techniques to management decision problems.

Decision Tree Analysis

In constructing a decision tree, one lays out choice alternatives, uncertain events, and outcome utilities as a series of branches. For each alternative, an expected value (EV) is defined as the average outcome over all possible events. The preferred choice is then the alternative with the highest EV. Decision trees have been used to aid such decisions as marketing strategy, plant expansion, and public policy planning.

DESCRIPTIVE ANALYSES

Most, but not all, descriptive analyses of decision making were initially concerned with discrepancies between normative rules (especially EV) and actual behavior. Edwards argued that it was necessary to substitute subjective probabilities and utilities for objective probabilities and payoffs in order to account for risky (gambling) decision behavior. This led to the Subjectively Expected Utility (SEU) model that has become standard in accounts of risky decision making.

Bounded Rationality
The concept of rationality has been questioned by Herbert Simon because of bounded rationality. This concept states that cognitive processing limitations leave humans with little option but to construct simplified models of the world.

Calibration
Questions have been raised about the ability of people to estimate probability and utility values. For instance, subjective probability values normally are not correctly calibrated in terms of "true" objective values. Research has generally shown that low probabilities are overestimated and high probabilities underestimated.

Heuristics
Kahneman and Tversky have suggested that decisions frequently are made using various psychological shortcuts or heuristics. However, the use of such heuristics frequently lead to biases in that relevant information tends to be ignored.

Averaging
Analyses of the psychological combination rules used in combining information have revealed that people usually average stimulus inputs in making judgments. Thus, people use information integration strategies that are often different from those assumed by formal analyses.

Experts
Although descriptive analyses frequently reveal that decision makers are limited and biased, there have been some instances where surprisingly good decisions by experts have been reported. Despite the numerous discrepancies between normative and descriptive approaches, there have been many successful applications of decision analysis in business and other settings. Although this may appear to be an anomaly, the successes in part reflect the importance of Benjamin Franklin's insights into problem decomposition: Decision making can almost always be improved by breaking the problem into parts.

GROUP PROBLEM SOLVING
INDUSTRIAL PSYCHOLOGY
LEADERSHIP STYLES
ORGANIZATIONAL DEVELOPMENT
WORK EFFICIENCY

J. SHANTEAU

MANAGEMENT DEVELOPMENT

Management development is a total, long-term off-the-job and on-the-job educational process. It is distinguished from supervisory training by its length. Guetzkow, Forehand, and James found that a year-long management development course changed behavior significantly more than shorter training courses. Management development can be a long and continuing process, proceeding from the time of entry into the organization at the lowest rung in the managerial ladder until near retirement at the top rung. In contrast to training, development refers to the education that further broadens practicing managers in coping with a variety of problems they are likely to face as they advance in their careers.

Management development occurs both on and off the job. In off-the-job schooling, it may include the same subject matter and processes required for the MBA degree such as accounting, finance, operations research, economics, and statistics. *Organizational psychology* usually figures strongly in required study of business policy, organizational theory, design of work, leadership, motivation, and morale.

Management development on the job can be seen, particularly in job rotation, coaching, and special assignments. Managers being groomed for high-level positions based on early identification by effective assessment programs systematically are moved diagonally upward through the organization, holding no positions for more than a few years at a time. The purpose is to provide the developing manager with an organization-wide perspective and identification as he or she gains experience coping with the problems in diverse units of the system. Coaching or mentoring provides developing managers with guidance and feedback from their superiors. Special assignments can provide needed experience.

An effective management development program is based on an analysis of the organization's objectives and its current and needed managerial resources. Dislocation of activities is minimized because the organization can promote from within rather than hiring from outside. Much of what an organization learns about coping with its internal and external environments is stored in the heads of its managers. Management development contributes to the maintenance of the organization's memory by making for efficient, orderly, internal succession.

The individual manager is served because management development makes career paths more explicit. It helps integrate the individual's needs with the organization's objectives and keeps the manager updated on advances. In the latter respect, it engages the manager in "career-long learning."

A particularly intriguing strategy for designing a management development program begins by asking a small set of the highest officers to identify their top performing managers. The preparation and approaches employed by these top performers are studied. Principles that emerge form the basis for the developmental efforts for other key managers in the organization.

A parallel analysis of the strengths and weaknesses of the current incumbents should follow. Concentration of development activities is indicated for those persons in areas where current and future requirements are unlikely to be met unless the relevant competencies are strengthened. Action plans for development emerge from examining the discrepancies between strengths and weaknesses. For planning, attention is directed to the most important discrepancies over which the manager has some control.

CAREER DEVELOPMENT
ORGANIZATIONAL DEVELOPMENT

B. M. BASS

MAN-TO-MAN SCALE
The man-to-man comparison method was developed in an effort to provide unambiguous anchor points for rating scales. It was used by the U.S. Army during World War I, but has seen only limited application since that time.

The man-to-man comparison method employs actual persons as scale anchor points. The rater constructs a five-point scale by ranking 12 to 25 of his subordinates on a trait (such as leadership ability).

The man-to-man method does provide relatively unambiguous scale anchor points, yet it has several disadvantages that limit its usefulness: (a) it results in an ordinal rather than interval or ratio scale; (b) it is cumbersome to use when many traits are to be rated because a different scale must be created for each trait; and (c) it is unlikely that the scale developed by one rater will be comparable to those developed by other raters because different persons are employed as anchor points.

RATING SCALES

W. I. SAUSER, JR.

MANIC-DEPRESSIVE PERSONALITY

All people experience some fluctuations in moods and emotions. Studies indicate that people whose moods are highly stable may be less healthy than those who experience mood variability. However, in a few people (perhaps 1% of the population) suffering from manic-depressive disorders, mood swings are so extreme that the person's ability to adapt to the requirements of daily living becomes seriously impaired.

DIAGNOSIS

According to the *Diagnostic and statistical manual of mental disorders,* manic-depressive disorders are classified as DSM 296: Major Affective Disorders: Bipolar Disorders. Subclassifications are made in terms of whether the person displays predominantly manic or depressive symptoms.

In the *manic* phase, the person generally displays a significant elevation in mood and activity. He or she often reports feeling confident, happy, and highly capable of undertaking nearly any task. The patient displays an increase in energy, often foregoing sleep while increasing work, sexual activity, and social interactions. Typically, such patients display a "flight of ideas" in which thoughts are poorly articulated and rarely followed to their logical conclusions. The patient is highly distractible and, when interfered with, may become abusive toward others.

In contrast, the *depressive phase* represents an extreme constriction of life activities. Typically, the patient reports extreme sadness and may weep continuously. The person loses interest in things that would ordinarily be pleasurable. The person may claim a loss of energy and spend a good deal of the day napping. Paradoxically, some depressed individuals will be agitated, especially at night when they are tormented by insomnia and early morning awakenings. The depressive phase brings feelings of worthlessness, hopelessness, and self-blame. Thoughts in this phase take on a brooding quality in which the person reports a great deal of indecisiveness and may express suicidal ideas.

The course of the swing from manic to depressive phases varies considerably from person to person. Thus, the popular notion of a sine wave or pendulum-like function in this disorder is overly simplistic. Most researchers and clinicians have noted that mania and depression are self-limiting in that, even without treatment, the episodes rarely last longer than 6 to 9 months. There is rarely any long-term physical or cognitive deterioration.

ETIOLOGY

Although manic-depressive disorders have been recognized since biblical times, there is still a great deal of debate as to their causes.

Physiological Approaches

Researchers who endorse a biological approach to affective disorders usually draw a distinction between *reactive* and *endogenous* disorders. In the endogenous disorders the disturbance seems to be independent of life events and to come from within the patient. Bipolar mood disorders appear more likely to fit the endogenous than the reactive pattern and therefore suggest a biological substrate.

Researchers such as John Price, David Rosenthal, and George Winokur have repeatedly found that close relatives of manic-depressive patients are significantly more likely to suffer from both unipolar and bipolar mood disorders than are the relatives of nonpatients. Furthermore, it seems that there is stronger evidence for the inheritance of bipolar than unipolar disorders. Winokur noted a "depressive spectrum" in which the male relatives of bipolar patients are likely to suffer from alcoholism, sociopathy, and depression, while female relatives are likely to suffer only from depression. This finding, coupled with the fact that father–son linkages are rare in bipolar disorders, suggested a possible X chromosome-linked disorder.

If genetic factors play a role in the bipolar disorders, then it would appear necessary to examine the biochemical mechanisms responsible for the disorder. The catecholamine hypothesis, advanced by Joseph Schildkraut states that depression is produced by an insufficiency of catecholamines, while mania may result from an overabundance of these substances. The indoleamine hypothesis, advanced by Alec Coppen, suggests that serotonin deficiency, rather than norepinephrine deficiency, leads to depression because tryptophan, the precursor of serotonin, elevates moods. Lithium, which seems to be effective in the treatment of mania and some depressions, affects both catecholamine and indoleamine metabolism.

Psychological Approaches

Biological factors undoubtedly play a role in bipolar disorders. However, it must be noted that there are also numerous other factors in these disorders. Among the first theories of manic-depressive disorders to take a psychological approach was the classic psychoanalytic theory of affective disorders jointly developed by Karl Abraham and Sigmund Freud. This theory states that depressive individuals are unusually dependent on others and have strongly incorporated the values and standards of others into their own personality structures. They therefore fail to form an adequate differentiation between the self and others. According to this viewpoint, mania is viewed as massive denial and reaction formation to underlying depression.

Among the neoanalytic theorists, Alfred Adler was the first to speak of depression as a tactic that could be used to manipulate others. According to this viewpoint, by avowing helplessness and self-condemnation, the depressed person can force others into supplying help, sympathy, and compliments.

Cognitive theorists such as Aaron Beck and Albert Ellis have stated that the locus of affective disorders lies in distorted and faulty cognitions concerning the self, the world, and the future. In terms of the self, the depressed person employs beliefs that overemphasize personal faults and inadequacies. In terms of the world, the depressed person construes the world as overbearing, hostile, and unrewarding. In terms of the future, the depressed person constructs a bleak picture of tragedies and sorrows to come and longs for a glorified but long-lost past. Theoreticians using this approach have not written much about manic states. However because manic patients demonstrate massive cognitive distortions, it may be possible to modify their cognitions.

Several learning theory explanations of depression have been proposed. One theory, advanced by Peter Lewinsohn and his colleagues, states that depressive behavior is analogous or perhaps identical to the extinction of learned responses. The depressed person may be trapped in a "vicious cycle": The less reinforcement received, the more behavioral withdrawal occurs. However, the more the person withdraws, the less reinforcement the person will receive. An explanation of mania, however, would be particularly challenging for this approach because it is difficult to see how too much reinforcement would lead to too much behavior, unless some additional elements were added to the theory.

A second variant of a learning approach that also considers cognitions can be found in Seligman's "learned helplessness" model. Having once learned to accept a helpless stance, individuals may limit or avoid future activities in which they may actually have a great deal of control and personal success.

In its more expanded form, a revision of the theory by Abramson, Seligman, and Teasdale draws a distinction between *external, universal helplessness* (no one can be successful) and *internal, personal helplessness* (*I* cannot function, although others can). In addition, a distinction is drawn between *stable* and *unstable* helplessness based on the length of time that the person has been exposed to uncontrollable circumstances. Like other approaches, this one has difficulty in explaining mania without the introduction of other factors.

In an attempt to integrate the vast literature on affective disorders, Akiskal and McKinney developed an integrative model of affective disorders that links genetic, biochemical, early child developmental, and current biological and social stress factors into a "final common pathway" of depression or mania. According to these authors, the final common pathway can be located in the action of the diencephalon, the subcortical area of the brain containing the thalamus, hypothalamus, and pituitary gland. Because numerous studies have implicated these brain regions as control centers for pleasure and pain, arousal, and physical growth, it would seem reasonable to assume that many of the biological and experimental factors in manic-depressive disorders may be at least mediated by events in the diencephalon.

TREATMENT

Although the bipolar affective disorders are among the most severe mental disorders, the prognosis for patients with these disorders is surprisingly good. These disorders have a limited duration and will change even when untreated. Regardless of treatment modality, however, therapists are aware of the potential suicide risks in the depressive phase and the potential "accidents" and mishaps that can occur in the manic phase. Patients should be reassured that, although they may be feeling hopeless, miserable, and out of control, they will not remain in that state.

Drugs, including the MAO inhibitors and the tricyclic antidepressants, have been useful for treating of depression, while lithium carbonate has been the treatment of choice in manic states. Some effectiveness has been established for lithium carbonate in depressive states as well.

Although its use is declining owing to increased drug usage, and its underlying mechanism is not fully understood, electroconvulsive (ECT) or "shock" therapy has been used since the 1930s.

Although there are only a few reports of the outcomes of well-controlled scientific studies of psychotherapy for depression and mania, those reports generally state that psychotherapy for depression often produces significant improvement over that found in control groups. Some studies have indicated that in some cases psychotherapy is more effective than drug therapy. There have been very few reports of the effects of psychotherapy for manic states. It may be that many manic patients do not seek therapy and, when in the therapy situation, they often view therapy as an intrusion in their lives.

LEARNED HELPLESSNESS
PERSONALITY DISORDERS

B. S. GORMAN

MARASMUS

Marasmus is the condition of extreme protein/calorie malnutrition in the first year of life, such that the infant not only fails to thrive but is in danger of dying. If the infant lives, he or she may suffer permanent loss of brain cells and less than normal growth.

Worldwide, the most common cause of marasmus is famine, a problem exacerbated if the mother does not breast-feed. In developed countries such as those of North America and Europe, marasmus is most often caused by neglect, when parents neither know nor care how to feed their infants. However, in some cases the mother appears to be feeding her baby with sufficient frequency and quantity, but a disruption of the usual mother–infant bond causes the baby to refuse nourishment, to vomit soon after eating, or to pass the food through the body without digesting it.

In the short term, marasmus is treated via intravenous feeding to keep the infant alive and restore normal weight. When the cause is neglectful or disturbed parenting, an experienced surrogate mother who meets the infant's need for love and care can usually restore the infant's trust, enabling it to eat normally.

INFANT DEVELOPMENT
MALNUTRITION AND HUMAN BEHAVIOR

K. S. BERGER

MARATHON THERAPY

Marathon therapy is a form of group psychotherapy involving sessions that may last from 5 to 48 hours, or over a weekend. Marathon group psychotherapy is embedded in the cultural and philosophical tenets of the encounter, sensitivity training, and human growth or potential movement. Two group leaders and from 10 to 14 participants use group pressure throughout extended sessions to attain intimacy in intense interactions among participants. The focus of the sessions is on the present ("here and now"), the primacy of direct experience and expression of self, and direct confrontation of psychological defenses. Techniques include nonverbal interactions and physical "games" or exercises.

Criticisms of marathon therapy include charges of "brainwashing" procedures, inadequate screening and subsequent breakdown of fragile patients, and lack of research substantiating claims made about marathon therapy's efficacy.

GROUP PSYCHOTHERAPY
INNOVATIVE PSYCHOTHERAPIES

A. K. HESS

MARIJUANA

Marijuana is a general term for preparation of the plant *cannabis sativa*, which has been cultivated for hundreds of years. Marijuana is usually smoked. It consists of more than 400 compounds. The psychoactive ingredient delta-9-tetrahydrocannabinol (THC) determines the potency of the substance. Hashish is a resin extracted from the plant that is smoked, and hashish oil is an extract of the plant sometimes used on the tip of a tobacco cigarette.

Marijuana became widely used in the United States in the 1960s; by 1979, 68.2% of adults between 18 and 25 had tried it at least once. The young adult age group demonstrated the highest rates of current use and lifetime prevalence.

The effects of marijuana depend on the potency, the amount used, past experience, and the circumstances in which one uses it. Initial intoxication includes feelings of euphoria and relaxation. Physiological effects include increased pulse and heart rate, reddening of the eyes, a dry mouth, and sometimes an increase in appetite. These experiences are followed by sleepiness.

Acute negative changes have been directly related to dose. Impairments in perceptual functioning, sensory motor coordination, short-term memory, and tracking ability have been reported. In addition, delta-THC has been linked to a reversible decrease of sperm production in males. There is evidence, however, of impaired respiratory functioning in chronic marijuana smokers. The most commonly reported negative emotional reaction has been panic anxiety attacks. In addition, paranoid reactions have been documented. Chronic usage has been associated with several psychosocial problems, but causality has not been determined.

Therapeutic use of marijuana has been suggested in the treatment of glaucoma and in the control of side effects (nausea and vomiting) from chemotherapy for cancer. Given the increasing usage of marijuana and the controversial claims regarding its potential use and abuse, it is clear that marijuana provides a fertile field for future research.

HALLUCINOGENIC DRUGS
PSYCHOPHARMACOLOGY
SUBSTANCE ABUSE

C. LANDAU

MARITAL ADJUSTMENT

In the early twentieth century, social scientists began to express their concern about marriage. With a few notable exceptions, not until the mid-1960s and early 1970s was marriage closely scrutinized as a unique phenomenon by psychologists. Many were clinical psychologists interested in improving marital therapy, although some social psychologists found the marital dyad a unique phenomenon in which to test their theories of interpersonal relationships. Much research had focused on demographic and global measures associated with marital success. Although probably the most frequently researched topic in family studies, the survey methodology and lack of precision in the measures has led some psychologically oriented researchers to decry the quality of research in the area.

The ultimate criterion of whether a marriage is successful is whether it ends naturally. A stable marriage is one in which the relationship ends with the death of one of the spouses. Divorce and separation define an unstable marriage. The United States has seen dramatic increases in the divorce rate. Projections have led some observers to predict that 4 out of 10 marriages contracted in the 1970s may end in divorce. The divorce rate of second and third marriages is even higher than that of first marriages.

A wide variety of terms has been applied to the evaluation of the degree to which existing marriages can be thought to be successful. "Marital adjustment" refers to the overall level to which the individuals have fit together into a smooth, functioning dyad. "Marital quality" is often used as a synonym for adjustment, but refers more to a detached evaluation of the characteristics of the relationship. "Marital satisfaction" refers to happiness with the relationship and desire for its continuance. These concepts are also dealt with separately as "marital happiness" and "marital commitment" respectively.

G. B. Spanier and C. L. Cole defined marital adjustment as a process, rather than a static state, that results from the degree of troublesome marital difficulties, tensions between spouses, marital satisfaction, dyadic cohesion, and consensus on matters of importance to marital functioning. A factor analytic study resulted in a 32-item scale. That scale, the Dyadic Adjustment Scale, contained four factors: *dyadic consensus,* the degree to which the spouses agree on matters of importance to the relationship; *dyadic cohesion,* the degree to which the spouses' lives are intertwined; *affectional expression,* the degree to which the individual spouse's needs for affection and sex are met in the relationship; and *dyadic satisfaction,* the happiness of the couple with the relationship, and the degree to which the couple entertains thoughts about ending it or is committed to its continuance.

CORRELATES OF MARITAL ADJUSTMENT AND STABILITY

R. A. Lewis and G. B. Spanier connected marital stability with marital adjustment. They list a number of premarital predispositions such as personality factors, values, social factors, and marital expectations that affect marital adjustment.

The predictors of marital adjustment and stability bear remarkable resemblance to the advice parents give their children concerning mate selection. Social homogamy, or similarity of social background, is positively associated with marital adjustment. Conversely, differences in social class, race, and religion are associated with lower marital adjustment and higher divorce rates. Social class itself is a predictor of marital adjustment. Traditional religious beliefs and church attendance are consistent predictors of marital success. In general, the more conventional the relationship, the higher the marital adjustment scores. Parental models are also important. Good communication and empathy skills in marital interaction are also associated with marital adjustment. R. L. Weiss suggests that egalitarian relationships are inherently more problematic than old-fashioned ones because norms for how the partners are to behave are absent. Traditional relationships are easier because there are norms guiding the interaction.

Marital distress refers to a level of maladjustment that has led the couple to actively consider termination of the relationship. Many developments in the field have been along the lines of distinguishing distressed from nondistressed couples. A number of sophisticated behavioral observation techniques have been developed, as well as data analysis procedures for analyzing them. Distressed relationships tend to have fewer positive and more negative communications. Distressed couples also have a negative reciprocity: A negative communication by one spouse is more likely to be followed by a negative communication by the other.

LOVE
SPOUSE SELECTION

E. E. FILSINGER

MARITAL INTERACTION STYLES

The style of relating that tends to form in marriage finds its pattern early in the dating period, possibly at the first meeting of a couple. As discussed by Rudolf Dreikurs, each dating partner, usually unconsciously, assesses the "fit" of personal values, attitudes, and behavior with the personal values and behavior of the other person. As both seek to define how they mesh, certain patterns of relating begin to occur repeatedly, almost as though a dance of interactional behavior were taking place. Raush reported that such patterns of behavior continued for years into the marriage and sometimes remained unchanging during the entire marital life cycle. These repetitive ways of relating, called *marital interactional styles,* fall into different types.

Two of these styles, vertical and level interactions, have been identified in some detail by G. Hugh Allred. The *vertical interaction style* is analogous to two people on a ladder who are climbing over each other in an effort to be superior, when there is only room for one person on each rung of the ladder. Often the patterns of relating in this type of relationship involve destructive criticisms.

By contrast, a *level interactional style* is characterized by cooperation. In this type of marriage a spouse's place does not depend on making the other partner feel left out. This way of relating is free from demeaning, critical comments, and love and trust are expressed openly. Most couples have some degree of both vertical and level behavior, but a marital interactional style is determined by the predominance of one or the other.

Three styles of interaction—complementary, symmetrical, and parallel—were originally identified by Gregory Bateson and have been researched by J. M. Harper and colleagues. In *complementary interaction* individuals exchange opposite behaviors. This kind of relationship is based on inequality of control, with one partner occupying a superior position and the other an inferior position.

In *symmetrical interaction* each person tries to avoid losing control of the relationship. Each person fights for the right to initiate action, criticize the other, offer advice, and so on. In *parallel interaction,* however, both partners know that neither will win at the expense of the other. Each person may employ similar or opposite behavior, but use it at the more appropriate and productive times.

Early family experiences have a tremendous impact on these marital interaction styles. The combination of the family situation and the child's interpretation of it gives rise to the child's creation of a mental "map" of ways to belong and find importance. In determining a "fit" with a potential mate, this blueprint guides each partner, usually unconsciously.

When choosing mates, people actually know more about each other than they consciously realize. Dreikurs believed that acceptance or rejection of a possible marriage partner is based on much knowledge and agreement that entirely escapes awareness. The identification of marital interaction styles can help them become more aware of their mutual behaviors. It is then possible to change ways of interacting to form more loving, lasting bonds.

EQUITY THEORY
PERSONALITY TYPES

J. M. HARPER
G. H. ALLRED
R. A. WADHAM

MARRIAGE COUNSELING

Marriage counseling refers to the systematic application of techniques intended to modify dysfunctional relationships. It arose somewhat uniquely in response to the social and family disorganization following World Wars I and II.

Three distinct clinical approaches emerged. The first was an extension of the pervasive psychoanalytic orientation of the period that focused on the individual dynamics of each respective spouse. The process was to generalize from the individual dynamics of each spouse to some resolution of the marital conflict, without diluting the transferential dynamics of the individual therapy. A second approach moved cautiously away from psychoanalytic concerns to focus on treating only the marital relationship. Although this represented the earliest form of couples therapy, it dealt only with conscious interactional material and avoided underlying personality dynamics. The third approach focused on the need to assess both the individual dynamics of each spouse and the particular manner in which the interface of these patterns led to relationship and interactional dysfunctions. This approach involved a blending of various clinical strategies including individual, conjoint, concurrent, and collaborative methods.

The development of marriage counseling represented much more than a clinical method. It marked the beginning of a major shift within the field of therapy toward recognizing that relationship disorders are linked to family processes, personal networks, and the social milieu. Since the late 1940s, the idea that an individual operates within a system had also been emphasized in family therapy. Many practitioners who primarily identify themselves as marriage counselors include children or grandparents in one or more sessions. Conversely, some family therapists prefer to work with the marriage relationship once the originally symptomatic children have become defocused.

A broadly defined systemic orientation is implicit throughout the field of marital and family therapy. This orientation is reflected in variable interpretations of structural, strategic, experiential, communicational, and psychodynamic models.

Systems theory is a general framework for a diverse range of therapies. Many therapists refer to "systems theory," but each sees it somewhat differently. A marriage relationship exists within a system of interpersonal interaction. An individual who comes to the attention of the therapist—the "identified patient"—is often symptomatic of the system's dysfunction, rather than the sole source of the difficulty. The relationship under study has detectable patterns of relating and communicating, although sometimes these are not clear to those involved. Once these patterns are differentiated, specific goals for change are established.

Behavior theorists see marital distress as interference with mutual reinforcement. By increasing positive actions and decreasing negative ones, partners will also experience changes in feelings and cognitions about relationships. Gerald Patterson and Richard Stuart are among the leading proponents of the social learning theory approach.

Rogerian theory has been used primarily with parent–child relationships and couples. The person-centered approach of expressing feelings through speaking and listening skills was pioneered by Bernard and Louise Guerney. Their emphasis on improving specific skills rather than on treating the overall relationship has been further developed by Sheron Miller. The Minnesota Couples Communication Program uses the "awareness wheel" model to teach specific skills such as "making feeling and intention statements."

Marriage counseling treatment methods have likewise moved toward a more integrative approach that assesses and works with individual, interactional, and family components. Many practitioners deal primarily with immediately identified communication problems. A smaller group of practitioners have focused on implementing behavioral techniques in an effort to change both role and interactional disorders. Some may work with multiple spouses in a group therapy setting, while others have indicated that they will treat the marriage only if each spouses' respective parents are available and involved in the therapy.

Practitioners who seek substantive change, beyond supportive or adjustment methods, recognize a broad range of factors contributing to marital dysfunction. These can be traced along developmental lines for each spouse, beginning with the earliest patterns of attachment and development. Subsequent premarital factors include the specific roles that each spouse plays with his or her own parents and siblings in their respective family of origin, their experience of family separation during adolescence, and the continuing patterns of intergenerational ties and loyalties. These elements become highlighted during the mate selection phase, which links dramatically complementary patterns of reciprocal needs, family loyalties, and idealized fantasies. The ensuing family formation issues of assuming parenting roles and evolving subsystems in the family, balancing intergenerational loyalties, and managing potential shifts in the complementarity represent other potential causes of dysfunction.

The actual style of marital treatment may vary widely. At certain stages it may be directed toward broadening the personal historical boundaries of each spouse. Another stage of marital treatment may be focused directly at increasing personal insight and awareness of relationship dynamics as they influence interactional dysfunctioning.

A further stage involves the therapist's direct intervention in the interactional process itself. This moves the therapy beyond insight or awareness into the direct use of the counselor/therapist's role to shift and often unbalance the couple's particular systemic interaction. In addition to managing the complexity of the various interactional components with the family system, the therapist must be alert to the typically subtle resistances of couple collusion and efforts to triangulate the therapist against the other spouse.

COUNSELING
DIRECTIVE COUNSELING
FAMILY CRISES
PSYCHOTHERAPY TECHNIQUES

C. A. EVERETT
G. R. LEDDICK

MARRIAGE COUNSELING IN GROUPS

When a husband and wife are counseled together in a group with other couples, each individual learns to empathize with the spouse and discovers how the other really feels, what the other really worries about, is upset about, and needs and expects. Both learn to recognize when lack of congruence is being experienced by the message sender or the message receiver and what each should do to improve communications. They learn to recognize clues that suggest a developing conflict or power struggle, a need to discuss a problem or share a success, or a need for affection and intimacy. They also learn to practice the interpersonal skills required to implement desired new behaviors.

Within such a group, participants also learn to differentiate between a support group and a rescue service, to use their fellow clients as a temporary support group during counseling, and to develop quality support groups with significant others outside of counseling. Seeing fellow clients discussing their pain and implementing new behaviors encourages them to take the risks required for change. Thus, fellow clients serve as models as well as helpers in such a counseling group.

DEFINITION OF THE PROCESS

This group's triad consists of three persons: wife, husband, and one or more helpers within the group. Those who have become proficient with this model have discovered that they can teach each client to pair up with the counselor or a helping client in their group so as to help rather than hurt the spouse.

Prior to the first session the counselor schedules an intake interview with each couple. First the counselor helps the couple discuss briefly their primary marriage and family problems, and whose cooperation is required for them to learn and implement desired new behaviors. Soon, however, the counselor encourages each to discuss his or her unproductive behaviors that require assistance and begins at once to teach the spouse to be the counselor's helper rather than to complain about the spouse's faults. Then the counselor meets with each spouse separately to clarify expectations and assess commitment to change. Finally, the counselor meets with the couple again for them to share reactions, assess the commitment of each to learn new behaviors, review the goals of each individual and of the couple, and decide whether or not to contract for membership in a counseling group.

When, for example, the wife speaks first, she is helped to discuss her own pain and unproductive and/or hurtful behaviors. While she discusses what about herself worries and upsets her, the counselor tries to detect precisely what is bothering her. During this process the counselor encourages other clients, and especially her husband, to listen empathically; to guess where she really hurts and use reflections to facilitate her discussion of her pain; to encourage her to decide what she must learn to do, and with whom, to improve the quality of her life; and to decide with whom she should share her goals and from whom she must solicit encouragement and reinforcement to achieve them.

Functioning as a counselor's helper increases the husband's sensitivity to her needs and his commitment to help her, decreases his needs for revenge and to win in a power struggle, and encourages him to negotiate for increased intimacy to learn new skills for managing conflict and to improve communication with his wife. Gradually, they discover that each must accept responsibility for defining and learning his or her desired new behaviors—that one can change only oneself. Each also learns to solicit the spouse's encouragement and reinforcement, to use the spouse's support, to seek her or his council in learning from mistakes, and to celebrate successes together.

The counselor watches for opportunities to teach the other clients to be both good clients and good helpers—at first, by reinforcing desired behaviors. During early group sessions the counselor also teaches precisely how in a specific instance each could have behaved differently to be a more effective helper or client. Video recordings can be used to help a client discover the impact of a particular behavior and with what it may be more appropriately replaced.

For some couples who are experiencing problems with their children, it is often desirable to schedule a family counseling session just prior to the couples' regular weekly session and arrange for the other couples to observe. Usually the counselor also describes the advantages of the family council and explains how to introduce and maintain one.

TENETS OF THIS MODEL

The effective counselor must be able to develop a good relationship with clients. The counselor achieves this objective by caring genuinely for prospective clients, conveying precisely what will be expected of them, teaching them to discuss their pain openly and to define precisely the new behaviors that must be learned, communicating how they will be helped to implement their new behaviors, and encouraging them to examine their doubts about counseling and ask questions about expectations prior to contracting for counseling. Thus, the counselor teaches them to decide for themselves whether or not to contract for counseling. Contracting has a positive influence on outcomes.

Moreover, counselors are obligated ethically to accept as clients only those whom they are competent to counsel and must review periodically whether or not each client is making adequate progress.

The more attractive a group is, the more it is apt to have an impact on its members. The extent to which its impact will be positive is determined by how well the counselor recognizes and uses therapeutic forces within the group. Instilling hope is crucial. However, no less important is the therapist's self-confidence in himself/herself and in the techniques used to help clients.

Though acceptance by fellow clients is not as predictable or as unconditional as that by the counselor, fellow clients communicate unique essential acceptance. When, therefore, clients discuss their deficiencies, they do not lose status in the group. On the contrary, they gain status for having the courage to discuss their pain and for their willingness to learn new behaviors.

Some clients must be helped to locate essential information and are taught new interpersonal skills to implement desired new behaviors. Role playing can be used within counseling sessions so clients can practice developing self-confidence and skills to implement new behaviors. Clients also can be assigned materials to read. Some clients require special instruction outside of counseling.

TERMINATION

Finally the counselor recognizes when it is time to terminate counseling and helps clients achieve closure. Effective termination helps clients say their goodbyes, appraise their growth in terms of their own criteria, and determine what each has left to do and from whom each will seek assistance in completing unfulfilled goals. Effective termination is used by the counselor to plan for follow-up evaluation sessions and to help clients discover the satisfactions that accrued to them from implementing their new behaviors.

EVALUATION

Unfortunately, most studies appraise only the general efficacy of a technique. Scholarly reviewers conclude that counseling does produce desirable changes in most clients. There is little evidence of any systematic differences in efficacy between individual and group counseling. However, clients can be hurt as well as helped. Marriage and family counseling are as effective as other treatments.

When a practitioner helps clients define precise criterion statements, clients can report their own, their spouses', and their fellow clients' growth on a behavior inventory developed out of all the clients' criterion statements (goals stated in terms of precise desired changes in behavior). Clients report on a Likert scale the degree to which they believe that each criterion statement describes each client's behavior at that particular time. Usually these reports are collected at three times: (a) at the end of the third group counseling session, (b) at the termination of counseling, and (c) during a follow-up meeting. Such an evaluation provides the counselor with three appraisals for every client: self, spouse, and fellow clients.

Even counselors and therapists who claim not to be interested in research must develop strategies for appraising each individual client's progress during treatment, at termination, and at follow-up. Moreover, it is not sufficient to assess whether a particular technique was effective. They must determine for whom it was effective, under what circumstances, when treated, by whom, and with what level of mastery of the technique.

CONJOINT THERAPY
FAMILY THERAPY
GROUP PSYCHOTHERAPY
MARRIAGE COUNSELING

M. M. OHLSEN

MASCULINE PROTEST

The term masculine protest was introduced by Alfred Adler in 1910 and confirmed by Sigmund Freud in his 1911 paper on the Schreber case. Undoubtedly, Freud as well as Adler had noted the frequent, often quite conscious or at least directly observable, phenomenon (often confirmed since then) that many women prefer to be men, while men want to be "real men."

Eventually, Adler subsumed this desire to be a "real man" under broader contexts and concepts such as the striving for power or perfection, for superiority, and finally for overcoming. Freud, in contrast, explained masculine protest as a function of the castration complex and penis envy.

ADLERIAN PSYCHOLOGY
PERSONALITY
TRANSSEXUALISM

H. L. ANSBACHER

MASS HYSTERIA

The term *hysteria* is used to describe any seemingly involuntary outburst of wild emotionalism as well as, in a more specialized sense, an emotional disorder in which physical symptoms such as nausea, fainting, and even blindness or paralysis occur in the absence of any organic basis. Mass hysteria—or "hysterical contagion," as it is more often referred to by psychologists—occurs when "uncontrollable" emotional frenzy or "hysterical" symptomatology spreads rapidly through a collectivity of people.

Individuals involved do not necessarily know or even have direct contact with one another.

History offers many instances of widespread mass hysteria. A biting mania spread through convents in Germany, Italy, and Holland in the eighteenth century. Dancing manias, in which afflicted individuals danced about furiously and erratically while screaming and even foaming at the mouth, swept through medieval Europe, recurring periodically from the fourteenth to the seventeenth century. As one of many modern examples, an epidemic of nausea and fainting spread among workers in an American textile plant in 1962.

A. C. Kerckhoff concluded that such outbreaks occur when a general sense of apprehension or dissatisfaction is experienced by members of a collectivity and when the prevailing social structure is inadequate to deal with it. Although different forms of collective response are possible in many such situations, in mass hysteria people typically do not take direct action but become "victims." This is most likely to happen when the source of the apprehension or tension is not readily identified, and thus there is no appropriate target against which action can be directed.

Suggestibility and rumor play important roles in the contagion of hysteria. When under extreme stress, individuals typically become much more suggestible and much less capable of critically examining the ideas and behaviors of others in their immediate environment.

Not everyone is equally affected by the spread of hysteria. Some individuals are more prone to emotional outbursts in general. They not only make rapid converts to any spread of hysteria, but also may serve as key propagators of it.

CROWDING
FIELD DEPENDENCY
HYPNOSIS
HYSTERIA
MOB PSYCHOLOGY

J. E. ALCOCK

MASTURBATION

Masturbation is the term used to signify any type of self-stimulation, usually of the external genitals, for sexual gratification. During adolescence, masturbation becomes one of the main sexual behaviors and remains so for many adults. McCary estimated that approximately 95% of adult males and between 50 and 80% of adult females have masturbated at one time or another.

Although in earlier historical periods masturbation was considered a sign of depravity or sinfulness, it is generally accepted today as a common and almost always benign practice.

HUMAN SEXUALITY

J. P. McKINNEY

MATERNAL DEPRIVATION

Deprivation means not receiving something that is needed or should be available. Maternal deprivation is experienced by the child who has no mother: for example, a child in an institution; the child whose mother works; the child who has to be hospitalized; and the child whose mother lacks parenting skills and neglects or possibly abuses the child. Deprivation can also result from an unstimulating environment, an unstable mother, an inadequate diet, or an inadequate sense of security.

Often when one form of deprivation is present, others are also present. Maternal deprivation can lead to reduced experiences in the environment, a form of cultural or sensory deprivation. The age at which a child is deprived, plus the length of time the deprivation continues, also need to be considered.

Early placement in an institution can lead to behavior that ranges from listlessness, loss of appetite, and retardation of normal development to a general wasting away that can continue even up to death (marasmus). Placement in an institution after 6 months of age is worse than earlier placement because of the bonds that have been established between mother and child.

Even brief separations of mother and infant, as in the case of hospitalization, can create disruptions in development. These disruptions are also greater after 6 months of age. Maternal deprivation always seems to be the primary factor.

Inadequate mothering can occur with a child who is difficult to respond to, a very young mother, a mother from a poor parenting background, or one who simply does not want the child. Any of these factors can lead to deficiencies in the way a child is fed, held, or responded to. Abused babies come from an inadequate mothering background; the abuse can take the form of neglect or physical or psychological attack.

Stimulation is necessary for the normal development of an individual. Sensory deprivation can lead to retardation in motor and mental development. One solution to deprivation found in many cultures is having several caregivers. The effects of multiple mothering depend on the specific patterns of interaction between the child and the maternal figures, and the type of social structure present.

The role of the father in a family constellation should not be overlooked. He can be a primary factor in multiple mothering. Sweden has attempted to let fathers participate equally in the raising of children, granting paternal leave so the father can have adequate time to interact with the infant after birth.

No particular parenting approach guarantees a healthy adult. Current research findings that most harmful effects level out as a child matures only indicate the absence of psychological disorder, and not that the individual is functioning at an optimal level.

LIFESTYLE
PARENT–CHILD RELATIONS

F. D. BRESLIN

MATHEMATICAL LEARNING THEORY

"Mathematical learning" theory reflects an increased reliance on mathematics as a tool in the construction and evaluation of psychological theory, and in particular of learning theory. Although there is a rather easily identified subgroup of experimental psychologists who may be called quantitative theorists, they most certainly do not share the same theoretical orientation. Rather, they share a way of doing things, a methodology of theory construction that is quantitative.

Mathematical learning theory has numerous advantages over its qualitative counterparts. It allows a finer division of the set of possible outcomes of an experiment into those that support or contradict the theoretical predictions. Thus, explicit unequivocal predictions can be made because deductive consequences exist. The theorist is forced to coordinate theoretical and observable dependent variables.

In evaluating quantitative theory, as opposed to qualitative theory, some additional factors must be considered. In a learning study, an equation tells us how to calculate some measure of behavior, the dependent variable, for any given trial number. The equation will have some constants or free parameters. The more free parameters (or constants) there are, the easier it is to predict the values of y, because the task reduces to a curve-fitting exercise. Ideally, we would like to estimate free parame-

ters in one situation and use them in another. But this is very difficult, if not impossible, in behavioral work. Consequently, we try to keep the number of free parameters as small as possible, ideally not more than two.

It is necessary in quantitative theory to identify the parameters, that is, to know what psychological process, mechanism, or variable is represented by the parameters of the theory. It is also necessary to specify the situations to which the theory applies.

Early attempts at quantitative learning theory reflected broad generalist views and seemed to ask questions regarding the shape of the learning curve. The most significant early attempt at quantitative learning theory was that of Clark L. Hull, subsequently extended and elaborated by Kenneth W. Spence. The Hull–Spence approach involved large numbers of free parameters, so that quantitative assessments often reduced to curve-fitting exercises. Another major problem was the lack of a clear relationship between observable and theoretical dependent variables.

This problem was avoided by William K. Estes, who used probability of response as his major theoretical dependent variable, measured by the relative frequency of occurrence of a given response. Estes is probably the single most important individual in developing mathematical learning theory.

Given relatively simple assumptions, the theory has been applied with relative success to time-dependent phenomena in learning and conditioning, choice behavior, discriminative situations, probability learning, concept identification, abstraction, and various human memory phenomena. Over the years, Estes' approach has undergone changes so that rewards and punishments are no longer seen to directly strengthen or weaken associative connections, but rather to modulate the flow of information in a given situation. The importance of contextual information has led Estes to a view that deals largely with the structure of information in a memory system.

LEARNING CURVES
LEARNING THEORIES

D. ROBBINS

MEASUREMENT

Psychological research focuses on the relationship among observable variables. Psychological theory is concerned with the relationship among constructs. These theoretical constructs are generally operationally defined by observable variables. In both theory and research these relationships are expressed most accurately and precisely when they are in quantitative terms. But if a relationship is to be expressed quantitatively, the variables also must be given quantitative values. In the most general sense, this is the purpose of measurement: to provide quantitative descriptions of the characteristics of objects or individuals.

A characteristic can be measured only if it (a) can be defined (at least tentatively), (b) is manifested in observable behavior, and (c) occurs in differing degrees. If these three requirements are not met, measurement is not possible.

Note that what are measured are the characteristics of individuals. Psychologists also assign quantitative values to stimuli and/or responses—a process usually called scaling.

MEASUREMENT DEFINED

There are various definitions of measurement. The most commonly used states that measurement is the process of assigning numerals to objects or events according to rules. In psychology the "objects or events" are individuals, and what are measured are the characteristics (attributes) of individuals. Thus, psychological measurement is the assignment of numerals to the characteristics or attributes of individuals according to rules.

This definition implies that three sets of factors are involved in measurement: the characteristics of individuals, the numerical values assigned, and the rules and procedures for relating the numerals assigned to the characteristics of the individuals.

The use of quantitative descriptions has several advantages over qualitative descriptions. Quantitative descriptions are more precise (they are finer and more accurate), are more objective (there is greater agreement between observers), facilitate communication, and are more economical (a set of data or a relationship can be expressed by one or a small number of quantitative values).

The Measurement Process

There are three basic elements in the measurement process: a dimension, a set of rules and procedures, and a scale. The dimension describes what property (or properties) is to be measured. The rules and procedures indicate how the measurement occurs—the conditions under which the measurement is obtained, the procedures used, and the mathematical model applied. The scale is the units in which the results are expressed.

The meaning of any measurement depends on the relations between these three elements. The relations between the operations and the scale determine the scale properties. The relations between the dimensions and the procedures, and between the dimension and the scale, determine the validity of the measurement.

What Is Measured?

Because the constructs used in psychological theories are often intangible or only vaguely defined, in empirical studies certain observable characteristics are used to operationally define these constructs. These attributes are what are measured. More precisely, what are measured are the indicants of attributes rather than attributes *per se.*

Consequently, psychological measurement always involves inferences. In all cases the attribute is inferred from its indicants. When dealing with theoretical constructs there is yet another level of inference: from the attribute to the construct.

Rules and Procedures

Although certain standards apply to all types of measurement (e.g., the procedures should be clearly specified, standardized, and replicable), the exact procedures used will vary, depending on the characteristic being measured. The definition of the attribute often suggests appropriate measurement procedures. Conversely, results obtained from (different) measuring procedures may suggest needed alterations in the definition of the attribute.

One other situation is frequently encountered in psychological measurement: A given characteristic can be measured by several different methods. Whether these various methods produce similar results, and thus can be used interchangeably, is an empirical question.

The Scale

The result of any measurement is a set of quantitative scale values representing the level of the attribute in each individual measured. With a few possible exceptions (like the IQ), psychological measurement does not have such widely accepted and clearly defined measurement scales.

Psychologists have usually sidestepped this problem by expressing performance in terms of the relative position in a comparison group (norm-referenced measurement) or in comparison to a standard of minimal proficiency or content mastery (content-referenced or criterion-referenced measurement), rather than on scales that have meaning in and by themselves.

Types of Errors

In psychological measurement, scores are not consistent over time, situations, or a sample of items. These inconsistencies are called measurement errors and result from variations in conditions or from fluctuations within the individual. The extent of these measurement errors determines the reliability of the measure.

Systematic errors are also important in measurement. These result from measuring characteristics that are stable facets of an individual's personality but which are irrelevant to the purpose of a particular measurement. Systematic errors reduce the validity of a measure.

TYPES OF MEASUREMENT SCALES

Because different sets of rules and procedures can be used to make a measurement, different types of measurement scales can be derived. These scales can be distinguished on several bases: the empirical operations used to construct the scale, their mathematical postulates, or their permissible transformations. The last is the most common basis of differentiation.

Stevens' Scale Types

S. S. Stevens distinguished between four basic types of measurement scales. In ascending order they are nominal, ordinal, interval, and ratio scales. These scales are hierarchical: The higher-level scales have all the properties of the lower-order scales plus additional ones. A *nominal scale* involves classification of objects into qualitatively different and independent categories. An *ordinal scale* involves classification and magnitude (greater or less); that is, objects can be ranked in order by the amount of the characteristic they possess. An *interval scale* involves classification, magnitude, and equal-sized intervals. In addition to indicating classification and magnitude and having equal-sized intervals, a *ratio scale* has a definable absolute zero point.

These are not the only types of scales. Other examples include log-interval scales, which involve power transformations; ordered-interval scales, where the intervals differ in size but the relative size of the intervals is known; summated scales, which combine items having nominal or ordinal properties to form a scale that approximates interval properties; and absolute scales, which involve only counting.

Issues

Several questions arise from the fact that different levels of measurement can exist, one being "which types of scales should be considered?" Many writers claim that only procedures that involve magnitude are truly measurement and that nominal scales should not be considered as such. Yet, others would require measurement scales to have fixed units; thus, only interval and ratio scales would properly be called measurement. Some have noted that, although one can assume that certain measurement procedures attain a given level of measurement, there is no empirical evidence that they do.

A related question concerns the scale level attained by psychological measurement. Gardner suggested that although specific items or observations may only have the properties of a nominal or ordinal scale, combining a large number of items or observations into a composite results in a scale whose properties closely approach those of an interval scale.

A third, heatedly debated question is the relationship between scale properties and the use of statistics to analyze data. Some psychologists have argued that the choice of a statistic is dictated by the nature of the measurement scale on which the empirical data is expressed. This argument has been refuted by Norman Anderson.

Although statistical methods do not make assumptions about measurement scale levels, the two are not unrelated. Even though the nature of the measurement scale does not dictate what statistical methods must be used to analyze the data, it must be considered when interpreting the data.

CRITERIA OF GOOD MEASUREMENT

As various sets of measurement operations can be used, how can one differentiate between good and poor measurement procedures or determine which of several alternative measurement models is best? One set of criteria is internal: Good measurement models have clearly specified and replicable procedures that are internally consistent and parsimonious, and result in reliable scores. A second set of criteria is external and concerns the empirical validity of the measurement model. Using this set, one is concerned with such questions as whether the model helps (a) explain the construct or phenomena being measured, (b) predict relations with other variables and external criteria, and (c) discover empirical or theoretical laws. Third, a good measurement model is generalizable: It can be used with different samples of people and in a variety of situations. Finally, the best measurement procedure is the one that is most practical, least costly, and most efficient.

CRITERION MEASURES
EMPIRICAL RESEARCH METHODS
OBSERVATIONAL METHODS
PSYCHOMETRICS
SCALING
STATISTICS IN PSYCHOLOGY

F. G. BROWN

MECHANISMS OF GROUP PSYCHOTHERAPY

The term *mechanisms* as used here refers to those processes that make group psychotherapy work. An investigation of over 300 articles by Corsini and Rosenberg led to the discovery of 166 cited mechanisms, such as "friendly environment," "sympathy," "watching others," "emotional release," and the like. Using a form of clinical factor analysis to find common patterns in these 166 specific mechanisms, the investigators located three major factors in the area of the emotions, one in the area of cognition, and one in the area of action or behavior. In each of these they found three submechanisms: in the emotional area, acceptance, altruism, and transference; in the cognitive area, spectator therapy, universalization, and intellectualization; and in the behavioral aspect, reality testing, ventilation, and interaction. The authors related these to love, understanding, and good works, and noted that religion and philosophy relate to these three classes of mechanisms of group psychotherapy.

EFFECTIVENESS COMPONENTS OF PSYCHOTHERAPY

N. KEFIR

MECHANISTIC THEORY

Mechanism in psychology is the doctrine that animals, including humans, may be regarded as machines. The contention is that, although living beings may be complex, they are nonetheless machines and require no special additional principles to account for their behavior.

Mechanistic theory is often linked—but should not be confused—with determinism and materialism. Denying that there is anything like soul or mind in living creatures, a mechanist is always a materialist, but a materialist need not be a mechanist. Similarly, a mechanist will be a determinist because machines are determined entities. However, a determinist need not be a mechanist, as in the case of Spinoza, a pantheist who nevertheless adhered to a rigorous determinism and denial of free will.

The roots of the psychological doctrine of mechanism lie in the mechanization of the world picture effected by the scientific revolution of the seventeenth century. Newton triumphantly established that the universe

is a celestial clockwork following precise, mathematically statable natural laws. Treating the universe as a machine was the first step in gaining usable knowledge about nature, and it is a model that has continued to serve physical scientists well. Following Newton, mechanism was inevitably carried from the celestial clockwork to a behavioral clockwork.

This process began with Descartes. When it came to the animal world, Descartes proposed that animals are mere machines, their behavior entirely determined by the mechanical functioning of their nervous systems. People, insofar as they are physical bodies, are likewise just machines. But people, Descartes maintained, also possess free souls exempted from bodily deterministic mechanism. Nevertheless, Descartes took a decisive step toward psychological mechanism, especially in reserving only a single function to the soul, that of thinking, while accounting for perception, memory, imagination, and other apparently "mental" activities in terms of physiological (i.e., mechanical) laws.

Julien Offroy de La Mettrie boldly concluded that "man is a machine." Although he banished the soul, La Mettrie was not a mechanist in the full modern sense because he was a vitalist, distinguishing between inorganic matter, of which machines are made, and organic matter, of which living beings are made and which gives them the special properties of life. But La Mettrie did open the way for later mechanists and other antireligious philosophers of the Enlightenment.

Two scientific obstacles then stood in the way of convincing presentations of mechanism. The first was the poor understanding of the nervous system and the relation of the brain to behavior. This obstacle was very gradually overcome in the nineteenth and twentieth centuries with the persuasive development of the sensory-motor conception of nervous function, which depicted the brain as a reflex-connecting machine linking incoming stimuli with outgoing motor responses. The second obstacle was the problem of vitalism—how to explain living, reproducing, and changing plants and animals in wholly mechanical, causal, nonteleological terms. This obstacle was overcome first by the theory of evolution, which showed that teleology was not necessary to describe organic evolution, and finally by the discovery of the DNA molecule, making possible the explication of an organism's life processes as the result of the mechanical reproduction, copying, and communication of information encoded on the double helix.

EMPIRICISM
FREE WILL
RELIGION AND PSYCHOLOGY
VITALISM

T. H. LEAHEY

MEDICAL MODEL OF PSYCHOTHERAPY

The traditional biomedical model of physical and psychiatric illness posits that the cause of a disease can ultimately be traced to the actions of one or more internal pathogens, causing discrete patterns of symptoms to emerge. To relieve symptoms and restore health, a biomedical practitioner must accurately diagnose patterns of presenting problems and provide treatments that arrest, inactivate, or reverse the action of underlying pathogens.

For example, a patient may report that the following problems have occurred for the first time and have persisted for several weeks: loss of pleasure or interest in many daily activities; fatigue; reduced activity levels; a disturbed appetite; a significant weight change; thoughts of death or suicide; difficulty concentrating; and feelings of hopelessness, guilt, and/or worthlessness. The patient's psychiatrist may determine that this pattern of symptoms is consistent with the *Diagnostic and statistical manual of mental disorders* (*DSM-IV*) criteria for a major depressive episode.

Operating under the assumption that the major depressive episode is a disorder caused by internal neurochemical and neuroendocrine abnormalities, the psychiatrist would most likely prescribe a medication designed to correct or modify the presumed pathogenic process.

A similar set of assumptions characterize the medical model approach to psychotherapy, although the hypothesized pathogenic processes differ. Like the biomedical model of illness, the medical model of psychotherapy posits that the primary cause of behavior problems lie within individuals. Replacing the biomedical model's assumption of biological causation, however, is the postulate of intrapsychic determinism, which states that dysregulation of hypothesized internal psychological processes give rise to problematic behavior. Many examples of such psychological "pathogens" (e.g., childhood trauma, unconscious motivations, unhealthy ego development, psychosexual fixations, unconscious defenses, and impaired object relations) can be found in psychoanalytic and psychodynamic explanations of psychopathology.

Given that intrapsychic factors are presumed to be the primary cause of behavior problems, assessment and treatment procedures typically focus on identifying and modifying dysfunctional internal psychological processes. Returning to the example of a major depressive episode, a mental health practitioner who espouses the traditional medical model might carefully interview the patient about recent stressors as well as childhood losses. A potential hypothesis guiding this assessment would be that specific recent stressors (e.g., a loss of a friendship) may have stimulated powerful unconscious drives and conflicts associated with a real or imagined childhood loss of great significance (e.g., abandonment or rejection from a parent). Thus, the psychological pathogen that caused the depressive symptoms is an unconscious conflict, triggered by a recent event but rooted in early childhood experience. To alleviate distress, the mental health practitioner might formulate a treatment designed to help the patient gain increased awareness of the childhood trauma and its associated intrapsychic conflict. Armed with insight, it would be expected that the patient could (a) more realistically appraise the severity of the recent stressors and (b) more effectively manage the consequent emotional responses. In addition, it would be presumed that an intervention that targeted symptom reduction without addressing the underlying conflict would fail to produce lasting improvement because the psychological pathogen would remain active.

EVALUATION OF THE MEDICAL MODEL OF PSYCHOTHERAPY

Several criticisms of the medical model of psychotherapy have been advanced in the behavioral assessment literature. First, because unobservable (and often unquantifiable) hypothetical constructs are cited as the primary causes of behavior, tautological explanations of behavior disorders are frequently encountered. Consider the following simple example of a tautological explanation:

Question: Why is that person drinking water? [behavior observed]
Answer: Because he is thirsty. [unobservable intrapsychic state cited as explanation]
Question: How do you know he is thirsty?
Answer: Because he is drinking.

Now, consider the two more sophisticated, yet equally circular, explanations of behavior problems shown in Table 1. As is apparent in these explanations, the problematic intrapsychic state is inferred because dysfunctional behavior is observed. At the same time, however, the only empirical evidence available to support the presence of the intrapsychic state is the observation of problematic behavior. Thus, use of unobservable hypothetical constructs can lead to pseudocausal explanations.

Table 1   Tautological Explanations of Behavior Problems

Potential Explanation for Nocturnal Enuresis

PARENT QUESTION:	Why is my child wetting the bed?
THERAPIST ANSWER:	Because she is fearful about the pending divorce and is unconsciously attempting to obtain nurturance by regressing to an earlier stage of development.
PARENT QUESTION:	How do you know she is unconsciously attempting to gain nurturance through regression?
THERAPIST ANSWER:	Because she is wetting the bed.

Potential Explanation for Self-Injurious Behavior

OBSERVATION:	A psychiatric inpatient has been repeatedly banging his head against walls resulting in detached retinas and possible blindness.
THERAPIST EXPLANATION:	I think that the patient probably witnessed a traumatic event as a child. This behavior represents an unconscious attempt to "undo" the memory through blindness.
BEHAVIORIST QUESTION:	What evidence do you have to support this hypothesis?
THERAPIST ANSWER:	The head banging and a theory.

A second criticism of the medical model is that little empirical evidence has been reported that supports the key assumptions that (a) intrapsychic factors (when adequately operationalized and measured) account for the greatest amount of variance in problematic behavior occurrence, (b) insight produces adaptive behavior change, and (c) modifying behavior without addressing underlying causes will result in symptom reemergence. A third criticism is related to patient diagnosis and labeling. Specifically, the medical model approach tends to label persons or personality rather than behavior. Consequently, adherents to this view may be more likely to perceive their patients as more dysfunctional, helpless, and less treatable. Finally, the medical model approach fails adequately to acknowledge the importance of situational and environmental determinants of behavior.

ANTABUSE
CLINICAL JUDGMENT
CONVULSIVE SHOCK THERAPY
NEUROCHEMISTRY
PHYSIOLOGICAL PSYCHOLOGY
PSYCHOENDOCRINOLOGY
SOMATOPSYCHICS

W. H. O'BRIEN

MEDIEVAL THINKING

It is usually said that medieval thinking was *symbolic*. Medieval people, however, strove to grasp the *meaning* of events, not their causes. We think of the world as a machine composed of causally interrelated parts, whereas the Middle Ages thought of the world as a book containing symbols meaningfully related to one another and to a transcendental, more perfect world of eternal reality. This symbolical attitude derives from Plato by way of Neoplatonism and its fusion with Christian belief at the beginning of the Middle Ages.

This world view was not uniform across the medieval population, however. Literacy was long the preserve of churchmen; the Bible was unknown in any living language; the laity generally experienced Christianity through the magical hocus-pocus (a corruption of *hoc est corpore*) of the Latin Mass. Research has revealed that ordinary people were likely to be pagans (perhaps barely Christianized), heretics, and even atheists. Nevertheless, at all social levels medieval thinking tended to be symbolic rather than causal, magical rather than scientific.

PHILOSOPHICAL PSYCHOLOGY
RELIGION AND PSYCHOLOGY

T. H. LEAHEY

MEDITATION

There are certain invariant ingredients in every system of meditation: concentration, mindfulness, and an altered state of consciousness. These common experiences and goals, however, are achieved through different techniques in different systems of meditation: by the silent chanting of a mantra; by gazing at an object such as a candle flame; by counting one's breaths; and by dealing with the inevitable distractions of life by striving for a one-pointedness that brings a sense of self-control and inner calm. Customarily the meditator sets aside at least two periods a day, morning and evening, of from 10 to 30 minutes each, and sits or lies in a quiet, comfortable environment while going through whatever procedures the particular system requires.

The physiological benefits indicate lowered levels of tension: slower heart rate, decreased blood pressure, lower oxygen consumption, and increased alpha brain wave production. The benefits experienced in 20 minutes of meditation exceed those of deep sleep, thus indicating the regenerative power of meditation and the saving of wear and tear on the body.

Cautions and contraindications must be observed in the psychotherapeutic use of meditation, and careful supervision by the therapist is ordinarily essential, although some people embark on a self-managed program with highly beneficial results.

The maximum benefits of meditation, of course, are realized in transferring the learning to the daily world of stress, remaining relaxed and controlled in the midst of anxiety-producing stimuli. Such voluntary control of the involuntary nervous system was considered impossible until recently. Paradoxically, the control is achieved not by striving to attain it.

MORITA THERAPY
NAIKAN THERAPY
YOGA
ZEN BUDDHISM

S. MOORE

MEMORY

Memory is usually thought of as a faculty or a capacity by which past experiences can be brought up, thought about, or described at the present time. Whatever else memory may be, it is not a tape recorder that has recorded all the sights, sounds, experiences, and so on that we might remember under appropriate circumstances. Some writers on the subject believe something very close to this. Wilder Penfield, a neurosurgeon, has reported detailed recall of past experiences from people whose brains he was able to stimulate with an electric probe while they were on the operating table. As there was no attempt made to verify the truth of the recalls, the reports must be accepted with some reservations. Even if the reports were accurate, they would not be proof that everything previously experienced had been "stored" in the brain.

Memory is also thought of as something that can be "exercised" or strengthened by practice. There seems to be no evidence that one can improve one's memory by repeated memorizing, although one can learn to use more effective methods of learning. Mnemonic devices may help. People who fail to remember some items might complain about having a "poor memory," but probably they only learned something poorly and should not have expected to remember it.

It is easier to deal with learning and forgetting without talking about memory because we do learn and forget, but whether we possess and use a memory may be scientifically doubtful. No one can study a memory, as it cannot be seen or manipulated in any way.

Sometimes forgetting happens all at once, without the passage of time, as when an accident to the head leaves one stunned or unconscious. Such amnesia may be permanent or temporary. Children sometimes seem to show amazing retention of events or situations. Such detailed recall is especially astonishing to adults because, as we grow older, we seem to lose the ability to recall many events and kinds of information. Old people sometimes seem unable to remember contemporary events, while having allegedly firm recalls of childhood experiences. It should be observed that the recall of childhood experiences might be strengthened by frequent rehearsals and retellings, or even constitute quite distorted recollections made to sound reasonable by confabulation and extraneous knowledge.

The failure of retention of recent events might be due to a lack of interest and failure to learn or observe. In laboratory studies, when old people are motivated to learn to the same criteria as young people, they frequently remember as well as the young learners.

KINDS OF MEMORY

The reference to memory of current events suggests that memory can be divided according to how long ago something happened. *Short-term memory (STM)* might better be regarded as the results of a first learning trial. The more often something is rehearsed, the more of it will be retained, and the longer. Researchers in short-term memory usually refer to anything remembered after 30 seconds as the function of *long-term memory (LTM)*, but as that is the only kind of retention that concerns most people, LTM becomes too general to be of any descriptive value.

Endell Tulving has described what he calls "episodic" and "semantic" memories. *Episodic* memory is the retention of specific events or particulars like names of different people. *Semantic memory* refers to general knowledge—for instance, the ability to speak English or to multiply. We may not remember when and where we learned to multiply fractions, for example, but we may remember how to do so.

PROCEDURES FOR ASSESSING MEMORY

In the laboratory, retention is usually measured in one of three ways: recall, recognition, and relearning.

Recall

In recall studies persons are asked to report on what they have just seen or heard either after each trial or after several trials. They may be asked to report verbatim (in order or sequence), or "freely"—that is, to report anything they think of in any order at all (free recall). Sometimes a first recall is not as complete as a later subsequent recall. In such instances the term *reminiscence* is employed to describe the additional recall. When persons are unable to recall all the material presented on their own, they can frequently be guided, aided, or " cued" with associated stimuli and report more material. Such operations are called "cued recall."

Recognition

A more direct method of prompting is to present the person with the original material embedded in a collection that includes material not originally seen. If a list of 20 words was used as the original material, the subject might be asked to pick out those 20 words from a new list of 40 words. It is commonly found that under fair conditions of distraction, subjects can recognize much more than they can recall.

Relearning

It is a strong finding in learning studies that material once learned and now forgotten can be relearned in a fraction of the original learning time. The difference in the two learning times, called a "savings score," was originally described by the first psychologist to study learning experimentally—Hermann Ebbinghaus. The savings-score finding has stood for 100 years. The fact that there is a savings in almost any situation tested has led to the generalization that one never really forgets something that has been learned—at least, not completely.

THEORIES OF MEMORY

The prominent current theories of memory or forgetting are (a) the theories of disuse or decay, and (b) the theory of interference, which may not be completely contradictory. Both are based on the passage of time.

Disuse Theory

The disuse theory is commonly accepted by laymen as intuitively correct. With the passage of time material things corrode, weaken, or disappear. It might be the same for memory, as it is commonly observed that events of the past begin to appear dim and fade with time and are less and less well recalled. If material is to be retained it must be practiced. The disuse theory, like its competitor, suffers from lack of physiological support and is usually opposed on the grounds that time, by itself, accomplishes nothing. It is what happens during the passage of time that is important. Such logical arguments encourage support for the interference theory.

Interference Theory

In the interference theory it is assumed that if something is learned to any criterion it will be retained to that criterion, unless something else either previously or newly learned interferes with the particular experience under consideration.

Retroactive Inhibition

In retroactive inhibition studies, a group of subjects first learns some material, material A. They then learn another list, material B. Subsequently they are tested for recall of A, and it is regularly found that if material B is somewhat similar to material A, there will be a drop in retention over that of a control group that learns only material A and is tested after the same interval.

Proactive Inhibition

If material B is similar to material A, the learners will have more trouble learning B than a control group that has not learned A. This is called proactive inhibition. In many instances past experience *helps* us to learn new things (perhaps at the expense of some retention of the old), and many new learnings are so unrelated to old experience that no interference can occur.

Retroactive and proactive inhibition apply only to situations where two sets of materials or habits have interference potential; such potential usually resides in the similarities of the two habits or materials. It sometimes appears that the more we learn or know, the more we forget. Our past experience is cumulative, and much of it may contain similar elements to materials or operations in new learning. Proactive inhibition is therefore more likely than retroactive inhibition to be a source of interference. Such has been found to be the case.

SUMMARY

Memory might best be thought of as a change in the ability of an individual to react in some particular way to some stimulus or signal. When we do not know something, it is because our nervous systems are not able to process some stimulus input with a particular output. When we have learned whatever is concerned, we have been changed so that we now produce the appropriate response. With other changes we may come to be unable to respond in the desired way: Again, we have changed so that the stimuli are not processed as they formerly were. When some responses or skills are practiced over a very long time, we become quite resistant to change. Even an amnesiac who has forgotten his name and address will remember to speak English in telling you that he cannot remember.

COGNITIVE ABILITIES
INFORMATION-PROCESSING THEORY
MEMORY EXPERIMENTS

B. R. Bugelski

MEMORY DISORDERS

Information learned and events experienced are considered to be more or less permanently stored in memory. To understand memory, an information-processing analogy may be helpful. Information is entered through the senses, operated on, stored, retrieved, and utilized. The operations stage has functions of attaching appropriate cues to information, linking related events, setting priority, and selecting information to avoid confusion.

Obviously, efficient retrieval is the objective of any memory system, but achieving it is not always easy. Retrieval can be hampered by lack of *availability.* When too much information is taken in, memory capacity can be exceeded and information is lost. When too much time elapses between instances of retrieval, old memories fade. Retrieval can also be hampered by lack of *accessibility.* Attaching inappropriate priority to information may lead to failure to recall the highest priority information; poor attention and highly similar cues applied to other information can cause confusion and interference during retrieval. Memory loss due to lack of availability and/or accessibility results in the most frequent, nonpathological form of memory disorder: *forgetting.*

Forgetting due to loss of availability of stored information can occur with too little rehearsal or repetition of the information to be remembered, or when recently acquired information receives priority over previously learned information, making the old information no longer available. A common cause of forgetting is confusion or interference from acoustically or semantically similar information.

Amnesia, or the loss of memory, can be either anteriograde or retrograde and is caused by emotional or cortical trauma and by alcohol or barbiturate abuse. Amnesia can be (a) *localized,* so that specific features of the time frame around the trauma fail to be both accessible and available for recall; (b) *selective,* as evidenced in the failure to recall particular events like the death of a loved one, an automobile accident, or war experiences; (c) *generalized,* as evidenced by the inability to recall all one's life events up to and surrounding the time of a traumatic experience; and (d) *continuous,* where there is failure to recall events around the traumatic event and into the present. Generalized and continuous types are much less frequent than localized and selective types.

Memory disorders evidenced during *senility* indicate a clarity in memory for events from the distant past interjected inappropriately into the present. The information recalled is frequently viewed as somewhat trivial by others, but has emotional and situational importance for the person.

Memory disorders are also evidenced by *confabulation* or story telling to fill in for periods of blanking caused by alcohol or substance abuse.

Here, substance abuse seems to interfere with the encoding and storage capabilities, so that both availability and accessibility are disrupted for periods that may exceed 48 hours. Similar blanking appears during epileptic episodes and schizophrenic catatonic stupors.

Special cases of memory disorders are evidenced in the intellectually retarded. With them, despite highly rehearsed motor and elemental intellectual exercises, memory is frequently short-term; rarely is it available for the past 24 hours. Other special cases of memory disorders are evidenced by the aphasias. Here, previously learned and frequently used abilities such as reading, speaking, writing, and picture recognition are lost through a neurological disorder that may be precipitated by cortical trauma, stroke, and so on. In such cases, formerly competent readers become *alexic* and lose the ability to read. Others who had had fine motor skills now become *apraxic* and lose the capacity for fine motor movement, and still others who were highly adept socially become *prosopagnostic* and lose the ability to recognize faces.

ATTENTION
ATTENTION SPAN
FORGETTING
MEMORY

D. F. FISHER

MEMORY EXPERIMENTS

In an early paper, W. H. Burnham described experimental methods for measuring memory of verbal or visual material that included reproduction, introduced by Hermann Ebbinghaus, and recognition, used by Ernst Weber, when judgments were made on line lengths and weights and on description. Recent studies of memory and remembering have also measured the time to compare an item, figure, or sentence as compared to serial recall of materials, partial report, probed recall, rates of learning, and savings scores (time to relearn). Researchers have investigated the effects on memory, remembering, or forgetting of a multitude of experimental variables including the following: types of materials learned or memorized (verbal words, sentences, stories, still and moving pictures, abstract and concrete forms); sensory modality of presentation of stimuli (e.g., visual, auditory, tactile, smell); and rate and form of presentation of materials (slow to fast, simultaneous compared to serial, partial or degraded compared to whole, multidimensional and complex compared to single dimensional).

Memory experiments have included studies of the effects of intervening or prior activities, everyday activities, laboratory-contrived situations, anomalies ("perfect" memories), and pathological losses due to surgery, amnesia, or other brain changes (e.g., drugs, alcohol, old age), as well as studies concerned with unique "sensory" memory (iconic or acoustic), primary or working memory, and long-term memory. Theoretical considerations to explain memory processes have stimulated research into the influence of a multitude of additional variables on memory: massed as compared to distributed repetition or practice; semantic meaning or organizational factors of verbal materials; processing strategies in perceiving to-be-remembered events (depth of processing); the length of time materials can be remembered; and influences of group or social factors on memory. Memory experiments have been conducted using apparatus such as cards, pencils, paper, and stop watches; more complex tachistoscopes that control the speed of presentation with elaborate key-press devices or devices to record verbal response time; and advanced minicomputers and microcomputers programmed to automatically present materials visually or verbally, with appropriate response-recording keys for voice or finger press that also analyze the recall correctness as well as the speed of response.

FORGETTING
MEMORY
RESEARCH METHODOLOGY

N. S. ANDERSON

MEMORY RETRIEVAL PROCESSES

Retrieval is the reclaiming of information previously stored in memory. Usually this consists of the restoration to conscious awareness of such information, although some aspects of stored memory may be retrieved and used without conscious awareness, a phenomenon known as implicit memory. This article considers the conscious retrieval of information.

RECOGNITION AND RECALL

In exploring memory retrieval, consider those factors that influence the degree to which information that has been encoded and stored is made available. One perspective is the mode of retrieval. For example, when retrieval occurs through recognition, an individual need only identify material previously learned or encountered. Recognition memory is used to answer a multiple-choice item on a test, to spot a familiar face in a crowd, and to recognize, in a museum, a painting that had been studied in a textbook.

Another form is recall. Recall is used, for example, to answer fill-in items on a test, to recite a poem learned earlier, and to describe a past vacation.

RETRIEVAL CUES

An important factor in retrieval is the presence of retrieval cues, or associative links that lead to the information to be recalled. One way to think of the difference between recognition and recall is in the extent to which each mode of retrieval provides retrieval cues. In general, a test question asking one to recall information provides fewer retrieval cues than a multiple-choice question in which one is given several alternative answers from which to choose.

Contextual Retrieval Cues

Information learned in one environment is more accurately recalled when the individual is in the same environment, whether the learning context is a room, a crib, or someone dressed in scuba gear 10 feet under water.

Internal States as Retrieval Cues

Retrieval cues may be provided by internal states present when the material was initially encoded, a phenomenon known as state-dependent memory. Evidence suggests that a variety of internal states can act as cues. Retrieval has been found to be better when a person is in the same mood during retrieval as when the memories were encoded, although these effects have not always been replicated. Surprisingly, state-dependent memory also seems to occur when in drug-induced states, although this does *not* mean that information can be learned better with the influence of drugs than without them.

One interpretation is that as information is initially encoded it becomes associated with the network of stimuli that make up the external environment or internal state. When this network is activated by a return to the same environment or physiological state, it provides a means of access to the originally learned material. Simply remembering the original learning environment, without actually returning to it, is sufficient to demonstrate improved retrieval.

Sometimes retrieval cues introduced at the time of retrieval can inadvertently influence the information retrieved. Consider the case of someone who witnessed an event and is called on to provide testimony. Eyewitness testimony is often convincing to a jury, and it seems plausible to assume that an eyewitness can give an accurate account of what was seen. However, information contained within a lawyer's questions may act as retrieval cues that alter the eyewitness' memory of an event. Subjects' estimates of the speed of cars in a filmed accident were higher when the question included the words *smashed into* rather than *hit*.

RETRIEVAL FAILURE

Much has been learned about retrieval processes by studying instances in which retrieval has not been wholly successful. Errors made when attempting to recall information provide clues as to the categories in which information is stored.

The Tip-of-the-tongue Phenomenon

The tip-of-the-tongue phenomenon (TOT state) occurs when a person searches his or her memory for a familiar word but, unable to retrieve it, recalls words of similar form and meaning. One of the examples noted by Brown and McNeill was an attempt to remember the street where a relative lived (Cornish) and, unable to remember it, retrieving instead *Congress, Corinth,* and *Concord*. As this example illustrates, incorrect words may be retrieved that bear similarities to the word being sought, such as the beginning letter and/or number of syllables. Or if complete words are not recalled, there may still be partial knowledge of the target word, such as the number and stress pattern of syllables.

Repression and Retrieval Failure

Another perspective on retrieval processes is provided by the psychoanalytic point of view. In *The psychopathology of everyday life,* Sigmund Freud gathered and analyzed a number of examples of errors in memory, including slips of the tongue, the forgetting of foreign words, and the recall of incorrect words. Some of the errors he analyzed were his own, made while writing the *Interpretation of dreams*.

Of these and other examples, Freud proposed that "where an error makes its appearance, a repression lies behind it." Thus, Freud emphasized the importance of motivation in retrieval failure and proposed that free association would provide a retrieval pathway back to the repressed material that led to the error. However, it is of interest that a number of Freud's examples of words recalled in error bear striking resemblances to the sorts of errors made in the tip-of-the-tongue (TOT) state.

RETRIEVAL CUES IN THE RECOVERY OF REPRESSED MEMORIES

Repression has been found to block far more than the retrieval of words and phrases. In a number of examples reported in the news media, for example, incidents of severe sexual abuse during childhood were not remembered until well into adulthood. In one instance, a woman recalled that her father had sexually assaulted and then had murdered a childhood friend some 20 years before. While psychotherapy played a role in retrieving the memory, the actual moment of recall had been triggered by a moment of deep eye contact with the woman's own daughter, who reminded her of the friend who had been brutally murdered so many years before.

Both these incidents illustrate how seemingly minor events or physical characteristics can serve as retrieval cues that restore to conscious awareness long-repressed memories of earlier traumatic events. There are a number of similarities found in laboratory studies, theoretical analyses, and anecdotal observations of retrieval processes. Ultimately, a complete theory of memory must account for not only the successes but also the failures in retrieval of the many forms of information stored in long-term memory.

MEMORY
MEMORY EXPERIMENTS
MEMORY SPAN
REHEARSAL

F. M. CAUDLE

MEMORY SPAN

Memory span refers to the maximum number of unrelated items that can be retained and repeated or grasped at one time. Memory span does not refer to the duration of retention, but only to the quantity of material that can be consciously held at the same time.

MEASURING THE MEMORY SPAN

A method for the assessment of memory span was described more than a century ago and various approaches to its measurement have been in use ever since. A common method of determining memory span is to read aloud a list of items to the person being tested. The list of items might consist of unrelated numerical digits, letters, or words. Items are presented at a steady rate, one at a time. At the end of the string of items, the person is asked to repeat them. The series is gradually lengthened until the individual can no longer succeed in the task.

CLINICAL ASSESSMENT

A number of psychometric tests use measures of the memory span to aid in evaluation and diagnosis. Memory span is one of a wide array of interacting abilities that contribute to an overall level of functioning measured by some intelligence tests. The Stanford–Binet Intelligence Scale is primarily used in the assessment of IQ in children. At various levels of the test, the child is asked to repeat digits in order; children are expected to be able to repeat an increasing number of numerical digits with increasing age. At 2.5 years of age, the child is expected to be able to repeat two digits, three digits at 3 years, four digits at 4.5 years, five digits at 7 years, and six digits at 10 years of age. The normal adult memory span is about seven digits.

A digit span test is one of several components of the Wechsler Intelligence Scales that may contribute to the assessment not only of intellectual functioning but also of some personality characteristics. A digit span test may be combined with other measures to assess what has been called freedom from distractibility. Persons who are easily distracted have difficulty with accurate reception and encoding. In addition, a digit span task requires not only accurate recall and sequencing but also vocalization of the digits. Performance on the digit span subtests, particularly when the examinee is asked to repeat digits backward, is significantly affected by anxiety or tension.

Tests of memory span also are used in the clinical assessment of impaired adults, such as those with Alzheimer's disease, an illness in which memory disturbance is one of the earliest symptoms. Although there seems to be minimal change in memory span during normal aging, people with Alzheimer's disease do show such deterioration. A digit span test is a useful tool in the overall evaluation of learning disabilities, brain damage, and mental retardation.

MEMORY SPAN IN THE LABORATORY

The laboratory study of memory span has been assimilated into the study of information-processing models of memory. Memory span also is referred to as short-term memory, a stage in the processing of information from sensory memory through short-term memory to long-term memory.

The capacity of the memory span was one focus of an influential article by Miller, titled "The magical number seven: Some limits on our capacity for processing information." The views expressed in this article presaged the emergence of the cognitive perspective in psychology.

MEMORY SPAN IN DAILY LIFE

Memory span plays a principal role in any activity for which it is necessary to retrieve information from long-term memory. As it happens, it is possible to retrieve at any given time only about as many items as can be held in short-term memory. Furthermore, memory span is essential to the ability to understand language (it is necessary to remember the beginning of the sentence long enough to make sense of the end of it), to take notes, and to perform a multitude of tasks, from dialing a telephone number to remembering what one is looking for in the kitchen.

It should be kept in mind that the limits imposed by short-term memory serve a highly useful function. Imagine for a moment that it was possible to remember every telephone number you had ever dialed. The amount of information would eventually become overwhelming. Limiting the information that is eventually passed on to long-term memory, the memory span in effect reduces cognitive clutter.

MAGICAL NUMBER SEVEN
MEMORY
REHEARSAL

F. M. CAUDLE

MENTAL HEALTH PROGRAMS

Historical changes in the major theories of psychopathology have been accompanied by changing views of appropriate treatment. Perhaps the oldest of these theories, demonological theories of the etiology of psychopathology, were accompanied by trephining the skull to permit the escape of evil spirits, by exorcism, and by brutal physical punishment. In the pre-Christian era, psychopathology was considered the result of a disease process. More recently, the moral treatment movement led by Philippe Pinel, and the state hospital movement led by Dorothea Dix, have enjoyed periods of popularity.

In the early 1900s community psychopathic hospitals, community aftercare services, psychiatric diagnostic clinics in general hospitals, psychiatric outpatient clinics, and community child guidance clinics began to emerge. The citizen's mental-hygiene movement worked to inform the public that mental illness and mental health are on a single continuum, that social factors should be considered in the investigation of the etiology of psychopathology, and that early identification and treatment of such disturbances would reduce the magnitude of society's mental health problems.

After World War II, with the influx of returning soldiers into mental hospitals, the federal government became much more involved in issues of mental health. In 1946 the National Mental Health Act was passed by Congress, creating the National Institute of Mental Health (NIMH). Subsequently, NIMH became an intellectual and financial source of much of what was innovative in American mental health training, research, and practice. Through the Community Mental Health Centers Act of 1963 such centers were required to provide (a) inpatient care including observation, diagnosis, and intensive treatment; (b) outpatient care including direct services such as those previously listed, but in a nonresidential setting on an ongoing basis; (c) partial hospitalization such as day treatment programs; (d) emergency care-oriented to crisis intervention; and (e) consultation, education, and information programs to provide indirect services to fellow professionals, community agencies, and nonmental health caregivers, so as to facilitate prevention. Beyond these programs, many other mental health programs can be found in the community mental health center such as diagnostic services, precare and aftercare programs, social, vocational, and physical rehabilitation programs, training programs for all members of the helping professions, and various research and evaluation programs.

HALFWAY HOUSES
PRIMARY PREVENTION OF PSYCHOPATHOLOGY
WALK-IN CLINICS

R. D. FELNER

MENTAL HEALTH TEAMS

The work of Gerald Caplan has been a dominant influence in defining mental health consulting. John Altrocchi adapted Caplan's basic statement and subsequent refinements into the following definition: Mental health consultation is "an interaction between two or more people—the consultant or consultants, who are mental health specialists, and the consultee or consultees, who play roles in community mental health and who invoke the consultant's help, within the consultees' usual work or professional functioning, in regard to a current work problem which is relevant to mental health and with which the consultee or consultees are having some difficulty."

Teams are generally interdisciplinary in makeup and include degreed professionals as well as paraprofessional, technical, and support personnel. Team members typically include psychiatrists, psychologists, psychiatric social workers, nurses, teachers, clergy, occupational and rehabilitation counselors, art therapists, and others. Consulting has been consistently differentiated from other professional activities such as providing psychotherapy, supervising, educating, and collaborating.

Caplan has devised a classification of four categories of mental health consulting on the basis of the type of problem and focus. In client-centered case consultation, the specialist provides services directly to a client referred by a clinician with whom there is a secondary relationship. Consultee centered case consultation focuses attention on the consultee's work, with the consultant remaining outside the clinical relationship. In program-centered administrative consultation, the concern lies with some element of the consultee's organization or program. Consultee-centered administrative consultation focuses on the consultee's work within the organization or program.

Attempts at orderly categorizing have been considered important. Once distinctions can be drawn, then differing expectations, consulting contract terms, and purposes can be better delineated. Distinctions also maintain the clarity of the consulting enterprise, which has numerous characteristics. Sheldon Korchin has succinctly described these characteristics: Consulting is a voluntary relationship; the consultant must accept an outsider's status; the relationship is time-limited; and the approach is problem-focused. An economical statement of consulting goals has been provided by Maclennan, Quinn, and Schroeder. The goals are to assist consultees in one or more of the following ways: to understand the mental health dimensions of their programs and problems; to resolve interpersonal conflicts and program crises; to acquire or improve skills relevant to their jobs; and to research, plan, develop, and evaluate their work. The aim of consultation is to enable consultees to function independently in a more efficient manner so that long-term dependency will not be fostered.

Consultees represent a diversified group of individuals who are active in providing human services. Given the multifaceted population of consultees, it has always been considered appropriate for consulting interactions to occur in a variety of sites.

A number of factors have been described by Caplan as being pivotal in establishing consulting relationships. Caplan has asserted that the interaction must be a joint dealing with a superordinate goal, that of resolving a complex problem. He has strongly urged consultants to be attuned to a consultee's self-respect in the side-by-side problem-solving enterprise.

Numerous theoretical models have been applied to mental health consulting. In general, the clinical-individual orientation such as Caplan's psychodynamic emphasis has dominated. However, other approaches that consider the individual–environment interphase have emerged. Among these theoretical models are principles of organizational theory, applications from the ecological view, open systems terms, and behavioral modification principles.

Much has been written about the experiences consultants undergo. Kaplan and Roman described a number of these stressors. They observed that questions of professional identity arise when mental health and social welfare services are combined in a teamwork approach. Career identity is an important element in self-esteem, therefore role image and definition have to be carefully coordinated and defined among team members. Kaplan and Roman have also identified a tendency to "overprofessionalize" the "nonprofessional" members of a team. This, they assert, engenders stress and ambiguity for both the worker and the team. Henry Grunebaum recommended interdisciplinary cooperation and differential role assignments as remedial measures.

While consultants may wrestle with the question of whether they will be found acceptable to consultees, they also wrestle with the problem of whether they can accept the limitations of their assignments. Relinquishing final decision-making responsibilities and ultimate responsibility for a consultee's client is difficult. Consultants are also faced with the special challenge of having to go beyond thinking primarily about a client's welfare and must consider how others such as coworkers will be affected by the individual under consideration. Finally, consultants face the challenge of reformulating their caregiver role as one member of a team that will have multiple views of a client.

Both John Altrocchi and Beryce Maclennan have underscored numerous difficulties in consulting. Altrocchi has identified personal pitfalls such as a consultant's aloofness, lack of diplomacy, sense of omnipotence, and ignoring of negative feedback. Maclennan has observed situational problems such as an inadequately negotiated consulting contract, gaining access for consulting, and difficulties in transferring a consultee.

Formalized training programs exist typically in academic settings where a defined course of study is presented. Trainees may range from graduate students to senior postgraduate professionals. Courses, seminars, a practicum, and supervised field placement work are included in a training program. Informal training occurs among self-study groups wherever professionals are so inclined. This format tends to include analogous components of formalized programming.

PROFESSIONAL CONSULTATIONS

J. BINDER
W. KARLE

MENTAL ILLNESS: ATTITUDES TOWARD

Sheldon Korchin has observed that attitudes toward mental illness were more directly related to the observing of severe abnormalities. In earlier centuries the afflicted were thought to be possessed by demons and so were incarcerated and tortured. During the Roman Empire, physicians advocated a more scientific view combined with humane treatment. But after Rome's demise the belief in possession revived, lasting until the Enlightenment.

Phillipe Pinel spoke against punishment and advocated treatment by direct confrontation, scientific study, and the use of case records and life histories. He even suggested that some conditions may have psychogenic origins. Prior to the first half of the twentieth century, the mentally ill were still viewed for the most part as simply "mad." The "insane" continued to capture people's imaginations, and it was not uncommon to see "crazy people" on display in circuses and freak shows.

An important influence on attitudes toward mental illness was the emergence of the "medical model," which removed mental illness from the realm of witchcraft and placed it in the field of medical study and treatment. The following characteristics of the medical model have been noted by Korchin: Mental illnesses are diseases having etiology, course, and outcome; they have organic bases; like physical ailments, there is an underlying state with surface symptoms; cure depends primarily on medical intervention; and the disease process is within the person.

Thomas Szasz has been one of the major critics of the model. Szasz stated that mental illness symptoms cannot be related to nervous system lesions, but should be viewed as communications by the patients concerning their belief about themselves and the world.

Korchin quoted the psychological model as evolving with the discovery that behaviors could be driven by unconscious processes and psychological determinants. Psychologists and other researchers have shown that mental illnesses can be learned social responses and are treatable by various psychotherapy approaches. Like the medical model, the psychological model has had a significant impact on public attitudes toward mental illnesses. The prevailing public attitude toward the mentally ill in the second half of the twentieth century is that they are sick people deserving treatment and humane care.

As more ailments have come under the purview of the mental health practitioner, there has been a tendency to evaluate complaints in the direction of illness. Charles Bowden and his colleagues showed that patients sometimes also had detrimental attitudes. Those with harsh and pessimistic views about mental illness had more severe psychopathology and tended to improve less.

There has been a shift in emphasis from psychological illness to psychological health. The mentally ill, who used to be treated in "insane asylums," are now being cared for in psychiatric hospitals and "mental health centers," and even as outpatients.

Changing attitudes have produced a variety of effects. Joan Brockman and Carl Darcy have noticed a reduced social distance between the public and the mentally ill. Korchin has seen a significant increase in the number of conditions falling within the realm of abnormal psychology and a subsequent increase in the range of the clinician's work. However, Szasz noted that social stigma is an unfortunate by-product of the label "mental illness" and that an individual's good qualities tend to be ignored.

Modern attitudes toward mental illness have also produced many legislative changes. Efforts have been made to produce a patient's "bill of rights" to ensure proper treatment. Laws have been established to safeguard dangerous individuals from themselves and to protect those around them. The mentally ill are no longer held automatically responsible for acts committed during an illness. Various studies have shown how different treatment methods yield attitude changes about mental illness. Ronald Fieve suggested that pharmacological outpatient treatment has enhanced positive attitudes toward the mentally ill because of a reduced need for inpatient care. Educational seminars designed to demythologize mental illness successfully reduce fears about it.

Korchin has identified two major goals of a public education program: to improve care for the mentally ill and to foster prevention. He mentioned that the most effective educational programs with attitude change as a goal are those in which learners actively participate. Korchin has identified three target groups: those vulnerable to emotional disorder, those holding power in the community, and those with caregiving functions. Korchin has emphasized that correct information reduces fears and reassures people, provides standards for self-evaluation, and inoculates against oncoming stress.

LABELING THEORY
PSYCHOLOGICAL HEALTH

W. KARLE
J. BINDER

MENTAL ILLNESS: EARLY HISTORY

HIPPOCRATES

Hippocrates (c. 460–377 B.C.), the towering figure of ancient medicine, first introduced mental aberrations into medical literature. His writings on psychopathology were as polemical and provocative as they were original.

Hippocrates is noted primarily for his shrewd clinical observations, his rational biomedical approach, and his forthright, stoical presentation of his views. He believed that disease resulted from an imbalance of the humors, a notion first encountered in the writings of Empedocles.

Lyons and Petrucelli sum up Hippocrates' contribution to the understanding of mental illness: "Concerning the emotional state of the patient and mental illness in general, the writings are especially astute and accurate in terms of modern understanding. Assignment of the brain as organ of thought and sensation is an important indication of a high state of understanding."

SOCRATES AND PLATO

In view of Socrates' devotion to ethics and epistemology, rather than rational science, it is not surprising that Socrates was said to attribute his own inspirations to demons. Zilboorg conjectured that Socrates' demons may have been auditory hallucinations and the man himself schizophrenic. Socrates' pupil Plato (429–347 B.C.) adopted a system of psychopathology that was, in many respects, Hippocratic and set forth the first clear body–soul dualism. According to Plato, the soul is made up of three parts. The rational part of the soul is immortal and divine. The irrational soul is mortal and includes the whole gamut of affect. The rational soul presides over the irrational soul. When the irrational soul becomes disturbed it falls out of the rational soul's control. The result is madness, of which there are three forms: melancholia, mania, and dementia.

ARISTOTLE

Aristotle (384–322 B.C.) was in no sense a disciple of Plato. A rational philosopher of natural (principally biological) and mathematical interests, he rejected mysticism and is regarded by many as the founder of scientific psychology. Certainly a pioneer in sensation and perception, he held that we perceive and hence comprehend our physical world through our senses. Aristotle devised logic to comprehend a reality that, although not mystical, often defied mortal understanding.

Aristotle divided the human soul into the rational, including wisdom, logic, reason, and discretion, and the irrational, comprising virtues such as self-control, dispassion, morality, and courage. Unlike Plato, Aristotle held that the various ingredients constituting the soul are inseparable and function in concert. Human behavior is not an isolated event, but is the consequence of integration.

According to Aristotelian psychology, mental illnesses have organic etiologies. No afflictions are entirely "psychological." Illnesses may lead to mental aberrations, hence the origin is physical. Furthermore, reason exists independent of mortal beings and is thus immune to the deteriorative effects of illness. Because reason is both creative and insulated from the effects of illness, illness may coexist with creativity. Aristotle's logic led to the conclusion that mental illness was of physical origin and was peculiar to the human species.

CELSUS AND THE ROMAN EMPIRE

Aulus Aurelius Cornelius Celsus (30 B.C.–50 A.D.) was primarily a scholar, chronicler, and historian of medicine. His medical writings spanned a wide range of topics, including mental illness. Included in his writings on mental illness were therapeutic measures for treating phrenitus (delirium).

A contemporary of Celsus is Pliny the Elder (23–79 A.D.). He was a notable Roman scholar whose imaginative writings were influential in his day. If there is one theme throughout his writings, it is the Greek teleological notion that everything has a purpose. Pliny believed there would be a cure for all diseases.

GALEN

Claudius Galen of Pergamum (129–199 A.D.), after Hippocrates, was the most famous of the ancient physicians an probably the most influential writer on medical topics of all time. Galen's physiology was based, in good measure, on Hippocrates' humoral theory. When the four elements of the blood were in correct proportion, the organism was healthy. There were also three spirits, one of them responsible for growth (natural), one for generation and dissipation of heat (vital), and one for sensation and movement (animal). Galen's physiology varied from Aristotle's cardiocentric notions, and he invested considerable energy in refuting Aristotle.

Galen, like Pliny, held strong anthropocentric convictions. Such a view held that any plant or animal that did not serve a useful function for humans (such as food, clothing, or medicine) existed only to teach a moral lesson. Although Galen's teleology was not in the Hippocratic tradition, his treatment certainly was, assisting nature in the healing process with diet, rest, and exercise. He was particularly sensitive to and concerned with the effect of emotional states on bodily symptoms. Galenic medicine was unquestionably a monumental forward step that influenced the next 15 centuries of treatment.

THE MIDDLE AGES

There were few substantive improvements in the treatment of mental illness until about the tenth century. One interesting figure, however, was the fifth-century physician Caelius Aurelianus, who translated Soranus of Ephesus, a revered Greek physician, into Latin. Soranus' writings were organized by Aurelianus into "Acute diseases" and "Chronic diseases." The writings of Soranus/Aurelianus provide excellent insights into current thinking on the diagnosis and treatment of mental illness. Both men vigorously opposed the then popular ways of treating mental illness.

Perhaps the greatest of all medieval physicians was Avicenna. His theory that mental illness was attributable to physical disturbances in the brain was as novel—and as ignored—as the heliocentric hypothesis of Aristarchus.

There were two noteworthy figures of the eleventh century. The recipient of Avicenna's medical mantle was Maimonides (1135–1204). His writings clearly reflected Hippocrates, Galen, and Avicenna, though he himself exerted considerable influence on European medicine. Maimonides discussed the problem of mental illness, classifying "psychic dispositions" among "moral imperfections."

A little-known figure is Roger Frugardi, who developed the technique of trephination around 1150. Another landmark in the treatment of the mentally ill was the establishment of the first mental institution at Valencia, Spain, in 1410. The first three asylums were all in Spain, the second being at Saragossa and the third at Granada.

PARACELSUS AND THE REBIRTH

One of the most extraordinary figures in medical history, as well as a seminal figure in psychiatry, was the Swiss physician and alchemist known as Paracelsus ("better than Celsus"), who marked the beginning of a gradual transition from iatrochemistry (alchemy) to chemistry. A committed mystic and astrologer, he also believed in the four elements of the Greeks and the three elements of the Arabs (mercury, sulfur, and salt), and spent much of his life in search of the philosopher's stone. Paracelsus opposed three qualities of Galenic medicine: (a) It was too inflexible and systematized, adhering to a rigid biogenic model; (b) it precluded all "psychological" aspects of the individual, relying instead on the unassailable influence of the humors; and (c) it represented the conservative vested interests and the respectability of the professional establishment.

The authoritative text on mental illness in Paracelsus' time was the *Malleus maleficarum* (Witches' hammer). The *Malleus maleficarum* was essentially the product of a papal bull of Innocent VIII. It appeared throughout Europe in 30 editions over a period of 200 years, flourishing during the Renaissance, a period otherwise characterized by a rebirth and blossoming of the arts and sciences.

Paracelsus determined that health and disease were accountable to five spheres: *ens astrale* (the stars or passage of time; diseases that are fatal today may be prevented tomorrow); *ens veneni* (the environment, providing food that nourishes as well as poisons that kill); *ens naturale* (the individual "nature" or personality); *ens spirituale* (the spiritual sphere or psyche that may lead to or protect from mental illness); and *ens Dei* (the sphere of God).

Paracelsus revolutionized psychiatry by providing the first descriptive *observational* approach to the understanding of mental illness. He associated head injury with paralysis, cretinism with thyroid dysfunction, and sexuality with hysteria. He dismissed the divine intervention of St. Vitus in the etiology of epilepsy and was probably the first to recognize the role of unconscious forces (*unwussende*) in illness, and he distinguished between "natural" (physical) illness and psychological (*spiritus vitae*) illness. Apparently he was the first to conceive the notion of individual personality, a concept not formally developed until the mid-nineteenth century.

GALILEAN/ARISTOTELIAN THINKING
HISTORY OF PSYCHOLOGY
MEDIEVAL THINKING
SUPERSTITIONS WITCHCRAFT

R. A. PRENTKY

MENTAL IMAGERY

Around the turn of the century, mental images were frequently mentioned in controversies concerning cognitive experiences. Whether images were crucial to thinking became a significant issue of contention among both theoretical and empirical psychologists in Germany at this time. John B. Watson, the father of behaviorism, regarded mental images as nothing more than mere ghosts of sensations with no functional significance. Subsequently, experimental psychologists ignored the existence of images and worked almost exclusively with linguistic and behavioral associations.

More recently, however, mental imagery has become one of the most significant issues in current cognitive psychology. Researchers such as Hobart Mowrer, Silvan Tomkins, and others had paved the way for the "return of the ostracized." For almost two decades Allan Paivio has been at the forefront of both research and theory relating memory processes to imagery. His research has led to the conclusion that "imagery variables are among the most potent memory factors ever discovered." Paivio has interpreted his results in terms of a coding model that contains the underlying assumption that there are two main modes of coding experience: verbal and imaginal. The dual coding hypothesis has generated a great deal of research, in which high imagery has been defined in three different ways: (a) according to the image-eliciting quality of the stimulus

as assessed by subjects' ratings or reaction time, (b) by instructions that increase the probability that imagery processes will be used, or (c) in terms of measures of individual differences utilizing spatial manipulation tests and questionnaires dealing with imagery ability.

CURRENT IMAGERY RESEARCH AND THEORY

Allan Paivio and his associates have demonstrated that imagery plays an important role in learning, memory, language, thinking, problem solving, perception, emotion, motivation, creativity, sexual behavior, and numerous other aspects of human behavior. This research has also revealed the functional characteristics that distinguish imagery from verbal symbolic processes. This differentiation has been further supported by neurophysiological and clinical work. The imagery system, because of its concrete and contextual nature, appears more akin to perception.

Although interest and research in imagery have mounted, there certainly is less than complete agreement concerning the nature and function of images. In addition to dual-coding models, several other significant theories have been devised: U. Neisser's percept analogy; D. Hebb's cell assemblies; T. Moran's propositional model; Kosslyn, Schwartz, and Pinker's array theory; A. Trehub's neural networks; R. Finke's levels of equivalence; R. Shepard's psychophysical complementarity; Z. Pylyshyn's tacit knowledge account; and G. Hinton's structural descriptions. These theorists fall into one of two groups: to use Dennet's terms the "*iconophiles*, those attributing a special nature to mental imagery representations and giving the reported special nature of images some important theoretical status, and the *iconophobes*, those who believe that images are mentally represented in the same way as other forms of thought with no special status accorded to some intrinsic 'spatial' or 'pictorial' nature." In R. Shepard's words "current controversy concerning mental imagery seems to have focused on two closely related questions: (a) Do the mental images that some of us undeniably experience, play a significant functional role in our thinking, or are they mere epiphenomenal accompaniments of underlying processes of very different, less pictorial character? and (b) What exactly are mental images or, more specifically, what sort of physical processes underlie them in the brain, and to what extent are these processes, like pictures, isomorphic to the external objects that they represent?"

Bugelski maintains that imagery is a neural phenomenon that may or may not be conscious. Data from Jerome Singer's research on the stream of consciousness support the notion that internal information is being generated and processed continuously.

A definition of imagery such as the one by A. Richardson is implicit in most of these approaches: "Mental imagery refers to all those quasi-sensory or quasi-perceptual experiences of which we are self-consciously aware, and which exist for us in the absence of those stimulus conditions that are known to produce their genuine sensory or perceptual counterparts."

CLASSIFICATION OF IMAGES

On the basis of twentieth-century investigations, A. Richardson has identified four classes of mental images that may be compared with respect to clarity, vividness, localization, fixedness or stability, completeness of detail, susceptibility to scanning, and degree of likeness to the sensory percept. The identified classes are (a) afterimages, (b) eidetic images, (c) memory images (or thought images), and (d) imagination images.

Afterimages

These images closely resemble percepts in that they have a strong sensory quality. Usually afterimages result from actual perception of a stimulus object: They are representations of the object's form and, positively or negatively, of its hue. They are usually less vivid than their percepts but have the sensory quality of literally being seen, like the percepts.

Eidetic Images

These are another form of perceptlike images. Two types of eidetic images are reported: those resembling prolonged afterimages occasioned by percepts and those originating in memory or the general process of imagination. Both types are characterized by clarity and detail. Eidetics are relatively fixed; one can scan them for details if examining a photograph. Existing studies accept the prevalence of eidetics among children, but among adults they are usually thought to be rare. The identification of an image as eidetic is not altogether reliable because investigators apply different criteria as well as different methods.

Memory Images

These images tend to be pallid, fragmented, indefinitely localized, and brief. However, they have the potential for extreme vividness and clarity, and conceivably could be cultivated for these qualities, and perhaps also for stability and external projection. Attention and affect appear to influence these qualities of memory images.

Imagination Images

These images are significantly influenced by motivational states and generally involve concentrated quasi-hypnotic attention along with inhibition of associations. Imagination images include relatively distinct forms. Some of these are very perceptlike and assume apparent independence.

ASSESSMENT OF MENTAL IMAGERY

Self-reports or questionnaires traditionally have been the most frequently utilized method of measuring individual difference in imagery ability. These measures have dealt with three aspects of imagery ability: (a) vividness or clarity of the images; (b) imagery types (whether subjects differ as to the modalities in which the clearest images occur); and (c) imagery control (whether some people willfully can manipulate their images better than others).

Vividness of Images

It was Francis Galton who developed the first instrument for imagery assessment: the famous "breakfast table questionnaire." Betts extended Galton's method. In contrast to Galton's test, which stressed visual images, Betts' instrument explored vividness of imagery in seven modalities: visual, auditory, cutaneous, kinaesthetic, gustatory, olfactory, and organic. Sheehan revised and shortened Betts' questionnaire into a version commonly called *Betts QMI.* Largely owing to its brevity and breadth, it is at present the most frequently used measure of imagery vividness.

Marks published an imagery test, called the Vividness of Visual Imagery Questionnaire (VVIQ), consisting of 16 items, 5 taken from the Betts QMI.

Types of Imaginal Ability

Galton is often given credit for introducing the terms *visile, audile,* and *motile* to describe persons whose habitual or preferred imagery mode is visual, auditory, or kinesthetic, respectively. Interest in this idea has been rekindled by Anne Roe's examination of Galton's theory that scientists have weak imagery powers. Roe discovered that scientists in different disciplines utilized different types of imagery, that is, visual or verbal imagery. Recently there has been a great deal of interest in the verbalizer–visualizer dichotomy. Paivio developed his Individual Differences Questionnaire (IDQ) to quantify this dichotomy. More recently A. Richardson, in an extension of Paivio's work, constructed a briefer instrument called the Verbalizer–Visualizer Questionnaire (VVQ).

Imagery Control

There are clear differences in the degree to which various subjects can control their visual memory images. The most widely used test of imagery control is the Gordon Test of Imagery Control, which involves oral instructions followed by 11 questions to which subjects answer either "yes" or "no," depending on their ability to manipulate imagery. A. Richardson introduced a tripartite scoring system—" yes," "no," or "unsure"—and recommended that printed rather than oral instructions be used.

Other Measures of Imagery

Another group of methods measures the facets of consciousness that reflect experience more directly. Examples of such measures are the thought-sampling method introduced by Eric Klinger, which aims to assess subjects' "current concerns," and the Experiential Analysis Technique of Sheehan, McConkey, and Cross. The main difference between these types of assessment and self-report inventories is that the former draws from the ongoing stream of consciousness rather than from retrospective comments on experience. Thus, they may be more valid for assessing the facets of cognition that distinguish current everyday thought.

The methods reported so far are self-report measures. Attempts have also been made to infer imaging ability from behavioral performances.

Akin to this type of ability tests are those that are spatial in nature. These tests often are clearly intended to arouse imagery, but this imagery is generally concerned with the mental manipulation of spatial relationships.

CLINICAL USES OF MENTAL IMAGERY

Although imagery has been an instrument of therapeutic intervention throughout recorded history, recently interest in imagery techniques has greatly expanded and intensified. Several writers have indicated numerous characteristics of the imagery mode that make it an eminently suitable vehicle for clinical work. A number of these are listed as follows:

1. A number of studies indicate that imagery and perception are experientially and neurophysiologically comparable processes and cannot be distinguished from each other by any intrinsic qualities.

2. Several contemporary psychologists contend that images are capable of representing situations or objects and consequently act as motivators for future behavior.

3. It appears that meaning is largely dependent on images.

4. Mental images provide a unique opportunity to examine the integration of perception, motivation, subjective meaning, and realistic abstract thought.

5. Imagery may be the main access to important preverbal memories or to memories encoded at developmental stages at which language, although present, was not yet predominant.

6. Klinger believes that the imaginal stream observed in image therapies tends to overrepresent the client's problem area or "current concerns."

7. Klinger also points out that images are accompanied by emotional responses to internal and external cues present in the situation.

8. Numerous studies have demonstrated the power of imagery to produce a wide variety of physiological changes.

9. It has been observed that spontaneous images occur in some individuals at times of verbal blockage; the images fill in with perceptual, usually pictorial, representation when the individual is unable to continue to formulate experiences verbally.

10. It has been demonstrated that free imagery, an analog of free association, is extremely effective in circumventing even very stubborn defenses and uncovering repressed material.

11. Horowitz states that the image mode is the medium most sympathetic to unconscious organization. It permits the spanning of the conscious–unconscious continuum more readily than does overt or

covert language; elements from the unconscious more easily "slip into" imagoic cognition, and image forms more readily act as symbols.

12. Jellinek notes the intrapsychic prophetic function of imagoic cognition: Ideas and responses often occur in imagery and appear only later in verbal cognition and behavior.

13. Guided daydream images in many cases are likely to produce therapeutic consequences in the absence of any interpretation by the guide or intellectual insight by the client.

14. Solutions rehearsed at the imaginal level during therapy appear to generalize outside the therapy situation.

Over the years, numerous widely varied imagery-based therapies have emerged both abroad and in this country. Evidence is also accumulating that spontaneous and induced visual images are also a rich and readily accessible source of diagnostic information.

IMAGELESS THOUGHT
IMAGERY
PSYCHOIMAGINATION THERAPY

A. A. SHEIKH

MENTAL MEASUREMENTS YEARBOOKS

Originating in 1938, the various mental measurements yearbooks (MMYs) published over a span of 40 years have provided an invaluable service to a broad array of test consumers.

According to Buros, the objectives of the MMYs were: (a) to provide a current bibliography of all tests available in English-speaking countries; (b) to provide a comprehensive and accurate bibliography for specific tests; and (c) to provide critical test reviews by qualified reviewers to help test consumers select suitable tests for specific purposes. Other goals cited by Buros include exerting pressure on test publishers to produce fewer tests of greater quality and providing more complete information about published tests. It was also hoped that test users would become more discriminating consumers of standardized tests.

PSYCHOMETRICS

G. J. ROBERTSON

MENTAL RETARDATION

HISTORY OF THE CONCEPT

The concept of mental retardation is relatively new, having first appeared in the mid-nineteenth century. Formerly, there was little awareness of individual differences with respect to intelligence. By the late seventeenth century, observers had begun to perceive a basic difference between the mentally ill and the mentally deficient. The French scientist Esquirol postulated that the essential difference between mental retardation and madness lay in the developmental character of the former. Esquirol proposed the first classification system for the retarded that roughly corresponds to the modern day profound, severe, and moderate levels of mental retardation.

In the early twentieth century, the French Ministry of Public Education commissioned Alfred Binet to develop a method to determine which children could not profit from public education. Binet's method, developed as a screening device for mental retardation, became the first test

of intelligence. The first Binet–Simon scale was published in 1905. The 1908 revision introduced the concept of "mental age."

Lewis Terman at Stanford University revised and translated the Binet–Simon Scale and published the Stanford–Binet Intelligence Scale in 1916. Herein was introduced the "intelligence quotient" or IQ: the ratio of the individual's mental age divided by chronological age and multiplied by 100 ($IQ = MA \div CA \times 100$). Individual comparisons of intelligence were thus made technically quite simple.

The importance of this early work in intelligence testing cannot be overestimated. First, it produced a concrete, reliable, practical method for evaluating a person's mental functioning. Second, this method allowed for the quantitative determination of differences among individuals. Third, the fine graduations made possible by the use of the IQ test indicated that there were many people whose intelligence fell between severely mentally retarded and average. Graduation of mental retardation was thus officially discovered and recognized.

In the 1930s and 1940s, a debate began regarding the causes of mental retardation. A long series of "twin studies"—comparing the intellectual abilities of identical and fraternal twins, or of identical twins raised apart—suggested that heredity was the dominant factor. Other researchers, such as Nancy Bayley and R. A. Spitz concluded that IQ is not fixed or constant and that one's environment may have a profound impact on the development of intelligence. By the 1950s, an interactionist position was generally accepted.

THE CONCEPT OF MENTAL RETARDATION

According to the American Association of Mental Deficiency (AAMD), mental retardation refers to "significantly subaverage general intellectual functioning existing concurrently with deficits in adaptive behavior, and manifested during the developmental period." Three criteria must be present before a diagnosis of mental retardation can be made.

Significantly subaverage general intellectual functioning. This first requirement relates to the person's level of general intelligence. This level is defined and measured by performance on an individually administered standardized test of intelligence. The upper cutoff for mental retardation is usually an IQ of 70: All persons with IQs below this cutoff point satisfy the first requirement for a diagnosis of mental retardation.

Deficits in adaptive behavior. Adaptive behavior is defined as the degree to which one meets the standards of personal independence and social responsibility expected for one's age and cultural group. Because those standards are age-related and culturally variable, this criterion is difficult to satisfy and measure reliably. Fortunately, fairly good normative developmental data are available and, generally speaking, there is an expectation for increasing independence, self-mastery, and conformity to societal demands and conventions as the person progresses from one developmental level to the next.

Manifested during the developmental period. This third requirement is included primarily to distinguish mental retardation from a variety of other disorders where low IQ and adaptive deficits are present. These disorders include such conditions as brain damage resulting from stroke or trauma, and emotional disorders. It is important to distinguish between persons who had ability but lost it and those who never really developed it.

The AAMD definition of mental retardation has several important implications. First, this definition refers only to performance at a given time and does not explicitly imply irreversibility. Second, the two-dimensional definition (low intelligence and adaptive deficit) is important because it precludes diagnosing a socially competent individual as mentally retarded simply because he or she performs poorly on an IQ test. Lastly, the AAMD definition is developmental and emphasizes the assessment of a person in terms of success with developmental tasks appropriate for that individual's age group.

LEVELS OF MENTAL RETARDATION

Since the advent of the intelligence test, the classification of mental retardation has been based almost exclusively on IQ levels. H. J. Grossman has developed a universally recognized system that employs the terminology *mild, moderate, severe,* and *profound.* The *mildly* retarded individual's IQ falls between 55 and 69. These persons usually look and act normal and display no overt, obvious signs of retardation. As adults they are frequently able to find and keep a semiskilled job, but often need supervision in social and financial affairs. They are generally able to care for themselves adequately and travel about familiar locales with ease. Intellectually they are at the level of a fourth- or fifth-grade child. Motor slowness and poor reading skills make competitive employment difficult for them. One of the common problems with mildly retarded adults is their inability to handle leisure time.

The *moderately* retarded person has an IQ of 40 to 54, with an approximate mental age of from 6 to 8 years. These people frequently look as though something is wrong with them. The chief focus of training is on self-care and other practical skills, and the majority become fairly proficient in such skills as dressing, toileting, eating, and grooming. Although the moderately retarded may be able to recognize some written words or even read some simple sentences, essentially they are functionally illiterate. They have few friends outside the immediate family, and any employment they obtain is usually of a repetitive, unskilled nature, perhaps in a sheltered setting where income is not dependent on production.

Severely retarded persons have an IQ of 25 to 39, with a mental age of from about 3 years and 9 months to 6 years. Although neurological damage is common in this group, they tend to be ambulatory. Special training can teach them to talk and care for simple personal needs. Academic training, however, is not effective. The focus of training is on self-care skills, and little independent behavior occurs. These individuals need constant supervision and care. They are apt to be openly friendly in the manner of little children and attach themselves to persons with whom they come in contact.

Profoundly retarded persons have an IQ below 25, with an estimated adult mental age of 3 years 8 months or less. The probability of concomitant neurological damage is high and many are nonambulatory. They are often multiply handicapped, but may learn to walk and speak a few words. Until recently, most of these persons were unable to feed and toilet themselves, but the widespread use of behavior modification techniques has increased the number who have such skills. For this group, total supervision is necessary, usually in an institutionalized setting.

PREVALENCE AND CAUSATIVE FACTORS

L. Allman and K. Jaffe estimate that approximately 7 million persons in the United States may be classified as mentally retarded. Presently, less than 10% of these persons are in institutions, and most of those institutionalized are severely or profoundly retarded.

Less than 15% of mental retardation cases have a known organic or medical cause. Most cases with a known cause, or etiology, fall into the severe or profound range. Organic causative factors include genetic abnormalities such as Down syndrome, maternal infections or disorders during pregnancy such as rubella or drug ingestion, birth difficulties that deprive the fetus of oxygen, or postnatal factors such as infections (e.g., encephalitis or meningitis), head injuries, asphyxiation, or toxins (e.g., poisoning).

GENETIC DISORDERS
INDIVIDUAL DIFFERENCES
NORMAL DEVELOPMENT

M. P. MALONEY

MERRILL–PALMER SCALES

Two editions of the Merrill–Palmer Scales are currently available: the Merrill–Palmer Scale of Mental Tests and the Extended Merrill–Palmer Scale, a revised version. The original edition was designed for use with children age 18 months to 6 years; the revision is restricted to ages 3, 4, and 5. Both scales were designed to provide a broader assessment of the preschool child's abilities than a conventional intelligence scale such as the Stanford–Binet.

The Merrill–Palmer Scale of Mental Tests consists of 93 tasks grouped into nine 6-month age groups, beginning with ages 18 to 23 months. Four broad clusters of tests are cited: Language, All-or-None, Form Board and Picture, and Motor Coordination. Content is heavily weighted with gross and fine motor tasks and with perceptual-motor items. Total point scores may be converted to mental ages and within-age percentile ranks. Ratio IQs may be computed. Norms were derived during the 1920s.

The Extended Merrill–Palmer Scale consists of 16 tasks, four for each of four dimensions: Semantic Production, Figural Production, Semantic Evaluation, and Figural Evaluation. Guilford's Structure of Intellect Model provided a taxonomy for structuring the content. The first descriptor for each dimension defines the type of content (semantic or figural), while the second term describes the process (production or evaluation). The authors advocate the separate interpretation of each dimension; norms consist of within-age percentile ranks.

INTELLIGENCE MEASURES
STRUCTURE OF INTELLECT MODEL

G. J. ROBERTSON

METAANALYSIS

Metaanalysis represents the attempt to integrate, by means of various statistical techniques, findings obtained from different studies focusing on the same research question. It allows for a quantitative assessment of the extent to which results are consistent or divergent across a variety of studies. As noted by Glass,

> Meta-analysis refers to the . . . statistical analysis of a large collection of analysis results from individual studies for the purpose of integrating the findings. It connotes a rigorous alternative to the casual, narrative discussions of research studies which typify our attempts to make sense of the rapidly expanding research literature.

Moreover,

> Contemporary research reviewing should be more technical and statistical than it is narrative. . . . The findings of multiple studies should be regarded as a complex data set, no more comprehensible without statistical analysis than would hundreds of data points in one study.

Metaanalysis has been applied in a vast array of settings, only partially illustrated by the following examples: an inquiry into the validity of survey questions, a determination of the effect of pretest sensitization on psychological and educational performance, and the consideration of the impact of school desegregation on academic achievement. The range in topics of these examples indicates the broad-based relevance of metaanalysis. Although interest in metaanalysis has recently increased substantially, the predominant method of integrating and comparing research findings in the behavioral sciences continues to be the narrative literature review. However, with further application and refinement of metaanalytic techniques, the narrative literature review may no longer be regarded as the only appropriate or acceptable means by which findings are compared, summarized, and integrated.

ADVANTAGES OF METAANALYSIS

A review of findings from any of the fields within the behavioral sciences could benefit from metaanalytic procedures for two reasons. The first pertains to the complexity and diversity of findings. In contrast to more paradigmatic scientific disciplines in which knowledge appears to accumulate in an incremental and progressive manner, the complexity of human behavior *per se* coupled with the difficulty of implementing effective and meaningful control measures in behavioral studies contribute to diverse and divergent findings. In addition, the general way in which behavioral studies are conducted further augments the variability of findings. Inquiry is commonly characterized by studies that employ different definitions of critical concepts, methods of study, sample characteristics, different sets of predictor variables, and different techniques of analysis. It is not surprising that questions concerning the validity and reliability of narrative literature reviews have been raised. The subjectivity and potential bias of narrative reviews are especially problematic in three specific areas: (a) the selection of specific studies, (b) the weighing of studies in terms of relative importance, and (c) the interpretation of the overall salience of study findings. In addition, when the number of study findings to be reviewed becomes sizable, the adequacy of narrative reviews is further questioned.

The second reason that a review of behavioral science findings could benefit from metaanalytic procedures relates to the capacity for recognizing previously unspecified patterns in the findings. Metaanalysis results in a more accurate assessment of the extent to which findings within specific research domains vary or are consistent. The recognition of possible differences in the significance, directionality, and magnitude of relationships among identified variables of interest can increase awareness of heretofore unrecognized patterns. Moreover, because metaanalysis is able to examine differences in the characteristics of the studies themselves as potential sources of variations in findings, consideration is not limited to a review of findings *per se* but also is expanded to include the context in which findings are obtained. Consequently, with a more acute awareness of variations in findings provided by metaanalysis, research efforts can focus on more precise and deliberate conceptualizations and measures of behavioral phenomena.

CRITIQUE OF METAANALYSIS

Despite its viability as an alternative to traditional literature review processes, metaanalysis has been the object of criticism. This criticism can be illustrated, in part, by three categories of concern pertaining to (a) the "file drawer" problem, (b) qualitative differences across studies, and (c) the question of multiple findings from the same study. In addition to describing these three types of criticism briefly, the ways in which metaanalytic procedures have been modified in response to each type of criticism will be noted.

First, the *file drawer problem* refers to the tendency for statistically nonsignificant findings not to be published and to remain in the files of researchers. Published studies would then incline to be biased toward positive findings, thereby increasing the likelihood of Type I error. As a corrective response, unpublished study findings obtained from private and professional sources can be incorporated into the analysis. Not all unpublished findings are available for analysis. Rosenthal has offered a partial resolution to this dilemma by providing an estimate of the required number of nonsignificant findings that would have to occur to nullify a noted significant effect. If the required number of additional study findings is comparatively large, then the results of analysis based on available findings can be confidently accepted. In this way, metaanalysis can, at least implicitly, address the problem of publication bias.

Second, metaanalysis has been criticized as a procedure inattentive to variations in the quality of the studies under review. Thus, the results of the analysis may be difficult to interpret if findings from studies with strong design features are combined with the results from studies with poor designs. Metaanalytic procedures can address this issue by coding the studies in accordance with design quality and then having this coded variable entered into the analysis. Consequently, it can be noted whether the results of the analysis differ according to variations in the quality of study design. In this way, metaanalysis can accommodate the possible impact of variations in the design of the studies.

Third, studies frequently report multiple findings. The question of how to deal with these nonindependent findings has raised concern. Some researchers perform separate analyses for each distinct dependent variable identified in the studies, whereas others combine, in the same metaanalysis, findings pertaining to the significance and effect of a predictor variable on all outcome measures. However, if multiple findings of studies are included in the analysis, the results of the analysis may appear to be more reliable than warranted because not all findings contained in the analysis would be independent. Although there is no rule determining the appropriate method to follow, the way in which this issue is empirically handled can have an impact on the results of the metaanalysis. If multiple findings from the same studies are included in the analysis, the number of tests of significance and size effects would be greater than the number of independent studies. Although such a procedure would increase the power of the metaanalysis, it would not only complicate the determination of error associated with the statistical findings of the analysis but, more important, may contribute to conceptual ambiguity and confusion. It is informative to know the overall significance and effect of a specified predictor variable on a range of dependent variables, but an awareness of the differential significance and effect of a predictor variable on separate groups of dependent variables may have a greater consequence for understanding behavioral phenomena. However, debate on the relative merits of the opposing positions on this issue of multiple dependent variables continues.

COMPUTATIONAL PROCEDURES FOR COMBINING STUDY FINDINGS

Before outlining computational procedures in metaanalysis, it is important to recognize two uses of the method: (a) the integration or combination of study findings and (b) the comparison of study findings. Each respective use involves different sets of metaanalytic procedures. For a discussion of procedures in which study findings are explicitly compared, in either a diffuse or focused manner, consult Rosenthal.

Within the context of combining study findings concerned with the same specific research question, two basic strategies are involved: (a) a determination of the overall level of significance of the combined findings and (b) a specification of the size of the noted effects. A variety of procedures have been developed for each of these two strategies.

Overall Significance of Findings

In combining the results obtained from independent studies evaluating the same directionally specific hypothesis, the researcher has available a variety of procedures known as combined tests. In this article, consideration will be limited to the methods developed by Fisher, Winer, and Stouffer et al.

Known as the adding logs method, the Fisher combined test is one of the most popular and frequently employed testing procedures and is indicated by the following equation:

$$\chi^2 = \Sigma - 2\log_e p$$

This procedure involves the summation of minus two times the natural log transformation of the respective one-tailed p values reported in the studies analyzed. The resultant test statistic has a χ^2 distribution with the degrees of freedom (df) equal to two times the number of studies (N)

included in the analysis (i.e., df $= 2N$). The Fisher method is used effectively when the number of studies under review is relatively small (five or less). Although this procedure has been demonstrated to be more asymptotically optimal than other combining methods, it does exhibit a rather severe deficiency whenever two studies report equally significant results in opposite directions. In this situation, the Fisher procedure yields equivocal results, supporting the significance of either outcome. Thus, when only a few studies are under review, it is recommended that this procedure not be used routinely. However, more generally, it is questionable whether the value of metaanalysis can be realized whenever diverse findings are obtained from such a limited number of studies. When the number of studies within a domain are few and the findings are noticeably different, questions are raised not only concerning the appropriateness of metaanalysis as a method of review but, whether the studies under review are indicative of any viable research domain.

The Winer combined test, referred to as the "adding ts" method, is expressed as follows:

$$Z_c = \frac{\Sigma t}{[\Sigma(df/(df-2))]^{1/2}}$$

Based on the sampling distribution of independent t statistics, this procedure involves the calculation of a standard normal deviate equivalent to the summation of t values divided by the square root of the variance of a t distribution, $(df/(df-2))$. These t values are obtained either directly from the studies under review or, if only p values are cited, converted from the reported p values. The variance of a t distribution is approximately normally distributed when the degrees of freedom (df) for each t value is greater than or equal to 10. Therefore, in situations in which the degrees of freedom for each t value are less than 10, this method will not yield good approximations. Thus, although the Winer method has the advantage of being unaffected by the number of studies under review, its effective use is ultimately contingent on the degrees of freedom associated with each study.

Finally, the Stouffer method, referred to as the "adding Z's" method, represents perhaps the most widely usable method of combining findings and is illustrated by the following equation:

$$Z_c = \frac{\Sigma z}{\sqrt{N}}$$

this procedure involves relatively straightforward computation. After the conversion of reported p values to corresponding standard normal deviates, or Z values, these Z values are summed and then divided by the square root of the number of studies being combined (N). This procedure is predicated on the fact that the sum of normal deviates is itself a normal deviate, with variance equal to the number of studies included in the analysis. The only notable limitation of this procedure is that unit variance is assumed for each of the combined studies when under some circumstances Type I or Type II errors may be increased.

When the number of study findings to be combined is small, it may be prudent to use more than one procedure in the assessment of the overall significance of the findings. Even when the number of study findings is large, the use of a second combining procedure as a check on the results of the metaanalysis is suggested. Although appreciable differences in the results of metaanalytic procedures occur only rarely, the calculation of test statistics using different methods would lend confidence to the findings of the analysis. Depending on the circumstance of the analysis, the researcher should consider other procedures, including Edgington's adding probabilities and testing mean p models, the adding weighted Zs and testing mean Z models, and various counting and blocking methods.

Estimation of Effect Size

As the second general metaanalytic strategy in combining study findings, assessments of the strength of the effect of interest are made. In contrast to the first strategy, which involved determining the overall significance of study findings, an assessment of effect size focuses more specifically on the extent to which a hypothesized relationship appears to have an effect. As Cohen noted

> Without intending any necessary implication of causality, it is convenient to use the phrase effect size to mean the degree to which the phenomenon is present in the population or the degree to which the null hypothesis [zero effect size] is false.

Effect size estimations can be made using a variety of procedures. In the following discussion, consideration will be limited to statistical tests appropriate for an assessment of (a) correlational relationships and (b) group differences based on Student's t test. In assessing the effect of correlational relationships, the intent is to integrate study findings pertinent to the relationship between two variables of interest measured on interval- or ratio-level scales, whereas the evaluation of group differences refers to an assessment of the extent to which a specified outcome varies across two identified groups, most commonly defined in reference to some kind of control–experimental or pretest–posttest condition.

Studies vary in design and the type of test statistic used in reporting findings. Findings related to the association between variables may be expressed in terms of the Pearson product moment correlation (r), chi-square, or some other statistic, whereas group difference findings may be reported using t, F, or other statistics. Therefore, before assessing the overall effect size, the different summary statistics reported in the studies under review must be converted to a common measure. Among the most frequently used measures for this purpose are the Pearson product moment correlation for correlational findings and the d statistic for group differences assessed by Student's t test. Although these two statistics will be used in the following presentation, metaanalysis is obviously not limited to the use of these particular statistics. For conversion procedures involving various statistics, consult Rosenthal. Once the statistics reported in the studies under review are converted to a common metric, the analysis of effect size can begin.

Correlation Relationships. An assessment of the effect size between two variables of interest involves straightforward arithmetic and is indicated by the following equation:

$$\bar{r} = \frac{\Sigma r}{n}$$

an average of the correlations between the variables reported in the studies is calculated by dividing the sum of the correlation coefficients reported in each study by the number of coefficients (n) involved in the summation. As an alternative to the use of r values, Fisher Z values may be averaged as stipulated in the following:

$$\bar{Z}_r = \frac{\Sigma Z_r}{n}$$

After the reported r values are changed into corresponding Z values using Fisher's r to Z transformation, the sum of the Fisher Z values is divided by the number of correlation coefficients included in the analysis. Once the mean Fisher Z score is obtained, it is converted to a corresponding r value, which is then reported as the summary statistic of the analysis.

In further assessing effect size, cross-study differences related to (a) variation in the size of the samples and (b) the use of different measurement techniques or procedures may need to be considered. Because the two procedures outlined previously are not adjusted or weighted for differences in the sample size of the studies, a correlation coefficient (or Fisher Z) derived from a study with a sample size of 10 would have the same weight in the calculation procedure as would another coefficient based on a sample of 500. In recognizing the potential salience of this type of variability, Hunter et al. and Rosenthal recommend that the analyses of effect size employ average r values weighted for differences in study sample size. It would be advisable to report findings of effect size based both on weighted and unweighted mean values.

Regarding the measurement of the variables involved in the effect size metaanalysis, it must be acknowledged that, at a general conceptual or theoretical level, the variables targeted in the analysis refer to the two same phenomena across study settings (e.g., social class and psychological well-being). However, at a more refined and detailed measurement level, the respective variables may have been measured using different techniques or procedures. Although this source of potential difference would be included in the analysis of the overall significance of findings, it also needs to be considered when interpreting the meaning of effect size estimates. In fields of study in which particular scales of measurement have been accepted as standards and thus routinely used, this issue may not be as salient as it would be when measurement scales are not conventionally recognized and used. However, it is in these later areas of study that substantial benefits from metaanalysis can accrue, provided the analysis reflects thoughtful inquiry.

Group Differences. In evaluating group differences assessed on the basis of Student's t test, a two-step process is involved. First, a standardized scale-invariant estimate of the size of the hypothesized effect is determined for each of the study findings reviewed. Thus, for example, if seven studies are under review, a standardized effect size estimate is calculated for each of the seven different sets of groups contained in the studies. These group sets most commonly represent either control–experimental or pretest–posttest situations. The following equation is used to calculate the standardized estimate of effect size (d) within each study:

$$d = \frac{|\bar{x}_1 - \bar{x}_2|}{SD}|$$

In this procedure, the absolute difference between the mean values reported in each group set is divided by the standard deviation (SD). The standard deviation used in this procedure is either the control or pretest group standard deviation or the within (pooled)-population standard deviation. After these standardized differences between the group means (d values) are determined, each d value is given a positive or negative sign, depending on the differential effect registered within the two types of groups. If, as hypothesized, the group mean value is greater for the experimental or posttest group compared with the control or pretest group, then the d value corresponding to that study is positive. If, contrary to the hypothesis, the group mean value for the experimental or posttest group is less than that of the control or pretest group, then the corresponding d value is negative. Once the signs are determined, the overall summary measure for the combined study findings can be calculated. This procedure is illustrated by

$$d_{\text{average}} = \frac{\Sigma d}{n}$$

in which the positive and negative d values for each study under review are summed and then divided by the number of studies (n). The final summary statistic (the average d) would then represent the effect size between the two group conditions measured in standard deviation units.

CONCLUSION

The expanded use of metaanalytic procedures critically depends on the availability of requisite test statistic information. Without the reporting of precise test statistic information (e.g., p, t, Z, d, or r values) and other necessary information, the future use of metaanalysis will be profoundly restricted. With an increased availability of requisite test statistic information, metaanalysis will continue to expand substantively and methodologically.

As metaanalysis has developed over time, a number of issues, previously regarded as limitations in the use of this type of procedure, have commanded the attention of researchers. This attention has led to the identification and resolution of some of the problematic features of metaanalysis. Illustrated by such issues as the mediating impact of other variables and the use of nonparametric methods, metaanalysis represents a dynamic, multifaceted set of procedures whereby study findings can be integrated in a theoretically and methodologically compelling manner.

The future direction of metaanalysis appears to depend not so much on the resolution of technical problems as on the development of an understanding of the conceptual basis for metaanalysis.

ALGORITHIC–HEURISTIC THEORY
CHI-SQUARE TEST
CORRELATION METHODS
INFORMATION-PROCESSING THEORY
NULL HYPOTHESIS TESTING
STRUCTURAL EQUATION MODELING
TIME SERIES ANALYSIS

D. NICKINOVICH

METAPSYCHOLOGY

Literally speaking, metapsychology means "after" or "beyond" psychology in the same sense that metaphysics is "after" or "beyond" physics. The two connotations are related but not identical. To be "beyond" psychology usually has systematic or theoretical implications and means that one is dealing with problems and issues that, strictly speaking, do not belong in the domain of psychology but are relevant to it. Usually the problems or issues referred to are foundational or philosophical and are presupposed by psychology.

The most frequent use of metapsychology in this sense lies within psychoanalysis. Sigmund Freud used this term frequently, first to refer to the fact that his psychology dealt with what was beyond the realm of conscious experience, but later to refer to the assumptions of psychoanalysis. Rapaport and Gill have developed the notion of the metapsychology of psychoanalysis by demonstrating that a complete understanding of it would involve five perspectives: (a) the dynamic (positing of psychological forces); (b) the economic (understanding the posited forces in terms of their amount of energy); (c) the structural (the positing of abiding psychological structures); (d) the genetic (the origin and development of psychological phenomena have to be understood); and (e) the adaptive (understanding psychological phenomena in relation to the environment).

To say that metapsychology comes "after" psychology is a meaning that emerged later—one tied to developments in the philosophy of science. From this perspective, metapsychology is but one of numerous specializations that try to discover the most proximate set of principles, presuppositions, concepts, taken-for-granted practices, or explanatory factors that render a specific science intelligible. For this meaning to be actualized, the science itself would have to have been in existence for a while, so that the metascience could come after it.

A different sense of metapsychology was employed by Georges Politzer. Picking up on the implied connotation "beyond psychology," Politzer criticized "classical psychology" for going beyond its proper subject matter—human action—to posit an erroneous metapsychological "soul substance" or "internal life." In this sense metapsychology is understood pejoratively because its assumptions force psychology to go beyond its proper subject matter and posit fictive entities like soul, mental processes, and facts of consciousness.

THEORETICAL PSYCHOLOGY

A. P. GIORGI

MICHIGAN PICTURE TEST

The Michigan Picture Test, originally published in 1953, was revised in 1980. It is designed to evaluate aspects of personality adjustment in children between the ages of 7 and 16 years by eliciting stories about standardized pictures. The test cards involve personal and social situations considered critical in child development. Administration is facilitated through the use of four "core cards" that are the sole basis on which four scores and norms are based: tension index, verb tense, direction of forces, and combined maladjustment index. The four core cards and the remaining cards may be utilized for content and qualitative analysis. Validation studies on the four test variables indicate that these scores are both reliable and valid in discriminating poorly adjusted from well-adjusted children.

PROJECTIVE TECHNIQUES

M. L. HUTT

MICRODIAGNOSIS

Microdiagnosis represents both a refinement and an extension of the diagnostic process in clinical psychology and related psychological disciplines. It is a process of evaluating behavior whereby the outcome can be more effectively evaluated both in terms of the intervening processes (or routes) leading to the outcome (product in behavior or test score) and the potential for change or improvement in the behavior.

Clinical psychologists, among others, have long recognized that test scores (and norms derived from test scores) do not necessarily or validly measure each individual's ability or behavior. Two of the most common "corrections" have involved reevaluating the obtained score in light of the individual's sociocultural history and/or evaluating the qualitative aspects of the test behavior (i.e., making informal, sophisticated analyses of unusual behavior during the test).

The individual who has suffered some organic brain insult can be evaluated for amount of impairment in some functions by means of standardized tests, but such findings may improperly represent either the person's potential for recovery/improvement or capacity to utilize compensatory "routes" in performance. Hutt and Gibby have documented research evidence, as well as case illustrations, to demonstrate the limitations and dangers of standardized testing in evaluating mentally retarded individuals.

Microdiagnosis, in contrast to diagnosis based on scores from standardized tests, consists of exploratory procedures to test the present potential limits of scores on tests by means of experimental investigation of all relevant parameters. Moreover, it attempts to determine alternate paths for meeting the requirements of a specified task. Evaluating the particular individual's history (physical, social, educational) and behavior during the testing session, the clinician develops alternate hypotheses concerning the individual's particular difficulties in the testing situation. Thus, the test score is regarded only as a starting point in clinical evaluation and is not necessarily taken to be validly indicative of that individual's ability or potential.

A number of psychologists have developed approaches to more effective and in-depth diagnosis to replace or supplement traditional assessment procedures. Some have adapted the methods of the experimental laboratory. Others have used trial learning and retesting procedures.

CLINICAL ASSESSMENT
DIAGNOSES
EMPIRICAL RESEARCH METHODS

M. L. HUTT

MICROTRAINING

Microtraining is a specialized instructional technology that has evolved to train individuals in the execution of complex behaviors. Behaviors to which this training system has been applied are teaching, counseling, firefighting, sales techniques, and a variety of sports activities such as skiing and golf. The technology was developed as a training method for teachers and has perhaps had greater impact in the training of counselors and interviewers.

The initial step in designing a microtraining program involves the breakdown of the complex behavior of concern into a sequence of single skills that, when integrated, will result in competent performance of the complex behavior by trainees. Training sequences are then developed for each of the constituent skills and the integration of those skills. The basic format for each training sequence is similar, with three essential phases. The *training phase* involves instruction in the definition, performance, and (frequently) measurement of the skill in question. The second or *practice phase* involves trainees in brief practice (5 to 10 minutes) of the skill in a simulated context (role-play interview, small class demonstration, and so forth). In the final or *feedback phase* the trainer provides feedback that will assist the trainee to improve performance of the skill. The emphasis is toward the competent integration of the skills.

There is considerable information available on the constituent skills in teaching, counseling, and interpersonal communication. Microtraining has been found to be efficient, enjoyable to trainees, and frequently conducive to more competent performance of the behavior in question. Most research supports the need for an instructional phase, an experiential phase, and a feedback phase.

APPROACHES TO LEARNING

D. R. EVANS

MIDDLE AGE

Although some students of human development delineate the middle-age period of the life cycle as beginning roughly in the late 20s and extending approximately into the late 40s, others extend it from 40 to 60. To gain a concept of what the middle-age person is like, it is best to define this period developmentally, physiologically, intellectually, sexually, socially and politically, and psychologically.

Developmentally. Erik Erikson postulated that middle age, like other periods of life, presented people with developmental tasks and skills that must be mastered if one is to experience some comfort and serenity in the next stage of life. For Erikson the developmental task of middle age centered in choosing what he called generativity over ego stagnation—namely, the expansion of ego interests from those of the self to broader spheres of identification with other people, with the group at large, and with future generations. Elsie Frenkel–Brunswick concluded from her Austrian study that middle-age people were experiencing the most stabilizing period of life, reaping the benefits from earlier periods of insecurity and heightened personal concern. In middle age, they have settled into long-term love relationships, established a permanent home, decided on a life occupation, and experienced their most fruitful periods of professional and creative work. Her findings confirm Erikson's beliefs about this stage.

Physiologically. Evidence suggests that middle age is a period in which all sensory thresholds decrease. After 30, basal metabolism begins to decrease, as does brain weight. The diminished blood supply to the pituitary, thyroid, adrenals, pancreas, and gonads results in gross histological changes, and while the calcium content of tissues increases, middle age sees a decrease in physical strength, physical stamina, and youthful attractiveness. Height declines after 30, at which time men's weight seems to stabilize, while women seem to gain up until the age of 54, very likely as a consequence of hormonal changes.

Intellectually. Although Thorndike's later studies showed the peak of learning capacity to be at ages 22 to 25, Soddy and Kidson's summary of numerous research studies that chart the changes in mental ability suggests that, with some small variation, a maximum is achieved roughly between the ages of 15 and 29, with all studies showing a slow, continuous decline in most abilities until the age of 60, at which time the decrease in learning ability markedly accelerates. The decline is considerable in rote memory, digit symbols, and block design, but small in vocabulary and information.

Sexually. Sexual activity does not begin with fertility or stop with infertility. Men stimulated to a high level of sexual output in their formative years maintain high levels of sexual output in their postclimactic years. Similar findings with women have led to the conclusion that the psyche plays a part at least equal to, or more likely greater than, that of the endrocrine system in determining the sex drive and sexual behavior of women during the postmenopausal period.

Socially and politically. Although we live in a society that may be oriented toward youth, it is controlled by the middle-age who have money, social position, knowledge, and skills to compensate them for their diminishing physical assets. Middle age is a period in which women gain dominance and importance as holders of power, skills, and money both within and outside the home, in comparison to their younger selves and middle-age men with whom they reverse roles. Contrary to popular belief about the devaluation of the elderly in technological societies, anthropological studies of aging in many cultures show that universally in all cultures women—specifically middle-age and older women, if healthy and able to care for themselves physically—become objects of affection and veneration in their kinship networks and are perceived as making important contributions to the quality of life in technological as well as agrarian cultures.

Psychologically. The so-called midlife crisis that some middle-age people experience may result from having had the benefits of longevity and success, and the opportunity to realize dreams and ultimately find them wanting. The finiteness of life becomes increasingly clear in middle age, and for many the awareness that one is past the point of starting again, that one is stuck with the choices one has made of life work, life mate, and lifestyle is distressing.

ADULT DEVELOPMENT
HUMAN DEVELOPMENT
LIFE-SPAN DEVELOPMENT

N. R. HAIMOWITZ

MIDDLE CHILDHOOD

Middle childhood is a chronological period of childhood from about age 6 to age 11 or 12, when children develop important competencies and skills.

PHYSICAL DEVELOPMENT

The average North American 6-year-old measures about 118 centimeters (46 inches) and weighs about 20 kilograms (44 pounds), and gains about 6 centimeters and 3 kilograms per year over the next 5 years. This growth rate is relatively slow and steady, compared to growth in infancy, early childhood, and adolescence.

Less visible, but psychologically more important, growth occurs in the child's central nervous system, digestive system, visual capacity, and hand coordination, as the child's brain and body become more mature. These changes allow children in middle childhood to benefit from formal instruction.

Gross motor skills (skills that involve large body movements) also mature during this period. As long as an activity does not demand too much strength and judgment, most children at this age enjoy developing their competence.

COGNITIVE DEVELOPMENT

During middle childhood children become much better at thinking logically about specific experiences. The best-known example of this ability is the development of the concept of conservation, as demonstrated by Jean Piaget.

Some psychologists believe there is a sudden improvement in cognitive ability at the beginning of middle childhood—an improvement that Sheldon White called a *five-to-seven shift.* However, most psychologists feel that these abilities develop more gradually throughout middle childhood and are dependent on specific instruction and varied experiences as well as brain maturation.

There is no disagreement, however, as to the impressive capacity of children to learn during middle childhood. Much of the motivation to learn comes from the children themselves. Erik Erikson calls this the period of industry versus inferiority, when children experience "the pleasure of work completion by steady attention and diligence." If the culture does not meet the child's willingness to learn with appropriate instruction, the child will develop a life-long sense of inferiority, according to Erikson.

PSYCHOSOCIAL DEVELOPMENT

Middle childhood brings a marked expansion of the child's social world, as children become less dependent on their parents for the details of daily care and more capable of forming close friendships. Hence, 6- to 11-year-olds enter "the culture of childhood."

Partly because the culture of childhood is strong, children at this age value friendship a great deal. The child who is rejected by other children, whether because of behavior, appearance, or family background, is likely to suffer from low self-esteem and lack of confidence. This is not to say that parents are unimportant during middle childhood. Parental encouragement of school achievement, restriction of television viewing, and overall warmth toward the child are clearly beneficial to the child's ego and achievement.

MORAL DEVELOPMENT

During middle childhood, children become able to understand—and follow—the standards of their society, often becoming quite rigid and narrow in their interpretation of those standards before becoming more open to change again as adolescence approaches. Much of the children's actual moral behavior depends on the role models they see and the values of their culture.

SEX DIFFERENCES

During middle childhood boys and girls are much more similar to each other than they are different. However, a few interesting sex differences emerge. Girls are physiologically more mature than boys throughout development.

Girls' play patterns are different, as they are less likely to be physically aggressive and more likely to play relatively inactive games. In addition, girls tend to rely on a small circle of friends, especially one "best friend"; boys tend to have a somewhat larger group or gang to play with. Both boys and girls play most often with same-sex peers. The girl "tomboy" who plays with boys is much more accepted than the boy "sissie" who plays with girls. The extent to which these play patterns are biological or cultural is a subject of debate among social scientists.

Another controversial question is why girls, by the end of middle childhood, are more skilled at reading and writing, while boys are more skilled at math and science. As Jeremy Finn learned in a cross-national study, at least part of the reason for this difference is cultural, for the emphasis of the educational system is reflected in the skills boys and girls within that system develop.

PROBLEMS

Compared to other periods of the life span, middle childhood is relatively free of serious problems. However, two types of difficulties merit attention. The first is school-related. Many children have difficulty mastering schoolwork at the same rate as their peers. In some cases this is a developmental delay in maturation, and the child will catch up later. In other cases the home or school is at fault. In yet other cases the child has a specific learning disability.

The second problem is delinquency and vandalism, which usually begin in middle childhood. Consequently, minor misdeeds should not be ignored; instead, an attempt should be made to understand the reasons and to restructure the destructive behavior patterns. Simply punishing the miscreant is inadequate and may be counterproductive.

CHILD PSYCHOLOGY
HUMAN DEVELOPMENT

K. S. BERGER

MILITARY PSYCHOLOGY

Military psychology concerns the utilization of psychological principles and methods for military applications. It involves traditional psychological specialty areas such as personnel (selection, classification, and placement), learning (training), experimental human factors, and social, clinical, and organizational psychology. Many countries have institutes of military psychology. Typically, such institutes employ both civilian psychologists and psychologists who are members of a military service.

TESTING

Sometimes the work accomplished by psychologists for the military has provided the impetus for advancements in psychology in the civilian sector. Group testing was developed by military psychologists during World War I in response to the need for the rapid classification of recruits. This type of testing served as a model for group intelligence tests and stimulated the development of the group testing movement in the 1920s. During World War II, the Army General Classification Test (AGCT) was developed to replace the earlier Army Alpha. A variety of tests were constructed for specialized purposes. The Office of Strategic Services (OSS) developed performance-oriented tests to select operatives. This OSS work, which contrasted sharply with the usual pencil-and-paper selection procedures, was a precursor of present-day assessment centers.

Since World War II, interest and activity in military testing research and development has been continuous. Work has also continued on computerized adaptive testing, in which examinees receive a set of test items tailored to their ability level, rather than the complete set of items contained in the usual lengthy group test. In addition to mental aptitude and interest testing, research is conducted on physical abilities required for military jobs.

TRAINING

Another major focus of military psychology, closely allied to testing, is training. The American military operates the largest educational and training program in the world, and the training function is an important one in military establishments the world over. Military psychologists both develop and assess training programs. There has been a shift from lecture-oriented to experiential or performance-oriented training.

EXPERIMENTAL/HUMAN FACTORS AREAS

Human factors concerns the relationship of people to their machines, their tasks, and their environment. The human factors field emerged as a composite of specialties in enhancing human performance, training, safety, and the design of person–machine interfaces. Designing equipment and systems for effective military training and operations is a continuing effort. Basic research has been required in vision, hearing, physiological reactions to stress, and so on. The design of cockpits, practice targets, clothing, weapons, and information-processing systems illustrates the diversity of human factors applications in the military. Here again, computer technology is increasingly used, especially in aircraft, weapons, and information systems.

CLINICAL/SOCIAL AREAS

The roles of military clinical psychologists are similar to those of civilian clinicians. In addition, military psychologists may work in stress and other specialization clinics, and collaborate closely with orthopedists and neurologists. Clinical psychologists in the military may also be assigned to locations where they have sole responsibility for mental health services, including inpatient management.

There have been numerous investigations of the social psychology of military groups, especially on the battlefield. The combat soldier's relationship with his primary group (the small group with which he works and fights) has been identified as an important factor in determining a soldier's ability to withstand the hardships and dangers of combat.

Studies have also been conducted on the processes and effects of brainwashing, interrogation, and sensory deprivation. Related research has investigated the effects of closely confined environments such as submarines. Other research has focused on the role of the family, as for instance the impact on personnel of family separations caused by shipboard duty or the relationship of family attitudes to reenlistment. The integration of racial minorities and women into the military has commanded considerable interest on the part of military psychologists. Research on the integration of black males into the U.S. Army indicated that increased contact with members of a minority group led to increased acceptance of them by the majority group. Results of research on the integration of women into the military have been more equivocal.

ORGANIZATIONAL PSYCHOLOGY

Leadership has long been a primary interest of military psychologists. Concerns relating to the selection, development, and evaluation of leaders have broadened to include situational and organizational factors. Increased performance/productivity and enhanced quality of life have become increasingly important goals for military organizational interventions.

APPLIED RESEARCH
HUMAN FACTORS
LEADERSHIP TRAINING

L. W. OLIVER

MILL'S CANONS

The extended title of John Stuart Mill's *A system of logic* declared it to be "a connected view of the principles of evidence and the methods of scientific investigation." Five canons (rules or laws) are stated as "regulative principles" of those experimental methods. These canons prescribe methods of discovering and proving causal laws and causal connections.

THE METHOD OF AGREEMENT

An example of an inference that proceeds according to this first method is the following one from J. Dollard and N. E. Miller.

It is interesting to note that one of the frequent symptoms of extreme combat anxiety cases is an interference with speech that may run from complete muteness to hesitation and stuttering. Similarly, the sufferer from acute stage fright is unable to speak. Many animals tend to stop vocalizing when frightened, and it is obvious that this tendency is adaptive in preventing them from attracting the attention of their enemies. In the light of this evidence one might suspect that the drive of fear has an innate tendency to elicit the response of stopping vocal behavior.

Mill's formulation of the abstract pattern of this mode of argument is this:

If two of more instances of the phenomenon under investigation have only one circumstance in common, the circumstance in which alone all the instances agree, is the cause (or effect) of the given phenomenon.

THE METHOD OF DIFFERENCE

An illustration of the Method of Difference is the following from R. Buchsbaum.

The primitive brain, as we saw it in the planaria, served chiefly as a sensory relay—a center for receiving stimuli from the sense organs and then sending impulses down the nerve cord. This is also true of the nereis, for, if the brain is removed, the animal can still move in a coordinated way—and, in fact, it moves about more than usual. If it meets some obstacle, it does not withdraw and go off in a new direction but persists in its unsuccessful forward movements. This very unadaptive kind of behavior shows that in the normal nereis the brain has an important function which it did not have in flatworms—that of *inhibition* of movement in response to certain stimuli.

Mill's formulation of the pattern of inference is this:

If an instance in which the phenomenon under investigation occurs, and an instance in which it does not occur, have every circumstance in common save one, that one occurring only in the former; the circumstance in which alone the two instances differ, is the effect, or the cause, or an indispensable part of the cause, of the phenomenon.

THE JOINT METHOD OF AGREEMENT AND DIFFERENCE

The Joint Method of Agreement and Difference is frequently regarded as merely the joint use of the Method of Agreement and the Method of Difference, so that it can be applied only where the first two methods are applied separately. But Mill's own statement of the method does not support this interpretation:

If two or more instances in which the phenomenon occurs have only one circumstance in common, while two or more instances in which it does not occur have nothing in common save the absence of that circumstance, the circumstance in which alone the two sets of instances differ, is the effect, or the cause, or an indispensable part of the cause, of the phenomenon.

As stated, it would seem to be merely a double use of the Method of Agreement. A more common interpretation of the joint method appears explicitly as the separate employments of the first two methods, one of agreement and one of difference.

There is a third interpretation of the joint method that makes it a considerably more powerful tool for induction where it is clear that neither the Method of Agreement nor the Method of Difference can be directly applied. In classifying inductive inferences, those falling under any of the three patterns described previously are generally regarded as examples of the Joint Method of Agreement and Difference.

THE METHODS OF RESIDUES

Mill's formulation of his fourth canon proceeds as such:

Subduct from any phenomenon such part as is known by previous inductions to be the effect of certain antecedents, and the residue of the phenomenon is the effect of the remaining antecedents.

The Method of Residues is sometimes said to be a strictly deductive pattern of inference and not inductive at all. Each of the other methods requires the examination of at least two instances, whereas the Method of Residues can be used with the examination of only one case. None of the other methods, as formulated by Mill, requires an appeal to any antecedently established causal laws, while the Method of Residues definitely does depend on such laws.

THE METHOD OF CONCOMITANT VARIATION

All the first four canons are readily seen to be *eliminative:* They proceed by considering situations either in which phenomena occur in the absence of circumstances that are thereby eliminated as possible causes of those phenomena, or in which phenomena fail to occur in the presence of circumstances that might have been thought to be possible causes of such phenomena.

There are situations, however, in which some circumstances cannot possibly be eliminated. One of Mill's own examples in discussing this problem concerns the cause of the phenomenon of the tides. Of such situations, Mill writes this:

But we have still a resource. Though we can not exclude an antecedent altogether, we may be able to produce, or nature may produce for us some modification in it. By a modification is here meant, a change in it not amounting to its total removal . . . when we find that all the variations in the *position* of the moon are followed by corresponding variations in the time and place of high water, the place being always either the part of the earth which is nearest to, or that which is most remote from, the moon, we have ample evidence that the moon is, wholly or partially, the cause which determines the tides.

Mill's general statement of this method is as follows:

Whatever phenomenon varies in any manner whenever another phenomenon varies in some particular manner, is either a cause or an effect of that phenomenon, or is connected with it through some fact of causation.

The Method of Concomitant Variation utilizes our ability to observe changes in the degree to which circumstances and phenomena are present, and admits a vastly greater amount of data as evidence for the presence of causal connections. Its chief virtue lies in admitting more evidence, for thereby the new method widens the range of inductive inference. This method is important as the first *quantitative* method of inductive inference, the preceding ones having all been qualitative.

CRITICISMS

Mill's canons have been criticized on several different grounds. One is that they say nothing about the *analysis* of circumstances. If the circumstances enumerated are not adequately analyzed or divided, the methods will not work. For example, if the circumstances are imbibing bourbon and water, scotch and water, brandy and water, and vodka and water, the Method of Agreement will lead one to conclude that water causes inebriation. But the analysis of using the several liquors and other ingredients to make alcohol requires *prior* knowledge of causal connections.

Another requirement for the canons to produce useful conclusions is that no relevant circumstances can be ignored. But here again, the relevance of circumstances can be discovered only by prior investigation.

Needed for any fruitful use of Mill's canons are hypotheses about what circumstances might be causally related to the phenomenon under investigation. Granted the hypotheses are present, the canons are useful in eliminating possible causal circumstances.

CORRELATION METHODS
HYPOTHESIS TESTING

I. M. COPI

MILLER ANALOGIES TEST

This test consists of 100 verbal analogy items drawn from a wide range of academic areas. It is a highly regarded test with reasonably substantial prediction of academic success of potential graduate students in graduate schools in a variety of departments. It measures verbal and reasoning ability and has the technical characteristics of being able to differentiate among high-ability students of varying potential. This test has been the subject of considerable research to support its claims. The Miller Analogies Test was carefully built, and access to it is strictly controlled. It has a high level of difficulty and good aids to help users interpret their test scores.

INTELLIGENCE MEASURES

W. ASHER

MILLON BEHAVIORAL HEALTH INVENTORY

The Millon Behavioral Health Inventory (MBHI) instrument derived its initial impetus from a theory of personality formulated by Theodore Millon. It was developed as an aid to psychologists, physicians, and other professional health care personnel who deal with physically ill and behavioral medicine patients. The MBHI also provides information concerning a patient's characteristic coping style and attitudes toward illness and treatment, as well as other psychological tendencies, such as compliance, that often influence the course of a patient's illness or response to treatment. Comprising 150 self-descriptive statements to be marked true or false, the MBHI is completed by most patients in about 20 minutes.

BEHAVIORAL MEDICINE

T. MILLON

MILLON CLINICAL MULTIAXIAL INVENTORY

The Millon Clinical Multiaxial Inventory (MCMI) inventory, developed by Theodore Millon, utilized as its model the Minnesota Multiphasic

Personality Inventory (MMPI). Including 175 self-descriptive statements, it is linked both to the clinical theory presented by Millon and to the *Diagnostic and statistical manual of mental disorders (DSM-V)*. The 20 clinical scales fall into four major categories: Basic Personality Patterns (Axis II); Pathological Personality Syndromes (Axis II); Moderate Clinical Syndromes (Axis I); and Severe Clinical Syndromes (Axis I).

Validation was an integral element of construction. In addition to programs for rapid machine scoring of answer forms, a computer-synthesized interpretive report that integrates both personological and symptomatic features of the patient is available. In line with current psychodiagnostic thinking, the interpretive report follows a multiaxial framework of assessment.

MINNESOTA MULTIPHASIC PERSONALITY INVENTORY
PERSONALITY ASSESSMENT

T. MILLON

MIND–BODY PROBLEM

For centuries, scholars in all disciplines have struggled to define the nature of the human being. One of the key problems is that which deals with the mind, the body, and the relationships between them.

There is general agreement that "body" refers to the material, physical characteristics of the organism, the activities of which can be studied by the traditional empirical methods of science.

It is mind (psyche, soul), the question of whether such an entity even exists, and how to define it, that is the crux of the mind–body problem. For some thinkers, the immediate experience of self-awareness constitutes evidence that mind is qualitatively different from the physiological body. At one extreme, the term "mind" or "mental" has been defined as a nonphysical, noncorporeal entity. Such an entity would not necessarily function according to the same laws as matter.

Being nonmaterial and nonphysical, the mind cannot be verified or studied by means of input from the physical senses. This feature of mind causes the "mind–body problem" for those who study human behavior by empirical methods.

Three major approaches to defining mind in a different manner have been directed toward solving this dilemma. The first is an extreme reductionism. From this viewpoint, mind *per se* does not exist: It is simply a label for a particular level of biological functioning.

A second approach tries to in some way relate the qualitatively unlike mind and body, learning about the former from empirical knowledge of the latter. All these approaches leave the psychologist with the problem of evolving a means for relating the internal activity of the mind to the physically observable behavior of the body.

A third approach, in some ways similar to reductionism, is not as simplistic. In this perspective, neither mind nor body is viewed as being an independent entity. Instead, the human being is viewed as a single composite or mind and body, neither of which has existence without the other. Such viewpoints have come to be called "double aspect." The deciding factor appears to depend on whether the particular definition of the mind aspect best lends itself to study by the method of rationalism, the method of empiricism, or some combination of the two. Thus, the necessity for interpreting psychological and behavioral data in terms of their correlates with the laws or physics and biology (as contrasted with independent laws of their own) will depend on the nature of mind and its relationship, if any, to body.

PHILOSOPHICAL PSYCHOLOGY

M. E. REUDER

MINDLESSNESS–MINDFULNESS

Mindlessness may be defined as a state of reduced cognitive activity in which the individual processes cue from the environment in a relatively automatic manner without reference to potentially novel (or simply other) aspects of those cues. Mindfulness, in contrast, is a state in which environmental cues are consciously manipulated, and the individual is engaged in actively constructing his or her environment. This is in marked contrast to the mindless state in which one deals with an already constructed environment.

Mindless information processing may arise either after many repetitions of a particular experience or, in certain instances, after a single exposure. In the former case, as an individual's experience with certain situations accumulates, a cognitive structure of the situation is formed that represents its underlying "semantics." The appearance of similar cues on subsequent occasions will then trigger a mindless sequence of behaviors. Once an activity becomes mindless, the underlying semantics may no longer be available for conscious cognitive manipulation or even for examination. In the latter single-exposure case, reduced cognitive activity does not result from reliance on cognitive structures built up over time, but from reliance on a cognitive structure that one has appropriated from another source.

Mindlessness is pervasive. In fact, for the typical individual, *mindfulness* is expected to occur only (a) when significantly more effort is demanded by the situation than was originally demanded, (b) when the external factors in the situation disrupt initiation or the mindless sequence, (c) when external factors prevent the completion of the behavior, or (d) when negative or positive consequences are experienced that are sufficiently discrepant with the consequences of prior enactments of the same behavior.

Although research has addressed reduced levels of cognitive activity (e.g., automaticity, preattentive processing, and overlearning), a newer theory and a newer term are needed for several reasons. First, mindlessness suggests a more molar unit of analysis than has been examined in the past. Second, mindlessness may come about with and without repeated exposure. Third, mindlessness and mindfulness appear to be qualitatively different, not just quantitatively different (e.g., that which has been processed mindlessly may no longer be available for active conscious cognitive work). Fourth, researchers studying automaticity, e.g., have focused on the adaptive function automatic processing serves in freeing conscious attention. Although this is certainly true, all research conducted thus far on mindlessness–mindfulness suggests that it may also be quite maladaptive.

The study of mindlessness has been pursued in several domains: its consequence for competent performance, for the perception of deviance, and for the course of physical disease, as well as its implications for the very study of social psychological processes.

Research has revealed that whether interactions between people were face to face or through written communications, and whether they were semantically sound or senseless, they occasioned behavior that appeared mindless as long as the structure of the interaction triggered some overlearned sequence of behavior. With respect to potentially relevant information, people failed to hear what was said and to read what was written.

Because the individual components of the activity progressively drop out with each repetition of an activity, the result is not only that the individual is responding to some abstracted structure but also that the steps of the task become relatively inaccessible. Thus research has found that counter to an analysis that ignored the mindless–mindful distinction, a great deal of practice at a task may render the individual more vulnerable to external factors that bring competence into question. When these factors led subjects to question whether they could do the task, groups that were moderately practiced were able to supply the steps or the activity as evidence of competence and, therefore, did not show performance decrements. Unpracticed and overpracticed groups could not supply the task components and, therefore, showed clear debilitation.

Regarding the perception of deviance, it was reasoned, first, that deviance (novelty) breeds mindfulness. If people are typically mindless vis-à-vis normal individuals, then the people who are deviant in any respect may be perceived as deviant in many respects (and, therefore, labeled, avoided, etc.) not so much because of their deviance but because of the thorough scrutiny prompted by the mindful state. Such a close examination of *any* individual would lead one to notice characteristics that typically go unnoticed and to inappropriately judge these characteristics as extreme or unusual. As predicted, it was found that the perception of the deviant was accurate, but the typical characteristics and gestures that were noticed were evaluated as extreme and unusual. This occurred whether the deviance was positive (e.g., a millionaire) or negative (e.g., an ex-mental patient) but did not occur when the same stimulus person was not given a deviant label.

Additional research investigated mindlessness on initial exposure, that is, mindlessness that results from the formation of premature cognitive commitments to information. A premature cognitive commitment is considered premature because the individual makes a commitment to information and freezes its meaning before considering alternative uses to which the information could be put.

Research found that encouraging decision making in nursing home residents resulted in these residents being happier, healthier, and more alert. A follow-up study also found that they lived longer than comparison groups. Initially, it was thought that the experimental group was a group for whom the researchers had induced a sense of control and responsibility. Because the elderly, especially the institutionalized elderly, are a group for whom routine is the rule, where there is very little to think about, the experimental group might be better seen as a thought-encouraged group, which would suggest that mindfulness may be necessary for survival. Its primary effectiveness in health-related issues, however, may be due to its ability to provoke mindfulness.

Work on mindlessness also has been conducted in an education setting. Here was found that when information is initially given in absolute language (e.g., "this is an X"), people form premature cognitive commitments to the information and are oblivious to future creative uses of that information. When instead people are instructed conditionally (e.g., "this could be X"), alternative uses of the information remain available to them.

Research on mindlessness and mindfulness has yielded a wealth of results, spanning a number of diverse issues—all unified by a common theme: the consequences of reduced cognitive activity. The findings thus far suggest that mindlessness–mindfulness is a central dimension in human functioning, the study of which may perhaps even yield basic laws of human behavior.

ABSTRACT INTELLIGENCE
ATTENTION
AUTOMATIC THOUGHTS
CONSCIOUSNESS
IMPLICIT LEARNING
MENTAL IMAGERY

E. J. LANGER

MINIMAL BRAIN DYSFUNCTION (DIAGNOSIS)

The syndrome of minimal brain dysfunction was first defined by Samuel Clements, referring to a sizable group of children whose behavioral and learning difficulties were puzzling and for whom typical interventions had not been effective. Follow-up studies indicate that this syndrome is not confined to childhood. These deficits, compensatory personality difficulties, and educational disabilities persist through adolescence and adulthood.

Clements defined the syndrome as consisting of near-to or above-average general intelligence accompanied by certain learning or behavioral disabilities, ranging from mild to severe, associated with deviations of function of the central nervous system. These deviations may manifest themselves by various combinations of impairments in perception (visual and auditory), conceptualization, language, and memory, and in the control of attention, impulse, motility, or motor function. Clements further holds the view that certain categories of deviant behavior, developmental dyscrasia, learning disabilities, and visual motor perceptual irregularities must be accepted as valid indices of disturbed brain functioning.

Symptoms associated with the syndrome now include poor or inaccurate body image, generalized immaturity, disturbances in kinesthetic integration, hypoactivity as well as hyperactivity, dysgraphia or agraphia, dyscalculia, speech and communication difficulties, cognitive difficulties, and reactive social, affective, and personality disturbances.

This syndrome has been referred to by various names over the years: hyperkinetic syndrome, hyperactive child syndrome, minimal brain damage or dysfunction, minimal or minor cerebral dysfunction, and chronic brain or organic syndrome. It has also been referred to by specific symptom formations: developmental lag, perceptual and neurological deficits, dyslexia, learning difficulties, specific learning or developmental difficulties, and so forth. It subsumed hyperkinetic and minimal brain dysfunction syndromes under this classification. Learning difficulties, usually associated with this syndrome, are listed under specific developmental disorders such as reading, arithmetic, and/or language disorders. An eloquent protest against this approach was made by Duncan.

There is resistance to the concept that these symptoms constitute a neurological or a psychoneurological syndrome or diagnostic category. The two major symptoms are specific or generalized learning disabilities or hyperactivity.

The estimated prevalence of the disturbance will vary, depending on whether one focuses on the syndrome as a whole or on specific symptom clusters. Children exhibiting either the overall syndrome and/or the symptom clusters have been estimated to constitute 3 to 45% of the school-age population, and 6 to 10 boys afflicted, one girl is also afflicted.

Hypotheses concerning etiology focus on genetic predisposition and familial origins; poor nutrition, exposure to toxic substances (including medications), and illness during gestation; perinatal stress; and illnesses of early childhood. Impoverished children have a greater exposure to debilitating circumstances and a higher vulnerability. Although delays in developmental milestones are usually present from a very early age, the disorder does not usually become apparent until the child enters school.

An area of difference among writers is the importance or the presence of an impaired neurophysiological substrate. Educators and teacher trainers have tended to ignore or minimize the fact that learning and behavior difficulties are symptomatic of disturbances in central nervous system functioning. Psychologists, psychiatrists, or pediatric neurologists have tended to emphasize the general neurological/developmental approach. They have further written about "soft neurological signs," disturbances in cognition and central perceptual processing, and other organic factors such as atypical EEG rhythms and vestibular dysfunctions—all as the neurophysiological substrate to learning disabilities.

The development and wider use of highly sensitized, noninvasive electronic scanning devices and more sophisticated electroencephalograms have revealed data that indicate that neurophysiological and neuropsychological factors play a major role in the syndrome. This is further supported by recent advances in brain chemistry, metabolism, and physiology.

Studies of children with the broad range of MBD symptoms defined previously indicate the presence of a number of additional disturbances in general metabolism, allergic reactions, physical growth, psychological maturation, and social development. These findings suggest that the cerebral dysfunctions may reflect some systemic disturbance affecting vegetative as well as central nervous system function. The child, then, can be beset by difficulties in general body functioning as well as by the visual perceptual, auditory, cognitive, and language processing deficits that cause learning disabilities.

Personality, social, and emotional difficulties are a frequent concomitant of the syndrome. Many of these children seem to have a basic predisposition to anxiety with an exaggerated "startle" response and also seem to overreact to both physiological and psychological stress with very severe anxiety attacks that have been labeled "catastrophic reactions." They frequently are impulsive and immature, or rigid and perfectionistic.

The assumption of an underlying neurological disturbance with a range of symptom formations—as opposed to isolated symptom clusters—and with reactive coping and psychological difficulties necessitates that diagnosis as well as intervention must be performed by an interdisciplinary team.

There is no standard battery. The tests used must vary and will depend on the age of the child, the relevance of tests for the presenting problems, the tests then in fashion, the psychologist's preference, and the length of time allotted for the examination. Present research indicates that attempted testing shortcuts do not produce specific profiles that identify learning disabled individuals, as the population is too heterogeneous.

The minimal brain dysfunction syndrome is reflected in a various behavioral, functional, and learning difficulties. The instruments used, therefore, must test for each major operational area to obtain a rounded picture. Judgments must be made about the individual's gross and fine motor coordination, control of motility, visual motor functioning, graphomotor skills, awareness of body image, auditory functioning, motor speech activity, language processing, cognitive functioning, personality, and academic skills.

In making the diagnosis, it is important to differentiate between (a) the child who is hyperactive but has adequate to good gross and fine motor coordination, is adequate to bright intellectually, and performs adequately at school and socially; (b) the child who has a specific isolated deficit (visual, auditory, motor, or speech) but is adequate to bright intellectually and performs adequately at school and socially; and (c) the child who exhibits difficulties across the range of symptoms described previously. This third child could properly be diagnosed as suffering from minimal brain dysfunction. The psychological consequences are less devastating and the prognosis brighter for the first two than for the third.

These children usually need several types of services, and timing is essential. The different types of services can include medication, special diet, optometric retraining, movement therapy, work with a learning disability specialist, and individual, group, and/or family therapies.

So far, the outcomes of the major interventions—medication, special education, and therapy—have not been encouraging. There is a need for increased communication and integration among and within the disciplines, and for a team approach to intervention.

Studies on the results or stimulant drug therapy indicate that while hyperactivity may be reduced, the children do not achieve academic competence or freedom from behavior disorders. Furthermore, questions have been raised about possible interference in the child's growth, the child's negative reactions to having to take the medication, and later drug and alcohol abuse.

The unclear outcomes of special education programs underscore the need to seek different formats and approaches. Also, "mainstreaming" so far has not fulfilled the hopes and expectations once held for it.

The child's and family's needs for psychological help has been repeatedly emphasized because of their increased vulnerability to emotional stress and because of the personality difficulties that reflect the child's poor self-image and sense of defeat. A variety of treatment modalities have been offered. They include behavior treatment, biofeedback, cognitive control, imitation, modeling, special play therapy, psychotherapy, and social skills training. Some of these techniques focus on helping the child change behaviors and learning patterns in the classroom, and others focus on helping the child and family shift ways of relating and interacting.

Follow-up studies indicate that even though some specific neurological deficits may disappear with maturity and the hyperactivity may decrease, either through medication or with the onset of adolescence, the adolescent or young adult is left with poor work or study habits, poor social skills, a sense of incompetence, and mild to marked personality difficulties. In view of these discouraging results, it seems evident that programs for early identification should be strengthened and that multifaceted early interventions and support systems should be made available to the child and parents.

**BRAIN
DIAGNOSES
MINIMAL BRAIN DYSFUNCTION (INTERVENTION)**

R. OCHROCH

MINIMAL BRAIN DYSFUNCTION (INTERVENTION)

Longitudinal studies of and follow-ups on young adults who as children suffered minimal brain dysfunction (learning disabilities or dyslexia) indicate that, although some of the earlier neurophysiological deficits may have disappeared, adaptive and psychological problems continue into adulthood. They are frequently left with immature ego development, a sense of incompetence, and poor study/work habits and social skills. They are beset with a myriad of negative self-images that reflect their past as well as present social and psychological realities. More often than not, they also suffer from crystallized personality disorders reflective of their efforts to cope with their developmental and learning difficulties, frustrations, and sense of despair. These personality disorders and negative self-images create substantial barriers to the ability to develop good social relationships or reliable job skills, or to deal with work pressures. The problems these young adults face are multidimensional and mutually reinforcing and formidable. As such, they require both multidimensional and innovative interventions. The need for early identification and intervention is crucial.

It is well established that one's sense of self must reflect a mental image of one's physical body, posture, control of movements, sensory acuity, skills, and so on. The personality development of the young child with physical deficits will initially reflect the child's efforts to cope with developmental and neurophysiological difficulties. Frustration and anxiety then develop in response to the child's inability to meet the increased demands for achievement and behavior from the parents and from the world beyond the home. Children who suffer from disturbances in metabolism and delayed growth and maturation may have atypical appearances. These disabilities are incorporated into the child's psychological sense of self, realistically add to the painful sense of difference, and make for further personality difficulties.

Further, in struggling to cope and to avoid the anxiety of failure, the child will develop pervasive self-defeating defenses. Some of these children develop patterns of impulsive behavior with remarkable ability to evade situations that impinge on their deficits and bring on anxiety reactions. Others develop powerful defenses of avoidance that make for automatic shut-off of learning or of approaching difficult or challenging tasks in which they feel doomed to failure. Another frequent pattern is the development of compulsive defenses, as the children struggle to impose some order on the buzzing confusion around them and on their own behavior. The resultant rigidity may in part reflect organic perseveration or necessary coping mechanisms, rather than a behavioral manifesta-

tion of dynamically based compulsivity. In the adolescent or adult, these types of personality or character formations, if not ameliorated, become the matrix of self-defeating patterns that reinforce the individual's sense of frustration and despair.

The neurophysiological developments and deficits cannot alone account for the child's psychological difficulties. The reactions of parents to their atypical child are a major factor in the child's subsequent personality development. The child's sense of self must reflect the parent's bewilderment, disappointment, and pain, as well as concerns for and anxiety about the child. Therefore intervention with the family as well as with the child is imperative, and work with the parents may become the primary focus.

The individual who works with the parents and child will have to anticipate a long-term relationship, as the family and child will need brief to moderately long contacts over a long period of time, probably into the child's adulthood. This is necessitated by the difficulties children with minimal brain dysfunction face at every developmental stage, and by the need for careful planning. The professional will also have to provide the parents and child access to a network of supportive services that the family can use.

Adolescents with minimal brain dysfunction or a history of minimal brain dysfunction may be in greater turmoil than the typical adolescent. The adolescent is therefore less prepared to deal with the usual developmental tasks of this stage—the greater independence from the parents, social/sexual involvement, and future planning. These adolescents are more vulnerable to both emotional disturbances and substance abuse. They may turn to drugs to control their hyperactivity, or to alcohol to lessen their depressed reactions, and marijuana may be their tranquilizer of choice.

They are more often than not overly dependent on their parents and are socially and psychologically immature and socially isolated.

The parents must also be involved, to a far greater degree, in helping the adolescent plan realistically for completion of school, for work or, if indicated, for college. Completion of high school or college may take longer for certain adolescents because of their background of learning difficulties. Furthermore, many of them will continue to need specialized educational help and other ancillary services.

Work with young and older adults with a history of minimal brain dysfunction also presents formidable difficulties. Individuals who seek help are those who have continued to struggle with their deficits and are trapped by the combination of their disability and their self-defeating patterns. Many of these young people suffer from crystallized personality disorders and chronic low-grade depression, and may present borderline and more serious features.

The young adults, like the adolescents, suffer from loneliness and despair, and also are in need of peer support groups.

**BRAIN
COUNSELING
MINIMAL BRAIN DYSFUNCTION (DIAGNOSIS)**

R. OCHROCH

MINNESOTA MULTIPHASIC PERSONALITY INVENTORY

The Minnesota Multiphasic Personality Inventory (MMPI, revised in 1989 to the MMPI-2) has emerged as the most widely used pencil-and-paper personality test among several hundred available personality assessment techniques. Hathaway and McKinley set out to create an objective diagnostic instrument for the comprehensive assessment of psychiatric patients. From a large pool of affirmative statements, Hathaway and McKinley selected a set of 504 self-description personality items to which the subject was asked to respond "true," "false," or "cannot say."

Table 1   MMPI Scale Numbers, Abbreviations, and Names

Number	Abbreviation	Name
	L	Lie
	F	Validity
	K	Correction
1	Hs	Hypochondriasis
2	D	Depression
3	Hy	Hysteria
4	Pd	Psychopathic-Deviate
5	Mf	Masculinity-Femininity
6	Pa	Paranoia
7	Pt	Psychasthenia
8	Sc	Schizophrenia
9	Ma	Mania
10	Si	Social introversion

These true–false items were administered to persons described as normal and to patients with various psychiatric diagnoses in order to develop a scale to represent each diagnostic group tested.

The original intentions of the MMPI were never realized. Individuals with a specific diagnosis often obtained high scores on several scales, and those obtaining a high score on a particular scale were a heterogeneous, not a homogeneous, group of individuals. Although its original plan of detecting a specific psychiatric disorder with a specific MMPI scale did not work out as expected, the MMPI scores nonetheless proved to be effective diagnostically when high or abnormal scores were used in combination or patterns.

The MMPI self-description statements, later increased from 504 to 566 items, are printed on cards or in a test booklet, and the responses are recorded on an answer sheet. The test is designed for adults 16 years of age or older; at least 6 years of successful education are desirable because of the reading requirements of this inventory. The test items consist of a wide variety of psychological characteristics such as health; social, sexual, political, and religious values; attitudes about family, education, and occupation; emotional moods; and typical neurotic or psychotic clinical manifestations, such as obsessive-compulsive behavior, phobias, delusions, and hallucinations. The MMPI provides scores on the three "validity" scales and 10 clinical scales listed in Table 1.

The three validity scales L, F, and K are a special feature of the MMPI. By including obviously favorable self-descriptions, very rare psychopathological symptoms, or subtle defensiveness items, the MMPI is able to assess test-taking attitudes, carelessness, misunderstanding, and malingering. In addition to the three validity and ten clinical scales, several hundred new scales have been developed that serve diffuse purposes and seem to vary in empirical validity. The Ego Strength Scale and Taylor Manifest Anxiety Scale are examples of special scales derived from the MMPI items.

PERSONALITY ASSESSMENT

W. T. TSUSHIMA

MIXED STANDARD SCALE

The mixed standard scale is usually credited to Friedrich Blanz and Edwin Ghiselli, although the method has earlier roots in F. Blanz's work in Finland. This method was developed as a potential control of halo and leniency errors in psychometric ratings, especially within the context of employee performance appraisal.

To develop a mixed standard scale, it is first necessary to generate clearly defined dimensions along which performance is to be assessed. An implicit assumption is made that these performance domains are unidimensional and related to overall success or performance on the job in question.

For each performance dimension, three brief behavioral examples of performance are written. These examples must be clearly related to the dimension intended, must discriminate between good and poor employees, and must represent good, mediocre, and poor levels of performance for the dimension.

After writing three standards per dimension, it is necessary to randomize their sequence for inclusion in the questionnaire. This tends to obscure the fact that items reflect a smaller group of distinct dimensions and also obscures the order of merit represented by items for each dimension. This random sequence of behavioral examples constitutes a "mixed standard scale."

Raters respond to the mixed standard scale by indicating whether the ratee is "better than," "equal to," or "worse than" the behavior represented by each standard. Scoring then involves looking at a rater's responses across the three standards for a given dimension and assigning points accordingly.

Scoring a mixed standard scale can be time-consuming; users may want to use a computer for this purpose.

SCALING

P. G. BENSON

MNEMONIC SYSTEMS

The typical individual usually learns by making materials meaningful. In using an available association or past learning to help learn new material (positive transfer), the individual finds that this strategy can qualify as a memory aid or mnemonic. For example, when learning a list of paired associates, the nonsense syllable pair *ros-lac* might be transformed into *rose-lake,* which might be a real place that is familiar to the learner. Another example might be that to facilitate learning and recall of the word pair *fox-sled,* one might conjure up the image of a fox coasting down a snowy hill on a sled.

There are several special mnemonic devices. One is the *pegword* method for memorizing lists of items or events. A person first memorizes a rhyme for, say, 20 integers: one is a bun, two is a shoe, three is a tree, four is a door, five is a hive, and so on. One then associates an item on the list, say, *sugar,* with bun (e.g., an image of sugar heavily sprinkled all over the bun). For the next item, one might image two *bananas* sticking out of a shoe, and so on through the list. The images can be as bizarre as one chooses, but it is not clear that bizarre images are always superior mnemonic devices. Later, when one recites the poem each cue word triggers a correct item on the list. The pegword method permits one to recall any item by its position in the list, such as the third or tenth, as well as items in their original order.

In general, concocting mental images to aid in the learning of arbitrary verbal associations facilitates memory by a sizable amount.

The method of *loci,* used in Ancient Greece, resembles the pegword method and is especially useful for recalling a long sequence of words or digits. It exploits one's familiarity with an itinerary or well-traveled route that contains many distinctive loci or landmarks. For example, a high school student memorized and recalled a list of 40 digits by this method, using the daily walk to school as the learned sequence of loci. Opening the front door to leave for school was the first cue and was associated in imagery with the first item to be remembered, the fire hydrant in front of the house was the second cue and was associated with the second item, the hill to climb to reach the main street was next, and then came the radio store on the corner, and so on. (Note: Almost 60 years later the images are still pretty vivid to that individual.) To recall the list, one simply runs through the route in imagery, and each locus cue triggers the correct digit. One only learns single, isolated associations. There is no information overload or span limitation; the task is relatively simple.

The learning of foreign language vocabulary is facilitated by using the keyword method. A keyword is an English word that sounds like some part of the foreign word. For example, the Russian word *zvonok* means "bell." The last syllable is emphasized and sounds like oak. Using *oak* as the keyword the memorizer erects some imagery to connect the two English words, for example, a transparent bell with an oak leaf-shaped clapper hanging inside. When confronted with either the Russian word or its English equivalent the appropriate response is elicited.

Some mnemonics are effective for remembering how to differentiate between two similar terms like the *abscissa* and *ordinate* of a graph or *stalactites* and *stalagmites*. To distinguish between the two geological terms, remember that the stalactite that hangs from the ceiling of a cave contains the letter *c*, the same as the initial letter for *ceiling*, and the stalagmite that protrudes from the *ground* contains the letter *g*. Some appreciate this mnemonic for remembering abscissa as the horizontal axis and ordinate as the vertical: When the word *ordinate* is said aloud, the lips extend in a vertical direction, whereas when the word *abscissa* is spoken, the lips remain practically horizontal.

Signalers in the U.S. Navy have been taught the phonetic alphabet (e.g., alpha for *a* and bravo for *b*) and the Morse code together, using a mnemonic of appropriate visual stimuli that elicit both the phonetic letter and the corresponding Morse code symbol. For example, a simple line drawing of a building with four dots (windows) in a row represents both the phonetic symbol (a hotel) and the Morse code symbol (four dots in a row) for the letter *h*. Later, the letter simply elicits the visual image that cues the correct phonetic and Morse code response. All of the images used are adequately straightforward.

When introduced to a person, many people cannot recall the name later. Typically this is because the name was not learned in the first place. To remember a name, it must be rehearsed and related to names already known or to something the name suggests from experience. The name can be related to the person by observing what is unusual or distinctive about his or her manner or appearance or whether he or she resembles someone else. Meaningful procedures like these are not time-consuming but are remarkably effective.

ASSOCIATIONISM
MNEMONICS
TRANSFER OF TRAINING

M. R. DENNY

MNEMONICS

Early mnemonic systems were aids to memory. Their use was attributed to the Greek poet Simonides and to the Romans as well, who used them as an aid to oratory. The modern devices, strategies, and aids to remembering use methods of localization (loci) and imagery. Most psychologists agree that imagery aids elaboration, mediation, and organization, so that materials are more easily remembered. In some sense, mnemonic aids are a practical demonstration of the positive effects of deeper "levels of processing on memory."

INFORMATION PROCESSING
MEMORY

N. S. ANDERSON

MOB PSYCHOLOGY

Roger Brown defined crowds as "co-acting, shoulder-to-shoulder, anonymous, casual, temporary, and unorganized collectivities." Crowds can be further subdivided according to whether they are active or passive, the former being a *mob* and the latter an *audience*. Mobs are further classified according to the dominant behavior of participants. *Aggressive* mobs, which include riot and lynch mobs, involve a display of aggression toward persons or objects. The dominant behavior of *escape* mobs is one of panic, as during a fire in a theater. *Acquisitive* mobs are similar to escape mobs in that both involve a competition for some object that is in short supply. *Expressive* mobs represent a wastebasket category that includes all mobs not in the first three categories.

Although there is no universal agreement among theorists, certain features tend to be attributed to mobs: (a) like-mindedness or "mental homogeneity," (b) emotionality, and (c) irrationality. Le Bon explained the mental homogeneity of mobs in terms of *contagion*—a mechanical, disease-like spreading of affect from one member to another. Others, like Milgram and Toch, suggested that the mechanism of *convergence* may also account for the seeming mental homogeneity of mobs: Like-minded individuals tend to converge and join mobs, thus homogeneity precedes rather than follows from membership in the mob. Two mechanisms are presumed to account for the emotional and irrational nature of mobs: (a) the loss of responsibility through anonymity, and (b) the impression of universality.

BYSTANDER INVOLVEMENT
DEINDIVIDUATION
MASS HYSTERIA
PEER INFLUENCE
VIOLENCE

M. S. GREENBERG

MODELS

A substantial portion of the research efforts in all areas of psychology involves the use of models. Examples include artificial cochlear models for audition, layered network models of brain function, computer models of thinking, and animal models of psychopathology.

Models are basic and powerful tools in science. The aeronautical scientist builds a miniature airplane for testing in a wind tunnel; the chemical scientist imagines electrons in shared planet-like orbits around atomic nuclei. These two types of models—one physical, one conceptual—aid in the discovery of useful principles for addressing real-world problems such as optimal wing shape for speed or how smooth a shape molecules will take when bonded to the wing's surface.

Models also are important in the biological and behavioral sciences, and this accounts in part for why so much research is done with animals in psychology. In spite of their wide use and demonstrated usefulness, models—and animal models in particular—are not well understood. However, they are used; for example, they aid understanding of how neurons produce learning, or how to develop new therapies for phobias. The most common use of animal models in psychology is in research on learning, memory, drug abuse, and psychopathology.

A model is not considered a claim of identity with that which is being modeled. Rather it is a convergent set of several kinds of analogies between the real-world phenomenon and the system that is being studied as a substitute for the real-world phenomenon. The kinds of analogy involved are (a) initial analogy, (b) material analogy, and (c) formal analogy.

Any phenomenon is not "just a thing" but the consequence of causal relationships between levels of factors in the real world. Similarly, any potentially useful model will involve a set of causally related factors. These causal chains of factors in both the real-world domain and the model domain may be several steps long. Models arise from the claims of correspondence between factors in the two domains. The two domains can have obvious similarity, as between a miniature airplane and a Boeing 747, or they can be dissimilar, as between the ball-and-stick arrays in chemistry and the molecular compound itself.

Consider a case in which there are both similarities and differences. One might note that some set of dysfunctional physiological and behavioral symptoms characterize patients with a given psychiatric disorder; one might further note that animals exposed to some drug exhibit behaviors similar to the behavioral symptoms of the patients. A hypothesis that the dysfunctional behavior of the animal and the dysfunctional behavior of the patient were similar would constitute an *initial analogy* in the modeling process. An additional hypothesis might be that the patient's dysfunctional physiological symptom is related to the animal's drug-induced physiological state; this would be a second initial analogy. The degree of *descriptive* similarity between the two sets of behaviors or between the two physiological states would constitute the degree of *material analogy*.

If a relation between the patient's physiology and the patient's behavior is demonstrated that parallels the empirical *causal* relation between the animal's physiology and its behavior, a *formal analogy* can be drawn between these two parallel, within-domain relations. This is how many models in psychology have arisen, such as the amphetamine-based model of schizophrenia and the cholinergic depletion model of Korsakoff's syndrome. Development of other models emphasized environmental-learning history rather than drug history, for example, the avoidance model of phobias and the learned helplessness model of depression.

An initial analogy alone is not a model; this is a common mistake. A true model involves both initial analogies and formal analogies. Also, the power of the modeling process is that it is possible to use the known and explicated causal relations in one domain (typically the model domain, but it can work both ways) as a guide to finding parallel relations in the second domain. Some scientists require that a large number of formal analogy parallels be proven, all involving substantial material analogy, before a claim of a model is made. Material analogy is not critical to the functional validity of a model; mathematical equations are often powerful models that when processed by computers generate knowledge about a system's behavior—even a living system—but without material analogy. Material analogy is akin to face validity; it ensures nothing. If a researcher waits until all the causal relations in each domain are fully and independently explicated before setting them into formal analogies, then the model yields little or no evidentiary power for new understanding.

The psychological models noted previously all began with an initial analogy made between behaviors. However, one might well argue that finding such similarities in behavior between species is a chancy process—possibly a misleading one, although subject to empirical test within the modeling process. This is because each species brings its own evolved propensities and biological constraints on its behavior to the test arena. Thus it is conceivable that two different species might have opposite dysfunctional behavioral manifestations from the same underlying physiological or psychological state. Although this has not proved a common problem, it does suggest an alternative approach to choosing the initial analogy. One might well choose to put into initial correspondence etiological factors rather than symptoms. This strategy is common in medical research and is based on the assumption that etiology and therapy are necessarily linked. In psychology, the sustaining conditions for some behavioral processes are often different from those that led to their development. Korsakoff's syndrome and phobias seem to be good examples. Posttraumatic stress disorder (PTSD) may prove to be a case requiring an approach of an etiological initial analogy, if one seeks an animal model of the consequences of stress, because the reported symptoms tend to take the form of thought disruptions, flashbacks, and other symptoms that are not directly observable in animals.

Although the elucidation of the modeling process here has used exemplars from animal models, the analysis is indeed a general one applying to physical models, computer-processing models, or quantitative models of psychological processes. Each has proved its value in giving insight into psychological processes of humans.

ALGORITHMIC-HEURISTIC THEORY
ANIMAL MODELS
GENERAL SYSTEMS
HOLISM
ISOMORPHISM
MOLAR–MOLECULAR CONSTRUCTS
RESEARCH METHODOLOGY

J. B. OVERMIER

MODERATED MULTIPLE REGRESSION

Moderated multiple regression is a type of multivariate analysis that examines whether the relationship between a dependent variable (Y) and a predictor variable (X) is influenced or moderated by a third variable (M). Consider the formula for regular linear regression:

$$Y + a + b_1X \tag{1}$$

where a is the intercept and b_1 is a regression weight associated with predictor X. In comparison, Equation 2 includes a predictor variable (M) whose moderating effect is represented by a product term (XM):

$$Y = a + b_1X + b_2M + b_3(XM) \tag{2}$$

where the subscripted bs represent regression weights associated with their corresponding predictors.

The inclusion of a moderator in Equation 2 permits the data analyst to address the question of whether the association between the dependent variable (Y) and the predictor variable (X) depends on a third variable. For example, is the relationship between life expectancy (a dependent variable) and being overweight (a predictor variable) influenced by another factor such as blood pressure (a moderator variable)? Is the association between student learning (a dependent variable) and instructor teaching style (a predictor variable) influenced by class size (a moderator variable)?

Similarities exist between moderator effects in multiple regression and interaction effects in analysis of variance. For example, an experimental design with two between-subjects factors, X and M, represents a special case of Equation 2 for which the predictor variables are categorical and uncorrelated. Equation 2, however, is more general in that it also is capable of incorporating continuous and correlated predictors and moderators. Furthermore, with appropriate coding, Equation 2 may also include repeated measures factors that have usually been analyzed through analysis of variance. Multiple regression analysis subsumes analysis of variance, and an interaction term in analysis of variance may be regarded as a moderator variable in multiple regression.

Consider the situation in which a new drug is being evaluated as a potential treatment for depression. Within each sex, eight depressed psychiatric inpatients are randomly assigned to either a *drug* or a *no drug* condition so that there are equal numbers of subjects in each condition. Following treatment, scores on a self-report depression scale are used as an outcome measure. In addition to evaluating whether the drug has an effect on scores on depression, it is of potential interest to determine

Table 1   An Example of Data Analyzed Using Traditional Analysis of Variance Calculations

Sex	Data Drug Condition	
	Drug	No Drug
Male	19, 19, 21, 24	33, 35, 36, 37
Female	23, 29, 27, 29	28, 33, 32, 34

Traditional Analysis of Variance Calculation

Source	SS	df	MS	F-Ratio
Sex	7.56	1	7.56	1.29
Sex	370.56	1	370.56	63.30
Sex × drug	95.06	1	95.06	16.24
Error	70.25	12	5.85	

whether the drug might be differentially effective for men and women. Hypothetical data are given in Table 1. Data are analyzed using traditional analysis of variance computations. These data are reformatted in matrix terms, using effect coding for the predictor (i.e., independent) variables, and analyzed using multiple regression analysis (Table 2). Tests of significance for corresponding factors in the analysis of variance (i.e., the F-

Table 2   Multiple Regression Reanalysis of Data from Table 1

Multiple Regression Data Matrix Using Effect Coding

Dependent Variable: Depression	Predictor Variables		
	Sex[a]	Drug[b]	Sex × Drug
19	1	1	1
19	1	1	1
21	1	1	1
24	1	1	1
33	1	−1	−1
35	1	−1	−1
36	1	−1	−1
37	1	−1	−1
23	−1	1	−1
29	−1	1	−1
27	−1	1	−1
29	−1	1	−1
28	−1	−1	1
33	−1	−1	1
32	−1	−1	1
34	−1	−1	1

Multiple Regression Results

Equation: depression score = $28.69 - 0.69 \times \text{sex} - 4.81 \times \text{drug} - 2.44 \times (\text{sex} \times \text{drug})$

Multiple $R = 0.93$

$R^2 = 0.87$

Tests of Predictor Weights in Above Equation

Predictor	b	t	t^{2c}
Sex	−0.69	−1.14	1.29
Drug	−4.81	−7.96	63.30
Sex × drug	−2.44	−4.03	16.24

[a] 1, male; −1, female.

[b] 1, drug; −1, no drug.

[c] These t^2 values are identical to the F-ratios in Table 1.

ratios) and predictor weights in the multiple regression (i.e., the t^2 values) are equivalent.

Although interactions in traditional analysis of variance computations may be regarded as special instances of moderator variables in multiple regression, regression approaches are more general because their applications include both continuous as well as categorical predictors, and both correlated in addition to uncorrelated predictors. Where correlated predictors and moderators are used, a hierarchical regression approach is recommended for evaluating the statistical significance of moderators.

CAUSAL REASONING
CORRELATION VERSUS CAUSATION
DOUBLE-BLIND RESEARCH
PROBABILITY
RESEARCH METHODOLOGY
STATISTICS

R. R. HOLDEN

MOLAR–MOLECULAR CONSTRUCTS

Theoretical constructs are the conceptual inventions or concepts devised to explain empirical observables as manifestations or instances of underlying theory. Thus they constitute the basic units or elements of substantive theory.

The molar–molecular distinction was first proposed by Tolman in an attempt to clarify psychology's molar character. It was his view that behavior can take place only in a whole organism. Tolman characterized behavior as both purposive and cognitive, and proposed that the primary job of the theoretical psychologist is to identify such molar phenomena as goals and the intervening means-objects in achieving goals. Although Tolman originally introduced these terms to distinguish between the functioning of the entire organism as a unit (molar construct) and its parts as units (molecular construct), the terms were subsequently applied widely and took on many additional meanings.

A theoretical construct is described as molecular to the extent that it involves: (a) the interaction of a small number of variables; (b) a brief unit of time; (c) concepts from the lower or reduced-to discipline; (d) limited generalizability; (e) an analytically devised phenomenon; (f) socially irrelevant problems; and (g) a small segment or fragment of the total organism. However, a theoretical construct is described as molar to the extent it involves: (a) a large number of interacting variables; (b) a long time interval; (c) concepts from the higher or reduced-from discipline; (d) broad generalizability (i.e., it applies to many contexts or situations); (e) a naively observed phenomenon (i.e., direct observation in the laboratory, the clinic, or the natural environment); (f) socially relevant problems; and (g) the whole organism.

Although all of these meanings can be found in the literature, the original meaning occurs most frequently. This multidimensionality led Littman and Rosen to the conclusion that these constructs should be discarded. However, a more realistic alternative is to retain the molar–molecular distinction, but to restrict its use to the originally intended meaning—namely, the size of the theoretical construct.

THEORETICAL PSYCHOLOGY

J. R. ROYCE

MONISM–DUALISM

Monism–dualism refers to a traditional classification of the types of solutions variously proposed for the mind–body problem. Such solutions assume that the human being comprises either a single, unified entity (monism) or two qualitatively different, independent entities (dualism). Adherents of the two types of solution also tend to differ in epistemology. Monists tend to view empiricism as the primary and/or only acceptable method of knowledge. Dualists, however, accept empiricism and rationalism as equally appropriate and valid, each in its own sphere.

Because monists tend to equate knowledge with empiricism, all of their definitions try in one way or another to reduce or equate mind (or mental functions) to the activity of the brain and nervous system. Thus, in effect, mind and body become "one." Mind is defined as being of the materialistic order of things. In the field of psychology, this position gives neuroscience a central locus of importance in the understanding and explanation of behavior.

Dualists, in contrast, are faced with the problem of in some way relating the activities of the nonmaterial mind and the material body. Two primary patterns of dualism appear to prevail throughout history. The first are the interactionist theories, of which the views of Descartes are considered classic. Modern dualists have not had much success in replacing Descartes' explanation in terms of modern neurological knowledge.

A form of dualism that avoids the difficulty of explaining an interaction is psychophysical parallelism. Mind and body are viewed as acting in concert such that events that affect the one affect the other. Thus knowledge of the one provides information about the other. The isomorphism of mental activity and brain functions, as well as the applications of the concepts of topology and field theory by Gestalt psychology, represent a modern version of psychophysical parallelism in present-day thinking.

A key element of dualistic positions as they affect psychology is that in defining the mind as being a totally separate entity from the materialistic body, conceptualizations of the activity of the mind are not constrained by the laws of materialism. Laws unique to mental activity become acceptable and appropriate.

Traditionally, American psychology has been heavily monistic since the days when Watsonian behaviorism made its great impact. Monism still prevails in this discipline. However, the rise in popularity of existentialism, humanism, and other "self-oriented" philosophies and their effects on the thinking of psychologists, particularly psychotherapists, have led to revived interest in problems that logically require dualistic positions.

MIND–BODY PROBLEM
PHILOSOPHICAL PSYCHOLOGY

M. E. Reuder

MONTESSORI METHOD

At the turn of the twentieth century a new and revolutionary educational method swept across Europe: the Montessori method, based on the original ideas of Maria Montessori, the first woman physician of Italy. Her love for teaching began while she was educating retarded children and later unmanageable children at her first school.

She viewed the central problem in education as the need to establish a new and better relationship between children and adults during the various stages of the children's development. She recognized the rights of children and respected them as human beings having a sense of personal dignity. The job of the teacher, she explained, was to facilitate the pupil–teacher relationship. This was accomplished by manipulating the classroom setting and by introducing materials that captivated the children and enabled them to teach themselves at their own rates. The school building became the Children's House, complete with child-sized furniture and equipment specially built to meet the intellectual and physical needs of youngsters.

Children have the freedom to select any materials to which they are spontaneously attracted. Each learner's choices reveal the child's unique potentialities. The children may work independently or in groups. The class is ungraded, and rules are intended to encourage mutual cooperation instead of competition. Since children become absorbed in their work, they do not have time for mischief. Instead, they acquire self-discipline.

Montessori materials are designed to provide the preschooler with practical life experiences, sensory activities, and language and school skills. Writing is introduced before reading by tracing sandpaper letters. By 4 or 5 years of age, Montessori children burst spontaneously into writing. Spelling is learned with a movable alphabet.

To round out the curriculum, science, history, geography, geometry, and arithmetic are explored. The curriculum is based on the finding that preschool children can solve problems and can accomplish a great amount of intellectual work before entering formal schooling. Montessori referred to the absorbent mind from birth to 6 years of age.

ALTERNATIVE EDUCATIONAL SYSTEMS
DISCOVERY LEARNING
INDIVIDUAL EDUCATION
LEARNING OUTCOMES I, II

S. S. Brown

MOONEY PROBLEM CHECKLIST

This personality problem instrument is not a test, but more of a form for communicating simply, quickly, and succinctly with a counselor what counselees perceive their problems to be. The instrument is composed of lists of common problems of students from grade nine through the college years and of adults. These problems are in areas such as health, school, home and family, money/work/occupation, courtship/sex/marriage, religion/morals, relations with people, social/recreational activities, personal/psychological relations, and curriculum/teaching.

PERSONALITY ASSESSMENT QUESTIONNAIRES

W. Asher

MORAL DEVELOPMENT

The central issue in the study of moral development is the process by which an individual internalizes socially approved rules and restrictions and comes to orient his or her behavior vis-à-vis these rules. Research and theory has focused on three conceptually distinguishable aspects of these developments: moral judgment (how one reasons about moral situations), moral behavior (how one behaves), and moral emotions (what one feels).

MORAL JUDGMENT

Since early in the twentieth century, psychologists such as James Mark Baldwin and William McDougall have studied the process of moral development. The seminal investigations Jean Piaget published have, however, inspired most contemporary research. According to Piaget's cognitive developmental account, a two-stage progression was involved; a shift from a heteronomous morality of constraint to an autonomous morality of cooperation is said to occur. Most research has focused on whether moral judgments are based on objective consequences or subjective intentions. In general, research supports an age-related shift from an objective to a more subjective (intentional) conception of responsibility.

Kohlberg built on and extended, in nontrivial ways, Piaget's earlier structural view that the progressive internalization of rules and principles may extend throughout adolescence and into adulthood. Moral development is postulated to be hierarchical in nature; each subsequent stage reorganizes and integrates the preceding one and consequently provides a more comprehensive basis for moral decisions. Kohlberg's invariant sequence is composed of three general levels—preconventional, conventional, and postconventional morality, each of which is divided into two specific stages. Although the order in which a person can proceed through the six stages is viewed as fixed and universal, the rate and final level of development may vary.

Preconventional morality is externally based. At the stage one *punishment* orientation, moral decisions focus on the power of authorities and the avoiding of punishing consequences. Stage two judgments are *hedonistically* oriented: acts that satisfy one's personal needs are deemed moral. Although preconventional morality emphasizes the aversive (punishing) or positive (reward) effects of immediate external consequences, conventional morality is said to be mediated by internalized rules and values. At stage three, *interpersonal concordance* is involved: One adheres to rules that have been internalized in order to please and be approved of by significant others. At stage four, morality is defined as "doing one's duty" and the now internalized rules of the existing *social order* are maintained for their own sake.

Postconventional reasoners attempt rationally to understand the abstract moral principles on which more concrete rules and laws are based. A personal effort is made to define principles that have applicability and validity separate from a given authority or social order. At stage five, a legalistic or *contractual* orientation is employed: People appreciate the relativistic nature of rules and laws, but realize that a contractual agreement is necessary to ensure the protection of individuals, including themselves. At stage six, *personal commitment* rather than social consensus underlies one's choice among moral principles. Conduct is dictated by a self-selected ideal, regardless of the reactions of others; violation of these principles is said to produce self-condemnation.

Research does reveal that an invariant level-to-level sequence may occur; preconventional morality is a prerequisite for conventional reasoning and both must precede the development of postconventional morality. However, the highest level may not necessarily be found in all samples of adolescents or adults. Critics have underscored the role that social–cultural factors may play in promoting postconventional reasoning, especially experiences within the context of a jurisprudence system of justice. Thus although Kohlberg's model may not provide the universal view of a moral person, it does seem to be relevant to an individual living in a country such as the United States, with a constitutionally based legal system.

MORAL BEHAVIOR

The theoretical link between moral cognition and action is elusive: People can exhibit the same behavior for different reasons, and individuals at the same level of moral reasoning may act in different ways.

In the 1920s, an even more fundamental issue of moral behavior was addressed by Hartshorne and May. They devised numerous behavioral indices of the extent to which subjects would actually resist the temptation to lie, cheat, and steal in experimental settings. Correlational analyses provided little evidence for a general personality trait of honesty; they advanced the position that moral behavior was situation-specific.

Knowing that a person is a conventional moral reasoner may not be sufficient; we also have to know the particular rules he or she conforms to before making behavioral predictions.

MORAL EMOTION

The psychoanalytic theory of guilt-motivated morality was presented by Sigmund Freud. Briefly stated, Freud believed that the children experienced Oedipal feelings. The anxiety that children feel over anticipated punishment is said to result in the repression of Oedipal feelings and hostilities. More important, fear of parental retaliation prompts an introjection of parental rules and prohibitions: The superego or conscience is formed. In subsequent situations children are said to experience self-punishment or guilt when tempted to violate these internalized rules. Research summarized by Martin Hoffman indicates that a more internalized morality is apt to result when discipline (especially withdrawal of love) is coupled with parental explanations about the harmful consequences of the child's behavior for others: other-oriented inductive techniques. Such inductions may contribute to moral development by enhancing a child's tendency to experience another's emotional state empathically.

ALTRUISM
CONFORMING PERSONALITY
CRIME
DEVIANCE

M. D. BERZONSKY

MORALE IN ORGANIZATIONS

The study of morale in organizations often concentrates on two major dimensions: work motivation and job satisfaction. Work motivation research has generated several theories that have influenced organizational management. Job satisfaction research often concentrates on the validity of such theories.

MAJOR THEORIES OF WORK MOTIVATION

According to J. C. Gray and F. A. Starke, theories of work motivation may be categorized into two broad areas: universalistic theories and contingency theories. Universalistic theories attempt to posit widespread applicability to the work environment, while contingency theories focus on individual differences that influence motivation levels.

Universalistic Theories

Perhaps the most widely cited theory of motivation is Abraham Maslow's Hierarchy of Needs, which proposes that human behavior is a result of people's attempts to satisfy currently unsatisfied needs. Such needs are arranged in a hierarchial order such that the satisfaction of a prior level of need leads to a need for satisfaction at a succeeding level.

Another often cited theory is Herzberg's Two-Factor Theory, which asserts that job satisfaction and dissatisfaction are conceptually different, being caused by different work-related factors. The variables that cause job satisfaction are labeled *motivators*. Those that cause dissatisfaction are called *hygienes*. Herzberg concludes that job satisfaction can be increased without reducing job dissatisfaction and vice versa.

A third notable theory is McClelland's Achievement Motivation Theory. Focusing on Murray's list of human needs, McClelland and his associates selected three needs that they considered most salient: (a) *power* (deriving satisfaction from controlling others); (b) *affiliation* (deriving satisfaction from social and interpersonal activities); and (c) *achievement* (deriving satisfaction from reaching one's goals).

Contingency Theories

The most notable contingency theory is B. F. Skinner's Stimulus-Response Theory. Also known as operant conditioning, this view argues that human behavior is not motivated by needs within an individual but by the external environment and the manner in which it doles out rewards and punishments. For the behavior of the individual to be conditioned (or shaped), attention must be given to (a) the consequences of one's behavior and (b) the schedules of reinforcement affecting one's behavior.

Equity Theory, originally presented by J. S. Adams, assumes that individuals are motivated by a desire to be treated equitably on their jobs. Essentially, work motivation is seen as the result of the person comparing his or her Inputs/Outcomes ratio with the identical ratio of the Comparison Other. When a discrepancy (i.e., inequity) exists between the two, this motivates the person to act so that equity may be achieved.

The last major contingency theory is V. H. Vroom's Expectancy Theory, which states that a person's motivation to perform an act is a function of (a) the outcomes the person perceives as desirable and (b) the person's belief that such outcomes can be attained.

JOB SATISFACTION AND MORALE

J. L. Gray and F. A. Starke note that theories of motivation have practical implications for the operation of an organization so as to maximize job satisfaction and morale. They cite four job-related areas that influence morale.

Job Design and Content

To increase employee motivation, the suggestion is often made that there be job enrichment, defined as changing the content of the job so as to make greater and fuller use of each employee's abilities.

Organizational Rewards and Punishments

This area, which has caused a good deal of debate, arises from operant conditioning research. The practical challenge for organizational managers appears to be one of deciding when and how to reward and punish.

Compensation

Although pay is seen as an important determiner of job satisfaction, such compensation is clearly seen as relative by most workers and therefore is not very useful as a primary motivator. A number of other dimensions related to compensation are important, including job security, supervision, working conditions, fringe benefits, and status.

Organizational Climate

Organizational climate is both a consequence and a determinant of motivation. Climate is typically defined in terms of a particular set of values espoused by the organization that can either facilitate or hinder an individual's performance.

ORGANIZATIONAL CLIMATE

A. BARÓN, JR.

MORITA THERAPY

Morita psychotherapy is a Japanese treatment form developed around the turn of the twentieth century by the Tokyo psychiatrist Shoma Morita. Basically Buddhist in orientation, the theory recognizes the inevitability of some anxiety, fear, and other discomfort in human living. The therapy aims, therefore, not at a symptom-free existence, but at a realistic acceptance of immediate suffering while doing what needs to be done from moment to moment. The Morita therapy client learns to respond to what reality brings simply because reality requires such response, not because doing so will lead to a cure in the sense of feeling better. Merging the "self" with the requirements of reality is the goal.

Moritists clearly distinguish between feelings and behaviors. Feelings are considered to be uncontrollable directly by the will. They cannot be maneuvered by wishing or thought or physical effort, but must be accepted as they are, without useless struggle. Although they may be experienced as pleasant or unpleasant, they are neither good nor bad and there is no moral responsibility attached to them.

Behavior, in contrast, is considered to be controllable by will. Behaviors are right or wrong in terms of the client's moral sense. Action always carries moral responsibility. Furthermore, behavior provides an indirect means of influencing thoughts and feelings. Nothing, however, provides absolute deterministic control over feeling states.

Inpatient treatment begins with 1 week of isolated bedrest, during which the patient must come to terms with changing thoughts and feelings. No distractions other than eating and natural bodily functions are permitted. Subsequent periods of increasingly difficult work, group sessions, and diary guidance prepare the patient for discharge some 2 months or so after admission.

Outpatient treatment in Japan and the United States generally includes directive counseling, diary guidance, reading and other assignments, and personalized education during weekly meetings. It appears that the principles of this way of life can be learned in a few months with immediate short term benefits, but it takes a somewhat longer period to put the practice into everyday life.

PSYCHOTHERAPY
ZEN BUDDHISM

D. K. REYNOLDS

MOTIVATION

In simple terms, motivation deals with the "why" of behavior. It refers to internal states of the organism that lead to the instigation, persistence, energy, and direction of behavior. Ordinarily, motivation includes goal direction and energizing of behavior, and a distinction is made between motivation *disposition* and motivation *arousal*. An organism may be likely to become fearful or anxious or hungry in certain circumstances as a motivational disposition, but motivation as an active state occurs only in a given moment or situation when the organism is actually aroused, that is, *motivated*. Because psychologists seek laws that include the behavior of lower animals as well as humans, the literature in the field of motivation has covered topics that deal with shared characteristics of all animal life, such as hunger, as well as topics that focus on uniquely human characteristics, such as the striving for achievement and excellence. Motivation is said to be an *organismic variable* in that it is a condition of the individual and not of the environment.

Motivation is said to be directing or steering, in that it leads to goal-directed behavior. This emphasizes the specificity of motivation: thirsty animals look for water, or a person in a stressful job tries to escape from this unpleasant work situation. Goals have been identified in two ways. One way describes goals as objective events or tangible environmental outcomes.

The second sense in which the term *goal* has been used is as an internal abstraction rather than an objective external event. For example, the goal of finding a less stressful job is an idea, a thought the person has about future events when motivated to leave a stressful work situation. Goals direct or steer, because in moving toward them the person makes some responses rather than others, and goals are functional at any given moment because they are internal here-and-now representations of the future and not objective, actual, future events.

Motivation can also be identified in terms of specific antecedent events and not merely in terms of outcomes (actual or cognitively representational outcomes). Antecedent events lead to different kinds of motivational states, and very often the behavior of the individual differs according to what specific antecedents have occurred.

INTENSITY

Motivation differs not only in kind, but also in intensity. We can speak of being more or less thirsty, more or less fearful. It is generally agreed that motivation excites or energizes, but theories differ as to how motivation energizes.

Different sources of motivation may have a summating effect on behavior. Heightened motivational arousal may occur as a result of increased intensity in any one kind of motivation or as a function of the summation of different sources of motivation. In many cases, the energizing effect of heightened motivational intensity can be observed by means of physiological measures rather than overt responses.

Measures of brain waves, skin conductance, heart rate, and muscle tension have been used to identify the intensity dimension of motivation. Under conditions of drowsiness and low excitation, electroencephalographic recordings generally show slow and large brain waves with a regular pattern, while under excited alertness the pattern is one of fast, low, irregular waves. As a result of increased excitation individuals also tend to show increase in muscle potential, as measured by electromyographic recordings, and decrease in skin resistance.

Overall, studies have demonstrated that organisms are more active the more they are motivated. Especially in naive subjects, response output of simple behaviors like running or bar pressing increases directly with increased motivation. For animals and humans, heightened motivation tends to increase effort, persistence, and responsivity.

Another demonstration of the energizing aspect of motivation is the fact that subjects under heightened motivation display increased stimulus generalization, which refers to a broadening in the range of stimuli to which an organism responds.

The reticular activating system (RAS) has been cited as a physiological explanation for the diffusely energizing effects of increased motivation. The early work of Moruzzi and Magoun and, later, Lindsley pointed to a system that involved the reticular formation, thalamus, and cortex, and this appeared to explain how organisms can show both specific and general arousal. However, a single arousal system has been questioned at both physiological and behavioral levels by a number of investigators.

DIFFERENCES BETWEEN PSYCHOLOGICAL AND PHYSIOLOGICAL NEEDS

Although at first glance it might appear that psychological needs as types of motivation are closely tied or are identical to physiological needs, the differences between the two are often dramatic. Physiological needs ordinarily pertain to the survival or health of the individual and are often described as "tissue" needs. Studies with a variety of mammals and especially with nonhuman primates have shown that psychological and physiological needs are different. For example, evidence exists that young laboratory rats require activity and environmental stimulation, which do not reflect "tissue needs," for optimum development and for facilitated learning of new behaviors.

That humans require emotional, intellectual, and social satisfactions for optimum development and effective living illustrates general or species-wide psychological needs. Sometimes motives that are called "needs" by researchers, such as the "need for achievement," are objectively measurable and function in predictable ways but are not potent among people in general. Such a motive may be very strong and have the quality of a "need" for a particular person, yet fail to represent a basic psychological need characteristic of all humans; in addition, it differs from physiological needs that pertain to survival or the physical health of the individual.

Just as psychological needs may be independent of physiological needs, so the reverse can be true. Many toxic effects that create physiological needs fail to relate to psychological needs. Another example in which physiological and psychological states differ is hunger. As problems of both obesity and anorexia nervosa become more prevalent in current society, this distinction is gaining increasing prominence in medical science and public awareness. Overall it is evident that, particularly for

humans, although physiological needs may be powerful sources of motivation, they are neither necessary nor sufficient as the basis for motivation.

DIFFERENCES BETWEEN BEHAVIOR AND MOTIVATION

One cannot infer the existence of a motivation merely by the presence of certain behaviors. Behavior may be due to many factors. Because motivation is an intervening variable, a state inferred to occur within an individual, how such a variable relates to behavior requires careful study and observation.

Animal aggression has been studied by animal behaviorists (often called *ethologists*), and in many cases the assumption has been made that animals have an innate drive or motivation for aggression. One line of support for this view is the evidence that when animals are deprived of the opportunity to display aggressive behavior they are more likely to behave aggressively later, and that animals raised in isolation display species-specific aggressive behavior even if not exposed to other animals of their species. However, evidence that aggression is not due to an innate drive comes from many sources. For example, laboratory studies have shown that socially isolating a rat makes it more emotional and more likely to be a killer.

Aggression has often been described as a reaction to frustration or pain. From many kinds of studies it is evident that early life experiences and learning shape the way an animal responds to stressful events.

FEAR AND ANXIETY

Motivations of fear and anxiety are usually learned. Some investigators have pointed to instances of innate fears in animals and human infants, but in general, human fear and anxiety are learned. Research has focused on how these motivations are learned, what kinds of situations induce them, and how these motivations affect behavior. Learning plays a dual role, since fear is learned and the behavior engendered by that motivation is also learned. A wide variety of animal and human behaviors occur toward painful or fear-arousing stimuli, such as attack, "freezing," crouching, running, and fleeing, and some of these behaviors follow species-specific patterns. Stimuli associated with pain come to evoke fear. Fear occurs when painful stimulation is anticipated. Fear and anxiety, although related, are distinguished in terms of their specificity. Fear occurs to a specific event while anxiety is more generalized and nonspecific. Because in humans painful events are often symbolic and not merely physical, researchers have explored conceptual processes such as "fear of failure" and "fear of success."

If painful stimulation can be terminated (escape) or prevented (avoidance), an animal or a person can learn new behavior that leads to such escape or avoidance. Behavior acquired through avoidance learning is typically acquired more slowly, but persists much longer, than behavior acquired through escape learning. Human anxiety has been thought to maintain avoidant behaviors.

That anxiety has far more negative than positive consequences was noted long ago by Sigmund Freud, who postulated that human neurosis has its roots in anxiety. Clinical, field, and laboratory findings have demonstrated that defensive motivations like fear and anxiety are likely to lead to behaviors that interfere with effective task performance and creative problem solving. Although in humans simple behaviors like eyeblink conditioning have been found to be facilitated by anxiety, complex behaviors are typically not facilitated. As motivations, anxiety and fear energize behavior, and in some situations or on some tasks they may lead to appropriate behavior. However, since direction as well as intensity of motivation is important, the way anxiety and fear affect behavior ordinarily varies according to the given circumstance and the given individual.

Anxiety has been measured as both a trait and a state, and usually the two show a strong positive correlation. However, in certain situations persons who have a disposition to be anxious (high trait anxiety) may have low state anxiety, and likewise, under specific circumstances persons of low trait anxiety may be very high in state anxiety. Anxiety and fear not only affect behavior but also may themselves result from a person's actions, so that a two-way rather than unidirectional relationship exists between motivation and behavior.

Although it appears that anxiety and fear arise only in response to aversive external events, in human beings these motivations can also be self-generated. According to Adlerian theory and clinical evidence, emotions serve a goal and are generated for a purpose. Emotions that typically disrupt a person's performance or adaptive behavior can also be used as a vehicle for behavioral control.

EXPECTANCY, CONTROL, AND APPROACH MOTIVATION

Cognitions and beliefs play a dominant role in human motivation. Beliefs are involved in values, expectation of future outcomes, and apperceptions of environmental events. Human motivation has been studied in terms of such cognitive processes. For example, literature on the achievement motive indicates that people who have a high "need to achieve" learn to strive to achieve excellence in performance at an early age. Self-reliance is a key aspect of their motivational disposition.

Many theorists have postulated that people function effectively when they believe positive outcomes are possible, and when they believe they have control over the nature of events that happen to them. An early theory that emphasized the importance of teaching children self-reliance and courage (willingness to try new things and to expend effort even when success is not guaranteed) was that of Alfred Adler. The literature on "locus of control of reinforcement" indicates that people who believe they have little control over events that happen to them are more anxious, and also less likely to behave in ways that lead to positive outcomes. Children trained with encouragement and self-reliance rather than with praise and rewards are more likely to maintain socially con structive behaviors. Laboratory studies with children and adults have shown that intrinsic motivation and self-direction maintain behavior more effectively than do extrinsic motivation and externally administered rewards.

Social motivation, expectancy, effort, and performance have been found to interrelate in a wide variety of settings. Realistic and moderately high goal setting has been found to occur in children with a high need to achieve, and moderately high goal setting leads to improvements in performance in adults as well. Children who fear failure, moreover, have been consistently found to set unrealistic goals that are either too high or too low. Thus social motivation and task motivation alter the kinds of expectancies individuals have, and expectancies have been found both to shape behavior and to be its consequence.

Studies of learned helplessness have found that animals also may alter their behavior as a result of the degree of control possible in a situation. Thus control over negative as well as positive outcomes has far reaching effects on behavior and motivation in animals as well as humans. Especially in humans, self-direction and symbolic processes are fundamental in determining motivation and its effects on behavior. Moreover altruism, love, and the many positive ways that human beings approach one another give a wide range and direction to human motivation and action.

ACQUIRED DRIVES
REWARDS
SELF-DETERMINATION

E. D. FERGUSON

MOVEMENT THERAPY

Movement therapy is a form of psychotherapy based on the premise that there is a direct and reciprocal relationship between the body and mind.

Distortions in the body, posture, breathing, and movement are seen as reflective of distortions in the psyche and the balanced state of the organism.

Since physiological and psychic behavior are codetermined, movement therapy is a psychotherapeutic approach that works to dissolve both muscular rigidity and tensions and psychic resistance.

Limits to mobility, spontaneity, and freedom are released through the use of movement and movement interaction as diagnosis, assessment, and treatment. The aim is for individuals to be able to tap their own inner resources and creativity.

Movement therapists work as primary and adjunctive therapists in clinical, health-care, and educational settings and in private practice. Movement therapy operates effectively in both therapeutic and growth-oriented settings.

MUSIC THERAPY
NONVERBAL THERAPIES
PSYCHOTHERAPY

D. G. ECKSTEIN
S. F. WALLOCK

MULTICULTURAL COUNSELING

Counseling strategies that disregard the cultural context are unlikely to be accurate or appropriate. Culture in this context is defined as "social stimuli that are the products of the behavior of other people."

Multiculturalism emphasizes both the ways in which groups are different from one another and the ways in which groups are similar at the same time. Overemphasis on similarity has resulted in the error of the "melting pot," which assumes differences do not matter. Overemphasis on differences has resulted in isolation of groups from one another. Multicultural counseling is a generic theory based on "both the culture-specific characteristics that differentiate and the culture-general characteristics that unite." Multiculturalism has been called a "fourth force" to supplement psychodynamic, behavioral, and humanistic psychology.

Interest in multicultural counseling grew out of the civil rights and feminist movements. Many minority writers have contributed to and shaped the multicultural perspective, which initially was focused on the oppression of minorities by the majority culture. Sue and Sue, Casas, Axelson, and Pederson, Draguns, Lonner, and Trimble have documented the ways in which the counseling profession has assumed the status quo values of a dominant culture. Wrenn pointed out the cultural encapsulation of counseling through ethnocentrism ("mine is best") or through relativism ("to each, his or her own"). Encapsulation resulted from defining reality according to dominant culture assumptions, being insensitive to cultural variations in society, protecting the status quo against change, and relying on a technique-oriented job description.

Lee and Richardson point out the pitfalls of a broad perspective of multiculturalism. The term may be defined so broadly and vaguely that it loses any meaning. Stereotyping each minority group may ignore within-group differences. Ignoring similarities across cultures could result in a new form of racism. There is the danger of discarding *all* traditional counseling as culturally biased. Possibly, counseling will never be accepted as credible by minorities because of past injustices.

D'Souza views affirmative action programs generally as unfair, ineffective, and inappropriate and so reflects a point of view that opposes multiculturalism in counseling and other fields generally as unfairly enforcing politically correct behaviors. Critics of multiculturalism, however, claim that imposing politically correct behavior has resulted in the destruction of traditional values. Patterson opposes efforts to modify counseling to fit other cultures in favor of a universalist viewpoint, by which all cultures are evaluated according to how well they promote self-actualization among their members. Patterson rejects the need for different skills, emphasis, and insights for use in each culture. Draguns responds to this criticism by pointing out that cross-cultural counselors do not try to change the culture but rather enable change to take place in the counselee, the goals of counseling are not limited to self-actualization across cultures, and it is not necessary to discard existing theory and practice to respond appropriately in different cultures.

Ridley points out that unintentional racism continues in counseling. There are counselors who claim to be color blind and to treat everyone alike. This implies that the counselor is uncomfortable differentiating between groups. Some counselors contend all a client's problems derive from the cultural background. When clients or therapists transfer positive or negative feelings to the client or therapist from previous relationships misinterpretations may occur. Some counselors have ambivalent motives in working with minorities that demonstrate a need for power and dominance, leading to inappropriate assessment. Therapists may respond inappropriately when a client accurately identifies racist behaviors in the therapist. Culturally appropriate nondisclosure may be misinterpreted by the therapist.

Support for multicultural issues in counseling have not until recently been reflected in the counseling profession. Racial and ethnic minorities are underrepresented in the profession. There is pressure to recognize the importance of culture by the National Institute of Mental Health, the American Psychological Association, (APA), and elsewhere. Casas credits the new interest in multiculturalism to the pragmatic acceptance of demographic changes favoring minorities, increased visibility of minorities, pressure by civil rights groups, and economic incentives for providers to attract nonwhite clients. The discovery of multiculturalism may also be the result of heightened group consciousness, government-mandated affirmative action in employment and education, court-ordered busing to achieve racial integration in schools, and demands for bilingual education.

The militancy of civil rights movements in the 1950s combined with the community mental health movement of the 1960s to affirm that mental health care was a right of all citizens. The popular dissent from the anti-Vietnam War movement and issues of feminism promoted discontent where protest against inequity was accepted and encouraged by the media. By the 1970s underuse of mental health services by minorities had become a serious issue. By the 1980s large numbers of refugees demonstrated the importance of a multicultural perspective in counseling. By the 1990s the rapidly changing demographic balance predicted that more than one-third of the nation's school students would be nonwhite by the year 2000, further highlighting the need for multiculturalism in counseling.

Baruth and Manning characterize research on multicultural counseling as focusing primarily on black–white pairs rather than other minority populations, using survey or archival designs, and drawing subjects from mental health clinics or psychiatric hospitals. Ponterotto criticized multicultural research citing 10 different weaknesses of that research: (a) no conceptual theoretical framework; (b) overemphasis on simplistic counselor–client process variables while disregarding important psychosocial variables; (c) overreliance on analogue research outside the real world setting; (d) disregard for intracultural within-group differences; (e) overdependence on student samples of convenience; (f) continued reliance on culturally encapsulated measures; (g) a failure to describe adequately the sample according to cultural background; (h) a failure to describe the limits of generalizability; (i) a lack of minority cultural input; and (j) a failure of responsibility by researchers toward minority subject pools.

Members of the APA's Division 17 (Counseling) Education and Training Committee developed a position paper of competence for multicultural counseling, divided into competencies emphasizing awareness, knowledge, and skill. The awareness competencies were: (a) the need for counselors to become aware of their own personal cultural heritage while valuing and respecting differences; (b) to be aware of how their own values may affect culturally different clients; (c) to become comfort-

able with differences in race and belief between clients and counselors; and (d) to know when a minority client should be referred elsewhere. The four knowledge competencies were: (a) to have a good understanding of the sociopolitical dynamics between minority and majority cultures; (b) to have specific knowledge and information about the client's particular culture; (c) to have a clear and explicit knowledge of generic and traditional counseling theory and practice; and (d) to be aware of institutional barriers that prevent minorities from using mental health services. The three skill competencies were: (a) all culturally skilled counselors should be able to generate a wide variety of verbal and nonverbal responses appropriate to the cultural setting and skill level; (b) counselors should be able to send and receive both verbal and nonverbal messages accurately and appropriately in each culturally different context; and (c) counselors should be able to advocate for or change the system or institution appropriately, when changes are necessary, on behalf of their culturally different clients.

BILINGUALISM
COUNSELING
CROSS-CULTURAL COUNSELING
CROSS-CULTURAL PSYCHOLOGY
CROSS-CULTURAL TRAINING PROGRAMS
CULTURAL DIFFERENCE
CULTURE SHOCK
SOCIAL INFLUENCE

P. B. PEDERSEN

MULTIDIMENSIONAL SCALING

Multidimensional scaling (MDS) most typically refers to a family of models and associated methods for representing data on similarities or dissimilarities of stimulus objects or other entities in terms of a spatial model. Essentially the aim of MDS, in a narrower meaning, is to simplify a large and complex set of observations by devising a spatial representation that will show the relationships among the stimuli. In such a spatial model the *proximities* data (similarities, dissimilarities, association indices, or other measures of closeness or proximity) are assumed to relate in a simple and straightforward way to *distances* between pairs of stimuli. Of course, with real data, subject to error and systematic distortion, a perfect relationship will not generally be possible.

One example frequently used to illustrate MDS reverses the standard process of reading distances from a map of cities so as to reconstruct the map knowing only the distances among the cities. In fact, in some forms of MDS—the *nonmetric* MDS procedures—only the *rank order* of the intercity distances need be known to reconstruct the map.

The rotation of coordinates just mentioned is not a trivial issue in MDS, but an important one in practical applications. The object of MDS is not merely to construct the spatial map or representation of the stimuli, but to interpret it in terms of meaningful psychological (or other) dimensions.

These dimensions correspond to the coordinates of the map. In psychological applications certain coordinate systems correspond to "natural" or easily interpretable psychological dimensions, whereas others do not. The particular coordinate system provided by an MDS computer program may be highly arbitrary and require rotation for reasonable interpretability. With regard to individual differences, we discuss later how "three-way" MDS, and the INDSCAL approach in particular, may help solve this rotational problem.

We now focus on MDS models and methods for one-mode (e.g., stimuli), two-way (i.e., pairwise) proximities data. These proximities data can arise from direct human judgments of similarity or dissimilarity, from such data as confusability of pairs of stimuli, or from various types of derived measures of similarity or dissimilarity (e.g., a "profile dissimilarity" measure computed between stimuli over rating scales, or various measures of similarity derived from word association tasks). In some cases matrices of correlations can be used as measures of similarity (of variables, people, stimuli, or other entities), so that MDS, when used this way, can be viewed as an alternative to factor analysis for deriving multidimensional structure from correlational data.

Once defined, the proximities can be thought of as comprising a two-way square table (or matrix). This table will usually (but not always) be symmetrical.

An important distinction frequently made is between *metric* and *nonmetric* approaches to MDS. In the metric approaches the proximities are assumed to be measured on at least an *interval scale*. In *nonmetric* MDS, the function is typically assumed to be only monotonic, or order-preserving. Thus nonmetric scaling assumes proximities measured only on an *ordinal scale*.

INDIVIDUAL DIFFERENCES MULTIDIMENSIONAL SCALING

The first approach to individual differences multidimensional scaling was the "points of view" approach proposed by Tucker and Messick. This was soon followed by the now dominant approach, generally called INDSCAL, for *in*dividual *d*ifferences multidimensional *SCAL*ing. INDSCAL accounts for individual differences in proximities data in terms of a model assuming a common set of dimensions underlying the stimuli (or other objects), while assuming that different subjects (or other data sources) have different patterns of saliences or importance weights for these common dimensions. Assuming for now that the "three-way" proximities data correspond to similarity judgments by different human subjects, the model makes the quite plausible assumption that each subject simply has a different set of scale factors (which can be thought of as amplifications or attenuations) applied to a set of "fundamental" psychological stimulus dimensions common to all individuals. It is as if each individual subject has a set of "gain controls," one for each of the fundamental stimulus dimensions, and that these are adjusted differently for each subject. The different settings might be due to genetic differences or to environmental factors re-rated to different experiential histories, or most likely, to a combination of nature (genetics) and nurture (environment).

One strength of this model for individual differences in perception is that the psychological dimensions assumed for the stimuli are uniquely determined by the similarities judgments of the subjects (based on the patterns of individual differences in similarities judgments). A second and equally important, advantage is that the saliences, or perceptual importance weights, can provide quite useful individual difference measures for the subjects.

The data for individual differences MDS generally comprise a number of symmetric proximities matrices, one for each subject (or other data source). Such data are generally designated as two-mode (stimuli and subjects) but three-way (stimuli × stimuli × subjects). A "mode" is a specific set of entities (e.g., the stimulus mode). The number of "ways" can be thought of as the number of "directions" in the data table (e.g., rows, columns, and "slices" for a three-way table, even though both rows and columns may correspond to the stimulus mode, while "slices" correspond to the subjects mode). The purpose of INDSCAL analysis is, given the three-way proximities data, to solve simultaneously for the stimulus coordinates and the subject weights so as to optimize the fit of the INDSCAL model to the (transformed) proximities data.

The INDSCAL method makes metric assumptions and entails a kind of three-way generalization of the "classical" method for two-way MDS.

The most efficient approach for implementing this analysis is provided by a program called SINDSCAL offered by Pruzansky.

Of particular interest among these alternative models and methods is one usually called Three-Mode Scaling proposed by Tucker, which is an adaptation of Tucker's three-mode factor analysis model and method to the case of three-way proximities data.

BROAD DEFINITION OF MDS

In its broadest definition, MDS includes a wide variety of geometric models for representation of psychological or other behavioral science data. Such models can include *discrete* geometric models such as tree structures (typically associated with hierarchical clustering), overlapping or nonoverlapping cluster structures, or other network models. More typically, however, MDS is associated with continuous spatial models for representation of data. In the broad definition of MDS such spatial models can include—in addition to the distance model for proximities data discussed previously—other geometric structures, such as what are called the vector model or the unfolding model for representation of individual differences in preference (or other dominance) data, or even the factor analysis model.

INDIVIDUAL DIFFERENCES
MULTIVARIATE ANALYSIS METHODS
STATISTICS IN PSYCHOLOGY

J. D. Carroll

MULTIMODAL THERAPY

Many clinicians embrace multidimensional and multifaceted assessment and treatment procedures that they frequently term "multimodal therapy." Yet although the majority of therapists are eclectic and multimodal in outlook, only a few are multimodal therapists. The distinction is important. An effective therapist will make some modifications in clinical procedures, depending on any of a large number of variables. Multimodal therapy, in a sense, is the therapy that competent therapists actually do, rather than what they say they do. Since multimodal therapy has a relevant systematic theory, a well-defined history, and a broad repertoire of techniques it may replace systems that restrict therapists' freedom and initiative, and dispense with the eclecticism that so many therapists appear to employ.

The multimodal framework provides an integrative assessment and treatment plan that considers the whole person in one's social network. This is achieved without sacrificing precision. People are troubled by a multitude of specific problems that call for a wide and diverse range of particular interventions. By attending to idiosyncratic variables, multimodal therapists avoid fitting clients to preconceived treatments; instead, they tailor treatment processes to meet clients' expectancies and other personalistic requirements. They employ operational means for "talking the client's language."

A multimodal assessment examines each area of a person's BASIC I. D. (B = behavior, A = affect, S = sensation, I = imagery, C = cognition, I. = interpersonal relationships, D. = drugs/biological factors.) A thorough assessment of each of these seven modalities readily provides the principal ingredients of one's psychological makeup. To appreciate the interactions among the various modalities—for example, how certain behaviors influence and are influenced by affects, sensations, images, cognitions, and significant relationships—is to know a great deal about individuals and their social networks.

One of the most important tactics used in multimodal therapy is called *tracking*. Some people tend to generate negative emotions by dwelling first on sensations (S) (e.g., slight dizziness and palpitations), to which they attach negative cognitions (C) (e.g., ideas of illness and death), immediately followed by aversive images (I) (e.g., mental pictures of hospitals and suffering), culminating in maladaptive behavior (B) (e.g., unnecessary avoidance). The foregoing SCIB sequence calls for different treatment strategies from, for instance, a BICS pattern. By tracking the precise sequence of events that results in the affective disturbance, the therapist enables the client to gain insight into the antecedent events, and also enables the client to intercede appropriately.

The well-trained multimodal therapist constructs Modality Profiles, which serve as a "blueprint for therapy," and when treatment impasses arise, Second Order BASIC I. D. Profiles are used to facilitate resolution. Additional multimodal methods are used with hospitalized patients.

INNOVATIVE PSYCHOTHERAPIES
PSYCHOTHERAPY

A. A. LAZARUS

MULTIPLE CORRELATION

Multiple correlation is a multivariate analysis method widely used in psychology and other behavioral sciences. It can be considered an extension of bivariate correlation, and indicates the degree of association between one variable and an optimally weighted combination of several other variables. The weights are determined by the principle of least squares so as to minimize the residual, or unrelated, variance.

The multiple correlation ranges in value from zero to one, and is interpreted similarly to a bivariate correlation, if rectilinearity and the other assumptions of the bivariate intercorrelations from which the multiple correlation is computed are reasonable.

In psychology the squared multiple correlation (R^2) frequently is used to estimate the proportion of variance in a dependent variable that is related to a set of independent variables. A related method, multiple regression, is used for predicting a dependent (or criterion) variable from a set of independent (or predictor) variables.

CORRELATION METHODS
MULTIPLE REGRESSION
STATISTICS IN PSYCHOLOGY

B. FRUCHTER

MULTIPLE FAMILY THERAPY

Multiple family therapy (MFT) is an approach to problems developed by the late H. Peter Laqueur, based on his work with hospitalized schizophrenic patients and combining features of group therapy and conjoint family therapy. He hypothesized that bringing several families together would enable each of the family members to possibly achieve identification with others, which could lead to a solution of practical problems.

In MFT, the medium of change is not transference but identification, which means that one person seeks to become like or to emulate another. The need for identification and acceptance is most important in the schizophrenic family, because individuals feel isolated by reason of having a hospitalized member. This fact often creates special problems among family members and forces them to seek outside resources. Multiple family therapy seeks to put the process of therapeutic change between one family and another, whereas individual therapy uses the therapist as the medium.

Although MFT began with work by Laqueur and schizophrenic families, its scope has widened into other areas and is not limited to this population. Underlying MFT are two premises: (a) there are strengths as well as weaknesses in families; and (b) people can learn from others by identification or though indirect learning.

STRUCTURE OF MFT

Families have the power to heal as well as to hurt. Many things are learned in the process of growing up in a family. Multiple family therapy emphasizes that, although a person or family may be deficient in one area, they may be strong in another. Laqueur and his colleagues suggest that five or six families be brought together for six to ten sessions of 90 minutes each and be allowed to talk about the issues that trouble them. The therapist acts as facilitator, guiding the discussion and asking various members for their comments or reactions.

PROCESS OF THERAPY

Multiple family therapy, like most therapies, goes through a series of stages. However, unlike most therapies, MFT is more limited in time and scope. There are three stages: observation, intervention, and consolidation. In the first stage various members are encouraged to talk to one another and themes are elaborated.

Multiple family therapy is interested in problem solving—not in personal dynamics. In stage two, the stress is put on interactions, and it is assumed that changes will be mutual and not made by only one person. This is a difficult stage because people often feel the problem rests with others; the therapist must point out mutually destructive behaviors. The strength of MFT is seen at this stage, when others in the group lend support to the therapist, pointing out faulty interactions. Role playing is often used.

Stage three involves termination and consolidation, evaluating progress and movement and deciding if sufficient changes have been made. More important, it is a time to realize that change will take place if family members are motivated to continue working on their relationships.

SUMMARY

Multiple family therapy has been found to be particularly effective with urban Black families and with aftercare patients. It lets a therapist be innovative and produce change in a relatively short time. This approach can be readily taught and does not rely solely on the intuition of the therapist.

BEHAVIOR THERAPY
CHANGE INDUCTION GROUPS

V. FOLEY

MULTIPLE PERSONALITY

Multiple personality has been defined as a condition characterized by "the existence within the individual of two or more distinct personalities, each of which is dominant at a particular time." Each personality is independent, autonomous, apparently existing as a separate and complete self. Transition from one personality to another is usually sudden. During the period when a secondary personality is overt or "executive," the original or primary personality is not conscious, and on its return is usually amnesic as to what has occurred.

The heart of the multiple syndrome is the psychological process of dissociation, wherein one segment of behavior and experience is kept separate and noncommunicative from another. A secondary personality is usually aware of the existence of the primary personality, but regards it as object and itself as subject. In some cases, the interactions between the various entities become extremely complex.

When "discovered," these cases usually have a long record of misdiagnosis and mistreatment. Although uncommon, they definitely are not "extremely rare." Published descriptions of several hundred cases are now available.

Most striking is the observation that in their feelings, attitudes, perceptions, and behaviors, secondary personalities are very different from the major self—often the exact opposite. This is not surprising when one recognizes that secondary personalities were created precisely out of unacceptable feelings and behaviors that were cognitively dissonant with the major self as—especially during childhood—it tried to adjust to the demands of its world.

Not only do the various personalities differ in many modalities— perceptual, motivational, affective, and behavioral—but also they respond differently on psychological tests such as the Minnesota Multiphasic Personality Inventory and the Rorschach. They may even show different patterns on electroencephalographic tracings.

There is some evidence to indicate that dissociation, like other psychological processes, lies on a continuum, and that true multiple personalities simply represent the extreme of the continuum.

Most cases of multiple personality reported in the older literature lasted for many years and were very difficult to treat. However, as a result of more recent experience, certain general principles of therapy have emerged.

In spite of a recent increase of interest in dissociation, multiple personality is still one of the least understood of personality disorders.

HYPNOTHERAPY

J. G. WATKINS

MULTIPLE REGRESSION

Multiple regression is a multivariate analysis method that relates a dependent (or criterion) variable (Y) to a set of independent (or predictor) variables (X) by a linear equation.

$$Y' = a + b_1X_1 + b_2X_2 + \cdots + b_kX_k$$

The regression or b weights are usually determined by the principle of least squares, to minimize the sum of the squared deviations of the dependent values from the corresponding predicted values.

In a "stepwise" approach, variables are added (or removed) one at a time from the independent variable set until there is a nonsignificant change. Also, sets of variables may be added (or removed) to evaluate their contribution to the multiple correlation, and an F-test done to determine if their effect is statistically significant. Nonlinear relationships may be evaluated by including higher order terms and/or multiplicative terms on the right-hand side of the equation.

The regression weights are determined most reliably when the independent variables are relatively uncorrelated. The situation in which some of them are highly intercorrelated is "multicollinearity," and tends to yield regression coefficients whose values may fluctuate markedly from sample to sample. Some common uses for multiple regression are:

1. To obtain the best linear prediction equation.

2. To control for confounding variables.

3. To evaluate the contribution of a specific set of variables.

4. To account for seemingly complex multivariate interrelationships.

5. To perform analysis of variance and covariance by coding the levels of the independent variables.

MULTIPLE CORRELATION
MULTIVARIATE ANALYSIS METHODS

B. FRUCHTER

MULTIPLE SCLEROSIS

Multiple sclerosis (MS) is a chronic and progressive degenerative neurological disease that attacks the myelin sheath (coating on the nerves) and conduction pathways of the central nervous system. Characterized by periods of remissions and exacerbations, the severity and duration of each exacerbation increases as the disease progresses, with symptomatic management possible.

The *etiology* of MS is unknown. The highest rate of incidence is between the ages of 20 and 40 years, with about 20% of patients experiencing first symptoms in their 40s and 50s. Multiple sclerosis is neither contagious nor hereditary.

The *signs and symptoms* of MS sclerosis are widely varied and often vague, with manifestations occurring alone or in any combination.

The *clinical course* usually is within one of the following categories, with progression from one pattern to a more serious one not uncommon: (a) a benign course, with mild remitting attacks and long symptom-free periods; (b) an exacerbating–remitting course, with periodic acute onset of symptoms followed by partial or complete recovery and plateaus of stable disability; (c) a slowly progressive course, with no clear exacerbations and remissions and a slow but steady deterioration of function; or (d) a rapidly progressive course, with a continuous functional deterioration over several months or years and a high susceptibility to further disabling or life-threatening complications.

Diagnosis is established primarily by neurological examination and patient history.

Treatment is symptomatic and supportive. Treatments to alter the course are experimental and often controversial. Drug therapies to alleviate symptoms and prevent complications include medications for spasticity and urinary dysfunction and steroids for exacerbations. Physiotherapy programs are designed to postpone the ultimate bedridden phase for as long as possible. Although lost motor power cannot be regained, muscles that are not being used can be prevented from weakness by strengthening exercises.

NEUROMUSCULAR DISORDERS
NEUROPSYCHOLOGY

R. T. GIUBILATO

MULTIVARIATE ANALYSIS METHODS

Psychological data tend to be inherently multivariate, that is, they tend to consist of more than a single observation on one or more individuals. Multivariate analysis methods have been developed to deal with such data in a simultaneous way, for example, as by exploring the data to discover important underlying features or, more deductively, by testing or evaluating *a priori* hypotheses about the data. At its best, multivariate analysis represents a generalization of univariate analysis, so that when the data consist of only a single variable, the multivariate method will yield the same result as the corresponding univariate method. Thus there are statistics based on multiple variables that can be specialized to such well-known univariate statistics as chi-square and the t-test.

Multivariate analysis covers a wide span of mathematical and statistical techniques, and there is no universally agreed-on definition of its correct domain. By convention, however, specialized topics such as reliability theory or latent trait theory are not considered a part of multivariate analysis, because of their separate traditions in psychological research. Methods for the analysis of multiple dichotomous variables are often studied under separate designations such as log-linear models. Similarly, the study of repeated observations on a single subject or another unit such as a classroom is typically described as time-series analysis.

MODELS

Multivariate analysis requires the joining of three different types of information into a single method that can be applied in practice. From the point of view of the psychologist, the substantive ideas and knowledge drawn from the field must be distilled and applied to the given data analytic situation. This knowledge, especially if formal, is called the *psychological model*. The psychological model provides the context for choosing among multivariate or other methods of data analysis or statistical description.

The second type of model used is the *mathematical* or *structural model,* which relates key variables, observations, parameters, and so on. The structural model is a formal mathematical representation that is presumed to be relevant to the multivariate situation by virtue of the psychological model. In general, multivariate methods are based on models that are linear in nature. Since psychological theories often involve nonlinear relations, the linearity assumption may be troubling to make. However, it may be reasonable to make this assumption if most of the dependent variables—the variables to be predicted—are approximately continuous in nature. If the variables are dichotomous or ordinal, the assumption may be more difficult to justify except as a convenience or an approximation.

The third type of model is the *statistical model.* Such a model must be developed if one is doing more than data description. In this case, one may be interested not only in describing the data, but also in drawing inferences about the larger population from which the data may have been drawn. A major point of contact between the structural model and the statistical model is the error structure of the observations. Recently the generalization of the multivariate normal distribution that allows variables to have nonzero but constant kurtosis has become valuable as providing a basis for extending traditional methods and some distribution-free methods have been introduced.

In addition to describing the distribution of variables, the statistical model must describe the sampling model that is used to generate the observations. Typically, this model is taken to be one of independent random observations, where a given individual's scores are not influenced by those of other individuals. Finally, the statistical model must specify the range within which certain statistical or random processes are thought to be operating.

Although multivariate methods can and should be used in an exploratory fashion to gain an insight into one's data and hypotheses about how the data might have been generated, a large class of methods are confirmatory in nature, designed to test theories. In general, the confirmatory approach to multivariate analysis attempts to do the following: (a) estimate the parameters of a distribution to test hypotheses about the parameters; (b) to establish confidence regions around the observed values by judicious use of standard errors and sampling theory; (c) evaluate the goodness of fit of a hypothesized structural model; (d) compare contrasting models; (e) attach probability statements to various results; and (f) evaluate the confidence that can be placed in one's inferences.

METHODS

The major multivariate methods can be categorized as linear model methods, linear compound methods, and linear structural methods. This classification depends on the extent to which random rather than fixed or known variables are involved in an analysis, and the extent to which small sample theory rather than only large sample theory can be relied on, with linear model theory being best developed and structural methods the least well developed statistically. As mentioned previously, there are also nonlinear methods.

CORRELATION AND REGRESSION STATISTICS IN PSYCHOLOGY

P. M. BENTLER

MUNCHAUSEN SYNDROME BY PROXY

Munchausen syndrome by proxy (MSP), a potentially fatal form of child abuse in which parents feign or create illnesses in their children and then present the children to medical personnel for assessment and treatment, was first described by Meadow. This syndrome is considered difficult to diagnose or treat.

Typically, the syndrome involves mothers as perpetrators. Common features are repeated efforts by mothers to secure medical treatment for children in several medical settings, mothers' perceptions of their children as vulnerable, mothers' willingness for their children to undergo diagnostic procedures and medical treatment of an invasive nature, and mothers inducing laboratory findings.

The child's medical history as related by the mother is usually long, detailed, and dramatic. The mother may present herself as anxious, angry, or paranoid and is not reassured by a negative finding. It is not uncommon for the mother to "mishear" findings or to draw illogical conclusions from information given. The mother also generally appears to be an exemplary caretaker.

The warning signs of MSP include the following:

1. Unexplained or unusual persistent or recurrent illnesses.
2. Discrepancies between clinical findings and history.
3. Signs and symptoms that do not make sense clinically.
4. Laboratory results at variance with apparent health of the child.
5. The working diagnosis is "a rare disorder."
6. An experienced physician states, "I have never seen a case like it."
7. Signs and symptoms do not occur in the mother's absence.
8. An extremely attentive mother who refuses to leave the child alone and may offer to take over some of the medical care of the child, including obtaining vital signs or laboratory samples.
9. Unusual or repeated treatment intolerance.
10. Mother's level of concern discordant with medical personnel's.
11. Seizures or apnea spells witnessed only by mother.
12. Atypical cases of sudden infant death syndrome (SIDS) or near SIDS.

13. Mother with previous medical or nursing experience.

14. Mother with a history of Munchausen's syndrome or victimization in MSP.

15. Mother relates a history of personal illness similar to the child's.

Excluded from the diagnosis are *help seekers,* that is, mothers whose primary motivation appears to be a need for outside intervention obtained through a sick child. These nonpathological mothers typically react with relief and cooperation when confronted or when help is offered.

Active inducers are considered prototypical MSP in which there are active and direct efforts by mothers to induce dramatic symptoms of illness in their children. Typically, the victims are infants or young children. The mothers are believed to gain attention through being perceived as excellent mothers, by "fooling" the "powerful" medical system, and by nurturance received as the mother of an ill child. *Doctor addicts* are obsessed with obtaining medical treatment for nonexistent illnesses for their children. Mothers remain convinced of illness inspite of repeated negative evidence. These mothers also report false history and symptoms, but the victims typically are school age or adolescent children. Such mothers may appear to be outwardly angry and distrustful, occasionally paranoid in regard to the medical system. *Illness exaggerators* differ from doctor addicts in that there is some documented but mild illness in the child. In the latter two types, there is likely to be a conflictual relationship between the mother and the medical staff.

Detection of MSP is extremely difficult and requires coordination of care and careful documentation. The diagnosis may be met with disbelief by other members of the care system. Close observation of the mother with the child is necessary, with some advocating surreptitious videotaping and searching of mother's belongings. Laboratory samples must be protected and the mother not allowed to obtain or come into contact with the samples. Toxicological screening and sophisticated knowledge of pharmacokinetics may be required. Most important, however, is clear, thorough, and detailed documentation. Managed health care systems and tertiary care systems may be vulnerable to being drawn into this abuse. Legal intervention is usually required, but difficult to obtain. Serial abuse of other children in the family is not unusual, but may not provide adequate evidence for legal intervention. Removal of the child from the home or required approval for medical care are effective in prevention of future abuse.

Perpetrators are resistant to treatment. Many mothers remove their children from the particular medical system and repeat the abuse in a different setting. Psychotherapy for the mother is always indicated but seldom successful. Munchausen syndrome by proxy results in psychological trauma to the victim, with resulting morbidity ranging from separation and feeding disorders in infants to development of MSP in adolescents.

BEHAVIORAL INTERVENTION
CHILD ABUSE
CLINICAL JUDGMENT
DECEPTION
DIAGNOSES
FACTIOUS DISORDERS
HEALTH CARE SERVICES
PARENT–CHILD RELATIONS

J. S. HOFFMAN

MUSCLE RELAXATION

Muscle relaxation may be viewed as a technique under the more generic term "relaxation," designed to enable an individual to achieve complete muscle and "mental" relaxation. Progressive relaxation is probably the most frequently employed procedure in the United States.

Jacobson, a physician concerned with the fact that many people are typically overstressed, tense, and unable to effectively relax, published a book detailing a series of exercises focused on tensing and relaxing one muscle or muscle group after another.

Joseph Wolpe presented a theoretical and practical analysis of a psychotherapeutic technique called Systematic Desensitization, which used an abbreviated form of progressive relaxation quite effective in inducing complete relaxation.

One common abbreviated procedure is to have the patient assume a comfortable position on a couch or recliner. After a few minutes, relaxation of the arms is initiated by instructing the patient to tense his or her fists, hold the tension for a few seconds, then relax the fists and permit them to rest gently. This tension–relaxation instruction is then applied to the forearms as well as the upper arms. Sequentially, relaxation instructions may then be directed to the facial area, neck, shoulders, and upper back, followed by the chest, stomach, and lower back. Finally, attention is given to the muscles of the hips, thighs, and calves.

In addition to specific instruction regarding muscle tension and relaxation, the patient is also told to breathe deeply and rhythmically. Concomitant with deep breathing, the practitioner also provides suggestions pertaining to feelings of warmth, comfort, and tranquillity. These suggestions appear to complement or enhance the relaxation achieved through the tension–relaxation exercises. With most people, progressive relaxation seems to be one of the more effective means of achieving muscle relaxation. It is used quite widely either directly or adjunctively as a therapeutic intervention technique.

BIOFEEDBACK
INNOVATIVE PSYCHOTHERAPIES
STRESS

W. W. WENRICH

MUSIC THERAPY

Music has been used since prehistoric times to produce ecstasy and enthusiasm, to incite aggression for battle, to soothe or express feelings, to help communication, to effect healing, and so on.

Research has found that certain feelings—joy, sadness, love, longing, and calm—are frequently elicited by music, although feelings like anger, fear, jealousy, and envy are not. The effects of major and minor chords, tempo, pitch, rhythm, harmony, and melody on human affect and behavior have also been studied. The fast tempo seems to be the most powerful element in creating excitement. The expressiveness of music seems to be due less to melodies than to rhythm and tempo. Tonal and rhythmic patterns affect coordination, equilibrium, bodily rhythm, and creative or aesthetic response, as well as different moods. Music is also credited with extending the attention span, reducing stress, facilitating self-expression, stimulating associations and imagery, and helping the process of memorizing.

In music therapy the patients may be listening or performing. Music has also been used in combination with dance movements. Even severely disturbed individuals benefit from music therapy.

In hospitals and the offices of psychologists, counselors, physicians, and dentists, music calms, reduces anxiety, and facilitates a therapeutic mood. Depth therapists use music to help the personality exploration. Yet the most frequent use of music therapy is with retarded and physically handicapped children. A wide range of programs has been developed for use with populations of varying ages and abilities.

D. MOTET

MYERS–BRIGGS TYPE INDICATOR

The Myers–Briggs Type Indicator is a personality assessment measure the purpose of which is to ascertain how individuals perceive and judge. The instrument was devised to implement Carl Jung's theory of *type*. Specifically, the Myers–Briggs Type Indicator was developed to measure four bipolar dimensions as follows:

1. *Extraversion versus introversion:* whether a person's attention is directed to people and things or to ideas.
2. *Sensing versus intuition:* whether a person prefers to perceive information by the senses or by intuition.
3. *Thinking versus feeling:* whether an individual prefers to use logic and analytic thinking or feelings in making judgments.
4. *Judgment versus perception:* whether an individual uses judgment or perception as a way of life. That is, does the individual evaluate events in terms of a set of standards, or simply experience them?

The value of the Myers–Briggs Type Indicator lies in the integration of the four bipolar dimensions to yield 16 combinations, each reflecting the unique and individual character of the score pattern. These 16 interpretations have been subjected to many studies, some of which are informal or of questionable design.

Other studies have established significant relationships of the individual's type with personality, interest, and measures of scholastic performance for college students. Still other studies have explored the relationship of the individual's type with creativity among incumbents in a variety of occupations.

The Myers–Briggs Type Indicator is a pencil-and-paper inventory with no time limit, but it usually takes about 1 hour to complete. Scoring may be by machine or manually. Norms for the instrument's results are based on college, noncollege, and high school prep students, with appropriate breakdowns by sex and college major. Split half reliabilities range from 0.66 to 0.91 for males, and from 0.74 to 0.93 for females on six samples of 100 students each.

ANALYTICAL PSYCHOLOGY
PERSONALITY ASSESSMENT

R. S. ANDRULIS

MYTH OF MENTAL ILLNESS

The proposition that mental illness is a myth—first advanced by Thomas Szasz—was intended to challenge the assumption that mental illness "exists" and is "like any other illness." Since the idea of mental illness is fundamental not only to psychiatry and the mental health professions but also to contemporary thought, the claim that mental illness does not exist undermines the very ground on which psychiatric diagnoses and treatments rest.

The view that mental illness is a myth is based partly on a conceptual analysis and partly on a consequential analysis of the terms used to portray mental illness or psychopathology.

Central to the conceptual critique of mental illness is an analysis of the historical development of this idea. Before the present idea of mental illness there were the ideas of psychosis and mania, and prior to that the ideas of madness and insanity. One of the important discoveries of modern medicine was that some persons considered to be mad, insane, maniacal, or psychotic were in fact suffering from brain diseases such as neurosyphilis or senile or traumatic dementia.

Actually, countless "problems in living"—many of which, *prima facie*, are the consequences of conflicting personal aspirations, moral values, social controls, and similar psychological and social factors—are categorized as mental illnesses. However, these can no more reasonably be reduced to or "explained" by abnormal neurological or neurophysiological processes than can the many patterns of human behavior not labeled as mental illnesses.

The consequential critique of mental illness emphasizes the need to scrutinize the strategic or tactical uses of mental illness terms and the importance of inferring the meaning of such terms from their practical consequences. For example, mental illness terms may be used to incriminate and exculpate persons as well as to obscure and evade painful moral and personal conflicts.

According to the view that mental illness is a myth, only diseases of the body are real, literal illnesses. Clearly, this does not mean that mental suffering, economic problems, and social dissensions do not exist or are not real. It means only that they are metaphorical diseases, and that we categorize and treat them like medical diseases at great peril to our integrity, responsibility, and liberty.

DIAGNOSIS
MEDIEVAL THINKING
THEORETICAL PSYCHOLOGY

T. SZASZ

MYTHS

Myths are traditional stories, usually originating in the timeless past of primitive, prerational, prescientific societies that reflect serious concerns recurrent in human consciousness, such as the creation of the universe, life, death, and rebirth, with reference to the supernatural, to ancestors, and to heroes. In psychology, myths have been useful as source material that enriches our understanding of human behavior.

No single theory, however valuable, fully explains the entire range of myths or even a single myth. Sigmund Freud said that myths, like dreams, are the royal road to the unconscious. Jung postulated that myths represent an inherited collective unconscious with universal symbolism and archetypes, and not a personal unconscious.

LITERATURE AND PSYCHOLOGY
PHILOSOPHICAL PSYCHOLOGY

R. W. ZASLOW

NAIKAN THERAPY

Naikan is a Japanese psychotherapy based on Jodo Shinshu Buddhism. Developed by a lay priest, Ishin Yoshimoto, Naikan became known for its success within the Japanese prison system. It is now used in the treatment of addictions, psychosomatic disorders, neuroses, delinquency, family disharmony, and a variety of other psychosocial problems. In addition, it has become part of the employee training programs of some companies, schools, and hospitals. Naikan is also undertaken by some clients who seek self-development and/or a religious experience. It has been introduced into the United States and Europe.

The premise of Naikan is that our existence is supported in countless concrete ways by the world in which we live, particularly the social world, yet we take from others without acknowledging or even recognizing their contributions to our daily living. Naikan theory holds that we suppress recognition of this support because we fear the sense of obligation and the demolishing of our fragile sense of self-sufficiency that would follow from a reappraisal of our existence.

The practice of Naikan is designed to rebalance the misperceived past. During intensive (shuchu) Naikan the client (Naikansha) sits in any comfortable position isolated from early morning until night, usually from 5:00 A.M. until 9:00 P.M. for 1 week, reflecting on the past. At intervals of approximately 1 to 2 hours during the day the Naikan guide visits the client. During these periodic interviews (mensetsu), the client tells the guide what has been recalled and the guide suggests the next topic for reflection. Generally, the assigned topic is a particular person and a particular period of the client's life. Specific events from the past are to be remembered and reported during mensetsu using three themes: What that person did for the client, what the client did in return for that person, and what troubles and worries the client caused that person. Approximately 60% of the time should be spent on the third theme.

There are a variety of styles of Naikan. In addition to the intensive Naikan there is nichijo, or everyday Naikan. Short periods in the morning and evening are devoted to Naikan, with normal daily activities carried on between. The morning reflection follows the same pattern as in intensive Naikan. The evening reflection concerns what was received from others during that day, what was returned to them, and what worries and troubles were caused them during that day.

At the week's end of shuchu, Naikan clients generally report a sense of guilt and repentance, along with an increased recognition of having been loved and cared for by others and a desire to repay the world for its ongoing support. A rich literature, including case studies and psychological testing, is available in Japanese.

ASIAN PSYCHOLOGIES

D. K. REYNOLDS

NARCISSISTIC PERSONALITY

The Diagnostic and statistical manual of mental disorders (DSM-IV) describes this personality as possessing a grandiose sense of self-importance. Notable are the individual's exhibitionism and desire to gain attention and admiration from others. A sense of entitlement is also characteristic of the narcissist. Achievement deficits and social irresponsibilities are justified by a boastful arrogance, expansive fantasies, facile rationalizations, and frank prevarications. Marked rebuffs to self-esteem may provoke serious disruptions in the more characteristic unruffled composure. In spite of the insouciant air of indifference and imperturbability, the

individual is often quite preoccupied with how well he or she is regarded. When faced with criticism or failure, there is either an attitude of cool disdain or feelings of intense rage, humiliation, or emptiness.

Havelock Ellis first gave psychological significance to the term "narcissism." Sigmund Freud's major contribution was devoted exclusively to development and pathology.

More recent analytic conceptions include those of Otto Kernberg and Heinz Kohut. Kernberg characterizes narcissistics as possessing an "unusual degree of self-reference in their interactions," as well as a great need to be admired, a shallow emotional life, and an exploitative and sometimes parasitic relationship with others.

In a social-learning formulation that avoids psychoanalytic concepts, Theodore Millon presented the following criteria for review by the committee developing the DSM-III. It served as the basis for the manual's diagnostic description and criteria for the narcissistic personality.

1. Inflated self-image.
2. Interpersonal exploitativeness.
3. Cognitive expansiveness.
4. Insouciant temperament.
5. Deficient social conscience.

DIAGNOSTIC AND STATISTICAL MANUAL OF MENTAL DISORDERS (DSM-IV)
PERSONALITY DISORDERS

T. MILLON

NATIONAL CHARACTER

National character represents the personality characteristics of the average member of a national population that differ from the averages of other nationalities. Operationally, national character is simply the differences in personality scores between samples of different national populations. Some authorities attempt to draw a composite picture from these different scores, which they label "French character," "American character," and so on. Some studies contrast child-rearing methods of different cultures and attempt to correlate adult personality with these methods.

A number of psychologists and anthropologists have used psychological tests to try to determine national differences.

The work of David McClelland and associates on the achievement motive suggests that national character may differ in what is the predominant value held, but most of the research has concerned changes within a given culture over a period of time, as in England. Some research has been done on changing motivation within a culture.

Almost all the research on national character, however, suggests that what is being observed is trends or tendencies. Stereotyping is something almost always to be cautioned against.

INFANT SOCIALIZATION
PERSONALITY TYPES
STEREOTYPING

W. E. GREGORY

NATIONAL COLLEGE OF PROFESSIONAL PSYCHOLOGY

In the 1980s people using psychological services began to require more definition of the provider, the processes, and the products of mental health service delivery. Consumers and purchasers of mental health services began to rely on procedural designations for the treatment of specific mental disorders. Insurance companies, government agencies, and managed care organizations focused on expertise in the management of disorders, such as alcohol and other drug abuse, depression, anxiety, and issues related to stress management. As the demand for more specific delineation of services increased, the broad competencies encompassed by psychology licensing laws reduced the ability of licensure to define adequately the many and varied skills possessed by psychology providers. Licensure alone was not adequate as a mechanism for the appropriate recognition of the expertise that could be offered by a given psychologist.

Furthermore, as purchasers of treatment, employers focused increasingly on short-term procedures that would diminish absenteeism and increase productivity. Reimbursement concerns influenced trends toward treating specific disorders rather than attempting extensive character change. This trend, along with the development of a flurry of "new" professions claiming exclusive rights over the expert treatment of particular complaints led to further reductions in the ability of psychologists to maintain their practices in traditional ways.

In 1981, the National Residency Training Program was proposed for psychologists that would provide training for specialties and proficiencies as they related to specific needs of society, and, more emphatically, to areas likely to be funded by third-party payers in the system of health delivery. Such training would enable psychologists to deliver services that were becoming more specialized. It was suggested that groups like the National Register or the Association of Psychology Internship Centers (APIC) should begin to evolve such designations and training programs. In 1983, a program was formally submitted to the Council of Representatives of the American Psychological Association (APA). An APA presidential task force was established to study the issues. The proposed program has evolved along two paths.

One initiative has moved toward the establishment of academic centers of excellence that would provide postdoctoral programs offering specialty training to psychologists, leading to the development of a cadre of experts and researchers. Some 14 specialty areas and designations were identified in initial discussions, including such areas as neuroscience, psychopharmacology, and forensic psychology. At the APA conventions in 1990 and 1991, the task force conducted workshops. Subsequently, experts were convened to begin to evolve protocols. Investigations were undertaken to develop structures for the delivery of the coursework. In Minnesota psychologists met with the hope of developing a consortium of graduate programs that would evolve specified fellowship training programs similar to the suggestion of residency proposals. These groups should reside in the universities directed by experts capable of training teachers and researchers in these several fields.

Most psychologists in 1991—about 60,000 or 70,000 of them—were in midcareer and would find it difficult in terms of time and funding to return to a university setting to fulfill requirements to achieve postdoctoral status of some specialty in the delivery of services and research. For this reason, an alternate path of training leading toward a credential of proficiency was proposed in the form of the National College of Professional Psychology. The proposal was described as a credentialing mechanism designed to recognize the specific proficiencies of already qualified psychologists. Acknowledging that the extensive education and professional experience leading toward the doctorate and licensure had already provided psychologists with a comprehensive knowledge of the field, the National College proposed to offer a program of courses delivered as a continuing education sequence that would allow psychologists to develop proficiencies in circumscribed areas.

Psychologists have begun to meet the demand to define their activities with greater specificity and identifiable qualifications. The concept is related to suggestions by Jack Wiggins for a national referral service. With services identifiable to the major purchasers of mental health services, a national referral service could assist in bringing specifically trained psychologists together with the foci of need in business, government, and community sectors.

ACADEMIC ABILITY GROUPING
ALTERNATIVE DOCTORAL PROGRAMS
AMERICAN PSYCHOLOGICAL ASSOCIATION
CLINICAL PSYCHOLOGY GRADUATE PROGRAMS
CONSUMER PSYCHOLOGY
HEALTH CARE SERVICES
JOB ANALYIS
PERFORMANCE APPRAISAL
PUBLIC POLICY

S. R. GRAHAM

NATIONAL EDUCATION ASSOCIATION

The National Education Association (NEA) was founded in 1857 as the National Teachers Association to promote the profession of teaching and to advance the interests of education in America. Although chartered by Congress, it is an independent and voluntary organization, neither supervised nor funded by the federal government. Through its affiliated state associations, the NEA represents nearly 1.8 million professional educators.

Throughout its history the NEA has played a crucial role in the development of educational policies and professional practices.

The general goals of the NEA include: economic and professional security for all educators; significant legislative support for public education; human and civil rights in education; leadership in solving social problems; and the pursuit of professional excellence. The association's growth and expansion over the years has led to its becoming a multifunctional organization as well as a powerful influence on the educational and legislative issues facing public education.

L. V. PARADISE

NATIONAL TRAINING LABORATORY

Based on the work of Kurt Lewin and others, the goals of the National Training Laboratory were originally to improve the quality of social participation and to evaluate new methods of changing behavior in group settings. Over time, however, the participants in the National Training Laboratory also became interested in individual psychological growth.

The concept of a training laboratory involves a temporary community designed to provide an educational experience for its members. Through formal and informal processes, individual participants can learn the skills necessary for productive group participation in a democratic society. One of the key elements is the basic skills training group or T-group, which was created to provide an environment where members could learn group dynamics and examine the reactions they themselves produced in others.

The ideas and techniques of the National Training Laboratory have been used in education, organizational development, and clinical as well as social psychology.

CHANGE INDUCTION GROUPS
GROUP PSYCHOTHERAPY
T-GROUPS

C. LANDAU

NATURAL SELECTION

Natural selection refers to Darwin's account of evolution in terms of the differential survival and reproduction of the members of a population: The environment selects the individuals who pass their characteristics on from one generation to the next and thereby shapes the characteristics of those in later populations. This article first briefly reviews the facts of evolution, then deals with the major features of the Darwinian account, and finally considers how selection is relevant to the study of behavior.

EVOLUTION

An explosion in the diversity of multicellular life occurred about 570 million years ago, during the geological period called the Cambrian, and was followed by a weeding out; the survivors provided the major groupings from which contemporary species evolved.

One such grouping was the vertebrates. The evolution from fish to amphibians to reptiles included many significant events, such as the colonization of land. The dinosaurs were a spectacular part of the story, but by 65 million years ago they were gone. Their passing allowed the evolution of large mammals.

In the geologic time scale of the period just reviewed, the 4 million years or so since the ancestors of hominids began walking upright is very short. Even shorter, however, is the time since the emergence of *Homo sapiens.* Human genealogy can be sketched only roughly, because the lines that separate different hominid populations are often hard to define. The genus *Homo* appeared roughly 2.5 million years ago, in the hominid species called *Homo habilis,* at about the same time as the earliest evidence of tool use. The appearance of *Homo erectus* and the use of fire has been dated at about 1.7 million years ago, in eastern Africa. The appearance of *Homo sapiens* has been dated at about 250,000 years ago. The expansion of some groups, such as the Cro-Magnons, was accompanied by the extinction of others, such as the Neanderthals. Anatomically modern humans emerged about 40,000 years ago, which is also a plausible though controversial date for the origin of human language.

The most successful theory in accommodating the facts of evolution is Charles Darwin's account in terms of natural selection.

Natural and Artificial Selection

Natural selection refers to the differential survival and reproduction of the members of a population; according to this account, the environment selects the individuals who pass their characteristics from one generation to the next and thereby shapes the characteristics of those in later populations. Evolution by natural selection requires variation within populations.

Selection was well known before Darwin because it was used in horticulture and animal husbandry. People knew how to breed plants or livestock selectively for hardiness, yield, or other characteristics. Such selective breeding was called artificial selection, and it created new varieties of vegetables, flowers, and so on. Workhorses were selected for strength and racehorses for speed. One part of Darwin's insight was that natural selection occurred in nature.

Darwin's main arguments were first published in *On the origin of species.* In some quarters his arguments were warmly received, but in others they were strongly resisted. Resistance grew, and by the end of the nineteenth century the belief was widespread that Darwinism was dead. It did not recover until well into the twentieth century. The half

century or so that preceded that recovery has been called the eclipse of Darwinism.

Alternative Theories

The reason for the eclipse was not that evolution itself had been discredited but that other theories had become dominant. The principal alternatives were Lamarckism, orthogenesis, and the combination of Mendelian genetics with mutation theory. Lamarckism was based on the work of an eighteenth-century French scientist who theorized that characteristics acquired during an organism's lifetime could be passed on to its offspring, through changes in its own genetic material or germ plasm. One problem with this theory was why advantageous acquired characteristics should be any more likely to be passed on than disadvantageous ones.

According to the theory of orthogenesis, evolution was directed by forces within organisms, without reference to the demands of the environment; it could be likened to a developmental unfolding. One manifestation of this unfolding was supposed to be the recapitulation of phylogeny by ontogeny. Ontogeny is the development of the individual organism, and phylogeny is its evolutionary history. During ontogeny, the embryo was thought to pass through stages corresponding to its phylogeny. This idea of recapitulation, however, had severe limitations and is no longer central to evolutionary theory.

The problem with Mendelian genetics was that it provided no mechanism for variation. In strict Mendelian descent, dominant and recessive genes in one generation determined their proportions in the next. Without variation, there was nothing on which natural selection could work. To provide for the appearance of new forms, Mendelian accounts added mutation theory, which held that evolution proceeded through spontaneous and usually large genetic changes.

In the nineteenth century, genes were theoretical entities; they had not yet been seen. The techniques of cell biology only later reached the point at which genes could be identified in actual cells. Nevertheless, all of these evolutionary theories assumed that hereditary material of some sort was passed on from one generation to the next and that evolution was determined by the properties of this material. A major flaw in some theories was the assumption that genetic material constituted a representation or copy of the organism. In the earliest versions of orthogenesis, called *preformationism,* the embryo was a homunculus, a tiny individual complete in all its parts; in later variations it took on ancestral forms, as ontogeny was said to recapitulate phylogeny. As for Lamarckism, the transmission of acquired characteristics required that they be preserved in the germ plasm in some way, so the germ plasm had to contain some kind of plan of those parts of the organism that were to be altered in subsequent generations. In either case, the germ plasm could be regarded as a representation or copy of the organism.

A recipe is a sequence of procedures or instructions. It describes how to create a product, but it does not necessarily incorporate a description of the product (a recipe for a cake does not look like a cake). A recipe can be informative, but it is not likely to contain information about its origins, such as the number of attempts it took to make it work. A blueprint, however, does not ordinarily say how to construct the structure. Like a recipe, it can be informative, but it is likely to omit information about its origins, such as the order in which different parts were designed. A blueprint is a representation or copy, but a recipe is not, and Lamarckism and the preformationist orthogenetic accounts treated genetic materials as blueprints rather than recipes.

The Modern Synthesis

A principal achievement in contemporary biology was the reinterpretation of genetic material, not as a blueprint for the organism's structure, but rather as a recipe for its development. The modern formulation demanded rethinking of the sense in which genetic material can be said to contain information, whether about evolutionary history or about the structure of the organism. Genetic material provides limited information about the past environments in which it has been selected, because it does not include the genetic materials of all those other organisms that did not survive. Also, such material provides limited information about the eventual structure of an organism because it is a recipe for the production of proteins rather than a blueprint for body parts. The implications of this line of thought were profound. One is that Lamarckism and at least some varieties of orthogenesis became untenable alternatives to Darwinian selection because their implicit copy theories were inconsistent with what had been learned about how the genetic material worked.

The integration of Mendelian genetics with Darwinian selection in the 1920s and 1930s, known as the modern synthesis, became the core of contemporary biology. Genetic experiments with *Drosophila* (the fruit fly) not only elaborated on genetic mechanisms but also brought mutations into the laboratory. With fruit flies, many generations could be studied within a relatively short time. The research gave evidence on natural rates of mutation and on the magnitude of mutation effects, which were relatively small compared to the changes that had been assumed in prior mutation theories. The combination of Mendelian genetics with the facts of mutation provided the variability needed for the workings of natural selection.

The Darwinian view had to face and overcome other hurdles besides competing theories. The incompleteness of the fossil record was mentioned previously. Understanding of prehistoric life depends on the accidental preservation of occasional members of earlier species, but the circumstances of their preservation and discovery inevitably leave gaps. Furthermore, hard parts such as bones and shells are more likely to be preserved than soft parts. Even if all of the parts are found intact, information about how these creatures behaved is limited. It is usually necessary to resort to indirect evidence (e.g., analogies with living species and fossil records of behavior such as fossil footprints).

The age of the earth had been another problem. That age was revised vastly upward during the twentieth century, but in the nineteenth century the estimate was so short that it did not seem that there had been enough time for evolution to have come about through natural selection. The likelihood of improbable events when these events have many opportunities to occur over an extended period of time had also been misunderstood. For example, suppose that some organic molecule is a crucial prerequisite for life, that it occurs in nature only when lightning creates it by passing through some mixture of the gases present in the early atmosphere of the earth and that the odds of this happening are 1 million : 1. The creation of that organic molecule might seem very much a long shot under those conditions. Now assume now that there were many lightning storms during the early history of our planet that over a few million years, those conditions were repeated many millions of times. Given these assumptions, it is a virtual certainty that the molecule would have been created not just once but many times, even though the particular moment of its creation would not have been predictable.

Variation and Selection

An example of natural selection: Conceive of a population of prey animals (e.g., zebras) the members of which vary in the speed at which they can run; the reasons might include individual differences in zebra anatomy, such as bone length or muscle size, sensory differences that will allow some to get off to a quicker start than others, and/or indirect factors that slow some down, such as susceptibility to disease. If these animals are preyed on by predators, the ones most likely to be caught are the slowest ones.

At any time during its history, this prey population has some mean or average speed. Some members are above that mean and others are below it. The ones below are those most likely to be caught and so are less likely to pass their genes to the next generation. The next generation will then include more descendants of those above the mean than of those below; that is, it will include fewer of the previous slow and more of the previous fast runners. Likely the mean speed will be higher in the new generation than in the prior one. Over many generations, therefore, the mean speed becomes faster.

According to these arguments, the source of selection is in the environment (the environments of predators include their prey and the environments of prey include their predators). Selection creates the features of organisms, but selection is necessary to maintain them as well as to create them. For example, the ancestors of whales were once land mammals. After they moved back into the sea, the environmental contingencies that had made legs advantageous no longer maintained the selection of well-formed legs. Instead, selection began to favor limbs that were effective for movement through water. The legs of the ancestors of whales gradually disappeared; in a sense it is appropriate to say that the legs had extinguished or become extinct. Selection operates on species, but it does so by acting on particular organs and systems and body parts.

Environments that include tall trees with edible leaves are environments in which long necks may be advantageous, especially if shorter trees are scarce or if their leaves are often depleted by competitors. Giraffes arose through the natural selection of relatively long necks; such selection could not occur in environments that lacked tall trees (the tall trees set the occasion for the selection of long necks). Yet the selection also depended on what there was to start with. In one species, variations among individuals might allow the selection of those with longer necks, but in another they might allow the selection of those who climb trees more efficiently. The environment selects from populations of organisms, but that selection can only operate on the range of variations available within those populations. Structural factors must be included among the constraints on possible variations. In the human species, for example, our four-limbed mammalian ancestry precludes the evolution of a pair of wings emerging from human shoulder blades.

Gradualism Versus Punctuated Evolution

The kind of phylogenic selection discussed involves gradual changes taking place over long periods of time. Some controversies about evolution have been about whether evolution takes place gradually or in fits and starts (punctuated evolution or saltation). The fossil record includes evidence of major changes in species over periods of time that are relatively short by evolutionary standards, for example, the explosion of multicellular life in the Cambrian period or, at the end of the Cretaceous period, the extinction of the dinosaurs (perhaps as a result of the impact of a comet or some other planetary catastrophe) and the later proliferation of large mammals. Given the strong evidence for both kinds of evolutionary change, it is most reasonable to conclude that evolution can take place either way.

Organized Complexity

Natural selection along a single dimension such as running speed seems straightforward enough, but evolution involves more than changes along single dimensions. It results in organized complexity, such as the intricate structure of the human eye. Is it reasonable to believe that natural selection could have produced such organized complexity? If the eye is a product of natural selection, it could not have emerged full blown. Yet what good is part of an eye? What selective advantage could it confer? The answer is that even 1% of an eye is a substantial advantage if all of one's contemporaries have even less.

Once a complex system such as an eye has evolved in a given species, it becomes exceedingly unlikely that it will ever be displaced by another system that has the same function. For example, the 1% of seeing that might be an evolutionary precursor of a complete human eye provides considerably less of an advantage if the complete eye already exists than if the alternative is not seeing at all. Selection does not replace existing mechanisms with others that do the same job, so it is probably safe to assume that a third eye will never evolve in the middle of our foreheads.

By-Products of Selection

Resemblance to sticks is an unusual property, and it is, of course, only one of many possible directions of selection. Selection can operate on different features in different populations, and not every feature that seems adaptive is necessarily a product of natural selection. Darwin regarded natural selection as the most important mechanism of evolution, but he took pains to point out that natural selection was not the only possible one: "I am convinced that Natural Selection has been the main *but not exclusive* means of modification" (emphasis added). Selectionist accounts of the features of a population demand more than just a plausible story about how those features might be advantageous.

Some phylogenic features might come about as incidental byproducts of selection. Some features of contemporary populations may not be direct products of natural selection; instead they may be incidental byproducts of other unrelated features that have arisen through selection.

SELECTION AND BEHAVIOR

In the Darwinian account, natural selection operates on successive populations of organisms, but selection can also operate on successive populations of responses within the lifetime of an individual organism. Shaping, for example, can produce changes in behavior by arranging consequences for some responses but not others. If only the strongest forces exerted by a hungry lever-pressing rat produce food, stronger presses will occur more often and weaker ones will occur less often, and over time the rat's presses will increase in force. Such selection has been called selection by consequences. It is ontogenic rather than phylogenic selection. In the lever-pressing example, food is the consequence that selects some responses and not others. Responses that produce food survive, and others are extinguished. Parallels between these two varieties of selection, natural selection and the selection of behavior by its consequences, have been explored in considerable detail.

Like Galileo's displacement of the earth from the center of the universe to an orbit around a star, accounts in terms of selection challenge traditional ways of thinking about ourselves. Some of the substantive issues have also been similar. As noted earlier, artificial selection was familiar in Darwin's time; what was questioned was whether such selection could operate naturally. The procedure called shaping is also an artificial selection procedure, as when an experimenter shapes the force of a rat's lever pressing or as when a behavior therapist shapes the vocalizations of a nonverbal institutionalized child. In such cases, the effectiveness of shaping is self-evident. However, this kind of selection is artificial, and the question is whether it also operates naturally to produce some of the varied patterns of behavior that occur in everyday life.

Typically, only outcomes are available, after the natural contingencies have already done their work. For example, it can be assumed that ontogenic selection was involved in shaping the skill with which grizzly bears catch salmon in the rivers of the Pacific Northwest, but what is seen are the differences between the inefficient performances of the young novices and the well-coordinated actions of the experienced adults. The shaping itself is not seen, because it continues over too long a time (the phylogenic analogy is in the incompleteness of the fossil record). The question of the extent to which natural selection operates in the production of behavior within the lifetime of an individual remains open, but the analogies in the history of the Darwinian account suggest that the question must be taken seriously.

ECOLOGICAL PSYCHOLOGY
EVOLUTION
HERITABILITY

HUMAN DEVELOPMENT
OPERANT CONDITIONING
RACIAL DIFFERENCES

A. C. CATANIA

NATURALISTIC OBSERVATION

Naturalistic observation refers to unobtrusive nonreactive study of organisms in their native habitat or environment devoid of manipulation or control by the researcher. The scope of such studies extends from individuals to entire social structures and cultures. Such studies are used in a variety of settings, and in a wide range of disciplines, using a multiplicity of techniques and extending beyond the study of human beings to include insects, birds, and other animals. Jane Goodall's study of chimpanzees in their natural habitat is an example of naturalistic observation. The range, variety, and heterogeneity of naturalistic observation studies in distinct disciplines and different social, cultural, and physical settings is reflected in the diversity of topics studied and richness of its findings.

Naturalistic observers often use other research methods, such as interviews, to verify their findings from observational studies and to gain an understanding of the culture and society they are studying. Throughout the evolution of naturalistic observation in different disciplines, this methodology was often identified with other techniques of inquiry. Fieldwork, ethnography, participant and nonparticipant observation, case studies, ethology, and qualitative research are examples of techniques often identified or used interchangeably with naturalistic observation. Naturalistic observation methods are considered a subcategory of a broader rubric of research methods and perspectives—referred to in the literature variously as naturalistic research, naturalistic inquiry, naturalistic methods, naturalistic perspectives, and naturalistic viewpoints—that avoid manipulation of antecedent conditions or imposition of constraints on outputs by experimenters. They include a host of other methodologies such as clinical methodology, life histories, and case studies.

Naturalistic observation is one of the oldest methodologies in science. Its origins date back to prehistoric times and are rooted in oral traditions. Recorded observations, such as those by Herodotus comparing people from Greece with people from other countries, go back to fifth century B.C. Explorers, travelers, journalists and literary figures have contributed observational accounts. From approximately the middle of the nineteenth to the early twentieth centuries, systematic observational studies were carried out, often by amateurs. Famous works during this period include William Booth's study of London, LePlay's study of the working class in France, Lewis Henry Morgan's pioneering anthropological study of the Seneca in 1851, and publication of W. H. R. Rivers's study of the Toda in 1906. A parallel development of systematic observations of animal behavior by Charles Darwin and other scholars popularized the study of ethology, or animal behavior. The period from the 1920s to the 1950s is marked by the use of naturalistic observation methods in a number of additional disciplines and specialties. However, except in cultural or social anthropology, these methods were either ignored or faced criticism from other groups in their respective disciplines. The influence of Franz Boas and the pioneering work in the 1920s by Bronislaw Malinowski on the Trobriand islanders set the tone for anthropological research. At the same time, sociologists in the United States were engaged extensively in naturalistic observation through participant observation and case studies under the guidance of Robert Park and W. I. Thomas. The works of K. Z. Lorenz and Nikolas Tinbergen provided additional impetus and examples for development of ethology in the fields of psychology and physical anthropology. Observational methods were introduced by Jean Piaget in developmental psychology through his studies of child development during this period.

The period after the 1950s witnessed basic comprehensive changes in naturalistic observation methods, which continue to evolve. Two developments that had a major impact are: (a) the introduction of unobtrusive measures and (b) the availability of versatile audiovisual tools for recording observations and dissemination of the observations to larger audiences.

Unobtrusive measures are an ingenious extension of naturalistic observation procedures. They consist of physical trace analyses, archival records, and simple observations. Physical trace analyses include erosion methods that measure signs of wear and tear. For example, book covers can be examined to find out their popularity. Accretion methods measure deposits or accumulation. Dust accumulated on books may be measured to assess the frequency of use. Archival records can be used to gain access to the problems faced by explorers, through their journal entries. Simple observations consist of subcategories that focus on physical signs, body movements, spatial analysis, language, and time-sampling analysis.

Data-gathering capacity has been greatly enhanced with the introduction of audiovisual or video equipment. Video provides a permanent observational record, allowing researchers repeated access to data and providing a potential for significant impact on viewers. Video accounts provide corroboration of accounts of direct observation. They are highly effective in the training of naturalistic researchers and in testing the reliability and validity of observational data, in spite of the fact that the data so gathered are subject to researcher selection bias in topics, choice of presentation, and camera angles. Such records can be submitted to other researchers for their interpretations. These tools have radically altered the roles of researchers. Observers are no longer the sole instrument of observation or necessarily the sole authors of data interpretation.

Ecological perspectives and human ethology were introduced after the 1950s. Behavior therapists used direct observation in collecting specific behavioral data in natural settings. Clinicians extended the scope of their observations from individuals to the study of organizations. Naturalistic observation methods were adopted in the fields of education in the 1960s and in educational program evaluation in the 1970s.

CONDUCTING NATURALISTIC OBSERVATION STUDIES

The diversity and complexity of naturalistic observation allows only for a general description of the methods and procedures involved. In chronological order, focus, access, entry, and role negotiation are the initial steps. Each study starts with a topic or focus of interest and a general idea of location or settings for the study. It is a common experience for naturalistic researchers to find that their interests expand or change during the course of their research. Researchers also must have consent or permission from individuals and/or authorities to conduct their study. In addition to the role of an observer, a number of other roles that may emerge later in the course of the research, such as guest, friend, and neighbor, must be defined.

The next phase consists of observation, interpretation, recording, analysis, and reporting, all affected by the researcher's theoretical stance. The researcher may prefer to emphasize purely descriptive studies or opt for a theoretical approach. One option is a grounded theory approach, emphasizing discoveries directly from data. Analytic induction is another approach to theory building. Here the emphasis is on verification hypotheses. For example, the idea that power always corrupts can be studied in the context of union organizations and reformulated until a fit is achieved.

A researcher has a choice between direct and indirect modes of observation. Similarly, a researcher might choose to be a participant or a nonparticipant observer, or vary between roles on different occasions. Gender, age, ethnicity of the observer and the observed, and the social and political climates are relevant factors. For example, female researchers have greater access to the study of women individually or as a group in most cultures. Time and event sampling is critical to observational

studies, because of the sheer volume of available data. Sampling of subjects becomes necessary if a large number of subjects are to be observed. Many different methods are used by researchers to abstract, record, analyze, and summarize observational data. The range of such records varies from anecdotes to coded records of events, and from specimen records to visual records of behavior.

Reliability, validity, credibility, and trustworthiness of their findings is a major concern of observers. A number of techniques are used to achieve these goals, such as repeated observations, multisite studies, comparisons of the findings with findings of other researchers, and informant interviews to validate their findings through triangulation.

Disengagement from a site needs to be arranged so that, ideally, doors will be open for a return study if the researcher is so interested. Typically, detailed analyses and report writing take place afterward.

The use of observational methods does not preclude the use of other tools such as interviews, projective techniques, and content analysis. Clinical psychologists favor using a multidimensional approach such as rating scales and interviews in addition to observation of behavior.

CRITICISM, CONTROVERSIES, AND REBUTTALS

At varying periods of time naturalistic methods have been subjected to controversy and criticism about their importance, utility, and methodology. Criticisms have stemmed from proponents of philosophical perspectives originating mainly from positivism and operationalism. Positivists believe that the scientific method, modeled after the natural sciences, is the most appropriate method for gaining knowledge. Operationalism aims to limit the scope of scientific studies to measurable entities. Quantitative data, experimental studies, deductive theory testing, and assumption of an objective reality apart from the observer are the bases of this traditional research model.

Naturalistic inquiry adheres to a combination of diverse philosophical perspectives such as phenomenology and humanism that explain and justify knowledge as a subjective process and interpret it with a contingent relationship to the environment. These differences in perspectives are related to the following issues: (a) observation and objectivity; (b) the anatomy of inquiry; (c) qualitative and descriptive approach to data; (d) criteria for assessment; (e) the high cost of naturalistic studies; and (f) concerns about ethical considerations.

Objectivity is difficult to maintain because of the effect of the observer on the observed. The researcher is an intrusive factor, likely to affect the observed and their behavior. Observing with one-way mirrors is an example of minimization of the impact of observation. Interpretation of another culture or behavior of other species by researchers who have their own personal and cultural biases is a second concern. Interpretations of pagan rituals in the nineteenth century were distorted by prejudices of missionary observers. If the same culture is studied by researchers whose interpretations are divergent, should both studies be suspect or should they be regarded as contributions to a more complete understanding of that culture? If one believes, as the positivists do, that there is a singular, true explanation of an event, divergent interpretations are attributed to errors of interpretation.

Naturalistic perspectives accept such discrepancies, because psychological interactions and social events are subject to varied interpretations. It is now generally recognized that social and behavioral sciences are not always devoid of researcher selectivity and bias. For example, differential research emphases in the studies of monkeys of Arashiyama reflect the distinctive values and beliefs held by Japanese and Western researchers. Naturalistic observation studies have been criticized for their lack of replicability and validity as well as their limited generalizability to other groups or cultures, which limits their use. A response to this criticism has been that a naturalistic observer is in search of understanding, rather than of universal laws. Defenders of naturalistic observations emphasize different criteria such as perspective, credibility, and lack of internal contradictions. Careful naturalistic observers identify the context of the research, codify their techniques, use cross-cultural validation, define behavioral units of analyses, conduct comparative studies, and test for universals. Unobtrusive measures are nonreactive, there is minimal observer effect, and measures can be replicated in many cases and are ideally suited for triangulation methods.

Another issue involves the relationship between theory and research procedures. Naturalistic researchers are engaged in the discovery of theory and theory building. The dominant traditional experimental method adheres to theory testing and verification. Naturalistic method is inductive, engaged in generalizations based on a study of individual cultures.

The legitimacy of the inductive method has not been widely accepted in the dominant research tradition, in spite of historical examples of the successful use of the inductive method, such as Darwin's theory of evolution, and extensive use of this method in the day-to-day lives of all people.

Although naturalistic observation studies are descriptive, there is no reason why observations and the environment cannot be coded and quantified. There are many good examples of this in the field. If classics in the field like Margaret Mead's account of Samoa are criticized for being erroneous, how are such issues to be determined? Naturalistic researchers expect interpretations of other cultures to be challenged, viewing the broader context of naturalistic inquiry as a tradition of reporting borrowed from social history, investigative journalism, and textual criticism that usually consist of more than one point of view.

The researcher's role may elicit ethical issues. For example, with disguised observation, how does a researcher draw the line between the need for privacy and the needs of research?

TRENDS AND CONCLUSIONS

The rigid natural science model is being challenged internally as well as externally. This has occurred even in physics, which has been held up as the archetypal discipline of scientific objectivity. Instead of the belief in an objective reality and the dualism of the object and the observer, the term *natural phenomenon* is now used by many physicists to include both the object of the study and the method of observation. Niels Bohr wrote, "It is wrong to think that the task of physics is to find out how nature is. Physics concerns what we can say about nature."

The emergence of narrative ethnography as a reflexive presentation of the nature and process of observation includes both the observer and observed in an interactive involvement, creating a further shift from traditional norms of objectivity and the duality between the observer and the observed. The observer and the observed are not necessarily separated in narrative ethnographic accounts and the emphasis is on reflexivity rather than detachment or value-free objectivity. It is a process described as observation of participation. Other perspectives such as critical feminism and microethnography advocate similar points of view about inclusion of the social milieu and the interaction and communication between the observer and observed in research studies to gain a realistic perspective.

It is reasonable to expect that naturalistic observation methods will eventually be accepted and used in their own right and as a supplement or complement to experimental research, survey research, and other research techniques even more widely.

ACTION RESEARCH
APPLIED RESEARCH
CROSS CULTURAL PSYCHOLOGY
ENVIRONMENTAL PSYCHOLOGY
OPERATIONS RESEARCH
PERFORMANCE APPRAISAL

RESEARCH METHODOLOGY
SAMPLING
SOCIAL CLIMATE RESEARCH

S. R. SONNAD

NATURE–NURTURE CONTROVERSY

The so-called "nature–nurture controversy" is really a family of controversies about the relative roles of heredity (nature) and environment (nurture) in shaping human characteristics.

These controversies exist not so much because the scientific questions involved are difficult—although many are—but because the proposed alternative solutions are perceived as having profound implications for cherished beliefs (often with religious or political overtones) concerning such matters as human equality, social justice, individual responsibility, and the character of civilization itself.

The several controversies subsumed under the general heading of the "nature–nurture controversy" may be differentiated in various ways. One is by the aspect of behavior involved. Some controversies such as that over instinct have focused largely on drives or motives, while others such as the IQ controversy have dealt mainly with abilities. Another way of distinguishing among nature–nurture controversies is by whether the emphasis is on individual, group, or species characteristics. The history of the nature–nurture controversy has involved irregular shifts in emphasis among these various aspects of the problem from time to time, often without a clear sense of the distinctions.

Locke invoked the metaphor of the mind as a blank sheet of paper on which all of knowledge is written by the hand of experience. His political view that all men are by nature equal and independent and that society is a mutual contract entered into for the common good had an immense influence through Jefferson, Voltaire, Rousseau, and the other theorists of the American and French revolutions.

In Locke's own view, human political equality was not inconsistent with an inborn diversity of human tendencies and capabilities. Nevertheless, Locke judged the bulk of human variation to be the result of differences in experience.

Charles Darwin gave the nature side of the controversy its modern form by placing the human mind solidly in the framework of biological evolution. Darwin made it clear that human behavior shared common ancestry with the behavior of other animal forms, and that behavioral as well as physical characteristics were subject to the basic evolutionary mechanism of hereditary variation followed by natural selection of the variants most successful in their environments. The English social philosopher, Herbert Spencer, found it easy to assimilate Darwin's views into his own developing theory of social evolution and may be considered the first of the so-called "Social Darwinists," who argued that the successful and unsuccessful in society represented the fit and the unfit in a Darwinian sense.

Francis Galton enthusiastically extended Spencer's ideas of genetic variation and natural selection to the interpretation of human variability. Obviously familial resemblances are potentially explainable by either heredity or environment, but Galton believed them to be largely hereditary. He also discussed racial differences, which he believed to be largely hereditary also. Galton saw clearly the political implications of his theories and founded the eugenics movement.

Galton's emphasis on individual and racial differences burgeoned in the United States in the mental testing movement. The psychologists Lewis M. Terman and Robert M. Yerkes were important figures whose own beliefs, on the whole, lay toward the nature side of the controversy. Yerkes organized the enormously successful intelligence testing for military selection purposes in World War I. Terman organized a massive study of genius. Genius was identified by a high IQ, which Terman assumed to be a fairly direct measure of inborn intelligence. Also, on the nature side of the equation, the social psychologist William McDougall developed an instinct-based theory. Its emphasis on the importance of inherited tendencies in shaping human social life aroused vigorous opposition among psychologists, sociologists, anthropologists, and others in the Lockean tradition. Both McDougall's instinct doctrine and the Galtonian notion of inherited individual differences in capacities were vigorously rejected in the radical behaviorism of the psychologist John B. Watson.

The decades from the 1920s to the 1950s were marked by a gradually decreasing salience of the nature–nurture controversy in psychology, although it never dropped entirely out of view. Concurrently, there was an increasing accumulation of relevant empirical studies with identical and fraternal twins, adoptive families, orphans, and so on, in both the United States and Europe. These studies, based on research designs that to some extent were able to separate genetic from environmental factors, were focused mainly on individual variation in ability, specifically the ubiquitous IQ, but they dealt to some extent with other psychological traits as well. An active research literature also developed on psychopathological conditions, such as neurosis and psychosis, criminality, and mental deficiency. However, for most ability and personality traits, normal and abnormal, it remained the case that overall estimates of the relative importance of genetic and environmental influences, so-called *heritability coefficients,* were the best that could be achieved. Since such estimates have rarely been made using adequate samples, and since the methods of measuring psychological traits still leave a good deal to be desired, the estimates tend to vary a good deal from study to study even in similar populations, leaving scope for persistence of the nature–nurture controversy, at least in a quantitative sense.

One answer seemed obvious: better measures and larger samples to narrow the gap of uncertainty. Another was to investigate the actual mechanisms by which genes and environments, have their effects. In a broad sense, the geneticist, T. Dobzhansky, elegantly integrated Darwinian concepts with an appreciation of the role of culture in human evolution and Lockean democratic ideals. By 1960, with the publication of the textbook *Behavior genetics* by J. L. Fuller, a biologist, and W. R. Thompson, a psychologist, it appeared that the controversy might at last be becoming ordinary science.

The calm was illusory. In 1969, Jensen surveyed various lines of evidence, and took a fairly strong hereditarian position, estimating about 80% of individual variation in IQ to be genetic. Worse, he conjectured that at least part of the persistent disadvantage of U.S. Blacks in IQ test performance was also genetic in origin. A furor arose in academic circles and the popular press—a furor exacerbated in 1971 by the publication of an article entitled "IQ" by the psychologist Richard J. Herrnstein. This article emphasized genetic differences arising among social classes in a mobile society, a theme introduced earlier by the British psychologist Cyril Burt.

A strong counterattack was launched with perhaps the most extreme environmentalist position being taken by the U.S. psychologist Leon Kamin. Then in 1975, Edward O. Wilson outlined a modern population–genetic basis for the notion that biological instincts might play a central role in human affairs in his theory of sociobiology.

More attacks and counterattacks followed. The earlier participants brought out further works. In Britain, H. J. Eysenck crossed swords with Kamin. On the environmentalist side, many of Kamin's suspicions about the trustworthiness of Burt's data were substantiated. S. J. Gould blasted away at hereditarians and IQ testing. The topic of race differences in IQ provoked several books. Works in sociobiology, pro and con, have been multiplying at an even faster rate.

It would not do to conclude, however, from the fact that the controversy is still active that no progress has been made. Modern views of biological evolution, although deriving from Darwin, are much more complex, differentiated, and mathematical, and incorporate a much more

adequate genetics. Modern psychology takes—at its best—a vastly more sophisticated view of the organism–environment interplay than did the instinct lists of McDougall or the behavioristic battle cries of John B. Watson. Finally, nature–nurture controversialists now must accommodate their prejudices to a much larger body of established fact.

**CULTURAL BIASES IN TESTING
HEREDITY AND INTELLIGENCE
HUMAN INTELLIGENCE**

J. C. LOEHLIN

NATURWISSENSCHAFTLICHE PSYCHOLOGIE

Psychology today is listed officially in some universities as a social science and in some as a biological science. This artificial division of psychology into social sciences (*Geisteswissenschaften*) and biological or natural sciences (*Naturwissenschaften*) has a long history. It was formulated in various degrees by a number of German psychologists, especially Wilhelm Hindelband, Heinrich Rickert, and Wilhelm Dilthey.

In later years this dichotomy produced different expressions. The structuralists were in the *Geisteswissenschaftliche* tradition, while the behaviorists were in the *Naturwissenschaftliche* camp.

This dichotomy has other implications. As a general rule, those in the natural sciences tend to be nomothetically oriented and to be number conscious. However, those in the social or human sciences tend to be phenomenologically oriented, concerned with the single individual, and ideographic in orientation. Biologically oriented theoreticians take the general view of determinism, while socially oriented theoreticians view the individual as capable of making independent decisions.

Modern day psychology is essentially functional. Some individuals like B. F. Skinner are in the biological tradition, while others such as Carl Rogers are in the social science tradition. Yet interestingly enough, Skinner, like Rogers, believes in concentrating on a single individual.

**GEISTESWISSENSCHAFTLICHE PSYCHOLOGIE
THEORETICAL PSYCHOLOGY**

W. S. SUTTON

NEAR-DEATH EXPERIENCES

Near-death experiences (NDEs), once regarded as meaningless hallucinations, have become the subject of serious study by medical and other researchers. To some extent, this growing professional concern is the result of the inescapability of the NDE. The progressive sophistication of biomedical advances has allowed increasing numbers of patients who otherwise would have died to be resuscitated. The accounts of experiences that many of these patients attempt to relate to medical personnel are so consistent and so real to them that the medical community has found them increasingly difficult to ignore.

Although different investigators have emphasized different aspects of the experience, the NDE is now generally accepted to be a profound subjective event with transcendental or mystical elements that many people experience on the threshold of death. Once thought to be rare, the NDE is now acknowledged to be reported by at least 33% of people who come close to death. A Gallup poll estimated that about 5% of the American population, or about 13 million Americans in 1992, had reported NDEs.

Raymond Moody, the psychiatrist who coined the term *near-death experience,* used it to refer to an ineffable experience on the threshold of death that may include hearing oneself pronounced dead, feelings of peace, unusual noises, a sense of movement through a dark tunnel, a sense of being out of the physical body, meeting other spiritual beings, meeting a being of light, a life review, a border or point of no return, a return to the physical body, frustrated attempts to tell others about the experience, profound changes in attitudes and values, elimination of one's fear of death, and independent corroboration of knowledge gained while out of the body. Moody emphasized that no two individuals' NDEs are exactly the same, and that few NDEs contain all these features.

Near-death experiences are reported by individuals who had been pronounced clinically dead but then resuscitated, by individuals who actually died but were able to describe their experiences in their final moments, and by individuals who, in the course of accidents or illnesses, feared that they were near death. Although initial studies suggested that how one came close to death—or how close one actually came to death—did not influence the occurrence or type of NDE, more recent research indicates that physiological details of the close brush with death may play a role.

It appears, for example, that NDEs dominated by cognitive features, such as loss of a sense of time, thought acceleration, and a life review, are more common when the near-death event is sudden and unexpected than when it may have been anticipated. Near-death experiences associated with cardiac arrest resemble out-of-body experiences, while those without cardiac arrest are more similar to depersonalization; experiences occurring to intoxicated persons tend to be bizarre and confused, like hallucinations. Furthermore, although all elements of the NDE can be reported by individuals who merely perceive themselves to be near death, certain features—such as an encounter with a brilliant light, enhanced cognitive function, and positive emotions—are significantly more common among individuals whose closeness to death can be corroborated, as by medical records.

Researchers have yet to find personal traits or variables that can predict who will have an NDE or what kind of NDE a person may have. Retrospective studies of near-death experiencers (NDErs), have shown them to be psychologically healthy individuals who do not differ from other people in age, gender, race, religion, religiosity, or mental health.

Several psychological hypotheses have been proposed to explain NDEs and their consistent features. A plausible explanation suggests that NDEs are products of the imagination, constructed from our personal and cultural expectations to protect us from facing the threat of death. However, empirical data do not support this theory. Cross-cultural studies do not show the expected variations in content of NDEs, and individuals often report experiences that conflict with their specific religious and personal expectations of the passage to death. Furthermore, people who had never heard or read of NDEs describe the same kinds of experiences as do people who are quite familiar with the phenomenon, and the knowledge individuals had about NDEs previously does not seem to influence the details of their own experiences.

Another problem for the expectancy model of NDEs is that children too young to have received substantial cultural and religious conditioning about death report the same kinds of NDEs as do adults. Several researchers have now published collections of childhood near-death experiences, including some reported to have occurred before the child could have acquired any language skills. Although NDEs are recounted by a large proportion of children who survive critical illnesses—in some studies, more than half—they are not recounted by children who suffer serious illnesses that are not potentially fatal. Interestingly, children generally do not report the life review typical of adults' NDEs, and they report meeting fewer deceased friends and relatives—two differences that might be expected from their brief experience with life.

Because NDErs report events that others around them cannot see or experience, some authors have suggested that NDEs are elaborate hallucinations produced either by drugs given to dying patients or by metabolic disturbances or brain malfunctions as a person approaches

death. However, patients who are given drugs when near death report fewer and less elaborate NDEs than do patients who remain drug-free. That finding may suggest that drugs, rather than causing NDEs, in fact prevent them from occurring or it may suggest merely that patients who are drugged tend not to recall their experiences.

Several neurochemical models have been proposed for the NDE, invoking the role of endorphins or various neurotransmitters, and neuroanatomical models have linked the NDE to specific sites in the brain. At this point, such models are not testable, but they offer the hope that scientists may someday bridge the gap between mystical experience and physiological events. Although correlating the NDE with physical structures or chemicals in the brain would not necessarily tell us what causes the NDE, it would potentially open up new tools and techniques for investigating the mechanisms and aftereffects of these experiences.

The most promising aspect of NDEs for future research is its role in personal transformation, as this is certainly the most easily measured and arguably the most important feature of the experience. Typical aftereffects, reported by many independent researchers, include increases in spirituality, concern for others, and appreciation of life and decreases in fear of death, materialism, and competitiveness. Persons who have NDEs tend to see themselves as integral parts of a benevolent and purposeful universe in which personal gain, particularly at another's expense, is no longer relevant. These profound changes in attitudes and in behavior have been corroborated in long-term studies of NDErs, in interviews with their significant others, and in research comparing NDErs with survivors of close brushes with death who do not recall NDEs.

COGNITIVE COMPLEXITY
DEATH ANXIETY
DELUSIONAL DISORDERS
HALLUCINATIONS
ILLUSIONS
IMAGERY
PARAPSYCHOLOGY

B. GREYSON

NEED–PRESS THEORY

Need–Press Theory is a personality theory developed by Henry Murray based on Kurt Lewin's definition of behavior as a function of the person and the environment. Walsh states that two fundamental assumptions underlie Murray's need–press model. First, the psychological significance of the personality can be inferred from behavior. Needs are viewed as the organizational tendencies that give a sense of unity and direction to a person's behavior. Thus an individual's behavior may be understood in terms of the dynamics of satisfying such needs. Second, the psychological significance of the environment can be inferred from the individual's perceptions of it. The environment is defined in terms of a variety of press that depend on the individual's interpretation of the environment.

Murray postulated two types of press: alpha and beta. *Alpha press* denotes those environmental stimuli that can effect a behavioral response and that can be perceived and reported by an objective, knowledgeable observer. *Beta press* are divided into two subtypes, *private beta press* and *consensual beta press*. The former is defined as the unique and private views that each individual has of the environment, while the latter refers to the interpretations shared by a group of individuals about the same environment.

The relationship between needs and press is isomorphic, but these concepts are not necessarily reciprocal.

Perhaps the single most important exponent of Need–Press Theory is George Stern, who has developed a number of measurement instruments.

Stern labels a congruent person–environment fit (i.e., complementary need–press) as anabolic, and the converse (uncomplementary need–press) catabolic. The anabolic relationship is said to stimulate and the catabolic to hinder self-enhancement and self-actualization.

Taking this dichotomy of congruency–incongruency into account, Stern developed a needs inventory based on Murray's classification of needs that included some 30 different need–press variables. The Activities Index (AI) provides a self-report of preferences that indicate a person's life goals and coping behavior. The items are geared to college-age subjects.

To facilitate the measurement of environmental press, Stern developed the College Characteristic Index (CCI). Using the AI and CCI together, one can obtain a measure of person-environment "fit" or congruence.

Walsh outlines several limitations of Need–Press Theory. Chief among these are the following:

1. The theory does not give adequate attention to the influence of learning on behavior change.
2. The process of need development is not explained.
3. The theory is difficult to test empirically, chiefly because some of the need–press scales are not parallel. Furthermore, need–press congruency research on the whole does not support the underlying assumption of the theory.

Walsh concludes, however, that Need–Press Theory seems to have heuristic and practical value in spite of such limitations.

PERSONALITY THEORIES

A. BARÓN, JR.

NEEDS ASSESSMENT

Needs assessment is an applied research tool used as an aid in planning human services. It emerged about 1975, during a period that saw many related developments in applied research, including program evaluation, community psychology, social epidemiology, and social indicators. This period also marked a shift toward more responsive and planful approaches to the provision of human services in the community—often mandated by legislation. Finally, public recognition of many social and psychological problems grew, as did expectations that relevant services be provided to deal with them.

There are several obstacles to planning and providing services in a manner responsive to community needs. As Warheit and coworkers have noted, these include inertia or active resistance on the part of the community or service providers, the number and diversity of community problems, disputes about which problems are most pressing, and the dynamic nature of community change. With the goal of overcoming such obstacles, needs assessment involves empirical measurement of community problems, existing services, use patterns, and potential services. Such data serve to distinguish serious from apparent problems, to identify service gaps, and to uncover barriers to use. The general goal of needs assessment, then, is to use empirical data on needs to aid decisions about what, when, and where services should be provided.

DEFINITION OF NEED

An implicit assumption of needs assessment is that there is a problem that has a solution; indeed, McKillip defines need as "the value judgment that some group has a problem that can be solved." Yet neither component is straightforward. Problem recognition usually depends on a perceived discrepancy between the current situation and some expectation.

Expectations may derive from standards set by experts (e.g., accreditation guidelines), the beliefs of the target population (e.g., residents' views on crime), high use of existing service (e.g., waiting lists), or relative performance (e.g., high rates of drug use by teenagers). Bradshaw terms these normative, felt, expressed, and comparative need, respectively. Problems may be serious but unsolvable or moderate but readily resolved; as McKillip notes, the identification of solutions—too often ignored in needs assessment—involves assessment of cost, impact, and feasibility. In short, empirical data on need can facilitate the decision-making process, but ultimately it involves the exercise of value judgments.

MODELS OF NEEDS ASSESSMENT

McKillip has presented three models of needs assessment that reflect different conceptualizations of need. The discrepancy model emphasizes normative expectations, is widely used, and has been adapted to many needs assessment contexts. Generally, it involves measurement of three elements: goals, actual performance, and the discrepancy between the two. Typically, the magnitude or judged significance of discrepancies is used to determine which preset solution will be implemented; thus the approach focuses on problems rather than solutions. Because goals typically are set by experts, the method has been criticized as elitist and insensitive to felt needs.

The marketing model may be seen as emphasizing felt and expressed need and is relatively new to human services. A marketing strategy involves finding a market niche and offering the range, mix, and quality of services that maximize "consumption," that is, use. At its best, this approach escapes the limitations of experts and empowers those in need. At its worst, it promotes ineffective services to those in no position to choose or offers only lucrative services. Clearly, the utility of the model depends on context—service alternatives, informed consumers, and so forth.

The decision-making model adapts multiattribute utility analysis (MAUA) to needs assessment. Multiattribute utility analysis is a technique used to minimize bias in complex decisions. Each option (alternative problem or service) is scored on multiple attributes (indicators of need such as use rates, problem prevalence, and survey data); attribute scores are converted to utilities (e.g., cigarette and cocaine use would be scaled differently); each attribute is given a weight (making explicit the value placed on it by experts, providers, and/or others); and weighted attribute scores are summed for each option to determine need. Technically, this model might reflect any or all facets of need, depending on the particular application—it is a complex but extremely flexible strategy.

NEEDS ASSESSMENT STRATEGIES

A number of different methodological approaches have been proposed for the conduct of needs assessment, each with advantages and disadvantages. Several methods focus on existing services and their use. Resource inventories are conducted to provide a comprehensive description of service resources—cataloging agencies, staff, type and quantity of service, types and number of clients served, and so forth—within some region. Resource inventories are solution oriented; they can reveal underused or hard-pressed services and service gaps (e.g., no services available for children or low-income clients), but cannot identify novel needs.

Service utilization analyses vary in complexity. Most useful are comparisons of rates under treatment with data on service capacity and predicted use, the latter being derived from epidemiological estimates, use at comparable agencies, or expert standards. Appropriate analyses may indicate that some group experiences barriers to service; problems include awareness, accessibility, and acceptability of services. Removal of barriers may increase use and decrease need. However, as McKillip notes, use and need may be related positively, negatively, or not at all.

Without information on nonuse, service-use data can be a misleading indicator of need.

Other approaches to needs assessment attempt to focus on the problems underlying need. Social indicators often are used when more direct information on problems is unavailable or too costly to collect. Social data for a given geopolitical area (often available from government sources) may relate to a target problem directly or indirectly. For example, national high school survey data on drinking and mortality statistics (including deaths related to alcohol) may provide leading and trailing indicators of alcohol abuse problems. Indirect indicators of risk might include demographic, socioeconomic, and social factors known to be related to alcohol problems. Often, estimation techniques must be used to apply existing data to a particular target area or group. The problem focus of this approach serves to complement solution-focused approaches discussed above. Disadvantages include the sometimes questionable assumptions underlying estimation procedures and inferences across levels of aggregation (cf. ecological fallacy).

Needs assessment questions often are best tackled more directly, through need surveys. Provided the relevant issues have been clearly articulated, surveys can be tailored to obtain relevant data from relevant samples. Surveys may focus on problems, expectations underlying needs, service use, preferences, barriers to service, and so forth. A wide variety of methods may be used—mail, telephone, and personal surveys. Data may be collected from a formal sample of the community, from specific client groups, or from community representatives thought to reflect the range of relevant opinion, as in key informant surveys. Alternative methods seek opinions less formally through community forums and structured groups such as focus groups, delphi panels, and nominal groups. These methods vary greatly in time required, cost, and the quality of information generated; used thoughtfully, each may be a useful tool in needs assessment.

ACTION RESEARCH
CLINICAL ASSESSMENT
COMMUNITY PSYCHOLOGY
FIELD RESEARCH
SOCIAL CASEWORK
SURVEYS

A. VAUX

NEGLECTED CHILDREN

Child neglect occurs when "a caretaker responsible for the child either deliberately or by extraordinary inattentiveness permits the child to experience avoidable present suffering and/or fails to provide one or more of the ingredients generally deemed essential for developing a person's physical, intellectual and emotional capacities." Neglected children differ from abused children. Although neglect may be considered a form of abuse, it is usually caused by poverty or ignorance. Abuse, in contrast, is more likely to be related to psychological factors in the caretaker.

Not a great deal is known about the causes of child neglect. Social stress factors that appear to contribute include a home where the father is absent or where family income is low. Cultural values affect child-caring practices as well. The level of emotional maturity of the caretaker is also an important factor. Neglected children typically have parents who themselves were neglected, suggesting that a cycle of neglect exists across generations.

The primary indicators of neglect are: frequent absence from or tardiness at school; inadequate clothing or hygiene; bruises or other injuries; extreme hostility; excessive withdrawal; inadequate medical attention; insufficient nourishment; frequent sleepiness; parental apathy; socially isolated parents; and irrational or unusual behavior by parents.

Neglected children tend to be either apathetic and listless or overly aggressive. They are below normal in physical and intellectual development. They often display attitudes of hopelessness and defeat, become suspicious of others, and do not trust themselves. When faced with the problems of life, neglected children tend to overrate their difficulty and underrate their own capacity to meet these problems with the help of others.

CHILD ABUSE
PARENT–CHILD RELATIONS

R. R. KOPP

NEGOTIATION

Negotiation is used in reference to interactions involving complex social units such as companies or nations with multiple issues. Rubin and Brown ultimately define bargaining and negotiation as "the process whereby two or more parties attempt to settle what each shall give and take, or perform and receive, in a transaction between them."

Rubin and Brown present five structural and social psychological characteristics of negotiating relationships, which are as follows:

1. At least two parties must be involved.

2. A conflict of interest involving one or more issues exists between or among the parties involved.

3. A voluntary relationship exists between or among the parties, regardless of prior experience or acquaintance with each other. Furthermore, the parties must believe that they have more to lose than to gain by not interacting with each other.

4. The negotiation actively involves the division or exchange of one or more specific resources and/or the resolution of one or more intangible issues. The negotiation outcome involves an interdependence or "give and take."

5. The negotiation activity is sequential rather than simultaneous. That is, the presentation of demands and proposals by one side is likely to be followed by an evaluation of these by the party (or parties), followed by concessions or counterproposals.

The most widely used paradigm for the study of negotiation has been some form of game that simulates a "real life" bargaining situation. Rubin and Brown discuss four such games that have been employed extensively in social psychological research.

Because of the structural differences in each situation, the games simulate actual negotiating conditions to varying degrees. Within their limitations, they provide paradigms by which to study a multitude of dependent and independent variables affecting bargaining situations, including the number of parties involved in negotiations, location of the bargaining site, communication options available to the parties, time limitations, and reward structures.

LABOR–MANAGEMENT RELATIONS

A. BARÓN, JR.

NEOBEHAVIORISM

Beginning in the 1930s, the psychologists who built on J. B. Watson's views, together with those of A. P. Weiss, revised their behavioristic position to make it more sophisticated and elaborate; the prominent neobehaviorists were E. C. Tolman, C. L. Hull, E. R. Guthrie, B. F. Skinner, and K. W. Spence. Skinner, who eventually became the most prominent, was the last to die. Their followers or students, to name only a few, were B. F. Ritchie and H. E. Gleitman (Tolman), N. E. Miller and O. H. Mowrer (Hull), F. D. Sheffield and N. E. Miller (Guthrie), M. Sidman and A. S. Catania (Skinner), and F. A. Logan and A. Amsel (Spence); they also made substantial contributions to neobehaviorism. J. R. Kantor, with his theory of interbehaviorism in which the response determines the stimulus as well as conversely, should also be mentioned. Although Kantor's following has been small, it is still quite viable.

Neobehaviorism is often seen as allied with the philosophy of science school of logical positivism, or operationism, and this is especially true of Spence's writings with Gustav Bergmann, who was his colleague at Iowa. That psychology as a natural science had to be empirical and objective was the main philosophical point for all neobehaviorists, but beyond that few were completely in sympathy with the logical positivism of Rudolf Carnap, H. Feigl, and C. G. Hempel. However, Sigmund Koch, a severe early critic of neobehaviorism, considered them closely related, and because of the demise of logical positivism, according to Koch, behaviorism was also dead or dying. From another perspective, behaviorism has just changed its clothes and taken a new name.

The learning theories of the neobehaviorists differ in certain respects, mainly with reference to the concept of reinforcement and the use of intervening variable concepts. Many other apparent internal differences are terminological. In the broadest and least controversial sense, stimulus and response are basic concepts in all these theories. Although Tolman emphasized the learning of S–S relations instead of S–R associations, these "what leads to what," or sign-significate, cognitions directed—at least intuitively—what a reasonable organism would do or where it would go. Although Skinner eschewed the concept of eliciting stimuli, his concept of a discriminative stimulus (S°) still controls emitted behavior. Skinner's definitions of stimulus and response are functional, which means that like all the other neobehaviorists he was chiefly concerned with molar behavior rather than specific movements. This he labeled *operant behavior,* while Guthrie termed it *acts* and Tolman, Hull, and Spence simply called it *molar behavior.*

ACT PSYCHOLOGY
APPROACHES TO LEARNING
BACKWARD CONDITIONING
BEHAVIORISM
CLASSICAL CONDITIONING
OPERANT CONDITIONING
POSITIVISM
STRUCTURAL LEARNING THEORY
THEORETICAL PSYCHOLOGY

M. R. DENNY

NEONATAL DEVELOPMENT

Following the prenatal period and birth, human development continues with the neonatal period encompassing the first few weeks of the newborn's life. On the average, weight at birth is 7 pounds and height is 20 inches. The rapid physical growth of the prenatal period continues during the first year. The sensory and motor capacities that evolve prenatally are ready for operation at birth.

To protect the infant from harm and to assure survival, a child is born with a repertory of *reflexes* consisting of breathing, sucking, blinking, sneezing, coughing, and vomiting, as well as defensive reactions to prevent obstruction of air passages, plus others. With the groundwork of reflexes, the child can learn to master the environment and grow intellectually. The sucking reflex leads to seeking the nipple. The palmar reflex leads to grasping an object and transferring it from hand to hand. Reflex heralds

the beginning stage of intellectual development called sensorimotor by Piaget.

The newborn is well equipped with *sensory skills.* The baby follows objects and perceives size, shapes, contours, contrasting colors, brightness, movement, and depth, and shows a preference for patterns like a checkerboard. The infant is able to distinguish between a real and a discrepant face and also between the mother's face and that of a stranger. A 2-week-old infant can stick out its tongue and clench its hands by imitating someone making those gestures.

Newborns appear to discern from which side a sound is coming. They discriminate among smells, including the odor of the mother. Tasting sweets brings a positive response, whereas a negative response is made to salty, sour, and bitter solutions. There is sensitivity to pain.

Touch is the most highly developed sense, particularly in the areas of the lips, tongue, ears, and forehead: stimulating these areas brings a positive response. By stroking the infant, attending to its needs, and comforting, parents convey the message of love, which is so essential to the psychological well-being of their offspring. Parents promote a bonding relationship with their infant by means of touching, eye-to-eye contact, a high-pitched voice, and signaling. The infant shows reciprocal bonding behaviors by eye contact, crying, smiling, rooting, and signaling.

John Bowlby calls the affectional tie between mother and child "attachment." Parenting has become a joint responsibility shared by father and mother alike, and both are of equal importance. The infant perceives the necessity of both parents by seeking comfort from either.

In addition to the senses, the child explores the world through *body movements.* Motor behavior proceeds in the same direction as the fetus grows in the uterus. The direction is cephalocaudal, or from head to toe.

Each child is *unique* from birth and requires its own amount of time for sleep and wakefulness. Wolff found that the newborn experiences a series of six states: regular sleep, irregular sleep, periodic sleep, alert inactivity, waking activity, and crying. The timing of these states and the cycles of eating, sleeping, and elimination are influenced by the child's innate nature and also by the environment, principally by the parents. The most frequent ways in which parents try to modify their infant's states are feeding and rocking.

Individual differences in temperament emerge as early as birth. Thomas, Chess, and Birch observed three distinct types of newborns: easy, slow, and difficult. The two-way interaction between the child of a particular temperament and the environment leads to the formation of personality. The researchers found that temperament tends to remain constant as the person grows older, and suggested that caregivers adapt their child-rearing practices to it.

BONDING AND ATTACHMENT
INFANT DEVELOPMENT

S. S. BROWN

NEOPSYCHOANALYTIC SCHOOL

Seven theorists originally influenced by Sigmund Freud developed a number of basic differences with the orthodox psychoanalytic approach, and some broke away from Freud because of these differences. Each modified and in some way extended psychoanalysis as it had been conceived by Freud. At times, some of these seven theorists have been called "neo-Freudians." The seven theorists form a historical link between Freud and certain contemporary personality/psychotherapy theorists.

The first five—Carl Jung, Alfred Adler, Karen Horney, Erich Fromm, and Harry Stack Sullivan—shared views that separated them from Freud's orthodox psychoanalytic view. They agreed that social and cultural factors were of great significance in shaping personality, and reacted against what they considered to be Freud's narrow insistence on the biological determinants of personality, especially the role of sex and aggression. They also gave less emphasis than Freud to unconscious factors as a determinant of human personality and behavior. Although most of them accepted the notion that early childhood experiences play a significant role in one's current psychological functioning and development, they rejected the notion that personality is fixed and determined by earlier experiences.

A central feature of Carl Jung's analytic theory and view of the person was his emphasis on the role of purpose and goals. Jung focused on the optimistic or creative side of humanity, the striving for completeness, and the role of living for purpose and meaning. Jung also broadened the Freudian notion of the unconscious, describing unconscious forces as both creative and destructive.

A central feature of Alfred Adler's individual psychology is emphasis on the social determinants of personality. He stressed that behavior is purposeful and goal-directed, and that humans are pushed by the need to overcome feelings of inferiority and pulled by strivings for superiority.

Karen Horney's central idea was *basic anxiety,* the child's feeling of being isolated in a potentially hostile world. Her theory of personality focused on the role of anxiety that grows out of disturbed parent–child relationships.

Erich Fromm contended that humans shape social forces themselves and thus create their own natures. In his writings Fromm stressed an existential view of humans, which included dealing with loneliness, isolation, a sense of belongingness, and the meaning of life.

Harry Stack Sullivan developed a theory of personality that emphasized interpersonal relations and the study of humans in relationship with significant others. As applied to psychotherapy, Sullivan saw the therapist as a participant/observer bringing objective and subjective reactions to the client.

Erik Erikson, identified as an ego psychologist, has developed an approach to personality that moves considerably beyond Freud's. Erikson's theory of development holds that psychosexual and psychosocial growth occur together, and that each stage of life is characterized by a crisis or major turning point at which individuals either achieve or fail to achieve successful resolutions.

Wilhelm Reich pioneered body-oriented psychotherapy by putting the body at the center of psychology. His central idea was that emotions are an expression of the movement of body energy, and that chronic muscle tensions block this flow of energy and thus block the expression of emotions such as rage, fear, pain, joy, and anxiety.

ADLERIAN PSYCHOLOGY
ANALYTICAL PSYCHOLOGY
HORNEY'S THEORY
PSYCHOANALYSIS
SULLIVAN'S INTERPERSONAL THEORY

G. COREY

NEURAL MECHANISMS OF LEARNING

Packed within 1 kg or so of mass in the brain are thousands of billions of computing elements, connected to each other in a seemingly random manner. Each element converts thousands of chemical signals into electrical signals every second, compares their value, and then reconverts them into chemical signals. From all of these computations comes the richness of human behavior: thoughts, actions, and emotions.

The function of these computing elements changes with experience, so that humans are not constrained to perform the stereotyped behaviors they were capable of at birth. Learned behaviors are what make humans unique in the animal kingdom.

Research in this area makes extensive use of model systems; examinations of either relatively simple behaviors or relatively simple nervous systems (or both). In addition, clinical literature from people whose brains have been damaged by accident or illness has provided insight into which parts of the human brain are involved in learning and memory. The combination of these approaches is beginning to reveal what, where, and how the brain changes when learning occurs.

EFFECTS OF BRAIN DAMAGE IN HUMANS AND MONKEYS

Examining the behavioral deficits of human subjects who have experienced brain damage has increased understanding of how behavioral functions are localized in the central nervous system. Since the first evidence that even higher functions are localized to specific parts of the brain, it has been apparent that understanding the mechanisms of learning and memory requires knowledge of where these changes are to be found. Several prominent clinical case studies of individuals who sustained brain damage as a result of surgical intervention or accidents as well as experimental studies on monkeys suggest that there are two important learning and memory systems in the primate brain: one in the medial temporal lobes of the cerebral cortex and one in the diencephalon, near the midline of the brain.

Effects of Damage to the Medial Temporal Lobes

The importance of the structures in the medial temporal lobe (including the hippocampus, amygdala, and surrounding neocortex) was demonstrated dramatically in the case of H. M., an individual of above normal intelligence who received a bilateral medial temporal lobectomy in 1954 to relieve intractable epilepsy. Following the surgery, H. M. exhibited a severe deficit in the ability to learn new information about facts or events, which has not shown any improvement for nearly 40 years. This anterograde amnesia (a memory deficit for the period of time after brain damage) exists in the absence of any other changes in H. M.'s personality or general intelligence (he scored slightly higher on IQ tests after the surgery, in spite of the amnesia).

ANALYSIS OF SIMPLE LEARNING IN VERTEBRATES

Human case studies and lesion experiments in monkeys have provided invaluable information about the role of some brain structures in learning and memory and the nature of human memory. Much of the data are difficult to interpret, however, in terms of defining a specific role for any part of the human brain in the learning process or identifying which neurons or synapses within these structures are the most likely to change as a result of experience. The difficulty is intrinsic to the fact that both the neural circuitry and the behaviors involved in these studies are quite complex. For this reason, many researchers in the field have chosen to study simpler forms of learning and memory in mammals that are likely to involve relatively less complex neural circuits.

I. P. Pavlov was the first researcher to develop a physiologically based theory of learning and memory. Pavlov proposed that the cerebral cortex, particularly well developed in humans, was the site of interactions between associable stimuli and thus the part of the brain in which learned responses were initiated. Karl Lashley conducted a long and detailed study of the effects of cerebral cortical lesions on the ability of rats to learn and remember complex mazes. Based on his observations, Lashley concluded that learning could not be localized to any one part of the cerebral cortex, because sufficiently large ablations of any part of the cortex produced equivalent deficits on mazes of equal difficulty. More recently, however, studies that have employed lesions restricted to brain regions other than the neocortex, examining a variety of different behaviors, have begun to suggest that investigations into the cellular and molecular basis of learning will be most productive if they focus on some especially important parts of the brain.

Role of the Hippocampus in Rapid Learning

Experimental data derived from lesion studies are in general agreement with the clinical literature cited previously; the hippocampus appears to play an important role in learning and memory. Although the exact nature of this role is a matter of debate, lesion of the hippocampus disrupts the learning or remembering of several different behavioral tasks, in rodents as well as primates.

Most of the literature on the effect of hippocampal lesions in rats relates to its hypothesized role in spatial learning. There has been, however, a considerable amount of research into the role of the hippocampus in other forms of learning, some of which relate more directly to the amnesic syndrome seen in humans with medial temporal lobe damage, and to experimental lesion effects in monkeys. Many of these studies suggest a role for the hippocampus in either short-term memory or in the relatively short-term storage of information required for the establishment of long-term memory.

In addition to the evidence from lesion experiments implicating a role for the hippocampus in learning and memory, recordings of the electrical activity of hippocampal neurons also suggests that the structure is particularly active during behaviors associated with learning, for example, the exploration of novel or complex environments or the repeated pairings of discrete sensory stimuli. Although the precise role of the hippocampus in learning and memory remains elusive, the accumulated evidence suggests that it will be an important structure in which to test theories of the biological mechanisms of learning.

Role of the Amygdala in Conditioned Emotional Responses

The amygdala is another important medial temporal lobe structure. Historically, it has been credited with a critical role in the generation of emotional behavior. This theory dates back to the pioneering work of Klüver and Bucy, who found that temporal lobe lesions (later restricted to amygdala) in monkeys produced a syndrome of bizarre behaviors all associated with inappropriate processing of emotional stimuli. More recently, research efforts have focused on the extent to which emotional behavior is learned, and there is a growing consensus that the amygdala is critically involved in emotional learning.

Investigations into the function of the amygdala in primates has also supported a role for this structure in learning and memory. Although some of these have confirmed a role for the amygdala in the detection of novelty of stimulus significance, others have proposed that by virtue of its anatomical connections, it is well designed to serve as an integrator of information from different sensory modalities. Indeed, lesions of the amygdala in monkeys severely impair the ability of the animals to learn a short-term recognition task that involves choosing an object by sight that they have never seen before, but have touched in the dark. As with the hippocampus, the precise role of the amygdala awaits definition, as does its importance in neural circuits, including other medial temporal and midline diencephalic structures.

Role of the Cerebellum and Brainstem in Conditioned Motor Responses

Since the early 1960s, the conditioned nictitating membrane response (NMR) in the rabbit has served as an effective model system for studying the neural mechanisms of simple learned motor responses. The study of simple forms of learning offers the advantage of allowing more precise quantification of the learned response and (theoretically) a reduction in the complexity of brain circuitry required to perform it. Once the neural mechanisms of simple learning have been elucidated, it will be possible to determine whether more complex forms of learning are elaborations of these basic, elemental changes.

The results of a series of experiments have suggested that a neural circuit consisting of brainstem nuclei and the cerebellum may be necessary and sufficient for producing learned eyeblink responses. Lesions restricted to the deep nuclei of the cerebellum produce complete and irreversible impairment of the conditioned NMR. Moreover, recording the electrical activity of neurons in the cerebellum indicates that at least some significant percentage of these cells change their pattern of activity during the learning of the conditioned NMR. Electrical stimulation of brainstem structures that send information to the cerebellum also can produce conditioned NMR, in the absence of any other stimuli.

As is the case with the investigations into the nature of hippocampal and amygdaloid involvement in learning and memory cited previously, studies of NMR circuitry have given us an exciting glimpse of where learning might occur, but not yet how it might. Two different lines of research have provided evidence of what changes might occur between neurons during learning. One of these lines has used an even simpler form of learning in a much simpler organism. The other has concentrated on the mechanisms of change in the nervous system that occur during activation of the brain without consideration of their behavioral relevance.

LEARNING AND NEURONAL PLASTICITY IN AN INVERTEBRATE

Some of the most impressive advances in the field have come from examinations of conditioned defensive responses in the marine mollusc *Aplysia*. Eric Kandel and associates at Columbia University have examined the cellular and molecular correlates of the conditioned gill and siphon withdrawal in *Aplysia* for more than 20 years. They have described an elegant system whereby learned increases in reflex responding produce increases in the strength of synaptic communication between identified neurons, whereas decreases in responding are associated with weakened synaptic communication.

Behavioral Responses of *Aplysia*

The learned responses are, of necessity, simple. *Aplysia* have a defensive reaction to tactile stimulation that involves the retraction of a fleshy spout (called the siphon) and the gill, both of which are used by the animal for respiration. The reflex shows both nonassociative and associative modulation. If the siphon is repeatedly stimulated mechanically (by a jet of seawater), the withdrawal reflex will habituate, so that after approximately 10 such stimuli, the *Aplysia* will no longer show any response to the tactile stimulus. If, in contrast, the tail is shocked, the animal will show both sensitization (by increasing the duration of a nonhabituated withdrawal) and dishabituation (the reinstatement of a habituated response). Furthermore, if the tail shock is repeatedly presented immediately after siphon stimulation (a Pavlovian conditioning paradigm), *Aplysia* will show an increase in the duration of the withdrawal response to siphon stimulation that is greater than that seen in sensitization. In other words, this incredibly simple animal, with only about 1000 neurons in its central nervous system, is capable of habituation, sensitization, and associative Pavlovian conditioning.

Changes in Neuronal Communication in *Aplysia*

Due in large part to the relative simplicity of *Aplysia*'s central nervous system, it has proven possible to determine the nature of the changes that occur during learning, in identified neurons known to participate in generating learned responses. Sensory neurons in the siphon form synaptic contacts with motor neurons responsible for siphon and gill withdrawal, that is, activation of these sensory neurons causes them to release chemical neurotransmitter, which is received by the motor neuron and causes it to fire an action potential, which in turn causes its target muscles to contract. E. R. Kandel has presented strong evidence that the sensory neuron to motor neuron contacts are modified during learning.

When habituation occurs, the strength of the response in the motor neuron elicited by activation of the sensory neuron decreases. In other words, the same stimulus given to the siphon produces the same response in the sensory neuron that, due to a decrease in the amount of neurotransmitter released, becomes unable to affect the motor neuron after repeated activation. By contrast, sensitization is associated with an increase in transmitter release from the sensory neuron, as a result of the modulatory action of the neurotransmitter serotonin, released by facilitatory interneurons by the sensitizing tail shock.

The neural mechanism for associative conditioning appears to be an elaboration of the mechanism for sensitization. Behaviorally, the difference between the two procedures is that a touch to the siphon precedes the tail shock only in the Pavlovian procedure. At the neuronal level, this means that siphon sensory neurons are active just before the release of serotonin by facilitatory interneurons. The result is an amplification of the mechanism by which sensitization enhances reflex responding to tactile stimulation.

LONG-TERM POTENTIATION: CHANGING THE STRENGTH OF NEURON-TO-NEURON COMMUNICATION

Is a change in the strength of synaptic connections the mechanism whereby learning occurs in mammals as well as in *Aplysia?* The question is more difficult to answer, because researchers do not have access to identified neurons that are unquestionably part of a neural circuit responsible for learning. The accumulated evidence does suggest, however, that certain brain regions are important for at least some forms of learning. A strategy that has shown great promise is to examine the mechanisms by which synapses change in these structures and then attempt to exploit that information to make inferences about the mechanisms of learning.

Evidence supporting the hypothesis that long-term potentiation is the mechanism of learning in mammals goes beyond surface similarities and comes in two categories. First, measurements made during several behavioral tasks indicate that increases in the size of the synaptic response correlate with learning. Moreover, the decay of long-term potentiation (LTP) of a period of weeks is highly correlated with forgetting, suggesting that LTP lasts as long as learning does. Second, pharmacological or genetic manipulations that block or attenuate LTP also block or attenuate learning. This does not prove a common mechanism, but as further investigations reveal more treatments that affect LTP and learning identically, the case becomes stronger.

Researchers are still a long way from developing a complete understanding of how experience changes the adult brain. Data from invertebrates, rodents, monkeys, and humans are, however, converging. These data suggest that learning and memory are processes that result from activity in specialized parts of the nervous system. Moreover, alterations in the strength of synaptic communication within networks of connected neurons can be induced, and this synaptic plasticity remains the best candidate mechanism for learning.

P. F. CHAPMAN

NEURAL NETWORK MODELS

Models containing networks of neuronlike elements have become prominent in psychology and its allied disciplines in both cognitive science and neurobehavioral science. Such models also have appeared under the headings of connectionist models and parallel distributed processing. In the area of cognition, networks have been used to explain phenomena as diverse as word recognition, categorization, visual pattern perception, coordinated motor action, and neurological disorders. In this regard, neural network models represent a dramatic departure from older theories that assume grammarlike manipulations of symbolic information. The nongrammatic and nonsymbolic features of neural networks also have made them suitable for explaining nonhuman learning and its neural underpinnings.

Neural networks are intended to produce a system of computation that is cooperative and self-organizing. Thus a neural network does not contain any explicit executive or supervisory subsystem. Behavior that appears to follow a rule, hypothesis, or strategy is supposed to emerge from the interactions among the elements, no one of which contains the rule, hypothesis, or strategy. Although network models have been inspired by the neuron, the bulk of the models have been constrained only weakly by the known architecture and functioning of real nervous systems. Stripped of their surplus meaning, neural networks are one type of quantitative model, subject to the conventional criteria for testing any model in psychology. The extensive use of computer simulations has required that these models be fully specified in terms of their own inner workings and their generation of outputs, thus yielding clear behavioral predictions.

BASIC FEATURES

The elements of a typical neural network can be described by two equations, namely an activation rule and a learning rule. The activation rule combines inputs to an element and generates an output level. The computations of a network entail the transmission of output activation levels from one element to the inputs of other elements. The learning rule alters the strengths of active inputs through variables called *connection weights*. The input level to the receiving element is usually the product of the received activation level and the current connection weight at the receiving element.

Linear Threshold Unit

The source of modern activation rules lies in the work of McCulloch and Pitts concerning the ability of neurons to act as logic gates. Figure 1 depicts a linear threshold unit. On the left side of the element are the input variables characterized as input activation levels (X_i) and weighted connections (V_i). Either variable can assume any real value. However, the activation levels are commonly assumed to be binary ($X_i = 0, 1$) and the weights fall between -1 and $+1$. The total input level at any moment

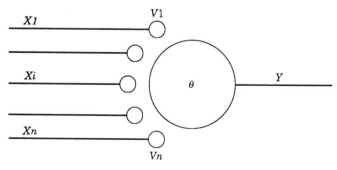

Figure 1. Linear threshold unit, in which X_i denotes input activation levels, V_i denotes connection weights, Θ denotes the threshold value, and Y denotes the output activation level.

of time is the sum of the active input weights ($\Sigma [V_i X_i]$). Like the input activations, the output of the unit is a binary level ($Y = 0, 1$). The activation of the output is determined by a comparison of the total input level with a threshold value (Θ) according to the following formula:

$$Y = 1 \text{ if } \Sigma (V_i X_i) > \Theta, \text{ otherwise } Y = 0.$$

By manipulating the connection weights or the threshold values, it is possible to produce common logic functions. For example, an *and* gate can be constructed in the following fashion. Assume that an element has two inputs (X_1, X_2), each with a connection weight of 0.50 ($V_1 = V_2 = 0.50$), and that the element's threshold is 0.75 ($\Theta = 0.75$). Under the McCulloch–Pitts activation rule, both inputs must be active ($X_1 = X_2 = 1$) for the total input level to exceed the threshold and thereby trigger the output (Y). The same element can be converted to an *or* gate by lowering the threshold to a value less than 0.50 or by raising the input weights to values greater than 0.75. Finally, for a complete logic system, a *not* operator can be constructed by inverting the activation rule so that when the total input level exceeds threshold, a unit that is otherwise on ($Y = 1$) will turn off ($Y = 0$). This inverse activation rule can be written as:

$$Y = 1 \text{ unless } \Sigma (V_i X_i) > \Theta, \text{ then } Y = 0.$$

Synaptic Facilitation

The source of learning rules for networks lies in an idea originally sketched by Hebb. In brief, he applied the ancient law of contiguity at a neural level and contended that synaptic transmission would undergo a gain in efficiency whenever presynaptic activity was contiguous with postsynaptic activity. Figure 2 shows an example of a Hebbian element. This Hebbian element has two input connections. One input (X_i), here called the "cue" input, has no initial connection weight and thus is unable to trigger the element. The other input (X_o), commonly called a "teacher" input, has a fixed, large weight ($V_o = 1$) that is capable of triggering the element and producing the "response" output. If there are simultaneous inputs, then the cue input will provide the presynaptic activity (X_i) and the teacher input will induce postsynaptic activity (Y). In mathematical terms, the change in connection weight (ΔV_i) is represented as a product of the two levels of activity. This learning rule can be written as $\Delta V_i = cX_iY$, where c is a rate parameter ($0 < c < 1$).

Although learning under the Hebbian rule depends strictly on the contiguity of activation levels, other rules assume that learning depends on the error in the ability of the cue's input weight to match the teacher's input. One of the most frequently used rules of this variety is known variously as the delta rule, the Rescorla–Wagner rule, the Widrow–Hoff rule, and the least-mean squares rule. When there are multiple, simultaneous cue inputs, this rule can be written as $\Delta V_i = c(V_oX_o - \Sigma [V_iX_i]) X_i$. Inspection of this rule reveals that when total input ($\Sigma [V_iX_i]$) differs greatly from the activation induced by the teacher input (V_oX_o), then the connection weight of each eligible input (ΔV_i) will change dramatically. Conversely, when the difference is small, the change will be small.

The error-correction rule is more complex than the Hebbian contiguity rule but has three key advantages in simulating associative learning, which are as follows:

1. *Self-Limiting Increments.* Whereas the contiguity rule produces connection weights that grow linearly, the error-correction rule is self-limiting. This feature reproduces the negative acceleration seen in most learning curves.

2. *Reversibility.* The contiguity rule produces only increments in learning, but the error-correction rule produces both increments and decrements. Specifically, in the contiguity rule, the absence of the teacher input (X_o) precludes any increments but has no decremental effect. However, for the error-correction rule, the absence of the teacher input means that the difference term becomes negative ($-\Sigma [V_iX_i]$), thus producing a decrement in the connection weight (V_i). In this way, the error-correction rule can track changes in the predictive value of a cue for the teacher input.

3. *Selectivity.* When there are multiple cues, the Hebbian contiguity rule is applied independently to each input. In contrast, the error-correction rule presupposes that a change in associative strength for each input depends on the net error over all the active inputs. For example, if one set of cues has already attained high weights, then the difference term ($V_oX_o - \Sigma [V_iX_i]$) will be near zero and thus will prevent additional concurrent cues from gaining weight. In this way, redundant cues will effectively be ignored. By the same token, when no one cue has a preexisting advantage, the total connection weight will be spread across the concurrent cues. In this way, an element can be "tuned" so that it will be triggered by only a certain configuration of inputs rather than any single input.

BASIC ARCHITECTURES

Although the individual elements provide the building blocks for a neural network, the architecture of their interconnections determines many of the emergent features of a network. There are two basic architectures that appear in many models, namely networks that contain multiple layers of elements and networks that feed their outputs back as inputs to the network.

Layered Networks

An example of a simple layered network is shown in Figure 3. The network has two inputs (A, B), each of which project to two elements (X, R). The X element that intervenes between the input events and the output element is known as a hidden element. This small network contains five modifiable connections, namely A-X, A-R, B-X, B-R, and X-R.

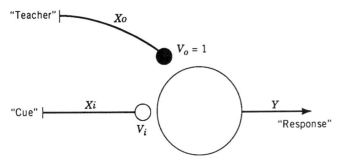

Figure 2. Hebbian adaptive unit, in which X_i denotes the cue input level, V_i denotes an adaptive connection weight, X_o denotes the teacher input level, V_o denotes the fixed connection weight, and Y denotes the response output level.

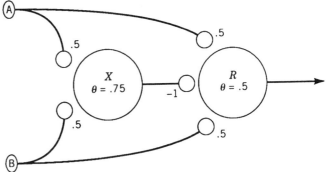

Figure 3. A layered network configured to obey the XOR rule.

Layered networks have proved crucial in resolving issues of stimulus representation and concept formation that have been intractable to conventional psychological theories and to single-layered network models. In particular, layered networks provide a basis for learning arbitrary mappings from stimulus input patterns to response output patterns. The key issue has concerned nonlinear mappings. In such mappings, the desired response to a combination of inputs is not an additive function of the responses to the separate inputs. For example, the simplist nonlinear mapping is the exclusive-OR (XOR) rule. The XOR rule requires a response to each of two inputs presented separately but not to their joint occurrence. For example, many people show XOR behavior in their taste preferences. A person may readily eat potatoes and readily eat licorice but refuse to eat licorice-flavored potatoes. If the separate stimulus–response mappings were strictly additive, licorice-flavored potatoes would be eaten with great pleasure.

It is possible to convert a nonlinear problem into a linear problem by postulating a special input for the joint occurrence of the basic stimulus inputs. However, when there is more than a handful of inputs, this tactic creates an explosion of special inputs. A more general solution is a learning mechanism that forms specialized encodings of joint inputs as the need arises. Layered networks have this ability. In brief, establishment of appropriate connection weights from the stimulus inputs to the hidden elements yields units specialized for particular combination of inputs. The connections between the hidden elements and the output elements provide the mapping of the specialized units to the appropriate response outputs.

The small network shown in Figure 3 is configured to display XOR behavior. In this configuration, the *A* input by itself cannot trigger the *X* element, because the *A-X* connection weight is less than the threshold of *X*, but the *A* input can trigger the *R* element, because its threshold is just low enough for the *A-R* connection to be effective. Likewise, the *B* input can only trigger the *R* unit. Thus the separate *A* and *B* inputs can each trigger the output of the network. However, as required by the XOR rule, the *A* and *B* inputs together will suppress an output. This is because the summed connection weights of the *A* and *B* inputs will trigger the *X* unit, and the *X* unit has a large negatively valued connection with the *R* element. Consequently, the joint occurrence of the *A* and *B* inputs cancels their individual positive connections with the *R* element.

Autoassociative Networks

An example of a small autoassociative network is shown in Figure 4. Each of five elements (*A, B, C, D, E*), receives one external input (*a, b, c, d, e*). These external inputs have fixed connections, each of which is capable of triggering an output from their respective elements. Furthermore, each element receives five recurrent inputs, one from each element's output including its own. For example, as shown in Figure 4, the *C* element has five connections, designated as *Ac, Bc, Cc, Dc,* and *Ec*. These connections are modifiable and operate according to the same learning rules as a single element or layered network. In brief, whenever an output and an input are both active, an effective connection can arise at their intersection.

Among other things, autoassociative networks can perform three functions that are of particular interest in psychology:

1. *Pattern Completion.* If a set of interconnections has been well established in an autoassociative network, then only a portion of original inputs can retrieve the entire set of outputs. For example, suppose that, for the network in Figure 4, the inputs a and e had repeatedly presented. As a consequence, four interconnections would been established, namely *Aa, Ae, Ea,* and *Ee,* which are located in four corners of the matrix of intersections. Subsequently, the a input by itself would trigger both the *A* and *E* outputs through the *Aa* and

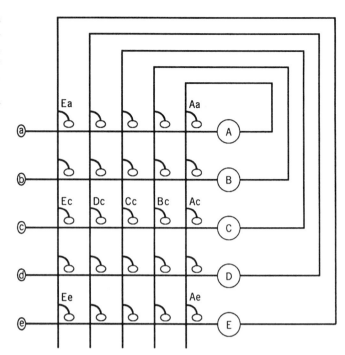

Figure 4. An autoassociative network, in which all output levels can be associated with input levels.

Ae connections. Likewise, the e input would trigger both outputs through the *Ea* and *Ee* connections.

2. *Noise Tolerance.*

3. *Superimposed Storage.* Autoassociative networks can store a large number of input sets. This feature allows for the retrieval of both prototypic patterns and specific exemplars. For example, McClelland and Rumelhart showed that a network with 24 units and 552 potential interconnections could store and reliably retrieve three different prototypical patterns each based on 50 different exemplars. They also showed that the pattern for at least one particular exemplar also could be retrieved when the network was presented with a subset of inputs corresponding to the exemplar's name tag. In a similar fashion, Kohonen demonstrated that a network containing 3024 elements could store and retrieve the digitized photographs of 100 different faces.

CURRENT STATUS

At present, it is difficult to predict where and how much solid achievement will occur through the use of neural network models. Much of the first flush of enthusiasm has passed. A more sober view of such models is appearing as they are tested against each other and against more traditional theories in different research areas. In the short term, the clearest trend is a diversification in the features of the elements as neural networks are applied in different areas. On the one hand, where neural network modeling is being merged with models of actual neuron functioning, the elements are becoming more faithful to the chemical, electrical, and structural features of neurons. On the other hand, where neural network modeling is being applied to cognitive phenomena, the elements are themselves depicted as having semantic or symbolic content. For example, an individual element might be triggered only by a specific letter or word.

LEARNING
MEMORY RETRIEVAL PROCESSES
NEURAL MECHANISMS OF LEARNING

E. J. KEHOE

NEUROCHEMISTRY

Communication between nerve cells in the brain and in the peripheral nervous system involves both electrical and chemical processes. Once stimulated, ionic changes occur within the intracellular and extracellular fluid of the cell, which result in the propagation of a nerve impulse or action potential. The electrical charge travels along the dendrite and subsequently the axon of the neuron, until it reaches the terminal portion of the axonal process. Swellings or boutons, situated at the terminal portion of the axon as well as along the axon itself, contain synaptic vesicles within which the chemical transmitter is stored. The cytoplasm of each bouton also contains the enzymes involved in the synthesis and degradation of the transmitter. Each neuron thus has the capability of producing only one neurotransmitter substance.

The arrival of the action potential at the axonal terminal triggers changes that culminate in the release of the neurotransmitter from the vesicle (exocytosis). Once released, the neurotransmitter diffuses across the synaptic cleft to stimulate receptors situated on the dendrites or soma of adjoining cells. In contrast to the presynaptic neuron, which contains only a single type of neurotransmitter, a variety of receptors sensitive to different types of transmitters may be present on the postsynaptic neuron. In addition, receptors present on the presynaptic neuron (autoreceptors) are stimulated, resulting in altered synthesis of the neurotransmitter substance. The action of the transmitter substance is terminated by enzymatic degradation and by the reuptake of the transmitter into the axon terminal.

Characterization of endogenous substances as neurotransmitters requires that several criteria be met. It is necessary, of course, to demonstrate that the neurotransmitter candidate be present in nerve terminals and be released on stimulation of the neuron. In addition, enzymes for synthesizing and catabolizing the substance should be present in the vicinity of the nerve ending. It should also be possible to mimic the effects of the putative neurotransmitter by exogenous substances, and drugs that potentiate or block synaptic responses should simulate or antagonize the effects of endogenously or exogenously administered materials. Several substances appearing in the brain have met the criteria established and are thought to act as junctional transmitters. These include acetylcholine, dopamine, norepinephrine, 5-hydroxytryptamine (serotonin), gamma aminobutyric acid (GABA), glutamic acid, and glycine. Additionally, evidence has accumulated that suggests that neuroactive peptides might also act as neurotransmitters in the brain. In the peripheral nervous system it seems that the major neurotransmitters are acetylcholine and epinephrine.

Although the various neurotransmitters appear throughout the brain, the specific pathways for some of the transmitters have been mapped rather extensively.

Considerable attention has been devoted to determining the contribution of various neurotransmitters to behavior, and to assessing the neurochemical concomitants of aberrant behaviors.

Pharmacological studies in humans, together with the analyses of transmitter metabolites in blood, urine, and cerebral spinal fluid, as well as in brains of suicide victims, have implicated neurotransmitter involvement in the mediation of a variety of psychological disorders. The elaboration of the mechanisms subserving such disorders has been instrumental in the development of new therapeutic agents that may be useful in the management of such illnesses.

BRAIN
CENTRAL NERVOUS SYSTEM
ENDORPHINS/ENKEPHALINS
PSYCHOPHARMACOLOGY

H. ANISMAN

NEUROLINGUISTICS

Broadly defined, neurolinguistics is a theory of language and brain. A formal theory of neurolinguistics is developing through interaction in the fields of neurology, psychology, and linguistics. Larnendella urged a simultaneous integration of three distinct perspectives in the formal theory of language and brain: *overt speech and language behavior, covert neuroanatomy and neurophysiology,* and the *functional organization of speech and language systems* as a contingent reality. He emphasized the need to incorporate into neurolinguistic theory implications of nonverbal communication systems of human behavior, of cultural and individual variables developed through environmental modification, and of cognitive information processing and a theory of human cognition.

Neurolinguistics may be described as a study of how information is received through the senses, processed in the neurons and neural pathways of the brain (including the language areas), and expressed in language and behaviors. The most salient sensory modalities for information processing into language are the visual, auditory, and kinesthetic modalities. Optimally, information is received and expressed in all channels with consistency and equal efficiency.

Information processing is concerned with two types of symbols: *theoretical,* related to language, and *qualitative.* Processing the different types of symbols is believed to depend on functions occurring within the left and right hemispheres of the brain. Theoretical symbols such as visual linguistic elements (e.g., the written word), auditory linguistic elements (e.g., the spoken word), visual quantitative elements (e.g., written numbers), and auditory quantitative elements (e.g., spoken numbers) are processed primarily in the left hemisphere of the brain.

Qualitative symbols of a sensory nature, such as sounds, taste, or pictures, are associated with cultural codes or the meanings received from nonverbal expressions, role playing, social distance, or time constraints, and are processed primarily in the right side of the brain. The bilateral symmetry of the brain provides that sights and sounds bringing in information from the external environment will be processed by both hemispheres together.

Neurolinguistic evidence is contributing to the understanding of communication, cognition, culture, and their practical applications. In addition to the study of disordered brain function, experimental techniques have been applied to speech and language processing in individuals who are considered normal. Research has indicated varying responses of individuals who are considered normal in the sensory modalities of vision and audition.

Electrophysiological experiments using auditory and visual stimuli show that auditory responses are significantly greater in the left hemisphere, and visual responses are significantly greater in the right hemisphere.

The right ear outperforms the left ear in hearing and identifying competing digits—a reflection of left-brain dominance for language. A clear left-ear advantage was found for melodies and environmental sounds. The left ear has direct access to the right hemisphere, and the right brain is dominant for music, chords, and nonverbal sounds.

Individuals tend to look up and away when a question has been posed and the answer must be retrieved. The same neurological pathways and structures seem to be used for both external stimulation in a given sensory modality and internal fantasies in that same modality.

Human beings who are considered normal are all endowed with essentially equivalent sensory organs and structures, both anatomically and physiologically. Each individual learns to depend on one sensory system or another as a means of perceiving and understanding the world. The Sensory Modality Checklist assesses an individual's preferred sensory modality for learning and self-expression.

Neuro-Linguistic Programming (NLP) is the study of the structure of subjective experience, or how individuals perceive and understand the world. Neuro-Linguistic Programming is a trademark name for a model of techniques and strategies for interpersonal communication based on some elements of transformational grammar and on the identification of preferred sensory representations for learning and self-expression.

Bandler and Grinder identified the process indicating that the predicates people use are representative of their preferred sensory modalities. An individual who highly values the visual system uses visual process words and predicates (verbs, adjectives, adverbs) such as "clear," "bright," "see," "perspective."

Bandler and Grinder also describe the nonverbal and physiological cues that people unconsciously use. Eye movements, breathing patterns, body postures, and body types give clues to an individual's preferred sensory modality.

N. A. HAYNIE

NEUROMUSCULAR DISORDERS

Neuromuscular disorders refer generally to disease processes that affect motor neurons, including axons and the innervation of the motor neurons with muscle fibers. A great many neuromuscular diseases are inherited, although it is common to find no genetic link in some types of neuromuscular diseases. When the disorder is transmitted genetically, the mother typically is the carrier. At onset of symptoms, neuromuscular disease manifests itself by an asymmetrical weakness with intact sensation. As the disease progresses the symmetry of wasting becomes apparent, with each side of the body manifesting similar rates of muscle atrophy.

It is easiest to conceptualize neuromuscular disorders and diseases according to the level and degree of motor neuron involvement. Upper motor neuron neuromuscular diseases may include progressive spastic bulbar paralysis, in which there is damage to the intracerebral corticobulbar and corticospinal tracts of a bilateral nature. Demyelinating diseases such as multiple sclerosis (MS) or amyotrophic lateral sclerosis (ALS), as well as cerebrovascular disease, can contribute to the type of neuromuscular disease. Owing to the bulbar involvement, speaking and swallowing may be affected and occasionally there is a lack of emotional control. Death usually occurs within 2 to 3 years as a result of intercurrent illness.

Often ALS affects both upper and lower motor neuron tracts. Females are usually less affected than males; victims tend to be middle aged (35 to 55 years). Wasting of the muscles of the hand is frequently a first symptom. Further wasting of the extremities occurs over time, followed in turn by spasticity. Survival time varies from 1 to 5 years. No known etiology exists for ALS. Lower motor neuron diseases include Werdnig-Hoffmann disease and Oppenheim's disease; progressive neuropathic muscular atrophy might be included in this category. These diseases occur primarily in infants, with the exception of the Oppenheim's disease, which usually occurs in adolescence. Survival time varies from 1 to 2 years, with a normal life expectancy not unusual for Dejerine-Sottas disease, which can also be included here.

Other neuromuscular diseases occurring with some frequency include myasthenia gravis and Duchenne's muscular dystrophy. Myasthenia gravis results from an acetylcholine deficiency due to an impairment of the synaptic transmission. Onset usually occurs in the third decade of life. The early symptoms include ptosis of the eyelids and difficulty swallowing, breathing, and speaking; the peripheral muscles become involved. Muscular dystrophy of the Duchenne's type is inherited as an X-linked recessive gene. The female carries the gene and the disease is manifested in the male. Weakness does not occur until the third, fourth, or even fifth year of life. Once muscle weakness occurs, there is progressive deterioration until death, which may not take place until late in the second decade.

Treatment of the neuromuscular diseases focuses on avoiding infection and controlling the spasticity. Psychological intervention should center around counseling and the maintenance of patient support mechanisms.

CENTRAL NERVOUS SYSTEM DISORDERS
MULTIPLE SCLEROSIS
PSYCHOPHYSIOLOGY

G. W. HYND

NEUROPSYCHOLOGICAL ASSESSMENT

Neuropsychological assessment is the evaluation of the various psychological functions governed by the brain. As with all psychological evaluations, neuropsychological assessment involves a process of answering clinical questions and responding to unique clinical situations that vary somewhat from patient to patient and across practice settings.

OVERVIEW

A wide variety of cognitive and intellectual abilities are typically assessed during a neuropsychological evaluation. Attention and concentration; learning and memory; sensory–perceptual abilities; speech and language abilities (sometimes including academic skills such as reading, spelling, and math); visuospatial and visuoconstructional skills; overall intelligence; executive functions (such as abstraction; reasoning; problem solving; behavioral self-monitoring; response discrimination, selection, and inhibition; and mental-processing efficiency and flexibility); and psychomotor speed, strength, and coordination all would be addressed in some fashion. Included are measures of sensory–perceptual input, the two principal central processing systems (verbal–language and nonverbal–visuospatial), executive organization and planning, and response output (motor abilities). In addition, underlying all the evaluations of these abilities, attention, concentration, arousal, and motivation also are measured. Although this list of cognitive functions might be organized or labeled differently by different neuropsychological schools of thought, these behaviors would generally be evaluated in most comprehensive neuropsychological evaluations. Frequently, aspects of psychological functioning (psychopathology, behavioral adjustment, and interpersonal issues) also are included in a neuropsychological evaluation.

Neuropsychological evaluation differs from other neurodiagnostic procedures such as computed tomography (CT) or magnetic resonance imaging (MRI) scans that examine the anatomical structure of the brain. With a neuropsychological evaluation, cognitive capabilities, from which inferences about the brain and its function can be derived, are examined. In this regard it is similar to neurodiagnostic tests that assess other functional capabilities of the brain. For example, the electroencephalogram (EEG) and event-related potentials (ERPs) measure the electrical activity of the brain; and positron-emission tomography (PET) scans or single-photon–emission tomography (SPECT) scans assess anatomical patterns of cerebral blood flow or metabolic activity. Among these, the neuropsychological evaluation is the only neurodiagnostic procedure that can evaluate how a person functions cognitively and behaviorally in real life.

Neuropsychologists must be aware of the anatomic considerations and behavioral sequelae associated with various etiological conditions in the evaluation and interpretation of data. For example, some cognitive functions depend on well-defined anatomic structures (e.g., lower-level sensory–motor skills and even higher level perception, such as recognition of familiar faces located in the sensory–motor strip and bilateral basal occipital–temporal regions, respectively). Other abilities (e.g., new learning, abstract reasoning, and speed of information processing) are diffusely organized or rely on complex interacting cortical and subcortical networks. The effects of brain injury can result not only in deficits in various cognitive abilities but also in the emergence of new behaviors or symptoms such as perseverations, unilateral neglect, or confabulations.

Lezak has suggested that mastery of four areas is essential to competent neuropsychological practice: (a) clinical psychotherapeutic and assessment skills; (b) psychometrics; (c) neuroanatomy and functional neuroanatomy; and (d) neuropathologies and their behavioral effects. A fifth essential knowledge area is a theoretical and understanding of how these four content areas interrelate and interact. This latter knowledge base might best be viewed as a overarching model or knowledge of brain–behavior relationships that is applicable across settings and diagnoses. It is only within this conceptual framework that the neuropsychologist can integrate the historical information, medical material, and current cognitive abilities; provide an accurate description of a person's cognitive strengths and deficits; arrive at correct diagnoses (etiological conditions and anatomic localization); outline the implications of the results for that person's functional living potential; formulate prognostications; and make clinically useful recommendations.

THE EVALUATION PROCESS

There are three general reasons for conducting a neuropsychological evaluation: differential diagnosis, patient care, and research. The first step in the assessment process is defining the questions that need to be answered to meet particular clinical needs. Next, the neuropsychologist must determine what information is required and how best to obtain it. Neuropsychological testing might be only one of several methods used. In fact, a psychological test is simply a sample of behavior obtained under controlled or standardized conditions. Other methods of obtaining information about a person's past and present behavioral capabilities include the case history, clinical interview, mental status examination, direct behavioral observations, and reports of other people who are involved with the patient (spouse, children, friends, employer, and other professionals such as nursing staff). If testing is to be conducted, then test selection must be competently addressed. Structuring the testing session, administration procedures, scoring, and clerical issues also are important factors in the overall competent completion of the data-collection phase of the evaluation process. Following data collection come the interpretation and application phases of the evaluation process.

Two major fixed batteries employed in current clinical neuropsychological assessment practice, the Halstead–Reitan Neuropsychological Test Battery and the Luria–Nebraska Neuropsychological Test Battery. In a fixed battery approach the issue of test selection is moot, because the set of tests is predetermined. The philosophy is to use a set of tests that has previously been developed, organized, and validated to assess the clinically important or relevant aspects of brain-related behaviors. Fixed battery approaches are typically psychometrically and quantitatively oriented. Their advantage is that they are comprehensive and standardized. However, they are generally quite time-consuming and inflexible. Futhermore, fixed battery approaches are incapable of being easily adapted as new knowledge emerges regarding brain–behavior relationships and cognitive functions.

Flexible battery approaches to assessment are more numerous and varied. Neuropsychologists variously describe themselves as clinically oriented, flexible–adjustive, hypothesis testing, or process oriented. However, underlying all such distinctions is the philosophy that assessments should be designed uniquely for each patient (or type of patient) and should answer particular referral questions. Although quantitative information is certainly used, an emphasis also is placed on qualitative information, such as how patients pass or fail particular tasks (process approach). The advantages are that assessments are more focused and relevant to individual patients and particular clinical questions and, consequently, are less time-consuming. New knowledge and better designed or normed

tests can easily be incorporated into the assessment. With a flexible approach, evaluations are not standardized across patients, assessments, or facilities. Specific problems or deficits may be missed because they were not a focus of the evaluation.

PRACTICE SETTINGS

As the field of clinical neuropsychology has grown, practice settings have diversified. Neuropsychological evaluations historically have been used to help determine lesion location in neurology and neurosurgical settings. That function has decreased in importance with the advent of such neuroradiological procedures as the CT and MRI scans. However, evaluations remain a frequently requested procedure to help identify the pattern and severity of deficits associated with various brain lesions or neurological conditions. They also play an important role in diagnosis of conditions such as Alzheimer's disease or acquired immunodeficiency syndrome (AIDS) dementia complex. Neuropsychological evaluations are often an important factor in helping medical staff, patients, and families make decisions about treatment issues and placement after hospitalization.

Neuropsychological evaluations also play a role in the differential diagnosis between neurological and psychiatric conditions that may appear clinically similar (e.g., dementia versus a pseudodementia secondary to depression or anxiety) but that have different prognostic implications and require divergent treatments. Finally, neuropsychological evaluation are increasing in forensic settings where they document the present or absence of behavioral impairments secondary to injuries (personal injury or medical malpractice cases) or in helping to evaluate issues of diminished capacity and competency.

SUMMARY

The field of clinical neuropsychology has become increasingly prominent over the past several decades, with the neuropsychological evaluation as its core. The unique contribution of the neuropsychological evaluation is that it is the only available diagnostic procedure that can assess brain–behavior relationships in terms of real-life behaviors.

Various approaches to assessment have been espoused and evaluations, are being requested in a wide variety of settings to meet a spectrum of clinical needs. Evaluations are useful in differential diagnosis among similarly appearing neurological disorders or between psychiatric and neurologic conditions. Neuropsychological assessments often serve as the nucleus of rehabilitation and educational intervention plans and are instrumental in the evaluation of their effectiveness.

ALZHEIMER'S DISEASE
COMPUTED TOMOGRAPHY
DEMENTIA
ELECTROENCEPHALOGRAPHY
HALSTEAD–REITAN BATTERY
LOBOTOMY
LURIA–NEBRASKA NEUROPSYCHOLOGICAL BATTERY
NEUROTRANSMITTERS
PSEUDODEMENTIA
SENILE PSYCHOSIS

R. D. VANDERPLOEG

NEUROPSYCHOLOGICAL DEVELOPMENT

The initial lure of developmental neuropsychology was the belief that children are neurologically simpler than adults and would provide clearer data as to the relationship between brain function and behavior. This turned out to be a simplistic view, and the study of the developing nervous system raised questions, such as: Why does the young brain appear to be so flexible in compensating for injury? How do environmental factors influence the developing brain? How do functional and structural asymmetries develop, and what are the behavioral implications of these? Before such questions can be answered, however, it is important to get an overview of the process of the neural developmental process.

NEURAL DEVELOPMENT

The growth of the brain and nervous system can be described as a series of changes that occur at particular ages. Although some changes are rapid and dramatic, others are more gradual. Regardless of the rapidity of change, however, these changes occur in a generally fixed sequence. The first of these stages of brain development is cell migration, during which nerve cells are formed in the inner or ventricular lining of the brain. After formation, they migrate from the inner lining through the layers that already exist, eventually to form a new outer layer. This means that structures such as the cortex actually mature from the inner to the outer surfaces.

During the cell migration stage, axonal growth manifests itself as axons begin to sprout from the migrating cells. Axons are the elongated neural processes that carry information away from the cell body to be received by other cells down the line. Each axon has a specific target it must reach if the neuron is to be functional. How each axon locates its target is still an unsolved question, although electrical or chemical gradients or preexisting physical structures may provide the needed map or blueprint to guide this targeted growth process.

The growth of dendrites is the next major change in the system. This growth does not start until after the cell reaches its final location after migration. The process of dendritic growth is much slower than axonal growth and involves much more branching and elaboration. At some stages of dendritic growth, there appears to be an overabundance of dendritic branches. Some of these excess or unused branches are eventually lost in a process referred to as *pruning*.

Although most people tend to think that neural development has finished after about 2 years of age, growth continues well beyond this point. Epstein suggested that brain growth occurs at irregular intervals, called growth spurts. Such spurts occur at around 3 to 18 months and 2 to 4 years, 6 to 8 years, 10 to 12 years, and 14 to 16 years. Except for the first (rather long) spurt, during which brain weight increases by about 30%, each subsequent growth spurt increases brain mass by 5 to 10%. It is tempting to try to correlate these growth spurts with overt changes in development. Thus it may be significant that the first four episodes of rapid brain growth seem to coincide with the four principal stages of cognitive development according to Piaget.

Other changes in the neural system continue well beyond adolescence. Thus, although myelination begins prenatally and is well advanced by 15 years of age, myelin continues to develop as late as age 60. However, all of the later changes are not associated with growth. An important factor in the later stages of neuropsychological development is cell losses. For instance, the area of the occipital cortex that receives projections from the fovea of the eye contains about 46 million neurons per gram of tissue in a 20-year-old person. In an 80-year-old person, however, the neuronal density is reduced by nearly 50, to only 24 million neurons per gram of tissue. This cell loss is believed to account for some of the loss of visual acuity in older individuals. Similar losses in other areas of the brain might also be expected to affect normal functioning.

ENVIRONMENTAL AND EXPERIENTIAL EFFECTS

The nervous system is affected by the environment and the activities of the developing organism. The general principle that describes the interaction between the environment and the developing nervous system

is functional validation. According to this principle, some form of stimulation or neural activity is needed to "validate" the usefulness of sections of the nervous system. In the absence of such validation, these units will cease to function and will not continue their growth and maturation.

Experimentally, the easiest way to observe how stimulation and activity affect brain function involves variation of an animal's sensory experience followed by direct monitoring of changes in the cortical areas that are used to process information from that sensory modality. For instance, a number of studies have looked at the effects of restricting visual experience on the growth of the occipital cortex, which is the primary processing site for visual information. In a classic series of studies, Hubel and Wiesel showed that in young kittens whose eyes had not yet opened, the general response patterns of the cells of the occipital cortex were similar to those of the adult (although somewhat sluggish and easily fatigued). They next showed that for the cells to continue in their normal functioning they needed stimulation (functional validation). They next reared cats for several months without any patterned visual stimulation. Although they found that there was no effect on the retina or lower visual centers, the occipital cortex showed massive disturbances. Many of the neural cells in this region showed disturbed or abnormal functions. Anatomically they have fewer and shorter dendrites and 70% fewer synapses than found in normally reared cats. Some of these abnormalities do correct themselves over time, when the animals are restored to normal visual stimulation.

The ability of restricted experience to disrupt normal function is reduced in older animals. If an animal has normal visual experience during the first few months of life, and then is reared for the same amount of time without visual stimulation, the degree of abnormality observed is much less. This suggests that there is some critical period during which stimulation is needed for normal and continuing neural development of the affected areas of the brain. More recent experiments suggest that these results from vision studies can be generalized to other sensory systems and hence to other areas of the brain. These results lead to the conclusion that although the basic functional pattern is innately determined and available early in the developmental process for normal function to be maintained adequate stimulation of the appropriate neural systems is necessary.

Environmental effects, in the form of traumas that affect the developing fetus (which might include the influence of toxic agents, mechanical injury, or chemical imbalances), can cause dramatic disturbances in neural development.

Contrasted to visible disruptions in neural development, less pronounced pathological conditions only show up in terms of behavioral changes, such as learning disabilities, reduced intelligence, personality disturbances, motor insufficiencies, and so forth. Many of these behavioral indicators of disrupted neuropsychological development are quite subtle. In these instances, atypical behaviors may serve as soft signs, which are nonphysiological indicators of disturbed neuropsychological development.

ASYMMETRY AND NEUROPSYCHOLOGICAL DEVELOPMENT

One way to illustrate the nature of neuropsychological development is to focus on a specific research area. As an example of how developmental issues and neuropsychological issues interact, consider functional asymmetries between the left and right sides of the body.

The differences in the functional properties of the two cerebral hemispheres are well known (e.g., language function is predominantly in the left hemisphere and spatial function is predominantly in the right hemisphere). These differences may come about because of differences in the rate of development of the two hemispheres. One suggestion by Corballis is that there is a left-to-right maturational gradient during development. This means that the left hemisphere develops earlier than the right, at least during the time when language functions are being acquired, and the right hemisphere catches up later. According to this theory, the left hemisphere gains control over language functions, not because it is intrinsically specialized for them, but simply because it is more developed and dominant when language is learned. In addition, there is the suggestion that if the left hemisphere is damaged, there is enough plasticity for the right hemisphere to take over language function, but only if this situation occurs early in development. If the right hemisphere has developed beyond some critical stage for language acquisition, this form of compensation would not be possible.

One persistent idea in neuropsychology is that the functional properties of the nervous system become more fixed and specialized over time. In the context of cerebral asymmetry this means that more evidence of lateralization should be expected with increasing age. This prediction has some experimental support, but the situation is complex. In general, research on the development of speech functioning after damage to the left hemisphere suggests that there are three critical age ranges: younger than 1 year of age, 1 to 5 years of age, and older than 5 years of age. If the damage occurs before 1 year of age, disruption of speech is quite extensive. If damage occurs between 1 and 5 years of age, the recovery of speech is usually possible, with the right hemisphere reorganizing to take over most of the functions lost by the left. Injuries to the left hemisphere after 5 years of age, however, show no recovery of function. Presumably, all of the right hemisphere functions are now set and fixed, and there is not enough plasticity left to replace the functions lost by the other hemisphere.

As is the case of many aspects of neuropsychological development, in the case of handedness there are indications that a bias toward a particular functional pattern exists quite early in development. There also is evidence that there is a gradual loss of plasticity with age, with a greater degree of specialization or asymmetry in older individuals. At birth there are indications that functional asymmetry correlated with handedness exists. This can be seen, for example, in the tonic neck reflex in infants, in which the head is turned to one side and the arm and leg on that side are extended. This reflex, which is limited to infants younger than 20 weeks of age, shows a strong bias to the right side for the majority of subjects tested. This demonstrates an early functional bias toward the right.

Hand preference continues to evolve with age. For tasks such as reaching, handedness is not reliable before 6 months of age and gradually becomes more stable and consistent up to about the age of 8 years. Thus handedness is much more variable in preschool-aged individuals than in adolescents or young adults. Attempts to change handedness demonstrate the loss of plasticity of function with increasing age. Although the success of changing handedness is not high at any age, there is a precipitous drop in the number of successful changes of handedness after about age 9 years.

In the previous example handedness was noted as a typical function dependent on the usual sequence of events found in neuropsychological development. The general pattern that emerges begins with an innate or early predisposition toward a particular behavioral pattern (e.g., toward right-handedness). Disruption of the normal developmental pattern can cause changes in the observed behavior (the emergence of left-handedness). The functional specificity becomes more set with chronological age (consistent handedness begins to emerge) and there is a gradual loss in functional plasticity (handedness becomes set and relatively unchangeable). This same sequence of stages (initial developmental predisposition, period of environmental vulnerability, period of plasticity, and fixed functional properties) appears in neuropsychological development, whether they be neurological structures, complex patterns of cerebral organization, or functional manifestations of behavior.

BRAIN TRAUMA
BRAIN LATERALITY
HANDEDNESS
NEONATAL DEVELOPMENT
NEURAL NETWORKS MODEL
NEUROCHEMISTRY
SPEECH DISORDERS
SPLIT-BRAIN RESEARCH

S. Coren

NEUROPSYCHOLOGY

Neuropsychology is the clinical and experimental field devoted to the study, understanding, assessment, and treatment of behaviors directly related to the function of the brain. Although the field works most commonly with individuals who have brains that are in some way abnormal, neuropsychology also looks at individual differences within persons who are considered normal due to differences in brain functions or organization. Neuropsychology is a branching field between psychology and neurology, and is closely related to behavioral neurology. Many individuals in the field are trained by neurologists in medical settings, rather than receiving their primary training in psychology.

HISTORICAL DEVELOPMENT

The relationship between brain function and behavior was recognized as early as 3500 B.C. in the Edwin Smith Papyrus, with some evidence suggesting that this relationship had been observed since the Upper Paleolithic period. Although ancient theorists agreed that human thought and intellectual abilities were found in the brain, there was disagreement over which brain structures were responsible for intellect. Not until the nineteenth century did modern concepts about brain function begin to develop.

Gall was the first major investigator to suggest that specific psychological functions are localized in specific organs or areas of the brain a theory that was given credibility by the French surgeon Paul Broca. On the basis of autopsies completed on two patients who had lost the ability to use expressive speech, Broca reported that he had found the brain area where motor speech is localized. Hailed by many as a major advance, Broca's work led to countless investigations attempting to localize specific psychological functions.

Inspite of the popularity of localization theories in the nineteenth century, many scientists rejected them. Flourens mounted a series of attacks, advocating instead an equipotentialist theory whereby intellectual and psychological skills are a product of the brain as a whole, rather than of specific localized areas. In the early twentieth century many neurologists adopted an equipotential viewpoint. Although these theorists agreed that basic motor and sensory functions are localized, they believed that higher intellectual functions were products of the brain as a whole. Any injury to the brain, no matter where located, will impair these higher intellectual skills.

Both theories have had a substantial impact on the assessment of brain impairment in clinical neuropsychology. Individuals advocating an equipotential viewpoint have concentrated on finding a test or tests that can measure the underlying higher intellectual skills impaired in all forms of brain injury. Psychologists assuming a localization position have concentrated on finding tests that measure each of the psychological skills mediated by the brain, thus allowing one to assess not only the psychological skills so mediated, but also localization in specific areas of the brain.

ROLE OF THE NEUROPSYCHOLOGISTS

Since the 1960s, neuropsychology has become an increasingly specialized field, practiced by individuals with training beyond that usually given to a clinical psychologist. Once involved only in discriminating brain-injured patients from other patients, the psychologist is now becoming more involved in precisely defining the nature and extent of brain damage, assessing treatment programs, determining patient prognosis, and planning rehabilitation programs.

New X-ray techniques visualize brain atrophy without pain or significant threat to the patient's life. Thus many discriminations once asked of the psychologist have become the province of the neuroradiologist. This, many have argued, suggests that the psychologist should perform a different role in neurodiagnostics.

One alternate role involves a detailed analysis of the brain syndrome as expressed in the individual patient. This includes the evaluation of such skills as general intelligence, perceptual-motor functioning, language, flexibility, speed of response, attention, and concentration.

ORIENTATIONS OF NEUROPSYCHOLOGY

Adoption of this new role has caused significant questions to arise concerning the relationship of neuropsychology to traditional training models in psychology. Some neuropsychologists are coming to recognize themselves as belonging to a subspecialty, much in the same way that clinical psychology is recognized as a subspecialty. Alternatively, others see neuropsychology (especially that aspect of the field dealing with assessment and treatment) as a subspecialty of clinical psychology. In this model, training in clinical psychology is supplemented with additional specialty training in neuropsychology.

Individuals from the different orientations may also see populations and practice in ways that are very different. Psychologists trained in the more neurological tradition most often see patients with clear deficits in brain function, especially those with aphasia because of the emphasis many prominent behavioral neurologists place on language disorders. Their examinations tend to be highly qualitative, based on how the patient does something rather than on scores achieved on more traditional psychological tests. Test procedures may be standardized but are often modified to meet the perceived needs of the patient and the impressions of the examiner.

In contrast, other psychologists may adopt a more quantitative approach to these problems, drawing on the rich history of quantitative psychometric assessment. These approaches may vary from the single-test approach now relatively in eclipse to the test battery approach, which has gained increasing popularity. These approaches emphasize establishing normative guidelines for test scores and allowing an objective analysis of the deficits shown by the patient, rather than relying on a purely intuitive assessment. However, the approach still demands a knowledgeable and skillful clinician to be effective, since patterns of test scores can be changed by a large number of variables including the area of the brain injured, the speed at which the injury occurred, the process causing the injury, the premorbid intellectual level, degree of recovery, and numerous other considerations.

ISSUES IN NEURODIAGNOSTIC TESTING

There are a number of significant issues in neuropsychology, including individual versus standardized testing, quantitative versus qualitative testing, single tests versus test batteries, the role of the clinical psychologist, and rehabilitation.

Individual Versus Standardized Testing

Proponents of the individualized approach generally advocate choosing tests for a patient on the basis of the referral question, initial historical information, and initial and subsequent clinical impressions. Neuropsychologists using this approach argue that an individualized examination allows the clinician to concentrate the testing efforts in those areas of greatest deficit for the patient. Theoretically, this approach allows the

clinician to arrive at a detailed evaluation of the patient in the smallest amount of time. Individuals not using the approach point out that the accuracy of the procedure is highly dependent on the skill of the individual clinician. If the correct tests are given on the basis of the clinician's judgment, then a highly effective examination may result. However, if the tests selected fail to measure the patient's deficits appropriately, then the examination will be inadequate at best and misleading at worst. In addition, opponents contend, this approach does not allow for the collection of systematic data across patients and disorders; as a result, the conclusions that can be reached from series of patients, or at least the scientific validation of those conclusions, are limited.

Because of these limitations, many clinicians use a standard test or test battery selected to represent what they see as the major dimensions deemed relevant in the evaluation of the suspected brain dysfunction. All patients are evaluated on these dimensions. The standardized approach has limitations. First, the more comprehensive the examination, the longer it will take; some of the more comprehensive test batteries may take 1 day or more to complete. Also, a standardized test battery may fail to address areas significant for a given patient but not for patients in general.

An effective compromise for dealing with the limitations of a standardized examination is to combine this approach with more flexible additional testing.

Quantitative Versus Qualitative Testing

The quantitative approach attempts to reduce all test performance to a set of numbers that can be used in comparisons with performance by groups considered to be normal and impaired normative groups. On the basis of such comparisons, a diagnostic decision may be made. Proponents of the quantitative approach emphasize its reliance on objective indices that are reproducible across investigators and clinicians, and its emphasis on research results gathered under controlled conditions.

The qualitative approach emphasizes the way in which a person attempts to complete a test rather than the individual's score. This allows the clinician to understand the underlying processes that cause a patient's performance. Once these underlying processes are understood, the clinician can identify the source of the brain dysfunction and its importance to the individual's recovery and rehabilitation treatment.

These approaches need not be mutually exclusive. A combination of these procedures is used most often by effective practicing clinicians.

Single Tests Versus Test Batteries

Traditionally, many psychologists have used only a single test in the evaluation of brain-related disorders. It is now recognized, however, that a single-test approach is generally not effective. Thus many clinicians have chosen a multi-test approach, with decisions based on the patient's overall performance. Ideally, the tests in a test battery represent different abilities affected in brain damage.

The use of test batteries also allows for more complex interpretive approaches. A test that represents right-hemisphere performance may be compared with a test that represents left-hemisphere performance. Verbal tests and tests of right-side motor and sensory functions are considered representative of left-hemisphere performance; nonverbal tests and left-side motor and sensory tests are considered representative of right-hemisphere performance.

With test batteries, a pattern analysis of test results may also be employed. Pattern analysis may represent one of the most powerful tools available to the clinical neuropsychologist in more difficult, subtle cases of organic brain syndrome.

The variety of tests employed for neuropsychological evaluation are quite extensive, whether single tests or batteries of tests are employed. Among the single tests, some of which are representative of the others include the Bender–Gestalt, Memory for Designs, Token Test, Benton

Visual Retention Test, subtests from the Wechsler Adult Intelligence Scale, the Boston Diagnostic Aphasia Examination, the Purdue Pegboard, the Stroop Color and Word Test, and the Wisconsin Card Sort Test.

A number of test batteries also exist, but most are used in only one or a relatively few settings. The two batteries that have attracted the most widespread attention are the Halstead–Reitan Neuropsychological Battery and the Luria–Nebraska Neuropsychological Battery. The Halstead–Reitan is the older of the two batteries, having been in use since the 1950s. More so than anything else, this battery was probably responsible for the increased popularity of clinical neuropsychology.

The Luria–Nebraska Neuropsychological Battery is a newer test, first introduced in 1978. This battery was a departure from standard tests in that it attempted to meld the qualitative, behavioral, and neurological approach of Luria, with the standardized and quantitative approach of Reitan. The test emerged as a unique approach to neuropsychological assessment and raised a considerable amount of controversy. In spite of this controversy it has become one of the major tests employed in the field and is currently taught in an increasing number of programs. Interpretation is done through pattern analysis, augmented by observations on the way in which the patient performed the items. These qualitative observations are currently being organized into a frequency evaluation to formalize these findings as well. The strength of the test lies in the integration of these approaches, as well as the research opportunities offered by the quantitative scores.

Rehabilitation

The design and implementation of rehabilitation programs based on neuropsychological findings is still in its infancy. There is little research in the area, although there has been increasing interest in the problems of the patient with cerebrovascular disorders and the patient with head trauma. Much has been done for the physically handicapped individual with peripheral disorders. The work of people like Diller, Ben-Yishay, Gertsman, Goodkin, Gordon, and Weinberger points to the potential high level of aid that can be offered by cognitive retraining techniques even in individuals with relatively serious disorders.

THEORETICAL CONSIDERATIONS

There are major theoretical schools within neuropsychology. Localizationist and equipotential positions form the basis for the major schools of thought.

Equipotential Theory

Equipotential theory, as mentioned previously, involves the assumption that all areas of the brain make an equal contribution to overall intellectual function. Thus the particular area of brain injury is unimportant; only the amount of brain injury determines the behavioral deficit. Many equipotential theorists place a strong emphasis on deficits in abstract or symbolic ability, which are presumed to accompany all forms of brain damage.

The equipotential view has heavily influenced the development of psychological tests. Although tests have been found on which brain-injured persons reliably do more poorly than persons who are not brain-injured, the tests have not been discriminating enough for day-to-day clinical work.

Localization Theory

Localization theory assumes that each area within the brain is responsible for specific psychological skills. Thus *where* an individual is injured becomes the primary concern of the organic brain assessment. Extent of injury is important only insofar as a larger injury will involve more areas of the brain and thus disrupt more skills. However, similarly sized lesions in different parts of the brain produce significantly discrepant effects. In evaluating an individual patient, a psychologist working from this theory must recognize that few injuries are truly limited to a specific area. Tumors, for example, may cause increased intracranial pressure, thus impairing areas of the brain far removed from the tumor itself. Head traumas disrupt functions in the hemisphere that is hit as well as in the opposite hemisphere, which is thrust against the skull. Stroke victims often have impaired cerebral circulation in general. In almost any injury there is likely to be impairment in many skills in areas removed from the injury, especially during the acute phases of the disorder.

Alternatives

Psychological research has not wholly supported either the localization or the equipotential theory. The equipotential theory cannot account for the specific, limited deficits that occur in some patients without any general impairment in abstract abilities or other similar skills. Localization theories are hard pressed to explain why a specific deficit, such as dysgraphia (inability to write), may occur with deficits almost anywhere in the left hemisphere and with many injuries in the right hemisphere.

Unable to accept either theory, many have looked toward an alternative. The creation of one such model has been credited to J. Hughlings Jackson, an English neurologist. Jackson observed that most psychological functions are not unitary abilities but are made up of more basic skills. According to Jackson, although very basic skills can be localized, all observable behavior is a complex interaction of numerous basic skills, so that the brain as a whole is involved in most actual behavior. Thus his theory combines both localization and equipotential viewpoints to form a theory that can account for the experimental evidence generated to support both views.

Jackson's views can be seen in their most developed form in the theories of the Russian neuropsychologist A. R. Luria. In Luria's view, all behavior is based on functional systems, patterns of interaction among the localized areas of the brain necessary to produce a given behavior. Any injury that interrupts any part of a functional system will disrupt all behaviors based on that system. Consequently, highly complex intellectual skills such as the ability to abstract are most sensitive to brain injury, because a great many functional systems must be involved to produce the behavior.

FACTORS AFFECTING NEUROPSYCHOLOGICAL ASSESSMENT

Neuropsychological assessment is aimed at the delineation of changes that occur due to brain changes. Ideally, conclusions from these tests should be independent of factors that are not aspects of brain function. Unfortunately, this is not always the case, as a variety of outside factors may influence test results. These can include a whole host of variables such as age, education, physical disorders, intelligence, and emotional status.

Age

Tests sensitive to brain injury also tend to be highly sensitive to the effects of aging. Some believe that age effects are caused by changes in the brain that accompany aging, thus providing a theoretical basis for the observed sensitivity of neuropsychological tests. This sensitivity makes it important for the neuropsychologist to consider age effects in analyzing test performance. It is also important to look closely at the results for patterns of test performance suggesting brain injury that may be masked by age-corrected scores. The patterns seen with various conditions are not altered by age.

Neuropsychological test performance of children is highly dependent on age. In addition, injuries to children have significantly different effects depending on age. Boll has observed that, in general, the earlier the injury, the more severe the neuropsychological effects.

Another significant problem in children is separating problems caused by delayed development and mental retardation from those caused by actual brain injury. In many cases the distinction cannot be made, and in practice the distinction is often not important in terms of treatment.

Education

The role of educational levels in test results has been controversial. On inspection, it is clear that many tests require a minimum level of education. The educational effects being observed may be related to general IQ, since individuals who go on to each succeeding level of education tend to have a higher average IQ. This relationship, as well as the effects of educational level on commonly used tests, needs more extensive research.

Physical Disorders

Peripheral disorders that impair motor movement, especially the movement of the hands and mouth, can in many instances seriously affect the accuracy and validity of many neuropsychological tests. In such patients it is often necessary to substitute tests requiring little motor coordination for many of the tests used in neuropsychology.

Intelligence

Individuals with lower intelligence levels perform less adequately on neuropsychological tests than do individuals whose level of intelligence is considered to be normal. Interpretation of the results must be adjusted on the basis of the patient's expected level of performance.

Emotional Problems

A major problem in the assessment of organic brain dysfunction has been separating deficits caused by brain injury from deficits caused by functional disorders. In many cases the level of performance exhibited by an individual with a chronic functional disorder is indistinguishable from the performance of the patient whose disorder is organic. Thus alternative diagnostic processes often must be used in making this discrimination.

One important difference between brain-injured and schizophrenic patients is the consistency of performance. Organic patients are highly consistent in the areas in which they have a deficit. Functional patients, in contrast, may show highly variable performance. Another important strategy is examining the test results for patterns of performance consistent with brain injury. Although the schizophrenic may show impaired performance, rarely will that performance suggest a specific organic disorder, as it should in the case of the true organic brain syndrome patient. A final strategy attempts to minimize the performance deficit in functional patients by scheduling shorter testing sessions to maximize performance motivation and minimize fatigue. In addition, changes in the patient's medication may also improve performance significantly.

EXPERIMENTAL NEUROPSYCHOLOGY

Clinical neuropsychology has received considerable attention, but an equally important area is experimental neuropsychology, which deals with both human and animal models and attempts to delineate the relationship between the brain and behavior. To the extent that the research involves humans, there is only a fine line between experimental human neuropsychology and clinical neuropsychology. However, the goals of the two areas are significantly different: Although clinical neuropsychology attempts to find rules and procedures effective in working with large numbers of patients, often with ill-defined (and undefinable) disorders, experimental human neuropsychology works with patients having precisely determined and restricted disorders to further our knowledge of brain–behavior relationships.

APHASIA
BRAIN INJURIES

BRAIN LATERALITY
CENTRAL NERVOUS SYSTEM DISORDERS
HALSTEAD–REITAN NEUROPSYCHOLOGICAL BATTERY
LURIA–NEBRASKA NEUROPSYCHOLOGICAL BATTERY
ORGANIC BRAIN SYNDROME

C. J. GOLDEN

NEUROSURGERY

Archaeological ruins offer ancient evidence of therapeutic intervention aimed at the nervous system. Trephining—the boring and scraping of the skull to release "evil spirits"—in fact relieved intracranial pressure caused by tumors, hemorrhages, and skull fractures. In a craniotomy, an extension of trephining, a flap of skull is removed entirely, exposing the fibrous coverings of the brain (meninges) overlying the outermost brain structures (cerebral cortex) and enabling visual examination of cortical structures and excision of pathological tissue. In 1947, the first stereotaxic device for humans was developed, allowing neurosurgery on deeper brain structures without serious damage to outer structures. This device locates hidden brain structures by using three-dimensional anatomical maps (atlases) and X-rayed reference points in the brain (such as the pineal gland or cerebral ventricles). The stereotax can be used for electrical stimulation at various tissue levels to test function before removing tissue, for testing the effect of temporarily halting tissue activity, and for facilitating circumscribed lesioning with electrolytic or radio frequency currents.

Several procedures are available for diagnostic use before surgery, including X rays of the skull (radiograph), of blood supply in the brain or spinal cord (angiograph, venograph), of ventricles in the brain (pneumoencephalograph, ventriculograph), or of spaces in and around the spinal cord (myelograph). Spinal (lumbar) punctures permit the collection of cerebrospinal fluid (CSF), evaluation of intracerebral pressure, and injection of contrast medium, and are necessary for one or more of the previously mentioned techniques. These procedures may be painful or risky. Computerized axial tomography (CAT) scanning, a 2-minute procedure with little risk or discomfort, reduces the need for more perilous tests. Other techniques to assess cerebral blood flow and glucose utilization provide access to ongoing regional brain function. In positron emission tomography (PET), the brain absorbs and utilizes radioactively tagged glucose, which emits particles (positrons) affecting the passage of X rays from a scanning device. The electroencephalogram produces waveforms from greatly amplified signals of electrical activity generated by neural firing in the cortex; abnormal waveforms indicate dysfunction and possible cellular pathology.

Most neurosurgery is for treatment of pathological conditions. Neurosurgery performed to ameliorate symptoms where no pathology is found is called functional. Functional neurosurgery is controversial and includes surgery for epilepsy with no apparent scar tissue, alleviation of motor disturbances with no manifest pathology, interruption of pain transmission, and surgery to control behavior and emotion.

Techniques used in psychosurgery (damage to nonpathological brain tissue to alter behavior or emotion) developed from animal experiments, observations of people with head injuries, and results of brain operations to control seizures and pain. Use of psychosurgery peaked in the 1950s and was performed throughout the world. Since then its popularity has declined, although removal of circumscribed nuclei in the brain is still performed.

BRAIN INJURIES
COMPUTERIZED TOMOGRAPHY
PSYCHOSURGERY

B. E. THORN

NEUROTOXIC SUBSTANCES

Neurotoxins are substances that are poisonous or destructive to nerve tissue. The damage may be produced selectively to certain areas of the brain or spinal cord. One of the most common sources of neurotoxins is industrial compounds.

Metals. Among the metals that are recognized neurotoxins are *lead, mercury,* and *manganese.* Industrial settings in which lead exposure can occur include ore smelters, foundries, battery factories, and paint plants. It is suspected that lead selectively affects motor neurons of the spinal cord. Lead has been suspected to cause mental impairment in urban children, but cause and effect cannot be definitely established.

Mercury. Mercury-containing fungicides for use on seed grains have caused major outbreaks of mercury poisoning. Mercuric chloride wastes, which appear as methyl mercury in fish and shellfish, led to serious outbreaks of mercury poisoning in Japan. The initial symptoms include cerebellar disorders, visual impairment, deafness, and mental disturbance.

Manganese. In the United States, manganese intoxication has been recognized among workers in mining, ore crushing, and ferromanganese alloy industries. Exposure primarily is from inhalation of dust particles or fumes. Toxicity may develop from 4 months to 15 years after onset of exposure. Acute mental disorder is often the initial symptom in manganese miners: They become irritable, emotionally unstable, and often have visual and auditory hallucinations. Other symptoms include apathy, memory impairment, progressive problems with walking and motor control, and speech disturbances.

Solvents. Chronic exposure to some industrial solvents may cause nerve damage with characteristic patterns. Some harmful solvents are n-hexane, Methyl-n-butyl ketone (MBK), and toluene. In cases of industrial exposure, symptoms begin as early as 2 months after exposure. Muscle weakness first develops in the lower extremities and then progresses to the upper limbs. Sensitivity to touch has also been noted with sensations of numbness. Relatively mild muscle atrophy occurs, with reflexes affected in the legs. The chemical causes nerve degeneration as shown in slowing of motor and sensory nerve function.

Methyl-n-butyl ketone (MBK) has been used for years as a solvent and cleaning agent. Contamination can occur through inhalation or skin contact. Tingling sensations often appear first in the hands and feet. Motor involvement occurs as foot drop or weaknesses in the hands and fingers. No clinical involvement of the central nervous system (CNS) or cranial nerves has been found. After cessation of exposure, neurological deficits disappear within 5 to 16 months.

Toluene is used as a cleaning agent, in insect sprays, and in rubber and ink solvents. It can be inhaled or absorbed through the skin. Acute effects include headache, nausea, and poor coordination.

Organic chemicals. Acrylamide is used in the manufacture of paper and as a waterproofing agent. Nervous system disorder has been noted in persons exposed to acrylamide dust. The disorder develops over several weeks with symptoms of sweating, limb weakness, and weight loss. There is evidence of nerve degeneration, but regeneration and recovery take place in from 2 to 12 months.

Carbon disulfide is used in the manufacture of rayon. The effects of poisoning include loss of vision, muscle tremors, and mild neuropathy.

Gases. Among gases, carbon monoxide and methyl chloride have neurotoxic effects. *Carbon monoxide* poisoning is a serious problem in the United States, accounting for 50% of fatal intoxications. Chronic carbon monoxide exposure has led to symptoms similar to Parkinsonism with muscle tremor, facial immobility, and rigidity. Peripheral nerve functions may also be affected by carbon monoxide. *Methyl chloride* is used in the production of foamed plastics. Acute exposure can produce drowsiness, blurred vision, confusion, unsteady gait, slurred speech, double vision, and convulsions. In most cases the effects are transient. Recovery may require up to 3 months.

Insecticides. There are 39 separate compounds employed as insecticides which account for large numbers of poisonings among agricultural and industrial workers. Peripheral neuropathies can be produced by *malathion, methylparathion,* and *mipafox.* After recovery from acute poisoning, CNS effects may persist for months; they consist of impaired memory, depression, or psychotic behavior. Survivors of acute *diazinon* poisoning had evidence of neuropathy with nerve degeneration in the extremities.

PSYCHOPHYSIOLOGY

J. L. ANDREASSI

NEUROTRANSMITTERS

A typical neuron consists of a soma or cell body, dendrites, and an axon. At the end of the axon there are even smaller extensions called terminal buttons, or end feet. These end feet make functional contact with other neurons, and the point of functional contact between neurons is called the *synapse.* The synapse is a narrow gap, and transmission of a nerve impulse across the synapse is nearly always chemical; the chemical messenger is called a *neurotransmitter.* Neurotransmitters are manufactured in the cell body and stored in tiny sacs called *synaptic vesicles.*

The chemical nature of synaptic transmission was demonstrated by Otto Loewi. Loewi isolated a frog's heart with an attached nerve. Stimulation of the nerve caused the heart's rate to decrease, and when Loewi extracted some of the fluid around the heart and applied it to a second heart that had not been electrically stimulated, the fluid made the second heart slow. He concluded that stimulation of the nerve to the first heart had released a chemical at the synapse between the nerve and the heart, and it was this chemical that carried the message to the heart to slow down. Because he had stimulated the vagus nerve, he called the mysterious chemical *Vagusstoff.* It is now called acetylcholine (ACh).

When a neurotransmitter such as ACh filters across the synapse, it comes into contact with receptors on the neuron on the other side. The neuron across the synapse is called the *postsynaptic neuron,* and the receptors are found mostly on its dendrites and soma. The transmitter substance causes either some depolarization (excitation) of the postsynaptic neuron or some hyperpolarization (inhibition).

Whether the postsynaptic neuron generates an action potential (passes on the message) depends on the total of influences on it from presynaptic neurons. That is, each neuron may have hundreds of synapses on it, some bringing excitatory messages and others bringing inhibitory messages. The neuron integrates all these influences and either does or does not produce an action potential.

If the neurotransmitter stayed around in the synapse for any length of time, it would reduce the number of messages that could be passed from one neuron to another. Thus, almost as soon as it is released, the transmitter substance is inactivated. In the nervous system, the most common means of inactivation is *reuptake,* by which the neurotransmitter is taken back into the presynaptic neuron. The other method of inactivation is used for only ACh and is called *enzymatic degradation.* In this case acetylcholinesterase (AChE) breaks the ACh molecule into two parts, neither of which has the action of the whole molecule.

Because it was the first transmitter substance discovered and because of where it is found, ACh is probably the best known of the neurotransmitters. Among other places, it is found in the brain and the spinal cord, and it is the chemical that carries messages from the motor nerves to the skeletal muscles. Studies of the brains of people who have died after having Alzheimer's disease have revealed an enormous depletion of ACh, particularly in the neural areas thought to have something to do with memory.

The brain uses dozens of neurotransmitters. For many years, it was believed that each neuron released only one particular neurotransmitter from all its end feet. It is now known that most neurons release two or three transmitters, and some may release as many as five or six.

The three major categories of neurotransmitters are biogenic amines, amino acids, and peptides. Acetylcholine is an example of a biogenic amine. Other important biogenic amines are dopamine, norepinephrine, and serotonin. Dopamine has been implicated in two brain disorders: schizophrenia and Parkinson's disease. In the case of Parkinson's disease, cells die in a brain area called the *substantia nigra.* Because the nigral cells make dopamine and send it to a part of the brain controlling motor activities, the person begins to develop characteristic symptoms such as tremor at rest and a lack of movement. Replacement therapy—giving a person drugs to increase the amount of dopamine in the brain—works for a time, but the disease is progressive. One of the main treatments is L-dopa.

Norepinephrine (also called *noradrenaline*) is the transmitter substance at the neuromuscular junctions in the sympathetic nervous system, and it also is found at many places in the brain. A decreased amount of norepinephrine and/or serotonin is believed to be responsible for depression. Drugs used to treat depression increase either norepinephrine, serotonin, or both.

ACETYLCHOLINESTERASE
ALZHEIMER'S DISEASE
HUNTINGTON'S CHOREA
NEUROCHEMISTRY
PARKINSON'S DISEASE

B. M. THORNE

NOISE EFFECTS

Noise is defined as unwanted sound. Its intensity is measured in decibels (dB). Zero dB is defined as the weakest noise that a person with normal hearing can just barely detect in quiet surroundings; 55 dB is equivalent to light traffic sounds, and 120 dB to jet takeoff from 200 feet away. Most behavioral studies use a modified dB scale, called the *dBA scale,* devised to approximate perceived loudness. This scale assigns higher weights to high-frequency sounds, since they are perceived as louder than low-frequency sounds of equal sound pressure.

Noise pollution is a worrisome problem in the United States. The Environmental Protection Agency (EPA) has estimated that more than 70 million Americans live in neighborhoods noisy enough to be annoying and to interfere with communication and sleep. More than 50% of production workers are exposed to workplace noise loud enough to damage hearing.

Noise is by definition unwanted and therefore frustrating and tension-inducing. As a stressor, it alters the functioning of cardiovascular, endocrine, respiratory, and digestive systems, and is also suspected of having damaging effects on mental health.

The hearing loss effects of noise are well established. The EPA estimates that 1 out of every 10 Americans is exposed to noise levels of sufficient intensity and duration to create permanent hearing losses. Hearing losses do not hurt and are not immediately apparent, but even minor hearing impairments seem to enhance susceptibility to further injury in the middle and late years.

The consequences of noise on performance cannot be easily predicted. They depend on the noise, the performance, the meaning of the sound, and the social context of the person performing. If people have clear warning of the need to react and receive easily visible cues, loud noise shows little or no overall effects on their work. In general, novel or unusual noises are more bothersome than familiar noise. However, familiar noises louder than 95 dBA—especially if unpredictable, uncontrollable, and

intermittent—are disruptive. Typically, noise leads to variable performance—moments of inefficiency interspersed with normal and compensatory spurts of efficient performance. The lapses make workers more accident prone.

In academic settings, adverse effects have been documented repeatedly by well-controlled studies that take into account the socioeconomic and racial characteristics of the participants and use comparison groups. Among the effects of noisy homes and schools are impairment of auditory and visual discrimination, reading and visual–motor skills, overall scholastic achievement, and of persistence in the face of frustration. One explanation for these effects is that noise disrupts the teaching–learning process, resulting eventually in cumulative deficits. Some investigators believe that the stressful effects of noise are ameliorated when people have accurate expectations about or (at least perceived) control over the noise.

Noise levels influence people's social conduct, as well. A number of experimental studies find that individuals exposed to noise tend to be less helpful than those not exposed. Sheldon Cohen has suggested that noise causes subjects to focus their attention on salient aspects of the situation and fail to notice interpersonal cues. Alternatively, decreases in helping might result from feelings of anger or frustration.

STRESS

L. L. DAVIDOFF

NONCONFORMING PERSONALITY

People placed in the category of nonconforming personality are diagnosed primarily in terms of society's values and their degree of conformity with the prevailing cultural context. Relevant factors may also include personal discomfort and difficulties with relationships, but of primary importance is some aspect of conflict with the person's social network, employment, and means of coping with stress. The label identifies behavior that is clearly at variance with accepted social norms but is not totally unacceptable. A value judgment on the net effect of the behavior is a significant criterion for the label.

Characteristics of these individuals include superficial charm, generally good intelligence, an absence of irrational thinking of a psychotic nature, and a lack of nervousness of a neurotic type. An outward facade of normality hides an underlying disturbance in maintaining good relationships at critical life endeavors like school, work, and family. When the disturbance reaches a critical level, various aspects of the social system intervene. At the extreme end, criminal legal sanctions may be applied. Most frequently, however, these people change schools, jobs, and mates in a never-ending effort to justify their belief system.

Treatment is rarely initiated by such individuals. Rather, the social system forces them to change. The treatment approach that stands the greatest success is based on social learning theory and behavior modification.

PERSONALITY DISORDERS

R. C. MARVIT

NONDIRECTIVE PSYCHOANALYSIS

This approach to psychotherapy is a blend of traditional psychoanalysis and client-centered therapy. It retains the principal conceptions of psychoanalytic clinical theory (resistance, regression, transference, and catharsis), but the therapist remains nondirective by being neutral and impersonal while relying primarily on interpretation as the therapeutic tool. The therapist strives to be nonauthoritarian, tries to express high regard for the patient's individuality and autonomy, and gives the patient maximum feasible independence in treatment.

This system of therapy was developed by I. H. Paul, who obtained training first in client-centered therapy and then in psychoanalysis. He was able to adopt client-centered attitudes and to reduce or eliminate psychoanalytic procedures of interrogating, probing, confronting, and diagnosing.

Treatment carried out on an individual basis may take from 2 to 4 years. Candidates for treatment must be capable of self-inquiry, reflection, and introspection. Since persons undergoing nondirective psychoanalysis should not be passive and submissive where the therapist is concerned, it is vital that the patient freely choose and actively decide whether to enter this kind of treatment.

CLIENT-CENTERED PSYCHOTHERAPY
PSYCHOTHERAPY

V. RAIMY

NONPARAMETRIC STATISTICAL TESTS

Nonparametric statistical methods are based on weaker assumptions about data than standard parametric procedures rely on.

ADVANTAGES AND COSTS OF NONPARAMETRIC STATISTICS

There are certain trade-offs involved in the use of nonparametric statistical tests rather than parametric tests. The major motivation for the use of nonparametric methods is a reluctance to make the assumptions necessary for the use of parametric procedures. A secondary motivation for the use of nonparametric statistical tests by some investigators is that some (although certainly not all) of these procedures are computationally quite simple and easy to conduct.

There are, however, several disadvantages or costs associated with the use of a nonparametric test. First, the null hypothesis tested generally will not be exactly the same as that tested by the "corresponding" parametric test. The null hypothesis for the independent groups t-test is that the means of the two populations are equal. The null hypothesis for the median test or the Mann–Whitney test, each of which might be applied to the same data to determine whether the two groups of scores "differ significantly from one another," is that the two populations are identical. This suggests that the finding of a significant difference could result from some unknown combination of differences in central tendency, variability, and symmetry. Nonparametric tests may also be insensitive to certain kinds of differences between the populations.

A second major cost is that nonparametric tests will tend to have relatively low statistical power compared to the standard parametric tests. The power of a statistical test is defined as the probability of rejecting the null hypothesis when the null hypothesis is false. Nonparametric tests generally will require larger sample sizes in order to achieve the same statistical power as parametric tests. If the assumptions of the parametric tests are more or less met by the data under consideration, these tests should probably be used.

No simple prescription can be applied to tell us exactly when nonparametric tests should be used. To make the optimal choice in a given situation, the investigator must be aware of the characteristics of the data and the available parametric and nonparametric tests.

RATIONALES FOR AND SOME EXAMPLES OF NONPARAMETRIC TESTS

In most nonparametric statistical tests, the original scores or observations are replaced by another variable containing less information. An important class of nonparametric tests employs the ordinal properties of the data. Another important class of tests employs only information about whether an observation is above or below some fixed value such as the median.

Yet another class of tests is based on the frequency of occurrence of "runs" in the data. A *run* is a series of events of one type occurring together as part of an ordered sequence of events. The ordering can occur temporally or can be based on the magnitudes of scores. A study of runs can be useful in deciding on the randomness or nonrandomness of sequences of observations.

Although there are a great many nonparametric tests that can be applied in various situations, only a few of the more commonly encountered tests are described briefly.

Sign Test for Matched Groups

In contrast to the parametric t-test for two matched differences, which employs the actual values of the paired differences, the sign test uses only the sign of the differences. The aim is to determine whether there is a preponderance of either sign, and the null hypothesis tested is that the probability of occurrence of a plus is the same as that of a minus.

Median Tests for Independent and Matched Groups

The median tests involve the comparison of several samples on the basis of deviations from the median. The null hypothesis tested is that the different populations from which the samples are drawn are identical. Forms of the median test exist for both independent and matched groups.

Mann–Whitney Test for Two Independent Groups

The Mann–Whitney test uses the ranks of observations to test hypotheses about the two populations from which the observations are sampled.

Wilcox Test for Matched Groups

The Wilcox test employs the ranks of the absolute values of the differences between members of the matched pairs. It is a good alternative to the correlated t-test.

Kruskal–Wallis Analysis of Variance by Ranks

This test can be considered a generalization of the Mann-Whitney test to more than two independent samples. The null hypothesis is that the k independent samples of size $n_1, . . . , n_k$ are sampled from identical populations.

Friedman Test for Matched Groups

The Friedman test can be considered a generalization of the Wilcox test to more than two groups. The test represents a good alternative to the parametric repeated measures analysis of variance.

PARAMETRIC STATISTICAL TESTS
STATISTICS IN PSYCHOLOGY

A. D. WELL

NONPROFESSIONALS IN MENTAL HEALTH

In 1961, the Joint Commission on Mental Illness and Health suggested that nonmedical personnel, including nonprofessionals, be accepted as having a role in service delivery. Although nonprofessionals had been used in the mental health fields for many years, particularly as aides in mental hospitals, the Commission's report marked the beginning of a dramatic increase in their deployment.

Nonprofessionals are people who provide direct human services but who do not hold an academic degree in the professional field in which they are working. Many different types of nonprofessionals are included in this definition, and various terms have been used in the literature to identify them. One of the more complete classification systems includes five categories. *Community caretakers* are individuals such as police and clergy, who provide essential community services. *Paraprofessionals* are paid middle-level mental health workers who have titles such as psychiatric aide, child care worker, or ward attendant. Such individuals may receive brief training that prepares them for a circumscribed role, or extensive preparation that allows them to function in positions of considerable scope and responsibility. The largest group of nonprofessionals is the *volunteers,* who donate their time without pay. *Self-help nonprofessionals* are generally laypeople who come together to create a mutual support system to meet their own needs, such as participants in Alcoholics Anonymous and Synanon, the drug rehabilitation program. Finally, the *natural nonprofessionals* are indigenous helpers whose position and interpersonal skill lead others to seek them out for various kinds of support. Among these five types of nonprofessionals, the most widely used in the mental health system have been the paraprofessionals and volunteers.

There are a number of reasons for the acceptance of nonprofessionals in the mental health fields. Probably the most important is the recognition that there is a shortage of professionally trained helpers and that this shortage is unlikely to be remedied in the near future. In addition, the distribution of mental health professionals is uneven and has resulted in inequities in service delivery, particularly with respect to race, social class, and geography. Nonprofessionals are often willing to work in places and with populations that professionals find relatively unattractive. Many professionals have begun to realize that the qualities that enable one person to be helpful to another are not the exclusive property of those with academic credentials.

Nonprofessionals have performed a number of different activities that vary with respect to scope and the degree of specialized skill required. Volunteers with minimal training and supervision have frequently served as companions to hospitalized mental patients. Nonprofessionals may also be trained to perform specific tasks, such as administering and scoring psychological tests, that assist professionals in their activities. Sometimes nonprofessionals are extensively trained to take on responsibilities very similar to those traditionally performed by professionals.

The attractiveness of nonprofessionals arises not only from their abundance and willingness to do things professionals tend to avoid, but also from several assets they are assumed to possess. Often nonprofessionals bring to their work great enthusiasm and high expectations for change, which can raise the morale of staff and patients. Although the nonprofessionals' lack of extensive training may be a limitation, it may also leave them with greater flexibility and willingness to innovate than professionals. When nonprofessionals are recruited from the population to be served, their understanding of the viewpoints and lifestyle of the people they are trying to help can be a great advantage. Also, when social distance between helper and helped is reduced, helpers are often perceived as more approachable.

There is good evidence that nonprofessionals of various types have been able to stimulate withdrawn hospitalized mental patients. Although there are studies indicating the effectiveness of nonprofessionals in providing crisis intervention, preventing delinquency, improving behavior problems in children, and treating mild behavior problems in college students, insufficient sound empirical research has accumulated to draw firm conclusions about most of these activities.

EFFECTIVENESS COMPONENTS OF PSYCHOTHERAPY
HUMAN SERVICES
MENTAL HEALTH PROGRAMS

S. G. FISHER

NONVERBAL BEHAVIOR

Nonverbal behavior is of interest because it involves nonlinguistic transmission of information between people. Nonverbal communication may include mass communication by such means as television, art, and graphics of various kinds. The analysis of nonverbal behavior and communication concerns visual, auditory, and tactile channels of face-to-face interaction. Most encounters in everyday life involve several channels at the same time; for instance, a mother in a store rebuking her child for taking candy from a shelf may point to the objects, make sharp voice tones, and shake her finger in a "no-no" signal.

Scientists and practitioners have long been aware of the importance of nonverbal behavior. Much of this interest has related to emotion, stemming from Charles Darwin's *The expression of the emotions in man and animals.* Sigmund Freud eloquently observed, "He that has eyes to see and ears to hear may convince himself that no mortal can keep a secret. If his lips are silent, he chatters with his finger-tips; betrayal oozes out of him at every pore." However, the amount of empirical research was not large until the 1970s and 1980s, when recording technology and rating procedures had reached refinement. Methods for nonverbal behavioral research now range from the social to the physiological, and include descriptive systems and measures of individual differences in sending and receiving cognitive and emotional information.

The visual channel for nonverbal communication includes appearance, distance, gestures, posture, facial expression, and eye contact. It is common for people all over the world to provide cues for status and beliefs by their clothing, hairstyle, and body decoration. Gender, age, group affiliation, and individual identity are displayed for others to recognize and differentiate quickly.

Behavioral use of space, sometimes called *proxemics,* varies across individuals and cultures. For instance, Arabic and Latin American people tend to stand much closer to each other in conversation than Northern Europeans, and within the North American culture, friends stand closer than strangers.

The body language of gestures, movement, and posture (sometimes called *kinesics*) is an important nonverbal signal. Early in life, children are taught in the United States to wave bye-bye, and adolescents have learned many nonverbal ways to express themselves, ranging from friendly handshakes to obscene insults. For example, in an extensive study of 25 gestures in 40 localities in various European countries, Desmond Morris and coworkers found that thumbing the nose was used extensively as a sign of mockery, but the ear touch or the ring made by the thumb and forefinger had several different meanings, depending on the locality.

The majority of research studies on visual aspects of nonverbal communication have been concerned with facial expression of emotion. Using reliable rating techniques with photographs, Ekman and others have demonstrated that six basic emotions are recognized widely across cultures: happiness, sadness, surprise, fear, anger, and disgust. A variety of studies have shown that emotional expressions are related to attractiveness, liking, dominance, and other variables, and threatening faces seem to stand out in a crowd.

The study of vocal cues (sometimes called *paralinguistics* or *prosody*) involves the meanings and connotations conveyed by aspects of speech aside from explicit content. Some researchers analyze sound waves mechanically and obtain voice prints. Some eliminate recognizable words from voices through altering audiotapes in various ways. Researchers also may retain the content but ask for judgments about emotions or subtle meanings. As any actor or theater-goer knows, a word or sentence may imply many different meanings by varying stress, tone, and so on. One instance of the latter approach, the test of implied meanings (TIM), has shown utility in differentiating between skilled therapists and others as well as gender differences favoring women. Judith Hall, in a metaanalysis of many studies, showed that females are better at sending and receiving nonverbal emotional messages than males.

The most prominent paralinguistic test that has been developed is the profile of nonverbal sensitivity (PONS). The PONS, which includes both visual and auditory stimuli, was given to more than 200 samples in the United States and other countries. Among the many findings were the superiority of facial expression in adding to accuracy over other channels, the relative importance of the audio channel with less educated people and young children, the moderately greater accuracy of females over males in using emotional cues, greater accuracy in more modernized cultures, and a low correlation between the PONS and measures of intellectual and academic ability.

Channels of communication other than vision and hearing have been explored rather little. There is some evidence from research that acceptable touching (excluding controversial or offensive touch) results in generally positive relationships. Crusco and Wetzel instructed waitresses to touch customers lightly and briefly on the hand or shoulder during normal service; the results showed that touched customers left larger tips. Hall identified four different personal zones from the intimate (less than 18 inches) to the public (25 feet or more), each calling for different behaviors and providing different channels of communication between people.

Existing empirical literature has many implications for applied social science, such as training in social skills and psychotherapy, but these have yet to be explored and studied extensively. As theories and methods become more sophisticated, they may be applied increasingly to the challenges of the multichanneled complexity of everyday activities in natural settings.

BEHAVIOR ANALYSIS
COMMUNICATION THEORY
CROSS-CULTURAL PSYCHOLOGY
CROWDING
CULTURAL DIFFERENCES
FACIAL EXPRESSIONS
VISUAL PERCEPTION

N. D. SUNDBERG

NONVERBAL INTELLIGENCE TESTS

These are tests presenting nonlanguage tasks, and/or administered with minimal or no use of language, and presumably measuring intellectual capacity.

TERMS AND ILLUSTRATIVE TASKS

The term *nonverbal* is closely related to other test labels. A *performance* test connotes manipulation tasks, such as block design or assembling objects, rather than paper and pencil tests. A *nonlanguage* test requires no use of oral or written language by examinee or tester. A *nonreading* test requires no reading or writing by examinee, but may require some verbal comprehension such as understanding oral directions to identify a picture. The distinction *verbal versus nonverbal* connotes language-laden, especially education-dependent, tasks versus tasks lifted out of a verbal–educational context. The difference should not be confused with the *verbal versus quantitative* distinction, since many quantitative tests sample school-acquired skills (e.g., computing prices of products). Certain cognitive tests yielding verbal, quantitative, and nonverbal subscores attempt to tap these different (but not wholly independent) abilities.

The terms just reviewed are reflected only roughly in the names of tests or in the structure of nonverbal items. Substituting symbols for digits may be called a "performance" measure, for example, although it is a paper-and-pencil task, while a figure–analogies task may combine nonverbal content with instructions the examinee must read. In addition to types of questions already named, tasks typically called "nonverbal" have included picture arrangement, picture completion, drawing persons or animals, embedded figures (finding a geometric pattern in a larger pattern field), and matrices. In the present discussion, *nonverbal (NV)* refers to task content.

Developmental tests are a category of measures related to NV tests, since infant and preschool testing must eliminate or control the role of language. Developmental tests often sample sensory, motor, attentional, perceptual, and manipulatory capabilities as well as cognitive functions. Piagetian scales assess qualitative functions such as imitation and the purposeful use of objects.

RELATION TO THEORY OF INTELLECT

The idea of a "pure," context-free ability to discern abstract relationships—distinct from schooled abilities and pervading performance on diverse intellectual tasks—goes back to Charles Spearman, who named this analytical talent *g*. Nonverbal tests have been significant in theoretical work on intelligence because tasks such as figure analogies, matrices, and embedded figures (all of which can range vastly in difficulty) have been considered good measures of a *g*-like ability. In the United States, theories of intellect departed from Spearman to stress separate abilities rather than a pervasive general ability, but "analytical" ability remained of interest. The evolution of this theory had several phases. After about 1940, when tests yielding both verbal (V) and NV or performance (P) subscores become available, the conception of a "performance IQ" gained popularity. Bilingual children and mild retardates, for example, were found to score better on P measures than on V-loaded tests. The V-P distinction lost credibility on empirical grounds, and was supplanted by the idea of an ability continuum with "crystallized" (education-dependent) abilities at one end, "fluid" (analytical) abilities at the other, and mixed cognitive tasks in between. Analytical ability was also theorized to be similar to Piaget's formal-operations level of intellect. During the 1960s and 1970s, when both concern for fair test use and interest in cross-cultural testing increasingly dominated the U.S. testing scene, NV test tasks were drawn into the design of tests intended to be unlinked, or somehow "fairly" linked, to culture and subculture.

USES

Performance, nonlanguage, and nonreading measures have contributed to evaluation work with special populations, such as infants and preschoolers, the retarded, the handicapped, and nonreaders. Demonstration, pantomime, and translation are among the means used to construct or adapt tasks so as to minimize the role of language, education, or culture in test performance. Some NV measures first designed to be "culture-fair" came to be helpful in clinical testing.

The effort to use NV tasks in the search for "culture-free" tests, then for "culture-fair" tests, met with much less success than had been hoped. Research usually showed that: (a) NV scores rise with socioeconomic level, as do V scores; (b) tests standardized on members of a culture or subculture favor persons of similar background; and (c) in a given cultural milieu, predictive validity of a test drops as cultural loading drops. Nonverbal tests sometimes have their applied uses when testers wish to minimize language-related advantages of some subjects over others, because NV performance depends less on verbal–educational shaping than V performance does. No test performance, however, is independent of culture; NV tasks cannot measure some "real" intellectual ability unrelated to experience in a human community.

CULTURAL BIAS IN TESTING
INTELLIGENCE MEASURES

A. B. PRATT

NONVERBAL THERAPIES

Nonverbal therapies are therapies whose effects are produced without a primary focus on verbal exchange between the therapist and client. Intended to produce emotional relief, personality growth and development, and the elimination of neurotic and psychotic symptomatology, they include art therapy (dance, drawing, music, painting, and sculpture); biofeedback training; breathing awareness techniques (yoga, Zen, and rebirthing); diet and megavitamin therapies; emotional release techniques (aqua-energetics, bioenergetics, LSD treatment, neo-Reichian, orgone, primal, and radix); energy balancing techniques (acupressure, polarity, reflexology, shiatsu, and Touch for Health); massage and deep tissue work (postural integration, Rolfing, and Trager); movement awareness techniques (Aikido, tai chi, and Feldenkrais); perception training; and sensory deprivation and sleep therapies.

Such nonverbal therapies are based on the nondualistic philosophy maintaining that body and mind are one, and thus that any emotional suffering that was not relieved by open display at the time of occurrence and that has not been released since then is represented not only mentally and emotionally but also physically. Most nonverbal techniques conceptualize a block in the free energy flow throughout the tissues of the body part involved in the original suffering—a block caused by holding on to the tension rather than relieving it by appropriate emotional display.

Many nonverbal techniques have been originated by, and are taught to and practiced by, people whose background and training are outside the mental health professions. This may account for the relative absence of methodically collected data.

ART THERAPY

Prior to the 1960s, art therapy was generally regarded as an adjunct to verbal-process psychotherapy in the traditional mental health treatment facility.

As the value of art productions by patients for diagnostic purposes was substantiated, the use of art in the treatment setting expanded. Art therapy has now gradually emerged as a primary treatment mode in its own right: Art therapists are specialized mental health professionals whose education usually includes graduate training in psychology and supervised clinical practice. The patient is encouraged to produce art works as active and creative expressions of personality dynamics and problem solutions.

BIOFEEDBACK TRAINING

Evidence of the beneficial effects of training the autonomic nervous system responses first appeared in scientific journals during the 1960s, although similar training had been carried out for more than 6000 years in the guise of yogic training. The major advance made possible by modern biofeedback training is the use of an external visual or auditory signal to inform the subject that specific bodily changes are being produced. Initially, such signals were used primarily to train patients with psychosomatic diseases such as hypertension or gastric ulcers to curtail activities that contributed to their ailments, frequently by entering voluntarily into particular brain-wave states. Also, the signals are increasingly in use to facilitate control over neurotic symptoms, such as anxiety or depression, and to promote the detailed learning of optimal mental and physical sets, as in training an athlete to keep certain muscles relaxed.

BREATHING AWARENESS TECHNIQUES

Particular patterns of breathing involving measured lengths of inhalations, pauses, and exhalations have been in use for 6000 years to produce particular energy flows and mind states associated with healing. Such techniques were brought into use in the United States for therapeutic purposes by Zen therapy and rebirthing. They utilized relaxed slow breathing to countercondition neurotic symptom states.

DIET AND MEGAVITAMIN THERAPIES

The basic premise of these therapies, also referred to as aspects of orthomolecular psychiatry, is that the brain's functions of healthy feeling and thinking can be accomplished only if the brain is receiving the nutrition it needs.

Combined with a diet free of refined carbohydrates and high in natural fiber foods and proteins, the megavitamin approach has become widely used in private-practice psychiatry and is advised for the public at large by health food advisers.

EMOTIONAL RELEASE TECHNIQUES

Practitioners discovering that therapeutic effects were produced simply by release sought to create a womblike setting and establish highly vulnerable body positions so as to promote open emotional release without verbal interaction. These techniques were based on the premise that emotional disturbance is directly related to the depth of repression of old emotional reactions. LSD and other psychoactive drugs have also been used to promote emotional release.

ENERGY-BALANCING TECHNIQUES

These techniques are based on ancient Oriental concepts of channels, called *meridians,* through which life energy is constantly traveling. Illness of every sort, including emotional disorders, is caused by blockage in such channels or by overemphasis of certain channels and underemphasis of others. Stimulation of certain points along appropriate meridians tunes and balances the energy patterns, with concomitant relief of both physical pain and psychological disturbance. Unlike acupuncture, which utilizes needles to stimulate such points, modern techniques like acupressure, polarity, reflexology, shiatsu, and Touch for Health use only finger massage.

MASSAGE AND DEEP TISSUE WORK

These techniques are designed to lengthen fascial coverings of skeletal muscles that have been held in neurotic contraction and to loosen fascial adhesions between muscles that have caused them to react as a group rather than independently. Deep tissue work is often accompanied by spontaneous emotional release, but this is regarded as secondary to the main aim of freeing the body armor and restoring the body's healthful alignment with the forces of gravity.

MOVEMENT AWARENESS TECHNIQUES

These procedures are often combined with regulated breathing patterns. Aikido and tai chi, the best known of the nonmartial Oriental practices, trace their beginnings to ancient disciplines originally designed to allow monks and prisoners to maintain good mental and physical health even if confined to very small spaces for long periods. As in dance therapy, the discipline requires specific emotional expression for proper performance.

Within the Western scientific tradition, Moishe Feldenkrais developed his technique from extended study of the way the body is structured and allowed to move when stressed and when functioning optimally.

PERCEPTION TRAINING

This kind of training operates on the premise that healthy personality development, including healthy learning capacity, is based on healthy perceptual development that, in turn, is founded on development of healthy balance and movement skills. These skills can be taught effectively to both schoolchildren and adults, not only to release inherent good learning capacities but also to bring about profound changes in personality, including major personality problems.

SENSORY DEPRIVATION AND SLEEP THERAPIES

These therapies are based on the clinical finding that many emotionally disturbed people respond favorably to the lessening or elimination of daily stimulation, however routine, and are further supported by evidence that basic belief systems associated with limbic system values change in the absence of stimulation. Prolonged bed rest and sleep produced by sedatives have been recommended as treatment for neurotic and psychotic patients, but are difficult to manage medically, and so have lost favor to shorter periods of total sensory deprivation. Commercially produced tanks, called Sarnadhi tanks, are available for hourly rental without any specialized supervision and are reported to be extremely refreshing and therapeutic. The Japanese system of Morita therapy is in this genre.

ART THERAPY
PSYCHODRAMA
YOGA

E. JONES

NORMAL DEVELOPMENT

Development refers to the functional adaptation of the individual resulting from the interaction of normal physiologic growth with environmental experience as mediated by the individual. The sequence of stages does not represent an automatic unfolding of precoded events.

Development evolves in an interpersonal setting. The family transmits culture, which provides differential access to knowledge and mental structures. They provide the interactions during the critical first 5 years.

BIRTH TO ONE MONTH

Adaptation

The main task of the newborn period is maintenance of an equilibrium akin to intrauterine life. Actions often appear reflexive to this end. However, newborns purposely adapt their primitive reflexes to produce novel experiences. Sucking is a pleasurable activity, transcending the feeding role. With existing abilities, newborns produce self-stimulation. Practicing consolidates and generalizes the skill. Newborns are creative participants in their own experiences.

Uniqueness

Participation partially reflects temperament. Traits such as activity level, irritability, response to stimuli, and cuddliness differentiate newborns and characterize subsequent development. Newborns protect their immature nervous system from stimulus overload by individual preference for crying, shifting of attention, or falling asleep.

Sensory Endowment

Sensorily, newborns are well-endowed. They distinguish a variety of patterns, focus within 8 inches, track a focused object, respond to differential illumination, and distinguish human voices. The alert waking state optimizes exercise of these perceptual skills. Babies who effectively convey

to family members their preference for holding positions facilitating alert waking learn more. Through their active participation babies are better able to connect life events. The mother helps to interpret events to the infant.

ONE TO FOUR MONTHS

Mastering Experience

Infants create their environment through attention to movement, contour, contrast, and moderate novelty. They shift attention rapidly from one detail to another. They experiment with their bodies, trying to master their experiences. With beginning myelinization of the nervous system, children who are 2-months old raise their heads toward new perspectives. At 4 months, perceptual abilities are coordinated. On hearing a sound, the infant turns to see the source. Sucking no longer is interrupted to attend to other stimuli; curiosity grows, and temperament determines interest. However, infants do not connect things with their actions. There is no existence apart from themselves.

Infant Interaction

The immediate response of the family to novel actions produces ideal learning. Babies learn best when other people are part of the outcome. There appear to be biological proclivities for people. Infants demonstrate preference for faces over other patterns. Short focal lengths and the contrast of the eyes encourage gazing at the cuddler's face. The baby moves rhythmically in concert with human voices. By 3 months, infants discriminate facial features and expressions, and the 4-month-old babbles incessantly only if someone will converse. Infants now recognize their captive audience.

FOUR TO TEN MONTHS

Emerging Self-Identity

Infants are fascinated by and seek anything which responds to their manipulations. Between the ages of 4 and 10 months they explore extensively by sitting, crawling, then standing. A new toy is grasped with one hand. Transferring it from hand to hand, rotating and banging it, comparing it to another toy in the other hand, they perceive differences. Similar toys may be grouped. Gradually infants discover that these things exist separate from themselves and their actions. Motivated youngsters search actively when a toy disappears.

People too are attributed a separate existence. The infant dislikes being alone. An absent parent is missed. Tenacious preferences for primary caretakers develop. Bedtimes are refused. A possession of the caretaker may console the infant.

Independent feeding provides a paradigm of this period. The infant coordinates into the new pattern of feeding several previously mastered motions such as grasping, moving a hand to the mouth, and chewing. Since these eating behaviors increasingly resemble those of the family, the infants join the family at mealtime. Infants now observe others *in vivo* instead of centered about themselves. They imitate family movements and sounds. Occasionally they contribute to the conversation, but still with attention-seeking behaviors. Then they return to practicing their new independent skills.

TEN TO TWELVE MONTHS

Independence

The first birthday celebrates the infant's walking. Fearlessly the infant takes on new tasks over and over until mastered. Children have clear goals; they intelligently modify existing skills in a purposeful manner to achieve their goal. They do not wait for chance discovery. Choices are made; they are not always popular.

Paradoxically, children develop autonomous skills while displaying their strongest attachment. Independence with intimacy leads to cooperative tasks as dressing and games such as peek-a-boo.

TWELVE TO EIGHTEEN MONTHS

Adventure
Toddlers ascend steps while holding onto an adult with one hand, oblivious to the dangers. The intensive search for novelty begins. Different styles of exploration determine what they will learn. Active searchers do not manipulate quietly, nor do quiet manipulators search actively. Boys tend to be searchers, while girls tend to be manipulators. While one toddler diligently overcomes obstacles, another may shift to a more easily attained task.

Eighteen-month-old children are creative. Coordinating perspectives shrink the world but also organize it.

Language
With the appearance of language, intelligence correlates positively with social class. Regardless of social class, girls are more verbal than boys throughout adolescence. Achievement of language competency is not well understood. Rates of acquisition vary, but the order is uniform. Perceptual and functional models for word meaning have been supported. From the beginning, children use correct sequence. Subjects and predicates correspond to children's experience as producers of actions. No known environmental factors—not even parental models—affect grammar development. Toddlers do not imitate speech—they create their own sentences. They telegraph sentences into one or two words, choosing the correct words to retain meaning. At all ages comprehension far exceeds expression. With only a 10-word vocabulary, toddlers effectively perform sequential commands.

The Family Medium
Diffuse familial attachments provide a rich medium for practicing new skills. Family influence is clear. Eldest children speak sooner and are more verbal throughout the life span. Toddlers with older siblings eager to interpret for them are late talkers. Increasingly, children reflect their parenting. A fine balance is sought between encouraging independence and fostering personal responsibility.

EIGHTEEN TO TWENTY-FOUR MONTHS
"No!" yells the toddler, running upstairs to escape Mother's control. Within minutes Mother is sought to share a new discovery. Such inconsistencies typify the latter half of the second year. Here again, a new phase in development of self is accompanied by behaviors to engage others, especially Mother.

Tolerance and Empathy
The senior toddler tolerates falls and frustrations poorly. Moods vary greatly. Struggles are routine with other children over toys and with parents over toilet training. An understanding of parental attitudes is poignantly demonstrated by the love given a new sibling rival. Independent exploration gives way to empathic social interactions. A preliminary morality is evident. Self-concept now includes gender identity; children refer to themselves by name.

Verbal communication gradually replaces physical intimacy for social relating. With their 50-word vocabulary and three-word sentences, toddlers demonstrate a purposiveness in behavior that is increasingly obvious to adult observers.

TWO TO FOUR YEARS

Rudimentary Conceptualization
The 3-year-old understands more than 1000 words and is adding another 50 words monthly. The 4-year-old fluently describes a picture story. Parents do not often realize that conceptual understanding behind this vocabulary is very rudimentary; their social demands increase greatly. Place in sibship affects sociability. Control over behaviors is expected. Toilet training provides a paradigm for the ensuing struggles.

Yet cognitively children still think egocentrically, unable to imagine another's viewpoint. Their mental symbols represent personal experience. Conceptualization is just beginning, evidenced by emerging classification abilities. Only one aspect of a problem is in focus at a time.

Motivation
Immediate gratification is postponed. There are many incentives. Cooperative play attests to a desire to be a part of the group. They are eager to please and master their surroundings. Between the ages of 3 and 4 years children ask "Why?" Motivation as well as consequence constitutes morality.

From successful interactions with their family, children develop pride in their behavior. With self-control they initiate cooperative play and share affection. The exclusive possession of parental attention is relinquished with the formation of equitable family ties. Children verbalize right and wrong behaviors consistent with family values.

FOUR TO TWELVE YEARS
The crucial stages in development of self-estimate occurred within the restricted home setting. Cooperative peer relationships have prepared them for social integration with the world beyond the family.

School Years
A new perspective greets egocentric 5-year-olds on entering school. No longer are they as special as at home. Being a group member can be disconcerting. School exemplifies the tasks for this period. Demands for social cooperation and academic learning foretell future emotional and educational success.

Transference of Social Learning
Children communicate effectively with unfamiliar adults and peers, appropriately varying their jargon to fit the situation. Gradual grammatical changes reflect new life roles. Overall language is increasingly conceptual. However, although children of upper socioeconomic families relate a story conceptually, those of lower classes describe it in a correct but more contextual style. Expectations of the two groups widen, as does achievement.

Ability to See More of the Whole
Cognitively, the 7-year-old focuses on several dimensions simultaneously. The cup of sausage-shaped clay retains its quantity and substance when the child rolls it into a ball. Similar appreciation of weight does not develop until age 10 years, and that of volume not until age 12 years. Thinking is still concrete, without ability to generalize.

Empathy and Morality
Children can also focus on other viewpoints socially with gradual increases over time. Moral dilemmas are approached at first with rigidity, but they may not follow their own guidelines as they snatch the larger piece of candy. Children are not by nature competitive; cooperation is readily learned. By age 11 years they recognize the flexibility of rules, but will nevertheless adhere more strictly to them. Slowly they recognize their own motives as determining moral responsibility. By 12 years of age,

children proudly offer the larger share to a same sex friend. Boys may appear more aggressive than girls, and therefore less socialized, but there are no sex differences in developing social responsibilities.

ADOLESCENCE

Adolescence greets boys and girls with the adult tasks of life. They are expected to be independent with vocational plans, yet remain within the family. Relating to the other sex is encouraged, but curiosity is tempered by parental morals. The family yields to peers as the principal socializing agent.

Adolescence is an artifact of twentieth-century technological culture. In other cultures, puberty imposes the expectations of adult functioning.

Continually trying on new behaviors, attempting to create new images of themselves, adolescents question and requestion their life role. To adults they seem egocentric. Worried about their adequacy, they move among peer groups, seeking approval. A sense of competency comes with involvement in social tasks. Open conflict develops with parents who attempt to dominate or control them, or still treat them as children. Boys especially see family rules as unfair. Sexual differences manifest themselves in every area of functioning.

"What if . . . ?" adolescents ask. They have taken a quantum leap from concrete thinking to abstraction. Scientifically, they hypothesize possibilities. Often they appear intrigued by their new skills, imbue their language with double entendres, seek extensive philosophical and political discussions. Much to the family's dismay, they often practice their new argumentative style at home. Yet sensitive personal concerns are expressed within social expectations. Ethics are important goals.

ADULTHOOD

Physical abilities reach a plateau shortly after adolescence and then recede. Personality formation has traditionally been considered complete by early in the second decade of life. However, this tenet has become controversial because of the emphasis on self-improvement in American culture.

How does personality relate to development? Perhaps self-esteem, desired control over one's life, and basic life values better reflect the character structure determining life adaptation. Handling life changes may be more developmentally significant than personality traits over time. Herein lies the controversy in adult development.

Marriage and parenthood are the two greatest tasks of early adulthood. The realities of cooperation, however, require new skills. Increasing divorce rates in American culture indicate a failure to cooperate successfully. Contentment with the parent role can bring a new self-esteem with a more positive outlook on life or more commonly stress the marriage equilibrium. Premature job advancement may reintroduce questions of self-worth.

For the elderly, who may have fewer physical and external resources and are deprived of the respect granted them in other times, cultural bias has fostered the mistaken belief that development has ceased. Aging is a natural part of the life span.

CHILD PSYCHOLOGY
HUMAN DEVELOPMENT

K. M. MYERS
J. W. CROAKE

NUDE GROUP THERAPY

Abraham Maslow stated that nudity might enhance sensitivity training groups. Paul Bindrim, following this suggestion, conducted the first nude group therapy session in 1967.

To determine whether genital nudity was the primary factor responsible for positive results, groups wearing bathing suits were compared clinically with groups that went through the same sessions totally naked. Many of the beneficial effects occurred without genital nudity.

While on the one hand it is quite clear that massage, body contact, Reichian work, and other aqua-energetic procedures do not require genital nudity, it is equally evident that under certain circumstances genital nudity is important and may even be indispensable to the therapeutic process. This is true, for example, when it is used in the following ways:

1. *As a therapeutic facilitator for participants who have never experienced group nudity.* For these persons, genital nakedness implies that there is nothing left to hide and fosters emotional openness.

2. *As a means of improving self-esteem.* Low self-esteem is frequently the result of a negative body image centering around the normally hidden breasts and genitals, which are thought to be inadequate, misshapen, or dirty. Their physical exposure allows for desensitization and reappraisal through open discussion. This is particularly valuable for persons who have experienced mastectomies and other genital deformities that have become greatly exaggerated in their own thinking.

3. *As a means of improving sexual functioning.* Acceptance of their genitals as a beautiful part of their bodies may be the first step in enabling participants to use and enjoy them sexually. Fear of the opposite sex is also lessened by physical exposure and discussion.

CHANGE INDUCTION GROUPS
INNOVATIVE PSYCHOTHERAPIES

P. BINDRIM

NULL HYPOTHESIS TESTING

Scientific research starts with the idea that a certain proposition is probably true. The proposition, regardless of form or complexity, is known as the *original hypothesis.*

Every such proposition has an opposite proposition. This opposite proposition is called the *null hypothesis.* When research data are analyzed, a decision is made to either reject or accept the null hypothesis. (Strictly speaking, the null hypothesis is not really accepted; one merely fails to reject it. The distinction is often blurred.)

Consider a proposition that fewer people given treatment A would meet a criterion (learn something, get well, or get a reward) than those given treatment B. The null hypothesis is that there is no difference in the percentages meeting criterion in the two groups. It cannot literally be supported. There comes a point when intuition is not enough: Informed analysis, based on probability theory, is required.

The illustration permits the identification of some basic principles and terms as follows:

1. The people constitute a sample of a larger population. The null hypothesis refers to the population, not the sample. In the population, the hypothesis of precisely no difference is either true or false.

2. A difference is *significant* if the probability of obtaining it in the sample when the null hypothesis is true is low enough.

3. The researcher decides whether a finding is significant enough by considering two risks of error. There are four possible outcomes of the decision: (a) a true hypothesis is properly accepted; (b) a true hypothesis is erroneously rejected (called a *Type I error*); (c) a false hypothesis is erroneously accepted (called a *Type II error*); and (d) a false hypothesis is properly accepted. In making the decision, the researcher should consider the relative importance of the two

kinds of error and the two probabilities, rather than casually accepting a Type I error of 0.05 or less as significant.

4. The null hypothesis has no direction, but the original hypothesis might. Some controversy exists concerning the proper determination of the significance levels under the two conditions (directional or nondirectional original hypotheses).

HYPOTHESIS TESTING
PROBABILITY
STATISTICAL INFERENCE
STATISTICS IN PSYCHOLOGY

R. M. GUION

NYMPHOMANIA

Broadly speaking, nymphomania refers to the condition of a woman whose sexual desire and/or behavior is referred to by terms like "insatiable," "abnormally intense," "unquenchable," "unrestrained," or "uncontrollable." In practice, the term is poorly defined and often loosely applied. It is usually distinguished from *sexual promiscuity,* but many proposed definitions obviously use the two expressions interchangeably.

A woman who has many sexual encounters, whose lovers are culturally considered to be inappropriate, who is anorgasmic despite frequent sexual contacts, and whose sexual behaviors rarely take place within the context of an intense emotional relationship fits the classical and folkloric stereotype. Furthermore, Levitt points out that the various conceptions of nymphomania neglect the potentially important factor of opportunity as reflected in physical attractiveness, place of residence, type of occupation, and marital status.

Albert Ellis and Edward Sagarin distinguish between *controlled promiscuity* and *endogenous nymphomania.* The former refers to the not-too-unusual, multipartnered existence of a woman who is completely functional, while the latter is "seldom found outside the disturbed wards of mental hospitals." Ellis adds that he has not encountered a single endogenous nymphomaniac in his extensive clinical practice.

SEXUAL DEVIATION

E. E. LEVITT

OBEDIENCE

Obedience is said to occur when the person does what he or she is told. Obedience is thus, by definition, a sociopsychological concept rooted in the relationship between two or more persons, one of whom prescribes a line of action that the other carries out. The psychological character of obedience varies, depending on the nature of the relationship between the subordinate and superordinate figures. Obedience, however, refers specifically to the overt act of compliance. From one situation to the next, different psychological processes may animate the obedient act.

Obedience may be given willingly or compelled by coercion. Often, voluntary obedience and coercion subtly coexist. In advanced forms of social life, coercion is typically replaced by compliance to legitimate authority. Thus obedience is given not simply to a person, but to a position or office; obedience also may be owed to the products of authority, such as traffic lights and systems of law. Obedience is ordinarily mediated through the assumption of roles that are mutually related in hierarchical terms and that constitute, in Parsons' terminology, "a social system."

SOCIALIZATION

The inculcation of obedience begins in the earliest years. Born into a state of biological dependency, the child is confronted with numerous parental demands, enforced with greater or lesser degrees of discipline. A further phase of socialization for obedience occurs in the school, where children are exposed to an institutional system of authority in which compliance is learned not only to specific persons, but also to an impersonal organizational framework.

Such learning is generally deemed essential for mature functioning within the hierarchical systems that characterize the adult social world.

THEORIES

Freud argued that obedience is rooted in libidinal bonds that develop between members of a group and its leader. These are not reciprocated because the leader cannot love all members with total love. Since the object choice of members is to this extent frustrated, their libidinal ties with the leader come to be based on the more primitive process of identification.

Erich Fromm's neo-Freudian treatment of obedience emphasizes the interplay between psychodynamic and sociohistorical factors. The erosion of security-conferring structures in modern times leaves the individual anxious and isolated; as one solution to this problem, individuals escape into totalitarian submission, renouncing the insecurities of freedom.

RECENT APPROACHES

Stanley Milgram reported an experimental study on the conflict between conscience and authority. The purpose of the experiment was to see how far the naive subject would proceed before refusing to comply with the experimenter's instructions. The results of the experiment showed that it was far more difficult to defy the experimenter's authority than was generally supposed.

The crux of Milgram's inquiry is a set of experimental variations that examine the variables that increase or diminish obedience. Among other things, his studies found the following: (a) closeness of the victim leads to diminished obedience; (b) group forces, depending on whether they support or oppose the experimenter's commands, create widely varying levels of disobedience; and (c) incoherence in the authority structure eliminates all obedience. Thus these studies demonstrate the dependence of obedience on the precise arrangement of factors in the situation.

H. Kelman approaches the problem of destructive obedience with a tripartite analysis, focusing on factors that remove inhibitions against violence. In his system, *authorization* legitimates a set of destructive actions toward others; *routinization* reduces the destructive procedure to a set of mechanical and administrative routines that discourage the introduction of moral considerations; and *dehumanization* facilitates action against the victim by depriving the victim of personhood.

The significance of obedience for society cannot be overstated; it is the means whereby autonomously functioning individuals are integrated into larger systems of coordination and control. It is thus a key concept in linking the psychological processes of the individual to the social structures of the larger world.

BYSTANDER INVOLVEMENT
DEINDIVIDUATION
EXPERIMENTER EFFECTS
GROUP PRESSURE

S. Milgram

OBESITY

S. M. Jourard considers obesity the primary appearance problem in the United States. L. P. Ullman and L. Krasner state that overeating can symbolize progressive suicide. Ari Kiev adds that obesity can hide depression. According to M. E. Moore, A. Stunkard, and L. Stole, people of the lower economic classes more readily become obese than middle-class individuals, who in turn are more apt to be overweight than wealthier people, who can afford a better quality balanced diet. Obese individuals were found to be more immature and had more psychological problems and poor impulse control. Excess weight causes shortness of breath and fatigue, joint trouble, high blood pressure and heart attacks, organ damage, and greater risk of diabetes.

Children's weights correlate with those of their parents. According to Alvin Eden, the appestat (at the base of the brain, controlling appetite) is possibly "set" higher genetically in some people, or they inherit more fat cells. Children of one obese parent are six times more likely and children of two obese parents 13 times more likely to become overweight, although parental influence as well as heredity could explain this.

Only two factors lead to normal weight loss: (a) *reduced food intake* of low calorie foods, avoiding the excess carbohydrates, and (b) *exercise sufficient to cause loss of breath.*

Eating is a function of (a) physiological signals ("hunger") and (b) attractive food. The overeating of obese individuals is governed almost entirely by the enticing appearance of food. Since a higher level of satiation is needed for them to feel satisfied, obese subjects eat even without hunger. Oversensitivity to environmental stimuli prompts them to eat without physiological need.

Schachter found that fat students eat more than needed because they ignore internal cues; they eat more as their environment improves, but are discouraged when eating is difficult, as through a tube, proving they need less food than they take in.

Skovholt, Resnick, and Dewey list some secondary "gains" of being overweight: (a) one can remain mother-dependent; (b) people expect less from fat people; (c) obesity can express defiance; and (d) obesity can be a "chastity belt" for those who fear sex.

The disadvantages of being overweight are numerous: (a) fat people tend to be sicker, more accident-prone, and die at a younger age; (b) the obese child is the last to be chosen for a school team, and the chances for college, following an interview, are reduced; (c) fat makes it harder to get an executive job, and fat executives earn less and advance more slowly; (d) fat individuals have fewer marital choices; and (e) the over-

weight sufferer has more problems in sports, in buying and wearing clothes, and in gaining respect and admiration.

A woman's fat insulates her from exhibitionistic tendencies and masculine approach. The "happy fat person" is a myth that masks frustration. Fat individuals may blame failures on appearance, robbing themselves of desire to resolve them. For many people, food is a tranquilizer. Susanne Orbach believes that women may use being overweight to rebel against a male-dominated society that wants women to be slim, perfect, feminine, passive sex goddesses.

Boredom, loneliness, frustration, and feeling unloved contribute to food indulgence, as do media advertising and food store displays. Fat people overfeed their pets because food means love. Other fat family members may sabotage one's efforts to get and stay thin. Overweight husbands escape chores and sex and find emotional stability in their impregnable fortress of flab.

Eating is inhibited by the ventromedial region of the hypothalamus, and encouraged by the lateral section. The hypothalamus may contain glucoreceptors sensitive to blood sugar. Norman Joliffe coined the term *appestat* for the hypothalamic appetite regulator. When people get used to overeating, they no longer feel satisfied with a sufficient amount.

The newborn associates safety, comfort, love, and pleasure with suckling, but bottle feeding tempts the mother to make her baby finish the bottle. Stuffing children through adolescence establishes a lifelong habit. The fat babies studied by J. Mayer and T. G. Harris ate the same or less than thin babies but were more inactive. The thin babies moved three times as much as the fat babies. Hilde Bruch concluded that overeating is caused mostly by: (a) a response to tension; (b) a substitute gratification in frightening situations; (c) emotional illness; and (d) food addiction.

Ultrasensitive fat people are unable to stand much physical and emotional pain. To the timid child, physical bulk represents safety and strength, a defense against the world and its responsibilities. Since exercise and social contacts appear dangerous, the fat child generally lacks sources of satisfaction outside food.

APPETITE DISORDERS
BEHAVIORAL GENETICS
EATING DISORDERS
PSYCHOPHYSIOLOGY

H. K. Fink

OBESITY TREATMENTS

Obesity, the presence of excess adipose tissue, is a problem for millions of people. In the United States, for example, the Metropolitan Life Insurance Company has estimated that 30% of males and 40% of females between the ages of 19 and 40 years are obese. The problem is not limited to the United States: many of the industrialized nations around the world show similar statistics.

Because of the physical, psychological, and social disadvantages of obesity, it has become the target for substantial treatment effort. Attempts to solve this problem have included dietary regimens, gastric bypass operations, mouth wiring, pharmacologic interventions, and exercise programs, all of which have either limited effectiveness or can be applied to only highly select populations. Two major contributions from psychology to the understanding and treatment of this refractory condition are psychoanalysis and behavior modification.

Psychoanalysis has contributed substantially to present knowledge of the psychological factors associated with obesity, and much of the early work in this area was done by Hilde Bruch. Her clinical observations of obese children were pioneering studies that formed the foundation for current understanding of obesity. The classic psychoanalytic view of obesity is that this condition is a product of dysfunctions occurring during the oral stage of development.

Gluckman indicated that inappropriate eating patterns may find their derivation in a postoral phase of development. Gluckman further emphasized the complexity of these problems and the limitations of the purely psychoanalytic perspective. The psychoanalytic treatment of obesity is, in general, indirect; that is, the presenting symptom of obesity is not the problem on which treatment is focused. Instead, attention is given to the underlying psychological conflicts. Presumably, when these conflicts are understood and resolved, the client's difficulties with overeating and overweight subside.

Little is known of the clinical applications of psychoanalysis in the treatment of obesity, including methods, results, and extent of use. Rand and Stunkard suggest that psychoanalysis apparently was effective as an indirect treatment of obesity. Additionally, they found that clients undergoing this treatment decreased in their feelings of body disparagement. Interestingly, improved body image was not found to be related to weight loss. Further studies may help determine whether these results are replicable, and may more accurately determine the overall effectiveness of this method.

BEHAVIOR MODIFICATION

The use of behavior modification in the treatment of obesity has been a relatively new occurrence. Its theoretical foundation was laid by Ferster, Nurnberger, and Levitt. Stuart, using the ideas of Ferster and his colleagues, reported that eight outpatients lost an average of 17 kg over a 1-year period, a heretofore unheard-of loss using psychological techniques. Stuart's phenomenal success provided the impetus for the rapid growth and development of behavior modification as a weight control treatment. It is the most widely used method of treating mild to moderate obesity.

Stimulus control, eating management, contingency management, and self-monitoring have generally formed the "core" of most behaviorally based weight control therapies because of their assumed efficacy. However, more recent research findings have placed the former assumptions in doubt. The possibility that these components of behavioral treatment are not particularly effective may help explain the limited weight losses obtained through this approach.

The ultimate objective of any weight control therapy is to produce substantial weight loss and to maintain the loss. Behavior modification has not been highly successful in achieving either objective. Considerable research effort has been engendered to find a more successful "formula."

Recent trends in the behavioral treatment of obesity derive primarily from the growing appreciation of the complexity of this problem. Obesity is a problem of numerous dimensions; its origins can be psychological, physical, social, and cultural. Behavior therapists have begun to recognize the complexity of this problem and have attempted to make the basic behavior modification approach to weight control more sophisticated. Research has examined the influence of various additions to the treatment, which additions include the use of very low calorie diets, social support, pharmacotherapy, relapse-prevention strategies, exercise, and cognitive interventions.

CONCLUSION

Psychoanalysis and behavior modification have made major contributions to the understanding of obesity, but both are limited in the ability to help clients achieve and maintain significant weight loss.

The future direction of weight control treatment seems to lie in a multidisciplinary approach commensurate with the complexity of the problem.

The extreme difficulty of losing weight in adulthood also suggests the logic of interventions that prevent rather than cure. The target of such

prevention efforts should be children, a group much neglected in obesity research even though substantial evidence suggests that much of adult obesity begins in childhood. A concerted effort with this group and their parents might prevent many of the problems of obesity in later life. Prevention efforts should also extend to developing an environment that promotes a healthy way of life. Nutrition, exercise, and stress management can be promoted in schools, workplaces, and communities. By doing so, we can assist in the maintenance of normal weight as well as the achievement of overall health. In such an effort, psychoanalysts and behavior therapists can play major functions in the multidisciplinary teams that plan and implement the intervention programs.

BEHAVIOR THERAPY
OBESITY
PSYCHOANALYSIS

J. P. FOREYT
A. T. KONDO

OBJECTIVE PSYCHOLOGY

Objective psychology refers *narrowly* to the psychologies of I. M. Sechenov, I. P. Pavlov, and V. M. Bekhterev, whose studies of reflexes and conditioning led them to represent psychological events—including higher mental processes—as dependent on reflex patterns in the central nervous system, especially the brain. Bekhterev first named his work objective psychology, then "reflexology." More *broadly,* objective psychologies are those psychologies taking a skeptical and naturalistic approach to phenomena traditionally called conscious or mental. In the *broadest* sense, objective psychologies are psychologies committed to the rules of science as a public, empirical effort, especially the principle that studies will be shared in the research community in ways that enable others to repeat them. In usual parlance, "objective psychology" refers not to a school of thought but to outlooks common to several twentieth-century psychologies—mainly, but not exclusively, behavioristic schools.

The objectivist sees behavior itself as worthy of study in its own right, suspecting that psychological terms for inner states or conditions reveal prescientific thinking.

Initially, objective psychology was entwined with animal psychology, associationism, and experimental psychology. These traditions are not the same as the objectivist tradition, although many people confuse them. Similarly, common notions have overidentified objective psychology with various theoretical preferences such as (a) determinism and (b) reductionism (the idea that psychological processes are "nothing but" physiological events). Objective psychologists have been determinists, but so have the Gestaltists. Skinner's and Kantor's systems are among objective schools that do not reduce psychological events to the physiological, as the Russian school seemed to do.

BEHAVIORISM
THEORETICAL PSYCHOLOGY

A. B. PRATT

OBSERVATIONAL METHODS

Observations, whether formal or informal, consist of taking note of events or occurrences and making a record of what is observed. Observation is basic to all science, and special methods have been devised to make observations of behavior objective and reliable.

In *controlled observation,* a situation is prearranged or contrived to study the responses of people or animals to certain stimulus conditions.

Because controlled observation involves special procedures, *uncontrolled observation,* in which the observer exerts no control over the situation and merely takes note of behavior *in situ,* is more common.

Much of what is known about the dynamics of personality and mental disorder is the result of observations made by people in clinical settings. The *clinical method* is not completely objective; not only does the therapist–observer affect the patient's behavior, but the patient also affects the reactions of the therapist.

In scientific research it is usually considered advisable for the observers to remain as unobtrusive as possible, not interacting in any way with those being observed. However, if the researcher elects to become a part of the observational situation and be a *participant observer,* the effects of the observer's presence on the behavior of the performers need to be considered in interpreting the research findings.

An important first step in improving the accuracy of observations is to train the observers. Observers must be made aware of the effects of their own biases, conduct, and condition on what is being observed, and of the tendency to confuse fact with interpretation. Furthermore, the influence of the situational context in which observations are made should be taken into account in interpreting the findings.

Obtaining meaningful results from an observational study also demands that the sample of observed behavior be representative, which is usually time-consuming and expensive. To reduce the time, expense, and volume of data obtained from continuous observations of behavior, special data-sampling procedures are employed. In *incident sampling,* only specified behavioral incidents are noted and recorded. A second procedure, *time sampling,* involves making a series of observations, each lasting only a few minutes, over a period of a day or so. Finally, the use of an *observational schedule,* such as a rating scale or checklist filled out during or shortly after the behavioral occurrence, can improve the reliability of observations.

Observations are also made in developmental research, surveys, correlational studies, and even experiments. For example, periodic observations of the development of the same age group of individuals over a period of months or years (*longitudinal investigation*), or of different age-groups of people at a specific point in time (*cross-sectional investigation*), are common in developmental research. Content analysis of self-observations recorded in diaries, autobiographies, letters, and other personal documents also provide insight into personality dynamics.

PSYCHOLOGICAL ASSESSMENT
UNOBTRUSIVE MEASURES

L. R. AIKEN

OBSESSIVE-COMPULSIVE PERSONALITY

From Sigmund Freud's description of the anal character to the twentieth-century problem of workaholism, the obsessive-compulsive personality—also referred to as the anankastic personality—has posed a dilemma for mental health professionals. The characteristics of this disorder are troublesome, yet are often highly valued in our society.

The *Diagnostic and Statistical Manual of Mental Disorders* recommended the term "compulsive personality disorder" for the syndrome that has been called obsessive-compulsive personality. The diagnostic criteria include a limited ability to express warm emotions, perfectionism, a rigid insistence on one's plans, excessive commitment to work to the detriment of personal relationships, and indecisiveness.

The overcontrolled adherence to unrealistic standards, combined with an inability to make decisions, leads to chronic unhappiness in the obsessive-compulsive personality. The disorder is more common in men than women.

Psychoanalytic explanations of etiology emphasize disordered development in the anal stage. Theoretically, then, the defense mechanisms of isolation, undoing, and reaction formation are necessary in order to defend against anal-sadistic impulses. Yet Pollak found little evidence supporting the psychoanalytic beliefs concerning etiology.

With respect to differential diagnosis, the obsessive-compulsive personality can be distinguished from the obsessive-compulsive disorder by the absence of obsessions (recurrent unwanted thoughts) and compulsions (repetitive behaviors that are driven, but not pleasurable).

COMPULSIVE PERSONALITY
PERSONALITY TYPES

C. LANDAU

OCCULTISM

The term "occultism," derived from the Latin *occulere,* meaning "to hide or conceal," refers to doctrines and rituals believed to lead to the attainment of higher mental or spiritual powers, but that are not accepted by either modern science or institutionalized religion. Mysticism, spiritualism, dowsing, numerology, Rosicrucianism, yoga, natural magic, Freemasonry, witchcraft, astrology, and alchemy are among the many occultisms that have had and in some cases continue to have an impact on Western civilization.

A basic tenet of such belief is that there exist secret and mysterious ("hidden") forces of nature that can be understood and manipulated only by those properly instructed in the necessary arcane knowledge, which is usually said to derive from ancient sources of wisdom. These forces can supposedly be employed to control the environment and foretell the future.

Although such magical beliefs are rejected by modern science, the natural sciences all have roots in occultism.

Occultism carried a certain intellectual respectability at least as late as the end of the seventeenth century, and astrology was still being taught in universities, alongside astronomy, as late as 1800.

Although most occultisms make empirical claims about the real world that are not accepted by modern science or by institutionalized religion, the boundaries between science, the occult, and religion are not always clear.

Parapsychology straddles the border between science and the occult. Although many of its scientific critics consider it to be squarely in the realm of the occult, devoted parapsychology researchers seek to apply rigorous scientific methodology in their studies and to reject any occultist ties. Yet their basic beliefs about supposed natural forces such as those said to give rise to mental telepathy, precognition, and so on are beliefs that have always been fundamental in most occult belief systems.

To distinguish occultisms that attempt to provide scientific evidence for their beliefs from those that do not, M. Truzzi proposed a five-category classification. He used the term *proto-scientific occultism* to refer to those instances where scientific validation is desired and attempted but where, owing to a lack of sufficient evidence, the claims have not been accepted by the scientific community. *Quasi-scientific occultism* comprises those occultisms in which the attempt is made to appear to be scientific, although little effort is made actually to be so, as in the case of astrology.

Pragmatic occultism is Truzzi's term for occultisms in which the grounds for the belief are close to those of science, yet scientific status is not claimed. *Shared mystical occultism* refers to mystical beliefs validated by the reports of others who have had similar private experiences, as in transcendental meditation. Finally, *private mystical occultism* refers to purely private validation of the mystical belief, as when an individual apparently receives a revelation of some sort from a deity or extraterrestrial beings.

To Truzzi's set of categories, Zusne and Jones advocated adding the category *philosophical occultism*. This is described as being similar to Truzzi's pragmatic occultism, except that the individual, rather than being concerned with practical results in the real world, focuses, through the beliefs of esoteric philosophy, on personal results that are spiritual advances on the path to perfection.

Although modern society places great emphasis on the importance of rational thinking, research suggests that human beings are as prone to magical thought as were their primitive ancestors. Although occultisms reflect an attempt, through magical thinking, to understand the workings of nature, they have their basis in powerful psychological needs and processes that operate by and large outside conscious awareness, and often may serve the needs to increase personal power and to find solace in the face of existential anxiety. It is unlikely that human beings will ever be free of such needs or of the propensity for magical thought.

PARAPSYCHOLOGY
RELIGION AND PSYCHOLOGY

J. E. ALCOCK

OCCUPATIONAL ADJUSTMENT

Occupational adjustment is a complex and continuous process that begins with entry into the labor force and continues through the life span. Applied psychologists study motivation and needs of the individual worker in relation to job satisfaction, and examine the effects of certain individual and organizational attributes on worker performance.

THEORIES OF OCCUPATIONAL ADJUSTMENT

Several theories have been advanced to explain occupational adjustment. A vocational development theorist, Donald Super, and colleagues suggested three stages in occupational adjustment (establishment, maintenance, decline). Super described developmental tasks that must be accomplished in each stage. In the initial or establishment phase of careers, the first task is to implement a vocational preference and to recognize the need to stabilize in a career. Next, the individual actually obtains a stable job, or becomes resigned to a more or less permanent instability. Finally, the individual consolidates and advances in a career pattern. Other stages were hypothesized by Miller and Form—trial period, stable period, retirement period—and by Robert Havighurst—becoming, maintaining, and contemplating.

Problems or styles of work adjustment have also been studied. Neff described five types of work maladaption or pathology, including lack of work motivation, fear or anxiety in response to productivity demands, hostility and aggression, dependency, and social naiveté. Finally, Holland and Schein showed how individual traits and environmental characteristics interact to produce occupational adaptation and advancement.

A complete and well documented formulation of occupational adjustment has been outlined by Lofquist and Davis in *Adjustment to work*. According to this theory, occupational environments provide different patterns of reinforcement that interact with an individual's needs and abilities. Correspondence, or harmony between an individual and the work environment, will result in satisfaction, satisfactoriness, and as a result, some level of tenure or work stability. Satisfaction and satisfactoriness are complementary outcomes of work adjustment.

Thus individual and environmental factors contribute to work adjustment. Psychological inventories are available to measure individual needs (Minnesota Importance Questionnaire, MIQ), and patterns of occupational reinforcers for different occupations have been compiled, consistent with the theory.

Warr and Wall suggest that general mental health and work adjustment are closely related. The authors agree that the satisfaction of personal needs through work is essential to self-esteem and therefore to overall health. In general, research evidence supports the tie between general and occupational adjustment. Crites is careful to point out that the connection is a complex one that probably depends on individual and organizational moderators.

INTERVENTIONS TO FACILITATE OCCUPATIONAL ADJUSTMENT

Treatment and prevention programs have been employed by industry to promote occupational adjustment and occupational mental health, and these include improvements in selection and training procedures. Research has found that balanced (positive and negative) job information given to a candidate results in more realistic expectations and lower turnover.

Other programs have been designed to train managers to be more effective in handling career development issues of employees. Additionally, counseling and employee assistance centers designed to provide services for workers have become increasingly popular in business, industrial, and government settings. These and other programs like them are designed to improve the individual's and the organization's ability to manage problems of occupational adjustment.

CAREER DEVELOPMENT
INDUSTRIAL PSYCHOLOGY
JOB SATISFACTION

A. R. SPOKANE

OCCUPATIONAL CLINICAL PSYCHOLOGIST

A specialist concerned with the psychological adaptation of persons to the workplace, this psychologist, whether acting as an external consultant or as an in-house specialist, addresses employee and organizational well-being through programs and services provided to and at the expense of the sponsor, such as an employer or a union.

An occupational clinical psychologist generally holds a doctoral degree from an accredited program, has had supervised experience with an employed population in an adult mental health facility, and meets licensing requirements under applicable state laws. Skilled in applying psychological principles to the management of the mental health of both employees and employers, this psychologist is trained in diagnosis and assessment; counseling and psychotherapy methodology, especially brief models; crisis intervention; stress management; management and organizational consultation; job disciplinary procedures; and program development and evaluation. Such professionals should have a working knowledge of federal, state, and local employment regulations and testing and privacy legislation, as well as of the special impact of the legislation on women, ethnic minorities, and the older worker.

INDUSTRIAL CONSULTANTS
OCCUPATIONAL CLINICAL PSYCHOLOGY

H. V. SCHMITZ

OCCUPATIONAL CLINICAL PSYCHOLOGY

Occupational clinical psychology is the field of inquiry, practice, and education concerned with the psychological functioning of persons in the workplace—in individual differences in terms of emotional, behavioral, cognitive, and motivational adaptation. Its intent is to stimulate healthy levels of employee and organizational well-being through organizationally sponsored psychological services, and embraces the evaluation, prevention, and treatment of the psychological difficulties that exist in all organizations.

Clients are employees of the sponsoring organization and their dependents. An additional client relationship exists with the corporation, labor union, or other sponsoring organization: The common goal is to enhance mental health and prevent mental illness in the workplace, which is of critical importance to an organization's well-being, its human resource capability, and the achievement of business goals. Specific employee problems addressed include emotional, marital, family, career, job, lifestyle, and substance abuse; interpersonal difficulties; and job changes. Specific organizational problems include organizational adaptive patterns, psychological work climate, supervisory problems, and motivational systems.

Occupational clinical services are effective when tailored to fit assessed organizational needs. Among key areas to be assessed are employee demographics, attitudes, productivity measures, health insurance utilization, medical costs, accidents, and substance abuse. Services include employee counseling and psychotherapy, information and referral concerning social service needs, crisis intervention, career planning, executive selection, vocational guidance, clinically based employment screening, accident prevention, worker's compensation evaluations, outplacement counseling, retirement planning, labor arbitration consultation, stress management, biofeedback, quality of working life programs, and health and parenting education. The services provided adhere to all standards and laws that govern privacy and confidentiality.

Applications of psychology to work settings had its formal beginnings during the beginning of the twentieth century. Early concepts regarding the psychological value of work were developed by Sigmund Freud.

During World War I, the work of psychologists in the classification and assignment of army personnel represented a significant achievement. In 1924, the classic Hawthorne experiments at the Western Electric Company expanded psychological applications from employee selection and placement to the more complex areas of employee relations, motivation, morale, and employee counseling. Employee counseling programs actually started much earlier, however.

Employee counseling programs, which focused on alcoholism recovery, were pioneered during the 1930s and 1940s at a number of companies. A clinical psychologist was hired by Detroit Edison in 1943 to assist employees with personal problems. Many programs that began during this period developed into models that were considerably more sophisticated and complex than the initial programs.

Labor unions also contributed to the developing awareness that proper attention be given to employees with personal problems. Some labor unions developed mental health services through their health centers.

Throughout the 1970s, many companies began new programs or professionalized existing services by adding state-licensed psychologists. Employee counseling programs are currently available in corporations representing all types of business and industry.

These developments paralleled the human relations movement, which began during the 1960s in American business and industry and led to the development of wider occupational applications of psychology. The writings of David McClelland, Frederick Herzberg, and Abraham Maslow regarding work motivation and satisfaction played a significant role in the early development of this movement.

It is generally accepted in industrial psychology that organizational problems, high employee turnover rates, chronic absenteeism and lateness, costs of replacing trained employees and valued executives, work-related accidents, premature death, and high utilization of medical insurance coverage are based in large part on the personal and interpersonal difficulties experienced by individual employees. Research indicates that more than 75% of important stress reactions experienced by individuals originate in their private lives. These stress reactions are transferred to the work setting, where performance suffers because of preoccupations with outside problems.

JOB SATISFACTION
LABOR/MANAGEMENT RELATIONS
OCCUPATIONAL CLINICAL PSYCHOLOGIST

H. V. SCHMITZ

OCCUPATIONAL COUNSELING

Occupational counseling is best distinguished from other similar forms of career and vocational assistance (i.e., vocational counseling, career counseling, vocational guidance) by its purpose and content. Typically the focus of occupational counseling includes the clients' preparation for entry into and progress in an occupation, as well as the fundamental emphasis on problems of occupational choice found in other forms of work-related counseling. In addition, occupational counselors work with clients from all levels of the occupational structure (e.g., skilled trades). Placement and follow up are thus important extensions of the professionals' role in occupational counseling.

The purpose of occupational counseling is to assist an individual to formulate occupational goals, select an array of possible occupations consistent with those goals, and implement a choice in the face of the realities of the marketplace. The addition of job finding as a counseling goal and the use of occupational information as a counseling tool distinguish occupational counseling from its more choice-oriented counterparts.

Occupational counseling had its roots in the social reform movement of the late 1800s. Its formal beginnings are credited to Frank Parsons. Parsons outlined a three-step process in which the client learned about self and about occupations and then combined the two in a process of "true reasoning."

Occupational counselors work in a variety of settings, including schools, rehabilitation agencies, counseling centers, career planning and placement centers, the Veterans Administration, state employment agencies, and community agencies, and increasingly in government, business, and industry.

THEORY AND TECHNIQUE

The practice of occupational counseling has been governed in part by theories of occupational choice. Crites divided existing theories into those that are principally nonpsychological, including (a) accident theory, (b) economic theory, and (c) cultural and sociological theory; and those that are principally psychological, including (a) trait-factor theories, (b) psychodynamic theories, (c) developmental theories, and (d) decision theories. For the most part, however, counselors have been guided by the practical problems involved in assisting the client to make and implement a reasonable occupational choice.

The most common method employed in occupational counseling has been face-to-face counseling involving one counselor and one client. Recently, however, there has been a dramatic increase in the use of other strategies.

These popular treatments seem to have several common elements, which make them successful and which could be incorporated in all treatments:

1. *Information* about self and about the world of work.
2. *Support,* including social support from a counselor, friends, family, or professional contacts.

3. *Cognitive structure,* or the acquisition of some framework for understanding self and the world of work, and for making occupationally related choices.

4. *Rehearsal of aspirations* to clarify and reinforce choices and to stimulate occupational exploration.

Information as Treatment

Information about the world of work can be derived from print or media sources, and also can be gathered through exploratory experience, such as plant or site tours, personal interviews, cooperative education programs in which the student works part time while studying, and through work experience.

Occupational psychologists have also commented on the necessity for developing self-knowledge as a goal in counseling. Donald Super called this the *self-concept;* Holland, the *vocational identity;* and Tyler, the *vocational construct.* The client uses information about occupational interests, values, skills, and abilities to formulate interpretations about which occupational options might be suitable. The client then tests the options by exploring them directly.

Assessment

Standardized measures of ability have been found to have some utility in occupational counseling. In general, moderate relationships were found between ability and success in training (0.39) and ability and job performance (0.22). Multiple tests or combinations of tests (batteries) were found to have better predictive validity than single tests.

Measures of occupational interests, however, have been more widely used in occupational counseling. Among the more popular and carefully validated of these interest inventories are the *Strong–Campbell Interest Inventory* (*SCI*), the *Kuder Occupational Interest Survey* (*KOIS*), and the *Self-Directed Search* (*SDS*). Inventories of values and job skills have also been developed, but their validation has been less complete. Computer-assisted versions of some interest inventories are now available and can be combined with interactive computer counseling programs. Results of research studies suggest that, as a rule, about 50% of those who take interest inventories tend to be in the occupations indicated by the inventory 10 to 15 years after they take the test. In general, however, the exact relationship between interests, abilities, and occupational choices is still not clear.

One area of assessment, the determination of decisional status, continues to attract increasing research attention. Three inventories, developed by Samuel Osipow, John Holland, and Vincent Harren, measure the state of the clients' decision-making ability (Career Decision Scale, My Vocational Situation, Assessment of Career Decision-Making). All three of these scales have direct links to occupational counseling interventions.

Job Search/Job Finding

How people find and secure jobs is an important but often neglected topic in occupational counseling, and one about which relatively little is known. Becker classifies job-search strategies as formal (want ads, employment services, schools, unions), informal (contacts with friends, relatives, job associates), or as direct applications (to firms). Becker concludes that young people tend to find jobs with assistance from friends or relatives and through direct applications.

Behavioral approaches to teaching job-search and job-finding skills have also been popular and effective. Mock interviews using videotape feedback and resumé-writing practice are commonly used to promote job-search skills. One particularly effective version of a job-search activity has been developed by Azrin. Called Job Clubs, these structured interventions provide group support, information, and skills training. Careful evaluation studies have shown these groups to be highly effective with a wide range of client populations.

Employee Assistance

Major employers in government, business, and industry now provide an array of mental health services for their employees. Since alcohol abuse, drug abuse, and marital, family, and personal problems may contribute to lost productivity, absenteeism, or job stress, employee assistance counseling is directed at such problems. The occupational counselor's role is changing to include more of this on-the-job counseling. In addition, occupational counseling incorporates midcareer and preretirement counseling activities as well.

CAREER DEVELOPMENT
COUNSELING
INDUSTRIAL PSYCHOLOGY

A. R. SPOKANE

OCCUPATIONAL INTERESTS

Because of the extensive concern of career development and career counselors with systematic measurement of career interests and adjustment, a general assessment of interests has become of major importance in the field. Among the issues involved have been the adequacy of psychometric approaches to measuring career interests; problems associated with sexism and/or racism in measuring career interests, particularly as these affect the language of the instruments; assumptions underlying the development of the instruments; and the norms on which the scores are based.

Interests are usually operationally defined by the instrument used to measure them. Four generic types of interests are usually assumed to exist. *Manifest interests* are represented by the activities in which an individual actually engages; *expressed interests* are those identified by an individual when asked about his or her interests; *inventoried interests* are those measured by various instruments, such as the Strong–Campbell inventory or the Kuder survey; and *tested interests* are inferred on the basis of the knowledge possessed by an individual about various fields of endeavor on the assumption that the knowledge reflects involvement in pertinent activities.

It is generally agreed that among adolescents occupational interests as measured by inventories predict about as well as expressed interests, and that adolescents' interests change over time. One reason interests do not predict occupational entry and satisfaction in adolescents well is that such variables as aptitudes, performance, and opportunity intervene significantly to determine occupational entry and achievement.

Most interest inventories are based on the general assumption that individuals who enter and find the same occupations satisfying share numerous characteristics, and so the interest measures strive to measure relevant personal characteristics. Unfortunately, little is known about how interests actually develop.

Most measures of career interest have followed highly successful examples used by the two leaders in the field—the *Strong–Campbell Interest Inventory* and the *Kuder Occupational Interest Survey.* Many counselors used both instruments together because one provided information about the person and the other provided information about the world of work as it relates to the person; as a result, the two instruments complemented each other.

Recognizing that each instrument had its limitations, their developers modified them over the years. Potential users also may have their own preferences for the psychometric underpinnings of one or the other instrument, but theoretically they measure fundamentally the same sets of attributes.

These two measures have dominated the field of interest measurement for almost half a century; other instruments have been developed but none have had anywhere near the influence on measuring career interest that these two have had.

Other measures, such as the *Self-Directed Search* (*SDS*) of J. L. Holland, have been used widely. The SDS assesses interests differently than the Strong–Campbell or the Kuder Occupational Scales. The SDS is probably the third most widely used device for measuring occupationally related interests.

SEXISM AND RACISM IN MEASUREMENT

All these instruments have met with difficulties as concern with racism and sexism heightened among test users. Most obvious in the earlier versions were sexism and the assumptions that particular occupations were deemed to be male as opposed to female, as well as the associated questions that resulted, the norms for the instruments, and the language used to describe interests. The Kuder and the Strong–Campbell measures now have same-sex and separate-sex normative approaches and sexism has been deleted from the language of the measures. Sexism in language is not a problem with the SDS, but there is a single set of norms, and given the items and their various representations on the scales, there are some systematic differences in the probability with which females versus males will score on different types that might not necessarily be related to eventual occupational membership and satisfaction.

Racism is more subtle and has been less directly addressed because the items are not necessarily racist themselves. However, the normative base, the language pattern, and the experience base may be substantially different for various ethnic groups, and thus may subtly affect the responses of individuals being assessed and their resulting score. Inappropriate inferences thus may be made.

INTEREST INVENTORIES
KUDER PREFERENCE INVENTORY
STRONG–CAMPBELL INTEREST INVENTORY

S. H. OSIPOW

OCCUPATIONAL STRESS

Occupational stress arises from interactions between people and their jobs and is characterized by changes within people that force them to deviate from their normal functioning.

Numerous personal consequences of occupational stress have been identified. Cardiovascular disease, gastrointestinal disorders, respiratory problems, cancer, arthritis, headaches, bodily injuries, skin disorders, physical strain or fatigue, and death are some of the purported physiological responses.

Psychological responses to occupational stress include anxiety, depression, dissatisfaction, boredom, somatic complaints, psychological fatigue, feelings of futility, inadequacy, low self-esteem, alienation, psychoses, anger, repression, and loss of concentration.

Dispensary visits, drug use and abuse, over- or undereating, nervous gesturing, pacing, risky behavior, aggression, vandalism, stealing, poor interpersonal relations, and suicide or attempted suicide are examples of potential behavioral consequences of occupational stress. It is important to note, however, that, in general, the data regarding any particular reaction are sparse. It is safest to conclude, therefore, that occupational stress can adversely affect an individual's well-being; precisely how these negative outcomes may manifest remains an open question. Furthermore, given the same level of exposure, different types of people respond differently to the occupational stressors they encounter.

With regard to the sources of occupational stress, three major categories can be identified: (a) organizational characteristics and processes; (b) working conditions and interpersonal relationships; and (c) job demands and role characteristics. Among organizational characteristics that have been suggested as stressful are high degrees of centralization, formalization, and specialization, as well as large size and a low rate of upward mobility. Organizational policies and processes that lead to pay inequities, frequent relocations, poor communications, ambiguous or conflicting task assignments, shift work, and inadequate feedback on performance also are seen as likely sources of stress.

Crowding, lack of privacy, noise, excessive heat or cold, inadequate lighting, glaring or flickering lights, and the presence of toxic chemicals and other air pollutants distinguish some working conditions identified as occupational stressors. Interpersonal relationships at work characterized by a lack of recognition, acceptance, and trust, as well as by competition and conflict, are seen as stress inducing.

With regard to job demands, likely stressors include repetitive work, time pressures and deadlines, low skill requirements, responsibility for people, and under- or overemployment. Finally, research on the roles people perform at work has suggested role conflict and ambiguity, role under- or overload, and role–status incongruency as potential stressors.

STRESS
STRESS CONSEQUENCES

A. P. BRIEF

OEDIPUS COMPLEX

A fundamental concept in the psychoanalytic theory of personality developed by Freud is the Oedipus complex. It derives its name from the legendary Greek king who, unknowingly, killed his father and married his mother.

MALES

The young boy's Oedipus complex consists of a double set of attitudes toward both parents: (a) An intense love and yearning for his mother is coupled with a powerful jealousy of and rage toward his father. This set is usually the stronger one. (b) He feels affection for his father, together with jealousy toward his mother. This occurs because all human beings are inherently bisexual (therefore the boy also behaves to some extent like a girl), and may become dominant if there exists an unusually strong constitutional tendency toward femininity.

The Oedipus complex may well be the most intense emotional experience of one's life, and includes all the characteristics of a true love affair: heights of passion, jealous rages, and desperate yearnings. His father becomes a rival to be done away with in order that the son may enjoy sole possession of his mother.

Ultimately, however, the Oedipus complex leads to severe conflicts. The boy fears that his illicit wishes will cost him his father's love and protection, which Freud characterizes as a child's strongest need. The boy concludes that girls originally possessed a penis but had it taken away as punishment, and fears that his seemingly all-powerful father will exact a similar penalty if the Oedipal wishes persist. To alleviate this intense castration anxiety, the boy eventually surrenders his conscious Oedipal strivings. At about age 5 to 6 years, he intensifies his identification with his father. The boy also develops internal prohibitions against doing certain things that his father does (such as enjoying special privileges with his mother). These identifications and prohibitions are incorporated into the component of personality that Freud called the superego.

FEMALES

Like the boy, the girl forms a powerful attachment to her mother during infancy. At about age 2 to 3 years, however, her discovery that she lacks a penis evokes strong feelings of inferiority and jealousy (penis envy). She responds by intensifying the envious attachment to her father, who possesses the desired organ; and by resenting the mother who shares her apparent defect, who allowed her to be born in this condition, and who now looms as a rival for her father's affection. Thus, while the girl is also inherently bisexual and has twofold attitudes (love and jealousy) toward both parents, her complex (sometimes called the Elektra complex) typically takes the form of desire for her father and hostility toward her mother.

The girl eventually seeks to compensate for her supposed physical deficiency by having her father's baby, preferably a boy baby who will bring the longed-for penis with him. Because the girl lacks the immediate and vital threat of castration anxiety, she remains Oedipal longer than the boy, and the superego that forms as a result of her less traumatic Oedipus complex is weaker than the boy's. Thus the girl has greater difficulty in sublimating her illicit strivings, and is more likely to become neurotic.

Whereas Freud regarded the Oedipus complex as a monumental discovery, this evaluation finds little support today outside of orthodox psychoanalytic circles. In particular, Freud's views about the relative inferiority of women have been roundly rejected by most psychologists. Freud's family consisted of a beautiful, indulgent mother and a cold and indifferent father, and hence his perception may have been overly influenced by the experiences of his own childhood.

PSYCHOANALYSIS

R. B. EWEN

OLDER ADULTS: MOOD AND MEMORY

A conservative estimate is that more than 50% of all adults older than 60 years of age complain about difficulties with remembering. However, memory complaints may represent an individual's feeling of impairment rather than an objective loss of memory. Research evidence suggests that there are age-related changes connected to memory and to overall intellectual functioning.

Studies comparing younger and older subjects frequently show greater within-subject variability for older participants. Other findings note that older adults often perform more slowly on cognitive tasks. There appears to be a relationship between how fast one can perform intellectual tasks and the agility of one's memory processes. Normal adults do show a significant decline of recent memory functions, but they do not share the demented adult's impairment of remote memory. In addition, older adults are more vulnerable to depression, especially in relationship to poor health. LaRue, Dessonville, and Jarvik point out that community surveys as well as studies of hospitalized patients have confirmed this relationship between physical health and depression. Whether the physical illness causes depression or whether depressed individuals are more predisposed to physical illness is still being debated. In addition to physical illness as a link to depression, these authors note that loss of social support related to bereavement, retirement, and relocation all contribute to depression, although depression as a function of these factors may be as crucial as are the availability of confidants.

Salzman and Gutfreund discovered that depression can produce decreased attention spans, increased errors of omission, decreased recall of new information, less access to pleasant memories accompanied by an increased access to sad memories, and less effective coding and memory strategies as well as decreased ability to organize information.

Scogin and Bienias report that memory training tends to have short-term positive effects. They assessed the effects of memory training on 27 memory-trained participants and 13 nontrained participants after a period of 3 years. They noted no differences in the number of memory complaints between the two groups at the 3-year follow-up, although the memory-trained participants initially had more memory complaints.

A later study by Flynn and Storandt compared several groups of 60- to 80-year-old memory-trained participants. Two of the groups studied a self-training manual, but the second group also attended group discussions dealing with problems of the elderly and the use of coping methods. The third group served as a wait-list control group. Results indicated that the group that attended the supplemental discussion improved memory performance, whereas those who only studied the self-instruction manual did not.

There is considerable literature to the effect that older adults are much more vulnerable to depression and are, in effect, more depressed than younger adults.

It is reasonably safe to conclude that there are changes in memory as one gets older, especially for the very old (older than 80 years). It also is safe to conclude that depression does have an effect on memory, attention span, and concentration, but the effects depend on the definition of attention span and the overall quality of one's intellectual and cognitive processes. Furthermore, such factors as physical health, social support, and overall life satisfaction also have an impact on psychological and cognitive functioning. Finally, it is still not known what the effectiveness is of memory workshops for normal older adults with memory complaints.

COGNITIVE COMPLEXITY
DEPRESSION
GERIATRICS
MEMORY DISORDERS

N. ABELES

OLFACTION

Olfaction literally means the act of smelling, and the term is commonly used to denote the sense of smell. For a number of reasons, less is known about olfaction than about the other major senses. First, the olfactory receptors are very tiny and are located deep in the head, which makes them difficult to study. Additionally, it is difficult to present a known quantity of an odorant to the receptors, both because of the aerodynamics of the nasal cavity and because of the nature of the stimulus itself. Although attempts have been made to define primary odors, researchers have not been successful in identifying a limited number of categories in which all odorants can be placed.

Olfaction is important for the behavior of a variety of animals, including mammals. For example, olfaction may be involved in predator–prey relationships—that is, a predator might use it to detect prey while a prey animal might rely on its sense of smell to avoid predation. The mating behavior of many species is guided, at least in part, by olfactory cues, and this is also true for parental behaviors.

Odorant stimuli are airborne molecules of volatile substances that are either water or fat soluble. In general, greater volatility means more odor, but there are important exceptions.

Several properties of odorant molecules may be related to their smell. Suggested possibilities are the shape of the molecule, its vibration frequency (movement of atoms in the molecule), and the rate of its movement across the olfactory receptors.

STRUCTURE OF THE OLFACTORY SYSTEM

The receptor cells are located in the olfactory epithelium (smell skin) at the top of the nasal cavity. The roof of the nasal cavity is formed by bone called the *cribriform plate*. Openings in the cribriform plate permit the passage of the *olfactory nerve*, which is composed of the axons of the receptor cells. The olfactory nerve ends in the *olfactory bulb*, a neural structure at the base of the brain.

At the other end of each receptor cell are hairlike structures called *cilia*. The sensitivity of an animal's olfactory system seems to be related both to the total number of receptor cells and to the number of cilia per receptor. By this measure, humans are low on the scale of sensitivity.

After leaving the olfactory bulbs, the olfactory pathways affect several structures in an area of the brain called the *rhinencephalon* (literally, nose brain). Some structures that receive olfactory input are the amygdala, hippocampus, pyriform cortex (located at the base of the temporal lobes), and the hypothalamus. A neocortical area responding to olfactory input, and in the lateral postero-orbital frontal cortex (LPOF), has been discovered by Tanabe and coworkers.

OLFACTORY PHENOMENA

The perceived intensity of an odor is greatly affected by adaptation. Only a brief period of exposure is sufficient to render an odor undetectable.

Adaptation occurs to the stimulus to which one is exposed and also to similar stimuli (cross-adaptation). The amount of cross-adaptation depends on the similarity between the adapting odor and other stimulus odors.

ACCOMMODATION
TASTE PERCEPTION

B. M. THORNE

ONLY CHILDREN

"Only children" are defined, in terms of ordinal position, as children without siblings, raised singly by their parent(s). In terms of psychological position, a child with a large (more than 7-year) age difference with regard to siblings nearest in age, or the only child of one sex in a family of opposite sex siblings, may be seen to function as an only child.

In keeping with his theoretical view of family constellation and birth order as strong potential influences on the child's strategy for fitting in and in the creation of personality and lifestyle, Adler suggested that: "The only child has a problem of his own. He has a rival, but his rival is not a brother or sister. His feelings of competition go against his father. An only child is pampered by his mother." It is also suggested that, from the Adlerian perspective, only children may have difficulties in interpersonal relations, with competing, and with sharing.

Little empirical research focusing on only children has been published; much of such information is imbedded in comparative birth-order research, with many contradictory findings.

BIRTH ORDER AND PERSONALITY

G. J. MANASTER

OPEN EDUCATION

Educators commonly disagree in their definitions of what conditions make a school "open." Some maintain that any practice that differs from traditional and formal classroom routines is sufficient; others hold that a truly open classroom is one in which pupils move about and talk at will, generate many of their own learning materials, and make many, if not all, decisions as to what they will learn and when they will learn it. Probably most proponents of open education would express preference for teaching/learning situations that lie somewhere between the two extremes.

The major themes in open education appear to be as follows:

1. *Encouragement and facilitation of student-initiated learning activity.* If students are not actively involved, they are not really learning.

2. *Individualization of learning.* Study materials are varied according to student needs, interests, and backgrounds. Students are taught in small groups, so that teachers can provide more individualized attention to special needs.

3. *Variety of instructional methods.* Classroom activities are not limited to the traditional lecture, reading, recitation, and testing.

4. *Openness of structure.* There may be experimentation with ungraded classes, team teaching, and architectural arrangements that permit fluidity of movement and accessibility.

5. *Relevance to everyday life.* Students' interests and experiences are a starting point for learning experiences, and attempts are made to relate whatever is being studied or discussed to the real world outside the classroom.

6. *Humaneness.* Teachers take pains to make students feel encouraged, supported, rewarded, understood, respected, and accepted. Warmth, openness, and group cohesiveness are encouraged.

7. *Application of principles of social psychology.* Teachers are sensitive to the principles of group dynamics and use them for group problem solving and for activities designed to increase patterns of mutual acceptance among students.

The open-education movement has its greatest following in English-speaking countries and in Europe.

Evaluation of open-education programs has produced mixed results. Some studies show that students who have had open-education experiences over a number of years have more positive attitudes toward themselves and others, as well as toward school and learning activities, and are more creative than students in more traditional programs. Other studies show that students in traditional classrooms attain higher levels of academic achievement, are less anxious, and are no less creative than those with open-education experiences. Students who have behavior problems, learning problems, or unusually high or low levels of anxiety appear to do better in more traditional settings. It may be that the outcomes of either style of education are too complex and varied to be adequately evaluated by the usual methods.

ALTERNATIVE EDUCATIONAL SYSTEMS
INDIVIDUAL EDUCATION

H. C. LINDGREN

OPERANT BEHAVIOR

It has long been known that behavior is affected by its consequences. We reward and punish people, for example, so that they will behave in different ways.

In *operant conditioning* behavior is also affected by its consequence, but the process is not trial-and-error learning. It can best be explained with an example. A hungry rat is placed in a semi-soundproof box. For several days bits of food are occasionally delivered into a tray by an automatic dispenser. The rat soon goes to the tray immediately on hearing the sound of the dispenser. A small horizontal section of a lever protruding from the wall has been resting in its lowest position, but it is now raised slightly so that when the rat touches it, it moves downward. In doing so it closes an electric circuit and operates the food dispenser. Immediately after eating the delivered food the rat begins to press the lever fairly rapidly. The behavior has been strengthened, or *reinforced,* by a single consequence. The rat is not "trying" to do anything when it first touches the lever and it does not learn from any "errors."

To a hungry rat, food is a natural reinforcer, but the reinforcer in this example is the sound of the food dispenser, which was conditioned as a reinforcer when it was repeatedly followed by the delivery of food before the lever was pressed. In fact, the sound of that one operation of the dispenser would have had an observable effect even though no food was delivered. When food no longer follows pressing the lever, the rat stops pressing. The behavior is said to be *extinguished.*

An operant can come under the control of a stimulus. If pressing the lever is reinforced when a light is on but not when it is off, responses continue to be made in the light but seldom if at all in the dark. The rat has formed a *discrimination* between light and dark. When one turns on the light, a response occurs, but that is not a reflex response.

The lever can be pressed with different amounts of force, and if only strong responses are reinforced, the rat presses more and more forcefully. If only weak responses are reinforced, it eventually responds only very weakly. The process is called *differentiation.*

A response must first occur for other reasons before it is reinforced and becomes an operant. It may seem as if a very complex response would never occur for the first time in order to be reinforced, but complex responses can be *shaped* by reinforcing their component parts separately to put together the final form of the operant. Operant reinforcement not only *shapes* the topography of behavior, it *maintains* it in strength long after an operant has been formed. *Schedules of reinforcement* are important in maintaining behavior. If a response has been reinforced for some time only once every 5 minutes, for example, the rat does not begin to respond immediately after reinforcement but responds more and more rapidly as the time for the next reinforcement approaches (called a *fixed-interval* schedule of reinforcement). If a response has been reinforced on the average every 5 minutes, but unpredictably, the rat responds at a steady rate (*variable-interval* reinforcement). If the average interval is short, the rate is high; if it is long, the rate is low.

If a response is reinforced after a given number of responses have been emitted, the rat responds more and more rapidly as the required number is approached (a *fixed-ratio* schedule of reinforcement). The number can be increased by easy stages up to a very high value: The rat will continue to respond even though responses are very rarely reinforced. When reinforcement occurs after an average number of responses but unpredictably, the schedule is called *variable-ratio.* It is familiar in gambling devices and systems, which arrange occasional but unpredictable payoffs. The required number of responses can easily be stretched, and in a gambling enterprise like a casino the average ratio is such that the gambler always loses in the long run.

Reinforcers may be positive or negative. A positive reinforcer reinforces when it is presented; a negative reinforcer reinforces when it is withdrawn. Negative reinforcement is not punishment. Reinforcers always strengthen behavior; that is what the word "reinforced" means. Punishment is used to suppress behavior. It consists of removing a positive reinforcer or presenting a negative one. It seems to operate by conditioning negative reinforcers. The punished person henceforth acts in ways that reduce the threat of punishment, and these ways are incompatible with, and hence take the place of, the behavior punished.

The human species is distinguished by the fact that its vocal responses can be easily conditioned as operants. There are many kinds of verbal operants because the behavior is reinforced through the mediation of other people, who do many different things. The reinforcing practices of a given culture compose what is called a language. Humans, however, tell each other what to do. We acquire most of our behavior only with that kind of help. We take advice, heed warnings, observe rules, and obey laws, and our behavior then comes under the control of consequences that otherwise would not be effective. Most of our behavior is too complex to have occurred for the first time without such verbal help. By taking advice and following rules we acquire a much more extensive repertoire than would be possible through a solitary contact with the environment.

Responding because behavior has had reinforcing consequences is very different from responding by taking advice, following rules, or obeying laws. We do not take advice because of the particular consequence that will follow: We take it only when taking other advice from similar sources has already had reinforcing consequences. In general, we are much more strongly inclined to do things if they have had immediate reinforcing consequences than if we have merely been advised to do them.

The innate behavior studied by ethologists is shaped and maintained by its contribution to the survival of the individual and species. Operant behavior is shaped and maintained by its consequences for the individual. Both processes have controversial features. Neither one seems to have any place for a prior plan or purpose. In both, selection replaces creation.

Personal freedom also seems threatened. It is only the feeling of freedom, however, that is affected. Those who respond because their behavior has had positively reinforcing consequences usually *feel* free. They seem to be doing what they *want* to do. Those who respond because the reinforcement has been negative and who are therefore avoiding or escaping from punishment are doing what they *must* do and do not feel free. These distinctions do not involve the fact of freedom.

The experimental analysis of operant behavior has led to a technology often called behavior modification. It usually consists of changing the consequences of behavior, removing consequences that have caused trouble or arranging new consequences for behavior that has lacked strength. Historically, people have been controlled primarily through negative reinforcement—that is, they have been punished when they have not done what was reinforcing to those who could punish them. Positive reinforcement has been less often used, partly because its effect is slightly deferred, but it can be as effective as negative reinforcement and has many fewer unwanted by-products.

BEHAVIOR MODIFICATION
CLASSICAL CONDITIONING
THORNDIKE'S LAWS OF LEARNING

B. F. Skinner

OPERANT CONDITIONING

The term *operant conditioning* is used in two senses in the field of learning. In its narrower sense it refers to a set of techniques used for the study of instrumental conditioning. In its broader and more fundamental sense, operant conditioning denotes a general theoretical orientation that applies these techniques and the concepts that arise from them to the full range of human and animal behavior.

OPERANT TECHNIQUE

The primary features of operant conditioning techniques may be illustrated by the following example. A rat is placed in a dimly illuminated small chamber contained in a sound-attenuating, lightproof enclosure. A lever protrudes from one wall of the otherwise barren chamber, and when the rat presses the lever, a small pellet of food sometimes drops into a cup located beside the lever. Such an arrangement is often called a Skinner box after psychologist B. F. Skinner, who first devised it.

The example illustrates the single feature that most clearly distinguishes operant procedures from other instrumental conditioning procedures: The behavior of interest may be executed repeatedly by the learner. Unlike discrete-trial procedures such as maze learning, in which behavior occurs in distinct episodes, the response is continuously and freely available in operant procedures.

Because repeated responding is possible, two further characteristics of operant conditioning techniques may be noted. First, responding is measured by its rate of occurrence. The rate of responding is taken as an approximation to the fundamental index of response strength—probability of response. On a cumulative record, the slope of the curve provides a direct measure of the momentary rate of responding. Second, with repeated responding possible, the relationship between various properties of the response (such as its number or time of emission) and the occurrence of the critical event that maintains the response (such as food) may be manipulated. The rule that describes the properties of the response that are required for the occurrence of the critical event is called the *schedule of reinforcement*. Different schedules yield characteristic patterns of responding. The high rates of responding and the complexity of many schedules of reinforcement usually require that operant conditioning experiments be implemented by automatic equipment, often computers.

OPERANT THEORY

In its broader sense, operant conditioning is a subdivision of biology that seeks to identify the environmental determinants of behavior by means of an experimental analysis. All behavior of both humans and animals is assumed to have its ultimate origins in the environment. The ancestral environment of the individual affects behavior through genetic mechanisms the effects of which are summarized by the principle of natural selection. These antecedents of behavior are the province of evolutionary biology. The past and present environments of the individual affect behavior through largely unknown neurochemical mechanisms, the effects of which are summarized by the principle of reinforcement. The analysis of the effects of the individual environment on behavior is the province of operant conditioning.

Both natural selection and reinforcement hold in common the belief that future behavior may be understood by examining the consequences of past behavior. In the case of natural selection, behaviors (and structures) are selected if they enhance reproductive fitness. In the case of reinforcement, behaviors are strengthened if they have been followed by critical events, which are technically termed *reinforcers*.

As the environmental origins of behavior are identified and their functional relationships to behavior are described, environmental changes may be instituted that affect the course of behavioral change as genetic engineering may affect the course of evolution.

A number of methodological implications flow from the basic assumption that the behavior of all organisms, including humans, is ultimately shaped by the environment. First, as people and animals both have been confronted with ancestral environments that have selected for the capacity to modify behavior within the lifetime of a single organism (i.e., the capacity to learn), a common functional statement of the reinforcement principle is likely to emerge from the study of any of a large number of species.

Second, since behavioral change results from the contact of the organism with its environment, and since the ancestral and individual environments vary somewhat from one organism to the next even under the best controlled circumstances, the process of change must be studied in a single organism. Conclusions based on averaging the performance of groups of organisms may obscure and distort the behavioral processes occurring in the individual.

Third, although a neurochemical description of the mechanisms underlying behavioral change will be obtained eventually, and will be a welcome addition to knowledge, operant conditioning seeks to analyze behavior as the product of environmental antecedents without appeal to postulated inferred processes or structures. Theoretical constructs of this type are regarded as diverting attention from the task of an experimental analysis, and as having the form but not the substance of explanations, since they often lead to errors of hypostatization (assuming an entity exists because it has been named) and logical circularity.

Operant conditioning attempts to analyze the interaction between the organism and its environment into a three-term sequence or contingency. The product of a successful experimental analysis is an identification of the environmental events (discriminative stimuli) that determine the occurrence of the behavior (operant) and of the environmental events (reinforcing stimuli, or reinforcers) necessary for the acquisition and maintenance of the behavior. The behavior whose emission is required for the occurrence of the reinforcer is called an operant to emphasize that it operates on the subsequent environment to produce certain consequences.

Finally, the changes in the environmental control of behavior that result from operant conditioning are not necessarily confined to the particular stimulus and response characteristics identified in the original experimental analysis. As the result of operant conditioning, it is most common for a class of stimuli to have acquired control over a class of responses.

BEHAVIOR MODIFICATION
OPERANT BEHAVIOR
REINFORCEMENT SCHEDULES

J. W. Donahoe

OPERATIONAL DEFINITION

Few topics in the area of scientific communication have been as troublesome as that of operational definition. Psychologists have done their share both to clarify and to muddy the waters on this problem, and this article outlines some of the principal facets they need to consider.

OPERATIONISM

Operationism was initiated by Harvard University physicist P. W. Bridgman, who had reviewed the history of definitions of fundamental physical concepts like length, space, and time as they were used before Einstein to learn why they required such drastic revisions in Einstein's revolutionary theorizing. Bridgman concluded that the traditional Newtonian definitions had contained substantial amounts of meaning not related to their actual physical measurements (e.g., the assumption of an absolute scale for time); it was this kind of excess meaning that was responsible for Einstein's need to make radical reformulations in these concepts.

Bridgman suggested that to avoid similar roadblocks in the development of physical theory it would be necessary to impose more stringent requirements on the making of definitions. His proposal was that concepts should be defined strictly in terms of the operations used to measure them. As he put it, "The concept is synonymous with the corresponding set of operations."

Bridgman found that nothing was quite as simple and straightforward as it had seemed at first. He subsequently made some strategic retreats from his initially monolithic position, such as acknowledging at least the temporary admissibility of paper-and-pencil operations and accepting the usefulness of abstract concepts.

The idea that the meaning of all concepts should be restricted to the necessary operations underlying them had an immediate appeal for psychologists. Operationism was promulgated early in psychology by S. S. Stevens. Stevens was careful to point out that the operational-definition movement was simply a formalization of the methodology that had always been used by effective scientists, including psychologists.

Unfortunately, the balanced position advanced by Stevens did not quite prove to be the norm. Probably the single most important negative factor was the overselling of the operational ideal, especially as applied to situations in which perfectly operational definitions of psychological concepts were clearly not even approximately feasible. Also, there was the continuing persistence of the more grandly conceived operationism, and the consequent overloading of what should have been merely a fundamental methodological principle with essentially less relevant substantive issues of one kind or another. The net result has been that far too little attention has been paid to the central principle.

A good example of the communication difficulties that await the unwary user or reader is afforded by the word *frustration*. Quite apart from the further complications of theoretical nuances, this word is used in at least three distinct ways, which are usually but by no means always kept clearly separated: (a) as a kind of blocking operation that prevents a motivated organism from obtaining a goal or persisting in goal-directed behavior; (b) as the kind of behavior that appears when such a goal-oriented organism is thus blocked; and (c) as some hypothetical inner process that is assumed to be responsible for the overt behavioral responses to the blocking operation.

None of the secondary and tertiary disputes over operationism can eliminate the fact that psychologists all too often are simply failing to communicate adequately with each other because they continue to use key terms in a variety of loosely defined and highly ambiguous ways. Some basic considerations need to be emphasized. First, operational definitions are not all-or-none achievements; rather, there is a continuum of operational clarity in definitions, that is, in the degree to which ambiguity and excess meaning have been eliminated. Second, full operational clarity needs to be an objective to be kept clearly in mind throughout all phases of theoretical and empirical research; acceptance of ambiguity must be regarded in many situations as a necessary but, it is hoped, not a permanent condition, and it is important that scientific communicators explicitly recognize this state of affairs rather than simply ignore it and gloss over the problem. Third, substantive issues involving defined concepts must not be allowed to intrude on and confuse the primarily methodological criteria associated with operational definitions. Fourth, it is hoped that recognition of the importance of these considerations serves as a spur to improve definitional clarity and ultimately to help make improvements in theoretical development. Taking this kind of positive approach to the definitional problem should also serve to help free psychologists from the semantic quagmires in which so many of the key concepts are still entangled.

COMMUNICATION THEORY
GENERAL SYSTEMS
LOGICAL POSITIVISM
MILL'S CANONS

M. H. Marx

OPERATIONALISM

Operationalism is the demand that all theoretical terms in science—that is, those that do not refer to something directly observable—be given operational definitions. The goal of operationalism was to eliminate from science any concepts that were metaphysical (and to positivists, meaningless), ensuring that science would ask only questions that had empirical answers, and would have theories that referred only to meaningful entities.

As empiricists, operationists assume that there is never doubt when talking about things that can be observed. Uncertainty arises for theoretical terms such as mass, drive, anxiety, and superego. None of these is publicly observable, even though anxiety and hunger have been experienced, and two terms, mass and superego, are entirely abstract. In an operational definition, a theoretical term is defined by linking it to some publicly verifiable operations measurement or a manipulation that can be performed on the environment.

The operationalist contends that the operational definition supplies the full meaning of a concept by linking it to unproblematic observation terms; anything more is unscientific "surplus meaning." Moreover, operationalists question the scientific legitimacy of any term not operationally definable.

It has proved difficult, if not impossible, to "operationalize" all the terms even of physics, leading positivists gradually to abandon operationalism. In psychology, operationalism has been criticized for unduly narrowing psychology's focus, making behaviorism the only acceptable psychology by methodological fiat rather than by superiority of results. That terms be operationalized remains, however, a common requirement of psychological theory.

EMPIRICISM
POSITIVISM
SCIENTIFIC METHOD

T. H. Leahey

OPERATIONS RESEARCH

Operations research is a relatively new field, the short history of which can be traced to the early years of World War II. This precise mathematical science has an articulated set of general guidelines that provides researchers with a plan for conducting an operations research study. The stages are as follows:

1. Formulating the problem.
2. Constructing a mathematical model to represent the system under study.
3. Deriving a solution from the model.
4. Testing the model and the solution derived from the model.
5. Establishing controls over the solution.
6. Putting the solution to work: implementation.

FORMULATING THE PROBLEM

Considerable attention must be given to establishing the general nature of the problem and, of even more importance, to the objectives for the study. These objectives should be stated in behavioral terms to minimize or eliminate ambiguity.

Sufficient care also should be given to prioritizing the objectives that can be realistically attained. A list of too many objectives can present potential operational difficulties, especially if these objectives are not clearly articulated in a logical sequence.

CONSTRUCTING A MATHEMATICAL MODEL

The second phase of an operations research study is the depiction of a model. The nature of a model is to represent the real world. In operations research, such models are symbolic, expressed in mathematical terms. The classical $E = mc^2$ is an example of a mathematical model. The usual forms for such models are algebraic equations, which not only are more economical than verbal expressions, but also entail precision of definition so that the particular elements, as well as their interrelationships, can be more clearly expressed and understood.

The most important concern in building the model is the clear and unambiguous development and definition of the objective function. This function expresses the relationship between the independent variables and the dependent variable.

DERIVING A SOLUTION FROM THE MODEL

The third phase of the operations research study demands that a solution be sought. Typically an optimal or best solution is desired, but it must be recognized that such a solution has value only to the model in question. Since the model is but a representation of the real-world problem, there are numerous situations in which an optimal solution would not entail the best direction to take.

However, when an optimal solution is combined with less than optimal or more realistic alternative solutions, all testable against the real problem, the use of an optimal solution does have benefits. One of these benefits extends to establishing, at the end of the study, the relative distance between the ideal solution and the accepted alternative.

A by-product of such a methodology of using operations research is the suggestion that less than optimal solutions might be conceived as stepping stones. This case of successive approximations can lead the operations researcher to a more fruitful conclusion.

There are numerous mathematical procedures for deriving solutions to an operations research model. These procedures are based on probability theories.

TESTING THE MODEL AND THE SOLUTION

There are two steps involved in testing the model and the solution. The first is the careful analysis of all of the model's elements, including a reexamination of the model's algebraic factors for simplistic cosmetic errors that can affect the validity. The more important step is reestablishing the relationship of the model to the premises that were used to develop the model in the first place.

A more systematic plan also includes the introduction of historic data that can be readily introduced into the model so that a prototype solution can be generated. The data must be inspected to assure the operations researcher of the validity of the test. It should be pointed out that since the model, for all practical purposes, is constructed on the basis of prior historic data and needs, it may behave quite differently in the future. Another common pitfall is the introduction into the model of factors that were not present in the historic database.

ESTABLISHING CONTROLS

The fifth stage, establishing controls over the solution, arises when the model is used repeatedly. Controls are established over the model when the operations researcher acknowledges the differences in the values of the historic data and how the relationships among the model's elements and solutions are affected by these differences. A more important step may be the construction of limits on selected key parameters of the model to establish a range of acceptable values given the real-world data.

IMPLEMENTING THE MODEL

The final step is the introduction of the real-world data into the model. Implementation of the model carries with it the obvious step of entering

real data and determining the solution. Furthermore, it is also important to determine the proximity to the historic solutions derived previously and also the implications of the solution for developing operating procedures. These steps provide an important link between the mathematical nature of operations research and the practical results arising from the study. Finally, these solutions and their management implications are used by the astute operations researcher to finalize the model for possible future use.

RESEARCH METHODOLOGY

R. S. ANDRULIS

OPINION POLLS

A distinction may be made between two varieties of public opinion polls—in one, the accuracy of the poll can be ascertained by a subsequent event; in the other, views are assayed but the results can be checked only by internal consistency or by another poll. Forecasting elections is the prime example of the first type; investigating current thinking on such issues as taxation, abortion, limitation of nuclear weaponry, and control of immigration is of the second type.

Only occasionally is there a formal referendum on any public issue. This means that polls in which respondents take clear-cut positions on matters of concern provide legislators with an important means of learning the views and wishes of their constituents.

The public opinion poll probably has its greatest social justification as an antidote to the influence of pressure groups since a good evaluation of public sentiment can be found from a scientifically conducted poll.

The crucial principle, first recognized by innovators in the 1930s, was that better deductions about what would happen in an election could be drawn from a small sample with defined characteristics than from a large sample with unknown characteristics. Current methods of the construction of samples are by no means uniform, but essentially there are three phases, and are as follows:

1. Clearly defining the group about which the prediction is to be made.
2. Deciding on the size of the sample to be studied.
3. Devising a scheme by which every person in the population has equal probability of being included in the sample.

Methods have been worked out that yield good approximations to random samples. The Gallup organization has successfully used a three-tier randomization in election polls. First there is a random selection of election districts; then within each election district there is a random selection of households; and finally within each household there is a random selection of the individual to be interviewed. Samples developed by this method tend to be both representative of the population and reasonably accessible to interviewers. In addition to views on candidates or issues, interviewers record demographic data, observed or in reply to questions: sex, age, education, occupation, income level, race, religious preference, and, when pertinent, political affiliation and vote in a recent election.

The use of modern computers permits adjustment of findings within an observed sample to what would probably be observed in the population, using statistics collected in the current population surveys of the U.S. Census Bureau.

When the group of individuals questioned in a poll closely approximates a truly random sample of the population under investigation, it need not be large. The Gallup organization has often used samples of only 1500, a size that can be shown to be accurate within 2 or 3 percentage points.

Two kinds of questions are used in polling: the open-ended or free-response variety, in which the respondent formulates the answer in his or her own words; and the structured-answer type, in which the interviewee chooses from two or more suggested answers. Both classifications are useful. The open-ended question is essential when exploring respondents' knowledge in an area, overall opinions, and reasons for their views. The "objective" item, involving a choice of stated alternatives, is useful in predicting elections, in ascertaining divisions on public issues, and in following trends.

Polling organizations committed to the use of the scientific method give much attention to the selection of the questions and to their precise wording.

Some officeholders conduct opinion surveys by mailing questionnaires to a sample of voters in their constituency. If a list of eligible voters is available, sampling is not difficult. Sometimes a 100% sample is used. The use of reply cards that can be read and tabulated by machine greatly reduces the cost of such surveys.

Another method of polling is by telephone. In some cases, the telephone numbers of individuals in a defined group can be ascertained and contacts made. However, some bias may be introduced in the sample because, for various reasons, the numbers at which some individuals may be reached are not in the telephone directory. There exists a computer-based dialing system by which a completely random selection of residential telephones (including unlisted numbers) in any desired area code can be contacted. Where the defined population is that of households having telephones, the procedure is useful.

ATTITUDE MEASUREMENT
CROSS-SECTIONAL RESEARCH
SURVEYS

P. H. DuBois

OPTIMAL FUNCTIONING

The area of optimal functioning was introduced into modern scientific psychology by Marie Jahoda. The persons contributing most heavily to the area of optimal functioning are humanistic psychologists who see optimal functioning as qualitatively different from normality or lack of pathology.

Simply stated, this area of psychology is a scientific investigation of what the person is capable of becoming, of the best the person can be, of the way the person can realize any number of personal potentials. It has been the task of workers in this area to examine these phenomena in systematic and scientific ways.

SELF-ACTUALIZATION

Abraham Maslow's empirical and theoretical investigation of optimal functioning asserts that there are two basic realms of human need. One, called the D or deficiency realm, is composed of the things we need to be functioning persons. These include the *physiological needs* for food, water, and other biological requirements; the *safety needs* to be protected from fear and chaos; the *belongingness and love needs* to be included in a family or friendship group to protect us from loneliness; and our *esteem needs* for self-respect and self-esteem, for a sense of accomplishment and worth. These needs are states of deficiency that must be met for us to be minimally adequate as human beings.

The B needs represent the needs that enable us to be optimally functioning human beings. These are our needs for self-actualization and our aesthetic needs. Maslow posited that these B-level needs, or meta-needs, are just as necessary as the D-level needs. If D needs are not met,

one becomes ill physiologically and psychologically. If the B-level need is not met, one develops meta-pathologies.

For Maslow, self-actualized persons are aided in their development by intense moments of ecstasy, joy, and insight called "peak experiences." There are moments of transcendence that take a person beyond self-actualization to what Maslow called the Z realm, a realm beyond the self that transcends both space and time.

Beautiful and Noble Persons
Working within the tradition of Maslow's approach, Landsman develops a system for describing and empirically investigating the optimal functioning person, whom he describes as the Beautiful and Noble Person. Placed on a continuum that begins with normality (meaning persons who are free of abnormality and are reality perceptive), Landsman describes his Beautiful and Noble Person as the development of a self that proceeds from (a) the passionate self, a self-expressive, self-enjoying state, to (b) the environment-loving self, where the person cares deeply for the physical environment and the tasks to be accomplished in the world, and finally (c) to the compassionate self, which enables the person to be loving and caring toward other persons.

FULLY FUNCTIONING PERSON
Rogers described what he considered to be the optimally functioning or, as he preferred, the "fully functioning person." In contrast to Maslow's approach, Rogers emphasized the process of being fully functioning as it occurs moment by moment in every person's life, rather than being primarily concerned with describing characteristics of persons. His work has been of the greatest influence in the field of psychotherapy, with less attention being devoted to formal research investigation of healthy persons outside the therapy situation.

Rogers starts with the assumption that every person has the capacity to actualize or complete his or her own inner nature. The key to this is for the person to remain in contact with his or her deepest feelings, which Rogers called *organismic experiences* or experiences of the organism. Optimal functioning is promoted when the person is able to know in awareness exactly what is happening at this deeper, direct organismic level. The person must be able to develop the kind of self or self-structure that is able to be congruent or in harmony with the person's own deep feelings or experiences.

This kind of personal development can take place most easily when the person has other people who are able to provide unconditional positive regard; a type of love, acceptance, and understanding of the individual's innermost being. This is a respect for the person's own internal frame of reference or way of understanding the world. When this happens, the person can develop a number of desirable characteristics. First, the person can be open to a wide range of experiences without being defensive, and will be almost totally aware of these experiences. The person will be able to be flexible and to maintain a constant state of growth and change. It not only enables the person to see experiences clearly, but also serves as a guide for evaluating these experiences. One's inner self can serve as a guide for living.

Psychology of Optimal Persons
Another formulation of optimal functioning centering on the concept of process that emphasizes constant change is Kelly's formulation of "A psychology of the optimal man." The unit of analysis is the *personal construct,* which is a meaning dimension or conviction a person might hold, such as seeing people as loving versus rejecting. The personality of the individual is made up of a number of these personal construct dimensions. One essential feature of optimal functioning for Kelly was for people to be able to make use of this system of personal meaning in

such a way that they complete what he called "full cycles of experiences." By this he meant that they must take up their conceptions of the world in such a way that these conceptions are tested and evaluated so that the total system will keep changing and developing to keep pace with an ever-changing world.

In this way, people are truly changed by the nature of their experience, and are kept in a continual mode of orderly change. The work within this framework has centered on ways to evaluate each of the steps and to promote a progression through these steps. The concern in construct theory is more with the way in which people invent or create themselves rather than uncover or discern an inner self.

OPTIMAL PERSONALITY TRAITS

Coan undertook a multivariate study of optimal functioning persons, and later elaborated the theoretical implications of this work.

In this empirical approach, Coan employed a battery of tests that took university students 6 hours to complete. This battery included measures pertaining to phenomenal consistency, cognitive efficiency, perceptual organization, the experience of control, the scope of awareness, openness to experience, independence, the experience of time, reality contact, self insight, logical consistency of the attitude–belief system and various other aspects of attitudes, beliefs, and adjustments. The final factor analysis yielded 19 obliquely rotated factors.

Of primary importance was the fact that no single general factor was found that could represent a global personality trait of self-actualization. Instead the picture that emerged appeared to contain a number of independent dimensions and a number of dimensions that seemed to be mutually exclusive.

Coan further suggests that a common theme in most of these polarities may be a general one of either being open to experience or having an attitude that we must maintain efficient control over life and world affairs. Coan suggests, from his own factor analysis and from his reading of the Eastern and Western theories of optimal functioning, that five basic characteristics can be isolated that characterize the "ideal human condition": (a) efficiency, (b) creativity, (c) inner harmony, (d) relatedness, and (e) transcendency.

OTHER SIGNIFICANT CONTRIBUTIONS

For the serious student of optimal functioning, special attention should be given to a number of other important systems of thought. These include (a) Jung's concept of individuation, (b) Fromm's productive character, (c) Allport's conception of appropriate functioning, (d) Erikson's conception of maturity, (e) Adler's formation of Social Interest, (f) Horney's sense of a real self and self-alienation, (g) Reich's notion of the genital character with self regulation, (h) Jourard's concept of self-disclosure, and (i) White's concern with competence and interest.

EGO DEVELOPMENT
PEAK EXPERIENCE

F. R. EPTING
D. I. SUCHMAN

ORGANIC PSYCHOSES

The term *organic psychoses* encompasses a host of disorders that have in common the fact that the particular etiology interferes with the individual's general mental functioning. Labeling some psychoses as organic and others as functional does not imply that there is no organic basis for the latter, but rather that a known and specifiable organic disorder is associated with the former.

Organic psychoses can be associated with any of a number of organic changes that directly or indirectly affect brain functioning: endogenous or exogenous toxic substances (alcohol, drugs, heavy metals, etc.), infections (paresis, meningitis, encephalitis, etc.), primary convulsive disorders (epilepsy), head trauma (concussions and resulting subdural hematoma), intracranial neoplasm (tumors), arteriosclerosis and cerebrovascular disorders, nutritional deficits (niacin, thiamine, Wernicke's syndrome), endocrine disorders (e.g., myxedema), and senile and presenile disturbances (e.g., Alzheimer's disease, Pick's disease, Huntington's chorea).

Symptomatically, many of the organic psychoses begin mildly enough with symptoms of fatigue, headache, moodiness, drowsiness, and distractibility and complaints of the inability to concentrate. Occasionally insidious personality changes take place, along with disturbances of sleep, and the appearance of increasing irritability and a loss of inhibitions, leading to behavioral changes such as increasing aggression, restlessness, and impulsiveness. Depending on the particular etiology and its time course, aphasia, apraxia, hemiparesis, emotional instability, depression, disorientation, perceptual disturbance, hallucinations, memory disturbances, delirium, dementia, and even convulsions may ensue. A number of patients, particularly those who have suffered trauma, display a "catastrophic reaction" in which the patient becomes very agitated, anxious, and upset when faced with a difficult problem.

Treatment of the organic psychoses depends on the specific etiology. It is important, therefore, to establish the correct diagnosis as early as possible so that appropriate medical and/or surgical treatment can be initiated.

ORGANIC SYNDROMES
SENILE PSYCHOSES

W. E. EDMONSTON, JR.

ORGANIC SYNDROMES

An organic syndrome is a clinical diagnostic label for symptom clusters manifested on mental status examination and attributed, directly or indirectly, to disturbed brain structure or function. In the American Psychiatric Association's *Diagnostic and Statistical Manual of Mental Disorders* (*DSM-IV*), a distinction is made between organic brain syndromes and organic mental disorders. *Organic brain syndrome* is a descriptive label that refers to a certain cluster of mental and behavioral symptoms related to brain dysfunction, but without reference to a specific cause. *Organic mental disorder,* however, refers to both a specific organic syndrome and a specific etiological agent.

A number of ramifications and implications imbedded in this distinction must be remembered. The first is that no single symptom or cluster of symptoms is uniformly associated with brain dysfunction. The brain is a highly complex organ, and disruption of its normal functioning can result in a myriad of psychological and behavioral deficits. Furthermore, the same etiological agent (e.g., head injury, tumor, vascular infarct) affecting one individual may manifest quite differently in another, depending on the brain lesion's size and location, whether the lesion is acute or chronic, the person's age, and premorbid personality and health.

A second point is that organic brain syndrome is a behavioral construct and not a neurological one. Failure to acknowledge this distinction can lead to the erroneous assumption that brain dysfunction and organic syndromes are reciprocally related.

Finally, although many organic symptom constellations (hallucinosis, organic affective syndrome, etc.) are similar to those found in such "functional" mental conditions as schizophrenia and the major affective disorders, they are distinguished in that they are directly related to a specific transient or permanent dysfunction of the brain. The distinction between organic and functional disorders is a somewhat gray area, and probably reflects more the limitations of our current knowledge of brain-behavior relationships than a hard and fast reality.

Thus the diagnosis of an organic versus functional syndromes largely rests on whether a known or presumed organic etiology can be identified.

SPECIFIC ORGANIC SYNDROMES

The *DSM-IV* describes 10 major organic syndromes: delirium, dementia, amnestic syndrome, organic hallucinosis, organic delusional syndrome, organic affective syndrome, organic personality syndrome, intoxification, withdrawal, and atypical or mixed organic brain syndrome. The specific symptoms constituting each syndrome may vary from individual to individual and even within the same person over time. Moreover, an individual may have more than one syndrome at the same time. Diagnosis is made on the basis of those symptoms that predominate in the clinical picture during mental status examination, and requires evaluation of the patient's general orientation, memory, intellectual functions, emotional stability, inner reality, and social behavior.

ALZHEIMER'S DISEASE
BRAIN INJURIES
CENTRAL NERVOUS SYSTEM DISORDERS
COMPUTERIZED TOMOGRAPHY
HUNTINGTON'S CHOREA
MINIMAL BRAIN DYSFUNCTION
MULTIPLE SCLEROSIS

G. J. CHELUNE

ORGANIZATIONAL CLIMATE

Organizational climate refers to an organization's characteristics as perceived by members. Climate is, therefore, the sum of *shared* organizational perceptions. It is a subjective concept that may not be related to actual properties of the organization.

Historically the concept of organizational climate may be traced to Tolman's description of "cognitive maps" of the environment, which are the schemas individuals create to make sense of their surroundings. Later, Lewin suggested that the atmosphere or climate of any group might be defined as the shared perceptions of individuals, or how individuals' cognitive maps are like each other.

Many research studies have focused on the subjective and intangible quality of climate in organizations. Measurements have usually involved questionnaires that elicit individual perceptions of organizational characteristics. These characteristics most frequently include the degree to which individuals are involved in the decision-making process, whether employees are informed of objectives, whether individual effort is recognized and rewarded, and whether superiors support those who work for them.

Other characteristics may include the sense of constraint experienced by workers, the sense of riskiness and challenge in work assignments, the degree to which conflict is tolerated or resolved, a sense of "forward motion" in the organization as a whole, and a sense of "belonging."

Climate is influenced by leadership style, formal systems and structures, administrative procedures, and decision-making rules. Climate has been shown to influence job satisfaction and performance, motivation, and creativity.

Resulting climates have then been characterized as participative versus directive, benevolent versus exploitive, production versus people oriented, and related to either power, achievement, or affiliation.

There are several controversial issues in organizational climate research. Two issues result from the difficulty in defining climate. First, climate has often been confused with culture, defined as "the set of habitual and traditional ways of thinking, feeling, and reacting that are characteristic of the ways a particular society meets its problems at a particular point in time." Most researchers assume, however, that climate is a subset of the larger culture, related to descriptions of organizational properties rather than descriptions of beliefs and values as a whole.

Psychologists who argue that climate refers to how people feel about their culture are touching on the second definitional issue. How people feel about their work situation is defined as job satisfaction. Some psychologists have argued that climate is just another name for satisfaction. Again, most climate researchers argue, however, that climate is descriptive (although subjective) while satisfaction is purely an affective and subjective concept.

Two other issues involve the relationship of climate to satisfaction and performance (or productivity). Clear relationships between climate and satisfaction have been consistently reported, but there are conflicting interpretations of these relationships. Some psychologists argue that climates that are participative in nature (supportive with decentralized decision making) consistently increase satisfaction. Others argue that this is not necessarily true, and that satisfaction results when the expectations of the individual match those of the climate.

The relationship of climate to performance (or productivity) also is not agreed on consistently. Some argue that a participative climate increases productivity; others say that the degree of fit between employees and the climate is the salient variable. In the case of performance, it would appear that the "degree of fit" argument is much stronger, and more psychologists have theorized that high performance is a result of individual/climate synchrony. Again, there is evidence from a recent study that performance is higher when the climate fits the person, rather than in prescribing one climate for all persons.

Finally researchers have concluded that because climate is based on perceptions, there are many climates within an organization. Climate is one result of the interaction between persons and environments and is influenced by the nature of the people involved as well as the setting.

EMPLOYEE PRODUCTIVITY
JOB SATISFACTION
MORALE IN ORGANIZATIONS

B. FORISHA-KOVACH

ORGANIZATIONAL DIAGNOSIS

When a consultant undertakes to help an organization change, there is a need to understand the organization as an organic system, adaptive and capable of change with a life of its own that transcends that of the people in it and with the capacity to perpetuate itself. Building on an open-system model, organizations may be seen as being made up of subsystems.

All organizations strive toward some goal. They mobilize the energies of their people and their financial, production, and technical resources. In the service of attaining that goal, they attack their respective environments and seek advantage in competition with other organizations. They also strive toward a stable regularity. These patterns of organizational behavior are consistent and observable.

PATTERNS OF BEHAVIOR

Value System

All organizations have a history, a culture, and a tradition. They strive toward some ideal, some standard of performance. They have rules, regulations, policies, procedures, norms of behavior, codes of conduct, and methods for monitoring all of those standards and controls. Much of an organization's activity is an outgrowth of the manner in which its leadership has constructed it, the kinds of people who have been attracted to it, and what it has done before, particularly its ways of having adapted to its unique crises.

History

All organizations, as a product of their history, culture, and traditions, also evolve a folklore. They have legendary heroes, recall certain competitive victories, develop certain repetitive ways of producing or selling or serving that characterize and differentiate them from other organizations in the same field.

Information

All organizations must obtain, process, and act on information. They must sense their socioeconomic realities. They get information both from within themselves and from the marketplace, as well as from the broader world, more or less systematically, which they then process and integrate into their ongoing activities. There is an organizational memory. There is a history of how the organization mobilizes its skills, knowledge, and capacities to solve various problems. There is a pattern to how it acts on them.

Communications

Organizations have methods of internal communication and modes of communicating with the outside. The communication system, together with the accounting control system, constitute what might be called the sensory and motor aspects of the organization.

Power

All organizations have leadership, which in turn exercises power and distributes it to the rest of the organization. The components of the organization may have their own power either because they possess knowledge or resources or organizational advantages. In those cases, the leadership must often interact with other power centers. The leadership must also interact with various constituencies outside the organization.

Key Figures

All organizations have, in addition to leadership, key figures who possess certain knowledge or social power and who interact in certain ways. The interaction of these key figures has a significant impact on the way the rest of the organization operates.

Groups

All organizations are comprised of varied groups. These may be functional groups such as sales, accounting, manufacturing, or engineering; or they may be disciplinary groups such as physicians and nurses, or teachers and principals; or they may be task groups such as different production and service facilities. These groups have relationships with each other and are continuously engaged in intergroup and intragroup adaptation.

Adaptation

All organizations adapt in certain consistent ways. These may be more or less successful, but they tend to be characteristic. Adaptation patterns may change with an infusion of new and different leadership, or new

and different organization membership, or changes in product or service orientation. However, by and large, barring such radical change, the adaptation processes are evolutionary and discernible.

THE DIAGNOSIS

Anyone who is to change any organization must have an understanding of the manner in which each of these systems operates, how they interact with each other and with the whole, and the interaction of the whole with its external environment. From that understanding the consultant may derive inferences concerning the disclosed gaps and inefficiencies and their effects. The consultant then uses his or her own discipline (sociology, psychology) and theory (social learning, psychoanalysis) to arrive at the meaning of the inferences. Proceeding from facts to inference to interpretation, the consultant may then come to a logical understanding of the organization and formulate a specific mode of action for dealing with its problem. That change effort then should be uniquely appropriate to a given problem, in a unique organization, under defined conditions, at a specific point in time.

The formulation of a diagnosis also requires the formulation of a prognosis. A prognosis enables the consultant to put boundaries around his or her work and to arrive at realistic expectations.

JOB ANALYSIS
ORGANIZATIONAL CLIMATE

H. LEVINSON

ORGANIZATIONAL PSYCHOLOGY

Organizational psychology aims to improve performance and satisfaction at organizational settings. It studies a wide range of topics, from work motivation, morale, and productivity to leadership and organizational effectiveness, and from small groups to large multinational corporations. The classical Hawthorne studies initiated in 1925 constitute the specific historical root of organizational psychology. Among the principles demonstrated by these experiments were that changes in the productivity of workers could not be explained simply as a function of objective factors such as physical and working conditions. Subjective factors such as morale, leadership style, employees' attitudes toward the company, and social relationships were important in understanding work behavior.

Organizational psychology also is influenced by the changing societal view of the nature of work and the responsibility of work organizations for the quality of work life of their employees. It overlaps with personnel psychology, which focuses on individual differences and selection. New areas of inquiry include the design and evaluation of training programs, performance appraisal, the measurement of employee morale and job satisfaction, and organizational diagnosis and assessment. Organizational psychology has many subareas. Among them are job satisfaction, work attitudes, career development, work motivation, group process, group dynamics, leadership behavior, organizational decision making, and organization development.

WORK ATTITUDES AND CAREER DEVELOPMENT

Because individual processes are important in developing an understanding of organizational psychology, work attitudes, job satisfaction, and attributions are extensively studied in relation to the organizational context. The work attitudes often reflect employees' reactions to jobs, groups, leaders, and the whole organization as well as guide work behavior. Job satisfaction has been the primary area of attitudes over the years. E. A. Locke's taxonomy of job dimensions represents job characteristics typically relevant to job satisfaction, including work itself, pay, promotion, recognition, work conditions, benefits, supervision, coworkers, customers, and family. Several dimensions of job satisfaction interactively determine the overall satisfaction. Therefore, multiple indicators should be used in measuring job satisfaction. A related topic is attribution. Attributions of internal causes (e.g., ability and effort) and external causes (e.g., task difficulty and luck) are influenced by information available, beliefs, and motivation. The attributions that people make regarding the causes of task performance may have significant effects on their work behavior in organizations. Most people also exhibit different managerial problem-solving styles, according to whether sensation or intuition dominates and whether feeling or thinking methods are used in evaluating information. Organizational psychology research reveals that people tend to integrate the four psychological functions in solving problems in varying situations.

E. H. Schein identified three basic career patterns in organizations: (a) engineering-based careers, with needs for challenging opportunities for higher earnings and advance; (b) scientific-profession based careers, which are more oriented toward the intrinsic challenges of tasks; and (c) pure professional careers. Studies show that both employees' prior orientation and subsequent occupational socialization affect the values of career development. J. L. Holland's career theory described six dimensions of the patterns between personal orientations and occupational environments: realistic, intellectual, social, conventional, enterprising, and artistic. D. E. Super and D. T. Hall's developmental theory suggests six major stages for occupational choice: exploration, reality testing, experimentation, establishment, maintenance, and decline. Career identification is formed on the basis of the organizational characteristics and the individual's self-concept.

WORK MOTIVATION

There are three general categories of motivation theories: need–motive–value theories, cognitive-choice theories, and self-regulation–metacognition theories. The need–motive–value theories attempt to explain motivational factors in terms of stable dispositions such as personality, need structures, and values. Among these theories are A. H. Maslow's need hierarchy theory and C. P. Alderfer's existence–relatedness–growth theory. Some intrinsic motivation theories focus on higher-order motives, such as E. L. Deci's cognitive evaluation theory and J. R. Hackman and G. R. Oldham's job characteristics theory, which concentrates on how job and organizational events affect task interest and perceptions of personal control as critical psychological states in work behavior. J. S. Adam's equity theory deals with the cognitive and social exchange relationships based on the feelings of how fair the employee is treated compared with others. Other well-known theories in this category include F. Herzberg's motivator–hygiene theory and D. C. McClelland's achievement motivation theory.

The cognitive-choice theories focus on the cognitive process involved in choice. V. H. Vroom's valence–instrumentality–expectancy theory represents the framework of those theories, emphasizing the perceived probability of successful performance given certain effort. B. Weiner's three-dimensional attribution theory (locus, stability, and controllability) emphasizes the motivational influence of attributions on behavior. Z. M. Wang's attributional model of motivation demonstrates that the goal structures (individual versus team) of the work system affect the attributional patterns, which in turn largely determine workers' subsequent affect, expectation, and work motivation.

The self-regulation–metacognition theories emphasize the motivational processes in goal-directed behavior. Locke's goal-setting theory intends to increase task efficiency and effectiveness by specifying the goal attributes and desired outcomes.

GROUP PROCESS AND GROUP DYNAMICS

The studies on group process and dynamics are influenced by the pioneering work of Kurt Lewin. Variables such as group norms, group pressure, intergroup conflicts, group leadership styles (democratic versus authoritarian), group cohesiveness, and interpersonal communication were carefully studied. Moreno's sociometric method is a popular technique for measuring group cohesiveness, which is often defined as forces that lead an individual to remain in or to leave a given group. Group cohesiveness is considered a significant factor influencing group effectiveness.

Group decision making is one of the major topics in group psychology. There are two lines of research in this area: a social psychological approach, dealing with role perception, participation, power sharing, and groupthink factor; and a cognitive approach, emphasizing goal structures, creative problem solving, cognitive resource use, uncertainty assessment, information distribution, and decision support. Another aspect of group dynamics is intergroup behaviors. Goal conflicts, resource sharing, task relations, and substitutability are found to be the principal factors affecting intergroup relationships.

LEADERSHIP AND ORGANIZATIONAL DECISION MAKING

Leadership is considered as a process of influencing group activities toward the achievement of goals. It is the product of interactions among leaders, subordinates, and organizational goals. The sources of leadership power include legitimate power, reward power, coercive power, referent power, and expert power. The effective use of power relies on the match between leadership styles and situations. There are three kinds of leadership models in organizational psychology. The traits models focus on the important personality traits responsible for the leadership success, but they neglect the crucial influence of leader's behavior and situations on leadership effectiveness. The behavioral models suggest that the relationship between leaders and their subordinates be a determinant for the effective leadership and that certain leadership behaviors be important for the accomplishment of group and organizational goals. Ohio State University leadership studies, begun in the late 1940s, resulted in the two-dimensional model of leader behavior: consideration (oriented toward good job relationships) and initiating structure (oriented toward formal standards and rules of performance). However, these models paid much attention to the relationship but little to the effects of the situations and, therefore, failed to establish a systematic relationship between leadership behavior and organizational performance. Contingency models of leadership, in contrast, emphasize the compatibility among contingency characteristics of leaders, subordinates, groups, and organizational situations. Fiedler's contingency model is among the important leadership theories. The model has three contingency variables: leader–member relations, task structure, and leader position power, which in combination create eight situations. The model shows the effectiveness of either relationship-motivated leadership or task-motivated leadership among different situations. Other main contingency models are R. J. House's path-goal model and V. H. Vroom and P. W. Yetton's normative model. A related active topic in organizational psychology is the assessment of leadership. The popular measures consist of two dimensions: the task- and relation-oriented leadership styles and the performance and maintenance styles. A useful approach to leadership assessment is the multilevel evaluation involving supervisors, coworkers, subordinates, and the leaders themselves.

Organizational decision making is important in organizational psychology. H. A. Simon regarded administrative decision making as a process of information processing and examined human rationality within the limits of a psychological environment using the concept of bounded rationality. F. A. Heller and B. Wilpert adopted a new approach and used influence–power–sharing as a core variable for understanding competence use and managerial success in organizational decision making.

ORGANIZATION DEVELOPMENT

An important aspect of organizational psychology is the rapidly growing field of organization development (OD), which includes human-processual interventions, technostructural interventions, and human resource management interventions. Many OD techniques have been developed, such as organizational diagnosing, sensitivity training, group consultation, managerial grid, and team training, for the purposes of moving organization members toward higher morale and better organizational performance. The ultimate aim is to improve the total organizational system. Other aspects of organization development and change include the job redesign for higher task variety, better task identity, more meaningful and stimulating tasks, the development of organizational structures that permit better distribution of influence–power and information, and the design of more equitable systems of rewards. A major approach to organization development is action research, which focuses on planned change as a cyclical process involving close cooperation between organizational members and psychologists. It usually includes diagnosis for problem identification, feedback to key members or groups, joint diagnosis and planning for change actions, and evaluation after action.

Several recent studies suggest three OD strategies that have proved to be effective: (a) expertise strategy, focusing on the strengthening of training in knowledge, competence, and skills among employees necessary for higher performance; (b) systems strategy, emphasizing the improvement of networking of management systems for information sharing, communication, and more adaptable organizational structure; and (c) participation strategy, facilitating the high involvement of various groups and employees at all organizational levels in the planning, designing, and implementation of new objectives of production and technological change. Technological innovation is closely related to organization development. A significant approach of organization development and technological innovation is the sociotechnical model, which was originally developed from the studies at the Tavistock Institute of Human Relations in London. The model focuses simultaneously on the technical system and the social system, emphasizing the interaction and the fit between those two systems in achieving organizational objectives.

Given the rapid development of international corporations and multinational joint ventures, the cross-cultural psychology approach is becoming more popular in the studies of organizational psychology. Z. M. Wang suggested adopting a cross-cultural–socioeconomic perspective in the understanding of organizational behavior and organizational culture in the context of the world's economic, social, and technological development.

APPLIED RESEARCH
FIELD RESEARCH
INDUSTRIAL PSYCHOLOGY
LABOR–MANAGEMENT RELATIONS
LEADERSHIP EFFECTIVENESS
OCCUPATIONAL STRESS
ORGANIZATIONAL CLIMATE
TEAM PERFORMANCE
WORK EFFICIENCY
WORK-SPACE DESIGNS

Z.-M. WANG

ORGONE THERAPY

Orgone therapy, developed by Wilhelm Reich, is based on a concept of health involving the functioning of biological energy (*orgone,* as Reich named it, from "organism" and "orgasm") in the body. It flows freely and fully in the healthy organism. When this energy is blocked, psychopathology, and at times physical pathology, can evolve. Orgone therapy is the technique Reich evolved to achieve emotional health by removing obstacles to the free flow of this energy in the organism.

Early in his analytic career, Reich found that patients who had had successful analyses developed a satisfactory genital life. He showed that a specific type of capacity for sexual satisfaction, heretofore undescribed, was necessary, and he called this *orgastic potency.* Orgasm was far more than a local climax; rather it involved total bodily convulsions of an involuntary nature. There was also complete cessation of psychic activity; there were no conscious fantasies whatsoever, but a blurring of consciousness at the moment of acme.

Reich also showed that the character itself, as well as the manifestations of symptoms, could be neurotic. He coined the term *character armor* to denote character traits serving as resistance in analysis. With thorough release of affects, there occurred changes—in bodily attitudes, expressions, and tonus. Repressed feelings were bound in the body as well as being in the unconscious. This led to a new addition to therapeutic technique—that of attacking the neurosis somatically. Somatic armor, with its psychic concomitants, functions to bind energy, interfering with the free flow of energy through the organism. The armor is removed by evoking and discharging repressed emotions in an orderly and consistent fashion. One or a combination of either physical or character-analytic methods can be used. This work is based on psychoanalytic precursors; one, of major importance, is psychosexual development paired with the vicissitudes of the libido.

Individual character development is, then, dependent on the degree and constellation of fixations (read "armoring") at any particular erogenous zone where libido (read "energy") is bound. Resultant symptoms or traits form personality but, most important, interfere with complete genital discharge, and thus with emotional health. When armoring is totally removed, one sees a unique physiological event that is an objective criterion of therapeutic success. There occurs a spontaneous tilting forward of the pelvis at the end of complete respiratory expiration, together with a moving forward of the shoulders. Reich called this phenomenon the *orgasm reflex.* It signifies that the patient is "orgastically potent."

INNOVATIVE PSYCHOTHERAPIES
SEX THERAPIES

A. NELSON

OUTPLACEMENT COUNSELING

Outplacement counseling is the process by which a person with terminated employment is provided professional advice, coaching, guidance, and education to enhance self-awareness, refine career objectives, and secure new employment in accordance with appraised needs and abilities. As a systematic procedure, it encourages constructive activity by the client in adjusting to the job loss, making decisions, planning effective strategies, and implementing the job search.

Outplacement counseling services are provided through the employing organization at no cost to the terminated employee. Outplacement services are valued by organizations as positive and cost-effective means for resolving personal, legal, and public relations aspects of the organization's termination policies and actions.

COUNSELING
EXIT INTERVIEWS

H. V. SCHMITZ

P

PAIN

Pain typically is regarded as a warning signal that something harmful or damaging is happening. Until recently, medical practitioners maintained the belief that pain was always the result of some discrete anatomical impairment that could be treated with a procedure, a device, or a pill. Such a medical model led to a sequential approach for intervention.

When pain persists into chronicity (defined as of 6 months' duration and not responding to medical treatment), this "disease model" has little significance. Wilbert Fordyce has proposed a new concept—a learning model—that pain behaviors are conditioned. Personal, emotional, and cognitive factors, although playing a role in the pain experience, are far from the sole source of chronic pain. It is no longer a sensory event, but has become part of one's habits and lifestyle.

Experience in recent years suggests that effective intervention of these pain patients can be accomplished best by a multidisciplinary team doing a thorough assessment of the various factors influencing the patients' pain behavior. The core of rehabilitation for many chronic pain patients is an operant conditioning program, where reinforcers are given for "well behavior" and withdrawn for such activities as bed rest, medication abuse, and pain verbalization. Physical and occupational therapists assess the patients' capacity for exercise and activities of daily living. They then train patients in adaptive behaviors and have them graph their responses, and other staff socially reward the patients' progress.

When appropriate, other aspects of treatment are incorporated, such as vocational counseling, biofeedback or hypnosis, individual and group psychotherapy, administration of analgesics, and occasionally the use of a transcutaneous nerve stimulator.

The coordinated efforts of such programs appear to be successful in returning patients to functional capacity while providing some pain relief.

ENDORPHINS/ENKEPHALINS
OPERANT CONDITIONING

J. C. ROOK

PAIN: COPING STRATEGIES

From an early age, virtually everyone has experience with brief, relatively mild pain caused by cuts, insect bites, minor burns, bruises, toothaches, stomachaches, and routine medical and dental procedures. In addition to these relatively minor painful experiences, some individuals also will experience acute pain from major trauma, surgery, and invasive medical procedures. Others may even experience persistent pain such as chronic back pain, headaches, or pain secondary to chronic illness such as arthritis. Whenever a person is confronted with a painful situation, there are demands or requirements placed on that individual for certain responses. For example, a child receiving an injection must hold his or her arm still while a needle is inserted into the arm. Individuals spontaneously react in these situations and use various strategies to deal with pain and the demands of the situation.

COGNITIVE COPING STRATEGIES

Mental strategies or ways to use thoughts or imagination to cope with pain are usually called *cognitive coping strategies.* Distraction involves thinking about other things to divert attention from pain and can be internal, such as imagining a pleasant scene, or external, such as focusing on a specific aspect of the environment. Reinterpreting pain sensations is imagining that the pain is something else such as numbness or a warm feeling. Calming self-statements refers to statements that one might tell oneself to provide comfort or encouragement (e.g., "I know I can handle this"). Ignoring pain is denying that the pain exists. Wishful thinking, praying, or hoping involves telling oneself that the pain will go away some day by faith, an act of God, or something magical. Fear and anger self-statements are statements one might tell oneself that promote fear or anger such as "I am afraid I am going to die." Catastrophizing refers to the use of negative self-statements and overly pessimistic thoughts about the future (e.g., "I can't deal with the pain"). Cognitive restructuring refers to a process of recognizing negative thoughts and changing them to more realistic and rational thoughts.

BEHAVIORAL COPING STRATEGIES

Overt things that a person might actually do to cope with pain are called *behavioral coping strategies.* Increasing behavioral activity involves actively engaging in activities such as reading or visiting with friends to stay busy and unfocused on pain. Pacing activity involves taking regular planned rest breaks to avoid overdoing and experiencing increases in pain. Isolation refers to withdrawing from social contact to cope with pain. Resting refers to reclining in bed or on the couch. Relaxation involves attempting to decrease physiological arousal by remaining calm and relaxing muscles. Relaxation also is sometimes referred to as a physiological coping strategy, because it may include direct physical benefits.

Some coping strategies are effective and facilitate good adjustment, whereas other strategies are ineffective and may promote additional pain and suffering. Although intuitively certain strategies appear effective and others seem ineffective, empirical studies are needed to demonstrate the relationship between coping strategies and adjustment. This is especially important, because some strategies are effective in one situation but not the next, or for one person but not another.

CHRONIC PAIN

Most individuals probably begin to develop strategies for coping with pain from an early age and from exposure to relatively minor painful experiences. Yet the research in this area has progressed almost backward, with initial studies focusing on coping strategies used by chronic pain populations such as patients with chronic back pain or pain secondary to disease (e.g., arthritis and sickle cell disease).

One of the first instruments designed to assess pain coping strategies systematically was the coping strategies questionnaire (CSQ) developed by Rosensteil and Keefe. The CSQ measures the frequency with which individuals use various cognitive and behavioral coping strategies to deal with pain. Research using the CSQ with chronic pain patients has found that pain coping strategies can be reliably assessed and are predictive of pain, psychosocial adjustment, and functional capacity. Chronic pain patients who are high on catastrophizing and perceived inability to control and decrease pain have higher levels of depression and anxiety and overall physical impairment. Chronic pain patients who take a more active approach to managing pain by using a variety of cognitive and behavioral strategies have been found, in at least some studies, to have better functional adjustment (i.e., remain more active in work and social activities). These results have been replicated across several research laboratories and with several populations of chronic pain patients (chronic back pain, headaches, osteoarthritis, rheumatoid arthritis, and sickle cell disease).

Taken together, the studies with chronic pain populations have generally concluded that although there seems to be some positive effects due to active coping efforts, negative thinking appears to be a more potent adverse influence on adjustment. Also, longitudinal studies have shown that coping strategies measured at one point in time are predictive of adjustment at follow-up. Thus maladaptive copers may continue to be at risk for future adjustment problems.

STABILITY AND CHANGE IN COPING STRATEGIES

Because of the significance of coping style in adjustment to chronic pain, researchers have attempted to determine whether the strategies used by individuals to cope with pain tend to be stable or to change over time.

Two approaches have been used to study this issue. The first approach has been to compare coping strategies assessed during a baseline assessment to coping strategies measured at follow-up (e.g., 1 year later) with no systematic intervention occurring between the two assessment periods. Results have shown that without intervention, coping strategies are relatively stable over time, suggesting that some individuals persist in ineffective coping efforts. This stability in coping style appears to be unrelated to changes in disease severity. That is, although disease severity may lessen, this does not automatically translate into improved coping efforts, and even if there is an increase in disease severity over time, this does not necessarily mean that there will be further deterioration in adjustment. Although coping tends to be relatively stable, individuals who do become more and more negative in their thinking may experience even further deterioration in functional capacity and psychosocial adjustment over time.

The second approach to examining changes in pain coping strategies in chronic pain patients has been intervention studies. These studies have attempted to improve pain coping by training individuals in cognitive and behavioral pain coping skills. These studies have shown that with intervention, pain-coping skills can be improved, and improvements in pain-coping skills translate into improvements of psychosocial and functional adjustment. For example, in one study, Keefe and coworkers trained a group of patients with osteoarthritic knee pain to use relaxation, imagery, distraction, cognitive-restructuring, and pacing activity. Compared with a control group, trained subjects had lower levels of pain and psychological disability. Furthermore, individuals in the pain coping skills group who had greatest positive change in their coping strategy use (i.e., increased perceived effectiveness) had the most improvements in physical abilities. Similar findings have been reported across several types of pain problems.

Taken together, these results suggest that without intervention, the strategies an individual uses to cope with chronic pain are relatively stable over time. Change in pain coping skills is possible, however, and cognitive-behavioral approaches appear to provide an effective means to train individuals with various chronic pain problems to use more effective coping strategies.

ACUTE PAIN

Acute pain may result from events ranging from minor experiences to pain secondary to surgery or invasive procedures. As with chronic pain, when an individual is confronted with acute pain, he or she reacts spontaneously and uses various strategies to cope. Because acute pain situations are often also stressful and anxiety provoking, coping strategies used in these situations often include both strategies to deal with pain and to deal with anxiety.

Among the earliest attempts to examine coping strategies used in acute pain situations were studies that described preoperative and postoperative adults as either active or avoidant copers. Active copers were considered persons who approached the painful stimulus (i.e., surgery) by seeking out information, dealing with it rationally, and using cognitive strategies to cope. Avoidant copers (or those high on denial) were those who preferred not knowing information about their surgery or medical procedure, and actually became anxious and experienced more pain when provided with information. Conclusions based on these early studies are limited, however, because studies often attempted to categorize subjects into one of these patterns of coping based on informal interviews of questionable reliability.

More recently, systematic measures for assessing pain coping strategies in acute pain situations have been developed. Butler and coworkers developed the cognitive coping strategy inventory (CCSI) for use with postoperative pain populations. The inventory consists of subscales that are similar to dimensions found to be important in the measurement of chronic pain coping (i.e., catastrophizing, attention diversion, and imaginative inattention). Items, however, are more relevant to the acute pain experience. Research using the CCSI has found that this questionnaire is reliable and valid, and coping strategies used by postoperative patients to deal with pain are related to recovery. For example, adults who are high on catastrophizing have higher levels of pain and functional disability after surgery.

CHILDHOOD PAIN

The investigation of coping strategies in children confronting painful experiences is a relatively new area of research. In contrast to the work with adults in which questionnaires are primarily used to assess pain coping, most studies with children use interviews and observational methods to examine pain coping strategies.

Interview studies have used both open-ended and semistructured formats to gather information on how children experience pain and what they do in response to it. For example, Ross and Ross interviewed a large sample of school-age children and asked them about the strategies that they used to cope with pain. Some of the children had chronic diseases such as sickle cell disease or hemophilia, but most had no major medical problems and responded in regard to their coping with more minor pain (e.g., cuts and bruises). Responding to open-ended questions, few children reported using self-initiated strategies to cope with pain. Of the small proportion that reported using strategies, distraction, thought stopping, and relaxation were among the more commonly reported strategies.

Observational studies of children coping with pain have focused primarily on children's reactions to painful procedures such as burn therapy or cancer-related treatments (e.g., venipunctures, bone marrow aspirations). In these studies, observers record the frequency of behaviors exhibited by the child such as crying, seeking social support, information seeking, and verbal and motor resistance. Although these behaviors are usually considered a measure of distress, some of the behaviors also can be conceptualized as coping efforts exhibited by the child to manage the pain and stress of the situation.

A few recent studies have found that coping strategies could be reliably assessed using questionnaires in school age children. Using a modified version of the CSQ that was developed for adults, Gil and coworkers found that children who engaged in negative thinking and relied passively on strategies such as resting had more adjustment problems. This pattern of coping was associated with greater reductions in school and social activity, more frequent health care contacts, and more depression and anxiety. Children who took an active approach to managing pain by using a variety of cognitive and behavioral coping strategies were more active and required less frequent health care services.

The KIDCOPE developed by Spirito, Stark, and Williams is a questionnaire that has been designed specifically to assess coping strategies used by children to deal with stressful situations. The child identifies a recent stressful event to provide a context for responding to the coping strategy items. Given that pain is a common problem identified by children with medical problems, the KIDCOPE can be a useful instrument to assess pain coping strategies, especially because it is relatively brief and simple to complete.

Child Age and Sex

Although there appear to be almost no major differences in coping between girls and boys, differences in coping strategy use have been found across different ages. Older children tend to have more coping skills in their repertoire, especially more cognitive coping skills. Some data suggest that older children with chronic pain secondary to disease may rely more on negative thinking and passive coping strategies as they get older. By adolescence, some of their maladaptive coping patterns may become entrenched and resistant to change.

Parents

The relationship of the parent to coping and adjustment in children also has been a recent target of study. A number of studies have evaluated the effects of parent presence versus absence on child coping during painful procedures. Most of these studies have shown that although children exhibit less overt distress when their parents are absent, they may be physiologically and psychologically disturbed by their parents' absence and merely inhibiting their behavioral reaction. Thus, rather than removing the parents, researchers may need to investigate which behaviors of the parent are related to effective versus ineffective coping by children during painful procedures.

Coping strategies used by parents to cope with their own (the parent's) pain also may be related to adjustment in children with pain problems. One study found that parents who took an active approach to managing their own pain had children who remained more active during episodes of sickle cell pain. Furthermore, there appear to be significant relationships between pain coping strategies in parents and in their children, suggesting that children might learn how to cope with pain, in part, by observing their parents' reactions.

CLINICAL IMPLICATIONS

Coping skills training is now a regular part of most comprehensive approaches to chronic pain management. Multidisciplinary pain programs now often include groups or individual sessions in which patients are trained to use active coping skills and cognitive restructuring techniques to manage pain. Although this type of approach is not routine for the management of most acute pain problems, there is a growing recognition for the need to train coping strategies to those undergoing medical procedures. Perhaps the area that has received the most attention has been in preparing children for surgery or for repeated invasive medical procedures such as burn therapy or cancer-related treatments. Although this is usually not done until after the child has developed a significant problem coping with pain, some clinicians are beginning to recognize the need to help prepare children to cope with painful experiences before they become oversensitized.

FEAR
INTERNALIZATION
PAIN
SELF-CONTROL

K. M. GIL

PANIC DISORDERS

DEFINITION

Five criteria have been established as defining panic disorder in the *Diagnostic and statistical manual of mental disorders* (*DSM-III-R*) and are as follows:

1. At some time a panic attack occurs that is unexpected, that is, not tied to a specific situation.

2. Four such attacks occur within a 4-week period, or one such attack is followed by a period of at least 1 month of fear of having another attack.

3. Four of the following symptoms accompany at least one of the attacks:
   - (a) shortness of breath
   - (b) dizziness, unsteadiness, faintness
   - (c) heart palpitations
   - (d) trembling
   - (e) sweating
   - (f) choking
   - (g) nausea or abdominal distress
   - (h) depersonalization or derealization
   - (i) numbness or tingling sensations
   - (j) flushes or chills
   - (k) chest discomfort
   - (l) fear of dying;
   - (m) fear of going crazy or doing something uncontrolled

4. In one or more attacks, four symptoms reach maximum intensity within 10 minutes of onset.

5. No organic factor can be found to account for the attacks.

Panic attacks have two primary features—the physiological symptoms and the thoughts that accompany these symptoms. Although physiological symptoms are generally accepted as required to define a panic attack, there is some debate regarding whether cognitions are also required. Research from mental health settings consistently supports the conclusion that cognitions nearly always accompany symptoms, whereas research from medical settings indicates that 20% to 40% of panic attack sufferers do not have accompanying cognitions.

During the American Civil War, Jacob Mendes Da Costa coined the term *irritable heart* to describe a syndrome similar to panic disorder. In England during World War I, Sir Thomas Lewis defined a problem similar to panic disorder and called it *effort syndrome,* because the symptoms were noted to arise after the slightest physical effort. Finally, in 1917 Sigmund Freud defined *anxiety attacks* in terms, both descriptive and causal, similar to the current understanding of panic attacks.

CAUSAL FACTORS

Numerous causal factors have been suggested as being related to panic disorder. They are generally divisible into two groups: biological and psychological. Biological factors include a genetic predisposition leading to a physiological vulnerability to certain substances, such as adrenaline, sodium lactate, and caffeine, and the physiological changes that accompany hyperventilation. Psychological factors include increased levels of stress and cognitive interpretations of physiological changes. Of special importance is information-processing theory, which holds that cognitive, situational, physiological, and behavioral cues that accompany emotional states are stored together in the brain. Because panic is an emotional state, the presence of such cues at a later time increases the likelihood that a full panic attack will be experienced.

A genetic basis for panic disorder has been supported by studies in which family members of individuals with panic disorder were compared with family members of individuals who did not have the disorder. Such studies demonstrated that family members of panic-disordered individuals were much more likely to have a diagnosis of panic disorder than were family members of individuals in the control group. Stronger evidence for a genetic link comes from comparing comorbidity rates for diagnosis of panic disorder in identical twins with fraternal twins. This study and others demonstrate a significantly higher rate of concordance for identical than fraternal twins. Taken together, the data support a conclusion that for some individuals a vulnerability to developing panic disorder is inherited. Because of the low concordance rates found in such studies, it is unlikely panic disorder per se is inherited. Rather, it is likely that a vulnerability to respond to stress with increased levels of physiological arousal is inherited.

TREATMENT

Treatments for panic disorder have targeted both the panic attacks and the avoidant behavior that develops secondarily to the attacks. Both pharmacologic and psychological treatments have been identified that effectively reduce panic attacks and avoidant behavior.

Psychological treatments that have been shown to be effective in controlled outcome studies are of two primary types: cognitive–behavioral and exposure. The former include techniques of relaxation training, breathing retraining, and cognitive restructuring, whereas the latter involves exposing individuals to previously avoided situations until comfort in those situations is restored. Research summarizing the effectiveness of these procedures indicates that the most effective treatments—cognitive–behavioral plus exposure and the high potency benzodiazepines—produce marked improvement in more than 80% of individuals suffering from this problem.

ANXIETY
CATHARSIS
CHILDREN'S FEARS
FEAR
LIFE EVENTS
MENTAL IMAGERY
VIOLENCE

G. A. CLUM

PARADIGMS

Paradigms are rules or regulations that set boundaries and direct actions toward accomplishing a goal successfully. Kuhn, a scientific historian, focused the attention of paradigms to the scientific world, believing paradigms only fit the physical scientific world. Paradigms in action amount to a basic set of ideas or concepts that directs an individual's behavior, therefore setting parameters to the individual's standard way of functioning toward a goal or work pattern and becomes his or her way of doing something or solving a problem.

Paradigms are found in every culture. Norms within every culture govern the boundaries of accepted behavior and become the proper way of doing things. When pattern changes occur, thus deviating from the established operating norms of any given situation, Barker referred to this as "a paradigm shift, . . . a change to a new game, a new set of rules."

In every generation changes have been initiated by nonconformists who took risks to make paradigm shifts, because paradigms equal conformity and the paradigm shifts create confusion. A simple example of a paradigm shift is if a person would want pie instead of the usual cake for his or her birthday; breaking from the traditional cake is a paradigm shift.

FAMILY INSTITUTION

Before the 1940s, a small percentage of women were in the job market, mostly doing office-type work. The basic paradigm before World War II was that women belonged at home with the children and the men were the breadwinners. This was an acceptable way of life. By 1950, a paradigm shift occurred. More women were entering the professional world. Many women entered the labor market so the family could have some "extras," but later the second income became a necessity to survive the economic crunch.

RELIGION

Many changes have taken place in religious practices, for example, in the Roman Catholic Church since Vatican II. Some changes were saying the Mass in the vernacular, the concept of healing of reconciliation, fasting before taking Communion, fewer statues, face-to-face confession, and increased lay ministeries. Such changes met considerable resistance. Ritzer stated that "the paradigm that emerges victorious is the one that is able to win the most converts," in his interpretation of Kuhn's original work. As new concepts gain more followers, the resistance to paradigm changes slows down and acceptance emerges.

Some of the now generally accepted theories of cognitive growth and development that were originally paradigmatic are those by Erik Erikson, Sigmund Freud, Jean Piaget, and Lev Vygotsky. Another paradigm in education concerning intelligence is based on the theories of Charles Spearman, J. P. Guilford, L. L. Thurstone, R. J. Sternberg, H. Gardner, and many more. Each presents guidelines and boundaries in methodology, standards, models, and procedures, and each specialty is under the whole umbrella of education.

Barker stated that "the interrelationship of all these paradigms is crucial to the success and longevity of any culture or organization." Some new paradigms take years to accept and others are accepted rapidly. If the need is great for a change, the paradigm shift will emerge quickly.

Paradigm shifts have occurred throughout the centuries, since the beginning of humankind. As new concepts and ideas are born, paradigm shifts will continue to occur and the needs of people will be met.

AUTOMATION
CAUSAL REASONING
CODING
CULTURAL DETERMINISM
HUMAN FACTORS
INFORMATION PROCESSING THEORY
INTUITION
PHILOSOPHY OF SCIENCE
SYSTEMS THEORY
THEORETICAL PSYCHOLOGY

P. CARICH

PARADOXICAL INTERVENTION

Paradoxical interventions are psychotherapeutic tactics that seem to contradict the goals they are designed to achieve. In the classic definition of a therapeutic double-bind or paradox, "an injunction is so structured that it (a) reinforces the behavior the patient expects to be changed, (b) implies that this reinforcement is the vehicle of change, and (c) thereby creates a paradox because the patient is told to change by remaining unchanged."

References to resolving problems with paradoxical interventions appear as early as the eighteenth century. In the twentieth century, Dunlap applied the technique of negative practice to problems such as stammering and enuresis. Rosen, through direct psychoanalysis, encouraged psychiatric patients to engage in aspects of their psychosis to prevent relapse, and Frankl used paradoxical intention to help his patients revise the meaning of their symptoms. The most influential literature on therapeutic paradox, however, derives from Gregory Bateson's project on communication. Bateson, Jackson, Haley, Weakland, and others explored the role of paradoxical double-bind communications in resolving as well as creating problems. Influenced by systemic–cybernetic ideas and by the work of master-hypnotist Milton Erickson, descendants of the Bateson project such as Haley, Weakland, Watzlawick, Fisch, and Selvini-Palazzoli went on in the 1970s to develop family therapy models with paradox as a central feature. Around the same time, Frankl's paradoxical intention technique was adopted by behavior therapists who demonstrated its usefulness with specific symptoms such as insomnia, anxiety, urinary retention, and obsessions.

Although paradoxical interventions have been associated historically with particular theoretical frameworks, the current literature tends to treat them as techniques that can be applied and explained apart from the models in which they were developed. Indeed, paradoxical interventions cut across theoretical boundaries insofar as paradoxical elements can be found in virtually all schools of psychotherapy.

There are striking differences in how therapists of different theoretical orientations use paradoxical intervention. Behavior therapists use paradoxical intention to interrupt within-person exacerbation cycles, whereas strategic–systems therapists use a wider variety of paradoxical interventions and more often focus on between-person (family) interaction. Another difference is that behavior therapists make their rationale explicit, although strategic therapists typically do not. In behavioral applications of paradoxical intention, the therapist typically teaches the client to adopt a paradoxical attitude, explaining, for example, how the client's intention to force sleep is actually exacerbating the problem and why a paradoxical intention to stay awake might make sleep come easier. The intention here is clearly the client's, not the therapist's, and the client is expected to do (or at least to try to do) what he or she is told. In strategic applications, however, the therapist sometimes expects a patient or family to do the opposite of what is proposed, and in this sense the therapist's intention is paradoxical. In contrast to the openly shared, educational rationale of a behavior therapist, strategic therapists attempt to maximize compliance (or defiance) by framing suggestions in a manner consistent (or deliberately inconsistent) with the client's own idiosyncratic language.

TYPES AND APPLICATIONS

Several schemes for classifying paradoxical interventions have been offered in the literature. Of the many types, the most commonly used are symptom prescription and restraint from change. Variations of these two techniques—asking clients to engage in the behavior they wish to eliminate or restraining them from changing—have been applied in both individual and family therapy. However, nearly all controlled studies of therapeutic paradox have involved symptom prescriptions with individuals. Based on these studies, Shoham-Salomon and Rosenthal reported that outcome largely depends on how these interventions are administered.

Most paradoxical interventions involve some combination of prescribing, reframing, and positioning. *Prescribing* means telling people what to do (giving tasks, suggestions, etc.) either directly or indirectly. For example, a therapist might ask a patient to have a panic attack deliberately, or prescribe that an overinvolved grandmother take full responsibility for a misbehaving child, expecting she will back off and let the mother take charge. *Reframing* involves redefining the meaning of events or behavior in a way that makes change more possible. Although reframing resembles interpretation, its goal is to provoke change rather than provide insight—and the accuracy of redefinition is less important than its impact. Thus Haley described a case in which a woman becomes more sexually responsive after her frigidity is reframed as a way of protecting her husband from the full force of her sexuality, and Selvini-Palazzoli, Boscolo, Cecchin, and Prata pioneered the use of positive connotation, a technique for changing dysfunctional family patterns by ascribing noble intentions to both the identified patient's symptom and the behaviors of family members that support it. *Positioning* is a term for altering the therapist's own role, or potential role, in a problem-maintaining system. For example, when a patient's pessimism is reinforced by an optimistic

or encouraging response from others, the therapist can do "less of the same" by defining the situation as even more dismal than originally supposed. In practice, prescribing, reframing, and positioning are interwoven, with each at least implicit in any paradoxical strategy or intervention. Thus prescribing that someone be deliberately anxious reframes an involuntary symptom as controllable, reframing problem behavior as a protective sacrifice carries an implicit (paradoxical) prescription not to change, and warning against dangers of improvement sometimes helps reverse or neutralize a therapist's role in a problem cycle.

Applications of paradox tend to be most varied and complex in marital and family therapy. In one case, where the focus was on reversing family members' well-intentioned but self-defeating attempt to solve a problem, a therapy team coached the relatives of a depressed stroke victim to encourage him by *dis*couraging him. In another case, a therapist asked a depressed husband to *pretend* to be depressed and his wife to try to find out if he was really feeling that way. For extreme marital stuckness, Todd recommends paradoxical interventions such as proscribing indecision about whether a couple should separate. The most dramatic examples of paradox with families come from the early work of the Milan team (Selvini-Palazzoli et al.): After complimenting a severely obsessional young woman and her parents for protecting each other from the sadness associated with the death of a family member several years earlier, the team prescribed that the family meet each night to discuss their loss and suggested that the patient behave symptomatically whenever her parents appeared distraught.

Clinical reports describe successful applications of paradoxical intervention with a wide variety of problems, including anxiety, depression, phobia, insomnia, obsessive–compulsive disorder, headaches, asthma, encopresis, enuresis, blushing, tics, psychosomatic symptoms, procrastination, eating disorders, child and adolescent conduct problems, marital and family problems, pain, work and school problems, and psychotic behavior. Paradoxical strategies appear least applicable in situations of crisis or extreme instability, such as acute decompensation or grief reactions, domestic violence, suicide attempts, or loss of a job, but there have been too few controlled studies to list indications and contraindications with any degree of certainty.

CHANGE MECHANISMS

Explanations of how and why paradoxical interventions work are as diverse as the interventions themselves. Behavioral, cognitive, and motivational processes—alone and in combination—have been proposed to explain change in both individuals and families. At the individual level, a behavioral account of why symptom prescription helps involuntary problems such as insomnia, anxiety, and obsessional thinking is that, by attempting to *have* the problem, a patient cannot continue in usual ways of trying to prevent it, thus breaking an exacerbation cycle. Cognitive explanations of the same phenomena emphasize that symptom prescription redefines the uncontrollable as controllable, decontextualizes the problem, and in a fundamental way alters the symptom's meaning. A third change mechanism has been suggested for situations in which clients appear to defy or oppose a therapist's directive. Here the client presumably rebels to reduce psychological reactance, a hypothetical motive state aroused by threats to perceived behavioral freedom.

Not surprisingly, explanations of how paradoxical interventions promote change at the family systems level are more diverse and more abstract. Some paradoxical interventions are assumed to interrupt problem-maintaining interaction cycles between people, and some, like Milan-style positive connotation, presumably operate by introducing information into the system or by changing the meaning of the symptom and the family interaction that supports it. Motivational explanations of systems-level change suggest that paradoxical interventions work by activating relational dynamics, such as compression and recoil, or by creating disequilibrium among systemic forces aligned for and against change.

Some theories of paradoxical intervention attempt to combine or integrate various change processes. For example, Rohrbaugh and coworkers proposed a compliance–defiance model distinguishing two types of paradoxical interventions. Compliance-based symptom prescription is indicated (a) when an unfree (involuntary) symptom like insomnia is maintained by attempts to stave it off and (b) when the potential for reactance is low (i.e., when clients are unlikely to react against attempts to influence them). Defiance-based interventions, however, work because people change by rebelling. These are indicated when clients view the target behavior as relatively free (voluntary) and when the potential for reactance is high.

Another model of therapeutic paradox originally proposed by Watzlawick and coworkers incorporates behavioral and cognitive explanations of change. The therapeutic double-bind—a directive deliberately to engage in involuntary symptomatic behavior—is a mirror image of the pathogenic "be spontaneous" paradox. The only way to obey such a directive is by disobeying it. According to Watzlawick and associates, two possible consequences follow: If the client is not able to produce the symptom on demand, she or he will show less of the problem; or, if the client does produce the symptom, it will be with a greater sense of mastery and control. In this way clients are "changed if they do and changed if they don't" (Watzlawick et al.): If the symptomatic behavior itself does not change, at least the client's perception of it changes. Also as Raskin and Klein wrote, behaviors over which one has control might be sins but they are not neurotic complaints.

EFFICACY

When paradoxical interventions are part of a broader therapeutic strategy, their specific contribution to clinical outcome is difficult to evaluate. Nevertheless, dramatic and seemingly enduring effects on individuals and families have been documented in numerous clinical reports and case studies and in qualitative literature reviews.

Controlled experimental studies of paradoxical interventions with individual clients have yielded mixed results. Two independent meta-analytic reviews indicate that paradoxical interventions compared favorably with no-treatment control conditions, but comparisons with nonparadoxical treatments have been equivocal. Whereas Hill's metaanalysis found paradox to be superior, Shoham-Salomon and Rosenthal found that the overall effect of paradoxical interventions was as large (but no larger than) the average effect size of psychotherapy in general.

Perhaps the most interesting metaanalytic result is that some forms of paradoxical intervention appear to be far more effective than others. In Shoham-Salomon and Rosenthal's analysis, the effect sizes of two positively connoted symptom prescriptions were significantly greater than those of other nonparadoxical treatments or of symptom prescriptions that did not include a positive frame. Paradoxical interventions were most effective when the therapist either (a) reframed the symptom positively before prescribing it (e.g., praising a depressed client's tolerance for solitude or his or her willingness to sacrifice for the good of others) or (b) explained the paradoxical intention (exacerbation-cycle) rationale. Both can be considered to include a positive connotation of the symptom, either by reframing or by explaining how the client is not sick, but stuck.

ETHICAL ISSUES

As the popularity of paradoxical therapy increased during the 1980s, concern also grew about ways in which these techniques can be misused. Strategic applications in which therapists do not make their rationale for particular interventions explicit to clients have been criticized as manipulative and potentially harmful to the client–therapist relationship. Defenders of strategic therapy, however, argue that good therapy is inherently manipulative and that therapeutic truth telling can be not only naive but discourteous. Responsible therapists of all persuasions agree that paradox should not be used for the shock value or power it promises: Encouraging a symptom or restraining people from changing can be disastrous if done sarcastically or from a sense of frustration ("There's the window—go ahead and jump!"). It is also significant that therapists like Haley, Weakland, Palazzoli, and Hoffman, all pioneers in the use of paradoxical methods, now give them less emphasis; even therapists well-versed in strategic methods find the term *paradoxical* confusing, inaccurate, and overly loaded with negative connotations. Of particular concern is that the term *paradoxical intervention,* cut loose from its theoretical and clinical moorings, is too easily seen as a quick fix or a gimmick.

Three guidelines may decrease the potential for misusing paradoxical interventions: first, define behavior positively. When prescribing a symptom or restraining change, avoid attributing unseemly motives to people (like needing to control, resist, or defeat one another); ascribe noble intentions not only to the symptom but also to what other people are doing to support it. Second, be especially cautious with challenging or provocative interventions. When restraining, for example, it is safer to suggest that change may not be advisable than to predict it will not be possible. Finally, have a theory. In other words, have a clear formulation of how the problem is being maintained and how a paradoxical intervention may help to change that. The most important guideline for paradoxical (or any other) intervention is having a coherent rationale for its use.

ACTUALIZING THERAPY
ALTERNATIVE PSYCHOTHERAPIES
CLINICAL JUDGMENT
COGNITIVE THERAPIES
FACTITIOUS DISORDERS
INTERNALIZATION
PSYCHOTHERAPY
PSYCHOTHERAPY EFFECTIVENESS

V. SHOHAM
M. ROHRBAUGH

PARADOXICAL SLEEP

According to the record of electrical activity of the brain, measured by the electroencephalograph (EEG), humans go through various cycles or stages during a night's sleep. Probably the simplest way to classify these stages is into S-sleep and D-sleep. S-sleep is so named for its characteristic slow-wave EEG pattern (large amplitude, slow activity). S-sleep is usually divided into four stages: Stage 1 has the least slow-wave activity, stages 2 and 3 have intermediate amounts, and stage 4 has the most slow-wave activity. At the beginning of a normal night's sleep, a person cycles successively through the stages of S-sleep before entering a period of D-sleep. For the rest of the night, periods of S-sleep alternate with periods of D-sleep. As the night progresses, stage 4 of S-sleep becomes less frequent, and the periods devoted to D-sleep tend to grow longer.

D-sleep, in contrast to S-sleep, is characterized by a desynchronized EEG pattern (low voltage, fast activity), rapid eye movements (REMs), and twitches of the fingers, toes, and other body parts. D-sleep is also called paradoxical sleep or REM sleep. The term *paradoxical* refers to the fact that this stage of sleep is characterized by an awake EEG pattern, yet the person or animal is behaviorally harder to arouse than during S-sleep. This stage of sleep also has been associated with periods of dreaming in humans. Specifically, if people are awakened either during or immediately after paradoxical sleep, they almost invariably report dreams. The term *paradoxical sleep* was introduced in an article on the stages of sleep published in *Scientific American* in 1967 by the French research physician Michel Jouvet.

What accounts for these two types of sleep and for their alternation during the night? The answer to this question is closely linked to the function of sleep itself. According to one explanation, sleep is an adaptive mechanism developed to conserve energy at night when food-gathering would be difficult for a diurnal animal. However, the evolution of many animals has resulted in regular patterns of locomotor activity, thought to occur approximately every 2 hours, during which food gathering and other activities related to the animal's survival might occur. If this 2-hour cycle continued around the clock, the animal would have its sleep periodically interrupted. Thus to get a full night's sleep *and* continue with the 2-hour activity cycle, the animal enters a period of D-sleep in which only the brain is awake.

PHYSIOLOGICAL NEEDS
SLEEP
SLEEP DISORDERS

B. M. Thorne

PARAMETRIC STATISTICAL TESTS

Parametric statistical tests, as opposed to nonparametric or distribution-free tests, require the postulation of assumptions regarding the characteristics, properties, and form of the distributions of populations from which samples are drawn for the tests. Among the most frequently required assumptions are those relating to the normality of the underlying distributions (t, F, r/R), homogeneity of variance (t, F), linearity of regression ($bx·y$, r/R), continuity of measures/variables, and equality of intervals of measures. Compared with nonparametric tests of the null hypothesis, parametric tests are more powerful, all other factors being equal. However, it is more for their versatility than for their power that they have become the most common tools of the researcher in psychological investigations.

In multivariate statistics, parametric tests are based primarily on two important assumptions: (a) that the measures involved in the data analyses assume a multivariate normal distribution; and (b) that the dispersion matrices (basically, variance–covariance) are the same for all groups. Central to the performance of parametric tests in multivariate statistics are the Wilks' lambda (Λ) and Bartlett's approximation to chi square (V), which involves Λ. Wilks' lambda is a general statistic for testing the significance of differences among group centroids.

Bartlett's V statistic is a natural logarithmic function of Λ that can be used as a parametric test statistic for testing the null hypothesis regarding equality of several group centroids. The statistic V is distributed as chi square with $n(G - 1)$ degrees of freedom. Variations of Λ and V are employed in performing parametric tests of the null hypothesis in multivariate statistics, for example, MANOVA, Multiple Discriminant Function Analysis, and Canonical Correlation Analysis.

NONPARAMETRIC STATISTICAL TESTS
STATISTICS IN PSYCHOLOGY

P. F. Merenda

PARANOIA

Paranoia has existed as a concept in Western thought since the ancient Greeks coined the word from *para,* meaning "beside," and *noia,* meaning "the mind." Although it often is used as a general word for madness, the verbal form of the word, *parano-so,* means "to think amiss," and thus it differs in implication from other words for madness, such as *mania,* which refers to emotional frenzy.

In 1783, *paranoia* was brought into English by William Cullen, a Scottish neuropathologist, who followed the German use of the word as a general term for madness. In 1818, the term was applied to a specific syndrome, also called *Verrücktheit,* by Heinroth, and it was established by Emil Kraepelin in the 1896 and later editions of his textbook as the name of a major psychosis, distinct from manic–depressive illness and dementia praecox (schizophrenia). Kraepelin described paranoia as a system of insidiously developed and unshakeable delusions of persecution, jealousy, or grandeur involving religion, inventions, or eroticism, all accompanied by clear and orderly thinking, willing, and acting, and sometimes by hypochondriacal complaints. Usually permanent, it could also be acute and curable.

Sigmund Freud used the Kraepelinian classification of paranoia with considerable frequency in his own diagnoses, classifying it as a psychosis of defense against unacceptable and repressed thoughts and feelings, homosexual in nature, which were then projected onto other people. The most famous case of paranoia he analyzed was of Joseph Schreber, a former judge and president of the senate of Dresden, Germany.

Other early investigators of paranoia and related disorders included Adolf Meyer, who saw the development of paranoia as a gradual transformation of the personality; Eugen Bleuler, who classified paranoia as a type of schizophrenia; and Ivan Pavlov, who suggested that paranoia represents abnormal signal transmission, which increases the elaboration and stability of the conditioned reflex. Later investigators included Norman Cameron, who distinguished between paranoia and paranoid states; Theodore Millon, who has described paranoid personality in detail; Swanson, Bohnert, and Smith, who authored a text on paranoid disorders from a psychodynamic viewpoint; Aubrey Lewis, who wrote a brief history of the use of the words *paranoia* and *paranoid* and concluded that they referred only to a symptomatic, toxic, or schizophrenic condition; Kenneth Colby, who developed a computer simulation of paranoid processes, based on the perception of statements as malevolent rather than benevolent or neutral; and George Winokur, who, in his presidential address to the American Psychopathological Association in 1977, replaced the term *paranoid disorders* with *delusional disorder,* declaring that it was useless to continue to explore the fine points of delusional illnesses, and that patients referred to as paranoid have nothing more or less than a delusion.

Investigations of paranoid and delusional disorders greatly increased in the 1980s. A 1981 issue of the *Schizophrenia bulletin* included articles that showed differences between paranoid and schizophrenic persons in cognitive style, in genetic and biochemical makeup, and in the formation of personality, thus laying to rest the old contention that paranoia should be subsumed under schizophrenia.

Meanwhile, the *Diagnostic and statistical management* series both reflected and shaped developments in the field, going from relatively simple entries in the first two editions to a complex one in *DSM-III,* in which the criteria for diagnosis included persecutory or jealous delusions, grandiosity, anger, ideas of reference, isolation, and suspicion. The types included paranoia per se, shared paranoid disorder (*folie a deux*), and acute paranoid disorder.

In *DSM-III-R,* however, Winokur's position became the official one for diagnosis, and paranoid disorders were reduced to delusional disorder with a persistent, nonbizarre delusion as the sole criterion. Types of the disorder were traditionally labeled erotomanic, grandiose, jealous, and persecutory and a somatic type was added as well as a residual category, with the former distinguishable from body dismorphic disorder or hypochondriasis only by the patient's degree of conviction that something was wrong with his or her body.

The shared type of paranoid disorder was renamed and reclassified as induced psychotic disorder, and the acute type as "psychotic disorder not otherwise classified (atypical psychosis)." Paraphrenia—a mild disorder of later life long described as exhibiting characteristics of both paranoia and schizophrenia—continued to be excluded as an official diagnosis.

In the wake of these changes, research on delusions increased, and has generally indicated that they are not readily defined, measured, or separated from other psychological phenomena, particularly strong emotions. Their content appears to be situation dependent, although the attributional style characteristic of them is relatively stable.

In spite of the divergencies in the history of paranoid or delusional disorders, it is possible to find a core concept running through the official definitions and descriptions, and the theoretical and research literature: Paranoia (delusional disorder) is a mental disorder characterized by the presence of persistent nonbizarre delusions of persecutory, grandiose, or other self-referential content, not caused by other mental or organic disorders. Social and marital functioning may be impaired, although nondelusional intellectual and occupational functioning may be satisfactory.

Excessively self-defensive or aggressive and violent behaviors related to the delusions may occur.

DELUSIONAL DISORDERS
HALLUCINATIONS
PARANOID PERSONALITY
RELIABILITY OF DIAGNOSES

A. D. SCHEUER

PARANOID PERSONALITY

This well-known syndrome is described in the *Diagnostic and statistical manual* (*DSM-IV*) as exhibiting a pervasive and unwarranted suspiciousness and mistrust. Viewed by others as guarded, secretive, and devious, paranoids foster these perceptions by their tendency to question the loyalty of others, by searching for hidden motives in their behavior, and by expecting to be tricked or duped. They "make mountains out of molehills," are argumentative, and are always ready to counterattack at the slightest hint of potential threat or criticism. Stubborn and defensive, they are rigid in the views they hold and are unwilling to compromise their position. Not only is there a mistrust of others, but there is also a vigilant resistance to external influences and an ever-present fear of losing the power of self-determination. The inclination to misinterpret incidental actions and statements as signifying deception or malevolence borders on the irrational, yet falls short of being a full-fledged delusional system. They display minimal affect, and are described by others as "cold" and lacking in humor. From their perspective, they take pride in being objective, rational, and unemotional. Quickly disposed to be critical of others, they are unusually sensitive to criticism directed at them.

The following criteria were derived from a biosocial-learning, rather than a psychoanalytic or constitutional model:

1. Vigilant mistrust (e.g., exhibits edgy defensiveness against anticipated criticism and deception; conveys extreme suspicion, envy, and jealousy of others).

2. Provocative interpersonal behavior (e.g., displays a disputatious, fractious, and abrasive irritability; precipitates exasperation and anger by hostile, deprecatory demeanor).

3. Tenacious autonomy (e.g., expresses fear of losing independence and power of self-determination; is grimly resistant to sources of external influence and control).

4. Minidelusional cognitions (e.g., distorts events into personally logical but essentially irrational beliefs; embellishes trivial achievements to accord with semigrandiose self-image).

5. Persecutory self-references (e.g., construes incidental events as critical of self, reveals tendency to magnify minor and personally unrelated tensions into proofs of purposeful deception and malice).

DIAGNOSTIC AND STATISTICAL MANUAL
PERSONALITY DISORDERS

T. MILLON

PARAPSYCHOLOGY

Parapsychology is the scientific study of "psi," the generic term for the various types of "psychic" phenomena that can be studied empirically. Basically two forms of psi are distinguished: (a) extrasensory perception (ESP) and (b) psychokinesis (PK). Extrasensory perception is the ability to acquire information shielded from the senses. It can be time displaced, in that the information may relate to past events (retrocognition) or future events (precognition). Traditionally, ESP is further classified into telepathy and clairvoyance. In telepathy, the information or target is a thought in someone else's mind; in clairvoyance, it is an external event or object. Psychokinesis is the ability of the mind to affect external systems outside the sphere of its motor activity.

BACKGROUND

The belief in psychic phenomena is as old as recorded human history. Even in contemporary industrialized societies, psychic experiences are reported to be widespread.

Along with belief there has also been persistent skepticism, the basis for which appears to be twofold. First, the phenomena are sporadic and elusive. Second, the phenomena, if genuine, have always appeared to defy natural explanation and to conflict with commonsense assumptions concerning the way we interact with our environment.

Evidence for psi is of two kinds—qualitative and quantitative. Qualitative psi comprises those events that have a naturalistic basis and includes episodes of spontaneous psychic occurrences in everyday life (e.g., premonition of an impending catastrophe) and field manifestations such as poltergeist disturbances (technically, recurrent spontaneous psychokinesis, or RSPK). Quantitative evidence for psi is, of course, the evidence obtained in laboratory settings under controlled conditions and evaluated statistically.

The most extensive collection of spontaneous experiences is the U.S. collection of L. E. Rhine of some 15,000 cases. The Rhine collection did not involve any effort to authenticate the cases. Its purpose was not to prove the existence of psi, but only to see whether the cases would throw any light on the psi process and thus generate fruitful hypotheses for laboratory testing.

Parapsychologists generally recognize the weakness of case material as evidence of psi.

The early experimental work was largely concerned with thought transference, or telepathy.

The first serious attempt to study psi experimentally in the United States was made by J. E. Coover. Coover's conclusion was that his results failed to support the hypothesis of telepathy. Among other early experiments in American universities were those by Troland and Estabrooks at Harvard University. Estabrooks' experiments are of special interest because, in the last series, when the agent and the subject were kept in separate rooms, the scores dropped significantly below what would be expected by chance.

DUKE EXPERIMENTS: SYSTEMATIC RESEARCH

The publication of Estabrooks' results of experimental telepathy coincided with Rhine's arrival at Duke University to work with William McDougall, who had a long-standing interest in psychical research.

Rhine set out to answer, by means of mathematically indisputable evidence, the question of the occurrence and range of ESP.

Among his ESP experiments, the Pearce–Pratt series is the best known. In this experiment, Hubert Pearce was the subject and J. G. Pratt was the experimenter. Working in two separate buildings, the subject and experimenter synchronized their watches and set an exact time for the start of the experiment. The experimenter randomly chose a deck of ESP cards from several available to him, shuffled it well, and gave it a final cut. He then picked the top card, placed it face down on a book, and allowed it to remain there for 1 minute. At the end of the minute, he picked the next card, and so on, until he was through with all the cards. The subject, working in his cubicle in the library, attempted to identify the targets, minute by minute, and recorded his responses. Pearce obtained hits in excess of what might be expected by chance. The probability of obtaining such a result by chance is less than 10^{-22}.

Rhine and his coworkers also carried out extensive experiments to test the possibility of psychokinesis, in which the subjects' task was to mentally influence falling dice to land with a desired face up. After 9 years of testing, Rhine claimed that he had sufficient evidence in support of PK. A significant aspect of the evidence came from an unexpected finding, a chronological falling off in the hit rate. The records of 18 independent experiments showed a highly significant tendency for the upper-left-hand quarter of the record page to show the highest percentage of hits and the lower-right-hand quarter, the lowest. This distribution of hits relating to chronological declines in scoring is labeled "quarter distribution" (QD).

Soon after convincing themselves that psi is real, Rhine and his associates set out to determine whether psi is constrained by such physical variables as size and shape of the targets, and by space and time. Having discovered no such restrictions, they moved on to relate psi to psychological variables. Notably Stuart and Humphrey at the Duke Laboratory and Gertrude Schmeidler at the City College of New York pioneered in the study of personality and ESP correlation.

Some Confirmations

Rhine and associates reviewed all experimental reports on ESP published between 1882 and 1939 and dealt with a variety of criticisms of them. Of the 145 studies, 82 gave results that would be considered significant by the statistical criterion generally adopted in psychological literature. Since 1940, several hundred successful psi experiments have been reported.

PROCESS-ORIENTED RESEARCH

Researchers convinced of the reality of psi have turned their attention to studies that may throw light on the psi process. These studies are important for several reasons: (a) any evidence in support of certain lawfulness of psi would also be evidence in support of its existence; (b) since much of the skepticism is prompted by the manifest bizarreness of psi, understanding of its relationship with other and better understood phenomena may lessen intellectual resistance to its acceptance; and (c) significant understanding of the process will provide the basis for obtaining a measure of control, or at least a degree of predictability and replicability.

H. J. Eysenck hypothesized that, if ESP is an ancient and primitive form of perception, extroverted subjects who are in a lower state of cortical arousal should do better in ESP tests than introverts, because conditions of high cortical arousal would be unfavorable to ESP. A fairly comprehensive review of the relevant literature in parapsychology convinced Eysenck that extroverts did perform better in ESP tests than introverts. Later Kanthamani and Rao reported the results of four series of experiments that lent further support for an ESP-extraversion relationship.

Another personality relationship explored somewhat extensively in relation to ESP test scores is neuroticism. In the sense of "maladaptive behavior caused either by anxiety or defense mechanisms against anxi-

ety," neuroticism scores tended generally to correlate negatively with ESP scores.

Belief in the possibility of ESP seems to be related to ESP scoring. The pioneer in this area of research, Schmeidler, divided her subjects into "sheep," or those who believed in the possibility of ESP, and "goats," or those who rejected such a possibility. She found that sheep generally tended to obtain more hits than goats.

Palmer published a review of the sheep–goat studies and found that in 13 out of the 17 experiments that employed standard methods and analyses, the sheep obtained better scores than the goats.

Psi and Sensory Noise Reduction

Most of the traditional procedures of psychic development emphasize the importance of reduced attention and awareness to sensory input. Parapsychologists have experimented with a variety of procedures designed to enhance internal awareness and reduce external attention. These include ganzfeld stimulation, hypnosis, relaxation, and meditation.

Considering the legendary elusiveness and annoying unpredictability of psi, the number of successful experiments that involved procedures for sensory noise reduction is indeed encouraging. In this context, it is worthwhile to note that ganzfeld stimulation is reported to increase electroencephalogram (EEG) alpha activity. Meditation and relaxation have a similar effect on the subject's EEG.

Several studies in parapsychological literature have attempted to relate EEG alpha activity to ESP scoring. These studies suggest that psi is related to alpha abundance as well as alpha frequency shifting from the pretest to posttest periods, indicating that some kind of noneffortful or relaxed attention may be basic in the psi process.

PSI-MISSING AND THE DIFFERENTIAL EFFECT

Psi-missing is the misdirecting of psi, which results in a significant avoidance of the target the subject is consciously attempting to hit. Rhine suggested "negative motivation and systematic cognitive error both operating unconsciously" as possible explanations for psi-missing. It was observed that subjects with negative attitudes toward psi tend to psi-miss. Situations that cause frustration and boredom and those that create conflict in the subject's mind are also associated with psi-missing. These findings support the negative motivation hypothesis. However, the case of consistent missing, in which the subject consistently mistakes or confuses one target symbol with another, fits better with the systematic-cognitive-error hypothesis.

One of the more frequently observed psi effects is the tendency for subjects to score differentially when tested under two contrasting conditions, such as two types of targets or two kinds of response modes. Rao labeled it the "differential effect."

Psi-missing in general, and the differential effect in particular, point to the bidirectional nature of psi. It is because of its bidirectionality that psi appears elusive and unreliable.

For the same reason, any hope of achieving predictability lies in an understanding of the mechanisms involved in psi's apparent self-obscuring process.

THEORIES OF PSI

It is often said that parapsychology has no paradigm of its own and that its data conflict *prima facie* with the paradigm of what Kuhn calls "normal science." This does not mean, however, that there is any lack of theorizing in the field.

The primary thrust of parapsychological theorizing so far has been directed toward explaining how psi may function in a manner relatively unaffected by space–time limitations. These theories represent what may be considered a vitalistic model. A few theorists have expressed the hope that an extension of the principles of the physical sciences will suffice to explain psi. A third, the acausal model, does away with the notion of interaction between the subject and the target. The best known theory in this category is Jung's concept of synchronicity, which postulates a noncausal linking of two events in a meaningful way.

Two influential theoretical attempts have generated meaningful research in recent years. Stanford proposed a "conformance behavior model." According to this model, the nervous system or the brain is a complex and sophisticated random event generator (REG). The ESP subject (or the experimenter), insofar as there is a wish or need to succeed in the test, is a "disposed system." A disposed system is contingently linked to an REG under circumstances that are favorable, such that the outputs of the latter fulfill the dispositions of the former. When such conformance behavior manifests, ESP exists. Stanford argues that his theory is more than a mere description and that it has important testable implications.

The observational theories of psi make use of quantum physics; the best known is by Walker. Walker's theory, an extension of his theory of consciousness, is based on the concept of hidden variables in quantum mechanics. Hidden variables are postulated to reconcile the demands of deterministic and stochastic conceptions of the development of the state vector. These hidden variables are conceived to be essentially inaccessible to physical measurement and to function independently of space–time constraints.

CRITICISM

Although a major problem for parapsychologists is the difficulty in finding a paradigm, their critics find one with ease that readily gives them a number of *ad hoc* hypotheses to explain away the "alleged" psi phenomena. If the world is what we think it is, parapsychological events ought not to occur. Therefore, any claim for psi, if examined thoroughly, would be found to involve some kind of error or fraud.

One of the most biting criticisms of psi was that published by G. R. Price. Price agreed that some ESP experiments cannot be explained away by "clerical and statistical errors and unintentional use of sensory cues," but since ESP is incompatible with scientific theory, these results must be attributed to "deliberate fraud or mildly abnormal conditions" on the part of those reporting them.

Notwithstanding the fact that Price later withdrew his accusation and apologized to Rhine, much of the criticism of psi research still emphasizes the possibility of fraud on the part of the subject or the experimenter.

The claims and criticisms in psi research raise interesting questions for the sociology and philosophy of science—how we do science and what constitutes evidence. The critical questions raised against parapsychology are quite uncommon in other sciences. The critics' justification is that parapsychology makes extraordinary claims and thus they are right to demand extraordinary evidence. To the extent that psi phenomena are difficult to replicate and harmonize with the rest of our knowledge of the universe, the demand for better and more evidence is likely to continue.

EXTRASENSORY PERCEPTION
PSEUDOPSYCHOLOGY

K. R. Rao

PARASYMPATHETIC NERVOUS SYSTEM

The parasympathetic nervous system (PNS) is one division of the autonomic nervous system; the other division is the sympathetic nervous system. The PNS is composed of neurons, the cell bodies of which are located in the brain stem and in the sacral segments of the spinal cord. These are uniformly preganglionic neurons, since they all synapse in

ganglia either in or near the effector organ. Preganglionic neurons in the cranial division descend to local ganglia, from which postganglionic fibers innervate the heart and thoracic and abdominal viscera, while neurons in the sacral division innervate the genitalia and organs of the pelvic cavity. The postganglionic synaptic transmitter in the parasympathetic division is acetylcholine.

The PNS dominates the functioning of the autonomic nervous system during periods of rest or relaxation. The restoration of energy supplies and slowing of metabolism that occur during PNS dominance is called *anabolism*. During such a period, cardiovascular functions are reduced: heart rate decreases and the volume of blood pumped with each stroke is less. Blood flow to the periphery is minimal, but blood flow to the gastrointestinal tract and other abdominal organs increases. These responses are largely the opposite of what occurs during sympathetic nervous system dominance.

CENTRAL NERVOUS SYSTEM
SYMPATHETIC NERVOUS SYSTEM

R. M. Stern

PARENT EDUCATION

Parent education refers to a systematic program designed to impart information, attitudes, and skills that will facilitate appropriate parenting. These programs most often are conducted with groups of parents and usually consist of weekly meetings of several hours' duration that take place over 4 to 12 weeks.

Miller and Swanson have traced the gradual change in attitudes toward parenting from the eighteenth-century idea of "breaking the child's will" to the post-1945 era in which children are allowed more freedom. However, there has been an increasing recognition that this freedom must be subject to limits lest the child fail to learn consideration for the needs of others.

Dreikurs attributed these trends to a revolution in attitudes regarding human relationships from authoritarian to democratic. In a democratic system, all people, including children, are seen as having a need to be treated with dignity and respect by others. Thus spanking and other forms of humiliating punishment are increasingly ineffective as methods of child management.

VARIETY OF APPROACHES

There are many systems in parent education. There are also many similarities between these systems. This has resulted in several "packaged" programs that combine elements from two or more of the original systems.

Dreikurs refined the ideas of Alfred Adler in developing an approach to family relationships based on mutual respect. Parents must give children a sense of belonging and a feeling of significance. He believed that this was fostered if parents believed in the ability of children to learn from their mistakes and allowed them to contribute to family functioning. He called this *encouragement*. In addition, Dreikurs advocated that punishment, wherein children are humiliated and made to feel "bad," be replaced by consequences, in which firm limits are established to discourage behavior that denies respect to others. He saw the misbehavior of children as a sign of discouragement, which resulted in attempts to belong through inappropriate behavior designed to gain them attention, power, revenge, or withdrawal from the tasks of life.

Parent effectiveness training by Thomas Gordon is the basis of a successful and widely disseminated program of parent education. This approach is based on Rogers' client-centered therapy, which emphasized acceptance of and active listening to both the content and the feelings being expressed in the communication between people. Gordon teaches that parents must end the use of such one-way communication patterns as blaming, lecturing, and commanding. Children are encouraged to resolve their own problems and a "no-lose" method of conflict resolution is advocated to ensure that the needs of all parties are met in a dispute.

A variety of parent education programs are based on the principles of behavior management pioneered by B. F. Skinner. This approach emphasizes the systematic application of positive reinforcement by ensuring that the child receive something rewarding after appropriate behavior. In addition to this approach, parents are counseled to ignore negative behavior when appropriate and to use nonhumiliating forms of punishment. Consistency and a thorough retraining of one or two behaviors at a time are emphasized. Rehearsal of new parent behavior before application with the child is a feature of this approach.

There is no legislative requirement that leaders of parent groups obtain training or have minimum qualifications.

Leaders should possess some knowledge of the milestones in child development, good interpersonal communication skills, social feeling for others, group process skills, and knowledge of appropriate referral resources in the community.

FUTURE DEVELOPMENTS

Parenting programs for special populations such as single parents, parents of exceptional children, and parents from low socioeconomic and minority groups need to be developed or further refined. Also, a lack of involvement by men is a problem that must be addressed. Groups that focus on development of a positive self-concept are also necessary for parents to provide the confidence and assertive skills necessary to good parenting.

Further research is needed to determine what factors make parent education most effective. Changes in attitudes, values, and behavior of both parents and children are just some of the factors that need further research.

PARENT–CHILD RELATIONS
PARENTAL PERMISSIVENESS

R. B. ARMSTRONG

PARENT–CHILD RELATIONS

When individuals become parents through pregnancy, adoption, or stepparenting, they find themselves facing a disequilibrium that requires a great deal of adaptation. The parents want to develop a strong bond with their infant or child, but they still want to maintain a healthy marital relationship and adult friendships and possibly to continue their careers. A new baby places restrictions on marital partners that did not previously exist.

More fathers have become sensitized to the important role they play in the child's development. Studies of human fathers and their infants confirm that many fathers can act sensitively and responsively with their infants, and that infants form attachments to both their mothers and fathers at roughly the same age. Probably the strongest evidence of the plasticity of male caretaking abilities is derived from studies in which the males from primate species notoriously low in male interest in offspring are forced to live with infants whose female caretakers are absent. Under these circumstances, the adult males show considerable competence in rearing the infants.

RECIPROCAL SOCIALIZATION AND SYNCHRONY IN PARENT–INFANT RELATIONSHIPS

Bell reviewed a number of studies related to caretaker effects on children and suggested that the effects may have been caused by the child's behavior as much as by the caretaker's. The fact that parents differ widely in

sensing the needs of their infants is one of the remarkable discoveries of the past decade. Some quickly note their child's moods and periods of distress and act to comfort the infant. This is called *synchrony*. Others may not notice the need for action or may be slow to respond. This is called *asynchrony*. In the psychoanalytic perspective, synchrony will generate a sense of trust in the infant; asynchrony will breed distrust. Learning theory stresses the presence or absence of clear reward contingencies. Clear contingencies make learning easier.

Recently a group of researchers demonstrated that mothers' synchrony with their infants' needs prompts physiological responses, and that these biological indices predict how mothers rate the temperament of their infants. Thirty-two middle-class mothers, each of whom had a 3-month-old infant, were shown short videotape sequences of an unknown infant (also 3 months old) alternately smiling and crying. The mothers who described their infants as "difficult" responded less sensitively to the infants on the videotapes.

Thus either the mother may learn very quickly (within 3 months in this case) to respond differently to a "difficult" than to an "easy" infant, or the infant's temperament may partially stem from the way in which the child is handled by the mother. It is likely that these findings evidence a little of both effects. Not only should the reciprocal nature of parent–child relations be considered when explaining the child's social behavior, but also the entire system of interacting individuals in the family should be considered when evaluating the child's development.

THE FAMILY AS A SYSTEM

As a social system, the family can be thought of as a constellation of subsystems defined in terms of generation, gender, and role. Divisions of labor among family members define particular subunits, and attachments define others, each family member being a participant in several subsystems, some dyadic, some polyadic.

As fathers become recognized as important socialization agents, it has become obvious that we should be studying more than two-party social interactions. Children interact with more than one parent or adult most days of their lives, yet we know very little about how parents serve each other as sources of support as well as sources of dissatisfaction.

One attempt to understand the link between spouse relationships and parent–infant relationships was conducted by Frank Pederson and his colleagues.

There was little relationship between measures of positive husband–wife interaction and their positive interaction with the infant. However, when negative social interaction between the husband and wife was observed (e.g., verbal criticism, blame), it was strongly linked to the negative affect shown by the father toward the infant. These findings suggest that the family is a network of interacting individuals functioning as a system.

Belsky developed an organizational scheme of the family system that highlights the possible reciprocal influences that marital relations, parenting, and infant behavior/development may have on each other.

PARENTAL PERMISSIVENESS

J. W. SANTROCK

PARENTAL PERMISSIVENESS

Parental permissiveness is the practice and rationale of someone in a parental role who allows, authorizes, encourages, and tolerates an extremely wide range of activities, behaviors, and values of a child. The underlying premise of this rationale is that children grow and flourish by their explorative experiences. This approach to child rearing was highly influenced by Freudian ideas, which stressed attention to children's instinctive needs.

Rudolf Dreikurs, a student of Alfred Adler, delineated a more democratic method of parenting. "The popular practice of letting children have unrestricted freedom has made tyrants of children and slaves of the parents. . . . Well-defined restrictions give a sense of security and a certainty of function within the social structure."

Dreikurs advocated that the best way to teach children the concepts of freedom and responsibility was through the use of encouragement and natural and logical consequences. Therefore, children are encouraged by experiencing the consequences of their own behavior. He frequently wrote that the natural and logical consequences of misbehavior were fundamentally different than punishment. The consequence of a misbehavior should be arranged by the parent so that it expresses the rules of the family, is related to the misbehavior, involves no judgment or reproach of the child, and is concerned with what will happen in the present and future. Thus the logical consequence is concerned with the child being responsive to the social order and is not intended to restrict the child's freedom.

Albert Pesso was concerned with the emotional ramifications of the issue between permissiveness and restrictiveness. He believed that the child should be permitted to experience and explore emotional and physical feelings. Yet, Pesso believed, it is up to the parents to limit the child when the child moves in a way that is destructive to self or others.

Diana Baumrind developed a typology that separated parents on the degree of control over their children: authoritarian (high control), permissive (low control), and authoritative (minimally restrictive but with firm control manifested at points of parent–child divergence). Baumrind concluded that either unrealistically high or low standards leave the child insecure and dependent on the outside world. Related support for this position has been reported by Coopersmith, who found that self-esteem is highest when the parents set limits without excessive control.

The majority of the theories and related research that study the issue of parental permissiveness assert the need for an authoritative parenting style. Thus the task of parenting becomes an artful balance between freedom and responsibility, as opposed to a parental stance that is overly restrictive or overly permissive.

CONSEQUENCES
PARENT–CHILD RELATIONS

R. A. Haber

PARKINSON'S DISEASE

Parkinson's disease is a chronic degenerative disorder of the central nervous system. The disease usually begins slowly, with only a few apparent symptoms. Because the onset is slow and the population affected is elderly, symptoms are frequently disregarded as consequences of the aging process.

The etiology is unknown. The epidemiological profile includes the facts that (a) it is a disease of the elderly, (b) first symptoms are usually noted in the patient's sixth decade of life, and (c) males are affected slightly more often than females. It has been noted that the neurotransmitter dopamine normally stored in the cells of the substantia nigra tissue in the brain are greatly depleted in Parkinson's disease. The reason is unclear.

Because symptoms develop slowly, years may pass before the diagnosis is made. The disease is progressive, so that eventually the patient's ability to perform the activities of daily living and other independent functions is reduced. Manifestations may include the following:

1. Muscle rigidity associated with slowness of voluntary movement, with the muscles feeling stiff and requiring much effort to move and the trunk of the body tending to stoop forward.

2. A masklike face with the patient appearing to stare straight ahead and assuming an expressionless look, with the eyes blinking less frequently than normal.

3. Tremors of the upper extremities, including activity of the thumb and fingers resulting in a characteristic "pinrolling movement" when the hand is motionless (resting tremors).

4. Resting tremors of the foot, lip, tongue, and jaw.

5. Rigidity or rhythmic contractions on passive stretching of the muscles in the arms (cogwheel phenomenon).

6. Restlessness, including a compelling need to walk about constantly.

7. Disturbances in free-flowing movement that result in jerky and uncoordinated movements.

8. General weakness and muscular fatigue with slow initiation of movement for purposeful acts.

9. Frequent muscle cramps of the legs, neck, and trunk.

10. A weak voice, resulting in a monotonic whispering speech pattern.

11. A loss of postural reflexes that results in difficulty in maintaining balance.

12. Inability to sit erect.

13. Walking in a stooped-over position with small shuffling steps, frequently accelerating almost to a trot.

14. Mental depression related to an abnormal physical appearance, a weakened voice, which affects communication, and a frequent tendency to withdraw from normal interaction because of self-consciousness and embarrassment.

15. Common autonomic manifestations that include drooling (due to decreased frequency of swallowing), oily skin, excessive perspiration, constipation, and urinary hesitation and frequency.

Management is directed toward control of the symptoms of the disease with drug therapy, supportive therapy and maintenance, and a physiotherapy program. Most patients manage well at home with an effective drug program that often allows maintenance of a normal lifestyle.

CENTRAL NERVOUS SYSTEM
NEUROMUSCULAR DISORDERS

R. T. Giubilato

PASSIVE–AGGRESSIVE PERSONALITY

The *Diagnostic and statistical manual of mental disorders (DSM-IV)* stresses as the prime characteristic of these personalities their resistance to the demands by others for adequate performance. Ostensibly those with this disorder express a form of covert aggression through their behavior, evident in such actions as procrastination, stubbornness, forgetfulness, and inefficiency. They are also characterized by a capricious impulsiveness, an irritable moodiness, and a grumbling, discontented, sulky, unaccommodating, and fault-finding pessimism. Often anguished and discontented, these personalities are generalized and perennial in their complaints, never satisfied either with themselves or with others. An intense conflict appears to exist within them between being dependent and being self-assertive, resulting in ever-present ambivalence and persistently erratic moods. Personal relationships are also fraught with wrangles and disappointments, provoked repeatedly by their characteristic complaining and negative, fretful behaviors.

Theodore Millon proposed a biosocial-learning framework for this disorder. The following diagnostic criteria were enumerated as a guide to this syndrome:

1. Labile affectivity (e.g., is frequently irritable and displays erratic moodiness; reports being easily frustrated and explosive).

2. Behavioral contrariness (e.g., frequently exhibits passively aggressive, petulant, and fault-finding behaviors; reveals gratification in demoralizing and undermining the pleasures of others).

3. Discontented self-image (e.g., reports feeling misunderstood, unappreciated, and demeaned by others; is characteristically pessimistic, disgruntled, and disillusioned with life).

4. Deficient regulatory controls (e.g., expresses fleeting thoughts and impulsive emotions in unmodulated form; external stimuli evoke capricious and vacillating reactions).

5. Interpersonal ambivalence (e.g., assumes conflicting and changing roles in social relationships, particularly dependent acquiescence and assertive independence; uses unpredictable and sulking behavior to provoke edgy discomfort in others).

DIAGNOSTIC AND STATISTICAL MANUAL
PERSONALITY DISORDERS

T. MILLON

PASTORAL COUNSELING

Pastoral counseling is a modern and psychologically sophisticated form of religious caring. Usually offered by a minister, priest, rabbi, chaplain, or other religious worker, pastoral counseling seeks to combine skilled counseling methods with an understanding and application of the moral guidelines and spiritual values of religion.

In contrast to the term *religious counseling,* which is not limited to Christian pastors or to Western systems of belief, the term *pastoral counseling* usually is limited to the help given by religious leaders whose beliefs are based in Judaic/Christian traditions.

The Bible is filled with examples of dedicated men and women who encouraged, guided, supported, confronted, comforted, advised, and in other ways helped people in need. Throughout the Christian era, pastors and other religious workers have engaged in what have come to be known as the four pastoral functions: (a) healing (restoring individuals to wholeness and leading them to advance beyond their previous conditions); (b) sustaining (helping hurting people to endure and to rise above difficult circumstances); (c) guiding (assisting perplexed individuals as they face difficult decisions); and (d) reconciling (reestablishing relationships between people and between individuals and God).

The modern pastoral counseling movement began in the 1920s as a reaction against both traditional theological education, which tended to have little practical and pastoral emphasis, and early psychiatric treatment, which had little place for religious perspectives on healing.

Clinical Pastoral Education (CPE) has developed into a highly organized movement. Much of its work has been in providing standards and guidelines for the training of pastoral counselors; demonstrating to both hospital personnel and theological educators that pastoral involvement is relevant and effective in the treatment of psychological and physical illness; investigating ways in which theology and the psychological sciences can be related; and showing that the personal and spiritual development of seminarians is at least as important as intellectual training for the ministry.

Pastoral counselors of all theological persuasions deal with personal, social, marital, family, and religious problems. Much of the emphasis in pastoral counseling is on coping with present problems, helping those who suffer, and giving spiritual guidance.

Pastoral counseling takes place not only in pastors' offices and church settings but also in hospital rooms, prison cells, parishioners' homes, restaurants, military settings, and funeral homes. Hospital and military chaplains usually identify themselves as pastoral counselors, as do college chaplains and chaplains associated with major league sports teams.

As pastoral counseling has become more popular and its effectiveness more recognized, increasing numbers of pastors are finding themselves swamped with requests for counseling. To meet these needs, several trends have become apparent within the pastoral counseling movement. These include increased communication and cooperation among pastors and professionals in the helping fields; the development of better training programs in seminaries; the stimulation of lay counseling within and through the local congregation; the establishment of pastoral counseling centers; the involvement of pastors in new and established counseling clinics and community centers; the consideration of ways in which problem prevention can be stimulated by and through the church or synagogue; the increased use of sermons and small study groups as ways of stimulating mental and spiritual health; and the development of films, seminars, and training programs that can supplement, replace, and prevent the need for counseling.

COUNSELING
RELIGION AND PSYCHOLOGY

G. R. COLLINS

PEABODY PICTURE VOCABULARY TEST

The Peabody test is presented in a 175-page booklet, with each page containing four illustrations of common objects, such as toys, kitchen appliances, and animals. The test is administered as follows: The examiner says the stimulus word (for example, "candle"). The subject is asked to point to or otherwise indicate the correct answer. The range of this test is considerable. However, the pictures are not spaced at psychologically meaningful intervals. The subject receives a total score in terms of correct replies, which can be converted to a standard score, a percentile, and, if one wishes, to an IQ.

The Peabody test has considerable versatility as well as range. Even retarded children like and can function on this test. It can be viewed as a test of general intelligence on the basis of the argument that (keeping environmental conditions constant) children who are inherently brighter are more likely to do well on this test than children who are not as bright. The test comes in two forms. Validity and reliability levels are considered acceptable for individual clinical use, and this test is frequently employed in combination with other tests, such as the Wechsler tests and the Stanford–Binet.

INTELLIGENCE MEASURES

A. SIMPKINS

PEACE PSYCHOLOGY

Peace making was linked with both political science and psychology by Aristotle (c. 300 B.C.), who wrote the first Western treatise on psychology and declared in his *Ethics* that human nature is primarily political, that statecraft (*politike*) is above all other arts and sciences in providing the greatest good for human beings, and that we make war only to obtain peace.

Following World War I, Sigmund Freud, among others, wrote of his disillusion with war as a highway to peace, and Alfred Adler condemned all violence and proposed that psychologists oppose war and everything else that is contrary to the interests of the family, the school, and society in general. Following the use of nuclear weapons in World War II and the continued development and proliferation of such weapons, various psychologists and psychiatrists as well as other professionals actively opposed the further design, stock-piling, and potential use of nuclear weapons. In addition, numerous groups were organized to prevent war and to promote peace and other conditions favorable to human development. These groups included Physicians for Social Responsibility (PSR), which was awarded the Nobel Peace Prize in 1985, and Psychologists for Social Responsibility (PsySR). The work of PsySR includes analyzing the psychology of the war system and other violent conflicts, changing prejudicial attitudes that instigate them, and teaching alternative nonviolent means for settling disputes. Workshops and information materials are offered to the general public and to specific groups, including mental health professionals, educators, military personnel, and policymakers.

In 1989, the American Psychological Association (APA) formally recognized peace psychology by establishing it as Division 48. This division emphasizes research and scholarship in addressing peace issues and was designed to collaborate with PsySR and with Division 9, which studies social issues in general.

GRIT
SOCIOPSYCHOLOGICAL DETERMINANTS OF WAR AND PEACE

A. D. SCHEUER

PEAK EXPERIENCES

The discoverer of peak experiences, Abraham Maslow, described them as rare, exciting, oceanic, deeply moving, exhilarating, and elevating experiences that generate an advanced form of perceiving reality, and are even mystic and magical in their effect on the experimenter.

THE NINETEEN CHARACTERISTICS

Maslow's concept of "self-actualizing" and of Being Cognition was sometimes used interchangeably with peak experiences. The 19 characteristics found in the original paper constitute perhaps the best available description of that oceanic and positive experience.

Those most pertinent may be summarized as follows: There is an experience of wholeness, of unity, and in the perceptual process, the person attends fully. The perceptions are richer. There is a disorientation in time and space—the person loses sight of the present environment. It is a positive experience; never an evil or negative one. The self-actualized person lives comfortably with polarities. The person at the peak is godlike, particularly in the complete, loving, uncondemning, compassionate, and perhaps amused acceptance of the world and of the person. The peak experience chases away fear and there is a healthy childishness in the person's behavior.

POSITIVE EXPERIENCE

Maslow paid less attention to the entire range of positive experience but acknowledged the existence of "foothill" or lesser, yet still positive, experiences making their own contribution to the self-actualizing personality. Seven categories are often used to describe the positive experiences: divine experiences, conquest of a skill, excitement, human relationships, beauty, earned success, and completion.

OTHER PEAK-EXPERIENCE RESEARCHERS AND THEORETICIANS

Many humanistically oriented and even some behavioral psychologists found peak experiences quite researchable. The literature shows the response to Maslow's propositions to be quite varied. A large number of theoretical and philosophical questions were raised.

However, experience of any kind has not been welcome in U.S. psychological laboratories. Maslow argued, along with others, for a "respectable place for experiential data." Phenomenology as the study of perceptual data in contrast to objective data is the true home of the peak experience. Howard Rosenblatt and Iris Bartlett found a relationship of peak experience to two major phenomenological concepts, paradoxical intention and intentionality, and Thomas Armor supported the position that the peak experience constitutes "a transcendence of the usual form of consciousness common to all mankind."

PEAK EXPERIENCES IN EDUCATION AND THE ARTS

Maslow suggested that the two easiest ways of triggering peak experiences were through classical music and sex. Beyond music itself as a trigger for the peak experience, Maslow was enthusiastic about rhythm exercises, athletics, and dancing. However, he also saw the possibility of mathematics education as peak producing.

Support for some of these propositions was not slow in coming in the form of empirical studies. Responding to Maslow's challenge to education, Nancy Wilgenbusch saw the possibility of developing Maslow's call for a human potential in teacher education.

Researchers in music also answered the Maslovian call. J. A. Pennington developed a quantitative measurement of the peak experience in music.

The empirical data and case studies reported lend credibility to the relationship between art and peak experience.

THE DRUG EXPERIENCE

Early in his descriptions of the peak experience, Maslow permitted himself to consider drug experiences as possibly having some similarity to the peak experience. However, he clearly rejected this as reported in a later paper by Mildred Hardeman. Peak experiences that really change the person come about where they are earned.

EMOTIONS
PHENOMENOLOGY

T. LANDSMAN

PEDIATRIC PSYCHOLOGY

Pediatric psychology exists at the intersection of developmental psychology, health psychology, and child psychopathology. The term was originally developed by Logan Wright in 1967 when he defined a pediatric psychologist as "any psychologist dealing primarily with children in a medical setting that is non-psychiatric in nature." The *Journal of Pediatric Psychology* defines pediatric psychology as "an interdisciplinary field addressing the full range of physical and mental development, health and illness issues affecting children, adolescents and families."

The need for this area of psychology was first articulated in 1930 by John Anderson, a pediatrician. The first psychologist to suggest a marriage of psychology and pediatrics was Jerome Kagan, with Logan Wright's 1967 paper in the *American Psychologist* being credited as formally marking the birth of the field. The Society of Pediatric Psychology, formed in 1968, is Section 5 of Division 12 of the American Psychological Association.

Pediatric psychology differs from child psychology in that the point of intervention usually is medical rather than psychiatric. Much of the work in pediatric psychology occurs in university medical centers, but the field has spread gradually from tertiary care sites to community hospitals, as well as primary care settings of private medical groups and individual practices.

The need for this field results from the increasing successes of pediatric medicine as well as a growing sophistication of both pediatrics and psychology. As physicians are able to save more children, morbidity increases. Progress in medicine has transformed many formerly fatal illnesses to chronic diseases. Thus there is a growing population of children who must cope with residual distress, prolonged or chronic treatments, and the sequelae of treatment. Each such child lives in a matrix of family, health care systems, educational system, and community, all affected by the child's physical and psychological health status.

Pediatricians especially have come to appreciate that behavioral psychological, and social issues must be addressed to effectively treat disease. Currently research has shown that more than half of visits to a pediatrician involve behavioral or academic questions, two-thirds of children admitted to a pediatric ward could benefit from a psychiatric consultation, and that children with multiple hospital admissions are more likely to have psychiatric symptoms, learning problems, or conduct disorders.

The pediatric psychologist functions as a member of a treatment team. The role played by the psychologist can be a adjunctive, consultative, or as an equal member of the team.

SERVICES PROVIDED BY PEDIATRIC PSYCHOLOGISTS

Psychological Evaluation

In the context of the medical setting, not only do psychological factors need to be evaluated, but also consideration must be given to the child's medical status, its impact on the child's behavior, its psychological impact, and the requirements of treatments and their impact on the child. Relevant family factors needing to be assessed include social and financial resources, health beliefs, changes in the family due to the illness, and the family's view of the illness. Health care system variables are relevant, including availability of care and patient and family functioning within the system as well as variables in the larger sociocultural environment (i.e., the culture's view of a particular diagnosis such as acquired immuno-deficiency syndrome, or AIDS).

Improvement of Compliance

A frequent role of the pediatric psychologist is to help the patient achieve medical compliance. Although compliance is an issue in all of medical psychology, pediatric psychology often deals with patients who do not understand the necessity for their treatment and may be experiencing developmental needs for achieving independence that are counter to the need to comply. In this role, the psychologist can be thought of acting as an agent of the medical system for the benefit of the patient.

Pain Control

Psychologists possess skills that provide an alternative or adjunct to pharmacologic pain control. Relaxation training, biofeedback-assisted relaxation and hypnosis can be used to provide pain prophylaxis. In children, pain-induced behaviors may be ambiguous (such as irritability, withdrawal, or regression). As behavioral experts, pediatric psychologists can work with health care workers so that pain can be recognized and treated in the most appropriate and effective manner.

Treatment of Psychogenic Illness

Physicians are frustrated and frequently made angry when patients present psychologically "caused" illnesses. The physician knows the illness has no organic base and has few tools to help the patient who is clearly in distress. Patients are usually equally convinced of the "reality" of their illness and also become angry and frustrated when their distress is ignored or denigrated. When the physician views the psychologist as a member of the health care team, the patient's confidence in the system to recognize and treat their distress is confirmed.

Ethicist and Child Advocacy

Medical advances have brought with them complex ethical issues. The pediatric psychologist is in a unique position to help the medical system as well as the patient and the family. In instances such as deciding whether to continue treatment, helping the medical system understand the psychological impact of its treatment, or recognizing the more subtle forms of abuse or neglect, the pediatric psychologist is able to fulfill a need met by no other person within the system.

Research

Any new scientific field must prove itself not only through service but also through research. Psychologists are trained as scientists as well as practitioners, the only professional in the medical system benefiting from this particular training model. Thus, psychologists bear the responsibility of increasing the knowledge base of pediatric psychology.

A number of personal skills are demanded of the pediatric psychologist. First there must be an understanding of personal and professional stimulus values because pediatric psychologists frequently work with people who have no mental health problems per se yet still require services. A pediatric psychologist must possess a high frustration tolerance, as referrals are sometimes received with no preparation to patient or parents, or are made as the patient is about to leave the hospital, or there may be failure to acknowledge the psychologist's expertise, and occasionally there may be failure of other professionals to carry out recommendations. The pediatric psychologist must avoid professional fanaticism in treatment teams. Others within treatment teams such as nurses, social workers, and physiotherapists hold different conceptual models that must be acknowledged and understood. There must be a tolerance for an unpredictable work schedule with need for services occurring emergently. The psychologist often works with hostile patients, unable to understand their need for referral to and treatment by a psychologist.

Training is a most important issue within pediatric psychology. Periodic conferences are held by the Society of Pediatric Psychology specifically to develop training standards. Four areas of knowledge have been defined as necessary for the competent practice: basic psychology, clinical psychology, developmental psychology, and health psychology. Training in the 1990s is almost always obtained at the internship or postdoctoral level, although several graduate programs in pediatric psychology do exist. A directory of available practica, internships, and fellowships is available through the Society of Pediatric Psychology.

CHILD ABUSE
CHILD PSYCHOLOGY
CHILDREN'S FEAR
EMOTIONAL CONTAGION
FAMILY CRISES
LOSS AND GRIEF

J. S. HOFFMAN

PEDOPHILIA

Pedophilia (from the Greek, meaning "love of children") is a psychosexual disorder essentially characterized by the act or fantasy of engaging in sexual activity with prepubertal children as a repeatedly preferred or exclusive method of achieving sexual excitement. Pedophiliac sexual activities may vary in intensity and include stroking the child's hair, and, when initiated by a male, holding the child close while covertly masturbating, manipulating the child's genitals, encouraging the child to manipulate his, and, less frequently, attempting intromission. Youngsters of any age up to puberty may be the object of pedophiliac attention; force seldom is employed.

Compared with most other paraphilias or "sexual deviations" there is more research available on the characteristics of those manifesting this particular disorder. Perhaps this situation is understandable in that pedophilia is viewed as an outrage by society, can result in obvious psychological damage to the victim, frequently leads to the arrest of the pedophiliac, and consequently creates an incarcerated group that can be readily studied. On the basis of what has been found empirically, pedophiliacs typically know the children they molest—neighbors, family, friends, relatives.

Although the disorder occurs predominantly in males, instances of pedophilia in females have been reported. Moreover, about twice as many pedophiliacs are oriented toward opposite-sexed children as are oriented homosexually. Pedophiliac individuals range in age from adolescence through the 70s, with a significant percentage in their mid- to late 30s. Further, there is some evidence that etiological factors in this disorder may vary, depending on the age of the offender.

Other research has further bolstered the position that persons who commit pedophiliac offenses fall into a variety of categories. By far the most common category is the psychologically immature offenders—individuals with chronic difficulties in relating to persons of their own age and who thus are sexually comfortable only with children. In most cases, these individuals know the child in question. A second category contains persons who impulsively regress to pedophilia under stress. Acting impulsively, this type of offender is usually not acquainted with the victim. A third category is comprised of men who have had powerful early sexual experiences with young boys (e.g., in reformatories) and have never progressed sexually much beyond that point. These pedophiliacs are typically callous and exploitative in their sexual behavior. A final category consists of antisocial personalities who prey on children in quest of new sexual thrills. Not infrequently, the pedophiliac behavior in this instance is motivated by both aggressive and sexual components, with the child often being physically harmed during the sexual act.

Other investigators have noted additional severe psychopathology in some pedophiliac offenders (e.g., alcoholism, schizophrenia, organic mental disorders) in which lowered inhibitory controls appeared to underlie the sexual act.

SEXUAL DEVIATIONS

D. J. ZIEGLER

PEER COUNSELING

Peer counseling is defined as the performance of limited counselor functions, under counselor supervision, by a person of approximately the same age as the counselee. The majority of peer counseling programs are conducted at the college level, although secondary and elementary schools are also involved. Community mental health agencies and penal systems have developed paraprofessional models using indigenous "natural" leaders and mediators in self-help programs for change.

Peer counselors have been used four ways: (a) as clerical help; (b) as an adjunct to the counseling program, usually in a narrowly defined role such as tutor or information provider; (c) as an aide in a group setting under direct supervision of a counselor; and rarely (d) as an independent agent with the responsibilities of a counselor.

A group counseling model for peer training emphasizes self-awareness, interpersonal and communication skills, and an introduction to counseling skills for higher levels of involvement. The model is theoretically grounded in applied and social learning theory, with attention being given to affective and cognitive development. The training program is based on principles of peer group behavior; the power of peer influence is directed toward positive, effective, and rewarding life skills. Peer coun-

selors are models for their peers; positive behavior is encouraged and developed in the training and exhibited by the peer counselors to influence their contemporaries.

V. Delworth evaluated peer counseling programs to ascertain why they are not more effective in school settings. He concluded that the major failure lies in the fact that these individuals are trained to maintain the status quo of the school. In most of the programs surveyed, peer counselors operate under the direct supervision of the counselor and within the formal hierarchical school structure. This makes it difficult to have an effect on "problem" students whose values are different from those represented by the peer counselors.

The necessary elements for an effective paraprofessional or peer program are that (a) the selection process must identify the natural leaders and helpers, (b) the training must provide access to "system entry" skills, (c) involvement in all aspects of the organization must be encouraged, (d) this involvement must be developmental, and (e) community among the peers must be built.

PEER GROUP THERAPY
PEER INFLUENCES

N. A. HAYNIE

PEER GROUP THERAPY

Therapy done in a group by lay people who share common problems is known as peer group therapy. Peer group therapy was lifted to major importance with the beginning of Alcoholics Anonymous (AA).

Peer group therapy uses a high level of self-disclosure, rigorous honesty about personal responsibility for actions done, admission of past wrongs to a member of the group or the group itself, readiness to give up old ways of behaving, the making of amends to people who have been harmed, the turning over of one's will and life to the care of some higher power, and assistance to others as a means of helping the member stay sober.

Other peer groups use much the same format, with some requiring more confrontation. Some groups reported on in the literature are simply peers, but most, other than AA and AA-type groups, also have lay leaders who are minimally trained by someone with a psychology background.

All told, approximately 1,500,000 people are involved in peer group therapy in AA and AA-type groups.

Peer group therapy is also practiced in groups such as Synanon, Daytop, and other communities set up to free people of drug use and to provide continuous living support thereafter. They are structured around an environment of deep love and concern but have a highly confrontative atmosphere with a constant demand for rigorous honesty in every aspect of the ex-addicts' daily lives. Communal living and constant confrontation seem to be required for addicts, whereas alcoholics do not find this necessary.

Many other self-help groups practice peer group therapy: Make Today Count (for cancer sufferers) and Grow groups (started in Australia and now in the United States for people who want to improve their emotional functioning) are two of the larger organizations. In addition, there are groups organized by parents or adults who need help facing a problem with an illness or handicap. Examples are United Cerebral Palsy and the Muscular Dystrophy Association.

A national clearinghouse for all self-help organizations is the Self Help Center of Evanston, Ill. There are nearly 40 other self-help centers in various stages of operation or development across the country. An estimated 500,000 self-help groups in the United States serve as many as 5 million people.

CHANGE INDUCTION GROUPS
GROUP PSYCHOTHERAPY
PEER COUNSELING

J. LAIR

PEER INFLUENCES

Healthy peer relationships are a necessity for human development. Since children and adolescents live in an expanding social world, it is important that they learn to develop effective relationships. High-quality relationships with others are important for all aspects of the development of children and adolescents. Constructive relationships stimulate learning; the internalizing of values, attitudes, and competencies; and effective socialization. Such relationships may be with adults or with other children and adolescents. Traditionally the relationship between adults and children has been viewed as the most important vehicle for ensuring effective socialization and development.

The fact is that peer relationships with a wide age range of other children or adolescents are a critical element in human development and socialization. Young people must (a) acquire competencies, attitudes, values, and perspectives in encounters with peers, and (b) occupy a comfortable niche within their peer culture. Compared with interaction with adults, interactions with peers tend to be more frequent, more intense, and more varied throughout childhood and adolescence.

INFLUENCES ON VALUES, ATTITUDES, PERSPECTIVES, AND SOCIAL COMPETENCIES

In their interactions with other children, children directly learn attitudes, values, skills, and information unobtainable from adults, such as how to deal with conflict or temptation. Peers actively explain to one another how and why certain things are right and wrong and which social competencies are appropriate and why. Peers provide powerful models of appropriate and inappropriate behavior. The socializing importance of peers does not end during adolescence. Friends and colleagues have a critical impact on one's values, attitudes, perspectives, and social competencies throughout one's life. Peer relationships also often fulfill a need for social comparison.

Prosocial and Antisocial Behavior

Interaction with peers provides support, opportunities, and models for prosocial behavior. If children perceive their peers as admiring prosocial actions such as honesty, altruism, cooperation, and respect for individuals, they will tend to engage in such behavior. It is while interacting with other children that one has the opportunity to help, comfort, share with, take care of, and give to others.

Whether adolescents engage in problem or transition behaviors such as the use of illegal drugs, sexual intercourse, and delinquency is related to their perceptions of their friends' attitudes toward such behavior. If adolescents perceive of their friends as disapproving of such actions, they will tend *not* to engage in them. The wide-scale rejection of a child by peers, furthermore, tends to promote antisocial actions by the child, such as aggressiveness, disruptiveness, and other negatively perceived behavior.

Impulsiveness

Children frequently lack the time perspective needed to tolerate delays in gratification. However, as they develop and are socialized, the focus on their own immediate impulses and needs is replaced with the ability to take longer perspectives. They can also view their individual desires from the perspectives of others.

Perspective-Taking Ability

Children learn to view situations and problems from perspectives other than their own through their interaction with their peers. Such perspective taking is one of the most critical competencies for cognitive and social development. It has been related to a number of important characteristics, including the ability to present and comprehend information, constructively resolve conflicts, willingly disclose personal information, help group problem solving, and display positive attitudes toward others in the same situation. Primarily through interaction with one's peers, egocentrism is lost and increased perspective-taking ability is gained.

Autonomy

Autonomy is the ability to understand what others expect in any given situation and to be free to choose whether to meet their expectations. In making decisions concerning what behavior is appropriate, autonomous people tend to consider both their internal values and the expectations of other people, and then to respond in flexible and appropriate ways. Peer relationships have a powerful influence on the development of values, social skills, and social sensitivity and the internalization of acceptance and support that form the basis for self-approval.

Loneliness

Children need constructive peer relationships to avoid the pain of loneliness. Although adults can provide certain forms of companionship, children need close and intimate relationships with peers.

Identity

Throughout infancy, childhood, adolescence, and early adulthood, a person moves through several successive and overlapping identities. In peer relationships, children become aware of the similarities and differences between themselves and others, they experiment with a variety of social roles that help them integrate their own sense of self, they clarify their attitudes and values and integrate them into their self-definition, and they develop a frame of reference for perceiving themselves.

Coalitions

For humans, banding together has survival value against enemies and environmental problems. In childhood, most people make friends and form attachments. Coalitions are formed that provide help and assistance not only during childhood and adolescence, but also throughout adulthood as well.

Productivity, Aspiration, and Psychological Health

In both educational and work settings, peers have a strong influence on productivity and aspirations. Supportive relationships with peers are also related to using abilities in achievement situations. Furthermore, the ability to maintain interdependent and cooperative relationships is a prime manifestation of psychological health. Poor peer relationships in elementary school predict psychological disturbance and delinquency in high school, and poor peer relationships in high school predict adult pathology.

PROMOTING POSITIVE PEER RELATIONSHIPS

Unfortunately, many modern schools, families, and other institutions are not managed in a way to foster healthy peer relations among children and adolescents. Fostering constructive peer relationships may be one of the most important challenges facing parents, educators, and other adults who wish to promote healthy development and effective socialization.

ADOLESCENT IDENTITY FORMATION
DEVELOPMENT OF HUMAN SOCIAL BEHVAVIOR
MIDDLE CHILDHOOD

D. W. JOHNSON
R. T. JOHNSON

PEER TUTORING

Any use of students to coach or tutor one another is usually called "peer tutoring," although when their ages differ, the students are not really members of the same peer group.

Comenius, the sixteenth-century Czech educator, observed what is a routine finding on peer tutoring today, that those doing the tutoring learn more than those who are tutored.

The appeal of peer tutoring for modern educators lies in its effectiveness as a teaching/learning method, rather than in its potential economies. Research studies have been universally supportive of the method.

In a review of research, A. Elliott arrived at the following explanations for the efficacy of peer tutoring:

1. Peer tutoring increases the percentage of time spent on teaching in the classroom period.

2. Peer tutoring provides learners with more feedback as to their performance and provides it promptly.

3. Peer tutoring increases time spent in student talk and decreases time spent in teacher talk.

4. Tutors enjoy an enhanced sense of competence and personal worth.

5. Tutors are enabled to view the teaching/learning situation from the teacher's position and thus are led to make the classroom psychological climate more cooperative and less suppressive and authoritarian.

6. Tutors are able to identify problems of learning and adjustment that have been overlooked by teachers.

ACADEMIC UNDERACHIEVEMENT
INSTRUCTIONAL THEORY

H. C. LINDGREN

PENCIL-AND-PAPER INTELLIGENCE TESTS

Pencil-and-paper intelligence tests, unlike their individually administered counterparts, result in savings of time and cost because they can be administered to groups of individuals. In addition, group intelligence tests can be scored quickly and objectively, thus enabling users to obtain considerable interpretive information within a relatively short span of time.

ORIGIN OF GROUP TESTING

Group intelligence testing resulted from an effort to duplicate the results of individual intelligence tests such as the Stanford–Binet Intelligence Scale. Otis, a graduate student of Lewis Terman, devised paper-and-pencil group test versions of certain Binet tasks for his doctoral dissertation. Otis completed his graduate studies at about the time a procedure was needed to screen and classify large numbers of World War I Army draftees. Otis joined Terman, Yerkes, and other distinguished psychologists of the day to develop a classification device. It was Otis' material that formed the basis for the Army Alpha Test, the first group intelligence test. The large-scale "experiment" with the Army Alpha Test validated the feasibility of the group test method. Within a short time, group intelligence tests were in widespread use in U.S. schools in an attempt by educators to deal with large increases in school enrollment.

CONTENT

Early group intelligence tests developed for use in the schools typically contained one or two levels, with a number of separately timed subtests. These tests were usually heavily loaded with vocabulary, general information, and school-taught skills. Many of these early measures seemed to overlap school achievement measures. Present-day critics, like their predecessors, contend that intelligence tests assess little more than verbal and mathematics achievement. One popular misconception is worthy of special mention: the belief that intelligence tests measure innate ability that is fixed at birth.

One well-known scholastic aptitude series is the Otis–Lennon School Ability Test. The two primary levels of this series, for grades K–3, yield a total score based on three subtests: classification, analogies, and verbal omnibus (several different types of items measuring the following of directions, quantitative reasoning, and verbal comprehension). The three levels for grades 4–12 contain a number of different item types in a cyclical, or spiral omnibus, arrangement, which facilitates administration and scoring. The item types include verbal analogies, opposites, figure analogies, figure series, arithmetic reasoning, number series, sentence completion, and inference. A single score is obtained for interpretation. The series is designed to predict academic success.

Another widely used test series is the Cognitive Abilities Tests. Three batteries, which may be used separately or as a comprehensive assessment, are available in a multilevel format for grades 3–12. The Verbal Battery contains four subtests (vocabulary, sentence completion, verbal classification, and verbal analogies); the Quantitative Battery, three subtests (quantitative relations, number series, and equation building); and the Nonverbal Battery, three subtests (figure classification, figure analogies, and figure synthesis). Each battery yields a single score for interpretation. According to the authors, this test series measures scholastic aptitude and abstract reasoning ability with the verbal, numerical, and figural symbol systems of our culture.

INTERPRETATION

Current tests usually provide within-age normalized standard scores and percentile ranks by age and by grade. Mental ages, a vestige of earlier tests, are sometimes provided for those users who want an age-related measure of cognitive development. Standardization samples for the current measures are usually based on a total of 100,000 or more examinees carefully selected to represent the national population at the target ages or grade levels. Norms for these tests are generally of better quality than those of individually administered tests.

UNRESOLVED ISSUES

From their inception, group intelligence tests have been the focus of much debate and controversy. Misconceptions about their interpretation and use have abounded. The complex and, as yet, little understood interrelation of hereditary and environmental factors as they are manifested in test performance has resulted in frequent vitriolic attacks by opponents of intelligence testing. The finding of generally lower performance of minority group members has resulted in charges that the tests are inherently biased in favor of middle-class whites. Entire cities have banned the use of group intelligence tests on the grounds that minority pupils are unduly penalized.

With all their limitations, standardized ability tests do provide an objective and cost-effective means for performing such functions. Psychologists, in particular, have a special professional responsibility to use tests wisely and to educate clients and other professionals in the correct use and interpretation of test results.

ARMY TESTS, WORLD-WAR I
CULTURAL BIASES IN TESTING
GROUP INTELLIGENCE TESTS
INTELLIGENCE MEASURES

G. J. ROBERTSON

PEPTIC ULCER

Peptic ulcer is a common ailment whose origin and course often include a strong psychosomatic contribution. Ulcers form when excessive amounts of acidic digestive juices erode the protective mucous lining of the duodenum, the stomach (less frequently), or (rarely) the esophagus. Ulcers are more common in middle-aged and older people than in young people, and are more common in men than women in twentieth-century Western society. Primary symptoms include pain and vomiting.

A predisposition to ulcers is associated with a family history of ulcers and with a "stressful" lifestyle.

Several factors can modify the ulcer-producing potential of a stressor in laboratory conditions. Electric shock produces more ulcers if it is unpredictable than if there is a warning signal. It produces fewer ulcers if the animal can make some active response to the shock, such as by fighting other animals. Brief exposure to restraint, enforced running, or another stressor reduces the probability of ulcer when that same stressor is later repeated with greater intensity. However, "immunization" by exposure to a mild stressor does not generalize strongly to other stressors.

Treatment for ulcers includes sleep, rest, antacids, and a controlled diet. Alcohol, aspirin, and highly acidic foods are seldom a cause of ulcers, but they may aggravate an ulcer; people with ulcers are advised to minimize their use.

DIGESTIVE SYSTEM
STRESS CONSEQUENCES

J. W. KALAT

PERCEPTION

Perception refers both to the experience of gaining sensory information about the world of people, things, and events, and to the psychological processes by which this is accomplished.

THE CLASSICAL THEORY

The idea that all of our thoughts and experiences are composed of a finite set of sensory ideas was developed systematically by a succession of British philosophers (empiricist and associationist) from Hobbes and Locke through Berkeley to James Mill and John Stuart Mill. The scientific study of perception began with physiological psychology, with Johannes Müller's efforts in 1838 to divide sensory experience into such modalities as vision, touch, and smell. The apparently seamless world perceived is found, on analysis, to comprise separable channels of experience, each of which depends on the action of some specific and identifiable part of the sensory nervous system, and which therefore reflects only indirectly on the actual state of the physical world.

Hermann von Helmholtz undertook to subdivide the modalities themselves into elementary sensations, each of which reflects the action that normally results from the stimulation of specific receptor nerve cells by the particular physical energies to which the receptors are specialized to respond. At about the same time, G. T. Fechner devised psychophysical

methods to measure the effects on experience of small differences in stimulation, providing psychological tools to match the physiological tools in sensory research.

Guided by these and rival theories, sensory research continues in several scientific fields. The primary test of the psychological relevance of such sensory inquiries, however, is how well they account for the properties of the perceived world. The account to this point has omitted most of the important properties of things and events—shape, lightness, distance, movement, melodic line, voice quality, and the meaning of utterances. According to classical theory, such important attributes of the world that are seen and heard are not sensations; rather they are complex learned perceptions.

This sets the stage and purpose of perceptual inquiry, best displayed in the visual perception of space.

Space Perception

The perception of the third dimension poses a special problem for philosophers, physiologists, and psychologists, because three dimensions cannot be specified by the two-dimensional array of light entering the eye. Normal environments present characteristic patterns within the two-dimensional array, however, that tend to be associated with different nearness and farness, and that therefore offer clues about the third dimension. One old and durable theory is that depth perception rests on these clues. Because their use entails no conscious process of inference, these are called *depth cues*, implying a direct psychological response rather than one mediated by conscious deduction.

In the early versions of the classical perceptual theory, it was assumed that depth perception was achieved through the learned association of such visual cues with memories of previous muscle-stretch and touch sensations. However, Thorndike showed that some animals can respond appropriately to visual depth cues even without any prior visual experience, a finding since corroborated and extended by E. J. Gibson and R. Walk. Thus, in addition to the fundamental sensations of color and shade assumed by the classical theory, there is a need to identify some innate visual mechanism for depth response, and a fundamental revision of that theory seems in order.

The Constancies and the Illusions

Our perceptions usually accord more with objects' stable properties than with the momentary sensory stimulation they offer. For example, our perceptions of an object's size normally remain quite constant, whereas its retinal image size increases as we approach it. In the geometrical illusions, however, the perceived size of some object, unchanged both in fact and in the retinal image, is drastically changed by adding a few slanting lines to it. Illusions of size, shape, color, and so on are extremely pervasive and usually robust phenomena.

The classical explanation of the constancies is that we have learned to take depth cues into account in judging objects' sizes, that we have learned to take the cues to illumination into account in judging their lightnesses, and so on. Although such learning, from our experiences with the world, to perceive things correctly sounds plausible as an explanation of the constancies, it is not self-evident why such experience should cause us to perceive illusions.

Organizational Phenomena

Organizational phenomena offer the final major challenge to classical theory. They rest on the distinction between figure and ground. A figure is a region of space, or set of contours, that has a recognizable shape. The factors that determine figure and ground thus are critical to what object will be perceived. These factors were studied mainly within the most famous systematic opposition to the classical theory—the Gestalt theory.

GESTALT THEORY

In this theory, propounded mainly by Wertheimer, Kohler, and Koffka, the configuration (the *Gestalt*) of the stimulating energies, not the energies themselves, is the essential stimulus attribute to which the nervous system responds. Between stimulus pattern and response stand such "laws of organization" as the "law of good continuation," which is that we perceive the figure–ground organization that interrupts the fewest smoothly continuing lines. Although neither quantitatively nor objectively studied, such demonstrations seem relevant to the casually observable facts of perception.

To forge a theory from these demonstrations, Gestaltists offered radically different notions of the nervous system. These by now have been thoroughly abandoned, but attempts at objective formulation of the laws of organization have continued, based on the principle that the viewer perceives the simplest organization that can be fitted to a particular pattern of stimulation. Such attempts have not done well, however, and current versions of the classical approach can better explain the Gestalt demonstrations than can Gestalt theory or its successors.

CLASSICAL THEORY REVISITED

An old view that has gained increasing support in recent years is that both the constancies and the illusions are aspects of one process, namely that we perceive those objects or events that would most normally be responsible for the sensory stimulation we receive. This requires the viewer to do something such as make perceptual inferences about the world, inferences that usually are right, but sometimes are wrong.

Given its unobservables, the theory is difficult to test. As Brunswik restated it, the light received by the eye normally contains packets of cues that provide information about the regular physical properties of the environment. Any individual cue has some probability of being correct—its "ecological validity"—and viewers learn to rely on each cue according to its probability.

In this version of classical perceptual theory, the Gestaltists' figure–ground phenomenon is merely a perceptual inference about which side of a contour is part of the object's surface, and the laws of organization are merely the probabilistic cues on which those inferences are based.

To test this theory, the ecological validities of the various cues must be known, obtained by "ecological surveys" of the environments to which viewers are normally exposed. To make such surveys meaningful, however, to which features of stimulation the sensory system is attuned must be known, a question that is very much at issue.

MODERN SENSORY PHYSIOLOGY

Ewald Hering and Ernst Mach, contemporaries of Helmholtz, proposed that the structure of the sensory nervous system might account explicitly and directly for at least some perceptual constancies and for the perception of objects' relative depths. In recent decades, networks of lateral connections that could serve such complex sensory functions have been found to exist between the receptors, as well as in the higher levels of the nervous system. Particularly important for current thinking in sensory science, Hering proposed receptor structures organized into opponent pairs; for example, structures that provide either red or green sensations, but not both, and others that provide blue or yellow. Structures that act as opponent pairs and that plausibly would serve this function have been identified by neurophysiological techniques, and have greatly influenced current thinking about color vision, and about sensory science in general.

It is not yet known whether, or to what extent, such pattern-sensitive networks actually contribute to the constancies, illusions, and organizational phenomena, but the fact that they have been demonstrated to exist makes it more plausible that many of the apparent properties of the physical world depend on the direct response of some specific sensory mechanism.

DIRECT PERCEPTION

The light that confronts the eye is called the *optic array,* as distinguished from the retinal image actually formed within the eye. As a consequence of motion parallax, objects at different distances in the world are displaced to different extents in the optic array by any movement of the viewer. In the most radical of direct theories, Gibson proposed that the optic array of a moving viewer in a normal environment contains sufficient information to specify for the nervous system the properties of the scenes and events in the physical world, and that our perceptions of these properties are direct responses to that information. One can find aspects of stimulation that reflect an object's size, shape, and so on, and remain invariant, even though its distance and slant—and therefore the retinal image it provides—may vary.

This theory's attraction lies in its offer to make the inference-like mental processes of the Helmholtzian explanation, with its theoretical encumbrance of unconscious inference, quite unnecessary. Although there are a few mathematical analyses of motion parallax, no evidence that such information actually is used ("directly" or otherwise) has been offered, and there is certainly at least some evidence that motion-produced information is not as effective in human perception as this theory would require.

TESTING THE CLASSICAL THEORY

Three lines of continuing research seemed, at their inception, particularly well suited to test or amend the classical theory.

Infant Perception and Perceptual Development

Some sensory structures that respond directly to some depth cues do exist—in some species. Recent research with human infants has pushed back the stage at which the infant is considered to be perceptually competent, including research that seems to show size constancy in infants a few weeks old. These results are insufficiently corroborated, however, since the infants have already had too much perceptual experience with the third dimension to provide solid evidence that distance and size perception are innate in humans.

Because conclusive research with very young human infants is extremely difficult, perceptual relearning has often been offered as a substitute, using rearranged sensory input.

Adaptation to Rearranged Sensory Input

Helmholtz argued that if a perceptual response to some stimulus were innate, it could not be changed through learning. An immense body of research now exists on adaptation and aftereffects to the altered relationship between sensory input and the physical world, or between some action and its sensory consequence. Although the research is important in its own right, however, it cannot prove that some particular perceptual response is learned, because the assumption that relearnability directly refutes innateness is itself invalid. Visual direction is indeed innately determined in chicks—prisms cause them to displace their pecking *even if they have had no prior visual experience*—yet they show adaptation and aftereffects after prolonged prism wearing.

The Search for Complex Sensory Channels

After looking at a waterfall, a viewer is less sensitive to downward motion (adaptation), and stationary objects appear to move upward (aftereffect). Such phenomena have long been taken as evidence of sensory receptors that detect motion—in this case, detectors of downward motion, which have been fatigued and weakened relative to detectors of upward motion. There is now good direct and indirect evidence of such mechanisms.

Many other types of channels have been proposed in recent years, each responsive to some complex property of stimulation, ranging from edge detectors and looming detectors to detectors of gratings of a particular spacing ("spatial frequency channels") by which the visual system performs a Fourier analysis on the retinal image. Virtually nothing has been done, however, that shows that such mechanisms actually contribute to our perceptions of the world, nor could they serve to simplify perceptual theory by making it unnecessary to deal with the inference-like components at the heart of the classical theory, because such components are themselves directly demonstrable.

EVIDENCE OF MENTAL STRUCTURE AND INFERENCE IN PERCEPTION

Three main lines of evidence set upper bounds on how completely our perceptions of the world might be explained as direct sensory response.

Perceptual Couplings and Computations

In the classical theory, certain perceived attributes, such as size and distance, are not free to vary independently, but are coupled, and vary together in ways that cannot be attributed either to sensory mechanisms or to the pattern of stimulation itself. Such couplings have been demonstrated. Although the extent, nature, and structure of perceptual couplings are not well explored, the mere fact that such inference-like processes can be demonstrated to exist at all limits what one can hope to explain in terms of direct response to stimulation.

Integration Across Successive Glances

One sees detail only in the fovea, a small region in the center of the retina. The eye makes rapid preaimed movements, called *saccades,* at different parts of any object, scene, or text from which the viewer seeks detailed information. Whenever the eye moves, the image of any object that is stationary in the world is correspondingly displaced on the retina. This fact raises two intertwined questions: Why do we not perceive the world to have moved with each such displacement? Also, how do we fit the contents of successive glances into a unified percept of object or scene?

With regard to the first question, Helmholtz had proposed that we take into account the direction and extent of the movement that the eye was ordered to execute, and some version of that proposal still seems viable. The second question has as yet received little attention, but studies of how people read and look at pictures and how they are able to construct spaces and events from the piecemeal sequences provided by motion pictures and television show clearly that we use our knowledge about the world to store the input from successive glances and to direct subsequent perceptual inquiry to places that have not yet been examined. Such abilities simply cannot be explained as direct response to stimulation.

The Response to Single Glimpses

Studies using brief (tachistoscopic) glimpses show that the information picked up by sensory mechanisms, no matter how sophisticated the latter may be, cannot account completely for what subjects report having seen in such short exposures. Words or pictures with which the viewer is more familiar, that are more expected, or that accord with his or her interest and concerns, are detected at briefer exposures. The effects are clear, even though the explanation is not.

CONTEXTUAL ASSOCIATIONS
ILLUSIONS
PERCEPTUAL ORGANIZATION
UNCONSCIOUS INFERENCE

J. HOCHBERG

PERCEPTUAL DEVELOPMENT

VISION

Infants have some visual skills at birth, but improvement during the first year of life is substantial. Infants younger than 1 month old can distinguish between black and white stripes 1/8 inch wide and a gray patch of similar brightness; by 1 year of age, their acuity is comparable to adult acuity. Young infants often have poorly controlled eye movements, and their eyes occasionally move in different directions from each other. However, their accommodation skills are better than was once thought; they show equivalent acuity for distances varying from 1 foot to 5 feet.

Infants have color vision by the age of 3 months. They can make discriminations among hues in the spectrum. Furthermore, they sort colors, using the same categories that adults use.

As infants mature, they prefer curved lines to straight lines, three-dimensional designs to flat designs, and designs with many small elements to designs with few large elements.

Infants can also perceive depth or distance. Infants as young as 2 months old show a greater change in heart rate when they are placed on the deep side of a visual cliff (on a sheet of glass with a patterned surface far below) than when they are placed on the shallow side.

It is unclear whether infants demonstrate constancy (the tendency for an object's size and shape to remain constant, inspite of changes in retinal size and shape).

Children are less sensitive than adults to the orientation of a shape. For example, adults are inaccurate in recognizing upside-down faces, whereas children younger than 10 years old can recognize a face that is upside down as accurately as a face that is upright.

Children appear to have good size constancy for distances up to about 10 feet. They show less constancy for objects at greater distances. Many of the common illusions, such as the popular Müller–Lyer line-length illusion, are stronger in children than in adults. The reasons for these developmental changes are not clear.

As children grow older, they develop the ability to pay attention to useful information and to ignore unwanted information. Their search strategies also become more systematic.

The visual system undergoes several changes during the aging process. The lens of the eye becomes somewhat yellow, so that the elderly are less sensitive to colors such as green, blue, and violet. The lens also becomes less elastic, so that its shape cannot be changed to view nearby objects (presbyopia). Acuity decreases after the age of 50 years, particularly for moving objects.

After age 50 years, binocular depth perception shows some decline. However, monocular depth perception remains relatively stable. There is no consistent trend in susceptibility to illusions as people approach old age.

There is some evidence that the elderly have difficulty in suppressing irrelevant stimuli and are more easily distracted by details.

OTHER PERCEPTUAL SYSTEMS

The auditory system is quite well developed at birth, and newborns are sensitive to a variety of noises. Infants can distinguish their own mothers' voices from strangers' voices at an early age, possibly several days after birth.

Young infants are sensitive to a wide variety of odors. They can smell the difference between mother and a stranger, possibly as early as a week after birth. A baby just a few hours old shows different facial expressions in reaction to sweet, sour, and bitter substances. Preference for sweet substances appears to be unlearned.

One-year-olds can recognize the shape of objects by touch alone. Also, 2-week-old infants can imitate an adult's gestures, such as tongue protrusion.

About 13% of Americans over the age of 65 years show advanced signs of presbycusis, a progressive loss of hearing in both ears for high-frequency tones. Elderly people are particularly likely to have problems in speech perception in a noisy environment that distorts speech.

There is little information about smell and taste in the elderly. Smell appears to be unaffected by age per se, once confounding variables associated with age changes are eliminated. Some studies indicate that taste sensitivity decreases with age, but other studies do not. There is some evidence, albeit controversial, that elderly people dislike bitter tastes more than do young people.

There are mixed reports about the relationship between pain sensitivity and age, the relationship being partly dependent on instructions provided to the subjects. Decision criteria for reporting pain appear to change during the aging process; elderly people seem to endure more pain before reporting it.

DEVELOPMENTAL DIFFERENCES
HUMAN DEVELOPMENT
INFANT DEVELOPMENT
LIFESPAN DEVELOPMENT

M. W. MATLIN

PERCEPTUAL DISTORTIONS

Distortions of perception are of three kinds: those coming from within the individual, those due to the medium between the person and the stimulus object, and those attributable to properties of the object itself.

Perceptual distortions from within the individual might arise from properties of the individual, as insanity or personality factors, or from temporary induced states, as from drugs.

Sound suffers many distortions that depend on the medium. Divers breathe helium or nitrogen and may sound like "Donald Duck," a squeaky type of speech hard to understand. The Doppler effect is a distortion produced by an approaching sound, as from a siren on an ambulance, that suddenly drops as the vehicle passes. Echoes sound different depending on the angle from which they bounce off an object. Auditory mirages in the open environment can make sounds appear to come from more than one direction.

Perceptual distortions from the object itself include the well-known visual illusions where objects may appear to be different than their true size or length. Auditory, tactual, and taste illusions are also important.

M. H. Pirenne showed visual distortions produced by photographing objects from a fixed point. Columns of equal size may appear so elliptical as to look egglike.

ILLUSIONS
PERCEPTION

R. D. WALK

PERCEPTUAL ORGANIZATION

For most psychologists, the topic of perceptual organization means Gestalt psychology. Kurt Koffka's message was that perception is organized. Koffka inveighed against the "constancy hypothesis," the notion that sensations have one, and only one, meaning. The chick picks the larger of two pieces of grain even though the larger one is farther away and so projects a smaller image on the eye than the nearer one. Many experiments were cited to show that children, animals, and adults pick relationally, that is, that they respond to the total situation.

The Gestalt psychologists noted that the perceptual field is composed of the figure or object of attention and of a background, or of figure and ground. They formulated figure–ground principles and principles of perceptual grouping. For example, things close together or proximal are grouped; similar things are grouped together; things that move together or have a "common fate" are grouped. Also included is a principle of good continuation or of continuing natural meaningful lines. These are, in brief, proximity, similarity, common fate, and good continuation, and they are examples of grouping principles relevant in a wide variety of contexts.

The Gestalt psychologists also believed that perception is natural and innate, not dependent on complex learning processes. This contrasts with the nineteenth century view of Hermann von Helmholtz, who believed that perception was constructed out of elementary sensations.

The study of perceptual organization since 1935 has been aided by many technical advances. Computers can build complex perceptual stimuli; oscilloscopes can present complex patterns; speech and other complex sounds (such as bird songs) can be analyzed with a sound spectrogram; a speech synthesizer can present complex speech stimuli; and the motion picture, the tape recorder, and the television camera are instruments for research.

A minor recurring theme is the debate over whether perception is a direct process as compared with a more constructed process based on cognitive processes. The Gestalt psychologists took a more direct approach and Helmholtz a more cognitive one. James Gibson describes the perceiver as actively responding to the invariant relations in the environment.

PICTURE PERCEPTION

Can the two-dimensional projection of a scene shown in a picture be naturally decoded by the observer? Must we learn to see pictures?

Research has focused on special populations of limited experience with pictures outside the Western tradition, such as animals, natives of primitive cultures, and children. Although all easily identify objects in pictures, space perception in pictures is more complex. Four-year-old children pick as the best picture one with literal perspective, but adults picked a more modified perspective in one study, while in another study neither schoolchildren nor adults accepted a literal perspective view.

EVENT PERCEPTION

Research on event perception has revealed amazing capabilities of the visual system in its organizing capabilities in a minimum of time. The research also agrees with the Gestalt claim that natural perception is three-dimensional.

Suppose a wire coat hanger was elongated and then bent in half twice. If a strong light were to project its shadow onto a translucent screen, a mass of lines would be seen. If the wire mass were rotated, a three-dimensional tangle of wires would be seen—no longer a flat, meaningless mass, but its true form. This is known as the *kinetic depth effect*. In another demonstration, a large square is shrunk to the size of a smaller square, but the observer does not see a large square shrinking in size. The square seems to recede from the observer and, as it gets larger, to approach the observer. The square shrinks and expands in a two-dimensional plane but the observer's nervous system seems to prefer the three-dimensional interpretation.

MOTION PICTURES

The perception of motion pictures has interesting problems of perceptual organization. The motion picture must reproduce the motion from the living environment in a realistic way, and it must tell a story that is compelling and imaginative. Sequential action means cutting from scene to scene, close-ups, distance shots, and different angles. Bad cutting can mean perceptual and conceptual jumpiness and unintended motion effects. The context is of overriding importance in deciding the meaning of a scene. Because many conceptual factors enter into film making, we cannot interpret a film in a direct perceptual manner on the basis of the immediate action taking place.

MUSIC PERCEPTION

Music tends to be grouped by frequency, the higher frequencies separately from the lower. In competition of frequencies into each ear, the tendency for right-handed people is to hear high frequencies in the right ear (which projects to the left or speech hemisphere) and lower frequencies in the left ear, projecting to the right or more spatial hemisphere. This is the perceptual experience even though it is contrary to the physical stimulus relationships. If a musical series is played with ascending and descending scales so that one ear receives an ascending note and the other ear a descending note, subjects hear two melodies, a higher one and a lower one, and also tend to hear higher frequencies in one ear and lower ones in the other. Diana Deutsch calls these "musical illusions," and they illustrate the strong tendency for proximity in frequency of tones to prevail, of high tones grouped together and lower tones grouped together. "Good continuation" would allow the subject to follow the ascending series and the descending one, but grouping by pitch prevails. Subjects recognize a melody played in a different key. None of the individual notes are the same, but the same relationships are preserved. This is transposition. Many musical relationships are built around this basic phenomenon and its relations.

SPEECH PERCEPTION

The acoustic stimulus for speech perception is perceived categorically. A speech signal of many variations is perceived as one sound. The analogy is to the color spectrum, where physical wavelengths vary continuously from 400 to 700 millimicrons, but we perceive discrete bands of color—red, green, blue, and yellow.

Silence is important in integrating our speech percepts. The function of small segments of silence is to provide emphasis, to produce stoplike consonants. Increasing the fricative duration (as in *shh*) also helps produce stop consonants. Silence helps to organize speech perception.

Speech perception is influenced by vision, an intersensory effect. McGurk and MacDonald showed that a speaker mouthing one sound while the voice spoke another made for a compromise. The sound *ba* while the speaker mouthed *ga* would be heard as *da*. The auditory sound was heard easily by itself, but the sight of a speaker mouthing a conflicting sound provided the compromise. Children were not as affected as adults, and thus the visual–audition effect must be based on experience.

INTERSENSORY RELATIONS

Perceptual organization extends to the relationships among the senses. Infants can recognize that a felt shape is equivalent to one they have seen. A dramatic demonstration of cross-modal equivalence without prior experience comes from an experiment by White and colleagues. Blind adults learned to use a device that translates a visual pattern into impulses delivered to vibrators on their back. An approaching visual object loomed large, and more and more vibrators were activated. Some blind subjects ducked to this looming tactual object, a real example of cross-modal equivalence in a second sense modality, the tactual one, where objects cannot loom. This is a dramatic demonstration of the unity of the senses.

ALARM SYSTEMS

The organization of the alarm system for audition and that for olfaction have some interesting similarities. Alarm calls used by small birds are high-pitched sounds that begin gradually. Such a call is very difficult to localize. Both the species that makes the call and many other species hear the alarm, and all can take cover from a predator, such as a diving hawk. However, mating calls are more specific. They permit individual

identification of a species, and the short clucks and chirps are easy to locate. Olfactory pheromones used by insects to signal alarm show great similarities, whereas sex pheromones are narrowly specific and highly potent. The broadness of the alarm system as contrasted with the specificity of the sex attractant system is a remarkably similar principle of organization in two different modalities.

CONCLUSIONS

Post-Gestalt understanding of the principles of perceptual organization has ties with the earlier Gestalt work, but it is best understood as a different focus on similar problems. Research on speech perception, event perception, music perception, and olfaction, and with sensory substitution systems is representative of research based on technology not available to the Gestaltists. Nevertheless the central Gestalt theme, that of the natural organization of all perceptual processes, is strongly upheld.

APPARENT SIZE
CONSTANCY
CONTEXTUAL ASSOCIATIONS
PERCEPTION
PERCEPTUAL DISTORTION
PERCEPTUAL TRANSACTIONALISM

R. D. WALK

PERCEPTUAL STYLE

A perceptual style means that a person has a characteristic way of perceiving the world. The idea that people perceive the world in different and individual ways is an intriguing one. The uses of color and form by some modern painters in highly individual and somewhat distorted ways have been hypothesized to be based on possible visual defects, so that the artist is truly copying his or her own subjective experience into art. However, this is difficult to prove—as are other hypotheses. Is it a truly perceptual influence or simply a cognitive interpretative one? Somehow, cognitive styles, meaning the way people think, seem a more neutral concept than perceptual styles. Additionally, there is always the problem of reliable and repeatable information.

Young children do seem to perceive the world more globally and as less differentiated than adults do. Not only do they have less developed verbal descriptions, but also their eye and hand movement search patterns are much less differentiated and precise than are those of older children and adults.

Herman Witkin used the concepts of "field independence" and "field dependence" in the 1950s and 1960s to describe individual differences on perceptual tasks. Witkin had three major tasks: an embedded figures task, a rod-and-frame task, and a tilted room task. Field-independent people can ignore the conflicting visual surround to find a hidden figure (embedded figures) or the true vertical (rod-frame, tilted room). The field-dependent subjects are more influenced by the visual surroundings, leading to worse performance on the embedded figures or dependence on the visual framework rather than the true gravitational one in the other tasks. Performance on the three tasks is related. Witkin also related the results to various personality measures. Field independence and field dependence are still heavily researched areas.

The most reliable "perceptual style" is that of immaturity. Children are less able to differentiate the visual field than are adults. In addition to children, brain-injured adults show these same effects.

CONTEXTUAL ASSOCIATION
PERCEPTION
PERCEPTUAL TRANSACTIONALISM

R. D. WALK

PERCEPTUAL TRANSACTIONALISM

Perception is guided by past experience, assumptions of the perceiver, and individual differences from past experience.

The best known demonstrations are all based on the ambiguities of literal projective perspective. They are the distorted room, the rotating trapezoidal window, and familiar objects whose projected size is manipulated in empty space.

The distorted room is based on simple geometry: An infinite number of planes in a static display from varying distances can project the same object. The Ames' distorted room is constructed to project the image of a normal room even though one corner may be far away. A person standing at the near corner of the room looks like a giant and the individual at the far end like a midget. The illusion depends on the person looking with one eye and keeping the head still. Such curiosities of literal perspective are well known and date back to at least the sixteenth century.

In this room individuals with whom one has an emotional bond (a spouse or loved one) do not look as distorted as strangers when viewed within the room.

The rotating trapezoidal window is the frame of a window painted on a trapezoid with the long side, for example, toward and the short side away from the observer. When the window rotates, it appears to oscillate back and forth while a normal rotating rectangular window appears to go round and round, to rotate normally. This effect has been held to be due to experience with windows.

Objects viewed in a visual void, meaning that only the object is visible with no intervening or surrounding cues, appear to be at a distance appropriate for their familiar size. The half-size playing card looks farther away than the normal-size playing card, though both are at the same physical distance.

APPARENT SIZE
ILLUSIONS
PERCEPTION
PERCEPTUAL DISTORTION

R. D. WALK

PERFORMANCE APPRAISAL

Organizations are concerned with performance. Indicators such as profits, sales, number of widgets produced, number of defective widgets, costs of production, downtime, number and severity of accidents, number and length of absences, and so forth are used in evaluating an organization and the units within an organization. Similarly performance appraisals evaluate performance of individual employees.

Performance appraisals are used in making administrative decisions, for counseling employees, in training and developing employees, for human resources planning, and in the validation of selection procedures. They are utilized in determining pay increases, in making promotional decisions, and in deciding whether an employee is to be discharged.

There is much discontent with performance appraisal systems. Frequent changes in the methods used for making appraisals, and even abandonment of them, are common occurrences.

HISTORY

Informal appraisals of performance have been universal throughout history. Formal appraisal systems have been used since at least the third century A.D. Industrial applications can be traced back to Robert Owens, who introduced them in Scotland early in the nineteenth century. The military forces of the United States adopted performance appraisals in 1813, and the federal government did so for its civilian personnel in 1842.

During the twentieth century, the growth of performance appraisal systems has been relatively rapid. Psychologists have played an active role in the development and application of these systems. In recent years, psychologists have become concerned with the applications of such systems and have been involved in efforts to improve their use.

Subsequent to the passage of the Civil Rights Act of 1964, performance appraisal systems have been subjected to legal challenges. In a number of rulings, federal court judges have found that such systems discriminate against minorities and other groups protected by the law.

METHODS

For appraising performance, a variety of methods have been developed. From the results of surveys of business and of government organizations, those in use can be classified as essay, rating scales, combined essay and rating scales, and objectives-based. Essays are essentially narrative reports on the performances of individual employees. They describe and evaluate performance. Rating scales are designed to quantify performance, either overall, on separate dimensions, or on a combination of both. Objectives-based appraisals are used in concert with management-by-objectives (MBO) approaches that have been adopted by many organizations in recent years.

Several varieties of rating scales have been developed. The most prevalent are known as "graphic" rating scales and are characterized by requiring the rater to indicate a ratee's performance as to some characteristic—for example, "integrity."

Another, more complex, method of rating is referred to as "forced choice." In using this method, a rater is required to select a word or phrase from two or more that best describes the person being rated. The words or phrases composing such combinations are statistically determined, as are the numerical values assigned each word or phrase.

A third rating method, developed during World War II, is known as "critical requirements" or, more commonly, as "critical incidents." The method is based on descriptions of behaviors that reflect either effective or ineffective performance. Once these critical incidents have been collected and edited for a particular occupation, they form the basis for a checklist of behaviors, the critical requirements that can be used in evaluating performance.

Behaviorally anchored rating scales (BARS) are a relatively recent addition to rating scale methods. They emphasize participation by the raters in developing the scales, a procedure called "retranslation," mathematical scaling, careful observations of performance, and logging of observations by the raters.

Behavioral observation scales (BOS) are the most recent addition to rating scale methods. Using critical incidents, behaviors important to effective performance in an occupation are first identified. They are grouped into categories by persons familiar with the work or by a statistical method called "factor analysis." The items describing the behaviors are designed so as to obtain estimates of the frequency with which the behaviors occur. A scoring method provides for total scores by categories of performance and for a total score across categories. Raters using the method are forced to focus on specific behaviors crucial to effective performance in making their observations and recording their observations.

All rating scale methods depend on some person or persons making judgments of performance. Consequently they are essentially subjective. In contrast, objectives-based appraisal methods focus on collecting information that furnishes objective information concerning performance, for example, sales, quantity and quality of goods produced, or frequency of absences.

RESEARCH

It is generally recognized that raters tend to make many errors. Among the common errors is the "halo effect," which is a tendency to rate a person the same on all characteristics being rated even though the ratee may perform differently on different aspects of a job. Another common error is referred to as "leniency," a tendency to rate all ratees more favorably than their individual performances would warrant.

It is a common practice in organizations to have supervisors rate their subordinates. Alternative sources, for example, peers, subordinates, outsiders, and the ratee himself or herself, are available.

To develop and validate an appraisal system properly, considerable research is required. The procedures are highly technical and require professional expertise. Unfortunately, many appraisal systems are developed by persons who lack essential knowledge and skills, and thus the validity of such systems is subject to challenge.

After an appraisal system has been implemented, an organization may want to determine the extent to which the system is meeting its objectives. Such an evaluation requires research that may entail extensive collection and analysis of data.

The use of performance appraisals in counseling employees is a relatively recent development. That both judging employee performance and counseling them on how to improve performance can produce difficulties for a manager seeking to accomplish these objectives became apparent in a series of studies conducted in the General Electric Company. The studies clearly showed that mutual goal setting by a supervisor and a subordinate and avoidance of criticizing the latter's performance are essential if improved performance is to be achieved.

APPLICATION

Implementing and maintaining a performance appraisal system requires much effort and involves many of the resources of an organization. Performance appraisal poses many issues, considerable mutual education may be required if both practitioners and researchers are to function as teams.

Appraisal systems tend to depend on ratings of performance, which are inherently subjective. The many attempts to objectify ratings have had little, if any, success. However, objective methods for appraising performance also have many limitations.

The legal issues involving discriminatory aspects of performance appraisal systems are relatively recent. Though future developments with respect to the legal aspects of performance appraisals are difficult to predict, it would appear that organizations and others concerned with such systems, psychologists in particular, must familiarize themselves with viewpoints expressed by the courts and keep abreast of pertinent developments.

APPLIED RESEARCH
JOB ANALYSIS
MORALE IN ORGANIZATIONS

D. L. GRANT

PERFORMANCE TESTS

Performance tests require overt and active responses, such as motor or manual behaviors. Such tests frequently measure motor coordination, speed, or perceptual or motor skills. Because of their usual deemphasis on language skills, performance tests have proved useful in the assessment of the physically handicapped, particularly the deaf.

Performance tests have been used extensively by the military (for example, flight training simulators to measure pilots' skills) and business (for example, typing tests). In nonacademic settings, performance tests, when obviously related to job skills, generally are acceptable to those being tested for hiring, placement, retention, or promotion considerations. Academic settings also use performance tests, for example, tests of pen-

manship, oral reading, and writing skills (based on assessing "work samples").

Although performance tests frequently have greater face validity, nonperformance paper-and-pencil tests remain the most commonly used test format. The paper-and-pencil tests, when administered to people sufficiently experienced in this format, can provide measurements that are valid, less expensive, and more conducive to group testing.

BLOCK DESIGN TEST
WECHSLER INTELLIGENCE TESTS

M. J. ALLEN

PERSONAL CONSTRUCT THEORY

Personal construct theory was formulated originally by George A. Kelly in *The psychology of personal constructs.*

It is essentially a cognitive theory of personality, applied primarily to problems in clinical assessment and psychotherapy. Research based on personal construct theory has addressed issues in a variety of different areas, including psycholinguistics, experimental aesthetics, cross-cultural psychology, social cognition, program evaluation, the analysis of political behavior, and environmental perception.

CONSTRUCTIVE ALTERNATIVISM

An explicit philosophical premise that underlies personal construct theory is "constructive alternativism." According to this principle, reality does not reveal itself to us directly, but rather is subject to as many different constructions as we are able to invent. Any given event is open to a variety of alternative interpretations. Kelly assumed that most, if not all, of our current constructions are subject to continual revision and ultimate replacement by more useful ones.

Constructive alternativism has definite implications in terms of how human actions relate to other kinds of events. It presupposes that we have the capacity to represent events, not merely respond to them *qua stimuli.* The nominal stimulus can often be identified as a physical event (i.e., described adequately by a physicist); however, the functional stimulus (i.e., what requires explanation by a psychologist) is constituted by the constructions of the person.

Kelly derived the name of his theory from his basic unit of analysis, the personal construct, defined as a bipolar dimension that represents a single dichotomous distinction, for example, happy/sad, tall/short, odd/even. He proposed that each individual develops a unique system of hierarchically related personal constructs to interpret and anticipate events. These constructs serve as the basis of perceived similarities and differences among the events to which they are applied.

BASIC THEORY

The content of personal construct theory has evolved gradually within the general axiomatic framework set out by Kelly. It consists of a single postulate and 11 corollaries derived from it. The fundamental postulate asserts that "a person's processes are psychologically channelized by the ways in which he anticipates events." This proposition implies that all psychological processes are anticipatory in nature.

The construction corollary states that "a person anticipates events by construing their replications." This does not mean that the same event ever actually recurs, but rather that personal constructs are used to abstract certain similarities and differences among events, and then organize these features into coherent patterns of representation, within the context of which we are able to detect recurrent themes in our experience over time.

According to the organization corollary, "each person characteristically evolves for his own convenience in anticipating events, a construction system embracing ordinal relationships between constructs." A particular construct seldom, if ever, stands alone in our experience, because usually it is deployed together with one or more other related constructs in interpreting and predicting events.

Kelly's range corollary states that "a construct is convenient for the anticipation of a finite range of events only." Each construct is viewed as having a specific range of convenience in the sense that it is useful for representing a single aspect of a limited domain of events.

The fragmentation corollary suggests that psychological development involves the gradual differentiation of a personal construct system into a number of independently organized and functionally specialized subsystems. However, development could not consist of differentiation alone. Otherwise an individual's construct system eventually could become so fragmented in structure that one aspect of experience could not be related to any other, and the system could no longer operate as a whole. According to Kelly, the degree of differentiation of a personal construct system is limited by the permeability of relatively superordinate constructs.

Specifically, the modulation corollary states that "the variation in a person's construct system is limited by the permeability of the constructs within whose range of convenience the variants lie."

Whereas the fragmentation and modulation corollaries together specify the parameters of progressive variations within a personal construct system, the mechanism of change is defined by the experience corollary. According to this proposition, "a person's construction system varies as he successively construes the replication of events." Predictive failure can lead to change even when we are relieved or pleased that what we expected did not happen. Constructs that are related closely to the construct(s) on which our original anticipations were based will be affected by disconfirmation more than will remotely related constructs.

Kelly's choice corollary specifies that "a person chooses for himself that alternative in a dichotomized construct through which he anticipates the greater possibility for extension and definition of his system." When an individual chooses how to behave in a given situation, the specific implications of each alternative course of action will be defined in terms of the relationships among constructs. Kelly saw people as continuously using their own behavior as the independent variable in conducting experiments that are designed to test hypotheses, not always explicitly formulated ones, derived from the specific relationships among constructs that articulate the structure of their thinking.

The individuality corollary asserts that "persons differ from each other in their constructions of events." Not only do people often apply different constructs to the same events, but also it is unlikely that any two persons ever put their constructs together in terms of the same set of relationships.

If we assume, with Kelly, that the personal construct system of each individual is unique, then it follows that an important aspect of interpersonal relations will be making inferences about both the content and structure of other persons' construct systems. His sociality corollary stipulates that "to the extent that one person construes the construction processes of another, he may play a role in a social process involving the other." The term *role*, in the context of this proposition, refers specifically to a course of activity undertaken in the light of one's understanding of another's point of view. This does not imply that accurate empathy is a necessary condition for establishing a role relationship with another person. This novel definition of role provides the rationale for Kelly's fixed-role therapy.

Kelly's commonality corollary states that "to the extent that one person employs a construction of experience which is similar to that employed by another, his psychological processes are similar to those of the other person." The commonality and sociality corollaries taken together imply that similarity between two persons in terms of the characteristics of their construct systems can facilitate communication and interpersonal understanding between them.

APPLICATIONS

Kelly devised a technique for brief psychotherapy, which he called fixed-role therapy. This is essentially an experimental procedure for inducing personality change in which the client enacts the role of a hypothetical personality for a period of several weeks.

COGNITIVE COMPLEXITY
PERSONALITY THEORIES
REPERTORY GRID TECHNIQUE

J. R. ADAMS-WEBBER

PERSONAL DOCUMENTS

Gordon Allport was the major advocate for the use of personal documents within psychology. In his 1942 monograph, he defined personal documents as "any self-revealing record that intentionally or unintentionally yields information regarding the structure, dynamics, and functioning of the author's mental life."

Allport identified six basic forms of documents: autobiographies, open-ended questionnaires, verbatim recordings, diaries, letters, and artistic and projective documents. He also provided the following list of basic motives for producing (intentional) personal documents: special pleading or self-justification, exhibitionism, desire for order, literary delight, personal perspective, catharsis, money, assignment, assisting in therapy, redemption, scientific interest, public service, and desire for immortality. Awareness of such motives aids researchers in going beyond common sense in their interpretations.

Allport adopted six criteria for assessing the validity of a particular interpretation: feelings of subjective certainty, conformity with known facts, mental experimentation by judging whether a particular factor is indispensable to the interpretation, predictive power, social agreement, and internal consistency.

BIOGRAPHICAL INVENTORIES
CRITICAL INCIDENTS TECHNIQUE
QUESTIONNAIRES
UNOBTRUSIVE MEASURES

J. B. CAMPBELL

PERSONALITY AND ILLNESS

At the turn of the century, the leading causes of death in the United States were attributable, directly or indirectly, to infectious diseases. Now, however, the chief causes of death are the degenerative diseases, many of which have been associated with psychological factors and misbehaviors such as substance abuse, sedentariness, and overeating. Infectious diseases require contact with viri or bacteria, while degenerative diseases result from excessive wear and tear on systems of the body.

Genetics predispose persons to certain degenerative diseases. Certain illnesses tend to run in families, presumably as a result of members sharing a common gene pool. Most researchers agree that there is ample evidence to assume genetic involvement in such diseases as coronary heart disease, hypertension, diabetes mellitus, and migraine headaches.

THE CONCEPT OF STRESS

Cumulative life demands, personality traits, and emotions lead to stress, which can contribute to disease. Hans Selye defined stress as a nonspecific response of the body to demands placed on it. He emphasized that the sources of the demand are unimportant. The demand may originate in life events, in social relationships, or in private events such as thoughts and emotions. All demands, regardless of their source, mobilize certain neurological and hormonal structures, which, if chronically induced, can lead to degenerative disease. Playing prominent parts in stress mobilization are the sympathetic nervous system and the endocrine hormones such as cortisol, cortisone, adrenaline, and noradrenalin. In small doses, stress serves as a tonic to enrich life, but in larger doses it overloads and wears out one system after another.

LIFE EVENTS

It has long been recognized that the clustering of life events—such as divorce, marriage, pregnancy, changes in living conditions, changes in careers or type of work, and retirement—is associated with illness. In 1897, Sir William Osler, in *Lectures on angina pectoris and allied states,* wrote: "I believe that the high pressure at which men live and the habit of working the machine to its maximum capacity are responsible for [arterial degeneration] rather than excesses in eating and drinking." Adolf Meyer researched the relationship between significant life demands and resulting illness by carefully charting life changes preceding illness. In *Contributions to medical and biological research,* published in 1919, he related how he tediously recorded his patients' life situations and their emotional responses to them. It soon became evident in a surprising number of cases that the clustering of these demanding situations were followed by illness. The pioneering work of Meyer was followed by a succession of researchers interested in the same idea, culminating in the *Schedule of recent experience* by Thomas Holmes. The schedule is a self-report questionnaire eliciting information about the occurrence of particular events in the person's recent life experience. Scores on the instrument are believed to be predictive of upcoming illness. Marion Amundson and colleagues refer to numerous prospective studies supporting the validity of the instrument, which is purported to measure the amount of adaptation energy occasioned by the clustering of life events, irrespective of their psychological meanings to the respondent.

LIFESTYLE AND PERSONALITY

The causal relationship between personality and illness has been recognized for a very long time. A quotation attributed to Hippocrates, the father of medicine, around 400 B.C., and to the ancient English physician, Parry of Bath, reads: "It is more important to know what sort of person has a disease than what sort of disease a person has." This quotation points up the importance of personal characteristics for the onset, course, and outcome of illness. Systematic attempts to explain the relationship of psychological factors to illness did not begin until the early 1900s. Alfred Adler, a contemporary of Freud, wrote about the emergence of certain personality characteristics as a result of efforts to compensate for physical disability in his *Study of organ inferiority and its physical compensation.* In this and later publications and lectures, he maintained that one's lifestyle, an organized set of beliefs about oneself and the world, determines the onset and severity of certain physical illnesses or disabilities.

Osler in 1910 and Dunbar in 1943 recognized a personality type related to heart attack. They noted that aggressive, driven, work-oriented attitudes were commonly seen among myocardial infarction patients. Meyer Friedman and Ray Rosenman in *Type A behavior and your heart* further documented the existence of a common personality type among cardiac patients. In their Western Collaborative Group Study they have produced evidence that persons with A-type characteristics—aggressive, competitive, and time-urged—are in a state of chronic sympathetic nervous system arousal in which the production of emergency-related hormones such as adrenaline and cortisol is increased. Sustained high levels

of these emergency hormones are related to the development of atherosclerosis, a premonitory of many forms of cardiovascular disease. Richard Lazarus emphasized the critical role of perceptions and cognitive appraisal in creating chronic emotional states. Thus persons with personalities organized to defend against threat are predisposed to anxious reactivity, which may result in hyperactivity of the sympathetic nervous system and lead to illness.

A-TYPE PERSONALITY
BEHAVIORAL MEDICINE
HEALTH PSYCHOLOGY
PEPTIC ULCERS
TEMPERAMENTS

K. B. Matheny
R. M. Kern

PERSONALITY ASSESSMENT

The measurement of personality traits has been an important function of clinical psychologists for many decades. Personality is not a matter to be guessed at or to be estimated by untried, unscientific, and unreliable methods. Rather it is an area that has been diligently investigated by psychologists with the result that proved and respected methods of assessing personality have been developed that are widely recognized and respected as having value far beyond the casual methods used during the prescientific era.

PURPOSES OF PERSONALITY ASSESSMENT

Determination of Responsibility in Legal Matters

It is difficult to answer the question of whether a person charged with some criminal offense should be held responsible for that offense or the person is suffering from a mental disease or defect that precludes such responsibility. In making such determinations, courts rely heavily on psychologists, who use measurement tools to determine whether the person can understand reality the way an ordinary person does, can think logically and rationally, and if he or she can plan and organize behavior in such a way as to be held responsible. The use of psychological tests to measure personality is considered fairly objective and thus more reliable than more subjective means of appraisal. A particularly knotty problem is that of "malingering." Sometimes an offender will attempt to feign mental illness to escape punishment for a crime. The public is suspicious of the ability of mental health professionals to detect such deception. The use of psychological tests, however, certainly enhances the capacity of professional teams to make accurate decisions.

Determination of Suitability for Child Custody

A very difficult matter to decide is to which parent custody of a child should be awarded where there is disagreement. Courts would like to have a parent who is responsible, nurturant, patient, and stable, and obviously everyone tries to appear so when applying for child custody. However, psychologists, with their sophisticated means of appraisal, may be able to determine more accurately than others whether someone really does have good parental characteristics or is just pretending.

Vocational Choices for Individuals Seeking Counseling

The question of what occupation to choose is crucial for all persons since it determines to a large extent their general feeling of competence and adequacy. Through personality assessment it is possible to determine whether one is better suited for a sedentary or an active occupation; for work involved with close contact with people, with more structured and formal contact, or perhaps with no contact at all.

Planning Psychotherapeutic Intervention

There are many different kinds of psychotherapies and not all are equally suited to everyone. Through assessment of personality, it can be predicted that some people will respond well to introspective techniques that lead to insight, that others can benefit from social skills training in a group, and that still others may benefit most from individual recordkeeping and behavioral assignments.

LEVELS OF PERSONALITY ASSESSMENT

The measurement of the personality is probably one of the most difficult and complex tasks. It can be measured at several distinct levels.

The Behavioral–Public Role

Most persons who come to the attention of psychologists have been referred because of characteristics that impinge unfavorably on others. For example, many people are involuntarily committed to hospitals because of abrasive and obnoxious behavior that other people cannot tolerate. Also, many children are brought to child guidance clinics because their parents or teachers cannot deal with their disruptive behavior. Similarly, when families appear for therapy, often one or more of them is there unwillingly, at the insistence of others who find their behavior intolerable.

Conscious Self-Concept

Obviously any personality assessment program must include some information provided by the individual based on conscious views of the self. The most common method for obtaining this kind of information is the clinical interview. Another is the personality inventory.

To comprehend the personality totally, most psychologists include some measure of the individual's fantasies, inner life, or unconscious. The most common method of doing this is through the administration of projective tests.

PRESENT STATUS OF PERSONALITY ASSESSMENT

The field of personality assessment is expanding as more uses for the assessment of personality are being found. Methods need to be quick and more efficient than those used in the past, as befits an expanding population.

Psychologists often form the apex of a pyramid in which they supervise paraprofessionals who supervise volunteers. Therefore, personality assessment methods need to be simplified, with only the interpretation remaining complex. This would tend to maximize the professional time of the skilled psychologist.

PROJECTIVE TECHNIQUES
RELIABILITY OF DIAGNOSES
TESTING METHODS

W. G. KLOPFER

PERSONALITY CHANGES

Behavior often changes across time and across situations; however, behavior change need not imply change in the underlying personality. The criteria for deciding whether behavior change reflects actual personality change or merely the joint effects of personality and the current situation or of two conflicting personality tendencies, the circumstances across which personality changes may be expected, the extent to which personality can change, and the mechanisms assumed to be responsible for the changes vary depending on one's theoretical orientation. The changes may be serendipitous or sought. The change may be abrupt, as with a religious conversion experience, or gradual, as is usual during therapy. Furthermore, the changes may take a variety of forms.

PERSONALITY THEORIES AND PERSONALITY CHANGES

It is not the case that personality theorists automatically advocate constancy of personality characteristics; rather, many have endorsed the concept and described the process of personality change. Thus personality theories provide an avenue for understanding personality changes. Perhaps the clearest example of this comes from the work of George Kelly. Kelly proposed that personality consists of "personal constructs," bipolar perceptual orientations used to construe the world and to anticipate the consequences of actions. These constructs are subject to revision on the basis of experience; that is, if a construct generates erroneous predictions, then it should and will be (in healthy individuals) modified. For Kelly, personality was analogous to a suit of clothes: If it does not fit, then it should be altered or exchanged.

Carl Rogers has argued that the "actualizing tendency," the innate motive to maintain and enhance one's "genetic blueprint" or potential, provides a basic force in the direction of personality change. This force is unhampered, permitting the self-concept to become a more accurate reflection of "true" tendencies, when one is exposed to an environment in which the need for affection from others is freely gratified. Rogers describes three conditions that produce this positive growth in a therapeutic relationship: (a) genuineness or congruence of the therapist; (b) caring or "unconditional positive regard" for the client; and (c) empathic understanding of the client by the therapist.

In a similar fashion, Abraham Maslow proposed that exposure to environmental conditions that permit or prohibit gratification of the basic needs (i.e., physiological, safety, love and belonging, esteem, and self-actualization) prompts movement up or down the hierarchy of needs. That is, since our behavior is governed by the lowest unfulfilled need, changes in job, family, or social conditions might alter fundamental motive structures. Such movement clearly would qualify as a personality change.

Freud's assumption of childhood determinism implied that personality is essentially formed at the conclusion of the phallic stage, around the age of 5 years. This position seems to be antithetical to the concept of personality changes, but it was tempered by the recognition that psychoanalytic therapy could effect substantial redistributions within the personality.

Jung, who repudiated the Freudian model in several important respects, proposed a general stage model of development that also incorporated the concept of personality change. Jung regarded puberty as the "psychic birth" of the individual. During the ensuing period, the motive forces of power and eros dominate; the person is oriented toward the external world and the tasks of finding a mate and establishing a vocation. Around the age of 40 years, however, a radical change occurs: A need for meaning ascends as the primary motive, and energy must be rechanneled as the individual turns inward to search for meaning in the unconscious.

MODELS OF PERSONALITY CHANGE

There have been various attempts to account for the process of personality change outside the context of classic personality theories. For example, Jerome Frank identified a set of characteristics common to psychotherapy, healing, "thought reform," and other systematic attempts to alter personality. The change agent is perceived as a powerful and effective authority, with a desire and a commitment to help the client. The agent provides a credible theoretical system, and both agent and client actively participate in the extended intervention program.

Donald Meichenbaum described the basic process underlying the change produced by psychotherapy as a "translation" from the client's pretherapy "internal dialogue" of negative self-statements to a new language and conceptualization system.

EMPIRICAL STUDIES OF PERSONALITY CHANGES

Numerous empirical studies have examined the relationship between personality change or stability and such occurrences as pregnancy, surgery, treatment for alcoholism, aging, and meditation. The *Psychological abstracts* listed 597 entries under "personality change" between 1967 and August 1980. Many of these articles report on restricted samples and limited aspects of personality; even more problematic is the general lack of a guiding theoretical orientation with respect to the process of change. Taken as a whole, however, the literature does demonstrate the existence of personality changes.

**CONVERSIONS
OPTIMAL FUNCTIONING
PERSONALITY TYPES
PSYCHOTHERAPY**

J. B. CAMPBELL

PERSONAL SPACE

Each person develops a "body-buffer zone," called the *personal space*—a surrounding invisible and portable boundary into which other people usually cannot enter without arousing psychological discomfort.

Perceived intrusions into personal space result in several behavioral and attitudinal manifestations of discomfort. One obvious reaction is simply to move away from the intruding person, and many studies have demonstrated this effect. Other studies have found that subjects report greater feelings of stress and lesser feelings of attraction for an intruder when tested under conditions that involve culturally inappropriate interpersonal distances. The gender of the intruder relative to that of the subject plays an important and complicated role in these reactions.

Researchers have used several techniques to measure the size of a subject's personal space. Preferred interpersonal distance can be measured by such methods as: (a) unobtrusively observing people in naturalistic settings; (b) allowing the subject to indicate when an approaching person should halt; (c) permitting free choice by the subject as to where to sit or stand when introduced into a social setting; and (d) using abstract techniques whereby the subject indicates how far apart hypothetical individuals would sit or stand by placing dolls on a board or marking on a piece of paper. Studies measuring preferred distance have shown that the size of one's personal space is not constant, but varies with the following:

Physical setting. Subjects in small rooms or in a corner of a room maintain greater interpersonal distances than those in large rooms or in the center of a room.

Similarity to and liking of the intruder. Although there is some contradictory evidence, most studies seem to indicate that people use smaller interpersonal distances with individuals they like and individuals they perceive as having attitudes similar to their own.

Age. Research on the development of personal space has generally demonstrated that interpersonal distance increases among grade-school children until about 12 years of age, when it approximates the adult distance. Children in preschools show preferences and variations in personal space even at 2 years of age.

Experience. Differences in personal space have been noted between people from different cultures, and this may reflect the role of experience.

**CROWDING
INTERACTIONALISM
TERRITORIALITY**

E. P. SARAFINO

PERSONALITY DISORDERS

Numerous attempts have been made to specify definitive criteria for distinguishing normal personalities from personality disorders. Central to an understanding of this distinction is the recognition that normality and pathology, at least as they relate to personality, are relative concepts, arbitrary points on a continuum or gradient.

Certain nonsymptomatological features do distinguish personality disorders from other clinical syndromes. Most notable are the pervasiveness and duration of their clinical signs. The characteristic traits that typify the disorders of personality tend to be enduring; they often are evident by childhood or adolescence and persist as notable features throughout the individual's life span. Further, they are expressed in a wide variety of settings, displaying themselves across the broad landscape of significant life situations—in social, occupational, and family contexts. This durability and omnipresence, rather than the specificity of particular behaviors, serve to distinguish personality disorders from other clinical states.

Eleven personality disorders comprise the list promulgated in the *Diagnostic and statistical manual-IV* (*DSM-IV*) and are as follows:

Dependent personality. This passive pattern of relating to others is characterized by a helplessness and clinging behavior, by compliance and lack of initiative, and by a search for attachments in which one can lean entirely on the leadership of others for affection and security.

Histrionic personality. This style is characterized by a lability of affect, by capricious and demonstrative behaviors, by an active solicitation and manipulation of others to gain attention, and by an insatiable and indiscriminate search for approval and stimulation.

Narcissistic personality. This pattern is noted by an air of egocentric self-assurance and a pretentious superiority, by a tendency to benignly exploit others for one's own advantage, and by immature fantasies and a careless disregard for the rights of others.

Antisocial personality. This individual is mistrustful of others, seeks autonomy and retribution for what are seen as past injustices, displays irritability, impulsiveness, and aggressiveness, and often engages in socially irresponsible behavior.

Compulsive personality. Characterized best by their inability to express feelings and by their rigid conformity to authority and regulations, these individuals appear joyless, value self-discipline, and are perfectionistic and overly organized.

Passive–aggressive personality. Noted by a pervasive, if passive, resistance to meeting the expectations that others have of them, this type voices ambivalent feelings toward most matters, and vacillates between social deference and conformity at one time, stubborn negativism at another, and guilt and contrition the next.

Schizoid personality. This style is typified by a social passivity, by minimal emotional and affectionate needs, a general listlessness and apathy, and a marked deficiency in both the capacity for and interest in maintaining warm and empathic human relationships.

Avoidant personality. This actively detached type reflects a pattern of social pan-anxiety and interpersonal mistrust, an alienation and devaluation of self and, despite longings for acceptance and affection, a pervasive hypersensitivity to potential derogation and humiliation.

Borderline personality. An advanced or dysfunctional pattern, this disorder is characterized by intense endogenous moods, an ambivalence or lack of clarity regarding self-identity and significant relationships, and recurring periods characterized by simultaneous feelings of rage, love, and guilt toward others.

Paranoid personality. This type displays a vigilant mistrust of others, an edgy defensiveness against anticipated criticism, a pervasive and usually unwarranted suspiciousness and expectancy of deception, a provocativeness, and a tenacious insistence on maintaining one's personal autonomy.

Schizotypal personality. This poorly integrated and dysfunctional type exhibits a variety of behavioral eccentricities, introduces personal irrelevancies into thought and communication, often appears self-absorbed, and displays either an ever-present air of anxious wariness or a total flattening of affect.

ANTISOCIAL PERSONALITY
AVOIDANT PERSONALITY
BORDERLINE PERSONALITY
COMPULSIVE PERSONALITY
DEPENDENT PERSONALITY
HISTRIONIC PERSONALITY
NARCISSISTIC PERSONALITY
PARANOID PERSONALITY
PASSIVE–AGGRESSIVE PERSONALITY
SCHIZOID PERSONALITY
SCHIZOTYPAL PERSONALITY

T. MILLON

PERSONALITY INTEGRATION

A number of theorists have put forth formulations of optimal functioning. Heinz Hartmann advanced the concept of an autonomous ego, suggesting that a person's mental development was not anchored to nonrational impulse life.

Abraham Maslow and Carl Rogers, two humanists, were influential in stimulating interest in optimal development. Maslow studied self-actualization and formulated descriptions of self-actualizing persons. Among the key attributes of self-actualizing persons, Maslow listed efficient perception of reality, acceptance of self and others, a sense of autonomy and a capacity for solitude, a capacity for intimacy and sharing, a sensitive feeling for ethics, and empathy for humankind.

Carl Rogers evolved a concept of the fully functioning person by studying the process of psychotherapy and observing how people changed through therapy. He noted three major attributes of fully functioning persons: (a) They were open to their experience; (b) they lived in an existential fashion through their awareness of immediate experience; and (c) they trusted their direct organismic experience as a basis for decision and action.

An influential contributor to the theory of competence is Robert White. His paper, "Motivation reconsidered: the concept of competence," has been widely reprinted and quoted, and stands as a model of theory building. White argued that an accurate view of human nature required that psychology go beyond drive theory and turn to concepts of positive motivation as explanations of behavior. In this connection, he put forth the concepts of competence, motivation, and effectance, which he defined as directed, systematic, positive self-rewarding behaviors that satisfied a need for environmental mastery.

RESEARCH CONTRIBUTIONS

Three research programs that have directed attention to effective functioning are summarized here. The earliest study in the Berkeley series was one by Frank Barron. The research participants were graduate students rated by their faculty and by an assessment staff on personal soundness. A wide range of observations and instruments was used, including extensive behavioral observations, self-descriptions, perception tasks, and personality measures. Observational data supported the view that students who ranked high in personal soundness were seen as having flexibility, good reality contact, high self-acceptance, and interpersonal effectiveness.

On the perception tasks, the high-ranking group showed flexibility, resistance to stress, and moderate accuracy in perception of size. In the life history variables, some of the most telling results were observed. Persons high in soundness had established positive relationships with siblings and had intimate and stable heterosexual relationships. They perceived their fathers as strong and positively valued, and showed early development of social facility. Health history was also quite significant. Persons high in soundness had early health records remarkably free from serious illness.

A research program by Douglas Heath employed a wide variety of variables to study mature men in three cultures: American, Italian, and Turkish. The main selection variable was a rating measure completed by faculty members and students who knew the research participants well. This measure identified groups of "more mature" and "less mature" men. What emerged from the data for the American sample was a coherent picture of maturity as seen from multiple frames of reference. The high-maturity groups showed superior intellectual skills and academic performance, even though the groups had been equated on verbal aptitude measures. Furthermore, the high groups showed greater capacity to withstand the effects of both distracting and personally disturbing information. These results in the cognitive sphere suggest efficiency in utilizing personal resources. In the interpersonal sphere, the men in the high groups were active in extracurricular activities, had high interaction with others, and were selected frequently for leadership positions.

Heath's cross-cultural study utilized essentially the same framework as the American study. Most important, the new study confirmed the major results of the earlier one, thus permitting the conclusion that the description of maturity was a pervasive phenomenon that encompassed multiple cultures.

The program by Julius Seeman took as its basic structure the concept of the person as a human system. The overarching concept was of organismic integration. The term *organismic* reflected inclusiveness, so that there was attention to all of the major behavioral subsystems: biochemical, physiological, perceptual, cognitive, and interpersonal. The term *integration* referred to the organization of these subsystems. Optimal functioning involved a coherent organization of these behavioral subsystems, such that information flow and information processing were maximized. The result was efficient functioning of the system. This overall concept is congruent with the definition of a system as put forth by Andras Angyal. According to Angyal, the defining characteristic of a system is *unitas multiplex*—that is, a system is characterized by multiple components that have an underlying unity of organization. Such unity necessarily involves connectedness and communication among the subsystem components. Failure in communication and information flow is understood to be disruptive to the system.

A summary view of the conceptual and empirical literature in personality effectiveness reveals major recurrent themes. A dominant theme refers to the organization of personality. Effective persons display an integrated organization, a harmonious and coherent blend of behavior dispositions. An equally dominant theme is that of self-definition. Effective persons accept and value themselves and trust their perceptions and judgments. The significance of this fact for effective behavior is that such attitudes foster maximal receipt and utilization of incoming sense data and perceptions, and thus provide a solid basis for decision and action. Effective persons are not only in good touch with themselves, but also with their interpersonal and physical environment. They have good environmental contact. In the cognitive domain, their efficient information-processing styles promote intellectual efficiency, a maximal use of their intellectual resources. Interpersonally, effective persons have the capacity both for autonomy and for intimacy, the accent on each being related to situations in which one or the other is appropriate. High functioning persons have the capacity for empathy and caring about others. They have minimal need to establish status hierarchies, but tend to establish horizontal peerlike relationships.

In developmental terms, the research reveals that these characteristics appear to have developmental continuity. They develop early. Many of these attributes are as clearly visible in persons 7 years old as in persons 27 years old. Such persons give us cause to conclude that there is a high ceiling on human potentialities.

CENTRAL TRAITS
HEALTH PSYCHOLOGY
OPTIMAL FUNCTIONING

J. SEEMAN

PERSONALITY RESEARCH

The major concern in personality research is the behavioral variance accounted for by internal (rather than situational) factors. To qualify as aspects of personality, these internal factors must be somehow mental (e.g., beliefs in internal versus external locus of control), although they may include a somatic substratum (e.g., Freudian instincts composed of wishes and metabolic energy). The particularistic tradition of personality research has studied the behavioral expressions of individual personality factors, whereas the holistic tradition has concerned the patterning of personality factors forming complete personalities.

The holistic tradition has been fueled by the applied concerns of clinical psychology, in which overall understanding of lifestyles is crucial to assessment and treatment. In contrast, the particularistic tradition, with its concern for rigor of conceptualization and method, has flourished in the academic world. To bring these traditions together, Henry Murray and coworkers extensively and systematically measured needs and their patterning in 50 male undergraduates. They called their approach *personology,* and it launched personality study as an accepted subdiscipline of academic psychology. Allport, in emphasizing the radical individuality of each person through his concept of ideographic (later, morphogenic) personality study, lent support to the attempt to bring together the holistic and particularistic traditions.

However, the integrated vision of personology has not held. Since 1938, academically based personality research has been dominated by the particularistic tradition, with its engaging simplicity and rigor. Employing middle-level theorizing, the particularistic approach involves defining a personality variable (e.g., dominance or negative affectivity) without concern for the rest of personality, measuring the variable (usually by questionnaires), and engaging in empirical study of its nomological network or behavioral expressions (such as competitiveness and job advancement for dominance or severity of physical illness symptoms for negative affectivity). If a study considers additional personality variables, they are as likely to be controlled out as considered along with the highlighted one. A comprehensive example of personality research in the particularistic tradition is the work of McClelland, Atkinson, Clark and Lowell.

The particularistic tradition has led to emphasis on personality variables that are either cognitive (e.g., internal versus external locus of control and hardiness), or affective (e.g., anxiety, depression, and negative affectivity). Occasionally, studies have emphasized defensive manifestations (e.g., socially desirable responding), and more complex amalgams

of cognition, affect, and behavior (e.g., needs for achievement and power). In general, however, individual investigators have not considered it part of their task to justify their emphasis by relating it to the rest of personality. If the particularistic tradition concerns itself at all with an overall view of personality, it includes the assumption that when enough individual and concrete facts are contributed by investigators, it stimulates integrative efforts in the field. That integrative efforts are still scant in academic psychology, in spite of thousands of particularistic studies since 1928, suggests this is a naive assumption.

The holistic tradition of personality study has continued to persist in relevant applied settings, notably clinical psychology. The impetus here has not been the accumulation of discrete facts, but rather the requirements imposed by trying to help people overcome lifestyle problems. To determine what is wrong with a person and implement a corrective plan necessitates comprehensive information about personality and lifestyle that can only be obtained through a holistic approach. It is in this context that the elaborate theories of personality that flourished in the first half of the twentieth century (e.g., Freud, Jung) have survived. Although particularists have been predictably disdainful of these grand efforts as hopelessly ambiguous and unscientific, there has developed discerning, systematic metatheorizing concerning the components of personality, how they interact, and their expressions in everyday life that lends rigor to the holistic approach.

The applied goals of clinical psychology are assessment and treatment of individual personality. True to the holistic nature of this assessment task are the comprehensive tests of personality. Some tests are structured in, typically, a questionnaire format and provide scales of many personality components that have adequate internal consistency, stability, and validity. Other tests are unstructured, usually employing projective format in which the subject's task is to clarify ambiguous stimuli by identifying them (e.g., Rorschach) or incorporating them in fantasy themes (e.g., Thematic Apperception Test [TAT]). Because of the greater difficulty in establishing subject and investigator reliability for unstructured tests, this format has been less accepted by academic psychologists than the structured format. Nonetheless, clinicians retain unstructured tests for the richness and depth of information they provide.

A holistic emphasis has also persisted in the less applied context of psychobiography, in which a life that is notable in some way is interpreted in terms of the psychosocial forces shaping it. Psychobiographers work from existing documentation and—if the person chronicled is still alive—additional interviews to integrate extensive observations into an overall picture of the person's lifestyle.

Personality research, even of the particularistic sort, has not always found ready acceptance in psychology. A typical debate involves explanations of behavior as forces emanating in the person versus in the situation. This issue flared early in this century in the debates between William McDougall and John Watson, the former emphasizing instincts (a person construct) and the latter, reinforcement (a situation construct). Another version of this debate took place in the 1950s, when Carl R. Rogers insisted that person-centered counseling operates by freeing the client to actualize inherent potentialities (a person construct) and B. F. Skinner countered by viewing the effects of this approach as shaping client behaviors of value to the counselor (a situation construct).

The latest version of the person–situation debate took place from the late 1960s through the mid-1970s. Instrumental in this debate was the critique of measures of particular personality variables for showing only modest stability and relationship to behaviors supposedly expressive of them. Soon social psychologists were insisting that most of the variance of behavior is situationally rather than personalistically determined. One response of personality psychologists emphasized that personality variables are best conceptualized as genotypes expressing themselves in patterns rather than literal repetitions of behavior; therefore, one should expect (rather than use as a critique) modest relationships to particular behaviors. In addition, such researchers indicated that because personality variables develop and change as a function of experience, their measures can be expected to show only modest stability. It was also demonstrated that when enough repeated measurements are available, stability is actually more than modest. A final rebuttal expressing the holistic traditions emphasized that because behaviors are complex enough to be jointly determined by several personality variables, it is only to be expected that the relationship between any particular variable and any particular behavior would be modest at best.

The most persuasive argument in the person–situation debate was the amassing of studies in which the explanation of behavioral variance by personality variables, situational variables, and their interaction could be compared. The evidence from these studies supported the interaction position, indicating that behavior is jointly determined by personal and situational forces, in the wake of which it behooves personality researchers to conceptualize and measure in a fashion that highlights the ways in which personality and situational forces combine to determine behavior.

This interactional accord has revitalized personality research, encouraging conceptualization and measurement of both person and situational forces and the personality variables that jointly express these forces. It is hoped that this will stimulate the study of sets of personality and social variables interacting together, hastening the time when a complex empirical appreciation of human behavior is possible.

DETERMINISM–INDETERMINISM
HOLISM
INTERACTIONISM
PERSONALITY ASSESSMENT
PERSONALITY THEORIES
PERSONOLOGY
RESEARCH METHODOLOGY

S. Maddi

PERSONALITY THEORIES

In essence, a theory of personality is a set of unproved speculations about aspects of human behavior. Established facts are often lacking in scientific work, but theories offer guidelines that serve in the absence of more precise information.

To this end, the personality theorist devises a variety of interrelated terms and concepts (*constructs*). Ideally, these constructs should satisfy several criteria. A good personality theory provides convenient descriptions, establishes a framework for organizing substantial amounts of data, and focuses attention on matters of greater importance. It also explains the phenomena under study, offering answers to such significant questions as the causes of individual differences in personality and why some people are more disturbed than others. The theory should also generate predictions, so that it may be evaluated and improved (or, if necessary, discarded). Finally, a valuable theory usually leads to important practical applications. It facilitates control and change of the environment, as by bringing about better techniques of parenting, education, or psychotherapy.

HUMAN NATURE

Personality is a comprehensive construct, and motivation is a fundamental aspect of behavior. Thus most theories of personality are in part theories of motivation, and make crucial assumptions about the basic nature of human beings.

The Quality of Human Motives

Many personality theorists have been intimately concerned with a challenging, if perhaps untestable, issue: Is human nature inherently malignant or benign?

At the most negative extreme is Sigmund Freud's psychoanalytic theory, which assumes that powerful human innate drives include incest and destructiveness. Since society will not tolerate such threats to its existence, it inevitably comes into conflict with the individual; and since the demands of society are conveyed through the parents and then internalized by the child at an early age, these conflicts eventually become intrapsychic. Freudian theory thus posits a rather pessimistic definition of mental health: the ability to resolve inescapable inner conflicts by channeling drives away from inborn illicit wishes and into less satisfying but more socially acceptable forms of behavior (sublimation). The parents facilitate the development of healthy behavior by nudging the reluctant child along the road to effective sublimations and socially acceptable satisfactions.

At the other extreme are theories that assume that human innate potentialities are wholly positive, and that we all have the capacity and the desire to develop them in constructive ways. These benign drives do not conflict with societal demands, so compromising them through sublimation is unnecessary. Thus to Alfred Adler, Karen Horney, and Carl Rogers, mental health consists of trying to satisfy our innate desires. Psychopathology occurs only if and when this healthy drive toward self-realization (actualization, self-perfection) is blocked by external social forces, the most notable of which is pathogenic parenting (e.g., pampering, neglect, overprotectiveness, overindulgence, humiliation, derision). Such parenting may create the belief that external obstacles and personal weaknesses cannot be overcome through one's best efforts (inferiority complex), or it may cause the child to become so profoundly anxious as to abandon the healthy quest for self-realization in favor of an all-out drive for safety. Adlerian theory rejects the idea of intrapsychic conflict altogether, concluding instead that conscious and unconscious are invariably united in the service of one's chosen life goals.

Between these extremes are theorists who attribute to humans both malignant and benign drives. Carl Jung assumes that some of our unconscious motives are indeed dark and frightening, although others can serve as wellsprings of creativity that guide us toward constructive solutions to problems. Abraham Maslow posits a weak inherent tendency toward positive growth and benevolence, which the far more powerful forces of learning and culture all too easily can convert into hatred and destructiveness. Gordon Allport theorizes that we all possess deeply rooted selfish and irrational tendencies, together with the inherent potential to outgrow this unreasonableness and become mature, considerate adults. Erich Fromm concludes that every human being has the capacity for love and responsibility toward others, but that fulfilling this potential is extremely difficult because we all begin life as wholly self-centered (narcissistic) infants. Erik Erikson has modified psychoanalytic theory by attributing to people important constructive motives actively supported by society, such as preserving a sense of individuality and inner wholeness (identity) and striving to master the environment in socially approved ways.

The Dynamics of Human Motives

Some theorists (e.g., Freud, Harry Stack Sullivan) posit that activated drives create a state of tension or excitation, which is experienced as unpleasant. Thus the basic objective of all human behavior is to reduce our drives and restore a state of equilibrium. However, many other theorists have taken exception to the drive-reduction model of motivation. They point out that numerous tension-increasing activities are also highly rewarding in their own right.

Freud posits that all mental and physical behavior is determined by prior causes (psychic determinism). However, most other theorists conclude that behavior must also be understood in terms of its purpose or goal (teleology).

There is general agreement among personality theorists that some degree of human motivation is unconscious and cannot be readily called to mind. Thus most would regard "know thyself" as a highly desirable goal, albeit a difficult and challenging one.

The Catalog of Human Motives

Both the number and the kind of human motives have been hotly disputed, although there are some areas of agreement. Freud limits the list to sexuality, which includes the whole range of erotic and pleasurable experience, and destructiveness. Jung stresses the importance of becoming one's true self by uniting the various opposites that comprise the human personality through some middle path (individuation), and also includes hunger, thirst, sexuality, power, activity, creativity, and feeling that one's life has meaning (as through religion). Adler emphasizes the quest to overcome the feelings of inferiority that inevitably result from our helplessness as infants, and that all of us have the innate potential to do so by striving to master our formidable environment in ways that promote the common good (social interest).

Other human motives cited by various theorists include developing our positive and unique potentialities in constructive ways, the need to feel a sense of identity and to master the environment, the need to be with other people and to develop mutually enhancing relationships with them, the need to reduce anxiety, the need for a unifying philosophy that gives meaning to one's life, the need to reduce such drives as oxygen deprivation and elimination, the need for sleep, the need to be tender to one's offspring, and the need to exist in the world in which we are born. At the opposite extreme from Freud are Raymond Cattell, who identifies some 10 to 15 human needs by means of the statistical technique of factor analysis; Henry Murray, who posits some 20 specific human needs; and Allport, who contends that motives vary so much from one individual to another that personality cannot be explained in terms of a number of universal drives or needs.

THE STRUCTURE OF PERSONALITY

Some theorists have sought to depict the complicated and often contradictory aspects of personality by devising appropriate structural constructs. Thus Freud refers to our "seething cauldron" of irrational, amoral, and unconscious innate motives as the *id;* to the more rational, partly conscious, problem-solving, and self-preservative aspect of personality as the *ego;* and to our partly conscious, learned standards of right and wrong as the *superego.* Erikson and Murray also utilize these three constructs but define them somewhat differently.

Jung's model of the psyche is particularly chaotic, with different components capable of gravitating between consciousness and unconsciousness, or even fusing into a single entity. The ego is wholly conscious, and represents the center of one's awareness and feelings of identity. The persona is wholly conscious, and represents the center of the protective facade that enables us to meet the demands of society while concealing our true inner nature. The personal unconscious includes material not within our awareness because it has been forgotten, repressed, or perceived subliminally. The collective unconscious, a major and controversial Jungian construct, consists of a storehouse of latent predispositions to apprehend the world in particular ways (archetypes) inherited from our ancestral past.

Other theories focus on the self as a primary structural construct. For example, Rogers concludes that we all try to actualize those abilities and goals that we perceive as our own. Ideally, this learned and conscious self-concept remains consistent with our healthy innate desires and capacities. However, it is all too easy to abandon our organismic drives in order to satisfy parental conditions for love and positive regard, and to accept the incorrect evaluations of ourselves that these significant others establish for us. The self-concept then becomes a distorted guideline that clashes with our true wishes (and makes it difficult even to recognize them), with this inner schism producing anxiety, confusion, and even psychopathology.

In contrast to the preceding theorists, Allport does not draw a clear distinction between motivational and structural constructs. He defines personality in terms of some 4000 traits, such as friendliness, ambition, cleanliness, enthusiasm, and seclusiveness. Every personality is a unique collection of personal traits, although a given culture does evoke roughly similar modes of adjustment that permit comparisons among different people (common traits).

Not all personality theorists regard structural constructs as necessary or even desirable. Some warn that in spite of often stressed cautions, structural constructs are likely to become reified: Continuous usage may well produce the belief that we all have, for instance, an id, ego, and a superego. This will make it more difficult to dispense with constructs that lose their utility in light of subsequent discoveries, a not unlikely occurrence in view of our relatively limited knowledge of the human personality.

Amid these various controversies, however, there is at least one island of agreement. The defense mechanisms that Freud attributes to the ego have been accepted and incorporated into virtually every theory of personality, if at times with some changes in terminology and in the underlying rationale.

THE DEVELOPMENT OF PERSONALITY

Freud defines personality development in terms of stages. During the first 5 to 6 years of life, particular regions of the body become both the child's primary source of pleasure and the main focus of conflict with the parents: first the oral stage (mouth and lips, feeding), followed by the anal stage (anus, toilet training), and then the phallic stage (penis or clitoris, Oedipus complex). Development ideally should culminate in the genital stage, characterized by effective sublimations and realistic enjoyments. However, if the child meets with excessive gratification or frustration during a pregenital stage, personality development to some extent will become fixated at that stage, and behavior will be influenced accordingly.

Freudian theory regards personality development as virtually complete by about the age of 6 years, a contention that has evoked considerable opposition. Thus Erikson argues that personality continues to change throughout one's life, and posits eight epigenetic psychosexual stages that range from infancy to age 50 years and beyond. Each stage is characterized by a specific psychosocial crisis brought on by increasing physiological maturity, and by correspondingly greater demands by the parents and society, and each should result in the emergence of a particular ego quality (e.g., trust, hope) if personality development is to proceed successfully. Sullivan agrees that significant changes in personality occur during later childhood and adolescence, and posits seven epochs through which personality may develop that range from infancy to adulthood.

The majority of personality theorists have rejected the idea of developmental stages. They prefer to concentrate on the goals of personality development (e.g., Adlerian socially interested striving for self-perfection, Horneyan self-realization, Rogerian actualization, Maslovian self-actualization), and to caution against parental pathogenic behaviors that prevent the child from reaching this ideal.

Character Typologies

Freud is by no means the only theorist who has devoted some attention to personality types. Jung describes individual differences in personality in terms of two dimensions: the typical way in which we interpret external stimuli (thinking, feeling, sensation, intuition), and whether we characteristically attend more to the external environment (extraversion) or to our own subjective world (introversion). There is an innate tendency for one aspect of each dimension to become dominant, which must be realized for personality development to be successful. Fromm refers instead to the desirable productive orientation, typified by a love of life, rational thought, and work that benefits others and oneself.

In contrast, Adler and Allport oppose the use of character typologies. Adler argues instead that we all develop our own particular style of life. This may involve such desirable and undesirable character traits as cheerfulness, social interest, and optimism, or selfishness, arrogance, vanity, hostility, and helplessness. However, every personality is at least somewhat unique, and the aforementioned terms are used solely because our language lacks sufficient precision to describe all of the subtle nuances that distinguish one human being from another.

Criteria of Mental Health

Freud's definition of mental health consists of two characteristics: the ability to love and the ability to work. Adler, Allport, Maslow, and Rogers have proposed more extensive criteria. These include social interest, a greater acceptance of others, and a greater capacity for deeper and loving relationships that are free of crippling possessiveness and jealousy; having a unifying philosophy that gives meaning to one's life; greater emotional security and self-acceptance; responding to innate needs and desires rather than to self-denying external standards; more accurate self-insight and perceptions of reality; greater creativity and spontaneity; and greater autonomy and resistance to enculturation.

PERSONALITY THEORIES: CONTRIBUTIONS AND CRITICISMS

Personality theorists have applied their constructs and principles successfully to numerous important areas and many specific constructs enjoy widespread acceptance. The course of personality theory has also been demarcated by major constructs that have been rejected by most modern psychologists, such as Freud's metaphysical and unmeasurable concept of libido (psychic energy). Given the essentially speculative nature of personality theory, however, such failures are to be expected. A more cogent criticism would be that not enough constructs have been discarded by the theorists who created them. Personality theorists have been far too free with neologisms, and have often duplicated each other's concepts without any apparent knowledge of having done so.

The inability of personality theorists to resolve the most fundamental of issues (e.g., the nature of human motivation) may lead one to question the merits of this field of endeavor. However, it is difficult to study subject matter that is capable of thought, lying to others, and even self-deception, and arrive at significant conclusions. The creative and broad scope of thought reflected in theories of personality represents an essential adjunct to the typically narrow findings of modern empirical research; and it offers rich rewards to anyone seeking to describe, explain, predict, or alter the behavior of human beings.

PERSONALITY

R. B. EWEN

PERSONALITY TYPES

Typal categorization is one of the oldest ways of distinguishing individuals with respect to personality differences. Numerous typologies have been proposed by writers, psychiatrists, and psychologists, and in these typologies people have been classified in terms of social behavior, pathology, modes of imagery, values, interests, attitudes, and various features of biological constitution assumed to be related to temperament. It is likely that every personality variable that has captured the interest of psychological theorists has been incorporated into a typology at some time. There is much overlap among typologies, however, and it is possible to recognize a small number of polarities that recur extensively.

The popularity of typologies can be understood in terms of the fact that they offer an economical way of summarizing complex configurations of variables—a way of characterizing the whole person in terms of a small number of broad categories. The critics of typological description, however, have long contended that the simplicity of the typology leads to inaccuracy, that the typal categories are artificial, and that the distinctive features of the individual are lost when one is lumped together with many other people with distinctive qualities of their own.

The imprecision of the typology is bound up with its simplicity. In principle, it is possible to achieve a high degree of descriptive precision with a typology, provided we are willing to sacrifice simplicity. If we wish to maintain comprehensiveness, we must cross-classify individuals in terms of a large number of very specific dichotomous variables. In this way, we can derive complex typal categories that are more univocally descriptive than any combination of scale scores resting on the same set of information.

The oldest known system of personality typing is that devised by ancient astrologers. Another ancient typology that has continued to receive attention for many centuries is based on the four humors of Hippocrates. Claudius Galen, who lived in the second century A.D., is usually given credit for developing a fourfold typology of temperaments based on this notion. These four basic temperaments are: sanguine, which arises from a preponderance of blood; phlegmatic, involving a preponderance of phlegm; choleric, involving a preponderance of yellow bile; and melancholic, involving a preponderance of black bile. In the eighteenth century, Immanuel Kant offered a more elaborate verbal description of these four types. Although the humoral doctrine itself can no longer be taken seriously, the work of Hippocrates and Galen may have inspired some modern investigators to look for biochemical sources of variations in human behavior and experience.

The idea that temperament is related to physique also has a long history. Hippocrates described two contrasting physical types, *habitus apoplecticus* and *habitus phthisicus.* The former type is relatively thick, and hence strong and muscular; the latter is thin, and hence more delicate and weaker.

Early in the nineteenth century, a threefold variant of the typology appeared in France. Leon Rostan characterized the types as digestive, muscular, and respiratory–cerebral. The threefold typology was subsequently adopted and modified by several German theorists. Some of these theorists were concerned primarily with constitutional predispositions to various diseases, but early in this century the work of the psychiatrist Ernst Kretschmer aroused renewed interest in the relationships between physique and temperament. Kretschmer (1925) revived the three French types, but called them pyknic, athletic, and asthenic (later called leptosomic). He also added a fourth type, the dysplastic, but this refers to an inconsistent mixture of the components of the three basic types.

Sheldon advocated the use of a somatotype, in which three numerals (each based on a 7-point scale) are used to express an individual's standing on three components of physique.

All the typologies noted thus far rest on an analysis either of cosmic events or of properties of the body, but typologies of a more strictly psychological nature also have a long history. People have often been classified in terms of their basic motives, interests, or values—in terms of the things that they seek or value or the things that arouse, attract, or please them. An early typology of this sort was offered by Plato in *The republic.* Plato regarded the human soul as possessing three basic principles or components. One is concerned with the appetites, or with a love of eating, drinking, sensual pleasure, or money. A second is concerned with passion or spirit. It may be expressed as courage, pugnacity, power, ambition, or a quest for honor. The third is the philosophic, reasoning element, which underlies the love of knowledge or learning. People differ with respect to the prominence of the three elements in their nature, and we can distinguish a type corresponding to the preponderance of each. One class of individuals would be those who seek wealth or gain. A second class would be those who seek honor. The third class would be the philosophers, the seekers of truth or wisdom.

Plato noted that each of the three orientations provides its own evaluative criteria. Thus, depending on one's own type, one may ascribe superiority to the wealthy individual, to the individual who achieves honor, or to the wise philosopher. At the same time, however, Plato argued that the philosopher is more highly developed than the other two types, having had the most comprehensive experience, and therefore is best qualified to be a ruler.

Early in the twentieth century, a related typology was suggested by the German psychologist Edouard Spranger. He categorized people in terms of the basic ways in which they seemed to experience meaning or value. He recognized six main kinds of evaluative attitude and six corresponding types of people. First, there is the cognitive attitude, which ascribes significance to ideas as such. This attitude is emphasized by individuals of the theoretical type. Similar to Plato's philosophers, such people value knowledge and truth. The economic attitude is more concerned with the relevance of objects to one's own bodily needs. This type corresponds roughly to Plato's appetitive type.

The aesthetic attitude emphasizes an empathic response to form and a concern with the expressive qualities of things and events. The aesthetic type attaches great value to form and harmony. The religious attitude seeks to relate each event to the all-embracing meaning of one's life as a whole. The type that stresses this attitude seeks a sense of unity in the universe and in his or her experience of it. Two other attitudes are concerned with one's relationship to other people. The social attitude, and hence the social type, affirms interest in other people and identification with them. The political attitude and the political type are concerned with the attainment of superiority or power over others. The political type, as described by Spranger, probably comes closest to the passionate or ambitious type depicted by Plato.

Of the many such typologies proposed by philosophers, two have been widely employed by people of other disciplines. One is the contrast between the Apollonian and the Dionysian styles of life proposed by Friedrich Nietzsche. The Apollonian individual favors control, balance, and restraint and is oriented toward inner images of beauty; the Dionysian favors unrestrained experience and expression. The other typology was proposed by William James, who distinguished two kinds of philosophers. He characterized the tender-minded philosopher as rationalistic, intellectualistic, idealistic, optimistic, religious, free-willist, monistic, and dogmatical, and the tough-minded type as empiricist, sensationalistic, materialistic, pessimistic, irreligious, fatalistic, pluralistic, and skeptical

Two major dichotomies proposed for psychiatric classification have also been widely influential. One was Emil Kraepelin's typology of the psychoses, involving a major division between manic–depressive psychosis and dementia praecox (later known as schizophrenia). The other was a comparable division proposed by Pierre Janet for the psychoneuroses, the major categories in this case being hysteria and psychasthenia.

The best known typology centering around the extraversion–introversion dichotomy is that of Carl Jung, who regarded these as two fundamental alternative attitudes underlying human experience. He believed that each of us has a constitutional predisposition toward one or the other.

ASTROLOGY
CENTRAL TRAITS

PERSONALITY
PHRENOLOGY

R. W. COAN

PERSON-CENTERED APPROACH FOUNDATIONS*

The central hypothesis of the person-centered approach can be stated briefly. Any individual has vast resources for self-understanding, for altering self-concept and basic attitudes, and for self-directed behavior. These resources can be tapped if a definable climate of facilitative psychological attitudes can be provided.

Three conditions constitute this growth-promoting climate. The first is genuineness, realness, or congruence. The term *transparent* describes this condition. There is a close matching or congruence at the gut level, what is present in awareness and what is expressed. The second attitude of importance in creating a climate for change is acceptance or caring or prizing—unconditional positive regard. The third facilitative aspect of the relationship is empathic understanding. As the person is empathically heard, it becomes possible for that person to listen more accurately to the flow of inner experiencing. These tendencies, the reciprocal of the therapist's attitudes, mean that the person is a more effective self-growth enhancer. There is a greater freedom to be the whole person that he or she inwardly is.

THE EVIDENCE

A body of research evidence supports the view that when these facilitative conditions are present, changes in personality and behavior do occur.

The person-centered approach rests on a basic trust in the organism. There is evidence from many disciplines to support an even broader statement: In every organism, at whatever level, an underlying flow of movement exists toward a constructive fulfillment of its inherent possibilities. The actualizing tendency can be thwarted or warped, but it cannot be destroyed without destroying the organism.

SOME CONFIRMING EXAMPLES

The most impressive fact about the individual human being seems to be the directional tendency toward wholeness, toward actualization of one's potentialities. Sometimes this growth tendency is described as if it involved the development of all the potentialities of the organism. This clearly is not true. The organism does not tend toward developing its own capacity of nausea, nor does it actualize its potentiality for self-destruction or its ability to bear pain.

The work in the field of sensory deprivation shows the organism's tendency to amplify diversities and to create new forms. Tension reduction or the absence of stimulation is a far cry from being the desired state of the organism. When deprived of external stimuli, the human organism produces a flood of internal stimuli, sometimes of the most bizarre form. The substratum of all motivation is the organismic tendency toward fulfillment.

There also appears to be a formative tendency at work in the universe. Physical scientists have focused primarily on entropy, the tendency toward disorder. By studying closed systems, they can give this tendency a clear mathematic description. They know that order or organization tends to deteriorate into randomness, with each stage less organized than the last. However, there is far less recognition of or emphasis on the more important formative tendency. Every form has emerged from a simpler, less complex form. This phenomenon is at least as significant as entropy.

---

* Adapted from Rogers, C. R. Foundations of the person-centered approach. In *A way of being.* Boston: Houghton Mifflin, 1980.

The Function of Consciousness

What part does awareness play in this formative function? The ability to focus conscious attention seems to be one of the latest evolutionary developments in our species. The human organism may be moving toward a more complete development of awareness.

In psychotherapy, we have been learning something about the psychological conditions most conducive to increasing this highly important function of self- awareness. With greater self-awareness, a more informed choice is possible, a conscious choosing in tune with the evolutionary flow. When a person is functioning in this way, it does not mean that there is self-conscious awareness of all that is going on within.

A HYPOTHESIS FOR THE FUTURE

It is hypothesized by person-centered theorists that there is a formative directional tendency in the universe that can be traced and observed in stellar space, in crystals, in microorganisms, in organic life, and in human beings. This evolutionary tendency is toward greater order, greater complexity, and greater interrelatedness. In humankind it develops from a single cell origin to complex organic functioning, to a conscious awareness of the organism and of the external world, to a transcendent awareness of the harmony and unity of the cosmic system including humankind. It is just possible that this hypothesis might be a basis on which we could begin to build a theory for humanistic psychology. It definitely forms a base for the person-centered approach.

CLIENT-CENTERED THERAPY
NONDIRECTIVE PSYCHOANALYSIS
PSYCHOTHERAPY

C. R. ROGERS

PERSONNEL EVALUATION

Personnel evaluations are formalized practices that provide information about the job performance of employees. Evaluations serve two general purposes—administrative and developmental. Administrative purposes are served to the extent that the evaluations are used to make personnel decisions about such things as salary increases, job assignments, promotions, and selection for training program participation. Developmental uses serve the individual employee by providing information about one's performance on the job and also information that can guide planning for future career roles.

The development of performance evaluation involves at least three major classes of processes and choices: (a) the specification of the performance criteria; (b) the development of performance evaluation measures; and (c) the choice of evaluators.

PERFORMANCE CRITERIA

The quality of any personnel evaluation system depends on the extent to which the major dimensions of performance on the jobs to be evaluated have been identified. These dimensions must be relevant to successful or unsuccessful performance of the job. Each dimension is called a *criterion;* collectively they are known as the *criteria*. The criteria are identified through job analyses.

Criteria can be classified in many different ways. However, psychologists usually think in terms of two general classifications, with the second of these subdivided once again. The first classification labels criteria as objective or subjective. Objective criteria are usually part of records kept on employees and, for the most part, are quite straightforward.

Subjective criteria are usually based on some individual's evaluation of the employee's performance. Subjective criteria can be further divided into trait-related and behaviorally related criteria. Examples of trait-related criterion dimensions are friendliness, honesty, aggressiveness, ambition, helpfulness, and hard work. Behaviorally referenced criteria would be relationships with customers, and knowledge and accuracy of transactions when working with the equipment on line with the central computer.

Psychologists almost always favor the use of objective criteria plus subjective ones that are behaviorally oriented. However, when the total evaluation is taken into account and it is necessary to compare employees across a wide variety of different types of jobs, the use of behaviorally based evaluation systems is more difficult.

PERFORMANCE MEASURES

Once the criteria have been identified, the next task is to construct ways in which to measure them. Objective criteria, by their very nature, have standards for their measurement, and thus the measurement problem is confronted directly when subjective performance evaluation scales must be developed. This task is one of constructing scales that are reliable, valid, unbiased, and as free as possible from contamination.

EVALUATORS

Because of the hierarchical nature of most organizations with the well-accepted control mechanism whereby supervisors are responsible for the work of their subordinates, most performance evaluations are done by employees' immediate supervisors. Also it is common for the next higher level of supervision to endorse the evaluations. In spite of this practice, there is no reason to believe that supervisors are in the best position to provide the evaluation. Peers are excellent sources of evaluations and are often better than supervisors. From the standpoint of the quality of the rating, the best generalization to be made is that this should vary as a function of the evaluator's ability to observe and judge the dimension in question. Thus, for some dimensions, supervisors may be best; for others, it may be peers. In other cases, there may be yet other individuals who can judge best.

PROCESS CONCERNS

Up until the mid-1970s, psychologists working in the area of performance appraisal concentrated almost all of their efforts on the development of performance rating scales and the procedures for using these scales. It was assumed that evaluators had well-formed notions about performance and that it was necessary to develop a way to measure their beliefs in an accurate fashion. Subsequently, there has been a recognition that the whole process of performance appraisal merits more attention. In particular, there is now the widespread belief that the limits in improvements that can be accomplished through scale construction alone have been reached. It is now time to turn attention to the process as a whole.

One of the most important aspects of this process was the recognition that the evaluator is faced with a person perception problem that requires the perception, memory, and recall of events related to the perception of a particular person—the employer. From this perspective, it is necessary to understand how people perceive others and what they remember about others; only after this understanding was reached could the question of how people retrieve from memory the information about others and record it on a scale be answered. This new focus promises to stimulate considerable work on the entire performance sequence and should lead to improvements in our ability to appraise performance.

Finally, in addition to looking at the evaluator, more attention must be paid to the characteristics of the performance setting. Although of utmost importance to the psychologists who develop evaluation systems, to the line manager with many other responsibilities the appraisal process is just another task that must be completed by a particular deadline. Thus more attention must be paid to the situational conditions under which appraisal takes place so that conditions can be established that increase the probability that accurate evaluations result. Again, the recent trend is to be more cognizant of the situational constraints and to attempt to deal with them in the personnel evaluation systems that are developed.

JOB ANALYSIS
JOB EVALUATION
PERSONNEL SELECTION

D. R. ILGEN

PERSONNEL SELECTION

Staffing organizations requires making decisions about people. In every organization, decisions must be made concerning whom to hire, to promote, to transfer, to terminate, to lay off, and probably less frequently, to demote.

Much organizational effort is involved in making selection decisions. Included are human resource planning, recruitment of personnel, choosing appropriate methods for making the decisions, and research on selection procedures.

The first applications of measurement principles in selecting people for occupations came early in the present century. Around 1911, Hugo Münsterberg developed a test for railway motormen and compared scores obtained on the test with records of performance in carrying out the work. Subsequently, he developed tests for telephone operators and related their scores to progress in training for the job. Somewhat later, the Bureau of Salesmanship Research was established at the Carnegie Institute of Technology and studies were made to improve the selection of sales personnel.

During World War I, psychologists working with the armed services developed the first tests that could be administered to large groups of people. The screening of nearly 2 million recruits on their intellectual abilities ensued. Following the war, the availability of large-scale testing made possible the expanded use of tests for selection purposes. The testing industry came into being.

Much research on personnel selection took place during the 1920s and 1930s. Included were many advances in the use of statistical procedures. World War II stimulated research on selection, with large numbers of psychologists either joining or being employed by the armed services to carry out this work.

With the passage of the Civil Rights Act of 1964 came challenges to traditional practices for selecting personnel. Psychologists began to examine the impact of selection procedures on the employment of minorities, women, and other groups protected by law.

SELECTION METHODS

No doubt the use of psychological tests in personnel selection has received more attention from psychologists than have other methods available for this purpose. Other methods are used, however, and have been subjected to considerable investigation.

Interviewing is the most widely used method for making selection decisions. Studies by psychologists, however, raise doubts as to its reliability and validity for this purpose.

Unlike interviewing, a relatively subjective process, psychological tests are standardized and are objectively scored. They are designed to measure characteristics of individuals, such as abilities (knowledge, aptitudes) and personality attributes (temperament, interests, values). Many are paper-and-pencil instruments, easy to administer and score, and relatively inexpensive.

Some tests are work sample tests. They are designed to measure abilities directly required in a particular job or occupation and are samples of functions found in diverse kinds of occupations.

The notion that a person's past behavior is indicative of future behavior is the basis for a method used in selecting people referred to as biographical information or, briefly, as biodata. The method originated with the application forms on which job applicants are asked to furnish information concerning educational background, work experience, marital status, home ownership, and so forth. Statistical analyses demonstrated that many items correlated with aspects of subsequent job performance.

Projective techniques, exemplified by the well-known Rorschach ink blot test, were designed by psychologists for use in psychodiagnosis. Psychodiagnosis is not, of course, limited to projective techniques. Many methods are used for this purpose.

A psychologist may use only one method—a lengthy interview, for example—or a variety of methods, including ability tests, personality tests, projectives techniques, and an interview. The psychologist then reviews the information obtained and evaluates the suitability of the applicant for the position in question.

The process is essentially a judgmental one, and generally is quite costly. As a consequence, it tends to be restricted to managerial and other higher level occupations. Because of the nature of the process, including the confidentiality of reports, research on its utility in predicting job performance has been limited. In spite of the absence of supporting data, however, many organizations have faith in and continue to use the process.

Another procedure for making selection decisions, also essentially judgmental, is the Assessment Center method. In this case, several assessors are used. This method focuses on the use of simulations, which are exercises in which the behaviors of applicants are observed.

Application of the method tends to be costly, although cost varies considerably depending on the length of the assessment, number of assessors involved, and other factors. Consequently its use tends to favor, but is not limited to, higher level occupations.

RESEARCH

The development of a science of personnel selection requires research. Furthermore, applications of selection methods frequently require that studies be made to evaluate their utilities. Many aspects of selection are thus involved, including validity and validation, job analysis, job performance measurement, selection practices, and recruiting.

Validity and validation are a primary concern of psychologists using selection methods. All selection decisions are predictions of future behavior, and all involve error. People may be accepted for employment yet subsequently fail, whereas those who would have succeeded if accepted may be rejected. The aim is to minimize selection error.

The traditional approach used to accomplish this purpose is known as *criterion-related validation*. The criterion-related validation approach can lead to inaccurate estimates of prediction error. The sample of applicants or job incumbents may not be representative of the applicant population or the number of people in the sample may be insufficient. The measure(s) of job performance may be inaccurate. Commonly used supervisory ratings of performance, for example, can be unreliable or biased. Extraneous influences may distort the performance measure(s). In conducting validation research, psychologists seek to control these and other sources of potential inaccuracy in obtaining estimates of prediction error.

ISSUES

Debates over the validity of selection procedures are common. Limitations of the traditional criterion-related approach to determining the validity of selection methods have been noted, and alternative approaches have gained both professional and legal recognition. They are referred to as *content validity* and *construct validity*.

Content validity refers to the relevance of the tasks, items, and other aspects of a selection method. In contrast, construct validity is theory oriented. To establish the construct validity of a selection procedure, a psychologist seeks evidence to support or refute hypotheses on which the method is based. Both approaches to determining the validity of a selection procedure focus on the method rather than on the criterion of job performance and the relationship of the selection procedure to the criterion, as does criterion-related validity. Both content and construct validity approaches to establishing the validity of a selection procedure are controversial.

Related to issues concerning the validities of selection procedures are issues with respect to bias, especially of psychological tests, criticized as being "culturally biased" and discriminatory to minorities. These criticisms arise from the fact that minority groups tend to obtain lower scores on many tests, paper-and-pencil ability tests in particular. Attempts have been made to develop "culture-free" tests, but they have not been successful. Psychologists have conducted many studies to ascertain whether tests are biased against minorities when used in vocational selection. Debate over the results of such studies has been lengthy. Whether the use of ability tests in personnel selection is fair, however, raises issues that pertain to how tests are used in selection. Legal issues have emerged that involve not only psychologists, but also many persons outside of the profession. These issues stem from the passage of the Civil Rights Act of 1964, which permits employers to use professionally developed ability tests as long as they do not use them to discriminate against minorities, women, and other groups protected by law.

VALIDITY GENERALIZATION

The assumption that selection procedures are specific to each situation and thus must be proved valid for each situation has long concerned psychologists involved in personnel selection.

The implications of research on validity generalization for employers who wish to use ability tests in selecting employees are clear. Acceptance, professional and legal, of methods for establishing the validity of tests without requiring validation studies for each situation would relieve employers of costly, and frequently not feasible, research. The employer, using appropriate job analysis methods, would be required only to demonstrate the comparability of jobs in his or her organization to those for which validity has been established.

EMPLOYMENT TESTS
INDUSTRIAL PSYCHOLOGY

D. L. GRANT

PERSONOLOGY

Henry A. Murray combined biological science, academic psychology, and clinical practice with the humanities to develop personology, a name that represents his focus on individuals in all their complexity. Also known as the need-press theory, it holds that the inner world of the individual (i.e., needs) interacts with environmental demands (i.e., press), leading to differentiated activity. Although simple in its general structure, personology is complex in its details, especially its emphasis on both the organic quality of behavior and its field orientation (i.e., the environmental context of human activity). In addition, personology sees the history of individuals and their present situation as equally important and emphasizes the unconscious basis of much human motivation. All of this is reflected in personology's complicated taxonomy and the multitude of classifications that Murray established.

Personology is replete with terms. For example, needs are inferred forces that organize perception, cognition, and action so as to transform an existing and unsatisfying condition. There are 20 such needs (e.g., achievement, affiliation, aggression, dominance, nurturance, order, sex).

The α press is the reality of the outside world, whereas the β press is that world as subjectively interpreted by an individual. Units of behavior, or actones, are a function of the individual and the environment. They are expressed by means of vectors, or particular patterns and modes of behavior, and are influenced by individual values. The total picture of an individual's functioning is referred to as his or her thema. It deals with the interaction between the need that is operating as well as the instigating press. Murray collaborated with Christiana Morgan to develop the Thematic Apperception Test (TAT), a widely used projective technique, to identify thema. Personology also bases its assessment of personality on personal documents—autobiography, correspondence, and creative works—especially in some of the research it has stimulated.

Personology emphasizes the study of ordinary individuals in natural settings, holding that its ultimate concern is the explanation and prediction of an individual's activities in everyday life. Personology holds that researchers themselves are instruments in psychological research, and that attention must be paid to their precision and rigor. Personology's research efforts have ranged from cross-cultural studies and literary analyses employing the TAT to Murray's psychological assessment of two Melville novels: *Moby Dick* and *Pierre*. It has been used to study the Freud–Jung relationship and the life narratives of, among others, Nathaniel Hawthorne, Eleanor Marx, and Richard Nixon.

From a critical point of view, personology has been described as a theory of motivation rather than a complete theory of personality, failing to account for ways in which motives are learned and developed. Personology contains no set of explicitly stated psychological assumptions linked to its concepts in a way that would produce testable consequences. Its applications to counseling and psychotherapy are indirect; nevertheless, it is frequently cited by humanistic psychologists and narrative psychotherapists who focus on the client's script, personal mythology, or life story. The TAT and its many adaptations are widely used projective techniques, suggesting that such concepts as needs, presses, and themas have a practical utility, at least for some practitioners. Some so-called postmodern psychologists find personology's taxonomy stultifying but resonate with its interest in literature and mythology, its sequence of analysis (or "deconstruction") followed by "reconstruction," and its refusal to focus on trivial issues in psychology. Indeed, Murray and his followers have spearheaded the study of creative imagination's role in addressing the problems of contemporary life—human relationships, value construction, and world peace.

IDEODYNAMICS
IDIOGRAPHIC–NOMOTHETIC PSYCHOLOGY
PERSONALITY THEORIES

S. KRIPPNER

PERSUASIVE COMMUNICATIONS

Most of civilization is the result of persuasive communication. Political leaders, preachers, parents, and advertising in its various forms all depend on creating "imprints," or communications that last. True persuasive communication exists only among humans and a few of the higher apes.

One can establish a rank order of persuasion techniques, ranging from logic to emotions. The highest form of persuasive communications is based on inspiration. It can be offered in the forms of hope, of giving courage, and of believing in oneself. When an appeal achieves this emotional experience, it has reached the most convincing form of communication.

Facts and logic are poor as persuasion methods because any change of belief requires readjustment, a most painful and highly emotional trauma.

Persuasive communication is much more a matter of the heart than of the brain. Good communication, no matter what the medium, must mobilize the senses. The people communicated with must smell, feel, and hear the message in a direct fashion. Understanding is not enough. Identification, empathy, and shared emotions are the keys to persuasiveness in almost every field.

ADVERTISING
MOTIVATION

E. DICHTER

PETS

Interspecies social interaction, whether predator–prey, curiosity–companionship–play, cooperation, or contact, has occurred throughout history. Dogs, adopted about 10,000 years ago, were perhaps the first pet species for *homo sapiens,* serving as co-hunters, as protectors of fields and granaries, and as meat. The human–pet bond is a unique relationship. Pets permit almost total freedom to relate, and they offer faithful, intimate, noncompetitive, and nonjudgmental associations. They may provide comfort and security against intruders, darkness, physical attack, boredom, and perhaps loneliness. A pet can serve as a silent interlocutor. A pet can also stimulate spontaneity and creativity; release pent-up energy and tension in the role of playmate; and help teach responsibility and human values in the role of dependent other. Most important, pets serve as vehicles for clear, direct responses—being loved and giving love go hand in hand, while abuse and neglect result in avoidance and rejection. Also, by acting out biological functions and sexual interactions, a pet can help educate children to understand natural phenomena.

ANTISOCIAL PERSONALITY
LONELINESS

F. DEUTSCH

PHENOMENOLOGICAL METHOD

Phenomenology looks at immediate experience and attempts to describe it with as little bias or interpretation as possible.

Phenomenology, phenomenological psychology, and the phenomenological method have many meanings. These stem from independent developments in philosophy (e.g., Husserl), psychotherapy, clinical assessment, psychiatry, and humanistic psychology. Phenomenology is empirical to the extent that it studies observable phenomena.

The phenomenological method maintains that personal experience can be scientifically studied and hence be a source of reliable data. The method consequently is not antagonistic to, or a replacement of, the natural science model of empirical psychology. Phenomenological data compensate for scientific psychology's lack of experiential content, undervaluation of subjective phenomena, and overdependence on behavior.

GENERAL FEATURES

The phenomenologically oriented psychologist, especially when beginning to study a phenomenon, is open to and trusts experience. Technical expertise and sophisticated training are put aside or reduced temporarily; implicit assumptions are made explicit and then suspended. Experiential accounts of others (clients, students, children, and subjects in a study) are listened to and taken seriously.

Phenomenological puzzlement leads to good questions. A question is good because, first, it reveals a grasp of what is already known, and second, it is sensitive to gaps in this knowledge.

Good questions initiate inquiry (we appreciate a phenomenon); they serve as a guide (we feel we are on the right—or wrong—track); and

they act as a check (we wonder if we are answering the question that began the research). Good questions can take different forms: "Why is that so—and does it matter enough to find out?"

The phenomenological method describes things as they are—not as we think they are. The phenomenological psychologist asks "What is it?" before asking "Why is it so?" The "stimulus error" is minimized because experience is not described in terms of what we know about physiology, childhood sources, or environmental determinants.

THE CONTRIBUTION OF GESTALT PSYCHOLOGY

The Gestalt psychologists championed the strategy of beginning with, relying on, and constantly referring to their own and other's phenomenology. The tradition continues in perception. The viewpoint is also represented in social psychology and cognition.

To solve a problem, there first has to be a realization that there is a problem. Then the problem has to be restated in a way that directs, guides, and maintains the search for a solution. "A question well put is a question half-answered."

PHENOMENOLOGICAL METHODS

Phenomenological accounts are subjective and hence open to distortion. Nevertheless, experiential content can be captured with some reliability. Several empirical methods transform qualitative experience, through systematic procedures, into quantitative data.

The most frequently used phenomenological method is the case study. A few people (or even just one), purposely chosen because they clearly exemplify a phenomenon, are studied in detail. Open and unstructured interviews and introspective reports are typical procedures. Other methods use brief self-reports (protocols). These illuminate quantitative details. Debriefing statements at the end of a study, another type of phenomenological account, inform the investigator of efforts, omissions, and misinterpretations that otherwise might be overlooked.

These phenomenological accounts, by remaining close to their experiential sources, capture the richness and uniqueness of the individual. Experiential qualities, lost in the usual aggregation of statistical data, are restored.

The phenomenological method can be faulted for only marginally fulfilling the criteria of precise definition, strict control, manipulable variables, and exact measurement. Personal feelings and thoughts are hard to know, express, and understand. The method is not easy to carry out or to teach to others, and it is difficult to know whether you have succeeded. There is the paradox of using experience to examine itself.

ETHOLOGY
IDIOGRAPHIC–NOMOTHETIC PSYCHOLOGY
ILLUSIONS
IMAGELESS THOUGHT
PHYSIOGNOMIC PERCEPTION
STRUCTURALISM

M. S. LINDAUER

PHENYLKETONURIA

Phenylketonuria (PKU) is a rare genetic metabolic disorder (about 1 in 16,000 births in the United States) in which the incomplete oxidation of an amino acid (phenylalanine) can lead to brain damage and severe mental retardation. Symptoms of PKU are usually absent in the newborn period. Later, mental retardation becomes the most important symptom. The majority of untreated phenylketonurics show mental retardation, usually severe. They tend to have lighter skin, hair, and eyes than unaffected family members. Many neurologic symptoms and signs, especially affecting reflexes, occur. Both petit and grand mal epileptic seizures are common in older children. Also common are hyperactivity, psychotic states, and an unpleasant body odor caused by the presence of phenylacetic acid in the urine and sweat.

GENETIC DISORDERS
MENTAL RETARDATION
SEX CHROMOSOME DISORDERS

J. L. ANDREASSI

PHILOSOPHICAL PROBLEMS IN PSYCHOLOGY

There are two philosophical problems in psychology around which the remaining problems cluster—the problem of the nature of human beings and of the philosophy of science. The attempts of individual scholars to develop a theory of humankind are not adequate in spite of the impressive scholarship so evident in these one-person efforts.

The complexity and scope of the problem are so great that its resolution will require a large team of generalist researchers whose expertise covers the full range of knowledge, from the physical, biological, and social sciences to the humanities. If we view a human being as a machine, which tends to be the view from the natural sciences, then a deterministic description typically follows. However, if we view a person as an existential being, then a free-will position is typically taken. This contrast also lies behind the philosophic commitments that separate humanistic psychologists from scientific psychologists.

The part–whole problem and the problem of values also lie at the nexus of human nature. The relationship between the parts and wholes of complex phenomena is the critical point at issue in the part–whole problem. If a whole can be completely accounted for by its parts, then it is simply a conglomerate that is reducible to the parts (e.g., a pile of bricks). However, if a whole is not reducible to additive parts, it has emergent properties—that is, properties that cannot be accounted for by the properties of the parts (e.g., the wetness of water is not a property of either hydrogen or oxygen). Elementism claims that a whole is nothing but the sum of the parts, whereas holism claims that a whole is more than the sum of the parts. With regard to the nature of values, the major problem is whether values are relative or absolute. For example, is the value "Killing is wrong" to be viewed as a commitment that is correct regardless of the circumstances (the absolutist position), or does it depend on circumstances (the relativist position)?

The remainder of psychology's philosophical problems fall under the banner of the philosophy of science. These include such problems as the logic of discovery, the nature of induction, the nature of knowledge, how to characterize scientific progress, the concept of paradigm, and the appraisal of theories. The induction problem refers to the fact that philosophers have not been able to specify the logical–conceptual basis for the scientist's ability to make valid inferences from empirical observations. For example, there is no guarantee that the $n + 1$th observed sample will yield the same probability level as the previous n samples. The central epistemological issue is that of specifying the criteria that justify a knowledge claim. The evolutionary theory takes the view that science is a continuous activity that advances by trial and error and a large number of small, cumulative steps. The revolutionary theory says that science is a discontinuous activity that advances as a result of a relatively small number of large steps—steps involving a shift in paradigm or worldview that provide a broader and deeper view of reality. The proponents of both theories use historical events as the evidential basis for their claims. It seems likely that aspects of both theories will be required for a complete

account of scientific progress. In its broadest sense, the problem of appraising theories is a synonym for philosophy of science because the ultimate goal of philosophy of science is to clarify the conceptual foundations of science, and conceptual foundations are embodied in theories. However, the narrower sense of theory appraisal refers to the development of a set of criteria for ascertaining the relative merits and shortcomings of theories. Such appraisal includes all of a theory's properties, including its philosophical presuppositions. The major goal of theory appraisal is to provide a method for the selective retention of the relatively small number of theories having the greatest potential for advancing the science in question.

Since the full range of psychology goes beyond science, psychology has some problems that emerge from within the discipline in addition to those it has inherited from philosophy of science.

EPISTEMOLOGY
GENERAL SYSTEMS
LOGICAL POSITIVISM
MILL'S CANONS
PHILOSOPHY OF SCIENCE

J. R. ROYCE

PHILOSOPHICAL PSYCHOTHERAPY

Philosophical psychotherapy produces changes in behavior and acquires emotional control by modifying thought processes relative to one's life outlook. A person's belief system affects personality as forcefully as environmental stimuli. Philosophical beliefs can be called internal stimuli. Often beliefs and attitudes play a decisive role in directing actions and govern the manner in which people respond to a given situation or set of stimuli.

EXISTENTIALISM
PSYCHOTHERAPY

W. S. SAHAKIAN

PHILOSOPHY OF SCIENCE

Science is humanity's most effective way of understanding and benefiting from nature. The scientific approach to problems is applied to questions ranging from the fundamental constitution of matter to the existence of life after death. Its goal is to understand and make explicit the process of scientific inquiry, perhaps thereby improving the way science works, and helping its application to younger fields such as psychology.

Aristotle, Newton, and Descartes as practicing scientists wrote treatises on method, but it was not until after the scientific revolution and the success of science as an institution that a real need for a philosophy of science arose. In the nineteenth century, a philosophical movement called positivism arose, basing itself squarely on a Newtonian concept of science, and seeking to extend this scientific method to social science and social control. In the twentieth century, philosophy of science was started as a formal discipline by the Vienna circle of logical positivists. Their picture of science was a formal version of most people's picture of science: The scientist is a disinterested investigator whose extensive observations ultimately produce powerful mathematical theories that slowly improve with each scientific generation.

However, the positivist's explication of science has proved inadequate. Other philosophers and historians of science demonstrated that science was a more human and less austerely rational affair. T. S. Kuhn argued that scientists often see what they want to see and irrationally defend their positions. To Kuhn, science does not slowly accumulate an ever better understanding of the world, but undergoes periodic revolutions in which an old viewpoint is replaced by a new one, not just by weight of evidence and cogency of reasoning, but by winning more converts and replacing out the old guard.

GENERAL SYSTEMS
LOGICAL POSITIVISM
POSITIVISM
SCIENTIFIC METHOD

T. H. LEAHEY

PHOBIAS

A phobia is an irrational fear that may manifest as fears of specific animate or inanimate objects, such as fear of snakes (ophidiophobia); fear of a defined group or class of people (xenophobia, fear of foreigners; andro-phobia, fear of men); fear of impending or anticipated occurrences (astro-phobia, fear of lightning; school/test phobia, fear of school or of exams); or a fear of virtually anything else imaginable. Following are a few of the other major phobias frequently reported in the clinical literature:

Phobia	Fear of
Acrophobia	High places
Agoraphobia	Going out of the house
Claustrophobia	Closed spaces
Cynophobia	Dogs
Cypridophobia	Venereal disease
Electrophobia	Electricity, especially getting a shock
Genophobia	Sex
Gynophobia	Women
Hodophobia	Traveling
Hydrophobia	Water
Hypnophobia	Sleep
Kakorrhaphiophobia	Failure
Mysophobia	Dirt
Pathophobia	Disease
Thanatophobia	Death

Although the objective assessment of any fear typically is open to debate with regard to what extent and under what circumstances real dangers are posed by the feared object or event, two criteria, unrelated to the appraisal of potential danger, differentiate phobias from rational and nonneurotic fears.

First, phobias have an obsessive nature. A phobic individual is often compelled to dwell on the feared thing far more than is necessary under the objective circumstances.

A second characteristic that differentiates a phobia from a realistic fear concerns the way in which anxiety is handled. A phobia typically produces so high a level of anxiety that it is immobilizing, preventing the person from acting in a way that could prove effective in alleviating the anxiety. What delineates the diagnostic criterion between a phobic fear and generalized anxiety is not always agreed on, but seems to depend on the concreteness of the feared object or event.

CAUSES OF PHOBIAS

There is no single universal explanation of the etiology of phobias. It is generally agreed, however, that some phobias may have direct events preceding their onset and others may not. This kind of event is called

the precipitating trauma or traumatic event, and may or may not be viewed as the direct cause of the phobia, depending on the theoretical orientation of the psychologist making the judgment. Three chief models of phobia are the psychoanalytic, the behavioral, and the cognitive.

The Psychoanalytic Model

Freud categorized phobia as part of the constellation of symptomatic neuroses he called "anxiety hysteria" *(Angst hysterie),* which also includes conversion hysteria. A phobia is an expression of repressed sexual fantasies, usually of an Oedipal nature, in conflict with defenses mustered to help contain these feelings.

The Behavioral (Social Learning) Models

The behavioral, or social learning, explanations of phobia focus on how an individual learns an inappropriate anxiety-evoking response to a stimulus that was initially neutral or unexciting. There are three main paradigms used: classical conditioning, operant conditioning, and modeling.

The etiology of a phobia was the subject of investigation in one of the first major experiments in behavioral psychology, still a landmark decades after publication. John B. Watson and Rosalie Rayner induced a phobia in Albert, an 11-month-old boy, by using the classical conditioning model associated with Pavlov and his eponymous dog.

According to the operant conditioning paradigm of B. F. Skinner, phobias develop not only from adventitious, or even intentional, pairing of stimuli, but also from a person's intentional, voluntary operations on the environment and the consequences of these operations (or reinforcers).

The modeling (observational learning) paradigm, developed extensively by Albert Bandura, suggests that phobias are learned—at least in part—by direct exposure to the anxieties and irrational fears of another, especially one to whom we feel connected, or feel a certain empathic attachment.

The Cognitive Model

The cognitive–dynamic view of phobia represented by Albert Ellis further dissects and clarifies the thinking processes involved in the distortion. Connections that are associated with the idea of "This is good," argues Ellis, become positive human emotions, such as love or joy, and those associated with the idea that "This is bad" become negative emotions, colored with painful, angry, or depressive feelings. A phobia is an illogical and irrational connection, associating "This is bad" or "This is dangerous" with things that really are not.

Other Explanations

Existential thinkers, such as Rollo May and Victor Frankl, view phobia as a reflection of the alienation, powerlessness, and meaninglessness in modern life, a consequence in part of industrialization and impersonalization. Other humanistic psychologists, such as Abraham Maslow, see phobia as they do neurosis in general, as a failure in personal growth, a thwarting of the possibilities of human potential.

Some theorists have focused on the physiological and genetic aspects of phobia. Edward O. Wilson sees phobia as a remnant of our genetic evolution. "In early human history," Wilson says, "phobias might have provided the extra margin needed to insure survival."

TREATMENT OF PHOBIA

Partisans of each of the theories discussed use techniques and methods of treating phobia consistent with what they accept as its cause. Psychoanalysts, believing it to be a product of repressed memories hidden under layers of defense, use free association, dream analysis, and interpretation to strip away the layers and get to the core of the conflict. Then, through a catharsis—a sudden emotionally charged freeing of the repressed—the patient can overcome the phobia and recover.

Behavioral psychologists have developed an impressive armamentarium of techniques for treating phobia. Two of the widely used paradigms are systematic desensitization and flooding.

Systematic desensitization is a form of classical conditioning in which anxiety-evoking stimuli are paired with inhibitory responses, either through imagination (vicarious desensitization) or in real-life situations (*in vivo* desensitization).

Flooding "is a method of treating phobias by rapid exposure in real life to the feared object or situation, maintaining maximum tolerable anxiety until it begins to diminish, then continuing closer and closer exposure until the patient or client is comfortable in the situation which was previously feared." Although it is considered a rapid method and effective, at least in the short term, it does expose the patient to high levels of anxiety, levels that some consider too high and possibly dangerous.

The process of rational-emotive therapy is characterized by the therapist's communication (often highly dramatic) to the patient of the distortions in his or her thinking. This is much like a teaching technique and is, in fact, geared toward helping the patient learn about how illogical thinking leads to illogical and phobic behavior patterns.

All four methods—psychoanalysis, systematic desensitization, implosive therapy, and rational-emotive therapy—claim high rates of cure. Empirical evidence tends to support this, at least insofar as comparison with disorders such as depression and schizophrenia are concerned.

ANXIETY
PERSONALITY DISORDERS

G. S. BELKIN

PHRENOLOGY

Phrenology, an outmoded theory of personality, originated with the speculations of the physician–anatomist Franz Joseph Gall. Intrigued by a personal inference that individuals with bulging or prominent eyes had good memories, Gall began to look for personality correlates of other features, such as broad foreheads, prominent jaws, and the like. Ultimately, he focused his attention primarily on the brain and skull, and founded what he called the new science of craniology. Knowledge of the brain and nervous system during the late eighteenth through the early nineteenth centuries was, at best, vestigial. In consequence, much of Gall's early work in developing his theory went toward the development of new techniques of dissection, perfection of the construction of models of the brain and skull, and the amassing of a unique collection of skulls. His basic belief was that mental functions are located in the brain, and that their exercise and perfection would lead to localized brain development. This, in turn, would lead to appropriate enlargement of the related areas of the surrounding skull. Thus, by close scrutiny of the skull and its various prominences, one could obtain a detailed and individualized diagnosis of an individual's personal qualities and characteristics. He was thus the first researcher to postulate what has come to be known as localization of brain function.

Around 1800, a pupil of Gall, Johann Spurzheim, joined him on a lecture tour to espouse the new science of phrenology (a term never used by Gall). A dynamic and convincing lecturer, Spurzheim changed the emphasis to stress mostly the detection of the presence of positive faculties and their modifiability by means of strategic training. The approach to "reading bumps" became less akin to medical diagnosis and more to fortune telling and charlatanry. Correspondingly, phrenology lost its popularity and acceptance by medical groups, but simultaneously became popular with the general public.

ANTHROPOLOGY
PSEUDOPSYCHOLOGY
TRAIT PSYCHOLOGY

M. E. REUDER

PHYLOANALYSIS

Trigant Burrow developed an approach to the study of psychopathology and social relations, which he termed *phyloanalysis* or *group analysis,* during the period from 1921 to 1950. Phyloanalysis means the analysis of psychological disorders common to human beings as a species in contrast to psychoanalysis, which focuses on individual disorders.

The central idea of phyloanalysis is that psychopathology is primarily caused by the encroachment of the cerebral symbol system on basic feeling processes, resulting in a pathological substitution of image perception for real perception. The basic method of group analysis is the group examination of the "immediate moment" in social behavior to reveal disruptions in perception and cognition.

Burrow was one of the first clinical researchers in psychology to conduct psychophysiological research to demonstrate the physiological signs that accompany defensive and nondefensive perception (which Burrow termed *ditention* and *cotention*). Although Burrow regarded his approach as a "social laboratory" more than a method of therapy, his ideas and methods foreshadowed many later developments.

GESTALT PSYCHOLOGY
GROUP PSYCHOTHERAPY

J. T. HART

PHYSICAL ATTRACTIVENESS

Beginning with Charles Darwin, anthropologists have long tried to discover universal standards of attractiveness. Darwin's painstaking observations finally convinced most scientists that culture sets the standard, and thus it was futile to search for universals. Any lingering hopes of identifying sweeping standards were shattered in Clellan Ford and Frank Beach's landmark survey of more than 200 primitive societies. They, too, failed to find *any* universal standards of sexual allure.

Sociobiologists have revived hopes that more sophisticated sociobiological theory and research techniques may finally enable scientists to pinpoint some aesthetic universals. In one promising study, Judith Langlois and Lori Roggman found evidence that the Greek's golden mean may serve as the standard of appeal.

Other sociobiologists have tested the hypothesis that men and women prefer faces that, in a sense, have it all—faces that combine the innocence of childhood with the ripe sexuality of the mature. Early ethologists observed that men and women often experienced a tender rush of feeling when they viewed infantile "kewpie doll" faces—faces with huge eyes, tiny noses and mouths, and little chins. Symonds proposed that men and women should be aroused by faces that possess features associated with maturity, especially lush, adult sexuality (for example, thick hair, dewy skin, and full lips) and/or mature power (for example, high cheekbones or a firm jaw and chin). Most recent evidence finds that people like faces that possess both assets, which might have large eyes and a small nose, combined with full sexual lips and a strong jaw and chin. Whether these preferences will turn out to be universal is not yet known. Historians remind us that in any society standards of beauty often change at a dizzying rate.

EVIDENCE THAT PEOPLE ARE BIASED IN FAVOR OF THE PHYSICALLY ATTRACTIVE

Scientists find that most people, most of the time, are biased in their reactions to attractive people. There seem to be four steps in the stereotyping process, and they are as follows:

1. Most people know that it is not fair to discriminate against the unattractive (they would be incensed if others discriminated against *them*), and yet . . . .

2. Privately, most people take it for granted that attractive and unattractive people are different; generally, they assume that what is beautiful is good, and what is unattractive is bad.

3. Most people treat people who are considered to be attractive and people who are considered to be average better than they treat the people who are considered to be unattractive.

4. As a consequence, a self-fulfilling prophecy occurs. The way people are treated shapes the kinds of people they become.

There is evidence that people perceive attractive–unattractive people differently. In one classic experiment, researchers showed college men and women yearbook photographs of men and women who varied markedly in appearance and asked them their first impressions of the students. Young adults assumed that handsome men and beautiful women possessed nearly all the virtues. They assumed that the good-looking were more sociable, outgoing, poised, and interesting; that they were warmer, more exciting, and more sexually responsive; and that they had better characters, were more kind, nurturant, modest, strong, and sensitive. On only one dimension were young adults suspicious of good looks; they did not expect attractive people to make especially good parents.

Good looks might have a bit of a dark side. For example, Dermer and Thiel asked college students to rate college women who varied greatly in attractiveness. In general, subjects assumed that attractive and average women possessed more appealing personalities and were more socially skilled than unattractive women. In this study, however, researchers also documented some ugly truths about beauty. Subjects expected attractive women to be more vain and egotistical, more bourgeois, and less committed to their marriages (more likely to have extramarital affairs and/or to request a divorce) than homely women. Similar results have been secured by Eagley and coworkers.

Not only do people think that the attractive are special, but also they treat them that way. Teachers award good-looking grade school, high school, and college students with better grades than their less attractive counterparts for the same work. Executives are more likely to hire and promote good-looking men and women and to pay them more. Clinicians spend more time with good-looking clients, who get better care and do better in therapy. Unattractive people are more likely to be judged mentally ill. Attractive law-breakers are less likely to get caught, to be reported to the authorities, to be found guilty, and if convicted, to receive strict sentences. Good-looking people are less likely to be asked to help others, but more likely to receive assistance if they ask for help or are in trouble. Finally, society's biases ensure that good-looking men and women have a marked advantage at every stage of an intimate relationship.

There are some limits to people's preference for and biased treatment of the most attractive, of course. Some types of people seem to care more about looks than do others: Traditional men and women seem to care more about looks than do the less traditional, and men seem to care more about others' looks than do women. People care more about looks in some situations than in others: Appearance seems to matter most when people are getting acquainted; later, other things—intelligence, personality, and so forth—become more important. Appearance matters more in romantic settings than in others.

What effect does such stereotyping have on men and women? The evidence is mixed. The good looking and the unattractive are not as different as people assume them to be. Self-esteem and self-concept are positively related to how good-looking people *think* they are, but not to their *actual* appearance. The personalities of the attractive and unattractive differ only slightly, if at all.

Attractive and unattractive people do seem to differ in one respect. The good-looking appear to be more confident in romantic and social situations and to possess more social skills. People expect the good-looking to be socially appealing and treat them that way. The evidence suggests that a sort of self-fulfilling prophecy generally operates. People expect the good-looking to be charming, treat them that way, and as a consequence, they become more skilled. This self-fulfilling aspect of physical attractiveness was demonstrated in a study by Mark Snyder, Elizabeth Tanke, and Ellen Berscheid. Men and women at the University of Minnesota were recruited for a study on the acquaintance process. First, men were given a Polaroid snapshot and biographical information about their partners. In fact, the snapshot was a plant; it depicted either a beautiful or a homely woman. Men were asked their first impressions of her. Those who believed they had been assigned a beautiful partner expected her to be sociable, poised, humorous, and socially skilled. Those who thought they had been assigned to an unattractive partner expected her to be unsociable, awkward, serious, and socially inept. Such prejudice is not surprising: It is known that good-looking people make exceptionally good first impressions.

The next set of findings, however, was surprising. Men were asked to get acquainted with their partner using the telephone. Male expectations had a dramatic impact on the way they talked to their partners during the telephone call. That, in turn, created a correspondingly great impact on the response of the women. Men, of course, thought they were talking to a beautiful or homely woman; in fact, the women on the other end of the line varied greatly in appearance, although most were probably average in appearance. Nonetheless, within the space of a telephone conversation, women became what men expected them to be. After the telephone conversation, judges listened to tapes of the women's portion of the conversation and tried to guess what the women were like just from that conversation. Women who had been talked to as if they were beautiful soon began to sound that way. They became unusually animated, confident, and socially skilled. Those who had been treated as if they were unattractive also began acting that way. They became withdrawn, lacked confidence, and seemed awkward. The men's prophecies had been fulfilled.

No doubt this behavior caused the women to try harder, too. If the stereotypes held by the men became reality within the 10 minutes of a telephone conversation, one can imagine what happens when people are treated well or badly over a lifetime. In fact, researchers have found some evidence that the attractive are in fact unusually socially skilled and experienced.

The good-looking have an advantage and the unattractive have a disadvantage in life. However, a careful analysis of existing data makes it clear that the emphasis should be on the latter half of this sentence. If the relationship between appearance and a host of other variables—self-esteem, happiness, job opportunities, dating, and popularity—are examined, it is soon discovered that the relationship between appearance and advantage is not a monotonically decreasing one. The data make it clear that the extremely attractive have only a small advantage. What is really important is to be at least average.

DRESS
HALO EFFECT
PERCEPTUAL TRANSACTIONALISM
PYGMALION EFFECT

E. HATFIELD

PHYSICS AND THE BEHAVIORAL SCIENCES

In classical physics, the universe is considered to be a huge machine, running blindly on and on, with all of its parts, including humankind, functioning as mere cogs predetermined to play their roles. This has led to the belief that the future of any part of a system or any system itself could be predicted with perfect certainty, if its state at any time could be known completely in all of its details. In addition, scientists have concluded from these basic premises that they could observe and analyze the universe, including humans, in a completely objective fashion.

A NEW PHYSICS

One hundred years after classical physics reached its zenith, a new physics, based on relativity theory and atomic physics, shattered the major concepts of classical physics. Einstein responded to these new developments with the lament, "All my attempts to adapt the [classical] theoretical foundation to this [new type of] knowledge failed completely. It was as if the ground had been pulled out from under one, with no foundation to be seen anywhere . . ."

The classical foundation that the new physics undermined included (a) absolute space, (b) absolute time, (c) the notion of elementary solid particles, (d) the deterministic nature of the universe, and (e) the notion that one could investigate and describe nature in a completely impartial and detached manner.

One of the pioneering experiments that dealt a death blow to the classical foundation was the single-hole and double-hole experiment using light. In this experiment, light particles were sent against a barrier with a single hole through which they could pass, and then they were directed toward a barrier with two holes. Behind each barrier, a photographic plate measured the movement of light particles. Experimenters found that even though they knew the initial conditions exactly, and kept them the same in both experiments, they could not predict what would happen to a single light particle. Classical laws said that experimenters could calculate where each particle would land on the photographic plate. However, this experiment showed they could not predict the behavior of individual particles.

Research on subatomic particles suggests that matter cannot be separated from its activity. Subatomic particles can be understood only in their dynamic context, their dynamic movement, and their interaction with one another. It might be said that the essence of matter is its activity, or the processes of interaction. Consequently, movement and rhythm are essential properties of matter.

This leads to the notion that it is impossible to understand much about any one particle before understanding all other particles because of the basic interconnectedness of the subatomic world. There seems to be a universal interconnectedness of all things and events throughout the universe.

Another finding that has grown out of the research into subatomic physics is that there are methodological limits to our ability to know. It is theorized that if researchers are to determine exactly the position of a particle, then it is not possible for them to know anything about its momentum, and if they determine exactly the momentum of a particle, they cannot know anything about its position. This phenomenon is known as Heisenberg's uncertainty principle.

As scientists penetrate deeper into matter, they do not discover "basic building blocks," but rather complicated webs of relationships among the various parts of the whole, and these connections always include the observer in some basic way. The human observer is the dynamic link in the chain of observational processes. We can never speak about nature without, at the same time, speaking about ourselves, for we cannot talk of nature without interacting with it and, therefore, without becoming a part of it. Some physicists suggest that we call the researcher a "participating observer."

Another implication for the researcher brought about by the new physics is that there is no way to predict individual events. Group averages can be predicted with a certain degree of accuracy, but individual subatomic events cannot be determined accurately.

The new physics suggests that: (a) all things are interconnected; (b) all actions are interactions; (c) all things are fluid, dynamic, and evermoving; (d) nature cannot be reduced to fundamental entities; (e) the behavior of one thing is not determined by some fundamental law, but is influenced by all the properties of all the parts; (f) consciousness and motivation or purpose are integral parts of the world; and (g) to explain something means ultimately to show how it is connected to everything else. These tenets suggest that we move away from the classical mechanistic, deterministic view of the world to one that is holistic, where everything interacts and interinfluences everything else. This new view of the nature of things cannot be lightly dismissed, as it is based on experiments of great precision and sophistication, and on a consistent and strict application of mathematical rules. In addition, the new physics is founded on a more fundamental knowledge than the old classical physics because the new includes the old as a limiting case that is applicable to both the atomic dimension and the larger dimensions productively treated by classical physics.

A BEHAVIORAL SCIENCE CONSISTENT WITH THE NEW WORLD VIEW

Behavioral scientists who continue to divide human beings and their environment into ever smaller parts in their quests to understand and predict behavior (a term applied to this approach is *reductionism*) are out of synchrony with the world discovered by the new physics. Two approaches in the behavioral sciences consistent with the new physics are the Individual Psychology of Alfred Adler, who developed his theories during the early part of the twentieth century, and General Systems Theory described by Ludwig von Bertalanffy. These two approaches match the discoveries of the new physics in a comprehensive and consistent fashion. Human beings are viewed as conscious, purposeful, decision-making, dynamic, interacting persons interconnected with everything about them, who influence and are influenced by other people and things.

DETERMINISM
FIELD THEORY
GENERAL SYSTEMS
PHILOSOPHY OF SCIENCE
PHYSIOLOGICAL PSYCHOLOGY (NONREDUCTIONISM)

G. H. ALLRED
J. M. HARPER
R. A. WADHAM

PHYSIOGNOMIC PERCEPTION

Physiognomy refers to expressive perceptions of persons, events, and things. A red patch is not only small in size, among other physically measurable and literal attributes, but it is also "exciting, hot, and energetic." Metaphoric, figurative, and symbolic language often capture physiognomic meanings. A related but more sensory phenomenon is synesthesia. Stimulation in one sense (perceiving the color red) touches off another sensory mode ("hearing" a high note).

QUALITIES OF PHYSIOGNOMY

Physiognomic properties are felt to be inherent in the object itself, that is, perceptual rather than associative. A tree *is* sad—it does not just remind you of something sad or make you feel sad. Physiognomic feelings are direct, spontaneous, and immediate rather than calculated. Memory and reflection provide labels, and social custom guides reactions, but they usually do not originate the physiognomic experience.

THEORIES AND APPROACHES

Comments on physiognomy can be traced as far back as Homer, but the first comprehensive and still influential work was that of Charles Darwin. He argued that facial and other bodily signs of emotion were rudimentary fragments of the original emotional displays of our animal ancestors. Darwin had world travelers test his theory. They reported cross-cultural similarities in emotional expression.

The Gestalt psychologists referred to physiognomy as tertiary qualities. Perceptual experience goes beyond the sum of its physical and physiological parts. There are emergent properties such as unity or organization, *prägnanz* and closure, good form and good continuation, figure–ground, and the "demands" of field forces.

Heinz Werner considered physiognomy to be the first and most primitive kind of perception. It demonstrates syncretism (bringing unlike things together); the nonseparability of perception from feeling and from movement; and, most generally, the holistic character of perception.

Less theoretical approaches measure individual differences in physiognomy, for example among artists and between the sexes. There are also correlational studies between physiognomy and personal attributes, such as creativity, imagery, and aesthetic sensitivity. Most studies, however, are aimed at demonstrating the presence of physiognomy.

The innate basis of physiognomic perception is indirectly supported by cross-cultural studies of emotion recognition. Similar judgments are found for facial photographs of happiness, surprise, anger, and most other basic emotions. Emotions are universally recognized by both technologically advanced and quite isolated cultures.

Physiognomy differs from other topics in perception; it cannot be easily treated in either sensory- or information-processing terms.

Nevertheless, in spite of these difficulties, physiognomy has several attractive features. Its study is holistic (nonreductionistic), phenomenological (experiential–descriptive), and interdisciplinary. Physiognomy is also a key factor in interpersonal communication. Training in physiognomic perception, if possible, might help reduce misunderstandings between people and cultures.

COGNITIVE COMPLEXITY
DRESS
FACIAL EXPRESSIONS
GESTURES

M. S. LINDAUER

PHYSIOLOGICAL NEEDS

Human beings and other complex mammals have few essential physiological needs—mainly for water, food, oxygen, and, arguably, sleep. This discussion concentrates on the need for water and for food.

THIRST

Even lean individuals can survive 4 to 6 weeks without food, but will die of dehydration within 4 to 5 days. The average adult human loses about 21 quarts of water each day. Most of this "obligatory" water loss (about 11 quarts) is in the form of urine as part of a complex process that rids the body of toxic waste products of cellular metabolism. The rest is lost, in roughly equal proportions, through evaporation from the lungs, in sweat from the skin, and as moisture content of fecal matter.

How do we know when and how much to drink? From introspection, as well as Cannon's classic work on the subject, one would infer that thirst is related to dryness of the mouth and throat. Indeed this is so commonly associated with thirst that we undoubtedly respond to it as a conditioned stimulus. However, extensive research has shown rather unequivocally that one can be thirsty when the mouth and throat are wet, and that the elimination of sensory feedback from the mouth and throat does not alleviate thirst in a person in need of water.

The organism's water needs appear to be metered by brain mechanisms that give rise to the sensation of thirst when the body's water stores become depleted. These brain mechanisms seem to be sensitive to at least two different signals that may come into play under different circumstances. Short periods of water deprivation result primarily in a loss of water from the general circulation, producing a state of hypovolemia (low volume) and low blood pressure. When the deprivation is continued, water is drawn out of cells to compensate, at least in part, for the dangerously low volume in the circulatory system. With prolonged water deprivation, this "cellular dehydration" accounts for 65 to 70% of the body's water loss, and vascular hypovolemia for the remaining 30 to 35%.

Cellular hydration appears to be metered by osmoreceptors that have developed a special sensitivity to the movement of water across their membranes or may respond to changes in their total size (water loss results in cellular shrinkage).

HUNGER

Life requires energy (commonly measured in kilocalories, or kcal). We obtain energy from three principal food groups: (a) carbohydrates, which are converted into glucose (the principal fuel for nearly all cells); (b) proteins, which are broken down into amino acids that are recombined to build and rebuild muscle tissue and are used as fuel by the liver; and (c) fats, which are stored mainly in adipose tissue in the form of free fatty acids and glycerol until other nutrients have been used.

It appears that hunger and satiety originate in brain mechanisms that collect information about the body's energy supply. The most widely accepted theory holds that hunger is proportional to the neural activity in a "center" located in the lateral hypothalamus, a region also implicated in the regulation of thirst. Satiety, according to this theory, is caused by the activation of the immediately adjacent medial hypothalamus.

Over the years, many puzzling questions have been asked about this hypothalamic theory of hunger and energy regulation. Damage to the lateral hypothalamus abolishes eating in experimental animals (recovery may occur after weeks or months of intragastric feeding). However, it is not clear that the effect is necessarily attributable to destruction of a hunger center rather than to an interruption of some of the major pathways through the area. Nor is it certain the observed lack of eating reflects a loss of appetite.

Although the mechanisms that transmit relevant information are not yet understood, contemporary investigators generally believe that hunger and satiety may also reflect the availability of other nutrients, such as free fatty acids, ketone bodies, and glycerol, and/or the state of the body's fat stores.

CHEMICAL BRAIN STIMULATION
DIGESTIVE SYSTEM
HOMEOSTASIS

S. P. GROSSMAN

PHYSIOLOGICAL PSYCHOLOGY (NONREDUCTIONISM)

Any serious consideration of a nonreductionist approach to physiological psychology calls for a prefatory definition in an effort to achieve a thorough comprehension of the pivotal term *reductionism*. The order ranges

Levels of integration

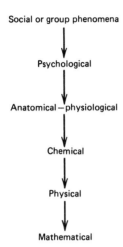

Social or group phenomena

↓

Psychological

↓

Anatomical–physiological

↓

Chemical

↓

Physical

↓

Mathematical

Figure 1. Hierarchy of the sciences arranged according to levels of complexity.

from physics, the simplest, to sociology, the most complex (Figure 1). The reductionist believes that all the diverse forms of nature are continuous and result from different combinations of the same basic elements. Reductionists conclude that the ultimate nature of the universe is reducible to those fixed and indivisible atomic building blocks. According to reductionists, that is the way to understand all aspects of nature.

At one time, the reductionist could have safely clung to the belief that at some time in the future, sociological, psychological, biological, and physical events would all be explained in terms of the fixed and eternal building blocks of physics. However, the absolutistic reductionist now is confronted by the embarrassing discovery of contemporary physics that atomic particles themselves have very elusive properties, hardly a dependable base on which to erect a firm theoretical structure.

REDUCTIONISM IN BIOLOGY

For its particular area of investigation, biology segregates living things, both plants and animals. Subdivisions of biology deal with cells (cytology), tissues (histology), anatomy or morphology, physiology, and embryology. Cells, tissues, organs, and organisms have properties beyond those found in molecules. Among them are organization, coordination, control, adaptation, growth or duplication, and repair. Although there are no phenomena in living systems that are not molecular, there also are none that are only molecular.

The cell shows a certain characteristic unity, pattern, order, and integration not found in the molecular constituents of cells. The organism also shows properties that cannot be inferred from its constituent organs. The word *organism* refers to organization, the hallmark of the living thing, plant or animal. It acts as a unit—as a system, not as a collection of independently acting, helter-skelter organs, tissues, cells, or molecules.

Opposed to the notion of reductionism is the concept of wholeness and levels of integration. According to holism, each cell, tissue, organ, or organism is more than the sum of its parts. A converse statement would say, in effect, that in describing a cell in terms only of its component molecules, some aspects of that cell would be left out. Knowledge of the individual parts would not yield understanding of the whole, except by seeing the role of the parts as an expression of the whole organism.

The concept of integrative levels may help to clarify a nonreductionistic approach to natural events. According to this notion, the order of sciences in Figure 1, from physics up to sociology, reflects levels of integra-

tion. Thus, in place of reductionistic continuity, there is discontinuity at each level, beginning at physics. At each higher level, new qualities emerge that were not apparent at lower levels. The implication is that events at each level must be studied at their own level instead of being forced into a lower mold. To reduce phenomena at a higher level to a lower level would be to lose the attributes and structure of the observations that initiated inquiry.

THE ROLE OF THE HYPOTHETICAL CONSTRUCT

In some sciences, such as physics and biology, some phenomena can be analyzed to the point at which sight and touch give out and the investigator is forced to resort to submicroscopical concepts, an undesirable situation, and certainly not one to be emulated. The relationship between what is perceived and what is conceived in explanatory terms sometimes becomes highly attenuated.

How can the troubles that reductionism presents be avoided? A different procedure is tried. This time, a field approach of the interbehavioral type is adopted in investigating psychological occurrences. A first requisite here will be to broaden views to include organism and stimulus object. With this change in orientation, the focus shifts away from the reductionist's concentration on the organism. The center of interest now concerns not what might be imagined going on inside the organism, but what transpires between the organism and stimulus object. Their interaction is of paramount, but not exclusive, preoccupation because there are additional observable variables. The interaction requires light to mediate visual and air for auditory interactions. No event occurs in a vacuum, so the setting factors or surrounding conditions in which the event occurs must be noted. All of these aspects of the total event must be seen in system, in their totality. It is hardly possible to overstress the equal emphasis given to the stimulus object, a view that certainly deglamorizes the organism.

Scientists come to accept certain events that fit a dependable regularity or "ideal of natural order" as self-explanatory. There is no need to go behind the scenes or to ask further questions. These occurrences are accepted as the starting point or base for explaining other things. Gravitation offers a convenient example. Note the gravitational interaction between the Earth and the Moon. It would not profit the astronomer to ask, "Why is there gravity?" The fact is that there is gravity, and the problem is to determine how, what, when, and where it operates. A rejection of the rock-bottom concept would be illustrated by an investigator who insisted on tearing apart the Earth and the Moon in an attempt to find the "cause" of gravity. Modern astronomers know better than to join such a foolish enterprise. They accept gravity as a fact that requires no further explanation, and go to work convinced that gravitation just *is*.

The concept of "rock-bottom" can be applied to psychological inquiry. For nonreductionistic physiological psychologists, the organism is rockbottom. They do not need to dissect it for some imaginary internal "cause" of behavior any more than the astronomer feels compelled to search within the bowels of the Earth or the Moon for the "cause" of gravity. Nonreductionists accept the organism as one of the variables and as a starting point for inquiry, an inquiry that relates the unitary, integrated organism to the stimulus and still other components of the total field. In summary, the difference between reductionistic physiological psychologists and the nonreductionistic variety is what they accept as rock-bottom. For the former, rock-bottom lies somewhere inside the organism's head; for the nonreductionist, the organism itself is rock-bottom.

THE ORGANISM AS A LOCUS OF VARIABLES

It would appear as if the nonreductionist's acceptance of the organism as rock-bottom implies a complete neglect of the biological aspects of the living copartner of a psychological event. This is not so. On the contrary, the nonreductionist looks on the organism as an important locus of variables than can affect the psychological event. An example using two scenarios in which a boy is reading a book can help make the point in a broad way. In both Event A and Event B, the boy and the book are interacting under definite and specific conditions. Among these are a certain illumination, quiet, 70°F temperature, and so on. However, prior to Event B the boy suffered damage to his brain. The important point is that Event A does not equal Event B. The brain concussion as a significant variable has changed the boy. Thus the boy in Event B is not the same boy as the one who participated in Event A. Therefore, the two events are not comparable. Reading that proceeded smoothly in Event A has been interfered with in Event B by a variable localizable within the biological matrix of the boy.

For the nonreductionist, such an explanation is rock-bottom and it is satisfying, but it only spurs the reductionist to search within the brain somewhere for a "why" kind of explanation for the boy's changed reading behavior. This procedure can only lead us back to "merely conceivable" explanations, which themselves call for verification before they can be used.

The difference between the reductionist and nonreductionist view of the nervous system can be summed up by characterizing the nervous system as a necessary but not a sufficient condition for proper verbal behavior.

Our consideration of the nervous system as a necessary but not sufficient condition of psychological occurrences paves the way for an expanded inquiry into the question of the organism as a locus of variables. Specifically, this calls for an inventory of the anatomical-physiological aspects of the organism that are involved in various psychological events. For example, in speaking, such parts as the oral cavity with lips, teeth, and vocal chords, and the trachea, lungs, and diaphragm participate in interactions. Yet even here there are no absolutes, as people without vocal chords or tongue have been able to produce speech. However, no amount of minute anatomical-physiological description explain how it is that one person speaks French, another speaks Swedish, and still another speaks Russian. Also, it is granted that a Beethoven born deaf would never have become the superb composer that he did. Yet the fact that he became deaf did not prevent him from composing the bulk of his work after his tragedy. There is a suggestion here of the domination of the flesh by the psychological. Certainly legs and arms are of crucial importance in football or baseball activities; but some leg amputees can swim. Nevertheless, any departure from an optimal intactness of the organism can act in a negative way. Blindness can prevent visual interactions, but so can absence of illumination. If we think of the former condition as more permanent, how about a sighted person's life imprisonment in a pitch-black dungeon? The two conditions are then equated, and, because either can have devastating consequences, neither condition is exalted above the other, as either can extinguish visual interactions. With the view of the organism as rock-bottom, the nonreductionist holds that a maximal intactness of the organism is desirable.

CONCLUSIONS

Because reductionism deals with imputed properties of the nervous system, we must take note of the circular reasoning underlying the hypothetical construct and reject theories that are "merely conceivable." As an alternative, the organism might be regarded as a locus of variables that can either facilitate or interfere with psychological events. As such, they are considered part of the total psychological event. A nonreductionist view avoids problems such as treating the nervous system (a) as causal (i.e., as producing psychological action) and (b) as having dual functions, biological and psychological—problems created by a reductionistic approach.

DETERMINISM
FUNCTIONAL PSYCHOLOGY
MIND–BODY PROBLEM

N. H. Pronko

PIAGET'S THEORY

Beginning in about 1960, a theory of the development of intellectual competence, formulated by Swiss biologist and philosopher Jean Piaget, came to dominate thought about the development of intellectual competence from infancy through adulthood. The theory focused on the development of the child's thinking; in particular, logical thinking. It maintained that, in the course of development, a child's thought undergoes a series of fundamental changes such that the later ways of thinking are dependent on, yet qualitatively distinct from, the earlier ones, and always moves in the direction of greater logical consistency. Subsidiary theories of Piaget's treated the development of moral judgment, perceptual development, the development of images, and memory development—from the perspective of how these are constrained by the various levels and sequences of our intellectual competence and functioning.

GENETIC EPISTEMOLOGY

Piaget's theory of intellectual development sought to make a contribution to another discipline, *genetic epistemology*. This discipline, originally named by American psychologist James Mark Baldwin, is more properly an interdisciplinary affair, drawing on philosophy, psychology, logic, biology, cybernetics, and structuralism. It treats all issues that bear on the questions: What is knowledge? From whence does it come? What conditions make it possible? The focus was on the development of knowledge within each life span, as well as the historical development of knowledge within the culture, particularly Western scientific cultures, over the course of the race's lifespan. Genetic epistemology, as seen by Piaget, attributed the development of knowledge and intelligence within the individual and within the culture to the same developmental and basically biological mechanisms and principles.

Piaget's contribution to genetic epistemology is largely methodological, since he proposed a way of resolving classical epistemological problems through the careful and prototypical observation of how infants, children, adolescents, and adults construct knowledge. The consistent motive behind his books on children's thought was inevitably the resolution of an epistemological problem through an analysis of how we come to think and know events in the various ways we do. For example, Piaget illuminates the classic epistemological question of whether, when no one is around, there is a noise when a tree falls in the forest by showing that our notion, firmly held as an adult, that objects exist and continue to exist independently of anyone perceiving them is a notion that takes about 2 years for each of us to construct. Indeed, the construction of the idea of the permanent object is one of the principal accomplishments of infancy. Similarly, as another example, the notion of *causality* is a complex epistemological matter, because we have no sure way of knowing which relationships between objects are caused and which are not. Piaget proposed that the causality issue can be clarified by an extensive description of how we construct our idea of causality in the first place.

Piaget's solution is *constructivism,* a position that holds that the fundamental categories and structures of our minds are not given *a priori*, but are constructed by us in the course of development through evolving systems by which we act on and transform the environment and our own minds. The succeeding levels or stages are always reformulations or reconstructions of the preceding way of acting on the world and validating knowledge and are always more consistent and more coherent than the preceding way.

THE EPISTEMIC SUBJECT

Since Piaget's theory of intellectual development is a competence theory, it follows that it is about an idealized person, a person who probably does not exist but who could exist and, if so, whose logical thinking would be indistinguishable from that of an ordinary person. The person is the *epistemic subject,* the pure knower who has no individual characteristics—no personality, sex, motivation (other than to know), culture, nationality—and the theory is about that person. Although the description of the child's competence to do logical problem solving may not tell us what the child in fact will do in a problem situation, it does say what the child can do if no other factors are present to mitigate the performance. In his later works, Piaget considered what procedures the child actually followed in solving problems and how these procedures or strategies utilized the child's competence. Although the epistemic subject merely understands and knows events, the ordinary person succeeds in any number of tasks, and often without any understanding of this success. In fact, the lag between success on a task and understanding the task is the typical finding.

The subject matter that the epistemic subject knows is restricted in the end to those truths that are necessarily true. Piaget's concern was in how we come to see many of the things that are true as necessarily true. For example, when $A = B$ and $B = C$, not only is it true that $A = C$, but it is necessarily true, it must be the case, and it could not possibly be otherwise. As another example, the whole is necessarily greater than any of its parts, and we know this, or deduce this, from knowing which is the whole and which is the part, and not in the end out of any need to measure or empirically compare the two in any way. At its core, the theory is about how we construct the truths we take to be necessary truths—the truths that have to be as they are and could not conceivably be different from what they are.

THE CLINICAL METHOD

In virtually all Piaget's research, the child is seen individually, given some materials or apparatus to manipulate, questioned about what he or she did in a relaxed clinical attitude with the questions tailored to the child's responses. What the child says or believes about what was done is important, but great emphasis also is placed on what the child actually does, how the problem is tackled, what errors the child makes, and so forth. Invariably, the child is asked to think about a common childhood in a new way, or to consider a new possibility in an ordinary childlike task such as lining sticks up in order by their lengths, and so on.

The tasks or problems set for the children are usually designed to reveal the structure of the child's reasoning about some significant epistemological question—nature of causality, necessity, implication, time or space, and so forth.

THE STAGES OF INTELLECTUAL DEVELOPMENT

The result was that all he claimed, at the end, was that he had developed a general outline or skeleton of a theory, one full of gaps to be filled in by others. Even with respect to the number of stages of intellectual development, there was some variation in his work from time to time, but most accounts set forth four main stages—the *sensorimotor stage* (0–2 years), with six substages; the *preoperational stage* (2–7 years), with two substages; the *concrete operational stage* (7–12 years), with two substages; and the *formal operational stage* (12 years and up). Within each stage and substage, Piaget frequently distinguished three levels: failure, partial success, and success.

In the final versions of the theory, development was viewed not as a linear progression through the stages, but as a spiral in which the differentiated forms and content at one level are reworked, restructured, integrated, or synthesized at the higher levels of the spiral. Invariant quantitative aspects of the clay ball are known before others.

Sensorimotor Stage

The six substages of this stage, covering roughly the first 2 years of life, show that the child exhibits the following characteristics and developments: (a) innate reflexes and inability to think, have purpose, or distinguish him- or herself from the surroundings; (b) reflexes extended into repetitive actions; (c) the ability to reproduce fortuitous, pleasant, and interesting events; (d) increased coordination of procedures to make the interesting things last; (e) discovery of new ways to produce interesting results; and (f) ability to represent absent events to him- or herself symbolically. The principal accomplishments are the construction of coordinated movements, which have a grouplike mathematical structure, the construction of representation, and intentionality. A specific tangible accomplishment is the construction of the permanent object.

Preoperational Stage

This stage, covering roughly the years between ages 2 and 7, has often been characterized more by what the child cannot do. During the first part of the stage, the newly emerging representational capacity is assimilated to the sensorimotor structures, and they are to accommodate it. The child also establishes a number of functional regularities, truths, and associations about the environment; for example, the aforementioned identity notion and certain functions and correlations. The children of this stage are distinguished by the surprising limitations in their thinking. Their thought, however, seems rigidly focused on only one aspect of a situation, often their own point of view (egocentrism), to the exclusion of other dimensions or perspectives. Preoperational thought, besides being centered on a single salient feature of an event, seems to flow in sequences of simple juxtaposition rather than sequences of logical implication or physical causality. Thus, children's reasons for their responses are often preposterous fabrications or justifications at any price.

Concrete Operational Stage

The errors the child makes during the preoperational stage are corrected in the following stage, but not uniformly or all at once. The sense of the qualifier, *concrete* in the title of the stage, is that the operational solution to the problems (that is, one based on a system of reversible mental actions) is worked out separately for the various contents of the problems. For example, the conservations are acquired by the child in the following order: number, length and mass, area, weight, time, and volume.

Formal Operational Stage

The system of reversible operations becomes further coordinated and extended in the next stage, the formal operational stage, which begins at about 11 or 12 years of age. The prior classification competence is extended to the combinatorial competence of the child's being able to consider all possibilities and to vary all but one in an analysis of a physical event. The ability to vary, mentally and hypothetically, all but one of the possible aspects of a situation means that the child can invent objects and situations that could not possibly exist in reality. Thus reality is subjected to possibility, and form can be considered and manipulated apart from its content, unlike with the concrete operational child.

The fundamental problem for the theory, and one for which no convincing answer was found, is the problem of novelty and spontaneity. How does new knowledge arise out of a cognitive structure that did not, in any discernible way, contain the new knowledge? Moreover, once new knowledge emerges, how does it come to be seen as necessarily linked to other knowledge?

COGNITIVE LEARNING STYLES
CONCEPTUAL LEARNING AND DEVELOPMENT

EPISTEMOLOGY
LEARNING THEORIES

F. B. MURRAY

PICK'S DISEASE

Pick's disease is a relatively rare form of atrophy of the cerebral cortex typically circumscribed to the frontal and/or temporal regions. Similar to Alzheimer's disease, Pick's disease develops in middle life, usually between the ages of 50 and 60 years, and is classified as a presenile or idiopathic dementia. The behavioral syndromes of Pick's disease and Alzheimer's disease are fairly similar, and the only way to differentiate conclusively between the two entities is through microscopic studies of diseased tissue, although sometimes computed tomography (CT scan) may help to pinpoint the focal atrophy characteristic of Pick's disease.

The early stages of Pick's disease are characterized by lapses in social conduct, a loss of normal inhibitions, and a tendency to either overactivity or apathy. The more abstract intellectual functions, such as reasoning and memory, show a decline early on, while more concrete functions are initially preserved. Capacity for self-care and ability to cope with the environment become increasingly compromised. In later stages of the disease, intellectual deterioration is more general, and speech and movement are reduced to a few stereotyped sequences. In the terminal stages, mutism and contractures may develop, there is significant weight loss, and the patient is bedridden.

ALZHEIMER'S DISEASE
ORGANIC SYNDROMES
PARKINSON'S DISEASE

S. P. URBINA

PITUITARY

The pituitary (hypophysis) is a glandular structure located beneath the hypothalamus of the forebrain in a depression of the skull known as the *sella turcica* (Turk's saddle). For descriptive, embryological, and functional reasons, the pituitary is divided into two lobes: the anterior, or adenohypophysis; and the posterior, or neurohypophysis. The gland is connected to the hypothalamus by the infundibulum, or hypophyseal stalk. A schematic drawing of the pituitary is shown in Figure 1.

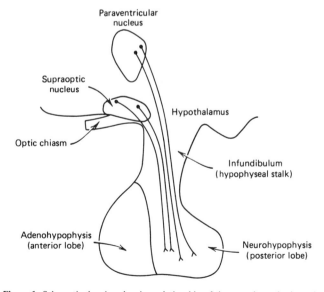

Figure 1. Schematic drawing showing relationship of the neurohypophysis to the hypothalamus. The adenohypophysis is functionally connected to the hypothalamus by blood vessels (not shown) called the hypothalamic–hypophyseal portal system.

The pituitary is often called the master gland of the body in recognition of its role in the control of many other endocrine glands. Actually, the portion of the pituitary for which this designation is appropriate is the adenohypophysis (the prefix *adeno* means gland).

ADRENAL GLANDS BRAIN
PITUITARY DISORDERS

B. M. THORNE

PITUITARY DISORDERS

The anterior pituitary secretes six hormones and the posterior pituitary secretes two hormones, all of which are important for human functioning. The anterior pituitary hormones include: (a) the growth hormone, which promotes growth; (b) adrenocorticotropin (ACTH), which controls secretions of another gland, the adrenal cortex; (c) thyroid-stimulating hormone (TSH), which controls the rate of secretion of thyroxine, a thyroid gland hormone; (d) prolactin, which promotes mammary gland development and milk production; (e) follicle-stimulating hormone (FSH); and (f) luteinizing hormone (LH). The last two are both important in reproductive activities. The two hormones secreted by the posterior pituitary are the antidiuretic hormone, which controls the release of body fluids, and oxytocin, which promotes labor contractions. Disorders in growth hormone secretion can be either in the direction of over (hypersecretion) or under (hyposecretion). Hyposecretion in childhood leads to dwarfism. Gigantism is often caused by a tumor of the pituitary gland, which, if diagnosed, can be treated by gamma irradiation. When hypersecretion of growth hormone occurs in the postadolescent period, the person does not grow taller, but the bones enlarge. This produces a condition known as "acromegaly," in which bone enlargement occurs in bones of the nose, the lower jawbone, the forehead, the hands, and the feet.

Overproduction of ACTH can lead to Cushing's disease. The face and body become puffy because of excess fat deposits; acne and excess facial hair growth also occur.

BEHAVIORAL GENETICS
BRAIN
PITUITARY

J. L. ANDREASSI

PLACEBO

The term *placebo* is derived from the Latin "to placate or please." A comprehensive definition has been given as "any therapy (or that component of any therapy) that is deliberately used for its nonspecific psychologic or physiologic effect, or that is used for its presumed effect on a patient, [symptom or illness] but which, unknown to patient and therapist, is without specific activity for the condition being treated."

The placebo response has been documented in pharmacological studies related to adrenal gland secretion, angina pain, blood cell counts, blood pressure, cold vaccine, common cold, cough reflex, fever, gastric secretion/motility, headache, insomnia, measles vaccine, oral contraceptives, pain, pupil dilation/constriction, rheumatoid arthritis, vasomotor function, warts, and so on.

Placebo effects are not limited to pharmacological agents, but have been well documented in studies of psychotherapy, acupuncture, hypnosis, and behavioral treatments for insomnia and pain (without in any way implying that these procedures do not have specific as well as documentable nonspecific effects). Surgical procedures such as ligation of mammary arteries for angina pain (in which electrocardiac changes were found with sham surgery) and dental procedures such as bruxism have been shown to be only placebo effects. The placebo response has been viewed as a nuisance variable in methodological studies. It can have powerful positive therapeutic effects.

THE PLACEBO EFFECT IN DOUBLE-BLIND TRIALS

The placebo response is best known as a methodological control procedure in pharmacological studies; medication is given double-blind so that neither the patient nor the researcher/clinical observer knows whether a medication or a placebo has been administered. Because of the reactive nature of all research and the effects of the interpersonal doctor–patient relationship and the drug-giving ritual, the expectation that relief of symptoms is imminent is communicated.

There are a number of methodological difficulties with the classic double-blind procedure, particularly in the so-called crossover design. Even in double-blind studies, either the observer or the patient may break the code (because of side effects or attribution of symptoms) and recognize which agent has been given. To prevent this from occurring, active placebos may be employed in which substances are used that mimic the side effects of the active drug. It is incumbent on the researcher to collect impressionistic data from both patient and observer concerning which agent they believe was administered. These perceptions often influence the patients' response more than their drug/placebo status. In spite of these and other limitations, the placebo control is still the method of choice in evaluating the specific effects of new pharmacological agents.

The placebo response is apparently mediated in all treatment contexts by expectancy, anxiety reduction, and so on that stem from the doctor–patient relationship. It is not related to suggestibility, gullibility, conformity, or related traits.

CLINICAL APPLICATIONS OF PLACEBO

Under what circumstances, if any, should placebos be actively prescribed? Most physicians admit that they have occasionally used placebos knowingly, but less than their colleagues, particularly those in other specialties. This unfortunate negative view of the placebo denies the significance of the doctor–patient relationship. Some critics argue that placebos are inherently unethical because deception is involved. From the point of view of the patient's contract with the physician to get better, any prescription or treatment, even if it is nonspecific, that may achieve this goal is reasonable. Indeed, it is unethical to deny the patient a treatment that may well be effective, inexpensive, and relatively safe.

The placebo has a number of clinical applications. First, it involves mechanisms that, once understood more efficiently, will lead to more rational methods of treatment in behavioral medicine. Placebo may also be a powerful diagnostic tool. Some physicians have learned to equate response to a placebo diagnostic test with the belief that the symptom (e.g., pain) is psychological and nonorganic. From the patient's point of view, there is no such thing as psychological pain. Rather, viewed in a positive light, successful placebo response indicates that the patients have the resources to manipulate and control their symptoms at some level.

The placebo effect is a significant part of the total treatment context. The nature of the doctor–patient relationship and the expectations of treatment and cure that are communicated in this context provide the basis for powerful nonspecific therapeutic interventions.

ACUPUNCTURE
BEHAVIORAL MEDICINE
HYPNOSIS
SELF-FULFILLING PROPHECIES
SUBLIMINAL PERCEPTION

F. J. Evans

PLANT BEHAVIOR

In recent years, some poorly controlled studies of sensitivity and responsiveness of plants to emotional stimuli have been given flamboyant publicity, thus arousing popular interest. Careful efforts to replicate the studies under conditions with better controls have failed to provide confirmation of the original findings, but the effects of the original reports on the lay public have not been eliminated.

The receptor processes of plants provide for responses to light, temperature, moisture, contact, gravity, and a variety of chemical stimuli, including both noxious and nutrient substances. The sensory processes of the plants are frequently diffuse and generalized throughout the individual, but often they are specific and narrowly localized.

The existence of "connector" functions between the receptor and effector foci in plants is readily confirmed by the distance between the two. The effector may be inches away from the receptor. The precise nature of the connector process has been the subject of conflicting theories. Some theories emphasize the diffusion of plant hormones; others stress plant nerves, and so on.

There are several different types of plant movements. Some of the microscopic plants glide along, probably as a result of protoplasmic streaming; others are propelled by the whiplike structures called flagella. Larger plants display movement (motor responses, effector behavior) as a result of growth patterns and turgor movements. In a planting where too many individuals are concentrated, the "competition" for light seems to lead to accelerated heightening of the plants—their elongation in the direction of the overhead sun. This is clearly a growth response. Such patterning of plant responses to light has been explained by the fact that the light reduces the concentration of the growth hormone "auxin," with the result that growth is inhibited on the brighter side while being facilitated on the shady side, and hence the bending. Twining movements by vines and tendrils seem to be responses to pressure effects as well as growth. Turgor movements are caused by changes in the concentration of water in the strategic cells; they provide support when cells are inflated by water and cause drooping when deflated.

"Fatigue" is demonstrated in plants when recovery after stimulation is incomplete. If the flytrap is prevented from closing and one of the hairs is repeatedly touched, the overstimulated receptor will no longer facilitate closure when the interference is removed—until after a lapse of time during which recovery occurs.

The behavior of the sensitive plant has given rise to efforts by psychologists to undertake controlled conditioning experiments. Such studies either have failed to establish conditioning or have presented positive findings that were not confirmed in replications.

In spite of the lack of uniform success in the conditioning studies conducted, plants do learn. The evidence reported in studies examining photoperiodicity in plants makes this abundantly clear. It may well be that the learning is a form of canalization rather than conditioning. Studies that demonstrate plant possession of "higher" mental faculties have received mixed receptions. Reports have been made of plants responding differentially to music, with classical music provoking positive responses and "acid" rock causing negative reactions. Similarly we find reports of plants responding differently, depending on how people talk to them. In the scientific community, these reports generally evoke profound skepticism. Other cultures are more acceptant and the ideas are strongly rooted in folk beliefs.

CANALIZATION
CIRCADIAN RHYTHM
CONDITIONING

E. L. Hartley

PLAY

Play is variously regarded as a "cobweb," an "omnibus term," or even as a category not useful for psychology. This is probably so because play manifests itself in so many forms that it is difficult to find a commonality of purpose or of form in all of these activities.

Play is used by some therapists as a treatment modality. A number of therapists have argued that children are generally unable to express their discontent and anxiety verbally, but, when allowed to express these in an unstructured milieu rich in fantasy-producing material such as toys, will work through their feelings in play.

Regardless of its form or structure, play is motivated by an interaction of the conditions of the player with those of the environment. The environment must contain elements conducive to an interchange with elements in the motivational state of the individual. This produces activity characterized by pleasure, interest, and reduction of tension. The elements that produce playful behavior may be similar to those that evoke curiosity and produce exploratory behavior.

Piaget, basing his taxonomy of play on his theory of cognitive development, argued that at each stage of development, certain types of play become predominant. Thus, in the sensorimotor stage (the first 2 years of life), practice play is common. This consists of repetition of patterns of movement or sound, beginning with sucking and babbling, finally developing into reacting with the environment in ways in which activities are varied systematically and their effects are monitored.

After the second year, the child moves into the preconceptual stage with an ability to master symbolic functions. Games reflect this change by becoming symbolic—games of make-believe. This is exemplified by the child's use of objects as things different from their apparent intention. Children also begin to place themselves in symbolic relationships with the external world.

During the intuitive stage (ages 4 to 7), children become interested in games with rules, structured situations, and social interactions with others. Gradually types of rules move from sensorimotor to collective, in that although rules are accepted earlier because they tend to lend structure and repetition, they later become accepted because of social constraints and demands of the group. Codification of rules appears about age 11 or 12, when competitive games become the norm.

Day identified five types of play and argued that overt characteristics do not always distinguish these types, but that they differ mainly in their source and telicity (goal). The five types are as follows:

1. *Exploratory play.* This type of play is motivated by uncertainty concerning objects and events in the environment.
2. *Creative play.* This is a more complex manifestation of exploratory play and requires the ability to symbolize as well as familiarity with the superficial or physical characteristics of the stimulus (toy).
3. *Diversive play.* Such play is seen as aimless interaction with the environment in general when boredom has set in.
4. *Mimetic play.* This play tends to be repetitious, structured, and symbolic. Its purpose is the achievement of competence and mastery.
5. *Cathartic play.* Therapeutic in goal, it may take any form or shape. Although intrinsic in the sense of arousal reducing, it does not seem to be associated with positive hedonic affect or pleasure.

PLAYFULNESS

Playfulness may be a method of comparing all forms of activity, including jobs and games, with the object of identifying the motivation to participate in these activities.

INFANT PLAY BEHAVIOR
PLAY DEVELOPMENT

H. I. DAY

PLAY DEVELOPMENT

Play is activity for its own sake and can be viewed, relative to children, as what they do when allowed to choose activities freely.

Play is a vehicle for learning that enables a child to grow cognitively, socially, physically, and emotionally. It is more than simply "a child's work," as within the context of play the child learns about interrelationships and is afforded the means to become an effective participant.

The development of play proceeds through stages that coincide with the child's cognitive and social development. Children initially pass through a period of solitary play, in which play is independent of activities of others and there is minimal communication. Parallel play is characterized by children playing beside, but not really with, each other. Cooperative play, the most complex form of play, occurs when children engage in organized activities, where leadership and elaborate social roles are assumed.

Regardless of age, boys tend to be more overtly aggressive than girls. Entrance into male groups is easier to achieve but harder to sustain; entrance to female groups is more difficult to attain but more long-lasting once achieved.

One predominant theory approaches play as the developmental opportunity to practice cognitive and social skills representational of the more stringent demands that are made at later ages. This developmental theory of play encourages varied, early, and controlled childhood experiences as precursors of optimum development.

The recapitulation theory conceptualizes play as an evolutionary link between the child and all biological and cultural stages that have preceded human beings on the phylogenetic scale. Human beings, the most complex of biological and social animals, require a longer time for the young experimentally to master the various demands imposed by the environment.

Observation, interpretation, and structuring of a child's play are methods of understanding the unique manner in which a child communicates with and perceives the world. Such approaches utilize play as a therapeutic method for treating behavioral or emotional disorders of children.

CHILDREN'S BEHAVIORAL STAGES
INFANT PLAY BEHAVIOR

A. THOMAS

PLAY THERAPY

Although children cannot easily describe their thoughts and feelings clearly to a therapist, they are often able to "show" their conceptions, experiences, wishes, and fears through their play. Common themes in children's play include (a) wish fulfillment, in which children play out interactions or experiences that they wish they could have, and (b) repetition of a negative experience, in which they continue to play a particular experience over and over again often with (c) reversed roles so that they take an active (often antagonistic) role where in real life they were a passive recipient. Initially a therapist may simply observe and allow the child to play. This play may serve both to help the therapist establish a positive relationship with the child and as a basis for the therapist to formulate an impression of the child's developmental skills, emotional conflicts, and interpersonal style. The content of the child's play, along with the level of conceptual complexity and organization demonstrated, the nature of interpersonal relationships and characters portrayed, and the conflicts, preoccupations, and affects emphasized may all serve an informative and diagnostic function for the therapist.

The actual mode of therapist intervention during play therapy varies widely. In nondirective play therapy, the therapist is fairly passive and supports the child with reflective statements to help the child play out personal conflicts and reach resolutions. Therapists with an ego-analytic orientation are more likely to make interpretations for the child at play to help the child understand and accept at a conscious level those emotional conflicts that have been repressed or denied. At another extreme are therapists with a social learning theory orientation, who would be more likely to focus on teaching a child how to play prosocially with others rather than on the affective content of the child's play. Depending on the particular needs and problems of various children, therapists may use more or less structure in their play therapy and may supplement this therapy with other types of intervention.

INFANT PLAY BEHAVIOR
PLAY
PLAY DEVELOPMENT

K. L. BIERMAN

POETRY THERAPY

Poetry therapy is a tool that every school of therapy may find room for in its armamentarium. The addition of poetry to therapy does not change the essential nature of either. All types of individuals can be involved, ranging from the mildly disturbed to the schizophrenic. However, the highly disturbed and those who are unable to comprehend what is going on are poor risks for this method.

BIBLIOTHERAPY
LITERATURE AND PSYCHOLOGY

A. LERNER

POLICE PSYCHOLOGY

Police psychology in its most primitive form began in 1916 when Lewis Terman attempted to use the then-current Stanford–Binet first edition to select police officers in California. Nothing much more happened until the middle of the twentieth century, when a few psychologists began to offer services to various local, state, and federal law enforcement organizations. The rapidly growing interest in providing psychological services to law enforcement began in the early 1980s and has been blossoming ever since. Given the considerable growth during the 1990s, police psychology is likely to be one of the principal directions of professional activity by the beginning of the twenty-first century.

WHAT IS IT?

Professional clinical psychology services (and eventually industrial–organizational services) to law enforcement involves new applications of the traditional activity of professional psychologists.

Assessment

Some psychologists are involved in selection of recruits for police training and selection of trainee graduates for positions in law enforcement. Psychologists also conduct fitness-for-duty evaluations of police officers who have been in stressful or damaging interactions while on the job. Psychologists have participated in the assessment procedures for promotion within the law enforcement community. They have particularly provided expertise in assessment centers. Psychological assessment techniques have been used to ensure that members of special teams (SWAT, hostage negotiation, undercover narcotics, and so forth) have the stability and stress tolerance for these jobs.

Intervention

Psychologists provide therapeutic services for police officers who are under stress (most of them), and crisis intervention services when police officers are involved in critical incidents, as well as grief counseling for police officers and families who are close to those officers who die in the line of duty. In addition, psychologists have begun to provide family counseling, counseling services for the children of police officers, drug and alcohol counseling, and development of peer counseling teams within the law enforcement agency.

Operations

Clinical psychologists have begun to provide such operational services as investigative hypnosis, dealing with mentally disturbed suspects, hostage negotiation, and serial offender psychological profiling.

Training

Psychologists provide training in police academies with respect to mentally disordered offenders, proper methods of dealing with citizens, impulse control, and understanding group behavior.

Psychologists also provide continuing education for police officers who must earn a certain number of credits every several years to maintain their sworn status. These presentations range from the psychology of driving to stress inoculation.

Strategic Planning

Some law enforcement departments have even begun to look to the future. Law enforcement has always been reactive to the stresses that crime places on the community. Modern police managers are beginning to look ahead to try to anticipate what community needs may eventually be for law enforcement. Psychologists, primarily industrial and organizational psychologists, have been providing consultations to police management in this new area of proactive response. Sensitivity training, restraint training, and politically correct anticipatory policy and training are just some of the areas that are being explored.

Research

All areas will work better when research involving local norms, base rates, and predictive effectiveness can be accomplished. Funding has now become available for such research, because all levels of law enforcement are becoming more aware that research and development funding pays long-range dividends in cost-effectiveness and cost-efficiency.

WHY IS THIS DEVELOPING NOW?

One of the greatest incentives for seeking psychological services by police agencies is that departments that have such services show a marked decrease in litigation against the department. Psychologists are helpful in insuring that people who will do the best possible job are selected as law enforcement officers and those already working are helped to maintain their skills and emotional stability in an extremely stressful work setting.

Modern police managers realize that for every dollar spent for psychological services, they will receive many hundreds of dollars in cost benefits.

WHAT IS NEXT?

As of 1993, there were probably fewer than 400 police psychologists in the United States. The numbers have been growing steadily. Division 18 of the American Psychological Association (APA) (Public Service) has a subsection of Police Psychology and Public Safety. Starting in about 1989 with 20 or so members, there were, in 1992, more than 300 members of this subsection. Standards are being developed and graduate institutions are beginning to offer courses in police psychology. The future for police psychology seems sure and certain.

BATTERED PEOPLE
BURNOUT
COMMUNITY PSYCHOLOGY
CRISIS INTERVENTION
DEPROGRAMMING
HUMAN RELATIONS TRAINING
MORALE IN ORGANIZATIONS
WORK EFFICIENCY

T. H. BLAU

POLITICAL VALUES

Rokeach defines "value" as "an enduring belief that a specific mode of conduct or end-state of existence is personally or socially preferable to an opposite or converse mode of conduct or end-state of existence." From this definition, it follows that "political values" pertain to conduct or end-states that relate to individual political behavior or to the political system in general, and whose preference may also be political in nature.

Many conceptual distinctions are made in applying the value concept. Lasswell and Kaplan, for example, differentiate two sets of values, *welfare values* (i.e., well-being, wealth, skill, and enlightenment) and *deference values* (i.e., power, respect, rectitude, and affection). Moreover, these values are associated with specific institutions through which they are achieved.

According to Lane, "the term *value* has two referents: what one desires, the object of a need or motive; and what one feels one 'ought' to desire, that which may be said to be the desirable."

In discussing the individual's core belief system, Lane links 10 needs, all psychological, with their associated values:

Needs	Values
Cognitive needs	Self-orientation, knowledge, enlightenment
Consistency, balance	Emotional harmony, self-consistency
Social needs	Affection, friendship, love
Moral needs	Rectitude, honesty, trustworthiness
Self-esteem	Self respect, respectability, status
Personality integration	Character, freedom from conflict, well-being
Expression and restraint of aggression and other impulses	Spontaneity and control
Autonomy, freedom	Autonomy, freedom
Self-actualization	Growth, development, maturation
Guides to reality	Security and safety; wealth, power, fame, respect

Lane then draws the connection between such values and the political system: "The values a person wants for himself, and for those he cares about, represent features of the core belief system that shape his thoughts about society and politics. We speak of politics as the authoritative allocation of values in society; hence in ascertaining 'who gets what' and 'who should get what' we are at the heart of political discourse."

VALUE CATEGORIES

In addition to the value categories advanced by Lasswell and Kaplan and by Lane, Rokeach offers a list of human values that distinguishes between instrumental and terminal values:

Instrumental Values	Terminal Values
Ambitious	A comfortable life
Broad-minded	An exciting life
Capable	A sense of accomplishment
Cheerful	A world at peace
Clean	A world of beauty
Courageous	Equality
Forgiving	Family security
Helpful	Freedom
Honest	Happiness
Imaginative	Inner harmony
Independent	Mature love
Intellectual	National security
Logical	Pleasure
Loving	Salvation
Obedient	Self-respect
Polite	Social recognition
Responsible	True friendship
Self-controlled	Wisdom

VALUES AND POLITICAL IDEOLOGY

Rokeach argues that two values, freedom and equality, underlie both personal ideologies and systems of political philosophy concerning the political desirability or undesirability of freedom and equality.

Rokeach holds that major political orientations are basically founded on different emphases regarding freedom and equality. Communism, for instance, places a high value on equality but a low value on freedom, and socialism also values equality highly but values freedom highly as well; capitalism, however, rates freedom highly but does not place equal stress on equality, and fascism ranks both freedom and equality low.

According to Rokeach, this two-value scheme does not apply to U.S. politics, where, because of a universally high valuation of freedom, the fundamental liberalism–conservatism dimension is reducible to variations in the single value of equality. In this case, liberalism places a higher value on equality than does conservatism.

ALIENATION (POLITICAL)
CONSERVATISM/LIBERALISM

S. LONG

PORTEUS MAZE TEST

Stanley Porteus originally published the Porteus Maze Test designed to supplement the Stanford–Binet IQ Test by measuring nonverbal aspects of ability (prudence, planning, and foresight). Porteus, then working with mentally impaired children, desired a test that could identify from among these children those with sufficient nonverbal skills to benefit from special services. The test has been used by itself and as part of Arthur's Point Scale of Performance Tests, a performance IQ test first published in 1915 and revised in 1947.

CULTURAL BIAS IN TESTING
INTELLIGENCE MEASURES
PENCIL-AND-PAPER INTELLIGENCE TESTS

M. J. ALLEN

POSITIVISM

Positivism is a strong form of empiricism that emphasizes the philosophy of science. Positivism begins properly with Auguste Comte. Comte pictured human history as passing through increasingly less superstitious ("theological" and "metaphysical") stages until a modern ("scientific") stage was reached. Science, Comte argued, was a matter of description, prediction, and control. The scientist begins with an accurate *description* of observable events from which laws mathematically describing natural regularities may be extracted. Once the laws are in hand, future events may be *predicted*. Finally, confirmed scientific laws make *control* of nature possible, as established causes may be manipulated to effect desirable and predictable ends. The good scientist should avoid attempting to give *explanations* of why things happen, particularly if these involve reference to unobserved entities. Postulation of unseen causes was regarded as a dangerous relapse into religious or metaphysical superstition.

In psychology, positivism has influenced behaviorism and given rise to operationalism. The positivistic psychologist aims to eliminate reference to mind from scientific psychology, believing that only thus can psychology avoid superstition. For the positivist, minds are unscientific, and psychology must be the description, prediction, and control of that which can be seen, behavior.

BEHAVIORISM
EMPIRICISM
OPERATIONALISM
PHILOSOPHY OF SCIENCE

T. H. LEAHEY

POSTMODERNISM

In the Age of Enlightenment, humans were in the center. Psychology as a science was founded on a conception of individual subjects, with internal souls and later internal psychic apparatuses. Psychology as science has been stongly entrenched in modern thought, most extreme in behaviorism and some trends of cognitive psychology. There has been a common search for extrinsic legitimation, the quest for universality, and abstract rationality, and the idea of commensurability.

Modernity encompasses not only the rationality of the Enlightenment but also the counterreaction of romanticism. The humanistic psychology, which originated at the time of the counterculture of the 1960s, has remained within the structures of modern thought, caught in a polarization to behaviorism. This concerns the quest for external legitimation, the dichotomy of the universal and the individual, the opposing of a technical rationality to a romanticist emotionalism, and the issue of quantitative commensurability versus qualitative uniqueness.

Behaviorism and humanism became two sides of the same modern coin—the abstraction of humanity from its specific culture. Here appears a double abstraction: The psyche studied by modern psychology—as consciousness or behavior—is abstracted from its cultural content as well as from its social and historical context. The cultural content and context are then taken as the accidental and local, and the psychological processes as the essential and universal.

PSYCHOLOGY IN A POSTMODERN CONDITION

In a postmodern age humans are decentered, the individual subject is dissolved into linguistic structures and ensembles of relations. The question arises as to the status of psychology as the science of the individual when the individual has been dethroned from the center of the world.

A postmodern discourse emphasizes the rootedness of humankind in a specific historical and cultural situation. There is a focus on the interrelations of a local context, on a linguistic and social construction of reality, and on the self as a network of relations. Postmodern thought involves a conception of knowledge as open, perspectival, and ambiguous; legitimation of knowledge through practice; and a multimethod approach to research, including qualitative descriptions of the diversity of men's and women's relation to the world.

There have been few discussions among psychologists on the consequences of a postmodern culture for the discipline. Three possible implications of a postmodern approach to the discipline of psychology may be outlined here as follows:

1. The very conception of a psychological science may be so rooted in modernist assumptions that it becomes difficult to understand men and women in a postmodern culture. Other disciplines, such as anthropology, have been more sensitive to the embeddedness of human activity in a cultural context and today provide the insightful knowledge of the relation of human beings to their world. If psychology has been the privileged way of modernity to understand human beings, a postmodern age may also mean a postpsychology age.

2. At the other extreme, contemporary psychology can be seen as a postmodern conceptual collage—a pastiche of recycled ideas and methods borrowed from other disciplines and combined according to the most recent consumer demands of a mass culture.

3. A third alternative would be that a postmodern discourse leads to a metatheoretical reconceptualization of the subject matter and opens new vistas for psychology.

A POSTMODERN PSYCHOLOGY?

With the emphasis on diversity and heterogenity in postmodern thought, it would give little meaning to outline a program for a postmodern psychology. Some implications of a postmodern discourse for the science and profession of psychology may, however, be outlined. They concern a reconceptualization of knowledge and research and a rehabilitation of professional knowledge. They involve deconstruction and social constructivism in psychology, a reinterpretation of the self, and systemic therapy.

Knowledge and Research

The recognition of the heterogeneous and noncommensurable contexts of the practical world involves a loss of hegemony for formalized experimental and statistical methods research. There is an acceptance of diverse ways of producing knowledge, with a move from knowledge as abstract, objective, and universal to ecologically valid, socially useful, and local. More practical forms of knowing are advocated, elevating the embodied knowledge of everyday life over theoretical knowledge. There is also a move from the knower to the known, from the knowing subject to the subject known, from the psychology of cognitive processes to epistemological investigation of the nature of the knowledge sought.

Narrative, hermeneutical, and deconstructive approaches are advocated. There is a multimethod approach with an emphasis on qualitative, interactive, and involved research. The research process is not a mapping of some objective social reality; research involves a coconstitution of the objects investigated with a negotiation and interaction with the very object studied. Conversation and social practice become the ultimate contexts in which the validity of knowledge is negotiated and ascertained.

A Rehabilitation of Professional Knowledge

The professional practice of psychologists is regarded as an important generator of psychological knowledge. Although generally discarded by academic psychology, the insights produced by these practices are, however, in line with philosophic analyses of knowledge in a postmodern age—given that they focus on local and narrative knowledge; on acceptance of the openness of practical knowledge; on the study of heterogeneous, linguistic, and qualitative knowledge of the everyday world; and on validation through practice. Knowledge becomes the ability to perform effective actions; the test for pragmatic knowledge is whether it serves to guide human action to intended goals. This does not imply a practice devoid of theory, but involves a shift in the focus of theorizing in psychology—from the interior of the individual to its relation to society, with the epistemological, ethical, and political issues involved.

A Deconstructive Social Psychology

There are a few trends within academic psychology that relate explicitly to a postmodern discourse, mainly in social psychology. Parker and Shotter thus argued for deconstructing social psychology, focusing on the deconstruction and rhetorics in text about humankind. The term *deconstruction* is a hybrid of *destruction* and *construction* and represents an effort to construct by destruction. Old and obsolete concepts are demolished to erect new ones. Deconstruction focuses on the self-contradictions in a text, on the tensions between what the text means to say and what it is nonetheless constrained to mean. Parker and Shotter follow Derrida, Foucault, and Lacan in looking at the internal contradictions of these texts and their social formation, uncovering the power relations at work and bringing forth the voices not expressed, such as the feminist work on the social construction of gender.

The Vanishing Subject

Postmodern authors reject a substantialized conception of the self at the center of the world, decentering it with a relational concept of subjectivity—the self exists through its relations with others as part of the text of the world. The focus on linguistic structures implies a decentering of the subject. The self no longer uses language to express itself; rather, the language speaks through the subject.

The unified subject of a humanist discourse is discarded. This essentialized subject is replaced by a provisional, contingent, and constructed subject, a subject whose self-identity is constituted and reconstituted relationally. Ken Gergen emphasizes the social construction of personal identities, in particular with the new communication technologies leading to a multiplicity of knowledge and a recognition of the perspectival nature of social reality. A saturation of the self occurs, transforming the self into a state of relatedness, to an embeddedness in a multitude of networks.

SYSTEMIC THERAPY

The professional field in which the implication of a postmodern linguistic shift has been taken up most explicitly is systemic therapy. There is a shift from the study of the psyche of the individual client to studying the family as a linguistic system. Pathology is no longer seen as residing in consciousness or in the unconscious but in the structures of language. The interactions and networks of a social group comes into focus. Indeed, the very term *psychotherapist* seems to be inadequate, for the therapist does not attempt to heal some interior "psyche" but works with language and, as a master of conversation, heals with words.

CONCLUSION

A postmodern discourse is at odds with the modernist base of modern psychology. The question that has been put forward here is whether the science of psychology is so rooted in modern thought that it cannot adequately grasp the relation of men and women to a postmodern world.

Some of the aspects of a psychology that addresses the postmodern condition have also been indicated.

A postmodern psychology would involve a move from studying the cognitive mechanisms of an internal psychic apparatus or inner experiences of a self-realizing self to examining the implications of practical activity in a linguistically constituted social world. This involves going beyond academic research to include the generation of knowledge by professionals and the epistemological, ethical, and political implications of this knowledge. In the current understanding of human beings, there is a move from the knower to the known, from the inwardness of an individual psyche to being in the world with other human beings.

The focus of interest is moved from the insides of a psychic container to the outside of the human world. Concepts such as consciousness and unconscious, self and the psyche, recede in the background, and concepts such as knowledge, language, culture, landscape, and myth appear in the foreground. There is a move from the archaeology of the psyche to the architecture of the current cultural landscapes.

ALIENATION (POLITICAL)
ECLECTICISM
EMPIRICISM
GENERAL SYSTEMS
HERMENEUTICS
METAPSYCHOLOGY
RATIONALISM
SYSTEMS THEORIES

S. KVALE

POSTTRAUMATIC STRESS DISORDER

The risk of exposure to trauma has been a part of the human condition since we have evolved as a species. Attacks by saber tooth tigers and twentieth-century terrorists have probably produced similar psychological sequelae in the survivors of such violence. Shakespeare's Henry IV appears to have met many, if not all, of the diagnostic criteria for posttraumatic stress disorder (PTSD), as have other heroes and heroines throughout the world's literature.

Posttraumatic stress disorder is unique among other psychiatric diagnoses because of the great importance placed on the etiological agent, the traumatic stressor. In fact, one cannot make a PTSD diagnosis unless the patient has actually met the stressor criterion, which means that he or she has been exposed to a historical event considered traumatic. Clinical experience with the PTSD diagnosis has shown, however, that there are individual differences regarding the capacity to cope with catastrophic stress so that, although some people exposed to traumatic events do not develop PTSD, others go on to develop the full-blown syndrome. Such observations have prompted a recognition that trauma, like pain, is not an external phenomenon that can be completely objectified. Like pain, the traumatic experience is filtered through cognitive and emotional processes before it can be appraised as an extreme threat. Because of individual differences in this appraisal process, different people appear to have different trauma thresholds, some more protected from and some more vulnerable to developing clinical symptoms after exposure to extremely stressful situations. Although there is a renewed interest in the subjective aspects of traumatic exposure, it must be emphasized that exposure to events such as rape, torture, genocide, and severe war zone stress are experienced as traumatic events by nearly everyone.

The diagnostic criteria for PTSD were revised in *DSM-IV* as shown in Table 1. Unfortunately, trauma is much more common than previously supposed, as shown by epidemiological research on Vietnam veterans, residents of a large American city, and female rape and incest survivors. These studies report current prevalence rates for PTSD as high as 15%.

Table 1   Posttraumatic Stress Disorder (*DSM-IV* Criteria)

A. The person has been exposed to a traumatic event in which *both* of the following were present:
  1. The person experienced, witnessed, or was confronted with an event that involved actual or threatened death or serious injury or a threat to the physical integrity of self or others
  2. The person's response involved intense fear, helplessness, or horror
  (NOTE: In children, this may be expressed instead by disorganized or agitated behavior)

B. The traumatic event is persistently reexperienced in *one or more* of the following ways:
  1. Recurrent and intrusive distressing recollections of the event, including images, thoughts, or perception
  (NOTE: In young children, repetitive play may occur in which themes or aspects of the trauma are expressed)
  2. Recurring distressing dreams of the event
  (NOTE: In children, there may be frightening dreams without recognizable content)
  3. Acting or feeling as if the traumatic event were recurring (includes a sense of reliving the experience, illusions, hallucinations, and dissociative flashback episodes, including those that occur on awakening or when intoxicated)
  (NOTE: In young children, trauma-specific reenactment may occur)
  4. Intense psychological distress at exposure to internal or external cues that symbolize or resemble an aspect of the traumatic event

C. Persistent avoidance of stimuli associated with the trauma and numbing of general responsiveness as indicated by *three or more* of the following:
  1. Efforts to avoid thoughts, feelings, or conversations associated with the trauma
  2. Efforts to avoid activities, places, or people that arouse recollections of the trauma
  3. Inability to recall an important aspect of the trauma
  4. Markedly diminished interest or participation in significant activities
  5. Restricted range of affect (e.g., does not expect to have a career, marriage, children, or a normal life span)

D. Persistent symptom of increased arousal (not present before the trauma) as indicated by *two or more* of the following:
  1. Difficulty falling or staying asleep
  2. Irritability or outbursts of anger
  3. Difficulty concentrating
  4. Hypervigilance
  5. Exaggerated startle response

E. Duration of disturbance (symptoms in Criteria B, C, and D) is more than 1 month

F. The disturbance causes clinically significant distress or impairment in social, occupational, or other important areas of functioning

Specify if:
  ACUTE: if duration of symptoms is less than 3 months
  CHRONIC: if duration of symptoms is 3 months or more

Specify if:
  WITH DELAYED ONSET: if onset of symptoms is at least 6 months after the stressor

Because of such findings, the *DSM-IV* no longer describes trauma as an *unusual* event.

The intrusive recollection criterion includes symptoms that are perhaps the most distinctive and readily identifiable symptoms of PTSD. For individuals with PTSD, the traumatic event remains, sometimes for decades or a lifetime, a dominating psychological experience that retains its power to evoke panic, terror, dread, grief, or despair as manifested in daytime fantasies, traumatic nightmares, and psychotic reenactments known as PTSD flashbacks. Furthermore, traumamimetic stimuli that trigger recollections of the original event have the power to evoke mental images, emotional responses, and psychological reactions associated with the trauma. Researchers, taking advantage of this phenomenon, can re-produce PTSD symptoms in the laboratory by exposing affected individuals to auditory or visual traumamimetic stimuli.

The avoidant–numbing criterion consists of symptoms reflecting behavioral, cognitive, or emotional strategies by which PTSD patients attempt to reduce the likelihood that they will expose themselves to traumamimetic stimuli, or if exposed, will minimize the intensity of their psychological response. Behavioral strategies include avoiding any situation in which they perceive a risk of confronting such stimuli. In its most extreme manifestation, avoidant behavior may superficially resemble agoraphobia, because the PTSD individual is afraid to leave the house for fear of confronting reminders of the traumatic event(s). Dissociation and psychogenic amnesia are included among the avoidant–numbing symptoms by which individuals cut off the conscious experience of trauma-based memories and feelings. Finally, because individuals with PTSD cannot tolerate strong emotions, especially those associated with the traumatic experience, they separate the cognitive from the emotional aspects of psychological experience and perceive only the former. Such "psychic numbing" is an emotional anesthesia that makes it difficult for people with PTSD to participate in meaningful interpersonal relationships.

Symptoms included in the hyperarousal criterion most closely resemble the symptoms seen in panic and generalized anxiety disorder. Whereas symptoms such as insomnia and irritability are generic anxiety symptoms, hypervigilance and startle response are more unusual. The hypervigilance in PTSD may sometimes become so intense as to appear like frank paranoia. The startle response has a unique neurobiological substrate and may actually be the most pathognomonic PTSD symptom.

The duration criterion specifies how long symptoms must persist to qualify for the (chronic or delayed) PTSD diagnosis. In *DSM-III*, the mandatory duration was 6 months. In *DSM-III-R*, the duration was shortened to 1 month. Based on longitudinal studies showing that acute recovery from trauma generally occurs within 3 months, the duration criterion in *DSM-IV* was shifted to 3 months. In other words, the complete PTSD syndrome will have to persist for at least 3 months before it can meet full diagnostic criteria.

Since 1980, there has been a great deal of attention devoted to the development of instruments for assessing PTSD. Keane and coworkers, working with Vietnam War veterans, developed psychometric and psychophysiologic assessment techniques that have proven to be both reliable and valid. Other investigators have modified such assessment instruments and used them with natural disaster victims, rape and incest survivors, and other traumatized cohorts. Research using such techniques has been conducted for the epidemiological studies mentioned earlier as well as in other studies.

Research indicates that PTSD may be associated with stable neurobiological alterations in both the central and autonomic nervous systems. Psychophysiological alterations associated with PTSD include hyperarousal of the sympathetic nervous system, increased sensitivity and augmentation of the acoustic-startle eyeblink reflex, a reduced pattern of auditory-evoked cortical potentials, and sleep abnormalities. Neuropharmacologic and neuroendocrine abnormalities have been detected in the noradrenergic, hypothalamic-pituitary-adrenocortical, and endogenous opioid systems. These data are reviewed extensively elsewhere.

Longitudinal research has shown that PTSD can become a chronic psychiatric disorder that can persist for decades and sometimes for a lifetime. Patients with chronic PTSD often exhibit a longitudinal course marked by remissions and relapses. There is a delayed variant of PTSD in which individuals exposed to a traumatic event do not exhibit the PTSD syndrome until months or years afterward. Usually, the immediate precipitant is a situation that resembles the original trauma in a significant way (for example, a war veteran whose child is deployed to a war zone, or a rape survivor who is sexually harrassed or assaulted years later).

If an individual meets diagnostic criteria for PTSD, it is likely that he or she will meet *DSM-IV* criteria for one or more additional diagnoses.

Most often these comorbid diagnoses include major affective disorders, dysthymia, alcohol or substance abuse disorders, anxiety disorders, or personality disorders. There is a legitimate question as to whether the high rate of diagnositc comorbidity seen with PTSD is an artifact of the decision rules for making the PTSD diagnosis, because there were no exclusionary criteria in *DSM-III-R*. In any case, high rates of comorbidity complicate treatment decisions concerning patients with PTSD, as the clinician must decide whether to treat the comorbid disorders concurrently or sequentially.

A book by Davidson and Foa reviews some of the remaining controversies about PTSD diasnostic criteria and some unanswered questions about the PTSD syndrome. Questions about the syndrome include: What is the clinical course of untreated PTSD? Are there different subtypes of PTSD? What is the distinction between traumatic simple phobia and PTSD? and What is the clinical phenomenology of prolonged and repeated trauma? In regard to the last, Herman has argued that the current PTSD formulation fails to characterize the major symptoms of PTSD commonly seen in victims of prolonged and repeated interpersonal violence such as domestic or sexual abuse and political torture. She has proposed an alternative diagnostic formulation that emphasizes multiple symptoms, excessive somatization, dissociation, changes in affect, pathological changes in relationships, and pathological changes in identity.

A final criticism comes from cross-cultural psychology and medical anthropology. For the most part, PTSD has been diagnosed by clinicians from Western industrialized nations working with patients from a similar background. Major gaps remain in the understanding of the effects of ethnicity and culture on the clinical phenomenology of posttraumatic syndromes. Researchers have only just begun to apply vigorous ethnocultural research strategies to delineate possible differences between Western and non-Western societies regarding the psychological impact of traumatic exposure and the clinical manifestations of such exposure.

The most successful interventions are those implemented immediately after a civilian disaster or war zone trauma. This is often referred to as *critical incident stress debriefing* (CISD), or some variant of that term. It is clear that the best outcomes are obtained when the trauma survivor receives CISD within hours or days of exposure. Such interventions not only attenuate the acute response to trauma, but often also forestall the later development of PTSD. Results with chronic PTSD patients are often less successful. Perhaps the best therapeutic option for mild to moderately affected PTSD patients is group therapy. In such a setting, the PTSD patient can discuss traumatic memories, PTSD symptoms, and functional deficits with others who have had similar experiences. This approach has been most successful with war veterans, rape and incest victims, and natural disaster survivors. For many severely affected patients with chronic PTSD a number of treatment options are available (often offered in combination), such as psychodynamic psychotherapy, behavioral therapy (direct therapeutic exposure), and pharmacotherapy. Results have been mixed, and few well-controlled therapeutic trials have been published to date. It is important that therapeutic goals be realistic, because in some cases, PTSD is a chronic and severely debilitating psychiatric disorder that is refractory to current available treatment. The hope remains, however, that growing knowledge about PTSD will enable the development of more effective interventions for all patients afflicted with this disorder.

**ANXIETY
CHILDREN'S FEARS
CRITICAL PERIODS
DESENSITIZATION AND REPROCESSING
DISASTER ANALYSIS
ENVIRONMENTAL STRESS
EYE MOVEMENT
FEARS THROUGHOUT THE LIFESPAN**

**MEMORY DISORDERS
STIMULUS GENERALIZATION**

M. J. FRIEDMAN

POWER

Power has been defined as a capacity or potential to influence others while resisting the influence of others and is described as an important motive in human action and interaction. In interaction with other variables (such as affiliation, inhibition, and aspects of maturity), according to De Charms and Muir, power can explain a great deal of human behavior. These authors emphasized the motivational aspects in their definition of power, describing it as a *need* to have impact and a *concern* over influencing others.

McClelland, for example, hypothesized an important relation between power and social maturity. He postulated four stages of power, which he felt were tied to levels of maturity within the individual.

Among other things, these efforts served to underscore an important consideration for objective psychology—that is, a concept such as power is neither good nor bad.

**AGGRESSION
LOCUS OF CONTROL
VIOLENCE**

S. BERENT

POWER OF TESTS

Hypothesis testing involves contrasting two rival hypotheses. The null hypothesis specifies that nothing unusual is happening. The alternative hypothesis specifies that something unusual is happening. For example, the null hypothesis might state that two groups have the same mean or that the correlation between two variables is zero. The alternative hypothesis can be directional or nondirectional. A directional hypothesis states the direction of the phenomenon: group 1 has a larger mean than group 2 or the correlation is larger than zero. A nondirectional hypothesis does not specify the direction of the effect, but states that the effect does exist: the two groups have different means or the correlation is not zero. Statisticians begin by assuming that the null hypothesis is true and reject the null hypothesis only if the observed results are quite unlikely under this assumption. Based on some assumptions concerning the study, for example, a random sample and a normally distributed dependent variable, the researcher can calculate the probability of rejecting the null hypothesis when it is true (α) and the probability of rejecting the null hypothesis when the alternative hypothesis is true (the power of the test). Because the researcher wants to reach the correct conclusion, good studies are designed to have low α and high power. A correct null hypothesis is unlikely to be rejected if α is low, and a correct alternative hypothesis is likely to be concluded if power is high.

Researchers generally use an α level of .05. They reject the null hypothesis only if the sample results are in the extreme 5% of the range of possible outcomes if the null hypothesis were true. When the null hypothesis is rejected, the researcher concludes that the results are significant and specifies the significance probability, that is, the α associated with the outcome. For example, the researcher may conclude that the correlation is significant at $p < .05$, meaning that the null hypothesis of a zero correlation could be rejected with an α less than .05. A more extreme result has a smaller significance probability, such as $p < .01$, or $p < .001$.

Because the traditional approach is designed to keep α low, researchers must be careful to ensure that the power of their tests is reasonably high. Power estimations can be made before data are collected, and research studies with insufficient power can be redesigned to improve power. There are four principal strategies to increase power: increase α, specify directional hypotheses, increase the sample size, and increase the effect size.

Increasing α increases power. Researchers are more likely to reject the null hypothesis when α is higher, so they are more likely to conclude that a correct alternative hypothesis is true. However, increasing α increases the risk of rejecting a true null hypothesis, an error that should be avoided. α levels above .05 traditionally are considered unacceptable, but higher levels can be used when power is extremely important and the ramifications of falsely rejecting the null hypothesis are not too costly.

A second way to increase power is to specify directional hypotheses. This allows the researcher to concentrate the α risk at only those outcomes that are consistent with the directional hypothesis. For example, a test on a correlation coefficient using a nondirectional hypothesis and an α of .05 might reject the null hypothesis for observed correlations below $-.60$ or above $+.60$. Outcomes between $-.60$ and $+.60$ are expected to occur 95% of the time for that study, whereas outcomes outside of this range are expected only 5% of the time when the null hypothesis is true. If the researcher could specify a directional hypothesis, such as a positive correlation, the decision might be to reject the null hypothesis for all correlations above $+.55$, because 5% of the expected correlations under the null hypothesis exceed this value. If the observed correlation were .58, the researcher could not reject the null hypothesis in favor of the nondirectional hypothesis but could reject the null hypothesis in favor of the directional hypothesis. By concentrating the α risk at one end of the possible set of outcomes, the researcher has a more powerful test. Unfortunately, if the directional hypothesis postulates the wrong direction, the researcher will not find significant results and will be in error. In the previous example, if the observed correlation were $-.63$, the researcher could reject the null hypothesis in the nondirectional test, but could not do so for the directional test that has been tailored for positive relationships. Researchers specify directional hypotheses only when the opposite result is inconceivable based on previous research, theory, or logic. For example, if all previous research has demonstrated a positive relationship between the two variables, the researcher would feel secure conducting a directional test.

A third way to increase power is to increase sample size. Statistics based on larger samples are more stable, allowing more precise estimation of population characteristics. This increased precision makes it more likely that correct alternative hypotheses are confirmed. In fact, research based on huge samples may have too much power because such studies may reject null hypotheses for trivial although statistically significant results. For example, a correlation of .02 may be significantly different from zero in a huge sample, but the relationship probably is too weak to be useful.

The effect size is the strength of the relationship being studied. Research on variables with large effect sizes has more power. For example, to demonstrate that different types of birds have different size eggs, one should compare ostriches and hummingbirds, with an enormous effect size, rather than compare chickens and ducks, with a smaller effect size. Studies investigating variables with a large effect size are more likely to reject the null hypothesis than studies designed to uncover small, more subtle effects. Researchers can select variables with strong relationships and choose ways to measure or control variables to maximize the effect size to have more powerful studies.

Researchers want studies with low α and high power, so they are likely to reach accurate conclusions. They generally control α by not allowing it to exceed .05, and they have strategies to increase power. A well-designed study may have a large α, a directional hypothesis, a large sample size, or a large effect size. The researcher considers all these options in designing a study that is likely to contribute meaningful information to the knowledge of psychology.

ERRORS (TYPE I AND II)
NULL HYPOTHESIS TESTING
SELECTION TESTS

M. J. ALLEN

POWER: STRATEGIES AND TACTICS

Power refers to the ability to make decisions that have an important impact and that involve others. Often, power involves controlling the behavior of others, although many times other people voluntarily accept the directives of power holders and do not feel any loss of independence. In everyday language, power refers to "getting one's way" and "having clout." Many people are socialized to distrust power, to feel that only evil and manipulative individuals are interested in acquiring it, and to feel that they themselves should avoid places where powerful people congregate. In reality, and like many complex issues such as economic incentives and government-sponsored housing programs, power is like fire. It can be used for good intentions, and it can be used to pursue evil goals. Power, especially the strategies and tactics for its implementation, can be viewed as a tool to be used in efforts toward the goals people set for themselves. Some individuals want to be associated with powerful people. Assume that an individual is one of four junior executives in line for a promotion to the senior executive ranks. Each of the four candidates has a sponsor at the vice presidential level in the large organization. The individual wants his or her vice presidential sponsor to have the power to have a decision implemented: the promotion to the higher level in the organization.

THE PLACE OF POWER IN PEOPLE'S PERSONALITY

Some people are more interested in acquiring power than others, and the most effective powerholders possess a combination of motives. Four motives or aspects of people's personality need to be analyzed. The need for power refers to people's desire to have an impact on the lives of others. The need for achievement refers to the desire to set and to work toward goals, such as starting a new business or inventing a new technology for personal computers. The need for affiliation refers to the desire to be with and to interact pleasantly with others. The fourth aspect of personality, impulse control, refers to the ability to set aside any of these motives when called for by the demands of the social situations in which people find themselves.

Leaders tend to be average to high in the power motive, and this should be higher than the affiliation motive. There must be limits to powerholders' need for affiliation because they inevitably make decisions that cause unhappiness among some people. However, there must be some affiliation motive, or powerholders run the risk of becoming tyrants who have no concern for the impact of their decisions on others. The achievement drive of powerholders must be high enough so that they set reasonable goals, but not so high that personal efforts to pursue the goals becomes paramount in their lives. Powerholders do not necessarily do all the work to accomplish their goals: they take steps to ensure that *others* do the work necessary to attain the goals. One reason why first-rate inventors or entrepreneurs sometimes become poor company presidents is that different motives are called for in different stages of a complex organization's development. To invent a new technology or to start a new business, a high achievement drive is necessary. If the technology or business is extremely successful, the power motive is necessary to manage the efforts of others involved in such organization efforts as accounting, finance, research and development, legal matters, manufacturing, marketing, and so forth.

USING POWER

The power motive alone is no guarantee of success. People must combine this motive with others so that there is a proper balance between power, achievement, affiliation, and impulse control. People must also learn strategies for the successful use of power. Although some of these strategies and tactics have a dark or manipulative side to them, many involve sensitivity to others, cooperative interaction, and the pursuit of goals that many people formulate in a democratic manner. When used in this positive manner, the intelligent and sensitive use of power can become part of effective leadership. At times, people without a power motive can become quite sophisticated about power. Often, these people learn that they need some knowledge of power to pursue their goals and that they are placed at a disadvantage if they avoid power and powerholders. For example, university professors who want a course of study introduced in their departments may find that even though they are uninterested in power they may find it necessary to know about it. These professors frequently learn that they must understand power to work through curriculum committees.

Stategies reflect people's careful planning about their future because they refer to complex sets of behaviors (e.g., resource and network development, developing the image of a winner) that will have many positive implications in their pursuit of power. Tactics, however, refer to more specific behaviors useful at a certain time and place in the pursuit of specific goals. Brislin developed an extensive list of both strategies and tactics useful in the acquisition and use of power, and examples of each are discussed.

SOME STRATEGIES IN THE ACQUISITION AND USE OF POWER

Most strategies involve the development of carefully thought out relations with others.

Developing a Network and Exchanging Favors

Power is an aspect of relationships among people, and most powerful individuals have cordial interactions with a wide variety of others. Although one image of a powerholder may be a deranged monarch ordering people to commit drastic deeds, reminiscent of a bad Hollywood movie, powerholders are most often cordial people who communicate well with others. This is especially true in a democracy, where people have various institutional supports such as the legal system, unions, and the media to complain about callous behavior emanating from leaders. Cordial relations with others are necessary because no one person has all the skills or knowledge needed to develop complex projects and to implement them. Assume that two executives want to suggest the development of a new product line. They must convince powerholders, necessitating communication skills. They must research the present marketplace, demanding a knowledge of survey methods, finance, production, and accounting. They must make predictions about the eventual consumption of the products, demanding a knowledge of distribution systems. In addition, legal concerns will be raised at many steps in the planning process. No two people can possess all this knowledge. The two will have to integrate the efforts and talents of others.

These efforts will be easier if the two executives know many other people who are part of a circle of acquaintances or network. People in one's network are not necessarily friends with whom one shares emotions. Rather, people in a network are useful to each other because they exchange favors. If people cease being useful to each other, they drop out of each other's network, although they may enter into a network relationship years later if they become mutually useful again. The exchanges of favors occur in a manner similar to that described by Cialdini. One person knows tax law. He or she exchanges a few key pieces of advice with a lawyer who knows what terms found in advertising can be considered part of the public domain. People who are knowledgeable about organizational developments through their active participation in the grapevine can exchange information learned for a variety of favors.

There is a sense of obligation in the exchange of these favors: people are expected to receive and to give. If people do not return favors, they are simply dropped from network membership and find themselves out of various information loops that formerly kept them up to date regarding developments in their organizations. Network development and maintenance may seem cold and unfeeling, and yet people must be able to exchange favors with others if they are to develop complex projects and if they are to keep themselves informed about goings-on in large organizations. Many powerholders know hundreds of people with whom they can exchange favors, but they cannot become deeply involved in the emotional lives of all of them. Becoming comfortable with network development is one of the necessities as people become more sophisticated about the nature of power in decision making.

Resource Development

To become an active participant in networks, people must have a resource that becomes the source of the favors they can offer. Seven categories of resources have been identified in the analysis of power: money, status, information, services, love and sex, goods, and the time and energy people can devote to various projects. Money may be the most easily understandable of the resources, because funds are almost always needed to start and to maintain projects. Furthermore, most people have competed for funds at some point in their lives (e.g., for a scholarship or a new project in their church) and so are aware of the power that access to money can bring. Money also represents one aspect of unfairness in the pursuit of power: Children who grow up with wealth and who are heirs to it have an advantage. Services are a possibility, especially in volunteer activities within people's communities. Individuals might ask themselves, "Where do influential people in my community meet?" Candidates (which differ from city to city) include the support guild for the opera or symphony, blood bank, youth sports, clubs, political action groups, college alumni organizations, and so forth. Then the individuals can exchange their services (e.g., editing a newsletter, volunteering for committee work) for access to the influential people, with the eventual possibility of calling on these people for favors. Another possibility for the nonwealthy is information. Individuals might make a point of developing knowledge about information that (a) everyone needs to know at some point but that (b) is not easily or widely available. Candidates include tax law, statistics, computer technology, and how to make effective presentations to the general public. At times, the information can be the names and unlisted phone numbers of influential people in one's network, as long as these people are not so widely known as to be easily accessible to everyone.

Developing a Positive Image and Becoming a Winner

People are better able to communicate with and integrate the talents of others if they have the positive image of a winner. A winner is someone with the reputation for being successful, for being able to get things done, and for being able to set and to achieve goals. When people have a reputation for getting things done, others want to become attached to them. In developing this positive image, Karl Weick suggests that people be aware of the strategy known as small wins. Instead of setting goals so ambitious that people run the risk of failure and becoming known as losers, Weick suggests that people divide projects into a set of winnable steps. As people achieve success in attaining these steps, they develop good reputations. A positive reputation allows them access to resources that in turn permits them to set the next, somewhat more ambitious goal.

Because one aspect of human nature is that others like to be associated with winners more than losers, people who achieve success in their winnable goals will attract individuals willing to become involved in future efforts. With these additional resources and colleagues, more work can be done along the route to the accomplishment of ambitious goals. A subtle aspect of this strategy is that the key people may want to keep their eventual goals a secret and to behave as if each of the smaller steps is the only objective they have at any one time. If the eventual goal becomes widely known, that will become the focus of people's attention, and a failure to attain it will tarnish reputations. If the smaller and attainable goals are in the forefront, the key people can claim success as each is achieved.

For example, an assistant professor in a psychology department may want to introduce a multicourse curriculum aimed at increasing sensitivy to cultural, ethnic, racial, and gender issues. If he or she proposes such a program as the first action, the plan may be turned down because of budget restrictions and because the program does not include the concerns of certain powerful and tenured professors. Instead, the professor might propose a set of steps, keeping the eventual goal to him- or herself. He or she might develop a unit on race or gender and integrate it into the current introductory, social, or developmental course. If the class has 30 students, 5 of them may be good public speakers. The professor could ask each of these students to prepare a short presentation on a concept in psychology that has been informed by the study of race or gender and have these students present their ideas in a departmental colloquium. Influential professors may receive a personal invitation. After this experience, the assistant professor can propose a new course and can later suggest that other courses be added as enrollment figures demonstrate the demand. With success achieved in these steps, the assistant professor becomes known as a winner and the likelihood of finding support for the more ambitious goal is increased.

SOME TACTICS IN THE ACQUISITION AND USE OF POWER
Tactics refer to specific and identifiable behaviors that allow people to gain the support of others and to deal with opposition to their proposals.

Trial balloons are similar to leaks, but the sources of ideas are usually attached to any communication with others. The ideal trial balloon contains the essence of a proposal but is presented in such a way that it can be disavowed if necessary. Furthermore, the potential of a disavowal has to be thought through so that it can be done in a manner that does not damage the image of powerholders. In national politics, trial balloons can be launched by a *former* cabinet officer or other former high ranking official. The official appears on a political talk show and says that the administration is considering a policy change. If the later response from political commentators and elected representatives is favorable, then the president can later introduce the formal proposal. If the response is highly unfavorable, the current administration can disavow the ideas by saying that they are not being considered and that the former official is simply stating the ideas of a private citizen.

Clear Images and Firsthand Experiences
In communicating with others to enlist their support, messages should contain clear images that will remain in their memories. People are exposed to so much information through newspapers, television, magazines, and interpersonal exchanges that they can easily be overwhelmed. Potential powerholders, who want attention to their proposals, have to compete for people's attention. One tactic is to personalize one's message.

Clear images can often be conveyed through firsthand experiences. People who become involved in firsthand experiences develop clear memories because their own actions and observations become part of their image of a policy issue. Firsthand experiences have more impact than reading or hearing about an issue because people become actively in-

volved, can ask questions that reflect personal concerns (in contrast to a journalist's personal concerns), and can reflect on others' responses to their concerns. For example, if there is a proposal to raise funds for a new leukemia treatment center, potential supporters could be given a tour of the current hospital facilities. There, they would meet several children carefully chosen for their attractiveness and articulateness. The people seeking support should stress that the prognosis for some of these children is good as long as modern medical treatment is readily available. The potential supporters would be encouraged to see for themselves that these children could receive much better treatment if the proposal could be implemented. As another example, recall the assistant professor who wants to increase course offerings in race, gender, ethnic, and cultural issues.

Sandboxes and Boogeymen
Some tactics are useful for dealing with opposition for one's proposals. One is to give the opponents a "sandbox," or a seemingly important task that has no long-term implications for policy development in an organization. The opponents become so busy playing in the sandbox that they leave the powerholders alone. This is a common tactic found on university campuses. Department chairs sometimes find themselves faced with an angry group of students who are opposing a policy change that will add more required courses. The chair then asks the students to do a study on the types of courses that university alumni have found most helpful both in job searches and career development. The students may busy themselves with this important-sounding study, but in actuality the department chair can make recommendations for required courses no matter what the results are of the study. If the chair finds that the report presents results consistent with his or her recommendations, then the study can be included in any formal proposal. If the chair finds that the report supports the students' recommendation for no new courses, then the study can be dismissed. Favorite reasons for the latter action include sample sizes too small, sampling biases, and the fact that the students had insufficient time for a definitive study.

Appealing to boogeymen is another tactic to deal with an opposition. Children learn about boogeymen as the source of severe punishment if they do not share their candy with friends or if they engage in behaviors that are interpreted as slights by other children. When applied to adult interactions, boogeymen are vague sources of power, not clearly visible, to which a powerholder can appeal.

BECOMING MORE SOPHISTICATED
Some people learn about power as part of their socialization when they see their lawyer and politician parents participating in networks, exchanging favors, developing complex plans, and working on their strategies and tactics. Others do not have access to the application of power when they are young and must learn about it as adults. One way to become more sophisticated is to participate in voluntary community activities. In addition to developing a network, people can observe the processes of coalition formation, communication of ideas, creation of a winning image, and so forth. A further possibility is to obtain a seat on the community activity's budget committee. No matter what proposal for the use of money is put forward, there is a guarantee that some people will prefer another use. In observing how successful people use skills, strategies, and tactics to push forward their preferred plans, careful observers can learn a great deal about the use of power. They can also learn that the most sophisticated approach is not to view power as an end in itself. Rather, power should be looked on as a tool to be used in compassionate and intelligent leadership.

ACTION RESEARCH
APPLIED RESEARCH

CONTROL THEORY
HUMAN FACTORS
INTERACTIONISM
SOCIAL EXCHANGE THEORY

R. W. BRISLIN

PRAISE

Praise, defined as warm approval, implies both information about the correctness of an action and a positive evaluation of the action. It is commonly accepted that praise has an effect on behavior. It is one of the most frequently used reinforcers in a variety of settings.

Most research on praise has been conducted in school settings and has concerned the variables that affect the effectiveness of praise as a reinforcer. In general, praise is most effective with students in the lower grades. At these grade levels, it is particularly effective with students of low ability and those from low socioeconomic backgrounds.

Researchers in the field of attribution theory note that praise affects our attributions of our own and others' ability. Low ability is attributed to individuals who are praised for success but receive neutral feedback for failure. High ability is attributed to individuals who are criticized for failure, but receive neutral feedback for success.

A number of psychologists and educators, including John Holt, Maria Montessori, Jean Piaget, and Donald Tosti, suggest that praise is harmful to the educational process. They argue that praise interferes with intrinsic motivation, and hence has a negative effect on the student's learning in the long run. Praise is an example of a commonsense construct that is found to be more complex than generally supposed when it is subjected to empirical research.

APPROACHES TO LEARNING
ENCOURAGEMENT
INSTRUCTIONAL THEORY
REWARDS AND INTRINSIC INTEREST
SCHOOL LEARNING

R. A. SHAW

PRECOCIOUS DEVELOPMENT

Precocity refers to an earlier than expected maturation level. Early development can be general or specific in its manifestation. Specific precocity is more often the case, and this typically does not present any adverse conditions for the child. However, precocity symptomatic of biological untimeliness is often pathologic in that the biological patterns are highly regulated by genetic composition.

Precocity of cognitive functions has been reported in the literature for centuries. It is difficult to discern whether such precocity is a result of biological factors or of outstanding parental training.

EARLY CHILDHOOD DEVELOPMENT
GENETIC DISORDERS

R. A. LEARK

PRECOCIOUS MATHEMATICAL REASONERS

Boys and girls who, compared with their age mates, are unusually advanced in their mathematical reasoning ability, knowledge of mathematical concepts, and/or computational skill, have a talent or talents likely to be valuable for learning school subjects that require quantitative aptitude or mathematical skills. Generally, most important of these is reasoning based more on keen analytic skill than on knowledge of learned concepts or facile manipulation of figures.

Distinctions between "aptitude" and "achievement" are hotly debated by individual-differences psychologists; of course, trying to separate mathematical reasoning ability from mathematical achievement partakes of that controversy.

PREDICTIVE VALUE OF SAT

Being able to do high-level analytical thinking with simple mathematical subject matter before having studied much formal mathematics is a powerful predictor of ability to learn mathematics fast and rigorously. For example, most students 12 years old or younger who score better than do 50% of college-bound twelfth-graders on SAT-M (i.e., 500) can learn the first year of high school algebra with an expert, fast-pacing mentor in from 0 to 15 hours. This compares with the 180 to 190 45- to 50-minute school periods of Algebra I usually required for that subject, typically in the ninth grade, when the student is 14 or 15 years old.

Youths who reason extremely well mathematically are one of the nation's most valuable natural resources. They have the potential to earn Ph.D. degrees at early ages—the late teens or early 20s—with distinction in difficult fields at leading universities. It is crucial that they be found early, and that each be helped in every feasible way to proceed at the speed and in the ways optimum for his or her combination of talents. Both they and the society in which they live stand to benefit enormously from this special attention.

ABSTRACT INTELLIGENCE
ACADEMIC APTITUDE TESTS
PRECOCIOUS DEVELOPMENT
PROJECT TALENT

J. C. STANLEY

PREJUDICE AND DISCRIMINATION

The terms *prejudice* and *discrimination* possess distinct meanings for most social scientists. The former denotes the possession of *negative attitudes* of a particular kind regarding members of a specific group or category; the latter is applied to the *negative actions* directed against the targets or victims of prejudice.

More specifically, social scientists view prejudice as the possession of negative attitudes that give rise to negative or unfavorable evaluations of individuals seen as belonging to that group. Prejudiced individuals may fall victim to errors in the processing and recall of information regarding the objects of their negative feelings: Over time, such individuals come to think of their "targets" in a certain way, and effectively filter out or ignore information inconsistent with or contrary to what they have come to believe about those targets.

As an attitude, prejudice is seen as having a tripartite nature, as possessing cognitive, affective, and behavioral components.

A person's beliefs and expectations regarding a particular group constitute the cognitive component of the prejudicial attitude. The term *stereotype* has come to designate networks or clusters of such beliefs and expectations. At the basis of all stereotypes is the assumption that all who belong to a specific category or group manifest similar behaviors and possess similar attitudes.

Individuals who are prejudiced against specific groups tend to experience intense negative feelings when they come into contact with these groups, either directly or indirectly. The affective component of the prejudicial attitude comes into play here, with profound negative emotional feelings tending to accompany cognitive reactions to objects of prejudice.

The behavioral component of prejudice has engendered the most research interest. Here the concern is the tendency of prejudiced individuals to act in a negative manner toward targets of their prejudice. When such tendencies become manifest in overt behavior, discrimination is said to occur.

The magnitude of the social problem represented by prejudice and discrimination has given rise to a subset of new terminology. *Tokenism* refers to a form of subtle discrimination marked by a tendency on the part of prejudiced individuals to behave in an overtly positive and accommodative manner toward the objects of their prejudice when such behavior extracts little cost or involves minimal effort. Tokenism can be used to rationalize discriminatory behavior at higher levels of social significance. Other terminology includes *sexism* and *ageism.*

The cognitive, affective, and behavioral components of prejudice all have been the object of research directed at assessing the nature and extent of prejudice in the population at large. The cognitive or belief component of prejudice, the assessment of stereotypes, is generally tapped through a trait-selection procedure. Information on the affective or feeling component of prejudice is generally derived through the use of attitude scales engineered to measure the level of an individual's positive or negative feelings toward specific groups. The *social distance scale* is an important tool in research into the behavioral component of prejudice. Subjects are presented with a series of hypothetical relationships between themselves and members of specific groups. The series of items represents increasing levels of closeness or intimacy between respondents and members of various groups (ranging from residing in the same country at the lowest level to intermarriage at the highest level), with the subjects being asked to indicate, for a given group, their willingness to accept individuals from that group into a given level of intimacy.

ATTITUDES
ETHNOCENTRISM
EQUITY THEORY
LABELING THEORY
SCAPEGOATING
STEREOTYPING

F. L. DENMARK

PREMARITAL COUNSELING

Premarital counseling can be viewed as "counseling" only in the broadest sense of the term. The function remains, for the most part, an advisement and educational intervention designed primarily to provide information typically to a young couple.

The foremost pioneer in implementing the educational instructional approach to premarital development was Ernest R. Groves who, in 1924, instituted a college course at Boston University entitled "Preparation for marriage and family living."

Another development that had a large impact on premarital counseling was the movement within psychology from a purely intrapsychic view of problems to a broadened look at interpersonal systems and cultural aspects of problem situations. This gave impetus for mental health professionals and pastoral counselors to begin looking more carefully at relationship variables in marriage and marriage preparation.

Beginning in the 1950s, the *Journal of pastoral psychology* began to reflect a wider interest in the relationship dimensions of premarital counseling as indicated by greater numbers of articles devoted to the subject. The increase in courses of study in pastoral counseling in many U.S. seminaries is a further indication that religious organizations are expanding their efforts in the interpersonal area.

The medical profession initially became involved in premarital examinations through the efforts of the U.S. Public Health Service to identify and control venereal diseases. Although most physical examinations tend to be perfunctory and mandated by state laws, some physicians have perceived the need to go beyond the routine and provide information and counseling to young couples. Much of the counseling furnished by physicians has focused on sex and sexuality.

There is growing evidence that at least some of the failed relationships are resulting in more constructive second marriages. Counseling after a failed marriage can help the new couple avoid the kinds of problems that caused their initial marriages to fail. Previously married people would also be expected to have gained some insight into the demands that marriage makes on them and to take a more rational approach to a new relationship.

The current literature on premarital counseling suggests that marriage and family counselors are being encouraged to assist those planning marriage to appraise realistically many of the romantic illusions and motivating forces associated with marriage. They can explore the psychosocial dimensions of the dynamics of marriage, the process of bonding, and commitment. Additionally, many are aware of the need to explore the family of origin and the grieving process of separation and saying goodbye.

COUNSELING
FAMILY COUNSELING
HUMAN SEXUALITY
SPOUSE SELECTION

R. C. BERG

PRESCRIPTION PRIVILEGES

In Slife and Rubenstein's *Taking sides,* prescription privileges for psychologists was chosen as one of ten new controversial issues that can lead to spirited debate. Some might argue that prescription privileges are a natural extension of present laws already on the books (e.g., California) that "establish that psychologists should be knowledgeable about psychopharmacological effects of populations at risk and are encouraged to seek additional education in the area of geriatric pharmacology" (Chap. 1539 of the statutes of 1990). Also, in Hawaii, State House Resolution 334-90 recommended a series of roundtable discussions dealing with Hawaii's unserved mental health needs and included "the possibility of allowing appropriately trained psychologists to prescribe psychotropic medications . . . under certain conditions."

Jansen and Barron asserted that biofeedback techniques, alarm bells for bed-wetting, galvanic skin responses, and polygraph assessments are examples of physical interventions already used by psychologists. Direct involvement of physical interventions by psychologists have included behavior management procedures with children. The American Psychological Association's (APA's) Task Force on Physical Interventions had two reports on this topic. In 1986 the task force concluded that research and clinical training must take account of physical interventions by psychologists, including psychopharmacology. Jansen and Barron pointed out that even though psychologists have been active in the development of physical interventions, they have been excluded automatically from giving medications because they do not have the title of physician. They agreed that medication providers must have adequate training but some psychologists question whether the "right" training is permitted to some professions whereas others are denied that training. DeLeon noted that development of model curricula in psychopharmacology was the subject of a special retreat of the APA's Board of Professional Affairs in 1989. That board gave high priority to the consideration of psychopharmacological interventions by psychologists to meet the public's need. Smyer summarized the reasons for including psychopharmacology in the curriculum for psychologists who work with older adults. Older adults have significant contact with psychotropic medications (as well as with prescription medications in general), and he emphasized that psychopharmacological agents are useful in mental disorders of older adults. He also noted that psychopharmacology is a principal factor in the treatment of elderly persons who suffer from mental illness.

MEETING SOCIETY'S NEEDS—THE PUBLIC POLICY PERSPECTIVE

DeLeon, Fox, and Graham argued that prescription privileges for psychologists are necessary and essential to meet the needs of quality care for the mentally ill and to deal with the problems of excessive medication for the elderly. They noted that, as of 1992, 28 states permitted nurse practitioners to prescribe and that optometrists could prescribe in all 50 states. Overall, it is the power of the individual states to determine which health practitioners have prescriptive authority. Physician-extenders (nurses, nurse practitioners, physicians' assistants, etc.) require supervision by physicians to prescribe, although health practitioners such as dentists, optometrists, and podiatrists are usually given independent status without physician supervision.

At the federal level, psychologists have legally prescribed medications within the Indian Health Service. Floyd Jennings, director of Mental Health Programs at the Santa Fe, New Mexico, Indian Hospital, wrote, "the single compelling warrant for prescription privileges is desperate need for services, desperate need to add another agent to psychology's therapeutic armamentarium that may contribute to the relief of human suffering. . . . Privileges granted to psychology are not seen as a threat either to income or professional territory" (p. 2). The Department of Defense authorized a demonstration pilot project permitting military psychologists to receive training to administer some psychotropic medications. The APA's *Practitioner* discussed congressional endorsement of a 2-year demonstration program wherein four military psychologists receive psychopharmacology training at the Uniformed Services University of the Health Sciences in Bethesda, Maryland.

DeLeon, Fox, and Graham pointed out that more than half of outpatient mental health visits are conducted by general medical practitioners and that nursing home residents are often medicated, using drugs designed to treat mental disorders in spite of the fact that most of these elderly patients are not mentally ill.

On the other side of the age continuum, there is widespread discussion among professionals as to the justification for medicating children. DeLeon, Folen, Jennings, Willis, and Wright indicated that proper diagnosis is crucial in using medications for children with attention deficit disorder and with attention deficit hyperactive disorder, but that they may not be necessary with other psychological disorders. A policy implication raised by these authors has to do with whether medications are sometimes prescribed for children whose parents are not able to manage their child's behavior. It is possible that the child's activity level is not the primary concern but rather the parents' inability to cope with children. Evaluating the stress level of the parent may lead to a productive course of action without necessarily subjecting children to medications. The authors pointed out that further research regarding the effects of medications on adolescents and youths who are mentally impaired is needed. Clinical child psychologists need to know more about the efficacy of psychoactive drugs with children and the general area of psychopharmacology. The authors emphasized that the power to prescribe also is the ability to use medications judiciously or not at all, depending on the circumstances. In a report chaired by Barkley and coworkers on the role of clinical child psychologists, it was argued that because child psychologists are already participants in decisions to medicate children they should be familiar with child psychopharmacology.

Breggin argued that the administration of drugs by psychiatrists is a political and financial issue encouraged by the "psychopharmacological complex" that "pushes biological and genetic theories, as well as drugs, on the society." He argued that psychiatry as a profession must discontinue its financial collaboration with drug companies and must not make inaccurate claims regarding genetic and biological causes of mental illness. Breggin insisted that love, understanding, and psychotherapy are the answers to psychiatric problems. His concerns revolve around the addictive and damaging aspect of drugs, especially if the patient has not been apprised in advance of the effects and consequences of psychotropic medications. Breggin also took to task psychologists who advocate precription privileges. He noted that some psychologists have become envious of the status accorded to psychiatrists and states that drug companies are sponsoring and funding seminars at meetings of psychologists to discuss the advantages of prescription privileges.

Fox suggested that prescription privileges for psychologists are in the public interest because the research training of psychologists makes them uniquely competent to evaluate the effects of medications. Furthermore, the good of society would be advanced because psychologists with prescription privileges would find it easier to work with nonpsychiatric physicians. A physician who is not a psychiatrist may not use certain medications for the treatment of emotional disorders or may not be familiar with the overall course of many emotional disorders. Fox suggested that many physicians prefer working with a psychologist rather than a psychiatrist and many physicians would probably have little difficulty in letting a nonmedical practitioner knowledgeable about mental disorders prescribe appropriate medications. Fox argued that it may not be wise for psychologists to restrict their roles, as restrictions ultimately diminish their ability to be helpful to their patients.

POLITICAL AND IDENTITY CONSIDERATIONS

DeNelsky pointed out that efforts to obtain prescription privileges would involve psychology in a full-scale war with psychiatry. Jancin reported that when, at the meeting of the APA, Patrick DeLeon predicted that psychologists will eventually gain prescription privileges there was "fussing and fuming" by the psychiatrists. Steven J. Kingsbury, a psychologist who is also a psychiatrist, claimed that psychiatry currently is less interested in psychotherapy although continuing to stay up to date on psychopharmacology. He argued that psychopharmacology is primarily medical, has little to do with psychological principles, and does not really belong within the armamentarium of psychologists. Arthur Shechet, worried that psychology will be merged with psychiatry in the public's mind, noted that the move to seek prescription privileges will be opposed not only by psychiatry but also by the entire American Medical Association (AMA). Barron analyzed the prescription privileges effort as a "me-too" effort to imitate the powerful (M.D.) father figure. Leonard Handler insisted that clinical psychology has advanced, because it is different from psychiatry in that psychologists are more broadly trained in contrast to the "biologically reductionistic model of mainstream medicine." Handler zeroed in on a central argument: Psychologists focus on the self, and it is the relationship between the therapist and the patient that produces more self-control. He maintained that searching for the meaning of symptoms may be more important than the symptoms themselves. Handler stated that there may be times that medications are necessary. However, he objected to medications as the central change agents, because patients can learn more about themselves without medications and "have a more meaningful growth experience." He asked for a clear distinction between those who practice psychotherapy as opposed to those whose primary orientation is biological and, therefore, excludes psychotherapy. He cautioned that failing to stand up for one's professional identity and distinctiveness may be equivalent to giving up one's birthright.

Brentar and McNamara disagreed. They do not believe that prescription privileges represent a loss of identity and argued that psychology as a field is evolving and prescription privileges is a possible step. They suggested that there are often objections to changing the status quo and that psychologists may be waiting for empirical evidence before there is full support for changes in the field.

Fox recognized that psychology might have to decide on the best time to use its limited resources to seek changes such as prescription privileges. He suggested, however, that timing is not the real issue, but instead the right of a profession to decide its direction is at stake. Fox insisted that it is the job of psychologists to decide their own fate rather than having other professions decide what the boundaries of psychology should be.

May and Belsky speculated that prescription privileges are just another step toward the medicalization of psychology. They see this as too narrow a focus and believe that the problems of the elderly, the chronically mentally ill, and other underserved groups are social problems. They suggested that prescription privileges could be handled more effectively by those who already have at least some track record (e.g., the nursing profession).

The medicalization of psychology is addressed in detail by DeNelsky. He suggested that psychiatry made a decision in the mid-1990s to medicalize its status. Rather than increasing its growth, psychiatry has not increased its share of the mental health market. Instead, it appears that the general public has accepted psychology as a mental health discipline and psychologists are currently the largest group of doctoral-level mental health providers in this country. Perhaps, DeNelsky suggested, this has come about because psychology is distinctly different from psychiatry. Moving to prescription privileges, he warned, is likely to reduce that distinction and might affect psychology adversely. Kingsbury agreed that psychotherapy training for psychiatrists has diminished and psychology is probably the acknowledged leader in the field of psychotherapy.

Brentar and McNamara cautioned about the assumption that psychiatrists have given up on psychotherapy as a treatment method. This might be true in public settings in which funding limitations have placed restrictions on psychosocial interventions. In the private sector, however, they contend that psychiatrists are still quite active in providing psychotherapy either by itself or in addition to psychotropic medications.

DeNelsky and Arthur Kovacs raised concern about energy expenditures. If prescription privileges were to become a major priority for psychology, other efforts (e.g., hospital privileges, minimum mental health benefits, etc.) might well take a backseat. However, some might argue that prescription privileges might actually facilitate hospital privileges, as hospital administrators might prefer giving privileges to those who can provide a full range of services.

Prescription privileges require changes in licensing laws. Whenever changes are made in licensing laws, the laws are opened to a variety of changes, some of them not wanted by the various professions affected. DeNelsky suggested this could constitute a major political risk. Because there is no unanimity on the topic of prescription privileges, potential efforts to change licensing laws could be divisive. DeNelsky recognized that all psychologists would not be mandated to seek such privileges but he did note that there would be pressures on those without such privileges to obtain them.

MARKETING ISSUES

Fox argued that the development of specialized medical treatment programs have mushroomed even though psychologists do offer such treatments independently. He cited the growth of hospital-based treatment programs for alcoholism, pain management, and behavior disorders of children as examples. Characteristically, these programs do not use psychologists as equal or autonomous partners. DeNelsky agreed that this may well be true, but cites figures that show that psychiatry has actually been losing its market share over the past 5 years for outpatient visits of patients. Figures on this topic fluctuate, however, depending on changing standards of reimbursement for inpatient versus outpatient treatment.

A major concern of psychologists has been the topic of access to hospital patient populations. This includes the ability to admit and discharge patients, enhanced clinical privileges for psychologists working in medical settings, and obtaining full medical staff membership with vote. Some progress along these lines has occurred, but Boswell and Litwin noted that less than 6% of hospital-affiliated psychologists have obtained admission or discharge privileges, and only 16% have obtained full medical staff memberships.

TRAINING ISSUES

Brentar and McNamara discussed three types of training models that could provide psychologists with the competence needed to begin prescribing psychotropic medications. The first is postdoctoral intensive training for psychologists wishing to become competent. A second would be a continuing education model, using workshops or seminars that could provide intensive training and updating for individuals already trained. The third model would incorporate relevant training into existing graduate programs, a difficult and expensive venture that would also lengthen an already long graduate training program. The authors suggested that interdisciplinary training with institutions that already have training programs in place might be a solution. Thus schools of optometry, nursing, or osteopathic medicine could be sites at which psychologists would be trained.

As to the content of training programs, there are clear differences of opinion as to what is needed. Fox argued that training should be similar to that received in medical school courses. However, Brental and McNamara noted that some state boards of optometry use a 30-hour training program to certify optometrists to prescribe relevant ocular medications.

The training at the Uniformed Services University of the Health Sciences will consist of a 2-year effort with didactic training occurring in the first year and hands-on supervised training at a major medical treatment center, according to DeLeon. He emphasized that the entire topic of prescription privileges is basically an educational concern. The School of Psychology at Nova University's program to train psychologists in psychopharmacology is in the development stage. This will consist of a didactic component after which trainees will observe, gather patient information, and eventually recommend medications for the patient to a psychiatrist. This program is designed for psychologists with earned doctorates in psychology who possess sufficient prior relevant knowledge as determined by the director of training.

Jennings described the qualifications and experiences necessary to provide limited prescription privileges at the Indian Health Service Hospital. Requirements include at least 1 year of postdoctoral experience in assessment and treatment. Prior training must include familiarity with laboratory tests designed to assess patients who will be given psychoactive drugs, knowledge within the area of compliance with medications, and clinical psychopharmacology coursework, which must be clearly documented. At least 6 months of prior experience must include physician oversight.

Although this is clearly a postdoctoral effort, many psychologists suggest that training programs for prescription privileges would eventually need to be included within predoctoral settings. DeNelsky argued that the time required for psychologists to complete the doctoral degree would have to be extended and psychological training would be basically changed.

Fox and coworkers described a proposed curriculum designed to produce psychologists capable of functioning as limited practice prescribers similar to dentists and podiatrists. These psychologists can prescribe medications within their area of expertise and are not subject to physician oversight. The curriculum requires an undergraduate knowledge base in biology, chemistry, and preparation for graduate level courses in biochemistry, physiological psychology, psychopharmacology (beginning and advanced), physiological and biological aspects of drug interaction, current topics in psychopharmacology, clinical psychopharmacology and therapeutics, professional and ethical issues in psychopharmacology, clinical psychopharmacology laboratory, chemical dependency, neuropsychology and laboratory, and psychopathology.

FINANCIAL CONCERNS, PROFESSIONAL LIABILITY, AND OVERMEDICATION

Piotrowski speculated on what would happen if psychologists were successful in gaining prescription privileges. One possible concern might be whether all practicing psychologists would have to share in the financial burden of increased malpractice premiums. Fox stated that it is a common practice in other professions to stipulate that one will not perform certain procedures or will restrict one's practice in specified ways. Those who choose not to administer medications should not be required to pay for the increased costs involved.

Aside from financial concerns, the overall issue of risk for psychologists increases dramatically with the obtaining of prescriptive authority. Imagine the depressed patient for whom drugs are appropriately prescribed but who misuses the prescription to make a suicide attempt. In addition, professionals are often faced with patients who are insistent on obtaining medications to deal with troubling psychological symptoms.

Most psychologists agree that some patients do benefit from medications for their psychological problems. Many psychologists would even concur that some patients with severe psychological problems need psychotropic medications. Some of those psychologists also believe that providing medications is the domain of medicine and psychiatry and psychology should stick to psychotherapy.

There are those who argue that there are many underserved patient populations in this country who receive little if any psychosocial treatment and who are overmedicated. The perception, at times confirmed by psychiatrists, that psychotherapy is not a major focus within psychiatry has been noted. Because psychologists are well trained in research and are competent in offering psychosocial interventions (psychotherapy), they might be in a better position to use both prescription privileges and psychotherapy in the treatment of patients, as they are the least likely to overmedicate. These psychologists take the position that prescription privileges, similar to hospital privileges, are natural extensions of psychological practice, are in the best interests of the public and in effect represent sound public policy.

CONCLUSIONS

Opinions on this topic have appeared in letters to the editor of the *APA Monitor* and are heard in discussions with clinical psychologists. Clearly, there are public policy, training, and marketing issues involved in the controversial area of prescription privileges for psychologists. As of 1992, however, the overarching issues appear to focus on political and identity concerns. Currently, a significant number of psychologists believe that a battle with psychiatry will result in a more widespread war with organized medicine, which might not be in the best interest of organized psychology. Others worry about being viewed as "junior psychiatrists." They express concern that winning the prescription privileges war will result in the medicalization of psychology. Included here is the fear that confidence in psychosocial treatment modalities offered by psychologists will diminish, because some members of the public will be afraid that they will receive drug treatments from psychologists and thus will turn to other professionals (social workers, counselors, ministers) for psychological interventions. However, some psychologists are concerned that more patients will turn

to them for a quick fix through medication rather than taking the more arduous path of psychotherapy.

There are responses to these concerns. Psychologists are already involved in physical interventions, although these may not be as high profile compared with prescription privileges. To argue that psychologists rely exclusively on nonphysical interventions is simply not true. In addition, as Fox noted, psychology is not exclusively a mental health discipline, because it deals broadly with behavior change in such areas of health, interpersonal functioning, learning, vocational functioning, and rehabilitation. Psychology has an impact on, among others, families, the able elderly, the physically handicapped, and those with learning characteristics, be they children or adults. Psychology has made major strides in the area of neuropsychology and in health psychology. Prescription privileges can be seen as one more step in the education and training of psychologists to be helpful to society. For those who argue that some psychologists will misuse these privileges because of status, greed, or other reasons, the truth is that there will always be unscrupulous individuals in all professions. There is no evidence that prescription privileges will increase the number of unscrupulous providers.

Probably the core argument is that prescription privileges should not be allowed because they would change the nature of psychology fundamentally. Many psychologists believe that prescription privileges should never be permitted because they violate the fundamental tenets of psychology. Nevertheless, a majority of psychologists do believe that some patients need psychotropic medications at some time in their lives. The Task Force on Psychologists' Use of Physical Interventions did define the practice of psychology as including both physical and psychological interventions. Fox pointed out that the use of such physical interventions should occur within the context of improving the quality of services, within the competence of the provider, and in the service of consumer welfare.

Psychology is a relatively young profession and changes are part of development. It is too early to forecast whether prescription privileges will become part of the practice of psychology in the twenty-first century.

ALTERNATIVE PSYCHOTHERAPIES
BEHAVIOR TOXICOLOGY
BEHAVIORAL MEDICINE
MEDICAL MODEL OF PSYCHOTHERAPY
PSYCHOPHARMACOLOGY
TRANQUILIZING DRUGS

N. ABELES

PRIMAL THERAPY

In 1970, Arthur Janov published *The primal scream*. Although schisms have developed among those who call themselves primal therapists, there is general agreement that very early traumas and early unfulfilled needs are responsible for neurosis and psychosis in later life. The traumas and unfulfilled needs prevent normal progress through the developmental stages that each individual undergoes, and the person is cut off from normal access to his or her feelings.

Procedures for primal therapy vary somewhat with the therapist, but generally clients receive full-time therapy over several weeks, during which they are usually seen daily for sessions of up to 3 hours. Following the intensive period, they are seen weekly in either individual or group sessions for a further 8- to 12-month period.

During therapy sessions, memories are uncovered and early hurts are reexperienced in a physical way. Confrontation with feelings often results in much writhing and convulsive movements.

INNOVATIVE PSYCHOTHERAPIES
PSYCHOTHERAPY

V. RAIMY

PRIMARY MENTAL ABILITIES

One of the earliest accomplishments of the new science of psychology was the objective measurement of mental abilities. With the introduction of the new method of factor analysis, Charles Spearman argued that intelligence could be characterized as being composed of a general factor (g) common to all meaningful activity and specific factors (s) unique to the tasks used to measure intelligence. Commonly used test instruments that applied the concept of general intelligence were soon introduced through the work of Binet and Simon and, later, Terman. American psychologists engaged in educational and occupational selection activities found the concept of general intelligence less useful for predicting success in specific jobs or other life roles. In addition, work on transfer of training had suggested that the notion of generalizability of a single ability dimension was not justified.

Efforts soon began, therefore, to determine whether human abilities could be described along a parsimonious number of distinct substantive dimensions. Initial work along these lines began with the publication of T. L. Kelley's *Crossroads in the mind of man,* which advocated the determination of group factors representing distinct skills, such as facility with numbers, facility with verbal materials, spatial relationships, speed, and memory. These efforts were also aided by advances in factor analysis that allowed the determination of multiple factors, each representing a latent construct represented by sets of independently observed variables.

Most prominently associated with these developments, L. L. Thurstone expounded the hope that a careful scrutiny of the relations among a wide array of assessment devices, developed to reflect a given construct as purely as possible, would yield a limited number of dimensions that would reflect "the building blocks of the mind." He proceeded to administer a battery of 56 simple psychological tests to a large number of children in Chicago schools and applied multifactor analysis to determine the basic dimensions. Given the procedures available at the time, he was reasonably successful in showing that fewer than 10 latent constructs could be used to explain most individual differences variance in his measures. The factors obtained in this work were consequently labeled the *primary mental abilities.*

Most of the factors identified by Thurstone have subsequently been replicated in work by others. The most important factors, in order of the proportion of individual differences explained, are the following:

Verbal Comprehension (V). This factor represents the scope of a person's passive vocabulary and is most often measured by multiple-choice recognition vocabulary tests.

Spatial Orientation (S). The ability to visualize and mentally rotate abstract figures in two- or three-dimensional space. This ability is thought to be involved in understanding maps and charts and in assembling objects that require manipulation of spatial configurations. This may be a complex factor involving both visualization and the perception of spatial relationships.

Inductive Reasoning (R or I). This is the ability to determine a rule or principle from individual instances, probably involved in most human problem solving. The ability is generally measured by number or letter series that has several embedded rules; the subject is asked to complete the series correctly.

Number (N). This is the ability to engage rapidly and correctly in a variety of computational operations. The most simple measure of this ability is a test checking sums for addition problems.

Word Fluency (W). This factor represents a person's active vocabulary and is generally measured by free recall of words according to a lexical rule.

Associative Memory (M). Found primarily in verbal tasks involving paired associates or list learning. It is not a general memory factor, evidence for which has not thus far been established.

Perceptual Speed (P). This ability involves the rapid and accurate identification of visual details, similarities, and differences. It is usually measured by letter canceling, simple stimulus, or number comparison tasks.

Other organizational schemes to characterize multiple abilities have been developed by G. H. Thompson and P. E. Vernon in England and by J. P. Guilford in the United States. The latter system actually classified tasks along a three-dimensional higher order hierarchy in terms of content, product, and operations involved in each task, resulting in a taxonomy of as many as 120 factors, many of which remain to be operationalized.

For the purposes of educational application, Thurstone and Thurstone developed a series of tests at several difficulty levels suitable for students from kindergarten to high school designed to measure Thurstone's first five factors (V, S, R, N, and W). This battery was updated and revised by Thurstone in 1962. Measures of the other factors may be found in the *Kit of factor-referenced tests* developed by the Educational Testing Service.

Although work with the primary mental abilities in educational practice has not been popular in recent years, the primary abilities have experienced a revival as a useful measurement instrument for charting the course of abilities in studies of adult development. A special augmented version of the Thurstone tests particularly suitable for work with older adults has been developed (STAMAT). The validity of the primary mental abilities in adults has been examined with respect to its relation to measures of practical intelligence and subjective perception of competence as well as to specific occupational outcomes.

ABSTRACT INTELLIGENCE
CLERICAL APTITUDE TESTING
FACTOR ANALYSIS
STRUCTURE OF INTELLECT MODEL
TESTING METHODS

K. W. SCHAIE

PRIMARY PREVENTION OF PSYCHOPATHOLOGY

Primary prevention involves efforts to reduce the future incidence of emotional disorders and mental conditions in populations of persons not yet affected. The efforts are proactive. Primary prevention sometimes is directed at high-risk groups, or at groups approaching high-risk situations or potential life crises. Programs in primary prevention may involve the reduction of organic factors contributing to psychopathology, efforts to reduce avoidable stress, the building of competencies and coping skills, the development of improved self-esteem, and the enhancement of support networks and groups.

The logic of investing in efforts at primary prevention is supported in several ways. First, the incredible imbalance between the number of people suffering emotional distress and those with mental disorders makes it impossible for individual interventionists to reach those needing help, and this gap is impossible to bridge.

Most of the enormous improvement in the health and increasing longevity of members of our society has come about as a result of the successful application of the methods of primary prevention within the field of public health. Public health prevention methods involve "finding the noxious agent" and taking steps to eliminate or neutralize it, or "strengthening the host."

During the first enthusiasm for the application of public health methods in the field of mental disorder, it seemed just a matter of time until these "mental illnesses" could also be brought under control and eliminated. However, as time has passed, it is gradually becoming apparent that most of the so-called mental illnesses may not have a specific and unique cause.

A high level of stress-causing conditions (e.g., powerlessness, unemployment, sexism, marital disruption, loss of support systems) can cause any of several patterns of emotional disruption (e.g., depression, alcoholism, anxiety, hypertension). In brief, there is a nonspecific relation between causes and consequences.

If our purpose is to reduce the incidence of the different conditions or compulsive lifestyles we refer to as mental disorders, is there any way to think about organizing prevention efforts? The following formula may be helpful:

$$\text{Incidence} = \frac{\text{Organic factors} + \text{Stress}}{\text{Competence} + \text{Self-esteem} + \text{Support networks}}$$

To succeed in preventive efforts is to reduce the incidence of the various forms of emotional disturbance. There are several strategies for accomplishing that purpose: The first is to prevent, minimize, or reduce the number of organic factors. The more an organic factor can be reduced or eliminated, the smaller the resulting incidence will be. Specific examples are as follows:

1. Reduction of the amount of brain damage resulting from lead poisoning or from accidents reduces the resulting mental conditions.
2. Prevention of damaged genes from developing into damaged individuals (after amniocentesis, aborting a fetus with chromosomal abnormalities) prevents the birth of a mentally impaired or brain-damaged infant.
3. Provision of medication to reduce hypertension lowers the incidence of brain injury resulting from strokes.
4. Improvement of the circulation of blood to the brain reduces the rate of later cerebral arteriosclerosis.

A second strategy involves the reduction of stress. Here relationships become more complex. Stress takes many forms. Reducing stress requires changes in the physical and social environment. Environmental stress situations involve a whole complex of interacting variables. Some forms of social stress are a product of deeply ingrained cultural values and ways of life not easily susceptible to change. Stress may result from low self-esteem that becomes a kind of self-fulfilling prophecy. Women and members of ethnic minorities, who learn from earliest childhood that their sex or race is seen as inferior, grow up with lower self-esteem that may be exceedingly difficult to change. Preventive efforts take the form of public education, changes in the mass media, and the reshaping of pervasive value systems. Such efforts encounter the angry resistance of the power forces that get real benefit from the values being criticized.

An area of major research investigation in recent years has been the relationship between stressful life events and the onset of both physical illness and mental disturbance. Studies report correlations between severity of life stresses and the probability of the appearance of specific illnesses in the future. Statistically significant relationships have been found between the stresses of life change and diseases such as tuberculosis, heart attacks, accidents, leukemia, and diabetes. High life stress has been associated repeatedly with subsequent mental and emotional disturbances. Being part of a strong support network reduces the risk of exposure to stress.

The model described by the formula obviously has shortcomings. Often intervention results in changes in all areas. For example, training in a sport may involve regular practice with resulting improvement in physical coordination, bodily health, musculature, circulation, and a sense of physical well-being. At the same time, the subject may experience a reduction of stress as he or she burns up energy in physical activity; meanwhile, improvement in competence in performing the physical requirements of the sport may increase self-confidence and self-esteem. Thus improvement occurs at all levels.

Ultimately many prevention efforts will require societal change through political action. For this reason, the struggle to redistribute power as a strategy for the prevention of psychopathology has only begun.

HEALTH CARE SERVICES
HOT LINE SERVICES
HUMAN SERVICES
PSYCHOTHERAPY
SELF-HELP GROUPS

G. W. ALBEE

PRIMATE BEHAVIOR

Since the order *Primates* includes some 200 species ranging in size from less than 100 grams to more than 100 kg, in habitat from tropical rain forest to hot desert to mountain and temperate climates that include heavy snow cover for most of the winter months, in social group sizes from two to hundreds, and in both nocturnal and diurnal activity patterns, uniformity of behavior within the order is not to be expected. There are, however, some similar physical, growth, sensory, motor, and hence behavioral characteristics that many possess, so that some patterns of behavioral similarity can be discerned.

One such characteristic of primates is that, in general, they are born as singletons so that they usually do not have an age-comparable sibling either as a companion or as a competitor during the growth period. The infant is not without attention, however, for the newborn of many species attracts the interest of other adult and semiadult females and of other juveniles of both sexes. Moreover, primates generally have a long infancy and adolescence, several years in many species; therefore, dependence on the mother is close and protracted. During this time, the male protects the helpless and burdened mother. Intimate bonds are thus established between them that last throughout life. The long juvenile period affords the youngster the opportunity to learn the rules of social stratification and of communication, to acquire information about the environment (e.g., water-hole locations, home range limits, and nest construction, if it is customary for the species to make one), and to acquire physical skills needed in later life. Another characteristic of many primates is versatility of posture and locomotion, particularly among the simians.

The most outstanding characteristic of some species of primates is the upper limit of their capacity for cognitive achievement. They have the ability to represent and modify informational input internally, which allows them to respond to a signal after it has disappeared, to recognize a sign whose value (meaning) changes from one circumstance to another, to identify a stimulus (e.g., a sphere haptically [by active touch] after it has been shown to them [cross-modal transfer]). Other cognitive activity includes the use of symbols as means of communication. Whether this activity demonstrates the use of language in the human sense is a matter of some dispute; nevertheless, skill levels such as these have not even been approached by nonprimate species.

Ethologists have taught that much of the behavior of lower animals is regulated by genetic factors rather than by learning. Experiments in which closely related but behaviorally distinct species are interbred reveal that the behavior patterns of the offspring correspond to expectations based on Mendelian laws of inheritance.

ANIMAL INSTINCTIVE BEHAVIOR
ANIMAL SOCIOBIOLOGY
ETHOLOGY
HERITABILITY

A. J. RIOPELLE

PRIMITIVE MENTALITY

Early Western visitors to preliterate societies were often impressed by what seemed strange thought processes implied by religious practices or expressed in local explanations of those practices. Scholars who had not themselves visited preliterate societies collected accounts of such observations and developed the hypothesis of "primitive mentality"; that is, that individuals in primitive societies think in a manner not just quantitatively but qualitatively different from the thinking of individuals in civilized societies. Levy-Bruhl portrayed primitive mentality as prelogical (i.e., not avoiding contradictions) and mystic (i.e., implying belief in hidden forces). He eventually decided that this broad hypothesis was mistaken, and concluded that mystical thinking is present in everyone but "is more easily observable among 'primitive peoples.' "

Among writers who assumed thought processes to be radically different in primitive and civilized people, the difference was variously ascribed to genetic endowment, to the mode of thought conventional in the society, or to an ill-defined "developmental status."

ACCULTURATION
HUMAN INTELLIGENCE
SOCIAL INFLUENCE

I. L. CHILD

PRISONER'S DILEMMA

The prisoner's dilemma is the name given to an interpersonal game extensively investigated by social psychologists interested in social conflict and its resolution. "Game" in this sense refers to a social situation involving interdependent decision making; that is, a situation in which each party's welfare depends on not just what he or she does, but rather on the combination of responses made by the two parties. The prisoner's dilemma game is the best known mixed-motive game in psychology. Figure 1 represents a simple two-person, two-choice game in which each of the two parties has two choice alternatives and each party's welfare depends on the resultant combination of choices. The letters entered into the matrix represent payoffs to the two parties for each choice combination. The letter on the left side of each cell represents the payoff

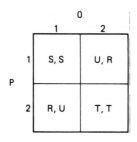

Figure 1. A game matrix.

to the party whose choices are labeled on the vertical axis (P); the letter on the right side of each cell represents the payoff to the person whose choice alternatives are labeled on the horizontal axis (O). A game meets the minimal criteria for a prisoner's dilemma if the following conditions are met for both parties: $U < T < S < R$ (criteria from mathematical game theory are more rigorous). The analogy involves two prisoners held by the police for a crime. The police separate the two and inform each prisoner that if he or she will give evidence against the other, he or she can go free. The prisoners are aware that if only one gives evidence, the other will receive the maximum penalty, for instance, 20 years; but if both give evidence, each will receive a moderate sentence, for example, 10 years. However, if neither gives evidence, each will be tried on a minor charge, with a penalty for each of a fine and less than 1 year in prison. Each would prefer to go free, but if both give evidence, both will go to jail for years. However, opting for the minor charge by refusing to give evidence may in fact result in the most severe penalty if the other gives evidence. Refusing to give evidence is defined as a cooperative response, since both must do so for the choice to yield mutually beneficial payoffs. Giving evidence may be seen as competitive—an effort to obtain the best outcome for oneself at the expense of the other, or as defensive—in an effort to thwart the competitive intention of the other. Experimental subjects who have played this game typically make competitive choices in spite of the collectively poor payoffs this strategy yields. Its extensive use by experimental social psychologists is attributable to its obvious parallels with recurrent problems of conflict, such as arms races.

CONFLICT RESOLUTION
COOPERATION/COMPETITION

W. P. SMITH

PRIVILEGED COMMUNICATIONS

The privacy of communication between a client and a psychologist is critical to the client's willingness to disclose personal information in a therapy or an evaluation setting. Lack of protection of the client's communication may therefore preclude the maximum benefits of the relationship.

Two major concepts address the issue of privacy of communication between client and psychologist. The first, confidentiality, holds that psychologists and others have the ethical responsibility not to reveal, except in certain special situations (e.g., a danger to someone), the disclosures of clients. The principle of confidentiality has been upheld in judicial and legislative actions of some states. The principle does not, however, protect client–psychologist communications from being revealed when the latter is a witness in a court action.

The second concept is that of privileged communication. Most states have established statutes that prevent psychologists from being forced to testify concerning information disclosed by the client in the professional relationship, except under certain conditions. Most states also cover physicians in their privileged communication statutes, while some also have laws that cover psychiatrists specifically, and some cover social workers.

The privilege—that is, the choice as to whether information will be made public—belongs to the client. This explicitly provides that no professional covered by a privileged communication statute has the legal right to reveal information independent of the client's consent. Should a client wish to have the information revealed, the psychologist is obligated to comply. In certain cases (e.g., competency hearings), a judge may deny the privilege whenever the evidence revealed by the professional is likely to be in the best interests of the client or of society.

Privileged communication is, therefore, a narrower concept than confidentiality. It is specific to the judicial process and not relevant to communication with other professionals, parents, and so forth, as are the constraints of confidentiality.

Criteria for exercise of the communication privilege often require licensure or certification of the psychologist and clarity of a professional relationship between client and psychologist. That is, the statute applies only if the person involved in the litigation is one with whom the psychologist has had a clear professional relationship. Information that the psychologist obtains outside the relationship is usually not protected.

There is a delicate balance between the individual's right to privacy, society's interests, and the necessity for revelation in court proceedings. Many states have dealt with these issues by describing exceptions to the privilege. One exception in several states exists whenever a judge believes that the importance of the proceeding outweighs that of the client's privacy. Others limit the privilege to civil actions, or exclude specific crimes (e.g., homicide, rape, child abuse) from the privilege. Danger to another individual is also used in some states as an exception to the communication privilege. In some states, a psychologist is not obligated to keep a client's communications privileged if the client files a legal complaint of malpractice against the psychologist. The privilege is waived in some states when clients use their own mental condition as a part of their claims, as in an insanity defense, or when examination of a client is ordered by the court. The final major exception included in some privileged communication statutes is if the professional determines that the client is in need of hospitalization for a mental disorder. The existing privileged communication statutes, therefore, vary as to which professionals are covered, the basis of the privilege, and the exceptions to the privilege.

PROFESSIONAL CONSULTATIONS
PROFESSIONAL ETHICS
PSYCHOLOGY AND THE LAW

T. S. Bennett

PROBABILITY

Probability theory is important to psychology because it is the foundation on which statistics is based, and statistics are the tools for conducting empirical research.

Suppose an event E can occur in M ways and fail to occur in N ways. Under the condition that M and N are equally likely to occur, the probability of success (i.e., the event will occur) is

$$p = \Pr\{E\} = \frac{M}{M + N}$$

The probability of failure (i.e., the event will not occur) is

$$q = \Pr\{\text{not } E\} = \frac{N}{M + N}$$

Hence

$$p + q = \frac{M}{M + N} + \frac{N}{M + N} = 1$$

and

$$q = 1 - p$$

Addition Theorem. If two or more events are mutually exclusive

the probability that either one of them or any combination of them will occur is the sum of their probabilities

$$\Pr\{E_1 + E_2\} = \Pr\{E_1\} + \Pr\{E_2\}$$

Multiplication Theorem. If two or more events are independent, the probability that the events will occur simultaneously or in succession is the product of the individual probabilities

$$\Pr\{E_1 \cdot E_2\} = \Pr\{E_1\} \cdot \Pr\{E_2\}$$

SAMPLING WITH AND WITHOUT REPLACEMENT

An important concept is sampling with replacement and sampling without replacement. In the former situation, the possibilities remain constant for all events because no case is last in the occurrence of any previous event. In the latter situation, the occurrence of a particular event precludes the possibility of that event happening again because the specific case is not replaced. In sampling with replacement, addition and multiplication theorems are usually applied. In sampling without replacement, the probability situation is considerably altered and the probability distribution assumes the form and properties of a mathematical distribution known as the *hypergeometric distribution.* Its probabilities are calculated as follows:

$$Pk = \frac{\binom{n_1}{k}\binom{n - n_1}{r - k}}{\binom{n}{r}}$$

where n = number of elements in set
n_1 = number of elements in subset
k = size of group k
r = size of group r

PROBABILITY DISTRIBUTIONS

Frequency distributions encountered in statistics are generally considered to be probability distributions, that is, in a general form of $(p + q)^n$. Although a probability distribution is discrete, it smooths out to a reasonably continuous one as n becomes increasingly large; that is, $n \to \infty$. If $p = q = 1/2$, then as $n \to \infty$, the probability distribution, as first shown by Bernoulli in the early nineteenth century, approximates the normal curve.

CONFIDENCE LIMITS
SAMPLING
STATISTICS IN PSYCHOLOGY

P. F. Merenda

PRODUCTIVE THINKING

Max Wertheimer devoted all of his scientific labor to two areas: perception and thought. He set forth a number of postulates that defined the parameters for "genuine, fine, clean, direct productive processes." First, external factors that inhibit these processes are blind habits, bias, special interests, and certain kinds of school drill. Second, certain operations, such as grouping, centering, and reorganization, characterize these processes. Third, these operations are part of nature. They are logically determined by the structural requirements of a problem and are related to whole-characteristics. Fourth, more traditional operations that also are involved in these processes similarly function in relation to whole-characteristics. Fifth, these processes are not characterized by an and-summative aggregation, that is, by a succession of piecemeal, chance occurrences in which associations or operations just arise. Thought processes are not arbitrary or capricious. Thought processes evidence a remarkable consistency of development that often can be witnessed only with the advantage of hindsight. Sixth, productive processes require "structural truth" as well as factual (piecemeal) truth. One of the cases that Wertheimer used to illustrate productive thinking was Johann Karl Friedrich Gauss, an infant prodigy in mathematics. At the age of 3 years, Gauss was already correcting his father's addition. The most widely recognized incident exemplifying Gauss' genius occurred when he was 6 years old. His teacher challenged the class to see which student would be the first to derive the sum of $1 + 2 + 3 + 4 + 5 + 6 + 7 + 8 + 9 + 10$. While all of the other students were busily adding up the numbers, Gauss observed that $1 + 10 = 11$ and $2 + 9 = 11$ and $3 + 8 = 11$, and so on. He determined that there were five such pairs and that 5 times 11 equaled 55. The example demonstrates reorganization of a series in light of a particular problem. Reorganization comes about as the individual begins to grasp the inner relations between the components and their overall structure.

In essence, thinking requires that all problems be viewed and dealt with structurally, that there be operations of structural grouping and segregation, that operations be viewed and treated in their structural place, that structural transposability be employed—separating structurally peripheral from fundamental features—and that structural rather than piecemeal truth be sought.

ABSTRACT INTELLIGENCE
COGNITIVE COMPLEXITY
PRECOCIOUS MATHEMATICAL REASONERS

R. A. PRENTKY

PROFESSIONAL CONSULTATIONS

Mental health consultation, as a major service modality, grew out of the community mental health movement. It is a way for mental health professionals to share their knowledge with other mental health workers or those in other professions (e.g., law, business) who are concerned with mental health-related issues.

Consultation and education constitute two major vehicles through which the community mental health center can share the responsibility for maintaining the mental health of the community with other agencies and with the public, and thus reduce the number of acutely and chronically disturbed individuals who require direct mental health services. Consultation and education also contribute significantly to assessment of the community's mental health needs, to the development of new resources, to the reshaping of service delivery systems, and to the improvement of interagency communication.

These activities can be divided into two broad categories—program consultation and human relations or case consultation. Program consultation deals with problems involved in the planning, development, implementation, and evaluation of services directly or indirectly affecting the mental health community. Participants in such consultations are generally administrators and planning staff. Initiatives for seeking consultation are taken by agencies, associations, and institutions in the community or by the community mental health centers. By contrast, human relations consultation and case consultation are concerned with the day-to-day functioning of an agency or service and its clients, and deals with the interpersonal relations of agency staff and the relationships between the consultees and their clients. In case consultation, the consultant is always in an advisory position.

Mental health consultation may take place in a wide variety of settings, including schools, hospitals, the justice system, and human service and welfare agencies. To operate in such diverse settings, consultants must maintain professional flexibility and be sensitive to the social ecology of the setting and the variety of social forces impacting on clients. Unlike a didactic teaching relationship or the therapist–client relationship, the consulting relationship is generally built on the consultant and client having coequal status.

CLINICAL JUDGMENT
MENTAL HEALTH TEAMS
TEAM PERFORMANCE

R. D. FELNER

PROFESSIONAL ETHICS

Ethics are standards that govern personal and professional conduct and are typically developed for the protection of consumers of services, professionals, organizations, research subjects, the profession, and society as a whole.

Ethical standards may be organized around the person or group to whom the professional is responsible or around broad classifications of principles. In either case, standards are usually general guidelines for making determinations about ethical actions both before and after they occur, rather than sets of rules for every possible professional action. When professional organizations develop standards of ethics, adherence to the standards is often held as one of the conditions of membership. The standards then become a basis for the adjudication of issues of alleged unethical conduct.

Systems of ethical principles are based on the goals, objectives, and fundamental values of the profession. They do not carry the weight of civil or criminal law, but may serve as guidelines for developing legislation or for determining whether accepted standards of practice have been violated in civil liability proceedings. Ethical principles are usually rewritten periodically to reflect the development of the profession, changes in the standards of society as a whole, or the results of judicial proceedings.

The APA's first formal ethical standards were published in 1953 and have since undergone several revisions.

The first area, "responsibility," emphasizes that psychologists should be extremely sensitive to the potential outcomes of their professional actions.

The principle of "competence" stresses that psychologists must engage in professional activity only in those areas for which they clearly have the ability, knowledge, training, and experience.

The principle of "moral and legal standards" requires psychologists to acquaint themselves with standards of behavior in the community and to apply this information to the development of their own systems of personal and professional values and conduct.

The principle governing "public statements" specifies ways of presenting an individual's or organization's professional qualifications, affiliations, and functions.

The principle of "confidentiality" is essential to effective psychological practice. Information communicated to psychologists in the context of professional relationships must not be communicated to anyone else in any manner without the consent of the person concerned, unless there is some clear danger to that person or others.

The principle concerned with the "welfare of the consumer" is designed to protect the rights of those who use psychological services.

The principle concerned with "professional relationships" emphasizes the obligations of psychologists in dealing with other professionals. Psychologists are expected to consider the needs and abilities of other professionals and to secure the best possible services for clients.

The principle governing the use of "assessment techniques" requires psychologists to observe relevant standards for such techniques, to maintain the security of the techniques, and to prevent their misuse.

The principle concerned with "research with human participants" is so complex as to require a lengthy separate publication. Ethical conflict is sometimes unavoidable in that the value of the research must be weighed against any potential risk to participants.

The final principle covers the "care and use of animals." Animal research subjects are to be treated humanely and in a manner that complies with existing laws.

These areas of ethical concern illustrate the types of issues with which psychologists and other professionals are concerned. It is clear that the emphasis is on protecting those with whom psychologists work. This emphasis helps to protect psychologists as well, by providing a framework in which to practice and the backing of a consensus of one's colleagues. In addition, it militates against intrusion from outside the profession.

Several major problems exist in developing and adhering to ethical standards. One is that there are widely varying methods for dealing with clients, many of which do not have clear standards of application. Second, the behavior of those seeking psychological services is often in conflict with societal expectations and the psychologist has responsibilities to both. A third problem is that of integrating the goals and values of the profession with those of society, as defined by statutory and case law. Yet another is that of psychologists in nonpsychological settings (e.g., business), where different organizational standards apply. These are but a few of the many problems involved in developing clear ethical guidelines.

There are several groups of clients for whom judgments about ethical practice are particularly difficult for psychologists. Persons who suffer from mental impairment constitute one group which, by virtue of its members' lack of ability to make their own effective decisions, places an extra burden of care on the psychologist.

A second group that requires special ethical consideration by virtue of inadequate self-protection skills comprises children, whose rights are particularly vulnerable to violation because these rights are limited under the law.

Family treatment also raises unusual ethical issues. Confidentiality is difficult to maintain, as therapists frequently find themselves in a position of communicating with some family members outside the family treatment setting, and these communications, even though they may be helpful to the family, must be kept confidential.

Therapy groups present special ethical problems in that members of such groups are bound only by their own moral standards and not by formal ethical or legal standards. Therefore, group members may behave in a potentially harmful way toward other members or may fail to keep information confidential.

Another group that creates difficult ethical issues consists of clients who use insurance coverage to pay for psychological services. Psychologists, to receive insurance payments, must communicate some information about the client (e.g., diagnosis, rationale for treatment, number of sessions) to the insurance company. That information is, therefore, no longer confidential.

It is evident that ethical principles do not resolve all problems encountered by psychologists. Exceptions to typical ethical judgment situations occur with changes in psychological theory and practice. Integration of societal and professional values with legal requirements and the unique needs of individuals is an ongoing process.

Ethical principles, therefore, are not static sets of rules, but rather are guidelines within which individual psychologists must still make continuous judgments in the best interests of all concerned.

PRIVILEGED COMMUNICATIONS
PROFESSIONAL CONSULTATIONS

T. S. BENNETT

PROGRAM EVALUATION

Program evaluation research uses the tools of inquiry from the social sciences to investigate social programs, decide on appropriate performance criteria, and assess program effectiveness. Its purpose is to aid rational decision making about social programs by consumers, program administrators, and policy makers.

Program evaluation research is most typically applied to sponsored activities implemented through an identifiable organizational structure with designated staff, appropriate facilities, defined budget, and so forth.

Program evaluation research was applied to many of the New Deal programs of the Franklin D. Roosevelt era, but it was catapulted forward during the 1960s under the influence of the "Great Society" programs of Lyndon Johnson. In that period, the federal government sponsored massive programs to eliminate poverty, reduce urban decay, and improve the education of minorities and the economically disadvantaged. Evaluation requirements were written into much of the supporting legislation, and numerous evaluation studies were commissioned to assess new program alternatives and, in some cases, to win political acceptance for new proposals.

APPROACHES AND TECHNIQUES

Program evaluation research does not constitute a unified field. It has no conceptual or methodological paradigm and only a few agreed-on principles and practices. The community of evaluation researchers is united more by common purpose than by common method.

The watershed distinction among the varieties of approaches to program evaluation research is between those with predominant emphasis on "evaluation" and those who stress "research." The evaluation perspective recognizes that to judge the value of a program adequately, all aspects of the program that contribute to its worth must be investigated. This includes goals, outcome, personnel, organizational structure, budget, morality, and need. Such a broad investigation, however, strains the capability of conventional social science methodology, at least the more rigorous requirements for tight experimental designs and validated quantitative measurement. Within the program evaluation perspective, therefore, there has been a steady growth in the application of broader and more flexible, if less definitive, methods. Such approaches permit what has been called "responsive" evaluation—that is, investigation of the particular concerns held by program decision makers and consumers and timely reporting of the results to make them optimally useful.

The research perspective views its task as determining, in the most methodologically sound fashion possible, whether a social program actually produces the effects expected. In this perspective, social programs are viewed as instances of organized social engineering intended to accomplish specific results. This cause-and-effect conception is quite compatible with the social science methodology of controlled experimentation and quantitative measurement. Properly done, such experimental comparisons provide relatively unequivocal estimates of the impact of the social program on the alleged beneficiaries and thus answer a central evaluation question, "Did the program have the desired effect?"

In addition to the relative extremes of controlled experimentation and qualitative ethnographic study, several other specific program evaluation techniques are worthy of mention. The issue occasionally arises, for instance, as to whether a program is appropriate to the needs of a community, a catchment area, or a clientele. For such situations, a set of techniques known collectively as "needs assessment" has been developed. Community or key informant surveys, records of existing service agencies, and analyses of social indicators (e.g., census data) are the most frequent components. Alternatively it may be questionable that the program is itself an appropriate candidate for evaluation research. "Evaluability assessment" provides a formal program definition and a specification of the evaluation approaches, if any, that might be appropriate. Another specialized technique is a benefit–cost analysis, adapted from economics. Its purpose is to monetarize the benefits of a program and compare them with the costs of various alternative programs or program implementations. Finally, there is a variety of management-oriented approaches that are distinguished by their applicability to the operational decisions that program administrators confront. Decision analysis applies statistical decision theory in support of management decision making in the face of uncertainty. Goal-attainment monitoring and generically similar procedures systematize program goals and establish information feedback systems that routinely inform program managers of progress toward those goals.

As numerous evaluation studies in a particular program area accumulate, they provide a valuable archive of information about contrasting program approaches and overall effects. One subspecialty of program evaluation research, known as "metaanalysis," addresses itself to the problem of integrating studies and identifying the broad patterns of results that emerge.

ORGANIZATIONAL ASPECTS

During the 1970s, program evaluation research began to consolidate as an organized field of specialization. Various professional organizations were founded and less formal evaluation groups were formed within several existing professional organizations. Professional journals devoted exclusively to program evaluation research and related issues arose. With this increased academic identity came training programs designated specifically for program evaluation research, largely as an area of specialization within a conventional social science program.

In spite of its increased disciplinary identity, program evaluation remains a multidisciplinary endeavor in terms of the primary affiliations of its practitioners. Furthermore, no discipline predominates, though most members are social scientists. Thus program evaluation research remains a bridging discipline—a varied but identifiable collection of concepts and methods spanning the traditional social sciences and the world of social programs and the problems they address.

APPLIED RESEARCH
MEASUREMENT
OBSERVATIONAL METHODS
ORGANIZATIONAL DIAGNOSIS
TREATMENT OUTCOME RESEARCH

M. W. Lipsey

PROGRESSIVE MATRICES (RAVEN'S)

Developed by British psychologist J. C. Raven, the *Progressive Matrices* (PM) tests measure the ability to educe relationships among figural elements contained in a matrix. Items employ either a complete pattern from which a piece has been removed, or figural elements placed in discrete rows and columns, with one element missing. These tests reportedly assess the ability to perceive and to think clearly, minimizing the influences of verbal communication and past experience. Some psychologists consider PM to be a relatively pure measure of Spearman's *g*.

INTELLIGENCE MEASURES
NONVERBAL INTELLIGENCE TESTS
PENCIL-AND-PAPER INTELLIGENCE TESTS
PSYCHOMETRICS

G. J. Robertson

PROJECTIVE TECHNIQUES

The common denominator of projective techniques may be contained in the following propositions:

1. Projective techniques present relatively ambiguous stimuli to the examinee.

2. The techniques are "response-free," in the sense that there are no right or wrong responses and the examinee is free to give whatever responses appear suitable.

3. Responses are interpreted as reflecting central personality tendencies and affective states.

4. The obtained records are also viewed, in varying degrees, as reflections of the cognitive processes and personality style of the subject.

Projective "techniques" or projective "tests" present a standard set of stimuli under specified conditions so that the responses obtained are attributable primarily to personality differences. Thus projection of personal needs and styles may be seen in much of human behavior and so interpreted, but only a limited number of methods or situations qualify for the designation of projective tests or techniques.

Some of the currently listed projective techniques date back to an era when the term was unknown. For example, the *word association* method, originally employed in Wundt's laboratory and subsequently used in the clinical setting by Jung, is retrospectively adopted as the "first projective technique."

The best known projective technique is the Rorschach test. The examinee's task is to respond with an interpretation of these unstructured visual stimuli.

The Thematic Apperception Test (TAT) is a picture story test, consisting of 20 pictures with alternatives for some of them, for women and men, girls and boys.

Still another illustration of a projective method is the *sentence completion technique*. This is a relatively structured verbal method whereby sentence stems or incomplete sentences are presented to the examinee, who is instructed to finish them as quickly as possible. The partial sentence presented limits the degrees of freedom of the respondent much more than the other methods do. Also the respondent has a much clearer awareness of the meaning of the responses. On the Rorschach, or even the TAT, respondents are not aware to what extent their "private worlds" are projected into their productions. In the case of sentence completion, the situation is much different in this respect, approaching the conditions of a questionnaire or a structured interview.

Projective drawings, doll play, and story completion, as well as adaptations of the Rorschach (e.g., the Holtzman inkblot method) and the CAT (Children's Apperception Test) models, are some of the methods that have further expanded the field of projective techniques. Numerous other adaptations and "tailor-made" methods have also been published.

Over the years, projective techniques have often been attacked by scientifically oriented critics. They have questioned the reliability and validity of the techniques employed. Literally thousands of research studies with the Rorschach, TAT, and other methods have been published subsequently. Much of the research supports the reliability of the Rorschach and some of the other methods, but a good deal of the field remains controversial in spite of the continued evidence of the clinical usefulness of the methods.

BLACKY PICTURES
EARLY RECOLLECTIONS
HIDDEN FIGURES TEST
HOLTZMAN INKBLOT TECHNIQUE
HOUSE–TREE–PERSON TEST

RORSCHACH TECHNIQUE
SENTENCE COMPLETION TESTS
THEMATIC APPERCEPTION TEST
WORD ASSOCIATION TESTS

A. I. RABIN

PROJECT TALENT

Project Talent was started in 1960 by John Flanagan and his associates to investigate the vocational attitudes and abilities, career objectives, and guidance services of high school students in the United States. More than 400,000 students in more than 1300 high schools across the country completed an extensive battery of tests and questionnaires designed to provide data on the following vocational and career issues: (a) the talent and capacities of youth; (b) standards for educational and psychological measurements; (c) how careers are selected; and (d) the effects of education on occupational preparation.

The project results have led to numerous publications on the vocational and occupational development of students, most notably Flanagan's *Design for a study of American youth*. Among the more important findings were that a great majority of students do not make appropriate career choices in high school, and career plans tend to be unrealistic in ninth grade, but become more realistic by grade 12, with dramatic career changes seen soon after graduation. Follow-up studies have provided considerable information to those in the field of vocational and career counseling.

GIFTED AND TALENTED CHILDREN
PRECOCIOUS MATHEMATICAL REASONERS

L. V. PARADISE

PROPAGANDA

Propaganda is the advancement of a position or view in a manner that attempts to persuade rather than to present a balanced overview. Propaganda can be contrasted with education, which seeks to communicate knowledge.

The first systematic analysis of war-time propaganda was by H. D. Lasswell. He studied each side's success in achieving four objectives: (a) demoralizing the enemy; (b) mobilizing hatred against the enemy; (c) maintaining the friendship of neutrals; and (d) possibly obtaining the cooperation of the neutrals.

In other countries, "propaganda" was used quite openly and nonevaluatively as a descriptor. Thus Josef Goebbels in Hitler's Germany was the head of the Propaganda Bureau. The United States has generally identified its agencies that do comparable work as "information" or "communication" agencies. In the United States, the term propaganda has had negative connotations since the 1930s, when it was identified with the efforts of Germany and Italy to obtain favorable views of their new political organizations.

In military propaganda, which seeks to subvert the morale of an enemy, the target is the potential waverer, the person who is still fighting but has lost any enthusiasm. To expect such persons to surrender on the basis of propaganda is unrealistic, but they might be encouraged to permit themselves to be captured, under appropriate circumstances.

One avenue in the study of propaganda involves the analysis of fear appeals in persuasion. Dependent variables studied include such issues as the intention to use seat belts and to obtain appropriate injections against disease. Although the results are not consistent, there is an overall tendency for a positive relationship between the intensity of fear arousal and the amount of attitude change that occurs from propaganda.

It is possible that influenceability or persuasibility by propaganda and other persuasive communications is a general trait, but research on the subject has had only moderate success in identifying its correlates. Propaganda is most likely to be effective with people who are already in favor of the views it is promoting. If they are not in favor they may not expose themselves to it. If they are not in favor but are exposed to it, they may not comprehend the message, by not identifying with it or changing its frame of reference. Therefore, propaganda efforts may start by preparing audiences to receive the message and to become advocates. This process involves appeals on the importance of an issue.

In marketing products or services, public relations and advertising activities represent a form of propaganda, since they are not necessarily interested in communicating the whole truth but in selective communication of information for the purpose of encouraging sales.

ATTITUDES
COMMUNICATION THEORY
PERSUASIVE COMMUNICATIONS
SOCIAL INFLUENCE THEORY

C. WINICK

PROSOCIAL BEHAVIOR

Prosocial behavior consists of responses that have no obvious benefits for the responder but are beneficial to the recipient. Both internal and external mechanisms have been proposed as determinants of prosocial behavior. As individuals mature, they understand more, are better able to grasp the consequences of their behaviors, and learn to accept and act on general principles of morality. External emphases have focused on the situational determinants of prosocial behavior. Two major theoretical approaches for understanding prosocial behavior have stressed the importance of the situation or setting: a reinforcement explanation of why persons sometimes help others, and a cognitive analysis of the manner in which perceptions and judgments can influence behavior. From the point of view of some learning theorists, prosocial responses occur because they have been rewarded in the past. In addition to direct experiences, individuals are also influenced by their expectations about future rewards or punishments.

Among factors found to affect prosocial behavior are external determinants such as the presence of bystanders. The presence of more than one bystander in an emergency situation tends to inhibit the responses of each person present. This bystander inhibition appears to be a function of individuals' uncertainty about the situation. People respond less when circumstances are ambiguous, when they are unfamiliar with the surroundings, and when they are unsure of the behavioral norms of a particular setting.

Internal factors found to affect prosocial behavior include such variables as the mood a person is experiencing. Helping behavior increases when individuals are in a positive mood. Prosocial behavior also varies as a function of the relative balance of perceived costs and perceived rewards.

ALTRUISM
BYSTANDER INVOLVEMENT
COOPERATION/COMPETITION
DEVELOPMENT OF HUMAN SOCIAL BEHAVIOR
SOCIAL CLIMATE EXPERIMENTS

C. H. HUBER

PSEUDODEMENTIA

The American Psychiatric Association's *Diagnostic and statistical manual of mental disorders*, (*DSM-III-R*) describes dementia as an organic mental syndrome characterized by global impairment in memory severe enough to interfere with the ability to work or severe enough to interfere with the ability to carry out social activities. Memory loss in dementia can be associated with faulty judgment, a tendency to avoid new tasks, and problems with impulse control. Friends and family may also note personality changes. The *DSM-III-R* generally assumes that dementia has an underlying organic cause.

For dementia to be diagnosed there must be evidence of impairment in short-term as well as long-term memory. In addition, one of the following must be present: (a) impairment in abstract thinking as noted, for example, by impaired performance in such tasks as defining words and concepts and finding similarities and differences in related words; (b) impaired judgment; (c) other impairments of higher cortical functioning, which can include problems in carrying out language or motor functions; and (d) changes in personality.

If no findings point to an organic basis for dementia, the manual advises that an organic cause can still be assumed if no other factors can be found as causative agents. *Pseudodementia* refers to nonorganic factors that can account for symptoms of dementia. Initially, this condition was named depressive pseudodementia under the assumption that depression will cause cognitive symptoms, including memory impairments. Andrew A. Swihart and Francis J. Pirozzolo pointed out that pseudodementia as a diagnostic category is not clearly defined, explaining that characteristic features of pseudodementia include reversibility of memory and other intellectual impairments once the nonorganic disorder has been diagnosed and treated accurately. In contrast, dementia is not reversible and is usually progressive, even though there may be long, plateau-like periods.

Most often, pseudodementia occurs in individuals older than 50 years of age, although it can occur at any age. Asenath LaRue, Connie Dessonville, and Lissy F. Jarvik noted that 30% of individuals may be incorrectly classified. Some individuals tend to improve without treatment, whereas others respond to treatment for depression. Although often difficult to apply clinical criteria to differentiate between demented and depressed individuals, there have been a number of attempts to do so. Memory loss for recent events is about the same as for distant events (patients with dementia often have greater memory loss for recent events). The emotional reactions (coping, affective state, concern about disability, and general complaints) of patients with pseudodementia tend to be emphasized in contrast to demented patients, and previous psychological problems are reported more frequently, although the ability to concentrate may be relatively intact. Overall performance on neuropsychological assessment tasks may be more variable, with a greater likelihood of "don't know" answers as opposed to "near misses." Most authorities agree that pseudodementia is especially difficult to diagnose. Furthermore, this diagnosis has not been demonstrated to be conclusive and is often based on an overall pattern of diagnostic signs and the overall clinical history of the patient, rather than on specifically pertinent symptom constellations.

Although depression has been noted as an important determinant in the diagnosis of pseudodementia, other conditions may produce nonorganic memory impairments. Individuals diagnosed as suffering from chronic schizophrenia or other psychotic disorders may have memory dysfunctions. Most often, the clinical history for such individuals is sufficient to rule out a dementing process. Malingering can also result in a diagnosis of pseudodementia (or dementia), but clinical history, overall patient symptoms, and careful psychological testing should minimize diagnostic dilemmas. Finally, the diagnosis of factitious disorder (the intentional production of symptoms without any evident outside incentives) could be consistent with pseudodementia. Psychological and neuropsychological assessment is helpful in making a differential diagnosis.

There is a lack of consensus for the diagnosis of pseudodementia. Carl Salzman and Janice Gutfreund stated that pseudodementia is neither pseudo nor dementia. They insisted that it is a genuine impairment of memory secondary to depression without impairment of other mental processes. They believe it is helpful to differentiate patients both on the basis of mood and cognitive functions as well as on age. They used a four-category descriptive system, starting with the young-old (younger than 80 years) who are mildly to moderately depressed. Then come the young-old who are severely depressed, followed by the old (older than 80 years) who are mildly to moderately depressed; this is followed by the old who are severely depressed. These authors contended that the assessment of memory loss as a function of depression is relatively easy for the first group and increasingly difficult for the other three groups. In their opinion, the older than 80 years of age, and severely depressed group may not be amenable to accurate assessment.

The importance of distinguishing between depression and dementia in the elderly is vital. Physicians prescribe antidepressant medications if they suspect that a patient may be depressed. Although this may be helpful for younger patients, it may be less than helpful for older patients because antidepressant medications may be toxic for the elderly, and, almost paradoxically, the chemical nature of some of the antidepressant drugs may in themselves produce memory impairment. Every effort should be made to differentiate dementia from pseudodementia, recognizing that neither dementia nor pseudodementia are clearly defined categories and that the assessment of pseudodementia is fraught with great difficulties, especially for those older than 80 years of age who are severely depressed.

ALZHEIMER'S DISEASE
BARNUM EFFECT
CENTRAL NERVOUS SYSTEM DISORDERS
DEPRESSION
SENILE PSYCHOSES
THOUGHT DISTURBANCES

N. Abeles

PSEUDOHERMAPHRODISM

The presence of male and female genitalia in one individual is commonly thought of as *hermaphrodism*. In many cases, however, the genitals are ambiguous or opposite to the genetic or gonadal sex. Pseudohermaphrodism occurs when only one type of gonadal tissue is present, but genital appearance is at least slightly at variance with gonadal sex. The cause of true or pseudohermaphrodism may be genetic, but anomalous sex organ development may also be caused by various prenatal hormonal factors.

Female pseudohermaphrodites, genetic females with ovaries and female sexual anatomy, have varying degrees of external genital masculinization. The most frequent cause of female pseudohermaphrodism is congenital adrenal hyperplasia (CAH), in which defective cortisone synthesis leads to overproduction of androgen, thus masculinizing the external genitalia. Genetically, gonadally, and internally female, CAH females are fertile, and, if the condition is discovered, are raised as females, with stereotypical female sex roles.

Male pseudohermaphrodites are genetic and gonadal males whose genitals do not masculinize; the disorder is called *testicular feminization*. Although the gonads secrete adequate amounts of androgens, the genitals differentiate as if no androgen were present, and the morphology is indistinguishable from that of the female. Usually discovered in adolescence, when the absence of menses causes concern, treatment involves removal of the testes and subsequent estrogen therapy.

BEHAVIORAL GENETICS
CHROMOSOME DISORDERS
GENETIC DISORDERS
HERITABILITY
NEONATAL DEVELOPMENT
SEXUAL DYSFUNCTIONS

B. E. THORN

PSEUDOPSYCHOLOGY

Work that superficially or deceptively resembles psychology can range from that of subprofessional quality to outright quackery. Some pseudopsychology is a harmless and entertaining pastime, but other forms can be harmful.

Professional and scientific psychology requires controlled observations under precisely specified and repeatable conditions. To the extent that its work depends on casual observation, anecdotes, and testimonial evidence, it is subprofessional or unscientific.

Why does pseudopsychology persist? One answer is that there is a handsome profit to be made in alleviating anxiety.

Given the diversity of approaches to psychology, it is difficult to distinguish developing subfields of psychology precisely from borderline pseudopsychology. Whether memory can be transferred from one organism to another or whether primates can acquire language is currently unclear, yet these are legitimate areas of research. Events such as voodoo death appear to exist, but the mechanisms are little understood.

EXAMPLES OF PSEUDOPSYCHOLOGY

The following examples of pseudopsychology, although they have some supporters, are without any currently demonstrable evidence of value.

Astrology

According to many astrologists, not only is an individual's basic temperament related to the moment of birth, but divination of future events is based on the current pattern of stars and planets. Specific contemporary criticisms of astrology include the fact that the moment of birth rather than that of conception is chosen as the focal point and astrology's failure to revise calculations in accordance with developments in modern astronomy.

Numerology

Although there have been extremely complex numerology systems such as the cabalistic, the usual practice comes from Pythagoras.

Color Preference

From the earliest times, color has symbolized various natural phenomena: red for fire, gold for sun, white for moon, green for crops, and so on. One recent practice is to ask the individual to rank 10 color chips in order of preference; without any research basis, it is claimed that the subject's personality can be deduced from the ranking.

Phrenology

In this eighteenth- and nineteenth-century movement, it was hypothesized that various human traits were associated with specific parts of the brain. Individuals with strong tendencies purportedly had enlargements of the corresponding brain area; these areas were detected by examining the shape of the skull.

Physiognomy

From the most ancient times, personality has been related to physical appearance. Basic body structure was used for personality predictions by people from Hippocrates of Cos to William Sheldon. Fat people are said to be jolly; tall, thin people are viewed as quiet thinkers. Other physiognomic variants include analysis of the shape of the head and face.

Palmistry

Divination using the hands is found in two forms. The more common, chirosophy, relates the lines on the palm to personality and fate. One method considers the dominant hand to indicate "natural" tendencies while the nonpreferred hand shows learned traits and the inclination to follow the natural traits. Chirognomy uses the shape of the hand and fingers, the way the fingernails are cut, and mannerisms in holding and moving the hands.

Graphology

The slant, size, letter formation, and other characteristics of handwriting are stated to be related to personality. Analysts disagree as to whether the signature or a sample of "casual" writing is more revealing. Handwriting analysis is more popular in Europe than in the United States. Research indicates too slight a relationship between personality and handwriting for practical prediction.

Cold Reading

"Cold" refers to lack of prior information about the client. The soothsayer first builds rapport by describing past events, and then moves to prediction. The technique involves placing the individual in one of seven categories, beginning with standard statements for the category, and modifying comments according to the subtle cues of the subject's body language and facial expression. A number of props may be used, such as playing or Tarot cards, dice, dominoes, tea leaves, a pendulum, a divining rod, a Ouija board, or a crystal ball.

Parapsychology

Clairvoyance is the instantaneous awareness of an event without the usual means of obtaining the knowledge. Telepathy is communication between two individuals without the use of obvious links. Precognition is the foretelling of future events in specific detail. Collectively, these three phenomena are referred to as extrasensory perception (ESP). Psychokinesis (PK) is the manipulation of physical objects by thought.

Even the best research designed to demonstrate the phenomena of ESP and PK is characterized by lack of adequate controls. J. B. Rhine and others have complained that stricter research standards are asked of parapsychology than of other areas, but selective stringency is entirely appropriate. Many instances of fraud are documented. The more unlikely the event, the more convincing must be the evidence.

Dream Analysis

Freud's notion of fixed symbols is now considered erroneous. Although many within a culture may use a common symbol, humans are too unique to apply an automatic interpretation without regard to individual differences. In the hands of a trained clinician, dream analysis is a useful tool that points to a person's traumas, anxiety, and wishes. However, it is the individual's hopes or expectations for the future that are discerned in some dreams, rather than simple prediction of the future.

ASTROLOGY
EXTRASENSORY PERCEPTION
PARAPSYCHOLOGY
PHRENOLOGY
PSYCHIC RESEARCH
SUPERSTITIONS
WITCHCRAFT

C. S. PEYSER

PSYCHIATRIC CLINICS

In 1909, the first community clinic for children was established with state funds in Chicago by William Healy. Healy's Juvenile Psychopathic Institute (later renamed the Institute for Juvenile Research) provided diagnostic and treatment services while simultaneously conducting research on the etiology of mental disorders. Following these initial efforts, with the hope of developing preventive programs and with encouragement of citizen groups such as the National Committee for Mental Hygiene, child guidance clinics developed rapidly, growing from an estimated seven in 1921 to more than 100 by 1927.

After World War II, the development of psychiatric clinics received another boost from a report by the interdisciplinary Joint Commission on Mental Illness and Health issued in 1961. Among its central recommendations, the Commission advocated replacing large state hospitals with the mental health services, such as outpatient clinics based in local communities, to maximize the patients' opportunities to maintain or develop social relations within their communities.

CHILD GUIDANCE CLINICS
MENTAL HEALTH PROGRAMS
REHABILITATION CENTERS
WALK-IN CLINICS

R. D. FELNER

PSYCHIATRIC SOCIAL WORK

Social work is a complex, diverse, and somewhat amorphous profession. The diversity of the tasks assumed by social workers requires an equally diverse knowledge base, one to which virtually all of the social and behavioral disciplines contribute.

DEFINITION

Psychiatric social workers are employed in mental health settings, usually hold a master's degree in social work, and are expert in social treatment (working with individuals, families, and small groups). Their education provides them with the following knowledge and skill:

1. An understanding of the common human needs of clients regardless of the setting in which they are encountered or the problems they present.
2. Knowledge about the effects of the help-giving systems as well as those systems in which the client interacts.
3. Knowledge about cultural diversity.
4. Knowledge about the environment with respect both to its effects on the individual and to the alteration of it.
5. Knowledge about social welfare policy, programs, and resources and how to obtain them.
6. Commitment to the underclass.
7. Ability to intervene with a range of problems, settings, and clients.
8. Research skills.

In 1974, 17% of the professional care staff in inpatient and outpatient, private and public mental health facilities were social workers. This is in contrast to psychiatrists and psychologists who represented 14% and 11%, respectively, of the full-time professional staff. Among such facilities, private mental hospitals hired the smallest percentage of social workers (3%) and outpatient clinics hired the largest percentage (26%). Assuming that staffing patterns adequately reflect service, social workers provide more mental health care than psychiatrists or psychologists do.

The formative years of social work include some of the currents that remain a part of the profession. Among them are concern for the basic survival needs of people, a tension between counseling and social reform, a concern for families and about the environments of the needy, and conflicting traditions of fact gathering, social control, and client advocacy. These divergent urges are of some consternation to the profession, and perhaps to educators in particular, as they struggle to define the needed curricular content. Since social work is largely the manifestation of society's altruism, and since social problems are unlikely to disappear but rather to transmogrify, depending on the economic and political conditions of the country, it is likely that the tensions will continue. Perhaps the strains are functional in that their continuous, and side-by-side existence allows various postures to achieve preeminence as needed.

APPROACHES TO INTERVENTION

During the 1960s, research into the effectiveness of social work began and the findings were disappointing. This decade also brought renewed interest in civil rights and poverty. As a result, an increasing number of social workers turned their attention to social reform and the clinical social workers began to develop, examine, and use approaches other than the dominant psychoanalytic one.

Psychosocial casework frequently is referred to as the diagnostic approach. The approach is characterized by a fairly lengthy assessment phase, during which facts are gathered for the purpose of accumulating a psychosocial history. The object of this endeavor is to understand the nature and dynamics of the client's personality. Attention to the environment or situation of the client is extolled, as it is in most approaches developed by social workers.

The *functional* model of practice was developed during the 1930s. In this approach, casework is seen as a process by which specific social services are delivered within the context of an enabling relationship. The helping process is emphasized, especially the aspects of initiating, sustaining, and terminating it. The function of the agency provides the focus for work and assessment or diagnosis is related to the client's use of service. The functional approach is employed by a very small percentage of social workers but many of its principles have influenced more recent scholarly contributions.

The *problem-solving* approach to casework evolved in the late 1950s. The differences between it and the psychosocial approach bordered on heretical at the time. The four major concepts within this approach are person, problem, process, and place. The process refers to that which occurs between social worker and client, and the place refers to the agency in which help is offered. The stress on the last three variables differentiates this approach from the psychosocial one. In other words, the coping capacities of the individual are given more recognition.

Task-centered casework is also a problem-solving approach. In this approach, the focus clearly shifts from the person to the problem. The target problem(s), that which is to be altered, is identified by the client rather than by the worker's assessment of personality deficits. Assessment is focused on the problem—the conditions that describe it, its frequency, duration, or severity—rather than on the person. This approach is a planned, short-term one. Intervention consists of helping the client engage in activities or tasks designed to reduce or eradicate the target problem.

A number of approaches based on *systems theory* have evolved. The ready acceptance of this framework for thinking is undoubtedly the promise it offers for a conceptual view of the environment. In these approaches, assessment consists of examining the various overlapping systems that might be causing or maintaining the problem. These approaches open up the question of who or what is to be changed and who is to do the changing.

The newly emergent *ecological perspective* is a variant on systems approaches. In this approach, stress is attributed to a lack of reciprocity between the individual and the environment. The adaptive capacities of clients are supported and environmental pressures are alleviated. One of the major advances explicated in the ecological approach is the recognition that most problems are neither solely the result of individual deficiencies nor of the social order.

Three other recent additions to our interventive tools are *empirical clinical practice, behavioral models,* and *eclectic approaches.* All are reflections of the profession's increasing concern for accountability. The eclectic models are conceptual tools for selecting the most effective interventions from a variety of approaches. Finally, behavioral procedures, described elsewhere, are being used increasingly by social workers.

The use of *family treatment* was evident from the inception of social work. It was not until the late 1950s, however, that models were articulated for intervening with families. The various approaches to family treatment have generally evolved from the work of interdisciplinary teams. Most work with families, regardless of the profession of the practitioner, tends to be eclectic. Social workers, like other helping professionals, employ the structural approach, communication and Bowenian theory, and psychodynamic and behavioral approaches.

Social group work, a method that consists of working with a small number of individuals collectively, emerged during the Settlement House movement. It was not until the 1940s that group work began to be used to help the emotionally troubled. The specific purpose and functions of social group work remain a matter of debate. Education, social reform, recreation, prevention, and therapy compete as *raisons d'etre.* Distinctions between various models for working with groups are not as clear-cut as those that exist among casework models. The same differences in emphasis do exist, however. Thus, paralleling the casework models, models for social group work have been developed around the following orientations: psychosocial, functional, systems, task centered, and problem solving. Distinctions among these approaches have been described.

COMMUNITY PSYCHOLOGY
MENTAL HEALTH TEAMS
SOCIAL CASEWORK

E. R. TOLSON

PSYCHIC RESEARCH

Psychic research is the controversial study of such phenomena as mediumship, telepathy, clairvoyance, telekinesis, and precognition. Sometimes the term is used to include a broader range of occult phenomena, such as poltergeists, UFOs, dowsing, and reincarnation; however, many psychic researchers exclude these from the field.

Historically, psychic research began in the nineteenth century among a circle of men concerned with the weakening of religion and faith in an afterlife. Science had eroded belief in traditional Christianity, and they turned to science to prove what for them was the central tenet of religion: the continued existence of the soul after death. In the background was the quasi-religious movement of Spiritualism. For the Christian conceptions of Heaven and Hell, the Spiritualists substituted a many-layered afterlife, envisioning the continued spiritual development of souls after death. Spiritualistic mediums—most of whom were outright frauds—purported to be able to communicate with departed persons, thereby furnishing "proof" of the existence of the soul and the eternity of life.

Psychic researchers set about investigating mediums, hauntings, and other evidences of the unseen.

The early psychic researchers focused on Spiritualistic mediums. Many were exposed as frauds, and others were charlatans who duped the investigators, whereas the feats of a few remain unexplained. In any case, from seances the researchers amassed alleged evidence of spirit communica-

tion. Unfortunately for the movement, investigation of mediums was often carried out in the most glaring public light, and the psychic researchers were ridiculed by skeptics and embarrassed by enthusiasts.

Psychic research entered a new phase in the 1930s with the work of J. B. Rhine and his colleagues at Duke University. Rhine substituted laboratory rooms for seance chambers, normal subjects for flamboyant mediums, and statistical tests for floating trumpets and ectoplasm, thereby revolutionizing psychic research and winning for it occasional grudging respect as a science.

The legitimacy of parapsychology is still questioned. From its beginning, psychic research has been championed by some eminent psychologists (e.g., William James, Gardner Murphy) and rejected by others (e.g., Wilhelm Wundt, Donald Hebb). It retains its popularity with the public at large, which links it with flamboyant occultism, often to the embarrassment of psychic researchers.

Parapsychologists are wont to couch their theories of paranormal phenomena in materialistic terms and to view their work as an extension of quantum physics or information-processing cognitive psychology. No longer are paranormal phenomena taken as necessary refutations of the materialistic worldview, but simply as anomalies—unexplained events—to be explained within established science.

OCCULTISM
PARAPSYCHOLOGY
PSEUDOPSYCHOLOGY
SUPERSTITIONS

T. H. LEAHEY

PSYCHOANALYSIS

The term *psychoanalysis* is used in three ways: (a) to designate a loosely knit body of *ideas on the nature of the human mind,* in particular, personality development and psychopathology; (b) to describe a *technique of therapeutic intervention* in a range of psychological disturbances; and (c) to designate a *method of investigation.* All were originated during the last decades of the nineteenth century by the Viennese-Jewish physician, Sigmund Freud (1856–1939). Freud was one of those great thinkers who "disturb the sleep of the world."

As therapy, psychoanalysis in its inception regarded as its central task the uncovering of pathogenic memories; this gave way to the search for fantasies, and with the theoretical shift away from "instincts and their vicissitudes" to the discerning of configurations of characteristically adaptive patterns of human relationships and of work in a particular society.

THE FIRST PHASE

Freud made his monumental discoveries in the context of a threefold crisis—in therapeutic technique, in the conceptualization of clinical experience, and in a personal crisis. All three crises were, in essence, one, and were the necessary dimensions of discovery in psychology.

As that other great nineteenth-century reviser of the human image, Charles Darwin, had used the Galapagos Islands as his laboratory, so the neurologist Freud, much influenced by Darwin, used his consulting room. The "dominant species" under investigation, at first, were mainly Victorian women diagnosed as suffering from hysteria. Freud had been deeply impressed by the work of internist Joseph Breuer. His later observations of the work of neurologists A. A. Liebault, H. Bernheim, and J. Charcot in France, who were also using hypnosis, confirmed his impression that this therapeutic technique offered better results than the then-fashionable electrotherapy. Unlike his colleagues, however, he became convinced that the source of difficulty ("forgotten mental contents") had not simply been "split off" but had been "pushed out" of, or "dragged down" from, immediate awareness by powerful *motivational* forces. This was a critical turn: to bring into focus the human psychological capacity to defend against pain. At first Freud called this process *defense,* and later *repression.* From the start, Freud underscored that repression is "not a premise, but a finding."

Freud's initial discovery of a level of mentation, not accessible to immediate awareness, but which, nonetheless, has observable effects on behavior and on experience, rests on this dynamic concept. Joseph Breuer theorized that there was a simple absence of communication between what he called a "hypnoid" mental state and waking consciousness. He assumed that, in such a hypnoid mental state, a real trauma—for example, a girl's seduction by her father—had occurred and had been "forgotten."

For a time, Freud tried to allow the older, more physiological theory to exist side by side with his new model. He became totally convinced that the "splitting off" of mental contents—often "converted" into symptoms—was deeply motivated in his cases of hysteria and was not simply an absence of communication between mental states. Of far greater significance for him than the etiology of hysteria was his growing conviction that *similar defensive processes were part of the psychology of ordinary normal human beings as well,* who, though they might be free of symptoms, did make slips of the tongue, tell jokes, and have dreams.

During this first phase (pre-1896), Freud came to the bold, and then bitterly contested, conclusion that the etiology of hysteria was psychological and not "neurological." Freud began to develop the hypothesis that there are three major determinants in hysteria: a *psychological trauma,* a *conflict of affects,* and a *disturbance in the sphere of sexuality.*

"The psychoses of defense" was published in 1896. This paper is actually the beginning of psychoanalysis, although Freud had not yet coined the word. The theory of this first phase collapsed when Freud discovered, to his dismay, that his patients' reports of infantile seduction were not necessarily reports of actual experiences, but of fantasies.

THE SECOND PHASE

The second phase of psychoanalytic inquiry began with Freud's discarding of the formal techniques of hypnosis and the introduction of his method of "free association": His patient, supine on a couch, was instructed by him—sitting behind on a chair—simply to say freely anything and everything that came to mind, without conscious censorship.

For purposes of inquiry into the workings of the mind, he used this method on the assumption that if conscious censorship is voluntarily suspended, the inner resistance (the concept is used as in electricity, not as in willful stubbornness) will lessen, thus permitting the emergence into awareness of "repressed" material or, at least, of its derivatives. Freud, early on, decided that the theory of psychoanalysis was an attempt to account for the "facts of transference and resistance." It was the method of free association, especially in the decoding of dreams, that Freud used, first in his self-analysis and later in his classic case of "Dora."

The conditions of dreaming provided a golden opportunity to study the difference between logical thought processes ("secondary thought process") and illogical—condensed, for example, or displaced—processes as in dreams, jokes, and poems.

From the beginning, Freud sought to put his general theory of the human mind "on psychological ground" and to free this theory from the constraints of the biology and neurology of his time. Indeed, in spite of the often dramatic successes of the hypnotic–cathartic "talking cure" in the first phase of his work (a phase with which many people, including clinicians, end their acquaintance with psychoanalysis), Freud increasingly believed that his discoveries might be ultimately more influential in general science than as a mode of therapy.

In this second phase of psychoanalysis, begun around 1897 and ending in 1923, Freud vigorously pursued not only the questions of "instincts and their vicissitudes" but also the central problem of the possible source for that dynamic (defensive–repressive) force that regularly—in patients and in normal people—keeps certain painful mental contents from awareness.

THE THIRD PHASE

Between 1900 and 1923, the psychoanalytic movement expanded organizationally, theoretically, and clinically, and experienced its major secessions as well. In his *Interpretation of dreams,* Freud pursued the universal inclination of dreams to "form fresh unities" out of disparate elements "which in our waking thoughts we should certainly have kept separate" (condensation). Again, that an element that was of no consequence in the dream thoughts "appears to be the clearest" and thus the most important feature of the manifest dream (or vice versa), he called displacement. These *condensations, displacements,* and *symbolizations* characterize a kind of thinking in which laws of formal logic have no place: This is the language and syntax of poetry, myth, magic, mysticism, and psychosis—the awesome *primary process.* This primary process is in contrast to the more familiar *secondary process,* governed by laws of logic. This was later linked by him to the "reality principle."

In 1923, Freud's *The ego and the id* crowned the third phase of psychoanalysis. In this book, Freud discussed the character and the evolution of the ego (the self, the "I"). He argued that when a person has to give up an "object" (i.e., a relationship), there ensues a modification within the "I" that can be described only as a *reinstatement* of that object, for example, as in melancholia.

Of central importance in the functional importance of the ego is the fact that control over the approaches to motility devolves on it. Thus, in relation to the id the ego is "like a man on horseback who has to hold in check the superior strength of the horse." The often-forgotten difference is that "the rider seeks to do so with his own strength while the ego uses borrowed forces."

There is little room for the experience of willing or choosing. Moreover, although some independent developmental roots are attributed to this ego, there is as yet no evolving and systematic (epigenetic) ground plan of a biopsychosocial nature.

Not until 1926 did Freud repudiate the idea that the ego (defensive, executive, and adaptive functions) is totally subservient to the id (drives).

Freud discussed the development of the ego ideal and the superego—roughly the conscience or an unconscious sense of guilt—only as a defensive internalization, an identification with the father by a male child, adding in a footnote, "Perhaps it would be safer to say 'with the parents,' " and acknowledging the "constitutional bisexuality of each individual." When the male child perceives his father as the obstacle to the carrying out of the child's (forbidden) desires toward his mother, the ego brings in this reinforcement (thus the term "superego") to help in carrying out the repression "by erecting this same obstacle within itself." The more intense the original conflict, the more exacting later on is the domination of the superego over the ego—in the form of conscience or perhaps of an unconscious sense of guilt.

It becomes the complex task of ego functioning to mediate—and to provide a delaying action—between the peremptory demands from the drives (id), these moral or spiritual restraints (superego), and the real world.

Jung (1875–1961)

In 1906, Freud, then almost 50 years old, received as a gift Carl Jung's account of his word–association experiments, highly sympathetic to psychoanalysis. In this experimental psychopathology, Jung introduced the *complex* as a link between an affect and an idea. During the next 7 years (1906–1913), over the protests of the leading Viennese psychoanalysts such as Adler and Wilhelm Stekel, Jung became the recognized political leader of the movement and Freud's heir apparent. The turning point between Freud and Jung came in 1912. Freud had already begun to be unhappy at the direction of Jung's thought into religion, mysticism, and mythology, finding his thinking confused. Direct reports from Jung's former patients persuaded Freud that the basics of psychoanalysis (resistance and transference) were being neglected in favor of fuzzy discussions of "archetypes" and "the collective unconscious."

Adler (1870–1937)

The Viennese psychoanalysts banded together to protest Freud's elevation of Jung to a position of leadership. The most prominent rebel was Alfred Adler, of whom Freud had held a high opinion in the early years. Adler's single-minded focus on the psychological effects of organ inferiority was the source of Freud's concern that Adler would soon deny the hard-won territory of the existence of unconscious mental processes and daimonic drives. Adler saw the aggressive drive as the source of energy when people compensate for their inferiorities, and his elaboration of this position precipitated the break with Freud.

By the time Freud placed the aggressive instinct within the death instinct (Thanatos) as opposed to the life instinct (Eros), Adler was no longer concerned with instincts. He considered the aggressive drive and the will to power as central means of defense and adaptation. Freud granted that Adler had indubitably brought "something new to psychoanalysis."

THE FOURTH PHASE

By the mid-1930s, Freud's dimly implied conception of the ego's relative autonomy from drives—and its integrative functions—had been made explicit. Ten years earlier, Freud, in *Group psychology and the analysis of the ego,* had begun to address the issues of the outside (social) reality.

In 1939, Heinz Hartmann published an essay, "Ego psychology and the problem of adaptation," in which he emphasized "those processes and working methods of the mental apparatus which lead to *adapted achievements.*"

By 1936, the basic theoretical tenets of psychoanalysis were being woven into American psychiatry by Harry Stack Sullivan. The destruction of self-esteem became a central problem for Sullivan and—because of his psychoanalytic inquiry into the schizophrenic process—he has been called the "theorist of the lonely."

The importance of the therapist's contribution to the transaction with a patient (countertransference) had been mentioned only glancingly by Freud (1910, 1915). Sullivan, following Sandor Ferenczi's lead, stated that Freud's great contribution was the "postulate of the unconscious," adding by 1937, "the crying need is for observers who are growing observant of their observing." Under the influence of William Alanson White and the Swiss psychobiologist Adolph Meyer, Sullivan moved decisively away from the orthodoxies of psychoanalysis and into an "American" psychiatry.

Karen Horney (1885–1952) shared Sullivan's emphasis on the social (interpersonal) and, in preference to genetic interpretation, she put the "here and now" at the center of therapy. She shared also his downgrading of instinct theory and sexuality and, along with Erik Erikson, although less systematically, saw people configurationally. Her main concern was not theory but therapy. She turned her attention to self-image and character structure as conditioned by social organization. The security operations that humans evolve are adaptive, she argued, as well as defensive.

Erikson (1902–1992)

Erik Erikson moved significantly beyond Freud. His revitalization of the Freudian tradition stems essentially from his systematic attempt to comprehend the simultaneous interweaving and evolution of the workings of the body, the psyche, and the society over the entire life cycle and into the sequence of generations.

Erikson's biopsychosocial model provides a locus for the various theories of object relations as well as for the emerging self-systems and self-psychologies. All of these bodies of observation had for many years remained outside the theoretical scope of psychoanalytic ego psychology. Clinicians were, of course, using these ideas all along.

SUMMARY

Although *psychoanalysis,* as investigative mode, therapy, and theory, is on the wane outside of psychoanalytic circles, the fundamentals of the Freudian revolution—as well as the post-Freudian revisions—since the late nineteenth century have been incorporated progressively into the mainstream not only of psychology and psychiatry, but also of the social sciences, the humanities, education, and history:

1. The postulate of a *level of mentation not accessible to immediate awareness,* but which has observable effects on experience and on behavior.

2. The concept of *psychological defense against pain,* which drives mental contents from awareness and seeks alternative solutions.

3. The *biopsychosocial and epigenetic view* that, from the start to the end of the life cycle (and into the sequence of generations), the "I" and the "we" (self-identity and group identity) are a product of the *simultaneous evolution of the body, the mind, and the society.*

4. The concept that, *along with the human propensity for conflict, there stands the potential for creative synthesis* in the service not only of survival, but also of genuine adaptation.

5. That beyond the pleasure principle stands repetition compulsion, which means the persistent effort to master actively that which has been (*painfully*) passively experienced.

On the assumption that a decisive step has been taken by the Freudian revolution toward an interpenetration of the psychological, the technological, and the political in the human order, a contemporary biopsychosocial theory permits the investigation of not only innovations in therapy, but also alternative modes of conflict–resolution within individuals, interpersonally and collectively.

M. BRENMAN-GIBSON

PSYCHOANALYTIC STAGES

Psychoanalytic stages, or psychosexual stages, are stages of psychosexual development postulated by Sigmund Freud to account for personality development in terms of changes in the biological functioning of the individual. Freud theorized that the central theme running through personality development is the progression of the sex instinct through four universal stages—oral, anal, phallic, and genital. A period of *latency* intervenes between the latter two psychosexual stages but, strictly speaking, it is not to be understood as a stage. Freud assigned crucial significance to the first three of these stages, termed *pregenital stages,* in the formation of adult character structure.

THE ORAL STAGE

During the oral stage of psychosexual development, which lasts approximately throughout the first year of life, the primary erogenous zone is the mouth. Through activities associated with the mouth—sucking, swallowing, biting—infants experience their first continuous source of pleasure, and thus the mouth region becomes a focal point of rudimentary psychosexual satisfaction. Fixation in the oral–aggressive phase (enter teeth), earmarked by biting and chewing activities, may result in a bitingly sarcastic, argumentative, and hostile adult personality.

THE ANAL STAGE

During the second and third years of life, the primary erogenous zone is the anus. Children at this stage are thought to derive considerable pleasure from temporary retention. With the onset of parentally controlled toilet training, however, the child's pleasures in this regard encounter the stiff opposition of social restraints, and various fixations may thus occur. Reflecting the assumption of the importance of early childhood experience in personality formation, Freudians believe that such an approach to toilet training forges the way for the development of adult productivity and creativity.

THE PHALLIC STAGE

The genitals become the primary erogenous zone during the phallic stage of psychosexual development, which extends from the fourth through the fifth years of life. During this stage, children can be observed examining their sex organs, masturbating, and showing interest in matters pertaining to birth and sex. However, perhaps more important, this period of life serves as the stage on which the most critical psychological drama of childhood is played out—the Oedipus complex. Freud theorized that every child unconsciously wishes to possess the opposite-sexed parent and simultaneously dispose of the same-sexed parent.

Freud believed that the boy experiences intense conflict over his incestuous desires toward the mother and fears retaliation from the father for such desires. Specifically, the small boy fears that the father will discover his sexual desires and retaliate by cutting off the boy's penis, a fear that, in psychotanalytic theory, is termed *castration anxiety.*

The little girl during the phallic stage is depicted as discovering that, unlike her father, she lacks a penis. Immediately following this anatomical discovery, the girl wishes she had one—a desire that, in psychoanalytic theory, is called *penis envy.* Penis envy in girls is roughly equivalent psychologically to castration anxiety in boys and, together, penis envy and castration anxiety are known as the *castration complex* in Freudian theory.

Failure to resolve the Oedipus conflict and unresolved Oedipal feelings lie at the root of many psychological disorders, when viewed from the perspective of psychoanalytic theory.

THE GENITAL STAGE

As the Oedipus complex becomes resolved, the child is presumed to move into a period of latency (lasting approximately from 6 to 12 years of age) in which the sex instinct remains relatively dormant and psychic energy is redirected into nonsexual activities, such as school and athletics. With the onset of puberty, however, genital sexuality is reawakened and the genital stage of psychosexual development, extending from puberty until death, begins. During the genital stage, narcissistic strivings become fused with, and largely transformed into, the seeking of heterosexual relationships involving mutual gratification. Thus the adult genital personality type, the successful product of psychosexual development in psychoanalytic theory, is characterized by capacity for mature heterosexual love, responsible concerns beyond the self, and productive living in society.

DEVELOPMENTAL STAGES
PSYCHOANALYSIS

D. J. ZIEGLER

PSYCHODRAMA

Psychodrama is a method of psychotherapy developed by Jacob Moreno. The approach makes use of dramatic techniques whereby the client acts out past, present, or anticipated life situations and roles in an attempt to gain deeper understanding and achieve catharsis.

Moreno firmly believed in the superiority of the therapeutic value of acting out one's problems rather than merely talking about them. Thus his techniques encourage action, personal interaction and encounter, expression of feelings in the present moment, and testing reality. This encounter occurs in the context of the here and now, regardless of whether the enactment relates to a past event or an anticipated one. Moreno considered spontaneity and creativity as basic characteristics of the healthy and alive person.

Psychodrama is both a lively and powerful method of therapy; by dealing with a past or an anticipated problem as though that conflict were happening now, intense feelings are typically brought up. This process is designed to be a corrective emotional experience; through the present-centered experience and enactment, catharsis occurs that is often followed by an increased level of insight. Anticipated events are played out in the present to give clients increased awareness of a range of choices.

There are five basic components of the psychodramatic method: a stage, a director, a protagonist, auxiliary egos, and the audience.

There are three phases of the psychodramatic process: (a) the warm-up phase, (b) the action phase, and (c) the discussion phase. Moreno wrote about the necessity for a *warm-up* period designed to get the participants ready for the experience. The group leader plays a key role in establishing this readiness and motivation needed to deal with real-life issues in a personal way. During this phase, members must be assured that the working environment is a safe one, and a climate of trust must be built. The techniques of accomplishing the warm-up are less important than its purpose; anything that leads to an increase of trust within the group is a useful tool for this initial phase.

The *action* phase consists of the acting out and working through of a past or present situation or of an anticipated event. The director uses a variety of dramatic techniques to guide the protagonist's exploration of new territory and gain fresh understanding without becoming overwhelmed. As acts are completed and as catharsis and insight are experienced, the action is allowed to wind down. Then the third phase of the psychodrama—the sharing, discussion, and postaction phase—consists of some attempt to integrate and provide meaning for the experience just acted out. The others in the group are asked to share personal observations by telling how the session related to them.

During the action phase of a psychodrama, there are many action-oriented techniques that are not ends in themselves but are aimed at the spontaneous expression of feelings. Some standard psychodramatic techniques include role reversal, the double technique, multiple doubling, the mirror technique, the magic shop, future projection, and dream work.

The key to successful psychodrama is the sensitivity and technical competence of the psychodrama director. Although psychodrama can be a powerful form of therapeutic intervention that can lead to a freeing of constricted feelings and a deeper self-understanding, which can eventually lead to constructive behavior changes, it can also lead to serious negative consequences for the participants.

GROUP PSYCHOTHERAPY
PSYCHOTHERAPY

G. COREY

PSYCHOENDOCRINOLOGY

In the middle of the twentieth century, the need for a fuller understanding of the biological basis and correlates of behavior and psychological processes led to the formation of new biobehavioral disciplines such as psychobiology, neuropsychology, psychopharmacology, and sociobiology. Psychoendocrinology can be defined as the study of the relationship between the endocrine system and behavior; that is, the influence of the secretions of the endocrine glands, called *hormones,* on behavior, and conversely, the effects of behavior and psychological stimuli on the functioning of the endocrine system. There is unequivocal experimental, clinical, and naturalistic evidence that hormones do indeed play a vital role in determining various behavior patterns in people and animals. It has also been demonstrated that behavior, experience, and psychological stimuli and states exert influence on the functioning of the endocrine system and the secretion of hormones.

The principal tasks of psychoendocrinology are: (a) establishment of covariation and correlation between endocrinological and behavioral events; (b) identification of the neuroendocrine mechanisms involved in the correlation; (c) identification of modifying variables and parameters of this correlation; and (d) understanding of the implication of the psychoendocrine influence for the adaptation of the organism to the environment as well as for physical and mental health.

ROOTS AND FOUNDATIONS

When internal secretion by ductless glands was established and the first hormones were discovered, some psychologists began to look into the possible role of endocrine secretions in emotions and temperament.

Experimental

The first experimental study was performed in 1849, half a century before the discovery of hormones, by A. A. Berthold in Germany. He concluded that "the testes release something into the blood that maintains male behavior and the secondary sex characters."

When the existence of endocrine secretion was established and various hormones were identified, experimentation, mainly on animals but later also on humans, began to flourish. In the 1930s, sex hormones and sex behavior patterns received most attention, but other hormones and behavior patterns were also studied. Adrenalin (or epinephrine), the hormone of the adrenal medulla, was the earliest and the most extensively studied hormone in humans.

Other endocrine systems began to be explored as well, and were found to be sensitive to a variety of psychological stimuli. The work on psychoendocrine relations steadily improved in precision and refinement, mostly because of considerable progress in the understanding of the chemistry and action of hormones as well as the breakthroughs in the measurement of minute quantities of hormones in the body tissues and fluids.

Clinical Observations and Studies

Principally medicine, psychiatry in particular, provided the strongest stimulus and support for psychoendocrine research. Physicians of the nineteenth century reported mental and behavioral changes in patients from disorders of organs that only later were recognized as endocrine glands. Other branches of medicine also pointed to the psychoendocrine component in certain diseases. Evidence was found that emotional disturbances and stress may affect the onset and severity of various medical conditions related to growth, sex functions, skin, nutrition, and sense organs. Studies showed that stress, because of its effect on the endocrine system and immunological responses of the organism, may be implicated in the etiology of cancer.

Neuroendocrinology

Several discoveries contributed to the origin and growth of neuroendocrinology, and consequently to its pivotal role in psychoendocrinology: (a) neurosecretion, that is, the ability of neurons to secrete substances

that possess characteristics of the hormone; (b) an intimate anatomical and functional link between the brain and the pituitary, a gland of central significance for the endocrine system; (c) the ability of the brain to synthesize and secrete hormones as well as the sensitivity of the brain to the circulating hormones; (d) existence of several neuroendocrine feedback loops, for example, between the adrenal cortex and the hypothalamus; (e) improvement of existing methods and introduction of new ones for the identification and measurement of hormones, such as radioimmunoassay; and (f) synthesis of several hormones and production of natural hormones by gene-splicing techniques.

PROGRESS AFTER 1950

Psychoendocrinology developed gradually from its foundations. Two orientations, represented by different groups of investigators, could be discerned within psychoendocrinology from the beginning: One focused primarily on the effects of psychological states on the endocrine system, and another concentrated on the hormonal determinants of various behavioral patterns. The investigators committed to the latter orientation prefer the term *behavioral endocrinology* as a more appropriate appellation for their research.

Although the objectives of psychoendocrinology were formulated around 1940, its consolidation as a scientific enterprise came only in the late 1950s, when neuroendocrine relations were sufficiently elucidated and more accurate research techniques became available. Before 1950, most of the data dealt with the relation of sex behavior to the gonadal hormones. Numerous studies also were carried out on the thyroid, epinephrine, and adrenocortical hormones with respect to behavior.

The scope of psychoendocrine studies has since greatly expanded and includes a wide range of endocrine glands, hormones, and hormonal analogs. The literature on hormones and behavior, which appeared after 1950, reflects the advances made.

PSYCHOENDOCRINE RELATIONS

Hormones have been found to be related to learning and memory, perception, motivation, mood and emotion, coping behavior, and aggression, and to such adaptive behaviors as sex, eating, drinking, and sleeping. Endocrine abnormalities seem to contribute to the etiology of some forms of mental retardation, learning disabilities, and affective disorders.

Hormones do not directly cause behavior. They affect behavior indirectly by their action on the nervous system, metabolism of the body, sensory receptors, muscles, and nonendocrine (exocrine) glands. The most important is the action on the nervous system.

Following are examples of the dependence of certain aspects of behavior on specific hormones—in these cases, on the sex hormones. Libido, or sexual arousability, is related to the hormone androgen in both men and women. Androgen is secreted by both sexes, though in different quantities. Libido is usually diminished when androgen secretion is reduced or absent. Sex hormones affect, among other functions, sensory capacities such as smell and vision. Cognitive functions may be affected by hormones.

Experimental and clinical data clearly indicate that the entire endocrine system is extremely sensitive, although each endocrine gland is sensitive in a different degree to psychological stimuli and states, such as emotions, as well as to certain activities and experiences.

Emotionally disturbed children often stop growing and do not develop normally. This happens because emotional disturbance inhibits normal secretion of the growth hormone. Such children may become dwarfs, or *psychosocial dwarfs,* as they are called in medicine.

The hormone–behavior interrelationship is intimate and pervasive. It is also most complex and subject to the interaction of both genetic and environmental factors. Investigators aim at studying the effect of a psychological event on as many endocrine responses as possible, or the effect of a hormonal event on as many psychological functions as can be assessed.

The relevance of psychoendocrine research to many problems of psychobiology and to several other disciplines, such as medicine, psychiatry, physiology, neuroendocrinology, social sciences, and education, forecasts for psychoendocrinology an increasing prominence among biobehavioral sciences. To the theoretical psychologist, psychoendocrinology offers new insights for the study and interpretation of the brain–mind relationship.

ADRENAL GLANDS
NEUROCHEMISTRY
PITUITARY DISORDERS
PSYCHOPHYSIOLOGY
PSYCHOPHARMACOLOGY
SOCIOPSYCHOPHYSIOLOGY

H. Misiak

PSYCHOKINESIS

Psychokinesis (PK) is the term commonly used in parapsychology for alleged effects of thought on physical events by unknown processes. The reality of PK is assumed in various aspects of the great religions, in the traditions of many preliterate societies, and in much of popular thought elsewhere. Persons whose modes of thought have been greatly influenced by science have tended to consider psychokinesis impossible or so unlikely as to merit no serious attention.

J. B. Rhine was apparently the first to use scientific procedures in a large-scale attempt to test for the occurrence of PK. A number of experiments he conducted or supervised in the 1930s led him to conclude that some individuals are able to exert a small but consistent influence on the fall of dice. A similar claim was later made for psychokinetic placement effects—that is, influence on where dice come to rest. In the 1960s and 1970s, most experiments were concerned with possible influence on random event generators whose randomization is effected by decay of radioactive substances. They, too, have found highly significant effects in some persons, but these were not repeatable dependably. Less adequate experimental controls have been possible in the study of gross psychokinetic effects claimed to be produced by a few exceptional persons.

EXTRASENSORY PERCEPTION
WITCHCRAFT

I. L. Child

PSYCHOLINGUISTICS

Psycholinguistics, a discipline specifically devoted to the psychological implications of language, is relatively new. For years, psychologists had been busy trying to conciliate structural linguistics with theories of learning using the techniques of word association, left-to-right analysis of sentences, and the statistical interpretation of frequency and order of words in speech.

THE IMPACT OF CHOMSKY'S THEORY

The speaker of any language can produce and understand an unlimited number of grammatically correct sentences and can decide whether any given sentence is grammatically correct, even if it is unfamiliar. This means, according to Chomsky, that human beings have the innate capacity to create grammatically correct sentences and that this capacity does not come from previous experience.

Underlying the surface structure of a spoken language is a deep structure of rules permitting the generation of all possible grammatically correct sentences. Some of these rules are specific to a given language, but there are also basic rules common to all languages and so one can speak of a "general grammar" closely linked with the structure of the mind and with human nature and its biological foundations. Because of this "natural" quality of the general grammar, and the fact that a child possesses a Language Acquisition Device (LAD) that enables the analysis of the linguistic productions heard in accordance with formal rules, the child develops linguistic competence. Thus Chomsky's theory is nativistic and directly opposed to the empiricism professed by behaviorists, and even by the mainstream of contemporary psychology.

NEW TRENDS

Some psychologists, inspired by Chomsky, set about the task of proving that children, from their first utterances, have a set of consistent rules that explains all their verbal productions, and that this initial grammar evolves according to an internal logic until it coincides with adult grammar. Taking into account the fact that the study of child language has been traditionally descriptive, or interested only in explaining the origin and meaning of words, the new approach proved encouraging and productive. However, the limitations of the new approach soon became evident also. Not surprisingly, researchers have gradually abandoned methodological limitations to place the verbal language of children in its real context, a behavioral and communicative situation.

Besides the codification processes and the formal rules of syntax, psycholinguistics deals with the physiological basis of language, the possibilities of verbal communication between animals, the functions of language in behavior, the relationship between language and thought, and the problems of meaning.

COGNITIVE COMPLEXITY
COMMUNICATION PROCESSES
LANGUAGE DEVELOPMENT

M. Siguan

PSYCHOLOGICAL ASSESSMENT

The purpose of a psychological assessment is to evaluate an individual generally relative to a specific problem or problems. These may include questions of sanity, intellectual functioning, learning disabilities, special abilities, personality functioning, school problems and behavior, and emotional and social areas. The assessment specialist develops hypotheses based on information of past behavior, present behavior, and predictions for future behavior as defined by given situations. Psychologists use past written reports, projective methods, objective methods, and interview material, and integrate these within a given framework in a report.

Assessment increased in importance during World War I. Psychologists undertook to assess intellectual functioning in large numbers of soldiers. The emphasis was on diagnostic techniques and improved statistical methods.

During World War II, the armed forces needed further methods of assessment in practical settings. These included pilot and officer candidate selections. A series of assessment methods were developed for the Office of Strategic Services to use in selecting agents. Psychologists were called on to develop and refine further assessment methods in these and other areas. There were parallel developments of refined statistical approaches to the analysis and understanding of the data.

Since World War II, development in assessment has continued. Intelligence scales have been refined, more carefully evaluated, and new ones developed. The culture-free approach has been emphasized in the evaluation of intellectual functioning of members of minority groups.

A further development has been the "behavioral assessment" approach. The individual's overt motor and verbal behavior constitutes the basic material for assessment and prediction of behavior.

Interviews are generally of two types. In the structured interview specific questions are asked to obtain specific information. There is a carefully designed order of presentation of the questions. The responses are checked to ascertain that the data obtained are clear and relevant. In the open-ended interview, the interviewer asks the interviewee to talk in general. The conversation may be about any topic and quite general at the start. The interviewer maintains either a mental or written checklist of material or areas to be covered. If any areas are omitted by the interviewee, the interviewer will ask more direct questions or lead the interviewee into discussing the specific area.

The use of psychological tests has been an important variable in the assessment process. Some tests are considered "objective." These tests are often called paper-and-pencil methods. The individual is asked to respond to specific questions and then the responses are evaluated. They are compared with the answers of known groups of individuals. The projective techniques are another group of assessment methods.

Another area of psychological assessment has been organic brain syndromes. The psychologist is often asked to determine whether there is evidence of brain dysfunction and, if the dysfunction is present, whether it has affected intelligence and/or personality and to what extent.

The Bender–Gestalt test measures the individual's ability to reproduce certain geometric designs by direct copying and from memory. The Bender–Gestalt has become a frequently used technique in assessing organic brain dysfunction.

Many assessment procedures have been adapted for both individual and group administration. Problems are encountered when the norms and the standards developed with one group are applied to a group with a different background or different educational opportunity. Group assessment methods are most effective when used for screening, which then may be followed by more individualized assessment.

Individuals who are part of a culture different from their original one are often found to be handicapped in responding with the information and knowledge needed in the new culture. For this reason, they may be considered intellectually deficient or emotionally disturbed. The results may be a function of a lack of information and experience rather than a basic lack of intellectual ability and personal maturity. In the late 1970s, a number of states limited the use of intellectual evaluation procedures with minority groups.

Research and experience in the 1970s and 1980s indicated that the behaviors that formed the basis for the behavioral assessment were often influenced by factors outside the directly observable. Motivation for specific behaviors is not always amenable to direct observation. The historical approach is also important in contributing to the understanding of present behavior as well as the prediction of future behavior. Therefore, assessment of intelligence, special abilities, and specific areas of functioning continues to be based to a large degree on specific test results.

BENDER–GESTALT TEST
CLINICAL ASSESSMENT
DIAGNOSTIC AND STATISTICAL MANUAL
INTELLIGENCE MEASURES
PERSONALITY ASSESSMENT
PROJECTIVE TECHNIQUES
QUESTIONNAIRES
RORSCHACH
STRONG–CAMPBELL INTEREST INVENTORY
RELIABILITY OF DIAGNOSES

TESTING AND LEGISLATION
THEMATIC APPERCEPTION TEST

B. Fabrikant

PSYCHOLOGICAL HEALTH

All psychotherapeutic systems have a view of human nature, a concept of disease etiology, and a vision of psychological health. This vision is the end point of "successful" therapy as defined by each particular orientation.

Reflecting a dissatisfaction with traditional pathology-based clinical and mental health classifications, some researchers are developing and empirically investigating models of positive health. There has also been an increasing interest in non-Western approaches to psychological health.

In the original constitution of the World Health Organization a view of health was stated in positive terms: "Health is a state of complete physical, mental, and social well-being and is not merely the absence of disease or infirmity."

There are problems with the study of psychological health. There is a gray area between science and values. Psychological health may be a cultural value. The balance is a tenuous one.

DIFFERENT VIEWS OF PSYCHOLOGICAL HEALTH

Theories of psychological health are often based on the views of the individual that each tradition has.

There are four broadly conceived beliefs about human nature, summarized in Table 1. Theory 1 states that the person is evil and basically amoral. Theory 2 says that people are good. Theory 3 includes the blank slate or *tabulae rasae* view. It is existence preceding essence. Theory 4 states that people have self-actualizing innate natures that not only are personal, as in Theory 2, but reflect a divine or cosmic or transpersonal spark intrinsic to everyone. Finally, there are combination theories.

The Goal of Teaching

The goal of "teaching" refers to the vision of psychological health and the model of human nature from which it springs (Table 2).

1. *The amoral theory of human nature.* Since people are basically evil, the vision can only be to make them less so. In Freudian terms, the goal is to give individuals more control over the id impulses; in traditional Christianity, the goal is to have people seek salvation and God, realizing their basically evil nature.

2. *The good theory.* This theory suggests that a concept of health is having the individual uncover his or her own self-actualizing nature. Rogers said "To move away from the facades, oughts, pleasing others, and to move toward self-direction—being more autonomous, increasingly trusting and valuing the process which is himself."

3. *The blank slate existence precedes essence theory.* The vision of this theory, in a relativistic world, is to choose one's self, to stand forth (existential), and to learn skills necessary for optimal cultural functioning (behavioral).

Table 1   Four Beliefs Describing Human Nature

Theory	View of Human Nature
1	Innately evil/amoral
2	Innately good, self-actualizing nature
3	Tabulae rasae: existence precedes essence
4	Innately good and in essence in harmony with the divine

Table 2   Goal of Teaching

Theory	View of Human Nature		Vision of Health
1	Innately evil/amoral	→	Lessen the evil and/or seek salvation
2	Innately good, self-actualizing nature	→	Uncover the self
3	Tabulae rasae: existence precedes essence	→	Create self
4	Innately good and, in essence, in harmony with the divine	→	Uncover the essence of self

4. *Transpersonal approach.* The vision is an awakening, nirvana, kensho to one's true self, which is "no self" but rather part of the larger Self.

VIEWS OF HUMAN NATURE

Goal of Therapy
For those who begin with the Theory 1 view of human nature, the best they can do is come to some kind of resolution—that is, the "best possible" conditions for the ego. The task of therapy is to uncover and understand initial traumatic events.

Ego Psychology
Ego psychology is used by different individuals and at different times to describe a wide variety of approaches. These range along a continuum from neoanalytic viewpoints of the conflict-free sphere of the ego to those believing in an innate, self-actualizing, intrapsychic ego.

View of the Individual
Theory 2, represented by Rogers, believes there is an innate, self-actualizing quality within each individual. Therefore, the goal of therapy is merely to provide a warm, supportive, trusting environment to allow the person to see and accept that innate self.

Behavioral Approach
This approach is used as an example of a Theory 3 viewpoint. Within a behavioral approach, there are many different groupings, and within each

of these groupings there are additional subgroupings. Behavior therapy consists of activities implying a contractual agreement between therapist and patient to modify a designated problem behavior with particular application to neurosis and affective disorders.

Behaviorists suggest that to be free, people need to have knowledge of the internal and external factors that control them. This means (a) having more accurate knowledge of the consequences of alternative behaviors, (b) learning more skills necessary for achieving objectives, and (c) diminishing anxieties that restrict participation in the alternatives chosen. Freedom also involves having precise awareness of the internal and external environments, and arranging these environments in such a way as to maximize individual choices.

Table 2 summarizes these three different viewpoints—id psychology, ego psychology, and behavior therapy—across the three dimensions. These viewpoints represent Theories 1, 2, and 3, respectively.

NONTRADITIONAL APPROACHES: THEORY 4—ZEN
These three approaches are contrasted in Table 3 with the religious/philosophical Eastern view of Zen Buddhism, representative of a Theory 4 viewpoint. The qualities of a healthy person as suggested by the Eastern tradition include determination and effort, flexibility and adaptability, a sense of meaning, an affirmation of life, dying to a finite ego, loss of self-importance, development of compassion and selfless service, increased depth of intimate relationships, development of control of one's mind and body, and ethical qualities such as the four illimitables or measureless states—compassion, sympathetic joy, all-embracing kindness, and equanimity.

SUMMARY
Not all of the innumerable views of psychological health fit into the four-theory model described. Other important theories include Jung's concept of the individuated self, Rank's use of creativity, and Maslow's self-actualizing people. Marie Jahoda has pointed out that most definitions of positive and mental health call attention to one or more of the following six aspects: (a) the attitude shown by a person to self; (b) the style and degree of self-actualization; (c) the degree of personal integration achieved by the individual; (d) the degree of autonomy achieved by the person; (e) the degree of the person's conception of reality; and (f) the degree of environmental mastery achieved by the person. Greater

Table 3   Comparison and Contrast of Four Schools of Psychotherapy

Topic	Psychodynamic (Id Psychology: Freud)	Client-Centered Therapy (Ego Psychology: Rogers)	Social Learning Theory (Behavioral Psychology)	Zen Buddhism
View of human nature	Aggressive; hostile, life out of control; ruled by unconscious	Innately good; intrapsychic self, which is self-actualizing	Person is tabulae rasa at birth; with no "essence"	A human being has pure, innate, good, unconscious "self" that is like Buddha nature and is within all
Goal of psychotherapy	To make the unconscious conscious; overcome childhood amnesia; recover warded-off memories	To let the person experience that self inwardly and knowingly	The target behavior: if deficit, teach it; if excess, decrease it; make it appropriate	To make the unconscious conscious; to hear the bird in the breast sing
Etiology of disease	Repression of sexual and hostile childhood wishes by superego and ego	Trying to meet external shoulds and oughts; inability to assimilate experiences into one's self-concept	Environmental variables; learning deficiency	Belief there is a "self"; greed; ego; attachments

knowledge of positive health can add considerably to clinical practice, and potentially to society at large.

BEHAVIORAL MEDICINE
COMMUNITY PSYCHOLOGY
HEALTH PSYCHOLOGY
HEALTHY PERSONALITY
MENTAL ILLNESS: EARLY HISTORY
PRIMARY PREVENTION OF PSYCHOPATHOLOGY
PSYCHOANALYSIS

D. H. SHAPIRO, JR.

PSYCHOLOGICAL LABORATORIES

It is generally believed that the first laboratory of psychology was established by Wilhelm Wundt at Leipzig University in Germany 1879–1880. On Wundt's arrival at Leipzig, the Royal Ministry set aside a small lecture room for his personal experimental work. In 1879, Wundt's students first began conducting experiments in this Leipzig room, and this almost certainly, in Wundt's mind, marked the beginning of the Leipzig laboratory. Of the 10 dissertations Wundt supervised during his first 4 years at Leipzig, only one was not clearly philosophical. In the academic year 1872 to 1873, William James was hired by Harvard to teach. In the academic year 1875 to 1876, he offered a course entitled The Relations Between Physiology and Psychology. This course included a laboratory housed in two ground-floor rooms of Lawrence Hall.

G. Stanley Hall received his degree from Harvard in 1878 under the joint supervision of James and the physiologist H. P. Bowditch, with the experimental work being done in Bowditch's laboratory at the medical school. The next year, Hall went to Germany, first to Berlin and then to Leipzig with Wundt. He returned to the United States in 1880, and in 1881 was invited to lecture at Johns Hopkins, where he remained until 1888. In 1883, according to a statement he made in an article in the *American Antiquarian Society* in 1894, Hall "founded" the first laboratory of experimental psychology in the United States at Johns Hopkins.

James did not let Hall's statement go unchallenged. In a note in *Science* for 1895, he replied: "I, myself, 'founded' the instruction in experimental psychology at Harvard in 1874–5, or 1876, I forget which. For a long series of years the laboratory was in two rooms of the Scientific School Building (Lawrence Hall), which at last became choked with apparatus, so that a change was necessary." There is no evidence that James' laboratory, in spite of its clear existence since the academic year 1875 to 1876, was anything more than a demonstration laboratory.

THE FIRST AMERICAN LABORATORY

Excluding James' demonstrational facility, when and where the first laboratory appeared in the United States is not clear. Hall claimed it for himself at Johns Hopkins in 1883, but the university never formally recognized it. In 1888, Joseph Jastrow went to the University of Wisconsin, where he "founded" a laboratory with official university recognition. However, this was a year after James McK. Cattell had started a laboratory at the University of Pennsylvania (Jastrow acknowledged Cattell's priority), and the same year that W. L. Bryan started a laboratory at the University of Indiana.

OTHER FIRST LABORATORIES

The first laboratories in other countries, up to the end of the nineteenth century, were: Copenhagen, 1886, by Alfred Lehmann; Tokyo, 1888, by Yozero Motora; Rome, 1889, by G. Sergi; Toronto, 1890, by James Mark Baldwin; Cambridge, 1891, by James Ward; Geneva, 1891, by Theodore Flournoy; Graz, 1894, by Alexius Meinong; Moscow, 1895, by A. Tokarsky; and Peking, 1897.

GROWTH OF THE LABORATORIES

By 1898, there were at least 48 psychological laboratories in the world, 26 in the United States. Laboratories continued to grow, especially in the United States, although many of the laboratories that appeared in the 1920s and 1930s were "testing laboratories," reflecting the post-World War I growth of psychometrics.

LABORATORY EQUIPMENT

The equipment of the very early laboratories centered around chronoscopes for measuring reaction times, tuning forks, and color mixers. Many of these pieces of equipment were works of art, being finished in beautifully tooled brass. In the early years, when much of the research was psychophysical in nature, the additional apparatus provided for increased accuracy in the presentation of sensory stimuli. Following the initiation of studies of memory and learning in the last 15 years of the nineteenth century, devices to provide stimulus control of these situations appeared—memory drums, mazes, and puzzle boxes. The development in the late 1930s by B. F. Skinner of his "Skinner box," in which an animal could press a bar to receive a reinforcement, led in the post-World War II years to the development of sophisticated electronic equipment for the presentation and scheduling of various stimulus conditions and for the automatic recording of responses. With the ever-increasing areas of specialization in psychology, there was a corresponding increase in the amount of sophisticated specialized equipment peculiar to the research interests of particular laboratories.

EMPIRICAL RESEARCH METHODS
EXPERIMENTAL PSYCHOLOGY
HISTORY OF PSYCHOLOGY
PSYCHOPHYSICS

R. S. HARPER

PSYCHOLOGICAL REPORT WRITING

When psychological reports are done well, they have considerable credibility. They are often decisive in diagnosing mental retardation, and are often of primary importance in borderline cases involving differential diagnoses between personality disorder and psychosis. However, consumer education has also resulted in a more critical attitude toward psychological reports among professionals and members of the general public.

SOURCES OF INACCURACY

Influences can exist on the psychological examiner arising from the social, professional, and interpersonal context in which he or she works. The writer should avoid confusion among (a) behavioral statements, (b) speculations about fantasies or inner processes of the person being described, and (c) data from an interview that report conscious thoughts and statements of the subject under review. The readers will be comparing statements from the report with other sources of information, and it should be made clear what the appropriate comparison should be.

Most writers on the subject seem to agree on certain points in preparing psychological reports. These include: (a) not giving information obtainable more easily from other sources; (b) listing the tests given, but not implying that each one is for the measurement of a specific function—most assessment instruments are comprehensive and not simply designed for a specific purpose; (c) avoiding quantitative statements such as citing norms if not particularly relevant; and (d) making sure that the conclusions and diagnostic findings bear some relationship to the rest of the report.

Complex interprofessional and interpersonal issues are involved in psychological reporting. A report can influence significant decisions and therefore deserves the best expertise that clinical psychologists can offer. Even though it may be safe to be vague, general, and usually accurate, it is much more helpful to be specific and precise. Psychological reports will continue to play an important part in structuring and influencing the public image of psychology.

CLINICAL ASSESSMENT
PERSONALITY ASSESSMENT

W. G. KLOPFER

PSYCHOLOGICAL SCIENCE

Psychological science is concerned with the application of scientific method and principles to the study of a set of questions that traditionally have been categorized as psychological in nature. It also is the body of theories and facts about the questions and issues that have emerged from this process. Psychological science is different from mere philosophical speculation about psychological questions. It also is different from the so-called self-help literature that deals in an intuitive way with problems of living. Psychological science requires empirical observation and experimental verification of its speculations that are often cast as, and considered to be, scientific theories. Defined in this way, psychological science is the discipline of all but a few university departments of psychology.

Psychological questions, at least historically, deal somehow with mental processes and conscious experience, a concept that is closely related to mind. Going back to antiquity, humans have speculated about the nature of mind, of the relationship of mind to the world in which they live, of the relationship of mind to the body of which it is a part, of the nature of knowledge and how it is acquired, and of the relationship between mind and human action. Through the ages, such philosophical speculation constituted a major focus of such notable thinkers as Plato and Aristotle, and of a range of philosophers following the Renaissance, including Descartes, Hobbes, Locke, Berkeley, and Kant. Of these, Kant is remembered for his insistence that there could be no science of psychology. This opinion was based on his belief that mental events were not measurable, thus there could be no mathematical analysis or description of them. Furthermore, according to Kant, mental events were brief and subject to distortion by the observation process itself, and mental events could not be produced by experimental means; they had their own existence and obeyed their own laws and whims. There simply could not be a science dealing with such an unmanageable and even nonphysical subject matter.

The development of psychological science required the emergence of a sophisticated view of science and then a demonstration of the capability of the scientific method to be relevant to psychological questions. These requirements seem to have been satisfied around the middle of the nineteenth century, at which time many of Kant's objections appear to have been surmounted by methodological advances leading to pertinent discoveries in physiology. If a date must be provided for the birth of psychological science, perhaps it would be 1874, the year that Wilhelm Wundt's *The principles of physiological psychology* was published. The preface to this work begins with this remarkable statement: "This work which I here present to the public is an attempt to work out a new domain of science."

Wundt's new science was to concern itself with the investigation of conscious processes and how they relate to physical events. Wundt's confidence that the time had come for a science of psychology was based on those advances touching on psychological subject matter that had been made in physiology, and many of the laboratory techniques of that physiology were employed in his laboratory, hence his term *physiological psychology*. Perhaps the most germane of these advances is that of Fechner, who seemed to have shown in 1860 that the conscious experience of sensations based on physical variables such as light or sound energy varied as the logarithm of the magnitude of the relevant physical variables. This relationship between the magnitude of sensation, a psychological quantity that is a part of conscious experience, and physical magnitude is the subject matter of the subdiscipline of psychophysics.

However, other advances had been made in physiology by the time Wundt proposed his new science. One of Wundt's goals was to establish a scientific basis for the analysis of mental content. Following the model of chemistry, he chose to ask: What are the elements of conscious experience and to what physical and biological variables are they to be related? For this purpose he employed a method called *introspection,* in which trained observers were required to analyze the changes that took place in their conscious experience when various stimuli were presented to them, an analogue of the procedure that Fechner and others had employed in studying sensory discrimination. Wundt's variation on this method, although seemingly scientific in that it occurred as a controlled experiment in a laboratory setting, lacked what is now recognized as an essential feature of science, namely objectivity. In science, it must be possible for scientists to agree on their basic observations. In Wundt's introspective method, what was being observed or interpreted was in the private conscious experience of observers who were trained to give analytic interpretations of their experience; a clearly subjective procedure. Wundt's program seems to have foundered on this subjectivity when observers in other laboratories found reason to disagree with Wundt's observers about details of the contents of conscious experience.

Later investigators seemed to have succeeded in overcoming many of these problems. The clue was in the original experimental task used by Fechner and others. Rather than asking the observer to make a complex analysis of the conscious experience occurring when a stimulus configuration was presented, all Fechner asked, in effect, was a simple question: "Did you detect a change?" This variation in procedure made possible the use of untrained observers, because the task was simple. All that was required was an assumption of the veracity of an observer who was paying attention to the task and who was motivated to perform adequately. The basic procedure often was even further simplified so as to require only the push of a button or other response by the observer to indicate that the change or other phenomena had occurred.

This simple procedural variation was sufficient to sustain a substantial amount of investigation after Wundt. The Gestalt movement made much use of it, and it was also the basis for much research in the psychological subfield of perception, which has been concerned largely with identifying and quantifying the relationship between stimulus input conditions and conscious experience and with the physiological mechanisms and processes that mediate these relationships.

Partly in response to the shortcomings of Wundt's introspective procedure and partly as an outgrowth of early successes in animal psychology, another methodological approach, the behaviorist movement, emerged in the first half of the twentieth century. In part, behaviorism has been seen as an outgrowth of what has been called *functionalistic psychology,* with a concern for explaining the function of mind and how mind could be implicated in the coping behavior of humans as well as other animals. However, it soon seemed apparent that human and animal behavior could be studied in their own right. The behaviorist approach, as enunciated by John B. Watson in 1913, was "a purely objective experimental branch of natural science. . . . Introspection forms no essential part of its methods." Mind and conscious experience were ruled out as topics of scientific investigation because they were not directly observable. Behaviorism, at least in the United States, became a dominant force in psychology and formed the basis for a substantial portion of research publications from 1920 through 1960.

Modern-day cognitive psychology emerged at about the 1960s and is almost synonymous with experimental psychology. Cognitive psychology's subject matter returns again to question of mind, but not in the form used by Wundt. Rather than examining the nature of conscious experience from the perspective of the observer of that experience, cognitive psychology focuses on theoretical mental processes as they are manifested in observable measures, such as accuracy and response time. In this approach, specific characteristics of mental processes are hypothesized and the observable consequences of assumptions about the characteristics are derived. Experiments are conducted then to determine whether the hypothesized consequences occur, with a positive result bolstering confidence in the power of the theoretical assumptions. This form of experimentation has as its empirical base observable responses made by the experimental subject, responses that depend on the activities of the hypothesized processes under investigation. From this perspective, cognitive psychology can be viewed as a return to an earlier view about the subject matter of psychological investigation but with the adoption of the sophisticated and objective methodology of behaviorism. Now, psychology's focus is not on the structure of conscious experience—rather, it is with the task of identifying and explicating the processes that are involved in attention, memory, pattern recognition, linguistic behavior (i.e., speaking, listening, and reading), thinking, problem solving, and associated problems.

The history of psychological science from its beginnings in the laboratory of Wundt to the present reveals a great broadening of its concern. Wundt's experimental procedures generally were limited to the question of identifying the elements of the structure of mind conceptualized as conscious experience. The behavioristic movement substituted a concern with the functioning of animal and human organisms interacting with an environmental context. Current cognitive psychology has returned to questions of mental activity but with a different goal than that of Wundt. However, along the way, psychology adopted a number of methodologies and procedures that extended its scope, and it grew by encompassing a number of areas related to its main goal. Psychology adopted the analytic methodology of statistics and in many areas was able to harness mathematical models to augment its growing methodological armament. The methods and goals of psychological science were applied to a wide variety of psychological questions and in a variety of settings. Current introductory textbooks in psychology display a wide array of applications of the methodology of psychological science, ranging from basic subfields of psychology such as perception, learning, cognition, social, and personality to such topics as drug abuse, mental illness, and gender differences, for all of which our knowledge has been extended through psychological science.

CLINICAL VERSUS STATISTICAL PREDICTION
CRUCIAL EXPERIMENTS IN PSYCHOLOGY
DOUBLE-BLIND RESEARCH
MILLS' CANONS
RESEARCH METHODOLOGY
SCIENTIFIC METHOD

C. A. BONEAU

PSYCHOLOGICAL TESTING: ITS SURVIVAL PROBLEMS

Psychological testing is a broad term that includes all types of professionally developed tests for evaluation of human abilities, aptitudes, educational achievements, skills, interests, attitudes, and personality characteristics. The term should not be limited, as is sometimes mistakenly interpreted, to refer only to tests related to personality and mental health adjustment.

Historically, psychological testing is closely identified with the origin of psychology as a science—objectively and quantitatively oriented, in contrast to earlier orientations of a more subjective and philosophical nature. Within psychology itself, psychological testing made early contributions to the application of psychological principles to practical problems. These applications grew rapidly after the establishment of psychological testing as a recognized and generally accepted procedure.

Before the 1960s, there were practically no significant threats to the survival of psychological testing as it had developed and as it was being used. For a test to survive, from the standpoint of scientific and professional standards, it has to be *reliable* and *valid*. The handling of these supports of reliability and validity was, and still is, in the hands of the professional developers of the tests. In the earlier days, the persons taking psychological tests rarely raised their voices. It was the developers' and users' heyday.

In the early days, there were some hotly argued questions involving psychological tests (IQ tests, in particular). However, these were not arguments that centered so much on the tests themselves as they were disagreements on the interpretations of results of the tests.

The "threats to survival" of psychological tests began to appear with growing and expressed concerns on the part of individuals about their rights in varied situations, including ones in which they may have been denied a job or admission to a school on the basis of a psychological test rating, or in which a child may have been placed out of the mainstream of education on the basis of a test. Emphasis began to shift to those below the critical-point (cutoff) score on the test and whether the test afforded them fair treatment.

The concern culminated in the Civil Rights Act of 1964. The fact that this Act involves a section relating to employment (Title VII) drew psychological tests into question as discriminating against disadvantaged groups. The U.S. Equal Employment Opportunity Commission (1978) has been viewed by many as a threat to psychological testing. The Federal Uniform Guidelines on Employee Selection Procedures aims mainly to protect minority and disadvantaged groups from discrimination in employment. Governmental regulatory measures also have been addressed to concerns related to the handicapped, some of which (especially education and employment) involve psychological testing.

SURVIVAL PROBLEMS

What are some of the threats to psychological testing?

1. Among the serious threats are those related to general ability testing. Except for achievement tests in schools, general ability tests are the most frequently applied and used of all tests. General ability tests have had various labels: intelligence tests, IQ tests, mental ability tests, general aptitude tests, and tests of learning potential. Many "specialized" tests that do not have these more general labels have large components of general ability evaluation.

Most general ability tests and specialized tests with strong general ability components are pencil-and-paper tests of a verbal nature. The threats stem from claims of unfairness of verbal tests to groups disadvantaged in the acquisition of the language, such as Blacks, Hispanics, Asians, and Native Americans.

Because written tests can hardly avoid the use of language, the vocabulary and reading levels of tests must be of concern to be sure that they alone do not deny opportunities to potentially successful students or job applicants. Relevant content also has to do with appropriate inclusion, related to the use of the test, of the various general ability factors, such as quantitative ability, spatial ability, reasoning ability, associative ability, and verbal fluency.

2. A second threat is differences in minority or disadvantaged group test scores as compared with the perceived advantaged group. A problem is the frequent assumption, on the part of test challengers, that a test that produces differential distributions of scores for disadvantaged groups versus the perceived advantaged group is by that fact, in and of itself, challengeable with respect to its validity. If women, for example, on the basis of their biological makeup cannot meet valid (realistically job-related) physical demands for firefighters in the same proportion that men can, differential distributions and eligibility must be accepted.

3. Is psychological testing helped or threatened by the regulatory measures that affect it professionally or legally? Any "guidelines" restrict the freedom of initiative, research, and experimentation that might otherwise take place. The governmental-related guidelines frequently confuse social is sues with professional–scientific issues related to testing. The professional–scientific guidelines are often too "academic" and do not always integrate sufficiently with the practical demands.

4. What are the threats from the courts to the survival of psychological testing? These threats have stemmed mainly from the intertwining of social problems with the scientific and professional advocacy of psychological tests. This comes from the use of psychological tests in many problems of social concern. In the educational admissions area, tests have been criticized for bias, coachability, and secrecy of results. In the personnel field, all techniques utilized in employment and other personnel decisions become threatened by the social problems and the court's commission to direct its attention to the social problems. When the court "throws out" a psychological test merely or mainly because it has adverse impact on the employing of minorities, there is little, if any, consideration of the test's validity. Nevertheless, the court decision is likely, in the minds of many, to reflect unfavorably on the validity of the test.

Psychological testing's survival in the "clinical" mental health field has not been challenged in court as much as it has been in the other two major fields of application (education and personnel administration). The reason is not entirely clear.

Threats to survival of psychological testing by the courts are diminishing with greater mutual understanding and mutually shared knowledge on the part of lawyers, judges, and professional psychometricians.

5. Can psychological tests survive the truth-in-testing threat? This is a label for demands requiring that tests that have been used become open and available, including details of questions and answers, to all test takers. Laws have been passed in New York state and California requiring such for tests used for educational admissions. A spread would markedly inhibit repeated uses of the same test, require frequent development and validation of new tests, and increase costs and decrease the likelihood of well-developed and validated tests.

6. What threats to survival are involved in the problems of establishing the validity of a psychological test? It has increasingly been demanded that validity be defended on the basis of statistically indicated relationships between test ratings and defined criteria of what the test is expected to accomplish. This demand is especially strong in educational and personnel uses and less strong in clinical psychological uses, where tests are more likely to be used and accepted as aids to clinical judgment. Inadequate and unreliable criterion measures have been a problem from the beginning of psychological test validity studies.

If criterion measures are unreliable and themselves not valid, a low correlation with psychological test scores may threaten the test erroneously. Perhaps the criterion is at fault, not the test.

None of the threats to survival of psychological tests are, in their basic nature, new. One or the other becomes more prominent with the era and its associated social demands. Also, there is the "state of the art," professionally, to be considered in the interpretation of threats to testing. The professionals concerned with testing will use the threats as stimuli to improvement.

CULTURAL BIAS IN TESTING
ITEM ANALYSIS
RELIABILITY OF DIAGNOSES TESTING AND LEGISLATION

T. HUNT

PSYCHOLOGISTS AS MENTAL HEALTH CONSULTANTS

The academic and experimental training of a psychologist usually takes place within the context of mental health and/or the psychological process. The depth to which specific areas are developed relates to the specialty of psychology studied. Generally, all psychological training includes a familiarity with personality dynamics, human relationships, organizational skills, sensitivity to others, conceptual skills, and assessment abilities.

Consultants are expected to facilitate, arbitrate, and offer direction. On occasion, they are expected to present materials in a didactic manner, as well as to address an issue in a group process format.

The primary aim is to attain a high level of credibility. Some focal areas include assessing the consistency of the communication regarding the reason(s) for bringing in a consultant, dispelling myths and fantasies related to the consultant's purpose, and displaying an interest in becoming oriented to and knowledgeable about the operation. A measure of one's level of credibility may well be the sense of trust experienced in the designated situation. It is also helpful to determine who will be the consultant's primary contact person.

A mental health consultant has the responsibility of determining the short-term as well as the long-term goals and objectives relative to an assignment. Typically, this is accomplished by meeting with key personnel within the organization in an effort to obtain background and current information. An action plan for the implementation of these goals and objectives tends to reinforce the credibility of the mental health consultant's role. These plans should be designed with ample flexibility to be responsive to needs of the organization that might surface.

The expertise of the mental health consultant lies in his or her specialty area, with regard to content. Of equal importance is the sensitivity and skill with which the consultant applies and conveys this knowledge.

LEADERSHIP AND SUPERVISION
MANAGEMENT DEVELOPMENT

S. S. CARDONE

PSYCHOLOGY AND THE COURTS

The metaphor of a courtship has been used to describe the historical and developing relationship between law and psychology. The growth of the discipline of psychology has led to new psychological knowledge and a variety of related treatments, and these, in turn, have provided the courts with new options and perspectives in dealing with its most vexing cases: the alleged "mentally ill," whose behavior is disturbing, potentially harmful, and seemingly inexplicable; the alleged "criminally insane," whose conduct violates the law, yet whose culpability is questioned; the so-called "juvenile delinquent," who defies supervision and limits, yet who needs both; and the alleged "incompetent," who needs paternalistic protection and relief in certain spheres of functioning, yet who protests benevolent interventions. The courts' courtship of psychology coincided, in good part, with their own shift in emphasis—moving increasingly from retribution to rehabilitation, from punishment to treatment.

Currently the psychological expert enters the courtroom, is accorded "expert witness" status, and is typically asked to render *clinical judgment* regarding specific questions as they relate to a *specific* individual: Is the defendant competent to stand trial? Was the defendant criminally insane at the time of the act? Is the individual currently dangerous to self or others? Is the person mentally ill? Is the person in need of treatment? Should the person be involuntarily committed to a mental hospital? In addition, a newer trend is discernible that promises even more psychologists in the courtroom. Behavioral scientists are now taking the stand to present *research expertise* that relates *generally* to a variety of matters and groups of individuals, such as eyewitness judgments; cross-racial accuracy; jury size, selection, and deliberation findings; brain chemistry and functioning; and mind–brain interactions.

When psychological experts take the stand to testify at an involuntary commitment hearing, they often are asked to render a judgment regarding mental illness, and a prediction regarding "dangerousness." These judgments and predictions are typically based on interviews (a mental status exam) and psychological testing. However, on critical cross-examination, questions about the psychologist's methods and inferences, their validity and reliability, and the psychologist's accuracy and "expertness" come to the fore. The psychological expert, through a technical language, draws a portrait that may help illuminate the seemingly bizarre and unintelligible behavior of the alleged mentally ill. However, to speak of "purposes," or to explain actions in terms of the defendant's thoughts, motives, fears, and emotions, the expert uses teleological and mentalistic concepts not at all dissimilar to the language of the law and the lay public.

The psychologist's skill, particularly in the area of treatment, has wedded the courts to mental health professionals with hope that therapy will set the courts and allegedly mentally ill free from their respective disorders. The promise has not yet been fulfilled. Involuntary treatment and hospitalization have not been effective remedies, and their failures have led patients back to the courts, where they assert their rights to treatment or to be free. More potent treatments, such as drugs, electroconvulsive therapy (shock treatment), behavior modification, and psychosurgery, also led patients back to the courts, this time asserting their right to refuse treatment. Therapists and patients, the community and the courts, find themselves entangled and confused as never before.

Disentanglement does not necessarily mean divorce: A separation may be healthy in order for psychologists to analyze their practices, ethics, and conceptions, their language and intents. A separation may also provide the time to examine what each can do well, what promises each can and cannot keep, and what each may reasonably expect from the other. Psychology and law can relate, do relate, and, in some sense, must relate. The search goes on, through action and reflection, for that sane, common ground.

COMPETENCY TO STAND TRIAL
CRIMINAL RESPONSIBILITY
ETHICAL PROBLEMS IN PSYCHOLOGY
EXPERT TESTIMONY
FORENSIC PSYCHOLOGY
PSYCHOLOGY AND THE LAW
RIGHT TO REFUSE TREATMENT
RIGHT TO TREATMENT

N. J. FINKEL

PSYCHOLOGY AND THE LAW

The involvement of psychologists in legal issues has expanded rapidly in recent years, as witnessed by the publication of numerous books, the establishment of a psychology and law division of the American Psycho-

logical Association (APA) and of such organizations as the American Psychology–Law Society, as well as by the development of educational and internship experiences. Universities have established joint degree programs in psychology and law in which both a Ph.D. and a law degree are obtained, and the American Board of Forensic Psychology has been set up to provide certification to qualified forensic psychologists.

EXPERT WITNESSES

Psychologists are now recognized in most courts as experts in a variety of criminal and civil issues and in class action suits with respect to mental patient and prisoner rights. The legal status of psychologists in the courtroom was established in *Jenkins v. United States*. Many of the areas of expertise are discussed.

The use of psychologists and other mental health professionals as experts to assist the court in making legal decisions has often been criticized. Perhaps the most articulate critic has been Judge David Bazelon. With respect to mental health issues such as competency and responsibility, Bazelon has objected to the way in which experts communicate the findings of their evaluations to the court. He is particularly concerned with the tendency of experts to testify in conclusory terms, rather than simply to testify on the substance of the evaluation.

There is little doubt that expert witnesses can have a major impact on legal decisions. In the area of competency to stand trial, for example, there is nearly certain court acceptance of the evaluator's conclusion. The potential power and influence of experts have led some mental health professionals to call on them to set limits on their testimony and to examine the effects of their power on the individual, the courts, and society.

One concern about expert testimony is the lack of preparation and training of the experts. Many experts are not able to keep up on the literature and are often relatively untrained in legal matters.

PREDICTION OF DANGEROUSNESS

The prediction of dangerous or violent behavior is an area in which psychologists have become heavily involved as expert witnesses. The ability of a psychologist, or any mental health professional, to predict violence, has been questioned. In fact, the APA Task Force on the Role of Psychology in the Criminal Justice System had as one of its recommendations:

> Psychologists should be exceedingly cautious in offering predictions of criminal behavior for use in imprisoning or releasing individual offenders. If a psychologist decides that it is appropriate in a given case to provide a prediction of criminal behavior, he or she should clearly specify (a) the acts being predicted, (b) the estimated probability that these acts will occur during a given time period, and (c) the factors on which the predictive judgment is based.

A major reason for cautionary statements such as this is that violent behavior is a low base rate event, which makes accurate predictions exceedingly difficult. Countless empirical studies have consistently shown error rates to be excessively high. In practice, this often means that the major concern for decision makers is to minimize the false negative rate. Thus parole boards, for example, are particularly concerned about releasing potentially violent offenders; consequently they are more conservative in their release criteria. This has the effect of increasing the false positive rates and the detention of a large number of persons who would not have been violent.

EYEWITNESS TESTIMONY

The reliability and validity of eyewitness testimony constitute an area in which psychologists have often served as researchers and expert witnesses in both criminal and civil cases. Involvement as expert witnesses has increased substantially in recent years. The research tends to show that the testimony of eyewitnesses is often unreliable. In particular, memory of an event can be altered in numerous ways, through fabrication, and forgetting and in even more subtle ways.

JURY RESEARCH

The involvement of social scientists in the selection of jurors has become a controversial issue. The premise is that American juries are often biased because certain groups are underrepresented on such variables as race, age, and education. Social scientists have conducted surveys of communities to determine demographic composition, attitudes about the defendant, or key issues involved in a particular case, such as the appropriateness of capital punishment or the influence of pretrial publicity. Social scientists, however, have sometimes gone beyond simply ensuring that a jury represents a fair cross section of a community by attempting to select jurors who would be biased in favor of a particular outcome. The ethical and legal implications of social science's involvement in juror selection have been debated, of course. Opponents have argued that selection is costly, is biased against indigent and other defendants who are unable to afford social scientists, and could be used as easily to provide jurors in favor of the prosecution as it could for the defense.

Perhaps the most persuasive argument against social science's involvement in jury selection is that there is little empirical support for the idea that the composition of the jury is a major factor influencing the verdict. In fact, there is considerable evidence that the verdict is based more on the evidence presented than on demographic characteristics of the jury or on characteristics of the defendant.

COMPETENCY AND RESPONSIBILITY

Several types of competency are relevant to and centrally involve psychologists interested in legal issues. Competency to stand trial is a legal term that refers to procedures allowing for the postponement of the trial of defendants who are determined to be incompetent—that is, not able to communicate properly with their attorney and/or to participate fully in their defense.

Grisso found that more than one-half of 10- to 16-year-olds did not adequately understand at least one of the four Miranda warnings and they also had difficulty in understanding the intended nature of the attorney–client relationship. Children's competency to testify has been studied by G. R. Melton. He concludes that the available data support the use of children's testimony. He adds, however, that the data come primarily from laboratory research, thus limiting the confidence with which this conclusion can be made. As with jury research, studies are needed that evaluate the extent to which the findings can be generalized to actual courtroom behavior of children.

Finally, the competence of mental patients and prisoners to consent to treatment as well as to participate in research is a matter of some concern and debate. For most of the history of the treatment of such individuals, the issue of consent was not even considered. It was assumed that commitment to a mental hospital or sentence to a prison gave the institutional authorities the right to treat individuals in whatever manner was deemed appropriate. This view has been challenged in the courts, with several decisions holding that institutionalized persons do indeed have the right to refuse treatment.

The issue of responsibility is involved in determining the appropriateness of a defense of insanity for criminal defendants. Although state laws vary, the basic philosophy is that to convict persons charged with a crime, they must be considered responsible for their behavior, including criminal behavior. If a defendant's behavior was not a product of free will, then he or she should not be held responsible for any crime. The American Law Institute, Section 4.01, translates this to a legal test in proposing

that: "A person is not responsible for criminal conduct if at the time of such conduct as a result of mental disease or defect he lacks substantial capacity either to appreciate the criminality (or wrongfulness) of his conduct or to conform his conduct to the requirements of law." Defendants found not guilty by reason of insanity are technically acquitted of their crime, but most states automatically confine these defendants to an institution for an indefinite length of time.

Some critics have suggested that the insanity defense should be abolished, while others have suggested less radical reform, such as the introduction of a diminished responsibility as an alternative to the insanity defense. This would allow for a finding of guilt but a reduction in either the seriousness of the charge or the severity of the punishment if mental disorder appeared to have influenced the criminal act.

There are many unanswered research questions regarding the issue of responsibility. Central among these are the following:

1. The validity of legal and mental health models for determining responsibility.
2. The treatment of acquitted defendants, including whether treatment must occur in an institution.
3. The need for an insanity defense to ensure the fairness of the legal system.
4. The appropriateness of alternative models such as diminished responsibility.

TREATMENT

A frequent role of psychologists is providing a variety of treatments to persons in the mental health and criminal justice systems.

In mental health, the concept of a right to treatment has received a great deal of attention. A number of legal decisions have established the right of mental patients in institutions to a certain minimum standard of treatment. The decisions did not specify standards with respect to the nature or potential effectiveness of the treatments. If a treatment is not likely to be effective or does not have to be given in an institution, then the establishment of a right to such treatment is a hollow victory.

One of the most significant changes in mental health law was the reform of civil commitment statutes. Psychologists who provide treatment either in institutions or in outpatient settings are obviously affected by these changes, and in fact were sometimes instrumental in achieving reform. The changes have been in two areas. First, the involuntary commitment of individuals to mental hospitals was made more difficult. Persons who were simply mentally ill no longer could be committed routinely. Rather, there had to be a finding that they were also dangerous to themselves or to others. Second, because of the availability of psychoactive drugs that reduce psychotic symptoms, many long-term patients were released from the mental hospitals. The long-term impact of the changes may not be as substantial as the reformers had hoped.

Many of the patients discharged as a consequence of the deinstitutionalization policy were "consigned to bleak lives in nursing homes, single-room-occupancy hotels and skid-row rooming houses." As a consequence, the deinstitutionalization movement may not have significantly affected the lives of previously hospitalized individuals. This consequence of deinstitutionalization should become a major research topic for psychologists.

The approach to criminals has been quite different, especially for those convicted of violent crimes. The view that criminals should be treated is a long-standing one, based largely on the writings of psychiatrists. They viewed all criminal behavior as symptomatic of mental illness, and hence psychiatric intervention was considered appropriate. This view has been met with considerable challenge, both as applied to adult and to juvenile offenders for abandoning the therapeutic model and replacing it with a more punishment-oriented model.

The often fierce debate about the effectiveness of treating prisoners is perhaps made pointless when one considers the amount of treatment a given prisoner is likely to receive. Furthermore, even when treatment has been made available, it is often inadequately or insufficiently applied by untrained or inexperienced persons or does not have sufficient theoretical integrity to support the assumption that the treatment would indeed have an impact on a particular problem.

The tendency of psychologists to focus almost entirely on individual change has also been criticized. Psychologists working in the criminal justice system have typically operated from an individual perspective, which holds that abnormal behavior, in this case criminal behavior, is a function of some deficit within the individual. Consequently it follows that the appropriate intervention is one that will change the individual in some way. However, if the literature on the inappropriateness of such interventions for most offenders is correct, then this strategy is likely to prove fruitless. Psychologists may have a greater impact if they put more emphasis on other potential causes of criminal behavior, such as situational or environmental factors that may promote or facilitate deviant behavior.

THE IMPACT OF PSYCHOLOGY

Has psychological research and theory had an impact on the legal system? It no doubt has, but the degree to which it has is unknown. The influence of any social science data on policy decisions is often indirect, and it is rare that a single study, or even an entire body of research, would dictate a legal decision or policy. Even in the *Ballew v. Georgia* case, which cited the jury research heavily, the decision may well have been the same in the absence of the research. The Justices may have decided that for pragmatic rather than empirical reasons a six-person jury was adequate. It is quite possible that legal and policy decisions are made quite independently of data, with research being used to make the decision appear more scientific. Methodological limitations of a study may be ignored, as they were in the case of *Ballew,* in that the findings that had some influence on the decision were based on laboratory or simulated jury research. Furthermore, as Monahan points out, the same body of research can be used to support two very different policies.

Although social scientists typically do not have control over the way in which their data are applied, there is little doubt that empirical data can be useful in legal decision making. Steadman discusses several examples of how studies in the area of forensic psychiatry and psychology can be used to effect policy and statutory changes. Tanke and Tanke suggest that to have greater impact, "social scientists must (a) identify empirical questions relevant to judicial decisions, (b) consult with legal experts to develop experimental research and criticism designed to produce information relevant to legal issues, and (c) present such information in a manner that is timely and merits acceptance by the judicial process." M. J. Saks provides an excellent example of how psychologists can become more active in the legislative and policy making process.

CONCLUSIONS

In the coming years, psychologists are likely to increase their involvement, and potentially their impact, in the legal arena. From an empirical perspective, research addressing a number of questions arising out of legal decisions or procedures will be needed. The effects of deinstitutionalization, greater external validity of jury decision-making studies, the effectiveness and appropriateness of treatment of offenders, the issues of consent and the right to refuse treatment, and the ability to predict dangerousness are but a few of the important questions that should be addressed in the form of empirical research.

COMPETENCY TO STAND TRIAL
CRIMINAL RESPONSIBILITY

EXPERT TESTIMONY
FORENSIC PSYCHOLOGY
JURY PSYCHOLOGY
PSYCHOLOGY AND THE COURTS
RIGHT TO REFUSE TREATMENT
RIGHT TO TREATMENT

R. ROESCH

PSYCHOLOGY OF MONEY

The attraction that money holds in virtually all societies is based on an acquired drive—one that is learned. The acquisition of the money drive generally occurs fairly early in life, usually as soon as children discover that money enables them to attain a wider range of goals than any other medium. As a result of many experiences in which money is directly or indirectly involved, it assumes value as a reinforcer or as an incentive for the majority of people. Many researchers have taken advantage of money's universal appeal.

The fact that money can be exchanged for a wide range of goods, services, and privileges gives it a high degree of arousal value. When subjects are only minimally aroused, as they are likely to be early in an experiment, the introduction of money tends to facilitate appropriate behavior. However, when subjects have been brought to a relatively high level of arousal, additional arousal resulting from the introduction of money rewards appears to have a distracting effect and therefore interferes with performance.

Money is especially useful in such experiments, because it may be expressed in quantifiable terms. Callahan-Levy and Messé asked men and women subjects to perform a task and then to indicate how much they or others should be paid for doing it. They found that men tended to pay themselves more than they paid other men or women, whereas women paid themselves less than they paid other women or men. The investigators interpreted their results as reflecting a general tendency for women to place a lower economic value on their services than men do on their own.

There are a number of folk sayings to the effect that "money cannot buy happiness," but most people talk and act as though they believed that money can give them a significant increase in pleasure and satisfaction—happiness, in everyday terms. Research studies present contradictory results as to whether money facilitates or inhibits positive emotional states. In favor of the more-money-brings-happiness paradigm are the results of many surveys that show that income is positively correlated with positive attitudes toward oneself and others and that pay level is positively correlated with job satisfaction. However, similar correlations emerge from the pairing of measures of positive attitudes and educational level. Inasmuch as monetary status and educational level are themselves positively correlated, it is not clear which of the two makes the more significant contribution to positive mental states. The results of these studies suggest that getting or having more money at least does not appear to *interfere* with "happiness."

A few studies sound a negative note, however. One of these is an investigation by Brickman and colleagues, who conducted a survey of individuals who had won between $50,000 and $1,000,000 in lotteries. Contrary to what might be expected, the winners' ratings of their past, present, and future happiness were not significantly different from those made by members of a comparison sample of nonwinning lottery ticket buyers who lived in the same neighborhoods. Furthermore, people in the comparison group rated their enjoyment of everyday pleasures— talking to friends, eating breakfast, watching television—significantly higher than did the lottery winners. Indeed, lottery winners said that they enjoyed everyday pleasures actually less than did a group of patients who were wholly or partially paralyzed as a result of accidents. Some of the winners also complained about strains that had developed in their relations with others after winning the big prize.

In everyday life, money paid as a surety deposit affirms the personal responsibility of the payer. People who paid a deposit on enrolling in a weight-reduction seminar tended to have better attendance records and rated instructional materials more highly than those who paid nothing. In another weight-reduction program, patients who paid the therapist's usual fee lost more weight than those who received the treatment gratis.

INCENTIVES
JOB SATISFACTION
REWARDS AND INTRINSIC INTEREST
TOKEN ECONOMIES

H. C. LINDGREN

PSYCHOLOGY OF MUSIC

The field of the psychology of music has been defined in a number of different ways. Seashore wrote about the "musical mind," which could respond to the elements of sound. The mind also possessed certain innate aptitudes or talents, which, with proper nurturing, could enable the person to be a proficient artist. There were, of course, variations in the degrees of these talents.

THE DIMENSIONS OF TONE

From a physical standpoint, a sound wave has various properties, such as frequency (number of cycles per second), intensity (amount of pressure on the ear), quality (the shape of the wave created by overtones), and duration (how long the tone is sounded). On the psychological or behavioral dimension, one responds to frequency in terms of *pitch*—that is, how high or low the tone is judged to be. In *loudness*, the concern is with how strong or weak the tone is. *Timbre* relates to the quality of the sound. The *duration* of the tone refers to time in music, whether the tone is short or long. The human ear can respond to frequencies from about 20 to about 20,000 Hz, and is most sensitive to tones in ranges of 2000 to 4000 Hz. Thus both pitch and loudness are dependent on both frequency and intensity, and are not simple correlates of each other.

Rhythm must also be taken into account as one of the basic components of music. It consists of various patterns of tones in terms of how long they are played and which are accented (greater loudness).

Another area of concern to psychologists of music involves the kinds of emotions and feelings that occur when listening or playing various kinds of music. These reactions can be measured by changes in physiological functions, such as heart rate, blood pressure, breathing, or the galvanic skin response. Music that stressed strong beats in the rhythmic pattern were described as dignified and vigorous; the smoother flowing rhythms were described as happy and playful.

The rise and fall of affective judgments (pleasant to unpleasant) on frequent hearings of various selections tend to vary with the nature of the composition, as well as the number of repetitions of a selection. So-called popular music rises rapidly in affective value with repetition, and then rapidly declines. For the musically educated, works of the great masters may rise more slowly in value at first, but continue to increase with repetition. More modern dissonant and atonal music tends to have generally less affective value, except for the most sophisticated musical listeners.

What constitutes musical ability or talent? Psychologists such as Seashore have maintained that musical ability consists of many separate talents, which may or may not be related. These would include the ability to make fine discriminations in pitch, loudness, timbre, time, rhythm, and tonal memory.

The heredity–environment issue also applies to musical talent. Most researchers tend to agree that musical appreciation is strictly acquired. When the concern is with talent for performing or composing, disagreements arise.

A variety of standardized tests of musical aptitude are currently available. Although they have some predictive validity, in general, their predictions have not been as successful as those of tests of intelligence.

Other areas of interest to psychologists of music include measures of musical performance and the effects of music on industrial production, as well as in offices and music therapy. There is experimental evidence that music can have positive effects. Music is used in occupational therapy where patients in mental hospitals can play or can perform together in bands, orchestras, and choruses. Listening to music can alter some emotional behaviors. For example, stimulating music, such as marches and lively dances, can have stimulating effects on the depressed, whereas calm music can help relieve excitement and anxiety. There is also strong evidence that music generally aids the digestive processes.

EXPRESSIVE ARTS
MUSIC THERAPY
RHYTHM

R. W. LUNDIN

PSYCHOLOGY OF THE ARTS

The arts rely on every ability of the mind—perceptual, cognitive, and motivational. Therefore, all branches of psychology contribute to the study of the arts.

Art derives from a property of percepts that has been almost totally neglected in experimental research even though it is one of the most impressive aspects of actual perceptual experience. It is the "dynamic quality" by which visual shapes or movements exhibit directed tensions and by which color relations entail harmony or discord. Dynamic properties are essentially transmodal.

It is particularly relevant for the psychology of art that these dynamic properties of percepts have recognizable analogies in the other realms of human experience, so that, for example, harmony and discord in music are spontaneously symbolic of types of social relation or a person's state of mind. Rigidity and flexibility apply to behavior as directly as they do to shapes or melodies. By being "expressive," the dynamic qualities of percepts turn into propositional statements about human experience in general. The expressiveness of percepts is the fundamental prerequisite of art.

Much experimental work has been devoted, especially by Gestalt psychologists, to the rules that govern the organization of visual and musical patterns. These rules determine which elements of a picture or melody are connected or segregated in perception, they control the difference between two- and three-dimensional appearance, and so forth.

All elements of the perceptual world have expressive dynamics, but they have it to a different degree. Some trees or clouds carry visual expression more clearly than others, but the mind's spontaneous sensitivity to the expressiveness of whatever is perceived in the environment constitutes the raw material of aesthetic experience. The means by which artistic statements are obtained do not differ in principle from the perceptual qualities observed everywhere outside the realm of the arts.

The motivational factors responsible for why art is produced and why peoples of all cultures have felt a need for it have greatly puzzled psychologists and philosophers during recent centuries. This is so because in the middle class society that developed in the West since the Renaissance the arts lost much of the well-defined function they had in the religious and social institutions of other ages. As the works of the visual arts and music were increasingly reduced to means of entertainment, stimulation, and diversion, the true significance of the arts, although still discernible in the works of the great, was no longer evident to common understanding. Aesthetic theory, therefore, came to favor a doctrine of hedonism: Art was said to be desirable because it aroused pleasure, although it should have been clear that this question-begging assertion abandoned the psychological problem instead of solving it.

Representational art serves basic cognitive needs. The artwork of children demonstrates that the making of pictures is a vitally important means of understanding the nature of the objects and actions the young mind is facing in the environment. The complexity of a tree, a bicycle, or a human figure is reduced in early drawings to a diagrammatic simplicity, which interprets shapes, connections, and causal relations. In principle, the same remains true at the highest level of representational art. A successful painting or sculpture presents relevant human experiences through patterns of shape and color that translate psychological, social, or physical facts into visual analogies. This ability of art to refer individual appearances to underlying generalities has encouraged Jungian psychologists to see works of art as reflections of archetypes, supposed to inhabit the "collective unconscious."

Cognitive enlightenment can be offered by the arts at any level of abstraction. Realistic portrayal keeps the artist's statement close to the particular connotations of a special situation or event. At the highest level of abstraction, painting and sculpture can abandon the representation of subject matter entirely and rely only on the expressive qualities inherent in shapes, textures, and color. Such nonfigurative art can be compared to the ways in which architecture, music, or dance can describe the dynamics of humanly relevant situations through the expression of pure visual or auditory form.

Art serves not only to enlighten the viewer, listener, or reader about the nature of existence, but also provides substitutes for valued objects, persons, or situations. What makes such substitutes particularly pleasing is that the artist has the power to shape them in any desirable manner and thereby to create embodiments of human wishes. This induced Freud to describe artistic activity as a neurotic mechanism, similar to wish dreams, by which satisfaction can be obtained while the challenges of reality are avoided.

The double function of the arts is particularly evident when they are used in therapy. The various techniques of drawing, painting, or modeling serve cognitively to let clients make tangible images of the mental state of affairs they are trying to understand and to handle. Storytelling and the writing of poetry can be used for a similar purpose. The clients' attempts to describe their psychological situation by perceivable means provide the diagnostician with valuable data. In addition, art activity can work as therapy. Less frightening than the real situation, yet furnished with the relevant expressive properties, the art object or activity offers an arena in which to cope with problems, face an adversary, obtain needed benefits, and so on, at a sufficiently lifelike level of reality. "Acting out" in musical or dance performance or on the theater stage can provide a desirable release of tension.

The specific functions of the arts become understandable when they are compared with those of purely cognitive activity best exemplified by science. Art and science differ psychologically in two essential ways. First, pure cognition, the instrument of science, limits itself to obtaining factual knowledge. For aesthetic purposes, such knowledge is also welcome, but only to the extent to which it contributes to the expressive perceptual qualities that constitute the data of art. These data of expression, however, are not simply absorbed as factual information, but are perceived as actual dynamics. The recipient does not merely take cognizance of a thunderstorm described in a picture, story, or symphony, but is directly affected by the kind of impact that characterizes such an event.

Equally fundamental is a second difference between science and art. Science is entirely object-oriented. It is geared to discovering the objective truth about the phenomena it investigates. In the arts, however, the artist's particular way of perceiving and shaping human experience is a necessary and valuable aspect of every aesthetic statement. Hence there are as many different ways of describing the same experience artistically as there are styles of representation. Psychologists know from projective tests that the more ambiguous the target, the broader is the range of interpretation. The work of art, to serve its purpose, must meet two conditions: It must look at the world in an original and profoundly significant way, and the representation thus obtained must be recognizable as valid.

Finally, a remark on the role of the arts in education may serve to illustrate once more the particular place of the arts in the functioning of the mind. The value of art education in schools and colleges goes far beyond training the young in yet another skill. When properly conceived, work in the art room and studio serves to develop the capacity for understanding facts and events through the perception of sensory dynamics. This capacity is vital not only for the artist, but also to help generate the imagery needed for all cognitive activities. Natural and social scientists, physicians, and engineers do their productive thinking by visualizing configurations of forces. Psychologists, for example, theorize on the dynamics of processes in the human personality or in social groups by means of models derived mostly from visual imagery.

ARTISTIC MORPHOLOGY
ART THERAPY
GESTALT PSYCHOLOGY

R. ARNHEIM

PSYCHOMETRICS

The field of psychometrics considers test data from a quantitative perspective. Two divisions might be identified: theoretical and applied. Psychometric theory provides researchers and psychologists with mathematical models used in considering responses to individual test items, entire tests, and sets of tests. Applied psychometrics is the implementation of these models and their analytic procedures to test data.

The four areas of psychometric consideration include norming and equating, reliability, validity, and item analysis. There are both theoretical formulations regarding these four categories and actual procedures to be performed in estimating the usefulness of a test in a specific instance.

NORMING AND EQUATING

Norming tests, part of test standardization, generally involves administration of an examination to a representative sample of individuals, determination of various levels of test performance, and translation of the raw test scores into a common metric.

Tests are sometimes equated when there are different forms of the same test. Equating brings all forms to a common scale. Four basic strategies exist. In the first, each test form is administered to an equivalent (e.g., randomly sampled) group of examinees and scores on the various forms are adjusted so that equal scores have equal percentile ranks (the same proportion failing at or below the score). In a more precise method, all examinees take all forms of the test and equations are used to estimate the score equivalencies among the various forms. A third frequently used method involves the administration of a common test or fraction of a test to all examinees. This common assessment serves as a "bridging" test that permits all measurements to be placed on a single scale; on many multiform examinations, a few "anchor" items are placed on each form to serve as the bridging test. The relatively recent family of statistical models of test scores, called item-response theory models, have proved especially useful for test equating.

Norming and equating have taken on new importance with recent advances in testing and with the greatly increased use of pass–fail decisions. These tests, frequently referred to as *criterion-referenced tests,* have been required by some states as minimum competency examinations to warrant high school graduation and as certification examinations to permit entry into various occupations and professions.

RELIABILITY

Reliability and validity refer to the generalizability of test scores—the determination of what inferences about test scores are reasonable (Cronbach et al., 1972). Reliability concerns inferences about consistency of measurement. Consistency is defined variously as temporal stability, similarity among tests proposed to be equivalent, homogeneity within a single test, and comparability of assessments made by raters. In the "test–retest" method, the reliability of a test is established by administering the test and then waiting a short period before administering the same test again to the same group. The two sets of scores are then compared to determine how similar they are. In the alternate-forms method, two parallel measures are administered to a sample of examinees. Using raters essentially as parallel forms is called *interrater reliability* and is often used when expert judgment is needed and is of unknown value.

VALIDITY

Validity refers to the quality with which a measurement procedure permits the desired inferences. Predictive validity assesses the ability of measurement devices to infer future success, such as on the job or in advanced education. Typically, the predictive measure is correlated with some quantified assessment of job or school success, called a *criterion.* Thus tests used for admission to graduate or professional schools are frequently correlated with grades at that school. The resultant correlation coefficient is called the *validity coefficient.* These coefficients may be adjusted when the range of criterion scores is narrow or when the criterion is unreliable, for example. When data are collected at essentially the same time as the predictor, this is a concurrent validity study. Since a single instrument is often not able to predict a criterion as well as would be desired, multiple predictors may be used, often with the statistical procedure of multiple regression, which weights the various tests to achieve maximal prediction of the criterion.

Content validity involves judging how well the domain to be tested has been covered and is especially useful for tests of educational achievement. Such judgments are generally made by those who are expert in the test domain.

In recent years, it has become accepted that construct validity subsumes predictive and content validity. The critical question asked with construct validity is: How well does a given test measure the trait(s) it is supposed to be measuring?

ITEM ANALYSIS

Most item analysis procedures either (a) look at the number of examinees answering the item correctly and incorrectly, (b) correlate individual items with other variables, or (c) check items for bias. The proportion of examinees answering an item correctly is perhaps inappropriately called *item difficulty.* A means of improving items is to check the proportion who select each option of a multiple-choice item; computing the mean test score of individuals selecting each option is also useful. These procedures check that options appear plausible to naive examinees while not appearing correct to the most knowledgeable. Selecting items that correlate highly with total test score maximizes internal consistency reliability in a test; selecting items that correlate highly with an external criterion maximizes predictive validity. A descriptive analog of these correlations is known as the *item characteristic curve;* typically, this is a graph that plots the proportion of examinees answering a question correctly against their total test scores (or some other estimate of their ability level). For effective items, these graphs are positive ascending lines that do not descend as ability increases. Item analysis procedures concerned with item bias attempt to identify items that are *differentially* difficult for various groups. In other words, these procedures control for overall differences in tested ability and then search for items that are differentially difficult for minority groups. The aim is that, if these items are eliminated from subsequent forms of the test, the test will be considered fair. Presently, these procedures are being subjected to initial scrutiny and are of yet undetermined value.

CLUSTER ANALYSIS
CONSISTENCY
CULTURAL BIASES IN TESTING
ITEM ANALYSIS
SELECTION TESTS
STATISTICS IN PSYCHOLOGY

K. F. GEISINGER

PSYCHONEUROIMMUNOLOGY

For many decades, a considerable number of psychologists believed that they had solved the mind–body problem by concluding that all "mental events" could be reduced to "physical events" occurring in the brain. This was a reaction to earlier philosophical speculation that one set of laws governed mental events, whereas another set governed physical events. More recently, however, psychologists have begun to realize that both the division of mind and body and the reduction of mind to body were socially constructed notions that began to lose their use as advances in the neurosciences began to favor models that illustrated the identity of mind and body, or at least the close interaction of the two processes.

One of the most important events in reframing traditional ideas of mind and body has been the development of psychoneuroimmunology (PNI), a term coined by Ader, although the concept was presaged by Salk when he included the immune system along with genetic, behavioral, and neurological systems in his interfactoral model of disease. This field encompasses studies on the effects of stress on immune functioning, the nature of the stressor as an experimental variable, and the ability to cope with stress. It studies the interaction of the body's central nervous system (in both its neurological and its psychological aspects) and the body's immune system (e.g., the role of the nervous system in regulating immune system functions, the ways in which stress and distress affect the nervous and immune systems). The endocrine system often is included as well, giving the field the somewhat cumbersome name of psychoneuroendocrinoimmunology (PNEI), making it one of the longest words in the English language.

The immune system defends the organism against such foreign invaders as bacteria, fungi, viruses, and toxic chemicals. It also acts as a regulatory and surveillance infrastructure (e.g., preventing its components from turning against each other, identifying and then killing mutant cells that might develop into cancer). One way of describing how the immune system achieves these ends is to divide it into two branches, each with different active agents and assignments. One branch can be referred to as the antibody-mediated, or humoral, subsystem, which operates through the bloodstream by means of antibodies produced by B cells (i.e., bone marrow-derived). (Both B and T cells are referred to as *lymphocytes,* which in turn are a category of white blood cells or leukocytes, along with phagocytes and natural killer, or NK, cells.) When activated by a foreign intruder or antigen, B cells produce any of five known types of antibodies, or immunoglobulins. For example, one type of antibody tends to increase during stress and is responsible for allergic reactions. If house dust or pollen is injected into the skin of a person sensitive to those substances, there could be an immediate reddening and swelling caused by antibodies going into action. The affected cell appears to secrete substances that affect the original signaling, completing a loop.

The action of B cells in the antibody-mediated subsystem is influenced by T (i.e., thymic-derived) cells and by macrophages, a type of phagocyte that consumes the invaders. Macrophages and T cells belong to the immune system's other branch, the cell-mediated subsystem, and produce messenger substances (i.e., cytokines, lymphokines, and monokines) that influence other immune cells. A tumor cell can be attacked by macrophages after being covered with antibodies or can be killed directly by cytotoxic T cells, also called killer T cells. Other T cells, called helper cells and suppressor cells, enhance or suppress the functions of the killer T cells and the B cells.

The capacity for memory is found in both the immune and central nervous systems, as are the use of chemical messengers and the capacities for adaptation, defense, and distant communication (i.e., cell traffic); perhaps these similarities facilitate the linkage of the two systems. The underlying basis for the memory of immune system cells is a change in their specific composition and their corresponding antigen-specific products. However, NK cells, the first line of defense against tumorous cells and cells infected by viruses, are natural killers in the sense that they do not have to learn by prior exposure or be programmed to do their work.

The antibody-mediated and the cell-mediated subsystems constantly interact with each other and with the nervous and endocrine systems in what Rossi describes as "a system of information transduction." The antibody-mediated subsystem provides an instant reaction against toxic, viral, and bacterial foreign proteins; it also is responsible for transfusion reactions against incompatible blood types when they occur. The cell-mediated subsystem is concerned with fighting virus-infected cells and foreign or abnormal cells. When a transplant reaction occurs, it is a result of the cell-mediated immune response. Cell-mediated immunity also is responsible for delayed types of allergy or hypersensitivity, for example, a person sensitive to tuberculin as a result of exposure to tuberculosis develops an area of skin reddening and hardness a day or so after the injection.

Another way of conceptualizing the immune system is to focus on its interrelationships with other bodily systems, contrasting the psychoneuroimmunological macrosystem with the psychoneuroendocrine macrosystem. In regard to the psychoneuroimmunological macrosystem, Wickramasekera has observed that PNI assumes that the immune system, the primary mechanism of healing, works in tandem with the central nervous system and the psychosocial environment. For Wickramasekera, the evidence suggests that central nervous system events can potentially and reliably alter immune responses. More specifically, there is evidence that anxiety and depression can inhibit the immune system as well as evidence that Pavlovian conditioning procedures can modestly but reliably reduce immunocompetence. The implications of these data are profound: for example, through such central nervous system mechanisms as emotional and expectancy learning (Pavlovian conditioning), the immune system may be influenced by placebo stimuli.

Neuropeptides are one type of neurotransmitter (another type being acetylcholine, a mediator of synaptic information flow). In reference to the psychoneuroendocrine macrosystem, Wickramasekera points out that there are descending pain inhibitory pathways from the medial brainstem. These pathways may involve both opiate (i.e., those with an action that resembles the effects of the opiates) and nonopiate neuropeptide mechanisms. Opiate mechanisms can be activated by endogenous neuropeptides (e.g., endorphins) and apparently also by electrical stimulation of certain brain sites (e.g., periaqueductal gray matter). Whether certain types of state-specific cognitive–affective activities (e.g., hypnotic analgesia) can

stimulate these brain sites is not known, but it appears that the opiate mechanisms can be activated within seconds of central nervous system stimulation, that the analgesic effects extend beyond the period of stimulation, and that this stimulation is particularly effective with clinical as opposed to experimental pain. Pert adds that access to periaqueductal gray matter to control pain is regularly demonstrated by yogis, athletes, and women in labor.

Wickramasekera notes that the activation of the endorphins may be one of the primary chemical mechanisms of pain reduction in the placebo response. However, other cognitively initiated (hypnotic analgesia), but chemically mediated psychoneuroendocrine pain inhibitory systems may also exist. For example, there is evidence that depression potentiates chronic clinical pain, and it has been suggested that decreased functional activity in the endogenous opioid neuropeptides may be linked to the manifestation of depression. Pain sensitivity and deficits to pleasure (depression susceptibility) may be mediated through the catecholamines, serotonin, norepinephrine, and dopamine, all of which are known to alter opiate action. Hence, there are psychoneuroendocrine mechanisms through which a placebo stimulus may reduce depression and pain sensitivity; one of the most rapid of these is through the recruitment of the endorphins.

Deficiencies in the immune system may increase the organism's susceptibility to infection or allow mutant cells to divide and become malignant. An overactive immune system may fail to differentiate between body cells and foreign cells and start attacking itself, giving rise to the so-called autoimmune diseases (e.g., rheumatoid arthritis, hyperthyroidism, lupus). There is increasing evidence that both conditions may be linked to psychosocial stressors and with overproduction or underproduction of particular hormones. In addition, the regulation of the immune system is due, in part, to the activity of the neuropeptides, as they consist of amino acid strings that connect the nervous system, endocrine system, and immune system.

Neuropeptides are secreted by the brain, the immune system, and nerve cells in various other organs. The areas of the brain that regulate emotional responses are particularly rich in receptor sites for these chemicals. At the same time, the brain contains receptor sites for protein molecules produced by the immune system alone (e.g., lymphokines, interleukins). This allows for a two-way communication framework linking the brain, the immune system, and potentially all other systems, providing for a pathway through which emotional reactions can affect the body's ability to defend itself.

The role of the neuropeptides is so important that they have been referred to as the "conductors of the immune orchestra." Pert proposes that the more that is known about neuropeptides, the more sense it makes to speak of "bodymind" than to use such traditional terms as mind and body. She adds that as the role of neuropeptides in information flow has become more apparent, the role of cell-to-cell synapses has become less important. Rossi sees this concept of information flow "as the common denominator that enables us to bridge mind and matter, psyche and soma, for a new science of mind/body healing."

RESEARCH ISSUES

The same neurological structures involved in the immune system are also implicated in emotional responses; as a result, physical stressors and emotional distress consistently influence the nervous system. The endocrine system produces hormones (e.g., gonadal steroids, thyroid hormones, adrenal hormones) that affect immune responses. In addition, such opioid neuropeptides as the endorphins and enkephalins can enhance the immune system's functioning. There is considerable evidence that emotions, attitudes, and negative stress can adversely affect the functioning of the immune system. There is far less evidence, however, concerning the effectiveness of psychological factors in fighting illness and enhancing immune functioning. A. S. Relman, as editor of the prestigious *New England Journal of Medicine,* stated "It's a well established fact that emotions can be reflected in pulse rate, respiration, skin temperature, [and] gastric secretion. . . . As for whether mental states can influence the course of disease, there is simply no hard scientific evidence." The executive editor of the journal, Marcia Angell, added, "It has not been shown unequivocally that someone's state of mind can cause or cure a specific disease."

Perhaps the data do not "show unequivocally" that mental and emotional conditions can "cause or cure" disease, but several investigators have produced evidence demonstrating that attitudes and affect can interact with and accompany disease in unusual ways. A review of the empirical literature linking stressor events with human immune reactivity found that acute stressor events had mixed effects on immunity, whereas the impact of chronic stressors was consistently linked with immune function suppression (relationships between psychosocial factors and immunity have been identified for several diseases, including cancer and acquired immunodeficiency syndrome (AIDS), and psychosocial interventions have had variable results in enhancing immunocompetence). Some specific areas of research indicate the relevance of PNI and PNEI to these issues.

1.   Work has been reported showing that the brain, particularly the structures involved in emotion (e.g., hypothalamus, pituitary gland) can be stimulated artificially to increase or decrease immune system activity.

2.   Testing relatives of patients with rheumatoid arthritis, Solomon and Moos found that some had the rheumatoid antibody in their blood and some did not. Those who did not have the antibody reflected the expected range of mental health found in the general population. However, those who had the antibody were exceptionally healthy emotionally, suggesting that this prevented them from contracting the disease.

3.   Achterberg and Lawlis's Imagery of Disease Test asks patients to draw images of their disease, their immune system, and their current treatment. The images are given scores from 1 to 5 on 14 dimensions (e.g., activity level, symbolism, vividness, frequency of positive images). The total score on the Imagery of Disease Test was found to predict the degree of speech clarity among patients with laryngectomies as well as rehabilitation qualities in mastectomy patients. This score predicted the status of cancer with 93% accuracy for those in total remission from cancer, and 100% accuracy for those who had died or who had rapid deterioration at a 2-month follow-up. Patients who were to experience new tumor growth often drew their cancer cells as large, hard, impregnable objects (submarines, crabs, lobsters, scorpions, etc.); however, snails and slugs were related to a better prognosis. Negative symbols for the immune system's white blood cells (lymphocytes) were snowflakes, clouds, and similar weak and amorphous objects. Positive symbols for white blood cells were white knights, Vikings, and religious figures.

Solomon proposed 14 hypotheses regarding the links between the central nervous system and the immune system. Each hypothesis is amenable to empirical testing, and some have already been supported by research data. For example, one hypothesis reads, "Enduring coping style and personality factors (so-called trait characteristics) should influence the susceptibility of an individual's immune system to alteration by exogenous events, including reactions to those events." In support of this hypothesis, a number of studies of cancer patients revealed personality traits similar to those in patients with autoimmune diseases; many of these traits exemplify alexithymia—the inability to find words for feelings—which typifies many people psychologically disposed to physical illness. Another list of research hypotheses has been proposed by Rossi and Cheek based on their thesis that messenger molecules mesh the mind and the body, modulating learning, memory, and emotional behavior.

Solomon has suggested that the term *immunosuppression prone* is a more accurate term than *cancer prone* or even *autoimmune prone.*

CLINICAL IMPLICATIONS

In Pavlovian terms, an antigen can be thought of as an unconditioned stimulus that elicits an immune response. On the basis of this premise, Ader and Cohen conducted research establishing that rats and mice could be conditioned to either suppress or augment their immune responses as measured by antibody levels and development of lethal complications of autoimmune disease. For example, they paired a conditioned stimulus (saccharin-flavored water) with an injection of an unconditioned stimulus (an immunosuppressive drug). When animals subsequently were exposed to the conditioned stimulus, they revealed a significant decrease in immune activity. These data may have clinical applications, assisting the understanding of how immune activity can decrease as a result of exposure to stimuli that are not ordinarily immunosuppressive.

There are existential life situations that appear to effect immune suppression. In one study of divorced and recently separated couples, the more recent the separation, the greater the depression of the percent of NK cells that was observed. Similarly, widows and widowers were observed to manifest a critical suppression of B cell and T cell activity 2 to 3 weeks after the death of their spouses, and (over an 11 year period) experienced a significantly higher rate of morbidity compared with nonbereaved controls. In another study, the caregivers of Alzheimer's patients had significant immunologic suppression of total T cells, helper T cells, and percent of NK cells. In addition, there was evidence of increased replication of the Epstein-Barr virus, which has been partially implicated in some types of chronic fatigue syndrome. However, when the Alzheimer's patient caregivers participated in support groups, there was a detectable improvement in the percent of NK cells. In addition, geriatric residents of independent living facilities showed a significant increase in cellular immunocompetence and resilience (e.g., an increase in NK cell activity) as a result of relaxation training; no change was supported for a control group or a group receiving social contact instead of progressive relaxation and guided imagery. Additional data have been reported with provocative clinical implications for psychotherapists, health educators, and family counselors; some examples follow.

1.   Cancer and other autoimmune diseases rarely coexist with schizophrenia. For example, both rheumatoid arthritis and schizophrenia affect about 1% of the U.S. population, but there is virtually no overlap. Because autoantibodies of all kinds are significantly higher in the blood of schizophrenics than in the general population, it has been speculated that autoantibodies stimulate the receptor for dopamine, a neuropeptide that has been implicated in schizophrenia.

2.   Allergies can be thought of as inappropriate defenses; allergic individuals react to such substances as pollen as if they were dangerous, when they are not. Similar overreactions to supposed danger manifests itself in the nervous system as phobias or extreme anxiety. When the immune system turns on itself, the result is an autoimmune disease; some psychotherapists hold that when the nervous system turns its aggression inward, the result is depression. However, both systems are able to learn by experience; immunization can lead to tolerance or immunity, and success in handling stress early in life can lead to increased resistance to it later.

3.   AIDS-related diseases are accompanied by a variety of immunologic abnormalities, including a decreased number of helper T cells. The human immunodeficiency virus (HIV) retrovirus is referred to by Solomon as a "necessary but probably not sufficient causal factor" for such opportunistic infections as *pneumocystis carinii* and Kaposi's sarcoma. These infections are likely to occur more rapidly if the patient suppresses

anger, uses denial as a coping style, manifests guilt, and has a history of recent stressful events.

4. Multiple personality disorder (MPD) has been found to be associated with marked psychophysiologic alternations, many of which involve the immune system (e.g., unexplained pain, insensitivity to pain, dermatological conditions, differential response to medication, allergies). About one out of four MPD patients exhibits a differential allergic response across personalities. For example, patients have been identified who experience allergic responses to such stimuli as citrus juice and cats in some personalities but not in others.

5. The enhancement of immune functioning by various interventions has been reported by several investigators. Relaxation exercises have increased the production of antibodies, an interleukin, and NK cell activity. Positive emotional states, brought about by humor and accompanied by laughter, have increased a salivary immunoglobulin. Psychological intervention with advanced breast cancer patients not only improved the quality of their survival but also the quantity, the treatment group living twice as long as the control group. This finding aroused controversy, although the principle author has criticized those who claim that "patients are able to wish away their cancer" and that "terminal cancer patients unconsciously want their disease to spread."

6. Although the research literature is inconsistent, there is some evidence that hypnosis can modify the activity of the immune system in several ways. If initiated within 2 hours of the injury, hypnotic treatment for second- and third-degree burns often can reduce the amount of blistering, reduce fluid loss, and diminish secondary infection, apparently through modification of interleukin activity. Conversely, some hypnotic subjects can simply be told that they are being touched with a hot object and develop blisters and redness in the area touched, even though the object used was at room temperature. Patients who are tuberculin positive have been given the suggestion, in hypnosis, that they will develop a reaction on one forearm and not the other. When a biopsy is performed at the site of the tuberculin reaction, an increased number of lymphocytes is revealed—but there is no evidence of the hemorrhage or swelling ordinarily induced by the interleukins produced by these cells on encountering an antigenic stimulus.

CONTINUING CONTROVERSIES

The most controversial area of PNI and PNEI involves the concept of intentional modification of immune responses. Evidence of the immunosuppressive effects of stress leads to the logical step of modifying the stress response as a way to potentially enhance immune function. Although the literature contains some contradictory data, promising results have been obtained from a variety of training programs. Hypnosis, biofeedback, and relaxation exercises have been used successfully to help patients control such immune responses as phagocytic, T cell, and NK cell activity. However, the lack of normative data on many immune parameters impedes understanding of the significance of many of these reported changes. In addition, other potential modifiers of the immune system (e.g., psychological health, diet, exercise) may be important interactive factors.

Some writers have commented on the difficulty in identifying the neural links between the brain and various component parts of the immune system, although at the cellular level there appears to be a definite relationship between the nerve cells and the immune system cells. Bulloch and Moore have identified neural projections from the spinal cord and the medulla to the thymus gland in rats and mice, suggesting that these nervous system structures play a role in the regulation of thymic stimulation of T cell production. Pert attributes communication to the neuropeptides, noting the importance of receptor specificity. Rossi has proposed a downward–upward informational model based on Bulloch's findings that a downward brain–body communcation link takes place by way of the autonomic nervous system that can modulate the activity of lymphoid

tissue (one of the basic mechanisms of PNE), and Pert, Ruff, Weber, and Herkenham's findings that an upward communication link from the body to brain takes place through information-carrying molecules produced in the white blood cells that modulate the brain.

Becker has suggested that this link may also involve the body's direct current (DC) electrical control system, the "current of injury" that exists at the site of injured cells and that seems to play a role in their recovery, perhaps through the stimulation of a massive amount of calcium ions. Becker suspects that this DC system plays a role in starting, maintaining, and suspending healing. In both Pert's and Becker's speculations, the glial cells play an important role in the internal networking process, and are seen as more important than linear cell-to-cell communication. These investigators, and many others involved in PNI and PNEI, contend they have discovered ways in which mind and body communicate, ways that undercut the dualistic and physicalistic concepts, supporting instead new information-based, bidirectional models of bodymind and healing.

ENDOPHINS–ENKEPHALINS
GENERAL ADAPTATION SYNDROME
GENETICS AND PERSONALITY TRAITS
HERITABILITY
HORMONES AND BEHAVIOR
MIND–BODY PROBLEM
NEUROCHEMISTRY
PSYCHOSOMATICS

S. Krippner

PSYCHONEUROLOGY

"The moral and active principles of the mind are strongly perverted or depraved; the power of self-government is lost or greatly impaired and the individual is found to be incapable not of talking or reasoning upon any subject proposed to him, but of conducting himself with decency and propriety in the business of life." Thus did the English psychiatrist J. C. Prichard define the new concept of "moral insanity" in his *Treatise* published in 1835. The same idea is embodied in the *manie sans dé lire* described by the father of French psychiatry, Phillipe Pinel, in 1812. In that same year, the first American psychiatrist, Benjamin Rush, referred to persons possessed of an "innate preternatural moral depravity." The great German systematists were concerned with accounting for that large and heterogeneous group of persons whose behavior is bizarre, perverse, or outlandish—and only in some cases immoral or antisocial—but who are neither deranged nor delusional. J. L. A. Koch, in 1891, organized them under the heading of "psychopathic inferiorities." In the successive editions of his influential textbook *Psychiatrie*, Emil Kraepelin plowed and replowed the same ground but, during the span of the seventh edition, he employed for the first time the term *psychopathic personality* as a label for the sort of people Prichard had in mind. The German nosologists, however, were reluctant to base their classifications on criteria that were sociological, or even political; one person's definition of an antisocial psychopath might be defined from another perspective as, for instance, a freedom fighter. Karl Schneider's monograph, *The psychopathic personality,* first published in 1923, defined 10 varieties of deviant personality, several of which might, but did not necessarily, predispose toward antisocial behavior.

The opposite approach was taken by G. E. Partridge in 1930, who concluded that a subgroup of the persons called psychopathic had as their dominant symptom an inability or unwillingness to conform to the demands of society, and he proposed the new term *sociopathic personality.* This designation was adopted by the American Psychiatric Association (APA) in the first edition of its *Diagnostic and statistical manual (DSM).*

With the publication of *DSM-III* in 1980, however, there was a reversion to the Germanic model. "Psychopathic personality" was dropped as too general and vague; "sociopathic personality," which had never really caught on, was also discarded. In their place were defined a dozen varieties of *personality disorder,* not unlike Schneider's 10 psychopathies, of which several might embrace persons hitherto called psychopathic (the "histrionic," "narcissistic," and "borderline" personalities) and one, the "antisocial personality," is more explicitly tailored to Prichard's prototype.

Unfortunately, there is no evidence that there really are 12 types of personality disorder rather than, for example, 9 or 19, or indeed, that a typological scheme is better than a dimensional one for analyzing this problem. Moreover, it is a reasonable certainty that not all of the persons who meet the descriptive criteria of the antisocial personality are etiologically or psychiatrically homogeneous. We can agree with Sir Aubrey Lewis' observation in 1974 that: "The diagnostic groupings of psychiatry seldom have sharp and definite limits. Some are worse than others in this respect. Worst of all is psychopathic personality, within its wavering outlines. Its outline will not be firm until much more is known about its genetics, psychopathology, and neuropathology." Yet if the outlines are too wavering, the research required to provide the needed knowledge may instead yield only additional confusion. By adopting criteria that are descriptive but essentially arbitrary, *DSM-III* has opted for diagnostic reliability at the cost of validity. It is doubtful that summary statistics compiled on the heterogeneous individuals who meet the criteria specified for "antisocial personality" will ever provide real illumination of this large category. More prevalent than schizophrenics, these people are a considerably greater social burden; whether they are labeled "moral imbeciles," "antisocial personalities," "sociopaths," or "psychopathic personalities," they constitute an important social, forensic, and psychiatric problem.

A FAMILY OF DISORDERS

The psychiatric problem is to understand why an intelligent and rational person might persist in antisocial behaviors in the face of risks and actual punishments that would inhibit most similar impulses in a normal individual. Defined thus generally, psychopathic personality can be regarded as a family of disorders, comprising at least four "genera" that are themselves divisible into "species." Thus the genus *dissocial psychopath* consists of persons who "do not show significant personality deviations other than those implied by adherence to the values or code of their own predatory, criminal or other social group," in the words of *DSM.* These are Fagin's children, the members of *cosa nostra* families, the ghetto guerrillas. In 1936, Karl Menninger, in *Man against himself,* described a second genus, the *neurotic character,* in whom antisocial behavior constitutes the acting out of neurotic conflict or the manifestations of an unconscious need for punishment. One must be careful here because a committed psychodynamicist can find unconscious or neurotic explanations for nearly any behavior abberration. In *The impulsive personality,* Howard Wishnie attributes the deceitful manipulativeness of the psychopath to a deep lack of confidence in the individual's own ability and in the good will of others; thus the "con artist" protagonist of the movie *The music man* becomes a self-doubting sufferer who might be cured by love and psychotherapy.

A third genus would include species of organic dysfunction or abnormality. Some pathologically impulsive individuals seem to have a specific defect of inhibitory control. Some hyperactive children mature into impulsive psychopaths. Other persons have tyrannical sexual hungers or explosive and uncontrollable tempers or an apparent short-circuiting of aggressive and sexual instincts. The premenstrual tension syndrome can lead some women to periodic outbursts of pathological aggressiveness. These affective disturbances appear to be constitutional in origin and would obviously predispose toward antisocial behavior. However, in an influential paper published in 1948, Benjamin Karpman insisted that, "when all the cases that I group under symptomatic or neurotic psychopathy are removed and accounted for, there would still remain a small group which may be designated as primary or idiopathic psychopathy."

THE PRIMARY PSYCHOPATH

The primary psychopath is the chronic offender who is not neurotic or dissocially reared or a victim of some organic dysfunction of emotional or impulse control. Without intending that this zoological classification be taken too seriously, at least two species and several "subspecies" can be identified provisionally within this genus.

Alienation Syndrome

Positive social attitudes and feelings do not spring full blown into the normal adolescent breast. They must be learned through the experience of nurturant parenting, rewarding affiliations with a variety of other persons, and the example of some admired and socialized adult. It is possible that there is a "critical period" within early childhood during which some minimum amount of cuddling and comforting must be experienced if the normal ability for love and attachment to others is ever to develop.

Among those persons who are capable of loving someone—members of their immediate family, for example—there are great individual differences in the radius of what might be called the "circle of empathy." Some people who will unhesitatingly swat a fly would be dismayed to run over a squirrel. Some squirrel hunters would mourn to see a dog suffer. There are citizens who quickly call the dogcatcher to euthanize a stray animal and yet oppose capital punishment and contribute to UNESCO. In the crowd watching a prospective suicide teeter on the high ledge of a building, there are some with their hearts in their throats, awash with feeling, and others whose eyes gleam with the happy anticipation of a child at the circus. Other things equal, it is likely that circles of empathy are smallest for those most often exposed to the sufferings of others because they have learned to desensitize themselves to vicarious discomfort.

Anger and hostility seem to be natural reactions to feelings of envy, frustration, and dissatisfaction with one's lot. Although we think of anger as a dysphoric emotion, it is certainly less unpleasant to feel angry than frightened or impotent or vulnerable or worthless. Some people seem to cultivate anger as a protection against these alternative and even more uncomfortable states of mind, and it is possible that this mechanism can become habitual, leading to a diffuse hostility that, in turn, may encourage antisocial actions.

Thus, in these disaffiliated, disempathic, and choleric individuals, three "species" of the alienated psychopath have been suggested. One should emphasize again that these descriptions are not offered as a genuine typology but merely to illustrate ways in which the normal emotions that prevent most of us from yielding to aggressive impulses, or from having such impulses in the first place, might fail to develop or be overmastered in certain individuals as a consequence of the deprivation of love, security, opportunity, and good example, especially in early childhood.

The Cleckley Psychopath

A thoughtful and influential essay on the clinical characteristics of the psychopathic personality, *The mask of sanity* by Harvey Cleckley, was first published in 1941 and evolved through five editions, the last appearing in 1976. In this monograph, distinguished by a vivid literary style, an extensive series of case histories is brought to life in such a way as to make it clear that Cleckley is referring to a distinctive subgroup of primary psychopaths who cannot be understood in terms of any of the etiological considerations discussed briefly here. From his own assessment of his material, Cleckley formulated a list of some 16 specific attributes that his cases seem to have in common. These attributes are not all equally important and a few (e.g., "suicide rarely carried out") appear to be derivative from others. The 10 or so core features can be summarized as follows.

Cleckley was persuaded that this syndrome results from some deep and probably constitutional defect involving an inability to experience the normal affective accompaniments of experience. People who are color-blind cannot appreciate how another will experience a rainbow. They might learn to simulate the comments others make about the chromatic beauties of a scene and to discriminate well enough for most purposes by remembering, for example, that "red" (whatever that means) is used as a descriptor of apples; they might never discover for themselves that this aspect of their experience is qualitatively different from the norm. The Cleckley psychopath, similarly, may simply be unable to experience normal guilt, remorse, frightened apprehension, or cherishing affection. Like the raw feel of the experience of color, these emotions are inherently private and unavailable to intersubjective comparison. The psychopath can learn what other people say in emotional situations; protestations of love or of regret may ring as true as those of any actor yet be equally hollow. It is also possible that this individual's indignation, if he or she is not believed, is both genuine and, in a sense, justified—how can one know that other people utter such statements only at the prompting of strong emotions that one has never felt?

Another approach has been to seek to understand the Cleckley psychopath in terms of a more focal and specific defect, one abnormality or difference from which the other features of the syndrome might derive as consequences. In particular, it has been suggested that this type of psychopath is distinguished by nothing more exotic than a low "anxiety IQ." All mammals can experience fear and can learn to associate anxiety with impulses that have been punished or with other stimuli that signal danger. Some people who develop conditioned fear responses much more readily than do other people have high anxiety IQs. A child at the low end of this same continuum will be difficult to socialize by the usual techniques of discipline that depend so heavily on the use of fear and punishment. The child may frustrate and antagonize his or her parents so as to be deprived of the important experience of that prototypic love relationship (this deprivation may begin quite early if the parents are themselves psychopathic). It is possible that the average child learns to identify with others as part of a self-protective effort to predict their behavior. Being relatively unconcerned with what others might do or think, the relatively fearless child may invest less effort in this aspect of social learning, and one who does not readily identify with others may not readily empathize with others or introject their values as required for the normal development of superego and the capacity for guilt. Fear and its allies (shame, guilt, and embarrassment) seem to be largely responsible for preventing most of us from now and then committing some of the same misdemeanors that constitute the antisocialism of the psychopath. The absence of fear, the happy-go-lucky insouciance that emerges when shyness, self-consciousness, guilt, and apprehension are dispelled, is a cardinal attribute of "charm." An important and paradoxical corollary of the anxiety IQ hypothesis is that the child at risk for psychopathy should not be considered sick or defective. This is the stock from which heroes are made. With the right sort of parenting—patient, perceptive, emphasizing rewards over punishment, consistently guiding so that the child is sure to achieve these rewards, cultivating a sense of pride and self-respect to substitute for the weak inhibitions of fear and guilt—these children may grow up to be explorers and adventurers, test pilots, and astronauts of the kind Tom Wolfe admired in his book *The right stuff.*

In 1957, D. T. Lykken showed that the Cleckley psychopath is slow to condition fear to warning signals, tends to ignore painful electric shock in a situation where normals learn to avoid the shock, and seems generally to be less influenced than the average person is by reactions of fear or embarrassment. These findings have been replicated and extended by other investigators, most notably by Robert Hare in a series of studies spanning 20 years. Hare has shown, for example, that the Cleckley psychopath displays abnormally little electrodermal arousal in anticipation of a painful shock or a loud blast of noise. In this same situation, however, the psychopath shows a higher than normal elevation of heart rate. Other research suggests that increased heart rate can reflect the operation of an adaptive control mechanism that attenuates central nervous system arousal and, perhaps in this situation, the impact of the anticipated shock itself. The psychopath's pain tolerance is not greater than normal as ordinarily measured but, if real incentives are offered, the psychopath will tolerate greater pain than will a control subject to achieve them.

Family studies by C. R. Cloninger and his colleagues indicate that psychopathy fits very nicely a threshold model that posits an underlying predisposition that, above some threshold (a lower threshold for males than for females), leads to the disorder. A genetically determined anxiety IQ, interacting with environmental influences (the style and consistency of parenting, etc.), could constitute this underlying variable of liability to psychopathy. Twin and adoption studies both indicate a significant genetic component; however, the vast majority of biological relatives of psychopathic offspring are *not* psychopaths. Even among monozygotic twins reared together, if one twin is psychopathic, there is less than a 50% chance that the co-twin will be psychopathic also. The evidence suggests that extrafamilial environmental differences, experiences peculiar to the individual, are most important of all in determining who will develop a psychopathic personality.

ADOLESCENT IDENTITY FORMATION
ANTISOCIAL PERSONALITIES
BONDING AND ATTACHMENT
CHARACTER DISORDERS
MORAL DEVELOPMENT
PERSONALITY DISORDERS

D. T. Lykken

PSYCHOPATHIC PERSONALITY

"The moral and active principles of the mind are strongly perverted or depraved; the power of self-government is lost or greatly impaired and the individual is found to be incapable not of talking or reasoning upon any subject proposed to him, but of conducting himself with decency and propriety in the business of life." Thus did the English psychiatrist J. C. Prichard define the new concept of "moral insanity." The same idea is embodied in the *manie sans délire* described by the father of French psychiatry, Phillipe Pinel. The first American psychiatrist, Benjamin Rush, referred to persons possessed of an "innate preternatural moral depravity." Emil Kraepelin employed the term *psychopathic personality.*

A FAMILY OF DISORDERS

The problem is to understand why an intelligent and rational person might persist in antisocial behaviors in the face of risks and actual punishments that would inhibit most similar impulses in a normal individual. Defined thus generally, psychopathic personality can be regarded as a family of disorders, comprising at least four "genera" that are themselves divisible into "species." Thus the genus *dissocial psychopath* consists of persons who "do not show significant personality deviations other than those implied by adherence to the values or code of their own predatory, criminal or other social group," in the words of *The diagnostic and statistical manual.* Karl Menninger described a second genus, the *neurotic character,* in whom antisocial behavior constitutes the acting out of neurotic conflict or the manifestation of an unconscious need for punishment.

A third genus would include species of organic dysfunction or abnormality. Some pathologically impulsive individuals seem to have a specific defect of inhibitory control. Some hyperactive children mature into impulsive psychopaths. Other persons have tyrannical sexual hungers or explosive, uncontrollable tempers or an apparent short-circuiting of aggressive and sexual instincts.

THE PRIMARY PSYCHOPATH

The Cleckley Psychopath

In his book *The mask of sanity,* Harvey Cleckley, formulated a list of some 16 specific attributes that his cases seemed to have in common.

Cleckley's psychopath "while not deeply vicious, carries disaster lightly in each hand." These persons may be intelligent and often display great charm, enhanced no doubt by a lack of nervousness or other neurotic manifestations. Yet they are fundamentally unreliable, with a remarkable disregard for truth, and seem incapable of real love or emotional attachment. This antisocial behavior often appears to be inadequately motivated; these individuals take needless risks, give the appearance of poor judgment, and show an indifference to punishment by failing to learn from unpleasant experience. They lack genuine remorse or shame, often rationalizing their behavior or laying the blame on others. They have a "specific loss of insight," that is, an inability to appreciate how others feel about them or to anticipate how others will react to their outrageous conduct. In perhaps three cases out of four, they are likely to be males.

Cleckley was persuaded that this syndrome results from some deep and probably constitutional defect involving an inability to experience the normal affective accompaniments of experience. The Cleckley psychopath simply may be unable to experience normal guilt, remorse, frightened apprehension, or cherishing affection.

An approach has been to seek to understand the Cleckley psychopath in terms of one abnormality or difference from which the other features of the syndrome might derive as consequences. In particular, it has been suggested that this type of psychopath is distinguished by nothing more exotic than a low "anxiety IQ." All mammals can experience fear and can learn to associate anxiety with impulses that have been punished or with other stimuli that signal danger. Some people who develop conditioned fear responses much more readily than other people do have high anxiety IQs. Fear and its allies, shame, guilt, and embarrassment, seem to be largely responsible for preventing most of us from now and then committing some of the same misdemeanors that constitute the antisocialism of the psychopath.

ADOLESCENT IDENTITY FORMATION
ANTISOCIAL PERSONALITIES
BONDING AND ATTACHMENT
CHARACTER DISORDERS
MORAL DEVELOPMENT
PERSONALITY DISORDERS

D. T. LYKKEN

PSYCHOPHARMACOLOGY

The word *psychotropic* derives from the Greek *psyche* (mind) and *tropikos* (turning); thus a turning or changing of the mind is the essential meaning of the term. Disorders from such drugs appear to be neurological in nature, primarily revealing themselves as disturbances in the central nervous system (CNS). Two early psychoactive tranquilizing agents were introduced at approximately the same period: reserpine, an alkaloid derived from the root of the *Rauwolfia serpentine* plant, and chlorpromazine, a synthetically developed phenothiazine compound. Numerous other tranquilizers followed rapidly, as the pharmaceutical companies foresaw a ready market for the use of such drugs.

Drugs per se cannot cure mental or emotional illness but evidence indicates that florid psychoses can be controlled and severe psychotic anxiety abated. Schizophrenic behavior can be managed more effectively, and manic–depressive states and other affective disorders, such as depressions, also frequently become responsive to appropriate medication. Debilitating anxiety, as a symptom of severe neurosis, is usually ameliorated through the administration of carefully selected and monitored tranquilizers. Effective dosages vary from one person to another since blood levels are not constant even with equal dosage and body weight.

Both the function and response of neurotransmitters have gained much prominence in recent years as potential avenues for dramatic breakthroughs in the understanding and treatment of mental disorders. In particular, the metabolites of serotonin, noradrenalin, and dopamine have been the focus of the study in depressive disorders.

ANTIPSYCHOTIC DRUGS

The most commonly used types of antipsychotic medications are aliphatics and piperazines. The best known aliphatic is chlorpromazine (Thorazine). Its early and widespread use had led to its being employed as a standard for dosage measurement for other antipsychotic drugs.

Mental hospitals with severely disturbed and chronically ill patient populations have employed potent piperazines; for example, fluphenazine (Prolixin) and butyrophenones, especially haloperidol (Haldol).

Although these drugs have been useful in controlling irrational thinking, combative–aggressive behavior, and hyperactivity, serious side effects have surfaced with increasing prominence. Tardive dyskinesia began to proliferate in the late 1970s. This disorder results from high dosages of neuroleptic drugs over periods of 6 months or more, as a rule, and appears primarily in adults and the elderly, although it can manifest itself in children as well. The body areas especially affected are the lips, jaws, eyes, arms, legs, and the trunk, Movements in these parts of the body are involuntary and irregular, and initially may be confused with Parkinsonism in adults. Protruding tongue, lip and facial contortions, eye blinking, and wide, unplanned openings of the jaws are common in the face. The fingers, wrists, and arms display both athetoid (slow, writhing movements) and choreiform (rapid, jerky but coordinated) expressions. A rocking motion of the trunk also may be present. In some adult cases, the disorder appears to become irreversible, although this unfortunate result is not likely to occur with children. Dystonia (muscle tone malfunction), akinesia (absence of movement or muscle paralysis), and akathisia (restlessness and/or inability to sit or lie down) are frequent additional accompanying symptoms of this distressing neurological malady, which characteristically appears after discontinuance of neuroleptic drugs.

Among the commonly used phenothiazines, and their basic dosages, are the following:

Generic Name	Commercial Name	Basic Dosage (mg)
Chlorpromazine	Thorazine	100
Triflupromazine	Vesprin	25
Promazine	Sparine	50
Trifluoperazine	Stelazine	5
Fluphenazine	Prolixin	2
Prochlorperazine	Compazine	16
Thiopropazate	Dartal	12
Butaperzine	Repoise	10
Perphenazine	Trilafon	10
Thioridazine	Mellaril	100

ANTINEUROTIC AND ANTIANXIETY DRUGS

Pharmacological agents used to control tension and anxiety may be regarded essentially as antineurotic. Three common types of anxiety drugs were: (a) the glycerols and meprobamates (Miltown, Equanil); (b) deprol (which combined meprobamate with benactyzine); and (c) the benzodiazepines, chlordiazepoxides (Librium), and hydroxyzine (Atarax), a diphenylmethane derivative.

Some of these drugs are, in effect, muscle relaxants and operate on the internuncial/neurons (meprobamates), although others also work through the midbrain and reticular activating system. Because of their structure and the metabolic activity of the minor tranquilizers, suicide is unlikely with overdose when they are taken alone. However, when mixed with alcohol or other CNS depressants, a number of these drugs may become hypotensive and result in death. Every drug varies in effective dosage and average daily amounts of many of the antianxiety compounds are difficult to substantiate. In any event, rough estimates of average daily doses for adults are listed here for some representative drugs for each type cited:

Generic Name	Commercial Name	Basic Average Dosage
Meprobamate	Miltown, Equanil	1600 mg
Meprobamate + benactyzine	Deprol	4 tablets
Diazepam	Valium	5 mg
Chlordiazepoxide	Librium	30 mg
Oxazepam	Serax	40 mg
Flurazepam hydrochloride	Dalmane	30 mg
Hydroxyzine hydrochloride	Atarax	400 mg

Physicians and patients may justifiably feel that these dosages represent too much or too little for their particular set of experiences. The placebo effect often operates in conjunction with drug ingestion, since the mere expectation that a given amount of a drug will be effective aids the process.

ANTIDEPRESSIVE DRUGS

Affective disorders account for disturbances in mood or emotional tone and include excitability, as well as depression. Some drugs that help to control anxiety are of value in dealing with heightened emotional states, such as mania and hypomania. Ideally, then, all medications for the affective states should be grouped together.

Antidepressants are generally classified into two principal groups, tricyclic agents and monoamine oxidase (MAO) inhibitors. Stimulants are sometimes still used to combat depression. The principal stimulants employed are amphetamines (Benzedrine), dextroamphetamine (Dexadrine), and methylphenidate (Ritalin), but, for the most part, they have given way to the tricyclics and MAOs.

LITHIUM SALTS

Lithium salts were used in Europe for several years prior to their adoption for treatment in the United States. Initially thought to be useful largely for manic states, they have been shown to be of some value for depressive states as well. Produced in the form of lithium carbonate, the primary use of lithium is probably best for the states of acute mania and for long-term administration in manic–depressive conditions. Precautions for its use are especially important in persons with renal or cardiovascular disorders, individuals on diuretics, and those who are debilitated or dehydrated where sodium is depleted. Toxicity is a likely serious consequence in such cases. Pregnant women and nursing mothers should not be given lithium because it has been shown to have adverse effects on the embryos of mammals and can appear in human milk. In depression, it presumably affects neuronal activity of the catecholamines, but its biochemical action in manic patients is still not fully understood.

SOPORIFICS AND HYPNOTICS

Sleep-inducing and sedative drugs were used before the new crop of psychoactive drugs came on the market. These medications are still prescribed for nighttime use when sleep is desired. Although they help to exert a calming effect and control anxiety, they are usually reserved for purposes of inducing sleep rather than for daytime use. Some barbiturates are short-acting and others long-acting in terms of both onset of action and duration.

It is important for persons taking drugs to understand these actions as well as the potential side effects, so that tragic errors in judgment do not occur regarding their ingestion. Legally, the psychotherapist and/or physician is on firmer ground if he or she has discussed various aspects of medications with the patient than if no information or warnings were

Generic Name	Commercial Name	Average Daily Dosage (mg)
Monoamine Oxidase Inhibitors (MAOs)		
Isocarboxazid	Marplan	20
Phenelzine sulfate	Nardil	45
Pargyline hydrochloride (HCl)	Eutonyl	25
Tranylcypromine sulfate	Parnate	20
Tricyclic Drugs		
Amitriptyline HCl	Elavil, SK-Amitriptyline	150
Nortriptyline HCl	Aventyl	75
Amoxapine	Asendin	300
Imipramine HCl	Tofranil, Imavate, Presamine, SK-pramine	200
Desipramine HCl	Norpramine, Pertofrane	150
Perphenazine and amitriptyline HCl*	Etrafon	6–75*
Protriptyline HCl	Vivactil	40
Doxepine HCl	Sinequan, Adapin	150
Cyclobenzaprine HCl	Flexeril	30
Maprotiline HCl	Ludiomil	150
Trimipramine maleate	Surmontil	150

* Tablets contain perphenazine 2 mg and amitriptyline HCl 25 mg each, hence a daily dosage T.I.D. equals 6 and 75 mg, respectively.

offered, even in suicidal cases. Patient cooperation should always be sought.

ACETYLCHOLINESTERASE
AMPHETAMINE EFFECTS
ANTABUSE
ANTIANXIETY DRUGS
ANTIDEPRESSIVE DRUGS
ANTIPSYCHOTIC DRUGS
CHEMICAL BRAIN STIMULATION
ENDORPHINS/ENKEPHALINS
NEUROCHEMISTRY
STIMULANTS
TRANQUILIZING DRUGS

C. J. FREDERICK

PSYCHOPHYSICAL LAWS

The term *psychophysics* refers to functional relations between variables on a physical continuum and corresponding sensory responses. A quantitative statement of such a relationship is termed a *psychophysical law*. These laws are intended to explain the functioning of sensory systems and to permit the prediction of sensory behavior. Psychophysical laws have been established for two major classes of events: (a) threshold or detection phenomena and (b) suprathreshold or discrimination phenomena.

For many psychological phenomena, time is a critical variable and temporal summation appears to be a fundamental principle in all sensory modalities. Temporal summation implies that the intensity and duration of a given stimulus interact reciprocally to maintain a given sensory response, such as the absolute threshold.

Vision

When the duration of a light stimulus is very short, a high intensity level is required for its detection; but, as the duration of the flash increases, the required intensity level decreases. This reciprocity between time (t) and intensity (I) demonstrates temporal summation and is known as Bloch's law: It = constant. The law holds at the absolute threshold of vision for durations up to about 0.1 second, often termed the *critical duration*. Beyond this value, temporal summation continues to occur, but perfect reciprocity no longer holds.

Audition

Within certain temporal limits, the intensive threshold of audibility decreases as the duration of the auditory stimulus is increased. However, the relationship at threshold is more complex than $It = c$ and is dependent on the frequency of the test tone and the age of the subjects. Although reciprocity occurs for certain frequencies and durations, it does not hold beyond 100 ms.

Other Sensory Modalities

Critical durations in the basic reciprocity principle have also been obtained for the minor senses. In gustation, the time varies according to the specific taste stimulus: Sweet stimuli require approximately 2 seconds; salt, 3 seconds; bitter and acid, 3.5 seconds each. For olfaction, time is no longer a significant factor at thresholds beyond 5 seconds. For thermal stimuli, temporal summation occurs up to 10 seconds; cold responses produced by a current of air striking the forehead involve reciprocity up to approximately 1.5 seconds.

SUPRATHRESHOLD PHENOMENA

As with threshold phenomena, the measurement of suprathreshold phenomena is dependent on behavioral responses. Accordingly, psychophysical theories attempt to explain the relations between stimulus variables and associated responses mediated through corresponding sensory modalities. Fundamental to these theories is the concept of three separate but related dimensions or continua: (a) a physical (stimulus) continuum; (b) an inferred subjective or sensory continuum; and (c) a judgmental or behavioral response continuum.

Differential Threshold

The differential threshold is a measure of the observer's ability to discriminate suprathreshold differences between stimuli. In 1834, E. H. Weber, in *De pulsu, resorptione, auditu et tactu*, reported that sensory discrimination is relative; that is, the amount by which the intensity of a stimulus must be increased or decreased ($\Delta\phi$) for a sensory change to be reported is a constant fraction of the intensity of the original stimulus (ϕ). In mathematical form, it is given as $\Delta\phi = k\phi$, where k is a constant of proportionality. This relationship is known as Weber's law. The law is intended as a general statement of the discriminability of stimuli in all sensory modalities and has been verified by numerous investigators. However, the Weber ratio does not hold at low levels of stimulus intensity and, depending on experimental circumstances, it may fail also at high intensities. Accordingly, various modifications have been proposed in which $\Delta\phi$ is made proportional to ϕ plus a constant, rather than ϕ alone.

Classical Psychophysical Scales

In 1860, Gustav T. Fechner introduced several psychophysical methods by means of which he claimed to be able to determine the magnitude of sensation as a function of stimulus magnitude. Starting with Weber's law and a set of assumptions, Fechner proceeded to use the minimal detectable change (termed "just noticeable difference, or jnd) to formulate a basic logarithmic law: $\psi = k \log (\phi/b)$, where ψ stands for psychological magnitude, ϕ refers to the physical value of the stimulus, b is the stimulus magnitude at the absolute threshold, and k is a constant of proportionality. Fechner's law states that as stimulus intensity increases geometrically, the magnitude of the sensation increases arithmetically; thus equal stimulus ratios produce equal intervals of sensation.

Numerous objections were raised for more than a century over Fechner's logarithmic law. The objections covered three main arguments: (a) that sensations do not have magnitude and, therefore, cannot be measured; (b) that Weber's law was only an approximation and did not hold over the entire stimulus range; and (c) that all jnds are not equal in subjective magnitude. Consequently, numerous modifications of Fechner's law were proposed.

Revised Psychophysical Scales

If the validity of Fechner's law is assumed and two adjacent sensory intervals are marked by three consecutive stimuli, the intensity of the middle stimulus (the bisection point) should equal the geometric mean of the two extreme stimuli. However, data from numerous studies have yielded central values closer to the arithmetic mean than the geometric mean. Thus the Fechnerian measurement of sensory responses by the indirect approach of discriminability of stimuli has not been verified by the direct determination of equal sense distances.

Comparison of Psychophysical Scales

Psychophysical scales can be derived from two major classes of experimental methods: (a) direct methods, or those in which there is an isomorphic correspondence between the judgments of an observer and the scale values assigned by the experimenter, as in magnitude estimation; and (b) indirect methods, or those in which there is no one-to-one correspondence between the judgments and the assigned scale values, as in category estimation. If a method were selected from each of these two classes and applied to the same set of stimuli, the obtained scales would be expected to be linearly related, so that a plot of one scale against the other should yield a straight line.

Typically, however, such a relationship is seldom obtained for intensive continua. A partition scale (indirect method of category production) plotted against its corresponding proportionality scale (direct method of magnitude production) almost always produces a curve that is concave downward and lies between a logarithmic function and a power function. The failure to find the predicted linear relationship suggests an increase in judgmental variability as the stimulus values progress from low to high on the test continuum. It is also possible that the lack of linearity is related to differences in the range of available responses or other factors within each scaling method, thereby affecting adaptation level.

Interpretation of Psychophysical Laws

When an observer is presented with two stimuli and is required to bisect the sensory distance between them by adjusting the value of a third stimulus on the same continuum, the adjusted value will depend on the directional order in which the two stimuli are presented: ascending or descending. The bisection will be set higher for the ascending pair than for the descending pair.

Since scale values can be influenced by various nonsensory factors such as stimulus order, stimulus range, range of responses, the value of the standard stimulus, and other conditions may be raised—about the interpretation of psychophysical scales and derived psychophysical laws. Strictly, psychophysical laws do not directly incorporate sensory magnitudes, but rather the relations between stimuli and associated judgmental responses from which postulated sensory magnitudes are inferred.

Some investigators believe that psychophysical scales specifically reflect a given aspect of sensory neural activity and consider psychophysical functions as "transducer" functions that describe how sensory mechanisms transform stimulus energy into neural activity. From a theoretical view, the transducer position complicates the formulation of psychophysical laws inasmuch as four, rather than three, continua are then implicated in the scaling situation—(a) physical, (b) physiological, (c) sensational, and (d) judgmental response. If the third continuum (sensational) were to be considered as theoretically nonessential, psychophysical laws no longer would contain the potential of reference to subjective magnitudes.

Whether psychophysical theory encompasses three or four continua, the nonlinearity of empirical psychophysical scales (logarithmic or exponential) may occur between any two adjacent continua.

It is also possible that the nonlinearity may occur not in the peripheral functions of the sensory system, but in the central information processing system of the brain. Accordingly, the judgmental responses in sensory scaling experiments could be influenced by prior learning experiences and by exigent contextual factors, including stimuli, responses, and procedures.

AUDITORY DISCRIMINATION
EMPIRICAL RESEARCH METHODS
HEARING
FECHNER'S LAW
PSYCHOPHYSICAL METHODS
VISUAL PERCEPTION
WEBER'S LAW

J. F. Corso

PSYCHOPHYSICAL METHODS

Psychophysics is the quantitative study of the relation between stimulus and sensation or sensory response. As such, it is concerned with the following questions: (a) How much stimulation is required to produce a sensation or sensory response? (b) How much must a stimulus be changed for the change to be detected? (c) In what way or ways must a stimulus be changed to be perceptually equivalent to another? (d) How does the sensation or sensory response change with changes in stimulus magnitudes? Psychophysical methods are used to answer these (among other) questions. They consist of the three classical methods advanced by Gustav Fechner for use in determining thresholds, numerous suprathreshold psychophysical scaling methods used for deriving measures of sensation magnitude, and signal detection theory methods used in providing measures of basic sensory sensitivity, minimally contaminated by motivational and attitudinal biases.

The method of limits, adjustment, and constant stimuli were initially collected and presented in 1860 by Fechner. They are used to determine absolute and difference thresholds (or limens). The absolute threshold (*Reiz Limen*, or *RL*) is the stimulus magnitude that is perceived 50% of the time. Similarly, the difference threshold (*Differenz Limen*, or *DL*) is the smallest change in stimulation detectable 50% of the time. Exact procedures vary somewhat but the following descriptions of the three methods are representative.

Method of Limits

This method presents to the observer on each trial a series of either increasing (ascending trials) or decreasing (descending trials) stimuli that change in incremental steps until there is a change in the observer's responding from yes to no (descending trials) or no to yes (ascending trials). The level of stimulation midway between the change is taken to be the threshold for that trial.

Method of Adjustment

In contrast to the method of limits, this method has the observer adjusting a continuously variable stimulus so that it will be equal to a standard stimulus. Each trial consists of an adjustment from a point of obvious inequality to a level that appears to be subjectively equal. Ascending and descending trials alternate with starting distances from the standard varying randomly.

Method of Constant Stimuli

On each trial of the method of constant stimuli, the observer receives one stimulus selected from a set of from four to nine stimuli. For determination of the RL, the observer responds with a "yes" or "no" on each trial. For the DL, the observer responds with "greater than" or "less than" to the comparison between the test stimulus of the set and the standard stimulus presented on each trial. Members of the set of stimuli are chosen, after some preliminary testing, such that they bracket the threshold and are such that (ideally) all are perceived some of the time and none is perceived all of the time.

SUPRATHRESHOLD PSYCHOPHYSICAL SCALING METHODS

Psychophysical scaling methods consist of a collection of different methods that have in common the feature that they prescribe rules by which subjects (directly or indirectly) assign numerical scale values to physical stimuli. These methods have frequently been used to test certain psychophysical laws. Some of the methods used in this way are bisection, equal appearing intervals, fractionation, and magnitude estimation.

In the method of *bisection*, the subject is instructed to adjust a variable stimulus so that the resulting sensation is equally distant from (or midway between) the sensations produced by two stimuli that are presented for bisection. The procedure is repeated, and the mean of the adjustments is computed. The method of *equal-appearing intervals* is one of the category methods and has the observer assign stimuli to one of a fixed number (e.g., five) of "equal-width" categories. The extreme values of the stimuli are presented first and identified as such to permit anchoring of judgments. After all judgments have been made, the mean or median category selected for each stimulus value is graphically plotted as a function of stimulus magnitude. *Fractionation* requires the observer to produce on each trial (by adjustment) a stimulus that is some specified part (e.g., one-half) of a given stimulus. This is done for each of several stimulus magnitudes. *Magnitude estimation* is a widely used procedure that has the observer estimate the magnitude of a stimulus by assigning a number to it. Stimuli greater than the comparison stimulus would receive larger numbers; those smaller would receive smaller numbers. For a group of subjects, the mean or geometric mean response to each stimulus is computed. These magnitude estimates are graphed as a function of the stimulus values estimated.

SIGNAL DETECTION THEORY

Motivation, expectation, and attitude are biases possessed by the observer in psychophysical threshold determinations. On trials in which no stimulus is presented ("catch trials") in the method of constant stimuli, "yes" responses occur. This circumstance in signal detection theory (SDT) is called a *false alarm*. Correct detection of the stimulus (responding with "yes" when the stimulus is present) is termed a *hit*. Changes in motivation, expectation, or attitude can increase the hit rate, but at the expense of elevating the false alarm rate.

In each of the three basic procedures used in SDT, the yes–no, rating, and forced choice, a series of trials (e.g., 200) is given with a signal present on some (signal plus noise trials) and not on others (noise trials). The observer's task in the yes–no procedure is to respond with "yes" on trials with a signal and "no" on others. In the rating procedure, categorized responses indicating degree of belief that a signal was present are given. The forced-choice task presents two or more alternatives (e.g., in separate intervals of time) with only one consisting of signal and noise. The observer decides which alternative most likely contained the signal.

The motivational, expectancy, and attitudinal biases are collectively treated as the observer's criterion, which is estimated from the false alarm rate. The criterion can be manipulated by changing the proportion of signal trials (and so informing the observer) by instructing the observer to be more lenient or strict, or by changing the payoffs for different decisions. When data are plotted with hit rate along the ordinate and false alarm rate along the abscissa, different levels for the observer's criterion yield different data points along what is called a receiver operating characteristic (ROC) curve. Different ROC curves are generated by different signal levels, but all points on the same ROC curve represent the same level of detectability. Thus sensory and nonsensory factors can be identified separately.

APPLICATIONS

In addition to being used to answer questions in theoretical psychophysics, the various psychophysical methods have had numerous practical applications within and outside psychology. Normal human visual and auditory thresholds (and, to a lesser extent, thresholds in other senses) are used in equipment design and human factors in engineering psychology and for comparison in clinical diagnosis in medicine. Suprathreshold scaling methods are used in industry and commerce in evaluating preferences. Signal detection methods can be applied to problems ranging from the evaluation of basic sensory capabilities to medical decision making.

AUDIOMETRY
EMPIRICAL RESEARCH METHODS
PSYCHOPHYSICS
SCIENTIFIC METHOD

G. H. ROBINSON

PSYCHOPHYSICS

Fechner attempted to devise a precise and quantitative way of measuring the mind by providing a measure of sensation magnitude. The idea that strong stimuli generate strong sensations and weak stimuli generate weak sensations was not new. The task was to determine how strong the corresponding sensation was for a given stimulus. Quantitative attempts to do this date back, at least, to the time of the Greek astronomer Hipparchus (160–120 B.C.), who invented the stellar magnitude scale categorizing visible stars into six categories, from faintest (sixth magnitude) to brightest (first magnitude).

However, once into consciousness, how intense is the resulting sensation? This is the basic question of psychophysics. Fechner proposed one answer: $R = k \log (I/I_o)$. The sensation magnitude (R) in Fechner's law varies directly with the logarithm of the stimulus intensity (I)-to-threshold (I_o) ratio. Much experimental work has been done using numerous psychophysical methods in an attempt to determine which fits the data better.

EMPIRICAL RESEARCH METHODS
FECHNER'S LAW
PSYCHOPHYSICAL METHODS
WEBER'S LAW

G. H. ROBINSON

PSYCHOPHYSIOLOGY

Psychophysiology is the study of mental or emotional processes as revealed through involuntary physiological reactions that can be monitored in an intact subject. It is helpful to distinguish psychophysiology from physiological psychology, which is the study of the physiological substrate of mental events.

For the psychophysiologist the independent variables usually will be psychological manipulations: The subject—most often a human subject—may be asked a question, given a problem to solve, be put under emotional stress, instructed to perform some task or to attend to a series of simple stimuli, and so on. The dependent variables will be physiological changes that can be recorded peripherally either as electrical signals (e.g., brain waves, muscle potentials, the electrocardiogram) or as pressure, volume, or temperature changes (e.g., breathing movements, blood pressure, skin temperature). Rarely, the psychophysiologist might use biochemical changes in urine, blood, or sweat as dependent variables.

Psychophysiology must be distinguished also from the field of psychosomatic medicine, since workers in both areas share an interest in many of the same physiological manifestations of mental and emotional events. For the psychophysiologist, the physiological reaction is a medium that carries a message about events occurring in the mind or brain. The fact that fear can produce peripheral vasoconstriction and a rapid heart beat is a concern to the student of psychosomatic medicine who is interested in these physical reactions in their own right. It is the fact that cold hands and tachycardia *betoken* fear that is of interest to the psychophysiologist.

PSYCHOPHYSIOLOGICAL MEASUREMENT

The immediate object of psychophysiological measurement is to generate an electrical signal that faithfully mimics the manner in which the physiological phenomenon being measured varies over time. Once the phenomenon has been represented as an electrical signal, it can easily be amplified or filtered, visualized as a tracing on a polygraph chart or on the face of a cathode-ray tube (CRT), recorded for later playback and analysis on a tape recorder, or fed into a computer. Some psychophysiological phenomena, such as the electroencephalogram (EEG), the electromyogram (EMG), and the electrocardiogram (ECG), are already electrical signals generated in the body, and their measurement requires only a pair of electrodes appropriately placed to pick up the biological voltage, connected to the input of an amplifier that will boost this voltage until it is strong enough to be recorded in some way. The most versatile method of recording is one that allows the original signal to be reproduced later, as a tape recording can be played back, but most psychophysiology laboratories also make a permanent visual record of the signal using an electrically driven pen that moves up and down with changes in the signal, writing on a paper chart that moves laterally.

Some psychophysiological phenomena that do not produce signal voltages directly may involve changes in the electrical properties of tissue that can be measured by passing an external sensing current through the tissue.

Noise

The modern world is literally full of electrical "noise," such as electromagnetic emanations from television transmitters, electric motors, passing autos, fluorescent lights, and so forth, which the human body picks up as does an antenna. Bioelectric signals originating in the body similarly become noise when they are not the signal to be measured but appear nonetheless in one's recordings.

Noise of biological origin, as when eye movements that affect the EEG or the ECG show up unwanted in the electrodermal channel, requires special solutions. Sometimes reorientation of the electrodes will suffice. If the noise consists mainly of frequencies outside the bandwidth of the desired signal, a bandpass filter may provide the solution. A third approach is to measure the noise directly in a separate channel and then subtract it from the signal channel by electronic inversion and summation.

Recorders

All modern polygraphs have standard outputs at which an amplified representation of each signal channel is available for connection to the input of a recorder or other device.

Computers

Most psychophysiology laboratories now employ small computers for online control of experiments and immediate analysis of data, and also for more complex subsequent analyses. Laboratory interface systems are available that make it possible to turn things on and off under computer control, to generate stimuli, to time events, and also to provide to the computer data, command signals, and other information from the laboratory. The computer can present pictorial or alphanumeric information to the subject by means of a CRT display or a variety of auditory stimuli including spoken words that have been digitally recorded and stored in the computer's memory. Psychophysiologists of the past have required a working knowledge of electrical principles, physiology, and statistics, and a more than rudimentary understanding of psychology; competent psychophysiologists of the present require a working knowledge of the computer as well.

ANALYZING THE DATA

The variance of a sample of scores on some psychophysiological variable can be partitioned thus:

$$\sigma_\omega^2 = \sigma_\psi^2 + \sigma_\phi^2 + \sigma_\varepsilon^2 \tag{1}$$

where σ_ψ^2 is due to individual differences in the underlying psychological variable of interest, σ_ϕ^2 is the orthogonal component of variance due to physiological differences, and σ_ε^2 represents measurement error. If skin conductance level (SCL), represented by ω, is being measured, ϕ for example, ψ might be central nervous system (CNS) arousal or "energy mobilization," ϕ would reflect ψ individual differences in the density and activity of volar sweat glands, and so forth, and ε would increase with

variation in cleaning the skin surface, in positioning the electrodes, in the area of skin contacting the electrolyte, and so on.

Underlying most psychophysiological measurement is the implicit assumption that ω is a monotonically increasing function—and, it is hoped, a simple linear function—of the underlying variable of interest:

$$\omega = a + b\psi + \varepsilon \tag{2}$$

Using SCL again as the example, the parameter a would represent this subject's minimum SCL when sudomotor activity is zero, while b would be determined by the reactivity of the entire electrodermal system, that is, the increase in conductivity produced by a unit increase in ψ. (Very similar assumptions are implicit in most psychological measurement.) The problem is that the parameters a and b also vary, often within the same individual from time to time, and certainly from one individual to another. This is the variation represented by σ_ϕ^2 in equation (1). The job of the psychophysiologist is, first, to ensure that the physiological variable chosen (ω) is linearly related to ψ, at least approximately, and then to try to minimize both measurement error σ_ε^2, and also σ_ϕ^2, the variance due to physiological variability, within subject or between subjects, which also must be regarded as error variance in this context.

The Linearity Assumption

Consider an experiment in which the subject is intensely stressed at the outset, then allowed to relax and go to sleep, while skin potential level (SPL) is continuously monitored. The SPL will be fairly low under intense stress, then will rise to a maximum while the subject is, for example, listening to an interesting story, then will fall again to a minimum when the subject goes to sleep. These individual curves show us that SPL has an inverted U-shaped relationship to CNS arousal and is therefore a poor index of that variable. Suppose that, in this same experiment, we also measure electrodermal responses, SCRs from one hand and resistance changes or SRRs from the other hand. Because they are being elicited over widely varying levels of tonic SCL and SRL, the SCRs will be poorly correlated with the corresponding SRRs. There is both theoretical and empirical support for the view that conductance is more simply related to central events than is resistance.

Minimizing Extraneous Variance

Minimizing variance resulting from error of measurement is largely a matter of competent and consistent technique; the details will depend on the variable being measured. To minimize variance due to extraneous physiological differences requires a statistical correction for individual differences in range. The basic idea is to estimate the parameters a and b of equation (2) for each individual subject and then obtain a range-corrected score for each subject:

$$\omega_{rc} = \frac{\omega - \hat{a}}{\hat{b}} \tag{3}$$

In the case of SCL, for example, $\hat{a}$ would be the subject's minimum SCL obtained when relaxed or asleep. The estimate of $\hat{b}$ might be obtained by subtracting $\hat{a}$ from that subject's maximum SCL shown under high stress. In the case of phasic changes such as the SCR, $\hat{a}$ or the minimum value is always zero. Phasic response values can therefore be range corrected merely by dividing by an estimate of that subject's maximum response amplitude.

THE CHANNELS OF PSYCHOPHYSIOLOGY

A number of organ systems provide the psychophysiologist with a variety of (clouded) windows through which to observe mental events. This section reviews the most widely studied of these systems, the channels that are recorded, and the variables quantified from each channel.

The Cardiovascular System

People have been drawing inferences about each other's mental and emotional processes from cardiovascular changes since the dawn of history because some changes—blushing and blanching of the skin, pounding of the heart, cold hands, and the like—can be detected without instrumental assistance. The important channels are the ECG, arterial pressure, finger-pulse pressure, and perhaps digital temperature.

In the intact subject, blood pressure can be measured only intermittently by ausculation. A pressure cuff on the upper arm is inflated until the brachial artery is sufficiently compressed to occlude the flow of blood. With a stethoscope over the artery distal to the cuff, the pressure is gradually released until the first Korotkoff sounds are heard. These sounds are caused by the spurting of blood through the arterial occlusion during the peak of the pressure cycle just after ventricular contraction. The first sounds mark the peak or *systolic blood pressure*. As pressure is relaxed further, the sounds wax and wane until a point is reached where blood flow continues even at the minimum of the pressure cycle; this is the *diastolic pressure*.

Heart rate and blood pressure tend to obey the Law of Initial Values, which states that the change in either variable produced by a stimulus will be correlated with the prestimulus level of that variable; a pressor stimulus will cause a smaller increase in the rate of an already racing heart than in one beating slowly and calmly.

The Electrodermal System

Compared with subdermal tissues, the skin has a relatively high resistance to the passage of electric current. In the latter part of the nineteenth century, it was discovered that the resistance of the thick skin of the palms and soles was extraordinarily reactive to psychological stimulation. It is known that the sweat glands in these volar regions subserve a special function; instead of helping with thermoregulation, they moisten grasping surfaces in preparation for action. Dry palmar skin is both slippery and more subject to abrasion. Neural circuits arising in the activating systems of the midbrain control volar sweating, which increases tonically with CNS arousal, and which also shows wavelike, phasic increases in response to any stimulus important enough to produce an orienting response. In part because the sweat gland tubules provide a low-resistance pathway through the epidermis, the electrical resistance of the skin varies with sweat gland activity. Since, in fact, resistance varies inversely with sweating, current practice is to measure skin conductance, the reciprocal of resistance. Skin conductance level (SCL) is lowest in a drowsy or somnolent subject, rises sharply with awakening, and rises still further during mental effort or emotional stress.

Electromyography

An electrode on the skin over any muscle mass, referenced against an electrode in some quiescent region such as an earlobe or over the shin, will pick up a high-frequency signal (10–500 Hz) produced by the repeated firing of hundreds or thousands of muscle fibers. This signal can be electronically integrated to yield a simpler curve representing average muscle tension. Except perhaps in rapid eye movement (REM) sleep, the striate muscles maintain a degree of tonus even at rest, with individual fibers firing asynchronously at a low rate. In a "tense" individual, this resting tonus may be quite high, either generally or in specific muscle groups. Surface electromyography provides a means of monitoring such subactive muscle tension.

Eye Movements and the Pupillary Response

The eyes are also "windows of the soul" through which one gets glimpses of the workings of the brain. Eye movements and the direction of gaze can be monitored by electrooculography (EOG). The eye is like a little battery with the cornea about 1 mV positive with respect to the back of the retina. If electrodes are positioned adjacent to the outer canthus of each eye, then, when both eyes are turned to the right, for instance, the electrode on that side becomes electropositive to the one on the left. Another pair of electrodes above and below one eye record vertical eye movements. The sensitivity of the EOG is illustrated by the fact that when a subject tracks a target moving sinusoidally from side to side on an oscilloscope screen, the EOG recorded on the polygraph will be a nearly perfect sine wave; if the target is then driven by a triangular waveform, the EOG record will reproduce this change.

The EOG has been used to study the saccadic eye movements employed in reading or in searching a visual display. It has also been used in the study of nystagmus and the smooth following movements with which the eyes track a moving target.

The size of the pupil, which can vary from about 2 to 8 mm in diameter, is regulated by the autonomic nervous system so as to tend to hold constant the intensity of light admitted to the retina. However, the pupil is also reactive to psychological stimulation with small (<1 mm) but regular changes (usually dilations) following a stimulus with latencies of the order of 0.2 second.

Electroencephalography

The electrical activity of the brain is far more complex than the most elaborate manufactured computer; only a billionth part of this information is available at the brain's surface, and still less at the scalp. Since an electrode on the scalp integrates electrical activity over a considerable area of cortex, a reasonably comprehensive record of the total EEG can be obtained from about 20 electrodes distributed systematically over the head. A set of standard placements has been defined, called the International Ten-Twenty System. The complete montage will be used by clinicians looking for EEG evidence of tumors or epileptiform activity, whereas the researcher more commonly uses only one or a few EEG channels. The most common use of the spontaneous EEG is in sleep research, where, with additional channels recording lateral eye movements and muscle tension, it is possible to identify, with considerable reliability, the five stages of sleep.

Event-Related Cortical Potentials

Virtually any stimulus sensed by the subject will produce an effect on the EEG; indeed, much of the apparently spontaneous EEG may be simply the composite effect of the flux of stimulation, external and internal, that continuously bombards the sensorium. To detect the effect of all but the most intense stimuli amid the background of EEG activity, requires repeated presentations of the stimulus so that the immediate poststimulus segments of the EEG record can be averaged together. If 100 0.5-second EEG segments are randomly selected and then averaged, the mean will tend toward a straight line. However, the 100 0.5-second segments that follow 100 presentations of, say, an auditory click will each contain the ERP elicited by that click, a relatively complex train of waves time-locked to the stimulus.

The earlier components of the ERP seem to represent earlier stages of cerebral processing. Recent evidence suggests the possibility of a relationship between the speed (latency) of these components and some basic dimension of intelligence. Later components, especially a positive wave about 300 msec poststimulus, seem to reflect the completion of a process of stimulus identification or classification. The actual latency of this wave varies with reaction time and its amplitude varies with the information content of the stimulus; unexpected, important, or possibly "memorable" stimuli produce larger "P" components.

The study of the psychological correlates of components of the ERP and the use of these data in formulating and testing models of the way in which the brain processes information constitute one of the most active and promising areas of current psychophysiological research.

AUTONOMIC NERVOUS SYSTEM
BRAIN WAVES
CENTRAL NERVOUS SYSTEM
COMPUTERIZED TOMOGRAPHY
ELECTROENCEPHALOGRAPHY
NEUROPSYCHOLOGY

D. T. LYKKEN

PSYCHOSEXUAL STAGES

In Sigmund Freud's personality theory, development is described in terms of stages defined by the specific expression of sexual, or libidinal, urges. Those areas of the body—the erogenous zones—that give rise to libidinal pleasure at specific ages are identified as the focus of each developmental stage.

The pregenital stages are followed by a period of supposed psychosexual quiescence, the *latency period,* which lasts from the end of the phallic stage at approximately age 5 years until the onset of puberty. During the latency period, libidinal urges are said to be repressed. Puberty, however, brings with it a resurgence of the pregenital urges, which now focus specifically on the pleasure deriving from the genital organs; thus the name of this final developmental period, the *genital stage.*

Libidinal urges in Freudian theory are not equatable with genital sexuality. For example, three of the psychosexual stages are "pregenital." The term *libido* is meant to define a broad concept of mental sexual energy occurring even in infancy. Nor do the stages refer only to male sexuality, in spite of the masculine language.

ORAL STAGE

In Freud's theory, the oral stage of development is characterized by a need for nurturance and an acquisition of pleasure derived primarily from the process of being nurtured and centering on the main avenue of nurturance, the mouth and lips.

ANAL STAGE

The anal stage extends approximately from 1 year to 2 years of age, and refers to the period of a child's life in which learning bowel and bladder control is a primary task and the pleasure and pain derived from expelling and retaining feces are the main libidinal outlet. The toddler in the anal period is growing in independence and self-assertion.

PHALLIC STAGE

Between 2 years and 3 years of age, the child begins more active exploration of his or her body. The locus of erotic pleasure shifts from the anus to the genitals as the young child discovers the pleasurable effect of masturbation.

GENITAL STAGE

After a period of psychosexual quiescence, termed latency, puberty brings with it a resurgence of the phallic strivings and more realistic capabilities for their expression. Masturbation becomes a source of erotic satisfaction, and appears so nearly universal and urgent that Freud called this adolescent impulse *onanism of necessity.* Armed with full adult genitalia and sexual drives, the growing adolescent shifts his or her affection from parents to peers, first of the same sex (a brief homosexual phase, just after puberty), and then of the opposite sex. In the fully integrated adult,

the psychosexual urges find expression in activity with an opposite-sexed partner of roughly the same age. More important, these urges no longer are purely narcissistic, as they were in the pregenital stages. The psychosexual urges now extend and generalize to altruism, friendship, sharing, and loving of a more adult nature.

HUMAN SEXUALITY PSYCHOANALYSIS

J. P. MCKINNEY

PSYCHOSOMATIC DISORDERS

The term *psychosomatic disorder* generally refers to a type of physical illness in which the etiology or course is related to significant psychological factors. Psychosomatic disorders usually include such illnesses as gastric ulcer, asthma, and essential hypertension, and are not limited to a single physiological system.

Scientific medicine achieved major progress toward the end of the nineteenth century, with an emphasis on physical disease, as a result of the discoveries in morbid anatomy, microbiology, and biochemistry. Freud's elaboration of the unconscious, Pavlov's studies of the conditioned reflex, and Cannon's notion of fight and flight reactions offered important psychological concepts that stimulated the growth of the psychosomatic approach in health care.

Early psychosomatic methodology consisted mainly of clinical observations. By the late 1950s, an increasing number of psychologists were engaged in laboratory and clinical psychosomatic experiments. There was a declining interest in researching psychoanalytic concepts in psychosomatic problems, while there was a growing trend toward experimental research studying human biological response to hypnotic techniques, conditioning, and sensory input and deprivation. Psychosomatic research with animals provided a large body of scientific information, with relevant implications for human physiology and clinical practice.

THEORETICAL CONCEPTS

Freud stressed the role of psychic determinism in somatic conversion hysteria. Freudian followers provided further refinement of psychoanalytic concepts vis-à-vis psychosomatic phenomena, including Dunbar's description of personality profiles (e.g., the ulcer personality, the coronary personality, the arthritic personality), as well as Alexander's analysis of psychodynamic patterns underlying asthma, ulcers, arthritis, hypertension, and other disorders.

Corticovisceral theory has prevailed in Eastern Europe, dominated by Pavlovian neurophysiology and conditioning research. In the United States, psychological stress theory, such as Cannon's concept of bodily homeostasis, Harold G. Wolff's research on the adaptive biological responses, and Hans Selye's work on pituitary adrenal responses, formed the foundation for psychosomatic research and clinical approaches. Social or ecological concepts have also been elaborated.

TYPE OF DISEASE

In 1950, Alexander listed seven classic psychosomatic diseases: essential hypertension, peptic ulcer, rheumatoid arthritis, hyperthyroidism, bronchial asthma, colitis, and neurodermatitis. More recently, the extensive classification system of the ninth *International classification of diseases* provided a comprehensive list of psychosomatic disorders, including the following:

1. Psychosomatic disorders involving tissue damage, such as asthma, dermatitis, eczema, gastric ulcer, mucous colitis, ulcerative colitis, urticaria, and psychosocial dwarfism.

2. Psychosomatic disorders not involving tissue damage, such as psychogenic torticollis, air hunger, psychogenic hiccough, hyperventilation, psychogenic cough, yawning, cardiac neurosis, cardiovascular neurosis, neurocirculatory asthenia, psychogenic cardiovascular disorder, psychogenic pruritus, aerophagy, psychogenic cyclical vomiting, psychogenic dysmenorrhea, and teeth grinding.

TREATMENT

The early roots of psychosomatic medicine consisted of psychoanalytically oriented therapies, such as those of Alexander and his associates. In more recent decades, nonanalytic psychotherapies have become more prominent. With the increasing sophistication in pharmacotherapies, psychiatrists find the use of psychotropic medications helpful, including various tranquilizers and antidepressants. Group psychotherapy is especially suitable for certain psychosomatic patients, such as those with bronchial asthma, who find relief in meeting others with similar concerns and learn to identify and verbalize significant feelings related to this condition.

In cases where psychosomatic reactions may be the result of learned patterns of behavior—for example, certain sexual dysfunctions—behavior therapy is an effective therapeutic method. One of the oldest forms of psychosomatic therapies, hypnosis, has been found to be effective in disorders such as hyperventilation, peptic ulcer, and headaches.

The past decade has seen a rapid growth in psychologists' employment of relaxation therapies, such as Jacobson's progressive relaxation, Luthe's autogenic training, and biofeedback to treat headaches and other stress-related disorders. In addition, principles and methods of transcendental meditation, yoga, and Morita therapy have also been used with psychosomatic disorders.

BEHAVIORAL MEDICINE
MENTAL ILLNESS: EARLY HISTORY

W. T. TSUSHIMA

PSYCHOSOMATICS

Psychosomatics, in its broadest sense, includes all interactions between behavior—thoughts, feelings, actions—and physical illness. Such relationships have been recognized for centuries. In fact, the bulk of medical treatments operated on psychological principles until the modern era emerged in the late nineteenth century.

Physicians rarely ask for psychological help when they treat "psychosomatic" patients. Consultation liaison is a "poor relation" division in most psychiatry departments. One of the reasons for this is that the claims for the psychosomatic approach run contrary to the way in which physicians traditionally prefer to proceed—by interpreting symptoms as manifestations of disturbances in various organs. If the real trouble lies in the functioning of the whole person, traditional medical procedures tend to grind to a halt. The usual "solution" at this point is to turn to a psychological explanation. Patients are often convinced by this sequence of events that "psychological" means not really worthy of serious concern.

This tendency to diagnose by exclusion also leads professionals to label symptoms as psychosomatic when they do not know what causes them.

SPECIFICITY THEORIES

A specificity theory holds that definite psychological constellations produce each psychosomatic disorder. Specificity hypotheses fall into four general groups: (a) personality specificity theory; (b) conflict specificity theory; (c) emotion specificity theory; and (d) response pattern specificity theory.

Personality specificity theory is associated primarily with Flanders Dunbar. This approach holds that definite personality traits lead to specific physical symptoms. These ideas have recently reappeared as "risk factors" said to represent predispositions to disease.

A conflict specificity theory is an extension of the psychoanalytic notion of conversion, according to which unconscious conflicts are resolved by being "converted" into somatic symptoms.

All specificity theories seek to solve the "symptom choice" problem on psychological grounds. Symptom choice means simply: "Why does patient A develop asthma while patient B is hypertensive?" The emotion specificity hypothesis suggests that specific emotions lead to definite somatic changes, and eventually to particular somatic disturbances.

Response pattern specificity theory rests on individual differences in stress–response patterns. Gastric reactors are prone to ulcers; blood pressure reactors are prone to hypertension. These notions place symptom choice at the physiological level and anticipate, to some extent, more recent developments.

NONSPECIFICITY THEORIES

The nonspecificity position maintains the etiological primacy of psychological factors in at least some cases of certain physical diseases but abandons the attempt to explain symptom choice. The explanatory burden is carried by the vaguely defined construct "organ vulnerability."

The *alexithymia* hypothesis is in the nonspecificity tradition. Certain people, alexithymics, find it difficult to experience or express emotions as others do. They are said to be particularly subject to psychosomatic disturbances. Although these ideas have received a good deal of attention, they remain controversial.

None of these theories have been extensively validated, although all can explain some phenomena. Psychosomatics is a complex area; multiple causation seems more likely than linear sequences. This complexity makes investigations likely to be misleading or fruitless when based on simple correlations between poorly measured psychological elements and physical symptoms. Studies of intervening events and mediating factors are necessary.

A useful organizing notion is the concept of stress. Modern psychophysiology extends and amplifies Cannon's work employing the psychological stress concept. The findings to date suggest the following likely conclusions: (a) Different emotions are associated with different patterns of changes; (b) there are considerable individual differences in these patterns; and (c) the patterns are often such that one can begin to see that physical diseases might arise from their continuation over long periods.

It is now so obvious that psychological events influence somatic phenomena that many experts reject Cartesian dualism altogether and think of mind and body as one. Family physicians report that 20 to 50% of their patients suffer from functional complaints. Mental health professionals specializing in behavioral medicine are demonstrating replicable results from treatment.

BEHAVIORAL MEDICINE
HEALTH PSYCHOLOGY
MIND–BODY PROBLEM
PSYCHOLOGICAL HEALTH
SOMATOPSYCHICS

H. A. STORROW

PSYCHOSTIMULANT TREATMENT FOR CHILDREN

Medical management usually pursues a simple logic. A prescription is issued. Compliance is assumed and at regular intervals the patient is provided the opportunity to declare him- or herself better, the same, or worse. The patient's judgment is taken at face value, which in turn guides the clinician's decision to continue, adjust, or discontinue the treatment regimen. When applied to children with attention-deficit hyperactivity disorder (ADHD)—for whom psychostimulant medication (primarily methylphenidate, e.g., Ritalin) is considered the first-line defense among treatment regimens and used in an estimated 750,000 children annually—the basic logic of medical management is flawed. The primary reasons for this fall into two broad categories: characteristics inherent to the child or patient and characteristics of the medication itself.

Child Characteristics

Children with ADHD are usually unaware of the nature or extent of their behavioral and learning difficulties. Parents and teachers bring their difficulties to the attention of mental health experts and request treatment. To complicate matters, many if not most children with ADHD are relatively insensitive to the effects of treatment, even when such effects are glaringly obvious to others in the environment. Thus when the patient does not complain—which is usual in ADHD—or complains only of others (also usual in ADHD), other means must be found to evaluate treatment effects.

Treatment Characteristics

The basic psychopharmacological properties and clinical usefulness of psychostimulants in treating children with ADHD is well established. Clinical trials have been conducted since the 1930s, and over the course of more than 60 years, positive treatment effects have been reported consistently for a wide range of outcome variables.

Nevertheless, several misconceptions concerning both the initial titration of and dosage effects associated with psychostimulants prevail. Popular among these is the notion that a child's gross body weight should be used to establish initial dosage parameters using a milligram of medicine per kilogram of body weight (mg/kg) ratio—the implicit assumption being that heavier children require more medicine than do lighter-weight children. Two studies have addressed this issue, with both reporting no relationship between children's body weight and clinical response to methylphenidate (MPH).

A more complicated issue concerns the dose–response nature of psychostimulants. Due largely to the pivotal work by Sprague and Sleator there is widespread belief that different behavioral domains are optimized at widely discrepant dosage levels in children. In brief, lower dosages are thought to optimize cognitive performance while higher dosages are required to optimize behavior and manageability in the classroom. Neither comprehensive reviews nor direct observations of children receiving psychostimulant treatment while working in classroom or laboratory environments have supported this allegation. Instead, both classroom behavior and cognitive performance (including academic productivity) have been found to be affected at similar dosage levels, usually within the middle to higher dosage range when using MPH. It should be stressed, however, that these results are at the *group* level of analysis and may not apply to any particular child undergoing treatment.

CONCLUSIONS

The use of psychostimulants as a therapeutic regimen to treat children with ADHD remains a highly controversial topic. A majority of children derive clear and sustained benefit from this therapeutic modality, although most experienced clinicians and researchers concur that neither this nor any treatment regimen used alone adequately addresses the multifaceted difficulties associated with ADHD. When used, controlled medication trials across a wide dosage range are strongly recommended owing to the individual responsivity or unique response children exhibit to the psychostimulants. Assessment of outcome should, at the very least, in-

clude multiple, standardized, treatment sensitive measures across settings (home and school) throughout the duration of the clinical trials as well as at scheduled intervals thereafter to assess continuity and maintenance of treatment effects. Finally, clinical indices of improvement should ideally include measures from both the behavioral *and* cognitive (academic) domains, owing to the latter variable's relationship with long-term academic achievement and adult outcome.

A-TYPE PERSONALITY
ACADEMIC UNDERACHIEVEMENT
ANTIPSYCHOTIC DRUGS
ATTENTION SPAN
MIDDLE CHILDHOOD
PSYCHOENDOCRINOLOGY

M. RAPPORT

PSYCHOSURGERY

Psychosurgery, by definition, implies the destruction of healthy brain tissue for the relief of severe, persistent, and debilitating psychiatric symptomatology. Although Elliot S. Valenstein, in *The psychosurgery debate: scientific, legal and ethical perspectives,* traces its use to early archeological evidence of trepanation in 2000 B.C., the first widespread application of psychosurgical procedures to psychiatric patients began in the late 1930s, reached its peak in the 1960s, and began to decline in the 1970s.

In the first half of the twentieth century, the technique most frequently used for creating lesions was frontal lobotomy, wherein fibers in the frontal lobes were cut bilaterally. Initially, this was accomplished by placing a cutting instrument into burr holes drilled through the skull, or through the bony orbits above the eyes, and then rotating the instrument. More precise placement of lesions became possible during the 1950s as a result of the invention of a stereotaxic instrument that held the head in a fixed position; a knife or electrode could then be lowered into the brain at a point predetermined by a set of three-dimensional coordinates as defined by a brain map or atlas. In this manner, well-localized lesions could be made.

The most effective targets for relief of psychiatric symptoms appeared to involve the medial and ventral areas of the frontal lobes (represented by triangles in Figure 1). Subsequently, other regions of the brain with well-defined connections to specific frontal areas were selected as targets for psychosurgery.

Because psychosurgery usually is performed on apparently normal brain tissue, its practice has generated considerable controversy. The National Commission for the Protection of Human Subjects of Biomedical and Behavioral Research supported several intensive investigations on the use and efficacy of psychosurgery.

On the basis of the diverse and extensive information reviewed by the Commission, recommendations were made to the U.S. Department of Health and Human Services (DHHS) regarding the use of psychosurgery. One recommendation encouraged DHHS to support evaluative studies of the safety and efficacy of the procedures, and two other recommendations detailed conditions for, and approval of, their limited use with institutionalized individuals. Obviously, psychosurgery is a topic that involves many ethical, scientific, and legal concerns, and there is no easy resolution of the controversy associated with its use.

BRAIN
BRAIN INJURIES

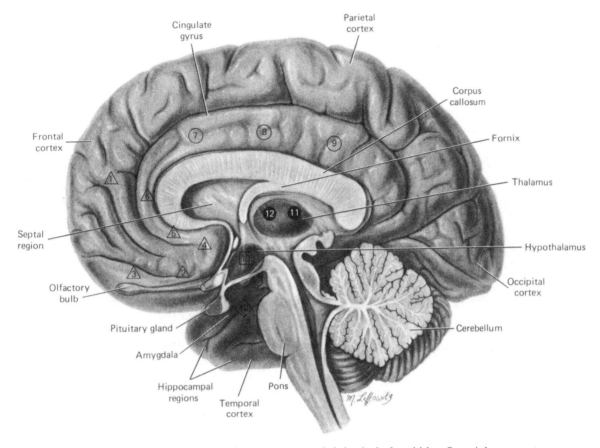

Figure 1. Targets of psychosurgery. Triangles represent surgical sites in the frontal lobes. Open circles represent sites for cingulotomy. Filled circles are thalamic targets. Additional sites are in the amygdala (diamond) and the hypothalamus (square).

LOBOTOMY NEUROSURGERY

M. Oscar-Berman

PSYCHOSYNTHESIS

Robert Assagioli's psychosynthetic approach is based on the notion of unifying one's personality expression with a deeper source of purpose and direction called the transpersonal Self. Psychosynthesis, more than most therapies, is concerned with values, inspiration, meaning, and service.

Assagioli had a complex view of the personality, which included not only a lower unconscious, a middle unconscious, and a superconscious, but also the transpersonal Self and the collective unconscious. During treatment, there first is an effort to guide the client in integrating the different aspects of the person that are viewed as "subpersonalities." After such integration and harmonization have occurred, a transpersonal psychosynthesis is undertaken to align the personality with the transpersonal Self to transcend the boundaries of the ego and to achieve fulfillment, purpose, and meaning in life.

PSYCHOTHERAPY

V. Raimy

PSYCHOTHERAPY

Psychotherapy is a method of working with patients/clients to assist them to modify, change, or reduce factors that interfere with effective living.

It involves interaction between psychotherapist and patients/clients in accomplishing these goals. Specific methods used depend on presenting symptoms and difficulties, as well as the theory followed by the psychotherapist.

People discouraged with their lives and depressed about their inability to attain their goals may experience anxiety about their frustration and deprivation. One aim in psychotherapy might be to help such people see their assets and liabilities realistically. To learn to cope with their frustrations and deprivations in a nondamaging manner might be a next step. Another goal in psychotherapy might be to help such people "actualize" or live to the fullest extent of their assets. Complete actualization is seldom achieved, but the closer a person comes to this goal, the more is attained out of living. Psychotherapy then may be seen as a method to aid individuals in recognizing potential, learning how to utilize this potential, and removing or reducing handicaps or blocks.

The therapeutic goal might be to aid the individual to modify or remove symptoms and behaviors that make it difficult to live satisfactorily and happily. People sometimes have difficulty living in our society as a result of many factors. Some are a consequence of inadequate early upbringing. Some are a result of current factors, poor relationships in interpersonal situations, or a distorted view of the world.

A further purpose would be to aid individuals in reducing or eliminating anxiety, and to cope with stress and the effects of stress. The stress and anxieties may be long standing or a result of current situations.

HISTORY OF PSYCHOTHERAPY

The practice of psychotherapy goes back to antiquity. Among the earliest psychotherapists were the witch doctors or shamen. Rituals, dances, ceremonies, and incantations were used in helping people who believed they were seriously ill, ills that were often emotional rather than physical. The goal of the witch doctors was to achieve relief and return their patients to more effective functioning. Even today some people believe in the effects of witchcraft, black magic, and voodoo. During the Middle Ages, emphasis was on the belief that the devil or devils possessed the affected individual. A more formal approach to psychotherapy began when the belief changed from devils to emotions as causative of emotional disturbances.

In individual therapy, there is a one-to-one relationship between the psychotherapist and the patient/client. The psychotherapist might meet with the patient/client infrequently or as frequently as three or more times a week and the time per session may vary from 30 to 60 minutes. In group therapy, there may be one or more psychotherapists who work with a group of people, usually with something in common. Groups usually meet one or more times a week for a period of approximately 90 to 120 minutes. A variation of group psychotherapy is the marathon, which meets for an extended period of time and works through or explores specific questions.

The family therapy approach may be thought of as a bridge between the individual and the group approaches. In the "systems" approach, each member of the family is considered coequal in importance to all other members of the family. The psychotherapist looks for the breakdown in the system's functioning. Family members are helped to reorganize the system and to reconstitute themselves as an effective family unit.

Various psychotropic medications, such as antianxiety and antipsychotic drugs, are often used as adjuncts to psychotherapy. These medications help reduce the anxiety that interferes with a person's ability to verbalize, concentrate, and discuss. Antipsychotic drugs may reduce severe disturbances to the level where the patient is able to cooperate in the process of psychotherapy.

SCHOOLS OF PSYCHOTHERAPY

The dynamic or reconstructive schools of psychotherapy emphasize the patient's history—the importance of understanding the individual's past and of exploring the effects of the past on present functioning.

Harry Stack Sullivan developed an interpersonal school of psychotherapy, which held that interpersonal relationships were most important in a person's life. Sullivan's interpersonal psychotherapy included the process of working through the relationships between the patient and the people held important by the client or patient.

Carl Rogers, an American psychologist, developed a theory that individuals strive for growth and perfection but run into blocks in their attempt to attain this growth. The psychotherapist's function is to help the individual overcome these blocks. Rogerian psychotherapy focuses more on the here and now and on ways of directly approaching the stumbling points in the person's life.

Behavior therapy developed in the 1950s. The approach was mainly based on the work done by Joseph Wolpe and B. F. Skinner. The behavioral approach focuses on the overt measurable behavior of the individual. The pure behaviorist contends that the only important thing is measurable behavior. Individuals exhibit anxiety as a consequence of learned maladaptive behavior. Remove this maladaptive behavior and they no longer have emotional difficulties.

THE FOCUS OF RESEARCH

At the outset, the major focus of research was on patient variables. Emphasis was on the patient's cooperation and response to the psychotherapeutic process. Researchers found that patients who were relatively young adults, verbal, and intelligent, and who had already attained a measure of success, had the most favorable outcome. Research clinicians then focused on effective techniques of psychotherapy.

As research became more sophisticated, psychotherapists became aware that the focus on specific techniques was not productive; it then turned to the variables in the psychotherapist. Research workers found that the variables of warmth, empathy, patience, openness, and honesty were among the more important to success in psychotherapy, regardless of the specific techniques or the school of psychotherapy.

The focus of research in the 1960s and 1970s was on the factors in the interaction between the psychotherapist and the patient/client that enhance or interfere with favorable outcome. In studies on patient variables, research workers discovered that the motivated patient who experiences anxiety and a willingness to change worked well in psychotherapy. The individual also was patient and accepted the idea that emotional factors influenced behavior. In the interaction variables, trust, a degree of openness, and motivation to become involved in the relationship were among the factors that increased the probability of a favorable outcome.

Research has indicated that all psychotherapy is effective. Psychotherapy reduces absenteeism from work and is cost effective as both a preventative and a rehabilitative measure. Research has focused on obtaining favorable results within a shorter time span. Crisis intervention techniques have been developed that are useful in emergency situations and in reducing immediate stress. Experimentation has continued with the intensity of psychotherapeutic experience, frequency of visits, and depth of exploration, based on the various theories and schools of psychotherapy. Different approaches in psychotherapy work for different types of individuals with varying problems.

ACTUALIZING THERAPY
ADLERIAN PSYCHOTHERAPY
ANALYTICAL PSYCHOLOGY
ART THERAPY
ASSERTIVENESS TRAINING
BIBLIOTHERAPY
BIOENERGETICS
BRIEF THERAPY
COGNITIVE BEHAVIOR THERAPY
COGNITIVE THERAPY
CONJOINT THERAPY
CREATIVE AGGRESSION THERAPY
CRISIS INTERVENTION
CURRENT PSYCHOTHERAPIES
ECLECTIC PSYCHOTHERAPY
EXPERIMENTAL PSYCHOTHERAPY
FAMILY THERAPY
FEMINIST THERAPY
GESTALT THERAPY
GROUP PSYCHOTHERAPY
IMPASSE-PRIORITY THERAPY
IMPLOSIVE THERAPY
INNOVATIVE PSYCHOTHERAPIES
MARATHON THERAPY
NAIKAN THERAPY
ORGONE THERAPY
PLAY THERAPY
POETRY THERAPY
PSYCHOANALYSIS
REALITY THERAPY
REEVALUATION THERAPY
TRANSACTIONAL ANALYSIS

B. FABRIKANT

PSYCHOTHERAPY: COMMON FACTORS

Common factors of psychotherapy refers to effective aspects of treatment shared by various and sundry forms of psychotherapy. Some writers have argued that they may be more important than factors unique to specific treatments held by advocates of these treatments to be the important agents of change. This argument is bolstered by the fact that whereas psychotherapy has been shown to lead to beneficial effects, no specific type of treatment has been proved consistently superior to any other. The argument is that if a multitude of different systems can legitimately claim equal success, then their diversity may be illusory and they share core features that are in fact the curative elements responsible for therapeutic success.

EARLY EFFORTS TO IDENTIFY COMMON FACTORS

The idea that common factors exist and that they are activated in diverse treatments is not a new one. Rosenzweig questioned whether the factors alleged to be operating in particular types of therapy were in fact the relevant ameliorative factors. He pointed out that, in addition to these identified factors, unrecognized events may be critical to therapeutic progress. Moreover, he suggested that these factors may be common to different forms of therapy.

The next major step was a paper by Alexander and French wherein they coined the term *corrective emotional experience* (CEE). This referred to having the patient behave in ways that he or she may have previously avoided so as to realize that feared consequences do not occur. Originally, CEE was placed within a psychoanalytic context. Alexander later explicitly expanded this notion to learning theory. Thus it was put forth as a factor common to both psychoanalysis and learning theory based treatments.

Work on common factors continued to appear sporadically through the 1950s but in an unsystematic manner. This changed with the pioneering work of Jerome Frank, who asserted that when a person enters any type of psychotherapy he or she is in a demoralized state. Because the person believes that the therapist can be of service, he or she has hope. This sets up an expectation that things will improve. This expectation in and of itself is ameliorative. Frank cited a good deal of research supporting this notion.

Investigators also demonstrated the importance of expectancies in behavioral and psychodynamically oriented psychotherapy outcomes. Shapiro has argued that psychotherapy effects are *entirely* due to the arousal of expectancies. Kirsch has developed a model called *response expectancy,* providing supporting evidence from the placebo, phobia, and hypnosis literatures. Work by Bandura on self-efficacy also underlines the importance of expectancies.

Frank identified four common factors he concluded led to improved morale, presumably by generating positive expectancies:

1. *An Intense, Confiding Relationship with a Helper.* The core of this relationship is the therapist's ability to inspire the patient's confidence in him or her as competent and concerned with the patient's welfare. This serves to increase expectations or hope of success, which in turn improves morale. Frank believes that without a good relationship, any procedure will fail; with it, most patients and probably any procedure will succeed. Thus, Frank attributes enormous importance to the therapeutic relationship.
2. *A Healing Setting.* This refers to the physical location in which the treatment takes place.
3. *A Rationale.* A rationale includes an explanation of the person's difficulties and a method for relieving it. Frank has referred to this rationale as a myth to highlight the fact that its objective reality is less important than its believability. The explanations embodied in the myth are held to provide the patient with a framework through which he or she can better understand personal distress, conferring meaning to previously inexplicable experiences. This new framework

carries with it the implicit understanding that change is possible and likely. This then enhances hope.
4. *A Set of Prescribed Treatments or Rituals for Alleviating the Problem.* This provides concrete prescriptions derived from the myth for alleviating the difficulties. Participation in such rituals enhances expectations of relief because the patient is actually doing something about his or her problems. To the extent that the experiences provided by these techniques lead to actual mastery or success experiences, self-esteem and morale are further enhanced.

COMMON FACTORS AS A TREND IN THINKING ABOUT THERAPY

In spite of the work of Frank and others, the features shared by all treatments were still relatively neglected through the mid-1970s. Within a decade, however, the identification of common factors across therapeutic perspectives was hailed as a major trend in therapy research and thinking.

Two intimately related sets of events seem to account for this change: the emergence of efforts at rapprochement between diverse schools of psychotherapy and the findings of various well-conducted psychotherapy outcome reviews.

Psychotherapy outcome studies generally show that no one form of therapy is superior to any other. Parallel to this development and partly fueled by it in the 1970s, the issue of rapprochement between different therapeutic modalities had gained momentum and had begun to develop into a clearly delineated area of study. Paul Wachtel's classic book on integrating psychoanalysis and behavior therapy was a major force in this movement. The Society for the Exploration of Psychotherapy Integration was formed to focus on issues related to such rapprochement. The Zeitgeist changed and the time became ripe for exploration of these issues. Different writers focused on different domains or levels of treatment. This led to diverse conceptualizations of how these commonalities should be understood as well as to different lists of common factors. As a result, there has been a veritable explosion in proposed common factors. Moreover, the trend is expanding. There is a positive relationship between year of publication and number of commonalities and change processes being proposed. Two papers have offered partial solutions to this problem. The first is a theoretical paper; the second employs a purely empirical approach.

Goldfried conceptualized the task of looking for common factors in terms of *levels of abstraction* from what is directly observable. Furthest removed from actual observation is the theoretical framework and philosophical stance that seeks to explain how and why change occurs. Goldfried concluded that rapprochement at this level is not yet possible because there is presently no agreed-on model of personality or human functioning. The lowest level of abstraction that comes closest to actual observations involves the therapeutic techniques employed in treatment. Goldfried rejects this as well, because he concludes similarities yielded at this level would be trivial.

Between these two extreme levels of abstraction lies the level favored by Goldfried, the level of clinical strategies. He argues that any such strategy that emerges across varying orientations is likely to be robust and genuine because it survived the distortions imposed by clinicians' varying theoretical biases. These strategies can then function as clinical heuristics that implicitly guide the therapist's treatment efforts.

An example of efforts to describe common factors at the intermediate level of abstraction recommended by Goldfried is the work of Orlinsky and Howard, who argue that any theory of psychotherapy must include an explication of five components (see following) as well as their interrelationships. Their comprehensive review of psychotherapy process research indicated what then extant research had to say about each component.

The first component identified by Orlinsky and Howard is the therapeutic contract. This defines the purpose, format, terms, and limits of psychotherapy. The most effective therapeutic contract calls for collaboration between patient and therapist. More specifically, this translates into therapist encouragement of patient initiative and patient assumption of an active role in resolving his or her problems.

The next component is termed *therapeutic interventions*. These comprise the official "business" of therapy, carried out under the terms of the therapeutic contract. Therapeutic interventions found to be effective include confrontation, immediacy of affective expression (together these sound similar to the aforementioned CEE), and therapist skillfulness.

The therapeutic bond was said to be an emergent aspect of the relationship that forms between the patient and therapist as they become involved with each other and perform their respective roles in treatment.

Orlinsky and Howard also discuss patient self-relatedness. This refers to the manner in which the patient experiences and manages his or her thoughts, feelings, and self-definitions in treatment relative to openness versus defensiveness. Research shows that lack of defensiveness is strongly and positively related to outcome.

Finally Orlinsky and Howard cite therapeutic realizations, helpful impacts generated within the therapeutic sessions. Within-session positive changes are associated with positive outcomes.

Grencavage and Norcross had a different approach to the multiplicity of common factors. They collected articles concerned with common factors and counted the number of times each common factor was discussed. The most consensually agreed-on commonalities were, in order of their frequency:

1. The development of a therapeutic alliance.
2. The opportunity for catharsis.
3. The acquisition and practice of new behaviors.
4. Patient positive expectations.
5. Beneficial therapist qualities.
6. Provision of a rationale for the patient's problems.

THE THERAPEUTIC ALLIANCE

The therapeutic relationship was the most often noted variable in Grencavage and Norcross's survey, in the form of a therapeutic alliance. All views of this alliance, in spite of some differences, see it as a collaboration between therapist and patient, often thought to be activated through the therapist's manifestations of variants of the Rogerian triad of unconditional positive regard, accurate empathy, and genuineness. Reviews of research have found that it is the *patient's* sense that these variables are operative rather than the therapist's or an objective observer's that is critical to their effectiveness. With this proviso, the empirical data support the importance of the therapeutic alliance.

CORRECTIVE EMOTIONAL EXPERIENCE

Confrontation and immediacy of affective expression were identified by Orlinsky and Howard as related to positive outcome in psychotherapy. The Menninger Foundation Psychotherapy Research Project, which examined psychodynamic psychotherapy, found that corrective emotional experiences resulted in long-lasting therapeutic changes. The largest and most systematic number of empirical investigations of this variable has been undertaken by behaviorally oriented researchers in their investigations of exposure. Exposure can be seen as providing a CEE because the patient faces the troublesome issue and learns that it is not as devastating as imagined or feared. This work shows that the emotional component of the CEE may not be necessary. Exposure in and of itself seems to be ameliorative. That is, neither increasing nor deadening anxiety altered the effectiveness of exposure. Moreover, the trappings that often accompany exposure and that exist to control affective arousal, such as relaxation, graduated scenes, and so on, seem to be of lesser importance.

This suggests that affective arousal may not be necessary for a corrective emotional experience. This does not correspond with Orlinsky and Howard's finding that immediacy of affective expression is a positive correlate of outcome, however. It may be that affect has usually covaried with confrontation but is not necessary to its effectiveness or, alternatively, it may be that it has beneficial effects independent of exposure. Clearly, more research is required. Whatever the underlying means whereby the CEE works, however, it seems clear that patient practicing of new behaviors and/or confronting fears, especially through techniques like exposure, is ameliorative.

THE THERAPIST'S PERSONALITY

Surprisingly, little of substance has been demonstrated empirically as regards therapist personality attributes. In their authoritative review of therapist variables, Beutler and coworkers state: "Collectively, the influence of the therapist's personality on psychotherapy is inconclusive." Some relatively well-established findings were discussed by the aforementioned authors (e.g., that therapists with the lowest levels of emotional disturbance produced the best outcomes). Similarly, therapist expertness or competence was found to be positively related to outcome.

VALUES

Although not identified by Grencavage and Norcross, values may be something that therapists have in common and teach to their patients. Jensen and Bergin demonstrated empirically that therapists share a common set of values. They found this to be generally true across a range of helping professions, theoretical orientations, and demographic variables. Other research has shown that convergence of therapist and patient values may be associated with positive therapeutic outcome. If therapists in fact share a common set of values, this convergence is probably toward that common set and, therefore, to a common outcome. In this view, common outcome is partly attributable to a shared set of values. Common factors models of psychotherapy will probably have to tackle the issue of values.

CREATING A COMMON FACTORS MODEL OF PSYCHOTHERAPY

The therapeutic alliance is a critical aspect of therapy that cuts across different treatment modalities. Expectations also are factors that seem to be effective in different clinical contexts. The corrective emotional experience generally, and exposure particularly, are clearly ameliorative, although the role of affect remains unclear.

Weinberger proposed a common factors model of psychotherapy based on the extant empirical literature. He termed it the REMA model because the proposed critical factors are the relationship, exposure, mastery, and attribution. In this model, all factors interact and are of equal importance. All must operate for positive change to occur and to be maintained. The relationship is ameliorative in its own right but insufficient in and of itself. Exposure to critical issues is only effective in the context of a therapeutic relationship and only works if it leads to mastery experiences, which together make up a corrective emotional experience. That is, trying out a new behavior can potentially lead to failure rather than mastery. This could then retraumatize the individual. Only when exposure leads to mastery is it therapeutically beneficial. Finally, change will last only if the patient attributes improvement to him- or herself.

THE RELATIVE IMPORTANCE OF THE DIFFERENT COMMON FACTORS

A further issue concerns the relative importance of these factors. There are several possible ways of addressing this matter. Weinberger offered four.

First, the factors can be thought of in terms of logical priority. In such a conceptional scheme, the therapeutic relationship would assume greatest importance. This is so because the relationship is necessary before the CEE can occur and possibly even before therapeutic expectancies can form. This seems to be the perspective taken by those who stress the relationship as the sine qua non of psychotherapy.

If, however, the factors are looked at from the point of view of sufficiency, expectancy assumes the greatest importance. Research has shown that expectations can lead to improvement even in the absence of other factors. Bandura showed that expectations of success or failure are sufficient for lasting therapeutic change. Without positive expectations, change was shown to be ephemeral, if it occurred at all. This emphasis on sufficiency is the perspective taken by those who see expectancy and/or self-efficacy as the key to psychotherapeutic success.

When the factors are seen as interacting reciprocally, no factor stands out as primary. All interact with one another. No one aspect of the model is more important than any other in principle; all should occur for therapy to prove maximally effective. Such a view was taken by Appelbaum, who suggested that an interaction of factors contributes to therapeutic effectiveness in a synergistic manner. In this conception, no factor assumes the mantle of cause or effect or even of necessity or sufficiency, because all operate as part of a total configuration. Weinberger's REMA model takes this perspective.

Finally, it is conceivable that any or all of the factors could operate in a particular treatment to similar effect. Rosenzweig took this position, suggesting that as long as a factor has an impact on some aspect of the personality, the interdependence of the personality subsystems would communicate this effect to the personality as a whole. Thus similar change could be initiated by any of the different common factors, either alone or in combination.

BEHAVIOR THERAPY
ECLECTIC PSYCHOTHERAPY
PERSUASIVE COMMUNICATIONS
PSYCHOTHERAPY EFFECTIVENESS
PSYCHOTHERAPY RESEARCH
PSYCHOTHERAPY TECHNIQUES

J. L. WEINBERGER

PSYCHOTHERAPY EFFECTIVENESS

Measuring the effectiveness of psychotherapy is a complex activity that can be best understood from its historical context and from the questions posed and the methods used to answer these questions.

GROWTH OF IMPORTANCE OF EFFECTIVENESS RESEARCH

Psychotherapy research growth has paralleled that of psychotherapy. Social and economic conditions have played a role in shaping the evolution of psychotherapy research. Following World War II, psychotherapy gained acceptance by the public as a treatment for mental disorders. Decreasing the stigma associated with receiving mental health treatment has caused greater numbers of people to want it. Because mental health care is included within third-party health benefits, its practice has come under greater scrutiny, with critical questions being posed about its effectiveness. Third-party reimbursers, policymakers, and other payers ask that practitioners identify the value of psychotherapy to justify claims for payment. Psychotherapists are asked to demonstrate that costly treatments have reliable effects. Practical and economic necessity as well as the search for scientific truth have helped to stimulate significant methodological and conceptual advances made in this area of research. Methodological sophistication makes it possible to provide empirical

support that psychotherapy is a socially useful, clinically effective, treatment method.

HISTORY

When psychoanalysis reigned as the dominant form of psychotherapy in the early 1900s, the single-case study represented the standard method for studying psychotherapy outcome. As psychotherapy moved out of its infancy into adolescence, multiple forms of psychotherapy proliferated to such a point that now more than 250 exist. To study psychotherapy appropriately, large samples of subjects and reviews of multiple investigations were more appropriate ways of studying psychotherapy effectiveness.

A key event or stimulus to the growth of the study of psychotherapy effectiveness occurred in 1952. In an article critiquing the effects of psychotherapy, H. J. Eysenck questioned the assumption that psychotherapy was an effective treatment. He studied outcome data for 8053 clients reported in 24 research articles. His key dependent measures consisted of discharge data from New York State hospitals and amount of improvement from patients seeking insurance settlements. Patients who received psychotherapy did not improve any more than controls. Eysenck interpreted his data to show that two-thirds of all neurotics who enter psychotherapy improve substantially within 2 years, but that two-thirds of neurotics who do not enter therapy improve within the same period of time. In additional reviews of studies, Eysenck noted that no conclusive research evidence existed to support the notion that psychotherapy with neurotics was more effective than no psychotherapy at all. Eysenck's findings incited much controversy. A number of studies were launched aimed at answering the fundamental question of whether psychotherapy is beneficial.

Numerous investigators conducted additional reviews of the literature and reanalyses of the original articles on which Eysenck based his conclusions. Those who disagreed with Eysenck's conclusions attacked his methodology. Bergin recalculated Eysenck's data, omitting various categories of patients such as premature terminators. He found a greater rate of improvement than that reported by Eysenck and a much lower rate of spontaneous remission. New interpretations of Eysenck's findings and other psychotherapeutic reviews led authors to conclude that the results of psychotherapy are positive, with a minority of patients showing no improvement or deterioration effects.

METHODOLOGICAL EVOLUTION

The controversy over whether psychotherapy was effective spurred closer scrutiny of the methodology used. Making meaningful comparisons was fraught with difficulty. Wide variations but little specificity or standardization of measurement existed. Critics found major deficiencies in the methodology of many outcome studies. Early group studies often failed to have proper or adequate control groups, using noncomparable samples and outcome criteria. Researchers realized that to draw valid conclusions about the effectiveness of psychotherapy, a number of factors must be equivalent to make appropriate comparisons of outcome studies. Some variables included nature of the sample; amount and quality of therapy; nature and onset of duration of disturbance; preciseness of definitions of disorder; cases comparable across studies; duration and thoroughness of follow-up; and patient, therapist, and process variables. Furthermore, to ensure methodological soundness, methods of outcome assessment must be independent of therapists' evaluation, calling for independent confirmations of the accuracy of reported data.

Once consciousness had been raised and awareness had increased about what a complex process it was to compare studies of psychotherapy outcome to arrive at an overall picture of the effectiveness of psychotherapy, conceptual gains were made and methodological sophistication and precision increased. In the 1980s, metaanalysis was employed, a quantitative procedure that allows a statistical analysis of groups of studies and provides a relatively objective way of evaluating an existing body of data. Metaanalysis allows summary statements to be made about the statistical significance of the size of the effects across multiple studies and the drawing of conclusions about aggregate results.

Smith and Glass, who conducted the first major study of significance using metaanalytic techniques, provided the most convincing challenge to the claim that psychotherapy was not an effective treatment. In a review of more than 475 studies, they computed an effect size statistic and concluded that those who received treatment were better off than 80% of those who did not receive treatment.

A later Smith, Glass, and Miller study was followed by a number of other metaanalytic reviews. The conclusions reached were that psychotherapy is helpful and has clinically significant effects. Not everyone benefits from psychotherapy and some even suffer from iatrogenic or negative effects, but based on numerous reviews of the literature, using both traditional and metaanalytic methods, one conclusion was undebatable: Planned and systematic efforts of trained therapists to relieve psychological distress were more effective than placebo control groups, waiting lists, or no treatment control groups. An additional finding of metaanalytic studies about the effectiveness of psychotherapy indicated that patients who show change initially in therapy maintain the change.

Although metaanalysis represents improved methods of studying psychotherapy outcome, it is not a perfect statistical procedure, limited to addressing differences in between study comparisons, and there is difficulty translating statistical information into clinically meaningful data.

Once psychological treatment was established as beneficial, the next question posed was: Which psychotherapeutic method is most effective or helpful? Researchers put considerable effort into trying to prove the superiority of one form of therapy over another. Whereas the well-established therapy orientations of psychodynamic, client-centered, behavioral, and cognitive have been shown to be effective, outcome differences were not consistent or pronounced. No one type of therapy has been found to be superior to any other on a long-term basis. Some studies show that some specific techniques (behavioral, cognitive, and eclectic mixtures) are helpful in the treatment of specific and circumscribed disorders such as stuttering, phobias, compulsions, childhood aggression, and sexual problems. However, overall, there is no clear evidence for the effectiveness of one type of psychotherapy over another.

With the general positive effects of psychotherapy having been established and with no single form of therapy having established itself as significantly better than any other, new research questions included: What are the specific effects of specific interventions by specified therapists on specific symptoms or patient types? Although much of psychotherapy research addresses a plethora of issues other than effectiveness per se, there is pressure to demonstrate that any form of therapy is clinically effective and cost-effective compared with alternate forms of intervention, such as purely pharmacological treatments.

Demonstrating that any form of psychotherapy is effective is necessary to have psychotherapy accepted by the scientific community, consumers, and payers. A number of controversial and important issues are focused in the effectiveness research. One is how short-term and long-term therapy compare on the dimension of efficacy. A second concern is how much psychotherapy is optimal to obtain maximum clinical and cost-effectiveness. A number of studies have shown that brief methods are quite effective and generally have a similar success rate to longer-term treatment.

In the 1980s, a new generation of psychotherapy research began becoming a potentially significant force in the development of the study of psychotherapy effectiveness. The use of high-speed computers has made it possible to conduct sophisticated epidemiological research and to examine the psychotherapy delivery system. The psychotherapy attrition curve (indicating that 30 to 50% of people do not return after the first session)

means that consideration must be given to how natural attrition in the samples studied in past effectiveness research affects the outcome of the studies and the interpretation of results. By studying large-scale trends in the national and international patterns of psychotherapy use, researchers are gaining a new understanding of the aggregate effects of psychotherapy, making it possible to see effectiveness from a new perspective.

ALTERNATIVE PSYCHOTHERAPIES
ECLECTIC PSYCHOTHERAPY
OPTIMAL FUNCTIONING
PERFORMANCE APPRAISAL
PSYCHOTHERAPY
PSYCHOTHERAPY RESEARCH
PSYCHOTHERAPY TECHNIQUES
RESEARCH METHODOLOGY
TIME-LIMITED PSYCHOTHERAPY
TREATMENT OUTCOME

C. S. Austad

PSYCHOTHERAPY RESEARCH

All of the more established psychotherapy orientations—psychoanalytically oriented, client centered, cognitive, and behavioral—have been shown to be effective, but none have been demonstrated to be generally more effective than the others. Different types of therapy, such as individual and group, time limited and time unlimited, drug, and interview, obtain positive results, with no clear superiority over contrasting types. The variables that have been found to correlate most significantly with successful outcome are client factors, such as ego strength and motivation for change and personal therapist factors, such as trust, warmth, and acceptance. Technique and technical proficiency appear to be less important. The results of psychotherapy are usually positive, with a minority of clients showing no improvement, but there can also be a "deterioration effect." These are some of the main conclusions of psychotherapy research.

HISTORY

Psychotherapy research was greatly facilitated by the demystification efforts of Carl Rogers, who pioneered in the verbatim recording of complete cases of psychotherapy in the early 1940s and advanced a lucid theory of attitude and behavior change associated with the provision of client-centered conditions. This lent itself to the formulation of many testable hypotheses. He developed client measures that could be applied to recorded data. Such measures were correlated with test results, client and therapist ratings of outcome, and assessments by external judges.

METHODOLOGICAL COMPLEXITY

Psychotherapy research is extremely difficult to carry out because of the multiplicity of theories and the tremendous complexity of the subject. A significant number of therapists believe that it is not possible to control and isolate all the pertinent variables in a way that fulfills the requirements of traditional scientific method. At the same time, there is mounting pressure from those who pay for psychotherapy, including government and insurance companies, that therapists demonstrate that their work is effective and that they be increasingly specific about the application of treatment.

RESEARCH ON PSYCHOTHERAPY OUTCOME

Most serious researchers have concluded that, in general, the evidence for the efficacy of psychotherapy is very strong. Smith, Glass, and Miller reported that in 475 controlled studies of psychotherapy involving tens of thousands of subjects and at least 18 different approaches, the average person who receives psychotherapy is better off at the end of therapy than 80% of people who need therapy but do not get it.

Janet Tracy Landman and Robyn M. Dawes reanalyzed a random sample of 42 studies judged methodologically adequate and found a somewhat larger treatment effect than in the original sample, which contained studies of mixed methodological quality. In general, "the better the quality of the research, the more positive the results obtained."

Hans J. Eysenck and S. Rachman are among dissenters who have taken the position that, although most neurotic patients benefit during the course of psychotherapy, an equivalent number improve without it. The majority of therapy researchers, however, disagree with their conclusions.

In the course of assessing the efficacy of treatment, psychotherapy researchers have concerned themselves also with negative results. Bergin proposed the term *deterioration effect* and presented empirical results from seven studies to substantiate the phenomenon. Other investigators have been gathering data to determine the prevalence of negative outcomes and their association with possible causal agents. Rates of deterioration in untreated groups have been found to vary widely.

In general, psychotherapy researchers are open to the possibility that psychotherapy may have powerful negative as well as positive consequences, motivating them to continue their efforts to throw light on a very complex process and to join with clinicians in discussing implications for selection, training, and the continuing education of practitioners.

CORRELATES OF OUTCOME

There remains the question of which variables account for or are correlated with therapeutic outcome. It is easier to list characteristics that have been found to bear no relationship to results, or where the research findings are mixed or inconclusive. Bergin has concluded that client variables such as level of personality integration and motivation for change are significantly related to outcome, but Sol Garfield has observed that this is true if *amount* of change is the criterion; the relationship between outcome and variables such as ego strength is not so clear. Morris Parloff and colleagues concluded that most therapist variables–such as personality, mental health, experience, sex, race, and socioeconomic status—are so simplistic and global that they result in what they term "terminal vagueness." The most substantial generalization deemed warranted by these reviewers was that the emotional problems of therapists may interfere with effective treatment.

PSYCHOTHERAPY RESEARCH IN PERSPECTIVE

Beyond the substantial conclusion that psychotherapy in general is effective, it might be said that 40 years of laborious research on more specific issues have brought forth a mouse. Rogers described psychotherapy as being in a state of chaos, "not however a meaningless chaos, but an ocean of confusion, teeming with life, spawning vital new ideas, approaches, procedures, and theories at an incredibly rapid rate."

CRITERION MEASURES
EFFECTIVENESS COMPONENTS OF PSYCHOTHERAPY
GROUP PSYCHOTHERAPY
PERSONALITY CHANGES
PSYCHOTHERAPY

N. J. Raskin

PSYCHOTHERAPY SUPERVISION

Early forms of psychotherapy supervision were closely tied to therapeutic orientations. Behaviorists, for example, saw client problems as learned maladaptive behavior; the trainee was responsible for promoting adaptive client behaviors. The goals of therapy were (a) identification of the problem and (b) selection of appropriate learning techniques. Behavioral supervision consisted of participating as cotherapist with each of several skilled therapists and engaging trainees in behavioral rehearsal (with coached clients) before their solo performance as therapists. Behaviorists reported various methods employed in supervision: (a) an apprenticeship relationship that was the "treatment of choice," but very time consuming; (b) a "continuing seminar" that met weekly or biweekly for several months and consisted of instruction on learning theory and case presentations; and (c) an "intensive institute" that involved a daily training session for several weeks and stressed theory discussion, demonstration of techniques, role-playing with peers, and a supervised session with clients.

EARLY FORMS

Psychoanalytic models of supervision were developed by Ekstein and Wallerstein. Trainees were encouraged to undergo analysis. Supervision presupposed a thorough grounding in psychoanalytic theory, including a knowledge of (a) defense patterns, (b) transference, (c) countertransference, (d) insight, and (e) resistance. Using a chess game analogy, Ekstein and Wallerstein described a sequence of supervision stages. In the "opening" the trainee and supervisor assessed each other for signs of expertise and weakness. The "midgame" was characterized by interpersonal conflict: attacking, defending, probing, and/or avoiding. During the "endgame," the supervisor was frequently silent to encourage the trainee to be more independent in dealing with clients.

Charles Truax and Robert Carkhuff were largely responsible for refining Carl Rogers' client-centered model of supervision. Rogers outlined a program of graduated experiences that gave trainees an opportunity to see "congruence," "empathy," and "unconditional positive regard" used by their supervisors and to practice these attributes themselves. The program included listening to audio tapes of experienced therapists, role-playing therapy with other students, observing live demonstrations with the supervisor acting as therapist, participating in a practicum with a client-centered supervisor, participating as a member of group therapy, and participating in individual therapy. Truax and Carkhuff saw three dimensions to the supervisor role: Supervisors provide high levels of empathy, congruence, and positive regard; trainees get specific didactic training in implementing these "necessary and sufficient conditions" of therapy; and trainees participate in group therapy in which they engage in self-exploration of their roles as therapists.

In each of these three orientations—behavioral, psychoanalytic, and client-centered–an important assumption was that the trainee would be sensitive enough to perceive and integrate the behaviors of the supervisor. It was also assumed that every supervisor would be an excellent therapist. Concomitantly, it was assumed that a person facile in the performance of therapy would be equally adept at directing the performance of others.

CURRENT PRACTICE

Although some therapists continue to link supervision to one brand of therapy, there is a growing trend for supervisors to integrate several supervision models. This is due in part to the depolarization of theoretical orientations and the predominance of the "eclectic" orientation among therapists. Norman Kagan's "Interpersonal Process Recall" model of supervision gives the supervisor a very specific structure for helping the trainee become aware of internal processes and specific thoughts occurring during therapy. Allen Ivey's "microcounseling" identifies specific skills in isolation, attempting to increase the trainee's behavioral repertoire in a systematic way. Janine Bernard's "discrimination model" trains supervisors to view supervision as a series of choice points in a 3 × 3 matrix of process skills/conceptualization skills/personalization skills by delivery approaches as a teacher, counselor, or consultant. Other theorists emphasize developmental stages in the trainee's growth during supervision, identifying specific tasks in each stage that must be resolved.

Supervision currently involves the use of direct observation for the provision of feedback to trainees and a systematic combination of modeling, didactic skill training, and consultation. The supervisor develops an individualized plan for the growth of each trainee, from anxious ambivalence toward autonomous collegiality.

CLINICAL PSYCHOLOGY GRADUATE TRAINING
COUNSELING
MENTAL HEALTH CONSULTATION TEAMS

G. R. Leddick

PSYCHOTHERAPY TECHNIQUES

The following are specific examples of the types of techniques that therapists use to change the behaviors/cognitions/affects of clients.

TALKING—FOCUS ON THE INTELLECT

Free Association. The therapist listens nonjudgmentally to the report of mental images in whatever order the client prefers to use. Interpretation is done at a later time. The client is asked to respond to words selected and sequenced by the therapist; responses range from a single word to a brief sentence. Both the content of the response and any delay in giving it are interpreted.

Dream Analysis. The story of the dream as recalled is the manifest content; interpretation is based on the underlying or latent content that expresses a wish. Because the wishes often involve past trauma, the person attempts to disguise the true meaning of the dream and thereby to minimize pain.

The underlying meaning of dreams may be a recommendation of the inner Self to the conscious person. Many dreams end with a solution to a current problem.

Nondirective Interview. The client is asked to talk with minimal guidance from the therapist. The therapist limits comments to repeating or rephrasing the statements made and describing the degree of expressed feeling. The client is encouraged to confirm or to correct the therapist's understanding.

Imagination. In Eidetic Psychotherapy, the client may be asked to imagine the humiliation of failure and then the pride of success. Detailed descriptions of the feelings in both circumstances are required. The underlying message is that the client is in control and can choose the feelings of success or of failure.

Directive Interview. The client is asked a fixed sequence of questions or asked to respond to a standard scale.

Analysis of Videotaped Behavior. The client is asked to interpret the behavior shown along stipulated dimensions. The behavior segment shown is usually of the client. A variation occasionally used is to confront the client in the immediate moment: Monitors are placed in view; the therapist remotely controls the camera and focuses on various body parts.

Interpretation. In the Conflict Resolution Therapy, the therapist helps the client conceptualize the nature of the conflict beneath the problem and then asks the client to produce a solution.

Rumpelstiltskin. The therapist occasionally can affect behavior dramatically by the "magic" of the right word or interpretive phrase. A receptive client can be vastly changed by giving a name to the core problem.

Confrontation. The therapist points out the client's failure to accept responsibility for the cure in a momentary "attack." Less general errors such as exaggeration of complaints or overgeneralizations are pointed out and labeled irrational.

Humor. Various styles of humor may be used to confront the client. Exaggeration to absurdity, mimicry of self-defeating behavior, ridicule of idiotic behavior, and sarcasm carefully combined with nonvocal warmth and acceptance are used.

Contradictory Messages. In Provocative Therapy, the therapist vocally agrees with the pessimism expressed by the client but nonvocally supports the notion that the client can be helped. Further *reality testing* is encouraged by taking the client's negative statements to their logical extreme or by immediately and superficially agreeing with a statement of "I'm no good."

Telephone Interview. Conversations over the telephone reduce the social cues and seem particularly useful to anxious and unstable individuals for whom a therapist is highly threatening. Others report similar advantages to having clients "converse" at computer terminals.

Silence. Alfred Adler often folded his hands and said nothing to force the client to reconsider conclusions and motivations. Many other therapists include silence as an important technique.

TALKING—FOCUS ON THE AFFECT

Supportive. The client is considered not to be sick but simply discouraged. The mistakes made are not fatal; one must enhance one's faith in oneself. The therapist supports the client while the coping ability is increased.

Feeling Talk. In assertiveness training, the client is taught to utter spontaneously felt emotions deliberately. Deliberate use of the word *I* is encouraged.

Poetry. The clients express emotion by reading poems selected by both the therapist and themselves.

Pets. The presence of pets in the office is suggested, especially for child clients. Not only are dogs an immediate source of comfort, but they can also become an opening topic of conversation.

Displacement. The client is taught to channel a desire or need into a more adaptive behavior. In Alcoholics Anonymous, for example, the supportive friendship of members replaces alcohol.

Relaxation. The client is taught exercises that may be done in any setting to reduce the level of anxiety.

Hypnosis. Sometimes hypnosis is used as an adjunctive procedure to decrease the inhibition or censorship of anxiety-arousing material.

Emotional Reliving. Many systems stress the benefit of vivid recollection of the detail of traumas.

Haircut. During an agreed period, the client must listen to a tirade on faults and errors without any attempt at a defense.

Scream. In New Identity Process, the client is taught to show emotion with the voice.

TALKING—FOCUS ON REHEARSAL OF BEHAVIOR

Fixed Role. This technique begins with the client writing a description of the self in the third person. Another sketch is prepared, this one with at least one major alternative trait. The client is told that the true role is "going on vacation" for a fixed period, such as

2 weeks. During this period, the alternative role is to be adopted as fully as possible. At the end of the time, the alternative role is abandoned, but the client probably will modify the original role somewhat.

Imagination. The client relaxes with eyes closed and then imagines a scene suggested by the therapist. In Systematic Desensitization, the scenes are presented in a graded series from least to most anxiety arousing. This is in direct contrast with Stampfl's Implosive Therapy, in which only the most anxiety-arousing scenes are used.

Consequences. In Covert Conditioning, the client is asked to imagine the positive, negative, and neutral consequences of specific behavioral acts.

Group Therapy. The group becomes a rehearsal for the client's regular environment. It is also comforting to see that other people have anxieties. Most groups are composed of relatively homogeneous clients—the same level of vulnerability, a common problem, or a natural group.

Psychodrama. This procedure borrows heavily from the theater. The client portrays him- or herself, with another member of the group moving, acting, and behaving as the patient would.

ACTIVELY BEHAVING

Modeling. Appropriate behavior is demonstrated live or on videotape, by the therapist or by others. The focus is on specific skills, such as asking for a date or being interviewed for a job.

Play Therapy. The client, particularly a young child, is provided many human figures and other objects, perhaps in a sand box. The therapist may ask questions about the characters and events.

Physical Activity. Activities include massage, jogging, movement awareness, and physical attack with rubber bats.

Art therapy. Drawings or other creative exercises are done. For those who have trouble communicating with others, a group mural is often constructed.

Negative Practice. The technique asks the client to repeat the maladaptive behavior or thought to fatigue.

SETTING FACTORS

Transference. The client places trust and confidence in the therapist and readily accepts the suggestions made.

Social Role. The therapist must be careful to avoid the conventions of society in giving or accepting gifts, changing appointment times, and other apparently "after-the-hour" comments.

Triad Counseling. The sessions are conducted by the counselor but with an anticounselor or devil's advocate present in addition to the client.

INDIRECT CONTACT WITH CLIENTS

Training Parents or Peers. The intervention is designed by the professional but is executed by others naturally present in the client's environment.

Bibliotherapy. Both self-help and professionally oriented works may have far- reaching impact.

Prevention. The therapist consults with laypeople and paraprofessionals in the design of systems that intervene before the difficulties become major distresses.

BEHAVIOR THERAPY—PROBLEMS AND ISSUES
COGNITIVE THERAPIES

EFFECTIVENESS COMPONENTS OF PSYCHOTHERAPY
HISTORICAL ROOTS OF PSYCHOTHERAPY
PSYCHOTHERAPY

C. S. PEYSER

PSYCHOTHERAPY TRAINING

Psychotherapy training has taken various forms across the different professions and over the years within psychology. Less formal training occurred in the early years of psychology, when there were fewer specialties. A particular type of therapy could be learned by a more formal program of several years of didactic and practical study at the particular institute.

Following World War II, psychologists grew in number and psychology expanded the domain and specialization of its activities. Between 1947 and 1965, a number of conferences were convened by the American Psychological Association (APA) to examine the training programs of psychologists.

SCIENTIST–PRACTITIONER MODEL

This model has the graduate student engaging in limited clinical, practical tasks, such as listening to clinicians conduct interviews, during the first 2 years of training. In the third and fourth years of graduate training, the student engages in practicum training during which the therapy is supervised by a faculty member or an agency staff member. Completion of course work and doctoral examinations precede a year-long clinical internship during which the trainee typically engages in supervised psychotherapy with a variety of clients.

Concurrent with the clinical training, the student–intern's program includes research activities, such as a master's thesis and doctoral dissertation. These are intended to create in the student an attitude of scientific inquiry toward clinical problems.

Training

Students tend to receive 1 hour of supervision for every 3 hours of psychotherapy they conduct. One-to-one supervision, with the supervisee recounting the previous hours of therapy to the supervisor, is the dominant supervision style, with audiotapes, group meetings, and videotapes following in frequency of use.

Stages of Supervision

Several stage theories of supervision have been presented, including that of M. J. Rioch, in which the trainee deals with the beginner's anxieties, progressing to using techniques to help the client cope, and learns about him- or herself as a helping agent for the client. S. Yogev posits a three-stage sequence, in which stage one is concerned with learning the role of the therapist, stage two concerns skill acquisition, and stage three involves solidification of stages one and two, where both experimental and didactic skills are refined in supervision.

MODELS OF PSYCHOTHERAPY TRAINING

Several types of models have been developed. One involves a teacher–student model, in which the teacher is deemed knowledgeable and conveys certain critical skills to the novice. Acquisition of skills results in the student accumulating mastery of psychotherapy. Another model is more of a case review model, in which the learner is more an apprentice who models on the experienced clinician, and whose work is reviewed at staff meetings by the clinician. Again, the weight of accumulated experience, plus the passage of program requirements in a formal program, results in the novice gaining journeyman status.

A third model is more collegial in nature. This model includes the latter stages of a training program in which a less formal relationship between the trainer and trainee is marked by more of a collegial–peer interaction. This model allows for a continual learning situation to evolve since this model blends into an ongoing peer consultation that can result in lifelong learning.

A focus on psychotherapy training in terms of building a theoretical base, considering it a professional practice, and discerning a need for research, has emerged only recently. The elements in psychotherapy training—the supervisors, the trainees, the relationship, the setting, the teaching process, the modalities (videotapes, groups), and the models of training—are only beginning to be conceptualized and empirically investigated. Ultimately, studies varying these aspects of training psychotherapists may be related to effectiveness of psychotherapeutic care rendered to clients.

CAREERS IN PSYCHOLOGY
PSYCHOTHERAPY
PSYCHOTHERAPY SUPERVISION
SOCIAL CASEWORK

A. K. HESS

PUBLIC POLICY

During the last half of the twentieth century, psychology matured as a profession and the behavioral sciences captured the public's interest. In 1950, there were 7273 members of the American Psychological Association (APA); in 1994, there was in excess of 110,000. In 1945, Connecticut adopted the first psychology "scope of practice" act; by 1977, psychology had obtained licensure-certification in all 50 states. The "health promotion and disease prevention" orientation was first brought into the public policy domain in 1974 by Marc Lalonde, the then-minister of National Health and Welfare for Canada. The health policy messages enumerated in that statement subsequently have been adopted by surgeons general since President Carter released *Healthy people*.

Since the 1970s, professional psychology has developed a significant presence in public health policy. During the 1970s and 1980s, psychology enjoyed increasing success in systematically modifying a wide range of federal statutes recognizing the profession's clinical and research expertise, thereby gaining autonomous inclusion under almost all programs in which the federal government serves as "the payer" for health (including mental health) services rendered to federal beneficiaries. Although psychology's active involvement in the political process is definitely expected to continue, training institutions have been slow to recognize the importance to psychologists of becoming intimately involved in the process.

Psychologists have long been active in the public policy-political arena. William James was a tireless advocate about psychology's potential contributions to society. Nicholas Hobbs and William Bevan (the seventy-fourth and ninetieth presidents of APA, respectively) constantly urged their colleagues to "give psychology away," as did APA presidents George Albee and M. Brewster Smith (the seventy-eigth and eighty-sixth presidents). Psychologists also have held important positions of public trust, including secretary of the former Department of Health, Education, and Welfare (HEW); commissioner of Children, Youth, and Families; director of the National Institute on Disability and Rehabilitation Research; and directors of various state mental health administrations.

Organized psychology has never really understood the all-important personal nature of the public policy-political process. Many psychologists do not sufficiently appreciate the long-term significance to psychology's clinical, educational, and research endeavors of being an integral component within the totality of the nation's federal health programs. As a learned profession, psychology has not used its breadth of knowledge and clinical skills, nor has it systematically sought ways directly to link the strengths of its training programs to society's needs. While medicine constantly creates administrative opportunities and support for its students and graduates, psychology virtually ignores health delivery and policy formulation.

THE APA CONGRESSIONAL SCIENCE PROGRAM

One of the most exciting developments within professional psychology has been the establishment of APA's Congressional Science Fellowship Program. Since its inception in 1974, this APA-sponsored program has been responsible for facilitating the active involvement of psychologists in the policy-making–political process, thereby bringing psychology's expertise directly to bear on a wide range of society's priorities. This program provides fellows with an intimate appreciation for the potential interrelationship between the profession and the nation's evolving policy agendas.

Starting with a single fellow (Pam Flattau), the APA has sponsored 35 fellows, 22 women and 13 men from practically every psychological specialty area. On completing their Capitol Hill experience, about half of the fellows have taken policy-related positions with various federal agencies, the Congress, and/or with public interest or policy research organizations. The remaining fellows have returned to positions similar to that which they held before accepting the APA assignment.

Historically, psychologists have viewed their profession as a "mental health specialty" that has only limited applications to the delivery of health care. Consequently, psychologists have allowed the discipline to evolve with little awareness of federal health policy developments.

The profession of psychology possesses much of value to society, especially its potential contributions to the nation's health delivery system. However, for the field to become one of the recognized "health professions," not only must its scientists and practitioners become more involved in the public policy process but its training institutions in particular, must give greater recognition to their involvement. Progress is occurring; however, there is still much to be accomplished.

NATIONAL HEALTH INSURANCE
PSYCHOLOGY AND THE LAW
SOCIAL INFLUENCE

P. DELEON

PUNISHMENT

Punishment is a topic that psychologist and layperson alike find difficult to discuss in objective or neutral terms. Not long ago, corporal punishment was widely approved. Both educational and legal systems depended on punishment. Punishment now has fallen into some disfavor. Within the family, what once was approved of as punishment may be considered "child abuse" or "spouse abuse." However, in spite of the trend in public attitudes towards disfavor regarding some types, punishment or potential punishment is still pervasive in the world today. People are questioning the use of punishment, raising issues such as: Does punishment work? When, how, and why?

WHAT IS PUNISHMENT?

Psychologists define punishment as the addition of an aversive consequence that results in a reduction of tendency to behave in a certain way; or as a consequence of behavior that reduces the probability of that behavior occurring again.

IS PUNISHMENT EFFECTIVE?

Early works on punishment seemed to demonstrate that it was ineffective in eliminating behavior. However, more recent work on punishment makes it clear that punishment can suppress or eliminate behavior. How effective punishment is in accomplishing this depends on various factors that vary from situation to situation, including characteristics of the punishing stimulus, characteristics of the behavior being punished, and characteristics of the subject being punished.

Intensity of Punishment

In general, research on punishment intensity has found that the greater the intensity of the punishing stimulus, the greater is the suppression of the punished behavior. A stimulus applied at too low an intensity may arouse and reinforce rather than punish.

Temporal Proximity

In general, for punishment to be maximally effective, it should follow immediately the behavior to be suppressed.

How punishment is first introduced can be critical. Punishment that has been introduced at a low intensity and gradually increased over a period of time has considerably less effect than does punishment presented suddenly at full intensity.

In general, it appears that increased frequency of punishment results in increased effectiveness of punishment, and that continuous punishment is more effective than intermittent punishment.

Effectiveness depends on the strength of the punished response. Continued reinforcement of a punished behavior appears to compete and to interfere with the suppression effects of punishment. Effectiveness also depends on whether the behavior being punished was originally established by reward or by punishment.

Subject Characteristics

There is some evidence indicating that punishment is decreasingly effective as the subject's motivation for the punished behavior increases. Effectiveness also varies with familiarity of the subject with the punishment being used, with species, and with age and developmental stage within species of subjects. Human cognitive abilities (e.g., reasoning, imagination) can also influence effectiveness of punishment. Verbalization of rationale seems to facilitate discrimination and generalization of punishment effects in humans. Descriptive verbalization and recall of what is being punished appear to reduce the impact of time delays between behavior and punishment. In some cases, observation of punishment by humans seems to have some effects, as though the punishment were experienced vicariously. Finally, punishment of humans appears to be most effective within a context of love.

THEORIES OF PUNISHMENT

Various theories have been used to explain how and why punishment results in a reduction of the frequency of the punished behavior. J. A. Dinsmoor explained punishment effects in terms of simple stimulus–response (S–R) principles of avoidance learning. Basically, this explanation holds that punished behaviors decrease in frequency because of an increase in frequency of behaviors that compete with or interfere with the punished response. Another theory explains punishment effects in terms of fear conditioning and reinforcement of whatever action or inaction eliminates or controls the fear.

Relevant Questions

Why do some subjects seem to enjoy and seek punishment? Occasionally a punishment procedure actually increases rather than decreases the frequency of the behavior being punished. As noted earlier, this can occur when the punished behavior was originally established by punishment.

Sometimes it appears that the parent has paid attention to the child primarily in response to misbehavior, and has unwittingly transformed the "punishment" into reinforcement. The result may be a situation in which punishment not only does not appear to be effective, but also in which the child or individual appears to seek more "punishment." Rather than contradict the effectiveness of punishment, such phenomena confirm the effectiveness of reinforcement.

Experiments on monkeys clearly show that punishment can have neurotic or seemingly harmful emotional side effects. Although such side effects are indeed frightening and should not be ignored, they do not appear in all experiments involving use of strong punishment. Punishment may also result in termination of a social relationship, operant aggression directed toward the punishing agent, and/or elicited aggression against individuals who had nothing to do with the original punishment.

SUMMARY

Punishment can be effective in reducing or eliminating undesirable behaviors. How effective a given punishment situation is depends on various factors, including characteristics of the punishing stimulus, the behavior being punished, and the subject being punished. Potential side effects of punishment, such as termination of social relations, should be considered in any application, especially when humans are involved.

ACQUIRED DRIVES
COUNTERCONDITIONING
LEARNING THEORIES
REINFORCEMENT
REWARDS

J. W. ENGEL

PURPOSIVE BEHAVIOR

William McDougall described the human organism as a purposive, self-regulating machine. He held that the concept of purpose implied the construct of "mind," and that purposes control both organic and behavioral functioning at fully conscious, marginally conscious, and/or subconscious levels. Edward Chase Tolman maintained that a response demonstrates a purpose if it shows a "teachable" quality; that is, the organism has a readiness to learn to select this response, sooner or later on successive occasions, because the response is more efficient in getting the organism to some end or objective.

According to Alfred Adler, behavior is directed by unconscious purposes. In contrast to Sigmund Freud, Adler maintained that since drives have no direction, it is a mistake to construct a psychological system based on drive psychology. Emotions also serve a purpose in Adler's system.

Behavioral scientists interested in cybernetics and systems theory have used these frameworks to understand the role of purpose in directing behavior. Purposive behavior is characterized by "negative feedback," in which signals for the goal modify and direct behavior. Thus, teleological or goal-directed behavior refers to purposeful reactions controlled by the difference between the state of the organism at any time and the "final" state or purpose toward which the organism is moving. This difference is "fed back" into the system, which then modifies its behavior, causing a progressive reduction of the "difference" until, finally, the difference between the current behavior and the goal state is zero (Rosenblueth).

ACQUIRED DRIVES
ANTICIPATION METHOD
DISCOVERY LEARNING
LEVELS OF ASPIRATION

MOTIVATION
REWARDS AND INTRINSIC INTEREST
SELECTIVE ATTENTION

R. R. KOPP

PYGMALION EFFECT

The term *Pygmalion effect* was taken from George Bernard Shaw's play. It is used as a synonym for self-fulfilling prophecy.

Robert Rosenthal and Lenore Jacobson were the first to use the concept of Pygmalion effect in their book, which described the effects of teachers' expectations on students' behavior. The original study involved an experimental manipulation of teacher expectations and an assessment of its effects on students' IQ scores. In this study, 20% of randomly selected students in 18 classrooms were described to teachers as having shown remarkable potential for academic growth (bloomers). Students in early grades for whom teachers' high expectations had been induced showed significant gains in total IQ and reasoning IQ when compared with other students in their school. Although the original study was criticized on methodological grounds, it directed much attention to the effects of teachers' expectations on students' performance in schools.

These findings were found to have special implications for the education of disadvantaged children. Disadvantaged children were found to perform poorly in schools because of low expectations by their teachers.

Two explanations were offered for the Pygmalion effect. Cooper suggested that teachers believe that they have less control over low-expectation students than over high-expectation students. Thus, to increase their control, teachers frequently give affective feedback to the former students, while the latter students more frequently receive feedback based on their effort expenditure. These different evaluation contingencies may lead low-expectation students not to believe that effort influences academic outcomes. Bar-Tal suggested that teachers' expectations regarding students' performance are based on the causal perceptions of teachers regarding the academic successes or failures of their students. If the teachers believe that the causes for a student's failure are unchangeable, then they do not expect future success on the part of the student and behave in accordance with this belief.

The formation of expectation is a human phenomenon and cannot be prevented. Only inaccurate and/or rigid expectations are maladaptive for educational practices of teachers. One way of diminishing the possible negative effect of the Pygmalion effect is to make the teacher aware of the phenomenon and its consequences.

EARLY CHILDHOOD EDUCATION
LABELING THEORY

D. BAR-TAL

Q-SORT TECHNIQUE

The Q-Sort is a technique used to describe an individual so as to yield a variable that can be related to other variables similarly derived, It has been utilized to compare a person's self-description with his or her ideal, to compare self-perceptions with the perceptions of the self by others, and to find the intercorrelations of the descriptions of a number of people, as made by themselves or by others. It can be used to divide a group of individuals into more or less homogeneous subgroups or types. When dealing with opinions and beliefs, the Q-Sort can be helpful in identifying panels of like-minded persons.

Characteristically the variable is based on a forced-choice classification of a fixed number of items or elements, which may be sentences, adjectives, or verbs with modifiers. The subject who is to perform the Q-Sort is given instructions as to how to respond to the items, generally presented on cards.

With most Q-Sorts, the prescribed distribution approximates the normal. The subject assigns values to his or her choices by apportioning the cards in the piles, in accordance with the assigned frequency of each. The Q-Sort technique dates back to about 1935, when it was proposed independently by G. H. Thomson and by William Stephenson.

FORCED-CHOICE TESTING

P. H. DuBois

QUADRIPLEGICS: PSYCHOLOGICAL ASPECTS

A whole new world of experience results from a sudden spinal cord injury. Injuries of this kind are caused primarily by falls, automobile or motorcycle accidents, and gunshot wounds. They have greater lifetime consequences for quadriplegics than for paraplegics, as the former lose much more mobility. A quadriplegic has had the spinal cord partially or wholly severed at one or more of the cervical levels. Many quadriplegics retain some degree of muscular function in the upper part of the body, such as the shoulders, arms, or wrists. Those injured at the two uppermost cervical levels have no voluntary motor function below the head. But there is often somewhat less sensory than motor deprivation.

The injured go into shock immediately after the initial trauma. The great majority have no recall of the accident or of the events that took place hours or even days later, although a few do retain these memories. Pain can last for many days, or even for weeks, and, in addition, quadriplegics have particularly disturbed sleep patterns.

During the recovery period, many variables can affect adjustment to the paralysis: the patient's age, socioeconomic level, financial worries, worry about loss of job, or loss of skills such as athletic ability. Perhaps as important are the attitudes and the behavior of physicians, nurses, aides, physiotherapists, and other hospital staff members, as well as spouses and families. Cultural background can also play a role; for example, in some cultures, the accident may be attributed to carelessness, fate, or evil spirits.

Professionals working with quadriplegics generally state that patients go through a definite sequence of emotions and attitudes (in addition to shock and pain). The general consensus has been that, at first, there is denial of the disability, followed by hope of recovery. Then comes depression, anxiety, mourning, guilt, and finally anger. Hard work on both physical and psychological rehabilitation, and the motivation to become as independent as possible, do a tremendous amount toward better readjustment for quadriplegics.

Both bowel and urinary control are lost in quadriplegics. There also can be varying degrees of sexual dysfunction. Sexual desire continues in all cases, and ways of obtaining sexual satisfaction can often be worked out with a partner.

Abel and Wilson concluded that family therapy could be an effective part of a hospital's routine procedure. In this way, the patient's family could be accurately informed about the injury and its effects as soon as possible. The patient and family could also be helped to express their feelings about the accident, the injury, and each other, thus gaining greater understanding and mutual support.

Quadriplegics have a particularly difficult time adjusting to life outside the hospital, whether in the family home, in a nursing home, or in independent living with aides. Those with some use of the upper limbs can learn a variety of tasks, such as using a motorized wheelchair, getting in and out of a van, driving a van, answering the telephone, and doing certain manual tasks with supports to the arm and hand. The more completely paralyzed cases can learn to carry on such activities as typing or running a motorized wheelchair by using their mouths and chins with special devices.

Quadriplegics need help in developing all possible physical skills. They must learn how to function in daily living, school situations, vocational training, and work. But they also need help in overcoming anxieties, worries, fears, and loss of self-esteem, and in gaining the confidence needed to face a new life.

HANDICAPPED (ATTITUDES TOWARD)
REHABILITATION CENTERS

T. M. ABEL

QUALITY OF LIFE

While a considerable amount of research and practice in psychology has been directed toward negative behaviors, such as depression, anxiety, stress, and aggression, there frequently has been a belief that the more positive aspects of human behavior should be a concern. Edward Tolman in his 1941 presidential address to the American Psychological Association stressed the need for a shift in emphasis from the economic to the psychological facets of people's behavior. The theoretical positions of Carl Rogers and Abraham Maslow stress the more positive factors involved in human development and functioning. However, it was R. A. Bauer who set the stage for subsequent research into the quality of life.

During the early 1970s, many government agencies began to develop methods of reporting social indicators. The types of measures reported were rather gross and included such data as the number of schools per person, the number of hospital beds per person, and the number of health care professionals per person. While these regional measures reflected the well-being of community units, they did not reflect the well-being of the individuals comprising the communities.

The next set of studies consisted of large sample studies aimed at measuring the quality of life of the particular samples studied. N. M. Bradburn provided the first data of this type. The affect balance score, the sum of positive affect minus the sum of negative affect, was used as the measure of life satisfaction. This measure was found to be normally distributed and was assumed to be indicative of quality of life. A second large sample study was reported by Campbell and colleagues. Survey data were obtained from a sample selected to be representative of the national population. Those sampled were asked to rate their degree of

satisfaction with particular areas of their life, family, work, friendships, housing, and health. They were also asked to rate how satisfied they were with their life in general. The latter ratings approximated a normal distribution but were skewed toward the "very satisfied" end of the scale.

The work of Bradburn, Campbell, Converse and Rodgers, and Flanagan provided a valuable beginning to the measurement of quality of life. However, a number of assessment issues have been raised by their work. First, the subjective nature of satisfaction measures has been recognized and efforts are being made to develop more objective, criterion referenced measures. Second, the early research quickly suggested that a global measure of quality of life was of little value. A number of authors have developed taxonomies of life domains that make up an individual's overall quality of life. The interest of industrial groups and unions in the quality of working life has spurred considerable interest and development in this specific area. Research in other domains, such as family, leisure, and environment, is also developing rapidly. The third and final issue is the contribution of cognitive, affective, and behavioral factors to the report of quality of life in each domain.

The developing interest in quality of life coincided with a trend in psychology toward primary prevention as advocated by Caplan. A second result of the growing interest in quality of life has been the work of industrial psychologists in redesigning working environments so that individuals are both productive and have a good quality of working life. One final area in which quality-of-life concerns have been raised is in the evaluation of treatment programs. T. H. Blau advocates that the end point of treatment should not be symptom relief but enhanced quality of life.

ENVIRONMENTAL PSYCHOLOGY

D. R. EVANS

QUESTIONNAIRES

Questionnaires are inventories used by researchers to gather various kinds of information from responding individuals. They are typically self-administered, so-called "self-report" devices. As such, they are similar to interviews. Among the advantages of questionnaires are their relatively low cost as a means of gathering data, a general freedom from bias on the part of an interviewer, the large number of individuals who may be asked to respond, the sense of anonymity that respondents may feel, the temporal flexibility afforded the respondent, the possibility of directly linking research questions and survey results, and the ease of data coding and analysis for interpretation of the results. A major disadvantage of questionnaires relates to "return rates"; frequently only a small fraction of those originally provided with a questionnaire complete it, and those who do may not be representative of the population of interest. Also, respondents may not be honest or may permit subtle biases to influence their responses. Another disadvantage of questionnaires is that individuals may write answers that do not, in fact, adequately address a question. Furthermore, many Americans are unable to read and write well enough to complete a questionnaire.

Questionnaires are used in both basic psychological research and applied research. In applied research, questionnaires are often used in program evaluations, job analyses, needs assessments, and market research. Most behaviors elicited by questionnaires are of the "typical behavior" variety. Furthermore, because most questionnaire research is correlational, causal attributions are, for the most part, inappropriate.

TYPES OF QUESTIONNAIRES

Most questionnaires are composed of numerous questions and statements. Statements are frequently used to determine the extent to which respondents agree or disagree with a given thought, concept, or perspective. Questions may be of two general types: free response and response selection. The chief advantage of response-selection questions is that responses may be easily keypunched or transferred to computer files via optical scanners for data-analytic purposes. Answers to free-response questions, on the other hand, first must be categorized, scored, and coded. Also, respondents may find the work required of them to detail their answers in writing laborious and therefore choose not to respond, or to give short, largely inadequate responses.

CONSTRUCTING A QUESTIONNAIRE

A number of steps are involved in performing a study involving a questionnaire. These steps may include the following:

1. Specifying the objectives of the study
2. Designing the questionnaire itself
3. Drafting the questionnaire
4. Editing the questionnaire
5. Developing instructions for administering the questionnaire
6. Pretesting the questionnaire
7. Revising the questionnaire
8. Developing a sampling plan for administering the questionnaire
9. Executing the survey/data collection
10. Analyzing the data
11. Reporting the results

For the sake of brevity, only the first six of these steps are mentioned here. It is essential that goals of the study be carefully detailed; such work may lead to the elimination of unnecessary items from the questionnaire and result in a higher response rate. These objectives are then operationalized in an outline of the questionnaire. T. J. Bouchard reported that there are various "rules of thumb" based on both research evidence and experience that may improve the decision making at this stage. These suggestions include involving the respondent population in as many stages of the construction process as possible; avoiding ambiguity at all costs; limiting questions to a single idea; keeping items as short as possible; writing questions using a level of language appropriate for the respondent population; wherever possible, using response-selection questions rather than free-response questions; and implementing procedures to reduce the influence of social desirability and other response sets. Editing should be performed by specialists in questionnaire construction as well as by members of the respondent population. In addition, "readability" checks can ensure that the wording is appropriate to the educational level of the respondents. The ordering of questions within the survey is important and must be performed with care.

Both introductions and instructions are advisable. If the survey is to be returned in the mail, a stamped, addressed envelope should be included.

Pretesting the questionnaire is essential. Interviews with or written comments from these respondents may highlight potential difficulties that can be avoided.

Data-analytic issues cannot be detailed in a brief recitation. However, analyses used for other psychological measures (interitem correlations, reliability and validity studies) are frequently appropriate for questionnaires.

Achieving an adequate and unbiased sample is perhaps the biggest problem in questionnaire research. The nonresponse problem is twofold. First, many individuals do not respond to surveys. Furthermore, these nonrespondents frequently differ from respondents. Strategies to increase return rates help: appeals and offers of small rewards, for example. Another strategy is to interview a random sample of nonrespondents.

K. F. GEISINGER

RACE BIAS IN TESTING

Race bias in testing represents the most common form of the cultural test bias hypothesis, which is the contention that racial and ethnic group differences in mental test scores are the result of inherent flaws in the tests themselves. Mean differences in scores among races are then interpreted as artifacts of the test and not as reflecting any real differences in mental abilities or skills.

Mean differences in mental test scores across race are some of the most well-established phenomena in psychological research on individual differences. The primary explanations of these differences are that they are produced by people who are reared in very different environments, with lower scoring groups having been relatively deprived as to the quantity and quality of stimulation received in the formative years, or, alternatively, that lower scoring groups reflect a difference in the genetic potential for intellectual performance. Most contemporary views take an environment X genetic interaction approach. Although race bias in testing has existed as a potential explanation at least since it was raised by Cyril Burt, with occasional papers on the issue appearing over the years, it was not widely accepted as a serious hypothesis until the late 1960s, when the Association of Black Psychologists (ABP) called for a moratorium on the use of psychological tests with minorities and disadvantaged students.

These actions by the ABP had several very positive effects. Prior to the call for a moratorium on testing of minorities, little actual research existed in the area. Much research was prompted by the ABP position as it brought the race bias hypothesis to the forefront of explanations of race differences in intelligence. Also in response to this call for a moratorium, the American Psychological Association Board of Scientific Affairs had a committee appointed to study the use of tests with disadvantaged students.

Research on race bias in testing was, and continues to be, of major importance to psychology as well as to society. The cultural test bias hypothesis is probably one of the most crucial scientific questions facing psychology today. If this hypothesis ultimately is accepted as correct, then the past 100 years or so of research in the psychology of individual differences must be dismissed as artifactual, or at least as confounded, since such research is based in standard psychometric methodology. Race bias in testing also is being tested in the judicial courts, not just in the scholarly court of open inquiry. Two major court decisions have given conflicting opinions regarding the issues.

Contrary to the position of the late 1960s, considerable research is now available regarding race bias in testing. For the most part, this research has failed to support the test bias hypothesis, revealing that (a) well-constructed, well-standardized educational and psychological tests predict future performance in an essentially equivalent manner across race for U.S.-born ethnic minorities; (b) the internal psychometric structure of the tests is essentially invariant with regard to race; and (c) the content of these tests is about equally appropriate across these groups.

Race bias in testing is one of the most controversial and violently emotional issues in psychology and will not be resolved entirely on the basis of research and data, as tests have unquestionably been abused in their past use with minority groups. Special consideration thus must be given to ensure that the misuse and abuse of the past are thwarted by "intelligent testing."

CULTURE FAIR TESTS
HERITABILITY
RACIAL DIFFERENCES

C. R. REYNOLDS

RACIAL DIFFERENCES

Classifications from Linnaeus onward distinguished between "races" if members of groups could be distinguished from one another with a high degree of accuracy. To be distinguished reliably requires that races differ from others in the incidence of alleles of some genes influencing observable attributes. This criterion can be met with regard to the major subgroups of humanity. One commonly used categorization of races is Caucasoid, Mongoloid, and Negroid. Other, more refined, differentiations of humanity include Garn's nine races and Lewontin's seven major races.

All people, regardless of race, share a common evolutionary history. It seems highly improbable that selection varied much across groups. All humans faced the same general variety of problems for nearly all of their evolutionary history. About 6% of the genetic diversity of humankind is accounted for by race membership, 8% by differences across populations within racial groups, and over 85% between individuals of the same populations within racial groups.

In the Western world, racial categorization is often based on skin color. However, Charles Darwin cogently remarked long ago, "Color is generally esteemed by the systematic naturalist as unimportant." Other differences, such as morphology, physiology, and behavior, are considered more important.

Physical differences may result from natural selection, basically through adaptive evolution. For example, most groups from the high Arctic are short and broadly built. This type of body results in a good deal of weight for the amount of surface area and, in consequence, there is low caloric loss from the maintenance of body temperature. However, the tall, lean, long-legged tribesmen of the Sudan, who maintain the same body temperature as the Eskimo, but inhabit a very hot and humid environment, have evolved a body build in the direction of maximum surface area to weight. This body type is best suited to dissipate the heat that otherwise would raise body temperature beyond the normal level.

Other physical differences among groups may result from nonadaptive, neutral evolutionary changes across groups. For most of the history of humanity, people lived in small breeding populations (dernes) in which chance variation in the gene pool provided by the founders of the deme became fixed attributes of their descendants. Mutations occurring within a deme, if adaptive, would spread within the deme, then to closely contiguous demes, but probably not to physically distant groups.

In the area of metabolic/physiology, sickle cell anemia is a good example of how genetic influences on race differences can be interpreted. Sickle cell anemia is found among West African blacks. Since the ancestors of American blacks resided in West Africa, this disorder is found among American blacks as well. Afflicted individuals have a foreshortened life expectancy. Why is the frequency of sickle cell anemia so high in certain groups? Allison discovered that persons who are heterozygous on the sickling gene pair (one member of the gene pair producing sickling, the other not) are quite resistant to malaria. Persons with two "normal" genes are at substantially greater risk of malaria, persons with two "sickling" genes develop anemia, and heterozygotes are at far lesser risk for either disorder. This "balanced polymorphism" has developed independently—presumably through selection of chance mutations—in a number of different racial/ethnic groups in malaria-infested regions. The various types of anemia resulting from sickle celling are not genetically the same across racial/ethnic groups, but all have the same basis—a heterozygote advantage.

While all of the data are not yet in, such reports serve as a cautionary note: Although race differences may exist, the bases of these differences require thorough investigation. Supposed genetic differences may be chiefly, or solely, environmental in origin.

It has long been known that American blacks score lower on intelligence (IQ) tests than do American Whites. However, persons of Asian ancestry have been reported to score higher on IQ tests than the Whites on which these tests, for the most part, were standardized. The question, at least with regard to Black–White differences, is not whether differences in test scores exist, but what might be the causes of these differences.

The IQ controversy was revived after a period of quiescence following Arthur Jensen's article. While Jensen accurately reported data available to him regarding within-group heritability, later research suggests that within-group differences are under substantially less genetic control than indicated by Jensen. In addition, Hirsch and others pointed out that even if within-group differences have a genetic basis, these differences really have no relevance when assessing the degree of genetic influence on differences among groups.

A paper by DeFries et al. is particularly germane since it shows differences across generations of the same ethnic groups that are close to the magnitude of the difference reported between Blacks and Whites. Generational and sex differences were highly consonant with changes in status (e.g., parental education, occupation) that occurred across generations—a strong argument for substantial environmental influences on cognitive test performance.

Personality is more difficult to measure than intelligence. The results of personality tests, which assess ongoing characteristics, are potentially confounded with mood and the fluctuations in feelings and behavior. Racial differences in personality (e.g., aggressiveness, nurturance) may exist. These differences are usually believed to be solely attributed to environmental influences. However, this is probably an oversimplified view of the subject. Freedman and Freedman provided data indicating the existence of genetically based race differences in personality. Other evidence suggests that there is a genetic component of variation in personality within given racial/ethnic groups. Group differences may exist, although probably at the subgroup rather than the racial level.

The basic message of contemporary research on race differences is that race differences do exist and may have a genetic basis. However, differences between races are less than the differences within subgroups of races, and differences between races and also between subgroups of races (whether genetic or environmental or a result of gene–environment interactions or correlations) are basically trivial, as compared with the differences between individuals within groups.

CROSS-CULTURAL PSYCHOLOGY
HERITABILITY
NATIONAL CHARACTER

S. YUEN

RANDOM NUMBERS

Random numbers are numbers generated by a random process—one that generates each number in such a way that each of the ten digits $(0, 1, 2, \ldots 9)$ is equally likely to occur. In general, any specific n-digit random number sequence has a probability of one divided by ten to the nth power. Published tables of random numbers are readily available and appear as an appendix in most statistics books.

Psychologists use random numbers in a variety of ways. For example, a random sample can be selected by numbering the potential subjects in a population and using a table of random numbers to select the subjects to be included in the sample. Such a random process would guarantee a random (unbiased) sample, a necessary prerequisite for virtually all statistical analyses.

Random numbers also could be useful for assigning subjects to treatment conditions in an experiment, for selecting levels of a treatment or for empirically deriving sampling distributions of statistics by randomly drawing samples from a known population distribution.

PROBABILITY
STATISTICS IN PSYCHOLOGY

M. J. ALLEN

RANKIAN PSYCHOLOGY

The influence of Otto Rank on psychological theory and professional practice has been institutionalized to a much lesser degree than has that of Freud, Jung, or even Adler. This lack of institutionalization seems consistent with the individualized and antidoctrinaire character of Rank's writings.

DIRECT INFLUENCES

Rank regularly taught, in the 1930s, at the Pennsylvania School of Social Work, where he analyzed several of the faculty members, and he also lectured at two schools of social work in New York City.

Carl Rogers, in the early years of his therapeutic work, was influenced by Rank. His subsequent innovations in theory and practice, especially his reliance on brief therapy and his orientation toward growth and self-actualization, have been harmonious with the spirit of Rank's writings and may be seen as a creative development out of the starting point provided by Rank.

Ernest Becker has presented an explicitly Rankian psychology of the ills of human society. Instead of Freud's implausible attribution of human suffering primarily to sexual repression demanded as a precondition of culture, Becker attributes it to the insatiable quest for symbols of immortality, arising from the universal fear of death.

ANTICIPATIONS

Rank's theory of personality and therapy, it has often been noted, bears marked similarity to psychoanalytic theory and treatment of narcissistic disturbances. Rank's acumen, and his long acquaintance with narcissistic problems in himself, enabled him to anticipate—perhaps, to some degree, to help bring about—substantial broadening and improvement of psychoanalytic theory.

Rank's view of self-actualization as a dominant aim in a typical individual's life helped open the way for him to consider men and women with an attitude of complete equality. His own work thus avoided the male-dominated strain in Freudian thought.

Rank's acceptance of and respect for irrationality, and his orientation of therapy more toward experiencing than toward explaining, show great resemblance to major aspects of transpersonal psychology. Again, the relationship appears to be an instance of anticipation rather than direct historical connection.

I. L. CHILD

RATER ERRORS

Rater errors refer to mistakes made by raters when they use a rating scale to indicate the performance of an individual. The task competence of the rater, as well as the rater's sex, social position, race, religion, and age, have all been found to have effects on the rating given. While many of these errors are idiosyncratic, the following types of rating errors are common across many situations.

The *leniency* error occurs when average ratings tend to be higher than the midpoint of a scale because of pressure on the rater to rate subordinates high, a perception that subordinate rating reflects that of the rater, and the prescreening of students or subordinates before evaluation time. The effect of this error is to reduce variability between individuals. The harshness error is the same situation in reverse.

The *central tendency* error occurs when the rater checks the midpoint of the scale continuously. This can come about because of a hesitancy to "play God" or because extreme ratings (unsatisfactory or poor) require additional support and may have drastic effects on the rater's relationship with the subordinates.

The *halo effect* occurs when one trait affects the way all others are measured. Halo effect implies a positive generalization to other traits; devil implies a negative one.

The *sequential* error occurs when the particular order of traits has a special effect on the following ones, such as the halo effect.

The *logical* error occurs when a rater correlates specific traits in a manner believed to be consistent with the performance on others. The logical error is more complicated than the halo error.

The *recency* error occurs when an incident close in time to the rating has a greater effect on the rater than it would have had it happened much earlier. This is especially a problem when the incident is an emotional one such as a grievance, accident, or fight.

Rater errors pose special problems for the issues of reliability and validity. Furthermore, ratings that differ in time may accurately reflect a change in behavior even though this difference would demonstrate an artificial lack of reliability. High inter-rater reliability is a useful tool if both raters are knowledgeable about the individual being rated.

The problem caused by rater error for rating validity is the most serious problem of all because ratings are frequently used when a more objective measure cannot be developed. To the extent that rater errors exist, and are not statistically adjusted out, the validity of the ratings is seriously contaminated.

Many strategies have been developed to reduce the impact of rater errors. These include training raters, statistical adjustment for systematic differences between raters (e.g., leniency), and development of alternative evaluation strategies such as behaviorally anchored rating scales, ranking methods, forced choice, and the force distribution techniques.

HALO EFFECT

L. BERGER

RATING SCALES

In contrast to the items on a checklist, which require only a "yes-no" decision by the respondent, on rating scale items the respondent (rater) must make an evaluative judgment on some multicategory continuum. Introduced by Francis Galton in the last century, rating scales have been widely employed in business, industry, educational institutions, and other organizational contexts to evaluate various behavioral and personality characteristics. Such ratings are usually made by another person (e.g., a supervisor or peer), but individuals can also rate themselves.

TYPES OF RATING SCALES

On a numerical rating scale, the rater assigns to the person being rated (ratee) one of several numbers corresponding to particular descriptions of the characteristic being rated. A simple example of a numerical scale for rating a person on "friendliness" is to assign an integer from 0 to 4, depending on how friendly the person is perceived as being. Also illustrative of a numerical rating scale is the semantic differential technique, used extensively in studies of the connotative meanings of various concepts. Another widely used rating method is a graphic rating scale, in which the rater checks the point on the line corresponding to the appropriate description of the ratee.

On a standard rating scale, the rater supplies, or is supplied with, a set of standards against which ratees are to be compared. An example is the man-to-man rating scale, used for many years by the U.S. Army to rate officers on promotability. A man-to-man scale is constructed for rating individuals on a given trait, say leadership ability, by having the rater think of five people who fall at different points along a hypothetical continuum of leadership ability. Then the rater compares each person to be rated with these five individuals and indicates which of them the ratee is most like in leadership ability.

On a forced-choice rating scale, raters are presented with two or more descriptions and asked to indicate the one that best characterizes the ratee. If there are three or more descriptions, raters also may be told to indicate which description is least characteristic of the ratee.

ERRORS IN RATING

An advantage of the forced-choice rating method is that it does a better job than other types of scales in controlling for certain errors in rating. Two errors are giving ratings that are higher than justified (leniency error) or lower than justified (severity error). Other errors are checking the "average" or middle category too often (central tendency error) and rating an individual highly on a certain characteristic or behavior simply because he or she rates highly in other areas (halo effect). Raters may also make the contrast error of rating a person higher than justified merely because a preceding ratee was very low, or rating a person lower than justified because a preceding ratee was very high.

SCALING

L. R. AIKEN

RATIONAL–EMOTIVE BEHAVIOR THERAPY

Rational–emotive behavior therapy (REBT) (formerly rational–emotive therapy) is a theory of personality and a system of psychological treatment developed in the 1950s by Albert Ellis, an American clinical psychologist. It emphasizes the role of unrealistic expectations and irrational beliefs in human misery. Emotions, Ellis asserted, largely follow from cognitions not from events. The REBT *A-B-C* theory of personality holds that should an unfortunate event such as a family quarrel be followed by extreme anxiety or some other undesirable emotional consequence, in-quiry will disclose that consequence *C* was caused not by activating event *A* but rather by some irrational belief or beliefs *B* about the nature or meaning of the quarrel, such as "I am an awful person" or "They are awful and should be punished" or "Without their approval, I cannot go on."

Ellis traces the origins of this discovery about the nature of human upset back nearly 2000 years to the writing of the later Stoics, Epictetus and his disciple, Marcus Aurelius, emperor of Rome, who wrote, "It is not this thing which disturbs you, but your own judgment about it" (A.D. second century). "Take away the opinion and there is taken away the complaint." However, REBT seeks not only to overcome disturbances caused by false beliefs but also to ameliorate the human predisposition toward crooked thinking that permits false beliefs to flourish. REBT theory, therefore, considers emotional disturbance in the light of human nature, which is viewed as having both biological and social aspects of great significance for theories of personality and treatment.

BIOLOGICAL ORIGINS OF PERSONALITY

The lowest organisms may show complex behavior in the apparent absence of learning because of genetic preprogramming or instinct. Such behaviors tend to be found in all members of a species and are performed in fixed stereotypical ways. Humans are largely lacking in fixed, instinctive behaviors, but instead possess a highly evolved capacity to acquire new behaviors through learning and to retain them through habit. What is preprogrammed in humans is the clear predisposition to learn and form habits. Thus, *what* one learns to speak depends on culture, but *that* one learns to speak reflects a powerful predisposition to acquire language. Rational–emotive behavior theory holds that such predispositions make some sorts of things more easily learned than others. Children easily learn the desire to be loved rather than hated and readily prefer satisfaction of a want to its frustration. The theory stresses that the capacity to learn includes the capacity to learn nonsense and that the predisposition to think is often the predisposition to think crookedly.

Among human predispositions with unfortunate consequences are tendencies to become overwhelmed by events, to acquire desires for obviously hurtful things, to shed even grotesquely inappropriate habits only with great difficulty, and to think in terms of absolutes that distort even relatively accurate beliefs into disturbingly inaccurate ones.

SOCIAL ORIGINS OF PERSONALITY

Ellis found many faulty cognitions that appear throughout Western culture. Among these are the belief that to have value one must be loved or approved of by virtually everyone and, similarly, that one must be perfectly competent and productive and that it is a catastrophe when things go other than the way one wishes them to. In each instance, the irrational belief is absolutistic and establishes impossible expectations. Thus, while people tend by nature to be happiest when their interpersonal relationships are best, most emotional disturbances result from caring too much about the opinions of others and from holding catastrophic expectations about the consequences of breached relationships.

PERSONALITY AND DISTURBANCE

Rational–emotive behavior theory regarding the biosocial origins of the predisposition to irrational thinking and emotional upsets holds that *because we are human,* it is easy to learn to disturb ourselves and very hard to stop. Accordingly, REBT devotes considerable attention to the mechanisms by which disturbance is perpetuated, because it is by disrupting these mechanisms that change might occur. If thoughts are the cause of emotional upsets, then thinking is the means by which disturbance is perpetuated. The theory holds that regardless of where an irrational belief comes from or how it was learned, it is maintained only by use.

People disturb themselves and perpetuate their own misery through habitual internal verbalizations of their irrational beliefs. When confronted by an action or event that might fairly be called unfortunate, the person goes beyond an accurate, rational cognitive response to an exaggerated, absolutistic one that elicits emotional upsets and self-defeating behavior.

The theory finds in the human tendency toward self-reindoctrination a significant access point into the self-defeating patterns of thought and action of its clients: Eliminate the irrational thought and the upset dissipates. Eliminate the irrational thinking and the problem will not recur. People tend to be happier and more effective when they are thinking and behaving rationally.

REBT APPROACHES TO TREATMENT

Although REBT therapists may employ a wide variety of specific techniques in therapy, the intent is to minimize or eradicate irrational beliefs and to foster a more rational lifestyle. The therapist seeks to reeducate the client, to break down old patterns and establish new ones, using logic, reason, confrontation, exhortation, teaching, prescription, example, roleplaying, behavioral assignments, and more. The central technique is disputation, a logicoempirical analysis through which irrational beliefs are identified and challenged.

The initial goal of therapy is to help the client achieve three insights in the course of therapy. Insight number one is that while self-defeating behaviors and emotional malfunctions have understandable origins in the past and provocations in the present, their current and proximal cause lies with one's irrational beliefs and not with one's parents, history, or circumstances. Insight number two is that these irrational, magical beliefs remain in force only in consequence of the continued mixed-up thinking and foolish behaviors that actively reinforce them. People remain disturbed because, and for only so long as, they continue to reindoctrinate themselves. Insight number three is that insights do not correct crooked thinking. Only hard work and practice can do this. Of the process of establishing these insights, Ellis has said that the essence of effective psychotherapy is "full tolerance of the client *as an individual* combined with a ruthless, hard headed campaign against his self-defeating *ideas, traits, and performances.*"

Fundamental to REBT is a broad campaign to push clients to work against their major irrational premises. This work is done on several fronts. Because humans can think about their thinking, it is possible to use cognitive methods to show clients the flawed nature of their expectations, demands, and beliefs, and to teach them to think more rationally. The REBT practitioner mainly relies on cognitive methods, but emotive procedures also may be used that, through role playing and otherwise, may set the stage for the actual occurrence of irrational beliefs and their attendant upsets and behavioral tendencies, which can then be analyzed and corrected. They also may be used to counteract such beliefs at the level of demonstrations, as when the therapist, or perhaps the therapy group, accepts clients in spite of "unacceptable" traits or attributes. Emotive methods are also employed to evoke feelings and reactions leading directly to changes in attitudes or values. As an active, directive, educative approach, REBT also uses behavioral methods, both in the office and through homework assignments. Perfectionistic clients may be instructed to fail deliberately at some real task to observe the noncatastrophic nature of the consequences, or shy persons may be required to take progressively larger risks in social settings to learn that failure is neither inevitable nor intolerable. Once clients begin to behave in ways that challenge their major behavioral beliefs, they are encouraged to continue to do so, because actions may in fact speak louder than words in maintaining change. Ellis observed that "humans rarely change and keep disbelieving a profoundly self-defeating belief unless they *act* against it."

REBT has continuously evolved and grown since its inception in the 1950s. Along the way, Ellis has twice changed the name from its original designation as rational therapy (RT). In part, the name changes were educative, intended to identify, first REBT's cognitive nature, then later to emphasize also the role of emotion in thinking and emotive methods to treatment. From 1961 through 1992, REBT was known by the now familiar title of rational–emotive therapy. But REBT has also included a behavior emphasis from the beginning, which now has been incorporated into its current "full title." In part, the name change also may reflect gradual changes in emphasis and scope. Ellis discusses his reasons for preferring REBT to RET in *Current psychotherapies.*

By whatever name it is known, REBT often incorporates cognitive, emotive, and behavioral elements within a single complex intervention. Regardless of the methods used, the goal remains constant: to help clients to foster their "natural human tendencies to gain more individuality, freedom of choice and enjoyment," and to help them discipline themselves against their "natural human tendencies to be conforming, suggestible and unenjoying."

**COGNITIVE BEHAVIOR THERAPY
MILL'S CANONS
PERSONALITY THEORY
PSYCHOTHERAPY**

R. E. ENFIELD

RATIONALISM

Rationalism is the philosophical position that emphasizes the faculty of reason as the primary guide for determining truth. It can be contrasted with empiricism, which holds that experience is necessary to gain knowledge. For the rationalist, ideas are innate; for the empiricist, ideas are acquired.

The impact of the rationalist movement on science can be noted early on in the deductive geometry developed by the Pythagoreans and Aristotle's formalized rules of logic. Today, rationalism continues to be influential in fields such as mathematics and has been espoused by thinkers such as Jules Poincaré, who argued that the concept of number is purely intuitive and cannot be apprehended on an empirical basis. Others take an even more fundamental position, maintaining that even the rules of inductive science rest on underlying rationalistic assumptions. For example, Alfred North Whitehead pointed out "that the very baffling task of applying reason to elicit the general characteristics of the immediate occasion, as set before us in direct cognition, is a necessary preliminary if we are to justify induction."

As far as modern science is concerned, a purely rationalistic approach to problem solving has been eroded by two considerations. First, the history of science has amply demonstrated that the scientific endeavor involves making observations, venturing predictions, and checking to determine whether results are in accord with theory. Patently, insofar as science depends on gathering facts, it is empirical, not strictly rational. It must be acknowledged that Descartes' grand design for deriving all knowledge from a few irrefutable ideas was an abject failure. The role of experience in verifying and correcting postulates seems necessary for scientific advancement. The test of truth is evidential, and the appeal is to facts not to inherent knowledge. Laws must be confirmed by the senses, not by reason alone.

Second, rationalistic certainty has been assailed in its citadel, mathematics, where it has been demonstrated by Kurt Gödel that logical consistency cannot be proved for nondenumerable sets. That is, the rules of mathematics cannot be guaranteed on rational grounds alone.

Psychology, in its desire to be scientific has eschewed dyed-in-the-wool rationalistic explanations, except for the periphery of the discipline where religious and existential assumptions about the nature of humanity and the meaning of life sometimes take on a strong rationalistic coloring. For example, Sartre's psychology, based on a closely reasoned analysis of the consequences of the relationships between the "in itself" and the "for itself," revealed a strongly rationalistic strain. Given certain self-evident intuitions, Sartre argued deductively to explain the development of personality and psychopathology in the individual.

Psychologists have attempted to confirm theory through observation, regardless of whether the data are based on introspective reports or direct observations of overt behavior. The impact of rationalism on modern psychology, therefore, is usually detectable only in modified form.

Titchener, one of the leading exponents of Introspectionism, understood mind to mean "simply the sum total of mental processes experienced by the individual during his lifetime." The study of psychology for Titchener consisted of asking subjects to report what was taking place in their minds under various situations and conditions. He believed, as did other introspectionists, that there were three classes of mental elements: sensations, images, and feelings. This tripartite division of mental experiencing would seem to qualify as a largely rational conclusion arrived at introspectively.

Another example of the rationalistic influence on psychological theory is Maslow's motivational approach, which established a hierarchy of values under the presupposition that lower needs must be assuaged before higher needs can be satisfied. The hierarchy itself appears to have been devised intuitively, and its appeal is mostly rational. Presumably, any reasonable person would agree with this ordinal arrangement of human needs.

The influence of rationalism also can be detected in one of psychology's bread-and-butter enterprises, the construction of personality inventories. Burisch discussed three basic approaches to test construction: external (empirical, criterion group), inductive (internal, internal consistency, itemetric), and deductive (rational, intuitive, theoretical). The deductive or rational method is espoused by psychologists who "believe that one can construct a scale for any personality trait for which there is a name in everyday language." That is, there is a presumption that reason will permit the rational test builder to decide what kind of items are likely to measure a given personality characteristic.

It should be noted that rational analysis also can be applied to areas that normally are considered to be outside the realm of scientific inquiry. How do we know what is "good" or what is "ethical"? The rationalists believe that at least some questions of ethics or value cannot be scientifically addressed but are nevertheless meaningful from a philosophical point of view. For example, Moore distinguished between instrumental good, which can be studied scientifically because it has consequences, and intrinsic good, which deals with concepts that are ultimately simple and cannot be operationally defined. The rationalists maintain, therefore, that reason holds sway in answering questions regarding inherent value.

EMPIRICAL RESEARCH METHODS
EMPIRICISM
LOGICAL POSITIVISM
OPERATIONALISM
POSITIVISM

E. E. Wagner

REACTANCE THEORY

People frequently react against attempted restrictions on their behavior. J. W. Brehm proposed that such oppositional behaviors can be understood as manifestations of a single motivational state—to restore a freedom that has been threatened or eliminated. Subsequent work on reactance theory has demonstrated considerable empirical support for the theory

and extended its range of applicability to a wide variety of psychological issues.

OVERVIEW OF THE THEORY

Psychological reactance is the motivational state aroused when an individual perceives that a specific behavioral freedom is threatened with elimination or is eliminated. When reactance motivation is aroused, the person desires to restore the threatened or eliminated freedom.

The theory asserts that every individual possesses a finite number of specific behavioral freedoms. A behavior is considered to be free if the individual is currently engaging in it, and/or expects to be able to engage in it in the future. "Behavior" in its broadest sense refers to emotions, attitudes, and beliefs as well as overt acts. This notion of perceived, specific freedoms is to be distinguished from ideas concerning freedom as a general state. Reactance theory does not assume any need or desire for freedom *per se*.

Any event that makes it more difficult for a person to exercise a freedom constitutes a threat to that freedom. Sometimes, of course, events will occur that make it impossible to exercise a freedom. In such cases, the freedom has been eliminated. Threats to freedom typically should produce reactance arousal. Eliminations of freedom, however, should only produce reactance arousal initially. Once the individual perceives that the elimination of a freedom is irrevocable, reactance arousal also should be eliminated.

In general, the more important the freedom and the greater the number of freedoms threatened, the greater will be the reactance aroused. Reactance arousal is also determined by the magnitude of the threat. Some threats pose but a minor difficulty to be overcome to exercise the freedom, some pose considerable difficulty, and some eliminate the possibility of exercising the freedom.

The most direct behavioral effect of reactance arousal is action to restore the threatened or eliminated freedom. Two counterforces, however, will reduce such attempts at direct freedom restoration. First, as the magnitude of pressure to comply increases, both reactance arousal and the motive to comply by relinquishing the freedom will increase. Moreover, there will be some situations in which the freedom to engage in the behavior is not irrevocably eliminated, but where costs of direct restorative action are sufficiently high to prevent direct opposition.

These two counterforces both act to reduce or eliminate direct restorative action, but their internal psychological consequences are quite different. Compliance motives counteract reactance arousal to determine the resulting behavioral tendency. Costs of direct opposition, however, should act mainly as a suppressor of overt action. Given a chance to restore freedom without incurring prohibitively high costs, the person should do so.

REPRESENTATIVE RESEARCH

Communicator Attractiveness

A study by J. W. Brehm and Mann found that subjects who believed that their individual judgments on a group task were highly important and who were pressured to change these judgments by a highly attractive group experienced considerable reactance arousal and tended to move in the direction opposite to the position advocated by the group.

Hostility

Worchel found that denying subjects their expected freedom of choice in regard to selecting one of three gift items for themselves created considerably more hostility than did either disconfirming their expectation of receiving the most attractive alternative or simply giving them a less attractive alternative in the absence of any expectancies. These results indicate the significant role of reactance arousal in generating hostility when important anticipated freedoms are arbitrarily eliminated.

ATTRIBUTION THEORY

S. S. BREHM

REACTION TIME

The measurement of reaction time (RT) is probably the most venerable subject in empirical psychology. It began in the field of astronomy, in 1823, with measurements of individual differences in the speed of perception of a star's transit across the hairline in a telescope. These measurements were called the personal equation and were used to correct astronomical timings for differences between observers. The term *reaction time* was introduced in 1873 by Sigmund Exner, an Austrian physiologist.

In psychology, RT has had a dual history. Each branch can be traced back to the latter half of the nineteenth century, and Cronbach has referred to them as "the two disciplines of scientific psychology"—experimental psychology and differential psychology. These branches originated in the laboratories of Wilhelm Wundt, the father of experimental psychology, and Sir Francis Galton, the father of psychometrics and differential psychology. In experimental psychology, RT was of interest primarily as a technique for analyzing mental processes and discovering general laws governing the mechanisms of perception and thought. In differential psychology, RT was of interest as a technique for measuring individual differences in mental abilities, particularly general mental ability, stemming from Galton's supposition that the biological basis of individual differences in ability is the speed of mental operations (along with sensory acuity and discrimination). These two branches of research on RT have been treated more or less separately in the literature throughout the history of psychology. However, the past decade has witnessed considerable cross-fertilization of the two fields, since researchers both in experimental cognitive psychology and in differential psychology have adopted the methodology of mental chronometry, or measurement of the time information is processed in the nervous system.

Research on RT cannot be explained without mentioning its specialized terminology for describing the essential features of its paradigms and methodology. In a typical RT experiment, the observer (O) is alerted by a preparatory stimulus (PS), which is usually in a different sensory modality than the following reaction stimulus (RS), to which O makes some overt response (R), such as pressing or releasing a telegraph key or a push button, typically with the index finger. The elapsed time between the termination of the PS and the onset of the RS is the preparatory interval (PI). It is usually between 1 and 4 seconds and varies randomly, so that O cannot learn to anticipate the exact moment of onset of the RS. The interval (usually measured in milliseconds) between the onset of the RS and the occurrence of R is the reaction time, also called response time (RT). In some RT paradigms, the O's R is really a double response with two distinct actions: (a) releasing a push button, and then (b) pressing another button that terminates the RS. In this case, the interval between the onset of the RS and the release response is the RT, and the interval between the release response and the response of pressing another button is the movement time (MT), also measured in milliseconds. (MT is typically much shorter than RT.) The apparatus for measuring RT and MT is generally quite simple, but the crucial aspect is the precision and reliability of the timing mechanisms. The older mechanical chronoscopes were fairly accurate, but they needed to be recalibrated frequently. In modern times, microcomputers with electronic timers make possible great accuracy and consistency of RT measurement; the O's variability from trial to trial is much greater than any measurement error attributable to the RT apparatus *per se*. Precise measurement of RT has proved valuable

in psychophysics, for the scaling of sensory strength and discrimination in RT units, and for providing an objective ratio scale with internationally standardized units.

From this simple RT paradigm other more complex RT paradigms have been elaborated, with the aim of distinguishing between the sensorimotor and the cognitive aspects of performance. The fundamental elaborations were introduced in 1862 by the Dutch physiologist Frans C. Donders, whose variations of the RT paradigm permitted measurement of the speed of particular mental processes as distinct from the sensorimotor components of RT. He is, therefore, properly credited as the father of mental chronometry. Donders distinguished three paradigms, which he labeled A, B, and C reactions: (A) simple RT (SRT) (i.e., a single R to a single RS); (B) choice RT (CRT), also termed disjunctive RT (i.e., two (or more) different RSs and two (or more) distinctive Rs), requiring O to discriminate between different RSs and choose the appropriate R from among a number of alternatives (e.g., different push buttons); and (C) discrimination RT (DRT) (i.e., two (or more) stimuli that O must discriminate) are presented in a random sequence, but there is only a single R to just one of the stimuli (designated by the experimenter), while O must inhibit response to the other(s).

The typical procedure on any one of these paradigms is a number of practice trials to ensure O's understanding of the requirements of the task, followed by a large number of test trials to ensure a fairly stable and reliable measurement of the RT. Because there is a physiological limit to the fastest speed of reaction (about 180 ms for visual and 140 ms for auditory stimuli), the distribution of an O's RTs is markedly skewed to the right. Hence the preferred measure of central tendency of an O's distribution of RTs obtained over n number of trials is the median, because it is less sensitive to skewness than the mean. A logarithmic transformation of the RTs is frequently applied, as the log of RT has an approximately normal, or Gaussian, distribution. RTs that are shorter than the best estimates of the physiological limit of RT for a given sensory modality are generally discarded as anticipatory errors. Another measurable feature of RT data is the *intra*individual variability of RT, measured as the standard deviation (SD) of an O's RTs obtained in n trials (labeled RTSD). It has interesting properties, both experimental and organismic, that are distinct from those of RT per se. More complex paradigms than SRT, such as Donder's disjunctive and discriminative reactions, obviously allow the possibility of error responses and hence the possibility of O's adopting a speed-accuracy trade-off strategy, whereby correctness in responding is sacrificed for sheer speed. Errors may be considerably minimized by instructions to O that emphasize accuracy as well as speed of response.

A central consideration in RT theory and research is that SRT and all of the more complex RT paradigms involve two sources of time, which may be categorized as peripheral and central. Duncan Luce, a leading researcher on mathematical models of decision processes, explains it as follows:

The first thing that simple reaction-time data seem to suggest is that the observed reaction times are, at a minimum, the sum of two quite different times. One of these has to do with decision processes, invoked by the central nervous system, aimed at deciding when a signal has been presented. The other has to do with the time it takes signals to be transduced and transmitted to the brain and the time it takes orders issued by the brain to activate the muscles leading to responses.

A basic assumption of mental chronometry is that information processing takes place in real time in a sequence of stages, and the total measured time from the initiation of a mental task can be analyzed in terms of the time required for each stage. This essentially follows Donder's subtraction method. But the assumption that information processing progresses sequentially in clear-cut stages has since proven rather too simple in many cases, because of parallel processing of information and interactions between elemental processes when additional processes are called for by increasing task complexity. Hence, statistical methods, such as Saul Sternberg's additive factor method, based on the analysis of variance, were devised to determine whether the processing stages are temporally discrete, overlap, or interact for any given task.

Some of the main experimental variables that influence RT are the nature of the PS and length of the PI, the sensory modality of the RS, the intensity and duration of the RS, the nature of the response, the degree of stimulus–response compatibility (e.g., spatial proximity of RS to the response button), amount of practice on the task, and the effect of the experimenter's instructions on the degree of incentive or motivation for quick-and-accurate reactions. Some of the organismic factors are the subject's age, intelligence, concentration on the task, finger tremor, anoxia (as at high altitudes), stimulant and depressive drugs (caffeine, tobacco, alcohol), physical fitness, diurnal fluctuations in body temperature (higher temperature means faster RT), and O's physiological state at a particular time of the day (e.g., recent food intake slows RT). In general, factors that slow down RT also increase RTSD. These organismic variables apparently have a greater effect on the central, or cognitive, component of RT than on the peripheral component, as inferred from their relative effects on SRT and CRT.

One of the more robust and theoretically tempting phenomena in the RT field that has been subjected to much investigation by experimental psychologists is the linear relationship between RT and the logarithm of the number (n) of choices or response alternatives in a CRT task. Although discovered in 1934 by a German psychologist, G. Blank, this relationship has been termed Hick's law, because of a seminal paper by W. E. Hick, which argued that the linear slope of RT as a function of the binary logarithm (i.e., log to the base 2) of n reflects the rate of information processing, measured as the amount of information processed per unit of time (e.g., 40 ms per bit of information). The reciprocal of the slope ($\times 1000$) expresses the rate of information processing in terms of number of bits per second. One bit (for binary digit), the unit of information used in information theory, is the amount of information that reduces uncertainty by one-half; the number of bits in a CRT task is the binary log of n. Hick and others have suggested neurological and mathematical models of the linear relationship between RT and information.

What might be called the Galtonian use of RT is seen in the study of individual differences, particularly in mental abilities, although RT has also been used in research in abnormal psychology (schizophrenics, e.g., have peculiarly slower and more variable RT than normal persons of the same age and IQ). In 1862, Galton was the first to suggest that the biological basis of individual differences in general mental ability (later known as g, the general factor in any collection of complex mental tests) could be measured by means of RT. Galton tested thousands of persons on visual and auditory RT as well as on a variety of other sensory-motor tasks. His measurements of RT, however, were based on far too few trials to have sufficient reliability to permit significant correlations with any external criteria of mental ability, such as educational and occupational level. (IQ tests did not exist at that time.) Other attempts near the turn of the century to demonstrate Galton's hypothesis were disappointing, and so the use of RT in research in differential psychology lost favor and the enterprise was prematurely aborted.

The RT research at that time was methodologically naive, and the reasons for concluding that there was no relationship between RT and intelligence were equally naive. These early studies were so extremely flawed by inordinate measurement error, restriction of the range of talent in the samples tested, inadequate and unreliable criterion measures of intelligence, and lack of any powerful methods of statistical analysis and inference that no scientifically worthy results could have been possible. The premature abandonment of RT as a tool in research on human

mental abilities was an historic case of what statisticians term a Type II error—acceptance of the null hypothesis when it is false.

A half a century later, with the invention of information theory, the development of experimental cognitive psychology, and the resulting conception of individual differences in intelligence as reflecting the speed or efficiency of elementary information processes, the Galtonian hypothesis was revived and examined anew. Around 1970, its time had come. Microcomputers with precision timing mechanisms, sophisticated measurement theory, and advanced statistical techniques of multivariate analysis offered advantages not available to Galton and his immediate followers. Since the 1970s, there has been an accelerating rate of published research on the relationship between RT and mental abilities, especially g. The majority of these studies have appeared in two psychological journals: *Intelligence* and *Personality and Individual Differences*. Some of the theory and empirical research is summarized in books edited by Eysenck and Vernon.

Unlike Galton and his early followers, modern investigators employ a wide variety of tasks, called elementary cognitive tasks (ECTs), in which RT (and often RTSD, MT, and MTSD) is the dependent variable. These ECTs differ in the number or complexity of their cognitive demands and are intended to reflect components of time taken for certain hypothesized information processes, such as stimulus apprehension, discrimination, choice, visual scanning of a number of items to find a designated "target" item, scanning of information held in short-term memory (e.g., the S. Sternberg paradigm), retrieval of information in long-term memory (e.g., the Posner paradigm), categorization of words and objects, and semantic verification of brief declarative statements. Although it is not possible here to describe the research on any one of these ECTs in any detail, the RTs obtained in every one of the them have shown significant correlations with psychometric intelligence, or IQ.

Some of the main findings in this field have been replicated with sufficient consistency to permit a number of empirical generalizations:

1. RT, MT, RTSD, and MTSD decrease from infancy to maturity and increase in later maturity and old age. The age differences are more strongly related to the central or cognitive components of these variables than to the peripheral or sensory-motor components.

2. Negative correlations between RT and IQ on single ECTs range between about -0.1 and -0.5, averaging about -0.35. The correlation is not a function of the speededness of the IQ test, and what is remarkable about these correlations is that the RTs were measured with ECTs that have virtually no intellectual content and bear no resemblance to the specific knowledge and skills called for in IQ tests. Apart from their sensory-motor components, RT and RTSD appear to be virtually content-free measures of speed and efficiency of information processing.

3. RT is more highly correlated (negatively) with the g factor than with other factors (independent of g) that constitute part of the variance of psychometric tests, such as verbal, spatial, numerical, memory, clerical speed, and specific factors.

4. Variability of the correlations between RT and psychometric abilities is related to the g loadings of the particular psychometric tests, differences in restriction of IQ range in the samples, and the degree of complexity of the ECT used for measuring RT, which is presumably a function of the number of different information processes involved in the task and the amount of information that needs to be processed to achieve a correct response.

5. There is an inverted U function of the relation between the size of the RT–IQ correlation and task complexity. RT tasks of moderate complexity show the largest correlations with IQ; further increases in task complexity invite individual differences in cognitive strategies, which are often unrelated to g.

6. RT is more correlated with IQ than is MT. The sensory-motor or peripheral component of RT, which is a relatively larger proportion of the variance in SRT than in CRT and other more complex forms of RT, is unrelated to IQ. Hence, given sufficient reliability of the RT measures, removal of the peripheral components from CRT and DRT by subtracting SRT increases their correlation with IQ.

7. RTSD (i.e., intraindividual variability in RT) is more negatively correlated with IQ than is RT itself. Besides a large proportion of variance that RT and RTSD have in common (which is negatively correlated with IQ), both RT and RTSD also have unique components that are negatively correlated with IQ. It is theorized that RTSD reflects errors, or "noise," in transmission of information in the nervous system.

8. Although correlations of RT and RTSD based on a single ECT are generally low (i.e., mostly -0.2 to -0.4), when a number of ECTs that involve different cognitive processes are used, their multiple correlation (R) with IQ (and especially g) goes up to as high as .70 (with correction for shrinkage); the size of R depends on the number of different ECTs included. The fact that the shrunken R based on a number of different ECTs is substantially greater than the zero-order r based on any single ECT suggests that IQ (or psychometric g) reflects a number of different information processes that are to some degree uncorrelated with one another. Persons differing in IQ also differ, on average, in the speed or efficiency of those brain processes that mediate the given ECT.

Edwin G. Boring stated in 1926 that "if the relation of intelligence (as the tests have tested it) to reaction time of any sort can finally be established, great consequences, both practical and scientific, would follow." Today there is no *if* about it: The relationship of intelligence to RT is now firmly established. Boring's prediction, however, remains to be realized.

ANTICIPATION METHOD
ERGO PSYCHOMETRY
PHYSIOLOGICAL PSYCHOLOGY
SENSORIMOTOR PROCESSES

A. R. JENSEN

READING DISABILITIES

Reading disability is a condition in which "reading is significantly below expectancy for both age and intelligence and is also disparate with the learner's cultural, linguistic, and educational experience." This definition does not imply any particular kind of causation.

Alexia means inability to read; it usually signifies loss of reading ability as a consequence of brain injury or disease. Dyslexia means partial (but usually severe) reading disability. Some writers use dyslexia broadly as a synonym for reading disability; others specify some form of central nervous system dysfunction.

The term *learning disability* is both more and less inclusive than reading disability. It is more inclusive in that a learning disability may relate to oral expression, listening comprehension, written expression, or mathematical calculation and reasoning, as well as reading. It is less inclusive in that it requires a severe discrepancy between achievement and potential and assumes a constitutional, neurological base. Also, it excludes cases primarily the result of visual, hearing, or motor disabilities; mental retardation; emotional disturbance; or environmental, cultural, linguistic, or economic disadvantage. Federal rules governing the classification of children as learning disabled were published in the *Federal Register,* December 29, 1977.

A group of professional organizations, dissatisfied with the federal definition, has sponsored the following definition: "Learning disabilities is a generic term that refers to a heterogeneous group of disorders manifested by significant difficulties in the acquisition and use of listening, speaking, reading, writing, reasoning or mathematical abilities. These disorders are intrinsic to the individual and presumed to be due to central nervous system dysfunction. Even though a learning disability may occur concomitantly with other handicapping conditions or environmental influences it is not the result of those conditions or influences."

About one-third of the school population is above average in reading, about one-third is in the average range, and about one-third is below average. The below-average readers divide up about as follows: About 2 to 3% are disabled learners; another 2 to 3% are mentally retarded; about 1% fall into other special education categories; about 7 to 13% are disabled readers; and about 20% are slow learners (IQs of 69 to 89) who are unable to maintain educational performance within the average range but are not low enough to qualify for special education.

Because of differences in the criteria employed and populations studied, definitive information on the incidence of reading disabilities is not available. National estimates range from a low of 1% in Japan to as high as 22% in Austria. Best available estimates for the United States are that 10 to 15% of school children have reading disabilities (including the disabled learners).

SUBTYPES OF READING DISABILITY

Since the beginning of the study of reading disabilities, physicians (mainly neurologists) have postulated a basic constitutional condition of the central nervous system, often hereditary and usually accompanied by other difficulties in communication. In contrast, educational psychologists have tended to be impressed by a wide range of physical, cognitive, emotional, sociological, linguistic, cultural, and educational disabilities found in readers, and have tended to favor a pluralistic view of causation.

Those who believe that all or most cases of reading disability can be attributed to a single cause vary widely in their views of what that cause is. Among the causes suggested are heredity; minimal brain dysfunction; maturational lag, a slowness in specific aspects of neurological development; rivalry between the two cerebral hemispheres; perceptual–motor deficits; visual–motor deficits; verbal deficits; disturbance of the cerebellar–vestibular system; and deficiency in attention and concentration.

Recent research has stressed efforts to discover meaningful subgroups within the reading disability population. They have utilized a variety of research designs and have studied populations selected by the use of differing criteria. It is not surprising that the resulting subtypes vary somewhat from study to study.

There is substantial agreement that severely disabled readers include a large group with deficits in a variety of linguistic abilities; a smaller group with deficits in visual perception and visual–motor ability; a group with specific difficulty in sequencing, and a variable number showing mixed patterns and no special deficits other than in reading and writing.

The verbal group shares a common difficulty in the segmentation of words into phonemes and in blending or synthesizing sounds into words. Other specific difficulties found in some with verbal deficits include slowness in naming colors or objects, weakness in short-term verbal memory, and poor motor control for speaking and writing; difficulty in listening comprehension may be present or absent.

Gaddes emphasized the importance of tying the diagnosis of reading disabilities to what is known about adult alexia and aphasia. However, only a small percentage of reading disability cases show definite evidence of brain damage, and the diagnosis of "minimal cerebral dysfunction" is usually based on "soft" neurological signs and/or the results of psychological tests and is therefore somewhat speculative.

All of the recent studies report sizable numbers of cases that do not fit neatly into any of the identified subgroups. The percentage ranges from as low as 15% to as high as 70% in various studies. These are probably cases in which causation is to be found in health and sensory deficiencies, emotional complications, poor educational experiences, or deviant linguistic and cultural backgrounds. In clinical practice, cases with a mixture of constitutional and environmental disabilities are far more common than are pure cases of constitutional origin.

Diagnosing Deficient Reading Skills

As yet there is no clear evidence linking subtypes of reading disability with specific remedial procedures. Reading specialists should concentrate on educational diagnosis, using formal and informal tests of word recognition, decoding, oral and silent reading, and comprehension, to develop tentative teaching plans and then employ intelligent and observant trial and error to modify the program as needed.

TREATMENT

Corrective reading means special help given to a poor reader by a classroom teacher within the regular classroom setting. Sometimes the teacher is helped in diagnosis and corrective planning by a reading specialist on the school's staff. In many school systems, this is the only kind of help available to disabled readers, and it is often inadequate.

Remedial reading occurs away from the regular classroom, in or outside the school, and should be conducted by a teacher with special training in remedial reading (or by tutors supervised by a reading specialist). The International Reading Association publishes a set of competencies needed by reading specialists, and many states certify qualified teachers as reading specialists.

The recent emphasis on a psychoneurological approach involves a general trend to try remedial teaching first. However, it should not be overlooked that some disabled readers have emotional problems severe enough to require psychotherapy.

PROCESS TRAINING

During the 1960s, the extremely new field of learning disabilities placed major emphasis on process training—the use of procedures intended to improve basic abilities that underlie learning difficulties. It was widely assumed that once the basic abilities were strengthened, academic learning would improve.

Unfortunately, evidence accumulated that such training sometimes improved the target abilities but was usually highly specific; and improvement in reading and other academic skills was usually poorer than in control groups given direct academic instruction. While some learning disability teachers still stress process training, the trend has been to emphasize direct remedial instruction and to embed process training within it. Specific procedures have been developed for correcting a wide variety of specific reading difficulties.

OUTCOMES OF REMEDIAL READING

Follow-up studies have shown that when bright disabled readers were given enough high-quality remedial help to enable them to handle school reading assignments, many of them were able to complete high school, college, and even graduate programs.

LEARNING DISABILITIES
MINIMAL BRAIN DYSFUNCTION

A. J. HARRIS

READING MEASURES

Something readable is identified as legible, easy to read, pleasurable, and/or interesting. The assessment problem is a complex one; while most

agree on the need for quantitative measures of readability, not everyone agrees on the essentials of readability.

Widely used measures include the Dale–Chall Readability Formula, the Flesch Formulas, the Farr–Jenkins–Patterson Formula, the Fry Readability Formula, the Fog Index, the Lorge Formula, and the SMOG Grading.

The Flesch Formulas have served as a standard for validating most other measures of reading level. There are, however, several problems with these indexes.

Yet such formulas do provide a basis for comparing the absolute complexity of various samples of reading, if they are applied cautiously with awareness of their limitations. The two major problems with all reading formulas remain how to quantify easiness and how to assess human interest. The standard solution is to equate easiness with appearance on old (dated) lists of familiar words or brevity of individual words as well as the sentences they compose. Interest (when it is assessed) is usually equated with easily quantifiable measures such as the number (or percentage) of personal pronouns, proper nouns, and person-oriented words. Most measures are highly quantified, and their calculation is rather mechanistic. Their usefulness is largely determined by the rationality of the person who applies the measures, the materials tested, and the interpretation of the results with the limits of such measures firmly in mind.

FLESCH FORMULAS

R. A. KASSCHAU

REALITY THERAPY

The concepts of reality therapy, developed by William Glasser, were first published in 1965. While the principles have remained the same, the original ideas have been continuously expanded and refined. The latest major expansion has been to relate the concepts to the way our brain works as an input control system.

The theory of reality therapy is based upon Glasser's belief that all living creatures are driven by powerful needs that must be satisfied. Human beings, the most complex creatures evolution has produced, have the most complex needs: to survive, to become secure, to belong and love, to gain self-esteem and power, to have fun, and to be free. Although these specific needs probably evolved from the basic survival need, they are all equal in potency at this time in our evolution. If they are able to satisfy them, humans behave in ways to maintain or increase the resulting pleasure. But if they are unable to satisfy these needs, pain occurs and, paradoxically, people may behave in ways to maintain, or even increase, the pain even though the ultimate purpose is to reduce suffering.

Reality therapy is a psychological system designed to help people to satisfy their needs in more efficient ways. Because all are driven by the same needs built into genetic structures, the main differences between people are the degrees of effectiveness by which they are able to satisfy these needs.

Reality therapists care little about standard psychological diagnoses and they generally describe people by the general behaviors chosen to attempt to satisfy their needs.

Essentially two broad classes of people defined by their similar behaviors are (a) those who generally fulfill themselves and are successful and happy much of the time and (b) those unable to do so and who suffer much pain and failure. Those who fail are further divided into several groups. First are those who give up. Because of forces built into genetic structures, people who give up and stop trying temporarily begin compensatory behavior no matter how ineffective it may be. Second, some who attempt to give up find that they cannot do so. They then choose a wide variety of symptomatic behaviors, mostly painful and ineffective, but the best that they are capable of at the time. Examples are behaviors with powerful feeling components, such as anger, which lead to acting out, or depressed behaviors that lead to misery and apathy. Even though humans are usually not aware of it, these behaviors are chosen as their best attempt to fulfill their needs.

Addictions are chosen behaviors, attempts to gain pleasure, and can be divided into two groups: *positive,* in which addicts become addicted to the pleasure of a repetitive strengthening behavior; and *negative,* in which they become dependent on the pleasure of chemicals such as alcohol or morphine even though the chemical is almost always eventually harmful. Finally, there are psychosomatic diseases in which real tissue damage occurs. Some people begin to behave in so creatively aberrant ways that they are judged insane. To fulfill needs, the human brain acts as a control system, continually acting on the world in an attempt to fulfill the needs built into it.

Reality therapy is an attempt to help people take better or more effective control of what they choose to do with their lives—to choose better behaviors and, in doing so, better fulfill their innate needs.

PSYCHOTHERAPY

W. Glasser

REDUCTIONISM

Auguste Comte proposed a hierarchy of the sciences with mathematics at the apex followed by astronomy, physics, biology, ethics, and sociology. Although by present standards Comte's ranking is questionable, his intent is clear: The simpler the units of measurement, the more fundamental the science. Today a more accurate ordinal representation of Comte's notion might be physics, chemistry, biology, psychology, sociology, and perhaps economics. Reductionism can be viewed as the philosophical position that reduces complex phenomena to simpler and presumably more basic elements. For logical positivists, reductionism takes on an additional, technical meaning, namely the requirement that directly observed sense data be used as reference points for factual statements.

Reductionism appeals to those seeking harmony among the sciences inasmuch as all units of observation can be conceptualized as resting on smaller, more fundamental entities, ultimately regressing to the smallest building blocks of physics. If the billiard ball analogy illustrates the mechanist view of causality, then the hierarchical interdependence among the sciences can perhaps be pictured as successive agglomerations of building materials (e.g., sand, bricks, walls, houses).

Usually, reductionists have not insisted on a recursion to physics to satisfy the requirements of science but have been content to drop down to the immediately preceding level of explanation. That is, the biological reductionist might look to biochemistry rather than physics for explication. The point remains, however, that theoretically all phenomena depend on the activity of the smallest physical particles in the universe, whatever they may be.

The reductionistic philosophy in psychology is well represented by behaviorists who believed in the primacy of the physical sciences. Watson and McDougall, for example, asserted, "We need nothing to explain behavior, but the ordinary laws of physics and chemistry." Just as the logical positivists stressed definitions derived from the operations performed when relevant observations were made, some experimental psychologists also became "operational," defining sensations in terms of the organism's ability to discriminate (i.e., deriving all inferences from actual behavior). The behaviorist, then, typically rejected the mind, having accepted the reductionist assumption that behavior is the result of underlying physiological and biochemical laws.

Although the behaviorists usually assumed that neurological changes were taking place when behavior was modified, they typically observed behavior as behavior, leaving it to the physiological psychologist to establish the causal links between physiological changes and overt activity. Furthermore, some experimental psychologists distanced themselves from reductionist assumptions and attempted to put the "mind" back into psychology. Edward Tolman spoke of the formation of cognitive maps in maze-running rats and distinguished between the "molecular facts of physics and physiology" and the "molar properties of behavior acts."

Tolman's position introduced a discontinuity in the reductionist worldview, asserting that, in principle, analyses must be made at their own descriptive levels and explanations cannot be regressed to simpler elements. Thus four attitudes toward the reductionist position can be discerned: (a) all scientific explanations are reducible to the basic elements of physics; (b) all scientific explanations are reducible, in principle, to the basic elements of physics, but it is impractical to do so; (c) at least some scientific explanations are not, in principle, reducible to the basic elements of physics; and (d) each scientific discipline must maintain its own level of analysis and prediction and only physics is reducible to physics. The stance taken toward reductionism, therefore, affects not only the kinds of explanations that are sought out but also one's view of the interconnectedness among the sciences.

Some psychologists such as E. R. Guthrie and John B. Watson have been unequivocal in their endorsement of reductionism and have maintained this position throughout their professional careers. Others, such as Sigmund Freud, appear to have started out as reductionists but ended up modifying their views when faced with the enormous problem of trying to understand and change human behaviors as molar phenomena. As a neurologist, Freud set out to establish a correspondence between the brain and mental events. However, as Parisi observed, "Over the course of his career, Freud successfully detached himself from the presupposition that biology is primary." In fact, despite Freud's exposure to Charcot's view that hysterical symptoms were due to dynamic brain lesions during his sojourn at Salpêtrière, Freud was constrained to remark that "the lesion in hysterical paralyses must be entirely independent of the anatomy of the nervous system." Apparently, fairly early in his career, Freud's experience with patients led him to reject the reductionist position. He was confronted by psychopathology that was not directly attributable to brain malfunction and was, therefore, constrained to give up on a reductionist explanation.

The difficulty that Freud faced is continually being confronted by the psychologist who must respond to typically human questions. How can an anxiety reaction be "cured"? How can production-line workers be motivated? How can at-risk children be helped? Therefore, it is little wonder that for psychologists reductionism has enjoyed more success as an orienting theoretical position than as a prescription for action. When it comes to praxis, psychologists tend to be pragmatic rather than reductionistic.

BEHAVIORISM
HOLISM
LOGICAL POSITIVISM
MECHANISTIC THEORY
MOLAR-MOLECULAR CONSTRUCTS

E. E. Wagner

REEVALUATION COUNSELING

Reevaluation counseling is a self-help movement to deal with emotional problems. The basic tenet of reevaluation counseling states that when individuals experience emotional distress, part of their "intelligence" or energy is tied to the distress and so they are less able to function sensibly and rationally.

The recovery process involves "discharging," or thoroughly expressing the painful emotions during one-to-one peer counseling. When discharging is completed, the individual's "intelligence" or energy is no longer tied down to the distressing experience, so that the individual reemerges as a more aware and rational being.

Counselors are trained by experienced teachers through classes and workshops. Each counselor must also follow specific guidelines presented in the reevaluation counseling manual. Although reevaluation counseling is an innovative approach, published information is scarce and the impact of this movement is difficult to evaluate.

INNOVATIVE PSYCHOTHERAPIES

T. I. Moon

REFLECTIVE LISTENING

The term *reflective listening* refers to a way of responding to another person as a means of creating empathy. Empathy is widely believed to be an important element of psychotherapeutic interaction.

Rogers considers empathy a complicated way of perceiving, being with, and communicating with another person. Clark believes that empathy is a human capacity based on the most recently evolved part of the brain that acts as a counteracting force to egocentric power drives. Other writers point out that most of the research on empathy has been based on the verbal expression of empathy, and that this is not a direct measure of the degree to which the person is deeply feeling the meanings being expressed. They emphasize the importance of the bodily experience of empathy, which is difficult to measure.

R. Schuster elucidates several similarities in the attitudes of empathy and those involved in some types of meditation. Rogers cites evidence that a person's empathic ability is not associated with academic or diagnostic proficiency. Corcoran suggests that it may involve right-hemisphere brain function rather than left (dominant) verbal functioning.

Reflective listening has been examined and taught in other than therapeutic contexts. Thomas Gordon teaches it to parents as a means of maintaining open and trusting relationships with their children. Aspy and Roebuck found that more empathic teachers had greater student involvement in the learning situation.

Listening involves holding a set of special attitudes toward the person being listened to. There is an acceptance of the content of the person's awareness. The listener trusts the resources of the speaker to evaluate and analyze and decide about the situation, and therefore does not jump in with advice and suggestions about what to do or how to perceive things. The aim of listening is to be in the other person's perceptual world, not to fit the other into one's own perceptual world.

Related to this is an expectation that this way of being with someone does something useful for the other person. The expectation is that the person's feelings and ideas, in the process of being listened to, will change in a problem-solving, insight-producing, tension-releasing, responsibility-building, conflict-reducing way.

Eugene Gendlin's theories of personality change provide some theoretical basis for this expectation, and some clarification of this kind of listening process. His work clarifies the "object" to which the listener listens and the nature of the personality processes stimulated in this way. Gendlin defines the "bodily felt sense" as the basic stuff of personality. The bodily felt sense is more inclusive than what a person is clearly aware of consciously. It includes everything felt at the moment, even if only vaguely and subliminally. The bodily felt sense of the speaker is the fluid object to which the listener attends.

Listening involves making an interactional opportunity for the other to experience one's own capacity for solving problems, for identifying the part he or she contributes to interpersonal difficulties, for building self-esteem, for sorting out complicated personal concerns and motives. The familiar attitudes of evaluation and diagnosis and advice seem to have the opposite effect, that of stopping this kind of process.

Gendlin's work suggests that the listener helps the other extend, toward his or her own complex experiencing, the attitudes that were found to promote a change process. Empathic communication, when it occurs, is an intimate relationship event.

CLIENT-CENTERED THERAPY
EMPATHY

J. R. Iberg

REFLEX ARC CONCEPT

John Dewey's paper *The reflex arc concept in psychology* was published in 1896. Even now it is considered one of the classics in the development of the functionalist school of psychology.

In Dewey's own time, psychologists had taken over the physiologist's model of the reflex arc and adapted it to the study of psychological action. The sensory neurons were said to conduct the stimulus to the central portion where "ideas" or "central processes" were alleged to occur, which, in turn, programmed the motor response that followed. Dewey saw such an explanation as highly abstract and splintered.

In comparing the preferred reflex arc theory with such an event as a child seeing a flame and reaching for it, Dewey saw a comprehensive unity in which stimulus and response were phases of a common event, one in which "seeing and grasping have been so often bound together to reinforce each other, to help each other out." For Dewey, seeing and reaching guide each other throughout the event instead of occurring as three separate and successive acts as dictated by the reflex arc model.

Above all, Dewey seemed to be reaching for an interpretation of behavior in terms of an organism—stimulus object interaction. He was also veering away from an organism-centered approach to a broader view, one that no longer sought for an explanation of psychological events within the skin of the organism.

Another split that troubled Dewey was the contemporaneous cleavage of the organism into a body and a mind. In his paper on the reflex arc, he struggled to rid psychology of the ancient dualism. He suggested that, instead of treating body and mind as separate entities, we learn to view behavior as so integrated that it is impossible to split it up into two things. He did not consider mental acts as simply psychical events, but as acts in which both the physical and psychical interpenetrated.

HISTORY OF PSYCHOLOGY
MIND–BODY PROBLEM
SOCIOPSYCHOPHYSIOLOGY

N. H. Pronko

REFLEXES

A reflex is the central nervous system's least complex, shortest latency motor response to sensory input. The expression of a reflex is an involuntary, stereotyped act determined by the locus and nature of the eliciting stimulus. However, conscious control may be exerted over many reflexes. Reflexes may be elicited by stimulation of any sensory modality. There are many reflexes and an exhaustive listing will not be provided here.

Rather, the principles that apply to all reflexes will be described using a few examples.

The simplest reflex is the myotactic, or muscle stretch, reflex. This reflex can be elicited from any skeletal muscle but the best known example is the patellar, or "knee-jerk," reflex. The anatomic basis of the myotactic reflex is the monosynaptic (one synapse) reflex arc. This includes the sensory end organ, the sensory nerve fiber with its cell body in the dorsal root ganglion, the α motor neuron on which the sensory axon synapses, and the axon of that α motor neuron returning to the muscle from which the sensory fiber came. The sensory end organ for the muscle stretch reflex is the muscle spindle. The muscle spindle has muscular endings called intrafusal fibers and a central, nonmuscular region contacted by the sensory ending. The intrafusal fibers are innervated by the γ motor neurons of the ventral spinal cord. Higher brain centers may bias the stretch reflex through modulation of the γ motor neuron. The reflex is initiated by stretch on the muscle that increases the length of the muscle spindle and consequently the rate of action potential production in the sensory (afferent) nerve fiber. Increased activity in the afferent fiber increases discharge of the target γ motor neuron, causes contraction of the extrafusal fibers of the muscle from which the afferent originated. When the extrafusal fibers contract, the muscle shortens and afferent fibers become less active.

More complex reflex arcs also exist. These reflex arcs include the interposition of one or more interneurons between the afferent and efferent limbs of the reflex. The Golgi tendon organ reflex provides an example—the simplest polysynaptic (more than one synapse) reflex. The sensory end organ is found in the tendon. Increased tension on the tendon, usually produced by contraction of the muscle to which it is attached, is the eliciting stimulus that increases activity in the tendon organ afferent fiber. The tendon organ afferent fiber ends on an interneuron in the spinal cord. This interneuron inhibits an α motor neuron, thus decreasing activity in its efferent axon. Because this axon returns to the muscle to which the stretched tendon is attached, the muscle relaxes and the tension on the tendon is reduced.

The muscle stretch reflex and the Golgi tendon organ tension reflex work in concert to provide the basis for rapid regulation of the degree of contraction of the muscle. These reflexes are useful for quick adjustments to change in position of the foot as a person hikes across uneven ground. Of course other polysynaptic spinal reflexes are involved in locomotion. These reflexes incorporate many more interneurons. The divergent (from one neuron to several) and convergent (from several neurons to one neuron) connections of the interneurons form the basis of these complex reflexes.

An example of the action of these reflexes is provided by a person who steps barefooted on a sharp object and reflexively withdraws the injured foot. The sensory input is pain. The pain afferents enter the spinal cord and synapse on interneurons. Some of these interneurons excite α motor neurons that cause the flexor muscles of the affected leg to contract to lift the foot, but other interneurons serve to inhibit the motor neurons that supply extensor muscles of the same leg. This permits the leg to lift quickly and smoothly. Other neurons receiving pain input send axons across the midline of the spinal cord, excite the motor neurons for extensors of the opposite leg, and inhibit those innervating its flexors. This causes that leg to stiffen and provide support as the damaged foot is lifted. Furthermore, interneurons also relay information up and down the spinal cord to produce intersegmental reflexes that coordinate muscle contraction of the truck and upper limbs.

The spinal cord monosynaptic and polysynaptic reflexes form the basis for maintenance and adjustment of posture. Brain motor systems influence spinal cord reflexes via input to interneurons and the γ motor neurons. Thus, changes in spinal cord reflexes may indicate pathology in motor systems originating from the brain. The hyperreflexia associated

with trauma to the motor pathways of the lateral spinal cord or to damage of the motor regions of the frontal lobe provides an example of this.

Several optic reflexes exist. Examples of these include the direct light reflex, which is the constriction of the pupil to light. It requires an intact retina, optic nerve, midbrain, and third cranial nerve but not the lateral geniculate nucleus or visual cortex.

Reflexes also may be elicited by stimulation of sensory input from the viscera. The baroreceptor reflex is an example of such an autonomic reflex. An increase in blood pressure stretches receptors in large vessels near the heart. This increases afferent input to nucleus tractus solitarius of the medulla. Neurons in the nucleus tractus solitarius relay activity to the motor nucleus of the vagal nerve, as well as to the spinal cord and heart rate and blood pressure decrease. Voluntary control over this reflex is difficult to obtain, but the reflex may be conditioned using classical conditioning paradigms.

ACETYLCHOLINESTERASE
ELECTRICAL NERVOUS SYSTEM STIMULATION
ENDORPHINS-ENKAPALINS
NEURAL NETWORK MODELS
NEUROTRANSMITTERS
SENSORIMOTOR PROCESSES

M. L. WOODRUFF

REHABILITATION

Rehabilitation is a process aimed at achieving certain defined objectives for an individual who has suffered an injury, disease, or debilitating condition. Rehabilitation assumes that the person to be rehabilitated was once capable of functioning appropriately in the area(s) of debilitation, since rehabilitation implies the return to a prior state or capacity of functioning.

Rehabilitation as a concept is relatively new in human history. Scott Allan reminds us that most cultures used banishment or killing as the means of dealing with the disabled. Although we now espouse a much more humanitarian view of disability, many people continue to respond to the disabled with strong aversion. Thus it is often difficult to establish certain types of rehabilitation centers near populated areas because the community is concerned that the people in the center will adversely affect the community.

As Gerald Caplan states, successful rehabilitation programs should begin with prevention of disability. Caplan's model of three-stage prevention includes, first, education and alteration of the physical environment to prevent the occurrence of disease; second, early detection and treatment to prevent permanent disability; and finally, treatment and rehabilitation to prevent further deterioration and to provide as much restoration of function as might be possible. Rehabilitation centers focus primarily on Caplan's third stage of prevention.

The earliest work in rehabilitation in the United States was the result of private interest groups that perceived a problem in their community and sought a remedy. The Shriners, for instance, were formed to aid physically disabled children. At times, the rehabilitation effort was part of a larger reform effort. For example, the Salvation Army focused its attention on the destitute, and in particular, persons with drinking problems.

Physical and mental rehabilitation took on greater significance with the occurrence of World Wars I and II. As modern medicine increased in quantity and quality, the more seriously injured were saved only to become seriously disabled. This comparatively large body of disabled individuals needed to be returned to their community, thereby placing the United States in a difficult position.

The process of rehabilitation begins with the evaluation and treatment of the disease, injury, or condition itself. In addition, any deficit remaining after treatment must be evaluated as to its effect on the individual's social, psychological, and vocational abilities. The acute care of the condition focuses upon the injury or disease—the disability. Rehabilitation, in contrast, begins to focus on ability, either the abilities that remain or those that can be developed using residual capacity.

Many types of diverse services are offered under the term *rehabilitation center*. There are rehabilitation centers for most types of physical and mental conditions as well as for personality disorders. Rehabilitation centers for the physically disabled are probably the largest and the most interdisciplinary and comprehensive with regard to services offered. This is attributable to the diversity of skills needed effectively to treat the conditions present, as well as to the trend in medicine to use specialty services as a means of optimizing health care.

Centers aimed at rehabilitating specialized problem areas are more likely to be single-discipline units or to use the services of other disciplines as adjunctive treatment called in on request for limited treatment input. However, the more comprehensive the treatment approach, the more interdisciplinary the treatment team needs to be.

Programmatic offerings of rehabilitation centers need be specific enough to alter effectively the primary dysfunction of the client while broad enough to deal with the interrelated problems of the disability. On occasion, a service may not be available within a center. In such situations an appropriate allied health service facility is contacted to provide the specialized service needed. If such service is not available or provided, the overall rehabilitation effort is likely to fail despite the success achieved in the other areas of the center.

Rehabilitation center programs vary greatly from region to region, even for the same disorder. This is attributable to a number of factors, including financial considerations, size of treatment population, availability of professionally trained specialists, and community attitude toward rehabilitation. In addition, there is significant variation that arises solely because of disagreement among treatment specialists as to which treatment method(s) work best. In truth, it is likely that a variety of approaches work for a majority of those afflicted while certain specific approaches work best with one or another individual within a treatment population.

Staffing of rehabilitation centers usually includes a mixture of professional, paraprofessional, and administrative personnel. There is often heavy reliance on paraprofessionals, partly because of the financial considerations involved in operating such a facility. However, there is perhaps equal support for the use of paraprofessionals whose training in the field is having experienced the particular disability in question and, through various means, having been able to effect their own rehabilitation.

HEALTH CARE SERVICES
HUMAN SERVICES

R. P. KAPPENBERG

REHEARSAL

Rehearsal is the deliberate, or effortful, processing of information to retain it in memory. Rehearsal in the broader sense of repetition leading to some form of strengthening has figured prominently in the history of psychology. Before the beginning of scientific psychology in the nineteenth century, philosophers such as Alexander Bain and John Stuart Mill proposed that greater frequency of repetition resulted in stronger associations among ideas. Repetition also has been central to many modern theories of learning. For example, Clark Hull and B. F. Skinner conducted empirical investigations of relationships among the repetitions of behaviors and the frequency with which they were rewarded.

Since the investigation of cognitive processes in memory became a major focus of psychology, repetition has been studied in the form of deliberate rehearsal of materials to determine its role in retention. Many of these studies have explored the role of rehearsal in the retention of verbal materials, although there have been an increasing number of studies of rehearsal in the retention of nonverbal materials.

PIONEERING STUDIES OF REHEARSAL IN MEMORY

The empirical studies of Hermann Ebbinghaus investigated the relationships between rehearsal and a number of characteristics of verbal materials that are still of interest. Using lists of nonsense syllables (consonant–vowel–consonant trigrams that formed a nonword such as *vop*), Ebbinghaus found that as the number of syllables in a series increased so did the number of repetitions, or amount of rehearsal, necessary for one errorless reproduction of the list. Ebbinghaus also found that the more repetitions during original learning the greater the savings in time (and number of repetitions) when lists were relearned, 24 hours later, to the same performance criterion.

REHEARSAL AND SHORT-TERM MEMORY

One distinction between memory systems that should be considered in relation to rehearsal is that of short-term memory versus long-term memory. The existence of long-term memory is intuitively easier to understand because one can readily call to mind events that happened a long time ago.

However, the existence of short-term memory is less obvious. Imagine that you are in a telephone booth to make an important call. You have just called Information for the number, an unfamiliar one, and dialed it. The fact that you could remember the number long enough to dial it, a few seconds, was made possible by short-term memory. To continue with this scenario, after dialing the number, you hear an unwelcome sound, a busy signal. It is probable that the number would have been forgotten *unless* something else happened (i.e., rehearsal, during which you kept repeating the number to yourself). Information held in short-term memory long enough to use it may be forgotten unless it is rehearsed further. This suggests the following question: How long can information be held in short-term memory without rehearsal?

In a classic experiment designed to answer this question, subjects were asked to remember a single item (e.g., a three-letter combination such as *chj*). It might appear that remembering a single item is a simple matter; however, once the item to be remembered was presented, subjects were then asked to count backward for 3 to 18 seconds (the retention interval). At the end of this period, subjects were asked to remember the item. The longer the retention interval, the greater the decline in performance, and after about 12 seconds, items were seldom recalled. In effect, counting backward prevented the rehearsal of the item so that it was lost from memory.

In everyday life, people do not go around counting backward, but they do encounter distractions (other stimuli to which they pay attention). In the telephone booth, for example, someone outside might have gestured to you to hurry up. Even the busy signal itself could have distracted you so that you no longer rehearsed the number and forgot it. In other words, it was not stored in long-term memory. This suggests another question: How might one have avoided forgetting the number and transferred it from short-term memory to long-term memory?

MAINTENANCE REHEARSAL VERSUS
ELABORATIVE REHEARSAL

In considering transfer from short-term to long-term memory, one issue concerns whether there are different types of rehearsal that have differing effects on retention. According to one point of view, known as the levels of processing theory, the simple repetition of items, such as in the telephone number example, results in shallow processing. Such repetition has become known as maintenance rehearsal, generally thought to keep information available from moment to moment but not to result in more permanent storage in long-term memory. For this to occur, deep processing is needed, and this is brought about through a different form of rehearsal known as elaborative rehearsal.

Elaborative rehearsal is a process by which associations are formed between the new information and the already stored information. This deep processing incorporates the new information into existing patterns of associative linkages in long-term memory. If you had simply repeated the telephone number over to yourself as you waited to redial the number, you would have been performing maintenance rehearsal. However, if you had elaborated on the telephone number so as to associate it with something already known, such as a familiar street address or a date, then the new telephone number could have been integrated into information already stored. Had you made a deliberate effort to do this when you were first given the number by the operator, then you could have remembered the number at a later time.

Elaborative rehearsal can take many forms, ranging from the search for an associative link with previously learned information to the deliberate use of mnemonic devices or memory aids. In any case, the more associations that new information has with information previously stored, the more meaningful the new information is and the more easily it can be retrieved at a later time. However, other factors, such as the uniqueness of the information and its similarity to information already stored, will also influence ease of retrieval. Returning to Ebbinghaus, it is possible too that he was employing maintenance rehearsal rather than elaborative rehearsal, because he deliberately avoided any meaningful analysis of the material he learned.

IS REHEARSAL ALWAYS NECESSARY?

It would appear reasonable to assume that at least some form of rehearsal is needed for information to be stored permanently. Thus, the question "Is rehearsal always necessary for information to be stored in long-term memory?" would seem to require a straightforward affirmative answer. However, this seemingly simple question turns out to be not so simple at all.

Thus far, the focus has been on memory for forms of information, such as numbers or words, that do require effortful processing, either to be temporarily maintained beyond the brief time limits of short-term memory or to be stored permanently. However, it also is the case that one remembers a great deal of information seemingly with little or no effort. A person may remember exactly where to find a particular piece of paper among several chaotic piles in his or her office. Or, after encountering the same person several times during the day, a coworker might remark, "I see you so seldom but today we've met three times?"

These examples suggest the existence of a form of automatic processing that seems to occur most readily in connection with information such as spatial locations and the frequency of events. These examples of automatic processing fall within an emerging area known variously as unconscious or involuntary processing or implicit memory. In contrast with studies of explicit memory, in which intentional retrieval of information follows a period of rehearsal, implicit memory involves unintentional, nonconscious retention that seemingly does not require deliberate rehearsal.

FUTURE DIRECTIONS FOR THE STUDY OF REHEARSAL

Just as Ebbinghaus created a new tool for the study of rehearsal when he invented the nonsense syllable, other new technologies are at hand. One promising direction for future research is the cognitive neuroscience approach, which combines cognitive research with neuropsychological and neurobiological observations. Using a variety of technological advances, a number of studies have examined brain functioning during the processes of rehearsal and retrieval as well as exploring memory not only in normal persons but in those who have impaired memory functions, resulting from disease or injury. Such an approach promises to provide new insights into distinctions between explicit and implicit memory. As can be seen, exploration of memory without rehearsal is rapidly becoming a new frontier.

MEMORY
MEMORY EXPERIMENTS
MEMORY RETRIEVAL PROCESSES
MEMORY SPAN

F. M. CAUDLE

REINFORCEMENT

Thorndike's statement of the "law of effect" reads as follows:

The law of effect is that: Of several responses made to the same situation, those which are accompanied or closely followed by satisfaction to the animal will, other things being equal, be more firmly connected to the situation, so that, when it recurs, they will be more likely to recur; those which are accompanied or closely followed by discomfort [annoyance] to the animal will, other things being equal, have their connections to that situation weakened, so that, when it recurs, they will be less likely to occur. The greater the satisfaction or discomfort, the greater the strengthening or weakening of this bond.

With the development of reinforcement theory, chiefly at the hands of Clark L. Hull, the key terms in the law of effect, "*satisfaction*" and "*discomfort*," became positive and negative reinforcement. Positive and negative reinforcement are theoretical concepts just as Thorndike's satisfaction and discomfort were. These effects are created by the manipulation of more objective conditions, positive reinforcers (rewards, satisfiers in Thorndike's terms) and negative reinforcers (punishers, annoyers in Thorndike's terms). Whether the effect is positive or negative, reinforcement depends on whether the positive or negative reinforcer is delivered or withheld. Positive reinforcement may be produced either by the presentation of a reward or by withholding a punishment when a particular response occurs; negative reinforcement may be produced either by the presentation of a punisher or by withholding a reward when a particular response occurs. These four arrangements define a basic classification of types of operant conditioning: (a) *reward training*—food is delivered when the rat presses the lever in the Skinner box; (b) *active avoidance training*—the rat avoids electric shock by crossing to the opposite side of a shuttle box; (c) *passive avoidance training*—the rat receives electric shock if it steps down from a platform onto a grid; (d) *omission training*—the rat receives food only if it fails to press the bar in the Skinner box.

CLASSICAL CONDITIONING
OPERANT CONDITIONING

G. A. KIMBLE

REINFORCEMENT SCHEDULES

In operant conditioning theory, a behavior is maintained by its consequences, that is, by the reinforcing or punishing events that follow the behavior. The relationship between a behavior and its consequences is called a contingency. Reinforcement generally operates on an intermittent schedule of some sort. Skinner pointed out that reinforcement may be scheduled in many ways and demonstrated that subtle differences in scheduling can generate dramatic differences in behavior.

Four basic schedules of reinforcement have been studied in detail. Two are ratio schedules, in which the presentation of a reinforcer is contingent on the number of responses emitted by the organism. In a fixed ratio (FR) schedule, every nth response is reinforced. In a variable schedule (VR), responses are reinforced on a certain average ratio, but the number of responses required for reinforcement varies unpredictably from reinforcement to reinforcement. The other two basic schedules are interval schedules, which are defined by the length of time that must elapse between reinforcements. The first response to occur after this time has elapsed is reinforced. In fixed interval (FI) schedules, this interval remains constant from reinforcement to reinforcement; in variable interval (VI) schedules, the intervals between reinforcements vary randomly about some mean interval.

In addition to these four basic schedules, there are a number of other schedules, such as differential reinforcement of low rates of response (DLR), differential reinforcement of other behaviors (DRO), and various complex and concurrent schedules, which are combinations of the four basic schedules.

Each schedule has a particular effect on behavior. Ratio schedules generally produce high rates of response, and interval schedules produce lower rates of response. Variable schedules, particularly variable interval schedules, produce a remarkably stable pattern of behavior. Behaviors maintained under variable schedules are also highly resistant to extinction. This fact helps to explain why it is so difficult to extinguish undesirable behaviors, since most behaviors are maintained under variable schedules.

**OPERANT CONDITIONING
REINFORCEMENT**

R. A. SHAW

REINFORCERS

In operant conditioning theory, the likelihood that a behavior will occur is determined by the consequences of that behavior. A positive reinforcer is any contingent stimulus that increases the likelihood of a behavior; a negative reinforcer is any contingent stimulus that decreases the likelihood of a behavior. Negative reinforcers are sometimes called punishers or aversive stimuli. The likelihood of a behavior will increase if the behavior is followed either by a positive reinforcer (positive reinforcement) or by the removal of a negative reinforcer (negative reinforcement). Conversely, the likelihood will decrease if the behavior is followed either by the removal of a positive reinforcer or by the introduction of a negative reinforcer (both are types of punishment).

There have been many approaches to the definition of a reinforcer. One approach has been developed by David Premack. He noted that we can measure the amount of time an organism engages in various behaviors, and then arrange these behaviors along a continuum from those with the highest probability to those with the lowest probability. The essential feature of his theory is called the Premack principle: Access to a high-probability behavior will serve as a positive reinforcer for a low-probability behavior, and engaging in a low-probability behavior will serve as a punishing stimulus for a high-probability behavior. There is considerable evidence from empirical studies in support of the Premack principle.

In planning and implementing contingency management in practical settings, it is useful to classify reinforcers into various types. The first basic classification is between unconditioned and conditioned reinforcers, that is, between primary physiological reinforcers, such as food and water, and stimuli whose reinforcing properties have been learned, such as grades and money. One common system divides reinforcers into five types: edible, tangible, exchangeable, activity, and social. Donald MacMillan

suggests that reinforcers can be arranged along a continuum of maturity, with primary rewards being the least mature and a sense of mastery being the most mature. It is the responsibility of the teacher or therapist to lead the student or patient along the continuum to more mature levels of reinforcers.

**APPROACHES TO LEARNING
OPERANT CONDITIONING**

R. A. SHAW

RELATIONSHIP THERAPY

Relationship therapy refers to several different types of psychotherapy, each of which focuses on the relationship between the therapist and the client as the effective change element.

Buber sees the essence of human living in the "encounter" between a person and the other as direct experiencing (I–Thou) rather than as seeing each other solely as objects or reduced by the filters of social roles (I–It). Psychotherapy involves the authentic encountering of the other individual, as an antidote to the social and mechanistic objectifying of others.

Sullivan sees the human as an accumulation of the reactions he or she has toward other people. This collection of reactions ("reflected appraisals") forms the "self," an "envelope of energy transformations." Abnormality results from the tendency to respond in stereotyped ways to people for whom that response is inappropriate. Psychotherapy consists of exploration by the therapist of the client's significant life events, with a keen awareness of the emotional tone between the client and therapist. The emotional tone and any stereotyped responses ("parataxic distortions") made by the client that were unwarranted during this exploration (termed *inception* and *reconnaissance*) are noted and subsequently scrutinized in the "detailed inquiry" phase of psychotherapy. The essence of psychotherapy is the detailed examination of the client's life, which will reveal, during the interviews, the client's insecurities or anxieties. These will be seen in the interaction with the therapist, most commonly through various indirect communications (stuttering, "misused" words, silences, a gesture that is inconsistent with a verbal statement) and through the feelings the therapist experiences with the client. The latter occurs by a process of "reciprocal emotion," or the sensing of the other's needs, and development of patterns of responding to gratify or frustrate these needs. Psychotherapy examines these needs of the client and the anticipation by the client of such needs in the therapist.

NEO-SULLIVANIANS

Marshall Duke and Stephen Nowicki focused on three concepts. The first, complementarity, is when a friendly or hostile response elicits a similarly friendly or hostile response from another, while a dominant or submissive response elicits the opposite response, submissive or dominant, respectively. The second concept, congruence, refers to the degree to which one's statements reflect one's "true" feelings. Duke and Nowicki incorporate Rotter's social learning theory concept of "situation" to illustrate how complementarity and congruence operate over time in differing situations. Their third concept (multiphasic relationship) holds that congruence or complementarity may or may not be appropriate in a given instance.

Sheldon Cashdan views relationship as the medium for personality change through a five-stage process. His system uses object-relations theory to embellish the basic Sullivanian model.

Clinton McClemore and Phillis Hart focus on the development of intimacy through a course of psychotherapy that sees its climax in the "disclosure."

David Young and Ernst Beier, following the Sullivanian model, see the critical ingredient in psychotherapy as responding asocially to the client's stereotyped communications.

The Palo Alto group has influenced the practitioners of relationship therapy by specifying various behavioral sequences between people in individual, family, and group formats. Cultural (transpersonal), interpersonal, and intrapsychic sources of communications styles that lead to maladaptive interactions were identified by the Palo Alto group.

Other psychotherapies use the concept of relationship in one of several senses. Postel's primary relationship therapy, based on Adler's theories, focuses on those clients who have been parentally rejected, have experienced parental loss, and are restricted in emotional expression.

Various psychoanalytic and process theories could claim to be relationship focused, with such concepts as the "corrective emotional experience" or living in the "here and now" central to the curative core of treatment. Relationship therapy has been used generically to indicate the establishment of a supportive relationship with the client.

INNOVATIVE PSYCHOTHERAPIES
SULLIVAN'S INTERPERSONAL THEORY

A. K. HESS

RELAXATION TRAINING

In an age of high-level stress and anxiety reactions, it may be difficult to see relaxation as a natural body state. It can be understood more readily if it is noted that stress activates the sympathetic nervous system and reactions of increased heart rate, higher blood pressure, and rapid breathing, the so-called fight-or-flight syndrome. This reaction has had evolutionary survival value, but is less appropriate in our age than it was in prehistoric eras. The body also has an opposite reaction to bring it back within normal limits: The parasympathetic nervous system slows the heart and reduces blood pressure, and the breathing rate decreases. Relaxation training helps the parasympathetic rebound to occur, and thus avoids chronic triggering and maintenance of high-level sympathetic arousal.

Highly useful and effective in itself as a corrective to the stress-induced anxiety of modern living, relaxation is also used in connection with various other techniques: hypnosis, yoga and Zen Buddhism, meditation, biofeedback, autogenic training, and some modes of psychotherapy. A number of systems of relaxation are available, most of them evolving in some way from Jacobson's progressive relaxation system.

Progressive relaxation starts with one muscle group and helps the client progress through the other groups. The client lies in a comfortable position on the back, eyes closed, first tensing and then relaxing one set of muscles at a time, noting the feeling of tension and of relaxation. Separate muscle groups are worked on before proceeding to other groups. Because of the extensive time necessary for this process, many therapists have altered and shortened Jacobson's method.

To be effective, relaxation must be applicable to the places where clients meet the stress of their work day. They cannot always sit down in a quiet room and close their eyes to relax. Through practice, they must first bring those places into their imagination while they relax at home; and then gradually bring the home-practiced relaxed state into the workplace. Thus, the learning is transferred into coping with the real world.

Relaxation must be attainable within a reasonably short time to be effective in one's daily life. The actual practice periods can utilize 10 to 30 minutes to achieve a state of complete relaxation; but one must be able to relax under stress in the workplace within a matter of seconds, or else relaxation remains a means of resting on withdrawal from the world rather than a means of coping with the stresses of the world. This time element is dealt with by practice in becoming fully aware of the deep state of relaxation achieved morning and evening at home, noting all the dimensions of it, and then transferring that deep state to the point of stress within a matter of a few seconds. It is not a simple accomplishment; it requires much practice.

Also, it helps to engage in a number of "mini" relaxation periods throughout the day, taking advantage of minutes wasted while waiting or riding or that are otherwise relatively unoccupied. Differential relaxation is another helpful device: One cannot relax the entire body while working or otherwise active, but those muscles not immediately used can be relaxed. While walking, we can relax our arms; while at a desk, we can relax our legs.

Relaxation training is not indicated for everyone, nor is it a cure-all. The most likely clients are those with high stress responses that interfere with their lives. Insomniacs, clients with tension headaches, and those tense and tight with cases of "nerves" are among those who would qualify for consideration. Relaxing in the face of certain intolerable situations may be an inappropriate response. Asserting oneself or working for realistic change may be indicated. Setting aside regular times and working at relaxation with good humor are important.

Most relaxation training programs, once the trainee has gained proficiency in both tensing and relaxing the muscles, dispense with the need for tensing, and allow the person to proceed directly into relaxing at each session. Another mark of the proficiency of the trainee is the ability to transfer the learning from the therapy milieu to his or her daily life of stressful situations.

AUTOGENIC TRAINING
BIOFEEDBACK
HYPNOTHERAPY
MEDITATION

S. MOORE

RELIABILITY OF DIAGNOSES

The reliability of clinical psychiatric diagnoses has been an issue of great concern ever since Emil Kraeplin's early attempts at systematic classification of mental disorders in the late nineteenth century. Diagnosis and classification fulfill several important functions: (a) administrative, including statistical record keeping; (b) clinical, as an aid in indicating etiology, choice of treatment, and prognosis; and (c) research, particularly in those studies where psychiatric diagnosis defines membership in an experimental or control group or where diagnosis in general is used as the dependent or independent variable. The usefulness of a diagnosis for these purposes depends, in part, on its reliability.

Reliability of diagnosis refers to the consistency with which different clinicians will apply the same diagnostic label to the same individual (interrater reliability) or the consistency with which a single clinician will apply the same diagnostic label to the same individual on two separate occasions (test–retest reliability). Clearly, in any measurement or descriptive procedure, there exists the potential for some "error" in measurement. In the case of clinical diagnosis, such error may derive from many different sources, including a bored, fatigued, careless, or unmotivated observer; a subject with a limited memory or one who tries to conceal or distort information; a confusing or undiscriminating diagnostic rating instrument; and noisy or distracting diagnostic conditions.

Two major experimental methods have been employed to investigate diagnostic reliability. The first method examines the relative frequency with which different clinicians assign different diagnoses to apparently similar patients. Studies have shown that clinicians often have "preferred" diagnostic categories; that is, each tends to classify most clients in a limited number of categories to the exclusion of others.

The second method for studying reliability compares diagnoses made by two or more clinicians of the same client (i.e., interrater reliability). Ash's examination of the extent of agreement among two or three clinicians who interviewed clients jointly but arrived at a diagnosis independently suggested that the diagnosis depended as much on the clinician making it as it did on the client being diagnosed. Agreement on the major diagnostic category of clients (mental deficiency, psychosis, neurosis, psychopathic personality, and normal range) was 51% between two clinicians and 46% among three clinicians. But with more specific diagnostic subcategories, agreement between two clinicians occurred in 49% of the cases, and among three clinicians in only 20% of the cases. Another study used a much larger sample than Ash (*N*-153 instead of *N*-52) and controlled for the experience of the diagnosticians. The results, though improved, still indicated considerable disagreement.

Ward and colleagues attempted to isolate those factors that accounted for the disagreement in diagnosis among the clinicians in the Beck et al. study. Three major sources of error were found: inadequacies in the diagnostic system's categories (*DSM-I*), which accounted for 62.5% of the disagreement; inconsistency among diagnosticians, which accounted for 32.5% of the disagreement, and inconsistencies in client behavior across interviews, which accounted for only 5% of the disagreement.

Current efforts to improve the reliability of diagnosis are reflected in the new APA *Diagnostic and statistical manual* (*DSM-IV*). Extensive field testing on the ability of clinicians to employ the diagnostic categories in the manual were, for the most part, encouraging, with kappa coefficients of agreement among judges as high as 0.87—although, for some categories, results were significantly poorer than others. Further studies of the reliability with which specific diagnostic categories may be employed are underway.

CLINICAL AND STATISTICAL PREDICTION
CLINICAL ASSESSMENT
DIAGNOSTIC AND STATISTICAL MANUAL

R. D. FELNER

RELIGION AND PSYCHOLOGY

Why are some people deeply religious whereas others have no belief in God and never attend religious services? Why do some people become Presbyterians while others are Episcopalians, Pentecostals, Roman Catholics, or Buddhists? Why do some believers have highly emotional religious experiences while others experience religion as a "dull habit?" Why are some people comforted and helped by their religious beliefs while others are plunged into overwhelming guilt and self-condemnation? What is the role of religion in mental health, psychotherapy, value clarification, and moral conduct?

These are some of the issues that concern psychologists who study religion. Although many have attempted to define *psychology of religion,* perhaps no definition is better than that of Cambridge professor Robert H. Thouless. He wrote that the psychological study of religion seeks "to understand religious behavior by applying to it the psychological principles derived from the study of non-religious behavior." Although the psychology of religion sometimes studies parapsychological phenomena, the emphasis tends to focus on more traditional forms of religious experience, including prayer, conversion, mystical experiences, worship, and participation in religious communes and cults. Such study also raises issues of counseling, but the psychology of religion is more concerned with understanding religious behavior or experience.

Historically, the psychology of religion began with a great and productive burst of interest and enthusiasm near the beginning of this century, almost faded from existence during the 50 years following the birth of behaviorism, and more recently has reemerged as a legitimate and respectable field of study for psychologists.

Although he described religion as an "illusion," a "universal neurosis," and a "narcotic" he hoped "mankind will overcome," Freud nevertheless had a great interest in religious behavior and wrote several papers and three major books on the subject. Carl Jung, Alfred Adler, and others in the early psychoanalytic movement continued the study of religion, often from a perspective that was less critical and more accepting of the psychological value of theological beliefs.

In the United States, the study of religion was considered an important branch of early general psychology. G. Stanley Hall, for example, applied scientific methods to the study of religion. Better known and much more influential were the Gifford lectures of William James. Published in 1902 under the title *Varieties of religious experience,* James' book has become perhaps the only classic psychological study of religion.

SOME AREAS OF INTEREST

Methodology
The complexity of religious behavior and experience has led psychologists to use a diversity of measuring tools. These include the analysis of personal reports and introspections; clinical, natural, and participant observation; the use of surveys, questionnaires, and in-depth personal interviews; the analysis of documents such as diaries and autobiographies of religious people; the use of personality tests; examination of religious documents, including the Bible; and use of experimental techniques. The scientific study of religion is progressing, but such progress is slow and difficult because human religious phenomena (such as "faith," "belief," "conversion," and "commitment") are not easy to define or to measure with precision.

Psychological Origins of Religion
Religion is a widespread phenomenon; it is long lasting and highly influential. Freud proposed that it began with primitive people struggling with guilt and sexual impulses. More recent psychologists have abandoned a search for the historical origins of religion and have concentrated, instead, on finding psychological roots for the origins and continuation of religion in modern individuals.

Religious Development
As individuals pass through the life cycle, they change in their views of the world and in their perceptions of God. The child's faith is likely to be simple and magical. As one grows older, moral values, concepts of the supernatural, and involvement in religious practices all change.

Religious Experience
This is a major area of interest for psychologists who study religion. William James analyzed the causes and influences of conversion, mystical experience, saintliness, and prayer. Later research has added studies of glossolalia, religious content in dreams, the psychological nature of meditation, the influence of religious persuasion and ritual, faith healing, altered states of consciousness, the power of confession and forgiveness, the influence of occult and cult phenomena, the explanation of miracles, the use of drugs to stimulate religious experiences, and religious influences in psychopathology.

The Dynamics of Religious Behavior
Pruyser proposed that religion influences, and is influenced by, human perception, intellectual processes, thinking, linguistic functions, emotion, motor behavior, interpersonal relations, and relationships with things, ideas, and the self. Although it currently appears to occupy a minimal

place in the psychology of religion, the study of the relationship of general psychology and religion holds interesting potential for future research.

Religion and Social Behavior

Social psychologists have a special interest in the social organization of churches and synagogues, the social structure and influence of religious bodies, the roles of religious leaders, and the nature of religious cults and study groups.

PHILOSOPHICAL PSYCHOLOGY
RELIGIOUS BEHAVIOR

G. R. COLLINS

RELIGIOUS BEHAVIOR

Religion deals with so many intangibles that science finds it almost impossible to study religion as such. About the only way in which science can comfortably approach religion is to confine itself to the study of religious behavior. Even here, however, there are many pitfalls. Almost any behavior becomes "religious behavior" for some individuals under some circumstances.

It is relatively easy to define religious behavior where supernatural beings are involved. Any behavior directed toward affecting the behavior and attitudes of such beings thus is clearly religious behavior. Any behavior directed toward a divinity or "spirit" would clearly belong to this category, but behavior directed toward more amorphous objects also belongs here—as feeling oneself "on sacred ground" or in the presence of "the numinous" or "mana." Rudolph Otto has made a great deal of this latter in "idea of the holy" or "mysterium tremendum." A work of nature or a work of art may produce this feeling.

Places and objects are central to religious behavior. They produce behavior that the given culture would describe as "religious" or "devotional." These vary from culture to culture—ranging from ecstasy to extreme humility, from joyful to serious. Even within a major culture there may be differences, as between the Pentecostal, who may shout and dance when worshiping, and the Episcopalian, who would never think of shouting in church. Church is a place for reverence, but one views this as indicating wild enthusiasms while the other sees it as showing the deepest seriousness. Nevertheless, one is able to identify such places as sacred and behaves in them as if convinced special powers were present. But there seems to be little that is not culturally defined in such behavior.

One of the difficulties in an objective study of religious behavior is the necessity for differentiating between magical and religious praxes. Objectively they may be much the same, but magic sees the praxis itself as compelling results, whereas the other sees the praxis as *influencing* the ultimate power (deity). Again, *intention* becomes a major factor in determining what is religious behavior.

Not all religious behavior is aimed at influencing ultimate power, however. Some of it is simply awe in the presence of the "mysterium tremendum." Still more of it is simply gratefulness for our very existence and the marvels of the world. And for the more mystical, religious behavior is an effort to increase identification with "the ultimate," or, as some would say, "the core of the universe." The problem for the objective scientist is that these are all subjective. The observed behavior may thus be magical, technical, or religious, depending on its meaning to the behavior.

Some of the behavior, however, may have no meaning, but simply be conditioned responses to specific stimuli. One would hardly describe Skinner's superstitious behavior in pigeons as religion! Some human behavior that might be labeled "religious" is similar—such as tapping on wood as a precaution when one has boasted of something.

Religious behavior thus differs from some other behaviors (magic, conditioned responses, etc.) only in the intent with which it is performed; although some argue that even behavior that was purely "conditioned" originally may become religious after sufficient usage.

A further difficulty comes in the matter of "private" experience, as contrasted with "public" experience. Often observable behavior has little relationship to the private experience. Pope Pius XII's visions of Christ are a good illustration. On his deathbed the Pope was heard talking with someone, although no one present saw this other person or heard the person's replies. The Pope reported this other person as Christ.

We are left with the observed data of the Pope's behavior and the unanswerable question as to whether it was religious behavior or behavior resulting from sensory pathology. Still, one has to conclude that in the eyes of the pontiff, the behavior was religious—again defining behavior in terms of the intent of the behaver, even if the stimuli were hallucinations.

Psychologists interested in this field, then, attempt to study behaviors that are either culturally or individually (or both) defined as "religious." They are concerned with finding the common denominators of such behavior. They want to know the antecedent conditions that trigger (stimulate) such behavior. They need information on the experiential factors by which such behavior is "learned"—although they also need to know whether this behavior is innate or unlearned. They also desire to know the emotional concomitants of the behavior and the motivation. All of this involves constant awareness of the distinctions between objective data and subjective states. All of the social sciences (and some biological sciences) are involved.

RELIGION AND PSYCHOLOGY

W. E. GREGORY

REPERTORY GRID TECHNIQUE

All forms of repertory grid derive from George Kelly's Role Construct Repertory Grid Test, described originally in the two-volume work in which he formulated the basic principles of personal construct theory. Repertory grid technique has played an integral role in the development of Kelly's theory since its introduction as both a clinical assessment procedure and a research instrument.

A repertory grid is essentially a method of quantifying and statistically analyzing relationships between the cognitive dimensions used in performing a complex sorting task. Kelly's original procedure, still widely used, was designed to elicit from each subject a representative sample of "personal constructs" (bipolar dimensions of judgment such as "happy/sad") and to assess the relationships between these constructs as they are employed in categorizing a list of personal acquaintances. Other investigators have devised grid tests in which either a standard set of constructs is supplied to subjects or some combination of elicited and supplied constructs is used. In all forms of repertory grid, however, the data elicited from each subject are entered into a separate two-dimensional matrix wherein there is a row for every construct and a column for every element.

The statistical procedures used to analyze individual repertory grids in both research and clinical settings include principal component analysis, multidimensional scaling, hierarchical cluster analysis, and nonparametric factor analysis, among others. Related methods of analysis have been applied to pooled repertory grid data elicited from groups of subjects.

The most widely used standardized repertory grid test is Bannister and Fransella's Grid Test of Schizophrenic Thought Disorder. Other standard grid tests in current use include James Bieri's Grid Test of Cognitive Complexity; the Bipolar Implications Grid, described by Fransella; and the Dyad Grid and Double Dyad Grid, described by Anthony Ryle.

PERSONAL CONSTRUCT THEORY

J. R. ADAMS-WEBBER

RESEARCH METHODOLOGY

Research design methodology in psychology follows the principles of research methodology in the sciences as exemplified by John Stuart Mill's Method of Difference. It states that if *A* is always followed by *a,* and *not-A* is always followed by *not-a,* then *A* is certainly the cause of *a.* In psychology, there are many special considerations in addition to this basic principle. Most of the variables are abstract and often have few direct referents to the biological or physical world. The very act of observing or measuring psychological variables can cause the subjects to react or change. In addition, actively placing persons into or excluding them from the "advantages" or "disadvantages" of receiving or not receiving a psychological treatment or condition may cause these subjects to differ from people in the day-to-day world. The consideration of scientific inquiry methods is the domain of research methodology in psychology.

As a start to understanding the problems of research methodology in psychology, an axiom and three basic facts are listed. A general axiom of science is that there is no knowledge without comparison. That this is true can be seen from Mill's Method of Difference. Note that comparison is basic to understanding the observations under the conditions of *A* and *not-A.* Comparisons between pairs of several differing conditions are necessary for fuller understanding of a phenomenon.

The first fact is that measurement in psychology generally is rather imprecise and in reality never can be as precise as many typical measurements of variables in the physical and biological domains.

The second fact is that a relatively large number of variables are relatively independent, perhaps of the order of 400 or more. Some psychologists believe that there are many more; others, a markedly fewer number of variables. Nevertheless, attempting to maintain control of or keep under observation even as few as 200 psychological variables presents a research methodology problem rather different from the handful of basic variables in physics (time, space, mass, charge, etc.).

The third fact is that these dimensions of human behavior vary over time; some not as much (such as intelligence) as others, which, by definition, are highly volatile (such as one's mood).

The purpose of psychology is to discover new psychological variables and to show the relationships among these new variables with already determined variables and, of course, new relationships among already known variables. The definition of a psychological variable is that it is a conceptual entity in the field of psychology.

It is in this context that research methodology is important. In science, the definition of a "fact" is the statement of the relationship between two variables. However, to have an understanding of the meaning of facts, researchers must have a context of comparative relationships in which to understand their data's scientific significance. It is the set of comparative relations, the context of the observations, that gives fuller meaning to the statements of relationship among variables. This context of comparative relationships is the domain of research methodology and design.

Because the purpose of most science is to understand why and how relationships occur, ultimately the strength, size, and causative direction statements (mutual cause, mutual effect, or reciprocal cause and effect) of these relationships must be determined. This quality, to be able to infer a causal relationship, is called the *internal validity* of the research design. Finally, these research relationships and cause-and-effect statements must be shown to generalize, to occur in the "real" world outside of the psychological laboratory or the somewhat controlled environment of a research study. These generalizations are called the *external validity* of the research design.

EXPERIMENTAL VERSUS PASSIVE OBSERVATIONAL RESEARCH DESIGNS

Research designs in psychology can be divided into two broad types: *experimental research designs* and *passive observational designs.* In the first type of design, variables are systematically imposed on or withheld from the subjects, either by the experimenter or by naturally forming conditions in society. Comparisons are then made on variables of interest among the groups of subjects that have had and have not had the imposed treatment variables or conditions. In the second broad type of research design, passive observational, the researcher merely observes subjects under many natural conditions and records the subjects' scores (or status) on a number of variables. Later these scores and status conditions under which the observations were made are interrelated. No attempt is made by the researcher to impose conditions or make systematic changes. Indeed, in a broad range of psychological research, it is difficult or not possible for the researcher to change the status of variables. Many of these variables are of great importance in psychology, such as age, gender, socioeconomic status, and intelligence.

True Experiments

Within the first broad type of research design, experimental designs are of two major subtypes—true *experiments* and *quasi-experiments.* The classification "true experiments" contains just one type of research design, although that design can have many variations. In true experiments, the subjects involved in the research are *randomly* allocated to experimental groups and control groups. The research groups formed by allocation of subjects to groups with the use of random numbers can be said to be not unequal on any variable except as expected by chance—and the amount of expected differences can be determined with some precision.

Note that there are always three parts in all experiments: (a) subjects' groups, (b) experimental treatments, and (c) results (or criteria). In the true experiment, as the result of randomly assigning subjects to groups, it can be assumed that all variables initially, and for all time to come, will be equal unless some systematically different treatments or conditions are applied. If, after seemingly different treatments are applied, it can be shown that a difference on any variable exists between groups, the primary inference is that the treatments or conditions *caused* that effect, and the treatments are indeed different. This is a very strong statement and an important one in the development of an understanding of theory in psychology where cause-and-effect statements are ultimately necessary for full understanding of phenomena. For research where variables can be applied or withheld, the true experiment, with its initial random allocation of subjects to groups, is a powerful research design. Its internal validity is unsurpassed.

Quasi-Experiments

Quasi-experiment groups are formed naturally or via the intervention of others (but not at random), and the treatments or conditions imposed on these groups and criteria measures are described. Further, to be a quasi-experiment, pretreatment measures also must be available. A major difference in the quasi-experiment is that initial equality of groups *cannot* be assumed as it can be in the true experiment. In fact, in a major type of quasi-experiment (there are several types), groups clearly are unequal initially.

Initial status (equal groups or unequal groups) in quasi-experiments then must be determined by actual assessment. If the groups in a quasi-experiment can be demonstrated to be initially equivalent on one or more variables of interest to the researcher, then the research logic is nearly the same as it is in the true experiment. However, many times in quasi-experiments groups do differ initially. In these cases, the cause-and-effect research design logic takes a different form. Groups are initially different. After experimental treatment, they must be either more different or less different on the criteria than they were initially. Either way suggests that the treatment may cause the greater or lesser differences in the criteria.

There are three major types of research designs within the major category of quasi-experiments, and literally hundreds of variations within the three types. The three types can be labeled: (a) *strong quasi-experiments*—in which the initial measures show the groups to be equal; (b) *weak quasi-experiments*—in which the groups are shown to be initially unequal; and (c) *interrupted time series designs*. The strong quasi-experiments emulate the cause-and-effect logic of true experiments rather well. Further, they are far more widely available to be done in the real world than true experiments where the researcher must have a major degree of ability to control the activities of those being studied and of those imposing the treatment conditions.

The problem with quasi-experiments is that even in the ones where initial equality on several variables is established, it is difficult to determine that all prior conditions probably influencing the subjects were also equal, or even that all variables in the subjects' groups were equal prior to the application of the treatment. Important unmeasured variables influencing the criteria may not be equal in the research groups.

At this point, two of the three basic facts will be applied to show problems in the research design validity of experiments. One fact is that psychological variables change over time. Another fact is imprecise measurement. These both suggest that one cannot ever be absolutely sure of experimental research findings—even in the true experiment. Findings in any given experiment can occur by chance alone as the result of naturally occurring variability over time and by random fluctuations in measurement systems. This threat to internal validity, called instability, is controlled by statistical analysis.

In the quasi-experiment, these problems of inferring cause-and-effect relationships are compounded. Even in strong quasi-experiments, the researcher must also assume that all important variables operated in all groups equally and that all important prior conditions were the same. Both of these assumptions may be difficult to accept. In the weak quasi-experiment, where groups are known not to be initially equal, even more problems arise. As a direct consequence of the first fact stated (the inability to measure variables precisely), it is known that all observed scores on variables (except average scores) are biased. For highly precise measures and those in the group not too distant from the average score, the bias is small, but for many of the more typical measures commonly used in psychological research, when used to measure rather atypical subjects, the bias can be rather marked. The result is that for these latter subjects, when using rather imprecise measures, future observations are expected to change and to be nearer to the average even when no treatments or unusual conditions intervene between the initial measurement and later measurements, such as those on a criterion after treatment in a quasi-experiment. This phenomenon is called *regression toward the mean*. The conclusion is that while weak quasi-experiments are a common design in psychology, they can be fraught with major interpretation difficulties, and their results must be viewed with some caution.

The third major type of quasi-experiment is the interrupted time series design. It occurs when subjects are observed periodically over time and a treatment is applied or a condition arises at some point or at several specified points in that time span. In essence, the subjects serve as their own control in that they are observed before a treatment is given and then observed again after the treatment is given. Although this research design model works rather well in the classical areas of the physical sciences and in those areas of biology where the phenomena are fairly stable, it is one of the three basic facts presented in the foregoing that psychological variables vary over time—even when no treatments are applied. Therefore, it is imperative that a number of observations be made both before and after the application of the treatment to assess the inherent stability—or lack of it—of the phenomenon being studied. Systematic application and withdrawal of the treatment and consequent observation of the results aid in more firmly establishing the cause-and-effect relationship.

PASSIVE OBSERVATIONAL RESEARCH DESIGN

The second major classification of research designs is the passive observational—those that are not experimental and often involve intrinsic variables that cannot be applied and withheld, such as socioeconomic level, grade point average, and intelligence level. Cause-and-effect relationships are much more difficult to establish, and in fact may not be possible to determine. The analyses are typically in terms of strength of relationships among a number of variables. Treatment or condition variables may be difficult to distinguish from criteria variables. Often all observations are made at one interval in time, although the teasing out of the direction of effects is facilitated by observations made over time and in longitudinal studies where they are done over long developmental periods.

The passive observational types of studies can be categorized into four major types of research designs: prediction and classification, sampling and survey, quantitative descriptive, and qualitative descriptive. These last two categories especially encompass a very large number of variations and methods. A major key to interpretation of the results of passive observational research is the development of elaborate theory about the nature of the relationships among variables, and indeed what variables are important. In the passive observational studies, the three basic facts about psychological variables begin to play a major role in the interpretation of research data.

Prediction and Classification

These involve K variables, $K - 1$ of which are used to predict the future (or even current) status, and the Kth variable is the predicted, or criterion, variable. The analytic method usually is statistical and involves multiple correlation and regression techniques or discriminant analysis. Prediction is also useful in selection processes when people are to be selected for entry into a program or for jobs, and the number applying for entry or the jobs is larger than the number to be accepted. The major limitations of the method are that (a) descriptive prediction is not necessarily a cause-and-effect prediction, and (b) limits on the precision of measurement distinctly limit the degree of prediction possible. Conversely, if a prediction reaches these limits, then no other variable added to the prediction set of variables can increase the level of the prediction.

Sampling and Survey Studies

The purpose of this type of passive observational research design is to describe a large population of people on a relatively small number of variables. It is done by selecting a representative group, called the sample, from the population and making the descriptive observations. The averages and variability of these observations are then calculated and estimates are made for the larger population of the ranges within which the averages for these variables are likely to fall.

Quantitative Descriptive Design

This type of research design also includes a large number of variations. Typically the observations are made at or near one interval of time on a group or several groups of subjects. All observations are quantified via the use of ratings, scales, test scores, and the like. The basic major analytic method used as a starting point in determining the degree of relationships between each pair of variables usually is correlational.

Strength of support of various hypotheses and alternative hypotheses are determined and, it is hoped, theory is advanced. Problems from a research design standpoint are the basic facts of imprecise measurement and difficulty in the ability firmly to determine cause-and-effect relationships. However, the quantitative descriptive procedures are fundamental to the development of good-quality experimental research designs. Furthermore, they are often the only design available where variables are intrinsic in subjects and cannot be manipulated, where it is unethical to manipulate variables, or where it is too expensive to manipulate variables.

Qualitative Descriptive Design

Qualitative research, if anything, is a category of research method that has even more variations, approaches, and themes than quantitative descriptive research. Qualitative descriptive research includes much of basic research where the aim is to discover new variables and new relationships among old and new variables. These observational procedures are typically inculcated in a theoretical system that suggests dimensions in the observational areas to be recorded. A clear objective is to conceptualize new dimensions of behavior, thought, feelings, and aspects of the inner and exterior environments that elicit them. It is of major use where only one or a small number of subjects (or if group behavior is of interest, one or a small number of groups) are involved. Nor is the method independent of other types of research. It is almost inevitably a forerunner to all the other methods because it is often here that the new variables are developed that are more fully developed in the quantitative descriptive method and later more rigorously studied in the experimental methods. The results are typically lengthy narratives.

THREATS TO INTERNAL VALIDITY

"Threats to internal validity" is the phrase in research design that interpreters of data use to describe the set of questions they have about possible inaccuracies in interpretation of cause-and-effect relationships among research variables. Some of these threats already have been suggested, particularly in the description of quasi-experiments. *Regression-toward-the-mean* score was the phrase used to describe the effect of imprecise measurement on present and future observations, and it is a major threat to internal validity in research design in psychology.

Maturation is another threat because subjects grow and develop on their own with the passage of time irrespective of what a researcher does to them. It is partly the result of this last hypothesis that control groups are used for comparisons with maturing subjects.

Mortality is another threat. The systematic reduction of groups of subjects because of dropouts, absences, people moving away, unanswered criterion questionnaires, and so on can make those who do not do well, as the result of a treatment or influence, less visible. Thus, the more visible do better on the criteria, making the treatment influence look better.

The threat of *selection* works at the beginning of the researcher's time sequence. The systematic choosing or a passive choice (those who select themselves) of people for a treatment or condition may be different for some groups before the treatment. These groups would still be different from others after the treatment—*even if no treatment or condition had been imposed.* Again, the alternative hypothesis question as to what the effects of no treatment or condition would be must be asked and tested to develop strong internal validity (cause-and-effect statements) among variables.

History involves changes in conditions surrounding the research such that those changes are intermixed with the research treatments. This confusion results in the inability to ascribe changes in subjects to the research treatment or to the external changes.

Instrumentation is a threat to internal validity somewhat unique to psychology because it involves changes in observers' standards over time or as the result of observational conditions. These changes result in different scores. The problem is that these differences in measurement standards may be mistaken for changes resulting from treatments.

Testing is another threat to internal validity almost entirely unique to psychology. It involves the distinct effect of gains in subjects' scores simply as the result of previously taking a test.

Instability, as has been indicated, results from attempts to interpret the naturally occurring changes in subjects and measurements both immediately or over longer periods of time.

There are also four affective Threats to Internal Validity: *imitation, compensatory rivalry, compensatory equalization,* and *demoralization.* These, too, are unique to the psychological sciences in that they result from emotional changes in subjects and administrators to adjust for the fact that they were not "favored" by receiving an experimental treatment.

EXTERNAL VALIDITY AND METAANALYSIS

Finally, there is the concept of *external validity* that is the sum of the characteristics of research that allow the cause-and-effect statements made (as the result of good internal validity) to be generalized to subjects, treatments, and criteria not used in the research, but similar to them.

Metaanalysis

The external validity of research findings is markedly enhanced when a number of studies of the same general treatment variable can be combined and summarized. This procedure is called *metaanalysis.* In metaanalysis, the strength of treatment effect and major conditions of the research on the criterion variables are determined. These variables are developed as the result of the theoretical interests of the metaanalysis researcher. Again, the basic analysis is comparing the relationship of all pairs of variables but the set of relationships of most interest is the set of research condition variables and the criterion variable that is research treatment effect size on the criteria variables, This Effect Size for each research study is determined simply by dividing the difference between the average scores on the criterion variable from the experimental groups and the control group by a measure of individuals' variability within these groups. As the result of this analysis, numerous research condition variables may be shown to have no influence on a set of criteria, and therefore researchers can generalize the results from a number of studies without regard to these now determined extraneous conditions.

Finally, the strength of each treatment variable and of combinations of all the treatment variables can be determined with respect to their influence on criteria. This is most important with regard to applied areas where simply saying that one variable influences another is not sufficient, but the *size* of that influence is.

CONTROL GROUPS
EXPERIMENTAL METHODS
HYPOTHESIS TESTING
MEASUREMENT
STATISTICS IN PSYCHOLOGY

J. W. ASHER

RESIDENTIAL ALTERNATIVES

Throughout the course of one's life, there may arise the need for residential care. This need may be generated by a variety of reasons, such as for physical rehabilitation, or because of mental or physical illness, loss of shelter, or old age.

Following is a listing of some residential alternatives.

Boarding home. A boarding home is one in which unrelated individuals reside with no supervision. The term *hospice is* often used interchangeably with boarding home.

Convalescent hospital. Convalescent hospitals afford long-term residential care for those requiring extensive rehabilitation or nursing care, or who are terminally ill.

Foster care. Foster care homes are provided by families who open their houses to children who require shelter. Most children who receive foster care require such service because of the loss of parents or guardians.

Group home. Group homes are provided by public and private agencies for children and adults who require supervised residential care.

Halfway house. A halfway house, by its very name, connotes a transition home. Generally halfway houses are operated by public or private agencies for the express purpose of facilitating a person's movement from a highly supervised residential setting to independence in the community.

Intermediate care facility. An intermediate care facility (ICF) offers residential services to people with developmental disabilities. Unlike group homes, many intermediate care facilities are located on institutional grounds, and follow a medical model.

Nursing home. A nursing home is a private or publicly operated long-term care setting for the terminally ill, disabled, or elderly. Unlike convalescent hospitals, nursing homes do not have ready access to all the necessary life-support services that some long-term convalescent patients require.

Orphanage. An orphanage is a residential care center designed to offer shelter to homeless children. Unlike foster care settings, orphanages generally serve large numbers of children.

Psychiatric hospital. A psychiatric hospital is a residential hospital, designed primarily for persons requiring psychiatric care. Most psychiatric hospitals are publicly operated.

Residential school. A residential school is one in which the educational/training programs are located on the same premises or under the same auspices as the residential program.

Respite care. Respite care is a short-term residential service provided to individuals who require temporary shelter, primarily in cases of emergency, family crisis, family vacation, or trial separation.

Retirement home. A retirement home is a residential alternative designed specifically for senior citizens. Retirement homes can follow many different models, including boarding homes, residential cottages, and apartments.

Sanitorium. A sanitorium is a residential alternative designed for the treatment of chronic disease and disorders such as tuberculosis and various forms of mental illness.

State school. A state school is an institutional school for children with special needs. Not unlike many residential schools, state schools have residences and educational/training opportunities located on the same site.

Supervised apartment. Supervised apartments are living alternatives for adults with special needs who are "capable of independent living." Supervised apartments can be found either in clusters or randomly located in an apartment complex. People residing in supervised apartments are regularly monitored by human services personnel to make certain that their personal and social needs are being met.

COMMUNITY PSYCHOLOGY

D. L. HOLMES

RESPIRATORY DISORDERS

Both emotional states and overt behavior have a profound impact on the respiratory system. The rapid breathing that accompanies fear and the pulmonary damage that results from smoking illustrate these points. Furthermore, respiratory disturbances have emotional consequences, as anyone who has had trouble breathing can testify.

Bronchial asthma is an episodic difficulty in breathing that occurs when the smaller air passages in the lungs become partially obstructed by constriction, swelling of their linings, and excessive secretions. The difficulty is primarily in expiration, and the lungs become hyperinflated.

Asthma was one of the seven "psychosomatic disorders" studied by Franz Alexander and his associates, who believed that the condition was,

in part, attributable to specific psychological conflicts. Numerous studies through the years, however, have generated confusing results that have seriously weakened the conflict specificity position.

Some conclusions seem to have current support: (a) Asthma is a syndrome, not a single disorder; (b) clear-cut results from psychological investigations must probably await more homogeneous samples of patients; (c) allergic, infectious, and psychological factors play varying roles in causation; and (d) psychological treatments may be of some benefit in some cases, but not alone.

The hyperventilation syndrome is a cluster of signs and symptoms produced by excessively deep and rapid breathing and the associated loss of blood carbon dioxide. The symptoms include, among others, dizziness, anxiety, palpitations, shortness of breath, trembling, numbness and tingling in the extremities, and muscle spasms. The importance of the syndrome lies in the following two facts: (a) Patients often hyperventilate without being aware they are doing so; and (b) the syndrome can mimic other psychological conditions, such as anxiety, panic, and phobic disorders.

BEHAVIORAL MEDICINE
PSYCHOSOMATIC DISORDERS

H. A. STORROW

RESPONSE BIAS

A response bias is any method or pattern of responding to test items that results in test takers making different responses than they would if the items were presented in a different manner. This different pattern of responding may be due either to the content and wording of the item or to the format of the item or the response.

The interest in response biases began with Lee Cronbach's studies of achievement tests. Cronbach reasoned that students who chose not to answer true–false items when unsure of the correct answer would obtain lower scores than students who attempted each item. Furthermore, even when scores were corrected for guessing, if there were unequal numbers of true- and false-keyed items (as there usually are), students would be differentially penalized depending on whether they selected "true" or "false" when uncertain. In a series of studies, Cronbach found that there were individual differences in the tendency to select "true" responses (that is, be acquiescent) from test to test. This tendency, combined with the fact that poorer students guess more than better students, resulted in scores on false-keyed items being more variable, reliable, and valid than scores on true-keyed items.

Since these original studies, hundreds of other response bias studies have been conducted. The largest number have used self-report personality inventories and focused on acquiescence (the tendency to answer "true" or "yes") and social desirability (the tendency to endorse items rated as reflecting socially desirable behaviors).

BASIC CONCERNS

Response biases are important at three levels of analysis. One is the interpretation of scores of individual test takers. To the extent that response biases affect an individual's scores, the interpretation of these scores will be changed. Second, when considering the scores of a group of test takers, response biases may affect the score distribution (e.g., mean, variance) as well as the test's reliability and validity. Third, if a response bias operates consistently from test to test, it will represent an individual differences dimension that may be worthy of study in its own right. In addition, if response biases are sources of reliable individual differences, the question of how to separate the effects of response biases from the effects of the trait or characteristic measured becomes an important issue.

TYPES OF RESPONSE BIASES

Response biases can occur on all types of assessment instruments. Leonard Rorer made a useful distinction between response sets and response styles. Response sets are content dependent and occur when individuals want to present a particular picture of themselves. In contrast, response styles are relatively content independent and occur when the stimuli or tasks are ambiguous or the test taker is unsure or undecided about the appropriate response.

IDENTIFYING AND CONTROLLING RESPONSE BIASES

Given that response biases occur, test constructors must develop methods to identify and control their effects. One class of such methods focuses on the structure of the task. Some response styles can be minimized by balancing item formats; for example, by including equal numbers of true and false items, by reversing the ends of rating scales, and by using both positively and negatively phrased attitude items. On projective methods, the use of ambiguous stimuli minimizes response sets but does not eliminate response styles. Conversely, highly structured procedures, such as rating specific behaviors rather than more general personality traits, can decrease the effects of both response sets and styles. Another approach is to use a forced-choice format. This approach forces test takers to respond on the basis of the item content rather than social desirability. Forced-choice formats are also used on rating scales.

A second class of methods involves the construction of special scales to detect biased responses. The simplest approach is to count the number of omitted items. Other approaches include repeating items and counting the number of atypical responses chosen. Both of these methods identify people who did not follow directions, and the latter can also identify people who are attempting to fake bad.

A more common method is to develop content-dependent scales to identify response sets. A number of social desirability scales have been developed. The Minnesota Multiphasic Personality Inventory (MMPI) contains several "validity scales" designed to identify response biases. The L scale contains items that reflect desirable behaviors that few people exhibit; thus high scores on the L scale suggest an attempt to fake good. The F scale contains items that are infrequently responded to in a particular direction. High scores on this scale (that is, many atypical or infrequent responses) identify people who are faking bad, who did not follow directions, or who exhibit many abnormal feelings and behaviors. The K scale measures more subtle test-taking defensiveness. Scores on the K scale are used as a correction factor on several diagnostic scales, to increase their validity. Another method is the subtle–obvious keys. By comparing responses with the subtle and obvious items, persons attempting to fake good or bad often can be identified. When several sources of assessment data are available, inconsistencies across assessment modes may suggest biased responding.

To summarize, response biases can and do occur on psychological tests, particularly on typical performance measures, and thus must be considered when interpreting scores. Their effects on validity, however, are still an open question.

F. G. BROWN

RESPONSIBILITY AND BEHAVIOR

Responsibility has been a concern of social scientists for many years, as reflected in the early penal codes and the writings of such eminent scholars as Emile Durkheim and Paul Fauconnet. Durkheim suggested that responsibility is a necessary constituent of moral life. Fauconnet expanded Durkheim's views and concluded that to be responsible is to be justly punishable. Somewhat later, Jean Piaget identified the evolution of responsibility as central in the development of moral judgment. But it was the seminal work of Fritz Heider that provided the impetus for extensive studies of the attribution of responsibility and its consequences for interpersonal behavior.

Heider proposed that whether and to what degree one person (the attributor) holds another (the actor) responsible for a given effect (outcome) depends on both the developmental stage of the attributor and the circumstances in which the effect occurs. The relevant circumstances may be labeled association, commission, foreseeability, intentionality, and justification. As the attributor matures and becomes more "sophisticated," he or she considers more and more of the relevant conditions surrounding the event.

Attribution of responsibility to others has behavioral consequences for both the actor and the attributor. The consequences of attributions of responsibility for criminal justice and the legal system are probably self-evident. Jury members may ask whether the person who is charged with a violation did in fact commit the offense (commission). If so, then questions about foreseeability, intentionality, and justification arise. The answers to these questions determine the degree of culpability (responsibility) and the sanctions (punishment) that should be administered to the violator.

In contrast with informal interpersonal situations, legal systems ordinarily do not hold persons responsible for outcomes when they are merely associated with the event, and, therefore, they are not open to sanctions. However, parents are sometimes held responsible for the behavior of their children, or persons may be held responsible for events that involve property ownership. In a similar fashion, military officers may be held responsible for the actions of soldiers under their command.

The many ways in which responsibility and behavior are related have been analyzed and documented in several carefully controlled studies. In an early investigation, J. W. Thibaut and H. W. Riecken created a situation in which one person (called the communicator) attempted to influence the behavior of two other persons (confederates of the investigator) who played roles having different degrees of status or prestige. Following a series of influence attempts, both confederates complied with the communicator's requests. The communicator attributed the high-status person's compliance to internal motivation (the person was responsible for his or her actions), whereas the low-status person's compliance was attributed to the communicator's influence. Furthermore, the person who was seen as responsible for his or her own behavior was rated as more acceptable to the communicator than the person whose behavior was seen as being controlled by the communicator.

Negative reactions to persons may occur when they suffer undesirable consequences, even when the objective circumstances ordinarily do not indicate that they are personally responsible for the bad outcomes. Lerner and Matthews asked female pairs to participate in a learning task. Each person was led to believe that her partner would receive strong electric shock, and that she would be in a more desirable position than her partner. When the person believed that her partner was responsible for her own suffering, later descriptions of the person were relatively objective. However, when the person believed herself to be responsible for the other person's fate, she devalued her as a person. Curiously, when the partner was seen as being responsible both for her own fate *and* for the person's own desirable position, the partner's attractiveness was enhanced.

The preceding investigations have emphasized the reactions of persons to the perceived responsibility of others for both positive and negative outcomes relevant to those others, but there is evidence that the attribution of responsibility to a person also affects that person's behavior. Schlenker has shown how people react when situational cues permit the inference that they may be responsible for negative events. In such instances, people attempt to account for the situation by offering *excuses* designed to minimize their responsibility for the event *or justifications* intended to reduce the negativity of the event and or its consequences.

These several investigations document, under relatively controlled conditions, those phenomena that can be observed in everyday life, and provide more precise specifications of those variables that determine attributions of responsibility and the consequences of such attributions. When persons are seen as being responsible for bad outcomes, they are judged negatively by others and their interactions with others are adversely affected. Others are less willing to interact with them, and when they do, the interaction process is modified, leading to less effective group products. On the positive side, responsibility for positive events leads to praise, liking, and increased desire for interaction. Unfortunately these positive effects do not occur as predictably as the negative ones.

FORENSIC PSYCHOLOGY
MORAL DEVELOPMENT

M. E. SHAW

RETICULAR ACTIVATING SYSTEM

The reticular formation (RF) extends from the caudal medulla to the rostral midbrain. Its neurons form the meshwork of the brain stem in which are embedded the specific nuclear groups that supply the cranial nerves with axons. The ascending and descending long tracts of the brain stem pass through and around the reticular formation. Its neurons tend to have long axons and a single RF neuron may have an axon that branches to reach the dorsal column nuclei, the spinal cord, and the hypothalamus. Because of such extensive branching, the neurons of the RF are capable of exerting profound effects on the general level of activity of the brain and spinal cord.

The RF is neither functionally nor structurally homogeneous. It can be divided into nuclear groupings according to anatomic and neurochemical criteria. The most convenient anatomic categorization is made along the medial-lateral dimension. The raphé nuclei are found along the midline of the structure. A large-celled region is found in the core of the RF and a small-celled division is located in the lateral portion of the RF. These large medial-lateral divisions may be subdivided along the rostral-caudal length of the RF. For example, the nucleus gigantocellularis is the large-celled nucleus of the medulla. It gives rise to reticulospinal axons that influence the activity of gamma motor neurons. In the pons, the nuclei pontis caudalis and oralis take the place of the nucleus gigantocellularis, and also give rise to reticulospinal axons. However, these nuclei, especially the rostral-lying pontis oralis, have many ascending projections and are involved in regulation of cortical arousal.

Some reticular nuclei may also be defined according to neurotransmitter content. Discrete neuronal cell groupings that contain the putative neurotransmitter norepinephrine have been identified in the medullary and pontine RF. The most extensively studied of these has been the locus coeruleus. Projections from this nucleus distribute throughout the forebrain, as well as the cerebellum, and have been shown to be involved in rapid-eye-movement sleep, as well as in maintenance of intracranial self-stimulation. Dopamine-containing neurons are found in the midbrain tegmentum and also have extensive projections to the forebrain. The best known of these dopaminergic projections arises from the substantia nigra. Loss of this pathway causes Parkinson's disease. The raphé nuclei give rise to serotonergic projections. Forebrain projections from the raphé are involved in slow-wave sleep, while spinal cord projections from the raphé may block transmission of pain impulses to the brain and effect changes in autonomic functioning. Finally, cell groups in the midbrain RF give rise to an ascending cholinergic projection that is involved in modulating neocortical electrographic arousal.

BRAIN

M. L. WOODRUFF

RETIREMENT

Retirement has been defined as a process involving "the separation of an individual from a job role—a role performed for pay—and the acquisition of the role of retired person." The aspect most often emphasized is the separation of the individual from employment that is monetarily rewarded, that is, a movement from, or withdrawal from, the labor market to outside of the labor market. This withdrawal from the labor force may be involuntary or voluntary, depending on the conditions of withdrawal.

INFLUENCING FACTORS

The main variables influencing retirement (of any type) are health and income, with health a more important factor prior to age 62, and economic factors as more influential after. Early retirement, which appeared to be on the increase in the 1970s, is influenced by these variables—that is, quality of health and adequacy of postretirement income. Of those individuals who retire on time (at age 65), the majority do so for economic reasons as well. That is, at age 65, many employees are entitled to full pension benefits, as well as full Social Security. Those who continue working, opting for partial or late retirement, may do so because they perceive their income as insufficient to allow full retirement. A small percentage continue working for personal satisfaction, although most individuals who can afford to retire, do so. A relatively small number of workers retire involuntarily because of mandatory retirement provisions. Changing economic factors, such as unemployment and inflation, influence (either positively or negatively) the timing and nature of retirement decisions over time.

ADJUSTMENT

Atchley reports that less than a third of the retired population has difficulty adjusting to retirement—40% of these because of reduced postretirement income, 22% because of loss of job, and 38% because of situational factors such as declining health or death of spouse. Studying five areas of life satisfaction (housing, area of residence, health, standard of living, leisure activity), Parties and Nestel report that most of the retirees studied said they were reasonably happy with their lives. Other researchers have also found satisfaction among the majority of retirees in their studies, although those who are involuntarily retired are often less satisfied than voluntary retirees.

There are conflicting views as to the qualities of retirement style that are most successful for adjustment, such as activity, disengagement, and continuity. Walker et al. conclude, however, that there is no single retirement style that leads to universal satisfaction; rather, it varies from person to person. Adjustment to retirement is most satisfactory when income is adequate, health is good, and loss of job is seen as an acceptable change in the individual's life.

COUNSELING AND INTERVENTION

Adjusting to change is an important task in later adulthood, and retirement is a substantial change. Preretirement counseling can assist individuals in preparing for such changes. Managing postretirement finances, accurately assessing the adequacy of resources prior to retirement, and acquiring preventive and instrumental health care are prime concerns in retirement counseling. In addition to assistance with adjustment, retirement counseling can aid retirees in locating employment and developing leisure activities. Numerous studies indicate a desire for part-time work among some retired individuals. The need for postretirement work may well increase with increases in inflation and unemployment. Leisure-time activities are also important for the life satisfaction of retirees, therefore, this is an area of concern in retirement preparation.

AGING: BEHAVIOR CHANGES
GERONTOLOGY

G J. MANASTER

REWARDS

The ancient theory of hedonism is based on the attractive assumption that behavior is regulated by pleasure and pain. We do what brings us pleasure and avoid painful stimuli or situations. So stated, the pleasure–pain principle is a motivational one. Thorndike, seeking a theory that would account for adaptive behavior (in parallel with the evolutionary selection of physical features), applied the principle of rewards and punishments to learning. He proposed that animals (and people) learn. If an organism repeated a response, whatever followed that response on a prior trial could be called a reward; if it did not repeat a response, whatever had followed it on the previous trial must have been a punishment. Thus, if a child were spanked for some misdeed, the spanking might not result in restraint—it might turn out that the child had found the spanking "satisfying" in some hypothetical need for attention.

Experimental confirmations that punishment weakened stimulus–response connections was never developed in a satisfactory manner, and eventually Thorndike dropped the notion that annoyers had any bearing on learning other than that of possibly leading organisms to try other responses. Learning was a matter of rewarding desirable responses. By 1938, two outstanding psychologists of the period followed up on Thorndike's theory, but both felt it desirable to change his terminology. For both Clark L. Hull and B. F. Skinner "satisfiers" became "reinforcements." Hull defined reinforcement in terms of decreasing degrees of drive stimulation. Rewards or satisfiers now became drive reducers and learning could occur only when drives were diminished. Thus, food, for a hungry rat, would reduce the drive of hunger and, somehow, this reduction in drive would add strength to a stimulus–response connection.

For Skinner, the term "drive" was too vague and/or subjective and he substituted the term "deprivation." A rat that had not eaten for some time could be considered to be in a deprived state, and, in such a state, it would learn (or perform) some act that was followed by food (a reinforcer). For Skinner, as for Thorndike, a reinforcer was anything that would result in a stronger or faster rate of performance of some activity that previously would occur only by chance. Skinner, like Thorndike, saw no virtue in punishment as he was able to demonstrate that once a response had been reinforced, subsequent punishment would not affect the likelihood of future repetitions, and it might only delay them.

SECONDARY REINFORCEMENT

For both Hull and Skinner, it was clear that people do not act or behave because they are rewarded with immediate biological drive reducers. People act when they receive praise, gold stars, money, or other nonbiological rewards. To bridge the gap between people and hungry rats, the concept of secondary reinforcement was introduced. A secondary reinforcer was alleged to acquire its reinforcing power by association with a primary reinforcer. Note that in establishing secondary reinforcers, no response is required—a *stimulus* is followed by the appearance of the reward.

PARTIAL REINFORCEMENT

Skinner discovered that if rewards or reinforcers were omitted occasionally, rats and pigeons (and people) would work even harder or longer than if rewards uniformly followed each response. Thus, to establish some behavior strongly and make it more consistent, it is advisable to intersperse nonrewarded trials with the rewarded ones rather frequently, but not so frequently as to result in "extinction" (the weakening of stimulus–response connections).

CRITICAL VIEWS

In the period when Hull and Skinner were emphasizing the importance of rewards for learning, there were serious attacks against the notion that rewards had any direct bearing on learning. Rewards might play a motivational role but learning could go on without them.

In the 1940s and 1950s, a large number of studies involved so-called "incidental learning." In such studies, subjects were instructed to learn one thing but were tested on another. It was found that they often learned things they had not been instructed to learn, and even things they were instructed not to learn. In such studies, subjects definitely were not reinforced for the unrequested learning.

By the 1970s, the subject of reward as related to learning began to drop in interest, but a new role was found for it in its perhaps original nature, that of a motivational factor. Behavior therapists began to follow Skinner's techniques in modifying human behavior—rewarding people when they behaved in some desired manner and withholding rewards when undesired behavior was exhibited. This ancient practice of all parents was brought into the clinical arena with presumably more systematic and standardized, or regulated, administration.

The presentation of rewards is now viewed largely as a matter of behavior control and it appears to work effectively. Parents frequently fail to establish control because they are not systematic and commonly do not spell out exactly what behavior they want to establish. Parents should recognize that rewarding desired behavior is probably the only procedure that will result in desired effects. Skinner's cautions about punishment should also be recognized, as the side effects (anger, resentment), along with the general ineffectiveness of punishment, might prove most unwelcome.

INCENTIVES
MOTIVATION

B. R. BUGELSKI

REWARDS AND INTRINSIC INTEREST

It is usually assumed that giving rewards for performing a task increases future motivation for and engagement in that activity. A large body of research supports this assumption. But recent studies have shown that sometimes the opposite effect occurs: Under some conditions, external rewards for performance of an intrinsically interesting activity *undermine* subsequent interest in the task.

One explanation for the undermining effect of rewards is called the "overjustification" hypothesis: If an external reward is offered and provided for engaging in an initially enjoyable task, the target activity is perceived by the person as overjustified because a reward is not necessary, and the individual infers that engaging in the activity was "basically motivated by the external contingencies of the situation, rather than by any intrinsic interest in the activity itself."

INFLUENTIAL CONDITIONS

Rewards generally do not reduce motivation. Several conditions for the occurrence of an undermining effect have been determined.

Interest Level

Research has shown that rewards can undermine high initial levels of intrinsic interest, but when the task involves less initial interest, rewards enhance motivation.

Reward Factors

Rewards do not always undermine high intrinsic interest. The *type* of reward seems to be an important factor: Whereas motivation is not reduced, and may be enhanced, by verbal praise of task performance, interest tends to be undermined by rewards that are more concrete or tangible, such as candy or money. These differential reward effects have usually been interpreted in terms of the subjects' perception of (a) personal competence and (b) whether they or others are in control. Praise conveys information that the subject is competent at the task, and thereby may enhance motivation; tangible rewards may provide clearer information that another party is controlling the subject's behavior, and this lack of personal control may have a depressing effect on task involvement.

Two other reward factors are also important. First, decrements in intrinsic interest occur when the rewards are made *contingent* on performance of the target activity, but not when task performance is not tied to the reward. Second, intrinsic motivation is more likely to be undermined when the reward is *salient,* that is, when the subject's attention is focused on it.

THEORIES

A wide variety of explanations have been offered for the undermining effect, and research has disconfirmed several of them. Among the more widely accepted theories are those that propose the mediation of cognitive processes in the undermining effect, particularly attributional processes. Characteristic of attributional theories (of which the overjustification hypothesis is one) is the proposal that the undermining effect results from complex cognitive inferences involving an evaluation of internal and external reasons for engaging in the target activity.

APPLICATIONS

The relevance of the undermining effect of rewards on motivation in applied settings is obvious, and discussion in the literature has focused on work and school, and on the reward procedure called "token economies," in which appropriate behavior is rewarded with tokens that can be exchanged later for desired goods or activities.

But the real world provides complications that have not been thoroughly investigated, and we need to determine what those complications are. Also, one study has shown that rewards reduce motivation only when there is a *norm for no payment.* More research is needed to determine how best to disentangle and apply the effects of rewards to promote effective behavior.

MOTIVATION
REACTANCE THEORY
REWARDS

E. P. Sarafino

RHYTHM

The concept of rhythm has many meanings. The broadest definition that covers all meanings of the word seems to be that of Plato: "Rhythm is order in movement." One might instead propose: "Rhythm is order in succession."

Patterns of temporal order can be found in areas greatly diverse. Here we consider temporal order in three of these—cosmology, biology, and perception. There are similarities between the first two areas, but neither relate to the third.

Cosmic rhythms are known on the basis of experiences independent in time, such as the rhythm of the seasons; the rhythm of the moon, which affects tides; and especially the rhythm of day and night, which has considerable repercussion on our daily lives.

Biological rhythms are numerous in the vegetable and animal kingdoms. If one considers the organism of the human being alone, almost all the body functions are rhythmical.

These rhythms comply with the different systems whose periodicity is endogenous, but they can play the role of synchronizer as one relates to another. Clearly, as the foundation, there is the nightly rhythm. However, humans can transcend the nightly rhythm for a time, either by living in artificial conditions, or in the far North, or even as astronauts. This circadian rhythm differs for its natural duration in being somewhat longer than 24 hours.

The waking–sleeping rhythm, which is more flexible, also would appear to comply with an oscillating system. One finds it in persons in "free-running" situations, without the influences of the nightly rhythm. It is used to regulate the lives of astronauts in space where the successions of light and darkness are much more rapid.

Yet, although the waking–sleeping rhythm is profoundly altered by social conditions (night work) or geographic considerations (transmeridian flights), one can ascertain that these new rhythms in the long run can serve as *synchronizers* for the body temperature rhythm, which then adjusts itself to the rhythm of the activity.

These adaptations are important; not only do feelings of well-being or weariness depend on the temperature rhythm, but also degrees of alertness and often levels of performance are affected.

These rhythms then are defined as endogenous; their period of time scarcely varies, but their phases can be displaced through synchronization with a rhythm of the same time period (e.g., the influence of activity rhythm on temperature).

Next we find rhythms acquired through habit (conditioning). Thus, it is with the rhythms of hunger, linked to our eating habits with repercussions on our degree of alertness. Weekly rhythms also exist, related in particular to weekend resting, which, come Monday morning, causes slight difficulties with readaptation to the routine of work, whether in the classroom or in the factory.

PERCEPTUAL RHYTHMS

When one speaks of rhythm, one thinks immediately of music and poetry; that is, of the recurrence at equal intervals of one or several elements organized in unified structures. This simple description means that, in these cases, there is a perception of the order in the succession.

The perception of rhythm leads us to ask two fundamental questions: (a) What are the temporal limits in which succession is perceived?, and (b) What is the nature of structures that lend themselves to repetition?

TEMPORAL LIMITS OF PERCEIVED RHYTHM

As the basis for the perception of rhythm, there is the capacity for apprehending successive elements in a unity analogous to our capacity for apprehending a portion of space in a visual angle.

This capacity for apprehending is often called *psychic present* because it corresponds to a perception in which there are simultaneously successive elements. Such is our ability to perceive a simple phrase, such as a telephone number. The psychological present has limits that relate both to the duration and the nature of the elements. Thus one can perceive the succession of two identical sounds that go from the threshold of 0.1 second to a duration of 1.8 seconds. Beyond this duration, the sounds become elements perceived as independent of each other.

But how many elements can one perceive in this present?

Here one must distinguish discrete elements from those that form a structure. Although we are able to apprehend about five letters of the alphabet presented out of order, we can perceive 12 syllables forming a verse. In a perceived structure, be it repeated or not, we perceive subgroups called chunks. The more a perceptual unity is subdivided, the longer the psychic present can be, under the condition that no internal interval exceeds 1.8 seconds. The regular repetition of equal situations thus no longer gives the perception of merely a unity (as that of a phrase) but of a rhythm, as is the case in music, poetry, and dance.

This leads us to consider the rapidity of succession, or tempo. Tempo is referred to as the rapidity with which the elements of a structure succeed themselves and the structures within themselves.

For the rhythmic unity to be clearly perceived, it is necessary that the duration between elements be sufficiently rapid. In significantly slowing the poetic diction or musical execution, one suppresses the perception of the rhythm.

RHYTHMIC STRUCTURES

Consider the simplest example, in which a single sound is repeated at intervals of 0.4 second. These sounds are perceived as linked to each other. When listened to with care, they are perceived as grouped in twos (more rarely in threes). If one analyzes this perception, one begins to see that these groups appear distinct from each other in one or two aspects—either a lengthening of the duration between the groups (pause) or the accentuation of one of two elements.

Artistic Rhythms

Clearly, artistic rhythms are, in the order of temporality, perceived rhythms. It is important to see whether there is a connection between what is done spontaneously by creative artists and the laws of rhythm derived through experimental procedures.

Temporal Limits

Rhythms produced in poetry and music have periods of duration that register perfectly in the indicated perceptual limits. The average length of the rhythmic measures is 3.2 seconds. For lines of poetry, according to J. E. Wallin, the average duration is 2.7 seconds.

For a number of elements of substructures in music, the composer rarely exceeds six beats, and the listener generally hears units of two or three beats. In poetry, the number of syllables rarely exceeds 12, and each line is scanned in two, three, or four parts by accents or pauses.

The structure of rhythmical units perfectly illustrates the preceding analyses. For want of documents, we know through Aristoxene de Tarente (fourth century B.C.) that rhythm is a succession of durations and that these durations are not arbitrary. There is a minimum of indivisible duration and multiples of this duration by two or three, so that rhythm is analyzed as a more or less complex series of shorts and longs, that is, of series of durations. This is also true of dance, music, and chant—arts that were not dissociated. Such was the case in Greek and Latin poetry. Today, depending on the language and customs, poetry is more of the syllabic type, with regular sequences of accents, and in classical poetry, rhyme provides a supplementary indication.

In the classical music of our time, the composer disposes of a set of durations that are exceedingly numerous because the possible durations are binary divisions of a very long note, the semibreve. This is divided into minims, crotchets, quavers, and so on, without counting further gradations. A composer, in a piece that is homogeneous from the point of view of tempo, makes principal use of two notes that stand in a ratio of two or three (quaver and crotchet, or double quaver-quaver, sometimes double quaver-semiquaver), and this in a proportion of 70 to 80%. Evidently there are short notes, long notes, and silences. We believe that these accidents are the creations of the artist, who seeks to escape the determinisms that demand the preferential use of only two periods of duration, the shortest of which is the most frequent.

How might one explain this spontaneous prevalence, perpetuated by usage, of only two durations in rhythmical structures? One might recall a general law that one often finds working in the domain of perceptions: the understanding of a simplification through a double process of assimilation of the elements only slightly different from each other, and of a distinction that tends to overestimate the differences not reduced by assimilation. But in the case of durations used in rhythms, one must remember the notion of transmitted information. In the scale of absolute perceived durations, it has been established that one cannot distinguish a number of durations greater than two or, at most, three.

Here we see a constraint on temporal perception that has imposed itself on artists of all times. It also imposed itself on those who created an alphabet on the basis of intermittent lengths, such as the Morse code based on a system of dots and dashes.

RHYTHMS OF MOVEMENTS

To study the laws of rhythm, we have made use of perceptions as well as aspects of motor production. One must first note that perceived rhythms, especially in the arts, are rhythms produced by human motor or verbal activities. There is, in effect, a harmony between the rhythms produced and the rhythms perceived. This harmony manifests itself, in particular, in the fact that heard rhythms elicit a very real motor induction whose movements also are periodic. The phenomenon is observable from the earliest age. A child at the age of 1 year can rock gently upon hearing a rhythmical musical piece, and even adults must tend to restrain spontaneous movements upon hearing music.

This spontaneity is also revealed by our difficulty in stressing a beat that, for example, lies between two normal accents, or what is called syncopation. Normally it takes considerable practice to execute two different rhythms with separate hands, to create a polyrhythm.

To return to the spontaneous synchronization of music, one clearly sees that the movement accompanies the principal accent point, but if the structure is long and complex, synchronal movements are created with secondary accent points. It all works as though the induced accompanying movements are to remain interlocked, which means that the interval that separates them must be distinctly less than 1.8 second.

Motor induction and synchronization give other than perceptual qualities to the rhythms. The audiomuscular harmony brings about emotional reactions characteristic of the perception of rhythm. Besides, spontaneous synchronization allows for the socialization of rhythmical activities, such as in dance, orchestral music, and choral singing. This socialization of activities is always a source of stimulation.

Spatial Rhythms

One speaks less of spatial rhythm than one does of auditory rhythm. In describing a monument, for example, one speaks more readily of form or proportion. Quite naturally there are successions, but they register in a three-dimensional context, which gives rise to further problems.

When considering only linear successions, it is observed that they often are like rhythmic structures with regular repetitions of identical elements, as a tree-planted avenue, or by a repetition of binary, or even tertiary, structures with regular spacings between the groupings. One may even find in rows of windows, for example, more complex structures with elements that are varied but of a repetitive nature.

AUDITORY PERCEPTION
CIRCADIAN RHYTHMS
PERCEPTUAL ORGANIZATION

P. Fraisse

RIGHT TO REFUSE TREATMENT

Past failures and current successes in the area of treatment have led to a paradoxical state of affairs: We involuntarily commit individuals for treatment, yet these very individuals frequently assert a right to refuse treatment.

Past failures regarding the hospitalized and involuntary patient have been well documented. Hospitalization *per se,* the "therapeutic milieu of the hospital," and traditional "talk therapy" have not led to recovery, cure, and discharge rates. The patient rights movement, the right to treatment, and the right to treatment in the least restrictive setting have been endorsed by several courts and legislatures.

The legal roots of such a right to refuse derives from both common law, where, under tort law, informed consent is needed before medical or psychological treatments are initiated, and from constitutional law. Constitutionally, the first, fourth, eighth, and fourteenth amendments have been offered to establish such grounds.

The implications and questions, and dilemmas, for the continued treatment of involuntary patients are many, and the reactions of therapists are being heard. For one, is informed consent possible? Can an involuntarily hospitalized patient, who may have been institutionalized for many years, give competent, knowing, and voluntary consent? Might not the therapist be a "double agent"—also concerned with ward management or invested in a research project, as well as in the welfare of the patient? Are therapists not in a double bind—faced with suits for not treating and suits for treating? Will patients now be entrapped by both their psychoses and their rights? Will this lead to a challenge to psychology to develop nonmedical treatments that are both effective and consent worthy? At this stage, the questions and issues have surfaced far faster than the solutions.

PROFESSIONAL ETHICS
PSYCHOLOGY AND THE LAW
RIGHT TO TREATMENT

N. J. Finkel

RIGHT TO TREATMENT

In 1960, Morton Birnbaum, a physician and lawyer, proposed "The Right to Treatment." Although the Constitution does not speak directly about such a right, nor does it mention hospitalization, involuntary commitment, or treatment, Birnbaum reasoned that the eighth and fourteenth amendments, those dealing with cruel and unusual punishment and deprivation of liberty without due process and equal protection, could be construed to imply such a right. The issue is this: When states commit individuals to psychiatric hospitals on *parens patriae* grounds (i.e., because they are mentally ill and in need of treatment), or because they are incompetent to stand trial, is there not also the promise and obligation to provide treatment?

The first test case was *Rouse v. Cameron,* in which Judge Bazelon argued that such a right does exist. More recent cases bring to light the many complicated questions, issues, and implications facing the courts, communities, patients, mental health practitioners, legal advocates, and other branches of government.

The 1970s brought the revolution and litigation of "patients' rights" to the foreground; along with it have come a fresh examination of involuntary commitment procedures and hospital practices, and the knowledge that our treatments have not fulfilled our promises.

PSYCHOLOGY AND THE LAW
RIGHT TO REFUSE TREATMENT

N. J. Finkel

RIGIDITY

Although the term *rigidity* has no precise definition, it can be said that rigidity is especially apparent when the person's behavior fails to change even though the demands of a new situation require different behavior.

Many terms in psychology refer to rigidity, including perseveration, conservatism, dogmatism, anality, intolerance of ambiguity, and compulsiveness. Terms such as flexibility, lability, tolerance of ambiguity, and, to some degree, creativity have served as labels for tendencies contrasted with rigidity.

RIGIDITY AS PERSEVERATION

Goldstein believed that, under ordinary circumstances, the healthy person functions as a whole system with well-integrated and articulated subsystems. However, in brain damage, the integrity of the system is destroyed and the person is unable to handle the complexity required by abstract problems. Goldstein stated that the rigid, concrete behavior shown by brain-damaged patients was not a simple loss, but rather was an attempt to reduce complexity and to make a potentially overwhelming situation more manageable.

Laboratory studies indicated that when subjects were repeatedly presented with problem-solving tasks that, at first, had a fixed solution formula, they often rigidly continued to use the same solution formula for subsequent problems, even though these new tasks could be solved in a variety of ways.

INTOLERANCE OF AMBIGUITY

A number of researchers and theoreticians have noted a fairly consistent constellation of traits that includes strict obedience to authority figures, intolerance of opposing opinions, prejudice, a tendency to construct an oversimplified view of the world, a tendency to employ sharply polarized cognitive constructs, and a cynical view of human nature.

Discussions of rigid, authoritarian, and dogmatic belief systems have been extended to psychopathology. Clinically, highly dogmatic and rigid behaviors can be observed in obsessive-compulsive and paranoid patients.

AN INTEGRATION OF APPROACHES

Piaget had shown how early thought is characterized by overassimilation and overaccommodation and cogently demonstrated that young children and mentally retarded adults employ one-dimensional, rigid, "centered" cognitive strategies in comparison with the multidimensional, flexible, "decentered" strategies employed by older children and normal adults. According to Piaget, affective and moral development is inseparable from cognitive development. Therefore, the rigid behaviors found in intellectual tasks have their parallels in the lack of autonomy, perseveration, and rigid constructions of personal and interpersonal values found in social behaviors.

It may be that rigidity, in both the intellectual and affective domains, is a manifestation of unbalanced schemes in which either accommodation or assimilation predominates. As many factors, including cognitive immaturity, neurological damage, and authority-oriented child-rearing practices, may hinder the development of adequately equilibrated schemes, rigidity may stem from many different roots.

OBSESSIVE-COMPULSIVE PERSONALITY

B. S. Gorman

RITES DE PASSAGE

The concept as well as the term *rites de passage* is attributable to the anthropologist Arnold van Gennep. Van Gennep dealt with common features of transitions in the life course, which ritualize the move from one status to another. Each status is anchored in certain group and interpersonal relationships; the ritual of the change makes it possible for the individual, as well as the society, to accept an individual in a new status. Van Gennep reached his theory by the analysis of a whole series of status transitions in a number of societies. Comparisons showed three common stages in these transitions, even though there may be different emphases on some stages in different situations: separation, transition, and incorporation.

The concept of transition corresponds to the similar events in nature—rites de passage can be found in celebration of the passage of the year. The first and third stages of the rituals can then be seen as an assurance of safe passage out of the old and into the new status. The crucial stage is the second, where the person concerned is not a member of any particular status, in a liminal stage, really not a member of any particular part of society, and in this stage is exposed to danger, as well as being dangerous to society. The most important part of the ritual, therefore, is concerned with containing these individuals and assuring the occupancy of this stage with the least risk.

In contrast to this general, socio-centered theory stands the psychoanalytic approach. Psychoanalysts center their interest around one rite, the puberty rites, and consider the others as derivatives or secondary.

Contemporary society is considered to be least dependent on ritual, which is why theories of ritual depend on data from far places and times. However, some rudimentary rites do exist, and we also find complete rituals, but they have lost importance and universality.

Another way of looking at rites de passage in current society is the explanation of substitutes and revivals of rites. If there is a social or individual necessity for making transitions, then we have to find evidence for the effects of their lack or for their reappearance in societies where the sacred has been rejected. The rituals of the so-called countercultures, especially, demonstrate a striving for new rituals.

The value of the concept lies in drawing attention to the intersection of personal, life course conditions and maintenance of the social order, and in its insistence on the uncanny, threatening, and threatened condition of the person undergoing these transitions.

CULTURAL DETERMINISM
NATIONAL CHARACTER
RITUAL BEHAVIOR

K. W. Back

RITUAL BEHAVIOR

Ritual is a conventionalized joint activity, given to ceremony, involving two or more persons, endowed with special emotion and often sacred meaning, focused around a clearly defined set of social objects, and when performed confers upon its participants a special sense of the sacred and the out of the ordinary. Ritual may grow out of any sector of group life. Rituals permit few variations and are subject to the pressures of interactional normalization. Ritual performances have the features of drama and involve the reenactment of cultural and world views held to be salient and central by human groups.

Emile Durkheim divided ritual into two categories: positive and negative, or sacred and profane. Positive rituals bring interactants together in ways that support their social relationship and permit offerings of various kinds, including the giving of gifts and greetings. Negative or avoidance rituals protect the individuals and their properties from the intrusions of others. They are commonly termed taboos. According to many observers, interpersonal rituals have replaced sacred rituals in contemporary western societies.

Rituals may be performed for purely magical, mystical, or religious reasons, so as to gain some control over or mark the uncontrollable, often occurrences in the natural world, transgressions of the group's moral code, or the existential certainties of birth, death, and the life-cycle transitions. Although social relationships cannot be studied directly, the interactions that occur between individuals can be, and to the extent that these interactions are ritualized and conventionalized, ritual becomes a principal means for studying social relationships.

CONCLUSIONS

The import of ritual in everyday life may be summarized in terms of the following three assertions: (a) That which a group takes to be problematic will be subjected to pressures to make those problematic objects, acts, and events predictable and routine. This is necessary if orderly actions are to be taken toward them. (b) Groups and relationships display constant negotiated struggles over what is problematic, routine, and predictable. (c) At the heart of organized group life lies a complex network of rituals—interpersonal, positive, negative, sacred, and secular—that are communicated to newcomers to the group and that, when taught and successfully performed, lead to systematic ways of making everyday group life predictable, ordinary, and taken for granted. An understanding of the everyday, taken-for-granted features of group life requires the systematic study of ritual. The understanding of how persons are connected to others and to the society at large demands similar study. Rituals stand at the intersection of persons and society and require detailed examination by the disciplines of social anthropology, sociology, social psychology, psychology, religion, and philosophy.

CROSS-CULTURAL PSYCHOLOGY
SYMBOLIC INTERACTION

N. K. Denzin

RIVALRY

Rivalry has several different meanings in psychology. In the area of visual perception, the concept of binocular rivalry refers to certain phenomena that can accompany the simultaneous presentation of different images to each eye of an individual.

In animal psychology, the term rivalry refers to competition between individuals, usually for a mate. The term has a similar usage in developmental psychology, where in the form of sibling rivalry it refers to the competition between children, typically for the attention of their parents.

W. P. Smith

ROLE EXPECTATIONS

Roles are prescribed ways for people to divide the labor of society and to interact with others. Social roles maintain the social system, and they prevent it from changing. Interpersonal relationships do not simply occur in random fashion, but follow certain social conventions, somewhat similar to the script for a play. Since the stability of society is important, people are carefully trained and their behavior is shaped by a process of socialization. To deviate drastically from one's social role(s) is to invite social sanctions, which can interfere with effective living and the attainment of one's goals. People continue to learn a variety of roles for various social situations. All of these roles enable the individual to interact with a variety of persons in many social contexts in appropriate ways.

Although people must perform certain functions, there is the danger of getting lost in these functions. It is possible for people to limit them selves by restricting the development of aspects that do not fit neatly with their roles.

Role expectations tend to be modified with time, as can be evidenced by the major changes during the past decade in the area of sex roles. Although people have mistakenly assumed that the differential behavior of women and men was mostly a function of biological factors, there have been challenges to this point of view. Socialization factors and cultural aspects have been found to be of critical importance in determining sex-role behavior.

ACCULTURATION

G. COREY

ROLE-PLAY TESTS

One of the fundamental premises of behavior therapy is that the most valid way to assess behavior is by direct observation in the natural environment. Unfortunately it often is uneconomical or impractical to conduct this form of assessment. This is especially true when the focus is interpersonal behavior. Many of the most clinically important social interactions, such as assertion situations and conflicts, occur infrequently and unpredictably. Many others, such as sexual interactions, are private and cannot be observed. Consequently behavior therapists have turned to analog strategies as a next best alternative.

Role-play tests are the most widely employed analog procedures. The subject/patient is seated next to an experimental assistant. The experimenter/clinician describes an interpersonal scenario. The assistant, portraying a protagonist, delivers a prompt line. The subject then responds as if he or she were actually confronting the assistant in the described situation.

The typical role-play test contains 6 to 12 scenarios, selected to represent typical encounters within a problem area (e.g., assertiveness, dating). The interactions generally are audio- or videotaped for subsequent behavioral ratings. Raters are carefully trained to evaluate the responses reliably on various dimensions found to be important for the skill being assessed.

PSYCHODRAMA

A. S. BELLACK

ROLE PLAYING

Although terminology in the area of role analysis (role theory) is nonstandardized, *role playing* most often refers to enactment; what individuals say and do insofar as such behaviors are expected and evaluated by others qualifies as role enactment, as opposed to the process of *role taking* where an individual imaginatively constructs the role of self or other so as to provide directives for ongoing behavior.

Moreno and Zeleny summarize the role drama (psychodrama, sociodrama, axiodrama) as introduced and developed by Moreno; although his interests were largely in the growth and development of the human personality, much has also been done in the area of personality assessment.

PSYCHODRAMA

M. S. BLOOMBAUM

ROLE TAKING

The concept of *role* is central in social psychology, connecting personal and social levels of organization. Expected behavior is performed and evaluated by self and others with reference to personal and social norms; these cohere in meaningful units termed roles. Interpersonal and conventional social roles constitute analytically separable contexts in terms of which behavior is anticipated, performed, and evaluated. Although terminology in this area is not standardized, *role taking* generally refers to the imaginative construction of a role to be enacted by someone else; role taking is a process that, in the ongoing give and take of social interaction, provides directives for behavior. In the self–other context, role taking is present to the extent to which self's behavior is influenced by self's conception of other's role.

A major distinction is between role taking and enactment. Any behavior displayed and evaluated in accordance with interpersonal and/or conventionalized expectations therefore may be termed *role playing* rather than role taking. Nevertheless it has been suggested that there is no such thing as role taking without role playing or role playing without role taking.

ROLE PLAYING

M. S. BLOOMBAUM

ROLFING

Ida Rolf, a biochemist and physiologist, is the founder of Rolfing or Structural Integration, a short-term therapy that involves direct physical manipulation of the body, particularly of connective and muscle tissue. The primary goal of the technique is structural change, "structure" referring to the relatively stable but malleable relations among segments of the body, such as parts of the torso and the pelvis.

Influenced by yoga and other Eastern body disciplines, Rolf adopted what she referred to as a monistic position. One's body consists of structures that mirror changes in one's world. Aspects of culture, of personal history and lifestyle, and of both psychological and physiological traumas are bodily borne as rigidities, imbalances, asymmetries, and rotations of the body structures.

K. J. SHAPIRO

RORSCHACH TECHNIQUE

The Rorschach technique was launched by the publication in 1921 of Hermann Rorschach's *Psychodiagnostik*. He viewed mental disorders as disease entities and liked to speak of the faculties of the organism such as will, emotions, intellect, and imagination. He was primarily a Jungian analyst and his original purpose in experimenting with inkblots was to discover a means of predicting whether patients would be introversive or extratensive.

The Rorschach technique became popular during the time in the history of clinical psychology when the psychoanalytic view was preeminent, when inner processes and the unconscious were the assessment target for clinical psychologists.

The Rorschach technique is no longer considered a magical instrument with a mysterious capacity for probing beyond the immediate, mystically revealing the inner essence. Part of this is due to the fact that one's inner essence is no longer sought after in the same manner as before. Rather, most clinicians currently are interested in predicting behavior under specified conditions. Exner, after reviewing various Rorschach interpretation systems and culling the valuable essence of each, composed a comprehensive system that has begun to create more uniformity in the administration, scoring, and research use of the test.

PROJECTIVE TECHNIQUES

W. G. KLOPFER

ROSENZWEIG PICTURE–FRUSTRATION (P–F) STUDY

The Rosenzweig Picture–Frustration (P–F) study is a semiprojective technique consisting of a series of 24 cartoonlike pictures, each depicting two persons involved in mildly frustrating situations of common occurrence. Facial features and other expressions of emotion are deliberately omitted from the pictures. The figure at the left is always shown saying certain words that help to describe the frustration of the other individual. In the blank caption box above the frustrated figure on the right, the subject is asked to write the first reply that enters his or her mind.

It is assumed that the examinee unconsciously or consciously identifies with the frustrated individual in each picture and projects his or her own bias in the responses given. To define this bias, scores are assigned to each response under two main dimensions: direction of aggression and type of aggression. Under *direction* are included extraggression (EA), in which aggression is turned onto the environment; intraggression (IA), in which it is turned by the subject on him- or herself; and imaggression (MA), in which aggression is evaded in an attempt to gloss over the frustration. It is as if extraggressiveness turned aggression *out,* intraggressiveness turned it *in,* and imaggressiveness turned it *off.* Type of aggression includes obstacle dominance (OD), in which the barrier occasioning the frustration stands out in the response; ego (etho) defense (ED), in which the ego of the subject predominates to defend itself; and need persistence (NP), in which the solution of the frustrating problem is emphasized by pursuring the goal despite the obstacle. From the combination of these six categories, there result for each item nine possible scoring factors.

Aggression is generically defined as assertiveness, which may be either affirmative or negative in character. Need persistence represents a constructive (sometimes creative) form of aggression, whereas ego (etho) defense is frequently destructive (of others or of oneself) in import. This point is particularly noteworthy because in many technical theories of aggression this distinction is overlooked and aggression is practically synonymous with hostility or destructiveness. Common parlance, when not contaminated by psychoanalytic or other psychological conceptualizations, comes close to the broader usage of the term *aggression,* which the P–F study employs.

Although the scoring of the P–F is always phenotypic (according to the explicit wording used in the response), interpretation is genotypic, involving three kinds of norms: universal (nomothetic), group (demographic), and individual (idiodynamic). Statistical data used in interpretation refer to group norms (i.e., the extent to which the individual performs vis-à-vis the group to which he or she belongs—age, sex, etc.). Individual (idiodynamic) norms, which derive from the unique wording of the responses and in interrelation of the scored factors in the protocol, complement the group norms. Universal (nomothetic) norms are represented by the constructs on which the instrument is based, and these underlie both group and individual norms. A Group Conformity Rating (GCR) measures the subject's tendency to agree with the modal responses of a normal population sample.

The P–F has been studied for both construct (criterion-related) and for pragmatic validity with significantly positive results. In addition to the clinical purposes for which the study was originally intended, it has been used as a screening or selection device in business and industry, schools, and research on cultural differences. In particular, the GCR has proved to be of value. The categories etho-defense and need-persistence also have been shown to have differentiating potential, and some positive results have been obtained for obstacle-dominance. P–F results in hospital and clinic settings have proved useful, but an exclusive reliance on the P–F as a symptom-differentiating tool in such contexts is not recommended. Used in conjunction with other tests or as part of a configuration index, the technique has significant potential.

The published evidence for P–F reliability and validity are summarized in the *Basic manual* and discussed in detail in the book *Aggressive behavior and the Rosenzweig picture–frustration (P–F) study.*

CLINICAL ASSESSMENT
IDIODYNAMICS
PERSONALITY ASSESSMENT
PROJECTIVE TECHNIQUES

S. Rosenzweig

ROTE LEARNING

Rote learning refers to a change in behavior that results from forming arbitrary, verbatim associations between a stimulus and response.

David Ausubel and colleagues suggest that all learning tasks can be conceptualized on a rote-meaningfulness continuum. Ausubel suggests further that, in school, most learning material should be conceptualized as meaningful and presented in a such a way as to facilitate meaningfulness with the students.

Rotely learned material is likely to be forgotten very quickly for two reasons. First, because the learning process is limited to associations that are formed, any material learned before or after that is similar will interfere, and reduce retention. Second, such associations are more susceptible to decay and disuse because they are not related to existing anchors within the memory system.

MEMORY EXPERIMENTS

J. M. McMillan

RUNAWAY BEHAVIOR

Runaway behavior, defined as children leaving home without parental permission, has been noted through history. In the United States, runaway behavior is seen as a problem of some magnitude. Estimates vary as to the number of runaways per year—from approximately half a million to 1 million.

Runaway behavior is stressful, even tragic, for the family; it often eventuates in criminal behavior or victimization of the runaway; and, societally, it is seen as a waste of potential and a drain on resources. Parent–child conflict—overcontrol as seen by girls, undercontrol as seen by boys—is typical of families from which children run. A majority of runaways have little involvement in school and high absenteeism prior to running away. The list of reasons runaways give for this behavior is long, and includes parents, police, dope, responsibility, bad food, city, teachers, love, hatred, bad friends, very good friends, embarrassing situations, and junior high school.

Runaways have more contact with the police and higher rates of drug abuse prior to leaving home than do nonrunaways. After leaving home, they experience even greater exposure to crime and drugs, and, if they are apprehended and put under the juvenile justice system, delinquent behavior increases.

ADOLESCENCE

G. J. Manaster

S

SADISTIC RITUALISTIC ABUSE

Sadistic ritualistic abuse (SRA), also known as satanic ritualistic abuse or ritual abuse, has been defined as a brutal form of abuse of children, adolescents, and adults, consisting of physical, sexual, and psychological abuse, and involving rituals. Retrospective investigations of a number of cases, typically involving convictions of adults abusing preschool children, have attributed the charges and even convictions to public hysteria and overzealous, leading interrogations. (Editorial update by AA.)

LEVELS OF SATANISM

Satanism has been defined in four levels.

1. The experimental–dabbler, typically a young person (age range between 9 and 28), is the fastest growing level within the ritual abuse/satanic belief system according to Sinandi. The dabbler may use fantasy role-playing games, heavy-metal music, and movies to enhance rituals. Rituals may involve drinking blood, wine, and/or urine mixtures, taking drugs as well as mutilating and sacrificing animals. These rituals may progress to human sacrifice.

2. Nontraditional, self-styled satanists are described as "individuals with psychotic personality disorders . . . obsessed with satanic themes . . . who may practice their gruesome rituals alone or in small groups." Hicks sees these satanists as social isolates who invented ideologies to affirm their behavior.

3. Organized traditional satanists are organized religious groups worshipping Satan. They are protected by religious freedom under the law and reportedly not linked to ritualistic crime. The Church of Satan, The Temple of Set, and The Process Church of the Final Judgment are typical examples of organized traditional satanists.

4. The final level is known as occultic networking or transgenerational cults. Ryder describes this group as "those perpetuated through family generations." Children raised in such environments tend to view cult activities as a normal part of the family. This category of satanism, often identified as SRA, is the focus of this chapter.

THE SRA CONTROVERSY

The FBI first received reports of possible SRA activity in 1983. Since then there has been an explosion of interest in and controversy surrounding SRA in Christian, professional, and law enforcement circles.

The basic controversy is over whether such cults exist, should they exist, how they are organized, and how they conspire to abuse people. It would seem that the phenomenon of SRA allegations from many independent sources requires more study. Research must go from anecdotal and unconfirmed (uncollaborated) accounts to more scientific research. Nurcombe and Unutzer noted there were too many unanswered questions and, therefore, the book on "ritual abuse" could not be closed or answered until pornographic sex rings and satanistic cells are penetrated by law enforcement professionals.

Greaves states that apologists believe on clinical grounds that satanic cult survivors' (SCS's) productions are actual experiences. Greaves reached this conclusion because SCS's productions in therapy appear to be "congruent in affect, cognition, behavior, symptom, process, and symptom reduction." This impression seems to be confirmed when these patients also display prominent posttraumatic stress disorder (PTSD) symptoms.

Commonly reported satanic symbols include the pentagram, inverted pentagram, hexagram (Star of David), cross of Nero (peace symbol or broken cross), swastika, anarchy, thaumaturgic triangle, udjat (all-seeing eye), scarab, lightning bolts, 666, ankh, inverted cross, black mass indicator, an emblem of Baphomet, church of Satan, and the cross of confusion.

RITUAL ABUSE OF CHILDREN

Snow and Sorensen conducted a study of ritualistic child abuse in five separate neighborhood settings. The subjects were 39 children, age 4 to 17. In four out of the five neighborhoods, three distinct components of the sexual abuse appeared: incest, juvenile perpetration, and the adult ritual sex ring.

Finkelhor et al. conducted a study of sexual abuse in day care centers in America. Over a 3-year period, they identified 270 day care centers with a total of 1639 victims of sexual abuse. They noted that 13% of the cases involved ritualistic abuse. Kelly examined the effects of sexual and ritualistic abuse in day care centers. Compared with the victims of sexual abuse, ritualistically abused children "experienced significantly more types of sexual abuse," more severe physical abuse, and along with the sexual abuse group was "extremely frightened by threats made by the offenders." Kelly found that there were significantly more victims per day care center and more offenders per child when ritualistic abuse was involved. "The children were also threatened with threats that supernatural powers such as Satan would always know where they were and what they were doing."

THERAPEUTIC ISSUES

Catherine Gould noted that for three reasons seldom do ritually abused children spontaneously disclose their abuse. These children are often drugged before the abuse. Hypnosis is often used to implant posthypnotic suggestions that they would not remember and, if they should, that they would have to harm or kill themselves. The abuse is so intolerable that dissociation usually occurs. These three factors combined in the ritualistic abuse of children before the age of 6 often create "amnestic barriers," making spontaneous disclosure unlikely.

Gould developed a checklist for signs and symptoms of ritualistic abuse in children that includes 12 categories: (a) sexual behavior and beliefs; (b) toileting and the bathroom; (c) supernatural, rituals, occult symbols, religion; (d) small spaces or being tied up; (e) death; (f) the doctor's office; (g) certain colors; (h) eating; (i) emotional problems, including speech, sleep, and learning problems; (j) family relationships; (k) play and peer relations; and (l) other fears, references, disclosures, and strange beliefs. The recommended form of therapy includes "a combination of play therapy and the disclosure [by the child] of the abuse to the therapist and the parents (when the abuse is extrafamilial)." The therapist is to be active in the treatment in structuring the therapeutic activities and providing motivation to the child to address issues that otherwise the child may avoid. Play therapy can be adapted to address possible multiplicity that may have resulted from the ritual abuse. Gould stresses that the four components of each traumatic incident be addressed using the acronym BASK, namely the (a) behavior, what occurred during the abuse; (b) affect, what the child experienced emotionally; (c) sensation, being able to "surface, identify, and experience the body trauma"; and (d) knowledge, the "meaning of the abusive event to the child and to the perpetrator."

Gould and Cozolino identify four mind-control programs that cults typically try to establish. They note ritualistic abuse is designed to cause dissociation, and the altered personalities thus created are exploited to serve cult functions. The process is described as follows: A victim is severely abused to the point that his or her emotions and cognitions are separated or split apart, creating a negative window, the cult program is then inserted, the abuse is then stopped, effectively closing the negative window. The cult program would now be in place but usually unconscious to the victim. These programs reportedly are (a) recontact programs, whereby a trigger signal causes the survivor to make contact with the cult or allow contact by a cult member; (b) reporting programs, whereby the survivor in one of his or her alters reports activities to the cult; (c) self-injury and suicide programs, to be enacted if "cult injunctions" are broken; and (d) therapy disruption programs, intended to disrupt therapy that may free a survivor from cult influences.

RITUAL ABUSE OF ADOLESCENTS

Most relevant research is focused on survivors of childhood ritualistic abuse. Tennant-Clark, Fritz, and Beauvais focused on the impact of occult participation on adolescent development. They noted a psychosocial profile of "high occult participants": chemical substance abuse, low self-esteem, negative feelings about school, poor self-concept, low desire to be considered a good person, negative feelings about religion, high tolerance for deviance, negative feelings about the future, low social sanctions against drug use, and feeling blamed.

ADULT SURVIVORS OF RITUAL ABUSE

Young et al. reported a study of 37 adult dissociative disorder patients who reported satanic ritual abuse as children. The types of abuses reported were, in order of decreasing percents: sexual, witnessing and receiving physical pain or torture, witnessing animal mutilation or killings, death threats, forced drug usage, witnessing and forced participation in human adult and infant sacrifice, and forced cannibalism, marriage to Satan, buried alive in coffins or graves and forced impregnation and sacrifice of own child. The marriage to Satan and forced impregnation percentages were based on 33 female patients.

ADULT SURVIVORS OF RITUAL ABUSE: THERAPEUTIC CONSIDERATIONS

Most adults with a history of SRA do not present themselves for therapy as adult survivors. They commonly will present highly developed dissociative disorders of varying complexity, frequently including Multiple Personality Disorder. Memories are well defended, usually by dissociative, amnesic layers uncovered through psychotherapy.

The phases of treatment involve (a) developing a therapeutic alliance, (b) evaluation and assessment, (c) clarifying the dissociative system, (d) discovering repressed information and dissolving dissociative barriers, (e) reconstructing memory and reframing beliefs, (f) countering indoctrinated beliefs, (g) desensitizing triggers and cues (programming), and (h) coming to terms with the past and finding new meaning and purpose in life. Young discusses different modes of treatment, including abreaction; hypnosis; expressive therapies such as journaling, art, and sand tray; medication; and hospitalization, including voluntary restraints. Shaffer and Cozolino also reported the benefit of 12-step groups as an adjunct to therapy.

It is common for SRA survivors to become depressed and suicidal subsequent to uncovering traumatic memories. This can be the result of suicidal programming or an inability to integrate the often horrific memories. It is critical to help patients to reframe their memories in the context that they were not responsible but were in fact victims of intimidation and abuse.

AMNESIA
ASSESSING CHILDREN FOR PSYCHOTHERAPY

CHILD ABUSE
DEPROGRAMMING
DEVIANCE
EXORCISM
FEARS THROUGHOUT THE LIFE SPAN
LIFE EVENTS
MEMORY DISORDERS
OCCULTISM
SADOMASOCHISM
SEXUAL DEVIATIONS
STRESS CONSEQUENCES
TREATMENT OUTCOME
WITCHCRAFT

G. F. Rhoades

SADOMASOCHISM

The reason for the composite term *sadomasochism* is that most individuals who have sadistic inclinations also harbor masochistic desires. Exclusive sadists are rare. Toch reported that the large majority of the men he studied obtained no *direct* gratification from the use of force. It was simply a mechanism by which various desires were gratified and different purposes fulfilled. Less than 6% obtained direct satisfaction from the employment of violence.

According to a survey of a self-defined S/M (sadomasochistic) sample, less than 9% of men inclined to sadomasochism prefer the dominant (sadistic) role exclusively, and less than 8% prefer the submissive (masochistic) role exclusively. The data for women were somewhat different, with less than 7% preferring the dominant role but more than 17% preferring the submissive role.

SEXUAL DEVIATIONS

E. E. Levitt

SALES PSYCHOLOGY

The field of sales psychology is often broadened beyond personal selling, which involves direct contact between the salesperson and the customer, to include marketing, which uses media advertising to attract potential customers.

Selling is divided into areas according to the customer and the product or service sold. Research has shown that characteristics correlated with success in one kind of sales are not necessarily predictive for other kinds.

A function for the psychologist who acts as a consultant to sales executives, sales managers, and sales trainers is to make them aware of the best and latest research knowledge that can be applied in the selection, training, follow-up, and performance evaluation of salespeople.

HISTORY OF SALES PSYCHOLOGY

Sales psychology was directly influenced by the three major systematic approaches: functionalism, behaviorism, and psychoanalysis. The functional emphasis was the first and the most important. Hugo Münsterberg launched the functional approach to applied psychology. In Münsterberg's 1913 book, he included a review of experiments on the effectiveness of advertising.

The table of contents of Strong's 1925 book shows a coverage of most topics included in modern textbooks on sales psychology: buyer motivation, market surveys, theories of selling, analyses of prospecting, strategies for opening–presenting–closing sales interviews, selection and training, sales management, and connections among selling, marketing, and advertising.

J. McKeen Cattell was another functional psychologist in the field of sales and marketing psychology. His creation, the Psychological Corporation, devised many tests used in sales personnel selection, conducted numerous market surveys, and developed much of the methodology of survey research now routinely applied by advertisers.

The behavioral approach was represented in the early history of sales and marketing psychology by J. B. Watson. Watson contributed significantly to the use and development of market survey methods. He frequently addressed sales and business conventions at which he tried to counter negative attitudes the public had toward sales as a profession and he taught salespeople to learn and apply the basics of stimulus–response psychology.

The psychoanalytic influence in sales and advertising was sketched by Donald Laird. He believed that sales resistances could be understood and overcome in the same ways that Sigmund Freud and other analysts understood and worked with clinical resistances. However, the most influential application of psychoanalytic ideas to advertising was made by Ernest Dichter. Dichter urged advertisers to attempt to understand the "deeper meanings" of products and services.

SAMPLES OF SALES RESEARCH AND MANAGEMENT APPROACHES

Most major managerial approaches have been applied to sales training and sales management. Among the most widely used are Blake and Mouton's managerial grid method; systems analysis; behavioral analyses; Drucker's management by objectives (MBO); Jackson and Aldag's managing the sales force by objectives; and Herzberg's analysis of job enrichment and work satisfiers.

Test results indicate that the most successful salespeople usually show these key characteristics: drive, energy, believability, assertiveness, emotional independence, self-sufficiency, self-assuredness, optimism, social outgoingness, a willingness to persuade and confront, a need to succeed, and a tendency to admit and accept limitations. All agree that different kinds of sales situations require different personality characteristics.

Many programs of sales training could benefit by an emphasis on broad sales education rather than narrow sales training and by conceptualizations about adult education. All too often, sales programs are not designed for independent, self-directing, adult learners.

ADVERTISING
INDUSTRIAL PSYCHOLOGY

J. T. Hart

SAMPLING

Sampling procedures are ways of selecting a small number of units from a population to enable researchers to infer the nature of that population from the sample. Sampling is used in public opinion and consumer polling to make inferences from the responses of the sample as to how the population will vote on election day or how consumers will react to a new product or a television program. Sampling as a concept is pervasive not only in experimental research, but in daily life, as when we judge a new supermarket by our first shopping visit there, or decide that the whole roast is underdone from the portion on our plate.

PROBABILITY AND NONPROBABILITY SAMPLES

Sampling procedures are divided into those yielding probability samples that involve random sampling and, therefore, probability theory, and those yielding nonprobability samples that do not involve random sam-

pling. Types of probability sampling, in addition to simple random sampling, are systematic, stratified, and cluster sampling. By using the mathematical theory of probability, one is able to infer the characteristics of the population from a probability sample within a determinable margin of error. Further, one can set that margin of error at any level of precision or certainty desired. More certainty requires larger samples, more complex designs, or both.

Quota, panel, and convenience samples (using whatever cases are handy) are nonprobability samples. Nonprobability samplers also make estimates of population values, but since they do not involve random sampling, their estimates do not have the same convincing probability theory base and are viewed with suspicion by those committed to probability sampling. Yet nonprobability samples are widely used because of their comparative convenience and economy.

BASIC SAMPLING CONCEPTS

Basic to sampling procedures is an understanding of the nature of the population and its relation to the sampling frame, the unit of sampling, and sample size.

The Population or Universe and the Sampling Frame

A first decision is to determine the population or universe to which one wishes to generalize. Ideally it should be identical with the sampling frame, which is the complete list of units in the universe from which the sample will be drawn. However, the population and frame may not be identical, either because the listing is incomplete or because it cannot be complete as the units to be sampled are not available.

Size of Sample

It may seem that the larger the sample, the better—but this is not necessarily true. One may obtain more precision than is needed, and thus waste resources. In many instances, resources concentrated on carefully gathering data thoroughly from a sample will yield better data than a census that could not be as thorough or as carefully controlled. If one has prior information about the variability of the characteristic being studied, one can estimate the size of the sample required for any desired level of precision. The size of the population bears no relation to the required sample size.

SAMPLING PROCEDURES

Following is a brief description of the most commonly used sampling procedures and their advantages and drawbacks. The choice of an appropriate procedure requires one to balance such considerations as level of desired certainty, availability of complete sampling frame list, geographic dispersion if interviews are involved, and available resources. Because of this complexity, specialists are often consulted regarding the design of sampling plans and procedures.

Simple Random Sampling

In simple random sampling, every unit must have an equal chance of being drawn in each selection, and each selection must be made independently of the others.

Systematic Sampling

The drawing of every nth person from the frame is a simple way of getting a random sample if there is no periodicity to the list. In contrast, if the list is ordered with respect to a pertinent property, it ensures representativeness with respect to that characteristic. Further, it gives a stratification effect that yields increased precision for the same size sample.

Stratified Random Sampling

Stratifying requires breaking the frame into two or more parts on the basis of some characteristic that, if not properly represented in the sample, might bias our inferences.

Stratified sampling requires that, in addition to correct enumeration of the frame, there be both information correctly allocating units to strata and correct information on the proportion each stratum is of the whole. If systematic sampling is used to extract cases from within strata, the problem of determining correct strata proportions is eliminated, since by taking every nth case, the strata are correctly represented.

If we wish to maximize the information gained from a given size of sample, there is still a better strategy than proportional stratified sampling. In general, the most efficient use of a sample of a given size is made by varying the proportion of the sample assigned to any given stratum in relation to that stratum's homogeneity or variability in comparison with the other strata; the more variability, the larger proportion of the cases are taken from it. This is called optimum allocation sampling. It requires knowledge of the variability of each stratum on the stratifying characteristic. One may stratify on more than one characteristic at the same time. Stratifying on too many variables, however, gains little and wastes resources unless each variable is largely independent of the other.

Cluster and Multistage Sampling

Particularly for interview studies of a widely dispersed population, simple and stratified random sampling can require considerable travel and be quite expensive. Cluster sampling reduces this cost considerably by geographically clustering the cases. It involves placing a grid over the geographic area of the population, randomly selecting squares (clusters) from the grid to represent it, and then using the cases in each cluster for the study. Because there may be more cases in a cluster than needed, cluster sampling is often used as the first stage of a multistage procedure.

Sequential Sampling

If the characteristics or opinions being studied will not change over the time the study is being done, and if it is easy and efficient to return to the field to gather additional data, sequential sampling has advantages. It permits use of any of the foregoing sampling plans. Each successive sample is added to the previous samples until stability of estimates within the desired range of precision is attained. This method recently has been of increased interest for telephone surveys.

Quota Sampling and Panels

Quota sampling and panels are nonprobability samples. Their goal is basically to establish a replica of the population to be sampled. Thus quotas are established for the important features of the population likely to affect the characteristic being studied. Characteristics commonly used are sex, education, socioeconomic status, ethnicity, and residence location.

Sometimes nonprobability sampling designs are combined with probability designs as, for example, in a political poll that uses a cluster sample procedure to select neighborhoods and then a quota sample to assure representation of age, sex, and political party affiliation within the neighborhood.

Snowball Sampling

Snowball sampling is a nonprobability sampling procedure used to define a social group or those in a network of communication. Once a few members of the group are identified, they are asked for names of others in that group. That same question is then asked of the persons newly identified, and the process continues until few new names are received and the group or community appears to be identified.

PROBABILITY

D. R. KRATHWOHL

SCALING

During the latter part of the nineteenth century, several investigators studied the relationship between stimulus intensity and the intensity of the sensation produced by that stimulus. According to G. T. Fechner, for example, sensation intensity is proportional to the logarithm of the stimulus intensity. L. L. Thurstone pointed out that one class of psychophysical methods, such as the method of average error, required that the experimenter be able to obtain and control some physical measurement of stimulus intensity, whereas another class of methods, for example, the method of paired comparisons, could easily be applied where precise measurement and controlled variation of the stimulus intensity were not possible. He pointed out further that by developing and utilizing methods of this type, one would have a powerful set of tools for the quantitative measurement of subjective qualities for which there are no relevant stimulus measurements.

Measurement may be defined as the assignment of numerals to represent certain nonnumerical properties of a set of objects. Four basic types of scales may be classified in a two-by-two system with respect to origin, or zero point, and unit of measurement, as follows:

	No Natural Origin	A Natural Origin
No unit of measurement (ordinal)	1	2
A unit of measurement (distance between two points)	3	4

An illustration of type 1, an ordinal scale with no unit and no origin, would be the Mohs' scale of hardness of objects. An illustration of type 2, an ordinal scale with a natural origin, would be a pleasantness–unpleasantness scale; the natural origin, or zero point, would be the zero point dividing pleasant from unpleasant. Scales of type 3 or 4 would occur in psychological scaling, for any situation in which it is reasonable to ask, regarding every set of three stimuli, a, b, and c, whether the difference between a and b is greater or less than the difference between b and c, where a, b, and c are all different, as in scales of value or preference.

PAIRED COMPARISONS AND THE LAW OF COMPARATIVE JUDGMENT

The basic method of experimentation for psychological scaling is the method of paired comparisons, also used in psychophysics. To use this method, it is not necessary that the experimenter obtain some relevant measure of stimulus intensity. It is only necessary that the experimenter be able to present the same stimulus a number of times, as, for example, a given work of art, or the word designating a given crime, could be presented a large number of times in combination with other stimuli of the same class. To utilize the *law of comparative judgment*, the subject must be presented, in turn, with all possible pairs of the set of objects being scaled, and for each pair, the subject gives a judgment with respect to the characteristic being scaled. The immediate purpose is to obtain the percentage of times one object in the pair is judged to exceed the other, either by a given subject, or by a group of subjects. This percentage is used as an estimate of the probability that one object will be judged to exceed the other.

One objection to paired comparisons as an experimental method is that $(n - 1)(n/2)$ judgments are required for n stimuli. For 10 stimuli, 45 judgments are required; if one wished to scale a set of 50 stimuli,

1225 judgments would be needed. Various time-saving procedures are described. One of these is the *multiple rank orders* method. Subsets of the stimuli larger than pairs are rank ordered, choosing appropriate subsets so that one gets information on all the pairs. Comparatively greater savings are obtained with larger sets of stimuli. Such arrangements have been termed *balanced incomplete block* designs.

An Experimentally Determined Zero Point

Another objection to the results obtained by the method of paired comparisons is that the scales obtained are of type 3. They have a unit of measurement, but no natural origin. Scales of type 4 have a natural zero point, which may be determined by the use of an *absolute judgment* section.

For single-ended attributes it is also possible to use the procedures of psychophysics for determining a stimulus limen to give a lower bound or zero point for such a scale. In situations where it is reasonable, the subject can be asked whether the quality is present or not. An absolute limen can then be determined by standard psychophysical procedures.

TOTAL CIRCULAR TRIADS

One advantage of the complete paired comparisons procedure is that it gives "total circular triads," a very good measure of the transitivity, or consistency, of the subject's judgments.

Successive Intervals and the Law of Categorical Judgment

This method is suitable for the situation in which one wishes to scale a large number of stimuli, and is willing to omit tests for transitivity, or linearity. It is, of course, possible to use a smaller subset of these stimuli for a paired-comparisons experiment to give total circular triads, as an indicator of the transitivity of the scale and the carefulness of the subjects. The subject is given each stimulus only once, and indicates its place on the designated scale, either by marking a point on a line, or by giving some number from 1 to 10, 20, or 30, for example, as directed by the experimenter. Frequently, descriptive names are used to designate some of the categories. Because this procedure requires only n judgments for n stimuli, while the paired comparisons method requires $(n - 1)(n/2)$ judgments, the saving in subject time is considerable. Data collected by the experimental method of successive intervals are analyzed by the law of categorical judgment.

MULTIDIMENSIONAL SCALING

The methods discussed so far are appropriate for dealing with any attribute of a set of objects that is one dimensional. The situation in which the single individual perceives the set of objects as differing in more than one dimension requires the development of new experimental methods, termed multidimensional scaling methods. The triadic judgments used by M. W. Richardson, presented subjects with a triad of stimuli *a, b,* and *c* and required each subject at each presentation to judge for which pair of stimuli the sense-distance was the greatest, and for which pair the sense-distance was the least. Since then there have been numerous developments in experimental and analytical methods for studying multidimensional scaling.

LAWS DETERMINED BY SCALING STUDIES

In the majority of scaling studies, the principal interest is in the scale values themselves, and how they may change from one stimulus to another, one person or group to another, or one time to another, as a result of exposing the judges to different types of influences, such as a movie or a lecture. However, the major scientific purpose of measurement is to establish laws relating the measured variables. Several studies have used various types of composite stimuli to determine the effect of combining stimuli of different types.

The majority of the situations dealt with so far in linear scaling of a set of objects by a group of persons, and multidimensional scaling, involve the analysis of a matrix. However, various situations arise that need three modes of classification to represent the data adequately. Three-mode analysis is the appropriate method to use whenever the data have three independent modes of classification.

MATHEMATICAL MODELS
MULTIDIMENSIONAL SCALING
PSYCHOMETRICS
PSYCHOPHYSICAL MEASUREMENTS

H. O. GULLIKSEN

SCAPEGOATING

Scapegoating is the process by which one finds a substitute victim on which to vent anger. By condemning the "scapegoat," one is able to vent one's feelings without attacking the real subject of one's ire or blaming oneself. In Biblical times, the Israelites cleansed their sins by allowing a goat, symbolically bearing their wrongdoings, to escape into the desert. In the modern psychological sense it is apt to be an unconscious projection.

The most obvious case of scapegoating in the modern world is that of Nazi Germany. Although the most dramatic examples of scapegoating are in intergroup relations, its most frequent use is probably individual.

VICTIMOLOGY

W. E. GREGORY

SCHEDULES OF REINFORCEMENT

Some stimuli, such as food when one is hungry or approval when one values the opinion of the audience, increase the frequency of the responses that produce (precede) them. A rat that receives food after pressing a lever is more likely to press the lever on future occasions, and a person whose words are greeted with approval is more likely to continue speaking. Technically, stimuli that strengthen the responses that precede them are called reinforcing stimuli, or simply reinforcers. Not every occurrence of a response need be followed by a reinforcer for the strength of the response to be affected (e.g., lever pressing by a rat might produce food only after the occurrence of five responses rather than after each response). A complete statement of the conditions under which a response is followed by a reinforcer is known as the schedule of reinforcement. Research has shown that the schedule of reinforcement critically determines the effect of the reinforcer on the response. Two aspects of the study of schedules of reinforcement are noted here: their behavioral effects and their theoretical treatment.

BEHAVIORAL EFFECTS

Three behavioral effects of schedules of reinforcement are considered: acquisition, maintenance, and persistence of responding. In general, acquisition (or learning) is slowed when only some occurrences of the response are followed by the reinforcer. Thus a rat learning to press a lever will acquire the response more rapidly if every occurrence of lever pressing is followed by food than if only some produce food. A schedule of reinforcement in which all occurrences of the response produce food is called a continuous, or consistent, schedule; one in which only some occurrences produce the reinforcer is called an intermittent, or partial, schedule.

Once the response has been acquired, intermittent schedules of reinforcement are generally sufficient to maintain responding, especially if the reinforcement schedule gradually changes from continuous to intermittent. Intermittent schedules maintain responding and, more important, determine the overall rate and temporal patterning of responding. For example, the same number of reinforcers may produce either high or low rates of responding, depending on the characteristics of the schedule. Traditionally, schedules of reinforcement have been classified in regard to two characteristics: the response requirements and the time requirements necessary for reinforcement. Schedules in which a number of responses are required to produce the reinforcer are known as ratio schedules; they specify a ratio of the number of responses to the reinforcer. For example, if a rat must emit four lever presses before the fifth press produces food, then the ratio schedule is 5 : 1. Schedules with time requirements in addition to the requirement for the one response that produces the reinforcer are known as interval schedules. For example, if 1 minute must elapse since the last occurrence of food before a lever press produces food again, then the interval schedule is 1 minute. In general, ratio schedules produce higher rates of responding than interval schedules. Both ratio and interval schedules may specify either a fixed or a variable amount of responses or time, respectively. Thus if food is presented after every fifth lever press, then the schedule is a fixed ratio schedule; if food is presented after an *average* of five responses (e.g., either three, five, or seven responses), then the schedule is a variable ratio schedule. In general, variable reinforcement schedules maintain steady rates of responding, whereas fixed schedules produce changing rates of responding. In fixed schedules, the rate of responding is low immediately after a reinforcer, when the response cannot produce the reinforcer, and increases thereafter.

The third behavioral effect of schedules of reinforcement is on the persistence of responding (i.e., on the extent to which the response continues to occur after the response no longer produces a reinforcer). In general, intermittent schedules of reinforcement greatly increase the persistence of responding (i.e., the resistance to extinction).

Because the rate and temporal patterning of responding is highly dependent on the schedule of reinforcement, many aspects of behavior that are conventionally discussed in motivational terms may be interpreted as the effect of schedules. For example, parents that buy candy for a child after a prolonged bout of pleading, begging, and whining have unintentionally reinforced such behavior on a ratio schedule of reinforcement. Whereas such behavior might otherwise be attributed to the child's "need" for candy or to some internal state such as the child being spoiled, a behavioral analysis attributes the behavior to the schedule of reinforcement on which it was acquired and maintained.

THEORETICAL TREATMENT OF SCHEDULES

The theoretical treatment of schedules of reinforcement has taken two complementary forms: molar approaches and molecular approaches. In molar approaches, efforts are made to account for the global aspects of behavior produced by the schedule (e.g., the overall rate of responding or the duration of responding during extinction). As an illustration, a common finding is that an organism confronted with two simultaneously available responses (a so-called concurrent schedule) will distribute its responses in proportion to the number of reinforcers available for those responses. Thus if three times as many reinforcers are available for one response as for the other during a given time period, then three times as many responses of the first type will occur. This molar relation between the number of reinforcers and the number of responses is summarized by the matching principle: The learner matches the relative number of responses to the relative number of reinforcers.

Alternatively, the behavior observed on a schedule of reinforcement may be analyzed in terms of the moment-to-moment, or molecular, rela-

tions among the particular stimuli, responses, and reinforcers occurring at each point in time. In this approach, the global relations studied by molar approaches are seen as the cumulative expression of molecular processes. That is, molar relations are the effects of molecular processes and do not themselves yield fundamental principles. The molecular approach to the interpretation of schedules of reinforcement was favored by B. F. Skinner. In contrast, in the molar approach, global relations are seen as fundamental because such relations are held to describe the behavior at the only level at which orderly functional relations may be observed. Current research indicates that some molar relations can, in fact, be interpreted as the net expression of molecular processes, but as yet others cannot. The molar molecular issue remains a matter of theoretical debate within the field. Regardless of which level is ultimately found most fruitful to interpret the effects of schedules of reinforcement, their study remains inescapable because of their important effects on the acquisition, maintenance, and persistence of behavior both in the laboratory and in the everyday world.

EXPERIMENTAL DESIGNS
LEARNING CURVES
LEARNING THEORIES
OPERANT CONDITIONING
REWARDS

J. W. DONAHOE

SCHIZOID PERSONALITY

The schizoid personality is a formal category of mental disturbance placed on Axis 11 of the classification system described in the *Diagnostic and statistical manual of mental disorders* (*DSM-III*). "Withdrawn" is the term one most frequently encounters in clinical descriptions of the schizoid personality. There is a marked impoverishment of social relations. These individuals are likely to have few friends and to occupy themselves with tasks and hobbies that can be performed alone. The seclusiveness seems to develop from an extreme sensitivity to the evaluative reactions of others. As a defense, the schizoid individual may retreat into excessive daydreaming. At the same time, the person appears relatively insensitive to the nonverbal cues used by others to communicate how they are feeling. The ability to express either humor or hostility is often notably lacking in schizoid types.

Occupationally, schizoid individuals tend to be characterized by narrow interests, unclear aspirations, and a poor work history involving frequent changes in jobs. These persons are often late, prone to mistakes, and unwilling to find productive activities when their regular work is insufficient to fill their time. Others report feeling uncomfortable when working around them. Schizoid types seem to do their best in positions requiring a minimum of social interaction.

A schizoid personality disorder in an adult individual is often preceded by a syndrome called "schizoid disorder of childhood or adolescence." These children have few close friends, and any friend they do have is likely to be another social isolate. Although often of above-average IQ, this individual is an underachiever in school, especially in mathematics. He or she is strongly attracted to television or movies, especially when plots have violent or supernatural themes.

Many schizophrenic patients will have displayed a schizoid personality prior to their psychotic break with reality, but it does not seem to be the case that most persons displaying a schizoid personality will progress to schizophrenia. A schizoid personality is more common among boys than girls.

The existence of a genetic predisposition toward development of a schizoid personality has been proposed by L. L. Heston. He calls the predisposition *schizoidia* and estimates that a third of those so afflicted will eventually become schizophrenic. The remainder will exhibit the schizoid personality to varying degrees due to the probable action of countervailing environmental or constitutional factors that may moderate expression of the underlying genetic predisposition. However, a review of research into the family backgrounds of schizoid and schizophrenic individuals has turned up many indications of environmental factors that may precipitate these mental disturbances.

PERSONALITY DISORDERS

W. Samuel

SCHIZOPHRENIA

Since earliest recorded history, there have been descriptions of human beings whose behavior, thinking, and feeling have been recognized as different, abnormal, sick, or possessed. Since biblical times, there have been descriptions of deviant behavior that have fallen into the three major categories: the depressions, the manias, and those disorders now called schizophrenia.

Diagnostic fashions have changed throughout time; these disorders have been termed paranoia, schizophrenic reactions, and dementia prae-cox, and now the official term is schizophrenic disorder. Today we think of schizophrenia as a complex psychobiological illness with resultant disorganization to such an extent that the individual experiences major changes in personality and major disabilities in the conduct of his or her life. The illness has a predictable course with a predictable outcome. At this point, we do not know the exact cause of schizophrenia, nor do we know how to cure it. We do know some of the genetic predeterminants, some of the biological reactions (windows), and also a good deal about the interpersonal and social situations that tend to precipitate exacerbations of symptoms in individuals who suffer from schizophrenia.

The modern diagnostic systems of schizophrenia begin with Eugen Bleuler's work at the turn of the twentieth century. He grouped these disorders and applied the name schizophrenia, referring to the split between thinking and affect.

A modern system for the diagnosis of schizophrenia was developed by Kurt Schneider, who developed a list of 11 first-rank symptoms. These included the perception of audible thoughts, voices arguing, voices commenting on one's actions, influence playing on the body, somatic passivity, thought withdrawal, thoughts ascribed to others (thought insertion), diffusion or broadcasting of thoughts, made impulses, made feelings, made volitional acts, and delusional perception. Although indeed these 11 first-rank symptoms are present in many of the individuals who suffer from schizophrenia, they represent end-stage symptoms and are only recognizable during the relatively acute stages of the illness.

In the system developed by Mendel based on the long-term observation of some 500 cases, the diagnosis of schizophrenia is made on the basis of the presence of three nuclear disabilities: the failure of anxiety management, the failure of interpersonal transactions, and the failure of historicity. In this system of diagnosis, all other signs and symptoms are either the consequences of these nuclear disabilities or attempts at restituting for the nuclear disabilities. During exacerbations of the illness, the consequential and restitutive symptoms appear; but during the quiescent periods of remission, or when good supportive therapy is available, only nuclear disabilities can be recognized and the other symptoms do not occur. In such an approach to the diagnosis, the purpose of helpful treatment, either through chemical or psychotherapeutic methods, is the elimination of the consequential and restitutive symptoms.

The official diagnostic system of the American Psychiatric Association known as *Diagnostic and statistical manual of mental disorders* (*DSM-*

IV) requires the existence of schizophrenic illness for at least 6 months, thus defining schizophrenia as a chronic illness. It also requires the presence of at least one of the following during the active phase of the illness, thus insisting on periods of acute exacerbation:

1. Bizarre delusions
2. Somatic, grandiose, religious, nihilistic or other delusions without persecutory or jealous content
3. Delusions with persecutory or jealous content
4. Auditory hallucination
5. Incoherence, marked loosening of associations, marked illogical thinking, or marked poverty of thought associated with one of the following:
   (a) Blunted, flat, or inappropriate affect
   (b) Delusions or hallucinations
   (c) Catatonic or other grossly disorganized behavior

The *DSM* also requires evidence of deterioration from previous level of function in such areas as work, social relations, and self-care. The diagnostic manual subdivides schizophrenia into the disorganized type, the catatonic type, the paranoid type, the undifferentiated type, and the residual type. The subtypes are characterized by various clusters of predominant symptoms.

The typical course of the illness begins with an acute episode, usually in adolescence (ages 13 to 17). Often this early episode is misdiagnosed. The initial episode is usually self-limiting, lasting a few weeks, followed by remission in which the patient appears near normal. The second episode usually occurs within 6 months to 1 year and tends to be more severe than the first, to last a few weeks, and to demonstrate more frankly psychiatric symptoms. It is the third episode that is usually seen as the first frankly definable episode of psychosis. This occurs within a year or two of the initial episode and results in major disruptions in the patient's life.

The subsequent course of the illness is marked by exacerbations and remissions. The number of exacerbations the patient experiences each year seems to be age related rather than related to the treatment received or the environment. Between the age of 20 and 30, the patient will experience an average of six exacerbations per year. Between the ages of 30 and 40, the patient will experience two exacerbations per year, and between 40 and 50, an average of one exacerbation per year. Usually after 50, the illness becomes quiescent in terms of exacerbations. During the exacerbations, the patient has frank psychotic symptoms, including delusions and hallucinations, disorganization of thought, and inability to function. During the remissions, the patient is quite often free of psychotic symptoms, particularly if given appropriate psychopharmacological agents. However, the nuclear symptoms remain and are demonstrable even during remissions.

There is one type of schizophrenia that has a somewhat later onset— paranoid schizophrenia. The usual age of onset is in the early 20s for that particular disorder. Paranoid patients tend to show less deterioration of function between the acute episodes.

Schizophrenia seems to occur in approximately 1% of the population. The incidence is very similar in all cultures and subcultures, in industrial as well as preindustrial societies, and in all human races. There is no evidence that social class differences affect the incidence of schizophrenia.

Starting in the 1980s, treatment of schizophrenia consisted of psychopharmacology, psychotherapy, and environmental manipulation. With good supportive therapy, the quality of life the schizophrenic patient leads can be markedly improved. The patient can spend most of his or her life in the community rather than in the hospital. Environmental manipulation consists of helping the patient to create, or have someone else create, a psychosocial milieu in which disabilities are minimized and the patient is most comfortable.

SUPPORTIVE CARE

W. M. MENDEL

SCHIZOTYPAL PERSONALITY

According to the *Diagnostic and statistical manual of mental disorders,* the prime characteristics of the disorder include various eccentricities in behavior, thought, speech, and perception. Although not invariable, periodic and marked social detachment may be notable, often associated with either flat affect or severe interpersonal anxiety. There is a tendency to follow a meaningless, idle, and ineffectual life, drifting aimlessly and remaining on the periphery of normal societal relationships. Some possess significant affective and cognitive deficiencies, appearing listless, bland, unmotivated, and obscure, and only minimally connected to the external world. Others are dysphoric, tense, and withdrawn, fearful and intentionally seclusive, inclined to damp down hypersensitivities and to disconnect from anticipated external threats. Notable also are their social attainment deficits, their repeated failure to maintain durable, satisfactory, and secure roles consonant with age. Many have experienced several brief and reversible periods in which either bizarre behaviors, extreme moods, irrational impulses, or delusional thoughts were exhibited. To many clinicians, the schizophrenic disorder is a syndromal prototype of which the schizotypal personality is a dilute and nonpsychotic variant.

PERSONALITY DISORDERS

T. MILLON

SCHOLARSHIP AND ACHIEVEMENT

Several studies have been made on the relationship between college grades and later (vocational) success. Some of these have been rather sketchy or confined to a single variable; others have attacked the problem more broadly.

Perhaps the earliest study was done by D. S. Bridgman on college grades and eventual salaries in the Bell Telephone Company. As decades passed, those who were in the top tenth or top third of their class at graduation grew farther and farther ahead of those who graduated down the line.

R. W. Husband followed up his class at Dartmouth 30 years later, when they were presumably at about the height of their careers, and found that those who barely graduated earned less at middle age than those who made between "B" and "C" averages, and that those who earned better than a "B" average had considerably higher incomes than those with lower grades. The "guesstimate" is that those with higher grades had formed more serious and better organized study habits at an early age and had retained these better habits into their working lives.

In Husband's study, not only scholarship, but also extracurricular activities, were compared with later success. He found that men with several outside interests, or marked supremacy in one or two, had definitely higher earnings at middle age than those with no outside activities. In addition, it did not seem to make much difference whether the activity was sports, dramatics, journalism, or campus politics—as long as there was the interest beyond the classroom, and the person worked hard enough to achieve top success.

R. W. HUSBAND

SCHOLASTIC APTITUDE TEST

The Scholastic Aptitude Test (SAT) is a 3-hour multiple-choice test that measures verbal and mathematical abilities important for success in college. All operational forms of the SAT in use at any one time are secure; administration is carefully controlled and takes place only at approved centers. Currently more than 1 million high school students take the SAT each year. A typical form of the SAT contains 85 verbal items (opposites, analogies, sentence completion, reading comprehension) in two 30-minute sections and 60 mathematics items (mathematics problems, quantitative comparison) in two 30-minute sections. In addition, there is a 30-minute Test of Standard Written English and a 30-minute section used to try out new items for future use.

Separate scores are reported for the Verbal and Mathematical sections on a scale ranging from 200 to 800. Current percentile rank norms for general high school students and college-bound students are available.

Evolution of the test has been carefully documented, and the procedures used in its development are rigorous and exacting. The SAT scores are typically used in conjunction with high school grade average to predict success in college.

APTITUDE TESTING
COLLEGE ACADEMIC PREDICTION

G. J. ROBERTSON

SCHOOL ADJUSTMENT

To the extent that a child has the skills and is able to meet the demands and expectations set forth in the school setting, that child is likely to be judged well adjusted. When a mismatch occurs between these two factors and the child fails to behave or perform in a manner expected by the school, he or she is likely to be judged poorly adjusted and in need of some intervention. This intervention, in turn, may be designed to remediate the child's skill deficits, or to modify the demands and characteristics of the school situation.

Adjustment may be judged across several domains. One may evaluate the extent to which a child achieves on academic tasks. In the behavioral domain, one may consider whether a child has the self-control skills, attention span, and other capabilities to control and direct behavior in the manner desired. Third, social-emotional adjustment depends on the child's social skills and norms of the peer group.

CLASSROOM DYNAMICS
EARLY CHILDHOOD EDUCATION
PYGMALION EFFECT
SCHOOL LEARNING

K. L. BIERMAN

SCHOOL GANGS

The term *gang* often connotes a group of persons associated together for some sinister purpose. Actually tightly knit friendship groups are quite common among adolescents and may serve many positive functions.

The formation of friendship groups, cliques, or gangs in school situations reflects a basic process of social development and emerges as children develop a more complex understanding of social systems and interpersonal relationships. During preadolescence, children's peer relationships begin to become more complex and hierarchically organized. Gradually throughout the early adolescent years, children become more aware of the various groups of friends with whom they are associated. They may maintain special friendships, now based on abstract attributes such as loyalty, trustworthiness, and intimacy. They also begin to recognize a second-order level of friendship based on association with a particular, self-defined group.

These self-defined peer groups often become organized around some central activity or shared goal. Regardless of the initial goal or task that brings certain individuals together, as they communicate with each other, they begin to establish a framework of shared attitudes, values, and consensual norms. Group members may dress, act, or behave in certain ways to distinguish themselves from other groups.

These peer groups or gangs play a major role in shaping the attitudes and self-conceptions of adolescents, particularly in the social domain. This peer influence may be particularly important in facilitating social development in areas such as sexual socialization and interpersonal relationships. In a minority of cases, these peer groups may have a negative influence on members, as when the group adopts a set of values and attitudes that are in opposition to the legal values ascribed by the greater society.

ADOLESCENT DEVELOPMENT
PEER INFLUENCES

K. L. BIERMAN

SCHOOL LEARNING

Over much of its history, a major preoccupation of psychology has been the study of learning. Many studies of learning have been conducted in the experimental laboratory, where conditions presumably can be well controlled, but it is also possible to study learning in the institutions where much learning in "real life" goes on—the schools. Even though it is not possible to control the conditions of learning in the school as well as in the experimental laboratory, it is reasonable to investigate how well laws of learning and other psychological findings apply in school learning.

This question has been the central concern of a major branch of psychology, traditionally called *educational psychology*. Recently the term *instructional psychology* has come into favor as a way of emphasizing the applications of educational psychology to the conduct of instruction at all levels of education. Instructional psychology has become what some have called an "educational technology," involving not only the use of computers and other technological devices as aids to instruction, but also application of the advances of behavioral and cognitive psychology in specifying how instructional materials should be prepared to promote optimal learning and how instruction can best be conducted.

At a microscopic level, such principles can give guidance as to exactly how materials should be prepared and presented, what learner strategies can be recommended, how learner responses can be rewarded or redirected in different ways, how learners can be helped to form associations and remember them (for example, through mnemonic techniques), and how learners' motivations can be increased.

At a macroscopic level, the whole process of school learning can be considered without attention to the details of particular learning tasks. Rather, school learning is viewed as a sequence of activities consisting of courses of instruction and other educational experiences lasting over many months, even years. The interest is in what major psychological variables influence the course of learning and affect the degree to which the learner achieves the overall goals of instruction.

Time has been viewed as a crucial variable in a "model of school learning." If the required time is not taken, learning will be incomplete. The degree of learning thus is some function of the ratio of the amount of time taken to the time needed.

The model proceeds to specify the major variables thought to influence the degree of learning attained by any given individual in a learning situation. Some of these variables are stated in terms of time. One is the individual's *aptitude*, which is regarded as being reflected in the amount of time the individual would require to learn the task under optimal conditions. Another variable expressed in terms of time is the individual's *perseverance*, the amount of time the individual is willing to spend in active learning of the task. According to the model, learning is not a function of "motivation" as such, but solely a function of the time during which active learning occurs. Also expressed in terms of time is the variable of *opportunity to learn*—the amount of time the individual (regardless of aptitude or perseverance) is allowed to spend in learning.

The model includes two additional critical variables that are not expressed as time. One is the *quality of instruction*, a term intended to summarize all variables associated with the manner in which instruction is presented (its clarity, comprehensibility, organization, sequencing, etc.) and the manner in which the student is given incentives, feedback regarding progress, guidance concerning the avoidance of error, and so forth.

The other variable of the model that is not expressed as time is student *ability to understand instruction*. It is assumed that this variable interacts with instructional quality in such a way that students with low ability to understand the instruction will need more time to learn when instructional quality is not sufficient for them to learn, whether because it is poorly presented and organized or because insufficient incentives and guidance are given. At the same time, students with high ability to understand instruction are less affected by poor quality of instruction, because they can, so to speak, instruct themselves. The model as a theoretical basis for analyzing school learning and interpreting causes of underachievement has served as a guide for practical programs of educational reform.

ALTERNATIVE EDUCATIONAL THEORY
INSTRUCTIONAL THEORY

J. B. CARROLL

SCHOOL PHOBIA

School phobia is generally defined as the unwarranted fear of school and/or inappropriate anxiety associated with leaving home. Several characteristics are present in school phobia: (a) severe difficulty in attending school, resulting in prolonged absence; (b) emotional distress, fearfulness, temper displays, or complaints of illness when faced with the possibility of school attendance; (c) parental knowledge of the school absence; (d) absence of any antisocial behaviors such as lying, stealing, or aggressive acting out. In other words, school phobia describes a situation in which there is irrational fear of some aspect of the school situation, with the understanding that the time away from school is spent at home. It is differentiated from truancy in that the truant deliberately avoids school and home to engage in some activity that is more enjoyable than being either in school or at home.

Data on the incidence of school phobia are somewhat sparse. The peak incidence appears to be around 11 years of age, with the likelihood that it is slightly more common for girls than boys. Most often, school phobia appears in the elementary school years. It is also found in children of all intellectual levels, often in children who are very bright. It is not, as one might expect, typically found in children destined for school failure, but quite the reverse. The occurrence of school phobia as a psychological problem is relatively small in relation to other psychological disorders of childhood. Researchers estimate that school phobia accounts for less than 8% of the cases seen in child psychiatric clinics.

It is generally believed that there are two different types of school phobia—acute and chronic. The acute type appears to demonstrate a rapid and dramatic onset coupled with adequate functioning in other areas of the child's life. Often the anxiety present is limited to attending school. The chronic type has a more incipient onset with prior episodes of refusal to attend school. Also, the chronic type displays disturbed personal functioning in other areas of social interaction.

There is no generally accepted view of the exact causes of school phobia. However, there is considerable agreement on the importance of the role that family relationship plays in the development of school phobia symptoms.

The psychodynamic theory views school phobia as separation anxiety. It is seen as the product of an overly dependent relationship between the child and the mother.

The learning theory explanation generally accepts the importance of separation anxiety but does not put much emphasis on the unresolved dependency issues of the mother. It generally emphasizes (a) the early learning that separation from mother can be dangerous and that home is a safe refuge from the fears of the outside world; (b) insufficiency of rewards from the school setting; and (c) actual anxiety-arousing experiences found in the school situation that contribute to the causes of the school phobia.

The psychodynamic approach to treatment emphasizes the necessity of treating the parent–child relationship through a process of psychotherapy. The behavioral approach, emphasizing rapid return to school, utilizes techniques from behavior therapy such as systematic desensitization or classical and operant conditioning procedures. Prognoses can vary from complete success to promises of continued psychological disturbance for many of the children. Younger children seem to have a better prognosis. Various forms of brief psychotherapy, focusing on the rapid return of the child to school, have consistently reported positive results.

ALTERNATIVE EDUCATIONAL SYSTEMS

L. V. PARADISE

SCHOOL PSYCHOLOGISTS

The applications of psychological assessment, consultation, and intervention within public school settings are the primary responsibility of school psychologists. More than 40 states designate specific criteria for certification as a school psychologist; most include a supervised internship in addition to prescribed academic course work. A majority of school psychologists have teaching certificates and have pursued graduate training after 1 or more years of teaching experience.

A 1982 study estimates that there are between 20,000 and 23,000 certified school psychologists, university-affiliated trainers of school psychologists, and students. Most school psychologists work within public educational settings, although some may be employed by community mental health agencies or by private schools, or may be in private practice.

The primary role of school psychologists is to ferret out the circumstances hindering optimum school performance for referred children and to assist the school system in the provision of educational plans for these children. This role relies on a knowledge of learning theories, psychometric assessment, child development, and family systems, in addition to a functional understanding of classroom analysis, school organization, and curriculum.

In addition to individualized student evaluations, a variety of other services may be provided by a school psychologist, depending on the school system's priorities and the personality and competencies of the psychologist. Psychological services may also include group appraisal of school children, coordination with community (child-serving) agencies, counseling and psychotherapy, coordination with other pupil personnel workers, preventative mental health consultation on programs for the gifted, participation on curriculum committees, research, provision of inservice training, collection and calculation of local normative data, and numerous other areas. Since school psychologists generally have the most

formal training in child development, research, and individual assessment in public education systems, consultation in these areas of expertise is often a major responsibility.

Ensuring compliance with Public Law 94-142 has resulted in a large proportion of time devoted to special education screening and assessment. Since its enactment, many school psychologists have less time for involvement in preventative mental health and other consultative functions. Despite these existent pressures toward a narrowing of role functioning there has been expansion of specialization within the field to include the areas of preschool education, vocational school psychology, urban and rural school psychology, and psychoneurological assessment as it relates to school-age children.

SPECIAL EDUCATION

A. THOMAS

SCHOOL READINESS

The concept of school readiness is applicable to learning throughout the school years, although it is usually associated with the primary grades, kindergarten through third grade. It can be defined as the ability of the child successfully to meet the cognitive, social, physical, and emotional expectations that accompany school attendance.

School readiness is determined by assessing the developmental level of children in such areas as listening comprehension, visual perceptual and fine motor skills, expressive and receptive vocabulary, and experiential knowledge. Readiness in these varied areas is generally considered to be the necessary foundation on which to base more diverse and complex learning skills. Many school districts have preschool clinics, conducted by multidisciplinary school personnel, to evaluate children's readiness.

Children who successfully meet school expectations continue to more complex learning activities. Children who are unable to meet these indices of successful performance are often deemed failures and may develop associated negative and defeatist attitudes toward learning in general and schooling in particular.

Research supports the finding that up to 20% of primary grade children are seen as not ready for their educational programs. The most common method of dealing with perceived lack of instructional readiness during the first years of school is retention in grade, or, for initial kindergarten attendance, requesting that the child remain home for an additional year. In addition to retention or delayed entry, school systems have attempted to accommodate differing levels of school readiness by providing differential curricula based on student assessment.

EARLY CHILDHOOD EDUCATION

A. THOMAS

SCHOOL TRUANCY

In its strictest sense, school truancy has been defined as students' absence from school without parents' knowledge or approval. In accordance with more common usage, truancy has referred to student absenteeism for unacceptable reasons, irrespective of whether it is known to, or approved by, the parents.

Research findings have been fairly consistent with regard to family factors associated with school truancy. Lower social class, higher than average family size, poverty, and poor housing conditions have all been significantly associated with school truancy. In general, the school behavior of truant students has been characterized by academic and behavioral failure, dislike for school, feelings of frustration, and frequent absenteeism beginning in the early school years. Dreikurs' theory of delinquency has been used as a focal point at which to establish remedial efforts regarding truancy, given the "coping mechanism" conceptualization. It states that problem behavior stems from feelings of inferiority and acting out behavior is a maladaptive attempt to compensate for lack of success in school.

SCHOOL ADJUSTMENT

C. H. HUBER

SCHOOLS OF PROFESSIONAL PSYCHOLOGY

Most psychologists are educated in academic departments of psychology. Even those entering such professional fields as clinical or counseling psychology usually pursue their graduate studies in departmental programs comparable in size and administrative structure with programs in experimental, developmental, or social psychology. Increasing numbers of psychologists preparing for careers of practice, however, are educated in schools of professional psychology administratively comparable with schools of law, medicine, engineering, or business. The earliest schools of professional psychology were freestanding institutions, unaffiliated with universities. Currently, many of the schools are situated in universities, although many others continue to operate independently.

Schools of professional psychology are distinguished by several characteristics. First, their explicit mission is to prepare students for careers of practice. Second, their organizational structure is that of a school or college rather than a departmental program. This status carries several consequences. Administrative resources and controls are relatively direct, usually through officers of the central administration in university-based schools and through boards of directors in freestanding schools. Enrollments are typically much larger than in departmental programs. A third characteristic of professional schools is that the curriculum is specifically designed to prepare people for professional work. Supervised experience in psychological practice is, therefore, emphasized throughout graduate study as well as in an internship. A dissertation is required in the programs of nearly all professional schools, but the inquiry is conceived as a form of practice and not as an end in itself. Fourth, the faculties include large numbers of practitioners, and all faculty members are ordinarily expected to maintain some involvement in professional activity. Finally, the degree awarded on completion of graduate study is most commonly the doctor of psychology (Psy.D.) degree rather than the Ph.D.

The forerunner of contemporary schools of professional psychology was the program in clinical psychology at Adelphi University. When the Adelphi program was approved by the APA Committee on Accreditation in 1957, it became the first accredited program whose primary objective was to educate clinicians for practice, instead of educating them as scientists or scientist-practitioners. Before that time, all clinical and counseling programs in the United States and Canada had followed the "Boulder model" of education, defined in a conference on the training of clinical psychologists at Boulder, Colorado, in 1949. The conference held that clinical psychologists were to be trained in academic psychology departments, prepared to conduct research as well as to practice psychology and awarded the Ph.D. degree upon completion of graduate studies. The early Adelphi program preserved the administrative structure that was common to other departmental programs, changed the curriculum mainly by introducing more supervised clinical experience than usual, and retained the Ph.D. as the terminal degree.

The first institution administratively organized as a school for practitioners of psychology was the Graduate School of Psychology in the Fuller Theological Seminary. Psychologists were initially brought into the seminary faculty to train clergy in pastoral counseling, but in time they expanded their activities to form a comprehensive doctoral program combining clinical psychology with theological studies. The Fuller Graduate School of Psychology was established in 1965.

Large-scale development of schools of professional psychology did not begin, however, until the California School of Professional Psychology was founded in 1969. In the 1960s, California suffered a shortage of professional psychologists. The population of the state was growing rapidly, community needs for mental health practitioners were severe, and the research-oriented clinical programs in the state produced few graduates. In 1970, the California School of Professional Psychology admitted students to its first two campuses, in San Francisco and Los Angeles. Additional campuses were opened in San Diego and Fresno over the next 2 years.

In 1973, another conference on professional training in psychology was held in Vail, Colorado. The conference concluded that psychology had matured sufficiently to justify creation of explicit professional programs, in addition to those for scientists and scientist-professionals. Professional schools were recognized as appropriate settings for training, and the Psy.D. degree was endorsed as the credential of choice on completion of graduate requirements in practitioner programs. Over the following years, schools of professional psychology were established in many locations throughout the United States, some in universities and some as freestanding institutions. The Graduate School of Applied and Professional Psychology, established at Rutgers University in 1974, was the first university-based professional school to award the Psy.D. degree. At Rutgers, as in the Illinois Psy.D. program that preceded it, a scientist-practitioner program leading to the Ph.D. degree was maintained for students interested primarily in research. This pattern—a relatively large school of professional psychology designed expressly to train practitioners and awarding the Psy.D. degree alongside a smaller Ph.D. program to prepare students for research careers—has since been adopted by several other universities and independent professional schools. By the early 1990s, more than 35 professional schools were in operation, approximately half in universities and half as freestanding institutions. In this period, more than one-third of students receiving doctorates in clinical psychology were graduated from professional schools.

As the schools have evolved, they have changed in several ways. Early faculties in freestanding schools were employed entirely or almost entirely on a part-time basis. Proportions of full-time faculty in the independent schools have increased over the years, and professional schools in universities employed large proportions of full-time faculty from the beginning. Psychological centers, analogous to the teaching hospitals of medical schools, are now an integral part of nearly all professional schools, and offer the controlled settings in which public services are offered by faculty and students, students are trained, and research is conducted. Dissertation requirements, which were eliminated completely in some of the early schools, are now an essential part of nearly every program, although the emphasis on direct education for practice and the view of systematic investigation as a form of professional service have been retained. The Psy.D. degree has replaced the Ph.D. degree in the practitioner programs of all but 2 of the 36 institutions listed by the National Council of Schools of Professional Psychology in 1991.

The council of professional schools was established by 1976 to provide a forum for exchange of information among professional schools, to develop standards for the education and training of professional psychologists, and in every way possible, to improve the educational process so that graduates would serve public needs most effectively. Through a series of conferences and reports, the council has conducted self-studies, defined curricula, and established means for quality assurance among its member organizations. Along with the Council of Graduate Departments of Psychology and the Council of University Directors of Clinical Psychology Programs, the National Council of Schools of Professional Psychology is an influential participant in shaping educational policy in American psychology.

AMERICAN PSYCHOLOGICAL ASSOCIATION
AMERICAN PSYCHOLOGICAL SOCIETY
DOCTOR OF PSYCHOLOGY DEGREE
PSYCHOTHERAPY TRAINING

D. R. PETERSON

SCHOOLS WITHOUT FAILURE

Schools without failure is the name given to a specific application of reality therapy in schools. Glasser discovered that the main obstacle to student success was the fact that large numbers of students who were failed in school gave up on attempting to learn. But as they did, to gain the feeling of involvement and worth that all people need, they turned increasingly to disruptive behavior. This often led them to band together against the school and become resistant to any attempt to teach them. Unless this was corrected by reducing and even eliminating failure, little could be done to get these students involved in education.

Glasser suggests that failure be eliminated by a school program based on the idea that students should be given credit for what they do and teachers should teach them until they learn, even if it takes longer than the standard period now allotted. Along with this basic change, Glasser also suggests that teachers incorporate a lot of class discussion to promote involvement and thinking and also make an effort to make the material at any level relevant to student needs. If this is done, then students, who are learning and are not angry and withdrawn because of failure, will follow reasonable rules, thus reducing discipline problems.

ALTERNATIVE EDUCATIONAL SYSTEMS

W. GLASSER

SCIENTIFIC METHOD

Psychology, as a science, uses the scientific method, which is a set of procedures designed to establish general laws through evaluating theories that attempt to describe, explain, and predict phenomena. The scientific method involves explicitly stated theories. Hypotheses are made from such theories, and their systematic, critical evaluation through objective, controlled, empirical investigations, and conclusions that are open to public scrutiny, analysis, and replication is the scientific method.

The scientific approach is analytical. Complex events are analyzed into relevant variables, relationships among these variables are investigated, and theories consistent with the empirical results are created and critically evaluated,

The scientific method involves a critical approach to data analysis and interpretation. Issues of observer bias (the researcher who only sees or emphasizes the results that are consistent with a theory), subject bias (the subject who cooperates with the researcher by conforming to the experimenter's expectations), and confounding or extraneous variables (alternative variables that could explain the observed phenomena) receive serious attention as scientists interpret the results of their studies.

The scientific method involves a broad array of alternative procedures ranging from carefully observing the variables as they naturally occur to collecting data under controlled situations with subjects randomly assigned to conditions. Scientific research design can be grouped into three major categories. Studies can be designed to describe events, to describe correlational relationships among events, or to establish cause-and-effect relationships between events. Descriptive and correlational studies can be used to provide information for theory construction and hypothesis testing. Causal research allows the researcher to establish the direct effect of one variable on another, rather than simply to establish that two variables may correlate.

An important maxim to remember is that "correlation does not imply causation." To establish a cause-and-effect relationship, the researcher must demonstrate that, by manipulating or controlling the causal variable, a change in the affected variable systematically occurs. This would constitute a scientific experiment. Sometimes, however, this is impossible. A single study, by itself, rarely is considered a sufficient basis on which to accept or discard a theory. Replication (producing duplicate studies) and cross-validation (conducting studies by defining variables in different ways or using different types of samples) are necessary for the scientific community to accept the validity of a scientific theory. They also provide evidence for refining theories, to delimit more carefully conditions under which the theory holds true.

Probably one of the easiest research methodologies is the archival method, which involves seeking information from public and private records, such as newspapers or diaries. Archival data are only as accurate as the original recorders, so that subjective judgments by these recorders may undermine the validity of the data.

Another type of scientific method involves a case study of a particular individual in depth. Although case studies can be used to evaluate hypotheses derived from theories about the etiology or the environmental influences on the patient, results from a single case may not be generalizable to other relevant cases, so that the need for cross-validation is particularly important when single-case studies are interpreted.

The systematic observation method can be extended from the case study of an individual to the study of entire groups. If the researcher does nothing intentionally to affect the group being observed, this technique generally is called the method of naturalistic observation.

Interpretation of data gathered through naturalistic observations must weigh the possibility that observer bias or subject bias affected the results. The very fact that an observer is present may alter the environment, inducing atypical behaviors. Observer bias may lead to misperceptions and misinterpretations.

An alternative research strategy is the use of surveys, questionnaires, and structured interviews. The questions can be presented in writing (such as an attitude survey or personality test) or orally (such as an individual IQ test or public opinion poll). The quality of the data depends on the cooperation and honesty of the subjects, as well as the quality of the questions asked. Construction of valid instruments for the survey method is complex because the questions must be unbiased, unambiguous, and at a vocabulary level appropriate for the population to be examined.

Although the survey method can provide large amounts of data inexpensively and allows subjects to volunteer to participate while their confidentiality is protected, it also has limitations. First, self-report data sometimes are of questionable validity. Because participation is voluntary, specific subgroups of the population may be over- or underrepresented in the sample, so that generalization of the results may be questionable.

All of these methods provide data for descriptive or correlational studies. Only an experiment in which the research manipulates the causal variable (the independent variable) and observes the effect on the affected variable (the dependent variable) can lead to conclusions about causality. It is crucial that all other variables that may affect the dependent variable (extraneous or nuisance variables) be controlled for, so that results can be unambiguously interpreted. It is also important that the operational definitions of the variables be reasonable, so that results can be generalized.

EXPERIMENTAL METHODS
HYPOTHESIS TESTING

M. J. ALLEN

SECOND-SIGNAL SYSTEM

The second-signal system refers to human verbal or inferential capabilities and denotes the ability to engage in abstraction from concrete objects and acts. Coined by I. P. Pavlov, the second-signal system is contrasted with the first-signal system, which has to do with the concrete effect of objects and actions on the living animal organism. While both humans and other animals respond—react to—concrete objects, only the human consistently responds to the verbal or linguistic representation of the object in a manner similar to that in which the human responds to the object itself. The ability of abstract notations (words) to call forth the concrete effect of the object or action named is achieved through conditioned reflex bonds, connecting the word with the first-signal system response (the concrete response). These connections are made in the cerebral cortex, and thus the dichotomy of first- and second-signal systems parallels the anatomic distinction of subcortical and cortical, in the same way that it parallels the dichotomies of concrete–abstract and nonverbal–verbal.

The second-signal system was the foundation of Pavlov's theory of hypnosis. It is through the second-signal system and its conditioned bonding with first-signal system responses that the verbal instructions during hypnosis are effective.

INDUSTRIAL/ORGANIZATIONAL PSYCHOLOGY
INFORMATION-PROCESSING THEORY
PSYCHOLINGUISTICS

W. E. EDMONSTON, JR.

SELECTION TESTS

Selection tests are psychometric instruments for the selection of job applicants or for an educational/training program. In a more restricted sense, selection refers to screening, by which suitable applicants are accepted and those considered unsuitable are rejected. Selection also refers to the classification or assignment of those selected to particular job categories and the placement of employees at a specific level of a job. Applicants are usually screened by only one test—a screening test, with only those falling above a specified cutoff score accepted. The placement of employees at a particular level of a job or class also usually involves only one test per placement test. However, classification decisions generally require taking scores on several tests into consideration.

Various types of psychological tests have been used for selecting applicants most likely to succeed on a job or in an educational/training program. The most useful tests vary with the specific nature of the criterion and the kinds of skills required for effective criterion performance. In general, psychological tests have proved most useful in selecting individuals for lower- or middle-level jobs than for higher level executive positions. Interest inventories and personality tests have fared less well than ability tests as selection devices, but they too have been used with some success in the selection of management personnel.

Because the validities of most selection tests are not very high, errors in selection are commonplace. Two types of selection errors, false positive and false negative, must be considered in deciding whether to use a test and at what point the cutoff score should be set.

EEOC GUIDELINES

The Uniform Guidelines on Employee Selection Procedures, as revised in 1978 by the Equal Employment Opportunity Commission (EEOC), were designed to require employers to produce evidence of the validity of selection tests that result in the hiring of a disproportionately lower number of minority group members and women. Employers must also demonstrate the fairness of such tests to minority groups, a demonstration not based on statistical evidence alone.

Because of the difficulties of adhering to the EEOC guidelines and of proving the validity and fairness of their selection tests, many employers have discontinued testing altogether. Unfortunately the alternative selec-

tion devices—interviews, letters of recommendation, application blanks, and the like—usually are even less reliable and valid than psychological tests.

INDUSTRIAL PSYCHOLOGY

L. R. AIKEN

SELECTIONISM

Selectionism is a general approach to the explanation of complex phenomena in which complexity is seen as the cumulative outcome of the repeated action of relatively simple processes. The first systematically developed instance of selectionism was the account of evolution through natural selection, independently proposed by Charles Darwin and Alfred Wallace in 1859. Evolution through natural selection views the complexity and diversity of life as the result of repeated cycles of variation in the characteristics of organisms, differential reproduction (natural selection) of life forms having certain characteristics, and retention of the products of differential reproduction that are responsible for those characteristics, which are now known to be the genes. In selectionism generally, repeated cycles of a three-step process—variation, selection, and retention—are held to be capable of producing both complexity and diversity as their "unintended" product. That is, complexity and diversity are emergent consequences of relatively simple processes and do not require higher-level principles to guide or direct them toward that end.

Within psychology, the most consistently selectionist approach is behavior analysis, the approach initiated and developed by B. F. Skinner. The selectionist stance of behavior analyses is most apparent in its claim that even complex human behavior is the cumulative product of selection by reinforcement. Reinforcers are stimuli that change (select) the probability that the environment will guide the responses that precede them. The selected responses then contribute to the variation available for subsequent selection, with complex behavior being the ultimate outcome. Complex behavior conventionally described by such terms as thinking, remembering, problem solving, and speaking are all seen as products of prolonged histories of selection by reinforcement (i.e., selection by the individual environment). Selection by reinforcement changes the behavior of the organism, which is itself the product of natural selection by the ancestral environments of the species of which the individual is a member. As a model for the changes wrought by natural selection across evolutionary time, Darwin appealed to artificial selection whereby animal husbandrymen bred domesticated animals to change some characteristics (e.g., the plumage of pigeons). Similarly, Skinner appealed to shaping, whereby the experimenter gradually changed the response criteria on which the occurrence of the reinforcer depended, as a model for how selection by natural contingencies may produce complex behavior within the lifetime of the individual.

One of the most important consequences of selectionist theories, whatever their realization, is that their constructs denote a range of variation rather than some fixed entity. For example, in evolution the concept of species is a statistical abstraction referring to a range of variation of characteristics. The "thing" species does not exist, only the differing individuals whose range of variation defines the concept species. The evolutionary biologist Ernst Mayr has most clearly articulated this characteristic of selectionist concepts. Similarly, in behavior analysis, a reinforcing stimulus does not select a single response but a range of responses whose characteristics meet the criteria for the occurrence of a reinforcer. The statistical nature of concepts in selectionist theorizing contrasts with concepts in essentialist theorizing, which is much more prevalent in psychology. For example, in the study of language, variations in the "grammaticality" of speech may be considered of little fundamental importance. Instead, variations are seen as the result of relatively unimportant "performance" variables (such as lapses in attention) that partially obscure the operation of an underlying invariant and universal essence, a "language acquisition device" or a "speech organ." For such linguistic theories, it is the invariant "universals" that are real and genuine, not the variations. The situation is similar to pre-Darwinian biology in which species were thought of as invariant and enduring entities of which the individuals were mere variations on the underlying species plan. In short, whereas selectionism regards variation within classes of phenomena as fundamental, essentialism regards variation as a troubling nuisance and misleading irrelevance. The distinction between selectionist and essentialist concepts has deep philosophical roots that may be traced to the British empiricists and Plato, respectively.

BEHAVIORAL GENETICS
BEHAVIORISM
EMPIRICISM
EVOLUTION
POSTMODERISM
REINFORCEMENT

J. W. DONAHOE

SELECTIVE ATTENTION

In animal learning experiments, an organism's behavior can often be shown to be controlled by only one element of a multielement compound stimulus. Such a demonstration has been taken as evidence for selective attention.

Theories of selective attention have often assumed that the probability of attending to one stimulus is inversely related to the probability of attending to another. However, the discovery of the phenomenon of "blocking" by Leon Kamin has led attentional theorists to propose changes in the inverse assumption. His evidence led N. J. Mackintosh to propose a new attentional theory. According to Mackintosh, animals "learn to ignore" stimuli, if those stimuli predict no change in the probability of unconditioned stimuli (US) predicted by other stimuli. The idea of learning to ignore stimuli has been further pursued by Pearce and Hall, who propose that a CS "loses associability" as its conditioned strength approaches the asymptote possible with the particular US under consideration.

LEARNING THEORIES

J. J. B. AYRES

SELF-ACTUALIZATION

Self-actualization pertains to the human need for self-fulfillment. It implies that individuals require and will work toward becoming everything they possibly can become. As a need, self-actualization is not a personal preference or inclination, but a biological and psychological imperative.

Most of the studies that pertain to self-actualization derive from the work of Abraham Maslow on the hierarchy of human needs. According to Maslow, there are five levels of human needs: basic physiological needs, safety needs, belongingness needs, esteem needs, and self-actualization needs. T. Roberts drew on the later writings of Maslow to suggest that there exists implicitly a sixth level of need—the need for self-transcendence.

People tend not to be content with being "normal," but strive toward being exceptional. Self-actualizing individuals tend to have a genuine desire to help the human race; they behave more kindly and less self-

consciously, and have closer interpersonal relationships than do non-self-actualizers. Self-actualizers demonstrate a strong belief in democratic principles while remaining highly discriminating in their friendships.

Self-actualizers tend to be more creative than other people. Such people transcend the culture within which they live and are part of a world culture practicing universal values.

A major limitation of Maslow's work was that he sought out specific subjects rather than random members of the general population. Also, his research approach was phenomenological. Such an approach gave tremendously rich data, but the generalizability of his findings has been questioned.

Shostrom's standardized questionnaire has become the most widely used instrument in the assessment of self-actualization. The Personal Orientation Inventory consists of 12 subscales: time competence, inner directedness, self-actualizing value, existentiality, feeling reactivity, spontaneity, self-regard, self-acceptance, nature of man, synergy, acceptance of aggression, and capacity for intimate contact. All subscales were derived from the writings of Maslow pertaining to self-actualizing individuals.

OPTIMAL FUNCTIONING

R. H. STENSRUD

SELF-CONCEPT

For centuries, theologians, philosophers, and laypersons have agreed that the origins and effects of self-conceptions merit serious attention. However, there have been few attempts to define self-conception terms rigorously enough to evaluate the extent to which philosophical, lay, and professional/scientific thinkers may all be considering the same idea(s).

Between the late nineteenth and mid-twentieth centuries, professional ideas concerning self-conceptions were kept alive and developed in an essentially abstract or theoretical way by a few psychologists, sociologists, and psychiatrists. At the beginning of this period, the most famous nineteenth century treatment of the topic of self by a psychologist was presented by William James, who based his statements on astute, uncontrolled, everyday observations, including his own perceptive brand of introspecting on his conscious processes. Mary Calkins attempted to bring the study of self-conceptions into the psychological laboratory. By 1935, Kurt Koffka was including the self as an important topic to be addressed by Gestalt psychologists, who used so-called phenomenological introspection in which observers reported their conscious experiences without the artificial restraints or analyses. Meanwhile sociologists such as Cooley and Mead were arguing for the importance of social interactions in shaping individuals' self-conceptions, which in turn were assumed to be crucial determinants of their social behavior; but these discussions were based on personal observations, not research.

Concurrently, a long line of clinicians in Europe and the United States were keeping alive various versions of the idea that self-conceptions are important in attaining a clinical understanding of individuals and in making the general statements that comprised their respective theories of personality. On the whole, however, their ideas, based almost entirely on uncontrolled clinical observations of single cases, seemed to lack rigor and testability, or even sometimes to repudiate the assumptions of scientific determinism. Accordingly their views were excluded for several decades from the mainstream of U.S. research psychology.

Child psychologists began to explore the development of social cognition—knowing about others and one's self in relation to others. This included such questions as whether qualitatively different developmental stages in social cognition may occur, and whether developmental trends in acquisition of ordinary language are associated with developing conceptions of self and others. In addition, the issue of the influence of parental characteristics and behaviors on self-conceptions was raised, and theory and research on moral development were obviously relevant to the acquisition of self-concept and ideals for self.

Social psychologists accorded importance to self-conception variables in their theories about interpersonal attraction, about humans' persuasibility and conformity behaviors, and about cognitive dissonance. Self-conception variables also figured in attribution theory. Also, social psychologists have joined sociologists in considering the effects of such variables as age, class, race, and gender on self-conceptions. Social learning theorists developed arguments about such variables as locus of control and learned helplessness, both of which are concerned (as is attribution theory) with the conditions under which a person sees his or her own characteristics or behavior as important factors in determining outcomes.

Psychologists interested in accounting for vocational choice and performance accorded theoretical importance to such ideas as the guiding role of prechoice self-conceptions and the eventual development of a vocational self-concept. Theorists and researchers thus far have considered almost entirely the *phenomenal* or *conscious self-concept,* not the so-called unconscious self-concept.

1. *Personal self-concept.* This is one's descriptive attributes or behavioral characteristics as seen from one's personal perspective. These characteristics may range from rather specific to quite broad. Note that the personal self-concept includes not only physical, behavioral, and internal characteristics, but also such aspects as gender identity, racial/ethnic identity, socioeconomic class identity, age identity, and a sense of self-continuity as being, in some respects, the same individual through time.

2. *Social self-concepts.* These are self-descriptive attributes or behavioral characteristics as one thinks they are seen by others.

They may or may not agree with the attributes one sees as characterizing one's self from one's personal viewpoint.

3. *Self-ideals regarding one's personal self-concept.* These are conceptions of what one would personally wish to be like.

4. *Self-ideals regarding one's social self-concepts.* These are conceptions of how one would like others to see one.

5. *Evaluations of descriptive personal self-conceptions in relation to the ideals for self regarding those attributes.* That is, these refer to evaluations of item 1, in relation to item 3.

6. *Evaluations of descriptive social self-concepts in relation to the ideals for one's social self-concept.* That is, these refer to evaluations of item 2 in relation to item 4.

SELF-ESTEEM

Most theoretical writing and research in the self-concept area concerns "self-esteem." The term *self-acceptance* also has been much used in the self-concept literature to refer to liking or respecting one's self while acknowledging one's shortcomings.

Although considerable agreement has been reached on the general idea of what to measure, progress in the measurement area has been slowed by (a) the intractable complexity of the set of variables involved; (b) the failure to attempt to disentangle the separate strands in self-conception and to develop respectively suitable measures; and (c) the neglect of acceptable procedures for establishing suitable reliability and construct validity of one's measures before using them in substantive research.

Wicklund has made the suggestion that the observable relationships between self-conceptions and respectively corresponding behaviors are stronger when the person is in a "self-aware" state. This state may be induced by working in the presence of a mirror or a tape recording of one's own voice, or it may be a generally characteristic state for some persons as compared with others.

Partly because hundreds of factors have been thought to be related to self-conceptions, the several thousand published research studies tend to be widely and thinly scattered across substantive areas. On the side of self-conception variables, the most frequent focus of published research studies has been on persons' characteristic levels of overall self-esteem or self-acceptance. The next most frequent focus has been on self-conceptions of relatively stable ability levels.

Regarding factors that researchers have tried to relate to self-conception variables, the greatest concentration of studies has been on achievement, ability, and creativity; age and developmental level; authoritarianism and dogmatism; family variables; gender; interpersonal attraction; psychotherapy; racial/ethnic status; and socioeconomic status.

It is most striking that zero or weak associations have been repeatedly obtained between self-esteem and each of several variables to which both theory and conventional wisdom confidently assumed self-esteem would be strongly related, for example, age, race, sex, socioeconomic level, psychotherapy, creativity, and persuasibility. It seems likely that a more sophisticated reformulation of theory could lead to more useful and interesting findings. For example, more attention should be paid to examining (a) the components of self-esteem, (b) the way(s) in which separate aspects of self-conception achieve differential salience in determining self-esteem (probably differing from individual to individual), and (c) the likelihood that neither children nor adults compare themselves with the very broad, generalized reference groups implicitly assumed to be important by researchers who look for sex, race, or class influences on self-esteem.

SELF-ESTEEM

R. C. WYLIE

SELF-CONTROL

Psychology has had a long and stormy relationship with concepts relating to issues of human agency. Willpower, will, and self-control have all been part of the battle. Over the past two decades, interest in self-control has again increased substantially.

INTEREST IN SELF-CONTROL AND SOME PROBLEMS

The theme of action with self-discipline and self-control arises in widely varying cultures and religious traditions. One reason why self-control will not just go away is the ubiquitousness and relevance of the term philosophically, societally, legally, and from a religious standpoint. A second reason for the current interest in self-control comes from reports from India and the Orient detailing extraordinary feats of bodily control and altered states of consciousness by meditation masters. These findings cause a reconsideration of the formulations of classical neurology that taught that the autonomic nervous system was beyond voluntary control. A third reason for the increased interest was the growing dissatisfaction among health care professionals who found themselves treating stress-related disorders exclusively with pharmacological solutions.

Within this context, one of the more promising areas in psychotherapy and the health sciences has been efforts toward the development and refinement of Eastern and Western self-control strategies for the amelioration of clinical problems. There has been a plethora of research studies showing the clinical effectiveness of these strategies with a variety of affective and physical disorders. A fourth reason for the current interest in self-control relates to the personal, social, and theoretical importance of control.

Control is mentioned in the *Diagnostic and statistical manual* under various guises, generally with absence of control or lack of voluntary ability being considered qualities of the impulse disorders, implicated in the depressive and anxiety disorders. Other related concepts in contemporary psychology include the social learning theorist's self-efficacy; delay of gratification; the existentialist's concept of will; Julian Rotter's internal/external locus of control; and the neoanalytic concept of competence suggested by Robert White. Furthermore, there are efforts to bring control theory from mathematics, systems and cybernetic theory to discussions of self-regulation.

A self-control strategy refers to a family of techniques an individual consciously practices in a regular, systematic manner to influence cognitive activity and/or behavioral activity in a desired direction. B. F. Skinner's view is that self-control is a behavioral sequence in which an organism manipulates environmental influences in accordance with learning principles to after a specific behavior.

M. J. Mahoney and D. B. Arrikoff define self-control as a social label differentially applied to some behavior patterns. Several characteristics are noted: A behavior pattern is not considered self-regulatory if it is apparent to the labeler that the behavior is receiving prompt reward or punishment; people do not receive credit for self-control if it is something they seem to have been doing effortlessly all their lives.

RESEARCH-COMPARING STRATEGIES

Preliminary research indicates the following differentiations among strategies that need to be taken into consideration:

1. For detecting a precise functional relationship between the patient's environment and stress, behavioral self-observation is the treatment of choice.
2. For tension headache, electromyography biofeedback is the treatment of choice; for migraine headache, it is temperature training.
3. Between meditation and biofeedback, for "general relaxation," meditation is the treatment of choice; for a specific stress area, biofeedback is preferable.
4. For cognitive stress, a cognitive strategy such as hypnosis or meditation appears more effective than a somatic strategy.
5. For somatic stress, exercise or progressive relaxation appears to be more effective.
6. For a person with a primarily auditory response system:
   a. When using biofeedback, a visual feedback stimulus is preferable.
   b. When using meditation or hypnosis, an auditory stimulus is preferred.

Almost all of the techniques involve attentional focusing, cognitive statements, and/or imagery. Furthermore, a general antistress response in the individual has been posited, which identifies a common pathway shared by all the self-control techniques that promotes a pattern of psychobiological responding antithetical to the stresses of daily living.

Free Will Versus Determinism

Self-control as a construct implies a process movement away from reflexive action to conscious choice and awareness. The belief system on which the construct is based is that individuals are not absolutely determined, can gain more autonomy and free choice, and do have the ability to effect change in their lives on some level. Thus, the concept of self-control is not possible without recourse to a view of individual choice and freedom, even if only an "as if" view. Further, this assumption of free choice, which is an existential given, may be increased as the individual learns additional skills of awareness, decision making, and so on.

Responsibility

Responsibility is also a critical underpinning of self-control, a movement away from blaming others and the environment and away from an external locus of control, toward an internal locus of control and assuming self-responsibility. Both Sigmund Freud and Carl Jung believed that, in the last analysis, it was up to the patient to change. In a sense, the issue becomes one of self-control: The choice is the individual's.

THE ROLE OF SELF

One of the most difficult and confusing philosophical issues regarding self-control is the question of who or what controls the mind and who or what is being controlled. There are many different and competing views with regard to this self, and at this point all they can provide are metaphors, analogies, or viewpoints, as there is as yet no definitive evidence suggesting any one right answer.

Some views suggest that the concept of self is not needed in understanding human behavior; others, that self needs to be seen as an interaction between the person and environment, whether field theory, social interaction theory, reciprocal determinism, or systems model. Some suggest that the vision of personal autonomy and self-control is located in this "self," whether it is called the centered self as in the existentialist view or the individuated self in Jungian terminology.

Some traditions stress the importance of controlling the "self," developing and enhancing this self so that there is an ability to overcome identity diffusion and low self-esteem. Several traditions discuss the importance of increasing the sense of congruence between self-concept and actual behavior, and increasing a positive sense of oneself (i.e., high self-esteem). Still other approaches center on the need to lose self-importance, to transcend self–other dichotomies, and to keep the self from becoming exclusively identified.

LOCUS OF CONTROL
PERSONALITY
RESPONSIBILITY AND BEHAVIOR

D. H. SHAPIRO, JR.

SELF-DETERMINATION

As a science, psychology has been built on the assumption that all behavior is lawful, that all behavior is *determined* by some set of complex, although ultimately understandable, forces. This assumption has always been seen as antithetical to the idea of free will. People, it is said, are not free to determine themselves; they are determined by forces outside of their control.

The issue is somewhat confusing. To be a science, psychology must proceed with the assumption that behavior is determined and as such must reject the free will position since free will implies freedom from causation. However, the idea of will (as opposed to free will) need not imply freedom from causation; it can be understood in terms of people's having the capacity, to some extent, to choose their own behavior on the basis of their thoughts and feelings. Following up on this point, Deci proposed the use of the term will to refer to people's capacity to decide how to behave and to have those decisions be causal antecedents of their behavior. Self-determination, he added, involves the process of utilizing one's will; in other words, it involves the process of deciding how to behave. This process can be seen as lawful because the principles by which people make choices are discoverable.

THE HISTORY OF WILL

William James discussed the concept of will in terms of voluntary behavior that follows from a mental image of a desirable outcome. Then, in the early part of the twentieth century, the advent of behaviorism shifted the focus away from ideas akin to will. All behavior was understood in terms of conditioned associations between stimuli and responses.

It was not until the 1950s and 1960s, when the cognitive movement gained credibility, that the stage was set for the reemergence of concepts such as will, intention, and self-determination. However, recent work has begun to emphasize the importance of affect and to integrate cognition and affect into a motivational analysis. This motivational analysis provides the basis for current conceptions of self-determination and will.

WILL AND ENERGY

In the theories of will proposed by James and Lewin, the energy source for willing was said to be the need that originally motivated the behavior that ultimately was willed. That, however, creates a problem. If those needs did not provide enough energy without calling will into play, how, one must wonder, can they provide energy for willing?

Deci's theory provides an answer to this previously unsolved problem. He proposed that intrinsic motivation, based in the innate need for competence and self-determination, provides the energy for willing.

FREE WILL
INTRINSIC MOTIVATION

E. L. DECI

SELF-DISCLOSURE

Self-disclosure is the process by which a person voluntarily and intentionally reveals authentic, important, personal, and hitherto private information to another person. Both the process of self-disclosure and research into that process are of considerable importance in understanding interpersonal relationships.

From a philosophical point of view, self-disclosure has been seen as the process by which one learns to understand oneself. Self-disclosure has also been seen as central in the development and maintenance of interpersonal relationships; others have seen the importance of self-disclosure in mental health, especially in the reduction of alienation from others. The literature is consistent that self-disclosure is a prerequisite for functioning effectively and avoiding psychological dysfunction.

The research on self-disclosure can be categorized into (a) the content or topic of the disclosure, (b) the characteristics of the person(s) to whom the disclosure is made, (c) the characteristics of the disclosure, and (d) the characteristics of the situation in which the disclosure is made.

In general, research has found that, regardless of gender, race, and nationality, people tend to be more willing to disclose information about their attitudes and opinions, tastes, and interests and less willing to disclose information about their finances, bodies, and personalities. People are most likely to disclose to individuals they know and like, although there is some tendency to disclose to total strangers, especially when it is assumed that they will never meet again. No general trends emerge from the published literature as to what kind of person is more likely to self-disclose. However, there is strong evidence to support the "dyadic effect," that is, that disclosures beget disclosures. To sum up the literature, it appears that self-disclosure is a function of situational variables, not personality variables.

OPTIMAL PERSONALITY

L. D. GOODSTEIN

SELF-EFFICACY

SOURCES OF EFFICACY

People's beliefs about their efficacy arise from four principal sources. The most effective way is through mastery experiences. Successes build a robust belief in one's personal efficacy. Failures undermine it, especially if failures occur before a sense of efficacy is firmly established. The second method is by social modeling. Models serve as sources of competencies and motivation. Seeing people similar to oneself succeed by perseverant effort raises observers' beliefs in their own capabilities. Social persuasion is the third mode of influence. Realistic boosts in efficacy can lead people to exert greater effort, which increases their chances of success. People also rely partly on their physiological state in judging their capabilities. The fourth way of altering self-efficacy beliefs is to reduce people's physiological overreactions or change how they interpret their physiological states.

EFFICACY-ACTIVATED PROCESSES

Self-efficacy beliefs regulate human functioning through four major processes: cognitive, motivational, emotional, and selection.

Cognitive Processes

The effects of self-efficacy beliefs on cognitive processes take various forms. Much human behavior, being purposive, is regulated by forethought embodying cognized goals. Personal goal setting is influenced by self-appraisal of capabilities. The stronger the perceived self-efficacy, the higher the goal challenges people set for themselves and the firmer their commitment to them.

Most courses of behavior are initially shaped in thought. Peoples' beliefs about their efficacy influence the types of anticipatory scenarios they construct and rehearse. Those who have a high sense of efficacy visualize success scenarios that provide positive guides for performance. Those who judge themselves as inefficacious are more inclined to visualize failure scenarios that undermine performance by dwelling on personal deficiencies and on how things will go wrong. A major function of thought is to enable people to predict the occurrence of events and to create the means for exercising control over those that affect their daily lives. Discovery of conditional relations between environmental happenings and between actions and outcomes requires effective cognitive processing of multidimensional information that contains ambiguities and uncertainties. The stronger the sense of personal efficacy, the more effective people are in their analytic thinking and in constructing successful courses of action.

Motivational Processes

Self-beliefs of efficacy play a central role in the self-regulation of motivation. Most human motivation is cognitively generated. In cognitive motivation, people motivate themselves and guide their actions anticipatorily through the exercise of forethought. They form beliefs about what they can do, they anticipate likely outcomes of prospective actions, they set goals for themselves and plan courses of action designed to realize valued futures. Different theories—attribution theory, expectancy-value theory, and goal theory—have been built around these various forms of cognitive motivators.

Perceived self-efficacy operates as a central factor in all of these variant forms of cognitive motivation. Self-beliefs of efficacy bias causal attributions for successes and failures. People act on their beliefs about what they can do as well as their beliefs about the likely outcomes of various actions. The effects of outcome expectancies on performance motivation are, therefore, partly governed by self-beliefs of efficacy. There are many activities that, if done well, guarantee valued outcomes, but they are not pursued by people who doubt they can do what it takes to succeed.

Affective Processes

The self-efficacy mechanism also plays a pivotal role in the self-regulation of affective states. There are three principal ways in which self-efficacy beliefs affect the nature and intensity of emotional experiences. Such beliefs create attentional biases and influence how potentially aversive life events are construed and cognitively represented; they operate in the exercise of control over perturbing thought patterns; and they sponsor courses of action that transform distressing environments into more benign ones. These alternative paths of affective influence are amply documented in the self-regulation of anxiety arousal and depressive mood.

People who believe they can exercise control over potential threats do not conjure up apprehensive cognitions and, hence, are not perturbed by them. But those who believe they cannot manage potential threats experience high levels of anxiety arousal. They dwell on their coping deficiencies, view many aspects of their environment as fraught with danger, magnify the severity of possible threats and worry about perils that rarely, if ever, happen. Through such inefficacious thought they distress themselves and constrain and impair their level of functioning. It is not the sheer frequency of perturbing cognitions, but the perceived inefficacy to turn them off that is the major source of distress.

Selection Process

The final way in which self-beliefs of efficacy contribute to human adaptation and change concerns selection processes. Beliefs of personal efficacy shape the course lives take by influencing selection of activities and environments. People tend to avoid activities and situations they believe exceed their coping capabilities, but they readily undertake challenging activities and pick social environments they judge themselves capable of handling. Any factor that influences choice behavior can profoundly affect the direction of personal development. This is because the social influences operating in selected environments continue to promote certain competencies, values, and interests long after the decisional determinant has rendered its inaugurating effect. Career choice and development is but one example of the power of self-efficacy beliefs to affect the course of life paths through choice-related processes.

The substantial body of research concerning the diverse effects of perceived personal efficacy can be summarized as follows: People who have a low sense of efficacy in a given domain of functioning shy away from difficult tasks, which they tend to perceive as personal threats; have low aspirations and weak commitment to the goals they choose; maintain a self-diagnostic focus rather than concentrate on how to perform successfully; dwell on personal deficiencies, obstacles, and adverse outcomes; attribute failures to deficient capability; slacken their efforts or give up quickly in the face of difficulties; are slow to recover their sense of efficacy after failures or setbacks; and are prone to stress and depression. In contrast, people who have a strong sense of efficacy approach difficult tasks as challenges to be mastered rather than as threats to be avoided; set challenging goals and sustain strong commitment to their goals; maintain a task-diagnostic focus that guides effective performance; attribute failures to insufficient effort or deficient knowledge and skills that are acquirable; heighten effort in the face of difficulties; quickly recover their sense of efficacy after failures or setbacks; and display low vulnerability to stress and depression.

**ACHIEVEMENT MOTIVATION
BEHAVIORAL INHIBITION
BURNOUT
DISPOSITIONAL SETS
ENCOURAGEMENT
FREE WILL
HEALTHY PERSONALITY
MOTIVATION**

A. Bandura

SELF-ESTEEM

Self-esteem is the way one feels about oneself, including the degree to which one possesses self-respect and self-acceptance. Self-esteem is the sense of personal worth and competence that persons associate with their self-concepts. The esteem needs were studied by Abraham Maslow, and he reported ways that self-esteem is related to the process of becoming a self-actualizing person. According to Maslow, all people have a need or desire for a stable, firmly based, sense of self-regard or self-respect, and they need the esteem from themselves and from others.

Alfred Adler developed his theory of personality largely on the concepts of the motivating power of basic inferiority and compensation. Adler did not view this process in negative terms; his contention was that individuals develop unique personalities by striving to overcome real or perceived inadequacies.

Karen Horney also wrote about the antecedents of self-esteem. She contended that children who did not receive adequate parental love, acceptance, and approval tend to develop a pattern of insatiable needs (which she saw as neurotic).

As might be expected, love, warmth, and acceptance have been demonstrated to be extremely important in terms of developing a high degree of self-esteem. This sense of trust becomes a major safeguard against anxiety in coping with the world, giving the infant the feeling of basic security needed to meet the challenges in the environment. In researching the basic components of self-esteem, Stanley Coopersmith found that high self-esteem results from parental acceptance, the setting of limits, and freedom for individual action within realistic limits. In summary, the critical factor as an antecedent to one's self-esteem is the quality and amount of parental attention and acceptance one received as a child.

Self-esteem is a multidimensional concept, as it exists in degrees. It is a vitally important component of one's self-concept. Thus, an individual might have high self-esteem in interpersonal relationships, yet lack esteem with regard to mastery of academics. Esteem is also related to one's personal identity. Having love and acceptance is directly related to a "success identity"; lacking love and acceptance is related to a "failure identity."

INFERIORITY FEELINGS

G. Corey

SELF-FULFILLING PROPHECIES

The social psychologist W. I. Thomas formulated the basic idea of the self-fulfilling prophecy: "If men define situations as real, they are real in their consequences." Since Thomas' pioneering work on the relationship between our actions and our subjective definition of the environment, the phenomenon of the self-fulfilling prophecy has been studied in a number of areas. In medicine, there have been many instances in which a patient's illness and/or cure have been brought about wholly or in part by the patient's expectations. In social science research, expectations of researchers have been shown to affect the results both of survey studies and of controlled experiments. This has been termed the *experimenter bias effect*. A related phenomenon is that subjects in behavioral experiments are motivated to perform according to perceived expectations of the experimenter. These perceived expectations have been termed the *demand characteristics* of the experiment.

Expectation effects can be particularly strong in clinical psychology settings, because subjects in such situations have generally been referred to the clinician as a result of some alleged maladaptive behavior. Several studies have found that an examiner's expectations for a subject can affect the subject's performance on a psychodiagnostic test. In other words, a person who is perceived as deviant will begin behaving in an even more deviant manner in reaction to others' perceptions. The expectations teachers hold for individual students, formed on the basis of socioeconomic status, race, sex, intelligence test scores, and even the child's first name, have been found to affect the academic achievement of these students.

Regardless of the area, the mechanisms of the self-fulfilling prophecy are the same. An initial expectation about one's own or another's behavior is formed on the basis of insufficient information. People then behave in ways consistent with the expectation. However, the self-fulfilling prophecy is not inevitable. Researchers, teachers, and clinicians have all been able to control expectation effects by seeking objective information that confirms or refutes initial expectations, and by controlling the dissemination of information that generates inappropriate expectations in the first place.

ROLE EXPECTATIONS
UNCONSCIOUS INFERENCES

R. A. SHAW

SELF-HELP GROUPS

Self-help groups are more or less formal organizations of nonprofessional people working toward a common goal to benefit each member of the group. The discussion centers instead on groups whose primary goal is to achieve psychological or behavioral gains for their members and that are committed to two principles: that people who are coping or have coped effectively with a personal problem are better helpers than professionals who do not have first-hand experience, and that such people help themselves by helping each other.

ORIGINS AND PRESENT STATUS

Various strains of ancestry have been cited for such self-help groups. Whatever their antecedents, contemporary self-help groups have evolved at least partly to meet therapeutic needs that are not, or are not adequately, dealt with by existing social institutions.

Alcoholics Anonymous (AA) is the oldest, largest, and best-known ongoing therapeutic self-help group. Founded in 1935, it is an organization of, by, and for alcoholics (with offshoots Al-Anon and Al-Ateen for relatives and friends). It now has more than 1 million members in 92 countries. Its 12-step program has been adopted by some 34 self-help groups, including Gamblers Anonymous, Overeaters Anonymous, Schizophrenics Anonymous, and Narcotics Anonymous. Other early and well-known self-help organizations are Recovery, Inc., for former patients of mental health institutions, and Synanon, for drug addicts (and, later, ex-convicts). Especially since the mid-1970s, the growth of self-help groups has been seen by some as a major movement in psychotherapy, a "fourth force" following the "third force" of humanistic psychotherapy.

TYPES OF GROUPS

Scholars have made a number of typologies of self-help groups. Leon Levy's four types are especially applicable to those with a therapeutic orientation.

Type I groups aim primarily at behavioral control or reorganization. Examples of such groups are AA, Gamblers Anonymous, and Parents Anonymous. Levy's Type II groups, whose members have in common a stressful status or condition, could be further divided into subtypes. Other Type II groups focus on such crises as rape, murder of one's child, and surviving a suicide victim. Still others deal with what might be called life transitions or transitions toward normality. Such groups work on coping with rather than changing the status of members. Type III groups are composed of people felt to be discriminated against because of sex, race, class, or sexual orientation, and finally, Type IV groups share no particular common problem but work toward general self-actualization and enhanced effectiveness.

THERAPEUTIC FACTORS IN SELF-HELP GROUPS

In spite of the great diversity of organizations already noted, it is possible to distinguish a number of generally common therapeutic features or processes that help members of self-help groups make attitudinal or behavioral changes.

Shared Experience

For most self-help groups, a particular kind of shared experience or situation is the basis and rationale for membership. This commonality has several benefits. People tend to feel immediately and thoroughly understood, and they thus are not psychologically alone. The commonality tends also to reduce defensiveness and encourage self-revelation, with its usual cathartic utility and reduction of shame.

Helping Others

The "helper therapy principle" of self-help groups posits that the more group members help others, the more they are helped themselves.

Ongoing Support Network

Members of self-help groups often receive supportive compliments or praise at their meetings. But typically the support extends virtually around the clock, with members on call. The support network becomes something like a concerned extended family.

Information Sharing

A good deal of benefit comes from receiving information, whether technical or part of folk wisdom.

Finding Models

Membership in a self-help group provides opportunities to observe how others cope effectively and to use them as models.

Gaining Feedback

In the openness and honesty that typify self-help groups, members' behaviors tend to be accurately observed and commented on.

Learning Special Methods

With some self-help groups such as AA, successful coping is closely linked to following special procedures or techniques. Members are trained to learn and perpetuate them, and the pattern provides a structure that many find valuable.

Other Cognitive Processes

Much of the helpful impact of self-help group processes seems related to other principles of cognitive therapy such as raising self-image, increasing self-understanding, expanding perceived alternatives, enhancing discriminations, and redefining norms.

SELF-HELP VERSUS PROFESSIONAL PSYCHOTHERAPY

The relationship between self-help groups and professional and institutional helpers has varied from close cooperation to antagonism. For some groups, independence from the authority, methods, and funding of professionals is a matter of principle. But even strong advocates of self-help groups make increasing acknowledgment of important ways in which professionals have started, advised, and legitimized some such groups. Research suggests that about a third of self-help groups started with at least the assistance of professional helpers. There is a fundamental interaction between professionals and laypersons in many of the groups related to physical health. Organizations such as AA are often strongly endorsed by psychiatrists and clinical psychologists.

CHANGE-INDUCTION GROUPS
DIRECTIVE COUNSELING
HUMAN POTENTIAL
PEER COUNSELING
SUPPORTIVE CARE

F. W. HANSEN

SELF—LOOKING-GLASS CONCEPT

The looking-glass concept of self is commonly attributed to C. H. Cooley who, in elaborating on William James' discussion of the social self, suggested that a reflected self arises when individuals appropriate a self-feeling on the basis of how they think they appear in the eyes of other individuals.

Cooley is credited with the looking-glass metaphor, but its appearance in the literature can actually be traced to the works of Adam Smith. This metaphor carries a double meaning in Smith's and Cooley's formulations. In everyday life, persons see their faces, figures, and dress in the glass. In interactions with others, it is necessary to *imagine* how we appear in the eyes of the other. The other becomes the mirror and their interpretation of us is given in their gestures, their facial expressions, and their statements.

The self-idea that incorporates self-feeling, according to Smith and Cooley, has three principal components—the imagination of the person's appearance to the other person, the imagination of the other's judgment of that appearance, and some sort of self-feeling, such as pride or mortification. Self-feelings move through these imputed and imagined reactions of each interactant to the other's real and imagined judgments of their social selves. Every interaction is peopled by many selves, and there are always more persons present in a situation than there are real bodies. The strength of Cooley's formulation lies in its emphasis on the multiplicity of definitions, feelings, and meanings that arise in any situation when two persons come together for interaction.

The looking-glass self-concept is basic to the symbolic interactionist theory of interaction and remains central to current social psychological theorizing on the social self and on emotion. The centrality of the self and of self-processes in the study of emotional feeling and emotional expression is pivotal in current neuropsychological formulations of emotion.

SYMBOLIC INTERACTION

N. K. DENZIN

SEMANTIC DIFFERENTIAL

The semantic differential was developed by C. E. Osgood as a measurement technique to assess meaning. Osgood assumed that meanings of words can vary in a considerable, but unknown, number of dimensions.

The semantic differential is a standardized procedure for eliciting a carefully devised sample of a subject's placement of a concept (word) on a series of continua. A typical example might involve the following problem: How would you rate *apple* on the following scales? Where would you position the meaning of *apple* along a continuum stretching between the two indicated points, where a 1 or 7 rating means extremely, 2 or 6 means strongly, 3 or 5 means slightly good (or bad), and a 4 rating means neither good nor bad or equally so?

Apple

good ____:____:____:____:____:____:____ bad
large ____:____:____:____:____:____:____ small
active ____:____:____:____:____:____:____ passive, etc.

Meaning in semantic space has two essential properties. One is direction from each scale's midpoint, and the other is distance from that origin (thought to be related to the intensity of the meaning).

Osgood found that semantic space could be conceptualized as having a minimum of three orthogonal dimensions: evaluative (e.g., good–bad); activity (e.g., active–passive); and potency (e.g., large–small). Thus, the semantic differential is a modified form of controlled associations, controlled primarily by the scaling procedures utilized and the rating scales selected.

The semantic differential has been used in cross-cultural studies of meaning, to study the development of meaning in children, as well as to assess moods and to detect both momentary and long-term changes in a subject's mood. It has also been used to assess attitudes, emotions, and changes in personality during psychotherapy, the latter being the most frequent use in modern times.

COGNITIVE COMPLEXITY
MEASUREMENT
PSYCHOLINGUISTICS
SCALING

R. A. KASSCHAU

SENILE PSYCHOSES

The senile psychoses are characterized by an insidious onset and a gradual and continual deterioration of mental functioning until death. Initially the individual's behavior may be only an exaggeration of his or her premorbid personality with increasing egocentrism, but as the disorder progresses, cognitive disability (e.g., memory impairment), increasing apathy and disinterest in the environment, withdrawal from interpersonal interactions, reduced alertness, increasing difficulty in handling change, personal carelessness, impaired judgment, delirium, and confusion and disorientation appear and worsen progressively. In some cases, depression, agitation, and/or paranoid ideation may be part of the symptom complex.

Senile deterioration occurs in 2 to 4% of the population over 65, the generally agreed upon age demarking the distinction between the senile and the presenile dementias. Women are at greater risk for senile psychoses than men, and the disorders have been shown to have higher concordance rates in monozygotic than dizygotic twins. Social factors appear to contribute to the development of the disorders in a given individual.

On autopsy, it is seen that the brain is atrophied, the ventricles are enlarged, the sulci have widened, and the gyri have narrowed. Although the brain is generally smaller in both weight and size than that of the presenile individual, deterioration is particularly evident in the frontal lobes and the *cornu ammonis*. Histopathological changes include a reduced number of cells, increased neurofibrillary density, and the presence of "senile plaques"—small, roundish areas of tissue deterioration.

CENTRAL NERVOUS SYSTEM DISORDERS
ORGANIC SYNDROMES

W. E. EDMONSTON, JR.

SENSATION SEEKING

Sensation seeking is a personality trait behaviorally expressed in the generalized tendency to seek varied, novel, complex, and intense sensations and experiences and to take physical risks for the sake of such experiences. Others have used different terms to describe what is essentially the same trait (e.g., monotony avoidance, venturesomeness, thrill seeking, arousal seeking).

PHENOMENAL EXPRESSIONS OF SENSATION SEEKING

Sports

High sensation seekers are more likely than lows to engage in sports providing novel sensations (like parachute jumping, hang gliding, scuba diving, cave exploring, and mountain climbing) or speed and excitement (like auto racing and skiing) or physical contact (like football and rugby). Low sensation seekers are more likely than highs to persist in sports or physical activities demanding endurance and training (like long-distance running or aerobic exercises) but not providing much intense excitement or exhilaration. Those who engage in sensation-seeking sports are generally higher on more than the one most relevant scale, TAS.

Sexual Attitudes and Behavior

Sensation seekers have permissive attitudes toward sexual behavior, and young, single college students who score high on sensation seeking tend to have had more varied types of sexual experiences with more partners than low sensation seekers. There seems to be no difference in sensation seeking between heterosexual and homosexual males in the same population.

Social, Love, and Marital Relationships

In casual social contacts, high sensation seekers are more inclined to engage in interaction with more eye gaze, vocalization, smiles, laughter, and self-disclosure. They are likely to dominate in a group situation. High sensation seekers are more likely to regard love as a game and their lack of commitment tends to lead to their having many more relationships. Despite their inconstancy, there is a mutual attraction based on sensation seeking in unmarried and married couples; their sensation seeking scores tend to be positively correlated. But there is a much lower correlation between sensation seeking scores of couples requiring marital therapy.

Drug and Alcohol Use

Sensation seeking is highly related to the use of illegal drugs as well as tobacco and alcohol in college and noncollege populations. Sensation seeking is related to the variety of drugs used rather than the specific class of drugs preferred. Users of illegal drugs score higher on sensation seeking than those who just use alcohol, and those who go beyond marijuana are even higher on the trait. Sensation seeking predicts drug and alcohol use from adolescence to young adulthood through its relationship with general deviance of behavior over time as well as certain specific pathways between SSS subscales and use of legal or illicit drugs.

Food Preferences and Eating Habits

High sensation seekers like to try novel foods and prefer spicy foods in both American and Japanese societies. Low sensation seekers tend to like foods that are familiar, bland, and sweet. Binge eating in bulimics is not related to sensation seeking. Sensation seekers tend to be gourmets rather than gourmands. Vegetarians tend to be low sensation seekers.

Psychopathology

Sensation seeking scores are elevated in antisocial personalities, compared with other criminals, and in manic–depressives (bipolar disorders) even when they are not in the manic state. Sensation seeking is even elevated in the children of those with bipolar disorders, indicating a probable genetic connection. There are several biological markers that sensation seeking and bipolar disorder have in common, including augmenting of the cortical evoked potential and low levels of the enzyme monoamine oxidase (MAO). The evidence on unipolar major depressive disorders is inconsistent, but a recent study suggests they are low on sensation seeking, even after recovery from a depressive episode. Schizophrenics, particularly those who tend to be inactive or catatonic, tend to be low sensation seekers.

Media, Art, and Music Preferences

High sensation seekers like designs that are novel, complex, and nonsymmetrical while lows like familiar, simple, and symmetrical designs. High sensation seekers like art that is impressionistic or expressionistic with high tension levels; lows like realistic, low-tension art. High sensation seekers like films with explicit sex and violence while lows avoid such themes in any form. High sensation seekers watch television less than lows but when they do watch they tend to be channel-switchers. Highs prefer loud and complex rock or jazz music; lows prefer quieter popular or background music.

Vocational Preferences

High sensation seekers like risky or even periodically stressful vocations, like air pilots, air-traffic controllers, and emergency-room hospital workers, or occupations providing a great deal of varied social contacts. Low sensation seekers are relatively more attracted to solitary business or clerical occupations. Female high sensation seekers tend to be interested in nontraditional occupations for women, like law, while female low sensation seekers prefer more traditionally feminine occupations like elementary school teaching and housewife. Job satisfaction was inversely related to sensation seeking in an industrial setting, and when these workers were put on a simulated job that was very monotonous their negative affect and satisfaction states were related to their sensation-seeking trait levels.

Risk Taking

Many but not all of the activities and substances preferred by high sensation seekers are risky. This does not mean that risk is the point of their activities, because most tend to minimize the risk to derive maximal enjoyment from the activity. Antisocial personalities and pathological gamblers may be exceptions to this generalization. For both of these, the risk adds a significant arousal factor that is essential to the enjoyment of the activity. Appraisal of risk varies inversely with sensation seeking and engaging in risky behaviors in most areas of risk taking. The inclination or disinclination to engage in risky activities is the outcome of an approach-avoidance conflict where the expected pleasure from the activity motivates the approach, and the anticipated fear or harm constitutes the avoidance motive. High sensation seekers have steeper approach gradients and flatter avoidance gradients than low sensation seekers. The theory explains why high sensation seekers are more likely than lows to volunteer for experiments perceived as risky but that promise some kind of novel experience.

Cognitive Styles and Attention

Despite a low, positive correlation between intelligence and sensation seeking, high sensation seekers often do not do well in conventional academic learning situations, presumably because of their competing interests in noncognitive experiences. Cognitive curiosity is not related to sensation seeking, although sensation seekers tend to be more open to experience and creative in open-ended problem solving. Sensation seekers tend toward broad cognitive generalizations and a tendency to use more complex cognitive categories. They are more accepting of unusual beliefs like paranormal phenomena. Low sensation seekers tend to be more narrow and dogmatic in cognitive judgments. High sensation seekers have a strong capacity for focused attention on a stimulus or task even with competing stimuli or task distractions. This strong attention may be reflected in their stronger orienting reactions to novel stimuli compared with low sensation seekers.

Psychophysiology

Sensation seekers have a strong orienting reaction to novel stimuli, particularly as measured by heart rate deceleration, while low sensation seekers tend to respond with defensive reactions (heart rate acceleration) when encountering novel stimuli of moderate intensity. However, the differences between high and low sensation seekers in orienting and defensive reactions tend to disappear when stimuli are repeated unless the stimuli are of special interest to the high sensation seekers. Thus it is primarily reaction to novel stimuli that is related to sensation seeking. The strong orienting tendency may represent part of the biological approach mechanism underlying sensation seeking.

Another difference between high and low sensation seekers lies in the capacity of the cortex to respond to intense stimulation. High sensation seekers tend to show augmented cortical evoked potentials in direct relationship to the intensity of visual or auditory stimuli. Low sensation seekers tend to show little augmentation, and often show a reduction of cortical response in reaction to high intensity stimuli. There is a direct relationship between this kind of cortical inhibition and behavioral inhibition in situations of uncertainty or overstimulation in both humans and other species.

Psychopharmacology

Information about psychopharmacology can be found in Zuckerman and Zuckerman et al.

Hormones. High sensation seeking males, particularly as defined by the disinhibition subscale, have high levels of plasma testosterone and estradiol compared with the average levels found in low sensation seekers. Testosterone also correlates with sociability, impulsivity, and extent of heterosexual experience in the same males. Cortisol in the cerebrospinal fluid (CSF) correlates negatively with sensation seeking, particularly that of the disinhibitory type, suggesting it may be a factor in the lack of behavioral inhibition in these sensation seekers.

Genetics of Sensation Seeking

Comparisons of identical and fraternal twins on the SSS yielded an uncorrected heritability of 58%, near the upper limit of heritability values found for personality traits. Recent data from the Minnesota twins study showed correlations of 0.54 between identical twins and 0.32 between fraternal twins separated at or shortly after birth and raised in different families. The first figure is a direct measure of heritability—54%. The correlation between separated fraternal twins must be doubled to obtain the heritability and thus yields a heritability of 64%. Averaging the two estimates yields a heritability estimate of 59%, almost identical with that obtained in the Fulker et al. study of twins reared together. The effects of shared environment are negligible in both studies. The implication is that the environmental influences affecting sensation seeking are specific ones that are likely to exist outside of the family such as differential peer experience. Although one has no choice in selecting his or her parents or siblings, the genotype is likely to influence one's selection of friends. As with other personality traits, genes may affect the development of personality not only by how they govern the construction of the nervous system but in indirect ways through two-way phenotype–environment influences.

BOREDOM
INTRINSIC MOTIVATION

PERSONALITY TYPES
TRAIT PSYCHOLOGY

M. ZUCKERMAN

SENSORIMOTOR PROCESSES

The control of human movement is located within the central nervous system (CNS), which consists of the brain and the spinal cord. With the exception of very simple reflex movements, neural impulses that initiate movements originate within the cortex of the brain. The area of the cortex from which the neural impulses originate is called the sensorimotor area and is primarily located within the two convolutions on either side of the central fissure. The sensorimotor area of the right hemisphere of the brain controls the left half of the body and that of the left hemisphere controls the right side of the body.

The anterior portion of the sensorimotor strip is primarily responsible for sending motor impulses. The posterior portion is primarily responsible for receiving sensory feedback. Since neither function alone is sufficient to produce purposeful movement, they are combined in the sensorimotor strip to work in harmony with each other. When the motor portion of the sensorimotor strip has been damaged, movement is not initiated and paralysis occurs. When the sensory portion of the sensorimotor strip has been damaged, movements cannot be executed correctly and ataxic or spastic movement results.

CENTRAL NERVOUS SYSTEM

D. E. BOWEN

SENSORY DEPRIVATION

Sensory deprivation is an experimental procedure in which an attempt is made to remove or restrict sensory stimuli with human subjects. Such experiments were initiated by Donald Hebb and colleagues. Studies of sensory deprivation suggest that a changing sensory environment is essential for normal human perceptual functioning. Severe sensory restrictions have serious psychological and physical effects.

ADAPTATION

J. L. ANDREASSI

SENTENCE COMPLETION TEST

The sentence completion test was first applied to personality assessment in 1928 by H. F. Payne. Since that time, such tests have become a regular part of most clinical test batteries and are commonly used in industrial and military personnel selection. The method consists of a set of uncompleted sentences (stems) that the subject is to complete. Sentence completion tests are simple to design and can be adapted to many purposes. The better known tests are those by Holsopple and Miale, Sacks and Levy, Rohde, Stein, Forer, and Rotter.

The Rotter Incomplete Sentences Blank (ISB) is the most rigorously standardized. Designed for the specific purpose of assessing the personality adjustment of college students, it contains 40 short stems, mostly in the first person. The scoring consists of classifying the responses in three categories—conflict, neutral, and positive—and assigning them weighted scores. The scores on the 40 stems are summed to obtain an overall adjustment total. Interscorer reliability is high.

Interpretation of the ISB is based on these total scores obtained for the content analysis. Although impressionistic or objective content analysis is the typical method of interpretation, formal analyses of the length of completions, use of personal pronouns, verb-adjective ratios, and so forth are sometimes used. Despite lack of agreement on the exact level of awareness at which the sentence completion test should be positioned, most clinicians agree that the bulk of the material elicited is closer to conscious control than that obtained in the TAT and Rorschach.

CLINICAL ASSESSMENT
PROJECTIVE TECHNIQUES

E. M. SIIPOLA

SEQUENTIAL METHODS

Sequential methods are quasi-experimental research designs applied to problems in developmental psychology and other developmental sciences designed to deal with the confounds implicit in the study of phenomena that involve the dimensions of chronological age, time, and generations (cohorts).

TRADITIONAL DESIGNS IN
DEVELOPMENTAL PSYCHOLOGY

Traditional research on the age variable in developmental psychology has employed either cross-sectional or longitudinal approaches. Both are fraught with internal validity problems that limit inferences that can be drawn from studies employing such designs. When individuals are compared with themselves or with others at different developmental stages, three parameters must be considered: the chronological age (A) of the individual when observed, the birth cohort (C) of that individual (date of entry into the environment), and the time (T) of measurement when the individual is observed. The traditional developmental research designs confound these parameters.

The cross-sectional (age-comparative) approach draws samples of individuals at different ages and compares their performance on a given dependent variable, assuming that samples are comparable in prior life history and all other variables except age. Groups of individuals measured at the same point in time but differing in age must by definition be born at different points in time also. Hence, cross-sectional studies confound the influences of chronological age and cohort. When comparisons are made over a wide age range, it has been argued that the resulting comparisons are most likely to reflect cohort (generational) variation rather than influences of chronological age. Cross-sectional studies are, however, appropriate to define age differences at a particular historical time for purposes of immediate policy decisions, and studies of limited age ranges in children or the very old may provide a first estimate of age change when cohort effects are unlikely to prevail.

The purpose of the classic longitudinal design, by contrast, is to study development within the same individuals. As such, the design explicitly represents a time series, with an initial pretest, a subsequent intervention (those maturational events that occur over time), and a posttest, that is applied to the same individual organisms. If there is more than one time interval, then there is a succession of alternating treatments (further maturational events) and posttests. The longitudinal design has usually been applied to a single group of individuals of relatively homogeneous chronological age when first tested and thus to a single birth cohort.

Several of the internal validity threats enumerated by Campbell and Stanley may be plausible alternative explanations for the observed behavioral change (or lack thereof) attributed to age in studies employing the traditional designs. In a single-cohort longitudinal study, time-of-measurement (period) and aging effects must be confounded, and the presence of period effects in the dependent variable will render estimates of age effects internally invalid. These period effects may either mimic or suppress maturational changes occurring over a particular age span,

depending on whether age and time-of-measurement effects covary positively or negatively.

The single-cohort longitudinal design does not directly control for, or allow assessment of the magnitude of, other internal validity threats. For example, pains are generally taken to eliminate the confound of instrumentation by taking steps to ensure that the measurement procedures remain as consistent as possible throughout the course of a study. Statistical regression effects are minimized at times by including at least two, and often more, retest occasions. Nevertheless, unless collateral control samples are employed for this very purpose, single-cohort longitudinal studies cannot circumvent the confounds of testing and experimental mortality. Single-cohort longitudinal studies were necessary and appropriate in the early stages of the developmental sciences. There continue to be instances when a single-cohort longitudinal design may be the best approach to providing preliminary evidence for developmental functions, which can later be replicated for additional cohorts and measurement occasions. Single-cohort studies may also be useful in applications such as defining typologies of developmental patterns in a specifically targeted population.

SEQUENTIAL STRATEGIES

To reduce the limitations inherent in both the cross-sectional and the single-cohort longitudinal designs, several alternative sequential strategies have been suggested. The term *sequential* implies that the required sampling frame involves a sequence of samples observed across several measurement occasions (periods). Sequential strategies can best be understood by differentiating between sampling design and analysis design, although both are closely related. Sampling design refers to the cells of a cohort-by-age matrix that are to be sampled in a particular developmental study. Analysis design refers to the manner in which the cells that have been sampled may be organized to analyze for the effects of age, cohort, and time of measurement. Figure 1 shows a typical cohort-by-age matrix, indicating all of the sequential designs and also illustrates the confounding of the three parameters of interest. A and C appear as the rows and columns of the matrix, whereas T is the parameter contained within the matrix cells. There has been a debate on whether and how these effects should be unconfounded. The issues involved are quite complex, highly technical, and beyond the scope of this introductory treatment.

SAMPLING DESIGNS

Two types of sequential sampling designs may be distinguished: those observing a panel of individuals repeatedly to fill the cells of the matrix and those using independent samples of individuals (each observed only once) drawn from the same cohorts to do so. The matrix shown in Figure 1 could have been produced by either approach. Employing Baltes's terminology, it is possible to denote the two designs as longitudinal and cross-sectional sequences, respectively. A cross-sectional sequence implies the replication of a cross-sectional study, the same age range being assessed for at least two different time periods, obtaining the estimate for each age level across multiple cohorts, where each sample is measured only once. A longitudinal sequence, by contrast, represents the measurement of at least two cohorts over the same age range. Again, estimates from each cohort are obtained at two or more points in time. The critical difference, however, is that the longitudinal sequence provides data that permit the evaluation of change within groups' individuals as well as individual differences in such change. An example of a data set containing both cross-sectional and longitudinal sequences may be found in Schaie and Hertzog.

ANALYSIS DESIGNS

Data collected according to schemes such as those indicated in Figure 1 permit a variety of alternative analysis strategies. Each row of this matrix

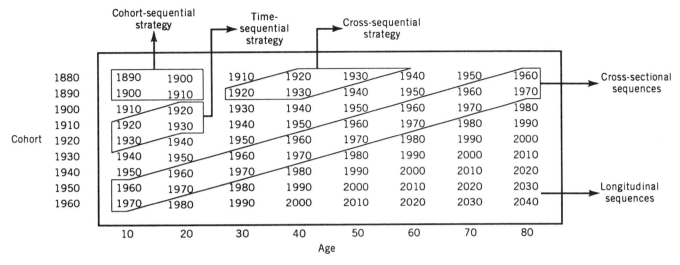

Figure 1. Schema of cross-sectional and longitudinal sequences and possible analytic designs derived from the general development model. Entries in this schema represent times of measurement.

can be treated as a single-cohort longitudinal study, each diagonal as a cross-sectional study, and each column as a time-lag study (comparison of behavior at a specific age across successive cohorts). Sequential sampling designs, unfortunately, do not permit complete disentanglement of all components of the $B = f(A, C, T)$ function due to the obvious linear dependency of the three factors. Nevertheless, it may be suggested that, given the model, three distinct analysis designs are available by considering the separate effect of any two of the components while assuming the constancy or irrelevance of the third on theoretical or empirical grounds.

Given the minimum designs displayed in Figure 1, Schaie suggests that the cohort-sequential strategy will permit separation of age changes from cohort differences, under the assumption of trivial time-of-measurement effects. The time-sequential strategy will permit the separation of age differences from period differences, assuming only trivial cohort effects. Finally, the cross-sequential strategy will permit separation of cohort differences from period differences. The time-sequential strategy, of course, does not allow a repeated measurement approach (i.e., the same individual cannot be the same age at two different points in time), but it does have merit for the estimation of age differences for social policy purposes, for those dependent variables for which cohort effects are likely to be minimal. It also is an appropriate strategy for estimating time-of-measurement (period) effects in studies covering a wide range of age/cohort levels.

Each of the sequential analysis strategies can be expanded further to control for the effects of experimental mortality and for testing or experimentation. One additional data collection will be required for each additional parameter to be controlled for.

When data are collected in the form of longitudinal sequences to examine intraindividual differences in change over time, it is possible to apply both cohort-sequential and cross-sequential strategies for data analysis. Developmental psychologists are likely to find the cohort-sequential design of greater interest because it explicitly differentiates intraindividual change within cohorts from average individual differences between cohorts. This design, in addition, permits a check of the consistency of age functions over successive cohorts, thereby offering greater external validity than would be provided by a single-cohort longitudinal design.

A critical assumption of the cohort-sequential design is that one postulates the absence of time-of-measurement effects contained in the data. This assumption may be parsimonious for many psychological variables, but others may still be affected by "true" period effects or the confounds

presented by occasion-specific internal validity threats of differences in instrumentation or experimenter behavior across test occasions. The question arises of how violations of the assumptions of no time-of-measurement (T) effects would be reflected in a cohort-sequential analysis. Logical analysis suggests that all estimated effects will be perturbed, albeit the most direct evidence would be shown by a significant C by A interaction. However, lack of a significant interaction does not guarantee the corresponding absence of T effects. Such effects could be localized in a small subset of occasions in extensive studies, in which case all effect estimates would be biased.

The essential consequence of the interpretational indeterminacy in sequential analysis is that all effect estimates will be inaccurate to some degree if the assumptions that justify the specific design are violated. The interpretational problem may be reduced, however, in estimating the relative likelihood of confounded T effects, given a strong theory about the nature and direction of estimated and confounded effects. The practical application of strong theory to sequential designs requires specification of confounds in an invalid design to obtain estimates of these confounded effects.

Although it is always preferable to estimate the "true" parameter effects from the appropriate design—one that makes the correct limiting assumptions—the developmental psychologist must often settle for something less than the optimal design, whether as a temporary expedient or because of the nature of the phenomenon that is being studied. The preferred design to be employed in a given study must, therefore, be guided both by the substantive literature as well as the investigator's theoretical assumptions.

COHORT DIFFERENCES
CONTAMINATION (STATISTICAL)
DOUBLE-BLIND RESEARCH
EXPERIMENTAL DESIGNS
LIFE EVENTS
LONGITUDINAL STUDIES
RESEARCH METHODOLOGY

K. W. SCHAIE

SET

The term *set* is used in a number of different contexts and problem areas in psychology—in areas as diverse as motor behavior, perception, and problem solving. There are many variants and synonyms of the term, although each tends to convey a specific theoretical orientation or to specify a particular application. Typical variants include the German word *Einstellung,* as well as more common and descriptive terms *readiness, determining tendency,* and *propensity.* A more problem-oriented variant sometimes encountered is *functional fixity.*

Set is a temporary condition that predisposes an individual toward a particular response, or class of responses. This condition can arise from the task requirements, in the form of overt or covert instructions, or from context, expectations, or prior experiences. At higher cognitive levels, it can alter the pattern of information pickup, the nature of what is perceived, or the probability that a particular problem may be solved.

One way in which set interacts with cognitive processes is called *attentional set,* which is a condition whereby the observer is prepared to receive information of a particular type, or from a particular channel. Such a set can have positive or negative consequences. In general, information of the type for which the observer is set is processed more accurately, and with shorter reaction times. There is a cost in that information for which the observer is not set may then be missed, or misinterpreted.

Another manifestation of set phenomena occurs when one perceives stimuli in accordance with expectations and context rather than on the basis of the actual physical stimulus in the environment. This is known as *perceptual set.* Perceptual set can also render certain stimuli functionally invisible, if one is not set for them.

Set may also affect problem-solving behavior. In this case, the term usually used is the German word *Einstellung.* To see this form of set in operation, consider the set of eight problems in Table 1. Here the subject is required to measure exactly a given quantity of water using several jars and a faucet. For instance, to obtain the 30 liters of water required in the first problem, one should fill the 39-liter jar first, then pour off 3 liters three times. It would be useful for the reader to try the remaining problems.

You probably would discover that problem 2 could be solved if one first filled jar II, and then poured off jar I once, and jar III twice. Notice that this same solution works for all of the remaining problems, and you probably used it all the way through, up to and including problem 8. In so doing, you actually missed the simpler solutions available in problems 7 and 8, both of which require only that you fill jar I and pour off jar III once. This demonstrates a *problem-solving set.* Notice that for problems 3 through 6, the set actually speeded your performance by biasing you toward the best solution, while in the last two cases it impeded performance by "blinding" you to the simpler, faster solution.

The last form of set to be discussed is evoked by common objects or techniques. It is known as *functional fixity.* This type of set often serves as a block to creativity and problem solving. In its simplest form, it embodies the fact that most objects and processes have a specific function. Thus, the function of a hammer is to pound things, of a knife is to cut, and of a trumpet is to make music, and so forth. Often this functional

Table 1   Water Jar Problem

Problem	Jar			Liters Needed
	I	II	III	
1	39	3		30
2	21	127	3	100
3	14	163	25	99
4	18	43	10	5
5	9	42	6	21
6	20	59	4	31
7	23	49	3	20
8	14	36	8	6

set provides a block to problem solving, since individuals tend to think of these objects as having only the familiar function. It is thus often shocking or amusing to see items used in unconventional ways. Therefore, although mental sets may make problem solving more routine and less effortful, the mark of creativity is often the ability to "break set."

COGNITIVE COMPLEXITY
CONTEXTUAL ASSOCIATIONS
PERCEPTION
PERCEPTUAL DISTORTION
SELECTIVE ATTENTION

S. Coren

SEX BIAS IN MEASUREMENT

Bias in measurement is an issue when groups respond differently to items in an achievement, ability, or aptitude test, or in other types of measures, such as interest inventories. Sex bias in measurement is an issue when men and women respond differently to such items. The issue has particularly important implications for women's educational and occupational choices, as it has for members of minority groups.

Although the terms *bias* and *unfairness* have often been used interchangeably, the consensus among those who have studied bias seems to be to use the term *bias* to refer to intrinsic features of a test—its content, the construct or constructs it purports to measure, and the context within which the content is placed. *Unfairness,* however, refers to ethical questions about how the test results are used. Shepard further defines bias as occurring when two individuals with equal ability but from different groups do not have the same probability of success on a test item.

Sex bias and sex fairness in measurement have been investigated mainly with reference to interest, achievement, and aptitude tests, and to a lesser extent with reference to personality measures. Many of the differences between men and women in test performance have been attributed to differences in the socialization process—different expectations regarding early childhood behavior, interests, and achievement; exposure to different sets of experiences, including courses each was encouraged to take in school; and the stereotyping of occupations as men's work and women's work, with the latter encompassing mainly low-level, dead-end occupations in which most women workers are found.

IN INTEREST MEASUREMENT

Until relatively recently, interest inventories—especially those with occupational scales—focused mainly on preferences for male-oriented activities. Only recently have there been attempts to build sex-balanced interest scales, with the number of items in a scale favored by one sex balanced by the number of items favored by the other sex. The National Institute of Education study of sex bias in interest measurement, included guidelines for sex-fair inventories such as the reporting of scores on all scales, regardless of sex of the criterion group, to both women and men; and more sex-fair interpretation of inventory results.

IN ACHIEVEMENT AND APTITUDE TESTING

After the ninth grade, item context as well as content and gender balance in testing are important variables in sex differences in performance, especially in mathematics and science. Carol Dwyer related findings that in tests of verbal ability, all other things being equal, males obtained higher scores when the material was set in the context of business, science, practical affairs, mechanical principles, or mathematics. Females scored higher when the material was drawn from the arts, the humanities, or understanding human relations. There was no conclusive evidence as to whether these differences were the result of familiarity with the context, or motivational considerations associated with the context, or some combination of the two. Tittle also described a study in which, while basic mathematical processes remained the same, when item context was manipulated experimentally to describe materials or settings more familiar to males or to females, sex differences in performance resulted. In aptitude testing, sex bias and fairness issues are perhaps best illustrated by Lee Cronbach's comments on the Armed Services Vocational Aptitude Battery. Cronbach pointed out that, among other weaknesses, the battery was poorly designed for use with women. Lack of trade and technical information (for instance, the ability to identify a carburetor) would be scored as low trade and technical aptitude, or ability to learn.

THE MAGNITUDE OF MALE–FEMALE DIFFERENCES

An important factor in dealing with questions of sex bias and sex fairness in measurement is the actual size of measured differences in ability. Janet Hyde describes a meta-analysis she applied to studies on verbal, quantitative, visual-spatial, and visual-analytic spatial differences between males and females. Although the differences had been described as "well established," Hyde found that they were, in fact, not large. Gender difference accounted for only 1% of the variance in verbal and quantitative ability, 4% of the variance in visual-spatial ability, and approximately 2.5% of the variance in visual-analytic spatial ability. These quantities, she concluded, were too small to account for the differences in the occupational distributions of men and women in occupations such as engineering.

A QUESTION OF SOCIAL JUSTICE

Messick pinpointed two critical questions: (a) Is the test good as a measure of the characteristics it is interpreted to assess? (b) Should the test be used for the proposed purpose in the proposed way? The first question is concerned with the psychometric properties of the test, especially construct validity. The second is an ethical question, and to answer it the proposed use of a test must be justified in terms of social values. These questions apply not just to matters of selection or personality assessment, but to all psychological and educational measurement, including construct-based ability tests and content-sampled achievement tests.

CULTURE-FAIR TESTS
RACE BIAS IN TESTING
SEXISM

E. E. DIAMOND

SEX CHROMOSOME DISORDERS

Normal sexual differentiation into genetic and phenotypic male and female takes place prenatally, and in various orderly stages. The first stage occurs at the time of conception; contribution of the XX or XY chromosomes determines genetic sex. In the second embryonic month, the gonads begin differentiation into ovaries or testes. During the third month of gestation, hormonal secretions by the testes (androgens) signal differentiation of internal and external male sexual organs. The absence of androgens, as in most genetic females, results in female internal and external differentiation. Occasionally genetic or hormonal disorders result in ambiguous differentiation and may cause confusion as to the sex of the child at birth. Behavioral observation of these individuals by John Money and his associates provides evidence that environment (i.e., whether one is reared and treated as a male or female) influences gender role and identity much more than do genetic or morphologic sex.

Disorders of the sex chromosomes can occur during meiosis (cell division producing gametes, cells with only half of the chromosomes

complement) or during mitosis (division of all cells past the gamete stage). Genetic errors during meiosis yield organisms with too few or too many sex chromosomes; mosaicism (combinations of more than one chromosomal pattern in the same individual) is caused by errors during mitosis. Breakage rather than total absence of sex chromosomes may also occur, resulting in a variety of gonadal and sex organ abnormalities. Missing or additional sex chromosomes are the most distinct sex chromosome disorders.

The only viable condition of sex chromosome loss is the occurrence of an X without a partner sex chromosome. The male counterpart of this syndrome (YO) is always lethal. Turner's syndrome (genetic karyotype 45/XO, indicating 45 total chromosomes with only one sex chromosome) occurs in one out of 7000 newborns, but is much higher in spontaneously aborted fetuses. Of Turner's syndrome females, about half are the "pure" genetic karyotype 45/XO; the other half have a variety of sex chromosome constitutions, usually caused by a defect in the second chromosome. Primary signs of this disorder are gonadal dysgenesis (undeveloped ovaries) and infertility. Phenotypically, internal and external sexual organs remain infantile, no menstruation occurs at puberty, and only with estrogen therapy can secondary sexual characteristics develop. These females also exhibit a distinctive cluster of congenital abnormalities, including short stature, webbed neck, and widely spaced nipples, giving their chests a shield-like appearance. Turner's syndrome females are assigned the sex role of female and reared as girls with stereotypically female gender role and identity.

Individuals with Klinefelter's syndrome, a disorder in which at least one X chromosome is added to the normal 46/XY karyotype (most commonly 47/XXY), are phenotypically male with a small to average penis size, extremely small nonfunctional testes, rounded hips, and some breast development. A high incidence of chronic medical disorders, including pulmonary and liver diseases and decreased intelligence, is common. A higher than normal incidence of psychopathology has been documented, and variations in sexual preference have been noted, although these individuals have a lowered sex drive, perhaps because of the lack of testosterone secretion. An increased frequency of this disorder is found in mental and penal institutions. Individuals with genetic karyotypes of more than one additional X (e.g., 49/XXXXY) have greater retardation, more severe genital immaturity, and other physical abnormalities. Incidence of Klinefelter's syndrome is one in 400 live-born males, and combinations of genetic abnormalities (mosaics) are not uncommon.

In the 47/XYY karyotype condition (referred to as "supermale"), there is also at least one extra sex chromosome. The phenotype is male. The extra Y results in increased height, but does not influence the expression of any other qualities that might be termed "super"-male. These males are often infertile and mentally retarded, and exhibit delinquent behavior, characterized by impulsive acting out and poor long-term planning. Although an increased incidence of this disorder is found in penal institutions, it is probably not accurate to conclude that a 47/XYY karyotype is a genetic marker for criminal activity. Its side effects of mental retardation, impulsivity, and physical stature (increasing visibility, and perhaps the perception of fearsomeness) may increase the likelihood of incarceration.

The 47/XXX females (called "superfemales") exhibit no definite physical stigmata, although IQ may be slightly lower. These females have stereotypic gender role/identity. Although fertile, they report greater than average menstrual problems and early menopause; their fertility increases the probability of producing XXY or XXX offspring. Additional Xs result in progressively more severe retardation, possibly linking chromosomal excesses of any kind with decreased intelligence.

CHROMOSOME DISORDERS
GENETIC DISORDERS

B. E. THORN

SEX DIFFERENCES

The study of sex differences derives from the field of differential psychology, introduced by Sir Francis Galton. Galton measured, quantified, and compared various physical and mental traits in men and women.

The field of sex differences received new impetus from a major study by Eleanor Maccoby and Carol Jacklin, in which they reviewed the psychological literature in over 50 content areas encompassing more than 1600 studies to determine what sex differences actually existed. They concluded that consistent sex differences could be found only in four areas: Girls have greater verbal ability than boys; boys excel in visual-spatial ability; boys show greater mathematical ability than girls; and males are more aggressive than females. Suggestive, but ambiguous, evidence of sex differences was found in the following areas: girls have greater tactile sensitivity; males are more active, especially in the company of others; girls are more likely or more willing to report fear, timidity, or anxious behavior; males are more competitive; males are more dominant; and girls tend to be more compliant. They failed to find consistent evidence of sex differences in other traditional areas of investigation.

Metaanalyses of the literature on sex differences in influenceability by Alice Eagly and Linda Carli and in cognitive areas such as verbal, quantitative, and visual-spatial abilities by Janet Hyde suggest that the variability accounted for by sex differences is typically very small. It has been estimated that approximately 1% of the variance in influenceability is accounted for by sex. Even in the area with the largest sex difference—spatial ability—Hyde reports that sex accounts for only about 5% of the variability found.

The area of sex differences is one in which the nature–nurture arguments still persist. Although most students of the area regard sex differences as the product of biological environmental interaction, in practice, researchers tend to concentrate on either biological or environmental variables. Moreover, a number of different interactions are possible in a given area, which may generate quite different research and policy decisions.

Criticism of biologically based theories of sex differences has been particularly evident in the newly emerging area of the psychology of women. Critics have focused on the effect of the sex of the experimenter or other evaluator of the person's performance in the production of sex differences. Other criticisms note that sex biases exist in the choice of what content area to study with what sex subject and in the selection of methodologies by which the "same" characteristic is evaluated in females and males.

Criticism of sex difference research may be conceptual as well as methodological. For example, no general theoretical framework exists to determine when a given sex difference should be examined or what it means if it is found. Therefore, findings on sex differences have tended to be scattered throughout the research literature. Since such findings also tend to be inconsistent and small in size, generalizations about sex differences have tended to be based either on arbitrary decision making or on stereotypic assumptions about what should be true. Descriptions involving sex, however, tend to be treated as explanations because biological processes are inferred whether explanatory mechanisms have been provided by the researcher.

SEX DIFFERENCES: DEVELOPMENTAL
SEX DIFFERENCES IN MATHEMATICS
SEXISM

R. K. UNGER

SEX DIFFERENCES: DEVELOPMENTAL

The best established sex differences are in the areas of life experiences and biology. They generally are considered to cause smaller and less well-established sex differences in the psychological areas of cognitive and social-emotional characteristics.

Cognitive areas showing sex differences include verbal and mathematics achievement and visual–spatial performance; the social-emotional area showing the most consistent sex difference is that of aggression. The developmental periods during which these sex differences occur vary somewhat by area.

Girls tend to excel at verbal tasks during infancy and young childhood. The existence of sex differences in verbal achievement during the elementary school years is not as clear, although many more boys than girls have trouble learning to read. Starting in early adolescence, females tend to achieve higher average scores than males on many kinds of verbal tasks, including lower level skills such as spelling and punctuation through high-level skills such as comprehension of difficult reading material and verbal analogies. The average female advantage continues through middle age and perhaps through old age, although there is very little relevant research on the elderly. Prior to adolescence, the sexes are quite similar in mathematics achievement. Starting some time during adolescence, males on the average tend to score higher than females on mathematics tests.

There are at least two major components to visual–spatial performance: analytic (including, for example, disembedding figures from backgrounds and constructing block designs) and nonanalytic (including mental rotations and reproducing spatial relations). Prior to adolescence, the sexes are similar in performance on both components. Starting in early adolescence, males tend to have higher average scores than females in both areas. The male advantage may continue into old age, although again there is little research in this area. The sexes, however, do *not* differ in spatial performance in nonvisual modalities such as touch or hearing.

Male children, on the average, are more aggressive than female children, from about age 2 through adolescence and college age. This pattern is found cross-culturally. The results for adults are not as clear. A review by Ann Frodi did not find that men always display more physical aggression; they did find, however, that men reported themselves as more aggressive and hostile than women.

LIFE EXPERIENCE DIFFERENCES

Starting at birth, girls and boys are treated differently in many socialization areas. Adults expect boys and girls, and women and men, to differ in the physical, personality, and cognitive characteristics contained in the sex-role stereotypes, although they profess to hold similar behavioral goals for their own children regardless of sex.

Education is differentiated by sex, with increasing differentiation occurring as educational level increases. Students are exposed to sex differentiation in the various occupations found in schools. Men fill most administrative and custodial jobs and tend to teach mathematics, social studies, and science in secondary schools. Women fill most of the clerical and secretarial jobs and teach most elementary school grades and language arts in secondary schools. Although about equal percentages of females and males graduate from high school, more males are encouraged to continue so the percentage of females continually drops as the level of the educational degree increases.

While in school, more boys than girls are encouraged and actually take the advanced mathematics and sciences courses, prerequisites to many majors in college, while more girls than boys take language courses. Correspondingly, in higher education, more females major in humanities and education while more males major in scientific fields. In vocational training, women are concentrated in the domestic, health, and office staff programs while men are enrolled in technical, agricultural, and trade/industry programs; these differences by sex lead to lower paying jobs for most women.

There also are sex differences related to family life and to work. All cultures have some division of labor by sex, usually based on mobility. Cross-culturally, men often are responsible for tasks that require travel; women usually are responsible for work that allows them to remain near home and take major child care responsibility. Both sexes perform tasks requiring strength.

There are sex differences in physical and mental health. Males have shorter average life spans and a higher proportion of males die prenatally and throughout life. However, women visit physicians and therapists more often. The largest sex difference for mental health problems is for depression.

Sex differences in health, both physical and mental, are mediated by marriage. Married men have lower average rates of death and illness than unmarried men. The healthiest women, however, are those who never marry.

As greater opportunities become available, some of the sex differences in life experiences are narrowing, primarily because increasingly more women are choosing to participate in activities, education, training, and jobs that have been considered culturally male appropriate. However, the gap in sex-differentiated pay scales has not narrowed; it appears to be widening.

BIOLOGICAL SEX DIFFERENCES

Several biological areas exhibit sex differences. These include genes, hormones, brain organization, and physical characteristics. Prenatal sexual development depends on a sequence involving chromosomes, hormones, and the environment. The sequence begins with the combination of an X or Y chromosome from the father paired with an X chromosome from the mother. Testicular hormones must be present prenatally to result in a biological male, regardless of the chromosomes present; without these hormones, a biological female develops. Genetic differences related to the sex chromosomes are one possible biological influence on sex-role development and on psychological sex differences.

Differences in brain structure and function also have been theoretically implicated in psychological sex differences and sex roles. Generally, the right hemisphere of the brain is related to performance on spatial tasks and to processing several items of information concurrently while the left hemisphere is linked to performance on verbal tasks and to individual processing of information items. There may be small sex differences in brain organization, but even if they do exist, they cannot explain psychological sex differences.

Sex hormones also have been proposed as one possible biological influence. Currently, however, hormonal sex differences do not explain psychological sex differences.

There may be monthly hormonal variations associated with some sex differences in perceptual and social-emotional characteristics. Some women experience changes in activity levels, sensory thresholds, and moods related to their menstrual cycles. However, there is no evidence, despite a great deal of research, that women's menstrual cycles are related to their cognitive performances.

There are several physical sex differences; for example, on the average, men are taller, heavier, and stronger than women. Girls, on the average, have higher physical maturation rates than boys, and the same may be true for the maturational rate of the central nervous system. Girls reach puberty between $1\frac{1}{2}$ and 2 years earlier, on the average, than boys. The rate of physical maturation does seem to be related to visual–spatial skills; for both sexes, later maturers have better visual–spatial skills than early maturers. There is no relationship between maturation rate and verbal skills.

CONCLUSIONS

Many psychologists studying the relationships among biological, life, and psychological sex differences conclude that biological sex differences do not explain psychological sex differences. Biological factors may set the potential for psychological characteristics. But the environment often overcomes the biological differences and controls the sex differences that do and do not appear in psychological characteristics.

C. G. Schau

SEX DIFFERENCES IN MATHEMATICS

Sex differences in mathematical aptitude favoring males have been reported for several years. Not until junior high school, however, do such sex differences become obvious. Girls then tend to excel on computational tasks, while boys excel on tasks requiring mathematical reasoning ability. Although the sex difference in overall mathematical reasoning ability is large, the sex difference in certain kinds of mathematics achievement is even larger. As compared with males, females complete fewer high school and college mathematics courses from a given competency level, have a lower rate of entry into quantitative fields in college for a given number of mathematics courses completed in high school, and have a lower rate of persistence in quantitative fields.

Several hypotheses have been proposed to account for these differences. The masculine-identification hypothesis states that it is necessary for one to identify psychologically with a male to have interest and ability in mathematics. The social-reinforcement hypothesis states that sex-related differences in mathematics achievement are due, at least in part, to differential social conditioning and expectations for boys and girls.

Fennema and Sherman proposed that the sex difference in mathematical reasoning ability is simply a function of the fact that boys take more mathematics than girls. Differential course taking is the result of socialization forces. Benbow and Stanley presented data that contradict this theory. They believe that some combination of endogenous and exogenous variables probably causes more boys than girls to reason well mathematically. What interactions of factors such as environment, female versus male hormones, physiologically induced differences in activity levels, and different brain-hemisphere lateralization might be responsible cannot as yet be ascertained.

C. P. Benbow

SEX-ROLE DEVELOPMENT

Sex roles are sets of attributes, including attitudes, personality traits, and behaviors, that a culture defines as appropriate for each sex. These beliefs generally are held, at least to some extent, by a majority of the culture's members. Sex-role beliefs become sex-role stereotypes when individuals use those attributes as rules and apply them to almost all females and males.

SEX-ROLE STEREOTYPES

Generally, the sex-role stereotypes of technologically advanced cultures are quite similar. The stereotypes for femininity include characteristics that can be categorized as expressive or communal. The masculinity stereotypes include characteristics generally associated with instrumentality or agency.

There are substantial variations in cultural sex roles and their accompanying stereotypes. For example, Margaret Mead studied the personality characteristics and behaviors of men and women in three cultures in New Guinea. Each culture had its own sex roles and stereotypes, but they did not match the feminine-expressive and masculine-instrumental ones of technologically advanced nations. This diversity among sex roles is one indication that many characteristics associated with them are not biologically determined but are transmitted by specific cultures.

Sex-role stereotypes, like all other stereotypes, are important for several reasons. First, many people expect others, as well as themselves, to act in accordance with the appropriate sex-role stereotype. Second, sex often determines the types of experiences to which people are exposed during their lives. Third, sex roles are a major source of many people's self-concepts.

THEORIES

Traditionally psychologists have used three general classes of theories to explain the processes involved in sex-role development: psychoanalytic, social learning, and cognitive. Psychoanalytic theory posits the child's defensive identification with the same-sex parent as the primary factor in sex-role development.

Social learning posits three basic primarily environmentally controlled mechanisms involved in learning sex roles and sex-role stereotypes. First, children learn the content of sex roles through direct instruction. Second, children learn about sex roles through direct reinforcement. Third, and most important, most sex-role learning, as well as all other kinds of learning, occurs from observing models. Social learning theorists have stressed the importance of parents as models and reinforcement agents, especially for young children.

There are two aspects to modeling in sex-role development: learning and performance. In the learning phase, children learn the content of both the feminine and masculine sex roles. However, children do not perform all of the behaviors that they have learned. Children tend to repeat or generalize behaviors that they have learned from models who received positive or avoided negative consequences.

Cognitive theories emphasize the cognitive processes involved in sex-role development, rather than the environmental input. Following Jean Piaget's model of cognitive development, Lawrence Kohlberg proposed a developmental progression in sex-role development starting with gender identification (the correct labeling of self and others for gender) at about 2 or 3 years of age and eventually developing into gender constancy (the understanding that gender does not change) at about age 7. Once gender constancy is attained, cognitive theorists maintain that it is self-reinforcing to behave in culturally sex-appropriate ways; basically, children self-socialize into culturally appropriate sex roles.

More recently, some cognitive theorists have switched the emphasis from the development of gender constancy to the use of information-processing constructs, especially cognitive structures called schemas that guide perception, in understanding sex-role development. Sandra Bem, for example, proposed that sex-role development results from the assimilation of a person's self-concept into the gender schema that provides a cognitive readiness to perceive information in sex-related ways.

DEVELOPMENT OF SEX ROLES

Development of Gender Identity

Gender identity, also called gender orientation, reflects people's private perceptions about themselves in relation to their assigned sex. Because it is a private perception, it is very difficult to measure. An abnormal gender identity is attributed to people, especially males, who behave in ways that are culturally inappropriate to their sex roles and so are frequently noticed; this often includes "feminine" boys, homosexuals, transsexuals, and transvestites.

For many years, John Money and his colleagues have worked with people whose gender identities, physical characteristics, and sex chromosomes do not match, primarily as a result of prenatal hormone effects. Through clinical experience, they have concluded that it is possible to change a child's sex assignment to that of the opposite sex, if that reassignment is done prior to about 18 months of age. Children who are reassigned after this age often experience severe psychological problems. Thus the establishment of a stable gender identity is set at about 18 months.

Development of Gender Constancy

Young children do not know that sex is a permanent attribute or that it usually is defined by the genitals. At about 2 years of age, children learn to label themselves accurately in regard to sex. At about age 3, they can label accurately the sexes of others. They next understand gender stability. At about age 7, children understand gender consistency or the concept that sex does not change with changes in name, dress, or behavior. Finally, between about 7 and 9, children understand that a person's sex is defined by genital appearance.

Sex-Role Knowledge

Sex-role knowledge refers to the accuracy of people's concepts about sex roles. It reflects a description, not a judgment.

As might be expected, children's sex-role knowledge increases with age. By 3 years of age, children have learned some of the conceptually simpler aspects of sex roles, especially those related to appearance (e.g., hair length, size, clothes), toys, common articles, and some occupations and activities. With increasing age, children's knowledge increases and broadens to include most occupations and other future roles, activities, appearance characteristics, and personality traits. By middle to late elementary school, children accurately know most aspects of the culture's sex-role stereotypes.

Sex-Role Attitudes

Unlike sex-role knowledge, sex-role attitudes include a judgmental component related to the "correctness" or "fairness" of the stereotypes. Sex-role aspects studied include attitudes about occupations, child and adult roles, personality traits, and activities, as well as people's own sex-role self-concepts.

During the developmental period from early preschool to early elementary school, children's sex-role attitudes tend to become increasingly sex-typed, probably at least in part due to their increasing sex-role knowledge. Individually, however, young children often exempt themselves from following rules derived from their own sex-role attitudes, although boys tend to be more consistent in following their own rules.

From early through late elementary school and into junior high school, many sex-role attitudes become increasingly less sex-typed. Developmental age trends from junior high through high school are not as clear, but it appears that at least some attitudes become increasingly sex-typed. These age patterns may be influenced by several factors, including cognitive maturity and socioeconomic status.

Adults who are involved in active parenting, with children still at home, are most traditional in their attitudes; childless young married couples and couples expecting children are intermediate; single adults and adults with no children at home are least sex-typed.

Throughout the life cycle, males' sex-role attitudes often are more sex-typed than females'. Home and child care roles show the greatest differences between the sexes; males, more than females, still attribute these roles primarily to women.

Sex-Role Behaviors

There are few well-established psychological sex differences in behaviors. Sex-role stereotypes imply that many more sex differences exist than actually do and that the differences are larger than they really are.

CONCLUSIONS

Most psychologists attribute sex differences and sex-role development to environmental and developmental cognitive effects, working in conjunction with small biological potentials. However, they conclude that the social environment has much more practical impact than underlying biological factors.

Although some people accept traditional sex-role stereotypes and the development of knowledge and attitudes that results from their pervasive presence as reasonable and natural, many psychologists do not. Traditional sex-role stereotypes are inconsistent with many sex differences and are maladaptive for most adult roles. Adults need the positive characteristics from both the masculine and feminine stereotypes to function well in society. Stereotyping itself is a normal cognitive process; people categorize many things on the basis of outstanding dimensions to help impose order on the tremendous amounts of information that they continually experience. But the environment prescribes the dimensions along which the stereotypes will be formed. Sandra Bern, like many other psychologists, objected to society's excessive use of the sex attribute that forces people to form and use stereotypes based on sex.

ACCULTURATION
ANDROGYNY
SEX DIFFERENCES
SEX ROLES
STEREOTYPING

C. G. Schau

SEX ROLES

Although a large number of books and articles have the term *sex roles* as part of their title, there is remarkably little consistency in the definition of this term. At the most general level, a sex role may be defined as "the set of behaviors and characteristics widely viewed as (a) typical of women or men (sex role stereotypes) and (b) desirable for women and men (sex role norms)." Characteristics that have been considered to be encompassed within one's sex role include personality traits, values, abilities, interests, and behaviors performed within the framework of familial or occupational roles.

Although sex-role stereotypes and norms represent beliefs about males and females as social groups, the term *sex typing* refers to the characteristics of a particular individual with respect to sex-related dimensions. It is measured by the way one rates one's own characteristics rather than those of others.

Beginning in the 1930s masculinity-femininity scales were designed to assess how individuals ranked on a hypothetical continuum ranging from typically and appropriately male to typically and appropriately female. In the 1940s and 1950s, psychoanalytic influences led theorists to make a distinction between conscious and nonconscious aspects of sex typing. The term most directly derived from psychoanalytic theory is sex-role identification. This concept relates to the extent to which an individual has internalized the traits and behaviors considered appropriate to an individual of one's own sex.

Lynn distinguished between sex-role preference (perceiving the characteristics of one sex as preferable to or more desirable than the other) and sex-role adoption (practicing aspects of behavior regarded as appro-priate for individuals of a particular sex without necessarily identifying with other aspects of the role).

More recent theories about sex roles have involved the conception of masculinity and femininity as two independent psychological dimensions. Two important instruments designed to measure sex roles in terms of this multidimensional formulation are the BSRI and the PAQ. Originally both formulations viewed the simultaneous possession of high numbers and/or levels of traits stereotypically considered masculine and feminine (androgyny) as the ideal sex-role identity in terms of mental health. Other new theories view sex roles in terms of developmental stages. These theories conceive sex roles as developing from a relatively undifferentiated stage through a phase of acceptance of traditional stereotypic sex roles to a state in which the individual reorganizes social norms in terms of his or her individual characteristics and needs. Rebecca and her associates have termed this stage *sex-role transcendence*.

SEX-ROLE SOCIALIZATION

Theories also differ in terms of how sex roles are acquired and on the differential implication of sex roles for males and females. The earliest treatment of sex-role socialization is that of Freud, a theory largely based on unconscious, instinctual, or maturational processes due to the possession of differential anatomical equipment by males and females.

Another important theoretical framework is based on social learning theory. This theory stresses the physical and social properties of the parent and the nature of reinforcement processes in children's acquisition of sex roles. Parents and other salient individuals in the child's environment reinforce the modeled behavior when it is considered sex appropriate and ignore or punish it when it is not.

Cognitive development theory stresses the role of the child's own behavior in the reinforcement of appropriate sex roles. This theory stresses the important role of self-categorization as a "boy" or "girl" rather than the passive acquisition of a behavioral repertoire via the reinforcement processes of others.

Both social learning and aspects of cognitive development appear to operate in the acquisition of sex-appropriate roles. For example, there is considerable cross-cultural evidence that there are consistent and persistent differences in the ways in which mothers and fathers treat their sons and daughters to enhance autonomy in the former and affective relationships in the latter. Nevertheless, parental behaviors may be inconsistent with reference to individuals. The impact of parental socialization practices may be modified by such variables as the physical characteristics of the child, his or her birth position, and the sex of siblings. Racial, ethnic, and social-class differences in parental behaviors have also been found, as well as differences in terms of the task investigated and the context in which it is studied.

Empirical studies find that children acquire various aspects of gender understanding in a rather invariant sequence. A given level of attainment is achieved first when the self is the referent, next when a same-sex other is the referent, and last when an opposite-sex other is the referent.

A major issue not resolved by social learning or cognitive development theory is the differential impact of sex-role socialization on girls and boys in our society. Although girls and boys may acquire concepts related to their own gender identity at about the same early age, throughout childhood many more girls than boys show a preference for aspects of the role of the opposite sex. There are several possible explanations for this sex asymmetry. One is that masculine characteristics are considered more useful and desirable to society as a whole.

Females do not appear to be penalized as much as males for deviating from their traditional sex role. These considerations suggest that changes in intrapsychic sex roles in the direction of greater androgyny cannot be evaluated without taking into account societal norms.

RECENT DEVELOPMENTS IN THE STUDY OF SEX ROLES

The concept of sex role as it has been used in psychology appears to be too global in nature. Spence and Helmreich have suggested replacing the term with four distinct categories: gender identity, sexual orientation, sex-role attitudes and behaviors, and personality characteristics. Sex or gender identity (there is some disagreement about which term should be used) appears to be an important factor in the processing of information about the self and others. The physical characteristics of that self and those of others are important indicators in the assessment of sex role. Various elements of sex role, however, may remain relatively independent of each other.

An overwhelming body of evidence indicates that sex labeling performs important cognitive functions in our society. Infants' personal characteristics undergo perceptual reorganization when they are labeled "male" or "female." Parents select sex-appropriate toys for their sons and daughters even when they express a belief in a sex-egalitarian ideology. Peers appear to be particularly important in the regulation of conformity to sex roles during early adolescence. Sex roles may be maintained during adulthood by situational factors and by the differential distribution of males and females into occupational and domestic contexts.

ANDROGYNY
DEVELOPMENT OF HUMAN SOCIAL BEHAVIOR
SEXISM

R. K. Unger

SEX THERAPIES

Sex therapy, like general psychotherapy, started largely with members of the clergy, philosophers, and physicians. By the time it began to become somewhat scientific—around 1920—it was mainly medical in nature, since it originated in the researches of clinicians and physicians.

Soon, however, popular writers began to give sex therapy away to the masses, so that ever since the 1920s much more sex treatment has probably been done through the reading of self-help books written by leading sexologists than has been accomplished in the offices of professional therapists.

In spite of its significant bibliotherapeutic applications, modern sex therapy did not begin to be scientific until the work of William Masters and Virginia Johnson in the 1960s. They particularly emphasized research and the use of follow-up studies and made such a powerful impression that their work has been followed up by many important investigators.

Sex disturbance covers many interrelated behavioral difficulties, including love, marriage, family, and general emotional problems. It seems preferable, therefore, that people with serious sex difficulties not be treated purely by applied sexologists but be seen, instead, by general psychotherapists who specialize in sex therapy as well.

COMMON KINDS OF SEX DISTURBANCES

Male Sex Problems

Males frequently come to sex therapy when afflicted with what Masters and Johnson call primary impotence—that is, an inability to achieve and/or maintain an erection quality sufficient to accomplish successful intercourse on any occasion; or when they have secondary impotence—that is, some but not complete inability to achieve and/or maintain erections. They also frequently have premature ejaculation. An infrequent, but difficult, problem of males is retarded ejaculation, or inability to have orgasm in a reasonably short period. Low sex desire is often exhibited by men who want sex therapy; and fear of being homosexual or otherwise "deviated" is another fairly common problem.

Female Sex Problems

Females often seek sex therapy because of orgasmic dysfunction: either primary orgasmic dysfunction, where a woman has never had orgasm in any kind of sex, or secondary orgasmic dysfunction, where she has difficulty coming to orgasm and has it only under special conditions. Women also frequently have low sex desire, vaginismus, and dyspareunia (painful intercourse). Occasionally they seek therapy because they think they are too highly sexed or because they have homosexual or other "deviant" tendencies.

Although most sex therapists now use a modified Masters and Johnson approach—which includes information giving, attitude reconstruction, the sensate focus, and activity homework assignments—several other major forms of sex therapy include additional or different methods.

MAIN FORMS OF SEX THERAPY

Psychoanalytic Therapy

This form of treatment emphasizes revealing the presumed early origins of sexual disturbance and the working through of these origins by prolonged psychoanalysis in an intensive relationship with an analyst. Psychoanalytic treatment has been seriously criticized but is still popular, particularly as an aspect of general psychotherapy with individuals with sex problems.

Experiential and Body-Work Therapy

Wilhelm Reich theorized that sexual inhibition and anxiety lead to general emotional disturbance and are incorporated into bodily armoring; and that the resolution of sex problems thus can be achieved only through a therapist's using considerable expressive-evocative and body-work techniques.

Behavior Therapy

Behavior therapists such as Andrew Salter, H. J. Eysenck, and Joseph Wolpe began to apply conditioning and deconditioning methods to the treatment of emotional and sexual problems, and by the end of the 1950s, this mode of sex therapy had made significant progress. A wide variety of techniques were tested and some have become popular, including operant conditioning, systematic desensitization, aversive conditioning, and skill training.

Cognitive Therapy

Cognitive therapy has been a popular form of psychological treatment. It largely consists of showing disturbed people that they are upsetting themselves by their unrealistic and irrational values and philosophies and that they can dispute and change these by a number of cognitive methods, including scientific thinking, refocusing, imaging, modeling, and psychoeducational techniques. Cognitive therapy is part of the Masters and Johnson method; is integral to sex bibliotherapy; and is explicitly or implicitly included in virtually all forms of sex therapy, even psychoanalysis. Its effectiveness is now backed by considerable clinical and research data.

Cognitive Behavior Therapy

Both RET and CBT not only acknowledge, explain, and uproot the philosophical and attitudinal underpinnings of sexual disturbances, but also teach clients many behavioral methods of changing their self-defeating cognitions and their dysfunctional actions. They view cognition, emotion, and behavior as interrelated and interactional systems of human functioning and use a multimodal approach to helping clients change all three of these modalities. Along with behavior therapy, it has become a significantly validated form of psychotherapy; and almost all modern sex therapists seem to employ important aspects of it.

Couple Sex Therapy

Sex therapy was originally applied mainly to single individuals with problems. But Masters and Johnson, pointing out the significant influence of one partner on the other's performance, work almost exclusively with couple therapy, and many of their followers imitate them in this respect. Although a therapist's simultaneously seeing both partners has distinct advantages, it also has practical and other limitations, thus much sex therapy is done with a single therapist seeing one partner alone. Masters and Johnson believe that both a male and a female therapist are required for optimal sex therapy, but many therapists find this procedure economically and otherwise impractical.

Group Sex Therapy

Group sex therapy, where men or women join together in regular therapy groups or a number of couples are seen in group therapy, has been pioneered by Arnold Lazarus and others. Its advantages are that group members see that other members have similar problems and that they can all help each other in revealing and working with their difficulties. A number of studies have shown it to be effective, sometimes more so than individual treatment.

Medical Sex Therapy

Early treatment of sex problems by medication was largely ineffective because it relied on hit-and-miss hormonal therapy. Similarly, a number of sex problems involve some medication problem—since several of the popularly used tranquilizers, antidepressants, vasodilators, vasoconstrictors, and other medications may interfere with sexual functioning, particularly in males. Adequate sex therapy, therefore, includes an investigation of general and special medical problems as well as possible recommendations for physical treatment.

Effectiveness of Sex Therapy

Hundreds of anecdotal and clinical reports of the effectiveness of sex therapy have appeared and many sound convincing. However, controlled experiments validating the efficiency, and particularly the long-term results, of different kinds of sex therapies are fairly scarce. From present indications, sex therapy will certainly survive; but more research is needed to back up or to discount the validity of the many different techniques now in use.

Certification Sex Therapists

Until recently, sex therapists have had no independent professional standing or certification. But now a good many training programs under professional auspices exist in clinics, hospitals, universities, and other centers. The American Association of Sex Educators, Counselors and Therapists is the main certification organization for sex therapists in the United States and Canada.

COGNITIVE THERAPY
FEMALE SEXUAL DYSFUNCTIONS
MALE SEXUAL DYSFUNCTIONS

A. ELLIS

SEXISM

Sexism is defined by David Stang and Lawrence Wrightsman as "any attitude, action, or institutional structure that bases a response to a person on the fact of his or her sex when sex should be irrelevant to the decision. Sexism usually is reflected in discrimination against women purely because of their sex." Personal sexism that reflects individual differences in negative attitudes toward women should be distinguished from societal or institutional sexism that reflects customary attitudes or behaviors that may not stem from an individual's personal biases.

PERSONAL SEXISM

Personal sexism is usually measured by attitude scales. The scale most frequently used currently is the Attitudes Toward Women Scale (AWS) developed by Janet Spence and Robert Helmreich. The present brief version of the AWS contains 15 items and measures attitudes concerning the political, economic, and social equality of women and men.

Researchers have found that women score as more profeminist than men, and that college students of either sex score as more profeminist than their same-sex parent. Philip Goldberg notes that negative attitudes toward females seem to exist in males almost universally. However, Robert Brannon points out that measures of sex prejudice share with measures of race prejudice little evidence of behavioral validity.

Nonverbal behaviors may be more indicative of personal sexism than are more reactive verbal indicators. Nancy Henley enumerates nonverbal behaviors used to connote power and status differences between the sexes, including eye contact, body orientation and interpersonal distance, and touching.

SOCIETAL SEXISM

Studies designed to determine that negative attitudes toward women exist as part of a general social reality have been more successful than those attempting to evaluate individual degrees of sexism. Philip Goldberg showed that women evaluated an identical essay more poorly if a female name was associated with it. Other researchers have demonstrated similar negative biases in the evaluation of works of art, poetry, and professional attainments.

Numerous studies of sex stereotypes indicate that perceptions of males and females can be distinguished by two major clusters of traits. Inge Broverman and her associates found that typical male traits as perceived by both sexes comprise independence, logic, objectivity, worldliness, and ability in mathematics, science, and business. Typical female traits include awareness of others' feelings, gentleness, and tact. Mental health experts perceived that the characteristics of the mentally healthy male and mentally healthy adult (sex unspecified) were similar, but that the mentally healthy female was more emotional and less mature than the mentally healthy adult. Such sex stereotypes appear to have created a double bind for women—they can be feminine or mature, but not both. Perceptions about males do not involve such contradictory trait prescriptions. Sources of sex stereotypes appear to be universal.

Sexism in language has been extensively documented. Studies indicate that the English language demeans women by trivializing female gender forms, by labeling female exceptions in occupations or behaviors defined as being in the male domain, and by excluding females, as in the generic use of masculine pronouns when both sexes are included. Much of the content of differential perceptions about males and females involves competence and achievement.

It has been estimated by Treiman and Terrell that most of the difference in the wages between the sexes can be accounted for by sex discrimination. Even when women hold positions equivalent to those of men, they may receive less reward for comparable achievements.

In summary, sexism exists in a number of forms: as individual attitudes that may be measured either by self-reports or nonverbally; as nonconscious societally based perceptions and attributions that are usually examined as stereotypes, but that actually may take the form of a social reality agreed upon by individuals of both sexes; and as institutionalized practices that stem from differential evaluation of the attainments of women and men and that lead to the occupational segregation of women and their cumulative disadvantage.

PREJUDICE/DISCRIMINATION
SOCIAL EQUALITY

R. K. UNGER

SEXUAL ABSTINENCE

Sexual abstinence means refraining from sexual activity, usually voluntarily. The compass of abstinence may include all sexual activity, from masturbation to intercourse, or may refer only to sexual relations with others. The related term *celibacy* is more precisely used to describe an individual who is both unmarried and sexually abstinent.

There are four main reasons to account for sexual abstinence: sociocultural, religious, interpersonal, and psychopathological. The two chief sociocultural reasons for sexual abstinence are prevention of intragroup conflict and population control.

The practice tends to lower the rate of reproductivity, to widen the spacing of siblings, and to control whose genes are contributed to the population gene pool. It is also used to reinforce gender-related divisions of labor.

In some interpersonal relationships, sexual abstinence is explicitly or implicitly agreed on by the partners. Yet may psychologists would consider a marital relationship devoid of a sexual component a dysfunctional relationship.

An individual who either cannot engage in any type of sexual relations or whose ostensibly voluntary decision is molded by irrational forces may indicate an psychopathological type of sexual abstinence. This may be indicative of a phobic reaction to all sexual activity (gynophobia) or a sexually related fear of the opposite sex (gynophobia or androphobia). Sexual abstinence may also represent a symptom of anhedonia—the inability to experience pleasure of any kind. Whatever the underlying pathology, a range of treatment procedures, from behavior modification to rational–emotive–behavioral therapy to psychoanslysis, has been shown to be successful in clinical settings.

HUMAN SEXUALITY

G. S. BELKIN

SEXUAL DEVELOPMENT

According to Sigmund Freud's psychoanalytic theory of personality, sexuality begins in infancy. The development of sexuality is a major part of the development of personality. According to Freud, the individual passes through several psychosexual stages.

Behaviorally, puberty marks the onset of human genital sexuality. Puberty begins between approximately 10 and 14 years of age for females and between 12 and 16 years of age for males. Hypothalamic stimulation of the pituitary gland causes secretion of pituitary hormones, including those directed to the gonads (gonadotropic) and to the adrenal glands (adrenocorticotropic). These glands, in turn, secrete the hormones responsible for the physical changes at puberty: a rapid increase in growth, the development of secondary sex characteristics, and the development of the reproductive capacity. In addition, the individual experiences an increase in sexual awareness and a heightening of sexual drives. Sexual activity, including kissing, petting, and even intercourse, is a frequent component of the adolescent experience.

Although intercourse is most often considered in the context of marriage, the incidence of premarital coitus has increased over the years. David Kallen noticed several major changes over the years from 1960 through 1980, including the following:

1. The percentage of adolescents reporting coitus. The data clearly indicate an increase in the number of high school and college students reporting having had intercourse.

2. The proportions of males versus females reporting coitus. In the past, the percentage of males reporting having had coitus was higher than the percentage of females. Kallen found that that had changed. Owing to the increased percentage of females reporting coitus, the proportion for males and females was almost identical by 1980.

3. The age at first coitus. Coitus is being reported at an earlier age.

4. The number of partners. There has been a growing tendency among adolescents to limit their sexual experience to one partner within a given time period.

5. The type of relationship. Not only are adolescents less promiscuous in terms of the number of their partners, but there is also a greater tendency to experience sexuality in a relationship of love and affection.

ADOLESCENCE
HUMAN SEXUALITY
PSYCHOSEXUAL STAGES

J. P. MCKINNEY

SEXUAL DEVIATIONS

Sexual deviations, or *paraphilias,* are psychosexual disorders characterized by sexual arousal in response to objects or situations that are not part of normative sexual arousal-activity patterns and that in varying degrees may interfere with capacity for reciprocal affectionate sexual activity. This term simply emphasizes that the deviation (para) is in that to which the individual is attracted (philia). It encompasses a number and variety of sexual behaviors that, at this time, are sufficiently discrepant from society's norms and standards concerning sexually acceptable behavior as to be judged "deviant."

In the *Diagnostic and statistical manual* from the American Psychiatric Association (APA), paraphilias are classified as of several types: (a) preference for use of a nonhuman object for sexual arousal; (b) repetitive sexual activity with persons involving real or simulated suffering or humiliation; and (c) repetitive sexual activity with nonconsenting partners.

Traces of paraphilias are commonly found in the realm of normal sexuality. It is only when such activities become the focal point of sexual gratification, and thereby displace direct sexual behavior with a consenting adult partner, that paraphilias may be said to exist.

The causes of paraphilias are seen as psychogenic rather than biogenic, and hence depend very much on the paradigm one adopts within psychopathology. For example, within the psychoanalytic paradigm, these disorders are viewed as a consequence of aberrations occurring during psychosexual development in early childhood; in the behavioristic paradigm, they are seen as unadaptive sexual behavior resulting from learning and conditioning experiences; in the humanistic paradigm, they presumably represent particular outgrowths of each individual's unique, albeit distorted, subjective world of experience.

TYPES OF PARAPHILIAS

What follows is a brief description of each recognized paraphilia, following the *DSM* categorization and description system.

Fetishism

Fetishism is essentially characterized by the use of nonliving objects or, less frequently, parts of the human body as the preferred or exclusive method of producing sexual excitement. These objects or body parts (called *fetishes*) are essential for sexual satisfaction in the fetishist and constitute the focal point of sexual arousal. Fetishists are almost always males. The objects involved in fetishism can be quite varied and commonly include women's underpants, shoes, stockings, and gloves; parts of the body that typically become fetishes include breasts, hair, ears, hands, and feet.

Transvestism

In the psychosexual disorder of transvestism, there is recurrent and persistent cross-dressing by a heterosexual male for the purposes of his own sexual arousal. The gamut of tranvestism extends from secretive and solitary wearing of female clothes, through sexually relating to one's spouse while so attired, to appearing in public cross-dressed and accompanied by extensive involvement in a like-minded subgroup.

Zoophilia

Zoophilia is marked by the use of animals as the repeatedly preferred or exclusive method of achieving sexual excitement. The animal may serve as the object of sexual intercourse or may be trained to excite the paraphiliac sexually by means of licking or rubbing. In this disorder, the animal is preferred regardless of other available sexual outlets.

Pedophilia

Pedophilia (from the Greek, meaning "love of children") is essentially characterized by a preference for repetitive sexual activity with children. Such activity may vary in intensity, and includes stroking the child's hair, holding the child close while covertly masturbating, manipulating the child's genitals, encouraging the child to manipulate his, and, less frequently, attempting intromission. A youngster of any age up to puberty may be the object of pedophiliac attention, with force seldom being employed.

Exhibitionism

Exhibitionism is characterized by repetitive acts of exposing one's genitals to an unsuspecting stranger for the purpose of producing one's own sexual excitement. Normally no further contact is sought.

Voyeurism

Voyeurism is fundamentally characterized by the repetitive seeking out of situations in which the individual looks ("peeps") at unsuspecting women who are either naked, undressing, or engaging in sexual activity. Voyeurs are almost always males and derive intense sexual excitement from their peeping behavior. They usually either masturbate to orgasm during the voyeuristic activity or immediately afterward in response to the scene witnessed. Further sexual contact with the observed woman (usually a stranger) is rarely sought, and most voyeurs, like exhibitionists, are not physically dangerous.

Sexual Sadism

The widely used term *sadism* derives from the infamous Marquis de Sade, who, for erotic purposes, perpetrated such cruelty on his victims that he eventually was committed as insane. Sexual sadism refers to a disorder essentially characterized by the infliction of physical or psychological suffering on another person as a method of stimulating one's own sexual excitement and orgasm. Moreover, persistent sexually stimulating fantasies of this nature are also experienced by the individual. In some instances, the sadistic activities function as stimulants in building up to sexual relations, while in others the sadistic practices alone are sufficient for complete sexual gratification. Although the partners of sadists may be consenting or nonconsenting, the majority of sadistic behavior seems to occur in a relationship with a willing partner.

Sexual Masochism

The essential feature of sexual masochism is sexual excitement produced in an individual by his or her own suffering. That is, in this disorder, the preferred or exclusive means of achieving sexual gratification is being humiliated, bound, beaten, whipped, or otherwise made to suffer. Such situations may be sufficient in themselves for full sexual gratification or they may be a necessary prelude to direct sexual behavior, such as intercourse. Like sadism, then, masochism essentially involves suffering; unlike sadism, the suffering here is inflicted on oneself rather than on others.

Atypical Paraphilia

In the *DSM* atypical paraphilia is a residual category for individuals with paraphilias that cannot be classified in any of the other categories. These disorders include coprophilia (feces), frotteurism (rubbing), klismaphilia (enema), mysophilia (filth), necrophilia (corpse), telephone scatologia (lewdness), and urophilia (urine).

HUMAN SEXUALITY
SEXUAL DEVELOPMENT

D. J. ZIEGLER

SEXUAL DYSFUNCTION

The term *sexual dysfunction,* used clinically, designates persistent and frequent disturbances of objective sexual performance coupled with subjective distress.

TYPES OF DYSFUNCTION

The classification system of specific sexual dysfunctions is based on location of a disorder within the sexual response cycle (arousal, plateau, orgasm, or resolution), as described by William Masters and Virginia Johnson. Kaplan described a phase preceding arousal, the desire phase. A distinction between primary (the problem has always existed) and secondary (the problem is of recent onset and currently present) is frequently made. The *Diagnostic and statistical manual of mental disorders* provides differential diagnostic criteria for disorders within three main areas of sexual dysfunction: inhibited sexual desire, inhibited sexual excitement, and problems related to orgasm.

Desire Phase Disorders

Sexual desire, an appetitive phase preceding any actual sexual stimulation, includes sexual fantasies and subjective wishes to engage in sex. Inhibited sexual desire (ISD), characterized by lack of interest in sex, does not always impair performance, but causes distress for the individual and may result in relationship conflicts. Sexual aversion, a more severe form of ISD than lack of interest, is viewed as a phobia in which sexual stimuli elicit disgust, anger, fear, and other emotional reactions.

Arousal Phase Disorders

Sexual arousal includes subjective sexual pleasure and physiological changes. Inhibited sexual excitement, a common disorder in both sexes, involves the inability to attain or maintain an erection in the male or vaginal lubrication in the female. Specific problems associated with arousal phase dysfunction in females are dyspareunia (painful intercourse) due to lack of vaginal lubrication, and vaginismus, spasmodic contractions of the outer third of the vagina, preventing insertion of the penis. Arousal phase dyspareunia also occurs in males and is associated with pain on erection or penile thrusting.

Disorders of Orgasm

An orgasm is a sudden release of vasocongestion and muscle tension, and subjective feelings of peak sexual pleasure. Orgasmic dysfunction is the most common sexual problem reported in women. Orgasmic dysfunction does not include women who experience orgasm through manual or oral stimulation but not through penile–vaginal thrusting. Premature ejaculation, a common orgasmic dysfunction in men, exists when ejaculation occurs before the man or couple desires it and with little voluntary control. A less common male orgasmic difficulty is inhibited ejaculation, in which sexual desire and erection are unimpaired but the ejaculatory reflex is inhibited in spite of adequate levels of stimulation. An uncommon orgasmic phase problem is painful ejaculation (dyspareunia).

Three points must be stressed when discussing and diagnosing sexual dysfunction. First, inhibition at any point in the sexual response cycle is not termed a dysfunction unless the individual or the couple is distressed. Second, occasional problems in sexual function are normal and do not denote dysfunction. Finally, although an individual or couple may experience various specific sexual dysfunctions, each phase in the sexual response cycle is physiologically independent, the most startling example being the fact that ejaculation can occur through a flaccid penis.

CAUSES OF DYSFUNCTION

Kaplan classifies factors that can contribute to sexual dysfunction as immediate or remote. Immediate refers to conditions occurring while the couple is engaging in sexual behavior that, if modified, obviate the problem. Sex therapists generally agree that the most common immediate causes of sexual dysfunction are performance anxiety and fear of failure. Psychoanalytic theorists propose that adult sexual dysfunction stems from childhood experiences that generate unconscious conflict, a remote cause.

A major contributing factor to sexual dysfunction is lack of sexual education or actual misinformation about sex. Misinformation about what constitutes normal sexual function and behavior leads to perpetuation of sexual myths and attempts to achieve unrealistic performance ideals.

Relationship variables also contribute to sexual problems. Dyadic causes of sexual dysfunction include distrust of the partner, fear of rejection, anger toward the partner over unmet expectations, dyadic power struggles, and actual physical or emotional repugnance for the partner. Poor communication pervades most sexually dysfunctional relationships at global and specific sexual levels. Because of the role of dyadic factors in sexual dysfunction, most sex therapists work with both partners, identifying dysfunction as a relationship problem rather than an individual problem.

Individual psychological factors also influence the development of sexual dysfunction. Basic attitudes about sexuality (pleasantness/unpleasantness, rightness/wrongness, and purpose), learned in the family environment, are carried into adulthood. Traumatic or unpleasant sexual experiences at any age may create negative feelings and responses in later sexual situations. Psychoanalytic theory views the intrapsychic element as most etiologically relevant in sexual dysfunction, pointing to unconscious sexual conflict arising from infantile incestual wishes.

Finally, organic factors may lead to sexual dysfunction, but they are rarely the sole etiology. A sexual dysfunction appearing as purely organic may be exacerbated by psychological factors (humiliation, frustration, or anxiety). Organic factors bearing on sexual dysfunction include physical fatigue, age, drugs, physical disability, and disease. Many drugs (alcohol, other central nervous system depressants and stimulants, narcotics, antihypertensive medication, high doses of antihistamines, antidepressants, and antipsychotics) disrupt the sexual response cycle at various points. As age increases, intensity and quality of sexual responses may change, and sexual desire may gradually diminish. In men, erection may take longer to achieve, ejaculation may be less forceful, and time between orgasms may increase. In women, vaginal lubrication and orgasmic inten-

sity may lessen. At no point, however, is a person rendered physically unable to enjoy all aspects of sexual function by aging. Physical disability may necessitate a drastic change in sexual technique, but need not preclude all options for sexual pleasure.

TREATMENT OF DYSFUNCTION

Masters and Johnson initiated sex therapy *per se.* Behavioral or direct-action modes of sex therapy work to remove immediate causes that maintain sexual dysfunction through behavioral exercises. Inhibited sexual desire and inhibited sexual excitement are treated by instruction in self-exploration, sexual fantasy, and exercises specifically strengthening the pubococcygeal (pelvic floor) muscles (Kagel exercises). Treatment for inhibited orgasm involves Kagel exercises and instruction in masturbation, use of vibrators, and role-play orgasm. Most behavior therapists believe that intensive psychotherapy is not necessary to alleviate sexual dysfunction. Jack Annon suggests that most sexual dysfunctions can be successfully treated by giving (a) permission to be sexual, (b) limited information about sexuality, and (c) specific suggestions about variations on traditional coitus. If intensive therapy appears necessary, approaches such as Kaplan's effectively integrate behavioral treatment specific to the dysfunction, treatment of dyadic problems, and psychodynamic or other approaches to intrapsychic issues.

ANXIETY
FEMALE SEXUAL DYSFUNCTIONS
MALE SEXUAL DYSFUNCTIONS
SEX THERAPIES

B. E. THORN

SEXUAL INTERCOURSE, HUMAN

Human sexual intercourse, or coitus, is one of the most common sexual outlets among adults. Although it is usually considered in the context of marriage, premarital and extramarital intercourse are also widely practiced. Adolescents appear to be engaging in sexual intercourse more frequently than was true in the past.

Reiss distinguished among four possible standards:

1. According to the ancient double standard, premarital intercourse was permissible for males, but not for well-bred females; thus a class of women existed (prostitutes) to satisfy men's desires.

2. The standard of permissiveness with affection means that premarital coitus is sanctioned, but only in an affectionate or loving relationship.

3. The permissiveness-without-affection standard means that premarital coitus is permissible whenever the two partners choose, regardless of the nature of their relationship.

4. The standard of abstinence suggests that premarital intercourse is not permissible, either for men or women.

In practice, North American sexual customs have changed from a double standard to a standard of permissiveness with affection, although many adolescents and adults adhere to a standard of abstinence until marriage as an ideal. Approximately one-third of all 17-year-olds report having experienced coitus, and there appear to be no sex differences in these data.

Cultures differ, too, in the preferred manner of experiencing intercourse. Although American partners prefer a face-to-face man-above position, this practice is by no means a universal preference.

CULTURAL DIFFERENCES
HUMAN SEXUALITY
SEX ROLE DEVELOPMENT

J. P. McKinney

SEXUALITY: ORIENTATION AND IDENTITY

DEFINITIONS

Sexual orientation refers to the sex of the erotic/love/affectional partners a person prefers. The terms *heterosexual, homosexual,* and *bisexual* are better used as adjectives, not nouns, and are better applied to behaviors, not people. In lay usage, however, one often speaks of a person as a homosexual or heterosexual; indeed people often refer to themselves the same way. Such casual usage often links together those whose regular sexual partners are of the same sex with those whose same-sex encounters are rare in comparison with heterosexual contacts. The term *homosexual* is best reserved for those whose sexual activities are exclusively or almost exclusively with members of the same sex, the term *heterosexual* for those whose erotic companions are always or almost always with the opposite sex, and the term *bisexual* or *ambisexual* for those with more or less regular sexual activities with members of either sex.

Sexual identity speaks to the way one views one's self as a male or female. This inner conviction of identification may or may not mirror the outward physical appearance or the gender role society imposes. These distinctions are crucial, particularly in regard to transsexualism. In the real world, the *transsexual,* as are others, is identified in terms of overt sexual anatomy. Transsexuals are reared as society views them. Nevertheless, the self-image of transsexuals is of the opposite sex. Their mirror images are in conflict with their mind's image. This aspect of life is separate from their sexual orientation, because a transsexual may be homosexually or heterosexually inclined. In everyday terms, anybody may "identify" themselves as homosexual or see their "identity" as homosexual. This use of the term is an affiliative sense. It is as if one might identify as an American Indian or a Unitarian.

One's *gender* or *gender role* is different, although related, to the concept of orientation and identity. Gender and gender role refer to society's idea of how boys and girls or men and women are expected to behave and should be treated. A *sex role* is the acting out of one's biological predisposition. The terms *boys* and *girls* and *men* and *women* are social terms; the terms *male* and *female* are biological terms. Gender has everything to do with the society in which one lives and may or may not have much to do with biology. Males, for instance, may live as women and females may live as men; a male may be reared as a boy but grow to live as a woman. For most people, their identity, orientation, and gender are in concert.

The typical male sees himself as such, acts in a masculine manner—a combination of biologically and socially determined behaviors—is treated as a male by society, and prefers to have sexual interactions with females. The typical female sees herself as such, acts in a feminine manner—also a combination of biologically and socially determined behaviors—is treated as a female by society, and prefers to have sexual interactions with males. Variations occur when an individual prefers erotic relations with someone of the same sex (male or female homosexuals) or when a male sees himself as a female (male transsexual) or a female sees herself as a male (female transsexual).

A heterosexual male sees himself as a male, lives as a male, enjoys his penis, and prefers erotic relations with a female. A homosexual male also sees himself as a male, lives as a male, and also enjoys his penis but prefers to have erotic relations with another male. In contrast, the male transsexual sees himself as a female, prefers to live as a women, wants

to have his penis removed and replaced with a vulva and vagina, and wants to have breasts. Usually he will prefer to have sexual relations with a male but sees this as a heterosexual encounter because he sees himself as a female. No male homosexual would want to have his penis removed and replaced with a vagina; this, however, is the frequent desire of the male transsexual. For a female transsexual the converse is true. Although she may not always opt to have a penis and scrotum constructed to replace her vagina and labia, she typically wants her breasts removed and her periods to cease, because they are constant and visible reminders of what she thinks she is not.

Transvestism is a related phenomenon. People who enjoy dressing in the clothing of the opposite sex are broadly termed transvestites or cross-dressers (TVs or CDs). The large majority of transvestites are male and heterosexual. If they are homosexual, they are usually called drag queens. The motivation behind such cross-dressing behavior is varied. For some there is erotic satisfaction, for others cross-dressing is an expression of a personality component comfortable in the clothes of the opposite sex. For some it is a response to a compulsion neither they nor science understands. The majority of homosexuals do not enjoy cross-dressing. Transsexuals cross-dress because it is in keeping with movement toward living in the sex they feel is them. Individuals that are primarily transvestites often express feelings of temporarily exchanging gender identity when cross-dressed.

These complexities are much more common than generally believed because all such individuals tend to live in "private closets." There is probably more variation in things sexual than in any other set of human behaviors. Because these combinations are usually private, they provoke neither comment nor criticism.

NUMBERS

The prevalence of all these behaviors is in dispute. Transsexualism is accepted as rare with rough estimates of 1 in 25,000 to 50,000, with male to female transsexuals outnumbering 2 to 1 to 5 to 1 those who go from female to male. Society recognizes that it is more advantageous in status, economics, and other ways to be a man and, therefore, more readily accepts a desire to change from female to male. People do not as easily understand the reverse: males wanting to be female.

To describe people's actions accurately, Kinsey devised a 7-point scale (0 to 6). Individuals whose behaviors were exclusively homosexual were classified as 6, or nearly so as 5. Those exclusively heterosexual were classified as 0, and those nearly so as 1. Intergrades were rated accordingly so that an individual with the same proportion of same-sex and opposite-sex encounters would be listed as a 3. Recognizing that people may wish one thing and do another, he simultaneously recorded people's orientation within their fantasies. A married woman exclusively having sex with her husband might be imagining she is with a female. A prisoner can have a homosexual encounter while fantasizing a heterosexual event. Kinsey and coworkers would average behavior and fantasy scores. Transsexual and transvestic behaviors also have been graded to reflect better the many types of individuals linked under these broad categories.

This discussion of population percentages and sexual activities, although of scientific import, also has sociopolitical implications. Some gay activists and homophobes assume that anyone who has engaged in any homosexual activity ought be counted as homosexual. Bisexuals are often seen as fence sitters who, for different reasons, would prefer not being identified as homosexual. Groups on both sides of this fence see the numbers as politically meaningful, abhorring the gray areas. These percentages have epidemiological and political implications. They affect the laws societies will enforce and social or medical issues like AIDS research and treatment for such illnesses as acquired immunodeficiency syndrome (AIDS) and whether openly gay individuals will be accepted in politics or the military.

SUBCULTURES

The term *homosexual* refers to private behavior, the term *gay* refers to public behavior and association with a subculture. Many homosexually oriented individuals are open about their sexual preferences and are identified by various mannerisms and activities. These observable traits may be effeminate by males or masculine ones by females. These may be natural expressions of self or part of highly formalized codes that signal group identity. Many of the social signals used to signal sexual interest are the same for homosexuals and heterosexuals. Yet, for homosexuals moving in a primarily heterosexual (straight) world, certain codes are useful: subtle uses of voice tone, stance and mannerisms, code words and eye contact, and frequenting known contact places such as gay bars, bath houses, or park areas.

Bisexual (ambisexual) behavior too was more openly discussed in the 1990s than in the past. There is again no evidence it was any more prevalent than at any other prior era. Ambisexuals more often congregate with homosexuals than heterosexuals but bisexuals see themselves, and are, in a category of their own. As lesbians have done before them, they call for recognition separate from homosexuals in general, with particular group needs and interests.

Women who prefer same-sex erotic and love activities exclusively or occasionally used to be called "romantic friends" in Victorian times. Even more than males they were a secret minority in the West whose visibility only became public after World War II. Into the 1960s they were lumped with males as "female homosexuals" or "female gays." Later, for political reasons they preferred to be called lesbians, because it gave them identity as a group.

Although many common needs exist among male and female homosexuals, lesbians have some special needs. In particular, they feel most strongly about not being stereotyped. As with individuals of any other orientation, they can be feminine or macho, conservative or liberal, devout or atheist, orgastically driven or not interested in orgasm, promiscuous or monogamous, in the closet or out of it, and attractive or plain. Their motivations or reasons for identifying with the lesbian community are often broader than those for male homosexuals. Some women will engage in same-sex activity for political reasons, although this is extremely rare or nonexistent among males.

In any culture, clothes are symbols of maleness or femaleness and mark affiliation or separateness. Clothes serve in obvious ways to keep the genders distinct and readily identifiable. There is demonstrably a great deal of psychic and social investment in vestments, and many people are disturbed that others do not keep inviolate the clothes, and thus group identity, that society prefers.

ROOTS OF SEXUAL BEHAVIOR

The interacting forces that lead to any type of behavior are not always clear. Why do some find it easy to obey social standards and indoctrinations and others find it difficult? No one is certain why a majority of individuals are heterosexual and a minority homosexual. Most clues, however, point to a genetic predisposition interacting with social training. Genetics set a bias, a predisposition, with which the individual meets society. This, in turn, has an effect on an individual's sexual orientation and sexual behavior. Not everyone, however, concurs that biology plays as strong a role.

The strongest evidence that sexual orientation has a genetic bias comes from studies of human families and twins. The classical studies in this area were done in the 1950s by Franz J. Kallmann working with 40 monozygotic and 45 dizygotic male twin pairs, in which at least one of the co-twins at the onset of the study admitted to homosexual behavior. Among these twins Kallmann found, without exception, that if one of the identical (monozygotic) twins was homosexual, so was his brother. Among the nonidentical (dizygotic) brothers, however, the twins were essentially similar to the general male population relative to sexual preference. Kallmann also found that if one member of a monozygotic twin pair of brothers rated a 5 or 6 on the Kinsey scale, then the chance that his brother also rated 5 or 6 was better than 90%. Kallmann reported that if the brothers differed in rating it was usually only within 1 or 2 points on the Kinsey scale.

Several research reports from the Netherlands and the United States indicate certain brain structures differ between heterosexuals and homosexuals. The Dutch researchers F. Schwaab and M. A. Hofman found a region of the brain called the suprachiasmatic nucleus is much larger in homosexuals than in heterosexuals, and Simon LeVay in the United States found a region of the hypothalamus (interstitial nucleus of the anterior hypothalamus #3) smaller in homosexuals and women than in male heterosexuals. The brains of lesbians are yet to be examined. Others also have found different areas of the brain differ between men and women and that these differences are associated with nonreproductive as well as reproductive functions. Such structural differences may yet be found to differ among heterosexual and homosexual individuals.

Critics of such sex research say scientists seldom look for causes of heterosexuality. For researchers, homosexuality and heterosexuality are two sides of the same coin; to learn the developmental forces of one type of behavior helps in understanding the other. The following studies document instances in which biological biases for heterosexuality and maleness override the social conditioning of rearing males as girls.

SOCIAL AND LEGAL INFLUENCES

Actually, what is postulated is not a nature–nurture dichotomy, but rather an interaction of both sets of forces. The rules, codes, traditions, and ideals of any society—the environment—also interact to structure an individual's behavior. These influences modify and work with or against any inherent behavioral bias. It is probably safe to say that acceptance of the idea of interaction effects is now generally the case among the scientific community world wide.

Genetic Bias + Social Influences = Behavior

Legal restrictions, generally a reflection of social attitudes, are strong modifiers of preferred behavior. It will take a strong-willed individual or one with a compulsive drive to display openly homosexual, transvestic, transsexual, or any divergent sexual behavior if the sanctions against the activity are strong enough. Stringent prohibitions against any overt sexual expression, even against public kissing or women displaying parts of their arms or legs, are seen in Arab Muslim countries. For such "minor" offenses the punishment may be caning or flogging. For homosexual behaviors, capital punishment or long-term imprisonment is often called for. Algerian liberals, for instance, have fought against the death sentence for homosexuality and adultery. Homosexuality and transsexuality rarely will be seen openly in these countries because to display such behaviors overtly would be risky.

There is no known culture where adult–adult homosexual behavior is encouraged or is a preferred mode of behavior. There are, however, societies in which adult–child same-sex activities are fostered. Although these are same-sex activities, they are not a preferred type of sexual outlet; the behaviors are with nonerotic motives. For example, among the Kaluli of New Guinea, all boys are the recipients of anal intercourse by the men. Among the Sambia of New Guinea, all boys fellate the adult men to obtain their semen. In these cultures it is believed such practices allow for the transmission of maleness from man to boy. When these boys attain manhood, despite years of same-sex "training" they switch to heterosexual erotic behaviors. Many cultures exhibit behaviors that would be considered sexual in the West but are not considered erotic within the society in question.

In some traditions, homosexual and/or transvestic activities were accepted with equanimity and even seen as practices of the gods. In the Mahabharata, the classical Hindu epic poem about good and evil, the god Krishna dresses as a woman and gives himself as the first sex experience for the first-born son of Arjun, the great warrior. Other gods in the Hindu pantheon are openly gay. In the days of precontact Hawaii, the island chiefs are known to have proudly had both same and opposite sex lovers.

COMING OUT AND OUTING

Among the more difficult processes of being different sexually is *coming out.* The precise meaning of the term keeps shifting but essentially means admitting to oneself that one is homosexually oriented, a transsexual, or transvestite, and then coming out of the denial and secrecy closet. After admitting this to the self, it means revealing this to others. However, much of society, even among the most tolerant, contains hidden minefields that not everyone wants to chance, so not everyone comes out. For those who do, it is usually a continuing, slow, and difficult process. Depending on how far one wants to go, others at work, sports, and the medical clinic will be informed. Friends are usually the first to know, and family, parents in particular, the last. No accurate estimate is available for that proportion of homosexuals, transsexuals, or transvestites that are out. Most activists in these subcultures believe that the more people that come out, the more difficult it will be for society to remain homophobic, heterosexist, and discriminatory. In the United States and elsewhere, national coming out days have been instituted to support this effort.

Outing is much more controversial. This was a phenomenon started in the 1990s. Seemingly born of frustration by the slow pace of societies' acceptance of gays, this is the practice of gay activists divulging the alleged or actual homosexual or transvestic behaviors of politicians, sports or media stars, and others. The argument is that doing so provides a host of role models for those ashamed of their own situation. It also reduces the power of those who would use secrecy to mask sexophobic activities they might use to hide their own behaviors. However, the process has been called philosophical rape, psychic violence, and ethical blackmail. Outing can certainly damage careers or lives.

THE MEANING OF BEING DIFFERENT

For some people, being different is a conscious decision. For others it is not a choice. They are different by birth or from events over which they have little control. Societies reject or accept them according to cultural myths, beliefs, and codes. From a worldview, there are many similarities among cultures in how they react but also dramatic differences. It is not a matter of right versus wrong, just different. Within any society there may be a neutral response, a reaction to a perceived threat, or a view that the behavior is a gift from god that needs special thanks.

The vast terrain of sexual behaviors may be likened to a United Nations feast. However, whereas those who appreciate different eating experiences for their subtle nuances may earn the title of gourmet, society is much less tolerant of those who appreciate different sexual experiences. This is true even when the participants are acting voluntarily and conduct their affairs in private. As with foods, some behaviors may never be tasted and some tasted once and never chosen again; but to dismiss them all without consideration or taste may be to deprive self and others not only of pleasure but also feelings of a secure ego.

ACCULTURATION
ADOLESCENT IDENTITY FORMATION
ANDROGENY
ANIMAL SEXUAL BEHAVIOR
BISEXUALITY

CULTURAL DETERMINISM
HOMOSEXUALITY
LABELING THEORY
SELF-CONCEPT
SELF-DISCLOSURE
SEX AFFERENCES
SEX ROLES
SEX-ROLE DEVELOPMENT
SOCIAL INFLUENCE
TABOOS
TRANSSEXUALISM
TRANSVESTISM

M. DIAMOND

SHAMANISM

Shamanism is probably humankind's oldest healing tradition, having survived for tens of thousands of years. Because of their psychological techniques shamans are sometimes described as the world's first psychologists and psychotherapists. Shamans are often confused with other healing practitioners such as priests, mediums, and witch doctors and do in fact often fill these roles. However, they can be distinguished and defined as practitioners whose activities include a method of gaining information by voluntarily entering alternate states of consciousness in which they experience themselves, or their "spirit(s)," traveling to other realms at will, and there obtaining information and power with which to benefit others.

There has been considerable confusion over the psychological status of shamans who have been dismissed as tricksters, pathologized as psychologically disturbed, or elevated to sainthood. Until recently, the conventional academic view was that shamans and shamanism were the products of primitive or pathological minds and diagnoses such as hysterical, epileptic, psychotic, and schizophrenic were applied liberally. However, this appears to reflect a number of unfortunate biases, including ethnocentrism, the well-known tendency to diagnose unfamiliar experiences, the "confusion of clinic and culture," the pathologizing tendency of psychoanalysis, and lack of researchers' personal familiarity with shamanic experiences and alternate states. Several studies describe shamans as being exceptionally healthy, effective, and powerful and many of their experiences and states as being carefully cultivated, culturally valued, and phenomenologically distinct.

The opposite view, namely that shamans are virtual saints whose experiences and states of consciousness are equivalent to those of advanced yogis and meditators, recently has become widespread in the popular culture. However, although many shamans are compassionate, others are wiley tricksters, and phenomenological analyses show that shamanic experiences are quite distinct from yogic and meditative ones.

Shamanic techniques include both physical and psychological approaches. One of their central and defining techniques is the shamanic journey in which they enter an alternate state of consciousness, experience leaving their body and roaming as free spirits throughout the universe, and acquire knowledge and power (especially from other spirits) to bring back to their tribespeople. To obtain the requisite state of consciousness, shamans employ preparatory ritual and ascetic practices, and then use a combination of ritual, rhythm (usually involving drums, rattles, singing, and dancing), and occasionally psychedelics. These shamanic journey experiences show certain similarities to lucid dreams and near-death experiences.

Shamans are ontological realists, meaning that they take the realms they visit and the spirits they meet to be objective independent realities. Contemporary psychological perspectives might view them as mind-created images akin to guided imagery, guided visualizations, or Jung's active imagination. Whatever one's philosophical interpretation, it seems that shamans can access valuable intuitive wisdom from their experiences.

Other techniques include physicalisms of diet, massage, manipulation, and herbal treatments (which are currently being researched by ethnobotanists). Psychological diagnostic techniques include an early projection test using a rock as a kind of projective technique and assessment of muscle tension as an index of conflict.

Psychotherapeutic approaches include specific techniques such as confession, catharsis, music, ritual, and trance induction. Nonspecific approaches include expectation, attention, and suggestion. The entire therapeutic process occurs within what Jerome Frank calls "a shared healing myth," meaning that both shaman and patient share beliefs concerning the nature, cause, and appropriate means for curing illness. The net effect of all these factors probably includes a strong placebo effect.

From the shaman's perspective the therapeutic factors are spiritual or psychic as much as, or more than, psychological or physical. Studies of psi in shamans have been inconclusive and most researchers decide the matter according to their personal belief systems.

ALTRUISM
CULTURAL DIFFERENCES
HERMENEUTICS
MYTHS
PHYLOANALYSIS
PSYCHOTHERAPY

R. WALSH

SHORT-TERM MEMORY

With the increased interest in information-processing models for learning, memory, and perception in the late 1950s, there rose a great deal of inquiry into the sequencing characteristics from intake to retention to retrieval of the information. Most information-processing approaches propose an iconic storage or sensory register as the initial stage, a short-term-memory intermediate stage, and then a long-term-memory stage in learning. Within and between these stages, attention and linguistic factors can intervene. Retrieval of information can be accessed from either the short-term- or long-term-memory phases.

Basically, short-term memory is a fleeting or transient, limited-capacity (five to nine items) memory storage. Its duration ranges between 20 seconds and 1 minute. The transfer of information from short-term to the more permanent long-term memory is by the process of rehearsal or memorial repetition. Short-term memory is very vulnerable. The memory trace has been shown to decay rapidly with *time* and *interference* from competitive acoustic (similar sounds) or semantic (similar meaning) information.

Common laboratory tasks, used to study short-term memory, involved the presentation of numerical, alphabetic, or word lists followed by the counting of the number of correctly remembered items. These included *distractor tasks, continuous or probe tasks,* and *paired associates.* Depending on the temporal or spatial parameters used in the experiment, these tasks contributed to either the decay of trace or interference notions.

Although short-term memory has limited capacity, researchers have found that this capacity can be enhanced through chunking. That is, each of six or seven items that can be remembered can serve as superordinate categories for six or seven other kinds of items or members of that superordinate category. Short-term-memory chunking, however, was found to be much more volatile than the long-term-memory superordinate categorization.

Although stimulus characteristics such as item similarity and meaningfulness can cause interference, so can the sequential placement of items.

Proactive interference causes information from previously learned material to reduce memory for new items, while *retroactive* interference causes poor recall of previously learned material because of the information recently learned. The effects of item interference can be seen in recall of lists of items. Here the performance curve of position of item recalled resembles a "U." The middle items seem to be the object of greatest interference, while the beginning list items have received much rehearsal and the ending items are still "fresh" in memory, so recall is enhanced.

Along with the quantitative assessments of short-term memory came the qualitative assessments of the information-processing sequence. Questions of whether short-term memory and long-term memory are independent processes or continuous processes were vigorously argued in the literature.

MEMORY
MEMORY DISORDERS

D. F. FISHER

SHORT-TERM THERAPY

Short-term therapy has experienced considerable change. New models have been developed, research measuring outcome and comparing techniques has been completed, and changes in the field of mental health care delivery have contributed to its metamorphosis, and these changes have had an impact on theraptists, clients, and those bearing the financial responsibility for therapy.

The goal in short-term therapy has been defined as using what clients bring to therapy to meet their needs in such a way that they can make a satisfactory life for themselves. What short-term therapies have in common begins with the brief nature of their interventions. There appears to have developed a consensus that the upper limit of short-term therapy is 20 to 25 sessions. Although there is some controversy regarding the length of short-term therapy, the common factor is that a limit exists.

Goals within short-term therapy models commonly reflect one or more of the following characteristics: (a) removal or amelioration of the client's most disabling symptoms as rapidly as possible, (b) prompt reestablishment of the client's previous emotional equilibrium, and (c) development of client's understanding of the current disturbance along with increased coping ability in the future.

The role of the therapist is critical to the short-term process. Although it has been long and widely acknowledged that a positive relationship between therapist and client is a necessary component for successful therapy, never has it been more critical than within the short-term model. Here one of the striking differences between long- and short-term therapy exists. Feelings of warmth, liking, and admiration for the therapist are often interpreted to the client by the long-term therapist. However, they are often actively sought in many of the short-term modalities.

The importance of focus, or staying on track during sessions, is another common element within the short-term psychotherapies; therefore, short-term therapists are more willing to direct the process. Ventilation of emotional material is encouraged. Intervention is swift, with the first interview often used for intervention as well as exploration and gathering of relevant information. In fact, focused single-session therapy is a model of short-term therapy based on one session. Therapists typically are more flexible due to the wide range of clients they see and, therefore, more often than not are seen as theoretically eclectic.

PSYCHODYNAMICALLY ORIENTED APPROACHES

Many short-term psychodynamic techniques use dynamic and object-related terminology to illuminate origins of psychopathology. Peter Sifneos described short-term anxiety-provoking psychotherapy (STAPP) as based on the notion that psychological problems begin during childhood while relating to family members and these patterns of relating are carried into adult life, where they continue to cause difficulty. The goal of STAPP is to induce a "corrective emotional experience" as the client gains insight into behavior, resulting in a dynamic resolution of childhood conflicts.

BEHAVIORAL APPROACHES

Behavior therapy, based on the experimental principles of learning, has developed a strong database that supports both its theory and practice. The techniques are widely used and lend themselves well to the limits of short-term therapy, although there are many examples of long-term behavior therapy. Typically, three steps are employed. First, target behaviors to be changed are identified. Second, reinforcers that maintain the target behaviors are identified, as are other commonly occurring reinforcers within the client's life. Finally, an experimental paradigm is developed that manipulates reinforcers to produce the new or target behaviors. The therapist and client receive information regarding the success of the intervention through the client's response.

COGNITIVE APPROCHES

One of the more potent of the early short-term therapies is rational emotive behavior therapy, is designed to help the client recognize that painful emotions and maladaptive behaviors are the result of irrational thought patterns and beliefs held by the client. Once these beliefs are revealed, challenged, and changed, the negative feelings and behaviors will diminish or cease. This therapy uses a powerful technique to identify and dispute irrational thinking. Ultimately, the client learns the system that the therapist is using so that when irrational thoughts reoccur, the client will not be dependent on the therapist.

STRATEGIC INTERVENTIONS

An example of a therapy based on strategic intervention is solution-focused brief therapy. This model conforms to the common elements of short-term therapy but offers its solutions in the observation that theoretically all presenting problems and symptomatic behaviors have exceptions or times when the problem does not occur. It is believed that paying a great deal of attention to these exceptions rather than analyzing the problem is a key to change. Interventions center on increasing exceptions and because these exceptions come from the client, they reflect the therapist's respect of and confidence in the client's ability to find solutions. This approach has been adapted for work with those suffering from alcohol abuse.

STATUS OF SHORT-TERM THERAPY

Possibly the most visible example of the current status of the short-term model is found in American Biodyne, Inc., a mental health maintenance organization. This privately held corporation provides mental health components to 5 million persons insured through various contractual health insurance agreements. The short-term therapy model employed is brief intermittent psychotherapy throughout the life cycle (BIT) as described by Nicholas Cummings.

The origins of short-term therapy coincided with the community mental health movement of the mid-1960s. It was seen as a method for reaching large numbers of clients while using fewer resources. The status of short-term therapy has evolved away from what was once thought of as a less effective practice used only by minimally trained therapists or when constraints prevented time-unlimited therapy. Many factors are driving this process, including a large body of research that demonstrates that short-term and unlimited therapy are indistinguishable in regard to their effectiveness. Increasingly, institutions are turning to the planned time-limited model due to resource constraints and the current state of

research and practice provide a sound rationale for the use of short-term therapy.

BEHAVIOR THERAPY
BRIEF THERAPY I
BRIEF THERAPY II
CURRENT PSYCHOTHERAPIES
ECLECTIC PSYCHOTHERAPY
INNOVATIVE PSYCHOTHERAPIES
TIME-LIMITED PSYCHOTHERAPY

F. E. DENISON

SHYNESS

The essential feature of shyness is being afraid of social interactions. It is a common phenomenon that almost everyone experiences occasionally. Typically, shy individuals are very self-conscious and preoccupied with potentially negative evaluations by others. By focusing on their shortcomings, shy people are usually anxious and often fulfill their worst expectations.

Shyness is a complex condition that spans a wide psychological continuum; it can range from occasional awkwardness in social situations all the way to neurosis that can completely disrupt an individual's life. Generally, unfamiliar situations and people who are perceived as different, powerful, or evaluative seem to elicit shyness. As a consequence of being shy, people experience varying degrees of loneliness, depression, poor self-esteem, and unassertiveness. Most shy people perceive shyness as an undesirable trait.

Although the specific origins of shyness vary from person to person, cultural values, social norms, and other environmental factors play a significant role in creating shyness. Philip Zimbardo recounts cross-cultural studies that show that social values of some cultures are more likely to foster shyness than others. In shyness-generating societies, love is contingent on performance, failures are magnified and internalized, rewards are few, and there is little encouragement to express ideas and feelings freely. For most shy individuals, shyness can be overcome through committing one's self to change, learning social skills, and building self-confidence.

ANXIETY
AVOIDANT PERSONALITY
INFERIORITY FEELINGS

T.-I. MOON

SIBLING RELATIONSHIPS

The sibling group consists of brothers and sisters in one's own nuclear family and is a nonvoluntary relationship. An individual's sequential position among siblings, known as *birth order* or *sibling status,* has been important in deciding the distribution of familial property.

SIBLING RIVALRY

Rivalry among brothers and sisters is displayed among less than half of all firstborns; is reported as most intense only among same-gender siblings who are close in age ($1\frac{1}{2}$ to 3 years apart); and is found primarily among children whose parents practice inconsistent discipline practices regardless of the form. It seems that children's personalities, especially their ability to adapt to the new, whether people, places, or things, contribute to reduced sibling rivalry. Moreover, parental behaviors can intensify a child's feelings of displacement, promote rivalry, and also interact with the child's personality to produce differing rates of sibling adjustment.

Besides parental behavior and children's personalities having an impact on sibling dynamics, especially militating against rivalry, social factors also have an influence. Firstborns who tend to assume dominant roles toward younger brothers or sisters exhibit less competition, and in many cases their influence has a greater impact than that of parents.

It seems that main effects of birth order or gender must be viewed with care because the dynamics of sibling interactions are affected by age spacing and parental behavior. Eldest children (those 9 months to 3 years older) tend to be bossier and more likely to interfere or ignore and to bribe or physically attack younger siblings, as contrasted with second borns with younger siblings or those whose spacing is farther apart. However, younger siblings are likely to be more tolerant. Mothers who encourage children to assume aspects of parental roles toward younger siblings are instrumental in promoting a higher quantity and better quality of sibling interactions in the family. Data also show that mothers with firstborn sons tend to explain and communicate more with their children in general than those with firstborn daughters, and their propensity seems imitated by older children in their relations with younger brothers and sisters. In some cases, older children even serve as attachment figures more so than parents for their younger siblings.

According to Zajonc, the oldest child, regardless of gender, has an advantage over younger children because of sharing a home with two adults for a period of time. When a sibling arrives, these children also benefit from serving as teachers of younger siblings. Again, reported effects are magnified when age spacing is greater than 3 years.

In addition, family size influences sibling dynamics. Although parents who expect and plan for large families often generate a warm and accepting climate for all their children to model, those who do not exude resentment, hostility, and anger. In fact, parents of large families, in general, tend to resort to authoritarian child-rearing techniques, and these in turn are displayed by older children toward younger siblings.

BIRTH-ORDER PORTRAITS

Sir Francis Galton observed that an exceptionally large number of prominent British scientists were firstborns. Initially, differences between firstborns and later borns were documented, but more recently researchers stressed the importance of differentiating among only children, firstborns, middle children, and last borns. Only children are the most dependent and achievement-oriented compared with children in the other positions. Their parents often make excessive demands on them, and the children view themselves as misunderstood and unfairly treated. They often seek the company of adults, have difficulty in relating to peers, and are less mature, partially because they missed the interactive learning involved in tutoring a younger sibling. Firstborns also have parents who expect much of them, and they receive and emit more behaviors than other children. They tend to be highly motivated, have high goals, adhere to rules, and are generally more likely to need social contacts and praise. They, however, are fearful, sensitive to pain, and seem less able to cope with anxiety compared with their birth-order counterparts. They tend to be conservative and cautious, are quite dependent on parents, and are often uncertain about their roles. Although middle borns may feel unloved and imposed on, they often turn to endeavors in which they can excel, and they show less anxiety and are more easy going. They also are more likely to attempt new tasks, activities, and behaviors, such as talking to strangers. More likely to support unconventional ideas, one study found that more than 90% of the scientists who initially supported Charles Darwin's evolutionary ideas during the nineteenth century were middle children. Last borns resemble firstborns in that they tend to be spoiled and are the focus of parental attention. They, however, remain quite babyish, are less likely to develop feelings of independence, and become discouraged with achievements or the lack of them. They are prone to high anxiety and personal problems that relate to their constant need to negotiate, accommodate, and tolerate. They also seldom have opportunities for assuming responsibility.

Since each of these birth-order patterns can be modulated by many factors—family size, age spacing, parental attitudes, economic conditions, and so on—they only represent composite averages. In addition, investigations tend to concentrate on middle class families, are cross-sectional rather than longitudinal, and rely on self-report retrospective data.

SIBLING RELATIONSHIPS ACROSS THE LIFE SPAN

Very few studies have been conducted to understand better sibling relationships during adulthood, middle age, and old age. Sibling ties tend to decrease with age, but often become strong during a family crisis or when there is an aged parent to provide a focus of common concern or interest.

BIRTH ORDER AND PERSONALITY
BIRTH-ORDER RESEARCH

F. Deutsch

SICKLE CELL DISEASE

CLINICAL FEATURES

Sickle cell disease (SCD) refers to a group of genetic disorders that affect approximately one of every 400 African American newborns. The disease results from the inheritance of two abnormal alleles responsible for hemoglobin formation, at least one of these alleles being the sickle cell allele (HbS). In SCD, vascular occlusion occurs when sickled red blood cells block small blood vessels. This can cause both acute and chronic complications, including acute chest syndrome, aseptic necrosis of hips or shoulders, retinopathy, leg ulcers, cerebral vascular accidents, and chronic anemia.

Repeated episodes of severe pain, often referred to as painful "crises," are the most common and disabling complication of SCD. Painful episodes are usually recurrent and unpredictable. Pain may be located in almost any area of the body, commonly the extremities, joints, low back, and abdomen. The frequency and severity of pain is highly variable, from long periods of almost no pain to painful episodes several times per month. Medical management attempts to minimize intravascular sickling and then reduce pain. This is often done with aggressive narcotic medications given orally for mild pain or intravenously for severe pain. Frequently, hospitalizations and emergency room visits are necessary.

Until recently, most parents of children with SCD did not know their newborn had the illness until their child began experiencing medical problems. Often the problems that occur in infants and young children with SCD are severe and can be life threatening. Without proper medical treatment, death may occur, and indeed, one of the periods in life in which individuals are at greatest risk for death from this disease is in the first 5 years of life. Recently, newborn screening has become more routine, and now newborns are often identified early. Although it is still common for some individuals to die suddenly and unexpectedly before age 40 years, many individuals live long and productive lives.

LIFESTYLE CONSEQUENCES

These individuals with SCD still encounter significant stressors related to their disease. In children, these include retarded growth, delayed puberty, and frequent clinic visits and hospitalizations. These stressors can affect peer relationships, self-concept, and school attendance. Given their cognitive development, young children may have difficulty understanding pain and the meaning of repeated hospitalizations. They may experience feelings of helplessness and fear of the unknown, and may have difficulty expressing feelings to their parents and medical professionals. Behavioral problems, especially internalizing behavioral problems, or the more silent forms of psychological distress (e.g., anxiety and depression) may occur.

As children enter adolescence and young adulthood, their disease may interfere with social relationships, academic performance, and occupational and family planning. Fears related to their illness may interfere with individualization, maturation, and separation.

Adults face decisions regarding selecting a partner and having children, issues that are often complicated by the fact that SCD is hereditary. Many adults may have problems meeting job and family responsibilities. Disability and unemployment are common and thus so are financial problems. As adults age, they may encounter more complications related to their illness and more frequent episodes of pain. As adults approach the average life span of someone with SCD, anxiety, depression, or even preoccupation with death may occur.

The emotional reactions that can occur in individuals with SCD are often complicated by inadequate recognition and treatment of pain by health care professionals. Many physicians and nurses have not had sufficient hands-on experience treating SCD pain, and thus they may be uncomfortable with aggressive medication management. Sometimes frequent hospitalization and emergency room visits are misinterpreted as drug-seeking behavior or faking pain. Although drug-related problems may occur in individuals with SCD, excessive concern over drug addiction by health care providers can lead to undermedicating and inadequate pain management. Some individuals who have frequent frustrating encounters with inexperienced health care professionals become discouraged and alienated from the health care system.

COPING WITH PAIN AND STRESS RELATED TO ILLNESS

Individuals with SCD cope well, are often able to work, remain active in social and recreational activities, and are well-adjusted psychologically. Many others, however, cope poorly, lead more limited lives, and become depressed and overly reliant on health care services for their pain management. Although some of the variability in adjustment is a result of disease severity, psychological factors, including coping strategies and social support, are significantly related to psychosocial and functional adjustment across the life span.

In adults, several factors have been related to good adjustment to SCD. Adults who have lower levels of daily stress, higher efficacy expectations, and high levels of family support have better psychological adjustment. Adults who take an active approach to coping with pain by using multiple cognitive and behavioral strategies such as diverting attention and calming self-statements are more active in household, work, and social activities. Other psychosocial factors have been associated with poorer adjustment to SCD. Adults from conflicted families and adults who use palliative coping methods for dealing with stress have poorer psychological adjustment. Overall poor psychosocial and functional adjustment also occurs in individuals who deal with pain by catastrophizing, engaging in fear and anger self-statements, and using passive strategies such as resting while neglecting to use other strategies when an episode of pain occurs. This pattern of pain coping has been associated with more severe pain; greater reductions in household, social, and occupational activities during painful episodes; and more frequent hospitalizations and emergency room visits.

In children and adolescents, there are similar relationships among these dimensions of coping, family support, and adjustment. Interestingly, factors in the parents such as maternal adjustment and the pain-coping strategies that parents use are also related to the child's adjustment. Furthermore, coping strategies in parents and their children are related,

possibly because children learn to cope with their own pain by observing their parent's reactions to pain.

There is a growing recognition for the need to treat individuals with this disease from a multidisciplinary perspective. There are now comprehensive SCD centers that emphasize the importance of integrating psychosocial and educational programs with clinical and basic science research. The goals of these centers often include providing multiple types of psychological treatments such as biofeedback and individual and family therapy along with traditional medical management approaches to enhance pain management and overall coping in patients and their families.

GENETIC DISORDERS
HERITABILITY
PAIN

K. M. GIL

SIGNS AND SYMBOLS

The systematic study of signs, in an effort to devise a unified science, is known as semiotics, and derives from the disciplines of philosophy and linguistics as well as psychology. These terms also have a further and more specialized meaning in medical practice—semiotics is the study of symptoms. In this case, in medical diagnosis, symptoms are signs presented for interpretation.

A sign is a stimulus that directs an organism to something other than itself, in the sense that we commonly say a clap of thunder is a sign of rain—the thunder signifies rain. Signs thus occur naturally within the environment, or within the organism (a neurophysiological transmission), or can be contrived in laboratory environments (a flashing light or sounding buzzer signifying food).

These examples of signs, as studied by behavioral scientists, are preverbal or prelinguistic. However, it has been the study of signs as a component of human language, the study of words as written or spoken signs, that has yielded the science of semiotics. Semiotic proposes the notion of human beings as the sign-using animals.

The Swiss linguist Ferdinand de Saussure conceived of language as a link between thought and sound. On the one hand, language requires concepts, which are nonverbal and purely psychological, and on the other hand, meaningful sounds, which are the expressions of the concepts. The union between concept and expression, between "the signified" and "the signifier," is a function rather than a thing. The function is to associate signifier with signified, and the resulting entity Saussure called the *linguistic sign.*

The essential distinction between a sign and a symbol was articulated by Walker Percy. "A sign is something that directs our attention to something else. A symbol does not direct our attention to something else, as a sign does. It does not direct at all. It 'means' something else." The recognition of symbolic content has been important in the creation and appreciation of art, poetry, and music since the nineteenth century, but as yet symbolization has been insufficiently recognized in our efforts at understanding human language.

A. QUAGLIANO

SIMULATION

Simulation is the imitation of natural situations in such a way that the subject deals with the simulation *as if* it were a real situation. This has the advantage of allowing the subject to respond to a situation *without facing the hazards* of the natural situation. In much psychological experimentation (particularly in social psychology), one simulates all but the crucial variable. The ultimate in simulation, however, is mathematical or computer simulation—when mathematical symbols (or computer codings) can be substituted for the elements and processes being investigated. Psychodrama is an example of simulation in psychotherapy wherein a person role-plays a simulated situation in social safety.

ROLE PLAYING

W. E. GREGORY

SIN

Sin is one of a group of concepts that refer to the violation of laws. Actions that violate human-generated laws are labeled crimes, offenses, or misdemeanors. Sins are actions that violate the laws of God. Experiences of guilt presumably arise from violations of either human-made or God-made laws.

In the Judeo-Christian tradition, the concept of "original" sin serves as an explanatory concept for the qualities of weakness and imperfection found in all human beings. *Actual sin* is the term more customarily applied to individual violations of the laws of God. These are often divided into two degrees of seriousness: mortal and venial. The importance of the concept of sin for psychology rests primarily on the role it plays in the understanding of personal guilt.

FREE WILL
RELIGION AND PSYCHOLOGY

M. E. REUDER

SINGLE PARENTHOOD

The number of single-parent families maintained by women in the United States increased by 131% between 1960 and 1978. This resulted in one in five children becoming a member of a single-parent family. Finer noted that single-parent families were faced with such problems as social isolation and loneliness, financial hardships, and pressure on children to be responsible for domestic duties that were beyond their capabilities.

IMPACT ON CHILDREN

A review of the literature suggests that single-parent children have a tendency to become poorly socialized, be cognitively deficient, and experience poor parent–child interactions. Hetherington and colleagues also found that during the first year following divorce, children are more aggressive, oppositional, distractible, and demanding than children from intact families. Several other studies support these findings.

Crossman and Adams described two social psychological theories that can be used to understand the potential negative effects of divorce on children. Crisis theory suggests that divorce is an undesirable and stressful event that can have undesirable consequences for a family member.

Zajonc's theory suggests that single parents tend to have less time to spend with their children because of additional role demands. The children's social and cognitive development thus tends to suffer because they do not have enough time to interact with their parent.

IMPACT ON PARENT

The most common initial reaction to single parenthood by a parent is depression. Often the parent feels victimized, alone, and angry. They tend to worry about unpredictable income, poor housing, and feelings of inadequacy. Other emotional reactions experienced by single parents include guilt or a sense of failure about a marriage breakdown, grief, fear, anxiety, confusion, and, in some cases, relief. The advent of single parenthood may also result in increased strain on the single parent's time, energy, emotions, and ability to work.

PARENT–CHILD RELATIONS

M. S. NYSTUL

SINGLE-SUBJECT RESEARCH DESIGNS

Single-subject research designs involve the intensive study of one organism continuously or repeatedly across time. The organism or subject may be a single animal or a single molar unit, such as an industrial organization. There are situations in which it is more meaningful, more convenient, more ethical, and/or less expensive to study one or very few subjects intensively than to study many subjects. A basic difference between group- and single-subject designs is that one or very few observations are generally obtained from each subject in group designs; with single-subject designs, many observations are obtained from one subject across time. The design categories of (a) correlational, (b) quasi-experimental, and (c) experimental that are used frequently to classify different types of group designs also can be used to classify various single-subject designs.

CORRELATIONAL DESIGNS

Single-subject correlational designs involve a collection of scores obtained across time (a time series) on some dependent variable of interest and, in addition, either (a) a series of scores on some other variable collected at the same time points (the concomitant series), or (b) a log of events that occur during the time series. An analysis is then carried out to determine whether changes in the dependent variable time series are associated with changes in the concomitant series or the occurrence of events that have been recorded. If an association is identified (through a visual or statistical analysis), this may lead to the hypothesis that variability in the dependent variable series has been caused by a concomitant variable. Unlike the single-subject quasi-experimental and experimental designs, the correlational design is not characterized by the experimental manipulation of some independent variable.

QUASI-EXPERIMENTAL DESIGN

The quasi-experimental AB design consists of two phases: the baseline (or A) phase and the intervention (or B) phase. Data are collected during the A phase to describe the behavior before the treatment is introduced. The amount of baseline data collected depends on the type of behavior studied, the type of subject, the situational variables, and other aspects of the experiment, but a useful guideline is to have sufficient data to obtain a clear picture of the stability of the behavior. After the baseline data are collected, the experimenter introduces an intervention, and data continue to be collected during the B phase. The intervention may be applied throughout this phase or applied only briefly at the beginning of the phase, depending on the nature of the intervention, the dependent variable, and the purpose of the study. If conditions other than the intervention change at the time the intervention is introduced, the change on the dependent variable from the A to the B phase will be confounded. A major weakness of the AB design is that it is often difficult to know if some condition other than the intervention has changed between the A and B phases.

EXPERIMENTAL DESIGNS

Four single-subject experimental designs are described here; others exist, but all are slight variants of these basic designs. Each of these designs provides greater certainty that a planned intervention is responsible for a change observed in time-series data than is provided by the AB quasi-experiment.

ABA and ABAB Designs

The direct extensions of the AB design are the ABA (baseline intervention-baseline) and ABAB (baseline-intervention–baseline-intervention) designs. The ABAB design is often referred to as a "reversal" design in the behavior modification literature because the intervention condition is reversed (more appropriately, withdrawn) after it is first applied. If the level of behavior during the second A phase in an ABA experiment returns to a level similar to that observed during the original A phase, the argument is strengthened that the intervention has caused a change. If the behavior is consistent within the two baseline conditions, consistent within the two intervention conditions, but clearly different between baseline and intervention conditions, a convincing case can be made that the intervention is effective and that the effect has been replicated within the subject. There are, however, many logical, ethical, and practical problems with these designs. Many interventions are one-shot treatments such as surgical ablation or teaching a skill. Once these treatments are applied, it may be illogical to expect the subject to revert to a preintervention level. Sometimes behavior is expected to revert to the baseline level but does not because conditions other than the intervention not present during the baseline phase maintain the behavior. In other situations, ethical arguments are incompatible with the design requirements; for example, an intervention may change a behavior that is harmful to the subject and consequently should not be withdrawn. These and related problems greatly reduce the number of situations in which ABA and ABAB designs are appropriate. Other single-subject designs can solve these problems.

Multiple Baseline Designs

Most of the difficulties associated with the ABAB design can be solved with some version of the multiple baseline design. This design is useful in a wide variety of basic and applied research settings. In a sense, this design is a collection of AB designs. Data are collected on two or more baselines (time series) and an intervention is applied to the first one. If the intervention appears to shift the time series to which it is applied but does not shift the other baseline series, it is then applied to the second series. If the application of the intervention to the second series has an effect on this series but not on any other series, the next series is then exposed to the intervention. Hence each available baseline series is exposed to the intervention, but the intervention is never initiated on more than one series at a time. Since the intervention is introduced in a staggered manner to the various baselines, it is implausible that some event unrelated to the intervention is the cause of the apparent effect on each series.

There are essentially three versions of the multiple baseline design; each version is identified by the nature of the baselines observed. The multiple baselines may be based on data collected across (a) several different behaviors (dependent variables) from one subject in one setting, (b) several different situations on one behavior from one subject, or (c) several different subjects on one behavior in one setting. A problem with the versions involving multiple baselines across behaviors is that the behaviors may be highly correlated and, as a result, will not provide independent sources of information on the intervention effects. Similar problems can occur with multiple baselines across situations or subjects, but the latter version is not as vulnerable to these problems because different subjects can often be isolated from each other. In general, multiple baseline designs avoid the ethical problem of withdrawing an effective intervention, are useful with interventions and behaviors that are either reversible or nonreversible, and are practical to implement in a wide variety of research settings.

Alternating Treatment Design

The differential effects of two or more treatments can be examined through the alternating treatments design. Multiple baseline data on one dependent variable (e.g., amount of pain experienced) are repeatedly collected from one subject in two or more situations (e.g., at home and at school) during the first phase. In the second phase, one treatment is applied in the first situation; then another treatment is applied in another situation. The treatments are alternated or presented in random order for each situation across time for the duration of the second phase. If one of the treatments is identified as most effective during the second phase, this treatment alone may be applied to all situations during a third phase to confirm the effect across situations. The basic advantages of this design are that several treatments can be studied within a short period of time and it is not necessary to withhold all treatments after baseline data are collected. A disadvantage is that the logic of the design dictates the use of treatments having very rapid effects that will not carry over long enough to contaminate the other treatments. Carry-over effects and multiple treatment interference are difficult to rule out as interpretation issues with this design. Other versions of this design involve the study of one treatment on multiple dependent variables and more complex arrangements in which multiple treatments, multiple dependent variables and/or multiple subjects are employed.

COMPARISON OF SINGLE-SUBJECT AND GROUP EXPERIMENTAL DESIGNS

Question Answered

At a general level, both single-subject and group designs provide an answer to the question of whether there is a treatment effect. They differ in terms of how the "effect" is defined and studied. The single-subject design provides important information on the form of the change across time whereas the between-group design provides an estimate of the intervention magnitude for a specified population of subjects.

A strong argument can be made that the nature of the treatment process should be investigated first with single subject designs. If an effective intervention is developed through the intensive study of a behavioral process in one subject, there is reason to hypothesize that it will be effective on others because the best guarantee of replication of results is an understanding of variables affecting the process. After the intervention or treatment package is developed using single-subject designs, it is often convincing then to employ a group design in an outcome study.

Data Collection Problems

Although it may be desirable to proceed from the use of single-subject designs for treatment refinement to group designs for outcome estimation, the realities of the research environment and the nature of the variables of interest usually dictate the design choice. Some single-subject design is feasible if (a) the subject is available repeatedly across a reasonable amount of time and is willing to participate, (b) the treatment is one that can be administered repeatedly or continuously, (c) the environmental context in which the subject is observed and treated is reasonably constant across the duration of the experiment, and (d) the dependent variable is a measure that can be obtained repeatedly or continuously. There are many variables (independent and dependent) that are not easily (or at reasonable cost) employed repeatedly. If the experimenter is not able to treat and measure repeatedly (for logical, practical, or political reasons), a group design may be the only choice. Group designs, however, are associated with other limitations. Randomized group designs, for example, are often impossible to carry out because random assignment of subjects to conditions may not be possible or there may be very few subjects available for the experiment. If continuous treatment and measurement are not possible but data from several treatment and measurement periods can be collected on a few subjects, repeated measurement group designs are appropriate.

Data Analysis

Historically, group designs have been associated with the use of statistical inference as the major form of data analysis. Single-subject designs have traditionally been analyzed using visual analysis of graphed data. Contemporary computer methods allow data from even very large group studies to be routinely plotted to simplify interpretation, and many methods are available for the statistical analysis of single-subject designs.

EXPERIMENTAL DESIGN
RESEARCH METHODOLOGY

B. E. HUITEMA

THE SIXTEEN PERSONALITY FACTOR QUESTIONNAIRE

The Sixteen Personality Factor Questionnaire, known simply as the 16PF, is a major technological outgrowth of the research on self-report data that Raymond B. Cattell directed over a period of more than 30 years. The research on which the 16PF is based proceeded by: (a) establishing, by factor analytic means, independent dimensions of personality within behavior-rating data; (b) writing self-report items to represent these dimensions; and (c) factoring to determine factors among the responses to these items.

Several forms of the 16PF have been produced over the last 30 years—some for different language culture groups (German, French, Japanese, Spanish, etc.), some for poor readers, and so forth. Several different norm tables are available.

Interpretations of the factors of the questionnaire derive from research and practical applications in a variety of social, clinical, industrial, and educational settings. Designated very briefly, the scales are as follows: A—Reserved to outgoing; B—Intelligent to obtuse; C—Emotional to calm; E—Compliant to assertive; F—Serious to enthusiastic; G—Nonconforming to socialized; H—Timid to bold; I—Practical to sentimental; L—Trusting to suspicious; M—Earnest to fanciful; O—Placid to concerned; Q_1—Conservative to experimenting; Q_2—Conforming to rebelling; Q_3—Careless to compulsive; and Q_4—Composed to tense. Commonly A, E, F, H, and Q_2 (−) have turned up as the major components of a second-order factor that represents concepts of extroversion–introversion; C(−); L, O, and Q_4 form another second-order factor of anxiety (versus ego control); G and Q_3 define a second-order factor of "good upbringing" or superego development; I and M indicate a second-order sensitivity–toughness dimension. Several factor analyses have provided support for these groupings and interpretations.

FACTOR ANALYZED PERSONALITY
QUESTIONNAIRES MEASUREMENT
MULTIVARIATE ANALYSIS METHODS

J. L. HORN

SKILL LEARNING

Skill learning is a term used by behaviorally oriented educators and psychologists, particularly those interested in special education and the remediation of academic or social–emotional school adjustment problems. A skill is defined as a coordinated series of actions that serve to attain some goal or accomplish a particular task. The goal or task may be academic, social, motor or a self-help or independent living task. The

particular skills that are identified and taught vary widely in scope and domain, depending on the needs and developmental level of a particular individual.

A skill-based educational program begins with a task analysis. The task to be taught is broken down into small, discrete, behavioral subtasks arranged in hierarchical order.

This kind of a task analysis can be used to guide assessment and intervention. Teachers can evaluate students' specific functioning levels on particular skills according to the level of mastery on the hierarchy of subtasks. Remedial intervention can then proceed by systematically teaching each behavioral task. Typically, procedures such as instructions, demonstrations, and modeling are used to introduce each new behavior. Behavioral rehearsal and repeated practice, along with performance feedback, are then employed to facilitate the individual's ability to adjust the sequence of behaviors into an integrated and smooth skill performance.

APPROACHES TO LEARNING
INSTRUCTIONAL THEORY
TASK ANALYSIS

K. L. BIERMAN

SLEEP

Formal speculations about sleep extend back to the Grecian times (Aristotle wrote a chapter on sleep), and research findings about sleep emerged as a part of the development of life science research in the nineteenth century. As findings about the circulatory system and the central nervous system (CNS) were developed, descriptions of the changes in these systems associated with sleep would be noted and often translated into theories of sleep.

A major technological development took place in 1937. The electroencephalogram (EEG), which measures brain waves, showed distinct and systematic pattern changes with the onset of and throughout sleep. For the first time, sleep could be measured objectively and continuously and could be viewed as an active process.

A second major breakthrough occurred in 1953, when Kleitman and Aserinsky discovered a regularly recurring "stage" of sleep characterized by rapid eye movements (REMs) and an active "awake" EEG pattern. This pattern, appearing spontaneously about every 90 minutes, was found to "index" the presence of the dream in human subjects.

Sleep research is an interdisciplinary effort. The researchers include biochemists, biologists, endocrinologists, neuroscientists, pediatricians, physiologists, psychiatrists, and psychologists. The particular studies range from single nerve cell activity to dream interpretation; the subjects include the entire phyla of organisms, infants, the elderly, and a full range of pathological states.

THE DIMENSIONS OF SLEEP

There are three measurement domains: sleep structure, sleep patterns, and subjective responses. Sleep structure refers to the dimensions of the ongoing sleep process; sleep patterns describe the amounts and placements of sleep within the 24 hours; and subjective responses include evaluative statements about sleep and dream recall.

Sleep structure is conventionally indexed by the EEG. In the young human adult, there are four "stages" of sleep (1–4) that are roughly related to sleep depth and the 1-REM (stage 1 plus REMs).

Figure 1 shows a typical night's sleep for a young adult indexed by stages. Each night, all humans approximate this record: 50% ($\pm5\%$) stage 2; 25% 1-REM ($\pm4\%$); 15% ($\pm3\%$) Stage 4; 7% Stage 3 ($\pm2\%$); and 3% Stage 1 ($\pm2\%$). The first REM period will occur after about 90 to 100 minutes and at intervals of 90 to 100 minutes thereafter with increases in the lengths of the bursts. Most of Stages 3 and 4 will occur in the early third of the night. There may be a few spontaneous awakenings.

Sleep patterns primarily index total sleep time, sleep onset, and termination times and the placement and number of episodes. In young adult sleep, this is typically a major nocturnal period with interjected naps.

Subjective responses may range from simple awareness of the time to get to sleep or within-sleep awakenings through evaluative terms, such as "light" and "deep" or "refreshing" sleep, to more global statements, such as "good" and "bad" sleep. Only limited research has been done on these responses, but that research has indicated a general looseness of the relationship between these responses and the objective measures of sleep. This is particularly true among persons who are expressing sleep complaints.

These measured properties of sleep may be viewed as dependent or independent variables, that is, we may ask what determines the variations in these measures or we may ask what the consequences are of variations in the measures.

Determinants of Sleep

A major determinant of sleep structure and patterns is species differences. The sleep of animals varies widely. Humans and primates have similar sleep structure, that is, four stages of sleep plus REM or "activated" sleep. However, the sleep of other species generally is comprised of two stages of sleep: slow-wave sleep, which resembles stages 3 and 4 of humans, and "activated" sleep, which involves cyclical episodes of brain activation within sleep equivalent to human 1-REM or dreaming sleep. The percentage and cycling vary. Major differences are seen in total sleep amounts, number of episodes, and placement. Grazing animals such as cattle tend to sleep only 2 to 4 hours each 24 hours, whereas small rodents sleep more than 12 hours per day. Primates generally have a long major sleep period, whereas most animals have frequent and limited sleep periods. Of course, some animals sleep during the day while others sleep at night. The varied sleep of animals is most useful in attempts to construct theories about the functions of sleep.

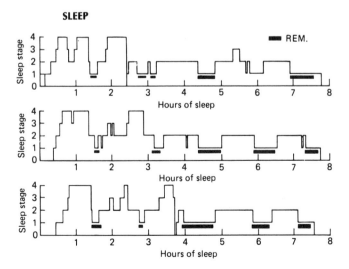

Figure 1. The sleep of a young adult described in stages. Stages 1 through 4 are indicated vertically and Stage 1-REM is indicated by the black bars. The horizontal indicates the passage of time across 8 hours. From W. B. Webb, *Sleep, the gentle tyrant* (New York: Prentice-Hall, 1975).

A second major determinant of sleep variations is age. In the human, age is associated with the largest changes in our lifetime. The stages of sleep develop quite rapidly and are intact by about 6 months of age. The major change is seen in Stage 1-REM, which constitutes about 50% of newborns' sleep and diminishes exponentially to approximately 25% by the end of the first decade. From this point, the distribution of stages remains remarkably constant into the sixth and seventh decades. The most dramatic changes are seen in the systematic developmental change in sleep patterns. The neonate averages about 16 hours of sleep in about six episodes equally distributed across the 24 hours. Within a few days, there begins a systematic consolidation of sleep into a major night period and a reduction of sleep within the waking period. The nighttime sleep amount remains relatively stable. With aging, in the fourth and fifth decade and beyond, the primary change in sleep is an increasing inability to sustain sleep, that is, awakening during the night and early sleep termination.

Another major determinant of the sleep dimensions is variations in time schedules resulting from voluntary or involuntary factors. All of these result in changes in sleep patterns per se—less total sleep, variations in the time of sleep, and length and number of sleep episodes.

Changes in sleep patterns have predictable effects on sleep structures. Because sleep stages are asymmetrically ordered in time, reducing nighttime sleep, for example, by one-fourth has little effect on Stages 3 and 4 and disproportionally reduces Stage 1-REM sleep. Displacing sleep from, for instance, 11 P.M. to 8 A.M. to 8 A.M. to 4 P.M. markedly affects the temporal order of the sleep structure. The latency of the first Stage 1-REM period is sharply reduced and may occur on sleep onset. Further, frequent awakenings and early sleep terminations are increased.

Sleep is a behavioral response system, and is at least partially determined by external stimulus conditions and psychological states. In very general terms, the determinants primarily affect sleep patterns and subjective responses with limited effects on sleep structure. Second, sleep is also mediated by the central nervous system, and variations imposed on that system by hypnotics, stimulants, or permanent alterations modulate the sleep response.

When sleep is considered as an independent variable, research has focused on the effects of sleep loss and on modified sleep structures, particularly variations in Stage 1-REM sleep. There are a few established physiological effects from even prolonged sleep deprivation of up to 10 days in humans. The performance effects are highly task dependent. The general picture is one of an inability to sustain performance rather than a loss of the capacity to respond.

Hundreds of studies have experimentally reduced or eliminated Stage 1-REM or activated sleep in humans and animals. These experiments have affirmed the development of a state "pressure," that is, Stage 1-REM or activated sleep is increasingly difficult to eliminate and there is a "rebound" in amounts in recovery sleep. However, behavioral effects are less certain. Substantial cognitive or personality effects have not been clearly demonstrated.

There has been an increasing and significant interaction between sleep research and biological rhythm research. Experiments with environments without time cues, modified time schedules, and displacement designs in which the time of sleep is shifted have established the fact that sleep is organized in a systematic circadian pattern. In short, sleep is a biological rhythm.

**CIRCADIAN RHYTH
DREAMS
HUMAN BEHAVIORAL RHYTHMS**

W. B. WEBB

SLEEP DISORDERS

Complaints regarding the quality and quantity of sleep are common, with perhaps as much as 15% of the adult population experiencing frequent and chronic disturbances of sleep. The most prevalent sleep disorders are the insomnias, or Disorders of Initiating and Maintaining Sleep. Three different types of insomnia have been identified, all of which involve chronic complaints of disturbed sleep and daytime fatigue: (a) Sleep-onset insomnia involves difficulty in falling asleep; (b) Sleep-maintenance insomnia is characterized by frequent awakenings at night; and (c) Terminal insomnia consists of awakening early in the morning and not being able to get back to sleep. These types may occur together or alone.

Insomnia is typically defined as a sleep-onset latency of more than 30 minutes, awakenings during the night that result in more than 30 minutes of wakefulness, or total sleep time of less than $6\frac{1}{2}$ hours. However, there are problems with the use of such standard criteria. Some individuals can function effectively with much less than the average amount of sleep. As people get older, the time it takes to fall asleep increases (especially for those persons older than 70 years of age), total sleep time decreases, the number of awakenings increases, and the percentage of deep sleep (stages 3 and 4) decreases. Quality and quantity of sleep must be evaluated on an individual basis in the context of chronological age.

Many cases of insomnia are associated with medical or psychiatric disorders. However, it is not always the case that sleep is improved when these conditions are treated. Furthermore, there is a considerable number of cases in which psychiatric or medical problems do not seem to play a part. A variety of etiological factors have been proposed for such cases, including anxiety, cognitive rumination, conditioning, and heightened physiological arousal.

The most common treatment for insomnia is hypnotic medication, such as the benzodiazepines and the barbiturates. Some of these drugs are addictive and others can be dangerous when mixed with alcohol. Tolerance develops with continued use, and larger doses are required to produce sleep. In addition, chronic use of hypnotic medication itself can produce disturbed sleep. Other treatments for insomnia include progressive muscle relaxation, stimulus control procedures, and paradoxical intention.

The second major category is Disorders of Excessive Somnolence, the most prevalent of which are narcolepsy and sleep apnea. The typical symptoms of narcolepsy are: (a) sleep attacks (brief, irresistible episodes of rapid-eye-movement sleep during the day); and (b) cataplexy (brief periods of muscle weakness without loss of consciousness). It is likely that narcolepsy is an organic disease of the central nervous system, probably transmitted genetically. Treatment consists of stimulant medication for sleep attacks (e.g., amphetamines) and tricyclic compounds for cataplexy.

In sleep apnea, the person repeatedly stops breathing while asleep and awakens suddenly to resume breathing. Such disrupted sleep typically leaves the individual feeling unrefreshed and sleepy on awakening in the morning. Sleep apnea may be considered a Disorder of Initiating or Maintaining Sleep or a Disorder of Excessive Somnolence. Complaints of insomnia, as well as complaints of marked daytime sleepiness, may have sleep apnea as their basis. Its cause is unknown, although it does tend to be associated with obesity, hypertension, and any condition that produces a narrowing of the upper airway. The most effective treatment of severe sleep apnea is tracheostomy.

Disorders of the Sleep–Wake Schedule are the third category and include transient disturbances due to "jet lag" and a change in work shift. A more persistent problem is Delayed Sleep Phase Syndrome, which is a chronic inability to fall asleep at a desired clock time. It appears that sleep onset and length are influenced by species-specific biological rhythms, and that in these individuals such rhythms may become unsynchronized, thus producing disturbed sleep.

The last classification is the Parasomnias, which are clinical conditions occurring during sleep, but in which the sleep process itself is not abnormal. An example is somnambulism, in which the person sits up in bed or may even leave the bed and walk around without gaining full consciousness. Other parasomnias include sleep terror, enuresis, and bruxism.

SLEEP
SLEEP TREATMENT

S. G. FISHER

SLEEP LEARNING

Sleep learning is planned learning while asleep, rather than incidental learning. In theory, material presented while the subject is asleep can be absorbed without competition and without the subject examining it critically. Audiotape and cassette programs have been developed to exploit this capacity.

Experimental results have been somewhat contradictory, with some subjects showing definite improvement in learning and others none. Most positive results apparently occur in semisleep or light sleep conditions ("semisomnolent states") and least positive results in states of deep sleep. Individual differences in sleep learning would probably be the result of individual differences in the length of these semisleep conditions. In this sense, it has most of the characteristics of suggestion and hypnosis. There is the capacity to receive input, but without evaluation. Therefore, unless the suggestion blatantly defies one's basic values, it is accepted.

One of the difficulties in evaluating sleep learning is that the definitions of sleep (any level of sleep) are so inconsistent. The situation is further complicated by the use of nonstandardized stimuli. Yet another variable is the use of tape recordings versus direct voice instruction. Sleep learning is, therefore, a very ambiguous term. To date there appears to have been no definitive experimentation or research on this topic.

LEARNING THEORIES
SLEEP

W. E. GREGORY

SLEEP TREATMENT

The specialized field of sleep treatment includes the application of pharmacology, psychotherapy, educational methods and electrosleep. Perhaps the major sleep disorder encountered is insomnia. The insomniac has difficulty in falling and/or remaining asleep and thus lacks sufficient sleep. Severity varies, but insomniacs usually show an elevated incidence of depression as measured on the Minnesota Multiphasic Personality Inventory (MMPI) scale, and are more often middle-aged and female. Pharmacological treatments include hypnotic and psychotropic drugs. The most effective psychotherapy interventions are active and direct rather than psychodynamic.

Narcolepsy and hypersomnia are conditions of excessive sleep. Antidepressants and dietary considerations are recommended for both disorders. Psychotherapy may also be of benefit since there is evidence of stress-related narcoleptic attacks.

Bruxism refers to teeth grinding during sleep. It can damage dental structures, is seen more frequently in females, can occur in response to life stress, and is associated with Stage 2 sleep. Hypnosis, electromyograph biofeedback, and a variety of behavioral interventions are used in treatment. Drug treatment is secondary and emphasizes muscle relaxants.

Sleep apnea is a potentially dangerous respiratory disturbance that involves a blockage of the upper airway and is frequently due to a loss of tonus of the pharyngeal constrictors with a resulting tendency of the tongue to relapse. The most extreme cases occur during rapid eye-movement (REM) sleep. Treatments include pharmacological and mechanical methods designed to regulate oxygen usage.

Webb and Cartwright have listed an entire class of sleep disorders that are often associated with childhood and show clear developmental peaks. They include sleepwalking, night terrors, nightmares, and enuresis. These disorders are usually outgrown, but some may persist into adulthood. They are associated with slow-wave sleep, and enuresis and sleepwalking are seen more in males. When a disorder is severe, Stage 4 suppressant drugs are used. Supportive psychotherapy can also benefit the child with enuresis as well as the parents. Sleep treatment methods have also enjoyed success in the adjunctive treatment of psychiatric and neurological disorders, internal medicine conditions, and other pathological conditions.

SLEEP DISORDERS

W. KARLE
J. BINDER

SLEEPER EFFECT

A sleeper effect in persuasion is a delayed increase in the impact of a persuasive message. It occurs when a communication shows no immediate persuasive effects, but, after a period of time, the recipient of the communication becomes more favorable toward the position advocated by the message. As a pattern of data, the sleeper effect is opposite to the typical finding that experimentally induced opinion change dissipates over time.

The first documented sleeper effects—although they were not termed that at the time—were obtained in studies conducted by Peterson and Thurstone and by Lewin. The Peterson and Thurstone study found that a film titled *Four Sons* proved to more effective in promoting pro-German attitudes after a 6-month delay than immediately after being shown to a group of Genoa, Illinois, high school students. They speculated that since Genoa did not have a movie theater at the time, their experiment created considerable discussion, which was responsible for the delayed opinion change. In the Lewin study, housewives were led in a discussion of the importance of serving nutritional foods (milk, orange juice, and cod liver oil) as part of the war effort. The results showed that more housewives served these foods 4 weeks after compared with 2 weeks after the discussion.

The term *sleeper effect* was first used by Hovland, Lumsdaine, and Sheffield to describe opinion change produced by the U.S. Army's *Why We Fight* films used during World War II. Specifically, Hovland and coworkers tested the effects of the film *The Battle of Britain* on U.S. Army recruits' confidence in the fighting ability of their British allies. They found that when the effect of this film was assessed 9 weeks after it was shown, some of the opinion items showed significantly more improvement in regard for the British than had been apparent at an earlier assessment that was given just 5 days after the film.

Although Hovland and coworkers proposed four explanations for their sleeper effect, it was their "source forgetting" interpretation, or what later was termed the dissociation discounting cue hypothesis, that set the stage for future sleeper effect research. According to a dissociation hypothesis, a sleeper effect occurs when a persuasive message is presented with a discounting cue (such as a low credible source or a counterargument). Just after receiving the message, the recipient recalls both message and discounting cue (i.e., both are associated in memory together), resulting in little or no opinion change. After a delay, as the association between message and discounting cue weakens, the recipient may "remember what was said without thinking about who said it." In other words, a sleeper effect occurs because of a spontaneous dissociation of a message and a discounting cue over time. Source information may be recalled, but it is not readily associated with the message content when opinions are queried.

Hovland and Weiss provided the first direct test of the dissociation hypothesis. Subjects received persuasive messages on such issues as the use of antihistamine drugs and the building of atomic submarines. These messages were attributed to either a trustworthy or an untrustworthy source. The results showed an increase in the percentage of people agreeing with the message given by the untrustworthy source 4 weeks after the presentation compared with immediately after the message was received. The sleeper effect was discussed in almost every social psychology textbook of the time, appeared in related literatures (such as marketing, communications, public opinion, and sociology), and even obtained some popular notoriety as a lay idiom.

However, in 1974, Gillig and Greenwald published a series of seven studies that would prove to be disconcerting for believers in the sleeper effect and the dissociation hypothesis. In their studies, more than 600 subjects received messages on such topics as the use of penicillin, medical checkups, and vitamin C. As in the Hovland and Weiss research, these messages were attributed to a low-credible source (a "nature" therapist). Unlike the Hovland and Weiss study, the results revealed no indication that a sleeper effect had occurred. Gillig and Greenwald were not alone in having difficulty producing a reliable sleeper effect. Other studies paired a discounting cue with an effective message and failed to produce a sleeper effect.

Is the sleeper effect a reliable phenomenon? Two sets of studies, one set by Gruder, Cook, Hennigan, Flay, Alessis, and Halamaj and one set by Pratkanis, Greenwald, Leippe, and Baumgardner, have answered yes and have specified one set of empirical conditions needed for producing a sleeper effect. In both the Gruder and coworkers' and Pratkanis and associates' studies, reliable sleeper effects were obtained when (a) message recipients were induced to pay attention to message content by noting the important arguments in the message, (b) the discounting cue came after the message, and (c) message recipients rated the credibility of the message source immediately after receiving the message and cue. For example, in a study conducted by Gruder and coworkers and replicated by Pratkanis and associates, subjects read a message arguing against the 4-day work week. As they read the message, subjects underlined the important arguments. After reading the message, subjects received a discounting cue stating that the previous message is false and then rated the trustworthiness of the source of the message. This set of procedures resulted in a sleeper effect—subjects were more opposed to the 4-day work week 6 weeks after (compared with immediately after) receiving the message.

The procedures developed by Gruder and coworkers and by Pratkanis and associates for reliably producing a sleeper effect are sufficiently different from earlier studies such as those conducted by Hovland and Weiss to warrant a new interpretation of the sleeper effect. As a replacement for the dissociation hypothesis, Pratkanis and coworkers proposed a differential decay interpretation. A sleeper effect occurs when (a) the impact of the message decays more slowly than the impact of the discounting cue and (b) the information from the message and discounting cue is not immediately integrated to form an attitude (and thus the discounting cue is already dissociated from message content). The procedures employed in the Gruder and coworkers' and Pratkanis and associates' studies are likely to produce these conditions; underlining important arguments, for example, strengthens the persistence of impact of the message, whereas presenting the cue after the message limits the message recipients' ability to think about the materials and integrate the content of message and discounting cue.

Ironically, although the earliest sleeper effects were obtained in field settings, the set of procedures for obtaining a sleeper effect identified by Gruder and associates and by Pratkanis and coworkers are not likely to occur with high frequency in everyday life. This does not diminish the theoretical importance of this research; however, it does raise the question of whether there are other ways of obtaining sleeper effects besides with procedures based on the forgetting of source hypotheses. Researchers have suggested the following techniques for producing sleeper effects: (a) delayed reaction to a fear-arousing message; (b) delayed insight into the implications of a message; (c) leveling and sharpening of a persuasive message over time; (d) dissipation of the effects of forewarning of persuasive intent; (e) group discussion of a message after a delay; (f) the dissipation of reactance induced by a message; (g) delayed internalization of the values of a message; (h) wearing off of initial annoyance with a negative or tedious message; (i) delayed acceptance of an ego-attacking message; and (j) delayed impact of minority influence.

**COGNITIVE ABILITIES
CONTEXTUAL ASSOCIATION
FORGETTING
IMPLICIT LEARNING
MEMORY RETRIEVAL PROCESSES**

A. R. Pratkanis

SMALL GROUP THERAPIES

In *Joining together: Group theory and group skills,* David Johnson and Frank Johnson provide a combined set of criteria to define a small group as:

Two or more persons who are interacting with one another; a social unit who view themselves as belonging to group; a collection of persons who are interdependent; a collection of individuals who join together to achieve a common goal or task; a collection of individuals who are all trying to satisfy some personal need through their joint associations; several persons who share norms concerning matters of common interest and participate in a system of interlocking roles; several persons who influence each other; and a collection of individuals who find the group rewarding.

Johnson and Johnson (1982) define a group as two or more individuals in face-to-face interaction, each aware of his or her membership in the group, each aware of the others who belong to the group, and each aware of their positive interdependence as they strive to achieve mutual goals.

In *Groups: Process and practice,* Gerald Corey and Marianne Schneider Corey present an overview of several types of therapeutic groups. In this sense, therapeutic groups have far broader purpose than being restricted to the treatment of emotional and behavioral disorder. Instead, such groups have the broad purpose of increasing people's knowledge of themselves and others, helping people to clarify the changes they most want to make in their daily lives, and giving people some of the basic tools needed to make these desired changes. By interacting with others in a therapeutic group in a climate of trust, participants are afforded the opportunity to experiment with new behaviors and to receive honest feedback from others in the group concerning the effects of their behavior. There are many types of specific therapeutic groups, a few of which are T-groups (or laboratory-training groups), encounter groups, personal growth groups, self-help groups, and many specific-focus groups. There are also groups composed of children, groups composed of adolescents, groups for various stages of adult development, and groups for meeting the concerns of the elderly. Kjell Erik Rudestam describes a variety of experiential groups, such as T-groups, encounter groups, Gestalt groups, psychodrama, body-therapy groups, dance therapy, art therapy, theme-centered groups, transactional analysis, and skill-training groups.

**GROUP PSYCHOTHERAPY
T-GROUPS**

G. Corey

SMALL-SAMPLE STATISTICS

Small-sample statistics, or "small-*n*" statistics, as it is often called, was given birth formally by W. S. Gosset's publication in the first decade of the twentieth century in which he posited the famous student's *t*-distribution. Gosset was then a statistician working at the Guiness Brewery in the United Kingdom. One of his duties was to analyze successive samples from barrels of freshly brewed stout. For a reason he never fully explained, he experimented with the idea of substantially reducing the number of samplings to be taken from the very large number of barrels of stout available at the brewery. This led to his postulation of the *t*-distribution. He published the results of his experiment in sampling with the *t*-distribution for small samples compared with the *z*-distribution (normal distribution) anonymously under the pseudonym "Student."

THE *t*-DISTRIBUTION

The *t*-distribution theory, like the *z*-distribution theory, applies to the testing of the null hypothesis that two samples are merely random ones selected from the same population; therefore, the calculated statistics (e.g., mean and standard deviation) are unbiased estimates of the population parameters. However, unlike *z,* the *t*-distribution theory for small samples does not require *a priori* knowledge or precise estimates of the population mean and standard deviation as is true for the *z*-distribution. Furthermore, although testing the mean difference between two large samples for statistical significance requires the underlying assumption that the population measures are normally distributed, the *t*-distribution theory does not require assumptions regarding parameters.

It is well known that normally distributed measures follow a single curve, the Gaussian curve, that satisfies the following equation:

$$y = \frac{N}{\sigma \sqrt{2\pi}} e^{-1/2 z^2}$$

In the *t*-distribution, a whole family of curves is represented by the following equation:

$$y = \frac{\Gamma\left(\dfrac{n+1}{2}\right)}{\Gamma\left(\dfrac{n}{2}\right)\sqrt{n\pi}}\left(1 + \frac{t^2}{n}\right)^{-(n+1)/2}$$

This is because the equation for *t* includes the σ function, which in mathematics signifies that a different curve satisfies the equation as *n* varies.

DEGREES OF FREEDOM

In the equation for *t*, *n* signifies degrees of freedom (df) involved in the estimate of the population variance (S^2), which is the second moment of any moment-generating function, such as the equation for the *t*-distribution. Degrees of freedom as applied in statistics refers to how many measures in the analysis are free to vary. In the *t*-distribution, one of the deviations from the sample mean is always fixed, because the sum of all of the deviations from the sample mean must equal zero. This fact has an effect on the sum of squares in calculating the sample variance as an unbiased estimate of the parameter S^2 and leads to df being equal to the number of measures minus one for each sample. Hence, in the development of the formulas and procedures for calculating the t-statistic in testing the null hypothesis, there are $n - 2$ degrees of freedom.

THE F-DISTRIBUTION

In the t-test, the null hypothesis to be tested is that *two* samples were drawn from the same population at random or randomly from *two* different populations with the same variance. What if there are more than two groups present in the analysis? This question began to be answered within two decades after Gosset developed the t-distribution. Two of the most prominent statisticians of the twentieth century were responsible for providing the answer. One was the great British statistician Sir R. A. Fisher, who proposed the first theoretical formulations that led to the development of the F-distribution and whose works in small-sample theory, following Gosset, were published in the mid-1920s (Fisher, 1925). The other was G. W. Snedecor, one of the first American statisticians, who developed the ratio of two variance estimates as a means of comparing two independent samples, irrespective of size. He named this ratio the F-ratio, in honor of Fisher. From these developments followed the postulation of the F-distribution as a distribution of the ratio of two χ^2 statistics, each in regard to their respective degrees of freedom:

$$ F = \frac{\dfrac{X_1^2}{df_1}}{\dfrac{X_2^2}{df_2}} $$

From this emerged the classic works of Fisher known as *the analysis of variance*, an explicitly small-sample statistical methodology.

The sampling distribution of F, with its dual $n = $ df equations is as follows.

$$ y = \frac{\Gamma\left(\dfrac{n_1 + n_2}{2}\right) n_1 n_1/2 n_2 n_2/2}{\Gamma\left(\dfrac{n_1}{2}\right)\left(\dfrac{n_2}{2}\right)} \times \frac{F(n_1 - 2)/2}{\left(n_1 F + n_2\right)(n_1 + n_2)/2} $$

Again, as in the case of t, it can be seen that there is a family of distributions that satisfies the equation for F. In this case, however, there are two separate degrees of freedom that become involved in the analysis; one for the numerator and one for the denominator in the F-ratio.

TABLES FOR EVALUATING THE t- AND F-STATISTICS

For large-sample statistics, normally only one table is necessary for reference in testing the null hypothesis. That table is the one involving the normal deviate, z, and showing the area under the normal curve between any two z-points on the abscissa. Tables for the t and F distributions, however, are necessarily complex, because these tables are based on multiple distributions that result from varying degrees of freedom. Although t and F are both frequency distributions, as is the normal distribution for large samples, they differ with respect to the four moments that describe them. The t-distribution, for example, is symmetrical (note the t^2 in its equation) for all df, but becomes increasingly leptokurtic as sample size decreases. Leptokurtic curves tend to be less asymptotic, (i.e., be higher at the tails) than mesokurtic curves such as the normal curve. This difference leads to marked discrepancies between the t and z points on the abscissa. For 5 df, the two-tailed α level of $p = 0.5$ is 2.57 for t, whereas for z it is 1.96. Hence, the t of 2.57 indicates statistical significance at the 5% level. However, for the normal curve, a z of 2.57 (2.58) would indicate statistical significance at the 1% level. Similar comparisons can be made with the F-distribution, because t equals F when the number of samples is two.

WHAT CONSTITUTES A "SMALL" SAMPLE?

The question has been raised of what size a sample must be to be considered small. There cannot be a definite answer to this question. However, it is conventionally accepted that the cutoff between a small and a large sample is set at df = 30. The reason for this somewhat arbitrary judgment stems from the comparison between the student t and the normal distributions. As noted earlier, the discrepancies between t and z tend to increase as df decreases, but decrease as df increases. In fact, t begins to approach z quite closely long before it reaches its limit at df = infinity when $t = z$. Inspection of tabled t-ratios reveals that the approximation becomes rather rapid at and beyond df = 30. The comparative values for t and z are, respectively: for a p of .05, 2.04 and 1.96; for a p of .01, 2.75 and 2.58; and for a p of .001, 3.65 and 3.29.

OTHER SMALL-SAMPLE STATISTICS

The t-test and the analysis of variance (F-test) statistical methodologies are explicitly designed for use with small samples, although they are applicable to large samples as well. There are, however, many other statistical methods applicable to small samples and frequently used for such purposes. These are the so-called nonparametric or distribution-free methods. Basically, the statistics involved in these methodologies were designed for use with measures that do not fit the definition of either ratio or interval of the measurement scales. Rather, they are either ordinal (rank) or nominal measures. For nonparametric statistics, no assumptions are made regarding parameters, especially that relating to variance estimates, because there is no variance in ordinal or nominal scales. For this reason, such statistical methods are used for ratio and interval scale measures when the samples are small and there is the likelihood that the underlying assumptions for large-sample statistics are being violated. Among such statistics that can be appropriately applied to small samples are Fisher's exact probability test; Friedman's ANOVA (2-group) for ranked data; Kendall's tau correlation method for ranked data; Kendall's coefficient (W) of concordance method; Kruskal–Wallis H-test for ranked data in single-group ANOVA; Mann–Whitney U-test; median test; sign test; Spearman's rho correlation method for ranks; and Wilcoxon's t-test.

PROBABILITY
STATISTICAL INFERENCE
VARIABLES IN RESEARCH

P. F. Merenda

SMOKING BEHAVIOR

The smoking of tobacco, particularly of cigarettes, has been the focus of considerable scientific study since the 1960s. Interest in tobacco, however, spans more than 400 years.

Although considerable public attention to the reports of dangerous aspects of cigarette smoking has apparently resulted in a slight decrease in per capita cigarette consumption in the United States, the tobacco consumed on a worldwide basis has increased considerably. This continued widespread use of cigarettes has raised many complex questions about the motivations for smoking, both in terms of initiation and maintenance of the habit, as well as its cessation.

INITIATION

Beginning the cigarette smoking habit is largely a phenomenon of adolescence in Western society. Most people who initiate the habit do so by age 20 years, but few report that the initial effect is enjoyable. Smoking was once traditionally a male venture, but female adolescents now smoke about as much as males. However, there does seem to be a steadily decreasing trend in the United States in the percentage of adolescents who initiate smoking.

Although there is almost certainly a very large number of personal reasons why certain individuals begin smoking and others do not, there are several fairly consistently observed influences. For example, starting to smoke seems to occur with greater frequency and earlier in lower socioeconomic settings and to be inversely related to academic performance. Although the strong influence of family smoking has been noted consistently, the exact nature of this influence is poorly defined.

One of the most important influences on smoking in adolescents appears to be peer pressure. Stress relief, tranquilization, or attempts to curb nervousness also have been suggested as important motives for the initiation of smoking behavior. There is also some evidence that early initiators tend to be more outgoing and arousal seeking than those who do not begin smoking. However, in spite of attempts to identify more completely the characteristics of initiators, the data in this area are unclear and inconsistent.

MAINTENANCE

The difficulties in understanding continuation of smoking appear to stem, at least in part, from its complex effects on both psychological and physiological levels.

On a physiological level, nicotine entering the bloodstream produces a number of short-term effects—most of them sympathomimetic. Effects on the circulatory system include increases in heart rate, blood pressure, heart stroke volume, and blood flow. Nicotine intake also leads to elevated blood glucose levels and dilation of blood vessels. The levels of several central nervous system chemicals (e.g., norepinephrine, serotonin, acetylcholine) also may be affected by nicotine, as are minor changes in electroencephalographic activity.

One of the most perplexing issues is that, although nicotine ingestion seems to act as a stimulant, most smokers consistently report a subjective relaxation or "tranquilizing" effect. Other reported positive subjective effects of smoking are feeling "comfort in social situations" and "flavor." In addition, there is evidence that smoking may have a positive effect on the performance of certain learning tasks and specific skills. However, how these and other apparent effects of smoking influence maintenance of the habit is far from clear.

Leventhal and Avis analyzed smoking behavior and reported seven factors associated with this habit: anxiety, addiction, fiddling, stimulation, social reward, pleasure/taste, and habit. Unfortunately, all of the classification schemes suffer from a lack of consistent empirical tests to support the categories as well as reliable and valid scaling to enable researchers to design experiments in which meaningful aggregations of data can be analyzed.

Because any frequently occurring behavior logically must have some sort of reward value, most researchers who have considered the motivational aspects of smoking conceive of the habit as serving a reinforcing role in one way or another. Various researchers have emphasized physiological, psychosocial, or even genetically related reinforcement functions.

Several researchers who have emphasized the importance of physiological reinforcement have taken the view that such reinforcement is mediated by "addiction." Addiction is usually defined by the presence of highly uncomfortable or debilitating symptoms and signs when the organism is deprived of the supposed addictive substance. However, the predictability of physiological and psychological reactions to smoking cessation is not high.

QUITTING SMOKING

Efforts to quit smoking are reflected in a variety of different techniques, the most frequent of which is probably a self-motivated decision to drop the habit. There are some data that suggest that quitting "cold turkey" may be a highly efficient method. Other methods of quitting include oral ingestion of nicotine, hypnosis, individual or group psychotherapy, and a variety of behavior modification techniques.

Regardless of method, and although no firm figures are available, the most thoughtful estimates suggest that between 10 and 25% of smokers are able to quit for long periods of time or permanently. In general, there has been little success in differentiating successful quitters from those who cannot or do not quit smoking. However, heavier smokers and those experiencing more stressful lives may have more difficulty.

ADDICTIVE PROCESSES
SELF-CONTROL

T. H. BLAU

SOCIAL CASEWORK

Social casework is the counseling method employed by the social work profession to assist individuals and families troubled by biopsychosocial problems. Casework consists of strategies for social reform and techniques of clinical practice. This method originated in charity organization societies of England and the United States during the late 1870s. Academicians, including G. Stanley Hall, were associated with the movement, and their ideas contributed to a new scientific philanthropy.

DEVELOPMENT OF THE CASEWORK METHOD

Mary Richmond's book *Social diagnosis,* published in 1917, reflected the spirit of the times by incorporating many concepts from the medical model. This influential text emphasized the need for social reform, along with the systematic collection of data on people's behavior and the assessment of facts to uncover the causes of social ills and their treatment.

The infusion of Freudian psychoanalytic concepts into casework theory and practice in the 1920s and 1930s directed caseworkers' attentions to individual processes and behavior within a framework of study, diagnosis, and treatment. This event diluted social work's traditional concern with environmental issues and social action.

Social casework was further influenced by various writings during the 1940s and 1950s. Gordon Hamilton focused on the connections between individual behavior and social situations, providing a psychosocial perspective. Another major theme was the active involvement of the client in the change process.

Helen Perlman presented a model of practice that gave prominence to client social roles, and the stages of the problem-solving process, based on the work of John Dewey. Casework practice, therefore, increasingly blended social reform with contributions from social science and concepts from psychoanalytic theory. Meanwhile, this theory had moved from a psychology of the id to an ego psychology.

CASEWORK AS A PROFESSIONAL DESIGNATION

The renewed concern with poverty and environmental issues during the 1960s and 1970s raised serious questions about casework's relevance and effectiveness. Fischer's disputed conclusion that casework was ineffective precipitated a major self-examination within the social work profession that resulted in a reconceptualization of casework as a professional rather than a methodological designation.

CURRENT APPROACHES TO CASEWORK

Most contemporary caseworkers integrate the functions of clinician, environmental change agent, and broker/advocate. The clinician role is often most prominent. The majority pattern their practice on one or more of the following approaches.

Psychosocial Treatment

This view emphasizes assessment, diagnosis, and treatment based on Freudian psychoanalytic theory, augmented by newer concepts related to communications and systems theory, family therapy, crisis intervention, and planned short-term treatment.

Family Therapy

Working with families is an important part of a caseworker's activity. Interventions are directed at bringing about change in the total family. Family therapy developed around a synthesis of ideas from psychoanalysis and theoretical constructs about communication, homeostasis, social systems, and roles. Many different models of family therapy are used, including experiential, structural, and behavioral approaches.

Crisis Intervention

Caseworkers often encounter clients in crisis who require short-term assistance. Crisis intervention is derived from studies of people in natural and human-generated disasters. A state of crisis is not viewed as an illness or pathology, but as an opportunity to promote growth in the client. This approach employs strategies and techniques from traditional and newer models of casework. However, the distinctive aspect is the focus on limited goals rather than attempts at deep personality change or other time-consuming activity.

Behavioral Approach

Social workers have adopted behavioral methods and procedures from psychology in response to the need for an empirically based approach to practice. Educators and practitioners have applied behavioral techniques in a variety of practice settings. The use of single-subject research designs and cognitive procedures has been of particular interest to the profession.

Task-Centered Practice

Based on casework research that established the greater effectiveness of short-term treatment, this approach was originally viewed as an overall structure that could employ procedures from a number of casework models. However, major features, such as specifying client tasks to be accomplished and the careful attention to outcome, are compatible with the behavioral approach.

Eclectic Casework

After proclaiming the ineffectiveness of the traditional model of practice, Fischer designed what he termed the *eclectic approach* to casework. Fischer's approach utilizes principles and procedures demonstrated by empirical evidence to lead to successful outcomes for clients. The four major components of eclectic casework are as follows: (a) structured procedures, such as the use of contracts, setting time limits, and planning and setting goals; (b) behavior modification techniques, including modeling, reinforcement, and systematic desensitization; (c) cognitive procedures aimed at correcting "faulty" thinking; and (d) core conditions of helping—therapist empathy, warmth, and genuineness.

The Life Model of Social Work Practice

The most recent addition to casework is the life model based on an ecological perspective. Carol Germain and Alex Gitterman developed this approach to be more suited to the broad purpose of social work rather than the more clinically oriented models. Their ecological perspective emphasizes the reciprocal relationship between organisms and their surroundings, as well as the ecosystem. The life model is directed to strengthening people's adaptive capacities and influencing their social settings.

This model provides the most comprehensive view to date of the person and environment as an integrated system. However, no original techniques have been developed to implement the particular perspective of the life model.

The rapid development of new casework approaches in recent years supports the view that a significant change is taking place in social work. The major feature of this change is the adoption of scientifically based approaches to practice.

CRISIS INTERVENTION
PSYCHIATRIC SOCIAL WORK

A. J. VATTANO

SOCIAL CLASS

All known societies have some type of stratification system that represents the hierarchical arrangement of status, prestige, resources, privileges, and power within the society. Social classes are the relatively homogeneous groupings that share similar levels of status and resources in the stratification system. Each class tends to develop its own ideology and social norms. As a result, social classes may differ on characteristics ranging from parenting style to political ideas. These differences between social classes make them of interest to psychologists.

DEFINITIONS

A number of interrelated terms can be employed in analyzing a social stratification system, which refers to the status hierarchy of the society. Social status is the prestige an individual has in a social system. It can be either achieved by the individual's effort or ascribed on the basis of who the individual is, and it is connected with the social role the individual possesses within the society. Each social role has rights, duties, and responsibilities. These social roles are either offered by the society or created by the individual. Most social roles have a reciprocal role, for example, doctor–patient, parent–child, and salesclerk–shopper. The social structure is made up of those interrelated roles that are necessary to carry out the work of the social system. Social norms are the rules for appropriate and inappropriate behavior held by the members of the society. Socialization involves training children into the roles and norms of the society. Status attainment refers to activities that confer status, such as education, marriage, and occupation. Social classes, as distinct from social castes, have permeable boundaries. Social mobility involves movement up and down the status hierarchy. Scholars who hold to the inevitability of systems of social stratification in human society can point to its presence within other animal species.

THEORIES OF SOCIAL CLASS

In the nineteenth century, Karl Marx offered a simple view of social classes now rejected as inadequate by social scientists. The single dimension he employed was economic structure. Society was divided into two classes—the owners of production and the workers they employ. Marx further held that cultural factors are determined by social class, for example, class ideologies. Max Weber offered a counterview of social stratification based on class, status, and party (power). He suggested that ideas, such as religion, could affect social class.

Emile Durkheim and other functionalists looked at society as a complex system of interrelated roles. To fill those roles, society must motivate its citizens by conferring status or prestige on the individuals' roles. Social analysts who hold this view are labeled structural–functionalists because of their emphasis on the functional aspects of social structure. They believe social stratification to be inevitable and basically good. Critics have suggested that the structural–functional position favors social stability over social change and that it does not include a full appreciation for the positive benefits of conflict.

MEASUREMENT OF SOCIAL CLASS

Individuals higher in the stratification systems have higher status, or prestige, and greater access to the rewards of society. Because of this, consumer items are often taken to be indicators of social class. However, the prestige component of social class is also important, and is most frequently tied to occupation. Frequently, social class is not treated as a categorical variable, but as a continuous variable labeled "socioeconomic status" and consisting of the weighted scores of education, occupational prestige, and income. In other cases, social class is treated as a dichotomous variable and the working class is compared with the middle class. Some writers have stated that social class is not a true psychological variable but is instead a "carrier variable" only loosely associated with true psychological variables. Within-class variances can be very great.

Correlates of Social Class

Warner and his colleagues located five social classes ranging from "upper-upper" to "lower-lower." Social class differences included attitudes, family interaction, and community involvements. Over the years social class differences have been found in variables ranging from marital adjustment to parenting styles to self-esteem to social and political attitudes. Cantril analyzed 13 different nations and found cross-cultural evidence of a positive relationship between personal happiness and education and income. Although analyzed at the level of the small group, social status has been found to affect interpersonal behavior. High-status individuals tend to speak more and are listened to more often.

In the Midtown Manhattan study, Srole and his colleagues found that the lower the socioeconomic level of their respondents, the greater the prevalence of psychological disturbance and the more severe the disturbance. Two explanations have been offered. The downward drift hypothesis suggests that disturbed individuals are not able to maintain higher status positions and slowly drift down. A second hypothesis suggests that the difficulty of living in the lower social status positions of society creates a higher level of stress, which in turn manifests itself in psychological disturbance.

Socioeconomic status is positively correlated with intelligence and the correlation is higher for adults than for children. R. J. Hernnstein has argued that because of the inheritability of mental abilities and the degree to which success is dependent on those abilities, social standing will increasingly be based on inherited abilities. He further argues that to the extent that environmental differences are minimized by the society, inherited characteristics will become more important.

B. Bernstein suggested that the social classes can be distinguished by how they use the language. Two linguistic forms are used: The middle class uses an "elaborated" code characterized by complex syntax. In contrast, the working class was thought to use a "restricted" code based on simple sentence structure and concreteness of expression.

Middle class mothers tend to hold values supporting curiosity and self-control in their children, whereas working class mothers tend to value obedience. These conditions are thought to favor the development of more cognitive complexity by middle class individuals.

Some researchers have argued that individuals hold so many different social statuses that it is not meaningful to talk about one social status. An individual who has high ascribed status (e.g., white Anglo-Saxon Protestant) and low achieved status (e.g., occupational prestige) tends to have more nervousness, rapid heartbeat, and shortness of breath than does a status-consistent person.

ENVIRONMENTAL PSYCHOLOGY
GROUP STRUCTURE

E. E. Filsinger

SOCIAL CLIMATE RESEARCH

In two experimental "social climate" experiments conducted by Ronald Lippitt and Ralph White under the supervision of Kurt Lewin, adult leaders of clubs of children behaved in three different ways, called autocratic, democratic, and laissez-faire. "Autocratic" implies a high degree of control by the leader without much freedom by the members or participation by them in group decisions. Both "democratic" and "laissez-faire" imply a low degree of control by the leader, but democratic is distinguished from laissez-faire by the fact that the leader of the former type is active in stimulating group discussion and group decisions, while in the laissez-faire pattern the leader plays a passive hands-off role of providing resources and a friendly supportive presence.

The data on leader behavior quantified the leader behavior comparisons and differentiated them on the basis of number of orders given, the number of disrupting commands, the type of criticisms, the number of guiding suggestions, the number of extending knowledge comments, the amount of stimulation of self-guidance, the pattern of praise and approval, and the number of fact-oriented comments.

The findings with reference to the impact of the different leadership roles have been summarized as follows:

1. *Laissez-faire was not the same as democracy.* There was less work done and it was of poorer quality. There was more time spent in disorganized horseplay and more discontent expressed about the meetings. In the postsession interviews, the boys expressed a preference for their democratic leader as compared with their laissez-faire leader.

2. *Democracy can be efficient.* The quantity of work done in the submissive response to autocracy was somewhat greater, but the originality of the work was greater in the democratic group situations. Also, the work motivation was stronger in the democratic situations as shown by the continuity of the group's behavior in the experimental situations when the leaders left the room.

3. *Autocracy can create open hostility and aggression.* This includes aggression toward scapegoats. In two of the autocratic groups, the members showed more assertive and hostile interpersonal behavior, and made more demands for attention from the authority figure. There was a higher frequency of scapegoat behavior and a pattern of destruction of their own property and creations.

4. *Autocracy can also create discontent that does not appear on the surface.* Four members dropped out of groups and all of them did so during autocratic club periods in which overt rebellion did not occur. Nineteen of the 20 boys preferred their democratic leader, and there was more discontent expressed in autocracy even when the general response in two of the groups was submissive rather than actively discontented.

5. *There was more dependence and less individuality in autocracy.* The observers coded more "submissive" and more "dependent" behavior. The content of the conversation was less varied and more confined to the immediate situation.

6. *There was more group-mindedness and friendliness in democracy.* The pronoun "I" was used relatively less frequently in the democratic group and the pronoun "we" more frequently. Spontaneous subgroupings were larger and lasted for longer periods. Friendly and group-minded remarks were quoted more frequently in the democratic atmosphere, as were mutual praise and friendly playfulness. In the democratic groups, the members showed a greater readiness to share property and to help each other.

A number of replications of these experiments in the U.S. culture have shown similar results. Perhaps the most extensive replications have been done in Japan by Misumi and his colleagues. On both tasks, the laissez-faire groups did the poorest work, but as between democracy and autocracy, the results depended on the nature of the task. In the more interesting task, the work done in democracy was superior; in the less interesting task, the work done in autocracy was superior.

In summarizing their findings and interpretations, White and Lippitt conclude that six basic psychological conditions foster and maintain a democratic social climate: (a) openmindedness to influence from others; (b) self-acceptance or self-confidence in initiating one's own contributions and expressing one's needs; (c) realism about the objective nature of the task and interpersonal situations; (d) freedom from status-mindedness; (e) fairness about equality of rights and opportunities; and (f) friendliness and good will in attitudes and actions toward others.

GROUP DYNAMICS
LEADERSHIP STYLES
TEAM PERFORMANCE

R. LIPPITT

SOCIAL COGNITION

The field of social cognition is concerned with the cognitive activity that mediates and accompanies social behavior. It provides an analysis of how stimulus information is initially encoded, organized (and transformed) in memory, and drawn on as the person moves through the social world.

Social cognition, which is neither a single theory nor a narrow empirical domain, refers instead to a particular conceptual level of analysis used in the joint explanation of human thought and social behavior. The level of analysis is molecular rather than molar. Theorists working within this orientation use "mental" constructs at the level of individual thoughts, categories, and concepts. These constructs are abstract enough to encompass a wide range of content domains (such as thoughts about people, traits, situations, animals, and works of art). Most researchers in this field, although mentalistic, do not restrict themselves to the study of "conscious" thought. The mental constructs are usually defined so as to leave open the question of consciousness.

Workers in the fields of cognitive psychology, psycholinguistics, and artificial intelligence became preoccupied with higher order cognitive processes, and interested in explaining complex types of human information processing, such as the comprehension and retention of stories, action sequences, and other thematically coherent stimulus ensembles.

The concept of a "schema" provided the initial meeting ground for the social and cognitive research groups. The elements of our cognitive world do not exist in some random, unrelated array. Rather, they are interassociated into higher order structures.

The schema concept was quite congenial to social psychologists because they already had been using a number of schema-like concepts. These included such terms as stereotype, norm, value, attitude, and implicit personality theory. Some workers in social cognition have developed taxonomies of schemas to aid in establishing conceptual similarities across different topics. Some of the categories proposed are person, role, event, trait, pictorial (or visual), and social group. Taxonomies have also been developed from the cognitive process point of view that classify schemas in terms of their conceptual properties.

INFORMATION-PROCESSING PERSPECTIVE

The social cognition approach views the human mind as an information-processing system. Information is received from the stimulus world, processed through the cognitive system, and drawn on when engaging in social behavior.

One stage of information-processing deals with the problems of encoding and organization.

A second information-processing topic area deals with the problem of cognitive retrieval. What determines the flow of thought, and how do we access prior information and inferences when engaging in social behavior?

There is also the problem of implicit retrieval that occurs in the case of more or less spontaneous social responses. A search for previously acquired information can be bypassed when a behaviorally relevant schema is available.

A third category of issues has to do with information integration. People often face situations for which they have no adequate schemas. Especially when people anticipate encountering such situations often in the future, it is in their interest to develop a new schema to deal with the kinds of variations found in this setting.

A fourth topic area is response selection. How do people survey their response alternatives, tacitly select one, and behaviorally implement it? Communication context and knowledge of the audience's point of view can affect how and when cognitive responses are transmitted.

UNRESOLVED ISSUES

Social cognition researchers have generally avoided the issue of how cognitive systems are energized. An allied concern is the role of cognitive systems in regulating motivational energies.

Social environments are exceedingly complex. The amount and diversity of information contained in a social interaction are enormous. How does the person arrive at a particular organizational mode? Does the mode fluctuate from one point in the conversation to another, and is it possible to encode (and/or store) the information in two or more ways simultaneously? This kind of question becomes salient when adopting the level of analysis characteristic of the social cognition perspective.

ATTENTION
COGNITIVE COMPLEXITY
CONTEXTUAL ASSOCIATIONS
IMPRESSION FORMATION
INFORMATION PROCESSING SOCIAL INFLUENCE THEORY

T. OSTROM

SOCIAL CONSTRUCTIONISM

Social constructionism is an account of knowledge-generating practices, scientific and otherwise. At this level, constructionist theory offers an orientation toward knowledge making in the psychological sciences, a standpoint at considerable variance with the empiricist tradition. At the same time, social constructionism contains the ingredients of a theory of human functioning; at this level, it offers an alternative to traditional views of individual and psychological processes. Constructionist premises also have been extended to a variety of practical domains, opening new departures in such fields as therapy, organizational management, and education.

SOCIAL CONSTRUCTION: ASSUMPTIONS AND ANTECEDENTS

Social constructionism is not wedded to a fixed set of principles. Rather, it is more properly considered as a continuously unfolding conversation in which various positions may be occupied, elaborated, or vacated as the dialogue proceeds. Several themes are typically located in writings that identify themselves as constructionist. It is typically assumed that accounts of the world—scientific and otherwise—are not dictated or determined in any principled way by what there is. Rather, the terms in which the world is understood are generally held to be social artifacts, products of historically situated interchanges among people. Thus the extent to which a given form of understanding prevails within a culture is not fundamentally dependent on the empirical validity of the perspective in question but rather on the vicissitudes of social process (e.g., communication, negotiation, communal conflict, rhetoric). This line of reasoning does not detract from the significance of various forms of cultural understanding. People's constructions of the world and self are essential to the broader practices of a culture, justifying, sustaining, and transforming various forms of conduct.

Although it has deep historical roots, contemporary social constructionism represents a convergence of several more recent movements within the social sciences and humanities. As philosophers grew increasingly discontented with attempts to ground empirical science in a set of foundational, or first, principles, the philosophy of science was gradually displaced by historical accounts of scientific practice. Kuhn and Feyerabend contributed to an expansion of inquiry into the communal bases of scientific knowledge claims. Historians of science were joined in this endeavor by sociologists of knowledge, ethnomethodologists, and scholars attempting to replace the deeply problematic presumptions of behavioral science with more interpretive or hermeneutic paradigms.

These inquiries also proved congenial in important respects, with a major evolution occurring in the literary and semiotic domains. Inspired by earlier writings of Saussure, Peirce, Wittgenstein, and others, literary theory turned from concerns with language as a means of representing the world (or the thoughts of an author), to language as a self-contained or self-referring system. In other words, the shift is from the object of the text to issues of intertextual relationship; genres through which objects are constructed; and the rhetorical conventions by which texts gain their sense of objectivity, rationality, or credibility. In the hands of theorists such as Jacques Derrida, that which is signified by the text is thereby deconstructed, replaced, as it were, by texts that gain their meaning only by an endless process of self-reference. For reader-response theorists, such as Stanley Fish, textual meaning is inherently social meaning. It is the interpretive community that enables textual strategies to gain legitimacy.

Simultaneous to the developments in social thought and literary theory, political events of the 1960s stimulated large numbers of scholars to reconsider the traditional scientific claims of value neutrality. With increasing degrees of sophistication and indignation, scholars influenced by critical school formulations demonstrated ways in which ordinary and unchallenged assumptions within the sciences lent themselves to unfair distributions of economic resources and political power. These concerns expanded exponentially as the feminist movement began to flourish, and inquiry mounted into the injurious implications of taken-for-granted assumptions embedded within theories, methods, and policies of the sciences. Scholars also became increasingly vocal over the ways in which social science assumptions carried racist values, championed selfish or narcissistic ways of life, or served as a means of subverting non-Western ways of life. For many such scholars, the works of Michel Foucault, which demonstrated the relationship between regimes of language and power relations, also proved pivotal. All of these endeavors demonstrated the extent to which accounts of the world are inseparable from broader social practices.

THE SOCIAL CONSTRUCTION OF KNOWLEDGE

The social constructionist views favored by this composite of developments has begun to furnish a replacement for traditional empiricist accounts of psychological science. In the process of this replacement, one may discriminate between two phases: deconstructionist and reconstructionist. In the former phase, pivotal assumptions of scientific rationality, along with bodies of empirically justified knowledge claims, are placed in question. Essentially, this work represents an elaboration and extension

of the early antifoundationalist arguments, now informed by the additional developments within the literary and critical domains. Thus an extensive body of literature has emerged, questioning existing commitments to scientific progress, empirical hypothesis testing, universal rationality, laws of human functioning, the impartiality of science, the exportation of Western scientific practices, and so on. Immersion in this literature alone, would lead to the conclusion that social constructionism is nihilistic in its aims. However, as many believe, the deconstructive process is only a necessary prolegomenon to a reconstructive enterprise.

Within the reconstructive phase, the chief focus is on ways in which scientific inquiry, informed by constructionist views, can more effectively serve the society of which it is a part. Although such issues are at the forefront of contemporary discussion, more a matter of debate than decision, several broad themes are apparent. When applied to the domain of psychological study, they suggest the following.

1. *Practical Empiricism.* Constructionists are critical of traditional claims that scientific knowledge, in the form of propositional networks, can yield logically derived predictions in a variety of practical settings. However, this is not to negate the possibility of practical prediction itself. Thus, for the constructionist the enormous array of empirical technologies are largely misused, serving primarily those who seek to sustain substantively empty theories within a community of scientific peers. In contrast, observational techniques, measuring devices, and statistical technologies can be used effectively to assess current conditions (e.g., cultural well-being, contours of conflict, homelessness), the efficacy of various programs (e.g., community shelters, job training, conservation), and to draw trend lines for deliberating the future (e.g., planning for day care needs, drug-counseling facilities, employment-retraining centers). Of course, the terms of such study would always be culturally constructed, but there is nothing about constructionism that demands the abandonment of intelligibilities (or ways of life) by virtue of recognizing their communally constituted character.

2. *Conceptual Innovation.* Although constructionism favors a shift of empirical efforts from the decontextualized setting of the laboratory to sites of practical activity, it also thrusts theoretical activity into a new and more significant role. For the constructionist, the traditional view that theories should provide accurate accounts of the world is placed in question. Rather, it is argued, language gains its meaning and significance from its function within relationships. Language is a major means by which relationships are carried out. Thus the theoretical language of psychology should be evaluated not in terms of verisimilitude but in terms of its contribution to cultural life. From this standpoint, the practical value of theoretical formulations does not await the drawing of derivative predictions; rather, as psychological discourse gains intelligibility within the culture (through education, the media, the mental health professions, and the like), it becomes a usable resource within the sphere of daily relationships. Thus scholarly work in psychology—in the form of innovative theorizing—may have enormous potential for the society. For as new theoretical lenses are made available, new options may open in problem domains of long standing. New ways of understanding conflict, of seeing the educational process, of appreciating group differences, and so on, may become available as a cultural resource. This is not to abandon empirical work at the level of scholarly inquiry. However, research procedures at this level primarily serve purposes of vivification; they give theoretical ideas—both descriptions and explanations—a sense of palpability. They enable others to see the world in particular terms.

3. *Valuative Reflection.* In the empiricist tradition, the primary criteria for critical assessment of scientific work were methodological. The chief question to be asked of a given formulation was whether it was a valid account of the phenomenon. For the constructionist, however, the crucial question to be asked of a theoretical formulation is how it can or will function within the broader society. What institutions and actions does the theory sustain, what is challenged by the formulation, and what new options are opened are all questions of paramount concern. To address such questions fully requires deliberation of a moral and political character. Does a given formulation sustain desirable or undesirable forms of cultural life? Does it undermine cherished institutions? Does it promote human welfare? Such questions necessarily move scientific deliberation from the realm of *is* to *ought*. From the constructionist standpoint, such deliberation should become a normal part of scientific training, and contributions to the dialogue should play a featured role in the books and journals of the field.

SOCIAL CONSTRUCTIONIST INQUIRY IN PSYCHOLOGY

Social constructionist views not only provide metatheory for the science of psychology but also are reasserted at the level of psychological theory itself. That is, in providing an account of the knowledge-making activities of scientists, they also offer a way of understanding patterns of human action more generally. Three active areas of inquiry are illustrative.

Major efforts are devoted to exploring the discursive construction of reality. Here investigators attempt to demonstrate the processes by which persons construct the world and self through language. Typically employing techniques of discourse analysis, many investigators explore patterns of existing construction (e.g., cultural assumptions about the developing child); the media construction of homosexuality; the public construction of acquired immunodeficiency syndrome (AIDS); or the available discourses for describing intelligence, the environment, or cultural conflict. Much of this research is used for purposes of generating social change. By elucidating common assumptions, investigators hope people may be emancipated from the taken for granted. In contrast, other investigators attempt to demonstrate the limits of our constructive frameworks. For example, Smedslund attempts to axiomatize cultural understandings of the mind, arguing that it is impossible for cultural participants—including scientific psychologists—to formulate an intelligible proposition that violates these assumptions. Still other scholars are concerned with the ways in which the cultural discourses and conversational positions are used to construct personal identity in ongoing relationships.

A second line of constructionist inquiry is into psychological processes themselves. However, rather than viewing such processes as universal and transhistorical, constructionists are more centrally concerned with individual functioning as it is socially constituted, both in history and culture. How is it that people come to account for their mental life in the ways they do and to perform in such a way that these constructions are made real to both self and others? Historical analysis thus attempts to reveal the ways in which psychological processes were constituted in previous eras and to assess the cultural conditions either favoring a given constitution of the mental world or rendering it dysfunctional. Such inquiry operates not only to enhance historical consciousness but also to unsettle comfortable assumptions of universality and psychological essentialism prevalent. Much the same end is achieved, as well, by inquiry into indigenous psychologies. Psychologically oriented anthropologists such as Katherine Lutz demonstrate "emotional patterns" in other cultures wholly unknown in the West, and explore the functions of these syndromes within the local cultural settings. Other investigators set out to explore the construction of the person within Western culture. For example, the work of Averill and colleagues elucidates the rules for performing emotions such as anger, love, and grief.

CONTROL THEORY
GEMEINSCHAFTGEFÜHL
HISTORY OF PSYCHOLOGY
LABELING THEORY
LOGICAL POSITIVISM

POSTMODERNISM
RATIONALISM
SOCIOMETRY
SYSTEMS THEORY

K. J. GERGEN

SOCIAL DESIRABILITY

Social desirability is the tendency for individuals to portray themselves in a generally favorable fashion. Within the field of psychological testing, the concept of social desirability has fueled heated debates for decades. Arguments have focused on the definition of social desirability, its pervasiveness, problems it presents for the interpretation of psychological tests, and methods for its control.

Social desirability has variously been defined as the tendency to give culturally sanctioned and approved responses, to provide socially desirable responses to statements in self-description, or to describe oneself in terms judged as desirable and to present oneself favorably. The emphasis is on a style of responding irrespective of the specific personality content measure intended to be measured by a psychological test. Consequently, a potential problem for a psychological test is whether an elevated score represents a high score on the test's content dimension or a greater tendency to present oneself favorably. To illustrate, does a high score on a certain measure of ambitiousness reflect the respondent's high level of ambitiousness or the respondent's tendency to answer items in terms of desirability? The possible existence of such ambiguous interpretations has led to a great deal of debate and research.

Research on measures of social desirability has led to the finding that there are two facets of social desirability. The first concerns the self and a belief in one's own ability. The second facet focuses on an orientation toward others and may represent either interpersonal sensitivity or deliberate impression management. It should be noted that individual tests designed to assess social desirability may measure either one or both of these facets.

Many researchers believe that self-report tests that have been developed without explicit attempts to minimize the influence of this stylistic responding will be saturated with social desirability. Consequently, any interpretations from such tests are ambiguous and suspect. In contrast to this objection is the belief that social desirability is itself a personality variable that may be a legitimate component of individual differences. For example, it might be argued that a strong belief in one's own abilities (i.e., social desirability) is a legitimate aspect of the concept of ambitiousness. This presents a problem: if social desirability is a component of many different constructs of personality and psychopathology (e.g., ambitiousness, friendliness, neatness), then these constructs are not truly and legitimately independent and should not be theorized, measured, or reported as such.

Methods have been proposed for coping with social desirability in self-report tests. First, a forced-choice response format could be built into a test. Options for any item should then be matched for social desirability. Second, test items could be selected that are more strongly representative of the psychological concept of interest than social desirability. This would involve a test-development strategy that used some form of item selection from a larger pool of test stimuli in which items have somehow been measured for appropriate content and inappropriate response bias (e.g., social desirability). Third, test instructions could be tailored to reduce the likelihood that test takers will respond in terms of social desirability. Possible instructions might include an emphasis on anonymity or a warning that inaccurate responses can be detected. Fourth, social desirability could be statistically removed from the score generated on the test. This would require the use of a social desirability scale whose score would then be used to correct the score for the psychological concept of interest.

R. R. HOLDEN

SOCIAL EQUALITY

The concept of social equality has had many meanings over the centuries. Social equality defined primarily from a political perspective focuses on rules of governance (who may vote, who may govern, by what rules leaders govern), while an economic focus describes processes that pertain to distribution of wealth (who has work opportunities, how economic resources are allocated). A psychological perspective focuses on rules that guide interpersonal relationships and status (who has value as a human being). Common constructs are used by the various perspectives, such as constructs of power, status, competition, cooperation, inferiority, and superiority, but these constructs have meanings that differ between the various points of view.

From a *psychological* point of view, the distinction needs to be made between equity, which refers to rules of allocation of rewards according to the extent of a person's effort or investment, and *social equality*. Social equality plays a central role in Adlerian theory. According to Adler and Dreikurs, without social equality and cooperation a win–lose "seesaw" pattern of competition occurs, with resultant feelings of inferiority that mar mental health and task performance. For Adler and Dreikurs, social equality refers to an ideal and intrinsic characteristic: Each human being has equality of value and worth. When social equality exists in an objective sense, democratic and cooperative human relationships are maximally possible. When individuals believe subjectively in social equality, they are more oriented to contributing to the human community and less likely to be preoccupied with personal prestige or with efforts to prove personal value.

Social equality does not mean identity, uniformity, or conformity. Gardner, like Adler and Dreikurs, distinguishes between equality of personal value and equality of performance. Gardner maintains that task performance and external attributes are not identical to the concept of social equality. As an ideal, social equality bears on questions of moral and ethical value concerning intrinsic human worth, dignity, and respect.

E. D. FERGUSON

SOCIAL EXCHANGE THEORY

Social exchange theory is based on the assumption that humans will form and sustain relationships if they believe that rewards they derive from such relationships will exceed costs. George Homans attempted to explain behavior, broadly defined as the outcome of interaction in which individuals trade or exchange resources. Although Homans derived his statement of modern exchange theory from behavioral psychology and microeconomics, analogous theories also are found in anthropology and political science. Although social exchange theory best explains interactions between two persons, the theory has also been extended to intergroup processes.

The five basic propositions of modern exchange theory were stated formally by Homans. He attempted to explain social behavior using basic notions of behavior originally developed by behavioral psychologists and neoclassic economists. The behaviorists' model of operant conditioning is based on the utilitarian principle that individuals will seek to maximize their pleasure and to avoid or minimize their pain. Individuals are expected to respond in predictable ways to rewards and punishments. Each interaction is an opportunity to exchange resources from which each participant attempts to receive resources of higher value than he or she has contributed or foregone. Generally speaking, social psychologists refer to things exchanged as resources. Although resources can be anything tangible or intangible, Foa and Foa have identified six classes of exchange resources: love, status, information, money, goods, and services. They further state that any resource falling into one of these six classes can be described with respect to one of two dimensions: particularism and concreteness. The particularism of resources is the extent to which its value depends on the particular person involved in the exchange. For example, an exchange of affection holds more value to a loved one than to a total stranger, although an exchange of money holds a more universal value. The second dimension, concreteness, refers to the degree to which the resource is tangible, such as a raise in salary as opposed to an increase in one's occupational status. From additional research, Foa and Foa found that particularistic resources tend to be exchanged for resources in the same class (e.g., love for love rather than love for money) but that less particularistic resources are commonly exchanged for resources in different classes. For example, money is often exchanged for goods or services.

Homans developed five general propositions concerning social behavior and the exchange of resources. Three of these propositions reflect the behavioral psychologists' model. The first proposition, directly derived from the model of operant conditioning, states: "for all actions taken by persons, the more often a particular action of a person is rewarded, the more likely the person is to perform that action." The second proposition acknowledges past learning: "If in the past the occurrence of a particular stimulus, or set of stimuli, has been the occasion on which a person's action has been rewarded, and the more similar the present stimuli are to the past ones, the more likely the person is to perform the action, or some similar action now." However, the third proposition states that "when a person's action does not receive the reward he expected, or receives punishment he did not expect, he will be angry; he becomes likely to perform aggressive behavior."

The last two propositions are more closely linked to economic theory. Microeconomic theory also is rooted in utilitarian traditions. One underlying assumption is that in the process of maximizing pleasure and avoiding pain, humans are utility maximizers. That is, "for each person each state of the world has a particular utility level, where utility is that which the person seeks to maximize through his actions." As such, the fourth proposition states that "the greater the profit a person receives as a result of his actions, the more likely he is to perform the action." In Homans's terms, profit is the net result of the benefits or rewards of an interaction less the costs associated with it.

The final proposition reflects the economic notion of declining marginal utility. Homans states that "the more often in the recent past a person has received a particular reward, the less valuable any further unit of that reward becomes for him." The idea is that one can become satiated with any given good such that additional units are no longer desired or hold the same value as they did initially.

Social exchange and economic exchange are further differentiated by the terms of the interaction. Whereas economic exchanges maintain explicit terms of the costs and benefits for each party involved, social exchanges are never explicit. In addition, the terms of the contract for an economic exchange are discussable, negotiable, and enforceable by law. For social exchanges, however, it would be considered in bad taste to attempt to negotiate a more profitable exchange and the terms of the exchange do not constitute an enforceable contract, create feelings of personal obligation, and have intrinsic significance for the participants. Social exchanges, it is said, entail unspecified obligations. "One person does another a favor, and while there is a general expectation of some future return, its exact nature is definitely not stipulated in advance."

Although Homans has gone a long way to provide powerful propositions to explain why an individual takes one course of action or maintains some relationships while dissolving others, he does not provide an explanation of what constitutes a benefit to one individual and a cost to another. Resources received are not necessarily valuable in the abstract but are valued in relation to anticipations given past association, current expectations, and comparisons to what others receive in similar interactions. Thibaut and Kelley present a description of preference hierarchies that takes into account individuals' histories and social comparisons.

DEVELOPMENT OF A PREFERENCE HIERARCHY

Social exchange theory can be seen as a theory of choice behavior. In choosing among alternatives, individuals need some standard or baseline by which to judge the relative reward of the alternatives. Individuals choose between alternatives "by evaluating the experiences or expected experiences with each in terms of a preference ranking and then selecting the best alternative." Thibaut and Kelley have addressed the issue of preference ranking in their theory of small group interaction. They suggest that individuals develop a scale of preferences against which they compare alternative choices. The midpoint of this scale is referred to as the *comparison level* (CL). Thibaut and Kelley state that individuals develop a CL that is a standard by which the person evaluates the rewards and costs of a given relationship in terms of what is felt to be "deserved." Relationships, the outcomes of which fall above the CL, would be relatively "satisfying" and attractive to the member; those entailing outcomes that fall below the CL would be relatively "unsatisfying" and unattractive. The location of the CL on the person's scale of outcomes will be influenced by all of the outcomes known to the member, either by direct experience or symbolically. The actual level of outcomes that yields this midpoint on the satisfaction–dissatisfaction scale will depend on the level of recently experienced outcomes or those outcomes for which the individual had major causal responsibility. They will be satisfied if they get more than they anticipate and dissatisfied if they get less.

Although each individual has a set CL for any resource, he or she also has a comparison level for alternative resources or exchange partners (CLalt). The value of a particular resource from one's exchange partner depends, to some degree, on the availability of alternative exchange partners or substitute resources. For example, if person A offers person B $10 to do a job, it is necessary to know if $10 for that job falls below or above the CL for person B and if person B has an alternative offer (CLalt) before it is possible to predict his or her response.

It is the conception of CLalt that leads to a discussion of power in social exchange relationships. To the extent that one exchange partner controls the access to scarce or desired resources, he or she has power over the other partner. In this case, there is no alternative exchange partner or the alternatives provide less desirable outcomes. Whichever person in a relationship has outcomes closer to his or her CLalt will have more power over the other. It is also assumed that the person least interested in maintaining the relationship, for whatever reason, has the power to dominate that relationship. This is referred to as the *principle of least interest* and leads to the conclusion that "power resides implicitly in the other's dependency." Emerson developed a theory of power-dependence relations based on the notion that because exchanges involve at least two parties, each is dependent on the other to some degree for interaction to occur. In a unilateral monopoly, person A can only obtain resources from person B. In terms of that resource, person B has ultimate power over A. The more different kinds of resources A gets from B, the more A is dependent on B, hence the more power B has over A. This

work has been extended to the study of coalition formation, power networks, and organizational linkages.

Even though subjects in research using payoff matrices are fully aware of the advantages of mutual cooperation, they tend to favor competitive choices. It appears that subjects are more interested in maximizing the differences between themselves and their game partners than maximizing their own rewards. Exceptions to this finding appear under conditions in which communication between the players was available or when the two players shared a close personal relationship. In both cases there is a basis for mutual trust, thus fostering cooperative strategies.

An additional source of power in social exchange relationships comes from when one exchange partner can influence the other's outcomes through his or her own actions. Thibaut and Kelley have argued that an individual can control the other's actions or behaviors by his or her own choice in two different ways. The first type of influential control or power is called *fate control*. "If, by varying his behavior, A can affect B's outcomes regardless of what B does, A has fate control over B." By initiating this type of control, one individual has narrowed the responses available to the other; B's fate depends on A's actions.

The second type of influential control is referred to as *behavior control*. "If, by varying his behavior, A can make it desirable for B to vary his behavior too, then A has behavior control over B." This is likely to occur when A can initiate a choice in behavior that increases the outcomes for B for a specific response or increases the costs of an alternative response from B. Although B still has a choice of behavior, A has the capacity to have a great deal of influence over B's outcomes and, as a result, a great deal of influence in B's behavior.

EXTENSIONS OF EXCHANGE THEORY

Although the discussion of a theory of social exchange within a dyadic relationship has benefited from the simplicity it afforded, it is widely recognized that extensions must be made to more complex social interactions. One extension has been the development of equity theory that suggests that the successes of other people will enter into the calculation of satisfaction with one's own success. One views their outcomes in relation to how others have done in addition to their own investments. Distributions of rewards, it is suggested, should be on the basis of individual effort and investment leading to the development of theories of distributive justice.

Exchange networks and the power of resource control have been another expansion of social exchange theory. As Thibaut and Kelley's discussion of fate and behavior control would suggest, one individual with control over a scarce resource maintains a source of power over others in an exchange network.

Social exchange theory has also been considered an important development in linking microprocesses with macrostructures. Blau initiated this work, which continues to gain attention. As was earlier noted, much of this interest crosses disciplinary boundaries, with all forms of the social sciences exploring derivations of social exchange theory.

ARBITRATION
CONTROL OF BEHAVIOR
SOCIAL EQUALITY
SOCIAL PSYCHOLOGY

L. RIES

SOCIAL INFLUENCE

All human interaction involves power and influence. Being skillful in influencing others and taking responsibility for such influence are important aspects of being human. Social influence may be discussed from two different points of view: the trait-factor perspective and the dynamic-interdependence perspective.

TRAIT-FACTOR PERSPECTIVE

From the trait-factor point of view, social influence is a function of the characteristics of (a) the person exerting the influence, (b) the person receiving the influence, and (c) the influence attempt itself. The major post-World War II application of the trait-factor approach to social influence was the Yale Attitude Change Program, headed by Carl Hovland. Most of the research in this program focused on the area in which the trait-factor view is strongest—the effects of a single attempt to influence delivered through the mass media. In each of these situations, the contact between the communicator and the receiver of the communication is brief and not repeated. Moreover, the communication is one-way; there is no interaction between the two parties. Because single instances of one-way communication are essentially static, a trait-oriented theory is quite helpful in analyzing them.

The exercise of social influence is seen as a credible and attractive communicator's delivery of an effectively organized message to a vulnerable or influenceable audience. Trait-factor researchers assume that people are rational in the way they process information and are motivated to attend to a message, learn its contents, and incorporate it into their attitudes.

Attempts to exert power over others are enhanced if one is credible and attractive; if one phrases one's messages so that they are two-sided, action-oriented, and discrepant with members' current beliefs; and if the receivers have low self-esteem, see their attitudes under modification as peripheral to them, have no forewarning of the influence attempt, role-play positions that agree with their own, have not practiced defending their position or are distracted while the message is being presented, and are not very intelligent. The trait-factor approach to influence, however, is weak both logically and empirically in situations where two or more individuals are constantly interacting.

DYNAMIC-INTERDEPENDENCE PERSPECTIVE

When interacting with others, one is constantly influencing and being influenced by the other individuals. People interacting with each other constantly modify and adjust their behavior to stay coordinated with one another.

From the dynamic-interdependence perspective, social influence is an attribute of a relationship, not of a person. Within a relationship, mutual influence exists to the extent that each can affect the goal accomplishment of the others. The more cooperative the relationship, the greater is the goal interdependence and the more influence individuals can exert on each other. Through mutual influence, the coordination of individuals' behavior necessary for successful goal accomplishment is achieved. Communication, decision making, leadership, conflict resolution, and all other aspects of interaction require mutual social influence. The engagement in social attempts is thus inevitable, and it is through the exercise of mutual influence that relationships are satisfying and productive.

Social influence can thus be defined as one person's control over resources valued by another. Social influence depends on a need–resource correspondence among individuals. Resources can be information, direct assistance in accomplishing a goal, the ability of others to affect one's costs of engaging in goal-directed behavior, and the ability to reward goal-directed behavior. It is the *perception* of a person's resources that determines the success of social influence attempts, not the person's actual resources.

Consciously planning how best to influence other people may seem to violate their freedom of choice and self-direction. There is, however, a difference between the use of influence and manipulation. All human interaction involves mutual influence; manipulation is a certain type of influence. *Manipulation* is the managing or controlling of others by a shrewd use of influence, especially in an unfair or dishonest way, and for one's own purposes and profit.

When discussing how social influence is developed and used, many behavioral sciences have given particular attention to its sources. There are six possible bases for a person's social influence: one's ability to reward and to coerce; one's legal position; one's capacity as a referent with whom others wish to identify; one's expertise; and one's information. Each of these sources enables one to influence others.

ADVERTISING
COMMUNICATION PROCESSES
PROPAGANDA

W. JOHNSON

SOCIAL INTEREST

Gemeinschaftsgefühl, or social interest, was one of the most original and unique concepts posited by Alfred Adler in his theory of Individual Psychology. It refers to an innate potential of the human being to develop an identification with and feeling for other people. It relates not only to people's feeling for their immediate community of loved ones and friends, but also to humanity at large, present and future. This quality, although innate, was presumed to develop only in a social context, and, in particular, through the infant's early interaction with the mother and father.

Social interest manifests itself in a variety of forms. One is the readiness of a person to cooperate and help even when circumstances are difficult and challenging. Another is one's inclination to give to others more than one demands. Finally, it may be demonstrated through one's capacity for empathic understanding of another's thoughts, feelings, and experiences. Adler viewed the primary tasks in life for each human being to be social in nature. Consequently, he believed that the successful resolution of the challenges of friendship, career, and intimacy depended on one's ability to make contact with and cooperate with others.

ADLERIAN PSYCHOLOGY
ALTRUISM
EMPATHY
PROSOCIAL BEHAVIOR

F. D. KELLY

SOCIAL INTERVENTIONS

DEFINITION

Social intervention can be defined broadly as any planned effort undertaken with the aim of improving the human condition, and goes far beyond the traditional concerns of psychology. It includes a wide array of activities undertaken by disparate professions, organizations, informal groups, or individuals. The goals are to meet basic material needs; to limit deviance; to resolve social conflict; to facilitate knowledge and enhance skill; to ameliorate psychological problems; to prevent or treat illness; and to promote cultural, spiritual, or intellectual life. The targets of such interventions are numerous and various: an entire nation, impoverished children, persons with specific disorders, decision makers, television viewers, burglars, spouse abusers, and so forth. Social intervention encompasses much activity by major institutions in society (systems of education, justice, health, mental health, religion, and politics) as well as groups or individuals that emerge as influential in a global, national, state, or local context.

The range of social interventions currently implemented by psychologists represents a much narrower field than that just outlined. Indeed, social interventions as *practiced* by psychologists have tended to expand somewhat cautiously from the secure base of traditional concerns (e.g., psychopathology) and methods (e.g., therapy). Yet psychologists in several areas (e.g., community, social issues, developmental, gender issues) have expressed an interest in social intervention more broadly, both as a source of new intervention methods and as an object of study per se. This interest reflects the view that "psychological" problems can neither be understood nor resolved independent of the social context in which they are embedded. Rather the social context—including extant social interventions—shapes problem definition and conceptualization, contributes to the problem, constrains intervention efforts, and is the necessary medium for sustainable solutions. Such views are more easily understood by examining community psychology.

COMMUNITY PSYCHOLOGY

Community psychology represents an evolving paradigm that traces its roots to the social reforms of the 1960s and the ensuing reappraisal of psychology's role in society. Key paradigmatic assumptions have been the subject of lively discussion. Themes include the following: a greatly expanded role for psychology in the promotion of human welfare; a shift to systemic and holistic epistemology; a blending of scientific, activist, and social critic roles; a shift from exclusively intrapsychic to social ecological models of problems; and an exploration of new modes of service delivery with an emphasis on prevention, collaboration, use of indigenous resources, cultural diversity, and empowerment. As Goodstein and Sandler so neatly put it, the focus of community psychology is on systems of deviance control, support, and socialization, rather than on troubled individuals.

Social Criticism

From this perspective, psychologists must engage in active social criticism rather than innocently accepting problem agenda and definitions perpetuated by power elites. Consider the recency of the "discovery" of family violence and other violence against women and children: This is difficult to understand except in the context of feminist changes to a patriarchal worldview.

Similarly, criticism of extant social interventions often reveals systemic failure (e.g., health care), misdirected effort (e.g., the war on drugs), perpetuation of problem myths (e.g., parental pathology in child neglect), or exacerbation of problems (e.g., official victimization of women alleging rape; encouraging citizens to protect themselves with handguns). However, when social interventions are entrenched, serve the interests of powerful constituencies, or give the political impression of decisive action, failures often are hidden, disguised, or dismissed.

Target Problems

Community psychology has promulgated an expanded view of what constitutes legitimate target problems (e.g., education, crime and safety, health, economic productivity, environmental quality, psychological well-being in addition to traditional areas of psychopathology). Perhaps more important, the paradigm has challenged the independence of these problems; rather they are seen as often interrelated. Consider, for example, the links between unemployment, health, academic achievement, housing, prejudice, teenage pregnancy, drug use, violence, crime, and child neglect. These problems are not only linked (it is impossible fully to understand or resolve one without consideration of the others), but they are also embedded in a context of social policies, institutional practices, and cultural norms.

Social Ecological Models

A central feature of community psychology is the shift from intrapsychic to social ecological models of problems. At a general level, such models emphasize the social context within which individuals function as well as the systemic and ecological properties of these contexts. Bronfenbrenner has presented a social ecological theory of human development that construes the social environment as a set of nested systems. Development—changes in understanding of, adaptation to, and competence regarding the world—is influenced by microsystems (e.g., home, school, work), mesosystems (e.g., relationship between home and work), exosystems (e.g., economic systems that influence work setting), and macrosystems (e.g., cultural norms and blueprints regarding family and work roles). Other models of social context fit into or complement this framework. Examples include models of behavioral interaction, social situations, behavior settings, social climate of settings, social support networks, organizations, community, and culture.

Ecological models have incorporated findings from social epidemiology regarding the distribution of psychological and other problems. Theories of life stress have served as an organizing framework for much of this literature and have been incorporated into community psychology.

In an ecological theory of stress, Hobfoll and Jackson have proposed that individuals seek to conserve, enhance, and protect resources in the face of threats. In an ecological model of social support, Vaux described conditions under which individuals or entire social networks might experience stressor-related need for support that exceeds the sustainable yield of their networks and suggested how gender, developmental stage, and social class might shape the support process. Theories of problems such as child abuse and neglect, child sexual abuse, and violence against women all have shown dramatic shifts from individual pathology to social ecological models that draw attention to cultural norms, gender- and family-role socialization, systems of deviance control, and family and community support resources.

In sum, the social ecological perspective briefly outlined here serves as a necessary background to understanding social intervention. No longer can psychologists limit their interventions to the treatment of individuals with specific disorders, innocent of the traumas (e.g., abuse), community change (e.g., plant closings), policies (e.g., day care), or service need (e.g., epidemiology of family violence) that serve as the context for these problems. These models suggest intervention goals (e.g., to reduce stressors and enhance personal or social resources). They also suggest how interventions might meet with resistance through homeostatic mechanisms in systems, how interventions might produce dramatic and unexpected effects through ecological perturbation, and how interventions must be integrated into the social ecology if they are to be sustainable.

GENERAL STRATEGIES OF SOCIAL INTERVENTION

The focus of community psychology is on systems of socialization, support, and deviance control. Social interventions might target any level of social organization: individuals, groups, organizations, collectivities, or cultural institutions. In their classic work, Chin and Benne outlined three general strategies evident in historical efforts to change human systems. Empirical-rational strategies emphasize information and appeal to the self-interest of rational beings (e.g., warning labels on cigarette packets). Normative-reeducative strategies seek to persuade and to change norms, values, or attitudes (e.g., public service announcements about AIDS, training programs, support groups, psychoeducational workshops, and socialization processes more generally). Power-coercive strategies use power ("legitimate" or otherwise) to force change (e.g., laws, protest groups, and terrorism). Each of these strategies has advantages and disadvantages and, to a greater or lesser degree, each may be manifest in any of the approaches discussed next.

Prevention Through Resource Enhancement

The prevention of problems has been prominent on the agenda of community psychology from its earliest days. Though problems persist, progress has been made. Many preventive programs build explicitly or implicitly on Dohrenwend's stress model. Viewing this in public health terms, the model suggests several approaches: reducing noxious agents such as stressors, enhancing host resistance by promoting personal resources, or altering the environment to make it more benign (i.e., less productive of stressors and more productive of support resources). Many interventions have sought to enhance personal or social resources.

An approach to building personal resources used in many programs with children and adolescents is to enhance social problem solving. Evidence is mixed regarding the effects of SPS training on adjustment, though program features associated with benefits are being identified. Competency-building programs have targeted at-risk groups, such as low-ncome, minority parents, with some success. Other programs have targeted adults or children who have recently experienced a stressful transition, such as divorce, again with some success.

Social support from family and friends appears to play an important role in psychological well-being. Despite the huge empirical literature on the topic, relatively few interventions have sought to promote this key social resource. Various promising strategies have been proposed. Programs have sought to teach individuals about social support, to promote support networks at school, to promote beneficial telephone friendships among elderly persons, and to seed the community with natural helpers; in general, results are encouraging but highlight the complexity of the support process.

Community psychologists have begun to examine support groups, which have emerged as an important third domain of helping that complements family and friend support and formal helping. Such mutual assistance may serve a number of functions.

In sum, social interventions have sought to prevent problems by enhancing personal and social resources along the lines proposed by Dohrenwend. Progress has been made in program development, and findings are quite encouraging. Yet it is still necessary to identify interventions that are reliably beneficial, even in the area of personal resources, where a good deal of work has been conducted. Moreover, these interventions are largely person-centered; psychologists have barely begun the task of trying to make social environments more benign (less stressful and more supportive), let alone drawing on other approaches to alter the social ecology. Some of these approaches are outlined briefly.

Consultation and Organizational Interventions

Consultation to community agencies was intended as a key role for community mental health centers, but never developed due to lack of training, guidelines, and funds. Nor has its potential been exploited fully by community psychologists, in spite of models adaptable to a range of focal problems, levels of social organization, and strategy. Organizational interventions have proved successful with respect to productivity but have less often addressed other goals. Even simple changes in work or school organizations may result in benefits.

Policy and Advocacy

Training in systems analysis and the synthesis of empirical findings makes community psychologists well suited for roles in policy analysis and advocacy. Illustrative efforts regarding policy have targeted unemployment, child care, gender and poverty, and adolescent employment. Advocacy involves efforts to change policies or practices that are injurious or unjust. Highly successful intervention efforts to counter drunk driving and dumping of toxic waste were initiated by victims: community psychologists might lead or facilitate such efforts.

Community Development

Several strategies of community development have been identified—social planning, locality development, and social action—that differ in their views of community, problem origin, and interventionist role. Potentially important roles for community psychologists within each approach have only rarely been explored.

PROBLEMS

The study and implementation of social interventions faces several major obstacles. Many of these reflect two common themes: cultural assumptions about the nature of relevant problems and disciplinary constraints. First, some views underlying the social intervention approach are radical, in the sense that they challenge powerful interests. Second, for good conceptual and pragmatic reasons, disciplinary specializations have evolved in terms of problems and level of analysis. Such specialization hampers the development of integrative social ecological theories to serve as frameworks for designing and choosing appropriate social interventions. Third, it has proved difficult to develop expertise in cross-disciplinary methodologies necessary to provide a knowledge-base for social interventions and demonstrate their effects. Fourth, the legitimacy of community psychology-based social intervention is yet to be established, and such interventions raise complicated ethical issues, many novel to psychologists. Finally, there is the sheer scope of social intervention broadly construed. The goal is gigantic: to shape and create social ecologies of socialization, support, and deviance control through the concepts and methods of an emerging community psychology. From this standpoint, the benefits, too, are considerable.

COMMUNITY PSYCHOLOGY
ENVIRONMENTAL MEASURES
ENVIRONMENTAL PSYCHOLOGY
EUTHENICS–EUGENICS
HOMELESSNESS
MAINSTREAMING (PSYCHOTICS)
NEEDS ASSESSMENT
SOCIAL INTEREST

A. VAUX

SOCIAL ISOLATION

Children who are isolated from positive interpersonal contact may be deprived of a number of important socializing experiences. Continued isolation may precipitate or increase inadequacies in social adaptation, thus leading to poor social adjustment in later years. Harry Harlow first showed the devastating effects that total isolation can have on the social development of young monkeys. Monkeys who are placed in isolation in the first 6 months of life later show extremely abnormal social behavior—they appear fearful and resist and withdraw from any social contact.

Although children are never raised in total isolation, milder forms of social deprivation may produce marked developmental delays and deficiencies. For example, young children who are institutionalized or lack a supportive primary caretaker often show marked retardation in many areas of development, including language and communication skills, physical abilities, responsivity, and affective expressiveness.

Children who are isolated from positive peer contact often show later difficulties in social adjustment. Quiet and withdrawn children who are disliked and ignored by classmates are more likely than their socially successful peers to suffer a number of adult problems, ranging from academic failure to delinquency to psychiatric illness. Social isolation in childhood may be exacerbated by anxiety and social skill deficits.

K. L. BIERMAN

SOCIAL LEARNING THEORIES

Social teaming theories of personality are first and foremost *learning* theories. Social learning theory heavily emphasized reinforcement ideas, but modern social learning theory has assumed a distinctly cognitive cast. The importance of reinforcement has been integrated with concepts that depict a thinking and knowing person who has expectations and beliefs. Thus the roots of modern social learning theory can be traced to theorists such as Kurt Lewin and Edward Tolman. From a social and interpersonal standpoint, the work of George Herbert Mead and Harry Stack Sullivan is probably also germane.

Currently, the major social learning theorists are considered to be Julian Rotter, Albert Bandura, and Walter Mischel. However, the social behaviorism of Arthur Staats bears some notable similarities to Bandura's work. Some would even include Hans Eysenck and Joseph Wolpe as social learning theorists because of the nature of their therapy methods, which follow a learning model.

ROTTER'S SOCIAL LEARNING THEORY

Several prime features characterize Rotter's theory. First, he adopts a construct point of view. This means that he is interested not in reconstructing reality through his theory, but in developing a series of concepts that provide predictive utility. Second, he is concerned with the language of description. He seeks to develop concepts free of vagueness or ambiguity. Third, he makes a strong effort to employ operational definitions that specify the actual measurement operations for each concept.

Rotter's use of the term *social learning* is a calculated one. He believes that much human behavior is acquired or learned. What is more, it takes place in a meaningful environment that is rife with social interactions with other people.

A major feature of the theory is the employment of both motivational (reinforcement) and cognitive (expectancy) variables. The theory is also distinctive in its use of an empirical law of effect. Anything is a reinforcement if it results in movement toward or away from a goal.

Finally, the emphasis of this theory is on performance rather than on the acquisition of behavior.

Basic Concepts

Rotter's theory requires four concepts or variables to predict an individual's behavior. First, there is behavior potential (BP). This refers to the potential for any given behavior to occur in a specific situation in connection with the pursuit of a specific reinforcement or set of reinforcements. Behavior here is defined broadly and includes motor acts, cognitive activity, verbalizations, emotional reactions, and so on.

The second major variable is expectancy (E). This is the probability held by an individual that a particular reinforcement will occur as a function of a specific behavior executed in a specific situation. Expectancies are subjective and do not necessarily coincide with any actuarial probability calculated objectively on the basis of prior reinforcement. One's perceptions are the crucial element.

The third major concept is reinforcement value (RV). This is defined as the degree of preference for any reinforcement to occur if the possibilities of their occurring were all equal.

Finally, there is the psychological situation, which, according to social learning theory, is an important predictive element. It is necessary to understand the psychological relevance of a given situation in affecting both reinforcement values and expectancies accurately to predict behavior in that situation.

Problem-Solving Expectancies

In recent years, a great deal of research has been devoted to problem-solving generalized expectancies. These cognitive variables are akin to attitudes, beliefs, or mental sets about how problem situations should be construed to facilitate their solution. Individuals differ widely in terms of these cognitions. Two generalized expectancies have been the focus of this research. They are internal versus external control of reinforcement (locus of control) and interpersonal trust. In the first instance, people differ in their beliefs about whether what happens to them is determined by their own behavior and attributes (internal) or is caused by luck, fate, chance, or powerful others (external). In the case of interpersonal trust, some individuals expect that others can be relied on to tell the truth, although others believe to the contrary. Again, which belief is held will be a powerful determinant of how people approach solutions to the problems they face.

BANDURA'S OBSERVATIONAL LEARNING

The social learning approach of Albert Bandura complements the social learning theory of Rotter. It accounts for the ways in which people acquire a variety of complex behaviors in social settings.

A basic notion of Bandura's is that of observational learning, a concept that can be traced to George Herbert Mead's work on imitation and vocal gestures. The subsequent analysis of imitation by Neal Miller and John Dollard provided an important springboard for Bandura. The work of O. Hobart Mowrer on sign learning and reward learning was also influential.

Basic Concepts

Bandura argues for a reciprocal relationship among behavior, person variables, and environmental variables. We are not simply driven by inner forces, nor are we pawns of some set of environmental contingencies. We are influenced, but we also exert influence.

Bandura asserts that an enormous amount of human learning involves modeling, observation, and imitation. Consequently, he does not view the creation of a complex behavior as an additive product of tiny elements of conditioning.

In effect, Bandura is asserting that much human learning transpires without the customary reinforcement that operant and classical conditioning principles require. People can learn in the absence of both reward and punishment. This does not mean, however, that reinforcement is irrelevant. Indeed, once a behavior is learned, reinforcement is quite important in determining whether the behavior will occur. Furthermore, observational learning is neither inevitable nor automatic. Many factors influence whether such learning takes place in a given situation. Such factors include the model's age and competence. The person's level of motivation may also enhance or retard modeling, imitation, and observation. A variety of social responses, such as aggression, sex-typed behavior, and emotional reactivity, among many others, are observed and hence learned.

A Cognitive Emphasis

To account for observational learning phenomena, Bandura believes that we employ symbolic representations of environmental events. Without such symbolic activity, it is hard to explain the tremendous flexibility in human behavior. It is his thesis that behavioral changes that occur through classical and instrumental conditioning, as well as through extinction and punishment, are actively mediated by cognitions. Also critical in human behavior are self-regulatory processes. People regulate their behavior by visualizing the consequences of that behavior. Thus relationships between stimulus and response are affected by these self-control processes.

Mischel has continued this cognitive emphasis in his analysis of several cognitive social learning person variables. He asserts that people differ with respect to certain person variables, and it is these differences that give rise to the enormous range of personality characteristics observed in others. First, there are competencies. These are repertoires of abilities that influence our thoughts and actions. Second, people differ in their encoding strategies in the sense that they represent or symbolize environmental stimulation in different ways. Third, there are expectancies or learned probabilities, which refer to the likelihood that certain behaviors or events will lead to certain outcomes. A fourth variable, subjective values, indicates that people differ in the values they attach to various outcomes. Last, there are self-regulatory systems and plans. Here, behavior is regulated by self-imposed standards.

Behavioral Change

Bandura's work has been highly important in the development of new approaches to therapeutic intervention. In particular, the acquisition of new cognitive and behavioral competencies through modeling has been prominent.

IMITATIVE LEARNING

E. J. Phares

SOCIAL PHOBIA

Social phobia was first officially recognized diagnostically with the publication of the *Diagnostic and statistical manual, 3rd ed. (DSM-III)* (American Psychiatric Association [APA]) in 1980, when the disorder was included within the classification of anxiety disorders. In *DSM-III-R* in 1987, the diagnostic criteria describe social phobia as "a persistent fear of one or more situations (the social phobic situations) in which a person is exposed to possible scrutiny by others and fears that he or she may do something or act in a way that will be humiliating or embarrassing." In social phobia, a person fears one or a few distinct situations. In generalized social phobia, the person avoids most social situations. Examples of social phobia provided in the *DSM-III-R* criteria include an inability to continue talking in public-speaking situations, choking on food when eating with others, or saying foolish things in social situations. Other criteria include (a) an invariable "immediate anxiety response" when exposed to the specific phobic stimulus; (b) avoidance (or endurance with intense anxiety) of the phobic situation; (c) usually some interference with social activities and relationships, including one's job; and (d) a recognition that the fear is "excessive or unreasonable." A social phobia is diagnosed only if criterion c applies or if there is "marked distress about having the fear." The disorder usually appears in late childhood or early adolescence; an average age of onset of about 16 years of age has been reported repeatedly, with a mean age of those with the disorder at about 30 years of age. Social phobia appears with about the same frequency in both sexes.

Avoidant personality may coexist with social phobia. In the personality disorder the person will avoid "social or occupational activities that involve significant interpersonal contact," whereas in social phobia the individual mainly avoids certain situations. Others have suggested that the distinction may be one of degree—avoidant personality disturbances being the more severe and pervasive of the two and presumably the more generally debilitating. In addition, the person who is considered to be a social phobic desires to be able to function in the feared social situation and may even suffer the consequences of voluntarily repeated exposure, whereas the individual displaying avoidant personality more commonly adopts avoidance of interpersonal interactions as a general strategy.

There is a high likelihood that social phobia will coexist with other *DSM-III-R* Axis I disorders, and the most commonly diagnosed disorders along with social phobia were generalized anxiety disorder (33.3% of the patients), and simple phobia (11.1%). Although social phobics may report panic attacks in certain social situations, a fact that can lead to misdiagnosis, the individual afflicted with panic disorder appears to be more greatly concerned with losing control over bodily functions or becoming disabled psychologically. By contrast, the social phobic mainly fears negative evaluations by others, an important difference between this disorder and the social-related anxieties that appear in a wide variety of other anxiety disorders. In short, it is specifically *what* is feared that provides the most obvious basis for the distinction.

ASSESSMENT

Reviews of both cognitive and behavioral methods for the assessment of social phobia are available. Among broad fear surveys, the Fear Survey Schedule (FSS), a general survey of fears seen in clinics, contains selected items relevant to social anxiety in various versions. This portion of the survey has been related to treatment outcome for social skills training and to other indicators of anxiety, providing some demonstrations of the validity of the scale for use in the assessment of social phobia. The Fear Questionnaire (FQ) measures social phobia on a subscale that assesses avoidance of five social settings. The FQ inventory has been shown to differentiate successfully the effects of cognitive and behavioral interventions for social phobia.

Among the variety of questionnaires specifically directed at social anxiety, two that appear to be cited most often in clinical research are the Social Avoidance and Distress (SAD) scale and the Fear of Negative Evaluation (FNE) scale, both developed by Watson and Friend. A number of recent treatment outcome studies have documented the usefulness of both of these scales in assessing change in social phobics due to clinical interventions.

The Anxiety Disorders Interview Schedule (ADIS) is among the most widely used behavioral interview methods for assessment of anxiety and phobias. A revision by DiNardo and coworkers, the ADIS-R, also is in use, which has been shown to have high reliability among raters of social phobia.

The most common method for assessing the client in actual phobic situations is through self-monitoring. The self-monitoring instrument ideally provides information regarding the type of social interaction, degree of anxiety experienced, antecedents and consequences of specific behaviors, duration of interactions, who was involved, and other aspects of the social phobic's problem situations.

TREATMENT

In his overall review of 17 studies on the treatment of social phobia, Heimberg observed that all studies yielded positive treatment outcomes irrespective of the form of intervention. The wide variety of manipulations hamper further conclusions about relative effectiveness of procedures. Forms of treatment have included social skills training, systematic desensitization, self-control desensitization, *in vivo* and imaginal exposure (flooding), anxiety management training, and several types of cognitive restructuring.

In two treatment outcome studies, both social skills training (SST) and rational emotive therapy (RET) were found to be effective in treating social phobia, although there seemed to be a slight (nonsignificant) advantage for the former on some dimensions. Moreover, SST was no more effective for subjects classified as "behavioral reactors" than for those classified as "cognitive reactors"; nor was RET differentially effective for the two groups. Like all of the previous treatment outcome studies conducted with social phobics, these also showed that "there is not one treatment strategy that is superior to all others."

Wlazlo and coworkers also looked at effects on social phobia obtained with social skills training. Drug interventions with social phobia have been reviewed by Levin, Schneier, and Liebowtiz.

ANTIANXIETY DRUGS
COPING
FACTITIOUS DISORDERS
FEAR
PHOBIAS
SOCIAL SKILLS TRAINING

J. G. CARLSON

SOCIAL PSYCHOLOGY

Social psychology bridges the interest of psychology, with its emphasis on the individual, with sociology, with its emphasis on social structures. As a field, it is as old as the two disciplines from which it draws, but it did not have a well-structured identity until the beginning of the twentieth century.

The blossoming of the field of social psychology is usually associated with the joint appearance of two textbooks under that title, one by Ross and the other by McDougall. Ross' work reflected his prior involvement in the analyses of collective behavior, and did not emphasize the individual in the social context. By contrast, McDougall emphasized individual behavior, and dealt extensively with mechanisms and tendencies to behave.

Another thrust in this early period was in "formal" sociology, with the main exponent being Simmel. In many ways, Simmel's work is seen as the major inspiration for later efforts involving group dynamics and small-group research.

Many of the developments of the early period tended to be relatively isolated in impact.

In the post-World War II period, the field experienced virtually an explosion of growth reflected in the hundreds of journals devoted to social psychology and subspecialties and in the array of books and monographs. Additionally, the expansion was accompanied by developments that have broken down disciplinary barriers. More pointedly, in the modern period, there has also been a great move toward applied science, and social psychology has been critically involved. This has ranged from concern with questions of analysis of social, ethnic, racial, sex, and other factors in intragroup and intergroup relations to more explicit studies with regard to policies in the private and public sectors under the rubric of evaluation research.

Notable advances in social psychology were lacking until the 1930s. One exception was the work of Allport, who studied the effects of group participation on performance. The seminal period in the post-depression years included the work of Lewin and his students, which emphasized field theory and group dynamics. In this period, Moreno and his associate, Jennings, advanced the use of sociometric analysis, and with this a complex of additional procedures that included role-playing and psychodrama. The more analytic materials stemming from child development were interpreted through such scholars as Mead. Freudian theoretical interests were also beginning to enter social psychology through academic interpreters, and the works of Fromm, for example, were read quite widely by sociologists. Public opinion polls had come on the scene, and the academic basis of opinion and attitude research was becoming a strong basis for research. Possibly a landmark in the transition to the post-World War II period was a publication by Murphy and colleagues that summarized much of the basic research of the period and established clearly that, as an experimental field based on systematic research, social psychology had a fundamental core and a body with reasonable appendages.

From the point of view of the massive accumulation of findings and their integration into theory, social psychology suffers, as most of the social and psychological sciences do. Progress has been meager in spite of a substantial amount of activity, especially in the post-World War II period. At the same time, the availability of computers, acknowledgment of the limitations of relatively small-scale experiments and observation, and the growth of a more general fabric of communication among the disciplines suggest that social psychology provides both an opportunity and the potential for scientific progress.

DESCRIPTIVE PSYCHOLOGY
OBSERVATIONAL METHODS

E. F. BORGATTA

SOCIAL PSYCHOPHYSIOLOGY

Social psychophysiology is characterized by the use of noninvasive procedures to study the relationships between actual or perceived physiological events and the verbal or behavioral effects of human association. The field represents the intersection of social psychology and psychophysiology. Social psychology, the older of the two disciplines, is directed toward understanding the reportable and behavioral effects of human association, whereas psychophysiology employs noninvasive procedures to study the interrelationships between physiological events and a person's reportable or overt behavior. Social psychophysiology has emerged from these disparately focused disciplines for the purposes of understanding the psychological significance of physiological events and explaining complex behaviors in biological terms.

The perspective on human behavior epitomized by social psychophysiology is quite old. It dates back to at least the third century B.C.

Articles bearing the imprint of a social psychophysiological perspective began appearing in the psychological literature in the 1920s, with reports about the changes in the breathing of poker players when they were bluffing and about the galvanic skin responses (GSRs) of students finding themselves possessing attitudes shared by few peers. The first summary of empirical research in social psychophysiology was published by Kaplan and Bloom in 1960. The review dealt with the physiological concomitants of social status, social sanction, delineation of the situation, and empathy. Optimism was expressed that the field of social psychophysiology had come of age. At about the same time, John Lacey published a critical and cogent review wherein he argued there was little consistency in the literature on which to build bridges between psychophysiological data and psychological constructs.

Nevertheless, investigations of the reciprocal influence of social and physiological systems began to broaden in scope and increase in number. In 1962, Schachter and Singer published a paper concerning their influential two-factor theory of emotions in which they postulated that the sensations derived from a large and unexpected increase in physiological arousal could be experienced as widely different emotions, depending on the circumstances covarying with these sensations. Leiderman and Shapiro represented a different vein of research: Evidence was presented for the dramatic impact that social factors such as conformity pressures have on physiological responding.

The attractiveness of psychophysiological procedures was tempered, however, by three formidable barriers: (a) the paucity of conceptual links between the psychophysiological data and social psychological constructs; (b) the technical sophistication and expensive instrumentation required to collect, analyze, and interpret psychophysiological data in social psychological paradigms; and (c) the inevitable pitting of social psychological and psychophysiological procedures against one another in studies of construct validation.

Three distinct strategies developed for dealing with these barriers. One strategy was simply to dismiss physiological factors as irrelevant, at least at present, to the study of social cognition and behavior, and to dismiss social factors as too molar to contribute to an understanding of psychophysiological relationships. A second strategy was to view the physiological factor important in the study of social processes as being diffuse and perceptible changes in physiological arousal. This view provided the rationale for conducting research with little or no psychophysiological recording equipment and expertise, since it followed from this reasoning that any single physiological response, or even sensitive measures of interoceptive sensations, reflected a person's physiological arousal at any given moment.

The third approach more often involved collaborative efforts by psychophysiologists and social psychologists. The strategy followed was to narrow the breadth of the social issue under investigation while increasing the depth (level) of the analysis. Specific patterns of physiological responses were conceived as reflecting and/or influencing specific social processes. Experiments exemplifying this approach are characterized by the simultaneous measurement of multiple physiological, verbal, and/or behavioral responses in a single session, and by interpretations that entertain highly specific, reciprocal, and (at least initially) biologically adaptive influences between social and physiological systems.

The increasing utility for investigators to be informed about various levels of human behavior ranging from the physiological to the sociocultural resulted during the 1980s in a convergence among the three research strategies outlined as the barriers to social psychophysiological research were overcome. The nonelectrophysiological procedures developed by earlier investigators to study the effects of "arousal" on social processes, for example, posed interesting questions regarding the actual physiological basis for the obtained data. This, in turn, resulted in research on the symptoms and sensations people associate with various patterns of somatic and autonomic responses.

PHYSIOLOGICAL PSYCHOLOGY (NONREDUCTIONISM) SOCIAL PSYCHOLOGY

J. T. CACIOPPO

SOCIAL SKILLS TRAINING

Concern about social competencies had long been secondary to other social and educational endeavors. It was generally assumed that one learned appropriate interpersonal skills "naturally," through the traditional socializing institutions—home, school, church, and workplace. When social inadequacies were noted, they were attributed to faulty socialization: poor breeding, poor schooling, or poor religious and moral training. Even traditional mental health concepts viewed interpersonal inadequacies as symptomatic of more basic, underlying conflicts or psychopathologies.

Changes in social institutions effect changes in their traditional functions, including the teaching and nurturance of social competencies. By the early 1970s, a number of such changes were evident. Family structure had been modified, with a rapid rise in single-parent families, as well as families in which both mothers and fathers worked outside the home. Religious institutions no longer held the central position or support they once had. Schools were called on to educate a more heterogeneous group of youngsters, displaying a wider range of in-school behaviors. The impact of a new socializing agent, television, also began to be noted.

The two major fields particularly receptive to social skills training were education and psychology. Throughout the history of education, the teaching of interpersonal, social, and moral behaviors and values sometimes has been an explicit, but almost always an implicit, goal.

Psychology's involvement in social skills training can be traced through the emergence of the behavior modification movement. From that perspective, treatment efforts were reconceptualized in learning theory terms, with problematic behaviors viewed as examples of inadequate or faulty learning.

A favorite target population for the early behavior modifiers was institutionalized psychiatric patients. Many of the first behavior modification efforts were directed toward eliminating the bizarre, disturbed, and disturbing behaviors that often characterized patients and teaching skills necessary for adequate outside functioning.

Most such training efforts espouse the rationale that the individual is deficient in important interpersonal competencies, having never learned them adequately in the past. However, some (e.g., Wolpe) believe that the relevant skills may have been acquired but their appropriate usage is inhibited by conditioned anxiety. Still other researchers (e.g., Meichenbaum) emphasize cognitive factors, such as negative expectations and self-appraisals, as causal. This view parallels the broader introduction and acceptance of cognitive factors into more traditional behavioral approaches to treatment, emerging under the rubric of "cognitive-behavior modification."

COMPONENTS

Although not all social skills training programs are alike, there are many commonalities. Programs differ in the relative emphasis placed on particular components, as well as their presentation, sequence, and use. Components most frequently included in training programs are (a) rationale presentation, (b) modeling, (c) role playing, (d) feedback, and (e) homework/transfer of training.

Rationale

An overview of the skills to be taught generally precedes training proper. The meaning of the terminology used and the relevance of the skill(s) to trainees' lives are often dealt with. No standard taxonomy of social skills and their behavioral referents yet exists.

Modeling

A clear presentation of the behaviors to be learned is a part of most training programs regardless of whether the theoretical basis is skill deficit or conditioned anxiety. Many modeling presentations include cognitive behaviors (self-verbalizations) as well as overt behaviors.

Role-Playing

After trainees have been exposed to modeled examples, they are given opportunities to practice the behaviors. Trainees may role-play both overt and covert responses, with the expectation that individualized practice will increase adequate skills in real-life situations.

Feedback

An integral component of virtually all social skills training programs is feedback and social reinforcement. Feedback may be in the form of approval, praise, or encouragement, or it may be corrective in nature with concrete suggestions for improved performance. Some programs, particularly those with young children or chronic psychiatric patients, may also use tangible reinforcement, such as money, food, candy, or tokens.

Some social skills programs use self-reinforcement techniques. In a forthright effort at shifting the locus of evaluation from external to internal, attempts are made to teach self-monitoring, self-evaluation, and self-reward as an important aspect of skill acquisition and generalization.

Homework/Transfer of Training

A most neglected area is transfer of training. Some social skills training programs acknowledge and deal with the transfer problem directly. The most frequently used technique for facilitating transfer is homework. Another major approach to facilitating successful generalization is the incorporation of "transfer enhancers" that increase the likelihood that transfer of training will occur. Goldstein and colleagues present five transfer enhancers: (a) provision of general principles, or presenting trainees with appropriate concepts, rules, or strategies for proper skill use; (b) identical elements, or making the training setting, both physically and interpersonally, as much like the real-life application setting as possible; (c) overlearning, or providing repeated practice of successful skill enactment in the training session; (d) stimulus variability, or presenting trainees with opportunities to practice their newly learned social skills in a variety of physical and interpersonal settings; and (e) real-life reinforcement, or maximizing the likelihood that trainees will receive adequate (external) social reinforcement and/or (internal) self-reinforcement as they use their skills successfully in their real-life environment.

Most assessment approaches use some combination of questionnaire/self-report measures of behaviors, cognitions and/or affective responses, naturalistic observations, and role-play simulations. Traditional psychological tests typically have not been used. Since neither a standardized nomenclature of skills nor a uniform assessment package yet exists, it is not possible to compare training effectiveness specifically across training programs, although a recent study by Curran and coworkers offers encouraging possibilities for such comparisons.

ASSERTIVENESS TRAINING
BEHAVIOR THERAPY
COGNITIVE BEHAVIOR THERAPY

R. P. SPRAFKIN

SOCIAL SUPPORT

Social support concerns the benefits to well-being that people derive through their relationships with others. Empirical research on social support is quite recent, emerging in social epidemiology and community psychology. Since the late 1970s, a huge body of empirical literature has been published, yet much of this work was premature, preceding necessary conceptual analysis.

CONCEPTUAL AND MEASUREMENT ISSUES

Social support is a rich but nebulous idea. Initially, research progress was severely hampered by the failure to specify relevant constructs. Interpretations of social support differed dramatically in terms of the range of social relationships, the forms of assistance, and the actual or perceived aspects of support considered relevant. Conceptual confusion led to a proliferation of poor measures, vague theory, and imprecisely modeled and tested hypotheses.

Support as a Transactional Process

By the mid-1980s, several important conceptual distinctions had emerged. Vaux proposed that social support was best viewed as a metaconstruct with three components: support network resources, supportive behavior, and support appraisals. Respectively, these constructs refer to the network of persons who provide assistance, specific acts of assistance, and the focal person's evaluative appraisals of such resources and assistance. This position explicitly recognized the conceptual legitimacy of several "approaches" to social support: These were viewed not as mutually exclusive alternatives but as components in a complex process of transactions between person and social environment. That is, people actively develop and maintain network resources, mobilize them in time of need to get assistance, and appraise the consequences. Moreover, this process occurs in an ecological context that constrains how support resources are developed and used. In this emerging conceptualization, "social support" and its influence on well-being are much more complex than originally thought.

Modes of Support

Distinctions among types of support were common early on but often were confusing in their diversity and lack of common terminology. Reviews of support typologies suggest an emerging consensus on six modes of support: emotional, guidance, feedback, socializing, practical, and material.

Measurement

The early conceptual confusion that has been outlined seriously undermined measurement of social support. Early studies employed idiosyncratic measures of unknown reliability and validity. Conceptual clarification brought dramatic improvements in measurement. Measures with established reliability and validity have been published that assess support network resources, support behavior, and support appraisals. Persistent shortcomings include the paucity of support-behavior measures, the emphasis on global satisfaction in support-appraisal measures, and most important, the failure of most measures to distinguish distinct modes of support.

SOCIAL SUPPORT AND WELL-BEING

A key source of interest in social support has been its promise as a potentially important influence on psychological and physical well-being.

The Buffer and Direct Models

According to the buffer model, support moderates (or "buffers") the effect of stressors on well-being. This model was seen as helping to explain the relatively weak relationship between life stress and disorder. The direct model simply states that support has a benign effect on well-being independent of stressors. Evidence for the models has been mixed and unconvincing. Some reviewers found evidence for the buffer model, some did not, and others concluded that buffer or direct effects are evident only under certain conditions.

Kessler and McLeod sorted studies by type of support measure. They concluded that evidence for the buffer and direct model, respectively, was observed depending on whether measures reflected support appraisals or network resources. Not only does this pattern beg explanation but it also failed to emerge in a review of later studies, where effects sometimes emerged only for some samples or measures of distress. Some measures of support even show a positive association with disorder (see Schwartzer and Leppin's 1991 paper on metaanalysis). Finally, mobilization of support may be beneficial or detrimental to well-being, contingent on other resources. Such complexities have led many researchers to the opinion that the simple buffer and direct models can accommodate neither empirical findings nor emerging transactional models of social support; they appear to have outlived their usefulness.

Alternative Models

Several writers have discussed a variety of alternative models that do not assume independence of stressors and support (implicitly, earlier models do so). Such models allow that stressors may mobilize support, which in turn diminishes distress; that support networks may generate stressors as well as provide a benign resource; that support may prevent stressors in the first place; and that these effects may depend on the ecological balance between a network's sustainable yield and the demand for support. Such models account for a number of otherwise peculiar findings.

Specificity Models

Cohen and McKay offered a variant of the buffer model: Support will buffer stressors only if it specifically matches the coping demands of those stressors. In their review, Cohen and Wills used this model as an explanation for inconsistencies in evidence for buffer effects. Although classification of measures was problematic, most buffer effects were observed for "functional" measures (especially global functional; cf. appraisal measures), consistent with predictions. Cutrona has developed a more detailed model of optimal matching that builds on typologies of support and of stress. A review provided evidence for the model. Although not without problems, optimal matching is likely to be a guiding theme of much future research.

Mechanisms of Support Effects
Specificity models highlight the need to articulate how support might buffer stress effects. Several mechanisms have been proposed: Support might prevent stressor occurrence, facilitate accurate appraisal, promote benign reappraisal, act directly to meet the demand, suggest coping options, sustain efficacy, and facilitate recovery of emotional equilibrium. As yet, these mechanisms have rarely been subjected to empirical tests or been tested, possibly underlying direct effects of support.

PROSPECTS FOR FUTURE RESEARCH
A number of issues are likely to engage future research on social support. First, the transactional model has raised numerous questions about the development and use of support resources and about how such processes are shaped by personal and ecological factors. Second, future research will integrate social support concepts into more traditional areas of psychology, including personality, development, and personal relationships. Third, the negative aspects of social ties will be better integrated with models of support. Finally, social support interventions (other than the ubiquitous support group) will be implemented and evaluated. Through family and friends, individuals enhance their emotional, informational, physical and material resources. Researchers have just begun to unravel these complex processes of social support.

DEPENDENCY
DEPENDENT PERSONALITY
SOCIAL DESIRABILITY
SOCIAL ISOLATION

A. Vaux

SOCIOBIOLOGY
Sociobiology studies relationships between biological environments and social behavior in animals and humans. Its growth has proceeded along parallel paths within various scientific and social science areas. No event, date, or founder can be given sole credit for its inception and development as a special area of study and research. Edward Wilson has helped to shape some basic sociobiological principles. His books have created a conceptual framework for the field and controversy over its existence.

Some social scientists have taken the position that human behavior (and to a lesser degree, animal behavior) is infinitely malleable, depending on environmental alterations. Some biologists have taken an equally extreme position that the environment has little effect on behavior, which is largely a function of heredity. Sociobiology argues that a growing body of research appears to demonstrate that the two factors always interact.

Sociobiology not only attempts to predict and explain behavior of individuals, but also seeks to explain and predict evolutionary changes in the social and cultural behavior of groups. Sociobiology relies heavily on an extension of Darwin's genetic theory.

Common core principles of sociobiology include the belief in a natural order of development of social behavior, a multilevel explanation of behavior, purposefulness of behavior (which is to achieve adaptation and subsequently continuation of the gene pool), and a biological substrate to the behavior that follows predictable patterns. Beyond these common core principles, sociobiological theories vary considerably in terms of proposed mechanisms of action and the relative contributions that the environment provides. Altruistic behavior in humans was a particularly difficult problem for Darwinian genetics. From a genetic standpoint, it did not appear to make sense for an individual to engage in behavior that could result in death, and subsequently the death of genetic material that the person was carrying. However, such altruistic behavior has frequently been observed in social insects such as worker bees, who fulfill labor tasks for the bee colony even though they themselves are sterile. An understanding of this puzzle of altruism came from W. Hammilton's work on the concept of "inclusive fitness," which explains altruistic behavior in social insects is an act that, although jeopardizing the genetic material of the individual, assures the likelihood of survival of genetically related social partners. This has been referred to as "reciprocal altruism"—aiding others with an expectation of return.

Critics of sociobiological theories have been numerous, and in some cases quite vocal. Among the concerns voiced are those reflecting potential socioeconomic and political costs of the theory and the impossibility of validating it, a biological reductionism and deterministic view that negates the role of the environment. Many authors have argued that the complexity of human behavior is such that any attempt at reductionism is impossible. The complexity of any individual theory of sociobiology, however, determines whether it is a reductionistic theory. Some theories place more emphasis on the environment, while other, more complex and well-integrated theories take into account what is known of biology and the environment and couples such knowledge together in a reciprocal fashion. Such theories cannot be considered reductionistic.

It appears impossible, from either an ethical or a methodological standpoint, to validate the theories through anything other than largely implicit research with numerous conflicting and confounding explanations for the results. One major concern is that attention is being taken away from environmental theories, which can be validated to a greater degree. This shift in emphasis can be used deliberately or inadvertently to create a system that justifies racial and sexual prejudices.

ALTRUISM
COMPARATIVE PSYCHOLOGY
EVOLUTION
NATURE–NURTURE CONTROVERSY
PHYSIOLOGICAL PSYCHOLOGY
PROSOCIAL BEHAVIOR

S. D. Sherrets

SOCIODRAMA
Sociodrama is a group therapy technique originally developed by J. L. Moreno as an extension of his psychodrama. Torrance later reconceptualized and refined sociodrama not only as a group creative problem-solving technique based in Moreno's early work, but also incorporating many of the creative problem-solving principles of Osborn and his colleagues. Although the use of sociodrama extends across virtually all age levels, Torrance focused on its use as a method of primary prevention of problem behaviors with disadvantaged and other high-risk populations.

The primary distinctions between sociodrama and its forerunner, psychodrama, lie less in methods than in purpose, although audience participation is much more important in sociodrama. In sociodrama, potential problem or conflict situations are derived from group discussion until an appropriate problem is established. The problem or conflict situation typically is not one currently being experienced by a group member, but rather one that is likely to be common to all the group members. No direction is given regarding the direction the solution is to take, as this is a major task of the group.

Members of the group are cast into roles they will play as the conflict situation is acted out. To facilitate the solution of the conflict, a number of production techniques may be employed, such as the soliloquy, direct presentation, double, mirror, role reversal, or other audience-involved methods.

The director's role in the sociodrama is to keep the action moving in the direction of a resolution of the conflict, with each session ending with a series of possible positive resolutions to the problems involved. Sociodramas should always be evaluated on the basis of their purpose and ability to move toward conflict resolution and not for their dramatic qualities or other criteria that may be irrelevant to the goals of the therapy session. Directors need to keep the audience involved throughout the session and to highlight rather than reduce the conflict present in the problem situation. By teaching participants to brainstorm alternative behaviors and to act out and rehearse for real-life problem solving, sociodrama has proved a useful method for preventing problem behaviors in children and adolescents at risk.

GROUP PROBLEM SOLVING
PSYCHODRAMA

C. R. REYNOLDS

SOCIOLOGY OF PSYCHOLOGICAL KNOWLEDGE

The sociology of psychological knowledge may be defined as the study of the social, political, and ideological context within which psychology has developed, both as a profession and as a science.

The sociology of psychological knowledge is actually a more focused example of the more encompassing discipline known as the sociology of knowledge. This latter field attempts to study the relationship between knowledge as a cultural product (e.g., ideologies, ethical beliefs, science, technology) and existential factors in society. Human thought is recognized to be conditioned in part by social substructures or human interrelationships. Examples of this enterprise include the writings of such social thinkers as Karl Marx, Max Scheler, Max Weber, and Emile Durkheim, all of whom attempted to analyze the social conditions of their time arising from the interplay of capitalism, science, technology, and democracy.

The sociology of knowledge contains yet another specialized subarea known as the sociology of science, because science is one way of acquiring knowledge. Although the sociology of knowledge concerns itself with the social basis of thought, the sociology of science examines the specific structure and process of the scientific enterprise. Science itself is viewed as a social institution and thus amenable to a sociological analysis.

The sociology of psychological science focuses on the process whereby psychological knowledge is achieved and disseminated, including such issues as the professional communication process (e.g., the journal review process), sex issues in hiring and promotion, government support for psychology training and research, the socialization process in psychology graduate education, and the geographical allocation and distribution of psychologists.

In Buss' inaugural work, five examples of the sociology of psychological knowledge are discussed briefly to elucidate this type of analysis. They focus on differential psychology, humanistic psychology, developmental psychology, behaviorism, and social psychology. As one instance, Buss views the rise of the study of individual differences (i.e., differential psychology) as based on the growth of capitalism, democracy, liberalism, science, and technology in England during the late nineteenth century.

THE ACADEMIC ACHIEVEMENT TEST

In Murray Levine's example of a sociological analysis of psychological knowledge, he provides documentation for viewing academic achievement tests and other related measures as outgrowths of Social Darwinism. Such testing, in Levine's view, helped legitimate different educational experiences for lower-class and middle-class youth and a differential allocation of youth to positions in the social structure.

Along a parallel line, documentation is provided for the development of age–grade organizational schemes in the school systems. Achievement tests served to provide some basis for promotion from one grade to the next; consequently, such test measures established age–grade scores that were reified over time. He further notes the existence of evidence for the notion that learning disabilities may well have been an outgrowth of the academic achievement test movement.

With regard to item analysis, Levine makes a case for viewing intelligence tests and achievement tests as indistinguishable from one another. If general intelligence is something different from school learning, then Levine suggests that contemporary achievement tests do not accomplish the task of measuring what is taught and learned in school. Furthermore, achievement tests are unable to measure such aspects as interest in the subject matter, reading with enjoyment, developing interpersonal and social competence, and learning to learn. Nonetheless, these tests are used to evaluate school programs aimed at achieving such goals.

Although conclusions drawn from such sociological analyses are always open to debate, one conclusion has become increasingly inescapable: There is a clear interplay between society and the development and use of knowledge, be it psychological or otherwise.

DESCRIPTIVE PSYCHOLOGY
INTERNATIONAL PSYCHOLOGY
PHILOSOPHY OF SCIENCE

A. BARÓN, JR.

SOCIOMETRY

Moreno described a number of ways of gathering data about interpersonal relations in groups. One approach, termed *sociometry,* attracted a great deal of attention among behavioral scientists and educators, as it provided a simple method of measuring interpersonal attraction among group members. The method has been used extensively in studying the social structure of play, work, and classroom groups, and has also proved useful in assessing the interpersonal attractiveness of individuals.

Sociometric data can be reported as the number of choices (or rejections) received by an individual group member. They can also serve as the basis for a "sociogram," which is a "map" of the choices made in response to the question.

Sociometry may be used to study factors related to group morale, and sociometric methods may be employed in any research concerned with interpersonal evaluations, attitudes, beliefs, or impressions that have evolved in a group setting. Among the variables that have been studied sociometrically are leadership, honesty, aggressiveness, prestige, and personal adjustment.

FRIENDSHIPS
INGROUPS/OUTGROUPS
INTERPERSONAL PERCEPTIONS

H. C. LINDGREN

SOCIOPSYCHOLOGICAL DETERMINANTS OF WAR AND PEACE

Since the beginning of recorded time, humans have relied on violence as the ultimate arbiter of their disputes. The sudden emergence of nuclear weapons with their limitless destructive capacity makes this time-tested solution unworkable. Human survival depends on the ultimate outlawing of recourse to violence in international disputes. The achievement of this distant, difficult, and perhaps impossible goal depends on contributions from all fields of human knowledge, including psychology, since in the last analysis decisions leading to war are made by individual leaders and leadership groups. Considered here are some of the psychological forces that trap national leaders and their constituents into the pursuit of power and security through the accumulation of nuclear weapons—a pursuit that, if unchecked, will inevitably result in disaster.

Although no solution to this problem can be envisaged in our present state of ignorance, any solution will depend on understanding the psychological forces involved.

FORCE OF HABIT

A good point of entry for our inquiry is the almost incomprehensible behavior of the leaders of the nuclear powers. All state unequivocally that they dread a strategic nuclear exchange, yet they pursue policies of competition in nuclear arms that steadily increase the likelihood of such a catastrophe. The basic psychological reason for this is that they are trying to master the threat of nuclear weapons by using the same ways of thinking and behaving that worked tolerably well with conventional ones. In actuality, in spite of the looming threat that nuclear weapons will be used, all armed conflicts are still being fought with prenuclear weapons, so the old patterns continue to be reinforced.

National leaders seek to preserve the war system by fantasizing scenarios of limited or theater nuclear war, ending with victory for one side before both are destroyed. To keep a nuclear war limited would require, among other conditions, a tight, minute-by-minute control of operations in the midst of a chaotic and mutually terrifying situation. Furthermore, while the fighting was actually going on, both sides, operating with different information, different weapons, and diametrically opposed objectives, would have to agree to accept the same outcome. Under these circumstances, the possibility of limiting any nuclear war is exceedingly remote.

THE PSYCHOLOGICAL UNREALITY OF NUCLEAR WEAPONS

Thinking about nuclear weapons as if they were nonnuclear ones is facilitated by the fact that, for almost all humans, the destructiveness of nuclear weapons exists only in the imagination. Except for the survivors of Hiroshima and Nagasaki, no one has experienced their effects directly.

Abruptness of Emergence of Nuclear Weapons

It took human beings hundreds of thousands of years to progress from a spear or a club, with which one weapon could kill one person, to a bomb containing a ton of dynamite, one of which could kill thousands of people. It took less than a decade to progress from this level to the hydrogen bomb, one of which can kill millions of people—at least as great a leap in destructive power as that between the spear and the dynamite bomb.

Thanks to their powers of symbolization, humans can adjust their thoughts rapidly to unprecedented new problems. Unfortunately, emotions, which determine behavior, change much more slowly. Psychiatrists have discovered that intellectual insight is powerless to change behavior unless accompanied by a "corrective emotional experience." Our intellect may tell us what we should do, but our emotions too often prevent us from doing it.

The Trap of Words

Because the nuclear weapons poised for annihilation are located in distant countries, they do not impinge on any of the senses—psychologically they exist only in words and, as has been pointed out, words that gain their meaning only by reference to other words have little, if any, emotional impact.

In the absence of direct sensory experience, our perception of reality is shaped by the words we use to describe it. Unfortunately, because nuclear weapons have emerged so recently, the only words we have to describe their properties are those appropriate to conventional weapons.

By the same token, although it is still true that nuclear weapons in the hands of an adversary are a grave threat, nuclear weapons in one's own hands, beyond a point long since passed by the nuclear superpowers, contribute not to the security, but to the insecurity, of all concerned. Yet such is the power of words that a preponderance of nuclear weapons over those of any adversary has been perceived by a U.S. president as "a margin of safety."

Habituation

Humans, like all living creatures, stop attending to stimuli that persist unchanged. When they first emerged in the form of the bombings of Hiroshima and Nagasaki, and again with the explosion of the first hydrogen bomb, nuclear weapons commanded worldwide attention; but as testing has gone underground and no further visible explosions have occurred, we have ceased to react to the burgeoning nuclear stockpiles, which have become part of the usually ignored background of our lives.

Denial

When, as occasionally happens, the full extent of the horror of nuclear weapons threatens to break into consciousness, it is met by denial or defensive avoidance. Denial is a normal and appropriate response to threats about which one can do nothing, such as one's own eventual death, but it is tragically maladaptive when failure to face the danger prevents the person from coping with it, as with the nuclear threat.

LEADERSHIP GROUPS AND BUREAUCRACIES

So far we have considered some of the psychological blocks in individuals to full awareness of and appropriate action against the menace of nuclear weapons. These are reinforced by aspects of the psychology of small groups and bureaucracies.

Leadership Groups

Leadership groups, like all groups, exert strong pressures on their members to conform. Under prolonged or intermittently acute stress, members of such groups come to rely increasingly on the development and maintenance of their primary group ties. Since the group feels a need to present a united front against actual or potential outside dangers, the deviant is sensed as a threat to the group's cohesiveness and singleness of purpose, and thereby a threat to its power. As a result, members suppress individual judgments in the service of preserving group cohesiveness, a phenomenon that has been labeled "groupthink."

Bureaucratic Forces

All leaders have to rely on bureaucracies to supply them with the information on which to base and implement decisions. Thus bureaucracies exercise powerful constraints on leaders by filtering the information that leaders receive. This power is enhanced by the bureaucrats being experts, whom the leaders, as nonexperts, cannot effectively challenge.

Although subunits within bureaucracies compete for power, status, and resources, they all cooperate when so doing will increase the resources available to all. All military services join in presenting "worst-case" analyses to political leaders and in supporting each other's demands for new weaponry because this leads to greater funding for all the units. Thus a major reason for the accumulation of nuclear arms is the competition between military services within nations.

Bureaucracies are even more resistant than individuals to making the adaptations needed to deal with new conditions.

As long as nuclear weapons are psychologically assimilated to conventional ones, regardless of the realities, the country that has a smaller or less technically advanced stockpile will see itself as weaker and will be seen as weaker by its opponents and allies. As Admiral Stansfield Turner has stated: "But whatever we do, it must not only correct the actual imbalance of (nuclear) capability; it must also correct the perception of imbalance . . . ."

In short, the pursuit of security through accumulating nuclear weapons is in reality more a race for prestige than actual strength. It is an especially costly and dangerous form of psychological warfare in which each nation seeks to achieve psychological security at the cost of real security.

Because fear, like any strong emotion, impedes problem solving by increasing rigidity of thinking, hampering consideration of alternatives, and shortening time perspective, from a psychological standpoint the first prerequisite for achieving new patterns of international relations compatible with nuclear weapons would be to take steps that would reduce mutual fears. Since two major sources of mutual fear are the growing stockpiles of nuclear weapons and the breakneck pace of research and development, which constantly threatens new "breakthroughs," a promising first step would be to institute a mutual freeze on the production, research, and deployment of nuclear weapons. At a more fundamental level, it would be necessary to develop ways of reducing the recurrent mutual misunderstandings and miscommunications between nations and of fostering international cooperation.

AGGRESSION
CONFLICT RESOLUTION
GRIT
MOB PSYCHOLOGY
VICTIMOLOGY
VIOLENCE

J. D. Frank

SOFT DETERMINISM

A soft determinist takes an intermediate position between strict causality and complete indeterminism. This position was accepted by Alfred Adler in his personalistic, subjective, and phenomenological psychology, although he never used the term in his writings. Soft determinism means that behavior is not capricious or random, but rather is orderly, lawful, and predictable, but within the limits of individual creativity.

A soft determinist holds that behavior is mainly controlled by the individual in terms of future purposes, the teleological position in science. Goals and purposes are subject to change, and consequently any individual's behavior will change accordingly in relation to that person's private, subjective, phenomenological views.

Adler's psychology held the creative self to be a central construct. In the dispute between Freud and his followers and Adler and his colleagues, this theme became a central battleground.

In proposing the creative self as a major theoretical construct in his theory, Adler introduced a sort of principle of indeterminancy similar to the Heisenberg principle in physics. The environment and heredity acting together on the child provided only probabilities at most.

For large numbers of persons born under similar environmental conditions and with similar genetic inheritance, rather accurate probability predictions may be made. As an example, for a large number of slum children in a certain ghetto, all of whom are Black and who come from divided homes, one may predict accurately that 80% will not complete high school. However, for any one child selected from that larger group, accurate predictions based on heredity and environment simply cannot be made.

One must consider, when trying to predict for one child, the creative power of *that* child. The behavior of the child is certainly influenced by both heredity and environmental conditions. Children (and adults) do tend to draw similar conclusions from similar circumstances, but the one who wishes to predict the future of an individual must know what use that individual has made of his or her experience.

ADLERIAN PSYCHOLOGY
DETERMINISM/INDETERMINISM
FREE WILL
PHILOSOPHY OF SCIENCE

T. E. Edgar

SOMATOPSYCHICS

Somatopsychics refers to psychological or psychiatric symptomatology of primary physical etiology. In contrast to psychosomatic disorders, which are physical conditions resulting from psychological stress, somatopsychic symptoms or disorders are presentations of a psychological or psychiatric nature directly caused by a somatic condition.

In everyday life, somatopsychically relevant occurrences are familiar. Emotional side effects produced by a body that is overheated, tired, or hungry may show as irritability, short-temperedness, irrational behavior, listlessness, diminished attention span, and so on. Hormonal changes have been found to effect psychological changes in some individuals. Mood swings and specific emotional states have been considered characteristic of adolescent and climacteric individuals. Some women experience premenstrual tension resulting in complaints ranging from depression, apathy, and fatigue to irritability and even aggressive acting out. The "baby blues" (postpartum depression) are equally recognized as a somatopsychic condition, although, in some instances, psychogenic components cannot be definitely excluded. High fever can cause anxiety and hallucinations, primarily in children. Psychological concomitants of aging, such as paranoid ideation, impaired judgment, obsessions, compulsions, memory defects, and outright personality changes, are common knowledge. Comparable changes have been observed in alcoholics and, to a lesser extent, in temporarily intoxicated persons. Behavioral consequences of the use of other pleasure-inducing drugs have been widely publicized. Various toxic ingestions such as lead poisoning (leading to learning disabilities, lethargy, somnolence, manic behavior, etc.), carbon monoxide poisoning (resulting in memory deficits, apathy, or depression), and exposure to asbestos and Agent Orange have become a public concern. Awareness has also been raised about mental and emotional detriments caused by deficiencies of certain nutritional elements (vitamins, minerals, proteins, etc.) and by malnutrition in general. Transient or permanent damage as a result of physical trauma, especially impact on the brain, is recognized as a cause of mental deficiencies, adverse emotional reactions, and personality changes.

Many drugs have been implicated in causing side effects. Much of the information collected on the medically and psychologically ill person in the somatopsychic field has been presented by R. C. W. Hall. Anxiety is found as a side effect of many physical conditions: in neurological (25%) and endocrinological disorders (25%) (including parathyroidism, diabetes mellitus, ovarian dysfunction), chronic infections (12%) (e.g., tuberculosis, mononucleosis, viral hepatitis), rheumatic disorders (12%) circulatory disorders (12%) and other conditions (14%) (including nephritis and nutritional deficiencies). About one third of the chronic renal disease patients (hemodialysis and kidney transplants) have been reported to suffer from significant psychopathology. The combination of tension, nervousness, anxiety, and fatigue appears as a consequence of many conditions. Depression to a pathological extent is a concomitant of pernicious anemia, lymphoma, parathyroidism, and viral hepatitis, and also of treatment with reserpine, corticosteroids, diazepam, and chloroquin, as well as of preventive measures in the form of certain oral contraceptives.

Biological, especially biochemical, theories of mental illness and mental retardation and of combinations of these, as seen in autism, are gaining recognition. Some outcomes, such as the mental retardation resulting from untreated phenylketonuria, can be explained entirely on a biological basis. Advanced research is identifying certain (sub)types of mental illness as a somatopsychic effect of biological conditions, including genetic and/or biochemical/environmental (e.g., nutritional) conditions. The work has contributed fundamentally to the establishment of orthomolecular psychiatry, which offers a biological approach (e.g., megavitamin therapy, mineral therapy) to the treatment and prevention of mental illness.

ORGANIC SYNDROMES
PSYCHOENDOCRINOLOGY
PSYCHOPHARMACOLOGY

E. WICK

SOMATOTYPES

The basic notion behind the idea of a somatotype is that behavior or personality is determined by physical body characteristics. The process of somatotyping is the method by which physical aspects of a body are described. This process of somatotyping has been highly systematized in the work of William Sheldon.

HISTORICAL ANTECEDENTS OF SOMATOTYPE THEORY

The suggestion that a relation exists between body characteristics and behavior dates at least as far back as the Greek physician Hippocrates, who proposed a typology in which people could be divided into four basic temperamental types—choleric, phlegmatic, sanguine, and melancholic—depending on which of four liquid substances ("humours") in the body was predominant. Although there were others after Hippocrates who related body factors to temperament, not until the work of Ernst Kretschmer, beginning in the 1920s, was the stage set for somatotyping. Kretschmer arrived at a schema for classifying human physique as *pyknic* (plump), *athletic* (muscular), or *asthenic* (frail and linear). A fourth category, *dysplastic,* described individuals who deviated greatly from any of the basic categories. Kretschmer concluded that there was a clear relationship between manic–depressive psychosis and the pyknic body build, and a similar association between schizophrenia and the asthenic, athletic, and certain dysplastic body builds.

Influenced by Kretschmer's views, William Sheldon proposed a somatotype theory that associated body structure and temperament in a new way. Based on a careful examination of thousands of photographs of the naked male body, Sheldon identified three basic dimensions for assessing physical structure. When *endomorphy* predominates, there is a soft roundness throughout the various regions of the body and the digestive viscera are massive and tend to dominate. *Mesomorphy* refers to the relative predominance of muscle, bone, and connective tissue. The mesomorphic physique is normally heavy, hard, and rectangular, with a predominance of muscle and bone. *Ectomomorphy* refers to long, slender, poorly muscled extremities. Relative to mass, the ectomorph has the largest brain. In Sheldon's technique of somatotyping, each individual is ranked in terms of the extent to which each of the primary physical dimensions is present in the person's physique.

Parallel to the three basic physical components, Sheldon postulates three temperamental components. Extreme *viscerotonia* is characterized by love of comfort, gluttony, sociability, and affection. *Somatotonia,* when predominant, indicates a craving for muscular activity and is generally associated with a lust for power, a certain callous ruthlessness, and a love of risk and chance. *Cerebrotonia,* in extreme form, means excessive restraint, inhibition, and shrinking from social contact. Sheldon has developed temperament scales by which an average score is computed for each component. Most of Sheldon's research revolves around the question of how much association exists between his components of physique and components of temperament. Sheldon reported that although the somatotype and the temperamental type do not always agree perfectly, the instances of any reversal of order of dominance in the three components are rare. Sheldon has also performed somatotyping of female bodies. Although there has generally been support from other investigators of Sheldon's empirical findings, the relationships between the somatotypes and temperament ratings have not been nearly as high as those reported by Sheldon.

PERSONALITY TYPES
PHYSIOGNOMY
SOCIOBIOLOGY
TEMPERAMENTS

J. L. ANDREASSI

SPECIES-SPECIFIC BEHAVIOR

Many behavioral patterns of nonhuman animals are characteristic of all appropriate members of the species and develop in the absence of specific learning experiences. These patterns are sometimes referred to as *species-specific behavior*. However, there are various conceptual traps when dealing with species-specific behavioral patterns, so some sharpening of definitions and explorations of their implications is appropriate.

In the broad sense, species-specific behavior refers to the behavior displayed by all or most members of a species. Some researchers, however, use the term in a narrower sense, restricting it to patterns that characterize a particular species and no other. Such behavioral patterns are *specific* to the species in the much more real sense that they are exclusive to the species. An example would be the songs of many species of birds that provide us with reliable cues as to their species identity. Some researchers would use the terms *species-characteristic* or *species-typical* when referring to behavior that is species-specific in the broader sense (i.e., characteristic of the species under study but perhaps of other species as well).

DEVELOPMENT

One of the conceptual traps related to species-specific behavior relates to its development. The term often has been used as an alternative to innate or instinctive. The European ethologists often referred to such patterns as *fixed-action patterns*. All of these terms have excess meaning with respect to the nature of the factors important in the development of the behavior. They may suggest to the reader that the environment is unimportant in the development of the behavior. *Species-specific* is more neutral and sometimes has been preferred for that reason.

According to contemporary views, development entails epigenetic processes, suggesting that all behavior is the product of the continuous and dynamic interaction of the developing organism, its genotype, and the environment. The environment is as important for the development of the organism and its species-specific behavior as for any other behavioral patterns. What is unusual about many species-specific behavioral patterns is that they do not require specific input for the behavioral pattern that will develop.

Another example is provided by the patterns of copulatory behavior in different species of rodents. These patterns differ among related species with respect to fairly stable characteristics. For example, the pattern of a grasshopper mouse is different from that of a deer mouse. There are many environmental manipulations that can affect both whether an animal mates, and if so, the timing and frequency of various events in the sequences of the two species. However, there is no known manipulation that qualitatively alters the species-specific pattern: of male grasshopper mice that mate and of all deer mice that mate, all grasshopper mice mate like grasshopper mice and all deer mice mate like deer mice.

Some researchers believe that to call a behavioral pattern innate or instinctive suggests that it is preformed and need only unfold according to some predetermined plan, rather than developing through dynamic organism–gene–environment interactions. It is for these reasons that they prefer the term species-specific.

SPECIES

Another conceptual trap surrounding the concept of species-specific behavior concerns what is meant by *species*. If the concept of species-specific is to be clear, so must be the concept of species. Our common sense conception of species is both typological and morphological. Members of a species are often thought of as all being of some ideal type, and the type is thought of structurally. Thus one distinguishes between cardinals and bluejays on the basis of their appearance and thinks of them as representations of ideal type specimens. A more biological concept defines a species as a group of animals capable of interbreeding among themselves under natural conditions but reproductively isolated from individuals that belong to different species. Thus species are conceptualized in relation to the possibility of reproduction in nature, rather than structure. It is important that this refers only to natural conditions; lions and tigers can produce ligers and tiglons in zoos, but they would not do so if placed together in nature. The most critical aspect of this conception is that members of a species may look very different yet still belong to the same species if they are part of a potentially unified reproductive group. In some species, the males and females may look so different that they were previously classified as belonging to different species. In others, developmental stages, such as metamorphosis, may render them unrecognizable as members of the same species unless individuals are followed longitudinally. All are members of the species; there is no ideal type.

Application of the biological species concept to the problem of species-specific behavior enables one to make further refinements. Species-specific behavior is characteristic of all *appropriate* members of the species. Some species-specific patterns may be characteristic only of males or of females. This is true of territorial defense in stickleback fish. Other patterns may appear only under particular conditions. During the breeding season, behavior may be different from behavior at other times of the year. Behavior may be changed radically as animals metamorphose through different developmental stages. All of these kinds of behavioral patterns may be regarded as species-specific characteristics, as long as one remembers that they are displayed only by the appropriate animals and only under the appropriate conditions.

TAXONOMY

Although species are defined in relation to reproductive activities, individuals usually are classified on the basis of structure. Species-specific behavioral patterns can be so characteristic of a species as to be useful in determining the appropriate relationships among closely related species. Characteristics are said to be *homologous* when they constitute a resemblance between two species that can be explained by descent from a common ancestor possessing the character in which they are similar to each other. Thus the wings of all species of bats are homologous to those of all other bat species, but are not homologous with the wings of birds or insects, which evolved in different lineages.

In general, species that are more closely related evolutionarily have more homologous characteristics, including species-specific behavioral patterns. These can be useful in classifying species that are difficult to classify using morphological criteria. For example, some species of fireflies cannot be told apart on the basis of appearance, but display different courtship patterns and are reproductively isolated from each other. They are thus good biological species, but can be classified only on the basis of their species-specific behavior. Ethologist Konrad Lorenz developed a taxonomy of the Anatidae, ducks and geese, based on shared behavioral patterns. Because the resulting diagram resembled an old-fashioned shaving-brush, it sometimes is referred to as the shaving-brush model.

By classifying and comparing the motor patterns used by different species of snakes when applying constrictive coils to prey, Greene and Burghardt showed these patterns to fit a consistent pattern through the evolution of closely related species. A single pattern was displayed by members of 48 species in four different primitive families, suggesting that the pattern evolved no later than the early Paleocene. Such findings provide support for more traditional systems of classification and reveal the precise structure of the pattern found in the evolution of behavioral patterns. They also reveal how specific species-specific behavior can be.

CONCLUSIONS

Many behavioral patterns are characteristic of all appropriate members of a species. Some are so specific as to be characteristic only of members of that species. The latter clearly are species-specific. The former may be referred to as species-specific, species-characteristic, or species-typical depending on one's definitions. It is important to remember, however, that even though these behavioral patterns are common in virtually all appropriate members of a species, they have complex ontogenetic patterns that are the result of dynamic developmental relationships.

ADAPTATION
ANIMAL SEXUAL BEHAVIOR
EVOLUTION
INSTINCT
RITUAL BEHAVIOR

D. A. DEWSBURY

SPECIFIC HUNGERS

Specific hunger is an increased preference for foods that contain a specific nutrient, such as a mineral or a vitamin, under conditions of increased need for that nutrient. It is usually distinguished from pica, which is a specific preference for ingesting something useless or harmful, such as clay or dirt.

The phenomenon of specific hungers was first documented by Curt Richter, who found that rats would adaptively modify their intake of carbohydrates, fats, proteins, sodium, calcium, the B vitamins, vitamin E, and others.

The specific hunger for sodium chloride (NaCl), unlike other known specific hungers, apparently depends on an innately programmed mechanism that can be triggered by need. When a rat becomes deficient in NaCl, it immediately shows an enhanced preference for foods and liquids containing any concentration of NaCl, or containing the similar-tasting, but poisonous, LiCl. It also shows an exaggerated rate of an operant behavior that was reinforced by NaCl prior to the need state, but is in extinction after the need occurs. There is some evidence that the same principles apply to humans.

In contrast, other specific hungers appear to develop in a trial-and-error manner. Apparently the preference develops, at least in large part, by the process of elimination, as the animal learns aversions to each deficient food it tries. For some nutrients, such as vitamins A and D, rats learn neither aversions to deficient diets nor preferences for enriched diets.

In addition, learning of specific preferences does sometimes occur. D. M. Zahorik demonstrated that rats develop preferences for foods that facilitate recovery from vitamin deficiency, and that they prefer these foods even to old "safe" foods that neither caused nor relieved a deficiency.

ANIMAL INSTINCTIVE BEHAVIOR
MALNUTRITION AND BEHAVIOR

J. W. KALAT

SPEECH AND HEARING MEASURES

Clinical, industrial, and research purposes are among those served by speech and hearing measurement. The nature of the tests and procedures used depends on the purposes of the testing.

SPEECH–LANGUAGE MEASURES

Speech Communication Systems

For purposes such as development of telephone fidelity, speech may be measured by experimental psychologists or engineers in terms of sound-wave properties such as frequency, amplitude, and sound waveform. Licklider and Miller have mentioned graphical methods, which use mathematical Fourier analysis of the waveform for analyzing speech into its component frequencies. They have also described the use of electrical methods, such as the Sound Spectrograph, which notes the changes in intensity–frequency pattern as a function of time. Visual patterns (spectrograms) for various words or phrases may be obtained and compared.

Physiological Function

Physiological aspects of speech and voice production may be studied by such methods as electrophysiological and cinefluorographic methods.

Clinical Assessment of Speech–Language

Evaluation of speech–language function for clinical purposes entails assessment of one or more of a number of subareas of speech and language. These subareas may include articulation, or phonology (the production of speech sounds); voice, or phonation, and resonance; language perception, processing, and production; and fluency (which includes stuttering).

Personnel qualified to administer clinical evaluations include certified speech–language pathologists and certified audiologists. When determining etiology and planning treatment of voice and hearing problems, medical evaluation should always be included in the assessment plan.

Although a number of standardized tests have been developed, speech–language evaluation frequently includes informal assessment by qualified professionals, because of the variability of cultural and regional norms.

HEARING MEASUREMENT

Electrical responses from the central auditory system yield information that may be of both experimental and clinical interest. Pure-tone audiometers generate vibrations that may be adjusted to vary the intensity (loudness) of tones ranging from low to high frequency (pitch). By indicating when each tone is heard, an individual may be assessed for the threshold of hearing throughout the audible range of frequencies. An *audiogram* is used to graph the results of the test. Hearing loss, in decibels, is recorded for frequencies tested. The type of hearing loss may then be determined by evaluating the data obtained from audiometric and other clinical tests.

AUDIOMETRY
HEARING
PSYCHOPHYSICS

B. B. MATES

SPEECH DEVELOPMENT

Until the 1960s, most students of speech–language development viewed the child as a relatively passive learner, hearing and absorbing the language patterns of older speech emitters. Two "insights" have changed this viewpoint. The first is that children speak their own languages with their own sets of rules and patterns. A child's speech is not merely a garbled simplification of the language of adults. Second, children must be their own linguists, listening to the speech of others and hypothesizing the rules of language. They then test those hypotheses by using them to try to understand the speech of others and to formulate their own speech.

The rapidity of speech and language learning is unmatched by the acquisition rate for other kinds of cognitive learning, in spite of the complexity and abstractness of linguistic structure. According to McNeill, a basis for the rich and intricate competence of adult grammar must emerge in the short span of 24 months.

STAGES OF DEVELOPMENT

The development of speech in young children typically follows a sequential pattern. What varies is the *rate* at which each child progresses through the various stages. Occasionally, children move so quickly through a stage that they appear to have skipped it altogether. The *prelanguage* stage extends through the first year of life, and encompasses the cooing and babbling periods. Usually during the third month of life, the child moves out of the crying-noises-only stage into the cooing stage. By the fifth month, most children are at the babbling stage, producing an increased variety of sounds. There is no convincing evidence that cooing and babbling are in any way essential to subsequent speech development. In the later months of the babbling stage, the child's linguistic environment begins to assert itself, so the babbling slowly takes on some of the intonational characteristics of the language to which the child is exposed.

The child's first words normally appear around the beginning of the second year of life. This begins the *holophrastic* stage, when the child uses single words usually meant to convey the meaning of a whole sentence.

At age 18 to 20 months the child begins to put words together. New combinations appear with increasing frequency, and the repertoire burgeons. These early efforts to communicate by combining words result in *telegraphic speech,* which is effective in spite of the lack of articles, prepositions, affixes, and other formative aspects of language.

THEORETICAL CONSIDERATIONS

Researchers, theorists, and students of speech and language development have tended to divide into two basic camps in the search for answers to some vexing fundamental questions. On the one side are the empiricists, generally committed to the concept of language as a learned skill.

Contrasted with this is the rationalist position, which assumes some innate knowledge of the basic structure of language. The rationalists maintain that the ease and speed with which children progress in language development can come about only through some genetic bioprogramming. D. Bickerton supports the general rationalist position on the basis of conclusions from his studies of Creole languages.

COMMUNICATION PROCESSES
EARLY CHILDHOOD DEVELOPMENT

O. G. JOHNSON

SPEECH DISORDERS

Speech is disordered when it interferes with communication, creates a problem for the listener, or causes maladjustment in the speaker.

Speech disorders are classified into four broad symptom types: (a) rhythm, (b) phonation, (c) articulation, and (d) symbolization. *Disorders of rhythm* essentially comprise various types of stuttering (stammering). Most modern speech pathologists make no distinction between stuttering and stammering. In this disorder, the flow of speech is interrupted by difficulty encountered at the initial part of a word or by sudden breaks and spasms once the sound begins. Children often begin to stutter at around 3 years of age or when entering school. Without undue pressure to speak, the problem ordinarily abates and disappears. When attention is called to children's malfunctioning speech or they are labeled as stutterers, generally then secondary symptoms of avoidance, struggling, and grimacing develop.

In disorders of rhythm, anxiety plays a prominent role. The relearning and deconditioning of feared situations can be of value in treating the psychological aspects of the problem while reducing the intensity and frequency of stuttering spasms. Disorders of rhythm are largely psychological in nature, but on occasion they can result from cerebral vascular accidents or neurophysiological disturbances.

Phonation disorders are characterized by disturbances in timbre, intensity, and pitch. Stereotyped inflections, hypernasal sounds, falsettoes, guttural speech, marked foreign accents, and cleft-palate speech all comprise examples of disturbances in phonation. These disorders lend themselves to treatment by a speech correctionist, whereas stuttering, with its highly charged emotional conflicts, may require the services of a professional psychologist knowledgeable in speech pathology or of other individuals with similar training and expertise.

Articulatory disturbances involve patterns where distortion, omission, substitution, and addition of speech sounds are evident. Characteristic illustrations are *delayed speech,* where a paucity of sounds or unintelligibility prevails; *lalling,* where sluggish use of the tongue tip occurs; *lisping* of all varieties (frontal, lingual, lateral, and occluded), when sibilant sounds and the t or d letters are involved; and *baby talk,* where infantile letters and sounds continue past the age of 2 to 3 years.

Disorders of symbolization occur largely in aphasia or dysphasia. Expressive problems predominate, although sensory disturbances often influence aphasic speech as well. Anatomical physical insults and organic brain disorders may operate in combination with psychological problems, or as an initial cause in and of themselves, to produce symbolic disorders. Aphasia, in particular, is the result of organic brain impairment, most frequently resulting from a cerebral vascular accident.

COMMUNICATION PROCESSES
SPEECH PERCEPTION

C. J. FREDERICK

SPLIT-BRAIN RESEARCH

Systematic split-brain research was initiated by Roger Sperry. A "split-brain" patient or experimental animal is produced when the main connecting link of millions of nerve fibers between the two halves of the cerebral cortex of the brain is severed. This most prominent connecting link is called the *corpus callosum.* Observations of human patients and experimental animals who had undergone this type of hemispheric deconnection led to little noticeable disruption of brain function, but experiments by Sperry and his associates revealed that the split brain is not entirely normal in function. For example, it was found in experimental animals that when the corpus callosum was cut, information learned by one side of the brain was not transferred to the other hemisphere. Subsequent studies using visual and touch discriminations and motor learning supported this basic finding.

There is evidence that the right hemisphere is generally superior to the left in spatial, motor, and other nonverbal activities. Evidence has also accumulated to support the conclusion that the left hemisphere of most human brains is concerned with numerical and analytic as well as linguistic activities.

BRAIN
BRAIN LATERALITY
LATERAL DOMINANCE
NEUROPSYCHOLOGY
PSYCHOSURGERY

J. L. ANDREASSI

SPORTS PSYCHOLOGY

Sports psychologists are concerned with the application of psychological theories and methods to sports, play, and recreational activities and with the discovery of more effective ways to further the learning and enjoyment of sports.

Modern sports psychology has broadened considerably from the early focus on motor learning, perception, and biomechanics. John Salmela includes a listing in which the professionals list their major areas of interest in the field. The most cited listings include motor skill learning, personality, anxiety and stress, conflict and competition, imagery training, relaxation training, hypnosis, attention training, motivation, socialization, development, team building, play and leisure, mental training, coaching, counseling, and fitness. The specific sports concentrations of these professionals range all the way from dance to baseball and basketball, and from soccer and fencing to volleyball, tennis, golf, and many others.

EXAMPLES OF SPORTS PSYCHOLOGY RESEARCH

In the early development of the field, psychologists simply attempted to apply general systems and methods of psychology to sports.

Rainer Martens applies general social psychology theories and methods to sports. There are limits, however, as to how directly and completely instruments from the field can be applied to another field. Martens found that general anxiety tests could not effectively discriminate athletes who experienced high anxiety during competition from those who did not. However, when he devised a special *Sport competition anxiety test,* discriminations were possible.

A long continued line of research has been the study of the role of mental practice in sports learning. B. R. Bugelski reports that most investigations show (a) that subjects who do physical practice followed by mental practice usually do just as well as subjects who do all physical practice, and (b) that subjects who are visual imagers do better than those who are low in imagery. This kind of research continued successfully when most experimental psychology was ignoring imagery and cognition. Bugelski cites a classic study of basketball free throws reported by R. Vandell and colleagues. Group I practiced every day for 20 days; group II, the control, did not practice; and group III engaged in mental practice for 20 days. The improvement in free-throw shooting was 41% for the physical practice group, 2% for the control, and 43% for the mental practice group. Innumerable studies of the same design have been conducted for all kinds of physical skills (high jumping, piano playing, dart throwing, gymnastics, and others), with generally similar results. Richard Suinn has suggested that these findings can be applied to counseling.

Many sports psychologists have applied batteries of personality tests to athletes and nonathletes and to athletes of different levels of skill to examine whether there is an "athletic type." Although there is considerable variability in the findings, a guarded conclusion is that the male athlete tends to be characterized by extroversion and emotional stability and to be self-assertive, self-confident, and capable of enduring stress. Female athletes tend to show lower extroversion scores than males, but higher emotional stability scores.

SPORTS COUNSELING AND SPORTS CONSULTING

When applied to individual athletes, sports counseling is designed to improve the athlete's performance. Problems such as precompetition anxiety, the fear of winning, slumps, and sustaining practice motivation are considered. Team sports consultants are concerned with team building, communication, and coaching problems.

APPLICATIONS OF SPORTS PSYCHOLOGY

As a field of study matures, it begins to borrow less from more established fields and to develop its own methods and theories, and is itself applied by professionals working in other contexts. Within the past decade, sports psychology has begun to be applied more widely.

Mental Health Applications

There are many research reports about the beneficial effects of jogging, running, and other sports to offset mental illnesses. John Greist and coworkers report that running is as effective in alleviating depressive symptoms as either time-limited or time-unlimited psychotherapy. However, there has also been a clinical recognition that sports can become the negative focus for a neurosis.

Business Applications

Robert Nideffer has devised a Test of Attentional and Interpersonal Style (TAIS), which has been used to identify the preferred style of attending (external–internal and broad–narrow) of athletes. The test identifies which situations are likely to overload the athlete's concentration and lead to performance errors. Nideffer has also devised a system of attentional control training that teaches athletes how to recognize and compensate for their attentional errors. Pratt and Nideffer describe how these measures and techniques of attention control training have been applied in business (with managers and executives) and in other organizational settings (e.g., police officers, fire fighters).

CONCLUSIONS

Richard Bolles, as well as other vocational counselors, have pointed out that men and women today are unwilling to delay recreation and leisure until their retirement years. Instead, they want to blend recreation, work, education, and social activities throughout their lifetimes.

These trends, along with the continued appreciation of lifestyle factors for health and well-being, are likely to widen the role of the sports psychologist in the future. Sports, especially competitive sports, provide for psychology a social laboratory in which people voluntarily undertake to master extremely difficult skills and subject themselves to intense physical stress and social pressure. For recreation and leisure, sports relate to essential features of the human biological inheritance— emotions, movement, competition, cooperation, and play. For applied

psychology and therapy, sports psychology can offer both a testing ground for ideas and methods and, in return, new role models of fitness, coaching, and training for the applied psychologist.

HEALTH PSYCHOLOGY
LEISURE COUNSELING

J. T. HART

SPOUSE ABUSE

Gelles and Straus report that between 20 and 40% of all murders in the United States involve domestic relationships. Police reports indicate that the majority of calls for help are from spouses involved in domestic disputes, and a high percentage of police fatalities result from investigation of such domestic disputes. Violence also appears to be a major complaint of spouses seeking a divorce and to be common even in the average intact U.S. marriage.

What is spouse abuse? People who experience marital violence, as well as theorists and researchers, must face this definitional issue. Spouse abuse is usually defined in terms of violence directed at a spouse. Violence is assumed to be physical, relatively severe, and sometimes repeated over time. Verbal abuse, less severe physical acts, and once-in-a-lifetime occurrences may not be considered to be spouse "abuse."

What causes spouse abuse? Various causes have been hypothesized and studied, including psychopathology, social class, and sex drives. Although violent spouses may appear to be mentally ill at the time of the violence, spouse abusers, with rare exceptions, are not mentally ill. More violence is reported by or about lower class couples, but this may be true because middle class couples tend to have more resources and more privacy, so that violent acts are less likely to involve the authorities or the public record. The fact remains that spouse abuse occurs among all classes of people. Other causal explanations involving biology, violence and sex connections, or sex drive have been generally discounted. Husbands may be more violent, but both husbands and wives resort to violence and are abused. Although not necessarily causal, use of alcohol has been found to be related to spouse abuse.

Straus proposed a more comprehensive theory of spouse abuse causation. According to this theory, the causes of abuse are to be found "in the structure of American society and its family system," and include such factors as a high level of family conflict, high level of violence in society, family socialization to violence cultural norms legitimizing violence, sexual inequality, and coping resources of women.

What keeps spouses in abusive marriages? Wives generally report four factors: (a) economic dependency; (b) presence of young children; (c) fear of living alone; and (d) perceived stigma of divorce. Severity and frequency of violence, history of physical punishment in childhood, and relative resources and power also are factors related to wives remaining with abusive husbands.

BATTERED PEOPLE
CHILD ABUSE
VICTIMOLOGY

J. W. ENGEL

SPOUSE SELECTION

In a society that places high values on individualism, we are inclined to believe that we choose our spouses on the basis of love-inspired free choice. The average adult has several love affairs before choosing a partner, and love may be secondary to other considerations when the choice is made. Factors such as vocational readiness and the approval of significant others in one's life have great influence on the decision to marry. Review of the data on heterogamy versus homogamy sheds much light on the process and outcome of mate selection.

HETEROGAMY

R. F. Winch has been the most vigorous proponent of the view that courting individuals seek partners whose needs complement rather than duplicate their own.

Although an appealing concept, research has generally failed to support the complementarity hypothesis. Not only have partners been shown to be generally unaware of each other's compensatory strengths, but there also has been no support for the notion that complementarities that are serviceable for one sex are equally so for the other and no formulas have been developed for determining the values that suitors would place on compensatory strengths and weaknesses in any complementarity-determining equation.

HOMOGAMY

Although virtually every culture prohibits incest and requires familial exogamy, many subcultural groups prescribe endogamy as a means of preserving the integrity of their social organizations. This may explain the fact that there is a preponderance of evidence showing that suitors are likely to choose partners of their own race, educational level, socioeconomic status, and ethnic subgroup. When concessions are made and a party from a higher status group chooses a partner with lower social standing, concessions are usually made in age and beauty, although within strata, men and women typically choose partners with age and appearance characteristics that match their own. This is consistent with what Murstein has termed an "exchange theory" of mate selection, in which each prospective partner seeks to enhance his or her social and psychological standing by choosing the most outwardly desirable mate possible.

The fact that education and other overt social characteristics do predict mate selection may be explained by the fact that these factors influence the range of potential partners that each suitor will encounter. This "propinquity factor" in mate selection recognizes the fact that residential and occupational segregation strongly determine the field of eligibles one will meet by virtue of time, distance, cost, and opportunity. The fact that religious integration exists at virtually every level of U.S. society may explain the fact that interreligious marriage is fast becoming the norm.

The less discernible similarity in values, attitudes, and behavior that we tend to seek in friends have also been shown to be highly valued criteria in the choice of mates. The motivation for selecting as intimates those who share one's frame of reference undoubtedly is the resulting ease in achieving consensus on the myriad decisions that must be made each day, as well as the validation of one's own beliefs and actions. Therefore it is not surprising that literally hundreds of studies have shown that couples appear to display greater consensus as they advance from casual acquaintanceship through marriage.

Errors in assumed similarity are explained by several factors. First, courtship has been regarded as a time of maximal human deception as each party seeks to gain the other's acceptance by attempting to make the most positive impression possible, often at the price of honesty. Beyond working from faulty data, the processes that courting partners use to organize their impressions of others tend to be more *psychological* than *scientifically* logical, very often leading to false conclusions.

The choice of partners in marriage has great significance for the stability of societies and their subgroups as well as for the long-term happiness of individuals. Social constraints on opportunities to meet prospective mates and barriers to certain unions considered objectionable are the means through which macrosocial bodies control who will marry whom. Within the pool of eligibles, each person must determine the

criteria that he or she will use to select a mate, must gather the data necessary to apply each criterion, and must weigh each datum in an overall go–no-go decision-making matrix.

EXCHANGE THEORY
HUMAN COURTSHIP PATTERNS
TABOOS

R. B. Stuart

STANFORD ACHIEVEMENT TEST

Stanford is a group-administered achievement battery for measuring fundamental learning levels of U.S. primary and secondary school pupils in reading, mathematics, language, science, social studies, and listening skills. The seventh edition of Stanford is for kindergarten through the 13th grades and contains 10 levels with more than 170 subtests and 7000 items.

Successive editions of the Stanford chronicle both the changing curricular emphases of U.S. schools and the evolution of the science of educational measurement. The achievement battery innovation facilitated the interpretation of intersubtest strengths and weaknesses. Machine scoring was introduced in the 1940 edition, and various refinements in scaling, norming, and sampling technology have appeared in successive editions.

Interpretation of the Stanford has typically relied on national norm-referenced derived scores such as grade equivalents, grade-based percentile ranks, and stanines. The seventh edition also offers criterion-referenced test interpretations for test content clusters.

ACADEMIC ABILITY GROUPING
ACADEMIC ACHIEVEMENT TESTS
PSYCHOMETRICS
SCHOOL LEARNING

G. J. Robertson

STANFORD–BINET INTELLIGENCE SCALE

More than any other psychological instrument, the Stanford–Binet Intelligence Scale has had an impact on U.S. society. It entered into the thinking of legislators and business people. As its use expanded in the education of bright and dull students and in the treatment of persons who are considered to be mentally handicapped, controversies developed as to its constancy, the relative contributions of heredity and environment, and its pertinency in theoretical differential psychology and in practical decisions affecting the future of individuals.

As a device useful in classifying children for instructional purposes, the intelligence scale was invented by Alfred Binet, a French psychologist. He was the first to apply psychological tests to children. Binet originated the concept of mental age and eventually arranged his tests in age groups.

The 1916 Stanford–Binet was definitely a revision of Binet's scale, with many tests taken from it directly. However, it included a number of new tests, mostly from Terman's work. The scale as a whole was carefully standardized, using extensive and representative samples of children and adults. The most important innovation, the IQ, was defined as the ratio of mental age to chronological age, with the maximum chronological age at a point where measured mental ability tends to level off.

In 1937, Terman and Maud A. Merrill published two carefully equated scales, Form L and Form M, each containing 129 tests with minimal overlap. The third revision, *The Stanford–Binet Intelligence Scale,* by Terman and Merrill, appeared in 1960. The two 1937 forms were consolidated into Form L-M, with many items eliminated and some relocated. A major change was the redefinition of the IQ as a standard score with a mean of 100 and standard deviation of 16. In 1972, revised norms were published, covering the age range from 2 to 18 years of age and taking into account the impact on test performance of recent social and cultural developments.

INTELLIGENCE MEASURES
WECHSLER INTELLIGENCE TESTS

P. H. DuBois

STATE-DEPENDENT LEARNING

The phenomenon of state-dependent learning relates principally to the use of drugs and their effects on memory or performance. When subjects are trained to perform a particular task followed by an injection of either a drug or saline solution during a test session, any impairment caused by the drug cannot necessarily be attributed to the direct effect of the drug on the nervous system. Overton demonstrated this with a simple experiment. One-half of the rats received a drug before training, while the other half received saline before training. Each of these groups was subdivided so that one subgroup was tested with the drug and the other subgroup was tested with saline. Rats trained with the drug and tested with saline showed definite impairment, as did rats trained with saline and tested with the drug. Rats that received saline during both sessions or drug during both sessions showed perfect retention. In short, impairment was not caused by the action of the drug on the nervous system but instead was due to the difference in the state of the organism between sessions, which Overton called *state-dependent* or *dissociated learning.* The conclusion is that in order to remember it is necessary for the organism to be in essentially the same physiological state as during acquisition.

One explanation of this phenomenon relates to McGeoch's point that any change in stimulus conditions between acquisition and recall produces poorer retention. This is true for both internal conditions or set and external context. Presumably, this effect is simply another example of the principle of stimulus generalization decrement, namely that stimuli out on the generalization gradient away from the original stimulus to which the response was learned have a weakened response tendency. That is, the internal state of the organism is a critical component of the total stimulus context for the learned response, and altering it produces forgetting.

An alternative interpretation of state-dependent learning has been called *subsystem replacement.* The drugs that affect the central nervous system are usually selective with reference to which group of neurons is involved. Under normal conditions a particular population of neurons mediates the learning of a particular task, but other neurons are also capable of doing this. So, if the action of the dominant group of neurons is blocked by a drug, the next population in line would mediate the acquisition of the task. Testing for retention with the subject under the influence of the drug should yield good performance; but retention without the drug should be poor, for that part of the nervous system now in control was not involved in the acquisition of this task.

Although there is some experimental evidence in favor of the subsystem replacement interpretation, the notion of generalization decrement is still quite viable; it is certainly possible that both interpretations can apply, although probably for different situations.

State-dependent learning also occurs with the use of electroconvulsive shock (ECS) and hypothermia, and here it is quite clearly related to stimulus similarity or generalization decrement. It has been demonstrated that ECS-induced retrograde amnesia for a punished response can be alleviated simply by presenting a noncontingent foot shock that makes recall more similar to acquisition conditions. Amnesia for a learned appetitive response was eliminated by the presentation of food but not by foot shock, whereas the reverse was true with amnesia for a punished response.

With hypothermia-induced retrograde amnesia, studies have shown that the subject must reach a critical level of recooling during recall before the learned response occurs. That is, the internal stimulus contexts for acquisition and recall must match well.

It also is possible that state dependency can help explain the Kamin effect. In shuttlebox avoidance learning, performance deteriorates with the passage of time and is poorest after about an hour away from the task (Kamin effect). This sort of forgetting can be eliminated by treatments administered just before testing. These reminders (stressors) are designed to reduce the contextual "mismatch" between acquisition and recall. Thus injections of adrenocorticotropic hormone (ACTH), forced swimming, and noncontingent foot shock all improve the rat's performance during testing.

CENTRAL NERVOUS SYSTEM
CONTEXTUAL ASSOCIATION
CRITICAL PERIODS
FIELD DEPENDENCY
VARIABLES IN RESEARCH

M. R. Denny

STATISTICAL INFERENCE

The process of drawing conclusions about a population on the basis of samples (in effect, subsets) drawn randomly from the population is statistical inference. It is widely used in psychology because whole populations can rarely be measured. The logic of statistical inference is the same regardless of the particular problem and techniques employed. On the basis of a sample, the researcher wishes to make statements about what is probably true of the population.

Measures taken on samples are called *statistics;* comparable measures of the population are called *population parameters.* A statistic is calculated on a specific and finite set of data. It will not necessarily equal the population parameter unless the sample is infinitely large, thus including the whole population. Instead, any sample is likely to yield statistics that differ from the true population parameters. The problem becomes one of deciding how accurately each statistic reflects the corresponding population parameters. The application of statistical inference, therefore, requires knowledge of probability theory.

The actual process of statistical inference often begins with setting up the *null hypothesis* (H_0): The researcher assumes that a sample statistic (commonly a mean) was drawn from a population with known parameters. If comparisons between samples are required, the researcher assumes each group (and its corresponding statistics) was sampled from the same population.

The null hypothesis is retained or rejected on the basis of how likely is the observed outcome. Standardized *test statistics* (such as z, t, F, and chi square), whose values have known probabilities, are used to evaluate sample statistics in relation to variability. If the difference between groups is largely relative to the amount of variability in the data, the researcher rejects the null hypothesis and concludes that the observed difference was unlikely to have occurred by chance alone: The result is statistically significant. In psychology, researchers customarily reject the null hypothesis if the observed outcome (in effect, the computed test statistic) is so extreme that it could have occurred by chance with a probability of less than 5% ($p < 0.05$).

Because statistical inferences are based on probability estimates, two incorrect decisions are possible: type I errors, in which the null hypothesis is rejected although true, and type 2 errors, in which the null hypothesis is retained although invalid. The former results in incorrect confirmation of the research hypothesis and the latter in the failure to identify a statistically significant result.

STATISTICS IN PSYCHOLOGY

A. MYERS

STATISTICAL SIGNIFICANCE

Researchers often employ statistical tests to evaluate the results of their studies. These tests permit the researcher to assess the probability that such results might have been due to chance. The term *statistical significance* is used in relation to the use of these tests.

The term *statistically significant* is applied to results in which the probability of chance is *equal to or below* an agreed on level. Most psychologists accept a 5% (or lower) probability of chance as being statistically significant. This is typically reported as $p < 0.05$ or $p < 0.01$, which means that if the study were replicated 100 times, we would expect to observe these results less than five times (or one time) due to chance. Statistical significance may be determined for both tests of difference and tests of relationship.

STATISTICS IN PSYCHOLOGY

C. J. DREW

STATISTICS IN PSYCHOLOGY

The first use of statistics in psychology is often credited to Sir Francis Galton. The term statistics in psychology refers to the application of quantitative measures and techniques to reporting and analyzing the results of psychological studies. The use of statistics is essential to psychology as a science. Observing, recording, and analyzing quantitative data permit meaningful comparisons based on objective standards. Statistics in psychology is commonly divided into two branches—descriptive and inferential.

DESCRIPTIVE STATISTICS

Descriptive statistics are procedures used to organize, summarize, and describe data. Such indicators describe relatively large bodies of data in quick, efficient ways. The most commonly used descriptive procedures are frequency distributions, measures of central tendency, and measures of relative standing. Regression and correlation are techniques used to describe relationships between variables.

Frequency Distributions

A frequency distribution shows the tally of how many times each score or value (or interval of scores or values) occurred in a set of data. Relative frequencies, the percent of responses of each value, are also often reported. The frequency distribution provides quick insight into the pattern of results, insight that would be difficult to achieve by working directly with raw data. Graphics are often used to provide visual representations of frequency data.

Measures of Central Tendency

Measures of central tendency are summary statistics that describe what is typical of a distribution. The *mode* is the most frequently occurring score. The *median* is the score that divides the distribution in half, so that one-half the distribution falls above the median and one-half the distribution falls below the median. The *mean* is the arithmetic average of all the scores. Whether the mean, median, or mode provides the best description depends on the shape of the distribution. If the distribution is symmetrical and has one mode (*unimodal*), the mean, median, and mode will coincide. The mean is pulled in the direction of extreme scores, making it the least useful measure of distributions that are badly skewed (*asymmetrical*).

Other useful descriptions of distributions are provided by measures of *variability,* or the degree to which scores in a distribution differ. Two distributions may have the same mean, median, and mode, but differ greatly in the degree of variability. Variability is measured by two statistics, the variance and the standard deviation.

Measures of Relative Standing

Measures of relative standing include percentiles and standard scores and are used to describe where a particular score falls in relation to the rest of the distribution. Welkowitz and colleagues defined a percentile as "a single number that gives the percent of cases in the specific reference group with equal or lower scores." The percentile is thus more precise than reporting simply that a score falls above or below the mean, median, or mode.

Standard scores (commonly called z scores) express the deviation from the mean in standard deviation units. Standard scores are useful because they can be interpreted by reference to the *standard normal curve* (z distribution), a symmetrical bell-shaped curve with known properties: a mean of 0 and a standard deviation of 1. Because the z score is signed, it is a quick indicator of whether a score fell above or below the mean. Because it expresses scores in terms of standard deviations, it indicates how unusual each score is—34% of all scores fall in the interval of 1 standard deviation below and 1 standard deviation above the mean ($z = \pm1$); 16% fall beyond $z = \pm1$; only $2\frac{1}{2}$% fall beyond $z = \pm2$.

Relationships Between Variables

Regression and correlation are procedures commonly used to describe relationships among variables. Two measures obtained on each subject in a sample can be plotted on xy coordinates to create a graphic representation of the relationship between the measures. Often this will yield approximately a straight line, reflecting a *linear relationship.* Numerical procedures are used to obtain the *regression line,* the mathematical equation of the line of best fit through the observed data points. Once the regression line has been derived, it is possible to predict the value of one variable when the other is known and to estimate the accuracy of the prediction.

The correlation coefficient is a quantitative index of the degree of linear relationship between two variables. The computational procedures eliminate the problem of comparison among different units. The values of r can vary between -1 and $+1$. The sign reflects the direction of the relationship. A negative correlation represents an inverse relationship: As one variable increases, the other decreases. A positive correlation represents a direct relationship: As one variable increases, the other also increases. The absolute value of r represents the strength of the relationship. Thus, ±1 represents perfect relationships. An r of 0 indicates no linear relationship. The value of r^2 indicates the percent of variance in one variable that can be accounted for by the other. Psychologists use this value to gauge how useful a particular measure is for prediction.

The Pearson r is designed for interval data on dimensions assumed to be distributed normally. A variety of other correlational procedures are available to handle other types of data: point biserial, phi coefficient, and Spearman's rho, for example. Correlations are often used in psychology as sources for experimental research hypotheses. Multiple regression, factor analysis, and canonical correlation are more recent relational techniques made practical by advances in computer technology. These procedures permit analysis of relationships among large numbers of variables.

INFERENTIAL STATISTICS

Inferential statistics are procedures for drawing inferences about large groups (in effect, whole populations) on the basis of observations made on smaller subsets called *samples*. Statistical inference serves two main purposes in psychology: to estimate population parameters from sample statistics and to assess the odds of obtaining a particular pattern of research results, given the characteristics of the data sampled.

The mean is the most commonly estimated population parameter. Because of the way in which the standard error is computed, larger samples generally yield smaller standard errors, making statistics computed on larger samples somewhat more accurate indicators of population parameters. By working with the *standard error* of the mean and standardized probability distributions (such as *t* distributions), it is possible to construct confidence intervals, ranges of values with known odds of containing the true population mean.

Evaluating Research Results

Inferential statistics may be used to assess the likelihood that particular samples belong to a known population. The process of statistical inference begins with a statement of the null *hypothesis* (H_0), which states the assumption that the observed statistics were drawn from a particular population. The null hypothesis is retained or rejected on the basis of how likely the observed outcome is. If the observed differences are large relative to the amount of variability in the measures taken, the researcher will reject the null hypothesis and conclude that the observed differences were unlikely to have occurred by chance. The result is then *statistically significant*. Test statistics with known frequency distributions are calculated to express the relationship between observed differences and variability.

Parametric Statistics

Parametric statistics can be used when two criteria are met: The variable under study is known or can be assumed to be normally distributed, and the data are interval or ratio.

If the mean and standard deviation of the population are known, or can be hypothesized, the exact odds of obtaining the observed difference between the known population parameter and a sample statistic can be determined. The *z* score can be evaluated by comparison with *the standard normal curve* (also called the *z* distribution).

Because researchers often rely on small samples, and because population parameters are rarely known, standardized Student *t* distributions are used more often than *z*. The exact shape of the *t* distribution varies roughly as a function of the number of cases sampled (more precisely, with the *degrees of freedom,* the number of values free to vary in the sample). The family of *t* distributions can be used to test the null hypothesis, which states that *two* samples were drawn from the same population. This is commonly done in research involving two groups of subjects, typically an experimental and a control group.

When more than two treatment groups are used, the Analysis of Variance (*F* test) may be applied. The *F* is an omnibus test that evaluates differences among all the possible pairs of treatment groups at once. The relative amounts of variance within versus between groups are compared. A variety of *post hoc* procedures are available to pinpoint the pairwise source of a significant *F* test.

Nonparametric Statistics

When the assumptions of the parametric tests cannot be met, or when ordinal (rank) or nominal (categorical) data are collected, *nonparametric* procedures are used. These techniques parallel parametric techniques in application and purpose. Nonparametric alternatives to the *t* test include the Mann–Whitney U test, the Wilcoxon (W) test, and the chi square test for nominal data. Nonparametric alternatives to the Analysis of Variance include the Kruskal–Wallis, Friedman, and chi square tests. The logic of each inferential test is the same: The appropriate null hypothesis is rejected if the computed test statistic is more extreme (less likely) than a predetermined critical value.

Because all statistical inferences are based on probability estimates, two incorrect outcomes are possible: type 1 errors, in which the null hypothesis is rejected although true, and type 2 errors, in which the null hypothesis is retained although invalid. The former results in incorrect confirmation of the research hypothesis, and the latter in the failure to identify a statistically significant result.

ANALYSIS OF VARIANCE
CENTRAL TENDENCY MEASURES
FACTOR ANALYSIS
MEASUREMENT
MULTIVARIATE METHODS
NULL HYPOTHESIS TESTING
PROBABILITY
STATISTICAL INFERENCES

A. Myers

STEPCHILDREN

Studies of stepfathers suggest that the entrance of a stepfather into a previously father-absent home has a positive effect on boys' cognitive and personality development; the effects on girls' cognitive and personality development are virtually uncharted. In one observational study of family interaction in stepfather, divorced-mother custody, and intact families, boys in stepfather families showed more competent social behavior than boys in intact families. By contrast, girls in stepfather families were observed to be more anxious than girls in intact families. Boys showed more warmth toward their stepfather than did girls. Boys in stepfather families also tended to show more mature behavior than did boys from divorced homes.

In a recent comparison of children in father custody, stepmother, and intact families, observations indicated some consistent sex differences— boys were observed to be less competent during social interaction with both their stepmother and their biological father than were girls. Combined with the data collected by Santrock and colleagues on stepfather families, an intriguing scenario of sex of child, sex of custodial parent, and type of stepparent family unfolds. During the early years of the stepfamily, children are confronted with many changes, adjustments, and possible new attachments. The disequilibrium created by the father's remarriage seems to produce a positive effect for his daughter but a negative effect for his son. His children have already undergone at least one major traumatic change in their lives, that is, the severing of their parents' marriage. Several years after the divorce, boys whose fathers have obtained custody seem to have adjusted well, and the same is true for girls whose mothers have custody. The entrance of a stepmother may produce conflict for a boy, and the entrance of a stepfather may do the same for girls.

DIVORCE
PARENT–CHILD RELATIONS

J. W. Santrock

STEPPARENTS

The number of remarriages in which children are involved has been steadily growing. Approximately 10 to 15% of all households in the United States are comprised of stepfamilies. A review of the stepparent literature presents mixed findings. Some researchers have found no differences between stepparent and intact families, while others have found significant differences that suggest stepparent families have more difficulties and problems.

Although an extensive amount of information about divorced families has been obtained in recent years, the efforts to understand the psychological climate of stepparent families have not been as extensive. One recent investigation represents the first attempt to observe actual social interaction in stepparent families. The most consistent findings suggested that the stepfather and biological mother showed more competent parenting when the child was a male than was the case for comparable intact families. Further analyses indicated that, in the sample studied, marital conflict was greater in the intact family boy's home than in the stepfather boy's home. These data clearly suggest that parenting techniques in stepparent families are not necessarily inferior to those in intact families.

There are virtually no data that compare stepfather or stepmother families with divorced mother or father custody families. Mothers with custody seem to have a particularly difficult time with sons, and some evidence suggests that fathers with custody may be more competent in rearing sons than daughters.

**DIVORCE
PARENT–CHILD RELATIONSHIPS**

J. W. Santrock

STEREOTYPING

Studies of prejudice directed toward ethnic groups often mention the important role played by stereotypes—those generalized and usually value-laden impressions that members of one social group use in characterizing members of another group.

The difficulty that arises when "stereotype" is given a purely negative meaning is that the social and cognitive mechanisms that underlie stereotyping are misunderstood. As a result, there is a tendency to overlook the fact that stereotyping normally and naturally occurs whenever social groups interact. Any socially identifiable group may be characterized in an almost infinite number of ways. It is impossible to know all there is to know about an ethnic group, for example, nor can more than a few variables be remembered when interacting with members of that group. Inevitably, what is done is to focus on a few variables believed to characterize the group in question and work them into a frame of reference used when observing, interacting with, or making decisions about members of the group. These frames of reference, or *working stereotypes,* enable people to predict, rightly or wrongly, how members of a given group will behave or react in a given situation.

The fact that people become dependent on stereotypes is a major source of difficulty. Stereotypes may dominate expectations of other group members and ignore or suppress evidence that indicates that the stereotype may be incorrect or inappropriate in a particular instance. There is a danger that stereotypes will be shaped by unconscious needs to project.

Donald T. Campbell pointed out that the most pernicious fault with stereotypes lies not so much in their fallacious elements, as in the causal explanation made for an inadequacy on the basis of a stereotype. Another danger inherent in stereotypes lies in the human tendency to use them as "self-fulfilling prophecies."

**ATTITUDES
DEINDIVIDUATION
ETHNIC GROUPS**

H. C. Lindgren

STIMULANTS

In low doses, stimulants result in mood elevation, euphoria, increased alertness, reduced fatigue, appetite suppression, and motor excitation, whereas higher doses may provoke irritability and anxiety. The more commonly used stimulants, such as cocaine, amphetamines, and methylphenidate, have been found to elicit a number of untoward side effects, and may induce schizophrenic-like symptoms, particularly paranoia. These compounds induce stereotyped behavior patterns in a wide variety of species, and it appears likely that their behavioral effects are due to the release of dopamine in the central nervous system. Clinically, stimulants such as methylphenidate, d-amphetamine, and pemoline have been used in the treatment of hyperactivity in children.

Stimulants that inhibit the degradation of biogenic amines (monoamine oxidase inhibitors) or block the neuronal uptake of amine (tricyclic antidepressants) have been used extensively in the treatment of affective disorders. Unlike amphetamine and cocaine, the therapeutic effects of these compounds appear to descend from their action on norepinephrine and serotonin concentrations, or by the down regulation of catecholamine receptors.

The two most widely used stimulants are caffeine and nicotine. Owing to its action on the cerebral cortex, caffeine produces wakefulness, alertness, and restlessness. In relatively high doses, brain-stem stimulation occurs, and respiration is stimulated. For this reason, caffeine may be used to offset the effects of sedative–hypnotic agents, such as alcohol and barbiturates. Finally, caffeine increases cardiac output and provokes constriction of blood vessels in the brain, an effect that has made caffeine useful in the treatment of some forms of migraine. Nicotine has pronounced effects on the central and peripheral nervous systems. Peripherally, low doses of nicotine stimulate ganglion cells and the neuromuscular junction. In addition, nicotine has been shown to stimulate salivation, delay gastric emptying, and inhibit stomach contraction. In higher doses, a functional blockade of receptors may occur. In addition, the release of peripheral catecholamines is produced by nicotine, and as a result, vasoconstriction, tachycardia, and elevated blood pressure may ensue. Centrally, nicotine is thought to influence the activity of neurons in the reticular formation, cortex, and hippocampus, and it excites vagal and spinal afferent neurons.

**CENTRAL NERVOUS SYSTEM
PSYCHOPHARMACOLOGY
SUBSTANCE ABUSE**

H. Anisman

STIMULUS

The word *stimulus* refers to whatever produces an effect. Psychology studies the human as a person, attempting to account for how the individual behaves as a unit.

The psychologist as a scientist studies human activity at the personal level as determined by the physics, physiology, pharmacology, and so forth of energistic events within the individual and those evoked by external events. The definition of stimulus in psychology must be in accord with this.

The human organism is responsive to a limited number of forms of energy. This responsiveness is mediated by ten senses or sense modalities—namely, the chemical senses of taste and smell; the mechanical sense of proprioception in muscles and tendons; touch, pain, and temperature receptors in the skin; vision, activated by photic radiation; and hearing, activated by vibrating energy over a limited range of frequencies. There is also what is called a common chemical sense whose function is seldom studied.

Although these modalities can be isolated from each other experimentally, in everyday life they function in groupings called *perceptual systems.* J. J. Gibson was the first to describe these systems as the visual system, the auditory system, the savor (taste–smell) system, the haptic system, and the vestibular system. S. H. Bartley called attention to the homeostatic system, which had failed to be described as a system, although for many years the components had been separately identified by physiologists.

The concept of perceptual *systems* is a factor in implying that cause–effect (stimulus–response) is a relationship that involves a great deal more activity within the organism following the impingement of energy on sense organs than is generally made explicit. For a perceptual system to be a system, certain individual sense modalities must interact neurally with each other, while the terminology gives the label to the major sense department in the system. When following the ramifications of the internal cause-and-effect activities, psychologists use the term *stimulus* as physiologists would use it. Only when the final outcome, the personalistic response, is achieved would the psychologist's label of stimulus be applicable.

Ames made a useful distinction. He called the energy reaching sense organs an *impingement.* In some cases, the impingement is not effective beyond the sense organ itself. Hence, for the purposes of physiologists, the impingement could be called a stimulus as it produced results in the category that was part of their subject matter. For psychologists, however, the impingement was not effective if it did not result in consequences in which psychologists are interested. It did not produce actions of the organism as a person. However, when it did, the input was a stimulus as well as a mere impingement.

Some psychologists have distinguished between the *distal* stimulus and the *proximal* stimulus. What they are referring to as the first kind of stimulus is the object perceived. Although the perceiver does see objects, they are not the causes of the seeing, but are its results or content.

Proximal stimuli are the forms of energy that reach sense organs and therefore are potential stimuli. They are stimuli if the energy is effective beyond the sense receptors and personalistic responses result. It is better to call them impingements if the result does not go beyond the sense organ.

HEARING
VISION

S. H. BARTLEY

STIMULUS GENERALIZATION

As the name implies, stimulus generalization refers to the capacity of a response that has previously been conditioned to a specific stimulus to be elicited later by a similar stimulus. Pavlov and his associates first demonstrated this phenomenon in laboratory experiments with dogs. After the dog experienced a succession of pairings between a stimulus and a response, such as a tone and food reinforcement, a stimulus similar in character and yet discriminably different from the original tone would be presented without reinforcement. This procedure resulted in the establishment of the well-known excitatory gradient of generalization, which showed that the intensity of the animal's response to the test stimulus was directly proportional to its similarity to the training stimulus.

Pavlov placed considerable importance on stimulus generalization. He regarded it as crucial for survival. Animals generalized responses to stimuli other than the original one to compensate for the instability of the environment. This early emphasis on the adaptive value of stimulus generalization led later theorists to treat it as a fundamental and irreducible process of learning. Later, however, other psychologists challenged

the validity of this view of generalization. For them, generalization was an artifact of the discrimination process.

Spence's theory of discrimination learning is a major representative of this first approach. It is based on the notion that excitation (a tendency to respond) develops to a stimulus paired with reinforcement and that this excitation generalizes to similar stimuli.

Lashley and Wade offered a view of generalization that contrasts sharply with the Hull–Spence approach. Lashley and Wade argued that a stimulus acquires control over a response only when that stimulus is contrasted with another one. Most often, the animal experiences only the training stimulus before generalization testing. Because the training stimulus represents only one value on the stimulus continuum, the animal fails to discriminate between training and test stimuli. The failure to discriminate between them results in a gradient of generalization.

Although much of the evidence contradicts the failure-to-discriminate hypothesis, there have been attempts to reconcile these interpretations.

Recently a cognitively oriented explanation of stimulus generalization has appeared to rival these earlier interpretations. This approach regards stimulus generalization as a special case of stimulus classification. The organism categorizes discriminably different events as equivalent and responds to them in terms of their class membership rather than their peculiarities.

CLASSICAL CONDITIONING
LEARNING

E. J. RICKERT

STRESS

In the most general sense, the term *stress* is used to refer to a situation in which a person is overtaxed in some way. However, within this very general framework, a number of specific definitions have evolved, each emphasizing a different aspect of the *overtaxing* situation, but basically consistent with one another. Each of these definitions also involves some explicit or implicit reference to strain—the negative, or pathological, outcome of stress.

The first type of definition is stated in terms of the organism's response to some situation. In Hans Selye's formulation, he pointed to stressors as being stimuli, which, because of their great magnitude, lead to the reaction he termed the General Adaptation Syndrome. The first part of the syndrome is the alarm reaction, that is, the individual responds to a signal by going into a state of alarm. The next stage is that of resistance, with the body attempting to limit the effects of the stressor. This stage prepares the organism for either fight against or flight from the stressor. If either reaction is unsuccessful, the individual moves into a state of exhaustion, from which tissue breakdown and even death can result. In other words, continued stress can lead to bodily damage. The body manifests the stress reaction by a rise in blood pressure, increased adrenaline, changed heartbeat, more red blood cells, slower digestion, and so on. However, Selye argued, some stress can be a positive experience; too little stress is also negative.

A second type of definition of stress focuses on the situation, or the stimuli, defined independently of the reaction of the person, even independently of the person's perceptions. Typically, the situations are of such gravity that they obviously tax most people, so that overlooking the variation in the perceptions of the situation by different people is not a serious shortcoming. The variety of such situations tends to defy unambiguous conceptualizations and measurement. Regardless, these stresses have been found to lead to such forms of strain as afflictions like ulcers and heart attack; as changes in body chemistry, such as in uric acid level and blood pressure; and as depression, anxiety, alcoholism, and even death.

A third definition focuses on the perceptions that people have of the demands of various situations. Thomas Holmes and R. H. Rahe measured individuals' perceptions of various types of events by having them rate the amount of readjustment each one demanded. The individuals also were asked to indicate the recent frequency of occurrence of these events in their own lives. For each individual, the frequency of each event was multiplied by its adjustment rating and the products were summed. These sums, called Social Readjustment Scores, have been found to be correlated with, and in some instances predictive of, such forms of strain as chronic illnesses, including coronary heart disease, diabetes, and ulcers; alcoholism; accidents and injuries; poor academic performance; and professional and competitive failures.

The fourth approach, the interactive, exemplified in the formulations of Joseph McGrath, Richard Lazarus, and John French, goes even further in considering the individual's own responses in dealing with a taxing situation. This approach has been formulated in its most general form by French as a poor fit between an individual's resources and the demands of one's environment. This conception of stress appears to be similar to Selye's notion that too low a level of stimulation can also cause stress. French and his colleagues found that workers whose abilities were underused experienced dissatisfaction.

At the other extreme, the situation may impose demands beyond the individual's capacity to meet them, even given the resources available in the situation. Obviously the degree of stress is a function of the ability of a given individual to meet these demands in the situation. Poor fits can have their locus either in the individual's perceptions of his or her inability to meet the demands of the situation and to satisfy personal motives, or in the individual's actual inability.

Some challenge-minded individuals may generate stress for themselves by setting themselves extraordinarily high goals. Some researchers have classified people as A type and B type, with the former striving with great energy and focus on greater and greater achievement. Such persons suffer more strain, including early fatal heart attacks, than do the more relaxed B types.

The exact process by which stress leads to strain is not well understood. Furthermore, little is understood as to why strain takes such different forms for different people. For some, it might involve specific, transitory, physiological changes, such as changes in blood pressure and in the acids in the blood. Others may develop some health problem such as heart disease, cancer, high blood pressure, or ulcers. Still others might have mental problems, such as anxiety attacks, depression, or even psychosis. Behavior problems, such as alcoholism, crime, drug addiction, or suicide, might occur in other lives. The form the strain takes may depend on the type of stress or each individual may have a propensity to show strain in specific ways. The relationships among these various forms of strain are also not well understood.

Several influences in an individual's life have been found to reduce the incidence of strain, although it is not known whether these influences reduce stress or strain or both. Most prominent among these ameliorative factors is social support from peers, from spouses, or even from supervisors. Another is exercise, or, more generally, physical exertion.

A-TYPE PERSONALITY
B-TYPE PERSONALITY
GENERAL ADAPTATION SYNDROME
STRESS CONSEQUENCES

E. STOTLAND

STRESS CONSEQUENCES

The recognition by Claude Bernard, and subsequently by Walter Cannon and Hans Selye, that stressful events influence the internal milieu of the organism ultimately led to concerted efforts to evaluate the contribution of physical and psychological insults to the induction or exacerbation of pathological states. Indeed, substantial attention has been devoted not only to the analysis of the effects of stressors on the classical psychosomatic illnesses (e.g., gastric ulceration), but also to pathologies related to affective disorders, cardiovascular illness, and immunologically related diseases such as neoplasia.

On inception of physical insults, the rate at which neurotransmitters are synthesized and used is increased. The enhanced activity of these transmitters is thought to increase the organism's preparedness to deal behaviorally with the aversive stimuli, and, in addition, may be fundamental to protect the organism from health risk. Soon after exposure to the stressor, the concentrations of the amines may rise, thereby assuring adequate supplies of the neurotransmitter, at least for the short run.

If aversive stimulation is relatively intense and protracted, excessive use of the neurotransmitter may occur. Under such conditions, rates of synthesis may not keep pace with use, thus resulting in a net reduction of amine levels. In the case of norepinephrine levels, the reductions have been noted in a wide variety of brain regions, such as hypothalamus, locus coeruleus, hippocampus, and cortex, although it appears that reductions occur more readily in some regions than in others. Alterations of dopamine activity appear to take place in a fairly restricted number of brain regions, such as the arcuate nucleus of the hypothalamus, the nucleus accumbens, and the mesofrontal cortex. Given the connections between the arcuate nucleus and the pituitary gland, it is likely that alterations of dopamine in this region are fundamental to the secretion of hormones from the pituitary. Moreover, in view of the potential involvement of the nucleus accumbens and mesocortex in emotional and psychotic disorders, the contribution of the dopamine variations to pathological states may be profound. Likewise, it is thought that stress-related alterations of epinephrine neurons in the hypothalamus may be related to hypertension.

It appears that aversive stimulation per se is not responsible for the reductions of norepinephrine that take place. Rather, the organism's ability to cope behaviorally with the insults is the prime determinant of the depletion. It seems that when behavioral control over a stressor is possible, the burden of coping is shared between behavioral and neurochemical methods.

Some theorists have proposed that failure to deal with a stressor through behavioral methods may result in cognitive transformations in which one perceives oneself as being "helpless" in determining one's own destiny, and this in turn may lead to depression. An alternative view is that depression is a consequence of neurochemical alterations, and these may be brought about in some individuals when behavioral control over aversive events is not available. According to the latter view, feelings of helplessness and hopelessness may be brought about by the neurochemical changes, and these cognitive processes, together with self-referent rumination and brooding, may further exacerbate neurochemical lability. This vicious circle of neurochemical and cognitive events ultimately may be responsible for the maintenance of the affective disorder.

In addition to genetic differences in response to aversive stimulation, it appears that various organismic, environmental, and experiential factors influence the extent of neurochemical change promoted by stressors.

A particularly critical factor in determining neurochemical lability concerns the chronicity of stress application. Although acute stress reliably provokes reductions of norepinephrine concentrations, control levels of norepinephrine are seen among animals that receive repeated exposure to aversive stimulation. If the stressor persists, the continued neurochemical activity may be excessive, and still further changes with adaptive significance may occur. Specifically, down regulation (subsensitivity) of norepinephrine receptors may occur, thereby antagonizing the effects of the increased use.

Although chronic exposure to stress results in adaptation, previous experience with a stressor may result in the sensitization or conditioning of neurochemical change. In effect, vulnerability to stress-provoked neurochemical variations may be increased by trauma experienced earlier. In addition to variations in neurochemical activity, pronounced changes of hormonal activity and steroids are produced by stressors.

Although the functioning of the immune system has traditionally been considered independent of the central nervous system (CNS), the possibility that psychological factors influence immune responsivity has received increasingly greater attention. In fact, there is a great deal of evidence pointing to a relationship between the activity of the CNS and immune functioning, and variables such as stress are recognized as factors that may influence vulnerability to immunologically related illnesses.

It has been reported that aversive stimulation may influence immunoresponsivity among animals and in humans. It appears that acute exposure to aversive stimuli results in suppression of B- and T-lymphocytes, as well as macrophages and natural killer (NK) cells. In view of the potential involvement of NK cells, as well as T- and B-cells, in host defense against *in vivo* tumors, some viruses, and microbial diseases, the contribution of aversive stimulation to a broad range of disease states seems quite likely.

As in the case of CNS neurotransmitters, the effects of stressors on immune functioning may be modified by several experiential and environmental factors. For instance, although acute application of a stressor induces immunosuppression, following chronic exposure to a stressor immunofacilitation is observed. The source for the differential effects of acute and chronic stressors remains to be determined; however, the contribution of CNS neurotransmitters cannot be overlooked, particularly in light of the neurochemical adaptation that occurs after repeated stress application.

In accordance with the neuroinummomodulation provoked by stressors, there is considerable evidence indicating that stressful events may influence neoplasia. It has been found that the application of acute stress enhances tumor development. An apparently essential feature for the tumor enhancement to occur is the controllability of the stressor. Moreover, social factors and housing conditions influence tumor development. Finally, it seems that application of a stressor also enhances metastases. Whether the tumor enhancement produced by stressors is mediated by changes in neurotransmitters, hormones, and corticoids, or metabolic changes remains to be determined.

HOMEOSTASIS
NEUROCHEMISTRY
PSYCHOPHYSIOLOGY
STRESS

H. ANISMAN

STRONG–CAMPBELL INTEREST INVENTORY

The Strong–Campbell Interest Inventory (SCII), first published in 1974 by David Campbell and Jo-Ida Hansen, was a revision and combination of the Strong Vocational Interest Blank for Men and the Strong Vocational Interest Blank for Women. It contains 325 questions that require the test taker to respond "like," "indifferent," or "dislike" to a variety of occupations, activities, school subjects, and types of people. The test is useful for people aged 16 or older.

The 1981 revision has 162 occupational scales, six general occupational themes (adventure, artistic, enterprising, investigative, realistic, and social), 23 basic interest scales, two special scales (academic comfort and introversion–extroversion), and a number of administrative indexes that are used to verify the validity of the test scores before they are interpreted. The test must be computer scored. Although all people take the same test, there are separate male and female norms, since sex differences in interest patterns frequently occur.

The purpose of the SCII is to provide information to the person and the professional counselor or personnel officer to aid in academic and career decision making. Scores reflect the person's interests rather than abilities. People who choose careers consistent with their interests have been shown to stay with their career choices longer than people who enter careers inconsistent with their interests.

The SCII is widely accepted by academic and career counselors as one of the best and most useful tests available for this purpose. It should be used and interpreted in conjunction with trained counselors.

VOCATIONAL INTEREST MEASUREMENT

M. J. ALLEN

STRUCTURAL EQUATION MODELING

Used in an array of topics ranging from the study of scholastic achievement to the investigation of mood states, structural equation modeling represents the systematic analysis of causal relationships. Alternately referred to as *demand analysis, multitrait multimethod analysis, path analysis, linear causal analysis,* or *simultaneous equations,* the expanded use of structural equation modeling is attributable, in large measure, to two features of research in the behavioral sciences. First, since many behavioral studies are not experimental, analysis of nonexperimental data requires the use of statistical procedures as alternatives to experimental manipulation and control. The intent of the statistical procedures inherent in structural equation modeling is to achieve some of the assessment potential of experimental research. Second, the focus of many studies is on hypothetical constructs not directly observable but that have a decisive impact and order relationships among measured variables. Consequently, models accommodating both the latent aspect of these variables and their empirical relationship to measured variables have been developed.

Regression equations report the degree of empirical association between variables of interest exemplified by a statement of finding such as "as *x* changes, so does *y*." Structural equations represent a higher level of abstraction in which, given the empirical association among the variables, specific causal linkages are the focus. Notwithstanding this distinction, regression equations can be used to estimate structural equations if certain conditions are met. First, the causal variables identified in the model must be independent of other unspecified causes or, alternatively, all important causal variables related to the phenomenon under study must be specified. Consequently, a high level of conceptual and theoretical exactitude is required in structural equation modeling. Second, the variables of the model are either dichotomous or linearly interrelated. Linear structural models can be used effectively in the investigation of nonlinear relationships if appropriate transformations are performed. Third, either the causal variables are measured without error or explicit procedures for the estimation of measurement error are implemented, as exemplified by the multitrait multimethod approach of multiple indicator models.

Fourth, causal direction and order among the variables of interest must be specified clearly. Although this may not be particularly problematic in a recursive model, the modeling of reciprocal causality necessitates the deployment of more elaborate and involved analytic procedures. If these four conditions are satisfied, then a causal interpretation of the meaning of the respective structural coefficients can be proposed.

In the behavioral sciences, few phenomena of interest can be adequately described and analyzed in terms of a single cause and effect. Usually, behavioral phenomena are embedded in a network of causal relations, requiring more demanding and exacting analytical procedures. Because the linear regression model provides the foundation for virtually all statistical procedures used in the behavioral sciences, as the level of substantive and theoretical complexity exceeds the limitations of the bivariate recursive model, other linear models can be incorporated in the analysis. If multiple predictor variables are to be recognized in the analysis, then a multiple regression model can be employed. If, in addition, multiple dependent variables are involved, then multivariate regression can be used. Finally, if reciprocal causality among endogenous variables is indicated, then a general linear structural equation model can be deployed.

To illustrate the form of the general linear structural equation model, a nine-variable example is examined briefly. The relations among these nine hypothetical variables can be diagrammed as follows:

$$A \rightarrow D \leftarrow u_D$$
$$\nearrow \quad \downarrow$$
$$B \rightarrow E \leftarrow u_E$$
$$\Updownarrow$$
$$C \quad F \leftarrow u_F$$

These nine variables represent three distinctive categories of variables: endogenous variables, exogenous variables, and disturbance terms. Analogous to the Y variable in the bivariate model, endogenous variables are variables whose values are completely determined by the causal relations specified by the model under consideration. In this illustration, the D, E, and F variables represent endogenous variables. Exogenous variables, represented by the variables A, B, and C, are variables that are reported to have a theoretically salient impact on the endogenous variables but values of which are determined by processes outside the model currently considered. Disturbance terms (u) associated with each endogenous variable indicate the extent to which variability in the respective endogenous variable is not explained by the other variables in the model. As can be noted in the diagram, several logically possible causal relationships are not specified (e.g., A–E, B–F, and C–D).

The causal model can be translated into the following three structural equations:

$$D = b_{DA}A + b_{DB}B + u_D$$
$$E = b_{EB}B + b_{ED}D + b_{EF}F + u_E$$
$$F = b_{FC}C + b_{FE}E + u_F$$

These three combined equations would thus represent a structural equation model of behavioral and stochastic processes believed to produce a specified set of data.

Although a series of additional technical issues must be addressed when using structural equation modeling (e.g., model identification, parameter estimation), the role of theory is quite evident. Thus although statistical procedures are inexorably required in the analysis of the proposed causal relationships, the initial impetus as well as guiding focus of structural equation modeling is provided by the interplay of theory and design considerations.

ALGORITHMIC–HEURISTIC THEORY
CAUSAL REASONING
COGNITIVE COMPLEXITY
GENERAL SYSTEMS
HUMAN FACTORS
MULTIPLE REGRESSION
SCIENTIFIC METHOD

D. G. NICKINOVICH

STRUCTURAL LEARNING THEORY

The Structural Learning Theory is a natural extension of earlier research, which provides a unifying theoretical framework from which to view interactions between individual learners and their environment (e.g., teaching and learning).

In structural learning theories, what an individual does and can learn in any particular situation is assumed to depend directly on what the person already knows. It is assumed that human cognition may be characterized in terms of specific individual knowledge (represented in terms of rules) and universal characteristics of the human information processor.

Knowledge refers to an individual's potential for behavior (under prespecified test conditions). Universal characteristics, by way of contrast, are best thought of as those aspects of human cognitive functioning inherent to people generally; they need not, and in some cases cannot, be learned. Nonetheless, universal characteristics impose important constraints on the way knowledge may be usefully represented and measured.

Two universal characteristics of human cognition are assumed in structural learning theories: one pertains to control (allowable interactions among rules) and the other to processing capacity and speed. In structural learning research, control mechanisms have been the subject of direct empirical study. This research has demonstrated that a wide variety of behavioral phenomena, ranging from problem solving and learning to motivation, memory, and skill development, may be explained and predicted by introducing appropriate lower and higher order rules and assuming the following control mechanism: When confronted with a problem, the learner is assumed to check each rule available (e.g., in working memory) to see if it applies. If exactly one such rule is found, it is actually applied. When no solution rules are immediately applicable, or when there are more than one, the search moves to the next level to check for higher order rules that have the potential to generate a unique solution rule that applies, and so on as necessary. Once a rule has been selected and applied, the output of such application, possibly a newly generated rule, is added to the set of available rules. Control then reverts to the next lower level where the search continues, this time to a rule set that contains the new rule.

Processing capacity is the second hypothesized cognitive universal. In contrast to most cognitive theories, working memory in the Structural Learning Theory is assumed to hold not only the data (the stuff on which rules operate), but also the rules (processes) themselves. This difference has a number of implications pertaining to a variety of memory and performance phenomena, only some of which have been investigated empirically.

In contrast to universal cognitive constraints, specific knowledge is assumed to vary over individuals. The first step in constructing a particular structural learning theory is to identify the prototypic competence underlying the given problem domain and to represent this competence in terms of a finite set of rules. These underlying rules must be represented in sufficient detail that all of the specified components make direct contact with assumed minimal capabilities of (all) students in the target population.

In structural learning research, a general method of analysis called *structural analysis* has evolved for the purpose of generating such competence. The theory tells how, through a finite testing procedure, one can identify what parts of which rules individual students do and do not know. In the theory, a number of important but sometimes subtle interrelationships exist among content, cognition, and individual differences.

Completing the circle, goal-switching control not only has found strong and direct empirical support in its own right, but it also makes possible a pragmatically useful basis for identifying what must be learned in instructional situations.

LEARNING THEORIES

J. M. SCANDURA

STRUCTURALISM

As a school or system of psychology, structuralism had its antecedents in British philosophy of the eighteenth and nineteenth centuries. Structuralism began formally with the teachings and writings of Wilhelm Wundt in the late nineteenth century. Many important experiments were performed in Wundt's laboratory: reaction time, color mixing, afterimages, psychophysics, and word associations. Wundt delineated the nature of psychological events, what the psychologist should be studying, and how to handle the results of experimental investigations.

Titchener took Wundt's psychology to the United States, where he named the system *structuralism.* He modified and enlarged on Wundt's basic tenets.

Both Wundt and Titchener defined psychology as the study of consciousness or conscious experience. This definition limited the true subject matter of psychology to human experience. Whatever was to be said of lower animals was left to the domain of biology. Throughout the first three decades of the twentieth century, structuralism was a dominant school in American psychology. By the early 1930s, the system was beginning to decline in popularity. Other systems grew up in opposition to it, such as functionalism, behaviorism, and Gestalt psychology.

Wundt and Titchener believed the task of the psychologist was to analyze the contents of consciousness into its elements. For Titchener, there were three classes of elements of experience: sensations, feelings, and images.

Titchener also believed the elements had dimensions or attributes. There was *intensity,* which referred to how strong or weak the sensations were—a loud or soft tone, a bright or dim light, a strong or weak odor or taste. *Quality* referred to the kind of experience, as in a particular pitch of tone; the color of an object (red or green); the sweetness or sourness of something tasted; hot, cold, pain, or tickle in the sense of touch. *Duration* referred to how long the experience lasted. *Clarity* involved the place an experience had in consciousness. Those experiences at the focus of consciousness would be very clear, while those at the fringe would be vague. The element of feelings lacked the dimension of clarity. Finally, Titchener described the attribute of *extensity* or volume, which he believed applied only to visual experience.

Attention referred to the arrangement of conscious elements. It could be voluntary, as when one intentionally directs one's attention to a particular object.

In experience, the elements were combined. The means whereby this combination could occur was *association.* Ideas could be associated by contiguity: things happening together in space or time and by similarity.

Both Wundt and Titchner had distinguished the two worlds of experience, the mental (consciousness) and the physical.

One aspect of experience that Wundt failed to explain was the meaning of a particular idea or set of experiences. Therefore, Titchener constructed his *context theory of meaning.* Here, meaning was divided into *core* and *context.* The core was the raw experience as it came to consciousness: a blue light or a high-pitched sound. It was context that gave the experience meaning. Context constituted the various associations conjured up by that core.

The methodology of structuralism was introspection and experimentation. Introspection was of special importance in analyzing experiences. Titchener maintained that science was dependent on observation and introspection was one of the methods. The person doing the introspective analysis had to be trained in the method.

Structuralism no longer exists as a systematic position. It died because it had nowhere to go. This methodology very much limited what psychologists could study in their minds and had no applications. It set psychology out as a discipline separate from philosophy with a methodology of investigation, at least in part, experimental.

HISTORY OF PSYCHOLOGY

R. W. LUNDIN

STRUCTURE-OF-INTELLECT MODEL

The structure-of-intellect (SOI) model shows strong ties with what is known as *cognitive psychology,* illuminating a wide range of the major concepts of perception, learning, memory, reasoning, creative thinking, problem solving, and decision making.

The structure of intellect defines intelligence as a systematic collection of abilities or functions for processing different kinds of items of information in various ways. The term *ability* is used in the context of individual differences and the term *function* in the context of the behaving individual.

Each basic SOI ability has three qualities or *facets.* It has a unique kind of *operation,* a kind of informational *concept,* and a kind of informational *product* or form. Each ability has its unique combination of one kind of operation, of information, resulting in a certain kind of product.

A set of five different operations times a set of five kinds of informational content times a set of six kinds of products (produced by the brain) yields 150 possible unique abilities, about two-thirds of which have been demonstrated by factor analysis. Mathematically, this kind of model is known as a *product of sets.*

Besides providing a logical and systematic view of intelligence, the model offers information regarding the use of tests and interpretations of scores in the assessment of intellectual levels of individuals. It also illuminates many aspects of cognitive psychology in general, providing a system of unambiguous concepts, because its concepts refer to well-defined features of intellectual events. There is evidence that SOI abilities are distinguishable even in very young children.

Because there are small correlations among many pairs of basic or first-order SOI abilities, there are higher order factors indicating somewhat broader abilities at the second- and third-order levels of generality. No completely general factorial ability is evident.

DIFFERENTIAL PSYCHOLOGY
FACTOR ANALYSIS
THEORETICAL PSYCHOLOGY

J. P. GUILFORD

STUDY METHODS

Outside the classroom, the primary means by which students learn have long been the preparation of homework assignments, other guided-study activities monitored by a teacher, and independent study on special projects. The requisite studying typically involves reading and remembering written materials, drilling on exercises so as to master specific skills, and preparing and presenting materials for evaluation by a teacher. In addition to textbooks, students often use library resources to acquire specialized information from printed reference materials or from audiovisual sources. Most studying involves working alone, although students often join together to clarify and plan assigned study activities, to obtain feedback or help on assignments, to review completed homework material, or to review for an upcoming examination. Studying traditionally has required a wide variety of activities. The advent of new educational technology based on televised and computer-assisted instruction likely will bring about changes in these traditional study approaches.

Observers have noted wide variations in the study methods typically employed by students. The time and place for studying, the physical conditions of the study environment, and the employment of specific study mechanics were some of the many factors observed. In spite of the lack of consistency seen, a large number of how-to-study books, guides, and tests have been published to assist students in improving study skills. Many schools and colleges offer study skills instruction.

Robinson, originator of the SQ3R method for reading textbooks, presented the approach following several years of research on the reading problems encountered by failing, average, and superior students. This study method, or some variation of it, has been included in most how-to-study books published subsequently. Five steps comprise the SQ3R method, and are as follows:

1. *Survey* the chapter.
2. *Question* by turning headings into questions to be answered while reading.
3. *Read* actively by underlining key phrases and marking main points.
4. *Recite* the main points to yourself in your own words to check your learning.
5. *Review* periodically to refresh your memory and assure retention.

Pauk developed the five-step Cornell system for taking notes, as the product of extensive trial and experiment based on learning theory. The steps are as follows:

1. During the lecture, *record* as many meaningful facts and ideas as possible in the main column of the notes.
2. After the lecture, *reduce* these ideas and facts into key words and phrases listed in the recall column.
3. Cover the main column and *recite* the main facts and ideas to yourself using the cues provided by the recall column.
4. *Reflect* on the material and write your own ideas and opinions in a separately organized summation.
5. Periodically *review* the notes quickly to assure that the material is remembered.

Brown and Holtzman employed direct observation, interviews, and questionnaires to develop the *Survey of study habits and attitudes* (SSHA). Specific suggestions for implementing efficient study skills and effective academic attitudes were derived directly from the SSHA

Many how-to-study guides and study skills inventories have been published but there appears to be considerable disagreement as to what constitutes "good" study habits. Some researchers have turned to the investigation of motivational factors. Following an intensive review of existing how-to-study literature, Brown concluded that attitudinal and motivational characteristics were of potentially greater importance than the purely mechanical procedures of studying. More important was what motivated the student to acquire or not acquire, and to use or not use, methods for effective studying.

The following topics are included in most study skills courses: using time efficiently; developing concentration skills; organizing the study area; reading and marking textbooks; skimming articles; summarizing concepts; organizing and outlining material; improving remembering; building vocabulary; taking lecture notes; taking reading notes; setting meaningful goals; conducting library research; writing in-class themes; writing topic reports; studying mathematical material; studying scientific material; preparing laboratory reports; making oral reports; reviewing for examinations; desensitizing test anxiety; taking objective tests; writing essay examinations; and taking problem tests.

Beginning in the early 1960s, the rapid expansion in educational opportunity for the economically disadvantaged resulted in the admission of large numbers of nontraditional students who were relatively ill-prepared for the academic demands of higher education. Without effective assistance in acquiring needed learning skills, these students found that the open door to educational opportunity quickly became a revolving door to academic oblivion. Concern about their low level of academic preparedness led to the creation of special learning centers with programs designed to help these students acquire the learning skills necessary for academic success.

Since its introduction, the concept of a college-wide learning assistance center to provide broad-based services for all students appears to have been widely accepted. Fiscally, however, the movement is struggling for full administrative recognition and acceptance. In the future, the development and implementation of new educational technologies, including computer-based instructional systems, should further expand the role and scope of learning assistance activities in both secondary and higher education.

ACADEMIC UNDERACHIEVERS
APPROACHES TO LEARNING
SCHOOL LEARNING

W. F. Brown

STUTTERING

Historically, Aristotle and Demosthenes were plagued by stuttering (dysphemia). The latter allegedly cured himself by speaking with pebbles in his mouth and shouting more loudly than the noise of the sea. Although historians cannot be certain about the exact nature of his dysphemic speech, some form of stuttering, previously called stammering, may well have occurred in ancient populations. It is a ubiquitous phenomenon found among all ages, races, sexes, and cultures throughout the world, occurring four to five times more frequently among males than females. Reasons for this disparity have never been clear. Stuttering is no respecter of socioeconomic status or position in life, as exemplified by King George VI of England, who stuttered markedly. The bulk of systematic studies published to date support the view that stuttering is a disorder related to anxiety and self-concept. Blocking and spasmodic efforts to speak constitute its essence. Descriptively, it may be defined as a disruption of verbal expression, characterized by involuntary audible or silent repetitions and prolongations in the utterance of short speech elements. In terms of the traditional classification of speech disorders, stuttering is designated as a disorder of rhythm. It is set apart from the three other categorical disorders of speech: articulation (e.g., lisping, lalling, baby talk), phonation or voice (e.g., falsettos), and symbolization (e.g., aphasias).

Early authors proposed a number of theories for the cause of stuttering that were later discarded. A litany of factors such as inadequate cerebral dominance, decreased leukocytes, increased carbon dioxide intake, elevated serum calcium, and abnormal salivary pH were put forth as causes. A nineteenth-century theorist who believed stuttering resulted from a large tongue proposed surgical reduction as a cure. Lack of cerebral dominance as the primary cause was related to the view that changing handedness could precipitate stuttering. This concept was based on the notion that the evocation of competing neural impulses in the brain were transmitted to the masseter muscles of the jaw, thereby eliciting stuttering.

The data attempting to ascribe a neurological, biochemical, or physiological cause of stuttering have been equivocal at best. Although Lindsley observed more blocking and unsynchronized α brain waves among stutterers than normal speakers, Scarborough found no difference in the electroencephalograms of stutterers and normal control subjects. In an effort to establish a hereditary link to stuttering, Nelson compared 204 stutterers with an equal number of controls and found more stuttering in families of the experimental group. This finding, however, does not prove causality or heredity, as other factors were not fully considered. Family members create stress and pressure on the stutterer unwittingly. They often insist that the individual can speak better and ask him or her to slow down and take deep breaths conveying a message of unacceptability of the condition. Psychoanalysts have proposed either oral or compulsive fixations as the root cause. These theorists maintained that stuttering represents continuing oral eroticism in narcissistic infantile persons who compulsively retain early oral equivalents of nursing and biting. Johnson classified stuttering into primary and secondary types. The former occurs in young children and is characterized by little awareness of its effects, whereas the latter is fraught with numerous signs, such as struggle, avoidance, and grimaces. This suggests that perceived reactions from others evokes anxiety, leading to severe secondary symptoms. Ingham contends the role of anxiety per se is overemphasized.

Stuttering is not a unitary phenomenon and has no single cause. The majority of recent controlled studies have supported the view that stuttering is learned, usually originating in childhood. Frederick assessed the effects of reward and punishment on stuttering behavior. Subjects read equated word lists under conditions of an increase and decrease in electric shock. High-anxiety subjects stuttered more under punishment, while low-anxiety subjects stuttered more under reward. When the groups were combined, these differences obscured each other. There were significant personality differences, indicating that people stutter for various reasons in spite of the presence of a common symptom.

Prominent among modern learning theories is an approach–avoidance conflict theory proposed by Sheehan, who successfully mastered his own stuttering problem. Approach and avoidance tendencies reach a state of equilibrium in which competing drives are present, one to speak and the other to hold back so as not to stutter. Stuttering occurs when the desire to speak fluently and the fear of stuttering come into balance. Accordingly, to resolve the conflict, a form of negative practice as an aspect of behavior modification is employed. Fear of stuttering is reduced by doing the thing feared most, namely stuttering, voluntarily and deliberately in a relatively easy, effortless way by prolonging the first syllable of the word. This is done with nonfeared words followed by a lesser number of feared words. Because stuttering has already occurred and there is nothing left to fear, tension and anxiety lessen and more fluent speech ensues.

Most speech pathologists and psychologists concur that it is of paramount importance for stutterers to accept the condition and cease trying to cover up speech blocks through a pseudosense of self as fluent. Stuttering is seen as a false role disorder. Trying to portray oneself as a fluent speaker becomes self-defeating. A vicious circle develops whereby stuttering is followed by shame and disgust, which lead to increased fear that stuttering will recur. As fear mounts, the tension created results in more stuttering. The cycle then repeats itself. The more the individual tries not to stutter, the more likely it is to occur.

A variety of treatment methods have focused on reducing or eliminating stuttering per se, such as delayed speech feedback and altering the flow of air from the mouth. However, these procedures appear to have produced disappointing long-term results. Effective treatment seems to require addressing the fear and shame of stuttering rather than the stuttering itself. Jacobson stated he experienced relief when stuttering was no longer perceived as a monolithic but rather a multifaceted behavior, requiring self-acceptance. When a feared situation is avoided it gains strength, and because the act that reduced the fear also becomes reinforced, a doubling effect results further perpetuating the problem. A combination of behavior-oriented speech therapy and psychotherapy is regarded as the most effective means of dealing with this troublesome disorder. Although the stuttering may not be eliminated entirely, it need not continue to be handicapping.

ACHIEVEMENT NEED
ANXIETY
BLOCKING
COPING
CYBERNETICS
DYSJUNCTIVE THERAPIES

C. J. FREDERICK

SUBLIMATION

Freudian theory holds that all human beings are motivated by powerful and innate sexual and destructive instincts (drives), including incest and murder. Because society will not tolerate such threats to its existence, it inevitably comes into conflict with the individual. Initially, this takes the form of conflict between the child and the first representatives of society whom it encounters, its parents. Subsequently, the socializing demands and prohibitions imposed by the parents are internalized by the child, leading to intrapsychic conflicts. To Freud, therefore, mental health consisted of resolving these conflicts by channeling one's drives away from inborn illicit wishes and into more socially acceptable forms of behavior (*sublimating* them). However, these substitute activities are never quite as satisfying as the original ones would be. The individual is left with a residue of unfulfilled desire, which is the price one pays for living in (and enjoying the benefits of) a civilized society.

An alternative definition for sublimation has been the unconscious substitution of one behavior for another that not only would be more satisfying, but also more threatening. This conception implies that sublimation is not always healthy or advantageous, as it may deprive an individual of the maximum feasible satisfaction when strong (but irrational) anxiety has become associated with a desirable goal that is actually safe and socially accepted.

COPING
DEFENSE MECHANISMS

R. B. EWEN

SUBLIMINAL INFLUENCE

Subliminal influence is the use of persuasion tactics delivered below the threshold of awareness. Although the term *subliminal perception* is well defined in the psychological literature, *subliminal influence* is used to refer to techniques, ranging from flashing words quickly onto a movie screen to backward phrases in rock music to cleverly hidden images in advertisements. Research has failed to support claims for the effectiveness of subliminal persuasion. Researchers have found that people can process minimal subliminal messages (such as extracting meaning from a single word presented outside of awareness), but cannot process complex subliminal messages. Regardless of the level of processing, subliminal messages have not been shown to influence behavior.

SENSATIONAL CLAIMS FOR THE POWER OF SUBLIMINAL INFLUENCE

Most Americans believe in the power of subliminal messages to influence behavior. Much of this belief in subliminal persuasion has been stimulated by sensational claims that have appeared in the mass media.

For example, in the late 1950s, James Vicary, an advertising expert, circulated a story, claiming that he had secretly flashed, at a third of a millisecond, the words *eat popcorn* and *drink Coke* onto a movie screen. Vicary claimed an increase in Coke sales of 18% and a rise in popcorn sales of almost 58%. Key proclaimed that subliminal implants were routinely placed in print advertisements, and that the word *sex* was printed on Ritz crackers and appeared on the ice cubes in a Gilbeys Gin ad. In the 1970s, parents and ministers began to voice concerns that rock music contained backward messages often of a satanic nature.

In the late 1980s and throughout the 1990s, manufacturers of subliminal self-help tapes claimed their tapes could improve everything from self-esteem to memory, to employee and customer relations, to sexual responsiveness, to bowling scores, to overcoming the trauma of rape. In 1987, Americans purchased more than $55 million worth of subliminal tapes. In 1990, the rock band Judas Priest was placed on trial for allegedly putting the subliminal implant "do it" in its song "Better by You, Better than Me." This implant supposedly caused the suicide deaths of two teenage boys.

The public has shown much outrage and concern over the possible unethical use of subliminal messages. In 1957, the columnist Norman Cousins lamented, "If the device is successful for putting over popcorn, why not politicians or anything else?" He advocated that people should take "this invention and everything connected to it and attach it to the center of the next nuclear explosive scheduled for testing." This public outrage spurred regulatory and legal action. The Federal Communications Commission declared that the use of subliminal persuasion could result in the loss of a broadcast license. The National Association of Broadcasters prohibited the use of subliminal advertising by its members. Australia and Britain banned subliminal messages. The California State legislature passed a law stating that the distribution of material with backward messages without public notice is an invasion of privacy. A Nevada judge ruled that subliminal messages are not protected as free speech.

DO SUBLIMINAL MESSAGES PERSUADE?

Given the public outrage and civic action, it is useful to ask this question: How effective are subliminal messages in changing and motivating behavior? The conclusion from more than 100 years of research is that subliminal messages are incapable of influencing behavior. In a comprehensive review of the literature, Moore concluded, "There is no empirical documentation for stronger subliminal effects, such as inducing particular behaviors or changing motivation. Moreover, such a notion is contradicted by a substantial amount of research and is incompatible with experimentally based conceptions of information processing, learning, and motivation." Other reviewers of this literature have reached the same conclusion, noting that proclaimed subliminal effects often fail to replicate and that studies claiming to find subliminal influence are methodological flawed and unsound.

After Vicary's claim for increased sales of popcorn and Coke because of subliminal messages, research increased. In 1958, the Canadian Broadcast Corporation conducted a replication of the Vicary study by flashing the message "phone now" 352 times during a popular Sunday night television show. Telephone usage did not go up during the period; nobody called the station. When asked to guess the message, viewers sent close to 500 letters, but not one contained the correct answer. However, aware of the Vicary study, almost one-half claimed to be hungry or thirsty during the show. In response to such findings, Vicary admitted to *Advertising Age* that he had handled the affair poorly. He stated, "Worse than the timing, though, was the fact that we hadn't done any research, except what was needed for filing for a patent. I had only a minor interest in the company and a small amount of data—too small to be meaningful."

The work of Key has been criticized on methodological grounds. For example, Key reports a study in which more than 1000 subjects were shown a Gilbeys Gin ad that supposedly contained the word *sex* embedded in ice cubes. A total of 62% of the subjects reported feeling aroused, romantic, and sensuous. However, Key did not include a control group in the study (a group of subjects who saw a similar ad without the implant), and thus it is unclear if these subjects felt aroused, romantic, and sensuous because of the alleged implant, in spite of it, or for some other reason.

Canadian researchers Vokey and Read conducted an extensive program of research showing that backward messages are ineffective in altering behavior. In their studies they found that subjects could not (a) discriminate a backward question from a backward statement; (b) tell if two backward messages had the same or different meaning; (c) distinguish nonsense from meaningful backward messages; and (d) distinguish among backward nursery rhymes, Christian, satanic, pornographic, or advertising messages. Vokey and Read also found that listening to backward messages did not influence subjects' semantic judgments and that subjects could "hear" hidden messages in backward messages even when there were no such messages present.

Recently, several studies have investigated the efficacy of subliminal self-help audiotapes. For example, Pratkanis and coworkers had subjects listen to subliminal self-help tapes designed to improve either self-esteem or memory. Half the subjects received mislabeled tapes; in other words, some subjects thought they had a memory-improving tape but really had a self-esteem tape, whereas others thought they had a self-esteem tape but listened to a memory tape. After 5 weeks of listening, the results showed no improvement in self-esteem or memory abilities. However, about one-half of the subjects thought they had improved based on tape label, but not content. Subjects who thought they had listened to a self-esteem tape (regardless of whether they did) were more likely to believe that their self-esteem had improved, and those who thought they had listened to a memory tape were more likely to believe that their memory had improved because of listening. In actuality, nobody's self-esteem or memory improved as a result of listening. To date, there have been nine independent investigations of subliminal self-help tapes. All nine studies have failed to find an effect consistent with the manufacturers' claims.

In the 1990 trial of the rock band Judas Priest, Judge Jerry Carr Whitehead heard arguments for and against the power of subliminal influence. His ruling in favor of Judas Priest and CBS Records in many ways stands as a summary judgment of the power of subliminal persuasion.

In his ruling, Judge Whitehead stated, "The scientific research presented does not establish that subliminal stimuli, even if perceived, may precipitate conduct of this magnitude (i.e., suicide deaths). There exist other factors which explain the conduct of the deceased independent of the subliminal stimuli."

ADVERTISING
BARNUM EFFECT
COMMUNICATION PROCESSES
DECEPTION
MOTIVATION

A. R. PRATKANIS

SUBLIMINAL PERCEPTION

Toward the end of the 1950s, a great deal of public concern was expressed when it was claimed that a method existed for presenting advertising messages that could influence behavior at an unconscious level. The procedure involved flashing messages quickly on a screen at a size, speed, or brightness that was too insignificant to produce awareness. Such stimuli are called *subliminal*. *Subliminal perception* comes about when such stimuli, even though apparently unnoticed, appear to exert an effect on later behavior.

There is serious doubt as to whether subliminal stimuli have significant effects on behavior, let alone whether they can be used to direct individuals toward specific actions or attitudes. Most of the evidence seems to suggest that meaning is not readily extracted from subliminal presentations. Instead, such covert stimuli seem to act at an affective, or emotional, level.

Another aspect of how emotional factors play a role in subliminal perception appears in the case of *perceptual defense*. This process, whereby there is an emotional response but no conscious response to a stimulus, is sometimes also called *subception*.

PERCEPTION
SELECTIVE ATTENTION

S. COREN

SUBLIMINAL PSYCHODYNAMIC ACTIVATION

Subliminal psychodynamic activation (SPA) has been termed "the strongest body of evidence favoring a psychoanalytic view of the unconscious." However, Balay and Shevrin and Fudin saw little worth to SPA.

The SPA model begins with the understanding that psychoanalytic dynamic propositions refer to unconscious events, and that once these events become conscious, their effects are no longer predictable. Therefore, to legitimately test their veracity, an investigator must be capable of affecting behavior without alerting the subject to the exact nature of the manipulation. Silverman claimed to have solved this problem by using a tachistoscope to control speed and illumination of stimuli so as to render them unreportable. Such stimuli, he argued, could then be used to affect behavior without the subject's awareness.

A typical SPA study is conducted in the following manner. Verbal messages and/or pictures believed to represent unconscious wishes, anxieties, and/or fantasies deemed important in psychoanalytic theory are presented to subjects by a tachistoscope for 4 ms. Behaviors predicted by psychoanalytic theory to be related to these unconscious dynamics are then assessed. Many experiments have been followed by a 10- to 20-trial forced-choice discrimination task. Double-blind procedures are said to be in force throughout these experiments (i.e., neither the subject nor the experimenter is aware of what stimuli are being presented). The subject is kept ignorant by virtue of the claimed subliminal nature of the stimulation. The experimenter is said to have no awareness of stimulus content, because the stimuli were prepared and coded by another person. Under these conditions, the subliminal exposure of stimuli with psychodynamic content was believed to affect behavior in a way that the subliminal exposure of neutral stimuli did not. Moreover, in many of these studies, the same psychodynamic stimuli were presented supraliminally to no effect. Bornstein performed a metaanalysis that showed that the effect sizes of these two conditions were significantly different, with the 4-ms condition showing the larger effect size. These findings are in keeping with the psychoanalytic supposition that when psychodynamic content is brought into awareness, its links with psychopathology can be severed. It also satisfies Merikle and Cheesman's dual requirements for being below a subjective threshold (i.e., persons respond differently when claiming to see nothing than when they claim to have seen something).

Early work focused on stirring up libidinal and aggressive conflicts so as to examine associated defensive processes. The majority of this work investigated the psychoanalytic proposition that the ego pathology of schizophrenics is in part attributable to an unconscious conflict over aggression. Other propositions tested in this phase of the research were that anal conflicts play a role in stuttering, that aggression is implicated in depression, and that Oedipal issues are active in the dynamics of male homosexuals. (As Weinberger and Silverman pointed out, this does not mean, nor was it meant to imply, that homosexuality is inherently pathological. Incest conflict and, for that matter, unconscious conflicts of all kinds can be found in people at all points in any continuum bearing on mental health.) Some relatively recent SPA studies have focused on the relationship of male Oedipal dynamics to competitive performance.

The bulk of recent SPA work has concentrated on triggering positive fantasies held to be capable of engendering adaptation-enhancing effects. This set of investigations evolved from the psychoanalytically based idea that unconscious fantasies of oneness or merger with the "good mother of early childhood," when activated, can bring about positive behavior change. Silverman termed these fantasies symbiotic-like or oneness fantasies and attempted to activate them through the subliminal message "MOMMY AND I ARE ONE (MIO)," sometimes accompanied by a congruent picture. Subjects have included nonclinical ("normal" college students) as well as clinical (e.g., schizophrenics, depressives, phobics, persons who have habit disorders) populations. Dependent measures have ranged from thought disorder to depression, to anxiety, to assertiveness, to self-revelations, to habit changes. Most of these studies have shown that the MIO stimulus was capable of improving the outcome of psychotherapeutic and educational interventions.

Metaanalyses have indicated that SPA, especially MIO, effects are genuine. Thus, a metaanalysis of MIO studies yielded a respectable overall effect size of $d = 0.41$. Weinberger and Hardaway showed that these effects could not be explained through anomalous data-analytic procedures, were not exclusive to Silverman's lab, and could not be attributed to unpublished (nonpeer reviewed) studies. In addition, in what Rosenthal has termed a file-drawer analysis, it was revealed that it would require 2287 null findings to obviate the positive results thus far obtained.

FANTASY
SUBLIMINAL PERCEPTION
UNCONSCIOUS INFERENCE

J. L. WEINBERGER

SUBSTANCE ABUSE

Substance abuse has been a controversial issue since ancient times. Debates concerning the use of marijuana, for example, can be traced to Chinese documents dated several centuries B.C. In the United States, concern about the abuse of alcohol and other drugs has existed since the early nineteenth century.

Substance abuse involves the use of any chemical to modify mood or behavior in a way that differs from socially approved therapeutic or recreational practices.

DIAGNOSIS

The American Psychiatric Association's (APA's) fourth edition of the *Diagnostic and statistical manual of mental disorders (DSM-IV)* lists four criteria for the diagnosis of substance abuse: recurrent patterns of substance abuse; recurrent use under hazardous conditons; recurrent legal problems due to abuse; continued use in spite of social problems.

Accurate diagnosis of substance abuse must include attention to the individual's specific cluster of problems. Substance abuse disorders can be continuous, episodic, in remission, or unspecified. In addition, most drugs can cause a variety of organic brain syndromes. Polydrug use is quite common. Finally, substance abuse problems may coexist with other psychiatric disorders, such as personality or affective disorders.

TREATMENT

Just as substance abuse should be individually assessed, so must it be treated. In general, however, several stages of intervention are usually necessary. Immediate attention to emergencies requires treatment of acute medical conditions such as panic reactions or malnutrition. Detoxification necessitates reduction of the substance while monitoring withdrawal symptoms and performing additional laboratory tests and clinical assessment. Individual counseling is usually the next step in treatment.

Support is a critical component of all phases of intervention. Therapeutic communities such as Synanon and self-help groups such as Alcoholics Anonymous can provide group support as well as confrontation and can serve as long-term programs for treatment and maintenance of drug-free functioning. The involvement of family is also necessary to help the substance abuser, as well as the family members.

PREVENTION

Most substance abuse prevention has been tertiary prevention or treatment of existing cases and prevention of recidivism. Secondary prevention, or early diagnosis and referral, usually have taken place in crisis intervention clinics. J. P. Swisher has emphasized the need for greater primary prevention efforts, or the planning of activities before abuse occurs. Swisher suggests that the most effective primary prevention efforts involve coordination of various community institutions, combinations of informational materials with alternatives to drug use, and the synthesis and integration of existing materials within ongoing community activities.

ALCOHOLISM TREATMENT
HEROIN ADDICTION
SMOKING BEHAVIOR

C. LANDAU

SUGGESTION THERAPY

Suggestion is the process of inducing an uncritical acceptance of a change in cognition, affect, or behavior. Historically, the use of suggestion has been involved in such practices as magic incantations, religious rituals, faith healing, voodoo, and the placebo effect. Its modern use for therapeutic purposes is considered to have started with Emile Coué. Hypnotherapy is a form of suggestion therapy in which the suggestibility is enhanced by the induction of a trance state.

There are different types of suggestion: heterosuggestion (induced by another person) and autosuggestion (self-suggestion); direct suggestion and indirect suggestion (covert suggestion intended to elude the defenses of the client); and verbal and nonverbal suggestion (through changes in facial expression, body and hand movement, etc). Suggestion operates to a certain extent in all forms of therapy.

The present trend in suggestion therapy is greatly influenced by Milton Erickson's approach involving the skillful use of verbal and nonverbal communication sometimes to convey direct, but mostly indirect, suggestions.

HYPNOTHERAPY
PSYCHOTHERAPY

D. MOTET

SUICIDE

Baechler has proposed a definition that emphasizes the operational functions the suicidal act is meant to serve: "Suicide denotes any behavior that seeks and finds the solution to an existential problem by making an attempt on the life of the subject."

Traditionally, suicide is one of the four *modes*—as distinguished from the hundreds of *causes*—of death; the other three are natural, accident, and homicide, called acronymically the NASH categories of death. Shneidman has proposed a supplementary classification in which all deaths (whatever their NASH label or their cause) are identified as one of three kinds: intentioned, subintentioned (in which the individual has played some partial, latent, covert, or unconscious role in hastening the demise), or unintentioned.

VARIOUS APPROACHES TO SUICIDAL PHENOMENA

A number of different approaches to the assessment, understanding, and treatment of suicidal phenomena are delineated.

Theological

Neither the Old nor the New Testament directly forbids suicide. St. Thomas Aquinas emphasized that suicide was a mortal sin in that it usurped God's power over human life and death. The notion of suicide as sin took firm hold and for hundreds of years played (and continues to play) an important part in the Western view of self-destruction.

Philosophical

In general, the "philosophers of suicide" never meant their written speculations to be prescriptions for action, but simply to reflect their own intellectual debates.

David Hume was one of the first major Western philosophers to discuss suicide without the concept of sin.

The existential philosophers of the twentieth century—Kierkegaard, Jaspers, Camus, Sartre, Heidegger—have made the meaninglessness of life (and the place of suicide) a central topic.

Demographic

The demographic approach relates to various statistics on suicide. Currently, in the United States, the suicide rate is 12.6 per 100,000 and ranks as one of the ten leading causes of adult deaths. Suicide rates gradually rise during adolescence, increase sharply in early adulthood, and parallel advancing age up to the age bracket 75 to 84 years, when it reaches a rate of 27.9 suicides per 100,000. Male suicides outnumber female suicides in a ratio of 2 : 1, and more Whites than nonwhites commit suicide. Suicide is more prevalent among persons who are single, widowed, separated, and divorced.

The suicide rate in young people, aged 15 to 24 years, has risen sharply since the 1950s, from 4.2 per 100,000 in 1954 to 10.9 per 100,000 in 1974. The suicide rate for nonwhites has also increased significantly. Most people who commit suicide in the United States are over the age of 45, but a 1994 report (by Garland and Zigler) indicates that the rate in adolescents, especially white males, rose over 200% in the previous 3 decades.

Sociological

Emile Durkheim's giant book *Le suicide* demonstrated the power of the sociological approach. As a result of his analysis of French data on suicide, Durkheim proposed four kinds of suicides, all of them emphasizing the strength or weakness of the person's relationships or ties to society. *Altruistic* suicides are literally required by society. Here the customs or rules of the group "demand" suicide under certain circumstances; *hara-kiri* and suttee are examples. *Egoistic* suicide occurs when the individual has too few ties with the community and is not reached by demands to live. Anomic suicides take place when the accustomed relationship between an individual and society is suddenly shattered, such as the shocking and immediate loss of a job, a close friend, or a fortune. *Fatalistic* suicides derive from excessive regulation. Examples would be persons whose futures are piteously blocked, such as slaves.

In a major break with Durkheim, Douglas pointed out that the social meanings of suicide vary greatly and that the more socially integrated a group is, the more effective it may be in disguising suicide; further, social reactions to stigmatized behaviors can themselves become a part of the etiology of the very actions the group seeks to control.

Maris believes that a systematic theory of suicide should be composed of at least four broad categories of variables—those concerning the person, the social context, biological factors, and "temporality," oftentimes involving "suicidal careers."

Psychodynamic

The principal psychoanalytical position on suicide was that it represented unconscious hostility directed toward the introjected (ambivalently viewed) love object. Karl Menninger delineates the psychodynamics of hostility and asserts that the drives in suicide are made up of: (a) the wish to kill, (b) the wish to be killed, and (c) the wish to die.

Gregory Zilboorg stated that every suicidal case contained not only unconscious hostility, but also an unusual lack of capacity to love others. He extended the concern solely from intrapsychic dynamics to include the external world, specifically the role of a broken home, in suicidal proneness.

Litman traces the development of Freud's thoughts on the subject. These factors include several emotional states—rage, guilt, anxiety, and dependency—as well as a great number of specifically predisposing conditions. Feelings of abandonment, and particularly of helplessness and hopelessness, are important.

Psychological

The psychological approach can be distinguished from the psychodynamic approach in that it does not posit a set of dynamics or a universal unconscious scenario but, rather, emphasizes certain general psychologic features that seem to be necessary for a lethal suicide event to occur. Four features have been noted: (a) acute *perturbation,* that is, an increase in the individual's state of general upsetment; (b) heightened *inimicality,* an increase in self-abnegation, self-hate, shame, guilt, self-blame, and overtly in behaviors that are against one's own best interests; (c) a sharp and almost sudden increase of *constriction* of intellectual focus, a tunneling of thought processes, a narrowing of the mind's content, a truncating of the capacity to see viable options that would ordinarily occur to the mind; and (d) the idea of *cessation,* the insight that it is possible to put an end to suffering by stopping the unbearable flow of consciousness. In this context, suicide is understood not as a movement toward death (or cessation), but rather as flight from intolerable emotion.

Legal

In the United States, only two states considered *committing* suicide a crime, but there is no penalty for breaking this law. In several states, suicide attempts are misdemeanors, although these laws are seldom enforced. Thirty states have no laws against suicide or suicide attempts but every state has laws that specify that it is a felony to aid, advise, or encourage another person to commit suicide.

Preventional

Shneidman and colleagues are generally associated with approaching suicide from a preventive perspective. They concluded from their research there that the vast majority (about 80%) of suicides have a recognizable presuicidal phase.

ATTEMPTED SUICIDE

In general, it has been believed that two "populations" (those who commit suicide and those who attempt suicide) are essentially separate. Strictly speaking, a suicide attempt should refer only to those who sought to commit suicide and fortuitously survived. Over a 10-year period, the overlap of the percentage of individuals who commit suicide with those who previously attempted suicide is 40%, whereas the overlap of those who attempt suicide and those who subsequently commit it is only 5%. Any event that uses a suicidal modality is a genuine crisis, even though it might not, under strict semantic rules, be called a "suicidal" event.

INDIRECT SUICIDES AND SUBINTENTIONED DEATHS

Karl Menninger's concepts of chronic, focal, and organic suicides and Shneidman's concept of subintentioned deaths—the ways in which individuals can play covert, unconscious, partial roles in hastening their deaths—obviously include what have been called indirect suicides.

GLOBAL, POLITICAL, AND SUPERNATIONAL ASPECTS

Contemporary (self-disserving) national neuroses (amounting to an international insanity) may very well lead to the self-induced death of human life as we know it. We live in a death-haunted time. Overwhelmingly, the most important kind of suicide for everyone to know about and to prevent is the *global* suicide that threatens us all and which, by the very presence of that threat, poisons our lives. Lifton appropriately urges on our consciousness the fact that we are in great danger of breaking our psychological connections to our own sense of continuity, generativity, and fantasized immortality—connections that are necessary to sustain our human relationships.

ALTRUISTIC SUICIDE
SUICIDE PREVENTION

SOCIOPSYCHOLOGICAL DETERMINANTS OF WAR
AND PEACE
THANATOLOGY

E. S. SHNEIDMAN

SUICIDE PREVENTION

Primary prevention of suicide involves the radical reduction of national and global economic and social tensions and thoroughgoing beneficent changes in certain governmental and societal patterns. Most people, when they talk about suicide prevention, are referring either to health education or to suicide intervention (i.e., response to or treatment of a suicidal person).

The basic rationale of suicide prevention activities is that overt suicidal behaviors are almost always preceded by certain presuicidal signs, and that suicidal states, once identified, can be mollified (and suicidal acts prevented). Retrospective studies of committed suicide indicate that approximately 90% of cases contain some indications of the decedent's suicidal intentions. These "clues to suicide"—precursors, warning signals, prodromal signs, or premonitory indexes—are either verbal (e.g., "You won't be seeing me around") or behavioral (e.g., giving away prized possessions). Response to presuicidal clues is the pathway to prevention of suicidal deaths.

SUICIDE PREVENTION CENTERS

Organized suicide prevention efforts are a twentieth century development. As of the early 1980s, there were about 200 suicide prevention centers in the United States, covering almost every major city. The centers are independent of each other. Although many centers now also deal with drug rehabilitation, homicide prevention, response to battered spouses, rape, teenage hot lines, and general crisis intervention, suicide prevention centers have become a vital part of the independently operated mental health services in many countries throughout the world.

CRISIS INTERVENTION
HOTLINE SERVICES
SUICIDE

E. S. SHNEIDMAN

SULLIVAN'S INTERPERSONAL THEORY

Interpersonal theory is a theory of interpersonal relations, developed largely in the 1930s and 1940s by Harry Stack Sullivan.

KEY CONCEPTS

Sullivan emphasized the *social nature* of human nature. He defined psychiatry, personality, and key assessment and treatment concepts in interpersonal terms. He also emphasized the crucial role of *anxiety* in personality formation and disturbance. Finally, Sullivan emphasized actual interactions or *performances* in the interpersonal field as the process by which disturbances are formed, revealed, and treated.

The Social Nature of Human Nature

Sullivan defined personality as "the relatively enduring pattern of recurrent interpersonal situations which characterize a human life." Even hermits maintain, through imagery, memory, and fantasy, an interpersonal life. *Dynamisms,* defined in terms of characteristic patterns of internal or overt social behavior, are the smallest meaningful unit of study of an individual.

That behavior often reflects relationships with persons not actually present was a cornerstone of Sullivan's approach. He perceived in the troubled behavior of his patients the distorting effects of such relationships. The inner aspect of this distortion he called *personifications,* images one holds of self or others, with their attendant feelings, impulses, and ideas. Stereotypes are widely shared personifications, positive or negative. Personifications built up in one relationship may be triggered in another, with consequent distortions of thinking, feeling, and acting.

Anxiety

Anxiety can be the most crucial formative influence in the interpersonal field, and its origins are the origins also of personality and of self. Their common roots lie in the helpless nature of infants, who survive only if nurtured. Over time, such interactions acquire two consequences: *satisfaction,* arising from need reduction, and *security,* arising from the preservation of a necessary relationship.

Threats to biological survival bring fear. Threats to security bring *anxiety,* which may be devastatingly powerful for a being lacking the maturity and experience to manage or dampen it.

The growing dynamism of *self* (Sullivan's word for the complex of processes that come increasingly to monitor, evaluate, and regulate activities in the interpersonal field) seeks above all else to preserve security. Behaviors bringing approval from significant others are strengthened; behaviors bringing disapproval are inhibited and may be eliminated.

Performances

Children dominated by the preservation of security grow up to have very distorted understandings of their performances in the interpersonal field. When children are broadly, persistently, and intensely disapproved of by significant others, they become more than conforming: They become emotionally disturbed.

Sullivan developed numerous strategies for detecting distortions in interpersonal relations and the often subtle manifestations of anxiety that accompany them, and for relating to disturbed people in such a way that they could begin to experience the truths behind the evasions, thus expanding the self. Central to his methods was the conviction that all the therapist can know objectively is performance in interpersonal situations. Sullivan perceived the therapist as a participant in the performances of the patient, and considered that the data of assessment and treatment arise in this process of *participant observation.*

PERSONALITY THEORIES
PSYCHOTHERAPY

R. E. ENFIELD

SUPERSTITION

Superstition may be defined as the acceptance of beliefs or practices that are groundless and inconsistent with the degree of understanding shared by members of a particular group or community. Yet certain ancient beliefs now considered superstitions survive. For example, the ancient Northern European fertility rite of decorating a house with greens at Christmastime is still practiced because it is colorful and in keeping with custom. The superstitions of primitive people generally involved a belief in the causal effects derived from supernatural powers because no better naturalistic explanations were known.

Early in the twentieth century, Sigmund Freud wrote about superstitions. He did not believe in supernatural powers but theorized that such beliefs were the externalization of conflicts and repressions to be found in the unconscious mind.

More recently, B. F. Skinner interpreted the development of individual superstitious behavior in terms of "accidental" or "chance" contingencies. He demonstrated how this could occur in an animal experiment.

ANIMISM

R. W. Lundin

SUPPORTIVE CARE

American society and American psychology view dependency in pejorative terms, yet dependency is a normal event in the course of human affairs. Humans are born helpless and dependent; independence is gained at varying rates with regard to various functions. We maintain that independence, and even take care of others; some of us, if we live long enough, again become dependent on others for a variety of functions. When dependency becomes excessive or interferes with the normal maturation and development, it is seen as a problem that requires treatment. One of the most common problems for the practicing psychotherapist is the evaluation and treatment of dependency.

The ego ideal of the society requires rugged independence, being one's own person, and standing on one's own feet. The expectation of a rugged independence, derived from the U.S. nineteenth century agrarian-pioneering ethic, does not serve us realistically in a twentieth century urban middle class society. The disparity between the ego ideal of independence and the reality of the sick individual must be taken into account by the therapist who deals with the treatment, and therefore with the management of dependency. For patients who necessarily must remain dependent, such as those who are chronically ill, one of the vital functions of the therapist is to give them permission to be dependent and to help them to forgive themselves for a state of dependency that is both reasonable and unavoidable. The chronically psychotic patient usually requires a lifelong therapeutic relationship that must be carefully nurtured and supportive. Managing and treating dependency is further complicated by the fact that intensive psychotherapy fosters dependency.

The care given to patients who have conditions that cannot be cured and cannot be altered is called *supportive care*. The purpose of supportive care is to maximize function and minimize dysfunction, to maximize pleasure and satisfaction in life and minimize pain and discomfort.

Although the therapeutic relationship can be altered, and with time may be minimal, it can never be totally terminated; dependency in such patients, therefore, cannot and should not be terminated. Supportive care as a technique of treatment focuses its effort on the appropriate maintenance of a dependent relationship that the patient uses to improve function and to gain comfort. A crucial part of supportive care is to monitor dependency so that it is therapeutic and growth producing, rather than inhibiting and dysfunctional.

Supportive care, in both theory and practice, requires an ongoing supportive relationship, either with an individual therapist or with the individual as a representative of the helping agency. Patients who are chronically ill often rely on such relationships for survival. It is essential, particularly early in therapy, that these relationships stand up to the patient's frequent testing as to availability and reliability. A program of supportive care must focus on the patient's abilities rather than on disabilities; it must minimize dependency but, at the same time, not threaten to cut off dependency gratification entirely.

In the long term, the management problem becomes one of fulfilling the patient's dependency needs at minimum expense to the therapist and the therapeutic program. This must be done very carefully so that the patient never has the feeling of being rejected. On developing some skill in meeting any dependency needs in the general community, the patient will require less time with the therapist or the therapeutic system. Eventu-

ally the therapist can symbolize and handle much of the dependency need gratification for the patient. At that point, the chronically ill patient often can live with minimal distress and maximum ability while needing only limited contact with the therapist.

MAINSTREAMING (PSYCHOTICS)
MENTAL HEALTH PROGRAMS

W. M. Mendel

SURFACE TRANSPORTATION

Among the major sources of surface transportation, psychological research has focused mostly on the automobile. In this regard, research interest has concentrated mainly on automobile accidents. The driver and automobile are usually studied as a "human–machine system." The system's performance in matters of speed, distance, and stopping pertains to the capabilities of the operator and the automobile. Accidents are thought to be a failure of the system, since both human error and faulty automobile design are causes. Investigations into the human element have shed light on the so-called "accident-prone" person, and also the relationships between accidents and the driver's age, experience, and speeding, drinking, and drug-taking habits. Various environmental conditions have been explored, such as the design of the car, road conditions, weather, and illumination.

The automobile driving simulator used for analyzing driving behavior and accidents is effective in ascertaining the driver's reactions to emergency situations. To reduce accidents, psychologists have recommended a systematic accident prevention program by modifying both the operator and the vehicle.

SCIENCE OF SEATING

Safety and comfort of automobile seats are being studied by engineering psychologists who specialize in anthropometry, involving the measurement of the dimensions of the human body for the purpose of fitting the seat to the driver.

STRESS AND MENTAL HEALTH

Gardell has evaluated stress among bus drivers by physiological measures, accidents, and number of sick days taken. He found that many drivers were the best judges of ways to reduce stress on the job.

Some passengers experience anxiety when using public transportation because of broken-down vehicles, deteriorating stations, and lack of safety. Correction of this negative environment helps to alleviate the travelers' stress. Motion sickness may be reduced by tempering vibrations and acceleration and deceleration. The combination of other environmental stresses has an adverse effect on the traveler, such as exposure to loud noises and extreme temperatures.

PUBLIC TRANSPORTATION

Although the public shows a clear preference for the automobile, there is much concern over problems caused by the proliferation of cars and highways: accidents, pollution, traffic congestion, depletion of gasoline, and so forth. It is believed that a safe and reliable U. S. rail system would prove a viable alternative to automobiles. Cantilli suggests improvements in the form of additional escalators, clean stations and washrooms, attractive stations, functioning heating and air conditioning, proper ventilation, noise control, better illumination, and security of both vehicles and stations.

More research on the psychology of mass transportation is required to revitalize transit facilities in accordance with the needs of patrons. Travelers choose their means of transportation on the basis of such factors as reliability, convenience and comfort, travel time, cost, condition of vehicles, self-esteem and autonomy, traffic and congestion, and diversions.

ACCIDENT PRONENESS AND PREVENTION
APPLIED RESEARCH

S. S. BROWN

SURPRISE

Surprise is a highly transient reaction to a sudden and unexpected event. Ongoing activity is momentarily halted. The facial expression is distinctive, with eyes wide, eyebrows raised, brow wrinkled, and mouth opened round. With extreme surprise, and especially with startle, there are eyeblink and postural reactions. It is one of the most easily and universally recognized emotions. Its physiological correlates are, in general, those of increased arousal.

Surprise can be unpleasant, pleasant, or both at once. Tompkins describes surprise, as a "resetting" state because, for a fraction of a second, the mind is cleared of thought.

Surprise can range from the relatively reflexive to the highly cognitive. On the reflexive side, it is closely related to the startle and orienting reflexes. It is also closely related to cognitive inconsistency—or incongruity, imbalance, or dissonance. Specifically, it is a reaction to a sudden change in the level of consistency.

SURPRISE—A PRIMARY EMOTION

A number of criteria for distinguishing the primary emotions have been proposed, including universality of expression and recognition, a neurophysiological substrate, phylogenetic and ontogenetic primacy, an adaptive function, a consistent hedonic tone, and duration over time. If defined so as to include startle, surprise has no difficulty meeting any of these criteria except the last two. Most theorists override these two criteria, as surprise appears on virtually every prominent list of primary emotions. A representative list is that of Plutchik: joy, sadness, acceptance, rejection, fear, anger, anticipation, and surprise.

Startle and the Orienting Response

Pure startle is a complex involuntary reflex to a sudden and intense stimulus. Unexpectedness can intensify a startle reaction. A high stimulus intensity can increase surprise but is by no means necessary. Suddenness is necessary for startle or surprise.

Surprise is related to the orienting response (OR), a reaction to novel stimuli in which the animal or person orients the body and sense organs toward the stimulus.

LEARNING

Leon Caiman suggested that a stimulus must be surprising to produce conditioning. In support of this thesis, he provided dramatic demonstrations of blocking, a failure of conditioning in which valid but redundant (and thus unsurprising) cues are ignored. Counterblocking, or "superconditioning," has also been demonstrated in which, for example, a good event (food) is made very surprising by the expectation of a bad event (shock).

The surprise theory of conditioning was formalized as a simple linear operator model by Rescorla and Wagner. Blocking, counterblocking, and several other diverse and counterintuitive conditioning phenomena have been integrated successfully by this model. Wagner extended this model to include both simple habituation and complex information processing in humans. All levels of learning are thus interrelated in this model through the concept of stimulus surprisingness.

COGNITION

One area of research relating surprise to human cognition is that on the P300 component of event-related electroencephalogram potentials (ERPs). In general, ERP components with short latencies are related to physical stimulus events, while the later ones, including P300, are more closely related to information processing.

Research by Donchin and collaborators has demonstrated that surprise can be measured by the amplitude of the P300 wave, from which one learns how much the subject's expectations or schemas are revised; from its latency, one learns how quickly the revision occurs.

Social Cognition

The literature on social cognition, including that specifically on cognitive consistency, is not a rich source of research on surprise, largely because little attention has been directed to suddenness, a necessary antecedent of surprise. However, the direct correspondence between sudden shifts in consistency level and surprise has been demonstrated. The findings of interest are the following correlations, all highly significant:

Unpleasantness and inconsistency	0.89
Surprise and inconsistency shift	0.86
Surprise and unpleasantness	0.83

Although the first correlation is noteworthy for showing how accurately pleasantness can be predicted from the level of inconsistency, the second correlation demonstrates that surprise corresponds very closely to the magnitude of the consistency shifts. The third correlation shows that here, where all inconsistency shifts are upward, surprise is unpleasant.

Humor

Sigmund Freud distinguished between tendentious or "tendency" humor and "harmless" humor. Corresponding to these two kinds of humor are two families of theories of humor. The foremost motivational theory is the psychoanalytic, which sees humor as based on the indirect expression of taboo sexual and aggressive motives. Cognitive theories, addressed primarily toward "harmless" humor, usually take either incongruity (i.e., inconsistency) or surprise as the central construct.

The role of incongruity and surprise in "harmless" or cognitive humor can be seen easily in the joke scenario, which has three parts: (a) the "setup," in which a frame of reference and expectations are established; (b) the "punchline," in which incongruity is suddenly introduced; and (c) the "point" or solution, whereby the listener suddenly resolves the incongruity. If insight is delayed, the listener is surprised twice, first by the sudden incongruity of the punchline, and again when the point is seen.

There is much evidence that funniness is directly related to surprisingness for "harmless" or incongruity-based humor. There is also some evidence that tendency jokes are funnier if they are not especially surprising, suggesting that the most satisfying tendency humor confirms our expectations or prejudices rather than challenging them. Thus surprise plays contrasting roles in the two kinds of humor.

CONDITIONING
EMOTIONS
HUMOR

R. H. WILLIS

SURROGATE PARENTS (ANIMALS)

Naturally occurring surrogate animal parents rarely develop in the wild. Most biologists believe that natural adoption among animals would interfere with the evolutionary process of survival of the most adaptive animals. However, sociobiologists do recognize that such altruistic behavior could provide for protection of the large gene pool of related animals. As well, it can provide a means for adult animals to "practice" being parents prior actually to producing offspring of their own.

Researchers have forced various artificial parenting arrangements on primates to study the differential effects of early deprivation and stimulation. Such studies have been completed largely using rhesus monkeys. The deprivation caused by the absence of the tactile, auditory, and kinesthetic stimulation of parents, particularly the mother, produced abnormal infant monkeys.

Subsequent experiments were designed to learn exactly what aspects of the parental deprivation were the most damaging to the infants' development. To answer these questions, Harlow provided various surrogate "parents" for the infants. Surrogates were one of three types: a stationary or moving terry-cloth model or a stationary wire model. The moving terry-cloth surrogate provided the greatest contact, comfort, and tactile/kinesthetic feedback. This surrogate produced the least number of abnormalities, whereas the stationary wire model produced the greatest number of problems.

These studies demonstrated that emotional attachment is independent of the feeding relationship but is determined by the tactile comfort. When frightened, the monkeys ran to the terry-cloth surrogates as opposed to the wire substitute.

DEVIANT MATURATION
MATERNAL DEPRIVATION

S. D. SHERRETS

SURVEYS

Opinion, attitude, and interest surveys are unlike traditional tests in that they are self-report measures in which the persons responding indicate what they feel or think; there are no right or wrong answers. The person responding to the survey is generally asked to rate each item on some type of rating scale—from *most* to *least,* or *strongly agree* to *strongly disagree,* or simply on a scale of anywhere from 3 to 10 points.

The Gallup Poll and the Harris Poll are two of the better known opinion surveys. Much market research is also of the opinion survey variety.

Attitude surveys are generally used to measure such things as how people feel about social or personal objects or issues. Examples are the Job Attitude Scale and the Attitudes Toward Women Scale.

Interest surveys measure preferences for certain activities; these usually are work-related activities, but some also measure preferences for play or leisure activities, or for activities related to school subjects. Interest surveys are generally used for career and educational exploration and planning. There are two principal types—those with internally built, homogeneous scales; and those with externally, or empirically, built criterion scales. Surveys of the former type are based on clusters of internally related items, with each cluster representing a basic interest dimension, such as outdoor, artistic, mathematical, or literary interest. Examples are the Kuder Preference Record, Vocational; the American College Testing Program Interest Inventory; and the Self-Directed Search. Scores are based on a comparison between the individual's responses and those of a representative sample of people in various grade or age ranges. Criterion, or empirically developed, scales, however, are based on the item responses of people in the criterion group or occupation represented by the scale. Scores represent the degree of similarity with the responses of people in the criterion groups. The validity of an interest survey is generally measured by how well it predicts the occupation or activity a person will enter, or how well satisfied the person will be with that occupation or activity. Empirically developed interest surveys generally are expected to meet an additional requirement: They must be able clearly to discriminate, or distinguish, members of one occupation from members of other occupations. Examples of empirically developed interest surveys are the Kuder Occupational Interest Survey and the Strong–Campbell Interest Inventory.

ATTITUDE MEASUREMENT
OPINION POLLS

E. E. DIAMOND

SYMBOLIC INTERACTION

The term *symbolic interaction* refers to a distinctly sociological and social psychological approach to the study of human group life and human interaction. Within American sociology, the work of Herbert Blumer has been most commonly associated with the perspective. Philosophically, symbolic interactionisin is most closely aligned with American Pragmatism, German Idealism, and German and French Phenomenology. The perspective is opposed to the various versions of logical positivism, structural–functionalism, cultural determinism, biological determinism, stimulus–response behaviorism, exchange, and balance or equilibrium theories. There is a certain compatibility with various forms of Marxist thought, psychoanalytic theory, phenomenological sociology, ethnomethodology, semiotics, and humanistic and existential psychologies and philosophy.

BASIC ASSUMPTIONS

Symbolic interactionism rests on three basic assumptions. First, humans act toward things "on the basis of the meanings that things have for them." Second, the meanings of social objects arise out of social interaction. Meanings are not in objects. Third, meanings are "handled in, and modified through an interpretive process." As a consequence, the meanings of objects change in and through the course of action. Meanings are not fixed.

The central object with whom one must deal with is oneself. Persons are both objects and subjects to themselves. The division between subjective and objective worlds of experience is removed in symbolic interactionist thought. The world is in the person, just as the person is in the world.

Language is the means for interaction and the medium through which it occurs. Language, as a system of signs, symbols, oppositions, and meanings, permits persons to enter into their own and others' activities and to make those activities objects of meaning and action. The study of language lies at the core of social psychology, and symbolic interactionism makes language a fundamental point of departure in the study of human interaction.

The central object to be negotiated in interaction is identity and the meanings of identity, the persons and others, lie not in persons, but in the interaction itself. Hence the study of symbolic interaction requires constant attention to the study of a process—the process of interaction.

The methodology of symbolic interactionism is naturalistic, descriptive, and interpretive. The interactionist seeks to study symbolic interaction in the natural settings of the everyday world. Preferred methods include participant observation, life histories, unobtrusive methods, ethnographies, and thickly contextualized interaction episodes or behavior specimens. Interactionist interpretations seek to illuminate the phenomenon under investigation and to embed description in relational, interactional, historical, and temporal materials. Causal explanations are set aside in favor of processual interpretations.

APPLICATIONS

Symbolic interactionists have contributed understanding to such diverse fields as social deviance and mental illness, drug addiction, collective behavior, childhood socialization, death and dying, aging, illness and pain, and the sociology of art.

INTERACTIONISM
SOCIAL PSYCHOLOGY

N. K. DENZIN

SYMPATHETIC NERVOUS SYSTEM

The sympathetic nervous system (SNS) is one division of the autonomic nervous system; the other is the parasympathetic nervous system. Anatomically the sympathetic division is composed of those neurons that originate within the thoracic and lumbar segments of the spinal cord and project to ganglia, or groups of cell bodies and synapses, lying along the vertebral column just outside the cord. There is a ganglion for each spinal segment, from the first thoracic to the third lumbar segment. These spinal ganglia are interconnected by neurons to form a chain of ganglia on each side of the vertebral column.

Efferent fibers leaving the chain extend to innervate smooth muscles and glands in the skin and viscera. Those neuron-innervating surface structures (the cutaneous and subcutaneous blood vessels, sweat glands, and pilomotor muscles) extend directly from cell bodies in the chain ganglia to the target organ, and hence are called *postganglionic neurons.* Other fibers innervating the smooth muscles and glands of the abdomen and pelvic area are preganglionic, since they pass through the chain of ganglia without synapse. The chemical transmitter between postganglionic neurons and effectors in the sympathetic division is norepinephrine, with the single exception of the sweat glands, where acetylcholine is the transmitter.

The SNS is always active, but is particularly so during emergency situations. SNS responses are relatively diffuse and long-lasting. All the changes make additional oxygen available for the metabolism of the increased carbohydrates going to the muscles. The SNS functions are sometimes called *catabolic,* because they lead to the breakdown of stored supplies and then rapid increase of metabolism. These responses are largely the opposite of what occurs during parasympathetic dominance.

AUTONOMIC NERVOUS SYSTEM
PARASYMPATHETIC NERVOUS SYSTEM

R. M. STERN

SYMPTOM REMISSION THERAPY

Symptom remission therapy is a generic term referring to a variety of therapies that reduce symptoms or behavior problems without modifying the presumed cause of those problems.

The term *symptom remission therapy* is based on a "disease" conceptualization of behavior problems. Some treatments may modify only the manifestations of the underlying etiological factors or disease process.

Because the original causal factors remain, a recurrence of the same behavior problems or the emergence of other behavior problems would be predicted. However, there is now an overwhelming body of research to suggest that behavior problems can be modified successfully, that those changes can last a long time, and that they are not necessarily accompanied by adverse changes in other behaviors.

BEHAVIOR THERAPY
PSYCHOTHERAPY

S. N. HAYNES

SYNESTHESIA

It seems uncontroversial that seeing is what we do with lights, hearing is what we do with sounds, and so on. The experience of synesthesia, however, refers to sensory experiences that cross these various modalities, so that one "hears" colors, or "sees" sounds. Similar experiences can be evoked by words or even single letters, so that letters are seen as having a certain color.

For some individuals, known as synesthetes, these cross-modal perceptual experiences seem as clear and compelling as ordinary perception. For example, an individual identified as S reported seeing "puffs of steam or splashes" when he heard certain words. When S was presented with a specific tone, he reported seeing a "brown strip against a dark background." Presented with a different tone, he reported a specific color. In some cases, he could not understand what was being said, because he was so distracted by the "color of someone's voice."

A substantial number of people have been identified as synesthetes. For example, the composers Olivier Messiaen and Alexander Scriabin both had clear synesthesia. In fact, there is some suggestion that synesthesia is more common among creative individuals. In spite of some anecdotal suggestions, however, there appears to be no connection between synesthesia and intelligence or between synesthesia and personality dysfunction. Research has also documented circumstances that promote synesthesia. For example, synesthesia accompanies some forms of schizophrenia and also some drug reactions.

Many forms of synesthesia exist, but among these, links between sight and hearing seem far more common. Synesthesia often seems asymmetrical, so that a synesthete might experience photisms in response to sounds, but not the reverse (i.e., no experience of sounds in response to lights).

There is considerable variation, from one synesthete to the next, in the specific linkage between the modalities. For example, one synesthete might perceive a particular vowel sound as green, and another might perceive the same sound as red. However, the synesthetic reaction is not entirely idiosyncratic. For example, across the various synesthetes, darker colors are perceived in response to lower vowel pitches; brighter colors are perceived in response to higher vowel pitches.

Individual synesthetes also seem quite consistent in their reactions, from one test to the next. In one study, synesthetes were asked to select the color evoked by specific letters of the alphabet; they were then retested after 24 hours and again after 1 year. The subjects were impressively consistent in their selections, even after the year's delay; nonsynesthetic subjects were appreciably less consistent, even when retested after just 1 day. Similar stability has been documented in other cases of synesthesia, including a woman who showed a strong color response to words, or a man who showed strong color responses to specific musical notes. This last-mentioned synesthete also showed remarkable ability to learn new note–color associations, with the suggestion that his synesthesia may be the result of very strong cross-modal associative abilities; for other synesthetes, however, researchers have argued against explanations in terms of remembered associations.

Many synesthetes echo S's assertion that their synesthesia is both compelling and spontaneous—they certainly cannot choose not to experience this synesthetic response. For example, one female synesthete experienced strong color reactions in response to printed letters, and experienced strong interference when trying to read letters printed in ink colors different from those she spontaneously experienced! This synesthete was also able to name the colors she experienced, when presented with letters printed in black, just as rapidly as she could name the color of printed circles.

Synesthesia in its full form is relatively rare. Most of us do not experience the vivid and immediate sensations that are characteristic of synesthesia. However, a wide range of subjects do describe themselves as experiencing at least some synesthesia. In addition, a number of studies have asked subjects to select colors that go with certain sounds, or to choose sizes that match certain pitches, and so on. The sensory correspondences identified in these matching studies are near-identical to the sensory linkages observed by synesthetes, suggesting that the mechanisms underlying synesthesia may in fact be widespread in the population.

Recent studies have in fact scrutinized how *non*synesthetes perceive stimuli composed of synesthetically corresponding or noncorresponding attributes. For example, synesthetes and nonsynesthetes appear to agree that bright colors correspond to higher pitches. Thus subjects in one study were presented with a series of tones and had to press one button if the tone was high and a different button if the tone was low. Subjects sat facing a computer screen, and a colored dot was presented on the screen simultaneously with the presentation of the tone. Responses were faster in this task if the high tones were accompanied by a white dot, and the low tones were accompanied by a black dot. Responses were somewhat slower if the high tones were accompanied by a black dot, and the low tones by a white dot. Responses were also slower if dot color was independent of pitch. These patterns were largely unchanged by practice in the task, and remained in place even when subjects sought specifically to focus on just the sounds. All of this is possible only by virtue of dark having some connection, in subjects' minds, to low pitch, and so on. Moreover, the evidence suggests that this cross-modal interaction, between hearing and seeing, is to some extent mandatory—unchanged by practice, largely unchanged by instructions, and a source of interference even in a task for which, in fact, dot color technically is irrelevant.

Plainly, there are still many questions to be asked about results like these and, indeed, about synesthesia in general. Most important are what is the nature of the connection between these sights and sounds or (more broadly) the nature of these cross-modal connections? Is synesthesia a case of a learned association (albeit a compelling association) of some sort? Or does synesthesia reveal some peculiar leakage from the neural channels for one modality into neural channels for other modalities? Are the cross-modal interactions observed in the laboratory (e.g., between dot colors and pitches) served by the same mechanisms as those underlying synesthesia in its full form? These are questions actively under debate in the current literature, and as yet, no consensus answers are available.

Synesthesia is often discussed as a component of how artistic compositions are perceived. Language within poems, for example, is often supposed to elicit vivid sensory experiences; music is often designed to evoke visual scenes, and so on. It seems clear that these cross-modal evocations do take place; what is less clear is the relation between these and the experiences reported by synesthetes, or the relation between these and the cross-modal interactions observed in the laboratory. It seems plausible that the synesthesia observed in artistic settings is less perceptual in its quality, and mediated instead by metaphor comprehension or by prior associations.

ARTISTIC MORPHOLOGY
COGNITIVE COMPLEXITY

DEACHRONIC VERSUS SYNCHRONIC MODELS
IMAGERY
PERCEPTUAL DISTORTION

D. REISBERG

SYSTEMS AND THEORIES

In American psychology, systems and theories historically have been closely associated. For this reason it is important that students of psychology know at least the essence of the major systems that have influenced and, to a lesser degree, continue to influence psychological thought.

SYSTEMS

A system of psychology may be defined as "an organization and interpretation of . . . data and theories . . . with special assumptions (postulates), definitions, and methodological biases."

The systems that have been most influential in American psychology are generally agreed to be structuralism, functionalism, behaviorism, Gestalt psychology, and psychoanalysis. The first two are now mainly of historical significance, although the role of a continuing kind of diffuse functionalism is noted in the following.

Structuralism

Structuralism was primarily the product of Wilhelm Wundt, who is credited with establishing the first formal psychological laboratory. Its American form was almost single-handedly shaped by Titchener. Wundt and Titchener conceived of psychology as a kind of "mental chemistry." Their objective was to analyze conscious experience into its components, using a highly refined form of introspection.

Functionalism

Functionalism developed essentially as a protest against the inadequacies of structuralism. Its theme was that all sorts of behavior, along with the conscious experience analyzed by the structuralists, should be grist for the psychologist's mill.

Although clearly anticipated by William James, functionalism as a formal system was founded by John Dewey and James Angell. The system espoused such diverse conceptual and practical efforts as Darwinian evolutionary theory and the mental testing movement. The common element that bound these diverse interests together was their *function*—their role in determining both behavior and conscious experience, the two subject matters of psychology.

Behaviorism

The most colorful and influential figure in the development of systematic psychology during the early twentieth century in the United States was John B. Watson, the outspoken founder of the behavioristic system. He developed the position that all that psychology has to study is behavior. During the latter half of the twentieth century, B. F. Skinner replaced Watson as the focus of attention, both positive and negative. Like Watson, Skinner initially worked with animal subjects. His systematic behaviorism was implemented in *operant conditioning,* which stressed emitted behavior rather than the elicited behavior involved in Pavlovian, or classical, conditioning. Also like Watson, Skinner was concerned with practical applications; the best known of these is *behavior modification,* a clinical technique that ignores internal states of the organism and focuses on changes in behavior.

Gestalt Psychology

Gestalt psychology was founded by Max Wertheimer and his two junior colleagues, Wolfgang Kohler and Kurt Koffka. The basic theme was that naive and unsophisticated perceptual experiences should be taken as givens—that is, accepted as they are—rather than reduced to any presumed elements. Phrased differently, the basic and now familiar proposition was that "the whole is more than the sum of its parts."

Psychoanalysis

Sigmund Freud's enormously provocative psychoanalytic system left enduring marks on psychology as well as on many other disciplines. Although psychologists differ widely in their evaluation of psychoanalysis, there can be little doubt that Freud's contributions have greatly enriched our understanding of human behavior. The impact of psychoanalysis, with its stress on early development and largely, if not wholly, unconscious sexuality as determinants of neurosis and psychosis, has been greatest on clinical psychology.

THEORIES

A theory may be defined as an attempt to explain some set of empirical events, particularly when assumptions are made as to how to bridge gaps in available knowledge about underlying factors. Theories vary widely in their organization and scope, from the simplest of hunches, through hypotheses of various sorts that deal with specific empirical predictions, to large-scale systems of deductively related "laws." The role of the more informal "theorizing" is in special need of emphasis because of the much greater attention typically paid to the formal types of theory.

The term *model* has come to serve as a kind of synonym for theory. In its original usage, model referred to an explanatory effort that was based on some better supported explanatory framework in another discipline, such as the use of a mathematical formulation as a basis for deriving experimental tests in psychology.

Deductive theory is characterized by the derivation of propositions, to be tested empirically, on the basis of logically related prior premises.

Inductive theory operates in exactly an opposite manner. It allows disparate bits and pieces of data to accumulate, and to be gradually articulated into theoretical propositions, without any explicit guidance (in its ideal form at least).

Functional theory attempts to remedy the major faults of deductive and inductive theories. It proceeds cautiously with respect to the empirical basis from which it is generated, but at the same time it is explicitly guided.

BEHAVIORISM
FUNCTIONALISM
GESTALT PSYCHOLOGY
HISTORY OF PSYCHOLOGY
PSYCHOANALYSIS
STRUCTURALISM

M. H. Marx

SYSTEMS THEORY

A system is a set of interacting units with relationships among them. Such relationships include both structure and function. Structure refers to the organization of the units that consist of subsystems and subsubsystems as well as the suprasystem. Process refers to changes in structure over time. Systems theory, which was founded by L. V. Bertalanffy, encompasses both closed and open systems.

Although systems theory is of great potential value to psychology, its application to date is limited to man–machine intuitive rules of education leading to universally uniform systems and personality theory. It has been applied most extensively in the disciplines of communication engineering, biology, and the social sciences.

The most successful applications of systems theory have been in interdisciplinary domains. J. G. Miller presents evidence for the similarity in systemic structures at seven levels, ranging from the microstructure of the cell, through the intermediate levels of the organ, organism, group, and society, to the macrostructure of the entire planet, the supranational system.

GENERAL SYSTEMS
SYSTEMS AND THEORIES

J. R. Royce

T

TABOOS

The word *taboo* comes from a Polynesian word meaning "forbidden" or "dangerous" (Hawaiian: *kapu*). In Western usage the term has come to represent anything forbidden, as "a tabooed subject." Incest is one such topic. In Victorian England and America all references to sex were forbidden—but this did not prevent illegitimate sexual activity.

Reference to the dead is forbidden to some degree in almost all societies. In some cases, references to dead persons have to be accompanied by some "insulating act," such as exclaiming "God bless his soul" or crossing oneself.

Taking one's own life is taboo in most societies—although in some it is culturally sanctioned under specified conditions. In Western culture, even the discussion of suicide is frowned on. Mental health professionals have been aware of tendencies toward suicide in their patients for many years, but only recently has the taboo been sufficiently broken that these tendencies can be discussed.

CULTURAL DIFFERENCES

W. E. Gregory

TABULA RASA

One of the central tenets of the philosophical and psychological position known as Empiricism is that all knowledge derives from experience. This contrasts with the Rationalist position, which holds that knowledge derives at least in part from innate ideas or an innate potential for ideas. The *tabula rasa* is a metaphor used by Empiricists to describe the mind at birth—that is, a blank slate, with no innate ideas. The presentation of the concept in the works of Locke has had the greatest impact on the development of modern psychology.

The concept of the tabula rasa is by no means universally accepted. In Locke's time, the most active critic of this concept was the German Rationalist Gottfried Willhelm Leibnitz, who argued that without some inherent ability to process information, our minds would be unable to receive any ideas from the environment. The position advocated by Leibnitz is evident today in the cognitive developmental theories of such writers as Jean Piaget and Noam Chomsky.

Few psychologists today would accept a pure tabula rasa characterization of the human mind. Even Locke admitted the existence of an innate predilection to acquire and combine information. The debate concerns not whether there is structure inherent in the human mind, but the nature and extent of that structure.

PHILOSOPHICAL PSYCHOLOGY

R. A. SHAW

TANTRUMS

A tantrum is a violent outburst, often consisting of kicking, hitting, screaming, crying, detructiveness, and related behaviors. Although most common in children, tantrums also are commonly reported in older, developmentally delayed people. They are usually thought of as a reaction to frustration, and are often very distressing to adults, especially when they occur in public.

Frustration sufficient to precipitate a tantrum may result when children are thwarted from achieving their goals by parents or other adults. Therefore, tantrums often represent a type of power struggle between child and parent. The tantrums are often inadvertently maintained by the parent by meeting the child's wishes on some occasions.

Effective treatments of tantrums have included Hare-Mustin's approach of having the parents encourage the tantrums; use of a variety of operant conditioning techniques in treatment settings (e.g., time out, response cost, reinforcement of appropriate behavior, extinction); and structured behavior modification techniques imposed by the parents.

PARENT–CHILD RELATIONS

T. S. BENNETT

TASK

The task variable in an experiment refers to the small or large behavioral unit a subject has to perform on the basis of instructions received from others or of a self-set goal. From the subjective point of view, the task relates to the subject's awareness of what is to be done and to the motivation or intention to perform it. As a practical goal, the task orients the subject's attention and regulates the subject's activity as a whole. The term *open* versus *closed* task was introduced by Nuttin.

In closed tasks, subjects believe that by giving their first response to a task stimulus, the task with regard to that stimulus is completed; in open tasks, the subject assumes that, after giving a response, the same stimuli or situations will return, at which time they will have to be responded to again. Open tasks are persisting tasks.

OPEN TASK AND THE INFORMATION VALUE OF REWARD

By categorizating tasks into the classes of open and closed, a new factor was introduced in behavioral experiments—the subject's cognitive-dynamic directedness toward a further goal, or *task persistence* as opposed

to need reduction, a factor ignored in behaviorism. By manipulating the open- and closed-task variable, the experimenter is provided with the possibility of investigating the impact of that factor on current behavioral processes. Together with task persistence, a second major factor was introduced through the open-task concept—the *information value* of reward and punishment in learning experiments. Besides its affective value, inasmuch as it rewards the subject for the response given, it provides cognitive information about the *utility* or *instrumentality* of that response for further task completion. In a closed-task experiment, reward and punishment have no information value (because no further task is to be accomplished), whereas their affective reward value is completely preserved. In this way, informative reward can be separated experimentally from noninformative reward and their respective impact investigated. As a result of such investigations, the impact of reinforcement on performance often appears to be mediated by informational processes, and a persisting task—or a higher activity level in the subject—seems to favor retention of the items concerned.

In the framework of the motivation–learning issue as a whole, the introduction of the task factor emphasizes the necessity of manipulating the motivational variable, also in terms of cognitively processed motivations such as tasks, goals, intentions, plans, and behavioral projects.

OPEN TASK AND INTENTIONAL LEARNING

The open-*versus* closed-task paradigm is not identical with the intentional *versus* incidental learning problem. In fact, in everyday life outside the school situation, most learning is of the incidental type. Nevertheless, most behavioral situations in daily life are of the open-task type, as people are at least implicitly "interested"—that is, cognitively motivated—to gather information about their world and about the efficiency of their behavioral responses in dealing with the world. However, situations and responses completely outside the realm of a person's behavioral interests—such as most laboratory experiments—are "closed" with regard to the subject's life in general.

OPEN-TASK ORIENTATION AND ACHIEVEMENT

Implicit in the open-task concept is the importance of a subject's orientation toward further goals and tasks for present performance and motivation. In an earlier stage of the achievement motivation theory, the strength of a subject's tendency to achieve success in a particular activity was considered to be a function of expectations of success *in that particular activity.* It appeared, however, that important behavioral effects are dependent on whether a subject perceives present performance as instrumental for further goals (open task). In fact, a subject's achievement-related motives appear to be more strongly aroused by task outcomes that open the possibility for further successes, as compared with tasks without any implication for the future (closed task). In the former case, future successes are said to be "contingent" on the previous ones.

A HISTORICAL NOTE

The task concept was introduced in experimental psychology by the Würzburg School at the beginning of the twentieth century to supplement the purely associationistic laws of psychological functioning. It was labeled *Aufgabe* and set up in the subject by *instructions;* it created an *Einstellung* or mental set with a dynamic and regulating effect—a *determining tendency.* In contemporary psychology, a similar need for cognitive and dynamic processes was felt by some psychologists with regard to behavioristic connectionism that succeeded associationism. Mediating processes of a cognitive–dynamic nature (such as choice and decision as a function of information, task, goal setting, etc.) are required. The open-task concept refers to such processes.

ACHIEVEMENT MOTIVATION
COGNITION MOTIVATION

J. NUTTIN

TASK ANALYSIS

Task analysis is one of the many methods of job analysis, and usually begins with the development of a task inventory, an exhaustive list of all tasks performed by incumbents in one job. The major part of the task inventory questionnaire asks the incumbent to rate the job tasks on such various dimensions as importance, frequency, time spent, and difficulty. Other sections of the questionnaire may deal with biographical information, source of knowledge or competence, satisfaction, level of feedback, and so on. Incumbent responses are analyzed to determine such factors as similarity of job, possibility of career progression, and proper place in compensation.

Similar to other psychometric tools, the task analysis technique should be reviewed for validity and reliability. The basic advantages of the task analysis technique include a method that is understandable because of its job-specific nature and the use of incumbents. A criticism of this approach is the possible difficulty of comparing jobs across different job families.

EMPLOYMENT PRACTICES
JOB ANALYSIS

L. BERGER

TASK DESIGN

The simplification and standardization of the tasks comprising a job have long been advocated as means of enhancing the job incumbent's productivity. Indeed, this strategy has been shown to benefit employers in a number of ways, including simplified production scheduling, lowered training costs, and reduced expenditures for labor through the employment of more interchangeable, lower skilled, and cheaper labor.

However, simplified and standardized tasks purportedly are perceived by job incumbents as monotonous and as leading them to feel bored and dissatisfied with their work; in turn, this boredom and dissatisfaction have been seen as costing employers in terms of increased absenteeism and turnover and reduced production output. Thus the psychological costs of simplification and standardization may offset at least some of the engineering benefits derived from this strategy.

To counteract the purported psychological costs of simplification and standardization, job enlargement and job enrichment have been advocated as alternative task-design strategies. Enlargement is defined as the design of jobs to include a wider variety of tasks and to increase the job incumbent's freedom of pace, responsibility for checking quality, and discretion over method. Enrichment, a more diffuse and open-ended kind of strategy, involves giving the job incumbent more of a say about what he or she is doing and more responsibility for the excellence of completed products.

Hackman and Oldham asserted that five core job dimensions through various psychological states influence job incumbents' affective and behavioral reactions to their jobs. The core dimensions are: (a) skill variety—the degree to which a job requires a variety of different activities in carrying out the work; (b) task identity—the degree to which the job requires the completion of a whole and identifiable piece of work; (c) task significance—the degree to which the job has a substantial impact on the lives or work of other people; (d) autonomy—the degree to which the job provides substantial freedom, independence, and discretion to the incumbent in scheduling the work and in determining the procedures

to be used in carrying it out; and (e) feedback—the degree to which carrying out the work activities required by the job results in the incumbent obtaining direct and clear information about the effectiveness of his or her performance.

Critical reviews of the research generated by the Hackman and Oldham conceptual frame of reference indicate that the core job dimensions are likely to lead to more positive affective states on the part of job incumbents but do not appear to influence their behaviors significantly.

Salancik and Pfeffer have introduced an alternative approach to the study of incumbent reactions to tasks. Essentially, they assert that the social cues evident in the incumbent's work environment rival objective task properties as explanations for incumbent reactions. Also, Brief and Aldag have speculated that the motivational properties of tasks can be understood best by asking how task properties influence perceptions of personal mastery and of self-reinforcement systems.

EMPLOYEE PRODUCTIVITY
HUMAN FACTORS

A. P. BRIEF

TASTE PERCEPTION

Traditionally, the several senses were treated as functioning independently. All qualities of a given sensory experience were attributed to a single modality mechanism. Taste could be described as occurring from activation of the gustatory receptors and the specific pathway from them to and including the brain.

J. J. Gibson was the first to survey this matter and to identify perceptual systems. He listed them as the basic orientation system, the haptic system, the savor system (taste and smell), the auditory system, and the visual system. Thus, instead of possessing the traditional five senses, humans possess five perceptual *systems.*

There are four taste qualities—sweet, sour, bitter, and salty. Common classes of foods either have very little taste or are supposed to have one of the four tastes mentioned. Although it is generally supposed that there are only four tastes, Bartoshuk has shown that there is a fifth taste, that of water.

Beidler pointed out a distinction between *taste* and *flavor.* Flavor is the experience produced when material is placed in the mouth. This material activates temperature, tactile, pain, and taste receptors. Taste is the experience resulting from the taste receptors alone. Some foods seem better hot, and others seem better cold—that is, some foods taste different at different temperatures. So, although we generally talk about taste when we refer to foods, strictly speaking, it is flavor that is involved.

In exploring the tongue with pointlike applications of substances, it is found that the salt taste is evoked along the sides and tip of the tongue as well as toward the back, as if the sensitivity is fairly uniform, except at the center of the tongue, where it is absent. Sour is evoked more strongly at the sides. Sweet taste is evoked most easily at the tip of the tongue, and bitter is evoked most intensely at the back of the tongue.

PERCEPTION

S. H. BARTLEY

TAXONOMIC SYSTEMS

Taxonomy is the science of classification, that is, the assignment of individuals to groups within a system of categories distinguished by *a priori* characteristics. In essence, one may *form* homogeneous groups by assessing "similarities" or assign to mutually exclusive groups by assessing "dissimilarities."

Science has traditionally proceeded by classifying and analyzing. The importance of classification is maximal when the area of inquiry is diverse and amorphous, as is often the case in the behavioral sciences. Defined classes are *not* simply notational; they connect the content of science to the real world. In fact, one might argue that classification is a normal cognitive process of integration in which the content of experience is connected to the real world.

Classification is inherently temporary and artificial, an *a priori* structure serving a limited purpose. Like any substitute for the "real thing," surrogate systems replace one another as our understanding of the real world changes.

Successful systems of the past, from the classic taxonomies of Linnaeus and Mendeleev to the contemporary "stages" of Erik Erikson and the genetic epistemology of Jean Piaget, have provided sound heuristic models on which to base future inquiry. Although classification undeniably plays a critical role in the advancement of science, it is not strictly a benign procedure. A number of notable problems should be addressed.

A guiding mission of scientific classification, disclosing unforeseen relationships, may go awry if rationally labeled categories mask complexity by sweeping variance into arbitrary pigeonholes.

A second problem concerns the simplest and most frequently employed categorical procedure—*dichotomization*. Apparently, the tendency to bifurcate all aspects of human experience extends not only into antiquity, but also has its roots firmly entrenched in modern thinking.

Not everyone, however, has been content to bifurcate the human condition. The drive for simplicity lures one into the false belief that, for instance, one who is "objective" is objective in all aspects of human endeavor, and one who is "subjective" is subjective in all aspects of human endeavor. Furthermore, it may be assumed incorrectly that a dichotomy is discontinuous and bimodally distributed.

A third important issue in classification concerns "property–set taxonomies." Grouping properties rather than individuals encourages errors of commission. This is no better exemplified in the behavioral sciences than in efforts to classify psychiatric disorders, which typically has proceeded by negotiation and compromise among professionals over the grouping of signs and symptoms based on clinical experience, with little or no scientific rationale to the process. As a result of grouping symptoms rather than patients, individuals placed in the same diagnostic category may respond quite differently to the same psycho- and chemotherapeutic intervention. Primarily as a result of a property–set approach to classification, nosological systems in behavior pathology have been characterized by a noteworthy lack of validity, evidenced by a tenuous association with etiology and prognosis. At least as critical as the lack of validity is the often cited unreliability of psychiatric classification. Fortunately, there have been recent productive strides toward a remedy through the application of sound empirical techniques to sign and symptom classification.

The statistical procedures for classifying are many and varied. As a rule, classification procedures must evidence discrimination and reliability. *Discrimination* speaks to the number of categories to which representative proportions of the population are assigned. If everyone is assigned to the same category, there is no discrimination.

Reliability, or consistency across repeated categorizations, can be examined using the standard error of measurement and the reliability coefficient.

The mathematical and computer-based procedures presently available, as well as those in current stages of development, have made classification a highly sophisticated art with the potential for increasing substantially the regions of specificity and the resolution of our taxonomic systems. M. Polanyi remarked that "taxonomy is based on connoisseurship." The need for exceptional skill and devotion that Linnaeus was known for has given way to rational, objective, and empirically based

procedures that promise to vitalize, fortify, and upgrade the behavioral science repertoire.

CLINICAL ASSESSMENT
CLUSTER ANALYSIS
MEASUREMENT

R. A. Prentky

TEACHING MACHINES

A teaching machine operates on the principle that if a learner emits a correct response, an immediate reinforcement maximizes the likelihood that that response will be learned. Aiding students to learn specific facts can be done with greater reliability by a machine than by a teacher who must simultaneously monitor the responses of large numbers of students.

Materials that are to be learned are arranged in a teaching machine to proceed from the known to the less well known in a series of small and preplanned steps called programs. Branching programs may cycle a learner back through previously presented material if an erroneous response is emitted, while correct responses are reinforced immediately as the learner is encouraged to proceed.

Early mechanical devices have been supplemented by electronic teaching programs for use on a computer. The crucial elements are a series of objectives, a sequenced program of frames with each representing a small but significant advance over preceding frames, and a means of delivering reinforcement for (highly probable) correct responses soon after each such response has been emitted.

INSTRUCTIONAL THEORY

R. A. Kasschau

TEACHING UNDERGRADUATE PSYCHOLOGY

There are two aspects of this topic: content and procedure. Curricular issues center around either the content of a particular course, or the content of a particular program. At the course level, the content is determined largely by available texts.

Concern over curricular issues was not greatly expressed until the latter months of World War II, when Harvard University appointed its Commission to Advise on the Future of Psychology. The report concluded that psychology "is young, growing, extending especially in the direction of social psychology, and tending toward applied or clinical forms," and that "arrangements which encourage the exclusive domination of psychology by the laboratory would sacrifice the unity of the subject, belie its freedom, and limit its opportunity." Nevertheless, in the list of the 13 "indispensable" components of the introductory course, only contemporary social structure, social relations and reactions, socialization of the child, individual differences, and personality development could be considered as a part of the growing and extending field.

The so-called Wolfie report, released by Cornell University in 1952, considered undergraduate instructional objectives, a recommended curriculum, the problems associated with personal adjustment courses and with students who wanted to work as psychologists with just the bachelor's degree, and curricular implementation and research problems. Their core curriculum called for laboratory courses in motivation, perception, thinking, and ability, with the availability of such specialized courses in psychology as learning, social, physiological, comparative, and personnel.

The report of a University of Michigan conference showed increased sensitivity to the varieties of student backgrounds, interests, and goals, and suggested three varieties of curricula—the inverted pyramid, the hourglass, and the flexible—although each of these curricula tended to center around the scientific courses.

In May 1970, the journal *American psychologist* was a special issue devoted to the place of psychology in the university, under the editorship of M. H. Appley. Appley noted that psychology had become too large and complex to be considered a single discipline, although there was a common core of some content, methodology, and interests. An increased responsiveness to social needs, without abandonment of scientific heritage and pursuits, was suggested.

In 1900, E. B. Titchener published the first volume of his four-volume *Experimental psychology—The instructor's manual for the qualitative experiments.* The first 14 pages of this manual were admonitions and suggestions to the instructor concerning how to teach this course. This appears to be the first attempt in psychology to provide guidance to the teacher.

In 1953, W. J. McKeachie published a small booklet, *Teaching tips: A guidebook for the beginning college teacher.* In 1975, it went into its seventh and much larger edition.

Claude E. Buxton published *College teaching: A psychologist's view* in 1956. In addition to being a practical guide to the teacher, it also contained discussions of psychology in the curriculum and problems of higher education in general. By 1992, some graduate psychology programs were providing formal instruction in teaching for their teaching assistants.

R. S. HARPER

TEAM PERFORMANCE

Team performance quality depends on its competence and motivation. Its competence depends not only on the individual skills and abilities its members bring to the group, but also on the distribution of available individual capabilities on a team, the distribution of role assignments, and the organization of the parallel distributions of roles and individual capabilities. B. M. Bass has presented a model for connecting its performance causally with various capabilities of a team, its members, and its processes. Some of the most important causal linkages provide useful generalizations about what modifies the team's dynamics and contributes to its performance.

Interaction processes modify how the task performance of individual members contributes to the task performance of the team. A study of 224 management teams by Bass and colleagues strongly suggests that harmony in interaction is conducive to team effectiveness. At the same time, faulty interaction processes reduce team effectiveness.

On *additive* tasks, such as brainstorming, pooling the ideas of individuals working alone yields more in total quantity and quality than if those same individuals brainstorm in groups. However, on *disjunctive* tasks (tasks requiring a unique team product), particularly if the tasks are difficult, an *assembly bonus effect* is likely. The team product will be superior to that of the average team member, although not necessarily as good as that of the best team member.

Many studies suggest that groups that are heterogeneous in values, interests, abilities, and concerns will exhibit more conflict as well as more creativity in interaction than will homogeneous groups. Other properties of consequence to team interaction processes are the team's size and the congruence in the group of the team members' status, esteem, and ability.

Conditions imposed on the group determine its properties. For instance, higher authority may specify everyone's role in the group so that all are equal but unique in the sources of information required to accomplish the team task. Conditions imposed can also directly affect interaction processes. Thus imposing a more difficult task may generate more consultation among members.

Task performance of the team feeds back to affect conditions imposed on the group. Teams suffer if they must operate without knowledge of whether they are performing adequately.

Task proficiency of individuals may be attributable to the position to which they are assigned. Generally, the centrally located subjects make more relevant and larger contributions to the team task because they have a better understanding of what is happening.

Team motivation also depends on a variety of factors, such as the clarity of the team goals, acceptance of the leadership, satisfaction with the work to be done, the commitment of the individual members to the team's efforts, and the interpersonal trust among members. Particularly important to the team's motivation are its processes. On mature teams, members have learned to trust each other, to communicate openly and to participate and share in decision making about the team's efforts, and to identify their individual goals with those of the team. Involvement, loyalty, and commitment are enhanced by consensual decision making. The key to increasing team motivation is the encouragement of participation in the planning and organization of team efforts.

Team cohesion is likely to have strong effects on its performance. Team performance was accelerated or decelerated by its cohesiveness depending on whether members saw that being productive was in their self-interest.

GROUP PROBLEM SOLVING
INDUSTRIAL PSYCHOLOGY
WORK EFFICIENCY

B. M. BASS

TELEOLOGICAL PSYCHOLOGY

A *teleology* is a description of events, including the behaviors of organisms, based on the presumed functioning of purposes and/or intentions. A teleological psychology would therefore hold that the behavior of all or some organisms may be best understood through invoking concepts of purpose and intention.

To understand telic description we must first review what it means to assert that anything existing has a *cause* associated with it. Aristotle named four basic ways in which he could explain the responsibility for a thing's existence or an event's occurrence. First is the *material cause* or substance that "makes things up." The *efficient cause,* or impetus that assembles things or brings events about instrumentally, is Aristotle's second causal construct. Third, there is a *formal cause* or pattern in events as well as the various shapes that things assume in becoming recognizable. The fourth possibility in this theory of knowledge Aristotle termed the *final cause,* or "that, for the sake of which" events happen or things exist.

There are three variations of teleological theory in the history of thought. First is a human teleology, as when Socrates refers to businessmen risking dangerous sea voyages "for the sake of" a possible profit (the "end" sought). There is also a *natural* teleology, as when Aristotle suggests that leaves on the branches of trees exist "for the sake of" providing shade for the fruit that grows there, concluding thereby that nature operates for a purpose. Finally, we have various deity teleologies of theologians, in which it is argued that the natural order unfolds "for the sake of" a Divine Plan. This last use of final causation was to bring telic description into decline as a scientific metaconception.

Most philosophers in the empiricistic tradition retained their belief in a deity but they fashioned a rigorous method of practicing science that did not rely on such a deity teleology to make its descriptive case or to establish its validity. The aim of all "proper" natural scientists was to *reduce* observed identities and/or actions to underlying mechanical processes. In effect, *reductionism* means to reformulate formal and final causation into material and efficient causation.

Teleological description drew precedents from continental philosophy. The tie binding all these views is an appreciation of the role that human conceptualization (mind) plays in the understanding and creation of experience (reality).

It could be argued that psychology as a unique scientific discipline began with G. T. Fechner's desire to prove that human beings are in fact teleological organisms. His distinctive psychophysical methods (average error, constant stimuli, limits) and famous law (Weber–Fechner) were the combined fruits of Fechner's efforts to show that consciousness (telic mind) was the inner unity of a corporeal system (nontelic matter). However, he brought a deity as well as a human teleology into his explanations, which turned away colleagues and students alike.

Helmholtz more than anyone else influenced the early course of psychological explanation, sending it in the direction of reductionism. He argued that the constancy principle (conservation-of-energy principle) applied with equal validity to the explanation of human behavior as to the explanation of inanimate and physical events. Concepts of mass, energy, force, and thence motion were familiar to Newtonian physics, which construed them in terms of material/efficient causation—resulting in the mechanization of nature. In a fascinating historical parallel, the youthful Sigmund Freud was to be influenced by E. W. Brücke, so that we can see in the libido theory of psychoanalysis an effort to "reduce" thoughts to underlying forces in the constancy–principle sense.

Advocates of an openly teleological explanation of behavior have been prevalent in psychology. Both Adler and Jung advocated teleological explanations of the human being. Notable efforts to provide a telic side to behavioral description can be seen in G. W. Allport's *functional autonomy* and in Gardner Murphy's concept of *canalization*. A classic telic/nontelic confrontation occurred in the debates between Rogers and Skinner regarding freedom and control, but the underlying issue was actually whether a person can behave "for the sake of" self-induced alternatives.

Teleological psychology may be experiencing a resurgence. Difficulties with the mechanistic conception of *reinforcement* in conditioning have led many psychologists to question the assumption that behavior is manipulated without a subject's—particularly a human subject's—awareness and *intentional compliance* playing a major role.

There is a so-called "Third Force" approach to psychology underway in modern psychology—third in the sense of being neither behavioristic nor psychoanalytical in outlook. The phrase "humanistic psychology" has almost been preempted by this Third Force. In this sense, humanistic psychology may be thought of as a branch of teleological psychology in which the aim is to study the more positive aspects of the human experience. This outlook is tantamount to a teleological humanitarianism. However, in the larger view, teleological psychological description is equally applicable to the negative and nonhumanitarian aspects of behavior. People can and do intend to do harm, inflict pain, and denigrate others. The overriding aim of teleological psychology is, one way or another, to reintroduce formal/final causation to psychological explanations of a higher *or* lower sort.

ADLERIAN PSYCHOLOGY
EXISTENTIALISM

J. F. RYCHLAK

TELEPHONE COUNSELING

Telephone counseling is a specialized intervention that has its roots in two major developments in public health and mental health. The first was the unfolding of the suicide prevention movement. The second impetus arose from the establishment of poison information centers, providing immediate counseling regarding antidotes for harmful chemicals. These two types of telephone services provided models for immediate counseling that were later extended in a number of ways, including the following: (a) hot lines for specific populations such as teenagers, the elderly, and homosexuals; (b) telephone services for specific problems such as drug and alcohol concerns, sex counseling, and child and spouse abuse; and (c) other telephone-related services and informational programs in which tape recordings may be listened to by the callers.

Telephone counseling services, then, provide a wide range of services, including information, crisis-oriented counseling, and ongoing therapy for repeat callers. These agencies often employ volunteers to staff the telephone lines and consequently have contributed to the development of the paraprofessional movement in the mental health field.

TELEPHONE COUNSELING VERSUS FACE-TO-FACE COUNSELING

Regardless of the type of telephone service, there is general agreement that interventions by telephone differ from conventional face-to-face counseling in five major ways. First, because of the easy access to telephones, callers often telephone at the moment that their need is most intense. Thus callers are often quite receptive to the telephone counselor's interventions because of the immediacy of the situation. Second, the callers can retain some personal control in whatever difficulty they are encountering. Third, the caller can remain anonymous. Fourth, callers can remain in the security of their immediate environments and still make contact with a helper. Finally, the counselor can remain anonymous. This promotes what can be termed *positive transference;* that is, the telephone counselor can be whatever the caller wishes him or her to be. Such positive transference can aid in the establishment of trust and confidence early in the counseling contact.

Although telephone counseling has many advantages, there are certainly some disadvantages as well. For example, the lack of visual clues can be useful from the caller's perspective, but for the counselor it presents a unique challenge because such information is not accessible in assessing counseling goals and strategies. Also, there is an inherent propensity for rapid and succinct counseling since callers frequently make contact on a one-time basis. Sustained and developmentally oriented counseling thus is not always possible to implement. Nonetheless, telephone counseling has become an established intervention as a result of the convenience, anonymity, and cost effectiveness it offers to the public.

CRISIS INTERVENTION
HOT LINE SERVICES
SUICIDE PREVENTION

A. BARÓN, JR.

TEMPERAMENTS

Synthesizing ideas from classical Greek medicine and astronomy, a theory of temperaments prevailing well into medieval times held that, for example, a sanguine disposition reflected a particular combination of "humours" in the body and that, in turn, this combination had been fixed by a certain configuration of the stars at the time of an individual's birth. In more recent times, Ernst Kretschmer and, independently, W. H. Sheldon and S. S. Stevens gathered support for the proposition that temperament is a function at least of inherited body form or physique, if not of the four cardinal humors.

Although most psychologists emphasize the role of inheritance in the determination of temperament, and some make it definitional, more critical features are that temperament refers to a pattern of enduring traits characterizing an individual. Temperament fits between personality as a whole and a particular discrete trait in terms of breadth of phenomenon.

In a longitudinal study of individual differences in infants, S. A. Thomas and S. Chess described nine categories of behavioral and physiologic reactivity, such as activity level, rhythmicity, intensity of response, and persistence. They found consistent and stable individual patterns among these differences, thus constituting individual behavioral styles or temperaments from infancy.

In personality psychology, H. A. Witkin and associates identified a stable and superordinate individual difference in spatial orientation. Their field–dependence construct measured a temperamental difference among individuals across a broad band of psychological systems—perceptual, cognitive, emotional, and social. In cognitive psychology, beginning with George Klein's work, investigators described various cognitive styles, consistencies in individuals across more than one cognitive domain (e.g., reflection–impulsivity, leveling–sharpening). In psychoanalytic ego psychology, David Shapiro located several neurotic styles, each of which consisted of certain modes of perception and action, and a certain experience of self.

HERITABILITY OF PERSONALITY TRAITS
PERSONALITY THEORIES

K. J. SHAPIRO

TERMINALY ILL PEOPLE

Historically, in the health profession in general, little attention had been paid to the psychosocial care of the dying patient. However, the 1960s and 1970s saw a marked increase in interest in all facets of terminal illness, including the patient's reaction, the management and care of the dying patient, and the reaction of loved ones to the patient's illness and death.

Kubler-Ross describes five emotional "stages" that the terminally ill patient experiences, which are thought generally to occur in the following sequence: First, *denial and isolation,* followed by *anger,* then *bargaining, depression,* and finally *acceptance.* However, depending on the individual characteristics of the patient, many of these emotions stages may "overlap," or be experienced simultaneously. David Peretz explains individual differences in coping techniques and reaction to death as an outgrowth of the individual's enduring psychological style.

Current work in the United States is modeled after work in England that resulted in the development of hospices for the special care of the terminally ill. The hospice setting provides a homelike environment, with health care and mental health counseling for the patient and family. The focus of the hospice program is to consider the ill person's feelings, wishes, and opinions concerning death rather than the typical hospital focus on curing or maintaining the patient's physical body. Such programs also provide valuable emotional support to the family, even following the death of the patient, to promote the expression and understanding of the complex emotions associated with the process of death and dying.

HOSPICES
LOSS AND GRIEF THANATOLOGY

R. D. FELNER

TERRITORIALITY I

Territoriality refers to behavior associated with the acquisition, maintenance, and defense of a territory. In animals, territories are geographical areas that surround the home. These areas are protected from other members of the same species and normally conspecifics are not even allowed entry. In humans, the concept of territoriality is similar, but it often takes different forms.

In animals, territoriality is usually thought of as instinctive and adaptive behavior. Because each group is separated from the others, the density of a population can be maintained at a level that facilitates food gathering, reproduction, and the control of aggression. These spaces can change in size.

Territoriality in humans takes more flexible forms. It is unclear whether this behavior in humans has instinctual or learned origins, but it is certain that people's use of territories is different from that of animals. First, there are several different kinds of human territories. People typically have one or two *primary territories,* such as the home or office, which are places in which a great deal of time is spent and are owned and personalized on a more or less permanent basis. People also have *secondary territories,* defined as places where they spend less time and in which ownership is transient. People control secondary territories only when they are in them. Public territories are places that people use but that are not owned by an individual or a small group. Parks, beaches, and other such areas are public because they are owned by an extremely large group.

Humans are also more flexible than animals in their defense of territory. Social and cultural mechanisms that fulfill many of the survival needs provided by territoriality among animals make defense of territory less often necessary among people.

The ways in which animals and humans denote territorial control also differ. Many animals rely on scent to notify others that they own a space, for example, urinating along its boundaries to provide clear cues. Humans typically use visual markers. Studies have indicated that people paint and decorate territories to denote ownership.

Aggressive defense of territory does occur among humans, although less often than among animals. This defense often takes milder forms than fighting. In the case of defense of well-established territories, physical aggression is less likely to occur.

A. S. BAUM

TERRITORIALITY II

There is disagreement concerning the best way to define territoriality. Classically, a territory is any defended area.

Animals of many species occupy specific portions of their habitats from which they exclude other members of the species. A male stickleback fish in breeding condition will defend an area around a nest against intruding males. This is the essence of territoriality. What is remarkable is that an animal that might lose a contest in a neutral area or in the territory of another individual typically will win while in its own territory.

Perhaps the most important fact to remember concerning territories is the diverse nature of different patterns grouped together under this one term. Wilson lists five types. Type A territories are large, defended areas within which animals can mate, court, and gather most of their food. Various species of fishes, lizards, and birds occupy such all-purpose territories. Type B territories also are relatively large and are used for breeding, but the residents go elsewhere to feed. Nightjays and reed warblers occupy such territories. Type C territories are small defended areas around a nest, as found in many colonial birds. There is room for little more than breeding. Type D territories are pairing or mating territories; animals go to these territories to mate but, in contrast to the first three types, raise their young elsewhere. Birds such as the sage grouse and ungulates such as the Uganda kob form such "leks." Type E territories are the roosting positions or shelters used by many species of bats, starlings, and domestic pigeons.

Thus territories can be seen to vary along several dimensions. They may or may not be used for feeding, mating, or rearing of the young, depending on the species. The number of residents varies from a single male, a mated male–female pair, or a whole group of animals that defend the territory. Most territories relate to a fixed location. An interesting borderline case can be found with bitterlings, small species of fish that lays eggs in the mantle cavities of certain species of mussels and that defend the area around the mussels, even if they move. It is important when trying to generalize from "territory in animals" to similar phenomena in humans that one remembers the diversity of animal territoriality.

Territorial defense need not always entail overt fighting; song or odors can serve to mark an area as occupied. In a typical experiment on the function of bird song, some males are removed from their territories and replaced with loudspeakers that do or do not continue to emit the songs. Intrusion by conspecifics is delayed when songs are played. In other experiments, devocalized males have difficulty in keeping out intruders. It seems as though males must sing to keep their space.

The concept of territory often has been applied to humans in a variety of contexts. Members of a nation may defend a border, members of a gang may defend their "turf," and suburban homeowners may defend their property. Indeed, Sebba and Churchman looked within the homesite to view the dwelling unit as composed of segments of space appropriate for use by different individuals or clusters of individuals. In another experiment, androstenol was shown to be a human odor that functioned to space males. By treating half of the stalls in a public restroom with the chemical, the experimenters found males to avoid marked "territories." Models of economic defensibility in relation to resources have been applied to human populations by anthropologists.

ANIMAL AGGRESSIVE BEHAVIOR
ANIMAL SEXUAL BEHAVIOR
ANIMAL SOCIOBIOLOGY
GENETIC DOMINANCE AND RECESSIVENESS
INSTINCT

D. A. Dewsbury

TEST ANXIETY

Test anxiety refers to the psychological, physiological, and behavioral responses to stimuli an individual associates with the experience of testing or evaluation. It is a special case of general anxiety and is characterized by feelings of heightened self-awareness and perceived helplessness that often result in lowered performance on tests or, more generally, on all types of cognitive and academic tasks.

Test anxiety is usually conceptualized as having two components—worry and emotionality. The worry component involves self-perceptions. The emotionality component refers to the affective and physiological concomitants resulting from autonomic arousal: the feelings of tension and distress. A related conception, J. D. Wine's direction of attention hypothesis, suggests that highly test-anxious persons divide their attention between task-relevant and self-referent variables, whereas low test-anxious persons focus more on the task.

Test-taking anxiety is generally measured by self-report inventories that tap both the worry and emotionality dimensions. Numerous studies indicate that test anxiety is most prevalent on complex tasks and when the situation is viewed as stressful or evaluative, and that highly test-anxious persons are more self-preoccupied and self-deprecatory than low test-anxious persons, and that these tendencies are increased in testing situations. There is also evidence that worry is negatively related to performance but that emotionality is not.

Because test anxiety results in lowered test and academic performance, a variety of treatment programs have been developed. The most promising results for improving performance involve combining cognitive refocusing and/or study skills training with desensitization and relaxation training.

ANXIETY

F. G. Brown

TESTING AND LEGISLATION

During the spring and summer of 1964, while the Civil Rights Act of 1964 was being debated in the U.S. Senate, a case* was brought before the Illinois Fair Employment Practices Commission in which it was alleged that a Black job applicant was denied employment because he had failed a short psychological (IQ-type) test that was "culturally biased" against Blacks. Although the Commission dismissed this charge, the case drew widespread national press attention, particularly from business people who expressed the fear that governmental agencies would dictate selection procedures and hiring standards in private industry. To allay such fears, Senator John Tower of Texas introduced an amendment accepted by the Congress that became part of the law. This amendment states, "Notwithstanding any other provision of this [Act], it shall not be an unlawful employment practice for an employer . . . to give and act upon the results of any professionally developed ability test provided that such test, its administration or action upon the results is not designed, intended or used to discriminate because of race, color, religion, sex or national origin" (Civil Rights Act of 1964, Title VII, Section 703h). Many state legislatures, in states where fair employment commissions or commissions against discrimination existed, followed the Senate's lead and incorporated a version of paragraph 703h into their state laws.

Psychological tests used for employment selection, however, had an entirely predictable consequence, based on 50 years of data accumulated since World War I's Army Alpha: Blacks, and to some extent other minorities (e.g., Latinos), earned lower scores than Whites; and at any cutoff score, a smaller proportion of blacks than whites qualified or "passed the test." In this context, the Equal Employment Opportunity Commission (EEOQ) issued *Uniform guidelines on employee selection procedures.*

In general, in the early cases the defending companies prevailed. The major turning point came in the U.S. Supreme Court ruling in the case of *Griggs v. Duke Power Company* [401 U.S.424, 3 FEP175(1971)]. The court ruled in favor of the plaintiff Griggs in a landmark decision in which a number of standards for test use were set: First, the initial burden was on the plaintiff to offer evidence that the selection procedure had *adverse impact;* second, if the selection procedure did have an adverse impact, the defendant user had to assume the burden of demonstrating by appropriate means that performance on the test was related to performance on the job for which the test was used as a selection criterion. The Court also indicated that "great deference" must be given to the EEOC *Guidelines,* which outlined standards of and procedures for test validation.

About 70,000 complaints of discrimination are filed with the EEOC annually. Of these, 10 to 15% allege discrimination by unfair testing.

EMPLOYMENT PRACTICES
TESTING METHODS

P. Ash

* *Myart v. Motorola.* Hearings before the Illinois Fair Employment Practices Commission, April–June 1964.

TESTING METHODS

Psychological tests have been developed for such a wide variety of purposes that testing methods vary greatly from test to test. A number of continua exist along which individual tests can be classified.

Test content can measure maximum performance or typical performance, the best one can do versus how one typically performs. Maximum performance tests have correct or incorrect answers; typical performance tests generally assess stylistic differences, without specific answers being uniformly better than others.

Maximum performance tests can be classified into two broad categories: ability and achievement tests. Pure ability tests measure what a person is capable of doing and generally present problems with which the person is unlikely to have had direct experience. Pure achievement tests assess the amount of information one has learned from previous experiences. The distinction is not always clear, because ability tests generally involve making use of previously learned principles. Much of the controversy concerning test bias in ability tests revolves around the issue of whether or not all potential test takers have been equally exposed to these prerequisite skills.

Ability and achievement tests can be classified along a speed versus power continuum. Pure speed tests contain questions that are easy to answer correctly, but that must be completed quickly. Power tests contain items, usually graded in difficulty, that assess maximum performance without pressure to work quickly.

Another distinction is between performance and nonperformance tests. Performance tests generally require overt, active responses, such as motor or manual behaviors, while nonperformance tests generally involve written verbal responses to questions.

Personality tests tend to be of two major types, objective and projective. Objective personality tests, such as the Minnesota Multiphasic Personality Inventory (MMPI), generally ask true–false or multiple-choice questions that are objectively scored. These items frequently are grouped into scales that measure different aspects of personality. Although the scores are objectively obtained, the integration of the pattern of scores to describe the whole person generally requires subjective judgments. Projective tests involve ambiguous stimuli that the subject must interpret, presumably by "projecting" into the interpretation aspects of his or her own personality. Classic projective tests are the Rorschach Inkblot Test and the Thematic Apperception Test (TAT). Administering and scoring projective tests require extensive professional training.

Tests can be designed to be administered to individuals or to groups of people. Individually administered tests, such as the Wechsler IQ tests, require more use of the administrator's time, and thus are more expensive to use. Group-administered tests, such as the Scholastic Aptitude Test (SAT), are less expensive to administer, but generally do not allow the test administrator carefully to analyze an individual's test-taking attitude or strategy or to query about specific responses to seek additional, clarifying information.

Three major approaches to score interpretation involve norm-referenced, criterion-referenced, and ipsative scoring. Norm-referenced scoring occurs most often and involves comparing a person's score with the scores of a norm group. Criterion-referenced scoring relates an individual's performance to absolute standards or criteria. Ipsative scoring involves comparing individuals' scores with each other.

PSYCHOMETRICS

M. J. ALLEN

TEST STANDARDIZATION

The standardization of a test is the establishment of uniform procedures for the (a) administration and (b) scoring of that instrument. The first standardized tests appeared in the early part of the twentieth century, when E. L. Thorndike, an experimental psychologist, and others extended principles learned in the laboratory to psychological measurement.

The *Standards for educational and psychological tests* (American Educational Research Association, 1985) provides an outline of procedures that test publishers and users are urged to follow to ensure proper implementation of standardization procedures. Control of test administration procedures is largely accomplished by instructions specified in test manuals. Regarding scoring procedures, the *Standards* specify that it is desirable that detailed instructions for both subjective and objective tests be furnished in the test manual, and, in the case of subjectively graded tests, research as to the extent of agreement between scorers should be enumerated. Standardization should also provide detailed information as to who is qualified to administer and score the test.

A final aspect of test standardization is the development of test norms. These values, in conjunction with reliability and validity information, permit psychologists to interpret test scores properly. Tests can also be equated to other similar tests so that scores from one can be compared to those of others.

Three potential advantages of standardized psychological tests are evident. First, standardized tests are frequently of higher quality than locally constructed tests. Second, the utilization of standardized examinations may free psychologists and other professionals from spending time on test construction, test administration, and other evaluative activities and permit them to devote the time to more important matters—therapy, instruction, and score interpretation, for example. Last, the use of standardized measures facilitates communication among psychologists. One important disadvantage of standardized measures should also be noted; as a result of their availability, standardized tests may be used when they are inappropriate.

MEASUREMENT

K. F. GEISINGER

T-GROUPS

The T-Group or Training Group emerged in the summer of 1946 as the result of a serendipitous event in a workshop for intergroup relations. Kurt Lewin headed an action-research team.

At the end of the workshop, in a debriefing session, the four workshop leaders decided that the procedure of using the group process as the agenda for group study of its own development and action taking was an important discovery that needed much more study and development. The developers made a clear distinction between group therapy with its focus on intrapersonal dynamics and the T-group with its focus on the study of group development, leadership-membership dynamics, and the processes of interpersonal interaction.

During the 1950s, practitioners from several different professional disciplines began to make adaptations of the T-group to their own disciplines. Those with a clinical, person-centered focus developed the "encounter group," with special interest in the impact on personal development as a result of involvement in intensive group interaction and interpersonal peer feedback, facilitated by a professional trainer.

Other practitioners were interested in the small face-to-face work groups as a crucial unit in organizational productivity. A variety of experiments attempted to adapt the T-group process to working with intact work groups. During the 1960s and 1970s, the personal growth movement sought adaptations of the T-group for the purpose of self-exploration, of freeing individuals from blockages in personal and interpersonal functioning. These developments departed rather completely from the original T-group focus on the study of group and interpersonal dynamics. In the decade of the 1980s, there was a renewal of interest in Lewin's notion that the small face-to-face group is the critical linkage between the large system and the person. With the increased concern about quality of work life as it relates to both productivity and mental health, there is growing evidence that the face-to-face support group is the basic interface between system and person, and the skills and values facilitated by T-group experience seem to have a new importance.

GROUP DYNAMICS

R. LIPPITT

THANATOLOGY

Throughout human history, the idea of death has posed the eternal mystery at the core of many religious and philosophical systems. Yet, except for a few sporadic forays, the place of death in psychology was practically *terra incognita,* until the mid-twentieth century.

Probably a major reason for psychology's inordinate delay in coming to grips with such a universal concern was its need to raise its flag independently of philosophy and ethics. Scientific respectability meant occupying oneself with measurable stimuli and repeatable and public responses. A consequence was restraint in scrutinizing consciousness and neglect of personality. The assault of World War II and the ensuing press of urgent social problems, however, forced psychology to look beyond its traditional positivism.

EMPIRICAL AND CLINICAL FINDINGS

A major realization is that the psychological influence of death is not restricted to the dying, elderly, suicidal, or combat soldier. Young children distinguish between "being" and "nonbeing." Protecting children by shielding them from the realities of death hinders their emotional growth. At the other end of the chronological continuum, many older persons want to share thoughts and feelings about dying and death but are frequently restrained from doing so by society's general reluctance to examine death. A net result is that many elderly persons turn to regressive and inappropriate patterns of conduct in dealing with death. Although the meaning of death can change with maturation and life experiences, the theme remains a seminal one throughout life.

Death possesses many meanings for people. Fear of death is also far from being a unitary or monolithic variable. Various subcomponents are evident—fear of going to hell, fear of the unknown, loss of identity, and the pain inflicted on survivors. Furthermore, significant discrepancies exist in many persons between their conscious and unconscious fear of death. Members of the helping professions need to be circumspect in accepting at face value the degree of fear affirmed by persons on a conscious level. Apprehensiveness and concerns about dying and death themselves can assume dissembling guises and gain expression in such symptoms as insomnia and depressed mood, and in sundry psychosomatic and emotional disturbances.

TREATMENT OF THE DYING PERSON

As a consequence of medical advances, prolongation of the dying process is aggravating the problem of personal dignity and control. Both clinical and empirical findings underline that dying is not just a biological process, but a psychosocial process as well. The essential communication of dying patients is for open and honest dialog with caregiver and family, and the need for confirmation of care and concern.

An influential five "stages of dying" model has been presented by Kübler-Ross: denial and isolation, anger, bargaining, depression, and acceptance. The model has proved helpful as a lead in understanding the

dying experience. Stages have been found to coexist, be reversed, or even omitted.

A frequent drawback in treatment of the dying person is that many professionals lose interest and transfer their motivation and resources elsewhere when efforts to forestall the dying process fail. A major response to this state of affairs has been the emergence of the hospice movement. It has focused on the problem of chronic pain, regard for the quality of life, and inclusion of the patient's family in the treatment process.

New alternatives now available as a result of increasing medical expertise have heightened awareness that economic, legal, and ethical, as well as medical and psychological, aspects are inherent in dealing with the dying experience. This has been accompanied by a surging interest in such issues as living wills, informed consent, and euthanasia.

GRIEF

Expression of grief is not a sign of weakness or self-indulgence. Rather, it reflects a necessary, deep, and human need that normal persons have. The funeral and ritual involved in mourning are important because they underscore the reality of death, bring support and the warmth of other human beings when needed, and provide a transitional bridge to the new circumstances brought about by the death of someone close.

It is frequently difficult to distinguish between appropriate normal grief and abnormal bereavement. Clinicians suggest that it usually reveals itself in a number of ways, such as morbid preoccupation with worthlessness, prolonged and marked functional impairment, delay or arrest of mourning, exaggeration of symptoms, and deviant behavior that violates conventional expectations or jeopardizes the health and safety of self and others.

METHODOLOGICAL CONSIDERATIONS

Inconsistent findings reported in the death literature reflect the use of differing populations, ages, assessment devices, and failure to fully appreciate the complex and multifaceted nature of attitudes toward death. At this stage of development, major desiderata for the field are longitudinal studies, cross-validation and reliability analyses of prevailing procedures, more astute incorporation of multilevel aspects, extended examination of functional and behavioral correlates of attitudes toward death, alertness to sociocultural context, and the conversion of major assumptions about death-related cognitions, feelings, and coping styles into operationalized empirical inquiry.

LOSS AND GRIEF

H. FEIFEL

THEMATIC APPERCEPTION TEST

The Thematic Apperception Test (TAT), originally designed by Morgan and Murray, consists of 30 pictures, most of which depict single individuals or two or more persons in ambiguous social interactions. Different combinations of 20 pictures each (selected for age and sex from the total 30) are recommended for use with men, women, boys, and girls. The instructions stress imaginative fantasy by asking the subject to create dramatic stories about the picture. The subject is asked: (a) What has led up to the situation in the picture? (b) What is happening now? Describe the feelings and thoughts of the characters. (c) What will the outcome be?

Murray proposed a descriptive method of content analysis. The stories were analyzed in terms of motivational forces from within the individual (called *need*) and forces from the environment (called *press*). The combining of the press, need, and outcome of the story defined a *thema* (e.g., mother died—son is mourning—he commits suicide).

Murray's propositions place heavy demands on the interpreter of the TAT, who must face the question of what level of the personality is revealed by each significant thema. Although Murray believed that all three levels influence the content of a story, his focus of interest was in discovering the latent thema. From the evidence, the extent to which the TAT reveals latent thema depends on a number of variables: the type of subject, the type of motive, and the conditions under which the test is administered.

The clinician must also face still another difficult question. Do the TAT thema predict the actual, overt public behavior of the story teller? Murray believed that the fantasy material is more apt to be related by contrast to public conduct because of the defense systems built to guard against the overt expression of unconscious impulses.

From a psychometric point of view, the TAT has many weaknesses. First, no standardized method of administration is used since the clinician is encouraged to feel free to modify the instructions to facilitate similar understanding of the task by subjects varying in age and type. Second, few examiners use all 20 of the standard pictures, and some even substitute some favorite pictures of their own choice. Third, no standard objective method of scoring is used although several have been devised. Moreover, since objective norms for determining the uniqueness of a given story are not available for different types of groups, clinicians depend on their own subjective norms based on experience.

The validity of the TAT has also been questioned. Construct validity for the TAT means consistency with data from other sources and predictable psychodynamic congruence of the data from all sources.

Despite its weaknesses, the TAT has had considerable heuristic value. It has stimulated a tremendous amount of clinical and experimental research.

The sheer quantity and quality of the research on the TAT, using a wide variety of groups of all ages, colors, and cultures and with a broad variety of applications, mark the TAT as a highly useful contribution to the study of human motivation and personality.

CLINICAL ASSESSMENT PROJECTIVE TECHNIQUES

E. M. Siipola

THEORETICAL CONSTRUCTS

It is relatively easy to name directly observable behaviors like eating and running. What accounts for these behaviors is a much more difficult task. When the relevant antecedent conditions are known, such as the presentation of a noxious stimulus (for running) or the presentation of food after it has been withheld (for eating), researchers can begin to understand such behaviors. But there is more to the problem than simply identifying antecedent conditions. Attributing overt behaviors to presumed covert intraorganismic functions, such as fear and hunger, requires the naming of those functions. Such naming is essentially the problem of theoretical constructs.

HYPOTHETICAL CONSTRUCTS AND INTERVENING VARIABLES

Theoretical constructs within psychology are thus hypothesized internal processes presumed to underlie specified overt behaviors. An influential distinction between two types of such constructs was made by MacCorquodale and Meehl. Hypothetical constructs are defined as complex internal processes with meanings that are not entirely confined to the relationship between the stimulating conditions and the ensuing behaviors (i.e.,

they contain surplus meaning). The basic problem with the hypothetical constructs as thus defined is that the presence of such additional, unspecified meaning allows an indeterminate amount of ambiguity to cloud the fundamental definition of the construct and so reduce its theoretical usefulness.

Intervening variables, are more restricted concepts. Their meanings are strictly circumscribed by the specified stimulus-response relationships (i.e., the antecedent environmental conditions and the consequent behaviors). The intervening variable is whatever occurs within the organism (presumably within the brain) that accounts for the observed stimulus–response relationship.

Such narrow definitions are not easy for psychologists to live with. Intervening variables as thus defined have been criticized as being sterile. This criticism is rebutted by pointing out that it is not the intervening variable itself that should be so accused but the theoretical use to which it is put. That rebuttal notwithstanding, intervening variables were never popular in psychological theory construction and seem to have become less popular in recent years. Nevertheless, at least some approximation to a fully operational definition, such as provided by the intervening-variable type of construct, holds promise for more effective theorizing in psychology. Some examples may help to support this opinion.

EXAMPLES OF INTERVENING VARIABLES

Here, two uses of intervening variables are considered that illustrate their potential value, especially as tools in the development of theory. Mowrer and Viek kept all laboratory rats in their experiment hungry. They allowed rats in the experimental group to turn off noxious electric shock by jumping off the floor. The shock was given 10 seconds after the rats started to eat food offered on a stick pushed up through the floor bars. Matched controls in contiguous cages had a shock of exactly the same intensity and duration, but these rats were unable to turn it off. The rats in the experimental group ate more of the food and started to eat faster than the control rats. This difference could not be attributed to any physical difference in the shock. Mowrer and Viek explained the behavioral difference by attributing a sense of helplessness to the control rats. The subsequent development of the learned helplessness problem, in which first animal and later human subjects were used, illustrates the way in which more extensive experimental and theoretical work can have both broader and deeper ramifications than an initial experimental demonstration of an intervening variable.

In a second early experiment, modeled on the Mowrer and Viek experimental design, Marx and Van Spanckeren used seizure-sensitive laboratory rats (subjects that had been found to be susceptible to seizures—then called audiogenic—when stimulated by high-frequency, high-intensity sound in a physically restricted environment such as a cage). Vertical poles were placed in the centers of two contiguous cages. An experimental and a control rat, matched for susceptibility to seizure on the basis of prior tests, were then placed in the contiguous cages and the noxious sound stimulation presented. The experimental rat was able to turn off the sound by tilting the pole; the control rat could not do so. Because the sound stimulation came from a centrally located speaker, placed between the cages, any behavioral differences could not be attributed to strictly physical factors but could be attributed to the difference in treatment (i.e., to the more active role of the experimental rat in the management of the noxious stimulus). The results were that the control animals showed both quicker and more frequent seizures. Marx and Van Spanckeren attributed this difference to a presumed sense of control in the experimental rats, thus offering a positive internal function as an intervening variable to account for their greater resistance to seizure.

CONTRIBUTIONS OF TOLMAN AND HULL

The use of intervening variables in psychological theory was first suggested by E. C. Tolman. Tolman later stated that he had come to favor the more comprehensive, less restricted hypothetical construct. Looking back on his earlier theoretical work, he commented,

> My intervening variables are generally speaking mere temporarily believed-in, inductive, more or less qualitative generalizations which categorize and sum up for me various empirically found relationships. . . . And they are not primarily neurophysiological . . . but are derived rather from intuition, common experience, a little sophomoric neurology, and my own phenomenology.

Clark Hull, in developing a grandly conceived hypothetico-deductive behavior theory, attempted to use intervening variables (e.g., habit strength, reaction potential, and inhibition) in a much more systematic and formalized manner. He used them as both theoretical tools—stimulants to and directors of empirical research—and theoretical concepts embedded in the propositions of his formal theory. There was much criticism of these intervening variables, which were regarded as too specific for the theory (such as specifying the weight in grams of the food rewards in some of the research with rats).

AN OPERATIONAL CONTINUUM
It is helpful to think of the hypothetical concept and the intervening variable as belonging on opposite ends of an operational continuum rather than as discrete, absolutely different types of constructs. Progressive improvement in the operational clarity of theoretical constructs can then be regarded as a more reasonable objective in psychological theory construction than any quick-fix of constructs with ambiguous or unspecified meanings.

The intervening variable seems to be more appropriate when used as a tool in theory construction than when used as an element in a fully formalized theory. Scientists are well aware that the phenomena they investigate are complex and not readily reducible to such interpretations. If the more straightforward and simplified concepts, such as intervening variables as here defined, are to be of maximum value, they must be gradually introduced and carefully refined in preliminary types of theory construction or theorizing. Attempting premature placement in highly formalized theory, as Hull did, is to invite rejection.

CAUSAL REASONING
HYPOTHETICAL DEDUCTIVE REASONING
MILL'S CANONS
OPERANT CONDITIONING
OPERATIONAL DEFINITION
SCIENTIFIC METHOD

M. H. MARX

THEORETICAL PSYCHOLOGY
There are two major facets of theoretical psychology—the construction of substantive theory and metatheory. Whereas substantive theory focuses on explaining the facts, metatheory focuses on explaining the nature of theory.

SUBSTANTIVE THEORY
Scientific theory constitutes the attempt to explain the observables of a specifiable domain of investigation. However, because theoreticians vary in their cognitive styles, a wide range of theories has been produced over the five centuries of scientific endeavor. Joseph Royce has categorized these epistemic styles as rationalism (logical consistency), empiricism (observable repeatability), and metaphorism (universality of insight via symbols). Ernst Nagel provides a four-category taxonomy of theories: analogical (models), descriptive (concepts limited to observation terms),

instrumental (concepts are useful fictions, tools, or instruments), and realistic (concepts reveal the truth; i.e., they are real, not merely useful fictions). Melvin Marx describes the following three models of theory construction: inductive, deductive, and the inductive-deductive interactive or functional mode. Royce has combined these three taxonomic schemes.

During the first half of the twentieth century, the major contributions to theoretical psychology came in the form of all-pervading points of view. The major views of this period are those of the behaviorists, the Gestaltists, and the psychoanalysts. Perhaps the most important contribution of each of these "isms" or "schools" was to point out an important approach that others had neglected. Although the proponents of these schools thought they were proposing a theory that would unify the entire discipline, it became increasingly apparent that they all overgeneralized, that their "theories" were limited in scope, and that their proposals were highly programmatic. The early twentieth century period of "schools" (1890–1935) was followed by the mid-twentieth century period (1940–1960) of area theorizing. During this period, there was a conscious effort to confine the scope of theorizing to an area of psychology such as learning or perception. Analysis suggested that the most successful of these theories occurred in the areas of sensation, perception, and learning, and that the least adequate occurred in the more complex domains of psychology, such as motivation, personality, and social behavior.

Late twentieth century (1970–1980) theoretical psychology has moved still further in the direction of miniature theorizing, on the one hand (i.e., the development of theories of subareas or of a single class of behavior such as avoidance conditioning), but has also shifted from a behavioristic to a cognitive (i.e., information-processing) paradigm.

METATHEORY
The major activity of the metatheorist is conceptual-linguistic analysis, the attempt to clarify the meanings and implications of theoretical terms, thereby increasing the viability of a theory. The most critical aspect of scientific theory is its relative ability to explain or account for observables. This characteristic of a theory has been referred to as its theoretical power, a continuum that ranges from weak to strong.

Relative theoretical power is actually a complex concept composed of many characteristics of a theory, including empirical testability, degree of empirical-formal fit, comprehensiveness of scope, parsimony, degree of formalization, degree of cohesiveness, and explicitness of conceptualization. Thus, theoretical power (or degree of theoretical development) is some (unknown) optimally weighted combination of all (also unknown) the relevant dimensions. And, because of this complexity, theories of equivalent overall maturity can vary in their level on any one dimension.

The point is that increments in theoretical power are dependent on the interaction between conceptual-linguistic precision and maturity level.

Although increments in conceptual precision result in increments in theoretical power at all levels, the linguistic and maturity characteristics of a theory constitute limiting constraints on what can be accomplished via conceptual analysis.

PHILOSOPHICAL PSYCHOLOGY
SYSTEMS AND THEORIES

J. R. ROYCE

THEORIES OF SLEEP
Theories in sleep research range from partial theories that relate to particular aspects of sleep such as the relations of REM sleep to dreaming to more general theories that try to account for the necessity of sleep.

This article is about these latter type. The various theories can be divided into five general categories.

Restorative Theories. Sleep is a necessary period of recovery from depletions or noxious states that are developed during wakefulness. This is the oldest (proposed by Aristotle) and most widely held theory of sleep. Organisms go to sleep when they are tired and wake up refreshed. As Shakespeare put it, "sleep that knits up the ravelled sleeve of care."

Protective Theories. Sleep serves to avoid continued and excessive stimulation. Pavlov, for example, considered sleep to be a form of cortical inhibition that serves to protect individuals from overstimulation. Organisms do not sleep because they are exhausted but to protect themselves from exhaustion.

Energy Conservation Theory. This theory emerged from animal studies that found a strong relationship between high metabolic levels and total sleep time. Because sleep, like hibernation, reduces energy expenditure, animals with high metabolic levels reduce their energy requirements by greater total sleep time.

Instinctive Theories. Sleep is here considered a species-specific, hard-wired instinct elicited by environmental cues calling for the appropriate response of sleep.

Adaptive Theories. These are the most recent sleep theories, which view sleep as an adaptive behavioral response. This position considers sleep to be an appropriate time-out response in relationship to predator pressures and foraging requirements. Thus sleep is not seen as a dangerous behavior (as viewed by restorative theories) but as a survival-enhancing response.

These theories were often combined. Both the protective theories and the instinctive theories may include the restorative concept. For example, Pavlov accepted a restorative function within his protective theory. The energy conservation theory and the restorative theories could be viewed as protective theories. An early form of the adaptive theory contained the instinct theory as its mechanism.

The restorative and adaptive positions came to represent the principal focuses of opposition. The reasons for this were clear. Each fit certain domains of sleep phenomena well. The restorative position fit the major consequences of sleep deprivation: When one lost sleep there were negative effects, and when one slept these effects were reduced. The adaptive position fit the broad array of animal sleep that appeared to reflect appropriate timing and amounts in relation to evolutionary pressures of the environment. For example, grazing herd animals that are under heavy predator pressure tend to sleep in short intermittent bursts with only about 4 hours of total sleep time for every 24 hours. Gorillas, with few natural predators and limited foraging needs, sleep some 14 hours per day.

Both positions suffered empirical embarrassments. The restoration model must posit some direct relation between the time awake and its consequences. Yet it was apparent that sleep deprivation effects did not increase linearly but in a wavelike fashion. When individuals are sleep deprived for two nights, they perform better on the third day than on the second night. Time asleep should be directly related to recovery time. However, some animals only sleep 4 hours per day to recover from 20 hours of wakefulness, whereas others require as much as 18 hours of sleep per day. Within species, the individual differences in sleep patterns have the shortest recovery times for the longest wakefulness times each 24 hours. It also was clear, from studies of displaced sleep such as shift work schedules, that sleep and sleepiness were affected by the time of day. On the other hand, the adaptive positions simply offered no solutions to the effects of sleep deprivation and were faced with the imponderable question of why the animal did not simply "nonbehave" or rest instead of sleeping.

Both theoretical positions had difficulties with the mechanisms underlying their positions. Since the earliest systematic research on sleep, there has been a search for the "toxin" or "depletion" substance that systematically changed during waking and reversed during sleep. But this has not been identified and its time course has not been specified. The adaptive theories leaned heavily on a loosely conceived instinctive mechanism.

Since the 1960s, there has been an infusion of research on the chronobiology or timing of sleep. From studies of sleep in time-free environments and in designs in which sleep was displaced in the 24-hour schedule (e.g., shift work), it became apparent that sleep was a time-locked system. Sleep could be seen to be an endogenously timed biological rhythm organized on approximately a 24-hour or circadian (*circa,* "about"; *dies,* "day") basis. For the adaptive theoretical position, it became increasingly clear that the explanatory mechanism for the appropriate timing of sleep could be that of an endogenous biological rhythm.

Alex Borbely and colleagues introduced a two-factor theoretical model of sleep. This model combined a sleep demand-recovery component and a timing or circadian component. Sleep and waking were jointly determined by a sleep demand (S) that rose during waking and declined during sleep and a circadian biological rhythm of sleepiness (C) that is determined by the timing component. This model is illustrated in Figure 1, which is greatly oversimplified. For example, the tendencies are certainly curvilinear and the circadian component is likely to have a positive component. Nevertheless, the overall relationships are appropriately represented.

Figure 1 shows a 24-hour period extending from 8 A.M. to 8 A.M. It assumes that an individual was awake from 8 A.M. and slept from 12 midnight until 8 A.M. Along the ordinate are levels of sleep tendencies associated with either the sleep demand component (S) or the circadian component (C). In this instance, sleepiness associated with S rises from 8 A.M. to midnight and falls from midnight to 8 A.M. The peak of the sleepiness associated with the C effect is at 4 A.M. The numbers below the figure are approximations of the sleepiness tendencies contributed by the two components and their combined effects. If the sleepiness threshold is 1 for awakening and 10 for sleep onset, the diagram would predict high probability of awakening at around 8 A.M. and sleep onset at about midnight.

This inclusion of the two components, and the more detailed specification of their interrelationships and functional aspects of the theoretical

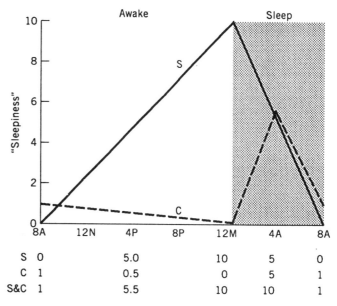

	8A	12N	4P	8P	12M	4A	8A
S	0		5.0		10	5	0
C	1		0.5		0	5	1
S&C	1		5.5		10	10	1

Figure 1. Relationship between sleep demand (S) and circadian timing (C) sleep tendencies in a 24-hour period.

constructs, moves theorizing from simply invoking general principles to permitting predictions and testing of the constructs. For example, using this model, if wakefulness is extended for, say 2 days, the interaction of these components will yield, in accord with data, a wavelike increase in sleepiness.

Figure 2 displays the operation of these constructs early in a shift work condition. The person is sleeping from 8 A.M. to 4 P.M. and working from midnight to 8 A.M. As in Figure 1, the sleepiness tendencies associated with the S and the C constructs are shown and their combined effects are indicated below the figure. Here, the sleep tendencies during the day period (8 A.M. to 4 P.M.), because they are not supplemented by the circadian tendency, diminish rapidly and approach the threshold of wakefulness. Because this is probably an exponential function, this predicts, as is the case, lighter sleep and early awakenings in the shift worker. Similarly, while attempting to work from midnight to 8 A.M., the rising sleepiness tendencies associated with the S factor in combination with the C factor predicts strong sleep tendencies and associated performance decrements. An elegant display of C–S modeling relative to sleep deprivation and varied time schedules is presented by Daan and Beersma.

Webb extended this two-factor model to include a third factor. The sleep responses to be predicted were the onset and termination of sleep and the sleep stage characteristics within sleep. According to this model, as with the two-factor model, the sleep response was predictable from the sleep demand level (defined as a positive function of wakefulness time and a negative function of sleep time) and circadian time (defined in terms of the time within a 24-hour sleep-wake schedule). The additional component was the presence or absence of voluntary or involuntary behaviors that were incompatible with the sleep response. Specifically, the model requires a specification of the time of prior wakefulness (or sleep); the time in the sleep–wake schedule (e.g., 10 P.M. or 10 A.M.); and the behavioral demands, (e.g., physically relaxed or activated, threatened or not threatened). Given these, the probability of sleep (or awakening) and the characteristics of sleep can be predicted. Or if two variables are held constant, say, 11 P.M. in a laboratory demand situation, then the sleep response (e.g., latency of sleep onset), and the subsequent sleep stages will be a direct function of time of prior wakefulness.

It is clear that each of the three major determinants of the sleep response are markedly modified by four additional factors: species differences, age, central nervous system variations (such as drugs or anomalies), and individual differences. For precise and extended predictions, each of the major parameters must be defined within species, within age levels, for specific central nervous system variations, and for established individual differences. Thus, the sleep demand and circadian parameters of a human infant are as different from those of a young adult as these are different from the rat. Within each of these groups there is a wide range of stable individual differences; and, of course, there are widely different behavioral demand components.

CIRCADIAN RHYTHM
SLEEP
SLEEP TREATMENT

W. B. WEBB

THERAPIES FOR INSTITUTIONALIZED ELDERLY PSYCHIATRIC PATIENTS

SOMATIC THERAPIES

R. K. R. Salokangas has characterized the past three decades of treatment for psychotic patients on first admission in three phases—1949 to 1958, the period of emphasis on shock therapies; 1959 to 1968, the era of neuroleptics; and 1969 to the present, intensive outpatient treatment. These three periods are not mutually exclusive and elements of the three major directions certainly coexist in practice in the past and present.

ELECTROSHOCK

The use of electroshock (ECT) for elderly patients has stirred controversy not only about this use, but also about unilateral versus bilateral electrode placement, which is a controversy as well in the treatment of younger depressed patients. R. M. Fraser and I. B. Glass conclude that there is no advantage in the use of bilateral ECT for the relief of depression, the alteration in behavior after five treatments or at 3 weeks, or the number of treatments required for "a satisfactory outcome," and the unilateral ECT resulted in a shorter recovery time.

Experience with younger patients contrasted with the Fraser-Glass study. It indicated that recovery times for elderly patients, mean age 72, were five times those of the younger patients for unilateral placement, and nine times the younger patients' times with bilateral ECT.

DRUG THERAPIES

The rationales for drugs for older patients vary widely and can be reviewed here only briefly. In 1975, the *Drugs and therapeutics bulletin* summarized the data on drug use for dementia, particularly those drugs claimed to be cerebral vasodilators and those purportedly cerebral "activators." The review concluded that none of the drugs could be recommended for routine use.

B. Pitt evaluated the use of tranquilizers and hypnotics in senile dementia and observed the trade-off of reduction in restlessness and aggressive behaviors for reduction in physical mobility and psychological independence.

The British use an unusual diagnosis, paraphrenia. Paraphrenia, or "paranoid states of late life," has been characterized by T. P. Bridge and R. J. Wyatt, who believe that about 10% of first admissions of elderly patients in England and Scandinavia for paranoid psychoses are not "old" schizophrenics because (a) their premorbid histories differ from those of younger schizophrenic patients and (b) the disease is a reactive rather than process disorder. These investigators state that paraphrenics are responsive to phenothiazine therapy and that the "treatment outcome

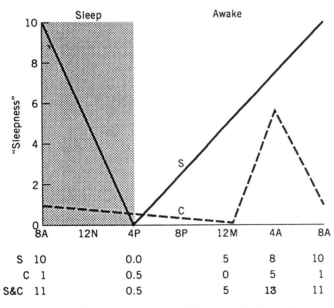

Figure 2. Relationship between sleep demand (S) and circadian timing (C) sleep tendencies in a shift work schedule.

S	10	0.0	5	8	10
C	1	0.5	0	5	1
S&C	11	0.5	5	13	11

. . . is almost invariably favorable, particularly when maintenance dosages are maintained." Bridge and Wyatt also observe that paraphrenics have a lower mortality rate than that for older patients with dementia or affective illness.

I. N. Mensh reviewed the risks in medication for older patients, citing the interactional effects of multiple drugs, the lower thresholds of response, and their unpredictability in older patients, producing acute and life-threatening episodes as well as chronic states such as tardive dyskinesia.

PSYCHOLOGICAL THERAPIES

R. A. Moline and P. Phillips instituted a reward system for inpatients. Maximum self-control earned a patient 120 points each weekday and permitted passes for leaving the ward or the grounds, or going home. The authors were enthusiastic that the reorganization of the ward system of control of behavior, implemented by staff and patients, was successful for many patients.

Reality orientation (RO) has been widely introduced into long-term care facilities for the elderly. H. Zepelin et al. evaluated a year-long RO program. The investigators were disappointed to note the lack of effectiveness of the program and observed that the positive effects "may have been limited by the advanced age of the residents . . . [these] continued with fairly severe disorientation and a high rate of disability."

In England, G. Smith was more positive, but with a different population. In four psychiatric hospitals, the number of beds was reduced by half by extensive utilization of group homes, halfway houses, supervised bungalows, and residential homes.

H. Harris et al., also in Great Britain, emphasize the architectural design and spatial location of things and people to enhance interactions of the institutionalized elderly. Verbal and other social interaction, and segregation of individual patients or groups of patients in large or small numbers, in institutional or in domestic living quarters, was a function much less of physical design of the living spaces than of "administrative and staff behavior" in determining patient behaviors.

J. Buch and co-workers estimated that about 5% of long-term patients 65 years or older have "declining physical and mental functions," such as communication problems, because of sensory impairment, dementia, or speech difficulty.

M. M. Katz studied therapies variously titled "a combination of modified" reality orientation, remotivation, activity, and milieu in a New York State extended-care facility with nearly 900 geriatric residents. He summarizes the ratings as 44% improved, 20% unchanged, 18% worse, and 18% not rated.

Nursing homes are different from other long-term institutions for the elderly but most studies have been done in nursing homes. Private versus public, size, and ethnic mix are among the variables that operate to limit generalizations.

R. J. Paul and G. L. Lentz probably have done one of the most intensive studies of institutionalized chronic mental patients. A social-learning program was recommended but it is important to emphasize one of the conclusions: "The absolute level of functioning achieved by residents who were able to move to the community was still sufficiently marginal that efforts to develop even more effective programs are clearly called for."

CONCLUDING REMARKS

A critical variable to consider in the treatment of chronic geriatric patients in long-stay institutions is the reliability of diagnosing older patients. More than 20 years ago, Mensh investigated the problem of confounding mental illness with physical illness among elderly patients. K. L. G. Nobbs has raised the same concerns: "Misplacement of physically ill patients in

mental hospitals produces mortality nearly three times that of correctly placed psychiatric cases."

L. J. Schmidt and colleagues have emphasized the effects of the reduction of state hospital populations, from 560,000 in 1955 to 250,000 in 1973, generally attributed to the establishment of community mental health centers and to the use of psychotropic drugs. However, the transfer of thousands to nursing homes has been a significant variable, especially for older patients. Finally, though the selection of patients for transfer to the various types of homes may have been the principal determinant, the course of these 1155 patients after transfer showed deteriorating or fluctuating physical and psychological states in 80% of the comprehensive care, 43% of the intermediate care, and 21% of the personal care patients.

GERONTOLOGY

I. N. MENSH

THERAPY TRAINEES

Carl Rogers identified the following attitudes as most important effectively to promote positive changes in clients: congruence or genuineness, unconditional positive regard, and accurate empathic understanding. Rogers asserted that therapists need not have any specialized knowledge, that accurate psychological diagnosis was not necessary for effective psychotherapy to take place, and that many conditions that other therapists commonly regard as necessary for effective psychotherapy are nonessential. Subsequent research seemed to support Rogers' bold assertion that personality characteristics of the therapist were the critical variables in determining constructive therapy outcomes.

James Palmer wrote that many trainers of psychotherapists agree that some form of psychotherapy is helpful and even necessary for the student psychotherapy trainee. According to Palmer, psychotherapy helps therapy trainees cope with their own anxieties, guilt, anger, depression, and other unfinished psychological business likely to intrude in establishing effective therapeutic relationships.

Of relevance to the issue of providing therapy trainees with experiences designed to promote the development of what has been referred to as the "therapeutic conditions" is the work of A. E. Ivey and J. Authier. Their approach to the training of counselors and therapists, known as *microcounseling,* is concerned with quantifiable measurable skills. Microcounseling breaks down the "therapeutic conditions" into smaller and definable components, and work on these skills is done systematically. The specific skills and attitudes that are the focus of counselor training are empathy, regard, respect and warmth, concreteness, immediacy, genuineness, and confrontation. G. Egan's model of effective helping skills includes the following: attending and listening as the bases of effective responding; accurate empathy and fostering of self-exploration through self-disclosure; respect and genuineness as the foundations of the helping relationship; the skills of summarizing, giving information, and challenging clients; the skills of confrontation, counselor self-disclosure, and immediacy; and learning to help clients develop action programs designed to lead to behavior change.

COMPETENCY IN PSYCHOLOGY
GRADUATE TRAINING IN PSYCHOLOGY

G. COREY

THORNDIKE'S LAWS OF LEARNING

Thorndike started his long career at Columbia University where he observed many kinds of animals in what he called "puzzle-box" problems.

An animal, say a cat, would be placed in a box from which it could escape in only one way, for example, by pulling a string that raised a door. In such a situation, a cat would initially engage in a variety of behaviors (sniffing, scratching, climbing the walls, etc.) before, in one way or another, getting the string in its claws and pulling away from it with the happy result of door opening. Upon replacement in the box, the cat would again wander about emitting chance responses until again the string was grasped in some way with the successful result. Over a series of such episodes, the cat would eventually pull the string earlier and earlier in the situation and would show what Thorndike called a gradual improvement in escape time.

Thorndike himself was satisfied that his studies had exposed the basic operations in learning that could be described as a gradual strengthening of some stimulus–response "connections" that at first occurred purely by chance and that happened to be "successful." There was no room in Thorndike's theory for anything like "insight" or intelligent or rational analysis. Learning was a matter of dumb luck. Sooner or later, if one tried one thing after another, one would stumble on the correct response. Because the correct response would be "satisfying," the "bond" between the stimulus and the response would be strengthened to some degree and eventually would be strong enough to occur first or early in a test situation. Thorndike was so convinced that he had discovered a basic rule or law of learning in the presumed importance of a satisfying state of affairs following upon a chance response that he formally proposed a summary of his belief in what he called the "law of effect."

THE LAW OF EFFECT

A stimulus–response connection or bond is strengthened when the response is followed by a satisfier. Thorndike attributed elimination of incorrect reactions to the occurrence of annoyers or annoying states of affairs. The two-part law of effect then amounted to the statement that one learned or retained whatever responses were followed by satisfiers and refrained from responses that were followed by annoyers.

OTHER LAWS OF LEARNING

Thorndike saw the law of effect as the basic principle governing learning but not quite sufficient to account for all learning that occurred or failed to occur. Two sublaws were regarded as necessary additions: These were the laws of *exercise* and of *readiness.*

The law of readiness was essentially a statement of the need to attend if one were to learn anything. Thorndike tried to offer a semineurological proposal in suggesting that the nervous system had to be tuned or "ready" for certain connections to be operative.

In many cases, the law of effect, being blind, could not accomplish complete learning in one trial. For some connections, many trials might be needed. Each successful trial added strength to a connection.

Although exercise, readiness, and effect at first seemed to cover the field, Thorndike found it useful to introduce additional laws from time to time. In 1931, for example, he modified the law of effect to drop the negative side. Punishment had been found, he believed, to have no effect on eliminating wrong responses. At best, punishment might create a temporary situation in which a correct response could be rewarded and strengthened. Thorndike also introduced the law of *belongingness.* This law was meant to suggest that some kinds of material were more readily learnable than others; some things seemed to go together more naturally than others. Another law, *associative shifting,* was introduced to meet the challenge from followers of Watson who were committed to the notion that all learning amounted to conditioning. The law of associative shifting was meant to incorporate conditioning into the law of effect. It amounted to a statement that stimuli associated with the original S–R bond could come, in time, to participate in the initiation of the response, even in the absence of the original stimulus.

LEARNING THEORIES
PUNISHMENT

B. R. BUGELSKI

THOUGHT DISTURBANCES

Thought, conscious and unconscious, serves the purposes of generating and monitoring communications, regulating activity, creating, proposing, and problem solving on both verbal and nonverbal levels. Thought disturbances can be observed in a continuum ranging in severity from the normally occurring breaks in attention to the pathological.

Some of the less serious thought disturbances are evidenced by hyperkinetic children whose attention is shortlived and whose tasks are interrupted by a seeming need to perform motor movement. Writers and composers also experience thought disturbances, such as blank periods during which, while all other normal functioning is intact, the ability to keep on with the writing or composing task seems impaired.

Frequently psychoneuroses such as phobic reactions and anxiety reactions can be attributed to irrational ideas. Many of these irrational ideas are accompanied by poor self-statements. Other psychoneurotic thought disturbances are evidenced in obsessive thoughts where frequently occurring judgmental thinking interferes with normal functioning. Disputation of these thoughts can lead to clear logical thinking.

Psychosomatic symptoms are thought disorders that reflect the inability of the individual to cope with anxiety and stress, which are transformed into physiological symptoms that can interfere with normal daily functioning as with many other psychoneurotic thought disorders.

Psychotic thought disturbances are usually accompanied by symptoms of *delusion,* where false beliefs of persecution or megalomania predominate, and *hallucinations,* where the organism generates its own stimulation in any or all of the sensory modalities. Though these thought disturbances are serious in their own right, they are generally attached to other types of pathological behavior, such as delirium, dementia, and schizophrenia.

Delirium is a disturbance of varying severity of consciousness. The subject may be in any state from fully awake to coma, and there is evidence of disorders in cognitive function, thinking, and perception. Delirium is a result of cerebral dysfunction without any destruction of tissue and seems to originate from metabolic, chemical, or toxic disturbances. Delirium is generally transitional and disappears with the removal of the metabolic, chemical, or toxic elements.

Dementia syndrome, however, is a thought disorder related to cortical tissue damage evidenced by diminished intellectual capacity during clear consciousness. There are personality, amnesiac, and disorientation changes that occur as well. Here the fully alert patient does not grasp the present. Memory deficits and poor concentration are in evidence. Language deteriorates to the point of being childlike and normal routine thoughts seem labored. Most disturbing is that many patients are aware of their cognitive difficulty and exhibit other secondary emotional disturbances.

Schizophrenia is an example of a psychogenic thought disorder. The schizophrenic's thought disorder seems to demonstrate a conscious sacrifice of physical and emotional life for some alternative "cocooned" existence for the perceived welfare of others. The thought disorder seems to direct an "escape for survival" as shown by a continual downward adjustment of functioning in an irrational struggle to stay alive. There is withdrawal from social contact and emotional involvement, as well as regression toward a lower level of intellectual function. This exclusionary nihilistic thought disturbance exhibits itself in paranoid, catatonic, hebephrenic, and simple types.

DEMENTIA
PERSONALITY DISORDERS

D. F. FISHER

THURSTONE SCALING

Thurstone scaling, also known as the method of equal-appearing intervals, is a technique devised by Thurstone for constructing quantitative attitude measurement instruments.

The first step is to gather a large number of statements representing a wide range of opinions about the attitude object (e.g., capital punishment). Statements ranging from extremely negative through neutral to extremely positive are drawn from persons holding varying viewpoints or from the popular literature. These statements are then independently sorted by judges into 11 piles of "equal-appearing intervals" ranging from (1) least favorable (toward the attitude object) through (6) neutral to (11) most favorable. The median and semi-interquartile range (Q) of the judges' scores for each statement are then calculated, and statements with large Q values are discarded as *ambiguous*. The remaining statements are item-analyzed for internal consistency, and inconsistent statements are discarded as *irrelevant*.

What remains from this process is a pool of consistent, unambiguous statements with scale values (median judges' scores) ranging from 1 to 11. The attitude scale itself is then constructed by including two or more statements from each of the 11 intervals on a questionnaire. Respondents check all of the statements with which they agree; the median scale values of the statements endorsed by respondents are their attitude scores. If the item pool is large enough, several parallel scales can be constructed and the reliability of the attitude score can be determined.

Thurstone's technique is time consuming and has been largely supplanted in popularity by newer techniques for developing measures of attitude. However, Thurstone scaling is a major step in the development of behaviorally anchored rating scales, mixed standard rating scales, and weighted checklists for measuring work performance.

**ATTITUDE MEASUREMENT
RATING SCALES**

W. I. SAUSER, JR.

TIME-LIMITED PSYCHOTHERAPY

Estimates of need have varied from 10 to 15% of the population of the United States in any one year, representing a potential of between 20 and 30 million applicants for psychotherapy, which, if acted on, would clog the service completely.

The juxtaposition between this vast potential need and the limited supply of trained psychotherapists has created a continuous pressure for brief modes of treatment. The experience of those offering services to the population at large is that most applicants for psychotherapy seek and are willing to commit themselves to no more than five or six interviews.

Certain classes of interventions, usually designated as crisis or supportive, are directed at helping the individual to recover from the effects of a temporary, often event-related, state. This kind of intervention is almost universally brief and directed toward helping the person to return to a previous level of functioning. Change in that level is not the goal. Brief and time-limited psychotherapies are used here to designate treatments in which the goals are enduring changes in the person's level of effectiveness and style of functioning. The most useful distinction between brief and time-limited psychotherapy is that in the latter there is an explicit setting of a limit in either calendar terms or in the number of sessions. J. N. Butcher and P. L. Koss state that most practitioners consider 25 sessions the upper limit of "brief" therapy.

Developments Within Psychoanalysis

The first responses to the ever-lengthening process of psychoanalysis took the form of modifications designed to reduce the austerity of the rule of free association and the strictures of the therapist as "blank screen." Sandor Ferenczi and Wilhelm Stekel are often cited as experimenters with various kinds of active interventions.

These developments were revived by Franz Alexander and Thomas French. Their direction was to control the frequency of visits to limit dependence on the therapist and actively to contravene the patient's transference (based on parental paradigms) distorted perceptions of the therapist. D. H. Malin proposed that the focus of attention should fall somewhere between the highly abstract formulation, for example, the oedipal conflict, and the pure pragmatic presenting problem. These formulations, which he labeled psychodynamic hypotheses, are to be stated in simple nontechnical terms. They seek to specify the kind of stress to which the patient is vulnerable, the criterion of recovery, and how this specific stress must be faced without developing new symptoms.

Developments Outside Psychoanalysis

Two of the most empirically tested brief treatments are operating under the umbrella of client-centered therapy and the even broader umbrella of the behavior therapies. Carl Rogers, the founder of client-centered therapy, evolved a method designed to keep responsibility in the client within an atmosphere in which he or she felt understood and accepted. While not explicitly designed to be brief, this therapy was seen as avoiding the kind of dependence on the therapist that can lengthen psychotherapy. Moreover, it was geared to whatever goals, limited or extensive, that the client set.

Similarly, the various versions of behavior therapy have tended toward the brief form. The learning theory ideology and the methodology based on it pushed in that direction. Thus, attention is concentrated on specific sets of actions as targets of the change process, which, under the circumstances of the voluntary entry in therapy, are represented by the person's complaints.

THEORY OF TIME-LIMITED PSYCHOTHERAPY

There are two theoretical roots from which James Mann's development of a pattern of 12 interviews can be traced. Rank advocated setting a fixed date for the termination of therapy to provide an important base for his will therapy.

Though acknowledging the relevance of Rank's ideas and their applications, Mann took his main inspiration from his analysis of the psychology of time. Pointing to observation of the evolution of the sense of time from the child-based feeling of infinite time to the increasing awareness of finiteness in any individual's life, he designed a pattern of treatment around this feature, geared to what he saw as one important component of psychopathology.

Psychotherapists have accumulated considerable favorable experience with this method. Comparisons of time-limited (18) and unlimited (averaging 37 interviews) client-centered and Adlerian treatments found essentially no differences in outcome. A similar result was obtained in limited (eight interviews) as compared with unlimited social casework.

**CRISIS INTERVENTION
INNOVATIVE PSYCHOTHERAPIES**

E. S. BORDIN

TIME PERSPECTIVE

Time perspective is the field of study that attempts to understand how and why we turn our thoughts beyond the present moment.

It is useful first to distinguish this process from *time perception*. Our "subjective clock" characteristically may be slower or faster than objective time, and it is also influenced by the situation—whom we are with, what we are doing, how we are feeling. H. Nichols observed that psychologists were hopeful of discovering a "time sense" comparable to other sense modalities. Instead it appears likely that sensing of time's passage is not a single, independent function, but emerges from multiple feedback as we respond to both our internal and external environment.

According to L. Frank, a disciple of Kurt Lewin, who defined time perspective as "the totality of the individual's views of his psychological future and psychological past existing at a given time," each of us has a distinctive position in society as well as a distinctive developmental history. This personal way of viewing the world is expressed in our interpretations of the past, present, and future. As we grow up, our time perspective becomes broader and more complex, Frank suggests, and represents the unique experiences we have had along the way. Furthermore, we are influenced every step of the way by society and social class.

Time perspective has been found to include several dimensions: *pretension,* the length of time in which thought is projected ahead; *retrotension,* the length of time in which thought is projected back into the past; *density,* the number of events thought about in past or future; *coherence,* the degree of organization within our past–present–future matrix; and *directionality,* the sense of perceived rate of movement toward the future. Individual time perspectives are complex, although some generalizations can be made.

One set of generalizations relates to our age and position in life. We tend to project further into the future as we move from childhood into adulthood. The sense of rapid movement from the present toward the future is at its keenest during adolescence, although pretension has not yet reached its peak. The past takes on new significance from the middle years of life onward, as the individual begins to seek a balance between what went before and what is yet to come. Increased concern for the past is a common finding for the years after youth. This does not necessarily mean that the future has lost its importance. Instead it suggests that people are making more use of their own more extensive experiences.

Elderly people often retain a strong sense of futurity even though objectively they may not have as much time ahead. The stereotype that older people "live in the past" has been refuted by researchers. Resourceful utilization of the past tends to be associated with high self-esteem and coping abilities in the second half of life.

A second set of generalizations centers on situational aspects. N. Israeli was perhaps the first to show that time perspectives tend to shrink when the economy is bleak and jobs hard to find. In fact, the sense of having "no prospects" is more typical for unemployed young adults than for the elderly. Seligman has called attention to another important situational influence on time perspective—one's sense of control or efficacy; that is, does what we do make any difference? Seligman's basic concept is expressed in the term *learned helplessness.*

LEARNED HELPLESSNESS

R. Kastenbaum

TIME-SERIES ANALYSIS

The statistical analysis of data that have been collected on a single unit (e.g., a person, a family, or a city) across time in either a continuous or a discrete form is a time-series analysis. As is the case for conventional parametric data analysis procedures, time-series methods are employed to describe the relationship between variables, predict future behavior, and test for treatment effects. There are two mathematically equivalent approaches to conceptualizing and computing time-series analyses. One approach, called a time-domain analysis, involves the use of concepts similar to those employed in conventional correlation and regression procedures. The second approach is called a frequency-domain analysis;

this involves the study of frequency components and is based on spectral analytic concepts. Some of the basic ideas associated with time-domain analyses are described here.

TIME-SERIES CONCEPTS

A time-series model is an equation that relates an observation obtained at some specified point in time to observations obtained previously on the same response measure and/or on other response measures. For example, if discrete body weight data are collected at equally spaced points in time on one subject, it might be of interest to know (a) the extent to which adjacent (or nonadjacent) observations in the time series are related, and (b) how to predict future body-weight scores. The answers to these two questions require the computation of the sample autocorrelation function, the identification of the time-series model, and the estimation of appropriate parameters.

An autocorrelation coefficient is essentially a conventional correlation computed between the dependent variable time series (body weight in the present example) and the lagged values of this time series. This coefficient (computed using a formula very similar to the Pearson correlation) is a measure of the linear dependence in the observations one time period apart; that is, it is a measure of the linear relationship between adjacent observations.

The collection of autocorrelation coefficients based on various lags is the estimated autocorrelation function; this is generally plotted in a graph known as a correlogram. Tests of statistical significance are applied to the coefficients.

Model Identification

If there is interest in predicting (forecasting) future scores from the available time series, it is necessary to identify the model that best describes the process that generated the sample series. The estimated autocorrelation function is useful in identifying the model. Three models among many that frequently describe time-series behavior are the white-noise model, the first-order autoregressive model, and the second-order autoregressive model. If the estimated autocorrelation function is a collection of nonsignificant autocorrelations, this is an indication that the variability in the series can be best characterized as "white noise" or random fluctuation.

The *first-order autoregressive model* frequently does a good job of representing time-series data; hence, the autocorrelation function pattern of this model should be compared with the estimated autocorrelation function pattern. It is known that the first-order autoregressive model is associated with autocorrelations that die out rapidly at higher order lags. If the lag-one autocorrelation of a first-order autoregressive model is known, the lag-two autocorrelation is the square of the lag-one autocorrelation, and any higher lag autocorrelation equals the lag-one autocorrelation raised to the Kth power where K is the lag.

Another useful model, the *second-order autoregressive model,* will fit some data better than the first-order autoregressive model just discussed. If this model fits the data better than the first-order autoregressive model, the behavior at time t can be predicted with less error by using information two steps back in addition to the information provided by the mean and the observation one step back.

The basic idea associated with the identification of any time-series model is the same with both simple and complex models: Match the structure of the observed data (as measured by various types of autocorrelation) with the structure known to be associated with a certain class of models. After a model has been tentatively identified, the parameters of the model are estimated.

Diagnostic Checking

Since the identification of a time-series model is based on a somewhat subjective procedure, it is sometimes advocated that the adequacy of the identified model be evaluated by estimating and testing the significance of the autocorrelation function of the estimated residuals of the model. This is sensible because the residuals of time-series models are assumed to not be autocorrelated. In fact, a basic purpose of time-series analysis is to discover what has to be done to the original data (i.e., what models must be fitted) to yield white noise residuals. Certain time series require very complex models to produce white-noise residuals. This frequently occurs when the series is not stationary. That is, the level, variance, and/ or autocorrelation structure may change over time.

INTERVENTION MODELS

A frequent problem in psychological research is to evaluate the effectiveness of an intervention. If data have been collected at equally spaced intervals before and after an intervention has been applied to some sampling unit such as a person, a group, or a county, it is often useful to describe and test the statistical significance of the apparent effect. There are two basic strategies for analyzing such effects.

The first approach is easily understood and very useful. It involves identifying a conventional time-series model on the preintervention data. The parameters of the model are estimated and then forecasts of the behavior expected to occur in the postintervention phase are made. These forecasts are based on the assumption that the preintervention process will not change after the intervention. If there is a discrepancy between the value forecast and the value observed in the postintervention phase, this difference can be tested. If the difference is statistically significant, this is evidence that the intervention is associated with a change. Since a test can be computed for each point in the postintervention phase, it is easy to evaluate the point at which the intervention begins to have an effect.

The second and more frequently used approach involves estimating and testing an intervention effect parameter. A difficulty with this approach is that the "effect" of an intervention is often of a complex form; it is appropriate to think in terms of an effect pattern rather than a mean difference.

BIVARIATE ANALYSIS

Time-series analysis can be used in the study of the relationship between two (or more) time series. The correlation between the time series (sometimes called the cross-correlation) can be of several forms because there are many ways in which the two series can be lagged. The motivation for studying such correlations is to find which of two series seems to be "driving" the other.

CORRELATION METHODS

B. E. HUITEMA

TOILET TRAINING

The practice of toilet training children is the cause of a great deal of anxiety and frustration for parents and has resulted in debates among professionals. Sigmund Freud suggested that inappropriate toilet training can result in lifetime trauma for the child. Still others submit that the process of toilet training reinforces the self-centered nature of the young child.

Foxx and Azrin suggest that there are four "preliminary considerations" to regard before commencing toilet training: age, bladder control, physical readiness, and instructional readiness. They submit that at age 20 months the child is "probably capable of being toilet trained." They further submit that a child is ready for toilet training when the child demonstrates bladder control by strength of urine stream as well as

quantity of urine eliminated. Readiness is also indicated when the child presents good "finger and hand coordination," enough to pick up objects, and also is capable of walking independently. Finally, Foxx and Azrin suggest that toilet training readiness is indicated when the child can follow simple directions and/or imitate actions.

PARENT–CHILD RELATIONS

D. L. HOLMES

TOKEN ECONOMIES

The generally acknowledged theoretical source of contemporary token economies is B. F. Skinner. Applications with severely disabled people in psychiatric hospitals is associated with the work of Ayllon and Azrin and Atthowe and Krasner, and the strongest documentation of the value of the procedure is presented by R. J. Paul and G. L. Lentz. Work with children was fostered by S. W. Bijou and his students and in classrooms by W. C. Becker and his colleagues. Another area of application is with delinquents.

All token economies have in common a target set of desirable responses and an explicit payoff for these acts. The responses selected are a picture of what any given dominant (i.e., teacher, parent, employer, therapist) group considers "normal." The responses are specified and, if complex, are broken down.

The token economy may start out with simple acts of self-care and self-feeding in the psychiatric hospital or simple academic tasks in the schoolroom. The instructor starts where the subject has a low rate of response but is capable of being successful. This is essentially the concept of shaping.

There is payoff for acts to be increased. With age and socialization, payoffs become more abstract and more delayed. The token economy is a preparation for this role, and all treatment decisions are made with this goal in mind.

Usually a token economy will have a contingency contract known to both subject and instructor. At the start, primary reinforcing stimuli may be used, but as soon as possible, acquired reinforcers, such as tokens or points, bridge the time between the act and the receipt of an explicit value, such as food, privacy, television, toys, or various privileges. As treatment progresses, the time between receipt of tokens and their exchange for the explicit backup reinforcers is increased. The acts for which there are payoffs are increased in complexity and difficulty—again, a process of shaping. Acts that originally led to payoffs are made necessary parts of or conditions for larger social acts. All behavioral procedures, such as shaping, prompting and fading, chaining, modeling, variable ratio schedules, reinforcer sampling, extinction, and time out from reinforcement, may be used in developing and maintaining new behaviors.

Rather than "do nots," the instructor in a token economy strives to find activities that are incompatible with the targets to be decreased. In extreme cases, to avoid injurious behavior or the like, there may be a fine or response cost or a rare use of aversive stimulation. As soon as possible, the incompatible, alternative behavior that is more socially useful is taught as a way to deal with the situation.

Since the goal is independent, socially successful reaction to situations, a person may well receive tokens for his or her own scheduling and evaluation of behavior. The ultimate goal is response in the extra-treatment environment, fulfilling because of intrinsic interest and naturally occurring social reinforcement. Although the token economy is a very useful set of applied procedures, it also has a major role in theoretical formulations of "normal" and "abnormal" behavior.

L. P. ULLMANN

TOOL USING

At one time researchers were surprised to learn that animals also could use tools. The use of an instrument to reach something, or to manipulate it in some way to achieve a goal, leads one to suspect that the act implies intelligence and adaptive capacity. If nothing else, a simple tool such as a stick in the hand extends one's range of activity and increases one's efficiency. Yet the use of a tool, in itself, does not tell us with certainty that intelligence was involved; simple species-typical behavior may be all that is concerned. Acts are not considered intelligent responses; they are characteristic of the species as a whole and not of individual animals. Moreover, these responses are always used in these situations, and thus they qualify as fixed action patterns.

The sea otter engages in tool using of a more complex type rarely seen in animals other than primates. When feeding on mussels, it brings to the surface a flat stone, perhaps 10 to 15 cm in diameter, which is placed on the chest. The mussel is then beaten against the stone until the shell is broken.

Chimpanzees have been observed obtaining termites in Africa. They first scrape away a thin layer of soil to expose a termite passage. Next they select a grass stalk, twig, or thin vine, which they poke into the hole. A moment later, they retrieve the stick and pass it between the lips, picking off the attached termites.

Agonistic tool using also occurs. Howlers, cebus, and spider monkeys of the New World and gorillas, orangutans, and gibbons of the Old World break off branches or nuts and throw them down at intruders, and baboons, macaques, and patas monkeys roll stones or rocks down hills toward intruders.

A. J. RIOPELLE

TOPOLOGICAL PSYCHOLOGY

Kurt Lewin hoped to find a general way to describe and explain psychological states and events precisely, using mathematical concepts. The mathematical field of topology deals with spatial relationships without attention to size, direction, shape, or even magnitude; the primary topological concepts are region, boundary, inclusion, adjacency, nonoverlapping, and the like. This made topology attractive for generating diagrams of the concrete dynamics both of the individual (the "person," in Lewin's terminology) and of the situation as seen by the person (the "life space," in Lewin's terminology).

A significant problem, however, as Lewin himself pointed out, is that such fundamental psychological facts as needs, tensions, or goals are often by their very nature quantitative, and often have a "direction"—concepts that are incompatible with pure topology. Lewin thus added the idea of "vector" to his system, and hoped to retain the advantages of both the mathematics of topology and the physical concept of a force that has direction and magnitude. He called this combination that permits vectors in a topological description *hodological space*, but did not complete the "vector" part of his system.

The situation as seen by the person is usually diagrammed by Lewin as an oval; everything outside the oval is not part of the individual's life space. The person is a region, usually represented by a small circle designated P, inside the oval of the life space. The life space is differenti-

ated into various additional regions with more or less permeable boundaries, indicating different features of the environment discriminated by P that are related in particular ways. The life space may also contain "barriers," or impermeable boundaries, which represent psychological borders that P considers impossible to cross. Psychological events involve movement, or "locomotion," within the life space.

Lewin further elaborated the region *within P*, suggesting, among many other things, that this region is much less differentiated in the child than in the adult. He also proposed that different levels of reality, including imagination, can be represented by several layers of superimposed life spaces.

The model generated a rich array of empirical research problems in such areas as psychological satiation, forgetting, substitution, memory, personality, and motivation, and became the medium of expression for Lewin's influential dynamic theory of personality, field theory, theory of group dynamics, and other theories in social psychology.

M. WERTHEIMER

TOXIC PSYCHOSES

Toxic psychoses are a loosely associated group of disorders whose main common element is that the aberrant behavior follows or coincides with either the intake of some exogenous substance, through inhalation, oral ingestion, or direct absorption, or the production of endogenous toxic substances in response to disease. Symptomatically, the toxic psychoses resemble one another by the presence of delirium manifested by attentional disturbances; perceptual disturbances, such as illusions and hallucinations; the inability to sustain clarity of thought; disorientations to time, place, and/or person; memory disturbances; and associated anxieties, fears, irritability, and occasional hyperactivity. Dementia to the point of social and occupational impairment may also be present with or without delirium, but is more common with chronic than with acute toxic conditions.

Exogenous toxic agents implicated in toxic psychoses include bromides, amphetamines, barbituric acid derivatives, *d*-lysergic acid diethylamide-25 (LSD), morphine, cocaine, marijuana, belladonna alkaloids, chloral hydrate, paraldehyde, and metals such as lead, arsenic, mercury, and manganese. In addition, psychotic reactions have been reported following the excessive use of antiparkinsonism drugs (e.g., Levodopa); anticonvulsants; lithium; cimetidine; phencyclidine (PCP); ergot, an alkaloid-containing fungus; alcohol; and over-the-counter diet aids (phenylpropanolamine) and nasal sprays (phenylephrine).

Endogenous psychosis-producing toxins can be the result of diabetes, kidney, and liver disease. Porphyrin increase, as the result of a genetically determined metabolic disorder, can also produce psychotic symptomatology. Differential diagnosis involves observation, a careful and complete history from both the patient and relatives and friends, and appropriate psychiatric and laboratory evaluations.

Treatment of the psychotic behavior begins with reducing the quantity of toxic substance present. In the case of abused medications, attention must also be given to the original disorder for which the patient was taking the substance that precipitated the psychotic behavior. Psychotherapy, directed toward both precipitating psychological factors and short- and long-range personal goals, is of value, concurrent with or following medical treatment.

W. E. EDMONSTON, JR.

TRAIT PSYCHOLOGY

Trait psychology is an approach to the theory and measurement of personality relying heavily on the concept of *trait* as a fundamental unit. Traits are defined in various ways. At the simplest level, they are seen as relatively enduring descriptive characteristics of a person. At a somewhat broader level, traits are defined as predispositions to behavior that are both enduring (i.e., having temporal consistency) and wide ranging (i.e., having cross-situational consistency). Gordon Allport asserted that traits also had a physiological basis. Allport also differentiated between common traits, found at some strength in all persons in a given culture, and unique traits, peculiar to an individual. The strongest, most pervasive dispositions within a person, he called cardinal traits.

A term frequently associated with trait is *type*. A trait is a single continuous dimension of personality, but a type is a more complex pattern of characteristics that serves as a model for categorizing people. Early in this century, Carl Jung identified sets of opposite personality types with extroverted versus introverted attitudes, and intuiting versus sensing and thinking versus feeling functions, now measured by the Myers–Briggs Type Indicator. Eysenck and most other trait theorists see personality as organized hierarchically with major predispositions encompassing a set of related traits; for instance the extroverted type includes traits such as sociability, impulsiveness, and activity.

Another term often contrasted with trait is *state*, which refers to a temporary condition, such as a mood, whereas trait refers to a long-range predisposition. In testing for state anxiety, for instance, C. D. Spielberger asks whether the person feels upset now; in testing for the corresponding trait, he asks if the person is generally, often, or constantly upset.

In many personality theories, traits occupy an important position as the basic units inferred from behavior. Several theorists use a trait-and-factor model; that is, they build systems empirically by factor analyzing a variety of items to produce basic scales or a variety of tests to produce higher level factors. The major personality theorists of this kind are Raymond Cattell, Eysenck and J. P. Guilford. Each has developed tests for constructs they see as basic traits.

Among several issues that might be discussed, two are particularly prominent. The first is the question of the number and kind of traits. Instead of Cattell's 16 factors for questionnaire data, Eysenck has identified three-extraversion, emotionality (neuroticism), and psychotism. Other widely used dimensional systems emphasizing interpersonal relations have identified two major axes—friendliness–hostility and dominance–submission, with many degrees of variation between them arranged in a circle. These two axes parallel the features frequently mentioned in organizational psychology—the socioemotional versus the task-oriented aspects of roles.

The other significant issue is the question of the cross-situational consistency of traits. The early work of Hartshorne and May temporarily shattered the belief in consistency of such traits as honesty by demonstrating that children who cheat on an examination do not necessarily lie or cheat in other circumstances. Yet intuitively we feel that people are consistent. By 1972, Eysenck had concluded that the trait position had been upheld and accepted. However, about that time the much greater attention to the environment and the rise of behavioral psychology led to further attacks on traits, especially by W. Mischel. However, Mischel and others subsequently have recognized that there is considerable consistency among some characteristics. Mischel and P. K. Peake noted that temporal and situational consistency should be separated. The former is high and the latter is low in reliability. Using a cognitive prototypical approach, they propose a resolution of the dilemma, saying that the perception and organization of personality consistencies depend on identifying the key features (the prototypes, or best examples of a characteristic) in personality rather than on behavioral-level consistency in situations.

CENTRAL TRAITS
PERSONALITY TYPES

N. Sundberg

TRANQUILIZING DRUGS

Tranquilizing drugs are usually placed into one of two categories. The "major tranquilizers," such as chlorpromazine (Thorazine), are drugs used primarily (although not exclusively) in the treatment of psychotic disorders, especially the various forms of schizophrenia. The "minor tranquilizers," such as diazepam (Valium), include those drugs used to treat nonpsychotic anxiety states.

Chlorpromazine is probably the best known of the antipsychotic drugs. Chlorpromazine represents the prototype of the phenothiazine group of antipsychotic. Many other agents with somewhat different chemical structures have been synthesized in this group since the advent of chlorpromazine. In addition, a closely related group of compounds, the thioxanthenes—such as thiothixene hydrochloride (Navane)—as well as the butyrophenones—such as haloperidol (Haldol)—are also widely used for their sedative and antipsychotic properties.

There are three principal applications of these drugs in psychiatry. Patients exhibiting acute behavioral and cognitive disturbances, especially excessive restlessness, excitement, and aggressive or destructive behavior attributable to a variety of causes may be managed with these agents. An antipsychotic can be used in a chronic regimen to prevent sudden relapses in schizophrenics and paranoid patients. Finally, these drugs are occasionally used to reduce anxiety in neurotic patients. Outside of psychiatry, they are effective as preanesthetic agents and in the treatment of vomiting.

As with almost any form of medication, the antipsychotic drugs produce unwanted effects. Sluggishness, feelings of heaviness, dry mouth, and blurred vision have all been reported, but typically abate with adjustment of dosage and passage of time. Because of their ability to block the action of the neurotransmitter dopamine in the extrapyramidal motor system, these drugs can produce changes in muscle tone, movement, and gait.

By far the most serious side effect of the antipsychotics is tardive dyskinesia. The incidence of this side effect may be as high as 50%. Tardive dyskinesia consists of involuntary, repetitive, jerky, and wormlike (athetoid) movements of the tongue, face, and limbs. It is unlike the other side effects described because it does not occur until the medication has been used for many years, and it is essentially irreversible. Frequent clinical reevaluation is a necessity and the status of the patient's motor system should be assessed frequently.

The antipsychotic drugs appear to interfere to some extent with the normal action of several neurotransmitters. For example, the side effects of blurred vision and dry mouth are due to their anticholinergic action. However, the most commonly accepted theory of the pharmacological basis of the antipsychotic effect of these drugs attributes their action to blockade of transmission in the dopaminergic systems of the brain.

Clinically the minor tranquilizers are used to control neurotic anxiety and psychological tension during acute stressful situations, and, because of their hypnotic effects, to combat insomnia. In addition, they have useful antiepileptic properties. The category of minor tranquilizer usually includes only the propanediols, such as meprobamate (Equanil), and the benzodiazepine derivatives, such as diazepam (Valium), with the term *sedative* being reserved for the barbiturates.

The barbiturates (e.g., amobarbital) were first introduced in the early part of the twentieth century. Pharmacologically they potentiate the inhibitory action of the neurotransmitter gamma-aminobutyric acid (GABA), but also depress all neurons, probably because of their effect on movement of the chlorine ion across neuron cell membranes. At high doses, the vital centers controlling respiration and cardiovascular reflexes are suppressed and death can result. Both accidental death from an overdose of barbiturates, especially when consumed in combination with alcohol, and their use in suicide constitute a significant danger. Moreover tolerance occurs rapidly, as does dependence.

The benzodiazepines were widely introduced into psychiatric practice in the early 1960s. Although they have essentially the same effects as the barbiturates, they are considered to be significantly safer. Unlike the barbiturates, the benzodiazepines do not have direct effects on nerve cell membranes. They produce a powerful potentiation of GABA, and also have their own receptors on neurons in the brain.

PSYCHOPHARMACOLOGY

M. L. WOODRUFF

TRANSACTIONAL ANALYSIS

Transactional analysis (TA) is an interactional therapy grounded in the assumption that people make current decisions based on past premises that at one time might have been appropriate for survival, but frequently are no longer valid. Although TA can be used in individual therapy, it is particularly suitable for groups. The approach emphasizes the cognitive, rational, and behavioral aspects of personality. The basic goal of the therapeutic process is to assist individuals in making new decisions regarding their present behavior and the direction of their lives.

The originator of TA, Eric Berne, based his personality theory on a framework of three separate ego states: parent, adult, and child. Clients are expected to learn how to identify the functioning of their ego states, so that they can make conscious choices as to how they will function in a given situation. Robert Goulding and Mary McClure Goulding have developed a modified version of TA that combines its principles and techniques with those of Gestalt therapy, family therapy, psychodrama, and behavior modification.

Transactional analysis focuses on injunctions, early decisions, strokes, games, rackets, the life script, and redecisions. Children grow up with certain parental messages (or injunctions) given both verbally and nonverbally.

Early decisions are aimed at receiving parental *strokes* (attention from parents). Transactional analysis pays attention to the manner in which people seek recognition and the kinds of strokes they ask for and receive. *Games,* which are a series of ulterior transactions with a predictable outcome and some type of payoff, develop as a way of supporting one's early decisions. Along with learning to detect games, group members learn about their *rackets,* which are the chronic bad feelings that flow from one's early decisions, are collected by people playing games, and justify one's basic decisions.

All of these elements fit into the *life script,* which includes one's expectations of how one's life drama will be played out. Members of TA groups learn how their life scripts influence their feelings, attitudes, and behaviors in the present. The Gouldings' approach to TA rejects the notion that we are passively "scripted" and that we are victims of early conditioning; rather they assert that we make decisions in response to real and imagined parental messages and that we basically "script" ourselves. A major contribution to TA theory and practice is the role of *redecisions.* A basic part of TA practice consists of the *contract* that sets the focus for therapy and determines the basis for therapeutic relationships.

CURRENT PSYCHOTHERAPIES

G. COREY

TRANSCENDENTAL MEDITATION

Various types of meditation have been practiced for over 2500 years. Many Eastern cultures have included forms of meditation as an important part of their religious and spiritual enrichment (e.g., Zen, Yoga).

More recently, the West has taken an interest in the practice of transcendental meditation (TM) as taught by Maharishi Mahesh Yogi.

It is promoted as a means to help increase energy, reduce stress, and have a positive effect on mental and physical health. The actual practice of TM involves sitting upright, with eyes closed, and silently repeating a mantra whenever thoughts occur. The meditation is said to be effortless, enjoyable, and relaxing. The individual is instructed to meditate for 20 minutes in the morning before breakfast and 20 minutes in the evening.

Numerous research reports relative to the effects of TM on physiological and psychological processes have been published. Many of these studies have been criticized for having a poor design or lacking control variables (e.g., controlling for dropout meditators). The following research findings therefore must be viewed with some caution. In 1970, Wallace published a research report that indicated that there is a significant decrease in respiration rate, heart rate, oxygen consumption, and skin conductance during TM. Wallace's findings were supported by several other researchers. West also noted that TM has been shown by several research studies to have a significant effect on electroencephalogram (EEG) readings.

Transcendental meditation has been associated with increases in self-control, happiness, self-actualization, self-concept, and decreases in psychopathology, such as anxiety and depression. West noted that several studies have shown TM practitioners either to stop or dramatically to decrease the usage of nonprescribed drugs. Transcendental meditation has also been used as an adjunct to psychotherapy. Meditation procedures similar to TM have also been used in the treatment of obesity and claustrophobia.

More than 50% of the individuals who begin TM stop practicing it after 1 year of training. There are several explanations for this high dropout rate. Otis noted that a significantly high percentage of neurotic individuals are attracted to TM. They appear to have high expectations and are looking for a quick solution to complicated psychological problems. When TM does not provide them with "the answers," they tend to stop practicing it.

There also may be some dangers associated with TM that could also account for the high dropout rate. For example, TM has been known to cause severe depression, attempted suicide, and schizophrenic breaks. The negative effects of TM most often result with individuals who overmeditate—for 3 hours or more at a time. People who do not overmeditate also may find the practice of TM too stressful. As one meditates, many suppressed and repressed thoughts and feelings may be brought into awareness.

M. S. NYSTUL

TRANSFER OF TRAINING

Transfer consists of some aspect of previous experience affecting subsequent performance. When such an influence occurs it can consist of either positive transfer, which enhances ability, or negative transfer, an impediment to performance.

The classical design for transfer testing is a procedure for determining whether and how subsequent performance is affected. In the experimental condition, subjects are trained in some preliminary activity (A) while controls are not given this experience. The testing phase then measures performance on a second task (B) and the ability of the two groups is compared. Numerous additional transfer designs have been proposed, as have techniques to specify the amount of transfer demonstrated.

Transfer is commonly observed in motor and verbal learning; for example, some positive motor transfer would be expected to accompany learning to play tennis after mastering racketball. Negative motor transfer frequently occurs when attempting to back a car with a trailer attached. Verbal learning has received considerably more attention and such studies indicate that transfer involves both nonspecific and specific components.

Negative transfer occurs when some aspect of previous experience functions to degrade subsequent learning. Thus a performance decrement may occur when identical stimuli are to be associated with differing responses. Negative transfer may also result in a situation in which the desired responses are similar though differing in important aspects.

CONCEPT LEARNING
TRANSPERSONAL PSYCHOLOGY (I)

J. L. FOBES

TRANSPERSONAL PSYCHOLOGY: AN EDITORIAL NOTE

Because of the importance of this topic, which relates to interpenetration of two conceptions and the creation of an emergent between Western and Eastern psychologies, I asked Dr. Norman Sundberg, a psychologist, and Dr. Roger Walsh, a psychiatrist, to write independent entries. They, in turn, took on collaborators, and so the reader is presented with two somewhat overlapping but nevertheless distinctive views of a phenomenon that may have considerable importance not only for psychology, but for humanity as well.

R. J. CORSINI

TRANSPERSONAL PSYCHOLOGY (I)

Transpersonal psychology has a short history but a long past. As a branch of psychology, it appeared in the late 1960s as an outgrowth of humanistic psychology. However, as an area of human concern, transpersonal psychology goes back to prehistoric times. In 1902, William James wrote about transpersonal phenomena. Carl Jung was apparently the first to speak of the "transpersonal unconscious," a term he used interchangeably with "collective unconscious." Many transpersonal psychologists see the emerging tradition as an integration of ancient wisdom and modern science and a rapprochement between Eastern mysticism and Western rationalism.

"Transpersonal" literally means across or beyond the individual person or psyche. It refers to an expansion or extension of consciousness beyond the usual ego boundaries and beyond the limitations of time and/or space and is concerned with aspects of psychology related to "ultimate human capabilities and potentialities that have no systematic place in positivistic or behavioristic theory ('first force') classical psychoanalytic theory ('second force'), or humanistic psychology ('third force')." This emerging "fourth force" covers empirical study, application, and theorization about a wide variety of topics, such as values, unitive consciousness, mysticism, the sacredness of everyday life, cosmic awareness, cosmic play, individual and species-wide synergy, the spiritual paths, theories and practices of meditation, compassion, and transpersonal cooperation. Belief systems are particularly important because they transcend the self and involve identification with the larger values and goals of groups and societies that often motivate a fully developed, unselfish human being. The transpersonal perspective is a metaperspective that suggests looking at the relative merits of different belief systems.

Much of the rationale for transpersonal psychology starts with a questioning of the basis for knowledge in orthodox scientific psychology. The transpersonal position is that there are several ways to obtain and prove knowledge and that there are many states of consciousness, all of which should be of importance for psychology. The altered states of consciousness may have special laws different from those of ordinary waking life. C. T. Tart, who equates the transpersonal with the spiritual, insists on the importance of studying phenomena that are mystical, subjective, and

ephemeral—phenomena that are readily accepted in many cultures. Some psychologists note that these are particularly difficult to describe or study, because they relate to the processing going on in the largely nonverbal, right side of the brain, whereas most science is ultimately communicated linearly in words and numbers.

Even in the natural sciences, transpersonal scientists raise possibilities for explanations of phenomena that differ from the common laws of causality by using such concepts as "formative causation" and "synchronicity." Although many eminent scientists have been intrigued by Jung's concept of synchronicity (a meaningful but acausal confluence of events), it was not until quite recently that science could consider such an unconventional phenomenon—an event outside of a space–time cause-and-effect sequence. This was made possible by dramatic findings in modern physics that presented a world view so radical and far-reaching in its implications as to alter the very foundations of science.

A coherent organization of research and theory in transpersonal psychology is yet to be developed. There are many possibilities for research. One aspect of Yoga that was once considered mystical and untested has already been moved into the "normal" arena of psychology, namely, control over autonomic body functions, which has spawned much research and application in biofeedback. Another common transpersonal topic that seems to be gaining acceptance is meditation. Walsh has reviewed the literature and advocates meditation as an inexpensive, self-regulated, and effective procedure, which may result in the deepest transformation of identity, lifestyle, and relationship to the world.

In alliance with its predecessor, humanistic psychology, transpersonal psychology takes an antireductionistic stance toward the sources of human experience and focuses on the phenomenology of consciousness—especially those states of consciousness that apparently transcend the impression of personal isolation, centrality, and self-sufficiency. As an interdisciplinary and cross-cultural movement, the transpersonal orientation presents many challenges to conventional psychology. With strong support from some areas in modern physics, it also presents many challenges to commonly held views of linearity, causality, fixed space–time relationships, and a purely mechanistic view of the universe. Needless to say, the fringes of transpersonal psychology engender much skepticism.

EAST/WEST PSYCHOLOGY
RELIGION AND PSYCHOLOGY
TRANSPERSONAL PSYCHOLOGY (II)

N. SUNDBERG
C. KEUTZER

TRANSPERSONAL PSYCHOLOGY (II)

Born out of a concern with pathology, Western psychiatry and psychology have only recently begun to turn their attention toward psychological health and well-being. In doing so, they have begun to appreciate that the study of the exceptionally healthy may suggest models of human nature and potential different from those derived from the study of pathology. Much of the new data are inconsistent with traditional models and transpersonal psychology draws on both Western science and Eastern wisdom in an attempt to integrate knowledge from both traditions concerned with the cultivation of psychological well-being.

The term *transpersonal* was adopted to reflect reports given by the exceptionally healthy and those involved in various consciousness disciplines such as meditation and yoga of experiences that extend *trans* (beyond) the *personal* (persona, personality, or ego). Transpersonal psychology emerged in the late 1960s largely out of humanistic psychology. Its emergence was also facilitated by a number of movements in psychology and the culture at large. These included a growing interest in the nature of consciousness and its alterations and the advent of psychedelics. At the same time, interest in Eastern cultures and disciplines was expanding. Gradually there emerged the recognition that certain non-Western psychologies were, in their own ways, as sophisticated as Western psychologies, and were especially concerned with well-being and human potential. The accumulation of empirical research in such areas as biofeedback, altered states of consciousness, and meditation gradually lent research support to the emerging transpersonal perspective—as did modern physics.

Transpersonal psychology recognizes that all psychologies are essentially models and as such that no one model is "the Truth," but rather only a necessarily limited image and pointer of reality. Moreover, it is suggested that these models may be complementary rather than oppositional. Transpersonal psychology is, therefore, particularly interested in broad integrations among psychologies—Eastern and Western, behavioral and dynamic, existential and social.

THE TRANSPERSONAL MODEL

Consciousness

The transpersonal perspective holds that a large spectrum of states of consciousness exists, that some are potentially useful and functionally specific and that some are true higher states. "Higher" is used here in the sense of possessing all the properties and capacities of lower states, plus additional ones. Furthermore, a wide range of literature from a variety of cultures and growth disciplines attests to the attainability of these higher states. However, the traditional Western view holds that a very limited range of states exists, for example, waking, dreaming, intoxication, delirium. Moreover, nearly all altered states are considered detrimental and "normality" is considered optimal.

Motivation

Transpersonal models tend to see motives as hierarchically organized in a manner similar to that first suggested by Maslow, who was the first Western psychologist explicitly to formulate a hierarchical model encompassing "higher" motives. Analogous models can be found in several Eastern psychologies.

The first of these higher motives is self-transcendence, a drive toward modes of experiencing and being that transcend the usual egoic states and limits of experience and identity—the drive toward the transpersonal realms. For the rare person who reaches these levels, such as the prototypic sage, master, or saint of Taoism, Buddhism, Zen, or Hinduism, all egoic identity and motivation are said to have been transcended.

In ascending this hierarchy, motives appear to shift from clearly physiological to apparently more psychological. They also appear to shift from strong to subtle, from prepotent to less potent and more easily disrupted, from deficiency to sufficiency, from egocentric to selfless, from avoidance to approach, from external to internal reinforcement, from field dependence to field independence, from spontaneous to requiring cultivation, from frequent to rare in occurrence in the population, and from older to more recently recognized in Western psychology.

Identity

Western psychologists usually assume that our normal, natural, and optimal identity is egoic. However, Eastern and transpersonal psychologies suggest that our sense of self potentially may be considerably more plastic than we usually recognize.

In addition, a variety of meditative and yogic practices aim at refining awareness and directing it to a microscopic examination of the self-sense. What has been reported for centuries by yogis and more recently by Westerners, including psychologists trained in meditation, is that under this microscopic examination, what was formerly thought to be the solid unchanging ego is recognized as a continuously changing flux of thoughts, images, and emotions. The egoic self-sense is revealed by this precise examination to be fundamentally an illusory product of imprecise awareness, and with the dissolution of the egoic self-sense, broader identification with humanity and the world may occur. In the deepest levels of insight, the highest reaches of transcendence, and the farthest limits of development, the me/not-me, self/other dichotomy is said to break down completely, resulting in a complete loss of egocentricity and a sense of identification with all people and all things.

PSYCHOTHERAPY

With its interest in exceptional degrees of well-being, the domain of transpersonal psychotherapy may extend beyond traditional therapeutic goals and adjustments. In acknowledging a greater potential for psychological well-being, it aims to afford those individuals who are ready to do so the opportunity of working at transpersonal levels.

Transpersonal psychotherapy, therefore, tends to be eclectic. Ideally, a transpersonal therapist would have available a broad range of techniques and approaches from traditional Western psychotherapies as well as skills such as meditation and yoga. In addition to eclecticism and adaptability, a transpersonal therapist would also be expected to be familiar with the potential for inducing states, experiences, and degrees of well-being beyond normal ego development.

SUPPORTIVE DATA

The transpersonal model is derived from and derives support from a convergent network of concepts derived, in turn, from overlapping aspects of several Western psychologies, Eastern psychologies and philosophies, states of consciousness, meditation, biofeedback, recent theorizing on health, and, perhaps, modern physics. Empirical data are as yet distressingly sparse, although no less so than in most other schools of psychology. There are considerable data on meditation, some on altered states of consciousness, and very little on exceptionally healthy individuals.

LIMITATIONS

First, there is clearly an inadequate empirical foundation. In addition, transpersonal models have not yet been widely integrated with other Western psychologies and therapies.

Transpersonal psychology may also be facing the two-edged sword of popularity. Increasing numbers of people are being attracted to it, some of whom do not appear to display an adequate rigor of theory and practice.

To anyone who has explored the transpersonal realms and experiences in depth, it is apparent that an adequate personal experiential foundation is clearly necessary for both deep intellectual comprehension and skillful therapy. Since the transpersonal realms and potentials for growth are so vast, far exceeding the explorations of most, it is probably safe to say that the limits of our personal understanding and growth represent one of the major limiting factors for this field.

EAST/WEST PSYCHOLOGY
RELIGION AND PSYCHOLOGY
TRANSPERSONAL PSYCHOLOGY (I)

R. WALSH
E. E. VAUGHAN

TRANSSEXUALISM

Transsexualism is a psychosexual disorder failing under the category of gender identity disorders.

The term *gender identity* refers to the person's sense of being male or female. In *gender identity disorders*, however, the individual (a) feels discomfort and inappropriateness about his or her anatomic sex, and (b) persistently engages in behaviors generally associated with the other sex.

It must be emphasized here that gender identity disorders do *not* refer to feelings of inadequacy about one's male or female role. In gender identity disorders, people feel that through a cruel trick of nature they have been placed in the body of one sex while actually belonging to the other.

More specifically then *transsexualism* is essentially characterized by a chronic sense of discomfort and inappropriateness about one's anatomic sex accompanied by a persistent wish to be rid of one's genitals and to live as a member of the other sex. The course of this disorder is chronic and almost invariably is evident in childhood; that is, the person always felt this way throughout his or her development. Frequently these individuals will complain that they are uncomfortable wearing the clothing of their anatomic sex, a feeling that often results in cross-dressing. Transsexuals also frequently engage in activities which, at least in terms of cultural sex-role stereotypes, are more closely associated with the opposite sex. But most of all, transsexuals yearn to be members of the opposite sex.

Males are more common than females among those persons seeking treatment for this disorder, with the estimated ratios varying from 8:1 down to 2:1. Three major types of developmental histories for transsexualism can be distinguished—asexual, homosexual, and heterosexual.

SOME DISTINCTIONS OF TRANSSEXUALISM

Transsexualism is sometimes confused with certain other conditions, so some distinctions are in order. First, it differs from *transvestism.* Although cross-dressing is involved in both psychosexual disorders, it is associated with sexual arousal in transvestism whereas in transsexualism it is not. Second, transsexualism is not the same thing as *homosexuality.* Moreover, comparisons of transsexuals and homosexuals reveal clear differences between the two groups in preferred sex objects and sexual fantasies. Third, although they insist that they are really members of the opposite sex, transsexuals are not suffering from delusions.

SURGICAL TREATMENT OF TRANSSEXUALISM

Since psychotherapeutic treatment of transsexualism has generally proved ineffective, more and more of these individuals have been requesting surgical sex reassignment. In the mid 1970s, it was estimated that more than 2500 Americans had had their sex altered surgically.

In males, this operation essentially consists of removal of the male organs and their replacement with an artificial vagina composed of the same tissue. In many cases, the vagina functions quite satisfactorily, even to the point of allowing the surgically transformed woman to experience orgasm. Frequent sex hormone injections are needed to stimulate breast development, create more feminine skin texture, and diminish beard growth. In females, breasts, ovaries, vagina, and uterus are surgically removed, and an artificial penis is substituted. The penis does not function normally, however, and the transformed man will also be sterile after surgery.

The follow-up studies of sex-change operations generally report favorable outcomes. That is, a majority of transsexuals are quite satisfied with the outcome and in no case wish to return to their original anatomic sex. Clearly, however, candidates for this surgery need to be carefully screened to be certain that they are actually transsexuals and are not suffering instead from some other psychological disturbance.

HUMAN SEXUALITY
TRANSVESTISM

D. J. ZIEGLER

TRANSVESTISM

In the psychosexual disorder of *transvestism,* there is recurrent and persistent cross-dressing by a heterosexual male for the purposes of his own sexual arousal. That is, the man achieves sexual satisfaction simply by putting on women's clothing, although masturbation (and heterosexual intercourse) is often engaged in once the individual is attired in female garb. Although anxiety, depression, guilt, and shame are often associated with the desire to cross-dress, the transvestite continues to do so because of the considerable satisfaction derived from the practice.

While transvestism is a comparatively rare disorder, some research has been conducted on it. To illustrate, it has been found that the "typical" transvestite is probably married (about two-thirds are), and if married, has children (about two-thirds do). Moreover, the overwhelming majority of transvestites assert that they are exclusively heterosexual, with the most common transvestic behavior consisting of privately cross-dressing at home in secret. Concerning their psychological makeup, transvestites as a group are no more neurotic or psychotic than matched control groups, although they do tend to be more controlled in impulse expression, more inhibited in interpersonal relationships, more dependent, and less involved with other people. Interestingly, more than three-fourths of transvestites consider themselves to be a different personality when cross-dressed, perhaps experiencing in female clothing a significant facet of their psychological makeup that cannot otherwise be expressed.

Finally, transvestism needs to be distinguished from transsexualism, fetishism, and homosexuality, since each of these is sometimes confused with this disorder. In *transsexualism,* there is a chronic sense of discomfort and inappropriateness about one's anatomic sex, a persistent wish to be rid of one's own genitals, a desire to live as a member of the opposite sex, and never any sexual arousal associated with cross-dressing; the great majority of transvestites consider themselves male, with erotic arousal being centered on dressing in women's clothing. Although articles of female clothing are involved in both *fetishism* and transvestism, fetishists do not dress in them whereas transvestites do. Finally, while some male *homosexuals* may occasionally cross-dress to attract another male or to masquerade in theatrical fashion as a woman, the act itself is not sexually stimulating for them. For transvestites, the cross-dressing itself is the focal point of sexual stimulation, and no attempt is made to invite the sexual attention of other males.

TRANSSEXUALISM

D. J. ZIEGLER

TREATMENT OUTCOME

The single most important issue in the scientific study of treatment is evaluation of effectiveness. The difficulties of conducting outcome research are monumental and have not been adequately solved. These difficulties in evaluative research must be understood in terms of four components. The first difficulty is contributed by the disorder itself and is the result of diagnostic inaccuracies, the self-limiting nature of the illness, the chronicity of many conditions, the periodicity of normally occurring exacerbations and remissions, and the general vagueness of the syndromes.

The second problem is in the area of defining what treatment is. Definitions range from viewing all events and experiences as treatment to the opposite approach of narrowly defining therapy as something done to an individual by someone with a specified degree or license. There is also great difficulty in accounting for differences in experience and skill among therapists in designing treatment outcome research.

The third factor that casts a giant shadow over all outcome studies is the public prejudice in popular psychology, economics, and politics.

No field of scientific inquiry is as burdened with these issues as is therapy outcome studies.

The final difficulty is in the way in which goals have been defined. The intrusion of customs, values, and societal and subcultural norms thoroughly confounds scientific design. In addition to these general areas of difficulty, the methodological problems of handling a large number of variables, and the necessary limitations on doing human research involving the lives of individuals over long periods of time, make it quite clear that the perfect research design, one resulting in definitive answers, is still considerably beyond the state of the art of outcome research in the 1980s.

THE DISORDER

To evaluate the effectiveness of any treatment intervention, it is necessary to understand and recognize the natural history of a disorder. We do have a wide variety of treatment interventions thought to be helpful in the hands of a variety of practitioners, which must be evaluated in terms of effectiveness against each other and against the null hypothesis. If the disorders are self-limiting, as with depression, this fact must be taken into account in outcome research. Much of the nonsense in the literature is the result of failing to do so.

The picture is even more complicated when studying a lifelong periodic illness such as schizophrenia. The natural history of the illness shows that the patient experiences periods of exacerbation and remission throughout most of life regardless of the kind of treatment received. If the patient improves, it is easy to fall into the research trap of assuming that whatever one was doing at the time the patient got better is the treatment that worked. Because many of the emotional and mental disabilities have as yet no demonstrable etiology and no clear biological window, it is difficult to be diagnostically precise.

THERAPY

The problem of defining treatment and identifying the specific variables that represent the significant interventions is complex. It is impossible to alter variables singly, or even to define all of the variables introduced in treatment interventions. Carefully designed placebo studies have shown how difficult it is to tease apart the psychological and pharmacological factors of medication response. There is much evidence to show that the effectiveness of a particular medication in the hands of one physician is statistically significantly different from the effectiveness of the same medication in the hands of another. The difference lies in the personality of the physician and the ability of the therapist to form a therapeutic alliance with the patient in producing a hopeful expectancy.

In psychotherapy, the multitude of variables is even greater. The nonspecifics of psychotherapy—including the personality of the therapist, the personality match of the patient and the therapist involved in the therapeutic alliance, hope, expectancy, and prior experience—are all part of the psychotherapy alchemy. Recent research has shown that there are psychotherapeutic therapists who can effectively function within the theoretical framework of a variety of approaches to treatment and who can use a variety of techniques effectively.

POLITICAL AND ECONOMIC ISSUES

When health care delivery becomes one of the largest industries in a country, the issues become economical and political rather than scientific. Unions, licensing and certification boards, and professional associations are involved in dividing up the economic pie. Therapy outcome in such a climate becomes less a scientific issue and more a political and economic debate.

Economic issues are an important part of outcome research. It is clear that society cannot afford unlimited resources for health care delivery.

If the resources are limited, how shall these be distributed? If these decisions are not to be made on the basis of political practice or economic pressure groups, then they must be based on cost effectiveness of treatment. Thus, cost effectiveness has now become an appropriate concern for outcome research.

GOALS

It is difficult but essential to be clear in the statement and definition of goals. Recent improvements in defining goals and measuring goal attainment have done much to improve outcome research design. In the past, treatment outcome research has been hampered by the vagueness of goals. Only now are we beginning to look at specific behavioral goals that can be observed as benchmarks in psychotherapy outcome research. These goals can be clearly defined and thoroughly understood by both the patient and the therapist. We have techniques to measure them, and even to quantify them.

Goals to some extent are determined by cultural norms. Should these be part of the treatment transaction? Is it the task of therapy to help the individual to adapt and fit in, or is it the task to help in being comfortable while being unadapted? In some therapeutic systems, a distinction is made between maladaptation and unadaptation that addresses this specific point. How do we take this into account in treatment outcome research?

METHODS AND TECHNIQUES OF RESEARCH

Methodological approaches are available that begin to approximate useful methodology for outcome research. What is needed, and what we are beginning to see, is increased precision and better techniques in addressing the four areas of ambiguity outlined. We are seeing much better precision and diagnosis. The development of specific measurable biological windows is near and will add tremendously to the researcher's ability to conduct outcome studies.

We can be much more precise in the definition of therapy. The nonspecific variables do exist and must be taken into account. With appropriate modern statistical techniques, and with a clear recognition of their presence in all therapies, these nonspecifics can be factored out, thus allowing us to compare the portion of the result that is specific for the treatment.

The largest improvement in outcome research has been made by a much improved attention to goals. Techniques for problem defining and goal stating have been clearly described in recent literature, and a number of approaches to quantification developed.

EFFECTIVENESS COMPONENTS OF PSYCHOTHERAPY PSYCHOTHERAPY RESEARCH

W. M. MENDEL

TWO-PROCESS LEARNING THEORY

The central premise of two-process learning theory is that the laws of classical and instrumental conditioning are not functionally equivalent. During the first half of this century, the general trend was to treat classical and instrumental learning according to a single set of principles. Nevertheless, even during its formative period, learning theory had expressed an alternative view: As early as 1928, S. Miller and K. Konorski had distinguished between two forms of conditioned response: Type I was Pavlov's secretary conditioned response (CR); it was formed by establishing a positive correlation between the CS and the unconditioned stimulus (US). The other, Type II, differed from the classical CR in that its occurrence was dependent on its consequences. Despite the early work of Konorski and others regarding the adequacy of uniprocess theories of learning, not until drive reduction theory encountered theoretical problems in dealing with avoidance learning did two-process theory emerge to challenge the prevailing view. For drive reduction theory, the motive for the avoidance response derived from the aversive unconditioned stimulus and the reinforcement of a successful response resulted from the termination of the aversive event. However, since the avoidance response prevents the US from occurring, the theory cannot account for how avoidance behavior is learned or maintained.

O. H. Mowrer's resolution of this problem was to propose that avoidance learning was the result of two processes. Fear instigated avoidance behavior and the behavior was maintained by fear reduction. In particular, classical conditioning served to establish the fear reaction to the CS by virtue of the contiguity of the CS and US. This position contrasted sharply with that of C. L. Hull, who had argued that the cessation of an aversive US was reinforcing. Mowrer had designated contiguity as the crucial process in classical conditioning. By contrast, reinforcement, a process common to instrumental learning, determined the selection of avoidance responses. Cast in this form, two-process theory assigned considerable importance to classical conditioning; the processes established by these procedures function either as motivators or as reinforcers to mediate instrumental behavior.

J. B. Trapold and M. A. Overmier have questioned the notion that classical and instrumental training procedures establish distinct Pavlovian and instrumental processes. They suggest instead the adoption of a neutral terminology, namely, response-independent and response-dependent learning. One implication of this usage is that response-independent learning is not necessarily a result of classical conditioning; another implication is that there is a greater reciprocity between the two forms of learning. Not only may response-independent learning affect the acquisition or the maintenance of response-dependent learning, but the representation formed during response-dependent learning may interact with the subsequent formation of stimulus–stimulus associations.

Although the current conceptual status of two-process theory is still in flux, many theorists argue that response-independent and response-dependent learning obey the same laws. They differ, however, in the sorts of associations established by the two training procedures. Classical conditioning promotes the formation of stimulus–stimulus associations, while instrumental conditioning results in the establishment of response–stimulus representations. This conceptual schema does not enjoy a substantial empirical base.

LEARNING THEORIES

E. J. RICKERT

U

THE UNCONSCIOUS

The unconscious is a hypothetical construct used to describe behaviors, phenomena, material, processes, and so on out of immediate awareness. Prior to Sigmund Freud, this concept had been used to explain a variety of behaviors such as dissociation and "mesmerism" or early trancework. Freud initiated using the formal term *unconscious*. Later, Milton H. Erickson and Ernest L. Rossi refined it via Ericksonian hypnotherapy and state-dependent memory learning and behavior systems or the mind–body approaches.

There are a variety of definitions and views of the unconscious, depending on one's theoretical background. The concept is difficult to define, and English and English found 39 distinct meanings.

HISTORICAL VIEWS

Because there is a variety of conceptualizations of the unconscious, a historical overview is appropriate.

Psychoanalysis

Sigmund Freud was the first modern-day theorist to explore personality in depth. One of his observations involved the unconscious. He divided awareness into three levels: (a) conscious awareness, (b) preconscious awareness, and (c) unconscious awareness. Conscious awareness is considered to include any materials, experiences, learnings, perceptions, feelings, or thoughts in immediate awareness. The preconscious—an intermediate level—consists of any materials that enter conscious awareness. The unconscious comprises all repressed thoughts, feelings, behaviors, memories, experiences, learnings, and so on remains totally out of aware-

ness. Defense mechanisms are considered to be unconscious dynamics that protect the ego by denying and distorting reality. The unconscious also has repressed sexual impulses—instincts, instincts, id impulses, wishes, dreams, and psychological conflicts.

Hypnotic and Ericksonian Views

Milton H. Erickson worked directly and indirectly with various processes of the unconscious. Erickson's view of the unconscious was developed through trancework. His view of the unconscious consisted of a reservoir of past memories, a storehouse of learning patterned from experiences. The unconscious is considered to be a positive constructive force by Erickson. Through the work of Erickson and others, the trance state has been connected to unconscious or subconscious functioning.

Trance is considered to provide a direct access to or a window into the unconscious process. Specific trance behaviors include age regression (remembering past memories without prior conscious recollection), age progression (experiencing futuristic scenarios before the actual events occur), hidden observer phenomena (imagining watching oneself doing something), dissociation, catalepsy (muscular suspension or immobility and rigidity in the limbs, based on concentration-suggestion), ideodynamic or psychomotor behaviors (involuntary behavioral movements—finger movements, hand movements, etc. out of the ordinary conscious awareness), autohypnosis, anesthesia (by suggestion and concentration), amnesia, automatic writing, imagery, time distortion, eye closure, and relaxation. Lankton and Lankton, furthered the Ericksonian view of the unconscious by emphasizing a right hemispheric physiological base along with behaviors such as spatial modes, pantamine (nonverbal movement), involuntary movements, imagery, sensory modalities, intuition, artistic-creative tendencies, literalism, psychophysiological functioning, music, symbolic representations-meanings, rhythmic patterning, and spontaneity.

Ernest L. Rossi took a psychophysiological view of the unconscious along with previously stated Ericksonian views. He postulated that the key not only to unconscious process but also to the issue of causality is state-dependent memory learning and behavior (SDML and B) systems. Rossi described state-dependent memory as "what is learned and remembered is dependent on one's psycho-physiological state at the time of the experience."

The SDML and B system is considered to stem from the limbic–hypothalmic system, which regulates much of human behavior and brain activity through information substances or messenger molecules. These regulatory processes are the substance of the unconscious. Rossi further contended that behaviors and/or learning consist of encoding perceptions into state-dependent memories at the limbic–hypothalmic level. More specifically, learning, memories, and/or perceptions are transduced into information via molecular processes within the brain, whereas sensory input is transduced through cellular interaction. This, then, is primarily the basis of the unconscious processsses. Rossi also related this with psychophysiological rhythms (circadian and ultradian cycles). Ultradian cycles are the natural rest cycles that facilitate natural rest states. These cycles provide a window into the unconscious. As an example, Rossi emphasized the similarities between ultradian cycles (20 minutes natural rest period occurring every 90 to 120 minutes) and trance states. These 20-minute periods are called basic rest activity cycles, in which the mind and body can be rejuvenated.

APPLICATIONS

Among the applications of the concept of the unconscious are changing behaviors and resolving problems. To accomplish these goals, the unconscious must be accessed and used. People are generally self-programmed through a series of choices based on a variety of experiences. Many problems are self-programmed at unconscious levels (unconscious choices or choices made at unconscious levels) and need to be reprogrammed at unconscious levels. Some methods of accessing and using the unconscious are internal visualization or imagery, fantasy and daydreams, dreams, self-talk, music, art, body rhythms (basic rest activity cycles), relaxation, and hypnotic techniques.

Imagery is the internal visualization of some image or scenario, with a theme and goal. Imagery enhances fantasies, dreams, and daydreams and adds a reality element to the experience. Similarly, imagination is related to imagery along with fantasy and dreams. By using imagery, fantasy, and daydreams, one gains the experience that something actually happened. When using imagery and/or imagination or fantasy, one should use sensory modes (auditory or hearing, kinesthetic or movement, taste, and smell). To prepare for upcoming events, one should develop a detailed image and/or scenario of the event and rehearse the scenario over and over, imagining successfully completing the task.

Araoz suggested that self-talk is a type of hypnotic suggestion that self-programs one's mind at an unconscious or subconscious level. By monitoring one's self-talk or self-statements and changing them, one can reprogram one's unconscious belief systems.

Another way to access unconscious processes and change dysfunctional behavior is through hypnosis and relaxation techniques that can directly access unconscious processes. Most people drift in and out of trance states all day long. These naturalistic trance states are considered part of the ultradian rest cycles. For more information on hypnotic techniques, see Hammond; Erickson, Rossi, and Rossi; Carich; Kroger; and Araoz.

Rossi emphasized the importance of the body's naturalistic rhythms. Rossi broke this into biomolecular exchanges of "housekeeping" genes (genes that regulate human metabolism). The unconscious can be accessed by taking advantage of these rest cycles.

Music, often a soothing method of relaxation, also can be a motivator and a stimulating source of creativity. Both music and art can serve as pathways to the unconscious, if one has learned to be receptive. Literally, most music and art work involve unconscious elements.

AUTOMATIC THOUGHTS
BLOCKING
DISPOSITIONAL SETS
FORGETTING
HYPNOSIS
MEMORY
STRUCTURAL INTELLECT MODEL

M. S. CARICH

UNCONSCIOUS INFERENCE

Since the beginning of experimental psychology, there has been a strong current of support for cognitive theories of perception, in which something like problem solving lies at the heart of the perceptual process. In Hermann von Helmholtz's original formulation, one perceives the object or event that would, under normal conditions, be most likely to produce the same impression on the nervous system.

In the past, arguments in opposition to the notion of unconscious inference were centered on specific issues and themselves included some element of contribution by perceptual system of the viewer. For example, in explaining the perception of an object's surface color, Ewald Hering rejected unconscious inference but admitted "memory colors"; and in explaining size and position constancy, the Gestalt psychologists rejected unconscious inference but admitted "laws of organization" supplied by the visual system of the brain. A much more radical and parsimonious alternative to unconscious inference was argued by J. J. Gibson, who maintains that our perceptions are direct responses to the information afforded to our perceptual system. For example, there is information in the stimulation that directly specifies the object's distance, and there is information that directly specifies the object's size, and there is no need for the viewer to use the information about distance in perceiving size.

We do not yet know whether the kind of information discussed by this "direct theory" is in fact used widely, or even used at all. We do know, however, that perceptual couplings can be demonstrated even when there is no possibility of attributing the relationship to information in the stimulus array and that the depth cues can be shown to be effective.

One might argue (as J. J. Gibson does) that unconscious inference will manifest itself only when stimulus information is for some reason inadequate—which leaves unconscious inference on the theoretical agenda in any case. Because as an explanation it subsumes so many other phenomena, many psychologists subscribe to some version of this notion. But even if we retain the Helmholtzian metaphor, the nature of the process of unconscious inferences, and of its premises, remains unexplicated. The nature of mental structure, central to the conception of unconscious inference and to any general theory of perception, remains to be explicated. Until it is, we are dealing only with a persuasive notion, and not with a predictive or a testable theory.

UNIVERSAL HEALTH CARE

Equal access to adequate health care for all Americans regardless of socioeconomic status, is an old idea that has received vigorous new interest in the 1990s. It is a nagging controversy that has spanned the six decades from 1932 to 1992. Defying resolution, it has rendered the United States the last industrialized nation to lack a nationalized health system and has resulted in a patchwork quilt of measures enacted over several decades that health economists regard as a nonsystem. The last decade of the twentieth century saw 30 to 40 million Americans who did not qualify for welfare, yet were too poor to afford health insurance. Almost half of these were children, which caused most Americans to change their attitudes about health insurance. By 1992, national polls showed that 70% of all Americans favored a government-sponsored national health insurance. This is the first time a majority of the people were so inclined.

The movement first received serious attention in the 1930s. Called "socialized medicine," it was vigorously opposed by the American Medical Association (AMA) over the next two decades, during which time it failed to obtain serious public support.

A movement for a nationalized health system emerged in the mid-1960s and throughout most of the 1970s. Advocates abandoned the term *socialized medicine* and championed the same concept of government-sponsored health care with the term *national health insurance.* This also was opposed by the AMA, but with less success. This second period of interest in a nationalized health care system resulted in the enactment of several federal health programs, though national health insurance itself did not come close to becoming a reality. Important programs are Medicare and Medicaid (Titles XVIII and XIX of the Social Security Act), which bring health care to the elderly and the indigent. The Hill-Burton Act stimulated the growth and expansion of hospitals throughout the nation, and the CHAMPUS legislation brought health care to the dependents of personnel in the armed forces. The HMO Act stimulated the founding of health maintenance organizations and helped usher in the era of managed care in the 1980s. The Veterans Administration received new vigor following the Korean and Vietnam wars.

These legislations resulted in public and private health schemes that fell short of a universal health system. Yet by 1992, the sum total of all government-sponsored health programs accounted for more than 50 cents of every health care dollar spent in the United States.

Although the United States had yet to adopt a universal health care system at the beginning of the last decade of the twentieth century, Hawaii enacted legislation to make health care available to all its residents. The state law requires all employers of a certain size to provide health insurance for their employees and establishes a category of the medically needy—persons who do not qualify for welfare but are too poor to afford health insurance. These are provided Medicaid benefits without necessarily participating in other aspects of the welfare system.

In 1987, Massachusetts enacted a similar system. However, the condition of the Massachusetts economy prevented implementation of this enactment, and Hawaii, as of 1992, was the only state with a universal health care system.

At the beginning of the 1990s, there emerged an awareness that there was a crisis in the U.S. health care system and that changes had to be made in terms of increasing access and controlling the inflation rate in providing those services. More than 400 bills were introduced into the 101st Congress designed to reform the health care system. In spite of the large number of bills pending in 1992, interest in universal health care crystallized into three main proposals: (a) an expanded employment-based insurance model as recommended by the (Claude) Pepper Commission, (b) a consumer-oriented model as preferred by the Heritage Foundation, and (c) a single-pay model in which the government would be the only payer for all health services.

The employment-based insurance model was intended to expand the private sector to cover the approximately 35 million Americans without coverage. Employers would be required either to provide coverage for their employees or to pay into a government fund. Because employers would be required to insure their employees ("play") or pay into a government fund, this proposal was dubbed the play-or-pay model.

The Heritage Foundation proposed the privatization of all health care in America. Consumers would choose from a large variety of competing private health care delivery systems, and the only role for the government in this "consumer-oriented" plan would be to pay the monthly insurance premium for the unemployed. Eventually, even Medicare and Medicaid would be dismantled. This concept would seek to reduce health costs by a highly competitive private system.

The third major proposal would make the government the only payer for all health care. There would be no role for the private sector other than providing supplemental benefits.

Whereas polls indicated that for the first time the majority of Americans favor nationalized health care, these same polls revealed that Americans were unprepared to accept increases in taxes and health care rationing. Every nation that had adopted universal health care has found that the tax burden became oppressive.

Members of Congress who grappled with health care issues looked to a system of government sponsorship of privatized care. Even those European nations with long-standing nationalized health systems sponsored experiments intended to bring back some measure of privatization. Confronting the 101st Congress was the budget deficit. Because of the lack of public funds and the inflation rate of health care costs, some experts saw managed care companies, which grew dramatically throughout the 1980s, poised to become the vehicle for universal health care.

With the beginning of the last decade of the twentieth century, all sectors of the economy, including organized medicine, agreed that reform of the health system was necessary. The controversy arose as to what shape this reform should take. Practitioners wanted to decide what and when health care should be dispensed. Hospitals wanted to be reimbursed for costs. Insurance companies favored a competitive bidding for all sectors of the system. But all sectors of the economy were in agreement that access to health care was the most critical issue facing the system.

The Health Care Financing Administration (HCFA) conducted a 6-year study of health care patterns in 36,000 welfare recipients as contrasted with 75,000 federal employees. It found that the employed population readily used health care services. In contrast, welfare recipients found access to the system to be difficult.

The study also confirmed the findings of a number of previous studies with employed populations that a comprehensive health system that includes a psychological benefit will increase access to health care and reduce medical costs by treating stress-related somatization with psychotherapy, a phenomenon known as medical offset. By 1990, a consensus had emerged that any comprehensive health care delivery system must include an equally comprehensive psychological component, otherwise the medical component would be overburdened by the 60%

of physician visits that reflect stress and somatization rather than physical disease.

History has taught psychology a valuable lesson. When Medicare was implemented in 1965, psychology was not included among the list of qualified providers. It took 25 years of active lobbying before the Congress adopted legislation in 1990 that specifically named psychology and social work as providers under Medicare. In anticipation of the eventual adoption of some form of universal health care, in 1990, the American Psychological Association launched a vigorous campaign to ensure that any system adopted would include a comprehensive psychological component.

BEHAVIORAL MEDICINE
MANAGED MENTAL HEALTH CARE
MENTAL HEALTH PROGRAMS
MENTAL HEALTH TEAMS
NEEDS ASSESSMENT
PUBLIC POLICY
SOCIAL CASEWORK
TREATMENT UTILITY

N. A. CUMMINGS

UNOBTRUSIVE MEASURES

Unobtrusive measures usually refer to dependent variables in a study that do not have subject reactivity. That is, the unobtrusive measure does not change the subject's response because the subject is usually unaware of the measure. Interest in unobtrusive measures increased after studies were published in the 1960s that demonstrated the pervasiveness of experimental artifacts such as the experimenter expectancy effect, evaluation apprehension, the volunteer subject effect, and the social desirability (good subject) effect. Furthermore, unobtrusive measures usually require very little modification of the natural environment so that results from studies using unobtrusive measures are more generalizable than results from a highly instrumental laboratory. Unobtrusive measures fit in handily with field studies often designed in social psychology. In short, unobtrusive measures trade off complete control over the dependent variable for ease of generalizability.

Physical traces include floor wear, waste baskets, missing pages, and location of objects. Archives include library records, speeches, budgets, films, and the use of records and patents. Simple observation includes nonverbal measures and location. Hardware includes photography, informal sensitive films, ultrasonic devices, movement recorders, photoelectric cells, and transmitters of various kinds.

One of the difficulties of using many of the unobtrusive measures is the dross rate, which is the volume of useless data (and time spent collecting it) often measured to get at the needed piece of information. The best use of nonreactive measures is not in lieu of the typical laboratory response measure, but in combination with it in another setting so as to support or dispute the generalizability of the laboratory studies.

MEASUREMENT

L. BERGER

UNSTRUCTURED THERAPY GROUPS

Unstructured therapy groups are used to help people work through personal problems and learn to develop intimate and caring interpersonal relationships. An unstructured therapy group may be defined as a group in which the facilitator uses no group exercises and the facilitator and members are free to express any feelings they desire. Unstructured therapy groups can be conducted successfully with a variety of populations. The dynamics of unstructured therapy groups conducted with different populations consist of elements common to these groups across populations.

LEADER CHARACTERISTICS

Yalom states that the leaders of therapy groups are responsible for highlighting significant group issues and for supporting the development of a cohesive group atmosphere characterized by interpersonal honesty and warmth. The facilitators of unstructured therapy groups additionally should be comfortable when the members express intense, and often negative, feelings about various subjects.

GROUP STAGES

Generally, unstructured therapy groups proceed through a series of stages that allow the members to gain trust and to benefit from participating. The following description represents one way of depicting the stages of unstructured therapy groups. Most groups conducted for ten or more sessions progress through a majority of these stages, although the order of the stages and the amount of time spent in each may vary.

Socializing Stage

During this stage the members generally discuss topics, such as the weather, related to the feelings of the members. At this stage the leader can encourage the members to discuss more personal topics.

Mistrust of Authority

As the members gain trust in the group, they will often first express anger toward outside authority figures and then will express anger directly to the group facilitator. At this stage, the facilitator can encourage members to express the anger they feel toward the leader openly and honestly in the group.

Self-Revelation

As the participants learn that they can freely express intense feelings during the group, they begin to disclose personal problems. The facilitator at this stage might encourage other members to discuss similar situations. They may be encouraged first to express the feelings they have about a problem and then to explore how they might best handle this problem.

New Ways of Relating

As different members begin to self-disclose in the group, most participants become concerned about the welfare of the other members. They begin to give more direct feedback to each other. The facilitator may help members learn how to give and receive appropriate feedback. Facilitators additionally need to be open to receiving feedback from the members.

Ending Stage

When unstructured therapy groups end, or when a member leaves the group, many of the members and the leader feel a sense of loss, and it is often appropriate for them openly to express such feelings of sadness. When a member is about to leave the group, the other participants and leader might review what the member learned in the group that can be applied outside.

GROUP PSYCHOTHERAPY

R. C. PAGE

VARIABLES IN RESEARCH

Kerlinger defines a variable as a "symbol to which numerals or values are assigned." This generic definition applicable, albeit, to psychological variables in research denotes a mathematical base. Any variable, *x* or *y*, therefore infers one of the four basic measurements scales: nominal, ordinal, interval, or ratio. The nature, type, and number of variables available to the researcher are numerous and variable. Their relative contributions in research investigations are not fixed but are related primarily to the experimental design(s) involved in the research study. Hence it is difficult, if not impossible, to order the research variables being discussed in this section with respect to importance or frequency of use or, as a matter of fact, any other categorical designation. The discussion of variables that follows should be reviewed in this context.

RESEARCH VARIABLES

Initially, variables are classified into one of two broad categories: those considered to be continuous and those considered to be discrete. Continuous variables can be measured along a continuum on points that are graduated (e.g., from low to high). These variables are those that are ordinarily measured by the interval or ratio scale. Examples in psychological research are scores on standardized tests, grade-point averages, and galvanic skin response. Discrete variables are categorical in nature, ordered or unordered, and measured by the nominal scale. Unlike continuous variables in which magnitude is involved in their measurement, discrete variables are evaluated simply in terms of either/or. Examples are gender, race, ethnic origin, and religious affiliation. A special note regarding discrete variables is that they may be classified into true dichotomies (e.g., male–female), true polytomies (e.g., eye color: brown, blue, and hazel), arbitrary dichotomies (e.g., pass–fail), or arbitrary polytomies (e.g., yes–no–undecided). Continuous variables are referred to as quantitative variables; discrete ones are qualitative variables.

Another important classification is of independent–dependent variables. The independent variable in a research study is presumed to be the cause of the dependent variable. Like variables, in general, these have a mathematical base. In the equation, $y = f(x)$, the dependent variable, *y*, is a function of the independent variable, *x*. This means that the outcome (*y*) depends on the manipulation of the *x* variable. In this context, it may be surmised that other variables exist in research: ones that may be manipulated and those that are not (nonmanipulated variables). Variables manipulated by the researcher are characteristic of a true experimental design. Those not manipulated are typical in a pseudoexperimental design or a correlational study in which attention is focused simply on the relationship extant between the independent and dependent variables. Kerlinger refers to these variables as active and attribute ones, respectively. Both types of variables assume an important and necessary role in research design in that they serve interactively to control extraneous systematic variance and minimize error variance in the experiment. This fact brings up the issue of drawing long-standing erroneous conclusions from faulty experiments. A classic example is the famous (or infamous, depending on which side of the fence the critic stands) Hawthorne experiments. The so-called Hawthorne effect—the unexpected impact of non-manipulated variables on manipulated ones—has since 1932 been accepted by researchers as an effect based on correct interpretations. Yet many researchers have been unaware that serious questions began to be raised in the 1940s about faulty designs involving the variables in the experiments that Kerlinger calls active and attribute that may have led to erroneous conclusions. Gillespie has written an extensive history of the Hawthorne experiments that should serve to clarify issues relating to the proper use of variables in research.

INTERVENING VARIABLES

It is well known within the discipline of psychology, and even beyond, that purely psychological attributes are elusive to the human senses; they are merely inferred concepts or constructs. As such they cannot be directly observed and measured; their latent manifestations in behavior can only be inferred from measurements of observable variables. Such attributes–constructs as assertiveness, sociability, and lability are rather elusive concepts, because they defy definite description in behavioral terms. However, observable variables relating to them play important roles in psychological research. Such variables are referred to as intervening variables, according to Tolman who first coined the term. Inferences regarding the presence and/or magnitude of intervening variables are presumed through the interpretation of such measures as psychological test scores and protocols designed to assess these constructs.

SPECIFIC TYPES OF VARIABLES

As stated earlier, innumerable variables can become involved in research designs. In addition to the more general ones discussed previously are many specific to the design of the experiments. Prominent among these are the following.

Predictor Variables. These are usually continuous variables used in the independent set of regression equations in correlational analyses. Most commonly the statistical methods involving such variables are multiple regression, canonical, and discriminant function analyses.

Predicted Variables. These are continuous or discrete variables, depending on the statistical method used, that represent the dependent variable(s) in the prediction equation(s). They are often called criterion variables.

Dummy Variables. On occasion a researcher may choose or be obliged, for some legitimate reason, to change a continuous variable to a discrete one, either independent or dependent. It also may occur that the researcher might wish to include a truly discrete variable among a set of continuous variables in a prediction equation. A common example is to include gender as a predictor variable in a regression equation. It also may occur that the dependent variable in the equation may be changed from being measured on the interval scale, as psychological measures usually are, to the nominal scale. A common use of this procedure is to substitute pass–fail or acceptable–marginal–reject for the underlying continuous measure. Such variables are referred to as dummy variables. Researchers who do employ them in their experiments should not lose sight of the true nature of such variables and take account of this in the interpretation of their results.

Before–After Variables. These are independent variables in experimental design in which the dependent variable is measured before and again after the behavior or action measured by the independent variable occurs.

Between-Subjects Variables. These variables are found primarily in analysis of variance (ANOVA) designs. They are independent variables having different subjects at different levels.

Within-Subjects Variables. These are independent variables again primarily in ANOVA designs in which the same subjects at all levels and each subject is measured repeatedly on the dependent variable.

CORRELATION METHODS
EXPERIMENTAL DESIGNS
EXPERIMENTAL METHODS
FACTORIAL DESIGNS
HAWTHORNE EFFECT
RESEARCH METHODOLOGY
STATISTICAL INFERENCE

P. F. MERENDA

VECTOR APPROACH TO PSYCHOTHERAPY

The vector approach to psychotherapy states that the multitudinous varieties of therapy basically deal with only six fundamental vectors or modalities through which human beings grow. By selecting one therapeutic method from the many found on each of these vectors, an eclectic therapist can achieve a highly potent balanced therapeutic integration and also be free to express his personal preferences and talents. The following therapies are grouped in terms of these vectors.

1. Rational vector—marked by insight, increased awareness, and learning
   a. Psychoanalysis
   b. Rational emotive therapy
   c. Transactional analysis
   d. Behavior therapy
2. Neuromuscular vector—marked by muscular tension, relaxation, and movement with the accompanying respiratory changes and emotional releases
   a. Reichian therapy
   b. Bioenergetics
   c. Rolfing
   d. Alexander technique
   e. Feldenkrais method
   f. Dance therapy
3. Interpersonal vector—marked by relationships between people
   a. Encounter groups
   b. Psychodrama
   c. Conjoint family therapy
   d. Gestalt therapy
4. Fantasy vector—marked by intrapersonal experiences when the individual closes out environmental stimulation
   a. Hypnotherapy
   b. Psychosynthesis
   c. Guided daydreams
5. Transpersonal vector—marked by transcendence of the individual's isolated state of consciousness
   a. Spiritual healing
   b. Parapsychological phenomena
   c. Jungian psychology
   d. Meditation
6. Biochemical vector—marked by changes in the body's chemistry, either internally or externally induced
   a. Orthomolecular treatment
   b. Carbogen
   c. Dietary procedures and exercise
   d. Psychedelic and psycholytic drug therapies
   e. Sedatives, stimulants, and tranquilizers

INNOVATIVE PSYCHOTHERAPIES
PSYCHOTHERAPY TECHNIQUES

P. BINDRIM

VICTIMOLOGY

Victimology has been defined by Drapkin and Viano as the study of "victims of crime and everything that is connected with such a victim," by S. Schafer as "the study of the criminal–victim relationship," and by I. L. Kutash et al. as "the science that deals with victims."

The first proponent of victimology as a science was Benjamin Mendelsohn. As early as the 1940s, however, interest in the victim was developing. Von Hentig held that a "nefarious symbiosis" often exists between victims and offenders, with the victim stimulating the offender toward a criminal response directed at the victim. He called these victims "activating sufferers," and felt such victims are of four kinds: (a) those who desire injury (submitting); (b) those who do so to achieve greater gain (conniving); (c) those who cooperate (contributing); and (d) those who provoke or instigate (soliciting). Mendelsohn developed the concept further, dividing victims into six categories on the basis of degree of culpability. Wolfgang confirmed this when he found that 26% of murder victims had precipitated their attacks. Kutash provided a basic aggression victimology vocabulary and classification system to establish a common nomenclature for this new science.

Victims of aggression can be divided into two distinct categories: (a) those who are victimized (play no role in becoming a victim) and (b) those who are victiming (promoting the victimage). The duration and frequency of victimage also can be classified.

The disorders that can develop in the situational aggression victim can be either acute or chronic; each type includes a discrete set of symptoms.

Acute situational aggression victim syndrome. A transient situational disturbance that follows a physical attack. Symptoms range from exhaustion, anxiety, grief, disorientation, hostility, remorse, regression, and denial to extreme cases that simulate hysterical neurosis of either a conversion type or a dissociative type. The military used to refer to these latter symptoms as "shell shock" or "battle fatigue."

Chronic situational aggression victim syndrome. A disorder of long duration that an individual develops over a prolonged period of being the victim of aggression. Symptoms range from neurasthenia, chronic anxiety, guilt, irritability, sleep disturbance, retrograde amnesia, extreme apathy, regression, low self-esteem, and weak ego strength to identification with the aggressor, massive hypochondriasis, somatization, and psychotic depressive reactions.

Whereas a situational aggression victim may develop disorders that weaken ego strength, promotional aggression victims have ego deficits to begin with. These disorders can be of three types—impulsive, compulsive, and characterological.

CHILD ABUSE
PSYCHOPATHIC PERSONALITY
SADOMASOCHISM

I. L. KUTASH

VIDEO PSYCHOLOGY

Video is used in psychology to gather and disperse information, to help people change (behavior, feelings, and attitudes), and as experimental stimuli. These uses are summarized here under seven headings.

ANALYZING AND DOCUMENTING

The most extensive use of video in psychology is to capture and analyze behavior. Video has been widely used in the analysis of motor activity, nonverbal communication, social interaction, and for medical diagnosis and for surveillance. Comparative psychologists have used video to study animal behavior from the courtship of the praying mantis to paw preferences in squirrels. Video analysis of facial expression is highly evolved, and this methodology is now being extended to examine the patterns of social interactions in families and other groups. The video allows whatever level of analysis there is time and patience for, once the coding system has been operationalized. It also is now possible to take "video X-rays" for diagnostic clarification in such situations as the inability to swallow by infants with disabilities. Video can be used in surveillance in sleep laboratories (using infrared lighting) and mounted in motor vehicles of drug-influenced drivers.

EDUCATIONAL VIDEOS

Videotapes and discs are often designed for instructing and informing. Research has been unsystematic, although some total systems have been thoroughly evaluated. Most information influencing production (style, length, pace, etc.) comes from the entertainment and public relations industries. The most promising applications can be listed under three headings. The first is classroom education for school-age children (e.g., interactive video for learning mathematics), in university settings (e.g., illustrations of attribution theory), and for on-the-job training (e.g., supported employment). The second is treatment preparation. Medical and dental patients or their family members are shown previews of intended therapeutic procedures. The third area is health and safety education, including consequences of drug use and childhood development. The most rapidly expanding strategy across all these areas involves the use of interactive video. Such a system combines computer technology and video discs to allow the student's responses to affect exposure to learning materials and tasks.

PEER MODELING

To help people change their behavior, one of the most prolific uses of video is to provide a client or trainee with demonstrations of effective behavior by a like person in a like situation. The range of training and therapeutic purposes is extensive. Applications in professional training range from divorce mediation to helping teaching assistants. Other productive areas are parent training and child self-management. In social skills and daily living, children and youth are most often featured. Motor performance (e.g., sport) is another area of extensive application. The potential for appropriately designed modeling videos for special populations (e.g., people with mental retardation) is promising but underdeveloped.

SELF-MODELING

Effective behavior also can be illustrated, for learning purposes, on videotapes by the clients or trainees themselves, through planning and editing in various ways. Self-modeling has been defined as a procedure in which people see themselves on videotapes showing only adaptive behavior. (Audiotapes, still photographs, stories in print, and individuals' imaginations also have been used for self-modeling.) Researched interventions exist for a wide variety of applications: disruptive behavior, selective mutism, depression, anxiety, sports, social skills, personal safety, self-control, physically challenging situations, the training of service providers, and others. The most effective form of self-modeling uses *feedforward*, a term coined to refer to video images of target skills not yet achieved, created by editing together components from the skill repertoire already available. For example, a boy cannot feed himself, but he can hold a spoon, dip it in the food, lift it to his mouth, and so on; these elements can be videotaped separately and edited together into a novel, complex activity, showing competence in a new but developmentally appropriate area. A simpler but not as dramatically effective strategy is *positive self-review,* which refers to compiling the best recorded examples of target skills already manageable but infrequently achieved. For example, a tennis player gets to review her best service, overhead volley, and so on after a full day of many attempts. In either form, self-modeling tapes are typically about 3 minutes long and are reviewed every 1 or 2 days, up to six times, for maximum effect; sometimes they are reviewed again every 2 or 3 months when a maintenance booster is desirable.

SELF-CONFRONTATION AND FEEDBACK

Viewing oneself on video in personally demanding situations can clearly lead to improved self-assessment. Video feedback is thus used in a wide variety of circumstances: competitive sports, professional skills, interpersonal communication, and so on. It appears to be most effective when the behavior required for correction or improvement is clearly indicated, and the behavior must be attainable or some other training or support (e.g., coaching and counseling) is provided. The other value of viewing oneself on unedited, unplanned videos may come from the motivational or emotional impact. The effect of seeing oneself perform badly on video, without being able to change or interact with the situation, can range from despair to anxiety to heightened sensitivity determination to succeed.

SCENE SETTING

The use of video to promote discussions, memories, emotions, or judgments is common but understudied in practice. The use of "interpersonal process recall" (reviewing videotapes to reexamine the thought processes and feelings associated with specific actions) has been developed as interviewing and counseling. The term *triggers* has been coined to refer to brief videos that provoke discussions as the basis for group learning experiences. These are typically short, unresolved vignettes, designed to promote discussion on contentious topics (e.g., child abuse or attitudes toward different cultures). Vignettes have been used surprisingly little in therapy. But there are promising uses documented in social skills training, exposure therapy, and sex therapy. A possibly related use of video, unsystematically referred to in the literature but nonetheless interesting, is the therapeutic and developmental impact for people (e.g., teens with emotional disturbance and criminal offenders) who take part in scripting and producing their own videos.

VIDEO AS EXPERIMENTAL STIMULI

A vast number of research studies mention the use of video vignettes, but the methodological principles are so far minimally defined. Video content may provide the independent variable (e.g., depressed affect in one vignette but not in another), or video may be contrasted with another medium (e.g., seeing oneself on closed circuit video versus a mirror). It is common to use a single vignette but to create different conditions by labeling (e.g., "she has an attention deficit" versus "she is disruptive") or to use subjects of different categories (e.g., experts versus novices). Video can even be a dependent variable, as when subjects adjust a distorted image to meet some criterion (e.g., assessment of body size in weight disorders).

The potential for using video in psychology has scarcely begun to peak. With advancing technology and increased user friendliness (with or without computer interface), the potential will increase.

ANIMAL MODELS
APPROACHES TO LEARNING
BEHAVIOR MODELING

CONSUMER PSYCHOLOGY
EDUCATIONAL PSYCHOLOGY
INSTRUCTIONAL SYSTEMS DEVELOPMENT
JOB ANALYSIS
OCCUPATIONAL COUNSELING
PERFORMANCE APPRAISAL
SELF-ACTUALIZATION
WORK EFFICIENCY

P. W. DOWRICK

VINELAND SOCIAL MATURITY SCALE

The Vineland Social Maturity Scale, originally developed by Edgar A. Doll, represented an early attempt to measure social competence. Doll defined social competence as "a functional composite of human traits which subserves social usefulness as reflected in self-sufficiency and in service to others." This aspect of human behavior has also been termed *adaptive behavior* and has been incorporated as a major component in the definition of mental retardation.

The Vineland Social Maturity Scale, which evaluates social competence from a developmental perspective, was normed on males and females from birth to 30 years of age. Eight categories of behaviors are assessed: (a) self-help general, (b) self-help eating, (c) self-help dressing, (d) locomotion, (e) occupation, (f) communication, (g) self-direction, and (h) socialization. A third party is interviewed who is familiar with the individual being assessed (e.g., parent, sibling). This interview is intended to determine the behaviors *customarily* performed by the target individual. Special procedures do, however, allow for the target individual to be interviewed or observed. Scores are derived from the number of acts or behaviors customarily exhibited by the individual and are computed in terms of social age (SA) and/or social quotient (SQ).

MENTAL RETARDATION

C. J. DREW

VIOLENCE

The study of violence has been an area filled with controversy. Even brief discussions of violence are laden with interpersonal and political as well as scientific overtones. Great concern is often expressed over the level of violence prevalent in U.S. society. Most debates are reduced to the question of the source of violence and whether it is inherent in human nature or part of the societies that have evolved. Part of the controversy alluded to surrounds the issues of alternative definitions of violence. As one proceeds to study violence and its correlates, different results emerge, depending on the definition adopted.

A second dimension along which definitions of violence vary involves legality. Some would define violence only in terms of illegal behavior. This excludes forms of sanctioned violence such as may occur in war or during social unrest. Others would place emphasis only on the form of the act (a more behavioral definition) and its intent. Our current legal system differentiates between personal or property destruction resulting from intentional violence and that caused by negligence.

The psychological study of violence has concerned itself with two primary approaches. The first has been the prediction of violence before its occurrence. The prediction approach involves a before-the-fact judgment from statistical profiles, personality tests, behavior patterns, demographic characteristics, and behavioral histories that an individual or group of individuals is likely to commit violent acts in the future. Monahan summarizes the following as being the best predictors of violence: lack of support from immediate family members, history of violence among

the family, violent behavior patterns among peers, the absence of steady employment, the availability of "willing" victims, the availability of weapons, the availability of alcohol, and the recency and prevalence of violence by the individual. The extent to which predictions are made over a long time period and across a variety of situations dramatically reduces their accuracy.

An area of somewhat greater controversy concerns the control procedures that follow the prediction of violence. Treatment approaches for remediating violence involve the loss of freedom for the individual about whom the violent prediction is being made. Psychology has played a role in providing data and occasionally expert testimony concerning the use of extensive control procedures. A great deal of controversy has arisen concerning the use of such procedures. The debate has centered on the way such predictions have been used for purposes of long-term incarceration, apparently without justification.

A related and insufficiently studied domain of violence involves that which is prevalent in the corporate world. Our society in particular allows corporate and automotive violence to occur at high rates. In the field of psychology and social science, little is known about such forms of violence. They have been surrounded by political sensitivities and hence have not been the topic of systematic investigation.

AGGRESSION

W. S. DAVIDSON, II

VISION (THEORIES OF)

Vision is the process of transducing (transforming) light energy into neural impulses that can then be interpreted by the brain. Light waves are the relatively small band of radiations to which the eyes are sensitive. The radiation can vary in intensity or wavelength. Variations in intensity are perceived as a difference in level of brightness. Variations in wavelength are perceived as a difference in color. The wavelengths that make up the visible spectrum range from roughly 400 manometers, perceived as violet, to about 750 manometers, perceived as red (1 manometer = 1 billionth of a meter).

The outermost layer of the eye is called the sclera. It is white with a tough, rubbery consistency that helps the eye hold its spherical shape. Light enters the eye through a transparent portion of the outer covering called the cornea and then passes through an aperture, called the pupil, which is surrounded by the iris, the colored portion of the eye. The iris has muscles that contract to change the size of the pupil, thus regulating the amount of light admitted to the inner chamber of the eye. In bright light, the pupil contracts, and in dim light, it expands. After the light has passed through the pupil, it enters the lens, which is a transparent focusing mechanism and focuses the light on the back of the eye, much as the lens of a camera focuses light on the film. The inner layer of the eye on which the light is focused is the retina, which contains the receptor cells that actually convert light to neural impulses through a photochemical reaction. There are two types of receptor cells—the rods and the cones.

The cone cells are responsible for chromatic (color) vision and visual acuity. They are most numerous in the fovea, a recessed area positioned almost exactly behind the lens. The rod cells are sensitive to minute amounts of light but are not sensitive to colors. There are no rod cells in the fovea. As the distance from the fovea increases, the concentration of rod cells also increases and the concentration of cone cells decreases.

The rod and cone receptor cells are called first-order neurons. They are connected to second-order neurons (bipolar cells), which, in turn, are connected to third-order neurons (ganglion cells). The ganglion cells are connected to the optic nerve fibers, which collectively form the optic nerve. The optic nerve fibers converge in the retina toward the optic disk, where they exit through the rear of the eye. This creates a small area with no receptor cells, resulting in a small blind spot in the visual field of each eye.

The two optic nerves from the eyes make a junction just in front of the pituitary gland and underneath the frontal lobes of the brain. This junction is called the optic chiasm. At the optic chiasm, the fibers from the nasal half of each retina cross over and the fibers from the temporal (outside) half of each retina leave the chiasm without crossing. This incomplete crossover has the effect of collecting in the left optic tract the fibers carrying neural impulses representing the right visual field of both eyes, and collecting in the right optic tract the fibers carrying neural impulses representing the left visual field of both eyes. Because of the decussation that occurred at the optic chiasm, the left visual field is represented in the right occipital lobe and the right visual field is represented in the left occipital lobe.

Understanding how the eyes and the brain interact to produce the perception of vision is a much more difficult task than tracing the visual pathway from the retina to the occipital lobes.

Besides responding directly to light, the receptor cells are also affected by the surrounding receptor cells. In addition to being connected to the second-order neurons, the receptor cells are connected to each other by what are called horizontal cells. Using the relatively simple eye of the horseshoe crab (*limulus*), F. Hartline and H. K. Ratliff found that neighboring receptor cells inhibited each other when they fired simultaneously, producing a much smaller degree of activity in each than when they were stimulated separately. S. W. Kuffler found a more complex interactive organization present in the vertebrate eye. Stimulated receptor cells interacted in both an excitatory and an inhibitory mode with the cells surrounding them. J. Y. Lettvin and colleagues found that different ganglion cells in a frog's retina responded maximally to different kinds of stimuli. They reported four different types of ganglion cells based on response to stimuli. One type responded most actively to contrast in the visual field. A second type responded only to small moving spots. A third type responded to moving edges, and the fourth class of ganglia responded to overall dimming of the visual field.

The major contribution of Lettvin et al. was the evidence that some organization of the visual field occurs in the cells within the retina rather than solely within the brain. D. H. Hubel and T. N. Wiesel found in the cells of the visual cortex of a cat a continuation and refinement of the selectivity that occurred in the ganglion cells of the retina. They also found that the cells of the visual cortex were arranged in columns perpendicular to the surface of the cortex and that the deeper the penetration, the more complex and sophisticated the cells were. They hypothesized the existence of four general types of cells organized in a hierarchical fashion. These were called simple, complex, lower-order hypercomplex, and upper-order hypercomplex.

VISUAL PERCEPTION

D. E. BOWEN

VISUAL IMAGERY

The nature of visual imagery is most easily described in subjective terms: Most people report a close resemblance between the subjective experience of visual imagery and the experience of actually perceiving. People often believe that they can "read" information from an image, much as they read information from an actual picture. Likewise, the image appears to depict the represented object as viewed from a specific distance and perspective, much as a picture does. Other modes of representation can be silent on how far away the object is or the angle from which the object is viewed. But these aspects must be specified for a picture—the picture must depict an object as seen from a specific point of view. It would seem that the same is true for a visual image.

These subjective qualities suggest that visual images depict much as pictures do and that one inspects visual images with processes related to those of visual perception. But psychologists are wary of self-reports about subjective experience. These reports cannot be literally true: There plainly is no "eye" inside the brain; nor are there pictures, or a projection screen, somewhere within the skull.

IMAGES, PICTURES, AND PERCEIVING

Most recent research has employed more objective means of studying imagery, and this research often turns out to corroborate self-reports: Visual images do have properties in common with pictures, and imagery does have much in common with perceiving. However, there also are important contrasts between images and pictures, or between imaging and perceiving, and these must be incorporated into our thinking as well.

Data indicate that images resemble pictures in regard to what information is included and what is excluded as well as what information is readily available and what is less available. For example, subjects inspecting a picture of (say) a cat can readily see the cat's head (because the head is large and up front), but may see the claws only with difficulty (because the claws are small and may be hidden from view). In contrast, subjects inspecting a description of a cat are likely to find prominent mention of the claws (because these are a salient feature of cats); the cat's head may be omitted from the description, on the grounds that it is too obvious to mention. Against this backdrop, visual images clearly follow the pattern of pictures, and not descriptions. Subjects inspecting an image of a cat (for example) give fast responses to questions like "Does the cat have a head?" and somewhat slower responses to questions about claws. (In contrast, subjects thinking about cats without an image show the reverse pattern: faster responses to *claws* than to *head*.) Evidence like this can be used to document the information included in, and also prominent in, visual images; the pattern generally reflects the pattern one would expect for pictures and not the pattern usually found with other forms of representation.

Research has also examined the processes used to read and to manipulate mental images. For example, in one experiment, subjects were asked to memorize the map of a fictional island. Subjects then imaged this map and, when they heard a tone, imagined a small speck moving from (say) the well shown on the (imaged) map to the palm tree. When the (imaged) speck reached the palm tree, subjects pressed a button, stopping a clock, and allowing researchers to measure how long this imagined travel took. On other trials, subjects imagined the speck moving from the palm tree to the rock and so on for all the other landmarks. The results showed a remarkably consistent linear relation between scanning time and imagined distance. Results like these provide strong indication that images preserve the pattern of spatial relations defined by the imaged scene or object, just as pictures do.

Similar results have been obtained with image rotation. That is, it takes twice as long to imagine an object rotated 40° as it does to imagine it rotated 20°; twice as long for 80° as for 40°, and so on. Other studies have measured how long it takes to zoom in on an imaged scene (to examine detail), or to zoom back (to examine larger objects). These studies also reveal a consistent relation between the amount of zoom and the time required, illustrating how image function is governed by distance relationships (i.e., more time required for moving greater distances).

VISUAL IMAGERY AND MEMORY

Visual imagery has a number of powerful effects on memory: Subjects more readily remember sentences or passages that can be visualized; specific instructions to visualize material also lead to improved memory.

This research is often conceptualized within the dual-code model. According to this model, visual imagery and verbal description provide distinct modes of mental representation; memory will be best if material is encoded in both manners.

It is worth mentioning that imagery's memory effects also may reflect the use of spatial imagery, rather than visual imagery. For example, instructions to visualize the to-be-remembered material also improve memory for those blind from birth. Likewise, instructions to visualize aid memory even for materials that would be difficult to see if literally visualized (e.g., an egg against a white background). It, therefore, may not be the pictorial properties of imagery that promote memory, but instead the organizing properties of imagery.

IMAGED PERFORMANCE

It is widely claimed that imaged performance, or imaged practice, has effects comparable with those of actual practice. By imagining one's golf stroke, one can improve one's performance. Related claims have been made for imagery's role in therapeutic contexts: If one is afraid of snakes, one can overcome this fear by imagining snakes at (gradually) closer and closer positions. If one has a tumor, one can diminish the tumor by visualizing the antibodies attacking the tumor.

Successes for these various techniques have been reported. It is difficult, though, to argue for reliable effects of these techniques. In many tests, imagined practice of motor skills has had no detectable effect. The more exotic uses of imagery (e.g., tumor reduction) have not been rigorously examined. When these effects are reported, crucial comparison data are often lacking (e.g., there is no way to ask how often, with other patients, imagery has not been followed by tumor reduction).

Most important, the mechanisms for these effects are quite unclear. At least some of these effects may be motivational, as the mere fact of thinking about the target performance may change one's attitude or motivation. Moreover, there are few indications that imagery itself is crucial here. Similar effects may be obtained if subjects think about the target performance in some other fashion, not drawing on imagery.

IMAGERY VIVIDNESS

Finally, research has attempted to unite the findings already described with the self-report about the imagery experience. Much has focused on subjects' descriptions of the vividness. Many subjects describe their imagery as clear and detailed, closely resembling the experience of actual seeing; other subjects describe their imagery as vague and undetailed, and not at all like seeing. Surprisingly, these two sorts of subjects perform equivalently on tasks of image scanning, image rotation, memorizing visualizable materials, and so on. This has encouraged many researchers to skepticism about these self-reports but also is consistent with the suggestion already made that imagery tasks like scanning or rotation draw on spatial imagery, whereas the self-reports may reflect the richness of visual imagery. In fact, imagery vividness does seem predictive of visual tasks such as memory for complex pictures, faces, and colors. However, this research is difficult to evaluate, especially given the absence of clear distinctions between visual and spatial imagery.

ARTISTIC MORPHOLOGY
IMAGELESS THOUGHT: THE WURZBURG SCHOOL
IMAGERY
INTERNAL REPRESENTATION
MENTAL IMAGERY
VISUAL PERCEPTION

D. REISBERG

VISUAL PERCEPTION

Visual perception is one of the systemwise ways of relating to the physical environment. It involves the organism's ability to make use of photic radiation. At the same time, it involves contributions to certain sense organs in addition to the eyes. Visual perception is partially made through the contribution of the vestibular mechanism in the ear and through the proprioceptive sense mechanisms in the muscles and tendons and temperature receptors.

Things can look hard or soft, rough or smooth, hot or cold, and yet there is nothing solely specific to the nature of photic radiation to provide such impressions. They come from what the other sense modalities can provide in conjunction with the experienced properties ordinarily considered as strictly visual. To provide the organism with the fundamental data that make vision the prime space sense, the sense organ for vision (the eye) has had to be more complex than any other.

Color and brightness are an additional dimension to position, form, and movement found in visual perception. The major system for depicting the color spectrum and the intensity and hue relations is the Munsell Color Solid.

EYE
VISION (THEORIES OF)

S. H. BARTLEY

VITALISM

Vitalism is the doctrine that living matter is suffused with a dynamic force not present in nonliving matter. The opposing position, called *biological mechanism,* goes back to René Descartes, who speculated that animals function as machines and that human functioning is substantially machine-like. Helmholtz and three of his group signed a legendary "pact against vitalism," asserting that the only forces active within organisms are physical-chemical forces.

Studies of neural functioning, optics, sensation, and psychophysical processes flourished as the century progressed, illuminating more and more organismic phenomena formerly seen as mysterious or inherently unstudiable. These developments helped provoke new statements of the vitalistic position, such as those by H. Driesch and H. Bergson, whose name for the elusive current of life was *elan vital* (the "vital force"). At about the same time, the mechanistic position was exemplified by the work of Jacques Loeb. A so-called mechanistic spirit dominated experimental psychology well into the twentieth century. Then the disputes akin to the vitalism-mechanism issue arose again among schools of psychology about what the subject matter and methods of psychology should be.

MIND–BODY PROBLEMS
PHILOSOPHICAL PSYCHOLOGY

A. B. PRATT

VOCABULARY TESTS

The 1994 *Tests in print IV* lists 40 English vocabulary tests (some being out of print). But these lists are only the tip of the iceberg. Along with vocabulary subsections of numerous intelligence and achievement tests are various verbal tests with high correlations with vocabulary, which require knowledge of words and which measure much the same function: verbal analogies, same–opposite, synonyms, verbal classification, and the like.

Vocabulary tests have many attractions. If it can be assumed that all respondents have grown up in the same general environment and have had similar opportunities to acquire words, vocabulary scores tend to reflect aptitude. However, much instruction is directed toward acquiring concepts in a special area, so that growth in vocabulary is an important aspect of growth in knowledge. Vocabulary is a basic component of reading and writing skills, and is a prerequisite for many forms of intellectual endeavor.

The high intercorrelations of vocabulary items result in high reliabilities, both by internal consistency and by alternate forms. Empirical validities in situations requiring intellectual abilities also tend to be high since many intellectual activities are almost synonymous with the manipulation of verbal concepts.

INTELLIGENCE MEASURES

P. H. DuBois

VOCATIONAL INTEREST MEASUREMENT*

The pioneer in this field was Edward K. Strong, Jr. The first edition of the Strong Vocational Interest Blank appeared in 1927.

The most recent derivative, the Strong–Campbell Interest Inventory, was published in 1974; the third edition of its manual was published in 1981. Thus, there is a history of more than 50 years of research and refinement for this instrument. It is estimated that as many as 21,300,000 people have taken one or another form of this test. In the most recent form there are 162 occupational scales representing 85 occupations; for 77 of these occupations there is a male and a female sample of successful workers, for four of them there is only a male scale, and for the remaining four there is only a female scale.

In the beginning, interest measurement was concerned with practical problems of vocational choice and vocational planning for individuals; it was highly empiric and with little theoretical foundation. But there was a beginning of theory; the first factor analysis of interest test scores was done by Thurstone. Using the intercorrelations among 18 occupational keys on the first edition, he derived four general factors: interest in science, interest in language, interest in people, and interest in commercial activities. Strong himself grouped his growing number of occupational keys by their patterns of intercorrelations.

J. L. Holland provided the typology that is now incorporated in the current edition of the Strong–Campbell Interest Inventory. He proposed that most persons can be categorized in terms of six broad personality types—realistic, investigative, artistic, social, enterprising, or conventional. An individual can be located in one, or some meaningful combination, of these six. The same six categories can also be used to define occupational environments or work settings. People will search out those environments that will let them use their skills and abilities, that will be consonant with their values and attitudes, that will let them take on satisfying roles and tasks, and that will permit them to avoid responsibilities they find distasteful or incongruent. Job performance, job satisfaction, and job stability will thus be the result of the interaction between the individual's personality structure and the characteristics of the work environment.

Notice the implications of these ideas: Occupational interests are determined *before* job experience occurs. Occupational interests are special cases of personality theory and motivational theory. *Within* types of interests, *levels* of performance can be postulated to take account of the different levels of ability required in occupations.

Parents will often insist that children can do anything they want to if they would "just get interested in it." Unfortunately this is an inaccurate assumption. The relation between claimed and measured interests is

significant for groups of individuals, but in individual cases the relation is not high enough to assume that claimed and measured interests are interchangeable.

G. T. Darley and T. Hagenah report several studies of test–retest reliabilities of earlier editions of the Strong Vocational Interest Blank, using subjects of differing ages at original testing and different intervals between test and retest, and using both Pearsonian and Spearman correlations. Their conclusions are as follows: "These interest test–retest correlations are a little lower than those in the literature for intelligence test–retest scores and somewhat higher than personality or attitude test–retest scores. Thus the behavior we measure with the occupational keys of the Strong Vocational Interest Blank seems to remain fairly stable over time . . ."

How well do scores on this test predict ultimate occupational participation for individuals? Strong determined the occupation-engaged-in for 663 Stanford University students who had been tested, on the average, 18 years earlier, while they were in college. He analyzed his data three ways: How well did the students score while in college on the keys for the occupations in which they were actually employed? How do the original scores of those engaging in an occupation compare with the original scores of those not engaging in that occupation? How do expert judges rate the degree of agreement between the original profile of scores and the occupation? On all three counts, the predictive validity of the Strong Vocational Interest Blank was powerful.

The most recent study of the predictive validity of the earlier forms of the Strong Vocational Interest Blank was completed by Robert Dolliver and his colleagues. They concluded that "The chances are about 1 to 1 that a man would end up in an occupation for which he received an A score . . . the chances are about 8 to 1 that a person will not end up in an occupation for which he received a C score." There is a low relation between measured interests and measured ability or scholastic achievement.

When instructed to "fake," respondents can bias their scores substantially, but when individuals respond to the items in ordinary administrations of the test, they usually answer truthfully, even in situations where they might be expected to bias their scores, as in applying for jobs or for admission to professional school programs. The detectable bias is not very many score points, and infrequently changes the broad interpretive band of scores from which similarity or dissimilarity of occupational interests is judged.

Do men and women show different patterns of vocational interests? Before answering this question, some historical considerations must be noted.

From the 1930s, when Strong published the first women's test, to the 1970s, the role of women in the labor force changed drastically. More women were in the workforce. More women were entering occupations hitherto viewed as "men's work." Campbell and J. C. Hansen devoted an entire chapter to the problem. Their conclusions were as follows:

1. Men and women, on the average, respond differently to almost half of the inventory items.

2. The size of the differences is considerable.

3. The differences do not disappear when only men and women who have made the same occupational choice are compared.

4. The differences have not lessened appreciably since 1930.

5. Attempts to develop combined-sex scales appear to be premature, and the validity of these scales varies from occupation to occupation.

6. Empirical scales constructed on the basis of same-sex criterion and reference samples work better (are more valid) than scales based on opposite-sex samples.

Another question: At what age do patterns of vocational interests begin to emerge in individuals? Studies of the earlier forms of the Strong

* The author wishes to thank Jo-Ida Hansen, Janet M. Hively, and Loralie Lawson for their careful review of this article.

Vocational Interest Blank indicated that meaningful and relatively stable patterns of interests can be seen in students averaging about the tenth-grade level, if they are of average general ability.

There have been many studies of the relations between vocational interests and personality measures. On the Strong–Campbell Interest Inventory, Campbell and Hansen have retained two nonoccupational measures: academic comfort and introversion–extroversion. It is to be noted also that Holland's typology is essentially a personality typing within his six themes.

As described by Ann Roe, personality factors played a large role in determining vocational direction for these eminent scientists. Further, S. J. Segal concluded that vocational choice is a resultant of the emotional development of the individual and is in part an expression of the individual's method of adjusting to his or her environment.

The development of vocational interests is affected by sex, age, and personality factors. But however they develop, measured vocational interests represent one of the three major elements to be identified in predicting job performance, job satisfaction, and job stability in our society's complex world of work. Levels of ability and available opportunity are the other two elements.

CAREER COUNSELING
INTEREST INVENTORIES

J. G. DARLEY

VOCATIONAL REHABILITATION

As reported by Richard Burk, the first Vocational Rehabilitation Act (Public Law 236) in the United States was passed by the Congress on June 2, 1920. This act placed a heavy emphasis on vocation and defined rehabilitation as "the rendering of a person disabled fit to engage in a remunerative occupation."

In theory, then, vocational rehabilitation would be directed to individuals disabled in some way and would be the endeavor of choice for those of incapacity. It would be distinguished from similar undertakings designed with initial training as a goal—such endeavors as career development, vocational guidance, and job training. In practice, however, many disabled persons select from available resources to meet their personal goals, often without regard to such formal definitions or the professionals' intentions.

Personal practices serve to obscure statistical trends and leave definitions imprecise. They occur not without reason, however. They reflect practical considerations. An individual might choose one program over another because it is closer geographically. The stigma associated with vocational rehabilitation, and the disability giving rise to its need, may represent another reason. S. Olshansky suggested that the disabled person often suffers from not one but a variety of types of stigma—relating to physical appearance, stereotypical ideas associated with receiving public assistance, and even attitudes regarding race, color, or religion. As medicine and science continue to produce results that increasingly prolong life, vocational rehabilitation may be called on more and more to contribute to the quality of that life.

REHABILITATION CENTERS

S. BERENT

WALDORF EDUCATION

Also known as "Steiner" education, Waldorf education is based on the philosophy of Rudolf Steiner, an Austrian scientist and scholar who was asked to create a school for the children of the workers at the Waldorf-Astoria cigarette factory in Stuttgart, Germany. The first school was organized in 1919, and the movement has since become international with more than 300 schools.

Teaching is based on Steiner's conception of humans as spiritual beings with repeated earthly incarnations. Thus, a child is not a blank slate to be filled with knowledge, nor an animal to be civilized, but is viewed by the teacher as bringing undisclosed potentials in various stages of development. The task of education is to allow these various potentials to develop to their full capacities.

Steiner's view of childhood development holds that the time at which a subject is introduced, as well as the manner in which it is presented, is of utmost importance. The curriculum integrates the arts, sciences, and humanities, and teaching is done from an artistic point of view, taking into account that individuals learn at different rates and in different ways. Grades are not given, and students create their own books from the teacher's presentation. The stress of Waldorf education is on the development of the "whole human being" socially, artistically, physically, and intellectually.

Waldorf schools may begin with a nursery class and go through high school, depending on the particular school. There is no principal or head, but all pedagogical decisions are made by a "College of Teachers." Teacher training consists of at least 2 years of postgraduate work at Waldorf institutes.

ALTERNATIVE EDUCATIONAL SYSTEMS
INDIVIDUAL EDUCATION

B. OZAKI-JAMES

WALK-IN CLINICS

Walk-in clinics provide short-term treatment and referral for individuals with psychological problems. These community mental health services are usually open 24 hours per day, do not require an appointment, and often include telephone hot lines.

Most walk-in clinics are operated by community mental health centers or emergency rooms within general hospitals. Specialized services dealing with problems of alcohol, drugs, suicide, and rape also include walk-in clinics. Taubman analyzed all the walk-in psychiatric patients seen in a hospital emergency room in a 70-day period. Results indicated that 25.8% of the patients were schizophrenic, 21.1% were alcoholic, 18.6% were depressed, and 24.7% had other diagnoses. With the guiding principle of being available when the person needs help and with the emphasis on short-term treatment, often by paraprofessionals, walk-in clinics are one answer to the great need for expanded mental health services.

C. LANDAU

WEBER'S LAW

Ernst Heinrich Weber on the basis of experiments with stimuli of pressure, lifted weights, and visual distance (line lengths), along with reported observations of others, concluded that, rather than perceiving simply the difference between stimuli being compared, we perceive the ratio of the difference to the magnitude of the stimuli. A similar finding had already been made by the French physicist and mathematician Pierre Bouguer for visual brightness. Gustav T. Fechner translated this conclusion into the familiar mathematical form used today. Thus, Weber's law is usually given as either $\Delta I/I = k$ or $\Delta I = kI$, where ΔI is the change required for a just noticeable difference in stimulation (JND), I is the stimulus magnitude, and k is a constant for the particular sense. The value of k is termed the Weber ratio.

Over the years since Weber's formulation, it has been observed that k is not strictly constant over the entire stimulus range, increasing for low and high intensities. It is, however, valid for the large range of intermediate intensities for the various senses.

PSYCHOPHYSICS

G. H. ROBINSON

WECHSLER INTELLIGENCE TESTS

Although the mental testing movement had been in evidence for decades, by the late 1930s there still was no successful well-standardized individual adult intelligence test. The continued dissatisfaction with the standardization and structure (mental age levels) of the Stanford–Binet served as a major stimulus for Wechsler in introducing the Wechsler–Bellevue Adult Intelligence Scales in 1939.

Wechsler's test was designed as a "point scale" rather than a mental age scale. It attempted to obviate the criticism leveled at the Stanford–Binet as being too verbal by including a large proportion of performance items and it used a sizable number of adults in the standardization sample. An attempt was made to control for education and occupational status. The final version of the test was intended for use with ages 10 through 60.

Some of the general factors that governed the final selection of the tests were the evidence that the particular tests correlated at a reasonable level with other intelligence test batteries, that they were sufficiently varied in their functions to prevent any special effects on examinees with particular abilities and disabilities, and that the characteristics of the tests allowed some diagnostic inferences based on the performance of the subjects examined.

After two revised editions Wechsler introduced a new and revised form, the *Wechsler Adult Intelligence Scale* (WAIS), in 1949. The WAIS was standardized on 1700 subjects (evenly divided between the sexes at the several age levels) between the ages of 16 and 64. In addition, a sample of 475 elderly (60 to 75+) subjects was included. All parts of the United States were represented in this standardization, urban and rural subjects at each age level, and 10% of "non-Whites." It was revised as the WAIS-R in 1981.

Wechsler defined intelligence as "an aggregate or global capacity of the individual to act purposefully, to think rationally and to deal effec-

tively with his environment." Considering the breadth of this definition and the great flexibility of the W-B and the WAIS, there is little wonder that a great deal of research on the diagnostic aspects of this test, beyond the mere reporting of IQs, has appeared in the literature. Some of the work involves quantitative research on the correspondence between test patterns and certain psychopathologic diagnostic groupings, while other writings concern the "clinical" and qualitative analyses of the test responses and the processes by means of which the subject arrived at them.

In his original work, Wechsler proposed a "deterioration index" based on the ratio between subtests that "do not hold" and those that "hold" up with age. Rabin generally concluded that group differences were obtainable with a number of patterns. However, the utility of scatter in individual diagnosis was questionable. Yet some positive findings are obtainable when careful definition of patient samples takes place. Thus it is clear from a number of studies that a markedly higher verbal than performance IQ is present in patients with right cerebral hemisphere lesions, while the reverse is true in patients with left hemisphere lesions. Fairly consistent results have been reported pointing to "performance greater than verbal IQ" in delinquents and adult sociopathic persons. Other findings point to a variety of additional relationships between WAIS patterns and diagnostic subgroups.

The *Wechsler Intelligence Scale for Children* (WISC) was published in 1949 as a "downward" extension of the W-B. It was revised as the WISC-R, then as the WISC-III. Still another scale, for younger children, the WPPSI (*Wechsler Preschool and Primary Scale of Intelligence*) was standardized on a stratified sample of 1200 children and published in 1967.

INTELLIGENCE MEASURES

A. I. RABIN

WEIGHT CONTROL

Ultimately the goal of weight control is to reach and maintain some ideal weight. Initially, however, the concern is either losing excess weight or adding needed weight. Almost all programs of weight control, whether formal or informal, are successful in the initial phase of changing weight. Unfortunately the ultimate goal of achieving a lasting weight change is much more difficult to attain.

Although the vast majority of individuals concerned with weight control wish to lose weight, there is a significant minority for whom weight gain is the focus of concern. One segment of this minority is made up of individuals who rarely seek professional help. Many of them are athletes and they wish to increase their weight to become bigger, stronger, or more competitive in some sport. Another segment of this minority for whom weight gain is of critical importance comprises those individuals who are so successful at weight loss that their health is endangered. Anorexia is characterized by a preoccupation with weight loss and an inability accurately to perceive the ideal weight. In the extreme, this condition is called anorexia nervosa and can become life threatening. About 10% of anorexic patients eventually starve themselves to death. The anorexic patient typically does not see a need for treatment and will resist efforts to get them to increase their weight. Most anorexics are female and the disorder is usually first manifested in adolescence. Treatment is most often a combination of medical intervention, to prevent nutritional deficiency, and psychotherapy. Therapy may consist of both behavioral programs designed to reinforce eating and individual psychotherapy to deal with concomitant emotional problems.

Concern with obesity is usually reserved for industrialized affluent societies that provide the luxury of chronic overeating and underexercising. Obesity is commonly defined as being 20% or more above the average weight for one's height and build. The health problems that follow obesity are widely recognized and obesity is frequently the focus for both formal weight loss treatment programs and informal diet and exercise plans. An enormous amount of time and money is spent each year on weight loss treatment programs and the range of treatments available is widely varied.

One reason for the difficulty in making permanent changes in weight may be the physiological role of the hypothalamus in controlling eating behavior. Early research suggested that the hypothalamus contained eating centers that either would trigger or suppress eating behaviors. More recent research suggests that the hypothalamus may determine a "set point" for body weight. The implication for treatment of obesity is that the "set point" determined by the hypothalamus needs to be altered before treatment can produce lasting results. It is not clear from current research how this can be accomplished.

Regardless of the disappointing outcome for weight loss programs reported in the literature, obesity continues to be a major focus for treatment. Hundreds of diets have been advertised to aid in weight loss. In addition, various exercise programs have been designed for use in conjunction with diet plans. Also available are various groups, such as Weight Watchers, in which the members help support each other in their common goal of reducing weight.

The weight control programs offered by the professional community and the commercial clinics usually encourage a multidimensional approach to treatment. Other methods of treatment are sometimes offered in conjunction with diet and behavioral management programs. Individual or group psychotherapy is helpful in dealing with emotional problems and resistance to treatment. Hypnosis is commonly used to aid in appetite suppression.

A final note should be added concerning the outcome of the various treatment programs. S. Schachter reported that in a survey he conducted, 63% reported that they were successful in losing weight, a percentage much higher than most experimental studies report. His explanation for this was that while experimental studies report the percentage of successes after one attempt to lose weight, most people make multiple attempts until they succeed.

APPETITE DISORDERS
OBESITY

D. E. Bowen

WITCHCRAFT

Witchcraft refers to a supposed malevolent influence of one person upon another by magical means. Anthropologists sometimes distinguish witchcraft from sorcery; sorcery involves practices deliberately performed, whereas witchcraft is the direct exercise—not necessarily deliberate—of supernatural power. In Western European tradition, witchcraft commonly embraces both concepts.

Efforts to practice witchcraft may be viewed as a form of aggressive behavior, capable of producing real injury if known to the victim, by processes such as are involved in psychosomatic illness. More accessible to study are *accusations* against supposed witches. Historians have studied the waves of accusations in Western Europe and in colonial America.

DEFENSE MECHANISMS
SUPERSTITIONS

I. L. Child

WOMEN, PSYCHOLOGY OF

The psychology of women has emerged as an interdisciplinary effort to understand the behavior of women. The various subdisciplines of psychology have explored the developmental paths that women follow and investigated the inner dynamics of their lives.

HISTORY

Philosophers, clergy, historians, biologists, and, more recently, psychologists have expressed opinions on the nature of womankind. Regardless of individual orientation, individuals from a given period of time have generally spoken with one mind, reflecting a cultural attitude of their era. Until recently, however, the opinions did not vary greatly. The general point of view was that women were both inferior and superior to men and that they were lacking in worldly capabilities but excelled in the spiritual spheres.

With the emergence of the psychology of women as an area of formal investigation in the late nineteenth century, research attempted to document this point of view with scientific fact. Each new argument enjoyed a moment of popularity before being superseded. First women were considered inferior to men, primarily in mental capabilities, because their brains were smaller. When this argument was demolished, scientists turned to specific areas of the brain and argued that men's frontal lobes—and later parietal lobes—gave them an advantage. As this argument became increasingly suspect, the argument of greater male variability was advanced—that men were both better and worse than women, but overall less mediocre. Finally, in the early 1900s, arguments focused on the "maternal instinct," that women were naturally preoccupied with pregnancy and lactation and had little energy for the development of other capabilities.

As each of these arguments moved in and out of vogue, few questioned the general assumption that in terms of worldly accomplishment, women were inferior to men. The prevalent attitude was challenged, however, by a small minority of some men and a few women scientists. It might as clearly be shown, said the opposition, that such differences as exist between men and women are due to cultural and social experiences as well as to biology, and are, therefore, the result of male and female experience and not the cause of such experience.

The dissenters in the early 1900s laid the foundation for much of the work on the psychology of women since the 1960s. First, they stated that behavior is not inevitably tied to biology, but is in part a result of the cultural context. Second, they questioned to what degree actual differences in behavior existed between men and women. Third, they laid the foundation for the social activism that is often closely allied with research in the psychology of women, by emphasizing cultural rather than biological causes of behavior.

The scientific interest in the behavior of women apparent in the beginning of the century largely disappeared in the following decades. With the advent of behaviorism, arguments that relied on such intangibles as "the maternal instinct" were ignored. Scientific psychologists occupied themselves with observable behavior—and generally ignored sex differences.

PSYCHOANALYTIC INFLUENCE

Psychoanalysts drew conclusions about human behavior from their experience with individuals in clinical settings. The psychoanalytic viewpoint strongly influenced popular conceptions of women and has sometimes been credited with originating the psychology of women. It is still one of the dominant viewpoints in the field.

Sigmund Freud's views on feminine psychology have had a powerful impact on modern knowledge of women. Although Freud disclaimed much knowledge of women, he proclaimed that woman was an inferior man.

Karen Horney, a neopsychoanalyst, in her own theoretical formulations strongly suggested that many of Freud's views on human beings in general, and women in particular, arose because he drew universalistic conclusions from specific cases. Furthermore, putting forth such conclusions actually tended to justify and increase the behaviors being described. The beliefs, or ideologies, about women thus served several purposes. Horney wrote: "It is fairly obvious that these ideologies function not only to reconcile women to their subordinate role by presenting it as an unalterable one, but also to plant the belief that it represents a fulfillment they crave, or an ideal for which it is commendable and desirable to strive."

Horney's argument was strengthened by the crosscultural work of Margaret Mead, which reported no particular behavioral differences between men and women in some other cultures—or reported differences that were the opposite of those in Western society. If male and female behaviors varied from culture to culture, it was easily concluded that male/female differences were unlikely to be either biological in origin or universal.

RECENT RESEARCH ON WOMEN

The 1960s saw an increase in empirical studies related to the psychology of women. The new research was spurred on, in part, by the emergence of the Women's Movement, which challenged psychoanalytic views. Psychologists (and those of other disciplines) set out to determine (a) what sex differences actually existed, (b) the causes of any such differences, and (c) the key issues in women's lives and how these developed over time.

SEX DIFFERENCES

Recent research has laid to rest a number of myths about male/female differences and taken a new look at existing differences. Research has found, for example, no support for the contentions that women are biologically weaker or less intelligent than men. There is also no evidence that women are more passive and dependent than men, or that they have lower achievement drives. Finally, women are not asexual but have sexual capacities that match or surpass those of men.

However, in each of these areas, certain previously assumed differences have been shown to exist. Women may not be weaker than men and may be more resilient, but on the average they are generally smaller and have less muscle tissue. Women are not less intelligent and, in fact, are more fluent verbally, but on the average they are less able in mathematical and spatial areas than men. Women may not be more passive than men, but they are less aggressive. They are not less achievement oriented, but focus their desires for achievement less often in public accomplishments. Finally, women have sexual capacities that in some ways surpass those of men, but at the same time they are more intent on interpersonal relationships and more attuned to "love and romance" than are men in general.

BIOLOGY VERSUS CULTURE

Current biological arguments are more sophisticated but not dissimilar to those from the 1890s and early 1900s. John Money has proposed that different levels of androgen in prenatal hormones may affect the neural patterns in the brain, thus predisposing individuals to "masculine" or "feminine" mental patterns. Another researcher suggested that since girls mature earlier than boys, the earlier maturation may foreclose certain possibilities for cognitive development, which would occur with later maturation.

Cultural arguments rely on the variability of male and female behavior in different settings and suggest that such variability would not occur if behavior were determined by biological differences between men and women. Even biologically, there is enormous variability; differences in hormone levels between men and women, on the average, are not nearly as great as between men and other men, or women and other women. Further, in many cases, cultural influences have been shown to override biology. Finally, many psychologists have pointed to the distress sometimes caused by men and women who adopt appropriate masculine and feminine behavior. These psychologists argue that if the behavior patterns associated with each sex were indeed "natural," then they would not be as dysfunctional as they often appear to be.

It is not possible, however, clearly to separate what is biological from what is cultural. Many psychologists are willing to admit to both biological and cultural influences on behavior, but most place greater emphasis on the cultural side.

POWER AND LOVE IN WOMEN'S LIVES

Since the time of Freud, psychologists have stated that individual well-being is signaled by the ability to work productively and to engage in meaningful interpersonal relationships. A considerable body of literature stresses the importance of both components in the lives of both women and men. Sandra Bern has termed this *androgyny*.

Much of the literature on women, however, has shown that love outweighs power and that women are often immersed in interpersonal relationships to the exclusion of individual achievement. Studies of modern marriages have shown that women often place such emphasis on their marital relationships that they are inevitably disappointed and suffer emotional and sometimes physical illness. In general, the emphasis on relationships in women's lives is attributed to the cultural injunctions (reinforced by psychoanalytic thought) that urge women to give up personal aspirations and to be a source of support for men.

Women who have entered the world of work, however, and demonstrated the capacity for high levels of achievement, have encountered numerous difficulties, some internal and some external. To the extent that women have internalized the injunctions of their culture, they have difficulty justifying their own achievement drives and retreat when the work environment poses obstacles. However, external obstacles do exist, often because women are viewed as outsiders within the workforce, and the perception of others, generally male, is that they do not belong and need not be afforded the same opportunities offered to male colleagues.

Women who are married, have children, and are pursuing careers appear to many to be "doing it all." Research reports have shown, however, that there are costs. For women who have undertaken career and domestic responsibilities, there is less time for friends and leisure activities. Stresses are associated with times of overload when conflicts between their varied roles become acute. Furthermore, when crises arise, the wife in the two-career family, more often than the husband, compromises her career objectives to meet domestic needs.

The ability of women to find a balance between power and love in their lives also depends on the individual, the time of life, and the historical setting. Numerous studies have reported that women who are able to succeed at work and maintain caring relationships have high energy and intelligence and personal resources to cope with unusual demands. Other work has shown that the balance of power and love may shift during the life cycle as women adjust their career goals around times of childbearing and child rearing.

ANDROGNY
CULTURAL DETERMINISM
SEX ROLES

B. FORISHA-KOVACH

WONDERLIC PERSONNEL TEST

The Wonderlic Personnel Test was one of the most popular, short (50-item, 12-minute) general intelligence screening tests used in industry during the post–World War II era. Many of its items were taken from the Otis Self-Administering Tests of Mental Ability. The types of items used were similar to those from the original Army Alpha used in World War I.

The reliability of the test varies from 0.70 to 0.94. Test validity for the Wonderlic is limited to correlations with the Otis (construct validity) and norms for over 30,000 workers based on highest grade level reached.

Overall, the test has not been factor analyzed but seems to represent a measure of general intelligence. This has been supported by study results that show the Wonderlic to be related to initial training performance or clerical-type work.

L. BERGER

WORD ASSOCIATION TEST

The word association test is a simple technique administered individually. The subject, upon hearing a stimulus word, is to reply as quickly as possible with the very first word that comes to mind. The examiner records the response, reaction time, and any peculiarities in the subject's behavior.

This grandfather of projective techniques has a rich history. E. Kraepelin applied the test to clinical diagnosis and reported the effects of fatigue, hunger, and drugs upon association.

Only later was the word association test influenced by the psychoanalytic movement. It was Carl Jung who first used word association as a clinical test procedure to discover complexes (centers of emotional disturbance) in patients. His major contribution was standardizing the method of administration and interpretation.

Jung used as stimuli a list of 100 words, which was selected to represent common emotional problems (e.g., anger, fear, death). He identified the following three signs of emotional disturbance (called complex indicators): (a) abnormalities in the content of the responses (e.g., egocentric responses, repetition of the stimulus); (b) long reaction times; and (c) affect shown by the subject's behavior (e.g., tension, laughter). These indicators are still often used in lie detection tests.

Later a radical modification of Jung's approach was introduced by D. Rapaport et al. They claimed that affect-laden areas of conflict could be inferred more readily from the stimulus words than from the content of the response word. Thus, the focus of analysis shifted to those stimulus words that aroused the most disturbance in the associative process and behavior of the subject.

The word association test has in general been disappointing both as a projective technique and as a diagnostic tool.

E. Siipola et al. used a modified technique that approximated the freedom from time pressure provided by other projective tests. This modification produced a fundamental change in the associative process. The subject delayed the response, deliberately searching for an associate that was personally satisfying. S. Dunn et al. found that such subject-bound associates were consistently related to the personality variables of impulsivity and values.

PROJECTIVE TECHNIQUES

E. M. SIIPOLA

WORD FREQUENCY

In psychology, word frequency is important not only in educational applications, but also in the control and analysis of stimulus and response attributes in experiments on perception, learning, memory, and language performance, and in characterizing the verbal repertoires of different populations of individuals—both normal and abnormal, and at different chronological and mental age levels.

The frequency of a word *type* is normally determined by counting the number of instances (*tokens*) of that type in a large sample of such tokens, either in spoken discourse or in written or printed texts. Computerized word counts generally define a type as a particular string of printed characters preceded and followed by a space. A *lemmatized* word count, in contrast, considers a word type as a defined class of words that includes its variant related forms (plurals, tense forms, capitalizations, etc.), and some lemmatized counts also distinguish between homographs (words spelled the same but different in meaning).

In two of the most widely used word counts in English, Edward L. Thorndike and Irving Lorge's *Teacher's word book of 30,000 words* and Henry Kucera and W. Nelson Francis' *Computational analysis of present-day American English,* word type frequencies are stated in frequency per million. The frequencies given in these sources will not be exactly comparable, not only because of noncomparability of the samples, but also because the former is lemmatized while the latter is not.

These counts are all based on printed materials. Few good counts of spoken language are available. Word frequencies from spoken and written word counts are fairly comparable; the major differences are likely to be for certain highly frequent personal pronouns.

There has been much interest in the mathematical form of distributions of word frequencies. Word frequency distributions can be used in estimating the size of vocabulary from which a sample has been drawn, but different assumed distributions yield somewhat different estimates.

Frequency is only one of a series of attributes of words that need to be controlled in psychological experimentation on verbal learning and memory processes. Frequency is positively related to the number of meanings a word has, but negatively related to word length. There are also relations of frequency with word familiarity, speed of recognition, intelligibility, association value, affective connotation, concreteness of meaning, the age when a word is likely to be acquired, and other important variables. In certain types of aphasia and other pathological conditions, word frequency, as well as the *type-token ratio* is a critical variable in characterizing vocabulary repertoires.

E. L. Thorndike was a pioneer in the study of the applications of word frequency studies in education—for example, in the selection of words for students' reading materials and dictionaries and in the measurement of the readability and comprehensibility of texts. Information on word frequencies has also played an important role in the teaching of foreign languages.

J. B. CARROLL

WORK AND PLAY

The technological character of advanced modern civilizations has tended to segregate work and play. A further extension of these segregations is to differentiate the motivations for work and play. This suggests that work is characterized by activities engaged in for the purpose of staying alive and that play refers to activities engaged in for their own sake. E. S. Bordin has proposed that work and play can be seen as involving various combinations of effort, compulsion, and spontaneity.

Effort and compulsion are intimately related. The greater the effort and the longer it endures, the stronger the pressure toward cessation and rest becomes. What sustains effort against the accumulating counterpressure is inner interest and involvement or externalized threats of punishment or annihilation, which, in turn, can be internalized and experienced as an inner compulsion, for example, to stay alive. Spontaneity refers to that element of interest, self-investment, and self-expression that transforms an effortful performance that might have been experienced as alienated toil into a creative, joyful self-expression. This transformed activity epitomizes play.

WORK AND PLAY IN CHILDHOOD

The bulk of the observation of play has been directed toward the immature. In young animals and children, observers stress the excess energy expended and the usefulness of play as a means toward mastery. Therapists working with children utilize this concept of play. Similarly, children are seen as using play to try out and prepare for anticipated adult roles.

The history of education has been marked by concern with preserving spontaneity concerned with maintaining appropriate levels of directed effort. Observers of children's play have noted that the fluid, spontaneous play of the young child soon gives way to formalizations of rules, which introduces restraining boundaries to spontaneity. The physical and intellectual development of the child is accompanied by more sophisticated play with its demands for mastery. Thus, growth and maturation are accompanied by ever-increasing participation by compulsion and effort. Play has become more than a simple joyful expression of energy in which effort is background.

WORK AND PLAY IN VOCATION

Virtually all persons face the necessity of securing the material means of staying alive or for additional comforts. In work-intensive societies, there was more room for men and women to mix the process of working for a livelihood with flexibility for self-expression. Our modern machine-dominated technological society challenges the preservation of these elements in work.

Is there any way to protect against work as alienated toil? Marxist philosophers such as Herbert Marcuse argue that under socialism in which the worker feels in control of the larger process of production, the greater economies in productivity afforded by the utilization of the machine can be converted into greater free time, making possible the assimilation of work into play. He argues that the experience of alienated labor is dictated by the excess repression exerted by capitalism to maintain that economic system.

Psychologists and industrial sociologists point out that many highly skilled jobs and professions require and permit long-term commitments and the flexible expressions of self that mix the compulsion, effort, and spontaneity marking the fusion of work and play. Research on personality development and the psychological characteristics and requirements associated with various occupations and occupational families has provided the base for helping individuals seeking vocational commitments to channel their choices toward optimal reconciliations of the wishes for material returns with their desires for satisfaction in work.

There remains the question of whether this can apply to all jobs. The Marxist answer accepts the antihumanistic element in the machine–human interface and only seeks to limit its duration. R. Blauner found that the worker's relation to the technological organization of the work process and the social organization of the factory determines whether he or she experiences a sense of control rather than domination, a sense of meaningful purpose rather than isolation, and a sense of spontaneous involvement rather than detachment and discontent. These views have spawned many efforts through job enlargement, job rotation, or drastic redesign to achieve for workers desirable levels of intrinsic satisfaction in their work life.

WORK AND PLAY IN LEISURE AND RETIREMENT

Surveys of workers' use of nonwork time finds them engaged in second jobs, educational activities, household chores, and child care. Some of this reflects the same economic pressures that make work a necessity. But these data also suggest that a major motivation in leisure time activity is not the removal of effort, but relaxation of the pressure of compulsion.

PLAY
WORK–REST CYCLES

E. S. BORDIN

WORK EFFICIENCY

Work efficiency refers to the study of productive human activity, and the physical and mental responses of individuals to energy expenditures in work and in nonwork settings. Fatigue, both mental and physical, that results from sustained work has been found to affect speed and accuracy of movements, strength and endurance, and quality (errors) and quantity of output. Studies of work efficiency, then, attempt to promote effective work performance, and to reduce stress, strain, boredom, and other negative consequences affecting individual health and well-being.

Efficient job performance is a principal goal of engineering psychology and human factors engineering, or ergonomics. The study of work efficiency has contributed to advances in job design aimed at improving output and reducing fatigue and accidents.

The beginnings of the study of work efficiency can probably be traced to Frederick Taylor who argued that work tasks should be studied in exact detail to improve efficiency and productivity. Taylor also suggested that workers should be matched to the job and trained to perform to the specifications of the scientific analysis. Other early work on fatigue by Frank and Lillian Gilbreth resulted in the design of special chairs for different types of work that reduced strain. Frank Gilbreth, a time–motion analyst, also outlined rules for motion economy that covered arrangement of the workplace, position of tools, and design of equipment that would enhance efficiency.

Physical Fatigue

Feelings of fatigue have been associated with lack of sleep, intense physical activity that results in muscular tiredness (soreness, stiffness, aches, etc.) and decreases in work performance. Generally, indicators of fatigue fall into three categories: chemical (e.g., blood or urine content, oxygen consumption), electrical (e.g., electroencephalogram, electromyograph), and physical (blood pressure, heart rate, body temperature).

Mental Fatigue

Mental fatigue is becoming more and more of a concern in studies of work efficiency. Mental fatigue may be especially problematic in situations involving sustained periods of concentration or vigilance. Mental fatigue may also be caused by too high a mental (information) work load.

Boredom and Monotony

Boredom is related to mental fatigue and can be generated by repetitiveness, lack of novelty, and monotony. Boredom depends on interaction of task characteristics, surroundings, and individual differences, but can be alleviated, under certain circumstances, by music, noise, or motivational incentives. A. Anastasi suggests that industry can counter the effects of boredom on workers by (a) proper selection and placement, (b) changes in work environment and surroundings, and (c) alterations in the work itself, such as job enrichment or job enlargement.

ERGOPSYCHOMETRY
INDUSTRIAL PSYCHOLOGY

A. R. Spokane

WORK–REST CYCLES

Any activity that involves work is measured physically in foot-pounds or physiologically in heat units. The usual physiological unit is expressed in kilocalories (kcal), where 1 kcal equals the amount of heat needed to raise the temperature of 1 kilogram of water from 15 to 16 C. Efforts have been made to relate such terms to kilocalories so that very heavy work might be rated as calling for 10 kcal/min, moderate work as 5 kcal/min, and light or very light work at about 2 kcal/min. A serious individual difference problem arises because what is heavy or moderate for one person might be light for another. Whatever activity is involved—for example, laying bricks (4 kcal/min) or mowing the lawn (7 kcal/min)—no one can continue working indefinitely without rest. The need for rest may arise more from boredom than from energy expenditure, but the need does arise. The nature of the rest is also difficult to define, as merely changing activities may serve the same function, that is, the restoration of the capacity for continuation of the original activity. In any case, work is regularly followed by rest in what might be described as a work–rest cycle.

The amount of rest required to recover from any activity is difficult to determine and depends on the criterion adopted. In the laboratory, a person might be willing to work on a treadmill or at other strenuous tasks to "exhaustion." Ordinarily, even in the laboratory, such a point can be exceeded by introducing motivational factors. In the workaday world no one works to exhaustion, as work is controlled by extraneous factors and people rest either formally or informally in various "breaks" and pauses.

In most activities, there are levels of expenditure of energy that one can continue more or less indefinitely if the rates are controlled so that sufficient rest is included between exertions to permit the next exertion. The problem resolves itself into a cost-efficiency one. As a rough rule, working four times as fast as some easily maintained standard will result in only twice the output before exhaustion is reached and longer rests are required to resume the prior level.

The work–rest cycle problem is complicated by great individual differences in motivation, attitudes toward work, relative susceptibility to boredom, the worker's physical and health characteristics, bargaining arrangements, and so on. In general, if left to one's self, one will develop a level of energy expenditure that will allow for the continuation of the work for some acceptable time.

ERGOPSYCHOMETRY
WORK EFFICIENCY

B. R. Bugelski

WORK-SPACE DESIGNS

The area surrounding a worker and the larger environment in which the worker operates is called the work space. The object of work-space design is to arrange the workplace to promote effectiveness and to enhance operator comfort and safety.

Similar in some respects to job design, work-space design focuses more specifically on the physical characteristics of the worker as the critical element in the design of the work station. Two related disciplines, anthropometry and biomechanics, have contributed important knowledge about the physical features and functions of the body, including linear dimensions, weight, volume and range of movements. Early research efforts revealed the importance of shape and design of hand tools and chairs, and arrangement of components in the work station to the workers' ability to use them efficiently. Frank Gilbreth and other motion-study analysts have outlined rules of motion economy that include arranging tools in the order in which they are to be used, having a regular place for each tool, and positioning tools for easy grasp.

J. McCormick and E. J. Tiffin view the immediate work space as a three-dimensional envelope around the operator, in which work tasks and activities are performed. The size and shape of the envelope are determined by observations of the nature of the task and the range of motion of the worker garnered from studies of operator movement.

Research has shown that the arrangement of the work station in a semicircle reduces excessive reaching required when components, bins, or controls are arranged end to end. According to A. Anastasi, the semicircular work space is appropriate for those tasks in which reaching must be done repeatedly. The savings over time of these small gains in efficiency is large, sometimes resulting in thousands of hours of work saved.

The ground-breaking work of Frank Gilbreth on the design of chair seats has led to a great deal of effort in designing seats with respect to optimum weight distribution, seat height, seat depth and width, trunk stabilization, and posture. Work surfaces (tables, benches, etc.) have also been the object of work design studies, as have tools and instruments (hand tools, surgical instruments). Finally, others have studied problems of the elderly and disabled in relation to work-space designs.

Environmental factors that impinge on the worker are an integral part of the design of the larger work situation. These include (a) illumination; (b) noise and vibration; (c) atmospheric conditions (humidity, temperature, negative ions); (d) pollutants and contaminants; (e) gravity and acceleration; and (f) radioactivity. A. Chapanis points out, however, that little is known about the compound effects of several of these environmental factors combined.

Elements in the work space may interact with one another. *Link analysis* is described by Anastasi as the investigation of the operational connections between elements within a work system. These data are then used to improve the arrangement of displays, controls, machines, and people.

INDUSTRIAL PSYCHOLOGY
WORK EFFICIENCY

A. R. Spokane

WORKING MEMORY

Virtually all mental activities require the coordination of several pieces of information, several ideas, or several inputs. Individuals often need to start by working on these ideas or inputs one at a time and only then integrate them into a full package. Consider the reading of any long sentence: One first must decipher the early words in the sentence, then place these words on hold while working on later words. Then, once several words have been identified, one must integrate the words to understand the full phrase. Likewise, consider a simple plan: One must first choose one's goal, but then must put this choice on hold to concentrate on the early steps needed to reach this goal. Then, once these early steps are taken, one must think about the goal again, to select the next steps.

These examples suggest an interplay between thought and memory: To devote attention to one aspect of a problem, one must set other aspects to the side. But these other aspects must remain available, so that they can be coordinated into a full package. The memory making this possible is called working memory (WM). When information is currently in use, or likely to be needed soon, it is stored within WM. In essence, WM functions as a mental scratchpad, although this metaphor suggests far too passive a role for WM. Information in WM must be quickly available to facilitate easy access to needed information. But to make easy access possible, WM is limited in size (so that the search through this memory is a trivial matter).

Secondary memory can hold vast quantities of information (namely all of one's remembered knowledge). But, as a consequence, considerable time and effort are needed to locate information within this huge warehouse. Secondary memory presumably holds material for a very long time and so, in some texts, is referred to as long-term memory (LTM). WM needs to store material only for as long as one is working on it and so, in older texts, is described as short-term memory (STM).

Many early studies of WM emphasized its role in the learning of new materials. Several principles are crucial for understanding this: One tends to think about material one has just noticed, and so newly arrived material is certain to gain access to WM. Information in WM is easily retrieved and so likely to be reported in any sort of memory test. In addition, the process of memorizing (i.e., placing material into secondary memory) is generally facilitated if one understands and actively thinks about the to-be-remembered (TBR) material. This engagement with TBR material will presumably take time and effort and so also will require the support of WM. Hence material that passes only briefly through WM is less likely to be remembered; material that is in WM for longer periods will be remembered if this time is spent in an appropriate fashion (i.e., engaging the TBR material in some active way).

Materials just heard or just seen are usually quite well remembered, an effect termed the recency effect. This reflects the fact that these materials can easily be retrieved from WM. However, the recency effect is disrupted if another task is interposed between the presentation of the TBR materials and the memory test, because the interpolated task will place demands on WM, displacing the previously arrived recency items. Likewise, the amount of time an item was in WM provides a reasonable predictor of the likelihood of subsequent recall from secondary memory, consistent with the claims that mental work is required to place materials into secondary memory, and that this work itself draws on WM.

More recent studies have examined WM's role in other tasks. Many of these studies have exploited the fact that WM's capacity varies somewhat among individuals. One can, therefore, ask about WM's function by asking what tasks or what processes are facilitated by a slightly larger WM and what tasks are compromised by a smaller WM. For example, research on reading reveals a crucial role for WM, with strong positive correlations observed between working memory's span (i.e., its overall capacity) and various measures of reading comprehension and reading speed, thus, an individual with a larger capacity WM is likely also to be a more efficient reader. Similar results have been obtained with assessments of reasoning skills.

This research draws attention to the importance of measuring WM's capacity. WM is generally spoken of as holding (on average) 7 ± 2 chunks of information. WM does seem to have about seven slots into which information can be placed, but there is flexibility in how information is packaged into these slots. WM's capacity is often measured with a span task, in which subjects are read a series of letters or digits, and must immediately repeat these back. With series of 6 or 7 items, performance is generally perfect. With longer series, errors occur, suggesting that WM's span has been exceeded. However, subjects can avoid this apparent limit on their memory by the following strategy. Consider a letter-span task in which subjects hear the series "H, O, P, T, R, A, E, G." Rather than thinking of these as individual letters, the subject might think of the list as a sequence of syllables ("ho, pit, rah . . . "). In this case, the subject will still remember seven items (syllables), but this will now include 14 letters! Likewise, a subject might form 3-letter syllables ("hop, tra . . . "). In this case, the subjects will remember close to 21 letters and so on. By assembling the TBR material into larger and larger chunks, subjects can make extraordinary use of the seven slots in WM.

WM's capacity actually reflects the combined contributions of WM's various components, because evidence indicates that WM is not a single, unitary entity. Instead, WM can be fractionated into several parts: a central executive, able to perform a wide range of complex functions, and then multiple slave systems, capable of short-term, rather mechanical storage. By using the slave systems for mere storage, the more powerful executive is freed for other, more demanding, aspects of a task.

The best-understood slave system is the phonological loop. In using this loop, the central executive initiates the covert pronunciation of the TBR materials. This activity by the inner voice causes a record of this pronunciation to be loaded into a phonological buffer (the inner ear). This record will gradually fade, and then the cycle must be restarted, with the executive again required to initiate action in the inner voice. Within each cycle, however, the functions of the inner voice and inner ear proceed more or less automatically, freeing the executive to work on other functions.

A wide range of evidence is compatible with this proposal. For example, short-term memory performance is worse if TBR materials are phonologically similar to each other ("man, map, mad . . . "). This reflects the confusability of these items within the phonological buffer, and this phonological similarity effect is, in fact, abolished if subjects are prevented from using the rehearsal loop. (Use of the loop can be blocked, for example, by requiring subjects to say, "ta, ta, ta . . . " aloud, while doing the main task. This use of speech occupies the control mechanisms needed for the inner voice, making this resource unavailable for use in rehearsal.) Likewise, measured span is slightly greater for shorter words than for longer ones. This is because shorter words can be more swiftly pronounced by the inner voice, allowing more efficient use of this resource. Again, this effect is abolished if use of the rehearsal loop is prevented.

Although there has been impressive progress in understanding WM's rehearsal loops, less is known about WM's central executive. Generally, the executive is presumed to be closely allied to systems monitoring and controlling attention, and crucial in initiating and coordinating action. These functions make it plain that the central executive is not a memory in the ordinary sense (i.e., it is not merely a means of storing information). Instead, the central executive embodies much active processing, emphasizing the work done in working memory.

ATTENTION SPAN
CONNECTIONISM
MEMORY
MEMORY RETRIEVAL PROCESSES
MEMORY SPAN
MNEMONICS

D. Reisberg

Y

YOGA

Yoga is a Sanskrit word with two roots. The first means "to meditate" and the second means "to join." The latter, more commonly accepted, implies the connecting of human nature with its cosmic source.

Historically, Yoga has developed in a Hindu and Buddhist environment and is, to some extent, influenced by the philosophies and practices of these religions. But in itself yoga is not a religion that depends on faith, ritual, and sacred scripture. It consists of methods developed by practicing yogis over thousands of years.

In general, yoga begins where medicine and psychotherapy leave off: helping otherwise healthy and adjusted people to achieve higher levels of functioning. It is an individualistic undertaking conducted under the careful supervision of a teacher who guides and monitors the student continuously.

Classic yoga philosophy is generally based on a rejection of worldly life as an illusion that must be overcome if the individual self is to become one with the universal spirit.

Because of its exotic origin and the general skepticism of Western scientists concerning extravagant claims made on its behalf, there has been relatively little scientific effort to study the practices and attainments associated with yoga. However, recent studies suggest that modern technology may be able to distinguish the relatively subtle effects produced by various meditative and yogic practices. Studies of brain wave activity and physiological stress indicators have produced quite different patterns when obtained from practitioners of Zen Buddhism, classical yoga, and Kriya yoga. The findings are in keeping with the claims made for the methods being tested.

Underlying yogic practices is a model of the individual unfamiliar to Western science, though traces can be found in most mystical traditions. It is often called *the subtle body* and roughly parallels such physiological systems as digestion. The subtle body consists of a series of interconnected centers called *chakras*. Each center has its own particular nature, but as in any system, it is the interaction of the parts that is important. When the subtle body is activated, it is able directly to process energy from the environment and refine it to a higher level that can nourish the inner development of the individual.

Seven major centers have been described in various mystical literatures, each with its own particular energy and function. All of these centers are ordinarily closed. It requires a conscious effort on the part of the individual to open them.

Various forms of yoga utilize different techniques, but the conception of the subtle body helps to clarify their ultimate purpose, namely, to help the individual experience a higher level of awareness and functioning through a conscious process of inner evolvement. This goal can be achieved only if people learn how to work with energy, conserving what they have and transmuting what they attract to more rarefied levels to nourish the more refined aspects of their inner natures.

EAST/WEST PSYCHOLOGY
RELIGION AND PSYCHOLOGY

J. H. MANN

Z

Z-PROCESS

The Z-process is a psychotherapeutic and attachment system, incorporating ethological and attachment principles, developed to overcome resistance to human bonding and growth. The autistic child shows self-destructive aggression and does not direct aggression toward other people. The Z-process treatment of autistic children led to the conclusion that such psychopathology results from a failure to develop two bonding behavior networks essential for the growth of viable attachment: (a) body contact, necessary for intimacy and basic trust; and (b) eye–face contact, necessary for the direction, integration, and focus of complex emotional and cognitive social behavior. A disturbance in these bonds is called the Medusa complex, which is corrected by "holding" the child in "protest" while maintaining eye–face contact. Niko Tinbergen and his collaborators have reported significant success in using the "holding" approach with autistic children.

AUTISM
BONDING AND ATTACHMENT

R. W. ZASLOW

z-SCORE

The letter z denotes a standard score referenced to a normal distribution; that is, a z-score is a measure of deviation from the mean in terms of the standard deviation as the unit.

If x is a normally distributed variable with mean μ and standard deviation σ, then

$$z = \frac{x - \mu}{\sigma}$$

Any value converted to a z-score is said to be normalized (i.e., rescaled to a value within a unit normal distribution with mean 0 and standard deviation 1). The advantage of normalizing disparate distributions is that doing so equates the various distributions to the same scale, thus permitting direct comparison of previously nonhomologous variables.

The area of the normal curve between $z = -1.96$ and $z = +1.96$ and contains 95% of all cases, between $z = -2.576$ and $z = +2.576$ contains 99% of all cases, so one of these two sets of z-scores is usually used to define the end points of the critical region for acceptance of the null hypothesis in psychological research.

MEASUREMENT
STATISTICAL SIGNIFICANCE
TEST STANDARDIZATION

H. Reich

ZEĬGARNIK EFFECT

Work by Bliuma Zeĭgarnik established the fact that subjects ranging widely in age tended to remember interrupted tasks better (and with greater frequency) than they did tasks they had completed. What amounted to common-sense observations constituted the impetus for a series of germinal experiments by Zeĭgarnik. For half of the activities, subjects were allowed to continue until they were finished. Following the activity or task session, the tasks were removed from the subjects' view and each was asked to recall and to jot down some of the activities in which they had been involved. Results of the study confirmed Zeĭgarnik's initial hypothesis. The number of *unfinished* or *incompleted* tasks (designated as *I*) that were recalled was significantly higher than was the number of completed tasks (designated as *C*). By and large, subjects taking part in Zeĭgarnik's research were twice as likely to recall incompleted tasks as completed ones.

A number of possible alternative explanations of the Zeĭgarnik effect have been advanced that do not emphasize the completion-incompletion variable *per se*. One such explanation is that it is the shock associated with the interruption or the cessation of work on a task that increases the salience of the task in the minds of subjects. Results revealed that the shock of task termination or interruption had little, if anything, to do with the difference in the frequency of recall. A second possible interpretation of Zeĭgarnik's original findings was that subjects may have assumed that the interrupted tasks would be completed later on (i.e., that they represented unfinished business). In another refinement of her original study, Zeĭgarnik successfully replicated her earlier findings, with an *I/C* ratio of 1.80, essentially the same as before.

In the series of Zeĭgarnik studies, the recall ratio for tasks interrupted at the middle or toward the end (tasks nearing completion) was higher than for tasks interrupted at or near the beginning of work on them. Ambitious subjects forgot completed tasks at a faster rate than did those of average ambitiousness. It may be concluded that the goal for these subjects was not merely task completion, but also some kind of success, thus giving rise to a higher *I/C* ratio. If task interruption were to be interpreted by subjects as signifying that they had failed, generating an ego-threatening situation, the *I/C* ratio would be further increased, with subjects tending to recall incompleted tasks with greater frequency than before.

Other explanations that might account for the Zeĭgarnik effect include the following: (a) Task interruption may actively set up a new motive involving resentment against the interruption itself or the interrupter and hence a better memory for the cause of the resentment. (b) The interruption may serve as an emphasizer of the interrupted task. (c) In Gestalt terms, the subject may strive for closure. (d) Subjects' persistence in attending to an unsolved problem may often have been rewarded in the past, hence giving rise to a higher rate of recall for unfinished tasks.

Studies have found that the Zeĭgarnik effect is sensitive to a number of factors that may be difficult, if not impossible, to control within the context of a laboratory study: (a) The Zeĭgarnik effect is less likely to appear if the subject is, to some extent, ego-involved in the task. (b) The effect is more likely to appear if the interruption of the task does not seem to be part of the experimental game plan. (c) The effect is most likely to appear if the subject has set a genuine level of aspiration in the interrupted task.

MEMORY EXPERIMENTS
SELECTIVE ATTENTION

F. L. Denmark

ZEN BUDDHISM

The Zen, or meditation, school of Mahdydna, or Northern Buddhism, first became generally known in the West in the decade following World War II. Its paradoxical training problems baffled and intrigued Western scholars. These problems have the avowed purpose of bringing the conceptual mind to an impasse or halt, to force students into direct perception of their own essential natures. Buddhism stems from the teachings of the Indian sage *Gautama Siddhartha*, called the *Buddha* ("Enlightened One") as embodying supreme wisdom and virtue.

He taught that suffering and dissatisfaction are inherent in the human condition, that all phenomena are in process of constant change, and that none possess a separate permanent self. Ignorance of these "signs of being" results in a vain attempt to cling to transient phenomena, which is the cause of suffering. Wisdom lies in relinquishment, as a consequence of clear perception, which leads to the cessation of suffering. He taught a method known as the "Noble Eightfold Path" as the means to this end. It consists of the practice of right understanding, aims, speech, action, livelihood, effort, mindfulness (awareness), and concentration. Gautama refused to express an opinion as to the existence of a deity, stating that it was "an unprofitable question."

Buddhism incorporated the older Indian concept of *Karma* (broadly speaking, "cause and effect"), which emphasizes responsibility for one's actions, and acceptance of their consequences. The concept of rebirth is taught. This has been variously interpreted as referring to the process of change occurring from moment to moment, or as change occurring through a series of lives. Buddhism does not believe in the existence of an "essence" or "soul," but states that the impetus of unfulfilled desire gives rise to other phenomena resulting from such craving. Rebirth has been described in India as being similar to a process in which a candle is lit from another; the flame is not the same, nor is it different. Contrary to popular Western belief, rebirth is viewed as undesirable, as it reactivates the onerous chain of suffering. Zen shares these basic tenets with general Buddhism, but emphasizes the necessity of living as a *Bodhisattva*, who selflessly devotes his or her life to the service of others, and helps them on the road to Enlightenment.

It is certain that Zen, as it is now known, contains many elements related to Chinese Taoism. H. Dumoulin has shown that its teachings are related to several Mahdydna sutra (scriptures) that emphasize the identity of form and emptiness.

Zen has made major creative contributions to the cultures of China, and of Korea, Manchuria, Vietnam, and Japan because it was taken by Buddhist missionaries. Particularly in the last country, it has influenced the training of warriors, administrators, poets, architects, and masters of the tea ceremony, of flower arrangement, of ink painting and calligraphy, and of judo, karate, kendo (swordsmanship) and other martial arts. It has profoundly influenced Japanese manners and social attitudes.

Traditional Zen practice centers around *Zazen* (seated meditation). The erect cross-legged posture favors alertness. Strength is centered in the lower abdomen. Silence is mandatory. The initial focus is often on counting inhalations and exhalations of breath. Later practice varies, but frequently involves concentration on a *Kōan*. Or the student may undertake the practice of *Shikan Taza* (silent, intense total awareness, resembling that of one facing a dangerous enemy). The student is required repeatedly to interview the master of the temple or monastery to demonstrate his or her understanding of the Kōan or experience of Shikan Taza. Such confrontations induce intense stress, and the student is urged to "become one" with the problem to break through to Enlightenment. As the student's answers are rejected again and again, he or she is brought to the brink of desperation. Finally, with total effort, the fortunate student may experience *Kensho* ("first seeing"), a form of direct unmediated perception, a taste of that *Satori,* or liberation, which is the aim of the practice.

Western commentators have viewed Zen as a means of breaking through social and personal conditioning and the limitation of conceptual categories. Erich Fromm (1960), in his essay in *Zen Buddhism and psychoanalysis,* has spoken of the integration of intellectual and affective knowledge aimed at by both those disciplines.

Carl Jung, Karen Horney, Fritz Perls, Claudio Naranjo, and Daniel Goleman have been among Western psychologists and psychiatrists interested in Zen.

In concluding, one is reminded that Zen masters have referred to the practice specifically as a cure for the disorders of "word sickness and mind wandering." It potentially provides potent additional means whereby contemporary psychologists may treat the troubled and the deluded.

MEDITATION
RELIGION AND PSYCHOLOGY

R. J. HEARN

ZWAARDEMAKER ODOR SYSTEM

Many attempts have been made to classify the various kinds of odors into a comprehensive system. One of the first was created by the eighteenth-century botanist/taxonomist Linnaeus, who used a sevenfold odor arrangement created as an aid to the classification of plants. But perhaps the best known system was devised by a Dutch otolaryngologist, Hendrick Zwaardemaker, who adapted and extended Linnaeus's scheme in his classic 1895 monograph, *The physiology of smell.* Zwaardemaker's system, which added two additional categories of smells and introduced several subclasses of each, remained the accepted scheme for classifying odors until well into the twentieth century. This widely adopted system categorized odors into the following nine classes: (a) ethereal (e.g., fruits, wines), (b) aromatic (spices, camphor), (c) fragrant (flowers, vanilla), (d) ambrosial (musk, sandalwood), (e) alliaceous (garlic, chlorine), (f) empyreumatic (coffee, creosote), (g) hircine or caprylic (cheese, rancid fat), (h) repulsive (bedbugs, belladonna), and (i) nauseating (feces, carrion).

Other classification systems include the Henning smell prism, which posits six primary odors (fragrant, ethereal, spicy, resinous, burnt, and putrid—one found at each corner of a triangular prism); the Crocker–Henderson system, with four primary odors (fragrant, acid, burnt, and caprylic or goaty); and the stereochemical model of Amoore, in which seven odor qualities are considered primary (camphoraceous, ethereal, floral, musky, pepperminty, pungent, and putrid). It should be noted that no classification of odors has received universal acceptance, largely because of the sizable contribution of subjective and associative elements.

CHEMICAL BRAIN STIMULATION
HUNGER
IMPRESSION FORMATION
SENSORIMOTOR PROCESSES
STIMULANTS

H. REICH

BIOGRAPHIES

ALLPORT, FLOYD HENRY (1890–1978)

Allport is considered to be the father of experimental social psychology. In his theories and research he set a direction in social psychology that was followed by psychologists in that area for several decades.

ALLPORT, GORDON WILLARD (1897–1967)

Allport regarded personality as the natural subject matter of psychology. His approach was eclectic, drawing on a wide variety of sources.

ALMEIDA, EDUARDO (b 1937)

Almeida conducted a program for the development of competence in school children from Mexico City. He also developed an instrument for studying public opinion.

AMES, LOUISE B. (b 1908)

Ames' books have been standard references relative to the developmental processes for both psychologists and parents.

ANASTASI, ANNE (b 1908)

Anastasi is most closely associated with the development of differential psychology. Her research centered chiefly on factor analysis, problems of test construction, and the interpretation of test scores.

ANGELL, FRANK (1857–1939)

Angell established a laboratory at Stanford University. His research centered on pyschophysics, especially auditory sensation.

ANGELL, JAMES ROLLAND (1867–1949)

Angell stated that functional psychology was the study of mental operations; that psychology should be considered a study of the functional utilities of consciousness; and that psychology is concerned with the relationship between the body and the environment.

ANGYAL, ANDRAS (1902–1960)

Angyal asserted that there are two basic patterns of motivation: striving toward mastery and striving toward love.

ANSBACHER, HEINZ L. (b 1904)

Ansbacher is the prime interpreter of Alfred Adler. His most important contribution is his clarification of Adler's concepts of lifestyle and social interest.

ANZIEU, DIDIER (b 1923)

Anzieu's main psychological concepts are "group delusion," "skin ego," "paradoxical transference," and "creative psychological work."

ASCH, SOLOMON (b 1907)

Asch is best known for performing a series of experiments on the effects of social pressures on single individuals.

AUSTAD, CAROL DONNA SHAW (b 1946)

Austad conducted research on the practice of psychotherapy in the managed-care setting.

AVENERIUS, RICHARD (1843–1896)

Avenerius hypothesized that there was a system "C" on which consciousness depended. The significance of this concept has to do with its influence on Titchener.

AZUMA, HIROSHI (b 1926)

Azuma's work centers around cognitive development of children, concept learning, and methods of instruction.

BACON, SIR FRANCIS (1561–1636)

Bacon stated that in science there are two kinds of experiments: those that shed light and those that bring fruit. He was the first to call a halt to medieval speculation and superstition.

BADDELEY, ALAN (b 1934)

Baddeley demonstrated that long-term memory tends to rely heavily on meaning, as opposed to short-term memory, which relies more heavily on sound or speech coding.

BAIN, ALEXANDER (1818–1903)

Bain stressed two basic laws of association: similarity and contiguity. He believed that sensations and feelings come together in close succession and in such a way that, when one of them is brought to mind, the other will most likely occur.

BAIRD, JOHN WALLACE (1873–1919)

Baird was regarded as Titchener's most representative follower. He made systematic experimental introspection of the higher mental processes the central research topic of Clark University.

BAKARE, CHRISTOPHER G. M. (b 1935)

Bakare devised a statistical technique for identifying the "kernel of truth" in interethnic stereotypes to understand the conflicts that plague Africa's development.

BALDWIN, JAMES MARK (1861–1934)

Known as a founding father of developmental psychology, Baldwin developed a thoroughgoing Darwinian genetic psychology. He stressed intentional action as the instrument of selection in mental development.

BALTES, PAUL B. (b 1939)

Baltes, a pioneer of life-span developmental psychology, emphasizes that individuals continue to maintain a capacity for change across the entire life span.

BANDURA, ALBERT (b 1925)

Bandura assigns a central role to cognitive vicarious, self-regulative, and self-reflective processes in human mastery and adaptation.

BARKER, ROGER G. (1903–1990)

Barker helped establish The Midwest Psychological Field Station, a pioneering center for research in environmental psychology that investigates relationships between environment and behavior.

BARTLETT, FREDERIC C. (1886–1979)

Bartlett is best remembered for his outstanding achievement in directing research. His work is best represented by his classic book, *Remembering.*

BASOV, MIKHAIL YAKOVIEVICH (1892–1931)

Basov was a Soviet psychologist who opposed a mechanistic point of view. He believed that heredity and environment both contributed to human growth and development, their roles changing from one phase of development to another.

BATESON, GREGORY (1904–1980)

Bateson conducted anthropological research with the Baining and the Sulka of the Gazelle Peninsula and with the Iatmul of New Guinea. Later in life he explored the causes of maladjustments and mental disorders.

BATESON, WILLIAM (1861–1926)

Bateson is best known for his contributions to the establishment of the Mendelian concept of heredity. Bateson named the new science "genetics" and extended his efforts to a study of chromosomes and genes.

BAYÉS, RAMÓN (b 1930)

Bayés is one of the founders of diverse entities in Spain, such as the introduction of behavior modification. He wrote the first Spanish book on behavioral pharmacology.

BAYLEY, NANCY (b 1899)

Among Bayley's seminal studies are longitudinal research on the life span; techniques for measuring behavioral, motor, and physical development; and assessment of interactions between behavioral and biological development.

BEACH, FRANK A. (1911–1988)

Known for his work in human and animal sexual behavior, Beach published his findings in *Patterns of sexual behavior.* In this book, sex is reviewed from cultural and evolutionary perspectives.

BEEBE-CENTER, JOHN G. (1897–1958)

Beebe-Center was an investigator of hedonic aspects. As a result of his studies of taste thresholds and the scaling of taste values, he developed a psychological scale of taste named the *gust scale.*

BEERS, CLIFFORD W. (1876–1943)

Beers developed manic-depressive disorder and for 3 years was a patient in several hospitals. Following his recovery, he organized the first Society for Mental Hygiene in 1908.

BÉKÉSY, GEORG VON (1899–1972)

Békésy is best known for his work in audition. He devised many new tools such as the Békésy audiometer for measuring loss of hearing.

BÉKHTEREV, VLADIMIR MIKHAĬLOVĬCH (1857–1927)

Békhterev is best known for his work on associated reflexes (usually referred to by Ivan Pavlov's term *conditioned reflexes*).

BELL, SIR CHARLES (1774–1842)

Bell is known for his discovery that the sensory fibers of a mixed nerve enter the spinal cord at the dorsal root, whereas the motor fibers of the same nerve leave the cord by a ventral root.

BENEDICT, RUTH F. (1887–1948)

Most of Benedict's research dealt with the origins of Native American cultures. She saw in each culture an assemblage of elements from many other cultures.

BIJOU, SIDNEY W. (b 1908)

Bijou was the director of the Child Research Laboratory and the Institute of Research in Exceptional Children at Champaign–Urbana Illinois, and the founding editor of the *Journal of experimental child psychology.*

BINET, ALFRED (1857–1911)

Binet acquired much of his data on intelligence by studying his daughters. He developed a test that became the first scale for the measurement of intelligence.

BINGHAM, WALTER V. (1880–1952)

During World War I, Bingham served as executive secretary of the committee on classification of personnel in the U.S. Army. He was one of a small group that developed intelligence testing for the Army.

BINSWANGER, LUDWIG (1881–1966)

Binswanger, an existentialist, rejected positivism, determinism, and materialism. In his view, we are completely responsible for our own existence, free to decide what we can and cannot do.

BLAKE, ROBERT R. (b 1918)

Blake has provided insight into group and intergroup dynamics, concentrating particularly on the organizational impact of group norms and the resolution of intergroup conflict.

BLAU, THEODORE H. (b 1928)

Blau has performed research on the nature and effects of mixed cerebral dominance. He proposed a neuropsychological/social influence theory of schizophrenia.

BLEULER, EUGEN (1857–1939)

Bleuler introduced concepts such as neologism, word salad, and negative speech into the descriptive vocabulary of schizophrenia, as well as the notion of autism and ambivalence.

BLONSKII, PAVEL (1884–1941)

Blonskii saw the necessity of replacing the scholastic methods of instruction due to the reality of industrialized society. He suggested making industrial work the cornerstone of the new education.

BOAS, FRANZ (1858–1942)

Boas wanted to make anthropology a rigorous and exact science. In many of his investigations he noted parallel developments in widely separated areas.

BODER, DAVID PABLO (1886–1961)

After the Russian Revolution, Boder traveled to Mexico where he was placed in charge of psychological research in penal institutions. Later, he established a psychological museum in the United States.

BOLLES, ROBERT C. (b 1928)

Bolles' research ranged over different areas of animal motivation and later focused on avoidance behavior. He developed the concept of species-specific defense reactions.

BONNET, CHARLES (1720–1793)

Bonnet and Condillac used the analogy of a human as a statue. Condillac had avoided physiology, but Bonnet wrote of nervous fluids and agitation of the nerve fibers. He may have anticipated the doctrine of the "specific energies of nerves."

BORGATTA, EDGAR F. (b 1924)

Borgatta's early research focused on role-playing techniques and sociometric analysis. Later, his research addressed the formal properties of small groups and the structure of interaction processes, as well as scaling and statistical analysis.

BORING, EDWARD G. (1886–1968)

Boring's *History of experimental psychology* is a widely accepted classic. It brought together the creative scientist and the *Zeitgeist*, or spirit of the times, and explained how their interaction affected the direction of psychology.

BOSS, MEDARD (b 1903)

Boss stressed man's freedom, denying all inferences to causality. His interpretation of "being-in-the-world" refers to man's possibilities for relating what he has encountered to his own existence.

BOWDITCH, HENRY PICKERING (1840–1911)

Bowditch was the first to demonstrate the all-or-nothing law of nerve transmission in heart muscle fibers. The principle that nerves cannot be fatigued is known as Bowditch's law.

BOWER, GORDON HOWARD (b 1932)

Bower's early research involved operant conditioning with lower animals. His interests then turned to problems in human learning, including mathematical models of learning.

BOWLBY, JOHN (1907–1990)

Bowlby is known for his work on the ill effects of maternal deprivation on personality development, and for formulating attachment theory as a way of conceptualizing a child's tie to his or her mother.

BRADLEY, FRANCIS HERBERT (1846–1924)

Bradley emphasized the importance of individuals to find themselves first as a whole and then bring themselves into line with the world of completely harmonized experience with an infinite coherent unity.

BRAID, JAMES (ca. 1795–1860)

Braid generally is credited to be the discoverer of hypnosis, although the phenomenon had been known and practiced earlier by Mesmer, Elliotson, and Esdale. His significance is that he removed the phenomenon from the realm of mystical explanation.

BRAY, W. CHARLES II (1904–1982)

Bray's research was mostly on hearing, especially on electrical potentials in the cochlea and auditory nerve action in response to sounds. His work initiated the field of auditory electrophysiology.

BRENMAN-GIBSON, MARGARET (b 1918)

Best known for her work on altered states of consciousness and their uses in psychoanalytic psychotherapy, Brenman-Gibson has extended this interest to the creative state in writers.

BRENTANO, FRANZ (1838–1917)

Brentano, in opposition to Wilhelm Wundt's views, proclaimed that the primary method of psychology was observation—not experimentation. He differentiated the act of seeing color from the sensory content of color.

BRETT, GEORGE S. (1879–1944)

Brett is primarily known for his monumental three-volume work, *A history of psychology*. He traced psychology from its earliest beginnings in ancient Greece to the twentieth century.

BREZNITZ, SHLOMO (b 1936)

Breznitz discovered and documented the phenomenon of "incubation of threat," whereby fear of danger grows with anticipation.

BRIDGMAN, PERCY W. (1882–1961)

Seeking to clarify the nature of physical concepts, Bridgman introduced the notion of operational definition: A concept is to be defined in terms of the operations by which it is observed.

CATANIA, CHARLES (b 1936)

As a behavioral pharmacologist Catania has written on topics in the experimental analysis of behavior, including learning, reinforcement schedules, and verbal behavior.

CATTELL, JAMES McKEEN (1860–1944)

The theme of Cattell's research was individual differences. His work contributed to the practical and applied psychology that was functional and uniquely American.

CATTELL, RAYMOND B. (b 1905)

Cattell derived his distinction in psychology from multivariate factor analysis and from numerous tests measuring various aspects of personality and intelligence that he developed.

CHA, JAE-HO (b 1934)

Cha was responsible for identifying a class of social perceptual phenomena, including dissonance effect and perceptual constancies that he named the discounting effect.

CHAPANIS, ALPHONSE (b 1917)

Sometimes called the father of human factors, or ergonomics, Chapanis acquired his taste for applied work while wrestling with the difficult problems encountered by the men who had to fly and fight in the military aircraft of World War II.

CHAVEZ, EZEQUIEL A. (1868–1946)

Chavez was considered by James Mark Baldwin to be the pioneer of Mexican psychology. He promoted educational reform that permitted him to teach the first psychology course in Mexico.

CHELPANOV, GEORGĬI IVANOVICH (1862–1936)

For Chelpanov, the brain was the seat of the soul through which psychology could be expressed. The soul was distinct from matter, but through proper experimental techniques it could be studied and understood.

CORNELIUS, HANS (1863–1910)

Cornelius maintained that the form quality was an attribute of experience and must be perceived as a whole (not broken down into individual experiences) as Wundt had suggested.

COUÉ, EMILE (1857–1926)

Coué, a chemist, studied hypnotism under Bernheim and Liébeault. He claimed that, by means of autosuggestion, ideas that caused illness might be suggested away. His statement, "Every day in every way I am becoming better and better," has become proverbial.

DARWIN, CHARLES (1809–1882)

Darwin's work influenced psychology in many ways. Two of them are that it changed the goal of psychology to the study of the organism's adaptation to its environment and placed increasing emphasis on individual differences among members of the same species.

DEWEY, JOHN (1859–1952)

Dewey's paper "The reflex arc concept in psychology" is usually credited with establishing functionalism as a defined school of psychology, rather than just an orientation or attitude.

DONDERS, FRANS C. (1818–1889)

Donders is most prominently known for his studies on reaction time. There were appreciable individual differences among observers. The particular reaction time, as it differed from one astronomer to another, became known as the "personal equation."

DOWNEY, JUNE ETTA (1875–1932)

Downey was the first psychologist to study individual differences in temperament. She developed the Will Temperament Test.

DREIKURS, RUDOLF (1897–1972)

Dreikurs, an Adlerian, pioneered group psychotherapy and developed the "double interview" in therapy. He was deeply concerned with social equality, which he viewed as the basis for mental health.

DUBOIS, PAUL-CHARLES (1848–1918)

Dubois may be considered the first psychotherapist in the modern tradition in that he believed in "moral persuasion" in dealing with the mentally ill—that is, in simply talking with patients in an attempt to reason with them.

DUNBAR, HELEN FLANDERS (1902–1959)

Dunbar demonstrated that psychosomatic disorders were emotional in origin and related the specific type of disorder to personality characteristics.

DUNCKER, KARL (1903–1940)

Duncker's publications cover a broad range of subjects, including problem solving, perception, motivation, systematic psychology, and philosophical issues.

DUNNETTE, MARVIN D. (b 1926)

Dunnette developed procedures for selecting and appraising research scientists, sales personnel, and clerical employees.

EBBINGHAUS, HERMANN (1850–1909)

Ebbinghaus was the first psychologist to investigate learning and memory experimentally. He invented the nonsense syllable procedure, which revolutionized the study of association and learning.

ECCLES, JOHN C. (b 1903)

Eccles, an interactionist and personalist, views the mind and brain as separate and distinct entities. He offered a "liaison between brain and mind hypothesis" to explain the interactive process.

EHRENFELS, CHRISTIAN VON (1859–1932)

Ehrenfels was a forerunner of the Gestalt movement. Asch credits Ehrenfels and Wertheimer as the major influences on his use of Gestalt in social psychology.

EISDORFER, CARL (b 1930)

Eisdorfer has specialized in research on aging. He was founding editor of the *Annual review of gerontology and geriatrics.*

ELKIND, DAVID (b 1931)

Elkind is perhaps best known for his attempt to extend, integrate, and apply Piagetian theories to educational and social problems of children and youth.

ELLIOTSON, JOHN (1791–1868)

Elliotson practiced mesmerism at the University College Hospital in London with positive results, and gave it professional acceptance. He treated patients suffering from a variety of nervous disorders and also employed hypnosis as an anesthetic.

ELLIS, ALBERT (b 1913)

After practicing psychoanalysis, Ellis rebelled against its dogma and inefficiency, experimented with several other methods, and started his own system, now known as Rational-Emotive-Behavior therapy (REBT).

ELLIS, HAVELOCK (1859–1939)

Ellis concluded that homosexual behavior was congenital. Masturbation, he stated, was a legitimate source of mental relaxation. Ellis also objected to Freud's application of adult sexual terms to infants.

ENDLER, NORMAN S. (b 1931)

Endler's interaction model of anxiety postulates that trait and state anxiety are multidimensional, and that interactions evoking state anxiety occur between persons and situations only when person factors and situational stress are congruent.

ENTWISTLE, NOEL J. (b 1936)

Entwistle implemented two 5-year programs of research on student learning in higher education. One involved psychometric tests to predict degree performance; another focused more on learning processes.

ERIKSON, ERIK H. (1902–1992)

Erikson is known for his work in developmental psychology. He coined the term *identity crisis* and described the human life cycle as being comprised of eight stages.

ESCALONA, SIBYLLE K. (b 1915)

Escalona's primary interest was normal development in infancy and early childhood. She was among the first to undertake extensive systematic studies of normal infant behavior in naturalistic settings.

ESDAILE, JAMES (1808–1859)

Esdaile, a British surgeon, began practicing hypnosis in India after having read of Elliotson's work. He used hypnosis to induce anesthesia. In operations to remove scrotal tumors, Esdaile reported reducing mortality rates from 50 to 5%.

ESQUIROL, JEAN ÉTIENNE (1772–1840)

A successor to Philippe Pinel, Esquirol was one of the first, if not the first, to apply statistical methods to clinical studies of the mentally ill.

ESTES, WILLIAM K. (b 1919)

Estes brought statistical theory to bear upon Guthrie's learning theory. He developed a statistical theory of learning predicated on the principle of contiguity.

EVANS, RICHARD I. (b 1922)

Evans is best known as a pioneer in oral history, instruction via film and television, and human problem-oriented research (prejudice, juvenile delinquency, health) in social psychology.

EWALD, JULIUS RICHARD (1855–1921)

Ewald was interested in the central nervous system and had a special interest in the physiology of receptor end organs. He developed the pressure-pattern theory of hearing, which challenged the resonance theory of Helmholtz.

EYSENCK, HANS J. (b 1916)

Eysenck has researched the areas of personality theory and measurement, intelligence, social attitudes and politics, behavioral genetics, and behavior therapy.

FABRE, JEAN HENRI (1823–1915)

Fabre described many aspects of insect behavior, including the relationship between the sex of the egg and the dimensions of the cell in the solitary bee. He opposed Darwin's theory of evolution.

FECHNER, GUSTAV THEODOR (1801–1887)

Fechner is best remembered for his development of psychophysics. For the first time scientists could measure the mind; by the mid-nineteenth century, the scientific methods were being applied to mental phenomena.

FERENCZI, SANDOR (1873–1933)

Ferenczi was interested in the relationship between biology and psychoanalysis and extended the work of Freud.

FERRIER, SIR DAVID (1843–1928)

Ferrier was noted for his contributions regarding the localization of brain functions. He was the first to locate the visual center in the occipital lobes, and his work led to important advances in brain surgery.

FERSTER, CHARLES B. (1922–1981)

Ferster was dedicated to a behavioristic approach to psychology. His writings and research ranged from basic behavioral research to its applications in education and clinical psychology.

FESTINGER, LEON (1919–1989)

Festinger further developed cognitive dissonance theory, which states that people whose behavior is in discord with their thoughts will restructure their thoughts and behavior to mutual agreement.

FICHTE, JOHANN GOTTLIEB (1762–1814)

Fichte was one of the successors to Kantian philosophy and psychology. He stressed the freedom of the human will in contrast to the determinism found in the physical sciences.

FISCHER, HARDI (b 1922)

Fischer is an experimental psychologist who is especially concerned with the relationships among visual perception, epistemology, and developmental psychology.

FISHER, RONALD A. (1890–1962)

Fisher gave psychology the analysis of variance, analytic techniques for small samples, the concept of null hypothesis, and the notion of significant/insignificant as a continuum rather than a dichotomy.

FLAMENT, CLAUDE (b 1930)

Flament's publications cover various topics: social influence, ingroup behavior, structural balance cognitive theory, qualitative data analysis, and ordered set theory.

FLAMMER, AUGUST (b 1938)

Flammer's research centers on question asking, selective memory, influence of titles, encoding, free discourse, perspective shifts, and individual differences.

FLAVELL, JOHN H. (b 1928)

Flavell's research style is to try to think of important cognitive competencies that others have not studied and then to investigate their development from childhood.

FLOURENS, PIERRE (1794–1867)

Flourens confirmed the Bell–Magendie law—the separation of the nervous system into sensory and motor divisions.

FLOURNOY, THÉODORE (1854–1920)

Flournoy was the initiator of scientific psychology in Switzerland, where he founded the first psychological laboratory. His research included studies on reaction time, imaging, sensation, and hypnosis.

FLÜGEL, JOHN CARL (1884–1955)

Flügel's best-known work is *A hundred years of psychology*, which reflects broad historical scholarship in psychology.

FOPPA, KLAUS (b 1930)

Foppa has worked mainly in the field of verbal communication, especially on the development of children's communicative skills, for which he developed several methods of analysis.

FOREL, AUGUSTE-HENRI (1848–1931)

Forel was the first to achieve biological preparations of human brain specimens and was also the first to describe parabiosis (the joining together of two animals for experimental research).

FOWLER, RAYMOND D. (b 1930)

Fowler is recognized for his innovative work in computer interpretation of the MMPI. His system has been translated into most major European languages and is considered a prototype for other computer-based testing systems.

FRAISSE, PAUL (b 1911)

Fraisse is best known for his contributions to time and rhythm psychology. He also has contributed considerably to the development of psychology as a science in France.

FRANK, JEROME D. (b 1909)

Frank's major research has led to the formulation of the demoralization hypothesis, the concept that the main healing power of psychotherapy lies in features that combat demoralization.

FRANKENHAEUSER, MARIANNE (b 1925)

Frankenhaeuser has approached human stress and coping problems by combining methods and concepts from biomedical and biosocial sciences.

FRANKL, VIKTOR E. (b 1905)

Frankl's logotherapy is predicated on "man's search for meaning," based to some degree on his experiences as an inmate of Nazi concentration camps.

FRANKLIN, BENJAMIN (1706–1790)

Franklin showed that the afterimage will be positive on the dark field of the closed eye and negative when the eyes are open and fixated on a white piece of paper.

FRANZ, SHEPERD I. (1874–1933)

Franz surgically removed parts of animals' brains to study the effects of their removal on behavior. Removing the frontal lobes of the animals' brains resulted in the loss of recently acquired habits.

FRENKEL-BRUNSWIK, ELSE (1908–1958)

Frenkel-Brunswik is best known for her major part in *The authoritarian personality* and for her empirical delineation of the concept of intolerance of ambiguity.

FREUD, ANNA (1895–1982)

The daughter of Sigmund Freud, she was a specialist in children's psychoanalysis who championed the needs of children, applying her father's theories.

FREUD, SIGMUND (1856–1939)

Freud developed a personality theory explaining human motivation and expanded his theory to include more than just treatment for the disturbed.

FRIJDA, NICO H. (b 1927)

Frijda developed a general theory of emotion, integrating the study of emotion into the information-processing framework, while still supporting phenomenological and clinical viewpoints.

FRISCH, KARL VON (1886–1982)

Von Frisch is best known for his study of communication in honeybees. He isolated the visual, olfactory, and gustatory cues involved in the communication, and demonstrated that honeybees navigate by using the sun for orientation.

FROEBEL, FRIEDRICH (1782–1852)

Froebel believed that the goal of education was to develop or unfold the innate potential of the individual. The child was assumed to be inherently good; thus, all human evil arises from wrong educational methods.

FROMM, ERICH (1900–1980)

Fromm acknowledged humankind's biological past but stressed humankind's social nature. The general theme of productive love permeates much of Fromm's writings.

GAGNÉ, ROBERT M. (b 1916)

Gagné performed a series of studies on the acquisition and distinguished motor and sensory nerves. He also identified learning hierarchies and mathematics learning.

GALEN (ca. 130–200)

Galen codified the then extant knowledge of medicine, anatomy, and medically pathological personalities into general personality theory (the humoral theory).

GALL, FRANZ JOSEF (1757–1828)

Gall is credited with being a pioneer in brain mapping or brain localization. Phrenology's basic premise, however, was invalidated when it was discovered that the skull and the brain's topography do not accord.

GALTON, FRANCIS (1822–1911)

Galton made seminal contributions in a variety of fields: classification of fingerprints, genetics, statistics, anthropometry, and psychometry. He was the first scientist to clearly formulate the nature–nurture question.

GALVANI, LUIGI (1737–1798)

Galvani investigated electrical phenomena in animal organisms. His work stimulated many further developments in the understanding of electrical phenoma in living organisms.

GARCIA, GUILLERMO DAVILA (1902–1968)

Garcia's fundamental research and teaching interest was in psychopathology. He founded the first Latin American group of cross-cultural studies.

GARCIA, JOHN (1917–1986)

Garcia is known for his studies on selective and adaptive learning mechanisms, and the modification of predatory behavior with conditioned taste aversions.

GEMELLI, AGOSTINO (1878–1959)

Gemelli was attracted to sociology, philosophy, and religion. He initiated and stimulated new areas of research and gave Italian psychology a stronger sense of identity and respectability.

GERMAIN, JOSÉ (b 1897)

Germain established scientific psychology in Spain in the early 1930s. He promoted the study, adoption, and application of psychological tests.

GESELL, ARNOLD L. (1880–1961)

Gesell greatly influenced child-rearing practices in the 1940s and 1950s. He took a strictly constitutional or physiological approach in which cultural or learning factors played little part.

GIBB, CECIL A. (b 1913)

Gibb's major contributions have been to university administration and educational leadership. His publications have been in the areas of personality, leadership, and executive behavior.

GIBSON, ELEANOR J. (b 1910)

Gibson's research has embraced learning in humans and animals, studies of controlled rearing in animals, development of reading skills, and especially perceptual development in infants and young children.

GIBSON, JAMES J. (1904–1979)

Gibson is primarily known for his research and theories of perception. He became a leader of a new movement by considering perception to be direct, without any inferential steps, intervening variables, or associations.

GILBRETH, FRANK B. (1868–1924)

Gilbreth analyzed bricklaying to determine the best way of doing it. In his book, *Motion study*, he extended the micromotion study to other areas of construction work.

GILBRETH, LILLIAN E. (1878–1972)

Gilbreth applied motion study to household management. She also offered seminars on general micromotion principles.

GLASSER, WILLIAM (b 1925)

Glasser formulated reality therapy, which states that persons are born with basic needs, the primary being the need to belong and to be loved, and the need to gain self-worth and recognition.

GODDARD, HENRY H. (1866–1957)

An early student of the causes of mental retardation, Goddard argued for hereditary intelligence and was an advocate of eugenics.

GOETHE, JOHANN WOLFGANG VON (1749–1832)

Goethe influenced psychology in two different areas: color vision and the theories of Sigmund Freud. He mistrusted experimentation but had great faith in intuitive observation.

GOLDSTEIN, KURT (1878–1965)

Goldstein developed a set of tests to measure the loss of abstract attitude in patients with organic brain disease. He observed that brain-injured patients tended to persevere when pushed to perform tasks they could no longer do.

GOODENOUGH, FLORENCE L. (1886–1959)

Goodenough was most widely known for the Draw-a-Man Test, which asks the child to draw a figure. This test is not scored for artistic ability, but for the presence of details.

GOSSETT, WILLIAM S. (1876–1937)

An English statistician and pioneer in the development of modern statistical methods, Gosset derived the statistic *t* (Student's *t*), widely used in tests of differences among means of small samples.

GOUIN DÉCARIE, THÉRÉSE (b 1923)

Gouin Décarie designed the first operational scale to assess cognitive development in infancy.

GRAHAM, FRANCES (b 1918)

Graham related physiological changes in autonomic and brain activity to perceptual–cognitive function, especially during early development.

GRAUMANN, CARL F. (b 1923)

Graumann maintained that any empirical manipulation, mathematical control, or theoretical account must remain retranslatable to the original evidence.

GREGORY, RICHARD L. (b 1923)

Gregory undertook studies on size constancy during motion. He developed the notion that perceptions are predictive hypotheses, somewhat like scientific hypotheses.

GRONER, RUDOLF (b 1942)

Groner's main work is a "generalized hypothesis theory" of cognitive activity. In its most general form, a series of model variants are constructed by specifying assumptions in a systematic and exhaustive way.

GUILFORD, JOY PAUL (1897–1987)

Guilford made numerous factor analytic investigations of personality traits, including intellectual abilities, culminating in his structure-of-intellect model.

GUILLAUME, PAUL (1878–1962)

Guillaume concentrated mostly on child psychology and on the study of anthropoids. He wrote on the epistemology of scientific psychology, which helped strengthen the foundations of this discipline.

GULLIKSEN, HAROLD O. (b 1903)

Gulliksen studied mathematical psychology. As an examiner in social sciences, he was part of a group developing objective tests for college-level courses.

GUTHRIE, EDWIN R. (1886–1959)

Guthrie was a learning theorist. He stated that learning is simply a matter of an S–R (stimulus–response) association by contiguity.

GUTTMAN, LOUIS H. (b 1916)

Guttman's positions relate to his major interest in psychometrics, nonparametric analysis, and social psychology.

GUTTMANN, GISELHER (b 1934)

Guttman's chief aim has been to find correlations between psychological variables and their biological basis.

HAGA, JUN (b 1931)

Haga incorporates the study of language into the theory and practice of teaching. He holds that meaning is conveyed by logical and emotive functions of language.

HALL, CALVIN S. (1909–1985)

Hall's contributions to the study of dreams are the application of quantitative content analysis to large samples of dreams and a cognitive theory of dreams and dream symbolism.

HALL, G. STANLEY (1844–1924)

Hall founded and promoted organized psychology as a science and profession. He also was involved in many aspects of child development and education.

HALL, MARSHALL (1790–1837)

Hall distinguished between voluntary and conscious activities, which are dependent on the higher centers of the brain.

HAMILTON, SIR WILLIAM (1788–1836)

In revolt against the British associationists, Hamilton held that the first principle of psychology was the unity and activity of the human mind.

HARA, KAZUO (b 1929)

Hara has been interested in two lines of research: physiological psychology and the measurement of social attitudes.

HARLOW, HARRY F. (1905–1981)

Harlow is best known for his studies on infant monkeys raised with surrogate mothers. He found that extended social deprivation led to severe disruption of later social behavior.

HARTLEY, DAVID (1705–1765)

Hartley is considered the founder of British associationism. He was one of the earliest physiological psychologists who attempted to relate association of ideas with brain vibrations.

HATFIELD, ELAINE C. (b 1937)

Hatfield's main contribution is theorizing and researching areas once thought to be impossible to investigate: passionate and compassionate love, intense emotion, and interpersonal equality.

HEALY, WILLIAM (1869–1963)

Healy developed performance tests to supplement the Stanford–Binet Intelligence Scale, of which the Healy Picture Completion Test is perhaps the most widely known and used, and pioneered in the establishment of guidance clinics for problem children.

HEBB, D. O. (1904–1985)

Hebb's experiments confirmed the importance of early experience in the growth of mind and intelligence, and at maturity, the continued need of exposure to a normal sensory environment for mental health.

HECHT, SELIG (1892–1947)

Hecht showed that the smallest amount of light that can be detected under the most ideal viewing conditions is very close to the physiological limit.

HECKHAUSEN, HEINZ (b 1926)

Heckhausen constructed TAT measures for the independent assessment of "hope of success" and "fear of failure." These measures became the base of the rapidly growing German achievement motivation research.

HEGEL, GEORGE FRIEDRICH (1770–1831)

Hegel saw reason, not experience, as the first principle. Modern notions of self-consciousness, self-actualization, consciousness raising, and self-concern are direct outgrowths of neo-Hegelian idealism.

HEIDBREDER, EDNA (1890–1985)

Heidbreder's varied interests included schools, systems, and theories of psychology; the psychology of cognition; and testing and measurement.

HEIDEGGER, MARTIN (1889–1976)

Heidegger is considered to be the bridge between existential philosophy and existential psychology. He believed that humans must accept that death is inevitable and nothingness will follow.

HEIDER, FRITZ (1896–1988)

Heider worked in Kurt Koffka's Research Laboratory on problems related to deafness. His concepts are found in his book, *The psychology of interpersonal relations*.

HELMHOLTZ, HERMANN VON (1821–1894)

Helmholtz formulated the mathematical foundation for the law of conservation of energy. He influenced the experimental approach to psychological problems, especially in perception and sensation.

HERBART, JOHANN FRIEDRICH (1776–1841)

Herbart believed that the mind could be a compound of smaller units. He brought to psychology the notion that the mind could be quantified and influenced Wundt and Freud with his book, concept of opposing forces.

HERING, EWALD (1834–1918)

Hering fostered the doctrine of nativism, the view that one can judge space and depth in an inherent way. This idea was later taken up by the Gestalt psychologists.

HERMANN, THEO (b 1929)

Herrmann is best known for his work in cognitive psychology, psychology of language, and philosophy of psychological science.

HILGARD, ERNEST R. (b 1905)

Hilgard's research interests were primarily in the psychology of learning and motivation, and since World War II he has focused his attention on social psychology and hypnosis research.

HINDE, ROBERT A. (b 1923)

Hinde's work on bird behavior entailed comparative studies of courtship behavior, analysis of motivational conflicts, and the study of habituation.

HIPPOCRATES (460–377 B.C.)

Hippocrates took Empedocles' four elements (earth, air, fire, water) and related them to their four corresponding bodily humors (black bile, blood, yellow bile, phlegm).

HOBBES, THOMAS (1588–1679)

Hobbes is considered the father of British empiricism and associationism. Influenced by Galileo's concept of motion, he concluded that psychological (mental) activities were motions in the nervous system.

HÖFFDING, HARALD (1843–1931)

Höffding believed that mental functions could best be understood through analysis and synthesis. He viewed the central fact of psychology as being the will.

HOLLINGWORTH, HARRY L. (1880–1956)

Hollingworth employed reintegration as a general principle and saw it as the basis of an improved association psychology.

HOLT, EDWIN B. (1873–1946)

An early behaviorist, Holt believed strongly that psychology should study "the specific response relationship."

HOLT, ROBERT R. (b 1917)

Holt strove to integrate the best of the two approaches of clinical and statistical prediction.

HORAS, PLÁCIDO A. (b 1916)

Horas endeavored to establish integrative bonds between discordant trends in contemporary psychology. He believed that psychology should emanate from a biophysical conception of human behavior, emphasizing its cognitive aspects.

HORNEY, KAREN D. (1885–1952)

Horney abandoned the standard Freudian orthodoxy because of the issue of female sexuality. She stated that Freud's stress on the sexual instinct was completely out of proportion.

HORST, A. PAUL (b 1903)

Horst's goal was to solve complex human problems using rigorous mathematical and quantitative techniques, rather than rhetoric and semantics.

HOSHINO, AKIRA (b 1927)

Hoshino is best known for his study of "culture shock," a review and critical theory of sojourners' assimilation and adjustment to a new culture and reentry into their own culture after a long stay abroad.

HOVLAND, CARL I. (1912–1961)

Hovland is credited with numerous contributions to psychology, among them the sleeper effect, communicator credibility, the preferred value of stating a conclusion, and valuable effects due to the order of presenting propaganda.

HULL, CLARK L. (1884–1952)

Hull's most important contribution to psychology lies in his theory of learning, considered one of the most important theories of the twentieth century.

HUME, DAVID (1711–1776)

Hume wrote the *Treatise of human knowledge*, in which he wrote: "Mind is nothing but a bundle or collection of different perceptions unified by certain relations and suppos'd tho' falsely to be endowed with a perfect simplicity and identity."

HUNT, THELMA (1903–1992)

Hunt's research was in the personnel psychology field, where she developed tests to meet problems stemming from the Civil Rights Act and government regulatory and court measures relating to tests.

HUNTER, WALTER S. (1889–1953)

Hunter believed that an objective, behavioristic approach to psychology should not continue to be used with a subject matter imposed on it by philosophy.

HUSSERL, EDMUND (1859–1938)

Husserl was the founder and most prominent exponent of *phenomenology*, which affirmed that philosophical inquiry begins with the phenomena of consciousness, and only phenomena of consciousness can reveal to us what things essentially are.

IKEDA, HIROSHI (b 1932)

Ikeda believes that the most essential thing in psychological study is scientific data collection and measurement, and because Japanese psychology needed more systematic disciplines, he devotes himself to promoting the scientific ideas of research.

IRITANI, TOSHIO (b 1932)

Iritani launched a new field of psycholinguistics. In his *New social psychology,* he proposes a broad, integrative unification of social psychological phenomena in the areas of politics, economy, population, geography, and history.

ITARD, JEAN MARIE-GASPARD (1775–1838)

Itard was a pioneer in the study of mental deficiency, having attempted to train Victor, the so-called wild boy of Averyron. Although his efforts with Victor met with little success, he developed methods that proved useful in training retardates.

IWAO, SUMIKO FURAYA (b 1935)

Regarding the relationship between the knowledge about and attitude toward foreign people, Iwao's findings suggest a linear positive relationship between knowledge and attitude, whereas if the amount of knowledge is large, the relationship is negative.

JAENSCH, ERICH R. (1883–1940)

Jaensch is best known for his work on eidetic imagery. He proposed two biotypes: The B-type was a vivid memory image under voluntary control; the T-type, not under voluntary control, was related to underactivity of the parathyroid.

JAHODA, MARIE (b 1907)

Two connecting threads are inherent in Jahoda's professional life: preventing social psychology from splitting into psychological and sociological branches and engaging in problem-centered rather than method-centered work.

JALOTA, SHYAM SWAROOP (b 1904)

Jalota is best known for his pioneering work for standardized tests of "general mental ability" in Hindi. He formulated a hypothesis that "each human experience carries within it the active or latent seeds of contrary impulses."

JAMES, WILLIAM (1842–1910)

James is considered America's greatest psychologist because of his brilliant clarity of scientific writing and his view of the human mind as functional, adaptive mental processes, in opposition to Wundt's analysis of consciousness into elements.

JANET, PIERRE (1859–1947)

Janet developed a system of psychology and psychopathology that he called "psychologie de la conduite" (psychology of conduct or behavior). A decrease in psychic energy was a central belief in Janet's explanation of mental disorders.

JANIS, IRVING LESTER (1918–1990)

According to the Janis–Feisrabend hypothesis, an argument is most effective when the pro side is advanced before the negative. Also, he demonstrated experimentally that hostile individuals are less susceptible to persuasion.

JASPERS, KARL (1883–1969)

Jaspers distinguished three modes of being: being-there, being-oneself, and being-in-itself. Being-there referred to the objective, real world. Being-onself meant one's personal existence. Being-in-itself involved an ability to transcend the known world and to know other worlds.

JASTROW, JOSEPH (1863–1944)

Jastrow wrote on the occult, psychic research, mental telepathy, spiritualism, and hypnosis. He was, at least in part, a believer in psychic phenomena. He attacked Freudian theory, likening it to a house built of playing cards.

JENNINGS, HERBERT S. (1868–1947)

Jennings' work was particularly important to psychology in two areas: He disproved the local action theory of tropisms and also demonstrated that mutations were likely to involve very small changes in organisms.

JENSEN, ARTHUR R. (b 1923)

Jensen hypothesized that both individual and racial differences in abilities are in part a product of the evolutionary process and have a genetic basis. His ideas came to be termed *jensenism,* often pejoratively.

JING, QICHENG (b 1926)

Jing's books *Colorimetry* and *Human vision* were the first books on visual science in China. He also has published studies of psychological development of Chinese children.

JOHN, ERWIN R. (b 1924)

John is known for his material theory of memory. He hypothesized a statistical configuration theory of learning based on Lashley's conclusions. John also argued for mass action rather than learning centers in the brain.

JONES, MARY COVER (1896–1987)

Jones is most prominent as the first researcher to remove a fear in a child—the case of Peter.

JUDD, CHARLES H. (1873–1946)

Judd studied the process of reading by photographing eye movements. He described how number consciousness was a function of reasoning and other high mental processes.

JUNG, CARL (1875–1961)

Jung's personality system included three levels of the *psyche:* (a) the *ego,* (b) the *personal unconscious,* and (c) the deeper *collective unconscious.*

KAGAN, JEROME (b 1929)

Kagan has researched various aspects of the development of children, including variation in the cognitive styles called reflectivity and impulsivity, and the maturation of memory, self-awareness, and moral sense over the first 2 years of life.

KAMIYA, JOE (b 1925)

Kamiya's research involves the psychophysiology of consciousness and heightened awareness, altered states of consciousness, and transpersonal consciousness.

KANT, IMMANUEL (1724–1804)

Kant rejected the view of the mind as mental substance. For him, mental processes could not be measured because they had only the dimension of time, not space. Psychology could never be an experimental science.

KANTOR, JACOB R. (1888–1984)

Kantor proposed a systematic psychology called interbehaviorism. It shares with the behavioristic tradition a denial of mind or mental activity in favor of an objective approach.

KATONA, GEORGE (1901–1981)

Katona's major contributions are his studies of consumer expectations and behavior found in such works as *Aspirations and affluence, A new economic era,* and *Essays on behavioral economics.*

KATZ, DAVID (1884–1953)

The same color, Katz discovered, can appear to the viewer in different modes such as surface or film color, or as bulky, shiny, transparent, or luminous. His findings demonstrated the influence of the total visual field on color perception.

KELLEY, HAROLD H. (b 1921)

Kelley's major contributions, all in social psychology, have been to the theory of small groups, including attribution theory dealing with the perception of causes of behavior, and to the study of close relationships.

KELLOGG, WINTHROP N. (1898–1972)

When their son Donald was 10 months old, Kellogg and his wife Luella obtained a 7-month-old chimpanzee, who was then raised as a sibling. Despite equal treatment, the son surpassed the ape after 9 months.

KELLY, GEORGE A. (1905–1967)

Kelly's theory of *personal constructs* is a broad, inclusive personality theory based on the notion that each individual attempts to anticipate and control his or her environment.

KELLY, LOWELL E. (1905–1986)

Kelly instituted a longitudinal study of 300 engaged couples that lasted from 1939 to 1980. One of his conclusions was that marital compatibility is due to only a small function of sex and social attributes.

KEREKJARTO, MARGIT (b 1930)

Kerekjarto's major research work has been in neuropsychology. She also developed the first major curriculum work in medical psychology education for Germany.

KIERKEGAARD, SOREN A. (1813–1855)

Kierkegaard anticipated depth psychology, depersonalization, and the crisis of the will. He understood the peculiar modern malaise of "spiritlessness."

KIESOW, FEDERICO (1858–1940)

Among the many areas researched by Kiesow are taste, sensitivity, thermic and tactile points, geometric illusions, the Weber–Fechner Law, eidetic imagery, psychophysics, and the specific function of the sense organs.

KINSEY, ALFRED C. (1894–1956)

The Kinsey reports provided the first quantified, thorough description of many diverse human self-reports of sexual experience. The data also put to rest many misconceptions about sexuality.

KLAGES, LUDWIG (1872–1956)

Klages believed that the body and soul interacted and that the point of this interaction was the human personality. An individual personality was a system of dynamic relationships.

KLINEBERG, OTTO (1899–1992)

Klineberg described differences in various psychological characteristics such as intelligence, emotions, and personality in various races including the Chinese, Native Americans, and American Blacks. His general conclusion was that these differences are by and large culturally determined.

KLOPFER, BRUNO (1900–1971)

Klopfer's major work was *The Rorschach technique.* It became the single most authoritative source on the Rorschach test.

KLÜVER, HEINRICH (b 1897)

Klüver developed the method of equivalent and nonequivalent stimuli for studying behavior and determined the role of the brain, particularly the striate cortex, in vision.

KOFFKA, KURT (1886–1941)

Koffka was a founder of the Gestalt psychology movement; of the three (Koffka, Köhler, and Wertheimer), he was particularly noted for his extensive publications.

KOHLBERG, LAWRENCE (1927–1987)

Kohlberg is best known for his research on moral development in children. Following the lines of Piaget, Kohlberg stated that children followed moral development in three stages.

KÖHLER, WOLFGANG (1887–1967)

Köhler, along with Wartheimer and Koffka, was a founder of the Gestalt psychology movement, of which he was particularly noted as the public spokesman.

KONORSKI, JERZY (1903–1973)

Konorski pursued his life's pervading goal, to learn "how the brain works," formulated when he was about 20 years of age. His most important book is *Integrative activity of the brain.*

KORNADT, HANS-JOACHIM (b 1927)

Kornadt has specialized in cross-cultural research, particularly concerning the development of aggression.

KRAEPELIN, EMIL (1855–1926)

Through careful observation of many patients and statistical tabulation of symptoms, Kraepelin concluded that there were two major mental disorders: demential praecox and the manic-depressive psychosis.

KRAFFT-EBING, RICHARD VON (1840–1902)

Psycholopathia sexualis is Krafft-Ebing's best-known work. He took a purely constitutional approach. All sexual variations are based on genetic defects, but masturbation could hasten or even produce disorders.

KRETSCHMER, ERNST (1888–1964)

Kretschmer is best known for his typology within the framework of constitutional psychology: Body structure/physiology determines personality.

KÜLPE, OSWALD (1862–1915)

Külpe began to believe that the analysis of consciousness involved more than what Wundt had suggested. He concluded that thinking could occur in the absence of mental images or sensations and termed this *imageless thought.*

LA METTRIE, JULIEN OFFROY DE (1709–1751)

La Mettrie saw humans as machines, which gives him a place in the history of behaviorism. In his later years he developed the doctrine of hedonism, asserting that pleasure is the goal of life and that all motivation is selfish.

LADD, GEORGE TRUMBULL (1842–1920)

Ladd believed that consciousness should operate to solve problems, although he granted that there is a biological side to the nervous system. From his view, the function of the mind is to adapt, and in adapting it must look to the future. Psychology should be practical.

LADD-FRANKLIN, CHRISTINE (1847–1930)

Ladd-Franklin is best known for her theory of color vision. Her theory is based on that of F. C. Donders, but with a developmental or genetic focus.

LAMARCK, JEAN-BAPTISTE DE MONET DE (1744–1829)

Lamarck developed the theory of evolution. One of his views accounted for the inheritance of acquired characteristics, which Lamarck thought was necessary to explain cumulative changes.

LASHLEY, KARL (1890–1958)

Lashley formulated two principles of brain functioning: mass action and equipotentiality.

LAZARUS, ARNOLD A. (b 1932)

Lazarus is the developer of multimodal therapy based on the simultaneous consideration of Behavior, Affect, Sensation, Imagery, Cognition, Interpersonal relations, and Drugs (BASIC-ID) for both diagnosis and treatment of mental disorders.

LAZARUS, RICHARD S. (b 1922)

Lazarus mounted efforts to generate a comprehensive theoretical framework for psychological stress and undertook programmatic research based on these formulations.

LE BON, GUSTAVE (1841–1931)

Le Bon developed a doctrine of the hierarchy of races. The criteria he set up involved the degree of reasoning ability, power of attention, and mastery of instinctual needs.

LEE, CHANG-HO (b 1936)

Lee has been developing an Oriental model of counseling and psychotherapy. The emphasis in his model includes educative dialogue, integrational approach, tolerance training, assets reinforcement, and enhancing social interest.

LEIBNITZ, GOTTFRIED WILHELM (1646–1716)

Leibnitz believed that mind and body followed their own laws in perfect agreement. Leibnitz's parallelism was one solution to the mind–body problem that has concerned philosophers and psychologists for centuries.

LEONTIEV, ALEKSEI (b 1903)

Leontiev believed in the cultural–historical theory, which attempted to use Marxist doctrine as a basis for human development. Besides accounting for human psychological processes, the theory held that when persons interact, psychological processes develop.

LERNER, ARTHUR (b 1915)

Lerner regards all literary genres as vital sources for understanding behavior; he holds that one's cognitive and unconscious understanding is shaped by the language, symbols, metaphors, and similes that influence one's growth and development.

LEWIN, KURT (1890–1947)

Lewin developed a topological vectoral psychology. Topology investigates the properties of space; vectors consider forces or dynamics.

LOCKE, JOHN (1632–1704)

Locke was the first of the British empiricists and bridged the gap between the rational continental philosophers such as Descartes, Leibnitz, and Spinoza. He helped to promote a new attitude toward knowledge that was fostered in the upcoming empirical tradition.

LOEB, JACQUES (1859–1924)

Loeb's theory of the tropism as applied to animal behavior represented a return to the mechanistic view set forth earlier by René Descartes, which stated that animals acted like machines.

LORENZ, KONRAD (1903–1989)

Lorenz never conducted a formal experiment, and his descriptive observations were often anecdotal. He infuriated his more conventional colleagues by saying, "If I have one good example, I don't give a fig for statistics."

LOTZE, HERMANN (1817–1881)

Lotze is known for his doctrine of local signs, typical of nineteenth-century thought, in which philosophical concepts, rather than empirical data, dominated the interpreted physiology of sense organs.

LUNDIN, ROBERT W. (b 1920)

Lundin's book, *An objective psychology of music*, was a protest against the mentalistic approaches to the psychology of music presented by Carl Seashore and Max Schoen. He attempted to establish musical behavior on firm empirical grounds.

MACH, ERNST (1838–1916)

Mach has been identified as a positivist who believed that sensations were the data of all science. In his view, all science is observational, and the primary data of observation are sensations.

MAGENDIE, FRANÇOIS (1783–1855)

Magendie contended that the seat of sensations was in the spinal cord and that the cerebrum perceived the sensations from the cord. This being

the case, the cerebrum could reproduce the sensations, thus accounting for memory.

MAIMONIDES, MOSES (1135–1204)

Maimonides rejected the notion of a personal immortality. For him, the capacity for individual thinking disappeared with the destruction of the body. Yet an individual might increase in understanding and knowledge, and so attain a kind of immortality.

MAKARENKO, ANTON SEMYONOVICH (1899–1939)

Makarenko's *The road to life* has been cited by most Soviet psychologists. His work developed a theory that became the basis of Soviet personality research and educational practices.

MALEBRANCHE, NICOLAS de (1638–1715)

De Malebranche rejected Descartes' interactionism in favor of the doctrine of occasionalism. According to this view, one event does not cause another but is simply an occasion for God, the cause of all things, to cause the second event to occur.

MARX, KARL HEINRICH (1818–1883)

The starting point of Marx's socialism is the doctrine of class struggle. This provided the key to two of his most widely known doctrines: a materialist conception of history and the theory of surplus value.

MASLOW, ABRAHAM H. (1908–1970)

Maslow considered his basic approach to psychology to fall within the broad range of humanistic psychology, which he characterized as the "Third Force" in American psychology, the other two being behaviorism and psychoanalysis.

MAY, ROLLO (b 1909)

May is known for his vanguard leadership in humanistic psychology, articulating existential tenets of the "encounter," "choice," "authenticity," "responsibility," "transcendence," and other existential hypotheses.

McCLELLAND, DAVID C. (b 1917)

McClelland developed a method of measuring human needs through content analysis of imaginative thought.

McDOUGALL, WILLIAM (1871–1938)

McDougall described an instinct as having three aspects: (a) a predisposition to notice certain stimuli, (b) a predisposition to make movements toward a goal, and (c) an emotional core.

McKEACHIE, WILBERT J. (b 1921)

Much of McKeachie's research has been concerned with attribute–treatment interactions, particularly with respect to those teaching variables interacting with student motivation, such as test anxiety.

MEAD, GEORGE H. (1863–1931)

For Mead, the self was an object of awareness rather than a system of processes. At birth there is no self because a person cannot enter one's own experiences directly.

MEEHL, PAUL E. (b 1920)

Meehl's monograph, *Clinical versus statistical prediction*, aroused wide interest (and dissent) and is considered a minor classic.

MERLEAU-PONTY, MAURICE (1907–1961)

Merleau-Ponty's primary concern was an understanding of the relationship between consciousness and nature. For him, nature referred to external events in their causal relationships. Consciousness, however, was not subject to causality.

MESMER, FRANZ ANTON (1734–1815)

Mesmer is commonly recognized as the founding father of modern hypnosis. He attempted to build on the rock of Newtonian ideas to find some basis for understanding human illness and cures.

MEYER, ADOLF (1866–1950)

Meyer is best known for his theory of psychobiology, which emphasized the importance of a biographical study for understanding all aspects of an individual's personality.

MILGRAM, STANLEY (1933–1984)

Milgram's best-known studies were on the dynamics of obedience to authority. As a result, he found an unexpectedly high rate of obedience. His obedience work became one of the best-known pieces of research in the social sciences.

MILL, JOHN STUART (1806–1873)

Mill believed that a combination of mental events resulted in something totally new that was not present in the original experiences, a notion that became identified as "mental chemistry."

MILLER, GEORGE A. (b 1920)

Miller was the first to demonstrate trial-and-error learning motivated by electrical stimulation of the brain.

MISIAK, HENRYK (1911–1992)

Misiak's experimental research focused on the perception of intermittent light, particularly on various parameters and applications of critical flicker frequency (CFF).

MISUMI, JYUJI (b 1924)

Misumi is known for his research that aims to classify leadership behavior by using combinations of the problem-solving or goal achievement-oriented functional dimension (P) and the group maintenance-oriented functional dimension (M).

MONTESSORI, MARIA (1870–1952)

Montessori used her scientific background to create universal principles and special methods and materials for a new pedagogy.

MORENO, JACOB L. (1892–1974)

Moreno developed the technique of psychodrama, a method of psychotherapy that depends on dramatic role playing.

MORGAN, CONWAY LLOYD (1852–1936)

Morgan is best known for the Lloyd Morgan's Canon, an application of the Law of Parsimony to an explanation of animal behavior.

MORITA, SHOMA (1874–1938)

Morita developed a new form of psychotherapy, generally known as Morita Therapy, that combined psychotherapy and Zen Buddhism. To gain insight, the patient must be in harmony with the universe.

MOWRER, O. HOBART (1907–1982)

Mowrer's best-known and probably most enduring practical contribution is a means of treating nocturnal enuresis known as the bell-and-pad method. His more substantive contributions were in learning, language, and interpersonal psychology.

MÜLLER, JOHANNES (1801–1858)

Müller is best known for his doctrine of the "specific energies of nerves," which states that regardless of how it is stimulated, each sensory nerve will lead to only one kind of sensation.

MÜNSTERBERG, HUGO (1863–1916)

Münsterberg exposed the fraudulence of popular mystics and occult figures, and generally applied psychology to everyday life.

MURPHY, GARDNER (1895–1979)

Murphy's biosocial approach to psychology was recognized as one of the most vital and influential movements in the field.

MURRAY, HENRY A. (1893–1988)

Murray developed his taxonomy of needs and presses to characterize people's directions in their lives and activities. Thus, he developed a systematic and dynamic approach to personality.

MYASISHCHEV, VLADIMIR N. (1893–1973)

Myasishchev suggested that conditioned reflexes might not be an adequate explanation of human motor behavior.

NEISSER, ULRIC (b 1928)

Neisser is best known for three books: *Cognitive psychology*, which helped to establish that field; *Cognition and reality*, which attempted to reorient it; and *Memory observed: Remembering in natural contexts,* which introduced the ecological approach to the study of memory.

NETTER, PETRA (b 1937)

Netter initiated research activities in the field of sensory suggestibility in relation to pain tolerance and placebo response.

NEWCOMB, THEODORE M. (1903–1984)

Newcomb was among the first psychologists to identify himself with social psychology. He showed that individual's characteristics and group memberships interacted to influence attitude changes after leaving college.

NIETZSCHE, FRIEDRICH WILHELM (1844–1900)

Nietzsche was convinced that psychology should consider the will to power as the primary human motive.

NOIZET, GEORGES (b 1925)

Noizet's main work deals with strategies in the comprehension of utterances and with evaluative judgments.

NORMAN, DONALD A. (b 1935)

The premise of Norman's research is that the unaided mind is limited in power, but that cognition, when distributed across people and objects, is powerful.

NÚÑEZ, RAFAEL (b 1921)

Núñez is best known for his research on Mexican personality characteristics. He searched for methods of understanding the psychological problems of the lower economic classes in Latin America.

NUTTIN, JOSEPH R. (1909–1988)

Nuttin was one of the first psychologists to formulate an integrated cognitive theory of human selective learning. He is also known for his theory of human motivation in terms of behavioral relations "required" for optimal functioning.

OKONJI, MICHAEL OGBOLU (1936–1975)

Okonji conducted research focused on child rearing, especially the relationship between the field-independence perspective of Herman Witkin and the intellectual perspective of Jean Piaget.

OLDS, JAMES (1922–1976)

Olds and Milner were able, by chance, to produce pleasurable effects by electrically stimulating the brain. This led them to assume that a "reward mechanism" exists in the brain and serves as a motivational apparatus.

OSGOOD, CHARLES EGERTON (1916–1991)

Osgood's experimental research has centered around the role of meaning within the context of learning theory. He developed the Semantic Differential Method while searching for a tool to quantify meaning.

OTIS, ARTHUR SINTON (1886–1964)

Otis developed the Otis Group Intelligence Scale that incorporated, for the first time, completely objective scoring and multiple-choice items, the keys to group testing and administration by minimally trained personnel.

PARAMESWARAN, E. G. (b 1935)

Parameswaran, known for his approach to the study of personality, is a pioneering researcher in the area of developmental psychology in India.

PAVLOV, IVAN PETROVICH (1849–1936)

Pavlov's methodology and his greatest scientific achievement was conditioning, a technique that significantly influenced the development of psychology.

PAWLIK, KURT F. (b 1934)

Pawlik developed a "trait-free theory of personality factors" in terms of interindividual difference covariations in developmental learning.

PEARSON, KARL (1857–1936)

Pearson contributed to the development of the biological, behavioral, and social sciences. His application of mathematical and statistical methods ranks among the great achievements of science.

PECJAK, VID (b 1929)

Pecjak studied concepts and conceptual interrelations and symbols and their cultural dependence. He found that some symbols are universal, whereas others were unique to individual cultures.

PEDERSEN, PAUL B. (b 1936)

Pedersen conducted research in Indonesia, Malaysia, and Taiwan that emphasized interdisciplinary area studies, with special attention to core values as they are influenced by cultural perspectives.

PEIRCE, CHARLES SANDERS (1839–1914)

Peirce held that the domain of knowledge could be so characterized that general assertions could be proven true of all knowledge and that all knowledge depended on logic that made such a characterization possible.

PENFIELD, WILBER GRAVES (1891–1976)

Among Penfield's contributions were the development of neurosurgical treatment of certain forms of epilepsy and the discovery that electric stimulation of certain parts of the cortex can evoke vivid memories of past life experiences.

PERLOFF, ROBERT (b 1921)

Perloff has contributed to psychology through his research on consumer behavior and evaluation studies relating to mental health and educational programs.

PERLS, FREDERICK (FRITZ) (1893–1970)

Perls' major contribution to psychology was the development of a new method of psychotherapy, which he named Gestalt therapy, an outgrowth and a rejection of psychoanalysis.

PFAFFMAN, CARL (b 1913)

Pfaffman conducted research on taste and other chemical senses and attempted to find basic relationships between the physiological and psychological aspects of organisms.

PFLÜGER, EDUARD FRIEDRICH WILHELM (1829–1910)

Pflüger's research involved studies of the nervous system. He became involved in the controversy over whether reflexes are conscious or unconscious.

PIAGET, JEAN (1896–1980)

Piaget studied the relationships formed between the individual knower and the world he or she endeavors to know. His two most important concepts of genetic epistemology are *functional invariants* and *structures.*

PIERON, HENRI (1881–1964)

Pieron's work focused on psychophysiology. During an early part of his career, he studied the mechanisms of sleep in animals. But the psychophysiology of sensations constituted the center of his scientific work.

PILLSBURY, WALTER BOWERS (1872–1960)

Pillsbury is probably best known as an historian of psychology. His *History of psychology* details the growth of psychology from philosophy.

PINEL, PHILIPPE (1745–1856)

Pinel made a plea for more humane treatment of the insane, who, at that time, were regarded by many as wicked and possessed by demons. He offered an alternative explanation that related disturbed behavior to brain malfunctions.

PINILLOS, JOSÉ (b 1919)

Pinillos is best known for his work on social attitudes and political stereotypes, and for his analysis of the *F*-scale.

PIZZAMIGLIO, LUIGI (b 1937)

Pizzamiglio contributed to the introduction of psycholinguistic models to explain aphasia and hemispheric dominance for cognitive abilities.

PLATO (427–347 B.C.)

Plato's influence on Western thought has been inestimable, extending to metaphysics, epistemology, ethics, politics, mathematics, and several branches of natural science.

PLOTINUS (204–270 A.D.)

Plotinus described the soul as a unitary entity, completely separate from the body, that is indestructible and immortal. He believed the soul's relation to the body was one of collateral existence, not mixing with the body but dwelling beside it, thus having an existence of its own.

PONZO, MARIO (1882–1960)

Ponzo's research was in general and experimental psychology, including the histology and psychophysiology of taste, and tactile and thermic stimulus localization in different regions of the skin.

PORTEUS, STANLEY DAVID (1883–1972)

Porteus began his best-known work in psychology, his Maze Test, as a supplement to Henry H. Goddard's 1909 translation of Alfred Binet's intelligence tests that would avoid the culture factor.

PRATKANIS, ANTHONY R. (b 1957)

Some of Pratkanis' research has demonstrated the conditions under which a sleeper effect will occur, the ineffectiveness of subliminal persuasion, and how the self influences information processing.

PRIBRAM, KARL H. (b 1919)

Pribram has investigated mind–brain problems with a focus on their philosophical implications, drawing on laboratory data to support his premises.

PRINCE, MORTON (1854–1929)

Prince described the biography of a multiple personality who had three distinct personalities that alternated with each other, characterized as the saint, the devil, and the woman. Two of the personalities had no knowledge of the others.

PURKINJĚ, JAN EVANGELISTA (1787–1869)

An extensive researcher of sensory elements in the phenomenological tradition, Purkinjě described how colors emerged from darkness at dawn.

QUETELET, LAMBERT ADOLPHE JACQUES (1796–1874)

Quetelet extended the notion of the normal distribution as being the true state of affairs rather than simply measurement error.

RAIMY, VICTOR (1913–1987)

Raimy proposed that changes in the self-concept would be used to chart the course of psychotherapy as well as general changes in personality.

In his theory, the self-concept is seen as a guide or map that persons consult when faced with choices.

RAINA, MAHARAJ K. (b 1943)

Raina has been involved in research on the National Talent Search Scheme in India. He has concentrated on longitudinal studies of the talented and the role of creativity in the talent search.

RAMON Y CAJAL, SANTIAGO (1832–1934)

Ramon y Cajal is called the father of present-day physiological psychology. His techniques for tracing neurons histologically remain a basic approach to physiological psychology.

RANK, OTTO (1884–1939)

Rank sought to develop an alternative scientific approach built on the person as both a voluntary interpreter of meaning and an initiator of action. His earlier conception of the birth trauma was largely replaced by more complex ideas. He also rejected the aim, shared by Freud and most of academic psychology, of mechanistic explanation of human behavior or experience with a cause–effect paradigm.

RAO, K. RAMAKRISHNA (b 1932)

Rao's contributions to psychology, both theoretical and experimental, focus mainly on aspects such as psi, which receive little attention in conventional psychology.

RATH, RADHANATH (b 1920)

After his early specialization in psychophysics, Rath turned to social psychology. While involved in the reorientation of primary school education and textbooks he performed intensive research in the area of early education.

RAVIV, AMIRAM (b 1939)

Raviv's research areas include prosocial behavior, pupils' attributions of success and failure, social climate in various settings, and issues related to the role of school psychologists.

RAZRAN, GREGORY (1901–1973)

Razran conducted extensive research in the area of classical conditioning by relating the various types of learning to levels of evolutionary development.

REICH, WILHELM (1897–1957)

Reich parted from psychoanalysis as his pursuits led him into realms the analysts could not or would not follow. For him, emotions came to mean the manifestation of a tangible, demonstrable biological energy (*orgone*).

REID, THOMAS (1710–1796)

Reid proposed that not only did people possess minds, but also that any individual mind knew more than it possessed. He also proposed *faculty psychology*.

REIK, THEODOR (1888–1969)

Although a believer in many psychoanalytical concepts, Reik disagreed with Freud over certain matters of love and sex. He believed that true romantic love has little to do with sex—that it is felt most strongly when the loved one is absent.

RESNICK, ROBERT J. (b 1940)

Resnick's clinical and research interests were attention-deficit disorders. He filed the landmark "Virginia Blues" litigation establishing the autonomous practice of psychology.

REUCHLIN, MAURICE (b 1920)

Reuchlin has asserted that, in research, the content of the data and the context of the research, as well as statistical findings, must be considered.

REVUSKY, SAM (b 1933)

Revusky helped pioneer an approach to learning that emphasized innate associative predispositions.

REYKOWSKI, JANUSZ (b 1929)

Reykowski is best known for developing a theory of intrinsic motivation applied to prosocial behavior.

RHINE, JOSEPH BANKS (1895–1980)

Rhine, considered the father of experimental parapsychology, spent over 50 years in active research that brought psychic research from closed séance rooms of mediums into open laboratories of scientists.

RIBES-IÑESTA, EMILIO (b 1944)

Partly responsible for the introduction of experimental psychology into Mexico, Ribes-Iñesta contributed to the development of the first professional and graduate research programs on behavior modification and behavior analysis.

RIBOT, THEODULE (1839–1916)

Together with Alfred Binet and Pierre Janet, Ribot was a founder of modern French psychology. He stressed motivational forces in personality development, which resulted in what we today would call a dynamic psychology.

RICHTER, CURT PAUL (1894–1988)

Richter's research included such areas as spontaneous behavior in rats, biological clocks, galvanic skin response, and rhythms, as well as nutrition and self-selection of diets in rats.

RIVERS, WILLIAM HALSE (1864–1922)

Rivers became interested in neurology and medical psychology during World War I. With Elliot Smith and T. H. Pear, he was the first to recognize "shell shock" as a distinct clinical entity.

ROGERS, CARL RANSOM (1902–1987)

Rogers developed a psychotherapeutic system, second in popularity only to that of Freud, in which the therapist acts as a facilitator.

ROKEACH, MILTON (1918–1988)

What people believe, why they believe, and what difference it makes are the recurring themes that have preoccupied Rokeach during his research career.

ROMANES, GEORGE JOHN (1848–1894)

Romanes, a student of behavior, chose to use the anecdotal method that he culled from both the scientific and popular literature. He criticized the tendency to attribute human characteristics, such as insight, to animals.

RORSCHACH, HERMANN (1884–1922)

Rorschach extended the inkblot technique to measure the entire personality.

ROSENZWEIG, SAUL (b 1907)

Rosenzweig is best known for his studies and theories of frustration and aggression. He has also studied tolerance for frustration and has noted that the spoiled child is ill equipped to handle frustration.

ROT, NIKOLA (b 1910)

Three areas are central in Rot's empirical research: psychological characteristics of judgments, attitudes, and problems connected to self-management.

ROTTER, JULIAN B. (b 1916)

Rotter's major contribution has been the development of social learning theory (SLT), in which he tried to integrate the two great traditions in psychology—the stimulus–response, or reinforcement, theories and cognitive, or field, theories.

ROYCE, JOSEPH R. (1921–1989)

Royce's major experimental research has focused on determining the gene correlates of factors of emotion.

ROYCE, JOSIAH (1855–1916)

Royce taught that truth could be proven, that an absolute mind exists, and that human beings can grasp truth.

RUBIN, EDGAR (1886–1951)

Rubin is best known for his dissertation: the figure/ground distinction. Under some circumstances, figure and ground can reverse.

RUBINSTEIN, SERGEI LEONIDOVICH (1889–1960)

Rubinstein formulated these principles of Soviet psychology: mind is a function of matter; and the human psyche is a function of historical evolution, the unity of consciousness, and the unity of theory and practice.

RUSSELL, ROGER W. (b 1914)

Russell was one of the first to search for neurochemical mechanisms underlying normal and abnormal behavior.

RUTHERFORD, WILLIAM (1839–1899)

Rutherford is known in psychology chiefly for his 1886 "Telephone Theory" of hearing.

SAKEL, MANFRED (1900–1957)

Sakel is primarily known for his discovery of the insulin coma treatment for schizophrenia.

SALTER, ANDREW (b 1914)

Salter's *Conditioned reflex therapy* founded behavior therapy. His *Case against psychoanalysis* offended many in the psychiatric establishment.

SANFORD, EDMUND CLARK (1869–1924)

As an innovator of psychological apparatus, Sanford developed the vernier pendulum chronoscope, which once was a standard instrument for studying reaction time.

SAPIR, EDWARD (1884–1939)

Sapir's study of language in Native American tribes was an early contribution to linguistic anthropology.

SCARR, SANDRA WOOD (b 1936)

Scarr explored genetic variability in human behaviors through twin, adoption, and intervention studies.

SCHACHTER, STANLEY (b 1922)

Schachter developed a cognitive theory of emotion in which he established that people cannot discriminate one emotion from another unless they have some cognitive indication as to what their feelings relate.

SCHAIE, K. WARNER (b 1928)

Schaie's principle contributions are long-term longitudinal research on adult intellectual development and study in the area of developmental research methodology.

SCHOPENHAUER, ARTHUR (1788–1860)

Schopenhauer stressed the redemption of the soul from its sensual bonds. According to him, human beings have an obligation to sensual things, but the final goal is to rise above the senses into the bosom of a peaceful Nirvana.

SCHUMANN, FRIEDRICH (1863–1940)

Schumann studied many visual forms and illusions without finding any necessity to appeal to the concept of form–quality. Instead, this could be accounted for by the laws of attention as well as eye movements.

SCOTT, WALTER DILL (1869–1955)

Scott transferred his psychological insights into the world of work and introduced the business uses of psychology into advertising, selling, and consumer behavior. Thus, he created a new field—industrial psychology.

SCRIPTURE, EDWARD WHEELER (1864–1945)

Scripture coined the term *armchair psychology* to describe those psychologies that state theories and speculations without experimental verification.

SEARS, ROBERT R. (1908–1989)

Sears' initial interests in physiological psychology shifted to personality and motivation. He performed numerous verification studies on psychoanalytic concepts.

SEASHORE, CARL EMIL (1866–1949)

For many years, Seashore devoted his experimental efforts to the study of music psychology. His thesis was that musical talent consisted of many different capacities.

SECHENOV, IVAN MIKHAILOVICH (1829–1905)

The founder of Russian physiology, Sechenov was a mentor to Ivan Pavlov and instrumental in bringing psychology and science together.

SEGUIN, EDOUARD (1812–1880)

Seguin originated sense and muscle training techniques whereby children with mental retardation were given intensive exercise in sensory discriminations and in the development of muscle control.

SELIGMAN, MARTIN E. P. (b 1942)

Seligman reformulated the helplessness model, claiming that attributions governed the expression of helplessness.

SELYE, HANS (1907–1982)

Selye formulated a code of behavior based on the laws that govern the body's stress resistance in dealing with personal, interpersonal, and group problems.

SERPELL, ROBERT (b 1944)

Serpell's research centered on the application of attention theory to various aspects of child development, notably perceptual errors on Western intelligence tests and second-language learning in Zambia.

SHELDON, WILLIAM HERBERT (1899–1977)

Sheldon developed an empirical basis for the structural theory of personality first suggested by Hippocrates and Galen. Sheldon refined what were essentially Kretschmer's three basic body types.

SHERIF, MUZAFER (1906–1988)

Sherif initiated a series of naturalistic experiments on group formation, intergroup conflict, and cooperation.

SHERRINGTON, CHARLES SCOTT (1857–1952)

Sherrington published studies on color vision and flicker, and wrote on the tactual and muscular senses. He introduced the terms *interoceptor*, *exteroceptor*, and *proprioceptor*.

SHIRAI, TSUNE (b 1910)

Shirai studied children and found their transposition behavior to be conspicuously different from that of the animals that had previously served as subjects in that field.

SHNEIDMAN, EDWIN S. (b 1918)

Shneidman is a suicidologist and thanatologist who has researched death and suicide.

SIGUAN, MIGUEL (b 1918)

Siguan has been a pioneer in the field of infant language, attempting to explain the origins of verbal language as arising from nonverbal communication.

SIMON, HERBERT A. (b 1916)

Simon has pioneered in creating information-processing psychology and has been active in the fields of mathematical economics and organization theory.

SINGER, GEORGE (b 1922)

Singer's major contributions to psychological research are in perception: eating, drinking and drug intake behaviors, and the application of biochemical methods to the assessment of stress programs.

SINGH, SHEO DAN (1932–1979)

Singh established India's first Primate Research Laboratory. His major areas of interest were the impact of urban conditions on the development of social, emotional, and cognitive behavior and the brain chemistry of rhesus monkeys.

SINHA, DURGANAND (b 1922)

Sinha's main research studies have focused on psychological dimensions of socioeconomic development, deprivation and poverty, and cognitive style and cross-cultural psychology.

SKINNER, BURRHUS FREDERICK (B. F.) (1904–1990)

Skinner took a completely objective approach to psychology. He contended that learning cannot occur in the absence of some kind of reinforcement, either positive or negative.

SMITH, M. BREWSTER (b 1919)

Smith studied antisemitism, race prejudice, and moral judgment in the student activists of the 1960s. He sought to link the complementarities of scientific and humanistic psychology by focusing on self-hood or personality.

SOLOMON, RICHARD LESTER (1919–1992)

Solomon's research has involved numerous areas of experimental psychology. Of particular importance have been his various studies of traumatic avoidance learning in dogs. In these studies, he explored many parameters of the problem.

SPEARMAN, CHARLES EDWARD (1863–1945)

Spearman discovered that individual differences on all tests of mental abilities are positively intercorrelated in representative samples of the general population.

SPENCE, JANET TAYLOR (b 1923)

Spence developed the Manifest Anxiety Scale as a vehicle for testing her and Kenneth Spence's theory about the interactions between task characteristics and drive or arousal level in determining task performance.

SPENCE, KENNETH W. (1907–1967)

In the philosophy of science and the tenets of logical empiricism, Spence sought the bases on which psychology could proceed as an objective, empirical science.

SPENCER, HERBERT (1820–1903)

Spencer considered associationism the most binding psychological principle. Along with his contemporary, Alexander Bain, he brought the entire movement of British associationism to an end.

SPERRY, ROGER WOLCOTT (1913–1994)

Sperry's finding, the split-brain phenomenon, created considerable discussion among neuropsychologists and led to the dual personality theory.

SPIELBERGER, CHARLES (b 1927)

Spielberger's research interests have focused on personality and learning, stress, anxiety, curiosity, and the experience, expression, and control of anger. With adaptations in 52 languages and dialects, his State-Trait Anxiety Inventory is the standard international measure of anxiety.

SPINOZA, BENEDICT BARUCH (1632–1677)

Spinoza's philosophy was rationalistic and deductive. Human beings, as a manifestation of God, reflect the psychophysical parallelism that prevails throughout the universe. People have two aspects, mind and body, which are basically one.

SPRANGER, EDUARD (1882–1963)

Spranger identified six types of people in terms of their life goals and values that operated apart from any biological drives or needs.

SPURZHEIM, JOHANN GASPER (1776–1832)

Spurzheim, a phrenologist, identified 37 faculties of the mind, each related to a specific cortical location. His grouping of the faculties into mental, motive, and vital types anticipated Sheldon's somatotypes.

STEINER, RUDOLF (1861–1925)

Steiner founded the first Waldorf School, now the largest nonsectarian private school system in the world. He taught that the development of humankind's intellectual and spiritual faculties could lead to a "spiritual science."

STEKEL, WILHELM (1868–1940)

Stekel stressed the teaching role of the analyst and saw the therapeutic relationship as an active partnership. He believed that the goals of the patient are important and that the patient should be led to distinguish between genuine and false goals.

STEVENS, STANLEY SMITH (1906–1973)

Stevens found that physical continua generally conform to a psychophysical power law rather than Gustav Fechner's logarithmic law.

STOUT, GEORGE FREDERICK (1860–1944)

Stout rejected mental chemistry and criticized Associationists for confusing the "presented whole" with the "sum of its presented components." Thus, Stout anticipated the Gestalt cry that "the whole is greater than the sum of its parts."

STRATTON, GEORGE MALCOLM (1865–1957)

Stratton wore special lenses that reversed the field of vision, up for down and right for left, during his waking hours for 8 consecutive days. After 3 days he was able to make relatively automatic and skilled movements and adjust to seeing an inverted world.

STRONG, EDWARD KELLOGG, JR. (1884–1963)

Strong spent most of his career measuring vocational interests. His later publications dealt with the variation of interests over time, including a large group studied 18 years after completing college.

STRUPP, HANS H. (b 1921)

Strupp viewed the nature of the psychotherapist's influence and the patient's susceptibility to that influence as one of the core problems in psychotherapy research.

STUMPF, CARL (1848–1946)

Stumpf's *Tonpsychologie* was the first work on the psychology of music. One of the most important aspects of this work was his theory of consonance and dissonance in music.

SULLIVAN, ARTHUR M. (b 1932)

Sullivan investigated teaching and learning at the remedial level as well as at the first- and second-year university level. The teaching and remedial programs that he devised resulted in dramatic increases in academic success.

SULLIVAN, HARRY STACK (1892–1949)

Not only is personality couched in interpersonal relations, Sullivan believed, but also the patient–therapist interpersonal relationship is critical for successful therapy.

SUNDBERG, NORMAN D. (b 1922)

Sundberg emphasizes both the "horizontal" and the "vertical": "horizontal" in the sense of knowledge across cultures, communities, and applied activities, and "vertical" in the sense of an appreciation of time, of the history and future of the life span.

SZASZ, THOMAS S. (b 1920)

Szasz is best known for his proposition that mental illness is a myth and for his uncompromising opposition to psychiatric coercions and excuses.

SZEWCZUK, WLODZIMIERZ L. (b 1913)

Szewczuk found three necessary conditions for any memorization: an active attitude, association with earlier experience, and association with emotional reactions.

TAKUMA, TAKETOSHI (b 1927)

Believing that the comparative study of twins is a reliable source for finding the determinants of development, Takuma has performed research on several hundred pairs of twins. Stratification theory is basic to this research.

TAYLOR, FREDERICK WINSLOW (1856–1915)

Taylor founded the area of industrial efficiency. He prescribed the time study with standardized tools and procedures organized by a planning department. Equipment was redesigned to be consonant with human abilities.

TEPLOV, BORIS MIKHAILOVICH (1886–1965)

Teplov related individual differences to the nervous system, stressing the importance of involuntary reflexes in a manner first studied by Ivan Pavlov.

TERMAN, LEWIS MADISON (1877–1956)

Terman's major research contribution to American psychology was his work in intelligence testing and his evaluation of gifted persons.

THOMAS AQUINAS (1225–1274)

In his *Summa theologica*, Thomas Aquinas stated that some things can be known by faith only, others by reason only, and still others by both revelation and rational proof. As humans seek truth, they are also seeking the final good.

THOMPSON, RICHARD F. (b 1930)

In collaboration with W. Alden Spencer, Thompson developed criteria for habituation and evidence that the basic process is a form of synaptic depression that occurs presynaptically.

THOMSON, GODFREY H. (1881–1955)

Thomson regarded the mind as comprising a very large number of "bonds," similar to Thorndike's "connections." Any mental act would draw on a sample of bonds, while other acts would draw on some of the same and some different.

THORNDIKE, EDWARD LEE (1874–1949)

Thorndike taught that psychologists should study behavior, not mental elements or conscious experience. He did fundamental work in understanding learning and also preceded Pavlov's *law of reinforcement* with his *law of effect*.

THURSTONE, LOUIS LEON (1887–1955)

Thurstone is best known for his contributions to factor analysis. His multiple factor theory has endured; however, with the advent of electronic computers, his centroid method of factor extraction has been replaced by more exact methods.

TILLICH, PAUL (1886–1965)

Tillich believed that religious questions arise from human situations and therefore are practical and not primarily theoretical. He was strongly influenced by existentialism.

TINBERGEN, NIKOLAAS (1907–1988)

Many of Tinbergen's works have become classics in both psychology and biology, including his work on courting behavior in sticklebacks, orienting behavior in wasps, and the behavior of grayling butterflies.

TITCHENER, EDWARD BRADFORD (1867–1927)

Titchener brought structuralism to the United States from Wundt's laboratory in Leipzig. He was a dominant figure in the early years of American psychology.

TOLMAN, EDWARD CHASE (1886–1959)

Tolman is primarily known for his theory of learning. Many psychologists consider this a "cognitive field theory," although in his many experiments, primarily with the white rat, he always stressed behavior. He is usually credited with introducing the concept of the "intervening variable" into psychology.

UZNADZE, DMITRII NIKOLAYEVICH (1886–1950)

Uznadze is best known for his theory of "set" as an objective approach to the unconscious.

VAIHINGER, HANS (1852–1933)

Vaihinger is known for his philosophy of "as-if": Something can work as if true even though it is false and recognized as false.

VERNON, PHILIP E. (1905–1987)

Vernon conducted a series of comparative studies of abilities in different parts of the world, from Tanzania to the Arctic.

VERPLANCK, WILLIAM S. (b 1916)

Verplanck showed that successive psychological judgments are not independent of one another, as theory dictated.

VITELES, MORRIS S. (b 1898)

Viteles structured the field of industrial psychology as it is today. His emphasis on the need for a solid experimental basis for industrial applications helped to counter conversion of industrial psychology into industrial psychotechnology.

VIVES, JUAN LUIS (1492–1540)

Vives stands alone as a forerunner of modern psychology. He believed that truths are to be discovered inductively rather than deductively, avoiding speculation.

VYGOTSKY, LEV SEMYONOVICH (1896–1934)

Vygotsky opposed the reflexology of Bekhterev, arguing that a study of mind was necessary because it distinguished humans from lower animals. However, he rejected introspection as a method.

WALLON, HENRI (1879–1962)

Wallon saw emotion as a physiological fact with humoral and physiological aspects, mediating between sensations and the social world.

WANG, ZHONG-MING (b 1949)

Wang has been active in the areas of reward systems design, group attributional training, high-tech innovations, judgment and decision making, and decision support systems.

WARD, JAMES (1843–1924)

Even though Ward was considered by many to be a philosopher more than a psychologist, he was instrumental in establishing the first psychological laboratory at Cambridge.

WARREN, HOWARD CROSBY (1867–1934)

Warren is best known as a writer and editor. He was a contributor to James Baldwin's *Dictionary of philosophy and psychology* and published the *Dictionary of psychology*, which was a standard work for many years.

WASHBURN, MARGARET FLOY (1871–1939)

Washburn's research included work on individual differences, color vision in animals, and aesthetic preferences by students for colors and speech sounds.

WATSON, JOHN B. (1878–1958)

The founder of American behaviorism, Watson established its two tenets: psychology as an objective science and psychology as the science of behavior.

WATT, HENRY JACKSON (1879–1925)

Watt's main contribution involved the study of experience as it occurred in word associations.

WEBB, WILSE BERNARD (b 1920)

Webb's research emphasized the role of individual differences and biological rhythms as determinants of sleep deprivation and performance, and also the effects of aging.

WEBER, ERNST HEINRICH (1795–1878)

Weber's main research concern was in the field of sensory physiology. He found that the point of just noticeable difference bears a constant relationship to the standard. This relationship is expressed in a formula by Gustav Fechner, who identified it as Weber's law.

WECHSLER, DAVID (1896–1981)

Wechsler applied his creative efforts to the development and standardization of intelligence scales that bear his name and to the substitution for Binet's Mental Age of a Deviation Quotient.

WERNER, HEINZ (1890–1964)

Werner held that development proceeds from the undifferentiated and unarticulated to the differentiated and articulated.

WERTHEIMER, MAX (1880–1943)

Wertheimer suggested that the whole is quite *different* from the sum of its parts—not just in that it is more, but *prior to* the parts.

WERTHEIMER, MICHAEL (b 1927)

Wertheimer's research career began with the study of sensory and perceptual processes, but soon broadened to include cognition, individual differences, psycholinguistics, person perception, and eventually the history of psychology.

WHIPPLE, GUY MONTROSE (1876–1941)

Whipple warned the American Psychological Association (APA) against charlatans and otherwise unqualified practitioners who were making their inroads into clinical psychology. As a result, the APA set forth procedures for qualifying psychologists.

WHITE, ROBERT W. (b 1904)

White made a timely contribution to theory when he published *Motivation reconsidered: The concept of competence*, soon followed by other papers on competence.

WHITE, WILLIAM ALANSON (1870–1937)

White abolished the various forms of physical restraint that had been used at St. Elizabeth's hospital, substituting them with concerned humane treatment.

WICKENS, DELOS D. (1909–1988)

Wickens' research activities were almost equally divided between work with human and animal subjects, a distribution expressing a bias toward addressing a basic psychology process by the most promising means.

WILLIAMS, JOANNA P. (b 1935)

Williams has performed research on beginning reading instruction, with a focus on phonemic skills and on reading comprehension (main idea and theme identification and critical reading).

WILSON, EDWARD OSBORNE (b 1929)

Wilson's sociobiology claims that the human body with its social behavior serves to perpetuate the genes. He believed that people exist for the sake of their genes. "The organism is only DNA's way of making more DNA."

WITKIN, HERMAN A. (1916–1979)

Witkin contributed greatly to the conceptualization of the relation between cognitive styles and personality. He believed people generally move from field dependence to field independence as they mature.

WITMER, LIGHTNER (1861–1956)

Witmer established the first psychological clinic at the University of Pennsylvania. He also founded *The psychological clinic*. In the first issue he called for the establishment of a new helping profession, to be termed clinical psychology.

WOLFF, CHRISTIAN VON (1679–1754)

Wolff stressed an active mind rather than one made up of the mere elements of experience as Locke had suggested. The mind consisted of faculties or functions such as knowledge, remembrance, feeling, and willingness.

WOLPE, JOSEPH (b 1915)

The centerpoint of Wolpe's research was experimental studies on the production and cure of neuroses in animals. Neuroses were produced by learning and were reversible by learning. Techniques for treating human neuroses were derived from these findings.

WOODWORTH, ROBERT SESSIONS (1869–1962)

For Woodworth, the subject matter of psychology was both behavior and consciousness. He believed that behaviorists such as John Watson, who had rejected consciousness or the mind, had left out part of a legitimate aspect of psychology.

WUNDT, WILHELM (1832–1920)

Wundt's systematic efforts established psychology as a new and recognized science in Germany during the nineteenth century. Using this method of introspection, students and researchers investigated the subject matter of immediate experience.

YELA, MARIANO (b 1921)

Yela's general theoretical view conceives of psychology as a multiparadigmatic science that is centered on behavior and considered a physical activity with biological and/or biographical significance.

YERKES, ROBERT MEARNS (1876–1956)

Yerkes invented an experimental maze to study animal learning and the evolution of intelligence through the animal species. From his experiments he formed the Yerkes–Dodson law.

YOUNG, PAUL THOMAS (1892–1978)

Young is known for his studies in sound localization using a pseudophone in which the auditory inputs are reversed. He found that auditory localization is significant, particularly when the sounding object cannot be seen.

YOUNG, THOMAS (1773–1829)

As a result of his interest in vision, Young became prominent in psychology. He described and measured visual astigmatism. By measuring the focal length of the eye, he demonstrated that the accommodation was attributable to the changing shape of the lens.

ZAJONC, ROBERT B. (b 1923)

Zajonc's interest has been drawn to the relationship between family structure and intellectual development.

ZAPOROZHETS, ALEXANDER (1905–1981)

Zaporozhets is best known for his concept of "perceptual action" and his theory of voluntary actions. He elaborated a concept of perceptual action that bound together the problems of sensorimotor skills and cognitive development.

ZAZZO, RENÉ (b 1910)

Zazzo has worked on three themes: mental deficiency, twins, and inverted images. He was concerned with solving experimentally the question of how a child achieves his or her own self-image and thus becomes a person.

ZEĬGARNIK, BLIÛMA (b 1900)

Zeĭgarnik is best known for her formal test of Lewin's theory that attainment of a goal or successful locomotion toward a positive valence relieves tension.

ZIMBARDO, PHILIP G. (b 1933)

Zimbardo simulated prison conditions at Stanford and discovered that student "inmates" became deindividualized and lost time perspective.

ZUBIN, JOSEPH (1900–1990)

Zubin was instrumental in developing techniques of observation and quantification of the behavior of mental patients. He also constructed behavior models in psychopathology from physiological, behavioral, genetic, and psychosocial perspectives.

APPENDIX

Ethical Principles of Psychologists and Code of Conduct

Reprinted with permission from *American Psychologist*, Dec. 1992.

CONTENTS

INTRODUCTION

The American Psychological Association's (APA's) Ethical Principles of Psychologists and Code of Conduct (hereinafter referred to as the Ethics Code) consists of an Introduction, a Preamble, six General Principles (A–F), and specific Ethical Standards. The Introduction discusses the intent, organization, procedural considerations, and scope of application of the Ethics Code. The Preamble and General Principles are *aspirational* goals to guide psychologists toward the highest ideals of psychology. Although the Preamble and General Principles are not themselves enforceable rules, they should be considered by psychologists in arriving at an ethical course of action and may be considered by ethics bodies in interpreting the Ethical Standards. The Ethical Standards set forth *enforceable* rules for conduct as psychologists. Most of the Ethical Standards are written broadly, in order to apply to psychologists in varied roles, although the application of an Ethical Standard may vary depending on the context. The Ethical Standards are not exhaustive. The fact that a given conduct is not specifically addressed by the Ethics Code does not mean that it is necessarily either ethical or unethical.

Membership in the APA commits members to adhere to the APA Ethics Code and to the rules and procedures used to implement it. Psychologists and students, whether or not they are APA members, should be aware that the Ethics Code may be applied to them by state psychology boards, courts, or other public bodies.

This Ethics Code applies only to psychologists' workrelated activities, that is, activities that are part of the psychologists' scientific and professional functions or that are psychological in nature. It includes the clinical or counseling practice of psychology, research, teaching, supervision of trainees, development of assessment instruments, conducting assessments, educational counseling, organizational consulting, social intervention, administration, and other activities as well. These work-related activities can be distinguished from the purely private conduct of a psychologist, which ordinarily is not within the purview of the Ethics Code.

The Ethics Code is intended to provide standards of professional conduct that can be applied by the APA and by other bodies that choose to adopt them. Whether or not a psychologist has violated the Ethics Code does not by itself determine whether he or she is legally liable in a court action, whether a contract is enforceable, or whether other legal consequences occur. These results are based on legal rather than ethical rules. However, compliance with or violation of the Ethics Code may be admissible as evidence in some legal proceedings, depending on the circumstances.

In the process of making decisions regarding their professional behavior, psychologists must consider this Ethics Code, in addition to applicable laws and psychology board regulations. If the Ethics Code establishes a higher standard of conduct than is required by law, psychologists must meet the higher ethical standard. If the Ethics Code standard appears to conflict with the requirements of law, then psychologists make known their commitment to the Ethics Code and take steps to resolve the conflict in a responsible manner. If neither law nor the Ethics Code resolves an issue, psychologists should consider other professional materials[1] and the dictates of their own conscience, as well as seek consultation with others within the field when this is practical.

The procedures for filing, investigating, and resolving complaints of unethical conduct are described in the current Rules and Procedures of the APA Ethics Committee. The actions that APA may take for violations of the Ethics Code include actions such as reprimand, censure, termination of APA membership, and referral of the matter to other bodies. Complainants who seek remedies such as monetary damages in alleging ethical violations by a psychologist must resort to private negotiation, administrative bodies, or the courts. Actions that violate the Ethics Code may lead to the imposition of sanctions on a psychologist by bodies other than APA, including state psychological associations, other professional groups, psychology boards, other state or federal agencies, and payors for health services. In addition to actions for violation of the Ethics Code, the APA Bylaws provide that APA may take action against a member after his or her conviction of a felony, expulsion or suspension from an affiliated state psychological association, or suspension or loss of licensure.

This version of the APA Ethics Code was adopted by the American Psychological Association's Council of Representatives during its meeting, August 13 and 16, 1992, and is effective beginning December 1,1992. Inquiries concerning the substance or interpretation of the APA Ethics Code should be addressed to the Director, Office of Ethics, American Psychological Association, 750 First Street, NE, Washington, DC 20002-4242.

This Code will be used to adjudicate complaints brought concerning alleged conduct occurring on or after the effective date. Complaints regarding conduct occurring prior to the effective date will be adjudicated on the basis of the version of the Code that was in effect at the time the conduct occurred, except that no provisions repealed in June 1989, will be enforced even if an earlier version contains the provision. The Ethics Code will undergo continuing review and study for future revisions; comments on the Code may be sent to the above address.

The APA has previously published its Ethical Standards as follows:

American Psychological Association. (1953). *Ethical standards of psychologists.* Washington, DC: Author.

American Psychological Association. (1958). Standards of ethical behavior for psychologists. *American Psychologist, 13,* 268–271.

American Psychological Association. (1963). Ethical standards of psychologists. *American Psychologist, 18.* 56–60.

American Psychological Association. (1968). Ethical standards of psychologists. *American Psychologist, 23,* 357–361.

American Psychological Association. (1977, March). Ethical standards of psychologists. *APA Monitor,* pp. 22–23.

American Psychological Association. (1979). *Ethical standards of psychologists.* Washington, DC: Author.

American Psychological Association. (1981). Ethical principles of psychologists. *American Psychologist, 36,* 633–638.

American Psychological Association. (1990). Ethical principles of psychologists (Amended June 2, 1989). *American Psychologist, 45,* 390–395.

Request copies of the APA's Ethical Principles of Psychologists and Code of Conduct from the APA Order Department, 750 First Street, NE, Washington, DC 20002-4242, or phone (202) 336-5510.

PREAMBLE

Psychologists work to develop a valid and reliable body of scientific knowledge based on research. They may apply that knowledge to human behavior in a variety of contexts. In doing so, they perform many roles, such as researcher, educator, diagnostician, therapist, supervisor, con-

---

[1]Professional materials that are most helpful in this regard are guidelines and standards that have been adopted or endorsed by professional psychological organizations. Such guidelines and standards, whether adopted by the American Psychological Association (APA) or its Divisions, are not enforceable as such by this Ethics Code, but are of educative value to psychologists, courts, and professional bodies. Such materials include, but are not limited to, the APA's *General Guidelines for Providers of Psychological Services* (1987), *Specialty Guidelines for the Delivery of Services by Clinical Psychologists, Counseling Psychologists, Industrial/Organizational Psychologists, and School Psychologists* (1981), *Guidelines for Computer Based Tests and Interpretations* (1987), *Standards for Educational and Psychological Testing* (1985), *Ethical Principles in the Conduct of Research With Human Participants* (1982), *Guidelines for Ethical Conduct in the Care and Use of Animals* (1986), *Guidelines for Providers of Psychological Services to Ethnic, Linguistic, and Culturally Diverse Populations* (1990), and *Publication Manual of the American Psychological Association* (3rd ed., 1983). Materials not adopted by APA as a whole include the APA Division 41 (Forensic Psychology)/American Psychology–Law Society's *Specialty Guidelines for Forensic Psychologists* (1991).

sultant, administrator, social interventionist, and expert witness. Their goal is to broaden knowledge of behavior and, where appropriate, to apply it pragmatically to improve the condition of both the individual and society. Psychologists respect the central importance of freedom of inquiry and expression in research, teaching, and publication. They also strive to help the public in developing informed judgments and choices concerning human behavior. This Ethics Code provides a common set of values upon which psychologists build their professional and scientific work.

This Code is intended to provide both the general principles and the decision rules to cover most situations encountered by psychologists. It has as its primary goal the welfare and protection of the individuals and groups with whom psychologists work. It is the individual responsibility of each psychologist to aspire to the highest possible standards of conduct. Psychologists respect and protect human and civil rights, and do not knowingly participate in or condone unfair discriminatory practices.

The development of a dynamic set of ethical standards for a psychologist's work-related conduct requires a personal commitment to a lifelong effort to act ethically; to encourage ethical behavior by students, supervisees, employees, and colleagues, as appropriate; and to consult with others, as needed, concerning ethical problems. Each psychologist supplements, but does not violate, the Ethics Code's values and rules on the basis of guidance drawn from personal values, culture, and experience.

GENERAL PRINCIPLES

Principle A: Competence

Psychologists strive to maintain high standards of competence in their work. They recognize the boundaries of their particular competencies and the limitations of their expertise. They provide only those services and use only those techniques for which they are qualified by education, training, or experience. Psychologists are cognizant of the fact that the competencies required in serving, teaching, and/or studying groups of people vary with the distinctive characteristics of those groups. In those areas in which recognized professional standards do not yet exist, psychologists exercise careful judgment and take appropriate precautions to protect the welfare of those with whom they work. They maintain knowledge of relevant scientific and professional information related to the services they render, and they recognize the need for ongoing education. Psychologists make appropriate use of scientific, professional, technical, and administrative resources.

Principle B: Integrity

Psychologists seek to promote integrity in the science, teaching, and practice of psychology. In these activities psychologists are honest, fair, and respectful of others. In describing or reporting their qualifications, services, products, fees, research, or teaching, they do not make statements that are false, misleading, or deceptive. Psychologists strive to be aware of their own belief systems, values, needs, and limitations and the effect of these on their work. To the extent feasible, they attempt to clarify for relevant parties the roles they are performing and to function appropriately in accordance with those roles. Psychologists avoid improper and potentially harmful dual relationships.

Principle C: Professional and Scientific Responsibility

Psychologists uphold professional standards of conduct, clarify their professional roles and obligations, accept appropriate responsibility for their behavior, and adapt their methods to the needs of different populations. Psychologists consult with, refer to, or cooperate with other professionals and institutions to the extent needed to serve the best interests of their patients, clients, or other recipients of their services.

Psychologists' moral standards and conduct are personal matters to the same degree as is true for any other person, except as psychologists' conduct may compromise their professional responsibilities or reduce the public's trust in psychology and psychologists. Psychologists are concerned about the ethical compliance of their colleagues' scientific and professional conduct. When appropriate, they consult with colleagues in order to prevent or avoid unethical conduct.

Principle D: Respect for People's Rights and Dignity

Psychologists accord appropriate respect to the fundamental rights, dignity, and worth of all people. They respect the rights of individuals to privacy, confidentiality, self-determination, and autonomy, mindful that legal and other obligations may lead to inconsistency and conflict with the exercise of these rights. Psychologists are aware of cultural, individual, and role differences, including those due to age, gender, race, ethnicity, national origin, religion, sexual orientation, disability, language, and socioeconomic status. Psychologists try to eliminate the effect on their work of biases based on those factors, and they do not knowingly participate in or condone unfair discriminatory practices.

Principle E: Concern for Others' Welfare

Psychologists seek to contribute to the welfare of those with whom they interact professionally. In their professional actions, psychologists weigh the welfare and rights of their patients or clients, students, supervisees, human research participants, and other affected persons, and the welfare of animal subjects of research. When conflicts occur among psychologists' obligations or concerns, they attempt to resolve these conflicts and to perform their roles in a responsible fashion that avoids or minimizes harm. Psychologists are sensitive to real and ascribed differences in power between themselves and others, and they do not exploit or mislead other people during or after professional relationships.

Principle F: Social Responsibility

Psychologists are aware of their professional and scientific responsibilities to the community and the society in which they work and live. They apply and make public their knowledge of psychology in order to contribute to human welfare. Psychologists are concerned about and work to mitigate the causes of human suffering. When undertaking research, they strive to advance human welfare and the science of psychology. Psychologists try to avoid misuse of their work. Psychologists comply with the law and encourage the development of law and social policy that serve the interests of their patients and clients and the public. They are encouraged to contribute a portion of their professional time for little or no personal advantage.

ETHICAL STANDARDS

1. General Standards

These General Standards are potentially applicable to the professional and scientific activities of all psychologists.

1.01 Applicability of the Ethics Code

The activity of a psychologist subject to the Ethics Code may be reviewed under these Ethical Standards only if the activity is part of his or her work-related functions or the activity is psychological in nature. Personal activities having no connection to or effect on psychological roles are not subject to the Ethics Code.

1.02 Relationship of Ethics and Law

If psychologists' ethical responsibilities conflict with law, psychologists make known their commitment to the Ethics Code and take steps to resolve the conflict in a responsible manner.

1.03 Professional and Scientific Relationship

Psychologists provide diagnostic, therapeutic, teaching, research, supervisory, consultative, or other psychological services only in the context of a defined professional or scientific relationship or role. (See also Standards 2.01, Evaluation, Diagnosis, and Interventions in Professional Context, and 7.02, Forensic Assessments.)

1.04 Boundaries of Competence

(a) Psychologists provide services, teach, and conduct research only within the boundaries of their competence, based on their education, training, supervised experience, or appropriate professional experience.

(b) Psychologists provide services, teach, or conduct research in new areas or involving new techniques only after first undertaking appropriate study, training, supervision, and/or consultation from persons who are competent in those areas or techniques.

(c) In those emerging areas in which generally recognized standards for preparatory training do not yet exist, psychologists nevertheless take reasonable steps to ensure the competence of their work and to protect patients, clients, students, research participants, and others from harm.

1.05 Maintaining Expertise

Psychologists who engage in assessment, therapy, teaching, research, organizational consulting, or other professional activities maintain a reasonable level of awareness of current scientific and professional information in their fields of activity, and undertake ongoing efforts to maintain competence in the skills they use.

1.06 Basis for Scientific and Professional Judgments

Psychologists rely on scientifically and professionally derived knowledge when making scientific or professional judgments or when engaging in scholarly or professional endeavors.

1.07 Describing the Nature and Results of Psychological Services

(a) When psychologists provide assessment, evaluation, treatment, counseling, supervision, teaching, consultation, research, or other psychological services to an individual, a group, or an organization, they provide, using language that is reasonably understandable to the recipient of those services, appropriate information beforehand about the nature of such services and appropriate information later about results and conclusions. (See also Standard 2.09, Explaining Assessment Results.)

(b) If psychologists will be precluded by law or by organizational roles from providing such information to particular individuals or groups, they so inform those individuals or groups at the outset of the service.

1.08 Human Differences

Where differences of age, gender, race, ethnicity, national origin, religion, sexual orientation, disability, language, or socioeconomic status significantly affect psychologists' work concerning particular individuals or groups, psychologists obtain the training, experience, consultation, or supervision necessary to ensure the competence of their services, or they make appropriate referrals.

1.09 Respecting Others

In their work-related activities, psychologists respect the rights of others to hold values, attitudes, and opinions that differ from their own.

1.10 Nondiscrimination

In their work-related activities, psychologists do not engage in unfair discrimination based on age, gender, race, ethnicity, national origin, religion, sexual orientation, disability, socioeconomic status, or any basis proscribed by law.

1.11 Sexual Harassment

(a) Psychologists do not engage in sexual harassment. Sexual harassment is sexual solicitation, physical advances, or verbal or nonverbal conduct that is sexual in nature, that occurs in connection with the psychologist's activities or roles as a psychologist, and that either: (1) is unwelcome, is offensive, or creates a hostile workplace environment, and the psychologist knows or is told this; or (2) is sufficiently severe or intense to be abusive to a reasonable person in the context. Sexual harassment can consist of a single intense or severe act or of multiple persistent or pervasive acts.

(b) Psychologists accord sexual-harassment complainants and respondents dignity and respect. Psychologists do not participate in denying a person academic admittance or advancement, employment, tenure, or promotion, based solely upon their having made, or their being the subject of, sexual-harassment charges. This does not preclude taking action based upon the outcome of such proceedings or consideration of other appropriate information.

1.12 Other Harassment

Psychologists do not knowingly engage in behavior that is harassing or demeaning to persons with whom they interact in their work based on factors such as those persons' age, gender, race, ethnicity, national origin, religion, sexual orientation, disability, language, or socioeconomic status.

1.13 Personal Problems and Conflicts

(a) Psychologists recognize that their personal problems and conflicts may interfere with their effectiveness. Accordingly, they refrain from undertaking an activity when they know or should know that their personal problems are likely to lead to harm to a patient, client, colleague, student, research participant, or other person to whom they may owe a professional or scientific obligation.

(b) In addition, psychologists have an obligation to be alert to signs of, and to obtain assistance for, their personal problems at an early stage, in order to prevent significantly impaired performance.

(c) When psychologists become aware of personal problems that may interfere with their performing workrelated duties adequately, they take appropriate measures, such as obtaining professional consultation or assistance, and determine whether they should limit, suspend, or terminate their work-related duties.

1.14 Avoiding Harm

Psychologists take reasonable steps to avoid harming their patients or clients, research participants, students, and others with whom they work, and to minimize harm where it is foreseeable and unavoidable.

1.15 Misuse of Psychologists' Influence

Because psychologists' scientific and professional judgments and actions may affect the lives of others, they are alert to and guard against personal, financial, social, organizational, or political factors that might lead to misuse of their influence.

1.16 Misuse of Psychologists' Work

(a) Psychologists do not participate in activities in which it appears likely that their skills or data will be misused by others, unless corrective mechanisms are available. (See also Standard 7.04, Truthfulness and Candor.)

(b) If psychologists learn of misuse or misrepresentation of their work, they take reasonable steps to correct or minimize the misuse or misrepresentation.

1.17 Multiple Relationships

(a) In many communities and situations, it may not be feasible or reasonable for psychologists to avoid social or other nonprofessional contacts with persons such as patients, clients, students, supervisees, or research participants. Psychologists must always be sensitive to the potential harmful effects of other contacts on their work and on those persons with whom they deal. A psychologist refrains from entering into or promising another personal, scientific, professional, financial, or other relationship with such persons if it appears likely that such a relationship reasonably might impair the psychologist's objectivity or otherwise interfere with the psychologist's effectively performing his or her functions as a psychologist, or might harm or exploit the other party.

(b) Likewise, whenever feasible, a psychologist refrains from taking on professional or scientific obligations when preexisting relationships would create a risk of such harm.

(c) If a psychologist finds that, due to unforeseen factors, a potentially harmful multiple relationship has arisen, the psychologist attempts to resolve it with due regard for the best interests of the affected person and maximal compliance with the Ethics Code.

1.18 Barter (With Patients or Clients)

Psychologists ordinarily refrain from accepting goods, services, or other nonmonetary remuneration from patients or clients in return for psychological services because such arrangements create inherent potential for conflicts, exploitation, and distortion of the professional relationship. A psychologist may participate in bartering only if (1) it is not clinically contraindicated, and (2) the relationship is not exploitative. (See also Standards 1.17, Multiple Relationships, and 1.25, Fees and Financial Arrangements.)

1.19 Exploitative Relationships

(a) Psychologists do not exploit persons over whom they have supervisory, evaluative, or other authority such as students, supervisees, employees, research participants, and clients or patients. (See also Standards 4.05–4.07 regarding sexual involvement with clients or patients.)

(b) Psychologists do not engage in sexual relationships with students or supervisees in training over whom the psychologist has evaluative or direct authority, because such relationships are so likely to impair judgment or be exploitative.

1.20 Consultations and Referrals

(a) Psychologists arrange for appropriate consultations and referrals based principally on the best interests of their patients or clients, with appropriate consent, and subject to other relevant considerations, including applicable law and contractual obligations. (See also Standards 5.01, Discussing the Limits of Confidentiality, and 5.06, Consultations.)

(b) When indicated and professionally appropriate, psychologists cooperate with other professionals in order to serve their patients or clients effectively and appropriately.

(c) Psychologists' referral practices are consistent with law.

1.21 Third-Party Requests for Services

(a) When a psychologist agrees to provide services to a person or entity at the request of a third party, the psychologist clarifies to the extent feasible, at the outset of the service, the nature of the relationship with each party. This clarification includes the role of the psychologist (such as therapist, organizational consultant, diagnostician, or expert witness), the probable uses of the services provided or the information obtained, and the fact that there may be limits to confidentiality.

(b) If there is a foreseeable risk of the psychologist's being called upon to perform conflicting roles because of the involvement of a third party, the psychologist clarifies the nature and direction of his or her

responsibilities, keeps all parties appropriately informed as matters develop, and resolves the situation in accordance with this Ethics Code.

1.22 Delegation to and Supervision of Subordinates

(a) Psychologists delegate to their employees, supervisees, and research assistants only those responsibilities that such persons can reasonably be expected to perform competently, on the basis of their education, training, or experience, either independently or with the level of supervision being provided.

(b) Psychologists provide proper training and supervision to their employees or supervisees and take reasonable steps to see that such persons perform services responsibly, competently, and ethically.

(c) If institutional policies, procedures, or practices prevent fulfillment of this obligation, psychologists attempt to modify their role or to correct the situation to the extent feasible.

1.23 Documentation of Professional and Scientific Work

(a) Psychologists appropriately document their professional and scientific work in order to facilitate provision of services later by them or by other professionals, to ensure accountability, and to meet other requirements of institutions or the law.

(b) When psychologists have reason to believe that records of their professional services will be used in legal proceedings involving recipients of or participants in their work, they have a responsibility to create and maintain documentation in the kind of detail and quality that would be consistent with reasonable scrutiny in an adjudicative forum. (See also Standard 7.01, Professionalism, under Forensic Activities.)

1.24 Records and Data

Psychologists create, maintain, disseminate, store, retain, and dispose of records and data relating to their research, practice, and other work in accordance with law and in a manner that permits compliance with the requirements of this Ethics Code. (See also Standard 5.04, Maintenance of Records.)

1.25 Fees and Financial Arrangements

(a) As early as is feasible in a professional or scientific relationship, the psychologist and the patient, client, or other appropriate recipient of psychological services reach an agreement specifying the compensation and the billing arrangements.

(b) Psychologists do not exploit recipients of services or payors with respect to fees.

(c) Psychologists' fee practices are consistent with law.

(d) Psychologists do not misrepresent their fees.

(e) If limitations to services can be anticipated because of limitations in financing, this is discussed with the patient, client, or other appropriate recipient of services as early as is feasible. (See also Standard 4.08, Interruption of Services.)

(f) If the patient, client, or other recipient of services does not pay for services as agreed, and if the psychologist wishes to use collection agencies or legal measures to collect the fees, the psychologist first informs the person that such measures will be taken and provides that person an opportunity to make prompt payment. (See also Standard 5.11, Withholding Records for Nonpayment.)

1.26 Accuracy in Reports to Payors and Funding Sources

In their reports to payors for services or sources of research funding, psychologists accurately state the nature of the research or service provided, the fees or charges, and where applicable, the identity of the provider, the findings, and the diagnosis. (See also Standard 5.05, Disclosures.)

1.27 Referrals and Fees

When a psychologist pays, receives payment from, or divides fees with another professional other than in an employer–employee relationship, the payment to each is based on the services (clinical, consultative, administrative, or other) provided and is not based on the referral itself.

2. Evaluation, Assessment, or Intervention

2.01 Evaluation, Diagnosis, and Interventions in Professional Context

(a) Psychologists perform evaluations, diagnostic services, or interventions only within the context of a defined professional relationship. (See also Standard 1.03, Professional and Scientific Relationship.)

(b) Psychologists' assessments, recommendations, reports, and psychological diagnostic or evaluative statements are based on information and techniques (including personal interviews of the individual when appropriate) sufficient to provide appropriate substantiation for their findings. (See also Standard 7.02, Forensic Assessments.)

2.02 Competence and Appropriate Use of Assessments and Interventions

(a) Psychologists who develop, administer, score, interpret, or use psychological assessment techniques, interviews, tests, or instruments do so in a manner and for purposes that are appropriate in light of the research on or evidence of the usefulness and proper application of the techniques.

(b) Psychologists refrain from misuse of assessment techniques, interventions, results, and interpretations and take reasonable steps to prevent others from misusing the information these techniques provide. This includes refraining from releasing raw test results or raw data to persons, other than to patients or clients as appropriate, who are not qualified to use such information. (See also Standards 1.02, Relationship of Ethics and Law, and 1.04, Boundaries of Competence.)

2.03 Test Construction

Psychologists who develop and conduct research with tests and other assessment techniques use scientific procedures and current professional knowledge for test design, standardization, validation, reduction or elimination of bias, and recommendations for use.

2.04 Use of Assessment in General and With Special Populations

(a) Psychologists who perform interventions or administer, score, interpret, or use assessment techniques are familiar with the reliability, validation, and related standardization or outcome studies of, and proper applications and uses of, the techniques they use.

(b) Psychologists recognize limits to the certainty with which diagnoses, judgments, or predictions can be made about individuals.

(c) Psychologists attempt to identify situations in which particular interventions or assessment techniques or norms may not be applicable or may require adjustment in administration or interpretation because of factors such as individuals' gender, age, race, ethnicity, national origin, religion, sexual orientation, disability, language, or socioeconomic status.

2.05 Interpreting Assessment Results

When interpreting assessment results, including automated interpretations, psychologists take into account the various test factors and characteristics of the person being assessed that might affect psychologists' judgments or reduce the accuracy of their interpretations. They indicate any significant reservations they have about the accuracy or limitations of their interpretations.

2.06 Unqualified Persons

Psychologists do not promote the use of psychological assessment techniques by unqualified persons. (See also Standard 1.22, Delegation to and Supervision of Subordinates.)

2.07 Obsolete Tests and Outdated Test Results

(a) Psychologists do not base their assessment or intervention decisions or recommendations on data or test results that are outdated for the current purpose.

(b) Similarly, psychologists do not base such decisions or recommendations on tests and measures that are obsolete and not useful for the current purpose.

2.08 Test Scoring and Interpretation Services

(a) Psychologists who offer assessment or scoring procedures to other professionals accurately describe the purpose, norms, validity, reliability, and applications of the procedures and any special qualifications applicable to their use.

(b) Psychologists select scoring and interpretation services (including automated services) on the basis of evidence of the validity of the program and procedures as well as on other appropriate considerations.

(c) Psychologists retain appropriate responsibility for the appropriate application, interpretation, and use of assessment instruments, whether they score and interpret such tests themselves or use automated or other services.

2.09 Explaining Assessment Results

Unless the nature of the relationship is clearly explained to the person being assessed in advance and precludes provision of an explanation of results (such as in some organizational consulting, preemployment or security screenings, and forensic evaluations), psychologists ensure that an explanation of the results is provided using language that is reasonably understandable to the person assessed or to another legally authorized person on behalf of the client. Regardless of whether the scoring and interpretation are done by the psychologist, by assistants, or by automated or other outside services, psychologists take reasonable steps to ensure that appropriate explanations of results are given.

2.10 Maintaining Test Security

Psychologists make reasonable efforts to maintain the integrity and security of tests and other assessment techniques consistent with law, contractual obligations, and in a manner that permits compliance with the requirements of this Ethics Code. (See also Standard 1.02, Relationship of Ethics and Law.)

3. Advertising and Other Public Statements

3.01 Definition of Public Statements

Psychologists comply with this Ethics Code in public statements relating to their professional services, products, or publications or to the field of psychology. Public statements include but are not limited to paid or unpaid advertising, brochures, printed matter, directory listings, personal resumes or curricula vitae, interviews or comments for use in media, statements in legal proceedings, lectures and public oral presentations, and published materials.

3.02 Statements by Others

(a) Psychologists who engage others to create or place public statements that promote their professional practice, products, or activities retain professional responsibility for such statements.

(b) In addition, psychologists make reasonable efforts to prevent others whom they do not control (such as employers, publishers, sponsors, organizational clients, and representatives of the print or broadcast media) from making deceptive statements concerning psychologists' practice or professional or scientific activities.

(c) If psychologists learn of deceptive statements about their work made by others, psychologists make reasonable efforts to correct such statements.

(d) Psychologists do not compensate employees of press, radio, television, or other communication media in return for publicity in a news item.

(e) A paid advertisement relating to the psychologist's activities must be identified as such, unless it is already apparent from the context.

3.03 Avoidance of False or Deceptive Statements

(a) Psychologists do not make public statements that are false, deceptive, misleading, or fraudulent, either because of what they state, convey, or suggest or because of what they omit, concerning their research, practice, or other work activities or those of persons or organizations with which they are affiliated. As examples (and not in limitation) of this standard, psychologists do not make false or deceptive statements concerning (1) their training, experience, or competence; (2) their academic degrees; (3) their credentials; (4) their institutional or association affiliations; (5) their services; (6) the scientific or clinical basis for, or results or degree of success of, their services; (7) their fees; or (8) their publications or research findings. (See also Standards 6.15, Deception in Research, and 6.18, Providing Participants With Information About the Study.)

(b) Psychologists claim as credentials for their psychological work, only degrees that (1) were earned from a regionally accredited educational institution or (2) were the basis for psychology licensure by the state in which they practice.

3.04 Media Presentations

When psychologists provide advice or comment by means of public lectures, demonstrations, radio or television programs, prerecorded tapes, printed articles, mailed material, or other media, they take reasonable precautions to ensure that (1) the statements are based on appropriate psychological literature and practice, (2) the statements are otherwise consistent with this Ethics Code, and (3) the recipients of the information are not encouraged to infer that a relationship has been established with them personally.

3.05 Testimonials

Psychologists do not solicit testimonials from current psychotherapy clients or patients or other persons who because of their particular circumstances are vulnerable to undue influence.

3.06 In-Person Solicitation

Psychologists do not engage, directly or through agents, in uninvited in-person solicitation of business from actual or potential psychotherapy patients or clients or other persons who because of their particular circumstances are vulnerable to undue influence. However, this does not preclude attempting to implement appropriate collateral contacts with significant others for the purpose of benefiting an already engaged therapy patient.

4. Therapy

4.01 Structuring the Relationship

(a) Psychologists discuss with clients or patients as early as is feasible in the therapeutic relationship appropriate issues, such as the nature and anticipated course of therapy, fees, and confidentiality. (See also Standards 1.25, Fees and Financial Arrangements, and 5.01, Discussing the Limits of Confidentiality.)

(b) When the psychologist's work with clients or patients will be supervised, the above discussion includes that fact, and the name of the supervisor, when the supervisor has legal responsibility for the case.

(c) When the therapist is a student intern, the client or patient is informed of that fact.

(d) Psychologists make reasonable efforts to answer patients' questions and to avoid apparent misunderstandings about therapy. Whenever possible, psychologists provide oral and/or written information, using language that is reasonably understandable to the patient or client.

4.02 Informed Consent to Therapy

(a) Psychologists obtain appropriate informed consent to therapy or related procedures, using language that is reasonably understandable to participants. The content of informed consent will vary depending on many circumstances; however, informed consent generally implies that the person (1) has the capacity to consent, (2) has been informed of significant information concerning the procedure, (3) has freely and without undue influence expressed consent, and (4) consent has been appropriately documented.

(b) When persons are legally incapable of giving informed consent, psychologists obtain informed permission from a legally authorized person, if such substitute consent is permitted by law.

(c) In addition, psychologists (1) inform those persons who are legally incapable of giving informed consent about the proposed interventions in a manner commensurate with the persons' psychological capacities, (2) seek their assent to those interventions, and (3) consider such persons' preferences and best interests.

4.03 Couple and Family Relationships

(a) When a psychologist agrees to provide services to several persons who have a relationship (such as husband and wife or parents and children), the psychologist attempts to clarify at the outset (1) which of the individuals are patients or clients and (2) the relationship the psychologist will have with each person. This clarification includes the role of the psychologist and the probable uses of the services provided or the information obtained. (See also Standard 5.01, Discussing the Limits of Confidentiality.)

(b) As soon as it becomes apparent that the psychologist may be called on to perform potentially conflicting roles (such as marital counselor to husband and wife, and then witness for one party in a divorce proceeding), the psychologist attempts to clarify and adjust, or withdraw from, roles appropriately. (See also Standard 7.03, Clarification of Role, under Forensic Activities.)

4.04 Providing Mental Health Services to Those Served by Others

In deciding whether to offer or provide services to those already receiving mental health services elsewhere, psychologists carefully consider the treatment issues and the potential patient's or client's welfare. The psychologist discusses these issues with the patient or client, or another legally authorized person on behalf of the client, in order to minimize the risk of confusion and conflict, consults with the other service providers when appropriate, and proceeds with caution and sensitivity to the therapeutic issues.

4.05 Sexual Intimacies With Current Patients or Clients

Psychologists do not engage in sexual intimacies with current patients or clients.

4.06 Therapy With Former Sexual Partners

Psychologists do not accept as therapy patients or clients persons with whom they have engaged in sexual intimacies.

4.07 Sexual Intimacies With Former Therapy Patients

(a) Psychologists do not engage in sexual intimacies with a former therapy patient or client for at least two years after cessation or termination of professional services.

(b) Because sexual intimacies with a former therapy patient or client are so frequently harmful to the patient or client, and because such intimacies undermine public confidence in the psychology profession and thereby deter the public's use of needed services, psychologists do not engage in sexual intimacies with former therapy patients and clients even after a two-year interval except in the most unusual circumstances. The psychologist who engages in such activity after the two years following cessation or termination of treatment bears the burden of demonstrating that there has been no exploitation, in light of all relevant factors, including (1) the amount of time that has passed since therapy terminated, (2) the nature and duration of the therapy, (3) the circumstances of termination, (4) the patient's or client's personal history, (5) the patient's or client's current mental status, (6) the likelihood of adverse impact on the patient or client and others, and (7) any statements or actions made by the therapist during the course of therapy suggesting or inviting the possibility of a posttermination sexual or romantic relationship with the patient or client. (See also Standard 1.17, Multiple Relationships.)

4.08 Interruption of Services

(a) Psychologists make reasonable efforts to plan for facilitating care in the event that psychological services are interrupted by factors such as the psychologist's illness, death, unavailability, or relocation or by the client's relocation or financial limitations. (See also Standard 5.09, Preserving Records and Data.)

(b) When entering into employment or contractual relationships, psychologists provide for orderly and appropriate resolution of responsibility for patient or client care in the event that the employment or contractual relationship ends, with paramount consideration given to the welfare of the patient or client.

4.09 Terminating the Professional Relationship

(a) Psychologists do not abandon patients or clients. (See also Standard 1.25e, under Fees and Financial Arrangements.)

(b) Psychologists terminate a professional relationship when it becomes reasonably clear that the patient or client no longer needs the service, is not benefiting, or is being harmed by continued service.

(c) Prior to termination for whatever reason, except where precluded by the patient's or client's conduct, the psychologist discusses the patient's or client's views and needs, provides appropriate pretermination counseling, suggests alternative service providers as appropriate, and takes other reasonable steps to facilitate transfer of responsibility to another provider if the patient or client needs one immediately.

5. Privacy and Confidentiality

These Standards are potentially applicable to the professional and scientific activities of all psychologists.

5.01 Discussing the Limits of Confidentiality

(a) Psychologists discuss with persons and organizations with whom they establish a scientific or professional relationship (including, to the extent feasible, minors and their legal representatives) (1) the relevant limitations on confidentiality, including limitations where applicable in group, marital, and family therapy or in organizational consulting, and (2) the foreseeable uses of the information generated through their services.

(b) Unless it is not feasible or is contraindicated, the discussion of confidentiality occurs at the outset of the relationship and thereafter as new circumstances may warrant.

(c) Permission for electronic recording of interviews is secured from clients and patients.

5.02 Maintaining Confidentiality

Psychologists have a primary obligation and take reasonable precautions to respect the confidentiality rights of those with whom they work or consult, recognizing that confidentiality may be established by law, institutional rules, or professional or scientific relationships. (See also Standard 6.26, Professional Reviewers.)

5.03 Minimizing Intrusions on Privacy

(a) In order to minimize intrusions on privacy, psychologists include in written and oral reports, consultations, and the like, only information germane to the purpose for which the communication is made.

(b) Psychologists discuss confidential information obtained in clinical or consulting relationships, or evaluative data concerning patients, individual or organizational clients, students, research participants, supervisees, and employees, only for appropriate scientific or professional purposes and only with persons clearly concerned with such matters.

5.04 Maintenance of Records

Psychologists maintain appropriate confidentiality in creating, storing, accessing, transferring, and disposing of records under their control, whether these are written, automated, or in any other medium. Psychologists maintain and dispose of records in accordance with law and in a manner that permits compliance with the requirements of this Ethics Code.

5.05 Disclosures

(a) Psychologists disclose confidential information without the consent of the individual only as mandated by law, or where permitted by law for a valid purpose, such as (1) to provide needed professional services to the patient or the individual or organizational client, (2) to obtain appropriate professional consultations, (3) to protect the patient or client or others from harm, or (4) to obtain payment for services, in which instance disclosure is limited to the minimum that is necessary to achieve the purpose.

(b) Psychologists also may disclose confidential information with the appropriate consent of the patient or the individual or organizational client (or of another legally authorized person on behalf of the patient or client), unless prohibited by law.

5.06 Consultations

When consulting with colleagues, (1) psychologists do not share confidential information that reasonably could lead to the identification of a patient, client, research participant, or other person or organization with whom they have a confidential relationship unless they have obtained the prior consent of the person or organization or the disclosure cannot be avoided, and (2) they share information only to the extent necessary to achieve the purposes of the consultation. (See also Standard 5.02, Maintaining Confidentiality.)

5.07 Confidential Information in Databases

(a) If confidential information concerning recipients of psychological services is to be entered into databases or systems of records available to persons whose access has not been consented to by the recipient, then psychologists use coding or other techniques to avoid the inclusion of personal identifiers.

(b) If a research protocol approved by an institutional review board or similar body requires the inclusion of personal identifiers, such identifiers are deleted before the information is made accessible to persons other than those of whom the subject was advised.

(c) If such deletion is not feasible, then before psychologists transfer such data to others or review such data collected by others, they take reasonable steps to determine that appropriate consent of personally identifiable individuals has been obtained.

5.08 Use of Confidential Information for Didactic or Other Purposes

(a) Psychologists do not disclose in their writings, lectures, or other public media, confidential, personally identifiable information concerning their patients, individual or organizational clients, students, research participants, or other recipients of their services that they obtained during the course of their work, unless the person or organization has consented in writing or unless there is other ethical or legal authorization for doing so.

(b) Ordinarily, in such scientific and professional presentations, psychologists disguise confidential information concerning such persons or organizations so that they are not individually identifiable to others and so that discussions do not cause harm to subjects who might identify themselves.

5.09 Preserving Records and Data

A psychologist makes plans in advance so that confidentiality of records and data is protected in the event of the psychologist's death, incapacity, or withdrawal from the position or practice.

5.10 Ownership of Records and Data

Recognizing that ownership of records and data is governed by legal principles, psychologists take reasonable and lawful steps so that records and data remain available to the extent needed to serve the best interests of patients, individual or organizational clients, research participants, or appropriate others.

5.11 Withholding Records for Nonpayment

Psychologists may not withhold records under their control that are requested and imminently needed for a patient's or client's treatment solely because payment has not been received, except as otherwise provided by law.

6. Teaching, Training Supervision, Research, and Publishing

6.01 Design of Education and Training Programs

Psychologists who are responsible for education and training programs seek to ensure that the programs are competently designed, provide the proper experiences, and meet the requirements for licensure, certification, or other goals for which claims are made by the program.

6.02 Descriptions of Education and Training Programs

(a) Psychologists responsible for education and training programs seek to ensure that there is a current and accurate description of the program content, training goals and objectives, and requirements that must be met for satisfactory completion of the program. This information must be made readily available to all interested parties.

(b) Psychologists seek to ensure that statements concerning their course outlines are accurate and not misleading, particularly regarding the subject matter to be covered, bases for evaluating progress, and the nature of course experiences. (See also Standard 3.03, Avoidance of False or Deceptive Statements.)

(c) To the degree to which they exercise control, psychologists responsible for announcements, catalogs, brochures, or advertisements describing workshops, seminars, or other non-degree-granting educational programs ensure that they accurately describe the audience for which the program is intended, the educational objectives, the presenters, and the fees involved.

6.03 Accuracy and Objectivity in Teaching

(a) When engaged in teaching or training, psychologists present psychological information accurately and with a reasonable degree of objectivity.

(b) When engaged in teaching or training, psychologists recognize the power they hold over students or supervisees and therefore make reasonable efforts to avoid engaging in conduct that is personally demeaning to students or supervisees. (See also Standards 1.09, Respecting Others, and 1.12, Other Harassment.)

6.04 Limitation on Teaching

Psychologists do not teach the use of techniques or procedures that require specialized training, licensure, or expertise, including but not limited to hypnosis, biofeedback, and projective techniques, to individuals who lack the prerequisite training, legal scope of practice, or expertise.

6.05 Assessing Student and Supervisee Performance

(a) In academic and supervisory relationships, psychologists establish an appropriate process for providing feedback to students and supervisees.

(b) Psychologists evaluate students and supervisees on the basis of their actual performance on relevant and established program requirements.

6.06 Planning Research

(a) Psychologists design, conduct, and report research in accordance with recognized standards of scientific competence and ethical research.

(b) Psychologists plan their research so as to minimize the possibility that results will be misleading.

(c) In planning research, psychologists consider its ethical acceptability under the Ethics Code. If an ethical issue is unclear, psychologists seek to resolve the issue through consultation with institutional review boards, animal care and use committees, peer consultations, or other proper mechanisms.

(d) Psychologists take reasonable steps to implement appropriate protections for the rights and welfare of human participants, other persons affected by the research, and the welfare of animal subjects.

6.07 Responsibility

(a) Psychologists conduct research competently and with due concern for the dignity and welfare of the participants.

(b) Psychologists are responsible for the ethical conduct of research conducted by them or by others under their supervision or control.

(c) Researchers and assistants are permitted to perform only those tasks for which they are appropriately trained and prepared.

(d) As part of the process of development and implementation of research projects, psychologists consult those with expertise concerning any special population under investigation or most likely to be affected.

6.08 Compliance With Law and Standards

Psychologists plan and conduct research in a manner consistent with federal and state law and regulations, as well as professional standards governing the conduct of research, and particularly those standards governing research with human participants and animal subjects.

6.09 Institutional Approval

Psychologists obtain from host institutions or organizations appropriate approval prior to conducting research, and they provide accurate information about their research proposals. They conduct the research in accordance with the approved research protocol.

6.10 Research Responsibilities

Prior to conducting research (except research involving only anonymous surveys, naturalistic observations, or similar research), psychologists enter into an agreement with participants that clarifies the nature of the research and the responsibilities of each party.

6.11 Informed Consent to Research

(a) Psychologists use language that is reasonably understandable to research participants in obtaining their appropriate informed consent (except as provided in Standard 6.12, Dispensing With Informed Consent). Such informed consent is appropriately documented.

(b) Using language that is reasonably understandable to participants, psychologists inform participants of the nature of the research; they inform participants that they are free to participate or to decline to participate or to withdraw from the research; they explain the foreseeable consequences of declining or withdrawing; they inform participants of significant factors that may be expected to influence their willingness to participate (such as risks, discomfort, adverse effects, or limitations on confidentiality, except as provided in Standard 6.15, Deception in Research); and they explain other aspects about which the prospective participants inquire.

(c) When psychologists conduct research with individuals such as students or subordinates, psychologists take special care to protect the prospective participants from adverse consequences of declining or withdrawing from participation.

(d) When research participation is a course requirement or opportunity for extra credit, the prospective participant is given the choice of equitable alternative activities.

(e) For persons who are legally incapable of giving informed consent, psychologists nevertheless (1) provide an appropriate explanation, (2) obtain the participant's assent, and (3) obtain appropriate permission from a legally authorized person, if such substitute consent is permitted by law.

6.12 Dispensing With Informed Consent

Before determining that planned research (such as research involving only anonymous questionnaires, naturalistic observations, or certain kinds of archival research) does not require the informed consent of research participants, psychologists consider applicable regulations and institutional review board requirements, and they consult with colleagues as appropriate.

6.13 Informed Consent in Research Filming or Recording

Psychologists obtain informed consent from research participants prior to filming or recording them in any form, unless the research involves simply naturalistic observations in public places and it is not anticipated that the recording will be used in a manner that could cause personal identification or harm.

6.14 Offering Inducements for Research Participants

(a) In offering professional services as an inducement to obtain research participants, psychologists make clear the nature of the services, as well as the risks, obligations, and limitations. (See also Standard 1.18, Barter [With Patients or Clients].)

(b) Psychologists do not offer excessive or inappropriate financial or other inducements to obtain research participants, particularly when it might tend to coerce participation.

6.15 Deception in Research

(a) Psychologists do not conduct a study involving deception unless they have determined that the use of deceptive techniques is justified by the study's prospective scientific, educational, or applied value and that equally effective alternative procedures that do not use deception are not feasible.

(b) Psychologists never deceive research participants about significant aspects that would affect their willingness to participate, such as physical risks, discomfort, or unpleasant emotional experiences.

(c) Any other deception that is an integral feature of the design and conduct of an experiment must be explained to participants as early as is feasible, preferably at the conclusion of their participation, but no later than at the conclusion of the research. (See also Standard 6.18, Providing Participants With Information About the Study.)

6.16 Sharing and Utilizing Data

Psychologists inform research participants of their anticipated sharing or further use of personally identifiable research data and of the possibility of unanticipated future uses.

6.17 Minimizing Invasiveness

In conducting research, psychologists interfere with the participants or milieu from which data are collected only in a manner that is warranted by an appropriate research design and that is consistent with psychologists' roles as scientific investigators.

6.18 Providing Participants With Information About the Study

(a) Psychologists provide a prompt opportunity for participants to obtain appropriate information about the nature, results, and conclusions of the research, and psychologists attempt to correct any misconceptions that participants may have.

(b) If scientific or humane values justify delaying or withholding this information, psychologists take reasonable measures to reduce the risk of harm.

6.19 Honoring Commitments

Psychologists take reasonable measures to honor all commitments they have made to research participants.

6.20 Care and Use of Animals in Research

(a) Psychologists who conduct research involving animals treat them humanely.

(b) Psychologists acquire, care for, use, and dispose of animals in compliance with current federal, state, and local laws and regulations, and with professional standards.

(c) Psychologists trained in research methods and experienced in the care of laboratory animals supervise all procedures involving animals and are responsible for ensuring appropriate consideration of their comfort, health, and humane treatment.

(d) Psychologists ensure that all individuals using animals under their supervision have received instruction in research methods and in the care, maintenance, and handling of the species being used, to the extent appropriate to their role.

(e) Responsibilities and activities of individuals assisting in a research project are consistent with their respective competencies.

(f) Psychologists make reasonable efforts to minimize the discomfort, infection, illness, and pain of animal subjects.

(g) A procedure subjecting animals to pain, stress, or privation is used only when an alternative procedure is unavailable and the goal is justified by its prospective scientific, educational, or applied value.

(h) Surgical procedures are performed under appropriate anesthesia; techniques to avoid infection and minimize pain are followed during and after surgery.

(i) When it is appropriate that the animal's life be terminated, it is done rapidly, with an effort to minimize pain, and in accordance with accepted procedures.

6.21 Reporting of Results

(a) Psychologists do not fabricate data or falsify results in their publications.

(b) If psychologists discover significant errors in their published data, they take reasonable steps to correct such errors in a correction, retraction, erratum, or other appropriate publication means.

6.22 Plagiarism

Psychologists do not present substantial portions or elements of another's work or data as their own, even if the other work or data source is cited occasionally.

6.23 Publication Credit

(a) Psychologists take responsibility and credit, including authorship credit, only for work they have actually performed or to which they have contributed.

(b) Principal authorship and other publication credits accurately reflect the relative scientific or professional contributions of the individuals involved, regardless of their relative status. Mere possession of an institutional position, such as Department Chair, does not justify authorship credit. Minor contributions to the research or to the writing for publications are appropriately acknowledged, such as in footnotes or in an introductory statement.

(c) A student is usually listed as principal author on any multiple-authored article that is substantially based on the student's dissertation or thesis.

6.24 Duplicate Publication of Data

Psychologists do not publish, as original data, data that have been previously published. This does not preclude republishing data when they are accompanied by proper acknowledgment.

6.25 Sharing Data

After research results are published, psychologists do not withhold the data on which their conclusions are based from other competent professionals who seek to verify the substantive claims through reanalysis and who intend to use such data only for that purpose, provided that the confidentiality of the participants can be protected and unless legal rights concerning proprietary data preclude their release.

6.26 Professional Reviewers

Psychologists who review material submitted for publication, grant, or other research proposal review respect the confidentiality of and the proprietary rights in such information of those who submitted it.

7. Forensic Activities

7.01 Professionalism

Psychologists who perform forensic functions, such as assessments, interviews, consultations, reports, or expert testimony, must comply with all other provisions of this Ethics Code to the extent that they apply to such activities. In addition, psychologists base their forensic work on appropriate knowledge of and competence in the areas underlying such work, including specialized knowledge concerning special populations. (See also Standards 1.06, Basis for Scientific and Professional Judgments; 1.08, Human Differences; 1.15, Misuse of Psychologists'

Influence; and 1.23, Documentation of Professional and Scientific Work.)

7.02 Forensic Assessments

(a) Psychologists' forensic assessments, recommendations, and reports are based on information and techniques (including personal interviews of the individual, when appropriate) sufficient to provide appropriate substantiation for their findings. (See also Standards 1.03, Professional and Scientific Relationship; 1.23, Documentation of Professional and Scientific Work; 2.01, Evaluation, Diagnosis, and Interventions in Professional Context; and 2.05, Interpreting Assessment Results.)

(b) Except as noted in (c), below, psychologists provide written or oral forensic reports or testimony of the psychological characteristics of an individual only after they have conducted an examination of the individual adequate to support their statements or conclusions.

(c) When, despite reasonable efforts, such an examination is not feasible, psychologists clarify the impact of their limited information on the reliability and validity of their reports and testimony, and they appropriately limit the nature and extent of their conclusions or recommendations.

7.03 Clarification of Role

In most circumstances, psychologists avoid performing multiple and potentially conflicting roles in forensic matters. When psychologists may be called on to serve in more than one role in a legal proceeding—for example, as consultant or expert for one party, or for the court and as a fact witness—they clarify role expectations and the extent of confidentiality in advance to the extent feasible, and thereafter as changes occur, in order to avoid compromising their professional judgment and objectivity and in order to avoid misleading others regarding their role.

7.04 Truthfulness and Candor

(a) In forensic testimony and reports, psychologists testify truthfully, honestly, and candidly and, consistent with applicable legal procedures, describe fairly the bases for their testimony and conclusions.

(b) Whenever necessary to avoid misleading, psychologists acknowledge the limits of their data or conclusions.

7.05 Prior Relationships

A prior professional relationship with a party does not preclude psychologists from testifying as fact witnesses or from testifying to their services to the extent permitted by applicable law. Psychologists appropriately take into account ways in which the prior relationship might affect their professional objectivity or opinions and disclose the potential conflict to the relevant parties.

7.06 Compliance With Law and Rules

In performing forensic roles, psychologists are reasonably familiar with the rules governing their roles. Psychologists are aware of the occasionally competing demands placed upon them by these principles and the requirements of the court system, and attempt to resolve these conflicts by making known their commitment to this Ethics Code and taking steps to resolve the conflict in a responsible manner. (See also Standard 1.02, Relationship of Ethics and Law.)

8. Resolving Ethical Issues

8.01 Familiarity With Ethics Code

Psychologists have an obligation to be familiar with this Ethics Code, other applicable ethics codes, and their application to psychologists' work. Lack of awareness or misunderstanding of an ethical standard is not itself a defense to a charge of unethical conduct.

8.02 Confronting Ethical Issues

When a psychologist is uncertain whether a particular situation or course of action would violate this Ethics Code, the psychologist ordinarily consults with other psychologists knowledgeable about ethical issues, with state or national psychology ethics committees, or with other appropriate authorities in order to choose a proper response.

8.03 Conflicts Between Ethics and Organizational Demands

If the demands of an organization with which psychologists are affiliated conflict with this Ethics Code, psychologists clarify the nature of the conflict, make known their commitment to the Ethics Code, and to the extent feasible, seek to resolve the conflict in a way that permits the fullest adherence to the Ethics Code.

8.04 Informal Resolution of Ethical Violations

When psychologists believe that there may have been an ethical violation by another psychologist, they attempt to resolve the issue by bringing it to the attention of that individual if an informal resolution appears appropriate and the intervention does not violate any confidentiality rights that may be involved.

8.05 Reporting Ethical Violations

If an apparent ethical violation is not appropriate for informal resolution under Standard 8.04 or is not resolved properly in that fashion, psychologists take further action appropriate to the situation, unless such action conflicts with confidentiality rights in ways that cannot be resolved. Such action might include referral to state or national committees on professional ethics or to state licensing boards.

8.06 Cooperating With Ethics Committees

Psychologists cooperate in ethics investigations, proceedings, and resulting requirements of the APA or any affiliated state psychological association to which they belong. In doing so, they make reasonable efforts to resolve any issues as to confidentiality. Failure to cooperate is itself an ethics violation.

8.07 Improper Complaints

Psychologists do not file or encourage the filing of ethics complaints that are frivolous and are intended to harm the respondent rather than to protect the public.

EDITOR'S NOTE

The United States Federal Trade Commission issued on December 16, 1992 a "draft of complaint" reprinted below (Docket C-3406) directed to the American Psychological Association claiming that the APA had violated the Federal Trade Commission Act (probably referring to the APA's *Ethical Principles for Psychologists and Code of Conduct*. The reader should examine the Ethical Principles and the Federal Trade Commissions statement, paying special attention to sections 3—*Advertising and other public statements* and 4–*Therapy*.

A careful reading of both items should be read by psychologists who offer their services via private practice to the general community.

Other related entries in the *American Psychologist* have been published on this topic that have appeared after the February 1993 issue.

R J C

In the Matter of: American Psychological Association, a corporation.
Docket No. C-3406
Decision and Order

The Federal Trade Commission having initiated an investigation of certain acts and practices of the respondent named in the caption hereof, and the respondent having been furnished thereafter with a copy of a draft of complaint that the Bureau of Competition proposed to present to the Commission for its consideration and that, if issued by the Commission, would charge respondent with violation of the Federal Trade Commission Act; and

The respondent, its attorney, and counsel for the Commission having thereafter executed an agreement containing a consent order, an admission by the respondent of all the jurisdictional facts set forth in the aforesaid draft of complaint, a statement that the signing of said agreement is for settlement purposes only and does not constitute an admission by respondents that the law has been violated as alleged in such complaint, and waivers and other provisions as required by the Commission's Rules; and

The Commission having thereafter considered the matter and having determined that it had reason to believe that the respondent has violated the said Act, and that a complaint should issue stating its charges in that respect, and having thereupon accepted the executed consent agreement and placed such agreement on the public record for a period of sixty (60) days, now in further conformity with the procedure prescribed in §2.34 of its Rules, the Commission hereby issues its complaint, makes the following jurisdictional findings and enters the following order:

1. Respondent American Psychological Association is a corporation organized, existing and doing business under and by virtue of the laws of the District of Columbia, with its office and principal place of business located at 1200 17th Street, N.W., Washington, D.C. 20036.

2. The Federal Trade Commission has jurisdiction of the subject matter of this proceeding and of the respondent, and the proceeding is in the public interest.

Order

I.

For the purpose of this order:

"Respondent" means the American Psychological Association, its directors, trustees, councils, committees, boards, divisions, officers, representatives, delegates, agents, employees, successors, or assigns.

"Members" means the Fellows, Members, and Associates classes of members of the American Psychological Association, and persons that hold Affiliate status with the American Psychological Association.

"Psychotherapy" means the therapeutic treatment of mental, emotional, or behavioral disorders by psychological means, and excludes programs, seminars, workshops, or consultations that address specific limited goals, such as career planning; improving employment skills or performance; increasing assertiveness; losing weight, giving up smoking; or obtaining non-individualized information about methods of coping with concerns common in everyday life.

"Current psychotherapy patient" means a patient who has commenced an evaluation for or a planned course of individual, family, or group psychotherapy, where the patient and the therapist have not agreed to terminate the treatment. However, a person who has not participated in psychotherapy with the psychologist for one year shall not be deemed a current psychotherapy patient.

II.

It is ordered that respondent, directly, indirectly, or through any corporate or other device, in or in connection with respondent's activities as a professional association, in or affecting commerce, as "commerce" is defined in Section 4 of the Federal Trade Commission Act, 15 U.S.C. §44, do forthwith cease and desist from:

A. Restricting, regulating, impeding, declaring unethical, interfering with, or restraining the advertising, publishing, stating, or disseminating by any person of the prices, terms, availability, characteristics, or conditions of sale of services, products, or publications offered for sale or made available by any psychologist, or by any organization or institution with which a psychologist is affiliated, through any means, including but not limited to the adoption or maintenance of any principle, rule, guideline, or policy that restricts any psychologist from:

1. Making public statements about the comparative desirability of offered services, products, or publications;

2. Making public statements claiming or implying unusual, unique, or one-of-a-kind abilities;

3. Making public statements likely to appeal to a client, patient or other consumer's emotions, fears, or anxieties concerning the possible results of obtaining or failing to obtain offered services, products, or publications;

4. Presenting testimonials from clients, patients, or other consumers;

5. Engaging in any direct solicitation of business from actual or prospective clients, patients, or other consumers or offering of services directly to a client, patient, or other consumer receiving similar services from another professional.

Provided that nothing contained in this order shall prohibit respondent from adopting and enforcing reasonable principles, rules, guidelines, or policies governing the conduct of its members with respect to:

1. Representations that respondent reasonably believes would be false or

deceptive within the meaning of Section 5 of the Federal Trade Commission Act;

2. Uninvited, in-person solicitation of business from persons who, because of their particular circumstances, are vulnerable to undue influence; or

3. Solicitation of testimonial endorsements (including solicitation of consent to use the person's prior statement as a testimonial endorsement) from current psychotherapy patients, or from other persons who, because of their particular circumstances, are vulnerable to undue influence.

Provided further that nothing in this order shall prohibit respondent from adopting and enforcing editorial, scientific, peer review, or display standards for its publications and conferences.

B. Prohibiting, restricting, regulating, impeding, declaring unethical, interfering with, or restraining any of its members, or any organization or institution with which any of its members is associated, from giving or paying any remuneration to any patient referral service or other similar institution for referral of clients, patients, or other consumers for professional services.

Provided that nothing contained in this order shall prohibit respondent from formulating, adopting, disseminating, and enforcing reasonable principles, rules, guidelines, or policies requiring that disclosures be made to clients, patients, or other consumers that the psychologist, or organization or institution with which he or she is associated, will pay or give, or has paid or given, remuneration for the referral of the clients, patients, or other consumers for professional services.

III.

It is further ordered that respondent shall:

A. Cease and desist for ten (10) years from the date at which this order becomes final, from taking any action against a person alleged to have violated any ethical principle, rule, policy, guideline, or standard, or taking disciplinary action on any other basis against a person, so as to restrain or otherwise restrict advertising, solicitation of business, or the payment of fees for the referral of clients, patients, or other consumers for services without first providing such person, at a minimum, with written notice of any such allegation and without providing such person a reasonable opportunity to respond. The notice required by this part shall, at a minimum, clearly specify the ethical

principle, rule, policy, guideline, or other basis of the allegation and the reasons the conduct is alleged to have violated the ethical principle, rule, policy, guideline, or standard or other applicable criterion.

B. Maintain for five (5) years following the taking of any action referred to in Part II.A. of this order, in one separate file, segregated by the names of any person against whom such action was taken, and make available to Commission staff for inspection and copying, upon reasonable notice, all documents and correspondence that embody, discuss, mention, refer, or relate to the action taken and all bases for or allegations relating to it.

IV.

It is further ordered that respondent shall:

A. Within thirty (30) days after the date this order becomes final, remove or amend to eliminate from the respondent's *Ethical Principles,* Bylaws, and any officially promulgated or authorized guidelines or interpretations of respondent's official policies any statement of policy that is inconsistent with Parts II and III of this order.

B. Within sixty (60) days after the date this order becomes final, publish in *The APA Monitor,* or any successor publication that serves as an official journal of respondent, a copy of this order with such prominence as is therein given to regularly published feature articles.

C. Within sixty (60) days after the date this order becomes final, publish in *The APA Monitor,* or any successor publication that serves as an official journal of respondent:

1. Notice of the removal of amendment, pursuant to this order, of any Principle, Bylaw, guideline, interpretation, provision, or statement, together with;

2. A copy of any such Principle, Bylaw, guideline interpretation, provision, or statement, as worded after any such amendment.

D. Within sixty (60) days after the date this order becomes final, distribute by mail a copy of Appendix A (cover letter) to this order, along with a copy of the order itself, to each of respondent's members and to each state psychological association affiliate.

E. Cease and desist for a period of one (1) year from maintaining or continuing respondent's affiliation with any state, regional, or other psychological association affiliate within one hundred

twenty (120) days after respondent learns or obtains information that would lead a reasonable person to conclude that said association has, following the effective date of this order, maintained or enforced any prohibition against:

1. advertising or making public statements concerning the comparative desirability of offered services;

2. advertising or making any public statement representing or implying unusual, unique, or one-of-a-kind abilities;

3. advertising or making any public statement intended or likely to appeal to a client's fears, anxieties, or emotions;

4. using a testimonial regarding the quality of a psychologist's services or products;

5. directly soliciting individual clients;

6. offering services directly to persons receiving similar services from another professional; or

7. making payments to patient referral services; where maintenance or enforcement of such prohibition by respondent would be prohibited by Part II of this order; unless, prior to the expiration of the one hundred twenty (120) day period, said association informs respondent by a verified written statement of an officer that the association has eliminated and will not reimpose such prohibitions(s), and respondent has no grounds to believe otherwise.

V.

It is further ordered that respondent

A. Within 90 days after the date of this order becomes final, and at such other times as the Commission may require by written notice to the respondent, file with the Commission a written report setting forth in detail the manner and form in which respondent has complied and is complying with the order;

B. For a period of five (5) years after the date this order becomes final, maintain and make available to Commission staff for inspection and copying, upon reasonable notice, records adequate to describe in detail any action taken in connection with the activities covered by Parts II, III, and IV of this order, including but not limited to all documents generated by the respondent or that come into the possession, custody, or control of respondent, regardless of the source, that discuss, refer to, or relate to any advice or interpretation rendered with respect to advertising, solicitation, or giving or receiving any remuneration for referring clients for professional services, involving any of its members.

VI.

It is further ordered that respondent shall notify the Commission at least thirty (30) days prior to any proposed change in respondent, such as dissolution, assignment, sale resulting in the emergence of a successor corporation or association, or any other change which may affect compliance obligations arising out of this order.

By the Commission.

Issued: December 16, 1992

CONTRACTS FOR PRACTICING PSYCHOLOGISTS

Whether a psychologist provider should offer clients a written contract, explicitly listing conditions and limitations, has been a matter of debate whether it should be required, recommended or ignored. The California licensure board at one point proposed a contract requirement, with a copy to be filed with the state, but energetic lobbying defeated the measure.

The author of this entry, Neal Pinckney, who served as a consultant to the licensing board in California and who was qualified as an expert witness in malpractice suits, studied more than 2,000 lawsuits and disciplinary hearing transcripts, and he came to the opinion that the single factor most likely to have prevented actions against therapists would have been a comprehensive contract. He wrote Law and Ethics in Counseling and Psychotherapy, Case Problems from which this section was adapted by Pinckney for this encyclopedia.

The sample contract here shown is a fictitious example of a contract based on Pinckney's recommendations.

CONTRACTS FOR PRACTICING PSYCHOLOGISTS

Although a comprehensive knowledge of and strict adherence to all applicable laws and ethical standards is the surest way to avoid problems of all kinds for psychologists in private practice, including lawsuits and licensing board actions; misunderstandings and imperfections of human memory frequently lead to adversarial actions which most often could have been prevented through a written agreement. A contract should be personalized to suit the needs and styles of each therapist, but should include, at a minimum, the following factors:

1. *Qualifications, training and experience of the provider.* Patients/clients may later assert you represented yourself to them as being other than what you are.

2. *A statement of your personal philosophy with an explanation of your procedures used and their purposes.* Answers the questions "Where are you coming from and how do you help people?"

3. *Discomforts and risks to be reasonably expected.* This should include a statement about risks to personal relationships as a result of changes in behavior, values, understandings. The patient/client may hold the change or loss of a relationship against you, and other persons may feel aggrieved by the changes effected.

4. *Benefits to be reasonably expected.* Promises are poison! They are the cause of many misunderstandings leading to malpractice suits and disciplinary hearings.

5. *Conditions and limits of confidentiality.* It does little good to inform a person that you must notify authorities *after* a disclosure is made. All states require reporting of abuse to minors, some also require notification of elder abuse. Following the *Tarasoff* decision, you are expected to notify any person who is the object of threatened harm (or family members and law enforcement authorities if the person cannot be reached).

6. *Alternatives to treatment of possible similar benefit.* This is to negate the "capture" effect. Alleged exploitation of a disoriented person can be defused.

7. *Freedom to withdraw from treatment, testing and activities at any time.* Allegations of coercive pressure are frequently claimed.

8. *Termination (both early and normal).* The bases for ending sessions and the responsibilities you assume following this.

9. *Policy regarding fees.* The statement should clarify how much is to be charged, how and when the practitioner–psychologist is to be paid, and how any differences in opinions about charges are to be handled.

10. *Recording of sessions: conditions, limits, uses, content, and storage.* Typically unclear, this issue is a common cause for lawsuits.

11. *Testimony in civil suits.* Having a clear-cut policy (to which you may make individual exceptions) can prevent you from wasting days in court, being involved in domestic disputes, or other lawsuits.

12. *Physical contact policy.* This is a major cause of malpractice and disciplinary actions. The safest practice is to refrain from all physical contact with clients. Disclosure of your position (and adherence to it) can prevent trouble.

13. *Availability: routine and emergency.* An understanding when and how clients are to contact you, especially during hours when your office is closed is essential, including how these calls will be handled and who else may respond. This is especially a problem presented by alcoholics.

14. *Statement of fees, charges, notice and cancellation of sessions, insurance, billing, telephone contact.* Absence of or vague statements may result in inability to collect for services and later anger leading to harassment allegations.

15. *Records release.* Release of records or notes, including to the patient/client.

16. *Drug or alcohol use during sessions.* Policy for first and subsequent attempts to services in an altered state.

17. *Concurrent therapy or treatment.* Disclosure requirements, communications with other practitioners.

18. *Other conditions.* All other special considerations, conditions and requirements which could become an issue of dispute or differing interpretation at a later time.

19. *Informed Consent.* Following an opportunity to discuss all points of concern in the contract, there should be an acknowledgement that the patient/client had read, understood and been able to clarify all the terms in the document, including the date and signature(s).

NEAL PINCKNEY

This contract, shown here with a fictional name and biography, is the author's personal therapy agreement. It reflects his professional philosophy and therapeutic style. Other psychologists may wish to create a personal contract which most closely reflects their own style and needs.

(LETTERHEAD HERE)
SAMPLE COUNSELING/THERAPY AGREEMENT

This clinical practice, as in any other professional office, best serves you when all communications and undertakings are clearly understood. We would like you to read this agreement carefully and make notes where you would like, so you can question or discuss any points which concern you or that are unclear. This agreement explains your rights as well as your obligations. When we have had an opportunity to discuss and clarify all the points, you will be asked to sign it. You will not be accepted as a patient (and no one at this clinic is considered to be your therapist) until we have both signed this agreement.

YOUR THERAPIST

Jane Doe, Ph.D., received her Bachelor of Science degree from the University of California, Berkeley in 1971. She was awarded a Masters of Science in Parapsychology from Duke University in 1972 and her Doctorate in Clinical Psychology from the University of Chicago in 1975. She was a member of the Simpkins Institute in Chicago from 1975 to 1979, did post-doctoral studies at the *Psychologishes Institut,* Vienna from 1979 to 1980, and was a member of the Client-Directed Therapy Group, Santa Barbara from 1981 to 1985. She has been in independent private practice since 1985. Dr. Rigney is licensed to practice psychology in Illinois and California. She is a fellow of the American Psychological Association and was chair of the Clinical Division in 1978 and 1979, and is a member of the California and Western Psychological Association and the National Association of Sexual Abuse Therapists. She has taught a number of courses at various universities in the area of clinical psychology and is the author of several published articles in professional journals, as well as the author of a chapter on Client-centered therapy in an edited book.

HOW YOUR THERAPIST WORKS

Therapy is a means of helping people. It can be through counseling or advising; in teaching you about yourself, your feelings, or of things you may not be aware; in examining your past; looking to your future; helping to deal with difficult situations and much more.

Just as there is no single prescription your physician can give you for all possible medical problems, there are as many different approaches to solving problems of personal growth, adjustment and behavior as there are therapists. What may be appropriate for others may not be best for you. Your therapist believes in setting goals which can be mutually agreed upon and holding you accountable for achieving them within a specified time. You will find that your therapist will not necessarily react to or judge you in many of the things you talk about, and that he or she may not always tell you how they feel about things you may wish some reaction to, but they will listen carefully to you. Their training and experience lead them to believe that some concerns of adulthood can be related to events of childhood but the focus may be on dealing with the present. We have found that what some people think is a major concern may, in reality, be keeping them from seeing the real problem. Understanding why we do things which cause us concern often aids us in changing problem behavior.

BENEFITS AND RISKS OF THERAPY

The ultimate goal of therapy is to render itself no longer necessary. How soon or completely this happens depends primarily on your willingness to cooperate, to be open and candid, and to take the steps (which can be risky) recommended. Relatively small steps in therapy may be the foundation to great leaps in future endeavors, but no promise of benefits or results can be guaranteed; the results may be influenced by factors often out of the control of the patient or the therapist.

There are some potential risks in the process. You may find your feelings about yourself and your relationships with others changed, and this can be the source of pain. Those close to you may resist your changes and react negatively to you. Some persons do not respond to the therapeutic process, and others may feel worse for the experience. As you begin to sense achievement of your goals and understandings of concerns which brought you here, you may feel you see some light at the end of the tunnel.

YOUR ALTERNATIVES TO THIS CLINIC

There are often other ways to meet your needs besides using this clinic. Some public agencies and hospitals offer free or low-cost counseling, individually and in group settings; services are provided by some religious organizations; and universities which train counselors and psychologists sometimes offer therapy at reduced cost. Other private practitioners use radically differing ways of achieving often similar results. Referral information is available on request.

YOUR RIGHTS

Whatever you may be asked to participate in is voluntary—you can choose not to take part in any activity, test, game, "homework" or response without upsetting our relationship, though you may be asked about your reasons. If at any time you do not want to continue, you have that right. You will be offered help in finding another person to help if you wish. But you may be asked to explain why you do not wish to continue, with no charge for that session.

You should feel free to ask questions at any time about treatment, fees, records, or any other matters that concern you. Time to clarify fees will not be billed to you.

What you disclose to your therapist is confidential; he or she cannot and will not reveal *anything*—even that you are a patient—unless required by law. We must notify appropriate authorities of information concerning abuse, neglect, or molestation of a minor (and in some places of an elderly person) and of threatened harm to a specific person (as well as notifying that person), and to testify and surrender records when ordered by a court of law.

When a patient is under 12 years of age, his or her parents or guardians have the right to be informed of the essence of therapy, but often it is in the best interests of the entire family to trust in the judgment of your therapist when patience is recommended. A minor 12 or older may request and be given confidential status to information as permitted by law. Parents paying for treatment should understand they may not have the right to know what is said in sessions.

Your personal records and files are kept in a secure place and will not be released to anyone without your written request or by court order.

In some situations you may be asked for permission to audio or video record sessions. You are free to refuse; but if you consent, a written agreement will be undertaken before any recording is made. You will never be recorded without your knowledge and consent.

Since the goal of therapy is to no longer need it, a time will come when you or your therapist feels this is the case. It might be that you do not agree—but it would be unethical for therapists to continue if they felt they could no longer be of benefit to you. You will be given at least a month to consider this, and following termination of therapy a follow-up contact will be requested.

Sometimes a patient does not participate fully or refuses suggestions or goals. In that case the patient is given notice that the sessions are terminated and he or she may only expect help in emergencies until time permits another source of help to be found, usually for a maximum of two weeks.

Therapists do not testify in divorce proceedings or civil cases unless action is brought against them or as ordered by a court.

While physical contact is not a policy of this clinic, an occasional clasp of support or hug may spontaneously occur. If this may concern you, please discuss it now and every effort will be taken not to offend you.

YOUR OBLIGATIONS

Fees are $— for a — minute therapy session, — minutes in direct contact plus — minutes reserved for review and notations to your records. You will be expected to pay for services at the time you make an appointment. While you may be eligible for insurance benefits, fees are your responsibility. Customary forms will be completed at no charge, but lengthy reports or forms will incur additional charges. When an insurance company authorizes direct billing, we will extend that courtesy. If you are forced to cancel an appointment, you must give three-working days notice.

If less notice is given but the hour can be scheduled for another patient, no fees will be lost. Otherwise, the hour will be charged to you. Telephone consultations are charged at $— for every interval of five minutes or less. Occasionally it becomes necessary to alter fees, but no fees will be increased until after three-months notice. The fee in this agreement is guaranteed for at least six months from the date you begin.

Patients who arrive in a state influenced by alcohol or drugs cannot participate in any type of sessions. After an initial refusal, subsequent appearance under the influence will result in termination of services.

If you are presently under the care of any other therapist, counselor or physician for a matter related in any way to your reason for being here, you cannot begin therapy here until you have disclosed that information and given consent for release of information to this clinic.

Office hours vary with demand and obligations elsewhere; usually the clinic is open on weekdays from (9 to 1) and (2 to 6,) but additional hours may be arranged. The telephone number, (555–5555) is answered (24) hours a day. If your therapist is not available to respond with the urgency your situation requires, another licensed therapist will contact you or you will be given assistance in meeting your needs.

The terms of this agreement are subject to change by mutual agreement, but nothing can be considered changed unless it is in writing and amended to this agreement.

YOUR ACKNOWLEDGEMENT

I have read this agreement carefully and have discussed all aspects which I felt concerned about or did not fully understand. I freely agree with the conditions.

I ☐ am / ☐ am not under the care of another therapist, counselor or physician or practitioner, or currently taking any medication which may effect my behavior. If you are, list names, addresses and medications on the attached form.

(Lines for Patients' and Therapists' signatures and dates here)

Adapted and reprinted from *Law & Ethics in Counseling & Psychotherapy; Case Problems*. California State University Press, Sacramento ©1986 Neal T. Pinckney, Ph.D.

NAME INDEX

This index is designed to locate names discussed in a substantive way in the encyclopedia. It is not meant to include every name cited in passing or as the author of a reference citation.

Abel, S. M., 77
Abel, T. M., 223, 763, 349
Abeles, N., 168, 207, 311, 342, 509, 706, 715
Abraham, K., 532, 540
Abrams, K., 410
Abramson, P., 514
Ach, N., 448
Adamopoulous, J., 393
Adams, J. S., 264, 578
Adams-Webber, J. R., 154, 667, 783
Adam-Terem, R. C., 497
Adler, A., 13, 14, 106, 130, 160, 169, 227, 228, 238, 263, 273, 276, 277, 299, 389, 403, 459, 466, 472, 479, 494, 497, 526, 540, 545, 580, 599, 631, 637, 651, 654, 668, 675, 685 , 719, 720, 758, 761, 781, 813, 852, 854, 865, 898
Adler.G., 227
Adler, P., 226
Adorno, T. W., 79, 186, 476, 506
Adrian, E. D., 36
Ahsen, A., 289
Aiken, L. R., 65, 352, 488, 502, 525, 767, 808
Ainsworth, M. D. S., 109
Ajzen, I., 76, 492
Albee, G. W., 430, 708, 761
Alcock, J. E., 84, 196, 364, 368, 500, 545, 626
Alden, L. E., 82
Alderfer, C. P., 640
Alexander, T., 6, 104, 136, 222
Alexander, F. G., 116, 909
Alexander, F. M., 261
Allen, M. J., 125, 230, 327, 496, 666, 695, 699, 766, 807, 878, 901
Allman, L., 560
Allport, F. H., 36, 127, 181, 365, 432, 445, 667, 672, 674, 675, 859, 941
Allport, G. W., 7, 447, 526, 673, 913, 941
Allred, G. H., 542, 543, 685
Almeida, E., 941
Alperson, E. D., 261
Altrocchi, J., 554, 555
Ames, L. B., 3, 31, 941
Amsel, A., 599
Amundson, M., 668
Anastasi, A., 2, 259, 935, 936, 941
Anderson, J. R., 71
Anderson, N. S., 150, 358, 359, 494, 547, 552, 573
Andreassi, J. L., 613, 655, 681, 690, 817
Andrews, I. R., 297, 513
Andrulis, R. S., 298, 410, 587, 635
Angell, F., 941
Angell, J. R., 366, 892, 941
Angell, M., 737
Angyal, A., 273, 671, 941
Anisman, H., 43, 451, 605, 875, 878
Ansbacher, H. L., 545, 941

Anzieu, D., 941
Appley, M. H., 897
Ardrey, R., 27
Argyle, M., 279
Ariès, P., 275
Aristotle, 45, 48, 128, 145, 339, 469, 556, 681, 726, 727, 768, 881
Arkes, H. R., 147
Armstrong, D. M., 307
Armstrong, R. B., 277, 652
Arnheim, R., 69, 378, 734
Arnold, M. B., 159, 160, 294
Arrikoff, D. B., 811
Asch, S. E., 180, 181, 392, 453, 456, 941
Aserinsky, E., 268
Ash, P., 417, 781, 900
Ashbrook, R. M., 132, 450
Asher, J., 785
Asher, W., 324, 568, 576
Assagioli, R., 751
Atkinson, J. W., 6
Auerbach, A. J., 465
Austad, C. S., 538, 756, 941
Ausubel, D. P., 64, 288, 795
Authier, J., 907
Avenerius, R., 941
Averill, J. R., 851
Ayllon, T., 87, 911
Ayres, J. J. B., 83, 476, 809
Azrin, N. H., 628
Azuma, H., 941

Bach, G. R., 261, 479
Back, K. W., 38, 163, 181, 392, 793, 303
Bacon, F., 220, 941
Baddeley, A., 941
Baechler, J., 885
Bain, A., 70, 777, 941
Baird, J. W., 941
Bakan, D., 433
Bakare, C. G. M., 941
Baldwin, J. M., 576, 688, 726, 941
Baltes, P. B., 942
Bandler, R., 606
Bandura, A., 27, 29, 61, 101, 152, 192, 433, 682, 753, 813, 857, 942
Bannister, D., 782
Bard, M., 165
Bard, P. A., 441
Barker, R. G., 280, 302, 304, 942
Barnum, P. T., 84
Barón, A. Jr., 533, 578, 597, 598, 863, 898
Baron, R. A., 164, 315, 366
Bar-Tal, D., 404, 405, 762
Bartel, N., 400

SUBJECT INDEX